The Dictionary of
DRINK

ALAN SUTTON

ALAN SUTTON PUBLISHING · PHOENIX MILL · FAR THRUPP
STROUD · GLOUCESTERSHIRE

First published 1988 under the title: *The Language of Drink*

Reprinted 1991, 1992

British Library Cataloguing in Publication Data

Edwards, Graham
The dictionary of drink.
1. Beverages—Dictionaries
I. Title II. Edwards, Sue
641.2′03′21   TX815

ISBN 0-86299-375-X

Whilst every care has been taken to ensure that all measurements and details given
in the recipes in this book are correct, the publishers cannot accept any
responsibility for any inaccuracies.

Typesetting and origination by
Alan Sutton Publishing Limited
Photoset in 8 on 8 point Melior
Printed in Great Britain by
The Guernsey Press Company Limited,
Guernsey, Channel Islands

The Dictionary of

Contents

Preface

As a lecturer, many hours can be spent searching for information, answering obscure questions from students or just satisfying one's own curiosity. I found, though, that quite often the word I was searching for could not be discovered in the index of any book but was hidden deep in the text, which often meant many hours of reading to find an elusive detail. In addition, the indexes of most books differ in their layout; for example, some books will have subject areas listed together in blocks, while others list everything alphabetically.

Added to this, was the problem of new releases which did not include previous historical beverage items when they were updated. As a result, I started to collect unusual snippets of beverage information and place them on an easy card-file system that could be used for quick reference while still being added to.

Before very long, I found that I had accumulated 3,000 entries and the file was growing daily. Being a food and beverage lecturer, it was not just alcoholic beverage information I needed but also that classed as non-alcoholic, for which there was very little written information available.

It was when my colleagues started using my file that I realised that it could be developed and turned into a book for use by everyone who drinks, whatever the beverage (including water), and especially by those who work with or serve drink.

The years which followed were spent travelling and searching for the relevant information to make this a comprehensive volume. Little did I realise that I would end up with a reference work of some 42,000 entries.

It was not until 1984, when I met Sue, that the book ever looked as though it would be finished. It had become my whole life but at no stage did it look as if it would ever be completed; now, thanks to her drive, the dream has been realised.

Graham Edwards

Guernsey

Acknowledgements

If we were to mention everyone who had assisted us in the compilation of this work then another book would be required to include them all. Over the last ten years we have solicited the help of countless in our quest for the correct information. So to all the thousands of trade and individual friends our deepest thanks.

We would, though, like to say a very special thanks to our families, our colleagues at work and the Tastevins de Guernesey, for their encouragement in seeing the work through, especially when our enthusiasm was flagging; also to Glad Stockdale for hundreds of hours of typesetting.

How This Book Works

This book is not meant to provide a *complete* answer to a question and was never designed to be an encyclopaedia (there are many excellent examples on the market to fill that role). It is as a comprehensive, single volume point of reference for a word, saying, name, etc., required quickly and sought alphabetically (regardless of subject area or word structure), that it serves its main purpose.

To this end 'Château X' or 'Clos X' appear under 'C' and not 'X' – the principle being that these are known and used in this form, the 'Château' or 'Clos' being a part of the name. Entries starting with 'Le', 'La' or 'Les', however, are not given under 'L' as many readers may be uncertain as to which form applies, or indeed as to whether or not the definite article is considered a part of the name.

Many of the words originating in the Eastern Bloc, Arabian and Asian countries have gained a variety of spellings derived during their phonetic transcription into anglicised or western forms. These variants have been included wherever possible.

In most instances information is very concise. The names of the vineyards, wineries and châteaux are entered principally for spelling and location purposes; further information can be obtained easily, either elsewhere in this book or in other specialist books on the relevant region, once this has been identified. For example, looking up 'Château Musar' will quickly identify it as a wine from the Lebanon. Similarly, once Château Tahbilk is known to be Australian, a book on Australian wines can be consulted for further information. There are also a number of entries for products which are no longer in production. These have been included because it is often difficult to find definitions in other reference books.

There are around 7,500 German vineyards listed, each having an individual entry giving its location. The entries are laid out as follows: first the *anbaugebiet* (one of the eleven German wine regions); then its *bereich* (a subdivision of this region); the *grosslage* (a grouping of villages within the *bereich*); and the vineyard itself (the einzellage). The abbreviations used are (aub), (ber), (gros), (vil). These entries are cross-referenced so that any one detail can help lead to a specific identification.

Cocktails are entered under the names by which they were given to the authors. Recipes vary greatly from barman to barman and where possible they have been averaged but, as the reader will see, some cocktail names embrace many different recipes. For most of the beer entries the original gravity (O.G.) is given as an average.

Finally, it is worth noting that entries can be deceptive in their brevity. In order not to waste space, maintain comprehensiveness and cater for all levels of expertise, entries are cross-referenced for beverage-related words and are not amplified where the additional information can be gleaned by following these up. In this way there is virtually no limit to the reading which could result from looking up one initial word, and a vast amount of knowledge can be gained from a start anywhere among the 42,000 or so entries.

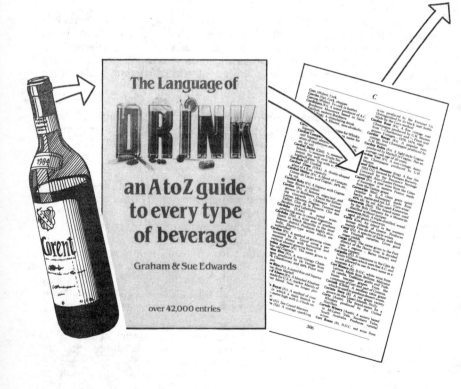

The Language of

DRINK

an A to Z guide
to every type
of beverage

Graham & Sue Edwards

over 42,000 entries

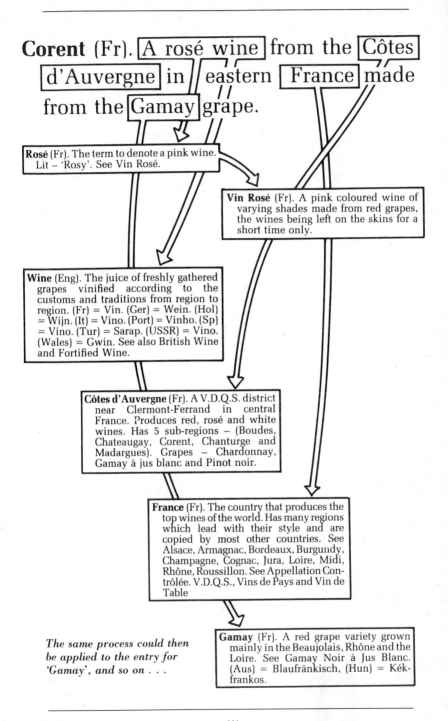

Corent (Fr). A rosé wine from the Côtes d'Auvergne in eastern France made from the Gamay grape.

Rosé (Fr). The term to denote a pink wine. Lit – 'Rosy'. See Vin Rosé.

Vin Rosé (Fr). A pink coloured wine of varying shades made from red grapes, the wines being left on the skins for a short time only.

Wine (Eng). The juice of freshly gathered grapes vinified according to the customs and traditions from region to region. (Fr) = Vin. (Ger) = Wein. (Hol) = Wijn. (It) = Vino. (Port) = Vinho. (Sp) = Vino. (Tur) = Sarap. (USSR) = Vino. (Wales) = Gwin. See also British Wine and Fortified Wine.

Côtes d'Auvergne (Fr). A V.D.Q.S. district near Clermont-Ferrand in central France. Produces red, rosé and white wines. Has 5 sub-regions – (Boudes, Chateaugay, Corent, Chanturge and Madargues). Grapes – Chardonnay, Gamay à jus blanc and Pinot noir.

France (Fr). The country that produces the top wines of the world. Has many regions which lead with their style and are copied by most other countries. See Alsace, Armagnac, Bordeaux, Burgundy, Champagne, Cognac, Jura, Loire, Midi, Rhône, Roussillon. See Appellation Contrôlée. V.D.Q.S., Vins de Pays and Vin de Table

The same process could then be applied to the entry for 'Gamay', and so on . . .

Gamay (Fr). A red grape variety grown mainly in the Beaujolais, Rhône and the Loire. See Gamay Noir à Jus Blanc. (Aus) = Blaufränkisch, (Hun) = Kékfrankos.

Abbreviations

A.C.	Appellation Contrôlée
Afr	Africa
Alb	Albania
Alc. by vol	Alcohol by volume
Alg	Algeria
Anb	Anbaugebiet
Arab	Arabia
Arg	Argentina
Aus	Austria
Austr	Australia
Bel	Belgium
Ber	Bereich
Bra	Brazil
Bul	Bulgaria
C.Am	Central America
Can	Canada
Ch.Isles	Channel Islands
Cktl	Cocktail
Cyp	Cyprus
Czec	Czechoslovakia
Den	Denmark
E.Asia	Eastern Asia
Egy	Egypt
E.Ind	East Indies
Eng	England
Euro	Europe
Fin	Finland
Fl.oz	Fluid ounce
Fr	France
G.B.	Great Britain
Ger	Germany
Gre	Greece
Gro	Grosslage
Hol	Holland
Hun	Hungary
Ice	Iceland
Ind	India
I.O.M.	Isle of Man
Ire	Ireland
Isr	Israel
It	Italy
Jap	Japan
Lat	Latin
Leb	Lebanon
Liq. Coffee	Liqueur Coffee
Lit	Literally
Lux	Luxembourg
Mad	Madeira

Mex	Mexico
M.East	Middle East
N.Am	North America
Non. alc	Non-alcoholic
Nor	Norway
N.Z.	New Zealand
O.G.	Original gravity
Pak	Pakistan
Pol	Poland
Port	Portugal
Rum	Rumania
S.Afr	South Africa
Scot	Scotland
Sp	Spain
Switz	Switzerland
Tur	Turkey
Vil	Village (*Weinbauert*)
Vin	Vineyard (*Einzellage*)

The Dictionary of

DRINK

A

A.A. (Eng) (abbr). Alcoholics Anonymous. An international body to help those people who have a 'drink' problem.

A.A.A. (Eng) (abbr). Action on Alcohol Abuse. A body who wish to raise the price on alcohol in a bid to cut consumption. Based in London. Advocates everything in moderation and more education regarding alcohol abuse.

Aalborg (Den). Town where Akvavit was first produced.

Aalborg Akeleje Snaps (Den). An Akvavit flavoured with herbs. 40% alc. by vol.

Aalborg Brewery (Den). A major brewery based in North Jutland.

Aalborg Esksport Akvavit (Den). An Akvavit with a slightly burnt taste due to the addition of Madeira wine. 45% alc. by vol.

Aalborg Fuselfri Akvavit (Den). A low strength caraway-flavoured Akvavit.

Aalborg Jubiloeums Akvavit (Den). A dill-flavoured Akvavit produced by DDS. 45% alc. by vol.

Aalborg Porse Snaps (Den). An Akvavit flavoured with bog myrtle. 45% alc. by vol.

Aalborg Taffel Akvavit (Den). A caraway-flavoured Akvavit produced by DDS.

Aan de Doorns Co-operative (S.Afr). Vineyards based in Worcester. Address = Box 235, Worcester 6850. Produces varietal wines.

Aan-de-Drift (S.Afr). A small vineyard that sells its grapes to the Mooiuitsig Wynkelders.

Aangeschoten (Hol). Tipsy. Drunken.

Aargau (Switz). Minor wine-producing district in north. Produces mainly white wines.

Aass Brewery (Nor). Based in Drammen, south-east Norway. Is noted for its Bayer, Bok and Jule Ales.

A.B. (Port) (abbr). An Aguardente Brandy produced by Caves São João. 43% alc. by vol.

Abadir-Dukem (Afr). One of the three main wine-producing regions in Ethiopia. See also Eritire and Guder.

Abafado (Mad). Pure grape juice fortified with up to 20% by vol. of alcohol. Used in the final blending of rich Bual (Boal) and Malmsey madeiras.

Ábalos (Sp). A Zona de Crianza in the Rioja Alta, north-western Spain.

Abanico (Sp). A straw-coloured, Fino Sherry with a tang of salt and flor produced by Bobadilla in Jerez de la Frontera.

Abarchage Traditionnel (Fr). Old method of stacking oak casks in the Cognac region whilst the spirit matures.

A.B.B. (Bra) (abbr). Associação Bradileira de Barmen. Brazil's Bartenders' Association. Address = Avenue Angelica, 845, C.E.P. 01227 São Paulo, Brazil

Abbaye (Bel). A strong, naturally-conditioned, bottled beer. Brewed by five Trappist abbayes.

Abbaye d'Aulne (Bel). An Abbaye-produced beer from south-east Belgium.

Abbaye de la Grâce de Dieu (Fr). A noted liqueur producer based in Doubs. Noted for its Trappistine liqueur.

Abbaye de la Moinette (Bel). An Abbaye beer brewed by the Dupont Brasserie in Tourpes.

Abbaye de Leffe Radieuse (Bel). An Abbaye-style beer brewed by the Stella Artois Brasserie in Louvain.

Abbaye de Leffe Triple (Bel). Was once an Abbaye brewery. Now a Golden beer brewed by the Stella Artois Brasserie.

Abbaye-de-Morgeot (Fr). See Morgeot (A Premier Cru A.C. Chassagne–Montrachet), Côte de Beaune, Burgundy. 10.92 ha.

Abbaye de Thélème (Bel). An Abbaye brewery produced beer.

Abbazia dell'Annunziata (It). A winery based at La Morra (a district of Barolo), Piemonte.

Abbey Ale (Eng). A strong cask conditioned Bitter brewed by the Cirencester Brewery in Gloucestershire.

Abbey Brewery (Eng). A small brewery near Retford, Nottinghamshire. Set up in 1981, it produces cask conditioned beers.

Abbey Brewery (Scot). The name for the

head office of the Scottish and New-castle Brewery, Edinburgh, Mid-lothian.

Abbey Cocktail (Cktl) (1). 1½ fl.ozs. Gin, juice ¼ lemon, dash Orange bitters. Shake well over ice, strain into a cocktail glass, top with a cherry.

Abbey Cocktail (Cktl) (2). ½ measure dry Gin, ¼ measure Lillet, ¼ measure orange juice, dash Angostura. Shake well over ice, strain into a cocktail glass.

Abbey Cocktail (Cktl) (3). 1 fl.oz. dry Gin, ½ fl.oz. sweet Vermouth, ½ fl.oz. orange juice, dash Angostura. Shake well over ice, strain into a cocktail glass. Dress with a cherry.

Abbey Knight (Eng). A dry, white wine made from the Müller-Thurgau grape by the Macrae Farms (Highwayman Vineyard), Bury St. Edmunds, Suffolk.

Abbey Well Water (Eng). A still mineral water produced by Waters and Robson in Morpeth, Northumberland. Sold in green glass bottles.

Abboc. (It) (abbr). For abbocato.

Abbocado (Sp). Medium sweet.

Abbocato (It). Lit – 'soft caressing'. Describes wines as either sweet or semi-sweet.

Abbot Ale (Eng). A strong Bitter ale brewed by the Greene King Brewery in either of their breweries at Biggles-wade, Bedfordshire or at Bury St. Edmunds, Suffolk.

Abbot's Aged Bitters (USA). Aromatic bitters produced in Baltimore since 1865.

Abbot's Choice (Scot). A blended Scotch whisky created by McEwan in Perth-shire. (part of the DCL group). 40% alc. by vol.

Abbots Lager (Austr). A Lager beer brewed by the Carlton and United Brewery in Victoria. 3.9% alc. by vol.

A.B.C. (Eng) (abbr). Aylesbury Brewery Company. Merged with Allied Breweries in 1972. Based in Ayles-bury, Buckinghamshire.

ABC (E.Asia). A medium Stout brewed by the Archipelago Brewery in Kuala Lumpur, Malaya.

A.B.C. (USA) (abbr). Alcoholic Beverage Control. (Board).

A.B.C.C. (USA) (abbr). Alcoholic Bever-age Control Commission.

Abdijbieren (Hol). A Trappist-produced Abbaye beer.

A.B.E. (Sp) (abbr). Asociación Barmen Españolos. Spain's Bartenders' Associ-ation. Address = Duque de Medinaceli-2, Madrid.

Abeille (Fr). Bee. See Bees.

Abel and Co (N.Z). A small winery based at Ponoma Road, Kumeu. Produces red and white wines including Beaunois and Ponoma Valley Claret.

Abele (Fr). Champagne producer. Address = 50, Rue de Sillery, 5100 Reims. Produces – Vintage and non-vintage wines. Vintages – 1975, 1976, 1982. Labels – Grande Marque Impériale and Sourire de Reims.

Abel-Musk (Ind). An aromatic plant, its seeds are often mixed with coffee as a stimulant and for flavour. It has a musk aroma.

Abelsberg (Ger). Vineyard. (Anb) = Württemberg. (Ber) = Remstal-Stuttgart. (Gro) = Weinsteige. (Vil) = Stuttgart (ortsteil Gaisburg).

Abendroth (Aus). An ancient red vine variety, rarely grown nowadays.

Aberdeen Ale Ltd (Scot). Formed in 1982 at the Devanha Brewery, Aberdeen. Brews Devanha XB 1036 O.G. and Triple 1043 O.G. See Devanha Brewery.

Aberdeen Angus (Arg). The brand-name of a red wine produced by the Bodegas Goyenechea.

Aberdeen Angus (Cktl). ⅔ measure Scotch whisky, ⅓ measure Drambuie, 1½ ozs. honey, juice ½ lime. Stir whisky, honey and lime juice in a warmed mug, add flaming liqueur. Stir and serve.

Aberdeen Cows (USA). A cream-based liqueur. Made from Scotch whisky and cream.

Aberfeldy (Scot). A single Malt whisky distillery based in Perthshire. A Highland malt whisky. 40% alc. by vol.

Aberlour (Scot). A 12 year old Highland malt whisky produced by the Aberlour-Glenlivet Distillery in Morayshire. 43% alc. by vol.

Aberlour-Glenlivet (Scot). A single Malt whisky distillery based south of Rothes, Morayshire (on the river Spey). A Highland malt whisky. 40% alc. by vol. Owned by Pernod-Ricard. See Campbell and Son.

Abf. (Ger) (abbr). For Abfüllung.

A.B.F. (Fr) (abbr). Association des Barmen de France. French Bartenders' Association. Address = 192, Boulevard Haussman, 75008, Paris, France.

Abfüller (Ger). Bottler.

Abfüllung (Ger). Bottling.

A.B.G. (Austr) (abbr). Australian Bar-tenders' Guild. Australia's Bartenders' Association. Address = c/o Catering Institute of Australia, P.O. Box A. 497, Sydney, New South Wales, 2000.

Abgebaut (Ger). A term used to describe a

wine that has lost its acidity.

Abimes (Fr). A wine village in the Savoie. Produces dry white wine of same name. Also spelt Abymes.

Abington Pub (Eng). A home-brew pub in Northampton, Northamptonshire. Owned by Clifton Inns, produces Cobblers Ale 1037 O.G. and Extra 1047 O.G.

A.B.I. Permit (USA) (abbr). Alcoholic Beverage Import Permit.

Abir Brewery (Isr). A famous Israeli brewery. Produces a Lager beer of same name at 11° Balling.

Abisante (USA). An aniseed-flavoured spirit. 40% alc. by vol.

Abocado (Sp). See Abbocado.

Abolengo (Sp). A 3 year old Brandy produced by Romate.

Abondance (Eng). A name given to wine that has been well diluted with water. The term can apply to the practice of adulterating the wine, or for the consumption by children by lowering the alcohol content. (Also makes it go further).

Abonnement (Fr). The practice of forming a contract on a fixed term basis to buy the complete harvest (vintage) of a Château for a number of years, at an agreed price in Bordeaux. A deal between the négociant and the grower (Château).

Abouriou (Fr). A red grape variety grown in the Côtes du Marmandais, Lot-et-Garonne, south-western France.

A.B.P. (Port) (abbr). Associação Barmen de Portugal. Portugal's Bartenders' Association. Address = Trav. da Fábricados Pentres 27, 1°-1200 Lisbon, Portugal.

Abra Farm and Winery [La] (USA). A winery based in Lovingston, Virginia. Produces French hybrid and vinifera wines.

Abran (USSR). A medium dry white wine from the Crimea.

Abrastol (Eng). An illegal additive to wine. Used as a preservative. Gives the wine a reddish colour.

Abrau-Dursso (USSR). A large wine-producing collective in southern Russia. Produces mainly sparkling wines.

Abre à Liqueur (Fr). See Toddy Palm.

Abricot d'Anjou (Fr). A brandy-based liqueur, flavoured with apricots. Produced in Angers, Loire. 31% alc. by vol.

Abricotine (Fr). An almond and apricot liqueur, yellow coloured. Has a slight taste of almonds acquired from the apricot stones used. Produced by Garnier at Enghien-les-Bains. 31.5% alc. by vol.

Åbro Brewery (Swe). A small brewery based in Vimmerby, south-east Sweden. Is one of the country's smallest.

Abrotonite (It). A wine consumed by the Romans. Was flavoured with artemisia (wormwood).

Abruzzi (It). See Abruzzo.

Abruzzo (It). A region east of Latium on east coast. Capital is L'Aquila.

Abruzzo Bianco (It). A white grape variety grown in Abruzzo. Known in Tuscany as the Trebbiano.

Abs. (Eng) (abbr). Acrylonitrile-butadiene-styrene.

Absinth (Fr). An alternative spelling of Absinthe.

Absinthe (Fr). Wormwood. (Artemisia absinthium).

Absinthe (Fr). A liqueur flavoured with wormwood, aniseed, angelica, cloves etc, coloured yellow. Invented by a Frenchman (Dr. Ordiniare) in Couvet, Switzerland. The recipe was sold to a Mr. Pernod in 1797. Was banned as Absinthe in 1915 because of toxic nature. Now known as Pastis at a reduced strength. 40–43% alc. by vol.

Absinthe–American Style (Cktl). 1 dash Angostura, 4 dashes syrup, ¼ gill Pastis, ¼ gill water. Shake over ice until frozen, strain into a cocktail glass, twist of lemon peel.

Absinthe Cocktail (Cktl) (1). 1 part Pernod, 1 part water, 1 dash sugar syrup, 1 dash Angostura. Shake over ice, strain into a cocktail glass.

Absinthe Cocktail (Cktl) (2). 1 fl.oz. Pastis, 2 dashes Angostura, dash Orgeat syrup, dash Anisette. Stir well over ice, strain into a cocktail glass.

Absinthe Cooler (Cktl). 3 dashes Pernod, ½ gill Whisky, ⅛ gill lemon juice, 2 dashes Angostura, ½ pint ginger ale. Stir in a tall glass with ice cube, serve with Pernod on top.

Absinthe Drip (Cktl). Made with a special drip glass. A cube of sugar and a cube of ice are placed in the dripper and a measure of Absinthe (Pastis) is placed in the glass. Ice cold water is poured over the sugar and ice to drip into the Absinthe. (A tea-strainer can be substituted for the dripper).

Absinthe–French Style (Cktl). See Absinthe Drip.

Absinthe Special (Cktl). ½ measure Absinthe, ½ measure dry Gin, dash Angostura, dash Grenadine. Shake over ice, strain into a cocktail glass.

Absinthe Suissesse (Cktl). ⅕ gill Pernod, 3 dashes Anisette, 3 dashes Orange flower water, 4 dashes Crème de Menthe, 1 egg white. Shake over ice, strain into a cocktail glass.

Absinthe–Swiss Style (Cktl). Also known as Mominette. ½ gill Absinthe in a tumbler, add syrup to taste, then top up with iced water. Grenadine may be used in lieu of syrup. (see – Tomate (Une), Purée (Une).

Absinthism (Eng). A disease condition caused by the over-drinking of Absinthe.

Absolut (Swe). A brand of neutral flavoured Vodka 40% alc. by vol.

Absolute Alcohol (Eng). 99% pure alcohol (Ethanol).

Abson (USA). An aniseed-flavoured liqueur.

Abstatt (Ger). Village. (Anb) = Württemberg. (Ber) = Württembergisch Unterland. (Gro) = Schozachtal. (Vins) = Burgberg, Burg Wildeck, Sommerberg.

Abstemious (Eng). Drinking only moderately.

Abstention (Eng). Refraining from drinking, giving up drinking any alcohol temporarily for some reason.

Abstich (Ger). Racking.

Abstinence (Eng). The carrying out of abstention.

Abstinent (Fr). Teetotal.

Abt. (Bel) (Abbr). Abbot. Strongest Trappist-style ale from St. Sixtus Abbaye, Westvleteren. Also Prior and Pater ales produced.

Abtei (Ger). Vineyard. (Anb) = Nahe. (Ber) = Schloss Böckelheim. (Gro) = Rosengarten. (Vil) = Sponheim.

Abtei (Ger). Vineyard. (Anb) = Mosel-Saar-Ruwer. (Ber) = Zell/Mosel. (Gro) = Rosenhang. (Vil) = Bremm.

Abteiberg (Ger). Vineyard. (Anb) = Mosel-Saar-Ruwer. (Ber) = Zell/Mosel. (Gro) = Rosenhang. (Vil) = Mesenich.

Abteilikoer (Ger). Lit – 'Abbot's liqueur'. Herb based liqueur, popular as a digestive.

Abtei Ruppertsberg (Ger). Vineyard. (Anb) = Nahe. (Ber) = Kreuznach. (Gro) = Schlosskapelle. (Vil) = Weiler.

Abtei Ruppertsberg (Ger). Vineyard. (Anb) = Nahe. (Ber) = Kreuznach. (Gro) = Schlosskapelle. (Vil) = Bingen-Bingerbrück.

Abtel (Ger). Grosslage. (Anb) = Rheinhessen. (Ber) = Bingen. (Vils) = Appenheim, Gau-Algesheim, Nieder-Hilbersheim, Ober-Hilbersheim, Partenheim, Sankt Johann, Sprendlingen, Wolfsheim. (See also – Orbel, Abtey).

Abtey (Ger). Grosslage. (Anb) = Rheinhessen. (Ber) = Bingen. (Vils) = Appenheim, Gau-Algesheim, Nieder-Hilbersheim, Ober-Hilbersheim, Partenheim, Sankt Johann, Sprendlingen, Wolfsheim. (See also Orbel, Abtel).

Abtsberg (Ger). Vineyard. (Anb) = Baden. (Ber) = Ortenau. (Gro) = Fürsteneck. (Vil) = Offenburg (ortsteil Zell-Weierbach).

Abtsberg (Ger). Vineyard. (Anb) = Franken. (Ber) = Mainviereck. (Gro) = Reuschberg. (Vil) = Hörstein.

Abtsberg (Ger). Vineyard. (Anb) = Mosel-Saar-Ruwer. (Ber) = Bernkastel. (Gro) = Münzlay. (Vil) = Graach.

Abtsberg (Ger). Vineyard. (Anb) = Mosel-Saar-Ruwer. (Ber) = Saar-Ruwer. (Gro) = Römerlay. (Vil) = Mertesdorf (ortsteil Maximin Grünhaus).

Abtsberg (Ger). Vineyard. (Anb) = Rheinpfalz. (Ber) = Südliche Weinstrasse. (Gro) = Herrlich. (Vil) = Impflingen.

Abtsfronhof (Ger). Vineyard. (Anb) = Rheinpfalz. (Ber) = Mittelhaardt Deutsche Weinstrasse. (Gro) = Schenkenböhl. (Vil) = Bad Dürkheim.

Abtsleite (Ger). Vineyard. (Anb) = Franken. (Ber) = Maindreieck. (Gro) = not yet assigned. (Vil) = Würzburg.

Abtswind (Ger). Village. (Anb) = Franken. (Ber) = Steigerwald. (Gro) = Schild. (Vin) = Altenberg.

Abtwingert (Euro). The famous vineyard of Rotes Haus (Red House) in Liechtenstein. Noted for its' white wines.

Abymes (Fr). See Abîmes.

Abyssinian Coffee (Eng). The old name for Ethiopian coffee.

A.C. (Fr) (abbr). Appellation Contrôlée.

Acacia (Eng). A gum used to prevent the premature depositing of red wine colouring matter.

Acacia Cocktail (Cktl). 1 measure dry Gin, ½ measure Bénédictine. Shake over ice, strain into a cocktail glass.

Acacia Winery (USA). A winery based in the Napa Valley, California. 21 ha. Grape varieties – Chardonnay and Pinot noir. Produces varietal wines.

Académie du Vin de Bordeaux (Fr). World famous Bordeaux wine school based in the town of Bordeaux, western France.

Acadian Distillery (Can). A Whisky distillery that produces a 100% Rye whisky. 40% alc. by vol.

Acampo Winery and Distilleries (USA). The former name for the Barengo Vineyards in Sacaramento Valley, California.

Acapulco (Cktl). 1½ ozs. white Rum, ¼ oz. Triple Sec, 1 barspoon sugar syrup, dash egg white. Shake well over ice, strain into an ice-filled old-fashioned glass, top with sprig of mint.

Acapulco Cocktail (Cktl). ½ measure Tequila, ½ measure white Rum, 1 gill pineapple juice, juice ½ lime. Shake well over ice, strain into an ice-filled collins glass, top with pineapple cube.

Acapulco Gold Cocktail (Cktl). ⅙ gill Golden Tequila, ⅙ gill golden Rum, ⅙ gill Coconut cream, ⅙ gill grapefruit juice, ⅓ gill pineapple juice. Shake well over ice, strain into an ice-filled highball glass.

Acariose (Eng). A vine pest. A species of mite that feeds on the leaves and fruit. Various species such as the Grape Rust Mite (Calepitrimerus vitis) and the Grape Bud Mite (Eriophyes vitis). Is treated with copper sulphite spray.

Acariosis (Eng). A vine condition due to attack from the vine mite. Symptoms are stunted growth and withered foliage.

Accademia Torregiorgi (It). Wine merchant and grower based at Neive, Piemonte.

Accra Brewery (Afr). A brewery based in Accra, Ghana which is noted for its Club beer.

Ace Lager (Eng). Federation of Newcastle keg Lager beer.

Acerbe (Fr). Immature, acid wine. Lit – 'bitter, sharp'.

Acerbité (Fr). Bitterness, sharpness.

Acerbitas (Lat). Bitterness.

Acerbity (Eng). Astringency or sharpness.

Acerbo (Port). Bitter, sharp.

Acérrimo (Port). Very bitter.

Acescence (Fr). To make the wine smell and taste like vinegar.

Acetaldehyde (Eng). Found in wine. Is formed during fermentation. The enzyme Zymase turns the acetaldehyde to alcohol. Has an apple taste and aroma.

Acetamide (Eng). Malady in wine. Caused by spoilage bacteria. Produces an unpleasant, mousy flavour.

Acetic Acid (Eng). CH_3COOH. Vinegar. Caused by Acetic fermentation.

Acetic Fermentation (Eng). Is caused generally by an infection with Acetobacter aceti, but several other species of organisms and certain types of film yeasts may initiate the process. Is detectable by smell and an oily sheen on top of the wine/beer.

Acetification (Eng). Turning into vinegar.

Acetify (Eng). Turn to vinegar.

Acétimètre (Fr). Acetimeter. An implement used to measure vinegar concentration.

Acétique (Fr). Acetic acid. Vinegar.

Aceto (It). Vinegar.

Acetobacter Aceti (Lat). A mould which after fermentation will break down the alcohol in the wine and produce vinegar in the presence of air. (Acetic acid).

Acetoin (Eng). A wine malady. Caused by Lactobacilli. Produces an off-flavour in the wine. Prevented by cleanliness.

Acetometer (Eng). An instrument for measuring the acetic acid content in vinegar etc.

Acetous (Eng). Having a taste of vinegar, vinegar tasting.

Acetum (Lat). Vinegar.

Acetylmethyl-Carbinol (Eng). A glycerine-related compound found in wine in small quantities.

Achaea (Gre). A province in the southern Peloponnese. Produces mainly red and white wines.

Achaia Clauss (Gre). Famous winery built in the 1860s by a Bavarian, Gustav Clauss on a hillside above Patras, Peloponnese.

Achaia-Clauss Wine Company (Gre). Company which makes Mavrodaphne (a dessert wine of Greece) and Brandy. See – Clauss (Gustav).

Achemeta (USSR). A sweet, white, dessert wine produced in Georgia.

Achentoul Spring Water Company (Scot). Produce a range of Caithness natural spring mineral waters.

Acheria Rouge (Fr). A red grape variety grown in the Madiran district of south-western France.

Achern [ortsteil Oberachem] (Ger). Village. (Anb) = Baden. (Ber) = Ortenau. (Gro) = Schloss Rodeck. (Vins) = Alter Gott, Bienenberg

Achkarren (Ger). Village. (Anb) = Baden. (Ber) = Kaiserstuhl-Tuniberg. (Gro) = Vulkanfelsen. (Vins) = Castellberg, Schlossberg.

Achromatous (Eng). Used to describe a white wine with little or no colour. (Achromic = colourless).

Achtarak (USSR). A wine-producing centre in Armenia, southern Soviet Union. Produces most styles of wines.

Achtaraque (USSR). A white, Sherry-style wine produced in Armenia, southern Soviet Union.

Acid (Eng). Imparts lasting qualities, adds bouquet and flavour. Too much acid makes wines sharp or sour. Too little makes wine flat. Gives wines freshness. (Fr) = Acide, (Ger) = Saüre, (Hol) = Zuur, (It) = Acido, (Lat) = Acidus, (Port) = Acido, (Sp) = Acido, (Tur) = Ekşi, (Wales) = Asid.

Acide (Fr). Acid.

Acidez (Port) (Sp). Sourness, acidity.

Acidification (Eng). The name given to the addition of acid to a must to correct a deficiency of acid or from infection from spoilage micro-organisms which increase the acidity.

Acidimetric Outfit (Eng). Equipment used to check the acid content of a liquid solution.

Acidity (Eng). In coffee gives a sharp, plumey taste. Necessary for a balanced style.

Acidity (Eng). The intensity of acid in a must or wine. Is measured on the pH scale. Also fixed or total acidity of combined acids measured by an Acidimetric outfit. In wine the acidity contributes to the bouquet, freshness, etc.

Acido (It). Acid.

Acido (Port) (Sp). Acid, tart, sour.

Acidulé (Fr). The term used for mineral waters that have been charged with carbonic gas (CO_2).

Acidus (Lat). Acid.

Acilik (Tur). Bitterness in wine or coffee.

Acinum (Lat). Grape/berry. See also Baca.

Acitité (Fr). Acidic taste in wines, etc.

Ackerman-Laurance (Fr). A wine-producer based in the Saumur, Anjou-Saumur, Loire. Noted for its Crémant de Loire produced by the méthode champenoise.

Ackerman Winery (USA). A winery based in Iowa. Produces mainly French hybrid wines.

Aconcagua Valley (Chile). A wine region of central Chile. Produces good quality red wines from the Cabernet and Malbec grapes.

Acorn Coffee (Eng). A coffee made from acorns by removing the cups, chopping flesh and roasting in oven. Cool, grind and infuse in boiling water for 10 minutes. Use same quantities as for ground coffee. See Ballota Oak.

Acqua (It). Water.

Acqua di Seltz (It). Soda water.

Acqua Gassosa (It). Soda water.

Acqua Minerale (It). Mineral water.

Acquavite (It). Brandy.

Acquette (Fr). A liqueur with gold or silver leaf added. Has a spicy aroma (from angelica, cinnamon, cloves and nutmeg) together with lemon peel. Resembles the Goldwasser and Silber-wasser of Germany.

Acquette d'Argent (Fr). Silver Acquette. Acquette with silver leaf.

Acquette d'Or (Fr). Acquette with gold leaf.

Acquit-à-Caution (Fr). The document that accompanies all shipments of wines and spirits for which French duties have not been paid.

Acquit Jaune d'Or (Fr). A yellow-gold certificate that accompanies every shipment of Armagnac and Cognac that is exported.

Acquit Régional Jaune d'Or (Fr). French Government certificate of authenticity of Cognac in Cognac.

Acquits Verts (Fr). The accompanying documents of wines.

Acre (Eng). 4840 square yards. 4046.86 square metres. 2.41 acres = 1 hectare.

Âcre (Fr). Denotes a harsh, acid or bitter wine.

Acrolein (Eng). An aldehyde found in wine which contributes to the bouquet.

Acrylonitrile-butadiene-styrene (Eng). Abs. A material often used for valves, pipework and containers used for wine. Is low in cost and easy to sterilise.

Action on Alcohol Abuse (Eng). See A.A.A.

Activated Carbon (USA). A method of purifying contaminated water or sewage by passing it through the acti-vated carbon so that after chlorination it is fit to drink.

Activated Charcoal (Eng). Used in Vodka production. A highly absorptive, porous form of carbon used to remove the colour and any impurities.

Activated Sludge (USA). The method of treating sewage water with bacteria to make it fit for drinking after it has been chlorinated.

Acuático (Sp). Water.

Acuoso (Sp). Watery.

Adabag (Tur). A medium dry red wine.

Adakarasi (Tur). A white grape variety grown in western Turkey.

Adam (Edouard) (Fr). Invented the pro-cess of redistillation in the seventeenth century at the University of Mont-pellier. See also Alambic Armagnaçais and Verdier.

Adamado (Port). Sweet.

Adam and Eve (Cktl) (1). ½ measure Gin, ⅕ measure Amaretto di Saronno, ⅕ measure Drambuie, 1 dash Grenadine, 1 dash Gomme syrup. Shake over ice. strain. Decorate with cherry and lemon slice.

Adam and Eve (Cktl) (2). 1 oz. Brandy, 1 oz. Forbidden Fruit, 1 oz. dry Gin, dash lemon juice. Shake over ice, strain into cocktail glass.

Adam and Eve Cocktail (Cktl). ⅓ measure Plymouth gin, ½ measure orange Curaçao, ⅙ measure Yellow Chartreuse. Stir with ice. Strain into a cocktail glass.

Adam Cocktail (Cktl). ½ measure Jamaican rum, ¼ measure Grenadine, ¼ measure lemon juice. Shake over ice, strain into a cocktail glass.

Adam-Garnotel (Fr). Champagne producer. Address = 51500 Rily-la-Montagne. Récoltants-Manipulants. Produces – Vintage and non-vintage wines. Vintages – 1973, 1975, 1976, 1979, 1982.

Adams (Port). Vintage Port Shippers. Vintages = 1935, 1945, 1947, 1948, 1950, 1955, 1960, 1963, 1966, 1967, 1970.

Adam's Ale (Eng). The nickname for water.

Adam's Apple Cocktail (Cktl). ¼ gill Calvados, ⅛ gill dry Gin, ⅛ gill Italian vermouth, 2 dashes Yellow Chartreuse. Stir all ingredients over broken ice. Strain into a cocktail glass, decorate with cherry, add twist lemon peel.

Adams County Winery (USA). A winery based in Orrtanna, Pennsylvania. Produces European and hybrid wines.

Adams [Leon] (USA). The founder of the Wine Institute in San Francisco in 1934.

Adam's Wine (Eng). A nickname for water.

Adana-Hatay (Tur). A vineyard based in southern Turkey which is noted for its medium-dry, white wines.

Addington Cocktail (Cktl). ½ measure sweet Vermouth, ½ measure dry Vermouth. Stir over ice, strain into an ice-filled highball glass. Top with soda water.

Addlestones Draught Cider (Eng). A draught traditional Cider produced by Showerings of Somerset. A cask conditioned Cider.

Adega (Port). A warehouse for storing wine, a wine cellar.

Adega Cooperativa Regional de Monção (Port). One of three commercial producers of Alvarinho.

Adega Cooperative de Palmela (Port). A large producer of Setúbal. Makes 10% of total region's production.

Adega Cooperative de Ponte da Barca (Port). Producer of the Aguardente Ponte da Barca.

Adega Cooperative de Ponte de Lima (Port). A co-operative in Peñafiel (a sub-region of Vinho Verde). Noted for its red Vinho Verde.

Adegas Exportadores de Vinhos de Madeira (Mad). Large firm that ships Madeira wines to the U.K.

Adega Velha (Port). A double distilled,

oak aged brandy produced by the Sociedade Agrícola da Quinta de Avelada.

Adelaide Metropolitan (Austr). Wine area in South Australia. Wineries include – Hamiltons, Penfolds and Woodley.

Adelberg (Ger). Grosslagen. (Anb) = Rheinhessen. (Ber) = Bingen. (Vils) = Armsheim, Bermersheim v.d.H., Bornheim, Ensheim, Erbes-Bürdesheim, Flonheim, Lonsheim, Nack, Nieder-Weisen, Sulzheim, Wendelsheim, Wörrstadt.

Adelberg (S.Afr). A blended red wine made from the Cabernet, Pinotage and Shiraz grapes. From the Simonsig Estate, Stellenbosch.

Adelgaçar (Port). To dilute, thin down.

Adelpfad (Ger). Vineyard. (Anb) = Rheinhessen. (Ber) = Bingen. (Gro) = Kaiserpfalz. (Vil) = Engelstadt.

Adelsberg (Ger). Vineyard. (Anb) = Nahe. (Ber) = Schloss Böckelheim. (Gro) = Paradiesgarten. (Vil) = Bayerfeld-Steckweiler.

Adelscott (Fr). A novelty beer brewed from malt kilned with peat by the Adelshoffen Brasserie.

Adelscott (Fr). A novelty beer brewed from peat kiln malt by the Fischer/Pêcheur Brasserie in Strasbourg, Alsace.

Adelsheim Vineyard (USA). A vineyard based near Dundee, Willamette Valley, Oregon. 8 ha. Produces Vitis vinifera and varietal wines.

Adelshoffen (Fr). A Pilsener lager beer brewed by the Schiltigheim Brasserie, Alsace.

Adelshoffen Brasserie (Fr). Brewery based in Alsace. Brews Adelscott.

Adel Seward S.A. (Fr). Cognac producer. Address = 45, Rue Grande, 16100 Cognac. Produces a range of Cognacs under the Adel label – ***, V.S.O.P. and Napoléon.

Adgestone Vineyard (Eng). Address = Upper Road, Adgestone, Sandown, Isle of Wight. Planted 1968, 10.5 ha. Soil = calcareous flinty loam. Grape varieties = Müller-Thurgau, Reichensteiner and Seyval blanc.

Adige [River] (It). A river which flows from the Alps in the north, south-east to the Adriatic sea. Flows through the Trentino-Alto Adige (Süd-Tirol) from which it gets its name.

Adios Amigos (Cktl). ⅓ gill white Rum, ⅙ gill Cognac, ⅙ gill Gin, ⅙ gill dry Vermouth, ⅙ gill lime juice. Shake well over ice, strain into an ice-filled highball glass.

Adissan (Fr). A wine-producing commune in the Clairette du Languedoc, southern France.

Adjuncts (Eng). The name given to the fermentable materials found in the Wort other than the Barley malt.

Adler (Ger). Vineyard. (Anb) = Mosel-Saar-Ruwer. (Ber) = Zell/Mosel. (Gro) = Schwarze Katz. (Vil) = Zell-Merl.

Adler Brauerei (Switz). An independent brewery based in Schwanden.

Administracion Geral de Alcool (Port). A.G.E. Body that receives grape spirit from the Comissão and disposes it to Port companies for brandying their wines or to firms for elaboration as brandy.

Admirable (L') (USA). An Altar wine (Angelica) produced by Novitiate in Los Gatos, California.

Admiral Cocktail (Cktl) (1). ⅓ measure Bourbon whiskey, ⅔ measure French vermouth, juice ½ lemon. Shake well over ice, strain into an ice-filled old-fashioned glass. Add squeeze of lemon peel juice.

Admiral Cocktail (Cktl) (2). 1 measure Gin, ½ measure Cherry brandy, ½ measure lemon juice. Shake over ice, strain into a cocktail glass.

Admiral's Ale (Eng). Cask conditioned premium Bitter 1048 O.G. brewed by the Southsea Brewery, Portsmouth, Hampshire.

Admiral's Sherry-Drake's Fino (Sp). A brand of Fino sherry produced by Lustau.

Adnams Brewery (Eng). Sole Bay Brewery, Southwold, Suffolk. Produces Smooth Bitter, Mild Ale, Olde Ale and Tally Ho Barley Wine. Also major wine mechants of note dealing in fine wines.

Adoc (Fr). An old term for sour milk.

Adolzfurt (Ger). Village. (Anb) = Württemberg. (Ber) = Württembergisch Unterland. (Gro) = Lindelberg. (Vin) = Schneckenhof.

Adomado (Port). Sweet.

Adom Atic (Isr). A semi-dry, red wine for the USA market made from French grape varieties. Produced by Carmel.

Adonis (Cktl). ⅔ measure dry Sherry, ⅓ measure sweet Vermouth, 1 dash Orange bitters. Stir over ice, strain into a cocktail glass, add twist of orange peel.

Adrianum (Lat). A white wine produced in Roman times in north-eastern Italy.

Adriatica (Yug). The brand-name for a co-operative association which markets wines in the USA.

Adrumenitanum (Lat). A full red wine which was produced in Sicily in Roman times.

Adry Cocktail (Cktl). ⅕ gill Bourbon whiskey, 4 dashes Cointreau. Shake over ice, strain into a cocktail glass with crushed ice. Dress with a cherry.

Adulterate (Eng). Denotes the addition of one (foreign) liquid into another liquid. e.g. water into spirits, beer, wine, etc. to illegally increase bulk. See Cut.

Ad Valorem Tax (Eng). A tax introduced for a year in 1924 that stated that the wealthy had to pay more for finer Champagne than the cheaper sparkling wines.

Advocaat (Hol). Liqueur of egg yolks, sugar, vanilla and brandy. Is of 15–18% alc. by vol.

Advocaat (Hol). Egg-nog.

Advocate Ale (Eng). A cask conditioned Ale 1032 O.G. brewed by the Crouch Vale Brewery, Essex.

Advocatenborrel (Hol). Advocaat drink. 17% alc. by vol.

Ad-vo-tizer (Cktl). 2 fl.ozs. dry Vermouth, 1 fl.oz. Advocaat, Tizer. Build Advocaat and Vermouth into an ice-filled highball glass. Stir in Tizer, add slice of orange.

Aegean Islands (Gre). Group of islands in eastern Greece. Samos, Limnos, Lesbos and Khios. Produce mainly sweet dessert wines from the Muscat grape.

Aegean Wines (Gre). Popular wines in ancient Greece.

Aeolian Islands (It). Also known as the Lipari Islands. Situated in the north of Sicily, within the jurisdiction of the province of Messina.

Aequicum (Lat). A red wine produced in central-eastern Italy in Roman times.

Aerate (Eng). To charge with gas i.e. CO_2 in beer and wines. See also Carbonated.

Aerobausqueador (Sp). An electric pump that helps to redistribute the cap and solids in the fermenting vat.

Aerobic (Eng). When applied to organisms denotes that they need air to respire and therefore reproduce (See Binary Fission). Wild yeasts in the grape musts are 'Aerobic' and are prevented from reproducing by the addition of SO_2. See also Anaerobic.

Aesculap Water (Hun). An Aperient mineral water from the Aesculap spring in Kelenföld, Budapest. High in sodium and magnesium sulphates.

Afames (Cyp). A deep red wine produced from the Mavron grape in the Troodos mountains around Platres, south-eastern Cyprus.

Aferrin (Eng). The alternative name for Calcium phytate (a fining agent) that removes excess iron, copper and zinc from wines.

Affalterbach (Ger). Village. (Anb) = Württemberg. (Ber) = Württembergisch Unterland. (Gro) = Schalkstein. (Vin) = Neckarhälde.

Affaltrach (Ger). Village. (Anb) = Württemberg. (Ber) = Württembergisch Unterland. (Gro) = Salzberg. (Vins) = Dieblesberg, Zeilberg.

Affchen (Ger). Vineyard. (Anb) = Rheinhessen. (Ber) = Bingen. (Gro) = Rheingrafenstein. (Vil) = Wöllstein.

Affecionados (Sp). Lovers of fine sherries or wines.

Affenberg (Ger). Vineyard. (Anb) = Rheinhessen. (Ber) = Wonnegau. (Gro) = Liebfrauenmorgen. (Vil) = Worms.

Affenflasche (Ger). Lit – 'Monkey bottle'. Bottle used for the Affenthal wines. (Affe means monkey).

Affenthaler Spätburgunder (Ger). A red wine produced in the Bereich of Ortenau in Baden from the Blauer spätburgunder grape variety and bottled in a monkey embossed bottle. Produced in a valley called Ave Thal.

Affile (It). See Cesanese di Affile.

Affinage (Fr). A term used to describe the long ageing of Banyuls Grand Cru wines in underground cellars at a constant temperature for a minimum of 30 months.

Affinity (Cktl) (1). ⅓ measure sweet Vermouth, ⅔ measure Scotch whisky, 2 dashes Angostura. Stir over ice, strain into a cocktail glass.

Affinity (Cktl) (2). ⅓ measure Scotch whisky, ⅓ measure Port, ⅓ measure dry Sherry, 2 dashes Angostura. Shake well over ice. Strain into an ice-filled old-fashioned glass.

Affinity Cocktail (Cktl). ⅖ measure French vermouth, ⅖ measure Italian vermouth, ⅕ measure Crème de Violette. Shake well over ice, strain into a cocktail glass.

Affligem Brasserie (Bel). An Abbaye brewery based in northern Belgium.

Aficionado (Port). Lover of Port.

Aficionado (Sp). A supporter of a particular wine.

Afonso III (Port). A brand of dry white wine produced in Lagoa, Algarve.

African Gin (Afr). A fairly bland, dry Gin.

African Lager (Eng) (slang). The nickname for Guinness stout.

African Teas (Afr). Main countries of production are Kenya, Uganda, Malawi, Tanzania and Mozambique.

Afrothes (Gre). Term for sparkling wine.

After Dinner (Cktl). ⅓ measure lemon juice, ⅓ measure Cherry brandy, ⅓ measure Prunelle. Shake over ice. Strain.

After Dinner Cocktail (Cktl) (1). 1 oz. Triple Sec, 1 oz. Apricot brandy, juice of a lime. Shake over ice, strain into a cocktail glass, add slice of lime.

After Dinner Cocktail (Cktl) (2). 1 measure Maraschino, 1 measure Kirsch, 3 dashes Curaçao, 3 dashes Angostura. Stir over ice, strain into a balloon glass. Top with 2 measures pineapple juice and a twist of lemon peel juice.

After Dinner Coffee (Eng). The name given to dark roasted, strong coffees.

After Eight (Cktl). ⅓ measure J&B Scotch whisky, ⅓ measure Royal Mint Chocolate liqueur, ⅓ measure cream. Shake well over ice. Strain, top with grated chocolate.

Afternoon (Cktl). ⅓ measure Cognac, ⅓ measure Fernet Branca, ⅓ measure Maraschino. Stir over crushed ice, pour into a Champagne saucer. Top with a dash of soda water, orange slice and serve with straws.

Afternoon Tea (Eng). Tea (usually China) and light refreshments served in the middle afternoon. Was started in the late eighteenth century by Anna Duchess of Bedford.

After One (Cktl). ¼ measure Campari, ¼ measure Gin, ¼ measure sweet Vermouth, ¼ measure Galliano. Shake over ice, strain, add a twist of orange peel and a cocktail cherry.

Afters (Eng). An illegal request for a drink after 'permitted hours'.

After Supper Cocktail (Cktl). 1 measure Triple Sec, 1 measure Apricot brandy, juice ¼ lemon. Shake over ice, strain into a cocktail glass.

After-taste (Eng). The taste left in the mouth after the wine has been spat out or swallowed.

Afuera (Sp). Denotes a wine produced from grapes grown on Albariza soil in south-western Spain.

Agave Cactus (Mex). Agave Tequilana Weber. The root is used for making Pulque from which Tequila is distilled.

Agave Tequilana (Mex). A sub-species of Agave cactus which is grown on Sierra Madre slopes by Tequila shippers.

Agave Tequilana Weber (Mex). See Agave Cactus.

Agawam (Can). A white grape variety grown in Niagara. Originates from the Vitis Labrusca.

A.G. Brandy (USA). A 'Gecht Brandy', produced and bottled by White Manor Liquor House.

Age (Eng). Refers to the maturing of wine.

A.G.E. Bodegas Unidas, S.A (Sp). Vineyard. Alta region, Rioja, north-eastern Spain. 50 ha. Address = Barrio Estracion 21, Fuenmayor, (La Rioja). Produces red, rosé and white wines from grape varieties – Tempranillo, Garnacha and Viura.

Aged Coffee (Eng). The name given to green coffee beans that have been held for 6–7 years to mature in warehouses.

Âge des Epices (L') (Fr). A 15 year old Cognac produced by L. Gourmel. Has a subtle flavour of cocoa and vanilla.

Âge des Fleurs (L') (Fr). A 12 year old Cognac produced by L. Gourmel. Has a subtle aroma of vine flowers.

Âge Inconnu (Fr). A grading for old brandies.

Âge Inconnu (Fr). An old Cognac brandy produced by Croizet.

Agenais (Fr). A Vins de Pays area in the Lot-et-Garonne Département in south-western France.

Agglomerate (Eng). See Aggloméré.

Agglomerated Cork (Eng). A cork built up from small pieces of cork glued and pressed together. Used for stoppering cheap table wines or as a firm base on sparkling wine corks to resist the wire cage and cap cutting into the cork. (Fr) = Aggloméré.

Aggloméré (Fr). Lit – 'Pressed together'. A cork made from cork pieces glued together. (Eng) = Agglomerated cork. In sparkling wines disks of cork are glued to the base of the agglomerated top. See Miroir.

Aggressività (It). Astringency or sharpness. Word used by Italian connoisseurs to describe sharp red wines.

Aghiorghitico (Gre). A red grape variety found especially in the Peloponnese islands.

Agiorgitiko (Gre). A red grape variety, also known as St. Georges. Produces dry red wines.

Agioritikos (Gre). The name given to white, rosé and red wines. The white made from the Assirtico and Athiri grapes, the rosé from the Grenache grape and the red from 40% Cabernet sauvignon and 60% Limnio grapes.

Agitated Wine (USA). A term used in California for sherry-style wines where flor is added to the wine and stirred through it to give a 'flor taste'.

Agker (Hun). State Wine Organisation.

Aglianico (It). A red grape variety of the Basilicata region of Southern Italy. Is also known as the Aglianico de Cassano and the Gaglioppo.

Aglianico del Vulture (It). D.O.C. red wine from the Basilicata region. Aglianico grape. Cannot be sold before November 1st. of year following the vintage. If total alcohol content is 12% by vol. and aged for 3 years (2 in wood) then it is graded 'Vecchio'. If 5 years (2 in wood) then graded 'Riserva'. The D.O.C. also applies to the natural sparkling wines.

Aglianico di Cassano (It). Local (Pollino, Calabria) name for the red Gaglioppo grape. See also Aglianico.

Agly [River] (Fr). A river in the Pyrénées Orientales within the Languedoc-Roussillon.

Agnesienberg (Ger). Vineyard. (Anb) = Nahe. (Ber) = Kreuznach. (Gro) = Kronenberg. (Vil) = Bad Kreuznach.

Agos Oro (Sp). White wine produced by Bodegas Lopez-Agos. Made from 100% Viura grapes, matured for 1 year in oak and 2 years in bottle.

Agostado (Sp). A method of pulling up the old vines in the Sherry region by digging up to 1¼ metres deep. This removes the old roots and brings the lower earth to the surface.

Agraço (Port). Unripe grape juice. Juice from unripe grapes.

Agrafe (Fr). A clamp which holds down the cork on a Champagne bottle during the second fermentation. Usually made of iron or steel. (Sp) = Grapa.

Agraffe (Fr). See Agrafe.

Agramont (Sp). The label used by Bodegas Cenalsa-Pamplona in the Navarra region for their red, rosé and white wines.

Agras (Alg). Sweet, almond-flavoured, unripe grape juice which is drunk ice cold.

Agraz (Sp). Unripe grape.

Agrazo (Sp). Unripe grape juice. Juice from unripe grapes.

Agreeable (Eng). A term which denotes that a wine, beer, cocktail, etc, has a pleasant, acceptable taste, aroma, etc.

Agressif (Fr). A term to denote a wine that is unharmonious, or made from unripe grapes.

Agresto (It). Unripe grape juice. Juice from unripe grapes.

Agrícola Castellana S. Cooperativa (Sp). A noted winery based in La Seca, Val-

ladolid, north-western Spain.
Agricola Alimentare (It). A Chianti Putto producer in Tuscany.
Agricole (Fr). The name given to Rum made from cane juice.
Agridulce (Sp). Bitter sweet.
Agrio (Sp). Sour, bitter, tart, rough,
Agritiusberg (Ger). Vineyard. (Anb) = Mosel-Saar-Ruwer. (Ber) = Saar Ruwer. (Gro) = Scharzberg. (Vil) = Oberemmel.
Agrokombinat (Yug). Co-operative.
Agronavarra (Sp). See CENALSA.
Agterkliphoogte Co-operative (S.Afr). Vineyards based in Robertson. Address = Agterkliphoogte Wynkelder Koöp Bpk., Box 267 Robertson 6705. Produces varietal wines.
Agterkliphoogte Wynkelder Koöp (S.Afr). See Agterkliphoogte Co-operative.
Agua (Sp). Water.
Agua (Port). Water.
Aguaceiro (Port). Water carrier.
Agua de Manatial (Sp). Spring water.
Agua Doce (Port). Fresh water.
Aguamanil (Sp). Ewer, water jug.
Aguamiel (Mex). Honey water. The sap of the Agave cactus used in the making of Pulque and Tequila.
Agua Pe (Port). Lit – 'Foot water'. A light red wine produced by adding water to the grape skins and refermenting. Produced in the Douro region. 4–5% alc. by vol.
Aguapié (Sp). Second pressing of the grapes which produces the juice after the Yema (1st pressing) when Gypsum is added.
Agua Potàvel (Port). Drinking water.
Aguar (Port). To water, to dilute.
Aguar (Sp). To dilute.
Aguardente (Port). A spirit distilled from wine made from grape pressings (pulp).
Aguardente de Cana (Bra). A spirit made from fermented sugar cane, known as Cachaça – the national drink of Brazil.
Aguardente de Cana-de-Acucar (Bra). The name used for white Rum in the nineteenth century.
Aguardente de Orujo (Port). A term for the French equivalent of marc.
Aguardente Medrohono (Port). Eau-de-vie popular in the Algarve.
Aguardiente (Sp). Brandy. Usually made by distilling the wine made from the grape pressings (pulp).
Aguardiente (W.Ind). In the distillation of Rum refers to the heart of the distillation. (See also Madilla).
Aguascalientes (Mex). A top wine-producing district in central Mexico.
Agueda (Port). Small region on the river Mondego. Produces wines similar to Dão wines and sparkling wines.
Agulha (Port). A fine, dry Vinho Verde which is slightly pétillant. Sold in stone bottles.
Ahachéni (USSR). A red grape variety grown in Georgia. Used in the making of dessert wines.
Ahlgren Vineyard (USA). A winery based at Boulder Creek, Santa Cruz, California. Produces varietal wines from Cabernet sauvignon, Petite syrah and Zinfandel grapes.
Ahméta (USSR). A white grape variety grown in Georgia. Used in the making of dessert wines.
Ahn (Lux). Village on the river Moselle. Vineyard sites are Palmberg and Vogelsang.
Ahr (Ger). Anbaugebiete. (Ber) = Walporzheim/Ahrtal. (Gro) = Klosterberg. (Vils) = Ahrweiler, Altenahr, Bachem, Bad Neuenahr, Dernau, Heimersheim, Heppingen, Marienthal, Mayschoss, Rech, Walporzheim.
Ahrbleichert (Ger). An old name for rosé wine made in the Ahr (Anb), from the Spätburgunder (Pinot noir) grape. The skins were removed very quickly from the must. Lit – 'Bleached wine'.
Ahrenberg (Ger). Vineyard. (Anb) = Rheinhessen. (Ber) = Bingen. (Gro) = Adelberg. (Vil) = Nach.
Ahr Information Service (Ger). Gebietsweinwerbung Ahr.e.V. Elligstr 14, 5483 Bad Neuenahr-Ahrweiler, W. Germany.
Ahr [River] (Ger). A tributary of the river Rhine. Flows through the Ahr wine Anbaugebiet.
Ahrtaler Landwein (Ger). One of 15 Deutsche Tafelwein zones.
Ahrweiler (Ger). Village. (Anb) = Ahr. (Ber) = Walporzheim/Ahrtal. (Gro) = Klosterberg. (Vins) = Daubhaus, Forstberg, Riegelfeld, Rosenthal, Silberberg, Ursulinengarten.
Ahr Wine Festivals (Ger). See Gebietsweinmarkt der Ahr. Winzerfest.
Ahsis (Isr). An aromatic wine often mentioned in 'The Bible'. Described as having a perfumed bouquet.
Ahus Taffel (Swe). A caraway-flavoured aquavit. 40% alc. by vol.
A.I.B.E.S. (It) (abbr). Associazione Italiana Barmen e Sostenitori. Italian Bartenders' Association. Address = Via Baldissera 2–20129 Milan, Italy.
Aichelberg (Ger). Village. (Anb) = Württemberg. (Ber) = Remstal-Stuttgart. (Gro) = Wartbühl. (Vin) =

Luginsland.

Aidani (Gre). A white grape variety grown mainly in southern Greece in the Cyclades Islands. Used to make a straw wine called Santorini on the Isle of Thira.

Ai Danil (USSR). A full-bodied red wine from the Crimea.

Aigéchate (USSR). A red, Port-style wine produced in the Armenia region.

Aigle (Switz). A white, medium-dry, table wine produced in the Chablais region.

Aiglon (L') (Ckl). ½ measure Mandarine Napoleon, ¾ measure Champagne. Serve 'On the rocks'. Garnish with a slice of orange.

Aigre (Fr). Sour wine. i.e. Vinaigre = vinegar.

Aigrots (Les) (Fr). A Premier Cru vineyard in the A.C. commune of Beaune, Côte de Beaune, Burgundy, 22ha.

Aiguebelle (Fr). A green liqueur made by white Monks (Cistercian) near Valence, from 35 different herbs, roots, flowers seeds and neutral spirit. There is also a sweeter yellow version. Also known as Liqueur de Frère Jean.

Aiguière (Fr). Lit – 'Ewer'. The name for a Claret jug with metal fittings. Also name for a water jug.

Ailenberg (Ger). Vineyard. (Anb) = Württemberg. (Ber) = Remstal-Stuttgart. (Gro) = Weinsteige. (Vil) = Esslingen.

Ailenberg (Ger). Vineyard. (Anb) = Württemberg. (Ber) = Remstal-Stuttgart. (Gro) = Weinsteige. (Vil) = Stuttgart (ortsteil Obertürkheim).

Ailric's Ale (Eng). A cask conditioned Old ale 1045 O.G. Brewed by Phillips Brewery, Marsh Gibbon, Bicester, Buckinghamshire.

Aïn-Bessem-Bouïra (Alg). Wine-producing area in Alger that produces full-bodied red and dry white wines.

Aîné (Fr). Senior partner.

Ain [River] (Fr). A tributary of the river Rhône which flows through the Jura region in the Département of Ain.

Ainslie and Heilbron (Scot). Whisky producer (part of DCL). Most of its Whisky is exported. Distillery based at Clynelish (Highland). Whiskies include – Ainslie's Royal Edinburgh and Clynelish (12 year old).

Ainslie's Royal Edinburgh (Scot). A blended Scotch whisky produced by Ainslie and Heilbron for export.

Aiola (L') (It). A Chianti Classico producer based in Tuscany.

Aiou-Dag (USSR). A red muscat dessert wine from southern Crimea.

Aird (L') (Ckl). ¹⁄₁₀ measure Scotch

whisky, ¹⁄₁₀ measure Kahlúa, ¹⁄₁₀ measure Bols Maraschino, ¹⁄₁₀ measure Ginger wine. Shake with ice, strain into a goblet.

Airén (Sp). A white grape variety of the central regions of Spain. Very productive and has a fine light bouquet and colour with a 12–14% by vol. of alcohol.

Airlock (Eng). A device used by home wine-makers to prevent air, bacteria or insects from contaminating the fermenting must. Made of glass or plastic and filled with water it allows the CO_2 gas to escape. See Bubbler.

Air Pressure (Eng). A system of dispensing beer. Used mainly in Scotland.

Aisne (Fr). A Département of which part is in the Champagne region that adjoins Marne.

Aït Souala (Afr). A red wine from the Aït Souala cellars at Aït Yazem in the Mekriés region of Morocco. Produced from the Carignan and Cinsault grapes and bottled by CVM. Also a rosé of same name produced.

Aiud (Rum). A wine-producing area noted for its medium-dry white wines.

Aiven (Asia). A spirit made from fermented mares' milk by the Tartars in Mongolia.

Aix-en-Provence (Fr). Red, white and rosé A.C. wine centre of Provence, south-eastern France.

Aix-la-Chapelle (Fr). An alkaline mineral water centre.

Aix-les-Bains (Fr). An alkaline mineral water centre.

A.J. (Cktl). 1½ ozs. Apple Jack, 1 oz. grapefruit juice. Shake well over ice, strain into cocktail glass.

Ajaccio (Fr). The capital of Corsica and name given to a range of non-vintage red, rosé and white A.C. wines.

Ajenjo (Sp). Wormwood. (Absinthe).

Ajudhia Distillery (Ind). A large Rum distillery based at Raja-Ka-Sahaspur, Distt Moradabad. Is owned by the National Industrial Corporation Ltd. (known as Nicol's), New Delhi. Produces – Black Bull XXX (5 year old), Field Marshal XXX, Himalayan XXX and Nicol's Standard XXX Rums.

Akadama (Jap). Lit – 'Symbol of the rising sun'. The first sweet white wine to be launched in 1907 by Shinjiro Torii. Made from Ume Shu plums.

Akavitte (Scan). Scandinavian gin. Stronger than Dutch gin. 40% alc. by vol.

AK Bitter (Eng). A light Bitter brewed by the Simpkiss Brewery, Brierley Hill,

A

Staffs in the West Midlands (Black Country).

Ak-Boulak (USSR). A sparkling, white wine produced in Kazakhstan.

Akeleje Akvavit (Den). Akvavit flavoured with many herbs. 43% alc. by vol.

Akevit (Scan). The name for rectified spirit distilled from grain or potatoes and flavoured with certain aromatic seeds, especially Caraway seeds. 45% alc. by vol. See Aquavit and Akvavit.

Akhaïa (Gre). A red wine produced in Peloponnese.

Akkerman (USSR). A wine-producing district of Moldavia (was formally part of Rumania known as Bessarabia).

AK Mild (Eng). A cask conditioned Mild brewed by McCullen Brewery of Hertford, Hertfordshire.

Akstafa (USSR). A dessert wine produced near Baku.

Akt. Ges. (Ger) (abbr). Aktiengesellschaft. (German Corporation).

Aktiebolaget Vin & Spritcentralem (Swe). State monopoly that makes 19 types of Brannvin including Explorer and Renat.

Akvaviittee (Scan). Aquavit.

Akvavit (Den). The name for a rectified spirit distilled from grain or potatoes and flavoured with certain aromatic seeds, especially Caraway seeds. See Aquavit, Akevit or Aalborg.

Akvavit Clam Cocktail (Cktl). ½ measure Akvavit, ¼ measure Clam juice, ¼ measure tomato juice, 4 dashes lemon juice, 2 dashes Worcester sauce, salt, pepper, cayenne. Stir well over ice, strain into an ice-filled old-fashioned glass.

A.K.W. Wines (S.Afr) (abbr). See Ashton Koöperatiewe Wynkelder.

Ala (It). A fortified wine made from herbs infused in alcohol and wine produced by the Corvo Winery in Sicily.

Alabama (USA). A wine-producing state in southern USA. Produces French and Muscat-style wines.

Alabama Cocktail (Cktl). 1½ ozs. Brandy, ½ oz. lemon juice, ¼ oz. Triple Sec, dash Gomme syrup. Shake over ice, strain into a cocktail glass.

Alabama Fizz (Cktl). 2 fl.ozs. Gin, juice ½ lemon, teaspoon powdered sugar. Shake over ice, strain into ice-filled highball glass. Top with soda and fresh mint.

A la Castellana (Sp). The term used to describe low and unsupported vine-training method.

Alaki (China). A type of Raki made from rice beer before 800 BC.

Alambic (Fr). A type of Pot-still. See also Alembic (an alternative spelling) and Alambique.

Alambicar (Port). To distill.

Alambic Armagnaçais (Fr). A specially modified continuous still used in the Armagnac region, invented by Edouard Adam. See also Verdier. Also spelt Alembic Armagnaçais.

Alambic Charentais (Fr). A special Pot-still used in the production of Cognac.

Alambie Winery (Austr). A winery based in the Murray Valley, Victoria.

Alambique (Fr)(Port)(Sp). Still. See Alambic.

Alambrado (Sp). The wrapping of fine wire mesh around some Spanish bottles with a lead seal to guarantee the contents. See Alambre.

Alambre (Sp). The light wire netting that is wrapped around some bottles of wine as an added seal to guarantee the authenticity of the contents. See also Alambrado.

Alameda (USA). A wine-producing region in central California.

Al-Anbīq (Arab). The Still.

Alanine (Eng). An Amino acid found in wines. Is formed by the yeasts.

Alarije (Sp). A white grape variety grown in Cáceres, south-western Spain.

Alasch Kümmel (Ger). The alternative spelling of Allasch Kümmel.

Alaska (Cktl). ⅔ measure dry Gin, ⅓ measure Yellow Chartreuse. Shake well over ice, strain into a cocktail glass.

Alateen (Eng). A group formed to help young people whose parents have a 'drink' problem. Started in the USA in 1957.

Alatera Vineyards (USA). Winery based in the Napa Valley, California. Grape varieties – Cabernet sauvignon, Chardonnay, Gewürztraminer, Johannisberg riesling and Pinot noir. Produces varietal wines and Paradis (a white wine from the Pinot noir).

Ala-Too (USSR). A red grape variety grown in the Kirghizian district. Produces Port-style red wines.

Alava (Sp). A wine-producing district in Chacolí, near Rioja, north-eastern Spain.

Alavesas S.A. (Sp). See Bodegas Alavesas.

Alayor (Sp). A wine-producer based in Minorca, Balearic Islands.

Albacete (Sp). A wine-producing province of upper La Mancha, central Spain.

Albachtaler (Ger). Vineyard. (Anb) = Mosel-Saar-Ruwer. (Ber) = Obermosel.

(Gro) = Gipfel. (Vil) = Wasserliesch.

Alba Flora (Sp). A medium-dry white wine produced on the island of Majorca.

Albariño del Palacio (Sp). The name given to a dry, pétillant, white wine produced in the Galicia region by Marqués de Figueroa.

Alba Iulia (Rum). A wine district in the Tîrnave, Transylvania. Noted for its medium-dry white wines produced from the Fetească, Italian riesling and Muskat-Ottonel grapes. Also spelt Alba Julia.

Alba Julia (Rum). An alternative spelling of Alba Iulia.

Albalonga (Ger). Early ripening white grape variety. Cross between the Riesling and Silvaner. Gives high must sugars.

Albán (Sp). The alternative name used for the Palomino grape.

Albana (It). A white grape variety from Emilia-Romagna.

Albana di Romagna (It). D.O.C. white wine from Emilia-Romagna region. Produced from the Albana grape, it is either Secco (dry) or Amabile (semi-sweet). The D.O.C. also applies to sparkling wines according to regulations within the provinces of Forli, Bologna and Ravenna.

Albania (Alb). A small wine-producing country producing average quality wines that are consumed locally.

Albanibräu (Switz). A strong Bier brewed by the Haldengut Brauerei.

Albani Brewery (Swe). Based in Odense. Produces – Giraf Beer 5.7% alc. by weight, Julebryg Christmas Beer 5.3% alc. by weight, Jule ØL (a low-alc, tax-free beer) and Påske Bryg.

Albano (It). A white wine from the Emilia-Romagna region.

Albanum (Lat). An ancient red wine produced in Roman times in central western Italy.

Alban Wine (It). The name for the wine of Alba in Roman times.

Albany Surprise (N.Z.). The most widely planted black table grape in New Zealand. Is a clonal selection of the American Isabella variety. Being very acidic, the wines are almost undrinkable.

Albarello (Sp). A red grape variety grown in western Spain.

Albariño (Sp). A white grape variety grown in the Ribeiro area of north-western Spain.

Albariza (Sp). Chalky soil found in the best Sherry country of Spain.

Albarizona (Sp). In the Sherry area a cross between the Barros and Albariza soils. Has 25% chalk. Found near Trebujena.

Albarizones (Sp). Same as Albarizona.

Albarolo (It). A white grape variety grown in northern Italy. Produces light dry wines. Also known as the Erbarola in Liguria.

Alben (Ger). An alternative name for the Elbling grape.

Alberello (It). The name given to the traditional low-yield, vine-training system.

Alberese (It). The name for limestone, marl and schistous clay soil in Chianti, Tuscany.

Alberga (Fr). An old mediaeval word for Inn or Tavern. See also Auberge.

Albergue (Port). Inn.

Albermarle Fancy Free (Pousse Café). In a liqueur glass pour in order – ⅓ measure Cherry brandy, ⅓ measure Cointreau, ⅓ measure Apricotine.

Albermarle Fizz (Cktl). 1 fl.oz. dry Gin, 2 dashes raspberry syrup, juice ½ lemon, dash Gomme syrup. Stir over ice, strain into an ice-filled highball, top with soda and 2 cherries. Serve with straws.

Albermarle Thirst Chaser (Cktl). Juice of ½ of orange and lemon, ⅓ of an egg white. Shake over ice, strain into a tumbler, top with lemonade.

Alberndorf (Aus). A wine village in the district of Retz, northern Austria. Produces mainly white wines. Is also known as Europadorf.

Albersweiler (Ger). Village. (Anb) = Rheinpfalz. (Ber) = Südliche Weinstrasse. (Gro) = Königsgarten. (Vins) = Kirchberg, Latt.

Alberta (Can). Small wine producing region.

Alberta Distillery (Can). A distillery noted for its 100% Rye whisky.

Albert Grivault (Fr). A cuvée based in the Premier Cru vineyard of Meursault-Charmes in the A.C. Meursault, Côte de Beaune, Burgundy. Is owned by the Hospices de Beaune. 0.5 ha.

Albig (Ger). Village. (Anb) = Rheinhessen. (Ber) = Nierstein. (Gro) = Petersberg. (Vins) = Homberg, Hundskopf, Schloss Hammerstein.

Albillo (Sp). A white grape variety grown in the central-southern regions of Spain. Also known as the Calgalon.

Albillo Castellano (Sp). See Abillo.

Albion Bitter (Eng). A bitter Ale brewed by Marston's Brewery, Burton-on-Trent, Staffordshire.

Albion Distillery (S.Am). A small Rum distillery based in Guyana. Is owned by the Guyana Distillers. (Government owned).

Albion Keg Mild (Eng). A Mild ale brewed by Marston's Brewery, Burton-on-Trent, Staffordshire.

Albisheim (Ger). Village. (Anb) = Rheinpfalz. (Ber) = Mittelhaardt = Deutsche Weinstrasse. (Gro) = Schnepfenflug vom Zellartal. (Vin) = Heiligenbrom.

Albling (Ger). An alternative name for the Elbling grape.

Albra Brauerei (Fr). The name derived from the merger of 4 breweries taken over by Heineken. Uses Ancre and Mutzig brand-names. Based in Alsace.

Albumen (Eng). A protein found in egg white, blood, etc. (Egg whites and blood are used for fining wines). See also Albumin and Albuminous Protein.

Albumin (Eng). Another spelling of Albumen.

Albuminous Protein (Eng). The protein found in blood and egg white, used to fine wines. The protein reacts with the tannin in the wine, leaving the wine clear. The particles fall to the bottom of the cask by gravitation.

Alc. (Eng)(abbr). Alcohol.

Alcaeus (Gre). A poet who wrote many songs and poems relating to wine and love in Ancient Greece.

Alcamo (It). D.O.C. white wine produced in the commune of Catarratto bianco in Sicily. Grape varieties used are Damaschino, Grecanico and Trebbiano toscano. Area of production is around Alcamo.

Alcanadro (Sp). A Zona de Crianza in the Rioja Baja, north-eastern Spain.

Alcañol (Sp). The alternative name for the Alcanón, Macabeo and Viura grape.

Alcanón (Sp). The alternative name for the Alcañol, Macabeo and Viura grape.

Alcayata (Sp). A black grape variety. Also known as the Monastrell.

Alcazar Amontillado (Sp). The brand-name for an Amontillado sherry produced by Bobadilla in Jerez de la Frontera.

Alcazar Cocktail (Cktl). ¼ gill Canadian Club whisky, ⅙ gill Bénédictine. Stir ingredients over broken ice, strain into a cocktail glass. Decorate with cherry and dash of orange peel juice. (A small dash of Orange bitters may be included.)

Alc. by vol. (Eng)(abbr). Alcohol by volume. 0% (pure water) and 100% (pure alcohol).

Al-Chark Brewery (Arab). A brewery which produces Pilsener-style beers in Syria.

Alchermes (It). Red liqueur made from Rose and Jasmine extract added to nutmeg, cinnamon and coriander distillation.

Alcobaa (Port). A district producing red and white wines from the Ramisco vine. Sited in 'The Ocean' of the river Tejo in the Estremadura region.

Al Cocktail (Cktl). ⅔ measure dry Gin, ⅓ measure Grand Marnier, dash Grenadine, dash lemon juice. Shake well over ice, strain into a cocktail glass. Dress with a lemon peel spiral.

Alcohol (Eng). Alcohol. (Fr) = Alcool. (It) = Alcool. (Hol) = Alcohol. (Port) = Alcohol. (Sp) = Alcohol. (Tur) = Alkol. (Wales) = Alcohol.

Alcohol Content (Eng). The amount of alcohol as a percentage of the total content of the bottle of beer, spirit, wine, etc. Is presented as Gay Lussac, Alc. by vol. or as OIML. See also Sykes Hydrometer, Proof, and U.S. Proof.

Alcohol Destillado de Vino (Sp). A spirit produced in a continuous still from wine. 95% alc. by vol.

Alcohol, [Ethyl] (Eng). C_2H_5OH, Obtained by the action of yeast on sugar during fermentation. Its strength can be further increased by distillation. Harmful only in large quantities.

Alcohol-Free Beer (Eng). Low-alcohol beers brewed for the motorist. Are mainly Lager-style beers. See Barbican, Birrell, Danish Lite, Gerstal, Hunter Ale, Kaliber, St. Christopher Lager, Swan Special Light.

Alcoholfreier Wein (Ger). Alcohol-free wine.

Alcoholic (Eng). A person who depends on alcohol, one who is addicted to alcoholic liquor.

Alcoholicity (Eng). Refers to the strength of an alcoholic liquor.

Alcohólico (Sp). Alcoholic.

Alcoholics Anonymous (Eng). A.A. Group to help alcoholics.

Alcoholic Strength (Eng). The measurement of alcohol by volume in a given quantity of an alcoholic beverage. See Gay Lussac, Sykes Hydrometer, OIML, U.S. Proof and Alcohol Content.

Alcoholic Yoghurt (Ire). A nickname for the cream liqueur Carolans.

Alcoholisation (Eng). Fermentation.

Alcoholisch (Hol). Alcoholic.

Alcoholise (Eng). To turn into an alcoholic liquor. To ferment. See Alcoholize.

Alcoholize (Eng). See Alcoholise.

Alcoholmeter (Eng). A calibrated instrument for measuring alcohol in a liquid.

Alcohol, [Methyl] (Eng). CH_3OH. A wood alcohol, obtained from the distillation of wood sugar by yeast. Is poisonous.

Alcoholometry (Eng). Measuring or calculating alcoholic strengths.

Alcool (Fr). The name given to a Cognac brandy that is over 84% alc. by vol.

Alcool (Fr)(It). Alcohol.

Álcool (Port). Alcohol.

Alcool Blanc (Fr). White alcohol. Defines clear liqueurs that have been matured in glass not wood so that no colour is gained. Usually distilled from fruit.

Alcool Denaturé (W.Ind). The local name used in Mauritius for denaturalised Rum.

Alcoolico (It). Alcoholic.

Alcoolique (Fr). Spirituous.

Alcoolisme (Fr). Alcoholism.

Alcools de Coeur (Fr). A name given to the middle part of the distillation. See Brouillis.

Alcool Vinico (Mad). Denotes brandy distilled from wine.

Alcudia (Cktl). ⅖ measure dry Gin, ⅕ measure Crème de banane, ⅕ measure Galliano, ⅕ measure grapefruit juice. Shake well over ice, strain, add twist of grapefruit peel.

Aldeanueva (Sp). A Zona de Crianza in the Rioja Baja, north-eastern Spain.

Aldehydes (Eng). Flavour elements, the result of alcoholic distillation.

Alderbro (Hun). A wine-producing village in the Debrö region. Noted for its Debroï Hárslevelü.

Alderic (Fr). The name of an A.C. Blanquette de Limoux produced by Producteurs de Blanquette de Limoux.

Aldermoor Vineyard (Eng). A vineyard, 2.5 ha. first planted in 1975. Grape varieties – Müller-Thurgau and Reichensteiner. Address = Poulner Hill, Ringwood, Hampshire.

Alderney Ale (Ch.Isles). A malt-extract brew 1035 O.G. from the Braye Brewery, St. Annes, Alderney.

Aldo Conterno (It). A wine-producer based in Monforte d'Alba (a district of Barolo), Piemonte.

Ale (Eng). An aromatic malt beer flavoured with hops. Types are Bitter Ale, Pale Ale, Brown Ale, India Pale Ale (IPA), Export Ale, Strong Ale, etc.

Aleatico (It). A red grape variety of the Muscat family. Produces sweet dessert red wines. See also Aleatico-Nero.

Aleatico (USA). See California Aleatico.

Aleatico di Gradoli (It). D.O.C. sweet red wine from Latium produced from Aleatico grape.

Aleatico di Gradoli Liquoroso (It). D.O.C. fortified wine made from slightly dried Aleatico grapes with a minimum alc. content of 12% by vol. Fortified to 17.5% by vol. then aged for six months from date of fortification. From Latium.

Aleatico di Portoferraio (It). A sweet, deep-coloured red wine from Elba in Tuscany, Aleatico grape, 14–15% alc. by vol.

Aleatico di Puglia (It). D.O.C. red wine produced from the Aleatico, Negro amaro, Malvasia nero and Primitivo grapes which are partially dried. Two styles – Dolce naturale and Liquoroso dolce naturale (fortified). From Puglia. If graded Riserva then must be aged for 3 years.

Aleatico-Nero (It). See Aleatico.

Aléatiko (USSR). A white grape variety grown in Uzbekistan. Produces white dessert wines.

Aleberry (Punch). Add 2 tablespoons of fine oatmeal to 1 pint Mild ale. Stand for four hours, strain and boil 5 minutes. Add 1 bottle Claret, juice of lemon and grated nutmeg. Serve hot in mugs with thin slices of toast.

Ale Carafe (Eng). Large glass carafes used in the eighteenth century for carrying ale from the cellar to the table of the gentry. Usually of ¼ gallon capacity.

Alec's Angel (Cktl). ¾ liqueur glass of Crème de Cacao, top with fresh cream.

Ale Flip [New Recipe] (Eng). 2 pints Ale, 4 fl.ozs. Brandy, 3 eggs, grated rind of 1 lemon, ½ barspoon ground ginger, 8 ozs brown sugar. Heat rind and ale. Beat rest of ingredients, pour heated ale into egg mixture, blend, return to pan until mix is creamy. Top with grated nutmeg.

Ale Flip [Old Recipe] (Eng). Old ale whisked up with egg yolk and sugar. Serve either hot or cold with grated nutmeg on top.

Alefons Giovanett-Weinkellerei Castelfeder (It). A large winery based in Neumarkt, Südtirol (Alto Adige).

Alegar (Eng). Malt vinegar.

Alegret (José) (Sp). A wine-producer based in Penedés. Address = Calle Sol 22, Vilafranca del Penedés, Barcelona. Produces fine red and white wines.

Ale House (Eng). A sixteenth-century establishment that sells ales only. (A public-house).

Alella (Sp). A Denominación de Origen of the Cataluña region of south eastern Spain. Produces mostly dry white wines.

Alella Cooperative Winery (Sp). A co-operative based in the Alella region. Has 153 members. Produces wines under the Marfil label.

Alemannenbuck (Ger). Vineyard. (Anb) = Baden. (Ber) = Markgräflerland. (Gro) = Lorettoberg. (Vil) = Mengen.

Alembic (Fr). An alternative spelling of Alambic.

Alembic Armagnaçais (Fr). See Alambic Armagnaçais.

Aleno (Sp). The brand-name of a Cream sherry shipped to the U.K. by John Buccleugh of Warrington, Lancashire.

Alenquer (Port). A sub-region of Oeste (western region). Produces red and white wines.

Alentejo (Port). A wine-producing region in southern Portugal. Produces red and white wines.

Ale Posset (Eng). Heat ale (½ pint) and milk (½ pint) with sugar, ginger and nutmeg to taste. Is served hot.

Alep Pine (Gre). See Aleppo Pine.

Aleppo (Arab). A hilly wine-producing region in northern Syria.

Aleppo Pine (Gre). Pine from which the resin is used exclusively for the making of Retsina. Also known as the Alep pine.

Ale Sangaree (Cktl). Dissolve ½ oz. of sugar into 5 fl.ozs. water. Place in a large tumbler, fill up with Ale. Top with grated nutmeg.

Alessano (It). A white grape variety of the Puglia region.

Alexander (Cktl)(1). 2 parts dry Gin, 1 part Crème de Cacao, 1 part double cream. Shake over ice, strain into a cocktail glass.

Alexander (Cktl)(2). ¾ measure Rye whiskey, ¼ measure Bénédictine. Stir over ice, strain into a cocktail glass. Add twist of orange peel on top.

Alexander Baby (Cktl). ⅓ measure Navy rum, ⅓ measure Crème de Cacao, ⅓ measure cream. Shake over ice, strain into a cocktail glass. Top with grated nutmeg.

Alexander Cocktail (Cktl). 1 oz. Brandy, 1 oz. (white) Crème de Cacao, 1 oz. cream. Shake over ice, strain into a cocktail glass. Top with grated nutmeg.

Alexander's Brother (Cktl). ⅓ measure dry Gin, ⅓ measure Crème de Menthe, ⅓ measure cream. Shake over ice, strain into a cocktail glass.

Alexander's Crown (USA). A vineyard based in the Alexander Valley, California. 25 ha. Grape variety – Cabernet sauvignon. Is owned by Sonoma Vineyards.

Alexander's Sister (Cktl) (1). ⅓ measure dry Gin, ⅓ measure (white) Crème de

Menthe, ⅓ measure cream. Shake over ice, strain into a cocktail glass.

Alexander's Sister (Cktl) (2). ⅓ measure Kahlúa, ⅓ measure Cognac, ⅓ measure cream. Shake well over ice, strain into a cocktail glass. Top with grated nutmeg.

Alexander Valley (USA). A small vineyard district of Sonoma County, north of Napa Valley, California.

Alexander Valley Vineyards (USA). A winery based in Alexander Valley, Sonoma County, California. 100 ha. Grape varieties – Cabernet sauvignon, Chardonnay, Chenin blanc, Gewürztraminer, Johannisberg riesling and Pinot noir. Produces varietal wines.

Alexandra Brewery (Eng). A brewery established in 1982 in Brighton, Sussex. Trades under the name of Becket's Bars and Ales. Produces beers and 'Old Snowy' 1054 O.G.

Alexandra Kingsley (Austr). A full-bodied white wine from the Chardonnay grape, has a soft dry finish. Produced by the Red Bank Winery, Victoria, Australia.

Alexandrakis (Afr). A winery based in northern Ethiopia. Produces medium-quality wines.

Alexandre (Serge) (Fr). A Cognac brandy producer. Address = Rue de Cagouillet, 16100 Cognac. Owns vineyards in the Fins Bois. Produces Vieux Cognac from Premier Cru (average age 12 years).

Alexandre d'Almeida (Port). A family-owned winery based near Lameira. Produces fine red, rosé and white wines.

Alexandria (Fr). A name for the Portuguese Moscatel do Setúbal grape.

Alexis Bailly Vineyard (USA). A bonded winery based in Minnesota. 4 ha. Produces hybrid wines.

Alexis Heck Cocktail (Cktl). ⅖ measure Cognac, ⅕ measure Grand Marnier, ⅕ measure golden Rum, ⅕ measure dry Vermouth. Stir over ice, strain into a Champagne saucer.

Ale Yeasts (Eng). Yeasts that stick together so they multiply so that they form a surface on top of the ferment. The ale results from top-fermentation.

Aleyor (Sp). A dark red table wine produced on the island of Mallorca.

Alezio (It). D.O.C. red wine from Salento, Apulia. Made from the Negro Amaro grape.

Alf (Ger). Village. (Anb) = Mosel-Saar-Ruwer. (Ber) = Zell/Mosel. (Gro) = Grafschaft. (Vins) = Arrasburg-Schlossberg, Herrenberg, Hölle, Kapellenberg, Katzenkopf, Kronenberg.

Alfa Brouwerij (Hol). Based in Schinnen, South Limburg. Noted for its

Super Dortmunder 7.5% alc. by vol. (the strongest beer in the Netherlands) and Alfa (an all-malt beer 5% alc. by vol).

Alfaro (Sp). A Zona de Crianza in the Rioja Baja, north-eastern Spain.

Alfie Cocktail (Cktl). 1½ ozs. Lemon vodka, ¼ oz. pineapple juice, dash Triple Sec. Shake over ice, strain into a cocktail glass.

Alfie Cocktail (Cktl) (Non-alc). ⅓ measure lemon juice, ⅓ measure pineapple juice, ⅓ measure orange juice. Shake over ice, strain into cocktail glass. Dress with cube of fresh pineapple.

Alföld (Hun). One of fifteen wine-producing regions situated on the 'Great Plain'.

Alfonso (Cktl). 1 fl.oz. Dubonnet, 1 lump sugar, 2 dashes Angostura. Place sugar in a Champagne glass, shake bitters onto sugar cube. Add Dubonnet, fill a glass with iced Champagne, stir slightly. Add twist of lemon.

Alfonso Maldonado (Sp). A noted wine-producer based in Rueda. See Viña Rebelde.

Alfonso Special (Cktl). ½ measure Grand Marnier, ¼ measure Gin, ¼ measure French vermouth, 2 dashes Italian vermouth, dash Angostura. Stir over ice, strain into a cocktail glass.

Alford Arms (Eng). A home-brew pub in Frithsden, Herts, England. Owned by Whitbreads. Produces Cherrypicker's, Rudolf's Revenge and Strong Amber ales.

Alforra (Port). Mildew.

Algarve (Port). A newly demarcated region. Produces light red wines and dry, white, apéritif wines.

Alger (Alg). One of the three wine-producing regions of Algeria. The main areas within the region are – Ain-Bessem-Bouira, Coteaux du Zaccar and Médéa.

Algeria (Alg). A Mediterranean wine producing country. 3 regions – Constantine, Oran and Alger. Produces mainly red, fat, soft and alcoholic wines 11–15% alc. by vol. Has an even climate, with consistent vintages.

Algonquin Cocktail (Cktl). ½ measure Rye whiskey, ¼ measure French vermouth, ¼ measure pineapple juice. Shake over ice, strain into an ice-filled old-fashioned glass.

Aliança Seco (Port). A dry white wine from Caves Aliana.

Alicante (Sp). A Denominación de Origen wine region of southern Spain. Produces red, rosé and white wines some-times sold under the appellation 'Montana'. Grape varieties – Bobal, Granacha, Monastrell, Moscatel romano and Tintorera.

Alicante (Sp). A red grape variety grown in north-western Spain.

Alicanté Bouschet (USA). A red grape variety producing red and dessert wines. Also known as the Petit bouschet. Has pink juice.

Alicanté Ganzin (USA). Red grape variety, produces dessert wines.

Alicanté Grenache (Afr). A red grape variety, producing full-bodied, soft, alcoholic (14% by vol) wines. Grown in Tunisia.

Alicantina (Sp). Another name for the Grenache grape.

Alice Brewery (Scot). A brewery in Inverness which produces Alice Ale 1040 O.G. Sixty 1060 O.G. Keg-Longman Lager 1040 O.G. and 80/– Export 1040 O.G. (a bottled beer).

Aligate (USSR). A medium dry white wine from the Moldavia region.

Aligoté (Fr). A prolific white grape variety. Used mainly in the Burgundy region, it produces mainly dry, acidic wines. See Kir and Sparkling Burgundy. Also known as the Blanc de Troyes, Chaudenet gras and Giboudot blanc.

Aligoté Ay-Danil (USSR). A dry white wine from the Crimean peninsula.

Aligoté des Hautes-Côtes (Fr). A light, dry, fruity wine from the vineyards of the A.C. Hautes-Côtes in Burgundy.

Alijo (Port). A small wine area in the Douro, north-east of Pinhão.

Alios (Fr). Ironstone soil. (Red sandstone, rich in iron).

Alises (Fr). An Eau-de-Vie produced from sorb-apples in Alsace.

Alize (Fr). A Pastis produced by Pernod-Ricard. 40% alc. by vol.

Aliziergeist (Fr). An Eau-de-Vie (fruit brandy) made from the berries of the wild Service tree. 45% alc. by vol.

Alkaline Water (Eng). Waters (natural spring) that are rich in minerals. Aix-la-Chapelle, Aix-les-Bains, Evian, Malvern, Perrier, Selters, St. Galmier, Vichy.

Alken (Ger). Village. (Anb) = Mosel-Saar-Ruwer. (Ber) = Zell/Mosel. (Gro) = Weinhex. (Vins) = Bleidenberg, Burgberg, Hunnenstein.

Alkermès (Fr). A red-coloured cordial. Dye is obtained from insects found in Mediterranean Kermes oak. Spirit is flavoured with cinnamon, cloves, mace, rose water and sugar. Popular in the eighteenth and nineteenth centuries.

Alkie (Austr) (Eng) (USA). See Alky.
Al Kohl (Arab). Alcohol.
Alkol (Tur). Alcohol.
Alkolik (Tur). Alcoholic.
Alkollü (Tur). Alcoholic liquor.
Alky (Austr) (Eng) (USA) (slang). An alcoholic.
Allandale Winery (Austr). Vineyard. Address = Allandale Road, Pokolbin, via Maitland, New South Wales, 23210. 7 ha. Grape varieties – Chardonnay, Pinot noir and Sémillon.
Allan's Special (Cktl). ½ measure Crème de Banane, 1 measure Gin, ½ measure lemon juice, dash egg white. Shake over ice, strain into a cocktail glass, add dash of Grenadine.
Alla Ruta (It). A green Grappa that has a herb plant in every bottle.
Allas-Champagne (Fr). A commune in the Charente-Maritime Département whose grapes are classed Petite Champagne (Cognac).
Allasch Kümmel (Ger). Style of Kümmel made in Stettin on the Polish-East German border. 41% alc. by vol.
Alla Sua (It). Lit – 'Your health'.
All Black Port (N.Z.). A Port-type wine produced by Mother's Cellar Winery in Henderson, North Island.
Allbright Brewery (Eng). Produces Welsh Brewer's keg Bitter plus Mitchells and Butlers bottled beer 1040 O.G.
Allegheny Cocktail (Cktl). 1 measure Bourbon whiskey, 1 measure French vermouth, ¼ measure lemon juice, ¼ measure Blackberry liqueur. Shake over ice, strain into a cocktail glass, add a twist of lemon peel.
Allegrini (It). A winery based in Verona, north-eastern Italy.
Allegro (Port). A red wine produced in Lafões.
Alleinbesitz (Ger). A wine-producer's monopoly.
Alleluia (Cktl). ½ fl.oz. Maraschino, ½ fl.oz. blue Curaçao, ½ fl.oz. lemon juice, 1½ fl.ozs. Tequila. Shake over ice into an ice-filled highball glass. Top with Bitter lemon and decorate with a slice of lemon, sprig of mint and a cherry.
Allen Cocktail (Cktl). 1 measure dry Gin, ½ measure Maraschino, juice ¼ lemon. Shake over ice, strain into a cocktail glass.
Allerfeinste (Ger). Lit – 'First of all' pre 1971 labelling term found on casks.
Allesverloren Estate (S.Afr). Vineyards based in Swartland. Address = Allesverloren, Riebeeck-Wes 6800. Produces varietal wines.
Allied Breweries (Eng). Ansell's, Ind Coope and Tetley's have five breweries producing a large variety of beers.
Allied-Lyons (Eng). A major company which owns many brand-name beverages both alcoholic and non-alcoholic. These include – Allied Breweries, Grants of St. James's, Showerings, etc.
Allies Cocktail (Cktl). 1 part dry Gin, 1 part French vermouth, 3 dashes Kümmel. Stir over ice, strain into a cocktail glass.
All in Cocktail (Eng). The nickname for a lethal mixture of glass 'slops' left in the bar that is often drunk by alcoholics.
Allmersbach a.W. (Ger). Village. (Anb) = Württemberg. (Ber) = Württembergisch Unterland. (Gro) = Schalkstein. (Vin) = Alter Berg.
All Nations (Eng). A pub which brews its own traditional ale. A light Mild. Address = Coalport road, Madeley (now part of Telford New Town), Shropshire.
All Nippon Bartenders' Association (Jap). A.N.B.A. Japanese Bartenders' Association. Address = Raionzu Mansion Dogenzaka 610, 2–19-3, Dogenzaka, Shibuya-Ku, Tokyo 150, Japan.
Alloa Brewery (Scot). Part of Allied Breweries. Based in Alloa, Clackmannanshire. Amongst its brews are Arrol's 70/- Ale, Diamond Heavy and Skol.
Allobrogia (Fr). A white grape variety grown in Roman times. Noted for its resin flavour.
Allogrogie (Fr). A Vins de Pays area in the Savoie Département in south-eastern France.
Allsach (Ger). A Kümmel flavoured with aniseed, almonds and spices. 40% alc. by vol.
All Saints Winery (Austr). A large winery based at Wahgunyah in north-east Victoria.
Allsopp Brewery (Eng). The revived name for Allied Breweries East Midand East Anglia Co. in 1985.
Allsopps (W.Ind). A Lager beer brewed by the Carib Co. in Trinidad under licence from Allied Breweries of England.
Allsopp's Pilsener (Afr). A Pilsener lager beer 1042 O.G. brewed by the East African Breweries of Tanzania under licence from Allied Breweries in England.
Allt-a-Bhainne (Scot). A new single Malt distillery built in 1974 in Speyside under Ben Rinnes in Banffshire. A

Highland malt whisky 40% alc. by vol. Part of Seagram.

Alluvial (Eng). Rich soil found on river banks. Not suitable for wine grape cultivation because it is too rich. Produces flabby wines.

Allwedd Costrell (Wales). Corkscrew.

All-White Frappé (Cktl). ¼ measure Peppermint schnapps, ¼ measure (white) Crème de Cacao, ¼ measure Anisette, ¼ measure lemon juice. Shake over ice, strain into a cocktail glass with a teaspoon of crushed ice.

Alma (Cktl). ³⁄₁₀ measure Mandarine Napoléon, ³⁄₁₀ measure Vodka, ¹⁄₁₀ measure Campari, ³⁄₁₀ measure grapefruit juice. Shake well over ice, strain into a cocktail glass.

Almacenista (Sp). The name given to a high-quality, old, unblended Sherry. Usually purchased by Aficionados who mature the sherries then sell them back to the shippers.

Almaden (USA). A wine-producing region in central California.

Almaden Vineyards (USA). A large winery based in California. 2,810 ha. Has vineyards in Alameda, Benito and Monterey with 5 wineries. Produces all styles of wines sold under Alamaden and Charles Lefranc labels. Owned by National Distillers.

Almansa (Sp). A Denominación de Origen in the province of Albacete in La Mancha, central Spain. Grape varieties – Aíren, Garnacha negra, Monastrell and Verdril.

Almansa (Sp). A Denominación de Origen wine-producing area in La Mancha, central Spain. Produces heavy styled wines.

Almansar (Sp). A Denominación de Origen of Levante in southern Spain.

Almarla Vineyards (USA). A small winery based in Matherville, Mississippi. Produces wines from French and American hybrid vines.

Almaza Brewery (Leb). A small brewery based in eastern Beirut.

Almeirim (Port). An area which produces red and white wines in the Estremadura region on the plains of the river Tejo.

Almendralejo (Sp). A red grape variety grown in the Estremadura and Léon districts. Produces good red wines.

Almendralejo (Sp). A wine-producing region in Estremadura.

Almeria (Cktl). ⅗ measure dark Rum, ⅖ measure Tia Maria, white of egg. Shake over ice, strain into a cocktail glass.

Almibar (Sp). Invert sugar solution used, mixed with wine, to sweeten pale sherries.

Almíjar (Sp). A yard in Jerez, where the grapes are placed on mats to dry in the sun. See Esparto Grass and Esparto Mats.

Almizcate (Sp). The name for the space between two bodega buildings.

Almog (Isr). A sweet red wine in the style of a Málaga. Produced for the USA market.

Almond Blossom (Cktl). ⅔ measure Perisco, ⅓ measure Cherry brandy. Shake over ice, strain into a cocktail glass. Dress with a cherry.

Almond Brewery (Eng). A former brewery in Wigan. Name revived by the Burtonwood Breweries in 1984. Used for a few pubs plus Almond's Bitter 1036.5 O.G.

Almond Eye Cocktail (Cktl). ⅓ measure Marsala, ⅓ measure Crème de Cacao, ⅓ measure cream. Shake over ice, strain into a cocktail glass.

Almondocato (Cktl). Fill a liqueur glass ⅘ full of Advocaat and top with a dash of Crème de Noyaux.

Almude (Port). A measure of 25 litres used for blending Port wine.

Alofat (Eng). An early English word for Ale. See also Alu and Ealu.

Aloha Coffee Liqueur (Scot). A Whisky-based, coffee liqueur. 29% alc. by vol.

Alois Lageder (It). A noted winery based in Bozen, Südtirol (Alto Adige).

Along the Shelf (Eng). Term used in drinking parties (usually 'Stag parties') where only spirits are consumed. Normally starting from one side of the bar and drinking a measure from each of the bottles 'On Optic' along the shelf.

Aloque (Sp). Red wines of the Valdepeñas region of Spain. Made from the Cencibel grape variety.

Alouchta (USSR). A red Port-style wine produced in the Crimean peninsula.

Aloxe Corton (Fr). An A.C. commune within the Côte de Beaune in Burgundy. Produces fine red and white wines. Vineyards – Grands Crus – Corton plus the name of vineyard – En Paulaud [part], Clos du Roi, La Vigne au Saint, Le Corton, Les Bressandes, Les Charlemagne [part], Les Chaumes [part], Les Combes [part], Les Fietres, Les Grèves, Les Languettes [part], Les Maréchaudes [part], Les Meix [part], Les Meix-Lallemant [part], Les Perrières, Les Pougets [part], Les Renardes, Voirosses. Premiers Crus – En Pauland [part], La Coutière, La Maréchaude, La Toppe-au-Vert, Les Chaillots, Les Fournières, Les Grandes – Lolières, Les Guérets, Les Maréchaudes [part], Les Meix [part] Les Petites-Lolières, Les Valozières [part], Les Vercots. See also vineyards of Ladoix-Serrigny and Château Corton Grancey.

Alpenbräu (Switz). A Bier brewed by the Hürlimann Brauerei in Zürich. Northern Switzerland.

Alpenkraeuter-Likoer (Ger). A liqueur based on Alpine herbs and roots, also with wormwood.

Alpes-Maritimes (Fr). A Département of Provence, south-eastern France. Produces red, rosé and white wines.

Alpha (USA). A red hybrid grape variety. Produces high acidity and can withstand low temperatures.

Alpha Acid (Eng). Found in the hop flower in the Alpha resin. Causes the bitterness in the beer.

Alphen Wines (S.Afr). Wines made by Gilbeys Ltd. with grapes grown by the Bairnsfather-Cloete Estate in Stellenbosch. Are varietal wines.

Alphonse Lavalee (N.Z.). A sweet red wine produced by the Fino Valley Winery in Henderson, North Island.

Alpina (It). See Fior d'Alpi.

Alpine Lager Beer (Can). A local brand of Lager beer produced by the Moosehead Brewery.

Alpine Punch (Punch). 1 bottle Elderberry wine, the peel and juice of 2 oranges, 8 cloves, ½ cinnamon stick. Stand for 2 hours, heat until near boiling, strain and serve with orange slices.

Alquitara (Sp). A pot-stilled spirit at 60%-65% alc. by vol.

Alsace (Fr). A wine region in north-east France. Lies in the foothills of the Vosges mountains between Mulhouse in the south and Strasbourg in the north. Noted for its fine 'Noble grape' dry white wines from the Gewürztraminer, Muscat, Riesling, Sylvaner and Tokay (Pinot). See Vendange Tardive.

Alsace Grand Cru (Fr). New A.C. laws introduced in 1971. Wines must be from named sites and from only the following grapes – Gewürztraminer, Muscat, Pinot Gris (Tokay), Pinot Noir, Riesling, Sylvaner. Min alc. 11% by vol. Passed by a tasting committee. Minimum alc. by vol. for Muscat and Riesling grapes is 10%.

Alsace Grand Vin (Fr). A term used when the wine has a minimum natural alcohol content of 11% by vol. Also called Alsace Réserve.

Alsace Réserve (Fr). See Alsace Grand Vin.

Alsace Willm (Fr). A noted wine-producer based in Alsace. Address = 67140 Barr. 12 ha.

Alsatia (Eng). The mediaeval name for Alsace, France.

Alsenz (Ger). Village. (Anb) = Nahe. (Ber) = Schloss Bockelheim. (Gro) = Paradiesgarten. (Vins) = Elkersberg, Falkenberg, Hölle, Pfaffenpfad.

Alsheim (Ger). Village. (Anb) = Rheinhessen. (Ber) = Nierstein. (Gro) = Krötenbrunnen. (Vin) = Goldberg.

Alsheim (Ger). Village. (Anb) = Rheinhessen. (Ber) = Nierstein. (Gro) = Rheinblick. (Vins) = Fischerpfad, Frühmesse, Römerberg, Sonnenberg.

Alsterwasser (Ger). A 'Hamburg shandy'. Consists of lemonade and Lager beer.

Alt (Ger). Old.

Alta (Can). A Beer brewed by the Carling O'Keefe Brewery, Toronto.

Alta Alella (Sp). A winery based in Alella region. 70 ha. Produces Marqués de Alella (a white wine produced from 60% Pansa and 40% Xarel-lo grapes).

Altarberg (Ger). Vineyard. (Anb) = Mosel-Saar-Ruwer. (Ber) = Zell/Mosel. (Gro) = Goldbäumchen. (Vil) = Ellenz-Poltersdorf.

Altärchen (Ger). Vineyard. (Anb) = Mosel-Saar-Ruwer. (Ber) = Bernkastel. (Gro) = Michelsberg. (Vil) = Trittenheim.

Altar Wine (Eng). Fermented juice of fresh grapes used for sacramental purposes.

Altavilla (Afr). A winery based in northern Ethiopia. Produces average table wines.

Alta Vineyard (USA). A small winery based in the Napa Valley, California. 3 ha. Grape variety – Chardonnay.

Altbier (Ger). A locally consumed over-fermented Bier of Dusseldorf. Equivalent of an English Ale 4.3–5% alc. by vol. and has a strong hop flavour. Name derives from old style of brewing. i.e. Top fermentation as opposed to lager which is bottom fermented.

Altdorf (Ger). Village. (Anb) = Baden. (Ber) = Breisgau. (Gro) = Burg Lichteneck. (Vin) = Kaiserberg.

Altdorf (Ger). Village. (Anb) = Rheinpflz. (Ber) = Südliche Weinstrasse. (Gro) = Trappenberg. (Vins) = Gottesacker, Hochgericht.

Altdörr (Ger). Vineyard. (Anb) = Rheinhessen. (Ber) = Nierstein. (Gro) = Gutes Domtal. (Vil) = Dalheim.

Altdörr (Ger). Vineyard. (Anb) = Rheinhessen. (Ber) = Nierstein. (Gro) = Gutes Domtal. (Vil) = Friesenheim.

Alte Burg (Ger). Vineyard. (Anb) = Baden. (Ber) = Breisgau. (Gro) = Burg Lichteneck. (Vil) = Mundingen.

Alte Burg (Ger). Vineyard. (Anb) = Baden. (Ber) = Breisgau. (Gro) = Burg Lichteneck. (Vil) = Köndringen.

Alte Burg (Ger). Vineyard. (Anb) = Hessiche Bergstrasse. (Ber) = Starkenberg. (Gro) = Rott. (Vil) = Zwingenberg.

Alteburg (Ger). Vineyard. (Anb) = Nahe. (Ber) = Kreuznach. (Gro) = Schlosskapelle. (Vil) = Waldlaubersheim.

Alte Ernte (Ger). A Kornbranntwein produced by Schlichte.

Alte Lay (Ger). Vineyard. (Anb) = Ahr. (Ber) = Walporzheim/Ahrtal. (Gro) = Klosterberg. (Vil) = Walporzheim.

Altenahr (Ger). Village. (Anb) = Ahr. (Ber) = Walporzheim/Ahrtal. (Gro) = Klosterberg. (Vins) = Eck, Übigberg.

Altenbamberg (Ger). Village. (Anb) = Nahe. (Ber) = Schloss Böckelheim. (Gro) = Burgweg. (Vins) = Kehrenberg, Laurentiusberg, Rotenberg, Schlossberg, Treuenfels.

Altenberg (Ger). Lit – 'Old hill'. Common vineyard name used in the German regions. There are 38 individual vineyard sites with the name in Germany.

Altenberg (Ger). Vineyard. (Anb) = Baden. (Ber) = Badische Bergstrasse/Kraichgau. (Gro) = Mannaberg. (Vil) = Heidelsheim.

Altenberg (Ger). Vineyard. (Anb) = Baden. (Ber) = Badische Frankenland. (Gro) = Tauberklinge. (Vil) = Lauda.

Altenberg (Ger). Vineyard. (Anb) = Baden. (Ber) = Badische Frankenland. (Gro) = Tauberklinge. (Vil) = Oberlauda.

Altenberg (Ger). Vineyard. (Anb) = Baden. (Ber) = Badische Frankenland. (Gro) = Tauberklinge. (Vil) = Oberschüpf.

Altenberg (Ger). Vineyard. (Anb) = Baden. (Ber) = Markgräflerland. (Gro) = Burg Neuenfels. (Vil) = Ballrechten-Dottingen.

Altenberg (Ger). Vineyard. (Anb) = Baden. (Ber) = Markgräflerland. (Gro) = Burg Neuenfels. (Vil) = Britzingen.

Altenberg (Ger). Vineyard. (Anb) = Baden. (Ber) = Markgräflerland. (Gro) = Burg Neuenfels. (Vil) = Britzingen (ortsteil-Dattingen).

Altenberg (Ger). Vineyard. (Anb) = Baden. (Ber) = Markgräflerland. (Gro) = Burg Neuenfels. (Vil) = Laufen.

Altenberg (Ger). Vineyard. (Anb) = Baden. (Ber) = Markgräflerland. (Gro) = Burg Neuenfels. (Vil) = Sulzburg.

Altenberg (Ger). Vineyard. (Anb) = Baden. (Ber) = Markgräflerland. (Gro) = Lorettoberg. (Vil) = Grunern.

Altenberg (Ger). Vineyard. (Anb) = Baden. (Ber) = Ortenau. (Gro) = Schloss Rodeck. (Vil) = Neuweier.

Altenberg (Ger). Vineyard. (Anb) = Franken. (Ber) = Steigerwald. (Gro) = Schild. (Vil) = Abtswind.

Altenberg (Ger). Vineyard. (Anb) = Franken. (Ber) = Steigerwald. (Gro) = Schlosstück. (Vil) = Ergersheim.

Altenberg (Ger). Vineyard. (Anb) = Mosel-Saar-Ruwer. (Ber) = Obermosel. (Gro) = Gipfel. (Vil) = Wellen.

Altenberg (Ger). Vineyard. (Anb) = Mosel-Saar-Ruwer. (Ber) = Saar-Ruwer. (Gro) = Römerlay. (Vil) = Trier.

Altenberg (Ger). Vineyard. (Anb) = Mosel-Saar-Ruwer. (Ber) = Saar-Ruwer. (Gro) = Scharzberg. (Vil) = Filzen.

Altenberg (Ger). Vineyard. (Anb) = Mosel-Saar-Ruwer. (Ber) = Saar-Ruwer. (Gro) = Scharzberg. (Vil) = Hamm.

Altenberg (Ger). Vineyard. (Anb) = Mosel-Saar-Ruwer. (Ber) = Saar-Ruwer. (Gro) = Scharzberg. (Vil) = Kanzem.

Altenberg (Ger). Vineyard. (Anb) = Mosel-Saar-Ruwer. (Ber) = Saar-Ruwer. (Gro) = Scharzberg. (Vil) = Mennig.

Altenberg (Ger). Vineyard. (Anb) = Mosel-Saar-Ruwer. (Ber) = Saar-Ruwer. (Gro) = Scharzberg. (Vil) = Oberemmel.

Altenberg (Ger). Vineyard. (Anb) = Nahe. (Ber) = Schloss Böckelheim. (Gro) = Paradiesgarten. (Vil) = Meddersheim.

Altenberg (Ger). Vineyard. (Anb) = Rheinhessen. (Ber) = Nierstein. (Gro) = Krötenbrunnen. (Vil) = Hillesheim.

Altenberg (Ger). Vineyard. (Anb) = Rheinpfalz. (Ber) = Mittelhaardt-Deutsche Weinstrasse. (Gro) = Mariengarten. (Vil) = Wachenheim.

Altenberg (Ger). Vineyard. (Anb) = Rheinpfalz. (Ber) = Mittelhaardt-Deutsche Weinstrasse. (Gro) = Rosenbühl. (Vil) = Weisenheim/Sand.

Altenberg (Ger). Vineyard. (Anb) = Rheinpfalz. (Ber) = Südliche Weinstrasse. (Gro) = Kloster Liebfrauenberg. (Vil) = Bad Bergzabern.

Altenberg (Ger). Vineyard. (Anb) = Württemberg. (Ber) = Kocher-Jagst-Tauber. (Gro) = Kocherberg. (Vil) = Dörzbach.

A

Altenberg (Ger). Vineyard. (Anb) = Württemberg. (Ber) = Kocher-Jagst-Tauber. (Gro) = Kocherberg. (Vil) = Weissbach.

Altenberg (Ger). Vineyard. (Anb) = Württemberg. (Ber) = Remstal-Stuttgart. (Gro) = Sonnenbühl. (Vil) = Weinstadt (ortsteil Strümpfelbach).

Altenberg (Ger). Vineyard. (Anb) = Württemberg. (Ber) = Remstal-Stuttgart. (Gro) = Wartbühl. (Vil) = Beutelsbach.

Altenberg (Ger). Vineyard. (Anb) = Württemberg. (Ber) = Remstal-Stuttgart. (Gro) = Wartbühl. (Vil) = Schnait i.R.

Altenberg (Ger). Vineyard. (Anb) = Württemberg. (Ber) = Remstal-Stuttgart. (Gro) = Weinsteige. (Vil) = Stuttgart (ortsteil Untertürkheim).

Altenberg (Ger). Vineyard. (Anb) = Württemberg. (Ber) = Württembergisch Unterland. (Gro) = Heuchelberg. (Vil) = Stockheim.

Altenberg (Ger). Vineyard. (Anb) = Württemberg. (Ber) = Württembergisch Unterland. (Gro) = Kirchenweinberg. (Vil) = Flein.

Altenberg (Ger). Vineyard. (Anb) = Württemberg. (Ber) = Württembergisch Unterland. (Gro) = Kirchenweinberg. (Vil) = Heilbronn.

Altenberg (Ger). Vineyard. (Anb) = Württemberg. (Ber) = Württembergisch Unterland. (Gro) = Salzberg. (Vil) = Ellhofen.

Altenberg (Ger). Vineyard. (Anb) = Württemberg. (Ber) = Württembergisch Unterland. (Gro) = Salzberg. (Vil) = Löwenstein.

Altenberg (Ger). Vineyard. (Anb) = Württemberg. (Ber) = Württembergisch Unterland. (Gro) = Salzberg. (Vil) = Sülzbach.

Altenberg (Ger). Vineyard. (Anb) = Württemberg. (Ber) = Württembergisch Unterland. (Gro) = Salzberg. (Vil) = Wimmental.

Altendorf Pilsener (Eng). A Pilsener lager beer 1034 O.G. brewed by the Watney Mann Brewery in London. Sold in cans.

Altenforst (Ger). Vineyard. (Anb) = Rheinpfalz. (Ber) = Südliche Weinstrasse. (Gro) = Bischofskreuz. (Vil) = Burrweiler.

Altenmünster (Ger). A strong Lager beer sold in a clamp-stoppered bottle.

Alter Berg (Ger). Vineyard. (Anb) = Franken. (Ber) = Maindreieck. (Gro) = Not yet assigned. (Vil) = Lengfurt.

Alter Berg (Ger). Vineyard. (Anb) = Rheinpfalz. (Ber) = Südliche Wein-

strasse. (Gro) = Trappenberg. (Vil) = Römerberg.

Alter Berg (Ger). Vineyard. (Anb) = Württemberg. (Ber) = Württembergisch Unterland. (Gro) = Schalkstein. (Vil) = Allmersbach a.W.

Alter Gott (Ger). Vineyard. (Anb) = Baden. (Ber) = Ortenau. (Gro) = Schloss Rodeck. (Vil) = Achern (ortsteil Oberachem).

Alter Gott (Ger). Vineyard. (Anb) = Baden. (Ber) = Ortenau. (Gro) = Schloss Rodeck. (Vil) = Lauf.

Alter Gott (Ger). Vineyard. (Anb) = Baden. (Ber) = Ortenau. (Gro) = Schloss Rodeck. (Vil) = Obersasbach.

Alter Gott (Ger). Vineyard. (Anb) = Baden. (Ber) = Ortenau. (Gro) = Schloss Rodeck. (Vil) = Sasbachwalden.

Alternative Wines (Eng). Wines sold instead of the well-known 'Great Wines'. e.g. Wines from the Côtes de Blaye and Côtes de Bourg instead of the Haut-Médoc.

Alte Römerstrasse (Ger). Vineyard. (Anb) = Nahe. (Ber) = Schloss Böckelheim. (Gro) = Rosengarten. (Vil) = Mandel.

Alte Römerstrasse (Ger). Vineyard. (Anb) = Rheinhessen. (Ber) = Bingen. (Gro) = Rheingrafenstein. (Vil) = Volxheim.

Altes Löhl (Ger). Vineyard. (Anb) = Rheinpfalz. (Ber) = Südliche Weinstrasse. (Gro) = Königsgarten. (Vil) = Landau.

Altesse (Fr). White grape variety grown in the Bugey and Seyssel regions of eastern France. Also known as the Roussette.

Althälde (Ger). Vineyard. (Anb) = Württemberg. (Ber) = Württembergisch Unterland. (Gro) = Salzberg. (Vil) = Ellhofen.

Althälde (Ger). Vineyard. (Anb) = Württemberg. (Ber) = Württembergisch Unterland. (Gro) = Salzberg. (Vil) = Lehreusteinsfeld.

Althälde (Ger). Vineyard. (Anb) = Württemberg. (Ber) = Württembergisch Unterland. (Gro) = Salzberg. (Vil) = Weinsberg.

Althof (Ger). Vineyard. (Anb) = Baden. (Ber) = Ortenau. (Gro) = Schloss Rodeck. (Vil) = Ottersweier.

Alt-Höflein (Aus). A wine village in the Falkenstein-Matzen district of northeastern Austria. Produces mainly white wines.

Al Tiempo (Mex). At room temperature.

Altise (Eng). A beetle pest that feeds on the vine leaves leaving them looking like lace. Treated by spraying with insecticide.

Altl (Aus). Denotes a taste of age in

wines.

Altlichtenwarth (Aus). A wine village in the Falkenstein-Matzen district of north-eastern Austria. Produces mainly white wines.

Altmannsdorf (Ger). Village. (Anb) = Franken. (Ber) = Steigerwald. (Gro) = Not yet assigned. (Vin) = Sonnenwinkel.

Alto (S.Afr). A red wine estate in the region of Stellenbosch.

Alto Adige (It). A part of the region of Trentino-Alto Adige. Also known as the Südtirol (South Tyrol).

Alto Adige Cabernet (It). D.O.C. red wine from the Cabernet grape produced in the Trentino-Alto Adige region. If aged for 2 years then can be called Riserva.

Alto Adige Lagrein Rosato (It). D.O.C. ruby red and rosé wine from the Trentino-Alto Adige. Made from the Lagrein kretzer grape. If produced from grapes from the Bolzano then entitled to the additional specification Lagreindi Gries.

Alto Adige Lagrein Scuro (It). D.O.C. red wine from the Trentino-Alto Adige. Made from the Lagrein dunkel (also known as the Lagrein Scuro) grape. If aged for 2 years then called Riserva. If grapes grown in Bolzano commune then entitled to the additional specification of Lagrein di Gries.

Alto Adige Malvasia (It). D.O.C. red wine from the Trentino-Alto Adige. Made from the the Malvasier (Malvasia) grape.

Alto Adige Merlot (It). D.O.C. red wine from the Trentino-Alto Adige. Made from the Merlot grape. If aged minimum 2 years then classed Riserva.

Alto Adige Moscato Giallo (It). D.O.C. white wine from the Trentino-Alto Adige. Made from the Golden muskateller (Moscato giallo) grape.

Alto Adige Moscato Rosa (It). D.O.C. rosé wine from the Trentino-Alto Adige. Made from the Rosenmuskateller (Moscato rosa) grape.

Alto Adige Pinot Bianco (It). D.O.C. white wine from the Trentino-Alto Adige. Made from the Weissburgunder (Pinot bianco) grape. D.O.C. also applies to sparkling wines.

Alto Adige Pinot Grigio (It). D.O.C. white wine from the Trentino-Alto Adige. Made from the Ruländer (Pinot grigio) grape. D.O.C. also applies to sparkling wines.

Alto Adige Pinot Nero (It). D.O.C. red wine from the Trentino-Alto Adige. Made from the Blauburgunder (Pinot nero) grape. If aged 1 year minimum then classed Riserva. D.O.C. also applies to sparkling wines.

Alto Adige Riesling Italico (It). D.O.C. white wine from the Trentino-Alto Adige. Made from the Welschriesling (Riesling italico) grape.

Alto Adige Riesling Renano (It). D.O.C. white wine from the Trentino-Alto Adige. Made from the Rheinriesling (Riesling renano) grape.

Alto Adige Riesling x Sylvaner (It). D.O.C. white wine from the Trentino-Alto Adige. Made from the Müller-Thurgau (Riesling x Sylvaner) grape.

Alto Adige Sauvignon (It). D.O.C. white wine from the Trentino-Alto Adige. Made from the Sauvignon grape.

Alto Adige Schiave (It). D.O.C. red wine from the Trentino-Alto Adige. Made from the Vernatschs (Schiave) grape.

Alto Adige Sylvaner (It). D.O.C. white wine from the Trentino-Alto Adige. Made from the Sylvaner grape.

Alto Adige Traminer Aromatico (It). D.O.C. white wine from the Trentino-Alto Adige. Made from the Gewürztraminer (Traminer aromatico) grape.

Alto Corgo (Port). Part of the Upper Douro where Port originates from.

Alto Couro (Port). Part of the Upper Douro where Port originates from.

Alt Oder Firn (Ger). A term used to describe a wine that has lost its freshness.

Alto Douro (Port). Upper valley of river Douro. Vineyards produce the only wine entitled to use the name Port.

Alto Estate (S.Afr). A vineyard based in Stellenbosch. Address = Alto Wynlandgoed, Box 184, Stellenbosch 7600. Produces varietal wines.

Alto Predicato (It). The generic name for both red and white wines produced from vineyards in the Chianti Classico zone.

Alto Wynlandgoed (S.Afr). See Alto Estate.

Altrheingauer Landwein (Ger). One of the 15 Deutsche Tafelwein zones.

Altschweier (Ger). Village. (Anb) = Baden. (Ber) = Ortenau. (Gro) = Schloss Rodeck. (Vin) = Sterenberg.

Altus (USA). A wine-producing area. The wineries of Mount Bethel, Post Sax and Wiederkehr are based there.

Altydgedacht Estate (S.Afr). Vineyard based in Durbanville. Address = P.O. Durbanville 7550. Produces varietal wines.

Alu (Eng). The mediaeval word for Ale (non-hopped beer).

Aluntinum (Lat). A red wine produced in Roman times in Sicily.

Alupka (USSR). A grape (red and white) variety grown in the Crimea. Produces Port-style wines.

Alupka (USSR). A pink dessert wine from the southern Crimea.

Alushita (USSR). A dry red wine from the Crimean peninsula.

Alushta (USSR). The alternative spelling of Alushita.

Alva (Port). A white grape variety grown in Beiras.

Alvarelhão (Port). A red grape variety used in the Dão region. Also called the Pilongo.

Alvarez Camp y Co (W.Ind). One of the main Rum producers in Cuba. Now state owned.

Alvarez y Díez (Sp). A noted winery based in Nava del Rey, Valladolid, north-western Spain.

Alvarinho (Port). A white grape variety used for making Vinhos Verdes. Only variety allowed to be used in Monção region.

Alvarinho Cepa Velha (Port). One of the best Vinhos Verdes. See Vinhos de Monção da and Adega Cooperativa Regional de Monção.

Alvear (Arg). The brand-name of a sparkling wine.

Alvear (Sp). A Brandy and wine producer in Montilla-Moriles.

Alvear Palace (Cktl). ⅝ measure Vodka, ⅛ measure Apricot brandy, ¼ measure pineapple juice. Shake over ice, strain into a cocktail glass.

Alves (João Camillo) Lda (Port). A wine producer based in Bucelas. Noted producer of Bucelas wine.

Alzey (Ger). Village. (Anb) = Rheinhessen. (Ber) = Wonnegau. (Gro) = Sybillenstein. (Vins) = Kapellenberg, Pfaffenhalde, Römerberg, Rotenfels, Wartberg.

Alzeyer Scheurebe (Ger). A white grape variety used mainly in the Rheinhessen.

a/M. (USA) (abbr). am Moselle. Found on a Moselle (Mosel) bottle label.

Amabile (It). Medium sweet.

Amabile Beone (Cktl). ⅔ measure (green) Crème de Menthe, ½ measure Drambuie, dash Pernod, 2 dashes Gomme syrup. Shake over ice, strain into a sugar-rimmed (Pernod) cocktail glass.

Amadé (S.Afr). A red wine from the Welgemeend Estate. Blended from Grenache, Pinotage and Shiraz grapes.

Amadeo I (Sp). A V.S.O.P. Brandy produced by Campeny in Barcelona.

Amador (USA). A north Californian county, uses mainly Zinfandel grapes.

Amalgamated Distilled Products (Scot).

The drinks division of the Argyll Group. Produce a wide range of Whiskies including Burberry's, Glen Scotia, Littlemill, Royal Culrose and Scotia Royale.

Amalia (It). A producer of sparkling wines (made by the cuve close method) based in Emilia-Romagna region.

Amalienstein (S.Afr). Vineyard based in the Ladismith area. Address = Box 70 Ladismith 6885. Grapes are vinified in the local co-operative.

Amance (Marcel) (Fr). A Burgundy négociant based at Santenay. An associate company of Prosper Maufoux q.v.

Amanda (Gre). A Dutch cream and Metaxa brandy-based liqueur produced by Metaxa. 17.5% alc. by vol.

Amandi (Sp). A wine-producing area based in Galicia. Produces red and white wines.

Amandiers (Les) (Fr). A vineyard of Dopff & Irion in Alsace. Named because of the almond trees that grow in the vineyard. Produces Muscat wines.

Amanzanillado (Sp). A style of aged Manzanilla sherry from Sanlúcar.

Amara (S.Am). See Amargo.

Amarante (Port). Wine region of the Entre Minho e Douro district. Produces both red and white pétillant wines.

Amarela (Port). A red grape variety grown in the Upper Douro district to produce Barca Velha.

Amaretto Coffee (Liq.Coffee). See Café Amaretto.

Amaretto Comforter (Cktl). ½ measure Amaretto, ½ measure Southern Comfort. Shake well together over ice, strain into a small wine goblet, float 1 fl.oz. whipped cream on top. Sprinkle with grated chocolate.

Amaretto di Amore (It). A well-known brand of Amaretto.

Amaretto di Saronno (It). A bitter, almond-flavoured liqueur with an Apricot brandy base. 28% alc. by vol.

Amaretto Florio (It). A bitter-sweet Sicilian almond liqueur produced near Trapini. 26% alc. by vol.

Amaretto Heartwarmer (Cktl). ½ measure Southern Comfort, ¼ measure French vermouth, ¼ measure Amaretto, 2 blanched almonds, 1 crushed peach stone, 2 dashes Gomme syrup. Warm the Southern Comfort, add nuts and syrup, stir and cool. Add Amaretto, stir, strain into an ice-filled old-fashioned glass.

Amaretto Sour (Cktl). 2 measures Amaretto di Saronno, 1 measure lemon juice. Stir with ice, strain over ice in an old-fashioned glass.

Amargo (Port) (Sp). Bitter, bitterness.
Amargo (S.Am). A style of apéritif produced in Uruguay. Is also known as Amara.
Amarit (E.Asia). A Lager beer brewed by the Thai Amarit Brewery in Bangkok, Thailand.
Amarit Brewery (E.Asia). A Brewery based in Bangkok noted for its beer of same name and Krating.
Amaro (It). Bitter. Used to describe very dry wines.
Amaro (It). Dark brown Bitters made from tree barks, herbs and other botanicals either with or without alcohol.
Amaro Cora (It). An Italian bitter apéritif.
Amarone (It). Bitter or very dry.
Amarone Della Valpolicella (It). A dry red table wine from Verona. Made from Reciotto grapes, 14–15% alc. by vol. See Reciotto.
Amaro Ramazzotti (It). A bitter apéritif wine produced in Milan. 30% alc. by vol.
Amarula (S.Afr). A fruit liqueur produced by Southern Liqueur Co. from the fruit of the Marula tree.
Amateur Winemaker (Eng). A monthly magazine produced for amateur winemakers.
Amathus (Cyp). The brand-name used by Loel of Limassol for a range of their wines.
Amatitan (Mex). The brand-name of a popular Tequila.
Amazens (Port). A name for the wine lodges in Vila Nova de Gaia.
A.M.B. (Mex) (abbr). Asociacións Mexicana de Barmen. Mexican Bartenders' Association. Address = 28,2 Piso, Mexico 1,D.F.
A.M.B.A. (Arg) (abbr). Association Mutual de Barman y Afines. Argentinian Bartenders' Association. Address = Avenue Juan de Garay 1927, Buenos Aires.
Ambassadeur (Fr). The brand-name of an aromatised wine flavoured with quinine and orange peel. 16% alc. by vol.
Ambassador (Cktl). ⅕ gill Tequila, juice of an orange, 2 dashes Gomme syrup. Stir over ice, strain into an ice-filled old-fashioned glass. Top with a slice of orange.
Ambassador (USA). The brand-name used by the Perelli-Minetti Winery in California for a range of their wines.
Ambelakia (Gre). A dry red table wine produced in eastern Greece.
Amber (Wales). A bottled Ale 1033 O.G. brewed by Crown Brewery Mid-

Glamorgan.
Amber (Eng). A bottled beer 1033 O.G. brewed by Newcastle Breweries in Newcastle, Tyne and Wear.
Amber (Eng). A keg Ale 1033 O.G. brewed by Whitbread Brewery.
Amber (Eng). A term used as a description for the colour of old (especially sweet) white wines.
Amber (USSR). A Beer at 19° brewed by the Yantar Brewery. Matured for 82 days.
Amber Dry (Eng). The brand-name for Clairette du Languedoc sold in the U.K.
Amber Fizz (Punch). ¾ pint dry Cider, ⅓ pint soda water, ⅕ pint Cognac, ⅙ pint Cointreau. Mix together. Chill well in a refrigerator. Serve in punch cups with apple slices.
Amber Gold (Fr). 3–4 year old *** Cognac from unblended, Estate-bottled, premier Fins Bois. Produced by Roullet et Fils.
Amber Green Cocktail (Cktl). ⅔ measure dry Gin, ⅓ measure sweet Vermouth, 2 dashes Yellow Chartreuse, dash Angostura. Shake over ice, strain into a cocktail glass.
Amber Malt (Eng). Malted barley added to the kiln and cooled slowly to obtain required colour.
Amber Moon (Cktl). Tabasco, raw egg, Whisky, blended together. Used as a 'Pick me up'.
Amber Road (Euro). The name given to the old Roman trade route from Italy to northern Europe. Was the main wine route from Italy to the Roman legions.
Amberton (Austr). Vineyard. Address = Henry Lawson Drive, Mudgee, New South Wales 2850. 24 ha. Grape varieties – Cabernet sauvignon, Chardonnay, Rhine riesling, Sauvignon blanc, Sémillon, Shiraz and Traminer.
Ambix (Gre). Cup.
Ambleville (Fr). A commune in the Charente Département whose grapes are classed Grande Champagne (Cognac).
Amboina Exotica (Cktl). 1 fl.oz. Pisang Ambon Henkes, 1 fl.oz. Gin, 1 fl.oz. lemon juice. Build into an ice-filled highball glass. Top up with apricot-orange drink.
Amboise (Fr). A commune in the Touraine district of the Loire. Allowed to use its name in the Touraine A.C.
Ambonnay (Fr). A Grand Cru Champagne village in the Canton d'Ay. District = Reims.
Amboss Lager (Eng). A keg Lager 1036 O.G. brewed by Hydes Brewery in

Manchester.

Ambra (It). A style of Marsala from Sicily. See also Oro and Rubino.

Ambrosette (Port). A 30 y.o. Tawny Port from the Sandeman Port shippers.

Ambrosia (Cyp). A red wine produced by the Keo Co. in Limassol.

Ambrosia (Eng). Lit – 'Food of the Gods'. Used to describe sweet drinks.

Ambrosia Cocktail (Cktl). ½ measure Calvados, ½ measure Brandy, juice of a small lemon, dash Triple Sec. Shake over ice, strain into an ice-filled highball glass. Top with iced Champagne.

AMCAF (Afr) (abbr). African and Malagasy Coffee Organisation.

Ameis (Aus). A wine village in the Falkenstein-Matzen district of north-eastern Austria. Produces mainly white wines.

Ameisenberg (Ger). Vineyard. (Anb) = Mittelrhein. (Ber) = Rheinburgengau. (Gro) = Burg Rheinfels. (Vil) = St. Goar-Werlau.

Améléon (Fr). A style of Cider (Scrumpy) from the Normandy region.

Amelioration (Eng). A name given to any treatment grape must has before fermentation (e.g. Chaptalisation, SO_2, etc.) which will improve the quality of the finished wine.

Améliorer (Fr). To improve by the addition of must or sugar before fermentation.

Amer (Fr). Bitters. Lit – 'Bitter'.

Amer Campari (It). A bitter liqueur produced by the Campari Co.

Amer. Gal. (USA) (abbr). American Gallon.

America (USA). A large wine producing country in the northern hemisphere. Has two distinct regions – the east coast which produces wines made from native grape species and the west coast where European grapes are used. Also has other small wine producing regions.

American Absinthe (Cktl). ½ gill Pernod, 1½ gills water, dash Gum syrup to taste. Shake over ice, strain. Soda water may be added.

American Aloe (USA). Name for Mezcal Cacti. See also Century Plant and Agave Cactus.

American Beauty (Cktl). ⅓ measure Brandy, ⅓ measure French vermouth, ⅓ measure orange juice, 2 dashes (white) Crème de Menthe. Shake over ice, strain into an old-fashioned glass. Float ½ fl.oz. Port on top.

American Beauty Cocktail (Cktl). ¼ measure dry Vermouth, ¼ measure Brandy, ¼ measure Grenadine, ¼

measure orange juice, dash (white) Crème de Menthe, Port wine. Shake all together except Port wine. Strain into 5 oz. goblet, top with Port wine.

American Beauty Special (Cktl). ⅓ measure Cognac, ⅓ measure Cointreau, ⅓ measure golden Rum. Shake over ice, strain into a Champagne saucer. Dress with a twist of lemon peel juice.

American Blended Light Whiskey (USA). A new category of Whiskey consisting of less than 20% of Straight whiskies at 100° U.S. Proof (50% alc. by vol) and more than 80% of American Light whiskey.

American Blight (USA). See Apple Blight.

American Coffee (USA). The coffee-producing region between Mexico and Uruguay. Most coffee produced is used for blending and includes both Arabica and Robustas.

American Cream Ale (USA). An Ale 4.75% alc. by vol. brewed by the Genesee Brewery in Rochester, New York.

American Distilling Company Inc (USA). A major Bourbon whiskey distillery based in Pekin, Illinois. Produces Bourbon Supreme 40% alc. by vol.

American Fizz (Cktl). ⅓ measure Gin, ⅓ measure Brandy, ⅓ measure lemon juice, dash Grenadine, dash Gomme syrup. Shake well over ice, strain into an ice-filled collins glass. Dress with a slice of lemon.

American Flyer Cocktail (Cktl). ⅓ gill white Rum, juice of a lime, ½ teaspoon sugar. Shake well over ice, strain into a Champagne flute. Top with iced Champagne.

American Gallon (USA). 128 American fl.ozs. 1 American fl.oz. = 0.960 U.K. fl.oz. 1 U.K. fl.oz. = 1.0416 American fl.ozs.

American Glory (Cktl). Place the juice of ½ an orange in a tumbler, add 2 ice cubes, fill with equal parts of Champagne and soda water. Stir and serve.

American Grog (Cktl). 1½ fl.ozs. dark Rum, ¼ fl.oz. lemon juice, cube of sugar. Place all into a warmed goblet, top with very hot water, stir.

American Legion Margarita (Cktl). ½ measure Tequila, ⅙ measure Cointreau, ⅙ measure lime juice, ⅙ measure lemon juice. Shake over ice, strain into a salt-rimmed (lime juice) cocktail glass.

American Lemonade (USA). Lemon squash with ¼ gill of Port wine poured on top.

American Light Whiskey (USA). See Light Whiskey.

American Market (Mad). The old-style

name used for Rainwater Madeira.

American Oak (USA). Wood used in the making of wine and spirit casks. Mainly from the forests in Kentucky and Ohio. Imparts sharp, dry flavours into the wines.

Americano (The) (Ckl). Place 1 measure of Italian vermouth into an ice-filled highball glass. Top with soda water and a twist of lemon peel juice.

Americano Cocktail (Cktl). 1 jigger Campari, 1 jigger sweet Vermouth. Pour over ice into a highball glass, fill with soda and add a twist of lemon.

American Rose Cocktail (Cktl). 1 measure Cognac, dash Grenadine, dash Pernod. Shake well over ice, strain into a balloon glass. Top with iced Champagne and a cherry.

American Vodka (USA). A style of spirit that is totally neutral in taste. 40% alc. by vol.

Amer Picon (Fr). Orange and Gentian bitters. A bitter tasting apéritif. 21% alc. by vol.

Amer Picon Cocktail (Cktl) (1). 1½ ozs. Amer Picon, teaspoon Grenadine, juice of a lime. Shake over ice, strain into a cocktail glass.

Amer Picon Cocktail (Cktl) (2). ½ measure Amer Picon, ½ measure Italian vermouth. Shake over ice, strain into a well-chilled cocktail glass.

Amer Picon Cooler (Cktl). ⅗ measure Amer Picon, ⅖ measure dry Gin, dash Gomme syrup, dash lemon juice. Shake over ice, strain into an ice-filled highball glass. Top with soda water.

Amer Picon Highball (Cktl). ⅔ measure Amer Picon, ⅓ measure Grenadine. Stir over ice, strain into an ice-filled collins glass. Top with soda water.

Amertume (Fr). Bitterness in wine when it throws a deposit and turns acid. See also Mannitol.

Amery Vineyards (Austr). Address = McLaren Vale, South Australia. 5171. 25 ha. Grape varieties – Cabernet sauvignon, Muscat à petit grain blanc, Pinot noir, Riesling, Shiraz and Traminer.

Amethustos (Gre). Sober, not intoxicated.

Am Gaisberg (Ger). Vineyard. (Anb) = Rheinpfalz. (Ber) = Südliche Weinstrasse. (Gro) = Herrlich. (Vil) = Herxheimweyher.

Am Heiligen Häuschen (Ger). Vineyard. (Anb) = Rheinhessen. (Ber) = Wonnegau. (Gro) = Liebfrauenmorgen. (Vil) = Worms.

Am Hohen Stein (Ger). Vineyard. (Anb) = Rheinpfalz. (Ber) = Mittel-

telhaardt-Deutsche Weinstrasse. (Gro) = Schnepfenflug vom Zellertal. (Vil) = Rittersheim.

Amigne (Switz). A white grape variety of old Valais and Vaud stock. It produces wines which are smooth, generous and well robed.

Amigo (Cktl). ½ fl.oz. Apricot brandy, 1 fl.oz. Vodka, 3 fl.ozs. lemon juice, 3 dashes Grenadine, 3 dashes Angostura. Shake over ice, strain into an ice-filled highball glass. Stir in pineapple juice.

Amigo Hnos & Cia (Sp). A wine-producer based in Reus, Tarragona.

Amilcar (Afr). A co-operative-produced wine from Tunisia.

Aminean Grape (It). A grape variety that was popular in Roman times. Had many species, both red and white.

Aminean Wine (It). A wine favoured in ancient times. Made from the Aminean grapes. See also Amminean Wine.

Amines (Eng). A name for the chemicals produced by spoilage organisms in beer and wines (especially home-made). Are identified by their fishy smell. This can be prevented by good hygiene.

Amis de la Chartreuse (Fr). Club Les Amis de la Chartreuse, 4 Boulevard Edgar Kofler, B.P. 102, 38503 Voiron, France.

Amity Vineyards (USA). A small vineyard based in Willamette Valley, Ohio. 3.5 ha. Produces vinifera-based wines.

Ammerlanden (Ger). Vineyard. (Anb) = Württemberg. (Ber) = Kocher-Jagst-Tauber. (Gro) = Kocherberg. (Vil) = Möckmühl.

Ammerschwihr (Fr). A wine-producing commune of the Haut-Rhin in Alsace.

Amminean Wine (It). A famous wine from the eastern half of the Roman Empire favoured by the Romans. See also Aminean Wine.

Ammostatoio (It). Wine press.

Amoltern (Ger). Village. (Anb) = Baden. (Ber) = Kaiserstuhl-Tuniberg. (Gro) = Vulkanfelsen. (Vin) = Steinhalde.

Amont (Sp) (abbr). Amontillado Sherry.

Amontillado (Sp). Fino sherries that have lost, due to age, the delicate character of Finos, but develop a nutty flavour of their own.

Amontillado Abolengo (Sp). A brand of Amontillado sherry produced by the Marqués de Misa.

Amontillado Cocktail (Cktl). ½ measure Amontillado sherry, ½ measure Dubonnet. Stir in an ice-filled highball glass. Top with a twist of lemon peel juice.

Amontillado Viejo (Sp). Very old, rare, mature Amontillado sherry.

A

Amorgiano (Gre). Red grape variety grown mainly in the southern regions. Produces medium bodied red wines.

Amoricano (Cktl). 1 measure Campari, 1 measure dry Martini. Stir with ice, strain into a highball glass, top with soda and decorate with a twist of lemon.

Amorosa (S.Afr). A popular medium sweet, rosé wine from Kellerprinz Wines S.F.W. Made from the Cinsault and Pinotage grapes.

Amoroso (Sp). Sweetened Oloroso sherry. Prepared for the British market. Unknown in Spain.

Amouille (Fr). The first milk of a cow after giving birth. See Beestings.

Amour Cocktail (Cktl). ½ measure Cream sherry, ½ measure French vermouth, dash Angostura. Shake over ice, strain into a cocktail glass. Top with a squeeze of orange peel juice and spiral of orange peel.

Amourette (Fr). A violet-coloured liqueur.

Amoureuses (Les) (Fr). A Premier Cru vineyard in the A.C. commune of Chambolle-Musigny, Côte de Nuits, Burgundy. 5.4 ha.

Ampainen Cocktail (Cktl). ½ measure Crème de Banane, ½ measure Vodka. Stir over ice in a highball glass. Top with ginger ale. Dress with a slice of orange.

Ampeau [Robert] (Fr). A leading wine producer in Meursault, Côte de Beaune, Burgundy.

Ampelidaceae (Lat). Botanical family of which the vine Vitis vinifera is a member.

Ampelographic (Eng). Vine growing.

Ampelography (Eng). The study of the vine.

Ampelopsis (Gre). The study of the vine.

Ampelos (Gre). Grapevine.

Ampelotherapy (Eng). The treatment of illness with wines or with grapes as part of the medicine. Mainly in mediaeval times.

Amphora (Gre). A two-handled vessel, jar or pitcher used in ancient times for holding wine or oil. See also Ampulla.

Ampulla (It). A two-handled bottle used for wine etc. in Roman times. See also Amphora.

Ampulla (Lat). A vessel in early Christianity for holding the wine and water for the Eucharist.

Ampurdán Costa Brava (Sp). A Denominación de Origen of the Cataluña region of south-eastern Spain on the French border. D.O. applies only to the rosé wines made from Cariñena and Garnacha grapes.

Amselberg (Ger). Vineyard. (Anb) = Baden. (Ber) = Ortenau. (Gro) = Fürsteneck. (Vil) = Reichenbach.

Amselfelder (Yug). See Yugoslav Amselfelder Spätburgunder.

Amstel Brouwerij (Hol). Famous Dutch brewery in Amsterdam. Taken over by Heineken.

Amsterdam Cocktail (Cktl). ½ measure Hollands Gin, ¼ measure orange juice, ¼ measure Cointreau, dash Angostura. Shake over ice, strain into a cocktail glass.

Amtliche Prüfungsnummer (Ger). The official German Government testing number given to the wines that have passed the most stringent examinations by tasting. Found on all quality wine labels. e.g. = 3–533–97–3–87. 3 (testing station N°), 533 (village N°), 097 (producers N°), 03 (N° of samples passed), 87 (year wine was bottled).

Amtliche Weinkostkommission (Aus). WKK. The name given to the official wine tasting commission who check the quality seal (the Weingütesiegel).

Amtsgarten (Ger). Vineyard. (Anb) = Mosel-Saar-Ruwer. (Ber) = Bernkastel. (Gro) = Kurfürstlay. (Vil) = Mülheim.

Am Wagram (Aus). A wine-producing area on the eastern side of the Kamp Valley.

Amyl Acetate (Eng). An ester found in wine. Has an aroma of pear drops. Formed from Acetic acid and Amyl alcohol.

Amyl Alcohol (Eng). $C_5H_{11}OH$. A higher alcohol. Part of the Fusel oils.

Amylolysis (Eng). The conversion of starch into sugar in barley malting.

Amylozyme 100 (Eng). The name for the Amylase enzyme which is used to convert starch into fermentable sugars.

Amynteon (Gre). Red wine made from the red Xynomavro grape. Grown mainly in the northern regions.

Anacreon (Gre). A poet who wrote many songs/poems on wine and love. 572–488 BC.

Añada (Sp). Single year. A vintage wine. Sherry of a single year before it goes into the Criaderas.

Añadas (Sp). The place where brandy matures before blending.

Anaerobic (Eng). Respiration without oxygen. Applies to wine yeasts that can multiply without oxygen. See also Aerobic.

Anaerobic Respiration (Eng). Term denoting the conversion of carbohydrate into alcohol and CO_2 by yeast fermentation.

Anagrus Epos (USA). A wasp species which feeds on the eggs of the Grape Leafhopper. Is encouraged by the Vignerons.

Anagrus Wasp (USA). See Anagrus Epos.

Anakie Cabernet (Austr). A red wine produced from the Cabernet sauvignon and Cabernet franc grapes. A well-balanced and well-flavoured wine, soft and with no bitterness. Produced by the Hickinbotham family vineyard, Victoria.

Analyser (Eng). The name given to the part of a continuous still that vaporises the fermented brew so that the alcohol can be extracted in the Rectifier.

Anapa (USSR). The chief wine centre of the Crimea Peninsular.

Anapa Riesling (USSR). A medium dry white wine from the Crimea. Made from the Welschriesling.

Añares (Sp). The brand label for red and white Rioja wines from Bodega Olarra.

Anatolia (Tur). Best Turkish wine producing area which has the districts of Ankara, Elazig and Gaziantep.

Anb. (Ger) (abbr). Anbaugebiet.

A.N.B.A. (Jap) (abbr). All Nippon Bartenders' Association. Address = Raionzu Mansion Dogenzako 610, 2–19–3, Dogenzaka, Shibuya-Ku, Tokyo 150.

Anbaugebiet (Ger). Cultivated territory or region for wines in Germany. 11 regions – Ahr, Mosel-Saar-Ruwer, Nahe, Rheingau, Mittelrhein, Rheinpfalz (Palatinate), Baden, Württemberg, Franken (Franconia), Rheinhessen, Hessische Bergstrasse. Each is divided into a number of Bereiche.

Ancellotta (It). A red grape variety grown in Emilia-Romagna.

Ancestor (Scot). A De Luxe blended Scotch whisky from John Dewar & Sons Ltd., Perth, Perthshire.

Anchialos (Gre). A white wine produced in the Thessaly region in northern Greece. Is made from the Rhoditis and Savatiano grapes.

Anchor Beer (Eng). A keg and canned beer brewed by North Country Brewery, Hull, Yorkshire.

Anchor Beer (E.Asia). A Pilsener-type beer brewed by the Archipelago Brewery in Kuala Lumpur, Malaya.

Anchor Beer (E.Asia). A Beer brewed by the Burgess and Maugham's Brewery in Singapore.

Anchor Bitter (Eng). A keg Bitter brewed by the Anchor Brewery, Salisbury, Wiltshire.

Anchor Bitter (Eng). A pale brew made from malt and hops but no sugar. Brewed by Godson's Brewery, Clapton, East London.

Anchor Brewery (Eng). Name for Gibbs Mew's brewery based in Salisbury, Wiltshire.

Anchor Keg (Eng). See Chairman's Choice.

Anchor Steam Brewery (USA). San Francisco brewery producing Anchor Steam beer and porter using clarifiers (long shallow pans) for fermentation.

Ancienne Méthode (Fr). An old method of making wine without the aid of any chemicals etc.

Ancient Age (USA). The brand-name of a Bourbon whiskey.

Ancient Druids (Eng). A pub set up in 1984 in Cambridge by Charles Wells Brewery of Bedford, Bedfordshire. The beer is brewed at the pub. Produces Kite Bitter 1038 O.G. and Druids Special 1045 O.G.

Ancient Proverb Port (USA). The brand-name used by the Llords and Elwood Winery in California for a range of their Port-style wines.

Ancre (Fr). The brand-name used by the Albra Breweries for their beers.

Andalusia (Sp). The region in south-west Spain that contains the Sherry and Montilla-Moriles regions.

Andalusia Cocktail (Cktl). ⅗ measure dry Sherry, ⅕ measure Bacardi White Label, ⅓ measure Brandy. Stir over ice, strain into a cocktail glass.

Andalusia Wines (S.Afr). See Vaalharts Co-operative.

Andean Vineyards (Arg). A major wine producer based in the central region.

Andechs Brauerei (Ger). A brewery in Erling-Andechs, Bavaria. Noted for its malty Bocks. See Bergbock Hell, Bergbock Dunkel, Doppelbock Hell, and Doppelbock Dunkel.

Andeker (USA). A Beer brewed by the Pabst Brewery in Los Angeles.

Andel (Ger). Village. (Anb) = Mosel-Saar-Ruwer. (Ber) = Bernkastel. (Gro) = Kurfürslay. (Vin) = Schlossberg.

Anderida (Eng). See Horam Manor from where it originates. A wine made from mainly Müller-Thurgau with some Seyval blanc. Bottled by Merrydown Wine Co. Ltd.

Anderson Cocktail (Cktl). ¾ measure dry Gin, ¼ measure Italian vermouth. Stir well over ice, strain into a cocktail glass, top with twist of orange peel.

Anderson Valley (USA). A wine-producing area in the Mendocino County, northern California.

Anderson Vineyards (USA). A winery

based in the Napa Valley, California. 9.5 ha. Grape variety – Chardonnay.

Andosilla (Sp). A Zona de Crianza in the Rioja Baja region of north-eastern Spain.

Andover Ale (Eng). A cask conditioned Ale 1040 O.G. brewed by the Bourne Valley Brewery, Hampshire.

Andrea da Ponte (It). A well-known brand of Grappa.

Andreasberg (Ger). Vineyard. (Anb) = Baden. (Ber) = Ortenau. (Gro) = Fürsteneck. (Vil) = Ortenberg.

Andreasberg (Ger). Vineyard. (Anb) = Mosel-Saar-Ruwer. (Ber) = Saar-Ruwer. (Gro) = Römerlay. (Vil) = Trier.

Andreas Bock (Ger). A fine, malty bock beer from the Aying Brauerei in Bavaria.

Andres Winery (Can). A winery based in Winona, Niagara. Produces hybrid wines.

Andros (Gre). An island in the northern Cyclades, Aegean sea. Long history of fame for the wines especially in ancient Greece.

Añejado Por (Sp). A term meaning 'aged by'.

Añejo (Sp). Old.

Anejo Cacique (S.Am). A Rum aged for 2 years in cask from Venezuela.

Anesone (It) (USA). Anis-liquorice flavoured liqueur. 45% alc. by vol.

Anesone Troduo (It). An absinthe-based spirit apéritif. 40% alc. by vol.

Anfora (It). Amphora or jar.

Anfora (Port). A red wine produced by Fonseca in Estremadura.

Angad (Afr). An A.O.G. area in the wine-producing region of eastern Morocco.

Angeac-Champagne (Fr). A commune in the Charente-Maritime Département whose grapes are classed Petite Champagne (Cognac).

Angeac-Charente (Fr). A commune in the Charente-Maritime Département whose grapes are classed Petite Champagne (Cognac).

Angel Face Cocktail (Cktl). ⅓ measure Calvados, ⅓ measure dry Gin, ⅓ measure Apricot brandy. Shake over ice, strain into a cocktail glass.

Angelica (Sp). A sweet yellow liqueur somewhat similar to Chartreuse. Made in the Basque country.

Angelica (USA). A fortified 'Altar wine', tawny in colour. Produced in California. See California Angelica.

Angelica Antigua (USA). A fortified 'Altar wine' produced by the East-Side Winery, Lodi, California.

Angelicant (Fr). An alternative name for the Muscadelle grape.

Angelikalikoer (Ger). An Angelica-based liqueur.

Angelo (Cktl). ½ fl.oz. Galliano, ½ fl.oz. Southern Comfort, 1 fl.oz. Smirnoff Vodka, dash egg white. Shake over ice, strain into an ice-filled highball glass. Top with orange and pineapple juice.

Angel's Delight (Pousse Café). Pour into an Elgin glass in order equal quantities of Grenadine, Crème d'Yvette and cream.

Angel's Dream (Pousse Café). Pour into an Elgin glass in order equal quantities of Maraschino, Crème d'Yvette and Cognac.

Angel's Kiss (Cktl). ¼ gill Bénédictine, ¼ gill cream. Put liqueur into a large Elgin glass, float cream on top.

Angel's Kiss (Pousse Café) (1). ¼ measure Crème de Cacao, ¼ measure Prunelle brandy, ¼ measure Crème de Violette, ¼ measure cream. Pour each carefully into a narrow glass in order.

Angel's Kiss (Pousse Café) (2). Equal measures poured in order into an Elgin glass of Crème de Cacao, Crème d'Yvette, Cognac and cream.

Angel Special (Cktl) (Non-alc). 1 egg yolk, 2 dashes Grenadine, 2 dashes Angostura, ⅓ pint orange juice. Blend with a scoop of crushed ice in a blender. Pour in a Champagne flute. Dress with a cherry.

Angel's Share (Eng). Term given to the spirit evaporation which occurs whilst it is maturing in cask. (Brandy, whisky etc). Up to 25% of the total may be lost.

Angel's Smile Cocktail (Cktl). ⅓ measure Kirsch, ⅓ measure Cointreau, ⅓ measure Vodka, dash Grenadine. Shake over ice, strain into cocktail glass. Dress with a cherry.

Angel's Tip (Cktl). ¾ measure brown Crème de Cacao, ¼ measure cream. Float cream on top of liqueur in a large Elgin glass.

Angel's Tit (Pousse Café). Pour into an Elgin glass in order, equal quantities of Maraschino and cream. Top with a cherry.

Angel's Wing (Cktl) (Pousse Café). 1 part Crème de Cacao, 1 part Brandy, 1 part cream. Pour in order into an Elgin glass.

Angel's Wing (Cktl) (Pousse Café). Another name for Angel's Kiss.

Angeou (Eng). The sixteenth-century spelling of Anjou.

Angereichert (Ger). Sugared.

Angern (Aus). A wine village in the Falkenstein-Matzen district in north-eastern Austria. Produces mainly white wines.

Angers Rose (Cktl). ⅓ measure Bourbon,

⅓ measure Cointreau, ⅓ measure pineapple juice, dash egg white, dash Campari. Shake over ice, strain into a cocktail glass. Decorate with a small slice of orange and cherry.

Angevine (Fr). A white grape variety. See also Madeleine Angevine.

Anghelu Ruju (It). Lit – 'Red Angel'. A rich, red, ruby wine similar to Port. Produced in Sardinia it has a pronounced bouquet and sweet, aromatic taste. Made from selected grapes partially dried in the sun.

Anglade (Fr). A commune in the A.C. Côtes de Blaye in north-eastern Bordeaux.

Angled Racks (USA). Name for Pupître-styled racks used for storing sparkling wines in a cellar.

Angler Cocktail (Cktl). ⅙ gill Vantogrio, ⅓ gill Gin, 2 dashes Orange bitters, 2 dashes Angostura. Stir over ice, strain into a cocktail glass. Add squeeze of lemon peel juice on top.

Angler Lager (Eng). A strong, bottled Lager 1054 O.G. brewed by the Charles Wells Brewery, Bedford, Bedfordshire for export.

Angler's Cocktail (Cktl). 1 measure dry Gin, 3 dashes Orange bitters, 2 dashes Angostura, 1 dash Grenadine. Shake well over ice, strain into an ice-filled old-fashioned glass.

Anglerwein (Ger). A brand of white Tafelwein produced by Deinhard in Koblenz.

Angles (Les) (Fr). A Premier Cru vineyard in the A.C. commune of Volnay, Côte de Beaune, Burgundy. 3.5 ha.

Anglet (Fr). A town near Bayonne. Noted for its Vin de Sable.

Anglian Ale (Eng). A strong, keg and bottled Ale 1048 O.G. brewed by the Anglian Brewery, Norwich, Norfolk.

Anglo-Australian Wine Company (Eng). Importer of Australian wines. Range available at 9, Greenways, Sandhurst, Camberley, Surrey, and at Will Logan Wine Agencies, Church Street, Hayfield, Stockport, Cheshire.

Anglo Vino de Sankta Georgo (Eng). Invented to celebrate the 100th anniversary of Esperato Society. From St. George's Vineyard, Waldron, East Sussex.

Angola (Afr). A wine made from palm sap. Produced in West Africa.

Angoris (It). A producer of sparkling wines (all methods) based in the Friuli-Venezia Giulia region. Labels include Modelet Brut.

Angostura (S.Am). A famous Rum-based Bitters. Flavoured with Gentian. Originally produced in Venezuela,

now produced in Trinidad.

Angostura (S.Am). Venezuelan town where Dr. J.G.B. Siegert invented the famous Bitters of the same name in 1824. The town is now called Ciudad Bolivar. 23% alc. by vol.

Angostura Aquavit (Swe). A flavoured Aquavit. Flavoured with Angostura.

Angostura Bark (S.Am). A tree of the genus Cusparia or Galipea which is the principal flavour of Angostura bitters.

Angostura Bitters (S.Am). See Angostura.

Angostura Fizz (Cktl) (Non-alc) (1). ¼ gill Angostura bitters, ⅛ gill plain syrup, ½ gill lemon juice, white of egg. Shake well over ice, strain into a tumbler. Top with soda water.

Angostura Fizz (Cktl) (Non-alc) (2). 1 fl.oz. Angostura, 1 egg white, dash Grenadine, dash cream. Shake over ice, strain into an ice-filled highball glass. Top with soda and dress with a lemon peel spiral.

Angoumois (Fr). Famous town in the north-east of the Cognac region whose wines are distilled into Cognac.

Angoves' St. Agnes Old Liqueur (Austr). Brandy aged in French oak casks for 7 years before blending. Produced at Angoves Vineyard.

Angoves Vineyard (Austr). Address = Bookmark Avenue, South Australia, 5341. 393 ha. Grape varieties – Cabernet sauvignon, Chardonnay, Chenin blanc, French colombard, Malbec, Rhine riesling, Sauvignon blanc, Shiraz, Sylvaner, Traminer.

Anguillula Aceti (Lat). See Vinegar Eel.

Anheuser-Busch (USA). The world's largest brewery. Producing Budweiser and Michelob beers. Address = St. Louis, Missouri.

Anice Forte (It). An absinthe-based spirit apéritif 41% alc. by vol.

Animador (Cktl). ⅓ measure Gin, ⅓ measure sweet Vermouth, ⅓ measure Apérital Delor. Shake over ice, strain into a cocktail glass.

Animator (Ger). A Doppelbock beer brewed by the Hacker-Pschorr Brauerei of Munich, West Germany.

Añina (Sp). An area within the Andalusia region. Chalk soil, grapes grown here make the best sherries.

Anis (Fr) (Sp). A popular liqueur or apéritif, flavoured with Star anis seeds. Was substituted for the banned Absinthe. Pernod is an example. 43% alc. by vol.

Anis (Port). Aniseed.

Anisado (Sp). Aniseed brandy.

Anis del Mono (Sp). An aniseed liqueur from Barcelona. Available in a sweet or dry form. 38% alc. by vol.

Anise (Eng). An umbelliferous plant of the Mediterranean (Pimpinella Anisum). Used in the making of aniseed-flavoured beverages.

Anise Chinchón (Sp). An anise-flavoured liqueur in Chinchón. 38% alc. by vol.

Anisetta Stillata (It). An aniseed liqueur from the Aurum Distillery in Pescara.

Anisette (Fr). An aniseed-flavoured liqueur with coriander and various other herbs etc. 25% alc. by vol.

Anisette Classique (Swe). An Anisette liqueur produced by Aktiebolaget Vin and Spritcentralem.

Anjou (Fr). Region of the Loire (western). Produces white, red and rosé wines. Noted for rosé and sweet white wines. (Coteaux du Layon and Quarts de Chaume).

Anjou Coteaux de la Loire (Fr). A.C. white wine from the Anjou region of the river Loire.

Anjou Coteaux de la Loire Rosé de Cabernet (Fr). A.C. rosé wine no longer produced. See Cabernet Rosé.

Anjou Coteaux de Saumur (Fr). An old A.C. wine classification no longer produced. Was for white, red and rosé wines.

Anjou Fillette (Fr). A 35 cl. bottle from the central Loire. A cross between a Champagne bottle and a Languedoc bottle. Also used in the Touraine, Loire.

Anjou Mousseux (Fr). A.C. white sparkling wine from the Anjou region of the river Loire.

Anjou Rosé (Fr). A highly popular A.C. rosé wine from the Anjou region of the river Loire. Slightly sweet and often pétillant.

Anjou Rosé de Cabernet (Fr). A.C. rosé from Anjou region on the river Loire. See Cabernet Rosé.

Anjou-Saumur (Fr). A.C. wine district within the Anjou region of the river Loire. Produces white, red and rosé wines. See Saumur.

Anjou-Saumur Rosé de Cabernet (Fr). An A.C. rosé wine produced in the Saumur district of Anjou region.

Anjoux S.A. (Fr). A négociant-éleveur based at Saint-Georges de Reneins, Burgundy.

Ankara (Tur). A vineyard area based in the Middle Anatolia region. Produces red and white wines.

Anker (Eng). 10 gallon cask.

Anker (Scot). An old Whisky cask of approximately 8 gallons capacity.

Anker Brasserie (Bel). A brewery that is noted for its Abbaye-style beers. See Floreffe.

Ankola Coffee (E.Ind). Coffee from Sumatra. Produces a mellow flavour with a good strong aroma.

Annaba (Alg). A red wine-producing region in eastern Algeria.

Annaberg (Ger). Vineyard. (Anb) = Mosel-Saar-Ruwer. (Ber) = Bernkastel. (Gro) = Probstberg. (Vil) = Schweich.

Annaberg (Ger). Vineyard. (Anb) = Rheinpfalz. (Ber) = Mittelhaardt-Deutsche Weinstrasse. (Gro) = Feuerberg. (Vil) = Kallstadt.

Annacquare (It). To dilute with water, watered-down wine.

Annata (It). Year, vintage.

Année Jalouse (Fr). Used to denote a year of greatly varying quality of wine production in Bordeaux.

Annie Green Springs (USA). The brandname used by United Vintners.

Anninger Perle (Aus). A white wine.

Anniversaire Très Ancienne Sélection (Fr). Cognac produced by Monnet.

Ann Street Brewery (Ch.Isles). A Jersey-based brewery. Produces beers under the Mary Ann label. Brews Skol under licence.

Annual Yield (Fr). Part of the A.C. laws. See 'Plafond Limité de Classement'.

Annular-Knopped Glass (Eng). An eighteenth-century glass consisting of a flat round based, swollen stem and trumpet bowl.

Año (Sp). Year. Seen on wine labels as 4°Año. = 4 years before bottled.

Anreicherung (Ger). Chaptalisation. Improvement of musts by addition of sugar. Also known as Anreichern.

Ansell's Brewery (Eng). A brewery based in Birmingham with 5 subsidiary companies.

Anselmi (It). A winery based in Monteforte, near Soave, Veneto.

Ansonica (It). A white grape variety used in Tuscany.

Ansprechend (Ger). Denotes an attractive engaging wine.

Antabuse (Eng). A drug (registered trademark) used to treat alcoholism. Induces nausea if alcohol is consumed. Contains Tetraethylthiuram disulphide.

Antarctica Paulista Cerveceria (Bra). A brewery based in São Paulo, south-eastern Brazil.

A.N.T.A.V. (Fr) (abbr). Association Nationale Technique pour l'Amélioration de la Viticulture. A research institute for the improvement of the vine. Based at the Domaine de l'Espiguette, Le Grau du Roi, Gard.

Antech (Edmond) (Fr). A producer of A.C. Blanquette de Limoux based at Limoux in southern France.

Ante Cocktail (Cktl). ⅖ measure Calvados, ⅖ measure red Dubonnet, ⅕ measure Triple Sec. Stir over ice, strain into a cocktail glass.

Ante Prandium (Lat). Lit – 'Before a meal'. An apéritif/cocktail.

Antequera (Sp). A wine-producing district based in north-western Málaga. Grows Pedro Ximénez grapes.

Anthocyanins (Eng). Blue, red or orange flower or fruit pigments. Are water soluble and are extracted during wine and liqueur production.

Anthocyanols (Eng). A group of pigments that give the red colour that is extracted from the grape skins by the action of alcohol.

Anthoxanthins (Eng). Important plant pigments for home-made wine production. Are responsible for the yellow and orange colour in certain wines. Also known as Flavones.

Anthracnose (Eng). The fungus that appears as stains on vine leaves, shoots and fruit. Holes then appear where the stains were. Treated with Bordeaux/Burgundy mixture.

Antialcoolique (Fr). Teetotal. See also Tempérance (De).

Antica Casa Vinicola Scarpa (It). A winery based at Nizza Monferrato, Piemonte.

Antica Confraria de Saint-Andu de la Galiniera (Fr). A wine society based in the Hérault Département.

Antica Querica (It). A producer of sparkling (méthode champenoise) wine based in the Veneto region, north-eastern Italy.

Anticipation Cocktail (Cktl). ⅓ gill Irish Velvet, scoop vanilla ice cream. Blend together in a blender with a little crushed ice. Pour in a Champagne flute. Top with grated chocolate.

Antier (Fr). An old, established Cognac house who united with Pomeral in 1949 to form the house of Gaston de Lagrange.

Antifogmatic (USA). An early colonial term for a cider or beer consumed early in the morning. See also – Phlegm Cutter, Fog Cutter Cocktail and Eye-Opener.

Antigua Coffee (W.Ind). A smooth mellow and somewhat spicy coffee with a smoky taste and aroma.

Antigua Distillery Ltd (W.Ind). A large Rum distillery based in Antigua. Produces light-bodied Rums. Is noted for its Cavalier Antigua Rum.

Antika (Gre). A dry white wine from Patras, Peloponnese.

Antillano (Cktl). ⅙ gill light Rum, ⅙ gill golden Rum, ⅙ gill grapefruit juice, ⅙ gill pineapple juice, dash Angostura, barspoon Grenadine. Shake over ice, strain into a highball glass with crushed ice. Decorate with pineapple, orange and a glacé cherry. Serve with straws.

Antilles Cocktail (Cktl). ⅗ measure Bacardi White Label, ⅖ measure white Dubonnet. Shake well over ice, strain into a cocktail glass. Dress with twist of orange peel juice.

Antinori (It). A noted Florence wine family who produce Chianti and Orvieto.

Anti-Oxidant (Eng). The name given to any chemical that stops wine musts from oxidising.

Antiqua (Sp). A Brandy produced by the Caves Alicança.

Antiquary (The) (Scot). A blended De Luxe Scotch whisky first produced by J. and W. Blackworth Hardie. Marketed by William Sanderson and Son Ltd.

Antique (Fr). Class for fine old Cognac. See Hine Antique.

Antique (Scot). A brand of De Luxe blended Scotch whisky from Hiram Walker. 40% alc. by vol.

Antique (USA). The brand-name of Kentucky bourbon whiskey. 6 y.o. distilled by Frankfort Distilling Co, Athertonville, Kentucky. 40% alc. by vol.

Antiquíssima (Port). On a label denotes 'Very old'.

Antler Bitter (Eng). A cask conditioned and keg Bitter brewed by Watney Mann.

Antoine Cocktail (Cktl). ⅔ measure Vodka, ⅓ measure lime juice, 2 dashes Crème de Cassis. Stir over ice, strain into an ice-filled highball. Top with orange juice and slice of orange.

Antoine Special (Cktl). ½ measure Dubonnet, ½ measure French vermouth. Float Vermouth onto the top of the iced Dubonnet in a 5 fl.oz. Paris goblet.

Antoine's Smile (Cktl). 1½ fl.ozs Calvados, ½ fl.oz. lemon juice, ½ fl.oz. Gomme syrup. Shake over ice, strain into a cocktail glass.

Antoinette (Fr). A dry cider apple grown in the Normandy region. Used to produce dry French ciders.

Antonio (Cktl). ⅓ measure Brandy, ⅓ measure dry Gin, ⅙ measure Maraschino, ⅙ measure (white) Crème de Menthe. Shake well over ice, strain into a cocktail glass.

Antonio Barbadillo (Sp). A noted Sherry bodega based in Sanlúcar de Barrameda, Andalusia.

Antoniolo (It). A major producer of Gattinara wine in northern Piemonte.

Antoniusberg (Ger). Vineyard. (Anb) = Mosel-Saar-Ruwer. (Ber) = Saar-Ruwer. (Gro) = Scharzberg. (Vil) = Serrig.

Antoniusbrunnen (Ger). Vineyard. (Anb) = Mosel-Saar-Ruwer. (Ber) = Saar-Ruwer. (Gro) = Scharzberg. (Vil) = Saarburg.

Anton Lindner (It). A small, private winery based in Eppan, Südtirol (South Tyrol).

Ants in the Pants (Cktl). ½ measure Gin, ¼ measure sweet Vermouth, ¼ measure Grand Marnier, dash lemon juice. Shake over ice, strain into a cocktail glass. Dress with a lemon peel spiral.

Antunes (Luiz) & Cia (Bra). One of Brazil's leading wine-producing companies.

Antuzzi's Winery (USA). A large winery based in Delran, New Jersey.

Antwerp Brasserie (Bel). A brewery based in northern Belgium, noted for its top-fermented draught Ales.

Anvil Strong Ale (Eng). A dark Winter beer brewed by Hyde's Brewery of Manchester.

A° (Sp) (abbr). Año. Year.

A.O.C. (Fr) (abbr). Appellation d'Origine Contrôlée. See Appellation Contrôlée.

A.O.G. (Afr) (abbr). Appellation d'Origin Garantie. The Moroccan wine quality grade which is only given to a wine if it meets very high standards (12% alc. by vol. recognised vines, etc).

A.1 (Cktl). ⅔ measure dry Gin, ⅓ measure Grand Marnier, 1 dash lemon juice, 1 dash Grenadine. Shake well over ice, strain into a cocktail glass.

A One (Cktl). See A.1.

Apagado (Sp). A term used to describe a Sherry with a weak bouquet.

Apaleador (Sp). The name given to the pole used to stir the wine during the fining process.

Apczer (Hun). The brand-name of a white table wine.

Apennines (It). A mountain range (volcanic) separating the regions of Emilia-Romagna in the east and Toscana in the west.

Aperient Waters (Eng). Waters that have high saline constituents mainly sulphate of magnesia and sulphate of soda. e.g. Cheltenham, Leamington Spa, Montmirail, Seidlity.

Aperire (Lat). Lit – 'to open'. Where the term apéritif originates from.

Aperital Delor (Fr). A fortified apéritif wine from Delor.

Apéritif (Fr). Pre-meal drink to encourage the gastric juices to flow. Can be a commercially made product or a mixed drink. e.g. Fino Sherry or a Dry Martini.

Apéritif Grill (Cktl). ⅓ measure (white) Crème de Menthe, ⅓ measure Fernet Branca, ⅓ measure sweet Vermouth. Pour gently into a cocktail glass in order. Do not stir. A 'Pick-me-up'.

Apéritif Perrier (Cktl). ⅙ gill Gin, ⅙ gill Noilly Prat, 2 dashes Rose's lime juice. Shake over ice, strain into a large goblet with 2 ice cubes. Add Perrier water, decorate with cucumber peel.

Apéritif Port (Port). A white Port in which the sugar has been fermented out. It is the driest Port possible.

Aperitivo (Fr). A low-alcohol bitters and herb flavoured drink. Is less than 1% alc. by vol. See Kattell-Roc.

Aperitivo (Port). Wine used as an apéritif.

Aperitivo Rosso (It). The brand-name of an Apéritif.

Aperol Aperitivo (It). A bitter apéritif, orange coloured and flavoured. 11% alc. by vol.

Apestoso (Sp). A term used to describe a Sherry that has an unpleasant smell and taste.

Apetlon (Aus). A wine village in Burgenland. Noted for its medium-sweet and sweet white wines which are produced on sandy soils.

APEVV (Port) (abbr). Associacão dos Produtores-Engarrafadores de Vinho Verde.

Apfelsaft (Ger). A non-alcoholic apple juice.

Apfelsinlikoer (Ger). A Brandy-based orange liqueur.

Apfelwein (Ger). Cider.

Aphrodes (Gre). Sparkling.

Aphrodite (Cyp). A dry white wine produced by Keo in Limassol.

Aphrodis (Fr). The brand-name of an A.C. Muscat de Rivesaltes, a VdN of the Roussillon, south-western France. Address = SIVIR Route des Crêtes, 66650 Banyuls-sur-Mer.

Aphrodisiac (Cktl). Heat 5 fl.ozs. Port wine with a dash of Curaçao until nearly boiling. Pour into a warmed, heat-proof glass. Dress with grated nutmeg and a slice of lemon.

Apiculate (Eng). Lemon shaped. Used to describe the shape of wild yeasts found in the Bloom on grape skins.

Apitiv (Port). The brand-name of a dry white Port and Sherry from Sandeman.

Aplostra (Cyp). The name for the mats used to dry the grapes for the production of fortified wines.

A.P. N° (Ger) (abbr). Amtliche Prüfungsnummer.

Apoferment (Eng). The start of fermentation.

Apollinaris (Ger). Naturally sparkling spring water from the Ahr Valley at Bad Neuerahr.

Apoplexy (Eng). A vine disease known as Esca. A Cryptogamic disease. The name derives from the way the vine dies.

Apostelberg (Ger). Vineyard. (Anb) = Nahe. (Ber) = Kreuznach. (Gro) = Schlosskapelle. (Vil) = Guldental.

Apostelgarten (Ger). Vineyard. (Anb) = Franken. (Ber) = Mainviereck. (Gro) = Not yet assigned. (Vil) = Michelbach

Apostles (Ger). Twelve large casks of old Rhine wine kept in cellars in Bremen.

Apostoles (Sp). The brand-name of a Sherry produced by Gonzales Byass.

Apostrophe Special 2000 (Cktl). ²/₁₀ measure Mandarine Napoléon, ²/₁₀ measure Curaçao (orange), ³/₁₀ measure Gin, ³/₁₀ measure dry Vermouth. Shake well over ice, strain into a cocktail glass.

Apotheca (Lat). Wine-cellar.

Apothecary Brandy (USA). A Brandy sold in an Apothecary-style jar. Is produced by Paul Masson, California.

Apotheke (Ger). Vineyard. (Anb) = Mosel-Saar-Ruwer. (Ber) = Bernkastel. (Gro) = Michelsberg. (Vil) = Trittenheim.

Appassire (It). The hanging of bunches of grapes to dry over the winter in the Abruzzi region to make dessert wines.

Appellation (Fr). Identifying name or title. See A.C.

Appellation Calvados Contrôlée (Fr). The top classification of Calvados produced within the Pays d'Auge in Normandy. See also Calvados Réglementée.

Appellation Calvados Réglementée (Fr). A classification of Calvados in Normandy other than the top A.C. Calvados of the Pays d'Auge.

Appellation Communale (Fr). Top appellations of the Premiers and Grands Crus of Burgundy.

Appellation Complète (Lux). Fine wine category. Label must indicate the grape variety, locality, vineyard site, name of grower and his domicile, vintage year and must complete a testing. See also Marque Nationale.

Appellation Contrôlée (Fr). A French law to protect names, improve the quality and limit production of wines from demarcated districts. Guarantees the name on label and the contents of container.

Appellation d'Origine (Fr). See Appellation Contrôlée.

Appellation d'Origine Contrôlée (Fr). A.O.C. See Appellation Contrôlée.

Appellation Régionale (Fr). A lesser appellation which often produces cheap, poor quality wines.

Appellation Réglementée (Fr). A.R. Spirituous equivalent of V.D.Q.S. See Appellation Calvados Réglementée.

Appellation Simple (Fr). Pre 1935 designation for wine of quality. See also A.C.

Appeltofftska Brewery (Swe). A brewery based in Halmstead, southern Sweden. One of the country's smallest.

Appelwijn (Hol). Cider.

Appelwoi (Ger). The name used in the Frankfurt area for Applewine.

Appendicitis (Cktl). ⅘ measure dry Gin, ⅛ measure lemon juice, ⅛ measure Cointreau, 1 egg. Shake well over ice, strain into a cocktail glass.

Appenheim (Ger). Village. (Anb) = Rheinhessen. (Ber) = Bingen. (Gro) = Abtel. (Vins) = Daubhaus, Drosselborn, Eselpfad, Hundertgulden.

A.P.P.E.R.A.M. (W.Ind) (abbr). Association Professionnelle des Producteurs Embouteilleurs de Rhum Agricole de la Martinique. An organisation formed to represent the interests of bottled Rum producers on the island of Martinique.

Appetiser (USA). See Appetizer.

Appetizer (Eng). A small amount of drink (or food) consumed to stimulate the appetite. See Apéritif. Also spelt Appetiser.

Appetizer Wines (USA). Apéritif wines. Vermouths etc.

Appleade (Eng). Pour 1 pint of boiling water over 3 sliced apples, stand 15 minutes, strain, add sugar to taste. Serve hot or cold.

Apple Blight (Eng). Insect (Aphid) Eriosoma Lanigera that infests apple trees with a waxy, powdery secretion. Also called American blight.

Apple Blossom Cocktail (Cktl). ½ measure Calvados, ½ measure Italian vermouth. Shake over ice, strain into a cocktail glass.

Apple Blow Fizz (Cktl). ½ gill Calvados, juice ½ lemon, 1 egg white, 1 teaspoon powdered sugar. Shake well over ice, strain into an ice-filled highball glass. Top with soda water.

Apple Brandy (Eng). Spirit distilled from Cider. (Fr) = Calvados. (USA) = Applejack.

Apple Brandy Cocktail (Cktl). 1 measure Applejack brandy, 1 teaspoon lemon juice, 4 dashes Grenadine. Shake over ice, strain into a cocktail glass.

Apple Brandy Highball (Cktl). Place ⅓ gill of Calvados into an ice-filled highball glass. Top with soda water, stir. Dress with a spiral of lemon peel.

Applecar Cocktail (Cktl). ⅓ measure Apple brandy, ⅓ measure Triple Sec, ⅓ measure lemon juice. Shake over ice, strain into a cocktail glass.

Apple Cocktail (Cktl). ⅓ measure Calvados, ⅓ measure Sweet Cider, ⅙ measure dry Gin, ⅙ measure Brandy. Shake over plenty of ice, strain into a large glass.

Apple Cooler (Cktl) (Non-alc). Place ½ pint apple tea, juice of a lemon, ½ pint lemonade and 1 fl.oz. Gomme syrup into an ice-filled jug. Stir, dress with apple slices and serve in ice-filled highball glasses.

Apple Gin (Scot). A colourless liqueur compounded in Leith. 40% alc. by vol.

Apple Jack (USA). American (New England) name for apple brandy. The distillation from cider. (Fr) = Calvados. 45% alc. by vol.

Apple Jack Cocktail (Cktl). ½ gill Apple Jack brandy, 2 dashes Gum syrup, 2 dashes Angostura. Stir over ice, strain into a cocktail glass. Add an olive and squeeze of lemon peel juice.

Apple Jack Highball (Cktl). 1 measure Apple brandy placed into an ice-filled highball glass. Top with ginger ale and a twist of lemon peel juice, stir.

Apple Jack Punch (Cktl). 1 bottle Apple brandy, 3 fl.ozs. Grenadine, 1 pint orange juice. Mix all well together in a Punch bowl with ice. Add 1½ pints ginger ale and apple slices.

Apple Jack Rabbit (Cktl) (1). 1½ ozs. Calvados, juice ½ lemon, juice ½ orange, teaspoon Grenadine. Shake over ice, strain into a cocktail glass.

Apple Jack Rabbit (Cktl) (2). ⅗ measure Applejack brandy, ⅕ measure lemon juice, ⅕ measure orange juice, ½ oz. maple syrup. Shake well over ice, strain into a sugared old-fashioned glass (with the maple syrup), add 2 ice cubes.

Apple Jack Rickey (Cktl). 1 measure Apple brandy, juice ½ lime. Place together in an ice-filled highball glass, top with soda, stir and add a slice of lime.

Apple Jack Sling (Cktl). See Hot Applejack Sling.

Apple Jack Sour (Cktl). 1 measure Apple brandy, ½ teaspoon powdered sugar, juice ½ lemon. Shake over ice, strain into sour glass. Dress with a cherry and a slice of lemon.

Apple Marc (Fr). Apple pomace pulp after the juice has been extracted.

Apple Mill (Eng). Used to cut up the apples before pressing for cider.

Applemony (W.Ind). The nickname for a blend of Appleton Estate Rum and Monymusk Rum in Jamaica.

Apple of Paradise (W.Ind). A liqueur made from local fruit on the island of Cuba.

Apple Pie Cocktail (Cktl). ½ measure white Rum, ½ measure sweet Vermouth, 2 dashes Grenadine, 4 dashes Brandy, 4 dashes lemon juice. Shake over ice, strain into a cocktail glass.

Apple Rum Punch (Punch). 6 oranges studded with cloves. Bake until brown. Add to a Punch bowl containing 1 bottle Rum, ½ bottle Brandy, 4 tablespoons sugar. Stir, then flame. Extinguish with 3 bottles Apple juice. Sprinkle with ground cinnamon and nutmeg. Serve warm.

Apple Rum Rickey (Cktl). 1 part Apple brandy, 1 part Rum, 4 dashes lime juice. Place Rum and Brandy into an ice-filled highball glass, top with soda water, stir, add lime juice on top.

Apple Spark (Eng). A sparkling apple drink from the Merrydown Co.

Apple Splitz (USA). A sparkling cooler made from white wine and apple juice. 1.2% alc. by vol.

Appletise (Eng). A non-alcoholic, carbonated apple drink from Schweppes.

Apple Toddy (Cktl). Bake an apple, peel, place piece of apple in an old-fashioned glass (or toddy glass). Add a cube of sugar, slice of lemon, ⅓ gill Calvados. Top with boiling water and stir with stick of cinnamon.

Appleton (W.Ind). Brand-name of a white Rum produced in Jamaica. Is produced by J. Wray Nephew. Sold in the U.K. by the United Rum Merchants. 40% alc. by vol. Brands include – Appleton Estate Special (5 y.o), Appleton Gold and Appleton White Classic.

Appleton Estate Distillery (W.Ind). A large Rum distillery based in the Black River Valley, Jamaica. Produces white and dark Rums.

Appleton Rums (W.Ind). Rums produced by the Appleton Estate Distillery. All styles are produced. Owned by J. Wray Nephew.

Appley (Eng). Term to describe young white wines where the malic acidity evokes a raw appley smell and tart flavour.

Âpre (Fr). Harsh or sharp. Excess tannin.

Apremont (Fr). A white wine of Savoie, eastern France.

Après Ski Cocktail (Cktl). ⅓ measure Pastis, ⅓ measure (white) Crème de Menthe, ⅓ measure Vodka. Shake over ice, strain into an ice-filled highball glass. Top with soda water and dress with mint and lemon slice. Serve with straws.

Apricot Anise Collins (Cktl). 1 measure dry Gin, 1 measure Anisette, ⅓ measure Apricot brandy, 4 dashes lemon juice. Shake over ice, strain into a collins glass. Top with soda, add 2 ice cubes and a slice of lemon.

Apricot Brandy (Eng). A liqueur made by maceration of fruit in base spirit, then re-distilling. 20–35% alc. by vol. See Barack Pàlinka.

Apricot Brandy Cooler (Cktl). Place 2 skinned fresh apricots, ⅓ gill Apricot brandy, ⅙ gill Gomme syrup and juice of a lemon into a blender with a scoop of crushed ice. Pour into a flute glass.

Apricot Cocktail (Cktl). 1 part Apricot brandy, 2–3 parts dry Gin, 4 dashes orange juice, 4 dashes lemon juice. Shake over ice, strain into a cocktail glass.

Apricot Cooler (Cktl). 1 liqueur glass Apricot brandy, 2 dashes of Grenadine, dash Angostura, juice of lemon or lime. Shake over ice (except bitters). Strain into a highball glass. Top up with soda water. Add bitters, spiral of lemon peel.

Apricot Daiquiri (Cktl). ½ measure white Rum, ½ measure lemon juice, ¼ measure Apricot brandy, 2 skinned and stoned apricots, scoop of crushed ice. Blend well together in a blender, pour into a Champagne saucer. Dress with an apricot slice and mint sprig.

Apricot d'Anjou (Fr). An Apricot brandy produced by Jacques Giffard in Angers, Loire.

Apricot Fizz (Cktl). 1 measure Apricot brandy, 1 teaspoon powdered sugar, juice ½ lemon and ½ lime. Shake over ice, strain into an ice-filled highball glass. Top with soda.

Apricot Flavoured Brandy (USA). A Brandy-based liqueur infused with apricots.

Apricot Gin (Eng). A liqueur Gin produced by Hawker's of Plymouth, Devon.

Apricot Lady (Cktl). 1 fl.oz. Apricot brandy, 1 fl.oz. golden Rum, ½ fl.oz. lime juice, 3 dashes orange Curaçao, 2 dashes egg white. Blend with ½ scoop crushed ice, pour into small wine glass.

Apricot Liqueur (USA). Also known as Apry, Abricotine. A liqueur made by the maceration technique.

Apricot Nog (Cktl). ⅓ measure Bacardi White Label, ⅙ measure Apricot brandy, ⅙ measure apricot juice, 3 dashes cream. Blend with scoop of crushed ice, pour into a collins glass.

Apricot Sour (Cktl). 1 fl.oz. Apricot brandy, 2 fl.ozs. lemon juice, dash Angostura, dash Gomme syrup, dash egg white. Shake over ice, strain into a Champagne flute. Add wedge of apricot.

Aprikose mit Whisky (Ger). See Kirsch mit Whisky.

Aprikosengeist (Ger). A Brandy-based liqueur flavoured with apricots.

Aprilia (It). D.O.C. red and white wines from Lazio. Red wines produced from Merlot, Montepulciano and Sangiovese grapes. White wines from Trebbiano grapes.

Apry (Fr). A tawny-coloured liqueur made of apricots soaked in sweetened brandy.

Apsinthion (Gre). Wormwood. From which Absinthe derives.

Apulia (It). The heel of Italy's 'Boot'. The region produces such wines as Bambino, Barletta, Guilia, Locorotondo, Martina Franca, Santo Stefano, Sansevero, Squinzano. Region also known as Puglia.

Aqua (Lat). Water.

Aqua Ardens (Lat). Fiery spirit, raw spirit.

Aqua Bianca (It). An Acquette using silver leaf. See Silver Acquette. (Fr) = Acquette d'Argent.

Aquadiente (Mex). A liqueur made from the Maquey aloe. Distilled from Pulque.

Aqua d'Oro (It). A version of the German Goldwasser. See Gold Acquette. (Fr) = Acquette d'Or.

Aquae Arnementiae (Eng). The Roman name for the Buxton Spring Water spring in the Peak district, Derbyshire.

Aquarius Cocktail (Cktl). ½ measure Bourbon whiskey, ½ measure Cherry brandy, ¼ measure cranberry juice. Shake over ice, strain into an ice-filled old-fashioned glass.

Aquavit (Scan). The name for a spirit distilled from grain or potatoes (rectified spirit) and flavoured with certain aromatic seeds, especially caraway seeds.

Aqua Vitae (Lat). Water of life. Early name given to brandy and other distillates.

Aquavit Fizz (Cktl). ⅕ gill Aquavit, 2 dashes Cherry brandy, 2 dashes lemon juice, 4 dashes Gomme syrup, 1 egg white. Shake well over ice, strain into an ice-filled collins glass. Top with soda.

Aqueduct Cocktail (Cktl). ⅓ measure Vodka, ⅓ measure Brandy, ⅓ measure Curaçao, 4 dashes lime juice. Shake over ice, strain into a cocktail glass. Top with a twist of orange peel.

A

Aqueous (Eng). Water-like.

Aqui (Switz). The brand-name of a still mineral water.

Aquila Rossa (Sp). A noted wine-producer based in the Penedés region of south-eastern Spain. Also produces Vermouths.

Aquileia (It). D.O.C. red and white wines from Friuli-Venezia Giulia. Wines named after main grape varieties – (reds) Aquileia merlot, Cabernet, Reposco, (whites) Aquileia tocai, Friulano, Pinot bianco, Pinot grigio.

Aquitani (Lat). The Roman name for Bordeaux.

A.R. (Fr) (abbr). Appellation Réglementée.

a/R. (Ger) (abbr). am Rhein. (on the Rhine).

Arabica (Afr). See Coffea Arabica.

Arabinose (Eng). A Monosaccharide found in wine that is unfermentable by yeast.

Arack (M.East). See Arak.

Arac Punsch (Nor). An Akvavit-based drink produced by A/S Vinmonopolet.

Arad (Rum). A wine producing district in the Siebenbürgen region of western Rumania.

Aragón (Sp). Denominación de Origen of northern Spain.

Aragon Cocktail (Cktl). ⅓ measure Cognac, ⅓ measure Crème de Banane, ½ measure cream. Shake well over ice, strain into a cocktail glass.

Aragón y Cía (Sp). A wine-producer based in Lucena, Montilla-Moriles.

Araignan (Fr). A white grape variety grown in Palette, Provence.

Arak (M.East). Any type of spirit made in the middle eastern countries from a variety of ingredients. See Arack, Arrack, etc.

Arak Cooler (Cktl). ⅕ gill Arak, ⅛ gill white Rum, dash Gomme syrup, dash lemon juice. Shake over ice, strain into an ice-filled highball glass. Top with iced Champagne.

Araki (M.East). A liqueur made from the juice of dates.

Aral (Tur). A noted large winery that produces red and white wines.

Arame (Port). The fine wire mesh seen on old Reserva bottles.

Aramon (Fr). A red grape variety grown in the south of France and USA. Has a high fruit level and produces average quality wines.

Arana (Sp). A 6 year old, light, red wine produced by Bodegas La Rioja Alta, Rioja.

Aranciata (It). Orangeade.

Aranzada (Sp). A land measure. 1 Aranzada = 0.475 ha.

Arataki (N.Z.). An area in Hawkes Bay where the second government vineyard was established in 1903.

Arawatta (Austr). A wine-producing area in Victoria.

Arbanats (Fr). A commune in the A.C. Graves region in south-western Bordeaux. Le Basque is the main vineyard.

Arbanne (Fr). A lesser white grape variety used in the production of some Champagnes.

Arbin (Fr). A deep-coloured, red V.D.Q.S. wine made from the Mondeuse grape in the Savoie region.

Arbois (Fr). The best known wine district of the Jura in south eastern France. Noted for its white wines.

Arbois Pupillin (Fr). An A.C. commune in the Jura region. Produces red, rosé and white wines.

Arbuissonnas (Fr). A commune in the Beaujolais. Has A.C. Beaujolais Villages or Beaujolais-Arbuissonnas status.

Arcen Brouwerij (Hol). A brewery based in Arcen, Limburg. Noted for its top-fermented beers. Arcen Triple 7.5% alc. by vol. Magnus 6.5% alc. by vol. and Oud Limburgs 5.5% alc. by vol.

Archanes (Gre). A wine region of the isle of Crete. Noted for its red wines of same name.

Archanes (Gre). A wine made in Crete from the Athiri, Kotsifali, Nandilari and Vilana grapes.

Archbishop (Eng). Mulled claret. The wine is heated together with sugar, oranges studded with cloves, then set alight before it is served.

Archer Daniels Midland Co (USA). A large distillery based in Peoria, Illinois. Is noted for its Cane Rums.

Archer's Brewery (Eng). Set up in 1979 in Swindon, Wiltshire.

Archer Stout (Eng). A Sediment beer (stout) 1042 O.G. from Manchester.

Archetto Toscano (It). A pruning method used in the Chianti district of Tuscany. Involves a hard pruning of the vines to give a small but high quality crop.

Archiac (Fr). A commune in the Charente-Maritime Département whose grapes are classed Petite Champagne (Cognac).

Archibald Arrow 70/- (Scot). A 70/- Ale brewed by Allied's Alloa Brewery, Clackmannanshire.

Archimedean Screw (Eng). A style of corkscrew where the cork-penetrating part of the corkscrew is shaped on the Archimedean screw (spiral blade) principle to aid the grip on the cork.

Archipelago Brewery (E.Asia). A brewery based in Kuala Lumpur, Malaya which produces ABC stout and Anchor beer.

Archway Bitter (Eng). A Bitter brewed by the Tooley Street Brewery in London.

Arcins (Fr). A lesser commune of the Haut-Médoc, Bordeaux.

Arcs (Les) (Fr). A wine-producing village in the Côtes de Provence.

Arctic Lite (Eng). A low carbohydrate Lager 1032 O.G. from Burton-on-Trent, Staffordshire.

Ardaillon (Fr). A Vins de Pays area in the Hérault Département of southern France. Red and rosé wines.

Ardanza (Sp). A 5 year old red wine produced by Bodegas La Rioja Alta, Rioja.

Ardbeg Malt (Scot). A single Malt whisky from the Ardbeg Distillery Ltd, Isle of Islay, Argyll. An Islay malt whisky. 40% alc. by vol. Part of Hiram Walker.

Ardeas (Lat). A red wine produced by the Romans in central-western Italy.

Ardèche (Fr). Département of the Côtes du Rhône.

Ardein Estate (S.Afr). A small vineyard in Robertson. Produces a medium sweet white wine from the Clairette and Raisin blanc grapes.

Ardein Vineyard (S.Afr). A small vineyard that sell its grapes to the Mooiuitsig Wynkelders.

Ardent Spirits (Eng). Brandy, Rum and Whisky. Denotes flavoured spirits with a burning sensation as well as flavour.

Ardillats (Fr). A commune in the Beaujolais district. Has the A.C. Beaujolais-Villages or Beaujolais-Ardillats status. Also known as Beaujolais-les-Ardillats.

Ardine (Fr). An Apricot brandy liqueur made by the firm of Bardinet.

Ardmore (Scot). A single Malt whisky distillery based east of Dufftown, Banffshire. A Highland malt whisky. 40% alc. by vol.

Ardon (Switz). A wine-producing village based near Sion in the Valais Canton. Noted for its Fendant wines.

Ardsley Cocktail (Cktl). ½ measure Sloe gin, ½ measure Calisaya. Shake well over ice, strain into a cocktail glass.

Ardsley Cooler (Cktl). 1 measure dry Gin stirred over ice in a highball glass, top with ginger ale. Decorate with sprig of mint.

Arealva (Port). A winery based in Lisbon. Produces red and white wines.

Arechabaia (W.Ind). A major Rum producer in Cuba. Now owned by the State.

Arecibo Distillery (W.Ind). A distillery based in Puerto Rico. Owned by the Puerto Rico Distillers Inc. (part of Seagram). Produces most styles of Rum.

Arena (Eng). The brand name sparkling white wine and tropical fruits drink 4% alc. by vol.

Arenaceous Soil (Eng). Sandy soil, sandstone.

Arenas (Sp). Sandy soil found in the Sherry region (Andalusia). Contains 10% chalk.

Arendal Brewery (Nor). A brewery based in Arendal, southern Norway. Brews Heineken under licence.

Aréni (USSR). A red grape variety grown in Armenia.

Arens (Lat). Thirsty.

Areometer (Eng). A device for measuring the S.G. of grape must. Other names include Oechsle, Baumé, Mustimeter.

Arequipa (Peru). An ancient Inca city where vineyards are planted. Produces mainly white wines.

Ares (Fr). An old measure of land.

Arévchean (USSR). A red, fortified wine produced in Armenia.

Arf an' Arf (Eng). Equal quantities of Pale Ale and Porter. See also Half and Half.

Arg. (S.Am) (abbr). Argentina.

Argal (Eng). See Argol and Argoil.

Argarth Plant (Mex). Another name for the Mezcal cactus. See also Century Plant.

Argens (Fr). A Vins de Pays area in Provence, Var Département, south-eastern France.

Argentina (S.Am). One of the largest producers of wine in the world. Little is exported. Main regions are Mendoza, Salta, San Juan and San Raphael. Criolla is the main grape variety.

Argile (Fr). Clay (soil).

Argile Rouge Bruyère (Fr). A sweet cider apple grown in the Normandy region. Used in the production of sweet ciders.

Argillaceous Soil (Eng). Sedimentary soil of fine ground material. i.e. Clay.

Argillats (Les) (Fr). A Premier Cru vineyard [part] in the A.C. commune of Nuits-Saint-Georges, Côte de Nuits, Burgundy. Also a vineyard in A.C. Nuits-Saint-Georges.

Argillières (Les) (Fr). A Premier Cru vineyard in the A.C. commune of Pommard, Côte de Beaune, Burgundy. 3.64 ha.

Arginine (Eng). An Amino acid found in wine. Is formed by the yeast.

Argoil (Eng). See Argol.

Argol (Eng). Tartaric deposit (Potassium hydrogen tartrate) thrown as the wine matures in cask.

Argonaut Winery (USA). A small winery based in the Sierra Foothills, Amador, California. Grape varieties – Barbera and Zinfandel. Produces varietal wines.

Argonne Oak (Fr). From the Ardenne forest. Used for Champagne casks.

Argyle Brewery (Scot). Edinburgh brewery, originally established as the Leith Brewery in 1982. Noted for its 80/- Ale 1043 O.G.

Aricinum (Lat). A red wine produced in Roman times in central Italy.

Arilli (Lat). Grape pips, raisins.

Arinto (Port). A white grape variety believed to be derived from the Riesling of Germany. Used in the making of Bucelas wines.

Arinto do Dão (Port). A white grape variety grown in the Dão region. Also known as the Assario branco.

Aris (Ger). A white grape variety. Cross between (Riparia x Gamay) and Riesling. Is early ripening and has a high sugar output.

Arise my Love (Cktl). Iced Champagne with 4 dashes of Crème de Menthe. Served in a Champagne flute.

Aristocrat Brandy (USA). The brand-name of a Brandy produced by the California Wine Association, Delano, California. 40% alc. by vol.

Aristophanes (Gre). A poet and playwright who wrote about wine and wine drinking in Ancient Greece.

Arizu (Arg). The brand-name of a noted sparkling wine.

Arjan (Asia). Another name for Koumiss (fermented mare's milk). Made by the Tartars.

Arjoado (Port). A system of vine training using wires stretched between trees.

Arkansas (USA). A small wine-producing region with vineyards mainly in the north of the state in the Ozark mountains.

Arkell's Brewery (Eng). Swindon brewery noted for its cask conditioned beers.

Armada Cream (Sp). A brand of Cream sherry produced by Sandeman.

Armadillo (Eng). A draught British Sherry distributed by Vine Products.

Armagnac (Fr). Brandy region in the Département of Gers in south-eastern France. A.C. is second only to Cognac, its brandies are more fiery than Cognac. Districts are Bas Armagnac, Haut Armagnac and Ténarèze.

Armagnaçais (Fr). A form of continuous still used for the making of Armagnac. See Alambic Armagnaçais.

Armagnac Blanc (Fr). A nickname for the Haut Armagnac. Derives from the chalk and limestone outcrops.

Armagnac Information (Fr). Address =

Maison du Tourisme, 32000 Auch, Haut Armagnac, Gers.

Armagnac Lafontan (Fr). Armagnac producer. Address = Castelnau d'Auzan, 32800 Eauze, Bas Armagnac.

Armagnac Marquis de Terraube (Fr). Armagnac producer. Address = Terraube, 32700-Lectoure, Haut Armagnac.

Armagnac Noir (Fr). A nickname for the Bas Armagnac. Derived from the local dark oak and pine woods.

Armagnac Samalens Sté V.E.V.A (Fr). Distillers of Armagnac. Address = Laujuzan, 32110, Nogoro. Produces ***, VSOP, Vintage 1930, 1939, Vieille Relique 15 y.o. Cuvée Anniversaire (consists of certain Bas Armagnacs which are almost 100 y.o).

Armagnac Sour (Cktl). ⅓ measure Armagnac, ⅔ measure fresh lemon juice, 1 teaspoon castor sugar, 1 teaspoon egg white, dash Angostura. Shake over ice, strain into a Champagne flute, top with a slice of orange.

Armagnac Vve Goudoulin (Fr). Armagnac producer. Address = Domaine de Bigor Courrensan, 32330-Gondrin.

Armazem (Port). Warehouse or wine store.

Armenia (USSR). An important wine region of the southern Soviet Union producing mainly dessert wines.

Armenias (S.Am). A noted coffee-producing region in Colombia.

Armentia y Madrazo (Sp). A red wine from the Haro district of Rioja.

Armillaria Mellea (Lat). A fungus that attacks the vine roots. See Armillaria Root-rot.

Armillaria Root-rot (Eng). A fungal disease which attacks the roots of the vines especially in sandy soils. Family = Pourridié. See also Armillaria Mellea, Dermatophora Necatrix and Rosellinia Necatrix.

A.R. Morrow Brandy (USA). The brand-name of a Brandy produced by the California Wine Association, Delano, California. In oak matured for 10 yrs.

Armsheim (Ger). Village. (Anb) = Rheinhessen. (Ber) = Bingen. (Gro) = Adelberg. (Vins) = Geiersberg, Goldstückchen, Leckerberg.

Arnberg (Ger). Vineyard. (Anb) = Franken. (Ber) = Maindreieck. (Gro) = Rosstal. (Vil) = Gössenheim.

Arnedo (Sp). A Zona de Crianza in the Rioja Baja region of north-eastern Spain.

Arneis (It). A white grape variety grown in Piemonte.

Arnes Journal (Ger). A wine and food

A

monthly magazine. Address = Arne-Verlag, Postfach 1247, 6203 Hochheim, West Germany.

Arnoison (Fr). Alternative name for the Chardonnay grape.

Arnstein (Ger). Village. (Anb) = Franken. (Ber) = Maindreieck. (Gro) = Rosstal. (Vins) = Assorted parts of vineyards.

Aroka (Asia). A fiery potent spirit made from mares' milk by the Tartar tribesmen with added grape juice.

Aroma (Eng). A distinctive fresh fragrance which is given off by the wine after being exposed to the air. Part of the bouquet.

Aroma (Eng). The smell/bouquet that the coffee grounds release when they are brewed.

Aromatic Geneva (Hol). A liqueur made with old Geneva which has been flavoured with aromatic herbs.

Aromatised Wines (Eng). Wines flavoured with herbs and other substances. Often fortified.

Arome (Fr). Odour or bouquet of wines or spirits.

Around the World Cocktail (Cktl). 1/3 measure white Rum, 1/3 measure orange juice, 1/3 measure lemon juice, 4 dashes Orgeat syrup, 2 dashes Cognac. Blend altogether in a blender with a scoop of crushed ice. Pour into a flute glass. Serve with straws.

Arpa (Tur). Barley.

Arpu (Egy). Old Egyptian word for wine.

Arquebuse (Fr). A white herb digestive liqueur. See also Eau d'Arquebuse.

Arraca (Fr). Old word to denote the removal of the wine off the lees. See Racking.

Arrack (M.East). The name derived from the Arabic for juice or sweet and designates native spirits. There are many types of Arrack, but they all have a spicy flavour. Other names are Arraki, Arak, Aruk, Raki, etc.

Arrack Punsch (Scan). Another name for Swedish Punsch. See also Caloric Punsch.

Arrack-Verschnitt (Ger). Verschnitt containing at least 10% Arrack.

Arraki (M.East). See Arrack.

Arrakverschnitt (Ger). A Rum and Arrak blend. (10% Arrack).

Arrata's Vineyard (USA). A small vineyard based in Santa Clara County, California. Grape variety – Cabernet sauvignon.

Arrasburg-Schlossberg (Ger). Vineyard. (Anb) = Mosel-Saar-Ruwer. (Ber) = Zell/Mosel. (Gro) = Grafschaft. (Vil) = Alf.

Arraubo (Mad). Boiled down grape must.

Also spelt Arrobe.

Arriba Kettle (Sp). A noted bodega based in the Penedés region. Produces Mont Marcel (a dry white wine).

Arrières Côtes (Fr). Communes in the Burgundy region that are to the west of the Côte d'Or, consisting of the Haut-Côtes de Nuits and the Haut-Côtes de Beaune. See Dijon.

Arrière-Gout (Fr). After-taste.

Arroba (Sp). A wine measure holding $16^2/_3$ litres. Can vary in other Spanish speaking countries.

Arrobe (Mad). See Arraubo.

Arrobe (Port). Fruit syrup.

Arrope (Sp). Boiling down the wine to sweeten and add colour to sherries. First made by the Moors. Boiled down to 1/5 quantity in Jerez and 1/3 in Málaga.

Arrosé (Fr). Watered.

Arrowfield (Austr). A winery based in the Hunter Valley, New South Wales.

Arrow Head (Cktl). 1/5 gill Bourbon whiskey, 2 dashes dry Vermouth, 2 dashes sweet Vermouth, 2 dashes lemon juice, dash egg white. Shake over ice, strain into a cocktail glass.

Arroyo, Rafael (W.Ind). A chemist who greatly improved the Rum distilling and ageing process in the early twentieth century in Puerto Rico.

Arroyo Seco (USA). Lit – 'Dry wash'. On a wine label denotes that the wine originates from a river-bottom area in Salinas Valley, Monterey County, California.

Arroyo Seco Vineyard (USA). A large vineyard based in Salinas Valley, Monterey County, California. 150 ha. Grape varieties – Cabernet sauvignon, Chardonnay, Merlot and Petite syrah. Produces varietal wines.

Arrumbador (Sp). The name for a bodega employee.

Ars (Fr). A commune in the Charente-Maritime Département whose grapes are classed Petite Champagne (Cognac).

Arsac (Fr). A commune within the district of the Médoc, Bordeaux. Château du Terre best wine. Red wines can use A.C. Margaux designation.

Arsenol (Cyp). Mis-spelling of Arsinoe.

Arsinoe (Cyp). A very dry white wine produced by Sodap. See Arsenol, Arsinol.

Arsinol (Cyp). Mis-spelling of Arsinoe.

Art (Ger). A term to denote character in a wine.

Art and Science of Brewing (USA). See Zymurgy.

Artemisia Absinthium (Lat). Wormwood.

Arthenac (Fr). A commune in the

Charente-Maritime Département whose grapes are classed Petite Champagne (Cognac).

Arthur Bell and Sons (Scot). See Bell's.

Arthur Cooper (Eng). The trading name used by Imperial Retail Shops Ltd. (division of Courage Ltd). Over 200 wine shops.

Arthur Girard (Fr). A cuvée (part of Marconnets) in the A.C. commune of Savigny-lès-Beaune, Côte de Beaune, Burgundy. Is owned by the Hospices de Beaune.

Arthur Narf (Eng) (slang). ½ bottled Guinness and ½ draught Guinness mixed together.

Arthur Rackham (Eng). 13 specialist wine shops in London's Thames Valley area. Runs the Vintner wine club. See Vintner (The).

Artichoke Brandy (Fr). Distillation of Jerusalem artichokes.

Artificiel (Fr). A term applied to a Kirsch made from a neutral alcohol which is diluted to normal strength and flavoured with essences.

Artig (Ger). Smooth rounded wine.

Artillery Cocktail (Cktl). ½ measure Gin, ½ measure Italian vermouth, 2 dashes Angostura. Stir over ice, strain into cocktail glass.

Artillery Punch (Punch). Juice of 2 pineapples, and 8 oranges, ½ pint light Rum, ½ pint Bourbon whiskey, 2½ pints dry Cider. Stir together and chill, add 3 pints iced Champagne (or sparkling wine).

Artimino (It). A Chianti Putto wine producer in Tuscany.

Artis (Fr) (abbr). Cru Artisans. Bordeaux classification.

Artist (Eng) (slang). A term used to describe an experienced drinker.

Artist Bitter (Eng). A light keg Bitter 1032 O.G. from Moorland's Abingdon, Brewery, Abingdon, Berkshire.

Artists Ale (Eng). A premium cask conditioned Bitter 1055 O.G. from Paradise Brewery, Hayle, Cornwall.

Artist's Cocktail (Cktl). ⅓ measure Whisky, ⅓ measure Sherry, ⅙ measure Groseille syrup, ⅙ measure lemon juice. Shake over ice, strain into a cocktail glass.

Artois Brasserie (Bel). A brewery based in Louvain. Noted for Abbaye De Leffe, Chevalier Marin, Ginder, Ketje, Loburg, Radieuse, Vieux Temps and Wielemans beers. See also Stella Artois.

Aruba (W.Ind). A small island off the coast of Venezuela. Produces light Rums.

Aruk (M.East). See Arrack.

Arunda Sektkellerei (It). A noted sparkling (méthode champenoise)

producer based in Mölten, Südtirol (South Tyrol).

Arva (E.Ind). A fermented liquor produced in Polynesia. See Ava and Ava Ava.

Arvelets (Les) (Fr). A Premier Cru vineyard in the A.C. Commune of Fixin, Côte de Nuits, Burgundy. 3.36 ha.

Arvelets (Les) (Fr). A Premier Cru vineyard in the A.C. commune of Pommard, Côte de Beaune, Burgundy. 8.5 ha.

Arvèze (Fr). A Gentian liqueur apéritif from Auvergne.

Arvine (Switz). A white grape variety. Old Valais and Vaud stock, giving a wine that is dry and full-bodied. Also dessert wines.

Arvino (It). A local name for the Gaglioppo grape in Savuto and Pollino, Calabria.

Arzelle (Fr). Decomposed mica soil found in the northern Rhône. In the Condrieu and Château Grillet estates.

Arzheim (Ger). Village. (Anb) = Rheinpfalz. (Ber) = Südliche Weinstrasse. (Gro) = Königsgarten. (Vins) = Rosenberg, Seligmacher.

Arzlay (Ger). Vineyard. (Anb) = Mosel-Saar-Ruwer. (Ber) = Zell/Mosel. (Gro) = Rosenhang. (Vil) = Cochem.

Asahi Brewery (Jap). A brewery based in Hokkaido. Has 6 divisions and produces light and dark beers. Also spelt Asaki.

Asaki Brewery (Jap). See Asahi Brewery.

Asali (Afr). An East African beverage fermented from honey.

Asbach Uralt (Ger). A famous German brandy matured in Limousin oak. 40% alc. by vol.

Asbestos Pulp (Eng). Originally used for filtering wines and beers. Now succeeded by cellulose pads and membrane filters.

Aschaffenburg (Ger). Village. (Anb) = Franken. (Ber) = Mainviereck. (Gro) = Not yet assigned. (Vin) = Pompejaner.

Asciato (It). Dry wine. See also Asciutto.

Asciutto (It). Dry wine. See also Asciato.

Ascorbic Acid (Eng). An additive to wines. Vitamin C. Acts as an antioxidant. SO_2 must be present. Used with caution.

Ascot Vineyards (Eng). First planted 1979. 1.7 ha. Address = Ascot Farm, Ascot, Royal Berkshire. Grape varieties – Madeleine angevine, Madeleine sylvaner, (3% each), Müller-Thurgau 50%, Pinot noir 3%, Reichensteiner 35%, Siegerrebe 3% and Zweigeitrebe 3%.

A.S.E. (USA) (abbr). American Society of Enologists.

Asenovgrad (Bul). A winery that

produces majority of red Mavrud wine in region of same name.

Asensio Carcelen (Sp). A small winery and wine museum based in Jumilla. Produces mainly Monastrell wines.

Asescence (Eng). A wine malady. Has a strong smell of nail varnish and tastes vinegary. Attacked by acetobacter, requires presence of air. Caused mainly by bad storage in vat or a faulty cork. See also Piqûre.

Ashanti Gold (Den). A chocolate liqueur produced by Peter Heering near Copenhagen.

Ashbourne (Eng). A natural spring water, carbonated or still, from Dovedale, Derbyshire. Agents = Nestlé & Co, St. Georges House, Croydon, Surrey.

Ashbrook Estate (Austr). Vineyard. Address = P.O.Box 263, West Perth, Western Australia. 6005. Grapes– Cabernet franc, Cabernet sauvignon, Chardonnay, Merlot, Sauvignon blanc, Verdelho. Winery address = South Harmans Road, Willyabrup, W. Austr.

Ash Drink (Eng). See Frénette.

Ashe Park Water (Eng). A mineral water. Still and carbonated varieties. Address = Ashe Park Estate, Steventon, Hampshire, RG25 3AY.

Ashford Brewery (Eng). Started in 1983 in Ashford, Kent. Produces – Challenger 1039 O.G. Kentish Gold 1035 O.G. Old Gold 1047 O.G.

Ashkelon (Isr). A Palestinian wine written about by the Romans.

Ashman's Winery (Austr). Part of Tyrell's, New South Wales.

Ashtarak (USSR). A dessert wine produced in Armenia.

Ashton Co-operative (S.Afr). Vineyards based in Robertson. Address = Ashton Koöperatiewe Wynkelder, Box 40, Ashton 6715. Produces varietals (known as A.K.W).

Ashton Koöperatiewe Wynkelder (S.Afr). See Ashton Co-operative.

Asid (Wales). Acid.

Asidig (Wales). Acidic.

Asindirmak (Tur). Vine grafting.

Asit (Tur). Acid.

Askalon (Isr). A noted Co-operative that produces red and white table wines.

Askeri (Iran). A small sweet white grape variety.

Askos (Gre). Wineskin. Skin bottle (bag) for holding wine. Used in Ancient Greece.

Asma (Tur). A word used to describe a hanging vine (trellised).

Asociación Barmen Españolos (Sp). A.B.E. Spanish Bartenders' Association. Address = Duque de Medin-

aceli-2 Madrid.

Asociación de Criadores Exportadores de Vino de Jerez (Sp). The Sherry growers' and exporters' association. Replaces the disbanded Grupo de Exportadores.

Asociación Mexicana de Barmen (Mex). A.M.B. Mexican Bartenders' Association. Address = 28,2 Piso, Mexico. 1, D.F.

Asociación Venezolana de Barmen (Ven). A.V.B. Venezuelan Bartenders' Association. Address = Nuevo Centro, Piso 11 Office 11b, Av. Libertador Chacao, Caracas.

Aspall Cyder House (Eng). A traditional family Cider-producing firm. Address = Debenham, Stowmarket, Suffolk.

Aspartic Acid (Eng). An Amino acid found in wines. Is formed by the yeast.

Aspenberg (Ger). Vineyard. (Anb) = Nahe. (Ber) = Schloss Böckelheim. (Gro) = Paradiesgarten. (Vil) = Bayerfeld-Steckweiler.

Aspenberg (Ger). Vineyard. (Anb) = Nahe. (Ber) = Schloss Böckelheim. (Gro) = Paradiesgarten. (Vil) = Oberndorf.

Aspen Ridge Winery (N.Z.). A small winery near Te Kauwhata in the North Island. 6 ha.

Asperg (Ger). Village. (Anb) = Württemberg. (Ber) = Württembergisch Unterland. (Gro) = Schalkstein. (Vin) = Berg.

Aspergillus Aryzae (Jap). Another spelling of Aspergillus Oryzae.

Aspergillus Oryzae (Jap). A special fungus called 'Malted rice fungus' used in the brewing of Saké. Also known as Koji mould.

Aspersion (Fr). A frost precaution used in Burgundy. The vines are sprayed with water to form a protective coating of ice.

Aspiran (Fr). A wine-producing commune in the A.C. Clairette du Languedoc, southern France.

Aspirating Valve (Eng). A valve which maintains the condition of beers which remain in cask for several days. Allows the beer to be drawn from cask and for CO_2 to replace it. Also called a 'Cask breather' or 'Demand valve'.

Aspisheim (Ger). Village. (Anb) = Rheinhessen. (Ber) = Bingen. (Gro) = Sankt Rochuskapelle. (Vins) = Johannisberg, Sonnenberg.

Asprinio (It). A white wine produced in Basilicata from a district of same name.

Aspro (Gre). The name given to lesser table wines produced by Tsantali.

Assaggiatore (It). Wine taster.

Assam (Ind). A major Indian tea-growing and producing region.

Assam (Ind). A variety of tea bush. Light leaved and dark leaved varieties. Single stemmed trees.

Assario (Port). A white grape variety grown in Alentejo.

Assario Branco (Port). Another name for the Arinto do Dão.

Assemat (J.C.) (Fr). A propriétaire-recoltant based at Roquemaure, 30150 Gard. Produces A.C. Lirac. See Rouge d'Eté, Lirac Rouge Classique and Domaine des Causses et Saint-Eynes.

Assemblage (Fr). The blending of wines of the same age, region, district, commune or vineyard of origin.

Assenovgrad (Bul). A delimited wine-producing area based in southern Bulgaria.

Assenzio (It). Absinthe.

Assetato (It). Thirsty.

Assirtico (Gre). A white grape variety used in the production of the white wine Agioritikos.

Assmannshausen (Ger). A village on the north west of the Rheingau region noted for its red wines made from the Spätburgunder grape.

Assmannshausen (Ger). Village. (Anb) = Rheingau. (Ber) = Johannisberg. (Gro) = Steil. (Vin) = Frankentha.

Assmannshausen-Aulhausen (Ger). Village. (Anb) = Rheingau. (Ber) = Johannisberg. (Gro) = Burgweg. (Vin) = Berg Kaisersteinfels.

Assmannshausen-Aulhausen (Ger). Village. (Anb) = Rheingau. (Ber) = Johannisberg. (Gro) = Steil. (Vins) = Hinterkirch, Höllenberg.

Associação Barmen de Portugal (Port). A.B.P. Portuguese Bartenders' Association. Address = Trav. da. Fábricados Pentres 27, 1°-1200 Lisbon.

Associação Bradileira de Barmen (Bra). A.B.B. Brazil's Bartenders' Association. Address = Avenue Angelica, 845 C.E.P. 01227, São Paulo. Brazil.

Associacão dos Produtores-Engarrafadores de Vinho Verde (Port). APEVV. An association of the single quinta estates in the Vinhos Verdes to protect and improve Vinhos Verdes wines. Founded in January 1985.

Assoiado (Port). Partner in a co-operative winery.

Associated Tavern Owners of America (USA). A.T.O.A. The USA equivalent of the Licensed House Managers Association in the U.K.

Associated Vintners (USA). Main wine producer in Yakima Valley, Washington, Pacific North-West. Produces wines from a 13 ha. vineyard based in Redwood.

Association de Propriétaires de Grands Crus Classés de Saint-Émilion (Fr) Address = Les Templiers, Rue Guadet. BP 46, 33330 Saint-Émilion.

Association des Barmen de France (Fr). A.B.F. French Bartenders' Association. Address = 192, Boulevard Haussman, 75008, Paris.

Association des Viticulteurs de la Côte d'Or (Fr). A body which advises the growers in the Côte d'Or, Burgundy.

Association Mutual de Barmen y Afines (Arg). A.M.B.A. Argentina's Bartenders' Association. Address = Avenue Juan de Garay 1927, Buenos Aires.

Association Nationale Technique pour l'Amélioration de la Viticulture (Fr). See A.N.T.A.V.

Association Professionnelle des Producteurs Embouteilleurs de Rhum Agricole de la Martinique (W.Ind). See A.P.P.E.R.A.M.

Association Technique Viticole de Bourgogne (Fr). A body whose aim is to improve vine growing and wine making in Burgundy.

Associazione Italiana Barmen e Sostenitori (It). A.I.B.E.S. Italian Bartenders' Association. Address = Via Baldissera 2–20129 Milan, Italy.

Assoiffé (Fr). Thirsty.

Assumption Abbey (USA). The brand name for Brookside Cellar wines in San Bernardino, California.

Assyrtiko (Gre). A white grape variety grown mainly in the southern Greek islands of Cyclades. Produces the straw wine Santorini.

Astenbecker (Der) (Ger). A wheat-based Branntwein produced by Furstlich Munster von Derneburgische Brennerei, Astenbeck.

Astheim (Ger). Village. (Anb) = Franken. (Ber) = Maindreieck. (Gro) = Kirchberg. (Vin) = Karthäuser.

Astinenza (It). Abstinence.

Asti (USA). A red wine-producing area based in the Italian Swiss Colony, California.

Asti Spumante (It). D.O.C. sparkling wine produced in the Piemonte region by natural fermentation using the Moscato naturale d'Asti grape. Has an aromatic taste which is characteristic of the Muscat grape. Delicately sweet. See also Moscato d'Asti Spumante.

Asti Spumanti (It). See Asti Spumante.

Astley Vineyards (Eng). Vineyards based at Stourport, Worcestershire. 1.7 ha. Grape varieties – Huxelrebe, Kerner, Madeleine angevine and Müller-Thurgau.

Aston Manor Brewery (Eng). A brewery set up in Birmingham in 1983.

Astoria Cocktail (Cktl). ⅕ gill Calvados, dash Amer Picon. Shake over ice, strain into a cocktail glass. Squeeze of lemon peel juice on top.

Astra Beer (Ger). The principal beer of the Bavarian St. Pauli Brauerei of Hamburg.

Astringency (Eng). Having an excess of tannin. See Astringent.

Astringent (Eng). A term used by a wine taster and applied to wines with an excess of tannin. Many red wines are astringent when young, but mellow and soften with age.

Astronaut Cocktail (Cktl). ⅓ measure Vodka, ⅓ measure white Rum, ⅓ measure lemon juice, dash passion fruit juice. Shake over ice, strain into an ice-filled highball glass. Top with a slice of lemon.

Asugar (Sp). See Muscavado.

A/S Vinmonopolet (Nor). State wine and spirits monopoly. See Lysholm (Jorgen B.) Distillery.

Aszar-Neszmely (Hun). One of fifteen wine-producing regions. Is situated in northern Transdanubia. Noted for its fine white wines.

Asztali Bor (Hun). Table wine.

Aszú (Hun). A term found on the labels of Tokay wines. Indicates a sweet, luscious wine made with botrytis attacked grapes. See Puttonyos.

Aszúbor (Hun). A sweeter type of Tokay wine. See Aszú.

Atacama (Chile). Noted vineyards based in northern Chile.

Atatürk (Kemal) (Tur). A statesman who built a winery in 1925 in the hope of encouraging more wine production amongst the Muslim people in Turkey.

Ataturk Farm Administration (Tur). A co-operative winery that produces fine, full wines.

Aţel (Rum). An important wine-producing area. Is part of the Tîrnave vineyard.

Athenaeus (Egy). A writer who lived in ancient Egypt and produced works on wine and gastronomy, notably the Deipnosophistae. Lived in the third century A.D.

Athiri (Gre). A white grape variety used mainly in southern Greece and Crete.

Athol Brose (Scot). A liqueur based on whisky mixed with honey and/or oatmeal and cream.

Athol Brose Number One (Cktl). 1 measure Athol Brose, 1 dessertspoon clear honey, 1 sherry glass cream. Mix well, warm slightly. Allow to cool before drinking.

Athol Brose Number Two (Cktl). 1 teaspoon clear honey into a tumbler containing 2 measures of Athol Brose. Top with heated milk, allow to cool before drinking.

Athos (Gre). A monastery that produces palatable local wines.

Atlantic Cognac Cocktail (Cktl). ⅔ measure Cognac, ⅓ measure Crème de Café. Shake over ice, strain into a collins glass. Top with orange juice, stir and decorate with a cherry and orange slice.

Atlantic Distillers (Can). A subsidiary of Seagram. Produces a range of Canadian whiskies.

A.T.O.A. (USA) (abbr). Associated Tavern Owners of America.

Atomic Cocktail (Eng). An aqueous solution of a radioactive substance such as sodium iodine which is drunk as part of the treatment for cancer.

Atta Boy Cocktail (Cktl). ⅗ measure dry Gin, ⅖ measure French vermouth, 4 dashes Grenadine. Shake well over ice, strain into a cocktail glass.

Attemporators (Eng). Spiral-shaped metal coils which are immersed in the fermentation vats and through which hot or cold water is passed. This regulates the temperature of the fermenting must.

Attenuate (Eng). Term used for the amount of sugar which has been used up by the yeast during fermentation.

Attica (Gre). A wine-producing area of the Kephesia district in central Greece where most of the Retsina is produced.

Attic Wine (Gre). The collective name which is used for the wines from the Attica region.

Attila Cocktail (Cktl). ⅔ measure Banyuls, ⅓ measure Vodka. Stir over ice, strain into a cocktail glass. Add soda water and dress with a spiral of lemon peel.

Attilafelsen (Ger). Grosslagen. (Anb) = Baden. (Ber) = Kaiserstuhl-Tuniberg. (Vils) = Gottenheim, Merdingen, Munzingen, Niederrimsingen, Oberrimsingen, Opfingen, Tiengen, Waltershofen.

Atzmauth (Isr). A sweet dessert wine.

Atzmon (Isr). A medium-dry, red, table wine.

Aubaine (Fr). An alternative name for the Chardonnay grape.

Aube (Fr). A Département that adjoins Marne in the south of the Champagne region. District = Château Thierry. See Canton de l'Aube.

Auberge (Fr). Inn or tavern. See Alberga.

Aubergiste (Fr). Innkeeper.

Aubin Blanc (Fr). A white wine produced in the Côtes de Toul, Lorraine.

Aucerot (Austr). A minor white grape used for blending, grown in the Hunter Valley, New South Wales.

Auch (Fr). A town in the Armagnac brandy region. Gers Département

Auchentoshan (Scot). A Lowland malt distillery noted for its triple distilled whisky. Address = Dalmuir, Nr Glasgow, Dunbartonshire. 40% alc. by vol. Owned by Stanley P. Morrison. Produces 10 and 18 years old malts. See Weaks and Strongs.

Auchere (Jacques et Fils) (Fr). A noted producer of A.C. Sancerre wines (white, rosé and red). Address = Le Bois de l'Abbaye, Bué, 18300 Sancerre, Loire.

Auchroisk (Scot). A single Malt whisky distillery north of Dufftown, Banffshire. A Highland malt whisky. 40% alc. by vol.

Auckland (N.Z.). A wine-producing area on the north west coast of the North Island.

Au Closeau (Fr). A Premier Cru vineyard of the commune A.C. Gevrey-Chambertin, Côte de Nuits, Burgundy. 0.5 ha.

Audacia Estate (S.Afr). Vineyard based in Stellenbosch. Address = Audacia Langoed, P.O. Box 50, Lynedoch 7603. Produces varietal wines.

Aude (Fr). A Département of the Languedoc-Roussillon in the Plaine de l'Aude.

Audit Barley Wine (Eng). A Barley wine brewed by the Greene King Brewery, Biggleswade, Bedfordshire.

Auen (Ger). Village. (Anb) = Nahe. (Ber) = Schloss Böckelheim. (Gro) = Paradiesgarten. (Vins) = Kaulenberg, Römerstich.

Auenstein (Ger). Village. (Anb) = Württemberg. (Ber) = Württembergisch Unterland. (Gro) = Schozachtal. (Vins) = Burgberg, Schlossberg.

Auersthal (Aus). A wine village in the Falkenstein-Matzen district of northeastern Austria. Produces mainly white wines.

Aufbesserung (Aus). The sugaring of the grape must to increase the alcohol content. (Fr) = Chaptalisation. (Ger) = Anreicherung.

Auf Dem Zimmerberg (Ger). Vineyard. (Anb) = Nahe. (Ber) = Schloss Böckelheim. (Gro) = Paradiesgarten. (Vil) = Oberstreit.

Auf Der Heide (Ger). Vineyard. (Anb) = Mosel-Saar-Ruwer. (Ber) = Bernkastel. (Gro) = Schwarzlay. (Vil) = Traben-Trarbach (ortsteil Wolf).

Auf Der Kupp (Ger). Vineyard. (Anb) = Mosel-Saar-Ruwer. (Ber) = Saar-Ruwer. (Gro) = Scharzberg. (Vil) = Konz.

Aufgesetzter (Ger). The name used for Kornbranntwein or pure alcohol that is flavoured with blackcurrant juice.

Auflangen (Ger). Grosslagen. (Anb) = Rheinhessen. (Ber) = Nierstein. (Vil) = Nierstein.

Aufwaerts Co-operative (S.Afr). Vineyards based in Goudini. Address = Aufwaerts Koöperatieve Wynkelder Bpk. Box 51, Rawsonville 6845. Produces Sherry-type and white wines.

Aufwaerts Koöperatiewe Wynkelder (S.Afr). See Aufwaerts Co-operative.

Augarant (Fr). A vineyard in the A.C. Fleurie, Cru Beaujolais-Villages, Burgundy.

Augenscheiner (Ger). Vineyard. (Anb) = Mosel-Saar-Ruwer. (Ber) = Saar-Ruwer. (Gro) = Römerlay. (Vil) = Trier.

Auggen (Ger). Village. (Anb) = Baden. (Ber) = Markgräflerland. (Gro) = Burg Neuenfels. (Vins) = Letten, Schäf.

Augier et Frères (Fr). The oldest Cognac house, formed in 1643. Now owned by Seagram.

Augsburger (USA). A Premium beer 5.5% alc. by vol. brewed by the Huber Brewery in Monroe, Wisconsin.

Auguardiente (Sp). Brandy.

Augusta (USA). An American grape variety. Both red and white varieties.

Augusta (USA). A small community based on the Missouri river. Has its own appellation. Wines given this appellation must contain 85% of Augusta grape.

Augustiner (Ger). A famous old brewery of Munich. Noted for its Bock beers. See Augustiner Dunkel and Maximator.

Augustinerberg (Ger). Vineyard. (Anb) = Baden. (Ber) = Kaiserstuhl-Tuniberg. (Gro) = Vulkanfelsen. (Vil) = Breisach a. Rh.

Augustiner Dunkel (Ger). A dark rich malty Bier from the Augustiner Brauerei of Munich.

August Schmidt (Ger). Address = 3000 Hannover, Hainholz. Distiller of Kornbranntweins and Weizenkorns.

Augustus Barnett (Eng). Specialist wine retail chain of shops owned by Bass.

Aujoux et Cie (Fr). A Burgundy négociant-éleveur. Address = 20 Bld Emile-Guyot, Saint-Georges-de-Reneins. Deals mainly in Beaujolais and Côte d'Or wines.

Aul (Scan). The name for the Viking beer brewed from barley. (Eng) = Ale, (Swe) (Den) = öl and (Nor) = Øl.

Auld Alliance (Cktl). ⅓ measure French

vermouth, ⅓ measure Glayva, ⅓ measure Cognac. Stir over ice, strain into an old-fashioned glass.

Auld Man's Milk (Cktl). ½ measure Jamaican rum, ½ measure Cognac, 1 teaspoon sugar, 1 egg, 2 measures boiling milk. Shake in a heated shaker, pour into a goblet. Top with grated nutmeg.

Auld Man's Milk (Scot) (slang). A term for whisky.

Auld Man's Milk (Punch). Heat a bottle of strong Ale in pan. Add ¼ teaspoon cinnamon, ¼ teaspoon nutmeg, ¼ teaspoon ginger. Add 2 beaten egg yolks and 2 teaspoons brown sugar when Ale has almost boiled. Stir slowly and well. Add 2 measures of Scotch whisky. Serve as hot as possible.

Auld Reekie (Scot). A cask conditioned Ale 1037 O.G. brewed by the Rose Street Brewery. An Alloa home-brew public house in Edinburgh.

Aulenberg (Ger). Vineyard. (Anb) = Rheinhessen. (Ber) = Nierstein. (Gro) = Krötenbrunnen. (Vil) = Ülversheim.

Aulerde (Ger). Vineyard. (Anb) = Rheinhessen. (Ber) = Wonnegau. (Gro) = Bergkloster. (Vil) = Westhofen.

Aultmore (Scot). A single Malt whisky distillery based near Keith, Banffshire. A Highland malt whisky. 40% alc. by vol.

Aum (Ger). A wine cask usually about 160 litres.

Aume (Fr). An Alsace cask of 114 litres. (25.1 gallons).

Aunt Jemima (Pousse Café). ⅓ measure each in order Brandy, (white) Crème de Menthe and Bénédictine.

Aupy (Henri) (Fr). A wine-producer based in Le Puy-Notre-Dame, Saumur, Anjou-Saumur, Loire. Noted for Saumur Mousseux.

Aurora (USA). White hybrid grape variety. Also known as Siebel 5279.

Aurore Cocktail (Cktl). ⅔ measure Bacardi White Label, ⅙ measure Mandarine Napoléon, ⅙ measure Crème de Framboise. Shake over ice, strain into a cocktail glass. Top with a spiral of orange and lemon peel.

Aurum (It). A pale gold liqueur with a flavour of oranges. 40% alc. by vol.

Aurum Cocktail (Cktl). ¼ measure Aurum, ¼ measure Gin, ½ measure sweet Vermouth. Stir over ice. Strain into a cocktail glass.

Aus (Ger) (Aus) (abbr). Aussle. (A wine from selected grapes).

Aus (Aus) (abbr). Austria.

Ausberger (S.Afr). A sweet white wine made from a blend of Steen and other grape varieties from the SFW produced

under the Autumn Harvest label.

Ausbruch (Aus). A wine category. Wines are made from over-ripe grapes attacked by Botrytis. (Min. must weight 27°KMW 150 Oechsle).

Ausbruchwein (Aus). See Ausbruch.

Ausdruckslos (Ger). A term used to describe an undistinctive wine.

Aus Eigenem Lesegut (Ger). Denotes 'From producer's own estate'.

Ausejo (Sp). A Zona de Crianza in the Rioja Baja region of north-eastern Spain.

Ausg'stecktist (Aus). Viennese daily paper from which can be found the list of the Heurigen open that day.

Aus Ländern Der E.W.G. (EEC). Table wine blended and bottled in Germany from wines produced by EEC member countries.

Auslese (Aus). A wine category. Must be made from fully ripe grapes, separated from any semi-ripe, imperfect or unhealthy grapes. (Min. must weight 21° KMW. 105 Oechsle).

Auslese (Ger). A wine quality category. Produced from late picked, selected ripe bunches of grapes. Makes a sweet white wine.

Ausleseweine (Ger). An old term for wine of Auslese quality. Pre 1971.

Ausone (Fr). A Premier Grand Cru Classé of Saint-Émilion. See Château Ausone.

Ausonius (Lat). A fourth century Roman poet from Bordeaux. Château Ausone was named after him.

Ausoniusstein (Ger). Vineyard. (Anb) = Mosel-Saar-Ruwer. (Ber) = Zell/Mosel. (Gro) = Weinhex. (Vil) = Lehmen.

Aussay (Eng). The old English name for Alsation wines. See also Osey.

Aussichtsterrasse der Deutschen Weinstrasse (Ger). 'Viewpoint of the German wine route' at the Schloss Ludwigshöhe near Edenkoben in the Rheinpfalz.

Aussle (Ger) (Aus). A wine from selected grapes.

Ausstich (Aus). A selection of the best finished Auslese wines, blended. Can be red or white.

Aussy (Les) (Fr). A Premier Cru vineyard (part) in the A.C. commune of Volnay, Côte de Beaune, Burguney.

Austr (Austr) (abbr). Australia.

Australia (Austr). A wine-producing country in southern hemisphere. Has been producing wines for 150 years. Wine regions in southern part of country. New South Wales, South Australia, Victoria and Western Australia. Main districts are – Adelaide, Barossa Valley, Clare Watervale, Coonawarra, Great Western, Hunter Valley, Margaret River, Mudgee, Murray Valley, Southern Vales, Swan Valley, Tasmania and Yarra Valley.

Australian Bartenders' Guild (Austr). A.B.G. Address = c/o Catering Institute of Australia, P.O. Box A.497, Sydney, New South Wales. 2000.

Australian Rum (Austr). Production commenced in the late nineteenth century. Both white and dark Rums produced. See Beenleigh and Bundaberg.

Australian Sherry (Austr). The name given to wines made in the style of true Spanish sherry. Most is of the Cream and Medium styles.

Australian Whiskey (Austr). A Grain whiskey distilled in a style which is a cross between Scotch and Irish whiskies.

Australian Wine Board (Austr). The governing body of the Australian wine industry. Government controlled.

Australian Wine Research Institute (Austr). An organisation based at Glen Osmond, near Adelaide, South Australia. Helps raise standards and promote Australian wines.

Austria (Aus). A major wine producing country in central Europe. Wines are produced to the same style as the German wines. Main regions are – Burgenland, Niederösterreich, Steiermark and Wien.

Austrian Rum (Aus). A blend of spirits and Rum similar to Rumverschnitt. (2% Rum). Known as Inländerrum.

Austried (Ger). A term to denote the first signs that the growers have of the condition of the vines after the winter and spring frosts.

Auténtico (Sp). A fresh, fruity, young red wine produced in Binisalem, Majorca. Made from the Montenegro grape.

Authental (Ger). Vineyard. (Anb) = Rheinhessen. (Ber) = Nierstein. (Gro) = Vogelsgärten. (Vil) = Guntersblum.

Autoclave (It). Name given to the 'Tank method' for sparkling wine production.

Autol (Sp). A Zona de Crianza in the Rioja Baja region, north-eastern Spain.

Autolysis (Eng). Yeast decomposition in wine. Is prevented by regular racking.

Automatic Red Wine Vinificators (Eng). Stainless steel vats specially made to encourage extraction of colour by a continuous juice sprinkler in rotating horizontal vats.

Autovac (Eng). An old style of Beer engine. Beer which has over-flowed into the drip-tray is recycled through the pump. Also known as an Economiser.

Autovinification (Port). A method of vinification in which the Mantle is moved to the bottom of the vat continuously. Also permits hygiene and temperature control. Uses pressure from the CO_2.

Autovinificator (Port). The name given to the special vat used in the production of Port. An automatic fermentation process using CO_2 pressure to syphon and circulate the must and extract the maximum colour and tannin quickly.

Autreau (G.E.) Père et Fils (Fr). Champagne producer. Address = 15 Rue Réné Baudet, Champillon, 51160 Ay. Récoltants-manipulants. Produces – Vintage and non-vintage wines.

Autrichen (Fr). French name for the red grape Portugieser.

Autumn Gold Cider (Eng). A draught/bottled cider from the Taunton Cider Co in Somerset.

Autumn Harvest (Eng). A Perry cider produced using pears from Continental Wine and Food.

Autumn Harvest Wines (S.Afr). The brand-name wines from the S.F.W.

Autumn Riesling Sylvaner (N.Z.). A dry white, blended wine from the Penfolds Winery, Henderson, North Island.

Auvergnac Gris (Fr). The French name for the Hungarian wine Szürkebaràt. Lit – 'Wine of the Grey Friar'.

Auvergne (Fr). A V.D.Q.S. wine-producing region. See Fronton.

Auvernat Blanc (Fr). An alternative name for the Muscadelle grape.

Auvernat Gris (Fr). An alternative name for the Pinot meunier grape grown in the eastern Loire and Champagne.

Auvernier (Switz). A Neuchâtel village noted for its Oeil de Perdrix.

Auvigue, Burrier, Revel et Cie (Fr). A small négociant-éleveur company based at Charney-lès-Mâcon, Mâconnais, Burgundy.

Aux Argillats (Fr). A Premier Cru vineyard [part only] of the A.C. commune of Nuits-Saint-Georges, Côte de Nuits, Burgundy. 2.5 ha.

Aux Beaux-Bruns (Fr). A Premier Cru vineyard of the commune A.C. Chambolle-Musigny, Côte de Nuits, Burgundy. 2.4 ha.

Aux Boudots (Fr). A Premier Cru vineyard in the A.C. Nuits-Saint-Georges, Côte de Nuits, Burgundy. 6.4 ha.

Aux Bousselots (Fr). A Premier Cru vineyard in the A.C. commune of Nuits-Saint-Georges, Côte de Nuits, Burgundy. 4.5 ha.

Aux Brûlées (Fr). A Premier Cru vineyard of the commune A.C. Vosne-Romanée, Côte de Nuits, Burgundy. 3.8 ha.

Aux Chaignots (Fr). A Premier Cru vineyard in the A.C. commune of Nuits-Saint-Georges, Côte de Nuits, Burgundy. 5.6 ha.

Aux Champs-Perdrix (Fr). A Premier Cru vineyard [part only] in the A.C. commune of Nuits-Saint-Georges, Côte de Nuits, Burgundy. 2.1 ha.

Aux Charmes (Fr). A Premier Cru vineyard of the commune A.C. Morey-Saint-Denis, Côte de Nuits, Burgundy. 1.2 ha.

Aux Cheusots (Fr). See Clos Napoléon.

Aux Clous (Fr). A Premier Cru vineyard [part] of the A.C. commune of Savigny-lès-Beaune, Côte de Beaune, Burgundy.

Aux Combottes (Fr). A Premier Cru vineyard of the commune A.C. Chambolle-Musigny, Côte de Nuits, Burgundy. 2.27 ha.

Aux Combottes (Fr). A Premier Cru vineyard of the commune A.C. Gevrey-Chambertin, Côte de Nuits, Burgundy. 4.9 ha.

Aux Coucherias (Fr). A Premier Cru vineyard [part] of the A.C. commune of Beaune, Côte de Beaune, Burgundy. 9.27 ha.

Aux Cras (Fr). A Premier Cru vineyard in the A.C. commune of Beaune, Burgundy. 5.02 ha.

Aux Cras (Fr). A Premier Cru vineyard in the A.C. commune of Nuits-Saint-Georges, Côte de Nuits, Burgundy. 3 ha.

Aux Crots (Fr). A Premier Cru vineyard [part only, including Château Gris] in the A.C. Nuits-Saint-Georges, Côte de Nuits, Burgundy. 8.9 ha.

Aux Échanges (Fr). A Premier Cru vineyard in the A.C. commune of Chambolle-Musigny, Côte de Nuits, Burgundy. 1 ha.

Auxerre (Fr). A city in the Yonne Département. Produces mainly red wines. Noted vineyards are Le Clos de la Chaînette, Coteau de Migraine and Trancy.

Auxerrois (Fr). A red grape variety grown in Cahors. Also known as the Malbec and Côt.

Auxerrois Blanc (Fr). A white grape variety also known as the Pinot Auxerrois. At one time grown as a lesser variety in Alsace but now no longer used.

Auxerrois Gris (Fr). An alternative name for the Pinot gris grape. See also Fauvet, Malvoisie, Pinot beurot and Ruländer.

Auxerroix (Fr). A red grape variety grown in the Lorraine district to produce the light pink Vin gris. Also known as the Malbec.

Auxey-le-Grand (Fr). A small wine-producing district in the Côte d'Or. Red wines only.

Aux Fourneaux (Fr). A Premier Cru vineyard [part] in the A.C. commune commune of Savigny-lès-Beaune, Côte de Beaune, Burgundy.

Aux Grand-Liards (Fr). A Premier Cru vineyard [part] in the A.C. commune of Savigny-lès-Beaune, Côte de Beaune, Burgundy.

Aux Gravains (Fr). A Premier Cru vineyard in the A.C. commune of Savigny-lès-Beaune, Côte de Beaune, Burgundy.

Aux Guettes (Fr). A Premier Cru vineyard [part] in the A.C. commune of Savigny-lès-Beaune, Côte de Beaune, Burgundy.

Auxiliary (Eng). Association of Publican's Wives, devoted to charitable activities.

Aux Malconsorts (Fr). A Premier Cru vineyard of the commune A.C. Vosne-Romanée, Côte de Nuits, Burgundy. 5.9 ha. Also known as Les Malconsorts.

Aux Murgers (Fr). A Premier Cru vineyard in the A.C. commune of Nuits-Saint-Georges, Côte de Nuits, Burgundy. 5 ha.

Auxois (Fr). An alternative name for the Pinot gris grape.

Aux Perdrix (Fr). A Premier Cru vineyard of the commune A.C. Nuits-Saint-Georges, Côte de Nuits, Burgundy. 3.4 ha.

Aux Petits-Liards (Fr). A Premier Cru vineyard [part] in the A.C. commune of Savigny-lès-Beaune, Côte de Beaune, Burgundy.

Aux Petits-Mons (Fr). A Premier Cru vineyard in the A.C. commune of Vosne-Romanée, Côte de Nuits, Burgundy. 3.7 ha.

Aux Reignots (Fr). A Premier Cru vineyard in the A.C. commune of Vosne-Romanée, Côte de Nuits, Burgundy. 1.7 ha.

Aux Serpentières (Fr). A Premier Cru vineyard [part] in the A.C. commune of Savigny-lès-Beaune, Côte de Beaune, Burgundy.

Aux Thorey (Fr). A Premier Cru vineyard in the A.C. commune of Nuits-Saint-Georges, Côte de Nuits, Burgundy. 6.2 ha.

Aux Vergelesses (Fr). A Premier Cru vineyard (including Bataillière) in the A.C. commune of Savigny-lès-Beaune, Côte de Beaune, Burgundy.

Aux Vignes-Rondes (Fr). A Premier Cru vineyard in the A.C. commune of Nuits-Saint-Georges, Côte de Nuits, Burgundy. 3.4 ha.

Auzonnet (Fr). A lemon and mint flavoured liqueur produced by Germain in southern France.

Ava (E.Ind). A fermented liquor made from the roots of a local pepper plant (Macropiper methysticum). High in alcohol is also known as Kava or Yava. See also Arva and Ava Ava. Produced in Polynesia.

Ava Ava (E.Ind). See Ava and Arva.

Ava-Ava (USA). An alternative name for Kava.

Avallon (Fr). A town in the Yonne Département. Produces red and white wines. See Côte Rouvre, Vézelay.

Avalon Vineyard (Eng). A vineyard based in East Pennard, Shepton Mallet, Somerset. Grape variety – Seyvel blanc.

Avaux (Les) (Fr). A Premier Cru vineyard in the A.C. commune of Beaune, Côte de Beaune, Burgundy. 13.4 ha.

A.V.B. (S.Am) (abbr). Asociación Venezolana de Barmen. Venezuelan Bartenders' Association. Address = Nuevo Centro, Piso 11 Office 11b, Av. Libertador Chacao, Caracas.

Avdat (Isr). Dry, light red and white wines produced by Carmel for sale in the USA.

Aveleda (Port). A Vinho Verde from near Penafiel in northern Portugal. The largest selling of the Vinhos Verdes.

Avelsbach (Ger). A fine wine area between the rivers Mosel and Ruwer in the Mosel-Saar-Ruwer.

Avelsbacher Hammerstein (Ger). A white medium dry table wine from Avelsbach on the Mosel.

Avenay (Fr). A Premier Cru Champagne village in the Canton d'Ay. District = Reims.

Avensan (Fr). A lesser Haut-Médoc commune in Bordeaux.

Aventinus (Ger). A dark, strong Wheat beer brewed by the Schneider Brauerei in Munich. 7.8% alc. by vol.

Avery's of Bristol (Eng). A large old established and famous firm of wine merchants based in Bristol. Address = 7, Part Street, Bristol BS1 5NG.

Avesso (Port). A white grape variety used in the making of Vinhos Verdes.

Aviation Cocktail (Cktl) (1). ⅔ measure Gin, ⅓ measure lemon juice, 2 dashes Maraschino. Shake over ice, strain into cocktail glass.

Aviation Cocktail (Cktl) (2). ½ measure sweet Sherry, ⅓ measure red Dubonnet. Stir over ice, strain into cocktail glass. Dress with a spiral of orange peel.

Avicenna (Arab). An Arab alchemist who wrote about alcohol strengths and distillation.

Avignon (Fr). A town which is in centre of southern Rhône vineyards.

Avignonesi (It). A winery based at Montepulciano, Tuscany. 86 ha. Noted for its Vino Nobile di Montepulciano.

Avillo (Sp). An alternative name for the Folle blanche grape.

Avinagrado (Port). A taste of vinegar, sour.

Aviner (Fr). The process of seasoning new oak casks for some wines so that they lose their 'wood' taste. Usually done with old wine. Lit – 'To season'. Is also applied to new oak vats.

Aviva (Isr). A leading wine-producing company in northern Israel.

Avize (Fr). A Grand Cru Champagne village in the Canton d'Avize. District = Épernay.

Avize (Fr). See Canton d'Avize.

Avo (Port). A sparkling wine made by the méthode champenoise by the Sociedade Agrícola dos Vinhos Messias.

Avonside (Scot). A De luxe Scotch whisky, blended and sold by Gordon and Macphail of Elgin, Morayshire.

Awatea Cabernet Merlot (N.Z.). A full-flavoured, deep coloured red wine, from the Te Mata vineyards, Hawkes Bay, North Island.

Awein (USSR). A milk-based, alcoholic spirit produced by the Tartars.

AWK (S.Afr). A producer of a range of sparkling wines produced by the cuve close method.

Axarquía (Sp). A wine-producing district in south-eastern Málaga. Grows Pedro Ximénez grapes.

Axas (Port). A lesser white grape variety grown in the Minho provence.

Axbridge (Eng). See Cheddar Valley Vineyard.

Axe Vale Brewery (Eng). A small brewery set up in 1983. Address = Colyton, Devon. Produces Battleaxe 1053 O.G. and Conqueror 1066 O.G.

Ay (Fr). A wine commune in the Marne Département. Noted for its fine Champagnes. See Canton d'Ay and Ay-Champagne.

Ayala (Fr). Champagne producer. Address = 2 Boulevard du Nord, 51160 Ay. Grande Marque. Produces – Vintage and non-vintage wines. Vintages – 1906, 1911, 1919, 1921, 1926, 1928, 1929, 1934, 1937, 1941, 1942, 1943, 1945, 1947, 1949, 1952, 1953, 1955,

1959, 1961, 1962, 1964, 1966, 1969, 1970, 1975, 1976, 1979, 1982, 1983.

Ay-Champagne (Fr). A Grand Cru Champagne town in the Canton d'Ay. District = Reims.

Ay-Danil (USSR). A very sweet wine from the Crimean peninsula from the Pinot Gris grape.

Ayguemortes (Fr). A commune in the A.C. Graves region of south-western Bordeaux.

Ayias Mamas (Cyp). A village on the south east end of the island that produces grapes for Commandaria dessert wine.

Ayilmak (Tur). To sober up. Become sober after a heavy drinking bout.

Aying Brauerei (Ger). A small brewery in Aying, Bavaria. Noted for its clean tasting, malty beers. See Platzl Special and Andreas Bock.

Ayios Georghios (Cyp). A village in the south eastern end of the island that produces the grapes for Commandaria dessert wine.

Ayl (Ger). Village. (Anb) = Mosel-Saar-Ruwer. (Ber) = Saar-Ruwer. (Gro) = Scharzberg. (Vins) = Herrenberger, Kupp, Scheidterberger.

Aylesbury Brewery (Eng). See A.B.C.

Ayran (Tur). Buttermilk.

Ayyaş (Tur). Denotes a drunkard, an alcoholic.

Ayze (Fr). An A.C. Vin de Savoie white wine. Is pétillant. Made from 75% Gringet and 25% Roussette grapes.

Azal (Port). A white grape variety used in the production of Vinhos Verdes.

Azal Branco (Port). A white grape variety of the Entre Minho e Douro. Used to produce Vinhos Verdes.

Azal Tinto (Port). A black grape variety grown in the Entre Minho e Douro. Produces deep red wines.

Azay-le-Rideau (Fr). Commune in the Touraine, Loire, which can add its name to A.C. Touraine.

Azedo (Port). Bitter, acidic.

Azedume (Port). Acid taste, acidic, bitter taste.

Azeitão (Port). Vineyards sited between Lisbon and Setúbal in southern Portugal.

Azerbaijan (USSR). A wine region that produces mainly dessert wines. Also part in Iran.

Azienda (It). Denotes a firm or business.

Azienda Agricola (It). When preceding producer's name, guarantees that the wine is made from his own grapes.

Azienda Agricola Attilio Simonini (It). A winery based at Donadoni in Puglia. Produces red, rosé and white wines.

Azienda Agricola Camigliano (It). A noted producer in Siena, Tuscany of Brunello di Montalcino.

Azienda Agricola di Angelo Gaja (It). A winery based in Barbaresco, Piemonte. 55 ha.

Azienda Agricola Greppo (It). See Biondi-Santi.

Azienda Agricola Italo Mattei (It). A principal producer of Verdicchio di Matelica.

Azienda Agricola M. & G. Fugazza (It). A winery based in Luzzano. 40 ha. in Romito and Luzzano. Wines bottled at Castello di Luzzano.

Azienda Vinicola (It). When preceeding the producer's name, guarantees that the wine is made from the producer's own grapes and purchased grapes.

Azijn (Hol). Vinegar.

Azores (Port). Islands in the North Atlantic that produced wines of note until vineyards were destroyed by Oidium and Phylloxera. See Fayal and Pico.

Aztali (Hun). See Tokay Aztali.

Azteca Cocktail (Cktl). ⅓ gill Tequila, juice ½ lime, 2 dashes Gomme syrup, slice of fresh mango. Blend with a scoop of crushed ice in a blender. Pour into a Champagne saucer and dress with 2 lime slices. Serve with straws.

Aztecato (Ch.Isles). The brand-name for the only commercially produced Tomato wine. Medium sweet and dry versions produced. Address = Guernsey Tomato Centre, Kings Mills, Câtel, Guernsey.

Aztec Punch (Cktl). 1 part Tequila, 5 parts grapefruit juice, ⅛ part strong tea, 1 part lemon juice, sugar syrup to taste. Stir all together, chill and serve.

B

Baach (Ger). Village. (Anb) = Württemberg. (Ber) = Remstal-Stuttgart. (Gro) = Wartbühl. (Vin) = Himmelreich.

Baar (Fr). A commune in the Bas-Rhin, Alsace. Produces mainly Riesling and Sylvaner grapes.

Baar Brauerei (Switz). An independent brewery based in Baar.

Baba Budan (Ind). The nickname for coffee. So called after the Muslim merchant who first introduced coffee to India in the seventeenth century.

Babbie's Special (Cktl). 1 measure Apricot brandy, 1 dash Gin, 1 dash sugar syrup, 1 dessertspoon cream. Shake over ice, strain into a cocktail glass.

Băbească (Rum). A pleasant red, acidic wine with a taste of cloves from the Nicoresti region. Made from grape of same name.

Băbească (Rum). A red grape variety from Focsani. Produces acidic wines with a slight taste of cloves. Also known as the Băbească Neagra.

Băbească Neagra (Rum). See Băbească.

Babeurre (Fr). Buttermilk.

Babic (Yug). An ordinary red table wine produced on the Dalmatian coast.

Babich Vineyard (N.Z.). Address = Babich Road, Henderson, Auckland. 30 ha. Grape varieties – Cabernet sauvignon, Chardonnay, Gewürztraminer, Müller-Thurgau, Palomino, Pinotage and Pinot noir.

Babo (It). A mustimetre used in Italy. Has the same scale as the Baumé system.

Babsi (Cktl). 1 fl.oz. Grand Marnier, ¾ fl.oz. Bourbon whiskey, 2 dashes lemon juice, 2 dashes orange juice. Build into a Champagne glass, top with iced Sekt.

Baby (Eng). Split, Nip or Quarter bottle.

Babycham (Eng). A sparkling perry drink produced by Showerings. Both dry and sweet styles sold in 100 mls. and 75 cls. bottles.

Baby Duck (Can). An ordinary sparkling wine. CO₂ injected.

Babylonians (M.East). The first real recorded wine-makers of any note, although wine was made long before them.

Baby Polly (Eng). The name given to a small 'split' Apollinaris mineral water.

B.A.C. (Can) (abbr). Bartenders' Association of Canada. Address = P.O. Box 1135, Adelaide Street, East Toronto.

Baca (Lat). Small round berried fruit. i.e. Grapes. See Bacciferous and Acinum.

Bacarat (Fr). Kattell-Roc, low alcohol red Vermouth. Is less than 1% alc. by vol.

Bacardi (W.Ind). A well-known brand of Bahamian, Brazilian, Cuban, Mexican and Puerto Rican white rums.

Bacardi Anejo (W.Ind). A cask aged white Rum produced by Bacardi. Is aged for six years.

Bacardi Blossom Cocktail (Cktl). ½ measure Bacardi, ½ measure orange juice, dash Maraschino. Shake over ice, strain into a cocktail glass.

Bacardi Cocktail (Cktl). 1½ fl.ozs. Bacardi White Label, juice of ½ lime, teaspoon Grenadine. Shake well together over ice, strain into a cocktail glass. Decorate with cherry.

Bacardi Collins (Cktl). 1½ fl.ozs Bacardi White Label, juice of ½ lime, 1 teaspoon sugar. Combine sugar with juice, add 2 or 3 ice cubes. Add Bacardi then fill glass with soda. Garnish with a cherry and slice of orange.

Bacardi Crusta (Cktl). ⅓ gill Bacardi, 1 teaspoon Pernod, ⅙ gill lemon juice, 2 dashes Angostura bitters. Shake over broken ice. Moisten inside of wine glass with lemon juice and sprinkle with ½ teaspoon powdered sugar. Put in lemon peel cut in a spiral then strain in mixture and add some sliced fruit.

Bacardi Cuba Libre (Cktl). Place some ice into a highball glass add 2 ozs Bacardi and top with Cola.

Bacardi Elixir Pousse (Pousse Café). In a liqueur Elgin pour Bacardi Elixir until the glass is ½ full. Fill the glass slowly with cream. Cross with a cherry on cocktail stick.

Bacardi Highball (Cktl). Fill highball glass with ice, add 2 ozs of Bacardi Anejo. Top with soda water.

Bacardi Mojito (Cktl). 2 ozs. Bacardi White Label, 1 teaspoon sugar, juice ½ lime, 2 dashes Angostura, 3 mint leaves. Combine sugar and juice, crush with mint leaves. Add 2 ice cubes and stir again. Add Bacardi and bitters. Top with soda water, add slice of lime.

Bacardi Old Fashioned (Cktl). 2 ozs. Bacardi Gold Label, 3 dashes Angostura, 1 teaspoon sugar, 1 teaspoon water. Muddle sugar, bitters and water well. Add ice and Bacardi. Mix well and garnish with a cherry, slice of orange, pineapple and rind of lime. Serve with straws.

Bacardi Pineapple Fizz (Cktl). 1½ ozs Bacardi White Label, 1 oz. pineapple juice, 1 teaspoon sugar. Shake well with ice, strain into 8 fl.oz. glass, fill with soda water.

Bacardi Sour (Cktl). 2 ozs Bacardi White Label, juice ½ lime, 1 teaspoon sugar. Combine juice with sugar, put Rum in a shaker, add ice, shake well, strain into a cocktail glass. Decorate with slice of pineapple, orange and a cherry.

Bacardi Special (Cktl). ⅔ measure Bacardi White Label, ⅓ measure Gin, juice of a lime, 1 dash Grenadine, 2 dashes Gomme syrup. Shake altogether over ice except the Rum, add Rum, shake again, then strain into a cocktail glass.

Baccarat (Eng). Style of glass of plain thin lead crystal. Various sizes.

Baccha (Lat). A priestess of Bacchus. Female devotee of Bacchus. See Bakkhe.

Bacchanal (Eng). Drunken or riotous celebration.

Bacchanal (Eng). Follower of Bacchus.

Bacchanal (Eng). Relating to Bacchus.

Bacchanalia (Eng). Denotes drunken revelry. i.e. A Bacchanalian party. (Rites associated with Bacchus).

Bacchanalis (Lat). Relating to Bacchus. See Bacchanal.

Bacchans (Lat). Devotee of Bacchus.

Bacchant (Eng). Priest of Bacchus. Male devotee of Bacchus.

Bacchante (Eng). Priestess of Bacchus. Female devotee of Bacchus.

Bacchari (Lat). To celebrate the Bacchanalia.

Bacchic (Eng). Relating to Bacchus.

Bacchic (Eng). Riotously drunk.

Bacchos (Gre). The name sometimes given to Dionysos (from which Bacchus derives). See also Bakkhos.

Bacchus (Ger). A white grape variety. Cross between the Riesling and Müller-Thurgau. Early ripening, gives fruity wines.

Bacchus (Lat). Roman god of wine. Jupiter (father) and Semele (mother).

Bacchus (USA). A small, black hybrid grape variety that produces good quality, full-bodied wines.

Bacchus Wines (S.Afr). The brand-name white wines from the S.F.W.

Bacciferous (Eng). Berry-bearing (applied to grapevines). From the Latin 'Baca'.

Baccio Punch (Punch). ½ bottle dry Gin, ½ bottle grapefruit juice, ½ bottle Champagne, ¼ bottle Anisette, ½ syphon soda water in a large bowl (not the Champagne) with ice. Add fruit in season and lastly the Champagne.

Bacco (It). Bacchus.

Bacco d'Oro (It). A sparkling (méthode champenoise) wine produced by Contratto in the Piemonte region.

Bacelo (Port). Denotes a newly planted vine.

Bacharach (Ger). Bereich. (Anb) = Mittelrhein. (Gros) = Schloss Reichenstein, Schloss Stahleck.

Bacharach (Ger). Rhine port which, together with Hockheim, was where most wines were shipped from in the middle ages. See Bachrag, Backrag.

Bacharach (Ger). Village. (Anb) = Mittelrhein. (Ber) = Bacharach. (Gro) = Schloss Stahleck. (Vins) = Hahn, Insel Heylessern Wert, Kloster Fürsteutal, Postern, Mathias Weingarten, Wolfshöhle.

Bacharach/Steeg (Ger). Village. (Anb) = Mittelrhein. (Ber) = Bacharach. (Gro) = Schloss Stahleck. (Vins) = Hambusch, Lennenborn, St. Jost, Schloss Stahlberg.

Bachelor's Bait Cocktail (Cktl). 1 measure dry Gin, 1 dash Amer Picon, 2 dashes Grenadine, 1 egg white. Shake over ice, strain into cocktail glass.

Bachem (Ger). Village. (Anb) = Ahr. (Ber) = Walporzheim/Ahrtal. (Gro) = Klosterberg. (Vins) = Karlskopf, Sonnenschein, Steinkaul.

Bacheroy-Josselin (Fr). Wine négocians based at Chablis, Burgundy.

Bachfischfest (Ger). A Rheinhessen wine festival held in Worms in August.

Bachrag (Eng). An old English pronunciation of Bacharach the wine port which together with Hockheim shipped most of the German wines associated with Mosel wines. See also Bacharach.

Bacigalupi Vineyard (USA). An

independent vineyard based in the west of Sonoma County, California.

Back-Blending (N.Z.). The addition of concentrated or unfermented grape juice to wine before bottling.

Backöfchen (Ger). Vineyard. (Anb) = Nahe. (Ber) = Kreuznach. (Gro) = Pfarrgarten. (Vil) = Wallhausen.

Backofen (Ger). Vineyard. (Anb) = Mittelrhein. (Ber) = Rheinburgengau. (Gro) = Herrenberg. (Vil) = Kaub.

Backrag (Eng). An old English pronunciation of Bacharach. See Bachrag.

Backsberg Estate (S.Afr). A wine estate in Paarl. Address = P.O. Box 1, Klapmuts 7625. Produces varietal wines.

Backus Vineyard (USA). A small vineyard based in the western part of the Napa Valley, California. Grape variety – Cabernet sauvignon.

Baco 1 (USA). The alternative name for the Baco noir.

Baco (Maurice) (Fr). A noted French grape hybridiser who has produced many varieties for both the USA and France.

Baco Noir (USA). A red hybrid grape variety. Also known as Baco 1.

Baco 22A (USA). A white hybrid grape variety. Cross between the Noah and Folle blanche. Is grown in USA, New Zealand and in Armagnac, France where it is known as the Plant de grèce.

Bacteria (Eng). Microscopic, single-celled organisms that generally cause spoilage in beer, wines and foodstuffs. Prevented by good hygiene.

Bacterial Haze (Eng). A condition in wine caused by Bacteria. Wine turns cloudy after being originally clear. Caused through poor hygiene and is found especially in home-made wines.

Bacterium (Lat). The singular of Bacteria.

Bacterium Gracile (Lat). The bacteria responsible for the Malo-lactic fermentation.

Bacterium Mannitopoem (Lat). A Bacteria that ferments Fructose into Mannitol, Ethanoic acid, CO_2 and Lactic acid.

Bacterium Tartarophtorum (Lat). See Tourne.

Badacsonki Rizling (Hun). A pale, dry, white full-bodied wine from Badacsony.

Badacsony (Hun). A district within the region of Lake Balatòn, North Transdanubia. Produces full-bodied white wines. Badacsonyi Szürkebaràt. Also spelt Badacsonyi.

Badacsonyer Burgunder (Hun). A red wine produced from Pinot gris grapes.

Badacsonyi (Hun). See Badacsony.

Badacsonyi Auvergnac Gris (Fr). The French spelling of the Hungarian Badacsonyi Szürkebaràt.

Badacsonyi Kéknyelü (Hun). A wine from the Lake Balatòn region known popularly as 'Blue Stalk'.

Badacsonyi Szürkebaràt (Hun). A wine made from the Pinot Gris grape in the Lake Balatòn region. Considered to be the best of the region, it is an aromatic, yellow-gold, fruity wine. See also Badacsonyi Auvergnac gris.

Badacsonytomaj (Hun). A wine-producing town in the south-west are of Lake Balatòn.

Badajoz (Sp). A large wine-producing region on the river Guadiana in south-western Spain.

Bad Bellingen (Ger). Village. (Anb) = Baden. (Ber) = Markgräflerland. (Gro) = Burg Neuenfels. (Vin) = Sonnenstück.

Bad Bergzabern (Ger). Village. (Anb) = Rheinpfalz. (Ber) = Südliche Weinstrasse. (Gro) = Guttenberg. (Vin) = Wonneberg.

Bad Bergzabern (Ger). Village. (Anb) = Rheinpfalz. (Ber) = Südliche Weinstrasse. (Gro) = Kloster Liebfrauenberg. (Vin) = Altenberg.

Bad Cannstatt (Ger). Village. (Anb) = Württemberg. (Ber) = Remstal-Stuttgart. (Gro) = Weinsteige. (Vins) = The following are near and are classified under the village of Stuttgart. Berg, Halde, Herzogenberg, Mönchberg, Steinhalde, Zuckerle.

Bad Dürkheim (Ger). Village. (Anb) = Rheinpfalz. (Ber) = Mittelhaardt-Deutsche Weinstrasse. (Gro) = Feuerberg. (Vins) = Herrenmorgen, Nonnengarten, Steinberg.

Bad Dürkheim (Ger). Village. (Anb) = Rheinpfalz. (Ber) = Mittelhaardt-Deutsche Weinstrasse. (Gro) = Hochmess. (Vins) = Hochbenn, Michelsberg, Rittergarten, Spielberg.

Bad Dürkheim (Ger). Village. (Anb) = Rheinpfalz. (Ber) = Mittelhaardt-Deutsche Weinstrasse. (Gro) = Schenkenböhl. (Vins) = Abstfronhof, Fronhof, Fuchsmantel.

Badel 70 (Cktl). 1/3 measure Cherry brandy, 1/3 measure Vinjak Cezar, 1/3 measure dry vermouth. Stir over ice. Strain into cocktail glass.

Badel-Vinoprodukt (Aus). A noted Rum-producer based at Zagreb. Brands include Rum Domaci.

Bad Ems (Ger). Village. (Anb) = Mittelrhein. (Ber) = Rheinburgengau. (Gro) = Lahntal. (Vin) = Hasenberg.

Baden (Aus). A town south of Vienna. Produces mainly white wines from the Zierfändler and Rotgipfler grape varieties.

B

Baden (Ger). Anbaugebiet. (Bers) = Badische Bergstrasse/Kraichgau, Badisches Frankenland, Breisgau, Bodensee, Kaiserstuhl-Tuniberg, Markgräflerland, Ortenau. Wine region in the south-west of Germany on the French/Swiss borders. Main grape varieties – Müller-Thurgau, Riesling, Ruländer and Spätburgunder. Produces 79% white wine and 21% red/rosé wines.

Baden-Baden (Ger). A Lithiated mineral water from the Baden region.

Baden-Baden (Ger). Village. (Anb) = Baden. (Ber) = Ortenau. (Gro) = Schloss Rodeck. (Vins) = Eckberg, Sätzler.

Badenheim (Ger). Village. (Anb) = Rheinhessen. (Ber) = Bingen. (Gro) = Sankt Rochuskapelle. (Vins) = Galgenberg, Römerberg.

Baden Information Service (Ger). Weinwerbezentrale Badische Winzergenossenschaften. Address = Ettlinger Strasse 12 7500 Karlsruhe, West Germany.

Badenweiler (Ger). Village. (Anb) = Baden. (Ber) = Markgräflerland. (Gro) = Burg Neuenfels. (Vin) = Römerberg.

Baden Wine Festivals (Ger). Freiburger Weintage, Kurpfälzisches Winzerfest, Kaiserstuhl-Tuniberg- Weinfest. See each.

Baden Wine Route (Ger). Badische Weinstrasse.

Badger Beers (Eng). The name for beers brewed by the Hall and Woodhouse Brewery based in Dorset. Badger Best Cask Bitter 1041 O.G. and Brock Lager 1033 O.G.

Bad Hönningen (Ger). Village. (Anb) = Mittelrhein. (Ber) = Rheinbergengau. (Gro) = Burg Hammerstein. (Vin) = Schlossberg.

Badia a Coltibuono (It). A Chianti Classico producer in Gaiole, Tuscany.

Badiane (Fr). A form of Anise from China, used in the making of Pastis. Botanical name = Illicium Anisatum.

Badische Bergstrasse/Kraichgau (Ger). Bereich. (Anb) = Baden. (Gros) = Hohenberg, Mannaberg, Rittersberg, Stiftsberg.

Badische Rotgold (Ger). A quality rosé wine from Baden. Is usually designated 'Rotling'. Made from grapes, juice or mash from the Grauburgunder and Spätburgunder grape varieties.

Badisches Frankenland (Ger). Bereich. (Anb) = Baden. (Gro) = Tauberklinge.

Badische Weinstrasse (Ger). Baden wine route.

Bad Kreuznach (Ger). Principle town in the Nahe anbaugebiet.

Bad Kreuznach (Ger). Village. (Anb) = Nahe. (Ber) = Kreuznach. (Gro) = Kronenberg. (Vins) = Agnesienberg, Berg, Breitenweg, Brückes, Forst, Galgenberg, Gutental, Himmelgarten, Hinkelstein, Hirtenhain, Hofgarten, Höllenbrand, Honigberg, Hungriger Wolf, In den Mauern, In den 17 Morgen, Junker, Kahlenberg, Kapellenpfad, Katzenhölle, Krötenpfuhl, Mollenbrunnen, Mönchberg, Monhard, Narrenkappe, Nonnengarten, Osterhöll, Paradies, Römerhalde, Rosenberg, Rosenheck, Rosenhügel, St. Martin, Schloss Kauzenberg, Steinberg, Steinweg, Tilgesbrunnen, Vogelsang.

Bad Krotzingen (Ger). Village. (Anb) = Baden. (Ber) = Markgräflerland. (Gro) = Lorettoberg. (Vin) = Steingrüble.

Badminton Cup (Cup). 1 bottle Claret, ¾ gill brown Curaçao, 2 bottles soda water, 3 ozs icing sugar, juice and rind of 1 lemon. Place all the ingredients (except soda) into a bowl with some ice chips. Leave ½ hour. Strain, add soda, serve rind and sliced cucumber on top.

Bad Münster a. St-Ebernburg (Ger). Village. (Anb) = Nahe. (Ber) = Schloss Böckelheim. (Gro) = Burgweg. (Vins) = Erzgrupe, Felseneck, Feuerberg, Götzenfels, Höll, Köhler-Köpfchen, Königsgarten, Luisengarten, Rotenfelser im Winkel, Schlossberg, Steigerdell, Stephansberg,.

Bad Neuenahr (Ger). Village. (Anb) = Ahr. (Ber) = Walporzheim/Ahrtal, (Gro) = Klosterberg. (Vins) = Kirchtürmchen, Schieferley, Sonnenberg.

Badoit (Fr). A natural sparkling water of Saint Galmier, Loire Valley.

Badplaats (Hol). Spa.

Badsberg Co-operative (S.Afr). Based in Goudini. Address = Badsberg Koöperatiewe Wynkelders Bpk., Grootvlakte, Box 72, Rawsonville 6845. Produces varietal wines.

Badsberg Koöperatiewe Wynkelder (S.Afr). See Badsberg Co-operative.

Badstube (Ger). Grosslage. (Anb) = Mosel-Saar-Ruwer. (Ber) = Bernkastel. (Vil) = Bernkastel-Kues.

Baere (Eng). An Anglo-Saxon word for barley from which Beer originated.

Baerenfang (Ger). A honey-based liqueur from Prussia. Flavoured with lime and Mullein flowers.

Baerlic (Eng). An old English word denoting 'made from barley'.

Bağ (Tur). Vineyard.

Baga (Port). The name for the elderberry

juice that was once used to colour Port wine. Now no longer used.

Baga (Port). A red grape variety grown in Bairrada region.

Bagaceira (Port). Brandy made from the residue of wine pulp. (Fr) = Marc. (It) = Grappa. (Sp) = Aguardiente.

Bagaço (Port). Grape brandy.

Baga de Louro (Port). A red grape variety grown in the Dão region.

Bagasse (W.Ind). The name given to residual sugar cane pulp after the juice has been removed in Rum production.

Bağbozumu (Tur). Vintage, grape harvest.

Bag, [Coffee] (Eng). Used for the transportation of the beans. 60 kilos.

Bag in the Box (Austr). The term given to the wines sold in polythene bags in cardboard box containers. Usually in litre (or multiples of) packs.

Bago (Port). A single grape.

Bagrina (Yug). A noted red wine produced in eastern Serbia.

Bahamas Cocktail (Cktl). ⅓ measure Southern Comfort, ⅓ measure light Rum, ⅓ measure lemon juice, dash Crème de Banane. Shake over ice, strain into a cocktail glass.

Bahama Sunrise (Cktl). 1 measure Galliano, 2 measures Mount Gay Eclipse Barbados Rum, 6 measures grapefruit juice. Stir over ice, strain into an ice-filled highball glass on top of ½ measure Galliano. Dress with mint sprig and serve with straws.

Bahamian Delight (Cktl). ½ measure Campari, ½ measure pineapple juice. Stir over ice, strain into an ice-filled club goblet. Top with a cherry.

Bahia (Bra). A liqueur that is a blend of grain spirit and coffee.

Bahia Cocktail (Cktl). ½ measure golden Rum, ⅙ measure coconut cream, ⅙ measure pineapple juice, ⅙ measure grapefruit juice. Blend in a blender with a scoop of crushed ice. Pour into a highball glass. Top with a cherry and pineapple cube. Serve with straws.

Bahlingen (Ger). Village. (Anb) = Baden. (Ber) = Kaiserstuhl-Tuniberg. (Gro) = Vulkanfelsen. (Vin) = Silberberg.

Bahnbrücken (Ger). Village. (Anb) = Baden. (Ber) = Badische Bergstrasse/Kraichgau. (Gro) = Stiftsberg. (Vin) = Lerchenberg (ortsteil).

B.A.I. (Ire) (abbr). Bartenders' Association of Ireland. Address = Jury's Hotel, Ballsbridge, Dublin 4.

Baie de Houx (Fr). A brandy-based liqueur flavoured with holly berries.

Baier (Nor). A Bavarian-style beer. Dark copper-brown in colour.

Baiken (Ger). Vineyard. (Anb) = Rheingau. (Ber) = Johannisberg. (Gro) = Steinmacher. (Vil) = Rauenthal.

Bailey Classification (USA). A scientist who produced alternate names for the American native vine species. See Vitis Argentifolia, Vitis Sola, Vitis Tilioefolia and Vitis Vulpina.

Baileys Brewery (Eng). A new brewery started in 1983. Address = Malvern, Worcestershire. Produces Best Bitter 1040 O.G. Super Brew 1047 O.G.

Bailey's Cream (Ire). A cream liqueur made in Dublin from Irish whiskey, cream, chocolate and neutral spirits. 15% alc. by vol.

Bailey's Irish Cream (Ire). See Bailey's Cream.

Baileys of Glenrowan (Austr). Vineyard, 102 ha. Address = Taminick Gap Road, Glenrowan, Victoria 3675. Grape varieties include – Aucerot, Brown muscat, Cabernet sauvignon, Hermitage, Muscadelle, Rhine riesling.

Bai Lin Tea (China). The brand-name of a China tea which, if drunk soon after a meal (it is claimed), will help to burn up the calories and so reduce weight.

Bain-de-Pied (Fr). A term used to describe the overflow of coffee (or tea) into the saucer. Lit – 'footbath'. Denotes the over-filling of a vessel.

Bairoque (Fr). A white grape variety grown in Tursan, Landes Département, south-western France.

Bairrada (Port). A small region on the river Mondego. Produces wines similar to red Dão and sparkling wines.

Baitz (Austr). A major spirit and liqueur producer of the country.

Baixo Corgo (Port). A district of the Alto Douro downstream of the Corgo river in the lowlands.

Baja California (Mex). A wine-producing area in northern Mexico. Contains the regions of Guadalupe, Santo Tomàs, Tañama and Valle Redondo.

Baja Montana (Sp). One of five D.O. wine-producing regions based in the Navarra region.

Bajulos Palos (Sp). A method of vine training on low stakes.

Bak (Tur). Drunk (consumed).

Bakano (N.Z.). A light, acidic, red, hybrid wine that is produced by the McWilliams Winery in Hawkes Bay.

Bakaver (N.Z.). A red wine produced by the Balic Winery, Sturges Road, Henderson, North Island. Produced from Baco and Seibel grapes.

Bak Beer (Hun). A strong dark beer brewed by the Kobànya Brewery.

Baked (Eng). A term used to describe wines with a high alcoholic content giving a taste of grapes gathered during very hot weather.

Bakersfield (USA). A noted wine town in the wine districts of Kern County and San Joaquin Valley, California.

Bakkhe (Gre). A priestess of Bacchus. Plural Bakkhai.

Bakkhos (Gre). Bacchus. See also Bacchos.

Baksmalla (Swe) (slang). A term used for a hangover.

Baku (USSR). A wine-producing region based in Azerbaijan. Produces mainly dessert wines.

Balaclava (Punch). 1 bottle Champagne, 1 bottle Claret, juice 2 lemons, bottle soda water. Stir gently over ice, dress with sliced cucumber. Serve in Champagne flutes.

Balaclava Punch (Punch). 3 pints tea, 1 bottle dry white wine, ½ pint Vodka, stick of cinnamon, 2 measures grapefruit juice, 1 measure Crème de Menthe. Heat all the ingredients together, strain, serve with slice of orange.

Baladí (Sp). A white grape variety grown in the Montilla-Moriles region.

Balagne (Fr). A wine-producing region in north-western Corsica.

Balalaika (Cktl). ⅓ measure Cointreau, ⅓ measure Vodka, ⅓ measure lemon juice. Shake over ice, strain into cocktail glass.

Balalaika (Eng). A proprietary brand of Vodka. 40% alc. by vol.

Balance (Eng). A term used to describe a wine which has all the good qualities expected combined in a wine. It has no deficiencies in its bouquet, flavour or character. A well-balanced wine is always a good wine, often a great wine.

Balatòn (Hun). Lake Balatòn. Area that produces mainly dry white wines.

Balatònfüred (Hun). A town on Lake Balatòn shore that is noted for its soft, white wines (sweet and dry styles).

Balatònfüred-Csopak (Hun). A wine-producing region in northern Transdanubia around Lake Balatòn.

Balatòn Furmint (Hun). A medium dry white wine with a fresh bouquet, from the Lake Balatòn region. Made with the Furmint grape.

Balatòni Riesling (Hun). A medium sweet white wine from the Lake Balatòn region. Made with the Welschriesling grape.

Balatònmellek (Hun). A wine-producing region based in northern Transdanubia around Lake Balatòn. Noted for its fine white wines.

Balatònudvari (Hun). A wine-producing town sited in the south-eastern area of Lake Balatòn.

Balavaud (Switz). A white wine produced in the Johannisberg district of the Valais canton.

Balbach (Anton) (Ger). A noted Rheinhessen wine Estate. Vineyards based in Nierstein.

Balbaina (Sp). A district within the Sherry region. Chalk soil, produces the best wines.

Balbino d'Altromonte (It). A sweet white wine from Calabria. 15–16% alc. by vol.

Balblair (Scot). A single Malt whisky distillery. Address = Edderton, Rossshire. A Highland malt whisky. 40% alc. by vol.

Baldear (Port). To decant.

Balderdash (Ire). A mixture of drinks which are generally unrelated. e.g. wine and milk. (It is also an Irish term for illogical conversation).

Baldinelli-Shenandoah Valley Winery (USA). Based in Amador, California. Produces red, rosé and white wines from Cabernet sauvignon and Zinfandel grapes.

Balearic Islands (Sp). A group of islands in the Mediterranean off the Levante coast of Spain. Islands are – Formentera, Ibiza, Majorca and Minorca.

Bale Mill Cellars (USA). The brand-name used by the Shaw winery in California for their varietal wines.

Balgarske Slantse (Bul). Lit – 'Bulgarian Sun'. Basic dry white wine made from the Furmint grape.

Balgownie Vineyard (Austr). Address = Hermitage Road, Maiden Gully, via Bendigo, Victoria 3551. 13 ha. Grape varieties – Cabernet sauvignon, Chardonnay, Pinot noir, Syrah.

Bali Coffee (E.Ind). A coffee of the Arabica category. Produces a mellow but strong aroma. Produced in Indonesia.

Balic Vineyard (N.Z.). Address = Sturges Road, Henderson, North Island. 15 ha. Grape varieties – Baco 22A, Müller-Thurgau, Palomino and Pinotage. Noted for its Bakaver and Vin Ché.

Balic Winery (USA). A winery based in Mays Landing, New Jersey. Produces mainly hybrid wines.

Bali Hai (USA). A popular 'Pop wine' produced by the Swiss Colony Co. (Part of United Vintners).

Balikesir (Tur). A noted vineyard based in the Thrace and Marmara regions. Produces white wines.

Balkan Gin (USSR). A light neutral Gin.

Ballabio (Angelo) (It). A producer of sparkling wines (by the méthode champenoise) based in Lombardy. Produces both white and rosé wines from the Pinot noir grape.

B

Ballantine (George and Son) (Scot). The main Scotch whisky brand of Hiram Walker (Canada). See also Ballantine's whisky.

Ballantine Ale (USA). A style of ale brewed by Falstaff's Narrangansett Brewery, Cranston, Rhode Island.

Ballantine Brewery (USA). A brewery that was based in Newark, New Jersey. Closed in 1972, beers are now brewed by the Falstaff's Narrangansett Brewery in Cranston, Rhode Island.

Ballantine's Whisky (Scot). A blended Scotch whisky produced by George Ballantine and Sons Ltd. in Dumbarton and in Elgin. Also 12, 17, and 30 year old De Luxe varieties. Sold in a square bottle. (Part of Hiram Walker). 40% alc. by vol.

Ballarat Bitter (Austr). The brand-name of beers brewed by the Carlton and United Breweries in Ballarat, Victoria.

Ballard Canyon Winery (USA). A small winery in Santa Barbara, Santa Cruz Valley, California. Grape varieties – Cabernet sauvignon, Chardonnay and Johannisberg riesling. Produces varietal wines.

Ballard's Brewery (Eng). Opened in 1980 in Sussex. Produces Wassail Ale 1060 O.G.

Balle (Ger). A brand of Rum produced by Hansen in Hensburg.

Baller Lager (Ind). A Lager beer 1040 O.G. brewed by the Mohan Meakin Brewery, Simla hills, Solan.

Balling (USA). A scale of sugar density in grape musts. Invented by a Czech scientist. Operated at 60°F. See also Brix and Sykes.

Ball of Malt (Ire). A request for a straight Malt whiskey.

Ballon (Fr). A Paris goblet. Plain round-bowled, stemmed glass.

Ballonge (Fr). An oval-shaped tub which can hold up to a ton of grapes which is used to carry them from the vineyard to the winery.

Balloon (Eng). A type of glass with a large bowl and narrow rim, used for Brandy in the U.K. and as a sampling (nosing) glass for immature wines in France.

Ballota Oak (Sp). A species of oak tree whose acorns are roasted and used as a coffee substitute. See Acorn Coffee.

Ballrechten-Dottingen (Ger). Village. (Anb) = Baden. (Ber) = Markgräflerland. (Gro) = Burg Neuenfels. (Vins) = Altenberg, Castellberg.

Balmenach-Glenlivet (Scot). A single Malt whisky, owned by Haig & Haig. A Highland malt whisky. 43% alc. by vol.

Balmes Dauphinoises (Fr). A Vins de Pays area in the Isère Département in central France. Produces red, rosé and white wines.

Balm Wines (Eng). A fermented brew produced from balm leaves infused in boiling water with sugar, strained and allowed to cool. Yeast is added, fermented and fined with egg white.

Balnot-sur-Laignes (Fr). A Cru Champagne village in the Canton de l'Aude. District = Château Thierry.

Baloes (Port). Pomegranate-shaped tanks of white concrete found in the Douro region. See also Igloos.

Balouzet (Fr). A local name for the Malbec grape in southern France.

Balsam of Herbs (Ger). An aromatic bitters from Wolfschmidt in Riga.

Balseiros (Port). Huge vats used for blending Port.

Balthasar (Eng). An alternative spelling of Balthazar.

Balthazar (Fr). A bottle notably of Champagne with a capacity of 16 standard bottles.

Baltimore Bracer (Cktl). ½ measure Anisette, ½ measure Brandy, 1 egg white. Shake over ice, strain into a cocktail glass.

Baltimore Egg Nogg (Cktl). 1 egg, 1 teaspoon sugar, 1 gill Madeira, ¼ gill brandy, ¼ gill dark rum. Shake well with a little fresh milk over ice, strain into a large tumbler with grated nutmeg on top.

Baltzinger, Robert (Fr). A wine-producer based in Alsace. Address = 68, Rue de l'Eau, Gertwiller, 67140 Barr.

Baluster Stem (Eng). A style of lead crystal glass with bubbles in the form of 'tear drops' in the stem.

Balvenie (Scot). A single Malt whisky distillery. Address = Dufftown, Banffshire. Owned by William Grant & Sons. A Highland malt whisky. 40% alc. by vol.

Balverne Vineyards (USA). A winery based in Sonoma Valley, California. Grape varieties – Cabernet sauvignon, Chardonnay, Gewürztraminer, Johannisberg riesling, Sauvignon blanc and Zinfandel. Produces – varietal wines.

Balzner (Euro). The name for the wines produced from Balzers in the state of Liechtenstein.

Bamako Beer (Afr). A light Beer brewed in Mali.

Bamberg (Ger). Dark 'smoked' beer from Bavaria. Also known as 'Rauchbier' it is brewed from malt that has been fire-dried over beechwood logs. Brewed in

Kaiserdom Brauerei and Schlenkerla home-brew house.

Bamboo Cocktail (Cktl). Also known as a 'Reform cocktail'. 1 dash Orange bitters, ¼ gill dry Sherry, ¼ gill French vermouth. Stir over ice, strain into cocktail glass. Squeeze of lemon peel on top.

Bamboo Cocktail (Cktl). ½ measure dry Sherry, ¼ measure dry Vermouth, ¼ measure sweet Vermouth. Stir well over ice, strain into a cocktail glass.

Bamboo Leafgreen Chiew (China). A speciality white wine.

Bamlach (Ger). Village. (Anb) = Baden. (Ber). Markgräflerland. (Gro) = Vogtei Rötteln. (Vin) = Kapellenberg.

Banadry (Fr). A banana-flavoured liqueur produced by Bardinet of Bordeaux. 26% alc. by vol.

Banana (Eng). A term used to describe the bouquet of a wine produced from frost attacked grapes. Also used to describe a wine that is in poor condition.

Banana Bird (Cktl). ½ measure Bourbon whiskey, ½ measure cream, 2 dashes Crème de Banane, 1 dash Triple Sec. Shake over ice, strain into a cocktail glass.

Banana Bliss (Cktl). ½ measure Banana liqueur, ½ measure Brandy. Stir over ice, strain into a cocktail glass.

Banana Cocktail (Cktl). ½ measure Crème de Banane, ¼ measure Gin, ¼ measure white Rum. Shake well over ice, strain into a cocktail glass.

Banana Cow Cocktail (Cktl). 4 fl.ozs. coconut milk, 1½ fl.ozs. golden Rum, 1 banana. Blend altogether in a blender with a scoop of crushed ice. Pour into a highball glass. Serve with straws.

Banana Daiquiri (Cktl). ½ fl.oz. Crème de Banane, 1½ fl.ozs. white Rum, juice ½ lime, ½ peeled banana, 2 scoops crushed ice. Blend on high speed in blender, pour into a glass unstrained. Serve with short, thick straws.

Banana Daktari (Cktl). See Daktari.

Banana Liqueur (Fr). See Banadry, Crème de Banane. 25–30% alc. by vol.

Banana Mint Cocktail (Cktl). ⅓ measure Crème de Banane, ⅓ measure (white) Crème de Menthe, ⅓ measure cream. Shake well over ice, strain into a cocktail glass.

Banana Punch (Cktl). 1 measure Vodka, ⅔ measure Apricot brandy, juice ½ lime. Pour ingredients into a highball glass over crushed ice, top with soda. Dress with sliced banana and mint sprig.

Banana Royal Cocktail (Cktl). ½ meas-

ure golden Rum, ½ measure coconut milk, 2 measures pineapple juice, 2 dashes cream, 1 banana. Blend together with a scoop of crushed ice in a blender. Pour into an old-fashioned glass. Top with toasted desiccated coconut.

Banana's Breeze (Cktl). ¼ fl.oz. Apricot brandy, ¾ fl.oz. Crème de Banane, 1 fl.oz. orange juice, 1½ fl.ozs orange juice, ½ fl.oz sweet and sour lemon juice, 3 drops Prothee. Shake over ice, strain into cocktail glass.

Banat (Rum). The largest wine-producing region. The best red is from the Kadarka grape.

Banater Riesling (Rum). An erroneous varietal name for the grape Creaca, Kreaca, Kriacza, Zakkelweiss. Known as the Grüzer in Austria.

Banatski Rizling Kreaca (Yug). A Riesling-style white grape variety grown in the Banat region Vojvodina.

Ban Bourguignone (Fr). A song sung at wine fraternities of Burgundy.

Banco Brewery (Swe). A co-operative brewery based in Skruv in south-east Sweden.

Banda Azul (Sp). A red wine produced by Federico Paternina of Rioja, Spain. Produced from the Tempranillo, Mazuelo and Garnacha grapes. It is matured for 1 year in oak and 1–2 years in bottle.

Banda Dorada (Sp). A white wine produced by Federico Paternina of Rioja from 70% Viura and 30% Malvasia grapes.

B and B (Cktl). ½ measure Brandy, ½ measure Bénédictine mixed together.

B and B (Fr). A liqueur produced by Bénédictine near Fécamp. A blend of Bénédictine and old Cognac. Is drier than the Bénédictine liqueur. 43% alc. by vol.

B and B Vineyards (USA). A winery based in Stockton, New Jersey. Produces mainly hybrid wines.

Bande à Côté (Fr). Turning the cask on its side so that the bung is on the side.

Bande Dessous (Fr). A term used to describe a full cask with the bung uppermost.

Bandeira (Sp). A wine similar in style to Port, produced in north-western Spain.

Ban des Vendanges (Fr). Official opening ceremony of the Graves and Médoc vintage. Allows the Confrères Vignerons to set a date for the harvest.

Ban de Vendange (Fr). Lit–'Proclamation of the harvest'. A proclamation of the date when the harvest may start, particularly in Champagne and Bordeaux.

Bandiera Winery (USA). Address = Cloverdale, Sonoma Valley, California.

Grape varieties – Cabernet sauvignon, Chenin blanc, Gamay, Petit syrah and Zinfandel. Produces varietal wines.

Bandol (Fr). A controlled place name for certain wines of Provence on the south coast of Aix. Produces A.C. red, rosé and white wines. Communes – Bandol, Beausset [part], Evenos [part], La Cadière d'Azur, Le Castellet, Ollioules [part], Saint-Cyr-sur-Mer [part] and Sanary. Main grape varieties – Clairette and Ugni blanc for the white wines and Cinsault, Grenache, Mourvaison and Mourvèdre for the red wines.

Banff (Scot). A 15 year old single Malt whisky produced by Slater Rodger and Co, part of the DCL. group. A Highland malt whisky. 45% alc. by vol.

Bang (Cktl). Half warmed Ale, half dry Cider, 1 wineglass Whisky. Stir well and sprinkle with ginger or nutmeg. Gin may be substituted in place of the Whisky.

Bang (Ind). See Bhang.

Banks and Taylor Brewery (Eng). A new brewery 1981 opened in Shefford in Bedfordshire. Noted for its Shefford Bitter 1038 O.G. Eastcote Ale 1041 O.G. and SOS 1050 O.G.

Bank's Beer (W.Ind). A light beer 5% alc. by vol. brewed by the Banks Brewery in Barbados.

Bank's Brewery (Eng). One of the remaining two breweries in the West Midlands belonging to the Wolverhampton & Dudley Breweries Ltd. Produces many fine beers. See also Hanson's Brewery.

Banks Brewery (W.Ind). A brewery based in Barbados. Brews Bank's beers and Ebony Lager (a dark Lager beer).

Banks DIH Ltd (S.Am). A Rum producer based in Guyana. Produces Gold Medal, Royal Liquid Gold, Super White and XM Standard.

Bannockburn Vineyard (Austr). Address = Midland Highway, Bannockburn, Victoria 3331. 16 ha. Grape varieties – Cabernet sauvignon, Chardonnay, Pinot noir, Sauvignon blanc and Shiraz.

Baños de Ebro (Sp). A noted wine-producing village based in the Rioja Alavesa, north-eastern Spain.

Banshee Cocktail (Cktl). ⅓ measure Crème de Cacao, ⅓ measure Crème de Banane, ⅓ measure cream, dash Gomme syrup. Blend altogether in a blender with a scoop of crushed ice. Pour into a cocktail glass.

Banskà Bystrica Brewery (Czec). A brewery founded in 1971 in eastern Czec. Noted for its light Pilsener beers.

Banvin (Fr). An old law which allowed the Lord of the manor to sell his wines first before his tenants (over a set period of time). Also old custom of fixing the date of the harvest. The fore-runner of the Ban de Vendange.

Banyuls (Fr). A Vin doux naturel from the Roussillon district of the Midi region. Made with the Grenache grape. Brown in colour. Consumed as an apéritif in France. Communes – Banyuls-sur-Mer, Cerbère and Port-Vendres. Must have a minimum alc. by vol. of 21.5% and a maximum of 7% unfermented sugar. See Banyuls Grand Cru.

Banyuls-Citron (Cktl). ½ gill Banyuls, ⅙ gill Sirop de Citron, soda water. Stir over ice, strain into a highball glass and top with soda.

Banyuls Grand Cru (Fr). A.C. Banyuls that must be aged for a minimum of 30 months in wood in under-ground cellars. See Affinage and Banyuls.

Banyuls-sur-Mer (Fr). A commune in the A.C. Banyuls region of south-western France.

Baobab (Afr). A north African drink produced from the fruit of the tree of same name.

Baptizer (Port). To water down wine (or milk) etc.

Bar (Eng) (abbr). Bar-counter where drinks are served/barrier between staff and the customer. Also applied to room where the bar is. See 'Public Bar' and 'Lounge'.

Bar (Eng) (abbr). Barred. To prevent entry into a Public house to undesirables.

Bar (Tur). A café serving alcoholic drinks. A drinking bar (place). See also Birahane.

Barack Pàlinka (Hun). A dry unsweetened Brandy made from the distilled juice of apricots. Sold in a short squat bottle with a long, fairly wide neck. Has a slight taste of almonds.

Barancourt-Brice, Martin, Tritant (Fr). Récoltants-Manipulants. Address = Place André, Tritant, Bouzy 51150, Tours sur Marne. Produces – Vintage and non-vintage wines. Vintages – 1969, 1970, 1971, 1973, 1975, 1976, 1979, 1982, 1983.

Baratke (Rum). A wine-producing area, is part of the Banat Vineyard.

Barbacarlo (It). Dry or semi-sweet red wine from Oltrepó Pavese, Lombardy.

Barbadillo (Sp). A noted Sherry producer of Jerez de la Frontera. Also in Sanlúcar de Barrameda. Owns many vineyards and a 415 ha. vineyard and winery with Harveys. Produces many

Sherries which include – Luis de Eguilas II. Pedro Rodriguez, Solear Manzanilla Pasada and a 60 year old Manzanilla.

Barbados Cream (Fr). See Crème des Barbades.

Barbados Distilleries (W.Ind). Major Rum distillers in the West Indies.

Barbados Rum (W.Ind). Medium coloured Rum with a light, slightly sweet flavour.

Barbados Water (W.Ind). An old seventeenth-century nickname for Rum.

Barbancourt (W.Ind). A famous Haitian rum distillery.

Barbantane (Fr). A Vin doux naturel produced in the commune of Barbantane in the Bouches-du-Rhône, southern France.

Barbara Cocktail (Cktl). 1 measure Vodka, ½ measure Crème de Cacao, ½ measure cream. Shake well over ice, strain into a cocktail glass.

Barbarella Cocktail (Cktl). (Non-alc). ½ measure Angostura, ½ measure Syrop de Fraises. Stir over ice in a highball glass. Top with grape juice.

Barbaresco (It). A famous D.O.C.G. red wine from Piemonte. Made from the Nebbiolo grape, aged 2 years (1 year in oak/chestnut casks). If aged 3 years = Riserva. 4 years or more = Riserva speciale.

Barbarian Beer (Eng). A cask conditioned Bitter 1045 O.G. brewed by the Pheasant and Firkin home-brew public house in London. Owned by the Bruce Co.

Barbarossa (It). A black grape variety grown in central eastern Italy.

Barbaroux (Fr). A red grape variety grown in south-eastern France.

Barbary Coast Cocktail (Cktl). ⅕ measure each of Gin, Scotch whisky, Crème de Cacao, Rum and cream, 1 dash Gomme syrup. Shake well over ice, strain into a cocktail glass.

Barbeillon J-C. (Fr). A producer of sparkling Touraine wines based at Oisly, Touraine, Loire.

Barbeito (Mad). A noted Madeira wine shipper.

Barbelroth (Ger). Village. (Anb) = Rheinpfalz. (Ber) = Südliche Weinstrasse. (Gro) = Kloster Liebfrauenberg. (Vin) = Kirchberg.

Barbera (It). A red wine grape grown principally in Piemonte, also to a small extent in California. The wine produced is deep-coloured, full-bodied and full flavoured.

Barbera (USA). See California Barbera.

Barbera Amabile (It). A slightly sparkling, sweet red wine from the Barbera grape.

Barbera d'Alba (It). D.O.C. red wine made from the Barbera grape in the commune of Alba in the province of Cuneo, Piemonte. Aged for 2 years (1 year in wood). 13% alc. by vol. If aged 3 years then classed Superiore.

Barbera d'Asti (It). D.O.C. red wine made from the Barbera grape in the commune of Asti, Piemonte. Aged for 2 years (1 year in wood). 13% alc. by vol. If aged 3 years then classed Superiore.

Barbera del Monferrato (It). D.O.C. red wine made from 75–90% Barbera and 10–25% Freisa, Grignolino and Dolcetto. If alc. content less than 12.5% by vol. and aged not less than 2 years then classed Superiore.

Barbero (It). A leading Bitters and Vermouth producer. Noted for their Diesus bitter apéritif. Also produce Moscato d'Asti. Based in the Piemonte.

Barberone (USA). See California Barberone.

Barbezieux (Fr). A noted town in the Charente Département in the Petite Champagne, Cognac. Its grapes are distilled into Cognac des Bois.

Barbican (Eng). A popular, alcohol-free Lager brewed by Bass Charrington.

Barbican Cocktail (Cktl). ¹/₁₀ measure Drambuie, ²/₁₀ measure Passion fruit juice, ⁷/₁₀ measure Scotch whisky. Shake over ice, strain into a cocktail glass.

Barbier (René) (Sp). A wine-producer based in Penedés. Grape varieties – Cabernet sauvignon, Cariñena, Garnacha, Monastrell, Parellada, Tempranillo and Xarello.

Bar Blender/Liquidiser (Eng). Used for making drinks that require puréed fruits.

Barbonne Fayel (Fr). A Cru Champagne village in the Canton de Sézanne. District – Épernay.

Barbosa (João T.) Lda (Port). A noted shipper of fine Dão wines.

Barbotage (Cktl). ½ measure orange juice, ½ measure lemon juice, dash Grenadine. Shake over ice, strain into a flute glass. Top with iced Champagne.

Barboteo (Sp). The name given to the art of 'chewing' the wine, i.e. retaining the wine in the mouth to warm it and improve the bouquet and flavour.

Barbotine (Fr). See Mugwort.

Barboursville Vineyard (USA). A winery based in Barboursville, Virginia. 100 ha. Produces vinifera wines.

Barca Velha (Port). A red wine produced by Ferreira from 15% Amarela, 60% Roriz and 20% Touriga francesa grapes grown at Meão in the upper Douro. Is matured at Vila Nova de Gaia.

Barcelo (Port). A white grape variety grown in the Dão region.

Barcelo (Luis) (Sp). A producer and exporter of Malaga.

Barclays (Jas) & Co (Can). A distiller of a range of Canadian whiskies. A subsidiary of Hiram Walker.

Barclay Square (Can). A blended Canadian whisky produced by Jas Barclay and Co. (A subsidiary of Hiram Walker). 40% alc. by vol.

Barco (El) (Sp). A large co-operative based in Galicia.

Barcos Rabelos (Port). Boats used to take down the casks of new Port wine from Pinhão to Oporto along the river Douro. Not used so much now as road and railway has been built.

Bardenheim Wine Cellars (USA). A winery based in St. Louis, Missouri. Produces vinifera and hybrid wines.

Bardinet (Fr). A liqueur and Rum producer based in Bordeaux. Produces – Ardine, Kümmel, Negrita (a brand of Rum), Parfait Amour and Triple Sec.

Bardinet (W.Ind). A noted Rum distillery based on the island of Martinique.

Bardo (Port). A system of vine training using wires stretched between granite pillars or wooden posts.

Bardolino (It). D.O.C. red wine from the Corvina veronese, Rondinella, Molinara, Negrara, Rossignola, Barbera and Sangiovese grapes. See also Bardolino Classico. If minimum alc. content 11.5% by vol. and aged minimum 1 year then classed Superiore.

Bardolino Chiaretto (It). D.O.C. rosé wine from grape varieties used in the making of Bardolino. See also Bardolino Chiaretto Classico.

Bardolino Chiaretto Classico (It). Wine from the central and best part of the region of production.

Bardolino Classico (It). A wine from the central and best part of the region of production.

Barea Velha (Port). Fruity wine.

Bärenblut (USA). A red wine produced by the Beringer Brothers Winery in the Napa Valley, California. Made from the Grignolino and Pinot noir grapes.

Bärenfang (Ger). A honey-flavoured lime and mullein flower liqueur. Made with neutral spirit.

Barengo Winery (USA). A large winery based in the northern part of the San Joaquin Valley, California. Owns vineyards in Fresno, Lodi and Modesto. Also buys in grapes. Produces most styles of wines. See also Cremocha.

Bärentrank (Ger). Lit – 'Bear's drink'. A

strong spirit from eastern Prussia, distilled from potatoes and flavoured with honey.

Barfly (Eng) (slang). A bar-hogger. A person who sits at the bar counter of licensed premises all the time, thus making it difficult for other customers to get served.

Bar Fly (USA). The nickname for a person who frequents bars (licensed premises).

Bargetto Winery (USA). A winery based in Soquel, Santa Cruz, California. Grape varieties – Barbera, Cabernet sauvignon, Chardonnay, French colombard, Johannisberg riesling and Zinfandel. Produces varietal wines.

Bar Glass (Cktl). A mixing glass for mixing cocktails. Also known as a Jigger.

Baril (Fr). Barrel, cask. 72 litres (16 gals) capacity. Used for spirits, wine, etc.

Baril (Wales). Cask, barrel.

Barile (It). Barrel, cask.

Barillet (Fr). Keg.

Bar-le-Duc (Fr). A red wine (Vin de table) producing town based in the Lorraine region.

Barley (Eng). Grain used in the production of beer and whisky. Ideal because of its high sugar, low starch content. See Two Row, Four Row and Six Row Barley.

Barley Corn (Eng). A single grain of barley.

Barleycorn Ale (Eng). A pale keg Ale 1033 O.G. brewed by Hall's Brewery, Burton-on-Trent, Staffs.

Barley Water (Eng). Wash 2 tablespoons of barley and boil for 2 hours in 2 quarts of water. Strain, add sugar to taste and allow to cool. Beneficial to the kidneys.

Barley Water (Eng). See Robinsons Barley Water.

Barley Wine (Eng). A dark, fruity beer with a very high alcohol content of over 1060 O.G. The strongest of ales it is normally sold in nips.

Bar Liquidiser/Blender (Eng). Used for making drinks that require puréed fruits.

Barlys (Wales). Barley.

Barm (Eng). In brewing the frothy head seen on the top of the fermenting vessel.

Barm (Eng). An old English name for yeast. See Barmr from which it derives.

Barmaid (Eng). A female who serves and operates behind a bar or counter to dispense drinks.

Barman (Eng). A man who serves and operates behind a bar or counter to dispense drinks.

Barmaster Cocktail (Cktl). ⅓ measure Mandarine Napoléon, ⅔ measure orange juice, dash Campari, dash Vodka, dash egg white. Shake well over ice, strain into a cocktail glass. Dress with slice of orange and a cherry.

Barmen (Tur). Barman, bartender.

Barmera (Eng). A range of Australian wines from Shaftesbury Vintners. Imported from the Consolidated Co-operative Wineries.

Barmr (Scan). The old Norse name for yeast. See Barm.

Barms (Ger). An old Gothic name for yeast.

Barna (Hun). A malty, dark beer 4% alc. by weight.

Barnes Winery (Can). A major wine producer based in Ontario.

Barnett (Fr). Cognac producer.

Barningham Vineyard (Eng). Planted 1972, 1.75 ha. Soil – Sandy loam over gravel. Grape variety – 95% Riesling x Sylvaner.

Barnsgate Manor Vineyards (Eng). A small winery based in Herons-Ghyll, near Uckfield, East Sussex. 8.25 ha. Grape varieties – Chardonnay, Kerner, Müller-Thurgau, Pinot noir, Reichensteiner and Seyval blanc. Is owned by Pieroth of Germany.

Barnstormer Ale (Eng). A strong Ale 1048 O.G. brewed by Stallion's in Chippenham, Berkshire.

Barnyard Fermented (Eng). A term used by coffee tasters to denote a poor coffee.

Barolo (It). D.O.C.G. red wine produced from the Nebbiolo grape in the Piemonte region. Aged for 3 years in oak/chestnut casks. If aged not less than 4 years then classified Riserva, if aged not less than 5 years then classified Riserva speciale.

Barolo Chinato (It). An apéritif of Barolo wine flavoured with quinine.

Baron (Ger). Vineyard. (Anb) = Rheinpfalz, (Ber) = Südliche Weinstrasse. (Gro) = Schloss Ludwigshöhe. (Vil) = St. Martin.

Barona Vermouth (Eng). The brandname of a Vermouth from Linfood Cash and Carry, Northamptonshire.

Baron B (Arg). A sparkling wine produced by the Bodegas Proviar.

Baron Cocktail (Cktl). 1 measure Gin, 1 measure Triple Sec, ¼ measure Italian vermouth, ¼ measure French vermouth. Stir over ice, strain into a cocktail glass, add a twist of lemon peel.

Baron de L' (Fr). See Ladoucette.

Baron de Rio Negro (Arg). The brandname of a sparkling white wine.

Baron et Fils (Fr). A Champagne producer. Address = Épernay.

Baron Vineyard (Le) (USA). A vineyard based in the Sonoma County, California. 6 ha. Grape variety – Rhine riesling. Owned by Sonoma Vineyards.

Baronial (Cktl). ⁷⁄₁₀ measure Lillet, ³⁄₁₀ measure Lemon gin, 2 dashes Angostura, 2 dashes Cointreau. Stir over ice, strain into a cocktail glass.

Baronne (S.Afr). A soft, red wine made from Cabernet and other grapes from the Nederburg Estate.

Baronoff (Eng). A proprietary brand of Vodka. 40% alc. by vol.

Baron Otard (Fr). An 8 year old V.S.O.P. Cognac produced by the Otard Co. in Cognac.

Baroque (USA). A red hybrid grape variety developed by the University of California. Grown in the Paul Masson Vineyards.

Barossa Co-operative (Austr). An estate in the Barossa Valley, South Australia. Uses the Kaiser Stuhl label for its wines.

Barossa Pearl (Austr). A sparkling wine of Barossa Valley from the Gramp Winery, South Australia.

Barossa Valley (Austr). A famous region near Adelaide, South Australia. Planted with ungrafted vines. Also spelt Barrosa.

Bar person (Eng). The designation given to barmen and women to comply with the Sex Discrimination Act of 1975.

Barquero (Sp). An extra dry Montilla produced by Pérez Barquero in Montilla-Moriles, southern Spain.

Barr (Fr). A famous old wine town in Alsace, north-eastern France.

Barr (Scan). An old Norse name for barley from which the word derives.

Barracas (Cktl). ⅔ measure sweet Vermouth, ⅓ measure Angostura. Shake well over ice, strain into an ice-filled cocktail glass.

Barracheiros (Port). Stalwarts who carry up to 75 kilo loads of grape bunches on their shoulders in baskets.

Barracuda (Cktl). 1 fl.oz. light Rum, ½ fl.oz. Grenadine, 1 fl.oz. pineapple juice, ¼ fl.oz. lime juice, 2 dashes Gomme syrup. Shake over ice, strain into a pineapple shell. Top with Champagne. Decorate with slice of pineapple and lime.

Barracuda Cocktail (Cktl). ½ measure golden Rum, ¼ measure Galliano, ½ measure pineapple juice, 1 dash lime juice, 1 dash Gomme syrup. Shake over ice, strain into an old-fashioned glass. Top with iced Champagne and a slice of lime.

Barraque (S.Afr). A dry, blended, white wine from Alpha Wines (part of Gilbeys).

Barre (La) (Fr). A Premier Cru vineyard in the A.C. commune of Volnay, Côte de Beaune, Burgundy. 2 ha. Also known as Clos de la Barre.

Barred (Eng). Term to denote that a person may not use certain licensed premises because they may have caused a disturbance (or other reason).

Barrelage (Eng). The term used to denote the number of barrels per week/year that are bought/sold.

Barrelage Agreement (Eng). A term by which a public house is obliged to purchase a certain annual barrelage from a brewery in return for a reduced interest loan.

Barrel, [Beer] (Eng). Holds 36 gallons (163.6 litres). (USA). 31.5 US. gallons.

Barrel Fermented (Eng). A term used when the fermentation process occurs in barrels as opposed to tanks, vats or in the bottle.

Barrelhouse (USA). A cheap drinking establishment which usually has unsavoury characteristics.

Barrel, [Rum] (W.Ind). Holds 40 gallons approximately.

Barrel, [Wine] (Fr). Holds 26½ gallons (119.5 litres), but can vary from country to country and from region to region.

Barret (Fr). A commune in the Charente Département whose grapes are classed Petite Champagne (Cognac).

Barriasson (Fr). Cognac producer.

Barricas (Sp). A 225 litre oak cask.

Barrier Reef (Cktl). 1 scoop ice cream, ¾ fl.oz. Cointreau, 1 fl.oz. Gin, dash Angostura. Stir together with ice. Add a few drops of blue Curaçao.

Barril (Sp). Barrel.

Barril del Gasto (Sp). Denotes a barrel of cheap wine from which the vineyard workers drink.

Barrique (Fr). Hogshead. A large barrel/cask. Bordeaux = 225 litres, Cognac = 205 litres, Loire = 213 litres and Mâcon = 210 litres.

Barrique à Vin (Ch.Isles). Wine cask.

Barrique Bordelaise (Fr). Cask, holds 49½ gallons (225 litres). Made of Limousin oak. 4 barriques equal 1 tonneau, 1 barrique equals 288 standard (75 cl) bottles.

Barrique de Transport (Fr). A specially strengthened cask which is suitable for despatching wine. Has metal rims at both ends.

Barriquot (Fr). The eighteenth-century name for a small cask or barrel.

Barrocão (Port). A producer of red and white Garrafeiras in Bairrada. Was founded in 1920.

Barron Brewery (Eng). A brewery opened in 1984 in Silverton, Devon. Noted for its Barron's Draught 1040 O.G.

Bar Room (Eng). A room in a building where alcoholic drinks are served (sold) for consumption on the premises. Must be licensed.

Barros (Port). Vintage Port shippers. Vintages – 1948, 1955, 1957, 1958, 1960, 1963, 1965, 1966, 1970, 1974, 1975, 1977, 1978, 1979, 1980, 1982.

Barros (Sp). The clay soil found in the Andalusia region. Also spelt Barrosa.

Barrosa (Sp). See Barros.

Barros Almeida (Port). Vintage Port shippers. Vintages = 1943, 1975.

Barrosa Valley (Austr). See Barossa Valley.

Barrydale (S.Afr). A wine-producing district within the region of Klein Karoo. Is noted for its brandy and its Burgundy-style table wines.

Barrydale Co-operative (S.Afr). Based in Klein Karoo. Address = Barrydale Koöperatiewe Wynmakery Bpk., Box 59, Barrydale 6750. Produces varietals and brandy. (The only co-operative Brandy distillery in South Africa).

Barrydale Koöperatiewe Wynmakery (S.Afr). See Barrydale Co-operative.

Barry Wine Company (USA). A winery based on the west bank of the Hemlock Lake, Finger Lakes, New York. 60 ha. Produces vinifera and hybrid wines.

Barsac (Fr). A famous commune of Sauternes in south-western Bordeaux on the west bank of the river Garonne. Can use the Sauternes A.C. or its own. Produces sweet white wines attacked by botrytis cinerea.

Bàrsonyos-Csàszàr (Hun). Northerly wine area. The town of Mór is noted for Ezerjó (one of the finest dry white wines of Hungary).

Bar Spoon (Eng). Long handled spoon with a disk base (muddler) on top. Made of stainless steel, silver or E.P.N.S.

Bar Syrup (Eng). Sugar and water mixture ratio 3–1. Used to sweeten cocktails.

Bart (André) (Fr). A Burgundy négociant based at 24, Rue de Mazy, 21160 Marsanny-la-Côte, Burgundy.

Bartels (USA). The brand-name used by the Lion Brewery in Wilkes-Barre, Pennsylvania for their range of beers.

Bartels Winery (USA). A winery based in Pensacola, Florida. Produces Muscadine wines.

Bartender (USA). See Barman, Barmaid, Barperson.

Bartender Cocktail (Cktl). ¼ measure dry Vermouth, ¼ measure Gin, ¼ measure Dubonnet, ¼ measure dry Sherry, dash Grand Marnier. Stir over ice, strain into a cocktail glass.

Bartenders' Association of Canada (Can). B.A.C. Address = P.O. Box 1135, Adelaide Street, East Toronto, Ontario.

Bartenders' Association of Ireland (Ire). B.A.I. Address = Jury's Hotel, Ballsbridge, Dublin 4.

Bartenders' Club of Iceland (Ice). B.C.I. Iceland's Bartenders Association. Address = P.O. Box 7114–127, Reykjavik.

Bartlett Beers (Eng). Home-brew public house beers from the Tavern in Newnham Bridge, Worcestershire. Produces Bartlett Mild 1040 O.G. Bartlett Bitter 1042 O.G.

Barton and Guestier (Fr). Wine négociants in Bordeaux who deal in fine Bordeaux wines. Wines are distributed by Seagram.

Barton Distillery (USA). A Bourbon whiskey based south-west of Frankfort in Kentucky.

Barton Manor Vineyard (Eng). First planted 1977, 2.5 ha. Address = Whippingham, East Cowes, Isle of Wight. Grape varieties – Gewürz-traminer, Huxelrebe, Müller-Thurgau, Reichesteiner and Seyval blanc.

Barton Special (Cktl). 1 measure Applejack, ½ measure Scotch whisky, ½ measure Gin. Shake well over ice, strain into an ice-filled old-fashioned glass.

Bartzch (Asia). A spirit made from hogsweed. Produced mainly in northern Asia. Made from a variety of 'weed' plants.

Barwell and Jones (Eng). A division of Tollemache and Cobbold Breweries. Has eight retail wine outlets in East Anglia.

Barzy-sur-Marne (Fr). A Cru Champagne village in the Canton de Condé-en-Brie. District = Château Thierry.

Basaltic (It). A basalt rich soil found in central Italy.

Bas-Armagnac (Fr). A sub-region of Armagnac in the Gers Département, where Armagnac brandy is made.

Bas-Beaujolais (Fr). The southern region of the Beaujolais. South of the Nizerand river. Also known as Bâtard-Beaujolais. Has chalky top soil with manganese subsoil. See also Haut-Beaujolais.

Bas-des-Duresses (Les) (Fr). A Premier Cru vineyard in the A.C. commune of Auxey-Duresses, Côte de Beaune, Burgundy, 5.9 ha.

Bas-des-Teurons (Le) (Fr). A Premier Cru vineyard in the A.C. commune of Beaune, Côte de Beaune, Burgundy, 7.32 ha.

Base (Eng). Another name for the Wash in Gin production.

Basedow Winery (Austr). A winery based in the Barossa Valley, South Australia. Buys in grapes (mainly Shiraz) to make table wine.

Basi (E.Ind). A spirit fermented from sugar cane, berries and bark in the Ilocos region of the Philippines.

Basic Wine (Eng). The name given to Vermouth after the blending wine with mistelle and before infusion with herbs.

Basic Yield (Fr). Rendement de base. The amount of wine that can be produced under the A.C. laws.

Basil Cocktail (Cktl). ¼ measure Grand Marnier, ¼ measure Tia Maria, ¼ measure Irish whiskey. Stir over ice, strain into a cocktail glass, float ¼ measure of cream on top. Add zest of lemon.

Basilicata (It). A mountainous region, surrounded by Puglia, Campania, and Calabria and reaching the Ionian and Tyrrhenian seas. The garnet red wine Aglianico de Vulture from the Monte Vulture vineyard is the most noted. Muscat and Malvasia grape varieties are the most predominant, and the 'Passito' treatment is used.

Baska (Fr). A coffee liqueur from Angers.

Bäska Dropper (Swe). Lit – 'Bitter drops'. A bitters flavoured with wormwood.

Basket Press (Fr). An old type of press now mainly out of date except for Champagne and other sparkling wines.

Basler Kirschwasser (Switz). A clear spirit-liqueur made from cherry stones. 40% alc. by vol.

Baslieux (Fr). A Cru Champagne village in the Canton de Châtillon-sur-Marne. District = Reims.

Bas-Médoc (Fr). The northern region of the Médoc, Bordeaux. Produces middle quality red wines.

Basquaise (Fr). A flat, fat, long necked flagon used for Armagnac brandy. Also called 'Pot Gascon'.

Basqueador (Sp). See Mecedor.

Bas-Rhin (Fr). Lit – 'Lower Rhine'. Region of Alsace.

Bass Ale (Ire). A keg Bitter 1036 O.G. brewed by the Bass Ulster branch in Ireland.

Bassareus (Lat). Word used for Bacchus. See also Dionysus, Euhan, Euan, Euhius, Euius, Lacchus, Lyaeus, Thyoneus and Bromius.

Bass Brewery (Eng). See also Charrington. Biggest English brewers who have merged with Worthington, Mitchells and Butlers, Charringtons. Produce Draught Bass 1044 O.G. a cask conditioned beer. Based at Burton-on-Trent, runs 13 breweries and has over 7,500 public houses.

Basse Normande (Fr). A straight sided, dumpy bottle. Especially used in the Rhône.

Basses-Alpes (Fr). A noted wine-producing Département which has the Provence region within its boundaries.

Basses-Mourettes (Fr). A Premier Cru vineyard in the commune of Ladoix Serrigny, A.C. Aloxe-Corton, Côte de Beaune, Burgundy. Produces red wines only.

Basses-Vergelesses (Fr). A Premier Cru vineyard in the A.C. commune of Savigny-lès-Beaune, Côte de Beaune, Burgundy.

Basses-Vergelesses (Les) (Fr). A Premier Cru vineyard in the A.C. commune of Pernand, Côte de Beaune, Burgundy. 17.5 ha.

Bassets (Les) (Fr). A vineyard in the A.C., commune of Montagny, Côte Chalonnaise, Burgundy.

Bassgeige (Ger). Vineyard. (Anb) = Baden. (Ber) = Kaiserstuhl-Tuniberg. (Gro) = Vulkanfelsen. (Vil) = Oberbergen.

Bassin de Vichy (Fr). A natural sparkling mineral water from Bassin de Vichy, Saint-Yorre. Royal French Spring.

Bass North (Eng). Part of Bass breweries, northern division. Includes Stone's Brewery, and breweries at Runcorn, Tadcaster and Sheffield.

Bass Special (Scot). A keg Ale 1035 O.G. brewed by Tennent Caledonian Brewery in Edinburgh and Glasgow.

Bass Worthington (Eng). A part of the Bass group. Has breweries all over Great Britain producing a large range of ales and lagers.

Bastard (Eng). A white to tawny-coloured wine produced in the seventeenth century.

Bastard Bottle (Eng). Another name for the Bladder bottle. Named so after the name of a family that first used them.

Bastard Lager (Eng). A term used in the brewing industry for the top fermented beer called Lager.

Bastardo (Mad). A rare type of Madeira which is light with a sweet taste.

Bastardo (Port). A red grape variety used in the making of red Dão.

Bastei (Ger). Vineyard. (Anb) = Nahe. (Ber) = Schloss Böckelheim. (Gro) = Burgweg. (Vil) = Traisen.

Bastel (Ger). Vineyard. (Anb) = Franken. (Ber) = Steigerwald. (Gro) = Schild. (Vil) = Greuth.

Bastia (Fr). Chief northern wine producing area of Corsica. Produces A.C. Patrimonio rosé.

Basto (Port). Region of the Entre Minho e Douro. Produces both red and white Vinhos Verdes.

Bâtard-Beaujolais (Fr). Other name for the Bas-Beaujolais.

Bâtard-Montrachet (Fr). Grand Cru A.C. vineyards in Chassagne-Montrachet, Côte de Beaune, Burgundy. Produces some of the finest white wines in the world.

Batavia (E.Ind). A noted coffee-producing region of Java.

Batavian Arak (E.Ind). Rum made on the island of Java. Dry and aromatic.

Bateman's Brewery (Eng). Address = Wainfleet, Lincolnshire. Family-owned brewery. Produces many brews. Noted for its Nut Brown 1033 O.G. Double Brown 1037 O.G. and Ploughman's Ale 1049 O.G.

Bates Brewery (Eng). Opened 1983 in Bovey Tracey, South Devon. Produces Bates Bitter 1045 O.G.

Bates Ranch (USA). A small independent vineyard based in Santa Cruz mountains, Santa Clara, California. Grape variety is mainly Cabernet sauvignon.

B.A.T.F. (USA) (abbr). Bureau of Alcohol, Tobacco and Firearms. (Department).

Bath [Water] (Eng). A spa mineral water from southern England.

Bath-Tub Gin (USA). An illegal spirit distilled during the Prohibition era. Also called Rotgut.

Batida (Cktl). Mixture of Cachaça, passion fruit juice, lemon juice, Tamarind and sugar shaken over ice, strained into an ice-filled highball.

Batida Abaci (Cktl). 1 measure Cachaça, 2 teaspoons sugar, slice of fresh pineapple. Blend with crushed ice. Serve unstrained in club goblet.

Batida Caju (Cktl). 1 measure Cachaça, 2 teaspoons sugar, dessertspoon cashew nuts. Blend with crushed ice, serve unstrained in a club goblet.

Batida de Côco (It). Coconut liqueur with milk. Produced by G. Burton & C.S.p.A. Trieste, under supervision of Mangaroca Liquores do Brazil Ltda, São Paulo. See Batida. 16% alc. by vol.

Batida Goiaba (Cktl). 1 measure

Cachaça, 2 teaspoons sugar, slice of fresh guava. Blend with crushed ice, serve unstrained in a club goblet.

Batida Limão (Cktl). 1 measure Cachaça, 2 teaspoons sugar, juice of fresh lime. Blend with crushed ice, serve unstrained in a club goblet.

Batida Mango (Cktl). 1 measure Cachaça, 2 teaspoons sugar, slice of fresh mango. Blend with crushed ice, serve unstrained in a club goblet.

Batida Maracuja (Cktl). 1 measure Cachaça, 2 teaspoons sugar, 2 ozs Fruit of Brazil. Blend with crushed ice, serve unstrained in a club goblet.

Batida Morango (Cktl). 1 measure Cachaça, 2 teaspoons sugar, 3 fresh strawberries. Blend with crushed ice, serve unstrained in a club goblet.

Batoque (Port). The cask bung-hole.

Batte (Fr). A wooden implement used to hammer home the corks into the necks of the wine bottle.

Battenburg (Ger). Village. (Anb) = Rheinphalz. (Ber) = Mittelhaardt-Deutche Weinstrasse. (Gro) = Höllenphad. (Vin) = Schlossberg.

Batterieberg (Ger). Vineyard. (Anb) = Mosel-Saar-Ruwer. (Ber) = Bernkastel. (Gro) = Schwarzlay. (Vil) = Enkirch.

Battersea Brewery (Eng). Pub Brewery, Prince of Wales, Battersea, London. Owned by Watney Mann. Noted for its Power House 1050 O.G.

Battleaxe Ale (Eng). A strong cask conditioned Ale 1053 O.G. brewed by Axe Vale Brewery in Devon.

Battlin Brewery (Ger). A small brewery based in Esch.

Batto Vineyard (USA). A small vineyard based in the southern part of the Sonoma Valley, Sonoma County, California. Grape variety is mainly Cabernet sauvignon.

Bauchet (Fr). A range of Champagnes imported by Augustin.

Baudes (Les) (Fr). A Premier Cru vineyard in the A.C. commune of Chambolle-Musigny, Côte de Nuits, Burgundy. 3.5 ha.

Baudot (Fr). Cuvées in the A.C. Meursault-Genevrières, Côte de Beaune, Burgundy. Les Genevrières Dessous 0.75 ha. and Les Genevrières Dessus 0.2 ha. Are owned by the Hospices de Beaune.

Bauerbach (Ger). Village. (Anb) = Baden. (Ber) = Badische Bergstrasse/Kraichgau. (Gro) = Stiftsberg. (Vin) = Lerchenberg.

Bauget-Jouette (Fr). Champagne producer. Produces – Vintage and non-vintage wines.

Baulne-en-Brie (Fr). A Cru Champagne village in the Canton de Condé-en-Brie. District = Château Thierry.

Baumann-Zirgel (Fr). A small wine estate based in Alsace. 5 ha.

Baumé (Antoine) (Fr). 1728–1804. Invented the Hydrometer. See Baumé Scale.

Baumé Scale (Fr). Hydrometer for measuring sugar in grape must. Invented by Antoine Baumé (1728–1804). 1° Baumé = 144.3 ([s-1]/s). 1° Baumé is approximately 1.8° Brix.

Baury (Fr). A vineyard in the commune of Arsac. A.C. Médoc, Bordeaux. Cru Bourgeois Supérieur.

Bausch (Ger). Vineyard. (Anb) = Franken. (Ber) = Steigerwald. (Gro) = Schild. (Vil) = Castell.

Bausch (Ger). Vineyard. (Anb) = Franken. (Ber) = Steigerwald. (Gro) = Herrenberg. (Vil) = Castell.

Bausendorf (Ger). Village. (Anb) = Mosel-Saar-Ruwer. (Ber) = Bernkastel. (Gro) = Schwarzlay. (Vins) = Herzlay, Hubertuslay.

Bava (It). A producer of sparkling wines (by the cuve close method) based in Piemonte, north-western Italy.

Bavaria Brouwerij (Hol). A brewery based in Lieshout, North Brabant. Is noted for its Dortmunder 5% alc. by vol.

Bavarian (N.Z.). A sweet, copper-coloured beer 1036 O.G. brewed by the Christchurch branch of the New Zealand Breweries.

Bavarian Beer (USA). A Lager beer brewed by the Duquesne Brewing Co. in Cleveland, Ohio.

Bavarian Glass (Eng). A patent design for a beer glass. 1 pint capacity, is slim, thick-based and waisted in centre. Produced by the Dema Glass Co.

Bavaria-St. Pauli (Ger). Brewery of Hamburg. Nothing to do with Bavaria (name only adopted). Produces fine beers such as Grenzquell and Astra, also has subsidiary breweries, notably Jever's in Friesland. There is no connection with St. Pauli beer in USA.

Bavaroise (Fr). An old nineteenth-century drink of egg yolk, sugar, milk, tea, with spirit. Was served hot and frothing. Chocolate was often substituted for the tea and citrus juices were also added.

Bavaroise aux Choux (Fr). A nineteenth-century drink of a mixture of Absinthe and Orgeat.

Baya (Sp). Berry.

Bayard Fizz (Cktl). 1½ fl.ozs. Gin, juice of a lemon, 1 barspoon sugar, dash Maraschino, dash Grenadine. Shake over ice, strain into a highball glass. Top with soda water.

Baycovin (Eng). Diethylprocarbonate. A preservative for wine.

Baye (Fr). A Cru Champagne village in the Canton de Montmort. District = Épernay.

Bayer (Nor). A dark, Bavarian ale 4.5% alc. by vol. brewed by the Aass Brewery in Drammen.

Bayer. Bodensee (Ger). Bereich. (Anb) = Franken. (Gro) = Lindauer Seegarten. (Vil) = Nonnenhorn. (Vins) = Seehalde, Sonnenbüchel. See also Bayerischer Bodensee.

Bayerfeld-Steckweiler (Ger). Village. (Anb) = Nahe. (Ber) = Schloss Böckelheim. (Gro) = Paradiesgarten. (Vin) = Adelsberg, Aspenberg, Mittelberg, Schloss Stolzenberg.

Bayerischer Bodensee (Ger). Bereich. Same as Bayer. Bodensee.

Bayerischer Bodensee Landwein (Ger). One of the Deutsche Tafelwein zones.

Bayern (Ger). A region which has 3 Untergebiete (table-wine sub-areas), Donau, Lindau and Main.

Bay of Plenty (N.Z.). A wine-producing area in the North Island.

Bayon (Fr). A commune based in the A.C. Côtes de Bourg in north-eastern Bordeaux.

Bayou Cocktail (Cktl). ⅓ gill Cognac, juice ¼ lime, 4 dashes peach juice. Shake well over ice, strain into a cocktail glass. Top with a squeeze of lime peel juice.

Bay Rum (W.Ind). A seventeenth-century Rum produced from bay leaves on the island of St. Thomas as an ingredient of a hair tonic.

Bay View Vineyard (N.Z.). Vineyard. 20 ha. Part of Glenvale Winery.

Bazas (Fr). A vineyard in the Gironde that produces mainly red wines.

B.B. (Eng) (abbr). West Country's Boys Bitter.

BBB [Three B's] (Eng) (abbr). Best Bitter Beer. Produced by Arkell's Brewery, Stratton St. Margaret, Nr. Swindon. 1038 O.G.

BBB [Three B's] (Eng) (abbr). Buster Brew Bitter. Produced by Gales of Hampshire. 1037 O.G.

BBBB [Four B's] (Eng) (abbr). Berrow Brewery Best Bitter. Produced by the Berrow Brewery, Somerset.

B.B.I. (Eng) (abbr). British Bottlers' Institute.

B.B. Martine (Fr). 5 year old V.S.O.P. Armagnac produced by Ducastaing.

B.C.I. (Ice) (abbr). Bartenders' Club of Iceland. Iceland's Bartenders' Association. Address = P.O. Box 7114–127, Reykjavik.

BDS (Eng). A cask conditioned Ale 1055 O.G. brewed by the Pig and Whistle home-brew public house in London. A Hampshire home-brew public house.

Bé (Fr) (abbr). Baumé. i.e. °Bé.

Beachcomber (Cktl). A mixture of 3 parts mineral water and 1 part Crème de Menthe. Serve in a highball glass over ice. Dress with a mint sprig.

Beachcomber (Eng). A liqueur of British wine, Jamaican rum and Coconut produced by the Goldwell Co.

Beachcomber Belle (Cktl). 1½ ozs. Jamaican rum, 3 ozs. grapefruit juice. Shake well with ice, strain into a highball glass. Top up with 3 ozs. ginger beer. Serve with straws and dress with sprig of fresh mint.

Beachcomber Cocktail (Cktl). ⅗ measure white Rum, ⅕ measure Triple Sec, ⅕ measure lime juice, dash Maraschino. Shake over ice, strain into a sugar rimmed (with lime juice) cocktail glass.

Beach's Borough Bitter (Eng). A cask conditioned Bitter 1038 O.G. brewed by the Market Brewery, Southwark, London.

Beacon Bitter (Eng). See Everards Beacon Bitter.

Bead (Eng). A term used to describe the stream of bubbles in sparkling drinks, especially wines. The smaller the bead, the better the quality of the wine.

Beadlestone (Cktl). ½ measure Scotch whisky, ½ measure French vermouth. Stir over ice, strain into cocktail glass.

Beaker (Eng). A cup with a wide mouth. Made of china, clay, glass or plastic. Also of waxed paper or wood.

Beals Cocktail (Cktl). ⅗ measure Scotch whisky, ⅕ measure French vermouth, ⅕ measure Italian vermouth. Stir over ice, strain into a cocktail glass.

Beam (USA). See Beam (James) Distilling Co.

Beamish and Crawford Brewery (Ire). Famous brewery of Cork. Noted for its Stout, but also brews Bass beers and Carling Black Label Lager under licence. Owned by Carling of Canada.

Bear Ale (Scot). A strong draught Ale 1050 O.G. brewed by the Traquair House Brewery, Scotland.

Beard Family (Eng). Public house chain in Sussex. Ceased brewing at their Star Lane Brewery in 1950s. Sell beers from the Harvey Brewery, Lewes.

Bearm (Eng). An old mediaeval name for yeast.

Bear Mountain Winery (USA). The former name of the Lamont Winery

Delano, Kern County, California.

Béarn (Fr). A region of south west France. Produces white, rosé and red wines. In Jurançon region in Béarn. Noted for Rosé de Béarn and red A.C. Madiran.

Bear's Drink (Ger). A name given to the Prussian 'Bärentrank', a beverage distilled from potatoes and flavoured with honey.

Beatnik (Cktl). Place a cube of sugar in goblet. Add 1 measure of fresh orange juice, 2 dashes Pernod, 1 measure Vodka. Stir and serve with a slice of orange.

Beatty Ranch (USA). A vineyard based east of St. Helena, Napa Valley, California. Grape varieties – Cabernet sauvignon and Zinfandel.

Beaufort (Herbert et Fils) (Fr). Champagne producers. Address = 32 Rue de Tours, 51150 Tours-sur-Marne. Récoltants-manipulants. Produces – Vintage and non-vintage wines. Member of C.V.C. Vintages – 1973, 1975, 1976, 1979, 1982, 1983.

Beaujeu (Fr). Commune in the Beaujolais. Has A.C. Beaujolais-Villages or A.C. Beaujolais-Beaujeu status.

Beaujeu (Fr). Commune in the Beaujolais. Has A.C. Beaujolais-Villages or A.C. Beaujolais-Beaujeu status.

Beaujolais (Fr). Large district in the south of Burgundy. Red wines A.C. produced from the Gamay (au jus blanc) grape, are fruity, light and early drinking. Separate A.C. Crus Villages are Brouilly, Côte de Brouilly, Chénas, Chiroubles, Fleurie, Juliénas, Moulin à Vent, Regnié, Saint-Amour and Cru Beaujolais Villages. 7,200 ha. Produces mainly red wines with a small amount rosé and white wines.

Beaujolais-Arbuissonnas (Fr). See Arbuissonnas.

Beaujolais-Ardillats (Fr). See Ardillats (Les).

Beaujolais-Beaujeu (Fr). See Beaujeu.

Beaujolais-Blacé (Fr). See Blacé.

Beaujolais-Cercié (Fr). See Cercié.

Beaujolais-Chânes (Fr). See Chânes.

Beaujolais-Charentay (Fr). See Charentay.

Beaujolais Cru Villages (Fr). See Beaujolais.

Beaujolais de l'Année (Fr). Latest Beaujolais vintage until next one.

Beaujolais-Denice (Fr). See Denice.

Beaujolais-Durette (Fr). See Durette.

Beaujolais-Emeringes (Fr). See Emeringes.

Beaujolais-Jullié (Fr). See Jullié.

Beaujolais-la-Chapelle-de-Guinchay (Fr). See Chapelle-de-Guinchay (La).

Beaujolais-Lancié (Fr). See Lancié.

Beaujolais-le Perréon (Fr). See Perréon (Le).

Beaujolais-les Ardillats (Fr). See Ardillats (Les). Also known as Ardillats.

Beaujolais-Leynes (Fr). See Leynes.

Beaujolais-Marchampt (Fr). See Marchampt.

Beaujolais-Montmélas-Saint-Sorlin (Fr). See Montmélas-Saint-Sorlin.

Beaujolais Nouveau (Fr). Wine from the latest vintage. Produced by the Macération Carbonique fermentation, used to be released on the night of 14th/15th November but now at midnight on 3rd Thursday in November (from 1985). See Beaujolais Nouveau race.

Beaujolais Nouveau Race (Eng). Race held in late 1960s and early 1970s from Beaujolais to Central London. Competition to get the first case of new wine to London. £1,000 prize. Ceased because of danger on roads through fast driving. Now held for charity, unofficially.

Beaujolais-Odenas (Fr). See Odenas.

Beaujolais Pot (Fr). A 50 cl. mug or half bottle from which the locals drink their wine.

Beaujolais Primeur (Fr). The name given to wines that are released before the general Beaujolais release date of December 15th following harvest. Only wines of Beaujolais and Beaujolais Villages can be released.

Beaujolais-Quincié (Fr). See Quincié.

Beaujolais Regnié (Fr). New Cru Beaujolais-Villages A.C. created 1985. See Regnié.

Beaujolais-Rivolet (Fr). See Rivolet.

Beaujolais-Romanèche-Thorins (Fr). See Romanèche-Thorins.

Beaujolais-Saint-Amour-de-Bellevue (Fr). See Saint-Amour-de-Bellevue.

Beaujolais-Saint-Étienne-des-Ouillières (Fr). See Saint-Étienne-des Ouillières.

Beaujolais-Saint-Étienne-la-Varenne (Fr). See Saint-Étienne-la-Varenne.

Beaujolais-Saint-Julien-en-Montmélas (Fr). See Saint-Julien-en-Montmélas.

Beaujolais-Saint-Leger (Fr). See Saint-Leger.

Beaujolais-Saint-Symphorien-d'Ancelles (Fr). See Saint-Symphorien-d'Ancelles.

Beaujolais-Saint-Véran (Fr). See Saint-Véran.

Beaujolais-Salles (Fr). See Salles.

Beaujolais Supérieur (Fr). Any wine from the communes of Beaujolais that has reached a minimum of 10% alc. by vol.

Beaujolais-Vaux-en-Beaujolais (Fr). See Vaux-en-Beaujolais.

Beaujolais-Vauxrenard (Fr). See Vauxrenard.

Beaujolais-Villages (Fr). Individual A.C. wines from within Beaujolais. Wines can be sold as their A.C., as Villages or as Beaujolais, plus the commune name (e.g. Beaujolais-Blacé). Communes are; Arbuissonnas, Beaujeu, Blacé, Cercié, Chânes, Charentay, Denice, Durette, Emeringes, Jullié, Lancié, La Chapelle-de-Guinchay, Lantigné, Le Perréon, Leynes, Marchampt, Montmélas-Saint-Sorlin, Odenas, Pruzilly, Regnié, Rivolet, Romanèche-Thorins, Saint-Amour-de-Bellevue, Saint-Étienne-des-Ouillières, Saint-Étienne-la-Varenne, Saint-Julien-en-Montmélas, Saint-Lager, Saint-Symphorien-d'Ancelles, Saint-Véran, Salles, Vaux-en-Beaujolais, Vauxrenard and Villié-Morgon. 5,300 ha. under vine. See Beaujolais and Beaujolais Nouveau.

Beaujolais-Villié-Morgon (Fr). See Villié-Morgon.

Beaulieu-sur-Layon (Fr). An A.C. commune in the Coteaux du Layon district of the Anjou-Saumur region in the Loire.

Beaulieu Vineyard (Eng). Planted 1958–61, 2.25 ha. Address = Brockenhurst, Hampshire. Grape varieties – 90% Müller-Thurgau with Huxelrebe, Seyve villard and Seibel. Soil – Gravel over loam.

Beaulieu Vineyard (USA). Vineyards of Rutherford, Napa Valley, California. Noted for full-bodied red wines from Cabernet sauvignon, and Pinot noir grapes. Also produces dessert and sparkling wines.

Beaumé (Fr). An alternative spelling of Baumé. See Baumé (Antoine).

Beaumes (Fr). A vineyard in the A.C. Hermitage, central Rhône, southern France.

Beaumes-de-Venise (Fr). A Côtes du Rhône-Villages A.C. famous for its Vin doux naturel white wine Muscat de Beaumes-de-Venise.

Beaumet (Fr). Champagne producer, Address – 3 Rue Malakoff 51200 Épernay. Produces – Vintage and non-vintage wines. De Luxe vintage cuvée is Cuvée Malakoff.

Beau Monde (Fr). A bottled sparkling wine cocktail made by the méthode champenoise.

Beaumonts-Bas (Les) (Fr). See Beaux-Monts (Les).

Beaumonts Hauts (Les) (Fr). See Beaux-Monts (Les).

Beaumont-sur-Vesle (Fr). A Grand Cru Champagne village in the Canton de Verzy. District = Reims.

Beaunay (Fr). A Cru Champagne village in the Canton de Montmort. District = Épernay.

Beaune (Fr). A wine town in the Côte d'Or, Burgundy. Also A.C. red wine commune around the town. Premier Cru vineyards are – À l'Écu, Aux Coucherais [part], Aux Cras [or Les Cras], Bélissaud, Champ Pimont [or Champimonts], Clos du Roi [part], En Genêt, En l'Orme, La Mignotte, Le Bas des Teurons, Le Clos de la Mousse, Les Aigrots, Les Avaux, Les Blanches Fleurs [part], Les Boucherottes, Les Bressandes, Les Cent Vignes, Les Chouacheux, Les Clos des Mouches, Les Epenottes [part], Les Fèves, Les Grèves, Les Marconnets, Les Montrevenots [part], Les Perrières, Les Reversées, Les Seurey, Les Sizies, Les Teurons, Les Toussaints, Les Tuvilains, Les Vignes Franches, Pertuisots, Sur-lès-Grèves and Tiélandry. 305.52 ha.

Beaunois (Fr). The local name in Chablis, Burgundy for the Chardonnay grape.

Beaunois (N.Z.). A Pinot chardonnay red wine produced by Abel and Co. of Kumeu.

Beauregard (Fr). A Premier Cru vineyard [part] in the A.C. commune of Santenay, Côte de Beaune, Burgundy.

Beauregard Brasserie (Switz). A brewery based in Fribourg. Part of the Sibra Group (Cardinal) Breweries.

Beauregard Ranch (USA). A small vineyard in Santa Cruz County, California Grape varieties – Johannisberg riesling and Zinfandel.

Beauregard Vineyard (USA). See Felton-Empire.

Beauroy (Fr). A Premier Cru vineyard in the A.C. Chablis, Burgundy.

Beausset (Fr). A commune [part] in the A.C. Bandol, southern France.

Beautiran (Fr). Commune in the A.C. Graves region of south-west Bordeaux.

Beauty Spot Cocktail (Cktl). 1 measure dry Gin, ½ measure French vermouth, ½ measure Italian vermouth, 4 dashes Orange bitters. Shake over ice, strain into a cocktail glass with a dash of Grenadine in the bottom.

Beau Val Wines (USA). A winery based in the Shenandoah Valley, Amador, California. Grape variety – Zinfandel.

Beauvoisin (Fr). An area of vinification for V.D.Q.S. wines of Costières du Gard, Languedoc, southern France.

Beaux-Champs (Les) (Fr). A vineyard in the A.C. commune of Montagny, Côte Chalonnaise, Burgundy.

Beaux-Monts (Les) (Fr). A Premier Cru vineyard in the A.C. commune of

Vosne-Romanée, Côte de Nuits, Burgundy. 2.4 ha. Consists of Les Beaumonts Hauts and Bas.

Beaux Vins (Les) (Fr). The fine (noble) wines label. e.g. Les beaux vins de Bordeaux. (The best wines of Bordeaux).

Beaver Bottle (Can). A brand of Canadian whisky produced by the Hudson's Bay Co. (A subsidiary of Seagrams).

Beaver Lager (Eng). An Export lager 1045 O.G. brewed by Greenhall Whitley, Warrington, Cheshire.

Beba (Sp). A red grape variety. Produces poor quality wines. Usually turned into raisins.

Bebedeira (Port). A drunken spree. A booze up.

Bebedero (Sp). A drinking vessel.

Bebedice (Port). Drunkenness.

Bêbedo (Port). Drunk, intoxicated.

Beber (Port) (Sp). To drink, swallow.

Bebida (Port). (Sp). Drink.

Bebida de Moderación (Mex). If seen on beer labels denotes that the alcoholic strength has been kept within the 5% alc. by vol. limit, satisfying the 1931 law that it is not an intoxicating drink.

Bechenheim (Ger). Village. (Anb) = Rheinhessen, (Ber) = Wonnegau. (Gro) = Sybillenstein. (Vin) = Fröhlich.

Becherbrunnen (Ger). Vineyard. (Anb) = Nahe. (Ber) = Schloss Böckelheim. (Gro) = Rosengarten. (Vil) = Mandel.

Becherovka (Czec). A herb-flavoured yellow liqueur produced in the Karlovanska factory at Karlsbad.

Bech-Kleinmacher (Lux). Wine village on the river Moselle. (Sites) = Roetschelt, Fousslach.

Bechtau (USSR). A white grape variety grown in Stavropol to produce dry white wines.

Bechtheim (Ger). Village. (Anb) = Rheinhessen. (Ber) = Wonnegau. (Gro) = Gotteshilfe. (Vins) = Geyersberg, Rosengarten, Stein.

Bechtheim (Ger). Village. (Anb) = Rheinhessen. (Ber) = Wonnegau. (Gro) = Pilgerpfad. (Vins) = Hasensprung, Heiligkreuz.

Bechtolsheim (Ger). Village. (Anb) = Rheinhessen. (Ber) = Nierstein. (Gro) = Petersberg. (Vins) = Homberg, Klosterberg, Sonnenberg, Wingertstor.

Becker (J) (Fr). A noted producer of Crémant d'Alsace in Zellenberg, Alsace.

Becket Beer (Eng). The brand-name of cask conditioned beers from the Alexandra Brewery, Brighton.

Beck's (Ger). The biggest exporter of German beers. Brewed in Bremen. Top of range is Beck's Bier, and St. Pauli brands. See also Haake-Beck Brauerei.

Beck's Bier (Afr). A Beer brewed under licence by the Intercontinental Breweries.

Beck's Bier (Ger). A popular Bier produced by Beck's of Bremen. 1045 O.G. 5% alc. by vol. It is a malty full beer.

Beckstein (Ger). Village. (Anb) = Baden. (Ber) = Badische Frankenland. (Gro) = Tauberklinge. (Vins) = Kirchberg. Nonnenberg.

Beclan (USA). A red grape variety.

Bédarrides (Fr). A noted wine commune of Châteauneuf-du-Pape, southern Rhône.

Bedford (Anna Duchess of) (Eng). Started the fashion of Afternoon Teas in the late eighteenth century to relieve the boredom between lunch and dinner.

Bed Tea (Afr). The name given to early morning tea in African hotels.

Bed Tea (Pak). Tea served to a house guest in bed in the morning.

Beechwood Beer (Eng). A top cask conditioned Bitter 1043 O.G. brewed by the Chiltern Brewery, Buckinghamshire.

Beefeater (Eng). Brand-name of a dry Gin produced by Burrough of London. 40% alc. by vol.

Beefeater Cocktail (Cktl). ¼ measure Royal Irish coffee liqueur, ¼ measure Royal Irish Mint chocolate liqueur, ½ measure Irish whiskey. Stir together, float cream on top.

Beef Tea (Eng). A stock made from minced lean beef, usually with nothing added to it. Used for invalids.

Beehive Beer (Eng). A keg Bitter 1032 O.G. brewed by Brakspear's Brewery, Henley-on-Thames.

Beelbangera Winery (Austr). A part of the McWilliams Winery, New South Wales.

Beenleigh (Austr). A noted Rum producer based in Queensland.

Beer (Eng). Fermentation of malted barley, liquor (water) and hops. See Ale and Lager. (Bel) = Bière, (Ch.Isles) = Bièthe, (Fr) = Bière, (Ger) = Bier, (Hol) = Bier, (Lat) = Cervisa, (Sp) = Cerveza. (Tur) = Bira. (Wales) = Cwrw.

Beer (USA) (Can). The name given to the brew after fermentation and before distillation for whiskey.

Beer Box (Eng). A disposable, air-sealed container (square) used to store up to 5 gallons of beer. Keeps it fresh for up to 1 month. Is easy to store.

Beer Buster Cocktail (Cktl). 1 measure Vodka, 1 bottle Malt liquor beer, 2 dashes Tabasco sauce. Place Vodka and Tabasco in a 12 'fl.oz. beer glass, add iced beer and stir gently.

Beer Crate (Eng). Container for holding beer bottles. Made of either wood or moulded plastic. 12 (1 pint) or 24 (½ pint) sizes.

Beerenauslese (Aus). Wine made from over-ripe grapes which have been affected by Botrytis, and which have been picked from the best parts of the vineyard. Minimum must weight of 25° KMW. (138° Oechsle).

Beerenauslese (Ger). Late picked selected over-ripe grapes which have been attacked by botrytis (edelfäule). Produces luscious sweet wines.

Beerenburg (Hol). See Beerenburg.

Beerenburg (Hol). A herb bitters of angelica, bay leaves, gentian, etc. Known as Friesengeist in Germany. 30% alc. by vol. Also spelt Beerenburg.

Beer Engine (Eng). A method of drawing cask conditioned ales from the cask in the cellar by suction. Each pull of the pump handle will deliver a full ½ pint.

Beer Engine (Eng). Pub near Exeter which brews its own cask conditioned ales. Produces Rail Ale 1037 O.G. and Piston Bitter 1044 O.G.

Beerenlay (Ger). Grosslagen. (Anb) = Mosel-Saar-Ruwer. (Ber) = Bernkastel. (Vil) = Lieser. (Vins) = Niederberg-Helden, Rosenlay, Süssenberg.

Beer Garden (Eng). Garden area outside of licensed premises set aside for drinking in the summer months.

Beermat (Eng). See also Dripmat, Coaster. Originally made of cork, now made of thin card, a mat used for soaking up spilt drinks. Are collected by enthusiasts. (Breweries etc. use them as an advertising medium).

Beer Muller (Eng). A copper conical container with a handle, used to heat (mull) the beer over an open fire.

Beer Octasphere (Eng). See Beer Sphere.

Beer Sangaree (Cktl). In a long glass dissolve a teaspoon of sugar in a little water. Top with chilled beer. Add grated nutmeg.

Beer Scraper (USA). Bone implement for removing dried beer slops off the bar top.

Beer Seidl (USA). A 16 fl.oz. beer glass.

Beer Shell (USA). An 8–10 fl.oz. beer glass.

Beer Sphere (Eng). A round container holding 20, 30 or 40 litres of Beer or Lager. Made airtight with a rubber seal and metal cap which is crimped over the neck. Will keep beer for seven days when opened. See also Beer Octash-

pere (an eight-sided Beer sphere).

Beer-Up (Austr) (slang). A heavy drinking bout.

Beery (Eng). Bad smell in the bottle caused by a secondary fermentation, resulting in an unsound wine.

Beery (Eng) (slang). A heavy smell of beer on the breath. Or tasting of beer.

Bees (Eng). Type of yeast which has the unique property of rising and falling in lumps during fermentation (like a bee) hence bee(s) wine.

Beesengenever (Hol). A blackcurrant-flavoured Genever (Gin).

Bee's Knees (Cktl). ⅓ measure dry Gin, ⅓ measure fresh lemon juice, ⅓ measure (clear) honey. Shake well over ice, strain into a cocktail glass.

Beestings (Eng). The name given to the first milk from a cow after parturition (giving birth).

Bees Wine (Eng). See Bee Wine. Also 'Fliers'.

Beeswing (Eng). Another name for the sediment thrown after maturation in red wines.

Beeswing (Port). The floating sediment that has not settled with the crust in Vintage Port.

Bee Wine (Eng). Made from the ginger-plant, a fungus which possesses peculiar properties. (see Bees). Brewed by adding bees to water with sugar, After fermentation it is ready in six weeks for drinking.

Bégadan (Fr). A commune in the Bas Médoc north-west Bordeaux.

Begg (John) (Scot). A Scotch whisky and Malt whisky producer owned by DCL. Brands include John Begg's Bluecap and Lochnagar.

Bègles (Fr). A commune in the A.C. Graves in south-western Bordeaux.

Begnins (Switz). A wine-producing area in La Côte on the western bank of Lake Geneva.

Behhari (Ger). An old name for a beaker, jug.

Behind the Wall (Cktl). 1½ ozs.Vodka, 1 oz. Mandarine Napoléon, 1 oz. Galliano, 1½ ozs. orange juice. Shake with ice, strain into a tall glass, add ice, top with ginger ale.

Beihingen (Ger). Village. (Anb) = Württemberg. (Ber) = Württembergisch Unterland. (Gro) = Schalkstein. (Vin) = Neckarhälde.

Beilberg (Ger). Vineyard. (Anb) = Baden. (Ber) = Badische Frankenland. (Gro) = Tauberklinge. (Vil) = Grossrinderfeld.

Beilberg (Ger). Vineyard. (Anb) = Baden. (Ber) = Badische Frankenland. (Gro) = Tauberklinge. (Vil) = Werbach.

B

Beilstein (Ger). Village. (Anb) = Mosel-Saar-Ruwer. (Ber) = Zell/Mosel. (Gro) = Rosenhang. (Vin) = Schlossberg.

Beilstein (Ger). Village. (Anb) = Württemberg. (Ber) = Württembergisch Unterland. (Gro) = Wunnenstein. (Vins) = Schlosswengert, Steinberg, Wartberg.

Beilstein (Ger). Village. (Anb) = Württemberg. (Ber) = Remstal-Stuttgart. (Gro) = Kopf. (Vin) = Grossmulde.

Beine (Fr). A Canton in the Reims district in Champagne. Has the Cru villages of Berru, Cernay-lès-Reims and Nogent-l'Abbesse.

Beines (Fr). A commune in the A.C. Chablis, Burgundy.

Beira Alta (Port). Region between Dão and the Spanish border. Produces red and white wines.

Beivre (Fr). Thirteenth-century word meaning 'to drink'. See Bevrage.

Bejaoua (Tun). A co-operative based in Tunisia. Belongs to the UCCVT.

Beker (Hol). Cup, beaker.

Bekka Valley (Arab). A noted wine-producing region in Lebanon. See Château Musar.

Bekond (Ger). Village. (Anb) = Mosel-Saar-Ruwer. (Ber) = Bernkastel. (Gro) = Sankt Michael. (Vins) = Brauneberg, Schlossberg.

Bel-Air (Fr). A Premier Cru vineyard in the A.C. commune of Gevrey Chambertin, Côte de Nuits, Burgundy. 3.72 ha.

Belan (Yug). A wine-producing region based in southern Macedonia.

Bel Arbres (USA). The brand-name used by the Fetzer Vineyards for a range of their table wines. Based in Redwood Valley, California.

Belbourie (Austr). A winery based in the Hunter Valley in New South Wales

Belchite (Sp). A wine-region based in Aragón. Produces red and white wines that are high in alcohol.

Beldi (Tun). A white grape variety.

Belemnitic (Fr). Chalk soil in Champagne.

Belfast Glass (Ire). Top Irish glass making centre in Northern Ireland.

Belgian Coffee (Liq.Coffee). Using a measure of Elixir d'Anvers.

Belhaven Brewery (Scot). Based in Dunbar, East Lothian is a major exporter to the USA and Italy. Brews a large selection of beers including Fowler's Wee Heavy 1070 O.G. Monkscroft House Ale 1070 O.G. Texas Ale 1056 O.G. Winston's Stout 1053 O.G.

Beli Burgundec (Yug). A local name for the Pinot blanc grape.

Belin, [J] (Fr). A négociant-éleveur based at Prémeaux, Côte de Nuits, Burgundy.

Beli-Pinot (Yug). A version of the Pinot blanc grape.

Beli Plavac (Yug). A white grape variety.

Bélissauds (Les) (Fr). A Premier Cru vineyard in the A.C. commune of Beaune, Côte de Beaune, Burgundy. 4.88 ha. Also known as Bélissaud.

Belji (Yug). A noted wine-producing town based in northern Croatia.

Belladonna Cocktail (Cktl). ⅓ measure Vodka, ⅓ measure Crème de Noyaux, ⅓ measure cream. Shake over ice, strain into a cocktail glass.

Bell'Agio (It). Brand-name of a sweet, white wine produced by Banfi from Moscato grapes.

Bella Napoli (USA). A winery in San Joaquin Valley, California. Produces wines under the Bella Napoli and Vine Flow brand labels.

Belland (Adrien) (Fr). A négociant-éleveur. Address = Place du Jet d'Eau, 21590 Santenay.

Bellapais (Cyp). A slightly sparkling white wine produced by the Keo Company based in Limassol.

Bellarmine Bottle Jug (Eng). A glazed jug of the seventeenth century in many sizes, with a bearded mask at the neck of the bottle to represent Bishop Bellarmine's (a Temperance man) face as a joke to ridicule him.

Bellaterra (Chile). The name of a white wine made from the Sauvignon blanc grape by Torres (of Spain).

Bell Canyon (USA). A brand-name used by the Burgess Cellars for their range of varietal wines.

Belle Epoque (Fr). See Perrier-Jouët Belle Epoque, Fleur de Champagne.

Bellegarde (Fr). A commune in the Languedoc in the Midi, southern France. Noted for its dry white wine Clairette de Bellegarde made from the Clairette grape.

Belle Isle (Ire). A cream liqueur flavoured with butterscotch.

Belle Poule (La) (Cktl). ½ oz. Mandarine Napoléon, 4 ozs. dry white wine, 1 oz. sweet Vermouth. Stir over ice, serve in a wine goblet with ice and a twist of tangerine peel.

Belle Sandarine (La) (Fr). A liqueur produced from Armagnac brandy and passion fruit.

Belle Strasbourgeoise (Fr). A Beer from the Fischer/Pêcheur Brasserie in Schiltigheim.

Bellet (Fr). A.C. wine area in Nice,

Riviera, Southern France. Produces dry red and white wines. Districts are – Candau, Cappan, Crémat, Golfan, Gros-Pin, La Tour, Le Grand-Bois, Le Pilon, Les Séoules, Lingestière, Mont-Bellet, Puncia, Saint-Romain-de-Bellet, Saint-Sauveur, Saquier and Serre-Long. The region is noted for its pebbly 'pudding stone' soil. Main grape varieties – (Red) Folle, Braquet and Cinsault. (White) Chardonnay, Clairette, Rolle and Rousanne,

Bellet de Nice (Fr). Another name for the Bellet area in south-eastern France.

Belle Terre Vineyard (USA). Vineyard in Alexander Valley, Sonoma County, California. Grape varieties – Cabernet sauvignon, Chardonnay and Johannisberg riesling. Produces varietal wines. See also Château St. Jean.

Belle Vue Beer (Bel). A Gueuze beer.

Bellevue Estate (Austr). A winery based in Hunter Valley, New South Wales. Owned by Drayton. Produces varietal and table wines.

Bellevue Vineyards (S.Afr). Based in Stellenbosch. Grapes vinified by the SFW.

Bellheim (Ger). Village. (Anb) = Rheinpfalz. (Ber) = Südliche Weinstrasse. (Gro) = Trappenberg. (Vin) = Gollenberg.

Bell Hill Vineyard (USA). A small vineyard based in Lake County, California. Grape variety – Cabernet sauvignon.

Bellingham (S.Afr). An estate based in Franschhoek. Produces white, rosé and red wines.

Bellingham Wines (S.Afr). The brand-name for the wines of Union Wines Ltd., Box 246, Wellington 7655. Varietal wines.

Bellini (Cktl). Champagne and peach juice. Fill a champagne flute ⅓ full with peach juice, top with iced Champagne.

Bellinzonese (Switz). A noted vineyard based in the Sopra Ceneri area of Ticino.

Bellone (It). A white grape variety grown in the Latium region.

Bellonie, Bourdillon et Cie (W.Ind). A Rum distillery based on the island of Martinique. Produces La Mauny Rum.

Belloe Vino (USSR). White wine.

Bellows Partners Choice (USA). The brand-name of a blended Whiskey.

Bell's (Scot). Arthur Bell & Sons Ltd. Distillers of Malt whisky (Blair Athol, Dufftown, Inchgower and Pittyvaich distilleries) and blenders of Scotch whisky (Bells, C & J. McDonald and The Real Mackenzie).

Owned by Guinness.

Belmont Cocktail (Cktl). 1 measure dry Gin, 4 dashes Raspberry cordial, ⅔ measure cream. Shake well over ice, strain into a cocktail glass.

Bel Normande (Eng). A sparkling non-alcoholic apple juice drink from Copak Drinks Ltd.

Belon (Tur). A sweet coffee. Also known as Sukar Ziada.

Belpais (Cyp). A white wine produced in the Middle Ages in eastern Cyprus by the Premonstratensian (white Canons) monks.

Belsenberg (Ger). Village. (Anb) = Württemberg. (Ber) = Kocher-Jagst-Tauber. (Gro) = Kocherberg. (Vin) = Heilig Kreuz.

Beninoise (La) (Afr). A Lager beer 10.5° Plato brewed in Benin.

Beltane Vineyard (USA). Vineyard based in the south-east of Sonoma County California. Grape varieties – Cabernet sauvignon and Chardonnay. Produces varietal wines.

Belval-Sous-Châtellon (Fr). A Cru Champagne village in the Canton de Châtillon-sur-Marne. District = Reims.

Belvinta Supreme (Cyp). The brand-name of a medium-sweet Cyprus sherry.

Belz (Ger). Vineyard. (Anb) = Rheinpfalz. (Ber) = Mittelhaardt-Deutsche Weinstrasse. (Gro) = Mariengarten. (Vil) = Wachenheim.

Benais (Fr). The top wine-producing commune in Bourgueil, Touraine, Loire.

Ben-Ami (Isr). The brand-name of a range of red and white table wines.

Benavides (Sp). A noted vineyard based in the Montilla-Moriles region.

Bench Grafting (Eng). The grafting of Vitis vinifera scions onto American root stock in nurseries and allowing them to set before planting in the vineyard. See also Field Grafting and Omega Grafting.

Benchmark (USA). Brand-name of a 6 y.o. Kentucky Bourbon whiskey produced by Seagram.

Bender (Eng) (slang). A heavy drinking bout. i.e. 'To go on a bender'.

Bendigo/Ballarat (Austr). Small vineyards based in Victoria.

Beneagles (Scot). A blended Scotch whisky, noted for its ceramic 'Eagle' bottles. Address = Peter Thompson (Perth) Ltd., Box 22, Crieff Road, Perth, Scotland. PH1 2SC.

Ben Ean (Austr). Light, dry white wine from Lindemans 'Ben Ean' vineyard New South Wales.

Benedict (Bel). An Abbaye-style beer brewed by the De Kluis Brasserie in Hoegaarden.

Benedict Cocktail (Cktl). ½ measure Bénédictine, ½ measure Scotch whisky. Stir over ice in an old-fashioned glass. Top with ginger ale.

Bénédictine (Fr). Distillery based in Fécamp, Normandy. Produces liqueur of same name. See also B and B. Also owns the Garnier liqueur distillery.

Bénédictine (Fr). A herb-flavoured, brandy-based liqueur, distilled in Fécamp, Normandy. See D.O.M. and B and B. 43% alc. by vol. Also produced in Madrid, Spain.

Bénédictine Cocktail (Cktl). ½ measure Cognac, ¼ measure Bénédictine, ¼ measure lemon juice. Shake well over ice, strain into a cocktail glass.

Bénédictine Scaffa Cocktail (Cktl). ¼ measure Bénédictine, ¼ measure Rum, ¼ measure Gin, ¼ measure Scotch whisky, dash Angostura. Stir over ice, strain into a cocktail glass.

Benediktinerberg (Ger). Vineyard. (Anb) = Mosel-Saar-Ruwer. (Ber) = Saar-Ruwer. (Gro) = Römerlay. (Vil) = Trier.

Benediktusberg (Ger). Vineyard. (Anb) = Franken. (Ber) = Maindreieck. (Gro) = Ravensburg. (Vil) = Retzbach.

Benesov Brewery (Czec). Brewery based in north-west Czec. Was founded in 1897. Noted for its fine clean beers.

Beneventanum (Lat). A red wine produced in central Italy in Roman times.

Bengal (S.Afr). A leading brand of double-distilled cane spirit.

Bengal Cocktail (Cktl). ½ measure Brandy, ⅛ measure Maraschino, ⅛ measure Curaçao, ¼ measure pineapple juice, 6 dashes Angostura. Stir over ice, strain into a cocktail glass.

Bengal Lancers Punch (Punch). ½ cup Cointreau, 2 pints lime juice, sugar to taste, ½ pint Claret, ½ cup Jamaican rum, ½ cup pineapple and orange juice, ice. Mix together, top with a magnum of Champagne. Garnish with lime slices.

Bengel (Ger). Vineyard. (Anb) = Baden. (Ber) = Bodensee. (Gro) = Sonnenufer. (Vil) = Meersburg.

Bengel (Ger). Village. (Anb) = Mosel-Saar-Ruwer. (Ber) = Bernkastel. (Gro) = Schwarzlay. (Vin) = sites not yet chosen.

Benicarló (Sp). A red grape variety grown in Valencia. Is known as the Mourvèdre in France.

Benicarló (Sp). A red wine from Valencia from the grape of same name.

Beni M'Tir (Afr). An A.O.G. area in the wine-producing region of Meknès-Fez, Morocco.

Benin (Afr). A Nigerian palm wine made from fermented palm sap.

Beni Sadden (Afr). An A.O.G. area in the wine-producing region of Meknès-Fez, Morocco.

Benisalem (Sp). A wine-producing area on the island of Majorca. Is noted for its full red wines.

Benmarl Vineyard (USA). A small estate winery based at Marlboro in the Hudson River Valley in eastern America. Produces mainly French-American hybrid grape wines.

Benmorven Müller-Thurgau (N.Z.). A light, fruity white wine from the Montana Wines.

Benmorven Riesling-Sylvaner (N.Z.). A slightly sweet white wine produced by Montana Wines. Was originally known as Bernkaizler.

Benn (Ger). Vineyard. (Anb) = Rheinhessen. (Ber) = Wonnegau. (Gro) = Bergkloster. (Vil) = Westhofen.

Benn (Ger). Vineyard. (Anb) = Rheinpfalz. (Ber) = Mittelhaardt-Deutsche Weinstrasse. (Gro) = Grafenstück. (Vil) = Obrigheim.

Bennets Strong Ale (Eng). A strong Ale 1057 O.G. brewed by the Five Towns Brewery, Stoke-on-Trent, Staffs.

Bennett Cocktail (Cktl). ⅓ gill Old Tom Gin, ⅙ fresh lime juice, 2 dashes Angostura. Shake well over ice, strain into a cocktail glass.

Ben Nevis (Scot). A single Malt whisky distillery. A Highland malt whisky. Also produce a Grain whisky. 40% alc. by vol.

Benningen (Ger). Village. (Anb) = Württemberg. (Ber) = Württembergisch Unterland. (Gro) = Schalkstein. (Vin) = Neckarhälde.

Bénovie (Fr). A Vins de Pays area in the Hérault Département, southern France. Produces red and rosé wines.

Benriach-Glenlivet (Scot). A single Malt whisky distillery produced by The Longmorn-Glenlivet Distilleries Ltd. A Highland malt whisky. 40% alc. by vol.

Benrinnes (Scot). A single Malt whisky distillery. A Highland malt whisky. 43% alc. by vol. (part of the DCL Group).

Benromach (Scot). A single malt whisky distillery. A Highland malt whisky. 40% alc. by vol.

Bensheim (Ger). Village. (Anb) = Hessische Bergstrasse. (Ber) = Starkenburg. (Gro) = Wolfsmagen. (Vins) = Kalkgasse, Kirchberg, Steichling,

Hernsberg, Paulus.

Bensheim-Auerbach (Ger). Village. (Anb) = Hessische Bergstrasse. (Ber) = Starkenburg. (Gro) = Rott. (Vins) = Höllberg, Fürstenlager.

Bensheim-Schönberg (Ger). Village. (Anb) = Hessische Bergstrasse. (Ber) = Starkenburg. (Gro) = Rott. (Vin) = Herrnwingert.

Benskins Brewery (Eng). A brewery belonging to Ind Coope. Beers brewed at Romford, Essex and bottled in Burton. Produces all types of ales.

Bentley (Cktl). ½ measure Applejack brandy, ½ measure Dubonnet. Stir over ice, strain into a cocktail glass.

Benton Harbor (USA). A wine district in the region of Michigan State. The main grape varieties – Catawba, Concord and Delaware.

Bentonite (Eng). A diatomaceous earth. See Bentonite Clay.

Bentonite Clay (USA). A fine clay from Wyoming. Used to clear wine as a fining. A Diatomaceous earth (hydrated silicate of aluminium). See Louisiana Clay.

Ben Truman (Eng). The brand-name of Watney's keg Bitter 1038 O.G. and Export 1045 O.G.

Ben Wyvis (Scot). A single malt whisky distillery sited north of Inverness. A Highland malt whisky. 40% alc. by vol.

Benzaldehyde (Eng). An Aldehyde found in wine which contributes to the bouquet and flavour of the wine.

Benzoic Acid (Eng). A chemical which may be added to stop fermentation and prevent all the sugar from being fermented out to produce a sweetish wine. Used mainly in home-made wines.

Beone (It). A drunkard.

Beor (Eng). A mediaeval word for beer.

Beotia (Gre). A wine region of Central Greece.

Ber (Ger) (abbr). Bereich.

Bérange (Fr). A Vins de Pays area in the Hérault Département, southern France.

Bérard (Victor) (Fr). A négociant-éleveur based in Varennes-les-Mâcon, Burgundy. Produces Beaujolais and Burgundy.

Berat (J. et Jacques) (Fr). Champagne producer. Address = 8 Rue St. Rich, Boursault, 51200 Épernay. Récoltants-manipulants. Produces Vintage and non-vintage wines. Vintages – 1971, 1973, 1975, 1976, 1979, 1982, 1983.

Berberana. S.A. (Sp). See Bodegas Berberana. S.A.

Bercy (Fr). Also known as Quai de Bercy. A part of Paris on the river Seine where most of the city's wines arrive and are distributed.

Bère (Ch.Isles). To drink.

Bere (Eng). The mediaeval name for barley from which beer derived.

Bere (It). Drink.

Bereich (Ger). An area within an Anbaugebiet. Chosen for its similar soil and terrain type. e.g. Bernkastel in the Mosel-Saar-Ruwer.

Berem (Wales). Yeast.

Berenberg (Hol). See Beerenburg.

Berenburg (Hol). A bitters from Holland.

Berentzen Appel (Ger). An apple and Whiskey-based liqueur produced by Berentzen. 25% alc. by vol.

Berg (Ger). Lit – 'hill or mountain'. A popular name used for vineyards in Germany, 23 individual sites have the name.

Berg (Ger). Vineyard. (Anb) = Ahr. (Ber) = Walporzheim/Ahrtal. (Gro) = Klosterberg. (Vil) = Heppingen.

Berg (Ger). Vineyard. (Anb) = Baden. (Ber) = Badische Bergstrasse/Kraichgau. (Gro) = Stiftsberg. (Vil) = Herbolzheim.

Berg (Ger). Vineyard. (Anb) = Baden. (Ber) = Badische Bergstrasse/Kraichgau. (Gro) = Stiftsberg. (Vil) = Neudenau.

Berg (Ger). Vineyard. (Anb) = Franken. (Ber) = Maindreieck. (Gro) = Kirchberg. (Vil) = Escherndorf.

Berg (Ger). Vineyard. (Anb) = Mittelrhein. (Ber) = Rheinburgengau. (Gro) = Burg Hammerstein. (Vil) = Unkel.

Berg (Ger). Vineyard. (Anb) = Nahe. (Ber) = Kreuznach. (Gro) = Kronenberg. (Vil) = Bad Kreuznach (ortsteil Winzenheim).

Berg (Ger). Vineyard. (Anb) = Nahe. (Ber) = Schloss Böckelheim. (Gro) = Rosengarten. (Vil) = Roxheim.

Berg (Ger). Vineyard. (Anb) = Rheinpfalz. (Ber) = Mittelhaardt-Deutsche Weinstrasse. (Gro) = Pfaffengrund. (Vil) = Diedesfeld.

Berg (Ger). Vineyard. (Anb) = Rheingau. (Ber) = Johannisberg. (Gro) = Daubhaus. (Vil) = Hochheim.

Berg (Ger). Vineyard. (Anb) = Rheingau. (Ber) = Johannisberg. (Gro) = Daubhaus. (Vil) = Kostheim.

Berg (Ger). Vineyard. (Anb) = Rheingau. (Ber) = Johannisberg. (Gro) = Landkreis Melsungen. (Vil) = Böddiger.

Berg (Ger). Vineyard. (Anb) = Württemberg. (Ber) = Württembergisch Unterland. (Gro) = Schalkstein. (Vil) = Aspreg.

Berg (Ger). Vineyard. (Anb) = Württemberg. (Ber) = Württembergisch Unterland. (Gro) = Schalkstein. (Vil) = Mark-gröningen.

Berg (Ger). Vineyard. (Anb) = Württemberg. (Ber) = Württembergisch Unterland. (Gro) = Staufenberg. (Vil) = Brettach.

Berg (Ger). Vineyard. (Anb) = Württemberg. (Ber) = Württembergisch Unterland. (Gro) = Staufenberg. (Vil) = Cleversulzbach.

Berg (Ger). Vineyard. (Anb) = Württemberg. (Ber) = Remstal-Stuttgart. (Gro) = Kopf. (Vil) = Hanweiler.

Berg (Ger). Vineyard. (Anb) = Württemberg. (Ber) = Remstal-Stuttgart. (Gro) = Kopf. (Vil) = Korb.

Berg (Ger). Vineyard. (Anb) = Württemberg. (Ber) = Remstal-Stuttgart. (Gro) = Kopf. (Vil) = Winnenden.

Berg (Ger). Vineyard. (Anb) = Württemberg. (Ber) = Remstal-Stuttgart. (Gro) = Weinsteige. (Vil) = Stuttgart (ortsteil Cannstatt).

Berg (Ger). Vineyard. (Anb) = Württemberg. (Ber) = Remstal-Stuttgart. (Gro) = Weinsteige. (Vil) = Stuttgart (ortsteil Feuerbach).

Berg (Ger). Vineyard. (Anb) = Württemberg. (Ber) = Remstal-Stuttgart. (Gro) = Weinsteige. (Vil) = Stuttgart (ortsteil Münster).

Berg (Ger). Vineyard. (Anb) = Württemberg. (Ber) = Remstal-Stuttgart. (Gro) = Weinsteige. (Vil) = Stuttgart (ortsteil Wangen).

Berg (Ger). Vineyard. (Anb) = Württemberg. (Ber) = Remstal-Stuttgart. (Gro) = Weinsteige. (Vil) = Stuttgart (ortsteil Zuffenhausen).

Bergamot Liqueur (Fr). A fruit liqueur made from a variety of Mediterranean oranges.

Bergamottelikoer (Ger). A liqueur based on Bergamot, an aromatic herb.

Berg Bildstock (Ger). Vineyard. (Anb) = Rheinhessen. (Ber) = Johannisberg. (Gro) = Steinmacher. (Vil) = Niederwalluf.

Bergbock Dunkel (Ger). A dark Bock bier from the Andechs Brauerei in Erling-Andechs, Bavaria.

Bergbock Hell (Ger). A malty Bock bier from the Andechs Brauerei in Erling-Andechs, Bavaria.

Bergborn (Ger). Vineyard. (Anb) = Nahe. (Ber) = Kreuznach. (Gro) = Sonnenborn. (Vil) = Langenlonsheim.

Bergel (Ger). Vineyard. (Anb) = Rheinpfalz. (Ber) = Mittelhaardt-Deutsche Weinstrasse. (Gro) = Höllenpfad. (Vil) = Grünstadt.

Bergel (Ger). Vineyard. (Anb) = Rheinpfalz. (Ber) = Südliche Weinstrasse. (Gro) = Schloss Ludwigshöhe.

(Vil) = Edenkoben.

Berger (Fr). A Pastis and Anisette producer who market under the Fournier label and Le Crystal.

Bergerac (Fr). Wine region of south-west France, 80 miles from the town of Bordeaux. Produces red, white and sweet white wines. A.C.'s of Bergerac, Côtes de Bergerac, Côtes de Montravel, Côtes de Saussignac, Haut-Montravel, Monbazillac, Montravel, Pécharmant and Rosette.

Berger Baron (Le) (Fr). A non-vintage red wine from the Mouton Rothschild stable under La Bergerie label.

Bergerbier (Bel). A Pilsener beer brewed in Mons.

Bergerdorf Brauerei (Ger). A subsidiary brewery of Holstein, based in Hamburg.

Bergères-les-Vertus (Fr). A Premier Cru Champagne village in the Canton de Vertus. District = Châlons.

Bergeron (Fr). A white grape variety grown in the Savoie region, south-eastern France.

Berghalde (Ger). Vineyard. (Anb) = Württemberg. (Ber) = Remstal-Stuttgart. (Gro) = Kopf. (Vil) = Grunbach.

Berghaupten (Ger). Village. (Anb) = Baden. (Ber) = Ortenau. (Gro) = Fürsteneck. (Vin) = Kinzigtäler.

Berghausen (Ger). Village. (Anb) = Baden. (Ber) = Badische Bergstrasse/Kraichgau. (Gro) = Hohenberg. (Vin) = Sonnenberg.

Bergheim (Fr). A commune of the Haut-Rhin in Alsace.

Berghof (Switz). A noted producer of Eau-de-vie.

Bergier (Jean) (Fr). A Cognac producer. Address = Brives S/Charente, 17800 Pons. 12 ha. in the Petite Champagne.

Berg Kaisersteinfels (Ger). Vineyard. (Anb) = Rheingau. (Ber) = Johannisberg. (Gro) = Burgweg. (Vil) = Assmannshausen-Aulhausen.

Bergkelder (S.Afr). A wine and spirit merchant of Stellenbosch. The wine arm of Oude Meester Group. Produces Fleur du Cap and Grünberger.

Bergkirche (Ger). Vineyard. (Anb) = Rheinhessen. (Ber) = Nierstein. (Gro) = Auflangen. (Vil) = Nierstein.

Bergkirchweih (Ger). A beer festival held at Erlanger in Franconia.

Bergkloster (Ger). Grosslagen. (Anb) = Rheinhessen. (Ber) = Wonnegau. (Vils) = Bermersheim, Eppelsheim, Esselborn, Flomborn, Gundersheim, Gundheim, Hangen-Weisheim, Westhofen.

Bergle (Ger). Vineyard. (Anb) = Baden. (Ber) = Breisgau. (Gro) = Burg Zäh-

ringen. (Vil) = Lehen.
Bergle (Ger). Vineyard. (Anb) = Baden. (Ber) = Ortenau. (Gro) = Fürsteneck. (Vil) = Offenburg (ortsteil Fessenbach).
Bergman's Lager (Wales). A Lager beer 1033 O.G. brewed by Peter Walker Brewery, Wrexham, North Wales.
Bergpfad (Ger). Vineyard. (Anb) = Rheinhessen. (Ber). Nierstein. (Gro) = Gutes Domtal. (Vil) = Dexheim.
Berg Rondell (Ger). Vineyard. (Anb) = Franken. (Ber) = Maindreieck. (Gro) = Honigberg. (Vil) = Dettelbach.
Berg Roseneck (Ger). Vineyard. (Anb) = Rheingau. (Ber) = Johannisberg. (Gro) = Burgweg. (Vil) = Rüdesheim.
Berg Rottland (Ger). Vineyard. (Anb) = Rheingau. (Ber) = Johannisberg. (Gro) = Burgweg. (Vil) = Rüdesheim.
Berg Schlossberg (Ger). Vineyard. (Anb) = Rheingau. (Ber) = Johannisberg. (Gro) = Burgweg. (Vil) = Rüdesheim.
Bergschlösschen (Ger). Vineyard. (Anb) = Mosel-Saar-Ruwer. (Ber) = Saar-Ruwer. (Gro) = Scharzberg. (Vil) = Saarburg.
Bergsig Estate (S.Afr). Vineyards based at Breede River. Address = Bergsig, Box 15, Breërivier 6858. Produces varietal wines.
Bergsträsser Weinmarkt (Ger). A Hessische Bergstrasse wine festival held in Heppenheim in June.
Bergsträsser Winzerfest (Ger). A Hessische Bergstrasse wine festival held at Bensheim in September.
Bergstrom (Austr). The name given to a pot-still designed by a coppersmith with same name.
Bergstrom Vineyard (USA). The Ranchita Oaks Winery in California. Grape varieties – mainly Cabernet sauvignon.
Bergwäldle (Ger). Vineyard. (Anb) = Baden. (Ber) = Badische Bergstrasse/Kraichgau. (Gro) = Mannaberg. (Vil) = Wiesloch.
Beringer Vineyard (USA). Large winery in the St. Helena district of the northern Napa Valley, California. Also has vineyards in Knights Valley, Sonoma County, California. Produces table and dessert wines. See Lemon Ranch.
Beriolo (It). A producer of Moscato d'Asti Spumante in the Piemonte region.
Berisford Solera (Sp). A 1914 Manzanilla Pasada sherry produced by José Pemartin in Jerez de la Frontera.
Berkane (Afr). An A.O.G. wine-producing area based in eastern Morocco.
Berkeley Wine Cellar (USA). The brand-name used by Wine and the People, California.
Berliner Kümmel (USA). A very dry Kümmel.
Berliner Weisse (Ger). A light coloured Wheat beer brewed in Berlin. It is known locally as 'The Cool Blonde'. The beer is bottle conditioned, is low in alcohol (3%) and is often flavoured with raspberry juice or woodruff when consumed. See Kindl Brauerei and Schultheiss Brauerei.
Bermatingen (Ger). Village. (Anb) = Baden. (Ber) = Bodensee. (Gro) = Sonnenufer. (Vin) = Leopoldsberg.
Bermersbach (Ger). Village. (Anb) = Baden. (Ber) = Ortenau. (Gro) = Fürsteneck. (Vin) = Kinzigtäler.
Bermersheim (Ger). Village. (Anb) = Rheinhessen. (Ber) = Wonnegau. (Gro) = Bergkloster. (Vin) = Hasenlauf.
Bermersheim v.d.H (Ger). Village. (Anb) = Rheinhessen. (Ber) = Bingen. (Gro) = Adelberg. (Vins) = Hildegardisberg, Klosterberg.
Bermersheim/Worms (Ger). Village. (Anb) = Rheinhessen. (Ber) = Wonnegau. (Gro) = Burg Rodenstein. (Vin) = Seilgarten.
Bermester (Port). A Vintage Port shipper.
Bermet (Yug). A locally made red Vermouth produced in the Vojvodina area of north-eastern Yugoslavia. Also a white version.
Bermondsey Beer (Eng). A cask conditioned Ale brewed by Bridge House Brewery.
Bermuda Bouquet (Cktl). 1 measure Gin, ⅔ measure Apricot brandy, ⅔ measure Grenadine, ⅓ measure Triple Sec, 1 teaspoon powdered sugar, juice ½ lemon, 4 dashes orange juice. Shake well over ice, strain into an ice-filled highball glass.
Bermuda Gold Liqueur (W.Ind). A liqueur produced by Somers Distilleries in Bermuda. 40% alc. by vol.
Bermuda Highball (Cktl). ⅓ measure Gin, ⅓ measure Brandy, ⅓ measure French vermouth. Stir over ice, strain into an ice-filled highball glass. Top ginger ale and twist of lemon peel.
Bermuda Rose (Cktl). 1 measure Gin, ¼ measure Apricot brandy, ¼ measure Grenadine. Shake over ice, strain into a cocktail glass.
Bermudiana Rose (Cktl). ⅖ measure dry Gin, ⅕ measure Apricot brandy, ⅕ measure lemon juice. Shake well over ice, strain into a cocktail glass.
Bernadino Spumante (N.Z). A fruity, sparkling white wine produced by Montana Wines from Dr. Hogg Muscat

grapes.

Bernard (It). A producer of Prosecco di Conegliano-Valdobbiadene in the Veneto region.

Bernardo Winery (USA). A small winery based in San Diego, California. Produces varietal and dessert wines.

Bernardus Pater (Bel). See St. Bernardus.

Bernard VII XO (Fr). A 10 year old Armagnac brandy produced by the Ducastaing Co.

Berneroy Calvados (Fr). The brand-name of a Calvados produced by UNGC.

Bernet (Yug). See Bermet.

Bernhoffen (N.Z). A medium-dry, white wine produced by the Pacific Vineyards, Mcleod Road, Henderson, North Island. Made from the Müller-Thurgau grape variety.

Bernice Cocktail (Cktl). ½ measure Vodka, ½ measure Galliano, juice of ½ lime, 2 dashes Angostura. Shake over ice, strain into cocktail glass.

Bernina Frizzante (It). A naturally sparkling mineral water, bottled at the spring at Piuro, Sondrio, in the Alps.

Bernina Naturale (It). A still mineral water from Piuro, Sondrio.

Bernkaizler Riesling (N.Z.). See Benmorven Riesling-Sylvaner.

Bernkastel (Ger). Bereich. (Anb) = Mosel-Saar-Ruwer. (Gros) = Badstube, Beerenlay, Kurfürslay, Michelsberg, Munzlay, Nacktarsch, Probstberg, Sankt Michael, Schwarzlay, Von Hessen Stein.

Bernkasteler Doktor (Ger). The greatest German vineyard. So named because of Archbishop Bomund 2nd, Elector of Trier (1351–62) who was so ill that, on his death-bed, he was given wine from this vineyard and so recovered. He bestowed the appellation on the Vineyard. See also Doctor.

Bernkasteler Docktor und Badstube (Ger). A 1971 designation of the Docktor wines in which grapes from the adjoining vineyard were used. Now no longer allowed.

Bernkasteler Docktor und Bratenhöfchen (Ger). A pre 1971 designation of the Docktor wines in which grapes from the adjoining vineyard were used. Now no longer allowed.

Bernkasteler Docktor und Graben (Ger). A pre 1971 designation of the Docktor wines in which grapes from the adjoining vineyard were used. Now no longer allowed.

Bernkasteler-Kues (Ger). Village. (Anb) = Mosel-Saar-Ruwer. (Ber) = Bernkastel. (Gro) = Kurfurstlay. (Vins) = Johannisbrünnchen, Kardinalsberg, Rosenberg, Schlossberg, Stephanus-Rosengärtchen,

Weissenstein.

Bernkasteler-Kues (Ger). Village. (Anb) = Mosel-Saar-Ruwer. (Ber) = Bernkastel. (Gro) = Badstube. (Vins) = Bratenhöfchen, Docktor, Graben, Lay, Matheisbildchen.

Bernstein (Ger). Vineyard. (Anb) = Mittelrhein. (Ber) = Rheinburgengau. (Gro) = Schloss Schönburg. (Vil) = Oberwessel.

Bernstein Vineyards (USA). A winery based at Mount Veeder, California.

Berón (Sp). A red wine produced by Bodegas Beronia, S.A. Rioja. Oakmatured and bottle-aged. 70–80% Tempranillo and 20–30% Viura.

Beronia (Sp). Red wines produced in Bodegas Beronia, S.A. Rioja. Oakmatured and bottle-aged.

Beroun Brewery (Czec). A brewery based in north-west Czec. Was founded in 1872. Noted for its fine beers.

Berri (Austr). A district of New South Wales that produces fine quality wines.

Berrie (Fr). A commune in the Vienne Département. Wines are under the A.C. Saumur, Anjou-Saumur, Loire.

Berri Estates (Austr). Vineyards in South Australia, is a part of Berri Remano. Address = Sturt Highway, Glossop, S. Australia, 5344. Grape varieties – Cabernet sauvignon, Gordo, Riesling and Shiraz. Produces varietal wines, a carbonated Passion wine and liqueurs.

Berri Renmano (Austr). A large vineyard estate, 3,000 ha. in South Australia. See Berri Estates. 34 varieties of grapes grown. Address = P.O. Box 238 Berri, South Australia, 5343.

Berrow Brewery (Eng). Opened in 1982 in Burnham-on-Sea, Somerset. Produces two cask conditioned beers BBBB 1038 O.G. and Topsy Turvy 1055 O.G.

Berru (Fr). A Cru Champagne village in the Canton de Beine. District = Reims.

Berry, Berries (Eng). Another name for the grape.

Berry Brothers & Rudd (Scot). Scotch whisky producers. Cutty Sark is one of their noted brands.

Berrywine Plantation (USA). A small vineyard based in Mount Airy, Maryland. 2.5 ha. Produces French hybrid wines.

Bersano (It). A noted producer of Moscato d'Asti Spumante in the Piemonte region, north-western Italy.

Berson (Fr). A commune in the A.C. Côtes de Blaye in north-east Bordeaux.

Bertani (It). A well-known Veneto wine producer. Noted for their cuve close sparkling wines.

Bertemati (Sp). A Brandy producer.
Bertero Winery (USA). A winery based in southern Santa Clara, California. Grape varieties – Barbera and Zinfandel. Produces varietal wines.
Bertier-Bichot (Fr). A producer of sparkling A.C. Vouvray based at Rochecorbon, Loire.
Bertins (Les) (Fr.) A Premier Cru vineyard [part] in the A.C. commune of Beaune, Côte de Beaune, Burgundy.
Bertins (Les) (Fr). A Premier Cru vineyard [part] in the A.C. commune of Pommard, Côte de Beaune, Burgundy. 3.7 ha.
Bertola (Sp). A Brandy and Sherry producer based in Jerez de la Frontera. Part of Bodegas Internacionales.
Bertolli (It). A famous Chianti Classico producer in Sienna, Tuscany.
Bertolli Fizzano (It). A Chianti Classico producer based in Tuscany.
Bertram Wines (S.Afr). Based in Stellenbosch. Address = Box 199, Stellenbosch 7600. Produces varietal wines.
Bertran (José López) (Sp). A large bodega based in Tarragona. 50 ha. Produces mainly white wines and Corrida table wine.
Bertrand (Fr). A distiller of Marc d'Alsace. Address = Wernach 67350, Pfaffenhoffen and Uberach.
Béru (Fr). A commune in the A.C. Chablis, Burgundy.
Berwangen (Ger). Village. See Kirchardt.
Berwick Glebe (Eng). A small vineyard based in Sussex. 1 ha. Address = Frensham College, Berwick, near Polegate, East Sussex. Grape varieties – Müller-Thurgau and Reichensteiner.
Berzamino (It). A variety of the red grape variety Marzemino.
Besigheim (Ger). Village. (Anb) = Württemberg. (Ber) = Württembergisch Unterland. (Gro) = Schalkstein. (Vins) = Felsengarten, Katzenöhrle, Neckarberg, Wurmberg.
Besitz (Ger). The sole owner of a vineyard.
Beso (Gre). A noted wine merchant based near Patras in Peloponnese.
Besotted (Eng). Intoxicated, incapable through alcoholic drink, stupefied through alcohol.
Bessans (Fr). A Vins de Pays area in the Hérault Département in southern France. Produces red, rosé and dry white wines.
Bessarabia (USSR). Now known as Moldavia, was part of Bulgaria until 1940. Produces fine table and dessert wines such as Negri de Purkar, Fetjaska, Romanesti, Trifesti and Gratasti.

Bessards (Les) (Fr). A vineyard in the Coteaux de l'Hermitage, northern Rhône. (red).
Bessay (Fr). A vineyard in the A.C. Juliénas Cru Beaujolais-Villages.
Bessen (Hol). A blackcurrant liqueur produced by De Kuyper. 20% alc. by vol.
Besserat de Bellefon (Fr). Champagne house. Address = BP 301, Allée du Vignoble, 51061 Reims. 10 ha. Produces – Vintage and non-vintage wines. Vintages – 1971, 1973, 1975, 1977, 1978, 1979, 1982. Owned by Pernod-Ricard.
Bessi (It). A producer of Chianti (Rufina district) who uses neither the D.O.C. or Classico designation but his own Chianti Superiore which is only used as a personal guarantee.
Best (Eng). The designation for top quality ales. See Best Bitter, Best Mild.
Best Bitter (Eng). The designation of the top ale in a brewery's portfolio.
Best Bristol Bitter (Eng). A cask conditioned Bitter 1045 O.G. from the Bruce home-brew public house.
Beste (Ger). Best.
Bestimmtes Anbaugebiet (Ger). Designated region. See Anbaugebiet.
Best Mild (Eng). The designation of the top Mild ale in a brewery's portfolio.
Best Scotch (Scot). See Lorimer and Clark.
Bests Great Western (Austr). Vineyards. Address = Concongello Vineyards, Great Western, Victoria 3377. 24 ha. Grape varieties – Cabernet sauvignon, Chardonnay, Chasselas, Pinot meunier, Riesling and Shiraz. Noted for its Hoch and sparkling wines.
Bethon (Fr). A Cru Champagne village in the Canton d'Esternay. District = Épernay.
Betschgräbler (Ger). Vineyard. (Anb) = Baden. (Ber) = Ortenau. (Gro) = Schloss Rodeck. (Vil) = Eisental.
Betsy Ross (Cktl). 1 oz. Port, 1 oz. Brandy, ¼ teaspoon Cointreau, dash Angostura. Shake over ice, strain into a cocktail glass.
Bettelhaus (Ger). Vineyard. (Anb) = Rheinpfalz. (Ber) = Mittelhaardt-Deutsche Weinstrasse. (Gro) = Kobnert. (Vil) = Ungstein.
Béttola (It). Public house, Tavern.
Betty James (Cktl). ½ measure Gin, ½ measure Maraschino, ¼ measure lemon juice, dash Angostura. Shake with ice, strain into a cocktail glass.
Between the Sheets (Cktl). ⅔ measure white Rum, ⅔ measure Brandy, ⅔ measure Cointreau, dash lemon juice. Shake over ice, strain into a cocktail glass.

Beugnons (Fr). An A.C. Premier Cru Chablis, often reclassified as the Premier Cru Vaillons.

Beuicarlo (Sp). A strong red wine from the region of Castellón de la Plana in Valencia.

Beulsberg (Ger). Vineyard. (Anb) = Mittelrhein. (Ber) = Rheinburgengau. (Gro) = Schloss Schönburg. (Vil) = Urbar by St. Goar.

Beuren (Ger). Village. (Anb) = Mosel-Saar-Ruwer. (Ber) = Zell/Mosel. (Gro) = Grafschaft. (Vin) = Pelzerberger.

Beuren (Ger). Village. (Anb) = Württemberg. (Ber) = Remstal-Stuttgart. (Gro) = Hohennenffen. (Vin) = Schlossteige.

Beurot (Fr). A local Burgundy name for the white grape Pinot gris. See also Burot.

Beutelsbach (Ger). Village. (Anb) = Württemberg. (Ber) = Remstal-Stuttgart. (Gro) = Wartbühl. (Vins) = Altenberg, Käppele, Sonnenberg. See Feuerwant.

Beutelsbach (Ger). Village. (Anb) = Württemberg. (Ber) = Remstal-Stuttgart. See Weinstadt and Feuerwant.

Beutelsstein (Ger). Vineyard. (Anb) = Nahe. (Ber) = Schloss Böckelheim. (Gro) = Paradiesgarten. (Vil) = Oberndorf.

Beuv'rie (Ch.Isles). Alcoholic liquor. See also Bév'rie and Litcheur.

Bévaeux (Ch.Isles). A boozer or drinker. See also Béveux.

Beva Fresca (It). A term for a very young wine or describing fresh grape juice which may be added to older wine before drinking.

Bevanda (It). Beverage, drink.

Bevee (Fr). An old word for a drink.

Beverages (Eng). The general term for all drinks. Non and alcoholic.

Beverage Testing Institute (USA). B.T.I. A body based in New York that promotes and developes the tastes in wines. See Hendonic Scale.

Beverage Wine (USA). Denotes an ordinary table wine.

Beveraggio (It). Beverage, drink.

Beveridge (Eng). A drink produced from white sugar, spring water and orange juice.

Beverly Hills Cocktail (Cktl). ½ gill Calvados, 2 dashes Angostura. Stir over broken ice, strain into a cocktail glass. Serve with a cherry and dash of lemon peel juice on top.

Bevernagie Brewery (Bel). A brewery based in Lichtervelde in west Flanders. Brews Oud Piro (a red beer).

Béveux (Ch.Isles). See Bévaeux.

Bevibile (It). Drinkable.

Bevitore (It). Drinker.

Bévottaïr (Ch.Isles). Booze, alcoholic drink.

Bévounnaïr (Ch.Isles). Tipple. See also Grogier.

Bevrage (Fr). An old word for drink other than water.

Bév'rie (Ch.Isles). Alcoholic liquor. See also Beuv'rie and Litcheur.

Bevvies (Eng). The plural of Bevvy. e.g. 'A few bevvies' (a few drinks).

Bevvy (Eng) (slang). Term for a drink. Abbreviation of Beverage. Term mainly used in and around Liverpool in north-western England.

Bévy (Fr). Old village not far from the Nuits-Saint-Georges, dating from tenth century. Produces red and white wines from the Pinot noir and Chardonnay vines. See Hautes Côtes de Nuits.

Beyaz (Tur). A semi-dry white wine.

Beyer (Léon) (Fr). A family wine business in Eguisheim, Alsace.

Beylerce (Tur). A red grape variety.

Bézique (W.Ind). The brand-name of a lemon-flavoured Bacardi rum.

Bhang (Ind). A beverage made from a fermentation of hemp leaves and twigs infused with water. See also Bang.

Bianca Fernanda (It). A white grape variety in Lombardy. Also known as the Cortese.

Biancame (It). A white grape variety grown in Abruzzi. Also known as the Passenna in the Marches.

Bianchello (It). A white grape variety grown in the Marches.

Bianchello del Metauro (It). D.O.C. white wine from the Marches. Produced from the Bianchello and Malvasia grapes. Metauro is a river which flows to the Adriatic.

Bianchetta Trevigiana (It). A white grape variety grown in the Trentino-Alto Adige.

Bianchi (Arg). The brand-name of the Hudson Winery, Ciovini, Buenos Aires. Produced in the San Rafael district of Mendoza.

Bianchi Borgogna (Arg). A red wine produced by Bodegas Bianchi.

Bianco (It). A golden white-coloured, medium-sweet Vermouth.

Bianco (It). The term used to describe a white wine.

Bianco (In) (It). A term which denotes that the juice is taken quickly from the skins.

Bianco Alcamo (It). See Alcamo.

Bianco Capena (It). D.O.C. white wine from Latium. Produced from the Malvasia di candia, Malvasia del lazio,

Toscano, Trebbiano toscano, Romagnolo, Giallo, Bellone and Bombino grape varieties.

Bianco d'Alessano (It). A white grape variety grown in Puglia. See also Alessano.

Bianco d'Arquata (It). A dry white wine from near Perugia in the Umbria.

Bianco dei Colli Maceratesi (It). D.O.C. white wine from the Marches. Produced from the Trebbiano toscano and Maceratino 50%, plus Malvasia toscano and Verdicchio grape varieties. Produced in the commune of Loreto in the province of Macerata.

Bianco di Alessano (It). A white grape variety grown in Puglia region.

Bianco di Custoza (It). D.O.C. white wine from the Lombardy region. Produced from the Trebbiano 5–15%, Garganega 20–30%, Trebbianello 5–15% and the Cortese 20–30%. The D.O.C. also describes the naturally sparkling wine produced from musts and wines according to regulations.

Bianco di Ostuni (It). D.O.C. white wine from the Puglia region. Produced from the Impigno, Francavilla, Bianco di Alessano and Verdeca grapes.

Bianco di Pitigliano (It). D.O.C. white wine from the Tuscany region. Produced from Trebbiano toscano, Greco, Malvasia bianca toscano and Verdelho grapes. The wine is produced 'Vinificato in bianco'.

Biancolella (It). A white grape variety grown on the island of Ischia on the southern tip of Italy.

Biancolella (It). A white wine from the grape of the same name produced on the island of Ischia.

Biancone (It). A white grape variety grown in Tuscany.

Biancosarti (It). The brand-name for an Apéritif produced in northern Italy.

Bianco Vergine Valdichiana (It). D.O.C. white wine from the Tuscany region. Produced from the Trebbiano toscano and Malvasia del chianti grapes. Vinification takes place without the skins.

Bianco Vermouth (It). A sweet, white Vermouth 16% alc. by vol.

Biane (USA). A brand-name used by the Brookside Winery of California.

Biar (Ger). An old local (Frisian) word for beer.

Biassa (It). One of the five towns in the Cinque Terre, Liguria, north-western Italy.

Bibber (Eng). Drinker, tippler, someone who likes alcoholic drink. See Winebibber and Bibbers.

Bibbers (Eng). An old name for heavy drinkers. See Bibber.

Bibbiano (It). A noted Chianti Classico producer.

Bibere (Lat). To drink. See Imbibe.

Bibita (It). Drink, beverage.

Bible Wines (Eng). A collective name used for the many wines mentioned in the Holy Bible. Ahsis, Khemer, Khometz, Mesech, Mimsach, Schechar, Soveh, Tirosh and Yayin.

Biblioteca (Sp). Wine cellars which are similar to libraries with samples of all vintages for reference tastings.

Bibulus (Lat). Fond of drink.

Bica Aberta (Port). A method of keeping the must from the skins in the making of White Port.

Bical (Port). A white grape variety grown in the Bairrada region.

Bical da Bairrada (Port). Another name for the Borrado das moscas grape.

Bicane Chasselas (Fr). A species of the white Chasselas grape. Is also known as the Napoléon.

Bicchiere (It). Drinking glass.

Bicentenary Pale Cream (Sp). A brand of Cream Sherry from Garveys of Jerez.

Bichot, (Albert et Cie) (Fr). A large Burgundy négociant-éleveur based in Beaune. Address = 6 Bld Jacques-Copeau, Beaune. Has many Sous-Marques. Owns – Domaine de Clos Frantin.

Bickensohl (Ger). Village. (Anb) = Baden. (Ber) = Kaiserstuhl-Tuniberg. (Gro) = Vulkanfelsen. (Vins) = Herrenstück, Steinfelsen.

Biddenden (Eng). Vineyard planted in 1969–70. 7.5 ha. Soil – loam over clay. Address = Little Whatmans, Biddenden, Ashford, Kent. Grape varieties – Müller-Thurgau 75%, Huxelrebe, Ortega, Pinot noir, Reichensteiner, Scheurebe and Seyval.

Bidon (Fr). An eighteenth-century wooden jug of approximately 5 litres capacity. Now made of metal.

Bidon (Fr). Can.

Bidon à Bière (Fr). Can of beer. Beer can.

Biebelnheim (Ger). Village. (Anb) = Rheinhessen. (Ber) = Nierstein. (Gro) = Petersberg. (Vins) = Pilgerstein, Rosenberg.

Biebelsheim (Ger). Village. (Anb) = Rheinhessen. (Ber) = Bingen. (Gro) = Sankt Rochuskapelle. (Vins) = Honigberg, Kieselberg.

Biela Sladka Grasica (Yug). A regional name for the white Welschriesling.

Bienenberg (Ger). Vineyard. (Anb) = Baden. (Ber) = Breisgau. (Gro) = Burg Lichteneck. (Vil) = Malterdingen.

Bienenberg (Ger). Vineyard. (Anb) = Baden. (Ber) = Ortenau. (Gro) = Schloss Rodeck. (Vil) = Achern (ortsteil Oberachem).

Bienenberg (Ger). Vineyard. (Anb) = Mittelrhein. (Ber) = Rheinburgengau. (Gro) = Schloss Schönburg. (Vil) = Niederburg.

Bienenberg (Ger). Vineyard. (Anb) = Mittelrhein. (Ber) = Rheinburgengau. (Gro) = Schloss Schönburg. (Vil) = Oberwessel.

Bienengarten (Ger). Vineyard. (Anb) = Baden. (Ber) = Ortenau. (Gro) = Fürsteneck. (Vil) = Durbach.

Bienengarten (Ger). Vineyard. (Anb) = Mosel-Saar-Ruwer. (Ber) = Zell/Mosel. (Gro) = Rosenhang. (Vil) = Sonheim.

Bienengarten (Ger). Vineyard. (Anb) = Mosel-Saar-Ruwer. (Ber) = Zell/Mosel. (Gro) = Weinhex. (Vil) = Güls.

Bienengarten (Ger). Vineyard. (Anb) = Rheingau. (Ber) = Johannisberg. (Gro) = Honigberg. (Vil) = Winkel.

Bienenlay (Ger). Vineyard. (Anb) = Mosel-Saar-Ruwer. (Ber) = Zell/Mosel. (Gro) = Grafschaft. (Vil) = Ediger-Eller.

Biengarten (Ger). Vineyard. (Anb) = Rheinpfalz. (Ber) = Mittelhaardt-Deutsche Weinstrasse. (Gro) = Meerspinne. (Vil) = Gimmeldingen.

Biengarten (Ger). Vineyard. (Anb) = Rheinpfalz. (Ber) = Südliche Weinstrasse. (Gro) = Königsgarten. (Vil) = Frankweiler.

Biengen (Ger). Village. (Anb) = Baden. (Ber) = Markgräflerland. (Gro) = Lorettoberg. (Vin) = Maltesergarten.

Bieninberg (Ger). Vineyard. (Anb) = Baden. (Ber) = Breisgau. (Gro) = Burg Lichteneck. (Vil) = Heimbach.

Bienteveo (Sp). A look-out post that is temporarily situated in the vineyard prior to the vintage (harvest).

Bienvenues-Bâtard-Montrachet (Fr). A Grand Cru vineyard in the A.C. commune of Puligny-Montrachet, Côte de Beaune, Burgundy. 2.3 ha.

Bier (Hol). Beer, ale.

Bierbrouwerij de Drie Hoefijzers (Hol). Three Horseshoes Brewery. Brews Breda and Skol lagers. See also Drie Hoefijzers and Breda.

Bier d'Alsace (Fr). Beer brewed in Alsace.

Bière (Fr). Beer, ale.

Bière de Garance (Fr). A local home-made Bier brewed from the madder plant.

Bière de Garde (Fr). Lit – 'Laying down beer'. Produced in wine shaped bottles with a cork. Made with a mixture of Pilsen and Munich-malt beers. 5½–6% alc. by vol. See also Jenlain and St. Leonard.

Bière de Garde de Saint Léonard (Fr). A high-strength Bière de Garde brewed by the St. Léonard Brasserie, 62200 St. Martin/Bologne. 6% alc. by vol.

Bière de Gingembre (Fr). Ginger beer.

Bière de Malt (Fr). Malt beer.

Bière de Ménage (Fr). Home-brewed beer.

Bière Panachée (Fr). Lit – 'Mixed beer'. Also Shandy.

Bière Rousse (Fr). Name for George Killan's Irish Red Ale brewed by the Pelforth Brewery under licence from Letts of Eire. See also Killan.

Bières de l'Abbaye (Bel). Abbey beers and Trappist beers.

Bieringen (Ger). Village. (Anb) = Württemberg. (Ber) = Kocher-Jagst-Tauber. (Gro) = Kocherberg. (Vin) = Schlüsselberg.

Bierkan (Hol). Beer can.

Bierkeller (Eng). A public house that is decorated in the German style and specialises in German beers (especially Lager) and served in Stein glasses.

Bierritz (Eng). The brand-name for malt liquor and orange wine drink. 7% alc. by vol.

Biersuppe (Ger). A beer eggnog. 1 pint Ale, 4 ozs. sugar, cinnamon and lemon zest. Heat, whisk into 4 egg yolks with a little milk. Strain and cool, serve with soaked raisins.

Bies Brewery (Den). A brewery based in Hobro in northern Jutland.

Bièthe (Ch.Isles). Beer.

Bietigheim (Ger). Village. (Anb) = Württemberg. (Ber) = Württembergisch Unterland. (Gro) = Schalkstein. (Vin) = Neckarberg.

Biferno (It). D.O.C. red wine from Molise. Produced mainly from the Montepulciano grape.

Biferno (It). D.O.C. white wine from Molise. Produced mainly from the Malvasia and Trebbiano grape varieties.

Biffy (Cktl). 1 measure Gin, ¼ measure Swedish Punsch, juice ½ lemon. Shake over ice, strain into a cocktail glass.

Big Apple (Cktl). ⅓ measure Scotch Apple, ⅓ measure Amaretto di Saronno, ⅓ measure Drambuie, dash Grenadine, dash lemon juice. Shake over ice, strain into an ice-filled highball glass. Dress with apple slice.

Big Apple Cocktail (Cktl). Hollow out the centre of an eating apple to form a glass. Chill well after firstly rubbing the inside with lemon juice. Blend pulp with ⅕ gill Cognac, ⅓ gill orange juice, ⅙ gill lemon juice and ½ scoop crushed ice. Strain into apple, serve with straws.

Big Bamboo Cocktail (Cktl). ⅓ measure golden Rum, ⅓ measure orange juice, ⅓ measure pineapple juice, ¼ measure Grenadine, 2 dashes lemon juice. Shake well over ice, strain into highball glass filled with ice. Dress with a mint sprig and orange slice.

Big Barrel Lager (Austr). A sweetish copper-coloured Lager brewed in 1974 by the Cooper's Brewery in South Australia for the Schützenfest.

Big Ben (Eng). A bottled strong Ale 1050 O.G. brewed by Thwaites Brewery, Blackburn.

Big Boy Cocktail (Cktl). ¼ gill dry Gin, ¼ gill Italian vermouth, ¼ gill French vermouth, dash Pernod, dash Angostura. Stir over broken ice, strain into a cocktail glass. Decorate with cherry and dash of lemon peel juice.

Bigbury Beer (Eng). A cask conditioned Best Bitter 1044 O.G. from the Summerskill Brewery, Devon.

Bigi (Luigi and Figlio) (It). Noted wine-producers in Tuscany and Umbria.

Big John's Chocolate Flavoured American Soda Pop (USA). A chocolate-flavoured, non-alcoholic drink produced by Vimto.

Big Lamp Brewery (Eng). Opened 1982 in Newcastle-upon-Tyne. Produces – Best Bitter 1040 O.G. Extra Special 1052 O.G. Old Genie 1070 O.G.

Bigny (Fr). An alternative name for the Merlot grape.

Bigot (Fr). A vineyard worker's two pronged hoe.

Big Ranch Road Vineyard (USA). Part of the Beringer Vineyards based in California.

Big 'T' (Scot). The brand-name of a blended Scotch whisky produced by the Tomatin Distillery Co.

Bihosteleagd (Rum). A wine-producing district in the Siebenbürgen region.

Bijeli Klikun (Yug). A white wine produced near Vukovar in south-eastern Croatia.

Bijeli Pinot (Yug). The local name for the Pinot blanc grape.

Bijelo (Yug). White.

Bijou Cocktail (Cktl). ⅙ gill Plymouth dry gin, ⅙ gill Italian vermouth, ⅙ gill Green Chartreuse, dash Orange bitters. Stir over ice, strain into cocktail glass, add an olive and a cherry. Squeeze of lemon peel on top.

Bikarr (Scan). An old Norse word for beaker or jug.

Bikos (Gre). Beaker, jug.

Bilbainas (Sp). See Bodegas Bilbainas.

Bilberry Grog (Cktl). 3 fl.ozs. Scotch whisky, 3 fl.ozs. Bilberry juice, 3 fl.ozs. water. Heat gently, stir constantly. When nearly boiling pour into a mug containing ½ oz. poached bilberries. Serve with a cinnamon stick and slice of orange.

Bildberg (Ger). Vineyard. (Anb) = Rheinpfalz. (Ber) = Südliche Weinstrasse. (Gro) = Trappenberg. (Vil) = Freimersheim.

Bildstock (Ger). Vineyard. (Anb) = Rheinhessen. (Ber) = Nierstein. (Gro) = Spiegelberg. (Vil) = Nierstein.

Bildstock (Ger). Vineyard. (Anb) = Rheinhessen. (Ber) = Wonnegau. (Gro) = Liebfrauenmorgen. (Vil) = Worms.

Bilecik (Tur). A vineyard based in the Thrace and Marmara region. Produces red wines.

Bilfingen (Ger). Village. (Anb) = Baden (Ber) = Badische Bergstrasse/Kraichgau. (Gro) = Hohenberg. (Vin) = Klepberg.

Bilge (Eng). The bottom of a beer cask where the sediment is retained as the beer is drawn off.

Bilge Beer Brewery (Eng). A brewery based at West Byfleet, Surrey. Promotes the Hacker Pschorr Premium beer range.

Bilina Brewery (Czec). A brewery in north-west Czec. Founded in 1674.

Billardet (Fr). A cuvée in the Les Arvelets 0.4 ha. Les Noizons 0.5 ha. Les Rugiens 0.33 ha. and Petits-Epenots 0.66 ha. Premier Cru vineyards in the A.C. Pommard, Côte de Beaune, Burgundy. Owned by the Hospices de Beaune.

Billecart-Salmon (Fr). Champagne producer. Address = 40, Rue Carnot, Mareuil-sur-Ay, 51160, Ay. Grande Marque. Produces – Vintage and non-vintage wines. Vintages – 1971, 1973, 1975, 1976, 1978, 1979, 1982, 1983. Brand labels include – Crémant des Moines and Rosé Millésmimé.

Billes (Fr). Small balls made of neutral alginate used in the Champagne region. Are porous and trap the yeasts, deposits and any cloudiness in the Champagne bottle. Help to shorten the length of time of the remuage. Still under trial.

Bill Gibb (Cktl). 2 ozs. Beefeater gin, 4 ozs. fresh orange juice, dash egg white. Shake with ice, strain into a highball glass, add 1 oz. Mandarine Napoléon, decorate with slice of orange and a cherry. Do not stir. Serve with straws.

Billigheim-Ingenheim (Ger). Village. (Anb) = Rheinpfalz. (Ber) = Südliche Weinstrasse. (Gro) = Kloster Lieb-

B

frauenberg. (Vins) = Mandelpfad, Pfaffenberg, Rosenberg, Sauschwänzel, Steingebiss, Venusbuckel.

Billy Hamilton (Cktl). ⅓ measure (brown) Crème de Cacao, ⅓ measure Brandy, ⅓ measure orange Curaçao, dash egg white. Shake over ice, strain into a cocktail glass.

Billy-le-Grand (Fr). A Premier Cru Champagne village in the Canton de Suippes. District = Châlons.

Billy Taylor Cocktail (Cktl). 1 measure Gin, juice ½ lime. Stir over ice, strain into an ice-filled highball glass. Top with soda water.

Biltmore Company (USA). A winery based in Ashville, North Carolina. Produces French-American hybrid wines.

Bilyara Vineyards (Austr). Address = P.O. Box. 396, Nuriootpa, South Australia 5355. 45 ha. Produces varietal wines.

Bin (Eng). A slot for holding a bottle of wine horizontally in a cellar.

Binary Fission (Eng). The term given to the method of reproduction which yeast may use to multiply. One cell divides into two, those two into four and so on. Needs warmth, food, moisture and time (20 minutes per division approximately) to reproduce.

Binau (Ger). Village. (Anb) = Baden. (Ber) = Badische Bergstrasse/Kraichgau. (Gro) = Stiftsberg. (Vin) = Herzogsberg.

Binaymina (Isr). A dry rosé wine produced mainly for the USA market.

Bine (Eng). The hop plant climbing stem made of twine.

Binelli-Mesthé (Fr). Armagnac producer. Address = 29, Rue Thierry Cazes, 32500-Fleurance.

Bin Ends (Eng). Small lots of wines sold off by wine merchants at a reduced cost because the lot is too small to include on new list.

Bin Eng (Ger). Small storage place for bottles of wine in a cellar.

Bingen (Ger). Bereich. (Anb) = Rheinhessen. (Gros) = Abtel (Abtey), Adelberg, Kaiserpfalz, Kurfürstenstück, Rheingrafenstein, Sankt Rochuskapelle.

Bingen (Ger). Village. (Anb) = Rheinhessen. (Ber) = Bingen. (Gro) = Sankt Rochuskapelle. (Vins) = Bubenstück, Kapellenberg, Kirchberg, Osterberg, Pfarrgarten, Rosengarten, Scharlachberg, Schelmenstück, Schlossberg-Schwätzerchen.

Bingen-Bingerbrück (Ger). Village. (Anb) = Nahe. (Ber) = Kreuznach. (Gro) = Schlosskapelle. (Vins) = Abtei Ruppertsberg, Hildegardisbrünnchen, Klostergarten, Römerberg.

Bingen Pencil (Ger). The name for a corkscrew in the Rheinhessen. Derived from when the Burgemeister of Bingen asked for a pencil at a council meeting but no one offered one. When later he produced some wine and asked for a corkscrew, everyone present offered him one!

Bingen Wine Cellars (USA). See Mount Elise Vineyards.

Bingerberg (Ger). Vineyard. (Anb) = Rheinhessen. (Ber) = Bingen. (Gro) = Adelberg. (Vil) = Flonheim.

Binger Rochusberg (Ger). A fine white wine produced in Bingen Rheinhessen.

Bingerweg (Ger). Vineyard. (Anb) = Nahe. (Ber) = Kreuznach. (Gro) = Schlosskapelle. (Vil) = Waldlaubersheim.

Bin Label (Eng). A label used to denote what wine is in a particular Bin to save disturbing the bottle. Has the name of wine, vintage, shipper, etc.

Binisalem (Sp). A major wine-producing region on Majorca, Balearic Isles.

Binning (Eng). The storing of wines in a cellar for development.

Bin Number (Eng). The number found on wine lists to denote which Bin the wine is held in. Also helps customers in that they don't have to pronounce the name.

Binson-Orquigny (Fr). A Cru Champagne village in the Canton de Châtillon-sur-Marne. District = Reims.

Bintang Brewery (E.Ind). A brewery based in Surabaja, Java which brews a Pilsener-style beer.

Binzen (Ger). Village. (Anb) = Baden. (Ber) = Markgräflerland. (Gro) = Vogtei Rötteln. (Vin) = Sonnhohle.

Bío-Bío (Chile). A noted wine-producing province and river based in the Southern Zone.

Biondi-Santi (It). A winery house on the Greppo estate at Montalcino in Tuscany. Noted for its Brunello wines.

Bior (Ger). The high German word for beer.

Biotin (Eng). A vitamin found in minute traces in wine.

Biou (Fr). The name given to the gigantic bunch of grapes that is carried during the procession of the Fête du Biou held annually in Arbois, Jura, eastern France.

Bira (Tur). Beer, ale.

Birac (Fr). A commune in the Charente Département whose grapes are classed Petite Champagne (Cognac).

Bira Fabrikasi (Tur). Brewery.

Birahane (Tur). Public house, bar. See also Bar.

Bir Bintang (E.Ind). A Lager beer brewed in the Dutch-style in Jakarta, Indonesia.

Birch Wine (Eng). A fermented wine produced from birch sap, sugar, water, yeast and dry white wine. Produced in Sussex.

Bird of Paradise Fizz (Cktl). 1 measure Gin, juice ½ lemon, 1 teaspoon powdered sugar, 4 dashes Grenadine, 1 egg white. Shake over ice, strain into an ice-filled highball glass. Top with soda water.

Bir Drassen (Afr). A wine co-operative based in Tunisia. Owned by the UCCVT.

Birdwood Vineyards (N.Z.). Old established vineyards based in Birdwood, Henderson, Auckland.

Bire (Ch.Isles). Beer, ale.

Birell Lager (Switz). A low-alcohol Lager 0.8% by vol. brewed by Hurlimann Brauerei.

Biri̇er (Ch.Isles). Brewer.

Birkenberg (Ger). Vineyard. (Anb) = Nahe. (Ber) = Kreuznach. (Gro) = Pfarrgarten, (Vil) = Sommerloch.

Birkenberg (Ger). Vineyard. (Anb) = Nahe. (Ber) = Schloss Böckelheim. (Gro) = Rosengarten. (Vil) = Roxheim.

Birkmyer Vineyard (USA). A small vineyard in the Napa Valley, California. Grape variety – mainly Johannisberg riesling.

Birkweiler (Ger). Village. (Anb) = Rheinpfalz. (Ber) = Südliche Weinstrasse. (Gro) = Königsgarten. (Vins) = Kastanienbusch, Mandelberg, Rosenberg.

Birl (Eng). A sixteenth-century word for plying a person with drink.

Birnengeist (Ger). A pear liqueur. (An eau-de-vie).

Birnenwasser (Ger). An eau-de-vie de poire.

Biron (Fr). A commune in the Charente-Maritime Département whose grapes are classed Petite Champagne (Cognac).

Birra (It). Beer, ale.

Birra Bellinzona Brewery (Switz). An independent brewery based in Bellinzona. Produces fine beers. See Chic.

Birra di Marzo (It). A Bock beer.

Birra Doppio Malto (Eng). An all-malt, strong, Pale ale brewed by the Gales Brewery, Horndean, Hants. Brewed for the Italian market.

Birraio (It). A brewer who brews Ales and Lager beers.

Birrell (Eng). A low-alcohol Lager beer brewed by the Watney Brewery.

Birreria (It). Brewery.

Birr'rie (Ch.Isles). Brewery.

Bisamberg (Aus). A wine-producing area based on the left bank of the river Danube.

Biscardo (It). A noted wine producer of Bardolino. Address = 37010, Calmasino di Bardolino, Verona.

Bisceglia Bros (USA). A winery based in San Joaquin, California.

Bischof (Fr). See Bishop (cocktail).

Bischoffingen (Ger). Village. (Anb) = Baden. (Ber) = Kaiserstuhl-Tuniberg. (Gro) = Vulkanfelsen. (Vins) = Enselberg, Rosenkranz, Steinbuck.

Bischof Frappé (Fr). See Iced Bishop.

Bischöfliches Weingut (Ger). A Mosel-Saar-Ruwer estate based at Trier. 94.5 ha. of vineyards at Ayl, Eitelsbach, Kasel, Piesport, Scharzhofberg, Trittenheim, Ürzig and Wiltingen.

Bischofsberg (Ger). Vineyard. (Anb) = Franken. (Ber) = Mainviereck. (Gro) = Not yet assigned. (Vil) = Grossheubach.

Bischofsberg (Ger). Vineyard. (Anb) = Rheingau. (Ber) = Johannisberg. (Gro) = Burgweg. (Vil) = Rüdesheim.

Bischofsgarten (Ger). Vineyard. (Anb) = Rheinpfalz. (Ber) = Mittelhaardt-Deutsche Weinstrasse. (Gro) = Schnepfenflug an der Weinstrasse. (Vil) = Forst.

Bischofsgarten (Ger). Vineyard. (Anb) = Rheinpfalz. (Ber) = Mittelhaardt-Deutsche Weinstrasse. (Gro) = Schnepfenflug an der Weinstrasse. (Vil) = Friedelsheim.

Bischofsgarten (Ger). Vineyard. (Anb) = Rheinpfalz. (Ber) = Mittelhaardt-Deutsche Weinstrasse. (Gro) = Schnepfenflug an der Weinstrasse. (Vil) = Wachenheim.

Bischofshub (Ger). Vineyard. (Anb) = Mittelrhein. (Ber) = Bacharach. (Gro) = Schloss Stahleck. (Vil) = Oberdiebach.

Bischofskreuz (Ger). Grosslagen. (Anb) = Rheinpfalz. (Ber) = Südliche Weinstrasse. (Vils) = Böchingen, Burrweiler, Dammheim, Flemlingen, Gleisweiler, Knöringen, Nussdorf, Roschbach, Walsheim.

Bischofstein (Ger). Vineyard. (Anb) = Mosel-Saar-Ruwer. (Ber) = Zell/ Mosel. (Gro) = Weinhex. (Vil) = Burgen.

Bischofstuhl (Ger). Vineyard. (Anb) = Mosel-Saar-Ruwer. (Ber) = Zell/ Mosel. (Gro) = Goldbäumchen. (Vil) = Cochem.

Bischofsweg (Ger). Vineyard. (Anb) = Rheinpfalz. (Ber) = Mittelhaardt-Deutsche Weinstrasse. (Gro) = Meerspinne. (Vil) = Mussbach.

Biscuity (Eng). A term used to describe the bouquet in some sparkling wines.

Derived from acetaldehydes owing to age in bottle or vinification method. Term can also apply to pasteurised beers.

Biser (Yug). Sparkling.

Bishop (Cktl). Juice ½ an orange, 2 dashes lemon juice, tablespoon powdered sugar, wine-glass soda water. Dissolve together in a tall glass, half fill with ice. Top with red Burgundy. Stir, add a little dark Rum. Garnish with fruits in season. Straws.

Bishop (Eng). Mulled Port. The Port is heated up with sugar, oranges, cloves and set alight before it is served. See also Archbishop.

Bishop Brewery (Eng). Opened in 1984 in Somerset. Produces Bishop's PA. 1037 O.G. and Bishop's Best Bitter 1041 O.G.

Bishop of Riesling Moselle (Ger). A medium-dry, white, Qba wine produced by Rudolph Müller.

Bishop Potter Cocktail (Cktl). ¼ measure Vermouth, ¼ measure sweet Vermouth, ½ measure dry Gin, 2 dashes Orange bitters, 2 dashes Calisaya. Shake well over ice, strain into a cocktail glass.

Bishop's Ale (Eng). A strong Barley wine 1080 O.G. from Ridley's Brewery, Essex.

Bishop's Anger (Eng). A strong bottled Ale 1053 O.G. brewed by Shepherd Neame Brewery, Kent.

Bishop's Tipple (Eng). A sweet Barley wine 1066 O.G. brewed by Gibbs Mews Brewery, Salisbury.

Bisingar et Cie (Fr). A Champagne producer. Address = Ay, Marne. Produces non-vintage wines.

Bismarck (USA). See Bismark. ½ pint Champagne, ½ pint Stout.

Bismark (Eng). A mixture of equal quantities of chilled Champagne and Guinness. Also known as Black Velvet.

Bisol (Desiderio & Figli) (It). A producer of sparkling (méthode champenoise) wines based in Veneto.

Bisquit Dubouché (Fr). A Cognac producer. Address = Ste Ricard, Domaine de Ligneres, 16170 Rouillac. 200 ha. in Fins Bois. Produce Extra Vieille Or. 40 year old.

Bisse (Switz). An aqueduct used for irrigating the vineyards in Valais.

Bisserheim (Ger). Village. (Anb) = Rheinpfalz. (Ber) = Mittelhaardt-Deutsche Weinstrasse. (Gro) = Schwarzerde. (Vins) = Goldberg, Held, Orlenberg, Steig.

Bisseuil (Fr). A Premier Cru Champagne village in the Canton d'Ay. District = Reims.

Bissig (Ger). Describes a wine with a strong tannin content, or a biting taste of acid.

Bissingen (Ger). Village. (Anb) = Württemberg. (Ber) = Württembergisch Unterland. (Gro) = Schalkstein. (Vin) = Neckarberg.

Bisson (Colonel) (Fr). An eighteenth-century colonel who made any of his troops 'present arms' when they passed the Clos de Vougeot vineyard in the Côte d'Or. The practice is still carried out to this day in honour of the great vineyard.

Bisţria (Rum). A wine-producing area noted for its medium-dry, white wines.

Bistro (Fr). Pub, Café, Tavern.

Bitartrates (Sp). Found in sherry. Gypsum is added to convert insoluble tartrates which will settle out. They make the wine go cloudy.

Bitburger Pils (Ger). A Pilsener lager brewed by the Simon Brauerei in Bitburg, Rhineland Palatinate.

Bite (Eng). A term given to the tannin taste of some red wines which are heavy in tannins.

Biter Cocktail (Cktl). 1 measure Gin, ½ measure Green Chartreuse, ½ measure lemon juice, dash Absinthe, sugar syrup to taste. Shake over ice, strain into a cocktail glass.

Bitola (Yug). A wine-producing district in Macedonia.

Bittall (Eng). The brand-name of a Port-based apéritif.

Bitter (Eng). Having a bad taste, unpleasant taste.

Bitter (Ger) (Hol). Bitter.

Bitter Ale (Eng). A copper-coloured beer. Has a high proportion of hops to give bitter taste. O.G. between 1030–1055. The most popular of beers in Britain.

Bitter Curaçao (Fr). An apéritif made from Bitter Français, Curaçao and soda water. Stir over ice, strain into a tall glass containing ice.

Bitter Disease (Eng). Also known as Tourne. Occurs in low-alcohol, sweet wines. Is caused by lactic acid producing bacteria and leaves the wine tasting bitter. Prevented by using sulphite.

Bitter Français (Fr). A noted French bitters.

Bitter Highball (Cktl). Put ⅕ gill Angostura into an ice-filled highball glass. Top with soda water (or ginger ale). Dress with a spiral of lemon peel.

Bitter Hour (Hol). Cocktail (apéritif) hour.

Bitterkeit (Ger). Bitterness, sharpness.

Bitterl (Aus). Lit – 'Little bitter one'. Denotes a very sharp, bitter wine.

Bitter Lemon (Eng). A · non-alcoholic sparkling 'mixer'. Contains quinine.

Bitter Melon (Cktl). 1 part Midori, 4 parts bitter lemon. Stir over ice in a highball glass.

Bitterness (Eng). An acrid taste, like the taste of asprin or quinine.

Bitter Pineapple (Cktl).(Non-alc). 1 measure pineapple juice, juice ½ lemon, 3 dashes Angostura. Shake over ice, strain into a highball glass. Top with ginger ale.

Bitter Rosso (It). A dry apéritif from Martini and Rosso. Pink in colour. 25% alc. by vol.

Bitters (Eng). Spirits of varying alcoholic strengths, flavoured with roots and herbs. Having in common only their bitterness and their claim to medicinal powers. Used in cocktails. Abbot's Aged Bitters, Amer Picon, Angostura, Beerenburg, Boonkamp's, Campari, Catz Bitters, Champion Bitters, Fernet Branca, Law's Peach Bitters, Orange Bitters, Pommeranzen, Sécrestat, Toni Kola, Underberg, Unicum and Welling's are examples.

Bitter Sécrestat (Fr). Bitters.

Bitter Sharp (Eng). A cider apple similar to the Bitter Sweet, but higher in acidity.

Bitters Highball (Cktl). Place selected bitters (½ fl.oz.) into an ice-filled highball glass. Top with ginger ale or soda and a twist of lemon peel.

Bitters Shaker (Eng). A glass decanter-shaped unit with a hole in the base (used for re-filling). Is used for mixing Bitters and spirits (mainly Whisky).

Bitter Stout (Ire). A style of Stout of which the Irish now produce the most. Beamish, Guinness and Murphy's are main breweries. Has between 4–7.5% alc. by vol.

Bitter Sweet (Cktl).(1). ½ measure Gin, ¼ measure Apricot brandy, ¼ measure Cerasella liqueur, ½ measure orange juice (sweet) or ¼ measure lemon juice (dry). Shake over ice and strain into a cocktail glass.

Bitter Sweet (Cktl).(2). ½ measure French vermouth, ½ measure Italian vermouth, dash Angostura, dash Orange bitters. Stir over ice, strain into a cocktail glass. Add a twist of orange peel.

Bitter Sweet (Eng). A cider apple of the West Country and West Midlands with a high acidity and plenty of sugar.

Bitter Sweet Orange (Cktl). 1 measure Yellow Izarra, 1 measure Campari, juice of orange. Shake over ice, strain into a cocktail glass.

Bitter-Sweet Punch (Punch). Heat 2 pints Cider, 1 cinnamon stick, pinch grated nutmeg and 4 ozs. cranberries until the berries burst. Add ¾ pint red wine, bring almost to the boil, strain and serve.

Bittertropfen (Ger). Lit – 'Bitter drops'. A herb liqueur used to season mixed drinks.

Bizanet (Fr). A wine-producing village based in the Corbières district of the Languedoc.

Bitzingen (Ger). Village. (Anb) = Mosel-Saar-Ruwer. (Ber) = Obermosel. (Gro) = Gipfel. (Vin) = Sites not yet choosen.

Bizerta (Tun). A town around which is produced most of the wines of the country. See Cap Bon.

Bizzy Izzy Highball (Cktl). ¼ gill Rye whiskey, ¼ gill pale Sherry, dash lemon juice, sugar to taste. Mix well together, top up with ice cold soda water.

Bjalo Vino (Bul). White wine.

Björnbärslikör (Nor). Blackberry liqueur.

Bjorr (Scan). An old Norse word for beer.

Blaauwkippen Agricultural Estates (S.Afr). Based in Stellenbosch. Address = Box 54, Stellenbosch 7600. Produces varietal wines.

Blacé (Fr). A commune in the Beaujolais. Has A.C. Beaujolais-Villages or A.C. Beaujolais-Blacé status.

Blackamoor Stout (Eng). A sweet Stout 1044 O.G. brewed by Hardys and Hansons Brewery, Nottingham.

Black and Black (Eng). Guinness and blackcurrant.

Black and Tan (Cktl). ½ measure sweet Vermouth, ¼ measure Pastis, ¼ measure Crème de Cassis. Shake over ice, strain into a cocktail glass. Top with a lemon slice.

Black and Tan (Eng). ½ pint Bitter ale, ½ pint Stout. Pour slowly together into glass. (Dry stout such as Guinness is best). See also Black Dash.

Black and White (Scot). A blended Scotch whisky created by James Buchanan. Produced at their Glentauchers Distillery, Mulben, Speyside. 40% alc. by vol.

Blackawton Brewery (Eng). A brewery in Devon. Brews Squires 1044 O.G. Devon Best 1036 O.G. and Blackawton Bitter 1037 O.G.

Black Beard (Ind). A Lager beer 1044 O.G. brewed by the Vinedale Brewery in Hyderabad.

Black Beer (Eng). A heavy Malt beer from the Mather Brewery, Leeds. A bottled beer 7% alc. by vol. If mixed with lemonade then called Sheffield Stout.

Blackberry Brandy (Eng). A liqueur made with blackberries, sugar and brandy. 20–30% alc. by vol.

Blackberry Flavoured Brandy (USA). A Brandy-based liqueur infused with blackberries.

Blackberry Julep (It). An apéritif wine made for the USA market.

Blackberry Liqueur (USA) (Pol) (Ger). Produced from blackberries by the maceration technique. Occasionally has a small amount of red wine added. 23% alc. by vol.

Blackberry Nip (N.Z.). A fortified wine produced by Mayfair Vineyards, Henderson, North Island.

Black Bess Stout (Eng). A bottled Stout 1043 O.G. brewed by Timothy Taylor's Brewery, Yorkshire.

Black Bottle Scotch Whisky (Scot). A blended Scotch whisky produced by Gordon Graham and Co. Ltd., Westhorn, 1780 London Road, Glasgow G32. 8XA. Sold in a black glass bottle. Now part of Long John International.

Black Brandy (USA). A liqueur (grape) brandy.

Black Bull (Ind). A wood-aged, 5 year old Rum distilled by the Ajudhia Distillery.

Black Bull Bitter (Eng). A keg Bitter 1035 O.G. brewed by Theakston's Brewery.

Black Bull Cider (Eng). The brand-name of a Cider produced by the Saffron Cider Company, Radwinter, Essex.

Black Bush (Ire). A soft, De Luxe Irish whiskey from the Bushmills Distillery. 8 years old. 40% alc. by vol.

Black Cockerel (It). The D.O.C. seal logo for the Chianti Classico wines in Tuscany. See Gallo Nero.

Black Coral (Eng). A blackcurrant-flavoured wine produced by Lamb and Watt of Liverpool, Lancashire.

Black Country Ale (Eng). A bottled Old ale 1052 O.G. brewed by the Simpkiss Brewery, West Midlands.

Black Country Bitter (Eng). A cask conditioned Bitter 1039 O.G. brewed by the Holden Brewery.

Blackcurrant Liqueur (Fr). See Crème de Cassis.

Blackcurrant Tea Cup (Cup). Place into a punch bowl ½ pint sparkling apple juice, ½ pint white wine, 1 pint blackcurrant tea and the juice of 2 lemons. Stir with ice, dress with apple slices and serve.

Black Dash (Austr). A mixed drink similar to a Black and Tan but with ⅔ pint Stout and ⅓ pint beer. Popular in South Australia.

Black Death (Eng). The popular nickname for Aquavit on the rocks.

Black Death (Ice). A Snapps presented in a wooden coffin. Launched by The Luxembourg Wine Co. The coffins are made by inmates of an Icelandic prison.

Black Devil Cocktail (Cktl). 1 measure dark Rum, ¼ measure Italian vermouth. Stir over ice, strain into a cocktail glass. Dress with a black olive.

Black Forest Cocktail (Cktl). ⅔ measure Cherry brandy, ⅓ measure Gin, dash Maraschino. Shake over ice, strain into a cocktail glass.

Black Forest Girl (Ger). A well-known brand of fruity, white wine made from the Müller-Thurgau grape by the ZBW in Baden.

Black Fox (Wales). A cask conditioned Bitter 1038 O.G. brewed by The Globe, a home-brew public house in Fishguard. Made with malt extract.

Black Friars Distillery (Eng). Produces Plymouth gin. The original Plymouth gin 'Coates' infused with Italian juniper. The name is protected by law from injunctions in the 1880s.

Black Frost (The) (Bra). The name given to a devastating frost that occurred on the 17th July 1975 which almost destroyed the Brazilian Coffee industry and raised the world price of coffee. Also known as 'The Great Frost'.

Black Glass (Eng). An expression that refers to the glass of the early bottles which were in fact olive green. Helped to hide the impurities the wine.

Black Gold (Fr). The name given to the volcanic cinder found in the soil of the Champagne region.

Black Half Hour (Eng). The name given in the eighteenth century to the half hour before dinner when guests arrived. No drinks were served and so the 'Apéritif' was invented to break the ice.

Black Hamburg (Ger). An alternative name for the Trollinger grape.

Black Hawk (Cktl). ½ measure Bourbon whiskey, ½ measure Sloe gin. Stir over ice, strain into cocktail glass. Top with a cherry.

Black Heart (W.Ind). A dark Jamaican rum matured in England by United Rum Merchants.

Black Hermitage (Austr). A red Claret-style wine made from the Syrah grape.

Black Horse Ale (USA). An Ale brewed by the Champale Brewery in Trenton.

Black Horse Ale (USA). An Ale brewed by the Koch Brewery in Dunkirk.

Black Horse Bitter (Eng). A cask conditioned Bitter 1048 O.G. brewed by Godson's Brewery, London.

Black Jack (Eng). A bottle made of leather used in Tudor times for carrying and storing wine.

Black Jack (Cktl). ⅓ measure Cointreau, ⅓ measure Kahlúa, ⅓ measure Scotch whisky, dash lemon juice. Shake over ice, Strain into a cocktail glass.

Black Jack (Eng). The name given to an eighteenth-century leather drinking mug of 1 pint capacity used for Cider or Ale. Tarred to make it water tight.

Blackjack Cocktail (Cktl). ⅖ measure Kirsch, ⅖ measure strong black coffee, ⅕ measure Brandy. Shake over ice, strain into an ice-filled old-fashioned glass.

Black July (Bra). A black grape variety.

Black July (Bra). See Black Frost (The).

Black Label (Austr). A red wine from the Seppelts Vineyard in South Australia.

Black Label (Scot). A top Brand de Luxe blended whisky of Johnnie Walker. 43% alc. by vol.

Black Magic (Cktl). 2 dashes Mandarine Napoléon, juice 2–3 grapes, dry sparkling wine. Pour grape juice and liqueur into Champagne flute. Top up with wine, decorate with 2 black grapes on side of rim.

Black Magic Cocktail (Cktl). 1 measure Vodka, ½ measure Kahlúa, dash lemon juice. Stir over ice, strain into an ice-filled old-fashioned glass. Top with a twist of lemon peel.

Black Malt (Eng). A specially malted barley used to add colour to beer.

Black Malvoisie (Austr). An alternative name for the Cinsault grape.

Black Mammy (Cktl). ¼ gill Brandy, juice of a small grapefruit, juice of a lemon, ¾ gill dark Rum, 2 cloves, 3 dashes sugar syrup. Shake over ice, strain into a highball glass. Decorate with orange and lemon peel.

Black Maria (Cktl). ¼ measure coffee liqueur, ¼ measure dark Rum, ½ measure strong black coffee, sugar to taste. Stir over ice, strain into a large balloon glass over ice.

Black Martini (Cktl). As for a Dry Martini but using a black olive in place of a green olive.

Black Monukka (USA). A white grape variety related to the Muscat grape. Used in the making of sweet fortified wines in California.

Black Mountain Vineyard (USA). A winery based in Alexander Valley, Sonoma County, California. Grape varieties – Chardonnay, Sauvignon blanc and Zinfandel. Produces varietal wines.

Black Mud (Eng). The nineteenth-century nickname for Turkish Coffee.

Black Muscat (USA). A black grape variety grown in California. Also known as the Muscat Hamburg.

Black Muscat (USA). Red wine produced in California from the Black muscat grape.

Black Nikka (Jap). A brand of Whiskey produced by the Nikka Distilleries.

Black of Alexandria (S.Afr). An alternative name for the Muscat Hamburg grape.

Black Pearl Cocktail (Cktl). ½ measure Cognac, ½ measure Tia Maria. Stir together over crushed ice in a tulip glass. Top with iced Champagne. Dress with a black cherry.

Blackpool Best Mild (Eng). A cask conditioned Mild 1036 O.G. brewed by Bass.

Black Prince (USA). A white grape variety used in the making of dessert wines in California.

Black Prince Mild (Wales). A keg dark Mild beer 1036 O.G. brewed by the Crown Brewery in South Wales.

Black Rot (USA). A vine disease (fungal) of American origin. Causes the grapes to shrivel. Treated with Copper sulphate.

Black Russian (Cktl). Place some ice into a tall glass, pour in 1 oz. coffee liqueur, 2 ozs. Vodka. Stir together.

Black Seal (W.Ind). A noted brand of dark Rum produced by the Wray and Nephew Group on the island of Jamaica.

Black Sheep (Cktl). 2 fl.ozs. dry Stout, 1 fl.oz. Kahlúa, 1 fl.oz. Glayva. Stir over ice, strain into an old-fashioned glass. Float double cream on top.

Blacksmith (Eng). ½ pint Guinness and ⅓ pint Barley wine.

Blacksmith Cocktail (Cktl). ⅓ measure Drambuie, ⅓ measure Crème de Café, ⅓ measure Cognac. Stir over ice in an old-fashioned glass.

Black Soil (Fr). The soil from the floor of the Montagne de Reims forest. Used to replace topsoil washed away in Champagne. See Black Gold.

Black Sombrero (Cktl). 1 measure Tia Maria placed into a narrow liqueur glass. Float 1 measure of cream on top.

Black Spot (Euro). A vine disease of the leaf. (fungal).

Black Stallion (Yug). A sweet red wine produced from the Vranac grape in the Titov Veles area of Southern Yugoslavia.

Blackstone Cocktail (Cktl). 1 measure Gin, ½ measure Italian vermouth, ½ measure French vermouth. Shake over ice, strain into a cocktail glass. Decorate with orange peel.

Blackstone Cooler (Cktl). 1½ fl.ozs. Jamaican rum poured into an ice-filled highball. Top with soda water and decorate with lemon peel.

Blackstrap (W.Ind). The local name given to molasses mixed with Rum.

Black Stripe (Cktl). Dissolve tablespoon of honey in a little hot water in a tumbler. When cool add 2 ice cubes, ¾ gill dark Rum and top with iced water. Stir, top with grated nutmeg and add a twist of lemon. Can also be served hot.

Black Tea (Eng). The designation for fermented teas. Is the main tea style.

Blackthorn Cocktail (Cktl). (1). ⅙ gill Sloe gin, ⅙ gill French vermouth, ⅙ gill Italian vermouth, 1 dash Orange bitters, 1 dash Angostura. Stir over ice, strain into a cocktail glass, add a squeeze of lemon peel juice on top.

Blackthorn Cocktail (Cktl). (2). ¼ gill Irish whiskey, ¼ gill French vermouth, 3 dashes Absinthe, 3 dashes Angostura. Stir over ice, strain into a cocktail glass, squeeze of lemon peel juice on top.

Blackthorn Cocktail (Cktl). (3). ⅙ gill Italian vermouth, ⅙ gill French vermouth, ⅙ gill Scotch whisky, ½ teaspoon Orange bitters, dash Angostura. Stir over broken ice, strain into a wine glass. Decorate with a cherry and dash lemon peel juice.

Black Tower (Ger). Brand-name for a Liebfraumilch Qba. from H. Kendermann of Bingen in the Rheinhessen. Sold in a black glass (stone-shaped) bottle. Bought by European Cellars in February 1987.

Black Velvet (Can). A Canadian rye whisky produced by Gilbey Canada Ltd.

Black Velvet (Cktl). A mixture of chilled Champagne and stout. Also known as Bismark/Bismarck.

Black Watch Cocktail (Cktl). ⅔ measure Scotch whisky, ⅓ measure Kahlúa. Stir over ice in an old-fashioned glass. Top with a dash of soda water and lemon peel spiral.

Black Widow Cocktail (Cktl). ⅔ measure Jamaican rum, ⅓ measure Southern Comfort, juice ½ lime, dash Gomme syrup. Shake over ice, strain into a cocktail glass.

Black Wine of Cahors (Fr). Name given to the wine made with the Malbec (Côt) grape in which the skins were left for a long period during fermentation, producing an astringent and tannic wine.

Bladder Shape (Eng). Early glass bottle 1715–1730 developed from the onion shape. Also known as the 'Bastard Bottle'.

Bladnoch (Scot). A single Malt whisky distillery in southern Scotland. Produces an 8 y.o. Lowland malt whisky. 43% alc. by vol. Produced by Bells.

Blagny (Fr). The only Burgundian communal place-name that has no accompanying commune. Blagny is a hamlet divided between Meursault and Puligny-Montrachet on the Côte de Beaune. Villages are La Jennelotte, La Pièce sous le Bois and Sous-le-Dos-d'Ane.

Blaignan (Fr). A commune in the Bas Médoc, north-western Bordeaux.

Blair Athol (Scot). A single Malt whisky distillery of Arthur Bell and Sons Ltd., Perth. An 8 year old Highland malt whisky. 40% alc. by vol.

Blairmhor (Scot). A single Malt whisky distillery. Owned by R Carmichael and Sons. A Highland malt whisky. 40% alc. by vol.

Blaison d'Or (Fr). An Armagnac produced by Chabot-Marquis de Puységur.

Blaj (Rum). A noted wine-producing area, part of the Tîrnave Vineyard.

Blanc (Fr). White.

Blanc (En) (Port). See Bica Alberta.

Blanc (Le) (USA). The label used by Californian Growers for their generic and varietal wines and Brandies.

Blanca-Roja (Sp). The alternative name for the white grape variety known as the Blancquirroja, Malvasia and Tobía.

Blancart Pastis (Fr). A low calorie, alcohol-free aniseed based drink. Has no colouring and has 1.8 calories per 100 ml. before dilution.

Blanc-Black Cocktail (Cktl). Place ⅕ gill Blackberry brandy into a flute glass. Top with chilled dry white wine.

Blanc d'Anjou (Fr). A local (Anjou-Saumur) name for the Chenin blanc grape variety.

Blanc de Blancs (Fr). White wines (still and sparkling) made with white grapes only.

Blanc de Cabernet Sauvignon (USA). A Californian white wine made from the Cabernet sauvignon grape (a Blanc de noir). Must have at least 51% of named grape.

Blanc de la Bri (S.Afr). A white wine made from 40% Sauvignon blanc and 60% Sémillon grapes by the La Bri vineyard.

Blanc de Marbonne (S.Afr). A dry Chenin blanc-based wine produced by the Koopmanskloof Estate in Stellenbosch.

Blanc de Morgex (It). A white grape variety grown in the Valle d'Aosta.

B

Blanc de Morgex (It). D.O.C. white wine from the Valle d'Aosta. Made from the Blanc de morgex grape.

Blanc de Noir (S.Afr). A dry, bottle-fermented, sparkling rosé wine from the KWV. Made from Cabernet and Pinotage grapes.

Blanc de Noir (Fr). A white wine made with black or red grapes. e.g. Champagne.

Blanc de Pinot Noir (USA). A Californian white wine made from the Pinot noir grape (a Blanc de noir). Must have at least 51% of the named grape.

Blanc de Savoie (Fr). A white grape variety of south eastern France.

Blanc de Troynes (Fr). A lesser name for the Aligoté grape.

Blanc d'Euvézin (Fr). A dry white wine produced in the Côtes de Toul in the Lorraine region, north-eastern France.

Blanc Doux (Fr). An alternative name for the Sémillon grape.

Blanc Foussy (Fr). Wine producer based in Touraine, Loire. Noted for Vin Vif de Touraine and Blanc Foussy (a sparkling méthode champenoise from the Chenin blanc grape).

Blanc Fumé (Fr). White grape variety also known as the Sauvignon. Used in the Pouilly region of the Loire. Lit – 'White smoke'.

Blanc Fumé (S.Afr). A superb dry white wine from the Sauvignon blanc grape produced by the Le Bonheur estate in Stellenbosch.

Blanc Fumé de Pouilly (Fr). An A.C. dry white wine from the Sauvignon grape in the Pouilly-sur-Loire, Central Vineyards, Loire.

Blanche Cocktail (Cktl). ⅓ measure Cointreau, ⅓ measure Anisette, ⅓ measure white Curaçao. Shake over ice, strain into a cocktail glass.

Blanche de Louvain (Bel). A white Wheat beer.

Blanche Feuille (Fr). An alternative name for the Pinot meunier.

Blanches-Fleurs (Les) (Fr). A Premier Cru vineyard [part] in the A.C. commune of Beaune, Burgundy. 1.16 ha.

Blanchots (Fr). An A.C. Grand Cru of Chablis, Burgundy. Produces supple, fragrant wines which are often quite heady.

Blanck (Marcel) (Fr). An Alsace négociant-éleveur based in Kientzheim.

Blanck (Paul et Fils) (Fr). An Alsace wine producer. Address = Domaine des Comtes de Lupfen, 32, Grand-Rue, BP.1, 68240 Kientzheim.

Blanco (Sp). White.

Blanco Abbocado (Sp). A medium-sweet white wine from Alella, Cataluña.

Blanco Añada (Sp). A full-bodied, dry white wine produced by Mont-Marcal in the Penedés region.

Blanco Reciente (Sp). A white wine from 100% Viura grapes produced by the Bodegas Olarra, S.A.

Blanco Selecto (Sp). A brand-label used by the Bodegas Bosch-Guell in the Penedés region.

Blanc Ramé (Fr). White grape variety used in the making of Cognac.

Blanc Sur Lie (Fr). 'Off the lees'. See Muscadet.

Bland (Eng). A tasting term that denotes a characterless wine.

Blando (Sp). A term used to describe a soft Sherry.

Blandy Brothers (Mad). A company that produces Duke of Sussex Sercial, Duke of Cambridge Verdelho, Duke of Cumberland Bual, Duke of Clarence Malmsey. All Madeira wines.

Blaner (Eng) (slang). For Blanquette de Limoux.

Blankenhornsberg (Ger). See Ihringen, Baden.

Blanket Pressure (Eng). Low pressure Carbon-dioxide (CO_2) applied to beer casks to prevent contact with the air.

Blanquefort (Fr). A commune of the A.C. Haut-Médoc, north-eastern Bordeaux.

Blanquette (Fr). An alternative local name for the white Colombard grape variety in the Dauphiné region. Also known as the Bon blanc and Piedtendre.

Blanquette de Limoux (Fr). An A.C. sparkling wine of the Languedoc. Made by the méthode champenoise from white Mauzac, Chardonnay and Chenin blanc grapes.

Blanquirroja (Sp). The alternative name for the Blanca-Roja white grape variety. Also known as the Malvasia and Tobía.

Blansingen (Ger). Village. (Anb) = Baden. (Ber) = Markgräflerland. (Gro) = Vogtei Rötteln. (Vin) = Wolfer.

Blanzac (Comte de) (Fr). A Champagne producer based in Epernay.

Blarney Stone (Cktl). ⅓ measure Irish whiskey, ⅓ measure green Curaçao, ⅓ measure dry Vermouth, 3 dashes Orange bitters. Shake with ice, strain into a cocktail glass.

Blarney Stone Cocktail (Cktl). 1 measure Irish whiskey, 2 dashes Pernod, 2 dashes Cointreau, 1 dash Maraschino, 1 dash Angostura. Shake over ice, strain into a cocktail glass. Add an olive and a twist of orange peel.

Blason de France Rosé (Fr). A non-vintage rosé Champagne produced by Perrier-Jouët.

Blason d'Or (Fr). A 15 year old Cognac produced by Château de la Grange.

Blason Fine Champagne (Fr). A V.S.O.P. 10 year old Cognac produced by Gilles Cosson.

Blasson Timberlay (Fr). Oak-aged, red and white Bordeaux wines produced by Robert Giraud at Saint-André-de-Culzac to celebrate the anniversary of Château Timberlay.

Blassfarbig (Ger). A term used to describe a Schillerwein that is pale pink in colour.

Blatina (Yug). A red grape variety. Produces a wine of the same name in Mostar.

Blatnà Brewery (Czec). A brewery based in Blatnà in western Czec. Founded in 1896. Produces fine light beers.

Blattenberg (Ger). Vineyard. (Anb) = Mosel-Saar-Ruwer. (Ber) = Bernkastel. (Gro) = Sankt Michael. (Vil) = Mehring.

Blau Arbst (Ger). A variety of the Blauburgunder grape grown in the Baden region. Used in the production of Affenthaler.

Blauburgunder (Aus). An alternative name for the Pinot noir.

Blauer Burgunder (Aus) (Ger). See Blauburgunder.

Blauer Malvasier (Aus). An alternative name for the Trollinger grape.

Blauer Portugieser (Aus). (Ger). A red grape variety. See Portugieser.

Blauer Spätburgunder (Ger). A red grape variety. Also known as the Pinot noir.

Blauer Trollinger (Ger). See Trollinger.

Blauer Wildbacher (Aus). A red grape variety only planted in Styria. Produces Krätzer or Schilder wines.

Blaue Zweigelt Rebe (Aus). A dry red wine, high in alcohol (11½–12% alc. by vol) from the Mailberg vineyards in the Weinvertal. Owned by the Order of Malta and administered by the Lenz Moser Co.

Blaufraenkischer (Aus). A red grape variety grown in Burgenland. Also known as the Gamay noir à jus blanc in France.

Blaufränkischer (Aus). An alternative spelling of Blaufraenkischer.

Blaulack (Ger). A Kabinett wine from the Herrgottströpfchen range of wines from Jakob Gerhardt.

Blaurock (Switz). A noted wine produced in Stein-am-Rhein.

Blaxland (Gregory) (Austr). The first vine-grower in Australia to export wine to London, England.

Blayais (Fr). The name given to the wines of the Côtes de Blaye district in north-eastern Bordeaux.

Blaye (Fr). A commune in the A.C. Côtes de Blaye in north-east Bordeaux.

Blaye (Fr). A district within Bordeaux on right bank of river Gironde. See Côtes de Blaye.

Blaye-Plassac (Fr). A commune in the A.C. Côtes de Blaye in north-east Bordeaux.

Blayney Vineyards (Ch.Isles). Planted 1972. Address = St. Mary, Jersey, Channel Islands. 2 ha. Grape varieties – Müller-Thurgau, Reichensteiner and Huxelrube. Wines sold under 'Clos de la Mare' label.

Blayney Wines (Eng). The trading name used by James Bell and Co. for their Off-Licences.

Blazquez (Sp). A Sherry bodega based at Jerez. Noted for its Carta Blanca and Carta Oro sherries. Also produces Felipe II and Toison de Oro brandies.

Bleasdale Winery (Austr). A family winery at Langhorne Creek and Clare-Watervale, Southern Vales.

Bleeding Heart (Cktl). In a liqueur glass pour in order ½ measure Advocaat and ½ measure Cherry brandy. The Cherry brandy will pursue a vein-like course. Hence the name.

Bleichert (Ger). A word used for rosé wines. Denotes a pale rosé wine.

Bleichheim (Ger). Village. (Anb) = Baden. (Ber) = Breisgau. (Gro) = Burg Lichteneck. (Vin) = Kaiserberg.

Bleidenberg (Ger). Vineyard. (Anb) = Mosel-Saar-Ruwer. (Ber) = Zell/Mosel. (Gro) = Weinhex. (Vil) = Alken.

Blend (Eng). Mixing together. e.g. wines in assemblage, drinks, fruit and ice in cocktails.

Blended Bourbon (USA). A mixture of Bourbon whiskey with a straight Whiskey or neutral spirit.

Blended Comfort (Cktl). Blend together 2 fl.ozs. Bourbon whiskey, 1 fl.oz. Southern Comfort, 1 fl.oz. orange juice, juice ½ lemon, 2 dashes French vermouth, ½ a fresh peach and a small scoop of crushed ice. Strain over ice into a highball glass decorated with a slice of peach and orange.

Blended Light Whiskey (USA). A light Whiskey which is mixed with less than 20% of straight whiskey on a Proof gallon (USA) basis.

Blended Straight Whiskey (USA). A mixture of two or more Straight whiskies.

Blended Whiskey (USA). An inexpensive whiskey being a blend of Straight whiskey and Neutral spirits. It is lighter in character and is especially useful as a cocktail ingredient.

Blender (Cktl). A machine with rotating blades that mixes and blends ingredients for cocktails. Mainly fruit cocktails.

Blender (Eng). A person who uses his nose to judge the qualities of the wines or spirits he uses in his final product.

Blending (Eng). The mixing together of different wines or spirits to produce a final product of best quality. See Assemblage.

Blending (Eng). The mixing of more than one type of green coffee bean or grades of roasted beans to obtain a particular flavour.

Blending (Eng). The mixing of teas of different grades and countries to obtain a standard taste.

Blending Materials (USA). Permitted materials such as Sherry, Peach juice, Prune juice etc. added to Whiskey up to 2½% by volume.

Blend 37 (Eng). The brand-name of a dark, continental instant coffee produced by the Nestlé Co.

Blenheim (Cktl). ½ measure Vodka, ¼ measure Tia Maria, ¼ measure fresh orange juice. Shake over ice, strain into cocktail glass.

Blenheimer (N.Z.). The brand-name used by Montana Wines for a dry white wine.

Blenheim Vineyards (N.Z.). Noted vineyards and a winery owned by Montana Wines.

Blénod-les-Toul (Fr). A commune in the Côtes de Toul, Lorraine region, north-eastern France. Produces Vins gris.

Blenton Cocktail (Cktl). ¼ gill Plymouth gin, ¼ gill French vermouth, dash Angostura. Stir over ice, strain into a cocktail glass. Also known as the Naval Cocktail.

Bleu-Do-It (Cktl). ½ fl.oz. Vodka, ½ fl.oz. Gin, ½ fl.oz. Tequila. ½ fl.oz. blue Curaçao, 1 fl.oz. lemon juice, dash egg white. Shake over ice, strain into an ice-filled highball glass. Top with a splash of soda.

Blezards Bitter (Eng). A cask conditioned Bitter 1039 O.G. brewed by the New Fermor Arms, a home-brew public house in Lancashire.

Bligny (Fr). A Cru Champagne village in the Canton de Ville-en-Tardenois. District = Reims.

Blind Drunk (Eng). A term used to describe a person whose vision is blurred through intoxication.

Extremely intoxicated.

Blind Tasting (Eng). A method of testing wines without an identification label so as not to be guided by the fame of the label. Does not mean with the eyes covered.

Blitz-Weinhard Brewery (USA). Producers of America's strongest beer, The 'Olde English 800' 7½% alc. by vol. Also a Lager 'Henry Weinhard's Private Reserve'. Address = Portland, Oregon.

Bliz's Royal Rickey (Cktl). Into a tumbler place 2 ice cubes, add juice of ½ a lime, juice of ¼ lemon, 1 teaspoon raspberry syrup, ½ gill French vermouth, ¼ gill Gin. Top up with ginger ale, stir, top with fruit and serve with spoon.

Block and Fall (Cktl). ⅓ measure Cointreau, ⅓ measure Apricot brandy, ⅙ measure Anisette, ⅙ measure Applejack brandy. Stir over ice, strain into a cocktail glass.

Blockesberg (Hun). A red table wine from Alderberg.

Bloemdal Wines (S.Afr). See Jacobsdal Co-operative.

Blonde (It). A sweet white vermouth also known as Bianco. Flavoured with vanilla and cinnamon.

Blondeau (Fr). A cuvée of the vineyards of En Champans, En l'Ormeau, Ronceret and Taille-Pieds in A.C. Volnay, Côte de Beaune, Burgundy. Owned by the Hospices de Beaune.

Blonde Dubonnet Thirst Quencher (Cktl). In a highball glass place 2 measures of Dubonnet blonde and top with chilled ginger ale. Dress with a lemon peel spiral.

Blondy Cocktail (Cktl). ½ measure Anisette, ½ measure Cointreau. Shake over ice, strain into a cocktail glass.

Blood (Eng). Used as a fining agent. See Ox blood. Is an albuminous protein which coagulates in the wine and as it sinks takes any fine particles down with it. Also helps to reduce the astringency and acidity of the wine.

Blood Alcohol (Eng). The alcohol in the blood produced by the body in the action of the gastric juices on the sugars and starches consumed. On average .003% alc. by vol. This is raised with the consumption of alcoholic beverages.

Blood Alcohol Level (Eng). The level of alcohol that has been absorbed by the body into the blood stream. Measured by many methods.

Blood and Sand (Cktl). ½ measure Scotch whisky, ½ measure sweet Vermouth, ½ measure Cherry brandy, ½ measure orange juice. Shake over ice, strain into a cocktail glass.

Blood Bronx (Cktl). ½ measure Gin, ½ measure French vermouth, juice of ¼ blood orange. Shake over ice, strain into a cocktail glass.

Bloodhound (Cktl). ⅙ gill dry Gin, ⅙ gill French vermouth, ⅙ gill Italian vermouth, ½ teaspoon sugar, 6 raspberries. Shake well over ice, strain into a cocktail glass.

Bloodiest Mary (Cktl). ⅓ Nicholoff Red Vodka, ⅔ tomato juice, juice of ½ lemon, 2 dashes Angostura. Shake over ice, strain into a highball glass. Add salt and pepper if required.

Bloodshot (Cktl). 1 fl.oz. Vodka, 2 fl.ozs. tomato juice, 2 fl.ozs. Beef bouillon, dash lemon juice, 2 dashes Worcester sauce, celery salt. Shake over ice, strain into a cocktail glass.

Bloody Bull Cocktail (Cktl). 1 fl.oz. Tequila, 2 fl.ozs. tomato juice, 2 fl.ozs. cold beef bouillon, dash lemon juice. Stir over ice in an old-fashioned glass. Dress with celery leaves and lemon slice.

Bloody Bullshot (Cktl). A combination of 2 cocktails – Bloody Mary and Bullshot.

Bloody Caesar (Cktl). 4 fl.ozs Clamato juice, 1 fl.oz. Vodka, dash lemon juice, 2 dashes Worcester sauce. Shake over ice, strain into a cocktail glass.

Bloody Maria (Cktl). As for a Bloody Mary but using Tequila in place of Vodka.

Bloody Marie (Cktl). ⅔ measure Vodka, ⅓ measure Blackberry brandy. Shake over ice, strain into a cocktail glass.

Bloody Mary (Cktl). 1 measure Vodka, 4 measures tomato juice, dash lemon juice, dash Worcester sauce, salt, pepper and celery salt. Place in old-fashioned glass, stir with stick of celery. Add ice if required.

Bloom (Eng). A term used to describe the wine yeasts that settle on the grape skins together with wild yeasts and acetobacters. Used in a natural fermentation or destroyed with SO_2 in a controlled fermentation.

Blossom (Cktl). ½ measure Bacardi White Label, ½ measure orange juice, dash Grenadine. Shake over ice, strain into a cocktail glass.

Blotto (Eng) (slang). Denotes a person who is unconscious (or semi-conscious) through alcohol. Very drunk.

Blowsy (Eng). A term used to describe an overblown, exaggerated, fruity bouquet on some wines.

Blücherhöhe (Ger). Vineyard. (Anb) =

Rheinpfalz. (Ber) = Südliche Weinstrasse. (Gro) = Schloss Ludwigshöhe. (Vil) = Edenkoben.

Blücherpfad (Ger). Vineyard. (Anb) = Rheinhessen. (Ber) = Wonnegau. (Gro) = Burg Rodenstein. (Vil) = Ober-Flörsheim.

Blüchertal (Ger). Vineyard. (Anb) = Mittelrhein. (Ber) = Rheinburgengau. (Gro) = Herrenberg. (Vil) = Kaub.

Blue (Can). The name used for a top Lager brewed by Labatt Brewery.

Blue (Eng). The name used for Ruddles Breweries' Rutland Bitter 1032 O.G.

Blue Anchor (Eng). A public house which brews its own beer. Situated in Coinagehall Street, Helston, Cornwall, is noted for its cask conditioned ales. Mild 1040 O.G. Medium 1050 O.G. BB 1053 O.G. Special 1066 O.G. Extra Special 1070 O.G. and Spingo.

Blueberry Tea (Cktl). In a heatproof glass place ⅛ gill Amaretto. Top with freshly brewed Ceylon tea, stir, add ⅛ gill Grand Marnier.

Blue Bird Cocktail (Cktl). ¾ measure Gin, ¼ measure Cointreau, dash Orange bitters. Stir over ice, strain into a cocktail glass. Add cherry and lemon peel twist.

Blue Blazer (Cktl). 2 fl.ozs. Scotch whisky (heated), 2 fl.ozs. boiling water, barspoon powdered sugar. Place Whisky in a silver 1 gill jigger, and the water into another silver 1 gill jigger. Ignite the whisky and mix both ingredients by pouring from one measure to the other. Sweeten and serve in an old-fashioned glass.

Blue Blazer Coffee (Eng). Stir 2 sugar cubes into a cup of hot, strong, black, freshly brewed coffee. Top with grated orange zest, then pour ⅕ gill of heated and ignited Irish whiskey on top.

Blue Bottle (Cktl). ½ measure Gin, ¼ measure blue Curaçao, ¼ measure Passion fruit liqueur. Stir over ice, strain into a cocktail glass.

Blue Bottle (Ger). Flute-shaped bottle made with blue glass used in the nineteenth century. Used now by some wine shippers as a gimmick.

Blue Boy (Gre). The name given to a medium-sweet, white table wine made by Tsantali.

Blue Curaçao (Fr). A liqueur made from Curaçao and natural blue colouring. Used mainly for cocktails.

Blue Danube (Aus). A dry, white wine produced by Lenz Moser from a blend of Gewürztraminer and Wälschriesling grapes.

Blue Danube (Cktl). ¼ measure blue Curaçao, ¾ measure dry Gin, dash

Absinthe. Shake over ice, strain into a cocktail glass.

Blue Danube (Eng). The brand-name of a Viennese coffee produced by the Walter Williams Co.

Blue Devil (Cktl). 1 measure Gin, ½ measure blue Curaçao, 2 dashes lemon juice, 2 dashes lime cordial. Stir well over ice, strain into cocktail glass with crushed ice. Serve with straws.

Blue Devil Cocktail (Cktl). 1 measure Gin, juice ¼ lemon, juice ¼ lime, ¼ measure Maraschino, 2 dashes Crème Yvette. Shake over ice, strain into a cocktail glass.

Blue Fining (Eng). Potassium Ferrocyanide. Used to clear excess metallic salts from the wine. If these salts were left they would tend to oxidise with air leaving the wine cloudy and bitter tasting. See Ferric Casse. (Ger) = Möslinger fining. Is poisonous if used in excess.

Blue Hanger (Scot). A De Luxe blended Scotch whisky produced by Berry Brothers and Rudd. 40% alc. by vol.

Blue Hawaiian (Cktl). ½ fl.oz. blue Curaçao, 1 fl.oz. coconut cream, 1 fl.oz. white Rum, 2 fl.ozs. pineapple juice, 1 scoop crushed ice. Blend, pour into a 5 oz. wine goblet.

Blue Jacket (Cktl). ¼ measure blue Curaçao, ½ measure Gin, ¼ measure Orange bitters. Stir over ice, strain into a cocktail glass.

Blue Label (Euro). A keg Ale brewed by the Farsons Brewery in Malta.

Blue Label (Eng). A bottled beer brewed by the Harveys Brewery, Sussex. 1033 O.G.

Blue Label (Eng). A bottled beer brewed by Timothy Taylor Brewery, West Yorkshire. 1043 O.G.

Blue Lady (Cktl). ½ measure blue Curaçao, ¼ measure Gin, ¼ measure fresh orange juice, dash egg white. Shake over ice, strain into a cocktail glass.

Blue Lagoon (Cktl). ½ fl.oz. blue Curaçao, ½ fl.oz. Vodka, lemonade. Pour vodka and Curaçao over ice in a highball glass. Top up with ice-cold lemonade.

Blue Maguey (Mex). Cactus from which Mezcal is made. Also known as the Mezcal Azul.

Blue Margarita (Cktl). ⅖ measure Tequila, ⅕ measure blue Curaçao, ⅖ measure lime juice. Shake over ice, strain into a salt-rimmed cocktail glass.

Blue Mezcal (Mex). The name for the Agave (cactus) plant.

Blue Monday (Cktl). ¾ measure Vodka, ¼ measure blue Curaçao. Stir over ice, strain into cocktail glass.

Blue Moon (Cktl). ¼ measure Crème Yvette, ½ measure Gin, ¼ measure lemon juice. Shake over ice, strain into a cocktail glass.

Blue Moon Cocktail (Cktl). ½ measure dry Gin, ½ measure Parfait Amour. Shake over ice, strain into a cocktail glass.

Blue Mountain Coffee (W.Ind). The finest of all the Jamaican coffees. An Arabica strain. The beans are a dull blue and give a rich full-bodied and full nutty flavour.

Blue Mountain Vineyard (USA). A vineyard based in western Texas (south of Fort Dans). 16 ha. Produces hybrid wines.

Blue Negligée (Cktl). ⅓ measure Green Chartreuse, ⅓ measure Parfait Amour, ⅓ measure Ouzo. Stir over ice, strain into a cocktail glass. Add a cherry.

Blue Nile Brewery (Afr). A brewery based in Kharthoum, Sudan. Owned by the State of Sudan, brews Carmel Beer 1044 O.G.

Blue Nun (Ger). Top selling Liebfraumilch Qba. from H. Sichel and Sons. A sparkling version is also available.

Blue Nun Gold (Ger). A Qmp. version of Blue Nun.

Blue Riband (Cktl). ⅕ measure blue Curaçao, ⅖ measure white Curaçao, ⅖ measure Gin. Stir over ice, strain into a cocktail glass.

Blue Ribbon (USA). A sweetish beer brewed by the Pabst Brewery, Newark, Peoria, Milwaukee.

Blue Ruin (USA) (slang). For Gin.

Blue Sea (Cktl). ¾ measure Bacardi White Label Rum, ½ measure blue Curaçao, 1 egg white, dash lemon juice, dash Pernod. Shake over ice, strain into a highball glass. Top with lemonade. Dress with sprig of mint and lemon slice.

Blue Seal (S.Am). The brand-name of Demerara rum produced in Guyana by the Guyana Distilleries.

Blue Stalk (Hun). Popular name given to the Badacsonyi Kéknyelü of the Balatòn region.

Blue Star (Cktl). ⅓ measure blue Curaçao, ⅓ measure Gin, ⅙ measure Lillet, ⅙ measure orange juice. Shake over ice, strain into a cocktail glass.

Blue Star (Eng). The logo of the Newcastle Brewery, Newcastle.

Blue Stripe White Burgundy Supreme (Austr). A full-bodied, rich and fruity white wine made with the Chardonnay grape by the Houghton Vineyard, Western Australia.

Blue Tasting Glass (Fr). A glass used by professional Cognac tasters. Is coloured blue so that they do not influence their judgement by looking at the colour.

Blue Train Special (Cktl). 1 measure Brandy, 1 measure pineapple syrup. Shake over ice, strain into a highball glass. Top with iced, dry Champagne.

Blue Triangle Ale (Eng). A top bottled Pale ale 1041 O.G. from Bass.

Blümchen (Ger). Vineyard. (Anb) = Mosel-Saar-Ruwer. (Ber) = Obermosel. (Gro) = Gipfel. (Vil) = Nittel.

Blume (Ger). Bouquet, aroma.

Blume (Ger). Vineyard. (Anb) = Ahr. (Ber) = Walporzheim/Ahrtal. (Gro) = Klosterberg. (Vil) = Rech.

Blume (Ger). Vineyard. (Anb) = Rheinhessen. (Ber) = Nierstein. (Gro) = Domherr. (Vil) = Stadecken-Elsheim.

Blumig (Ger). Denotes a wine with a good bouquet.

Blushing Barmaid (Cktl). 1 fl.oz. Campari, 1 fl.oz. Amaretto di Saronno, dash egg white. Shake together over ice, strain into large ice-filled goblet. Stir in bitter lemon. Decorate with apricot wedge

Blushing Bride (Cktl). ¼ measure Vodka, ¼ measure Cherry brandy, ¼ measure orange Curaçao, dash Orange bitters, dash egg white. Shake well over ice, strain into a cocktail glass.

Blushing Princess (Eng). A brand-name Cider cocktail from Symonds of Hereford. Contains cider, gin and damson wine.

Blush Wines (USA). A term used for rosé wines with a light pink colour.

Blythe Vineyards (USA). A small winery based in La Plata, Maryland. Produces hybrid wines.

B.N.I.A. (Fr) (abbr). Bureau National Interprofessionnel d'Armagnac.

B.N.I.C. (Fr) (abbr). Bureau National Interprofessionnel du Cognac.

B.N.I.C.E. (Fr) (abbr). Bureau National Interprofessionnel des Calvados et de-Vie-de-Cidre-et-de-Poire.

B.N.M.W.A. (Eng) (abbr). British National Mineral Waters Association.

Boag Brewery (Austr). A brewery based in Launceston.

Boal (Mad). A deep, golden-coloured, sweet, full-bodied Madeira. Has a fine balance of sugar, acid and tannin with a somewhat smoky taste. Also spelt Bual. Made from the Boal grape.

Boal di Madeira (USA). A white grape variety used in the production of dessert wines in California.

Boal do Porto Santo (Mad). A white grape variety used in the production of Madeira wine.

Boardroom Port (Port). A fine, Tawny Port from the Dow Port Shipping Co.

Boa Vista (Port). Port wine estate in the Alto Douro. Owned by Offley. See Offley Forrester Boa Vista.

B.O.B. (Eng) (abbr). Buyer's Own Brand. Champagne sold under a retailer's own brand name.

Bobadilla (Sp). The brand-name for '103' brandy made in Andalusia and 'Gran Capitán'. Also major Sherry producers, producing Alcazar Amontillado, Banico Fino, Capitan Oloroso, La Merced and Sadana.

Bobal (Sp). A black grape variety grown in south-eastern Spain. Is also known as the Tinto de requena and Requeno.

Bobal Blanco (Sp). An alternative name for the Tortosi grape.

Bobbin-Knopped Glass (Eng). An eighteenth-century glass whose stem is a series of balls of glass on a round flat base, with a trumpet bowl.

Bobby Ales (Ch.Isles). The brand-name for beers brewed by Randalls Brewery St. Peter Port, Guernsey.

Bobby Burns (Cktl). 1½ measures Scotch whisky, ½ measure sweet Vermouth, 2 dashes Bénédictine. Shake over ice, strain into a cocktail glass.

Bobby Burns Cocktail (Cktl). 1 measure Malt whisky placed into a liqueur glass. Top with double cream.

Bobby Mild (Ch.Isles). A Mild ale brewed by Randalls Brewery, St. Peter Port, Guernsey. 1036 O.G.

Bobenheim am Berg (Ger). Village. (Anb) = Rheinpfalz. (Ber) = Mittelhaardt-Deutsche Weinstrasse. (Gro) = Feuerberg. (Vins) = Kieselberg, Ohligpfad.

Boberg (S.Afr). A wine district. Produces Sherry-type wines noted for their natural Flor that produces good Finos.

Böbingen (Ger). Village. (Anb) = Rheinpfalz. (Ber) = Südliche Weinstrasse. (Gro) = Trappenberg. (Vin) = Ortelberg.

Boca (It). D.O.C. red wine from the Piemonte region. Produced from the Nebbiolo 45–70%, Vespolina 20–40% and Bonarda novarese 20%. Aged 3 years (2 years in chestnut/oak casks). Dry wine with an aftertaste of Pomegranates.

Boca Chica Carioca (W.Ind). A brand of Rum produced in Puerto Rico for export.

Bocal (Fr). Jar, bottle.

Boccale (It). Mug, jar.

Bocchino (It). A brand-name of a Grappa.

Boccie Ball (Cktl). 2 ozs. Amaretto di Saronno, 2 ozs. orange juice. Mix in a highball glass, add ice and top up with

B

soda.

Böchingen (Ger). Village. (Anb) = Rheinpfalz. (Ber) = Südliche Weinstrasse. (Gro) = Bischofskreuz. (Vin) = Rosenkranz.

Bock (Fr). A beer tankard made of glass which holds about ½ a pint (285 mls). Used for drinking draught beer.

Bock (Fr). A glass of beer.

Bock (Ger). A special brew of heavy, dark and sweetened beer. 6.25% alc. by vol. See Einbeck. Belgian Bock is less alcoholic. Lit – 'Buck beer'.

Bock Beer Day (Ger). A day when winter brews of Bock beers are consumed. When these beers are ready for drinking it is supposed to herald the arrival of Spring.

Bockbieres (Ger). Denotes beers with an original gravity of 16–18%.

Bockel (Fr). An Alsace wine producer. Address = 2, Rue de la Montagne, BP. 53, 67140 Mittelbergheim.

Bockenau (Ger). Village. (Anb) = Nahe. (Ber) = Schloss Böckelheim. (Gro) = Rosengarten. (Vins) = Geisberg, Im Felsneck, Im Neuberg, Stromberg.

Bockenheim (Ger). Village. (Anb) = Rheinpfalz. (Ber) = Mittelhaardt-Deutsche Weinstrasse. (Gro) = Grafenstück. (Vins) = Burggarten, Goldgrube, Hassmannsberg, Heiligenkirche, Klosterschaffnerei, Schlossberg, Sonnenberg, Vogelsang.

Bockrus (Nor) (slang). A hangover.

Booksbeeren (Euro). An East European name for Blackcurrant Liqueur.

Bocksberg (Ger). Vineyard. (Anb) = Nahe. (Ber) = Schloss Böckelheim. (Gro) = Paradiesgarten. (Vil) = Feïlbingert.

Bocksberg (Lux). A vineyard site in the village of Wasserbillig.

Bocksbeutel (Ger). An attractively shaped bottle for holding Franconian Steinwein. Now used extensively in Portugal, South Africa and Chile. See Boxbeutel.

Bocksbeutelstrasse (Ger). The Franken wine route.

Böckser (Aus). A wine with a foul smell or taste. See also Seniffeln.

Bockshaut (Ger). Vineyard. (Anb) = Rheinhessen. (Ber) = Bingen. (Gro) = Kurfürstenstück. (Vil) = Gau-Bickelheim.

Bockshoden (Ger). An erroneous varietal name for the red Trollinger grape. Lit – 'Male goat's testicles'.

Bockstein (Ger). Vineyard. (Anb) = Mosel-Saar-Ruwer. (Ber) = Saar-Ruwer. (Gro) = Scharzberg. (Vil) = Ockfen.

Bockstein (Ger). Vineyard. (Anb) = Rheinhessen. (Ber) = Bingen. (Gro) = Kaiserpfalz. (Vil) = Gross-

Winternheim.

Bockstein (Ger). Vineyard. (Anb) = Rheinhessen. (Ber) = Nierstein. (Gro) = Domherr. (Vil) = Stadecken-Elsheim.

Bockwingert (Euro). A single Domaine in Liechtenstein which makes up approximately half the vineyard area in Vaduz the capital.

Bocoy (Sp). A large cask used in the north of Spain of approximately 600 litres. (132 Imp. gallons) in capacity.

Bodagfährtle (Ger). A term used to describe the taste of the red wines whose grapes are grown on shell limestone soil. e.g. in the Württemberg Anbaugebiet.

Böddiger (Ger). Village. (Anb) = Rheingau. (Ber) = Johannisberg. (Gro) = Landkreis Melsungen. (Vin) = Berg.

Boddington's Brewery (Eng). An independent brewery in Manchester. Brews cask conditioned Mild 1033 O.G. and Bitter 1035 O.G.

Bodega (Port). A wine shop. Usually of a poor grade, selling cheap table wine.

Bodega (Sp). A Spanish winery, warehouse for wine storage or bar.

Bodega (Sp). A wine shop, shop selling wine.

Bodega Co-op. del Campo Nuestra Señora de Manjavacas (Sp). Wine-producers based in La Mancha. Labels include – Zarragon.

Bodega Co-op. del Valle de Ocón (Sp). A major co-operative based in the Rioja region.

Bodega Co-op. de Ribeiro (Sp). The largest co-operative in Galicia. Produces seven types of wine – Granel, Lar, Pazo (red, rosé and white) and Xeito (rosé and white).

Bodega Co-op. la Bastida (Sp). A large wine co-operative based in Rioja.

Bodega Co-op. Nuestra Señora de la Anunciación (Sp). A wine co-operative based in Rioja.

Bodega Co-op. Nuestra Señora de Valvanera de Cuzcurrita, Tirjo y Sajazarra (Sp). A major wine co-operative based in Rioja.

Bodega Co-op. Nuestra Señora de Vico (Sp). A wine co-operative based in the Rioja region.

Bodega Co-op. San Isidro (Sp). A major wine co-operative based in the Rioja region.

Bodega Co-op. San Miguel (Sp). A wine co-operative based in the Rioja region.

Bodega Co-op. San Pedro Apóstol (Sp). A major wine co-operative based in the Rioja region.

Bodega Co-op. Santa Daria (Sp). A wine co-operative based in the Rioja region.

Bodega Co-op. Sonsierra (Sp). A major

wine co-operative based in the Rioja region.

Bodega Co-op. Virgen de la Vega (Sp). A wine co-operative based in the Rioja region.

Bodegas Alavesas S.A. (Sp). Address = Carretera de Elciego, s/n Lauardia, Alva. Founded in 1972. Grape varieties – Tempranillo 80% and Viura 20%. Produces – Solar de Samaniego = red and white wine of Vintage, Reserva and Gran Reserva quality Rioja.

Bodegas Alvarez (Sp). A modern winery based in La Rueda. 100 ha. (also buys in grapes). Produces cask matured white wines under the Mantel label.

Bodegas Arias (Sp). A winery based in Nava del Rey, Valladolid region, north-western Spain.

Bodegas Ayuso (Sp). A winery based in La Mancha. Labels include – Mirlo and Viña Q.

Bodegas Bardón (Sp). A winery based in Corella, Ribera Baja. Produces – Don Luis, Togal and Zarums.

Bodegas Berberana S.A. (Sp). Address = Ctra. Eloego, s/n Cenicero, La Rioja. Alta region of Rioja. Grape varieties – Tempranillo 65%, Viura 20%, Garnacha, Mazuelo and Graciano 5% each. Produces red, rosé and white wines. 130 ha. See Carta de Plata, Carta de Oro and Preferido.

Bodegas Beronia S.A. (Sp). Address = Olauri Najera, La Rioja. Alta region of Rioja. Grape varieties – Tempranillo 85%, Viura, Garnacha and Mazuelo 15%. Produces red 90% and white 10% wines. 10 ha. See Berón.

Bodegas Bianchi (Arg). A wine producer at San Raphael. Owned by Seagram. Produces Cabernet wines under the labels of Don Valentin and Particular.

Bodegas Bilbainas S.A. (Sp). Address = Apartado 124, Particular del Norte 2, Bilbao 3. Alto region of Rioja, Grape varieties – Tempranillo, Garnacha, Viura and Malvasia. Produces red 60%, rosé 15%, white 25% wines. 250 ha. See Royal Carlton, Vendimia Especial (red and white), Viña Pomal and Viña Zaco.

Bodegas Bosch-Guell (Sp). A noted winery based in the Penedés region.

Bodegas Camacho (Sp). Producers of fine Montilla wines (Amontillado and Fino) in the Montilla-Moriles, south-eastern Spain under the Sombra label.

Bodegas Campillo (Sp). Address = Carretera de Logoño, s/n Oyon, Alava. Alavesa region of Rioja, Grape varieties – Tempranillo, Viura and Malvasia. 100 ha. in the Rioja Alavesa.

Bodegas Campo Blanco (Sp). Address = Avdo. Estación s/n Cenicero, Rioja. Do not own vineyards. 100% red wines bought in from Rioja Alta and Alavesa.

Bodegas Campo Viejo (Sp). Address = c/Gustavo Adolfo Bécquer, 3 Logroño, La Rioja. Alavesa region of Rioja. Grape varieties – Tempranillo 80%, Garnacha 15%, Mazuelo 5%. 350 ha. (275 ha. in the Rioja Alta and Rioja Baja). Produces Marqués de Villamanga.

Bodegas Cantabria (Sp). A winery based in Laguardia, Rioja Alavesa.

Bodegas Carlos Serres S.A. (Sp). Address = P.O. Box 4, Haro, La Rioja. Alta region of Rioja, own no vineyards. Produce red 70%, rosé 10% and white 20% wines. See Carlomango and Tercher Ano.

Bodegas Cenalsa-Pamplona (Sp). A new winery based in Navarra. Owned by the shareholders and Department of Agriculture in Navarra. Promotes the image of Navarra wines. Labels – Agramont and Campo Nuevo.

Bodegas Cooperativas el Barco (Sp). Wine co-operative in Galicia in north-western Spain. Produces Valdeorras Tinto.

Bodegas Cooperativas Sta. María la Real (Sp). A noted co-operative based in Nájera in the Rioja Alta.

Bodegas Cooperativa Vinícola de Labastida (Sp). A wine co-operative based in Labastida, Rioja Alavesa.

Bodegas Corral S.A. (Sp). Address = D. Florencio Corral Daroca, Presidente Ctra, Logroño, KM 10 – Navarrete, La Rioja. Alta region of Rioja, Grape varieties – Tempranillo, Garnacha, Viura and Malvasia. Produces red 90%, rosé 5% and white 5% wines under the Don Jacoba label. 40 ha. in the Rioja Alta.

Bodegas Crillon (Arg). A winery owned by Seagram that produces sparkling wines by the Tank method.

Bodegas de Crianza (Sp). Bodegas that are registered with the Consejo Regulador in Rioja that must age their wines in oak.

Bodegas de la Torre y Lapuerta (Sp). A winery based in Alfaro, La Rioja. Produces red and white wines under the Campo Burgo label.

Bodegas del Delfin (Mex). A winery based in Parras de la Fuente, Coahuila.

Bodegas Delicia (Sp). A noted winery based in Ollauri, Rioja Alta.

Bodegas del Romerol (Sp). A winery based in Fuenmayor, Logroño. Produces red and white wines.

Bodegas del Rosario (Mex). A winery

based in Parras de la Fuente, Coahuila.

Bodegas del Vesubio (Mex). A winery based at Parras de la Fuente, Coahuila.

Bodegas de Monte Casino (Mex). A winery based in Saltillo, Coahuila.

Bodegas de Perote (Mex). A winery based in Parras de la Fuente, Coahuila.

Bodegas de San Lorenzo (Mex). Casa Madero's winery based in Parras de la Fuente, Coahuila.

Bodegas de Santo Tomàs (Mex). A large winery founded in 1888. Based at Ensenda.

Bodegas de San Ygnacio (Mex). A winery based in Saltillo, Coahuila.

Bodegas Domecq S.A. (Sp). Address = Carretera Villabuena, s/n Elciego, Alva. Alavesa region of Rioja, Grape varieties – Tempranillo and Viura. 320 ha. in the Rioja Alvasa. Produces Privilegio del Rey Sancho and Viña Eguia.

Bodegas Don Ramos (Sp). A Sherry producer based in Jerez de la Frontera. Noted for its Don Ramos (a fine Fino sherry).

Bodegas El Coto S.A. (Sp). Address = Oyón, Alava. Alavesa region of Rioja, Grape varieties – Tempranillo 85% and Viura 15%. 123 ha. Produces Cotode Imaz.

Bodegas El Montecillo (Sp). Address = San Cristobal, 34 Fuenmayor, La Rioja. Alta region of Rioja. Owns no vineyards. Produces – red 85%, rosé 2.5% and white 12.5% wines. Cumbrero Viña Monty is their brand label.

Bodegas Familia Saviron (Sp). A noted winery based in La Mancha. Produces red and white wines.

Bodegas Faustino Martinez S.A. (Sp). Address = Carretera de Logroño, s/n Oyón, Alava. Alavesa region of Rioja, Grape varieties – Viura 10%, Tempranillo 80%, Mazuelo 5% and Graciano 5% wines. 350 ha.

Bodegas Federico Paternina (Sp). A large winery in Rioja. Address = Avenida Santo Domingo II, Haro, La Rioja. 480 ha. Produces a range of fine red, rosé and white wines.

Bodegas Felix Solis (Sp). A large winery based in Valdepeñas. Produces Valdoro (a cold fermented white wine), Viña Albali (an oak matured red wine) and a 100% Cencible red wine.

Bodegas Flichman (Arg). A winery based in Mendosa. Produces – Caballero de la Cepa (red and white) and sparkling wines. Grape varieties – Merlot and Syrah.

Bodegas Francisco Viguera (Sp). A winery based in Haro, Rioja Alta.

Bodegas Franco-Españolas S.A. (Sp).

Address = Cabo Noval, 2 Logroño, Rioja. 350 ha. Produces red 65%, rosé 10% and white 25% Part of the Rumasa Group. See Damante, Rioja Bordon and Viña Soledad.

Bodegas F. Rivero Ulecia (Sp). A noted winery based in Arnedo, Rioja. Produces Señorío de Prayla.

Bodegas García Carrión (Sp). A winery based in Jumilla. Produces – Chiquito, Covanegra, Don García, Fiesta, Puente Viejo and San Simón.

Bodegas Gómez Cruzado (Sp). A major wine co-operative based in Rioja.

Bodegas Gonzales Videla (Arg). A small winery that sells its wines under the Panquehua and Tromel labels.

Bodegas Goyenechea (Arg). A winery noted for its red Aberdeen Angus wine.

Bodegas Gracia (Sp). A winery based in the Montilla-Moriles region.

Bodegas Gurpegui (Sp). Address = Avda, Celso Muerza, 8 San Adrian, y Cuevas, 32/34/36, Haro. Baja and Alta regions of Rioja, Grape varieties – Tempranillo 40% and Viura 60%. Produces red 50%, rosé 30% and white 20%. 200 ha. See Viña Berceo.

Bodegas Internacionales (Sp). A winery that produces a range of Sherries under the Duke of Wellington label.

Bodegas Irache (Sp). A winery based in Estella, Navarra. Produces both Crianza and Reserva red wines.

Bodegas J. Freixedes (Sp). A winery based in Vilafranca del Penedés. Produces Viña Santa Marta range of red and white wines.

Bodegas José Palacios (Sp). Address = Apartado 1.152, Poligono de Cantabria, Logroño, La Rioja. Alta region of Rioja, Grape varieties – Tempranillo 40% and Garnacha 60%. Produces red, rosé and white wines. 350 ha. in a co-operative system in the Alta and Baja regions. See Eral, Herencia Remondo and Utero.

Bodegas Julián Chivite (Sp). A winery based in Navarra. Produces fine red, rosé and dry/sweet white wines.

Bodegas la Cuesta (Sp). See Cuesta.

Bodegas Lafuente (Sp). A winery based in Fuenmayor, Rioja Alta.

Bodegas Lagunilla S.A. (Sp). Address = Carretera de Victoria kms. 182/183, Fuenmayor, La Rioja. Alta region of Rioja. Owns no vineyards. Produces red 80%, rosé 14% and white 6% wines.

Bodegas Lan (Sp). See Bodegas Landalan.

Bodegas Landalan (Sp). Address = Paraje de Buicio, s/n Fuenmayor, Rioja. Alta region of Rioja, Grape varieties – Tempranillo, Mazuelo and Viura. 70 ha. Produces red, rosé and white wines under the Lancorta and Viña Lanciano labels. Also known as Bodegas Lan.

Bodegas la Rioja Alta (Sp). A winery based in the Rioja Alta. Produces – red, rosé and dry/sweet white wines.

Bodegas la Rural (Arg). A winery based at Coquimbito. Grape varieties – Riesling and Traminer.

Bodegas la Seca (Sp). A large winery based in León. Produces mainly red wines from the Prieto picudo grape.

Bodegas Latorre y Lapuerta (Sp). A winery based in Alfaro, Rioja Baja.

Bodegas Laturce (Sp). A large winery based in the Rioja Alta and Alavesa. Address = Logroño, La Rioja. 123 ha. Produces red wines.

Bodegas Lopez (Arg). A small winery noted for its Cabernet sauvignon wines.

Bodegas Lopez-Agos (Sp). Address = Carretera de Logroño s/n. Fuenmayor, La Rioja. Alta region of Rioja. 45 ha. Grape varieties – Tempranillo 190% and Viura 10%. Produces red 90%, rosé 5% and white 5% wines.

Bodegas los Curros (Sp). A winery based in Fuente del Sol and Rueda, Valladolid. See Queen Isabella.

Bodegas Magical (Sp). A Sherry producer based in Jerez de la Frontera. Labels include Cream Game Fair and Magical.

Bodegas Marqués de Cáceres (Sp). Address = Ctra. de Logroño s/n, Cenicero, La Rioja. Alta region of Rioja, Grape varieties – Tempranillo 80%, Mazuelo 5%, Graciano 3%, Garnacha 6% and Viura 6%.

Bodegas Marqués de Ciria (Sp). A winery based in the Rioja Alta. Address = Calle Gustavo Adolpho Becquer 3, Logroño, La Rioja. Produces red and white wines under the Marqués de Ciria label.

Bodegas Marqués del Puerto (Sp). A winery based in the Rioja Alta area. Address = Carretera de Logroño s/n, Fuenmayor, La Rioja. 40 ha. Produces a range of red, rosé and white wines including Señorio Agos.

Bodegas Marqués de Monistrol (Sp). A winery based in Catalonia. Owned by Martini and Rossi. Produces dry/sweet red and sparkling wines.

Bodegas Marqués de Murríeta (Sp). Address = Finca Ygay, Carretera de Zaragoza Km 5, Apartado, 109, Logroño. Alavesa region of Rioja, Grape varieties – Tempranillo 60%, Garnacha 10%, Viura 25%, Mazuelo, Malvasia and Graciano 5%. Produces red 60%, rosé 20% and white 20%. 160 ha. in the Rioja Alta. See also Castillo Ygay.

Bodegas Martinez Bujanda (Sp). A large

winery based in the Rioja region. Address = Camino Viejo de Logroño s/n, Oyón, Alava. 200 ha. Produces red and white wines under the Conde Valdemar and Valdemar labels.

Bodegas Martinez Lacuesta (Sp). A winery based in the Rioja region. Address = Calle la Ventilla 71, Haro, La Rioja. Owns no vineyards but buys in grapes mainly from the Rioja Alta. Produces red and white wines.

Bodegas Montecillo (Sp). A winery based in Fuenmayor, Rioja Alta.

Bodegas Montecristo (Sp). The brand-name of wines from Montilla-Moriles.

Bodegas Morenito (Sp). An old established winery based in Valdepeñas, central Spain.

Bodegas Muerza S.A. (Sp). Address = Vera Magallon Square 1, Apartado 44, San Adrián, Navarra. Baja region of Rioja. Owns no vineyards. Produces red 75%, rosé 15% and white 10% wines sold under the Rioja Vega label.

Bodegas Muga. S.A (Sp). Address = Barrio de la Estación, s/n Haro, Rioja. Alta region of Rioja, Grape varieties – Tempranillo, Garnacha, Mazuela and Viura. Produces red 95% and white 5%. 22 ha. in the Rioja Alta. See Prado Enea and Muga (red and white). Also Conde de Haro (a sparkling wine).

Bodegas Navarro S.A. (Sp). A winery based in the Montilla-Moriles region that produces Montilla wine.

Bodegas Norton (Arg). A well-established winery. Noted for its sparkling wines sold under the Consecha Especial and Norton labels. Also produces table wines under the Perdriel label.

Bodegas Ocha (Sp). A winery based in Olite, Navarra. Produces mainly light red and rosé wines.

Bodegas Olarra (Sp). Address = Poligono de Cantabria, s/n Logroño. Alta region of Rioja. Owns no vineyards. Produces red 65%, rosé 5% and white 30%. See Cerro Añon.

Bodegas Otero (Sp). A winery based in Benavente, Zamora.

Bodegas Palacio (Sp). A winery based in Laguardia, Alava. Produces red, rose and white wines. Owned by Seagram.

Bodegas Paternina S.A. (Sp). Bodegas based at Ollauri in the Rioja Alta. Produces fine red and dry white wines.

Bodegas Penaflor (Arg). Large old winery in Mendoza. Produces most styles of wines.

Bodegas Peñalba López (Sp). A winery based in Ribera del Duero. Uses the Torremilanos label.

Bodegas Perez de Albaniz (Sp). Bodegas

where Faustino 1 is produced. See Bodegas Faustino Martinez S.A..

Bodegas Prestige (Sp). A modern winery based in Villena, Alicante.

Bodegas Princesa (Sp). A noted winery based in Valdepeñas. Produces – Viña del Calar.

Bodegas Proviar (Arg). A winery noted for its sparkling wines sold under the labels of Baron B and M. Chandon (produced with the help of Moët et Chandon of France). Also produces fine red and white wines.

Bodegas Ramón Bilbao S.A. (Sp). Address = Apartado Postal N°.15, Haro, La Rioja. Produces red 85%, rosé 5% and white 10% wines. 10 ha.

Bodegas Real Divisa (Sp). A winery based in Abalos, Rioja Alavesa.

Bodegas Ribera Duero (Sp). A winery based in Peñafiel. Noted for its red wines.

Bodegas Riojanas S.A. (Sp). Address = Estación 4, Cenicero, Rioja Alta. Alta region of Rioja, Grape varieties – Tempranillo, Mazuelo, Graciano, Garnacha and Viura. Produces red 80%, rosé 6% and white 14% wines. 200 ha. See Canachales 2°Ano, Monte Real and Viña Albina.

Bodegas Rioja Santiago (Sp). Address = Barrio Estación s/n, Haro, Logroño. Alta region of Rioja, Grape varieties – Tempranillo 65% and Garnacha 35%. Produces red 50%, rosé 12% and white 38% wines. 27 ha. Owned by Pepsi Cola.

Bodegas Rivero (Sp). A winery based in Arnedo, Rioja Baja.

Bodegas Rojas y Cía (Sp). A winery based in Laguardia, Rioja Alavesa.

Bodegas Santa Ana (Arg). A noted winery based in Guaymallen, Mendoza. Produces red, rosé, sparkling and white wines.

Bodegas Schenk (Sp). A winery based in Valencia. Produces both red and white wines.

Bodegas Suter (Arg). A winery owned by Seagram. Noted for its Etiquette Blanca (white) and Marron (red) wines.

Bodegas Torres (Sp). See Torres.

Bodegas Vega Sicilia (Sp). A wine producer of the Valladolid region. 900 ha. Grape varieties – Albillo, Cabernet sauvignon, Garnacho tinto, Malbec, Merlot and Tinto aragonés. Produces Valbuena and Vega Sicilia (red wines only).

Bodegas Velazquez S.A. (Sp). Address = Azcárraga 27–29, Cenicero, La Rioja Alta region of Rioja, 50 ha. Grape varieties – Tempranillo 80% and

Garnacha 20%. Produces 100% red wine under the Monte Velaz label.

Bodegas Viña Salceda S.A. (Sp). A winery based in Elciego, Rioja Alavesa. Produces fine red wines.

Bodegas Vista Alegre (Sp). A winery based in Haro, Rioja Alta.

Bodegas Weinert (Arg). A small winery noted for its fine wines.

Bodeguero (Sp). A bodega owner. Wine maker.

Bodello (Sp). A white grape variety grown in north-western Spain.

Bodengeschmack (Ger). A term used to describe a wine that has an earthy taste.

Bodenham Reichensteiner (Eng). A dry white wine produced by the Broadfield Vineyard, Hereford.

Bodenheim (Ger). Village. (Anb) = Rheinhessen. (Ber) = Nierstein. (Gro) = Sankt Alban. (Vins) = Burgweg, Ebersberg, Heitersbrünnchen, Hoch, Kapelle, Kreuzberg, Leidhecke, Monchspfad, Reichsritterstift, Silberberg, Westrum.

Bodensee (Ger). Bereich. (Anb) = Baden. (Gro) = Sonnenufer.

Bodensee (Ger). Lake Constance. Bereich of Baden.

Bodental-Steinberg (Ger). Vineyard. (Anb) = Rheingau. (Ber) = Johannisberg. (Gro) = Burgweg. (Vil) = Lorch.

Bodenton (Ger). The taste of the soil. Used for some of the Württemberg wines.

Bodicote Brewery (Eng). Address = Plough, Bodicote, Banbury, Oxon. Noted for its cask conditioned Jim's Brew 1036 O.G. and N° 9 1043 O.G.

Bodman (Ger). Village. (Anb) = Baden. (Ber) = Bodensee. (Gro) = Sonnenfer. (Vin) = Königsweingarten.

Bodø Brewery (Nor). A brewery based in Bodø in north Norway.

Bodrum (Tur). Cellar.

Body (Eng). Description of strength and fullness in a wine from a high degree of alcohol and fruit.

Boeckel (E) (Fr) An Alsace wine producer. Address = 67140 Mittelbergheim. 21 ha.

Boeckser (Ger). A term used to describe a wine with a smell and taste of bad eggs.

Boeger Winery (USA). A winery based in Placerville, Eldorado, California. 8.5 ha. Grape varieties – Cabernet sauvignon and Chenin blanc. Produces varietals and house wine under the Hangtown label.

Boerenjongens (Hol). Lit – 'Farmer boys'. A raisin-flavoured Brandewijn.

Boerenmeisjes (Hol). Lit – 'Farmer girls'. An apricot-flavoured Brandewijn.

Bofferding (Lux). A noted Lager beer brewed by the Bofferding Brewery.

B

Bofferding Brewery (Lux). See Brasserie Nationale.

Boğazkarasi (Tur). A fine red wine produced in Anatolia.

Boğazkere (Tur). A white grape variety.

Bogdanuşa (Yug). A Dalmation white grape variety.

Bogen (Ger). The Guyot system of vine training. See Einzelbogen and Doppelbogen.

Bogey (Cktl). In a pint tankard containing ice cubes add 2 ozs. Vodka, 1 oz. lime juice cordial. Top up with ginger beer. Decorate with slice of lemon.

Boggs Cranberry Liqueur (USA). A cranberry-flavoured liqueur produced by the Heublein Co. in Hartford, Connecticut.

Bogle Vineyards (USA). A winery based in Clarksburg, Yolo, California. Grape varieties – Chenin blanc and Petit syrah. Produces varietal wines.

Bogota (S.Am). A fine grade of coffee beans from Colombia.

Bogotas (S.Am). A noted coffee-producing region in Colombia. See Bogota.

Boguzkere (Tur). A red grape variety used in the making of Buzbag.

Bohea (China). A black tea from the Wu-i Shan hills, much favoured in the eighteenth century. Now of little quality.

Bohemia (Czec). An old wine region that now produces only a little wine. Both red and white is made from the Blauer Burgunder, St. Laurent, Blaufrankirscher for the reds and Pinot, Traminer and Sylvaner for the whites.

Bohemian Maid (Can). The brand-name of a Malt beer.

Böhlig (Ger). Vineyard. (Anb) = Rheinpfalz. (Ber) = Mittelhaardt-Deutsche Weinstrasse. (Gro) = Mariengarten. (Vil) = Wachenheim.

Boil (Eng). 'The boil' is the term used in brewing when the Wort and Hops are boiled together in the Copper.

Boiled (USA) (slang). For intoxicated, very drunk.

Boilermaker (Eng). ½ pint Brown ale and ½ pint Mild ale mixed.

Boilermaker (USA). A neat whiskey with a beer chaser.

Boiling Water (Eng). The condition to which water must be heated 100°C (212°F) for the brewing of tea. Must be at a rapid, rolling boil to produce the best infusion.

Boillot (Fr). A cuvée in the A.C. vineyard of Les Duresses in the commune of Auxey-Duresses, Côte de Beaune, Burgundy. Is owned by the Hospices

de Beaune. 0.75 ha.

Boillot (Henri) (Fr). A Burgundy négociant-éleveur based at Volnay, 21190 Meursault

Boire (Fr). To drink.

Boire à la Santé de (Fr). Toast. 'Drink to the health of'.

Bois (Fr). Name given to the wood chips added to wine to replace cask aging but still give the wine a flavour of wood.

Bois (Fr). Wood. See 'Goût de Bois'. Woody taste.

Bois à Terroir (Fr). See 'Bois Communs Dits à Terroir'.

Bois Communs Dits à Terroir (Fr). The seven grades of Cognac.

Bois Dur (Fr). A lesser name for the red Carignan grape variety in southwestern France.

Boise (Fr). The addition of oak shavings, liquid or extract of powdered oak to Eau-de-vie as it is aging to help speed the process up. Also addition of a solution in which wood chips have been boiled to extract tannins (or hot water into new casks).

Bois Ordinaires et Bois Communs (Fr). Sixth Cru of Cognac. Covers 6% of area.

Bois Rosé (Cktl). ⅓ measure B and B, ⅓ measure Noilly Prat, ⅓ measure blackcurrant. Shake over ice, strain into a cocktail glass. Add a slice of lemon.

Boisseaux Estivant (Fr). A Burgundy négociant based at Beaune. A small company who ship fine wines.

Boisset [Jean Claude] (Fr). A négociant-éleveur of Nuits-Saint-Georges, Côtes de Nuits, Burgundy.

Boissière (Fr). A noted producer of Chambéry in south-eastern France.

Boissin (Ch.Isles). Public bar.

Boisson (Fr). Drink, beverage, booze.

Boisson Alcoolique (Fr). Liquor.

Boisson de Sureau (Fr). Elderberry cordial.

Boissons d'Orge (Fr). A non-alcoholic barley cordial (liquorice flavoured).

Boissons Fermentées (Fr). Fermented drinks (beverages).

Boîte (Fr). Cannister. e.g. Boîte à Bière.

Boîte à Bière (Fr). Beer can.

Boîte à Thé (Fr). Tea caddy.

Boizel (Fr). Champagne house. Address = 16 Rue de Bernon, 51200 Épernay. Produces – Vintage and non-vintage Champagne. Vintages – 1900, 1904, 1906, 1909, 1911, 1914, 1915, 1919, 1921, 1926, 1928, 1929, 1934, 1937, 1941, 1943, 1945, 1947, 1949, 1952, 1953, 1955, 1959, 1961, 1962, 1964, 1966, 1969, 1970, 1971, 1973, 1975, 1976, 1978, 1979, 1980, 1982, 1983. Labels include the De luxe cuvée –

Joyau de France.

Bok (Hol). A seasonal beer, available between October and December. Is reddish-black in colour with a strong malty taste and aroma.

Bokma (Hol). Distillery based in Leeuwarden. Owned by Heineken. Produces Jenevers and fine range of liqueurs.

Bok Øl (Nor). Bock beer.

Bol (Yug). A wine-producing region in Dalmatia.

Bolaffi Guide (It). An Italian wine guide compiled by Luigi Veronelli.

Bolanden (Ger). Village. (Anb) = Rheinpfalz. (Ber) = Mittelhaardt-Deutsche Weinstrasse. (Gro) = Schnepfenflug vom Zellertal. (Vin) = Schlossberg.

Bolandse Co-operative Wine Cellars (S.Afr). Based in Paarl. Address = Bolandse Koöperatiewe Wynkelders, Box 2, Hugenot 7645. Produces varietal wines. Merged with the Paarl-Valle Wynkoöperasie Beperk to form this large winery.

Bolandse Koöperatiewe Wynkelders (S.Afr). See Bolandse Co-operative Wine Cellars.

Bolée (Fr). An earthenware bowl used in Normandy for the drinking of Cider.

Bolée de Cidre (Fr). Cider bowl. See also Boulée and Bolée.

Bolero Cocktail (Cktl). 1 measure dark Rum, ½ measure Calvados, 2 dashes Italian vermouth. Stir over ice, strain into a cocktail glass.

Bolgheri (It). D.O.C. rosé wine from Livorno, Tuscany. Made from Cabernet, Montepulciano and Sangiovese grapes.

Bolivar (Sp). A dry Amontillado Sherry produced by Domecq. (Dating from 1898).

Bolivia (S.Am). A country that has some of the highest vineyards in the world in the Chuqisaca province. Has been producing wine since the sixteenth century. Most wine drunk locally.

Bolla (It). A well-known Veneto wine producer, including cuve close sparkling wines.

Bollène (Fr). A commune of the Principauté d'Orange Département in the southern Rhône.

Bolleponge (W.Ind). A word used for a drink made of spirit, lemon juice, sugar, mace and toast.

Bollinger (Fr). A Grande Marque Champagne house. Address = 4 Bld du Maréchal de Lattre de Tassigny, 51160 Ay. 140 ha. Produces – Vintage and non-vintage wines. Vintages – 1904, 1906, 1914, 1919, 1921, 1924, 1926, 1928, 1929, 1934, 1937, 1941, 1943, 1945, 1947, 1949, 1952, 1953, 1955, 1959, 1961, 1962, 1966, 1969, 1970, 1973, 1975, 1976, 1979, 1982.

Bollschweil (Ger). Village. (Anb) = Baden. (Ber) = Markgräflerland. (Gro) = Lorettoberg. (Vin) = Steinberg.

Bolo (Eng). A mixture of spirit (usually Rum), fresh fruit juices and spices drunk in the eighteenth century.

Bologna (Giacomo) (It). A winery based in Braida, Piemonte. Is noted for Brachetto d'Acqui and Grignolino d'Asti.

Bologne (W.Ind). A Rum distillery based in Guadeloupe.

Bols (Hol). A famous Dutch firm of liqueurs and spirit producers. See Bols (Lucas).

Bols (Lucas) (Hol). A Dutchman who was one of the first makers of liqueurs. The modern firm of Erven Lucas Bol are descendants of the original firm started in the sixteenth century.

Bolsberry (USA). A mild pleasant liqueur made from blackcurrants and other fruits. In Holland it is classed as an apéritif.

Bolscherwhisk (Hol). A Cherry brandy and Scotch whisky liqueur produced by the Bols Co.

Bolshoi Vodka (USA). A Vodka brand imported by Park Ave. Imports, New York. 40% alc. by vol.

Bolskaya (Can). A brand of Vodka produced by Hiram Walker. 40% alc. by vol.

Bolskümmel (Hol). The original Kümmel first produced in 1575 by Erven Lucas Bols.

Bolzano (It). Wine province of the Trentino-Alto Adige. Produces red and white wines. The best being Santa Maddalene.

Bomas (Eng). The seventeenth-century spelling used for Bommes (commune in the A.C. Sauternes).

Bomba (Sp). The name for the siphon used for racking in the bodegas.

Bombach (Ger). Village. (Anb) = Baden. (Ber) = Breisgau. (Gro) = Burg Lichteneck. (Vin) = Sommerhalde.

Bombard (Eng). A large leather jug used for carrying ale etc. up from the cellar to the bar. Up to 8 gallons in capacity.

Bombardier Bitter (Eng). A cask conditioned Bitter 1042 O.G. brewed by Charles Wells Brewery, Bedford.

Bombay (Cktl). ½ measure Brandy, ¼ measure dry Vermouth, ¼ measure sweet Vermouth, dash Pastis, 2 dashes orange Curaçao. Stir over ice, strain into a cocktail glass.

Bombay (Eng). A brand of Gin produced by Greenall Whitley at Warrington.

40% alc. by vol.

Bombay Cooler (Cktl). 2 measures dry Gin, ½ measure Curaçao, juice of ½ orange, dash Angostura. Shake over ice, strain into a highball glass. Top up with tonic water.

Bombay Punch (Punch). 2 quarts Champagne, 1 quart soda water, ½ gill orange Curaçao, ½ gill Maraschino, 1 pint Sherry, 1 pint Brandy. Stir together gently in a chilled punch bowl. Decorate with nuts and fruits in season.

Bombay Sherry Punch (Punch). 1 bottle Brandy, 1 bottle Sherry, 1 tablespoon Maraschino, 1 tablespoon Cointreau, 2 bottles dry sparkling wine, syphon of soda water. Mix with large ice cubes in a punch bowl. Decorate with fruit in season. Add wine and soda last.

Bombilla (S.Am). A silver tube with a strainer at the lower end which is used to drink Yerba Maté tea through. (The lower end being inserted into the gourd the tea is served in).

Bombino (It). A red grape variety grown in Puglia and Latium.

Bombino Bianco (It). A white grape variety grown in Latium. Also called the Ottonese or Trebbiano d'Abruzzo. See Bombino.

Bombino Nero (It). A black grape variety grown in Latium.

Bombo (El) (Sp). A noted vineyard based in the Moriles area of Montilla-Moriles, southern Spain.

Bombom Crema (W.Ind). A honey-flavoured liqueur produced in Cuba.

Bombonas (Sp). A pear-shaped glass bottle that some Priorato wines are aged in called Vino Rancios (they have a Sherry taste).

Bom Fim (Port). A noted quinta belonging to Dow's Port shippers.

Bomita (Sp). A white grape variety grown in Cáceres, south-western Spain.

Bommerlunder (Ger). A brand of Aquavit.

Bommes (Fr). A commune of Sauternes in Bordeaux. Wines sold under the A.C. Sauternes. A sweet white wine. The grapes are attacked by Botrytis. See Bomas.

Bömund II (Archbishop) (Ger). 1351–62 Elector of Trier. Recovered from serious illness by drinking the wines of the 'Doktor' vineyard in Bernkastel, Mosel-Saar-Ruwer.

Bonarda (It). A red grape variety grown in Piemonte.

Bonarda di Gattinara (It). A red grape variety used in the making of Gattinara

wine in Piemonte.

Bonarda Novarese (It). A red grape variety also known as the Uva rara.

Bonarda Oltrepo Pavese (It). D.O.C. red wine from Piemonte. Made from the Bonarda grape.

Bonardi (It), A producer of Moscato d'Asti Spumante in the Piemonte region.

Bon Blanc (Fr). The local Bugey and Seyssel area name for the Chasselas grape in south-eastern France. Also known as the Colombar and the Pied-tendre.

Bonbonne (Fr). Carboy.

Boncompagni Ludovisi (It). A noted winery based in the Latium region. Is noted for its red wines including Fiorana.

Bon Courage Vineyards (S.Afr). Vineyards based in Robertson. Address = Goede Moed. P.O. Box 22, Klass Voogds 6707. Produces varietal wines.

Bond (Eng). The storage of excisable liquor on which duty and taxes have not been paid.

Bonde (Fr). A word used for a bung or stopper.

Bonde Bordelaise de Sûreté (Fr). An unbroachable stopper used to seal wine that is maturing in barrels.

Bonded (Eng). Wines and spirits are bonded in a 'Bonded Warehouse' under Government supervision until Customs and Excise duties are paid by the owner.

Bonded (S.Am). A brand of Rum produced in Guyana by the Guyana Distilleries.

Bonded Warehouse (Eng). Premises where liquor is kept in Bond until Duty is paid.

Bonesio Winery (USA). A winery based in Santa Clara, California. Produces varietal wines.

Bondola (Switz). A red wine from the Ticino region, a smooth and fruity wine.

Bond 7 (Austr). A popular brand of Whiskey produced by Gilbeys. Part of International Distillers and Vintners.

Bond Stacking (Eng). A method breweries adopt for stacking beer crates to distribute the weight. Is similar to brick building.

Bone Dry (Eng). A light, dry, Fino sherry from Avery's of Bristol.

Bone-Dry (Eng). The term to describe a wine with no sugar and plenty of acidity.

Boneparte Shandy (Eng). Brandy and Lemonade.

Bone Structure (Eng). A description used to indicate the body in a red wine.

Bonfoi Estate (S.Afr). Vineyards based at

Stellenbosch. Address = Bonfoi Box 9, Vlottenburg 7580. Produces varietal wines.

Bon Goût (Fr). Good taste, flavour. Applicable to wines or spirits.

Bonhams Wine Auctions (Eng). Address = Montpelier Galleries, Montpelier Street, Knightsbridge, London SW1 1HH.

Bonheur Estate (Le) (S. Afr). Based in Stellenbosch. Address = P.O. Klapmuts 7625. Produces a fine Blanc Fumé from the Sauvignon blanc grape.

Bonhomme (Le) (Fr). A wine village in Alsace. (Ger) = Dieboldshausen.

Bonito (Sp). A term used to describe an elegant Sherry.

Bonnaire (Fr). Récoltants-Manipulants of Champagne. Address = 51200 Épernay. Produces – Vintage and non-vintage wines. Member of the C.V.C. Vintages – 1934, 1947, 1949, 1952, 1955, 1959, 1961, 1964, 1966, 1969, 1971, 1973, 1975, 1976. See Cramant Bonnaire.

Bonnaire-Bouquemont (Fr). A Champagne producer and grower. Produces a 100% Blanc de blanc Cramant Grand Cru.

Bonne Bouche (Fr). Good mouthful.

Bonne Chauffe (Fr). In Cognac the heart of the distillate. Lit – 'Good Fire'. Was supposedly invented by Chevalier de la Croix Maron in the sixteenth century.

Bonne Esperance (S.Afr). A red wine of the Bordeaux style produced mainly for the USA market by KWV. Also a rosé and white etc. sold under this label.

Bonnes-Mares (Fr). A.C. Grand Cru vineyard of the commune Morey-Saint-Denis in the Côte de Nuits. The smallest of the Grand Crus it is shared with the Chambolle-Musigny commune. 1.8 ha.

Bonnes-Mares (Fr). A.C. Grand Cru vineyard of the commune Chambolle-Musigny in the Côte de Nuits. Also in the Grand Cru Morey-Saint-Denis commune. 13.7 ha.

Bonnet (F. et Fils) (Fr). Champagne producer. Address = Rue de Mesnil, Oger, 51190 Avize. 9 ha. Produces – Vintage and non-vintage wines. Vintages – 1973, 1976, 1979, 1980.

Bonneuil (Fr). A commune in the Charente Département whose grapes are classed Grande Champagne (Cognac).

Bonnevaux (Les) (Fr). A vineyard in the A.C. commune of Montagny, Côte Chalonnaise, Burgundy.

Bonnezeaux (Fr). A site on the commune of Thouarcé, Coteaux du Layon. Produces sweet white wines, grapes attacked by Botrytis. A.C. from Pineau de la Loire. 125 ha. 13–16% alc. by vol. See Syndicat du Cru de Bonnezeaux.

Bonnie Prince Charlie (Cktl). ½ fl. oz. Drambuie, 1 fl.oz. Brandy, 1 fl.oz. lemon juice. Shake over ice, strain into a cocktail glass.

Bonnievale (S.Afr). A district within the Klein Karoo region. Noted for its brandy.

Bonnievale Co-operative Winery (S.Afr). Based in Breede River. Address = Box 206, Bonnievale 6730. Produces varietal wines.

Bönnigheim (Ger). Village. (Anb) = Württemberg. (Ber) = Württembergisch Unterland. (Gro) = Stromberg. (Vins) = Kirchberg, Sonnenberg.

Bonnonee Winery (Austr). Address = Box 145, Campbell Avenue, Irymple, Victoria. Grape varieties – Barbera, Chardonnay, Crouchen, Gewürztraminer, Rhine riesling, Ruby cabernet, Shiraz. Produces varietal and table wines.

Bon Père William (Le) (Switz). Au Eau-de-vie-de-poire. Pear-flavoured Eau-de-vie.

Bons Bois (Fr). The fifth Cru of Cognac. Covers 24.7% of area.

Bons Bourgeois (Fr). See Cru Bourgeois.

Bon Spuronza Vineyards (USA). A small winery based in Westminster, Maryland. Produces French/American hybrid wines.

Bontemps (Fr). A scoop or wooden pail used to hold the finings (egg whites).

Bonvedro (Austr). A red grape variety.

Bonvillars (Switz). A wine-producing area in northern Vaud. Produces both red and white wines.

Bonville (et Fils F.) (Fr). Champagne producer. Address = 9, Rue Pasteur, 51190 Avize. Récoltants-manipulants. Produces – Vintage and non-vintage wines.

Bonvin (Switz). A grower and merchant based in Sion, south-west Switz.

Bonvino (It). A red grape variety grown in Latium.

Bon Vivant (Can). A Canadian Rye whisky produced by the Canadian Gibson Distilleries.

Bonwin Wines (S.Afr). Wines made and sold by Mooiuitsig Wynkelders.

Booby Cocktail (Cktl). 1 measure Gin, ½ measure lime juice, dash Grenadine. Shake over ice, strain into a cocktail glass.

Boodles (Eng). The brand-name of a Gin produced by Seagram. 40% alc. by vol.

Boom Boom Punch (Punch). 1 bottle dark Rum, 1 pint orange juice, 1 bottle Italian vermouth, ½ bottle iced Champagne. Pour all (except the Champagne) into a large punchbowl. Chill down, add the wine, stir gently and decorate with banana slices.

Boomerang Cocktail (Cktl). ⅙ gill Gin, ⅓ gill French vermouth, ⅙ gill Italian vermouth, dash Angostura, 2 dashes Maraschino. Stir over ice, strain into a cocktail glass. Add cherry and squeeze of lemon peel on top.

Boomsma (Hol). Distillery based in Leeuwarden. Produces Genever and Beerenburg aromatic bitters.

Boon Brasserie (Bel). A brewery based in Lembeck. Noted for its Kriek beers.

Boonekamp (Hol). Aromatic bitters. 35% alc. by vol.

Boon Rawd Brewery (E.Asia). A brewery based in Bangkok, Thailand. Produces Singha Lager beer.

Booranga vineyard (Austr). Part of the College Winery, New South Wales. 13 ha. Mainly the Cabernet sauvignon grape grown.

Boor Brandy (S.Afr). Name used by English settlers to describe the Brandy that the Boer farmers drank.

Boordy Vineyard (USA). Vineyards in Ryderwood, Maryland and New York State on the south shore of Lake Erie. Produces fine wines.

Boos (Ger). Village. (Anb) = Nahe. (Ber) = Schloss Böckelheim. (Gro) = Paradiesgarten. (Vin) = Herrenberg, Kastell.

Booster Cocktail (Cktl). 2 ozs. Brandy, teaspoon Cointreau, 1 egg white. Shake well with ice, strain into a medium-sized glass. Grate nutmeg on top.

Boot (Eng). A part of the corking procedure. A cylindrical leather container. See Boot and Flogger.

Boot and Flogger (Eng). Old English method of corking bottles. The Boot was a cylindrical leather container to hold the bottle and the wooden Flogger used to drive home the cork. Still used in some small cellars.

Booth Brothers (Austr). A winery based in north-east Victoria.

Booth's Dry Gin (Eng). A famous London dry Gin produced by the Booths Distillery (part of The Distiller Co. Ltd). 40% alc. by vol.

Booth's Party Punch (Punch). 3 wine glasses Booth's Gin, ½ wine glass Cointreau, ¼ wine glass Brandy, juice of 1½ lemons, ½ teaspoon powdered sugar. Mix well with ice in a punch bowl. Add ½ flagon of lemonade. Decorate with sliced cucumber.

Bootlace Beer (Eng). Cask conditioned Ale 1038 O.G. brewed by the Bruce home-brew public house in Bristol.

Bootlegger (USA). A person who smuggled alcoholic liquor into America during the Prohibition.

Bootlegging (USA). The term used during Prohibition for the practice of carrying a flask of illegal Whiskey in the top of the boot.

Booze (USA) (slang). For alcoholic drink.

Booze Artist (Eng) (slang). A consistant drinker of alcoholic liquor.

Boozer (Eng) (slang). For a public house or reputed drinker.

Booze-Up (Eng) (slang). For a heavy drinking bout.

Boozy (Eng) (slang). A term used to describe a person, place, etc. that is associated with above the normal consumption of alcoholic liquor. e.g. 'A boozy place'.

B.O.P. (Eng) (abbr). Broken Orange Pekoe. A grade of tea.

Boplaas Estate (S.Afr). Vineyards based at Klein Karoo. Address = Boplaas Langoed, P.O. Box 156, Calitzdorp 6660. Produces varietal wines.

Boppard (Ger). Village. (Anb) = Mittelrhein. (Ber) = Rheinburgengau. (Gro) = Gedeonseck. (Vins) = Elfenlay, Engelstein, Fässerlay, Feuerlay, Mandelelstein, Ohlenberg, Weingrube.

Bopser (Ger). Vineyard. (Anb) = Württemberg. (Ber) = Remstal-Stuttgart. (Gro) = Weinsteige. (Vil) = Gerlingen.

Bór (Hun). Wine. See Borok.

Bora Sambuca (It). A Sambuca produced by Stock in Trieste, Piemonte. 40% alc. by vol.

Borba (Port). A district near the Spanish border in Alentejo. Noted for its full-bodied red wines.

Borba Cooperativo (Port). A co-operative based in Alentejo. Produces mainly red wines.

Bordeaux (Fr). Considered to be the most famous of all wine regions. Is situated in south-western France. Produces fine red wines (see Graves, Médoc, Pomerol and Saint-Émilion), dry white (see Graves) and the finest sweet white (see Barsac and Sauternes). Also produces rosé and sparkling wines. A.C.'s are – Barsac, Bordeaux, Bordeaux Clairet, Bordeaux Côtes de Castillon, Bordeaux Supérieur Côtes de Castillon, Bordeaux Côtes de Franc, Bordeaux Mousseux, Bordeaux Rosé, Bordeaux Supérieur, Cadillac, Cérons, Côtes Canon-Fronsac, Côtes de Blaye, Côtes de Bordeaux Sainte-Macaire, Côtes de Bourg, Côtes de Fronsac, Entre-Deux-Mers, Graves, Graves Supérieures, Graves de Vayres, Haut-Médoc, Lalande de Pomerol, Listrac, Loupiac, Lussac-Saint-Émilion, Margaux, Médoc, Montagne-Saint-Émilion, Moulis, Pauillac, Pomerol,

Premières Côtes de Bordeaux, Puisseguin-Saint-Émilion, Sainte-Croix-du-Mont, Saint-Émilion, Saint-Estèphe, Sainte-Foy-Bordeaux, Saint-Georges-Saint-Émilion, Saint-Julien and Sauternes.

Bordeaux (Fr). A.C. designation for basic wines of the region. Red and white. i.e. Bordeaux rouge and Bordeaux blanc. Minimum alcohol content red = 10% and white = 10.5% by vol.

Bordeaux Bottle (Fr). A tall bottle with full shoulders used in Bordeaux and most other wine producing countries. Green coloured for red wines and clear for white.

Bordeaux Clairet (Fr). A.C. designation for rosé wines from the region.

Bordeaux Cooler (Cktl). 2 fl.ozs. Claret, ¼ fl.oz. Cognac, juice of ⅓ lemon, 1 fl.oz. orange juice, ½ fl.oz. Gomme syrup. Stir well over ice, strain into a club goblet. Dress with a spiral of lemon peel.

Bordeaux Côtes de Castillon (Fr). A.C. designation for red wines. The district is sited south-east of Bordeaux. Most wines are sold as A.C. Bordeaux Supérieur.

Bordeaux Côtes de Franc (Fr). A.C. designation for red wines. District on the south-east of Bordeaux. Wines often sold as A.C. Bordeaux Supérieur.

Bordeaux Mixture (Fr). A mixture of copper sulphate, quicklime and water used to prevent mildew and other fungal diseases.

Bordeaux Mousseux (Fr). A.C. designation for the sparkling wines of the region. Produced mainly by the méthode champenoise. Grape varieties – (red) Cabernet franc, Cabernet sauvignon, Camenere, Colombard, Malbec, Mauzac, Merlot, Petit verdot and Ugni blanc. (white) Sauvignon blanc, Sémillon and Muscadelle. Minimum alc. content before second fermentation in bottle of 11% by vol.

Bordeaux Rosé (Fr). An A.C. dry rosé wine produced from permitted grapes and must have a minimum alcohol content of 11% by vol.

Bordeaux Supérieur (Fr). A.C. designation for red wines from the region. Has a higher alcohol content than A.C. Bordeaux. Minimum 11% alc. by vol. Also rosé and dry and sweet white wines.

Bordeaux Supérieur Côtes de Castillon (Fr). A.C. designation, higher in alcohol than A.C. Bordeaux Côtes de Castillon. Often sold as A.C. Bordeaux Supérieur. A.C. covers red wines from

permitted grapes with a minimum alcohol content of 11% by vol.

Bordeaux Supérieur Côtes de Francs (Fr). A.C. red and white sweet or dry wines from the region. Minimum alcohol content of red 11% and white 11.5% by vol.

Bordeaux Supérieur Haut-Bénauge (Fr). A.C. sweet white wines from the Haut-Bénauge region (in the Entre-Deux-Mers) produced from permitted grapes and a minimum alc. content of 11.5% by vol.

Bordeauxwijn (Hol). Claret.

Bordelaise Lourde (Fr). Another name for the Bouteille Bordelaise.

Bordeleau (Isr). A red grape variety.

Bordelesas (Sp). The name for the standard Bordeaux wine cask.

Bordeleza Belch (Euro). An alternative name for the Tannat grape in eastern Europe.

Border Brewery (Wales). Closed down in 1984 by Marstons in Burton. All their beers now brewed by Marstons in Burton.

Borderies (Fr). The third Cru of Cognac. Regarded as good as Petite Champagne. Covers 4.7% of the Cognac region. In the communes of Burie, Chérac, Chevres, Cognac, Javrezac, Louzac, Saint-André, Saint-Laurent-de-Cognac, Saint-Sulpice and Richemont.

Border Scotch Beer (Eng). A keg Beer 1035 O.G. brewed by Theakston's Brewery.

Bordes (Les) (Fr). A vineyard in the A.C. commune of Montagny, Côte Chalonnaise, Burgundy.

Bordo (Tur). Name for French red wine (usually from Bordeaux).

Bordo (USSR). A red grape variety grown in Bessarabia Combine.

Bordo Ay-Danil (USSR). A dry red wine from the Crimean Peninsula.

Bordón (Sp). The brand-name for the red Rioja wines from Bodegas Franco Españolas.

Borelli Winery (USA). A winery based in San Joaquin County, California. Grape varieties – Chenin blanc and Zinfandel. Produces varietal wines.

Borg Brewery (Nor). A brewery based in Sarpsborg, south-east Norway.

Borges (Port). Vintage Port Shippers. Vintages – 1914, 1922, 1924, 1963.

Borges and Irmão (Port). Producer of Gatão and Gamba brands of Vinhos Verdes and Trovador.

Borgogna Crna (Yug). A local name for the Gamay noir à jus blanc.

Borgogno (Giacomo) (It). A noted winery based in Barolo, Piemonte. Produces fine Barolo wine.

B

Borgoña (Chile). The name for a Burgundy style wine.

Borgonja (Yug). A red wine produced in Porec, north-western Slovenia.

Borg Special (Cktl). ⅓ measure Cherry brandy, ⅓ measure Drambuie, ⅓ measure Bacardi rum. Shake over ice, strain into a cocktail glass.

Borie (La) (S.Afr). A wine estate in Paarl owned by the KWV. Produces red, white and sparkling wines under La Borie label.

Borie-Manoux (Fr). A négociant-éleveur of Châteaux Batailley, Beau-Site, Haut Bages-Monpelou and Trottevielle and Domaine de l'Église.

Borinquen Cocktail (Cktl). 1 measure dark Rum, ½ measure Passion fruit syrup, 4 dashes high proof Navy Rum, ½ measure lime juice, ½ measure orange juice. Blend all the ingredients together with a scoop of crushed ice. Pour into an old-fashioned glass.

Borja (Sp). A demarcated area in the Aragón region. Produces wines that are high in alcohol.

Borj el Amrl (Afr). A noted co-operative based in Tunisia. Belongs to the UCCVT.

Borkülönlegességeszölögazdasàgànak (Hun). A speciality from the vineyards of the regions named.

Borlido (Port). A winery in Bairrada. Produces Garrafeira red and white wines.

Bornava Misketi (Tur). A red grape variety grown in the Aegean region.

Bornchen (Ger). Village. (Anb) = Rheinhessen. (Ber) = Baden. (Gro) = Adelberg. (Vins) = Hähnchen, Hütte-Terrassen, Kirchenstück, Schönberg.

Börnchen (Ger). Vineyard. (Anb) = Rheinhessen. (Ber) = Nierstein. (Gro) = Sankt Alban. (Vil) = Harxheim.

Bornchen (Ger). Village. (Anb) = Rheinpfalz. (Ber) = Südliche Weinstrasse. (Gro) = Trappenberg. (Vin) = Neuberg.

Borneret (Fr). A vineyard in the A.C. commune of Savigny-lès-Beaune, Côte de Beaune, Burgundy. Is owned by the Hospices de Beaune.

Bornich (Ger). Village. (Anb) = Mittelrhein. (Ber) = Rheinburgengau. (Gro) = Loreleyfelsen. (Vin) = Rothenack.

Borniques (Les) (Fr). A Premier Cru vineyard in the A.C. commune of Chambolle-Musigny, Côte de Nuits, Burgundy. 1.5 ha.

Bornóva (Tur). A wine-producing area at Izmir in western Turkey. Noted for its red and white wines.

Bornpfad (Ger). Vineyard. (Anb) = Rheinhessen. (Ber) = Nierstein. (Gro)

= Vogelsgärten. (Vil) = Guntersblum.

Borok (Hun). Wines. See Bór.

Boroka Vineyard (Austr). Address = RMB 2072 via Stawell, Victoria 3380 (Pomonal Road, Halls Gap, Victoria). 10 ha. Grape varieties – Cabernet sauvignon, Chardonnay, Colombard and Shiraz.

Borough Beer (Eng). A cask conditioned Bitter 1045 O.G. brewed by the Bruce home-brew public house: The Goose and Firkin, London.

Borough Brown Ale (Eng). Bottled Brown ale 1034 O.G. brewed by Shepherd Neame Brewery, Faversham, Kent.

Borovička (Czec). A water-coloured spirit similar to Gin. Also spelt Borovivika. 35% alc. by vol.

Borovivika (Czec). The alternative spelling of Borovička.

Borraçal (Port). A black grape variety grown in the Entre Minho e Douro to produce dark red wines.

Borraccia (It). Water-bottle.

Borracheiros (Mad). Men who carry the goat-skin containers (Borrachos).

Borracho (Port). A drunkard.

Borracho (Sp). Drunk, intoxicated.

Borrachos (Mad). Goat-skin back-sacks for carrying the grape juice to the wineries.

Borrachos (Port). Drunkard.

Borrado das Moscas (Port). A white grape variety grown in the Dão. Also known as the Bical da Bairrada.

Borra Winery (USA). A winery based near Lodi, San Joaquin Valley in California. 9 ha. Grape varieties – Barbera, Carignane and Zinfandel. Produces varietal wines.

Borrel (Hol). A small glass of liquor.

Borreluur (Hol). Apéritif hour.

Borret (Fr). The name given to the new wine of Armagnac prior to when it is placed in the still for distilling.

Borve House Brewery (Scot). A brewery based on the Isle of Lewis. Produces cask conditioned Pale ale 1038 O.G. Heavy 1043 O.G. and Extra 1085 O.G.

Borzoi (Eng). A British Gin and a Vodka distilled by Burroughs.

Bosador (Sp). The name given to a funnel that is inserted into a fermenting barrel of must. The must can rise in this during fermentation.

Bosca (It). A noted wine producer in Asti. Produces Spumanti and Vermouth. See Bosca (Giovanni).

Bosca (Giovanni) (It). A noted producer of a fine range of wines and Vermouths based in Canelli, Piemonte. Sold under the names of Gibó, Sereno and Tosti.

Bosca y Figli [Luigi] (It). A sparkling

(méthode champenoise) wine producer based the Piemonte region.

Boschendal Estate (S.Afr). Vineyards in the Drakenstein Valley, Paarl. Address = Groot Drakenstein 7680. Produces Lanoy and varietal wines including Le Barquet, Le Mirador and Le Pavillon.

Bosché Vineyard (USA). A vineyard based in Rutherford, Napa Valley in California. 6.6 ha. Grape variety – Cabernet sauvignon.

Bosch Guell (Sp). A winery based near Vilafranca, Penedés region. Noted for its table wines.

Bosco (It). A white grape variety of northern Italy.

Bosham Brewery (Eng). Opened in 1984 in Sussex. Produces cask conditioned Old Bosham 1044 O.G. and FSB 1058 O.G.

Boskydel Vineyards (USA). A small winery based in north Michigan that produces generic and hybrid wines.

Bosman and Co (S.Afr). A producer of Buchu brandy.

Bosmere (Eng). A vineyard based in West Tytherton, Chippenham, Wiltshire. First planted in 1976. 0.8 ha. Grape varieties – Madeleine angevine, Müller-Thurgau, Pinot noir, Seyval plus others.

Bosmere Vineyard (Eng). Address = Saxmundham, Suffolk. 4.5 ha. Grape variety – Müller-Thurgau.

Bosnia-Herzegovina (Yug). A lesser wine-producing State.

Bosom Caresser (Cktl). 1 egg yolk, ¼ gill Brandy, ¼ gill Curaçao, ¼ gill Madeira, ¼ gill Grenadine. Shake well over ice, strain into a wine glass.

Bossa Nova Special (Cktl). 1 fl.oz. white Rum, 1 fl.oz. Galliano, ¼ fl. oz. Apricot brandy, 2 fl.ozs. pineapple juice, ¼ fl.oz. lemon juice, dash egg white. Shake over ice, strain into highball with ice. Decorate with fruit in season.

Bosso (It). Distilleria Bosso Luigi and Co. A distiller of Grappa.

Bostandschi-Oglu-Kakour (USSR). A red wine from the Crimea region.

Boston Bullet (Cktl). As for Dry Martini but served with an olive stuffed with an almond.

Boston Cocktail (Cktl).(1). 1 oz. Bourbon, 1 oz. dry Madeira, 1 egg yolk, 1 teaspoon powdered sugar. Shake well with ice, strain into a wine goblet. Top with grated nutmeg.

Boston Cocktail (Cktl).(2). ½ measure Gin, ½ measure Apricot brandy, juice ¼ lemon, 4 dashes Grenadine. Shake over ice, strain into a cocktail glass.

Boston Cooler (Cktl).(1). Put into a highball glass the peel of a lemon and an ice cube. Add equal parts of ginger ale and Sarsaparilla.

Boston Cooler (Cktl).(2). Place juice of ¼ lemon, 1 teaspoon powdered sugar, 2 fl.ozs. soda water into a collins glass. Stir, top with 2 fl.ozs. Rum and 2 fl.ozs. ginger ale. Decorate with a spiral of orange peel over rim of glass.

Boston Eggnog (Cktl). ⅕ gill sweet Madeira, ⅕ gill milk, dash Cognac, dash Jamaican rum, 4 dashes Gomme syrup. Blend altogether in a blender with a scoop of crushed ice. Strain into a cocktail glass, top with grated nutmeg.

Boston Flip (Cktl). ¼ gill Madeira, ¼ gill Rye whiskey, 1 egg yolk. Shake well over ice, strain into a cocktail glass.

Boston Gold (Cktl). 1 measure Vodka, ½ measure Crème de Banane. Shake over ice, strain into an ice-filled highball glass. Top with orange juice.

Boston Shaker (USA). A cocktail shaker comprising of two cones, one made of glass the other stainless steel or silver.

Boston Sidecar (Cktl). ⅓ measure Jamaican rum, ⅓ measure Brandy, ⅓ measure Cointreau, juice ½ lime. Shake over ice, strain into a cocktail glass.

Boston Sour (Cktl). 1 measure Whiskey, juice ½ lemon, 1 teaspoon powdered sugar, 1 egg white. Shake over ice, strain into a sour glass, add a slice of lemon and a cherry.

Boston Tea Party (USA). 1773 Event when 342 chests of tea were dumped into the harbour after the Tea Act was passed.

Bosun Beer (Eng). A top grade Bitter 1048 O.G. Brewed by the Brewhouse Brewery, Poole, Dorset.

Bosun Beer (Eng). A cask conditioned dark Mild ale 1032 O.G. brewed by Southsea Brewery, Portsmouth.

Bota (Fr). An old provincial name for a cask.

Bota (Sp). Butt or cask. Holds 108 gallons (490 litres).

Bota (Sp). A leather wine bag made of goats-skin, pitch lined.

Bota Bodeguera (Sp). The name given to a very old butt now no longer in use.

Bota Chica (Sp). A shipping butt of 110 Imp. gallons. Also known as a Bota de Embarque.

Bota de Embarque (Sp). The alternative name for the Bota Chica.

Bota de Recibo (Sp). A butt of 111.63 Imp. gallons.

Bota Gordo (Sp). A storage butt of 132–146 Imp. gallons used in the wine bodegas.

Botaina (Sp). A brand of old Amontillado sherry produced by Domecq in Jerez.

Botanical Beer (Eng). Non-alcoholic

beers brewed in the days of the Temperance movement.

Botanicals (Eng). Herbs and peels used to flavour wines and spirits (liqueurs).

Botelha (Port). Bottle.

Botella (Sp). Bottle.

Botequim (Port). A bar, café bar.

Botenheim (Ger). Village. (Anb) = Württemberg. (Ber) = Württembergisch Unterland. (Gro) = Heuchelberg. See Brackenheim.

Botha Co-operative (S.Afr). Vineyards based at Breede river valley. Address = Botha Cooperative Wine Cellar, P.O. Botha 6857. Produces varietal wines.

Bothy (Scot). Distillery.

Bothy Vineyard (The) (Eng). A vineyard based at Bothy Cottage, Frailford Heath, Abingdon, Oxfordshire. 1.35 ha. Grape varieties – Huxelrebe, Optima, Ortega and Perle.

Botija (Port). A stone bottle, jar.

Botobolar Vineyards (Austr). Address = Botobolar Lane, Mudgee, New South Wales. 23 ha. Grape varieties – Cabernet sauvignon, Chardonnay, Couchen, Marsanne, Rhine riesling, Shiraz and Traminer.

Botrus (Lat). Bunch of grapes.

Botrys (Gre). Producer of Brandy and table wines (red and white).

Botrytis (Lat). A grey mould. See Pourriture Gris.

Botrytis Cinerea (Lat). Noble rot. The mould which in certain districts forms on the skins of grapes and penetrates the skin, so causing the water in the juice to evaporate. This concentrates the sugar to give high sugar musts. These produce luscious, sweet wines. e.g. Sauternes (Fr). Trokenbeerenauslesen (Ger). Known in (Eng) = Noble rot. (Fr) = Pourriture noble, (Ger) = Edelfäule, (Hun) = Aszú, (It) = Muffa nobile, (S.Afr) = Edelkeur, (Switz) = Flétri, (USA) = Noble mold. See also Passerillage and Marciume Nobile.

Bottaio (It). Cooper, cask maker.

Bottchen (Ger). Vineyard. (Anb) = Mosel-Saar-Ruwer. (Ber) = Bernkastel. (Gro) = Schwarzlay. (Vil) = Wittlich.

Botte (Fr). An old word for Butt, barrel.

Botte (It). Barrel, cask.

Bottelary Co-operative (S.Afr). Vineyards based in Stellenbosch. Address = Bottelary Koöperatiewe Wynkelder, Box 16, Koelenhof 7605. Produces varietal wines.

Bottelary Koöperatiewe Wynkelder (S.Afr). See Bottelary Co-operative.

Bottenau (Ger). Village. (Anb) = Baden. (Ber) = Ortenau. (Gro) = Fürsteneck. (Vin) = Renchtäler.

Bott-Geyl (Fr). An Alsace wine producer. Address = 68980 Beblenheim.

Botticino (It). A small commune in the Garda district of Lombardy. Derives it's name from Botte (barrel). Logo is also a small barrel.

Botticino (It). A red wine from the Garda district of Lombardy. Grapes used – Barbera 30–40%, Schiava gentile 20–30%, Marzemino 15–25% and Sangiovese 10–20%. D.O.C.

Böttigheim (Ger). Village. (Anb) = Franken. (Ber) = Maindreick. (Gro) = Not yet assigned. (Vin) = Wurmberg.

Bottiglia (It). Bottle.

Bottiglieria (It). A wine-shop.

Bottigua (It). Bottle.

Bottle (Eng). A glass container for holding liquids. Many shapes, sizes and colours. Standard wine bottle holds 75 cls.

Bottle Age (Eng). The time the wine has spent in bottle.

Bottle and Basket (Eng). Retail Off-licences owned by the Virani hotel and property group.

Bottle Bank (Eng). Organised points of collection where used, empty bottles can be deposited for recycling. Usually charity-organised and run.

Bottle Bib (Eng). An absorbant crêpe paper ring that encircles around the bottle neck to catch any drips that occur whilst pouring.

Bottle Brush (Eng). A thin wire handle with bristles intertwined with the wire at the one end. Used to remove stains and debris from used bottles (and decanters) before re-use. Used mainly by homemade wine makers.

Bottle Bursts (Fr). A term used in Champagne and other sparkling wine regions for bottles that have weakened glass and that burst during second fermentation when the pressure is increased.

Bottle Collar (Eng). Silver or other metal ring which fits over the neck of the wine bottle and rests on the shoulder. Has the name and the bottle contents engraved on it.

Bottle Conditioned (Eng). Applies to Ales that have a second fermentation in the bottle which leaves a sediment.

Bottle Cradle (Eng). See Cradle.

Bottled-in-Bond Stamp (USA). Treasury department's decision N°1299 reads 'Is no guarantee as to purity or quality of the spirits, and the government assumes no responsibility with respect to claims by dealers in this connection in advertising Bottled-in-Bond spirits'.

Bottled-in-Bond Whiskey (USA). These are straight whiskies bottled at 100° USA proof. Matured in cask for at least 4 years in warehouses controlled by the government. Hence the name.

Bottle Fermented (USA). Méthode Champenoise.

Bottle Fever (Eng). See Bottle Sickness.

Bottle Label (Eng). See Decanter Label.

Bottle-O (Austr). A dealer who specialises in empty bottles.

Bottle Party (Eng). A drinks party where each guest brings a bottle of alcoholic liquor.

Bottle Ripe (Eng). A term used for a wine that has been stored in bottle and gained bottle age and maturity and is ready for drinking. After it has reached this stage it will then slowly start to deteriorate.

Bottler's Code (Eng). A code of letters and numbers found on the capsule or cork to guarantee authenticity of the wine.

Bottle Safe (Eng). A device to put over the neck and cork of bottles of wines or spirits. This is locked in position to prevent any pilferage.

Bottle'scape (Eng). A wall-mounted cabinet which when closed appears to be a picture. Stores bottles and glasses. Popular in the nineteenth century.

Bottle Scent (Eng). Describes Saké that has deteriorated usually due to poor storage (i.e. in direct sunlight).

Bottlescrew (Eng). The name given to the first corkscrew.

Bottleship (Eng). A bookcase, magazine rack, cocktail cabinet and occasional table all-in-one. Held 6 bottles and several glasses. Popular in the nineteenth century.

Bottle Sickness (Eng). Happens to some newly bottled wines. Disappears after some months. Result of oxygen absorption and the formation of acetaldehyde. Causes loss of bouquet. (Ger) = Flaschentrank.

Bottle Stink (Eng). Hydrogen Sulphide. Smell that sometimes exudes from newly opened wines. Mainly due to the air between the cork and the wine. Treated by decanting and aerating.

Bottle Ticket (Eng). Also called Decanter labels, used to indicate the contents of the bottle or decanter. Made of parchment, wood, ivory or bone.

Bottling (Eng). The placing of beverages into clean, sterile bottles of various capacities. Mainly done automatically but some wines still bottled by hand (e.g. home-made wines)

Bottom Fermentation (Eng). Applied to those beers where the yeast falls to the bottom of the vat during fermentation. e.g. Lager, Bock, Pilsener, etc. Yeast = Saccharomyces Uvarum.

Bottom Rose (Cktl). ⅓ measure Cinzano Rossi, ⅓ measure Apricot brandy, ⅓ measure Genever gin. Shake over ice, strain into a cocktail glass.

Bottoms (Eng). The lees or dregs left after racking or decanting. In a 36 gallon (163.6 litres) barrel of beer the natural sediment (yeasts and hops debris) amounts to about 1 gallon (4.5 litres).

Bottoms Up (Eng). A chain of 18 Off-licences taken over by Peter Dominic in 1985. Now taken over by IDV.

Bottoms Up (Eng). An informal toast. A request to drain the glass of its contents.

Bottwar [River] (Ger). A tributary of the river Neckar in the Württemberg Anbaugebiet. Soil = red marl.

Bötzingen (Ger). Village. (Anb) = Baden. (Ber) = Kaiserstuhl-Tuniberg. (Gro) = Vulkanfelsen. (Vins) = Eckberg, Lansenberg.

Bouaki (USSR). A white grape variety used mainly as a table grape and for some dessert wines in Uzbekistan.

Boual (Mad). Another spelling of the Boal grape variety of Madeira.

Bou Á-Rkoub (Afr). A co-operative based in Tunisia. Belongs to the UCCVT.

Bouaye (Fr). A town in the Muscadet (Pays Nantais) region of the Loire.

Bouchaon (Ch.Isles). Cork.

Bouchard Aîné et Fils (Fr). A Burgundy négociant based at Beaune. Ships many fine wines. Address = 36, Rue Ste-Marguerite, 21203 Beaune.

Bouchard Père et Fils (Fr). A Burgundy négociant-éleveur based in Beaune. Has large holdings in the Côte d'Or including Beaune Grêves Vigne de l'Enfant Jesus and Beaune Marconnets.

Bouchard-Philippe (Fr). A Burgundy négociant-éleveur based at Saint Jean des Vignes. Owns a small domaine at Savigny-lès-Beaune and at Beaune.

Bouché (Fr). A term to denote that the bottle is closed with a cork.

Bouchemaine (Fr). A commune in the A.C. Savennières, Anjou-Saumur, Loire.

Boucher (Aimé S.A.) (Fr). A noted négociant in the Loire. Address = 279, Route de Chambourd, 41350, Husseau-sur-Casson.

Boucher Père et Fils (Fr). A Champagne producer. Produces vintage and non-vintage wines.

Bouchères (Les) (Fr). A Premier Cru vineyard in the A.C. commune of Meursault, Côte de Beaune, Burgundy. 4.25 ha.

B

Boucherottes (Les) (Fr). A Premier Cru vineyard [part] in the A.C. commune of Beaune, Côte de Beaune, Burgundy. 8.6 ha.

Boucherottes (Les) (Fr). A Premier Cru vineyard [part] in the A.C. commune of Pommard, Côte de Beaune, Burgundy. 1.7 ha.

Bouches du Rhône (Fr). A Vins de Pays area in the Languedoc-Roussillon region.

Bouchet (Fr). A red grape variety used in Saint-Émilion. Local name for the Cabernet franc. See Château St. Georges. Is known in the Loire as the Breton, Bouchy or Véron.

Boucheur (Fr). The name given to the person who inserts and hammers the cork into the neck of a Champagne bottle.

Bouchon (Fr). Stopper, cork.

Bouchon Couronne (Fr). Crown cork, used in some Champagne houses during the second fermentation.

Bouchon de Tirage (Fr). In Champagne, the temporary cork used during the second fermentation in the bottle and up to dégorgement. Many of the houses have now replaced it with a Crown Cork.

Bouchonné (Fr). Denotes a corked wine, from a defective cork.

Bouchots (Les) (Fr). A vineyard in the A.C. commune of Montagny, Côte Chalonnaise, Burgundy.

Bouchots (Les) (Fr). A Premier Cru vineyard in the A.C. commune of Morey-Saint-Denis, Côte de Nuits, Burgundy. 2 ha.

Bouchy (Fr). The local Loire (and Madiran) name for the Cabernet franc grape. See also Breton, Bouchet and Véron.

Bouchy (Fr). A red wine produced in the Jurançon region.

Boudalès (Fr). An alternative name for the Cinsault grape.

Boude (Fr). Bung.

Boudes (Fr). A sub-appellation of the V.D.Q.S. district Côtes d'Auvergne, southern France.

Boudriottes (La) (Fr). A Premier Cru vineyard [part] in the A.C. commune of Chassagne-Montrachet, Côte de Beaune, Burgundy. 17.81 ha. (red and white).

Bouéchage (Fr). A term that describes the manual digging around the vine where the plough cannot reach.

Bougneau (Fr). A commune in the Charente-Maritime Département whose grapes are classed Petite Champagne (Cognac).

Bougros (Fr). A.C. Grand Cru of Chablis, Burgundy. Produces a full wine with a long aftertaste.

Bougy (Switz). A wine-producing area in La Côte on the western bank of Lake Geneva.

Bouillage (Fr). The first fermentation in Champagne when the must literally foams and hisses. Imitates boiling.

Bouille (Fr). A milk churn.

Bouilleurs de Cru (Fr). Farmers in Cognac who only distil the wine from the grapes they grow.

Bouilleurs de Profession (Fr). Professional distillers in Cognac, those who sell their distillates to the Cognac houses.

Bouillie Bordelaise (Fr). Bordeaux Mixture. See.

Bouilloire (Fr). Kettle, copper.

Bouilly (Fr). A Cru Champagne village in the Canton de Ville-en-Tardenois. District = Reims.

Boukha (M.East). An Eau-de-vie made from figs. Also called Mahia.

Boulaouane (Afr). A wine-producing area in Morocco based south of Rabat. Produces red and rosé wines.

Boulard Mist (Cktl). ⅓ gill Calvados, juice of ½ lemon, 1 teaspoon sugar. Shake well over ice, strain into an old-fashioned glass.

Boulbène (Fr). The name given to the fine clay and sandy soils of the Armagnac region.

Boulder Brewery (USA). A brewery based in Boulder, Colorado. Noted for its top-fermented, bottle-conditioned beers.

Boulder Hill Vineyard (USA). A winery based in Laporte, Indiana. Produces hybrid wines.

Bouleuse (Fr). A Cru Champagne village in the Canton de Ville-en-Tardenois. District = Reims.

Bound SO₂ (Eng). Sulphur-dioxide added to wine which has combined with sugar or aldehydes, or has converted to Sulphuric acid (H_2SO_4).

Bounty (USA). The brand-name used by California Growers for a range of wines.

Bounty (W.Ind). The brand-name of a Rum produced on Saint Lucia by the St. Lucia Distillers Ltd.

Bouoillaon (Ch.Isles). Beef tea, Consommé.

Bouquet (Fr). Aromas. Collection of smells and aromas given off by wines which, in the right type of glass, can be concentrated at the top of the glass (at the rim) to give the scent of the grape, soil grown in, age and class (type) of wine.

Bouquet (Le) (S.Afr). A late harvest wine produced from Bukettraube, Gewürztraminer and Muscat grapes by the Boschendal Estate.

Bouquet Blanc (S.Afr). A fruity white wine made with the Steen grape by the Landskroon estate in Paarl.

Bouquet de Cissus (Fr). Co-operative in the Médoc. A.C. Haut-Médoc. Address = 33250 Cissac, Médoc. Commune = Cissac. 30 ha. Grape varieties – Cabernet sauvignon 50% and Merlot 50%.

Bouqueté (Fr). Fragrant.

Bouquet Rouge (S.Afr). A bland red wine from the Landskroon Estate.

Bourbon Cocktail (Cktl). ⅓ gill Bourbon whiskey, juice ½ lemon, 4 dashes Triple Sec, 4 dashes Bénédictine, dash Angostura. Shake over ice, strain into a cocktail glass. Top with twist of lemon peel juice.

Bourbon Coffee (E.Afr). Coffee beans from the island of Bourbon (also known as Réunion Island). Are oblong in shape and yellow in colour.

Bourbon Coffee (Afr). The alternative name for Coffea Arabica.

Bourbon Coffee (Liq.Coffee). Using a measure of Bourbon whiskey.

Bourbon Collins (Cktl). ⅓ gill Bourbon whiskey, ⅛ gill lemon juice, 1 teaspoon sugar. Stir over ice in a collins glass. Top with soda water. Dress with a lemon slice, serve with straws.

Bourbon Cooler (Cktl). Fill a tall glass with cracked ice. Fill half with lime juice, add 1 oz. Bourbon. Top up with pineapple juice. Stir, serve with straws.

Bourbon Créole Coffee (Fr). See Café Créole Bourbon.

Bourbon de Luxe (USA). The brand-name of a Bourbon whiskey produced in Kentucky.

Bourbonella (Cktl). ½ measure Bourbon whiskey, ¼ measure Orange Curaçao, ¼ measure Vermouth, dash Grenadine. Stir over ice, strain into a cocktail glass.

Bourbon Fog (Cktl). 1 quart Vanilla ice cream, 1 quart Bourbon whiskey, 1 quart cold strong black coffee. Stir together in a punch bowl until well blended. Serve in Champagne flutes.

Bourbon Highball (Cktl). Pour ⅓ gill Bourbon whiskey into an ice-filled highball glass. Top with soda water and dress with a lemon peel spiral.

Bourbon Mist (Cktl). ⅓ gill Bourbon whiskey into an old-fashioned glass filled with crushed ice. Dress with a lemon peel spiral.

Bourbon Santos (Bra). A top quality coffee bean from the Santos region. Produces fine coffees with good flavour and acidity.

Bourbon Sour (Cktl). 1 oz. Bourbon whiskey, juice ½ lemon, teaspoon of powdered sugar. Shake over ice, strain into a small tumbler.

Bourbon Supreme (USA). The brand-name of a Bourbon whiskey produced by the American Distilling Company Inc. in Pekin, Illinois.

Bourbon Whiskey (USA). Originally made in Bourbon County, Kentucky, must have not less than 51% maize spirit. Matured in new charred oak casks for at least four years. See Craig (Reverend Elijah).

Bourbouenc (Fr). Same as Bourboulenc.

Bourboulenc (Fr). A red grape variety used in the southern Rhône. Gives finesse to the wines.

Bourdin (Jean-Claude) (Fr). A wine-producer based at Jurquant, Saumur, Anjou-Saumur, Loire. Noted for their Saumur Mousseux.

Bourdon (W.Ind). A noted Rum distillery based in Guadeloupe.

Bourée Fils (Fr). Burgundy négociants based in Gevrey-Chambertin, Côte de Nuits, Burgundy.

Bourg (Fr). A commune in the A.C. Côtes de Bourg in north-east Bordeaux.

Bourg (Fr). An A.C. district within Bordeaux on the right bank of the river Gironde in the north-east of the region. See Côtes de Bourg.

Bourg-Bourgeais (Fr). A.C. for red, demi-sec, sweet and dry white wines from the right bank of the Gironde (opposite the Haut-Médoc).

Bourg-Charente (Fr). A commune in the Charente Département whose grapes are classed Petite Champagne (Cognac).

Bourgeais (Fr). The name given to the wines from the Côtes de Bourg.

Bourgeois (Fr). A term used in the Médoc. See Cru Bourgeois. Denotes that the wines are of medium quality.

Bourgignon Noir (Fr). An alternative name for the Gamay noir à jus blanc in south-western France.

Bourgneuf-Val d'Or (Fr). A noted wine commune in the A.C. Mercurey, Côte Chalonnaise, Burgundy.

Bourgogne (Fr). Burgundy.

Bourgogne (Fr). A Canton in the Reims district of Champagne. Has the Cru villages of Brimont, Cauroy-les-Hermonville, Cormicy, Merfy, Pouillon, Saint-Thierry, Thil and Villers-Franqueux.

Bourgogne Aligoté (Fr). A dry white wine of Burgundy made with the Aligoté grape. Minimum alc. content 9.5% by vol.

Bourgogne Aligoté de Bouzeron (Fr). An A.C. dry white wine produced from the Aligoté grape in the commune of Bouzeron.

Bourgogne Blanc (Fr). A dry white wine of Appellation Regionale category, minimum alcohol content 10.5% by vol.

Bourgogne Clairet de Marsannay (Fr). The A.C. of the light rosé produced in the commune of Marsannay-la-Côte in the Burgundy region. See also Rosé de Marsannay.

Bourgogne Grand Ordinaire (Fr). An Appellation Regionale which includes red, rosé and white wines. See Bourgogne Passe-Tout-Grains.

Bourgogne Hautes-Côtes-de-Beaune (Fr). A.C. designation granted on 4th August 1961. Red and rosé wines made with Pinot noir, white wines made from the Chardonnay and Pinot blanc.

Bourgogne Hautes-Côtes-de-Nuits (Fr). A.C. designation granted on 4th August 1961. Red wines made with Pinot noir, white wines made from the Chardonnay and Pinot blanc.

Bourgogne Irancy (Fr). A.C. red and rosé wines produced south-west of Chablis from the César, Pinot noir and Tressot grapes.

Bourgogne Marsannay (Fr). The A.C. of the red wines of the commune of Marsannay-la-Côte and Couchey.

Bourgogne Mousseux (Fr). Sparkling Burgundy. Applies to white and rosé wines, reds excluded (since December 1985). Minimum alcohol content 9.5% by vol. which must be natural.

Bourgogne Ordinaire (Fr). A rare Appellation Regionale of Burgundy which produces red, rosé and white wines.

Bourgogne Passe-Tout-Grains (Fr). A red or rosé wine which is made from ⅔ Gamay and ⅓ Pinot noir. Often has the A.C. Bourgogne Grand Ordinaire. Minimum alc. content of above 9.5% by vol.

Bourgogne Rosé (Fr). An A.C. rosé wine produced in the Yonne Département in the Burgundy region from César, Pinot noir and Tressot grapes.

Bourgogne Rosé de Marsannay (Fr). A rosé (the only one in the Côte d'Or) produced in the commune of Marsannay-la-Côte. Also known as Bourgogne Clairet de Marsannay.

Bourgogne Rouge (Fr). An Appellation Regionale wine which varies with each region it's produced in. Often of high quality for its price. Made with most of the red grape varieties grown in Burgundy.

Bourgogne Rouge de Marsannay (Fr). An A.C. red wine produced from the Pinot noir grape in Marsannay-la-Côte.

Bourgueil (Fr). A wine district of the Touraine in the middle Loire. Produces red and rosé A.C. wines from the Cabernet sauvignon and the Cabernet franc grapes. Minimum alc. content of 9.5% by vol.

Bourguignonnes (Fr). The name given to the 75 cls bottles with a long sloping shoulder and short necks used in Burgundy.

Bourne Valley Brewery (Eng). Opened in 1978 in Andover, Hampshire. Brews cask conditioned Weaver's Bitter 1037 O.G. Andover Ale 1040 O.G. Henchard Bitter 1045 O.G. and Wallop 1056 O.G.

Bournvita (Eng). A commercially prepared, powdered, malted chocolate drink. Usually reconstituted with hot milk. Produced by Cadburys (part of Kenco-Typhoo).

Bourret (Fr). A white grape variety used in the making of Vermouth.

Bourro (Fr). A spiced wine. See also Vin Bourro.

Bourru (Fr). A term to denote a rough, crude wine.

Boursault (Fr). A Cru Champagne village in the Canton de Dormans. District = Épernay.

Bousa (Afr). A Beer made from millet.

Bouscaut (Fr). An estate in the commune of Cadaujac in the A.C. Graves, Bordeaux.

Bouschet Sauvignon (Fr). Another name for the Cabernet sauvignon grape.

Bousse d'Or (Fr). A Premier Cru vineyard in the A.C. commune of Volnay, Côte de Beaune, Burgundy. 1.9 ha. Also known as La Bousse d'Or.

Boutari (Gre). Name given to wine merchants dealing in Macedonian wines.

Bouteille (Fr). Bottle.

Bouteille à Vin (Ch.Isles). Wine bottle.

Bouteille Consignée (Fr). A returnable bottle.

Bouteille Fantaisie (Fr). An unusually shaped bottle used for a special event or market.

Bouteille Nantaise (Fr). A long necked, dumpy bottle used in the Nantais region for Muscadets.

Bouteillerie (Fr). Bottle store.

Bouteille Tradition (Fr). Old Cognac bottle. Clear glass bottle used by Hennessey's (Cognac) to sell their brandies.

Bouteville (Fr). A commune in the Charente Département whose grapes are classed Grande Champagne (Cognac).

Boutière (La) (Fr). A Premier Cru vineyard in the commune of Cheilly-lès-Maranges. A.C. Santenay, Côte de Beaune, Burgundy.

Boutières (Les) (Fr). A vineyard in the commune of Solutré-Pouilly, A.C. Pouilly-Fuissé, Mâcon, Burgundy.

Boutinet (Bernard) (Fr). A Cognac producer. Address = 16360 Breville. 26 ha. in the Fins Bois.

Boutique Winery (USA). A small winery that only produces one or two styles of wine.

Bouvet-Ladubay (Fr). An A.C. sparkling Saumur, made by the méthode champenoise at St. Hilaire St. Florent, from the Chenin blanc, Cabernet franc and Cabernet sauvignon grapes. A.C. is owned by Taittinger.

Bouveur (Fr). Drinker.

Bouvier (Yug). A red grape variety used to make Plemenka, a wine from the Vojuodina region. Also grown in Hungary and Austria. Also known as Ranina.

Bouviertraube (Aus). A white grape (table) variety. Is used to produce Auslese, Spätlese and Prädikat wines due to its low acidity and early maturation.

Bouwland Wines (S.Afr). See Kanonkop Estate.

Bouzeron (Fr). A small village in the Chalonnaise near Chagny. Produces fine A.C. Bourgogne Aligoté.

Bouzouki (Gre). The name given to a medium-sweet, red table wine made by Tsantali.

Bouzy (Fr). A Grand Cru Champagne village in the Canton d'Ay. District = Reims. Is famous for its still red wines of same name.

Bouzy Brut (Fr). A 100% Grand Cru Champagne produced in Bouzy by the local vineyard of Barancourt.

Bouzy Rouge (Fr). A red wine made in the district of Bouzy in Champagne. Mainly used for the families of the proprietors of Champagne and also for mixing to make rosé Champagne.

Bovale Grande (It). A red grape variety grown in Sardinia, also known as the Girone.

Bovale Sardo (It). A red grape variety grown in Sardinia, also known as the Muristellu.

Bovlei Co-operative (S.Afr). Based in Wellington. Address = Box 82, Wellington 7655. Produces varietal wines. Has 66 members.

Bovril (Eng). The brand-name for a concentrated beef extract drink. Is diluted with boiling water.

Bowen (Arg). A wine-producing area

based in southern Argentina.

Bowen Estate (Austr). Vineyard. Address = P.O. Box 4B, Coonawarra, South Australia 5263. 30 ha. Grape varieties – Cabernet sauvignon, Rhine riesling and Shiraz. Winery address = Naracoote Road, 2 miles north of Penola.

Bowl (Eng). An old English term to denote a drink of intoxicating liquor. i.e. 'to partake in a bowl of Brandy'.

Bow Lane Reserve Fino (Eng). A light, dry Fino sherry from the Balls Brothers of London.

Bowle (Ger). A wine cup prepared with wine, herbs, fruit, liqueurs or brandy.

Bowlewein (Ger) (slang). A term for wines that are only suitable for cups and punches as a base.

Bowman Beer (Eng). A Brown ale 1030 O.G. and Strong ale 1054 O.G. brewed by Charles Wells, Bedford.

Bowman Vineyard (USA). A vineyard based in Amador County, California. Grape variety – Zinfandel.

Bowman Wine Cellars (USA). A winery based in Weston, Missouri. Produces hybrid wines.

Bowmore (Scot). A single Malt whisky distilled at the Bowmore distillery on the Isle of Islay by Stanley P. Morrison. An Islay malt whisky. 12 year old, 40% alc. by vol. Also as a 1965 bi-centenary version (as a limited edition).

Boxberg [stadtteil Unterschüpf] (Ger). Village. (Anb) = Baden. (Ber) = Badische Frankenland. (Gro) = Tauberklinge. (Vin) = Mühlberg.

Boxbeutel (Ger). See Bocksbeutel.

Boxer Brewery (Switz). An independent brewery based in Lausanne.

Boy (Eng) (slang). The term used for a bottle of Champagne in the Victorian/Edwardian eras.

Boyer (Fr). A commune in the Mâconnais where Mâcon Supérieur is produced.

Boy's Bitter (Eng). The other name for the Pale ale brewed by the Hall and Woodhouse Brewery at Blandford Forum, Dorset.

Boxton Vineyards (Eng). A vineyard based in Boyton End, Stoke-by-Clare, Suffolk. 2 ha. Grape varieties – Huxelrebe and Müller-Thurgau.

Boza (Yug). A Turkish-style, non-alcoholic brew made from corn.

Bozcaada (Tur). A wine-producing area. Growers make their own wine.

Bozner Leiten (It). See Colli di Bolzano.

B.P. (Eng) (abbr). Broken Pekoe. A tea grade.

Brabrux Brasserie (Bel). A brewery based in Wolvertem in north Belgium.

Brač (Yug). A wine-producing island off

the Dalmatian coast.

Bracer (Eng) (slang). A stiff drink e.g. Gin, Rum, Whisky, etc. to give a person courage to do a task. Or as a tonic.

Brace Up (Cktl). ½ gill Brandy, juice of small lime, 2 dashes white Anisette, 2 dashes Angostura, fresh egg. Shake well over ice, strain into a tumbler. Top up with Vichy water.

Brachetto (It). A red grape variety grown in the Piemonte region. Produces brilliant red, light wines.

Brachetto d'Acqui (It). A red pétillant wine produced from the Brachetto grape in Piemonte. D.O.C.

Brachetto d'Acqui (It). A term under the D.O.C. regulations used to describe the naturally sparkling wines obtained from the musts and wines produced in the region of Acqui Terme in Piemonte.

Brackenheim (Ger). Village. (Anb) = Württemberg. (Ber) = Württembergisch Unterland. (Gro) = Heuchelberg. (Vins) = Dachsberg, Mönchsberg, Schlossberg, Wolfsaugen, Zweifelberg.

Brackenheim [ortsteil Botenheim] (Ger). Village. (Anb) = Württemberg. (Ber) = Württembergisch Unterland. (Gro) = Heuchelberg. (Vin) = Ochsenberg.

Brador (Can). A hopped Ale that has been top-fermented. Produced by the Molson Brewery in Quebec. 6.25% alc. by vol.

Braes of Glenlivet (Scot). A single Malt whisky distillery in north-east Scotland. Owned by Seagram. A Highland malt whisky. 40% alc. by vol.

Braga (Port). A wine district in the region of Entre Minho e Douro. Produces red and white Vinhos Verdes.

Braggot (Eng). An old-fashioned beverage of spices, honey and ale wort.

Bragi (Ch.Isles). Intoxicated, tipsy, drunk.

Brahma Beer (Bra). A Beer brewed in Brazil by the Brahma Brewery in Rio and exported for sale in USA.

Brahma Brewery (Bra). A brewery based in Rio de Janeiro. Noted for its Brahma Chopp beer.

Brahma Chopp (Bra). A Pilsener-type beer 1048 O.G. brewed by the Brahma Brewery in Rio.

Brahms and Liszt (Eng). A bottle conditioned Sediment beer brewed by the Selby Brewery, Selby, North Yorkshire.

Brahms and Liszt (Eng) (slang). Cockney rhyming slang to denote a drunken person. Someone under the influence of alcohol.

Braine (Fr). A Canton in the Soissons district of Champagne. Has the Cru village of Cersauil.

Brain's Brewery (Wales). Old well-known brewery in the centre of Cardiff. Produces many fine beers including – Red Dragon 1035 O.G. Red Dragon Dark 1035 O.G. Red Dragon Bitter 1035 O.G. and keg Capital 1033 O.G.

Brainstorm (Cktl). 2 ozs. Irish whiskey, 2 dashes Bénédictine, 2 dashes dry Vermouth. Serve in an old-fashioned glass with ice, twist of orange peel. Stir.

Brain-sur-Allonnes (Fr). A commune in the A.C. Saumur, Anjou-Saumur, Loire. Produces red and white wines.

Brakspear's Brewery (Eng). Also known as the Henley Brewery, Henley-on-Thames. Produces – XXX Mild 1030 O.G. XXXX Old 1043 O.G. Beehive Keg Bitter 1035 O.G. and Special 1043 O.G.

Bramaterra (It). D.O.C. red wine from Piemonte. Made mainly from the Nebbiolo grape.

Branca Menta (Fr). A green, mint digestif produced by Fernet Branca. Uses many herbs, is aged for 1 year in Slovenian oak. Is softer than Fernet Branca.

Brancelho (Port). A white grape variety used in the production of Vinhos Verdes.

Brancellao (Sp). A red grape variety grown on the Ribeiro area of north western Spain. Produces deep-coloured acidic wines.

Branco (Port). White.

Branco Extra Seco (Port). A white Port produced by Quinta do Noval. The sugar is fermented out before the spirit (Brandy) is added.

Branco Lameiro (Port). A white grape variety grown in Lima for Vinhos Verdes.

Branco Seco (Bra). Dry white wine.

Branco Suave (Bra). Mellow white wine.

Brand (Lucien) (Fr). An Alsace wine producer. Address = 67120 Ergersheim.

Brand Brouwerij (Hol). See Brand's Brouwerij.

Brande Conde (Sp). A famous Brandy produced by Osborne.

Branded Wines (Eng). Wines sold on their brand name instead of the area/ region name. e.g 'Blue Nun', 'Mateus Rosé' etc.

Brandeln (Ger). A term used to describe a wine with a taste of caramel or brandy.

Branderij and Gistfabriek 'Hollandia 11' BV (Hol). A large Moutwijn producer. Part of Grist-Brocades NV group.

Brander Winery (USA). A small winery based in Santa Barbara, California. Grape variety – Sauvignon blanc.

Brandeston Priory (Eng). A vineyard based in Woodbridge, Suffolk. 2.5 ha.

First planted in 1975. Grape varieties Müller-Thurgau 90% plus small parcels of other varieties.

Brandevin (Fr). Brandy (unmatured clear wine spirit).

Brandevinier (Fr). A travelling distiller of Brandy or Eau-de-vie.

Brandewijn (Hol). Lit – 'Burnt wine'. Brandy. (Fr) = Vin brûlé.

Brandewyn (Hol). The same as Brandewijn.

Brandied Ginger (Cktl). ⅔ measure Cognac, ⅓ measure Stones Ginger Wine, 2 dashes lime juice, 2 dashes orange juice. Shake over ice, strain into a cocktail glass. Serve with a piece of preserved ginger and grated chocolate.

Brandied Madeira (Cktl). ⅙ measure Brandy, ⅙ measure Boal Madeira, 4 dashes French vermouth. Stir over ice, strain into an ice-filled old-fashioned glass. Add twist of lemon.

Brandied Port (Cktl). ⅙ measure Brandy, ⅙ measure Tawny Port, 4 dashes lemon juice, 4 dashes Maraschino. Shake over ice, strain into an ice-filled old-fashioned glass. Add slice of orange.

Brandig (Ger). Term used to describe a wine with a spirity, brandy taste.

Branding (Eng). Method of placing a mark with hot iron on the cork to give authenticity to the bottle's contents.

Brand Labelling (Eng). The names on wine labels that are to do with the producer and have no actual name of wine. e.g 'Mateus Rosé'.

Brand Name (Eng). See Branded Wines.

Brand's Brouwerij (Hol). A brewery based in Wijke, Limburg. Noted for its wide range of unpasteurised beers including Imperator and Brand Up '52. Granted the title Koninklijke (Royal) by the Queen of the Netherlands.

Brands Vineyard (Austr). A winery of Coonawarra in South Australia. Grape varieties – Cabernet and Shiraz. Wines sold under the Laira label.

Brand Up '52 (Hol). A well-hopped Pils beer brewed by the Brand Brouwerij in Wijke.

Brandvlei Co-operative (S.Afr). Vineyards based in Dornrivier, Worcester. Address = Brandvlei Koöperatiewe Wynkelder, Private Bag X3001, Worcester 6850. Produces varietal wines.

Brandvlei Koöperatiewe Wynkelder (S.Afr). See Brandvlei Co-operative.

Brandy (Eng). Distillation of wine made from grape must.

Brandy Alexander (Cktl). ⅓ measure Brandy, ⅓ measure (brown) Crème de Cacao, ⅓ measure cream. Shake over ice, strain into a cocktail glass. Grate

nutmeg on top.

Brandy Alexander Milk Punch (Cktl). ⅕ gill Cognac, ⅛ gill Crème de Cacao, 1 gill milk. Shake well over ice, strain into a highball glass. Top with grated nutmeg and serve with straws.

Brandy and Ginger Ale (Cktl). Place 1 measure Brandy in a tumbler containing 2 ice cubes. Top with ginger ale and stir.

Brandy and Soda (Cktl). Place 1 measure Brandy in a tumbler with 2 ice cubes. Top with soda water.

Brandy Antinori (It). A well-known Brandy from Antinori.

Brandy Balloon (Eng). The name given to the 'nosing glass'. Has a large bowl and narrow lip. Used for nosing wines during production. Is favoured by the British as a brandy glass. See Brandy Inhaler and Brandy Snifter.

Brandy Blazer (Cktl). 2 measures Cognac, 1 lump sugar, orange and lemon zest. Mix altogether in a pan, ignite, stir then extinguish. Strain into an old-fashioned glass. May add ½ fl.oz. Kahlúa.

Brandy Cassis Cocktail (Cktl). 1 measure Brandy, ½ measure lemon juice, 1 dash Crème de Cassis. Shake over ice, strain into a cocktail glass. Add twist of lemon peel.

Brandy Champerelle Cocktail (Cktl). ½ measure Cognac, ½ measure Curaçao, 2 dashes Angostura. Stir over ice in a balloon glass.

Brandy Cobbler (Cktl).(1). 1 gill Brandy, ¼ gill brown Curaçao. Shake over broken ice, strain into highball with ice. Decorate with dash lemon peel juice, 2 slices lemon, spoon and straws.

Brandy Cobbler (Cktl).(2). 1 measure Brandy, 4 dashes orange Curaçao, sugar to taste. Fill 5 oz. wine goblet with crushed ice, add brandy, sugar and Curaçao. Stir, decorate with fruit, add sprig of mint and serve with straws.

Brandy Cocktail (Cktl).(1). ½ gill Cognac, 3 dashes Curaçao, dash Angostura. Stir over ice, strain into a cocktail glass.

Brandy Cocktail (Cktl).(2). ⅓ gill Cognac, 1 dash Pernod, 4 dashes brown Curaçao, 10 drops Angostura. Stir over ice. Strain into cocktail glass, serve with a cherry and dash of lemon peel juice.

Brandy Cocktail (Cktl).(3). ¼ gill Cognac, ¼ gill dry Vermouth. Stir over ice, strain into a cocktail glass, decorate with cherry and a dash of lemon peel juice.

Brandy Cocktail (Cktl).(4). ⅓ gill Brandy, 2 dashes sugar syrup, 2 dashes

Angostura. Stir over ice, strain into a cocktail glass. Add twist of lemon peel.

Brandy Cocktail (Cktl).(5). ½ measure Cognac, ¼ measure Italian vermouth, ¼ measure Grand Marnier, 2 dashes Angostura. Shake over ice, strain into a cocktail glass. Squeeze of orange peel juice on top.

Brandy Collins (Cktl). See Collins, substitute brandy for spirit.

Brandy Crusta (Cktl). ⅓ gill Brandy, ⅙ gill lemon juice, dash Orange bitters, dash Angostura, ½ teaspoon powdered sugar, teaspoon plain syrup, teaspoon Maraschino. Shake over ice, strain. Moisten inside of wine glass with lemon juice and sprinkle with sugar. Add mixture and serve with fruit slices and lemon peel.

Brandy Daisy (Cktl). ½ gill Brandy, ½ gill lemon juice, ½ gill lime juice, ¼ gill Grenadine. Shake over ice, strain into a highball and fill up with soda water. Serve with slices of fruit on top and a spoon.

Brandy de Bayo (Ch.Isles). Cherry brandy. Home-made by soaking cherries and raspberries in brandy with cinnamon, cloves and sugar.

Brandy de Gengivre (Ch.Isles). Ginger cordial.

Brandy del Bourgogne (It). A Brandy produced by Gambarotta.

Brandy Egg Flip (Cktl).(1). 1 egg, 1 measure Brandy and sugar syrup to taste. Shake and strain into a cocktail glass. Add grated nutmeg.

Brandy Egg Flip (Cktl).(2). 1 measure Brandy, 1 teaspoon sugar, 3 measures hot water. Place ingredients into a tumbler, stir, float a toasted biscuit on top. Add grated nutmeg.

Brandy Egg Nogg (Cktl). ½ gill Brandy, ⅓ gill Rum, 1 teaspoon sugar, 1 egg, ¾ gill milk. Shake over ice, strain into a highball. Top with grated nutmeg.

Brandy Fix (Cktl). 1½ fl.ozs. Brandy, 4 fl.ozs. lemon juice, ½ fl.oz. Cherry brandy, 4 dashes Gomme syrup. Pour into a goblet filled with crushed ice, stir slightly. Add orange and lemon slices and a cherry. Serve with straws.

Brandy Fizz (Cktl). ½ gill Brandy, 4 dashes brown Curaçao, dash Grenadine, ¾ gill lemon juice, white of egg. Shake over ice, strain into a highball. Top with soda.

Brandy Flip (Cktl). See Brandy Egg Flip.

Brandy Float (Cktl). A measure of Cognac floating on top of a glass of water. Is achieved by placing a whisky glass of water over a pony glass of Brandy. The pony glass is gently removed leaving the Brandy floating on top of the water.

Brandy Gump (Cktl). ½ measure Brandy, ½ measure lemon juice, 2 dashes Grenadine. Shake over ice, strain into a cocktail glass.

Brandy Highball (Cktl). As for Gin Highball but using Brandy in place of the Gin.

Brandyhum (Cktl). Equal quantities of Van der Hum and brandy.

Brandy Inhaler (USA). The name often used for a Balloon glass (nosing glass).

Brandy Mac Cocktail (Cktl). ½ measure Brandy, ½ measure Ginger wine. Shake over ice. strain into an ice-filled highball. Top with soda.

Brandy Milk Punch (Cktl). 1½ fl.ozs. Brandy, 2 fl.ozs. milk, barspoon sugar. Shake over ice, strain into wine goblet. Top with nutmeg.

Brandy Punch (Cktl).(1). ¾ gill Brandy, juice ½ lemon, sugar syrup to taste. Shake well over ice, strain into a wine goblet. Top with iced soda water.

Brandy Punch (Cktl).(2). 1 measure Brandy, 4 dashes Curaçao. Stir with ice in a highball, top with ginger ale. Add mint and fruit.

Brandy Punch (Punch) (1). Juice of 12 lemons, 4 oranges, 1 gill Gomme syrup, 6 fl.ozs. Grenadine, 2 pints soda water, 6 fl.ozs. Cointreau, 2 bottles Brandy, ¾ pint strong cold tea. Stir well together, decorate with fruits in season.

Brandy Punch (Punch) (2). ½ bottle Cognac, 2 measures white Rum, 3 measures Cointreau, 1 measure Maraschino, juice 10 lemons, ¾ lb. sugar, 1 pint iced soda water. Stir the sugar in the lemon juice. Pour in remaining ingredients except soda. Leave to chill, add soda, decorate with fruit in season.

Brandy Rickey (Cktl). Place the juice of ½ a lime and 3 ice cubes into a highball glass. Add 1½ measures Brandy and top with soda. Serve with twist of lime peel.

Brandy Rum (W.Ind). Name given to the Haitian rum because it is lighter and less pungent than most rums. Also applied to Barbados rum.

Brandy Sangaree (Cktl). Equal parts of Brandy and water with barspoon of sugar. Fill glass with crushed ice, stir in ingredients. Top with grated nutmeg.

Brandy Scaffa (Cktl). Equal quantities of Brandy and Maraschino in a cocktail glass. Stir, add 2 dashes Angostura on top and serve.

Brandy Shamparelle (Cktl). ¼ measure Anisette, ¼ measure red Cointreau, ¼ measure Yellow Chartreuse, ¼ measure Brandy. Shake over ice, strain into a cocktail glass.

Brandy Shrub (Eng). Place the juice of 5

lemons and the zest of 2 lemons with 4 pints Brandy into a bowl. Cover and stand for 3 days. Add 2 pints sweet Sherry and 2 lbs. sugar. Stir well, strain through a jelly bag and bottle. Drink as required.

Brandy Sling (Cktl). Dissolve a teaspoon of powdered sugar into the juice of ½ a lemon and a little water. Add ⅓ gill Cognac. Place into an ice-filled old-fashioned glass. Top with a twist of lemon peel.

Brandy Smash (Cktl). 1½ fl.ozs. Brandy, 6 leaves mint, powdered sugar. Dissolve sugar in a little water in an old-fashioned glass. Add mint and bruise to extract flavour. Add brandy, fill with crushed ice. Stir, decorate with lemon slice. Serve with straws.

Brandy Snaps (Eng). Not a drink but a type of cake. Made with sugar syrup, butter, flour and ginger.

Brandy Snifter (USA). Name given to the nosing glass. (Brandy balloon).

Brandy Sour (Cktl). 1½ fl.ozs. Brandy, ¾ fl.oz. lemon juice, teaspoon powdered sugar. Shake well over ice, strain into a tall glass, top with soda, add a slice of orange and a cherry.

Brandy Squirt (Cktl). ⅓ gill Brandy, 2 barspoons powdered sugar, 4 dashes Grenadine. Shake over ice, strain into a highball glass, top with soda water. Decorate with a pineapple piece and a strawberry on a cocktail stick.

Brandy Swizzle (Cktl). Place the juice of a lime, 1 teaspoon powdered sugar and 2 fl.ozs. soda water into a collins glass over ice. Stir with a swizzle stick, add 2 dashes Angostura, ⅓ gill Gin, top with soda and serve with swizzle stick.

Brandy Toddy [cold] (Cktl). Place ½ teaspoon powdered sugar and 1 teaspoon water into an old-fashioned glass. Stir, add ⅓ gill Brandy and an ice cube. Stir, add twist of lemon peel juice on top.

Brandy Toddy [hot] (Cktl). Place a sugar cube into a warmed old-fashioned glass. Fill ⅔ full very hot water, add ⅓ gill Brandy. Stir, decorate with lemon slice, top with grated nutmeg.

Brandy Vermouth (Cktl). ⅘ measure Brandy, ⅕ measure Italian vermouth, dash Angostura. Stir over ice, strain into a cocktail glass.

Brandy Warmer (Cktl). Add 1 teaspoon of Cognac to ⅓ pint freshly brewed tea. Float a slice of lemon on top. Serve with a cinnamon stick.

Brandy Warmer (Eng). A silver pot with a handle used to heat brandy in the eighteenth century for serving as a toddy.

Branik Brewery (Czec). A small brewery in the north west of Prague. Noted for its dark beer called Tmavé 12°, served in a bar called 'The Cave' which is situated in the former monastry of St. Thomas. Founded in 1898.

Branntwein (Ger). Brandy. Lit – 'Burnt wine'.

Branntwein aus Wein (Ger). Lit – 'Made from wine'. When found on a label it denotes that the Brandy does not contain 38% alc. by vol. and may not have been oak matured.

Brännvin (Den) (Swe). Aquavit.

Branscourt (Fr). A Cru Champagne village in the Canton de Ville-en-Tardenois. District = Reims.

Brant Cocktail (Cktl). ¼ measure peppermint liqueur, ¾ measure Brandy, dash Angostura. Shake over ice, strain into a cocktail glass. Serve with dash lemon peel juice on top.

Brantini (Cktl). 1 measure Brandy, ⅔ measure Gin, dash French vermouth. Stir over ice, strain into an old-fashioned glass with an ice cube. Add a twist lemon peel juice.

Braquet (Fr). A red grape variety grown in the A.C. Bellet district in Provence, south-eastern France.

Bras Armé (Fr). The brand-name of a fine old Cognac from Hennessy.

Brasenose Ale (Eng). A hot drink served on Shrove Tuesday at the Brasenose College. Recipe = 6 pints hot Ale, sugar to taste with 6 roasted eating apples floated on top. Also known as Lamb's Wool.

Brasilian Night (Cktl). ¾ measure Vodka, ¼ measure blue Curaçao, ½ measure Batida de Coco. Shake well over ice, strain into a cocktail glass. Top with chocolate powder.

Brassage (Fr). Brewing.

Brasschaat Brasserie (Bel). A brewery noted for its Witkap Pater, light-coloured, bottle-conditioned, top-fermented beer.

Brasser (Fr). To brew.

Brasserie (Fr). Brewery, Ale-house. Also restaurant.

Brasserie Nationale (Lux). A brewery formed in 1974 by a merger of the Bofferding and Funck-Bricher breweries.

Brasseries du Logone (Afr). A brewery in Chad noted for its Gala Export Beer.

Brasseur (Fr). Brewer.

Bratenhöfchen (Ger). Vineyard. (Anb) = Mosel-Saar-Ruwer. (Ber) = Bernkastel. (Gro) = Badstube. (Vil) = Bernkastel-Kues.

Bratislava Brewery (Czec). A brewery

based in south-east Czec. founded in 1873.

Brau ag Brauerei (Aus). A brewery in Linz. Also owns the Schwechat Brauerei near Vienna.

Braubach (Ger). Village. (Anb) = Mittelrhein. (Ber) = Rheinburgengau. (Gro) = Marksburg. (Vins) = Koppelstein, Marmorberg, Mühlberg.

Braucol (Fr). A red grape variety grown in the Gaillac region.

Brauer (Aus) (Ger). Brewer.

Brauerei (Aus) (Ger). Brewery.

Brauhaase Brewery (Afr). A brewery based in Togo noted for its Pilsener beer.

Brauneberg (Ger). Village. (Anb) = Mosel-Saar-Ruwer. (Ber) = Bernkastel. (Gro) = Kurfürstlay. (Vin) = Hasenläufer, Juffer, Juffer-Sonnenhr, Kammer, Klostergarten, Mandelgraben.

Brauneberg (Ger). Vineyard. (Anb) = Mosel-Saar-Ruwer. (Ber) = Bernkastel. (Gro) = Michelsberg. (Vil) = Hetzerath.

Brauneberg (Ger). Vineyard. (Anb) = Mosel-Saar-Ruwer. (Ber) = Bernkastel. (Gro) = Michelsberg. (Vil) = Rivenich.

Brauneberg (Ger). Vineyard. (Anb) = Mosel-Saar-Ruwer. (Ber) = Bernkastel. (Gro) = Sankt Michael. (Vil) = Bekond.

Brauneberg (Ger). Vineyard. (Anb) = Mosel-Saar-Ruwer. (Ber) = Saar-Ruwer. (Gro) = Scharzberg. (Vil) = Konz.

Brauneberg (Ger). Vineyard. (Anb) = Mosel-Saar-Ruwer. (Ber) = Zell/Mosel. (Gro) = Goldbäumchen. (Vil) = Klotten.

Brauneberg (Ger). Vineyard. (Anb) = Mosel-Saar-Ruwer. (Ber) = Zell/Mosel. (Gro) = Weinhex. (Vil) = Oberfell.

Braune Kupp (Ger). Vineyard. (Anb) = Mosel-Saar-Ruwer. (Ber) = Saar-Ruwer. (Gro) = Scharzberg. (Vil) = Wiltingen.

Braunerde (Aus). The name for the brown clay soil found mainly in the Wachau region.

Bräunersberg (Ger). Vineyard. (Anb) = Rheinpfalz. (Ber) = Mittelhaardt-Deutsche Weinstrasse. (Gro) = Schnepfenflug vom Kellertal. (Vil) = Ottersheim/Zellerthal.

Braunfels (Ger). Vineyard. (Anb) = Mosel-Saar-Ruwer. (Ber) = Saar-Ruwer. (Gro) = Scharzberg. (Vil) = Wiltingen.

Braunweiler (Ger). Village. (Anb) = Nahe. (Ber) = Schloss Böckelheim. (Gro) = Rosengarten. (Vins) = Hell-

enpfad, Michaeliskapelle, Schlossberg, Welterkreuz.

Brautrock (Ger). Vineyard. (Anb) = Mosel-Saar-Ruwer. (Ber) = Zell/Mosel. (Gro) = Grafschaft. (Vil) = Bullay.

Brave Bull (Cktl). 1 fl. oz. Tequila, 1 fl.oz. Coffee liqueur. Pour over ice into a tall glass, stir, add a twist of lemon.

Braye Brewery (Ch.Isles). Opened in 1984 in Alderney. Brews from malt extract. Produces Alderney Ale 1035 O.G.

Brazil (S.Am). Grows mainly hybrid grape varieties. Wines consumed mainly locally. Also produces spirits (Pisco, Rum and grain spirits). Largest coffee-producing country in the world.

Brazil Cocktail (Cktl). ¼ gill dry Sherry, ¼ gill French vermouth, dash Orange bitters, 2 dashes Pernod, 2 dashes sugar syrup. Stir over ice, strain into a cocktail glass, squeeze of lemon peel juice on top.

Brazil [Coffee] (S.Am). The world's largest producer. Regions of Bahia, Parama, Santos (Bourbon Santos, Flat Bean Santos and Red Santos) and Victoria.

Bread Wine (USSR). The historical name given to Russian Vodka as it was traditionally made from grain.

Breaker (Eng). A Malt liquor 1047 O.G. brewed by Tennents (Bass).

Breaker (Eng). A small water cask used on a boat to carry drinking water in the eighteenth century.

Breakfast Cocktail (Cktl). ½ measure Port, ¼ measure Crème de Cacao, ¼ fresh lemon juice, 2 dashes light Rum, dash egg white. Shake over ice, strain into a cocktail glass. Top with nutmeg.

Breakfast Coffee (Eng). The name given to light, mild-roasted coffees.

Breakfast Cup (Eng). China drinking vessel of ½ pint capacity, used at breakfast for tea, coffee etc.

Breakfast Egg Nogg (Cktl).(1). ½ gill V.S.O.P. Cognac, ¼ gill orange Curaçao, 1 fresh egg, 1 gill milk. Shake well over ice, strain into a tumbler. Add grated nutmeg.

Breakfast Egg Nogg (Cktl).(2). ⅓ gill Apricot brandy, ⅛ gill Curaçao, 1 egg, 1 gill milk. Blend together, strain into a highball glass. Top with grated nutmeg.

Breaking Down (Eng). A term applied to the distillation of spirits to denote the adding of pure water to the spirit to reduce it to the required strength.

Breaky Bottom Vineyard (Eng). Planted in 1974. Sited at Rodmell, Lewes, Sussex. 1.75 ha. Grape varieties – Müller-Thurgau and Seyval blanc.

B

Breathalyse (Eng). To test on the Breathalyser.

Breathalyser (Eng). An instrument used by police forces in many countries to detect the alcohol level in motor vehicle drivers' blood. This is achieved by taking a breath sample with a variety of styles of equipment.

Breathalyze (Eng). See Breathalyse.

Breathalyzer (Eng). See Breathalyser.

Breathing (Eng). The action of wine as it matures in the bottle. Minute amounts of air pass between the cork and bottle neck during a long period of time. Also applies when the cork is drawn and the wine is allowed to 'Breathe' for a period of time before it is consumed.

Breath Test (Eng). The term for the taking of a breath sample on the Breathalyser.

Brebaje (W.Ind). The name given to an Aguardiente produced in Puerto Rico.

Breckenridge Cellars (USA). The brand-name used for a range of varietal wines produced by the Giumarra vineyards.

Breclav Brewery (Czec). Old brewery based in southern Czec. founded in 1522.

Brecon (Bel). A still and sparkling mineral water imported into the U.K. by Spadel.

Brecon Bubbly (Wales). A bottled carbonated mineral water from the Brecon Beacons in Mid-Wales.

Brecon Natural Spring Water (Wales). A bottled mountain spring water from the Brecon Beacons in Mid-Wales. Still and carbonated.

Brède (La) (Fr). A commune in the A.C. Graves region of central-western Bordeaux.

Breda Bier (Afr). A Lager beer brewed under licence from the Breda Brewery in Holland.

Breda Brouwerij (Hol). See Bierbrouwerij de Drie Hoefijzers.

Breda Royal Lager (Hol). A Lager beer brewed by the Bierbrouwerij de Drie Hoefijzers.

Brède, [La] (Fr). A moated estate in the Graves, Bordeaux. Produces dry white wine.

Brédif (Fr). A grower with cellars at Rochecorbon in Vouvray, Touraine.

Breed (Eng). A term used to describe a wine of fine quality distinguished for its kind.

Breedeberg (S.Afr). A varietal wine produced by the KWV.

Breede River Valley (S.Afr). A controlled region of origin in the Cape province. Noted for its fortified wines.

Breërriviervallei Wines (S.Afr). See De Wet Co-operative.

Breganze (It). A small town in Veneto. Name also applies to six types of wine.

Breganze Bianco (It). D.O.C. white wine from Veneto region. Made with the Pinot bianco, Pinot grigio, Riesling italico, Tocai, Sauvignon and Vespaiolo grape varieties.

Breganze-Cabernet (It). D.O.C. red wine from Veneto region. Made with the Cabernet franc and Cabernet sauvignon grape varieties. Is classified as Superiore if is 12% alc. by vol. minimum.

Breganze-Pinot Bianco (It). D.O.C. white wine from the Veneto region. Made from the Pinot bianco and Pinot grigio grape varieties. Is classified as Superiore if is 12% alc. by vol. minimum.

Breganze-Pinot Nero (It). D.O.C. red wine from the Veneto region. Made with the Pinot nero grape variety. Is classified as Superiore if is 12% alc. by vol. minimum.

Breganze Rosso (It). D.O.C. red wine from the Veneto region. Made with the Cabernet franc, Cabernet sauvignon, Freisa, Groppello, Marzomina, Merlot and Pinot nero.

Breganze-Vespaiolo (It). D.O.C. white wine from the Veneto region. Made from the Vespaiolo grape variety. Classified as Superiore if is 12% alc. by vol. minimum.

Breidecker (N.Z.). A white grape variety used in blending.

Breinsberg (Ger). Vineyard. (Anb) = Rheinpfalz. (Ber) = Mittelhaardt-Deutsche Weinstrasse. (Gro) = Schnepfenflug von Zellertal. (Vil) = Rüssingen.

Breisach a. Rh. (Ger). Village. (Anb) = Baden. (Ber) = Kaiserstuhl-Tuniberg. (Gro) = Vulkanfelsen. (Vins) = Augustinerberg, Eckartsberg.

Breiselberg (Ger). Vineyard. (Anb) = Nahe. (Ber) = Kreuznach. (Gro) = Schlosskapelle. (Vil) = Windesheim.

Breisgau (Ger). Bereich. (Anb) = Baden. (Gros) = Burg Lichteneck, Burg Zähringen, Schutterlindenberg.

Breit (Ger). A term used to describe a sound wine that has no finesse.

Breitenweg (Ger). Vineyard. (Anb) = Nahe. (Ber) = Kreuznach. (Gro) = Kronenberg. (Vil) = Bad Kreuznach.

Brela (Yug). A wine-producing region in Dalmatia.

Bremm (Ger). Village. (Anb) = Mosel-Saar-Ruwer. (Ber) = Zell/Mosel. (Gro) = Grafschaft. (Vins) = Calmont, Frauenberg, Laurentiusberg. Schlemmertröpfchen.

Bremm (Ger). Village. (Anb) = Mosel-Saar-Ruwer. (Ber) = Zell/Mosel. (Gro)

B

= Rosenhang. (Vins) = Abtei, Kloster Stuben.

Brenin Bitter (Wales). A light keg Bitter 1034 O.G. brewed by the Crown Brewery in South Wales.

Brenner (Ger). A fungal disease that browns the vine leaves between the veins on the basal leaves. Treated with copper sulphate.

Brentwein (Ger). Brandy. Lit – 'Burnt wine'. See also Branntwein.

Breque (Fr). A producer of Bordeaux Mousseaux based at Pain-de-Sucre, Côte de Bourg, north-eastern Bordeaux.

Bresparolo (It). Veneto name for the white Vespaiolo grape.

Bressande (La) (Fr). A noted vineyard in the A.C. commune of Rully, Côte Chalonnaise, Burgundy.

Bressandes (Les) (Fr). A Premier Cru vineyard in the A.C. commune of Beaune, Côte de Beaune, Burgundy. 21.8 ha.

Bressanone (It). A term used in the Trentino-Alto Adige region for the Valle Isarsco wines if produced in the communes of Varna and Bressanone.

Bressanone (It). A local name in the Trentino-Alto Adige region for the Austrian white Brixen grape.

Bresse-sur-Grosne (Fr). A commune in the Mâconnais district where Mâcon Supérieur is produced.

Breton (Fr). Touraine, Loire name for the Cabernet franc grape variety. Also known as the Bouchet, Bouchy and the Véron.

Breton Fils (Fr). Récoltants-Manipulants in Champagne. Address = 12 Rue Courte-Pilate, Congy, 51270 Montmort. Produces – Vintage and non-vintage wines.

Brettach (Ger). Village. (Anb) = Württemberg. (Ber) = Württembergisch Unterland. (Gro) = Staufenberg. (Vin) = Berg.

Brettanomyces Bruxelliensis (Bel). A wild yeast used for making Lambic beer.

Brettanomyces Lambicus (Bel). A wild yeast used for making Lambic beer.

Bretterins (Les) (Fr). A Premier Cru vineyard (including La Chapelle) in Beaune, A.C. commune of Auxey-Duresses, Côte de Beaune, Burgundy. 5 ha.

Bretzenheim (Ger). Village. (Anb) = Nahe. (Ber) = Kreuznach. (Gro) = Kronenberg. (Vins) = Felsenköpfchen, Hofgut, Pastorei, Schlossgarten, Vogelsang.

Bretzfeld (Ger). Village. (Anb) = Württemberg. (Ber) = Württembergisch Unterland. (Gro) = Lindelberg. (Vin) = Goldberg.

Bretz Winery (USA). A winery situated on Middle Bass Island, Ohio. Produces fine hybrid wines.

Breuil (Le) (Fr). A Cru Champagne village in the Canton de Dormans. District = Épernay.

Breuil (Le) (Fr). A vineyard in the A.C. commune of Montagny, Côte Chalonnaise, Burgundy.

Breuningsweiler (Ger). Village. (Anb) = Württemberg. (Ber) = Remstal-Stuttgart. (Gro) = Kopf. (Vin) = Holzenberg.

Breuningsweiler (Ger). Village. (Anb) = Württemberg. (Ber) = Remstal-Unterland. (Gro) = Wartbühl. (Vin) = Haselstein.

Breuwan (Eng). An old Saxon word for brewer.

Brevet Royal (Fr). A 4 year old Cognac produced by Rouyer.

Bréviaire (Fr). A bottle similar in style to the bocksbeutel.

Brew (Eng). The name given to the boiling wort by the brewer. See also Brewing

Brew (Eng) (slang). For drink.

Brew (USA). Applied to the ferment in beer or lager.

Brewer (Eng). A person who makes (brews) beer. (Fr) = Brasseur, (Ger) = Brauer. (Hol) = Brouwer. (It) = Birraio, (Port) = Fabricante de Cerveja, (Sp) = Cervecero. (Wales) = Darllawydd.

Breweriana (Eng). Collectable items associated with Public houses or Breweries – usually in the form of advertising for a brewery's products.

Brewer's Bitter (Eng). A cask conditioned Ale 1037 O.G. brewed by the Ind Coope Brewery, Romford, Essex.

Brewer's Choice (Euro). A top-fermented Bitter 1050 O.G. brewed by Farsons Brewery in Malta.

Brewer's Gold (Eng). A type of hop used in Britain for the 'Dry hopping' of cask conditioned beers. Heavy cloying aroma and flavour.

Brewer's Gold (USA). A style of Ballantine ale 1070 O.G. brewed by the Falstaff's Narrangansett Brewery, Cranston, Rhode Island.

Brewers Gold Ale (Eng). A bottled strong Ale 1078 O.G. brewed by the Truman's Brewery, London.

Brewers' Society (Eng). Address = 42. Portman Square, London, W1H 0BB.

Brewer Street Rascal (Cktl). 1 fl.oz. Mandarine Napoléon, ⅓ fl.oz. Vodka, 4 fl.ozs. grapefruit juice, dash egg white. Shake well over ice, strain into a large wine glass. Decorate with a wedge of grapefruit.

Brewery (Eng). A building for making beer. (Aus) = Brauerei, (Bel) (Fr) = Brasserie, (Hol) = Brouwerij, (Ger) = Brauerei, (It) = Fabbrica, (Port) = Fábrica de Cerveja, (Sp) = Cerveceria, (Tur) = Bira Fabrikasi, (Wales) = Darllawyd.

Brewery Bitter (Eng). A cask conditioned Bitter 1036 O.G. brewed by the Smiles Brewery in Bristol, Avon.

Brewery Conditioned (Eng). A term used for beer which is conditioned at the brewery. e.g. Keg.

Brewery Tap (Eng). The name given to the Pub/Bar usually found built into the Brewery premises.

Brewex (Eng). A brewing trade fair held every few years.

Brewhouse (Eng). Part of the brewery where the brewing of the beer takes place.

Brewhouse (Eng). A public house in Poole, Dorset. Owned by the Poole Brewery which brews its own beers. Produces cask conditioned High Street Mild 1035 O.G. High Street Bitter 1036 O.G. Bosun 1048 O.G. Dave's Lager 1048 O.G.

Brewhouse Ale (Eng). A top Bitter 1055 O.G. brewed by Reepham Brewery, Norfolk.

Brewing Kettle (USA). Fermenting vessel.

Brew Kettle (Eng). A vessel used to heat the Wort during the brewing process. Also known as a Copper.

Brewmaster Ale (Eng). An Export Lager 1042 O.G. brewed by Whitbread's.

Brewster (Eng). An old term for a female brewer. Now used for a brewer of either sex.

Brewster Sessions (Eng). Annual licensing court which meets in February. It is the main court for issuing, transferring and renewing of classes of drinks licences.

Brew Ten (Eng). A Beer brewed by Bass Worthington at their Bass North plant in Tadcaster, Yorkshire.

Brew X1 (Eng). A famous Midlands cask conditioned and keg Bitter brewed by Mitchells and Butlers Brewery, Birmingham.

Brey (Ger). Village. (Anb) = Mittelrhein. (Ber) = Rheinburgengau. (Gro) = Gedeonseck. (Vin) = Hämmchen.

Brezanky (Czec). A wine-producing town based north of Prague.

Brézé (Fr). A commune near Saumur, Anjou-Saumur in the Loire region.

Brezloff (Sp). A brand of Vodka produced by Cocal in Telde, Canary Islands.

Breznice Brewery (Czec). An old brewery based in Breznice, western Czec.

Bri (La) (S.Afr). A vineyard based in Franschhoek. Address = La Bri, Franschoek,

7690. Produces – Blanc de la Bri.

Brian O'Lynn (Eng). The London cockney rhyming slang for Gin.

Bricco Manzoni (It). A red wine from Monforte d'Alba in the Piemonte. Made from a blend of Barbera and Nebbiolo grapes.

Bricher Meisterbock (Lux). A Beer brewed by the Funck Brewery in Neudorf.

Brick Dust (Eng). The description given to the flavour of fine red Graves wines.

Brick Tea (China). Also known as Pressed Tea, a tea pressed into bricks for ease of transport. Is black in colour and stamped with a description of the tea. Are now rarely made although are still produced by the Tsaiao Liu Chiu Tea Brick Factory.

Bricout et Koch (Fr). Champagne producer. Address = 7, Route de Cramant, 51190, Avize. Produces – Vintage and non-vintage wines. Vintages – 1973, 1975, 1976, 1978, 1981. Labels include Bricout Rosé, Carte Noir, Carte Or and Charles Koch.

Bricout Rosé (Fr). A pale pink, non-vintage Champagne produced by Bricout et Koch from Chardonnay and Pinot noir grapes.

Bridal Cocktail (Cktl). ⁵⁄₁₀ measure Saké Gozenshu, ³⁄₁₀ measure Rosse liqueur, ²⁄₁₀ measure lemon juice, barspoon Maraschino. Shake over ice, strain into a cocktail glass.

Bride's Tears (Hol). The nickname for a Goldwasser and Silberwasser.

Bridge Bitter (Eng). A cask conditioned Ale 1042 O.G. brewed by Burton Bridge Brewery, Burton-on-Trent.

Bridge House (Eng). A Public house next to the Tower bridge in London that brews its own ales. Produces cask conditioned Bermondsey Bitter 1036 O.G. Special 1048 O.G. 007 1055 O.G.

Bridgewater Arms (Eng). A Public house in Little Gaddesden, Hertfordshire that brews its own beers. Produces cask conditioned Best Bitter 1035 O.G. Earl's Bitter 1048 O.G. Old Santa 1066 O.G.

Briedel (Ger). Village. (Anb) = Mosel-Saar-Ruwer. (Ber) = Bernkastel. (Gro) = Vom Heissen Stein. (Vins) = Herzchen, Nonnengarten, Schäferlay, Schlem, Weisserberg.

Briedern (Ger). Village. (Anb) = Mosel-Saar-Ruwer. (Ber) = Zell/Mosel. (Gro) = Goldbäumchen. (Vins) = Rüberberger-Domherrenberg.

Briedern (Ger). Village. (Anb) = Mosel-Saar-Ruwer. (Ber) = Zell/Mosel. (Gro) = Rosenhang. (Vins) = Herrenberg, Kapellenberg, Römergarten, Servatiusberg.

Briesgauer Riesling (Ger). An erroneous varietal name of the Ortlieber (Knipperlé) grape.

Brie-Sous-Archiac (Fr). A commune in the Charente-Maritime Département whose grapes are classed Petite Champagne (Cognac).

Brigg Beer (Nor). A low-alcohol beer 2.2% alc. by vol.

Brighams Creek Rhine Riesling (N.Z.). A dry, fruity, single vineyard white wine from Selaks.

Bright Beer (Eng). Also known as Brewery-conditioned beer. Usually it is chilled and filtered to remove the yeasts and solids.

Brighton Punch (Cktl). ⅓ measure Bourbon whiskey, ⅓ measure Brandy, ⅓ measure Bénédictine, juice ½ orange and lemon. Shake over ice, strain into a collins glass half-filled with crushed ice. Top with soda water, stir. Dress with an orange and lemon slice. Serve with water.

Brights (Can). The biggest winery in Ontario. Produces mainly French-American hybrid wines.

Brigitt (Cktl). ⅓ measure dry Vermouth, ⅓ measure Whisky, ⅓ measure Triple Sec, dash lemon juice. Stir over ice, strain into a cocktail glass. Decorate with an olive.

Briki (Gre). A pot for making Greek (Turkish) coffee. (Arab) = Kanaka, (Tur) = Ibrik.

Briljant (Hol). A premium Beer brewed by the De Kroon Brouwerij in Oirschot, Brabant.

Brillat-Savarin (Fr). An Armagnac distillery. Address = Distillerie Armagnaçaise SA, BP. 55, 32100 Condom.

Brillet (Fr). Cognac producer. Address = Les Aireaux, Graves, 16120 Châteauneuf. 40 ha. in Grande Champagne and 40 ha. in Petite Champagne. Produces – Très Rare Heritage and Poire au Cognac (extract of Poire Williams and Eau-de-vie de Cognac).

Brilliance (Eng). A term used to describe a star-bright or crystal clear wine.

Brilliant (Eng). A term used to describe an absolutely clear drink.

Brimmer (Eng). Term for a glass or bowl or other vessel full to the top (the brim) with liquid.

Brimont (Fr). A Cru Champagne village in the Canton de Bourgogne. District = Reims.

Brinay (Fr). A commune in the A.C. Quincy, Central Vineyards, Loire.

Brinckhoff's N°1 (Ger). A fine Lager beer brewed by the D.U.B. Brauerei in

Dortmund, Westphalia.

Brindar (Port) (Sp). To drink (to the health of). A toast. To toast one's health. Brinde = Toast.

Brindare (It). To drink a toast.

Bring Your Own (Austr). A nickname for restaurants in Melbourne which are un-licensed and customers have to bring their own alcoholic drink (wine etc) to drink with their meal. Known as B.Y.O's.

Briolet (Fr) (slang). A term used for wines of Brie which are very acidic. Is also used for other acidic wines.

Briones (Sp). A Zona de Crianza in the Rioja Alta, north-eastern Spain.

Briotett (Fr). A firm that produces Crème de Cassis liqueur and other fruit liqueurs in Dijon, Côte d'Or.

Brisbane (Austr). A wine region in Queensland in Eastern Australia.

Brissac (Fr). Commune in the A.C. Coteaux de l'Aubance, Anjou-Saumur, Loire. Produces fine rosé wines.

Bristol Blue (Eng). An eighteenth-century type of glass made in Bristol, using Colbalt oxide from Saxony to produce blue-coloured glass decanters etc.

Bristol Bottle (Eng). A mould for making bottles of claret (Bordeaux) shape. Invented by the Bristol glassmakers.

Bristol Brewery (Eng). The name for Hall's Brewery near Bristol. Produces Jacobs Best Bitter 1038 O.G. Bristol Pride 1045 O.G.

Bristol Cream (Sp). Brand name for a dessert Cream Sherry, produced in Jerez de la Frontera by Harvey's. Sweetened Oloroso.

Bristol Dry (Sp). A brand of dry Sherry produced by Harvey's in Jerez de la Frontera.

Bristol Fino (Sp). A brand of dry Sherry produced by Harvey's in Jerez de la Frontera.

Bristol Milk (Sp). A brand of sweet Sherry produced by Harvey's in Jerez de la Frontera.

British Bonded (Eng). A term used to describe Cognacs which travel in cask to England and are matured in London Dock warehouses. Aged in bond and a record kept. See also Old Landed.

British Bottlers' Institute (Eng). B.B.I. A body for the promotion and standards of glass bottling.

British Columbia (Can). A wine region in western Canada.

British Columbia Distillery Co (Can). A subsidiary of Seagram. Produces a range of Canadian whiskies.

British Compounds (Eng). Word used to describe the rectified, redistilled and

B

flavoured spirits.

British Institute of Innkeeping (Eng) Address = 121, London Road, Camberley, Surrey, GU15 3LF.

Britisher's Wine (Eng). A nineteenth-century nickname given to Port.

British Gallon (Eng). British Imperial Gallon. Equal to 1.20 American gallons. Contains 160 Imperial fluid ounces (fl.ozs).

British Institute of Innkeeping (Eng). Address = Ramsey House, Central Square, Wembley, Middlesex. HA9 7 AP.

British Natural Mineral Waters Association (Eng). BNMWA. Associated body of the NMWBWA. Formed to represent the interests of packers and importers of bottled natural mineral waters. See also BSDA.

British Navy Rum (Eng). See Pusser's.

British Plain Spirit (Eng). Spirit produced in the U.K. e.g. Gin, Vodka and Whisky before maturation.

British Sherry (Eng). A sherry style wine made in the U.K. from grape concentrate. Cream and medium styles produced.

British Soft Drinks Association (Eng). A body formed in Bristol on the 1st May 1987. Represents all makers of still, carbonated drinks, bottled waters, fruit and vegetable drinks. Includes the NASDM, NMWBWA and BNMWA.

British Soluble Coffee Manufacturers Association (Eng). Address = 6, Catherine Street, London EC4N 5AB.

British Wine (Eng). Wine made in the U.K. from grape concentrate that is imported and reconstituted. May have flavourings added.

Britvic (Eng). Firm that produces bottled fruit juices and squashes as mixers. Merged with Corona in 1987. See Britvic 55.

Britvic 55 (Eng). A sparkling fruit drink from Britvic. 55% fruit.

Britzingen (Ger). Village. (Anb) = Baden. (Ber) = Markgräflerland. (Gro) = Burg Neuenfels. (Vins) = Altenberg, Rosenberg, Sonnhohle.

Britzingen [ortsteil Dattingen] (Ger). Village. (Anb) = Baden. (Ber) = Markgräflerland. (Gro) = Burg Neuenfels. (Vin) = Altenberg, Rosenberg, Sonnhohle.

Briuwan (Ger). An old word for brewer.

Brives-sur-Charente (Fr). A commune in the Charente-Maritime Département whose grapes are classed Petite Champagne (Cognac).

Brix (USA). A scale of sugar density of grape must. Operates at 17.5°C or 20°C. Invented by A.F.W. Brix in Germany in the nineteenth century. See also Balling and Sykes.

Brixen (Aus). A term used to describe a white grape in the Südtirol. Known as the Bressanone in Italy.

Brizard (Marie) (Fr). A liqueur company that makes a wide range of liqueurs. Based in the Basque country.

Brno Brewery (Czec) A brewery based in Brno southern Czec. founded in 1872.

Broach (Eng). A tool for tapping casks of wine or spirits etc. Also to tap a cask.

Broaching (Eng). Opening, applicable to casks of wine, beer, spirits etc. Also denotes the opening of a cask to remove the contents.

Broadfield Vineyard (Eng). Planted 1972. Address = Broadfield Court Estate, Bodenham, Herefordshire. 4.2 ha. Grape varieties – 75% Reichensteiner and 25% Riesling. Vinified at Pilton Manor. See Bodenham.

Broadside Ale (Eng). A strong Pale ale 1068 O.G. brewed by the Adnams Brewery, Suffolk.

Broadsman Bitter (Eng). A cask conditioned Bitter 1035–1037 O.G. brewed by the Woodeforde Brewery in Norfolk.

Broadway Cocktail (Cktl). ½ gill dry Gin, ¼ gill Italian vermouth, 2 dashes Orange bitters. Shake over ice, strain into a small wine glass. Serve with a dash of orange peel juice on top.

Broc (Fr). A small earthenware brown jug used for wine in mediaeval times.

Brocard (Fr). A négociant based in Beaune, Côte de Beaune, Burgundy.

Brocca (It). Pitcher, jug.

Brochon (Fr). A village that was part of the A.C. Côte de Nuits Villages, but is now part of Gevrey-Chambertin. 53 ha.

Brock Lager (Eng). A Lager 1033 O.G. brewed by the Hall and Woodhouse Brewery, Dorset.

Brod Brewery (Czec). A brewery based in central Czec. founded in 1880.

Brodňanka (Czec). A Mild beer brewed in Uhersky.

Broggingen (Ger). Village. (Anb) = Baden. (Ber) = Breisgau. (Gro) = Burg Lichteneck. (Vin) = Kaiserberg.

Broiling (Eng). A term used for the roasting of coffee beans. See also Singeing.

Broken Leg (Cktl). Stir in a suitable mug 1 oz. Bourbon whiskey, 2½ ozs. hot apple juice, 4 raisins, stick of cinnamon, slice of lemon.

Broken Orange Pekoe (Eng). A type of broken leaf grade tea. Usually used in traditional packet teas.

Broken Pekoe (Eng). A type of broken leaf tea grade. Used in tea bags and in packet tea.

Broken Pekoe Souchong (Eng). A type of broken tea leaf grade, small and uneven.

Broken Spur (Cktl). ¼ measure dry Gin, ¼ measure sweet Vermouth, 1½ measures Port wine, dash Anisette, yolk of egg. Shake over ice, strain into a wine goblet.

Broken Spur Cocktail (Cktl). ⅓ gill Port, ⅙ gill Italian vermouth, 2 dashes Cointreau. Stir over ice, strain into a cocktail glass.

Broken Tea (Eng). A small size tea grade obtained from the sieving of tea leaf. e.g. Broken Pekoe, Fannings, Dust, Broken Orange Pekoe.

Brokenwood Vineyard (Austr). 20 ha. Address = McDonalds Road, Pokolbin, New South Wales 2321. Grape varieties – Cabernet sauvignon, Chardonnay, Hermitage and Sémillon.

Brolio Chianti (It). The most famous of the Chianti Classico estates, also where the Governo process was created.

Brombeergeist (Ger). Blackberry brandy.

Brombeerlikoer (Ger). Blackberry liqueur.

Bromista (Scot). A popular brand of white Rum bottled by Scottish and Newcastle Breweries.

Bromius (Lat). Another name for Bacchus.

Bronco Winery (USA). A winery based near Stanislaus in the Central Valley, California. Produces varietal and table wines.

Brøndums Kummenakvavit (Den). A caraway and cinnamon flavoured Akvavit produced by DDS.

Brøndums Snaps (Den). A low-strength Akvavit produced by DDS.

Brontë (Eng). A honey, spices, herbs and orange-flavouring, brandy based liqueur made in Yorkshire. Bottled in a squat pottery jug. 34% alc. by vol.

Bronte Winery (USA). A large winery based in Paw Paw, Michigan. Produces American and hybrid wines.

Bronx (Cktl). ½ measure dry Gin, ⅙ measure dry Vermouth, ⅙ measure sweet Vermouth, ⅙ measure orange juice, dash egg white. Shake over ice, strain into a cocktail glass.

Bronx Golden (Cktl). As for a Bronx with the addition of an egg yolk. Serve in a flip glass.

Bronx Silver (Cktl). 1 measure Gin, ½ measure dry Vermouth, juice ½ orange, 1 egg white. Shake over ice, strain into a cocktail glass.

Bronx Terrace (Cktl). ⅔ measure dry Gin, ⅓ measure dry Vermouth, dash lime juice cordial. Stir over ice, strain into a cocktail glass, decorate with cherry.

Bronze Port (Austr). A full-bodied, sweet, Port-style wine from West End Wines, New South Wales. Produced from the Hermitage grape.

Brooke Bond Oxo Ltd (Eng). Famous producers of a wide range of teas and coffees based in Croydon. Brands include P.G. Tips (tea) and Red Mountain (coffee).

Brookfields Vineyards (N.Z.). Address = Meeanee, Hawkes Bay, North Island. 3 ha. Grape varieties – Cabernet sauvignon, Chasselas, Gewürztraminer, Müller-Thurgau, Pinot gris and Rhine riesling.

Brooklyn (Cktl). 1½ measures Rye whiskey, ½ measure sweet Vermouth, dash Amer Picon, dash Maraschino. Stir over ice, strain into a cocktail glass.

Brooklyn Kümmel (Cktl). Into a 5 oz. wine glass place some shaved ice and a slice of lemon. Pour ⅕ gill Kümmel on top.

Brook's Club (Eng). An old eighteenth-century tea blend.

Brookside Winery (USA). A multi-owned winery based in Cucamonga, California. Wines sold under the Assumption Abbey, Brane and Brookside labels.

Brookvale Riesling (N.Z.). A brand of white wine produced by the Villa Maria Winery, South Auckland.

Brookvale Riesling Sylvaner (N.Z.). A medium, fruity, white wine from the Villa Maria Winery, South Auckland.

Broomelt (Lux). A vineyard site in the village of Ehnen.

Brother Dominic (N.Z.). An alcoholic beverage containing some grapes produced in 1979 by Montana Wines. (Had undergone process of Oenological Amelioration).

Brotherhood Winery (USA). A winery based in Hudson Valley, New York. Produces hybrid and sparkling wines.

Brotwasser (Ger). Vineyard. (Anb) = Württemberg. (Ber) = Remstal-Stuttgart. (Gro) = Wartbühl. (Vil) = Stetten i.R.

Brotwasser (Ger). Lit – 'Bread water'. A white wine of Stetten in (Anb) = Württemberg. (See). A delicate wine that gets its name from a lady who used to dip her bread into her wine year after year.

Brotzeit (Ger). Elevenses. Morning coffee.

Brou (Roger-Felicien) (Fr). A sparkling wine producer based in Vouvray, Touraine, Loire. Address = Clos de l'Epinay, 37210 Vouvray.

Brouette-Bassereau (Fr). A producer of Bordeaux Mousseux based at Pain-de-

B

Sucre, Côtes de Bourg, north-eastern Bordeaux. Wines made by méthode champenoise.

Broughton Brewery (Scot). Opened in 1980 near Biggar. Produces cask conditioned Greenmantle Ale 1038 O.G. keg Broughton Ale 1036 O.G. and bottled Old Jock 1070 O.G.

Brouillards (Les) (Fr). A Premier Cru vineyard [part] in the A.C. commune of Volnay, Côte de Beaune, Burgundy. 6.5 ha.

Brouillet (Fr). A Cru Champagne village in the Canton de Ville-en-Tardenois. District = Reims.

Brouillis (Fr). Denotes first distillate. The term used in Cognac for the 'heart' of the distillation, separated from the headings and tailings.

Brouilly (Fr). An A.C. Cru Beaujolais-Villages, Burgundy. 1,100 ha. under vine.

Brouwen (Hol). Brew.

Brouwer (Hol). Brewer.

Brouwerij (Hol). Brewery, Brew-house.

Brouwsel (Hol). Mash.

Brown Distillers (Robert) (Can). A subsidiary of Seagram. Produces a range of Canadian whiskies.

Brown Ale (Eng). A bottled sweet, mild ale, usually low in alcohol, lightly hopped and dark in colour.

Brown Betty (Cktl). Brandy, spices, lemon, brown sugar and strong ale. Pour into glass, top with toast cubes. Drunk hot or cold.

Brown Betty (Eng). The name given to the red-brown earthenware teapot.

Brown Bracer Ale (Wales). A Brown ale 1033 O.G. brewed by the Crown Brewery in South Wales.

Brown Brewery (Eng). A collection of four breweries in Blackburn, Carlisle, Masham and Workington. Produce a large range of ales.

Brown Bros (Austr). See Brown Brothers.

Brown Brothers (Austr). A large famous family winery in Milawa, Victoria. Vineyards at King Valley, Koombahla, Milawa, Mystic Park and Whitlands. Grape varieties – Cabernet sauvignon, Chardonnay, Gewürztraminer, Merlot, Muscat, Riesling and Sémillon. Produces varietal, dessert, botrytised and fortified wines. See Tarrango (a red cross between the Touriga and Sultana) and Flora (a sweet yellow-gold coloured dessert wine).

Brown Cocktail (Cktl). ⅓ measure dry Vermouth, ⅓ measure dry Gin, ⅓ measure Jamaican rum. Stir over ice, strain into a cocktail glass.

Brown Cow (Cktl). 1 part Kahlúa, 3 parts

full-cream milk. Stir together with ice, strain into a goblet.

Brown Curaçao (USA). An orange-flavoured liqueur, with orange-brown colour. e.g. Grand Marnier, Van der Hum, etc.

Brown-Forman (USA). A Bourbon whisky distillery based in Louisville, Kentucky.

Browning (Eng). A vine complaint. Usually occurs when careless pruning aimed at increasing production takes place. The vine leaves show brown stains and eventually fall off.

Browning (Eng). A wine complaint. Caused through oxidation by the enzyme Polyesterase. Fruit if rotten acts upon tannin with free oxygen when air is in contact with the wine. Also caused by contamination of wine with metal.

Brown [J.T.S] (USA). A Bourbon whiskey distillery based in Frankfurt, Kentucky.

Brown Muscat (Austr). A dark skinned Muscat grape variety used for making dessert wines in Victoria.

Brown Oxford Ale (Eng). A Brown ale 1032 O.G. brewed by the Morrell's Brewery, Oxford.

Brown Peter Ale (Eng). A Brown ale 1034 O.G. brewed by Peter Walker's Brewery, Warrington.

Brown Sherry (Eng). Sherries made by blending Olorosos with sweetening and colouring wines. Brown sherry was popular with the Victorians whom many have said invented it.

Brown Stout (Eng). A sweet Stout 1040 O.G. brewed by the Holt's Brewery, Manchester.

Brown Velvet (Eng). ⅙ measure Port wine, ⅚ measure sweet Stout. Stir lightly together in a tall glass until blended.

Brown Willy (Eng). An Ale brewed by the Min Pin home-brew public house (inn) at Tintagel, Cornwall.

Broyage (Fr). The crushing of the grapes.

Broyes (Fr). A Cru Champagne village in the Canton de Montmort. District = Reims.

Broyhan Alt (Ger). A noted malty, top-fermented Bier from the Lindener-Gilde Brauerei in Hanover. 5.25% alc. by vol. it has a strong hoppy flavour. Named after a sixteenth-century brewer.

Brözel (Günter) (S.Afr). A noted wine-producer of the Nederburg Estate.

Bruce Breweries (Eng). A chain of home-brew Public houses in London which are under the 'Firkin' banner.

Bruce [David] (USA). A winery in Santa Cruz, California. 10.5 ha. Grape varieties – Cabernet sauvignon, Petit syrah, Pinot noir and Zinfandel.

Bruchsal (Ger). Village. (Anb) = Baden. (Ber) = Badische Bergstrasse/Kraichgau. (Gro) = Mannaberg. (Vin) = Klosterberg.

Bruchsal [stadtteil Obergrombach] (Ger). Village. (Anb) = Baden. (Ber) = Badische Bergstrasse/Kraichgau. (Gro) = Mannaberg. (Vin) = Burgwingert.

Bruchsal [stadtteil Untergrombach] (Ger). Village. (Anb) = Baden. (Ber) = Badische Bergstrasse. (Gro) = Mannaberg. (Vins) = Michaelsberg, Weinhecke.

Bruck (Aus). A wine-producing area on the left bank of the river Danube below Vienna.

Brückchen (Ger). Vineyard. (Anb) = Rheinhessen. (Ber) = Nierstein. (Gro) = Spiegelberg. (Vil) = Nierstein.

Brückstück (Ger). Vineyard. (Anb) = Mosel-Saar-Ruwer. (Ber) = Zell/Mosel. (Gro) = Weinhex. (Vil) = Winningen.

Brüderberg (Ger). Vineyard. (Anb) = Mosel-Saar-Ruwer. (Ber) = Obermosel. (Gro) = Konigsberg. (Vil) = Langsur.

Bruderberg (Ger). Vineyard. (Anb) = Mosel-Saar-Ruwer. (Ber) = Saar-Ruwer. (Gro) = Römerlay. (Vil) = Mertesdorf (ortsteil Maximin Grünhaus).

Brudersberg (Ger). Vineyard. (Anb) = Rheinhessen. (Ber) = Nierstein. (Gro) = Rehbach. (Vil) = Nierstein.

Bruderschaft (Ger). Vineyard. (Anb) = Mosel-Saar-Ruwer. (Ber) = Bernkastel. (Gro) = Sankt Michael. (Vil) = Klüsserath.

Brugerolle (Fr). A Cognac producer. Address = Cognac Brugerolle, 17160 Matha près Cognac. Produces – Napoléon Aigle Rouge 10 y.o. Napoléon Aigle d'Or 25–30 y.o. Très Vieux Cognac Réserve Spéciale X.O. Owns no vineyards.

Brugga (Scan). An old Norse word for brewer.

Bruggeman Distillerie (Bel). A large distillery based in Ghent.

Brugnola (It). A red grape variety.

Brugny-Vaudancourt (Fr). A Cru Champagne village in the Canton d'Avize. District = Epernay.

Bruichladdich (Scot). A single Malt distillery on the island of Islay, owned by Invergordon Distillers. A strong peaty malt whisky. An Islay malt whisky. 10 years old. 43% alc. by vol.

Bruidstranen (Hol). Lit – 'Bride's tears'. A liqueur produced by Van Zuylekom of Amsterdam. A version of Goldwasser.

Bruin Bier (Hol). Brown beer. (Ale).

Bruisyard St. Peter Vineyard (Eng). First planted 1974. Address = Church Road, Bruisyard, Saxmundham, Suffolk. 4 ha. Grape variety – Müller-Thurgau.

Bruito (Port). Dry.

Brükes (Ger). Vineyard. (Anb) = Nahe. (Ber) = Kreuznach. (Gro) = Kronenberg. (Vil) = Bad Kreuznach.

Brûlets (Les) (Fr). A wine-producing village in the commune of Fuissé in A.C. Pouilly-Fuissé, Mâcon, Burgundy.

Bruley (Fr). A Vin gris from commune of same name in the Lorraine region.

Brûlot (Fr). Lit – 'Firebrand'. The action of placing spirit (or liqueur) into a spoon with a sugar cube, igniting it and pouring into a cup of hot black coffee. e.g. Café Brûlot au Rhum.

Brum (Fr). An old word for Rum.

Brummie (Eng). A bottled Brown ale 1032 O.G. brewed by Davenport's Brewery, Birmingham.

Brumov Brewery (Czec). An old brewery based in eastern Czec.

Bründelsberg (Ger). Vineyard. (Anb) = Rheinpfalz. (Ber) = Südliche Weinstrasse. (Gro) = Trappenberg. (Vil) = Schwegenheim.

Brune et Blonde (Fr). Two slopes on the Côte Rotie in the Rhône. The slopes named after the types of soils present. i.e. Brune has soil of iron oxide, Blonde has soil of limestone.

Brunello (It). A red grape variety of the Sangiovese family. Used to produce Brusco dei Barbi Colombini in Tuscany. Made by a unique and long fermentation process.

Brunello di Montalcino (It). A red grape variety grown in the Tuscany region to produce a wine of the same name. Also known as Sangiovese grosso.

Brunello di Montalcino (It). A famous D.O.C.G. red wine produced from the grape of the same name in Tuscany. Vinification and ageing must occur in commune of Montalcino. Must be aged for 4 years minimum. If aged 5 years is classified Riserva.

Brunet (Fr). A cuvée in the vineyard of Bressandes in A.C. Beaune, Côte de Beaune, Burgundy. Is owned by the Hospices de Beaune.

Brunette Cocktail (Cktl). 1/3 measure Bourbon whiskey, 1/3 measure Kahlúa, 1/3 measure cream. Shake over ice, strain into a cocktail glass.

Brunissure (Eng). Browning caused by a lack of pruning and hence overproduction. Brown stains appear on the leaves which then fall off the vine. Can be fatal if the vine becomes exhausted.

Brünnchen (Ger). Vineyard. (Anb) = Mittelrhein. (Ber) = Rheinburgengau. (Gro) = Loreleyfelsen. (Vil) = Nochern.

Brunnenhäuschen (Ger). Vineyard. (Anb) = Rheinhessen. (Ber) = Wonnegau. (Gro) = Bergkloster. (Vil) = Westhofen.

Bruno Colacicchi (It). A noted red wine-producer based in the Latium region. Noted for Torre Ercolana and Romagnano.

Bruno Giacosa (It). A winery based in Neive, Alba in Piemonte. Buys in the grapes from local vineyards.

Bruno Negroni (It). A producer of sparkling (méthode champenoise) wines based in Emilia-Romagna.

Bruno Paillard (Fr). A Champagne house. Address = Rue Jacques Maritain, 51100 Reims. Produces – Vintage and non-vintage wines. Owns no vineyards. Vintages – 1969, 1973, 1974, 1975, 1976, 1979, 1982.

Brunswick Cooler (Cktl). Place into a highball glass the juice of a lemon, 1 teaspoon of sugar syrup, 2 lumps of ice. Add cold ginger ale, stir and serve.

Brussannes (Les) (Fr). See Brussonnes (Les).

Brüssele (Ger). The name given to the wine of Kleinbottwar, Württemberg.

Brussels Lace (Eng). The name given to the foam pattern that is left behind on the sides of the glass after the beer has been consumed.

Brussonnes (Les) (Fr). A Premier Cru vineyard [part] in the A.C. commune of Chassagne-Montrachet, Côte de Beaune, Burgundy. 17.72 ha. (red and white). Also known as Les Brussannes.

Brut (Fr). A term used to describe the driest wines, Champagne and other sparkling wines. It is drier than 'Extra dry'.

Brut (Sp). Dry (for sparkling wines).

Brut de Brut Gran Reserva de Artesania (Sp). A soft, fruity, dry Cava wine produced by Cavas Hill.

Brut de Futs Hors d'Âge (Fr). A style of Cognac produced by Edgard Leyrat.

Brut di Concilio (It). A sparkling (méthode champenoise) wine produced by Lagariavini in the Trentino-Alto Adige region north-eastern Italy.

Brut Intégrale (Fr). Term sometimes used for a completely unsugared Champagne. Also known as Brut Non-Dosé and Brut Zéro.

Brut Natur (Sp). Extra dry (sparkling wine).

Brut Non-Dosé (Fr). See Brut Intégrale and Brut Zéro.

Bruto (Port). Denotes a very dry sparkling wine.

Bruto (Sp). Extra dry.

Brut Quatro Vecchio (It). A sparkling (méthode champenoise) wine made from Chardonnay and Pinot noir grapes by Castello di Bevilacqua. Min. alc. content of 12% by vol.

Brut Sauvage (Fr). A non-dosage Champagne from Piper Heidsieck.

Bruttig-Fankel (Ger). Village. (Anb) = Mosel-Saar-Ruwer. (Ber) = Zell/Mosel. (Gro) = Goldbäumchen. (Vin) = Götterlay.

Bruttig-Fankel (Ger). Village. (Anb) = Mosel-Saar-Ruwer. (Ber) = Zell/Mosel. (Gro) = Rosenhang. (Vins) = Kapellenberg, Langenberg, Martinsborn, Pfarrgarten, Rathausberg, Rosenberg.

Brut Zéro (Fr). See Brut Intégrale and Brut Non-Dosé.

Brympton d'Evercy (Eng). Planted 1974. 0.33 ha. Address = Yeovil, Somerset. Soil – loam pH7. Grape varieties – 50% Müller-Thurgau and 50% Reichensteiner.

BSDA (Eng) (abbr). British Soft Drinks Association.

BSN Bières (Fr). The largest bottle-maker. Has 17 breweries. 2 principal components – Kronenbourg and Société Europé de Brasseries. Tiger Scotch is a well-known brand.

B.T.I. (USA) (abbr). The Beverage Testing Institute.

Bual (Mad). A medium sweet Madeira. See also Boal.

Bubbler (USA). The glass fermentation valve known as an airlock in the U.K.

Bubbles (Eng). CO_2 gas released when sparkling wine or beer is opened.

Bubbly (Eng) (slang). Term for Champagne and other sparkling wines.

Bubeneck (Ger). Vineyard. (Anb) = Rheinpfalz. (Ber) = Mittelhaardt-Deutsche Weinstrasse. (Gro) = Feuerberg. (Vil) = Elflerstadt.

Bubenheim (Ger). Village. (Anb) = Rheinhessen. (Ber) = Bingen. (Gro) = Kaiserpfalz. (Vins) = Honigberg, Kallenberg.

Bubenheim (Ger). Village. (Anb) = Rheinpfalz. (Ber) = Mittelhaardt-Deutsche Weinstrasse. (Gro) = Schnepfenflug vom Zellertal. (Vin) = Hahnenkamm.

Bubenstück (Ger). Vineyard. (Anb) = Rheinhessen. (Ber) = Bingen. (Gro) = Sankt Rochuskapelle. (Vil) = Bingen.

Buçaco (Port). A top quality red wine produced by the Buçaco Hotel near Coimbra in Beira Alta.

Bucaramangas (S.Am). A noted coffee-producing region in Colombia.

Buccaneer Beer (Eng). A cask conditioned Bitter 1065 O.G. brewed by the

Pier Hotel, a home-brew public house in Gravesend.

Buccaneer Beer (Eng). A cask conditioned Bitter 1065 O.G. brewed by the Southeastern, a home-brew public house in Strood.

Buccaneer Punch (Punch). 1 pint Bacardi rum, ½ pint dry white wine, ½ pint orange juice, ¼ pint lemon juice, 1 vanilla pod, 1 cinnamon stick, 4 ozs. sliced fresh pineapple, grated nutmeg. Mix together, chill down, serve with orange and lemon slices.

Buccia Vineyard (USA). A winery based in Conneaut, Ohio. Produces French hybrid wines.

Bucelas (Port). A demarcated area of Portugal. Produces white wines in the Estremadura region on the plains of the river Tejo. See Camilo Alves.

Bucellas (Port). Old spelling of Bucelas.

Buchanan (Scot). Producers of Strathconon (a Vatted malt). Part of the DCL group.

Buchanan Blend (The) (Scot). An 8 year old blended De Luxe Scotch whisky produced by Buchanan and Co. 40% alc. by vol.

Buchbrunn (Ger). Village. (Anb) = Franken. (Ber) = Maindreieck. (Gro) = Hofrat. (Vil) = Heisser Stein.

Bucherburger (Switz). A red wine.

Buchholz (Ger). Village. (Anb) = Baden. (Ber) = Breisgau. (Gro) = Burg Zähringen. (Vin) = Sonnhalde.

Buchner Filter (Eng). A straight-sided funnel which is fitted with a perforated porcelain plate. Used for filtration of wines.

Buchu Brandy (S.Afr). A liqueur Brandy flavoured with the leaves of the Buchu plant.

Buck (The) (Cktl). ½ measure Cognac, ⅔ measure (white) Crème de Menthe, ⅙ measure lemon juice. Shake over ice, strain into an ice-filled collins glass. Top with ginger ale and dress with seedless grapes.

Buckaroo (Cktl). Into a highball glass put 1½ ozs. American Bourbon and several dashes Angostura. Add ice, Coca Cola and stir.

Buckeye Ontario Special Ale (Can). A Beer brewed by the Carling Brewery in Toronto.

Buckfast Wine (Eng). A tonic wine produced by Bénédictine monks in Devon from French wine, herbs and minerals.

Buckie's Brose (Cktl). ⅓ measure Scotch whisky, ⅓ measure Kahlúa, ⅓ measure cream, 1 teaspoon clear honey. Shake well over ice, strain into a cocktail glass. Top with toasted oatmeal.

Buckingham (Can). A brand of dry Gin produced by Hiram Walker.

Buckingham Valley Vineyards (USA). A small winery based in Buckingham, Pennsylvania. 4 ha. Produces French hybrid wines.

Buck Jones Cocktail (Cktl). ¾ measure Jamaican rum, ¼ measure Cream sherry, juice ½ lime. Place together in an ice-filled highball glass. Stir, top with ginger ale.

Buckley Brewery (Wales). The oldest Welsh brewery based at Llanelli. Produces cask conditioned Ales and other styles.

Bucks County Vineyards (USA). A winery based in New Hope, Pennsylvania. Produces Chardonnay, Riesling and French hybrid wines.

Buck's Fizz (Cktl). Place some ice in a highball glass. Add 1 oz. of fresh orange juice then top up with iced Champagne.

Buck's Fizz (Cktl).(Non-alc). In a highball glass mix equal quantities of chilled Ashbourne mineral water and fresh orange juice.

Bucktrout and Co (Ch.Isles). The largest wine and spirits merchants in Guernsey. Bottles own brands of spirits and sherries. See also Guernsey Brewery 1920 Ltd.

Buda (Hun). A red table wine from Budapest.

Budaer Riesling (Ger). An erroneous varietal name for the Kleinweiss white grape variety.

Budafok (Hun). The headquarters of the Hungarian State wine cellars.

Budai (Hun). A white grape variety.

Budding (Eng). The term given to the action of yeast multiplying.

Budějovice (Czec). The modern name for Budweis (Austro-Hungarian Empire name). See České Budějovice.

Budel Brouwerij (Hol). A small brewery based in Budel, north Brabant. Brews unpasteurised beers of same name.

Bud Mutation (USA). A natural mutation of the plant to produce different fruit than that of the parent strain.

Budos (Fr). A commune in the A.C. Graves district of south-western Bordeaux.

Budvar (Czec). A brewery in Bohemia in the town of České Budějovice. Produces the light-coloured beer Budweis. Founded in 1895.

Budweis (Czec). A light-coloured Beer brewed by the Budvar Brewery in České Budějovice.

Budweiser Beer (USA). Beer produced by Anheuser-Busch, St. Louis. Name originates from the Czech town of České Budějovice. Brewed with malted barley or rice and fined over beechwood chips. Brewed under licence by Watneys in England. 1044 O.G.

Budweiser Light (USA). A Malt beer from Anheuser-Busch, St. Louis.

Bué (Fr). A small commune in the A.C. Sancerre district of the Central Vineyards, Loire.

Buehler Vineyards (USA). A small vineyard and winery based in the Napa Valley, California. 25 ha. Grape varieties – Cabernet sauvignon and Sauvignon blanc. Produces varietal wines.

Buena Vida Vineyards (La) (USA). A large winery based in Springtown, Central Texas. Produces mainly hybrid wines.

Buena Vista (USA). A vineyard sited at Sonoma, north of San Francisco. Grape varieties – Cabernet sauvignon, Gamay, Gewürztraminer, Pinot noir and Zinfandel. Produces table and dessert wines.

Buffalo Valley Winery (USA). A winery based in Lewisburg, Pennsylvania. Produces French hybrid wines.

Buff Bitter (Lux). A Beer made according to Dr. Boerhare's formulae.

Buffelskroon Wines (S.Afr). See Calitzdorp Co-operative.

Buffet (Hol). Bar.

Buffeter (Fr). To draw off wine from a cask and replace with water. See Servir à Buffet.

Buffethouder (Hol). Bar-keeper, Barman.

Buffetjuffrouw (Hol). Barmaid.

Buff's Bitter (Eng). A cask conditioned Bitter 1050 O.G. brewed by the Canterbury Brewery, Kent.

Bugey (Fr). A V.D.Q.S. district in Savoie which produces dry white, rosé and red wines from the Altesse, Gamay, Jacquère, Mondeuse blanche, Pinot noir and Poulsard grapes.

Buggingen (Ger). Village. (Anb) = Baden. (Ber) = Markgräflerland. (Gro) = Lorettoberg. (Vins) = Höllberg, Maltesergarten.

Bugisu Coffee (S.Afr). A Ugandan coffee which produces a fine coffee with good flavour and aroma.

Bühl (Ger). Vineyard. (Anb) = Baden. (Ber) = Kairerstuhl-Tuniberg. (Gro) = Attilafelsen. (Vil) = Merdingen.

Bühlertal (Ger). Village. (Anb) = Baden. (Ber) = Ortenau. (Gro) = Schloss Rodeck. (Vins) = Engelsfelsen, Klotzberg.

Bühl [ortsteil Neusatz] (Ger). Village. (Anb) = Baden. (Ber) = Ortenau. (Gro)

= Schloss Rodeck. (Vins) = Burg Windeck-Kostanienhalde, Sternenberg, Wolfhag.

Build (Cktl). To pour the necessary ingredients into a glass without pre-mixing.

Buisson (Le) (Fr). The brand-name for a Vin de table from Henry Chouteau.

Buitenverwachting (S.Afr). A vineyard in Constantia. Produces varietal wines.

Buitzorg (E.Ind). A coffee-producing region in Java.

Buketreich (Ger). Rich pronounced bouquet.

Bukettriesling (Ger). A grape variety from a cross between the Red riesling X Muscat St. Laurent.

Bükkalja (Hun). A wine-producing region based in northern Hungary. Is noted for its white wines.

Bukkettraube (S.Afr). A white grape variety. Has a Muscat aroma, is light in acidity and is used for blending. Of German origin.

Bule (Port). Tea-pot.

Bulgaria (Bul). A large wine producing country. Wine production and sales are controlled by Vinprom. Produces fine wines and spirits (most are exported to USSR). Wine producing regions delimited in 1978 are – North region [Novo Selo, Pavlikeni, Pleven, Suhindol and Svishtov], South region [Assenovgrad, Chipan, Haskovo, Karlovo, Pazardjik and Stara Zagora], East region [Burgas, Burgas Prosenik, Shumen, Songulare, Targovishte and Varna] and the South-west region [Sandanski Melnik].

Bulk Gallon (Eng). A wine gallon. 160 Imperial fl.ozs. 128 US fl.ozs. A gallon of spirit, basis for charges of Customs and Excise.

Bulk Process (Eng). The fermentation of sparkling wines in long sealed tanks instead of by the méthode champenoise.

Bullace Grape (USA). An alternative name for the Muscadine grape.

Bullards Old Ale (Eng). A noted Old ale 1057 O.G. brewed by Norwich (Watney's) Brewery.

Bullay (Ger). Village. (Anb) = Mosel-Saar-Ruwer. (Ber) = Zell/Mosel. (Gro) = Graftschaft. (Vins) = Brautrock, Graf-Beyssel-Herrenberg, Kroneberg, Kirchweingarten, Sonneck.

Bulldog (Cktl). Place a lump of ice in a highball, add juice of ½ lemon, ¾ gill dry Gin, sugar syrup to taste and top up with ginger ale. Stir carefully and serve. Can substitute orange instead of lemon. Also known as Bulldog Cooler.

Bulldog Ale (Eng). A bottled Pale ale 1068

O.G. brewed by Courage. See also John Martin and Martin's Pale Ale.

Bulldog Cooler (Cktl). See Bulldog.

Bulldog Highball (Cktl). ⅓ measure Gin, ⅓ measure orange juice. Shake over ice, strain into a cocktail glass. Top with cold ginger ale. Straws.

Bullenheim (Ger). Village. (Anb) = Franken. (Ber) = Steigerwald. (Gro) =Schlosstück. (Vin) = Paradies.

Bullers (Austr). A vineyard based in north-east Victoria.

Bull Frog (Cktl). 1½ ozs. Apricot brandy, juice of a lemon. Shake over ice, strain into a cocktail glass.

Bullfrog Beer (Eng). A cask conditioned Bitter 1045 O.G. brewed at the Frog and Firkin Public house in London.

Bulligny (Fr). A commune in the Côtes de Toul, Lorraine region. Produces Vins gris.

Bull Pup Cooler (Cktl). 1½ fl.ozs. Gin, 1 pint ginger ale, juice ½ lemon. Place together into an ice-filled jug. Stir, serve in highball glasses with a thin strip of lemon peel.

Bull's Blood (Hun). Popular name given to the robust red wine from the Eger region called Egri Bikavér. Made from a combination of Kadarka, Kéfrankos and Médoc noir grape varieties. Name used on the label.

Bulls Eye Ale (Eng). A bottled Brown ale 1035 O.G. from the Greenhall Whitley Brewery, Warrington.

Bull's Eye Cocktail (Cktl). ⅓ measure Brandy, ⅔ measure dry Cider. Stir together in a highball glass with ice, top with ginger ale.

Bull Shot (Cktl). 1 measure Vodka, 4 ozs. clear beef bouillon, dash lemon juice, dash Worcester sauce, celery salt. Pour 'On the rocks' in an old-fashioned glass. Stir and serve.

Bull's Milk (Cktl). ¾ gill V.S.O.P. Cognac, sugar syrup to taste, 1 part milk. Shake well over ice, strain into a tumbler, add grated nutmeg and cinnamon on top.

Bully Hill (USA). A new winery based in the Finger Lakes region. Produces varietal wines from hybrid American grapes.

Bulmers (Eng). The largest cider makers in U.K. based at Hereford on the English/Welsh border. Produce Kiri and distribute Perrier water and Orangina. See Woodpecker, Strongbow and Pomagne.

Bumastus (Lat). A variety of vine.

Bumper (USA). A glass or tankard filled to the brim for a toast in the seventeenth and eighteenth centuries.

Bunce Brewery (Eng). Opened in 1984 in Netheravon, Wiltshire. Brews Bunce's Best 1043 O.G.

Bunches (Eng). The trading name used by Fuller Smith and Turner's, two large stores in Surrey and London. See also Fullers.

Bundaberg (Austr). A Rum producer based in Queensland. Brands include Endeavour.

Bundarra Vineyard (Austr). A part of Baileys of Glenrowen.

Bundenheim (Ger). Village. (Anb) = Rheinhessen. (Ber) = Nierstein. (Gro) = Domherr. (Vin) = Sites not yet chosen.

Bundes-Kellerei-Inspektor (Aus). Federal Cellar Controller Office where the vignerons have to state what type of wine and quantity was produced.

Bundesverband der Deutschen Spirituosen Industrie (Ger). A body which is associated with over 60 of the major distilleries.

Bundesweinpramierung (Ger). A competition run by the D.L.G. (German Agricultural Society) to find the top wines. Gold, silver and bronze awards are given to the best, the award to be displayed on the bottle label.

Bung (Eng). A stopper of cork, glass, metal, rubber or wood etc. used to block a bunghole.

Bungawarra Vineyard (Austr). 20 ha. Address = Marshall's Crossing Road, Ballandean, Queensland. Grape varieties – Cabernet sauvignon, Chardonnay, Malbec, Muscat, Pinot noir, Sémillon, Shiraz.

Bunghole (Eng). Hole through which a cask is filled with beer, wine, etc. It is closed using a shive (beer) or a bung. Also used for the removal of cask's contents.

Bunn (E.Asia). The Amharic word for coffee.

Bunnahabhain (Scot). A single Malt Islay distillery. Owned by the Highland Distilleries Company. An Islay malt. 12 year old. 40% alc. by vol.

Bunny Hug (Cktl). ⅓ measure Pernod, ⅓ measure Whisky, ⅓ measure Gin. Shake over ice, strain into cocktail glass.

Buntsandstein (Ger). The name for the sandstone soil found in Franken. (Franconia).

Burberry's (Scot). A De Luxe Scotch whisky 15 years old. Produced by A. Gillies and Co., a subsidiary of Amalgamated Distilled Products.

Burdigala (Lat). An old Roman name for the Bordeaux region.

Burdin (Fr). A famous French hybridiser. Noted for developing a red grape variety from a white grape original.

B

Burdock (Eng). A bur-like fruit from the genus Arctium, family Compositae. A weed used in the production of Dandelion and Burdock. Has heart-shaped leaves and purple flowers surrounded by hooked bristles.

Burdon (Sp). A Sherry producer based in Puerto de Santa Maria. Is part of Caballero.

Burdur Dimitiri (Tur). A white grape variety grown in southern Turkey.

Bureau Interprofessionnel des Calvados (Fr). Committee who regulates the making of Calvados.

Bureau National Interprofessionnel de l'Armagnac (Fr). Armagnac governing body. B.N.I.A.

Bureau National Interprofessionnel des Calvados et Eaux-de-Vie-de-Cidre-et-de-Poire (Fr). BNICE. Defines areas where Calvados apples and pears may be grown.

Bureau National Interprofessionnel du Cognac (Fr). Government body that controls the production and sale of Cognac. Fixed the prices for grapes, wine and new/aged distillations before 1984. B.N.I.C.

Bureau of Alcohol, Tobacco and Firearms (USA). See B.A.T.F.

Burette (Eng). A glass or plastic tube which is calibrated and fitted with a stopcock. Used in the testing of musts.

Burg (Ger). The old name for a fortified town.

Burg (Ger). Grosslagen. (Anb) = Franken. (Ber) = Maindreieck. (Vils) = Hammelburg, Ramsthal, Saaleck, Wirmsthal.

Burg (Ger). Vineyard. (Anb) = Baden. (Ber) = Badische Bergstrasse/Kraichgau. (Gro) = Mannaberg. (Vil) = Heidelberg.

Burg (Ger). Village. (Anb) = Mosel-Saar-Ruwer. (Ber) = Bernkastel. (Gro) = Schwarzlay. (Vins) = Falklay, Hahnenschrittchen, Thomasberg, Wendelstüch.

Bürg (Ger). Village. (Anb) = Württemberg. (Ber) = Remstal-Stuttgart. (Gro) = Kopf. (Vin) = Schlossberg.

Burgas (Bul). A delimited wine-producing area based in the Eastern region.

Burgas Prosenik (Bul). A delimited wine-producing area based in the Eastern region.

Burgberg (Ger). Vineyard. (Anb) = Ahr. (Ber) = Walporzheim/Arthal. (Gro) = Klosterberg. (Vil) = Mayschoss.

Burgberg (Ger). Vineyard. (Anb) = Mosel-Saar-Ruwer. (Ber) = Bernkastel. (Gro) = Schwarzlay. (Vil) = Lösnich.

Burgberg (Ger). Vineyard. (Anb) = Mosel-Saar-Ruwer. (Ber) = Saar-Ruwer. (Gro) = Römerlay. (Vil) = Trier.

Burgberg (Ger). Vineyard. (Anb) = Mosel-Saar-Ruwer. (Ber) = Zell/Mosel. (Gro) = Weinhex. (Vil) = Alken.

Burgberg (Ger). Vineyard. (Anb) = Nahe. (Ber) = Kreuznach. (Gro) = Schlosskapelle. (Vil) = Dorsheim.

Burgberg (Ger). Vineyard. (Anb) = Rheinhessen. (Ber) = Bingen. (Gro) = Kaiserpfalz. (Vil) = Ingelheim.

Burgberg (Ger). Vineyard. (Anb) = Württemberg. (Ber) = Württembergisch Unterland. (Gro) = Schalkstein. (Vil) = Steinheim.

Burgberg (Ger). Vineyard. (Anb) = Württemberg. (Ber) = Württembergisch Unterland. (Gro) = Schozachtal. (Vil) = Abstatt.

Burgberg (Ger). Vineyard. (Anb) = Württemberg. (Ber) = Württembergisch Unterland. (Gro) = Schozachtal. (Vil) = Auenstein.

Burg Bischofsteiner (Ger). Vineyard. (Anb) = Mosel-Saar-Ruwer. (Ber) = Zell/Mosel. (Gro) = Weinhex. (Vil) = Hatzenport.

Burgbronn (Ger). Village. (Anb) = Württemberg. (Ber) = Württembergisch Unterland. (Gro) = Heuchelberg. (Vin) = Hahnenberg.

Burg Coreidelsteiner (Ger). Vineyard. (Anb) = Mosel-Saar-Ruwer. (Ber) = Zell/Mosel. (Gro) = Goldbäumchen. (Vil) = Klotten.

Burgeff (Ger). The name of a large producer of Deutscher Sekt.

Burg Ehrenberg (Ger). Vineyard. (Anb) = Baden. (Ber) = Badische Bergstrasse/Kraichgau. (Gro) = Stiftsberg. (Vil) = Heinsheim.

Bürgel (Ger). Vineyard. (Anb) = Rheinhessen. (Ber) = Wonnegau. (Gro) = Burg Rodenstein. (Vil) = Flörsheim-Dalsheim.

Burgen (Ger). Village. (Anb) = Mosel-Saar-Ruwer. (Ber) = Bernkastel. (Gro) = Kurfürslay. (Vins) = Hasenläufer, Kirchberg, Romerberg,

Burgen (Ger). Village. (Anb) = Mosel-Saar-Ruwer. (Ber) = Zell/Mosel. (Gro) = Weinhex. (Vil) = Bischofstein.

Burgengau (Ger). An Untergebiet of the Oberrhein district.

Burgenland (Aus). A wine region containing the Eisenberg and the Neusiedlersee. Produces both red and white wines.

Burger (Ger). The name given to the white wines from Burg, Bernkastel.

Burger (USA). A white grape variety used to make white and dessert wines in

California.

Burger (Le) (Fr). The Alsace name for the Vins de table made from the Burger-Elbling grape variety.

Burger-Ebling (Fr). A white grape variety of Alsace

Bürgergarten (Ger). Vineyard. (Anb) = Rheinpfalz. (Ber) = Mittelhaardt-Deutsche Weinstrasse. (Gro) = Meerspinne. (Vil) = Haardt.

Burgerlich (Ger). Bourgeois, middle-class wines.

Bürgerspital (Ger). Holy Ghost Hospice of the Citizens in Franconia. Vineyards still support it. Produce white wines.

Burgess Best (Eng). A cask conditioned Bitter 1048 O.G. brewed by the Railway, a home-brew public house owned by Whitbread in Burgesshill, Sussex.

Burgess Brewery (S.E.Asia). A brewery based in Singapore.

Burgess Cellars (USA). A large winery based in St. Helena, Napa Valley. Owns 9.25 ha. Grape varieties – Cabernet sauvignon, Chardonnay, Chenin blanc, Johannisberg riesling, Petit syrah, Pinot noir and Zinfandel. Also buys in grapes. See Dutton Vineyard.

Burggarten (Ger). Vineyard. (Anb) = Ahr. (Ber) = Walporzheim/Ahrtal. (Gro) = Klosterberg. (Vil) = Dernau.

Burggarten (Ger). Vineyard. (Anb) = Ahr. (Ber) = Walporzheim/Ahrtal. (Gro) = Klosterberg. (Vil) = Heimersheim.

Burggarten (Ger). Vineyard. (Anb) = Rheinpfalz. (Ber) = Mittelhaardt-Deutsche Weinstrasse. (Gro) = Grafenstück. (Vil) = Bockenheim.

Burggraf (Ger). Vineyard. (Anb) = Baden. (Ber) = Badische Bergstrasse/Kraichgau. (Gro) = Mannaberg. (Vil) = Rauenberg.

Burggraf (Ger). Vineyard. (Anb) = Mosel-Saar-Ruwer. (Ber) = Zell/Mosel. (Gro) = Grasfchaft. (Vil) = Alf.

Burggräfler (Aus). A term used in the Südtirol region of Italy. Known as Burgravio in Italy. Specification given to a wine obtained in the land of the former county of Tyrol.

Burg Gutenfels (Ger). Vineyard. (Anb) = Mittelrhein. (Ber) = Rheinburgengau. (Gro) = Herrenberg. (Vil) = Kaub.

Burghalde (Ger). Vineyard. (Anb) = Württemberg. (Ber) = Remstal-Stuttgart. (Gro) = Sonnenbühl. (Vil) = Weinstadt (ortsteil Beutelsbach).

Burghalde (Ger). Vineyard. (Anb) = Württemberg. (Ber) = Remstal-Stuttgart. (Gro) = Sonnenbühl. (Vil) =

Weinstadt (ortsteil Schnait i.R.).

Burg Hammerstein (Ger). Grosslagen. (Anb) = Mittelrhein. (Ber) = Rheinbergengau. (Vils) = Bad Hönningen, Dattenberg, Hammerstein, Kasbach, Leubsdorf, Leutesdorf, Linz, Rheinbrohl, Unkel.

Burg Katz (Ger). Vineyard. (Anb) = Mittelrhein. (Ber) = Rheinburgengau. (Gro) = Loreleyfelsen. (Vil) = St. Goarshausen.

Burglay (Ger). Vineyard. (Anb) = Mosel-Saar-Ruwer. (Ber) = Bernkastel. (Gro) = Michelsberg. (Vil) = Minheim.

Burglay (Ger). Vineyard. (Anb) = Mosel-Saar-Ruwer. (Ber) = Bernkastel. (Gro) = Nacktarsch. (Vil) = Kröv.

Burg Layen (Ger). Village. (Anb) = Nahe. (Ber) = Kreuznach. (Gro) = Schlosskapelle. (Vins) = Hölle, Johannisberg, Rothenberg, Schlossberg.

Burglay-Felsen (Ger). Vineyard. (Anb) = Mosel-Saar-Ruwer. (Ber) = Zell/Mosel. (Gro) = Schwarze Katz. (Vil) = Zell.

Burg Lichteneck (Ger). Grosslagen. (Anb) = Baden. (Ber) = Breisgau. (Vils) = Altdorf, Bleichheim, Bombach, Broggingen, Ettenheim, Hecklingen, Heimbach, Herbolzheim, Kenzingen, Köndringen, Malterdingen, Mundingen, Nordweil, Ringsheim, Tutschfelden, Wagenstadt.

Burgmauer (Ger). Vineyard. (Anb) = Mosel-Saar-Ruwer. (Ber) = Bernkastel. (Gro) = Probstberg. (Vil) = Schweich.

Burg Maus (Ger). Vineyard. (Anb) = Mittelrhein. (Ber) = Rheinburgengau. (Gro) = Loreleyfelsen. (Vil) = St. Goarshausen.

Burg Neuenfels (Ger). Grosslagen. (Anb) = Baden. (Ber) = Markgräflerland. (Vils) = Auggen, Bad Bellingen, Badenweiler, Ballrechten-Dottingen, Britzingen, Britzingen (ortsteil Dattingen), Feldberg, Hügelheim, Laufen, Liel, Lipburg, Mauchen, Müllheim, Niedereggenen, Niederweiler, Obereggenen, Schliengen, Steinenstadt, Sulzburg, Zunzingen.

Burgomer Burgundec (Yug). A red wine from the Spätburgunder grape, made in the Kosovo Pilje vineyard in south Serbia.

Burgoyne and Company (Austr). A noted old-established wine exporting firm (c 1870) of Australia.

Burg Ravensburger Dicker Franz (Ger). Vineyard. (Anb) = Baden. (Ber) = Badische Bergstrasse/Kraichgau. (Gro) = Stiftsberg. (Vil) = Sulzfeld.

Burg Ravensburger Husarenkappe (Ger). Vineyard. (Anb) = Baden. (Ber) =

Badische Bergstrasse/Kraichgau. (Gro) = Stiftsberg. (Vil) = Sulzfeld.

Burg Ravensburger Löchle (Ger). Vineyard. (Anb) = Baden. (Ber) = Badische Bergstrasse/Kraichgau. (Gro) = Stiftsberg. (Vil) = Sulzfeld.

Burgravio (It). See Burggräfler.

Burg Rheinfels (Ger). Grosslagen. (Anb) = Mittelrhein. (Ber) = Rheinburgengau. (Vil) = St. Goar-Werlau.

Burg Rodenstein (Ger). Grosslagen. (Anb) = Rheinhessen. (Ber) = Wonnegau. (Vils) = Bermersheim/Worms, Flörsheim-Dalsheim, Mörstadt, Ober-Flörsheim.

Burgsponheim (Ger). Village. (Anb) = Nahe. (Ber) = Schloss Böckelheim. (Gro) = Rosengarten. (Vins) = Höllenpfad, Pfaffenberg, Schlossberg.

Bürgstadt (Ger). Village. (Anb) = Franken. (Ber) = Mainviereck. (Gro) = Not yet assigned. (Vins) = Centgrafenberg, Mainhölle.

Burgstall (Ger). Vineyard. (Anb) = Baden. (Ber) = Bodensee. (Gro) = Sonnenufer. (Vil) = Hagnau.

Burgstall (Ger). Vineyard. (Anb) = Baden. (Ber) = Bodensee. (Gro) = Sonnenufer. (Vil) = Immenstaad.

Burgstall (Ger). Vineyard. (Anb) = Baden. (Ber) = Bodensee. (Gro) = Sonnenufer. (Vil) = Kippenhausen.

Burgstall (Ger). Vineyard. (Anb) = Baden. (Ber) = Bodensee. (Gro) = Sonnenufer. (Vil) = Markdorf.

Burgstall (Ger). Vineyard. (Anb) = Württemberg. (Ber) = Kocher-Jagst-Tauber. (Gro) = Kocherberg. (Vil) = Criesbach.

Burgstall (Ger). Vineyard. (Anb) = Württemberg. (Ber) = Kocher-Jagst-Tauber. (Gro) = Kocherberg. (Vil) = Niedernhall.

Burgu (Tur). A corkscrew. See also Tirbuson.

Burguet (Alain) (Fr). A négociant-éleveur based at Gevrey-Chambertin, Côte d'Or, Burgundy.

Burgundac Bijeli (Yug). The name given to the Chardonnay grape that is grown in Vojvodina and Slavonia.

Burgundac Crni (Yug). A red grape variety grown in Banat, Serbia.

Burgundec (Yug). A full-bodied red wine produced in Serbia.

Burgunder (Fr). The name for the Pinot noir grape in Alsace. Also known as the Spätburgunder, Frühburgunder.

Burgundi (Hun). Hungarian name for the Pinot noir.

Burgundii (Euro). A fifth-century kingdom of which present day Burgundy was part.

Burgundy (Fr). Famous wine region of East Central France. Divided into 5 areas = Chablis, Côte de Nuits, Côte de Beaune, Côte Chalonnaise, Mâconnais and Beaujolais. See also Côte d'Or.

Burgundy (USA). See California Burgundy.

Burgundy Basket (USA). Wine cradle.

Burgundy Bishop (Cktl). 1 measure dark Rum, juice ¼ lemon, 1 teaspoon powdered sugar. Shake over ice, strain into an ice-filled highball glass. Top with red Burgundy and decorate with fruit in season.

Burgundy Cask (Fr). A wine cask of 114 litre capacity.

Burgundy Cobbler (Cktl). 1 teaspoon Gomme syrup, 4 dashes orange Curaçao, red Burgundy. Fill an ice-filled highball glass ⅔ with wine. Add liqueur and syrup, stir, decorate with fresh fruit and a mint sprig.

Burgundy Cocktail (Cktl). ¾ measure red Burgundy, ¼ measure Cognac, 2 dashes Maraschino. Stir over ice, strain into a cocktail glass. Add slice of lemon and a cherry.

Burgundy Cup (Punch). 1 bottle Burgundy (red), ½ gill Brandy, ½ gill Maraschino, ¼ gill brown Curaçao, 1 bottle soda water, 3 dashes Bénédictine. Stir all well together over ice in punch-bowl. Serve in large tumbler with slices of orange and lemon and fresh fruit.

Burgundy Mixture (Fr). Copper sulphate and Calcium carbonate (washing soda) used for spraying against pests and diseases.

Burgundy Mull (Punch). 1 bottle Burgundy (red), 1 wine-glass dry Sherry, 2 ozs. Brandy, ½ bottle Blackcurrant cordial, sugar to taste, juice 3 lemons, 1 quart water, ground ginger. Mix together, heat, strain and add sliced lemons. Serve in cups.

Burgundy Punch (Punch). ¾ pint Burgundy (red), ¾ pint iced water, 1½ fl.ozs. Port, juice ½ lemon, ½ fl.oz. Gomme syrup, 1 fl.oz. orange juice. Stir altogether, decorate with orange and lemon slices.

Burg Warsberg (Ger). Vineyard. (Anb) = Mosel-Saar-Ruwer. (Ber) = Obermosel. (Gro) = Gipfel. (Vil) = Wincheringen.

Burgweg (Ger). Grosslagen. (Anb) = Franken. (Ber) = Steigerwald. (Vils) = Iphofen, Markt Einersheim, Possenheim.

Burgweg (Ger). Vineyard. (Anb) = Mosel-Saar-Ruwer. (Ber) = Bernkastel. (Gro) = Schwarzlay. (Vil) = Traben-Trarbach.

B

Burgweg (Ger). Grosslagen. (Anb) = Nahe. (Ber) = Schloss Böckelheim. (Vils) = Altenbamberg, Bad Münster a. St-Ebernburg, Duchroth, Niederhausen an der Nahe, Norheim, Oberhausen an der Nahe, Schlossböckelheim, Traisen, Waldböckelheim.

Burgweg (Ger). Grosslagen. (Anb) = Rheingau. (Ber) = Johannisberg. (Vils) = Assmannshausen-Aulhausen, Geisenheim, Lorch, Lorchhausen, Rüdesheim.

Burgweg (Ger). Vineyard. (Anb) = Rheinhessen. (Ber) = Nierstein. (Gro) = Sankt Alban. (Vil) = Bodenheim.

Burgweg (Ger). Vineyard. (Anb) = Rheinhessen. (Ber) = Wonnegau. (Gro) = Liebfrauengarten. (Vil) = Worms.

Burgweg (Ger). Vineyard. (Anb) = Rheinpfalz. (Ber) = Mittelhaardt-Deutsche Weinstrasse. (Gro) = Grafenstück. (Vil) = Kindenheim.

Burgweg (Ger). Vineyard. (Anb) = Rheinpfalz. (Ber) = Mittelhaardt-Deutsche Weinstrasse. (Gro) = Rosenbühl. (Vil) = Lambsheim.

Burgweg (Ger). Vineyard. (Anb) = Rheinpfalz. (Ber) = Mittelhaardt-Deutsche Weinstrasse. (Gro) = Rosenbühl. (Vil) = Weisenheim/Sand.

Burgweg (Ger). Vineyard. (Anb) = Rheinpfalz. (Ber) = Mittelhaardt-Deutsche Weinstrasse. (Gro) = Schwarzerde. (Vil) = Grosskarlbach.

Burg Wildeck (Ger). Vineyard. (Anb) = Württemberg. (Ber) = Württembergisch Unterland. (Gro) = Schozachtal. (Vil) = Abstatt.

Burg Windeck Kastanienhalde (Ger). Vineyard. (Anb) = Baden. (Ber) = Ortenau. (Gro) = Schloss Rodeck. (Vil) = Bühl (ortsteil Neusatz).

Burgwingert (Ger). Vineyard. (Anb) = Baden. (Ber) = Badische Bergstrasse/Kraichgau. (Gro) = Mannaberg. (Vil) = Bruchsal (stadtteil Obergrombach).

Burgwingert (Ger). Vineyard. (Anb) = Baden. (Ber) = Badische Bergstrasse/Kraichgau. (Gro) = Mannaberg. (Vil) = Helmsheim.

Burg Zähringen (Ger). Grosslagen. (Anb) = Baden. (Ber) = Breisgau. (Vils) = Buchholz, Denzlingen, Emmendingen (ortsteil Hockburg), Freiburg i. Br. (ortsteil Lehen), Glottertal, Heuweiler, Sexau, Wildtal.

Burie (Fr). A commune in the Charente-Maritime Département whose grapes are classed Borderies (Cognac).

Burignon (Switz). A white wine from the Vaud canton of Chardonnes.

Buring, (Leo) (Austr). Wine specialists of the Barossa Valley. Owned by Lindeman.

Burkes Brewery (Eng). A public house brewery at the Lion in Croydon, Surrey. Produces cask conditioned Original 1034 O.G. and Best Bitter 1042 O.G.

Burke's Irish Brigade (Eng). A bottled Stout brewed by Greenhall Whitley, Warrington. For export.

Burkheim (Ger). Village. (Anb) = Baden. (Ber) = Kaiserstuhl-Tuniberg. (Gro) = Vulkanfelsen. (Vins) = Feuerberg, Schlossgarten.

Burkittsville Vineyards (USA). A small winery based in Burkittsville, Maryland. Produces hybrid wines.

Bürklin-Wolf (Ger). A family estate of the Palatinate (Rheinpfalz).

Burma (Asia). A hardy variety of the Assam tea bush.

Burmarrad (Euro). A wine-producing area on the island of Malta.

Burmester (Port). Vintage Port shipper. Vintages = 1873, 1878, 1887, 1890, 1896, 1900, 1904, 1908, 1912, 1920, 1922, 1927, 1931, 1935, 1937, 1940, 1943, 1945, 1948, 1954, 1955, 1958, 1960, 1963, 1977.

Burn (Scot). The name given to the streams in the Scottish Highlands of whose clear waters are often used to make Scotch whisky.

Burnay Sale (Eng). The largest auction ever held of wines. 10,000 pipes of Port. (565,000 dozen bottles). Held for 4 days in May 1892 at Christies.

Burnbrae (Austr). A. winery based in Mudgee, New South Wales.

Burnett Gin (Eng). A brand of Gin sold under the White Satin label. Part of Seagram. 40% alc. by vol.

Burnins (Les) (Fr). A vineyard in the A.C. commune of Montagny, Côte Chalonnaise, Burgundy.

Burns Ale (Scot). A keg Special ale 1036 O.G. brewed by Drybrough's Brewery, Edinburgh. Known as Burn's Scottish ale if canned.

Burn's Scottish Ale (Scot). See Burns Ale.

Burnt Ale (W.Ind). Same as Dunder.

Burnt Wine (Eng). Brandy.

Buronator (Ger). A dark Bock bier brewed by the Rosenbrauerei at Kaufbeuren, Western Germany.

Burot (Fr). The local Burgundy name for the white Pinot gris. See also Beurot.

Burrough's (Eng). A company that produces a range of 'Mixed doubles' drinks. See Beefeater Dry Gin.

Burrweiler (Ger). Village. (Anb) = Rheinpfalz. (Ber) = Südliche Weinstrasse. (Gro) = Bischofskreuz. (Vins) = Altenforst, St. Annaberg, Schäwer, Schlossgarten.

Bursins (Switz). A wine-producing area

in the La Côte district on the west bank of Lake Geneva.

Burslem Brewery (Eng). A subsidiary company of Ansell's Brewery.

Bursley Bitter (Eng). A cask conditioned Bitter 1040 O.G. brewed by the Five Towns Brewery, Stoke-on-Trent.

Burt Brewery (Eng). A brewery based at Ventnor, Isle of Wight. Produces cask conditioned LB. 1030 O.G. and a variety of other beers.

Burth Brewery (Switz). Brewery based in Liechtenstein. Part of the Sibra Group (Cardinal) Breweries.

Burton Ale (Eng). A bottled Ale 1031 O.G. brewed by Greene King Brewery, eastern England.

Burton Ale (Eng). A cask conditioned Bitter 1047.5 O.G. brewed by Ind Coope Brewery, Burton-on-Trent.

Burton Ale (Eng). The general name given to beers brewed in the town of Burton-on-Trent.

Burton Bitter (Eng). A cask conditioned Bitter 1037 O.G. brewed by the Marston's Brewery, Burton-on-Trent. Also a keg version.

Burton Brewery (Eng). Allied Breweries major brewery based at Burton-on-Trent.

Burton Bridge Brewery (Eng). Opened in 1982, in Burton-on-Trent. Produces cask conditioned Bridge Bitter 1042 O.G. Burton Porter 1045 O.G. Festival Ale 1055 O.G. Old Expensive 1065 O.G.

Burtonising (Eng). The process of adding chemicals to the brewing liquor to obtain an identical composition to true Burton liquor.

Burton Mild (Eng). A Mild beer 1033 O.G. brewed by Everards Burton Brewery.

Burton-on-Trent (Eng). The major brewing centre in England. Established because its water has a high mineral content. Ideal for the British beers. Based in Staffordshire.

Burton Porter (Eng). See Burton Bridge Brewery.

Burton Union (Eng). A system developed in the nineteenth century of fermentation where the beer rises out of oak casks, through swanneck pipes into troughs for use in pitching into following brews.

Burtonwood Brewery (Eng). A large brewery based at Warrington. Produces many styles of beer including a cask conditioned Mild 1032 O.G. and Top Hat 1047 O.G. Based at Bold Lane, Burtonwood, Warrington, Cheshire.

Burt's Brewery (Eng). A small Isle of Wight brewery that brews cask conditioned beers LB 1030 O.G. Dark Mild 1030 O.G. VPA 1040 O.G.

Buruk (Tur). Denotes an acidic, sour wine.

Burundi Coffee (Afr). A noted Arabica coffee produced in central Africa. Has good acidity and body.

Busch (USA). A Bavarian beer brewed by Anheuser-Busch.

Buschenschank (Aus). A Viennese tavern owner displaying a bunch of fir-twigs on the wall of his tavern to show that his Heurige are on sale. See Heurige and Heurigen.

Buschenschanken (Aus). An Austrian wine (Heurigen) Inn.

Busen (Hol). An old Dutch word for heavy drinking.

Busera (Afr). A rough beer made from millet and honey.

Bush Beer (Bel). A strong, copper-coloured Ale 9.5%-10% alc. by vol. brewed by the Dubuisson Brasserie near Tournai.

Bushcreek Vineyards (USA). A winery based in Peebles, Ohio. Produces French-American hybrid and native wines.

Bushel Basket (Eng). The hop-picking basket used by the Bushler to take the hops from the picker's crib into the large sacks.

Bushie (S.Am). The local name for 'Moonshine' in Guyana.

Bushler (Eng). A man who fills the large sacks with the hops from the hop pickers' cribs with his Bushel basket.

Bushmills Malt (Ire). A single Malt Irish whiskey produced by the Bushmills Distillery. 10 years old. 40% alc. by vol.

Bushmills Whiskey (Ire). A smoky-flavoured Irish whiskey. Named from Northern Ireland's oldest distillery. Part of Irish Distillers.

Bushranger Cocktail (Cktl). ⅓ gill dark Rum, ⅙ gill Dubonnet, dash Angostura. Stir over ice, strain into a cocktail glass.

Bush Tea (Afr). A beverage made from the dried beans of the shrub family Cyclopia in southern Africa.

Busslay (Ger). Vineyard. (Anb) = Mosel-Saar-Ruwer. (Ber) = Bernkastel. (Gro) = Schwarzlay. (Vil) = Erden.

Bus Ticket (S.Afr). The nickname for the wine certificate on South African wine bottles. The size of a postage stamp it gives authenticity to the wine's contents with a series of coloured bands. Blue = Wine's origin, Red = Vintage, Green = Grape variety. If coloured gold then of superior quality.

Butanoic Acid (Eng). C_3H_7COOH. A volatile acid found in wine.

Butcher (Austr). The name used in South Australia for a 6 fl.oz. glass.

Butcombe Bitter (Eng). See Butcombe Brewery.

Butcombe Brewery (Eng). Based in the Mendip Hills near Bristol. Produces cask conditioned Butcombe Bitter 1039 O.G.

Butiliram (Bul). To bottle.

Butler (Eng). The nineteenth-century servant who looked after the wine cellar.

Butler Nephew (Port). Vintage Port shippers. Vintages – 1922, 1924, 1927, 1934, 1942, 1945, 1947, 1948, 1955, 1957, 1958, 1960, 1975.

Butler's Friend (Eng). A corkscrew that works on the principle of two prongs that slip down each side of the cork between it and the bottle neck and ease the cork out without damage. So called because the dishonest butler would consume the good contents of the bottle and replace it with inferior wine, then replace the undamaged cork without the owner's knowledge.

Buton (It). A producer of Elixir di China (a style of bitter apéritif) and liqueurs.

Butt (Eng). Two hogsheads capacity.

Butt (Sp). A Sherry cask with a capacity of 108 gallons (490 litres). 132 U.S. gallons.

Butt (USA). A cask measuring 126 US gallons.

Buttafuoco (It). A sweet, red sparkling wine made from the Barbera grape (plus others) in Lombardy. Sold under the D.O.C. Oltrepo Pavese.

Buttage (Fr). A method by which the soil in the vineyard is ploughed up to the vine trunk in winter as a precaution against frost.

Butte (Hun). A measure used in Tokaj-Hegyalja. 13.6 litres.

Butteaux (Fr). An A.C. Premier Cru Chablis. Often reclassified as the Premier Cru Montmains.

Butte County (USA). A small wine producing county in Sacramento Valley, California.

Butte Creek Winery (USA). A small winery based in Butte County. Was closed in 1976.

Bütten (Ger). The name given to the grape picker's hod in the Rheingau.

Buttered Coffee (Eng). Put hot coffee in glass, add 1 measure of brandy, sugar to taste. Stir, add pat of butter on top and a stick of cinnamon to stir.

Buttered Rum (Eng). See Hot Buttered Rum.

Butterfly (Cktl). ⅖ measure Gin, ³⁄₁₀ measure dry Vermouth, ⅕ measure blue Curaçao, ⅕ measure Poire Williams. Shake over ice, strain into a flute, decorate with a twist of lemon and orange.

Buttermilk (Eng). The liquid left after the butter has been removed. Has a sour taste.

Buttig (Hun). See Butte.

Buttis (Lat). Cask.

Button Hook (Cktl). ¼ measure Pernod, ¼ measure Cognac, ¼ measure (white) Crème de Menthe, ¼ measure Apricot brandy. Shake over ice, strain into a cocktail glass.

Butyl (Eng). C_4H_9OH. A higher alcohol. Part of the Fusel oils.

Butylene Glycol (Eng). A glycerine-related compound found in wines in small quantities.

Butyrate Acid (Eng). See Cheesy.

Butyric Acid (Eng). C_3H_7COOH. An acid found in spirits and in wines in small quantities.

Buur (Den). A strong beer brewed by the Thor Brewery.

Buvable (Fr). Drinkable.

Buvee (Fr). Old word for drinking.

Buxentinum (Lat). A red wine produced in south-western Italy in Roman times.

Buxeuil (Fr). A Cru Champagne village in the Canton de l'Aube. District = Château Thierry.

Buxton (Eng). A mineral water from Buxton, Derbyshire. Both still and sparkling styles sold.

Buxy (Fr). A Premier Cru vineyard and town of the Côte Chalonnaise in Burgundy in the commune of Montagny.

Buza (Egy). An alcoholic beverage distilled from fermented grapes.

Buzau (Rum). A Wallachia wine-producing district.

Buzbağ (Tur). A rich, red, dry wine made from the Boguzkere grape.

Buzet (Fr). An A.C. region in the south-west of the country produces fine, full-bodied red wines.

Buziaş (Rum). A wine-producing area. Part of the Banat Vineyard.

Buzón (Sp). Bung.

Buzz (Eng). A term meaning 'Send the bottle round', refers to the passing of the Port.

Buzzer Cocktail (Cktl). ¼ measure dry Gin, ¼ measure sweet Vermouth, 4 dashes Crème de menthe, 2 dashes Angostura. Shake over ice, strain into a cocktail glass. Add cherry.

Buzzetto (It). Alternative name for the Trebbiano toscano grape.

BV (USA) (abbr). Beaulieu Vineyards. Appears on their labels.

BVA (Eng) (abbr). Birch Vale Ale 1037

O.G. brewed by the Winkle's Brewery, North Derbyshire.

B.V.C. (Eng) (abbr). Bulgarian Vintners Company Ltd. Address = Bridge Wharf, 156, Caledonian Road, London N1 9RD. The major Bulgarian wine importers to the U.K.

B.V.D. Cocktail (Cktl). ⅔ measure Bacardi rum, ⅔ measure dry Vermouth, ⅔ measure dry Gin. Shake over ice, strain into a cocktail glass.

BYB (Eng) (abbr). Bentley's Yorkshire Bitter. 1033 O.G. Brewed by Whitbread in Sheffield.

Bybline (Egy). A sweet white wine produced in Phoenicia.

Bynum Winery (USA). A winery based on the west side of the Russian River, Sonoma County, California. Grape varieties – Cabernet sauvignon, Chardonnay, Fumé blanc, Gewürztraminer, Pinot noir and Zinfandel.

B.Y.O. (Austr) (abbr). See Bring Your Own.

Byrd Vineyards (USA). A small winery based in Myersville, Maryland. 7 ha. Grape varieties – Cabernet sauvignon, Chardonnay, Gewürztraminer and Sauvignon blanc. Produces vinifera and also hybrid wines.

Byrrh (Fr). A bitter apéritif wine.

Contains quinine, Peruvian bark, oils and herbs. 17% alc. by vol. Produced by Violet Frères.

Byrrh-Cassis Cocktail (Cktl). 1 fl.oz. Byrrh, 3 dashes Crème de Cassis. Stir together in an ice-filled old-fashioned glass.

Byrrh-Citron (Cktl). ½ gill Byrrh, ⅙ gill Sirop de citron, Soda water. Stir over ice, strain into tall glass with ice. Top with soda water.

Byrrh Cocktail (Cktl).(1). 1 measure Byrrh, 1 measure dry Gin. Shake well with ice, strain into a cocktail glass.

Byrrh Cocktail (Cktl).(2). ⅓ measure Byrrh, ⅓ measure dry Vermouth, ⅓ measure Rye whiskey. Stir with ice, strain into cocktail glass.

Byrsa (Afr). A noted fortified wine-producing area in Tunisia.

Bytca Brewery (Czec). A brewery based in Bytca in eastern Czec.

By the Neck (Eng) (slang). The term for a bottle of beer with the Crown cork removed. Not served in a glass.

Byzantine Coffee (Eng). Another name for Turkish coffee.

Byzantis (Gre). The name of a red wine from the island of Zakinthos near Peloponnese.

Cab (Isr). An old Hebrew measure. Equal to ½ gallon, 2.3 litres. See also Kab.

Cabaceo (Sp). Blend of wine.

Caballero (Sp). A Sherry and Brandy producer. Is noted for Benito, Don Guisa (a Fino) and Gran Señor Choice Old Cream range of Sherries. Based in Puerto de Santa Maria. Also produces Ponche orange and brandy liqueur.

Caballero (Sp). A pale Amontillado sherry produced by Gonzalez Byass in Jerez de la Frontera.

Caballero (Luis) (Sp). A noted Sherry producer based in Jerez. Noted for its Fino Pavon.

Caballero de la Cepa (Arg). The brandname for red and white wines from the Bodegas Flitchman.

Cabana (W.Ind). The brand-name of a white Rum.

Cabana Soft Drinks (Eng). A soft drinks manufacturer based in Preston Lancashire. Produces soft drinks and mixers (on draught) through franchise.

Cabardès (Fr). V.D.Q.S. red and rosé wines produced in the Département of Aude, southern France. Grape varieties – Carignan, Cinsault, Grenache, Mourvèdre and Syrah.

Cabaret (Ch.Isles). Inn, public house.

Cabaret (Fr). A liqueur stand (decanter, glassware and tray) used for liqueur service. Also for a liqueur cabinet.

Cabaret (Fr). Tavern, public house or restaurant.

Caberat (Bra). The local spelling of the Cabernet sauvignon grape.

Caberet (Cktl). ⅓ gill Gin, 2 dashes Angostura, 1 dash Bénédictine, 2 dashes French vermouth. Stir over ice, strain into a cocktail glass. Top with a cherry.

Caberne (Bul). The name for the Cabernet sauvignon grape.

Cabernet (Fr). The famous, superb red wine grape from Bordeaux. Is related to the Cabernet sauvignon. See also Cabernet Franc.

Cabernet Brda (Yug). A mild red wine.

Cabernet Breton (Fr). The Touraine (Loire) district name for the Cabernet franc grape.

Cabernet d'Anjou Rosé (Fr). An A.C. rosé wine produced in the Anjou-Saumur district of the Loire. Produced from the Cabernet sauvignon or Cabernet franc grapes. Is a perfumed, slightly sweet wine. Min. alc. content 10% by vol.

Cabernet del Trentino (It). D.O.C. red wine produced in the Trentino region from Cabernet sauvignon and Cabernet franc grapes.

Cabernet de Piave Riserva (It). See Piave Cabernet.

Cabernet di Pramaggiore (It). D.O.C. red wine produced in Veneto. Grape varieties – Cabernet franc 90% and Merlot 10%. If aged for 3 years and 12% alc. by vol. then classed Riserva.

Cabernet Franc (Fr). A classic red grape variety used mainly in the Graves, Saint-Émilion and Pomerol districts of Bordeaux. Also to a lesser degree in the Médoc. Also known as the Bouchet, Bouchy, Breton and Véron. Produces wines with an aromatic bouquet. See also Cabernet Gris.

Cabernet Gris (Fr). The alternative name for the Cabernet franc red grape variety.

Cabernet Levodia (USSR). A dry red wine from the Crimean Peninsula.

Cabernet Rosé (Fr). An A.C. rosé wine from the Anjou-Saumur district of the Loire, made from the Cabernet franc grape. It replaces the Anjou Coteaux de la Loire Rosé de Cabernet.

Cabernet Rosé (USA). A rosé wine produced in California from the Cabernet sauvignon grape.

Cabernet Sauvignon (Fr). The classic black grape variety of the Médoc district of Bordeaux. Gives tannin, colour and body to the wine. Most widely grown grape in the world. See Gros Bouchet.

Cabernet Sauvignon di Miralduolo (It). A red Vini da Tavola wine from the Cabernet sauvignon grape produced in central Italy.

Cabernet Toso (Arg). A Cabernet-based wine produced by the Toso Winery at San José.

Cabeza (En) (Sp). The name for the Gobelet or Head pruning method of vine training.

C

Cabezuela (Sp). The name given to a second sedimentation of musts.

Cabido (Port). A Dão wine produced by Real Companhía Vinícola do Norte de Portugal.

Cabinet (Ger). See Cabinett and Kabinett.

Cabinett (Ger). Used to describe a special reserve wine one grade up from Qmp. A natural wine with no added sugar and is estate bottled. See also Kabinett.

Cabinett-Wein (USA). Kabinett. A wine of a Kabinett standard.

Cablegram Cooler (Cktl). Into a large tumbler put 2 ice cubes, juice of ½ lemon, ¾ gill Rye whiskey, dash Gomme syrup. Top up with ginger ale, stir gently and serve.

Cablegram Highball (Cktl). ⅓ gill Bourbon whiskey, 1 teaspoon of powdered sugar, juice ½ lemon. Stir well over ice, strain into an ice-filled highball glass. Top with ginger ale.

Cab Mac (Austr). A light, fresh wine made from the Cabernet sauvignon grape by macération carbonique fermentation.

Cabrière Estate (S.Afr). Vineyards based in Franschhoek. Address = Clos Cabrière, Cabrière Street, P.O. Box 245, Franschhoek 7690. Produces varietal wines.

Cabrières (Fr). A commune in the Coteaux du Languedoc district of southern France. Produces A.C. rosé Clairette du Languedoc wine (of same name) only from Carignan and Cinsault (min. 45% max. 50%) grapes. 11% alc. by vol.

Cacao (Fr). See Crème de Cacao.

Cacao (Hol) (It). Cocoa.

Cacao Disbor (Fr). A Crème de Cacao and vanilla-flavoured liqueur produced by Puerto Cabello.

Cacao mit Nuss (Ger). A white chocolate and hazelnut liqueur.

Cacao Torréfié (Fr). Roasted chocolate. A powder of fine roasted cocoa beans which produces a dark, slightly bitter-tasting drink.

Cacao Tree (S.Am). Species – Theobroma Cacao. Tree whose seeds produce cocoa and chocolate.

Cacatoes Cocktail (Cktl). 1 measure Cognac, ½ measure Mandarine Napoléon, ½ measure orange juice, 3 dashes Crème de Banane, 3 dashes lemon juice, dash Grenadine. Shake over ice, strain into cocktail glass. Top with a cherry and orange slice.

Cacc'Emmitte di Lucera (It). D.O.C. rosé wine from Lucera in the Apulia region.

Cacchione (It). A grape variety grown in Latium.

Cáceres (Sp). A wine-producing region in south-western Spain. Includes areas of Cañamero, Ceclavin, Cilleros, Hervós, Jerte Miajados and Montánchez.

Cachaça (Bra). A white sugar cane spirit. See also Caxaca.

Cachaça (Port). Rum. Also (slang). For 'Fire water'.

Cachaça de Cabeca (Bra). The name given to the Heads (first spirit out of the still) in Cachaça production.

Cachaça São Francisco (Bra). A premium sugar cane spirit (Rum style) produced by Seagram in Rio de Janeiro.

Cachapoal (Chile). The principal wine-producing region of central Chile. Produces good, sound wines.

Cachar (Ind). A tea-producing area in northern India.

Cachet (Fr). Seal or mark.

Cachet Blanc (Austr). A wine produced by the Quelitaler Estate, South Australia.

Cachiri (S.Am). A rough spirit that is produced from fermented cassava. Produced in Guyana. Is similar to Cajuada.

Cacho (Port). A bunch of grapes.

Cactus (Mex). The plant used in the making of Tequila. There are 2 types – Maguey and Blue Maguey (or Mezcal Azul).

Cadarca (Rum). An alternative spelling of Kadarka (a red grape).

Cadastro (Port). Vineyard register.

Cadaujac (Fr). A commune within the A.C. Graves district of south-western Bordeaux.

Cadaval (Port). A white wine from Torres Vedras.

Caddy (Eng). See Tea Caddy.

Ca'del Bosco (It). A well-known winery in Franciacorta, Lombardy. 31 ha. Produces sparkling (méthode champenoise) wines.

Cadenas (W.Ind). Originally one of the major Rum producers in the West Indies based on the island of Cuba.

Cadenasso Winery (USA). A small winery based in Fairfield, Solano, California. 38 ha. Grape varieties – Cabernet sauvignon, Chenin blanc and Zinfandel. Produces varietal and dessert wines.

Cadenhead (William) (Scot). A Malt whisky producer based in Aberdeen. Produces Putachieside Liqueur Whisky.

Cadet (Fr). Lit – 'younger'. Name that prefixes many vineyards in the Saint-Émilion district of Bordeaux. e.g. Château Cadet-Piola, Château Cadet-Soutard.

Cadet-Bon (Le) (Fr). A wine from the Cadet vineyards in Saint-Emilion. Is also known as Cadet-Pinaud-Bon.

Cadet-Pinaud-Bon (Fr). See Cadet-Bon (Le).

Cadière d'Azur (La) (Fr). A commune in the A.C. Bandol, Provence.

C

Cadillac (Fr). An A.C. of the Côtes de Bordeaux. Produces semi-sweet, white wines from the Sauvignon blanc, Sémillon and Muscadelle grapes.

Cadiolo Winery (USA). A small winery based in Escalon, Stanislaus, California. Produces table and dessert wines.

Cadiz Cocktail (Cktl). ⅓ measure Fino sherry, ⅓ measure Blackberry brandy, ⅙ measure Cointreau, ⅙ measure cream. Shake over ice, strain into an ice-filled old-fashioned glass.

Cadnam Bitter (Eng). See CB.

Cadres (Fr). A commune in the A.C. Côtes de Blaye in north-eastern Bordeaux.

Caecuban (It). See Caecubum Wine.

Caecubum Wine (It). A red wine originating from the days of the Roman Empire. From Ager Caecubus in south Latium. See also Caecuban.

Caeres (Lat). A red wine produced in central-western Italy during Roman times.

Caesarea (Isr). A Palestinian wine (red) written about by the Romans.

Café (Fr). Coffee shop in the seventeenth to nineteenth centuries. Was run with food.

Café (Fr) (Port) (Sp). Coffee.

Cafea (Rum). Coffee.

Café Alexander (Cktl). Blend with a scoop of crushed ice, ⅕ pint iced black coffee, ½ fl.oz. Cognac, ½ fl.oz. Crème de Cacao, 1 fl.oz. cream. Serve in a highball glass.

Café à l'Irlandaise (Liq.Coffee). Using a measure of Irish whiskey. Is also known as Gaelic coffee and Irish coffee.

Café Allemande (Liq.Coffee). Using a measure of Schnapps.

Café Amaretto (Liq.Coffee). Using ½ measure Amaretto and ½ measure Kahlúa.

Café Américaine (Liq.Coffee). Using a measure of Bourbon whiskey.

Café Anglaise (Liq.Coffee). Using a measure of Gin.

Café Borgia (It). Equal quantities of hot black Espresso coffee and hot chocolate. Pour into warmed cups, top with sweetened, whipped cream and grated orange peel.

Café Brizard (USA). A coffee-flavoured liqueur.

Café Brûlot (USA). See Creole Café Brûlot.

Café Brûlot Diabolique (USA). As for Creole Café Brûlot using a measure of Cointreau with the brandy.

Café Calypso (Liq.Coffee). Using a measure of Tia Maria.

Café Caribbean (Liq.Coffee). Using a measure of white Rum.

Café Carioca (Cktl). ⅕ gill iced black coffee, ⅙ gill Jamaican rum, ⅙ gill orange juice. Stir over ice, strain into a flute glass. Top with whipped cream, grated chocolate and orange zest.

Café Chimo (USA). Into a large wine goblet place 1 teaspoon of Instant coffee, ½ fill with hot fresh brewed coffee (leave spoon in the glass), add 1 oz. maple syrup, ½ fl.oz. Cognac. Top with crème chantilly (whipped, sweetened cream).

Café com Leite (Bra). Hot drink of ½ coffee and ½ milk drunk with plenty of sugar in the morning.

Café Créole Bourbon (Fr). A method of making coffee using a filter and bain-marie. The water is heated in the bain-marie and is then poured slowly over the grounds in a filter. The resulting coffee is heated in the bain-marie. Takes approximately 1 hour to brew.

Café Curaçao (Cktl). ½ measure Kahlúa, ½ measure Triple Sec. Stir over ice in an old-fashioned glass. Serve with spiral of orange peel and straws.

Café Curaçao (Liq.Coffee). Using a measure of Grand Marnier.

Café Décafeiné (Fr). Decaffeinated coffee.

Café d'Écosse (Liq.Coffee). Using a measure of Malt whisky.

Café de Olla (Mex). Coffee made with brown sugar, cinnamon and cloves. Boiled and served thick.

Café de Paris (Cktl). ⅓ gill dry Gin, ⅛ gill Pernod, ⅛ gill cream, 1 egg white. Shake well over ice, strain into a 5 oz. goblet.

Café de Paris (Fr). A sparkling wine produced by the cuve close method from CDC in Paris.

Cafeeiro (Port). The coffee bush (tree).

Café Fertig (Switz). Coffee served with a measure of Schnapps.

Café Filtre (Fr). Filter coffee. Method of brewing coffee using a filter (paper or other). Near boiling water (96°C) is poured over the grounds in the filter medium.

Café Galliano (It). Rub the rim of a wine glass with a lemon wedge and dip in castor sugar. Place a measure of Galliano in the glass and ignite. When the sugar has caramelised add hot coffee until ¾ full. Top with double cream.

Café Glacé (Fr). Iced coffee with vanilla-flavoured milk and cream (iced).

Café Gloria (Liq.Coffee). Using a measure of Cognac and a vanilla pod.

Café HAG (Hol). The brand-name of an instant, de-caffeinised coffee. Also a ground variety.

Café Impérial (Liq.Coffee). Using a measure of Mandarine Napoléon.

Café Italienne (Liq.Coffee). Using a measure of Strega.

Café Jamaique (Liq.Coffee). Using a measure of Jamaican (dark) rum.

Café Kahlúa (Liq.Coffee). Using a measure of Kahlúa and cream topped with grated orange zest.

Café Liégeois (Fr) (1). Iced coffee served with whipped cream.

Café Liégeois (Fr) (2). 4 fl.ozs. iced coffee blended in a blender with a scoop of coffee ice cream, served in a tall glass and topped with whipped cream.

Café Mexicaine (Liq.Coffee). Using a measure of Tequila.

Café Normandie (Liq.Coffee). Using a measure of Calvados.

Café-Oh (E.Asia). Hot, thick, black coffee served with sugar in glasses from Thailand. Is known as Oliang if cream is added.

Café Religieux (Liq.Coffee). Using a measure of Bénédictine.

Café Royal (Eng). Place into a saucepan 1 orange studded with cloves, 4 pieces of orange zest and lemon zest, 1 stick of cinnamon, ¼ pint Cognac, 3 fl.ozs. Cointreau. Heat and flame. Douse with 1½ pints strong, black coffee, sweeten with sugar cubes to taste. Serve in a demi-tasse.

Café Royal Appetizer (Cktl). 1 measure dry Gin, 1 measure Dubonnet, juice ½ lemon. Shake over ice, strain into a cocktail glass.

Café Royale (Liq.Coffee). Using a measure of Cognac.

Café Royale (USA). See Coffee Royale.

Café Russe (Liq.Coffee). Using a measure of Vodka.

Café Sanka (USA). The brand-name of a de-caffeinated instant coffee.

Cafeteira (Port). Coffee pot.

Cafeteria (USA). An old Spanish name for a coffee-shop. Now denotes a self-service restaurant.

Café Tia Sole (Sp). A brand of coffee liqueur made by Campeny in Barcelona.

Cafetière (Fr). Coffee pot.

Cafetière (Fr). The brand-name of the 'plunger pot' coffee-making method. Incorporates a glass jug and plunger. The grounds are placed into the jug, near boiling water (96°C) poured onto the grounds and the plunger placed on top. When the coffee reaches the required strength the plunger is pushed to the base of the jug to separate the coffee from the grounds.

Cafèzal (Port). A coffee plantation.

Cafezinho (Bra). Fill a cup ¾ full with brown sugar. Top with strong black coffee. Usually drunk in the afternoon and evening.

Caffè (It). Coffee.

Caffè Caraibi (It) (Liq.Coffee). Using a measure of white Rum. Also known as Café Caribbean.

Caffè Espresso (It). Lit – 'Pressed coffee'. See Espresso Coffee.

Caffè Della Casa (It) (Liq.Coffee). Using a measure of Sambuca.

Caffè Francese (It) (Liq.Coffee). Using a measure of Cognac. Also known as Café Royale.

Caffeina (It). Caffeine.

Caffeine (Eng). Constituent of coffee and tea. Stimulates the nervous system and respiration. $C_8H_{10}N_4O_2$.

Caffè Irlandaise (It) (Liq.Coffee). Using a measure of Irish whiskey. Also known as Gaelic coffee and Irish coffee.

Caffè Italiano (It) (Liq.Coffee). Using a measure of Strega.

Caffè Jamaique (It) (Liq.Coffee). Using a measure of Jamaican (dark) Rum. Also known as Café Jamaique.

Caffè Russo (It) (Liq.Coffee). Using a measure of Vodka. Also known as Café Russe.

Caffè Scozzese (It) (Liq.Coffee). Using a measure of Scotch whisky.

Caffettiera (It). Coffee pot.

Cafi (Ch.Isles). Coffee.

Caf'tchière (Ch.Isles). Coffee pot. See also Caf'tière.

Caf'tière (Ch.Isles). Coffee pot. See also Caf'tchière.

Cagazal (Sp). A white grape variety grown in Rioja. Is also known as the Calagraño, Jaén, Jaina and Navés.

Ca-Gera Agricola Vinhos Alto Douro (Port). Producers of Grandelite wine.

Cagliari (It). A vineyard centre in southern Sardinia. Campidano produces the best red and white wines.

Cagnassó Winery (USA). A winery based in Marlboro, Hudson Valley, New York. Produces hybrid wines.

Cagnina (It). A red grape variety grown in central-eastern Italy.

Cahors (Fr). An A.C. district in the Lot Département. Produces red and white wines (red from the Côt, also known as the Malbec grape variety). See also Black Wine of Cahors.

Cahors (Fr). A red grape variety grown in small quantities in the Bordeaux region. Is also known as the Côt and Malbec.

Cahouet (Fr). See Cahove.

Cahove (Fr). An early seventeenth-century name for coffee. See also Cahouet.

Cailleret (Le) (Fr). A Premier Cru vineyard

in the A.C. commune of Puligny-Montrachet, Côte de Beaune, Burgundy. 5.4 ha.

Cailleret (Les) (Fr). See En Cailleret.

Caillerets (Les) (Fr). A Premier Cru vineyard in the A.C. commune of Meursault, Côte de Beaune, Burgundy. 1.3 ha.

Caillerets-Dessus (Fr). A Premier Cru vineyard in the A.C. commune of Volnay, Côte de Beaune, Burgundy. 14.7 ha. Also known as Les Caillerets-Dessus.

Cailles (Les) (Fr). A Premier Cru vineyard in the A.C. commune of Nuits-Saint-Georges, Côte de Nuits, Burgundy. 3.8 ha.

Caillier (Fr). A sixteenth-century wooden drinking cup used for wine.

Caillottes (Fr). The Loire name for the dry limestone soil of the Sancerre district in the Central Vineyards.

Cailloux (Fr). The small gravel pebbles of the Haut-Médoc. Retain the heat of the sun.

Cainho Branco (Port). A white grape variety grown in the Lima (sub-region of Vinho Verde).

Caiño (Sp). A red grape variety grown in the Ribeiro region of north-western Spain. Produces deep-red, sharp tasting wines.

Caipirinha (Cktl). 1 measure Cachaça, 1 lime, sugar to taste. Cut the lime into small pieces, place into an old-fashioned glass. Sprinkle with sugar and crush together. Fill with ice, add the Cachaça. Serve with a spoon.

C.A.I.R. (Gre). A co-operative based on the Island of Rhodes. Is the main wine-producer there.

Cairanne (Fr). A.C. in the Côtes du Rhône-Villages. Produces mainly red wines (with a little rosé and white wine).

Cairns Bitter Ale (Austr). A Bitter beer brewed by C.U.B. in Cairns.

Caithness Spring (Scot). A natural mineral water produced by Achentoul Spring Water Company. Also a sparkling variety.

Cajuada (S.Am). A spirit produced from pulverised cashew nuts in Guyana.

Cake (Eng). The name given to the residue of the grapes after the juice has been extracted in a press.

Cakebread Cellars (USA). A winery based near Oakville, Napa Valley, California. 9 ha. Grape varieties – Cabernet sauvignon, Chardonnay, Sauvignon blanc and Zinfandel. Produces varietal wines.

Çakirkeyif (Tur). Denotes tipsy, merry.

Calabrese (It). A red grape variety grown in Sicily. Also known as the Nero d'Avoia.

Calabresi Frohlich (It). A red grape variety.

Calabria (It). The southernmost region of the Italian peninsula. Also a peninsula in its own right. Famous for its full red wines.

Calados (Sp). The underground cellars of Rioja for maturing wines.

Calafia (Mex). The label used by Luis Cetto Vineyards in Guadalupe, Baja California for a range of their wines.

Calagraño (Sp). A white grape variety grown in Rioja. Also known as the Cagazal, Jaén, Jaina, Navés and the Cayetana in the Estremadura.

Calahorra (Sp). A Zona de crianza in the Rioja Baja, north-eastern Spain.

Calanda Brewery (Switz). An independent brewery based in Chur.

Calaretto (It). A white grape variety used in the making of Marsala.

Calaveras (USA). A small wine-producing county in the Sierra Foothills, California. Covers approximately 26 ha.

Calcaire de Plassac (Fr). Calcareous subsoil combined with clay found in the commune of Margaux in the Haut-Médoc, Bordeaux. It is unique to the commune. On the top is gravel and gravillious.

Calcareous (Eng). Chalk soil. Found in Champagne, Cognac and Jerez de la Frontera. Contains calcium carbonate.

Calcinaia (It). A Chianti Classico estate based in Tuscany.

Calcium Carbonate (Eng). CACO₃. Used to de-acidify wines made from under-ripe grapes.

Calcium Phytate (Eng). A fining agent. Also known as Aferrin.

Calcium Sulphate (Eng). CASO₄. See Gypsum.

Calctufa (Eng). Another name for Tufa. See also Calctuff.

Calctuff (Eng). Another name for Tufa. See Calctufa.

Calcutta Cup (Eng). A mixture of ½ pint Guinness and ½ pint tonic water.

Caldaro (It). A dry red wine from the upper Trentino-Alto Adige. Produced around lake of same name. Also called Lago di Caldaro.

Caldaro (It). A small lake based south-west of Bolzano in the region of Trentino-Alto Adige. Produces a red wine of same name. See also Lago di Caldaro.

Caledon (S.Afr). A wine-producing district in the Cape Province.

C

Caledonia (Cktl). 1 fl.oz. Glayva, 1 fl.oz. Scotch whisky, juice of a lemon, dash Grenadine, dash egg white. Shake over ice, strain into cocktail glass. Dress with slice of lemon and a cherry. Serve with straws.

Caledonia Cocktail (Cktl). ⅓ measure Cognac, ⅓ measure Crème de Cacao, ⅓ measure fresh milk, 1 egg yolk. Shake well over ice, strain into an ice-filled highball glass. Serve with a cinnamon stick.

Caledonian (Scot). A Grain whisky distillery based near Edinburgh.

Caledonian Ale (Scot). A rich Ale 1077 O.G. brewed by the Lorimer and Clark's Caledonian Brewery, Edinburgh.

Cal'em and Filho (Port). Vintage Port shippers. Quinta da Foz. Vintages – 1935, 1947, 1948, 1955, 1958, 1960, 1963, 1966, 1970, 1975, 1977, 1980, 1982, 1983.

Calepitrimerus Vitis (Lat). The grape rust mite. See Phyllocoptes Vitis and Acorissis.

Calera (La) (Chile). A noted wine-producing area in the Aconcagua province, northern Chile.

Calera Wine Co (USA). A winery based in San Benito County, California. 9.5 ha. Grape variety – Zinfandel. Noted for its Zinfandel Essence (produced from Botrytised grapes).

Calgalon (Sp). A white grape variety grown in Jerez de la Frontera. Is also known as the Albillo and Castellano.

Calgary Export (Can). A noted brand of beer.

Calgrano (Sp). A white grape variety used for the white, dry wines of the Rioja.

Calice (It). Cup, chalice.

Calice (Port). A wine glass. A glass for Port wines and liqueurs. Also a Chalice cup.

Calichal (Mex). A mixture of Pulque and Lager beer at approximately a 4 to 1 ratio.

California (USA). A wine-producing state on the west coast of America. Main regions are – Alameda, Lake, Mendocino, Monterey, San Benito, San Joaquin Valley, San Luis Obispo, Santa Barbara, Santa Clara, Santa Cruz, Sierra Foothills and Southern California. See Serra (Friar Junipéro).

California Aleatico (USA). A medium sweet, red table wine with the Muscat aroma. A varietal which must contain 51% of the named grape variety.

California Angelica (USA). A blend of several dessert wines of the California region. Are blended to produce a very sweet wine of 10–15% unfermented sugar. See Angelica.

California Barbera (USA). A varietal, full-bodied, deep coloured red wine. Must have at least 51% of the named grape. See also California Barberone.

California Barberone (USA). Lit – 'Small Barbera', is a varietal with at least 51% of the Barbera grape but less than the California Barbera. See California Barbera.

California Brandy (USA). Produced by much the same method as Cognac. Sold at about 50% alc. by vol. Is blended and matured in oak casks. Has a good nose, but is more fiery than Cognac.

California Brandy Advisory Board (USA). The governing body for USA-produced brandies.

California Burgundy (USA). A deep, rich, ruby-red, full-bodied and flavoured wine. Is sold in traditional Burgundy bottles.

California Cabernet Sauvignon (USA). A varietal, full-bodied red wine of Claret type. Must have at least 51% of named grape.

California Carignane (USA). A varietal, full-bodied red wine with a full aroma. Must have at least 51% of the named grape.

California Chablis (USA). A delicate, straw-coloured wine made with the Chardonnay and Pinot blanc grapes. Other varieties are used such as the Burger, Chenin blanc, Golden chasselas, Green Hungarian, etc.

California Champagne (USA). A sparkling wine made by all methods (charmat, cuve close, méthode champenoise). Follows French labelling practices.

California Charbono (USA). A varietal, full-bodied red wine of the Burgundy style. Must have at least 51% of the named grape.

California Chardonnay (USA). A varietal, light, dry, medium-bodied white wine. Must be made from at least 51% of the named grape.

California Château Sauterne (USA). See Château Sauterne.

California Chenin Blanc (USA). A varietal, light, dry, medium-bodied, white wine. Must be made from 51% of named grape.

California Chianti (USA). A dry, medium-bodied, deep red and well-flavoured wine. Softer than its Italian original. Is sold in a straw-covered flask.

California Claret (USA). A dry, rich, red, medium-bodied wine bottled in the traditional Bordeaux bottle.

California Folle Blanche (USA). A dry,

straw-coloured, medium-bodied wine with Chablis characteristics. Must have at least 51% of the named grape.

California Gamay (USA). A light, red, fruity wine with a good bouquet in the Beaujolais style. Must have at least 51% of the named grape.

California Grappa (USA). Is distilled from grape pomace. A fiery Brandy with no colour, and no ageing. Also known as California Pomace.

California Grignolino (USA). A varietal, full-flavoured, red wine. Must have at least 51% of the named grape.

California Growers (USA). A large winery based at Cutler in Tulare, California. Grape varieties – Cabernet sauvignon, Emerald riesling, French colombard and Johannisberg riesling. Its varietal wines are sold under Bounty, Le Blanc and Setrakian labels. Also produces brandies. See Growers Old Reserve.

California Haut Sauterne (USA). See Haut Sauterne.

California Hock (USA). A light, dry, pale-coloured wine made from assorted grapes but having the characteristics of Hock wine.

California Lemonade (Cktl). ⅓ gill Bourbon whiskey, juice of a lemon, 2 teaspoons powdered sugar, 2 dashes Grenadine. Shake well over ice, strain into a collins glass with crushed ice. Top with soda water and decorate with slice of orange, lemon and a cherry. Serve with straws.

California Light Muscat (USA). A varietal Muscat wine. Varies from dry to very sweet but all have a Muscat aroma. Also sometimes labelled with the exact varietal. e.g. the Moscato canelli, Moscato hamburg, etc.

California Madeira (USA). Made to resemble the true Madeira but tends to taste like a sweet Sherry.

California Malaga (USA). A very deep, dark amber-coloured wine made from a blend of dessert wines.

California Marsala (USA). Made to resemble the true Marsala but tends to be like a very sweet Sherry.

California Mission (USA). A native red grape variety.

California Moselle (USA). A light, dry, pale-coloured wine made from assorted grapes but having the characteristics of the wines of the Mosel-Saar-Ruwer.

California Muscat Brandy (USA). Distilled from Muscat wines which give it its distinctive bouquet of the Muscat grape.

California Muscatel (USA). A rich, sweet,

highly perfumed, white wine. Made from any one of the eight Muscat varieties.

California Petite Syrah (USA). A varietal, full-bodied, red wine of the Burgundy style. Must contain at least 51% of the named grape.

California Pinot Blanc (USA). A light, dry, straw-coloured wine. Must contain at least 51% of the named grape.

California Pinot Noir (USA). A varietal, full-bodied, red wine made in the Burgundy style. Must contain at least 51% of the named grape.

California Pomace Brandy (USA). See California Grappa.

California Port (USA). A Port-type wine made in California but now no longer allowed to use the name Port through treaties of 1968.

California Red Pinot (USA). A varietal, full-bodied, red wine of the Burgundy style. Must contain at least 51% of the named grape.

California Rhine Riesling (USA). A light, dry, pale-coloured wine. Is made from assorted grapes but has the characteristics of a Rhine wine.

California Riesling (USA). A dry, acidic, white wine made from a variety of grapes including the Emerald riesling, Grey riesling, Johannisberg riesling, etc.

California Rosé (USA). A light-bodied, dry wine that ranges in colour from pale pink to light red. Grapes such as Cabernet, Gamay, Grenache and Grignolino are all used in the making.

California Sauterne (USA). A light, full-bodied, dry, golden wine. Is often sold as Dry Sauterne.

California Sauvignon Blanc (USA). A varietal, sweet, white wine. Must contain at least 51% of the named grape.

California Sémillon (USA). A varietal, dry, fruity, white wine. Must contain at least 51% of the named grape.

California Sherry (USA). A dessert wine which is baked in the sun in large vats to give it a slightly bitter tang and nutty flavour.

California Sparkling Burgundy (USA). A sparkling red wine made from red grapes. Semi-sweet to sweet.

California Sparkling Malvasia Bianca (USA). A carbonated version of the still table wine. Made by the Charmat method.

California Sparkling Moselle (USA). A carbonated version of the still table wine. Made by the Charmat method.

California Sparkling Muscat (USA). A carbonated version of the still table wine. Made by the Charmat method.

C

California Sparkling Sauterne (USA). A carbonated version of the still table wine. Made by the Charmat method.

California State Board of Viticultural Commissioners (USA). A Body formed in 1880 to help combat pests, improve grape cultivation and wine-making practices and to improve the economic status of the industry.

California Sweet Sauterne (USA). See Sweet Sauterne.

California Tokay (USA). An amber-coloured blend of sweet wines.

California Trebbiano (USA). See California Ugni Blanc.

California Ugni Blanc (USA). A varietal, light, dry, medium-bodied, white wine. Must contain at least 51% of the named grape. Also known as the California Trebbiano.

California Vermouth (USA). Made as in Europe. (French style is light in colour and dry, Italian style is amber in colour and sweet). Sold under brand names.

California White Chianti (USA). A dry, fruity, medium-bodied, white wine made from the Trebbiano and Muscat grapes. Is sold in the traditional straw-covered flasks.

California Wine Association (USA). C.W.A. A group of wineries based in Delano, California. Under the control of Perelli-Minetti Co. Varietal wines and brandies produced. See Aristocrat Brandy and Morrow Brandy.

California Wine Institute (USA). Founded in February 1934. Introduced standards and helps promote Californian wines.

California Zinfandel (USA). A varietal, red, fruity and spicy wine. Must contain at least 51% of the named grape.

Calimero Cocktail (Cktl). 1 measure Cognac, 1 measure orange juice, ½ measure Grand Marnier, ½ measure Tia Maria, 2 dashes lemon juice, ½ egg white. Shake well over ice, strain into a balloon glass. Dress with a slice of orange.

Câlin Cocktail (Cktl). ⅗ measure orange juice, ⅕ measure Anisette, ⅓ measure Mandarine Napoléon. Shake over ice, strain into a cocktail glass. Dress with a mint leaf, cherry and a slice of lime.

Calisay (Sp). A digestive liqueur made from herbs and aromatic roots, blended with pure alcohol. 32% alc. by vol.

Calisaya (Sp). A bitters flavoured with quinine and calisaya bark and with a brandy base. 33% alc. by vol.

Calisay Cocktail (Cktl). ½ measure Calisaya, ½ measure sweet Vermouth, 2 dashes Gomme syrup, 2 dashes lime juice. Shake well over ice, strain into a cocktail glass.

Calissano (It). A noted producer of Asti Spumante. Produced by the méthode champenoise. Labels include Realbrut.

Calistoga (USA). A noted wine town in the northern Napa Valley, California.

Calitor (Fr). A red grape variety grown in the southern Rhône.

Calitris Quadrivalvis (Gre). The pine tree from which the resin is used to make Retsina. Called the Aleppo pine.

Calitzdorp (S.Afr). A wine and brandy-producing region based in Klein Karoo, eastern Cape.

Calitzdorp Co-operative (S.Afr). A co-op. winery based in Klein Karoo. Address = Calitzdorp Vrugte en Wynkelders, Box 193, Calitzdorp 6660. Produces varietal wines sold under the Buffelskroon Wines label.

Calitzdorp Vrugte en Wynkelders (S.Afr). See Calitzdorp Co-operative.

Calix (Lat). Wine cup. See also Camella.

Calkarasi (Tur). A white grape variety grown in the Aegean.

Callao (S.Am). The word for a brewery in Peru.

Callaway Winery (USA). Vineyards and winery based in Temecula in Southern California. Grape varieties – Chardonnay, Chenin blanc, Petite syrah, Sauvignon blanc and Zinfandel. Produces varietal wines. See also Sweet Nancy.

Callet (Sp). A red grape variety grown on the Balearic Islands.

Call Time (Eng). Denotes that drinking time on licensed premises has come to an end. See Drinking Up Time.

Calmont (Ger). Vineyard. (Anb) = Mosel-Saar-Ruwer. (Ber) = Zell/Mosel. (Gro) = Grafschaft. (Vil) = Bremm.

Calmont (Ger). Vineyard. (Anb) = Mosel-Saar-Ruwer. (Ber) = Zell/Mosel. (Gro) = Grafschaft. (Vil) = Ediger-Eller.

Calmus (Ger). A liqueur wine produced near Frankfurt in the nineteenth century from Botrytis-attacked grapes.

Calm Voyage (Cktl). ⅓ measure Strega, ⅓ measure white Rum, ⅓ egg white, ⅙ measure Passion fruit liqueur. Blend altogether with a scoop of crushed ice in a blender. Pour into a flute glass.

Caloric Punch (Scan). A tonic liqueur with a Rum base.

Caloric Punsch (USA). Another name for Swedish Punsch. See also Arrack Punsch.

Calouères (Fr). A Premier Cru vineyard in the A.C. commune of Morey-Saint-Denis, Côte de Nuits, Burgundy. 1.3 ha.

Caluso Passito (It). D.O.C. white wine produced in Caluso, Piemonte region.

Grape variety – Erbaluce. Grapes are selected and then partially dried under natural conditions until sugar content in not less that 30%. Must be aged for a minimum of 5 years.

Caluso Passito Liquoroso (It). A fortified wine from Caluso, Piemonte. Made from the grapes, musts or wines suitable to produce Caluso passito. Must be aged for a minimum of 5 years.

Calva (Fr). Denotes an apple brandy other than A.C. Calvados.

Calvados (Fr). An apple brandy made from the double distillation of apple/pear wine in pot stills. Matured in oak casks. Produced in Normandy. See Calvados du Pays d'Auge, etc. 40% alc. by vol.

Calvados Cocktail (Cktl). ⅓ measure Calvados, ⅙ measure Cointreau, ⅓ measure orange juice, ⅙ measure Orange bitters. Shake over ice, strain into a cocktail glass.

Calvados Cooler Cocktail (Cktl). ⅙ gill Calvados, juice ½ lemon, 1 teaspoon sugar. Stir well over ice in a highball glass. Top with soda water.

Calvados de la Vallée de l'Orne (Fr). A lesser A.R. Calvados area. See Calvados.

Calvados de l'Avranchin (Fr). An A.C. Calvados area. See Calvados

Calvados-du-Calvados (Fr). A lesser A.R. Calvados area. See Calvados.

Calvados du Cotentin (Fr). An A.C. Calvados area. See Calvados.

Calvados du Domfrontais (Fr). An A.C. Calvados area. See Calvados.

Calvados du Mortainais (Fr). An A.C. Calvados area. See Calvados.

Calvados du Pays d'Auge (Fr). An A.C. Calvados area. See Calvados.

Calvados du Pays de Bray (Fr). An A.C. Calvados area. See Calvados.

Calvados du Pays de la Risle (Fr). An A.C. Calvados area. See Calvados.

Calvados du Pays du Merlerault (Fr). An A.C. Calvados area. See Calvados.

Calvados du Perche (Fr). An A.C. Calvados area. See Calvados.

Calvados Rickey (Cktl). ⅙ gill Calvados, juice ¼ lemon. Stir well over ice in an old-fashioned glass. Top with soda water. Dress with a slice of lime.

Calvados Sour (Cktl). ⅙ gill Calvados, ½ teaspoon sugar, 2 dashes lemon juice. Shake over ice, strain into a club goblet. Dress with an orange slice and a cherry.

Calvert Distilling Co (USA). A part of Seagram. Major distillers of Bourbon whiskey, Vodka and many other spirits.

Calvet (Fr). Major French négociants. Address = 75, Cours de Médoc, 33300,

Bordeaux. Ship both Bordeaux and Burgundy wines plus Cognac.

Calvet et Cie (Fr). A négociant based in Beaune, Côte de Beaune, Burgundy.

Calvi (Fr). A sub-region in the north of Corsica. Produces fine A.C. red and white wines.

Calviere (Eng). A lightly sparkling, medium dry, alcoholic pear drink produced by Showerings, Shepton Mallet, Somerset. (Owned by Allied Lyons).

Calypso (Eng). A Rum and banana cream liqueur produced by Goldwell and Company.

Calypso (S.Afr). The brand-name of a double-distilled cane spirit.

Calypso Cocktail (Cktl). Place ⅙ gill orange Curaçao into an ice-filled highball glass. Top with ginger ale.

Calypso Coffee (Liq.Coffee). Using a measure of Tia Maria.

Cama de Lobos (Mad). One of the island's top vineyards. Is also known as Camara de Lobos.

Camara de Lobos (Mad). See Cama de Lobos.

Camaralet (Fr). A red grape variety grown in the Bergerac region of south-western France.

Camarate (Port). A red grape variety also known as the Mortàgua.

Camarate (Port). A red wine made from a blend of Cabernet sauvignon, Merlot and Periquita grapes. Is produced by J.M. Fonseca in Azeitão.

Cambas (Gre). A dry, light-coloured Brandy. 40% alc. by vol.

Cambiaso Vineyards (USA). A Thai-owned winery based in Sonoma County, California. Grape varieties – Barbera, Cabernet sauvignon, Petite syrah and Sauvignon blanc. Produces varietal wines.

Cambodia (E.Asia). A single stemmed variety of tea bush which is used to cross with other varieties of tea bush to improve quality.

Cambrai (Austr). A winery based in Clare-Watervale, South Australia. Produces varietal wines.

Cambrian Brewery (Wales). A subsidiary brewery of Ansell's based in South Wales. Produces cask conditioned Dark Ale 1034 O.G.

Cambridge Ale (Eng). A bottled Pale ale 1052 O.G. brewed by the Paine Brewery, Cambridgeshire.

Cambus (Fr). A well-known Brandy producer. Produces a range of fine brandies and wines.

Camella (Lat). Wine cup. See also Calix.

Camel Lager (Afr). A Lager beer 1044 O.G. brewed by the Blue Nile Brewery in

Khartoum, Sudan.

Camellia Sinensis (Lat). The botanical name for the true Tea bush.

Camelot Spring (Cktl). 1 part Brandy, 2 parts Merrydown Mead, 4 parts Merrydown Apple Wine, sliced apples or whole strawberries. Marinate the fruit in the mead and brandy for one hour, add wine and ice cubes. Serve in goblets.

Camera Obscura (Sp). Describes a wooden structure that has a candle inside which is used to test the clarity of wines.

Cameron Brewery (Eng). A large brewery based in Hartlepool, Yorkshire. Produces many fine styles of beers including cask conditioned Lion Bitter 1036 O.G. Strongarm 1040 O.G. Crown 1040 O.G. Hansa 1036 O.G. and Strongarm Special 1046 O.G.

Cameronbridge (Scot). A Grain whisky distillery based in Fife, south of Dundee. Built in 1824. Owned by Haig. See Cameron Brig and Old Cameron Brig.

Cameron Brig (Scot). A famous single Grain whisky produced by Haig. See Cameronbridge and Old Cameron Brig.

Cameron's Kick (Cktl). ½ measure Scotch whisky, ½ measure Irish whiskey, juice ½ lemon, 2 dashes Orange bitters. Shake over ice, strain into a cocktail glass.

Cameroon Coffee (W.Afr). Both Robustas and Arabicas grown. Are both sweet and mellow in style.

Camilla (Cktl). ⅙ gill dry Gin, ½ gill Camomile tea, dash French vermouth, dash Italian vermouth. Shake over ice, strain into a cocktail glass. Dress with a green olive.

Camilo Alves (Port). Produces Bucelas (only firm to do so). Is sold under the Caves Velhas label. Also sells Dão wines.

Camina (Ger). A red grape variety. A cross between the Portugieser and the Spätburgunder. Has higher sugar and acidity than either of its parents.

Camino Real (Mex). A coffee-flavoured liqueur produced by Montini.

Cammarèse (Fr). A red grape variety grown in the southern Rhône.

Camomile Tea (Eng). A herbal (Tisane) tea, used as a stimulant. Helps relaxation.

Campagna (Lat). Lit – 'Open, un-forested land' from which Champagne derives.

Campagnola (It). A wine-producer based in Valgatara, Verona. Noted for his Valpolicella.

Campanas (Las) (Sp). Red, rosé and white wines sold under the Castillo de Tiebas label from Vinícola Navarra, northeastern Spain.

Campanàrio (Mad). A noted vine-growing area on the south coast.

Campania (It). A wine province that includes Naples. Lies south of Latium on the west coast. See Lacryma Christi del Vesuvio.

Campari (It). A famous Orange bitters. Is bright red in colour. Its base is an extract of capsicum. 24% alc. by vol.

Campari Apéritif (Cktl). Place a good measure of Campari in an ice-filled highball glass. Top with soda, stir, dress with a slice of orange.

Campari Shakerado (Cktl). ⅓ gill Campari shaken vigorously over ice, strained and served in a small goblet.

Campay Cocktail (Cktl). ⅕ gill Campari, ⅕ gill dry Gin, dash Gomme syrup, juice of a grapefruit. Shake well over ice, strain into a club goblet. Dress with a spiral of lemon peel. Serve with straws.

Campbell and Son (Scot). The former owners of Aberlour-Glenlivet Distillery. Has now been taken over by Pernod-Ricard.

Campbells Ales (Bel). Strong bottled Christmas and Scotch ales. Are brewed for the Belgiums by the Whitbreads Brewery in England.

Campbell's Glory (Jap). A white grape variety.

Campbells of Rutherglen (Austr). A winery based in north-east Victoria. Is noted for its dessert wines.

Campbeltown (Scot). A class of Malt whisky from Campbeltown on the Mull of Kintyre. Only 2 now produced (Springbank and Glen Scotia).

Camp Coffee (Eng). A coffee and chicory essence beverage drink. Is slightly sweetened.

Campden Tablets (Eng). Proprietary brand-name for small Potassium or Sodium Metabisulphide tablets used by amateur winemakers to stop the growth of bacteria, moulds and yeasts. Also prevents Malo-Lactic fermentation.

Campeaching Wood (Mex). Also known as Logwood. Produces a dye often used to improve the colour of wines and liqueurs.

Campeador (Sp). A red wine produced from the Garnacha 40% and the Tempranillo 60%. Is oak-matured for 3 years then bottle-aged for 2 years. Produced by Martinez Lacuesta.

Campelo (Joaquin Miranda & Filhos) (Port). Producers of Morgarinha-Bagaceira do Minho (an Aguardente).

C

Campeny (Sp). A spirits and liqueurs producer based in Barcelona.

Campidano (It). The top vineyard in Caglian, southern Sardinia. Noted for its red and white wines.

Campi Flegei (It). One of the areas in Campania where Falerno wine is produced.

Campiglia (It). One of the five towns in Cinque Terre, Liguria.

Campillo (Sp). The brand-name for the wines produced by Bodegas Campillo in Rioja.

Campobello (It). A Chianti Classico producer based in Tuscany.

Campo Blanco (Sp). A red wine produced by Bodegas Campo Blanco, Rioja. Made from the Garnacha and Tempranillo grape varieties.

Campo Burgo (Sp). The name of a range of red and white wines produced by Bodegas de la Torre y Lapuerta.

Campo Fiorin (It). A single vineyard Ripasso (a Vino da Tavola) red wine produced by Masi.

Camponac (Fr). The brand-name of Eschanauer. Red and white wines sold for export.

Campo de Borja (Sp). A Denominación de Origen based near Navarra in north-eastern Spain.

Campo de Tarragona (Sp). One of three sub-zones in Tarragona, south-eastern Spain. Main grape varieties – Cariñena, Garnacha, Paralleda and Xarel-lo.

Campo Nuevo (Sp). The brand-name label used by Cenalsa in the Navarra region, north-eastern Spain.

Campo Viejo (Sp). The brand-name for wines from the Bodegas Campo Viejo, Rioja. Red, red reserva and white wines are produced.

CAMRA (Eng) (abbr). CAMpaign for Real Ale. A British organisation to promote the production of traditional cask conditioned and bottle conditioned beers.

Camsie Spring (Eng). A recognised mineral water.

Camtrell and Cochrane (Eng). See C and C.

Camus (Fr). A noted Cognac producer. Address = Camus la Grande Marque SA, 29 Rue Marguerite de Navarre, BP 19, 16101 Cognac. 100 ha. 50% in the Grande Champagne and 50% in the Borderies.

Camus (Scot). A Grain whisky distillery based at the mouth of the river Forth, eastern Scotland.

Caña (S.Am). Rum.

Caña (S.Am). Sugar cane from which the molasses are obtained for the production of Rum.

Caña (Sp). A glass of beer.

Caña (Sp). A tall, straight-sided glass used for drinking Sherry in Jerez de la Frontera. See also Copita.

Canaan (S.Afr). A red grape variety.

Can Abadía (Sp). The brand-name of a dry, light, red wine produced by Raimat in Lérida.

Canada (N.Am). Main wine regions are around Niagara, with new regions appearing. Wines made from American vines and named after European types. e.g. Canadian Chablis, Canadian Claret, etc. Also produces noted Rye whiskies.

Canada (Port). A measure of 2 litres capacity used in the blending of Port.

Canada Cocktail (Cktl). 1½ fl.ozs. Canadian whisky, 2 dashes Cointreau, 2 dashes Angostura, 1 teaspoon powdered sugar. Shake over ice, strain into a cocktail glass.

Canada Cup (Can). The brand-name of a Canadian whisky produced by Schenley. 40% alc. by vol.

Canada Dry (Eng). See Canada Dry Rawlings.

Canada Dry Rawlings (Eng). Producers of Canada Dry (a popular brand of ginger ale) sold in a distinctive green bottle. Also other mineral mixers and fruit juices.

Canada House (Can). A brand of Canadian rye whisky produced by the Canadian Distillers Ltd. (a subsidiary of Seagram).

Canadaigua (USA). Producers of sparkling wines based in eastern USA.

Cañada Seca (Arg). A wine-producing area based in southern Argentina.

Canadian Cherry Cocktail (Cktl). ⅓ measure Rye whisky, ⅓ measure lemon juice, ⅓ measure orange juice, ⅙ measure Cherry brandy. Shake over ice, strain into an ice-filled old-fashioned glass (with the rim moistened with Cherry brandy).

Canadian Club (Can). A blended Canadian whisky produced by Hiram Walker and Sons Ltd. 40% alc. by vol.

Canadian Cup (Can). A straight Rye whisky produced by the Canadian Schenley Distilleries. 40% alc. by vol.

Canadian Distillers Ltd (Can). A subsidiary of Seagram. Produces a fine range of Canadian whiskies.

Canadian Double Distilled (Can). A brand of Canadian whisky produced by the Canadian Distillers Ltd. 40% alc. by vol.

Canadian Gibson Distilleries (Can). Produces a range of Canadian whiskies.

Canadian Lord Calvert (Can). A brand of Canadian whisky produced by Seagram. 40% alc. by vol.

Canadian Mist Distilleries Ltd (Can). Distillery based at Collingwood, Ontario. Produces Canadian Mist (a blended Canadian whisky). 40% alc. by vol.

Canadian Pineapple (Cktl). ½ gill Canadian Club whisky, juice ½ lemon, ¼ gill pineapple juice, 2 dashes Maraschino. Shake over ice, strain into an ice-filled highball glass. Dress with pineapple cubes.

Canadian Rye Whisky (Can). See Canadian Whisky and Rye Whisky.

Canadian Schenley Distilleries Ltd (Can). Producers of Canadian Cup, Five Thirty, OFC and Order of Merit brands of whiskies. Also produces liqueurs sold under the Henkes and Ross label.

Canadian Sunset Cocktail (Cktl). ½ measure Canadian whisky, ¼ measure Strega, ¼ measure Galliano, juice of a lemon, 2 dashes Grenadine. Shake all ingredients (except the Grenadine) over ice, strain into a cocktail glass containing the Grenadine. Do not stir.

Canadian Whisky (Can). A Whisky made mainly from rye but can be made from other cereals. Can be bottled at 2 years of age. It is usually matured in charred oak casks for 5 years. Varies in alcoholic strength.

Canado Saludo (Cktl). ⅕ gill Jamaican rum, ⅙ gill orange juice, ⅙ gill pineapple juice, 4 dashes Grenadine. Shake well over ice, strain into a club goblet with a pineapple chunk, orange slice and a cherry. Serve with straws.

Canaiolo Bianco (It). A white grape variety grown in Tuscany.

Canaiolo Nero (It). A red grape variety used in the making of Chianti in the Tuscany region. Known as the 'Grape of the Estruscans'. Has a good sugar content.

Canakin (Eng). See Cannikin and Canikin.

Canakkale (Tur). A vineyard based in the Thrace and Marmara regions. Produces white table wines.

Canakkale-Balikesir (Tur). A vineyard based in the Thrace and Marmara regions. Produces red wines.

Canal Street Daisy (Cktl). 1 measure Bourbon whiskey, ¼ measure lemon juice, 1 measure orange juice. Stir over ice, strain into an ice-filled highball glass. Top with soda water and orange slice.

Cañamero (Sp). A wine-producing village based near Guadaloupe in the Estremadura that produces Flor-attacked wines.

Canard-Duchêne (Fr). Champagne producer. Address = 1, Rue Edmond Canard, 51500 Ludes, Rilly-la-Montagne. A Grande Marque. Produces – Vintage and non-vintage wines. Vintages – 1943, 1947, 1949,1952, 1955, 1957, 1959, 1961, 1962, 1964, 1966, 1969, 1970, 1971, 1973, 1975, 1976, 1979, 1982. Produces – N.V. Patrimoire. Part of Veuve Clicquot.

Cañarroyo (Sp). A white grape variety grown in central Spain.

Canary Islands (Sp). A group of Spanish islands off the West African coast whose wines are only consumed locally. The wine of Palma was popular in England in the seventeenth century under the name of Palma Sack. Also produces Canary Sack.

Canary Sack (Sp). A sweet wine produced in the Canary Islands.

Canasta Cream (Sp). An old, sweet, premium Oloroso sherry produced by Williams and Humbert.

Canastas (Sp). The baskets used in Jerez to carry the cut grapes to the winery.

Can Casal (Sp). The brand-name of a light, dry, white wine produced by Raimat Bodegas in Lérida.

Canchales (Sp). Red and white wines produced by Bodegas Riojanas S.A. Cenicero, Rioja.

Canciller (Arg). The name given to a premium range of wines produced by Griol (the State co-operative).

Can Clamor (Sp). The brand-name of a red wine produced by the Raimat Bodega in Lérida.

Candau (Fr). A wine-producing district based in A.C. Bellet, Provence.

C & C (Eng) (abbr). A soft drinks producer. The third largest in the U.K. which markets under the 'Club' label. Camtrell & Cochrane (G.B.). Warwickshire.

Candes (Fr). A white wine produced in the Touraine district, Loire.

C and G (Eng) (abbr). City and Guilds. The examining body for the 717 (originally 707–3) Alcoholic beverages certificate.

Candia (It). The name for Crete in the thirteenth century. Wines were known as Candiae, Candy or Malvasia Candiae.

Candiae (It). See Candia.

Candida (Cktl). ⅓ measure Marie Brizzard, ⅓ measure Cognac, ⅓ measure double cream. Place with some crushed ice into a mixing glass. Stir until foaming, strain into a cocktail glass.

Candida Mycroderma (Lat). A variety of yeast. Is aerobic, grows on low alcohol wines.

Candy (It). See Candia.

Cane (Eng). The name used to describe a mature vine shoot.

Canebière Cocktail (Cktl). ⅔ measure Pernod, ⅓ measure Cherry brandy. Shake over ice, strain into cocktail glass.

C

Caneca (Port). A tankard, mug or large glass.

Caneco (Port). An oak jug that is bound with copper.

Cane Cutter (S.Am). A brand of Rum produced in Guyana.

Cane Garden Bay (W.Ind). A noted Rum distillery based in the Virgin Islands.

Canéjean (Fr). A commune in the A.C. Graves district in south-western Bordeaux.

Canella (It). Producer of sparkling (cuve close) wines in Veneto. Also produces Prosecco di Conegliano-Valdobbiadene.

Canellino (It). The name given to the sweet-styled Frascati Superiore.

Canepa [José] (Chile). A winery based at Valparaiso. Noted for its dry Sémillon, sweet Muscadel and Cabernet wines.

Canephora (Afr). Coffea Canephora. Also known as Robusta coffee. Hardy plant. Grows in low altitudes, indigenous in north-east and central Africa, Asia and South America.

Cane Spirit (Eng). A rectified spirit made from cane sugar in various countries such as South Africa, South America and the West Indies.

Canica (Mad). A hybrid grape variety also known as the Cunningham. Has been banned from use in Madeira production.

Canikin (Eng). See Cannikin and Canakin.

Canister Beer (Eng). Another name for Keg beer.

Canned (Eng) (slang). Drunk, intoxicated.

Canned Cocktail (Cktl). ⅓ measure Gin, ⅓ measure Vodka, ⅓ measure lime juice. Shake over ice, strain into a cocktail glass. Dress with a slice of lime.

Cannelle (Fr). A liqueur flavoured with cinnamon.

Cannellino (It). Term that means the same as Dolce (sweet) in Latium.

Cannicci (It). Special wicker frames in Tuscany. Used to partially dry the grapes (Governo) for Chianti. Also known as Castelli.

Cannikin (Eng). A small can used as a drinking vessel in the nineteenth century. See also Canakin and Canikin.

Cannonau (It). A red grape variety used to produce both dry and sweet fortified wines in Sardinia.

Cannonau di Sardegna (It). D.O.C. ruby red wine made in Sardinia from the Cannonau grape variety plus no more than 10% of Bovale grande, Bovale sardo, Carignano, Pascale di cagliari, Monica or Vernaccia di S. Gimignano grapes. Must be aged 1 year in wood. If three years then Riserva. Also produced – Superiore Natural Mente Secco (dry), Amabile (medium sweet) and Dolce (sweet).

Cannonau di Sardegna Liquoroso (It). D.O.C. vino liquoroso. 2 types are produced (secco and dolce naturale). Additional sub-denomination Oliena or Nepente di Oliena can appear on the label if grapes used are produced from Oliena or Orgosolo Rosé Cannonau di Sardegna, produced by the fermentazione in bianco.

Cano (Gaspar F. Florido) (Sp). A fine Sherry producer based in Jerez de la Frontera.

Canoa (Sp). A wedge-shaped funnel used to fill wine casks.

Cañocazo (Sp). The alternative name for the white grape Mollar blanco.

Canon (Fr). A wine measure of ¹⁄₁₆ of a litre used in the eighteenth and nineteenth centuries.

Canon-Fronsac (Fr). An A.C. red wine of Bordeaux. See Côtes Canon-Fronsac.

Canons Grélifuges (Fr). Nineteenth-century cannons designed to fire into the clouds to prevent hailstorms in the Burgundy region.

Canova (It). Cellar, cave or tavern.

Can Rius (Sp). The brand-name for a dry, rosé wine produced by Raimat Bodega in Lérida.

Canstatter Wasen (Ger). An Autumn beer festival held in Stuttgart in the Canstatt district which specialises in the beers of Baden and Württemburg.

Cant (Eng). The end piece of the top of a cask in which the two hold the middle stave.

Cantab Bitter (Eng). A sweet-style Bitter beer brewed by the Tolly Cobbold Brewery, Ipswich, Suffolk.

Cantaro (Ger). A white grape hybrid cross between Seibel 2765 and the Müller-Thurgau.

Canteiro (Mad). The name given to Madeira that has been through the Estufa system but has been heated in small casks. Used mainly in blending to improve wines.

Cantenac (Fr). A commune within the district of A.C. Haut-Médoc in north-western Bordeaux.

Canterbury (N.Z.). A wine-producing area in the South Island.

Canterbury Ale (Eng). A cask conditioned Ale 1038 O.G. brewed by the Wiltshire Brewery, Tisbury, Wiltshire for the Canterbury Brewery in Canterbury, Kent.

Canterbury Brewery (Eng). A brewery based in Canterbury, Kent which has its beer brewed under contract by the Wilt-shire Brewery of Tisbury. Produces cask conditioned Canterbury Ale 1038 O.G. and Buff's Bitter 1050 O.G.

Cantharus (Lat). Tankard.

Cantillon (Bel). A museum brewery in Anderlecht, Brussels. Produces Lambic beers.

Cantimplora (Sp). Water bottle.

Cantina (It). Cellar.

Cantina (Sp). Cellar, winery or bar.

Cantina Agricola (It). When preceded by the producer's name on the label it guarantees that the wine is made from the producer's own grapes.

Cantina Collavini (It). Noted wine-producers based in Grave del Fruili.

Cantina Co-operative (It). Denotes a wine-growers' co-operative.

Cantina Mascarello (It). A noted tradi-tional wine producer based in Barolo, Piemonte.

Cantina Sociale (It). Denotes a wine-growers' co-operative.

Cantina Sociale di Canelli (It). A noted producer of Moscato d'Asti Spumante in Piemonte.

Cantina Sociale di Dolianova (It). A wine co-operative based at Dolianova, Sar-dinia.

Cantina Sociale di Locorotondo (It). A wine co-operative based in Bari. Pro-duces a still and sparkling version of Locorotondo.

Cantina Sociale di Santa Maria Delle Versa (It). A producer of sparkling (méthode champenoise) wines in Lom-bardy.

Cantina Sociale di Soligo (It). Producers of sparkling (méthode champenoise) Pro-secco wines in Veneto.

Cantina Sociale di Valdobbiadene (It). Pro-ducers of Prosecco di Conegliano-Valdobbiadene in Veneto.

Cantina Sociale di Vo (It). Producer of sparkling (cuve close) wines in Veneto.

Cantina Sociale S.A. Della Versa (It). Pro-ducer of sparkling (méthode cham-penoise) wines in Lombardy.

Cantina San Marco (It). Producer of Frascati wines. Address = Via di Fras-cati 34, 00040, Monteporzio Cantone, Roma.

Cantina San Marco (It). Producer of spark-ling (cuve close) wines in Lazio.

Cantina Tollo Società Co-operative (It). A wine co-operative based at Tollo in Abruzzo.

Cantina Vinicola (It). When it precedes the producer's name on a label it guarantees that the wine is made from his own and bought in grapes.

Cantine (It). When it precedes the pro-ducer's name on a label it denotes that he is a commercial producer buying grapes from growers, possibly owning vineyards himself.

Cantinetta (It). Cellar, bar.

Cantois (Fr). A commune in the Haut-Benauge, central Bordeaux.

Canton (Fr) (Switz). An area of wine production, e.g. Vaud.

Canton d'Avize (Fr). An area in the Cham-pagne region. Contains the Grand Cru villages of Avize, Cramant, Le Mesnil-sur-Oger, Oger and Oiry. Premier Cru villages of Cuis and Grauves and the Cru villages of Brugny-Vaudancourt, Chavot-Courcourt, Mancy, Monthelon, Mor-angis and Moslins.

Canton d'Ay (Fr). An area in the Cham-pagne region. Contains the Grand Cru villages of Ambonnay, Ay-Champagne, Bouzy, Louvois and Tours-sur-Marne and the Premier Cru villages of Avenay, Bisseuil, Champillon, Cumières, Dizy, Hautvilliers, Mareuil-sur-Ay, Mutigny, Tauxières and Tours-sur-Marne and the Cru villages of Cormoyeux and Romery. Marne.

Canton de Beine (Fr). See Beine.

Canton de Bourgogne (Fr). See Bour-gogne.

Canton de Braine (Fr). See Braine.

Canton de Châtillon-sur-Marne (Fr). See Châtillon-sur-Marne.

Canton de Condé-en-Brie (Fr). See Condé-en-Brie.

Canton de Dormans (Fr). See Dormans.

Canton de Fismes (Fr). See Fismes.

Canton de l'Aube (Fr). An area in the Champagne region. Contains the Cru villages of Balnot-sur-Laignes, Buxeuil, Courteron, Gye-sur-Seine, Les Riceys, Montgueux, Neuville-sur-Seine and Polisy.

Canton de Montmort (Fr). See Montmort.

Canton d'Épernay (Fr). See Épernay.

Canton de Reims (Fr). See Reims.

Canton d'Esternay (Fr). See Esternay.

Canton de Sézanne (Fr). See Sézanne.

Canton de Suippes (Fr). See Suippes.

Canton de Vertus (Fr). See Vertus.

Canton de Verzy (Fr). See Verzy.

Canton de Ville-en-Tardenois (Fr). See Ville-en-Tardenois.

Canuto (Sp). A narrow pipe of mahogany or olive wood, driven into the Falsete prior to the wine being racked off.

Canvermoor (Eng). A company that pro-duces a range of soft drinks. Also is a major distributor of Bulmers Strong-bow Cider, Woodpecker Cider and Red Stripe Lager.

Can-y-Delyn (Eng). A Welsh whiskey-based liqueur produced by the Hall-

C

garten Company in London.

Canzem (Ger). The English spelling of the Saar vineyard of Kanzem.

Cao (Port). A red grape variety used in the production of Port to give it colour.

Caol Ila (Scot). A single Malt whisky distillery based on the Isle of Islay. Is used mainly for blending of Scotch whiskies. An Islay malt whisky. (Part of the DCL group). 43% alc. by vol.

Cap (Eng). The name given to the solid layer of skins and pips which floats on the top of fermenting red wine. Is usually broken up and submerged in the wine for maximum colour (and tannin) extraction. See also Chapeau and Capello Sommerso.

Capa Negra (Sp). A Brandy produced in Jerez. Is distilled from local wines. Address = Sandeman Hinos. y Cia, Pizzaro 10, Jerez de la Frontera. Produces Solera Reservada Capa Negra (3 year old), Brandy Reserva Capa Vieja (18 year old).

Capataz (Sp). The head cellarman of a Spanish cellar.

Cap Bon (Afr). A principal wine-producing area in Tunisia based around Bizerta. Produces a full-bodied, dark, red wine of same name.

Cap Corse (Fr). A full-bodied, sweet red wine apéritif flavoured with herbs and quinine from area of same name in the northern part of Corsica.

Cape Bouquet (S.Afr). A medium-sweet, white wine from KWV. Is made from the Muscadelle grape.

Cape Codder (Cktl). 1/3 measure cranberry juice, 1/6 measure Vodka, 1/6 measure lemon juice. Shake over ice, strain into an ice-filled old-fashioned glass. Top with soda water.

Cape Cod Jack Cocktail (Cktl). 1/2 measure Calvados, 1/2 measure bilberry juice, dash Gomme syrup. Stir over ice in an old-fashioned glass. Serve with the stirrer.

Cape Forêt (S.Afr). A dry, white, cask-matured wine made from the Chenin blanc grape by KWV.

Cape House (S.Afr). The brand-name for a South African sherry.

Capello Sommerso (It). Lit – 'Submerged cap'. A vinification method where the skins are kept submerged in the must for 3–5 weeks to extract maximum colour and tannin.

Capel Vale Winery (Austr). Address = P.O. Box 692, Bunbury, Western Australia. 9.5 ha. Grape varieties – Cabernet sauvignon, Chardonnay, Gewürztraminer, Merlot, Rhine riesling, Sauvignon blanc and Shiraz. Pro-

duces varietal and table wines. The vineyard address is = Lot 5, Stirling Estate, Capel Northwest Road, Capel, Western Australia 6271.

Cape Mentelle Vineyards (Austr). Address = P.O. Box 110, Margaret River, Western Australia. 17 ha. Grape varieties – Cabernet sauvignon, Sauvignon blanc, Sémillon, Shiraz and Zinfandel. Produces varietal and table wines. Vineyard address is = Off Walldiff Road, Margaret River, Western Australia.

Capena (It). D.O.C. dry white or sparkling wines from Latium.

Capenheimer (S.Afr). A sparkling, medium-sweet, white wine made from the Steen grape.

Cape Nouveau Black (S.Afr). A dry, fruity, pétillant, white wine produced by KWV.

Caperdonich (Scot). A single Malt whisky distillery based at Rothes. A Highland malt whisky. 43% alc. by vol.

Caperdonich Distillery Company Limited (Scot). A subsidiary of the Glenlivet Distillers Limited.

Cape Riesling (S.Afr). The name for the Crouchon grape of France.

Caperitif (S.Afr). A deep-coloured apéritif made from wine blended with spirit and herb-flavoured.

Cape Smaak (S.Afr). Lit – 'Cape taste'. See Kaapse Smaak.

Cape Smoke (S.Afr). Derivative of Kaapse Smaak. Used nowadays for inferior Brandy.

Cape Wine Centre (Eng). Address = South African Wine Trade Centre, 46, Great Marlborough Street, Longon W1V 1DB.

Cape Wines and Distillers (S.Afr). CW & D. A part of SFW. Produces varietal wines, brandies and liqueurs.

Capillaire (Eng). Sugar, water and egg white heated and flavoured with almond or orange flower water. Used to sweeten hot or cold drinks and punches.

Capireaux (Fr). A heady wine, high in alcohol. Goes to one's head.

Capitala (La) (Sp). A brand of Manzanilla sherry produced by Marqués de Real, Tesoro.

Capital Ale (Eng). A cask conditioned light Mild 1030 O.G. brewed by Marston's Brewery, Burton-on-Trent, Staffordshire.

Capital Ale (Eng). A keg Ale 1033 O.G. brewed by Brain's Brewery, Cardiff.

Capitan (Sp). An Oloroso sherry produced by Bobadilla in Jerez de la Frontera.

Capitel San Rocco Rosso (It). Ripasso wine produced by Renzo Tedeschi in Valpolicella, Verona.

Capogreco Winery (Austr). A winery based

in the Murray Valley, Victoria. Produces varietal wines.

Cappan (Fr). A wine-producing district based in A.C. Bellet, Provence.

Cappuccino (It). A red grape variety grown in Savuto, Calabria.

Cappuccino Coffee (It). Espresso coffee topped with hot frothy milk and grated chocolate mixed with ground cinnamon sprinkled on top. Also spelt Capuccino (English spelling).

Cappucino Cocktail (Cktl). ⅓ measure Kahlúa, ⅓ measure Vodka, ⅓ measure cream, dash Gomme syrup. Shake well over ice, strain into a cocktail glass.

Capraldehyde (Eng). An aldehyde found in wine which contributes to the bouquet and flavour of the wine.

Capri (It). An island off the west coast that produces red, rosé and white wines.

Capri Bianco (It). A white wine made on the island of Capri from the Greco and Fiano grapes.

Capric Acid (Eng). $C_9H_{19}COOH$. An acid that is found in wine in small quantities.

Capri Cocktail (Cktl).(1). ⅓ measure Cognac, ⅓ measure Campari, ⅓ measure sweet Martini. Stir over ice, strain into cocktail glass. Add ice cube and lemon peel spiral.

Capri Cocktail (Cktl).(2). ⅙ gill Crème de Banane, ⅙ gill (white) Crème de Cacao, ⅙ gill cream. Shake over ice, strain into an ice-filled old-fashioned glass.

Capricornia (Austr). A liqueur made from tropical fruits.

Caprilla (Cktl). ¾ measure Vodka, ⅕ measure dry Port, ⅕ measure Cherry brandy, 2 dashes Grenadine. Stir over ice, strain into cocktail glass. Top with a cherry.

Caproic Acid (Eng). $C_5H_{11}COOH$. An ester that is found in wine in small quantities.

Caprylic Acid (Eng). $C_7H_{15}COOH$. An acid that is found in wine in small quantities.

Capsule (Eng). The lead, foil or plastic covering over the top of a bottle to seal the contents from the air.

Capsule Blanche (Bel). Lit – 'White top'. A light-coloured beer with a very pronounced bitterness brewed by the Abbaye of Chimay Brasserie.

Capsule Bleu (Bel). Lit – 'Blue top'. A deep copper-coloured, well-hopped beer 8% alc. by vol. brewed by the Abbaye of Chimay Brasserie.

Capsule Rouge (Bel). Lit – 'Red top'. A beer 6% alc. by vol. brewed by the Abbaye of Chimay Brasserie.

Captain Collins (Cktl). ⅕ gill Canadian whisky, juice ½ lime, dash Grenadine. Shake over ice, strain into an ice-filled collins glass. Top with soda, stir and serve.

Captain Cook Brewery (N.Z.). A brewery based in Auckland. Introduced beer that was filtered, pasteurised and carbonated.

Captain Morgan (W.Ind). The brand-name of a dark Rum from Barbados, Guyana and Jamaica. 40% alc. by vol. Sold by Seagram.

Captain's Bitter (Eng). A cask conditioned Bitter 1037 O.G. brewed by the Southsea Brewery, Portsmouth, Hampshire.

Captain's Blood (Cktl). 1½ fl.ozs. dark Rum, 2 teaspoons lime cordial, dash Angostura. Shake over ice, strain into a cocktail glass.

Capua (It). An area in Campania where Fallerno wine is produced.

Caques (Fr). Willow baskets used in the Champagne region to carry the grapes. 375–393 kgs (150–175 lbs) can be held in each.

Capuccino (Eng). See Cappuccino Coffee.

Capuccino (It). A cream and brandy-based liqueur 17% alc. by vol.

Carabinieri Cocktail (Cktl). ⅖ measure Galliano, ⅖ measure Tequila, ⅕ measure Triple Sec, 3 dashes lime juice, 1 egg yolk. Shake over ice, strain into an ice-filled highball glass. Top with fresh orange juice, decorate with a green and red cherry and a slice of lime.

Cara Blanc (S.Afr). A dry, fragrant, light, white wine produced by Blaauwklippen Agricultural Estate from the Colombar grape.

Caracas (S.Am). A coffee-producing region in Venezuela.

Caracol (Eng). A small grade of green coffee bean. Also known as a Peaberry.

Carafe (Fr). A clear glass decanter used for serving wines or water at the table. Inexpensive wines are usually served 'en carafe'. Lit – 'Decanter'.

Carafe Clos-Vougeot (Fr). An urn-shaped, glass decanter with a short neck.

Caraffa (It). Decanter.

Carafino Wines (S.Afr). The brand-name for everyday drinking wines produced by Gilbeys Ltd.

Carafon (Fr). A small carafe of ½ a litre capacity or less.

Carajillo (Sp). The name given to a strong black coffee with a dash of Brandy. Drunk in the morning in northern Spain.

Caramalt (Eng). See Carapils.

Caramany (Fr). The name of a new appellation of part of the Côtes de Roussillon-Villages, south-western France.

Caramba Cocktail (Cktl). ½ measure dry Gin, dash Crème de Framboise, dash

Cherry Heering, 2 dashes grapefruit juice, 2 dashes pineapple juice. Shake over ice, strain into a club goblet. Dress with a spiral of grapefruit peel and a cherry.

Caramel (Eng). Used to colour spirits, wines and beers. Made from burnt sugar.

Caramelised (Eng). A term sometimes used to describe the flavour of Madeira wine which acquires this taste due to the Estufa system.

Carapils (Eng). Used in the production of Lager. A lightly kilned malt. Also called Caramalt.

Cara Sposa Cocktail (Cktl). 1/3 measure Cointreau, 1/3 measure Tia Maria, 1/3 measure cream. Shake well over ice, strain into a cocktail glass.

Caratello (It). A barrel of 50 litres capacity.

Carawdines (Eng). A noted blender and producer of fine teas and coffees based at Berkeley Square, Bristol, Avon.

Carbine (Austr). A bitter Stout brewed by the Castlemaine Perkins Brewery in Queensland.

Carbonated (Eng). Charged with CO_2 gas. i.e. soft drinks, bottled beers, cheap sparkling wines, etc. See Carbonates.

Carbonated Sparklers (USA). The cheapest grade of sparkling wine. The Government requires them to be labelled as such. e.g. Carbonated Hock.

Carbonated Wine (USA). Wines made by artificial carbonation. Both red and white wines are made in this way as well. Dry to sweet styles.

Carbonates (Eng). Term which denotes artificially gassed (carbonated) drinks.

Carbon-dioxide (Eng). CO_2 gas. A non-toxic gas given off by the action of yeast on sugar.

Carbone (It). Carbonate.

Carbonell y Cía, S.A. (Sp). A producer of fine Montilla wines based in Córdoba, Montilla-Moriles.

Carbonic Acid (Eng). A weak acid formed by Carbon-dioxide being soluble in water. Helps to prevent oxidation during racking. Disappears at the end of fermentation with the loss of CO_2.

Carbonic Acid Gas (Eng). CO_2. Carbon-dioxide.

Carbonic Maceration (Eng). See Macération Carbonique.

Carbónico (It). Carbon-dioxide.

Carbonnieux (Fr). See Château Carbonnieux.

Carboxylase (Eng). The name given to an enzyme secreted by wine yeasts. It removes the carbon from pyruvic acid and reduces it to acetaldehyde.

Carboy (Eng). A large glass container similar to a large Italian flask. Holds 5 gallons or more.

Carcavelos (Port). A demarcated region. Produces sweet, fortified white wines from the Galego dourado grape.

Cardamaro (It). A bitter, tonic liqueur produced from herbs and wine by Giovanni Bosca in Canelli.

Cardeal (Port). A Dão wine produced by Caves Dom Teodósio.

Cardenal (Sp). The brand-name of a Sherry produced by Valdespino.

Cardenal Cisneros (Sp). A Brandy over 10 years old produced by Romate.

Cardenal Mendoza (Sp). A De Luxe brandy over 10 years old produced by Romate.

Cardhu (Scot). A single Malt whisky distillery based at Knockando in Morayshire. A Highland malt whisky. 12 year old. 40% alc. by vol. Part of John Walker and Sons. (Owned by the DCL group). See also Cardow.

Cardicas (Cktl). 1/3 measure white Rum, 1/3 measure dry white Port, 1/3 measure Cointreau. Shake well over ice, strain into a frosted cocktail glass.

Cardinal (Fr). A variation of the dark Kir where the white wine is replaced by red wine. See also Communiste.

Cardinal Brewery (Switz). A brewery based in Fribourg. Part of the Sibra Group (Cardinal) Breweries. Brews Top.

Cardinal Cocktail (Cktl). 1/3 gill dry Gin, 2 dashes dry Vermouth, dash Campari. Stir over ice, strain into a cocktail glass. Dress with a lemon peel spiral.

Cardinal Punch (Punch) (Non-alc). 2 pints cranberry juice, 1 pint orange juice, juice of 2 lemons, 4 bottles chilled ginger ale. Stir altogether over ice and serve.

Cardinal Richard Muscadet de Sèvre et Maine (Fr). A Muscadet de Sèvre et Maine produced by Château du Cléray from a top wine tested by a team of tasters each year from a selection of vineyards.

Cardow (Scot). A single Malt whisky from the same distillery as Cardhu near Knockando, Morayshire. A Highland malt whisky. 40% alc. by vol. Part of the DCL Group.

Carelle-Dessous (Fr). A Premier Cru vineyard [part] in the A.C. commune of Volnay, Côte de Beaune, Burgundy.

Carelle-Sous-la-Chapelle (Fr). A Premier Cru vineyard in the A.C. commune of Volnay, Côte de Beaune, Burgundy.

Carema (It). D.O.C. red wine from Piemonte in a small commune near Turin.

C

Made from the Nebbiolo grape. Produced by leaving the grapes to macerate before pressing in a room saturated with natural CO_2. Aged 4 years (2 years in oak/chestnut casks).

Carême (Fr). Lent. The Roman Catholic fasting of 40 days from Ash Wednesday to Easter when only a little food and no alcoholic beverages are consumed.

Carey Cellars (USA). A winery based in the Santa Ynez Valley, Santa Barbara, California. 19 ha. Grape varieties – Cabernet sauvignon, Chardonnay, Merlot and Sauvignon blanc. Produces varietal wines.

Carey Winery (USA). A winery based in Alameda, California. Produces table and dessert wines.

Cargo (Mad). The old name for sweet Madeira wine.

Cariba (Eng). A carbonated, non-alcoholic, pineapple and grapefruit drink from Schweppes.

Caribbean Champagne (Cktl). ½ measure white Rum, ½ measure Crème de Banane. Shake over ice, strain into a Champagne flute and top with iced Champagne. Add a slice of banana.

Caribbean Coffee (Liq.Coffee). Using a measure of white Rum.

Caribbean Cool (Eng). A range of non-alcoholic, sparkling, fruit-flavoured drinks.

Caribbean Cup (Cup). ½ pint dry Cider, ⅕ pint white Rum, ½ pint orange juice. Mix together with ice. Decorate with mint sprigs and orange slices.

Caribbean Sunset (Cktl). ⅕ measure Gin, ⅕ measure blue Curaçao, ⅕ measure Crème de Banane, ⅕ measure cream, ⅕ measure lemon juice, dash Grenadine. Shake all (except the Grenadine) over ice, strain into a cocktail glass. Add the Grenadine. Do not stir.

Carib Brewery (W.Ind). A brewery based in Trinidad. Brews Allsopps, Carib Lager, F.E.S. and Skol.

Carib Lager (W.Ind). A Lager beer 1049 O.G. brewed by the Carib Brewery in Trinidad.

Carignan (Fr). A red grape variety grown in southern France. Is also known as the Bois dur, Carignane, Carignan noir, Cariñena, Catalan, Crujillón, Mataro, Mazuelo, Roussillonen and Tinto mazuela.

Carignane (USA). A red grape variety used for red wines and dessert wines. See also California Carignane and Carignan.

Carignano (It). A red grape variety grown in Latium and Sardinia.

Carine (Cktl). ¼ measure Mandarine Napoléon, ½ measure dry Gin, ¼ measure Dubonnet, 3 dashes lemon juice. Stir well over ice, strain into cocktail glass.

Cariñena (Sp). A Denominación de Origen region between Madrid and Barcelona. Produces heavy red wines. D.O. applies to red and rosé wines produced in the region in province of Zaragoza. Grape varieties – Cariñena, Garnacha blanca and Garnacha negra.

Cariñena (Sp). A red grape variety grown in the south-eastern regions of Spain. Also known as the Mazuelo and Carignan.

Carinera (Sp). A red grape variety grown in the Penedés region.

Carino (It). A producer of Moscato Spumante wines in Piemonte.

Cariño (Sp). A red grape variety grown in Ribeiro.

Carioca (Bra). A strong coffee drink. Is usually drunk watered down with hot or cold water.

Carioca (W.Ind). The brand-name of a Rum from a distillery of same name in Puerto Rico.

Carioca Cocktail (Cktl). ⅕ gill Cognac, ⅛ gill Kahlúa, ⅙ gill cream, 1 egg yolk. Blend together with a scoop of crushed ice in a blender. Pour into a saucer glass. Sprinkle with ground cinnamon.

Carleton Tower (Can). A blended Canadian whisky produced by Hiram Walker. 40% alc. by vol.

Carling Black Label (Can). A Lager beer 1037 O.G. brewed by Carling O'Keefe Brewery in Toronto. Brewed in Britain under licence by Bass Charrington.

Carling Brewery (USA). Noted breweries based in Baltimore, Belleville, Phoenix and Tacoma.

Carling O'Keefe (Can). A large brewery based in Toronto. Owns Beamish Brewery in Ireland. Famous for its Carling Black Label Lager.

Carlins (Les) (Fr). A vineyard in the A.C. commune of Montagny, Côte Chalonnaise, Burgundy.

Carlomagno (Sp). A red wine produced by Bodegas Carlos Serres S.A. in Rioja. Made by macération carbonique. Matured in oak 3¼ years and then in bottle. Made from 60% Tempranillo and 40% Garnacha grapes.

Carlonet (S.Afr). A Cabernet-based red wine produced by Uiterwyk.

Carlo Rossi (USA). The brand-name used by the Gallo Winery for a range of their table wines.

Carlos 111-1 (Sp). Brandies 6 and 12 years old respectively produced by Domecq.

Carlos Serres (Sp). A white wine produced by Bodegas Carlos Serres S.A., Rioja.

C

Vinification by macération carbonique then oak and bottle matured.

Carlowitz (Yug). The old name for a red wine produced in Sremski Karlovici, Vojvodina.

Carlsbad (Czec). A lithiated mineral water.

Carlsbad Becher (Czec). A herbal liqueur made with spa water from Carlsbad used for the aroma and taste.

Carlsberg (Czec) (Ger). A bitter herbal digestive liqueur.

Carlsberg (Ger). Vineyard. (Anb) = Mosel-Saar-Ruwer. (Ber) = Bernkastel. (Gro) = Kurfürslay. (Vil) = Veldenz.

Carlsberg Brewery (Den). A large, famous brewery based in Copenhagen.

Carlsberg Lager (Den). A famous Lager beer brewed by the Carlsberg Brewery. Brewed under licence in many countries. Calsberg Pilsener 1030 O.G. and Special Brew 1080 O.G.

Carlsberg 68 (Den). See Elephant Lager.

Carlsberg Special Brew (Den). A strong Lager beer 1080 O.G. brewed by the Carlsberg Brewery in Copenhagen.

Carlshama (Swe). A Swedish Punsch 55.5% alc. by vol. Produced by the Aktiebolaget Vin & Spritcentralem.

Carlsheim (S.Afr). A Sauvignon blanc blended, dry, white wine from the Uitkyk Estate in Stellenbosch.

Carlsminde Brewery (Den). A brewery based in Nyborg.

Carlton United Brewery (Austr). A brewery based in Melbourne. Produces Carlton, Victoria and Fosters beers.

Carmaralet (Fr). A white grape variety grown in the Jurançon region in south-western France.

Carmel (Isr). A large co-operative that produces wines and fruits. See Société Coopérative Vigneronne des Grands Caves.

Carmel Hock (Isr). A medium dry, white wine produced by the Carmel co-operative.

Carmeline (Fr). A liqueur cordial of herbs. Now no longer produced. Was originally made in Bordeaux.

Carmelitano (Sp). A herb-flavoured, brandy-based liqueur.

Carmelith (Isr). A semi-dry, red table wine produced by the Carmel co-operative.

Carmel Valley (USA). A small wine-producing district in Monterey County, California.

Carmenére (Fr). A lesser red grape variety grown in Bordeaux.

Carmenet (Fr). An alternative name for the Cabernet franc grape.

Carmes (Fr). A popular brand of Melisse liqueur made from balm-mint.

Carmignano (It). D.O.C. red wine from the communes of Carmignano and Poggio a Caiano in Tuscany. Produced from Sangiovese, Canaiolo nero, Cabernet, Trebbiano toscano, Canaiolo bianco and the Malvasia grapes. Cannot be sold before June 21st of the 2nd year of vintage. If aged minimum of 3 years then classed as Riserva.

Carnegie Porter (Swe). A Mild beer 3.5% alc. by vol. brewed by the Pripps Brewery.

Carnelian (USA). A black, hybrid grape variety developed by the University of California.

Carneros (USA). A wine-producing district based in the southern part of the Napa Valley, California.

Carneros Creek Winery (USA). A winery based in the Napa Valley, California. 4 ha. Grape varieties – Cabernet sauvignon, Chardonnay, Pinot noir and Zinfandel. Produces varietal wines.

Carnevale (Giorgio) (It). A Moscato d'Asti producer based in the Piemonte region of north-western Italy.

Carnival (Cktl). ⅓ measure Cognac, ⅓ measure Lillet, ⅓ measure Apricot liqueur, dash Kirsch, dash orange juice. Shake over ice, strain into a cocktail glass.

Carolans (Ire). A cream liqueur made from Irish whiskey, honey, Clonmel cream and chocolate. Produced in Tipperary. 17% alc. by vol. See Alcoholic Yoghurt.

Caroni (W.Ind). The brand-name of a white Rum from Trinidad that is matured in England.

Carousal (Eng). Lit – 'A merry drinking party'. A seventeenth-century word.

Carouse (Eng). A seventeenth-century word denoting a drinking spree. To drink freely.

Carousel (Ger). A wrought iron turntable used for wine tasting in the Rheinpfalz. Has spaces for up to 12 glasses. Different wines are poured into each and drinkers revolve the table to sample each.

Carpano (It). The brand-name of a famous Vermouth producer. Produces Punt & Mes.

Carpano (Antonio) (It). In 1786, the Italian purported to have invented sweet Vermouth. See also Noilly (Louis).

Carpathian Mountains (Rum). Occupies most of central Rumania. Wine regions are situated amongst their foothills.

Carpené-Malvolti (It). A famous wine and brandy producer based in the Veneto region.

Carpené-Malvolti Brut (It). A sparkling (méthode champenoise) wine produced in Veneto by Carpené-Malvolti from Chardonnay and Pinot grapes. 12.5% alc. by vol.

Carpineto (It). A Chiánti Classico producer based in the Tuscany region.

Carral (Sp). Wine butt.

Carras (John) (Gre). A hotelier based at Sithonia, Halkidiki. Produces red and white wines under the labels of Côtes du Meliton and Château Carras.

Carrascal (Sp). A district within Andalusia. Has chalky soil. Also spelt Carrascol.

Carrascol (Sp). The alternative spelling of Carrascal.

Carrère (Fr). An Armagnac producer. Address = Distilleries Carrère SA, 36, Rue des Alliés, 32500 Fleurance. Produces – Panache d'Or and Panache d'Or V.S.O.P.

Carricante (It). A white grape variety grown in Sicily to make dry white wines.

Carrington Distilleries (Can). The producers of Carrington Canadian Whisky. 40% alc. by vol.

Carrodilla Tinto (Arg). The brand-name of a red wine produced in central Argentina.

Carrol Cocktail (Cktl). ⅓ gill Brandy, ⅙ gill sweet Vermouth. Stir over ice, strain into a cocktail glass. Top with a cherry.

Carrousser (Fr). Old word denoting 'To drink freely', used in the sixteenth century.

Carr's Best Bitter (Eng). A cask conditioned Bitter beer 1041 O.G. brewed in a home-brew public house in Southampton, Hampshire. Is owned by Whitbreads.

Carr Taylor (Eng). A vineyard planted in 1973 at Yew Tree Farm, Westfield, Hastings, East Sussex. 8.5 ha. Grape varieties – Gutenborner 30%, Kerner 10%, Müller-Thurgau 20% and Reichensteiner 40%.

Carruades de Château Lafite (Fr). A red wine produced at Château Lafite from vines under 12 years old.

Cars (Fr). A commune in the A.C. Côtes de Blaye in north-eastern Bordeaux.

Carsebridge (Scot). A Grain whisky distillery based south of Dundee, Perthshire.

Carseolanum (Lat). A red wine produced in central Italy in Roman times.

Carso (It). D.O.C. red and white wines from the Friuli-Venezia Giulia region.

Carstairs (USA). A blended Whiskey bottled by the Calvert Distillers Co. of Baltimore, Louisville. 40% alc. by vol.

Carstens (Ger). A noted producer of Deutscher Sekt by the cuve close method.

Carta Blanca (Mex). The name of a Beer exported to the USA.

Carta Blanca (Sp). A Fino sherry produced by Agustin Blàzquez in Jerez de la Frontera.

Carta Blanca (W.Ind). A light-bodied Rum (white label) produced in Greater Antilles, Cuba and Puerto Rico.

Carta de Oro (Sp). A red wine produced by Bodegas Berberana S.A. Oak matured for 2 years minimum and for 1 year in bottle. Also a white wine of same name.

Carta de Plata (Sp). The brand-name for red and white wines produced by Bodegas Berberana S.A. in Rioja.

Carta Nevada (Sp). A non-vintage Cava wine produced by Freixenet in the Penedés region.

Carta Oro (Sp). An Amontillado sherry produced by Agustin Blázquez in Jerez de la Frontera.

Carta Oro (W.Ind). A brand of golden Rum (gold label) coloured with caramel and produced in the Greater Antilles, Cuba and Puerto Rico.

Cartaxo (Port). A red wine area in the Estremadura region on the plains of the Rio Tejo.

Carte Blanche (Fr). The name given to the sweeter style of Champagne from Pomméry et Greno.

Carte Blanche (Fr). A non-vintage Champagne produced by F. Bonnet et Fils.

Carte de Vin (Fr). Wine list.

Carte d'Or Riesling (Austr). A white wine from the Yalumba Vineyard. Is crisp, spicy and aromatic.

Cartègue (Fr). A commune in the A.C. Côtes de Blaye in north-eastern Bordeaux.

Carte Noir (Fr). A non-vintage Champagne produced by Bricout et Koch from 40% Chardonnay, 20% Pinot meunier and 40% Pinot noir grapes.

Carte Noire Extra (Fr). A Cognac (12 years old average) produced by Castillon Renault.

Carte Or (Fr). A non-vintage Champagne produced by Bricout et Koch from 40% Chardonnay and 60% Pinot noir grapes.

Carte Orange (Fr). A non-vintage Champagne produced by Napoléon from Chardonnay 40% and Pinot noir 60%.

Carte Verte (Fr). A non-vintage Champagne produced by Napoléon from Chardonnay 25% and Pinot noir 75%.

Cartoixa (Sp). The alternative name used in the Tarragona region for the Xarel-lo grape.

Carton (Eng). A cardboard box which normally holds 12 standard bottles of wine or spirits. See also Case.

Cartron (Fr). A liqueur producer based in Burgundy. Noted for Crème de Nuits

C

and a mandarine liqueur produced from brandy and tangerine peel.

Cartwright Brewery (USA). A brewery based in Portland, Oregon. Brews Cartwright Portland Beer 5% alc. by vol.

Caruso Cocktail (Cktl). ⅓ measure dry Gin, ⅓ measure dry Vermouth, ⅓ measure (white) Crème de Menthe. Stir over ice, strain into a cocktail glass.

Carvalho (Port). Oak.

Carvalho, Ribeiro and Ferreira (Port). Producers of Conde de Santar (a Dão wine). Founded in 1898. Does not vinify any wine. Is the largest Brandy maker in Portugal. Also produces Aguardente Preparada Reserva (brandy) and red and white Serraclayres (an Alentejo wine).

Carver Wine Cellars (USA). A winery based in Rolla, Missouri. Produces hybrid wines.

Carypton (W.Ind). A green-coloured swizzle drink. Is drunk as an apéritif.

Casa (It). If precedes producer's name on the label means he is a commercial producer who buys grapes from growers, possibly owning vineyards himself.

Casabello Wines Ltd (Can). A winery based in Penticton, Vancouver. Also imports grapes from Washington. Wines sold in vacuum-sealed litre carafes and bottles.

Casa Blanca (Cktl). ⅓ measure Jamaican rum, ⅛ measure Cointreau, ⅛ measure lime juice, ⅛ measure Maraschino. Shake over ice, strain into a cocktail glass.

Casablanca (Cktl). 1½ fl.ozs. white Rum, 1 fl.oz. coconut cream, 2 fl.ozs. pineapple juice, 2 dashes Grenadine, 2 scoops crushed ice. Blend well together in a blender, pour into a large balloon glass.

Casablanca (Afr). A wine-producing region of Morocco. Contains the A.O.G. areas of Doukkala, Sahel and Zenata. Soil is mainly sandy.

Casablanca Cocktail (Cktl). ⅔ measure Vodka, ⅓ measure Advocaat, 2 dashes Galliano, 4 dashes lemon juice, 2 dashes orange juice. Shake over ice, strain into a cocktail glass. Top with a slice of orange.

Casablanca Collins (Cktl). 1¼ fl.ozs. Vodka, ¼ fl.oz. Galliano, 1 fl.oz. Advocaat, ½ fl.oz. lemon juice, ¼ fl.oz. orange juice. Shake over ice, strain into an ice-filled highball glass. Top with a cherry.

Casa Compostela (Port). A small private firm that produces Vinhos Verdes. Has 28 ha. Grape varieties – Azal, Loureiro,

Pederña and Trajadura. Address = Requião, 4760 V.N. Familicão. Produces – Casa de Compostela.

Casa da Tapada (Port). A producer of Vinho Verde from the Loureiro grape. Address = Soc. Agricola Lda S-Miguel de Fiscal 4700 Amares.

Casa de Cabanelas (Port). A brand of Vinho Verde produced from Azal, Loureiro, Pederña and Trajadura grapes. Address = Bustelö 4560 Penafiel.

Casa de Calderón (Sp). A private bodega based in Utiel-Requena in the Levante region.

Casa de Cerca (Port). A pétillant rosé wine.

Casa de Compostela (Port). A brand of Vinho Verde produced from the Casa Compostela.

Casa de Penela (Port). A Vinho Verde produced from the Loureiro and Trajadura grapes. Address = Adaúfe, 4700 Braga.

Casa de Rendufe (Port). A Vinho Verde producer based in Resende. Grape variety – Avesso.

Casa de Santa Leocàdia (Port). A Vinho Verde produced mainly from the Loureiro grape. Address = Geraz do Lima, 4900 Viana do Castelo.

Casa de Sezim (Port). A Vinho Verde producer. Address = Nespereira, 4800 Guimarães. Grape varieties – Loureiro, Pederña and Trajadura.

Casa de Valdaiga (Sp). A light red wine produced by VILE in León.

Casa de Vila Boa (Port). A Vinho Verde producer. Address = Vila Boa de Quires, 4630 Marcode Canaveses. Main grape variety is the Azal.

Casa de Vilacetinho (Port). A Vinho Verde producer. Address = Alpendurada, 4575 Entre-Os-Rios. Grape varieties – Azal, Loureiro and Pederña.

Casa de Vila Nova (Port). A Vinho Verde producer. Wine made from the Avesso and Pederña grapes.

Casa de Vilaverde (Port). A Vinho Verde producer. Address = Caíde de Rei, 4620 Lousada. Grape varieties – Azal, Loureiro and the Pederña.

Casa do Landeiro (Port). A Vinho Verde producer. Address = Carreira, 4750, Barcelas. Grape varieties – Loureiro and Trajadura.

Casa dos Cunhas (Port). A Vinho Verde produced by the Quinta do Belinho, Antas, 4740 Esposende from Loureiro grapes. Also a red version from the Espadeiro and Vinhão grapes.

Casa Fondata Nel (It). On a wine label denotes 'Firm established in'.

C

Casa Larga (USA). A winery based near Rochester in the Finger Lakes, New York. 5 ha. Grape varieties – Chardonnay, Gewürztraminer and Riesling. Produces varietal wines.

Casal de Vale Pradinhos (Port). An Aguardente produced by Maria Pinto de Azevado.

Casal do Ermízio (Port). A Vinho Verde producer. Address = Ronfe, 4800 Guimarães. Grape varieties – Loureiro, Pederña and Trajadura.

Casaleiro (Port). Brands of Vinhos Verdes and Dão wines produced by Caves Dom Teodsio.

Casalinho (Port). The brand-name of a Vinho Verde from Caves do Casalinho.

Casal Garcia (Port). A brand of Vinho Verde from Quinta Avelada.

Casal Mendes (Port). A brand of Vinho Verde from Caves Aliança.

Casal Miranda (Port). A brand of Vinho Verde from Louro.

Casa Madero (Mex). See Bodegas de San Lorenzo.

Casamari (It). A Cistercian herb liqueur.

Casanis (Fr). A Corsican-made Pastis which is popular in France.

Casa Ranuzzi (S.Am). Producer of Inca Pisco in Lima, Peru. (Is made exclusively for McKesson Liquor Co. of New York).

Casa Romero (Sp). A producer and shipper of Málaga wine from Málaga, southern Spain.

Casa Santos Lima (Port). A winery based outside Silgueiros in the Dão region. Produces red and white Dão wines.

Casa Sola (It). A Chianti Classico producer based in Tuscany.

Casa Vinicola (It). When it precedes a producer's name on a label denotes that he is a commercial producer buying grapes and possibly owning vineyards as well.

Casa Vinicola Dosio (It). A wine-producer based in La Morra, Piemonte. Noted for their Barolo wine.

Cascade (USA). A hybrid red grape variety. Is also known as the Seibel 5409.

Cascade Brewery (Austr). Tasmania's main brewery.

Cascade Highball (Cktl). Equal quantities of sweet Vermouth and Crème de Cassis. Stir over ice in a highball glass.

Cascade Mountain Vineyards (USA). A small winery based in the Hudson Valley, New York. 6 ha. Produces hybrid wines.

Cascades (USA). A hop variety which has a minty, sweet and oily character often used for the dry-hopping of beers.

Cascade System (Fr). Old system now no longer used in which the wine producer sells his wines at various maximum grades. The method was open to abuse and allowed many inferior wines to be sold as top A.C. wines. Has now been replaced by the 'Rendement de Base'. See also 'Plafond Limité de Classement'.

Cascais (Cktl). ⅖ measure Smirnoff vodka, ³⁄₁₀ measure Campari, ³⁄₁₀ measure dry Sherry. Stir well over ice, strain into cocktail glass. Top with a twist of orange peel.

Cascal (Port). A white grape variety grown in Penafiel (a sub-region of Vinho Verde).

Cascalho (Mad). Stony soil found on the island of Madeira.

Cascarilla (S.Am). A popular liqueur, spirit-based and flavoured with spices and barks. 30% alc. by vol.

Cascastel (Fr). A noted wine-producing village in the Corbières area of Languedoc, southern France.

Cascastel (Fr). A commune in the A.C. Fitou, southern France.

Cascastel-de-Corbières (Fr). A commune in the Corbières area of the Languedoc region, southern France. Is allowed to use the A.C. Fitou.

Casco (Sp). Cask.

Case (Eng). A box made of wood or cardboard used to hold 12 full bottles or 24 half bottles of wines, beers or spirits. See also Carton.

Casea Nobre (Mad). Lit – 'Noble vine'. Denotes the permitted vines for use in the production of Madeira wines.

Casein (Eng). A protein used in the production of white wines. Used as a clarifier and as a preventative against oxidation and madeirisation. Also lightens the colour of wine.

Caseinogen (Eng). The principal protein in milk which is converted into casein by rennin.

Caseiri (Mad). See Caseiro.

Caseiro (Mad). Parcel of land cultivated under the old feudal system. A Caseiri pays half of his grape crop as his rent.

Casel (Eng). The spelling of Kasel (a village in the Bereich of Saar-Ruwer, Mosel-Saar-Ruwer, Western Germany) in the nineteenth century.

Casellas Winery (Austr). A winery based in Riverina, New South Wales. Produces varietal and table wines.

Casenallas (Jaime Lluch) (Sp). A wine producer based in the Penedés region. Address = Carretera de Ignalada-Sitges, Km 25, Barcelona. Produces Junot.

C

Casgen (Wales). Cask, barrel.

Casiene (Fr). An old-style fining agent still used in the vinification of méthode ancienne in the Palette, south-eastern France.

Casier à Bouteilles (Fr). Bin or bottle rack.

Casillero del Diablo (Chile). A red wine made from 100% Cabernet sauvignon grapes in central Chile by Concha y Toro. Is oak-matured 2–3 years and then bottle-aged for 2 years.

Casino (Cktl). ½ measure Gin, ¼ measure lemon juice, ¼ measure Maraschino. Shake well over ice, strain into a cocktail glass. Top with a cherry.

Casino (Hun). A brand of Rum.

Cask (Eng). Wooden (oak, chestnut, etc) container for beers, wines or spirits. Sizes = Pin 4½ gals. (20.45 litres), Firkin 9 gals. (40.90 litres), Kilderkin 18 gals. (81.80 litres), Barrel 36 gals. (163.60 litres), Hogshead 54 gals. (245.40 litres). Now are also made of metal and in metric sizes of 25 litres capacity and multiples thereof.

Cask Age (Eng). The time wines and spirits are left to mature in casks of wood to obtain some of the flavour of that wood. Helps to soften the wines or spirits.

Cask Breather (Eng). See Asperating Valve.

Cask Conditioned (Eng). Beer that is allowed to condition in the cask in the public house cellar after delivery from the brewery. Is primed with finings, sugar and dry hops and takes 2–3 days before it is ready for drinking. See also Primings, Tapping and Venting.

Casking (Eng). The placing of beer, wines or spirits into a cask. See Étonner.

Casorzo d'Asti (It). A small D.O.C. region based north-east of Barbera d'Asti in Piemonte.

Casque (Eng). A brandy-based, honey liqueur.

Cas-Rougeot (Le) (Fr). A Premier Cru vineyard of the A.C. commune of Mon-thélie, Côte de Beaune, Burgundy. 0.4 ha.

Cassan (Fr). A Vins de Pays area of the Hérault Département in southern France. Produces red and rosé wines.

Cassayre-Forni Winery (USA). A small winery based near Rutherford, Napa Valley, California. Grape varieties – Cabernet sauvignon, Chenin blanc and Zinfandel. Produces varietal wines.

Casse (Fr). An unhealthy haze or deposit in wines. See Copper Casse and Iron Casse.

Casse Bleu (Fr). Iron casse. Also known as Casse Ferrique.

Casse Brune (Fr). A condition that occurs in wines made from grapes that have

been attacked by Pourriture gris (grey rot). Is treated with tannin and bisul-phate.

Casse Ferrique (Fr). Iron casse. Also known as Casse bleu.

Cassillero del Diablo (Chile). See Casillero del Diablo.

Cassis (Fr). A blackcurrant liqueur made chiefly in the northern Côte d'Or (Dijon plains and Arrières Côtes), Burgundy. See also Crème de Cassis.

Cassis (Fr). A mainly white A.C. wine area in the Côtes de Provence on the south-eastern coast of France. Produces a little red and rosé wine. Minimum alc. by vol. of 11% for all A.C. wines.

Cassis Cocktail (Cktl). ⅔ measure Bour-bon whiskey, ½ measure dry Ver-mouth, 2 dashes Crème de Cassis. Shake over ice, strain into a cocktail glass.

Cassis de Dijon (Fr). A fine Crème de Cassis produced only on the plains of Dijon in Burgundy.

Cassis-Kirsch (Fr). An apéritif. Same as Polichinelle.

Cassovar (Czec). A Lager beer brewed in Kosice.

Casta (Port). A red grape variety.

Casta Predominante (Port). Lit – 'Predo-minant grape variety'.

Castarède (Fr). An Armagnac producer. Address = J. Castarède, Pont-des-Bordes, 47230 Lavardac. 20 ha. situated in the Bas Armagnac. Produces Château de Maniban Cuvée Spéciale.

Castas Nobres (Mad). Lit – 'Noble varie-ties'. The permitted grapes used in the production of Madeira (white) = Bual, Sercial, Terrantez and Verdelho (red) = Bastardo and Terrantez preto.

Castaway (Eng). The name of a sparkling 'Cooler' produced from white wine and tropical fruit juice.

Castay Frères (Fr). An Armagnac pro-ducer. Address = Château de Jaulin, Bretagne d'Armagnac, 32800 Eauze.

Casteja (Fr). An Armagnac producer. Pro-duces V.S.O.P. Grande Reserve.

Castelão (Port). A red grape variety grown in Bairrada.

Castel Chandon (Arg). The brand-name used by Bodegas Proviar for a range of their wines.

Castel Danielis (Gre). A dry red, table wine produced in Patras by Achaia-Clauss.

Castel del Monte Bianco (It). D.O.C. white wine from Puglia in the commune of Minervino Murge and in parts of Bari. Grape varieties – Bombino bianco, Palumbo, Pampanuto, Trebbiano giallo and Trebbiano toscano.

C

Castel del Monte Rosato (It). D.O.C. rosé wine from Puglia in the commune of Minervino Murge and in parts of Bari. Grape varieties – Bombino nero, Montepulciano and Uva di troia.

Castel del Monte Rosso (It). D.O.C. red wine from Puglia in the commune of Minervino Murge and in parts of Bari. Grape varieties – Bombino nero, Montepulciano, Sangiovese and Uva di troia. If aged for 3 years minimum and alc. by vol. of 12.5% then classed Riserva.

Castel de Monte (It). A light red, almost rosé wine from the Apulia (Puglia) region which has a velvety, dry, delicate taste.

Castelfiora (It). A noted producer of sparkling (cuve close) wines in the Marche region.

Castelino (Port). A red grape variety grown in Torres Vedras.

Castell (Ger). Village. (Anb) = Franken. (Ber) = Steigerwald. (Gro) = Herrenberg. (Vins) = Bauch, Feuerbach, Hohnart, Kirchberg, Kugelspiel, Reitsteig, Schlossberg, Trautberg.

Castell (Ger). Village. (Anb) = Franken. (Ber) = Steigerwald. (Gro) = Schild. (Vins) = Bausch, Kirschberg.

Castellana (Sp). A white grape variety.

Castellane (Vicomte de) (Fr). A Champagne producer based in Épernay. Produces – Vintage and non-vintage wines and liqueurs (See Vicomte Champagne Liqueur).

Castellberg (Ger). Vineyard. (Anb) = Baden. (Ber) = Kaiserstuhl-Tuniberg. (Gro) = Vulkanfelsen. (Vil) = Achkarren.

Castellberg (Ger). Vineyard. (Anb) = Baden. (Ber) = Kaiserstuhl-Tuniberg. (Gro) = Vulkanfelsen. (Vil) = Ihringen.

Castellberg (Ger). Vineyard. (Anb) = Baden. (Ber) = Markgräflerland. (Gro) = Burg Neuenfels. (Vil) = Ballrechten-Dottingen.

Castellblanch (Sp). Producers of Cava wines based in San Sardurní de Noya, Cataluña.

Casteller (It). D.O.C. light red wine from the Trentino-Alto Adige region. Produced from the Lambrusco, Merlot and Schiava grapes.

Castellet (Le) (Fr). A noted wine-producing commune in A.C. Bandol, Provence, south-eastern France.

Castelli (It). Another name for the Cannicci.

Castell'in Villa (It). A Chianti Classico producer based in Tuscany.

Castelli Romani (It). A delimited wine region in Lazio. Produces mainly white wines with some red. See Frascati.

Castelli Romani (It). A white grape variety grown in Lombardy. Also known as the Trebbiano toscano.

Castello (It). Castle. The Italian equivalent of a French Château.

Castello della Sala (It). A white wine produced by Antinori from the Grechetto and Sauvignon blanc grapes.

Castello di Bevilacqua (It). A producer of sparkling (méthode champenoise) wines in Veneto. Labels include Brut Quarto Vecchio.

Castello di Bornato (It). A noted producer of Franciacorta wine from Barbera, Cabernet franc, Merlot and Nebbiolo grapes.

Castello di Cacchiano (It). A Chianti Classico estate in Gaiole, Tuscany. Owned by Ricasoli.

Castello di Gabbiano (It). A Chianti Classico producer based in the Tuscany region.

Castello di Luzzano (It). See Azienda Agricola M.eG. Fugazza.

Castello di Montegufoni (It). A Chianti Putto producer based in the Tuscany region.

Castello di Nieve (It). A vineyard based in Nieve, Piemonte.

Castello di Nipozzano (It). A Chianti produced by the Frescobaldi Co.

Castello di Volpaia (It). A Chianti Classico producer based at Radda, Tuscany. 42 ha.

Castello Gabbiano (It). A Chianti Classico producer based in the Tuscany region.

Castello Montefioralle (It). A Chianti Classico producer based in the Tuscany region.

Castelmaure (Fr). A wine-producing village in the A.C. Corbières area of the Languedoc, southern France.

Castelnau (Fr). A commune in the A.C. Médoc, north-western Bordeaux. May use the A.C. Listrac designation.

Castel San Michele (It). A dry, red wine made from the Cabernet and Merlot grapes by the agricultural college in the Trentino-Alto Adige region.

Castelvecchi (It). A Chianti Classico producer based in the Tuscany region.

Castets (Les) (Fr). A Premier Cru vineyard in the A.C. commune of Saint-Aubin, Côte de Beaune, Burgundy.

Castiglione Falletto (It). A commune in the Barolo district of the Piemonte region.

Castilla la Vieja (Sp). A Bodega de Crianza based in Rueda.

Castillo de Cuzcurrita (Sp). A Bodega based in Rio Tirón, Rioja, north-western Spain.

Castillo de Manza (Sp). The label used by

Vinos de Castilla in the La Mancha region.

Castillo de Melida (Sp). The brand-name of a light, red wine produced by Julián Chivite in the Navarra region, north-western Spain.

Castillo de Tiebas (Sp). Label under which red and white wines of Vinícola Navarra, Las Campañas in Navarra are sold.

Castillo la Torre (Sp). A Cava wine produced by Freixedas in the Penedés region.

Castillon Renault (Fr). A Cognac producer. Address = 23 Rue du Port, 16101 Cognac. Has own distillery. Owns no vineyards, buys in wines. Produces – Carte Noire Extra (average 12 years old).

Castillo San Lorenzo Fino Clarete (Sp). A non-vintage red wine from Rioja.

Castillo Ygay (Sp). A red wine produced by Bodegas Marqués de Murrieta in Rioja.

Castle Ale (Eng). A bottled special Pale ale 1047 O.G. brewed by the McMullen Brewery, Hereford.

Castle Ale (Eng). A bottled special Pale ale 1041 O.G. brewed by the Morrell Brewery, Oxford, Oxfordshire.

Castle Cary Vineyard (Eng). A vineyard based at Honeywick House, Castle Cary, Somerset. 1 ha. Grape varieties – Huxelrebe, Madeleine angevine, Müller-Thurgau and Seyval blanc.

Castle d'Almain (Yug). A red wine from Pelješac in Dalmatia. Is also known as Dingač.

Castle Dip Cocktail (Cktl). ½ measure (white) Crème de Menthe, ½ measure Calvados, 3 dashes Pernod. Shake over ice, strain into a cocktail glass.

Castle Hill Sauvignon Blanc (N.Z.). A dry white wine made from the Sauvignon blanc grape, matured in wood and produced by the Te Mata Vineyard.

Castle Lager (Afr). A well-hopped Lager brewed by the South African Breweries.

Castlemaine-Perkins (Austr). A brewery based at 185 Milton Road, Brisbane. Brews XXXX.

Castlemaine-Tooheys (Austr). A new company formed by the merger of the Castlemaine Brewery of Brisbane and the Tooheys Brewery of Sydney in 1980.

Castlemaine XXXX (Austr). A keg Lager beer 1035 O.G. brewed by the Castlemaine-Tooheys Brewery. Brewed under licence in Wrexham by Allied Breweries. Canned version 1041–1045 O.G. 4.8% alc. by vol.

Castle Steamer Beer (Eng). A cask conditioned Ale 1045 O.G. brewed by the Three Tuns, a home-brew public house in Bishop's Castle, Shropshire.

Castletown Brewery (I.O.M). A brewery based in Castletown, Isle of Man that sells beers under the Castletown label. Brews Castletown Liqueur Barley Wine 1072 O.G. Nut Brown 1036 O.G. and Red Seal 1036 O.G.

Castle Wine and Green (S.Afr). Noted producers of a range of fine South African brandies.

Castra (Sp). A method of pruning useless buds on Sherry vines to help the growth of good healthy buds.

Castres (Fr). A commune in the A.C. Graves district of south-western Bordeaux.

Catador (Sp). Wine taster.

Catalan (Fr). A Vins de Pays area in the Pyrénées-Orientales Département, south-western France. Produces red, rosé and dry white wines.

Catalan (Fr) (Sp). A red grape variety also known as the Mourvèdre in France and Carignan in Spain.

Catalogue Raisonné (It). A catalogue of vines compiled by the Marchese Leopoldo (1790–1871).

Catalonia (Sp). The English spelling of Cataluña.

Cataluña (Sp). A Denominación de Origen region in south-eastern Spain. Produces red, rosé, white and Cava wines. Produces fine brandy (Mascaro) and is also famous for cork, the best in Europe. Has four D.O.s within its boundaries. They are – Alella, Penedés, Priorato and Tarragona (provinces of Barcelona, Gerona, Lérida and Tarragona).

Catalyst (Eng). A chemical agent which induces chemical changes in other substances by its presence but remains unchanged itself. Used in some wines to solidify unwanted elements in the wine.

Catalytic Agent (Eng). See Catalyst.

Catape (Fr). An alternative name for the Muscadelle grape.

Catarratto Bianco (It). A white grape variety grown in Sicily. Is used in the production of Marsala.

Catawba (USA). A large red American grape variety (Vitis Labrusca). Used for white and rosé wines and for blending in sparkling wines.

Catechol (Eng). A tannin found in fruit. Causes astringency in wine.

Catedral de León (Sp). The brand label for the red, rosé and white wines of VILE.

Catemario (It). See Collavini.

Catering Tea Grading Scheme (Eng). Body whose aim is to improve the standards of tea service in the catering sector. Applies quality standards to most of the catering tea drunk.

Catherine Blossom Cocktail (Cktl).(Nonalc). ⅓ pint orange juice, 2 scoops water ice, ½ measure maple syrup. Blend altogether in a blender. Pour into a highball glass. Top with soda water.

Catiniense (It). A red wine produced on the island of Sicily during Roman times.

Cat's Water (Eng) (slang). A term used for Gin.

Cattier (Fr). Récoltants-manipulants in Champagne. Address = 6 & 11 Rue Dom Pérignon, Chigny les Roses, 51500 Rilly la Montagne. Produces – Vintage and non-vintage wines.

Catto's (Scot). A blended Scotch whisky produced by James Catto & Co. Ltd. Renfrew. 40% alc. by vol. Part of the International Distillers and Vintners. Also available as a 12 year old.

Catturich-Ducco (It). A producer of sparkling (méthode champenoise) wines based in Lombardy.

Catty (China). The Chinese word for 'weight' from which tea 'caddy' derives.

Catz Bitters (Hol). An aromatic bitters.

Caucinianum (Lat). A white wine produced in central Italy during Roman times.

Caudin (Ch.Isles). Intoxicated, tipsy. See also Chiraï.

Caudle (Eng). Hot spiced wine or ale to which beaten egg yolk and sugar is added. Made from Gruel.

Caulinum (Lat). A red wine produced in central-western Italy during Roman times.

Cauquenes (Chile). A wine-producing region in southern Chile noted for its fine wines.

Caupo (Lat). Innkeeper, publican.

Caupona (Lat). Alehouse.

Cauro (Fr). A red wine produced on the island of Corsica.

Cauroy-les-Hermonville (Fr). A Cru Champagne village in the Canton de Bourgogne. District = Reims.

Cautivo (Arg). A Cabernet-based wine produced by Orfila at St. Martin, Mendoza.

Caux (Fr). A Vins de Pays area in the Hérault Département in southern France. Produces red, rosé and dry white wines.

Cava (Sp). Cellar.

Cava (Sp). The name for wines produced by the méthode champenoise. Has 28 separate Denominaciónes de Origen including Cava itself. Most are in the Cataluña region.

Cava Boutari (Gre). A four year old, oak-aged, red wine produced by Boutari from the Xinomavro grape.

Cava Cambas (Gre). A smooth, golden wine aged before bottling.

Cava Carras (Gre). A range of red, rosé and dry white wines.

Cavalier Cocktail (Cktl). 1½ measures strawberry juice, ½ measure Cinzano Bianco, ¼ measure Grand Marnier, ¼ measure white Rum. Shake well over ice, strain into a highball glass. Top with ginger ale, strawberry and orange slice.

Cavalier d'Asti et de Montferrato (It). A wine-brotherhood based in the Asti district of the Piemonte region, north-western Italy.

Cavalierii (Fin). A 'sparkling wine' made from whiteberries by the méthode champenoise.

Cavallino Rosso (It). The name for a brandy produced by Schweppes Italia.

Cavalotto (It). A winery based at Castiglione Falletto (district of Barolo), Piemonte.

Cavalry Bottle (Eng). A leather bottle with a long strap, shaped like a bocksbeutel. Was used by the cavalry in the eighteenth and nineteenth centuries.

Cavas Conde de Caralt (Sp). Catalonian sparkling wines produced by the Cava method.

Cavas del Ampurdán (Sp). A sparkling (Cava) wine producer based in Ampurdán-Costa Brava, Cataluña.

Cavas de San Juan (Mex). A winery based in the valley of Río de San Juan. Produces wines under the Hidalgo label.

Cavas do Barrocão (Port). Winery based in Bairrada. Produces fine red Dãos and Bairrada Garrafeiras.

Cavas Hill (Sp). A bodega based near Moja, Penedés. Produces both Cavas and table wines.

Cavas Masachs (Sp). A winery based in Vilafranca del Penedés. 55 ha. Produces sparkling (Cava) wines under the labels of Louis Vernier and Masachs.

Cavas Segura Viudas (Sp). A winery based in Cataluña. Was part of the Rumasa group. Produces sparkling (Cava) wines.

Cavatappi (It). Corkscrew.

Cavaturracciolo (It). Corkscrew.

Cave (Fr). Cellar (underground). See also Chais.

Cave à Liqueurs (Fr). Liqueur cellar. Usually a cabinet or chest which is lockable. Often glass-fronted.

Caveau (Fr). A small cellar. Often used for fine wines.

Caveau de Gustation (Fr). Tasting cellars.

Cave Bellevue (Fr). A vineyard. Address = Ordonnac, 33340 Lesparre, Médoc. 210 ha. Commune = Ordonnac. A.C. Médoc. Cave Coopérative Ordonnac. Grape varieties – Cabernet franc 5%, Cabernet sauvignon 45% and Merlot 50%.

Cave Canterayne (Fr). Cave coopérative. Commune = Saint-Sauveur. A.C. Haut-Médoc. Address = Saint-Sauveur 33250, Pauillac.

C

Cave Coopérative (Fr). Wine growers co-operative association. First introduced in 1907 in southern France.

Cave Coopérative Belle Vue (Fr). A co-operative based in the commune of Ordonnac-et-Potensac. A.C. Médoc, Bordeaux. 130 ha.

Cave Coopérative Condom (Fr). An Armagnac-producing co-operative. Address = Avenue des Mousquetaires, 32100 Condom.

Cave Coopérative de Bégadan (Fr). Vineyard. Address = Cave St. Jean, Bégadan 33340 Lesparre, Médoc. 567 ha. Commune = Bégadan. A.C. Haut-Médoc. Grape varieties – Cabernet franc, Cabernet sauvignon, Merlot and Petit verdot.

Cave Coopérative de Die (Fr). A co-operative winery based in southern France. Main producer of Clairette de Die.

Cave Coopérative de Liergues (Fr). A co-operative winery based in Villefranche, Beaujolais, Burgundy. Founded in 1929.

Cave Coopérative de Pauillac (Fr). A co-operative winery based in Pauillac, Médoc, north-western Bordeaux.

Cave Coopérative des Côtes-de-Castillon (Fr). A co-operatiye based in the commune of Saint-Étienne-de-Lisse. 3 ha. A.C. Saint-Émilion, Bordeaux.

Cave Coopérative des Grands Vins de Fleurie (Fr). Address = 699820, Fleurie. A noted co-operative based in Fleurie, Beaujolais, Burgundy.

Cave Coopérative des Grands Vins de Juliénas (Fr). Address = 69840 Juliénas. A large co-operative of 306 members based in Juliénas, Beaujolais, Burgundy. Sells direct to négociants.

Cave Coopérative des Grands Vins Rosés (Fr). A co-operative winery of 19 members. Address = 21 Rue de Mazy, 21160 Marsannay-la-Côte, Burgundy.

Cave Coopérative de St. Sauveur (Fr). A co-operative winery based in Canterayne.

Cave Coopérative de Vertheuil (Fr). A co-operative winery based in Châtellenie, Vertheuil.

Cave Coopérative de Vinification de Quinsac (Fr). A co-operative vineyard in the commune of Quinsac. A.C. Premières Côtes de Bordeaux. 140 ha. Address = 33360 Quinsac. Grape varieties – Cabernet franc, Cabernet sauvignon and Merlot.

Cave Coopérative la Chablisienne (Fr). A co-operative winery based in Chablis, Burgundy. Address = 89800 Chablis.

Cave Coopérative le Vieux Colombier

(Fr). A co-operative winery based at Lafon-Prignac, Prignac-en-Médoc, north-western Bordeaux.

Cave Coopérative St-Jean (Fr). A co-operative based in the commune of Bégadan. A.C. Médoc, Bordeaux. See Cave Saint-Jean.

Cave des Cordeliers (Fr). A Burgundy négociant based in Beaune, Côte de Beaune, Burgundy.

Cave des Producteurs Réunis (Fr). An Armagnac producer. Address = 32100 Nogaro.

Cave de Vinification des Grands Vins de Listrac (Fr). A vineyard. Address = Listrac, Médoc, 33480 Castelnau. 160 ha. Commune = Listrac and Moulis. A.C. Médoc. Grape varieties – Cabernet sauvignon, Merlot and Petit verdot.

Cave du Bourgogne (Fr). A Burgundy négociant based in Beaune, Côte de Beaune, Burgundy.

Cave Frères (Fr). An Armagnac producer. Address = 32520 Lannepax.

Cave Grand Listrac (Fr). A co-operative winery. Address = Listrac 33480 Castelnau-de-Médoc. A.C. Listrac. Commune = Listrac, Médoc, north-western Bordeaux.

Cave Harnois (Fr). A patent underground spiral wine cellar designed specifically for the home-owner. (U.K.) = The Spiral Cellar.

Cavekane (Tuk). Coffee.

Cave la Châtellenie (Fr). A co-operative winery. Address = Vertheuil 33250 Pauillac. Commune = Vertheuil. A.C. Haut-Médoc, north-western Bordeaux.

Cave la Paroisse (Fr). A co-operative winery. Address = St-Seurin-de-Cadourne, 33250 Pauillac. Commune = St-Seurin-de-Cadourne. A.C. Haut-Médoc, north-western Bordeaux.

Cave la Rose Pauillac (Fr). A co-operative winery. Address = Rue Maréchal-Joffre, 33250 Pauillac. Commune = Pauillac. A.C. Pauillac, Médoc, north-western Bordeaux.

Cave les Vieux Colombiers (Fr). A co-operative winery. Address = Prignac-en-Médoc, 33340 Lesparre. Commune = Prignac. A.C. Médoc, north-western Bordeaux.

Cave Marquis de Saint-Estèphe (Fr). A co-operative winery. Address = Saint-Estèphe, 33250 Pauillac. A.C. Saint-Estèphe, Commune = Saint-Estèphe, north-western Bordeaux.

Cavendish Cape (S.Afr). The name given to a range of South African sherries from KWV.

Cavendish Manor (Eng). A vineyard. Address = Nether Hall, Cavendish,

Suffolk. Planted 1972. 4.2 ha. Soil – Boulder clay. Grape variety – Müller-Thurgau. Vinification at Chilford Hall, Linton, Cambridgeshire.

Cave Pavillon de Bellevue (Fr). A co-operative based in the commune of Ordonnac 33340 Lesparre. A.C. Médoc, Bordeaux.

Caverna (Sp). Cavern, cellar.

Caversham Estate (Austr). A part of the Sandalford Winery, Western Australia.

Caves Acàcio (Port). The producer of Novo Mundo (a Dão wine).

Cave Saint-Brice (Fr). A co-operative winery. Address = Saint-Yzans-de-Médoc, 33340 Lesparre. A.C. Médoc. Commune = Saint-Yzans, north-western Bordeaux.

Cave Saint-Jean (Fr). Société Coopérative de Vinification. Address = Bégadan, 33340 Lesparre. A.C. Médoc. Commune = Bégadan, north-western Bordeaux. 500 ha.

Cave Saint-Roch (Fr). A co-operative winery. Address = Queyrac, 33340 Lesparre. A.C. Médoc. Commune = Queyrac, north-western Bordeaux.

Cave Saint-Sauveur (Fr). Vineyard. Address = 33250 Pauillac. 100 ha. A.C. Haut-Médoc. Commune = Saint-Sauveur-du-Médoc. Grape varieties – Cabernet sauvignon, Malbec, Merlot and Petit verdot. Owned by Coopérative Vinicole.

Caves Aliança (Port). Producers of Casa Mendes (a Vinho Verde) and Dão Aliança. Also red and white Garrafeiras in Bairrada and Aliança Seco.

Caves Borlida (Port). Producers of S. Vincente (a Dão wine).

Caves Coopératives de l'Appellation Haut-Médoc Cave la Paroisse (Fr). A co-operative winery based in the commune of St-Seurin-de-Cadourne. A.C. Haut-Médoc.

Caves da Raposeira (Port). Producers of sparkling wines in Lamego. Is owned by Seagram.

Caves da Silva (Port). Producer of Dalva (a Dão wine) and Isabel (a sparkling méthode champenoise wine).

Caves de la Reine Pédauque (Fr). A noted Burgundy shipper based in Beaune, Côte de Beaune.

Caves de Solar de S. Domingos (Port). Produces Dão wines under the Dão S. Domingos label. Also red and white Bairrada wines.

Caves-de-Teilles (Fr). A commune in the A.C. Fitou region, south-western France.

Caves do Casalinho (Port). The producer of Casalinho (a brand-name of Vinho Verde).

Caves d'Olt (Les) (Fr). A large co-operative based in Parnac, Cahors. It handles nearly half of the region's wine production.

Caves Dom Teodósio (Port). Producer of Dão and Vinho Verde wines under the label of Casaleiro. Also Cardeal (a Dão wine).

Caves Fundação (Port). Producer of Dão wines under the Dão Fundação brand-name.

Caves Império (Port). Produces – Painel (a Dão wine), red and white Garrafeiras, Bairrada and Impérial (a Dão wine).

Caves Pimavera (Port). Produces Dão wines under the Dão Primavera label. (Owns no vineyards).

Caves São João (Port). A winery based in Bairrada, Beira Littoral. Is noted for its full-bodied Bairrada wines.

Caves Solar das Francesas (Port). A noted shipper of Dão wines.

Cave St. Martin (Lux). A leading producer of sparkling wines based at Remich.

Cave Uni-Médoc (Fr). Union de Caves Coopératives. Address = Gaillan-en-Médoc, 33340 Lesparre. A.C. Médoc. Commune = Gaillan, north-western Bordeaux.

Caves Velhas (Port). A winery owned by Camilo Alves (who still produce Bucelas under this name). Also produce Dão Caves Velhas (a brand-name used for their Dão wines).

Cave Vinicole d'Eguisheim (Fr). An Alsace co-operative. Address = 6, Grand-Rue, 68420 Eguisheim.

Cave Vinicole de Pfaffenheim (Fr). An Alsace co-operative. Address = 68250 Rouffach.

Cave Vinicole de Puisseguin (Fr). A co-operative winery based in the commune of Puisseguin-Saint-Émilion. A.C. Saint-Émilion, Bordeaux. 570 ha.

Cave Vinicole de Turkheim (Fr). An Alsace co-operative. Address = 68230 Turkheim.

Cavicchioli (It). A winery based at San Prospero near Sorbara in the Emilia Romagna region. Noted for its Lambrusco (still and sparkling).

Caviros (Gre). A large, noted wine-producer of Greece.

Caviste (Sp). Cellar worker.

Cavit (It). A co-operative in the Trentino-Alto Adige region. Blends, matures and bottles wines made by other co-operatives.

Caxaca (Bra). The alternative spelling of Cachaça.

C

Çay (Tur). Tea.

Cayd (Sp). A noted Sherry-producer, Criadores Almancenistes' brand-name. Buidores de Vinhos de Jerez.

Çaydanlik (Tur). Tea-pot.

Cayetana (Sp). A white grape variety grown in western Spain to produce medium white wines. Is often blended with other varieties. Known as the Calagraño in Rioja.

Çay Fincani (Tur). Teacup.

Çayhane (Tur). Tea house, tea shop.

Caymus Vineyard (USA). A winery based near Rutherford, Napa Valley, California. 29 ha. Grape varieties – Cabernet sauvignon, Chardonnay, Pinot noir and Zinfandel. Produces varietals and table wines under the Liberty School label.

Cayo Verde (USA). A lime-flavoured liqueur.

Cazanove (Fr). The brand-name of a Cognac from Cazanove. Address = S.A. 17500 Jonzac. Also produces a range of liqueurs.

Cazeau (W.Ind). A Rum distillery based in Haiti that produces Rhum Marie Colas.

Cazes Frères (Fr). A noted producer of A.C. Muscat de Rivesaltes. VdN. Address = 4, Rue Francisco Ferrer, BP 61–1064, Rivesaltes.

Cazetiers (Fr). A Premier Cru vineyard in the A.C. commune of Gevrey-Chambertin, Côte de Nuits, Burgundy. 9.11 ha. Also known as Les Cazetiers.

C.B. (Fr) (abbr). Château Bottled.

CB (Eng) (abbr). Cadnam Brewery based in Cadnam, New Forest, Hampshire. Produces Cadnam Bitter 1031 O.G.

C.B.A.B. (USA) (abbr). California Brandy Advisory Board.

CC (USA). The label used by J.F.J. Bronco Winery, California for a range of its wines.

C.C.S.B. (Eng) (abbr). Coca Cola and Schweppes Beverages Company.

CDC (Fr). Producer of Café de Paris. Address = 30, Avenue Kléber, Paris.

C.D. Pils (Ger). A Pilsener Lager brewed by the Dinkelacker Brauerei in Stuttgart. 5.3% alc. by vol. Is unpasteurised and has a long lagering period.

Cebada (Sp). Barley.

Cecema Punch (Punch). 1½ pints white Rum, 1 pint orange juice, 1 pint pineapple juice, 2 pints iced lemonade, ¼ pint lemon juice, ½ pint Gomme syrup. Stir together (except lemonade). Chill down in a refrigerator. Add lemonade and 2 sliced oranges.

Ceclavin (Sp). A wine-producing area based in Cáceres, south-western Spain.

Cedar Hill Wine Company (USA). A winery based in Cleveland Heights, Ohio. Produces French-American hybrid and vinifera wines under the Château Lagniappe label.

Cedarwood (Eng). A term used to describe a certain bouquet associated with the bottle maturity of a wine which has previously been fermented or stored in wood.

Cederberg Kelders (S.Afr). A winery based at Cederberg. Address = Dwarsrivier, P.O. Cederberg 7341. Produces varietal wines.

Cederlunds Torr Caloric (Swe). A Swedish Punsch 55.5% alc. by vol. Produced by Aktiebolaget Vin & Spritcentralem.

Cédratine (Fr). A citrus-flavoured liqueur produced on the island of Corsica.

Cedres (Les) (Fr). A vineyard in the A.C. Châteauneuf-du-Pape in the southern Rhône.

Ceiling Yield (Fr). See Plafond Limité de Classement.

Celebes Islands Coffee (E.Ind). An Indonesian coffee which produces strong, full-flavoured coffees.

Celebrated Oatmeal Stout (Eng). A bottled strong Stout 1050 O.G. brewed by the Samuel Smith Brewery, Tadcaster, Yorkshire.

Celebration Ale (Eng). A sweet, heavy, strong Ale 1066 O.G. brewed by the Morrell's Brewery, Oxford, Oxfordshire.

Celebration Cream (Sp). A brand of Cream Sherry produced by Domecq in Jerez de la Frontera.

Celebration Wine (USA). The name often used for sparkling wines.

Cella (Lat). Cellar.

Cellah (Afr). An A.O.G. area in the wine-producing region of Gharb, Morocco.

Cellar (Eng). An underground room for the storage of beers, wines, etc. Must have a cool, constant temperature (10–16°C) with little or no vibration. (Fr) = Cellier [also Cave]. (Ger) = Keller. (Hol) = Kelder. (It) = Cantina. (Lat) = Cella. (Port) = Adega. (Sp) = Bodega. (Tur) = Mahzen. (USA) = Celler. (Wales) = Seler.

Cellarage (Eng). The area of a cellar.

Cellarage (Eng). The charges levied for storing wines etc. in a cellar.

Cellar Brewery (Eng). See Cirencester.

Cellarcraft (Eng). The name given to the tending of wines in a hygienic manner in order to mature them and keep them in peak condition. Includes storage, temperature and hygiene. In winemaking includes filtering, fining, blending and bottling.

Cellarer (Eng). In a monastery a monk who is responsible for the wine and food in the cellar.

Cellaret (Eng). A small cupboard, case or cabinet for storing bottles of wine. Has compartments.

Cellar Master (Eng). Person in charge of the cellars. (Fr) = Maître de Chai. (Ger) = Kellermeister. (Sp) = Capataz.

Cellatica (It). A small town in the Garda district of Lombardy, north-west of Brescia. Also the name of red wine.

Cellatica (It). D.O.C. red wine from the Lombardy region. Produced from Barbera 25–30%, Incrocio terzi 10–15%, Marzernino 20–30% and Schiava gentile 35–40% grapes.

Celler (USA). Cellar.

Cellerette (Eng). A large, lead-lined bucket designed to take bottles of wine and ice. Usually on a stand and lockable. Also called a wine cooler. Popular in the eighteenth and nineteenth centuries.

Celles (Fr). A commune in the Charente-Maritime Département whose grapes are classed Petite Champagne (Cognac).

Cellier (Fr). Cellar.

Cellier-aux-Moines (Fr). A vineyard in the A.C. commune of Givry, Côte Chalonnaise, Burgundy.

Cellier de Marrenon (Fr). A group of co-operatives based in the southern Rhône. Produce both red and white wines.

Celliers (Fr). Above-ground, wine stores in monasteries.

Celorico de Basto (Port). A small district in the Vinho Verde region that produces fine white wines.

Celtic Bright Bitter (Wales). A keg Bitter 1033 O.G. brewed by the Buckley's Brewery, Llanelli, South Wales.

Celtic Gold Lager (Wales). A Lager 1046 O.G. brewed by the Silverthorne's Brewery in Cwmbran, Gwent.

CENALSA (Sp) (abbr). Comercializadora Exportadora Navarra de Alimentación. S.A. A body owned by the government, savings banks and producers' co-operatives. Conducts viticultural research. Is based in Navarra, north-eastern Spain. Trade name = Agronavarra.

Cenanthaldehyde (Eng). An Aldehyde formed by oxidation of alcohols. Is found in wine in small traces. Contributes to the bouquet.

Cencibel (Sp). A red grape variety grown in the La Mancha region to produce dry red wines of 12–14% alc. by vol. Also known as the Tempranillo, Tinto fino and the Ull de llebre.

Cendré de Novembre (Fr). A rosé wine produced in the Arbois district of the Jura, central-eastern France.

Cenicero (Sp). A noted wine-producing village in the Rioja Alta, north-western Spain.

Cenizo (Sp). The local name for the first system of Oidium (a dark, fine, ash-like powder that gathers on the vine stem).

Centaure (Fr). Brand Cognacs produced by Rémy Martin. Either Napoléon, X.O. or Extra.

Centaurée Quinta (Fr). A proprietary brand of apéritif.

Centaury (Fr). An aromatic wine flavoured with majoram, hyssop, tea, coriander and citrus peels.

Centenario (Sp). A 3 year old Brandy produced by Terry.

Centenary Ale (Eng). A bottled Ale brewed by the Elgood Brewery in Wisbech, Cambridgeshire to celebrate 100 years of brewing. Is a strong, dark brew.

Centenary Ale (Eng). A bottled Ale 1080 O.G. brewed by the Mitchells Brewery, Lancaster to celebrate 100 years of brewing.

Centenary Ale (Eng). A bottled Ale 1060 O.G. brewed by the Home Brewery, Nottingham to celebrate 100 years of brewing.

Centerbe (It). Another name for the herb liqueur Mentaccia. Called so because 100 herbs are used in its production.

Centgericht (Ger). See Zentgericht.

Centgrafenberg (Ger). Vineyard. (Anb) = Franken. (Ber) = Mainviereck. (Gro) = Not yet assigned. (Vil) = Bürgstadt.

Centiliter (USA). Centilitre. $\frac{1}{100}$th part of a litre.

Centilitre (Euro). $\frac{1}{100}$th part of a litre.

Centine Rosso di Montalcino (It). A red wine produced from Brunello grapes by Costello Villa Banfi in the Tuscany region.

Central Coast (USA). A large Californian wine-producing area between Santa Barbara and San Francisco.

Central Otago (N.Z.). A wine-producing area based in the South Island.

Central Union of Wine Producing Co-operatives (Gre). See Keosoe.

Central Valley (Chile). A major wine-producing area in central Chile. Produces over half the country's wine.

Central Vinícola do Sul (Bra). A body who have helped in the development of the local wine industry. (abbr) = VINOSUL S/A.

Centrifugal Press (Eng). It works on the principle of a spin-dryer drawing the must through the sides of the drum as it spins, leaving the pomace behind. Does not crush the pips, skins or stalks.

Centrifuge (Euro). A unit which removes the solid matter out of grape juice. Is used in Germany in the preparation of Süss-reserve.

Centrifuging (Eng). See Centrifuge.

Centro de Estudos Vitivinícolas do Dão (Port). Research body in the Dão region that has laboratories in Nelas. Works with the Federação in the region.

Centurian (USA). A black grape variety developed by the University of California.

Century Plant (USA). The name for the Mezcal Cacti. See also American Aloe and Agave Cactus.

Cent Vignes (Les) (Fr). A Premier Cru vineyard in the A.C. commune of Beaune, Côte de Beaune, Burgundy. 23.5 ha.

Cep (Fr). Vine stock.

Cepa (Port). Grapevine, vine stock.

Cepa (Sp). Vine stock.

Cepa Borgona (Sp). A Riojan vine rootstock brought by the French in the nineteenth century. Thought to be the Pinot noir or Gamay from Burgundy.

Cepa Chablis (Sp). A Riojan vine root-stock brought by the French in the nineteenth century. Thought to be the Chardonnay from the Burgundy region.

Cépage (Fr). A vine variety. e.g. one of the leading 'cépages' of the Burgundy region is the Pinot noir.

Cépage Courant (Fr). The standard grape varieties for the region under the A.C. laws. e.g. Gamay in the Beaujolais.

Cépages Améliorateurs (Fr). Lit – 'Grape variety improvers'. Grape varieties that help to upgrade the quality of the finished wine.

Cépages d'Abondance (Fr). The name used to denote heavy cropping grape varieties.

Cépages Nobles (Fr). Noble grape varieties. e.g. the Riesling in the Alsace region.

Cepa Médoc (Sp). A Riojan vine root-stock brought by the French in the nineteenth century. Thought to be the Cabernet sauvignon from Bordeaux.

Cepa Velha (Port). The brand-name used by the Vinhos de Monção in the Minho for red and dry white wines.

Cep d'Or (Fr). A 15 year old Cognac produced by Jean Fillioux.

Cephalonia (Gre). An Ionian island in western Greece. Produces mainly country wines for local consumption.

Cerasol (Sp). A red grape variety grown in the Navarra, north-eastern Spain. Produces light red wines. See Ojo de Gallo.

Cerassella (It). A liqueur made from cherries in Pescara.

Cerasuolo (It). Lit – 'cherry coloured'.

Cerasuolo (It). D.O.C. red wine from the Abruzzi region. Made from the Montepulciano grape.

Cerasuolo di Vittoria (It). D.O.C. red wine from Sicily. Made from the Calabrese, Frappato, Grosso nero and Mascalese grapes. Is high in alcohol.

Cerbère (Fr). A commune in the A.C. Banyuls, south-western France.

Cerceal (Mad) (Port). A white grape variety grown in Madeira to make the fortified wine Sercial. Cerceal is the old spelling originally from the Rhine. Also grown in Bairrada and Dão in Portugal.

Cercié (Fr). A commune in the Beaujolais. Has A.C. Beaujolais-Villages or Beaujolais-Cercié status.

Cercle des Chevaliers du Cep (Fr). A wine society based in Châteauroux.

Cercles (En) (Fr). The name given to wines contained in casks (barrels).

Cerdon (Fr). A vineyard in the Ain Département of central-eastern France. Produces red and sparkling rosé wines.

Ceremony Brandy (USA). The brand-name of a 5 or 8 year old Brandy bottled by the Guild of Wineries and Distillers at Lodi in California. 40% alc. by vol.

Ceres (S.Afr). A wine-producing area in the Cape Province.

Ceres Brewery (Den). The largest, independent brewery in Denmark. Is based in Aarhus. Noted for its Ceres Danish Stout 7.5% alc. by vol.

Ceret (Sp). An old name for Sherry. Derived from Xera (the Greek name for Jerez).

Ceretene (It). The Roman name for Sherry.

Ceretto (It). A winery based in Alba, Piemonte, north-western Italy.

Cergal (Port). The brand-name used by a brewing company based at Belas for one of their beers.

Černà Hora Brewery (Czec). An old brewery based in south-western Czec.

Cernay (Fr). A wine-producing village of the Haut-Rhin at the southern extreme of Alsace. Known in German as Sennheim.

Cernay-les-Reims (Fr). A Cru Champagne village in the Canton de Beine. District = Reims.

Černý Kozel (Czec). Lit – 'Black billy goat'. A strong beer brewed by the Stankov Brewery.

Cérons (Fr). A commune in the A.C. Cérons in south-eastern Bordeaux.

Cérons (Fr). A commune [part] in the A.C. Graves district of south-eastern Bordeaux.

Cérons (Fr). A.C. district of south-eastern Bordeaux on the west bank of the river Garonne, between the communes of Graves and Sauternes. Produces sweet, white wines with a hint of Botrytis Cinerea. Contains the communes of

Cérons, Illats and Podensac. Minimum alc. content 12.5% by vol.

Cerro Añon Reserva (Sp). A red wine produced by Bodegas Olarra S.A. Made from the Tempranillo 60%, Garnacha 30%, Mazuela 5% and Graciano 5% grapes.

Cerseuil (Fr). A Cru Champagne village in the Canton de Braine. District = Soissons.

Certificate (Fr). A vintage De Luxe cuvée Champagne produced by A. Charbaut et Fils from 100% Chardonnay grapes.

Certificate of Age (USA). The Government certificate guaranteeing the age of spirits produced in the USA.

Certified (USA). The brand-name for a Brandy produced by Schenley Distillers.

Certosa (It). A green herb liqueur from Florence. Yellow and red versions are also produced which are sweeter. Made by the Carthusian monks.

Cervaro (It). An oak-aged, white wine produced by Antinori from the Chardonnay and Grechetto grapes.

Cerveceria (Sp). Brewery, bar.

Cervecero (Sp). Brewer, beer-seller.

Cerveja (Port). Beer, ale.

Cerveja de Fàbrica (Port). Brewery. See also Cervejaria.

Cervejaria (Port). A public house, bar. Also name for a brewery. See also Cerveja de Fàbrica.

Cerveteri Bianco (It). D.O.C. white wine from the communes of Cervelen, Ladispoli, Santa Marinella and Civitavecchia in Latium. Made from Barbera, Canaiolo nero, Carignano, Cesanese commune, Montepulciano and Sangiovese grapes.

Cerveteri Rosso (It). D.O.C. red wine from the communes of Cervelen, Ladispoli, Santa Marinella and Civitavecchia in Latium. Made from Barbera, Canaiolo nero, Carignano, Cesanese commune, Montepulciano and Sangiovese grapes.

Cerveza (Sp). Beer, ale.

Cerveza Negra (Sp). Dark beer.

Cervione (Fr). A wine-region based in north-eastern Corsica. Produces a full-bodied red wine of same name.

Cervisa (Lat). Ale, beer.

Cervisia (Fr). A Barley wine made from fermented barley malt in the middle ages.

Cervoise (Fr). A mediaeval, un-hopped beer.

Cesanese (It). A red grape variety grown in the Lazio region. Also known as the Cesanese commune.

Cesanese Commune (It). See Cesanese.

Cesanese di Affile (It). A red grape variety grown in Latium (Lazio).

Cesanese di Affile (It). D.O.C. red wine from the communes of Affile, Roiate and part of Arcinazzo in the Latium (Lazio) region. Made from Barbera, Bombino bianco, Cesanese di affile, Montepulciano, Sangiovese and Trebbiano toscano. Produced as Secco, Amabile or Dolce. D.O.C. also applies to the sparkling wines

Cesanese di Olevano Romano (It). D.O.C. deep-ruby red wine from the communes of Olevano Romano and parts of Genazzano in the Latium (Lazio) region. Made from Barbera, Bombino bianco, Cesanese di affile, Montepulciano, Sangiovese and Trebbiano toscano grapes. Produces Secco, Amabile and Dolce. D.O.C. also applies to sparkling and semi-sparkling wines.

Cesanese di Piglio (It). D.O.C. red wine from Latium. Made from the Barbera, Bombino bianco, Cesanese di affile, Montepulciano, Sangiovese and Trebbiano toscano grapes. Produced as either Secco, Amabile or Dolce. D.O.C. also applies to the sparkling wines.

César (Fr). A red grape variety. See Céssar.

Cesare (It). A brand of sweet Vermouth at 18% alc. by vol.

Cesarini-Sforza (It). Wine-producers based in Trentino-Alto Adige region. Produces sparkling wines from the Chardonnay and Pinot grapes.

České Budějovice (Czec). A famous Bohemian brewing town. Was known as Budweis in the Austro-Hungarian Empire.

České Krumlov Brewery (Czec). An old brewery based in České Krumlov in south-western Czec.

Céssar (Fr). A red grape variety grown in Burgundy in the Yonne Département. Used for the production of Bourgogne rouge.

Cessenon (Fr). A Vins de Pays area in the Hérault Département in southern France. Produces red and white wines.

C'est la Vie (Cktl). ⅓ gill Calvados placed into a liqueur glass, float ⅓ gill cream on top and decorate with finely grated dark chocolate.

C'est la Vie (Lux). A sparkling (méthode champenoise) wine produced by the House of Gales. White and rosé styles produced.

Ceti Standard (Fr). A type of bottle from Bordeaux. Is lighter than the Bordelaise Lourde.

Cevada (Port). Barley.

Ceylon Breakfast (Eng). A fine flavoured tea of Broken Orange Pekoe characteristics. Made from high-grown Uva Ceylon teas.

Ceylon Breweries (Sri.L). A brewery which

C

brews Lion Lager, Stout, Pale and Jubilee Ales.

Ceylon Tea (Sri.L). Although country now known as Sri Lanka, teas are known as Ceylon teas. Best regions are – Dimbula, Dikoya and Nuwara Eliya (all high regions). Are blended teas with a light, delicate, lemony flavour. Usually served with lemon.

Ceylon Tea Centre (Eng). Address = 22, Regent Street, London SW1. Does research and promotion of Ceylon teas.

Ceyras (Fr). A wine-producing commune in the A.C. Clairette du Languedoc, southern France.

Cezve (Tur). Coffee pot.

Ch. (Fr) (abbr). Château.

CH (Fr) (abbr). Chanteau. Found on barrels in Cognac. See Chanteau.

Cha (China). A fermented beverage made from palm sap.

Cha (Eng) (slang). Tea. e.g. 'A cup of cha'. Derives from the Cantonese word 'Tcha'.

Chà (Port). Tea.

Chabanneau et Cie (Fr). A Cognac producer. Address = Chabanneau et Cie, BP 8 16101 Cognac.

Chabiots (Fr). A Premier Cru vineyard of the A.C. commune of Morey-Saint-Denis, Côte de Nuits, Burgundy. 2.2. ha.

Chablais (Switz). A wine-producing district between the Vaud and Valais cantons. Produces dry, heady white wines.

Chablis (Fr). The most northerly district of the Burgundy region. Produces mainly white wines within the A.C. from the white Chardonnay grape, also some V.D.Q.S. red wines in the southern half of the district. Communes of – Beines, Béru, Chablis, Chemilly-sur-Serein, Chichée, Courgis, Fontenay, Fyé, La Chapelle-Vaupelteigne, Lignorelles, Ligny-le-Châtel, Maligny, Milly, Poilly-Poinchy, Préhy, Rameau, Villy and Viviers. Has four grades – Chablis Grand Cru, Chablis Premier Cru, Chablis and Petit Chablis.

Chablis (Fr). One of the four methods of pruning permitted in the Champagne region.

Chablis (USA). See California Chablis.

Chablis Cup (Cup). 1 bottle Chablis, 2–3 fl.ozs. Sherry, rind of a lemon, ½ fl.oz. Gomme syrup. Mix altogether in a large jug, add ice, serve in goblets.

Chablis Grand Cru (Fr). There are seven vineyards entitled to this appellation. Must have 11% alc. by vol. They are – Blanchots, Bougros, Les Clos, Les Grenouilles, Les Preuses, Valmur and Vaudésir.

Chablis Moutonne (Fr). A vineyard which is of Chablis Grand Cru standard but has no official grading.

Chablis Premier Cru (Fr). There are 22 individual vineyards that are entitled to this appellation. Must have 10.5% alc. by vol. They are – Beauroy, Beugnon, Butteaux, Chapelot, Châtain, Côte de Fontenay, Côte de Léchet, Fourchaume, Les Forêts, Les Lys, Mélinots, Mont de Milieu, Montée de Tonnerre, Montmains, Pied d'Aloup, Séchet, Troesme, Vaillon [also known as Côte de Vaillon], Vaucoupin, Vaulorent, Vaupulent and Vosgros [also spelt Vosgiras].

Chablis Simple (Fr). Chablis and Petit Chablis grades.

Chaboeufs (Les) (Fr). A Premier Cru vineyard in the A.C. commune of Nuits-Saint-Georges, Côte de Nuits, Burgundy. 3 ha.

Chabot-Marquis de Puységur (Fr). Armagnac producer. Address = Compagnie Viticole des Grandes Armagncs, Route de Bordeaux, 40190 Villeneuve de Marsan. 60 ha. situated in the Bas Armagnac. Produces – Chabot Blason d'Or, X.O. and Marquis de Puységur.

Chaboud (Jean-François) (Fr). A producer of A.C. Saint Péray Mousseux in the Rhône. Made from the Marsanne and Roussanne grapes.

Chacé (Fr). A commune in the A.C. Saumur, Anjou-Saumur, Loire. Produces red and white wines.

Ch'a Ching of Lu Yu (China). See Tea Scripture.

Chacolets (Les) (Fr). A vineyard in the A.C. commune of Montagny, Côte Chalonnaise, Burgundy.

Chacolí (Sp). A white, sharp, Basque wine. 8–9% alc. by vol. from area of same name in north-eastern Spain.

Chacón (Miguel Velasco S.A.) (Sp). A producer of Montilla based on Montilla-Moriles.

Chadely (Arab). A Mullah who, in the ninth century was purported to have discovered coffee. Also known as Scyadly.

Chadenac (Fr). A commune in the Charente-Maritime Département whose grapes are classed Petite Champagne (Cognac).

Chaffots (Les) (Fr). A Premier Cru vineyard in the A.C. commune Morey-Saint-Denis, Côte de Nuits, Burgundy. 1.25 ha.

Chagga Coffee (Afr). The alternative name for Kilimanjaro Coffee from Tanzania. Gets its name from the Tribe who cultivate it. See also Kibo Chagga Coffee.

Chagny (Fr). A wine-town in the Mercurey district, Côte Chalonnaise, Burgundy.

Chai A building used to store wines, usually above ground but similar to a Cave or Cellar.

Chai de Viellissement (Fr). Wine cellar used for ageing wines.

Chai de Vin (Fr). Winery.

Chaillots (Les) (Fr). A Premier Cru vineyard [part] in the A.C. commune of Aloxe-Corton, Côte de Beaune, Burgundy.

Chailloux (Les) (Fr). A vineyard in the commune of Solutré-Pouilly in the A.C. Pouilly-Fuissé, Mâcon, Burgundy.

Chaintré (Fr). A commune in the Mâconnais district which produces A.C. Pouilly Fuissé.

Chairman's Choice (Eng). A keg Bitter 1039 O.G. brewed by the Gibbs Mew Brewery, Salisbury, Wiltshire. Also known as Anchor Keg.

Chaix (Fr). Above ground cellars.

Chalambar (Austr). A brand of red wine produced by Seppelt in Victoria. A blend of Hermitage and other varieties.

Chaleira (Port). Kettle.

Chalenberg (N.Z.). A medium-sweet, white wine made from the Müller-Thurgau grape by the Pacific Vineyards, McLeod Road, Henderson, North Island.

Chalet Debonné Vineyards (USA). A winery based in Madison, Ohio. 16 ha. Produces French hybrid and Labrusca wines.

Chalice (Eng). A religious drinking vessel.

Chalino (N.Z). A medium-sweet, white wine made from the Chasselas and Palomino grapes combined with Muscat juice. Produced by the Te Mata Winery, Hawkes Bay.

Chalk (Eng). Fine calcareous soil found in the Champagne, Cognac and Andalusia (Jerez) regions. Also to a lesser extent in many other wine regions of the world. Produces fine wines.

Chalkers Cocktail (Cktl). ⅓ measure Vodka, ⅓ measure Batida de Côco, ⅓ measure cream, dash egg white. Shake over ice, strain into a cocktail glass.

Chalkhill Vineyard (Eng). Address = Bowerchalke, Wiltshire. 2.5 ha. Grape varieties – Bacchus, Kerner and Müller-Thurgau.

Chalk Hill Vineyard (USA). A vineyard based in the Russian River Valley, Sonoma County, California. Produces varietal wines.

Chalkis (Gre). A dry, white wine from Negropont.

Chalk Tufa (Fr). See Tufa.

Challenger Bitter (Eng). A cask conditioned Bitter 1039 O.G. brewed by the Ashford Brewery, Ashford, Kent.

Challes (Fr). A sulphurous mineral water.

Chalone Vineyard (USA). A winery based in Monterey County, south of San Francisco, California. 50 ha. Grape varieties – Chardonnay, Chenin blanc and Pinot noir. Produces varietal wines.

Chalonnaise (Fr). A red and white wine-producing district in the central Burgundy region. Has 4 communes of Givry, Mercurey, Montagny and Rully.

Chalonnes (Fr). A commune in the A.C. Savennières, Anjou-Saumur, Loire.

Chalon-sur-Marne (Fr). An important centre of the Champagne trade.

Chalons-sur-Vesle (Fr). A Cru Champagne village in the Canton de Fismes. District = Reims.

Chalumeau (Fr). Drinking straw.

Chalumeaux (Les) (Fr). A premier Cru vineyard in the A.C. commune of Puligny-Montrachet, Côte de Beaune, Burgundy. 7 ha.

Chalybeate Water (Eng). Mineral waters that are either carbonated or sulphated. Act as a stimulant and as a tonic. e.g. Passy, Vittel, St. Nectaire and Forges.

Chalybon (Gre). A biblical sweet wine made near Damascus and drunk in ancient Greece. Also known as Helbon.

Chalybon (Gre). The brand-name given to the wines from the Lebanon vineyards.

Chamakha (USSR). A red grape variety grown in Azerbaijan to produce dessert wines.

Chambard (Eng). A brand of wine from J.E. Mather and Sons.

Chambers' Rosewood (Austr). A winery based in north-eastern Victoria. Is noted for its dessert wines, especially Tokay.

Chambertin (Fr). A Grand Cru vineyard within the A.C. commune of Gevrey-Chambertin, Côte de Nuits, Burgundy. 12.5 ha. and is adjacent to the famous vineyard of Clos de Bèze. Has 8 Grand Crus that can use its name in prefix.

Chambertin Clos de Bèze (Fr). See Clos de Bèze.

Chambéry (Fr). An aromatic, fortified wine flavoured with herbs and sugar from the Haut-Savoie. See also Chambéryzette.

Chambéry-Citron (Cktl). ½ gill Chambéry, ⅙ gill Sirop de Citron. Stir over ice, strain into an ice-filled highball glass. Top with soda water.

Chambéry-Fraisette (Cktl). ½ gill Chambéry, ⅙ gill Fraisette. Stir over ice, strain into an ice-filled highball glass. Top with soda water.

C

Chambéryzette (Fr). A red, aromatic, fortified wine from the Haute-Savoie. Is made with the juice of wild strawberries. Top brands are Dolin and Gaudin.

Chamblanc (S.Afr). A demi-sec (and doux) sparkling wine made from the Clairette blanche and Colombard grapes by the Bertrams Estates.

Chambolle Musigny (Fr). An A.C. commune in the Côte de Nuits, Burgundy. Has Grand Cru vineyards of – Les Bonnes Mares [part] and Les Musigny 24.4 ha. and the Premier Cru vineyards of Aux Beau-Bruns, Aux Combottes, Aux Échanges, Combe d'Orveau [part], Derrière-la-Grange, La Combe d'Orveau, Les Amoureuses, Les Baudes, Les Borniques, Les Carrières, Les Chabriots, Les Charmes, Les Chatelots, Les Combottes, Les Fousselottes, Les Fuées, Les Grands Murs, Les Groseilles, Les Gruenchers, Les Haut-Doix, Les Lavrottes, Les Noirots, Les Plantes and Les Sentiers. 68.35 ha.

Chambraise (USA). The American spelling of Chambéryzette.

Chambre (Fr). Lit – 'room'. Denotes in wine language 'room temperature' for the service of red wines. Ideally at 18°C-22°C. See Chambrer.

Chambrer (Fr). From the French Chambre. The term is used for bringing red wines to room temperature from cellar temperature.

Chambre Syndicate des Courtiers (Fr). A syndicate of wine brokers in Bordeaux. Responsible for the 1855 classification of Sauternes wines in Bordeaux.

Chambrecy (Fr). A Cru Champagne village in the Canton de Ville-en-Tardenois. District = Reims.

Chamery (Fr). A Cru Champagne village in the Canton de Verzy. District = Reims.

Champagnac (Fr). A commune in the Charente-Maritime Département whose grapes are classed as Petite Champagne (Cognac).

Champagne (Fr). The top A.C. sparkling wine-producing region in the world. The method of making sparkling wine was invented by a monk Dom Pérignon. Is the most northerly wine region of France. Has chalk soil. Three major regions – Montagne de Reims [in the north], Vallée de la Marne [central] and Côte des Blancs [in the south]. Cantons of – d'Avize, d'Aÿ, de Beine, de Bourgogne, de Braine, de Châtillon-sur-Marne, de Condé-en-Brie, de Dormans, d'Épernay, de Fismes, de l'Aube, de Montmort, de Reims, de Sézanne, de Suippes, de Vertus, de Verzy, de Ville-en-Tardenois. See Dom Pérignon, Méthode Champenoise, Grande Marque and Widow Cliquot.

Champagne Gogo (Fr). Denotes that Champagne is flowing freely. Can drink as much as one likes.

Champagne Apple (Cktl). 1 part Champagne, 1 part dry sparkling Cider. Serve in the Champagne flute. Dress with an apple slice.

Champagne Bottle Sizes (Fr). Quarter = (20 cls), Half Bottle = (40 cls), Imperial Pint = (60 cls), Bottle = (80 cls), Magnum = 2 bottles (1.6 ltrs), Jereboam = 4 bottles (3.2 ltrs), Rehoboam = 6 bottles (4.8 ltrs), Methuselah = 8 bottles (6.4 ltrs), Salmanazar = 12 bottles (9.6 ltrs), Balthazar = 16 bottles (12.8 ltrs) and Nebuchadnezzar = 20 bottles (16 ltrs).

Champagne Cider (Eng) (USA). The name given to sparkling Cider.

Champagne Charlie (Eng). A song sung in Victorian days by George Leybourne when Champagne was very popular.

Champagne Charlie (Fr). The name given to a De Luxe vintage cuvée Champagne produced by Charles Heidsieck. Minimum of 45% Chardonnay and remainder Pinot noir grapes.

Champagne Cobbler (Cktl).(1). 1 gill Champagne, 2 dashes old Cognac, 1–2 dashes lemon juice, 3–4 dashes Gomme syrup. Stir gently over crushed ice, serve with dash of lemon juice, slice of lemon and straws.

Champagne Cobbler (Cktl).(2). Into a mixing glass place Champagne, 2 dashes sugar syrup and fruit syrup. Stir with ice, strain into highball glass filled with crushed ice. Top with a dash of lemon juice. Serve with straws and fruit in season.

Champagne Cocktail (Cktl). Into a Champagne saucer place a cube of sugar that has been soaked with a dash of Angostura and 2 dashes of Cognac. Add slice of orange and a cherry then top with iced Champagne.

Champagne Cooler (Cktl). Fill a highball glass ½ full of ice, add ½ measure of Nassau Orange Liqueur and ½ measure Martell Cognac. Top with iced Champagne.

Champagne Coupe (Fr). Champagne saucer glass.

Champagne Cup (Cup) (1). Into a large jug place ⅓ gill Abricotine, ⅓ gill Curaçao, ⅔ gill Cognac, 1 bottle iced Champagne and 1 pint soda water. Add ice, stir well and serve with slices of fruit in season, a sprig of mint or borage and some sliced cucumber.

Champagne Cup (Cup) (2). Into a large jug place 1 bottle of iced dry Champagne, ½ gill Cognac, ½ gill Maraschino, ⅓ gill Yellow Chartreuse, ¼ gill Gomme syrup. Stir well over ice, serve with slices of orange, lemon, cucumber and fruits in season. Top with sprig of mint.

Champagne Cup (Cup) (3). Into a large jug place 1 bottle iced dry Champagne, 4 fl.ozs. Cognac, 3 fl.ozs. Grand Marnier, 1 fl.oz. Maraschino, 1 teaspoon powdered sugar. Stir altogether with ice, add sliced fruits in season and sprig of mint.

Champagne de Courcy (Fr). See De Courcy.

Champagne des Princes (Fr). A De Luxe vintage cuvée Champagne produced by De Venoge from 100% Chardonnay.

Champagne Deutz, Deutz and Gelderman (Fr). See Deutz.

Champagne de Venoge (Fr). See De Venoge.

Champagne Flip (Cktl).(1). Shake a yolk of egg over ice, add iced Champagne and strain into a wine glass. Top with grated nutmeg.

Champagne Flip (Cktl).(2). 1 egg yolk, barspoon Gomme syrup, 1 fl.oz. orange juice, 3 dashes Grand Marnier. Shake well together over ice, strain into a wine goblet. Top with iced Champagne.

Champagne Flute (Fr). A tall slim glass for correctly serving all sparkling wines in to retain their (sparkle) bubbles.

Champagne Frappé (Fr). Champagne served very cold.

Champagne Humide (La) (Fr). The name given to the northern area of Champagne. Is the strip down towards Burgundy. Lit – 'damp'. Is extremely fertile.

Champagne Julep (Cktl). Place a cube of sugar in a tumbler, add 2 mint sprigs and crush together with a barspoon muddler. Add ice, and top with iced Champagne. Stir gently and serve with sliced fruits in season.

Champagne Napoléon (Cktl). 1 fl.oz. Mandarine Napoléon, dash orange juice. Pour into Champagne flute, top with iced Champagne.

Champagne of Teas (Ind). The finest teas. Said to come from the Himalayan foothills near Darjeeling.

Champagne-Orange (Cktl). An alternative name for Buck's Fizz.

Champagne Pick-me-up (Cktl). ½ gill Cognac, juice ½ orange, 4 dashes Curaçao or Grenadine. Shake well over ice, strain into a highball glass, top with iced Champagne. Add a dash of Pernod.

Champagne Pouilleuse (La) (Fr). The western Champagne where the soil is poor and chalky. Lit – 'Good for nothing'.

Champagne Punch (Cktl). 1 teaspoon Gomme syrup, juice of ½ lemon, ⅙ gill Curaçao. Shake over ice, strain into a wine glass, top with iced dry Champagne and decorate with fruits in season. (1 measure of Brandy can be used).

Champagne Rare (Fr). A De Luxe cuvée Champagne produced by Piper-Heidsieck from 60% Chardonnay and 40% Pinot noir.

Champagne Riots (Fr). See Champagne Wars.

Champagne Rosé-Gris (Fr). Lit – 'Grey rosé Champagne'. The Middle-ages name for still Champagne. Was of a light rosé colour.

Champagne Saucer (Eng). A saucer-shaped glass used for the serving of Champagne cocktails. This type of glass was popular in the USA at the turn of the century. See Champagne Coupe.

Champagne Société de Producteurs, Mailly-Champagne (Fr). A Champagne co-operative. Address = 51500 Rilly la Montagne. Wines made from members' grapes. Produces – Vintage and non-vintage wines. Owns 70 ha. Vintages – 1973, 1975, 1977, 1979, 1980, 1982. De Luxe cuvée – Cuvée des Échansons, also Mailly Rosé (a non-vintage rosé Champagne).

Champagne Trouillard (Fr). A family Champagne-producing firm based in Épernay. Produces vintage and non-vintage wines.

Champagne Velvet (Cktl). Another name for Black Velvet.

Champagne Wars (Fr). 1910–1911. Laws passed in 1911 after vignerons who were making wine exclusively from grapes grown in the province rose up in arms against those importing cheap grapes into the province. Riots broke out so that laws were introduced to fix boundaries within which grapes must be grown in order to be entitled to be made into Champagne.

Champagnisation (Eng). The name for the méthode champenoise sparkling wine-making method.

Champagnisation (Eng). A term used in the nineteenth century for the practice of making the cork shoot out of a Champagne bottle by firstly shaking the bottle so as to cause an 'explosive' effect.

Champagnon (Fr). A still apéritif wine from the Champagne region. Is fortified with Cognac. Also known as Ratafia de Champagne.

Champagny-Sous-Uxelles (Fr). A commune in the Mâconnais district whose grapes can be used for making Mâcon Supérieur.

Champale (USA). Beer 6–8% alc. by vol. brewed by the Champale Brewery in Trenton, New Jersey. Also citrus and Grenadine fruit flavours.

Champale Brewery (USA). A brewery based in Norfolk, Virginia.

Champale Brewery (USA). A brewery based in Trenton, New Jersey. Noted for its Champale 6–8% alc. by vol.

Champalimaud (Port). Producers of a single quinta Vintage Port (Quinta do Cotto) based at Cidadelhe near Regua. Also produces red and white wines including Vinhos Verdes.

Champan (Sp). The local Cataluña name for Cava wines.

Champaña (Sp). The name for Champagne.

Champanha (Bra). Sparkling wine.

Champ-Canet (Le) (Fr). A Premier Cru vineyard in the A.C. commune of Puligny-Montrachet, Côte de Beaune, Burgundy. 4.6 ha.

Champ-Clou (Fr). A vineyard in the A.C. commune of Rully, Côte Chalonnaise, Burgundy.

Champeaux (Fr). A Premier Cru vineyard in the A.C. commune of Gevrey-Chambertin, Côte de Nuits, Burgundy. 6.76 ha.

Champelle (N.Z.). The brand-name used by Selaks for their sparkling (méthode champenoise) wine.

Champerelle (Pousse-Café). Pour into a tall liqueur glass in order equal quantities of Curaçao, Anisette, Chartreuse and Cognac.

Champigneulles (Fr). A brand of Bière from Champigneulles.

Champigniser (Eng). Another name for the méthode champenoise.

Champigny (Fr). A light red A.C. wine from a small vineyard near Saumur, Anjou-Saumur, Loire.

Champillon (Fr). A Premier Cru Champagne village in the Canton d'Ay. District = Reims.

Champimonts (Fr). See Champ-Pimont.

Champinski (Eng). The name for Russian sparkling wines.

Champinski (USSR). A sparkling wine produced in the Don Valley.

Champion Ale (Eng). A bottled Pale ale 1032 O.G. brewed by the Adnams Brewery, Suffolk.

Champion Ale (Eng). A bottled Pale ale 1040 O.G. brewed by the Gales Brewery, in Hampshire. Brewed for the French market.

Champion Ale (Eng). A bottled Pale ale 1038 O.G. brewed by the Greenall Whitley Brewery in Warrington, Cheshire.

Champion Bitters (Fin). Bitters produced by the Marli Co.

Champitonnois (Fr). A Premier Cru vineyard in the A.C. commune of Gevrey-Chambertin, Côte de Nuits, Burgundy. 3.97 ha. Also known as Petite Chapelle.

Champlat-Boujacourt (Fr). A Cru Champagne village in the Canton de Châtillon-sur-Marne. District = Reims.

Champlieu (Fr). A commune in the Mâconnais whose grapes may be used in the production of Mâcon Supérieur.

Champlot (Fr). A Premier Cru vineyard in the A.C. commune of Saint Aubin, Côte de Beaune, Burgundy. 8 ha.

Champneys Chittern Hills (Eng). A natural mountain or carbonated water from Tom Hill, Hertfordshire (source).

Châmpogne (Ch.Isles). Champagne.

Champonnets (Fr). A Premier Cru vineyard in the A.C. commune of Gevrey-Chambertin, Côte de Nuits, Burgundy. 3.32 ha.

Champonnières (Les) (Fr). A Premier Cru vineyard in the A.C. commune of Pommard, Côte de Beaune, Burgundy. 3.3 ha.

Champoreau (Fr). The term used for a liqueur or spirit added to milky coffee.

Champ-Pimont (Fr). A Premier Cru vineyard in the A.C. commune of Beaune, Côte de Beaune, Burgundy. 18.07 ha. Also known as Champimonts.

Champs-Cains (Les) (Fr). See Champs-Gains (Les).

Champs Elysées (Cktl). ⅗ measure Brandy, ⅕ measure Yellow Chartreuse, ⅕ measure lemon juice, dash Angostura. Shake over ice, strain into a cocktail glass.

Champs-de-Coignée (Les) (Fr). A vineyard in the A.C. commune of Montagny, Côte Chalonnaise, Burgundy.

Champs-Fulliot (Les) (Fr). A Premier Cru vineyard in the A.C. commune of Monthélie, Côte de Beaune, Burgundy. 8.74 ha.

Champs-Gains (Les) (Fr). A Permier Cru vineyard [part] in the A.C. commune of Chassagne-Montrachet, Côte de Beaune, Burgundy. 4.24 ha. Also spelt Les Champs-Cains.

Champs-Toizeau (Les) (Fr). A vineyard in the A.C. commune of Montagny, Côte Chalonnaise, Burgundy.

Champtocé (Fr). A commune in the A.C. Savennières, Anjou-Saumur, Loire.

Champvoisy (Fr). A Premier Cru Champagne village in the Canton de Dormans. District = Epernay.

C

Champy Père et Fils (Fr). A noted Burgundy shipper. Address = 5, Rue du Greniera Sel, 21200 Beaune. A small company with some good vineyard holdings.

Chancay (Fr). A commune in A.C. Vouvray, Touraine, Loire.

Chancellor (USA). A red hybrid grape variety also known as the Seibel 7053.

Chancellor Cocktail (Cktl). ⅓ gill Scotch whisky, ⅛ gill French vermouth, ⅛ gill Port, 2 dashes Angostura. Shake well over ice, strain into a cocktail glass. Dress with a cherry.

Chancelord and De Vitis (Fr). Cognac producer. Address = Sarl Queron, Macqueville, 17490 Beauvais sous Matha. 50 ha. in the Fins Bois. Produces Napoléon Chancelord (a 15 y.o.), Antique De Vitis (a 20 y.o.) and Age d'Or De Vitis (a 50 y.o.).

Chandesais (Fr). A Burgundy shipper based in Fontaines, Côte Chalonnaise. Specialises in the wines of the Côte d'Or, especially of the Hospices de Beaune.

Chandits (Les) (Fr). A vineyard in the A.C. commune of Montagny, Côte Chalonnaise, Burgundy.

Chandon (USA). A sparkling (méthode champenoise) wine from Moët et Chandon's vineyards at Yountville, Napa Valley, California.

Chandon (M.) (Arg). A sparkling wine produced by Bodegas Proviar.

Chandos (N.Z.). A light, sweet white wine from the Ormond Vineyard.

Chânes (Fr). A commune in the Beaujolais district. Has A.C. Beaujolais-Villages or Beaujolais-Chânes status. Also sold as Mâconnais Blanc.

Chang (China). An old Chinese name for wine. See also Li and Chiu.

Changuirongo (Mex). A traditional drink of Tequila and a fizzy drink with plenty of ice.

Changuirongo (The) (Cktl). Place ice into a highball, add a measure of Silver Tequila and top with equal quantities of tonic and cola.

Chanière (La) (Fr). A Premier Cru vineyard in the A.C. commune of Pommard, Côte de Beaune, Burgundy. 10 ha.

Chanlin (Fr). A Premier Cru vineyard [part] in the A.C. commune of Volnay, Côte de Beaune, Burgundy.

Chanlins-Bas (Les) (Fr). A Premier Cru vineyard in the A.C. commune of Pommard, Côte de Beaune, Burgundy. 7.1 ha.

Channe (Switz). A tin receptacle which varies in shape in each of the cantons and which preserves in full the fresh taste of the wine.

Chanoyu (E.Asia). Buddist Tea Ceremony. Lasts 2 hours and includes lunch and green teas. See also Koicha and Ususha.

Chanrue (Les) (Fr). A wine-producing village in the commune of Solutré-Pouilly in Pouilly-Fuissé, Mâcon, Burgundy.

Chanson Père et Fils (Fr). A Burgundy négociant-éleveur based in Beaune, Côte de Beaune. Have existing holdings such as Beaune Clos de Fèves.

Chantagne (Fr). A noted wine-producing village in the Savoie region of south-eastern France.

Chantalouettes (Les) (Fr). A vineyard in the A.C. Pouilly Fumé, Central Vineyards, Loire.

Chant de Nuy (S.Afr). A very dry, fruity, white wine made from the Colombard, Steen and other varieties by the Nuy Co-operative.

Chante Alouette (Fr). A noted, white A.C. Hermitage vineyard in the northern Côtes du Rhône.

Chanteau (Fr). The name given to a partly empty barrel in Cognac production. It is used to replenish other barrels during the ageing process. Marked CH for identification.

Chante Bled (Afr). A brand of A.O.G. red wine from the Meknès in Morocco. Made from the Carignan and Cinsault grapes. Carries the A.O.G. Guerrouane. Bottled by CVM.

Chantecler (Cktl). As for a Bronx Cocktail but with the addition of 3 dashes of Grenadine.

Chantemerle (Fr). A Cru Champagne village in the Canton d'Épernay. District = Épernay.

Chantenière (La) (Fr). A vineyard in the A.C. commune of Saint-Aubin, Côte de Beaune, Burgundy. 10 ha.

Chante-Perdrix (Fr). A Rhône wine produced by Delas at Tournon.

Chantepleure (Fr). A tube used in the Anjou district of the Loire for removing the wine from the cask.

Chantovent (Fr). A well-known Vin de Table from the Minervois region.

Chantre (Ger). A Weinbrand produced by Eckes at Neider-Olm.

Chantré Brandy Cream Liqueur (Ger). A brand of German cream and brandy liqueur produced by a subsidiary of Peter Eckes. (Merrydown is the U.K. agent). 17% alc. by vol.

Chanturgues (Fr). A red wine from Clermont-Ferrand near the Côtes d'Auvergne. Made from the Gamay grape.

Chão de Areia (Port). Lit – 'sandy bed'.

Name of a wine of the Colares region, north of Lisbon. 11% alc. by vol.

Chão Rijo (Port). Lit – 'solid bed'. Name for a wine from the Colares region, north of Lisbon.

Chapala Cocktail (Cktl). ⅓ gill Tequila, ⅛ gill orange juice, ⅛ gill lemon juice, dash Orange flower water, 2 barspoons Grenadine. Shake over ice, strain into an ice-filled highball glass. Add a slice of orange.

Chapeau (Fr). Lit – 'Cap'. Applies to the skins on top of the fermenting must.

Chapeau et Landais (Fr). An Anjou and Crémant de Loire producer based at Chace, Loire.

Chapeau Soumergé (Fr). Grape cap (skins, pips, etc) which is submerged into the must by wicker racks so as to extract the maximum colour and tannin. See Chapeau.

Chapel Hill Cocktail (Cktl). ¼ gill Bourbon whiskey, ¼ gill Cointreau, juice ¼ lemon. Shake over ice, strain into a cocktail glass. Top with a twist of orange peel.

Chapelle (La) (Fr). A Premier Cru vineyard in the A.C. commune of Auxey-Duresses, Côte de Beaune, Burgundy. 12.8 ha. Is now split up to form Les Bretterins and Reugne.

Chapelle (La) (Fr). A vineyard producing red wines in the A.C. Hermitage, northern Rhône.

Chapelle (La) (Fr). A Premier Cru vineyard [part] in the A.C. commune of Auxey-Duresses, Côte de Beaune, Burgundy. 5 ha. Also known as Les Bretterins.

Chapelle (La) (Fr). A Premier Cru vineyard [part] in the A.C. commune of Auxey-Duresses, Côte de Beaune, Burgundy. 7.8 ha. Also known as Reugne.

Chapelle-Chambertin (Fr). A Grand Cru vineyard in the A.C. commune of Gevrey-Chambertin, Côte de Nuits, Burgundy. 4.06 ha.

Chapelle-de-Guinchay (La) (Fr). A commune in the Beaujolais. Has A.C. Beaujolais-Villages or Beaujolais la Chapelle-de-Guinchay status.

Chapelle-Vaupelteigne (La) (Fr). A commune in the A.C. Chablis, northern Burgundy.

Chapelot (Fr). A Premier Cru vineyard in the A.C. Chablis. Sometimes is reclassified as the Premier Cru Montée de Tonerre.

Chapiteau (Fr). Cognac still.

Chapître (Fr). A vineyard in the A.C. commune of Rully, Côte Chalonnaise, Burgundy.

Chaponnières (Les) (Fr). A Premier Cru vineyard in the A.C. commune of Pom-

mard, Côte de Beaune, Burgundy. 3.3 ha.

Chapoutier (Max) (Fr). A noted Rhône négociant-éleveur. Address = 18, Ave de la République, 26600 Tain l'Hermitage.

Chappellet Vineyard (USA). A winery based in the Napa Valley, California. 41.5 ha. Grape varieties – Cabernet sauvignon, Chardonnay, Chenin blanc, Gamay, Johannisberg riesling and Merlot. Produces varietal wines.

Chaptal (Fr). The name of the Minister of Agriculture in the time of Napoléon 1st. Gave his name to the system of Chaptalisation.

Chaptalisation (Fr). The addition of sugar to grape must to secure a higher degree of alcohol. The amount that can be added is strictly controlled by law. Invented by Dr. Chaptal. See Chaptal. (Eng) = Sugaring. (Ger) = Anreichern. See also Sucrage (Le).

Chaptaliser (Fr). The name for the sugar used for Chaptalisation.

Char (Eng) (slang). Tea (drink). See also Cha.

Character (Eng). Term used by wine tasters to denote wine with a definite and unmistakable, though not necessarily outstanding, quality.

Character Amoroso (Sp). A pale-gold Sherry based on an 1895 Oloroso Solera produced by Sandeman.

Charal (Can). A major wine-producer based in Ontario.

Charbaut (A et Fils) (Fr). Champagne producer. Address = 17, Avenue de Champagne, 35, Rue Maurice Cerveaux, 51205 Épernay. Produces – Vintage and non-vintage wines. Vintages – 1971, 1973, 1976, 1979, 1982. Label – De luxe cuvée is Certificate.

Charbono (USA). A red grape variety. Produces full-bodied red wines.

Charbono (USA). See California Charbono.

Charcoal (Eng). Used to take the excess colour out of wines, especially rosés. Done by filtering the wine through the charcoal. See also Activated Charcoal.

Chardon (N.Z.). A fruity, lightly sparkling, white wine produced by the Penfolds Winery from Müller-Thurgau grapes.

Chardonnay (Fr). One of the world's finest white grape varieties. Is used for the production of France's great dry white wines including Chablis, Champagne and Montrachet. Also known as the Arnoison, Aubaine, Beaunois and Melon blanc.

Chardonnay (USA). See California Chardonnay.

Chardonnay Blanc Musqué (Fr). A lesser variety of the Chardonnay grape which has a strong 'musky' aroma.

Chardonnay di Capezzana (It). A Chardonnay-based Vino da Tavola from central-western Italy.

Chardonnay di Miralduolo (It). A Chardonnay-based Vino da Tavola from central-western Italy.

Chardonnay Rosé (Fr). A lesser variety of the Chardonnay grape. Has a light red skin.

Chardonne (Switz). A wine-producing district based near Lavaux in the central Vaud canton.

Charentais (Fr). A Vins de Pays area in the Charente and Charente-Maritime Départements of western France. Produces red, rosé and dry white wines.

Charentais Still (Fr). An open-fired Pot still used to distil Cognac in the Charente Département. Holds not more that 30 hecto-litres.

Charentay (Fr). A commune in the Beaujolais district. Has the A.C. Beaujolais-Villages or Beaujolais-Charentay status.

Charente (Fr). A département of western France, north of Bordeaux where Cognac brandy is produced. The finest grapes grown for Cognac are in this département.

Charente-Maritime (Fr). A département of western France, north of Bordeaux where Cognac brandy is produced, Has part of the Petite Champagne area within its boundaries.

Charge de Bouteiller (Fr). A cellar master in the eighteenth and nineteenth centuries.

Charged Water (USA). Mineral water.

Charger Lager (Scot). A canned Lager 1032 O.G. brewed by the Tennants Brewery in Glasgow.

Charité (La) (Fr). A famous old vineyard at Pouilly-sur-Loire making A.C. Pouilly Fumé.

Charles (Cktl). ½ measure sweet Vermouth, ½ measure Brandy, dash Angostura. Stir over ice, strain into a cocktail glass.

Charles and Diana (Scot). A 12 year old blended De Luxe Scotch whisky from Whyte and Mackay. Sold in a royal blue bottle (stein-style) and a leather-style box which is satin-lined.

Charles Chaplin Cocktail (Cktl). 1½ fl.ozs. Sloe Gin, ½ fl.oz. Apricot brandy, 2 teaspoons lime juice. Shake over ice, strain into a cocktail glass.

Charles Coury Vineyards (USA). See Reuter's Hill Vineyard.

Charles de Batz de Montesquiou Fezenzac (Fr). The Patron Saint of the Armagnac. Also known as D'Artagnan.

Charles Dennery (Fr). A brut Champagne produced by Charbaut et Fils.

Charles et Fils (Fr). Récoltants-manipulants in Champagne. Address = 4 Rue des Pervenches, Montigny-sous-Chatillon, 51700 Dormans. Produces – Vintage and non-vintage wines. A member of the C.V.C.

Charles Gerard (S.Afr). A white wine produced by Fairview from a blend of Sauvignon blanc and Sémillon grapes.

Charles Koch (Fr). A vintage Champagne produced by Bricout et Koch from 60% Chardonnay and 40% Pinot noir.

Charles Lefranc (USA). The brand-name used by the Almaden Vineyards in California for a range of their fine wines.

Charles Le Roi (Lux). A sparkling (méthode champenoise) wine produced by Bernard Massard.

Charleston Cocktail (Cktl). ½ measure Mandarine Napoléon, ½ measure Cherry brandy. Stir over ice in a highball glass. Top with 7-Up.

Charley Goodleg (Cktl). ⅙ gill Galliano, ⅓ gill Tequila. Shake over ice, strain into an ice-filled sugar frosted (orange juice) highball glass. Top with orange juice.

Charley's White Label (W.Ind). A light, blended Rum produced in Jamaica in 1892. Now produced by Seagram.

Charlotte Dumay (Fr). Cuvées owned in the Renardes (2 ha), Clos du Roi (0.5 ha) and Les Bressandes (1 ha) of Corton, Côte de Beaune, Burgundy. Owned by the Hospices de Beaune.

Charm (Eng). A term used to describe an appealing wine.

Charmat (Fr). The 'cuve close' or 'tank method'. Invented by Eugène Charmat in 1910 for the production of sparkling wines.

Charmat (Eugène) (Fr). The inventor of the Tank method of producing sparkling wines. Originated from Bordeaux.

Charmelottes (Les) (Fr). A vineyard in the A.C. commune of Montagny, Côte Chalonnaise, Burgundy.

Charmes (Les) (Fr). A Premier Cru vineyard in the A.C. commune Chambolle-Musigny, Côte de Nuits, Burgundy. 6.ha.

Charmes-Chambertin (Fr). A Grand Cru vineyard in the A.C. commune of Gevrey-Chambertin, Côte de Nuits, Burgundy. 32.36 ha., of which 19.5 ha. of them is Mazoyères-Chambertin which can be sold as Charmes-Chambertin (since the name of Mazoyères-Chambertin is not well-known).

Charmes-Dessous (Les) (Fr). A Premier Cru vineyard in the A.C. commune of

Meursault, Côte de Beaune, Burgundy. 12.5 ha.

Charmes-Dessus (Les) (Fr). A Premier Cru vineyard in the A.C. commune of Meursault, Côte de Beaune, Burgundy. 15.5 ha.

Charmes-la-Côte (Fr). A commune in the Côtes de Toul, Lorraine, north-eastern France. Produces Vins gris.

Charmots (Les) (Fr). A Premier Cru vineyard in the A.C. commune of Pommard, Côte de Beaune, Burgundy. 3.6 ha.

Charneco (Port). The name given to a wine from a sub-district of Bucelas of the same name in the sixteenth and seventeenth centuries.

Charnières (Les) (Fr). A Premier Cru vineyard in the A.C. commune of Savigny-lès-Beaune, Côte de Beaune, Burgundy.

Charnu (Fr). Denotes a full-bodied wine.

Charpenté (Fr). Denotes a well-made wine.

Charpignat (Fr). An A.C. vineyard on the bank of Lake Bourget in the Savoie region, south-eastern France.

Charpoutier (Fr). A négociant based at Tain in the Côtes du Rhône. Produces Hermitage wines under the names of Chante Alouette (white wine) and La Sizeranne (red wine).

Charred Barrels (USA). Used in the making of American whiskey. Gives the whiskey colour and quality.

Charrier (Fr). A neutral and slightly pétillant mineral water.

Charrington (Eng). A large brewery that merged with Bass in 1967 to form the Bass Charrington Company. Brews Charrington IPA 1039 O.G., Prize Medal 1035 O.G. and Barley Wine 1064 O.G. Also many fine beers.

Charta (Ger). A group formed in 1984 to promote wine-drinking with food. The wines must conform to Halbtroken regulations.

Charter of Muri (Ger). A charter of the abbey of Mur near Zurich for viticultural practices such as planting, pruning, hoeing, etc.

Chartreuse (Fr). A herb-flavoured, green liqueur 55% alc. by vol. A yellow sweeter version 40% alc. by vol. is also made using orange and myrtle flavours. Also produced in Spain in the Tarragona region and at Voiron (Spain).

Chartreuse Cooler (Cktl). ⅕ gill Green Chartreuse, ⅙ gill lime juice. Blend together in a blender with a scoop of crushed ice. Pour into a flute glass and top with iced Champagne.

Chartreuse Diffusion (Fr). The name of the company which distributes the Chartreuse liqueurs.

Chartreuse Nun (Cktl). ⅕ gill Green Chartreuse in the large liqueur glass. Top with double cream and sprinkle with finely grated dark chocolate.

Chartreuse Tonic (Cktl). ⅕ gill Green Chartreuse, juice 1 lime. Stir well over ice in an old-fashioned glass. Top with tonic water and dress with a slice of lime.

Chasan (Fr). A crossed grape variety between the Chardonnay and the Palomino (Listán). Grown in the Languedoc region of southern France.

Chaser (Scot). The name given to a measure of spirits (usually Scotch whisky) consumed before a glass of beer. Both are purchased together. e.g. 'Bitter and Whisky chaser'.

Chassagne-Montrachet (Fr). A vineyard area in the A.C. commune of Chassagne, Côte de Beaune, Burgundy. Has the Grand Crus of Montrachet [part], Bâtard-Montrachet [part] and Criots-Bâtard-Montrachet [part]. 10.8 ha. Also the Premier Crus of Bois de Chassagne, Champgain, Clos de la Boudriotte, Clos Saint-Jean, L'Abbaye de Morgeot, La Maltroie, La Romanée, Les Boudriottes, Les Brussanes, Les Caillerets, Les Champs-Gain, Les Chaumées, Les Grande Montagne, Les Grandes Ruchottes, Les Macherelles, Les Ruchottes and Les Vergers. 163.92 ha.

Chassart Distillerie (Bel). A distilling company based in Chassart. Produces grain Elixer and Jenevers under own name.

Chasselas (Fr). A white grape variety grown in southern France. Is known as the Fendant in Switzerland and the Gutedel in Baden, Western Germany.

Chasselas Blanc (Fr). An alternative name for the Chasselas grape.

Chasselas Cioutat (Fr). A lesser variety of the Chasselas grape.

Chasselas de Fontainbleu (Fr). The local name for the Chasselas grape in central France.

Chasselas de Montauban (Fr). The local name for the Chasselas grape.

Chasselas de Thomery (Fr). A local name for the Chasselas grape.

Chasselas Doré (USA). Also known as the Golden Chasselas. A white grape variety used for white wines in California. Is also known as the Palomino in Spain and the Chasselas in France.

Chasselas Musqué (Fr). A white grape variety from the Chasselas species. Has a 'musky' spicy aroma.

Chasselas Rosé (Fr). The alternative name for the Fendant rosé grape.

Chasselas Violet (Fr). A black grape

variety. A variation of the white Chasselas grape.

Châtains (Fr). A Premier Cru vineyard of A.C. Chablis. Is often reclassified as the Premier Cru Vaillons.

Château (Fr). Castle, manor house or lodge. In a wine country it can only be used on a label if the vineyard exists, has produced wine, and has a traditional right to use the name.

Château Abel-Laurent (Fr). Where the white wine of Château Margaux called Pavillon blanc is vinified and aged.

Château à Lafitte (Fr). A vineyard in the A.C. Entre-Deux-Mers, Bordeaux.

Château Alphen (S.Afr). A wine-producer in Constantia.

Château Ambleville (Fr). The brand-name of Cognacs produced by Raymond Ragnaud.

Château Ambois (Fr). A vineyard in the commune of Saint-Georges-Saint-Émilion. A.C. Saint-Émilion, Bordeaux. 1 ha.

Château André-Lamothe (Fr). A.C. Graves. Commune = Portets. 6 ha. (red and white).

Château Andron-Blanquet (Fr). Address = Saint-Estèphe, 33250, Médoc. Cru Bourgeois. A.C. Saint-Estèphe. Commune = Saint-Estèphe. 15.9 ha. Grape varieties – Cabernet franc, Cabernet sauvignon, Merlot and Petit verdot.

Château Aney (Fr). Address = Margaux, 33460, Médoc. Cru Bourgeois. A.C. Haut-Médoc. Commune = Cussac-Fort-Médoc. 20 ha. Grape varieties – Cabernet franc, Cabernet sauvignon and Merlot.

Château Angludet (Fr). A vineyard in the commune of Cantenac. A.C. Haut-Médoc, Bordeaux. 30 ha.

Château Anniche (Fr). A vineyard in the commune of Haux. A.C. Premières Côtes de Bordeaux, Bordeaux. Address = 33550 Haux. Grape varieties – Cabernet 60%, Malbec 20% and Merlot 20%.

Château Anseillant (Fr). A vineyard in the commune of Pomerol. A.C. Pomerol, Bordeaux.

Château Anthonic (Fr). A vineyard in the commune of Moulis. A.C. Moulis, Bordeaux. Cru Bourgeois Supérieur. 5 ha.

Château Archambeau (Fr). A vineyard in the commune of Illats. A.C. Cérons, Bordeaux. 4 ha.

Château Archambeau (Fr). A vineyard in the A.C. Graves, Bordeaux. (white).

Château Arcins (Fr). A vineyard in the commune of Arcins. A.C. Haut-Médoc. Address = Arcins, 33460 Margaux. Cru Bourgeois.

Château Arnaud de Jacquemeau (Fr). Address = 33330 Saint-Émilion. A.C. Saint-Émilion. Commune = Saint-Émilion. 4.75 ha. Grape varieties – Cabernet franc 20%, Cabernet sauvignon 10%, Malbec 10% and Merlot 60%.

Château Arnauld (Fr). Address = Arcins, 33460 Margaux, Médoc. A.C. Haut-Médoc. Commune = Arcins. 20 ha. Grape varieties – Cabernet franc, Cabernet sauvignon, Malbec, Merlot and Petit verdot.

Château Arnauton (Fr). A vineyard in the commune of Fronsac. A.C. Côtes de Fronsac, Bordeaux. 11 ha.

Château Arricaud (Fr). A vineyard in the commune of Landiras. A.C. Graves, Bordeaux. 12 ha. (white).

Château Augey (Fr). A vineyard in the commune of Bommes. A.C. Sauternes, Bordeaux. 10 ha.

Château Ausone (Fr). Address = 33330 Saint-Émilion. Premier Grand Cru Classé. A.C. Saint-Émilion. Commune = Saint-Émilion. 7 ha. Grape varieties – Cabernet franc and Merlot.

Château Austerlitz (Fr). A vineyard in the commune of Sables-Saint-Émilion. A.C. Saint-Émilion, Bordeaux. 5 ha.

Château aux Roquettes (Fr). A vineyard in the A.C. Saint-Émilion, Bordeaux. 2 ha.

Château Badette (Fr). A vineyard in the A.C. Saint-Émilion, Bordeaux. 8 ha.

Château Badon (Fr). A vineyard in the commune of Saint-Émilion. A.C. Saint-Émilion, Bordeaux. 6 ha.

Château Bagnols (Fr). Grand Cru. A.C. Saint-Émilion. Commune = Saint-Étienne-de-Lisse. 6.5 ha. Grape varieties – Cabernet franc and Merlot.

Château Bahans (Fr). The vintage and non-vintage second red wine of Château Haut-Brion (Premier Grand Cru Classé) in the Graves.

Château Bahans-Haut-Brion (Fr). See Château Bahans.

Château Balac (Fr). Cru Bourgeois. Address = 33112, St. Laurent du Médoc. A.C. Haut-Médoc. Commune = St. Laurent. 13–14 ha. Grape varieties – Cabernet franc, Cabernet sauvignon and Merlot.

Château Baleau (Fr). See Château Côte Baleau.

Château Balestard-la-Tonnelle (Fr). Grand Cru Classé. A.C. Saint-Émilion. Commune = Saint-Émilion. 11.41 ha. Grape varieties – Cabernet franc 20%, Cabernet sauvignon 20%, Malbec 5% and Merlot 65%.

Château Balestey (Fr). A vineyard in the

C

commune of Cérons. A.C. Graves, Bordeaux. 10 ha.

Château Baleyron (Fr). A vineyard in the commune of St-Seurin-de-Cadourne. A.C. Haut-Médoc, Bordeaux.

Château Baloques-Haut-Bages (Fr). A vineyard in the commune of Pauillac. A.C. Pauillac, Bordeaux. Cru Bourgeois. 6 ha.

Château Balouet-Roailloy (Fr). Address = Langon 33210. A.C. Graves. Commune = Langon. 3.9 ha. Grape varieties – Cabernet, Merlot, Sauvignon and Sémillon. See also Clos Dumes.

Château Barateau (Fr). A vineyard in the commune of Saint Laurent. A.C. Médoc, Bordeaux. Cru Bourgeois. 7 ha.

Château Barbé (Fr). A vineyard in the A.C. Premières Côtes de Blaye, Bordeaux.

Château Barbe Blanche (Fr). A vineyard in the commune of Lussac-Saint-Émilion. A.C. Lussac-Saint-Émilion, Bordeaux. 8 ha.

Château Barbe Morin (Fr). A vineyard in the commune of Loupiac. A.C. Loupiac, Bordeaux. 5 ha.

Château Barberousse (Fr). A vineyard in the commune of Loupiac. A.C. Loupiac, Bordeaux. 4 ha.

Château Barbet (Fr). A vineyard in the commune of Cars. A.C. Côtes de Blaye, Bordeaux.

Château Barbey (Fr). A vineyard in the A.C. Saint-Émilion, Bordeaux. 2 ha.

Château Barbeyron (Fr). A vineyard in the A.C. Saint-Émilion, Bordeaux. 4 ha.

Château Barbier (Fr). A vineyard in the commune of Fargues. A.C. Sauternes, Bordeaux. 6 ha.

Château Barde-Haut (Fr). A vineyard in the A.C. Saint-Émilion, Bordeaux. 12 ha.

Château Bardins (Fr). A vineyard in the commune of Cadaujac. A.C. Graves, Bordeaux. 2 ha. (red and white).

Château Bardis (Fr). Address = Saint-Seurin-de-Cadourne, 33250, Pauillac. A.C. Haut-Médoc. Commune = Saint-Seurin-de-Cadourne. 8 ha. Grape varieties – Cabernet sauvignon 65% and Merlot 35%.

Château Bardon-Ferrand (Fr). A vineyard in the commune of St-Aignan. A.C. Côtes de Fronsac, Bordeaux. 2 ha.

Château Bardoulet (Fr). A vineyard in the A.C. Saint-Émilion, Bordeaux. 2 ha.

Château Baret (Fr). Address = Villenave d'Ornon, Graves. A.C. Graves. Commune = Graves. 40 ha. Grape varieties – Cabernet sauvignon, Merlot, Sauvignon and Sémillon. (red and white).

Château Barjumeau-Chauvin (Fr). A vineyard in the commune of Sauternes. A.C. Sauternes, Bordeaux. 3 ha.

Château Barker (Austr). Vineyard. Address = Albany highway, P.O. Box 102, West Barker, Western Australia, 6324. 17 ha. Grape varieties – Cabernet sauvignon, Gewürztraminer, Malbec, Merlot, Pinot noir, Rhine riesling, Sémillon and Shiraz.

Château Barrabaque (Fr). A vineyard in the commune of Fronsac. A.C. Côtes Canon-Fronsac, Bordeaux. 7 ha.

Château Barrail des Graves (Fr). Address = Saint-Sulpice-de-Faleyrens, 33330 Saint-Émilion. A.C. Saint-Émilion. Commune = Saint-Sulpice-de-Faleyrens.

Château Barraud (Fr). A vineyard in the commune of Montagne-Saint-Émilion. A.C. Saint-Émilion, Bordeaux. 4 ha.

Château Barrette (Fr). A vineyard in the commune of Sauternes. A.C. Sauternes, Bordeaux. 5 ha.

Château Barreyres (Fr). A vineyard in the commune of Arcins. A.C. Haut-Médoc, Address = Arcins, 33460 Margaux. Cru Bourgeois. 62 ha.

Château Barrieux (Fr). A vineyard in the commune of Samonac. A.C. Côtes de Bourg, Bordeaux.

Château Barthès-Pian-Médoc (Fr). A vineyard in the commune of Le Pian. A.C. Haut-Médoc, Bordeaux.

Château Bastor-Lamontagne (Fr). A vineyard in the commune of Preignac. A.C. Sauternes, Bordeaux. 38 ha. Cru Bourgeois.

Château Batailley (Fr). Grand Cru Classé (5th). A.C. Pauillac. Commune = Pauillac. 80 ha. Grape varieties – Cabernet franc, Cabernet sauvignon and Merlot.

Château Batsalle (Fr). A vineyard in the commune of Fargues. A.C. Sauternes, Bordeaux. 4 ha.

Château Batsères (Fr). A vineyard in the commune of Landiras. A.C. Graves, Bordeaux. 4 ha. (white).

Château Baudron (Fr). A vineyard in the commune of Montagne-Saint-Émilion. A.C. Montagne-Saint-Émilion, Bordeaux.

Château Baulac-Dodijos (Fr). A vineyard in the commune of Barsac. A.C. Barsac (or Sauternes), Bordeaux. 5 ha.

Château Bayard (Fr). A vineyard in the commune of Montagne-Saint-Émilion. A.C. Saint-Émilion, Bordeaux. 7 ha.

Château Bayard (Fr). A.C. white wine from Vienne in the Département of Isère. S. France.

Château Béard (Fr). A vineyard in the

A.C. Saint-Émilion, Bordeaux. 5 ha.

Château Béard le Chapelle (Fr). Address = Peyrelongue, Saint Laurent des Combes. Grand Cru. A.C. Saint-Émilion. Commune = Saint Laurent des Combes. 16 ha. Grape varieties – Cabernet franc, Cabernet sauvignon and Merlot.

Château Beauchêne (Fr). A vineyard in the commune of Beautiran. A.C. Graves, Bordeaux. 5 ha. (red and white).

Château Beauchêne (Fr). A vineyard in the commune of Pomerol. A.C. Pomerol, Bordeaux. 2 ha.

Château Beaufils (Fr). A.C. Bordeaux.

Château Beaulac (Fr). A vineyard in the commune of Illats. A.C. Cérons, Bordeaux. 3 ha.

Château Beaulieu (Fr). A vineyard in the commune of Pomerol. A.C. Pomerol, Bordeaux. 1 ha.

Château Beaulieu (Fr). A vineyard in the commune of Saint-Germain-d'Esteuil. A.C. Médoc, Bordeaux. Cru Bourgeois.

Château Beau-Mayne (Fr). A.C. Bordeaux.

Château Beau-Mayne (Fr). Grand Cru. A.C. Saint-Émilion. Wine is made from the young vines of the Grand Cru Classé Couvent des Jacobins.

Château Beau-Mazeret (Fr). A part of Château Grand-Mayne, A.C. Saint-Émilion, Bordeaux.

Château Beaumont (Fr). Address = 33460, Margaux, Médoc. Cru Grand Bourgeois. A.C. Haut-Médoc. Commune = Cussac-Fort-Médoc. 146 ha. Grape varieties – Cabernet franc, Cabernet sauvignon, Merlot and Petit verdot. The second wine is Château Moulin d'Arvigny.

Château Beauregard (Fr). A vineyard in the A.C. Corbières, Languedoc, southwestern France. (red).

Château Beauregard (Fr). A vineyard in the commune of Pomerol. A.C. Pomerol, Bordeaux. 13 ha. Grape varieties – Cabernet franc, Cabernet sauvignon, Malbec and Merlot.

Château Beauregard (Fr). A vineyard in the commune of Saint-Julien. A.C. Saint-Julien, Bordeaux. 4 ha.

Château Beau-Rivage (Fr). A vineyard in the commune of Macau. A.C. Bordeaux Supérieur.

Château Beauséjour (Fr). Address = 33330 Saint-Émilion. Premier Grand Cru Classé, A.C. Saint-Émilion. Commune = Saint-Émilion. 7 ha. Grape varieties – Cabernet franc, Cabernet sauvignon and Merlot. The second wine is Croix de Mazerat.

Château Beauséjour (Fr). A vineyard in the commune of Montagne-Saint-Émilion. A.C. Saint-Émilion, Bordeaux. 6 ha.

Château Beauséjour (Fr). A vineyard in the commune of Pomerol. A.C. Pomerol, Bordeaux. 2 ha.

Château Beauséjour (Fr). A vineyard in the commune of Puisseguin-Saint-Émilion. A.C. Saint-Émilion, Bordeaux. 14 ha.

Château Beauséjour (Fr). A vineyard in the commune of Saint-Estèphe. A.C. Saint-Estèphe, Bordeaux. 23 ha.

Château Beau-Séjour-Bécot (Fr). Address = 33330 Saint-Émilion. Grand Cru Classé, A.C. Saint-Émilion. Commune = Saint-Émilion. 18.5 ha. Grape varieties – Cabernet franc, Cabernet sauvignon and Merlot.

Château Beauséjour-Duffau-Lagarosse (Fr). A vineyard in the commune of Saint-Émilion. A.C. Saint-Émilion, Bordeaux. 6.5 ha.

Château Beausite (Fr). A vineyard in the commune of Lussac-Saint-Émilion. A.C. Saint-Émilion, Bordeaux. 3 ha.

Château Beausite (Fr). A vineyard in the A.C. Saint-Émilion, Bordeaux. 4 ha.

Château Beau Site (Fr). Cru Grand Bourgeois Exceptionnel. A.C. Saint-Estèphe. Commune = Saint Corbian. 22 ha. Grape varieties-Cabernet sauvignon 70%, Merlot 25% and Petit verdot 5%. Also known as Château Beau Site Haut Vignoble.

Château Beau-Site (Fr). A vineyard in the commune of Bourg. A.C. Côtes de Bourg, Bordeaux.

Château Beau-Site (Fr). A vineyard in the commune of Monprinblanc. A.C. Premières Côtes de Bordeaux, Bordeaux.

Château Beau Site de la Tour (Fr). A.C. Fronsac. Second wine of the Grand Cru. A.C. Saint-Émilion. Château Gueyrot.

Château Beau Site Haut Vignoble (Fr). See Château Beau Site.

Château Beau-Soleil (Fr). A vineyard in the commune of Pomerol. A.C. Pomerol, Bordeaux. 3 ha.

Château Béchereau (Fr). A vineyard in the commune of Bommes. A.C. Sauternes, Bordeaux. 12 ha.

Château Bedou (Fr). A vineyard in the commune of Cars. A.C. Côtes de Blaye, Bordeaux.

Château Bégadanet (Fr). A vineyard in the commune of Bégadan. A.C. Médoc, Bordeaux. 4 ha.

Château Bégot (Fr). A vineyard in the commune of Lansac. A.C. Côtes de Bourg, Bordeaux.

Château Bélair (Fr). Address = 33330 Saint-Émilion. Premier Grand Cru Classé, A.C. Saint-Émilion. Commune = Saint-Émilion. 14 ha. Grape varieties – Cabernet franc 40%, and Merlot 60%.

Château Bel Air (Fr). A.C. Bordeaux

C

Supérieur.

Château Bel Air (Fr). Address = Domaines Henri Martin, 33250, Saint-Julien, Médoc. A.C. Haut-Médoc. Commune = Saint-Julien. 35 ha. Grape varieties – Cabernet sauvignon 60% and Merlot 40%.

Château Bel-Air (Fr). A vineyard in the A.C. Côtes de Blaye, Bordeaux.

Château Bel-Air (Fr). A vineyard in the commune of Montagne-Saint-Émilion. A.C. Saint-Émilion, Bordeaux. 8 ha.

Château Bel-Air (Fr). A vineyard in the commune of Portets. A.C. Graves, Bordeaux. 2 ha. (white).

Château Bel-Air (Fr). A vineyard in the commune of Puisseguin-Saint-Émilion. A.C. Saint-Émilion, Bordeaux. 11 ha.

Château Bel-Air (Fr). A vineyard in the commune of Tresses. A.C. Entre-Deux-Mers. (white).

Château Bel-Air (Fr). A vineyard in the commune of Saint-Morillon. A.C. Graves, Bordeaux. 3 ha. (white).

Château Bel-Air (Fr). A vineyard in the commune of Vayres. A.C. Graves-de-Vayres, Bordeaux.

Château Bel-Air (Fr). A vineyard in the commune of Loupiac. A.C. Loupiac, Bordeaux. 5 ha.

Château Bel-Air (Fr). A vineyard in the commune of Camblanec. A.C. Premières Côtes de Bordeaux, Bordeaux. (red and white).

Château Bel-Air (Fr). A vineyard in the commune of Néac. A.C. Pomerol, Bordeaux. 10 ha.

Château Bel-Air (Fr). A vineyard in the commune of Sainte-Croix-du-Mont. A.C. Sainte-Croix-du-Mont, Bordeaux.

Château Bel-Air Lagrave (Fr). Address = Grand-Poujeaux, Moulis-en-Médoc 33480, Castelnau-en-Médoc. A.C. Moulis-en-Médoc. Commune = Moulis. 12 ha. Grape varieties – Cabernet sauvignon, Merlot and Petit verdot.

Château Bel-Air-Lussac (Fr). A vineyard in the commune of Lussac-Saint-Émilion. A.C. Saint-Émilion, Bordeaux. 12 ha.

Château Belair-Marignan (Fr). A vineyard in the commune of Saint-Émilion. A.C. Saint-Émilion, Bordeaux.

Château Bel-Air-Marquis-d'Aligre (Fr). A vineyard in the commune of Soussans. A.C. Haut-Médoc, Bordeaux. 17 ha. Cru Exceptionnel.

Château Belair-Sarthou (Fr). A vineyard in the A.C. Saint-Émilion, Bordeaux. 5 ha.

Château Belgrave (Fr). Grand Cru Classé (5th). A.C. Haut-Médoc. Commune =

Saint-Laurent. 76 ha. Grape varieties – Cabernet sauvignon 60%, Merlot 35% and Petit verdot 5%.

Château Bel-Horizon (Fr). A vineyard in the A.C. Saint-Émilion, Bordeaux. 2 ha.

Château Belingard (Fr). A vineyard in the A.C. Monbazillac, Bergerac, southwestern France. (sweet white).

Château Belingard (Fr). A vineyard in the A.C. Côtes de Bergerac. Address = 17 Rue Millet, 24100 Bergerac. (red and white).

Château Belle Assise Coureau (Fr). Address = Saint-Sulpice-de-Faleyrens A.C. Saint-Émilion. Commune = Saint-Sulpice-de-Faleyrens. 14.6 ha. Grape varieties – Cabernet franc 10%, Cabernet sauvignon 30% and Merlot 60%.

Château Bellefontaine (Fr). A vineyard in the commune of St-Pierre-de-Mons. A.C. Graves, Bordeaux. 3 ha. (white).

Château Bellefont-Belcier (Fr). Address = Saint Laurent des Combes, 33330 Saint-Émilion. Grand Cru. A.C. Saint-Émilion. Commune = Saint Laurent des Combes. 13 ha. Grape varieties – Cabernet franc 20%, Cabernet sauvignon 10% and Merlot 70%.

Château Bellegrave (Fr). A vineyard in the commune of Listrac. A.C. Haut-Médoc, Bordeaux. 9 ha.

Château Bellegrave (Fr). A vineyard in the A.C. Saint-Émilion, Bordeaux. 11 ha.

Château Bellegrave-du-Poujeau (Fr). A vineyard in the commune of Le Pian. A.C. Haut-Médoc, Bordeaux. Cru Bourgeois.

Château Bellegraves (Fr). A vineyard in the commune of Pomerol. A.C. Pomerol, Bordeaux. 4 ha.

Château Bellerive (Fr). A vineyard in the commune of Valeyrac. A.C. Médoc, Bordeaux. Cru Bourgeois. 9 ha.

Château Belleroque (Fr). A vineyard in the commune of Bourg. A.C. Côtes de Bourg, Bordeaux.

Château Belle-Rose (Fr). Address = 33250, Pauillac, Médoc. Cru Bourgeois. A.C. Pauillac. Commune = Pauillac. 7 ha. Grape varieties – Cabernet franc, Cabernet sauvignon, Malbec and Merlot.

Château Belles-Plantes (Fr). A vineyard in the A.C. Saint-Émilion, Bordeaux. 3 ha.

Château Bellevue (Fr). A vineyard in the A.C. Bergerac, south-western France. (red).

Château Bellevue (Fr). A vineyard in the commune of Blaye. A.C. Côtes de Blaye, Bordeaux.

Château Bellevue (Fr). A vineyard in the

C

commune of Cussac-Fort-Médoc. A.C. Haut-Médoc, Bordeaux. 1 ha.

Château Bellevue (Fr). A vineyard in the commune of Lussac-Saint-Émilion. A.C. Lussac-Saint-Émilion, Bordeaux. 11 ha.

Château Bellevue (Fr). A vineyard in the commune of Macau. A.C. Haut-Médoc, Bordeaux. Cru Bourgeois.

Château Bellevue (Fr). A vineyard in the commune of Montagne-Saint-Émilion. A.C. Montagne-Saint-Émilion, Bordeaux. 4 ha.

Château Bellevue (Fr). A vineyard in the commune of Pomerol. A.C. Pomerol, Bordeaux. 5 ha.

Château Bellevue (Fr). A vineyard in the commune of Quinsac. A.C. Premières Côtes de Bordeaux, Bordeaux.

Château Bellevue (Fr). Address = 33330 Saint-Émilion. Grand Cru Classé. A.C. Saint-Émilion. Commune = Saint-Émilion. 9 ha. Grape varieties – Cabernet sauvignon 25% and Merlot 75%.

Château Bellevue (Fr). A vineyard in the commune of Saint-Michel-de-Fronsac. A.C. Fronsac, Bordeaux.

Château Bellevue (Fr). A vineyard in the commune of Valeyrac. A.C. Médoc, Bordeaux. 9 ha.

Château Bellevue la Forêt (Fr). A vineyard in the A.C. Côtes du Frontonnais, Tarn-et-Garonne, south-western France. (red and rosé).

Château Bellile Mondotte (Fr). A vineyard in the commune of Saint-Hippolyte. A.C. Saint-Émilion, Bordeaux. 4 ha.

Château Belloy (Fr). A vineyard in the communes of Fronsac. A.C. Côtes Canon Fronsac, Bordeaux. 5 ha.

Château Belon (Fr). A vineyard in the commune of Saint-Morillon. A.C. Graves, Bordeaux. 3 ha. (white).

Château Bel-Orme-Tronquoy-de-Lalande (Fr). A vineyard in the commune of Saint-Seurin-de-Cadourne. A.C. Haut-Médoc, Bordeaux. Cru Bourgeois. 25 ha.

Château Benoit (USA). A winery based in Lafayette, near Dundee, Oregon. 8 ha. Produces vinifera wines.

Château Bensse (Fr). A vineyard in the commune of Prignac. A.C. Médoc, Bordeaux. Cru Bourgeois.

Château Béouran (Fr). A vineyard in the commune of Saint-Émilion. A.C. Saint-Émilion, Bordeaux. 1 ha.

Château Bergat (Fr). Address = 33330 Saint-Émilion. Grand Cru Classé. A.C. Saint-Émilion. Commune = Saint-Émilion. 3 ha. Grape varieties – Cabernet franc, Cabernet sauvignon and Merlot 70%.

Château Bergeron (Fr). A vineyard in the commune of Bommes. A.C. Sauternes, Bordeaux. 5 ha.

Château Berliquet (Fr). Address = 33330 Saint-Émilion. Grand Cru Classé A.C. Saint-Émilion. Commune = Saint-Émilion. 8.74 ha. Grape varieties – Cabernet franc, Cabernet sauvignon and Merlot 70%.

Château-Bernard (Fr). A commune in the Charente Département whose grapes are classed Grande Champagne (Cognac).

Château Bernard-Raymond (Fr). A vineyard in the commune of Portets. A.C. Graves, Bordeaux. 5 ha. (red and white).

Château Bernateau (Fr). Address = Saint-Étienne-de-Lisse, 33330 Saint-Émilion. Grand Cru. A.C. Saint-Émilion. Commune = Saint-Étienne-de-Lisse.

Château Bernisse (Fr). A vineyard in the commune of Barsac. A.C. Barsac (or Sauternes), Bordeaux. 3 ha.

Château Bernones (Fr). A vineyard in the commune of Cussac-Fort-Médoc. A.C. Haut-Médoc, Bordeaux. Cru Bourgeois.

Château Berthenon (Fr). A vineyard in the commune of St-Paul. A.C. Côtes de Blaye, Bordeaux.

Château Berthou (Fr). A vineyard in the commune of Comps. A.C. Côtes de Bourg, Bordeaux.

Château Bertin (Fr). A vineyard in the commune of Montagne-Saint-Émilion. A.C. Montagne-Saint-Émilion, Bordeaux.

Château Bertinat-Lartigue (Fr). A vineyard in the commune of Saint-Émilion. A.C. Saint-Émilion, Bordeaux.

Château Bertineau-Goby (Fr). A vineyard in the commune of Montagne-Saint-Émilion. A.C. Saint-Émilion, Bordeaux. 9 ha.

Château Bertineau St. Vincent (Fr). A vineyard in the commune of Lalande de Pomerol. A.C. Lalande de Pomerol, Bordeaux.

Château Bertranon (Fr). A vineyard in the commune of Loupiac. A.C. Loupiac, Bordeaux. 2 ha.

Château Beychevelle (Fr). Address = Saint-Julien, Beychevelle 33250, Pauillac, Médoc. Grand Cru Classé (4th). A.C. Saint-Julien. Commune = Saint-Julien. 72 ha. Grape varieties – Cabernet franc 8%, Cabernet sauvignon 60%, Merlot 28% and Petit verdot 4%.

Château Bézineau (Fr). A vineyard in the A.C. Saint-Émilion, Bordeaux. 13 ha.

Château Bicasse-Lartigue (Fr). A vineyard in the A.C. Saint-Émilion, Bordeaux. 3 ha.

Château Bicot (Fr). A vineyard in the communes of Fronsac and St-Aignan. A.C. Côtes de Fronsac, Bordeaux. 3 ha.

Château Bicot Latour (Fr). A vineyard in the commune of St-Aignan. A.C. Côtes de Fronsac, Bordeaux. 3 ha.

Château Bidou (Fr). A.C. Bourgeais et Blayais.

Château Bigaroux (Fr). Address = Saint-Sulpice-de-Faleyrens, 33330 Saint-Émilion. Grand Cru. A.C. Saint-Émilion. Commune = Saint-Sulpice-de-Faleyrens. 6 ha. Grape varieties – Cabernet 10% and Merlot 90%.

Château Billeron (Fr). A vineyard in the A.C. Saint-Émilion, Bordeaux. 8 ha.

Château Binet (Fr). A vineyard in the commune of Parsac. A.C. Saint-Émilion, Bordeaux. 9 ha.

Château Biston-Brillette (Fr). A vineyard in the commune of Moulis. A.C. Moulis, Bordeaux. Address = Moulis 33480 Castelnau-de-Médoc. Cru Bourgeois. 10 ha.

Château Blaignan (Fr). A vineyard in the commune of Blaignan A.C. Médoc, Bordeaux. Used to be known as Château Tafford-de-Blaignan. 45 ha. Cru Bourgeois.

Château Blissa (Fr). A vineyard in the A.C. Côtes de Bourg, Bordeaux.

Château Bodet (Fr). A vineyard in the commune of Fronsac. A.C. Côtes de Canon-Fronsac, Bordeaux. 10 ha.

Château Boënot (Fr). A vineyard in the commune of Pomerol. A.C. Pomerol, Bordeaux. 4 ha.

Château Boiresse (Fr). A vineyard in the commune of Ayguemortes. A.C. Graves, Bordeaux. 4 ha. (white).

Château Bois du Roc (Fr). A vineyard in the commune of Saint-Yzans. A.C. Médoc, Bordeaux. Address = St-Yzans-de-Médoc, 33340 Lesparre.

Château Bois-Grouley (Fr). A vineyard in the A.C. Saint-Émilion, Bordeaux. 3 ha.

Château Boismartin (Fr). A vineyard in the commune of Léognan. A.C. Graves, Bordeaux. (red).

Château Bois-Rond-Grand-Corbin (Fr). A vineyard in the A.C. Saint-Émilion, Bordeaux. 4 ha.

Château Boissac (Fr). A vineyard in the commune of Lussac-Saint-Émilion. A.C. Lussac-Saint-Émilion, Bordeaux.

Château Bonair (Fr). A vineyard in the commune of Mérignac. A.C. Graves.

Château Bon la Madeleine (Fr). Address = 33330 Saint-Émilion. Grand Cru Classé. A.C. Saint-Émilion. Commune = Saint-Émilion. 4 ha. Grape varieties – Cabernet sauvignon 40% and Merlot 60%.

Château Bonneau (Fr). A vineyard in the commune of Montagne-Saint-Émilion. A.C. Saint-Émilion, Bordeaux. 9 ha.

Château Bonneau-Livran (Fr). Address = St-Seurin-de-Cadourne, 33250 Pauillac, Médoc. Cru Bourgeois. A.C. Haut-Médoc. Commune = St-Seurin-de-Cadourne. 12 ha. Grape varieties – Cabernet sauvignon 50% and Merlot 50%.

Château Bonnet (Fr). A.C. Bordeaux.

Château Bonnet (Fr). A vineyard in the A.C. Entre-Deux-Mers, Bordeaux.

Château Bonnet (Fr). Address = Saint Pey d'Armens, 33330 Saint-Émilion. Grand Cru. A.C. Saint-Émilion. Commune = Saint Pey d'Armens. 23.1 ha. Grape varieties – Cabernet franc 27%, Cabernet sauvignon 11%, Malbec 2% and Merlot 60%. Second wine is Château d'Armens. A.C. Saint-Émilion.

Château Bonnet Réserve du Château (Fr). New wine, aged in new oak casks and fined with egg white from the Grand Cru. A.C. Saint-Émilion vineyard Château Bonnet.

Château Bord-Fonrazade (Fr). A vineyard in the A.C. Saint-Émilion, Bordeaux. 4 ha.

Château Bord-Lartigue (Fr). A vineyard in the A.C. Saint-Émilion, Bordeaux. 2 ha.

Château Borie-Lalande (Fr). A vineyard in the commune of Saint-Julien. A.C. Saint-Julien, Bordeaux. 18 ha.

Château-Bottled (Fr). Mise-en-bouteille-au-Château. These words on a wine bottle label guarantee the authenticity of the wine. Used mainly in Bordeaux. Does not guarantee quality.

Château Bouchaine (USA). A winery based in Carneros, Napa Valley, California. Grape varieties – Cabernet sauvignon, Chardonnay and Pinot noir. Produces varietal wines.

Château Bouchoc (Fr). A vineyard in the commune of Loupiac. A.C. Loupiac, Bordeaux. 2 ha.

Château Bouchoc (Fr). A vineyard in the commune of Sainte-Croix-du-Mont. A.C. Sainte-Croix-du-Mont, Bordeaux. 3 ha.

Château Boudgand (Fr). A vineyard in the A.C. Côtes de Bergerac, south-western France. Address = 17 Rue Millet, 24100 Bergerac. (red and white).

Château Boulerne (Fr). A vineyard in the A.C. Saint-Émilion, Bordeaux. 9 ha.

Château Bouqueyran (Fr). A vineyard in the commune of Moulis. A.C. Médoc, Bordeaux. Cru Bourgeois. 2 ha.

Château Bourdieu (Fr). A vineyard in the commune of Berson. A.C. Côtes de

C

Blaye, Bordeaux. Address = Berson, 33390 Blaye.

Château Bourgade (Fr). Is part of Château Rosemount in the A.C. Haut-Médoc, Bordeaux.

Château Bourgneuf-Vayron (Fr). A vineyard in the commune of Pomerol. A.C. Pomerol, Bordeaux. 8.5 ha.

Château Bournac (Fr). A vineyard in the commune of Civrac. A.C. Médoc, Bordeaux. Address = Civrac-en-Médoc, 33340 Lesparre. Cru Bourgeois. 3 ha.

Château Bournac (Fr). A vineyard in the commune of Saint-Estèphe. A.C. Saint-Estèphe, Bordeaux. 3 ha.

Château Bourseau (Fr). A vineyard in the commune of Lalande de Pomerol. A.C. Lalande de Pomerol, Bordeaux.

Château Bouscaut (Fr). Address = 33140 Pont de la Maye, Graves, Bordeaux. Grand Cru Classé. A.C. Graves. Commune = Cadaujac. 36.5 ha. Grape varieties – Cabernet franc, Cabernet sauvignon, Merlot, Sauvignon and Sémillon.

Château Bousclas (Fr). A vineyard in the commune of Barsac. A.C. Barsac (or Sauternes), Bordeaux. 3 ha.

Château Bousquet (Fr). A vineyard in the A.C. Graves, Bordeaux.

Château Boutisse (Fr). Address = Place du Marcardieu, Saint-Christophe-des-Bardes, 33330 Saint-Émilion. A.C. Saint-Émilion. Commune = Saint-Christophe-des-Bardes. 16 ha. Grape varieties – Cabernet 25% and Merlot 75%.

Château Bouyot (Fr). A vineyard in the commune of Barsac. A.C. Barsac (or Sauternes), Bordeaux. 6 ha.

Château Boyd-Cantenac (Fr). Address = Cantenac, 33460 Margaux. Grand Cru Classé (3rd). A.C. Margaux. Commune = Cantenac. 20 ha. Grape varieties – Cabernet franc, Cabernet sauvignon, Merlot and Petit verdot.

Château Boyrein (Fr). A vineyard in the commune of Roaillan. A.C. Graves, Bordeaux. 42 ha. Grape varieties – Cabernet franc, Cabernet sauvignon, Merlot, Sauvignon and Sémillon.

Château Bragard (Fr). A vineyard in the commune of Saint-Émilion. A.C. Saint-Émilion.

Château Brame-les-Tours (Fr). A vineyard in the commune of Leyssac. A.C. Saint-Estèphe, Bordeaux. Address = Saint-Estèphe, 33250 Pauillac. 6 ha.

Château Branaire-Ducru (Fr). Address = 33250 Saint-Julien de Beychevelle. Grand Cru Classé (4th). A.C. Saint-Julien. Commune = Saint-Julien. 48 ha.

Grape varieties – Cabernet franc 75%, Merlot 20% and Petit verdot 5%.

Château Branas Grand Poujeaux (Fr). Address = 33480 Moulis, Médoc. A.C. Moulis. Commune = Moulis. 8 ha. Grape varieties – Cabernet franc, Cabernet sauvignon, Merlot and Petit verdot.

Château Brane-Cantenac (Fr). Address = 33460 Margaux, Médoc. Grand Cru Classé (2nd). A.C. Margaux. Commune = Cantenac. 85 ha. Grape varieties – Cabernet franc, Cabernet sauvignon, Merlot and Petit verdot. See Domaine de Fontarney.

Château Branne (Fr). A vineyard in the commune of Montagne-Saint-Émilion. A.C. Saint-Émilion, Bordeaux. 6 ha.

Château Brassens-Guitteronde (Fr). A vineyard in the commune of Barsac. A.C. Barsac (or Sauternes), Bordeaux. 5 ha.

Château Breuil (Fr). A vineyard in the commune of St-Martin-Caussade. A.C. Côtes de Blaye, Bordeaux.

Château Briès-Caillou (Fr). A vineyard in the commune of Saint-Germain d'Esteuil. A.C. Médoc, Bordeaux.

Château Brillette (Fr). A vineyard in the commune of Moulis. A.C. Moulis. 30 ha. Grape varieties – Cabernet sauvignon, Merlot and Petit verdot. Cru Grand Bourgeois.

Château Brissac (Fr). A vineyard in the A.C. Anjou. Anjou-Saumur, Loire. (rosé and sweet white).

Château Brisson (Fr). A vineyard in the A.C. Saint-Émilion, Bordeaux. 4 ha.

Château Brochon (Fr). Address = Ch. Saint-Marc, Barsac, 33720 Podensac. A.C. Graves. Commune = Podensac. 27 ha. Grape varieties – Cabernet sauvignon, Merlot, Muscadelle, Sauvignon and Sémillon.

Château Brondelle (Fr). Address = 33210 Langon. A.C. Graves. Commune = Langon. 18 ha. Grape varieties – Cabernet franc, Cabernet sauvignon, Sauvignon 30% and Sémillon 70%.

Château Brousseau (Fr). A vineyard in the commune of Saint-Hippolyte. A.C. Saint-Émilion, Bordeaux.

Château Brousteras (Fr). A vineyard in the A.C. Médoc, Bordeaux.

Château Broustet (Fr). Address = 33940 Barsac. Grand Cru Classé (2nd). A.C. Barsac (or Sauternes). Commune = Barsac. 16 ha. Grape varieties – Muscadelle 15%, Sauvignon 35% and Sémillon 50%.

Château Brown (Fr). A.C. Graves. Commune = Léognan. 10 ha. Grape varieties – Cabernet sauvignon 65% and Merlot 35%.

C

Château Bruhaut (Fr). A vineyard in the commune of St-Pierre-de-Mons. A.C. Graves, Bordeaux. 2 ha. (white).

Château Brulesécaille (Fr). A vineyard in the commune of Tauriac. A.C. Côtes de Bourg, Bordeaux. Address = 33710 Bourg-sur-Gironde. Côtes de Bourg. Commune = Tauriac.

Château Brun (Fr). Address = Saint-Christophe-des-Bardes, 33330 Saint-Émilion. A.C. Saint-Émilion. Commune = Saint-Christophe-des-Bardes. 6 ha. Grape varieties – Cabernet sauvignon 10% and Merlot 90%

Château Brun-Mazeyres (Fr). A vineyard in the commune of Pomerol. A.C. Pomerol, Bordeaux. 3 ha.

Château Burlis (Fr). Address = Vignonet, 33330 Saint-Émilion. A.C. Saint-Émilion. Commune = Vignonet. 3.19 ha. Grape varieties – Cabernet franc, Cabernet sauvignon and Merlot 76%.

Château Busquet (Fr). Address = Château Sansonnet, 33330 Saint-Émilion. A.C. Lussac-Saint-Émilion. Commune = Lussac-Saint-Émilion.

Château Bzenec (Czec). A sparkling wine made in the Uzhorod region.

Château Cabannieux (Fr). Address = 33460 Portets, Graves. A.C. Graves. Commune = Portets. 21 ha. Grape varieties – Cabernet sauvignon 40%, Merlot 60%, Sauvignon 25% and Sémillon 75%.

Château Cadet-Bon (Fr). Address = 33330 Saint-Émilion. Grand Cru. A.C. Saint-Émilion. Commune = Saint-Émilion. 3 ha.

Château Cadet-Peychez (Fr). Address = B.P. 24, 33330 Saint-Émilion. Grand Cru. A.C. Saint-Émilion. Commune = Saint-Émilion.

Château Cadet-Piola (Fr). Address = B.P. 24, 33330 Saint-Émilion. Grand Cru Classé. A.C. Saint-Émilion. Commune = Saint-Émilion. 7 ha. Grape varieties – Cabernet franc 18%, Cabernet sauvignon 28%, Merlot 51% and Pressac 3%

Château Cadet-Pontet (Fr). Address = 33330 Saint-Émilion. A.C. Saint-Émilion. Commune = Saint-Émilion. 8 ha. Grape varieties – Bouchet 25%, Cabernet sauvignon 25% and Merlot 50%. Second wine of Château Pontet.

Château Cadet Soutard (Fr). Address = Saint Laurent des Combes, 33330 Saint-Émilion. Grand Cru. A.C. Saint-Émilion. Commune = Saint Laurent des Combes.

Château Cages (Fr). A vineyard in the commune of Illats. A.C. Cérons, Bordeaux. 5 ha.

Château Caillou (Fr). Grand Cru Classé (2nd). A.C. Barsac. (or Sauternes). Commune = Barsac. 15 ha. Grape varieties – Sauvignon 10% and Sémillon 90%. See also Cru du Clocher and Domaine Sarraute.

Château Calmeilh (Fr). A vineyard on the Île de Nord, Gironde. A.C. Bordeaux Supérieur.

Château Calon (Fr). A vineyard in the commune of Montagne-Saint-Émilion. A.C. Montagne-Saint-Émilion, Bordeaux. Address = 33570 Montagne-Saint-Émilion. 20 ha.

Château Calon Montagne (Fr). A vineyard in the commune of Saint-Georges-Saint-Émilion. A.C. Saint-Émilion, Bordeaux. 3 ha.

Château Calon Saint-Georges (Fr). A vineyard in the commune of Saint-Georges-Saint-Émilion. A.C. Saint-Émilion, Bordeaux. 3 ha.

Château Calon-Ségur (Fr). Grand Cru Classé (3rd). A.C. Saint-Estèphe. Commune = Saint-Estèphe. 60 ha. Grape varieties – Cabernet franc 15%, Cabernet sauvignon 65% and Merlot 20%.

Château Calvé-Croizet-Bages (Fr). The alternative name for Château Croizet-Bages.

Château Camarset (Fr). A vineyard in the commune of St-Morillon. A.C. Graves, Bordeaux. (red and white).

Château Cambes-Kermovan (Fr). A vineyard in the commune of Bourg. A.C. Côtes de Bourg, Bordeaux.

Château Cambon (Fr). A vineyard in the commune of Blanquefort. A.C. Haut-Médoc, Bordeaux. 5 ha.

Château Cambon-la-Pelouse (Fr). A vineyard in the commune of Macau. A.C. Haut-Médoc, Bordeaux. Cru Bourgeois. 40 ha.

Château Camensac (Fr). Grand Cru Classé (5th). A.C. Haut-Médoc. Commune = Saint Laurent. 60 ha. Grape varieties – Cabernet franc, Cabernet sauvignon and Merlot.

Château Cameron et Raymond-Louis (Fr). A vineyard in the commune of Bommes. A.C. Sauternes, Bordeaux. 9 ha.

Château Camino-Salva (Fr). A vineyard in the commune of Cussac. A.C. Haut-Médoc, Bordeaux. Cru Bourgeois.

Château Camperos (Fr). A vineyard in the commune of Barsac. A.C. Barsac (or Sauternes), Bordeaux. 12 ha. Also Château Mayne-Bert and Château Montalivet.

Château Camponac (Fr). A vineyard in the commune of Pessac. A.C. Médoc,

C

Bordeaux.

Château Cannon (Fr). A vineyard in the commune of Fronsac. A.C. Saint-Émilion, Bordeaux. Also the commune of Saint-Michel-de-Fronsac.

Château Canon (Fr). A vineyard in the commune of Fronsac. A.C. Côtes Canon-Fronsac, Bordeaux. 5 ha.

Château Canon (Fr). Address = 33330 Saint-Émilion. Premier Grand Cru Classé, A.C. Saint-Émilion. Commune = Saint-Émilion. 18 ha. Grape varieties – Cabernet franc, Cabernet sauvignon, Malbec and Merlot.

Château Canon-Boîtard (Fr). The former name for Château Canon-la-Gaffelière in Saint-Émilion.

Château Canon-Chaigneau (Fr). A vineyard in the commune of Néac. A.C. Pomerol, Bordeaux.

Château Canon de Brem (Fr). A vineyard in the commune of Fronsac. A.C. Côtes Canon-Fronsac, Bordeaux.

Château Canon la Gaffelière (Fr). Address = 33330 Saint-Émilion. Grand Cru Classé, A.C. Saint-Émilion. Commune = Saint-Émilion. 19 ha. Grape varieties – Cabernet franc 35%, Cabernet sauvignon 5% and Merlot 60%.

Château Canon-Saint-Émilion (Fr). The name that Château Canon (the Premier Grand Cru Classé Saint-Émilion) is usually sold under.

Château Cantalot (Fr). A vineyard in the commune of St-Pierre-de-Mons. A.C. Graves, Bordeaux. 7 ha. (white).

Château Cantau (Fr). A vineyard in the commune of Illats. A.C. Cérons, Bordeaux. 4 ha.

Château Cantebeau-Couhins (Fr). Once part of Château Couhins. A.C. Graves. Mostly white wines.

Château Cantegril (Fr). A vineyard in the commune of Barsac. A.C. Barsac (or Sauternes), Bordeaux. 14 ha.

Château Cantelaude (Fr). A vineyard in the commune of Macau. A.C. Haut-Médoc, Bordeaux. Cru Bourgeois.

Château Canteloup (Fr). A vineyard in the commune of Fours. A.C. Côtes de Blaye, Bordeaux.

Château Canteloup (Fr). A vineyard in the commune of Saint-Estèphe. A.C. Saint-Estèphe, Bordeaux. 15 ha.

Château Canteloup (Fr). A vineyard in the commune of Yuroc. A.C. Premières Côtes de Bordeaux, Bordeaux.

Château Cantelouve (Fr). A vineyard in the commune of Fronsac. A.C. Côtes de Fronsac, Bordeaux. 10 ha.

Château Cantemerle (Fr). A vineyard in the commune of Saint-Genès-de-Blaye. A.C. Côtes de Blaye, Bordeaux.

Château Cantemerle (Fr). Grand Cru Classé (5th). A.C. Haut-Médoc. Commune = Macau. 21 ha. Grape varieties – Cabernet franc, Cabernet sauvignon, Merlot and Petit verdot. See Château Royal Médoc.

Château Cantenac (Fr). Address = 33330 Saint-Émilion. Grand Cru. A.C. Saint-Émilion. Commune = Saint-Émilion. 14 ha. Grape varieties – Cabernet franc 15%, Cabernet sauvignon 10% and Merlot 75%. Second wine Château Piganeau.

Château Cantenac-Brown (Fr). Address = Cantenac, 33460 Margaux. Grand Cru Classé (2nd). A.C. Margaux. Commune = Cantenac. 32 ha. Grape varieties – Cabernet franc 6%, Cabernet sauvignon 77% and Merlot 17%.

Château Canterane (Fr). Address = Saint-Étienne-de-Lisse, 33330 Saint-Émilion. Grand Cru. A.C. Saint-Émilion. Commune = Saint-Étienne-de-Lisse. 10 ha. Grape varieties – Cabernet franc 20%, Cabernet sauvignon 20% and Merlot 60%.

Château Cantereau (Fr). A vineyard in the commune of Libourne. A.C. Pomerol, Bordeaux.

Château Cantin (Fr). A vineyard in the commune of Saint-Christophe-des-Bardes. A.C. Saint-Émilion, Bordeaux.

Château Canuet (Fr). Address = Margaux 33460. Cru Bourgeois. A.C. Margaux. Commune = Margaux. 11 ha. Grape varieties – Cabernet sauvignon 50% and Merlot 50%.

Château Capbern-Gasqueton (Fr). Cru Grand Bourgeois Exceptionnel. A.C. Saint-Estèphe. 36 ha. Grape varieties – Cabernet franc 20%, Cabernet sauvignon 40% and Merlot 40%.

Château Cap de Fouste (Fr). A vineyard in the A.C. Côtes du Roussillon, south-western France. Grape varieties – Carignan 30%, Grenache 66% and Syrah 4%.

Château Cap-de-Haut (Fr). A vineyard in the commune of Lamarque. A.C. Médoc, Bordeaux. Cru Bourgeois.

Château Cap de Mourlin (Fr). Address = 33330 Saint-Émilion. Grand Cru Classé. A.C. Saint-Émilion. Commune = Saint-Émilion. 15.2 ha. Grape varieties – Cabernet franc 25%, Cabernet sauvignon 12%, Malbec 3% and Merlot 60%.

Château Cap d'Or (Fr). A vineyard in the commune of Saint-Georges-Saint-Émilion. A.C. Saint-Émilion, Bordeaux. 5 ha.

Château Cap du Haut (Fr). A vineyard in the commune of Moulis. A.C. Moulis, Bordeaux. 7 ha.

Château Caperot (Fr). Is part of Château Monbousquet in A.C. Saint-Émilion, Bordeaux.

C

Château Capet-Bégaud (Fr). A vineyard in the commune of Fronsac. A.C. Côtes de Canon-Fronsac, Bordeaux. 3 ha.

Château Capet-Guillier (Fr). Address = Saint-Hippolyte, 33330 Saint-Émilion. Grand Cru. A.C. Saint-Émilion. Commune = Saint-Hippolyte. 15 ha. Grape varieties – Cabernet franc 30%, Cabernet sauvignon 10% and Merlot 60%.

Château Capet Pailhas (Fr). A vineyard in the commune of Saint-Émilion. A.C. Saint-Émilion, Bordeaux.

Château Cap-Léon-Veyrin (Fr). Address = Donissan, Listrac, Médoc, 33480 Castelnau, Médoc. Cru Bourgeois. A.C. Listrac-Médoc. Commune = Listrac. 12 ha. Grape varieties – Cabernet franc, Cabernet sauvignon, Merlot and Petit verdot.

Château Carbonnieux (Fr). Address = 33850 Léognan. Grand Cru Classé. A.C. Graves. Commune = Léognan. 70 ha. Grape varieties – Cabernet franc, Cabernet sauvignon, Malbec, Merlot, Muscadelle, Petit verdot, Sauvignon and Sémillon.

Château Carcanieux (Fr). Address = Terres Hautes de Carcanieux, 33340, Queyrac (Lesparre). Cru Bourgeois. A.C. Médoc. Commune = Queyrac. 25 ha. Grape varieties – Cabernet franc, Cabernet sauvignon and Merlot.

Château Cardinal Villemaurine (Fr). Address = Place du Marcardieu, 33330 Saint-Émilion. Grand Cru. A.C. Saint-Émilion. Commune = Saint-Émilion. 30 ha. Grape varieties – Cabernet 30% and Merlot 70%.

Château Careau-Matras (Fr). Address = 33330 Saint-Émilion. Grand Cru. A.C. Saint-Émilion. Commune = Saint-Émilion. 15 ha. Grape varieties – Cabernet franc 30%, Cabernet sauvignon 3% and Merlot 67%.

Château Carmes-Haut-Brion (Fr). A vineyard in the commune of Pessac. A.C. Graves, Bordeaux. 2 ha. (red).

Château Caronne-Sainte-Gemme (Fr). A vineyard in the commune of Saint Laurent. A.C. Haut-Médoc, Bordeaux. Cru Grand Bourgeois Exceptionnel. Also as Château Caronne-Ste-Gemme. 36 ha.

Château Carras (Gre). A red wine produced from 50% Cabernet franc and 50% Cabernet sauvignon grapes by Domaine Porto Carras.

Château Carruades Lafite (Fr). A vineyard (discontinued in 1967). The second growth of Château Lafite (Pauillac).

Château Carteau (Fr). Address = 33330 Saint-Émilion. Grand Cru. A.C. Saint-Émilion. Commune = Saint-Émilion. 12 ha. Grape varieties – Cabernet franc 30%, Cabernet sauvignon 20% and Merlot 50%.

Château Carteau-Bas-Daugay (Fr). A vineyard in the A.C. Saint-Émilion, Bordeaux. 4 ha.

Château Carteau-Côtes-Daugay (Fr). Address = 33330 Saint-Émilion. Grand Cru. A.C. Saint-Émilion. Commune = Saint-Émilion. 12.5 ha. Grape varieties – Cabernet franc 30%, Cabernet sauvignon 20% and Merlot 50%.

Château Carteau-Pin-de-Fleurs (Fr). A vineyard in the A.C. Saint-Émilion, Bordeaux. 3 ha.

Château Cartier (Can). A noted winery based south of Toronto.

Château Caruel (Fr). A vineyard in the commune of Bourg. A.C. Côtes de Bourg, Bordeaux.

Château Cassagne (Fr). A vineyard in the commune of St-Michel. A.C. Côtes Canon-Fronsac, Bordeaux. 4 ha.

Château Cassat (Fr). A vineyard in the commune of Puisseguin-Saint-Émilion. A.C. Puisseguin-Saint-Émilion, Bordeaux.

Château Cassevert (Fr). A part of Château Grand-Mayne, A.C. Saint-Émilion, Bordeaux.

Château Castel Viaud (Fr). A vineyard in the commune of Saint-Émilion. A.C. Saint-Émilion, Bordeaux.

Château Castéra (Fr). A vineyard in the commune of Cissac. A.C. Médoc, Bordeaux. 47 ha. under vines. Grape varieties – Cabernet franc, Cabernet sauvignon and Merlot 40%. Cru Bourgeois.

Château Castéra (Fr). A vineyard in the commune of St-Germain-d'Esteuil. A.C. Médoc, Bordeaux. 30 ha.

Château Catalas (Fr). A vineyard in the commune of Pujols. A.C. Graves, Bordeaux. 6 ha. (white).

Château Caudiet (Fr). A vineyard in the commune of Loupiac. A.C. Loupiac, Bordeaux. 10 ha.

Château Cauzin (Fr). A vineyard in the A.C. Saint-Émilion, Bordeaux. 4 ha.

Château Cazeau (Fr). A vineyard in the commune of Gomac. A.C. Entre-Deux-Mers, Bordeaux.

Château Cazeaux (Fr). A vineyard in the commune of St-Paul. A.C. Côtes de Blaye, Bordeaux.

Château Cazebonne (Fr). A vineyard in the commune of St-Pierre-de-Mons. A.C. Graves, Bordeaux. 7 ha. (white).

Château Certan-de-May (Fr). A.C. Pomerol. Once part of the estate of Vieux Château Certan. 4 ha.

C

Château Certan-Giraud (Fr). A vineyard in the commune of Pomerol. A.C. Pomerol, Bordeaux. 2 ha.

Château Certan-Marzelle (Fr). A vineyard in the commune of Pomerol. A.C. Pomerol, Bordeaux. 4 ha.

Château Chadène (Fr). A vineyard in the commune of St-Aignan. A.C. Côtes de Fronsac, Bordeaux. 6 ha.

Château Chaillou (Fr). A vineyard in the commune of St-Paul. A.C. Côtes de Blaye, Bordeaux.

Château Chalon (Fr). A.C. Château Chalon, Jura. A Vin Jaune, sold in a Clavelin bottle. Wine is attacked by Flor. Produced from the Savagnin grape.

Château Chambert-Marbuzet (Fr). Address = Saint-Estèphe 33250. Cru Bourgeois. A.C. Saint-Estèphe. Commune = Saint-Estèphe. 30 ha. Grape varieties – Cabernet sauvignon 55% and Merlot 45%.

Château Champion (Fr). Address = Saint-Christophe-des-Bardes, 33330 Saint-Émilion. Grand Cru. A.C. Saint-Émilion. Commune = Saint-Christophe-des-Bardes. Second wine of Château Vieux Grand Faurie. 5 ha.

Château Chante Alouette (Fr). A vineyard in the A.C. Côtes de Blaye, Bordeaux.

Château Chante-Alouette (Fr). A vineyard in the A.C. Saint-Émilion, Bordeaux. 6 ha.

Château Chantecaille (Fr). A vineyard in the A.C. Saint-Émilion, Bordeaux. 3 ha.

Château Chantegrive (Fr). A.C. Graves. 60 ha. Grape varieties – Cabernet franc, Cabernet sauvignon, Merlot, Muscadelle, Sauvignon and Sémillon. 5 ha.

Château Chantegrive (Fr). A vineyard in the commune of Saint-Émilion. A.C. Saint-Émilion, Bordeaux.

Château Chantelet (Fr). Is part of Château Larques, A.C. Saint-Émilion, Bordeaux.

Château Chanteloisseau (Fr). Address = 33210 Langon. A.C. Graves. Commune = Langon. 20 ha. Grape varieties – Cabernet sauvignon and Sauvignon.

Château Chantelys (Fr). A vineyard in the commune of Prignac. A.C. Médoc, Bordeaux. 4 ha.

Château Chapelle Madelaine (Fr). Address = 33330 Saint-Émilion. Grand Cru Classé. A.C. Saint-Émilion. Commune = Saint-Émilion. 1 ha.

Château Charmail (Fr). A vineyard in the commune of Saint-Seurin-de-Cadourne. A.C. Saint-Estèphe, Bordeaux. Cru Bourgeois. 12 ha.

Château Charron (Fr). A vineyard in the commune of St-Martin. A.C. Côtes de Blaye, Bordeaux. 30 ha. Grape varieties – Sauvignon and Sémillon.

Château Chasselauds (Fr). A vineyard in the commune of Cartelègue. A.C. Côtes de Blaye, Bordeaux.

Château Chasse-Spleen (Fr). Cru Grand Bourgeois Exceptionnel. A.C. Moulis. 42 ha. Grape varieties – Cabernet sauvignon, Merlot and Petit verdot.

Château Chatain (Fr). A vineyard in the commune of Néac. A.C. Pomerol, Bordeaux.

Château Châteaufort de Vauban (Fr). A vineyard in the commune of Cussac-Fort-Médoc. A.C. Haut-Médoc, Bordeaux. 3 ha.

Château Chauvin (Fr). Address = 137, Rue Doumer, Libourne 33500. Grand Cru Classé. A.C. Saint-Émilion. Commune = Saint-Émilion. 13 ha. Grape varieties – Cabernet franc 30%, Cabernet sauvignon 10% and Merlot 60%.

Château Chaviran (Fr). A vineyard in the commune of Martillac. A.C. Graves, Bordeaux. 4 ha. (red).

Château Chayne (Fr). A vineyard in the A.C. Côtes de Bergerac. Address = 17 Rue Millet, 24100 Bergerac. (red and white).

Château Chêne Liège (Fr). A vineyard in the commune of Pomerol. A.C. Pomerol, Bordeaux.

Château Chêne Vieux (Fr). A vineyard in the commune of Puisseguin-Saint-Émilion. A.C. Puisseguin-Saint-Émilion, Bordeaux. 8 ha.

Château Cheval Blanc (Fr). Address = 33330 Saint-Émilion. Premier Grand Cru Classé (A). A.C. Saint-Émilion. Commune = Saint-Émilion. 41 ha. Grape varieties – Cabernet franc, Malbec and Merlot.

Château Cheval-Brun (Fr). A vineyard in the A.C. Saint-Émilion, Bordeaux. 5 ha.

Château Chevalier (USA). A winery near St. Helena in the Napa Valley, California. 25 ha. Produces table wines from the Cabernet sauvignon, Chardonnay and Johannisberg riesling grapes.

Château Chevaliers d'Ars (Fr). A wine co-operative in the commune of Arcins. A.C. Haut-Médoc, Bordeaux. 25 ha.

Château Cheval Noir (Fr). A vineyard in the commune of Saint-Émilion. A.C. Saint-Émilion, Bordeaux. Grape varieties – Cabernet franc, Cabernet sauvignon and Merlot. 3 ha.

Château Chevrol Bel-Air (Fr). A vineyard in the commune of Néac. A.C. Pomerol, Bordeaux.

Château Chicane (Fr). A vineyard in the

C

commune of Toulenne. A.C. Graves, Bordeaux. 3 ha. (red and white).
Château Chichoye (Fr). A vineyard in the commune of Loupiac. A.C. Loupiac, Bordeaux. 2 ha.
Château Cissac (Fr). Address = 33250 Pauillac. Cru Grand Bourgeois Exceptionnel. A.C. Haut-Médoc. Commune = Cissac. Grape varieties – Cabernet, Merlot and Petit verdot. 26 ha.
Château Citran (Fr). Address = 33480 Avensac. Cru Grand Bourgeois Exceptionnel. A.C. Haut-Médoc. Commune = Avensan. 90 ha. Grape varieties – Cabernet sauvignon 40% and Merlot 60%
Château Clairac (Fr). A vineyard in the A.C. Côtes de Blaye, Bordeaux.
Château Clairfont (Fr). A vineyard in the commune of Margaux. A.C. Margaux, Bordeaux. 8 ha.
Château Clare (Austr). A vineyard estate in Clare-Watervale, South Australia. Owned by Taylors.
Château Clarke (Fr). Address = 33480 Listrac-Médoc. Cru Bourgeois. A.C. Listrac. Commune = Listrac. 170 ha. Grape varieties – Cabernet franc, Cabernet sauvignon, Merlot and Petit verdot.
Château Clauss (Gre). A red wine produced by the Achaïa Clauss Winery of Patras. Made with the Mavroutis grape.
Château Clauzet (Fr). A vineyard in the commune of Saint-Estèphe. A.C. Saint-Estèphe, Bordeaux. 3 ha.
Château Clerc Milon (Fr). Address = 33250 Pauillac. Grand Cru Classé (5th). A.C. Pauillac. Commune = Pauillac. 30 ha. Grape varieties – Cabernet franc, Cabernet sauvignon and Merlot.
Château Climens (Fr). Premier Grand Cru. A.C. Barsac. (or Sauternes). Commune = Barsac. 32 ha. Grape variety – Sémillon 100%
Château Clinet (Fr). A vineyard in the commune of Pomerol. A.C. Pomerol, Bordeaux. 6 ha.
Château Clos d'Amières (Fr). A vineyard in the commune of Cartelègue. A.C. Côtes de Blaye, Bordeaux.
Château Clos de Lacapère (Fr). A vineyard in the commune of Landiras. A.C. Graves, Bordeaux. 2 ha. (white).
Château Clos des Jacobins (Fr). A.C. Saint-Émilion. See Clos des Jacobins.
Château Clos Figeac (Fr). Address = 33330 Saint-Émilion. Grand Cru. A.C. Saint-Émilion. Commune = Saint-Émilion. 5 ha. Grape varieties – Bouchet 25%, Cabernet sauvignon 15% and Merlot 60%.
Château Clos Fourtet (Fr). Address = 33330 Saint-Émilion. A.C. Saint-Émilion. Commune = Saint-Émilion.

Château Clos Haut-Peyraguey (Fr). A vineyard in the commune of Bommes. A.C. Sauternes, Bordeaux. Address = 33210 Langon.
Château Closiot (Fr). A vineyard in the commune of Barsac. A.C. Barsac (or Sauternes), Bordeaux. 5 ha.
Château Clos Jean (Fr). A vineyard in the commune of Loupiac. A.C. Loupiac, Bordeaux. 12 ha.
Château Clos l'Église (Fr). A vineyard in the commune of Pomerol. A.C. Pomerol, Bordeaux.
Château Clos René (Fr). A vineyard in the commune of Pomerol. A.C. Pomerol, Bordeaux.
Château Clotte (Fr). Address = 33330 Saint-Émilion. Grand Cru Classé. A.C. Saint-Émilion. Commune = Saint-Émilion.
Château Colbert (Fr). A vineyard in the commune of Comps. A.C. Côtes de Bourg, Bordeaux.
Château Colombey (Fr). A vineyard in the A.C. Entre-Deux-Mers, Bordeaux. (white).
Château Colombier Monpelou (Fr). Address = 33250 Pauillac. Cru Grand Bourgeois. A.C. Pauillac. Commune = Pauillac. 14 ha. Grape varieties – Cabernet franc, Cabernet sauvignon, Merlot and Petit verdot.
Château Commarque (Fr). A vineyard in the commune of Sauternes. A.C. Sauternes, Bordeaux. 4 ha.
Château Comte des Cordes (Fr). Address = 33330 Saint-Émilion. Commune = Saint-Émilion. Second wine of Château Fonrazade. Grand Cru. Saint-Émilion.
Château Conseillant (Fr). A vineyard in the commune of Labarde. A.C. Médoc, Bordeaux.
Château Conseillante (Fr). A vineyard in the commune of Pomerol. A.C. Pomerol, Bordeaux.
Château Constant-Trois-Moulins (Fr). A vineyard in the commune of Macau. A.C. Haut-Médoc, Bordeaux. Cru Bourgeois.
Château Corbin (Fr). Address = 33330 Saint-Émilion. Grand Cru. A.C. Saint-Émilion. Commune = Montagne-Saint-Émilion. 13 ha.
Château Corbin-Michotte (Fr). Address = 33330 Saint-Émilion. Grand Cru Classé. A.C. Saint-Émilion. Commune = Saint-Émilion. 7.6 ha. Grape varieties – Cabernet franc 30%, Cabernet sauvignon 5% and Merlot 65%.
Château Corconnac (Fr). A vineyard in the commune of Saint Laurent. A.C. Médoc, Bordeaux. Cru Bourgeois.
Château Cormeil-Figeac (Fr). Address = 33330 Saint-Émilion. Grand Cru Classé.

A.C. Saint-Émilion. Commune = Saint-Émilion. 20 ha. Grape varieties – Bouchet 30% and Merlot 70%. Second wine is Château Magnan-Figeac. Grand Cru. Saint-Émilion.

Château Cormey Figeac (Fr). A vineyard in the commune of Saint-Émilion. A.C. Saint-Émilion. 10 ha.

Château Corton Grancey (Fr). Grand Cru. A.C. Corton. Côte de Beaune, Burgundy. Owned by Louis Latour. Is allowed to sell his wines under this name as he had done so before A.C. laws were introduced.

Château Cos d'Estournel (Fr). Address = Saint-Estèphe 33250 Pauillac. Grand Cru Classé (2nd). A.C. Saint-Estèphe. Commune = Saint-Estèphe. 60 ha. Grape varieties – Cabernet sauvignon 60% and Merlot 40%

Château Cos-Labory (Fr). Address = Saint-Estèphe, 33250 Pauillac. Grand Cru Classé (5th). A.C. Saint-Estèphe. Commune = Saint-Estèphe. 27 ha. Grape varieties – Cabernet franc, Cabernet sauvignon, Merlot and Petit verdot.

Château Côte-Baleau (Fr). Address = 33330 Saint-Émilion. Grand Cru. A.C. Saint-Émilion. Commune = Saint-Émilion. 17 ha. Grape varieties – Cabernet franc 16%, Cabernet sauvignon 16% and Merlot 66%.

Château Côte de Bonde (Fr). A vineyard in the commune of Montagne-Saint-Émilion. A.C. Saint-Émilion, Bordeaux. 7 ha.

Château Côte de Rol-Valentin (Fr). A vineyard in the A.C. Saint-Émilion, Bordeaux. 3 ha.

Château Côte-Mignon-la-Gaffelière (Fr). A vineyard in the A.C. Saint-Émilion, Bordeaux. 1 ha.

Château Côtes Bernateau (Fr). Address = Saint-Étienne-de-Lisse, 33330 Saint-Émilion. Grand Cru. A.C. Saint-Émilion. Commune = Saint-Étienne-de-Lisse. 18 ha. Grape varieties – Bouchet 25%, Cabernet sauvignon 6%, Merlot 65% and Pressac 4%.

Château Côtes de Blaignan [Cru Hontane] (Fr). A vineyard in the commune of Blaignan. A.C. Médoc, Bordeaux. 5 ha.

Château Cottière (Fr). A vineyard in the commune of Teuillac. A.C. Côtes de Bourg, Bordeaux.

Château Coubet (Fr). A vineyard in the A.C. Côtes de Bourg, Bordeaux.

Château Coucy (Fr). A vineyard in the commune of Montagne-Saint-Émilion. A.C. Saint-Émilion, Bordeaux. 11 ha.

Château Coudert (Fr). A vineyard in the A.C. Saint-Émilion, Bordeaux. 3 ha.

Château Coudert-Pelletan (Fr). Address = Saint-Christophe-des-Bardes, 33330 Saint-Émilion. Grand Cru. A.C. Saint-Émilion. Commune = Saint-Christophe-des-Bardes. 6 ha. Grape varieties – Cabernet franc 15%, Cabernet sauvignon 15%, Malbec 10% and Merlot 60%.

Château Coufran (Fr). Address = St-Seurin-de-Cadourne, 33250 Pauillac. Cru Grand Bourgeois. A.C. Haut-Médoc. Commune = St-Seurin-de-Cadourne. 64 ha. Grape varieties – Cabernet sauvignon 15% and Merlot 85%.

Château Couhins-Lurton (Fr). Address = Léognan 33850. Grand Cru Classé. A.C. Graves. Commune = Villenave d'Ornon. 1.75 ha. Grape variety – Sauvignon blanc.

Château Coullac (Fr). A vineyard in the commune of Sainte-Croix-du-Mont. A.C. Sainte-Croix-du-Mont, Bordeaux. 5 ha.

Château Couloumet (Fr). A vineyard in the commune of Loupiac. A.C. Loupiac, Bordeaux. 5 ha.

Château Couperie (Fr). A vineyard in the commune of Saint-Émilion. A.C. Saint-Émilion, Bordeaux.

Château Courant (Fr). A vineyard in the commune of Arcins. A.C. Médoc, Bordeaux.

Château Courant-Barrow (Fr). A vineyard in the commune of Arcins. A.C. Médoc, Bordeaux. Cru Bourgeois.

Château Court les Muts (Fr). A vineyard in the A.C. Bergerac. (white).

Château Coustet (Fr). A vineyard in the commune of Barsac. A.C. Barsac (or Sauternes), Bordeaux. 6 ha.

Château Coustolle (Fr). A vineyard in the commune of Fronsac. A.C. Côtes Canon-Fronsac, Bordeaux. 12 ha.

Château Coutelin-Merville (Fr). A vineyard in the commune of Saint-Estèphe. A.C. Saint-Estèphe, Bordeaux. 11 ha.

Château Coutet (Fr). A vineyard in the commune of Barsac. A.C. Barsac (or Sauternes), Bordeaux. 70 ha. Grape varieties – Muscadelle 10%, Sauvignon 20% and Sémillon 70%. A Premier Grand Cru. Separated from Château d'Yquem in 1922.

Château Coutet (Fr). Address = 33330 Saint-Émilion. Grand Cru. A.C. Saint-Émilion. 11 ha. Grape varieties – Bouchet 45%, Cabernet sauvignon 5%, Malbec 3%, Merlot 45% and Pressac 2%.

Château Couvent-des-Jacobins (Fr). See Couvent-des-Jacobins.

Château Crabitey (Fr). A vineyard in the

commune of Portets. A.C. Graves, Bordeaux. 15 ha. (red and white).

Château Cravignac (Fr). Address = 33330 Saint-Émilion. A.C. Saint-Émilion. Commune = Saint-Émilion. 8 ha. Grape varieties – Cabernet franc 35% and Merlot 65%.

Château Cremade (Fr). An A.C. wine based in Le Tholonet.

Château Croix-de-Justice (Fr). A vineyard in the commune of Puisseguin-Saint-Émilion. A.C. Saint-Émilion. Bordeaux. 5 ha.

Château Croix-du-Merle (Fr). A vineyard in the A.C. Saint-Émilion, Bordeaux. 3 ha.

Château Croix-Figeac (Fr). A vineyard in the A.C. Saint-Émilion, Bordeaux. 3 ha.

Château Croix-Peyblanquet (Fr). A vineyard in the A.C. Saint-Émilion, Bordeaux. 4 ha.

Château Croix-Villemaurine (Fr). A vineyard in the A.C. Saint-Émilion, Bordeaux. 1 ha.

Château Croizet-Bages (Fr). Grand Cru Classé (5th). A.C. Pauillac. Commune = Pauillac. 25 ha. Grape varieties – Cabernet franc, Cabernet sauvignon and Merlot.

Château Croque-Michotte (Fr). Address = 33330 Saint-Émilion. Grand Cru Classé. A.C. Saint-Émilion. Commune = Saint-Émilion. 14 ha. Grape varieties – Cabernet franc 10%, Cabernet sauvignon 10% and Merlot 80%.

Château Croûte-Charlus (Fr). A vineyard in the commune of Bourg. A.C. Côtes de Bourg, Bordeaux. Cru Bourgeois.

Château Croûte-Mallard (Fr). A vineyard in the commune of Bourg. A.C. Côtes de Bourg, Bordeaux.

Château Cru du Gravier (Fr). A vineyard in the commune of Arsac. A.C. Haut-Médoc, Bordeaux. 4 ha.

Château Cruscaut (Fr). A vineyard in the commune of Saint Laurent. A.C. Médoc, Bordeaux. Cru Bourgeois.

Château Crusquet de Lagarcie (Fr). A vineyard in the commune of Cars. A.C. Côtes de Blaye, Bordeaux.

Château Crusquet Sabourin (Fr). A vineyard in the commune of Cars. A.C. Côtes de Blaye, Bordeaux.

Château Cruzeau (Fr). A vineyard in the commune of St-Médard-d'Eyrans. A.C. Graves, Bordeaux. 47 ha. (red and white).

Château Cup (Cup). 1 bottle red Claret, 1 bottle soda water, 1 measure Cognac, 1 measure Cointreau, 2 dashes Gomme syrup. Stir over ice in a mixing glass. Dress with sliced lemon and cucumber.

Château Curé-Bon-la-Madeleine (Fr). Address = 33330 Saint-Émilion. Grand Cru

Classé, A.C. Saint-Émilion. Commune = Saint-Émilion. 5 ha. Grape varieties – Cabernet franc 10%, Malbec 10% and Merlot 80%.

Château Cusseau (Fr). A vineyard in the commune of Macau. A.C. Haut-Médoc, Bordeaux. Cru Bourgeois.

Château d'Aganac (Fr). A vineyard in the commune of Ludon. A.C. Haut-Médoc, Bordeaux. 30 ha. Grape varieties – Cabernet franc, Cabernet sauvignon and Merlot.

Château d'Agassac (Fr). A vineyard in the commune of Ludon. A.C. Haut-Médoc, Bordeaux. 34.8 ha. Cru Grand Bourgeois Exceptionnel.

Château d'Anchon (Arg). The brand-name of a dry white wine.

Château d'Angludet (Fr). Address = 33460 Cantenac. Cru Grand Bourgeois Exceptionnel. A.C. Margaux Commune = Cantenac. 75 ha. Grape varieties – Cabernet franc, Cabernet sauvignon, Merlot and Petit verdot.

Château d'Anice (Fr). A vineyard in the commune of Podensac. A.C. Cérons, Bordeaux. 12 ha.

Château d'Anseillan (Fr). A vineyard in the commune of Pauillac. A.C. Haut-Médoc, Bordeaux. Cru Bourgeois.

Château d'Arbanats (Fr). A vineyard in the commune of Arbanats. A.C. Graves, Bordeaux. 6 ha. (white).

Château d'Arboras (Fr). A vineyard in the V.D.Q.S. Saturnin. (red).

Château d'Arche (Fr). Address = 33290 Ludon, Médoc. A.C. Haut-Médoc. Commune = Ludon. 9 ha. Grape varieties – Cabernet sauvignon, Malbec, Merlot and Petit verdot.

Château d'Arche (Fr). Grand Cru (2nd). A.C. Sauternes. Commune = Sauternes. Grape varieties – Sauvignon 15%, Sémillon 80% and Muscadelle 5%

Château d'Arche-Lafaurie (Fr). Grand Cru Classé (2nd). A.C. Sauternes. Commune = Sauternes. 19 ha.

Château d'Arche Pugneau (Fr). A vineyard in the commune of Preignac. A.C. Sauternes, Bordeaux.

Château d'Arches (Fr). A vineyard in the commune of Ludon. A.C. Haut-Médoc, Bordeaux. 4 ha.

Château d'Arches (Fr). A vineyard in the commune of Sauternes. A.C. Sauternes, Bordeaux. 15 ha. Also Château Lamothe.

Château d'Arche-Vimeney (Fr). A vineyard in the commune of Sauternes. A.C. Sauternes, Bordeaux. 5 ha. Grand Cru Classé (2nd).

Château d'Arcins (Fr). A vineyard in the commune of Arcins. A.C. Haut-Médoc, Bordeaux. Cru Bourgeois.

C

Château d'Ardolou (Fr). A vineyard in the A.C. Corbières. Address = Ribaute, 31200 Lézignan-Corbières.

Château d'Arlay (Fr). A vineyard in the A.C. Jura. Produces the famous Vin Jaune (Vin de paille).

Château d'Armajan-des-Ormes (Fr). A vineyard in the commune of Preignac. A.C. Sauternes, Bordeaux. 7 ha.

Château d'Armens (Fr). A.C. Saint-Émilion. Second wine of Château Bonnet. Grand Cru. Saint-Émilion.

Château d'Arnauld (Fr). A vineyard in the commune of Arcins. A.C. Médoc, Bordeaux. Cru Bourgeois.

Château d'Arpayé (Fr). A.C. Fleurie. Cru Beaujolais-Villages, Burgundy. 15 ha. Address = 69820 Fleurie.

Château d'Arsac (Fr). A vineyard in the commune of Arsac. A.C. Médoc, Bordeaux. Cru Bourgeois.

Château d'Arthus (Fr). A vineyard in the A.C. Saint-Émilion, Bordeaux. 4 ha.

Château Dassault (Fr). Address = 33330 Saint-Émilion. Grand Cru Classé. A.C. Saint-Émilion. Commune = Saint-Émilion. 30 ha. Grape varieties – Cabernet franc 20%, Cabernet sauvignon 10% and Merlot 70%.

Château d'Augey (Fr). A vineyard in the commune of Bommes. A.C. Sauternes, Bordeaux.

Château Dauphine Rondillon (Fr). A vineyard in the commune of Loupiac. A.C. Loupiac, Bordeaux. 15 ha.

Château d'Auros (Fr). A vineyard in the A.C. Graves, Bordeaux.

Château Dauzac (Fr). Address = Labarde, Margaux 33460. Grand Cru Classé (5th). A.C. Margaux. Commune = Margaux. 40 ha. Grape varieties – Cabernet franc, Cabernet sauvignon, Merlot and Petit verdot.

Château d'Avallrich (Fr). A vineyard in the Côtes du Roussillon, south-western France. Address = 33270 Floirac.

Château David (Fr). Address = Vensac 33590 St. Vivien de Médoc. A.C. Médoc. Commune = Vensac. 10 ha. Grape varieties – Cabernet sauvignon 75% and Merlot 25%

Château d'Ay (Fr). The Château of the Grand Marque Champagne house of Ayala.

Château de Barbe (Fr). A vineyard in the commune of Villeneuve. A.C. Côtes de Bourg, Bordeaux. 61.5 ha.

Château de Bastard (Fr). A vineyard in the commune of Barsac. A.C. Barsac (or Sauternes), Bordeaux.

Château de Beaucastel (Fr). A vineyard in the A.C. Châteauneuf-du-Pape, Rhône. 72 ha.

Château de Beaulieu (Fr). A.C. Bordeaux rouge. Address = 33540 Sauveterre-de-Guyenne, Bordeaux.

Château de Beaulieu (Fr). An A.C. Cabernet d'Anjou rosé from the Anjou-Saumur, Loire.

Château de Beaulieu (Fr). A V.D.Q.S. red wine from the Coteaux du Languedoc, south-western France.

Château de Beaulon (Fr). A noted Pineau des Charentes from the Cognac region, western France.

Château de Beaune (Fr). The name for the cellars of négociants-éleveurs Bouchard Père et Fils, Burgundy.

Château de Beauregard (Fr). A.C. Bordeaux blanc.

Château de Bel Air (Fr). A vineyard in the commune of Lalande de Pomerol. A.C. Pomerol, Bordeaux.

Château de Bellet (Fr). A vineyard in the A.C. Bellet, Provence, south-eastern France. One of only two growers.

Château de Bellevue (Fr). A vineyard in the A.C. Morgon. Cru Beaujolais-Villages, Burgundy. Address = Côte de Py, Morgon.

Château de Bellevue (Fr). A vineyard in the commune of Lussac-Saint-Émilion. A.C. Lussac-Saint-Émilion, Bordeaux.

Château de Bensée (Fr). A vineyard in the A.C. Médoc, Bordeaux.

Château de Bertranon (Fr). A vineyard in the commune of Sainte-Croix-du-Mont. A.C. Sainte-Croix-du-Mont, Bordeaux. 2 ha.

Château de Berzé (Fr). A vineyard in the Mâcon, Burgundy. Produces A.C. Mâcon Supérieur.

Château de Beychade (Fr). A vineyard in the A.C. Côtes de Bourg, Bordeaux.

Château de Blissa (Fr). A vineyard in the commune of Bayon. A.C. Côtes de Bourg, Bordeaux.

Château de Blomac (Fr). A vineyard in the V.D.Q.S. Minervois. Address = 11700 Capendu. (red, rosé and white).

Château de Bluizard (Fr). A vineyard in the A.C. Beaujolais-Villages, Burgundy.

Château de Bousquet (Fr). A vineyard in the commune of Bourg. A.C. Côtes de Bourg, Bordeaux.

Château de Breuil (Fr). A vineyard in the A.C. Coteaux du Layon, Anjou-Saumur, Loire.

Château de Breuilh (Fr). A vineyard in the commune of Cissac. A.C. Médoc, Bordeaux. Cru Bourgeois.

Château de Brézé (Fr). A vineyard in the A.C. Saumur, Anjou-Saumur, Loire. Address = 19260 Brézé.

Château de Brochon (Fr). A vineyard in the A.C. Haut-Médoc, Bordeaux.

C

Château de Brugnac (Fr). A.C. Bordeaux Supérieur.

Château de Budos (Fr). A vineyard in the commune of Budos. A.C. Graves, Bordeaux. 9 ha. (red).

Château de Bussy (Fr). A vineyard in the A.C. Beaujolais-Villages, Burgundy.

Château de By (Fr). Address = Bégadan 33340 Lesparre. Cru Bourgeois. A.C. Médoc. Commune = Bégadan. 30 ha. Grape varieties – Cabernet franc 10%, Cabernet sauvignon 30%, Merlot 40% and Petit verdot 20%.

Château de Cabriac (Fr). A vineyard in the A.C. Corbières, Languedoc, south-western France.

Château de Cach (Fr). A vineyard in the commune of Saint Laurent. A.C. Médoc, Bordeaux. Cru Bourgeois.

Château de Cadillac (Fr). A.C. Bordeaux.

Château de Caiz (Fr). A vineyard in the A.C. Cahors, south-western France. Address = Luzech, Lot.

Château de Camensac (Fr). See Château Camensac.

Château de Cantenac Prieuré (Fr). See Château Prieuré Lichine.

Château de Caraguilhes (Fr). A vineyard in the A.C. Corbières, south-western France. Address = St Laurent de la Cabrerisse, 11220 Legrasse.

Château de Cardaillan (Fr). Address = Toulenne 33210 Langon. A.C. Graves. Commune = Toulenne. 50 ha. Grape varieties – Cabernet sauvignon 80%, Merlot 20%, Sauvignon 90% and Sémillon 10%

Château de Carignan (Fr). A vineyard in the commune of Carignan. A.C. Premières Côtes de Bordeaux. Address = 33360 Latresne. 110 ha. Grape varieties – Cabernet franc 25%, Merlot 50% and Sauvignon 25%.

Château de Carles (Fr). A vineyard in the commune of Barsac. A.C. Barsac (or Sauternes), Bordeaux. 6 ha.

Château de Carles (Fr). A vineyard in the commune of Fronsac. A.C. Côtes de Fronsac, Bordeaux.

Château de Carrasset (Fr). A vineyard in the commune of Lamarque. A.C. Médoc, Bordeaux. Cru Bourgeois.

Château de Castegens (Fr). A vineyard in the A.C. Côtes de Castillon, Bordeaux. Address = Belves de Castillon.

Château de Cayrou (Fr). A vineyard in the A.C. Cahors, south-western France. Grape varieties – Auxerrois, Jurançon, Merlot and Tannat.

Château de Cérons (Fr). A vineyard in the commune of Cérons. A.C. Cérons, Bordeaux. 15 ha. Grape varieties – Sauvignon and Sémillon.

Château de Chaintres (Fr). A vineyard in the A.C. Saumur-Champigny, Anjou-Saumur, Loire. Address = Dampierre-sur-Loire. (red, rosé and white).

Château de Chambert (Fr). A vineyard in the A.C. Cahors, south-western France.

Château de Chamboureau (Fr). A vineyard in the A.C. Savennières. Anjou-Saumur, Loire.

Château de Champagny (Fr). A V.D.Q.S. vineyard in the Côtes Roannaises, western France. Grape variety – Gamay. (red and rosé).

Château de Chantegrive (Fr). Address = Domaine de Chantegrive, Podensac 33720. A.C. Graves. Commune = Podensac. 60 ha. Grape varieties – Cabernet franc, Cabernet sauvignon, Merlot, Muscadelle, Sauvignon and Sémillon.

Château de Chasseloir (Fr). A vineyard in the A.C. Muscadet de Sèvre et Maine, Pays Nantais, Loire. Address = 44690 St-Fiacre-sur-Maine.

Château de Chatagnéréaz (Switz). A white wine produced in Rolle, La Côte, western Switzerland by Schenk.

Château de Chenbonceau (Fr). A vineyard in the A.C. Touraine, Loire. Address = Chenonceau, Touraine. (white and sparkling [méthode champenoise] wines).

Château de Clairfont (Fr). The second wine of Château Prieuré-Lichine, Grand Cru Classé (4th) Margaux, Bordeaux.

Château de Clary (Fr). A vineyard in the A.C. Côtes du Rhône, southern France.

Château de Cognac (Fr). The Château headquarters of the Otard Cognac company in Cognac, western France.

Château de Côme (Fr). A vineyard in the commune of Saint-Estèphe. A.C. Saint-Estèphe, Bordeaux. 2 ha.

Château de Cornneilla (Fr). A V.D.Q.S. red wine from the Côtes du Roussillon, south-western France.

Château de Coulinats (Fr). A vineyard in the commune of Sainte-Croix-du-Mont. A.C. Sainte-Croix-du-Mont, Bordeaux. 3 ha.

Château de Courvoisier (Fr). The headquarters of Courvoisier Cognac in Jarnac, Charente.

Château de Coye (Fr). A vineyard in the commune of Sauternes. A.C. Sauternes, Bordeaux. 1 ha.

Château de Crain (Fr). A vineyard in the A.C. Entre-Deux-Mers, Bordeaux. (white wine).

Château de Cremat (Fr). A vineyard in the A.C. Bellet, Provence, south-eastern France. One of only two growers.

C

Château de Cruzeau (Fr). Address = Château-la Louvière, Léognan 33850. A.C. Graves. Commune = Léognan 50 ha. Grape varieties – Cabernet sauvignon, Merlot and Sauvignon blanc.

Château de Cujac (Fr). A vineyard in the commune of Saint-Aubin. A.C. Médoc, Bordeaux. Cru Bourgeois.

Château de Dauzay (Fr). A vineyard in the A.C. Chinon, Anjou-Saumur, Loire.

Château de Dreiborn (Lux). A sparkling wine made by the méthode champenoise by St. Martin.

Château de Fargues (Fr). A vineyard in the commune of Fargues. A.C. Sauternes, Bordeaux. 7 ha.

Château de Fayolle (Fr). A vineyard in the A.C. Bergerac. (red and white).

Château de Ferrand (Fr). Address = Saint-Hippolyte, 33330 Saint-Émilion. Grand Cru. A.C. Saint-Émilion. Commune = Saint-Émilion. 28 ha. Grape varieties – Cabernet franc 15%, Cabernet sauvignon 15% and Merlot 70%.

Château de Fesle (Fr). A vineyard in the A.C. Bonnezeaux, Anjou-Saumur, Loire, Address = 49380 Thouarcé, Loire.

Château de Fieuzal (Fr). Address = Au Bourg, Léognan 33850. Grand Cru Classé. A.C. Graves. Commune = Léognan. 16 ha. Grape varieties – Cabernet sauvignon, Merlot, Petit verdot, Sauvignon and Sémillon.

Château de Fines Roches (Fr). A vineyard in the A.C. Châteauneuf-du-Pape, southern France. 46 ha.

Château de Fleurie (Fr). A vineyard in the A.C. Fleurie Cru Beaujolais-Villages, Burgundy.

Château de Fonscolombe (Fr). Address = 13610 Le-Puy-Sainte-Réparde, Aix-en-Provence. A.C. Coteaux d'Aix-en-Provence.

Château de Fontpinot Grande Champagne (Fr). A fine Cognac produced by Frapin et Cie in Cognac.

Château de Fouilloux (Fr). A vineyard in the Cru Beaujolais-Villages of Brouilly in Burgundy. Produced by Pasquier-Desvignes.

Château de Fourques (Fr). A vineyard in the A.C. Coteaux du Languedoc, south-western France. Address = 34980 Saint-Gely-du-Fesc.

Château de France (Fr). Address = 33850 Léognan. A.C. Graves. Commune = Léognan. 31 ha. Grape varieties – Cabernet 50%, Merlot 50%, Muscadelle, Sauvignon and Sémillon.

Château de Gasq (Fr). The old name for Château Palmer Grand Cru Classé (3rd). A.C. Margaux.

Château d'Égmont (Fr). A vineyard in the commune of Ludon. A.C. Haut-Médoc, Bordeaux. Cru Bourgeois.

Château de Gorsse (Fr). A vineyard in the commune of Margaux. A.C. Margaux, Bordeaux. Cru Bourgeois.

Château de Gourgazaud (Fr). A vineyard in the V.D.Q.S. Minervois, south-eastern France. Address = 34210 La Livinière, Minervois. (red).

Château de Grand Pré (Fr). A vineyard in the A.C. Fleurie Cru Beaujolais-Villages, Burgundy.

Château de Grissac (Fr). A vineyard in the commune of Prignac-Marcamps. A.C. Côtes de Bourg, Bordeaux.

Château de Guezes (Fr). A vineyard in the A.C. Côtes de Buzet, south-western France. (red).

Château de Haut-Gravat (Fr). A vineyard in the commune of Bourg. A.C. Côtes de Bourg, Bordeaux.

Château de Hilde (Fr). A vineyard in the commune of Bègles. A.C. Graves de Bordeaux, Bordeaux.

Château de Jau (Fr). A vineyard in the A.C. Muscat de Rivesaltes, southern France. Address = 66600 Cases-de-Pène. Also produces A.C. Côtes du Roussillon.

Château de Jaulin (Fr). See Castay Frères.

Château de Javernand (Fr). A vineyard in the Cru Beaujolais-Villages of Chiroubles in Burgundy. Address = 69115 Chiroubles.

Château de Junca (Fr). Address = Saint-Sauveur de Médoc, 33250. A.C. Haut-Médoc. Commune = Saint-Sauveur de Médoc. 9 ha. Grape varieties – Cabernet sauvignon 50%, Malbec 3% and Merlot 47%

Château de Labarde (Fr). The name given to the second wine of Château Dauzac. Also the former name of the Château.

Château de la Barde (Fr). Address = Saint Laurent des Combes, 33330 Saint-Émilion. Grand Cru. A.C. Saint Émilion. Commune = Saint Laurent des Combes. 3.65 ha. Grape varieties – Cabernet franc 20%, Cabernet sauvignon 10% and Merlot 70%.

Château de Labat (Fr). A vineyard in the commune of Saint Laurent. A.C. Haut-Médoc, Bordeaux. Cru Bourgeois.

Château de Labaude (Fr). Armagnac producer. Address = GFA de Labaude, Sorbets 32110 Nogaro. 100 ha. in Bas Armagnac.

Château de l'Abbaye (Fr). A vineyard in the A.C. Fleurie Cru Beaujolais-Villages, Burgundy.

Château de l'Abbé-Gorsse-de-Gorsse (Fr). A vineyard in the commune of Margaux. A.C. Haut-Médoc, Bordeaux.

Cru Bourgeois.

Château de Labégorce (Fr). A vineyard in the commune of Margaux. A.C. Margaux, Bordeaux. Cru Bourgeois.

Château de la Bidière (Fr). A vineyard in the A.C. Muscadet de Sèvre et Maine, Pays Nantais, Loire.

Château de la Bigotière (Fr). A vineyard in the A.C. Muscadet de Sèvre et Maine, Pays Nantais, Loire.

Château de la Bizolière (Fr). A vineyard in the A.C. Savennières, Anjou-Saumur, Loire.

Château de la Brède (Fr). A vineyard in the commune of La Brède. A.C. Graves, Bordeaux. 6 ha. (white).

Château de la Bridane (Fr). A vineyard in the commune of Saint-Julien. A.C. Médoc, Bordeaux. Grape variety – Cabernet sauvignon 100%. Cru Bourgeois.

Château de Lacarelle (Fr). A large vineyard in the A.C. Beaujolais-Villages, Burgundy. Address = 69460 St-Étienne-des-Oullières.

Château de Lacaze (Fr). Armagnac producer. Address = Parlebosq-en-Armagnac, 40310 Gabarret. Vineyards in Bas Armagnac. Produces – ***, V.S.O.P. and Hors d'Âge.

Château de la Chaize (Fr). A vineyard in the Cru Beaujolais-Villages of Brouilly in Burgundy.

Château de la Chartreuse (Fr). A vineyard in the commune of Preignac. A.C. Sauternes, Bordeaux. 5 ha.

Château de la Commanderie (Fr). A vineyard in the commune of Lalande de Pomerol. A.C. Saint-Émilion, Bordeaux.

Château de la Cour d'Argent (Fr). Address = Saint-Sulpice-de-Faleyrens, 33330 Saint-Émilion. A.C. Bordeaux Supérieur.

Château de Lacouy (Fr). Armagnac producer. 20 ha. in Bas Armagnac.

Château de la Croix (Fr). A vineyard in the commune of Lormont. A.C. Premières Côtes de Bordeaux, central Bordeaux.

Château de la Croix-Millerit (Fr). A vineyard in the commune of Bayon. A.C. Côtes de Bourg, Bordeaux.

Château de la Croix-Simard (Fr). A vineyard in the A.C. Saint-Émilion, Bordeaux. 1 ha.

Château de la Dauphine (Fr). A vineyard in the A.C. Côtes de Fronsac, Bordeaux.

Château de la Dimerie (Fr). A vineyard in the A.C. Muscadet de Sèvre et Maine, Pays Nantais, Loire. Address = G.F.A. Rouge Terre de la Viticulteurs au Loroux Bottereau, Loire Atlantique.

Château de la Font-du-Loup (Fr). A vineyard in the commune of Courthézon. A.C. Châteauneuf-du-Pape, southern Rhône. Grape varieties – Cinsault, Clairette, Grenache, Grenache blanc, Mourvèdre and Rousanne.

Château de la Fresnaye (Fr). A.C. Cabernet d'Anjou, Anjou-Saumur, Loire.

Château de la Galissonière (Fr). A vineyard in the A.C. Muscadet de Sèvre et Maine, Pays Nantais, Loire. Address = 6, Pallet, Loire Atlantique.

Château de la Gardine (Fr). A vineyard in the A.C. Châteauneuf-du-Pape, southern Rhône. Address = 84230 Châteauneuf-du-Pape.

Château de la Grange (Fr). A vineyard in the A.C. Premières Côtes de Blaye, north-eastern Bordeaux.

Château de la Grange (Fr). Cognac producer. Address = 17400 St. Jean d'Angely. Owns 90 ha. Produces – Bladon d'Or (15 year old) and Maxim's de Paris Cognacs.

Château de la Grave (Fr). A vineyard in the commune of Bourg. A.C. Côtes de Bourg, Bordeaux. Cru Bourgeois.

Château de la Gravière (Fr). A vineyard in the commune of Toulenne. A.C. Graves, Bordeaux. 7 ha. (white).

Château de la Guimonière (Fr). A vineyard in the A.C. Quarts de Chaume, Coteaux du Layon, Anjou-Saumur, Loire. (sweet white).

Château de l'Aiglerie (Fr). A.C. Anjou, Anjou-Saumur, Loire Atlantique. (white wine).

Château de la Janière (Fr). A vineyard in the A.C. Muscadet de Sèvre et Maine, Pays Nantais, Loire.

Château de la Jousselinière (Fr). A vineyard in the A.C. Muscadet de Sèvre et Maine, Pays Nantais, Loire.

Château de la Maisdonnière (Fr). A.C. Muscadet, Pays Nantais, Loire.

Château de la Maltroye (Fr). Estate in A.C. Chassagne-Montrachet, Côte de Beaune, Burgundy. (red and white).

Château de Lamarque (Fr). Address = 33460 Margaux. Cru Bourgeois. A.C. Haut-Médoc. Commune = Lamarque. 50 ha. Grape varieties – Cabernet franc, Cabernet sauvignon, Merlot and Petit verdot.

Château de la Mecredière (Fr). A vineyard in the A.C. Muscadet de Sèvre et Maine, Pays Nantais, Loire. Address = 44190 Clisson, Loire Atlantique.

Château de la Monge (Fr). A vineyard in the commune of Bourg. A.C. Côtes de Bourg, Bordeaux.

Château de Lamothe (Fr). The fifteenth-century name for Château Margaux.

C

Premier Grand Crú Classé Margaux.

Château de la Mouchetière (Fr). A vineyard in the A.C. Muscadet de Sèvre et Maine, Pays Nantais, Loire. Address = La Mouchetière, Le Loreux-Bottereau, Loire Atlantique.

Château de Lamourous (Fr). A vineyard in the commune of Le Pian. A.C. Haut-Médoc, Bordeaux. 4 ha.

Château de Lamouroux (Fr). A vineyard in the commune of Margaux. A.C. Margaux, Bordeaux. Cru Bourgeois. 7 ha.

Château de la Nauve (Fr). Address = Saint Laurent des Combes, 33330 Saint-Émilion. A.C. Saint-Émilion. Commune = Saint Laurent des Combes. 11 ha. Grape varieties – Cabernet franc, Cabernet sauvignon and Merlot 80%.

Château de la Nerthe (Fr). An old-established vineyard in the A.C. Châteauneuf-du-Pape, southern Rhône.

Château de la Nouvelle Église (Fr). A vineyard in the commune of Pomerol. A.C. Pomerol, Bordeaux.

Château de la Preuille (Fr). A vineyard in the A.C. Muscadet, Pays Nantais, Loire.

Château de la Princesse (Fr). A vineyard in the commune of Sainte-Croix-du-Mont. A.C. Sainte-Croix-du-Mont, Bordeaux. 2 ha.

Château de la Ragotière (Fr). A vineyard in the A.C. Muscadet de Sèvre et Maine, Pays Nantais, Loire.

Château de la Ramière (Fr). A vineyard in the A.C. Côtes du Rhône, south-eastern Rhône.

Château de la Rigodière (Fr). A vineyard in the A.C. Beaujolais, Burgundy.

Château de la Rivière (Fr). A vineyard in the commune of St-Michel. A.C. Fronsac, Bordeaux. Address = La Rivière, 33145 St-Michel-de-Fronsac.

Château de la Roche (Fr). A vineyard in the commune of Les Lèves et Thoumeyrogues. A.C. Saint-Foy-Bordeaux, Bordeaux. (red and white).

Château de la Roche aux Moines (Fr). A vineyard in the commune of Savennières, Anjou-Saumur, Loire. A.C. Savennières. Address = Savennières-Coulée de Serrant, Loire.

Château de la Roulerie (Fr). A vineyard in the commune of Saint-Aubin de-Luigne. A.C. Coteaux du Layon-Chaume, Anjou-Saumur, Loire. Grape variety – Cabernet franc.

Château de Laroze (Fr). A vineyard in the commune of Margaux. A.C. Margaux, Bordeaux. 2 ha.

Château de la Salagre (Fr). A vineyard in the A.C. Monbazillac, Bergerac, south-western France. (sweet white).

Château de la Tuilerie (Fr). A vineyard in the V.D.Q.S. Costières du Gard. Address = Route de Saint-Gilles, 30000 Nimes.

Château de l'Aulée (Fr). A vineyard in the commune of Azay le Rideau. A.C. Touraine, Loire. Grape variety – Chenin blanc.

Château de l'Émigré (Fr). A vineyard in the commune of Cérons. A.C. Graves, Bordeaux. Address = Route d'Illats, 33177 Cérons. 2 ha. Grape varieties – Merlot, Sauvignon 35% and Sémillon 65% (red and white).

Château de l'Ermitage (Fr). A vineyard in the commune of Loupiac. A.C. Loupiac, Bordeaux. 2 ha.

Château de l'Espérance (Fr). A vineyard in the commune of La Brède. A.C. Graves, Bordeaux. 12 ha. (red and white).

Château de l'Estagnol (Fr). A.C. Côtes du Rhône. Grape variety – Bourboulenc (Blanc de blancs).

Château de l'Estonnat (Fr). A vineyard in the commune of Margaux. A.C. Margaux, Bordeaux.

Château de l'Hospital (Fr). A vineyard in the commune of Portets. A.C. Graves, Bordeaux. 8 ha. (red and white).

Château de Ligré (Fr). A vineyard in the A.C. Chinon, Touraine, Loire. Address = Ligré, 37500 Chinon.

Château de l'Oiselinière (Fr). A vineyard in the A.C. Muscadet de Sèvre et Maine, Pays Nantais, Loire. Address = Aulanière, 44190 Clisson, Loire Atlantique.

Château de Lucquos (Fr). A vineyard in the commune of Barsac. A.C. Barsac (or Sauternes), Bordeaux.

Château de Lunes (Fr). V.D.Q.S. red wine from the Coteaux du Languedoc, southern France.

Château de Lussac (Fr). A vineyard in the commune of Lussac-Saint-Émilion. A.C. Saint-Émilion, Bordeaux. 20 ha.

Château de Luzies (Fr). A vineyard in the commune of Barsac. A.C. Barsac (or Sauternes), Bordeaux. 3 ha.

Château de Maco (Fr). A vineyard in the commune of Tauriac. A.C. Côtes de Bourg, Bordeaux.

Château de Madère (Fr). A vineyard in the commune of Podensac. A.C. Médoc, Bordeaux.

Château de Malendure (Fr). A vineyard in the commune of Loupiac. A.C. Loupiac, Bordeaux. 3 ha.

Château de Malgarni (Fr). A vineyard in the commune of Saillans. A.C. Côtes de Fronsac, Bordeaux. 3 ha.

Château de Maligny (Fr). A vineyard in the A.C. Chablis, Bordeaux.

Château de Malle (Fr). Grand Cru Classé

C

(2ⁿᵈ). A.C. Sauternes. Commune = Preignac. 20 ha. Grape varieties – Muscadelle 5%, Sauvignon 25% and Sémillon 70%

Château de Malleret (Fr). A vineyard in the commune of Le Pian. A.C. Haut-Médoc, Bordeaux. 60 ha. Grape varieties – Cabernet franc, Cabernet sauvignon and Merlot. Cru Bourgeois.

Château de Maniban Cuvée Spéciale (Fr). A vintage Armagnac produced by Castarède. Vintages – 1893, 1900, 1924, 1931, 1934, 1940.

Château de Manissy (Fr). A vineyard in the A.C. Tavel, southern Rhône.

Château de Marbuzet (Fr). Address = Saint-Estèphe 33250 Pauillac. Cru Bourgeois. A.C. Saint-Estèphe. 7 ha. Grape varieties – Cabernet sauvignon and Merlot.

Château de Marsan (Fr). An estate in the Armagnac that was run as a model farm and experimental station.

Château de Marsillac (Fr). A vineyard in the A.C. Côtes de Bourg, north-eastern Bordeaux.

Château de Mauves (Fr). Address = 25, Rue François Maurice, Podensac. A.C. Graves. Commune = Podensac. 16 ha. Grape varieties – Cabernet sauvignon 65% and Merlot 35%

Château de May (Fr). A vineyard in the A.C. Graves, Bordeaux. (red).

Château de Mendoce (Fr). A vineyard in the commune of Villeneuve. A.C. Côtes de Bourg, Bordeaux. Address = 33710 Bourg.

Château de Menota (Fr). A vineyard in the commune of Barsac. A.C. Barsac (or Sauternes), Bordeaux.

Château de Mercey (Fr). A.C. Hautes Côtes de Beaune, Burgundy. Vineyards situated near Cheilly-les-Maranges. (red and white).

Château de Meursault (Fr). An estate of 41.5 ha. in the A.C. commune of Meursault in the Côte de Beaune, Burgundy. (red and white).

Château de Moncontour (Fr). A vineyard in the A.C. Vouvray, Touraine. Is famous for its sparkling Vouvray.

Château de Mons (Fr). Address = Saint-Sulpice-de-Faleyrens,, 33330 Saint-Émilion. A.C. Saint-Émilion. Second wine of Château du Barry. Grand Cru. Saint-Émilion.

Château de Montdespic (Fr). A vineyard in the A.C. Côtes de Castillon, Bordeaux.

Château de Montmelas (Fr). A vineyard in the A.C. Beaujolais-Villages, Burgundy.

Château de Montmirail (Fr). A vineyard

in the A.C. Gigondas, Côtes du Rhône-Villages. Address = BP 12 – 84190 Vacqueyras.

Château de Montrabech (Fr). A vineyard in the A.C. Corbières, south-western France.

Château de Morgan (Fr). A vineyard in the A.C. Morgon. Cru Beaujolais-Villages, Burgundy.

Château de Musset (Fr). A vineyard in the Lalande de Pomerol. A.C. Lalande, Bordeaux.

Château de Myrat (Fr). A vineyard in the Commune of Barsac. A.C. Barsac (or Sauternes), Bordeaux.

Château de Nages (Fr). A vineyard in the V.D.Q.S. Costières du Gard, southern France. (red).

Château de Nairne (Fr). A vineyard in the commune of Barsac. A.C. Barsac (or Sauternes), Bordeaux.

Château de Neuville (Fr). A vineyard in the A.C. Saint-Émilion, Bordeaux. 1 ha.

Château de Nevers (Fr). A vineyard in the A.C. Brouilly. Cru Beaujolais-Villages, Burgundy.

Château de Nouchet (Fr). A vineyard in the commune of Martillac. A.C. Graves, Bordeaux.

Château de Nouguey (Fr). A vineyard in the commune of Langon. A.C. Graves, Bordeaux. 2 ha. (white).

Château de Nouvelles (Fr). A.C. Rancio de Rivesaltes. Address = 11350 Tucan.

Château de Pach-Lat (Fr). A vineyard in the A.C. Corbières, south-western France.

Château de Padère (Fr). A vineyard in the A.C. Côtes de Buzet, south-western France.

Château de Paillet-Quancard (Fr). A vineyard in the commune of Langoiran. A.C. Premières Côtes de Bordeaux. Address = 33550 Langoiran. Grape varieties – Cabernet sauvignon 35% and Merlot 65%

Château de Panisseau (Fr). A vineyard in the A.C. Bergerac. Address = Thénac, 24240 Sigoulés, Dordogne. Grape variety – Sauvignon blanc.

Château de Parnay (Fr). A vineyard in the A.C. Anjou, Anjou-Saumur, Loire Atlantique. (white wine).

Château de Peyre (Fr). A vineyard in the commune of Fargues. A.C. Sauternes, Bordeaux. 1 ha.

Château de Peyros (Fr). A vineyard in the A.C. Madiran, Pyrénées, south-western France. (red).

Château de Pez (Fr). A vineyard in the commune of Moulis. A.C. Moulis, Bordeaux. 40 ha.

Château de Pez (Fr). Address = Pez,

C

Saint-Estèphe, 33250 Pauillac. A.C. Saint-Estèphe. Commune = Saint-Estèphe. 23.25 ha. Grape varieties – Cabernet franc 15%, Cabernet sauvignon 70% and Merlot 15%

Château de Pick (Fr). A vineyard in the commune of Preignac. A.C. Sauternes, Bordeaux. 23 ha.

Château d'Epiré (Fr). A vineyard in the commune of Savennières, A.C. Savennières, Anjou-Saumur, Loire.

Château de Pizay (Fr). A vineyard in the A.C. Morgon. Cru Beaujolais-Villages, Burgundy.

Château de Plaisance (Fr). A vineyard in the commune of Chaume. A.C. Coteaux du Layon, Anjou-Saumur, Loire.

Château de Pommard (Fr). A vineyard in the A.C. Pommard, Côte de Beaune, Burgundy. 20 ha.

Château de Pommarède (Fr). A vineyard in the commune of Castres. A.C. Graves, Bordeaux. (red and white).

Château de Portets (Fr). A vineyard in the commune of Portets. A.C. Graves, Bordeaux. 42 ha. (red and white).

Château de Pressac (Fr). Address = Saint-Étienne-de-Lisse, 33330 Saint-Émilion. Grand Cru. A.C. Saint-Émilion. Commune = Saint-Étienne-de-Lisse. 55 ha. Grape varieties – Cabernet franc 40%, Malbec and Pressac 2% and Merlot 58%. Second wine is Château Tour de Pressac.

Château de Puisseguin (Fr). A vineyard in the commune of Puisseguin-Saint-Émilion. A.C. Saint-Émilion, Bordeaux.

Château de Puligny Montrachet (Fr). A cuvée in the Premier Cru vineyard of Les Folatières, A.C. Puligny Montrachet, Côte de Beaune, Burgundy.

Château de Puy-Blanquet (Fr). A vineyard in the commune of Saint-Étienne-de-Lisse. A.C. Saint-Émilion, Bordeaux.

Château de Raousset (Fr). A vineyard in the A.C. Chiroubles Cru Beaujolais-Villages, Burgundy.

Château de Ravignan (Fr). An Armagnac producer. Address = Domaine de Ravignan, Perique, 40190, Villeneuve de Marsan. 18 ha. in Bas Armagnac.

Château de Rayne-Vigneau (Fr). Premier Grand Cru Classé. A.C. Sauternes. Commune = Bommes. 65 ha. Grape varieties – Muscadelle 10%, Sauvignon 25% and Sémillon 50%

Château de Respide (Fr). A vineyard in the commune of St-Pierre-de-Mons. A.C. Graves, Bordeaux. (white).

Château de Ribaute (Fr). A vineyard in the A.C. Corbières, south-western France.

Château de Rochefort (Fr). A vineyard in the A.C. Muscadet de Sèvre et Maine, Pays Nantais, Loire. Address = Vallet, Loire Atlantique.

Château de Rochemorin (Fr). A vineyard in the commune of Léognan. A.C. Graves, Bordeaux. (red and white).

Château de Rol (Fr). A vineyard in the A.C. Saint-Émilion, Bordeaux. 5 ha.

Château de Rolland (Fr). A vineyard in the commune of Barsac. A.C. Barsac (or Sauternes), Bordeaux. 14 ha.

Château de Romefort (Fr). A vineyard in the commune of Cussac. A.C. Médoc, Bordeaux. Cru Bourgeois.

Château de Roquebert (Fr). A vineyard in the commune of Quinsac. A.C. Premières Côtes de Bordeaux. Address = Quinsac 33360 Latresne. 16.4 ha. Grape varieties – Cabernet, Malbec and Merlot.

Château de Roques (Fr). A vineyard in the commune of Puisseguin-Saint-Émilion. A.C. Saint-Émilion, Bordeaux.

Château de Roquetaillade (Fr). A vineyard in the commune of Mazères. A.C. Graves, Bordeaux.

Château de Roquetaillade (Fr). A vineyard in the commune of Ordonnac-et-Potensac. A.C. Médoc, Bordeaux. 3 ha.

Château de Rouillac (Fr). Address = 33170 Gradignan. A.C. Graves. Commune = Canéjean. 5 ha. Grape varieties – Cabernet sauvignon 85% and Merlot 15%. (red).

Château de Roux (Fr). A vineyard in the A.C. Côtes-de-Provence, south-eastern France. Address = Le Cannet-des-Maures, 83340 Le Luc. (red and rosé).

Château de Rozet (Fr). A vineyard in the A.C. Pouilly Blanc Fumé, Central Vineyards, Pouilly-sur-Loire.

Château de Ruth (Fr). A vineyard in the A.C. Côtes du Rhône. Grape varieties – Carignane, Grenache and Syrah.

Château de Saint-Julien d'Aille (Fr). A vineyard in the commune of Vidauban. A.C. Côtes-de-Provence. Address = BP 38, 83550 Vidauban.

Château de Saint-Philippe (Fr). A vineyard in the commune of Saint Philippe d'Aiguille, Côtes de Castillon, eastern Bordeaux. A.C. Bordeaux Supérieur. Address = 33350 Saint Philippe d'Aiguille.

Château de Saint Pey (Fr). Address = Saint-Pey-d'Armens, 33330 Saint-Émilion. Grand Cru. A.C. Saint-Émilion. Commune = Saint-Pey-d'Armens. 16 ha. Grape varieties – Cabernet franc 30%, Cabernet sauvignon 6% and Merlot 64%.

Château de Saint Pierre (Fr). Address =

Saint Pierre de Mons 33210. A.C. Graves.
Grape varieties – Cabernet 60%, Merlot
40%, Sauvignon 35% and Sémillon 65%

Château de Sales (Fr). A vineyard in the
commune of Pomerol. A.C. Pomerol,
Bordeaux. 48 ha. The second wine of
Château Chantalouette.

Château de Samonac (Fr). A vineyard in
the A.C. Côtes de Bourg, north-eastern
Bordeaux.

Château des Annereaux (Fr). A vineyard in
the commune of Lalande de Pomerol.
A.C. Lalande de Pomerol, Bordeaux.

Château de Sarenceau (Fr). A vineyard in
the A.C. Saint-Émilion, Bordeaux. 5 ha.

Château de Sarpe (Fr). A vineyard in the
A.C. Saint-Émilion, Bordeaux. 6 ha.

Château des Arrocs (Fr). A vineyard in the
commune of Langon. A.C. Graves,
Bordeaux. 3 ha. (white).

Château de Sassay (Fr). A vineyard in the
A.C. Chinon, Touraine, Loire.

Château de Savennières (Fr). A vineyard in
the commune of Savennières. A.C.
Savennières, Anjou-Saumur, Loire.

Château des Bachelards (Fr). A vineyard in
the A.C. Fleurie Cru Beaujolais-Villages,
Burgundy.

Château des Belles Graves (Fr). A vineyard
in the commune of Ordonnac et Podensac. A.C. Médoc, Bordeaux.

Château des Brousteras (Fr). A vineyard in
the commune of Saint-Yzans-de-Médoc.
A.C. Médoc, Bordeaux. Address = Saint-
Yzans-de-Médoc, 33340 Lesparre.

Château des Caperans (Fr). A vineyard in
the commune of Cussac-Fort-Médoc.
A.C. Haut-Médoc, Bordeaux. 4 ha. Grape
varieties – Cabernet 50% and Merlot 50%

Château des Capitans (Fr). A vineyard in
the A.C. Juliénas Cru Beaujolais-Villages, Burgundy. Address = BP 73 –
69822 Belleville Cedex.

Château des Carmes-Haut-Brion (Fr). A
vineyard in the commune of Pessac. A.C.
Médoc, Bordeaux.

Château des Chambrettes (Fr). A vineyard
in the commune of Pessac. A.C. Médoc,
Bordeaux.

Château des Charmes (Can). A main wine
producer based in Ontario.

Château des Combes (Fr). A vineyard in the
commune of Bégadan. A.C. Médoc,
Bordeaux. 4 ha.

Château des Combes-Canon (Fr). A vineyard in the commune of St-Michel. A.C.
Côtes de Canon-Fronsac, Bordeaux. 2 ha.

Château des Deduits (Fr). A vineyard in the
A.C. Fleurie Cru Beaujolais-Villages,
Burgundy.

Château des Desmoiselles (Fr). A vineyard
in the A.C. Saint-Émilion, Bordeaux. 1
ha.

Château des Ducs d'Epernon (Fr). See
Maison du Vin, Château des Ducs
d'Epernon.

Château de Segries (Fr). A vineyard in the
A.C. Lirac, Côtes du Rhône, southern
France.

Château de Selle (Fr). Address = Taradeau,
83460 Les Arcs. A.C. Côtes-de-Provence.
Grape varieties – Cabernet sauvignon,
Cinsault and Grenache. (red and rosé).
Owned by Domaines Ott.

Château des Fines Roches (Fr). A.C.
Châteauneuf-du-Pape. 50 ha. Grape varieties – Cinsault 5%, Grenache 70%,
Mourvèdre 5% and Syrah 10% with 10%
of 8 other varieties.

Château des Fougères (Fr). A vineyard in
the commune of La Brède. A.C. Graves,
Bordeaux. 2 ha. (white).

Château des Gauliers (Fr). A vineyard in
the A.C. Bonnezeaux, Coteaux du Layon,
Anjou-Saumur, Loire.

Château des Gondats (Fr). The second
wine of Château Marquis de Terme. A
'Palus' wine.

Château des Granges (Fr). A vineyard in
the A.C. Beaujolais, Burgundy.

Château des Graves (Fr). A vineyard in the
commune of Portets. A.C. Graves,
Bordeaux. (red and white).

Château des Graves (Fr). A vineyard in the
A.C. Saint-Émilion, Bordeaux. 4 ha.

Château des Graves-de-Mondou (Fr). A
vineyard in the A.C. Saint-Émilion,
Bordeaux. 4 ha.

Château des Gravettes (Fr). A vineyard in
the commune of St. Morillon. A.C.
Graves, Bordeaux.

Château des Gravières (Fr). A vineyard in
the commune of Portets. A.C. Graves,
Bordeaux. 5 ha. (red and white).

Château des Graviers d'Ellies (Fr). Address
= Saint-Sulpice-de-Faleyrens, 33330
Saint-Émilion. Grand Cru. A.C. Saint-
Émilion. Commune = Saint-Sulpice-de-
Faleyrens. 7 ha. Grape varieties – Caber-
net sauvignon 25% and Merlot 75%

Château des Guerches (Fr). A vineyard in
the A.C. Muscadet de Sèvre et Maine,
Pays Nantais, Loire.

Château des Guillemins (Fr). A vineyard in
the commune of Langon. A.C. Graves,
Bordeaux. 8 ha. (white).

Château de Simone (Fr). A vineyard based
in the A.C. Palette, Provence, south-
eastern France.

Château des Jacobins (Fr). A vineyard in
the commune of Pomerol. A.C. Pomerol,
Bordeaux. 1 ha.

Château des Jacques (Fr). A vineyard in the
A.C. Moulin-à-Vent Cru Beaujolais-
Villages, Burgundy. Address = 71570
Romanèche-Thorins.

C

Château des Jaubertes (Fr). A vineyard in the commune of St-Pierre-de-Mons. A.C. Graves, Bordeaux. 6 ha. (red).

Château des Labourons (Fr). A vineyard in the A.C. Fleurie Cru Beaujolais-Villages, Burgundy.

Château des Laurets (Fr). A vineyard in the commune of Puisseguin-Saint-Émilion. A.C. Puisseguin-Saint-Émilion, Bordeaux.

Château des Lucques (Fr). A vineyard in the commune of Portets. A.C. Graves, Bordeaux. 5 ha. (red and white).

Château des Mailles (Fr). A vineyard in the commune of Sainte-Croix-du-Mont. A.C. Sainte-Croix-du-Mont, Bordeaux. 6 ha.

Château des Mauves (Fr). A vineyard in the commune of Podensac. A.C. Cérons, Bordeaux. 7 ha.

Château Desmirail (Fr). Address = 33460 Margaux. Grand Cru Classé (3rd). A.C. Margaux. Commune = Cantenac. 18 ha. Grape varieties – Cabernet franc, Cabernet sauvignon, Merlot and Petit verdot.

Château des Moines (Fr). A vineyard in the commune of Lalande de Pomerol. A.C. Lalande de Pomerol, Bordeaux.

Château des Moines (Fr). A vineyard in the commune of Saint-Christophe-des-Bardes. A.C. Saint-Émilion, Bordeaux.

Château de Sours (Fr). A vineyard in the A.C. Entre-Deux-Mers, central Bordeaux.

Château Despagne (Fr). A vineyard in the commune of St-Pierre-de-Mons. A.C. Graves, Bordeaux. 4 ha. (white).

Château Despagnet (Fr). A vineyard in the commune of Saint-Émilion. A.C. Saint-Émilion, Bordeaux. 3 ha.

Château des Palais (Fr). A vineyard in the A.C. Corbières, south-western France.

Château des Peyrères (Fr). A vineyard in the commune of Landiras. A.C. Graves, Bordeaux. 4 ha.

Château des Peyteaux (Fr). A vineyard in the A.C. Côtes du Frontonnais, south-western France. (red).

Château des Religieuses (Fr). A vineyard in the A.C. Saint-Émilion, Bordeaux. 2 ha.

Château des Remparts (Fr). A vineyard in the commune of Preignac. A.C. Sauternes, Bordeaux. 1 ha.

Château des Richards (Fr). A vineyard in the commune of Mombrier. A.C. Côtes de Bourg, Bordeaux.

Château des Rochers (Fr). A.C. Bordeaux Supérieurs.

Château des Rochers (Fr). Part of Château Bonneau, A.C. Saint-Émilion, Bordeaux.

Château des Roches (Fr). A vineyard in the commune of Loupiac. A.C. Cérons, Bordeaux.

Château des Rochettes (Fr). A vineyard in the A.C. Anjou, Anjou-Saumur, Loire. Address = Concourson-sur-Layon, Loire.

Château des Rocs (Fr). A vineyard in the commune of Preignac. A.C. Sauternes, Bordeaux. 1 ha.

Château des Roziers (Fr). A vineyard in the commune of Montagne-Saint-Émilion. A.C. Saint-Émilion, Bordeaux. 4 ha.

Château des Templiers (Fr). A vineyard in the commune of Pomerol. A.C. Pomerol, Bordeaux. 3 ha.

Château Destieu (Fr). A vineyard in the commune of Saint-Étienne-de-Lisse. A.C. Saint-Émilion, Bordeaux.

Château Destieux (Fr). Address = Saint-Hippolyte, 33330 Saint-Émilion. Grand Cru. A.C. Saint-Émilion. Commune = Saint-Hippolyte. 8.27 ha. Grape varieties – Cabernet 35% and Merlot 65%.

Château Destieux-Verac (Fr). A vineyard in the A.C. Saint-Émilion, Bordeaux. 11 ha.

Château de St. Maigrin (Fr). Cognac producer. Address = Saint-Maigrin, 17520 Archiac. 50 ha. in the Bons Bois.

Château des Tonnelles (Fr). A vineyard in the commune of St-Aignan. A.C. Côtes de Fronsac, Bordeaux. 6 ha.

Château des Tourelles (Fr). Address = Blaignan 33340. Cru Bourgeois. A.C. Médoc. Commune = Blaignan. 21 ha. Grape varieties – Cabernet sauvignon 50% and Merlot 50%

Château des Tours (Fr). A vineyard in the A.C. Brouilly Cru Beaujolais-Villages, Burgundy. Address = 69830 St-Étienne-la-Varenne.

Château des Tours (Fr). A vineyard in the commune of Montagne-Saint-Émilion. A.C. Saint-Émilion, Bordeaux. 59 ha.

Château des Tours (Fr). A vineyard in the commune of Sainte-Croix-du-Mont. A.C. Sainte-Croix-du-Mont, Bordeaux. Also Ste Cle du Domaine du Château Loubens.

Château des Trois Chardons (Fr). Address = Cantenac, Margaux 33460. A.C. Margaux. Commune = Cantenac. 2.5 ha. Grape varieties – Cabernet sauvignon 60% and Merlot 40%

Château des Trois Moulins (Fr). A vineyard in the commune of Macau. A.C. Haut-Médoc, Bordeaux. Cru Bourgeois.

Château des Tuileries (Fr). A vineyard in the commune of Virelade. A.C. Graves, Bordeaux. 10 ha. (red and white).

Château de Suduiraut (Fr). Premier Grand Cru Classé. A.C. Sauternes.

Commune = Preignac. Grape varieties – Sauvignon 5% and Sémillon 95%.

Château de Suronde (Fr). A vineyard in the A.C. Quarts de Chaume, Anjou-Saumur, Loire.

Château de Tariquet (Fr). Armagnac producer. Address = P. Grassa et Fils, Château de Tariquet, 32800 Eauze. 60 ha. in Bas Armagnac.

Château de Taste (Fr). A vineyard in the commune of Lansac. A.C. Côtes de Bourg, Bordeaux.

Château de Tastes (Fr). A vineyard in the commune of Sainte-Croix-du-Mont. A.C. Sainte-Croix-du-Mont, Bordeaux. 6 ha.

Château de Terrefort-de-Fortissan (Fr). A vineyard in the commune of Villenave-d'Ornon. A.C. Graves, Bordeaux. Cru Bourgeois.

Château de Teuil de Nailhac (Fr). A vineyard in the A.C. Monbazillac, Bergerac.

Château de Teysson (Fr). A vineyard in the commune of Néac. A.C. Lalande de Pomerol, Bordeaux.

Château de Thau (Fr). A vineyard in the commune of Gauriac. A.C. Côtes de Bourg, Bordeaux.

Château de Tiregand (Fr). A vineyard in the commune of Pécharmant, A.C. Pécharmant, Bergerac. (red). Address = Comtesse F de Saint-Exupéry Creysse, 24100 Bergerac.

Château de Touilla (Fr). A vineyard in the commune of Fargues. A.C. Sauternes, Bordeaux. 3 ha.

Château de Tracy (Fr). A vineyard in the A.C. Pouilly Fumé, Central Vineyards, Loire.

Château de Trinquevedel (Fr). A vineyard in the A.C. Tavel. Grape varieties – Clairette, Cinsault and Grenache. Rosé wine sold in Véronique bottle.

Château de Valois (Fr). A vineyard in the commune of Pomerol. A.C. Pomerol, Bordeaux. 6 ha.

Château de Valpinson (Fr). A vineyard in the A.C. Côtes du Rhône, south-eastern France.

Château de Vanisseau (Fr). A vineyard in the A.C. Bergerac. (white).

Château de Vaudenuits (Fr). A.C. Vouvray, Touraine, Loire. (white dry and sweet sparkling [méthode champenoise] wines). Address = BP 23, 37210 Vouvray.

Château de Vaudieu (Fr). A vineyard in the A.C. Châteauneuf-du-Pape, southern Rhône.

Château de Viaud (Fr). A vineyard in the commune of Lalande de Pomerol. A.C. Saint-Émilion, Bordeaux.

Château de Viens (Fr). A vineyard in the A.C. Côtes de Bourg, north-eastern Bordeaux.

Château Villegorge (Fr). A vineyard in the commune of Avensan (and Moulis). A.C. Haut-Médoc, Bordeaux. Cru Bourgeois Exceptionnel.

Château de Villenouvette (Fr). A vineyard in the A.C. Corbières, south-western Bordeaux.

Château de Villerambert (Fr). A vineyard in the A.C. Minervois, south-western France. (red).

Château de Virelade (Fr). A vineyard in the commune of Arbanats. A.C. Graves, Bordeaux. 13 ha. (red and white).

Château de Vosne Romanée (Fr). A vineyard in the A.C. commune of Vosne Romanée, Côte de Nuits, Burgundy.

Château d'Eyguem (Fr). A.C. Bordeaux. (red).

Château Deyrem Valentin (Fr). A vineyard in the commune of Soussans-Margaux. A.C. Haut-Médoc, Bordeaux. 7 ha.

Château d'Hortevie (Fr). A vineyard in the commune of Saint-Julien. A.C. Saint-Julien, Bordeaux. Cru Bourgeois.

Château Dillon (Fr). Address = 33290 Blanquefort. A.C. Médoc. Commune = Blanquefort. 100 ha. Grape varieties – Cabernet franc, Cabernet sauvignon and Merlot.

Château d'Issan (Fr). Grand Cru Classé (3rd). A.C. Margaux. Commune = Cantenac. 32 ha. Grape varieties – Cabernet sauvignon 75% and Merlot 25%.

Château Divon (Fr). A vineyard in the commune of Saint-Georges-Saint-Émilion. A.C. Saint-Émilion, Bordeaux. 4 ha.

Château Doisy-Daëne (Fr). Grand Cru Classé (2nd). A.C. Barsac (or Sauternes). Commune = Barsac. Grape variety – Sémillon 100%

Château Doisy-Dubroca (Fr). Grand Cru Classé (2nd). A.C. Sauternes. Now part of Château Climens, Barsac.

Château Doisy-Védrines (Fr). Grand Cru Classé (2nd). A.C. Barsac (or Sauternes). Commune = Barsac. 20 ha. Grape varieties – Sauvignon 30% and Sémillon 70%.

Château Domaine de la Rose Maréchale (Fr). Cru Bourgeois. A.C. Médoc. Commune = St-Seurin-de-Cadourne.

Château Domeyne (Fr). A vineyard in the commune of Saint-Estèphe. A.C. Saint-Estèphe, Bordeaux. 2 ha.

Château Doms et Clos du Monastère (Fr). A.C. Graves. Commune = Portets. 15 ha. (red and white).

C

Château Donissan-Veyrin (Fr). A vineyard in the commune of Listrac. A.C. Haut-Médoc, Bordeaux. 6 ha.

Château Doumayne (Fr). Address = Château Sansonnet, 33330 Saint-Émilion A.C. Saint-Émilion. Commune = Saint-Émilion.

Château Doumens (Fr). A vineyard in the commune of Margaux. A.C. Margaux, Bordeaux. Cru Bourgeois.

Château Drouilleau Belles Graves (Fr). A vineyard in the commune of Néac. A.C. Lalande de Pomerol, Bordeaux.

Château Duarate (S.Am). A red wine produced in San Salvador.

Château du Barrail (Fr). A vineyard in the commune of Bégadan. A.C. Médoc, Bordeaux.

Château du Barrail (Fr). A vineyard in the commune of Eynesse. A.C. Saint-Foy-Bordeaux, Bordeaux.

Château du Barry (Fr). Address = Saint-Sulpice-de-Faleyrens, 33330 Saint-Émilion. Grand Cru. A.C. Saint-Émilion. Commune = Saint-Sulpice-de-Faleyrens. 16 ha. Grape varieties – Cabernet franc 20%, Cabernet sauvignon 10% and Merlot 70%. The second wine is Château de Mons.

Château de Basque (Fr). A vineyard in the A.C. Saint-Émilion, Bordeaux. 3 ha.

Château du Basty (Fr). A vineyard in the A.C. Beaujolais-Villages, Burgundy. Wine produced by Perroud in Lantignié.

Château du Beau Vallon (Fr). A vineyard in the commune of Saint-Christophe-des-Bardes. A.C. Saint-Émilion, Bordeaux. Address = Saint-Christophe-des-Bardes, 33330 Saint-Émilion.

Château du Biac (Fr). A vineyard in the commune of Langoiran. A.C. Premières Côtes de Bordeaux. Address = 33550 Langoiran. 10 ha. Grape varieties – Cabernet franc, Cabernet sauvignon, Merlot, Muscadelle, Sauvignon and Sémillon. (red 50% and white 50%).

Château du Bloy (Fr). A vineyard in the A.C. Bergerac, south-western France. Address = Bonneville, 24230 Velines. (red, rosé, sweet white and dry white).

Château du Bluizard (Fr). A vineyard in the A.C. Beaujolais-Villages, Burgundy.

Château du Bosquet (Fr). A vineyard in the A.C. Côtes de Bourg, Bordeaux. Cru Bourgeois.

Château du Bouchet (Fr). A vineyard in the A.C. Côtes de Buzet, south-western France.

Château du Boulay (Fr). A vineyard in the A.C. Montlouis, Touraine, Loire.

Château Dubraud (Fr). A.C. Bordeaux. (red).

Château du Breuil (Fr). A vineyard in the commune of Bayon. A.C. Côtes de Bourg, Bordeaux.

Château du Breuil (Fr). A vineyard in the commune of Cissac. A.C. Médoc, Bordeaux. 19 ha.

Château du Busca (Fr). Armagnac producer. Address = Château du Busca Maniban, 32310 Mansecome. 30 ha. in Ténarèze. Produces – Marquis de Maniban Napoléon.

Château du Calvaire (Fr). A vineyard in the A.C. Saint-Émilion, Bordeaux. 12 ha.

Château du Carles (Fr). A vineyard in the commune of Saillans. A.C. Côtes de Fronsac, Bordeaux. 13 ha.

Château du Cartillon (Fr). A vineyard in the commune of Lamarque. A.C. Haut-Médoc, Bordeaux. 20 ha. Cru Bourgeois.

Château Ducasse (Fr). A vineyard in the commune of Barsac. A.C. Barsac (or Sauternes), Bordeaux. 5 ha.

Château du Casse (Fr). A vineyard in the commune of Pomerol. A.C. Pomerol, Bordeaux. 2 ha.

Château du Castera (Fr). A vineyard in the commune of Saint-Germain d'Esteuil. A.C. Médoc, Bordeaux. Cru Bourgeois.

Château du Cauze (Fr). Address = Saint-Christophe-des-Bardes, 33330 Saint-Émilion. Grand Cru. A.C. Saint-Émilion. Commune = Saint-Christophe-des-Bardes. 23 ha. Grape varieties – Cabernet franc, Cabernet sauvignon and Merlot 60%.

Château du Cayron (Fr). A vineyard in the A.C. Cahors. Address = 46700 Puy-l'Évêque, Lot.

Château du Chatelard (Fr). A vineyard in the A.C. Beaujolais-Villages, (Lancié), Burgundy.

Château du Chayne (Fr). A vineyard in the A.C. Côtes de Bergerac, south-western France.

Château du Cléray (Fr). A vineyard in the A.C. Muscadet de Sèvre et Maine, Pays Nantais, Loire. Address = Sauvion Fils, 44330 Vallet, Loire. See Cardinal Richard Muscadet de Sèvre et Maine.

Château du Clocher (Fr). A vineyard in the A.C. Saint-Émilion, Bordeaux. 3 ha.

Château du Clos Renon (Fr). A vineyard in the commune of Portets. (Graves). A.C. Bordeaux Supérieur. (red).

Château Ducluzeau (Fr). A vineyard in the commune of Listrac. A.C. Listrac, Bordeaux. 4 ha. Grape varieties – Cabernet sauvignon 20% and Merlot 80%.

C

Château du Cognac (Fr). The premises of Otard, Cognac producers.

Château du Coing de St-Fiacre (Fr). A vineyard in the A.C. Muscadet de Sèvre et Maine, Pays Nantais, Loire. Address = 44 St-Fiacre, Loire.

Château du Comte (Fr). A vineyard in the A.C. Saint-Émilion, Bordeaux. 3 ha.

Château du Cros (Fr). A vineyard in the commune of Loupiac. A.C. Loupiac, Bordeaux. 21 ha.

Château du Croute (Fr). A.C. Bordeaux. (red).

Château Ducru Beaucaillou (Fr). Address = Saint-Julien, Beychevelle, Grand Cru Classé (2nd). A.C. Saint-Julien. Commune = Saint-Julien. 50 ha. Grape varieties – Cabernet franc, Cabernet sauvignon, Merlot and Petit verdot.

Château du Domaine de Descazeaux (Fr). A vineyard in the commune of Gauriac. A.C. Côtes de Bourg, Bordeaux.

Château Dudon (Fr). A vineyard in the commune of Barsac. A.C. Barsac (or Sauternes), Bordeaux. 8 ha.

Château Dudon (Fr). A.C. Bordeaux. (red).

Château du Ferrand (Fr). A vineyard in the commune of Saint-Émilion. A.C. Saint-Émilion, Bordeaux. Address = 33330 Saint-Émilion.

Château du Fronsac (Fr). A vineyard in the commune of Fronsac. A.C. Côtes de Fronsac, Bordeaux. 4 ha.

Château du Gaby (Fr). A vineyard in the commune of St-Michel. A.C. Côtes Canon-Fronsac, Bordeaux. 25 ha.

Château du Galan (Fr). A vineyard in the commune of Saint Laurent. A.C. Médoc, Bordeaux. Cru Bourgeois.

Château du Glana (Fr). A vineyard in the commune of Saint-Julien. A.C. Saint-Julien, Bordeaux. Cru Grand Bourgeois Exceptionnel.

Château du Grand Clapeau (Fr). A vineyard in the commune of Blanquefort. A.C. Haut-Médoc, Bordeaux. Address = 33290 Blanquefort. 11 ha. Cru Bourgeois.

Château du Grand Moine (Fr). A vineyard in the commune of Lalande de Pomerol. A.C. Lalande de Pomerol, Bordeaux.

Château du Grand Moulas (Fr). A vineyard in the A.C. Côtes du Rhône, south-western France.

Château du Grand-Saint-Julien (Fr). A vineyard in the commune of Saint-Julien. A.C. Saint-Julien, Bordeaux. Cru Bourgeois.

Château du Haire (Fr). A vineyard in the commune of Preignac. A.C. Sauternes, Bordeaux. 4 ha.

Château Duhart Milon (Fr). See Château Duhart Milon Rothschild.

Château Duhart Milon Rothschild (Fr). Address = 33250 Pauillac. Grand Cru Classé (4th). A.C. Pauillac. Commune = Pauillac. 50 ha. Grape varieties – Cabernet franc, Cabernet sauvignon and Merlot

Château du Haut-Gravier (Fr). A vineyard in the commune of Illats. A.C. Cérons, Bordeaux. 11 ha.

Château du Juge (Fr). A.C. Bordeaux Sec. Address = 33190 Yvon Mau.

Château du Juge (Fr). A vineyard in the commune of Preignac. A.C. Sauternes, Bordeaux 4 ha.

Château du Junca (Fr). A vineyard in the commune of St-Sauveur. A.C. Haut-Médoc, Bordeaux. Address = St-Sauveur, 33250 Pauillac.

Château du Magnum (Fr). A vineyard in the A.C. Graves, Bordeaux. (white).

Château du Marquisat (Fr). A vineyard in the A.C. Côtes de Bourg, north-eastern Bordeaux.

Château du Mayne (Fr). A vineyard in the commune of Barsac. A.C. Barsac (or Sauternes), Bordeaux. 7 ha.

Château du Mayne (Fr). A vineyard in the commune of Pomerol. A.C. Pomerol, Bordeaux. 2 ha.

Château du Mayne (Fr). A vineyard in the commune of Preignac. A.C. Sauternes, Bordeaux. 2 ha.

Château du Mirail (Fr). A vineyard in the commune of Portets. A.C. Graves, Bordeaux. Address = 33460 Portets. 23 ha. Grape varieties – Cabernet, Merlot and Sémillon

Château du Mont (Fr). A vineyard in the commune of Sainte-Croix-du-Mont. A.C. Sainte-Croix-du-Mont, Bordeaux. 7 ha.

Château du Mont (Fr). A vineyard in the commune of Preignac. A.C. Sauternes, Bordeaux. 4 ha.

Château du Monthil (Fr). A vineyard in the commune of Bégadan. A.C. Médoc, Bordeaux. Address = Bégadan, 33340 Lesparre. 20 ha. Grape varieties – Cabernet sauvignon, Malbec, Merlot and Petit verdot

Château du Moulin (Fr). A vineyard in the commune of Montagne-Saint-Émilion. A.C. Saint-Émilion, Bordeaux. 6 ha.

Château du Moulin du Bourg (Fr). A vineyard in the commune of Listrac. A.C. Haut-Médoc, Bordeaux. 7 ha.

Château du Moulin Rouge (Fr). Address = Cussac-Fort-Médoc, 44460 Margaux. Cru Bourgeois. A.C. Haut-Médoc. Commune = Cussac-Fort-Médoc. 15

C

ha. Grape varieties – Cabernet sauvignon, Malbec, Merlot and Petit verdot.

Château du Noble (Fr). A vineyard in the commune of Loupiac. A.C. Loupiac, Bordeaux. 7 ha.

Château du Nozet (Fr). See Baron de Ladoucette.

Château du Pape (Fr). A vineyard in the commune of Preignac. A.C. Sauternes, Bordeaux. 3 ha.

Château du Paradis (Fr). Address = Vignonet, 33330 Saint-Émilion. Grand Cru. A.C. Saint-Émilion. Commune = Vignonet. 25 ha.

Château du Pavillon (Fr). A vineyard in the commune of Roaillan. A.C. Graves, Bordeaux. 6 ha. (white).

Château du Pavillon (Fr). A vineyard in the commune of Sainte-Croix-du-Mont. A.C. Sainte-Croix-du-Mont, Bordeaux.

Château du Petit-Moulinet (Fr). A vineyard in the commune of Pomerol. A.C. Pomerol, Bordeaux. 3 ha.

Château du Peyrat (Fr). A vineyard in the commune of Cérons. A.C. Cérons, Bordeaux 8 ha.

Château Dupeyrat (Fr). A vineyard in the commune of St-Paul. A.C. Côtes de Blaye, Bordeaux.

Château du Peyrat (Fr). A vineyard in the commune of Saint Laurent. A.C. Médoc, Bordeaux. Cru Bourgeois.

Château Dupian (Fr). A vineyard in the commune of Le Pian. A.C. Haut-Médoc, Bordeaux. Cru Bourgeois.

Château du Pick (Fr). A vineyard in the commune of Preignac. A.C. Sauternes, Bordeaux.

Château du Planter (Fr). An A.C. Bordeaux Rouge. Address = 33540, Sauveterre-de-Guyenne.

Château Duplessis-Fabre (Fr). A vineyard in the commune of Moulis. A.C. Moulis, Bordeaux. Address = 33480 Moulis. Cru Bourgeois. 17 ha. Grape varieties – Cabernet franc, Cabernet sauvignon, Merlot and Petit verdot.

Château Duplessis-Hauchecorne (Fr). A vineyard in the commune of Moulis. A.C. Moulis, Bordeaux. 16 ha. Cru Grand Bourgeois.

Château du Pont du Bouquey (Fr). A vineyard in the A.C. Saint-Émilion, Bordeaux. 3 ha.

Château du Pontet (Fr). A vineyard in the A.C. Saint-Émilion, Bordeaux. 3 ha.

Château du Puy (Fr). A vineyard in the commune of Parsac-Saint-Émilion. A.C. Saint-Émilion, Bordeaux. 6 ha.

Château du Puynormand (Fr). A vineyard in the commune of Parsac-Saint-Émilion. A.C. Saint-Émilion, Bordeaux. 7 ha.

Château Durand-Laplagne (Fr). A vineyard in the commune of Puisseguin-Saint-Émilion. A.C. Puisseguin-Saint-Émilion, Bordeaux.

Château du Raux (Fr). Address = Cussac-Fort-Médoc. 33460 Margaux. A.C. Haut-Médoc, Bordeaux. Commune = Cussac-Fort-Médoc. 10 ha. Grape varieties – Cabernet sauvignon 50% and Merlot 50%

Château du Rayas (Fr). A vineyard in the A.C. Châteauneuf-du-Pape, southern Rhône.

Château Durfort-Vivens (Fr). Address = 33460 Margaux. Grand Cru Classé (2nd). A.C. Margaux. Commune = Margaux. 20 ha. Grape varieties – Cabernet franc 10%, Cabernet sauvignon 82% and Merlot 8%

Château du Roc (Fr). A vineyard in the commune of Barsac. A.C. Barsac (or Sauternes), Bordeaux 2 ha.

Château du Roc (Fr). A vineyard in the commune of Cérons. A.C. Cérons, Bordeaux. 5 ha.

Château du Roc de Boissac (Fr). A vineyard in the commune of Puisseguin-Saint-Émilion. A.C. Saint-Émilion, Bordeaux.

Château du Rocher (Fr). Address = Saint-Étienne-de-Lisse, 33330 Saint-Émilion. Grand Cru. A.C. Saint-Émilion. Commune = Saint-Étienne-de-Lisse. 14 ha. Grape varieties – Cabernet franc 20%, Cabernet sauvignon 30% and Merlot 50%.

Château du Roy (Fr). A vineyard in the A.C. Saint-Émilion, Bordeaux. 3 ha.

Château du Rozay (Fr). A vineyard in the A.C. Condrieu, northern Rhône.

Château du Seuil (Fr). A vineyard in the commune of Cérons. A.C. Cérons, Bordeaux. 3 ha.

Château du Seuil (Fr). A vineyard in the V.D.Q.S. Aix-en-Provence, south-eastern France. (red, rosé and white).

Château du Suduiraut (Fr). A Premier Grand Cru Classé vineyard in the commune of Preignac. A.C. Sauternes, Bordeaux.

Château du Tailhas (Fr). A vineyard in the commune of Libourne. A.C. Pomerol, Bordeaux. 9 ha.

Château du Taillan (Fr). Cru Grand Bourgeois. Address = Le Taillon-Médoc, 33320 Eysines. A.C. Haut-Médoc. Commune = Le Taillon-Médoc. 25 ha. Grape varieties – Cabernet franc, Cabernet sauvignon and Merlot.

Château du Tasta (Fr). A vineyard in the commune of Camblancs. A.C. Premières Côtes de Bordeaux. Address = 33360 Camblancs.

Château du Tasta (Fr). A vineyard in the

C

commune of St-Aignan. A.C. Côtes de Fronsac, Bordeaux. 12 ha.

Château du Tertre (Fr). A.C. Margaux. Commune = Arsac. 45 ha. Grape varieties – Cabernet franc, Cabernet sauvignon and Merlot.

Château du Testeron (Fr). A vineyard in the commune of Moulis. A.C. Haut-Médoc, Bordeaux. Cru Bourgeois.

Château Duthil-Haut-Cressant (Fr). A vineyard in the commune of Le Pian. A.C. Haut-Médoc, Bordeaux. Cru Bourgeois.

Château du Thyl (Fr). A vineyard in the A.C. Beaujolais-Villages, Burgundy.

Château du Touran (Fr). A vineyard in the A.C. Saint-Émilion, Bordeaux. 4 ha.

Château du Treuil de Nailhac (Fr). A vineyard in the commune of Monbazillac. A.C. Monbazillac, Bergerac.

Château Dutruch-Grand-Poujeau (Fr). Address = 33480 Moulis-en-Médoc. Cru Grand Bourgeois Exceptionnel. A.C. Moulis. Commune = Moulis. 30 ha. Grape varieties – Cabernet, Merlot and Petit verdot.

Château du Val-d'Or (Fr). A vineyard in the A.C. Saint-Émilion, Bordeaux. 3 ha.

Château du Vieux-Moulin (Fr). A vineyard in the commune of Loupiac. A.C. Loupiac, Bordeaux. 9 ha.

Château du Vigneau (Fr). A vineyard in the commune of St. Nicholas de Bourgueil. A.C. St. Nicholas de Bourgueil, Touraine, Loire.

Château du Violet (Fr). A vineyard in the commune of Preignac. A.C. Sauternes, Bordeaux. 7 ha.

Château du Vivier (Fr). A vineyard in the A.C. Fleurie Cru Beaujolais-Villages, Burgundy.

Château d'Yquem (Fr). A Premier Grand Cru Classé vineyard in the commune of Sauternes. A.C. Sauternes. 80 ha. Grape varieties – Sauvignon 20% and Sémillon 80%. Its dry white wine is Y Grec (a wine rarely seen).

Château Esterlin (Fr). A vineyard in the commune of Barsac. A.C. Barsac (or Sauternes), Bordeaux. 3 ha. Also Clos d'Espagnet.

Château Eyquem (Fr). A vineyard in the commune of Bayon. A.C. Côtes de Bourg, Bordeaux.

Château Fagouet-Jean-Voisin (Fr). A vineyard in the A.C. Saint Émilion, Bordeaux. 6 ha.

Château Faizeau (Fr). A vineyard in the commune of Montagne-Saint-Émilion. A.C. Saint-Émilion, Bordeaux. 7 ha.

Château Faleyrens (Fr). A vineyard in the A.C. Saint-Émilion, Bordeaux. 5 ha.

Château Falfas (Fr). A vineyard in the commune of Bayon. A.C. Côtes de Bourg, Bordeaux.

Château Fantin (Fr). A vineyard in the commune of Saint-Jean-de-Blaigrac. A.C. Entre-Deux-Mers, Bordeaux.

Château Fargues (Fr). A vineyard in the commune of Fargues. A.C. Sauternes, Bordeaux. 62 ha.

Château Farluret (Fr). A vineyard in the commune of Barsac. A.C. Barsac (or Sauternes), Bordeaux. 4 ha.

Château Fatin (Fr). A vineyard in the A.C. Médoc, Bordeaux. Cru Bourgeois.

Château Faurie de Souchard (Fr). Address = BP 24, 33330 Saint-Émilion. Grand Cru Classé. A.Ç. Saint-Émilion. Commune = Saint-Émilion. 12 ha. Grape varieties – Cabernet franc 26%, Cabernet sauvignon 9% and Merlot 65%.

Château Fayau (Fr). A vineyard in the A.C. Cadillac, Bordeaux.

Château Fayolle (Fr). A vineyard in the A.C. Bergerac, south-western France. (red).

Château Fellonneau (Fr). A vineyard in the commune of Macau. A.C. Haut-Médoc, Bordeaux. 1 ha.

Château Fernon (Fr). A vineyard in the commune of Langon. A.C. Graves, Bordeaux. 40 ha. (red and white).

Château Ferran (Fr). A vineyard in the commune of Martillac. A.C. Graves, Bordeaux. 3.5 ha. (red and white).

Château Ferrand (Fr). A vineyard in the commune of Pomerol. A.C. Pomerol, Bordeaux. 11 ha.

Château Ferrandat (Fr). A vineyard in the A.C. Saint-Émilion, Bordeaux. 4 ha.

Château Ferrande (Fr). Address = 33640 Portets, Castres, Gironde. A.C. Graves. Commune = Portets. 43 ha. Grape varieties – Cabernet franc, Cabernet sauvignon, Merlot, Sauvignon and Sémillon.

Château Ferrière (Fr). Grand Cru Classé (3rd). A.C. Margaux. Commune = Margaux. 26 ha.

Château Feytit-Clinet (Fr). A vineyard in the commune of Pomerol. A.C. Pomerol, Bordeaux. 6 ha.

Château Fieuzal (Fr). A vineyard in the commune of Léognan. A.C. Graves, Bordeaux. 1 ha. Grand Cru Classé. (white).

Château Figeac (Fr). Address = 33330 Saint-Émilion. Grand Cru Classé. A.C. Saint-Émilion. Commune = Saint-Émilion. 40 ha. Grape varieties – Cabernet franc, Cabernet sauvignon and Merlot.

Château Filhot (Fr). Address = 33210 Sauternes. Grand Cru Classé (2nd). A.C.

C

Sauternes. Commune = Sauternes. 60 ha. Grape varieties – Muscadelle 5%, Sauvignon 25% and Sémillon 70%

Château Fleur (Yug). The brand-name for full, sweet, red and white wines.

Château Fleur Cardinale (Fr). Address = Saint-Étienne-de-Lisse, 33330 Saint-Émilion. Grand Cru Classé. A.C. Saint-Émilion. Commune = Saint-Étienne-de-Lisse. 12 ha. Grape varieties – Cabernet franc 15%, Cabernet sauvignon 15% and Merlot 70%.

Château Fleury (Fr). A vineyard in the commune of Barsac. A.C. Barsac (or Sauternes), Bordeaux. 2 ha. Also Château Terre-Noble.

Château Fombrauge (Fr). Address = Saint-Christophe-des-Bardes, 33330 Saint-Émilion. Grand Cru. A.C. Saint-Émilion. Commune = Saint-Christophe-des-Bardes. 75 ha. Grape varieties – Cabernet franc 30%, Cabernet sauvignon 10% and Merlot 60%.

Château Fonbadet (Fr). Address = 33250 Pauillac. A.C. Pauillac. Commune = Pauillac. 18 ha. Grape varieties – Cabernet franc, Cabernet sauvignon, Malbec, Merlot and Petit verdot.

Château Foncet Lacour (Fr). The brand-name for Barton & Guestier red and white wines.

Château Foncla (Fr). A vineyard in the commune of Castres. A.C. Graves, Bordeaux. 13 ha. (red and white).

Château Foncroise (Fr). A vineyard in the commune of St-Selve. A.C. Graves, Bordeaux. 7 ha. (red and white).

Château Fond-de-Rol (Fr). A vineyard in the A.C. Saint-Émilion, Bordeaux. 1 ha.

Château Fond-Razade (Fr). A vineyard in the A.C. Saint-Émilion, Bordeaux. 4 ha.

Château Fongaban (Fr). Part of Château Mouchet A.C. Saint-Émilion, Bordeaux.

Château Fonpetite (Fr). A vineyard in the commune of Saint-Estèphe. A.C. Saint-Estèphe, Bordeaux. Cru Bourgeois.

Château Fonpiqueyre (Fr). The name under which Château Liversan is sometimes sold.

Château Fonplégade (Fr). Address = 33330 Saint-Émilion. Grand Cru Classé. A.C. Saint-Émilion. Commune = Saint-Émilion. 19.5 ha. Grape varieties – Cabernet franc 35%, Cabernet sauvignon 5% and Merlot 60%.

Château Fonrazade (Fr). Address = 33330 Saint-Émilion. Grand Cru. A.C. Saint-Émilion. Commune = Saint-Émilion. 15 ha. Grape varieties – Cabernet franc 10%, Cabernet sauvignon 20% and Merlot 70%. Second wine is Château Comte des Cordes.

Château Fonréaud (Fr). Address = 33480 Listrac-Médoc. Cru Bourgeois. A.C. Listrac. Commune = Listrac. 45 ha. Grape varieties – Cabernet sauvignon, Merlot and Petit verdot.

Château Fonroque (Fr). Address = 33330 Saint-Émilion. Grand Cru Classé. A.C. Saint-Émilion. Commune = Saint-Émilion. 18 ha.

Château Fontanet (Fr). A vineyard in the commune of Le Taillon-Médoc. A.C. Médoc, Bordeaux. Cru Grand Bourgeois.

Château Fontebride (Fr). A vineyard in the commune of Preignac. A.C. Sauternes, Bordeaux. 2 ha.

Château Fontesteau (Fr). A vineyard in the commune of Saint-Sauveur. A.C. Haut-Médoc, Bordeaux. 12 ha. Cru Grand Bourgeois.

Château Fontmurée (Fr). A vineyard in the commune of Montagne-Saint-Émilion. A.C. Saint-Émilion, Bordeaux. 8 ha.

Château-Fort (Lux). A large spirit distilling centre in Beaufort.

Château Fort de Vauban (Fr). Address = 33460 Margaux. Cru Bourgeois. A.C. Haut-Médoc. Commune = Cussac-Fort-Médoc. 6 ha. Grape varieties – Cabernet 40% and Merlot 60%

Château Fortia (Fr). A historic vineyard in the A.C. Châteauneuf-du-Pape, southern Rhône where the A.C. laws were conceived.

Château Fougeailles (Fr). A vineyard in the commune of Néac. A.C. Lalande de Pomerol, Bordeaux.

Château Fougères (Fr). A vineyard in the A.C. Saint-Émilion, Bordeaux. 9 ha.

Château Fouguetrat (Fr). A vineyard in the A.C. Saint-Émilion, Bordeaux. 19 ha.

Château Fourcas-Dupré (Fr). Address = 33480 Listrac-Médoc. Cru Grand Bourgeois Exceptionnel. A.C. Listrac. Commune = Listrac. 40 ha. Grape varieties – Cabernet franc, Cabernet sauvignon and Merlot

Château Fourcas-Hosten (Fr). Address = 33480 Listrac-Médoc. Cru Grand Bourgeois Exceptionnel. A.C. Listrac. Commune = Listrac. 40 ha. Grape varieties – Cabernet franc, Cabernet sauvignon and Merlot

Château Fourcas-Loubaney (Fr). Address = Moulin de Laborde, 33480, Listrac-Médoc. A.C. Listrac. Commune = Listrac. 5 ha. Grape varieties – Cabernet sauvignon 60% and Merlot 40%

Château Fourney (Fr). Address = Saint-Pey-d'Armens, 33330 Saint-Émilion, Grand Cru. A.C. Saint-Émilion.

Commune = Saint-Pey-d'Armens. 12 ha. Grape varieties – Cabernet franc 30%, Cabernet sauvignon 6% and Merlot 64%.

Château Fourtet (Fr). A vineyard in the commune of Saint-Émilion. A.C. Saint-Émilion, Bordeaux.

Château Franc (Fr). A.C. Saint-Émilion. Commune = Saint-Émilion. Second wine of Château Franc-Patarabet. Grand Cru. Saint-Émilion. 4 ha.

Château Franc-Beau-Mazerat (Fr). A vineyard in the A.C. Saint-Émilion, Bordeaux. 3 ha.

Château Franc-Bigaroux (Fr). Address = Vignonet, 33330 Saint-Émilion. Grand Cru. A.C. Saint-Émilion. Commune = Vignonet.

Château Franc-Cantenac (Fr). A vineyard in the A.C. Saint-Émilion, Bordeaux. 1 ha.

Château Franc-Cormey (Fr). A vineyard in the A.C. Saint-Émilion, Bordeaux. 2 ha.

Château Franc-Cros (Fr). A vineyard in the A.C. Saint-Émilion, Bordeaux. 4 ha.

Château Franc Grace-Dieu (Fr). Address = 33330 Saint-Émilion. Grand Cru. A.C. Saint-Émilion. Commune = Saint-Émilion. 8 ha. Grape varieties – Bouchet 41%, Cabernet sauvignon 7% and Merlot 52%.

Château Franc-Laporte (Fr). A vineyard in the A.C. Saint-Émilion, Bordeaux. 9 ha.

Château Franc-Larmande (Fr). A vineyard in the A.C. Saint-Émilion, Bordeaux. 3 ha.

Château Franc-la-Rose (Fr). A vineyard in the A.C. Saint-Émilion, Bordeaux. 4 ha.

Château Franc Maillet (Fr). A vineyard in the commune of Pomerol. A.C. Pomerol, Bordeaux. 4 ha.

Château Franc Mayne (Fr). Address = 33330 Saint-Émilion. Grand Cru Classé. A.C. Saint-Émilion. Commune = Saint-Émilion. 6.5 ha.

Château Franc-Mazerat (Fr). A vineyard in the A.C. Saint-Émilion, Bordeaux. 2 ha.

Château Francois (Austr). The name of a small vineyard based in New South Wales. Produces varietal wines.

Château Franc-Patarabet (Fr). Address = 33330 Saint-Émilion. Grand Cru. A.C. Saint-Émilion. Commune = Saint-Émilion. Grape varieties – Cabernet franc 27.5%, Cabernet sauvignon 27.5% and Merlot 45%. Second wine is Château Franc. A.C. Saint-Émilion.

Château Franc Peilhan (Fr). A vineyard in the A.C. Saint-Émilion, Bordeaux. 3 ha.

Château Franc-Petit-Figeac (Fr). A vineyard in the A.C. Saint-Émilion, Bordeaux. 3 ha.

Château Franc-Pineuilh (Fr). Address = Saint-Christophe-des-Bardes, 33330

Saint-Émilion. A.C. Saint Émilion. Commune = Saint-Christophe-des-Bardes. 8.5 ha. Grape varieties – Cabernet franc 35%, Cabernet sauvignon, Malbec and Merlot 60%.

Château Franc Pipeau (Fr). Address = Saint-Hippolyte, 33330 Saint-Émilion. Grand Cru. A.C. Saint-Émilion. Commune = Saint-Hippolyte. 4.5 ha. Grape varieties – Cabernet franc 15%, Cabernet sauvignon 25% and Merlot 60%.

Château Franc Pourret (Fr). A vineyard in the Côtes Saint-Émilion. A.C. Saint-Émilion, Bordeaux. 11 ha.

Château Franc Rosier (Fr). A vineyard in the commune of Saint Hippolyte. A.C. Saint-Émilion, Bordeaux. 11 ha.

Château Franquet Grand Poujeaux (Fr). Address = 6 Rue des Lilas, Moulis 33250. A.C. Moulis. Commune = Moulis. 6 ha. Grape varieties – Cabernet franc, Cabernet sauvignon, Malbec, Merlot and Petit verdot.

Château Froquard (Fr). A vineyard in the commune of Saint-Georges-Saint-Émilion. A.C. Saint-Émilion, Bordeaux. 3 ha.

Château Fuissé (Fr). A vineyard in the commune of Fuissé. A.C. Pouilly-Fuissé, Mâconnais, Burgundy.

Château Gaby (Fr). A vineyard in the commune of Fronsac. A.C. Côtes Canon-Fronsac, Bordeaux. 6 ha.

Château Gachet (Fr). A vineyard in the commune of Néac. A.C. Lalande de Pomerol, Bordeaux.

Château Gaciot (Fr). A vineyard in the commune of Avensan. A.C. Haut-Médoc, Bordeaux. 5 ha.

Château Gadeau (Fr). A vineyard in the commune of Plassac. A.C. Côtes de Blaye, Bordeaux.

Château Gadet-Plaisance (Fr). A vineyard in the commune of Montagne-Saint-Émilion. A.C. Saint-Émilion, Bordeaux. 4 ha.

Château Gagnard (Fr). A vineyard in the commune of Fronsac. A.C. Côtes de Fronsac, Bordeaux. 11 ha.

Château Gai (Can). A winery sited near the Niagara Falls. Produces a variety of wines.

Château Gaillard (Fr). A vineyard in the commune of Sables-Saint-Émilion. A.C. Saint-Émilion, Bordeaux. 4 ha.

Château Gaillard (Fr). Address = 33330 Saint-Émilion. Grand Cru. A.C. Saint-Émilion. Commune = Saint-Émilion. 20 ha. Grape varieties – Cabernet franc 20%, Cabernet sauvignon 40% and Merlot 40%.

Château-Gaillard (Le) (Fr). A Premier Cru

vineyard in the A.C. commune of Mon-thélie, Côte de Beaune, Burgundy. 0.9 ha.

Château Gaillard-de-Gorse (Fr). A vine-yard in the A.C. Saint-Émilion, Bordeaux. 3 ha.

Château Gallais Bellevue (Fr). A vine-yard in the commune of Potensac. A.C. Haut-Médoc, Bordeaux. Cru Bourgeois.

Château Garderose (Fr). A vineyard in the commune of Sables-Saint-Émilion. A.C. Saint-Émilion, Bordeaux. 5 ha.

Château Garraud (Fr). A vineyard in the commune of Néac. A.C. Saint-Émilion, Bordeaux.

Château Garreau (Fr). See Garreau.

Château Gastebourse (Fr). Part of Château Pontet Clauzure, A.C. Saint-Émilion, Bordeaux.

Château Gaubert (Fr). A vineyard in the A.C. Saint-Émilion, Bordeaux. 16 ha.

Château Gaudet-le-Franc-Grâce-Dieu (Fr). A vineyard in the A.C. Saint-Émilion, Bordeaux. 8 ha.

Château Gaury Balette (Fr). A vineyard producing A.C. Bordeaux wines.

Château Gaussan (Fr). A vineyard in the A.C. Corbières, south-western France. Grape varieties – Grenache and Syrah.

Châteaugay (Fr). A sub-appellation of the V.D.Q.S. region of Côtes d'Auvergne near Clermont-Ferrand in central France. Produces red wines made from the Gamay grape.

Château Gay-Moulins (Fr). A vineyard in the commune of Montagne-Saint-Émilion. A.C. Saint-Émilion, Bor-deaux. 7 ha.

Château Gazin (Fr). A vineyard in the commune of Plassac. A.C. Côtes de Blaye, Bordeaux.

Château Gazin (Fr). A vineyard in the commune of Léognan. A.C. Graves, Bordeaux. 7 ha. (red and white).

Château Gazin (Fr). A vineyard in the commune of Pomerol. A.C. Pomerol, Bordeaux. 25 ha.

Château Génisson (Fr). A vineyard in the commune of St-Germain-de-Graves. A.C. Premières Côtes de Bordeaux. 20 ha. Address = St-Germain-de-Graves, 33490 Saint-Macaire. Grape varieties – Cabernet 50%, Malbec 10% and Merlot 40%.

Château Genot-Boulanger (Fr). An estate in the A.C. commune of Pommard in the Côte de Beaune, Burgundy.

Château Gensonne (Fr). A vineyard in the commune of Sainte-Croix-du-Mont. A.C. Sainte-Croix-du-Mont, Bordeaux. 2 ha.

Château Gessan (Fr). Address = Saint-Sulpice-de-Faleyrens, 33330 Saint-Émilion. Grand Cru. A.C. Saint-Émilion. Commune = Saint-Sulpice-de-Faleyrens. 7.32 ha. Grape varieties – Cabernet 82% and Merlot 18%

Château Gigault (Fr). A vineyard in the commune of Mazion. A.C. Côtes de Blaye, Bordeaux.

Château Gilette (Fr). A vineyard in the commune of Preignac. A.C. Sauternes, Bordeaux. 14 ha. Cru Bourgeois. Also Domaine des Justices and Châteaux Les Rochers, Les Ramparts and Lamothe.

Château Gironde (Fr). A vineyard in the commune of Puisseguin-Saint-Émilion. A.C. Saint-Émilion, Bor-deaux. 4 ha.

Château Gironville (Fr). A vineyard in the commune of Macau. A.C. Médoc, Bordeaux. Cru Bourgeois.

Château Giscours (Fr). Address = 33460 Margaux-Labarde. Grand Cru Classé (3rd). A.C. Margaux. Commune = Lab-arde. 84 ha. Grape varieties – Cabernet sauvignon 75% and Merlot 25%

Château Glana (Fr). A vineyard in the commune of Saint-Julien. A.C. Saint-Julien, Bordeaux. 71 ha.

Château Gloria (Fr). Address = Saint-Julien Beychevelle. A.C. Saint-Julien. Commune = Saint-Julien. 45 ha. Grape varieties – Cabernet franc, Cabernet sauvignon, Merlot and Petit verdot.

Château Gobinaud (Fr). A vineyard in the commune of Listrac. A.C. Listrac, Bordeaux. 8 ha.

Château Godeau (Fr). A vineyard in the A.C. Saint-Émilion, Bordeaux. 3 ha.

Château Gombaude-Guillot (Fr). A vine-yard in the commune of Pomerol. A.C. Pomerol, Bordeaux. 6 ha.

Château Gombeau (Fr). A vineyard in the commune of Fronsac. A.C. Côtes de Canon-Fronsac, Bordeaux. 4 ha.

Château Gontet-Robin (Fr). Address = Château Sansonnet, 33330 Saint-Émilion. A.C. Puisseguin-Saint-Émilion. Commune = Puisseguin-Saint-Émilion.

Château Gontier (Fr). A vineyard in the commune of Plassac. A.C. Côtes de Blaye, Bordeaux.

Château Gorre (Fr). A vineyard in the commune of Martillac. A.C. Graves, Bordeaux. 3 ha. (red and white).

Château Goujon (Fr). A vineyard in the commune of Montagne-Saint-Émilion. A.C. Saint-Émilion, Bordeaux. 3 ha.

Château Gouprie (Fr). A vineyard in the commune of Pomerol. A.C. Pomerol, Bordeaux. 3 ha.

Château Grand Abord (Fr). Address = 33460 Portets. A.C. Graves. Commune = Portets. 17 ha. Grape varieties –

C

Malbec 10%, Merlot 90%, Sauvignon and Sémillon.

Château Grand Barrail (Fr). A vineyard in the A.C. Côtes de Blaye, Bordeaux.

Château Grand Barrail Lamarzelle Figeac (Fr). Address = 33330 Saint-Émilion. Grand Cru Classé. A.C. Saint-Émilion. Commune = Saint-Émilion. 19 ha. Grape varieties – Cabernet franc 20%, Cabernet sauvignon 20% and Merlot 60%.

Château Grand-Berc (Fr). A vineyard in the A.C. Saint-Émilion, Bordeaux. 4 ha.

Château Grand Bigaroux (Fr). Address = Saint-Sulpice-de-Faleyrens, 33330 Saint-Émilion. Grand Cru. A.C. Saint-Émilion. Commune = Saint-Sulpice-de-Faleyrens. 6 ha. Grape varieties – Cabernet 10% and Merlot 90%

Château Grand'Boise (Fr). Address = BP 2, 12530 Trets. A.C. Côtes-de-Provence, south-eastern France. (red and blanc de blanc wines) Grape varieties – Cabernet sauvignon, Cinsault, Grenache and Syrah.

Château Grand-Caillou-Noir (Fr). A vineyard in the A.C. Saint-Émilion, Bordeaux. 3 ha.

Château Grand Canyon (Fr). Address = 33250 Pauillac. Cru Bourgeois. A.C. Pauillac. Commune = Pauillac. 8 ha. Grape varieties – Cabernet franc, Cabernet sauvignon and Merlot.

Château Grand-Carretey (Fr). A vineyard in the commune of Barsac. A.C. Barsac (or Sauternes), Bordeaux. 1 ha.

Château Grand Chemin (Fr). A vineyard in the commune of Cérons. A.C. Cérons, Bordeaux. 4 ha.

Château Grand Chemin (Fr). A vineyard in the commune of Cérons. A.C. Graves, Bordeaux. 2 ha. (white).

Château Grand Clapeau Olivier (Fr). A vineyard in the commune of Blanquefort. A.C. Médoc, Bordeaux. Cru Bourgeois.

Château Grand Corbin (Fr). A vineyard in the commune of Saint-Émilion. A.C. Saint-Émilion, Bordeaux. Grand Cru Classé. 13.5 ha.

Château Grand-Corbin-Despagne (Fr). Address = 33330 Saint-Émilion. Grand Cru Classé. A.C. Saint-Émilion. Commune = Saint-Émilion. 31 ha. Grape varieties – Cabernet franc 25%, Cabernet sauvignon 5% and Merlot 70%. Second wine is Château Reine-Blanche.

Château Grand Corbin Giraud (Fr). A vineyard in the Graves-Saint-Émilion. A.C. Saint-Émilion, Bordeaux. Grand Cru Classé.

Château Grand Corbin Manuel (Fr).

Address = 33330 Saint-Émilion. Grand Cru. A.C. Saint-Émilion. Commune = Saint-Émilion. 12 ha. Grape varieties – Bouchet 30%, Cabernet sauvignon 30% and Merlot 40%.

Château Grand Duroc Milon (Fr). A vineyard in the commune of Pauillac. A.C. Pauillac, Bordeaux..

Château Grandes Murailles (Fr). A vineyard in the Côtes Saint-Émilion. A.C. Saint-Émilion, Bordeaux. 2 ha. Grand Cru.

Château Grandes-Vignes-Clinet (Fr). Part of Château Gombaude-Guillot A.C. Pomerol, Bordeaux.

Château Grand Gontey (Fr). A vineyard in the A.C. Saint-Émilion, Bordeaux. 4 ha.

Château Grandis (Fr). A vineyard in the commune of Saint-Seurin-de-Cadourne. A.C. Haut-Médoc, Bordeaux. 5 ha.

Château Grand Jacques (Fr). A vineyard in the A.C. Saint-Émilion, Bordeaux. 11 ha.

Château Grand-Jaugueyron (Fr). A vineyard in the commune of Cantenac. A.C. Haut-Médoc, Bordeaux. 3 ha.

Château Grand Jour (Fr). A vineyard in the commune of Yvrac. A.C. Premières Côtes de Bordeaux.

Château Grand-Jour (Fr). A vineyard in the commune of Prignac-Marcamps. A.C. Côtes de Bourg, Bordeaux.

Château Grand Lartigue (Fr). Address = 33330 Saint-Émilion. Grand Cru. A.C. Saint-Émilion. Commune = Saint-Émilion. 7 ha. Grape varieties – Cabernet 25% and Merlot 75%.

Château Grandmaison (Fr). A vineyard in the commune of Léognan. A.C. Graves, Bordeaux. 2 ha. (red).

Château Grand Mayne (Fr). Address = 33330 Saint-Émilion. Grand Cru. Classé. A.C. Saint-Émilion. Commune = Saint-Émilion. 21 ha. Grape varieties – Cabernet franc 40%, Cabernet sauvignon 10% and Merlot 50%.

Château Grand-Mayne-Qui-Né-Marc (Fr). A vineyard in the commune of Barsac. A.C. Barsac (or Sauternes), Bordeaux. 1 ha.

Château Grand Mazerolles (Fr). A vineyard in the A.C. Premières Côtes de Blaye, Bordeaux.

Château Grand-Mirande (Fr). A vineyard in the A.C. Saint-Émilion, Bordeaux. 6 ha.

Château Grand Moulin (Fr). A vineyard in the commune of Saint-Seurin-de-Cadourne. A.C. Médoc, Bordeaux. Cru Bourgeois.

Château Grand Moulinet A vineyard in

C

the commune of Pomerol. A.C. Pomerol, Bordeaux. 2 ha.

Château Grand Ormeau (Fr). A vineyard in the commune of Lalande de Pomerol. A.C. Lalande de Pomerol, Bordeaux.

Château Grand-Peilhan-Blanc (Fr). A vineyard in the A.C. Saint-Émilion, Bordeaux. 7 ha.

Château Grand-Pey-Lescours (Fr). Address = Saint-Sulpice-de-Faleyrens, 33330 Saint-Émilion. Grand Cru. A.C. Saint-Émilion. Commune = Saint-Sulpice-de-Faleyrens. 24 ha.

Château Grand-Pontet (Fr). Address = 33330 Saint-Émilion. Grand Cru Classé. A.C. Saint-Émilion. Commune = Saint-Émilion. 14.65 ha. Grape varieties – Cabernet franc 15%, Cabernet sauvignon 15% and Merlot 70%.

Château Grand-Puy-Ducasse (Fr). Grand Cru Classé (5th). A.C. Pauillac. Commune = Pauillac. 35 ha. Grape varieties – Cabernet franc and Merlot.

Château Grand Puy Lacoste (Fr). Address = 33250 Pauillac. Grand Cru Classé (5th). A.C. Pauillac. Commune = Pauillac. 45 ha. Grape varieties – Cabernet sauvignon and Merlot

Château Grand Renouilh (Fr). A vineyard in the commune of St-Michel. A.C. Côtes Canon-Fronsac, Bordeaux. 6 ha.

Château Grand-Rivallon (Fr). A vineyard in the A.C. Saint-Émilion, Bordeaux. 3 ha.

Château Grand-Seuil (Fr). Address = Puyricard, 13100 Aix-en-Provence. V.D.Q.S. Coteaux-d'Aix-en-Provence. (red and rosé wines).

Château Grand-Soussans (Fr). A vineyard in the commune of Soussans. A.C. Médoc, Bordeaux. 3 ha.

Château Grands Sillons (Fr). A vineyard in the commune of Pomerol. A.C. Pomerol, Bordeaux. 3 ha.

Château Grand Travers (USA). A winery based in Grand Traverse (City), North Michigan. 18 ha. Grape varieties – Chardonnay and Riesling.

Château Grange Neuve (Fr). A vineyard in the commune of Pomerol. A.C. Pomerol, Bordeaux. 4 ha.

Château Grangeneuve (Fr). Part of Château Figeac, A.C. Saint-Émilion, Bordeaux.

Château Grangey (Fr). A vineyard in the A.C. Saint-Émilion, Bordeaux. 5 ha.

Château Gravas (Fr). A vineyard in the commune of Barsac. A.C. Barsac (or Sauternes), Bordeaux. 8 ha.

Château Graves-d'Armens (Fr). A vineyard in the A.C. Saint-Émilion, Bordeaux. 3 ha.

Château Graves d'Arthus (Fr). A vineyard

in the A.C. Saint-Émilion, Bordeaux. 5 ha.

Château Graves-Richeboh (Fr). A vineyard in the commune of Moulis. A.C. Moulis, Bordeaux. 2 ha.

Château Gravet (Fr). A vineyard in the A.C. Saint-Émilion, Bordeaux. 12 ha.

Château Gravet-Renaissance (Fr). Address = Saint-Sulpice-de-Faleyrens, 33330 Saint-Émilion. Grand Cru. A.C. Saint-Émilion. Commune = Saint-Sulpice-de-Faleyrens. 9 ha. Grape varieties – Cabernet franc 30%, Cabernet sauvignon 2%, Malbec 3% and Merlot 60%. Second wine is Les Grandes Versannes.

Château Graveyron (Fr). A vineyard in the commune of Portets. A.C. Graves, Bordeaux. 10 ha. (red and white).

Château Gressier-Grand-Poujeaux (Fr). Address = 33480 Moulis-Médoc. A.C. Moulis. Commune = Moulis. 19 ha. Grape varieties – Cabernet franc 15%, Cabernet sauvignon 35% and Merlot 50%.

Château Greysac (Fr). Cru Grand Bourgeois. A.C. Médoc. Commune = Bégadan. 65 ha. Grape varieties – Cabernet franc, Cabernet sauvignon, Malbec, Merlot and Petit verdot. Address = Bégadan, 33340 Lesparre.

Château Grillet (Fr). A.C. Château Grillet. The smallest A.C. in France. Produces 3,000 bottles of white wine per year. 1.45 ha. Grape variety – Viognier. Sited near Condrieu, northern Rhône.

Château Grillon (Fr). A vineyard in the commune of Barsac. A.C. Barsac (or Sauternes), Bordeaux. 6 ha.

Château Gris (Fr). An estate in the A.C. Nuits-Saint-Georges. Côtes de Nuits, Burgundy.

Château Grivière (Fr). Address = 33340 Lesparre. A.C. Médoc. Commune = Blaignan. 19 ha. Grape varieties – Cabernet franc, Cabernet sauvignon and Merlot.

Château Gros Caillou (Fr). A vineyard in the commune of Saint-Sulpice-de-Faleyrens. A.C. Saint-Émilion, Bordeaux. 12 ha.

Château Gros Jean (Fr). A vineyard in the commune of St-Aignan. A.C. Côtes de Fronsac, Bordeaux. 4 ha.

Château Gros-Moulin (Fr). A vineyard in the commune of Bourg. A.C. Côtes de Bourg, Bordeaux.

Château Gruaud-Larose (Fr). Address = Saint-Julien-Beychevelle. Grand Cru Classé (4th). A.C. Saint-Julien. Commune = Saint-Julien. 76 ha. Grape varieties – Cabernet franc, Cabernet sauvignon, Merlot and Petit verdot. See also Sarget de Gruaud-Larose.

C

Château Guadet de Franc Grâce-Dieu (Fr). A vineyard in the A.C. Saint-Émilion, Bordeaux. 8 ha.

Château Guadet-Plaisance (Fr). Address = Montagne-Saint-Émilion. 33330 Saint-Émilion. A.C. Montagne-Saint-Émilion. Commune = Montagne-Saint-Émilion.

Château Guadet Saint-Julien (Fr). Address = 33330 Saint-Émilion. Grand Cru. A.C. Saint-Émilion. Commune = Saint-Émilion. 6 ha. Grape varieties – Cabernet franc, Cabernet sauvignon and Merlot 75%.

Château Guerande (Fr). A vineyard in the A.C. Muscadet de Sèvre et Maine, Pays Nantais, Loire. Address = 44330 Vallet.

Château Guerit (Fr). A vineyard in the commune of Tauriac. A.C. Côtes de Bourg, Bordeaux. Also known as Domaine de Guerrit.

Château Guerry (Fr). A vineyard in the A.C. Côtes de Bourg, Bordeaux. Address = Domaine Ribet, 33450 Saint-Loubès.

Château Gueyrosse (Fr). A vineyard in the commune of Sables-Saint-Émilion. A.C. Saint-Émilion, Bordeaux. 4 ha. Address = 33500 Libourne.

Château Gueyrot (Fr). Address = 33330 Saint-Émilion. Grand Cru. A.C. Saint-Émilion. Commune = Saint-Émilion. 8.33 ha. Grape varieties – Cabernet franc, Cabernet sauvignon and Merlot 66%. Second wine is Château Beau Site de la Tour. A.C. Fronsac.

Château Guibeau Lafourvieille (Fr). A vineyard in the commune of Puisseguin-Saint-Émilion. A.C. Saint-Émilion, Bordeaux. 25 ha.

Château Guienne (Fr). A vineyard in the commune of Lansac. A.C. Côtes de Bourg, Bordeaux.

Château Guillaumont (Fr). A vineyard in the commune of La Brède. A.C. Graves, Bordeaux. 13 ha. (red and white).

Château Guillemot (Fr). A vineyard in the commune of Saint-Christophe-des-Bardes. A.C. Saint-Émilion, Bordeaux. 7 ha.

Château Guillonnet (Fr). A vineyard in the commune of Anglade. A.C. Côtes de Blaye, Bordeaux.

Château Guillot (Fr). A vineyard in the commune of Pomerol. A.C. Pomerol, Bordeaux. 5 ha.

Château Guillotin (Fr). A vineyard in the commune of Puisseguin-Saint-Émilion. A.C. Saint-Émilion, Bordeaux.

Château Guillou (Fr). A vineyard in the commune of Saint-Georges-Saint-Émilion. A.C. Saint-Émilion, Bordeaux. 13 ha.

Château Guimbalet (Fr). A vineyard in the commune of Preignac. A.C. Sauternes, Bordeaux. 1 ha.

Château Guinot (Fr). A vineyard in the A.C. Saint-Émilion, Bordeaux. 4 ha.

Château Guionne (Fr). A vineyard in the commune of Lansac. A.C. Côtes de Bourg, Bordeaux.

Château Guiraud (Fr). A vineyard in the commune of St-Ciers-de-Canesse. A.C. Côtes de Bourg, Bordeaux.

Château Guiraud (Fr). Premier Grand Cru Classé. A.C. Sauternes. Commune = Sauternes. 55 ha. Grape varieties – Muscadelle, Sauvignon and Sémillon. (Also grows some Cabernet sauvignon and Merlot).

Château Guitard (Fr). A vineyard in the commune of Montagne-Saint-Émilion. A.C. Saint-Émilion, Bordeaux.

Château Guitteronde (Fr). A vineyard in the commune of Barsac. A.C. Barsac (or Sauternes), Bordeaux. 1 ha.

Château Guitteronde-Bert (Fr). A vineyard in the commune of Barsac. A.C. Barsac (or Sauternes), Bordeaux. 9 ha.

Château Guitteronde-Sarraute (Fr). A vineyard in the commune of Barsac. A.C. Barsac (or Sauternes), Bordeaux. 4 ha.

Château Hallet (Fr). A vineyard in the commune of Barsac. A.C. Barsac (or Sauternes), Bordeaux 10 ha.

Château Hanteillan (Fr). Address = Cissac-Médoc, 33250 Pauillac. Cru Bourgeois. A.C. Haut-Médoc. Commune = Cissac. 87 ha. Grape varieties – Cabernet franc 8%, Cabernet sauvignon 45%, Merlot 42% and Petit verdot 5%. See also Châteaux Larrivaux, Larrivaux-Hanteillan and Tour de Vatican.

Château Hauchat (Fr). A vineyard in the commune of St-Aignan. A.C. Côtes de Fronsac, Bordeaux. 1 ha.

Château Hauret (Fr). A vineyard in the commune of Illats. A.C. Cérons, Bordeaux. 4 ha.

Château Haut-Badette (Fr). Address = 37, Rue Pline-Parmentier, 33500 Libourne. A.C. Saint-Émilion. Commune = Saint-Christophe-des-Bardes. 6 ha. Grape varieties – Cabernet sauvignon 10% and Merlot 90%.

Château Haut-Bages Averous (Fr). Address = 33250 Pauillac. A.C. Pauillac. Commune = Pauillac. 5 ha. Grape varieties – Cabernet sauvignon, Merlot and Petit verdot.

Château Haut-Bages Libéral (Fr). Address = Balogues, 33250 Pauillac. Grand Cru Classé (5th). A.C. Pauillac. Commune = Pauillac. 28 ha. Grape

C

varieties – Cabernet sauvignon, Merlot and Petit verdot.

Château Haut-Bages Monpelou (Fr). Address = 33250 Pauillac. Cru Bourgeois. A.C. Pauillac. Commune = Pauillac. 15 ha. Grape varieties – Cabernet sauvignon 75% and Merlot 25%

Château Haut-Bailly (Fr). Address = 33850 Léognan. Grand Cru Classé. A.C. Graves. Commune = Léognan. 25 ha. Grape varieties – Cabernet franc 10%, Cabernet sauvignon 60% and Merlot 30%. See also La Parde de Haut-Bailly.

Château Haut-Ballet (Fr). A vineyard in the commune of Néac. A.C. Lalande de Pomerol, Bordeaux.

Château Haut-Barbeyron (Fr). A vineyard in the A.C. Saint-Émilion, Bordeaux. 4 ha.

Château Haut-Bastienne (Fr). A vineyard in the commune of Montagne-Saint-Émilion. A.C. Saint-Émilion, Bordeaux. 4 ha.

Château Haut Batailley (Fr). Address = 33250 Pauillac. Grand Cru Classé. (5th). A.C. Pauillac. Commune = Pauillac. 20 ha. Grape varieties – Cabernet franc 10%, Cabernet sauvignon 65% and Merlot 25%.

Château Haut-Bayle (Fr). An A.C. Bordeaux rouge from a co-operative winery at 33540 Sauveterre-de-Guyenne. (Les Vignerons de Guyenne à Blasinon).

Château Haut Bellevue (Fr). A vineyard in the commune of Lamarque. A.C. Haut-Médoc, Bordeaux. 3 ha.

Château Haut-Benitey (Fr). A vineyard in the A.C. Saint-Émilion, Bordeaux. 5 ha.

Château Haut-Bergeron (Fr). A vineyard in the commune of Preignac. A.C. Sauternes, Bordeaux. 4 ha. (Adjoins Château d'Yquem).

Château Haut-Bergey (Fr). Address = 33850 Léognan. A.C. Graves. Commune = Léognan. 13.5 ha. Grape varieties – Cabernet sauvignon 70% and Merlot 30%. (red).

Château Haut-Berthonneau (Fr). A vineyard in the A.C. Saint-Émilion, Bordeaux. 1 ha.

Château Haut Beychevelle Gloria (Fr). Part of Château Gloria A.C. Haut-Médoc, Bordeaux.

Château Haut-Blaignan (Fr). A vineyard in the commune of Blaignan. A.C. Haut-Médoc, Bordeaux. Cru Bourgeois. 7 ha.

Château Haut Bommes (Fr). A vineyard in the commune of Bommes. A.C. Sauternes, Bordeaux.

Château Haut Breton Larigaudière (Fr). Address = Soussans 33460. A.C. Margaux. Commune = Soussans. 5 ha.

Grape varieties – Cabernet sauvignon 70% and Merlot 30%

Château Haut-Brignon (Fr). A vineyard in the commune of Cenac. A.C. Premières Côtes de Bordeaux, central Bordeaux.

Château Haut-Brion (Fr). Address = 33600 Pessac. Premier Grand Cru Classé. A.C. Graves. Commune = Pessac. 43 ha. Grape varieties – Cabernet franc, Cabernet sauvignon, Merlot, Sauvignon and Sémillon. See Château Bahans Haut Brion.

Château Haut-Brisson (Fr). Address = 167, Avenue Maréchal Foch BP. 170, 33500 Libourne. Grand Cru. A.C. Saint-Émilion. Commune = Vignonet. 23 ha. Grape varieties – Bouchet 10%, Cabernet sauvignon 25% and Merlot 65%.

Château Haut-Cabat (Fr). A vineyard in the commune of Anglade. A.C. Côtes de Blaye, Bordeaux.

Château Haut-Cadet (Fr). Address = 33330 Saint-Émilion. A.C. Saint-Émilion. Commune = Saint-Émilion. 13 ha.

Château Haut-Caillou (Fr). A vineyard in the commune of Fronsac. A.C. Côtes de Canon-Fronsac, Bordeaux. 3 ha.

Château Haut-Canteloup (Fr). A vineyard in the commune of Couquèques. A.C. Médoc, Bordeaux. Cru Borgeois.

Château Haut-Carmail (Fr). A vineyard in the commune of Saint-Seurin-de-Cadourne. A.C. Haut-Médoc, Bordeaux. 5 ha.

Château Haut-Castanet (Fr). A.C. Bordeaux Rouge.

Château Haut-Chaigneau (Fr). A vineyard in the commune of Néac. A.C. Lalande de Pomerol, Bordeaux.

Château Haut-Chéreau (Fr). A vineyard in the commune of Lussac-Saint-Émilion. A.C. Saint-Émilion, Bordeaux. 2 ha.

Château Haut-Claverie (Fr). A vineyard in the commune of Fargues. A.C. Sauternes, Bordeaux. 4 ha.

Château Haut-Cloquet (Fr). A vineyard in the commune of Pomerol. A.C. Pomerol, Bordeaux. 1 ha.

Château Haut-Corbin (Fr). A vineyard in the commune of Saint-Émilion. A.C. Saint-Émilion, Bordeaux. 3.5 ha. Grand Cru Classé.

Château Haut de Baritault (Fr). A vineyard in the commune of Sainte-Croix-du-Mont. A.C. Sainte-Croix-du-Mont, Bordeaux. 5 ha.

Château Hauterive (Fr). A vineyard in the commune of Saint-Germain-d'Esteuil. A.C. Médoc, Bordeaux. Cru Bourgeois.

Château Hautes Combes (Fr). A vineyard in the A.C. Côtes de Bourg, Bordeaux.

C

Château Hautes-Graves-d'Arthus (Fr). A vineyard in the A.C. Saint-Émilion, Bordeaux. 9 ha.

Château Haut-Fonrazade (Fr). A vineyard in the A.C. Saint-Émilion, Bordeaux. 11 ha.

Château Haut Garin (Fr). A vineyard in the commune of Prignac. A.C. Haut-Médoc, Bordeaux. Cru Bourgeois.

Château Haut-Grâce-Dieu (Fr). Part of Château Peyrelongue A.C. Saint-Émilion, Bordeaux.

Château Haut-Grand-Faurie (Fr). A vineyard in the A.C. Saint-Émilion, Bordeaux. 4 ha.

Château Haut-Gueyrot (Fr). A vineyard in the A.C. Saint-Émilion, Bordeaux. 2 ha.

Château Haut-Guiraud (Fr). A vineyard in the A.C. Côtes de Bourg, Bordeaux.

Château Haut-Guitard (Fr). A vineyard in the commune of Montagne-Saint-Émilion. A.C. Saint-Émilion, Bordeaux. 4 ha.

Château Haut-Jean-Faure (Fr). A vineyard in the A.C. Saint-Émilion, Bordeaux. 7 ha.

Château Haut-Jeanguillot (Fr). A vineyard in the A.C. Saint-Émilion, Bordeaux. 4 ha.

Château Haut Laborde (Fr). A vineyard in the A.C. Médoc, Bordeaux.

Château Haut-Langlade (Fr). A vineyard in the commune of Parsac-Saint-Émilion. A.C. Saint-Émilion, Bordeaux. 4 ha.

Château Haut-Larose (Fr). A vineyard in the commune of Lussac-Saint-Émilion. A.C. Saint-Émilion, Bordeaux. 5 ha.

Château Haut-Lartigue (Fr). A vineyard in the A.C. Saint-Émilion, Bordeaux. 3 ha.

Château Haut-Lavallade (Fr). Address = Saint-Christophe-des-Bardes, 33330 Saint-Émilion. A.C. Saint-Émilion. Commune = Saint-Christophe-des-Bardes. 12 ha. Grape varieties – Cabernet franc, 20%, Cabernet sauvignon 25% and Merlot 65%.

Château Haut-Logat (Fr). Address = Cissac, 33250 Pauillac. A.C. Haut-Médoc. Commune = Cissac. 14 ha. Grape varieties – Cabernet sauvignon 75% and Merlot 25%.

Château Haut-Macô (Fr). A vineyard in the commune of Tauriac. A.C. Côtes de Bourg, Bordeaux. 35 ha. Address = 33710 Tauriac. Grape varieties – Cabernet 70% and Merlot 30%.

Château Haut-Madère (Fr). A vineyard in the commune of Villenave d'Ornon. A.C. Graves, Bordeaux. 2 ha. (red).

Château Haut Madrac (Fr). Address =

33250 Pauillac. A.C. Haut-Médoc. Commune = St-Saveur-du-Médoc. 40 ha. Grape varieties – Cabernet 75% and Merlot 25%

Château Haut-Maillet (Fr). A vineyard in the commune of Pomerol. A.C. Pomerol, Bordeaux. 5 ha.

Château Haut-Marbuzet (Fr). Address = 33250 Saint-Estèphe. Cru Grand Bourgeois Exceptionnel. A.C. Saint-Estèphe. Commune = Saint-Estèphe. 30 ha. Grape varieties – Cabernet franc 10%, Cabernet sauvignon 40% and Merlot 50%

Château Haut-Maurac (Fr). A vineyard in the commune of St-Yzans-de-Médoc. A.C. Médoc, Bordeaux. Address = St-Yzans-de-Médoc, 33340 Lesparre.

Château Haut-Mauvinon (Fr). A vineyard in the A.C. Saint-Émilion, Bordeaux. 8 ha.

Château Haut-Mayne (Fr). A.C. Graves. Commune = Cérons. 8 ha. Grape varieties – Cabernet franc 50%, Cabernet sauvignon 50%, Sauvignon 25% and Sémillon 75%

Château Haut-Mayne (Fr). A vineyard in the commune of Fargues. A.C. Sauternes, Bordeaux. 2 ha.

Château Haut Mazerat (Fr). Address = 33330 Saint-Émilion. Grand Cru. A.C. Saint-Émilion. Commune = Saint-Émilion. 12.5 ha. Grape varieties – Cabernet franc 30%, Cabernet sauvignon 10% and Merlot 60%.

Château Haut Mazeris (Fr). A vineyard in the commune of St-Michel. A.C. Côtes Canon-Fronsac, Bordeaux. 6 ha.

Château Haut-Merigot (Fr). A vineyard in the A.C. Entre-Deux-Mers, central Bordeaux.

Château Haut-Musset (Fr). A vineyard in the commune of Parsac-Saint-Émilion. A.C. Saint-Émilion, Bordeaux. 5 ha.

Château Haut-Nauve (Fr). A vineyard in the A.C. Saint-Émilion, Bordeaux. 3 ha.

Château Haut-Nouchet (Fr). Address = 33650 Labrède. A.C. Graves Supérieures. Commune = Léognan. 11 ha. (red and white).

Château Haut-Padarnac (Fr). A vineyard in the commune of Pauillac. A.C. Haut-Médoc, Bordeaux. Cru Bourgeois.

Château Haut-Panet-Rineuilh (Fr). A vineyard in the A.C. Saint-Émilion, Bordeaux. 2 ha.

Château Haut Pauillac (Fr). A vineyard in the commune of Pauillac. A.C. Médoc, Bordeaux. Cru Bourgeois.

Château Haut Peyraguey (Fr). A Premier Cru Classé vineyard in the commune of Bommes. A.C. Sauternes, Bordeaux.

Château Haut-Peyroutas (Fr). A vineyard

C

in the A.C. Saint-Émilion, Bordeaux. 2 ha.

Château Haut-Piquat (Fr). A vineyard in the commune of Lussac-Saint-Émilion. A.C. Saint-Émilion, Bordeaux. 9 ha.

Château Haut-Plaisance (Fr). A vineyard in the commune of Montagne-Saint-Émilion. A.C. Saint-Émilion, Bordeaux. 7 ha.

Château Haut Plantey (Fr). A vineyard in the commune of Listrac. A.C. Haut-Médoc, Bordeaux. 3 ha.

Château Haut-Plantey (Fr). Address = Saint Laurent des Combes, 33330 Saint-Émilion. Grand Cru. A.C. Saint-Émilion. Commune = Saint-Hippolyte. 9.10 ha. Grape varieties – Cabernet franc 28%, Cabernet sauvignon 2% and Merlot 70%.

Château Haut-Poitou (Fr). A vineyard in the commune of Lussac-Saint-Émilion. A.C. Saint-Émilion, Bordeaux. 2 ha.

Château Haut-Pontet (Fr). A vineyard in the A.C. Saint-Émilion, Bordeaux. 5 ha.

Château Haut-Pourret (Fr). A vineyard in the A.C. Saint-Émilion, Bordeaux. 5 ha.

Château Haut-Pourteau (Fr). A vineyard in the commune of Lussac-Saint-Émilion. A.C. Saint-Émilion, Bordeaux. 2 ha.

Château Haut-Rabion (Fr). A vineyard in the commune of Vignonet. A.C. Saint-Émilion, Bordeaux. Address = Vignonet, 33330 Saint-Émilion. 5 ha.

Château Haut-Rat (Fr). A vineyard in the commune of Illats. A.C. Cérons, Bordeaux. 16 ha.

Château Haut-Renaissance (Fr). Address = Saint-Sulpice-de-Faleyrens, 33330 Saint-Émilion. A.C. Saint-Émilion. Commune = Saint-Sulpice-de-Faleyrens. 3 ha.

Château Haut Rey (Fr). A vineyard in the commune of Fronsac. A.C. Côtes de Fronsac, Bordeaux. 8 ha.

Château Haut-Rocher (Fr). Address = Saint-Étienne-de-Lisse, 33330 Saint-Émilion. Grand Cru. A.C. Saint-Émilion. Commune = Saint-Étienne-de-Lisse. 15 ha. Grape varieties – Cabernet franc 25%, Cabernet sauvignon 15% and Merlot 60%.

Château Haut-Sarpe (Fr). Address = 37, Rue Pline-Parmentier, 33500 Libourne. Grand Cru Classé. A.C. Saint-Émilion. Commune = Saint-Christophe-des-Bardes. 15 ha. Grape varieties – Cabernet franc 30%, Cabernet sauvignon 10% and Merlot 60%.

Château Haut-Ségottes (Fr). Address = 33330 Saint-Émilion. Grand Cru. A.C. Saint-Émilion. Commune = Saint-Émilion. 8.6 ha. Grape varieties –

Cabernet franc 40%, Cabernet sauvignon 10% and Merlot 50%.

Château Haut-Serre (Fr). A vineyard in the A.C. Cahors, south-western France. Grape varieties – Cabernet sauvignon and Tannat.

Château Haut-Simard (Fr). A vineyard in the A.C. Saint-Émilion, Bordeaux. 20 ha.

Château Haut-Sociondo (Fr). A vineyard in the commune of Cars. A.C. Côtes de Blaye, Bordeaux.

Château Haut-St-Georges (Fr). A vineyard in the commune of Saint-Georges-Saint-Émilion. A.C. Saint-Émilion, Bordeaux. 2 ha.

Château Haut-Tayac (Fr). A vineyard in the commune of Soussans-Margaux. A.C. Haut-Médoc, Bordeaux. 6 ha.

Château Haut-Touran (Fr). A vineyard in the A.C. Saint-Émilion, Bordeaux. 3 ha.

Château Haut-Troquard (Fr). A vineyard in the commune of Saint Georges-Saint-Émilion. A.C. Saint-Émilion, Bordeaux. 3 ha.

Château Haut-Troquart (Fr). A vineyard in the A.C. Saint-Émilion, Bordeaux. 4 ha.

Château Haut-Tuquet (Fr). A vineyard in the commune of St-Magne-de-Castillon (Côtes de Castillon). A.C. Bordeaux Supérieur.

Château Haut-Veyrac (Fr). A vineyard in the A.C. Saint-Émilion, Bordeaux. 7 ha.

Château Hélène (Fr). Address = Barbaira, 11800 Trèbes. A.C. Corbières. (red wine).

Château Hennebelle (Fr). Address = 33460 Margaux. A.C. Haut-Médoc. Commune = Lamarque. 5.5 ha. Grape varieties – Cabernet sauvignon, Merlot and Petit verdot.

Château Hontemieux (Fr). A.C. Médoc. Commune = Blaignan. Grape varieties – Cabernet sauvignon and Merlot.

Château Hornsby (Austr). A small winery at Alice Springs, Northern Territory.

Château Hortevie (Fr). A vineyard in the A.C. Médoc, Bordeaux. Cru Bourgeois.

Château Hostein (Fr). A vineyard in the commune of Saint-Estèphe. A.C. Saint-Estèphe, Bordeaux. 3 ha.

Château Houbanon (Fr). A vineyard in the commune of Prignac. A.C. Médoc, Bordeaux. Cru Bourgeois.

Château Houissant (Fr). Cru Grand Bourgeois Exceptionnel. A.C. Saint-Estèphe. Commune = Saint-Estèphe. Also sold as Château Leyssac. 20 ha.

Château Hourbanon (Fr). A vineyard in the commune of Prignac. A.C. Médoc, Bordeaux. 6 ha.

Château Hourmalas (Fr). A vineyard in

C

the commune of Barsac. A.C. Barsac (or Sauternes), Bordeaux. 6 ha. Also Château St-Marc.

Château Hourtin-Ducasse (Fr). A vineyard in the commune of Saint-Sauveur. A.C. Haut-Médoc, Bordeaux. Cru Bourgeois.

Château Houtou (Fr). A vineyard in the commune of Tauriac. A.C. Côtes de Bourg, Bordeaux.

Château Huradin (Fr). A vineyard in the commune of Cérons. A.C. Cérons, Bordeaux. 8 ha. See Domaine du Salut.

Château Jacqueblanc (Fr). A vineyard in the A.C. Saint-Émilion, Bordeaux. 20 ha.

Château Jacqueminot (Fr). A vineyard in the A.C. Saint-Émilion, Bordeaux. 1 ha.

Château Jacquenoir (Fr). A vineyard in the A.C. Saint-Émilion, Bordeaux. 4 ha.

Château Jacques-Blanc (Fr). A vineyard in the commune of Saint-Étienne-de-Lisse. A.C. Saint-Émilion, Bordeaux.

Château Jamnets (Fr). A vineyard in the commune of St-Pierre-de-Mons. A.C. Graves, Bordeaux. 2 ha. (red and white).

Château Jany (Fr). A vineyard in the commune of Barsac. A.C. Barsac (or Sauternes), Bordeaux. 2 ha.

Château Jappe-Loup (Fr). A vineyard in the commune of Saint-Étienne-de-Lisse. A.C. Saint-Émilion, Bordeaux.

Château Jaubert-Peyblanquet (Fr). A vineyard in the A.C. Saint-Émilion, Bordeaux. 5 ha.

Château Jaugueblanc (Fr). A vineyard in the A.C. Saint-Émilion, Bordeaux. 5 ha.

Château Jean-Blanc (Fr). A vineyard in the commune of Saint-Pey d'Armens. A.C. Saint-Émilion, Bordeaux. 6 ha.

Château Jeandeman (Fr). A vineyard in the commune of Fronsac. A.C. Côtes de Fronsac, Bordeaux.

Château Jean du Mayne (Fr). A vineyard in the commune of Graves-Saint-Émilion. A.C. Saint-Émilion, Bordeaux. Grand Cru Classé.

Château Jean-Faure (Fr). Address = 33330 Saint-Émilion. Grand Cru. A.C. Saint-Émilion. Commune = Saint-Émilion. 20 ha. Grape varieties – Cabernet franc 60%, Malbec 10% and Merlot 30%.

Château Jean-Galant (Fr). A vineyard in the commune of Bommes. A.C. Sauternes, Bordeaux. 2 ha.

Château Jean-Gervais (Fr). A vineyard in the commune of Portets. A.C. Graves, Bordeaux. 25 ha. (red and white). Also Clos Puyjalon.

Château Jean-Laive (Fr). A vineyard in the commune of Barsac. A.C. Barsac (or Sauternes), Bordeaux. 4 ha.

Château Jean-Lamat (Fr). A vineyard in the commune of Sainte-Croix-du-Mont. A.C. Sainte-Croix-du-Mont, Bordeaux. 4 ha.

Château Jean-Marie-Cheval-Blanc (Fr). A vineyard in the A.C. Saint-Émilion, Bordeaux. 2 ha.

Château Jean Voisin (Fr). Address = 33330 Saint-Émilion. Grand Cru. A.C. Saint-Émilion. Commune = Saint-Émilion. 14 ha. Grape varieties – Cabernet franc 25%, Cabernet sauvignon 15% and Merlot 60%.

Château Jendeman (Fr). A vineyard in the commune of St-Aignan. A.C. Côtes de Fronsac, Bordeaux. 9 ha.

Château Joly (Fr). A vineyard in the A.C. Saint-Émilion, Bordeaux. 2 ha.

Château Jolys (Fr). A vineyard in the A.C. Jurançon, south-western France.

Château Joutan (Fr). Armagnac producer. Address = 40240 Betbezer, Labastide d'Armagnac. 6.5 ha. in Bas Armagnac.

Château Juliénas (Fr). A vineyard in the A.C. Juliénas Cru Beaujolais-Villages, Burgundy.

Château Junayme (Fr). A vineyard in the commune of Fronsac. A.C. Côtes Canon-Fronsac, Bordeaux. 13 ha.

Château Jupille (Fr). A vineyard in the A.C. Saint-Émilion, Bordeaux. 2 ha.

Château Jura-Plaisance (Fr). A vineyard in the commune of Montagne-Saint-Émilion. A.C. Saint-Émilion, Bordeaux. 8 ha.

Château Justice (Fr). A vineyard in the A.C. Saint-Émilion, Bordeaux. 3 ha.

Château Kirwan (Fr). Address = 33460 Cantenac, Margaux. Grand Cru Classé (3rd). A.C. Margaux. Commune = Cantenac. 32 ha. Grape varieties – Cabernet franc, Cabernet sauvignon, Merlot and Petit verdot.

Château la Barde (Fr). A vineyard in the commune of Tauriac. A.C. Côtes de Bourg, Bordeaux.

Château Labarde (Fr). A vineyard in the commune of Labarde. A.C. Médoc, Bordeaux.

Château la Barde (Fr). A vineyard in the commune of Saint Laurent des Combes. A.C. Saint-Émilion, Bordeaux. 3 ha.

Château la Barrière (Fr). A 'Vin Nouveau' produced by Château Peychaud. Commune = Teuillac (Côtes de Bourg). A.C. Bordeaux. Grape varieties – Cabernet sauvignon 20% and Merlot 80%.

Château la Barthe (Fr). A vineyard in the A.C. Saint-Émilion, Bordeaux. 4 ha.

Château la Bastide (Fr). The former name of Château Dauzac, Margaux.

Château la Bastienne (Fr). A vineyard in the commune of Montagne-Saint-Émilion, Bordeaux.

Château Labatut-Bouchard (Fr). Address = 33490 Saint-Maxant. A.C. Premières Côtes de Bordeaux. Commune =

C

Cadillac.

Château l'Abbaye (Fr). Address = 33330 Saint-Émilion. A.Ç. Saint-Émilion. Commune = Saint-Émilion.

Château l'Abbaye-Skinner (Fr). A vineyard in the commune of Vertheuil. A.C. Saint-Estèphe, Bordeaux.

Château l'Abbé-Gorsse-de-Gorsse (Fr). A vineyard in the commune of Margaux. A.C. Margaux, Bordeaux. 10 ha. Cru Bourgeois.

Château la Bécade (Fr). A vineyard in the commune of Listrac. A.C. Haut-Médoc, Bordeaux. Cru Bourgeois. 28 ha.

Château la Bécasse (Fr). A vineyard in the commune of Saint-Julien. A.C. Saint-Julien, Bordeaux. 4 ha.

Château Labégorce (Fr). Address = Margaux 33460. Cru Bourgeois. A.C. Margaux. Commune = Margaux. 29.5 ha. Grape varieties – Cabernet franc 5%, Cabernet sauvignon 60% and Merlot 35%

Château Labégorce-Zédé (Fr). Address = 33460 Margaux. A.C. Margaux. Commune = Soussans. 26 ha. Grape varieties – Cabernet franc 10%, Cabernet sauvignon 50%, Merlot 35% and Petit verdot 5%

Château la Berrière (Fr). Address = 44450 La Chapelle, Basse-Mer. A.C. Muscadet de Sèvre et Maine. See also Muscadet Saint-Clément.

Château la Bertonnière (Fr). A vineyard in the commune of Plassac. A.C. Côtes de Blaye, Bordeaux.

Château Labesse (Fr). A vineyard in the commune of Côtes du Castillon. A.C. Bordeaux Supérieur.

Château la Blancherie (Fr). A vineyard in the commune of La Brède. A.C. Graves. 20 ha. Grape varieties – Cabernet sauvignon, Merlot, Sauvignon and Sémillon.

Château la Bonnelle (Fr). Address = Saint-Pey-d'Armens, 33330 Saint-Émilion. Grand Cru. A.C. Saint-Émilion. Commune = Saint-Pey-d'Armens. 6.5 ha. Grape varieties – Cabernet sauvignon 35% and Merlot 65%.

Château Laborde (Fr). A vineyard in the commune of Lalande de Pomerol. A.C. Saint-Émilion, Bordeaux.

Château la Borderie (Fr). A vineyard in the A.C. Côtes de Bergerac, southwestern France. Address = Route de Marmande, Bergerac. (red, rosé and white).

Château la Borie (Fr). A vineyard in the A.C. Côtes du Rhône, south-eastern France.

Château Laborie (Fr). A vineyard in the commune of Sainte-Croix-du-Mont. A.C. Sainte-Croix-du-Mont, Bordeaux. 6 ha.

Château la Bouade (Fr). A vineyard in the commune of Barsac. A.C. Barsac (or Sauternes), Bordeaux. 12 ha.

Château la Bouygue (Fr). A vineyard in the A.C. Saint-Émilion, Bordeaux. 3 ha.

Château Labrède (Fr). A vineyard in the commune of Mombrier. A.C. Côtes de Bourg, Bordeaux.

Château la Bridane (Fr). Address = Cartujac, 33112 Saint Laurent, Médoc. Cru Bourgeois. A.C. Saint-Julien. Commune = Saint-Julien. 15 ha. Grape varieties – Cabernet sauvignon 55% and Merlot 45%

Château la Brouillère (Fr). A vineyard in the commune of Bommes. A.C. Sauternes, Bordeaux. 4 ha.

Château la Brousse (Fr). A vineyard in the commune of Saint-Martin-Caussade. A.C. Côtes de Blaye, Bordeaux.

Château Laburthe-Brivazac (Fr). A vineyard in the commune of Pessac. A.C. Graves, Bordeaux.

Château Lacabane (Fr). A vineyard in the commune of Saint-Martin-Caussade. A.C. Côtes de Blaye, Bordeaux.

Château la Cabanne (Fr). A vineyard in the commune of Soussans. A.C. Haut-Médoc, Bordeaux. Cru Bourgeois.

Château la Cabanne (Fr). A vineyard in the commune of Pomerol. A.C. Pomerol, Bordeaux. Grape varieties – Cabernet franc 20% and Merlot 80%. 9 ha.

Château la Cardonne (Fr). A vineyard in the commune of Blaignan. A.C. Médoc, Bordeaux. Cru Grand Bourgeois. 55 ha.

Château la Carte (Fr). A vineyard in the commune of Saint-Émilion. A.C. Saint-Émilion, Bordeaux. Grand Cru Classé. 4.5 ha.

Château la Caussade (Fr). A vineyard in the commune of Sainte-Croix-du-Mont. A.C. Sainte-Croix-du-Mont, Bordeaux. 5 ha.

Château la Cave (Fr). A vineyard in the commune of Blaye. A.C. Côtes de Blaye, Bordeaux.

Château la Chaise (Fr). A vineyard in the commune of Brouilly. A.C. Brouilly Cru Beaujolais-Villages, Burgundy.

Château la Chapelle (Fr). A vineyard in the A.C. Saint-Émilion, Bordeaux. 4 ha.

Château la Chapelle-de-Lescours (Fr). A vineyard in the commune of Saint-Sulpice-de-Faleyrens. A.C. Saint-Émilion, Bordeaux. 3 ha. Grape varieties – Cabernet franc, Cabernet sauvignon, Malbec and Merlot.

Château la Chapelle-Lariveau (Fr). A

C

vineyard in the commune of St Michel. A.C. Côtes Canon-Fronsac, Bordeaux. 5 ha.

Château la Chapelle-Lescours (Fr). A vineyard in the A.C. Saint-Émilion, Bordeaux. 3 ha.

Château la Chapelle-St-Aubin (Fr). A vineyard in the commune of Bommes. A.C. Sauternes, Bordeaux. 3 ha.

Château Lachesnaye (Fr). Address = Cussac-Fort-Médoc, 33460 Margaux. A.C. Haut-Médoc. Commune = Cussac-Fort-Médoc. 20 ha. Grape varieties – Cabernet sauvignon 50% and Merlot 50%

Château la Chichonne (Fr). A vineyard in the commune of Pomerol. A.C. Pomerol, Bordeaux. 2 ha.

Château la Clare (Fr). Cru Bourgeois. A.C. Médoc. Commune = Bégadan. 20 ha. Grape varieties – Cabernet franc, Cabernet sauvignon and Merlot.

Château la Closerie-du-Grand-Poujeaux (Fr). A vineyard in the commune of Moulis. A.C. Haut-Médoc, Bordeaux. Cru Bourgeois. 7 ha.

Château la Clotte (Fr). A vineyard in the commune of Barsac. A.C. Barsac (or Sauternes), Bordeaux. 5 ha.

Château la Clotte (Fr). A vineyard in the commune of Puisseguin-Saint-Émilion. A.C. Saint-Émilion, Bordeaux. 2 ha.

Château la Clotte (Fr). A vineyard in the commune of Saint-Émilion. A.C. Saint-Émilion, Bordeaux. Address = 33330 Saint-Émilion. Grand Cru. 4.5 ha.

Château la Clotte-Grande-Côte (Fr). A vineyard in the A.C. Saint-Émilion, Bordeaux. 4 ha.

Château la Clusière (Fr). Address = 33330 Saint-Émilion. Grand Cru Classé. A.C. Saint-Émilion. 4.78 ha. Grape varieties – Bouchet 20%, Cabernet sauvignon 10% and Merlot 70%.

Château la Clyde (Fr). A vineyard in the commune of Langoiran. A.C. Premières Côtes de Bordeaux. Address = 33550 Langoiran. 15.5 ha.

Château la Commanderie (Fr). A.C. Bordeaux Mousseux.

Château la Commanderie (Fr). A vineyard in the commune of Libourne. A.C. Pomerol, Bordeaux. 5 ha.

Château la Commanderie (Fr). A vineyard in the commune of Pineuilh. A.C. Saint-Foy-Bordeaux, southern Bordeaux.

Château la Commanderie (Fr). Address = 33330 Saint-Émilion. Grand Cru. A.C. Saint-Émilion. Commune = Saint-Émilion. 3.6 ha. Grape varieties –

Cabernet franc 10%, Cabernet sauvignon 5% and Merlot 85%.

Château la Commanderie (Fr). A vineyard in the commune of Saint-Estèphe. A.C. Médoc, Bordeaux.

Château la Condamine-Bertrand (Fr). A vineyard in the A.C. Clairette du Languedoc, south-western France.

Château Laconfourque (Fr). A vineyard in the commune of Saint-Julien. A.C. Saint-Julien, Bordeaux. 1 ha.

Château la Conseillante (Fr). A vineyard in the commune of Pomerol. A.C. Pomerol, Bordeaux. 12 ha. Grape varieties – Cabernet franc, Malbec and Merlot.

Château la Côte-Daugay (Fr). A vineyard in the A.C. Saint-Émilion, Bordeaux. 1 ha.

Château la Côte-Haut-Brion (Fr). A vineyard in the commune of Talence. A.C. Graves, Bordeaux. Cru Bourgeois.

Château la Couronne (Fr). A vineyard in the commune of Montagne-Saint-Émilion. A.C. Saint-Émilion, Bordeaux. 4 ha.

Château la Couronne (Fr). A vineyard in the commune of Pauillac. A.C. Haut-Médoc, Bordeaux. (Part of Château Haut Batailley). 3 ha.

Château la Couspaude (Fr). A vineyard in the commune of Saint-Émilion. A.C. Saint-Émilion, Bordeaux. Address = BP 40, 33330 Saint-Émilion. Grand Cru. 4.5 ha.

Château la Croix (Fr). A vineyard in the commune of Néac. A.C. Saint-Émilion, Bordeaux.

Château la Croix (Fr). A vineyard in the commune of Pomerol. A.C. Pomerol, Bordeaux. 8 ha.

Château la Croix (Fr). A vineyard in the commune of Fronsac. A.C. Côtes de Fronsac, Bordeaux. 11 ha.

Château la Croix (Fr). A vineyard in the commune of Teuillac. A.C. Côte de Bourg, Bordeaux.

Château la Croix Bellevue (Fr). A vineyard in the commune of Lalande de Pomerol. A.C. Lalande de Pomerol, Bordeaux.

Château la Croix-Chantecaille (Fr). A vineyard in the A.C. Saint-Émilion, Bordeaux. 6 ha.

Château la Croix-de-Blanchon (Fr). A vineyard in the commune of Lussac-Saint-Émilion. A.C. Saint-Émilion, Bordeaux. 5 ha.

Château la Croix-de-Gay (Fr). A vineyard in the commune of Pomerol. A.C. Pomerol, Bordeaux. 12 ha. Grape varieties – Cabernet franc 20% and Merlot 80%

C

Château la Croix-de-la-Bastienne (Fr). A vineyard in the commune of Montagne-Saint-Émilion. A.C. Saint-Émilion, Bordeaux. 2 ha.

Château la Croix du Casse (Fr). A vineyard in the commune of Pomerol. A.C. Pomerol, Bordeaux.

Château la Croix du Chabut (Fr). A vineyard in the A.C. Premières Côtes de Blaye, Bordeaux.

Château la Croix Gandineau (Fr). A vineyard in the commune of Fronsac. A.C. Côtes de Fronsac, Bordeaux. 5 ha.

Château la Croix-St-Georges (Fr). A vineyard in the commune of Pomerol. A.C. Pomerol, Bordeaux. 4 ha.

Château la Croix St. Michel (Fr). A vineyard in the A.C. Côtes de Bourg, Bordeaux.

Château la Croix-Taillefer (Fr). A vineyard in the commune of Pomerol. A.C. Pomerol, Bordeaux. 2 ha.

Château la Croix Toulifaut (Fr). A vineyard in the commune of Pomerol. A.C. Pomerol, Bordeaux. 1 ha.

Château la Croizille (Fr). A vineyard in the A.C. Saint-Émilion, Bordeaux. 4 ha.

Château la Cure (Fr). A vineyard in the commune of Cars. A.C. Côtes de Blaye, Bordeaux.

Château la Dame Blanche (Fr). Address = La Taillan-Médoc, 33320 Eysines. A.C. Bordeaux Blanc. Commune = La Taillan. 25 ha. Grape varieties – Colombard 33% and Sauvignon 67%

Château la Dauphine (Fr). A vineyard in the commune of Fronsac. A.C. Canon-Fronsac, Bordeaux. 6 ha.

Château la Dominique (Fr). Address = Route de Montagne, BP 160, 33500 Libourne Cedex. Grand Cru Classé. A.C. Saint-Émilion. Commune = Saint-Émilion. 21 ha. Grape varieties – Cabernet franc 15%, Cabernet sauvignon 15%, Malbec 10% and Merlot 60%.

Château Ladouys (Fr). A vineyard in the commune of Saint-Estèphe. A.C. Haut-Médoc, Bordeaux. 4 ha.

Château la Duchesse (Fr). A vineyard in the commune of Fronsac. A.C. Canon-Fronsac, Bordeaux.

Château la Fagnouse (Fr). A vineyard in the A.C. Saint-Émilion, Bordeaux. 5 ha.

Château la Faucherie (Fr). A vineyard in the commune of Montagne-Saint-Émilion. A.C. Saint-Émilion, Bordeaux. 3 ha.

Château la Faure (Fr). A vineyard in the commune of Saillans. A.C. Côtes de Fronsac, Bordeaux. 13 ha.

Château Lafaurie (Fr). A vineyard in the commune of Néac. A.C. Lalande de Pomerol, Bordeaux.

Château Lafaurie-Peyraguey (Fr). A Premier Grand Cru Classé vineyard in the commune of Bommes. A.C. Sauternes. 22 ha. Grape varieties – Muscadelle 10%, Sauvignon 30% and Sémillon 60%.

Château Laffite (Fr). A vineyard in the commune of Yvrac. A.C. Médoc, Bordeaux.

Château Laffite-Saint-Estèphe (Fr). A vineyard in the commune of Saint-Estèphe. A.C. Haut-Médoc, Bordeaux.

Château Laffitte (Fr). A vineyard in the commune of Bégadan. A.C. Médoc, Bordeaux.

Château Laffitte-Cantegric (Fr). A vineyard in the commune of Listrac. A.C. Haut-Médoc, Bordeaux. Cru Bourgeois.

Château Laffitte-Canteloup (Fr). A vineyard in the commune of Ludon. A.C. Médoc, Bordeaux.

Château Laffitte-Carcasset (Fr). Address = Saint-Estèphe 33250. A.C. Saint-Estèphe. Commune = Saint-Estèphe. 25 ha. Grape varieties – Cabernet franc 10%, Cabernet sauvignon 60% and Merlot 30%

Château Lafite (Fr). See Château Lafite Rothschild.

Château Lafite Rothschild (Fr). Address = 33250 Pauillac. Premier Grand Cru Classé. A.C. Pauillac. Commune = Pauillac. 100 ha. Grape varieties – Cabernet franc, Cabernet sauvignon and Merlot.

Château Lafitte-Bordeaux (Fr). A vineyard in the A.C. Graves, Bordeaux. (red).

Château Lafitte-Talence (Fr). A vineyard in the commune of Talence. A.C. Graves, Bordeaux. (red).

Château Lafleur (Fr). A vineyard in the commune of Pomerol. A.C. Pomerol, Bordeaux. 4 ha.

Château la Fleur (Fr). A vineyard in the A.C. Saint-Émilion, Bordeaux. 5 ha.

Château La Fleur-Cadet (Fr). A vineyard in the A.C. Saint-Émilion, Bordeaux. 4 ha.

Château la Fleur-des-Rouzes (Fr). A vineyard in the commune of Pomerol. A.C. Pomerol, Bordeaux. 4 ha.

Château Lafleur du Roy (Fr). A vineyard in the commune of Pomerol. A.C. Pomerol, Bordeaux. (Mainly Merlot grapes).

Château Lafleur-Gazin (Fr). A vineyard in the commune of Pomerol. A.C. Pomerol, Bordeaux. 4 ha.

Château la Fleur-Milon (Fr). Cru Grand Bourgeois. A.C. Haut-Médoc. Commune = Pauillac. 13 ha.

Château la Fleur-Perruchon (Fr). A vineyard in the commune of Lussac-Saint-Émilion. A.C. Saint-Émilion, Bordeaux. 5 ha.

Château la Fleur-Pétrus (Fr). A vineyard in

C

the commune of Pomerol. A.C. Pomerol, Bordeaux. 9 ha.

Château la Fleur Picon (Fr). Address = 33330 Saint-Émilion. Grand Cru. A.C. Saint-Émilion. Commune = Saint-Émilion. 5.58 ha. Grape varieties – Cabernet franc 35% and Merlot 65%.

Château la Fleur Pourret (Fr). Address = 33330 Saint-Émilion. A.C. Saint-Émilion. Commune = Saint-Émilion. 4.7 ha. Grape varieties – Cabernet franc 50%, Cabernet sauvignon 25% and Merlot 25%.

Château la Fleur-St-Georges (Fr). Part of Château St-Georges A.C. Saint-Émilion, Bordeaux.

Château Lafon (Fr). A vineyard in the commune of Listrac. A.C. Listrac, Bordeaux. Cru Grand Bourgeois. 7 ha.

Château Lafon (Fr). A vineyard in the commune of Sauternes. A.C. Sauternes, Bordeaux. 6 ha. Also Château le Mayne.

Château Lafon-Laroze (Fr). A vineyard in the commune of Sauternes. A.C. Sauternes, Bordeaux. 3 ha.

Château Lafon-Rochet (Fr). Address = 33250 Saint-Estèphe. Grand Cru Classé (4ᵗʰ). A.C. Saint-Estèphe. Commune = Saint-Estèphe. 55 ha. Grape varieties – Cabernet franc 8%, Cabernet sauvignon 70%, Malbec 2% and Merlot 20%

Château Lafont (Fr). A vineyard in the commune of Cartelègue. A.C. Côtes de Blaye, Bordeaux.

Château la Fontaine (Fr). A vineyard in the commune of Fronsac. A.C. Côtes de Fronsac, Bordeaux. 9 ha.

Château la Fortia (Fr). A noted vineyard in the A.C. Châteauneuf-du-Pape, southern Rhône.

Château la Fortine (Fr). A vineyard in the A.C. Saint-Émilion, Bordeaux. 12 ha.

Château la France (Fr). A vineyard in the commune of Blaignan. A.C. Médoc, Bordeaux. Cru Bourgeois. 6 ha.

Château Lafuë (Fr). A vineyard in the commune of Sainte-Croix-du-Mont. A.C. Sainte-Croix-du-Mont, Bordeaux. 10 ha.

Château la Gaffelière (Fr). Address = 33330 Saint-Émilion. Grand Cru Classé. A.C. Saint-Émilion. Commune = Saint-Émilion. 25 ha. Grape varieties – Cabernet franc, Cabernet sauvignon and Merlot.

Château la Galiane (Fr). A vineyard in the commune of Soussans-Margaux. A.C. Haut-Médoc, Bordeaux. 4 ha.

Château la Ganne (Fr). A vineyard in the commune of Pomerol. A.C. Pomerol, Bordeaux. 5 ha.

Château Lagarde (Fr). A vineyard in the commune of Saint-Seurin-de-Cursac. A.C. Côtes de Blaye, Bordeaux.

Château la Garde (Fr). Address = 45650 La Brède. A.C. Graves. Commune = Léognan. 39 ha. Grape varieties – Cabernet franc, Cabernet sauvignon, Merlot, Sauvignon and Sémillon.

Château la Garde (Fr). A vineyard in the commune of Martillac. A.C. Graves, Bordeaux. 13 ha. (red).

Château la Garde Roland (Fr). A vineyard in the commune of Saint-Seurin-de-Cursac. A.C. Côtes de Blaye, Bordeaux.

Château la Garelle (Fr). A vineyard in the commune of Saint-Émilion. A.C. Saint-Émilion, Bordeaux. 12 ha.

Château la Garlière (Fr). A vineyard in the A.C. Haut-Médoc, Bordeaux. Cru Bourgeois.

Château la Gigoterie (Fr). A vineyard in the A.C. Côtes de Blaye, Bordeaux.

Château la Girouette (Fr). A vineyard in the commune of Fours. A.C. Côtes de Blaye, Bordeaux.

Château Lagniappe (USA). The label used by the Cedar Hill Wine Co. based in Cleveland Heights, Ohio for their vinifera wines.

Château la Gomerie (Fr). A vineyard in the A.C. Saint-Émilion, Bordeaux. 2 ha.

Château la Gorce (Fr). Address = Blaignan, 33340 Lesparre. A.C. Médoc. Commune = Blaignan. 42 ha. Grape varieties – Cabernet 70% and Merlot 30%

Château Lagorce (Fr). A vineyard in the commune of Moulis. A.C. Moulis, Bordeaux. 3 ha.

Château la Gordonne (Fr). A vineyard in the A.C. Côtes de Provence (white wine).

Château la Gorre (Fr). A vineyard in the commune of Bégadan. A.C. Médoc, Bordeaux. 7 ha.

Château la Grâce-Dieu-les-Menuts (Fr). Address = 33330 Saint-Émilion. Grand Cru. A.C. Saint-Émilion. Commune = Saint-Émilion. 13 ha. Grape varieties – Cabernet franc 30%, Cabernet sauvignon 10% and Merlot 60%.

Château la Grande-Clotte (Fr). A vineyard in the commune of Lussac-Saint-Émilion. A.C. Saint-Émilion, Bordeaux. 5 ha.

Château Lagrange (Fr). A vineyard in the commune of Blaye. A.C. Côtes de Blaye, Bordeaux.

Château Lagrange (Fr). A vineyard in the commune of Bourg. A.C. Côtes de Bourg, Bordeaux.

Château Lagrange (Fr). Address = Sarl, 33250 Saint-Julien, Pauillac. Grand

C

Cru Classé (3ʳᵈ). A.C. Saint-Julien. Commune = Saint-Julien. 55 ha. Grape varieties – Cabernet 65% and Merlot 35%

Château la Grange (Fr). A vineyard in the commune of Pomerol. A.C. Pomerol, Bordeaux. 8 ha.

Château la Grange Neuve (Fr). A vineyard in the A.C. Bergerac, south-western France. (red).

Château la Graulet (Fr). A vineyard in the commune of St-Cier-de-Canesse. A.C. Côtes de Bourg, Bordeaux.

Château la Grave (Fr). A vineyard in the commune of Sainte-Croix-du-Mont. A.C. Sainte-Croix-du-Mont, Bordeaux. 6 ha.

Château la Graves (Fr). A vineyard in the commune of Fronsac. A.C. Côtes de Fronsac, Bordeaux. 3 ha.

Château la Grave Trigant de Boisset (Fr). A vineyard in the commune of Pomerol. A.C. Pomerol, Bordeaux. 8 ha.

Château Lagravette (Fr). A vineyard in the commune of Bommes. A.C. Sauternes, Bordeaux. 2 ha.

Château Lagravette-Peyredon (Fr). A vineyard in the commune of Listrac. A.C. Listrac, Bordeaux. 5 ha.

Château la Gravière (Fr). A vineyard in the commune of Sainte-Croix-du-Mont. A.C. Sainte-Croix-du-Mont, Bordeaux. 11 ha.

Château la Graville (Fr). A vineyard in the commune of Sainte-Croix-du-Mont. A.C. Sainte-Croix-du-Mont, Bordeaux. 4 ha.

Château la Grenière (Fr). A vineyard in the commune of Lussac-Saint-Émilion. A.C. Saint-Émilion, Bordeaux. 5 ha.

Château la Grolet (Fr). See Château la Graulet.

Château Lague Bourdieu (Fr). A vineyard in the commune of Fronsac. A.C. Côtes de Fronsac, Bordeaux. 4 ha.

Château la Gurgue (Fr). Address = Rue de la Tremoille, Margaux. Cru Bourgeois. A.C. Margaux. Commune = Margaux. 12 ha. Grape varieties – Cabernet 75% and Merlot 25%

Château la Hargue (Fr). A vineyard in the commune of Plassac. A.C. Côtes de Blaye, Bordeaux.

Château la Haye (Fr). Address = Saint-Estèphe, 33250 Pauillac. A.C. Saint-Estèphe. Commune = Saint-Estèphe. 10 ha. Grape varieties – Cabernet sauvignon, Merlot and Petit verdot.

Château Lahouilley (Fr). A vineyard in the commune of Barsac. A.C. Barsac (or Sauternes), Bordeaux. 3 ha.

Château la Hourcade (Fr). A vineyard in the commune of Preignac. A.C. Sauternes, Bordeaux. 4 ha.

Château la Houringue (Fr). A vineyard in the commune of Macau. A.C. Haut-Médoc, Bordeaux. Cru Bourgeois.

Château la Jaubertie (Fr). A vineyard in the commune of Monbazillac. A.C. Bergerac, south-western France (red and white).

Château la Lagune (Fr). Address = Ludon, Médoc 33290 Blanquefort. Grand Cru Classé (3ʳᵈ). A.C. Haut-Médoc. Commune = Ludon. 55 ha. Grape varieties – Cabernet franc, Cabernet sauvignon, Merlot and Petit verdot.

Château Lalande (Fr). Address = 33480 Listrac-Médoc. A.C. Listrac. Commune = Listrac. 12 ha. Grape varieties – Cabernet, Merlot and Petit verdot.

Château Lalande Borie (Fr). A.C. Saint-Julien. Commune = Saint-Julien. 18 ha. Grape varieties – Cabernet franc 10%, Cabernet sauvignon 65% and Merlot 25%.

Château Lalanette Ferbos (Fr). A vineyard in the commune of Cérons. A.C. Cérons, Bordeaux. 5 ha.

Château Lalibarde (Fr). A vineyard in the commune of Bourg. A.C. Côtes de Bourg, Bordeaux.

Château la Louvière (Fr). Address = Léognan 33850. A.C. Graves. Commune = Léognan. 55 ha. Grape varieties – Cabernet franc, Cabernet sauvignon, Merlot, Sauvignon and Sémillon. (red and white).

Château la Magdelaine (Fr). A vineyard in the commune of Saint-Émilion. A.C. Saint-Émilion, Bordeaux. 11 ha.

Château la Marche-Canon (Fr). A vineyard in the commune of Fronsac. A.C. Côtes Canon-Fronsac, Bordeaux. 2 ha.

Château la Maréchaude (Fr). A commune in the Lalande de Pomerol. A.C. Saint-Émilion, Bordeaux.

Château Lamarque (Fr). A vineyard in the commune of Lamarque. A.C. Haut-Médoc, Bordeaux. Cru Grand Bourgeois. 47 ha.

Château Lamarque (Fr). A vineyard in the commune of Sainte-Croix-du-Mont. A.C. Sainte-Croix-du-Mont, Bordeaux. 15 ha.

Château Lamartine (Fr). A vineyard in the commune of Cantenac. A.C. Bordeaux Supérieur, Bordeaux. Grape varieties – Cabernet sauvignon and Merlot. Vinified at Château Cantenac-Brown.

Château Lamarzelle (Fr). Address = 33330 Saint-Émilion. Grand Cru Classé. A.C. Saint-Émilion. Commune = Saint-Émilion. 15 ha. Grape varieties – Cabernet franc 20%, Cabernet sauvignon 20% and Merlot 60%.

Château la Mausse (Fr). A vineyard in the commune of St-Michel. A.C. Côtes Canon-Fronsac, Bordeaux. 7 ha.

Château la Mayne (Fr). A vineyard in the commune of Sables-Saint-Émilion. A.C. Saint-Émilion, Bordeaux. 3 ha.

C

Château Lambert (Fr). A vineyard in the commune of Pauillac. A.C. Médoc, Bordeaux. Cru Bourgeois.

Château Lambert (Fr). A vineyard in the commune of St-Aignans. A.C. Côtes de Fronsac, Bordeaux. 3 ha.

Château la-Mission-Haut-Brion (Fr). Address = 33400 Talence. Grand Cru Classé. A.C. Graves. Commune = Talence. 20 ha. Grape varieties – Cabernet franc, Cabernet sauvignon, Merlot, Muscadelle, Sauvignon and Sémillon.

Château la Mondotte (Fr). Address = Saint Laurent des Combes, 33330 Saint-Émilion. Grand Cru. A.C. Saint-Émilion. Commune = Saint Laurent des Combes. 4.2 ha. Grape varieties – Cabernet franc 30% and Merlot 70%.

Château Lamorère (Fr). A vineyard in the commune of Moulis. A.C. Médoc, Bordeaux. Cru Bourgeois.

Château Lamothe (Fr). A vineyard in the commune of St-Paul. A.C. Côtes de Blaye, Bordeaux.

Château Lamothe (Fr). A vineyard in the commune of Lansac. A.C. Côtes de Bourg, Bordeaux.

Château Lamothe (Fr). A vineyard in the commune of Cadaujac. A.C. Graves, Bordeaux. 4 ha. (red and white).

Château Lamothe (Fr). A vineyard in the commune of Saint-Medard-d'Eyrans. A.C. Graves, Bordeaux.

Château Lamothe (Fr). Address = 33250 Pauillac. Cru Grand Bourgeois. A.C. Haut-Médoc. Commune = Cissac. 50 ha. Grape varieties – Cabernet franc, Cabernet sauvignon 70%, Merlot 25% and Petit verdot.

Château Lamothe (Fr). A vineyard in the commune of Gatarnos Haut. A.C. Premières Côtes de Bordeaux, central Bordeaux

Château Lamothe (Fr). A vineyard in the commune of Sauternes. A.C. Sauternes, Bordeaux. 15 ha. Also Château d'Arches.

Château Lamothe (Fr). A vineyard in the commune of Sauternes. A.C. Sauternes, Bordeaux. 14 ha. Also Domaine des Justices and Châteaux Gilette, les Remparts and les Rochers.

Château Lamothe (Fr). Grand Cru Classé. A.C. Sauternes. Commune = Sauternes. Grape varieties – Sauvignon 20%, Sémillon 70% and Muscadelle 10%.

Château Lamothe Bergeron (Fr). A vineyard in the commune of Cussac-Fort-Médoc. A.C. Haut-Médoc, Bordeaux. Cru Bourgeois. 10 ha.

Château Lamothe-Bouscaut (Fr). A vineyard in the commune of Cadaujac. A.C. Graves, Bordeaux. Cru Bourgeois.

Château Lamothe-de-Bergeron (Fr). A vineyard in the commune of Cussac-Fort-Médoc. A.C. Haut-Médoc, Bordeaux. Cru Bourgeois.

Château la Mothe et Grand Moulin (Fr). A vineyard in the commune of Saint-Seurin-de-Cadourne. A.C. Haut-Médoc, Bordeaux. Address = Société Civile Cru Bourgeois, Saint-Seurin-de Cadourne, 33250 Pauillac. 30 ha.

Château la Mouleyre (Fr). A vineyard in the commune of Sainte-Croix-du-Mont. A.C. Sainte-Croix-du-Mont, Bordeaux. 4 ha.

Château la Mouline (Fr). Address = 33480 Castelnau-de-Médoc. A.C. Moulis. Commune = Moulis. 15 ha. Grape varieties – Cabernet franc, Cabernet sauvignon, Merlot and Petit verdot.

Château la Mourette (Fr). A vineyard in the commune of Bommes. A.C. Sauternes, Bordeaux. 3 ha.

Château Lamouroux (Fr). A vineyard in the commune of Cérons. A.C. Cérons, Bordeaux. 10 ha.

Château Lamouroux (Fr). A vineyard in the commune of Cérons. A.C. Graves Supérieur, Bordeaux. 8 ha. (white).

Château Landon (Fr). A vineyard in the commune of Bégadan. A.C. Médoc, Bordeaux. 25 ha.

Château la Nerte (Fr). A vineyard in the A.C. Châteauneuf-du-Pape, southern Rhône.

Château Lanessan (Fr). Address = Cussac-Fort-Médoc 33460 Margaux. Cru Bourgeois Exceptionnel. A.C. Haut-Médoc. Commune = Cussac-Fort-Médoc. 40 ha. Grape varieties – Cabernet franc, Cabernet sauvignon, Merlot and Petit verdot.

Château Lanessan (Fr). A vineyard in the commune of Pauillac. A.C. Pauillac, Bordeaux.

Château Lanette (Fr). A vineyard in the commune of Cérons. A.C. Cérons, Bordeaux. 5 ha.

Château la Nève (Fr). A vineyard in the commune of Loupiac. A.C. Loupiac, Bordeaux. 9 ha.

Château Lange (Fr). A vineyard in the commune of Gradignan. A.C. Graves, Bordeaux.

Château Lange (Fr). A vineyard in the commune of Bommes. A.C. Sauternes, Bordeaux. 5 ha.

Château l'Angélus (Fr). A vineyard in the commune of Pomerol. A.C. Pomerol, Bordeaux. 1 ha.

Château l'Angélus (Fr). Address = 33330 Saint-Émilion. Grand Cru Classé. A.C. Saint-Émilion. Commune = Saint-Émilion. 23 ha. Grape varieties – Cabernet franc 50%, Cabernet sauvignon 5%

C

and Merlot 45%.

Château Langlade (Fr). A vineyard in the commune of Parsac-Saint-Émilion. A.C. Saint-Émilion, Bordeaux. 6 ha.

Château Langlois (Fr). A vineyard based in Saumur, Anjou-Saumur, Loire. Produces sparkling (méthode champenoise) wines. Owned by the Bollinger Champagne house.

Château Langoa (Fr). See Château Langoa Barton.

Château Langoa-Barton (Fr). Address = Saint-Julien, Beychevelle 33250 Pauillac. Grand Cru Classé (3ʳᵈ). A.C. Saint-Julien. Commune = Saint-Julien. 25 ha. Grape varieties – Cabernet franc, Cabernet sauvignon, Merlot and Petit verdot.

Château Langueloup (Fr). A vineyard in the commune of Portets. A.C. Graves, Bordeaux. 2 ha. (red and white).

Château Laniote (Fr). A vineyard in the commune of Saint-Émilion. A.C. Saint-Émilion, Bordeaux. 5 ha. Address = 33330 Saint-Émilion. Grand Cru Classé.

Château la Noé (Fr). A vineyard in the A.C. Muscadet de Sèvre et Maine, Pays Nantais, Loire. Address = Clos de Ferré, Vallet, Loire Atlantique.

Château Laouilley (Fr). A vineyard in the commune of Roaillan. A.C. Graves, Bordeaux. 3 ha. (white).

Château la Paillette (Fr). A vineyard in the commune of Sables-Saint-Émilion. A.C. Saint-Émilion, Bordeaux. 3 ha.

Château la Papeterie (Fr). A vineyard in the commune of Montagne-Saint-Émilion. A.C. Saint-Émilion, Bordeaux. 9 ha.

Château la Patache (Fr). A vineyard in the commune of Pomerol. A.C. Pomerol, Bordeaux. 2 ha.

Château la Pelletrie (Fr). Address = Saint-Christophe-des-Bardes, 33330 Saint-Émilion. Grand Cru. A.C. Saint-Émilion. Commune = Saint-Christophe-des-Bardes. 15 ha. Grape variety – Merlot 100%.

Château Lapelou (Fr). A vineyard in the commune of Barsac. A.C. Barsac (or Sauternes), Bordeaux. 6 ha.

Château la Perotte (Fr). A vineyard in the commune of Eyrons. A.C. Côtes de Blaye, Bordeaux.

Château la Perrière (Fr). A vineyard in the commune of Lussac-Saint-Émilion. A.C. Saint-Émilion, Bordeaux. 5 ha.

Château Lapeyrère (Fr). A vineyard in the commune of Sainte-Croix-du-Mont. A.C. Sainte-Croix-du-Mont, Bordeaux. 5 ha.

Château la Picherie (Fr). A vineyard in the commune of Montagne-Saint-Émilion. A.C. Saint-Émilion, Bordeaux. 6 ha.

Château Lapinesse (Fr). A vineyard in the commune of Barsac. A.C. Barsac (or Sauternes), Bordeaux. 16 ha.

Château Laplagnotte-Bellevue (Fr). Address = Saint-Christophe-des-Bardes, 33330 Saint-Émilion. Grand Cru. A.C. Saint-Émilion. Commune = Saint-Christophe-des-Bardes. 6 ha. Grape varieties – Cabernet franc 20%, Cabernet sauvignon 20% and Merlot 60%.

Château la Plante (Fr). A vineyard in the commune of Sables-Saint-Émilion. A.C. Saint-Émilion, Bordeaux. 1 ha.

Château la Pointe (Fr). A.C. Pomerol. Commune = Pomerol. 20 ha. Grape varieties – Cabernet franc 20%, Malbec 5% and Merlot 75%.

Château la Providence (Fr). A vineyard in the commune of Ludon. A.C. Médoc, Bordeaux. Cru Bourgeois.

Château la Providence (Fr). A vineyard in the commune of Pomerol. A.C. Pomerol, Bordeaux. 3 ha.

Château la Rame (Fr). A vineyard in the commune of Sainte-Croix-du-Mont. A.C. Sainte-Croix-du-Mont, Bordeaux. 5 ha.

Château Larchevêque (Fr). A vineyard in the commune of Fronsac. A.C. Côtes Canon-Fronsac, Bordeaux. 5 ha.

Château Larcis-Ducasse (Fr). Address = Saint Laurent des Bardes, 33330 Saint-Émilion. Grand Cru Classé. A.C. Saint-Émilion. Commune = Saint Laurent des Combes. 12 ha. Grape varieties – Cabernet franc 30%, Cabernet sauvignon 5%, Malbec 5% and Merlot 60%.

Château la Renaissance (Fr). A vineyard in the commune of Pomerol. A.C. Pomerol, Bordeaux. 1 ha.

Château Laribotte (Fr). A vineyard in the commune of Preignac. A.C. Sauternes, Bordeaux. 5 ha.

Château Lariveau (Fr). A vineyard in the commune of Saint-Michel. A.C. Côtes Canon-Fronsac, Bordeaux.

Château la Rivière (Fr). A vineyard in the commune of Saint-Michel. A.C. Côtes Canon-Fronsac, Bordeaux. Address = 33145 Saint-Michel-de-Fronsac.

Château Larivière (Fr). A vineyard in the commune of Blaignan. A.C. Médoc, Bordeaux. 12 ha.

Château Larmande (Fr). Address = 33330 Saint-Émilion. Grand Cru Classé. A.C. Saint-Émilion. Commune = Saint-Émilion. 9 ha. Grape varieties – Cabernet franc 30%, Cabernet sauvignon 5% and Merlot 65%.

Château la Rocaille (Fr). A vineyard in the commune Virelade. A.C. Graves, Bordeaux. 9 ha. (red and white).

Château la Rocaille (Fr). A vineyard in the commune of Saint-Émilion. A.C. Saint-

Émilion. 5.47 ha. Address = Guey-rosse, 33500 Libourne. Grape varieties – Bouchet, Cabernet sauvignon 50% and Merlot 50%.

Château Laroque (Fr). Address = Saint-Christophe-des-Bardes. Grand Cru. A.C. Saint-Émilion. Commune = Saint-Christophe-des-Bardes. 44 ha. Grape varieties – Cabernet franc 20%, Cabernet sauvignon 15% and Merlot 65%.

Château la Roque (Fr). A vineyard in the commune of La Roque. A.C. Premières Côtes de Bordeaux, central Bordeaux.

Château la Roque de By (Fr). A vineyard in the commune of Bégadan. A.C. Médoc, Bordeaux. Cru Bourgeois.

Château Larose (Fr). A vineyard in the commune of Baurech. A.C. Entre-Deux-Mers, Bordeaux. (red and white).

Château la Rose-Capbern (Fr). Part of Château Capbern A.C. Haut-Médoc, Bordeaux.

Château la Rose Côtes Rol (Fr). Address = 33330 Saint-Émilion. Grand Cru. A.C. Saint-Émilion. Commune = Saint-Émilion. 8.5 ha. Grape varieties – Cabernet 35% and Merlot 65%.

Château la Rose de France (Fr). A vineyard in the commune of Saint-Julien. A.C. Saint-Julien, Bordeaux. 2 ha.

Château la Rose Garamay (Fr). See Château Livran. A.C. Médoc.

Château la Rose-Pauillac (Fr). A Cave Cooperative vineyard in the commune of Pauillac. A.C. Pauillac, Bordeaux. Cru Bourgeois.

Château Larose-Perganson (Fr). A vineyard in the commune of St Laurent du Médoc. A.C. Haut-Médoc, Bordeaux. Cru Bourgeois.

Château la Rose Pourret (Fr). Address = 33330 Saint-Émilion. Grand Cru. A.C. Saint-Émilion. Commune = Saint-Émilion. 8.26 ha. Grape varieties – Cabernet 50%, Merlot 50%

Château Laroseraie-du-Mont (Fr). A vineyard in the commune of Puisseguin-Saint-Émilion. A.C. Saint-Émilion, Bordeaux. 4 ha.

Château la Rose Trimoulet (Fr). Address = Puisseguin-Saint-Émilion. 33330 Saint-Émilion. Grand Cru. A.C. Saint-Émilion. Commune = Puisseguin-Saint-Émilion. 5 ha. Grape varieties – Cabernet franc 20%, Cabernet sauvignon 10% and Merlot 70%.

Château Larose-Trintaudon (Fr). A vineyard in the commune of Saint Laurent du Médoc-Gironde. A.C. Haut-Médoc, Bordeaux. Cru Grand Bourgeois. 157 ha.

Château Laroze (Fr). Address = 33330 Saint-Émilion. Grand Cru Classé. A.C.

Saint-Émilion. Commune = Saint-Émilion. 30 ha. Grape varieties – Cabernet franc 45%, Cabernet sauvignon 10% and Merlot 45%.

Château Larrieu-Terrefort (Fr). A vineyard in the commune of Macau. A.C. Haut-Médoc, Bordeaux. Cru Bourgeois. 3 ha.

Château Larrivaux (Fr). Address = Cissac, Médoc 33250 Pauillac. A.C. Haut-Médoc. Commune = Cissac. 100 ha. Grape varieties – Cabernet sauvignon, Malbec, Merlot and Petit verdot. (Bought by Château Hanteillan in 1979 and added to its name). See Château Hanteillan.

Château Larrivaux-Hanteillan (Fr). The name used by Château Hanteillan for its second wines.

Château Larriveau (Fr). See Château Larrivaux.

Château Larrivet-Haut-Brion (Fr). A.C. Graves. Commune = Léognan. 16.16 ha Grape varieties – Cabernet sauvignon 60%, Merlot 40%, Sauvignon 60% and Sémillon 40%.

Château l'Arrosée (Fr). Address = 33330 Saint-Émilion. Grand Cru Classé. A.C. Saint-Émilion. Commune = Saint-Émilion. 25 ha.

Château Lartigue de Brochon (Fr). A vineyard in the commune of St-Seurin-de-Cadourne. A.C. Médoc, Bordeaux. Cru Bourgeois.

Château Lartique (Fr). A vineyard in the commune of Saint-Estèphe. A.C. Saint-Estèphe, Bordeaux. 2 ha.

Château Larue (Fr). A vineyard in the commune of Parsac-Saint-Émilion. A.C. Saint-Émilion, Bordeaux. 4 ha.

Château la Salette (Fr). A vineyard in the commune of Cérons. A.C. Cérons, Bordeaux. 5 ha.

Château la Salle (Fr). A vineyard in the commune of Martillac. A.C. Graves, Bordeaux. 3 ha. (red and white).

Château la Salle (USA). A sweet, dessert wine made from the Muscat grape by the Christian Brothers at their Mont la Salle vineyards in California. Sold in a decanter-shaped bottle.

Château la Sartre (Fr). A.C. Graves. Commune = Léognan. 10 ha. Grape varieties – Cabernet franc, Cabernet sauvignon, Malbec and Merlot.

Château Lascombes (Fr). Address = 33460 Margaux. Grand Cru Classé (2nd). A.C. Margaux. Commune = Margaux. 137 ha. Grape varieties – Cabernet sauvignon, Malbec, Merlot and Petit verdot.

Château la Serre (Fr). Address = 33330 Saint-Émilion. Grand Cru Classé. A.C.

C

Saint-Émilion. Commune = Saint-Émilion. 7 ha. Grape varieties – Cabernet 20%, Merlot 80%. Second wine is Clos la Tonnelle.

Château la Solitude (Fr). A vineyard in the commune of Martillac. A.C. Graves, Bordeaux.

Château Lassale (Fr). A vineyard in the commune of St-Genès. A.C. Côtes de Blaye, Bordeaux.

Château Lassalle (Fr). A vineyard in the commune of Potensac. A.C. Médoc, Bordeaux. Cru Bourgeois.

Château Lassèque (Fr). Address = Saint-Hippolyte, 33330 Saint-Émilion. Grand Cru. A.C. Saint-Émilion. Commune = Saint-Hippolyte. 23 ha. Grape varieties – Cabernet franc 35%, Cabernet sauvignon 20% and Merlot 45%.

Château Lasserre (Fr). A vineyard in the commune of Saint-Émilion. A.C. Saint-Émilion, Bordeaux. 7 ha. Grand Cru Classé.

Château la Taure Ste-Luce (Fr). A vineyard in the commune of Blaye. A.C. Côtes de Blaye, Bordeaux.

Château la Terrasse (Fr). A vineyard on the Île Verte in the river Gironde. A.C. Bordeaux Supérieur.

Château la Tête-du-Cerf (Fr). A vineyard in the commune of Montagne-Saint-Émilion. A.C. Saint-Émilion, Bordeaux. 6 ha.

Château la Touche (Fr). A vineyard in the A.C. Muscadet de Sèvre et Maine, Pays Nantais, Loire. Address = André Vinet, Vallet, Loire Atlantique.

Château la Tour (Fr). A vineyard in the commune of Barsac. A.C. Barsac (or Sauternes), Bordeaux. 2 ha.

Château la Tour (Fr). A vineyard in the commune of Léognan. A.C. Graves, Bordeaux. 4 ha. (red and white).

Château Latour (Fr). A vineyard in the commune of Montagne-Saint-Émilion. A.C. Saint-Émilion, Bordeaux. 5 ha.

Château Latour (Fr). Address = 33250 Bordeaux. Premier Grand Cru Classé. A.C. Pauillac. Commune = Pauillac. 60 ha. Grape varieties – Cabernet franc, Cabernet sauvignon and Merlot. The second wine is Les Forts de Latour.

Château Latour (Fr). A vineyard in the commune of St. Martin-du-Puy Gironde. A.C. Bordeaux Supérieur, Bordeaux.

Château Latour à Pomerol (Fr). A vineyard in the commune of Pomerol. A.C. Pomerol, Bordeaux.

Château la Tour Baladoz (Fr). Address = Saint Laurent des Combes, 33330 Saint-Émilion. Grand Cru. Saint-Émilion. Commune = Saint Laurent des

Combes. 10 ha. Grape varieties – Cabernet, Merlot 65% and Petit verdot.

Château la Tour-Ballet (Fr). A vineyard in the commune of Montagne-Saint-Émilion. A.C. Saint-Émilion, Bordeaux. 1 ha.

Château la-Tour-Bicheau (Fr). Address = Portets Gironde 33640. A.C. Graves Commune = Portets. 20 ha. Grape varieties – Cabernet, Merlot, Sauvignon and Sémillon. (red and white).

Château la Tour-Blanche (Fr). A vineyard in the commune of Parsac-Saint-Émilion. A.C. Saint-Émilion, Bordeaux. 3 ha.

Château la Tour Blanche (Fr). Address = 33340 Saint-Christoly-de-Médoc. Cru Bourgeois. A.C. Médoc. Commune = Saint-Christoly. Grape varieties – Cabernet franc 10%, Cabernet sauvignon 40% and Merlot 50%. 26 ha.

Château la Tour Blanche (Fr). A Premier Grand Cru Classé vineyard in the commune of Bommes. A.C. Sauternes, Bordeaux. 27 ha.

Château la Tour-Cantenac (Fr). A vineyard in the commune of Cantenac. A.C. Haut-Médoc, Bordeaux. Cru Bourgeois.

Château la Tour-Carnet (Fr). Grand Cru Classé (4th). A.C. Haut-Médoc. Commune = Saint Laurent. 31 ha. Grape varieties – Cabernet franc, Cabernet sauvignon, Merlot and Petit verdot.

Château la Tour Castillon (Fr). A vineyard in the commune of Saint-Christoly-de-Médoc. A.C. Médoc, Bordeaux. Cru Bourgeois.

Château la Tour-de-Bessan (Fr). Part of Château la Tour-de-Mons, A.C. Haut-Médoc, Bordeaux.

Château la Tour-de-Boyrin (Fr). A vineyard in the commune of Langon. A.C. Graves, Bordeaux. 13 ha. (white).

Château la Tour-de-By (Fr). Address = 33340 Bégadan. Cru Grand Bourgeois. A.C. Médoc. Commune = Bégadan. 61 ha. Grape varieties – Cabernet franc, Cabernet sauvignon and Merlot.

Château la Tour de Fabrezan (Fr). A vineyard in the A.C. Corbières, south-western France. (red). Grape varieties – Carignan, Grenache and Syrah.

Château la Tour-de-Grenet (Fr). A vineyard in the commune of Lussac-Saint-Émilion. A.C. Saint-Émilion, Bordeaux. 30 ha.

Château la Tour de Leyssac (Fr). A vineyard in the commune of Saint-Estèphe. A.C. Saint-Estèphe, Bordeaux. 4 ha.

Château la Tour de Malescasse (Fr). A vineyard in the commune of Lamarque. A.C. Haut-Médoc, Bordeaux. 5 ha.

Château la Tour-de-Marbuzet (Fr). A vineyard in the commune of Saint-Estèphe. A.C. Saint-Estèphe, Bordeaux.

Château la Tour de Mons (Fr). Address = Soussans, 33460 Margaux. A.C. Margaux. Commune = Soussans. 40 ha. Grape varieties – Cabernet franc, Cabernet sauvignon, Merlot and Petit verdot.

Château la Tour-de-Pape (Fr). A vineyard in the commune of Mérignac. A.C. Graves, Bordeaux.

Château la Tour de Pez-l'Hétéyre (Fr). A vineyard in the commune of Saint-Estèphe. A.C. Saint-Estèphe, Bordeaux. 9 ha.

Château la Tour de Pressac (Fr). A vineyard in the commune of Saint-Étienne-de-Lisse. A.C. Saint-Émilion, Bordeaux.

Château la Tour-des-Combes (Fr). A vineyard in the commune of Saint Laurent des Combes. A.C. Saint-Émilion, Bordeaux.

Château Latour-de-Ségur (Fr). A vineyard in the commune of Lussac-Saint-Émilion. A.C. Saint-Émilion, Bordeaux. 8 ha.

Château la Tour des Ternes (Fr). A vineyard in the commune of Saint-Estèphe. A.C. Saint-Estèphe, Bordeaux. 12 ha.

Château la Tour du Haut-Caussan (Fr). A vineyard in the commune of Blaignan. A.C. Médoc, Bordeaux. 6 ha.

Château la Tour du Haut Moulin (Fr). A vineyard in the commune of Cussac-Fort-Médoc. A.C. Haut-Médoc, Bordeaux. Cru Grand Bourgeois. 24 ha.

Château la Tour du Mirail (Fr). A vineyard in the commune of Cissac. A.C. Haut-Médoc, Bordeaux. Cru Bourgeois.

Château la Tour-du-Pin-Figeac (Fr). Address = 33330 Saint-Émilion. Grand Cru Classé. A.C. Saint-Émilion. Commune = Saint-Émilion. 10.5 ha. Grape varieties – Bouchet 25% and Merlot 75%.

Château la Tour-du-Pin-Figeac-Moueix (Fr). Address = 33330 Saint-Émilion. Grand Cru Classé. A.C. Saint-Émilion. Commune = Saint-Émilion. 10.5 ha. Grape varieties – Cabernet franc 30% and Merlot 70%.

Château la Tour du Roc (Fr). A vineyard in the commune of Arcins. A.C. Haut-Médoc, Bordeaux. 9 ha.

Château la Tour du Roch Milon (Fr). A vineyard in the commune of Pauillac. A.C. Pauillac, Bordeaux. 18 ha.

Château la-Tour-du-Roi (Fr). A.C. Médoc. Second wine of Château Lagrange Grand Cru Classé (3rd) St-Julien.

Château la Tour-Figeac (Fr). Address = 33330 Saint-Émilion. Grand Cru Classé, A.C. Saint-Émilion. Commune = Saint-Émilion. 13.6 ha. Grape varieties – Cabernet franc 40% and Merlot 60%.

Château la Tour Gayet (Fr). A vineyard in the commune of St-Androny. A.C. Côtes de Blaye, Bordeaux.

Château la Tour Gilet (Fr). A vineyard in the commune of Montagne-Saint-Émilion. A.C. Saint-Émilion, Bordeaux. 6 ha.

Château la Tour-Guillotin (Fr). A vineyard in the commune of Puisseguin-Saint-Émilion. A.C. Saint-Émilion, Bordeaux. 6 ha.

Château la Tour Haut-Brion (Fr). Address = 33400 Talence. Cru Classé. A.C. Graves. Commune = Talence. 6 ha.

Château la Tour Haut-Caussan (Fr). Address = 33340 Blaignan-Médoc. Cru Bourgeois. A.C. Médoc. Commune = Blaignan. 9 ha. Grape varieties – Cabernet sauvignon 55% and Merlot 45%.

Château la Tour Haut Vignoble (Fr). A vineyard in the commune of Saint-Estèphe. A.C. Haut-Médoc, Bordeaux. 12 ha.

Château la Tour l'Aspic (Fr). A vineyard in the commune of Pauillac. A.C. Haut-Médoc, Bordeaux. 4 ha.

Château la Tour Léognan (Fr). A vineyard in the commune of Léognan. A.C. Graves, Bordeaux. 7 ha. Address = Léognan 33850. Grape varieties – Cabernet franc, Cabernet sauvignon, Malbec, Merlot, Sauvignon and Sémillon.

Château la Tour Lichine (Fr). Part of Château Capbern, A.C. Haut-Médoc, Bordeaux.

Château la Tour Marbuzet (Fr). A vineyard in the commune of Saint-Estèphe. A.C. Médoc, Bordeaux. Cru Bourgeois.

Château la Tour Marcillanet (Fr). A vineyard in the commune of Saint Laurent. A.C. Médoc, Bordeaux. Cru Bourgeois. 6 ha.

Château la Tour Martillac (Fr). Address = Martillac, 33650 La Brède. Grand Cru Classé. A.C. Graves. Commune = Léognan. 23 ha. Grape varieties – Cabernet franc, Cabernet sauvignon, Malbec, Merlot, Muscadelle, Petit verdot, Sauvignon and Sémillon. Also Kressmann la Tour.

Château Latour-Musset (Fr). A vineyard in the the commune of Parsac-Saint-Émilion. A.C. Saint-Émilion, Bordeaux. 10 ha.

Château la Tour-Paquillon (Fr). A vineyard in the commune of Montagne-Saint-Émilion. A.C. Saint-Émilion, Bordeaux. 8 ha.

Château la Tour Pibran (Fr). A vineyard in the commune of Pauillac. A.C. Haut-

Médoc, Bordeaux. Cru Bourgeois. 7 ha.

Château Latour-Pomerol (Fr). A vineyard in the commune of Pomerol. A.C. Pomerol, Bordeaux. 9 ha.

Château Latour-Pourret (Fr). A vineyard in the A.C. Saint-Émilion, Bordeaux.

Château Latour Prignac (Fr). A vineyard in the commune of Prignac. A.C. Haut-Médoc, Bordeaux. 115 ha.

Château la Tour Puyblanquet (Fr). A vineyard in the commune of Saint-Étienne-de-Lisse. A.C. Saint-Émilion, Bordeaux. 40 ha.

Château la Tour Saint-Bonnet (Fr). A vineyard in the commune of Saint-Christoly. A.C. Médoc, Bordeaux. Cru Bourgeois.

Château la Tour Saint Joseph (Fr). Address = 33250 Pauillac. Cru Bourgeois A.C. Haut-Médoc. Commune = Cissac. 10 ha. Grape varieties – Cabernet sauvignon 75% and Merlot 25%.

Château la Tour-Seguy (Fr). A vineyard in the commune of St-Ciers-de-Canesse. A.C. Côtes de Bourg, Bordeaux.

Château la Tour Sieujan (Fr). A vineyard in the commune of St Laurent. A.C. Médoc, Bordeaux. Cru Bourgeois.

Château la Tour-St-Georges (Fr). Part of Château St-Georges, A.C. Saint-Émilion, Bordeaux.

Château la Tour St. Pierre (Fr). A vineyard in the Côtes-Saint-Émilion. A.C. Saint-Émilion, Bordeaux.

Château la Tourte (Fr). A vineyard in the commune of Toulenne. A.C. Graves, Bordeaux. 6 ha. (white).

Château la Trezette (Fr). A vineyard in the A.C. Sauternes, Bordeaux.

Château Latrezotte (Fr). A vineyard in the commune of Barsac. A.C. Barsac (or Sauternes), Bordeaux. 7 ha.

Château Latte de Sirey (Fr). Address = Saint Laurent des Combes, 33330 Saint-Émilion. A.C. Saint-Émilion. Commune = Saint Laurent des Combes. 5 ha. Grape varieties – Cabernet franc, Cabernet sauvignon and Merlot 65%.

Château la Tulière (Fr). A vineyard in the A.C. Côtes de Bourg, Bordeaux.

Château la Tuque (Fr). A vineyard in the commune of Eyresse. A.C. Saint-Foy-Bordeaux, south-eastern Bordeaux.

Château l'Aubépin (Fr). A vineyard in the commune of Bommes. A.C. Sauternes, Bordeaux. Cru Bourgeois.

Château Laujac (Fr). Address = Bégadan, 33340 Lesparre-Médoc. Cru Grand Bourgeois. A.C. Médoc. Commune = Bégadan. 60 ha. Grape varieties – Cabernet franc, Cabernet sauvignon, Merlot and Petit verdot.

Château Launay (Fr). A vineyard in the

commune of Teuillac. A.C. Côtes de Bourg, Bordeaux.

Château Laurensanne (Fr). A vineyard in the commune of St-Seurin-Bourg. A.C. Côtes de Bourg, Bordeaux.

Château Laurenzane (Fr). A vineyard in the commune of Gradignan. A.C. Graves, Bordeaux.

Château Lauretan (Fr). The brand-name for red and white wines produced by the négociant-éleveur Cordier in Bordeaux. Red – Cabernet franc, Cabernet sauvignon, Merlot. White – Sauvignon blanc and Sémillon.

Château Laurette (Fr). A vineyard in the commune of Sainte-Croix-du-Mont. A.C. Sainte-Croix-du-Mont, Bordeaux. 15 ha.

Château la Vaisinerie (Fr). A vineyard in the commune of Puisseguin-Saint-Émilion. A.C. Saint-Émilion, Bordeaux. 8 ha.

Château La Valade (Fr). A vineyard in the commune of Fronsac. A.C. Côtes de Fronsac, Bordeaux. 15 ha.

Château Lavalière (Fr). A vineyard in the commune of Saint-Christoly. A.C. Médoc, Bordeaux.

Château Lavallade (Fr). Address = Saint-Christophe-des-Bardes, 33330 Saint-Émilion. Grand Cru. A.C. Saint-Émilion. Commune = Saint-Christophe-des-Bardes. 13 ha. Grape varieties – Cabernet 25% and Merlot 75%.

Château Lavaud la Maréchaude (Fr). A vineyard in the commune of Lalande de Pomerol. A.C. Lalande de Pomerol, Bordeaux.

Château la Venelle (Fr). A vineyard in the commune of Fronsac. A.C. Côtes de Fronsac, Bordeaux. 4 ha.

Château la Vieille Cure (Fr). A vineyard in the commune of Saillans. A.C. Fronsac, Bordeaux. Address = 331412 Villegouge. 14 ha.

Château la Vieille-France (Fr). A vineyard in the commune of Portets. A.C. Graves, Bordeaux. 16 ha. Grape varieties – Cabernet and Sémillon (red and white).

Château Lavignac (Fr). A vineyard in the commune of Preignac. A.C. Sauternes, Bordeaux. 3 ha.

Château Laville (Fr). A vineyard in the commune of Preignac. A.C. Sauternes, Bordeaux. 11 ha.

Château Laville Haut Brion (Fr). Address = 67, Rue Peybouquey, 33400 Talence. A.C. Graves. Commune = Talence. 6 ha. Grape varieties – Sauvignon 40% and Sémillon 60%.

Château Lavillotte (Fr). Address = 33250

C

Vertheuil-Médoc. A.C. Saint-Estèphe. Commune = Vertheuil. 13 ha. Grape varieties – Cabernet 75% and Merlot 25%.

Château Lavinot-la-Chapelle (Fr). A vineyard in the commune of Néac. A.C. Saint-Émilion, Bordeaux.

Château la Violette (Fr). A vineyard in the commune of Pomerol. A.C. Pomerol, Bordeaux. 2 ha.

Château le Amon Winery (Austr). Address = 140 km. Post, Calder highway, Big hill, Bendigo, Victoria 3550 (P.O. Box 487). 4.2 ha. Grape varieties – Cabernet sauvignon, Rhine riesling, Sémillon, Shiraz.

Château le Basque (Fr). A vineyard in the commune of Arbanats. A.C. Graves, Bordeaux. (red and white).

Château le Basque (Fr). A vineyard in the commune of Lussac-Saint-Émilion. A.C. Saint-Émilion, Bordeaux.

Château le Bécade (Fr). A vineyard in the commune of Listrac. A.C. Médoc, Bordeaux. Cru Bourgeois.

Château le Bedou (Fr). A vineyard in the A.C. Côtes de Blaye, Bordeaux.

Château le Bonnat-Jeansotte (Fr). Address = Saint Selve, 33650 La Brède. A.C. Graves. Commune = Saint Selve. 16 ha. Grape varieties – Cabernet 65%, Merlot 35%, Sauvignon and Sémillon.

Château le Bon Pasteur (Fr). A vineyard in the commune of Pomerol. A.C. Pomerol, Bordeaux. 6 ha.

Château le Boscq (Fr). Address = Saint-Christoly, 33340 Médoc. Cru Bourgeois. A.C. Médoc. Commune = Saint-Christoly. 24 ha. Grape varieties – Cabernet franc, Cabernet sauvignon and Merlot.

Château le Boscq (Fr). A vineyard in the commune of Saint-Estèphe. A.C. Saint-Estèphe, Bordeaux. 13 ha.

Château le Bourdieu (Fr). Address = Vertheuil 33250 Pauillac. A.C. Haut-Médoc. Commune = Vertheuil. 51 ha. Grape varieties – Cabernet franc 20%, Cabernet sauvignon 50% and Merlot 30%.

Château le Breuilh (Fr). A vineyard in the commune of Cissac. A.C. Haut-Médoc, Bordeaux.

Château le Brouillaud (Fr). A vineyard in the commune of St-Médard-d'Eyrans. A.C. Graves, Bordeaux. 5 ha. (white).

Château le Burck (Fr). A vineyard in the commune of Mérignac. A.C. Graves, Bordeaux.

Château le Caillou (Fr). A vineyard in the A.C. Côtes de Bourg, Bordeaux.

Château le Caillou (Fr). A vineyard in the commune of Pomerol. A.C. Pomerol, Bordeaux. 5 ha.

Château le Carillon (Fr). A vineyard in the commune of Pomerol. A.C. Pomerol, Bordeaux. 4 ha.

Château le Castelot (Fr). Address = Saint-Sulpice-de-Faleyrens, 33330 Saint-Émilion. Grand Cru. A.C. Saint-Émilion. Commune = Saint-Sulpice-de-Faleyrens. 8.7 ha. Grape varieties – Cabernet franc 20%, Cabernet sauvignon 20% and Merlot 60%.

Château le Cauze (Fr). A vineyard in the commune of Saint-Christophe-des-Bardes. A.C. Saint-Émilion, Bordeaux.

Château le Chais (Fr). A vineyard in the commune of Puisseguin-Saint-Émilion. A.C. Saint-Émilion, Bordeaux.

Château le Chatelet (Fr). Address = 33330 Saint-Émilion. Grand Cru Classé. A.C. Saint-Émilion. Commune = Saint-Émilion. 2.5 ha.

Château le Chay (Fr). A vineyard in the commune of Puisseguin-Saint-Émilion. A.C. Saint-Émilion, Bordeaux. 32.5 ha.

Château le Cône Moreau (Fr). A vineyard in the commune of Blaye. A.C. Côtes de Blaye, Bordeaux.

Château le Cône Sebilleau (Fr). A vineyard in the commune of Blaye. A.C. Côtes de Blaye, Bordeaux.

Château le Cône Taillasson (Fr). A vineyard in the commune of Blaye. A.C. Côtes de Blaye, Bordeaux.

Château le Coustet (Fr). A vineyard in the commune of Barsac. A.C. Barsac (or Sauternes), Bordeaux. 5 ha.

Château le Couvent (Fr). A vineyard in the Côtes-Saint-Émilion. A.C. Saint-Émilion, Bordeaux. Grand Cru Classé. 0.6 ha.

Château le Crock (Fr). Address = Marbuzet, Saint-Estèphe, 33250 Pauillac. Cru Grand Bourgeois Exceptionnel. A.C. Saint-Estèphe. Commune = Saint-Estèphe. 31 ha. Grape varieties – Cabernet sauvignon 65% and Merlot 35%.

Château le Cros Vernet (Fr). A.C. Bordeaux Supérieur.

Château le Fournas (Fr). A vineyard in the commune of Saint-Sauveur. A.C. Haut-Médoc, Bordeaux. 6 ha.

Château le Fournas Bernadotte (Fr). A vineyard in the commune of Saint-Sauveur. A.C. Haut-Médoc, Bordeaux. 20 ha.

Château le Gardera (Fr). The name for a red A.C. Bordeaux Supérieur produced by the négociants-éleveurs Cordier from Cabernet sauvignon and Merlot grapes.

Château le Gay (Fr). A vineyard in the commune of Pomerol. A.C. Pomerol, Bordeaux. 8 h.

Château l'Église-Clinet (Fr). A vineyard in the commune of Pomerol. A.C. Pomerol, Bordeaux.

C

Château l'Église Vieille (Fr). A vineyard in the commune of Lamarque. A.C. Haut-Médoc, Bordeaux. 3 ha. Grape varieties – Cabernet 50% and Merlot 50%.

Château le Grand-Mazerolle (Fr). A vineyard in the commune of Cars. A.C. Côtes de Blaye, Bordeaux.

Château le Grand Peyrot (Fr). A vineyard in the commune of Sainte-Croix-du-Mont. A.C. Sainte-Croix-du-Mont, Bordeaux. 5 ha.

Château le Gravier-Gueyrosse (Fr). A vineyard in the commune of Sables-Saint-Émilion. A.C. Saint-Émilion, Bordeaux. 7.5 ha.

Château le Hère (Fr). A vineyard in the commune of Bommes. A.C. Sauternes, Bordeaux. 6 ha.

Château Léhoul (Fr). Address = Route d'Auros, 33210 Langon. A.C. Graves. Commune = Langon. 5 ha. Grape varieties – Cabernet sauvignon, Malbec, Merlot, Muscadelle, Sauvignon and Sémillon.

Château le Huzet (Fr). A vineyard in the commune of Illats. A.C. Cérons, Bordeaux. 7 ha.

Château le Jurat (Fr). Address = 33330 Saint-Émilion. Grand Cru. A.C. Saint-Émilion. Commune = Saint-Émilion. 7.5 ha. Grape varieties = Cabernet sauvignon 35% and Merlot 65%.

Château le Landat (Fr). A vineyard in the commune of Cissac. A.C. Médoc, Bordeaux. Cru Bourgeois.

Château le Mayne (Fr). A vineyard in the commune of Preignac. A.C. Sauternes, Bordeaux. 13 ha.

Château le Mayne (Fr). A vineyard in the commune of Puisseguin-Saint-Émilion. A.C. Saint-Émilion, Bordeaux. 3 ha.

Château le Mayne (Fr). A vineyard in the commune of Sauternes. A.C. Sauternes, Bordeaux. 6 ha. Also Château Lafon.

Château le Menaudat (Fr). A vineyard in the commune of St-Androny. A.C. Côtes de Blaye, Bordeaux.

Château le Meynieu (Fr). Cru Grand Bourgeois. Address = 33250 Vertheuil-Médoc. A.C. Haut-Médoc. Commune = Vertheuil. 15 ha. Grape varieties – Cabernet 70% and Merlot 30%

Château le Monastère (Fr). A vineyard in the A.C. Côtes de Bourg, Bordeaux.

Château le Moulin-Rompu (Fr). A vineyard in the A.C. Côtes de Bourg, Bordeaux.

Château le Mouret (Fr). A vineyard in the commune of Fargues. A.C. Sauternes, Bordeaux. 6 ha.

Château Lemoyne-Lafon-Rochet (Fr). A

vineyard in the commune of Le Pian. A.C. Haut-Médoc, Bordeaux. 6 ha.

Château le Mugron (Fr). A vineyard in the commune of Prignac-Marcamps. A.C. Côtes de Bourg, Bordeaux.

Château l'Enclos (Fr). A vineyard in the commune of Pomerol. A.C. Pomerol, Bordeaux. 7 ha.

Château Lenoir (Fr). A vineyard in the commune of Sables-Saint-Émilion. A.C. Saint-Émilion, Bordeaux. 4 ha.

Château Leonay (Austr). Address = Para Road, Tanunda, South Australia, 5253. 80 ha. Grape varieties – Cabernet sauvignon, Chardonnay, Malbec, Pinot noir, Rhine riesling, Sauvignon blanc, Sémillion and Shiraz. Vineyards in the Barossa Valley, Hunter River and Watervale districts.

Château Léoville-Barton (Fr). Address = Saint Julien-Beychevelle 33250. Grand Cru Classé (2nd). A.C. Saint-Julien. Commune = Saint-Julien. 45 ha. Grape varieties – Cabernet gris, Cabernet sauvignon, Merlot and Petit verdot.

Château Léoville-Las-Cases (Fr). Address = Saint Julien-Beychevelle 33250. Grand Cru Classé (2nd). A.C. Saint-Julien. Commune = Saint-Julien. 135 ha. Grape varieties – Cabernet franc, Cabernet sauvignon, Merlot and Petit verdot. See Clos du Marquis.

Château Léoville-Poyferré (Fr). Address = Saint Julien-Beychevelle 33250. Grand Cru Classé (2nd). A.C. Saint-Julien. Commune = Saint-Julien. 61.3 ha. Grape varieties – Cabernet franc, Cabernet sauvignon and Merlot.

Château le Pape (Fr). A vineyard in the commune of Léognan. A.C. Graves, Bordeaux. 6 ha. (red and white).

Château le Pavillon (Fr). A vineyard in the commune of Loupiac. A.C. Loupiac, Bordeaux. 4 ha.

Château le Peillan (Fr). A vineyard in the commune of Saint Laurent des Combes. A.C. Saint-Émilion, Bordeaux.

Château le Pelletan (Fr). A vineyard in the commune of Saint-Quentin-de-Caplang. A.C. Saint-Foy-Bordeaux, south-eastern Bordeaux.

Château le Pin (Fr). A vineyard in the commune of Sainte-Croix-du-Mont. A.C. Sainte-Croix-du-Mont, Bordeaux. 3 ha.

Château Lépine (Fr). A vineyard in the commune of Sables-Saint-Émilion. A.C. Saint-Émilion, Bordeaux. 2 ha.

Château le Pont-de-Pierre (Fr). A vineyard in the commune of Lussac-Saint-Émilion. A.C. Saint-Émilion, Bordeaux. 3 ha.

Château le Prieuré (Fr). A vineyard in the

commune of Saint-Gènes-de-Blaye. A.C. Côtes de Blaye, Bordeaux.

Château le Prieuré (Fr). Address = 33330 Saint-Émilion. Grand Cru Classé. A.C. Saint-Émilion. Commune = Saint-Émilion. 6 ha. Grape varieties – Cabernet franc 30% and Merlot 70%.

Château le Puy (Fr). A vineyard in the commune of Parsac-Saint-Émilion. A.C. Saint-Émilion, Bordeaux.

Château le Puy-St-Georges (Fr). Part of Château St-Georges, A.C. Saint-Émilion, Bordeaux.

Château le Rauly (Fr). A vineyard in the A.C. Bergerac, south-western France. (red).

Château le Raux (Fr). A vineyard in the commune Cussac. A.C. Haut-Médoc, Bordeaux. 4 ha.

Château l'Ermitage (Fr). A vineyard in the commune of Preignac. A.C. Sauternes, Bordeaux. 7 ha.

Château le Roc (Fr). A vineyard in the commune of Bourg. A.C. Côtes de Bourg, Bordeaux.

Château le Roc (Fr). A vineyard in the commune of Saint-Estèphe. A.C. Saint-Estèphe, Bordeaux. Cru Bourgeois.

Château le Roc-de-Troquard (Fr). A vineyard in the commune of Saint-Georges-Saint-Émilion. A.C. Saint-Émilion, Bordeaux. 3 ha.

Château le Rose-et-Monteil (Fr). A vineyard in the commune of Preignac. A.C. Sauternes, Bordeaux. 5 ha.

Château le Sahue (Fr). A vineyard in the commune of Preignac. A.C. Sauternes, Bordeaux. 3 ha.

Château les Alberts (Fr). A vineyard in the commune of Mazion. A.C. Côtes de Blaye, Bordeaux.

Château les Arrieux (Fr). A vineyard in the commune of Preignac. A.C. Sauternes, Bordeaux. 5 ha.

Château les Baraillots (Fr). A vineyard in the commune of Margaux. A.C. Margaux, Bordeaux.

Château les Bardes (Fr). A vineyard in the commune of Montagne-Saint-Émilion. A.C. Saint-Émilion, Bordeaux. 3 ha.

Château les Bardes (Fr). A vineyard in the commune of Pomerol. A.C. Pomerol, Bordeaux. 2 ha.

Château les Bavolliers (Fr). A vineyard in the commune of St-Christ-de-Blaye. A.C. Côtes de Blaye, Bordeaux.

Château les Bertins (Fr). A vineyard in the commune of Valeyrac. A.C. Médoc, Bordeaux.

Château les Bouysses (Fr). The name used by Les Côtes d'Olt (Cahors) for a red wine.

Château les Brandines (Fr). A vineyard in the A.C. Bergerac, south-western France. (red).

Château l'Escadre (Fr). A vineyard in the commune of Cadre. A.C. Premières Côtes de Blaye, Bordeaux.

Château l'Escaley (Fr). A vineyard in the commune of Sainte-Croix-du-Mont. A.C. Sainte-Croix-du-Mont, Bordeaux. 5 ha.

Château les Capitans (Fr). A vineyard in the A.C. commune of Juliénas, Cru Beaujolais-Villages, Burgundy.

Château Lescarjeau (Fr). A vineyard in the commune of Saint-Sauveur. A.C. Haut-Médoc, Bordeaux. 5 ha.

Château les Carmes-Haut-Brion (Fr). A vineyard in the commune of Pessac. A.C. Graves, Bordeaux.

Château les Carrières (Fr). A vineyard in the commune of Montagne-Saint-Émilion. A.C. Saint-Émilion, Bordeaux. 2 ha.

Château les Charmettes (Fr). A vineyard in the commune of Budos. A.C. Graves, Bordeaux. 2 ha. (white).

Château les Chaumes (Fr). A vineyard in the commune of Fours. A.C. Côtes de Blaye, Bordeaux. Address = 33390 Blaye.

Château les Chaumes (Fr). A vineyard in the commune of Néac. A.C. Pomerol, Bordeaux.

Château les Combes (Fr). A vineyard in the commune of Saint-Estèphe. A.C. Saint-Estèphe, Bordeaux.

Château les Cônes-Sebizeaux (Fr). A vineyard in the commune of Blaye. A.C. Côtes de Blaye, Bordeaux.

Château les Côtes-de-Gardat (Fr). A vineyard in the commune of Montagne-Saint-Émilion. A.C. Saint-Émilion, Bordeaux. 5 ha.

Château Lescours (Fr). A vineyard in the commune of Saint-Sulpice-de-Faleyrens. A.C. Saint-Émilion, Bordeaux.

Château les Cruzelles (Fr). A vineyard in the commune of Lalande de Pomerol. A.C. Saint-Émilion, Bordeaux.

Château Lescure (Fr). A vineyard in the commune of Lerdelais. Produces A.C. Bordeaux Mousseux.

Château les Essarts (Fr). A vineyard in the commune of Lussac-Saint-Émilion. A.C. Lussac-Saint-Émilion, Bordeaux.

Château les Eyguires (Fr). A vineyard in the commune of Saint-Christophe-des-Bardes. A.C. Saint-Émilion, Bordeaux.

Château les Eyquems (Fr). A vineyard in the commune of Tauriac. A.C. Côtes de Bourg, Bordeaux.

Château les Faures Bellevue (Fr). A.C. Bordeaux. (red wine).

C

Château les Fines Roches (Fr). A vineyard in the A.C. Châteauneuf-du-Pape, southern Rhône.

Château les Grandes Murailles (Fr). Address = 33330 Saint-Émilion. Grand Cru Classé. A.C. Saint-Émilion. Commune = Saint-Émilion. 3.5 ha. Grape varieties – Cabernet franc 16%, Cabernet sauvignon 16% and Merlot 66%.

Château les Grandes Versaines (Fr). A vineyard in the commune of Néac. A.C. Lalande de Pomerol, Bordeaux.

Château les Grandes-Vignes (Fr). A vineyard in the commune of Montagne-Saint-Émilion. A.C. Saint-Émilion, Bordeaux. 2 ha.

Château les Grandes-Vignes (Fr). A vineyard in the commune of Pomerol. A.C. Pomerol, Bordeaux. 1 ha.

Château les Grands-Sillons (Fr). A vineyard in the commune of Pomerol. A.C. Pomerol, Bordeaux. 2 ha.

Château les Granges d'Or (Fr). A vineyard in the commune of Blaignan. A.C. Médoc. Cru Bourgeois. Address = Blaignan, 33340 Lesparre.

Château les Graves de Germignan (Fr). A vineyard in the commune of Le Taillan. A.C. Haut-Médoc, Bordeaux. 3 ha.

Château les Gravilles (Fr). Address = 33250 Pauillac, Médoc. A.C. Haut-Médoc. Commune = Saint Sauveur du Médoc. 4 ha. Grape varieties – Cabernet sauvignon 68% and Merlot 32%.

Château les Hautes-Rouzes (Fr). A vineyard in the commune of Pomerol. A.C. Pomerol, Bordeaux. 2 ha.

Château les Hauts de Granges (Fr). A vineyard in the commune of Salles-de-Castillon, Côtes de Castillon, eastern Bordeaux. A.C. Bordeaux Supérieur. (red).

Château les Jacquets (Fr). A vineyard in the commune of Saint-Georges-Saint-Émilion. A.C. Saint-Émilion, Bordeaux. 5 ha.

Château les Jouans (Fr). A vineyard in the commune of Saint-Sulpice-de-Faleyrens. A.C. Saint-Émilion, Bordeaux.

Château les Justices (Fr). A vineyard in the commune of Preignac. A.C. Sauternes, Bordeaux. 3 ha.

Château les Laurets (Fr). A vineyard in the commune of Puisseguin-Saint-Émilion. A.C. Saint-Émilion, Bordeaux. 75 ha.

Château les Maules (Fr). A vineyard in the A.C. Bergerac, south-western France. (red).

Château les Moines (Fr). A vineyard in the commune of Blaye. A.C. Côtes de Blaye, Bordeaux.

Château les Ormes de Pez (Fr). Address = Saint-Estèphe, 33250 Pauillac. Cru Grand Bourgeois. A.C. Saint-Estèphe. Commune = Saint-Estèphe. 30 ha. Grape varieties – Cabernet franc, Cabernet sauvignon, Merlot and Petit verdot.

Château les Ormes Sorbet (Fr). Address = 33340 Lesparre. Cru Grand Bourgeois. A.C. Médoc. Commune = Couquèques. 20 ha. Grape varieties – Cabernet franc, Cabernet sauvignon, Merlot and Petit verdot.

Château le Souley-Ste Croix (Fr). Address = 33250 Vertheuil. Cru Bourgeois. A.C. Haut-Médoc. Commune = Vertheuil. 20 ha. Grape varieties – Cabernet sauvignon 60% and Merlot 40%.

Château les Palais (Fr). A vineyard in the A.C. Corbières, south-western France. (red).

Château Lespault (Fr). A vineyard in the commune of Martillac. A.C. Graves, Bordeaux. 4.5 ha. (red and white).

Château les Petits Arnauds (Fr). A vineyard in the commune of Cars. A.C. Côtes de Blaye, Bordeaux.

Château les Plantes (Fr). A vineyard in the commune of Barsac. A.C. Barsac (or Sauternes), Bordeaux. 5 ha.

Château les Remparts (Fr). A vineyard in the commune of Preignac. A.C. Sauternes, Bordeaux. 14 ha. Also Domaine des Justices and Châteaux Gilette, Lamothe and les Rochers.

Château les Renardières (Fr). A vineyard in the commune of Saint-Georges-Saint-Émilion. A.C. Saint-Émilion, Bordeaux. 4 ha.

Château les Richards (Fr). A vineyard in the commune of Cars. A.C. Côtes de Blaye, Bordeaux.

Château les Rochers (Fr). A vineyard in the commune of Preignac. A.C. Sauternes, Bordeaux. 7 ha.

Château les Rochers (Fr). A vineyard in the commune of Preignac. A.C. Sauternes, Bordeaux. 14 ha. Also Domaine des Justices and Châteaux Gilette, Lamothe and les Remparts.

Château les Roches Rouges (Fr). A vineyard in the A.C. Saint-Émilion, Bordeaux.

Château Lestage (Fr). Address = 33480 Listrac-Médoc. Cru Bourgeois. A.C. Listrac-Médoc. Commune = Listrac. 56 ha. Grape varieties – Cabernet sauvignon, Merlot and Petit verdot.

Château Lestage (Fr). A vineyard in the commune of Parsac-Saint-Émilion. A.C. Saint-Émilion, Bordeaux. 8 ha.

Château Lestage (Fr). A vineyard in the commune of Saint-Seurin-de-Cadourne. A.C. Haut-Médoc, Bordeaux. 1 ha.

C

Château Lestage Darquier [Grand Poujeaux] (Fr). A vineyard in the commune of Moulis, A.C. Moulis, Bordeaux. Cru Bourgeois. Address = Moulis, 33480 Castelnau-de-Médoc. 4 ha.

Château Lestage Simon (Fr). A vineyard in the commune of St-Seurin-de-Cadourne. A.C. Haut-Médoc, Bordeaux. Cru Bourgeois. Address = St-Seurin-de-Cadourne 33250 Pauillac.

Château l'Estagnol (Fr). A vineyard in the A.C. Côtes du Rhône, south-eastern France.

Château les Templiers (Fr). A vineyard in the commune of Lalande de Pomerol. A.C. Lalande de Pomerol, Bordeaux.

Château les Trois Moulins (Fr). A vineyard in the Côtes-Saint-Émilion. A.C. Saint-Émilion, Bordeaux. Grand Cru Classé.

Château Lestruelle (Fr). A vineyard in the commune of Saint-Yzans. A.C. Médoc, Bordeaux. 21 ha. Grape varieties – Cabernet 30% and Merlot 70%.

Château les Tuileries-de-Bayard (Fr). A vineyard in the commune of Montagne-Saint-Émilion. A.C. Saint-Émilion, Bordeaux. 8 ha.

Château les Videaux (Fr). A vineyard in the A.C. Côtes de Blaye, Bordeaux.

Château les Vieux-Rocs (Fr). A vineyard in the commune of Lussac-Saint-Émilion. A.C. Saint-Émilion, Bordeaux. 3 ha.

Château les Vignes (Fr). A vineyard in the commune of Fronsac. A.C. Côtes Canon-Fronsac, Bordeaux. 2 ha.

Château le Tarey (Fr). A vineyard in the commune of Loupiac. A.C. Loupiac, Bordeaux. 5 ha.

Château le-Tetre-de-Perruchon (Fr). A vineyard in the commune of Lussac-Saint-Émilion. A.C. Saint-Émilion, Bordeaux. 3 ha.

Château le Tertre Roteboeuf (Fr). Address = Saint Laurent des Combes, 33330 Saint-Émilion. Grand Cru. A.C. Saint-Émilion. Commune = Saint Laurent des Combes. 5.5 ha. Grape varieties – Cabernet franc 20% and Merlot 80%.

Château le Teyssier (Fr). A vineyard in the commune of Puisseguin-Saint-Émilion. A.C. Saint-Émilion, Bordeaux.

Château le Thil (Fr). A vineyard in the commune of Léognan. A.C. Graves, Bordeaux. 3 ha. (red).

Château l'Etoile-Pourret (Fr). A.C. Saint-Émilion. Part of Château la Grâce-Dieu.

Château le Tréhon (Fr). A vineyard in the commune of Bégadan. A.C. Médoc,

Bordeaux. Address = Bégadan, 33340 Lesparre. 13 ha.

Château le Tuquet (Fr). A vineyard in the commune of Beautiran. A.C. Graves, Bordeaux.

Château l'Évangile (Fr). A vineyard in the commune of Pomerol. A.C. Pomerol, Bordeaux. 13.67 ha. Grape varieties – Cabernet franc and Merlot.

Château le Virou (Fr). A vineyard in the commune of St-Girons. A.C. Premières Côtes de Blaye, Bordeaux.

Château Leyssac (Fr). See Château Houissant.

Château Lezin (Fr). A.C. Bordeaux Supérieur.

Château l'Hermitage (Fr). A vineyard in the commune of Couquèques. A.C. Médoc, Bordeaux. 6 ha.

Château l'Hermitage (Fr). A vineyard in the commune of Martillac. A.C. Graves, Bordeaux.

Château l'Hermitage (Fr). A vineyard in the commune of Montagne-Saint-Émilion. A.C. Saint-Émilion, Bordeaux. 6 ha.

Château l'Hermitage-Mazerat (Fr). A vineyard in the A.C. Saint-Émilion, Bordeaux. 4 ha.

Château l'Hôpital (Fr). A vineyard in the commune of Saint-Estèphe. A.C. Saint-Estèphe, Bordeaux. 5 ha.

Château Libertas (S.Afr). A wine from Stellenbosch Farmers' Winery. Made from Cabernet and Pinotage grapes.

Château Lidonne (Fr). A vineyard in the commune of Bourg. A.C. Côtes de Bourg, Bordeaux. Address = 33710 Bourg-sur-Gironde.

Château Lieujan (Fr). A vineyard in the commune of St-Sauveur. A.C. Haut-Médoc, Bordeaux. Cru Bourgeois. Address = St-Sauveur, 33250 Pauillac.

Château Ligondras (Fr). A vineyard in the commune of Arsac. A.C. Margaux, Bordeaux. Address = Arsac, 33460 Margaux.

Château Limbourg (Fr). A vineyard in the commune of Villenave-d'Ornan. A.C. Graves, Bordeaux. 10 ha. (red and white).

Château Lionnat (Fr). A vineyard in the commune of Lussac-Saint-Émilion. A.C. Saint-Émilion, Bordeaux.

Château Lion Noble d'Or (Jap). A sweet white wine made by Suntory.

Château Liot (Fr). Cru Bourgeois. A.C. Barsac (or Sauternes). Commune = Barsac. Grape varieties – Sauvignon, Sémillon and Muscadelle. 11 ha.

Château Liot-Moros (Fr). A vineyard in the commune of Pujols. A.C. Graves, Bordeaux. 5 ha. (white).

C

Château Liouner (Fr). A vineyard in the commune of Listrac. A.C. Listrac, Bordeaux. Cru Bourgeois. Address = Listrac, 33480 Castelnau-de-Médoc.

Château Listrac (Fr). A vineyard in the commune of Listrac. A.C. Haut-Médoc, Bordeaux. Cru Bourgeois.

Château Liversan (Fr). Address = 33250 Pauillac. Cru Grand Bourgeois. A.C. Haut-Médoc. Commune = Saint-Sauveur-du-Médoc. 50 ha. Grape varieties – Cabernet franc, Cabernet sauvignon, Merlot and Petit verdot.

Château Livran (Fr). A vineyard in the commune of Lesparre. A.C. Médoc, Bordeaux. Cru Bourgeois. Address = Saint-Germain-d'Esteuil, 33340 Lesparre. 40 ha.

Château Lognac (Fr). A vineyard in the commune of Castres. A.C. Graves, Bordeaux. 5 ha. (red).

Château Lognac (Fr). A vineyard in the commune of Portets. A.C. Graves, Bordeaux.

Château L'Oiselinière de la Ramée (Fr). A vineyard in the A.C. Muscadet de Sèvre et Maine, Pays Nantais, Loire.

Château Loquey (Fr). A vineyard in the commune of Saint-Seurin-de-Cadourne. A.C. Haut-Médoc, Bordeaux. 12 ha.

Château l'Oratoire (Fr). A vineyard in the commune of Saint-Émilion. A.C. Saint-Émilion, Bordeaux. 6 ha. Grand Cru Classé.

Château Lorillard (USA). A ficticious Château used as part of a 'Kent' cigarettes advertising campaign in 1986, the Château being from the Médoc.

Château l'Ormeau-Vieux (Fr). A vineyard in the commune of Puisseguin-Saint-Émilion. A.C. Saint-Émilion, Bordeaux. 7 ha.

Château Loubens (Fr). A vineyard in the commune of Sainte-Croix-du-Mont. A.C. Sainte-Croix-du-Mont, Bordeaux. 10 ha. Grape varieties – Sauvignon blanc, Sémillon and Muscadelle. See Château des Tours.

Château Loudenne (Fr). Address = 33340 Saint-Yzans de Médoc. Cru Grand Bourgeois. A.C. Médoc. Commune = Saint-Yzans. 55 ha. Grape varieties – Cabernet franc, Cabernet sauvignon, Merlot, Sauvignon 50%, Sémillon 50%.

Château Loumède (Fr). A vineyard in the A.C. Côtes de Blaye, Bordeaux.

Château Loupiac-Gaudiet (Fr). A vineyard in the commune of Loupiac. A.C. Loupiac, Bordeaux. 10 ha. Grape varieties – Sauvignon and Sémillon.

Château Lousteau Vieil (Fr). A vineyard in the commune of Sainte-Croix-du-Mont.

A.C. Sainte-Croix-du-Mont, Bordeaux. 7 ha.

Château Loyac (Fr). Second wine of Château Malescot-Saint Exupéry.

Château Lucas (Fr). A vineyard in the commune of Lussac-Saint-Émilion. A.C. Saint-Émilion, Bordeaux. 9 ha.

Château Ludeman-Lacôte (Fr). A vineyard in the commune of Langon. A.C. Graves, Bordeaux. 7 ha. (white).

Château Ludon-Pomiés-Agassac (Fr). A vineyard in the commune of Ludon. A.C. Médoc, Bordeaux. Cru Bourgeois.

Château Lugagnac (Fr). A vineyard in the commune of Vertheuil. A.C. Médoc, Bordeaux.

Château Lussac (Fr). A vineyard in the commune of Lussac-Saint-Émilion. A.C. Saint-Émilion, Bordeaux.

Château Lusseau (Fr). A vineyard in the commune of Ayguemortes. A.C. Graves, Bordeaux. 4 ha. (red).

Château Lynch-Bages (Fr). Address = 33250 Pauillac. Grand Cru Classé (5th). A.C. Pauillac. Commune = Pauillac. 75 ha. Grape varieties – Cabernet franc, Cabernet sauvignon and Merlot.

Château Lynch-Moussas (Fr). Address = 33250 Pauillac. Grand Cru Classé (5th). A.C. Pauillac. Commune = Pauillac. 35 ha. Grape varieties – Cabernet sauvignon 70% and Merlot 30%.

Château Lyonnat (Fr). A vineyard in the commune of Lussac-Saint-Émilion. A.C. Saint-Émilion, Bordeaux. 49 ha.

Château Lyon-Perruchon (Fr). A vineyard in the commune of Lussac-Saint-Émilion. A.C. Saint-Émilion, Bordeaux. 4 ha.

Château Macau (Fr). A vineyard in the commune of Tauriac. A.C. Côtes de Bourg, Bordeaux.

Château Macay (Fr). A vineyard in the commune of Samonac. A.C. Côtes de Bourg, Bordeaux.

Château Mac-Carthy Moula (Fr). A vineyard in the commune of Saint-Estèphe. A.C. Haut-Médoc, Bordeaux. Cru Grand Bourgeois. 6 ha.

Château Macquin St-Georges (Fr). A vineyard in the commune of Saint-Georges-Saint-Émilion. A.C. Saint-Georges-Saint-Émilion, Bordeaux.

Château Macureau (Fr). A vineyard in the commune of Montagne-Saint-Émilion. A.C. Saint-Émilion, Bordeaux. 6 ha.

Château Madélis (Fr). A vineyard in the commune of Portets. A.C. Graves, Bordeaux. 4 ha. (red and white).

Château Madère (Fr). A vineyard in the commune of Podensac. A.C. Cérons, Bordeaux. 12 ha.

Château Madran (Fr). A vineyard in the

C

commune of Pessac. A.C. Graves, Bordeaux. 3 ha. (red).

Château Magdelaine (Fr). Address = 33330 Saint-Émilion. Grand Cru Classé. A.C. Saint-Émilion. Commune = Saint-Émilion. 11.5 ha. Grape varieties – Cabernet franc, Merlot.

Château Magence (Fr). A vineyard in the commune of Saint-Pierre-de-Mons. A.C. Graves, Bordeaux. 30 ha. Address = 33210 Langon. (white).

Château Magnan-Figeac (Fr). Address = Cormeil-Figeac, 33330 Saint-Émilion. Grand Cru. A.C. Saint-Émilion. Commune = Saint-Émilion. Second wine of Château Cormeil-Figeac. Grand Cru. Saint-Émilion.

Château Magnan la Gaffelière (Fr). Address = 33330 Saint-Émilion. Grand Cru. A.C. Saint-Émilion. Commune = Saint-Émilion. 8 ha. Grape varieties – Cabernet franc 40%, Cabernet sauvignon 10% and Merlot 50%.

Château Magnol (Fr). A vineyard in the commune of Blanquefort. A.C. Haut-Médoc, Bordeaux. Cru Bourgeois. Address = 33290 Blanquefort.

Château Magondeau (Fr). A vineyard in the commune of Saillans. A.C. Côtes de Fronsac, Bordeaux. 9 ha.

Château Maillard (Fr). A vineyard in the commune of Mazères. A.C. Graves, Bordeaux. 5 ha. (white).

Château Maine-Blanc (Fr). A vineyard in the commune of Lussac-Saint-Émilion. A.C. Saint-Émilion, Bordeaux.

Château Maine-Marzelle (Fr). A vineyard in the commune of Saint-Savin-de-Blaye. A.C. Côtes de Blaye, Bordeaux. Address = 33920 Saint-Savin-de-Blaye.

Château Maison Blanche (Fr). A vineyard in the commune of Montagne-Saint-Émilion. A.C. Saint-Émilion, Bordeaux. 30 ha.

Château Maisonneuve (Fr). A vineyard in the commune of Parsac-Saint-Émilion. A.C. Saint-Émilion, Bordeaux. 7 ha.

Château Maja (USA). The brand-name used by the Conn Creek vineyard in the Napa Valley, California for one of their Chardonnay wines.

Château Malanguin (Fr). A vineyard in the commune of Parsac-Saint-Émilion. A.C. Saint-Émilion, Bordeaux.

Château Malartic-Lagravière (Fr). Address = 39 Ave. de Mont-de-Marsan, Léognan. Grand Cru Classé. A.C. Graves. Commune = Léognan. 22 ha. Grape varieties – Cabernet franc, Cabernet sauvignon, Merlot and Sauvignon.

Château Malécot (Fr). A vineyard in the commune of Pauillac. A.C. Pauillac, Bordeaux. 7 ha.

Château Malescasse (Fr). Address = 33460 Lamarque. Cru Bourgeois. A.C. Haut-Médoc. Commune = Lamarque. 40 ha. Grape varieties – Cabernet franc, Cabernet sauvignon and Merlot.

Château Malescot Saint-Exupéry (Fr). Address = 33460 Margaux. Grand Cru Classé (3rd). A.C. Margaux. Commune = Margaux. 45 ha. Grape varieties – Cabernet franc, Cabernet sauvignon, Merlot and Petit verdot.

Château Malineau (Fr). Address = 33330 Saint-Émilion. Grand Cru. A.C. Saint-Émilion. Commune = Saint-Émilion. 4.89 ha. Grape varieties – Bouchet, Cabernet sauvignon and Merlot 66%.

Château Malleprat (Fr). A vineyard in the commune of Martillac. A.C. Graves, Bordeaux. 3 ha. (white).

Château Malleret (Fr). A vineyard in the commune of Le Pian. A.C. Haut-Médoc, Bordeaux. Cru Grand Bourgeois. 22 ha.

Château Malmaison (Fr). A vineyard in the commune of Moulis. A.C. Moulis, Bordeaux. 4 ha.

Château Mandelot (Fr). A.C. Hautes Côtes de Beaune. (Vil) = Mavilly-Mandelot, Burgundy. Grape variety – Pinot noir.

Château Marbuzet (Fr). A vineyard in the commune of Saint-Estèphe. A.C. Saint-Estèphe, Bordeaux. Cru Grand Bourgeois Exceptionnel. 12 ha.

Château Marchand (Fr). A vineyard in the commune of Montagne-Saint-Émilion. A.C. Saint-Émilion, Bordeaux.

Château Marcillan-Belle-Vue (Fr). A vineyard in the commune of Saint Laurent. A.C. Médoc, Bordeaux. Cru Bourgeois.

Château Margaux (Fr). Address = 33460 Margaux. Premier Grand Cru Classé. A.C. Margaux. Commune = Margaux. 99 ha. Grape varieties – Cabernet franc, Cabernet sauvignon, Merlot, Petit verdot and Sauvignon. See Pavillion Rouge du Château Margaux.

Château Margot (Fr). A vineyard in the commune of Pomerol. A.C. Pomerol, Bordeaux. 1 ha.

Château Marque (Fr). A vineyard in the commune of Saint-Seurin-de-Cadourne. A.C. Haut-Médoc, Bordeaux. 1 ha.

Château Marquey (Fr). Address = 33330 Saint-Émilion. Grand Cru. A.C. Saint-Émilion. Commune = Saint-Émilion.

Château Marquis-d'Alesme-Becker (Fr). Address = 33460 Margaux. Grand Cru Classé (3rd). A.C. Margaux. Commune

C

= Margaux. 15 ha. Grape varieties – Cabernet franc, Cabernet sauvignon, Merlot and Petit verdot.

Château Marquis-de-Terme (Fr). Address = 33460 Margaux. Grand Cru Classé (4th). A.C. Margaux. Commune = Margaux. 40 ha.

Château Marsac-Séguineau (Fr). A vineyard in the commune of Soussans. A.C. Médoc, Bordeaux. Cru Bourgeois. 7 ha.

Château Martinens (Fr). Cru Grand Bourgeois. A.C. Margaux. Commune = Cantenac. 30 ha. Grape varieties – Cabernet franc, Cabernet sauvignon, Merlot and Petit verdot.

Château Martinet (Fr). A vineyard in the commune of Sables-Saint-Émilion. A.C. Saint-Émilion, Bordeaux. 12 ha.

Château Martinon (Fr). A vineyard in the A.C. Entre-Deux-Mers central Bordeaux. (white).

Château Mascard (Fr). A vineyard in the commune of Saint Laurent. A.C. Médoc, Bordeaux. Cru Bourgeois.

Château Masereau (Fr). A vineyard in the commune of Barsac. A.C. Barsac (or Sauternes), Bordeaux. 7 ha.

Château Mathalin (Fr). A vineyard in the commune of Barsac. A.C. Barsac (or Sauternes), Bordeaux. 11 ha.

Château Matras (Fr). Address = 33330 Saint-Émilion. Grand Cru Classé. A.C. Saint-Émilion. Commune = Saint-Émilion. 8.5 ha.

Château Matsa (Gre). A soft, dry white wine produced by Boutari.

Château Maucaillou (Fr). Address = 33480 Castelnau de Médoc. Cru Bourgeois A.C. Moulis. Commune = Moulis. 55 ha. Grape varieties – Cabernet franc, Cabernet sauvignon, Merlot and Petit verdot.

Château Maucamps (Fr). A vineyard in the commune of Macau. A.C. Médoc, Bordeaux. Cru Bourgeois. 3 ha.

Château Maucoil (Fr). A vineyard in the A.C. Châteauneuf-du-Pape, southern Rhône.

Château Mauconseil (Fr). A vineyard in the commune of Plassac. A.C. Côtes de Blaye, Bordeaux.

Château Mauras (Fr). A vineyard in the commune of Bommes. A.C. Sauternes, Bordeaux. 13 ha.

Château Maurens (Fr). A vineyard in the commune of Saint-Étienne-de-Lisse. A.C. Saint-Émilion, Bordeaux.

Château Mausse (Fr). A vineyard in the A.C. Canon-Fronsac, Bordeaux.

Château Mauvesin (Fr). A vineyard in the commune of Moulis. A.C. Moulis, Bordeaux. 60 ha.

Château Mauvezin (Fr). Address = 33330

Saint-Émilion. Grand Cru Classé. A.C. Saint-Émilion. Commune = Saint-Émilion. 16.7 ha. Grape varieties – Cabernet franc 50%, Cabernet sauvignon 10% and Merlot 40%.

Château Mayence (Fr). A vineyard in the commune of Mazion. A.C. Côtes de Blaye, Bordeaux.

Château Mayne (Fr). A vineyard in the commune of Pomerol. A.C. Pomerol, Bordeaux. 3 ha.

Château Mayne-Bert (Fr). A vineyard in the commune of Barsac. A.C. Barsac (or Sauternes), Bordeaux. 12 ha. Also Châteaux Camperos and Montalivet.

Château Mayne d'Anice (Fr). A vineyard in the commune of Podensac. A.C. Cérons, Bordeaux. 4 ha.

Château Mayne de Bernard (Fr). A vineyard in the A.C. Côtes de Bourg, Bordeaux.

Château Mayne-Levêque (Fr). A vineyard in the commune of Podensac. A.C. Graves, Bordeaux. 15 ha. (red and white).

Château Mayne Vieille (Fr). A vineyard in the commune of Galgon. A.C. Côtes de Fronsac, Bordeaux. 16 ha.

Château Mazarin (Fr). A vineyard in the commune of Loupiac. A.C. Loupiac, Bordeaux. 16 ha. Grape varieties – Sauvignon and Sémillon.

Château Mazerat (Fr). A vineyard in the A.C. Saint-Émilion, Bordeaux.

Château Mazeris (Fr). A vineyard in the commune of Saint-Michel. A.C. Côtes Canon-Fronsac, Bordeaux. Address = 33145 Saint-Michel-de-Fronsac. 7 ha.

Château Mazeris Bellevue (Fr). A vineyard in the commune of Saint-Michel. A.C. Côtes Canon-Fronsac, Bordeaux. 6 ha.

Château Mazerolles (Fr). A vineyard in the commune of Cars. A.C. Côtes de Blaye, Bordeaux.

Château Mazeyres (Fr). A vineyard in the commune of Pomerol. A.C. Pomerol, Bordeaux. 10 ha.

Château Méaume (Fr). A vineyard in the commune of Maransin. A.C. Bordeaux Supérieur. 25 ha. Grape varieties – Cabernet franc 15%, Cabernet sauvignon 5% and Merlot 80%.

Château Médrac (Fr). A vineyard in the commune of Moulis. A.C. Moulis, Bordeaux. 1 ha.

Château Megnien (Fr). A vineyard in the commune of Sainte-Croix-du-Mont. A.C. Sainte-Croix-du-Mont, Bordeaux. 3 ha.

Château Meillant (Fr). A V.D.Q.S. wine of the Loire. (red, rosé and white). Produced in the Cher Département.

C

Château Melnik (Czec). A sparkling wine made in the Uzhorod region.

Château Mendoce (Fr). A vineyard in the commune of Villeneuve. A.C. Côtes de Bourg, Bordeaux.

Château Menota (Fr). A vineyard in the commune of Barsac. A.C. Barsac (or Sauternes), Bordeaux. 17 ha. Also Château Menota-Labat.

Château Menota-Labat (Fr). A vineyard in the commune of Barsac. A.C. Barsac (or Sauternes), Bordeaux. 17 ha. Also Château Menota.

Château Mercian (Jap). A 'Grand Cru Classé' wine produced by Sanraku Ocean based in Yamanashi near Tokyo.

Château Mercier (Fr). A vineyard in the commune of Barsac. A.C. Barsac (or Sauternes), Bordeaux. 2 ha.

Château Méric (Fr). Address = 33650 La Brède. A.C. Graves. Commune = La Brède. 12 ha. Grape varieties – Cabernet franc, Cabernet sauvignon, Malbec, Merlot, Muscadelle, Sauvignon and Sémillon.

Château Merissac (Fr). The second wine of Château Dassault. Grand Cru Classé, A.C. Saint-Émilion.

Château Merlet (Fr). An A.C. Bordeaux wine from the Entre-Deux-Mers, central Bordeaux.

Château Merlet (Fr). A vineyard in the A.C. Graves, Bordeaux.

Château Meynard (Fr). A vineyard in the commune of Sables-Saint-Émilion. A.C. Saint-Émilion, Bordeaux. 6 ha.

Château Meyney (Fr). Cru Grand Bourgeois Exceptionnel. A.C. Saint-Estèphe Commune = Saint-Estèphe. 74 ha. Grape varieties – Cabernet franc, Cabernet sauvignon, Merlot and Petit verdot. See also Prieur de Meyney.

Château Michel de Montaigne (Fr). A vineyard in the A.C. Bergerac, south-western France. (red).

Château Mille-Secousses (Fr). A vineyard in the commune of Bourg. A.C. Côtes de Bourg, Bordeaux.

Château Millet (Fr). Address = 33460 Portets. A.C. Graves. Commune = Portets. 58 ha. Grape varieties – Cabernet 40% and Merlot 60%.

Château Milon (Fr). Address = Saint-Christophe-des-Bardes, 33330 Saint-Émilion. Grand Cru. A.C. Saint-Émilion. Commune = Saint-Christophe-des-Bardes. 22.91 ha. Grape varieties – Cabernet franc, Cabernet sauvignon and Merlot 75%.

Château Minière (Fr). A vineyard in the commune of Restigné. A.C. Bourgueil, Touraine, Loire.

Château Minuty (Fr). A V.D.Q.S. rosé wine from the Côtes de Provence, south-eastern France.

Château Mirabel (Fr). A vineyard in the commune of Pujols. A.C. Graves, Bordeaux. 3 ha. (white).

Château Moderis (Fr). A vineyard in the commune of Virelade. A.C. Graves, Bordeaux. 5 ha. (red and white).

Château Monbazillac (Fr). A vineyard in the commune of Monbazillac. A.C. Monbazillac, Bergerac.

Château Monbousquet (Fr). Address = Place Guadet, 33500 Libourne. Grand Cru. A.C. Saint-Émilion. Commune = Saint-Sulpice-de-Faleyrens. 40 ha. Grape varieties – Cabernet franc 40% and Merlot 60%.

Château Monbrison (Fr). Address = Arsac 33460. Cru Bourgeois. A.C. Margaux. Commune = Arsac. 25 ha. Grape varieties – Cabernet franc, Cabernet sauvignon and Merlot.

Château Moncets (Fr). A vineyard in the commune of Néac. A.C. Saint-Émilion, Bordeaux.

Château Monconseil (Fr). A vineyard in the commune of Plassac. A.C. Côtes de Blaye, Bordeaux.

Château Moncontour (Fr). A vineyard in the A.C. Vouvray, Touraine, Loire. Produces sparkling (méthode champenoise) wines and pétillant Vouvray.

Château Mondou (Fr). A vineyard in the commune of Saint-Sulpice-de-Faleyrens. A.C. Saint-Émilion, Bordeaux.

Château Mongravey (Fr). A vineyard in the commune of Arsac. A.C. Margaux, Bordeaux. Cru Bourgeois. Address = Arsac, 33460 Margaux.

Château Monjou (Fr). A.C. Barsac (or Sauternes). Commune = Barsac. 9 ha. Also Château Terre Noble.

Château Monlot Capet (Fr). A vineyard in the commune of Saint-Hippolyte. A.C. Saint-Émilion, Bordeaux. 8 ha.

Château Monpelou (Fr). A vineyard in the commune of Pauillac. A.C. Pauillac, Bordeaux. 8 ha.

Château Monregard Lacroix (Fr). A vineyard in the commune of Pomerol. A.C. Pomerol, Bordeaux. 5 ha.

Château Montagne (Isr). A dry white table wine.

Château Montaiguillon (Fr). A vineyard in the commune of Montagne-Saint-Émilion. A.C. Montagne-Saint-Émilion, Bordeaux. 23 ha.

Château Montaiguillon (Fr). A vineyard in the commune of Saint-Georges-Saint-Émilion. A.C. Saint-Émilion, Bordeaux. 3 ha.

Château Montalivet (Fr). A vineyard in

the commune of Barsac. A.C. Barsac (or Sauternes), Bordeaux. 12 ha. Also Châteaux Camperos and Mayne-Bert.

Château Montauriol (Fr). A vineyard in the commune of Villaudric. A.C. Côtes du Frontonnais, south-western France. Address = 31620 Villaudric.

Château Montbelair (Fr). A vineyard in the A.C. Saint-Émilion, Bordeaux. 2 ha.

Château Montbenault (Fr). Address = 49380 Faye-d'Anjou. A.C. Coteaux du Layon. Commune = Faye-d'Anjou. Anjou-Saumur, Loire.

Château Montbrun (Fr). A vineyard in the commune of Cantenac. A.C. Haut-Médoc, Bordeaux. 9 ha.

Château Montchenot (Arg). The brand-name of red and white wines produced by Bodegas Lopez Hermanos, Mendoza.

Château Monteau (Fr). A vineyard in the commune of Preignac. A.C. Sauternes, Bordeaux. 9 ha.

Château Montelena (USA). Address = Calistoga, Napa Valley, California. Napa Valley Winery. 40 ha. Produces – varietal wines from the Cabernet sauvignon and Chardonnay grapes.

Château Montesquieu (Fr). A vineyard in the commune of Puisseguin-Saint-Émilion. A.C. Puisseguin-Saint-Émilion, Bordeaux. 14 ha.

Château Montfort (Fr). A noted wine brotherhood based in the Jura region of eastern France.

Château Monthil (Fr). A vineyard in the commune of Bégadan. A.C. Médoc, Bordeaux. Cru Bourgeois. 15 ha.

Château Montlabert (Fr). Address = 33330 Saint-Émilion. Grand Cru. A.C. Saint-Émilion. Commune = Saint-Émilion. 12.5 ha. Grape varieties – Cabernet franc 35%, Cabernet sauvignon 15% and Merlot 50%. Second wine is La Croix Montlabert.

Château Montlau (Fr). A vineyard in the commune of Branne. A.C. Bordeaux Supérieur. Address = 33420 Branne. (red).

Château Montremblant (Fr). A vineyard in the A.C. Saint-Émilion, Bordeaux. 5 ha.

Château Montrose (Fr). Address = 33250 Pauillac. Grand Cru Classé (2nd). A.C. Saint-Estèphe. Commune = Saint-Estèphe. 49 ha. Grape varieties – Cabernet franc 10%, Cabernet sauvignon 65%, Merlot 25%

Château Monturon (Fr). Address = Saint Laurent des Bardes, 33330 Saint-Émilion. A.C. Saint-Émilion. Commune = Saint Laurent des Bardes. Second wine of Château Rozier. Grand Cru. Saint-Émilion.

Château Montus (Fr). A vineyard in the A.C. Madiran, Pyrénées, south-western France. (red).

Château Moreau (USA). The brand-name of the Gibson vineyard of Fresno, California for a range of their wines.

Château Morillon (Fr). A vineyard in the A.C. Saint-Émilion, Bordeaux. 2 ha.

Château Morin (Fr). A vineyard in the commune of Saint-Estèphe. A.C. Haut-Médoc, Bordeaux. Cru Grand Bourgeois. 10 ha.

Château Mouchet (Fr). A vineyard in the commune of Puisseguin-Saint-Émilion. A.C. Puisseguin-Saint-Émilion, Bordeaux. 10 ha.

Château Mouchique (Fr). A vineyard in the commune of Puisseguin-Saint-Émilion. A.C. Puisseguin-Saint-Émilion, Bordeaux. 4 ha.

Château Moulerens (Fr). A vineyard in the commune of Gradignan. A.C. Graves, Bordeaux.

Château Moulin à Vent (Fr). A vineyard in the commune of Cérons. A.C. Cérons, Bordeaux. 4 ha.

Château Moulin-à-Vent (Fr). Address = 33480 Moulis-en-Médoc. Cru Grand Bourgeois. A.C. Moulis. Commune = Moulis. 30 ha. Grape varieties – Cabernet sauvignon, Malbec, Merlot and Petit verdot.

Château Moulin-à-Vent (Fr). A vineyard in the commune of Néac. A.C. Pomerol, Bordeaux.

Château Moulin-à-Vent (Fr). A vineyard in the commune of St-Michel. A.C. Côtes Canon-Fronsac, Bordeaux. 6 ha.

Château Moulin Bellegrave (Fr). Address = Vignonet, 33330 Saint-Émilion. Grand Cru. A.C. Saint-Émilion. Commune = Vignonet. 15 ha. Grape varieties – Cabernet franc 15%, Cabernet sauvignon 15% and Merlot 70%.

Château Moulin-Blanc (Fr). A vineyard in the commune of Néac. A.C. Pomerol, Bordeaux.

Château Moulin-Blanc (Fr). A vineyard in the commune of Montagne-Saint-Émilion. A.C. Saint-Émilion, Bordeaux.

Château Moulin de Bel Air (Fr). Address = Saint-Yzans-de-Médoc. A.C. Médoc. Commune = Saint-Yzans. 20 ha. Grape varieties – Cabernet franc, Cabernet sauvignon and Merlot.

Château Moulin de Buscateau (Fr). Address = Ordonnac, 33340 Lesparre, Médoc. A.C. Médoc. Commune = Ordonnac. 5 ha. Grape varieties – Cabernet sauvignon 50% and Merlot 50%.

Château Moulin de Cantelaube (Fr). A vineyard in the A.C. Saint-Émilion, Bordeaux. 3 ha.

Château Moulin de Castillon (Fr). Address

C

= Le Bourg, Saint-Christoly-de-Médoc 33340. A.C. Médoc. Commune = Saint-Christoly-de-Médoc. 13 ha. Grape varieties – Cabernet sauvignon, Malbec and Merlot.

Château Moulin de Ferregrave (Fr). A vineyard in the commune of Saint-Vivien-de-Médoc. A.C. Médoc, Bordeaux. Address = Jau Dignac et Loirac, 33590 St-Vivien-de-Médoc.

Château Moulin de Gassiot (Fr). A vineyard in the commune of Sauveterre-de-Guyonne. A.C. Bordeaux Rouge. Address = 33540 Sauveterre-de-Guyonne.

Château Moulin de Laborde (Fr). Address = 33480 Listrac, Médoc. A.C. Listrac. Commune = Listrac. 8 ha. Grape varieties – Cabernet sauvignon 60%, Merlot 30% and Petit verdot 10%.

Château Moulin de la Bridane (Fr). A vineyard in the commune of Pauillac. A.C. Pauillac, Bordeaux. 2.5 ha.

Château Moulin de Landry (Fr). A vineyard in the A.C. Côtes de Castillon, eastern Bordeaux.

Château Moulin de la Rose (Fr). Address = 33250 Saint-Julien, Beychevelle. A.C. Saint-Julien. Commune = Saint-Julien. 4 ha. Grape varieties – Cabernet franc, Cabernet sauvignon and Petit verdot.

Château Moulin de Pierrefitte (Fr). Address = Saint-Sulpice-de-Faleyrens, 33330 Saint-Émilion. Grand Cru. A.C. Saint-Émilion. Commune = Saint-Sulpice-de-Faleyrens. 7 ha. Grape varieties – Cabernet 10% and Merlot 90%.

Château Moulin des Carruades (Fr). The second wine of Château Lafite.

Château Moulin de St-Vincent (Fr). A vineyard in the commune of Moulis. A.C. Médoc, Bordeaux. Cru Bourgeois.

Château Moulin de Taffard (Fr). Address = Saint-Christoly-de-Médoc, 33340 Lesparre. A.C. Médoc. Commune = Saint-Christoly. 8 ha. Grape varieties – Cabernet sauvignon and Merlot.

Château Moulin du Cadet (Fr). A vineyard in the commune of Saint-Émilion. A.C. Saint-Émilion, Bordeaux. Grand Cru Classé. 5 ha.

Château Moulin-du-Jura (Fr). A vineyard in the commune of Montagne-Saint-Émilion. A.C. Montagne-Saint-Émilion, Bordeaux. 3 ha.

Château Moulin du Vilet (Fr). A vineyard in the commune of Saint-Christophe-des-Bardes, A.C. Saint-Émilion, Bordeaux. Address = Saint-Christophe-des-Bardes, 33340 Saint-Émilion.

Château Moulinet (Fr). A vineyard in the commune of Pomerol. A.C. Pomerol, Bordeaux. 13 ha.

Château Moulin Eyquem (Fr). A vineyard in the A.C. Côtes de Bourg, Bordeaux

Château Moulin Haut-Laroque (Fr). A vineyard in the commune of Saillans. A.C. Fronsac, Bordeaux. Address = Saillans, 33141 Villegouge.

Château Moulin Joli (Fr). See Château Les Ormes-de-Pez, A.C. Haut-Médoc, Bordeaux.

Château Moulin Neuf (Fr). A vineyard in the commune of Loupiac. A.C. Loupiac, Bordeaux. 10 ha.

Château Moulin-Pey-Labrie (Fr). A vineyard in the commune of Fronsac. A.C. Fronsac, Bordeaux. 4 ha.

Château Moulin-Riche (Fr). A vineyard in the commune of Saint-Julien. A.C. Saint-Julien, Bordeaux. Cru Bourgeois.

Château Moulin-Rose (Fr). A vineyard in the commune of Lamarque. A.C. Haut-Médoc, Bordeaux. 3 ha. Cru Bourgeois.

Château Moulin Rouge (Fr). A vineyard in the commune of Cissac-Fort-Médoc. A.C. Haut-Médoc, Bordeaux. Cru Bourgeois.

Château Moulins (Fr). A vineyard in the commune of Saillans. A.C. Côtes de Fronsac, Bordeaux. 16 ha.

Château Moulin Saint Georges (Fr). Address = 33330 Saint-Émilion. Grand Cru. A.C. Saint-Émilion. Commune = Saint-Émilion. 11 ha. Grape varieties – Cabernet franc 35% and Merlot 65%.

Château Moulins-de-Calon (Fr). A vineyard in the commune of Montagne-Saint-Émilion. A.C. Saint-Émilion, Bordeaux.

Château Moulins Haut Villars (Fr). A vineyard in the commune of Fronsac. A.C. Fronsac, Bordeaux.

Château Moulis (Fr). Address = 33480 Moulis-en-Médoc. Cru Bourgeois. A.C. Moulis. Commune = Moulis. 12 ha. Grape varieties – Cabernet sauvignon 50% and Merlot 50%.

Château Mounic (Fr). A vineyard in the commune of Fargues. A.C. Sauternes, Bordeaux. 1 ha.

Château Moura (Fr). A vineyard in the commune of Barsac. A.C. Barsac (or Sauternes), Bordeaux. 1 ha.

Château Mouteou (Fr). A vineyard in the commune of Portets. A.C. Graves, Bordeaux. 3 ha. (red and white).

Château Moutin (Fr). A vineyard in the commune of Portets. A.C. Graves, Bordeaux. 1 ha. (red).

Château Mouton Cadet (Fr). A famous branded Claret. Was originally sold as an off-vintage Château Mouton Rothschild. Now sold separately. See Mouton Cadet.

Château Mouton Baronne Philippe (Fr). See Château Mouton d'Armailhacq.

C

Château Mouton-Baron Philippe (Fr). Address = 33250 Pauillac. Grand Cru Classé (5ᵗʰ). A.C. Pauillac. Commune = Pauillac. 67 ha. Grape varieties – Cabernet franc 15%, Cabernet sauvignon 65% and Merlot 20%.

Château Mouton d'Armailhacq (Fr). Renamed Château Mouton-Baron Philippe. Cru Classé de la Baronne Philippe in 1975 in honour of his late wife the late Baronne Pauline.

Château Mouton-Rothschild (Fr). Address = 33250 Pauillac. Premier Grand Cru Classé. (Elevated from 2ⁿᵈ growth in 1973). A.C. Pauillac. Commune = Pauillac. 73 ha. Grape varieties – Cabernet franc, Cabernet sauvignon and Merlot.

Château Mouyet (Fr). A vineyard in the commune of Budos. A.C. Graves, Bordeaux. 2 ha. (red).

Château Musar (M.East). A red wine produced in the Bekkar Valley in the Lebanon from Cabernet sauvignon grape (plus minor quantities of other grape varieties). Also produces some white wine.

Château Musseau de Haut (Fr). A vineyard in the commune of St-Aignan. A.C. Côtes de Fronsac, Bordeaux. 2 ha.

Château Musset (Fr). A vineyard in the commune of Lalande de Pomerol. A.C. Lalande de Pomerol, Bordeaux.

Château Musset (Fr). A vineyard in the commune of Parsac-Saint-Émilion. A.C. Saint-Émilion, Bordeaux. 7 ha.

Château Myosotis (Fr). A vineyard in the A.C. Saint-Émilion, Bordeaux. 3 ha.

Château Myrat (Fr). Grand Cru Classé (2ⁿᵈ). A.C. Barsac (or Sauternes). Commune = Barsac. (Now no longer in production).

Château Naguet-la-Grande (Fr). A vineyard in the commune of Parsac-Saint-Émilion. A.C. Saint-Émilion, Bordeaux. 5 ha.

Château Nairac (Fr). Address = 33720 Podensac. Grand Cru Classé (2ⁿᵈ). A.C. Barsac (or Sauternes). Commune = Barsac. 13 ha. Grape varieties – Sauvignon 6%, Sémillon 90% and Muscadelle 4%.

Château Nairne (Fr). A vineyard in the commune of Barsac. A.C. Barsac (or Sauternes), Bordeaux.

Château Nallys (Fr). A vineyard in the A.C. Châteauneuf-du-Pape, southern Rhône.

Château Nardon (Fr). Part of Domaine Laroque, A.C. Saint-Émilion, Bordeaux.

Château Naude (Fr). A vineyard in the commune of Saint-Sulpice-des-Faleyrens. A.C. Saint-Émilion, Bordeaux.

Château Négrit (Fr). See Vieux Château Négrit.

Château Nénin (Fr). A.C. Pomerol. Commune = Pomerol. 28 ha. Grape varieties – Bouchet 30%, Cabernet sauvignon 20% and Merlot 50%.

Château-Neuf (Fr). A vineyard in the commune of Léognan. A.C. Graves, Bordeaux. Cru Bourgeois.

Châteauneuf (Fr). A commune in the Charente Département whose grapes are classed Petite Champagne (Cognac). Wines are made into Cognac des Bois.

Châteauneuf-Calcernier (Fr). The old name for Châteauneuf-du-Pape. Was changed in 1850 to present name by the Marquis de Nerthe.

Châteauneuf-du-Pape (Fr). A.C. rich, heady red and white wines produced in the southern Rhône. Produces both red and white wines from a variety of grapes including white varieties. See Mistral and Baron le Roy.

Château Nexon-Lemoyne (Fr). A vineyard in the commune of Ludon. A.C. Médoc, Bordeaux. Cru Bourgeois. 16 ha.

Château Noton (Fr). A vineyard in the commune of Arsac. A.C. Haut-Médoc, Bordeaux. Cru Bourgeois.

Château Nodot (Fr). A vineyard in the A.C. Côtes de Bourg, Bordeaux.

Château Nodoz (Fr). A vineyard in the commune of Tauriac. A.C. Côtes de Bourg, Bordeaux.

Château Olivier (Fr). Address = 33850 Léognan. Grand Cru Classé. A.C. Graves. Commune = Léognan. 36 ha. Grape varieties – Cabernet-sauvignon 70%, Merlot 30%, Sauvignon 30%, Sémillon 65% and Muscadelle 5%.

Château Pabeau (Fr). Address = 33250 Saint-Seurin-de-Médoc. A.C. Haut-Médoc. Commune = Saint-Seurin-de-Cadourne. 10 ha. Grape varieties – Cabernet 50% and Merlot 50%.

Château Padouen (Fr). A vineyard in the commune of Barsac. A.C. Barsac (or Sauternes), Bordeaux. 10 ha.

Château Pageot (Fr). A vineyard in the commune of Sauternes. A.C. Sauternes, Bordeaux. 5 ha.

Château Pailhas (Fr). Address = Saint-Hippolyte, 33330 Saint-Émilion. A.C. Saint-Émilion. Commune = Saint-Hippolyte. 25 ha. Grape varieties – Cabernet franc 8%, Cabernet sauvignon 20%, Malbec 2% and Merlot 70%.

Château Palmer (Fr). Grand Cru Classé (3ʳᵈ). A.C. Margaux. Commune = Cantenac. 41 ha. Grape varieties – Cabernet 60% and Merlot 40%.

C

Château Paloumat (Fr). A vineyard in the commune of Fargues. A.C. Sauternes, Bordeaux. 2 ha.

Château Paloumey (Fr). A vineyard in the commune of Ludon. A.C. Médoc, Bordeaux. Cru Bourgeois.

Château Panet (Fr). A vineyard in the commune of Fronsac. A.C. Côtes Canon-Fronsac, Bordeaux. 4 ha.

Château Panet (Fr). A vineyard in the A.C. Saint-Émilion, Bordeaux. 22 ha.

Château Panigon (Fr). A vineyard in the commune of Civrac. A.C. Médoc, Bordeaux. Cru Bourgeois. 20 ha.

Château Panniseau (Fr). A vineyard in the A.C. Bergerac, south-western Bordeaux. (red and white).

Château Pape-Clément (Fr). Address = Pessac, Gironde. Grand Cru Classé. A.C. Graves. Commune = Pessac. 27.3 ha. Grape varieties – Cabernet sauvignon 65%, Merlot 35%, Muscadelle, Sauvignon and Sémillon.

Château Papetterie (Fr). A vineyard in the commune of Néac. A.C. Saint-Émilion, Bordeaux.

Château Paradis (Fr). A vineyard in the commune of Vignonet. A.C. Saint-Émilion, Bordeaux. 19 ha.

Château Parans (Fr). A vineyard in the A.C. Saint-Émilion, Bordeaux. 7 ha.

Château Pardaillan (Fr). A vineyard in the commune of Cars. A.C. Côtes de Blaye, Bordeaux.

Château Pardanac (Fr). A vineyard in the commune of Pauillac. A.C. Médoc, Bordeaux. Cru Bourgeois.

Château Parempuyre (Fr). A vineyard in the commune of Parempuyre. A.C. Médoc, Bordeaux. Cru Bourgeois.

Château Paret Beauséjour (Fr). A.C. Bordeaux Supérieur.

Château Partarrieu (Fr). A vineyard in the commune of Fargues. A.C. Sauternes, Bordeaux. 8 ha.

Château Pasquier (Fr). A vineyard in the commune of Camblancs. A.C. Premières Côtes de Bordeaux. Address = 33360 Camblancs.

Château Patache d'Aux (Fr). Address = Bégadan, 33340 Lesparre, Médoc. Cru Grand Bourgeois. A.C. Médoc. Commune = Bégadan. 40 ha. Grape varieties – Cabernet franc, Cabernet sauvignon and Merlot.

Château Patarabet (Fr). Part of Château Paradis, A.C. Saint-Émilion, Bordeaux.

Château Patris (Fr). Address = 33330 Saint-Émilion. Grand Cru. A.C. Saint-Émilion. 10 ha. Grape varieties – Cabernet sauvignon 30% and Merlot 70%.

Château Paulet (Fr). Cognac producer. Address = Route de Segonzac, BP 24, 16101 Cognac. Produces – Écusson Rouge ***, Very Rare Âge Inconnu, Borderies Très Vieilles plus V.S.O.P. and X.O.

Château Paveil-de-Luze (Fr). Address = Soussans, 33460 Margaux. Cru Grand Bourgeois. A.C. Margaux. Commune = Soussans. 23 ha. Grape varieties – Cabernet sauvignon 65% and Merlot 35%.

Château Pavie (Fr). BP. 7 F, 33330 Saint-Émilion. Premier Grand Cru Classé. A.C. Saint-Émilion. Commune = Saint-Émilion. 41 ha. Grape varieties – Bouchet, Cabernet sauvignon and Merlot.

Château Pavie Décesse (Fr). Address = BP 7 F, 33330 Saint-Émilion. Grand Cru Classé. A.C. Saint-Émilion. Commune = Saint-Émilion. 9.9 ha. Grape varieties – Bouchet 25%, Cabernet sauvignon 15% and Merlot 60%.

Château Pavie-Macquin (Fr). Address = 33330 Saint-Émilion. Grand Cru Classé. A.C. Saint-Émilion. Commune = Saint-Émilion. 13 ha. Grape varieties – Cabernet franc 15%, Cabernet sauvignon 15% and Merlot 70%.

Château Pavillon Cadet (Fr). Address = 33330 Saint-Émilion. Grand Cru Classé. A.C. Saint-Émilion. Commune = Saint-Émilion. 3.5 ha.

Château Pavillon-Figeac (Fr). A vineyard in the A.C. Saint-Émilion, Bordeaux. 4 ha.

Château Pavillon-Fougailles (Fr). A vineyard in the A.C. Saint-Émilion, Bordeaux. 1 ha.

Château Pay-de-Lalo (Fr). A vineyard in the commune of Saint-Germain-d'Esteuil. A.C. Médoc, Bordeaux. 2 ha.

Château Pay de Pie (Fr). A vineyard in the commune of Fronsac. A.C. Côtes de Fronsac, Bordeaux.

Château Pébayle (Fr). A vineyard in the commune of Barsac. A.C. Barsac (or Sauternes), Bordeaux. 5 ha.

Château Pechon-Terre-Noble (Fr). A vineyard in the commune of Barsac. A.C. Barsac (or Sauternes), Bordeaux. 3 ha.

Château Pédebayle (Fr). A vineyard in the commune of St-Pierre-de-Mons. A.C. Graves, Bordeaux. 8 ha. (white).

Château Pedesclaux (Fr). Address = 33250 Pauillac. Grand Cru Classé (5th). A.C. Pauillac. Commune = Pauillac. 18 ha. Grape varieties – Cabernet franc 10%, Cabernet sauvignon 65% and Merlot 25%.

Château Peguilhem (Fr). A vineyard in the commune of Saillans. A.C. Côtes de Fronsac, Bordeaux.

Château Peillan-St-Clair (Fr). A vineyard

in the A.C. Saint-Émilion, Bordeaux. 6 ha.

Château Peillon-Claverie (Fr). A vineyard in the commune of Fargues. A.C. Sauternes, Bordeaux. 9 ha.

Château Pelletan (Fr). Address = Saint-Christophe-des-Bardes, 33330 Saint-Émilion. A.C. Saint-Émilion. Commune = Saint-Christophe-des-Bardes.

Château Pelletan (Fr). A vineyard in the commune of Saint Quentin-de-Caplang. A.C. Saint-Foy-Bordeaux, south-eastern Bordeaux. 5 ha.

Château Péran (Fr). A vineyard in the commune of Langon. A.C. Graves, Bordeaux. 8 ha. (white).

Château Perenne (Fr). A vineyard in the A.C. Côtes de Blaye, Bordeaux.

Château Pérey (Fr). A vineyard in the A.C. Saint-Émilion, Bordeaux. 8 ha.

Château Perin de Naudine (Fr). Address = Castres-Gironde, 33640 Portets. A.C. Graves. Commune = Castres. 4.52 ha. Grape varieties – Cabernet 50% and Merlot 50%.

Château Pernaud (Fr). A vineyard in the commune of Barsac. A.C. Barsac (or Sauternes), Bordeaux 17 ha.

Château Perrein (Fr). A vineyard in the commune of Mazion. A.C. Côtes de Blaye, Bordeaux.

Château Perron (Fr). A vineyard in the commune of Fronsac. A.C. Côtes de Fronsac, Bordeaux. 3 ha.

Château Perron (Fr). A vineyard in the commune of Roaillan. A.C. Graves, Bordeaux. 14 ha. (white).

Château Perron (Fr). A vineyard in the commune of Lalande de Pomerol. A.C. Lalande de Pomerol, Bordeaux.

Château Perroy-Jean-Blanc (Fr). A vineyard in the commune of Bommes. A.C. Sauternes, Bordeaux. 7 ha.

Château Perruchon (Fr). A vineyard in the commune of Lussac-Saint-Émilion. A.C. Saint-Émilion, Bordeaux.

Château Pesilla (Fr). A vineyard in the commune of Landiras. A.C. Graves, Bordeaux. 4 ha. (white).

Château Pessan (Fr). A vineyard in the commune of Portets. A.C. Graves, Bordeaux. 40 ha. Grape varieties – Cabernet franc, Cabernet sauvignon, Merlot and Sémillon.

Château Petit Bigaroux (Fr). A vineyard in the commune of Saint-Sulpice-de-Faleyrens. A.C. Saint-Émilion, Bordeaux. 5 ha.

Château Petit-Bois la Garelle (Fr). A vineyard in the commune of Saint-Émilion. A.C. Saint-Émilion, Bordeaux. 4.82 ha. Address = 33330 Saint-Émilion.

Château Petit Bord (Fr). A vineyard in the A.C. Saint-Émilion, Bordeaux. 1 ha.

Château Petit-Clos (Fr). A vineyard in the commune of Montagne-Saint-Émilion. A.C. Montagne-Saint-Émilion, Bordeaux. 8 ha.

Château Petit-Cormey (Fr). A vineyard in the A.C. Saint-Émilion, Bordeaux. 6 ha.

Château Petit Faurie (Fr). A vineyard in the A.C. Saint-Émilion, Bordeaux. 1 ha.

Château Petit-Faurie de Souchard (Fr). A vineyard in the commune of Saint-Émilion. A.C. Saint-Émilion, Bordeaux. 19 ha. Grand Cru Classé.

Château Petit-Faurie de Soutard (Fr). Address = 33330 Saint-Émilion. Grand Cru Classé. A.C. Saint-Émilion. Commune = Saint-Émilion. 8.88 ha. Grape varieties – Cabernet franc 30%, Cabernet sauvignon 10% and Merlot 60%.

Château Petit-Faurie-Trocard (Fr). A vineyard in the commune of Saint-Émilion. A.C. Saint-Émilion, Bordeaux. 4 ha.

Château Petit Figeac (Fr). Address = La Fleur Pourret, 33330 Saint-Émilion. Grand Cru. A.C. Saint-Émilion. Commune = Saint-Émilion. 1.5 ha. Grape varieties – Cabernet sauvignon 40% and Merlot 60%.

Château Petit-Frombrauge (Fr). A vineyard in the A.C. Saint-Émilion, Bordeaux. 2 ha.

Château Petit-Gravet (Fr). Address = 33330 Saint-Émilion. Grand Cru. A.C. Saint-Émilion. Commune = Saint-Émilion. 5 ha. Grape varieties – Cabernet franc 30%, Cabernet sauvignon 20% and Merlot 50%.

Château Petit-Mangot (Fr). A vineyard in the A.C. Saint-Émilion, Bordeaux. 5 ha.

Château Petit-Refuge (Fr). A vineyard in the commune of Lussac-Saint-Émilion. A.C. Saint-Émilion, Bordeaux. 4 ha.

Château Petit Val (Fr). Address = 33330 Saint-Émilion. Grand Cru. A.C. Saint-Émilion. Commune = Saint-Émilion. 9.5 ha. Grape varieties – Cabernet franc 30%, Cabernet sauvignon 5% and Merlot 65%.

Château Petit-Village (Fr). A.C. Pomerol. Commune = Pomerol. 11 ha. Grape varieties – Cabernet franc, Cabernet sauvignon and Merlot.

Châtrau Petray (Fr). A.C. Bordeaux Supérieur.

Château Pétrus (Fr). A.C. Pomerol. Commune = Pomerol. 11.5 ha. Grape varieties – Cabernet franc 5% and Merlot 95%.

Château Peychaud (Fr). A vineyard in the commune of Teuillac. A.C. Côtes de Bourg, Bordeaux.

Château Peychez (Fr). A vineyard in the

C

commune of Fronsac. A.C. Côtes de Fronsac, Bordeaux. 4 ha.

Château Peygenestou (Fr). A vineyard in the A.C. Saint-Émilion, Bordeaux. 2 ha.

Château Peymartin (Fr). A vineyard in the commune of Saint-Julien. A.C. Saint-Julien, Bordeaux. Cru Bourgeois. 15 ha.

Château Peymouton (Fr). A vineyard in the A.C. Saint-Émilion, Bordeaux. 3 ha.

Château Peyrabon (Fr). Address = Saint-Sauveur-du-Médoc 33250. Cru Grand Bourgeois. A.C. Haut-Médoc. Commune = Saint-Sauveur-du-Médoc. 70 ha. Grape varieties – Cabernet franc 23%, Cabernet sauvignon 50% and Merlot 27%.

Château Peyraguey-le-Rousset (Fr). A vineyard in the commune of Preignac. A.C. Sauternes, Bordeaux. 15 ha. Also Cru d'Arche-Pugnau.

Château Péyran (Fr). A vineyard in the commune of Landiras. A.C. Graves, Bordeaux. 4 ha. (white).

Château Peyrat (Fr). A vineyard in the A.C. Premières Côtes de Bordeaux, central Bordeaux.

Château Peyreau (Fr). Address = 33330 Saint-Émilion. Grand Cru. A.Ç. Saint-Émilion. Commune = Saint-Émilion. 13.5 ha. Grape varieties – Cabernet franc 25%, Cabernet sauvignon 10% and Merlot 65%. Second wine is Clos de l'Oratoire.

Château Peyrebrune (Fr). A vineyard in the commune of Cartelègue. A.C. Côtes de Blaye, Bordeaux.

Château Peyredon (Fr). A vineyard in the commune of Moulis. A.C. Moulis, Bordeaux. 3 ha.

Château Peyredon-Lagravette (Fr). Address = 33480 Listrac-Médoc. A.C. Listrac. Commune = Listrac. 7 ha. Grape varieties – Cabernet-sauvignon, Malbec, Merlot and Petit verdot.

Château Peyrelongue (Fr). Address = 33330 Saint-Émilion. Grand Cru. A.C. Saint-Émilion. 10 ha. Grape varieties – Cabernet franc 15%, Cabernet sauvignon 15% and Merlot 70%.

Château Peyron (Fr). A vineyard in the commune of Fargues. A.C. Sauternes, Bordeaux. 4 ha.

Château Peyrou (Fr). A vineyard in the commune of Saint-Étienne-de-Lisse. A.C. Saint-Émilion, Bordeaux. 5 ha.

Château Peyrouquet (Fr). A vineyard in the A.C. Saint-Émilion, Bordeaux. 1 ha.

Château Peyroutas (Fr). A vineyard in the commune of Vignonet. A.C. Saint-Émilion, Bordeaux. 8 ha.

Château Peyruchet (Fr). A vineyard in the

commune of Loupiac. A.C. Loupiac, Bordeaux. 12 ha.

Château Phélan Ségur (Fr). Cru Grand Bourgeois Exceptionnel. A.C. Saint-Estèphe. Commune = Saint-Estèphe. 59 ha. Grape varieties – Cabernet franc, Cabernet sauvignon and Merlot.

Château Phénix (Fr). A vineyard in the commune of Pessac. A.C. Graves, Bordeaux.

Château Piada (Fr). A vineyard in the commune of Barsac. A.C. Barsac (or Sauternes), Bordeaux. 11 ha. Also Clos du Roy.

Château Piaut (Fr). A vineyard in the commune of Barsac. A.C. Barsac (or Sauternes), Bordeaux. 9 ha.

Château Pibran (Fr). A vineyard in the commune of Pauillac. A.C. Haut-Médoc, Bordeaux. Cru Bourgeois. 7 ha.

Château Picard (Fr). A vineyard in the commune of Saint-Estèphe. A.C. Saint-Estèphe, Bordeaux. Cru Bourgeois.

Château Pichelebre (Fr). A vineyard in the commune of Fronsac. A.C. Côtes Canon-Fronsac, Bordeaux. 5 ha.

Château Pichon (Fr). A vineyard in the commune of Parempuyre. A.C. Haut-Médoc, Bordeaux. 3 ha.

Château Pichon Comtesse (Fr). A vineyard in the commune of Pauillac. A.C. Pauillac, Bordeaux.

Château Pichon-Lalande (Fr). See Château Pichon-Longueville Comtesse de Lalande.

Château Pichon-Longueville (Fr). Grand Cru Classé (2nd). A.C. Pauillac. Commune = Pauillac. 30 ha. Grape varieties – Cabernet sauvignon 70% and Merlot 30%.

Château Pichon-Longueville-Baron (Fr). See Château Pichon-Longueville.

Château Pichon-Longueville Comtesse de Lalande (Fr). Address = 33250 Pauillac. Grand Cru Classé (2nd). A.C. Pauillac. Commune = Pauillac. 62 ha. Grape varieties – Cabernet franc, Cabernet sauvignon, Merlot and Petit verdot. See also Réserve de la Comtesse.

Château Picon-Gravignac (Fr). A vineyard in the A.C. Saint-Émilion, Bordeaux. 4 ha.

Château Picque-Caillou (Fr). A vineyard in the commune of Pessac. A.C. Graves, Bordeaux. 14 ha. Grape varieties – Cabernet franc, Cabernet sauvignon and Merlot.

Château Picque-Caillou (Fr). Address = Route de Pessac, 33700 Mérignac. A.C. Graves. Commune = Mérignac. 7 ha. Grape varieties – Cabernet sauvignon 50% and Merlot 50%.

Château Pidoux (Fr). A vineyard in the

A.C. Saint-Émilion, Bordeaux. 2 ha.

Château Pierre Bibian (Fr). A vineyard in the commune of Listrac. A.C. Listrac, Bordeaux. Cru Bourgois. 14 ha.

Château Piganeau (Fr). Address = 33330 Saint-Émilion. A.C. Saint-Émilion. Commune = Saint-Émilion. Second wine of Château Cantenac. Grand Cru. Saint-Émilion.

Château Pignon-de-Gay (Fr). A vineyard in the commune of Pomerol. A.C. Pomerol, Bordeaux. 2 ha.

Château Pindefleurs (Fr). Address = 33330 Saint-Émilion. Grand Cru. A.C. Saint-Émilion. Commune = Saint-Émilion. 10.27 ha. Grape varieties – Cabernet franc and Merlot.

Château Pinet (Fr). A vineyard in the commune of Berson. A.C. Côtes de Blaye, Bordeaux.

Château Piney (Fr). A vineyard in the A.C. Saint-Émilion, Bordeaux. 6 ha.

Château Pingoy (Fr). A vineyard in the commune of Portets. A.C. Graves, Bordeaux. 8 ha. (red and white)

Château Pinon la Roquete (Fr). A vineyard in the commune of Berson. A.C. Côtes de Blaye, Bordeaux.

Château Pion (Fr). A vineyard in the A.C. Bergerac, south-western France (red).

Château Piot (Fr). A vineyard in the commune of Barsac. A.C. Barsac (or Sauternes), Bordeaux.

Château Pipeau (Fr). Address = Saint Laurent des Combes, 33330 Saint-Émilion. Grand Cru. A.C. Saint-Émilion. Commune = Saint Laurent des Combes. 25 ha. Grape varieties – Cabernet franc, Cabernet sauvignon and Merlot 65%.

Château Pipeau-Menichot (Fr). A vineyard in the A.C. Saint-Émilion, Bordeaux. 6 ha.

Château Pique-Caillou (Fr). A vineyard in the commune of Mérignac. A.C. Graves, Bordeaux.

Château Piron (Fr). A.C. Bordeaux.

Château Piron (Fr). A vineyard in the commune of Parsac-Saint-Émilion. A.C. Saint-Émilion, Bordeaux. 6 ha.

Château Piron (Fr). A vineyard in the commune of St-Morillon. A.C. Graves, Bordeaux. 15 ha. (red and white).

Château Pitray (Fr). A vineyard in the A.C. Côtes de Castillon, eastern Bordeaux.

Château Placette du Rey (Fr). A vineyard in the commune of Fronsac. A.C. Côtes de Fronsac, Bordeaux. 4 ha.

Château Plagnac (Fr). A vineyard in the commune of Bégadan. A.C. Médoc, Bordeaux. 38 ha. Grape varieties – Cabernet sauvignon 70% and Merlot 30%.

Château Plainpoint (Fr). A vineyard in the commune of St-Aignan. A.C. Côtes de Fronsac, Bordeaux. 12 ha.

Château Plaisance (Fr). A vineyard in the commune of Villeneuve-de-Blaye. A.C. Côtes de Bourg, Bordeaux.

Château Plaisance (Fr). A vineyard in the commune of Montagne-Saint-Émilion. A.C. Saint-Émilion, Bordeaux. 20 ha.

Château Plaisance (Fr). A vineyard in the commune of Parsac-Saint-Émilion. A.C. Saint-Émilion, Bordeaux. 9 ha.

Château Plaisance (Fr). A vineyard in the commune of Saint-Sulpice-de-Faleyrens. A.C. Saint-Émilion, Bordeaux.

Château Plantey de la Croix (Fr). A vineyard in the commune of St-Seurin-de-Cadourne. A.C. Médoc, Bordeaux. Cru Bourgeois.

Château Pleytegeat (Fr). A vineyard in the commune of Preignac. A.C. Sauternes, Bordeaux. 12 ha.

Château Plince (Fr). A vineyard in the commune of Pomerol. A.C. Pomerol, Bordeaux. Grape varieties – Cabernet 30% and Merlot 70%. 7 ha.

Château Plincette (Fr). A vineyard in the commune of Pomerol. A.C. Pomerol, Bordeaux. 1 ha.

Château Pointe-Bouquey (Fr). A vineyard in the A.C. Saint-Émilion, Bordeaux. 4 ha.

Château Pomeys (Fr). Address = Moulis-en-Médoc, 33480. A.C. Moulis. Commune = Moulis. 8 ha. Grape varieties – Cabernet sauvignon 65% and Merlot 35%

Château Pomiés-Agassac (Fr). A vineyard in the commune of Ludon. A.C. Médoc, Bordeaux. Cru Bourgeois.

Château Pommarède (Fr). A vineyard in the commune of Castres. A.C. Graves, Bordeaux. 3 ha. (red).

Château Pommarède-de-Bas (Fr). A vineyard in the commune of Castres. A.C. Graves, Bordeaux. 5 ha. (red and white).

Château Pomys (Fr). Address = Leyssac, Saint-Estèphe 33250. A.C. Saint-Estèphe. Commune = Saint-Estèphe. 15 ha. Grape varieties – Cabernet franc, Cabernet sauvignon, Merlot and Petit verdot.

Château Pontac (Fr). A vineyard in the commune of Loupiac. A.C. Loupiac, Bordeaux. 10 ha.

Château Pontac (Fr). See Château Pontac-Monplaisir.

Château Pontac-Lynch (Fr). A vineyard in the commune of Margaux. A.C. Margaux, Bordeaux. 22 ha.

Château Pontac-Monplaisir (Fr). Address

C

= Villenave d'Ornon 33140. A.C.
Graves. Commune = Villenave
d'Ornon. 14 ha. Grape varieties – Cabernet sauvignon 40%, Merlot 60%, Sauvignon and Sémillon.

Château Pont-de-Figeac (Fr). A vineyard in the A.C. Saint-Émilion, Bordeaux. 25 ha.

Château Pont-de-Mouquet (Fr). A vineyard in the A.C. Saint-Émilion, Bordeaux. 12 ha.

Château Pont-de-Pierre (Fr). A vineyard in the commune of Lussac-Saint-Émilion. A.C. Saint-Émilion, Bordeaux.

Château Pontet (Fr). Address = 41 Cours Victor-Hugo 33340. Cru Bourgeois. A.C. Médoc. Commune = Blaignan. 11 ha. Grape varieties – Cabernet 50% and Merlot 50%.

Château Pontet (Fr). A.C. Saint-Émilion. Second wine of Château Cadet-Pontet. Grand Cru. Saint-Émilion, Bordeaux. 4 ha.

Château Pontet-Canet (Fr). Address = 33250 Pauillac. Grand Cru Classé (5th). A.C. Pauillac. Commune = Pauillac. 120 ha. Cabernet franc, Cabernet sauvignon and Merlot.

Château Pontet Caussan (Fr). A vineyard in the commune of Blaignan. A.C. Médoc, Bordeaux. Cru Bourgeois.

Château Pontet-Clauzure (Fr). A vineyard in the commune of Saint-Émilion. A.C. Saint-Émilion, Bordeaux. Grand Cru Classé. 8 ha.

Château Pontoise-Cabarrus (Fr). A vineyard in the commune of St-Seurin-de-Cadourne. A.C. Médoc, Bordeaux. Cru Grand Bourgeois. 18 ha.

Château Pontrousset (Fr). A vineyard in the A.C. Premières Côtes de Blaye, Bordeaux.

Château Pontus (Fr). A vineyard in the commune of Fronsac. A.C. Fronsac, Bordeaux.

Château Potensac (Fr). Address = Ordonnac, 33340 Lesparre, Médoc. Cru Grand Bourgeois. A.C. Médoc. Commune = Ordonnac. 160 ha. Grape varieties – Cabernet franc, Cabernet sauvignon and Merlot.

Château Pouget (Fr). Address = Cantenac 33460 Margaux. Grand Cru Classé (4th). A.C. Margaux. Commune = Cantenac. 10 ha. Grape varieties – Cabernet franc, Cabernet sauvignon and Merlot.

Château Poujeaux (Fr). Address = Moulis, 33480 Castelnau. Cru Grand Bourgeois Exceptionnel. A.C. Moulis. Commune = Moulis. 50 ha. Grape varieties – Cabernet franc, Cabernet sauvignon, Merlot and Petit verdot.

Château Poujeaux-Theil (Fr). See Château Poujeaux.

Château Poumey (Fr). A vineyard in the commune of Gradignan. A.C. Graves, Bordeaux. 4 ha. (red and white).

Château Poyanne (Fr). A vineyard in the commune of Gauriac. A.C. Côtes de Bourg, Bordeaux.

Château Pressac (Fr). A vineyard in the A.C. Saint-Émilion, Bordeaux. 24 ha.

Château Preuilhac (Fr). A vineyard in the commune of Lesparre. A.C. Médoc, Bordeaux. Cru Bourgeois. Address = 33340 Lesparre. 26 ha.

Château Priban (Fr). A vineyard in the commune of Macau. A.C. Médoc, Bordeaux. Cru Bourgeois.

Château Prieuré-Blaignan (Fr). A vineyard in the commune of Blaignan. A.C. Médoc, Bordeaux.

Château Prieuré-Lescours (Fr). Address = Saint-Sulpice-de-Faleyrens, 33330 Saint-Émilion. Grand Cru. A.C. Saint-Émilion. Commune = Saint-Sulpice-de-Faleyrens.

Château Prieuré-Lichine (Fr). Address = 33460 Margaux. Grand Cru Classé (4th). A.C. Margaux. Commune = Margaux. 60 ha. Grape varieties – Cabernet franc, Cabernet sauvignon, Malbec, Merlot and Petit verdot. Second wine is Château de Clairefont.

Château Prost (Fr). A vineyard in the commune of Barsac. A.C. Barsac (or Sauternes), Bordeaux. 8 ha.

Château Pugnau (Fr). A vineyard in the commune of Preignac. A.C. Sauternes, Bordeaux. 3 ha.

Château Puy Beney (Fr). A vineyard in the commune of Mazion. A.C. Côtes de Blaye, Bordeaux.

Château Puy Beney Lafitte (Fr). A vineyard in the commune of Mazion. A.C. Côtes de Blaye, Bordeaux.

Château Puy-Blanquet (Fr). Address = Saint-Étienne-de-Lisse, 33330 Saint-Émilion. A.C. Saint-Émilion. Commune = Saint-Étienne-de-Lisse. 120 ha.

Château Puyblanquet-Carrille (Fr). Address = Place du Marcardieu, 33330 Saint-Émilion. Grand Cru. A.C. Saint-Émilion. Commune = Saint-Christophe-des-Bardes. 18 ha. Grape varieties – Cabernet 25% and Merlot 75%.

Château Puy-Bonnet (Fr). A vineyard in the commune of Parsac-Saint-Émilion. A.C. Saint-Émilion, Bordeaux. 5 ha.

Château Puycarpin (Fr). A vineyard in the Côtes de Castillon, eastern Bordeaux. A.C. Bordeaux Supérieur.

Château Puy Castéra (Fr). Address =

C

Cissac-Médoc, 33250 Pauillac. Cru Bourgeois. A.C.' Haut-Médoc. Commune = Cissac. 28 ha. Grape varieties – Cabernet franc, Cabernet sauvignon, Malbec and Merlot.

Château Puyfromage (Fr). A vineyard in the commune of Saint-Cibard, Côtes de Castillon, eastern Bordeaux. A.C. Bordeaux Supérieur. Address = 33570 Saint-Cibard, Gironde.

Château Puy Normand (Fr). A.C. Montagne-Saint-Émilion. Commune = Montagne-Saint-Émilion.

Château Puy-Razac (Fr). Address = 33330 Saint-Émilion. Grand Cru. A.C. Saint-Émilion. Commune = Saint-Émilion. 6 ha. Grape varieties – Cabernet franc 30%, Cabernet sauvignon 30% and Merlot 40%.

Château Quentin (Fr). A vineyard in the A.C. Saint-Émilion, Bordeaux. 35 ha.

Château Quercy (Fr). A vineyard in the A.C. Saint-Émilion, Bordeaux. 4 ha.

Château Queyrats (Fr). A vineyard in the commune of St-Pierre-de-Mons. A.C. Graves, Bordeaux. 34 ha. Also Château St. Pierre and Clos d'Uza.

Château Queyret-Pouillac (Fr). A vineyard in the A.C. Entre-Deux-Mers, central Bordeaux.

Château Queyron (Fr). A vineyard in the commune of Cérons. A.C. Cérons, Bordeaux.

Château Queyron (Fr). A vineyard in the commune of Cantois. A.C. Entre-Deux-Mers, central Bordeaux.

Château Queyron (Fr). A vineyard in the A.C. Saint-Émilion, Bordeaux. 4 ha.

Château Queyron-Pin-de-Fleurs (Fr). A vineyard in the A.C. Saint-Émilion, Bordeaux. 4 ha.

Château Quinault (Fr). A vineyard in the commune of Sables-Saint-Émilion. A.C. Saint-Émilion, Bordeaux. 12 ha.

Château Quinault (Fr). A vineyard in the commune of Saint-Émilion. A.C. Saint-Émilion, Bordeaux. Grand Cru.

Château 'R' (Fr). The dry white wine of Château Rieussec, A.C. Sauternes, Bordeaux.

Château Raba (Fr). A vineyard in the commune of Talence. A.C. Graves, Bordeaux.

Château Rabat (Fr). A vineyard in the A.C. Saint-Émilion, Bordeaux. 3 ha.

Château Rabaud-Promis (Fr). A vineyard in the commune of Bommes. A.C. Sauternes, Bordeaux. 30 ha. Premier Grand Cru Classé.

Château Rabion (Fr). A vineyard in the A.C. Saint-Émilion, Bordeaux. 5 ha.

Château Rahoul (Fr). Address = 33640 Portets. A.C. Graves. Commune = Por-

tets. 17.5 ha. Grape varieties – Cabernet sauvignon 30%, Merlot 70% and Sémillon 100%.

Château Ramage-la-Batisse (Fr). A vineyard in the commune of St-Sauveur. A.C. Haut-Médoc, Bordeaux. 60 ha. Cru Bourgeois. Grape varieties – Cabernet franc, Cabernet sauvignon, Merlot and Petit verdot.

Château Rasclet (Fr). A vineyard in the commune of Vignonet. A.C. Saint-Émilion, Bordeaux.

Château Raspide (Fr). A vineyard in the commune of Barsac. A.C. Barsac (or Sauternes), Bordeaux. 5 ha.

Château Rausan Ségla (Fr). Address = 33460 Margaux. Grand Cru Classé (2nd) A.C. Margaux. Commune = Margaux. 41 ha. Grape varieties – Cabernet franc, Cabernet sauvignon, Merlot and Petit verdot.

Château Rauzan-Gassies (Fr). Address = 33460 Margaux. Grand Cru Classé (2nd). A.C. Margaux. Commune = Margaux. 29 ha. Grape varieties – Cabernet franc, Cabernet sauvignon, Merlot and Petit verdot.

Château Rayas (Fr). A vineyard in the A.C. Châteauneuf-du-Pape, southern Rhône.

Château Raymond-Lafon (Fr). A vineyard in the commune of Sauternes. A.C. Sauternes, Bordeaux. 5 ha. Address = 33210 Sauternes.

Château Rayne-Vigneau (Fr). A vineyard in the commune of Bommes. A.C. Sauternes, Bordeaux. 62 ha. Premier Grand Cru Classé.

Château Real Martin (Fr). A vineyard in the A.C. Côtes de Provence. Address = 83143 Le Val.

Château Rebeymond-Lalibard (Fr). A vineyard in the commune of Bourg. A.C. Côtes de Bourg, Bordeaux.

Château Rebeymont (Fr). A vineyard in the commune of Bourg. A.C. Côtes de Bourg, Bordeaux.

Château Rebouquet (Fr). A vineyard in the commune of Berson. A.C. Côtes de Bourg, Bordeaux.

Château Redon (Fr). A vineyard in the commune of Cissac. A.C. Médoc, Bordeaux.

Château Régent (Fr). A vineyard in the A.C. Saint-Émilion, Bordeaux. 4 ha.

Château Reindent (Fr). Address = Saint Laurent des Combes, 33330 Saint-Émilion. A.C. Bordeaux Supérieur. (red).

Château Reine-Blanche (Fr). The second wine of Château Grand-Corbin-Despagne. Grand Cru Classé. Saint-Émilion. 5 ha.

C

Château Remy (Austr). A winery in the Pyrenees, Victoria. Produces both still and sparkling wines.

Château Renaissance (Fr). A vineyard in the commune of Saint-Sulpice-de-Faleyrens. A.C. Bordeaux. Address = Renaissance, Saint-Sulpice-de-Faleyrens, Saint-Émilion.

Château Renard (Fr). A vineyard in the commune of St-Arche-de-Fronsac. A.C. Fronsac, Bordeaux.

Château Renouil Franquet (Fr). A vineyard in the commune of Moulis. A.C. Moulis, Bordeaux. 4 ha.

Château Respide (Fr). A vineyard in the commune of Langon. A.C. Graves, Bordeaux. 34 ha. (red and white).

Château Respide (Fr). A vineyard in the commune of St-Pierre-de-Mons. A.C. Graves, Bordeaux. 4 ha. (white).

Château Respide (Fr). Address = 33210 Toulenne. A.C. Graves. Commune = Toulenne. 11 ha. Grape varieties – Cabernet 20%, Merlot 20%, Sauvignon 30% and Sémillon 30%.

Château Rêve-d'Or (Fr). A vineyard in the commune of Pomerol. A.C. Pomerol, Bordeaux. 5 ha.

Château Reverdi (Fr). Address = Donissan Listrac 33480. A.C. Listrac. Commune = Listrac. 8 ha. Grape varieties – Cabernet sauvignon, Merlot and Petit verdot.

Château Reynard (Fr). A vineyard in the A.C. Saint-Émilion, Bordeaux. 4 ha.

Château Reynella (Austr). A red wine produced by the Reynella Vineyards (from Cabernet sauvignon grapes) in Reynella, South Australia.

Château Reynon (Fr). A vineyard in the commune of Bequey-Cadillac. A.C. Premières Côtes de Bordeaux. Address = 33410 Bequey-Cadillac. Grape varieties – Cabernet sauvignon 50%, Merlot 50% (red) and Sauvignon blanc (white). 37 ha.

Château Reysson (Fr). A vineyard in the commune of Vertheuil. A.C. Haut-Médoc, Bordeaux. Cru Grand Bourgeois. 46 ha.

Château Ricadet (Fr). A vineyard in the commune of Cartelègue. A.C. Côtes de Blaye, Bordeaux.

Château Ricaud (Fr). A vineyard in the commune of Loupiac. A.C. Loupiac, Bordeaux. 36 ha.

Château Richautey le Haut (Fr). A vineyard in the commune of St-Aignan. A.C. Côtes de Fronsac, Bordeaux. 2 ha.

Château Richeterre (Fr). See Château la Tour-de-Mons, A.C. Haut-Médoc, Bordeaux.

Château Richodey (Fr). A vineyard in the commune of St-Aignan. A.C. Fronsac, Bordeaux. 2 ha.

Château Richon (Isr). Vin blanc d'Israel. A medium dry golden white wine produced for the USA market.

Château Richon (Isr). Vin rouge d'Israel. Grape variety – Alicanté. A medium-sweet red wine produced for the USA market.

Château Rider (Fr). A vineyard in the commune of Bourg. A.C. Côtes de Bourg, Bordeaux.

Château Rieussec (Fr). Premier Grand Cru Classé. A.C. Sauternes. Commune = Fargues. 60 ha. Grape varieties – Sauvignon 24%, Sémillon 75% and Muscadelle 1%. See also Château 'R'.

Château Rigaud (Fr). A vineyard in the commune of Puisseguin-Saint-Émilion. A.C. Saint-Émilion, Bordeaux. 3 ha.

Château Ripeau (Fr). Address = 169, Avenue Foch, BP.17, 33500 Libourne. Grand Cru Classé. A.C. Saint-Émilion. Commune = Saint-Émilion. 20 ha. Grape varieties – Cabernet franc 25%, Cabernet sauvignon 25% and Merlot 50%.

Château Rivallon (Fr). A vineyard in the A.C. Saint-Émilion, Bordeaux. 8 ha.

Château Rivereau (Fr). A vineyard in the commune of Côtes de Bourg, Bordeaux.

Château Robert (Fr). A vineyard in the commune of Pomerol. A.C. Pomerol, Bordeaux.

Château Robert Franquet (Fr). A vineyard in the commune of Moulis. A.C. Moulis, Bordeaux. 4 ha.

Château Robin (Fr). A vineyard in the commune of Saint-Christophe-des-Bardes. A.C. Saint-Émilion, Bordeaux. 4 ha.

Château Robin-des-Moines (Fr). A vineyard in the A.C. Saint-Émilion, Bordeaux. 5 ha.

Château Roc (Fr). A vineyard in the A.C. Saint-Émilion, Bordeaux. 4 ha.

Château Roc-de-Puynormand (Fr). A vineyard in the commune of Parsac-Saint-Émilion. A.C. Saint-Émilion, Bordeaux. 6 ha.

Château Rochebelle (Fr). Address = Saint Laurent des Combes, 33330 Saint-Émilion. Grand Cru. A.C. Saint-Émilion. Commune = Saint Laurent des Combes. 2.45 ha. Grape varieties – Cabernet 25% and Merlot 75%

Château Rochemorin (Fr). Address = Château la Louvière, Léognan 33850. A.C. Graves. Commune = Léognan. 55 ha. Grape varieties – Cabernet sauvignon, Merlot, Sauvignon and Sémillon.

Château Roche-Morin (Fr). A vineyard in the commune of Martillac. A.C. Graves, Bordeaux. 48 ha. (red and and white).

Château Rocher-Beauregard (Fr). A vineyard in the commune of Pomerol. A.C. Pomerol, Bordeaux. 2 ha.

Château Rocher-Bellevue-Figeac (Fr). A vineyard in the A.C. Saint-Émilion, Bordeaux. 8 ha.

Château Rocher-Corbin (Fr). A vineyard in the commune of Montagne-Saint-Émilion. A.C. Saint-Émilion, Bordeaux. 6 ha.

Château Rocher-Figeac (Fr). Address = 194, Route de St-Émilion, 33500 Libourne, A.C. Saint-Émilion. Commune = Saint-Émilion. 7 ha. Grape varieties – Cabernet 15% and Merlot 85%.

Château Rochet (Fr). See Château Lafon-Rochet. Alternative name used.

Château Rocheyron (Fr). A vineyard in the commune of Saint-Christophe-des-Bardes. A.C. Saint-Émilion, Bordeaux.

Château Rocs-Marchand (Fr). A vineyard in the commune of Montagne-Saint-Émilion. A.C. Montagne-Saint-Émilion, Bordeaux. 9 ha.

Château Roc-St-Michel (Fr). A vineyard in the commune of Saint-Émilion. A.C. Saint-Émilion, Bordeaux. 4 ha.

Château Roland (Fr). A vineyard in the commune of Pauillac. A.C. Pauillac, Bordeaux. 5 ha.

Château Roland (Fr). A vineyard in the commune of Saint-Émilion. A.C. Saint-Émilion, Bordeaux.

Château Rol de Fombrauge (Fr). A vineyard in the A.C. Saint-Émilion, Bordeaux. 4 ha.

Château Rolland (Fr). A vineyard in the commune of Pauillac. A.C. Médoc, Bordeaux. Cru Bourgeois.

Château Rollan de By (Fr). A vineyard in the commune of Bégadan. A.C. Médoc, Bordeaux. Cru Bourgeois. Address = Bégadan, 33340 Lesparre.

Château Rolland-Maillet (Fr). A vineyard in the commune of Saint-Émilion. A.C. Saint-Émilion, Bordeaux. Grand Cru.

Château Romain (Alg). A red wine produced in Zaccar, northern Algeria.

Château Romassan (Fr). A vineyard based in the A.C. Bandol, south-eastern France. Owned by Domaine Ott. Produces red and rosé wines from the Mourvèdre grape.

Château Romefort (Fr). A vineyard in the commune of Cussac-Fort-Médoc. A.C. Haut-Médoc, Bordeaux.

Château Romer du Hayot (Fr). A vineyard in the commune of Fargues. A.C. Sauternes, Bordeaux.

Château Romer-Lafon (Fr). A vineyard in the commune of Fargues. A.C. Sauternes, Bordeaux. 15 ha. Grand Cru Classé (2nd).

Château Rondillon (Fr). A vineyard in the commune of Loupiac. A.C. Loupiac, Bordeaux. 12 ha.

Château Roquebrune (Fr). A vineyard in the commune of Cenac. A.C. Premières Côtes de Bordeaux. Address = 33360 Cenac. Grape varieties – Cabernet franc 33%, Cabernet sauvignon 33% and Merlot 33%.

Château Roquefort (Fr). A vineyard in the commune of Haux. A.C. Premières Côtes de Bordeaux. Address = 33550 Haux. Grape varieties – Cabernet 60%, Malbec 20% and Merlot 20%.

Château Roquegrave (Fr). Address = Villeneuve Valeyrac 33340. A.C. Médoc. Commune = Valeyrac. 36 ha. Grape varieties – Cabernet 70% and Merlot 30%.

Château Roquetaillade (Fr). A vineyard in the commune of Mazères. A.C. Graves, Bordeaux. 3 ha. (white).

Château Roquetaillade la Grange (Fr). Address = Mazères, 33210 Langon. A.C. Graves. Commune = Mazères. 36 ha. Grape varieties – Cabernet franc, Cabernet sauvignon, Malbec, Merlot, Petit verdot, Sauvignon and Sémillon.

Château Rosario (Fr). A vineyard in the commune of Eyzines. A.C. Graves, Bordeaux. 1 ha. (white).

Château Rose de Pont (Fr). A vineyard in the A.C. Médoc, Bordeaux.

Château Rose-la-Riche (Fr). A vineyard in the commune of Macau. A.C. Médoc, Bordeaux. Cru Bourgeois.

Château Rosemont (Fr). A vineyard in the commune of Labarde. A.C. Médoc, Bordeaux.

Château Rose Ste-Croix (Fr). A vineyard in the commune of Listrac. A.C. Listrac, Bordeaux. 6 ha.

Château Rosevale Winery (Austr). A winery based near Tanunda, Barossa Valley, South Australia. Produces varietal wines. Also in Gomersal, Barossa Valley.

Château Rostang-Haut-Carré (Fr). A vineyard in the commune of Talence. 4 ha. (red and white).

Château Roubinet (Fr). A vineyard in the commune of Pujols. A.C. Graves, Bordeaux. 8 ha. (white).

Château Roucheyron (Fr). A vineyard in the A.C. Saint-Émilion, Bordeaux. 6 ha.

Château Roudier (Fr). Address = Château Balestard la Tonnelle, 33330 Saint-Émilion. A.C. Montagne-Saint-Émilion. Commune = Montagne Saint-Émilion. 30 ha.

C

Château Roudier (Fr). A vineyard in the commune of Montagne-Saint-Émilion. A.C. Montagne-Saint-Émilion, Bordeaux. 3 ha.

Château Rouet (Fr). A vineyard in the commune of Fronsac. A.C. Côtes de Fronsac, Bordeaux. 3 ha.

Château Rouget (Fr). A vineyard in the commune of Pomerol. A.C. Pomerol, Bordeaux. 11 ha.

Château Roullet (Fr). A vineyard in the commune of Fronsac. A.C. Côtes Canon-Fronsac, Bordeaux. 3 ha.

Château Roumieu (Fr). A vineyard in the commune of Barsac. A.C. Barsac (or Sauternes), Bordeaux. 18 ha.

Château Roumieu-Lacoste (Fr). A vineyard in the commune of Barsac. A.C. Barsac (or Sauternes), Bordeaux. 5 ha.

Château Rouques (Fr). A vineyard in the commune of Puisseguin-Saint-Émilion, Bordeaux.

Château Rousselle (Fr). A vineyard in the commune of St-Ciers-de-Canesse. A.C. Côtes de Bourg, Bordeaux.

Château Rousset (Fr). A vineyard in the commune of Samonac. A.C. Côtes de Bourg, Bordeaux. 25 ha.

Château Roustit (Fr). A vineyard in the commune of Sainte-Croix-du-Mont. A.C. Sainte-Croix-du-Mont, Bordeaux. 9 ha.

Châteauroux (Fr). A noted wine-producing town in the Indre Département, central France.

Château Royal-Médoc (Fr). The second wine of Château Cantermerle.

Château Royal Saint-Émilion (Fr). The brand name of a Co-operative in the Saint-Émilion district of eastern Bordeaux.

Château Rozier (Fr). Address = Saint Laurent des Combes, 33330 Saint-Émilion. Grand Cru. A.C. Saint-Émilion. Commune = Saint Laurent des Combes. 18 ha. Grape varieties – Bouchet 20%, Cabernet sauvignon 5% and Merlot 75%. Second wine is Château Monturon.

Château Rozier-Béard (Fr). A vineyard in the A.C. Saint-Émilion, Bordeaux. 6 ha.

Château Ruat (Fr). A vineyard in the commune of Moulis. A.C. Moulis, Bordeaux. 6 ha.

Château Sablons (Fr). A vineyard in the commune of Montagne-Saint-Émilion. A.C. Montagne-Saint-Émilion, Bordeaux. 5 ha.

Château Sahuc (Fr). A vineyard in the commune of Preignac. A.C. Sauternes, Bordeaux. 2 ha.

Château Sahuc-Latour (Fr). A vineyard in the commune of Preignac. A.C. Sauternes, Bordeaux. 4 ha.

Château Saige-Fort-Manoir (Fr). A vineyard in the commune of Pessac. A.C. Graves, Bordeaux. 5 ha. (red).

Château Saint-Agraves (Fr). Address = Artigues, Landiras, 33720 Podensac. A.C. Graves. Commune = Landiras. 10 ha. Grape varieties – Cabernet franc, Cabernet sauvignon and Merlot.

Château Saint-Amand (Fr). A vineyard in the commune of Preignac. A.C. Sauternes, Bordeaux.

Château Saint-Augustin-la-Grave (Fr). A vineyard in the commune of Martillac. A.C. Graves, Bordeaux.

Château Saint-Bonnet (Fr). A vineyard in the commune of Saint-Christoly. A.C. Médoc, Bordeaux. Cru Bourgeois. 30 ha.

Château Saint-Christoly (Fr). Address = Le Bourg, Saint-Christoly-de-Médoc A.C. Médoc. Commune = Saint-Christoly-de-Médoc. Grape varieties – Cabernet 65% and Merlot 35%. 4 ha.

Château Sainte Roseline (Fr). A vineyard in the A.C. Côtes de Provence. Address = 83460 Les Arcs-sur-Argens.

Château Saint-Estèphe (Fr). Address = Leyssac, Saint-Estèphe 33250. A.C. Saint-Estèphe. Commune = Saint-Estèphe. 12 ha. Grape varieties – Cabernet franc, Cabernet sauvignon, Merlot and Petit verdot.

Château Saint Estève d'Uchaux (Fr). A vineyard in the A.C. Côtes du Rhône, south-eastern France. Address = Uchaux-F-84100 Orange.

Château Saint Georges [Côte Pavie] (Fr). Address = 33330 Saint-Émilion. Grand Cru Classé. A.C. Saint-Émilion. Commune = Saint-Émilion. 5.48 ha. Grape varieties – Bouchet 33%, Cabernet sauvignon 33% and Merlot 33%.

Château Saint Jacques (Fr). Address = Annexe au Château Siran, Labarde, 33460 Margaux. A.C. Bordeaux Supérieur. Commune = Labarde-Médoc. 10 ha. Grape varieties – Cabernet franc, Cabernet sauvignon, Merlot and Petit verdot.

Château Saint Jean (USA). A small winery of Kenwood, Sonoma, California. Grape varieties – Cabernet sauvignon, Chardonnay, Gewürztraminer and Johannisberg riesling. Produces varietal and late-harvest wines.

Château Saint-Julien (Fr). A.C. Médoc. Second wine of Château Lagrange. Grand Cru Classé (3rd). Saint-Julien. 3 ha.

Château Saint Martin (Fr). A.C. Roussillon.

C

Château Saint-Paul (Fr). A vineyard in the commune of St-Seurin-de-Cadourne. A.C. Haut-Médoc, Bordeaux. Cru Bourgeois. Address = St-Seurin-de-Cadourne, 33250 Pauillac. 19 ha.

Château Saint Pierre (Fr). Address = 33250 Saint-Julien, Beychevelle. Grand Cru Classé (4ᵗʰ). A.C. Saint-Julien. Commune = Saint-Julien 20 ha. Grape varieties – Cabernet franc 5%, Cabernet sauvignon 70% and Merlot 25%.

Château Saint-Pierre-Bontemps (Fr). See Château Saint Pierre.

Château Saint-Pierre-Sevaistre (Fr). See Château Saint Pierre.

Château Saint-Roch (Fr). A vineyard in the A.C. Lirac, southern Rhône.

Château Saint-Saturnin (Fr). A vineyard in the commune of Bégadan. A.C. Médoc, Bordeaux. Cru Bourgeois. Address = Bégadan, 33340 Lesparre. 8 ha.

Château Saint Sorlin (Fr). A Cognac producer. Address = Saint Sorlin de Cognac, 17150 Mirambeau. 36 ha in the Fins Bois. Produces a range of Cognacs.

Château-Salins (Fr). A wine town in Alsace. (Ger) = Salzburg.

Château Samion (Fr). A vineyard in the commune of Saint-Georges-Saint-Émilion. A.C. Saint-Émilion, Bordeaux. 9 ha.

Château Sansonnet (Fr). Address = 33330 Saint-Émilion. Grand Cru Classé. A.C. Saint-Émilion. Commune = Saint-Émilion. 8 ha. Grape varieties – Cabernet franc 20%, Cabernet sauvignon 20% and Merlot 60%.

Château Saransot-Dupré (Fr). Address = Listrac-Médoc 33480. Cru Bourgeois. A.C. Listrac. Commune = Listrac. 40 ha. Grape varieties – Cabernet sauvignon 60% and Merlot 40%.

Château Sauman (Fr). A vineyard in the A.C. Côtes de Bourg, Bordeaux.

Château Saupiquet (Fr). A vineyard in the A.C. Saint-Émilion, Bordeaux. 1 ha.

Château Sauterne (USA). A sweet white wine made from Sauvignon blanc, Sémillon and Muscadelle grapes in California.

Château Sauvenelle (Fr). Address = Route de St-Émilion, 33500 Libourne. A.C. Saint-Émilion. Commune = Libourne. 70 ha. Grape varieties – Cabernet franc, Cabernet sauvignon and Merlot.

Château Segonzac (Fr). A vineyard in the commune of St-Genès-de-Blaye. A.C. Côtes de Blaye, Bordeaux.

Château Ségur (Fr). A vineyard in the commune of Parempuyre. A.C. Haut-Médoc, Bordeaux. Cru Grand Bourgeois. 30 ha.

Château Ségur d'Arsac (Fr). Address = 33460 Margaux. A.C. Haut-Médoc. Commune = Arsac. 260 ha. Grape varieties – Cabernet franc, Cabernet sauvignon and Merlot.

Château Ségur Fillon (Fr). A vineyard in the commune of Parempuyre. A.C. Haut-Médoc, Bordeaux. Cru Grand Bourgeois.

Château Semeillan-Mazeau (Fr). Address = Listrac-Médoc, 33480. Cru Bourgeois. A.C. Listrac. Commune = Listrac. 12 ha. Grape varieties – Cabernet sauvignon and Merlot.

Château Sénéjac (Fr). A vineyard in the commune of Le Pian. A.C. Haut-Médoc, Bordeaux. Cru Bourgeois.

Château Senilhac (Fr). Address = 33250 Pauillac. A.C. Haut-Médoc. Commune = Saint-Seurin-de-Cadourne. 14 ha. Grape varieties – Cabernet franc, Cabernet sauvignon and Merlot.

Château Sestignan (Fr). Address = 33590 Saint Vivien-de-Médoc. Cru Bourgeois. A.C. Médoc. Commune = Jau-Dignac-Loirac. 20 ha. Grape varieties – Cabernet sauvignon, Malbec, Merlot and Petit verdot.

Château Siaurac (Fr). A vineyard in the commune of Néac. A.C. Lalande de Pomerol, Bordeaux.

Château Sigalas-Rabaud (Fr). Premier Grand Cru Classé (2ⁿᵈ). A.C. Sauternes. Commune = Bommes. 14 ha. Grape varieties – Sauvignon 10% and Sémillon 90%.

Château Siglas-Rabaud (Fr). See Château Sigalas-Rabaud.

Château Sigognac (Fr). Address = 33340 Saint-Yzans-de-Médoc. Cru Grand Bourgeois. A.C. Médoc. Commune = Saint-Yzans. 73 ha. Grape varieties – Cabernet franc, Cabernet sauvignon and Merlot.

Château Simard (Fr). A vineyard in the A.C. Saint-Émilion, Bordeaux. 15 ha.

Château Simon (Fr). A vineyard in the commune of Barsac. A.C. Barsac (or Sauternes), Bordeaux. 4 ha.

Château Simon-Carretey (Fr). A vineyard in the commune of Barsac. A.C. Barsac (or Sauternes), Bordeaux. 4 ha.

Château Simone (Fr). A vineyard in the A.C. Palette. Address = 13590 Meyreuil, Aix-en-Provence. Grape varieties – Clairette, Cinsault, Grenache and Mourvèdre (red and white).

Château Siran (Fr). Address = 33460 Margaux. Cru Exceptionnel. A.C. Margaux. Commune = Labarde. 33 ha. Grape varieties – Cabernet franc, Cabernet sauvignon, Merlot and Petit verdot.

Château Smith-Haut-Lafitte (Fr). Grand Cru Classé. A.C. Graves. Commune =

C

Martillac. 51 ha. Grape varieties – Cabernet franc, Cabernet sauvignon, Merlot and Sauvignon 100%.

Château Sociando (Fr). A vineyard in the commune of Cars. A.C. Premières Côtes de Blaye, Bordeaux.

Château Sociando-Mallet (Fr). Address = 33250 Pauillac. Cru Grand Bourgeois. A.C. Haut-Médoc. Commune = Saint-Seurin-de-Cadourne. 30 ha. Grape varieties – Cabernet franc 10%, Cabernet sauvignon 60% and Merlot 30%

Château Soleil (Fr). A vineyard in the commune of Puisseguin-Saint-Émilion. A.C. Puisseguin-Saint-Émilion, Bordeaux. 5 ha.

Château Solon (Fr). A vineyard in the commune of Preignac. A.C. Sauternes, Bordeaux. 4 ha.

Château Soucarde (Fr). A vineyard in the commune of St-Seurin-de-Bourg. A.C. Côtes de Bourg, Bordeaux.

Château Soudars (Fr). Address = 33250 Pauillac. Cru Bourgeois. A.C. Haut-Médoc. Commune = Saint-Seurin-de-Cadourne. 14 ha. Grape varieties – Cabernet sauvignon 65% and Merlot 35%.

Château Soutard (Fr). Address = 33330 Saint-Émilion. Grand Cru Classé. Saint-Émilion. Commune = Saint-Émilion. 28 ha. Grape varieties – Cabernet franc 40% and Merlot 60%. Second wine is Clos la Tonnelle.

Château Soutard-Cadet (Fr). A vineyard in the A.C. Saint-Émilion, Bordeaux. 3 ha.

Château St. Ahon (Fr). A vineyard in the commune of Blanquefort. A.C. Médoc, Bordeaux. Cru Bourgeois.

Château St. Amand (Fr). A vineyard in the A.C. Sauternes, Bordeaux.

Château St-André (Fr). A vineyard in the commune of Saint-Georges-Saint-Émilion. A.C. Saint-Émilion, Bordeaux.

Château St-Anne (Fr). A vineyard in the commune of St-Christoly. A.C. Médoc, Bordeaux. 4 ha.

Château St-Antoine (Fr). A.C. Bordeaux. (red).

Château St. Bonnet (Fr). A vineyard in the A.C. Médoc, Bordeaux.

Château St-Christophe (Fr). A vineyard in the A.C. Saint-Émilion, Bordeaux. 7 ha.

Château St. Didier-Parnac (Fr). A vineyard in the A.C. Cahors, south-western France.

Château Ste. Chapelle (USA). A winery based near Caldwell, Idaho. 60 ha. Produces varietal wines.

Château Ste. Michelle (USA). A large winery in Washington, Pacific North-West. 1,280 ha. Grape varieties – Cabernet sauvignon, Chardonnay, Gewürztraminer and Riesling. Produces varietal wines.

Château St. Georges (Fr). A vineyard in the A.C. Côtes du Rhône, south-eastern France.

Château St-Georges (Fr). A vineyard in the commune of Saint-Georges-de-Montagne. A.C. Saint-Émilion, Bordeaux. Address = 33570 Lussac.

Château St-Georges (Fr). A vineyard in the commune of Saint-Georges-Saint-Émilion. A.C. Saint-Émilion, Bordeaux. 35 ha.

Château St-Georges-Macquin (Fr). A vineyard in the commune of Saint-Georges-Saint-Émilion. A.C. Saint-Émilion, Bordeaux. 17 ha. Is part of Domaine de Maisonneuve.

Château St-Germain (Fr). A vineyard in the commune of Berson. A.C. Côtes de Blaye, Bordeaux.

Château St-Germain (Fr). A vineyard in the commune of Saint-Germain-d'Esteuil. A.C. Médoc, Bordeaux. 2 ha.

Château St-Gérôme (Fr). A vineyard in the commune of Ayguemortes. A.C. Graves, Bordeaux. 4 ha. (red and white).

Château St. Haon (Fr). A vineyard in the commune of Blanquefort. A.C. Haut-Médoc, Bordeaux. 13 ha.

Château St-Hubert (Fr). A vineyard in the commune of Saint-Émilion. A.C. Saint-Émilion, Bordeaux. Grand Cru. Address = 33330 Saint-Émilion.

Château St-Jacques-Calon (Fr). A vineyard in the commune of Montagne-Saint-Émilion. A.C. Montagne-Saint-Émilion, Bordeaux. 6 ha.

Château St. Jean (USA). See Château Saint Jean. Vineyards Belle Terre and Rancho Alta Vista.

Château St-Julien (Fr). A vineyard in the commune of Saint-Julien. A.C. Médoc, Bordeaux.

Château St-Lô (Fr). A vineyard in the A.C. Saint-Émilion, Bordeaux. 8 ha.

Château St-Louis (Fr). A vineyard in the commune of Saint-Georges-Saint-Émilion. A.C. Saint-Émilion, Bordeaux. 4 ha.

Château St-Marc (Fr). A vineyard in the commune of Barsac. A.C. Barsac (or Sauternes), Bordeaux. 6 ha. Also Château Hourmalas.

Château St-Martial (Fr). A vineyard in the A.C. Saint-Émilion, Bordeaux. 2 ha.

Château St-Martin (Fr). A vineyard in the commune of Listrac. A.C. Listrac, Bordeaux. 2 ha.

C

Château St-Michel (Fr). A vineyard in the commune of Barsac. A.C. Barsac (or Sauternes), Bordeaux. 1 ha.

Château St-Michel (Fr). A vineyard in the commune of Montagne-Saint-Émilion. A.C. Saint-Émilion, Bordeaux. 2 ha.

Château St. Patrice (Fr). A vineyard in the A.C. Châteauneuf-du-Pape, southern Rhône.

Château St-Paul (Fr). A vineyard in the commune of Montagne-Saint-Émilion. A.C. Montagne-Saint-Émilion, Bordeaux. 5 ha.

Château St. Pey (Fr). A vineyard in the commune of Saint-Émilion. A.C. Saint-Émilion, Bordeaux. Grand Cru. 9 ha.

Château St. Pierre (Fr). A.C. Côtes du Roussillon. (red wine).

Château St. Pierre (Fr). A vineyard in the commune of St-Pierre-de-Mons. A.C. Graves, Bordeaux. 34 ha. (white). Also Château Queyrats and Clos d'Aza.

Château St. Pierre (Fr). A vineyard in the commune of Montagne-Saint-Émilion. A.C. Montagne-Saint-Émilion, Bordeaux.

Château St-Pierre-de-Pomerol (Fr). A vineyard in the commune of Pomerol. A.C. Pomerol, Bordeaux.

Château St-Roch (Fr). A vineyard in the A.C. Saint-Émilion, Bordeaux. 3 ha.

Château St. Roch (Fr). A vineyard in the commune of Saint-Estèphe. A.C. Médoc, Bordeaux. Cru Bourgeois.

Château St-Seurin (Fr). A vineyard in the A.C. Haut-Médoc, Bordeaux.

Château Suau (Fr). A vineyard in the commune of Barsac. A.C. Barsac (or Sauternes), Bordeaux. 7 ha. Grand Cru Classé (2nd).

Château Suduiraut (Fr). Grand Cru Classé. A.C. Sauternes. Commune = Preignac. 72 ha. Grape varieties – Sauvignon 15% and Sémillon 85%.

Château Sylvain (Fr). A vineyard in the commune of Cérons. A.C. Cérons, Bordeaux. 3 ha.

Château Taffard-de-Blaignan (Fr). See Château Blaignan.

Château Tahbilk (Austr). Address = Tahbilk, Victoria 3607. 75 ha. Grape varieties – Cabernet sauvignon, Chardonnay, Chenin blanc, Marsanne, Rhine riesling, Sauvignon blanc, Sémillon blanc and Shiraz.

Château Taillefer (Fr). A vineyard in the commune of Pomerol. A.C. Pomerol, Bordeaux. 21 ha.

Château Talbot (Fr). Address = Saint-Julien, Beychevelle 33250. Grand Cru Classé (4th). A.C. Saint-Julien. Commune = Saint-Julien. 85 ha. Grape varieties – Cabernet franc, Cabernet sauvignon, Merlot and Petit verdot. See also Connétable Talbot.

Château Tanesse (Fr). A vineyard based in central Bordeaux owned by the négociant-éleveurs Cordier. Produces fine wines from Cabernet sauvignon, Sauvignon blanc, Sémillon and Muscadelle grapes.

Château Tanunda (Austr). A winery in the Barossa Valley, South Australia. Produces mainly varietal wines.

Château Tarreyre (Fr). A vineyard in the A.C. Saint-Émilion, Bordeaux. 2 ha.

Château Tasta (Fr). A vineyard in the commune of Saint-Aignan. A.C. Fronsac, Bordeaux.

Château Taureau (Fr). A vineyard in the commune of Lussac-Saint-Émilion. A.C. Saint-Émilion, Bordeaux. 3 ha.

Château Tauzinat (Fr). A vineyard in the A.C. Saint-Émilion, Bordeaux. 3 ha.

Château Tauzinat L'Hermitage (Fr). Address = Saint-Christophe-des-Bardes, 33330 Saint-Émilion. A.C. Saint-Émilion. Commune = Saint-Christophe-des-Bardes. 12.5 ha. Grape varieties – Cabernet franc 40% and Merlot 60%.

Château Tayac (Fr). A vineyard in the commune of Bayon. A.C. Côtes de Bourg, Bordeaux.

Château Tayac (Fr). Address = Tayac, Soussans 33460 Margaux. Cru Bourgeois. A.C. Margaux. Commune = Soussans. 35 ha. Grape varieties – Cabernet franc, Cabernet sauvignon, Merlot and Petit verdot.

Château Teillac (Fr). A vineyard in the commune of Puisseguin-Saint-Émilion. A.C. Puisseguin-Saint-Émilion, Bordeaux. 7 ha.

Château Templiers (Fr). A vineyard in the commune of Lalande de Pomerol. A.C. Lalande de Pomerol, Bordeaux.

Château Terfort (Fr). A vineyard in the commune of Sainte-Croix-du-Mont. A.C. Sainte-Croix-du-Mont, Bordeaux. 3 ha.

Château Terrefort (Fr). A vineyard in the commune of Loupiac. A.C. Loupiac, Bordeaux. 8 ha.

Château Terrefort-Quancard (Fr). A vineyard in the commune of St-André de Cubzac. A.C. Bordeaux.

Château Terre-Noble (Fr). A vineyard in the commune of Barsac. A.C. Barsac (or Sauternes), Bordeaux. 2 ha. Also Château Fleury.

Château Terre Noble (Fr). A vineyard in the commune of Barsac. A.C. Barsac (or Sauternes), Bordeaux. 9 ha. Also Château Montjou.

Château Terre Rouge (Fr). A vineyard in

C

the A.C. Médoc, Bordeaux.

Château Terrey-Gros-Caillou (Fr). Address = Saint-Julien-Beychevelle, 33250. Cru Bourgeois. A.C. Saint-Julien. Commune = Saint-Julien. 14 ha. Grape varieties – Cabernet 65%, Merlot 30% and Petit verdot 5%.

Château Terrien (Fr). A vineyard in the commune of Lussac-Saint-Émilion. A.C. Saint-Émilion, Bordeaux. 3 ha.

Château Terrier Bergerac (Fr). A vineyard in the A.C. Bergerac, south-western France. (red).

Château Tessendey (Fr). A vineyard in the A.C. Côtes de Fronsac, Bordeaux.

Château Tetre Daugay (Fr). Address = 33330 Saint-Émilion. Grand Cru Classé. A.C. Saint-Émilion. Commune = Saint-Émilion. 18 ha. Grape varieties – Cabernet franc 30%, Cabernet sauvignon 10% and Merlot 60%. Second wine is Château de Roquefort.

Château Tetre-de-la-Mouleyre (Fr). A vineyard in the commune of Parsac-Saint-Émilion. A.C. Saint-Émilion, Bordeaux. 2 ha.

Château Tetre Roteboeuf (Fr). A vineyard in the commune of Saint-Émilion. A.C. Saint-Émilion, Bordeaux. Address = 33330 Saint-Émilion.

Château Teynac (Fr). A vineyard in the commune of Saint-Julien. A.C. Saint-Julien, Bordeaux. 5 ha.

Château Teynac [Clos St-Julien] (Fr). A vineyard in the commune of Saint-Julien. A.C. Saint-Julien, Bordeaux. 4 ha.

Château Teyssier (Fr). A vineyard in the commune of Puisseguin-Saint-Émilion. A.C. Puisseguin-Saint-Émilion, Bordeaux. 28 ha.

Château Teyssier (Fr). Address = Vignonet, 33330 Saint-Émilion. Grand Cru. A.C. Saint-Émilion. Commune = Vignonet. 18 ha. Grape varieties – Cabernet 35%, Merlot 60% and Petit verdot 5%.

Château Thibaut (Fr). A vineyard in the commune of Fargues. A.C. Sauternes, Bordeaux. 2 ha.

Château Thibéaud Maillet (Fr). A vineyard in the commune of Pomerol. A.C. Pomerol, Bordeaux. 2 ha.

Château Thieuley (Fr). A.C. Bordeaux Clairet.

Château Thivin (Fr). A vineyard in the A.C. Côte de Brouilly Cru Beaujolais-Villages, Burgundy.

Château Thomé-Brousterot (Fr). A vineyard in the commune of Illats. A.C. Cérons, Bordeaux. 8 ha.

Château Timberlay (Fr). A vineyard in the commune of Saint-André-de-Cubzac. Gironde. A.C. Bordeaux Rouge.

Château Tiregand (Fr). A vineyard in the A.C. Pécharmant, Bergerac, south-western France. 30 ha. (red).

Château Toinet Fombrauge (Fr). A vineyard in the A.C. Saint-Émilion, Bordeaux. 8 ha.

Château Tonneret (Fr). A vineyard in the A.C. Saint-Émilion, Bordeaux. 2 ha.

Château Toudenac (Fr). A.C. Bordeaux. (white).

Château Touilla (Fr). A vineyard in the commune of Fargues. A.C. Sauternes, Bordeaux. 3 ha,.

Château Toulifant (Fr). Part of Château Taillefer, A.C. Pomerol, Bordeaux.

Château Tournalin (Fr). A vineyard in the A.C. Canon-Fronsac, Bordeaux.

Château Tournilon (Fr). Address = Saint Pierre-de-Mons 33210 Langon. A.C. Graves. Commune = Saint Pierre-de-Mons. 13 ha. Grape varieties – Cabernet franc 30%, Cabernet sauvignon 35%, Merlot 35%, Sauvignon 40% and Sémillon 60%.

Château Tourans (Fr). A vineyard in the commune of Saint-Étienne-de-Lisse. A.C. Saint-Émilion, Bordeaux.

Château Tour Blanche (Fr). Address = Saint-Christophe-des-Bardes, 33330 Saint-Émilion. Grand Cru. A.C. Saint-Émilion. Commune = Saint-Christophe-des-Bardes. 12 ha. Grape varieties – Cabernet 30% and Merlot 70%.

Château Tour Carelot (Fr). A vineyard in the commune of Avensan. A.C. Haut-Médoc, Bordeaux. Cru Bourgeois. Address = Avensan, 33480 Castelnau-de-Médoc.

Château Tour-Coutely-Saint Louis (Fr). Address = Leyssac, Saint-Estèphe 33250. A.C. Saint-Estèphe. Commune = Saint-Estèphe. 5 ha. Grape varieties – Cabernet franc 10%, Cabernet sauvignon 50%, Malbec 5%, Merlot 30% and Petit verdot 5%.

Château Tour de Bardes (Fr). Address = Saint Laurent des Bardes, 33330 Saint-Émilion. A.C. Saint-Émilion. Commune = Saint Laurent des Bardes. The second wine of Clos Labarde.

Château Tour de Capet (Fr). A.C. Saint-Émilion. The second wine of Château Capet-Guillier. Grand Cru. Saint-Émilion.

Château Tour de Grenet (Fr). Address = Lussac-Saint-Émilion. 33330 Saint-Émilion. A.C. Lussac-Saint-Émilion. Commune = Lussac-Saint-Émilion.

Château Tour de Pressac (Fr). Address = Saint-Étienne-de-Lisse, 33330 Saint-Émilion. A.C. Saint-Émilion. Commune = Saint-Étienne-de-Lisse. The second wine of Château de Pressac.

C

Château Tour des Combes (Fr). Address = Saint Laurent des Combes, 33330 Saint-Émilion. Grand Cru. A.C. Saint-Émilion. Commune = Saint Laurent des Combes. 17 ha. Grape varieties – Cabernet franc 15%, Cabernet sauvignon 15% and Merlot 70%.

Château Tour des Termes (Fr). Address = Saint Codian, Saint-Estèphe 33250. A.C. Saint-Estèphe. Commune = Saint-Estèphe. 30 ha. Grape varieties – Cabernet franc, Cabernet sauvignon, Merlot and Petit verdot.

Château Tour du Haut-Moulin (Fr). Address = Cussac-Fort-Médoc. 33460 Cru Bourgeois. A.C. Haut-Médoc. Commune = Cussac-Fort-Médoc. Grape varieties – Cabernet sauvignon, Merlot and Petit verdot.

Château Tour du Mirail (Fr). Address = 33250 Pauillac. Cru Bourgeois. A.C. Haut-Médoc. Commune = Cussac. Grape varieties – Malbec, Merlot and Petit verdot.

Château Tour du Pas St-Georges (Fr). Address = Saint-Georges-Saint-Émilion. 33330 Saint-Émilion. A.C. Saint-Georges-Saint-Émilion. Commune = Saint-Georges-Saint-Émilion.

Château Tour du Roc (Fr). Address = Arcins, 33460 Margaux. Cru Bourgeois. A.C. Haut-Médoc. Commune = Arcins. 14 ha. Grape varieties – Cabernet sauvignon 50% and Merlot 50%.

Château Tour Fortin (Fr). A vineyard in the commune of Saint-Émilion. A.C. Saint-Émilion, Bordeaux. Address = 33330 Saint-Émilion.

Château-Tour-Grand-Faurie (Fr). Address = 33330 Saint-Émilion. A.C. Saint-Émilion. Commune = Saint-Émilion. 11 ha. Grape varieties – Bouchet 20%, Cabernet sauvignon 5%, Malbec 5% and Merlot 70%.

Château Tour Grand Mayne (Fr). A vineyard in the A.C. Côtes de Castillon, eastern Bordeaux.

Château Tour Granins (Fr). A vineyard in the commune of Moulis. A.C. Moulis, Bordeaux. Cru Bourgeois. Address = Moulis 33480, Castelnau-de-Médoc.

Château Tour Musset (Fr). Address = Montagne-Saint-Émilion, 33330 Saint-Émilion. A.C. Montagne-Saint-Émilion. Commune = Montagne-Saint-Émilion.

Château Tournefeuille (Fr). A vineyard in the commune of Néac. A.C. Lalande de Pomerol, Bordeaux.

Château Tour Prignac (Fr). A vineyard in the commune of Prignac. A.C. Médoc, Bordeaux. Cru Bourgeois. Address = Prignac-en-Médoc, 33340 Lesparre.

Château Tour Renaissance (Fr). Address = Saint-Sulpice-de-Faleyrens, 33330 Saint-Émilion. Grand Cru. A.C. Saint-Émilion. Commune = Saint-Sulpice-de-Faleyrens. 35 ha. Grape varieties – Cabernet franc 20%, Cabernet sauvignon 10% and Merlot 70%.

Château Tour Saint Christophe (Fr). Address = Saint-Christophe-des-Bardes, 33330 Saint-Émilion. Grand Cru. A.C. Saint-Émilion. Commune = Saint-Christophe-des-Bardes. 20 ha. Grape varieties – Cabernet franc, Cabernet sauvignon and Merlot 66%.

Château Tour Saint-Pierre (Fr). Address = 33330 Saint-Émilion. Grand Cru. A.C. Saint-Émilion. Commune = Saint-Émilion. 10 ha. Grape varieties – Cabernet franc 10%, Cabernet sauvignon 10% and Merlot 80%.

Château Tourteau-Chollet-Lafitte (Fr). A vineyard in the commune of Arbanats. A.C. Graves, Bordeaux. 13 ha. (red and white).

Château Tourteran (Fr). A vineyard in the commune of St-Sauveur. A.C. Médoc, Bordeaux. Cru Bourgeois.

Château Toutigeac (Fr). A.C. Bordeaux Rouge.

Château Touzinat (Fr). A vineyard in the A.C. Saint-Émilion, Bordeaux. 7 ha.

Château Tramont (Fr). A vineyard in the commune of Arcins. A.C. Haut-Médoc, Bordeaux.

Château Trapaud (Fr). Address = Saint-Étienne-de-Lisse, 33330 Saint-Émilion. Grand Cru. A.C. Saint-Émilion. Commune = Saint-Étienne-de-Lisse. 14.5 ha. Grape varieties – Bouchet 30%, Cabernet sauvignon 20% and Merlot 50%.

Château Trapeau (Fr). A vineyard in the A.C. Saint-Émilion, Bordeaux. 8 ha.

Château Trianon (Fr). A vineyard in the Côtes-Saint-Émilion. A.C. Saint-Émilion, Bordeaux. 5 ha.

Château Trillon (Fr). A vineyard in the commune of Sauternes. A.C. Sauternes, Bordeaux. 8 ha.

Château Trimoulet (Fr). Address = 33330 Saint-Émilion. Grand Cru Classé. A.C. Saint-Émilion. Commune = Saint-Émilion. 17 ha. Grape varieties – Cabernet franc 35%, Cabernet sauvignon 15% and Merlot 50%.

Château Trinité-Valrosé (Fr). A vineyard on the Île de Patiras in the river Gironde. A.C. Bordeaux Supérieur.

Château Trintin (Fr). Part of Château Boënot in A.C. Pomerol, Bordeaux.

Château Tristant (Fr). A vineyard in the commune of Pomerol. A.C. Pomerol, Bordeaux. 1 ha.

C

Château Trois-Moulins (Fr). A vineyard in the commune of Saint-Émilion. A.C. Saint-Émilion, Bordeaux. Grand Cru. 4.5 ha.

Château Tronquoy-Lalande (Fr). Cru Grand Bourgeois. A.C. Saint-Estèphe. Commune = Saint-Estèphe. 16 ha. Grape varieties – Cabernet sauvignon 50%, Merlot 45% and Petit verdot 5%.

Château Troplong-Mondot (Fr). Address = 33330 Saint-Émilion. Grand Cru Classé. A.C. Saint-Émilion. Commune = Saint-Émilion. 30 ha. Grape varieties – Bouchet, Cabernet sauvignon, Malbec and Merlot 70%.

Château Trotanoy (Fr). A vineyard in the commune of Pomerol. A.C. Pomerol, Bordeaux. 9 ha.

Château Trottevieille (Fr). Address = 33330 Saint-Émilion. Premier Grand Cru Classé. A.C. Saint-Émilion. Commune = Saint-Émilion. 11 ha. Grape varieties – Bouchet, Cabernet and Merlot.

Château Truquet (Fr). A vineyard in the A.C. Saint-Émilion, Bordeaux. 4 ha.

Château Tucau (Fr). A vineyard in the commune of Barsac. A.C. Barsac (or Sauternes), Bordeaux. 3 ha.

Château Tuquet (Fr). A vineyard in the commune of Beautiran. A.C. Graves, Bordeaux. 26 ha. (red and white).

Château Turon Lanère [Dalas] (Fr). A vineyard in the commune of Loupiac. A.C. Loupiac, Bordeaux. 3 ha.

Château Turon Lanère [David] (Fr). A vineyard in the commune of Loupiac. A.C. Loupiac, Bordeaux. 5 ha.

Château Tustoc (Fr). A vineyard in the commune of Toulenne. A.C. Graves, Bordeaux. 8 ha. (white).

Château Uferic (Fr). A vineyard in the commune of Cérons. A.C. Cérons, Bordeaux. 6 ha.

Château Val-Joanis (Fr). A vineyard in the V.D.Q.S. Côtes de Lubéron, southeastern France. (red, rosé and white).

Château Valley Red (N.Z.). A soft, fruity, full-flavoured red wine from Nobilo's vineyard.

Château Valmont-Mayne (Fr). A vineyard in the commune of Barsac. A.C. Barsac (or Sauternes), Bordeaux. 2 ha.

Château Valose (Fr). A.C. Bordeaux Supérieur (red).

Château Valoux (Fr). A vineyard in the commune of Cadaujac. A.C. Graves, Bordeaux. Cru Bourgeois.

Château Védrines (Fr). A vineyard in the commune of Barsac. A.C. Barsac (or Sauternes), Bordeaux.

Château Verdet (Fr). A vineyard in the commune of Libourne. A.C. Pomerol, Bordeaux.

Château Verdignan (Fr). Address = St-Seurin-de-Cadourne, 33250 Pauillac. Cru Grand Bourgeois. A.C. Haut-Médoc. Commune = Saint-Seurin-de-Cadourne. 50 ha. Grape varieties – Cabernet franc 5%, Cabernet sauvignon 50% and Merlot 45%.

Château Verdus et Bardis (Fr). A vineyard in the commune of St-Seurin-de-Cadourne. A.C. Haut-Médoc, Bordeaux. Cru Bourgeois. Address = St-Seurin-de-Cadourne, 33250 Pauillac.

Château Verger (Fr). A vineyard in the A.C. Côtes de Bourg, Bordeaux.

Château Vernous (Fr). A vineyard in the commune of Lesparre. A.C. Médoc, Bordeaux. 15 ha.

Château Vertheuil (Fr). A vineyard in the commune of Sainte-Croix-du-Mont. A.C. Sainte-Croix-du-Mont, Bordeaux. 10 ha.

Château Vésinerie (Fr). A vineyard in the commune of Puisseguin-Saint-Émilion. A.C. Saint-Émilion, Bordeaux.

Château Veyrac (Fr). A vineyard in the commune of Saint-Étienne-de-Lisse. A.C. Saint-Émilion, Bordeaux. 3 ha.

Château Veyres (Fr). A vineyard in the commune of Preignac. A.C. Sauternes, Bordeaux. 10 ha.

Château Veyrin (Fr). A vineyard in the commune of Listrac. A.C. Médoc, Bordeaux. Cru Bourgeois.

Château Veyrin-Domecq (Fr). See Château Veyrin.

Château Victoria (Fr). A vineyard in the commune of Vertheuil. A.C. Médoc, Bordeaux. Cru Bourgeois.

Château Videau (Fr). A vineyard in the A.C. Côtes de Blaye, Bordeaux.

Château Videlot (Fr). A vineyard in the commune of Libourne. A.C. Saint-Émilion, Bordeaux.

Château Vieille-Tour-la-Rose (Fr). A vineyard in the A.C. Saint-Émilion, Bordeaux. 3 ha.

Châteauvieux (Switz). The name of a red wine produced in Sion, Valais, western Switzerland.

Château Vieux (Arg). The brand-name of a red wine produced by Bodegas Lopez from the Cabernet sauvignon grape.

Château Vieux Blassan (Fr). A.C. Bordeaux Supérieur.

Château Vieux Bonneau (Fr). A vineyard in the commune of Montagne-Saint-Émilion. A.C. Saint-Émilion, Bordeaux. 4 ha.

Château Vieux Braneyre (Fr). Address = Les Gunes, Cissac-Médoc 33250 Pauillac. A.C. Haut-Médoc. Commune = Cissac. 10 ha. Grape varieties – Cabernet franc, Cabernet sauvignon, Merlot and Petit verdot.

C

Château Vieux Cantenac (Fr). Address = Cantenac, 33330 Saint-Émilion. Grand Cru. A.C. Saint-Émilion. Commune = Saint-Émilion. 5 ha. Grape varieties – Bouchet, Cabernet, Merlot.

Château Vieux-Castel-Robin (Fr). A vineyard in the A.C. Saint-Émilion, Bordeaux. 4 ha.

Château Vieux-Ceps (Fr). A vineyard in the A.C. Saint-Émilion, Bordeaux. 6 ha.

Château Vieux-Château-Certan (Fr). A vineyard in the commune of Pomerol. A.C. Pomerol, Bordeaux. 13 ha. Grape varieties – Cabernet franc 25%, Cabernet sauvignon 20%, Malbec 5% and Merlot 50%.

Château Vieux-Château-Landon (Fr). A vineyard in the commune of Bégadan. Bordeaux.

Château Vieux Château-St-André (Fr). Address = Montagne-Saint-Émilion, 33330 Saint-Émilion. A.C. Montagne-Saint-Émilion. Commune = Montagne-Saint-Émilion.

Château Vieux Chevrol (Fr). A vineyard in the commune of Néac. A.C. Saint-Émilion, Bordeaux.

Château Vieux Clos St-Émilion (Fr). Address = 33330 Saint-Émilion. Grand Cru. A.C. Saint-Émilion. Commune = Saint-Émilion. Grape varieties – Cabernet franc 25%, Cabernet sauvignon 20%, Malbec 5% and Merlot 50%.

Château Vieux Garouilh (Fr). A vineyard in the A.C. Saint-Émilion, Bordeaux. 5 ha.

Château Vieux Grand Faurie (Fr). Address = Saint-Christophe-des-Bardes, 33330 Saint-Émilion. Grand Cru. A.C. Saint-Émilion. 10 ha. Grape varieties – Cabernet franc 15%, Cabernet sauvignon 15% and Merlot 70%. Second wine is Château Champion.

Château Vieux Guadet (Fr). Address = Place du Marcardieu, 33330 Saint-Émilion. Grand Cru. A.C. Saint-Émilion.

Château Vieux-Guillou (Fr). A vineyard in the commune of Saint-Georges-Saint-Émilion. A.C. Saint-Émilion, Bordeaux. 4 ha.

Château Vieux-Guinot (Fr). Address = Saint-Étienne-de-Lisse, 33330 Saint-Émilion. Grand Cru Classé. A.C. Saint-Émilion. Commune = Saint-Étienne-de-Lisse. 12 ha. Grape varieties – Cabernet franc 45%, Cabernet sauvignon 5% and Merlot 50%.

Château Vieux-Larmande (Fr). A vineyard in the A.C. Saint-Émilion, Bordeaux. 4 ha.

Château Vieux-Logis-de-Cazelon (Fr). A vineyard in the commune of Montagne-Saint-Émilion. A.C. Saint-Émilion, Bordeaux. 2 ha.

Château Vieux-Maillet (Fr). A vineyard in the commune of Pomerol. A.C. Pomerol, Bordeaux. 1 ha.

Château Vieux Montaiguillon (Fr). A vineyard in the commune of Saint-Georges-Saint-Émilion. A.C. Saint-Émilion, Bordeaux. 3 ha.

Château Vieux-Mouchet (Fr). A vineyard in the commune of Montagne-Saint-Émilion. A.C. Saint-Émilion, Bordeaux. 1 ha.

Château Vieux Moulin (Fr). A vineyard in the commune of Fronsac. A.C. Côtes de Fronsac, Bordeaux. 5 ha.

Château Vieux-Moulin-du-Cadet (Fr). A vineyard in the A.C. Saint-Émilion, Bordeaux. 3 ha.

Château Vieux-Pourret (Fr). Address = 33330 Saint-Émilion. Grand Cru. A.C. Saint-Émilion. 4.2 ha. Grape varieties – Cabernet franc 25% and Merlot 75%.

Château Vieux Robin (Fr). Address = Bégadan, 33340 Lesparre. Cru Bourgeois. A.C. Médoc. Commune = Bégadan. 13 ha. Grape varieties – Cabernet sauvignon 65% and Merlot 35%.

Château Vieux-Sarpe (Fr). Address = 37, Rue Pline Parmentier, 33500 Libourne. Grand Cru. A.C. Saint-Émilion. Commune = Saint-Christophe-des-Bardes. 6.5 ha. Grape varieties – Cabernet franc 20%, Cabernet sauvignon 10% and Merlot 70%.

Château Vignelaure (Fr). A red wine estate near Aix-en-Provence, south-eastern France. A.C. Provence.

Château Vignes (Fr). A vineyard in the commune of Fronsac. A.C. Côtes de Fronsac, Bordeaux. 2 ha.

Château Villars (Fr). A vineyard in the commune of Saillans. A.C. Fronsac, Bordeaux. Address = 33141 Villegouge. 12 ha.

Château Villefranche (Fr). A vineyard in the commune of Barsac. A.C. Barsac (or Sauternes), Bordeaux. 6 ha.

Château Villegeorge (Fr). Address = 33480 Castelnau de Médoc. A.C. Haut-Médoc. Commune = Avensan. 20 ha. Grape varieties – Cabernet franc, Cabernet sauvignon and Merlot.

Château Villemaurine (Fr). Address = BP N°31 au Domaine de Louiseau, 33240 Saint André de Cubzac. Grand Cru Classé. A.C. Saint-Émilion. Commune = Saint-Émilion. 8 ha. Grape varieties – Cabernet 30% and Merlot 70%

Château Vincent (Fr). A vineyard in the commune of Cantenac. A.C. Haut-Médoc, Bordeaux. 1 ha.

Château Vincent (Fr). A vineyard in the commune of St-Aignan. A.C. Fronsac,

Bordeaux. Address = 33126 Fronsac, Gironde. 12 ha. Is jointly owned.

Château Vincent la Mouleyre (Fr). A vineyard in the commune of St-Aignan. A.C. Côtes Canon-Fronsac, Bordeaux. 2 ha.

Château Viramon (Fr). Address = Saint-Étienne-de-Lisse, 33330 Saint-Émilion. Grand Cru. A.C. Saint-Émilion. 11 ha. Grape varieties – Cabernet 30% and Merlot 70%.

Château Voigny (Fr). A vineyard in the commune of Preignac. A.C. Sauternes, Bordeaux. 6 ha. Cru Bourgeois. Grape varieties – Sauvignon and Sémillon.

Château Vrai Canon Bouché (Fr). A vineyard in the commune Fronsac, A.C. Côtes Canon-Fronsac, Bordeaux. 5 ha.

Château Vrai Canon Bourret (Fr). A vineyard in the commune of Fronsac. A.C. Côtes Canon-Fronsac, Bordeaux. 2 ha.

Château Vrai Canon Boyer (Fr). A vineyard in the commune of St-Michel. A.C. Côtes Canon-Fronsac, Bordeaux. 7 ha.

Château Vraye-Croix-de-Gay (Fr). A vineyard in the commune of Pomerol. A.C. Pomerol, Bordeaux. 6 ha.

Château Wente (USA). A white, Sauternes-style wine produced by the Wente Bros. in Livermore, California.

Château Windsor (Isr). A semi-dry, red table wine.

Château Woltner (USA). A winery based in the Howell Mountains, Saint Helena, Napa Valley, California. Produces varietal wines.

Château Yaldara (Austr). A winery in the Barossa Valley, South Australia. Produces varietal wines.

Château Yarrinya Winery (Austr). Address = Pinnade Lane, Dixons Creek, Yarra Valley, Victoria. 18 ha. Grape varieties – Cabernet sauvignon, Chardonnay, Gewürztraminer, Pinot noir, Sauvignon blanc and Shiraz.

Château Yelas (N.Z.). The brand-name used by Pleasant Valley Wines of Valley Road, Henderson.

Château Yon (Fr). A vineyard in the commune of Saint-Christophe-des-Bardes. A.C. Saint-Émilion, Bordeaux.

Château Yon-Figeac (Fr). Address = 33330 Saint-Émilion. Grand Cru Classé. A.C. Saint-Émilion. Commune = Saint-Émilion. 24 ha. Grape varieties – Bouchet, Cabernet sauvignon and Merlot.

Château Yveline (Fr). A vineyard in the commune of Lalande de Pomerol. A.C. Lalande de Pomerol, Bordeaux.

Château Xanadu (Austr). Address = P.O. Box 99. Margaret River, Western Australia 6285. 35 ha. Grape varieties –

Cabernet franc, Cabernet sauvignon, Chardonnay, Sauvignon blanc and Sémillon.

Châtelaine (Fr). A female Château (vineyard) owner.

Chatelots (Les) (Fr). A Premier Cru vineyard in the A.C. commune of Chambolle-Musigny, Côte de Nuits, Burgundy. 2.6 ha.

Châtenets (Les) (Fr). A wine-producing village in the commune of Fuissé in A.C. Pouilly-Fuissé Mâcon, Burgundy.

Chatenois (Fr). A wine town in Alsace. Known in German as Kestenholz.

Châtillon-en-Diois (Fr). V.D.Q.S. region of the Rhône. Produces red, rosé and white wines. Minimum alc. by vol. (red) = 11%, (white) = 10%.

Châtillon-sur-Marne (Fr). A Cru Champagne village in the Canton de Châtillon-sur-Marne. District = Reims.

Châtillon-sur-Marne (Fr). Canton in the Reims district of the Champagne region. Has the Cru villages of – Baslieux, Belval-sous-Châtillon, Binson-Orquigny, Champlat-Boujacourt, Châtillon-sur-Marne, Courtagnon, Cuchery, Cuisles, Jonquery, Montigny-sous-Châtillon, La Neuville-aux-Larris, Olizy-Viuolaine, Passy-Grigny, Pourcy, Reuil, Sainte-Gemme, Vandières and Villers-sous-Châtillon.

Chaucé Gris (USA). A white grape variety grown in Santa Cruz and in Livermore, California. Also known as the Grey riesling.

Chaudenet Gras (Fr). A lesser name for the Aligoté grape in eastern France.

Chaudière (Fr). An onion-shaped pot-still used in the Cognac region for distillation.

Chauffe Coeur (Fr). A 6 and 10 year old Cognac produced by Martayrol.

Chauffe Coeur Napoléon (Fr). A 10 year old Cognac produced by Martayrol.

Chaufferettes (Fr). A frost precaution used in the Burgundy region. The use of burners in the vineyards.

Chauffe-Vin (Fr). A type of holding tank (heat exchanger) used in the Cognac region.

Chaume (Fr). A vineyard in the Coteaux du Layon, Anjou-Saumur region in the Loire. Produces fine, luscious sweet (botrytis cinerea) white wines.

Chaumes (Les) (Fr). A Premier Cru vineyard in the A.C. commune of Vosne-Romanée, Côte de Nuits, Burgundy. 7.4ha.

Chaumuzy (Fr). A Cru Champagne village in the Canton de Ville-en-Tardenois. District = Reims.

C

Chautagne (Fr). A light red wine produced from the Gamay grape in the Savoie region, south-eastern France.

Chautauqua (USA). A wine region of eastern USA. A strip that follows along the south bank of Lake Erie from Buffalo west to Ohio. The Concord is the main grape variety used.

Chauvenet (Fr). A Burgundy négociant based in Nuits-Saint-Georges. Noted for Red Cap sparkling Burgundy.

Chauvet (Fr). Champagne house. Address = 11 Avenue de Champagne, 51150 Tours-sur-Marne. 10 ha. Produces – Vintage and non-vintage wines. Vintages – 1971, 1973, 1976, 1979, 1982.

Chauvet Vineyard (USA). A small vineyard based in Sonoma Valley, Sonoma County, California. Grape variety – Zinfandel.

Chave (Gérard) (Fr). A wine producer based in Hermitage, Rhône. Produces red and white Hermitage wines.

Chàvena (Port). Tea cup.

Chavignol (Fr). A wine-producing village in A.C. Sancerre, Central Vineyards, Loire. Includes the vineyard of Les Monts Damnés.

Chavot-Courcourt (Fr). A Cru Champagne village in the Canton d'Avize. District = Epernay.

Chazalettes and Co (It). Noted Vermouth producers based in Turin.

Chazelles (Les) (Fr). A vineyard in the A.C. commune of Montagny, Côte Chalonnaise, Burgundy.

Cheater (Can). A short glass that has a line marked on the side which shows ⅝ of an ounce short. It is a dishonest glass.

Cheb Brewery (Czec). A brewery based in western Czec.

Cheddar Valley Vineyards (Eng). Address = Townsend Farm, Axbridge, Somerset. Planted 1974. 1.25 ha.

Cheerio Cocktail (Cktl). 1/12 gill Italian vermouth, 1/12 gill French vermouth, ⅙ gill dry Gin, 1 tablespoon orange juice, dash Orange bitters, 2 dashes Absinthe. Shake over ice, strain into a cocktail glass.

Cheers (Eng). A salutation with a drink. Denotes 'Good health and thank you' (for the drink purchased for you).

Cheese (Eng). Milled cider apples layered between a fine mesh cloth for pressing. See Cheese Cloth.

Cheese Cloth (Eng). A fine mesh cloth used in cider making to contain the Cheese so it can be pressed to extract the juice. Hence the name 'Cheese' cloth.

Cheesy (Eng). A term used to describe the characteristic element in the bouquet of an old Champagne. Is caused by the presence of Butyrate acid.

Chef de Cave (Fr). The head cellarman.

Chef de Culture (Fr). The vineyard foreman.

Chef du Vignoble (Fr). The head of the vineyard. Chief vigneron.

Chef-Huisknecht (Hol). Butler.

Chefoo (China). The name given to a sweet red wine, similar in style to a light, fortified wine and to a strong, aromatic white wine.

Cheilly-lès-Maranges (Fr). A commune in the A.C. Santenay, Côte de Beaune-Villages, Burgundy. Has the vineyards of Maranges [part], La Boutière [part], Les Maranges [part] and Les Plantes. The red wines (from the Pinot noir grape) may be sold under the Côte de Beaune-Villages label.

Chelois (USA). A red hybrid grape variety.

Chelsea Gin (Eng). The brand-name of a dry Gin produced by International Distillers and Vintners Ltd., London.

Chelsea Reach (Cktl). In a highball glass place 2 ice cubes and add 2 ozs. Vodka, 2 ozs. orange squash. Top with medium-dry cider.

Chelsea Sidecar (Cktl). ½ measure dry Gin, ½ measure Cointreau, juice ¼ lemon. Shake over ice, strain into a cocktail glass.

Chelsea Sunshine (N.Z.). The name given to the sugar and water solution that is added to some grape musts to increase the alcohol content.

Cheltenham (Eng). A still aperient mineral water from mid-western England.

Chemakhinsk (USSR). A major wine-producing centre in Azerbaijan.

Chemical Additives to Wines (Eng). See Carbon-dioxide, Gypsum, Plâtage, Phosphotage, Salage, Shellisage, Sulphur-dioxide and Tanisage.

Chemical Beer (Eng). A mis-used term for many beers. Relates to the addition of minerals to waters that are mineral-deficient. The law does not allow any 'chemicals' to be added to beers. See German Purity Law.

Chemilly-sur-Serein (Fr). A commune in the A.C. Chablis, Burgundy.

Chemise (Fr). The name given to the coating or deposit that collects on the inside of red wine bottles.

Chénas (Fr). A commune of the A.C. Cru Beaujolais-Villages, Burgundy. 220 ha. under vines.

Chenay (Fr). A Cru Champagne village in the Canton of Fismes. District = Reims.

Chêne (Fr). Oak.

Chêne (Fr). A term used to describe the

oaky character that wine obtains from the wooden casks.

Chenel (S.Afr). A white grape variety. A cross between the Chenin blanc and Trebbiano.

Chénevery (Les) (Fr). A Premier Cru vineyard [part] in the A.C. commune of Morey-Saint-Denis, Côte de Nuits, Burgundy. 3.25 ha.

Chénevottes (Les) (Fr). A Premier Cru vineyard [part] in the A.C. commune of Chassagne-Montrachet, Côte de Beaune, Burgundy. (red and white).

Chenin Blanc (Fr). The chief white grape of the Anjou-Saumur and Touraine regions of the Loire. Makes both dry and sweet white wines.

Chenin Blanc (USA). See California Chenin Blanc.

Chenin Noir (Fr). A red grape variety. Also known as the Pineau d'Aunis.

Chenite (USA). A dark, rosé wine produced from the Chenin blanc and Petit syrah grapes. Produced by Cilurzo and Piconi in Temecula, California.

Chenôve (Fr). A Burgundy vineyard (1920) which used to be of 52 ha. but has now been absorbed into the suburbs of Dijon. Has almost disappeared.

Chenu (Fr). Lit – 'The white hair of old age'. A term used to denote a fine wine of old age.

Chequer Bitter (Eng). A keg Bitter 1036.5 O.G. brewed by the Davenports Brewery, Birmingham.

Chequers (Scot). A 12 year old De Luxe blended Scotch whisky produced by McEwan and Co. 40% alc. by vol.

Cher (Fr). A Vins de Pays area in the Loir-et-Cher Département, central-western France. Produces red, rosé and dry white wines.

Chérac (Fr). A commune in the Charente-Maritime Département whose grapes are classed Borderies (Cognac).

Chereau (Fr). A large producer of Muscadet in the Pays Nantais district of the Loire region.

Cheribon (E.Ind). A coffee-producing region in Java.

Cherinac (Sp). The alternative spelling of Jeriñac.

Cheri Sling (Cktl). 2 ozs. Chéri-Suisse, 1½ ozs. dry Gin. Shake over ice, strain into a highball glass, add a dash of lime juice, top with soda.

Chéri-Suisse (Switz). A cherry and chocolate liqueur.

Cheri Tonic (Cktl). 2 ozs. Chéri-Suisse, 1 oz. lime juice. Shake over ice, strain into a highball glass, top with soda water.

Cherristock (It). A cherry-flavoured liqueur.

Cherry (Eng). The name given to the fruit of the coffee tree because of its cherry-like appearance.

Cherry Alexander (Cktl). ½ measure Cherry brandy, ½ measure Crème de Cacao, ¼ measure cream. Shake over ice, strain into a cocktail glass.

Cherry 'B' (Eng). A cherry wine produced by Showerings.

Cherry B Cream (Eng). A Devon cream, Brandy and Cherry liqueur produced by Showerings.

Cherry Bestle (Den). A local cherry-flavoured liqueur.

Cherry Blossom Cocktail (Cktl). ⅔ measure Brandy, ⅓ measure Cherry brandy, dash lemon juice, dash Grenadine, dash Curaçao. Shake over ice, strain into a cocktail glass. The glass may be frosted with Cherry brandy and castor sugar.

Cherry Blossom Liqueur (Jap). A delicate pink liqueur with a strong fragrance of Japanese cherry blossoms.

Cherrybom (Port). A cherry liqueur produced by J.M. Fonseca.

Cherry Bounce (USA). A cordial made by boiling the strained juice of cherries. Add lemon peel, cinnamon, cloves, all-spice, mace and sugar to taste. Add ½ pint of Brandy to every 1 gallon (US) of juice. Drink hot or cold.

Cherry Brandy Liqueur (Euro). Produced by the maceration of fruit in spirit 22–25% alc. by vol.

Cherry Brandy Punch (Punch). 1 pint boiling water, juice of 2 lemons, ½ lb. sugar. Bring back to boil, simmer 5 minutes, add 1 bottle deep red wine, ¼ pint Cherry brandy. Heat slowly, add slices of orange and lemon.

Cherry Brandy Vichniovaia (USSR). A cherry-based spirit.

Cherry 'B' White (Eng). A white, cherry-flavoured wine from Showerings.

Cherry Cobbler (Cktl). Place ⅕ gill Cherry brandy into an ice-filled highball glass. Top with dry white wine. Dress with a slice of orange.

Cherry Cocktail (Cktl). ¼ gill cherry syrup, ¼ gill ginger syrup, 2 dashes lime syrup and 1 dash Angostura. Stir over ice, strain into a highball glass. Top with soda and serve with slices of orange and a cherry.

Cherry Coke (USA). A cola drink with a cherry taste produced by the Coca Cola and Schweppes Beverage Company.

Cherry Cooler (Cktl). 1½ ozs. Cherry brandy, juice of ½ lemon, ½ teaspoon castor sugar. Shake well over ice, strain into a highball glass over ice, top with soda.

Cherry Daiquiri (Cktl). ½ measure white

Rum, ¼ measure Cherry brandy, ¼ measure lemon juice. Shake over ice, strain into a cocktail glass.

Cherry Fizz (Cktl). ⅓ measure Cherry brandy, juice ½ lemon. Shake over ice, strain into an ice-filled highball glass. Top with soda water and a cherry.

Cherry Flavoured Brandy (USA). A brandy-based liqueur infused with cherries

Cherry Flip (Cktl). ⅓ gill Cherry brandy, 1 egg, 1 teaspoon powdered sugar, ⅛ gill cream. Shake well over ice, strain into a flip glass. Top with grated nutmeg.

Cherry Heering (Den). A very popular cherry-flavoured liqueur. Produced by Peter Heering.

Cherry Hill Vineyard (Eng). Address = Nettlestead, Kent. Planted 1966, 1 ha. Soil – Greensand. Grape varieties – Müller-Thurgau 98%, Siebel 13053 1% and Seyve Villard 1%. Vinified at Lamberhurst.

Cherry Julep (It). An apéritif wine produced for the USA market.

Cherry Karise (Den). A local cherry-flavoured liqueur.

Cherry Kirsberry (Den). A Danish brand-name cherry wine.

Cherry Liqueur (USA). Produced from small black wild cherries by the maceration technique.

Cherry Marnier (Fr). A Dalmatia black cherry liqueur. 23% alc. by vol. Produced in Paris.

Cherry Nalivika (USSR). A cherry liqueur.

Cherry Pepsi (USA). A cherry-flavoured cola drink produced by Pepsi-Cola World Wide Beverages Company.

Cherrypicker's (Eng). See Alford Arms.

Cherry Ricky (Cktl). Place some ice in a highball glass, add juice of a small lime, 2 measures Cherry brandy, stir and top with Perrier mineral water.

Cherry Rocher (Fr). A large liqueur producer. Address = La Côte St. André, Vienne. Produces Cherry Rocher (a cherry liqueur), Guignolet and many fruit and herb liqueurs.

Cherry Rum Cocktail (Cktl). ⅓ gill Jamaican rum, ⅛ gill Cherry brandy, ⅛ gill cream. Shake over ice, strain into a cocktail glass.

Cherrys (Ire). Part of the Guinness-controlled Irish Ale Breweries based in Waterford, south-eastern Eire.

Cherry Sling (Cktl). ⅓ gill Cherry brandy, juice ½ lemon. Stir over ice in an old-fashioned glass. Top with a twist of lemon peel juice.

Cherry Sour (Cktl). Place 1 measure

Cherry brandy into an ice-filled highball glass. Add 1 sugar cube and the juice of a lemon. Stir, top with soda water and decorate with a slice of orange and lemon.

Cherry Sour Simple (Cktl). ⅕ gill Cherry brandy in an ice-filled highball glass. Top with iced lemonade and a slice of lemon.

Cherry Stock (It). A cherry liqueur produced by Stock in Trieste. 24% alc. by vol. from the juice of maraska cherries.

Cherry Triple (Cktl). ⅔ measure Cherry brandy, ⅓ measure Triple Sec. Stir over ice in a highball glass. Add juice of ½ lemon. Top with soda water.

Cherry Whiskey (Fr). A cherry-flavoured whiskey liqueur. Also known as Chesky, Gean Whiskey, Geen Whiskey, Guyne Whiskey.

Cherry Whisky (Cktl). ½ gill Scotch whisky, ½ teaspoon Angostura, 1 teaspoon Grenadine. Stir over broken ice, strain into a wine glass. Decorate with a cherry and a dash of lemon peel juice.

Cherry Wine Cocktail (Cktl).(1). ¾ fl.oz. Danish cherry liqueur, ¾ fl.oz. dry Gin, juice ½ lime. Shake over ice, strain into a cocktail glass.

Cherry Wine Cocktail (Cktl).(2). ½ measure Danish cherry wine, ½ measure Vodka, juice ½ lime. Shake over ice, strain into a cocktail glass.

Cherry Wine Collins (Cktl). ¾ fl.oz. Danish cherry wine, ¾ fl.oz. dry Gin, juice ½ lime. Mix well over ice, strain into a highball glass. Top with soda.

Cherson (USSR). A wine-producing region based in the Ukraine.

Cherveno Vino (Bul). Red wine.

Cherves (Fr). A commune in the Charente-Maritime Département whose grapes are classed Borderies (Cognac).

Cheshire English Pub Beer (Eng). A bottled Ale 1045 O.G. produced by the Greenhall Whitley Brewery, Warrington, Cheshire for the USA market.

Chesima (E.Asia). A plant used in the production of Oolong teas which gives the tea a unique flavour. (Often flavoured with jasmine).

Chesky (Fr). A cherry-flavoured Whiskey liqueur produced by Fremy.

Chess (Swe). A light-styled Ale 5.6% alc. by vol. brewed by the Pripps Brewery.

Cheste (Sp). A Denominación de Origen wine-producing region within the province of Valencia in southern Spain. Grape varieties – Macabéo, Merseguera, Muscat, Pedro Ximénez, Planta fina and Planta nora. Produces mainly white wines.

Chester Brown (Eng). See Old Chester.

C

Chesterfield Ale (USA). A bottom-fermented, dry-hopped Ale brewed by the Yuengling Brewery, Pottsville, Pennsylvania.

Chester Gold (Eng). See Old Glory.

Chesters Brewery (Eng). A brewery of Whitbreads. Known as the Manchester Trading Company and Salford Brewery. Produces cask conditioned Chester Best Mild 1033 O.G. and Chesters Best Bitter 1034 O.G. Sold under the name of Duttons in the north of England.

Chestnut Mild (Eng). A dark, keg Mild 1033 O.G. brewed by the John Smith Brewery in Tadcaster, Yorkshire.

Cheurlin et Fils (Fr). Champagne producer. Address = Gye-sur-Seine, 10250 Mussysur-Seine. 25 ha. Produces – Non-vintage wines. All the remuage is done by hand. Top cuvée is Prestige Brut.

Cheval Blanc (Fr). See Château Cheval Blanc.

Chevalier (Yves) (Fr). A noted wine producer based at Turquant, Saumur, Anjou-Saumur, Loire. Noted for his Saumur Mousseux.

Chevalier d'Alsace (Fr). Alsatian white wines that have been made from noble grape varieties that have been gathered after the prescribed harvest date. See also Flambeau d'Alsace.

Chevalier de Stérimberg (Le) (Fr). the name of a white A.C. Hermitage produced by Jaboulet Aîné in the Côtes du Rhône.

Chevalier et Fils (Fr). A Burgundy négociant based in Charney les Mâcon, Mâconnais, Burgundy.

Chevalier Marin (Bel). A Pilsener-style Beer brewed by the Artois Brasserie in Louvain.

Chevalier-Montrachet (Fr). A Grand Cru vineyard in the A.C. commune of Puligny-Montrachet, Côte de Beaune, Burgundy. 7.1 ha.

Chevaliers Bretvin (Fr). A noted wine brotherhood of Nantes in the western Loire. Is the fourth oldest in France. Is mainly concerned with the wines of the Pays Nantais. Has branches world-wide. Its president is always the Marquis de Goulaine.

Chevaliers de la Chantepleure (Fr). A wine brotherhood based in Vouvray, Touraine, Loire.

Chevaliers de Sancerre (Fr). A wine society based in Sancerre, Central Vineyards, Loire.

Chevaliers du Sacavin (Fr). A wine brotherhood based in Angers, Anjou-Saumur, Loire.

Chevaliers du Tastevin (Fr). Burgundy growers' and wine merchants' body to promote the sale of their wines.

Cheverny (Fr). A V.D.Q.S. white wine district in the Loire Valley. Produces red, rosé and white wines.

Chevier (Fr). The local name for the Sémillon grape in Bordeaux along the river Dordogne.

Chevrets (Les) (Fr). A Premier Cru vineyard in the A.C. commune of Volnay, Côte de Beaune, Burgundy. 6 ha.

Chevrier Blanc (USA). A white wine produced by the Vichon Winery, Napa Valley, California. Made from a blend of Sauvignon blanc and Sémillon grapes.

Chewy (Eng). A term used to describe full-bodied wines. Similar to meaty.

Cheys (Fr). The name given to the walls that retain soil in the terraced vineyards of the Côte Rôtie in the northern Rhône. Also called Murgeys.

Chia Fan (China). A noted brand of Rice wine produced in Shanghai. See also Shao-Hsing Rice Wine.

Chiai Della Furba (It). A red Vini da Tavola wine made from ⅓ Merlot and other grape varieties in central-western Italy.

Chianti (It). D.O.C.G. red wine from Tuscany. (Arezzo, Florence, Pisa, Pistoia and Siena districts). Produced from the Canaiolo nero, Malvasia del chianti, Sangiovese (main variety) and Trebbiano toscano grapes. Made using the Governo process. If the minimum total alc. content is 12% by vol. and aged 2 years then called Vecchio. If 3 years then Riserva. See Chianti Classico, Chianti Putto and Ruffino.

Chianti (USA). See California Chianti.

Chianti Classico (It). See Classico and Chianti. Has a Black Cockerel (Gallo Nero) as it's symbol. Minimum alc. content 12.5% by vol. If aged 2 years in cask then called Vecchio. If 3 years then is called Riserva. Founded in 1924.

Chianti Colli Arentini (It). D.O.C.G. Chianti area that doesn't belong to either Chianti Classico or Chianti Putto.

Chianti Colli Fiorentini (It). D.O.C.G. Chianti area that doesn't belong to either Chianti Classico or Chianti Putto.

Chianti Colline Pisane (It). D.O.C.G. Chianti area that doesn't belong to either Chianti Classico or Chianti Putto.

Chianti Colli Senesi (It). D.O.C.G. Chianti area that doesn't belong to either Chianti Classico or Chianti Putto.

Chiantigiana (It). A special Chianti bottle of 175 centilitres.

Chianti Magni (It). A Chianti Classico producer based in Tuscany.

Chianti Montalbano (It). D.O.C.G. Chianti area that doesn't belong to either Chianti Classico or Chianti Putto.

C

Chianti Putto (It). ,D.O.C.G. Chianti Consorzio founded in 1927. Set up by producers similar to Chianti Classico. Has a Cherub as its logo.

Chianti Rufina (It). D.O.C.G. Chianti area that doesn't belong to either Chianti Classico or Chianti Putto.

Chianti Superiore (It). Produced in the Classico district, the wine uses neither the Classico or D.O.C.G. seals. Instead it sells under the name of the producer Marchese Vittorio Frescobaldi.

Chian Wine (Gre). A dark, red, sweet, heavy wine produced on the island of Chios. Has a long historical fame.

Chiaretto (It). Very light red wines. Lit – 'Claret'.

Chiaretto (It). Pale pink. Used when describing rosé wines.

Chiaretto del Garda (It). A deep-coloured, rosé wine of the Lombardy region produced on the southern shores of Lake Garda. Made from the Sangiovese grape.

Chiarire (It). Clarify.

Chiarli (It). Noted wine-producers based in Modena, Emilia-Romagna, north-eastern Italy.

Chiaro (It). Clear.

Chiavennasca (It). The Lombardy name for the Nebbiolo grape.

Chic (It). A De Luxe beer brewed by the Birra Bellizona Brewery of Ticino.

Chica (S.Am). A spirit produced from fermented maize by the Indians in Peru. Also made from molasses.

Chicago Bomb Cocktail (Cktl). ½ measure (green) Crème de Menthe, ½ measure (white) Crème de Cacao, 1 scoop vanilla ice cream. Blend together in a blender. Pour into a flute glass.

Chicago Cocktail (Cktl).(1). ½ gill Brandy, 3 dashes Curaçao, dash Angostura. Stir over ice, strain into a cocktail glass. Top with iced Champagne, add a squeeze of lemon peel juice on top. Also known as a Fancy Brandy Cocktail.

Chicago Cocktail (Cktl).(2). ⅓ gill Brandy, 2 dashes Triple Sec, 1 dash Angostura. Sugar the rim (with orange juice) of an old-fashioned glass. Shake ingredients over ice, strain into a glass.

Chicago Fizz (Cktl). ½ measure Port, ½ measure Jamaican Rum, juice ½ lemon, 1 teaspoon powdered sugar, 1 egg white. Shake well over ice, strain into an ice-filled highball glass. Top with soda water.

Chicama Vineyards (USA). A winery based on Martha's Vineyard Island, Massachusetts. Produces hybrid wines.

Chicco de Caffé (It). Coffee bean.

Chicha (S.Am). A local wine in Bolivia made from molasses and corn.

Chichée (Fr). A commune in the A.C. Chablis, Burgundy.

Chi Chi (Cktl). ½ fl.oz. Vodka, 1 fl.oz. Coconut cream, 4 fl.ozs. unsweetened pineapple juice. Blend with 2 scoops of crushed ice in a blender. Serve in a large highball glass and decorate with a pineapple slice, cherry and serve with straws.

Chicken (USA). The broad general name used to include various types of native American grapes used in wine production.

Chicken Drink (Cktl). ½ measure white Rum, ¼ measure Apricot brandy, ¼ measure orange juice. Shake over ice, strain into a cocktail glass. Dress with a slice of orange.

Chickering Hall (Eng). A vineyard. Address = Chickeringhall, Hoxne, near Eye, Suffolk. Grape variety – Müller-Thurgau.

Chiclana (Sp). An area in the Jerez Supérieur district.

Chicory (Eng). An additive to coffee blends when roasted. Makes the coffee bitter. See Cichorium Intybus and French Coffee.

Chicory Coffee (Eng). See Wild Chicory Coffee.

Chig-Ge (E.Asia). An alcoholic drink of fermented mare's milk made in Mongolia. Is similar to Koumiss.

Chignin (Fr). A white table wine from the vineyards of Chignin, Savoie, south of Chambéry. Made from the Jacquère grape.

Chignin-Bergeron (Fr). A wine-producing village based in the Savoie region of south-eastern France.

Chigny-les-Roses (Fr). A Premier Cru Champagne village in the Canton de Verzy. District = Reims.

Chihuahua (Mex). A district that contains the wine-producing area of Delicías.

Chile (S.Am). A south American wine-producing country along the south-eastern coast. Produces full-bodied wines from European vine species. Top regions are – Aconcagua, Bio-Bio, Colchagua, Curico, Maipo River, Santiago, Talca and Valparaiso. Country often is divided into three zones (north, central and south) for grape production.

Chilford Hundred (Eng). Vineyard. Address = Chilford Hall, Linton, Cambridgeshire. Soil – Loam gravel. 7.5 ha. Grape varieties – Huxelrebe, Müller-Thurgau, Ortega, Schönburger and Siegerrebe.

Chilled and Filtered (Eng). A part of the brewing process in which the beer is cooled which causes suspended proteins to separate out and then it is filtered out.

Chilled Cherry Tea (Cup). Place 75 mls. Cherry brandy, 250 mls. white sparkling wine and 250 mls. Wild Cherry Tea into jug over ice. Stir, serve in highball glasses with cocktail cherries.

Chill Haze (Eng). A condition which can appear in cask conditioned Ales. Caused when the beer becomes too cold and the proteins separate out. Does not alter the flavour but looks unsightly. Treated by filtering.

Chillier à Cidre (Ch. Isles). Cider cellar.

Chillproofing (Eng). A process of chilling wines to remove excess acid and proteins. Filtered afterwards.

Chilsdown (Eng). Vineyard. Address = The Old Station House, Singleton, Chichester. West Sussex. 5.3 ha. Soil – clay, silt loam over chalk. Grape varieties – Chardonnay, Müller-Thurgau and Reichensteiner. See also Chalklands and Grapple.

Chiltern Brewery (Eng). A brewery opened in 1980 near Aylesbury, Bucks. Produces cask conditioned Chiltern Ale 1036 O.G. and Beechwood Bitter 1043 O.G.

Chiltern Hills (Eng). A recognised English mineral water.

Chimay (Bel). A Trappist ale. Brewed by the Abbaye of Chimay. Is bottle-conditioned and vintage dated. Each style is distinguished by the bottle cap colour. See Capsule Blanche, Capsule Bleu and Capsule Rouge.

Chimay Brasserie (Bel). An Abbaye brewery based in southern Belgium. Brews beers of same name. See Chimay.

Chimay Glass (Bel). A specially designed glass (bell-shaped with an inturned rim on a short, stumpy stem) used to serve Chimay beers.

Chime (Eng). The end rim of a beer cask.

China (Asia). The main species of tea bush. Has the smallest leaves of the tea bush family.

China (E.Asia). Country which has the oldest wine making records (2,500 BC). Main wine-producing regions are – Hebei, Henan, Jiangsu, Liao River, Shanxi, Sinkiang and Yangste. Is also noted for its Rice wines and Tea. See C.N.C.O.F.I.E.C.

China (Fr). A liqueur produced from wild cherries in Grenoble, eastern France.

China Bisleri (It). Tonic wine.

China Black (China). A tea from the Anhwei province. A medium leaf that gives a good quality, delicate taste.

China-China (Fr). A tonic liqueur made from spices and other ingredients including quinine. Produced by Picard et Cazot Fils in Lyons.

China-Martini (It). A bitters-apéritif 31% alc. by vol. produced by Martini and Rossi. Contains quinine.

China National Cereals, Oils and Foodstuffs Import and Export Corp (E. Asia). The Chinese State monopoly that produces wines, spirits, etc. Based in Dairen, Fukien, Hupeh, Kwangsi, Kwangtung, Peking, Shanghai, Shantung and T'ien-Chin. (abbr) = C.N.C.O.F.I.E.C.

China Oolong Tea (China). The most expensive tea in the world. Has a fine flavour, body and aroma.

China Tea (China). See Oolong, Tea Bricks and China Black.

Chinato (It). An apéritif made from Barolo wine and quinine.

Chinchón (Sp). An aniseed-flavoured Aguardiente usually drunk diluted. Is similar to Ouzo and Pastis.

Chinese Cocktail (Cktl). ½ gill Jamaican rum, 3 dashes Maraschino, 3 dashes Curaçao, 3 dashes Grenadine, 1 dash Angostura. Stir over ice, strain into a cocktail glass, add a cherry and squeeze of lemon peel juice on top.

Chinese Egg Nogg (Cktl). See Itchiban.

Chinese Ginseng Port Wine (China). A Port-style red wine flavoured with ginseng root. Produced by the Talien Brewery.

Chinese Itch Cocktail (Cktl). ⅓ gill golden Rum, ⅙ gill Passion fruit juice, dash Orgeat syrup, juice of a lime. Blend with a scoop of crushed ice in a blender. Pour into a saucer glass. Dress with a slice of lime.

Chinese Lady (Cktl). ½ measure Yellow Chartreuse, ½ measure grapefruit juice, 1 measure Lemon gin. Shake well over ice, strain into a large cocktail glass.

Chinon (Fr). An A.C. wine-producing area in the Anjou-Saumur district, Loire. Produces red, rosé and white wines. Red wines have a distinct flavour of strawberries. Minimum alc. by vol. 9.5%

Chios (Gre). An island in the Aegean Sea noted for its white wines.

Chipan (Bul). A delimited wine-producing region in southern Bulgaria. Main grape varieties are – Aligoté, Cabernet sauvignon, Dimiat, Merlot and Pinot noir.

Chipiona (Sp). The Andalusian name for a Moscatel wine and the name of a district in Jerez Supérieur.

Chippewa Pride (USA). A light Beer 4.37% alc. by vol. brewed by the Leinentugel Brewery at Chippewa Falls, Wisconsin.

Chiquet (Gaston) (Fr). Champagne producer. Address = 912 Av du Général

Leclerc, 51318 Épernay. Récoltants-manipulants. Produces vintage and non-vintage wines.

Chiquito (Sp). The brand-name used by Bodegas García Carrión in Jumilla for red table wine.

Chira (Fr). An alternative name for the Syrah grape in south-western France.

Chiraï (Ch.Isles). Intoxicated. See also Caudin.

Chirine (USSR). A red grape variety grown in Kazakhstan for the making of dessert wines.

Chiroubles (Fr). A commune in the Cru Beaujolais-Villages, Burgundy. Has 320 ha. under vine.

Chispa Cellars (USA). A small winery based in Calveras, California. Grape varieties – Ruby cabernet and Zinfandel. Produces varietal red wines.

Chiswick Bitter (Eng). A cask conditioned Bitter 1035 O.G. brewed by the Fuller's Brewery, London.

Chitry (Fr). A small wine-producing district in the Yonne Département that produces red wines.

Chiu (China). A term for wine. See also Li and Chang.

Chivas Regal (Scot). A De Luxe blended Scotch whisky (12 year old) produced by the Chivas Brothers in Aberdeen. Part of Seagram. 43% alc. by vol.

Chivite (Julián) (Sp). A wine-producer based in Ribero del Ebro, Navarra. Noted for Parador (10 year old red wine), Cirbonero (5 year old red wine), Gran Fuedo (4 year old red wine) and Castillo de Melida (a young red wine). Also produces rosé and white wines.

Chlorophyl (Eng). Is sometimes found in white wines, it gives a distinct green tinge to the wine.

Chlorose (Eng). A yellowing of the vine leaves, leaving them unable to nourish the grape. Usually shows the vine is not suited to the soil. Fertilizers are sometimes a cure.

Chmelar (Czec). A Beer brewed by the Zătec Brewery. Lit – 'Hop grower'.

Choc Dream (Cktl). ½ measure Vodka, 1 measure Royal Mint Chocolate Liqueur, ⅔ measure cream. Shake well over ice, strain into a cocktail glass. Add dash of Tia Maria and sprinkle with grated chocolate on top. Serve with straws and a cherry on the rim of the glass.

Chocen Brewery (Czec). A brewery based in Chocen in northern Czec.

Chocks (Eng). The wooden wedges used to secure the beer casks on stillages.

Chocla Menthe (Hol). A peppermint and Cacao-flavoured liqueur produced by De Kuyper. 30% alc. by vol.

Chocolate (Eng). A beverage produced from the seeds of the Cacao plant. See Xocoatl and Drinking Chocolate.

Chocolate Cocktail (Cktl).(1). 1 teaspoon chocolate powder, yolk of an egg, ¼ gill red Port. Stir over broken ice, pass through a strainer into a wine glass.

Chocolate Cocktail (Cktl).(2). ¼ gill Port, ¼ gill Yellow Chartreuse, 1 egg yolk, 1 teaspoon chocolate powder. Shake over ice, strain into a cocktail glass.

Chocolate Daisy (Cktl). ½ measure Port, ½ measure Brandy, ½ teaspoon powdered sugar, juice ½ lemon, 4 dashes Grenadine. Shake over ice, strain into an ice-filled highball glass. Add sliced fruit in season.

Chocolate Flip (Cktl). ½ measure Sloe gin, ½ measure Brandy, 1 egg, 1 teaspoon sugar, 2 teaspoons cream. Shake over ice, strain into a flip glass. Top with grated nutmeg.

Chocolate Liqueurs (Euro). See Chéri-Suisse, Chocolate Suisse, Crème de Cacao, Royal Mint Chocolate Liqueur. Also Chokalu.

Chocolate Malt (Eng). A specially malted barley produced by roasting kiln-dried malt at a lower temperature than for Black malt.

Chocolate Manufacturing Association and American Cocoa Research Institute (USA). Address = 7900 Westpark Drive, Suit 514, McLean V.A. 22101.

Chocolate Punch (Cktl). ⅕ gill Kahlúa, 1½ teaspoons chocolate powder, 1 teaspoon coffee powder, 150 mls. milk, sugar to taste. Heat together, stirring until well mixed. Pour into a heat-proof glass, top with whipped cream and ground cinnamon.

Chocolate Rum (Cktl). ⅓ measure Jamaican rum, ⅙ measure (white) Crème de Menthe, ⅙ measure Crème de Cacao, 4 dashes high strength Rum, ½ fl.oz. cream. Shake over ice, strain into an ice-filled old-fashioned glass.

Chocolate Soldier (Cktl).(1). ⅓ measure Crème de Cacao, ⅓ measure Brandy, ⅓ measure dry Vermouth, 2 dashes Orange bitters. Shake over ice, strain into a cocktail glass.

Chocolate Soldier (Cktl).(2). ½ measure dry Gin, ¼ measure Dubonnet, ¼ measure lime juice. Shake over ice, strain into a cocktail glass.

Chocolate Suisse (Switz). A chocolate-flavoured liqueur with tiny squares of chocolate floating in it. 30% alc. by vol.

Chocolate Taste (Eng). A term applied to the taste of old Champagne that is past its best. Usually avoided.

Chodovà Planà Brewery (Czec). An old

established brewery based in western Czec.

Chodovar (Czec). A dark, special, strong Beer 13° brewed by the Chodovà Planà Brewery.

Choice Madeira (Mad). May use a brand-name or word 'Madeira' and a description. e.g. dry, medium, etc. but not the name of the grape. Must be minimum age 3 years after estufagem.

Choice Old Cameron Brig (Scot). The only single blended Grain whisky which is produced by John Haig & Co. Ltd.

Chokalu (Mex). A chocolate-flavoured, sweet liqueur. 26% alc. by vol.

Chollet (Fr). See Cognac Chollet.

Chondrus Crispus (Lat). A red algae used to clarify the wort during the brewing process.

Chope (Fr). A half a litre glass used for beer.

Chope (Fr). Tankard.

Chopine (Fr). A ½ litre mug, tankard. (Originally a ½ litre capacity measure).

Chopiner (Fr). Booze.

Chopineur (Fr). Boozer.

Chop Nut (Cktl). ½ fl.oz. Crème de Banane, ½ fl.oz. Coconut liqueur, 1 fl.oz. Vodka, 1 fl.oz. orange juice, dash egg white. Shake well over ice, strain into a large cocktail glass.

Chopp (Bra). A brand of beer.

Chorey-lès-Beaune (Fr). An A.C. wine-producing village in the northern Côte de Beaune, Burgundy. Has no Premier Cru vineyards. Wines usually sold as A.C. Côte de Beaune-Villages.

Chorherrenhalde (Ger). Vineyard. (Anb) = Baden. (Ber) = Bodensee. (Gro) = Sonnenufer. (Vil) = Meersburg.

Chorherrenstift Cellar (Aus). Wine cellars based at Klosterneuberg. Have their own shaped Sekt bottles.

Chorny Doktor (USSR). A red, sweet, dessert wine from the Crimean peninsula.

Chotapeg (Ind). The old Raj word for a glass of Whisky (or other style of spirits).

Chouacheux (Les) (Fr). A Premier Cru vineyard in the A.C. commune of Beaune, Côte de Beaune, Burgundy. 5.04 ha.

Chouao (S.Am). Often seen on a label of Crème de Cacao. Denotes that the Cacao bean comes from the Chouao region of Venezuela.

Chouilly (Fr). A Grand Cru Champagne village in the Canton d'Épernay. District = Épernay. Reclassified in 1985.

Choum (E.Asia). A digestif liqueur made from fermented rice in Vietnam. If it is

matured then known as Tchoung-tchoung.

Christian Brothers (USA). Religious brotherhood who produce wines in the Napa Valley, California. Also produce brandies. See Mont la Salle Vineyard. They also own the largest collection of antique and unusual corkscrews in the world. See also Mount Tivy Winery. Produces varietal wines.

Christian Brothers XO Rare Reserve (USA). A fine Brandy produced by the Christian Brothers. Introduced in 1972.

Christian Dupré (Eng). The brand-name of a Brandy produced for Linfood Cash and Carry, Northamptonshire. 40% alc. by vol.

Christianshavner Akvavit (Den). The brand-name of an Akvavit produced by Peter Heering.

Christina Wine Cellars (USA). A winery based in McGregor, Iowa. Produces mainly French hybrid wines.

Christmas Ales (Eng). Festive ales brewed for the Christmas period. Are usually high in alcohol.

Christmas Cheer (Punch). 1 pint water, ¼ bottle Jamaican Rum, 4 bottles red wine, 12 cloves, ½ teaspoon ground cinnamon, ½ teaspoon grated nutmeg. Heat water, wine, Rum and spices together with a lemon studded with the cloves and bake in a hot oven for approximately 15 minutes. Serve in cups.

Christmas Cracker (Eng). A dark-brew Ale 1080 O.G. brewed by the Woods Brewery in Shropshire.

Christmas Reserve (Eng). A Christmas brew 1065 O.G. brewed by the Mauldon Brewery in Suffolk.

Christmas Yule Egg Nog (Punch). 12 eggs, ⅓ pint dark Rum, 1 pint milk, 1 pint cream, 2 pints Scotch whisky, 2 lbs. sugar. Beat egg yolks and sugar together, beat egg whites separately and fold into yolks and sugar. Add remaining ingredients, chill and serve with grated nutmeg.

Christopher's Fino (Eng). A fine, dry, Fino Sherry from Christopher's and Co. London.

Christophorou (Cyp). A small, independent company who deal with wine production based in Limassol, south-eastern Cyprus.

Christwein (Ger). The name for a wine made from grapes gathered on December 24th and 25th.

Chronic Alcoholism (Eng). Causes the diseases of Cirrhosis, Gastritis, Nephritis and Neuritis.

Chuico (Chile). A wicker-covered demi-john of 5–10 litres capacity.

C

Chumai (USSR). A red, dessert wine from the Moldavia region. Made from the Cabernet grape.

Chun Mee (E.Asia). A green, unfermented tea produced in Taiwan.

Chupeta (Port). A drinking straw.

Chur Brauerei (Switz). A brewery based in Freuenfeld. Produces Weizenbiers.

Church Hill (Austr). The brand-name used by the Mildara Vineyards.

Churchill Cocktail (Cktl). 1 fl.oz. Scotch whisky, ⅓ fl.oz. Cointreau, ⅓ fl.oz. Italian vermouth, dash lemon juice. Shake over ice, strain into a cocktail glass.

Churchill Graham Lda (Port). Vintage Port shippers. Vintages – 1982. Produce – Quinta da Agua Alta.

Church Parade (Cktl). 1 measure Plymouth Gin, ½ measure dry Vermouth, dash orange Curaçao, ½ measure orange juice. Shake over ice, strain into a cocktail glass.

Churleur (Fr). A word used by the Champenois for 'a drunk'.

Churn (Eng). A large container used for transporting milk. 1–10 gallons in capacity.

Chusclan (Fr). A.C. Côtes du Rhône-Villages.

Chwart (Wales). A quart (2 pints).

Chwisgi Cymraeg (Wales). Welsh whiskey. See Swn y Don and Swn y Mor.

Chymos (Fin). A company that produces Lakka, Polar and Villman liqueurs.

Chyorniye Glaza (USSR). Lit – 'Black eyes'. A style of 'Port' wine that's produced near Krasnodar.

C.I.A. (The) (Cktl). ⅓ measure Armagnac brandy, ⅓ measure Cointreau, ⅓ measure Yellow Izarra. Shake over ice, strain into an ice-filled old-fashioned glass.

Cía Vinícola del Sur, S.A. (Sp). A producer of Montilla based in Montilla-Moriles, south-eastern Spain.

C.I.B. (Fr) (abbr). Comité Interprofessionnel de la Côte d'Or et de l'Yonne pour les Vins de Bourgogne.

C.I.B.M. (Fr) (abbr). Comité Interprofessionnel de Saône-et-Loire par les Vins A.O.C. de Bourgogne et de Mâcon.

C.I.B.V. (Fr) (abbr). Comité Interprofessionnel de Vins de Bordeaux. Address = 1, Cours du XXX Juillet, 33075 Bordeaux, Cedex.

C.I.C.D.R. (Fr) (abbr). Comité Interprofessionnel des Vins des Côtes du Rhône.

Cicero (Cktl). ⅓ measure Honiggoscherl, ⅓ measure dry Vermouth, ⅓ measure orange juice. Shake over ice, strain into a highball glass. Top with iced Champagne.

Cichorium Intybus (Lat). The botanical name of the chicory plant. Used as a substitute for coffee.

Ciclopi (It). Noted wine-producers based near Etna on the island of Sicily.

Cider (Eng). Fermented apple juice. Dry = 6% alc. by vol. Medium = 4% alc. by vol. Sweet = 2% alc. by vol. See also Scrumpy. (Fr) = Cidre. (It) = Succo di Mele.

Cider Cocktail (Cktl).(1). ⅓ measure sparkling Cider, ⅓ measure dry Gin, ⅓ measure orange juice. Stir over ice, strain into a goblet.

Cider Cocktail (Cktl).(2). ¾ gill Cider, 1 dash Angostura, 3 dashes Gomme syrup. Stir over ice, strain into a goblet. Top with a lemon slice.

Cider Cup (Cup).(1). Into a large jug place some ice, 1 gill pale Sherry, ½ gill Brandy, ½ gill blue Curaçao, 2 pints Cider, rind of a lemon. Stir with some ice and serve.

Cider Cup (Cup) (2). ⅙ gill Calvados, ⅙ gill Curaçao, ⅙ gill Maraschino, ⅙ gill Brandy, 2 pints Cider. Stir over ice in a large jug. Decorate with orange slices.

Cider Eggnog (Cktl). 1 egg, 1 teaspoon Gomme syrup, ⅓ pint milk. Shake over ice, strain into a collins glass. Top with sweet Cider and grated nutmeg.

Cider Glass (Eng). A stemmed, trumpet-shaped glass that was popular in the eighteenth and nineteenth centuries.

Cider Grog (Eng). Heat ⅓ pint Cider and ⅕ pint Jamaican rum together until nearly boiling. Add sugar to taste and decorate with a lemon studded with some cloves.

Cidéries Mignard (Fr). A noted Cider producer based in Bellot. Also produces Mignard (a sparkling white grape juice).

Cidéries Réunies (Fr). One of France's largest Cider companies based in Normandy, northern France.

Cidraie (La) (Fr). The brand-name for a range of Ciders produced by Cideries Réunies, Le Thiel, Normandy.

Cidre (Bel) (Ch.Isles) (Fr). Cider.

Cidre Bouché (Fr). Sparkling cider. Is fermented twice (naturally).

Cidre Brut (Fr). The most popular Cider in France. Is dry and of 4% alc. by vol.

Cidre Doux (Fr). A sweetish Cider up to 3% alc. by vol. Fermentation is stopped early so that not all the sugar is fermented.

Cidre Fermier (Fr). Lit – 'Farm cider' or 'Farmer's cider'. Home-produced cider, the equivalent of English 'Scrumpy'.

Cidrérie du Calvados (Le) (Fr). One of the largest Cider producing companies of Normandy.

Cidre Sec (Fr). Dry cider.

Cie des Grands Armagnacs (Fr). Armagnac producer. Address = Castelnau

C

d'Auzan, 32800 Eauze.

Cienega (USA). A wine-producing area of San Benito, California.

Cierzac (Fr). A commune in the Charente-Maritime Département whose grapes are classed Petite Champagne (Cognac).

Cigar Box (Eng). The term used to describe the aroma of some red wines (that of a wood bouquet). An example is Spanish Rioja.

Cignano (It). A Chianti Putto producer based in the Tuscany region.

Ciliegiolo (It). A red grape variety grown in the Tuscany region.

Cilleros (Sp). A wine-producing area in Cáceres, south-western Spain.

Cilurzo and Piconi (USA). A winery based in Temecula, California. 16.5 ha. Grape varieties – Cabernet sauvignon, Chenin blanc and Petit syrah. Produces Chenite and varietal wines.

Cima Corgo (Port). The upper area of the river Douro.

Cin (USA). A noted brand of Vermouth.

Cincher (Cktl). 1½ fl.ozs. Cherry brandy, 1½ fl.ozs. dry Gin. Pour over crushed ice in an old-fashioned glass.

Cinderella (Cktl).(Non-alc). ⅓ gill orange juice, ⅓ gill lemon juice, ⅓ gill pineapple juice. Shake over ice, strain into a cocktail glass.

Cinnamaldehyde (Eng). An Aldehyde found in wine which contributes to the bouquet and flavour of the wine. Is produced by the oxidation of alcohols.

Cinq-Saou (Fr). The alternative name for the Cinsault grape.

Cinqua (N.Z.). The alternative name for the black hybrid grape Seibel 5455.

Cinquantenaire (Fr). The brand-name of a blend of Armagnac brandies produced by Janneau. 40% alc. by vol.

Cinque Terre (It). Lit – 'Five villages'. A small region situated on the narrow coastal strip of the Italian Riviera between Savona and Spezia in the Liguria region. Produces full-flavoured white wines from the Albarola, Bianchetta boscovines and Vermentino grapes. D.O.C. towns are – Biasca, Campiglia, Monterosso, Riomaggiore and Vernazza.

Cinqueterre (It). The alternative spelling and presentation of Cinque Terre.

Cinque Terre Sciacchetrà (It). D.O.C. white wine from the Cinque Terre, Liguria. Made from partially dried grapes – Albarola, Bosco and Vermentino varieties. Can have on the label Vino dolce naturale (naturally sweet wine) when there is 4% sugar in suspension.

Cinque-Vie (Cktl). ¼ gill Kirsch de Zoug,

¼ gill Cointreau, ¼ gill Vodka, ¼ gill grapefruit juice. Shake well over ice, strain into a cocktail glass. Top with a cherry.

Cinquième Cru (Fr). Fifth growths. The 1855 Médoc classification. There are 18 Châteaux on the list.

Cinsault (Fr). A red grape variety grown in southern France. Also known as Espagna, Hermitage, Malaga and Picardin noir.

Cinsaut (S.Afr). A red grape variety.

Cinsaut (USA). A white grape variety used in the making of dessert wines in California. Also known as Malaga.

Cintana (It). A red grape variety grown in Sicily to produce red and rosé wines.

Cintiana (Bra). A red grape variety.

Cinzano (It). A noted large Vermouth-producing company based in Turin. Also produce Piemonte wines.

Cinzano Glass Collection (It). A magnificent collection of early glass in Turin.

Cinzano Winery (Austr). A winery based in Riverina, New South Wales.

Cirbonero (Sp). The brand-name of a 5 year old, full-bodied, red wine produced by Julián Chivite in Navarra, north-eastern Spain.

Circulatory Vat (Port). A method of fermentation in which stainless steel vats are used. Inside these is a central column with an Archimedian screw rotated by an electric motor which carries the Manta down to the bottom of the vat continuously.

Circumpotatio (Lat). To pass drinks around, passing drinks around.

Cirencester Brewery (Eng). A brewery based in Cirencester, Gloucestershire. Also known as the Cellar Brewery. Produces cask conditioned Down Moore Ale 1042 O.G. and Abbey Ale 1047 O.G.

Cirfandli (Hun). A white grape variety.

Ciriaco Borelli Winery (USA). See Borelli Winery.

Cirial (Sp). A white grape variety grown in the La Mancha region. It produces dry wines low in acidity.

Ciró (It). A Calabrian province of southern Italy. Noted for its red, rosé and white wines. Old wine district whose wines are a distant descendant of Cremissa (a wine offered to athletes at the Olympic games).

Ciró Bianco (It). D.O.C. white wine from Calabria. Produced from the Greco bianco and Trebbiano toscano grapes grown in the commune of Ciró.

Ciró Rosato (It). D.O.C. rosé wine from Calabria. Produced from the Gaglioppo, Greco bianco and Trebbiano toscano

C

grapes in the communes of Ciró Marina and part of Melissa Ceucoli (all in the province of Catanzaro).

Ciró Rosso (It). D.O.C. red wine from Calabria. Produced from the Gaglioppo, Greco bianco and Trebbiano toscano grapes. If produced in communes of Ciró and Ciró Marina then entitled to the Classico designation. If total alc. by vol. is 13.5% and aged 3 years then classed Riserva.

Cirrhosis (Lat). A disease of the liver associated with an excessive and continuous alcohol consumption.

Cisa Asinari dei Marchesi di Gresy (It). A noted vineyard based in the Barbaresco district of Piemonte.

Cisk Lager (Euro). A Lager beer 1042 O.G. brewed by the Farsons Brewery in Malta.

Cissac (Fr). A commune in the A.C. Haut-Médoc, north-western Bordeaux.

Citation Brandy (USA). The brand-name of a Brandy bottled by the Guild of Wineries and Distillers at Lodi, California.

Citeaux Monks (Fr). The owners of Clos de Vougeot, Côte de Nuits, Burgundy until the French revolution.

Citric Acid (Eng). $CH_2(COOH) C(OH) (COOH)CH_2 COOH$. Additive to wines. Prevents iron casse by complexing with iron ions.

Citroen (Hol). A lemon peel-flavoured liqueur produced by De Kuyper. 30% alc. by vol.

Citroengenever (Hol). A lemon-flavoured Jenever (Gin).

Citronen-Eis Likör (Ger). A yellow liqueur made from the juice and oil of lemon. Eis denotes that it should be drunk over ice.

Citrusdal (S.Afr). A dessert wine and brandy-producing region based north of Tulbagh.

Citrusdal Co-operative (S.Afr). Vineyards based at Olifants River. Address = Citrusdal Koöperatiewe Wynkelders Bpk., Box 41, Citrusdal 7340. Produces varietal wines.

Citrusdal Koöperatiewe Wynkelders (S.Afr). See Citrusdal Co-operative.

Citrus Spring (Eng). A sparkling spring water and 10% fruit juice (orange or lemon) drink produced by Britvic.

Citrus Teacup (Cktl). 1½ pints fresh brewed tea, rind of a grapefuit, lemon, orange and apple, 1 clove. Heat together, strain, sweeten with sugar syrup to taste. Serve hot or cold.

City and Guilds Alcoholic Beverages Certificate (Eng). Prefix 717. Was originally prefixed 150 (1960's) and 707–3

(1970's). The qualification for wine waiters (sommeliers).

City Gin (Eng). A dry Gin produced in 1986 by Nicholson & Co. for the 'Morning Advertiser' to raise monies for the L.V.A. schools (part of the sales donated). A limited production.

City Lager (Afr). A Lager 1042 O.G. brewed by the East Africa Breweries in Tanzania.

City Lights (Cktl). ½ measure Glayva, ¼ measure orange juice, ¼ measure lemon juice. Stir over ice, strain into an ice-filled highball glass. Top with soda water, slice of lemon and a cherry. Serve with straws.

Ciudad Real (Sp). A wine-producing area in the La Mancha region.

C.I.V.A. (Fr) (abbr). Comité Interprofessionnel des Vins d'Alsace.

C.I.V.A.S. (Fr) (abbr). Conseil Interprofessionnel des Vins d'Anjou et de Saumur.

C.I.V.B. (Fr) (abbr). Comité Interprofessionnel des Vins de Bordeaux.

C.I.V.C. (Fr) (abbr). Comité Interprofessionnel du Vin de Champagne. Was founded in 1942 to regulate the growing of the vines and the production of Champagne, Address = 5, Rue Henri Martin, 51-Épernay.

C.I.V.C.P. (Fr) (abbr). Comité Interprofessionnel des Vins de Côtes de Provence.

C.I.V.D.N. (Fr) (abbr). Comité Interprofessionnel des Vins Doux Naturels.

C.I.V.G. (Fr) (abbr). Comité Interprofessionnel des Vins de Gaillac.

C.I.V.O.P.N. (Fr) (abbr). Comité Interprofessionnel des Vins d'Origine du Pays Nantais.

Civrac (Fr). A commune in the Bas-Médoc, A.C. Médoc, north-western France.

C.I.V.R.B. (Fr) (abbr). Comité Interprofessionnel des Vins de la Région de Bergerac.

C.I.V.T. (Fr). (abbr). Comité Interprofessionnel des Vins de Touraine. Address = 19, Square Prosper Mérimée, 37000 Tours.

Clacquesin (Fr). A firm that produces Crème de Cassis, Extrait des Pins (pine needle liqueur) and Clacquesin liqueur.

Cladosporium Cellerae (Lat). The name given to the black-brown mould that grows on walls etc. in wine cellars. Lives off the alcoholic vapours (esters and volatile acids). See also Torula Compniacensis.

Claerkampster (Hol). A monastery-produced herb liqueur. 35% alc. by vol.

C

Claeryn (Hol). A young Genever produced by the Bols Co.

Clair-Daü (Fr). A large estate 41.5 ha. based in the Côte de Nuits, Burgundy.

Clairdie (Fr). A Clairette de Die sparkling (méthode champenoise) wine from the Cave Coopérative Clairette de Die, Rhône.

Clairdoc (Fr) (abbr). A.C. Clairette du Languedoc.

Clairet (Fr). Lit – 'Clear, bright, light'. Associated with the red wines of Bordeaux. Anglicised to Claret by the English when Bordeaux wines were first popular. See Claret.

Clairet de Moselle (Fr). A rosé wine produced in Metz, Lorraine, northeastern France.

Clairet-Schillerwein (Fr). Alsace rosé wine.

Clairette (Fr). See Clairette.

Clairette (It). A white grape variety grown in Sardinia.

Clairette à Grains Ronds (Fr). The alternative name for the Ugni blanc in southern France.

Clairette Blanche (Fr). A white grape variety grown in southern France to produce sparkling and still white wines usually low in alcohol and acidic. Also grown in Armagnac and other countries e.g. South Africa.

Clairette de Bellegarde (Fr). An A.C. full-bodied and flavoured white wine from the area of the Costières du Gard, 25 miles south-west of Avignon near the Rhône-Sète canal. Made from the Clairette grape. Minimum alc. by vol. 11%.

Clairette de Die (Fr). An A.C. dry, sparkling (méthode champenoise) wine produced from the Clairette and Muscat à petits grains (25% max) grapes. Has a fine Muscat flavour and bouquet. Minimum alc. by vol. 10% (Muscat-based) and 9% (Clairette-based).

Clairette de Die Mousseux (Fr). An A.C. sparkling (méthode champenoise, no liqueur de tirage added) wine. Made from the Clairette and Muscat (minimum 50%) grapes. Minimum alc. by vol. 10% (Muscat-based) and 9% (Clairette-based).

Clairette de Venice (Fr). An alternative name for the Ugni blanc.

Clairette du Gaillac (Fr). A slightly-sparkling, red-rosé wine produced in the Gaillac region, Tarn Département, southern France.

Clairette du Languedoc (Fr). An A.C. dry, white, acidic wine produced near Montpellier in the Midi region. Also a semi-sweet version (Rancio) aged 3 years minimum alc. by vol. 14%, (dry) 13%. Made from the communes of – Aspiran, Cabrières, Ceyras, Paulhan and Péret. See Clairdoc.

Clairette Egreneuse (Isr). A white grape variety.

Clairette Ronde (Fr). See Clairette à Grains Ronds.

Clairin (W.Ind). The local name for the white spirit (Rum) from the first distillation in Haiti.

Clairvaux Co-operative (S.Afr). Vineyards based at Robertson. Address =Clairvaux Koöperatiewe Wynkelders, Box 179, Robertson 6705. Produces varietal wines.

Clairvaux Koöperatiewe Wynkelders (S.Afr). See Clairvaux Co-operative.

Clam (Fr). A commune in the Charente-Maritime Département whose grapes are classed Petite Champagne (Cognac).

Clamato Cocktail (Cktl). 1 measure Vodka, ½ measure clam juice, 2 measures tomato juice. Shake over ice, strain into an ice-filled old-fashioned glass.

Clamato Juice (USA). A clam and tomato juice drink.

Clan Campbell (Scot). A 12 year old blended De Luxe Scotch whisky. 43% alc. by vol.

Clan Dew (Eng). The brand-name of a Whisky and ginger wine drink.

Clan MacGregor (Scot). A blended Scotch whisky produced by William Grant and Sons. 40% alc. by vol.

Clanrana (Scot). A herb-flavoured liqueur whisky.

Clansman Cocktail (Cktl). ½ measure white Rum, ½ measure Apricot brandy, 1 measure orange juice, ½ measure lemon juice, dash egg white. Shake over ice, strain into a cocktail glass. Dress with slices of orange, lemon and a cherry.

Clanwilliam (S.Afr). A Brandy and dessert wine-producing region based north of Tulbagh.

Clan-y-Delyn (Eng). A Whisky, honey and sugar-based liqueur produced by Hallgarten. 40% alc. by vol.

Clape (La) (Fr). An A.C. district in the Aude Département. Is classed as part of the Coteaux du Languedoc. Produces mainly white wines.

Clara (Mex). A term used to denote 'clear' when applied to Lager beers.

Clare (Austr). An area of South Australia near the towns of Clare and Watervale. Produces full, rich reds and full-bodied white wines.

Clare (Cktl). ½ measure Sloe gin, ½ measure Italian vermouth, dash

Cognac. Shake over ice, strain into a cocktail glass.

Claremont Winery (Can). One of the top wineries based in British Columbia.

Clarendon and Bakers Gully (Austr). Part of the Coolawin Estate in South Australia.

Clare Riesling (Austr). The erroneous varietal name for the white grape Crouchen.

Clares (Eng). Chaucer's way of spelling Clairet (from his Canterbury Tales).

Claret (Eng). The name given to the red wines of Bordeaux (especially those of the Médoc). A corruption of the French words Clairet and Clairette.

Claret (USA). See California Claret.

Claret Cobbler (Cktl). Place some ice into a large goblet, half fill with Claret wine, add a barspoon of Gomme syrup, 4 dashes Curaçao. Stir, decorate with fruit in season, sprig of mint. Serve with straws.

Claret Cocktail (Cktl). Dissolve 1 teaspoon powdered sugar in 2 fl.ozs. soda water. Add 3 fl.ozs. Claret. Stir over ice, strain into a highball glass with ice. Decorate with fruits in season, mint and cucumber peel.

Claret Cup (Cup). Juice 2 oranges, juice 2 lemons, 1 bottle Claret, ¼ pint water, 1 syphon soda water, rind of 1 orange and lemon. Boil 4 ozs. sugar in the water together with the rinds. Add the juices and wine and cool. Place ice into a large jug, add mix, top with soda, fruits in season, mint and sliced cucumber.

Clarete (Port). Light red wine.

Clarete (Sp). A term used to describe a light red wine from the Rioja region.

Clarete Campanas (Sp). A fine, light red wine produced by Las Campanas in the Navarra region, north-eastern Spain.

Claret Jug (Eng). A Georgian decanter-style glass container with a handle. Often has a silver neck band, lid and base.

Claret Lemonade (Cktl). Dissolve 2 teaspoons sugar in the juice of a large lemon in a highball glass. Top with 2 fl.ozs. Claret and soda water. Dress with an orange and lemon slice and a cherry. Serve with straws.

Claret Punch (Cktl). 4 fl.ozs. Claret, 1 fl.oz. lemon juice, 2 dashes orange Curaçao, 3 dashes Gomme syrup. Stir over ice, strain into an ice-filled highball glass. Top with ginger ale and a slice of lemon.

Claret Punch (Punch). 1 bottle Claret, 2 fl.ozs. Cognac, 2 fl.ozs. orange Curaçao, 1 sliced orange, ½ pint soda water. Stir together, add ice and serve.

Claret Sangaree (Cktl). 1 measure Claret, juice of a lemon, 1 teaspoon castor sugar. Fill a wine glass with crushed ice, add ingredients and stir. Top with an orange slice and grated nutmeg.

Claret Sangaree (Cktl). 1 measure Claret, juice of a lemon, 1 teaspoon castor sugar. Fill a wine glass with crushed ice, add ingredients and stir. Top with an orange slice and grated nutmeg.

Clarett (Eng). The old Georgian way of spelling Claret.

Claretto (It). Claret.

Clare-Watervale (Austr). A wine-producing region of South Australia. Is based 90 miles north of Adelaide. Planted mainly with Cabernet, Riesling and Shiraz.

Claridge (Cktl). ⅙ gill Cointreau, ⅙ gill dry Gin, ⅙ gill Apricot brandy, ⅓ gill dry Vermouth. Stir over ice, strain into a cocktail glass.

Clarificação (Port). The clarification (fining) of wines with egg white, bentonite, etc.

Clarificants (Eng). The name given to substances used to clear wines and make them bright. See Bentonite, Blood, Egg White, Gelatine and Isinglass.

Clarifiers (USA). Long shallow pans used in San Francisco to ferment the beer in the Anchor Steam Brewery.

Clarify (Eng). To clear wine and make it bright using fining agents such as ox blood, isinglass, egg white, gelatine or bentonite.

Clark and Randolph Fizz (Cktl). 1 gill Gin, 1½ fl.ozs. pineapple juice, 1 egg white. Shake well over ice, strain into an ice-filled highball glass. Top with soda water. Serve with straws.

Clark Brewery (Eng). A brewery opened in 1982 in Wakefield, Yorkshire. Produces cask conditioned Hammerhead 1050 O.G. and Henry Boon's Wakefield Ale 1038 O.G.

Clarkes Hydrometer (Eng). Invented in 1725 by John Clarke. Was the first accurate hydrometer using brass weights.

Clarksburg (USA). A wine-producing district in Yolo County, California.

Claro (Port). See Vinho Claro.

Claro (Sp). Bright wine.

Claro de Lias (Sp). Describes a clear wine obtained from the lees of the must.

Claros de Turbios (Sp). A wine made from the lees which accumulate in the casks and is used for blends in some cheaper sherries.

Clarry (Eng). The nickname for Clairet (Claret) in the seventeenth and eighteenth centuries.

Clary Wine (Eng). A wine made from

chopped Málaga raisins and Clary blossom.
Clásico (Sp). A term used in the Tarragona region for red or sweet white dessert wines up to 14–15% alc. by vol.
Classé (Fr). Denotes a wine of quality. See Grand Cru Classé.
Classement (Fr). Classification. e.g. Classement 1855.
Classic (Cktl). ½ measure Brandy, ⅙ measure Maraschino, ⅙ measure lemon juice, ⅙ measure orange juice. Shake over ice, strain into a sugar-rimmed (lemon juice) wine glass. Add a twist of lemon peel juice.
Classic (Eng). The term used to describe top quality wines which have finesse and style.
Classic (Ger). A fine Lager beer brewed by the Dortmunder Kronen Brauerei of Dortmund, Westphalia. 5.1% alc. by vol.
Classico (It). Lit – 'Classic'. The central and best area in relation to wine. To be labelled Classico the grapes must come from the delimited area. i.e. Chianti Classico, Frascati Classico, etc.
Classic Wine Glass (Czec). A fine glass design made of Barium crystal in Bohemia. Is similar to the Baccarat design. Supplied in U.K. by Classic Wine Club, 4, Mardon, Westfield Park, Hatch End, Middlesex. HA5 4JQ.
Clastidio (It). The name given to red or dry white wines from Lombardy.
Clastidium (Lat). A dry, white wine made from the Pinot grigio and the Pinot nero grapes. Is oak matured.
Clastido-Ballabio (It). A producer of sparkling (méthode champenoise) wines based in Lombardy.
Clauss (Gustav) (Gre). A Bavarian refugee who in 1861 set up business in Patras and introduced the Mavrodaphne dessert wine. The business is now called the Achaia-Clauss Wine Co.
Clausthaler Lager (Ger). A bottled, low-alcohol Lager beer 0.6% by vol. Brewed by the Binding Brauerei, Frankfurt.
Clavelin (Fr). A squat bottle used for the Jura (vins jaunes) wines of eastern France. Holds 60 cls. (20.5 fl.ozs).
Claverie (Fr). Armagnac producer. Address = Lannemaignan, 32240 Estang. 10 ha. in the Bas Armagnac.
Clavignon, Gamay Rouge (Switz). A red wine produced from the Gamay grape by Société Vinicole de Perroy in the Vaud canton.
Clavileño (Sp). A dry white wine produced by La Daimieleña in the La Mancha region.
Clay (Eng). Sedimentary soil, stiff, viscous earth.
Clayette (Fr). A wicker tray used in the Champagne region to hold the grape whilst épluchage takes place.
Claymore (The) (Scot). A blended Scotch whisky produced by A. Ferguson and Co. A subsidiary company of White Horse Distillers (part of DCL). 40% alc. by vol.
Clayson Report (Scot). A report on the Scottish licensing laws made in 1976 by Dr. Christopher Clayson who headed the government committee. It allowed public houses to apply for regular extensions to permitted hours and to be open all day.
Clayton's Original (Eng). A cask conditioned Ale 1048 O.G. brewed by the Fellows, Morton and Clayton Brewery (a Whitbreads home-brew public house) in Nottingham.
Clean (Eng). A term used to describe a wine which has no unnatural aroma or maladies present.
Clean Coffee (Eng). The name given to the coffee beans when they are ready for roasting.
Cleebronn (Ger). Village. (Anb) = Württemburg. (Ber) = Württemburgisch Unterland. (Gro) = Heuchelberg. (Vin) = Michaelberg.
Cleft Grafting (Sp). A style of grafting carried out on those vines which have previously been bench or field grafted and have not taken.
Clemenceau Cocktail (Cktl). ⅖ measure Gin, ⅖ measure French vermouth, ⅕ measure Cointreau, 2 dashes Orange bitters. Shake over ice, strain into a cocktail glass.
Clément Distillerie (W.Ind). A noted Rum distillery based on the island of Martinique.
Clément V (Fr). The first Avignon Pope (1305–13), built Châteauneuf-du-Pape and owned Château Pape Clément in the Graves (1216–1314).
Clerambault (Emile) (Fr). Champagne producer. Address = Neuville Buxeuil, Neuville-sur-Seine. 10250 Mussy-sur-Seine. Co-operative. Produces – Vintage and non-vintage wines.
Clerget (Fr). An important négociant-éleveur based in Saint Aubin, Côte de Beaune, Burgundy.
Clermont-Ferrand (Fr). A town in eastern France near the Côtes d'Auvergne where Châteaugay and Chanturgues are produced from the Gamay grape. Noted for its chalk soil.
Clés des Ducs (Fr). A brand of Armagnac made by the Izarra company.
Cleversulzbach (Ger). Village. (Anb) = Württemberg. (Ber) = Württembergisch Unterland. (Gro) = Staufenberg. (Vin) = Berg.

C

Clevner (Ger). The name given to the Frühburgunder grape (Pinot noir) in the Württemberg region.

Clicquot (Madame) (Fr). Inventor of Remuage and Dégorgement. See Veuve Clicquot.

Clicquot Rosé (Fr). A vintage rosé Champagne produced by Veuve Clicquot Ponsardin from 52% Pinot noir, 32% Chardonnay and Bouzy Rouge.

Cliff Hanger (Cktl). 1 measure Montezuma Silver Tequila stirred over ice in a highball glass. Top with bitter lemon and a slice of lemon.

Cliftonia (Cktl). ⅓ measure Swedish Punsch, ⅔ measure Grand Marnier, ⅓ measure dry Gin, ⅓ measure orange juice. Shake over ice, strain into a cocktail glass.

Clifton Inns (Eng). A company associated with Watney Mann running over 120 public houses.

Climat (Fr). A specific individual vineyard used mainly in the Côte d'Or, Burgundy. (Having individual climatic conditions).

Climat (Switz). A term designating a particular wine-growing area.

Climat de la Forge (Fr). The old name used for Clos de Tart, Côte de Nuits, Burgundy.

Climat-du-Val (Fr). A Premier Cru vineyard in the A.C. commune of Auxey-Duresses, Côte de Beaune, Burgundy. 23 ha. Also known as the Clos-du-Val.

Climate (Eng). Appertaining to the weather. The right climate is needed to produce grapes suitable for wine production. See Micro-climate.

Clim Cav (Fr). A wine rack made from Pozzolana (a volcanic lava) quarried near Auvergne. Address = Sogestel 17, Boulevard du Général de Gaulle, 49600 Beaupréau.

Clinch's Brewery (Eng). Now known as the Glenny Brewery.

Clinton (USA). A red grape variety.

Clinton Vineyards (USA). A small winery based in Hudson Valley, New York. 6 ha. Noted for its Seyval blanc wines.

Clip Joint (USA) (slang). An establishment that charges high prices for drinks, etc. Overcharges.

Clipper Beer (Eng). A cask conditioned Bitter 1040 O.G. brewed by the Pier Hotel in Gravesend, Kent, and the Southeastern in Strood, Kent.

Clisse (Fr). The name for the wicker covering wrapped around demi-johns.

C.L.O.C. (Den) (abbr). Cumin Liquidum Optimum Castelli. Lit – 'Best caraway in Castel'. A caraway-flavoured liqueur. 31.5% alc. by vol.

Cloc Brun (Den). A brown version of C.L.O.C. 38.5% alc. by vol.

Clohars (Fr). A noted growth of Cider produced in Brittany, north-western France.

Clone (Eng). The best of a species of vine which is usually resistant to disease and tolerant to climatic conditions. An improved specimen. Lit – 'A group of organisms or cells of the same genetic constitution that are descended from a common ancestor by asexual reproduction as by cuttings, grafting, etc'.

Clos (Fr). A walled vineyard especially in Burgundy.

Clos (Le) (Fr). A wine-producing village in the commune of Fuissé in A.C. Pouilly-Fuissé, Mâcon, Burgundy.

Clos (Les) (Fr). A grand Cru vineyard of A.C. Chablis, Burgundy.

Clos Abadía (Sp). A full, red wine produced by Raimat in Lérida from Cabernet 50%, Garnacha 20% and Tempranillo 30%.

Clos Arlots (Fr). A Premier Cru vineyard of the village Premeau in the southern end of the A.C. commune of Nuits-Saint-Georges, Côte de Nuits, Burgundy. 4 ha. Also known as Clos des Arlots.

Clos Avocat (Fr). A vineyard in the commune of Cérons. A.C. Cérons, Bordeaux. 4 ha.

Clos Barrail-du-Milieu (Fr). A vineyard in the commune of Pomerol. A.C. Pomerol, Bordeaux. 2 ha.

Clos Barreau (Fr). A vineyard in the commune of Fargues. A.C. Sauternes, Bordeaux. 1 ha.

Clos Barreyre (Fr). A vineyard in the commune of Virelade. A.C. Graves, Bordeaux. 3 ha. (white).

Clos Baudoin (Fr). A.C. Vouvray. Address = Prince Poniatowski, Vouvray 11 & LI. Central Vineyards, Loire.

Clos-Baulet (Fr). A Premier Cru vineyard in the A.C. commune of Morey-Saint-Denis, Côte de Nuits, Burgundy. 0.8 ha.

Clos Bayard (Fr). A vineyard in the commune of Montagne-Saint-Émilion. A.C. Saint-Émilion, Bordeaux. 5 ha.

Clos Beaufort-Mazerat (Fr). A vineyard in the commune of Saint-Émilion. A.C. Saint-Émilion, Bordeaux. 2 ha.

Clos Beauregard (Fr). Part of Château Taillefer. A.C. Pomerol, Bordeaux.

Clos Beau Rivage de By (Fr). A vineyard in the commune of Bégadan. A.C. Médoc, Bordeaux. 5 ha.

Clos Bel-Air (Fr). Part of Domaine la Pointe. A.C. Pomerol, Bordeaux.

Clos Belle-Vue (Fr). A vineyard in the

commune of Sainte-Croix-du-Mont. A.C. Sainte-Croix-du-Mont, Bordeaux. 4 ha.

Clos Bellevue-Figeac (Fr). A vineyard in the A.C. Saint-Émilion, Bordeaux. 3 ha.

Clos Bellevue-Peyblanquet (Fr). A vineyard in the A.C. Saint-Émilion, Bordeaux. 3 ha.

Clos Bernachot (Fr). Part of Château du Roy, A.C. Saint-Émilion, Bordeaux.

Clos Blanc (Fr). A Premier Cru vineyard in the A.C. commune of Pommard, Côte de Beaune, Burgundy. 4.3 ha. Also known as Le Clos Blanc.

Clos Blanc [de Vougeot] (Fr). A Premier Cru vineyard in the A.C. commune of Vougeot, Côte de Nuits, Burgundy. 1.8 ha.

Clos Bonalgue (Fr). A vineyard in the commune of Pomerol. A.C. Pomerol, Bordeaux. 3 ha.

Clos Bourgelet (Fr). A vineyard in the commune of Cérons. A.C. Cérons, Bordeaux. 7 ha.

Clos Brun (Fr). A vineyard in the A.C. Saint-Émilion, Bordeaux. 3 ha.

Clos-Bussière (Fr). A Premier Cru vineyard in the A.C. commune of Morey-Saint-Denis, Côte de Nuits, Burgundy. 3.1 ha.

Clos Cabanes (Fr). A vineyard in the commune of St-Pierre-de-Mons. A.C. St-Pierre-de-Mons, Bordeaux. 4 ha. (white).

Clos Cabannes (Fr). A vineyard in the commune of St-Pierre-de-Mons. A.C. Graves. Bordeaux. 1 ha. (white).

Clos Cantenac (Fr). A vineyard in the A.C. Saint-Émilion, Bordeaux. 6 ha.

Clos Cantermerle (Fr). A vineyard in the commune of Cérons. A.C. Cérons, Bordeaux. 3 ha.

Clos Caperot (Fr). A vineyard in the A.C. Saint-Émilion, Bordeaux. 3 ha.

Clos Casal (Sp). A dry, white wine produced by Raimat in Lérida from Chardonnay 37%, Macabéo 30% and Parellada 33%.

Clos Castelot (Fr). A vineyard in the A.C. Saint-Émilion, Bordeaux. 10 ha.

Clos Chantegrive (Fr). A vineyard in the commune of Podensac. A.C. Graves, Bordeaux. 15 ha. (red and white).

Clos Chante-l'Alouette (Fr). A vineyard in the A.C. Saint-Émilion, Bordeaux. 4 ha.

Clos Chaudron (Fr). A vineyard in the A.C. commune of Montagny, Côte Chalonnaise, Burgundy.

Clos Cherchy (Fr). A vineyard in the commune of Pujols. A.C. Graves. Bordeaux. 4 ha. (white).

Clos Cloziot (Fr). A vineyard in the commune of A.C. Barsac (or Sauternes), Bordeaux. 1 ha.

Clos Cormey (Fr). A vineyard in the A.C. Saint-Émilion, Bordeaux. 7 ha.

Clos Côtes-Roland-de-Pressac (Fr). A vineyard in the A.C. Saint-Émilion, Bordeaux. 2 ha.

Clos Darches (Fr). A vineyard in the commune of St-Pierre-de-Mons. A.C. Graves, Bordeaux. 4 ha. (white).

Clos d'Armajan (Fr). A vineyard in the commune of Budos. A.C. Graves, Bordeaux. 2 ha. (red).

Clos d'Armens (Fr). A vineyard in the A.C. Saint-Émilion, Bordeaux. 2 ha.

Clos Darrouban (Fr). A vineyard in the commune of Portets. A.C. Graves, Bordeaux. 2 ha. (red and white).

Clos d'Arthus (Fr). A vineyard in the A.C. Saint-Émilion, Bordeaux. 5 ha.

Clos Dauphin (Fr). A vineyard in the A.C. Saint-Émilion, Bordeaux. 2 ha.

Clos Daviaud (Fr). A vineyard in the commune of Parsac-Saint-Émilion. A.C. Saint-Émilion, Bordeaux. 5 ha.

Clos de Amandiers (Fr). A vineyard in the commune of Pomerol. A.C. Pomerol, Bordeaux. 2 ha.

Clos de Barail (Fr). A vineyard in the commune of Illats. A.C. Cérons, Bordeaux. 9 ha.

Clos de Bèze (Fr). The finest of the Grand Crus of Gevrey-Chambertin. Of 16 ha. and has 12 owners. Often regarded as the finest of the red Burgundies. Also classed as Chambertin-Clos de Bèze.

Clos de Bos-Lancon (Fr). A vineyard in the commune of Illats. A.C. Cérons, Bordeaux. 4 ha.

Clos de Chaumiennes (Fr). An old walled vineyard in the wine village of Pouilly-sur-Loire. Produces fine A.C. Blanc Fumé.

Clos de Ciron (Fr). A vineyard in the commune of Loupiac. A.C. Loupiac, Bordeaux. 4 ha.

Clos de Gamot (Fr). A vineyard in the A.C. Cahors. Address = Rayssac, Lot Département, southern France.

Clos de Gensac (Fr). A vineyard in the commune of Pujols. A.C. Graves, Bordeaux. 4 ha. (white).

Clos de Jeanlaive (Fr). A vineyard in the commune of Barsac. A.C. Barsac (or Sauternes), Bordeaux. 5 ha.

Clos de la Barre (Fr). A Premier Cru vineyard in the A.C. commune of Volnay, Côte de Beaune, Burgundy. 2 ha. Also known as La Barre.

Clos de l'Abbaye (Fr). A vineyard in the A.C. Bourgueil, Touraine, Loire.

Clos de l'Abbaye-de-la-Rame (Fr). A vineyard in the commune of Mazères. A.C. Graves, Bordeaux. 6 ha. (white).

Clos de la Bonneterie (Fr). A vineyard in the commune of Portets. A.C. Graves, Bordeaux. 4 ha. (red and white).

C

Clos de la Cavaille-Lescours (Fr). A vineyard in the A.C. Saint-Émilion, Bordeaux. 1 ha.

Clos de la Chaînette (Fr). A small, noted red wine vineyard based in Auxerre.

Clos de la Chapelle (Fr). A vineyard in the A.C. commune of Pouilly-Fuissé, Mâconnais, Burgundy.

Clos de la Commaraine (Fr). A Premier Cru vineyard in the A.C. commune of Pommard, Côte de Beaune, Burgundy. 4 ha.

Clos de la Coulée de Serrant (Fr). Address = Château de la Roche aux Moines, Savennières, Loire. A.C. Savennières-Coulée de Serrant, Anjou-Saumur.

Clos de la Cure (Fr). Address = 33330 Saint-Émilion. Grand Cru. A.C. Saint-Émilion. Commune = Saint-Émilion.

Clos de la Dioterie (Fr). A vineyard in the A.C. Chinon, Anjou-Saumur, Loire.

Clos de la Féguine (Fr). A cuvée of the Premier Cru vineyard Aux Cras in the A.C. Beaune, Côte de Beaune, Burgundy.

Clos de la Gravette (Fr). A vineyard in the commune of Pomerol. A.C. Pomerol, Bordeaux.

Clos de la Henri (Fr). Address = 'Le Vaud Godard', Benais, 37140 Bourgueil, Loire. A.C. Bourgueil.

Clos de la Maison Blanche (Fr). A vineyard in the commune of Budos. A.C. Graves, Bordeaux. 2 ha. (white).

Clos de la Mare (Ch.Isles). See Blayney Vineyards.

Clos de la Maréchale (Fr). A Premier Cru vineyard in the village of Prémeaux in the A.C. of commune Nuits-Saint-Georges, Côte de Nuits, Burgundy. 9.5 ha.

Clos de la Mousse (Fr). A Premier Cru vineyard in the A.C. commune of Beaune, Côte de Beaune, Burgundy. 3.36 ha.

Clos de Langres (Fr). A vineyard in the Côte de Nuits which forms the boundary with the Côte de Beaune. Belongs to La Reine Pedauque. Produces supple fruity wines.

Clos de la Perrière (Fr). A Premier Cru vineyard in the A.C. commune of Fixin, Côte de Nuits, Burgundy. 6.53 ha. Owned by Phillip Joliet.

Clos de la Perrière (Fr). A Premier Cru vineyard in the A.C. commune of Vougeot in the Côte de Nuits.

Clos de la Point du Jour (Fr). A vineyard in the A.C. Fleurie Cru Beaujolais-Villages, Burgundy.

Clos de la Poussie (Fr). A vineyard in the A.C. Sancerre, Central Vineyards, Loire. 30 ha. (red and white wines). Owned by Cordier.

Clos de la Roche (Fr). A Grand Cru vineyard in the A.C. commune of Morey-Saint-Denis, Côte de Beaune, Burgundy. 15.5 ha.

Clos de la Roilette (Fr). A vineyard in Fleurie, A.C. Cru Beaujolais-Villages, Burgundy.

Clos de la Sablette (Fr). A vineyard in the A.C. Muscadet de Sèvre et Maine, Pays Nantais, Loire.

Clos de la Tuilerie (Fr). A vineyard in the commune of Portets. A.C. Graves, Bordeaux. 5 ha. (red and white).

Clos de la Vieille Forge (Fr). A vineyard in the commune of Lalande de Pomerol. A.C. Lalande de Pomerol, Bordeaux.

Clos de l'Avocat (Fr). A vineyard in the commune of Cérons. A.C. Cérons, Bordeaux. 3 ha.

Clos de l'Écho (Fr). A vineyard in the A.C. Chinon, Anjou-Saumur, Loire.

Clos de l'Ecu (Fr). A Premier Cru vineyard in the A.C. commune of Beaune, Côte de Beaune, Burgundy. 5 ha. Also known as À l'Écu.

Clos de l'Église (Fr). A vineyard in the commune of Lalande de Pomerol. A.C. Lalande de Pomerol, Bordeaux.

Clos de l'Église (Fr). A vineyard in the commune of Saint-Jean-de-Blaignac. A.C. Saint-Émilion, Bordeaux. 17 ha.

Clos de l'Émir (Alg). A red wine produced in Mascara.

Clos de l'Oratoire (Fr). Address = Château Peyreau, 33330 Saint-Émilion. Grand Cru Classé. A.C. Saint-Émilion. Commune = Saint-Émilion. 9.45 ha. Grape varieties – Cabernet franc 30% and Merlot 70%.

Clos de l'Oratoire des Papes (Fr). A vineyard in the A.C. Châteauneuf-du-Pape, Rhône.

Clos de Mazeray (Fr). A vineyard in the A.C. Meursault, Côte de Beaune, Burgundy. (red and white).

Clos de Miaille (Fr). A vineyard in the commune of Barsac. A.C. Barsac (or Sauternes), Bordeaux. 1 ha.

Clos de Moines (Fr). A vineyard in the commune of Lalande de Pomerol. A.C. Lalande de Pomerol, Bordeaux.

Clos de Mons (Fr). A vineyard in the commune of La Brède. A.C. Graves, Bordeaux. 3 ha. (red and white).

Clos de Montibeux (Switz). A white wine produced in the canton of Valais.

Clos de Naudin (Fr). A vineyard in the A.C. Saint-Émilion, Bordeaux. 2 ha.

Clos de Nauton (Fr). A vineyard in the commune of Fargues. A.C. Sauternes, Bordeaux. 4 ha.

Clos de Nouchet (Fr). A vineyard in the commune of Castres. A.C. Graves, Bordeaux.

Clos d'Épenots (Fr). A Premier Cru vineyard in the A.C. commune of Pommard, Côte de Beaune, Burgundy. 3.64 ha.

C

Clos de Pierrefeu (Fr). A vineyard in the commune of Preignac. A.C. Sauternes, Bordeaux. 4 ha.

Clos de Places (Fr). A vineyard in the commune of Arbanats. A.C. Graves, Bordeaux. 1 ha. (red and white).

Clos de Princes (Fr). A vineyard in the commune of Barsac. A.C. Barsac (or Sauternes), Bordeaux. 2 ha.

Clos des Abbayes (Switz). A vineyard based near Lausanne in Lavaux. Noted for the auction of its wines every December.

Clos de Sainte-Catherine (Fr). A vineyard in the A.C. Coteaux du Layon, Anjou-Saumur, Loire.

Clos des Amandiers (Fr). A vineyard in Alsace which is one of the few that sells wine using its name (vineyard). A light muscat wine with a slight almond taste.

Clos des Argillières (Fr). A Premier Cru vineyard from the village of Premeaux in the southern part of the A.C. commune Nuits-Saint-Georges, Côte de Nuits, Burgundy. 4.2 ha.

Clos des Arnaud (Fr). A vineyard in the commune of Lalande de Pomerol. A.C. Lalande de Pomerol, Bordeaux.

Clos de Sarpe (Fr). A vineyard in the A.C. Saint-Émilion, Bordeaux. 3 ha.

Clos des Arvelets (Fr). A Premier Cru vineyard in the A.C. commune of Pommard, Côte de Beaune, Burgundy. 8.5 ha. Also known as Les Arvelets.

Clos des Avaux (Fr). A cuvée in the Premier Cru vineyard of Les Avaux in the A.C. commune of Beaune, Côte de Beaune, Burgundy. Is owned by the Hospices de Beaune.

Clos des Barillères (Fr). Address = Bouchereau Frères, Beauregard, Mouzillon, Loire Atlantique. A.C. Muscadet de Sèvre et Maine.

Clos des Batailles (Fr). A vineyard in the A.C. Sancerre, Central Vineyards, Loire.

Clos des Capucins (Fr). A fine, noted vineyard of Kayserberg-Weinbach in Alsace. Owned by Faller-Frères.

Clos des Chartrons (Fr). The second wine of Château Lagrange, Grand Cru Classé (3rd) A.C. Saint-Julien.

Clos-des-Chênes (Fr). A Premier Cru vineyard in the A.C. commune of Volnay, Côte de Beaune, Burgundy.

Clos des Corbières (Fr). A vineyard in the commune of Montagne-Saint-Émilion. A.C. Montagne-Saint-Émilion, Bordeaux. 2 ha.

Clos des Cordeliers (Fr). A vineyard in the commune of Souzay-Champigny, A.C. Saumur-Champigny, Anjou-Saumur, Loire.

Clos des Corvées (Fr). A Premier Cru vineyard in the village of Prémeaux in the southern part of the A.C. commune of Nuits-Saint-Georges, Côte de Nuits, Burgundy. 5.1 ha.

Clos des Ducs (Fr). A Premier Cru vineyard in the A.C. commune of Volnay, Côte de Beaune, Burgundy.

Clos de Seillas (Fr). A vineyard in the commune of Gauriac. A.C. Côtes de Bourg, Bordeaux.

Clos des Épeneaux (Fr). A cuvée in the Premier Cru Les Épenots, A.C. Pommard, Côte de Beaune, Burgundy.

Clos des Fiètres (Fr). A vineyard within the Grand Cru Corton, Côtes de Beaune, Burgundy. Also known as Les Fiètres.

Clos des Forêts (Fr). A Premier Cru vineyard in the village of Prémeaux in the southern part of the A.C. commune of Nuits-Saint-Georges, Côte de Nuits, Burgundy.

Clos des Fougères (Fr). A vineyard in the commune of Virelade. A.C. Graves, Bordeaux. 4 ha. (white).

Clos-des-Fourneaux (Fr). A vineyard in the A.C. commune of Mercurey, Côte Chalonnaise, Burgundy. Can use the designation Premier Cru on the bottle label.

Clos des Goisses (Fr). A single vineyard based at Mareuil-sur-Ay, owned by Philiponnat. Produce a De Luxe vintage cuvée Champagne of the same name from Chardonnay 30% and Pinot noir 70% grapes.

Clos des Grandes Vignes (Fr). A Premier Cru vineyard [part] of the village of Prémeaux in the southern part of the A.C. commune of Nuits-Saint-Georges, Côte de Nuits, Burgundy. 2.1 ha.

Clos des Grandes Vignes (Fr). A vineyard in the commune of Pomerol. A.C. Pomerol, Bordeaux. 6 ha. Also known as Clos des Grandes Vignes-Clinet.

Clos des Grands Sillons (Fr). A vineyard in the commune of Pomerol. A.C. Pomerol, Bordeaux. 3 ha.

Clos des Grands Voyens (Fr). Address = Rue de Jamproyes, 71640 Mercurey. A vineyard in the A.C. commune of Mercurey, Côte Chalonnaise, Burgundy. Can use the designation Premier Cru on the bottle label.

Clos des Gravières (Fr). A vineyard in the commune of Portets. A.C. Graves, Bordeaux. 3 ha. (red and white).

Clos des Gros-Chênes (Fr). A vineyard in the A.C. Saint-Émilion, Bordeaux. 5 ha.

Clos des Jacobins (Fr). Address = 33330 Saint-Émilion. Grand Cru Classé. A.C. Saint-Émilion. Commune = Saint-Émilion. Grape varieties – Cabernet

C

franc, Cabernet sauvignon and Merlot. 8 ha. Owned by Cordier.

Clos des Lambrays (Fr). A Grand Cru vineyard in the A.C. commune of Morey-Saint-Denis. Côte de Nuits, Burgundy. 6 ha. Promoted to Grand Cru status in 1981.

Clos des Magrines (Fr). A vineyard in the commune of Puisseguin-Saint-Émilion. A.C. Puisseguin-Saint-Émilion, Bordeaux. 3 ha.

Clos des Maraings (Fr). A vineyard in the commune of Preignac. A.C. Sauternes, Bordeaux. 3 ha.

Clos des Menuts (Fr). Address = Place du Chapitre, 33330 Saint-Émilion. Grand Cru. A.C. Saint-Émilion. Commune = Saint-Émilion. 22.5 ha. Grape varieties – Cabernet franc 10%, Cabernet sauvignon 20% and Merlot 70%.

Clos des Moines (Switz). A noted vineyard based near Lausanne in Lavaux.

Clos des Montaigus (Fr). A vineyard in the A.C. commune of Mercurey, Côte Chalonnaise, Burgundy. May use the designation Premier Cru on the bottle label.

Clos des Mouches (Fr). A premier Cru vineyard in the A.C. commune of Beaune, Côte de Beaune, Burgundy, 25.13 ha.

Clos des Moulins-à-Vent (Fr). A vineyard in the commune of Cérons. A.C. Cérons, Bordeaux. 5 ha.

Clos des Ormes (Fr). A Premier Cru vineyard [part] in the A.C. commune of Morey-Saint-Denis, Côte de Nuits, Burgundy. 4.8 ha.

Clos Despagne (Fr). A vineyard in the commune of St-Pierre-de-Mons. A.C. Graves, Bordeaux. 4 ha. (white).

Clos d'Espagnet (Fr). A vineyard in the commune of Sauternes. A.C. Sauternes, Bordeaux. 3 ha. Also Château Esterlin.

Clos des Papes (Fr). A vineyard in the A.C. Châteauneuf-du-Pape, Rhône.

Clos des Pyramides (Egy). The brandname for red and white wines usually exported to the USSR.

Clos des Réas (Fr). A Premier Cru vineyard in the A.C. commune of Vosne-Romanée, Côte de Nuits, Burgundy. 2.1 ha.

Clos des Religieuses (Fr). A vineyard in the commune of Puisseguin-Saint-Émilion. A.C. Puisseguin-Saint-Émilion, Bordeaux. 8 ha.

Clos des Roches (Fr). A vineyard in the commune of Illats. A.C. Cérons. Bordeaux. 2 ha.

Clos des Roches (Fr). A vineyard in A.C. Sancerre, Central Vineyards, eastern Loire.

Clos des Rois (Fr). A Premier Cru vineyard [part] in the commune of Sampigny-lès-Maranges, A.C. Santenay, Côte de Beaune, Burgundy.

Clos des Sarrazins (Fr). A vineyard in the A.C. Saint-Émilion, Bordeaux. 6 ha.

Clos des Templiers (Fr). A vineyard in the commune of Pomerol. A.C. Pomerol, Bordeaux. 1 ha.

Clos des Tonnelles (Fr). A vineyard in the commune of St-Aignan. A.C. Côtes de Fronsac, Bordeaux. 4 ha.

Clos de Tart (Fr). A Grand Cru vineyard in the A.C. commune of Morey-Saint-Denis, Côte de Nuits, Burgundy. 7.5 ha. Is owned by Maison Mommessin.

Clos de Tavannes (Fr). A Premier cru vineyard [part] in the A.C. commune of Santenay, Côte de Beaune, Burgundy.

Clos de Terrefort (Fr). A vineyard in the commune of Loupiac. A.C. Loupiac. Southern Bordeaux. 3 ha.

Clos de Toumalin (Fr). A vineyard in the commune of Fronsac. A.C. Côtes Canon-Fronsac, Bordeaux. 2 ha.

Clos de Triguedina (Fr). Address = 46700 Puy-l'Évêque, Lot. A vineyard in A.C. Cahors, southern France.

Clos de Varambond (Fr). A vineyard in the commune of Fuissé, A.C. Pouilly-Fuissé, Mâconnais, Burgundy.

Clos de Vougeot (Fr). The Grand Cru vineyard in the A.C. commune of Vougeot, Côte de Nuits, Burgundy. 50 ha. Has some 80 owners. See Bisson [Colonel].

Clos Domaine-Château-la-Bastienne (Fr). A vineyard in the commune of Montagne-Saint-Émilion. A.C. Montagne-Saint-Émilion, Bordeaux. 12 ha.

Clos du Alem (Fr). A vineyard in the commune of Saillans. A.C. Côtes de Fronsac, Bordeaux. 10 ha.

Clos du Barrail (Fr). A vineyard in the commune of Cérons. A.C. Cérons, Bordeaux. 8 ha.

Clos du Bois (USA). A large winery based in Sonoma County, California. 124.5 ha. in Alexander Valley and Dry Creek Valley. Grape varieties – Cabernet sauvignon, Chardonnay, Gewürztraminer, Johannisberg riesling and Pinot noir. Produces varietal wines.

Clos du Bourg (Fr). A vineyard in the A.C. Vouvray, Touraine, Loire.

Clos du Calvaire (Fr). A vineyard in the A.C. Saint-Émilion, Bordeaux. 2 ha.

Clos du Casrel (Fr). A vineyard in the commune of Néac. A.C. Lalande de Pomerol, Bordeaux.

Clos du Castel (Fr). A vineyard in the commune of Pomerol. A.C. Pomerol, Bordeaux. 2 ha.

C

Clos du Chapitre (Fr). A Premier Cru vineyard [part] in the A.C. commune of Fixin, Côte de Nuits, Burgundy. 4.79 ha. The remaining part is in the A.C. commune of Gevrey-Chambertin. Is entirely rented out to Domaine Gelin & Moulin

Clos du Chapitre (Fr). A Premier Cru vineyard [part] in the A.C. commune of Gevrey-Chambertin, Côte de Nuits, Burgundy. 0.97 ha. The remaining part is in the A.C. commune of Fixin.

Clos du Chatain (Fr). A vineyard in the commune of Néac. A.C. Lalande de Pomerol, Bordeaux.

Clos du Chêne Marchand (Fr). A vineyard in the A.C. Sancerre, Central Vineyards, Loire.

Clos du Chêne Vert (Fr). A vineyard in the A.C. Chinon, Anjou-Saumur, Loire.

Clos du Clocher (Fr). A vineyard in the commune of Pomerol. A.C. Pomerol, Bordeaux. 5 ha.

Clos du Commandeur (Fr). A vineyard in the commune of Pomerol. A.C. Pomerol, Bordeaux. 1 ha.

Clos du Crot de la Roue (Fr). A vineyard in the A.C. Sancerre, Central Vineyards, Loire.

Clos du Fagnard (Fr). A vineyard in the commune of Pomerol. A.C. Pomerol, Bordeaux. 2 ha.

Clos du Gratte Sabots (Fr). A vineyard in the A.C. Sancerre, Central Vineyards, Loire.

Clos du Gros (Fr). A vineyard in the A.C. Saint-Émilion, Bordeaux. 1 ha.

Clos du Jaugua (Fr). A vineyard in the commune of Illats. A.C. Cérons, Bordeaux. 4 ha.

Clos du Marquis (Fr). Address = 33250 Saint-Julien, Pauillac. A.C. Haut-Médoc. Commune = Saint-Julien. The second wine of Château Léoville-Las-Cases Grand Cru Classé (2nd) Saint-Julien.

Clos du Mas (Fr). A vineyard in the commune of Listrac. A.C. Listrac, Bordeaux. 5 ha.

Clos du Medouc (Fr). A vineyard in the commune of Sainte-Croix-du-Mont. A.C. Sainte-Croix-du-Mont, Bordeaux. 2 ha.

Clos Dumes (Fr). Address = Langon 33210. A.C. Graves. Commune = Langon. See Château Balouet-Roailly.

Clos du Mesnil (Fr). A single vineyard based in Mesnil-sur-Ogier. Owned by Krug. 1.9 ha. Produces a vintage Blanc de Blancs De Luxe Champagne of same name. Vintages – 1979, 1980, 1981, 1982, 1983, 1984, 1985, 1986.

Clos du Monastère (Fr). See Château Doms et Clos du Monastère.

Clos du Mont Olivet (Fr). A vineyard in the A.C. Châteauneuf-du-Pape, Rhône.

Clos du Moulin (Fr). A vineyard in the commune of Saint-Christoly. A.C. Médoc, Bordeaux. 8 ha.

Clos du Moulin (Fr). A vineyard in the commune of Saint-Estèphe. A.C. Saint-Estèphe, Bordeaux. 5 ha.

Clos du Moulin-à-Vent (Fr). A vineyard in the commune of St-Pierre-de-Mons. A.C. Graves, Bordeaux. 5 ha. (white).

Clos du Palais-Cardinal (Fr). A vineyard in the A.C. Saint-Émilion, Bordeaux. 5 ha.

Clos du Palmiers (Fr). A vineyard in the commune of Sainte-Croix-du-Mont. A.C. Sainte-Croix-du-Mont, Bordeaux. 3 ha.

Clos du Pape (Fr). A vineyard in the commune of La Brède. A.C. Graves, Bordeaux. 6 ha. (white).

Clos du Pape (Fr). A vineyard in the commune of Fargues. A.C. Sauternes, Bordeaux. 5 ha.

Clos du Papillon (Fr). A vineyard in the A.C. Savennières. Anjou-Saumur, Loire.

Clos du Pellerin (Fr). Part of Clos Barrail-du-Milieu, A.C. Pomerol, Bordeaux.

Clos du Roc (Fr). A vineyard in the A.C. Saint-Émilion, Bordeaux. 3 ha.

Clos du Roi (Fr). A Grand Cru vineyard [part] in the A.C. commune of Aloxe-Corton, Côte de Beaune, Burgundy. (red and white).

Clos du Roi (Fr). A Premier Grand Cru vineyard [part] in the A.C. commune of Beaune, Côte de Beaune, Burgundy. 8.44 ha.

Clos-du-Roi (Fr). A vineyard in the A.C. commune of Mercurey, Côte Chalonnaise, Burgundy. May use the designation Premier Cru on the bottle label.

Clos du Roy (Fr). A vineyard in the commune of Barsac. A.C. Barsac (or Sauternes), Bordeaux. 11 ha. Also Château Piada.

Clos du Roy (Fr). A vineyard in the commune of Pomerol. A.C. Pomerol, Bordeaux. 3 ha.

Clos du Roy (Fr). Address = 18, Rue F. Gambon, 58150, Pouilly-sur-Loire, Sancerre. A.C. Sancerre, Central Vineyards, Loire.

Clos du Sable (Fr). A vineyard in the A.C. Saint-Émilion, Bordeaux. 2 ha.

Clos-du-Val (Fr). A Premier Cru vineyard in the A.C. commune of Auxey-Duresses, Côte de Beaune, Burgundy. 23 ha. Also known as the Climat-du-Val.

Clos du Val (USA). A French-owned winery in the Napa Valley, California. Grape varieties – Cabernet sauvignon, Chardonnay and Zinfandel. Produces varietal wines.

Clos du Verger (Fr). A Premier Cru vineyard in the A.C. commune of Pommard, Côte de Beaune, Burgundy. 2.55 ha.

C

Clos du Vieux (Fr). Part of Château les Eyguires, A.C. Saint-Émilion, Bordeaux.

Clos d'Uza (Fr). A vineyard in the commune of St-Pierre-de-Mons. A.C. Graves, Bordeaux. 34 ha. (white). Also Château Queyrats and St. Pierre.

Closed Wine (Eng). A wine which has still to develop. Its bouquet is still closed in.

Close Encounters Cocktail (Cktl). 2 fl.ozs. orange juice, ¼ fl.oz. Cognac, ¼ measure Crème de Fraises, 2 dashes Curaçao, dash Angostura, Blend together with a scoop of crushed ice in a blender. Pour into a large goblet. Dress with an orange slice on the rim of the glass.

Clos Feurus (Fr). A jointly-owned vineyard in the A.C. Saint-Émilion, Bordeaux. 4 ha.

Clos Fonrazade (Fr). A vineyard in the A.C. Saint-Émilion, Bordeaux. 4 ha.

Clos Fontaine (Fr). A vineyard in the commune of Fargues. A.C. Sauternes, Bordeaux. 2 ha.

Clos Fontelle (Fr). A vineyard in the A.C. Saint-Émilion, Bommes. 4 ha.

Clos Fourney (Fr). A vineyard in the A.C. Saint-Émilion, Bordeaux. 4 ha.

Clos Fourtet (Fr). Premier Grand Cru Classé. A.C. Saint-Émilion. Commune = Saint-Émilion. 21 ha. Grape varieties — Cabernet franc, Cabernet sauvignon and Merlot.

Clos Franc-Larmande (Fr). A vineyard in the A.C. Saint-Émilion, Bordeaux. 3 ha.

Clos Gaensbroennel (Fr). A famous vineyard on a hill near Barr in Alsace.

Clos Gauthey (Fr). A Premier Cru vineyard in the A.C. commune of Monthélie, Côte de Beaune, Burgundy. 1.4 ha.

Clos Gerbaud (Fr). A vineyard in the A.C. Saint-Émilion, Bordeaux. 1 ha.

Clos Gilet (Fr). A vineyard in the commune of Montagne-Saint-Émilion. A.C. Montagne-Saint-Émilion, Bordeaux. 3 ha.

Clos Girautin (Fr). A vineyard in the commune of Barsac. A.C. Barsac (or Sauternes), Bordeaux. 1 ha.

Clos Gontey (Fr). A vineyard in the A.C. Saint-Émilion, Bordeaux. 32 ha.

Clos Grand-Faurie (Fr). A vineyard in the A.C. Saint-Émilion, Bordeaux. 4 ha.

Clos Grand-Gontey (Fr). A vineyard in the A.C. Saint-Émilion, Bordeaux. 4 ha.

Clos Gravet (Fr). A vineyard in the A.C. Saint-Émilion, Bordeaux. 11 ha.

Clos Gros-Caillou (Fr). A vineyard in the A.C. Saint-Émilion, Bordeaux. 3 ha.

Clos Guinot (Fr). A vineyard in the A.C. Saint-Émilion, Bordeaux. 6 ha.

Clos Haut-Bibey (Fr). A vineyard in the A.C. Saint-Émilion, Bordeaux. 2 ha.

Clos Haut-Cabanne (Fr). A vineyard in the A.C. Saint-Émilion, Bordeaux. 1 ha.

Clos Haut-Caillou (Fr). A vineyard in the commune of Fronsac. A.C. Côtes Canon-Fronsac, Bordeaux. 3 ha.

Clos Haut-Cavujon (Fr). A vineyard in the commune of Lalande de Pomerol. A.C. Lalande de Pomerol, Bordeaux.

Clos Haut-Jaugueblanc (Fr). A vineyard in the A.C. Saint-Émilion, Bordeaux. 1 ha.

Clos Haut-Listrac (Fr). A vineyard in the commune of Puisseguin-Saint-Émilion. A.C. Puisseguin-Saint-Émilion, Bordeaux. 4 ha.

Clos Haut-Mazerat (Fr). A vineyard in the A.C. Saint-Émilion, Bordeaux. 8 ha.

Clos Haut-Mazeyres (Fr). A vineyard in the commune of Pomerol. A.C. Pomerol, Bordeaux. 9 ha.

Clos Haut-Montaiguillon (Fr). A vineyard in the commune of Saint-Georges-Saint-Émilion. A.C. Saint-Émilion, Bordeaux. 5 ha.

Clos Haut-Peyraguey (Fr). Premier Grand Cru. A.C. Sauternes. Commune = Bommes. 25 ha.

Clos Haut-Peyraguey (Fr). A vineyard in the commune of Barsac. A.C. Barsac (or Sauternes), Bordeaux.

Clos Haut-Robin (Fr). A vineyard in the A.C. Saint-Émilion, Bordeaux. 4 ha.

Clos Haut-Troquard (Fr). A vineyard in the A.C. Saint-Georges-Saint-Émilion. A.C. Saint-Émilion, Bordeaux. 1 ha.

Closing Time (Eng). The time when the sale of alcoholic beverages is not permitted between licensing hours. After 'Time' has been called, (10 minutes for full on-licence and 30 minutes for restaurant licence) it is permitted to consume those drinks that were purchased during permitted hours, after which the licensed premises must be vacated.

Clos Jacqueminot (Fr). A vineyard in the A.C. Saint-Émilion, Bordeaux. 4 ha.

Clos Jamnet (Fr). A vineyard in the commune of La Brède. A.C. Graves, Bordeaux. 4 ha. (white).

Clos Jauguet (Fr). A vineyard in the commune of Barsac. A.C. Barsac (or Sauternes), Bordeaux. 1 ha.

Clos Jaumard (Fr). A vineyard in the A.C. Saint-Émilion, Bordeaux. 2 ha.

Clos Jean-de-Maye (Fr). A vineyard in the commune of Portets. A.C. Graves, Bordeaux. 5 ha. (red and white).

Clos Jean Dubos (Fr). A vineyard in the commune of Pujols. A.C. Graves, Bordeaux. 2 ha. (white).

Clos Jean Guillot (Fr). A vineyard in the A.C. Saint-Émilion, Bordeaux. 1 ha.

Clos Jean-Voisin (Fr). A vineyard in the A.C. Saint-Émilion, Bordeaux. 3 ha.

C

Clos la Barde (Fr). Address = Saint Laurent des Bardes, 33330 Saint-Émilion. Grand Cru. A.C. Saint-Émilion. Commune = Saint Laurent des Bardes. 4.5 ha. Grape varieties – Cabernet 40% and Merlot 60%

Clos la Bouade (Fr). A vineyard in the commune of Barsac. A.C. Barsac, (or Sauternes), Bordeaux. 3 ha.

Clos la Bourrue (Fr). Part of Château Haut-Jean-Faure, A.C. Saint-Émilion, Bordeaux.

Clos la Cabanne (Fr). A vineyard in the commune of Puisseguin-Saint-Émilion. A.C. Puisseguin-Saint-Émilion, Bordeaux. 4 ha.

Clos Lacombe (Fr). A vineyard in the commune of Pomerol. A.C. Pomerol, Bordeaux. 2 ha.

Clos la Coutale (Fr). Address = 46700 Puy-l'Évêque, Lot. A vineyard in the A.C. Cahors, southern France.

Clos la Croix (Fr). A vineyard in the A.C. Saint-Émilion, Bordeaux. 6 ha.

Clos la Croix-Figeac (Fr). A vineyard in the A.C. Saint-Émilion, Bordeaux. 4 ha.

Clos la Fleur-Figeac (Fr). Part of Château Haut-Jean-Faure, A.C. Saint-Émilion, Bordeaux.

Clos la Fleur Figeac (Fr). Address = Château La Tour du Pin Figeac, 33330 Saint-Émilion. A.C. Saint-Émilion. Commune = Saint-Émilion. 3.66 ha. Grape varieties – Cabernet franc 35% and Merlot 65%.

Clos Laforest (Fr). A vineyard in the commune of Saint-Christoly. A.C. Médoc, Bordeaux. 4 ha.

Clos la Glaye (Fr). A vineyard in the A.C. Saint-Émilion, Bordeaux. 4 ha.

Clos la Madeleine (Fr). Address = Château la Gaffelière, 33330 Saint-Émilion. Grand Cru Classé. A.C. Saint-Émilion. Commune = Saint-Émilion. 2 ha. Grape varieties – Cabernet franc and Merlot.

Clos Lamagine (Fr). A vineyard in the commune of St-Pierre-de-Mons. A.C. Graves, Bordeaux. 6 ha. (white).

Clos la Marche (Fr). A vineyard in the commune of Fronsac. A.C. Côtes Canon-Fronsac, Bordeaux. 2 ha.

Clos la Maurasse (Fr). A vineyard in the commune of Langon. A.C. Graves, Bordeaux. 8 ha. Grape varieties – Cabernet sauvignon 45%, Malbec 10%, Merlot 45%, Sauvignon 50% and Sémillon 50%.

Clos Lamothe (Fr). A vineyard in the commune of Portets. A.C. Graves, Bordeaux. 5 ha. (red and white).

Clos-Landry (Fr). A Premier Cru vineyard in the A.C. commune of Beaune, Côte de Beaune, Burgundy. 1.98 ha. Also known as Tiélandry.

Clos Lapachère (Fr). A vineyard in the commune of Barsac. A.C. Barsac (or Sauternes). 4 ha.

Clos l'Arabey (Fr). A vineyard in the commune of Sainte-Croix-du-Mont. A.C. Sainte-Croix-du-Mont, Bordeaux. 2 ha.

Clos l'Arieste (Fr). A vineyard in the commune of Preignac. A.C. Sauternes, Bordeaux. 3 ha.

Clos la Rose (Fr). A vineyard in the commune of Pomerol. A.C. Pomerol, Bordeaux. 3 ha.

Clos Larrivat (Fr). A vineyard in the commune of Sainte-Croix-du-Mont. A.C. Sainte-Croix-du-Mont, Bordeaux. 3 ha.

Clos la Soulatte (Fr). A vineyard in the commune of Pomerol. A.C. Pomerol, Bordeaux. 2 ha.

Clos la Tonnelle (Fr). The second wine of Château La Serre, Grand Cru Classé Saint-Émilion.

Clos la Tonnelle (Fr). The second wine of Château Soutard, Grand Cru Classé, Saint-Émilion.

Clos la-Tour-Cluchon (Fr). A vineyard in the commune of Portets. A.C. Graves, Bordeaux. 4 ha. (red and white).

Clos la Vallée-du-Roi (Fr). A vineyard in the commune of Montagne-Saint-Émilion. A.C. Montagne-Saint-Émilion, Bordeaux. 3 ha.

Clos l'Avocat (Fr). A vineyard in the commune of Cérons. A.C. Graves, Bordeaux. 3 ha. (white).

Clos le Couvent (Fr). A vineyard in the commune of Saint-Émilion. A.C. Saint-Émilion, Bordeaux. Grand Cru.

Clos L'Église (Fr). A vineyard in the commune of Pomerol. A.C. Pomerol, Bordeaux. 5 ha.

Clos l'Église Clinet (Fr). A vineyard in the commune of Pomerol. A.C. Pomerol, Bordeaux. 4 ha.

Clos le Haut-Crabitan (Fr). A vineyard in the commune of Sainte-Croix-du-Mont. A.C. Sainte-Croix-du-Mont, Bordeaux. 2 ha.

Clos Léhoul (Fr). A vineyard in the commune of Langon. A.C. Graves, Bordeaux. 4 ha. (white).

Clos le Pas-St-Georges (Fr). A vineyard in the commune Saint-Georges-Saint-Émilion. A.C. Saint-Émilion, Bordeaux. 6 ha.

Clos les Arrivaux (Fr). A vineyard in the commune Sainte-Croix-du-Mont. A.C. Sainte-Croix-du-Mont, Bordeaux. 3 ha.

Clos les Grands-Champs (Fr). A vineyard in the commune of Pomerol. A.C. Pomerol, Bordeaux. 5 ha.

Clos les Hautes Bretonnières (Fr). Address

C

= Joseph Hallereau, Les Chaboissières, Vallet, Loire. A.C. Muscadet de Sèvre et Maine, Pays Nantais, Loire.

Clos les Moines (Fr). A vineyard in the commune of Couquèques. A.C. Médoc, Bordeaux. 10 ha.

Clos les Perriers (Fr). A vineyard in the A.C. Sancerre, Central Vineyards, Loire.

Clos les Santenots (Fr). See Les Santenots.

Clos l'Étoile (Fr). A vineyard in the commune of Lalande de Pomerol. A.C. Lalande de Pomerol, Bordeaux.

Clos l'Évêque (Fr). Address = Château d'Estroyes, 71640 Mercurey. A vineyard in the commune of Mercurey. A.C. Mercurey, Côte Chalonnaise, Burgundy.

Clos Liché (Fr). A vineyard in the commune of St-Pardon-de-Conques. A.C. Graves, Bordeaux. 3 ha. (white).

Clos l'Oratoire (Fr). A vineyard in the A.C. Châteauneuf-du-Pape, southern Rhône.

Clos Louloumet (Fr). A vineyard in the commune of Toulenne. A.C. Graves, Bordeaux. 3 ha. (white).

Clos Magne Figeac (Fr). Address = 33450 Saint-Sulpice-et-Cameyrac. A.C. Saint-Émilion. Commune = Saint-Sulpice-et-Cameyrac. 5.5 ha. Grape varieties – Cabernet franc and Merlot.

Clos Maisonneuve (Fr). A vineyard in the commune of Parsac-Saint-Émilion. A.C. Saint-Émilion, Bordeaux. 2 ha.

Clos Mandillot (Fr). A vineyard in the commune of Saint-Christoly. A.C. Saint-Émilion, Bordeaux.

Clos Marcilly (Fr). A vineyard in the A.C. commune of Mercurey, Côte Chalonnaise, Burgundy. May use the designation Premier Cru on the bottle label.

Clos Mariout (Egy). A vineyard that produces fine, full-flavoured white wines.

Clos Matamir (Egy). A vineyard that produces fine, full-flavoured red wines.

Clos Maurice (Fr). A vineyard in the commune of Saint-Sulpice-de-Faleyrens. A.C. Saint-Émilion, Bordeaux. 1 ha.

Clos Mayne-Lamouroux (Fr). A vineyard in the commune of Barsac. A.C. Barsac (or Sauternes), Bordeaux. 2 ha.

Clos Mazeyres (Fr). A vineyard in the commune of Pomerol. A.C. Pomerol, Bordeaux. 6 ha.

Clos Mercier (Fr). A vineyard in the commune of Barsac. A.C. Barsac (or Sauternes), Bordeaux. 3 ha.

Clos Micot (Fr). A Premier Cru vineyard in the A.C. commune of Pommard, Côte de Beaune, Burgundy. 3.9 ha.

Clos Mireille (Fr). A Blanc de Blanc wine produced by Domaine Ott in the A.C. Côtes de Provence, south-eastern France. Grape varieties – Sauvignon, Sémillon and Ugni blanc.

Clos Monplaisir (Fr). A vineyard in the A.C. Saint-Émilion, Bordeaux. 2 ha.

Clos Montesquieu (Fr). A vineyard in the commune of Montagne-Saint-Émilion. A.C. Montagne-Saint-Émilion, Bordeaux. 3 ha.

Clos Morteil (Fr). A vineyard in the commune of Bégadan. A.C. Médoc, Bordeaux. 4 ha.

Clos Napoléon (Fr). A Premier Cru vineyard in the A.C. commune of Fixin, Côte de Nuits, Burgundy. 1.75 ha. Also known as Aux Cheusots.

Clos Nardin (Fr). A vineyard in the commune of St-Michel. A.C. Côtes Canon-Fronsac, Bordeaux. 1 ha.

Clos Nouchet (Fr). A vineyard in the commune of Castres. A.C. Graves, Bordeaux. 3 ha. (red).

Clos Pailhas (Fr). A vineyard in the A.C. Saint-Émilion, Bordeaux. 3 ha.

Clos Pasquette (Fr). A vineyard in the A.C. Saint-Émilion, Bordeaux. 3 ha.

Clos Patarabet (Fr). A vineyard in the A.C. Saint-Émilion, Bordeaux. 1 ha.

Clos Patarabet-la-Gaffelière (Fr). A vineyard in the A.C. Saint-Émilion, Bordeaux. 2 ha.

Clos Patris (Fr). A vineyard in the A.C. Saint-Émilion, Bordeaux. 1 ha.

Clos Petit Corbin (Fr). Address = 33330 Saint-Émilion. A vineyard in the commune of Saint-Émilion. A.C. Saint-Émilion, Bordeaux.

Clos Petit-Figeac (Fr). A vineyard in the A.C. Saint-Émilion, Bordeaux. 3 ha.

Clos Petit Mauvinon (Fr). Address = Saint-Sulpice-de-Faleyrens, 33330 Saint-Émilion. A.C. Saint-Émilion. Commune = Saint-Sulpice-de-Faleyrens. 4 ha. Grape varieties – Cabernet sauvignon 35% and Merlot 65%.

Clos Peyret (Fr). A vineyard in the commune of Preignac. A.C. Sauternes, Bordeaux. 1 ha.

Clos Pezat (Fr). A vineyard in the A.C. Saint-Émilion, Bordeaux. 1 ha.

Clos Piganeau (Fr). A vineyard in the A.C. Saint-Émilion, Bordeaux. 1 ha.

Clos Plaisance (Fr). A vineyard in the commune of Parsac-Saint-Émilion. A.C. Saint-Émilion, Bordeaux. 9 ha.

Clos Pleville (Fr). A vineyard in the commune of Pomerol. A.C. Saint-Émilion, Bordeaux. 1 ha.

Clos Plince (Fr). A vineyard in the Sables-Saint-Émilion. A.C. Saint-Émilion, Bordeaux. 1 ha.

C

Clos Pourret (Fr). Part of Clos Petit-Figeac, A.C. Saint-Émilion, Bordeaux.

Clos Pressac (Fr). A vineyard in the commune of Saint-Étienne-de-Lisse. A.C. Saint-Émilion, Bordeaux. 7 ha.

Clos Prieur (Fr). A Premier Cru vineyard [part] in the A.C. commune of Gevrey-Chambertin, Côte de Nuits, Burgundy. 1.98 ha.

Clos Puyjalon (Fr). A vineyard in the commune of Portets. A.C. Graves, Bordeaux. 25 ha. (red and white). Also Château Jean-Gervais.

Clos René (Fr). A vineyard in the commune of Pomerol. A.C. Pomerol, Bordeaux. 10 ha.

Clos Rol de Fombrauge (Fr). A vineyard in the commune of Saint-Christophe-des-Bardes. A.C. Saint-Émilion, Bordeaux. 4 ha.

Clos Roucheyron (Fr). A vineyard in the A.C. Saint-Émilion, Bordeaux. 1 ha.

Clos Rousseau (Fr). A Premier Cru vineyard in the A.C. commune of Santenay, Côte de Beaune, Burgundy.

Clos Saint-Denis (Fr). A Grand Cru vineyard of the commune of Morey-Saint-Denis. 6.5.

Clos Sainte Magdeleine (Fr). A vineyard in the A.C. Cassis, Provence, south-eastern France.

Clos Saint-Jacques (Fr). A Premier Cru vineyard in the A.C. commune of Gevrey-Chambertin, Côte de Nuits, Burgundy. 6.92 ha. Also sold as Village Saint-Jacques.

Clos Saint-Jean (Fr). A Premier Cru [part] in the A.C. commune of Chassagne-Montrachet, Côte de Beaune, Burgundy. 14.36 ha.

Clos Saint Julien (Fr). Address = 33330 Saint-Émilion. Grand Cru. A.C. Saint-Émilion. Commune = Saint-Émilion. 20 ha. Grape varieties – Cabernet franc, Cabernet sauvignon and Merlot.

Clos-Saint-Marc (Les) (Fr). A Premier Cru vineyard in the village of Prémeaux in the southern part of the A.C. commune of Nuits-Saint-Georges, Côte de Nuits, Burgundy. 0.9 ha.

Clos Saint Martin (Fr). Address = Château Côte-Baleau, 33330 Saint-Émilion. Grand Cru Classé. A.C. Saint-Émilion. Commune = Saint-Émilion. 3.5 ha. Grape varieties – Cabernet franc, Cabernet sauvignon and Merlot.

Clos Saint-Paul (Fr). A vineyard in the A.C. commune of Givry, Côte Chalonnaise, Burgundy.

Clos Saint-Pierre (Fr). A vineyard in the A.C. commune of Givry, Côte Chalonnaise, Burgundy.

Clos Salmon (Fr). A vineyard in the A.C.

commune of Givry, Côte Chalonnaise, Burgundy.

Clos Sentouary (Fr). A vineyard in the commune of St-Pierre-de-Mons. A.C. Graves, Bordeaux. 2 ha. (white).

Clos Sicard (Fr). A vineyard in the A.C. Saint-Émilion, Bordeaux. 4 ha.

Clos Simard (Fr). A vineyard in the commune of Saint-Émilion. A.C. Saint-Émilion, Bordeaux. 4 ha.

Clos Sorbés (Les) (Fr). A Premier Cru vineyard in the A.C. commune of Morey-Saint-Denis, Côte de Nuits, Burgundy. 3.3 ha.

Clos St-André (Fr). A vineyard in the commune of Pomerol. A.C. Pomerol, Bordeaux. 2 ha.

Clos St-Anne (Fr). Part of Château Taillefer, A.C. Pomerol, Bordeaux.

Clos St-Émilion (Fr). A vineyard in the A.C. Saint-Émilion, Bordeaux. 7 ha.

Clos St-Hilaire (Fr). A vineyard in the commune of Portets. A.C. Graves, Bordeaux. 6 ha. (red and white).

Clos St. Jacques (Fr). Address = Sté Civile du Domaine de la Folié, 71150 Chagny. A vineyard in the A.C. commune of Rully, Côte Chalonnaise, Burgundy.

Clos St-Jean (Fr). A vineyard in the commune of Pujols. A.C. Graves, Bordeaux. 8 ha. (white).

Clos St-Martin (Fr). A vineyard in the commune of Saint-Émilion. A.C. Saint-Émilion, Bordeaux. 6 ha. Grand Cru Classé.

Clos St-Robert (Fr). A vineyard in the commune of Barsac. A.C. Barsac (or Sauternes), Bordeaux. 1 ha.

Clos St-Robert (Fr). A vineyard in the commune of Pujols. A.C. Graves, Bordeaux. 30 ha. (red and white).

Clos St-Valéry (Fr). A vineyard in the A.C. Saint-Émilion, Bordeaux. 3 ha.

Clos Tasta (Fr). A vineyard in the commune of St-Aignan. A.C. Côtes de Fronsac, Bordeaux.

Clos Teynac-Rival (Fr). A vineyard in the commune of Lussac-Saint-Émilion. A.C. Saint-Émilion, Bordeaux. 3 ha.

Clos Toulifant (Fr). Part of Château Boënot, A.C. Pomerol, Bordeaux.

Clos Triguedina (Fr). A vineyard in the A.C. Cahors in south-western France.

Clos Trimoulet (Fr). Address = 33330 Saint-Émilion. Grand Cru. A.C. Saint-Émilion. Commune = Saint-Émilion. 8 ha. Grape varieties – Cabernet franc 10%, Cabernet sauvignon 10% and Merlot 80%.

Clos Valentin (Fr). A vineyard in the A.C. Saint-Émilion, Bordeaux. 4 ha.

Clos Verdet-Monbousquet (Fr). A vineyard in the commune of Saint-Émilion.

A.C. Saint-Émilion, Bordeaux. 5 ha.
Clos Vert Bois (Fr). A vineyard in the A.C. Saint-Émilion, Bordeaux. 4 ha.
Clos Viaut (Fr). A vineyard in the commune of St-Pardon-de-Conques. A.C. Graves, Bordeaux. 2 ha. (white).
Clos Viaut (Fr). A vineyard in the commune of St-Pierre-de-Mons. A.C. Graves, Bordeaux. 9 ha. (white).
Clos Vieux Capot (Fr). A vineyard in the commune of Fronsac. A.C. Côtes Canon-Fronsac, Bordeaux. 2 ha.
Clos Vieux-Maillet (Fr). A vineyard in the commune of Pomerol. A.C. Pomerol, Bordeaux. 2 ha.
Clos Vieux-Pontet (Fr). A vineyard in the A.C. Saint-Émilion, Bordeaux. 1 ha.
Clos-Voyen (Fr). A Premier Cru vineyard in the A.C. commune of Mercurey, Côte Chalonnaise, Burgundy. Is also known as Les Voyens.
Clotted Cream (Eng). See Devonshire Cream.
Clou (Le) (Fr). A vineyard in the A.C. commune of Montagny, Côte Chalonnaise, Burgundy.
Cloud Burst Cocktail (Cktl). 1 fl.oz. dry Gin, ¾ fl.oz. Crème de Noyau, juice ½ lime, juice ½ lemon, dash egg white. Shake over ice, strain into an ice-filled highball glass. Top with soda water, lemon slice and ¼ fl.oz. Parfait Amour.
Cloud Buster Cocktail (Cktl). Place ⅕ gill Vodka into a flute glass with 2 small ice cubes. Top with iced Champagne and spiral of lemon.
Cloudiness (Eng). Caused by either a drastic change in temperature, from unwanted continuation of fermentation, from excess protein or bacterial action. Treated by fining.
Cloud Mist (China). The name given to the tea grown in the Lu Shan Botanic Garden in the Szechwan Province. Is served to visiting Western VIPs. Was originally reserved for the Emperor's use only.
Cloud Seeding (Eng). The action of spraying clouds with silver iodide to create rainfall away from the vineyards which might turn into hail storms over the vineyards. Either practised with aircraft or rockets in those areas of greatest risk. (Burgundy in France and Penedés in Spain are examples.)
Cloudy (Eng). See Cloudiness.
Cloudy Sky (Cktl). Place 2 ice cubes into a highball glass, add juice of ½ lime, ¾ gill Sloe Gin, stir and top with ginger ale.
Clouseaux (Les) (Fr). A vineyard in the A.C. commune of Montagny, Côte Chalonnaise, Burgundy.
Cloux (Fr). A vineyard in the A.C. commune of Rully, Côte Chalonnaise, Burgundy.
Clovaillon (Fr). A Premier Cru vineyard in the A.C. commune of Puligny-Montrachet, Côte de Beaune, Burgundy. 5.5 ha.
Clove Cocktail (Cktl). ⅓ measure Italian vermouth, ⅙ measure Sloe Gin, ⅙ measure Muscatel wine. Stir over ice, strain into a cocktail glass.
Clover Club (Cktl).(1). ⅓ gill Gin, ⅙ gill French vermouth, 1 teaspoon raspberry syrup, juice of lime, egg white. Shake over ice, strain into a 5 oz goblet.
Clover Club (Cktl).(2). 2 measures Gin, 1 measure Grenadine, 1 measure lemon juice, 1 egg white. Shake well over ice, strain into a cocktail glass.
Clover Club Royal (Cktl). ½ gill dry Gin, ¼ gill Grenadine, ¼ gill lemon juice, 1 egg yolk. Shake well over ice, strain into a cocktail glass.
Cloverdale (USA). A wine-producing district in the Russian River Valley, California.
Clover Leaf Cocktail (Cktl). As for Clover Club but with 2 sprigs of mint shaken with the cocktail. Decorate with a sprig of mint.
Cloying (Eng). A term given to a sweet wine the sweetness of which tends to be overpowering to the other properties of the wine.
Club (Eng). Licensed premises that differ from full On-licenses. There are two classes – [a]. The club that operates the same as a public house with a full On-licence and the same licensing hours but the clientele must be members. e.g. Royal British Legion Clubs, Workingmen's Clubs. [b]. The club that has a Club licence and is owned by the members, opening to suit the club's activities. e.g. Golf Clubs, Rugby Clubs. All visitors to clubs must have been signed in by a paid-up member and must be accompanied by the member whilst on the club premises.
Club Amontillado (Sp). A brand of Amontillado sherry produced by Harvey in Jerez de la Frontera.
Club Bottle (Fr). The name given to the bottles used for the sparkling Blanc Foussy wine of Vouvray, Touraine, Loire.
Club Cocktail (Cktl).(1). ½ gill Whisky, 3 dashes Grenadine, 2 dashes Angostura. Stir over ice, strain into a cocktail glass, add a cherry and squeeze of lemon peel juice on top.
Club Cocktail (Cktl).(2). ⅓ gill dry Gin, ⅙ gill sweet Vermouth. Stir over ice,

strain into a cocktail glass. Add a cherry and olive.

Club Cooler (Cktl). ⅓ gill Italian vermouth, ⅙ gill Grenadine, dash lemon juice, ½ pint soda water. Stir over ice in a highball glass, serve with a squeeze of lemon peel juice.

Club des Amis du Vin de Bordeaux (Fr). A wine society based in Bordeaux.

Club de Viticulteurs Champenois (Fr). Founded in 1971 by a group of récoltants-manipulants to improve the quality of non-vintage wines by limiting the amount of vintage wines its members may produce. (abbr) = C.V.C.

Club Goblet (Eng). A short footed tulip glass 6⅔ fl.ozs. used for cocktails and fruit juices.

Club Lager Beer (Afr). A Lager beer brewed by the Accra Brewery in Ghana.

Club Licence (Eng). See Club.

Clubman (S.Afr). The brand-name of a mint-flavoured punch (a wine apéritif).

Clubman (The) (Cktl). 1 fl.oz. Irish Mist, 4 fl.ozs. orange juice, dash egg white. Shake over ice, strain into an ice-filled highball glass. Trickle blue Curaçao down the inside of glass.

Club Room (Eng). A private room within licensed premises where clubs and societies can meet and drink in private.

Club Rose (Cktl). ½ measure Calvados, 1 measure Rye whisky, ½ measure lime cordial, dash Grenadine, dash egg white. Shake well over ice, strain into a cocktail glass.

Club Soda (USA). The name for a Soda syphon.

Club Tawny Port (Port). A fine old Tawny Port from Graham's Port shipping company.

Club Weisse (Ger). A sparkling Wheat beer 5.2% alc. by vol. brewed by the Spätenbräu Brauerei in Munich.

Cluster (USA). A hop variety which has a mild bitterness and bland flavour.

Clyde Distillers Ltd (Scot). Based in Glasgow. Produces King's Royal blended Scotch whisky. 43% alc. by vol.

Clynelish (Scot). A single Malt distillery at Bora, Sutherland. A new distillery under the same name has recently been built nearby by the DCL. Group. 43% alc. by vol.

C.M. (Fr) (abbr). Coopérative-Manipulant. C.I.V.C. registered member's initials on a Champagne label. Name belongs to a co-operative of top producers.

C.N.C.O.F.I.E.C. (China) (abbr). China National Cereals, Oils, Foodstuffs Imports and Export Corp.

CO₂ (Eng). Chemical symbol for Carbondioxide. 1 Carbon atom and 2 Oxygen atoms.

Coaching Inn (Eng). An old picking-up or setting-down point for horsedrawn coach passengers. Usually offers food, drink and accommodation.

Coachman (Cktl). ½ measure Cognac and ½ measure Port.

Coa-Dor (USA). A cloth bag into which coffee grounds are placed and then are put into near-boiling water to brew the coffee.

Coahuila (Mex). A region that contains the wine-producing districts of Parras and Saltillo.

Coalporter Beer (Eng). A cask conditioned Ale 1048 O.G. brewed by the Bruce public house in Bristol.

Coarse (Eng). A term used in wine tasting for wines with a rough texture.

Coastal Belt (S.Afr). A major wine-producing area in the south west.

Coaster (Cktl). Place several dashes of Angostura bitters into a spirit glass. Swirl and discard. Add 1 measure of Gin. Serve with Soda water.

Coaster (Eng). A stand of silver, cork, cardboard, wood etc., used to stand bottles, glasses or decanters on to prevent drips of wine or beer staining the tables. (Fr) = Dessous.

Coatepec (Mex). A noted coffee-producing region in southern Mexico.

Coatepec Coffee (Mex). A coffee from Vera Cruz. Is a rich, full-flavoured coffee that can be drunk on its own.

Coates and Co (Eng). The distillers of Plymouth Gin at the Blackfriars Distillery in Plymouth, Devon.

Coates Gaymers (Eng). A major Cider-making firm based in Somerset.

Coating (Eng). A deposit that is sometimes found on the inside of red wine bottles. See Chemise.

Cobalt Oxide (Eng). A mineral from Saxony used in glass making to produces a blue glass called Bristol Blue. Used for decanters and wine glasses in the seventeenth and eighteenth centuries.

Cobbin (A.E. and Co) (Eng). Address = St. Mary's Road, Ealing. A wine and spirits retail outlet owned by J.T. Davies & Sons. See also Davisons.

Cobblers (USA). A drink for warm weather. Made from wine or spirits, fresh fruits and ice shavings. Served in a highball glass.

Cobos (Sp). A producer of Montilla wines, in Montilla-Moriles.

C

Coca (S.Am). A Peruvian shrub whose leaves are used for infusion in alcohol, wine or as a Tisane. Has strong stimulative (narcotic) powers.

Cocabelos (Sp). A wine-producing area in Galicia. Produces red and white wines.

Coca Cola (USA). A Cola created in America, now produced under licence world-wide. Non-alcoholic, carbonated. Invented by Dr. John Pemberton in 1886. Formed the CCSB with the Schweppes Co. in 1986.

Coca Cola and Schweppes Beverages Company (Eng). CCSB. Newly formed, a merger of Coca Cola and Schweppes. Is the largest soft drinks company in the U.K.

Cocal (Sp). Liqueur producers based in Telde, Canary Islands.

Cocao Shells (Eng). Used to make a substitute cocoa drink. The powder was infused (similar to coffee).

Cocchi (It). A noted producer of Moscato d'Asti based in Piemonte, northwestern Italy.

Coccocciola (It). A white grape variety grown in Abruzzi.

Cochem (Ger). Village. (Anb) = Mosel-Saar-Ruwer. (Ber) = Zell/Mosel. (Gro) = Goldbäumchen. (Vins) = Bischofstuhl, Herrenberg, Hochlay, Klostergarten, Pinnerkreuzberg, Schlossberg, Sonnenberg.

Cochem (Ger). Village. (Anb) = Mosel-Saar-Ruwer. (Ber) = Zell/Mosel. (Gro) = Rosenhang. (Vins) = Arzlay, Nikolausberg, Rosenberg.

Cochero (Hol). A banana and cream-based liqueur 14.9% alc. by vol.

Cochineal (S.Am). A grub (or beetle) that attacks the vine, feeding on its sap. This weakens the plant and eventually kills it. Oil emulsions prevent it.

Cochiry (S.Am). A Beer made from sweet potatoes in Guyana.

Cochylis (Lat). The eggs of a night-flying moth whose caterpillars eat the blossoms and later the bunches of grapes. Treated by lead arsenate and other insecticides.

Cock-Ale (Eng). A mixture of spirits fed to fighting cocks in the eighteenth century. This would also be consumed by the winning punters with a number of tail feathers in the drink showing the number of ingredients in the drink. Tale is often suggested as being the origination of Cocktail.

Cockburn (Port). Vintage Port shippers. Vintages − 1870, 1872, 1873, 1875, 1878, 1881, 1884, 1887, 1890, 1894, 1896, 1900, 1904, 1908, 1912, 1927, 1935, 1947, 1950, 1955, 1960, 1963, 1967, 1970, 1975, 1977, 1982, 1983, 1985. Single Quinta is the Quinta da Eira Velha (1978). Owned by Allied-Lyons.

Cockburn Smithies (Port). Vintage Port shippers. See Cockburn.

Cocked Ale (Eng). Yorkshire dialect. Denotes a fresh, foaming beer.

Cock-eyed (Eng) (slang). A nineteenth-century term for drunk, intoxicated.

Cock Robin Bitter (Eng). A keg Bitter brewed by the Robinson Brewery in Stockport.

Cocktail (Eng). A combination of mixed drinks. Can be alcoholic or non alcoholic. See Flanagan (Betsy) and Cock-Ale.

Cocktail Age (USA). 1920−1935.

Cocktail Carine (Cktl). ½ measure Gin, ¼ measure Mandarine Napoléon, ¼ measure Dubonnet, dash lemon juice. Shake over ice, strain into a cocktail glass.

Cocktail Cherry (Eng). Two kinds, red = Maraschino, or green = Curaçao or Crème de Menthe. Used as a cocktail decoration.

Cocktail Hour (USA). The name given to the apéritif hour (pre-dinner) when cocktails are normally consumed.

Cocktail Mixes (USA). Prepared cocktail mixes (fruit juices etc) that only need the addition of the spirit to complete them.

Cocktail Party (Eng). A pre-meal party where apéritifs (cocktails) are served with canapés (hors d'oeuvres) to stimulate the appetite.

Cocktail Shaker (Eng). An implement for mixing cocktails with ice to cool them quickly. Has a lid and strainer built in. Usually made of silver, EPNS or stainless steel.

Cocktail Sherry (USA). The name given to a dry, Sherry-type drink made from a variety of grapes.

Cocktail Stick (Eng). A small pointed stick of wood or plastic used either for impaling fruit (cherries, pineapple, etc) or onion, olive, etc. which are placed in a drink (cocktail) or used for canapés.

Coco (Ch.Isles). Cocoa.

Coco (Wales). Cocoa.

Cocoa (Eng). A commercially produced powdered drink made from the cocoa bean. It is mixed with hot milk or water and sweetened to taste. See also Chocolate.

Cocoa Association Ltd (Eng). Address = Cereal House, 58, Marks Lane, London EC3. Conducts research and promotion.

Coco Braziliana (W.Ind). A coconut-flavoured liqueur.

Coco Fresh (It). A coconut-flavoured liqueur from Francoli.

C

Cocogif (W.Ind). A coconut-flavoured liqueur.

Coco Loco Cocktail (Cktl). 2 measures coconut water, ½ measure white Rum, ½ measure Apricot brandy, ½ measure coconut milk. Blend with a scoop of crushed ice in a blender. Pour into a coconut shell. Dress with powdered cinnamon. Serve with straws.

Coconut Breeze (Cktl). 1½ fl.ozs. dark Rum, ¾ fl.oz. pineapple juice, ¾ fl.oz. coconut milk, dash Maraschino, dash Orgeat syrup. Shake over ice, strain into a cocktail glass.

Coconut Daiquiri (Cktl). 2 fl.ozs. lime juice, 1 fl.oz. Coconut liqueur, ½ fl.oz. white Rum, dash egg white. Shake over ice, strain into a cocktail glass.

Coconut Liqueur (W.Ind). A white Rum flavoured with essences from macerated coconuts.

Coconut Milk (Eng). The juice obtained by pressing the coconut kernel flesh.

Coconut Shell Cocktail (Cktl). A shell shaped as a cup, top quarter removed, flesh scooped out, blend with ⅓ gill Tequila, juice ¼ lemon, 1 oz. coconut cream, 2 dashes Maraschino and a scoop of crushed ice. Serve in the shell with straws and spoon.

Coconut Tequila Cocktail (Cktl). ⅓ gill Tequila, juice ¼ lemon, 2 dashes Maraschino, ⅙ gill coconut milk, scoop crushed ice. Blend together in blender, serve in a flute glass.

Coconut Tumble Cocktail (Cktl). 1½ fl.ozs. white Rum, 1 fl.oz. coconut milk, ¾ fl.oz. Cointreau, dash Grenadine. Stir well over ice. Pour into a coconut shell. Dress with cherries and serve with straws.

Coco Oco Cocktail (Cktl).(Non-alc). ½ measure coconut milk, juice of ¼ lemon, ¼ teaspoon Angostura, 4 dashes Maraschino, ⅙ pint milk. Blend with a scoop of crushed ice in a blender. Strain into a goblet. Dress with a cherry.

CocoRibe (USA). A coconut milk and white Virginian Rum liqueur from Cincinnati, Ohio. 23% alc. by vol.

Cocoron (Hol). A coconut-flavoured liqueur produced by De Kuyper.

Cocui (S.Am). See Cocuy.

Cocuy (S.Am). A brandy distilled from fermented sisal roots in Venezuela. See also Cocui.

Coda di Volpe Bianco (It). A white grape variety grown in the Campania region. Gives strong, vinous, straw-coloured dry wines.

Cod Bottle (Eng). A mineral bottle with a marble in the neck to retain the pressure, often coloured to stop being used by rival companies.

Code du Vin (Fr). In Burgundy forbids more than the addition of 9 kilogrammes of sugar per 3 hectolitres of must and 200 kilogrammes per hectare.

Códega (Port). A white grape variety.

Code of Hammurabi (Arab). The first wine laws of Babylonia in 2000 B.C.

CODERUM (W.Ind) (abbr). Comité de Défense et d'Organisation du Marché du Rhum.

Codex Laureshamensis (Ger). A list of vineyards donated to the abbey of Lorsch by St. Nazarius in 764 A.D. (consisted of vineyards of most of the present day regions along the Rhine).

Codlings (Eng). Old English Cider-making apples. Made very fine cider.

Codo (Port). A white grape variety grown in Beiras.

Codorníu (Sp). A producer of sparkling Cava wines by the méthode champenoise in south-eastern Spain.

Codswallop (Eng). The name for the mallet that was used to hammer the marble into the Cod mineral bottles.

Coebergh (Hol). A distillery that produces Jenevers and liqueurs. Part of Heineken.

Coefficient of Valorization (Port). Part of the method of scoring marks during a tasting of Vinhos Verdes by multiplying the points scored during the tasting according to the type of wine.

Coères (Les) (Fr). A vineyard in the A.C. commune of Montagny, Côte Chalonnaise, Burgundy.

Coeur de Lion (Cyp). A red table wine produced by Keo in Limassol.

Coeur de Rouge (S.Afr). A red wine blend of Cabernet 75%, Cinsault and Pinotage from the Audacia Estate in Stellenbosch.

Co-Ferment (Eng). Part of the complex proteins (enzymes) which together with the Apoferment form the Holoferment.

Coffea (Lat). A coffee tree species of the genus Rubiaceae of which there are 60–100 species.

Coffea Abeokutae (Lat). A variety of the coffee tree grown mainly in Africa. See Coffea.

Coffea Arabica (Lat). A species of the coffee tree. Grows mainly in hilly regions 600–2000 metres and produces the finest coffees. See also Bourbon Coffee and Coffea.

Coffea Arabusta (Lat). A hybrid coffee tree from Arabica and Robusta cross.

Coffea Canephora (Lat). A species of the coffee tree. Also known as the Robusta. See Coffea.

Coffea Congensis (Lat). A variety of the coffee tree grown mainly in West Africa. See Coffea.

Coffea Devevrei (Lat). A variety of the

coffee tree grown mainly in West Africa. See Coffea.

Coffea Eugenioides (Lat). A variety of coffee tree grown mainly in West Africa. See Coffea.

Coffea Excelsa (Lat). A variety of the coffee tree whose bean produces a dark roast. Grown mainly in West Africa. See Coffea.

Coffea Liberica (Lat). A variety of the coffee tree. Grown mainly in West Africa. See Coffea.

Coffea Robusta (Lat). A variety of Coffea Canephora. Produces a dark, bitter coffee. Is more resistant to disease than Arabica and grows at altitudes of sea level to 600 metres. See Coffea.

Coffea Stenophylla (Lat). A variety of the coffee tree grown mainly in West Africa. See Coffea.

Coffee (Eng). A beverage produced from the roasted and ground bean (kernel) of the Coffea tree. Strength of the roast and blending will influence the strength of brew. There are three main types – Brazil, Milds and Robustas. See also Pure Coffees.

Coffee Amaretto (Liq.Coffee). Using ½ measure Amaretto and ½ measure Tia Maria. Top with whipped cream.

Coffee and Brandy Liqueur (USA). A liqueur made from a blend of Colombian coffee and Brandy. 35% alc. by vol.

Coffee Bags (Eng). Fresh ground coffee in mesh bags. Usually of medium ground to prevent grinds escaping. Produces mainly medium brews.

Coffee Berry Disease (Eng). A strain of Colletotrichum Coffeanum. Major coffee disease. Lives in the bark tissue of the coffee tree. Is dispersed by rain splash.

Coffee Bestle (Den). A coffee-flavoured liqueur.

Coffee Borgia (Liq.Coffee). See Café Borgia.

Coffee Break (USA). The time allocated around mid-morning (11 a.m) when coffee (and biscuits) are consumed. See Elevenses and Tea Break.

Coffee Brewing Methods (Eng). Boiling, Filtering, Infusion, Percolating and Steaming. See Al Fresco, Automatic Drip, Espresso, Filter, Neapolitan Pot, Percolator, Turkish and Vacuum.

Coffee Bush Diseases (Lat). See Colletotrichum Coffeanum, Hemileia Vastatrix and Stephanoderes Hamjei.

Coffee Cherry (Eng). The name given to the fruit of the Coffea tree. Has an outer skin, parchment, silverskin and 2 beans (seeds).

Coffee Cobbler (Cktl). ⅕ gill Cognac, 2 dashes sugar syrup, fresh brewed coffee. Stir over ice, strain into an ice-filled highball glass. Top with a dash of Port wine. Serve with straws.

Coffee Cocktail (Cktl).(1). ⅔ measure Port wine, ⅓ measure Brandy, 2 dashes orange Curaçao, yolk of egg. Shake over ice, strain into a cocktail glass.

Coffee Cocktail (Cktl).(2). ⅙ gill Cognac, ⅓ gill Port, 1 egg yolk, 1 teaspoon Gomme syrup. Shake over ice, strain into a small wine goblet. Top with grated nutmeg. Also known as Law's Cocktail.

Coffee Diablo (Fr). Heat together 2 cloves, 1 fl.oz. Cognac, ½ fl.oz. Cointreau, piece of orange and lemon zest over a low flame until nearly boiling. Ignite and pour over hot black coffee in a heatproof glass or cup.

Coffee-Flavoured Brandy (USA). A Brandy-based liqueur infused with coffee beans.

Coffee Flip (Cktl). 1 egg, 1 teaspoon sugar, ⅕ gill Brandy, ⅕ gill Port, 2 teaspoons cream. Shake over ice, strain into a flip glass. Top with grated nutmeg.

Coffee Grasshopper (Cktl). ⅓ measure coffee liqueur, ⅓ measure Crème de Menthe (white), ⅓ measure cream. Shake over ice, strain into an ice-filled old-fashioned glass.

Coffee Grinds (Eng). See Grinds or Coffee Grounds.

Coffee Grounds (Eng). The roasted beans after they have been ground (cut up) for brewing. See also Grinds.

Coffee Leaf Rust (Eng). Hemileia Vastatrix. An obligate parasite to coffee. Forms orange pustules on the underside of leaves. The postules contain spores. Heavy infection can kill the plant.

Coffee Liqueurs (Eng). Spirit-based, coffee-flavoured liqueurs. Range in alc. content from 17–35% by vol. Best known are Bahia, Coffee Bestle, Kahlúa, Kamok, Pasha and Tia Maria.

Coffee Machines (Eng). Manual or automatic units which aid the brewing of coffee from the roasted, ground bean. See Coffee Brewing Methods.

Coffee Morning (Eng). An event organised to raise monies for charity where coffee is served for a nominal fee.

Coffee Nog (Eng). For two persons. 2 measures Cognac, 2 teaspoons cocoa powder, 2 teaspoons sugar, 1 measure Crème de Cacao, 2 egg yolks, 1 measure whipped cream. Pour ⅓ pint strong black coffee into a saucepan, add ingredients (except cream), heat slowly. Stir, pour into heat-proof glasses, top with cream and grated nutmeg.

Coffee Royale (USA). 5 ozs. strong hot black coffee, 1½ ozs. Brandy, sugar cube. Heat an 8 oz. goblet, place coffee into glass. Put bowl of a teaspoon over coffee, place sugar cube into bowl. Pour Brandy over sugar and then ignite sugar and Brandy in bowl of spoon. Stir into coffee and serve.

Coffee Sour (Cktl). ⅓ gill Tia Maria, ⅙ gill lemon juice, 1 teaspoon powdered sugar, ½ egg white. Shake well over ice, strain into a sour glass.

Coffee Sport (USA). A coffee liqueur which is similar in style to Crème de Café.

Coffee Substitutes (Eng). Ingredients that are roasted and ground and used as a substitute for coffee or as an additive to coffee to bulk out and flavour. Main ones are – Acorn, carrot, cereals, chick pea, chicory, dandelion root, date, fig, lupin and soya.

Coffee Syrup Nog (Eng). Hot milk mixed with coffee essence and golden syrup to taste.

Coffee Terminal Market Association of London Limited (Eng). Address = Cereal House, 58, Mark Lane, London EC3R 5AB.

Coffee Trade Federation (Eng). Address = Tamesis House, 9, Wapping Lane, London E1 9DA.

Coffee Tree (Eng). A name for the Coffea from the family Rubiaceae. 60–100 species.

Coffee Year (Eng). 1st October to 30th September.

Coffeina (It). Caffeine.

Coffey (Eng). The seventeenth-century word used for coffee.

Coffey (Aeneas) (Ire). An Irish Excise officer who in 1831 invented and registered the patent for the 'Coffey Still', a continuous still. See also Robert Stein.

Coffey Still (Ire). A continuous still invented by Aeneas Coffey. See also Robert Stein and Patent Still.

Coffi (Wales). Coffee.

Cognac (Fr). A commune in the Charente Département whose grapes are classed Borderies (Cognac).

Cognac (Fr). A commune in the Charente Département whose grapes are classed Grande Champagne (Cognac).

Cognac (Fr). A spirit distilled from wine in the Charente region of western France. Has own A.C. and rated the best Brandy in the world. Crus of Grande Champagne, Petite Champagne, Borderies, Fins Bois, Bons Bois and Bois Ordinaires. See also Fine Champagne.

Cognac Authentique (Fr). The name given to Cognac brandy that is less than four years old.

Cognac Chollet (Fr). Cognac producer. Address = Le Planty, Boutiers-Saint-Trijan, 16100 Cognac. 18 ha. in Fins Bois. Produces a wide range of fine Cognacs.

Cognac Coupling (Cktl). 1 measure old Cognac, ½ measure Tawny Port, ¼ measure Pernod, 4 dashes lemon juice. Shake over ice, strain into an ice-filled old-fashioned glass. Serve with straws.

Cognac des Bois (Fr). The name for the lesser Cognac areas of Borderies, Fins Bois, Bons Bois and Bois Ordinaires.

Cognac Grades and Ageing (Fr). Is classified according to age (of the youngest brandy in the blend). The blend must be at least two years old before it can be exported. Grades are – * * * and V.S. must be aged for 3 years in wood before bottled. V.S.O.P. must be more than 4 years old and Old Liqueur which will have been matured in wood for 20, 30 or 40 plus years. (Also known as X.O. Extra Vieille, Napoléon, etc). See Compte System

Cognac Mint Frappé Cocktail (Cktl). ½ measure Cognac, ½ measure Crème de Menthe. Stir well over ice, strain into an ice-filled highball glass. Add crushed mint leaves and serve with straws.

Cognac Orange Cocktail (Cktl). 1 measure orange juice, ½ measure Cognac. Stir over ice in a highball glass. Dress with a slice of orange and serve with straws.

Cognoscenti (It). Connoisseurs.

Coigns (Scot). A term used for chocks to hold casks in place.

Coing (Fr). Quince brandy. A stone fruit brandy.

Cointreau (Fr). A clear Triple Sec orange liqueur. Produced by Les Distilleries Cointreau, 49, St-Barthélemy d'Anjou, Angers. Also distilled in Vilafranca de Penedés, Spain. Made from dried bitter orange peel and sweet orange peel. 40% alc. by vol.

Cointreau Rocks (Cktl). In a small tumbler pour 3 ozs. Cointreau over ice cubes. Add 3 dashes of Angostura, stir, decorate with slice of lemon.

Cokanski Merlot (Yug). A red wine produced in north-eastern Yugoslavia near the Hungarian border.

Coke (Eng). (abbr). Of Coca Cola.

Coke High (Cktl). In a small glass put 1 measure Rye whiskey, add ice and a slice of orange. Top up with Coca Cola.

Cola (Afr). A seed which contains caffeine. Is used as a colouring agent and flavouring agent (bitter) in beverages.

Cola (USA). A non-alcoholic red-brown carbonated drink made from a secret blend of essences and other flavours. Top brands Coca Cola and Pepsi Cola.

Cola de Mono (Chile). A mixture of milk, coffee, vanilla and Aguardiente (flavoured with anis) served at Christmas. Drunk hot or cold.

Cola de Pescado (Sp). Isinglass.

Colares (Port). A demarcated area of Portugal. Produces red and white wines. Sited in 'The ocean' of the river Tejo in the region of Estremadura. See also Ramisco Vine.

Colas (Marie) (W.Ind). A Rum distillery based at Port au Prince, Haiti. Produces Rhum Citadelle.

Colatje (Hol). A term used if a Kleintje beer is served in a Colatje glass.

Colatje Glass (Hol). A small (baby) beer glass.

Colchagua (Chile). A province and wine-producing area in the Central Zone.

Colcord Winery (USA). A winery based in Paris, Kentucky. 14 ha. Produces French-American hybrids and Vinifera wines.

Cold Bottling (Eng). A term used to describe wines, beers, etc. that do not go through pasteurisation after bottling. The wines, beers, etc. are usually passed through a membrane filter or treated with SO_2 to ensure sterility (all equipment must be hygienically clean and sterile).

Cold Cactus Cocktail (Cktl). ⅖ measure Tequila, ⅖ measure Vodka, ⅕ measure blue Curaçao, juice ½ lemon, dash egg white. Shake over ice, strain into a highball glass. Top with soda.

Cold Compound Gin (Eng). A cheaply produced Gin by adding chemically-made juniper-flavoured essence to the alcohol.

Cold Deck Cocktail (Cktl). 1 measure Brandy, ½ measure (white) Crème de Menthe, ½ measure sweet Vermouth. Stir over ice, strain into a cocktail glass.

Cold Duck (Cktl). Equal quantities of red Burgundy and iced Champagne.

Cold Duck (Ger). Kalte Ente. Sparkling red wine.

Cold Duck (USA). A mixture of sweet pink sparkling wines from the mid-west.

Cold Duck 5ᵗʰ Avenue (S.Afr). A sparkling rosé wine made from Steen, Clairette blanche and Pinotage grapes by the SFW. (medium-sweet).

Cold Duck St. Louis (S.Afr). A rosé sparkling wine made from Grenache, Cinsault and Clairette blanche grapes by Gilbeys Ltd. (sweet).

Cold Ginger Tea (Cktl). ½ pint cold tea, ½ pint dry ginger ale, 1 oz. stem ginger syrup, 1 measure Whisky, 6 cloves. Infuse tea with cloves, cool, add remaining ingredients, cool, decorate with sliced stem ginger.

Colding (Ger). A brand of Rum produced by Hansen in Flensburg.

Cold Mix System (USA). A method of making Gin as an alternative to the Head System.

Cold Spring Brewing (USA). A brewery based in Cold Spring, Minnesota. Is noted for its Colonie, Fox De Luxe, Gameinde and Kegelbrau.

Cold Sterile Filtration (Eng). The process of filtering wine through fine sheet membrane filters to remove yeast cells. Does not affect the finished wine.

Cold Turkey (USA) (slang). A term used for giving up an addiction all at once instead of being weaned off the habit. i.e. An alcoholic.

Col du Cygne (Fr). The name given to the pipe that the Cognac vapours pass through before reaching the cooling coil (condenser).

Coleburn (Scot). A single Malt whisky distillery. Built in 1896 on Rothes road, outside Elgin. Owned by DCL company. 43% alc. by vol.

Coleraine (Ire). A light blend of Grain whiskey from Coleraine in north-eastern Ireland.

Coleraine Cabernet Merlot (N.Z.). A wine from Te Mata. Deep coloured, soft and elegant.

Cole Ranch Vineyard (USA). A vineyard based in Mendocino County in California. 16.5 ha. Grape variety — Johannisberg riesling.

Colheita (Port). Vintage.

Coligny (Fr). A Cru Champagne village in the Canton de Vertus. District = Châlons.

Coliseo Corregedor (Sp). The brand-name of a Sherry produced by the Valdespino Co.

Collage (Fr). Clearing wine of its sediment.

Collar (Eng). An area between the measure line of a glass and the beer surface.

Collar (Fr). To clarify a wine in cask.

Collar (USA). The name given to the foamy top to a glass of beer.

Collard Brothers (N.Z.). A vineyard and winery. Address = Lincoln Road, Henderson, North Island. Grape varieties — Cabernet franc, Cabernet sauvignon, Gewürztraminer, Merlot, Müller-Thurgau and Rhine riesling.

Collares (Port). The alternative spelling of Colares.

Collar Label (Eng). The label found on the

C

neck of a bottle of beer, spirits or wine. (Fr) = Collerette.

Collavini (It). A noted winery based at Corno di Rosazzo in the Friuli-Venezia Giulia region. Buys in grapes as it owns no vineyards. Also known as Catemario. Produces cuve close sparkling wines.

College Ale (Eng). A cask conditioned Ale 1073 O.G. brewed by the Morell Brewery of Oxford.

College Ale (Eng). A term formerly used to describe strong beers brewed in the colleges of the older universities.

College Bottles (Eng). Early bottles with the seal of the college embossed on them. Eighteenth and early nineteenth century.

College Fino (Eng). A fine, Fino sherry from the Dolamore stable in London.

College Winery (Austr). Address = P.O. Box 588, Wagga Wagga, New South Wales 2650. 13 ha. Grape varieties – Cabernet franc, Cabernet sauvignon, Chardonnay, Merlot, Pinot gris, Rhine riesling and Traminer.

Colle-Musquette (Fr). An alternative name for the Muscadelle grape.

Collerette (Fr). Describes the label seen on some wine bottle necks, known as the Collar label in England. See also Cravate.

Collery (Fr). Champagne producer. Address = 4 Rue Anatole, 51160 Ay. 8 ha. Produces – Vintage and non-vintage wines. Vintages – 1945, 1947, 1959, 1964, 1966, 1969, 1970, 1971, 1973, 1974, 1976, 1979, 1980, 1981, 1982.

Colletotrichum Coffeanum (Lat). The Coffee Berry Disease. A fungus that attacks the berry (cherry) of the coffee tree especially the Coffea Arabica variety.

Colli (It). Lit – 'Hill wine'.

Colli (It). An old term, that, when applied to Marsala, denotes 2 years of ageing and 18% alc. by vol.

Colli Albani (It). D.O.C. white wine from Latium. Made from Bonvino, Cacchione, Giallo, Malvasia del Lazio, Malvasia rossa, Trebbiano toscano and Verde grapes. Vinification has to take place in the area of production. Graded Superiore if total alc. by vol. is 12.5% D.O.C. also applies to the naturally sparkling wines.

Colli Berici (It). D.O.C. red wine from Veneto. 3 red wines are named after principal grape variety used. Colli Berici Cabernet, Colli Berici Merlot and Colli Berici Tocai Rosso.

Colli Berici (It). D.O.C. white wines of Veneto. 4 white wines are named after

principal grape variety used. Colli Berici Garganega, Colli Berici Pinot Bianco, Colli Berici Sauvignon and Colli Berici Tocai Bianco.

Colli Bolognesi dei Castelli Medioevali (It). See Colli Bolognesi di Monte San Pietro.

Colli Bolognesi di Monte San Pietro (It). D.O.C. red wines from Emilia-Romagna. 2 red wines are named after the principal grape variety used, Barbera and Merlot. If the Barbera has total alc. content of 12.5% and aged 3 years (1 year in wood) then graded Riserva.

Colli Bolognesi di Monte San Pietro (It). D.O.C. white wine from Emilia-Romagna. 3 white wines are named after the principal grape variety used, Pinot bianco, Riesling italico and Sauvignon. The Bianco is made from Albana and Trebbiano romagnola grapes.

Colli del Trasimeno Bianco (It). D.O.C. white wine from Umbria. Made from the Grechetto, Malvasia del Chianti, Trebbiano toscano 60%, Verdicchio and Verdello grapes. Produced by the Order of Malta monks at the Castello Magione, Perugia.

Colli del Trasimeno Rosso (It). D.O.C. red wine from Umbria. Made from Cigliegiolo, Gamay, Malvasia del Chianti, Sangiovese 60–80% and Trebbiano toscano grapes. Produced by the Order of Malta monks at the Castello Magione, Perugia.

Colli di Bolzano (It). D.O.C. red wine from Trentino-Alto Adige. Made from Lagrein, Pinot nero and Schiave grapes.

Colli di Catone (It). A winery based at Monteporzio Catone in the Latium region. Is noted for its Frascati wines.

Colli di Congeliano (It). A dry white wine from the Treviso provence of Venetia. Made from the Prosecco grape.

Colli di Tuscolo (It). A winery based in Latium. Noted for its Frascati Classico wines.

Colli Euganei (It). A district within the province of Padova in Veneto. Has 17 communes producing red and white wines. The vineyards are in the Euganean hills.

Colli Euganei Bianco (It). D.O.C. white wine from Veneto. Made from the Garganega, Pinella, Pinot bianco, Riesling italico, Sauvignon, Seprina and Tocai grapes. If total alc. content is 12% and aged for minimum of 6 months then graded Superiore. D.O.C. also applies to sparkling wines produced to specifications.

C

Colli Euganei Moscato (It). D.O.C. white wine from Veneto. Made from the Moscato bianco grape. D.O.C. also applies to sparkling wines produced according to specifications.

Colli Euganei Rosso (It). D.O.C. red wine from Veneto. Made from Barbera, Cabernet franc, Cabernet sauvignon, Merlot and Raboso veronese grapes. If total alc. content is 12% and aged minimum 12 months then graded Superiore. D.O.C. applies to sparkling wines produced according to specifications.

Colli Lanuvini (It). D.O.C. white wine from Latium. Made from Bellone, Bonvino, Malvasia bianca di candia, Puntinata and Trebbiano grapes. Produced in communes of Genzano and part of Lanuvio in the Alban hills.

Colli Morenici Mantovani del Garda (It). D.O.C. red, rosé and white wines from Lombardy. Red and rosé made from 30–60% Rossanella, 20–50% Rondinella and 10–30% Negrara trentina. White made from 20–25% Gargenega, 20–25% Trebbiano giallo and 10–40% Trebbiano nostrano. If rosé total alc. content equals 11.5% then graded Chiaretto.

Colline di Caldaro (It). A red wine produced near Lake Caldaro from the Pinot noir and Schiave grapes.

Collines de la Moure (Fr). A Vins de Pays area in the Hérault Département in southern France. Produces red, rosé and dry white wines.

Collines Rhodaniennes (Fr). A Vins de Pays area based in the northern Rhône valley in the Départements of Ardèche, Drôme, Isère and the Loire. Produces red, rosé and dry white wines.

Collins (USA). See John Collins and Tom Collins. Can also be made from other spirits. e.g. Whisky collins.

Collins Lemon Gin (USA). A lemon-flavoured Gin produced by Seagram.

Collio (It). A small area west of Goriza in Friuli-Venezia-Giulia on the border with Yugoslavia in the north. Produces white and some sparkling wines. See Collio Goriziano.

Collio Cabernet Franc (It). See Collio Goriziano.

Collio Goriziano (It). D.O.C. red and white wines from Friuli-Venezia-Giulia, 7 white wines named after the principal grape variety used – Collio Goriziano-Malvasia, Pinot Bianco, Pinot Grigio, Riesling Italico, Sauvignon, Tocai and Traminer. 3 red wines – Collio Goriziano Cabernet Franc, Merlot and Pinot Nero.

Collio Malvasia (It). See Collio Goriziano.

Collio Merlot (It). See Collio Goriziano.

Collio Pinot Bianco (It). See Collio Goriziano.

Collio Pinot Grigio (It). See Collio Goriziano.

Collio Pinot Nero (It). See Collio Goriziano.

Colli Orientali del Friuli (It). D.O.C. red and white wines from Friuli-Venezia-Giulia. 8 white wines named after the principal grape. Colli Orientali del Friuli – Picolit, Pinot Bianco, Pinot Grigio, Ribolla, Riesling Renano, Sauvignon, Tocai and Verduzzo. 4 red wines. Colli Orientali del Friuli – Cabernet, Merlot, Pinot Nero and Refosco. If reds are aged a minimum of 2 years then can be classed Riserva. If white Picolit aged for 2 years minimum can also be classed Riserva.

Collio Riesling Italico (It). See Collio Goriziano.

Collio Sauvignon (It). See Collio Goriziano.

Collio Tocai (It). See Collio Goriziano.

Collio Traminer (It). See Collio Goriziano.

Collioure (Fr). An A.C. red wine from Banyuls, Roussillon in the Midi. Produced from the Carignan and Grenache grapes.

Colli Piacentini Malvasia (It). D.O.C. white wine from the Emilia Romagna region. Made from the Malvasia grape. D.O.C. also applies to a Frizzante or Spumante version.

Collison's (S.Afr). A leading brand of double-distilled cane spirit.

Colli Tortonesi (It). D.O.C. district of Piemonte. Produces red, white and sparkling wines.

Colli Tortonesi Barbera (It). D.O.C. red wine from Piemonte. Made from Barbera plus up to 15% of Bonarda, Dolcetto and Freisa grapes. If alc. content is 12.5% by vol and aged 2 years (1 year in oak-chestnut) then graded Superiore.

Colli Tortonesi Cortese (It). D.O.C. white wine from Piemonte. Made from Cortese grapes. Has a slight bitter taste of almonds.

Colloids (Eng). Gelatinous substances that are used as finings. e.g. Bentonite, egg white, gelatine, isinglass and oxblood.

Colmar (Fr). A wine town of Alsace. Also the scene of an annual wine fair.

Cölner Hofbräu (Ger). A famous tavern in Cologne noted for its beers and hospitality. Originated in the sixteenth century.

C

Colne Spring Ale (Eng). A strong bottled Ale 1082 O.G. brewed by Benskins Brewery, Watford.

Colobel (USA). A red hybrid grape variety also known as Seibel 8357.

Colodra (Sp). Wine measure.

Cologne Spirit (Eng). See Silent Spirit.

Coloma Wine Cellars (USA). A small winery based near Lodi, San Joaquin, California. Produces varietal and dessert wines.

Colomb (Fr). The name for the Colombar grape used in the Armagnac region.

Colombar (Fr). A white grape variety that is sensitive to Oiidium. Needs much sulphur spraying which results in a harsh wine. It can produce highly alcoholic wines. Used mainly in Cognac where it is known as the Pied-Tendre. Also known as the Bon blanc in Dauphiné. See also Blanquette.

Colombard (Fr). Another spelling of Colombar.

Colombe Cathare (Fr). The name for an A.C. Blanquette de Limoux produced by Jean Demolombe.

Colombia (S.Am). A small wine-producing country with 1,000 ha. under vines. Produces mainly sweet dessert wines. Also produces Aguardiente, Rum, Brandy and rectified spirits. See also Colombia Coffee.

Colombia Coffee (S.Am). A rich, low-acid coffee with a winy flavour. One of the best coffees from the high Andes. Used mainly for blending. Main regional varieties are – Armenias, Bogotas, Bucaramangas, Excelso, Hibanos, Manizales and Medellins.

Colombier (Fr). An alternative spelling of the white Colombar grape.

Colombier (Fr). A commune within the A.C. Monbazillac in the Bergerac region. (sweet white).

Colombo Special (Cktl). 1 measure Gin, ½ measure Crème de Menthe, ½ measure lemon juice, dash egg white. Shake well over ice, strain into a cocktail glass.

Colona Winery (N.Am). The largest winery in British Columbia. Is owned by the Nabisco Company.

Colong (E.Asia). A semi-green, light, delicate tea with a fruity scented aroma. Should be drunk without milk or sugar.

Colonial Cocktail (Cktl). ¾ measure dry Gin, ¼ measure grapefruit juice, 4 dashes Maraschino. Shake over ice, strain into a cocktail glass. Top with an olive.

Colonial Sugar Refining Company (Austr). The largest Rum distillery in Australia. Is based in Pyrmont, Sydney. Rums are produced from Queensland molasses.

Colonie (USA). A light, malty beer brewed by the Cold Spring Brewery in Cold Spring, Minnesota.

Colonna (It). See Montecompatri-Colonna.

Colonnara (It). A noted sparkling (méthode champenoise) Verdicchio from the Marche region.

Colony Village Winery (USA). A winery based in Iowa. Produces mainly French hybrid wines.

Color (Sp). Colour wine. See also Paxerete.

Colorado Cocktail (Cktl). ½ measure Kirsch, ½ measure Cherry brandy, ¼ measure cream. Shake well over ice, strain into a cocktail glass.

Colorado Mountain Vineyards (USA). A winery based in Colorado. 8 ha. Grape varieties – Chardonnay, Gewürztraminer and Riesling. Also buys in grapes from California.

Colorino (It). A red grape variety used in Chianti to give colour to the wine.

Color Wine (Sp). See Arrope, Paxerete, Sancocho, Color, Vino do Color.

Colour Deposit (Eng). A wine malady. An almost black deposit, often adhering to the side of the bottle during natural maturation. Can be reduced by an extra addition of SO_2.

Col Sandago (It). An estate winery based in Veneto. Produces red, white and sparkling Prosecco wines.

Coltassala (It). A dry, red wine from Castello di Volpaia in Chianti (Classico) estate at Radda, Tuscany. Made from the Sangiovese grape.

Colt 45 (USA). A Malt beer 1047.O.G. brewed by the Colt Breweries of America. Brewed under licence by Courage's Brewery U.K.

Columbard (Fr). An alternative spelling of the white grape variety Colombar.

Columbia Cellars (USA). A winery based near Seattle in Washington. Grape varieties – Cabernet, Chardonnay, Gewürztraminer, Riesling and Sémillon. Produces table and varietal wines.

Columbus (Aus). A well-hopped Beer 5.4% alc. by vol. brewed by the Steigel Brewery in Saltzburg.

Columbus Cocktail (Cktl). 1½ measures dry Vermouth, ½ measure Angostura bitters. Shake over ice, strain into an ice-filled goblet.

Column Stacking (Eng). A method of stacking beer crates, one on top of the other. Used for certain wooden and plastic crates. See also Bond Stacking.

Comarca de Falset (Sp). One of the three sub-zones in Tarragona. The soil is of granite, limestone and loam. Main grape varieties – Carieña, Garnacha and Tempranillo.

C

Combeau/Normandin-Girard/de Laage (Fr). Cognac producer. Address = 28, Rue des Ponts, 16140 Aigre. Produces – Cognac Pascal Combeau, Cognac Normandin, Cognac Girard and Cognac de Laage.

Combe-aux-Moines (Fr). A Premier Cru vineyard in the A.C. commune of Gevrey-Chambertin, Côte de Nuits, Burgundy. 4.78 ha. Also sold as La Combe-aux-Moines.

Combe House (Eng). A vineyard based at Broad Oak, Heathfield, East Sussex. 0.8 ha. Grape varieties – ⅔ Müller-Thurgau and ⅓ Seyval blanc. First planted 1979.

Comber Distilleries (Ire). An old distillery based in Belfast, Northern Ireland that closed in 1953.

Combes (Fr). In Burgundy (the Côte d'Or) name for the minor valleys that deeply indent the Côte.

Combes (Les) (Fr). A vineyard in the A.C. commune of Montagny, Côte Chalonnaise, Burgundy.

Combes (Les) (Fr). A Premier Cru vineyard in the A.C. commune of Saint-Aubin, Côte de Beaune, Burgundy.

Combes Bitter (Eng). A cask conditioned Ale 1041 O.G. brewed by Watney's Brewery.

Combes-Dessus (Les) (Fr). A Premier Cru vineyard in the A.C. commune of Pommard, Côte de Beaune, Burgundy. 2.8 ha.

Combettes (Les), (Fr). A Premier Cru vineyard in the A.C. commune of Puligny-Montrachet, Côte de Beaune, Burgundy. 6.7 ha.

Combibloc (Eng). A patented carton packaging for beverages.

Combibo (Lat). I drink to the full. Also a fellow drinker.

Combinado (Sp). The alternative name for Mitad y Mitad.

Combination (Cktl). ½ measure dry Gin, ¼ measure French vermouth, ¼ measure Amer Picon, ½ measure lemon juice, ½ measure orange Curaçao. Shake over ice, strain into a cocktail glass. Sprinkle with grated nutmeg.

Comblanchien (Fr). A commune which is part of the Côte de Nuits-Villages. Isn't allowed to use name as its own A.C.

Comblizy (Fr). A Cru Champagne village in the Canton de Dormans. District = Épernay.

Combo Cocktail (Cktl). ⅓ gill French vermouth, 4 dashes Brandy, 2 dashes Curaçao, dash Angostura, 1 teaspoon powdered sugar. Shake over ice, strain into an ice-filled old-fashioned glass.

Combottes (Fr). A Premier Cru vineyard in the commune A.C. Gevrey-Chambertin, Côte de Nuits, Burgundy. 4.9 ha. Also sold as Aux Combottes.

Combottes (Les) (Fr). A Premier Cru vineyard in the A.C. commune of Chambolle-Musigny, Côte de Nuits, Burgundy. 0.65 ha.

Combustible Matter (Eng). The compounds of must. Starch, Protein, Pectin, Cellulose, Acids, Tannin, Colouring, Vitamins, Enzymes and other unknown substances.

Come Back Marion (Cktl). ⅗ measure dry Gin, ³⁄₁₀ measure grapefruit juice, ¹⁄₁₀ measure Orgeat syrup, dash Fraises du Bois. Shake over ice, strain into a cocktail glass.

Comédie (La) (Fr). The name of the Hennessy Cognac's Paradise cellar. Once used as a theatre hence the name. Has the largest collection of old Cognacs.

Comercializadora Exportadora Navarra de Alimentación. S.A. (Sp). An organisation to promote the produce and wines of the Navarra region. Is owned by the provincial government and companies. Trade name is Agronavarra. (abbr) = CENALSA.

Comercial Pirineos (Sp). A major wine-producer based in Rioja.

Comet (The) (Cktl). 1 measure Brandy, ⅓ measure Van der Hum, ⅔ measure grapefruit juice. Shake over ice, strain into a cocktail glass, add a drop of lemon peel juice.

Comfort American (Cktl). 1 fl.oz. Southern Comfort, ½ fl.oz. lime cordial, ½ fl.oz. Campari, dash egg white. Shake well over ice, strain into an ice-filled highball glass. Top with American ginger ale.

Comfort Coffee (Liq.Coffee). Using a measure of Southern Comfort.

Comforter (Cktl). 1 measure dry Gin, 1 measure Dry Martini. Shake over ice, strain into a cocktail glass, add a dash of dry sherry and zest of lemon.

Comissão de Viticultura da Região dos Vinhos Verdes (Port). The headquarters in Oporto of the Vinhos Verdes Commission. It analyses samples, researches into yeasts and bulk production of yeast which is distributed to co-operatives. (abbr) = CVRVV.

Comissão de Viticultura Região de Colares (Port). A body that has now been absorbed by the Junta Nacional do Vinho.

Comitato Nazionale Per la Tutela Delle Denominazione d'Origine (It). National committee. Consists of 28 members plus a chairman. Chosen by the Ministry of Agriculture in collaboration with the Ministry of Industry and Commerce.

Comité Consultatif Viti-Vinicole (EEC). Consultative committee for wine growing and wine making.

Comité d'Action Viticole, nous Arretêrons les Importations (Fr). A body of southern wine producers whose aim is to stop the importation of Italian wines. Based at Sète was first formed in the early 1970s.

Comité d'Aménagement des Hautes-Côtes (Fr). A group formed to promote the wines of the Hautes-Côtes by organising wine tastings and tourist routes etc.

Comité de Défense et d'Organisation du Maché du Rhum (W.Ind). A body formed in 1960 in Martinique to arrange contracts and prices between producers and importers. (abbr) = CODERUM. See also FENARUM.

Comité d'Experts (Fr). An old governing body of Alsace for control and production of Alsace wines.

Comité Interprofessionnel de la Côte d'Or et de l'Yonne Pour les Vins de Bourgogne (Fr). A body for the promotion and control of Chablis and Burgundy wines. (abbr) = C.I.B. Address = Rue Henri-Dunant, 21200 Beaune.

Comité Interprofessionnel de Saône-et-Loire Pour les Vins A.O.C. de Bourgogne et de Mâcon (Fr). A body for the promotion of the wines of Mâcon and Burgundy. (abbr) = C.I.B.M.

Comité Interprofessionnel des Vins d'Alsace (Fr). 1962 Protective committee of merchants and growers to control and promote Alsace wines. (abbr) = C.I.V.A. Address = 8, Place de Lattre-de-Tassigny, 68003 Colmar Cedex.

Comité Interprofessionnel des Vins d'Anjou (Fr). A body for the promotion of Loire wines. (abbr) = C.I.V.A.

Comité Interprofessionnel des Vins de Bourgogne et Mâcon (Fr). A body for the promotion of Mâconnais and Burgundy wines. (abbr) = C.I.B.M. Address = Maison du Tourisme, Ave du Maréchal-de-Latte-de-Tassigny, 71000, Mâcon.

Comité Interprofessionnel des Vins de Gaillac (Fr). A body set up to promote and control the wines of Gaillac. (abbr) = C.I.V.G. Address = 8, Rue du Père Gibrat, 81600 Gaillac.

Comité Interprofessionnel des Vins de la Région de Bergerac (Fr). A body formed for the promotion and control of Bergerac wines. (abbr) = C.I.V.R.B.

Address = 2, Place du Docteur-Cayla, 24100, Bergerac.

Comité Interprofessionnel des Vins des Côtes de Provence (Fr). A body for the promotion of the wines of Provence. (abbr) = C.I.V.C.P. Address = 3, Ave Jean-Jaurès, 83460 Les-Arcs-sur-Argens.

Comité Interprofessionnel des Vins des Côtes du Rhône (Fr). A body for the promotion of the wines of the Rhône. (abbr) = C.I.C.D.R. Address = Maison du Tourisme et du Vin, 41, Cours Jean-Jaurès, 84000 Avignon.

Comité Interprofessionnel des Vins de Touraine (Fr). A body for the promotion and control of the wines of Touraine, Loire. (abbr) = C.I.V.T. Address = 19, Square Prosper Mérimée, 37000 Tours.

Comité Interprofessionnel des Vins d'Origine du Pays Nantais (Fr). A body for the promotion of the wines of western Loire. (abbr) = C.I.V.O.P.N. Address = 17, Rue des États, 44000 Nantes. Branch for Muscadet based at Maison des Vins, Bellevue, 44690 La Haie Fouassière.

Comité Interprofessionnel des Vins Doux Naturels (Fr). A body for the promotion of VdN wines of southern France. (abbr) = C.I.V.D.N. Address = 19, Ave de Grande-Bretagne, 66000 Perpignan.

Comité Interprofessionnel du Vin de Bordeaux (Fr). A body for the promotion of Bordeaux wines. (abbr) = C.I.V.B.

Comité Interprofessionnel du Vin de Champagne (Fr). A body formed in 1942 to regulate the growing of the vines and the production of Champagne. (abbr) = C.I.V.C. Address = 5, Rue Henri Martin, 51-Épernay.

Comité National de Pineau (Fr). A body for the promotion of Pineau des Charentes based in Cognac. Address = 45, Avenue Victor Hugo, 16100 Cognac.

Comité Professionnel du Bourgogne (Fr). A body based in Burgundy for the promotion of Burgundy wines.

Comité Vin (Fr). Wine committee.

Command (Cyp). The brand-name used by the Loël Company for a range of Cyprus sherries.

Commander (Cktl). ⅓ measure Cognac, ⅓ measure Port, ⅓ measure lemon juice. Shake over ice, strain into an ice-filled highball glass. Top with sparkling mineral water.

Commanderia (Cyp). A rich, sweet, dessert wine made in south east of the island. Made from dried out grapes and then flavoured with cloves and resin

C

and with scented woods which are suspended in the wine in a bag. Becomes tawny as it ages. Matured 12 years or more. Not fortified.

Commanderia St. John (Cyp). The full title for Commanderia. Gets its name from the Crusades when it was given to any of the injured knights whilst they were recuperating in Cyprus.

Commanderie de Champagne (Fr). A wine brotherhood based in the Champagne region.

Commanderie de Champagne de l'Ordre des Coteaux (Fr). A wine society based in the Champagne region.

Commanderie de la Bargemone (Fr). A vineyard in the commune of St. Cannat. V.D.Q.S. Coteaux d'Aix en Provence, south-eastern France.

Commanderie de l'Île de France des Anysetiers du Roy (Fr). A noted wine brotherhood based in Paris.

Commanderie de Sauternes-Barsac (Fr). A wine brotherhood of the Sauternes and Barsac.

Commanderie des Chevaliers de Tursan (Fr). A wine brotherhood based in south-western France. Promotes the wines of the region.

Commanderie des Grands Vins d'Amboise (Fr). A wine brotherhood based in Touraine, Loire.

Commanderie des Nobles Vins du Jura et Gruyère de Comte (Fr). A noted wine society for the promotion of Jura wines.

Commanderie des Vins et Spiritueux de France (Fr). A society based in Paris for French wines and spirits.

Commanderie de Tavel (Fr). The wine brotherhood of Tavel in the Rhône.

Commanderie du Bontemps de Médoc et des Graves (Fr). A wine brotherhood of the Médoc and Graves.

Commanderie du Bontemps de Sainte-Croix-du-Mont (Fr). A wine brotherhood of the Sainte-Croix-du-Mont, Bordeaux.

Commanderie du Bontemps de Sauternes et de Barsac (Fr). A wine brotherhood for the wines of Sauternes and Barsac based in Bordeaux.

Commanderie du Taste-Saumur (Fr). A wine brotherhood for the wines of Baumur based in the Loire region.

Commando (S.Afr). The brand-name for a Brandy produced by Castle Wine and Green.

Comme (La) (Fr). A Premier Cru vineyard [part] in the A.C. commune of Santenay. Côte de Beaune, Burgundy.

Commende Majeure de Roussillon pour Garder le Devoir et le Droit de la Vigne et du Vin (Fr). A wine society for the promotion and improvement of the wines of the Roussillon.

Commerce (Fr). A term applied to a blend of Kirsch with an Eau-de-Vie or neutral alcohol.

Commercial Wines (Eng). A wine trade term for wines that can be bought and sold in large quantities at a reasonable profit.

Commerciante (It). Dealer, trader.

Comminutes (Eng). An alternative name for fruit drinks where the fruit is pulverised or 'comminuted'.

Commodore (Cktl). ⅗ measure Rye whiskey, ⅓ measure lime juice, 2 dashes Orange bitters, sugar to taste. Shake over ice, strain into a cocktail glass. Add sugar to taste.

Commodore (Fr). The name of the Grande Cuvée Champagne produced by the De Castellane Champagne house.

Commodore Cocktail (Cktl). 1 fl.oz. Bourbon whiskey, ½ fl.oz. lemon juice, 2 dashes Angostura, dash Gomme syrup. Shake over ice, strain into a cocktail glass.

Common (Eng). A term used to describe a wine as sound but lacking any finesse.

Common Clean (W.Ind). The name given to light-bodied styles of Rum produced in a continuous still.

Common Dry (Mad). An old-style name used for Sercial. Now no longer used.

Common Man's Glass (Eng). The term given to the continental glass of the seventeenth and eighteenth century that was mass-produced.

Common Rich (Mad). An old-style name used for Malmsey. Now no longer used.

Commonwealth Winery (USA). A winery based in Plymouth, Massachusetts. Produces hybrid and vinifera wines.

Commun (Fr). Denotes a wine with no character.

Commune (Fr). A township or the administrative council or parish in France.

Communiste (Fr). A variation of the drink Kir in Burgundy. Red wine replaces the white. Also known as a Cardinal.

Como (Gre). The name given to a red, fortified wine from the island of Syra.

Compagnie d'Honneur des Sorciers et Birettes (Fr). A wine society based in the Anjou, Loire.

Compagnie de la Vallée de la Loire (Fr). The largest producer of Muscadet wines in the Pays Nantais region of the Loire.

Compagnie des Mousquetaires d'Armagnac (Fr). A wine brotherhood based in the Armagnac region.

Compagnie des Produits de Gascogne (Fr). An Armagnac producer based in Ténarèze and Bas Armagnac. Noted for the De Montal brand of Armagnac brandy.

C

Compagnie du Sarto (Fr). A wine brotherhood based in the Savoie region of south-eastern France.

Compagnons de Bordeaux (Fr). A wine brotherhood based in Bordeaux.

Compagnons de Loupiac (Fr). A wine brotherhood for the wines of Loupiac, Bordeaux.

Compagnons du Beaujolais (Fr). A wine brotherhood for the wines of Beaujolais, Burgundy.

Compagnons du Loupiac (Fr). A wine society based in Loupiac, Bordeaux.

Compagnons du Pintou (Fr). A wine society based in Auvergne.

Compagnons Hauts-Normands du Gouste-Vin (Fr). A wine society based in Paris.

Companhia Cacique de Café Soluvel (Bra). The largest producer of instant coffee in Brazil.

Companhia dos Vinhos Messias (Port). Producers of Messias Seco.

Companhia União Fabril Potuense (Port). C.Ú.F.P. Company formed by a merger of Oporto Breweries. Brews Crystal (a Pilsener-style Lager beer).

Compañía Española Promotora de la Exportación, S.A. (Sp). A major wine-producer based in the Rioja region.

Compañía Mata (Sp). A noted producer and exporter of Málaga wines.

Compañía Ron Bacardi (W.Ind). Originally one of the main producers of Rum on the island of Cuba before the revolution.

Compañía Vinícola del Norte de España (Sp). C.V.N.E. Address = Costa del Vino 21-Haro, La Rioja. 480 ha. Grape varieties – Garnacha 10%, Graciano 5%, Mazuelo 10%, Tempranillo 60% and Viura 15%. Produces – red wine 65%, white wine 33%.

Compartimenti (It). Provinces.

Compléter (Switz). Late picked.

Completer (Switz). A rare white grape variety from Grison and Herrschaft. Produces a rich, sweet wine.

Complex (Eng). A term often used to describe wines that have many smells and tastes. Is usually applied to fine wines.

Complexa (Mad). A Vitis vinifera cross black grape variety used in the production of Madeira. A new variety of Tinta negra mole.

Complexity (Eng). A term used to describe the different nuances of bouquet and taste in a wine.

Comportes (Fr). Wooden containers used for transporting the grapes from the vineyard to the winery. Hold 40–50 kilogrammes of grapes. Are round with dowling handles.

Compotatio (Lat). A drinking party.

Compotation (Eng). A seventeenth-century term for drinking together in company.

Compotor (Lat). Fellow drinker. See also Combibo.

Compound Beverages (USA). These are made by combining either a fermented beverage or a spirit with flavouring substances.

Compound Gin (USA). A mixture of neutral spirits and extract or oil of juniper and other botanicals.

Compounding (Eng). A method of extracting flavours from ingredients to make spirits.

Comps (Fr). A commune in the A.C. Côtes de Bourg in north-eastern Bordeaux.

Compte O (Fr). A term used for distilled Armagnac on May 1st of the following year after Compte 00 and for Cognac on April 1st of the following year after Compte 00.

Compte OO (Fr). A term used for newly distilled Armagnac in September and October till April 30th of the following year and for Cognac till March 31st of the following year.

Compte System (Fr). A system devised for the ageing of A.C. Brandies (Armagnac and Cognac). Works on a series of numbers from 00 to 6. After 00 (see Compte 00) the brandy is raised one number per year spent in wood. e.g. a 'Compte 4' will have spent 4 years in cask. See also Aquit Jaune d'Or.

Comptoir (Fr). Bar or counter.

Comptoir des Vins du Maroc (Afr). CVM. A Belgo-Moroccan company which has sole marketing rights for Moroccan wines sold under names of – Chantebled, Ourika and Tarik.

Comte André de Montpezat (Fr). The brand name used by Les Côtes d'Olt for a red wine.

Comte de Champagne (Fr). The label used by Taittinger for their De Luxe vintage cuvée Champagne made from 100% Chardonnay and for a vintage rosé made from 100% Pinot.

Comte de Vogüé (Fr). A vineyard in the commune of Le Musigny in the Côte de Nuits. See Domaine Comte de Vogüé.

Comtesse de Roseval (Fr). The brand name of a Crémant de Bourgogne produced by Labouré Gontard, Nuits-Saint-Georges, Côte de Nuits, Burgundy.

Comte de Wormeldange (Lux). A producer of sparkling (méthode champenoise) and pétillant wines.

Comte Tolosan (Fr). A Vins de Pays area in the Haute-Garonne near Toulouse. Produces red, rosé and dry white wines.

C

Coñac (Sp). A brandy which is dark, sweet and high in alcohol.

Coñac Corriente (Sp). Rough, local brandy.

Cona Coffee (Eng). A brand-name unit for making coffee by the vacuum process.

Conca (It). A red wine produced near the Bay of Sorrento in the Campania region. Made from the Aglianico, Canaiolo, Malvasia and Sangiovese grapes.

Conca del Barbera (Sp). A Denominación de Origen wine-producing region in Priorato. Wines made mainly from Bobal, Macabéo, Pansa, Parellada and Sumoll tinto.

Conca del Huelva (Sp). A Denominación de Origen wine-producing region in south-western Spain on the Portuguese border.

Conca d'Ora (Cktl). ⅝ measure dry Gin, ⅛ measure Cherry brandy, ⅛ measure Maraschino, ⅛ measure Triple sec, orange peel. Shake over ice, strain into a cocktail glass.

Concannon (USA). A vineyard in the Livermore Valley, Alameda, California. 75 ha. Grape varieties – Cabernet sauvignon, Petit syrah and Zinfandel. Produces varietal wines.

Concentrated Wine (Hol). An old Dutch description of brandy which was shipped to Holland. Originally made to save freight charges. See 'Soul of the Wine'.

Concentrato (It). A concentrated grape must that is used for correcting wines.

Concha (La) (Sp). The brand-name of an Amontillado sherry from Gonzalez Byass in Jerez.

Concha y Toro (Chile). The largest wine firm with over 1040 ha. in the Maipo Valley (has several Bodegas). Noted brands it produces are Cassillero del Diablo, Marqués de Casa and St. Emiliana.

Conching (S.Am). The process of developing the flavour in the chocolate (cocoa) bean after fermentation.

Conchita Cocktail (Cktl). 1 fl.oz. Tequila, 1 fl.oz. grapefruit juice, 2 dashes lemon juice. Shake over ice, strain into a cocktail glass with 2 ice cubes.

Concierto (It). A herb liqueur made by the Maiori Nuns of Amalfi Riviera.

Conçillon et Fils (Fr). A major liqueur producer based in the Loire region.

Concise (Switz). A wine-producing area in the northern Vaud canton. Produces red and white wines.

Conclave Cocktail (Cktl).(Non-alc). ¾ measure orange juice, ¼ measure raspberry syrup, ½ measure milk. Shake over crushed ice. Strain into an ice-filled highball glass. Dress with a slice of orange and serve with straws.

Concoction (Eng). A mixture of drinks etc. that does not conform to a set recipe.

Concongello Vineyards (Austr). See 'Bests Great Western'.

Concord (USA). A blue-black grape variety of North America. Very sweet and can withstand severe winters. Used for blending and religious wines. American native vine stock.

Concord Cocktail (Cktl). ¼ measure Calvados, ¼ measure Grand Marnier, ½ measure orange juice. Stir with ice, strain into a club goblet. Top with iced Champagne, decorate with a cube of pineapple.

Concorde (Eng). A slightly sparkling British wine produced by Allied Lyons.

Concours Agricole (Fr). A wine classification competition.

Concurso Nacional de Vinhos Engarrafados (Port). A nationwide competition organised by the Junta in which the producers own wines take part and are awarded prizes by a qualified jury.

Condado (Sp). County.

Condado de Rosal (Sp). A wine-producing area on the river Miño in western Spain. Produces mainly red wines from the Caiño, Espadeiro and Tintarrón grapes.

Condado de Huelva (Sp). Denominación de Origen of Huelva province in South-western Spain. D.O. applies to white wines produced in the region. Grapes – Garrido fino, Listán, Mantúa, Palomino and Zalema.

Condado de Niebla (Sp). An old name for the D.O. Huelva province in south-western Spain. Lit – 'Country of mist'.

Condal (Sp). The brand-name for the wines of Bodegas Rioja Santiago.

Conde, S.A. (Rafael Cruz) (Sp). A producer of Montilla based in Córdoba.

Conde de Caralt (Sp). A bodega based in San Sadurní de Noya. Produces Cava and table wines.

Conde de Haro (Sp). A white Cava wine produced by Bodegas Muga in the Rioja region.

Conde de la Salceda (Sp). A wine from Viña Salceda S.A., Rioja. The Tinto is oak matured for 2–3 years and also 3 years in bottle.

Conde de Los Andes (Sp). A red 'Gran Reserva' Rioja wine produced by Federico Paternina at Ollauri.

Conde de Osborne (Sp). A 20 year old brandy produced by Osborne.

Conde de Santar (Port). An Estate-produced wine from the Dão region.

C

Conde Duque (Sp). An 8 year old brandy produced by Gonzalez Byass.

Conde-en-Brie (Fr). A Canton in the district of Château Thierry in the Champagne region. Has the Cru villages of – Aisne, Barzy-sur-Marne, Baule-en-Brie, Passy-sur-Marne and Trelou-sur-Marne.

Condemine (La) (Fr). A vineyard in the A.C. commune of Montagny, Côte Chalonnaise, Burgundy.

Condensed Milk (Eng). Milk which is evaporated in a vacuum to reduce the water content up to 50%. Usually sold canned, sweetened or unsweetened.

Condenser (Eng). The part of the distilling process that turns the vapour (alcohol) back into liquid.

Conde Valdemar (Sp). See Bodegas Martinez Bujanda.

Condition (Eng). Part of the beer-making process in which the newly made beer is 'primed' and conditioned. CO_2 gas is dissolved into beer during this process to give it 'condition'.

Condom (Fr). The commercial centre of the Armagnac brandy region, Gers Département.

Condomois (Fr). A Vins de Pays area in the Gers Département. Produces red, rosé and dry white wines.

Condrieu (Fr). A.C. region in the Rhône. Only white wines are produced from the Viognier grape on terraced vineyards. Wines are full-bodied, often with a touch of pétillance and sweetness in a good vintage. See Château Grillet.

Conestoga Vineyards (USA). A winery based in Birchrunville, Pennsylvania. Produces Labrusca and French hybrid wines.

Confraria dos Enofilos da Bairrada (Port). A Bairrada fraternity who help to promote and enhance the quality of the wines.

Confraternità della Cheer (It). A wine brotherhood.

Confraternità d'la Tripa (It). A wine brotherhood.

Confrérie (Fr). Brotherhood. A wine organisation in France for the promotion and enjoyment of the wines of a specific district or region.

Confrérie de Bacchus et d'Icare (Fr). A wine society based in Lyons.

Confrérie de Chevaliers du Cep (Fr). A wine society based in Verdigny.

Confrérie de Guillon (Switz). A wine brotherhood.

Confrérie des Alambics Charentais (Fr). A society for the promotion of Cognac brandy based in the Cognac region.

Confrérie des Baillis de Pouilly-sur-Loire (Fr). A wine society based in the eastern Loire; a wine brotherhood based in Pouilly-sur-Loire, Central Vineyards, Loire.

Confrérie des Chevaliers de la Canette (Fr). A wine brotherhood based in Deux Sèvres, Western Loire.

Confrérie des Chevaliers de la Chantepleure (Fr). A wine brotherhood based in Vouvray, Touraine, Loire.

Confrérie des Chevaliers de la Syrah et Roussette (Fr). A wine brotherhood of the Rhône.

Confrérie des Chevaliers des Cuers de Baril (Fr). A wine brotherhood based in Loches, Mâconnais, Burgundy.

Confrérie des Chevaliers du Sacavin (Fr). A wine brotherhood based in Angers, Anjou-Saumur, Loire.

Confrérie des Chevaliers du Tastevin (Fr). A wine brotherhood of Burgundy. See Tastevinage.

Confrérie des Chevaliers Rabelaisiens de Belgique (Bel). A wine brotherhood.

Confrérie des Compagnons de la Capucine (Fr). A wine society based at Toul.

Confrérie des Comtes de Nice et de Provence (Fr). A wine society based in Provence.

Confrérie des Échansons de Vidauban (Fr). A wine brotherhood based in the Provence region, south-eastern France.

Confrérie des Grandgousiers (Fr). A brotherhood of Touraine. Meetings held in Amboise in the Loire Valley.

Confrérie des Hospitaliers de Pomerol (Fr). A wine society for the promotion of Pomerol wines based in Bordeaux.

Confrérie des Trois Ceps (Fr). A wine society based in the Yonne.

Confrérie des Vignerons de la Canette (Fr). A wine society based in Bouille-Loretz.

Confrérie des Vignolants de Neuchâtel (Switz). A wine brotherhood of Neuchâtel, western Switzerland.

Confrérie des Vin Gousiers d'Anjou (Fr). A wine society based in Anjou, Loire.

Confrérie du Gosier-sec de Clochmerle (Fr). A fraternity founded in the Beaujolais in 1961.

Confrérie du Vin de Cahors (Fr). A wine society based in Cahors.

Confrérie Saint-Étienne (Fr). A wine society based in Alsace.

Confrérie Saint Vincent des Vignerons de Mâcon (Fr). A wine brotherhood based in the Mâconnais, Burgundy.

Confrérie Saint Vincent des Vignerons de Tannay (Fr). A wine brotherhood based in the Nièvre Département, central France.

Confrérie Saint-Vincent et Disciples de la

Confréries Vigneronnes (Fr). Wine brotherhoods.

Confrérie Vineuse des Piliers Chablisiens (Fr). A wine fraternity founded in 1952 which meets 4 times a year for the promotion of Chablis wines.

Confrérie Vineuse des Tire-Douzil (Fr). A wine brotherhood based in the Vienne Département, Loire.

Congé (Fr). Documents which indicate that internal taxes have been paid. These usually accompany wines and spirits. Different types of document are used for different styles of wines and spirits.

Congenerics (Eng). See Congeners.

Congeners (Eng). Composition of wines and spirits etc. Made up of alcohols, esters, acids, fusel oils etc. that give bouquet and flavour.

Conghurst Vineyard (Fr). A vineyard based in Conghurst Oast, Hawkhurst, Kent. 0.5 ha. Grape varieties – Chasselas and Regner.

Congius (Lat). A measure in Roman times approximately equal to an Imperial gallon.

Congo (China). See Congou.

Congou (China). A coarse-leaf grade of 'Black tea'. Also spelt Congo.

Congregazione (It). Co-operative.

Congy (Fr). A Cru Champagne village in the Canton de Montmort. District = Épernay.

Conhaque (Bra). A liqueur.

Conical Fermentation Vessel (Eng). A tall cylinder with a tapered lower end. The fermenting brew is kept agitated by air injection.

Conn Creek (USA). A winery based near Rutherford, Napa Valley, California. Grape varieties – Cabernet sauvignon, Chardonnay and Zinfandel. Produces varietal wines.

Connecticut (USA). Home to many small wineries producing mainly French hybrid wines.

Connétable Talbot (Fr). The second wine of Château Talbot. Grand Cru Classé (4th). A.C. Saint-Julien.

Connétablerie de Guyenne (Fr). A wine brotherhood for the wines of the Guyenne in south-eastern Bordeaux. Members are devoted to the promotion of sweet white wines.

Connoisseur (Fr). Lit. = One who appreciates and knows of the fine things of life.

Cono (Sp). The name used in Málaga and Valencia for Tino.

Conos (Sp). The name given to large wooden, truncated, conical-shaped vats. See also Tino.

Conqueror Ale (Eng). A cask conditioned Ale 1066 O.G. brewed by the Axe Vale Brewery, Devon.

Conradsminde Glassworks (Den). Glassworks which produced many of the early drinking vessels in the eighteenth and nineteenth centuries.

Conroi (Cktl). ⅔ measure Rye whiskey, ⅙ measure Apricot brandy, ⅙ measure Crème de Banane, ⅔ measure orange juice. Shake over ice, strain into a cocktail glass.

Conrotto Winery (USA). A winery based in Santa Clara, California. Produces ordinary table wines.

Consecha (Sp). See Consecho.

Consecha Special (Arg). A brand of sparkling wine produced by the Bodegas Norton.

Consecho (Sp). Crop or vintage.

Conseil des Échansons de France (Fr). A wine society based in Paris.

Conseil Interprofessionnel des Vins d'Anjou et Saumur (Fr). A body for the promotion of the wines of Anjou-Saumur, Loire. (abbr) = C.I.V.A.S. Address = 21, Boulevard Foch, 49000 Angers.

Conseil Interprofessionnel des Vins de Fitou, Corbières et Minervois (Fr). A body for the promotion of wines of the Midi. Address = R.N.113, 11200 Lézignan-Corbières.

Conseil Interprofessionnel du Vin de Bordeaux (Fr). A body for the promotion of Bordeaux wines. (abbr) = C.I.V.B. Address = 1 Cours du 30 Juillet, 33000 Bordeaux.

Consejo Regulador de la Denominación de Origen (Sp). Organisation for the defence, control and promotion of a Denominación de Origen.

Consentinum (Lat). A red wine produced in southern Italy during Roman times.

Conservato (It). A wine to which concentrated or boiled wine has been added.

Consoczio (It). See Consorzio.

Consort (Afr). A brand of double-distilled cane spirit.

Consorzio (It). A local growers' association with legal standing.

Consorzio Per la Difesa dei Vini Tipici Barolo e Barbaresco (It). A local consorzio. Seal is seen on some bottles of wine – Barbara = Ancient tower and Barolo = Golden lion in blue field.

Consorzio Vino Chianti Classico (It). Formed on 14 June 1924. Has a black cockerel as logo (the ancient crest of

Lega del Chianti)

Contact Process (Eng). The addition of finely ground tartrate crystals to cooled wine. This is stirred for 16 hours and the tartrates can then be removed. Reduces the wine's acidity.

Constantina (S.Afr). A coastal wine region. See Groot Constantina.

Constantina (S.Afr). An old name for a rich, sweet, liqueur-type wine from Groot Constantina vineyards.

Constantinovka (USSR). A wine-producing centre in the River Don area. Produces mainly white wines.

Constanza (Rum). A wine-producing region based in the Dobruja region.

Consulat de la Vinée de Bergerac (Fr). A wine society based in the Bergerac region.

Consulat de Septimanie (Fr). A wine brotherhood of the Languedoc.

Consumo (Port). Ordinary table wine. Vin ordinaire.

Contadino (It). Vineyard worker.

Container Beer (Eng). The brewery name for Keg or Bright beer.

Conterno (Giacomo) (It). A winery based in Monforte d'Alba, Piemonte.

Contessa Rosa Nature (It). A sparkling (méthode champenoise) wine produced by Fontanafredda in Piemonte. Made from Chardonnay and Pinot grapes. Minimum alc. by vol. 11.5%.

Conte Vaselli (It). Producers of Orvieto in the Umbria region.

Conteville Winery (Austr). A winery based in the Swan Valley. Grape varieties – Cabernet, Hermitage and Riesling.

Conthey (Switz). A wine-producing village based near Sion in the Valais Département. Is noted for its Fendant wines.

Contichinno (Austr). A coffee, cream and Rum liqueur produced by the Continental Distillers.

Conticream (Austr). A chocolate, cream and Scotch whisky liqueur produced by the Continental Distillers.

Contière (La) (Fr). A Premier Cru vineyard in the commune of Ladoix-Serrigny, A.C. Aloxe-Corton, Côte de Beaune, Burgundy.

Conti Forest Hill (Austr). Vineyard. Address = 18 Km, West Mount Barker Muir Highway, Forest hill, P.O. Box 49, Western Australia 6324 22 ha. Grape varieties – Cabernet sauvignon and Rhine riesling.

Contigu au (Fr). Lit – 'Adjoining the'. Seen on a bottle label.

Conti Loredan-Gasparini (It). A sparkling (méthode champenoise) wine producer based in Veneto.

Continental Blend Coffee (Eng). A dark, full roast which produces a strong, dark, rich coffee. Ideal for after dinner drinking.

Continental Cocktail (Cktl). ⅕ measure dark Rum, ⅓ measure Crème de Menthe (white), juice ¼ lemon, ½ teaspoon Gomme syrup. Shake over ice, strain into a cocktail glass. Top with a twist of lemon peel juice.

Continental Distillers (Austr). A large distilling company noted for its cream liqueurs. See Contichinno and Conticream.

Continental Flavoured Rum (W.Ind). A rum produced only in Jamaica. Is aromatic and has a 'pineapple' flavour. Germans use it for their Rum Verschnitt.

Continental Lager (Eng). A Lager beer 1034 O.G. brewed by Davenports Brewery, Birmingham.

Continental's Charter Oak (USA). The brand-name of a Bourbon whiskey. 40% alc. by vol.

Continental Sour (Cktl). As for Brandy sour but with a dash of Claret on top.

Continental Vineyards (USA). A vineyard based in San Luis Obispo County, California. Grape variety – Zinfandel.

Continental Winery (N.Ž.). Address = Okaika, Northland. 4.3 ha. Grape varieties – Baco 22, Breidecker, Grey riesling, Niagara and Reichensteiner.

Contino (Sp). The name given to a single-vineyard, red wine produced by the Compañía Vinícola del Norte de España in the Rioja Alta.

Continuato (It). Continuous still.

Continuous Fermentation (Eng). A process where the Wort is passed continuously through a concentration of yeast.

Continuous Screw Press (Fr). A rather harsh type of press that is only used for Vin de table and wines for distilling.

Continuous Still (Eng). See Coffey Still, Patent Still and Robert Stein.

Conti Royal (USA). The brand-name of a Brandy produced by the East-Side Winery Co-operative in Lodi, California.

Conti Royale (USA). The brand-name used by the East-Side Winery Cooperative in Lodi, California for their fine wines.

Conti Sanminiatelli (It). A Chianti Classico producer based in Greve in Tuscany.

Conti Serristori (It). A Chianti Classico producer based in Percussina in Firenze, Tuscany.

Contra Costa (USA). A northern district

C

of California. Produces fine white table wines, red and dessert wines. 395 ha.

Contraetiqueta (Sp). In Rioja the name given to the back label on a wine bottle that specifies the type of wine.

Contratto (It). Wine producers at Canelli, Piemonte. Also produce brandies and sparkling (méthode champenoise) wines including Sabauda Riserva and Bacco d'Oro.

Contrex (Fr). A still mineral water from Contrexville in the Vosges mountains, Alsace. Is high in minerals.

Controllata e Garantita (It). Controlled and guaranteed. See D.O.C.G.

Convalmore-Glenlivet (Scot). A single Malt whisky distillery based near Dufftown, Banffshire. Part of the DCL. Group. Produces – 18 year old Malt 45% alc. by vol.

Convenience Cask (Eng). Plastic bag containers in cardboard boxes, used for dispensing wine in large quantities. Helps to keep the air out.

Convento de Alpendurada (Port). A producer of Vinho Verde wine based at Alpendurada 4575 Entre-Os-Rios.

Cooch Behar Cocktail (Cktl). Shake together a small tomato juice with ⅕ gill Pepper vodka over ice. Strain into an ice-filled old-fashioned glass.

Cook Brewery (Eng). Now no longer brewing but is a distributor for Ridley's Brewery = Halstead, Essex.

Cooked (Eng). A term used in tasting to describe a sweet, heavy smell.

Cooks New Zealand (N.Z.). Vineyard. Address = Paddy's road, Te Kauwhata North Island. 400 ha. at Te Kauwhata and Fernhill. Grape varieties – Cabernet sauvignon, Chardonnay, Chauche gris, Chenin blanc, Müller-Thurgau, Pinot noir, Sauvignon blanc and the Sylvaner.

Cool (Eng). A brand of light-style, low-alcohol Cider produced by the Taunton Cider Co. Has no artificial colouring or flavouring.

Coolabah (Austr). The brand-name of a range of cask and flagon wines produced by the Orlando Winery, South Australia.

Coolawin (Austr). Vineyard. Address = Grants Gully road, Clarendon, South Australia 5157. 50 ha. at Clarendon and Bakers Gully in Adelaide Hills and at Woods Point. Grape varieties – Cabernet sauvignon, Rhine riesling and Shiraz.

Cool Banana (Cktl). 1 fl.oz. Crème de Banane, ¾ fl.oz. Triple sec, ¼ fl.oz. Grenadine, 1 fl.oz. double cream, dash egg white. Shake over ice, strain into a cocktail glass.

Cool Blonde (The) (Ger). The Berliners' name for their Champagne-like beer called Berliner Weisse.

Cool Breeze (Cktl). 1 fl.oz. Cognac, 3 fl.ozs. cream, ½ fl.oz. Grand Marnier, 2 dashes Maraschino cherry juice. Shake over ice, strain into a cocktail glass.

Cool Caribbean Cocktail (Cktl). ½ fl.oz. Crème de Banana, 1 fl.oz. Coconut liqueur. Stir over ice in a highball glass. Top with orangeade. Dress with a slice of orange and 2 cherries.

Cool Cup (Cup). ¾ pint sweet Sherry, 1 pint dry Cider, juice and zest of a small lemon, ⅓ gill sugar syrup, pinch grated nutmeg. Stir together, chill down, add mint and sliced cucumber. Top with a syphon of iced soda water and serve.

Cooler (USA). A mixed drink of spirit, ginger ale or soda, syrup and dressed with crushed ice and fruit in season.

Cooler Club (E.Ind). A slightly sparkling, pineapple and passion fruit flavoured drink produced by Mather in conjunction with a Bangkok firm in Thailand.

Coolgardie Safe (Austr). A cupboard or box with wetted hessian sacking draped over it used for keeping drinks (and food) cool by evaporation.

Coolserve (Eng). A refrigeration unit that chills bottles of white wines. Holds up to 14 litres. Marketed by Gilbeys.

Coolship (USA). In brewing a container for cooling the wort after it passes through the hop strainer.

Cool Spring (Can). A light, low-alcohol beer 3.9% alc. by vol. brewed by the Labatt Brewery.

Coomassie (Cktl). ⅓ gill dry Sherry, ⅙ gill Cognac, 1 barspoon icing sugar, 1 egg yolk, 2 dashes Angostura. Shake well over ice, strain into a highball glass. Top with grated nutmeg and cinnamon.

Coonawarra (Austr). A wine district in South Australia. 200 km south of Adelaide. Contains the Terra Rosa.

Coonawarra Cabernet Sauvignon (Austr). A full-flavoured red wine with a strong bouquet from the Rosemount Estate vineyards in New South Wales.

Coonawarra Shiraz (Austr). A full, peppery aromatic red wine with a touch of sweetness from the Rosemount Estate vineyards in New South Wales.

Cooper (Eng). Cask or barrel maker.

Cooper (Eng). A mixture of ½ pint Stout and ½ pint Porter.

Cooper (Eng). A merchant who is employed in the testing and bottling of wine.

Cooperage (Eng). The building where casks (barrels) are made. See also Coopery.

Cooperage (Eng). The craft of the Cooper.

C

Cooperage (Eng). The fee charged by a Cooper for his work.

Cooperativa (Sp). A co-operative winery.

Cooperativa de Manjavacas (Sp). A large bodega based in La Mancha. Uses the label Zagarrón for its wines.

Cooperativa de Ribero del Duero (Sp). A large co-operative winery based in Peñafiel. Is noted for Protos (a 5 year old, cask-aged red wine).

Cooperativa de Vila Nova Tazem (Port). A large winery belonging to SOGRAPE.

Cooperativa Interlocal de Alesanco (Sp). A modern winery based in Logroño, Rioja. Operates on a continuous vinification method (Torre Vinaria).

Cooperativa Jesus Nazareno (Sp). A winery based in Barco. Produces Gran Vino Godello (a white varietal wine) and Valdouro (a red wine from Garnacha and Vencia grapes).

Cooperativa la Purisima (Sp). A large co-operative winery in the Yecla region. Produces red, rosé and white wines.

Cooperativa la Seca (Sp). The only co-operative winery based in the La Rueda region. Produces Palido and Dorada (flor affected wines) and Cuatro Rayas and Veliterra (white wines).

Cooperativa San Raphael (Arg). A large co-operative which deals mainly in concentrated grape must and ordinary bulk wines.

Cooperativa Santa Rita (Sp). A winery based in Fuenterobles, Utiel-Requena, Levante.

Cooperativa San Valero (Sp). A co-operative winery based near Zaragoza in Cariñena. Produces mainly table wines.

Cooperativa Vinícola de Cenicero, B. 'Santa Daria' (Sp). Address = Ctra de Logroño, s/n, Cenicero (la Rioja). 800 ha. Grape varieties – Garnacha, Graciano, Malvasia, Mazuelo, Tempranillo and Viura. Produces Santa Daria and Valdemontan.

Cooperativa Vinícola de Labastida (Sp). See Labastida.

Cooperativa Vinícola del Penedés (Sp). COVIDES. Has wineries at San Cugat and San Sadurní in Cataluña, south-eastern Spain.

Cooperativa Vinícola del Ribeiro (Sp). A winery based in Rivadavia. Produces low-alcohol white wines.

Cooperativa Vinicola Produttori Verdicchio Monte Schiavo (It). C.V.P.V. A co-operative winery based at Moie di Maiolati in the Marche region.

Co-operative (Eng). A winery or cellar belonging jointly to a number of small producers.

Coopérative (Fr). Co-operative.

Coopérative d'Armagnac 'Gerland' (Fr). Armagnac co-operative. Address – Route de Bordeaux, 49190 Villeneuve-de-Marsan.

Coopérative de L'Union des Propriétaires de Vins Fins (Fr). A wine co-operative of the commune of Gevrey-Chambertin in the Côte de Nuits, Burgundy.

Coopérative de Montagne (Fr). A co-operative vineyard and winery in the çommune of Montagne-Saint-Émilion. A.C. Saint-Émilion, Bordeaux. 145 ha.

Coopérative des Vins Fins (Fr). A wine co-operative of the commune Morey-Saint-Denis in the Côte de Nuits, Burgundy.

Coopérative Intercommunale de Vinification (Fr). Address = Prignas en Médoc, 33340. A.C. Médoc. Commune = Lesparre. 290 ha. Grape varieties – Cabernet franc, Cabernet sauvignon and Merlot.

Coopérative-Manipulant (Fr). C.M. on a Champagne bottle label denotes a co-operative producer's wine.

Coopérative Régionale de Vins de Champagne (Fr). C.R.V.A. A Champagne co-operative consisting of 680 vignerons. Sells under the trade-name of Jacquart.

Coopératives de Pressurage (Fr). A Champagne co-operative that presses the grapes only.

Coopératives de Pressurage et Vinification (Fr). A Champagne co-operative that presses the grapes and makes the initial still wine.

Coopératives de Pressurage, Vinification et Champanisation (Fr). A Champagne co-operative that presses the grapes, produces the still wines and Champagne and sells it.

Co-operative Wine Farmers' Association (S.Afr). K.W.V. Formed in 1918 at the time of the two Gladstone acts.

Coopers Brewery (Austr). A brewery based in Adelaide. Produces bottle-conditioned beers fermented in wooden casks. Extra stout 6.9% alc. by vol. and Sparkling ale 5.3% alc. by vol.

Coopers Creek Winery (N.Z.). Address = Main road, Huapai. 4 ha. Grape varieties – Cabernet sauvignon, Chardonnay, Gewürztraminer, Merlot and Sauvignon blanc.

Coopers Fruit (Cktl). ⅓ measure Mandarine Napoléon, ⅓ measure Vodka, ⅓ measure Crème de Banane. Shake well over ice, strain into a cocktail glass. Dress with a slice of banana, lemon and a cherry.

C

Cooperstown Cocktail (Cktl).(1). A Martini cocktail, shaken with 2 sprigs of fresh mint.

Cooperstown Cocktail (Cktl).(2). As for (1) with addition of ½ teaspoon of Orange bitters.

Coopery (Eng). The alternative word for Cooperage.

Coorg (Ind). A coffee-producing region in central India.

Coors Brewery (USA). Based at Golden, Colorado, is the world's largest brewery. Brews Irish Red Ale under licence from Letts Brewery in Southern Ireland.

Cooymans (Hol). A noted liqueur producer. Address = P.O. Box 416, 5201 AK Den Bosch. Produces many fine liqueurs.

Copa (Lat). Barmaid.

Copa (Sp). Wine glass.

Copa de Oro (Cktl). 1 oz. Tequila, 1 oz. Grand Marnier, 1 egg, 1 teaspoon castor sugar. Shake well together, strain into a wine glass, top with round orange slice and straws.

Copenheering (Cktl). ⅓ measure Peter Heering Cherry Brandy, ⅔ measure Vodka, dash lime and lemon juice. Stir over ice, strain into a cocktail glass.

Copère (Bel). A top-fermented beer brewed by the Dinant Brasserie.

Copertino (It). D.O.C. red wine from the Apulia region. Is made from the Negramaro grape.

Copetin (Bra). A Vermouth served in Brazil as a gesture of hospitality usually in the 'Vermouth hour' between 5–6 p.m.

Cophe (USSR). Coffee. See also Kofé.

Copita (Sp). A rosebud-shaped Sherry glass. Also a name for a glass of Sherry. See also Caña.

Copo (Port). A tumbler, drinking glass.

Copo de Água (Port). Water glass. A glass of water.

Copo de Vinho (Port). Wine glass. A glass of wine.

Coppa da Sciampagna (It). A saucer (Champagne) glass.

Copper (Eng). See Kettle.

Copper Beech (Sp). The name of a rich, sweet, brown Sherry from Harveys.

Copper Casse (Eng). Wine malady. Orange brown deposit which dissolves when the wine is oxygenated. Wine has a high copper content. Treated with Blue finings.

Copperino (Cktl). ⅓ measure Kahlúa, ⅓ measure cream, ⅓ measure Galliano. Shake over ice, strain into a cocktail glass. Add grated nutmeg on top.

Copper Sulphate (Eng). CUSO₄. Used to

remove hydrogen sulphide smells in wine. Legal limit 1 mg per litre. Caution is required as it also promotes oxidation.

Copper Syrup (Eng). A concentrated malt extract used in the copper to extend the brew length or to alter the gravity.

Copus Cup (Punch). Place 2 pints Bitter ale, ½ pint Cognac, ¼ pint Crème de Noyau, ½ lb. sugar, juice ½ lemon into a saucepan and heat gently. Serve warm with a slice of toast coated with grated nutmeg and cloves floated on top.

Coq (Fr). 3–4 year old Cognac produced by Jean Fillioux.

Coques Courtes (Fr). The 2 short shoots on the main branches of the Taille-Genre Bordelaise vine training system.

Coquimbo (Chile). Northern vineyards in Chile.

Coquinero (Sp). A brand of dry, nutty Sherry produced by Osborne.

Coquito Cocktail (Cktl). Blend ½ fl.oz. Cherry Heering, 1 fl.oz. white Rum, ½ fl.oz. Coconut cream and 3 fl.ozs. fresh cream with a scoop of crushed ice in a blender. Pour into a highball glass. Serve with straws.

Cora (It). A Vermouth made in Turin.

Coral (Mad). The name for a local brand of beer brewed on the island.

Coral Reef (Cktl). 1 part Warnick's Advocaat, 2 parts pineapple juice, 1 part lime juice. Stir together over ice in a highball glass, dress with a cherry.

Cora Villa Costa (It). A producer of sparkling (cuve close) wines in the Piemonte region. Noted for Moscato d'Asti.

Corbans (N.Z.). Address = Great North Road, Henderson. Vineyards at Te Kauwhata, Tolga Bay, Gisborne, Hawkes Bay and Marlborough.

Corbeaux (Les) (Fr). A Premier Cru vineyard in the A.C. commune of Gevrey-Chambertin, Côte de Nuits, Burgundy. 3.12 ha.

Corbes (Fr). A red grape variety grown in the Bergerac region.

Corbet (Fr). A négociant based in Morey-Saint-Denis, Côte de Nuits, Burgundy.

Corbières (Fr). An A.C. wine area situated on the foothills of the Pyrénées with Carcassonne in the north-west. Produces mainly red wines at 11% alc. by vol. minimum.

Corbières du Roussillon (Fr). An A.C. red wine from the Corbières area in the Roussillon region of south-eastern France.

Corby Distillery (Can). A producer of Canadian whisky.

Corby's Reserve (USA). The brand-name for a blended Whiskey.

C

Corc (Wales). Cork.

Corcho (Sp). Cork, stopper.

Corcyn (Wales). To cork (a bottle).

Cordeliers (Fr). A noted producer of A.C. Bordeaux Mousseux based in Saint-Émilion, eastern Bordeaux.

Cordial (Eng). A stimulating drink.

Cordial (Eng). A filtered, non-alcoholic, fruit squash.

Cordial (Scot). The nickname for Whisky.

Cordial (USA). The American name for liqueurs.

Cordial Campari (It). A light-yellow dessert liqueur obtained from the distillation of raspberries and brandy. 37.5% alc. by vol.

Cordial Daisy (Cktl). ¾ measure Cherry brandy, ¼ measure Triple Sec, juice ¼ lemon. Stir well over shaved ice in a highball glass. Top with soda water.

Cordiale (It). Cordial.

Cordial Glass (USA). A thistle-shaped glass of 4 fl.oz. capacity.

Cordial Médoc (Fr). A blend of Curaçao, Crème de Cacao and Cognac. 44% alc. by vol.

Cordial Reby (Fr). A liqueur with Cognac base. Brown in colour.

Cordier (Fr). A famous négociant and grower in Bordeaux. Owns the following vineyards – Châteaux Gruaud Larose, Meyney, Plagnac, Tanesse and Talbot, Clos de la Poussie, Clos des Jacobins and Labottière.

Córdoba (S.Am). A noted wine-producing area in central Argentina.

Córdoba (Sp). A wine area of southern Spain in which Montilla is the most famous district. Produces highly alcoholic, Sherry-type wines which are unfortified.

Cordon (Fr). A method of growing vines invented by Dr. Guyot using a permanent stump with horizontal and vertical shoots growing from it.

Cordon Argent (Fr). The name given to fine old Cognacs.

Cordon Bleu (Fr). A non-vintage Champagne produced by De Venoge from 40% Chardonnay and 60% Pinot noir grapes.

Cordon Bleu (Fr). A noted fine old liqueur Cognac from Martell.

Cordon d'Alsace (Fr). A blended Alsatian wine made for U.S.A. market. Mainly of Sylvaner blend. Now no longer produced.

Cordon de Royat (Fr). A method of vine training in which a main branch is trained ⅔ metre high with 2–3 buds on each shoot.

Cordon Jaune (Fr). See Grand Marnier.

Cordon Negro (Sp). A vintage sparkling wine produced by the Frexinet Co. Distinguished by its black matt bottle. Made by the Cava method.

Cordon Rosé (Fr). A fine vintage rosé Champagne produced by G.H. Mumm from ⅓ Chardonnay and ⅔ Pinot noir grapes. Vintages – 1976, 1979, 1982.

Cordon Rouge (Fr). A popular non-vintage, brut Champagne produced by G.H. Mumm.

Cordon Rubis (Fr). A light-style Cognac produced by Martell in Cognac. Has an average cask-age of 20 years.

Cordon Vert (Fr). A non-vintage, demi-sec Champagne produced by G.H. Mumm.

Coref Ertach Pensans (Eng). A fine Ale 1055 O.G. brewed by Pensans Brewery, Cornwall for the Penzance Heritage fortnight. Also Charter Pensans.

Corent (Fr). A rosé wine from the Côtes d'Auvergne in eastern France made from the Gamay grape.

Corenwijn (Hol). A clean grain spirit (similar to Schnapps) made from barley, maize and rye. Lit – 'Corn wine'. 40% alc. by vol. Also spelt Korenwijn.

Corenwijn (Hol). The brand-name used by the Bols Company for a Moutwijn distilled without juniper.

Corenwyn (Hol). A triple-distilled, wood-aged, all-grain Corenwijn.

Corfu (Gre). An island in the western Ionian islands of Greece. Produces mainly Vins-de-Pays-style wines.

Corgi (Fr). A species of barley malt from the Triumph varieties. Gives good sugar yields.

Corgo (Port). The name given to the Port district of the Douro river. Is divided into 2 regions – Baixo (lower) and Clima (upper).

Corgolin (Fr). A commune in the Côte de Nuits-Villages which uses that A.C. and is not allowed to use its own name as a separate A.C.

Cori Bianco (It). D.O.C. white wine from Latium. Made from Bellone, Malvasia di candia, Trebbiano giallo and Trebbiano toscano grapes. From the commune of Cori and part of Cisterna.

Corinth (Chile). A seedless table grape which is used to produce dessert wines.

Corinto Nero (It). A red grape variety grown on the Lipari Islands, Sicily.

Corio (Austr). The brand-name for a Whiskey produced by the United Distillers.

Coriole Winery (Austr). A winery based in McLaren Vale, Southern Vales, South Australia. Produces varietal wines.

Cori Rosso (It). D.O.C. red wine from

C

Latium. Made from Cesanese, Montepulciano and Nero buono di cori grapes. From the commune of Cori and part of Cisterna.

Cork (Eng). Usually made from the bark of the Portuguese or Spanish cork oak (Quercus Suber).

Cork (Ire). A town in southern Ireland famous for its glass.

Corkage (Eng). A charge levied by restaurants to customers for bringing in their own wines to be opened and consumed in the restaurant.

Cork Borer (Eng). A brass instrument used for boring holes in cork, metal or plastic bungs (or stoppers) to enable any size of spile or airlock to be fitted to a cask.

Cork Distillery Co (Ire). Originally formed in 1867 by the amalgamation of the Daly, Green, North Mail, Old Middleton and Water Course Distilleries. Is now part of the Irish Distillers Group Ltd.

Cork Dry Gin (Ire). A dry Gin produced by the Irish Distillers Group at the Cork Distillery Co.

Corked (Eng) (slang). Drunk, intoxicated.

Corked Wine (Eng). A very rare occurrence. Caused by a diseased cork. Immediately detectable by an unpleasant smell in the cork and a fungus-like taste in the wine.

Corker (Eng). An instrument used by amateur wine makers to fit around cylindrical corks in home-made wines that need maturation and therefore need laying down.

Corkette (Eng). A patented device that is used to remove corks from bottles of wine. Consists of a hollow needle which is pushed through the cork into the bottle and then air is pumped into the bottle with the aid of the handle to build up pressure in the bottle to force out the cork.

Cork Flogger (Eng). The name given to a flat piece of hard wood used to ram a softened cork flush home in the neck of the bottle. See also Boot.

Corkiness (Eng). A wine malady. Smell of damp, autumnal woodlands, usually from a bad cork. Caused by the mould Aspergillus.

Cork Pin (Eng). A decorative pin and chain used to hold the extracted cork around the neck of the wine bottle or decanter for inspection.

Cork Press (Euro). An implement for compressing the corks before they are placed in the bottle (neck). Used in the late eighteenth and early nineteenth centuries.

Corkscrew (Eng). Implement for extracting the cork from a bottle of wine. There are many designs since its invention in the seventeenth century. (Fr) = Tire-Bouchon, (Ger) = Korkzieher, (Hol) = Kurketrekker, (It) = Cavatappi or Cavaturacciolo, (Sp) = Tirabuzón, (Tur) = Tirbuson, (Wales) = Allwedd Castrel.

Cork Weevil (Eng). An insect that attacks the cork wood. Sometimes found in wine-bottle corks.

Corky (Eng). A term to describe a wine that has been contaminated by a faulty cork.

Cormicy (Fr). A Cru Champagne village in the Canton de Bourgogne. District = Reims.

Cormondrèche (Switz). A noted vineyard in the Neuchâtel district of western Switzerland.

Cormoyeux (Fr). A Cru Champagne village in the Canton d'Ay. District = Reims.

Cornas (Fr). An A.C. red wine region of central-western Rhône, on the river Isère. Wines made from the Syrah grape. Minimum alc. by vol. 10.5%.

Cornell Cocktail (Cktl). 1 measure dry Gin, 4 dashes Maraschino, 2 dashes lemon juice, 1 egg white. Shake well over ice, strain into a cocktail glass.

Cornerea (La) (It). A white wine producer in southern Piemonte. Wines from the Arneis grape.

Cornevent (Fr). A vineyard in the A.C. commune of Montagny, Côte Chalonnaise, Burgundy.

Corney and Barrow (Eng). A noted, old-established firm of wine merchants. Address = 12, Helmet Row, London, EC1V 3QJ. Produce fine 'house wines'.

Corn Grits (USA). Cracked corn used for making beer.

Cornish Best Bitter (Eng). A cask conditioned and keg Bitter 1042 O.G. brewed by the Cornish Brewery Co. in Redruth, Cornwall. Was originally known as the Devenish Brewery.

Cornish Brewery Company (Eng). See Devenish Brewery.

Cornish Original (Eng). A Beer brewed by the Cornish Brewery Co.

Cornish Wreckers Scrumpy (Eng). A cask Cider produced by Countryman in Devon.

Corn Liquor (USA). Corn whiskey. Old western America name for it.

Cornwell Cocktail (Cktl). ⅓ gill dry Gin, ⅙ gill Seville orange bitters. Shake well over ice, strain into a cocktail glass, add peel of an olive and squeeze of lemon peel juice on top.

C

Corn Whiskey (USA). A fiery whiskey made from a mash containing 80% maize or more with little or no ageing.

Coromandel Valley (Austr). A wine-producing district based in South Australia.

Coronas (Sp). A red wine made from 25% Monastrell and 75% Ull de llebre grapes by Torres in Penedés. Is aged in American oak for 1 year.

Corona Soft Drinks (Eng). A famous soft drinks company that has merged with Beecham Soft Drinks Co. and then joined with Britvic. Now known as Britvic Corona.

Coronata (It). A white wine from Genoa in north-western Italy. Made from the Vermentino grape.

Coronation (Bel). A pale, strong Ale brewed by the Wielemans Brasserie in Brussels.

Coronation Cocktail (Cktl).(1). ½ gill Brandy, 3 dashes Curaçao, 2 dashes Peach bitters, 2 dashes peppermint. Stir over ice, strain into a cocktail glass, squeeze of lemon peel on top.

Coronation Cocktail (Cktl).(2). 1 oz. dry Vermouth, 1 oz. Dubonnet. 1 oz. dry Gin. Stir over ice, strain into a cocktail glass.

Coronation Cocktail (Cktl).(3). ¼ gill Sherry, ¼ gill French vermouth, 1 teaspoon Maraschino, 1 teaspoon Angostura. Shake over ice, strain into a cocktail glass.

Coronation Crystal (Cup). 1 bottle dry white wine, 3 glasses Marsala, 1 bottle Soda water, sliced lemon. Mix all together and leave for 2 hours. Sweeten to taste. Serve iced.

Coronet VSQ (USA). A premium label Brandy produced by the Schenley Distillers in California.

Coron Père et Fils (Fr). A négociant-éleveur based in Beaune. Owns 4 ha. in the A.C. Beaune.

Corowa (Austr). A wine-producing area based in New South Wales which produces mainly sweet, fortified wines.

Corps (Fr). Body. i.e. Richness in alcohol and other substances.

Corpse-Reviver (Cktl).(1). ½ fl.oz. Calvados, 1 fl.oz. Marc brandy, ½ fl.oz. sweet Vermouth. Stir over ice, strain into a cocktail glass. Add a twist of lemon peel.

Corpse Reviver (Cktl).(2). ¼ measure Gin, ¼ measure Triple Sec, ¼ measure lemon juice, ¼ measure Swedish Punsch, dash Pernod. Shake over ice, strain into a cocktail glass.

Corpse Reviver (Cktl).(3). ⅓ measure Cognac, ⅓ measure Fernet Branca, ⅓ measure Peppermint Schnapps. Shake over ice, strain into a cocktail glass.

Corpse Reviver (Cktl).(4). ¼ measure dry Gin, ¼ measure Cointreau, ¼ measure China Martini, ¼ measure lemon juice, dash Pernod. Shake over ice, strain into a cocktail glass.

Corpse Reviver (Cktl).(5). ½ measure Cognac, ½ measure Calvados, ¼ measure sweet Vermouth. Shake over ice, strain into a cocktail glass.

Corpse Reviver (Cktl).(6). ⅓ measure Cognac, ⅓ measure orange juice, ⅓ measure lemon juice, dash Grenadine. Shake over ice, strain into a flute glass. Top with iced Champagne and a slice of orange.

Corpse Reviver (USA). A pick-me-up cocktail.

Corquete (Sp). A knife with a curved tip used in the harvesting of the grape.

Corrales Winery (USA). A winery based in Corrales, New Mexico. Produces mainly table wines.

Corral Tinto Rioja (Sp). A red wine produced by Bodegas Corral S.A. Alta, Rioja. Is oak and bottle-matured.

Correct (Eng). A term used to describe a wine with all the right characteristics for its type and origin. Not necessarily a fine wine.

Correction (Eng). The addition of sugar, acid, tannin or the removal of excess acid or tannin in wines. Also the blending of wines. Practised to maintain uniformity and improve the wine. Strict laws relating to this practice vary from country to country.

Corredor (Sp). Wine broker.

Corretto (It). Cordial.

Corrida (Sp). The brand-name for a range of Spanish wines distributed in the U.K. by Stowells of Chelsea, London. Produced by José López Bertran, Tarragona. Are sold in Spain under the Vinate label.

Corroborar (Sp). To fortify, strengthen.

Corsé (Switz) (Fr). Full-bodied. High in alcohol.

Corsica (Fr). An island producing red and rosé wines usually strong and aromatic. A.C. Has six sub-regions (Calvi, Coteaux d'Ajaccio, Figari, Patrimonio, Porte Vecchio and Sartène).

Corsican Bounty Cocktail (Cktl). ½ measure Mandarine Napoléon, 1 measure Malibu, 1 measure lemon juice, dash Orgeat, dash egg white. Shake well over ice, strain into a cocktail glass. Top with a slice of lemon and a green cocktail cherry.

Cortado (Sp). A Sherry-style between an Amontillado and an Oloroso. Classified as Un, Dos, Tres, Cuarto.

C

Cortaillod (Switz). A red wine of the Neuchâtel region from the Pinot noir grape. Also a pink wine called Cortaillod Oeil de Perdrix.

Cortaillod Oeil de Perdrix (Switz). See Cortaillod.

Corte (Fr). A wine district of central Corsica that produces full flavoured wines.

Corte (Port). The name given to the process of treading grapes. Means the first treading which crushes the grapes to release the best juice.

Cortese (It). A white grape variety grown in Piemonte and Liguria.

Cortese (Giuseppe) (It). A small wine producer based in Barbaresco, Piemonte. (Has vineyards on Rabaya Hill).

Cortese di Galvi (It). D.O.C. white wine from Piemonte. Made from the Cortese grape. D.O.C. applies to the sparkling wine produced by the natural process from musts or wines according to the regulations.

Cortese Spumante (It). D.O.C. sparkling wine from Piemonte. See Colli Tortonesi Cortese.

Corton (Fr). A Grand Cru vineyard in the A.C. commune of Aloxe-Corton, Côte de Beaune, Burgundy. Many climats within the vineyard use the name. e.g. Corton-Bressandes, Corton-Charlemagne. Also known as Le Corton. Part lies in the A.C. commune of Pernand Vergelesses. (red and white).

Corton-Bressandes (Fr). A Grand Cru climat in the vineyard of Corton, A.C. Aloxe-Corton, Côte de Beaune, Burgundy. Also known as Les Bressandes.

Corton Charlemagne (Fr). A Grand Cru climat [part] in the vineyard of Corton, A.C. Aloxe-Corton, Côte de Beaune, Burgundy. Part is also in the A.C. commune of Pernand-Vergelesses. Is also known as Le Charlemagne. (red and white). 25 ha.

Corton-Chaumes (Fr). A Grand Cru climat [part] in the vineyard of Corton, A.C. Aloxe-Corton, Côte de Beaune, Burgundy. Is also known as Les Chaumes. (red and white).

Corton Clos du Roi (Fr). A Grand Cru climat in the vineyard of Corton, A.C. Aloxe-Corton, Côte de Beaune, Burgundy. (red and white).

Corton-Combes (Fr). A Grand Cru climat [part] in the vineyard of Corton, A.C. Aloxe-Corton, Côte de Beaune, Burgundy. Is also known as Les Combes. (red and white).

Corton En Pauland (Fr). See Corton-Pauland.

Corton-Fiètres (Fr). A Grand Cru climat in the vineyard of Corton, A.C. Aloxe-Corton, Côte de Beaune, Burgundy. Is also known as Les Fiètres.

Corton-Grèves (Fr). A Grand Cru climat in the vineyard of Corton, A.C. Aloxe-Corton, Côte de Beaune, Burgundy. Is also known as Les Grèves. (red and white).

Corton-Languettes (Fr). A Grand Cru climat [part] in the vineyard of Corton, A.C. Aloxe-Corton, Côte de Beaune, Burgundy. Also known as Les Languettes. (red and white).

Corton La Vigne-au-Saint (Fr). A Grand Cru climat in the vineyard of Corton, A.C. Aloxe-Corton, Côte de Beaune, Burgundy. (red and white).

Corton-Maréchaudes (Fr). A Grand Cru climat [part] in the vineyard of Corton, A.C. Aloxe-Corton, Côte de Beaune, Burgundy. Is also known as Les Maréchaudes. (red and white).

Corton-Meix (Fr). A Grand Cru climat [part] in the vineyard of Corton, A.C. Aloxe-Corton, Côte de Beaune, Burgundy. Is also known as Les Meix. (red and white).

Corton-Meix-Lallemant (Fr). A Grand Cru climat [part] in the vineyard of Corton, A.C. Aloxe-Corton, Côte de Beaune, Burgundy. Is also known as Les Meix-Lallemant. (red and white).

Corton-Pauland (Fr). A Grand Cru climat [part] in the vineyard of Corton, A.C. Aloxe-Corton, Côte de Beaune, Burgundy. Is also known as Corton-En-Pauland or En Pauland. (red and white).

Corton-Perrières (Fr). A Grand Cru climat in the vineyard of Corton, A.C. Aloxe-Corton, Côte de Beaune, Burgundy. Also known as Les Perrières. (red and white).

Corton-Pougets (Fr). A Grand Cru climat [part] in the vineyard of Corton, A.C. Aloxe-Corton, Côte de Beaune, Burgundy. Also known as Les Pougets. (red and white).

Corton-Renardes (Fr). A Grand Cru climat in the vineyard of Corton, A.C. Aloxe-Corton, Côte de Beaune, Burgundy. Also known as Les Renardes. (red and white).

Coruba (W.Ind). A brand of dark Rum produced in Jamaica by the Rum Company (Jamaica) Ltd.

Çorum (Tur). A wine-producing area in northern Turkey. Produces mainly white wines.

Corvée (La) (Fr). A vineyard in the A.C. commune of Montagny, Côte Chalonnaise, Burgundy.

Corvées-Paget (Les) (Fr). A Premier Cru vineyard of the village of Prémeaux in the southern part of the A.C. commune of Nuits-Saint-Georges, Côte de Nuits, Burgundy. 1.6 ha.

C

Corvina (It). A red grape variety grown in the Veneto region. Makes light red wines.

Corvina Veronese (It). A red wine grape used in the making of Bardolino wine.

Corvo (It). A large producer of red and white wines based near Palermo in Sicily.

Cos (Pol). Old term used to describe the Tokay wines of Hungary suitable for buying. (abbr). of Latin expression 'ut vinum habeat colorem, odorem et saporem' = 'Wine should have colour, scent and taste'.

Cosecha (Sp). Harvest or vintage.

Cosechero (Sp). Vineyard owner.

Cos-Labory (Fr). See Château Cos-Labory.

Cosmos Cocktail (Cktl). ⅔ measure fresh cream, ⅓ measure Coconut cream, 2 measures Tropical Fruit drink, 6 fresh strawberries. Blend altogether in a blender with a scoop of crushed ice. Strain into a goblet. Top with a strawberry.

Cossack (Eng). A Vodka produced by Booth's Co. 40% alc. by vol.

Cossack Cooler Cock). In a highball glass filled with ice, add 1 measure Cossack vodka, fill with equal amounts of ginger ale and medium dry Cider. Garnish with a slice of lemon and rub the glass rim with a mint leaf.

Cossart Gordon (Mad). A Madeira company that produces under the 'Good Company' label, as well as Cossarts.

Cosson (Gilles) (Fr). Cognac producer. Address = SARL La Grange Neuve, Guimps, 16300 Barbezieux. 50 ha. in Grande Champagne 35% and Petite Champagne 65%. Produces – Très Vieille Réserve Fine, Champagne 25 year old and Blason Fine Champagne 10 year old.

Costa Blanca (Sp). The name used by García Poveda in Alicante for a range of wines.

Costa Rica Coffee (W.Ind). A mild coffee with a strong nutty flavour. The beans are blue-green in colour. Gives a fine brew with low acidity, good body and flavour.

Coste [Pierre] (Fr). A négociant-éleveur based in Langon, Bordeaux.

Costières du Gard (Fr). A V.D.Q.S. red wine region of the Midi in the Gard Département.

Costmary (Euro). An old herb used for flavouring ale in the middle ages. Of the family Compositae, species – Chrysanthemum balsamita. Leaves only were used.

Costrel (Eng). A leather or earthenware flask which held water, wine or beer and was carried on a waist-belt in the middle-ages.

Costyn Vineyard (Wales). A vineyard based at Cosheston, Pembroke Dock, Dyfed. Planted 1978. 0.35 ha. Grape varieties – Madeleine angevine, Müller-Thurgau, Reichensteiner, Wrotham Pinot, plus others.

Côt (Fr). Alternative name for the Malbec grape in the Loire, Cahors and Auxerrois.

Côte (Fr). Slope, side of hill.

Côte [La] (Switz). A wine-producing district in the canton of Vaud, southwestern Switzerland.

Coteau de Migraine (Fr). A vineyard which produces red wine in Auxerre in the Yonne Département, northern Burgundy. 18.5 ha.

Coteaux (Fr). Hillsides, slopes.

Coteaux Cathares (Fr). A Vins de Pays area in the Aude Département in central-southern France. Produces red and rosé wines.

Coteaux Cévenois (Fr). A Vins de Pays area of the Gard Département in southwestern France. Produces red, rosé and dry white wines.

Coteaux Champenois (Fr). A new name for the still wine produced in the Champagne region. Was known as Vin Nature de Champagne but now EEC regulations prevent the use of the old name.

Coteaux d'Aix-en-Provence (Fr). An A.C. region in southern France. Produces red, rosé and white wines from the Carignan, Cinsault, Clairette, Counoise, Mourvèdre, Muscat and Ugni blanc grapes. Received A.C. status in 1984.

Coteaux d'Ajaccio (Fr). A.C. red, rosé and white wines of the Ajaccio region of Corsica.

Coteaux d'Ancenis (Fr). A Loire vineyard area around the town of Ancenis which produces red and rosé wines from the Gamay grape. V.D.Q.S. status. The same vineyard produces Muscadet Coteaux de la Loire.

Coteaux de Baronnies (Fr). A Vins de Pays area in the Drôme Département in south-eastern France.

Coteaux de Carthage (Afr). The brandname for red and rosé wines made by the UCCVT in Tunisia.

Coteaux de Cèze (Fr). A Vins de Pays area within the Gard Département in southwestern France. Produces red, rosé and dry white wines.

Coteaux de Fenouillèdes (Fr). A Vins de Pays area within the Pyrénées Orientales Département in south-western France.

Coteaux de Fontcaude (Fr). A Vins de

Pays area within the Hérault Département in southern France. Produces
red, rosé and dry white wines.

Coteaux de Glanes (Fr). A Vins de Pays
area within the Lot Département in
southern France.

Coteaux de Gresivaudan (Fr). A Vins de
Pays area in the Isère Département,
central-eastern France.

Coteaux de Ksara (Arab). A brand of
white wine produced in Lebanon.

Coteaux de la Cabrerisse (Fr). A Vins de
Pays area within the Aude Département
in central-southern France. Produces
red and rosé wines.

Coteaux de la Cité de Carcassonne (Fr). A
Vins de Pays area within the Aude
Département in central-southern
France.

Coteaux de la Loire (Fr). A separate A.C.
within the region of Anjou-Saumur,
Loire.

Coteaux de la Loire-Rosé de Cabernet
(Fr). A.C. rosé wine made from the
Cabernet franc grape in the Coteaux de
la Loire.

Coteaux de la Méjanelle (Fr). An A.C.
wine-producing district in the Hérault
Département. Produces white wines.

Coteaux de l'Ardèche (Fr). A Vins de Pays
area within the Ardèche Dèpartement
in south-east France.

Coteaux de l'Aubance (Fr). A.C. white
wines. Separate A.C. in the district of
Anjou-Saumur of the Loire. Produces
sweet white wines from the Chenin
blanc grape.

Coteaux de l'Aubance-Rosé de Cabernet
(Fr). A.C. rosé from the Anjou-Saumur
region of the Loire. Made from the
Cabernet franc grape.

Coteaux de Lézignanais (Fr). A Vins de
Pays area within the Aude Département
in central-southern France. Produces
red and rosé wines.

Coteaux de Libron (Fr). A Vins de Pays
area within the Hérault Département in
southern France. Produces red, rosé
and dry white wines.

Coteaux de Mascara (Alg). A fine wine-
producing area in the Oran Département. Produces red, rosé and white
wines.

Coteaux de Miramont (Fr). A Vins de
Pays area within the Aude Département
in central-southern France. Produces
red and rosé wines.

Coteaux de Murviel (Fr). A Vins de Pays
area within the Hérault Département in
southern France. Produces red and rosé
wines.

Coteaux de Narbonne (Fr). A Vins de Pays
area within the Aude Département in

central-southern France. Produces red
and rosé wines.

Coteaux d'Enserune (Fr). A Vins de Pays
area within the Hérault Départment in
southern France. Produces mainly red
wines.

Coteaux de Patras (Gre). A medium-dry
white wine made from the grape Rhoditis. Produced in Peloponnese.

Coteaux de Peyriac (Fr). A Vins de Pays
area within the Aude Département in
central-southern France. Produces red
and rosé wines.

Coteaux de Pierrevert (Fr). V.D.Q.S. red,
rosé, white and sparkling wines from
near Manosque in the Rhône.

Coteaux de Quercy (Fr). A Vins de Pays
area within the Lot Département in
south-western France. Produces red
and rosé wines.

Coteaux de Saint-Christol (Fr). A.C. red
wine-producing district in Languedoc-
Roussillon region, southern France.

Coteaux de Saumur (Fr). A.C. within the
Anjou-Saumur district of the Loire.

Coteaux de Saumur-Rosé de Cabernet
(Fr). A.C. rosé of the Saumur region of
Anjou-Saumur in the Loire. Made from
the Cabernet franc. Now sold as A.C.
Cabernet rosé.

Coteaux-des-Baux-en-Provence (Fr). A.C.
wine-producing region in south-
eastern France. Produces red, rosé and
a litle white wine. Received A.C. in
1985.

Coteaux des Fenouillèdes (Fr). A Vins de
Pays area in the Pyrénées-Orièntales
Département in south-western France.

Coteaux de Termenès (Fr). A Vins de Pays
area within the Aude Département in
the Languedoc-Roussillon region
southern France.

Coteaux de Tlemcen (Alg). A wine-
producing area in the Oran Département. Produces red, rosé and white
wines.

Coteaux de Touraine (Fr). A wine region
of the central Loire. Wines produced
are Bourgueil, St. Nicolas de Bourgueil,
Vouvray and Montlouis.

Coteaux de Touraine (Fr). A.C. red, rosé
and white wine designation which is
now no longer used.

Coteaux de Touraine Mousseux (Fr). A.C.
sparkling wine of the Touraine region
of the Loire. Now no longer used as A.C.
designation.

Coteaux de Vérargues (Fr). A.C. wine-
producing area in the Coteaux du Languedoc, southern France. Produces red
and rosé wines.

Coteaux du Cap Corse (Fr). A.C. red, rosé,
dry and semi-sweet white wines from

C

Corsica. Also VdN. (from Muscat and Vermentino grapes).

Coteaux du Cher et de l'Arnon (Fr). A Vins de Pays area in the Cher and Indre Départements of western France. Produces red, rosé and white wines.

Coteaux du Giennois (Fr). A V.D.Q.S. wine area of the Loire between Orléans and Pouilly-sur-Loire. Produces both red and white wines.

Coteaux du Khanguet (Afr). A noted wine-producing area in Tunisia.

Coteaux du Languedoc (Fr). A.C. of the Languedoc in the Midi, southern France. Grapes – Carignan and Cinsault (maximum 50%), Grenache, Mourvèdre and Syrah. Received A.C. in 1985.

Coteaux du Layon (Fr). Separate A.C. within the region of Anjou-Saumur of the Loire. Produces fine, sweet (botrytis cinerea) wines. See Coteaux du Layon-Chaume and Quarts de Chaume.

Coteaux du Layon-Chaume (Fr). A.C. sweet white wine of the Anjou-Saumur region. See Coteaux du Layon. Minimum alc. by vol. 13%.

Coteaux du Layon-Rosé de Cabernet (Fr). A.C. rosé wine made from the Cabernet franc grape in the Anjou-Saumur region of the Loire. Now sold as A.C. Cabernet rosé.

Coteaux du Littoral Audois (Fr). A Vins de Pays area within the Aude Département in central-southern France. Produces red and rosé wines.

Coteaux du Loir (Fr). See Coteaux de la Loire.

Coteaux du Loiret (Fr). Old A.C. red, rosé and white wines of the Loire.

Coteaux du Lubéron (Fr). See Côtes du Lubéron.

Coteaux du Lyonnaise (Fr). A.C. red, rosé and white wines produced near Lyons in the Rhône region.

Coteaux du Pont-du-Gard (Fr). A Vins de Pays area within the Gard Département in south-western France. Produces red, rosé and dry white wines.

Coteaux du Salagou (Fr). A Vins de Pays area within the Hérault Département in southern France. Produces red and rosé wines.

Coteaux du Salavès (Fr). A Vins de Pays area within the Gard Département in south-western France. Produces red, rosé and dry white wines.

Coteaux du Tessalah (Alg). A wine-producing area in the Oran Département. Produces red, rosé and white wines.

Coteaux du Tricastin (Fr). A.C. red wine district on the left bank of the Rhône. 12

communes produce light red wines. Grapes – Carignan, Cinsault, Grenache, Mourvèdre and Picpoul.

Coteaux du Vendômois (Fr). V.D.Q.S. red, rosé and white wines produced north of Blois in the Loire.

Coteaux du Vidourle (Fr). A Vins de Pays area within the Gard Département in south-western France. Produces red, rosé and dry white wines.

Coteaux du Zaccar (Alg). A wine-producing area in the Alger Département. Produces red, rosé and white wines.

Coteaux et Terrasses de Montauban (Fr). A Vins de Pays area in the Tarn-et-Garonne Département, south-western France. Produces red and rosé wines.

Coteaux Flaviens (Fr). A Vins de Pays area within the Gard Département of south-western France. Produces red, rosé and dry white wines.

Coteaux Mascara (Alg). A principal wine-producing area in the Oran Département.

Coteaux Varois (Fr). A Vins de Pays area within the Var Département in south-eastern France. Produces red, rosé and dry white wines.

Côte Blonde (Fr). The name for half of the Côte Rôtie district in the northern Rhône. So named because of the light-coloured soil, composed of Silico-Calcerous.

Côte Brune (Fr). The name for half of the Côte Rôtie district of the northern Rhône. So named because of the brown-coloured soil, a brownish clay.

Côte Catalane (Fr). A Vins de Pays area within the Pyrénées-Orientales Département in south-western France.

Côte Chalonnaise (Fr). A region in the southern half of Burgundy. Has 3 A.C. red districts – Givry, Mercurey and Rully. 1 A.C. white district – Montagny. The red wines made from the Pinot noir, the white from the Chardonnay and Pinot blanc.

Côte d'Azur de la Côte d'Or (Fr). See Domaine de Bévy.

Côte de Beaune (Fr). The southern half of the Côte d'Or in Burgundy. Noted for its Grand Cru white wines made with the Chardonnay grape and Premier Cru red wines made from the Pinot noir. See also Hospices de Beaune.

Côte de Beaune-Villages (Fr). A.C. red wines produced from the Pinot noir grape from communes within the Côte de Beaune in the southern half of the Côte d'Or, Burgundy. Minimum alc. by vol. of 10.5%.

Côte de Brouilly (Fr). A.C. Cru Beaujolais-Villages, Burgundy. Has 280 ha. under vines.

Côte de Dijon (Fr). An area based north of the A.C. Fixin, Côte de Nuits, Burgundy. Was once a top growth region. Now planted mainly with the Gamay grape.

Côte de Fontenay (Fr). A.C. Premier Grand Cru Chablis. Often is reclassified as the Premier Cru Fourchaume.

Côte de la Mouleyre (Fr). A vineyard in the A.C. Saint-Émilion. Address = Saint-Christophe-des-Bardes, 33330 Saint-Émilion. Commune = Saint-Christophe-des-Bardes.

Côte de Léchet (Fr). A Premier Cru vineyard in the A.C. Chablis, Burgundy.

Côte de Nuits (Fr). Northern half of the Côte d'Or in Burgundy. Noted for its Grand Cru red wines made with the Pinot noir grape.

Côte de Nuits-Villages (Fr). Previously known as Vins Fins de la Côte de Nuits. Consists of the communes of Brochon, Fixin, Prissey, Corgolin and Comblanchien. The latter three cannot use their commune names as a separate A.C. Grape variety – Pinot noir. Minimum alc. by vol. 10.5% red and 11% white.

Côte de Parnasse (Gre). The name for red and white wines from Hatikoi.

Côte des Blancs (Fr). A vineyard area of the Champagne region. Produces white grapes (Chardonnay) for Champagne production.

Côte des Colombes (USA). A vineyard based in Banks, Oregon. 4 ha. Produces vinifera wines.

Côte des Prés-Girots (Fr). A Premier Cru vineyard in the A.C. Chablis. Often reclassified as Premier Cru Les Fourneaux.

Côte d'Or (Fr). A top wine area of Burgundy. Consists of the Côte de Nuits in the northern half and the Côte de Beaune in the south. Lit – 'Golden hills'.

Côte Droit (Cktl). ⁷⁄₁₀ measure Mandarine Napoléon, ²⁄₁₀ measure orange juice, ¹⁄₁₀ measure Calvados, ³⁄₁₀ measure Dubonnet. Shake well together over ice, strain into a highball glass with ice, top with a cherry and slice of orange.

Côte Hyot (Fr). A red wine produced in the Savoie region in south-eastern France.

Coterie (Fr). Set or group. e.g. Group of vine growers.

Coterie des Closiers de Montlouis (Fr). A wine society based in the Touraine district of the Loire.

Côte Roannaise (Fr). V.D.Q.S. red and rosé wines produced in the Loire Département, central France. Produced from the Gamay grape. Minimum alc. by vol. 9%.

Côte Rôtie (Fr). A district in the northern Rhône. Made up of the Côte Blonde and Côte Brune. Villages – Ampuis, Tupin and Semons. Vineyards are terraced. Grape varieties – Syrah for red and Viognier for white.

Côte Rôtie (Fr). A Premier Cru vineyard in the A.C. commune of Morey-Saint-Denis, Côte de Nuits, Burgundy. 0.4 ha.

Côte Rouvre (La) (Fr). A large vineyard in Avallon, Yonne Département. Produces red and white wines.

Côtes (Fr). Hills, vineyard slopes.

Côtes Canon-Fronsac (Fr). An A.C. district in central-eastern Bordeaux on the right bank of the river Gironde. Grape varieties – Cabernet franc, Cabernet sauvignon, Malbec and Merlot. Minimum alc. by vol. 11%.

Côtes Catalanes (Fr). A Vins de Pays area in the Pyrénées-Orientales Département. Includes the canton of Rivesaltes.

Côtes d'Agly (Fr). A.C. Vin doux naturel from the Roussillon region on the Pyrénées border.

Côtes d'Auvergne (Fr). A V.D.Q.S. district near Clermont-Ferrand in central France. Produces red, rosé and white wines. Has 5 sub-regions – (Boudes, Chateaugay, Corent, Chanturge and Madargues). Grapes – Chardonnay, Gamay à jus blanc and Pinot noir.

Côtes de Bergerac Moelleux (Fr). A.C. sweet white wine from the Bergerac region of western France. 12–15% alc. by vol.

Côtes de Blaye (Fr). A.C. district in north-eastern Bordeaux. Also known as the Blaye. Communes = Anglade, Berson, Blaye, Blaye-Plassac, Cadres, Cars, Cartelègue, Eyrons, Fours, Mazion, Plassac, St-Androny, St-Christ-de-Blaye, St-Genès, St-Genès-de-Blaye, St-Girons, St-Martin-Caussaude, St-Paul and St-Seurin-Cursac. Red wines of minimum alc. by vol. 10.5%, also white wines. See also Premières Côtes de Blaye.

Côtes de Bordeaux (Fr). See Premières Côtes de Bordeaux and Côtes de Bordeaux Saint-Macaire.

Côtes de Bordeaux Saint-Macaire (Fr). A.C. white wine district in the southern region of Bordeaux. Sweet white wines. Minimum alc. by vol. 11.5%.

Côtes de Bourg (Fr). A.C. district in the north-eastern Bordeaux. Also known as the Bourg. Communes = Bayon, Bourg, Comps, Gauriac, Lansac, Samonac, Prignac-Marcamps, Monbrier, St-Ciers-de-Canesse, St-Seurin-Bourg, Pugnac, Tauriac and Teuillac. Red wines of minimum alc. by vol. 10.5%, also white wines. See also Bourgeais.

Côtes de Brian (Fr). A Vins de Pays area within the Hérault Département in southern France.

Côtes de Bruhlois (Fr). A Vins de Pays area within the Lot-et-Garonne Département in south-western France.

Côtes de Buzet (Fr). A.C. area based south-east of Bordeaux. Produces mainly red with some white wines. Minimum alc. by vol. 10%. See Cuvée Napoléon.

Côtes de Cabardès et de l'Orbiel (Fr). A V.D.Q.S. red-wine-producing area in the Languedoc. Lies in the Aude Département part of the Coteaux du Languedoc, south-western France.

Côtes de Castillon (Fr). A.C. red wine region in the south-eastern part of Bordeaux. Wines often sold under the A.C. Bordeaux Supérieur designation.

Côtes de Céressou (Fr). A Vins de Pays area within the Hérault Département in southern France. Produces red, rosé and dry white wines.

Côtes de Duras (Fr). A.C. red and white wine-producing region based east of Bergerac. Grape varieties – Cabernet, Malbec, Mauzet, Muscadelle, Sauvignon blanc and Sémillon. Minimum alc. by vol. 10.5%.

Côtes de Fronsac (Fr). A small A.C. district in eastern Bordeaux. Red wines only.

Côtes de Gascogne (Fr). A Vins de Pays area within the Gers Département in central-southern France.

Côtes de Gien (Fr). A V.D.Q.S. area between Orléans and Pouilly-sur-Loire in the Loire. Produces red and white wines.

Côtes de la Malepère (Fr). V.D.Q.S. red and rosé wines from the region of Carcassonne in the Aude Département.

Côtes de Lastours (Fr). A Vins de Pays area in the Aude Département in central-southern France.

Côtes de Montestruc (Fr). A Vins de Pays area within the Gers Département in central-southern France.

Côtes de Montravel (Fr). A.C. white (medium-sweet) wine-producing district of the Bergerac region. Minimum alc. by vol. 12%.

Côtes de Pérignan (Fr). A Vins de Pays area within the Aude Département in central-southern France.

Côtes de Prouille (Fr). A Vins de Pays area in the Aude Département in central-southern France.

Côtes de Provence (Fr). A.C. of Provence. Fine wines in which some 12 vineyards can use the designation Grand Cru. Red, rosé and white wines produced. Received the A.C. in 1977.

Côtes de Rol (Fr). A vineyard in the commune of Saint-Émilion. A.C. Saint-Émilion, Bordeaux. 4 ha.

Côtes de Saint-Mont (Fr). A V.D.Q.S. area within the Gers Département in central-southern France. Produces red, rosé and white wines.

Côtes de Saussignac (Fr). An A.C. commune in the Côtes de Bergerac, south-western France.

Côtes de Thau (Fr). A Vins de Pays area within the Hérault Département in southern France. Produces red, rosé and dry white wines.

Côtes de Thongue (Fr). A Vins de Pays area within the Hérault Département in southern France. Produces red, rosé and dry white wines.

Côtes de Toul (Fr). A V.D.Q.S. white wine produced in Lorraine near Nancy. Light red, rosé and white wines produced. Sited within the communes of – Blénod-les-Toul, Bruley, Bulligny, Charmes-la-Côte, Dongermain, Écouvres, Lucey and Mont-le-Vignoble.

Côtes d'Olt (Les) (Fr). The only large cooperative based in A.C. Cahors, south-western France. 512 members. Grapes – Malbec, Merlot and Tannat. Sells under the brand-names of Côtes d'Olt, Comte André de Montpezat and Château les Bouysses.

Côtes du Condomois (Fr). A Vins de Pays area within the Lot-et-Garonne Département in central-southern France.

Côtes du Forez (Fr). A V.D.Q.S. district in central Rhône, southern France. Grape variety – Gamay rouge à jus blanc.

Côtes du Fronton (Fr). A small V.D.Q.S. red-wine-producing district in south-western France. Grape variety mainly Negrette. Min. alc. by vol. 10.5%.

Côtes du Frontonnais (Fr). See Côtes du Fronton.

Côtes du Haut-Roussillon (Fr). A Vin Doux Naturel from the Roussillon region of southern France.

Côtes du Jura (Fr). A.C. wine region at the foot of the Jura mountains in eastern France. Noted for its Vin jaune (straw wine) from the commune of Arbois. Red, rosé and white wines produced.

Côtes du Jura Mousseux (Fr). Sparkling wines produced by méthode champenoise (or méthode gaillaçoise) in the Savoie region in south-eastern France. Made from the Chardonnay and Pinot blanc grapes.

Côtes du Lubéron (Fr). A A.C. region of the Rhône. Produces red, rosé and white wines.

Côtes du Marmandais (Fr). A V.D.Q.S. district near Marmande in the Lot-et-Garonne Département in south-western France. Produces red wines. Minimum alc. by vol. 10%.

C

Côtes du Meliton (Gre). An A.O.C. wine-producing area in Macedonia. Produces red, rosé and white wines. See Carras.

Côtes du Rhône (Fr). A large wine region in southern France. Noted for its heady red wines. Produces all styles of wines. Covers the Départements of Ardèche, Drôme, Gard, Vaucluse, Rhône and the Loire. Minimum alc. by vol. of 11%. See Château-Grillet, Châteauneuf-du-Pape, Cornas, Côte Rôtie, Crozes-Hermitage, Gigondas, Hermitage, Lirac, Saint-Joseph, Saint-Péray and Tavel.

Côtes du Rhône-Villages (Fr). A.C. designation of the central Rhône region. Communes can use their own name or Côtes du-Rhône-Villages A.C. 17 Villages – Beaumes-de-Venise, Cairanne, Chusclan, Laudun, Rasteau, Richegude, Roaix, Rousset-les-Vignes, Sablet, Seguret, St. Gervais, St. Maurice-sur-Eygues, St. Pantaléon-les-Vignes, Vacqueyras, Valreas, Vinsobres and Visan.

Côtes du Roussillon (Fr). A.C. wine-producing region in south-eastern France. Produces red, rosé, white and VdN wines. Grape varieties – Carignan, Cinsault, Grenache, Lledoner pelut, Macabéo and Mourvèdre.

Côtes du Roussillon-Villages (Fr). A.C. red wines from the better parts of the Roussillon region in south-eastern France. Minimum alc. by vol. 12%.

Côtes du Tarn (Fr). A Vins de Pays area within the Lot-et-Garonne Département in central-southern France.

Côtes du Ventoux (Fr). An A.C. district of the eastern Rhône. Produces red, rosé and white wines. Also A.C. Mazan (a VdL).

Côtes du Vidourle (Fr). A Vins de Pays area within the Gard Département in the Languedoc-Roussillon region.

Côtes du Vivarais (Fr). A V.D.Q.S. district in the south of the Massif Centrale. Produces light red, rosé and white wines.

Côtes et Pied de Côtes (Fr). A zone of production in the Saint-Émilion, Bordeaux. Lit – 'Hillsides and lower slopes'.

Côtes Frontonnaises (Fr). See Côtes du Fronton.

Côtes Roannaises (Fr). A V.D.Q.S. red and rosé wine-producing area in the Loire. Grape variety – Gamay St. Romain à jus blanc. Also known as Vins de Renaison.

Côtes Rocheuses (Fr). A Cave Coopérative based in Saint-Émilion, Bordeaux. Part of Royal Saint-Émilion. 775 ha. total.

Côtes Saint-Émilion (Fr). A district within the A.C. Saint-Émilion, Bordeaux.

Côte St. André (Fr). A white wine from Vienne in Dauphiny in the Isère Département, south-eastern France.

Coteşti (Rum). Focsani red and white table wines.

Cotignac (Fr). A quince-flavoured liqueur. 14.8% alc. by vol.

Cotleigh Brewery (Eng). Opened in 1979 in Wireliscombe, Somerset. Produces Old Buzzard 1048 O.G. Tawny Bitter 1040 O.G. Nutcracker 1036 O.G. and WB Bitter 1037 O.G. (all cask conditioned ales).

Cotnari (Rum). A noted wine region producing sweet dessert wines.

Cotnari (Rum). A strong natural wine based on the Grasă grape which is subject to botrytis cinerea. Produced in the Cotnari region.

Coto de Imaz (Sp). A red wine produced by Bodegas El Coto S.A., Rioja. Made from the Tempranillo grape. Oak-matured. A vintage style is also produced.

Cotswold Cottage Cider (Eng). A dry or medium-sweet Cider produced by the Frampton Village Cider Co.

Cottage Brand (Eng). A herb farm based near Canterbury, Kent. Produces a wide range of teas.

Cottage Vineyards (USA). A winery based in Marlboro, Hudson Valley, New York. Produces American and hybrid wines.

Cotte (La) (S.Afr). The Prestige label of the Franschhoek Co-operative.

Cotto (It). Cooked wine. i.e. Concentrated. A speciality of a few regions.

Cotturi and Sons (USA). A winery based in Sonoma County, California. Grape varieties – Cabernet sauvignon, Chardonnay, Gewürztraminer, Johannisberg riesling, Pinot noir, Sémillon and Zinfandel. Produces varietal wines.

Couche (Ch.Isles). The name given to the pulp (cheese) residue left from the apples after the juice has been extracted in Cider production.

Couchey (Fr). A commune which joins Marsannay-la-Côte and has its wines under the same A.C.

Couderc (Fr). A famous French hybridiser. A grape named after him is grown in Brazil.

Couderc (Sp). A rootstock used in Tarragona. A cross between Vitis riparia and Vitis berlandieri.

Cougar's Cooler (Cktl). ¼ fl.oz. Vodka, ¼ fl.oz. Oolgaard blueberry liqueur, ½ fl.oz. lemon juice. Shake well over ice, strain into a 12 oz. highball glass filled with ice. Garnish with a cherry and slices of citrus fruits.

Couillebaud (Rémy) (Fr). A Cognac producer. Address = Nle 141 Malvielle, Moulidars, 16290 Hiersac. 22 ha. in the Fins Bois. Produces***, V.S.O.P. and Napoléon.

Coulage (Fr). Leakage. Loss of liquid from a cask.

Coulange-la-Vineuse (Fr). A vineyard producing red wine in Auxerre in the Yonne Département in north-central France.

Coulant (Fr). Lit – 'flowing'. Term used to describe an easy drinking wine.

Coulée de Serrant (Fr). A.C. vineyard at Savennières which produces a light, rich white wine.

Couleuse (Fr). A term used in the Champagne region for a sparkling wine that has lost its gas.

Coulommes-la-Montagne (Fr). A Cru Champagne village in the Canton de Ville-en-Tardenois. District = Reims.

Coulonges (Fr). A commune in the Charente-Maritime Département whose grapes are classed Petite Champagne (Cognac).

Coulure (Fr). A vine malady caused by rain and mineral deficiency in the soil. Can have a disastrous effect at the crucial stage of blossoming. The blossoms fall off and berries become stunted. There is no real cure but careful fertilizing will help.

Couly Dutheil (Fr). A noted producer of Chinon wines in the Anjou-Saumur, Loire. Address = 12, Rue Diderot BP 234, 37502 Chinon.

Counoise (Fr). A red grape variety of the Rhône. Used for its vinosity, freshness and bouquet.

Counseil Interprofessionnel des Vins de Bordeaux (Fr). C.I.V.B. The controlling body for Bordeaux wines. Address = 1, Cours du XXX Juliet, 33075 Bordeaux, Cedex.

Count Currey Cocktail (Cktl). ⅓ gill Gin, 1 teaspoon powdered sugar. Shake over ice, strain into a Champagne flute. Top with iced Champagne.

Count Rossi (Cktl). Place 2 ice cubes in a small tumbler. Top with ⅓ gill dry Martini and ⅓ gill sweet Martini vermouths. Squeeze lemon rind over. Stir, serve with a slice of orange.

Country Bitter (Eng). A cask conditioned Bitter 1036 O.G. brewed by the Queen Victoria home-brew public house in London.

Country Bitter (Eng). A cask conditioned Bitter 1041 O.G. brewed by McMullen's Brewery of Hertford, Hertfordshire.

Country Bitter (Eng). A keg Bitter beer 1036

O.G. brewed by Usher's Brewery in Wiltshire.

Country Brew (Eng). A bottled Pale ale 1050 O.G. brewed by Ridley's Brewery in Essex.

Country Cider (Eng). A low-strength Cider produced by Merrydown Co. in Sussex.

Country Club Cooler (Cktl). Place 2 dashes of Grenadine into a collins glass with 2 fl.ozs. soda water. Stir, add 2 ice cubes, 2 fl.ozs. dry Vermouth. Top with ginger ale and a spiral of orange zest.

Country Girl (Gre). The name given to a range of medium-dry, red, rosé and white wines produced by Tsantali.

Countryman Cider (Eng). Address = Milton Abbot, near Tavistock, Devon. Company which produces fine Ciders. Is helped by the St. Austell Brewery who have shares in the company. Specialises in still Ciders. (Cornish Wreckers, Devon Gold, Ploughmans and Scrumpy).

Country Manor (Eng). A still Perry produced by the Goldwell Co.

Country Satin (Eng). A liqueur of Devon cream, Malt whisky and British wine produced by the Goldwell Co.

Count Thibaut IV (Fr). Purported to have brought the Chardonnay grape back to Champagne from the Crusades in the Middle-East.

County Ale (Eng). A cask conditioned Champion ale 1050 O.G. brewed by Ruddles Brewery. Has won the Brewex Supreme Championship on two occasions.

County Creek Winery (USA). A vineyard and winery based in Telford, Pennsylvania. Produces American and hybrid Vinifera wines.

County Hamley (Austr). Vineyard. Address = Bookmark Ave, & 28th street Renmark, South Australia 5341. 2 ha. Grape varieties – Cabernet sauvignon, Chardonnay, Merlot, Pinot noir, Ruby and Sauvignon blanc.

Coupage (Fr). The vatting or blending of wines to produce a good, standard wine.

Coup d'Après (Fr). A term for a large glass of wine consumed after the soup course at a meal in the nineteenth century.

Coup d'Avant (Fr). A pre-meal drink (apéritif) drunk just before the meal which began in the nineteenth century.

Coup de l'Étrier (Fr). Stirrup cup. An eighteenth- and nineteenth-century drink of wine given to a rider before his journey home.

Coup de Milieu (Fr). A drink of spirits served in the middle of a meal. i.e. Calvados (in Normandy) and Marc (in Champagne).

C

Coup de Vin (Fr). The amount of wine that can be drunk in a single swallow (gulp).

Coupé (Fr). A blended wine.

Coupe (Fr). A Champagne saucer.

Coupe à Champagne Américaine (Fr). A Champagne saucer glass.

Coupe à Thée (Ch.Isles). Teacup.

Coup en Vitesse (Fr). Lit – 'A quick one' (drink).

Coupé Souche (Fr). The name given to the large, long handled secateurs used to cut the shoots and fruit branches of the vine.

Couprie (Fr). Cognac producer. Address = Ets Couprie, La Roumade 16300 Ambleville/Barbezieux. 22 ha. in Grande Champagne. Produces – X.O. Très Vieille Réserve 20 year old and Très Vieux Cognac d'age 42 year old.

Cour Pavillon (La) (Fr). The brand-name used by Gilbeys for their red and white Bordeaux wines.

Courage Brewery (Eng). A large company that has 3 breweries at Bristol, Reading and Tadcaster (John Smiths). Produces many famous beers including cask conditioned Directors 1046 O.G. Simonds Keg Bitter 1036 O.G. Harp Lager 1032 O.G. Hofmeister 1036 O.G. Kronenbourg 1064 O.G. Colt 45 1047 O.G. Bulldog 1068 O.G. and Russian Stout 1100 O.G. Bought by Elders IXL in 1986. Also brews Festivale.

Courage Russian Imperial Stout (Eng). A strong, medium Bitter beer with a long history. Has a long bottle maturation of 2 years. Bottle conditioned 1100 O.G. Brewed by Courage's. See also Russian Stout.

Courant (Chile). A two year old wine.

Courant (Fr). A term used in Alsace to denote other than noble grapes.

Courantin (S.Am). A fruit Rum produced in Guyana with a taste and aroma of spices and fruit.

Courbu (Fr). A red grape variety grown in the Tursan region, south-western France. Also grown in the Jurançon.

Courbut Blanc (Sp). A white grape variety also known as the Ondarrubi zuria.

Courcelles-Sapicourt (Fr). A Cru Champagne village in the Canton de Ville-en-Tardenois. District = Reims.

Cour-Cheverny (Fr). A dry white wine from the Touraine district in the Loire.

Courgis (Fr). A commune in the A.C. Chablis, Burgundy.

Courjeonnet (Fr). A Cru Champagne village in the Canton de Montmort. District = Épernay.

Courmas (Fr). A Cru Champagne village in the Canton de Ville-en-Tardenois. District = Reims.

Court (Fr). Denotes a short, unbalanced wine.

Courtagnon (Fr). A Cru Champagne village in the Canton de Châtillon-sur-Marne. District = Reims.

Courtakis (Gre). A wine merchant who is noted for his dark red Nemean wine.

Courte à Cot (Fr). A style of pruning used in the Sauternes district in south-western Bordeaux. The vines are severely pruned.

Couteron (Fr). A Cru Champagne village in the Canton de l'Aube. District = Château Thierry.

Courthiézy (Fr). A Cru Champagne village in the Canton de Dormans. District = Épernay.

Courtier (Fr). A wine broker. One who visits vignerons and keeps them in touch with the market. A liaison between the vignerons and négociants.

Courtiers de Campagne (Fr). Country winebrokers. Send wines of interest to the wine merchants (négociants). Receives a percentage of the price of the purchase from their client.

Courtillier Musqué (Fr). Another name for the Huxelrebe grape. Also known as the Muscat courtillier.

Court Lane Vineyard (Eng). A vineyard based at Ropley, Hampshire. First planted 1979. 0.8 ha. Grape varieties – Huxelrebe, Madeleine angevine, Müller-Thurgau and Reichenteiner.

Court Noué (Fr). A virus that turns vine leaves yellow so that they become misshapen, shoots grow laterally and become short and stunted. Is transmitted in the soil by parasites. (Eng) = Fanleaf.

Courvoisier (Fr). Cognac producer. Address = BP 59, 16200, Jarnac. Largest seller of Cognac. Top is Extra Vieille 50–60 year old.

Cous (Lat). The name of an Aegean island noted for its wines in Roman times.

Cousinerie de Bourgogne (Fr). A wine fraternity founded in 1960 in Savigny-lès-Beaune in the Côte d'Or, Burgundy. Has members world-wide. Meets four times a year.

Cousiño Macul (Chile). A wine estate based near Santiago. Grape varieties – Cabernet sauvignon, Chardonnay and Sémillon. Wines are sold under Don Luis and Don Matias labels.

Couvent des Jacobins (Fr). Vineyard. Address = 33330 Saint-Émilion. Grand Cru Classé. A.C. Saint-Émilion. Commune = Saint-Émilion. 9 ha. Grape varieties – Cabernet franc, Cabernet sauvignon and Merlot.

Covadonga Cocktail (Cktl). 1½ fl.ozs. Campari, 1 fl.oz. Italian vermouth, ½ fl.oz.

Grenadine, 1 fl.oz. orange juice, dash Angostura. Shake over ice, strain into a club goblet. Dress with an orange slice.

Covanegra (Sp). The brand-name used by the Bodegas García Carrión in the Jumilla region for a range of their red, rosé and white wines.

Covered Wagon (Cktl). 1½ fl.ozs. Tequila, 1 fl.oz. French vermouth, juice ½ lime, dash Grenadine. Shake over ice, strain into a cocktail glass.

COVIDES (Sp) (abbr). Cooperativa Vinícola del Penedés.

Covino Special (Cktl). ½ measure Cognac, ½ measure Noilly Prat. Stir over ice, strain into a cocktail glass. Top with a twist of lemon peel juice.

Cow (Eng). A cream-based liqueur of low alcoholic strength.

Cowboy Cocktail (Cktl). ⅓ gill Scotch whisky, ⅙ gill cream. Shake over ice, strain into a cocktail glass.

Cowper (Wales). Cooper, cask maker.

Cowslip Tea (Eng). A herbal tea which is a good aid to sleep. See Tisanes.

Cow's Nipple (China). See Niunai.

Coxley Vineyard (Eng). Address = Coxley, Near Wells, Somerset. Grape variety – Seyval blanc.

Cox's Ruin (Cktl). 1 part Pimms No.1, 3 parts lemonade, dash Cointreau Mix over ice in a highball glass. Dress with a slice of cucumber and orange.

Crabbers' Nip (Eng). A Barley wine 1066 O.G. brewed by the Devenish Brewery. Now ceased being produced.

Crabbie (Scot). A De-Luxe blended Scotch whisky distilled and blended by John Crabbie and Co. in Edinburgh. 8 year old. 43% alc. by vol.

Crabbie's Green Ginger Wine (Scot). The only ginger wine matured in oak casks from Crabbie and Co. Edinburgh.

Crabutet Noir (Fr). An alternative name for the Merlot grape.

Crachoir (Fr). Spittoon.

Cracked Corn (USA). A cereal used in the making of some beers. See also Corn Grits.

Cracked Ice (USA). Broken ice from a block or from large cubes.

Crackling (S.Afr). A semi-sweet, pétillant wine from the SFW Centurin Harvest Wines.

Crackling Rosé (USA) (slang). For the pétillant rosés of Portugal.

Crackling Wines (USA). A North American name for sparkling wines made by CO_2 injection to give a slight sparkle.

Cradle (Eng). A wicker, straw or metal basket used for bringing red wines from the cellar for decanting. Allows the handler to keep the bottle horizontal whilst the cork is being removed. See Burgundy Basket and Wine Cradle.

Cragganmore (Scot). A single Malt whisky distillery based on the river Spey. A Highland malt whisky. 45% alc. by vol.

Craibillon (Fr). A small (0.65 ha) vineyard in the village of Brochon, now part of the A.C. Gevrey-Chambertin in the Côte de Nuits.

Craido en Cava (Sp). Lit – 'Born in the cellar'. Applied to Spanish sparkling wines. A poet's description of wine made by the masters of the craft.

Craie (Fr). Chalk (soil).

Craig (Elijah) (USA). A Baptist preacher. Reputedly the first man to have made Bourbon whiskey in Scott County, Kentucky in 1789.

Craigellachie-Glenlivet (Scot). A single Malt whisky distillery in Speyside. Produces a 16 year old whisky. Owned by Peter Mackie. 40% alc. by vol.

Craigmore (Austr). A winery based in Mudgee, New South Wales. Produces varietal and Port-style wines.

Craipillot (Fr). A Premier Cru vineyard in the A.C. commune of Gevrey-Chambertin, Côte de Nuits, Burgundy. 2.75 ha.

Cramant (Fr). A Grand Cru Champagne village in the Canton d'Avize. District = Épernay. Reknowned for its Blanc de Blancs.

Cramant Bonnaire (Fr). A vintage Champagne produced by Bonnaire. Vintages – 1934, 1947, 1949, 1952, 1955, 1959, 1961, 1964, 1966, 1969, 1971, 1973, 1975, 1976, 1979, 1982.

Crambambull (Cktl). Ale, rum, sugar and whisked egg. Served hot or cold.

Cranmore Vineyard (Eng). Opened in 1967 near Yarmouth in the Isle of Wight. 3 ha. Soil – Clay. Grape varieties – Gutenborner 15%, Müller-Thurgau 75% and Weisser burgunder 10%.

Crapula (Lat). Intoxication, drunkenness.

Crapulant (Eng). Drunken, suffering from intemperance.

Crapulentus (Lat). Drunk, intoxicated.

Crapuloso (Port). Drunken, intoxicated.

Crapulous (Eng). Denotes a person in an intoxicated state.

Cras (Les) (Fr). A Premier Cru vineyard [part] in the A.C. commune of Chambolle-Musigny, Côte de Nuits, Burgundy. 4.5 ha. Also known as Les Gras.

Cras (Les) (Fr). A Premier Cru vineyard in the A.C. commune of Meursault, Côte de Beaune, Burgundy. 4.8 ha.

Cras (Les) (Fr). A Premier Cru vineyard [part] in the A.C. commune of Vougeot,

C

Côte de Nuits, Burgundy. 4.2. Also known as Les Gras.

Crate (Eng). Container of wood or plastic holding 12 or 24 pint or half pint bottles of beer respectively. Usually applies to beers but cider, minerals, wine etc. can also be carried.

Crato Branco (Port). A white grape variety grown in the Algarve.

Crato Preto (Port). A red grape variety grown in the Algarve.

Cravate (Fr). See Courette.

Crawford (Scot). A noted Scotch whisky distillers based in Leith. Now part of DCL.

Crawford's Five Star Scotch Whisky (Scot). A De-Luxe blended Scotch whisky produced by Archibald and Aikman Crawford in Leith.

Crayère (La) (Fr). A co-operative winery in Bethon in the southern Marne Département. See Saint Simon.

Crayères (Fr). The chalk caves built by the Romans in Champagne.

Crazies (Eng). A white table wine from Joyous Garde vineyard, Wargrove, Berkshire.

Crazy (Eng). An egg-based drink produced by Townend of Hull, Yorkshire.

Crazy (Ind). A Lager beer 1064 O.G. brewed by the Vinedale Brewery in Hyderabad.

Crazy Horse (Cktl). ½ fl.oz. Crème de Banane, ½ fl.oz. Fraises des Bois, 1 fl.oz. Scotch whisky. Shake over ice, strain into a Champagne flute. Top with iced Champagne, decorate with slices of lime, orange and wild strawberries. Finish with a mint sprig.

Creaca (Rum). A grape variety also known as Banater riesling, Kreaca, Kriacza and Zakkelweiss.

Cream (Eng). The fatty part of milk.

Cream (Eng). The name given to the precipitation from a brew of tea when it cools. Contains caffeine, Theaflavins and Thearubigins.

Cream (Eng). A term given to Sherry that is heavily sweetened.

Cream Ale (USA). A blend of Ale and Lager beer. Main producers are the Genesee Brewery, Rochester, New York.

Cream Beer (USA). See Creamy Beer.

Creamer (Eng). A machine that removes (separates) the cream from the milk in a dairy.

Cream Fizz (Cktl). ¾ gill Gin, juice of lemon, ⅛ gill cream, teaspoon sugar syrup. Shake well over ice, strain into a highball glass and top with soda water.

Creaming (Eng). The term used to describe a wine that has a slight mousse (sparkle).

Cream Label Stout (Eng). A bottled Stout 1038 O.G. brewed by Watneys.

Cream Liqueurs (Eng). A combination of cream, spirit and flavourings. e.g. Bailey's Irish Cream, Devonshire Cream Liqueur, Merlyn.

Cream of the Barley (Scot). See Stewart's Cream of the Barley.

Cream of the Century (Sp). A deep-gold Sherry produced by Wisdom and Warter in Jerez de la Frontera.

Cream Puff (Cktl). ⅓ gill dark Rum, ⅙ gill Cream, 2 dashes Gomme syrup. Shake over ice, strain into an ice-filled highball glass. Top with soda water.

Cream Sherry (Eng). A very sweet Sherry. An Oloroso sweetened with Paxerete.

Cream Soda (USA). A vanilla-flavoured, non-alcoholic carbonated drink.

Cream Stout (Eng). A name often used for English stout. Now can no longer be used because of Trade Descriptions Act, as contains no cream. See also Milk Stout.

Cream Stout (Wales). A bottled sweet Stout 1040 O.G. brewed by the Felinfoel Brewery in South Wales. See Cream Stout.

Creamy Beer (USA). A carbonated beer, either bottled, canned or on draught.

Creamy Orange Cocktail (Cktl). ⅙ gill Cognac, ⅓ gill sweet Sherry, ¼ gill cream. Shake over ice, strain into a cocktail glass.

Creamy Screwdriver (Cktl). ⅓ gill Vodka, 1 gill orange juice, 1 egg yolk, 2 dashes Gomme syrup. Blend together with a scoop of crushed ice. Pour into a collins glass.

Creața (Rum). A white grape variety grown in the Banat Vineyard (Tomnatec and Teremia Mare) for the production of white wines. Is also known as Riesling de Banat.

Crébillon (Fr). An alternative spelling of Craibillon.

Crécelle (Fr). Lit – 'rattle'. The new method of mechanical riddling of Champagne bottles which is replacing remuage by hand. (Eng) = Gyropalette. (Sp) = Girasol.

Creedy Bitter (Eng). See Creedy Valley.

Creedy Valley (Eng). A brewery opened in 1984 in Crediton, Devon. Produces cask conditioned Creedy Bitter 1036 O.G. and Tun Bitter 1041 O.G.

Crema (Sp). A term used to describe a sweet Málaga wine.

Crema de Mandarine (Sp). A mandarine liqueur produced by the Cocal Co. in Telde, Canary Islands.

Crémant (Fr). A term denoting a creamy foam on top of wine in association with light sparkling wines which have less carbonation than Champagne. Associated with Cramant village in Champagne.

C

Crémant (Fr). A wine-producing district in Bellet, Provence, south-eastern France.

Crémant d'Alsace (Fr). A new A.C. sparkling wine made from Riesling, Pinot blanc, Pinot gris and Pinot noir grapes. Made by the méthode champenoise but has less CO_2 than Champagne. Aged for a minimum of 9 months before dégorgement. Minimum alc. by vol. 10% (8.5% must be natural). Introduced in 1976.

Crémant de Bourgogne (Fr). A light sparkling dry wine from Burgundy made by the méthode champenoise. Can be red, rosé or white with the white A.C. only being made from the Chardonnay grape.

Crémant de Cramant (Fr). A unique sparkling (méthode champenoise) wine produced by G.H. Mumm Champagne house in Champagne. Is a Blanc de Blancs with a lighter sparkle. Mumm use an agraffe to hold the cork in place as opposed to the usual wire cage.

Crémant de la Loire (Fr). A new title for sparkling wines of the Anjou-Saumur and Touraine districts of the Loire. A.C. Minimum alc. by vol. 10% (8.5% must be natural).

Crémant des Moines (Fr). A non-vintage Champagne produced by Besserat de Bellefon from 20% Chardonnay and 80% Pinot noir grapes.

Crémant F. Kobus (Fr). See St. Odile.

Crema Vinera (La) (USA). A winery based in the Sonoma County, California. Grape varieties – Cabernet sauvignon, Chardonnay and Pinot noir. Produces varietal wines.

Crème d'Almond (USA). Another name for Crème de Noyau.

Crème d'Amandes (Fr). A sweet almond-flavoured liqueur.

Crème d'Ananas (Fr). A pineapple liqueur made by maceration. 30% alc. by vol.

Crème de Banane (Fr). A banana-flavoured liqueur made by infusion and maceration. 30% alc. by vol.

Crème de Cacao (Fr). A cocoa-flavoured liqueur made from cacao beans. 25–30% alc. by vol. See Chouao.

Crème de Café (Cktl). ⅓ measure Coffee brandy, ⅓ measure cream, ⅙ measure dark Rum, ⅙ measure Anisette. Shake well over ice, strain into an ice-filled old-fashioned glass.

Crème de Café (Fr). A liqueur made from spirit extracts of coffee, coloured brown and sweetened. 26–31% alc. by vol.

Crème de Cassis (Fr). A blackcurrant liqueur produced in Burgundy. Made from both infusion and maceration methods. 18–25% alc. by vol. Fine Crème de Cassis has a vintage date because it will lose its fine flavour.

Crème de Ciel (Hol). An orange liqueur similar to Curaçao. Light blue in colour.

Crème de Fraises (Fr). A strawberry liqueur made from both cultivated and wild strawberries by both infusion and maceration.

Crème de Fraises des Bois (Fr). A liqueur made from wild strawberries.

Crème de Framboises (Fr). A liqueur made from raspberries by both infusion and maceration methods.

Crème de Gin (Cktl). ¾ measure dry Gin, ¼ measure (white) Crème de Menthe, juice ¼ lemon, 2 teaspoons orange juice, 1 egg white. Shake well over ice, strain into a cocktail glass.

Crème de Grand Marnier (Fr). A cream and Grand Marnier liqueur from the Grand Marnier company.

Crème de Guignolet (Fr). A cherry liqueur made in Dijon. Guignol = Punch.

Crème de Kobai (Jap). A liqueur produced from Japanese plums.

Crème de la Crème (Fr). Term given to the finest wines etc. Lit – 'Cream of the cream'.

Crème de Mandarine (USA). A liqueur produced from tangerine peel. Is produced by the infusion method. 30% alc. by vol.

Crème de Menthe (Fr). A peppermint-flavoured liqueur. Colourless when it leaves the still. Sold without colour or green. 30% alc. by vol.

Crème de Mokka (Fr). A light brown coffee-flavoured liqueur.

Crème de Myrtilles (Fr). A liqueur made from wild bilberries from the mountains of France.

Crème de Noisette (Fr). A hazelnut-flavoured liqueur made by the infusion method. 30% alc. by vol.

Crème de Noix (Fr). A walnut-flavoured liqueur from Périgord. Produced by the infusion method. 30% alc. by vol.

Crème de Noyau (Fr). A peach-kernel-flavoured liqueur. 30% alc. by vol.

Crème de Noyaux (USA). See Crème de Noyau.

Crème de Noyeau (Fr). An almond-flavoured liqueur. Pink or white in colour.

Crème de Nuits (Fr). A double Crème de Cassis liqueur produced by Cartron in Nuits-Saint-Georges, Burgundy. 17% alc. by vol.

Crème de Pecco (Hol). A tea-flavoured

C

liqueur, medium-sweet and colourless.

Crème de Poire (Fr). A pear-flavoured liqueur.

Crème de Prunelle (Fr). A plum-flavoured liqueur, is plum-green in colour. Made by infusion and maceration. 40% alc. by vol.

Crème de Rhum (Cktl). ½ measure white Rum, ⅓ measure Crème de Banane, ⅓ measure orange squash. Shake over ice, strain into a cocktail glass, add a cherry and slice of lemon.

Crème de Roses (Fr). A liqueur made from the oil of rose petals, vanilla and citrus oils. Pink in colour.

Crème des Barbades (Fr). An Eau-de-Vie, flavoured with spices (cloves, cinnamon and mace) and citrus peel.

Crème de Tête (Fr). A label term used in Sainte-Croix-du-Mont until banned in 1973. Denoted the use of botrytis cinerea-attacked grapes in the wine.

Crème de Thé (W.Ind). An old Martinique liqueur made in the nineteenth century from cane syrup sweetened with cane sugar and flavoured with tea.

Crème de Vanille (USA). A vanilla-flavoured liqueur made by the infusion method from Mexican vanilla beans. 30% alc. by vol.

Crème de Violette (USA). A violet-flavoured liqueur obtained from the oil of violets and vanilla by the infusion method and blending. 30% alc. by vol.

Crémerie (Fr). Dairy.

Crémeux (Fr). Creamy.

Crème Yvette (USA). A liqueur made from Parma violets. Is violet in colour. 32% alc. by vol.

Crémier (Fr). Dairyman, dairywoman (milkmaid).

Cremocha (USA). A sweet, coffee-flavoured liqueur produced by the Barengo Winery in San Joaquin, California.

Creole Café Brûlot (USA). 1 pint strong hot coffee, ¼ pint Brandy, 1 whole orange peel in spiral, cinnamon stick, vanilla pod, 12 cloves, 4 sugar cubes. Place all in bowl (except coffee), heat, ignite and baste with a ladle letting flaming liquor cascade into bowl. Add hot coffee, infuse 3 minutes, strain and serve.

Creole Cocktail (Cktl). 1 measure Jamaican rum, 4 dashes lemon juice, 1 dash Tabasco sauce, salt and pepper. Shake well over ice, strain into an ice-filled old-fashioned glass. Top with iced beef bouillon. Stir.

Creole Cooler (Cktl). 8 ozs. crushed pineapple, 1 pint milk, 2 fl.ozs. orange juice, 1 fl.oz. lime juice. Combine pineapple and juices in jug, add sugar to taste, add milk, mix well. Chill and serve.

Creole Lady (Cktl). ½ measure Bourbon whiskey, ½ measure Boal Madeira, 4 dashes Grenadine. Stir over ice, strain into a cocktail glass. Decorate with red and green cherries.

Crépitant (Fr). A term used to describe the slight fizz (pétillance) in some wines from Crépy in Savoie.

Crépy (Fr). A.C. white wine from Savoie in south-eastern France. The wine is often slightly pétillant. Made from the Chasselas grape. 9.5% alc. by vol. Is sold in tall green bottles. See Crépitant.

Crescenz (Ger). Growth. See also Kresenz.

Cressier (Switz). A noted vineyard based in the Neuchâtel district of western Switzerland.

Cresta Bella (USA). The brand-name used by the Gibson Vineyards in California for their wines.

Cresta Blanca (USA). Part of the Guild Co-operative, Livermore Winery the north coast of California.

Cresta Doré (N.Z.). The brand-name of a dry white wine produced by the McWilliams Winery in Hawkes Bay.

Creta (Gre). A dry white wine produced on the island of Crete.

Cretan Malvasia (Port). Another name for the Malmsey grape.

Crete (Gre). An isle which produces local red, rosé and white wines.

Crete (Gre). A dry white wine from the island of same name.

Crets (Les) (Fr). A vineyard in the A.C. commune of Montagny, Côte Chalonnaise, Burgundy.

Creu (Fr). Seventeenth-century spelling of Cru from the verb Croître (to grow).

Creusots (Les) (Fr). An old name for the Premier Cru vineyard Clos Napoléon in the A.C. commune of Fixin, Côte de Nuits, Burgundy.

Creux (Fr). Denotes a thin wine that lacks body.

Creux de la Net (Fr). A Premier Cru vineyard [part] in the A.C. commune of Pernand-Vergelesses, Côte de Beaune, Burgundy. 5 ha.

Creysse (Fr). A commune within the A.C. district of Pécharmant in northern Bergerac. (red wine).

Crezenz (Ger). 'The growth of'.

Criadera (Sp). The nursery. Contains the younger Sherries waiting to go into the Solera system.

Criado (Sp). Matured.

Criado y Embotellado Por (Sp). Grown and bottled by.

Crianza (Sp). Lit – 'Ageing'.

Crianza (Sp). Young brandy nursery.

Crianza Bajo Velo (Sp). Lit – 'Ageing under film'. Applied to Vino de Crianza wines.

C

A method of ageing wines in sealed casks or vats away from the air.

Crianza en Botella (Sp). Denotes the ageing in bottle of wine. Is applied to Vino de Crianza wines.

Crianza en Madera (Sp). Denotes the ageing in cask. Applied to Vino de Crianza wines.

Crianza en Roble (Sp). Denotes ageing in oak. Applied to Vino de Crianza wines.

Crib (Eng). A large sheet of cloth used in hop picking to collect the hops. See Bushler.

Cribari and Sons (USA). A label owned by the Guild Wineries and Distilleries in California.

Criesbach (Ger). Village. (Anb) = Württemberg. (Ber) = Kocher-Jagst-Tauber. (Gro) = Kocherberg. (Vins) = Burgstall, Hoher Berg, Sommerberg.

Crilles (Les) (Fr). A vineyard in the A.C. Sancerre, Central Vineyards, Loire.

Crillon Cocktail (Cktl). ⅓ gill Noilly Prat, ⅛ gill Campari, ⅛ gill Eau-de-Vie-de-Poire. Shake over ice, strain into an ice-filled old-fashioned glass. Dress with an orange and lemon spiral.

Crimea (USSR). See Crimean peninsula.

Crimean Peninsula (USSR). An important wine region which produces most styles of wines.

Crimmins Ranch (USA). A small vineyard based near Healdsburg, California. Grape variety – Sauvignon blanc.

Crimson Cocktail (Cktl). ⅓ gill Gin, ⅛ gill lemon juice, 4 dashes Grenadine. Shake over ice, strain into a cocktail glass. Float a little Port on top.

Criolla (Arg). A native grape variety that corresponds roughly to the Californian Mission.

Criots-Bâtard-Montrachet (Fr). A Grand Cru vineyard in the A.C. commune of Chassagne-Montrachet, Côte de Beaune, Burgundy. 1.4 ha.

Cripple Cock (Eng). The brand-name of a Cider produced by the Saffron Cider Co. in Radwater, Essex.

Crippledick (Eng). A Beer brewed by the St.Austell Brewery, Cornwall.

Crisp (Eng). A term to describe a white wine that has a pronounced acidity without being sharp. e.g. Mosel wines.

Cristal (Chile). A white grape variety.

Cristal (Port). A Pilsener-style Lager beer brewed by the C.U.F.P.

Cristal (Sp). The label used by Castellblanch for their 'brut' and 'extra' sparkling wines.

Cristal Aiken (Hol). The brand-name of a well-hopped Pilsener Lager beer 5% alc. by vol. brewed in Limburg.

Cristal Brut (Fr). A vintage De Luxe cuvée

Champagne produced by Louis Roederer from 45% Chardonnay and 55% Pinot noir grapes.

Cristal Floquet (Fr). An orange-flavoured colourless Curaçao made by the firm of Floquet.

Cristal Pinot Brut (It). A sparkling (méthode champenoise) wine produced by Maggi in Lombardy.

Cristo (El) (Sp). A nineteenth-century name given to a 3,500 gallon cask. Now known as El Maestro.

Criteuil-la-Magdeleine (Fr). A commune in the Charente Département whose grapes are classed Grande Champagne (Cognac).

Crni (Yug). Black. Also name of red wine grape variety. See Crno.

Crno (Yug). A red grape variety. See Crni.

Croaker Beer (Eng). A cask conditioned Ale 1050 O.G. brewed by the Frog and Frigate public house in Sheffield, Yorkshire.

Croatia (Yug). A northern wine region on the Dalmatian coast reaching around the Adriatic sea to the Italian border. Produces top quality red wines with some fine white wines.

Croatina (It). A red grape variety grown in the Piemonte region.

Crock Bottle (Eng). A stone bottle used since Roman times to keep wine cool in warm climates.

Crocked (Eng) (slang). Drunk, intoxicated.

Crodo Lisiel (It). A still mineral water bottled at the Crodo Springs in Formazzo.

Croeschen Riesling (S.Afr). Locally produced white grape variety. Produces light wines.

Croffta Vineyard (Wales). Address = Groes-Faen, Pontyclun, Mid-Glamorgan. Planted in 1975. 1.25 ha. Grape varieties – Madeleine angevine, Müller-Thurgau and Seyval blanc.

Croft (Port). Vintage Port shippers. Vintages – 1870, 1872, 1875, 1878, 1881, 1884, 1885, 1887, 1890, 1894, 1896, 1897, 1900, 1904, 1908, 1912, 1917, 1920, 1922, 1924, 1927, 1935, 1942, 1945, 1950, 1955, 1960, 1963, 1966, 1970, 1975, 1977, 1980, 1982, 1985. Owned by Gilbey's. Also produce a range of wines and sherries as well as Ports. Single quinta is the Quinta da Roeda.

Croft (Sp). A Sherry and wine producer. Address = Rancho Croft Ctra, Circunvalcion 636,3, Apartado 414, Jerez de la Frontera. Owns 290 ha. of vineyards and wineries. Brand-names include Palo Cortado and Delicado. Owned by Gilbey's.

Croître (Fr). See Creu.

C

Croix de Mazerat (Fr). A vineyard in Saint-Émilion. Address = 33330 Saint-Émilion. A.C. Saint-Émilion. Commune = Saint-Émilion. The second wine of Château Beauséjour. Grand Cru Classé Saint-Émilion.

Croix de Salles (Fr). Armagnac producer. Address = H. Dartigalongue et Fils, BP9 32110 Nogaro. 40 ha. in Bas Armagnac. Produces – Trésor de Famille.

Croix de Salles (Fr). A V.S.O.P. Armagnac produced by H. Dartigalongue et Fils at Nogaro in the Bas Armagnac.

Croix des Bouquets (W.Ind). A distillery based in Haiti. Produces Rhum Champion.

Croix de Touraine (Fr). A V.D.Q.S. wine no longer produced under this label.

Croix de Touraine Mousseux (Fr). A V.D.Q.S. sparkling wine now no longer produced.

Croix Maron (Chevalier de la) (Fr). Reputed to have invented the Bonne Chauffe (second distillation) for brandy in the sixteenth century in Cognac.

Croix Montlabert (La) (Fr). Address = 33330 Saint-Émilion, Commune = Saint-Émilion. A.C. Saint-Émilion. The second wine of Château Montlabert. Grand Cru Saint-Émilion.

Croix-Noires (Les) (Fr). A Premier Cru vineyard in the A.C. commune of Pommard, Côte de Beaune, Burgundy. 1.2 ha.

Croizet (Pierre) (Fr). Cognac producer. Address = Lantin, 16200 Jarnac. 30 ha. in the Fins Bois. Produces a range of Cognacs.

Croizet Eymard (Fr). Cognac producer. Address = BP 3. 16720 Saint Merne-les-Carrières, 16200 Jarnac. 150 ha. in the Grande Champagne. Produces – Age Inconnu and Réserve Royale.

Crombé Brasserie (Bel). A brewery based in Zottegem. Sells its beers under the brand-name of Oud-Zottegem.

Cromwell Bitter (Eng). A cask conditioned Bitter 1037 O.G. brewed by Marston Brewery near York.

Cross (Eng). A new variety of vine obtained by cross-pollination of 2 varieties of the same species e.g. Vitis vinifera. e.g. Riesling x Silvaner = Müller-Thurgau.

Crossbow (Cktl). 1/3 measure Cointreau, 1/3 measure Gin, 1/3 measure Crème de Cacao. Shake over ice, strain into a cocktail glass.

Crouchen (Austr). A white grape variety. Also known as the Clare riesling.

Crouch Vale Brewery (Eng). Opened in 1981 near Chelmsford in Essex. Produces SAS 1048 O.G. Woodham Bitter 1035.5 O.G. and Willie Warmer.

Croupe (Fr). A ridge where vines grow. e.g. Margaux.

Crow (Dr. James) (USA). Built the first distillery in Frankfurt Kentucky in 1835. Now a modern distillery making Old Crow bourbon.

Crow Light (USA). The brand-name of a light, blended Whiskey. 40% alc. by vol.

Crown (USA). The name for the Cap (Chapeau) during the fermentation process.

Crown Ale (Eng). An Ale brewed for the Queen's Silver Jubilee by the Cameron's Brewery in Hartlepool, County Durham. 1040 O.G.

Crown Ale (Eng). A Pale ale (bottled) 1039 O.G. brewed by Greene King Brewery East Anglia.

Crown Beer (E.Asia). A Lager beer brewed by the Oriental Brewery in Seoul, South Korea.

Crown Bitter (Eng). A Bitter beer brewed by Bass Charrington at their Cape Hill Brewery.

Crown Brewery (Wales). A brewery in south Wales that used to brew for the miners' clubs. Based in Mid-Glamorgan it still supplies the clubs in the area. Brews Brenin 1034 O.G. Brown Bracer 1033 O.G. Great Western 1041 O.G.

Crown Cork (USA). A patent metal bottle cap now used for most bottled carbonated beverages.

Crown Graft (Eng). A style of grafting where the Scion is inserted at the crown of the stock.

Crowning (USA). A term used to describe the using of the Crown corks to cap pressure beers in bottle.

Crown of Crowns (Ger). A famous brand-name Liebfraumilch from the firm of Langenbach.

Crown Point Bitter (Eng). A cask conditioned Bitter 1038 O.G. brewed by the Crown Point Inn, Seal Chart in Kent.

Crown Point Inn (Eng). A home-brew public house in Seal Chart, Kent.

Crown Royal (Can). A De Luxe blended Canadian whisky 40% alc. by vol. Produced by Seagram.

Crown Russe Vodka (USA). A Vodka produced by Calvert Distilling Co. (Part of Seagram). 30% alc. by vol.

Crown Viking (Eng). A brand-name used by Dema Glass for a popular style of their glassware.

Crozes-Hermitage (Fr). A.C. within the district of Hermitage in the central Rhône. Has 11 communes in 350 ha.

C

situated in the northern end of Hermitage. Red and white wines. Minimum alc. by vol. 11%.

Cru (Fr). Growth. The soil on which the vine is grown. See Premier Cru, Grand Cru, Creu and Crus.

Cru Abraham (Fr). A vineyard in the commune of Sainte-Croix-du-Mont. A.C. Sainte-Croix-du-Mont, Bordeaux. 4 ha.

Cru Arrançon-Boutoc (Fr). A vineyard in the commune of Preignac. A.C. Sauternes, Bordeaux. 3 ha.

Cru Artisan (Fr). A term no longer used in the Médoc for the rank below Cru Bourgeois.

Cru au Verre (Fr). See Cruover.

Cru Baboye (Fr). A vineyard in the commune of Fargues. A.C. Sauternes, Bordeaux. 2 ha.

Cru Barberousse (Fr). See Château Barberousse.

Cru Baret-les-Arrivaux (Fr). A vineyard in the commune of Sainte-Croix-du-Mont. A.C. Sainte-Croix-du-Mont, Bordeaux. 3 ha.

Cru Barjumeau (Fr). A vineyard in the commune of Sauternes. A.C. Sauternes, Bordeaux. 3 ha.

Cru Barraillot (Fr). A vineyard in the commune of Margaux. A.C. Margaux, Bordeaux. 3 ha.

Cru Barrette (Fr). A vineyard in the commune of Fargues. A.C. Sauternes, Bordeaux. 1 ha.

Cru Barrouet (Fr). A vineyard in the commune of Pujols. A.C. Graves, Bordeaux. 3 ha. (white).

Cru Bas-Peyraguey (Fr). A vineyard in the commune of Preignac. A.C. Sauternes, Bordeaux. 2 ha.

Cru Batsalle (Fr). A vineyard in the commune of Fargues. A.C. Sauternes, Bordeaux. 1 ha.

Cru Baylieu (Fr). A vineyard in the commune of Fargues. A.C. Sauternes, Bordeaux. 7 ha.

Cru Bel-Air (Fr). A vineyard in the commune of Illats. A.C. Cérons, Bordeaux. 3 ha.

Cru Bel-Air (Fr). A vineyard in the commune of Preignac. A.C. Sauternes, Bordeaux. 2 ha.

Cru Bel-Air Mareil (Fr). A vineyard in the commune of Ordonnac-et-Potensac. A.C. Médoc, Bordeaux. 3 ha.

Cru Bellevue-Mondotte (Fr). A vineyard in the A.C. Saint-Émilion, Bordeaux. 2 ha.

Cru Bergeron (Fr). A vineyard in the commune of Preignac. A.C. Sauternes, Bordeaux. 4 ha.

Cru Berlière (Fr). A vineyard in the

commune of Parsac-Saint-Émilion. A.C. Saint-Émilion, Bordeaux. 4 ha.

Cru Bernisse (Fr). A vineyard in the commune of Barsac. A.C. Barsac (or Sauternes), Bordeaux. 1 ha.

Cru Bibian Darriet (Fr). A vineyard in the commune of Listrac. A.C. Haut-Médoc, Bordeaux. 2 ha.

Cru Bichons (Fr). A vineyard in the commune of La Brède. A.C. Graves, Bordeaux. 5 ha. (red and white).

Cru Bignon (Fr). A vineyard in the commune of Bommes. A.C. Sauternes, Bordeaux. 1 ha.

Cru Bilbey (Fr). A vineyard in the A.C. Saint-Émilion, Bordeaux. 6 ha.

Cru Biquet (Fr). A vineyard in the A.C. Saint-Émilion, Bordeaux. 4 ha.

Cru Bordesouilles (Fr). A vineyard in the commune of Preignac. A.C. Sauternes, Bordeaux. 3 ha.

Cru Boritz (Fr). A vineyard in the commune of St-Pierre-de-Mons. A.C. Graves, Bordeaux. 4 ha. (white).

Cru Bourgeois (Fr). The classification of Médoc wines below the 5th growths of the 1855 classification. Wines are of good quality and carry A.C. Haut-Médoc (or A.C. communes) and A.C. Médoc. Since 1978 must not be less than 7 ha. in size, wine to be made on the property and submitted for official tasting before being awarded the designation.

Cru Bourgeois Exceptionnel (Fr). An old grading for top Cru Bourgeois wines grown within the A.C.s of the Haut-Médoc. Now no longer allowed by the EEC.

Cru Bourgeois Supérieur (Fr). A.C. Bordeaux. Aged in wood. Superior to a Cru Bourgeois.

Cru Bousclas (Fr). A vineyard in the commune of Barsac. A.C. Barsac (or Sauternes), Bordeaux. 4 ha.

Cru Boutoc (Fr). A vineyard in the commune of Preignac. A.C. Sauternes, Bordeaux. 5 ha.

Cru Boutoc (Fr). A vineyard in the commune of Sauternes. A.C. Sauternes, Bordeaux. 2 ha.

Cru Boutreou (Fr). A vineyard in the commune of Preignac. A.C. Sauternes, Bordeaux. 1 ha.

Cru Bouyon (Fr). A vineyard in the commune of Pujols. A.C. Graves, Bordeaux. 2 ha. (white).

Cru Brouillaou (Fr). A vineyard in the commune of Podensac. A.C. Cérons, Bordeaux. 11 ha.

Cru Calens (Fr). A vineyard in the commune of Beautiran. A.C. Graves, Bordeaux. 6 ha. (white).

Cru Camegaye (Fr). A vineyard in the commune of Landiras. A.C. Graves, Bordeaux. 2 ha. (white).

Cru Camelong (Fr). A vineyard in the commune of Bommes. A.C. Sauternes, Bordeaux. 1 ha.

Cru Canteloup (Fr). A vineyard in the commune of Blaignan. A.C. Médoc, Bordeaux. 2 ha.

Cru Capital Monte Fontana (It). A sweet Recioto wine produced by Renzo Tedeschi in Valpolicella, Veneto.

Cru Caplane (Fr). A vineyard in the commune of Bommes. A.C. Sauternes, Bordeaux. 2 ha.

Cru Caplane (Fr). A vineyard in the commune of Sauternes. A.C. Sauternes, Bordeaux. 5 ha.

Cru Carbonnieu (Fr). A vineyard in the commune of Bommes. A.C. Sauternes, Bordeaux. 6 ha.

Cru Cardeneau (Fr). A vineyard in the commune of Saillans. A.C. Côtes de Fronsac, Bordeaux. 10 ha.

Cru Castagnet (Fr). A vineyard in the commune of Virelade. A.C. Graves, Bordeaux. 3 ha. (white).

Cru Chanyeloisseau (Fr). A vineyard in the commune of Langon. A.C. Graves, Bordeaux. 5 ha. (white).

Cru Chauvin (Fr). A vineyard in the commune of Sauternes. A.C. Sauternes, Bordeaux. 2 ha.

Cru Chêne-Vert (Fr). A vineyard in the commune of Parsac-Saint-Émilion. A.C. Parsac-Saint-Émilion, Bordeaux. 7 ha.

Cru Chercy (Fr). A vineyard in the commune of Pujols. A.C. Graves, Bordeaux. 2 ha. (white).

Cru Classé (Fr). Classified growths. In Bordeaux the ratings that the vineyards were given. Médoc 1855 (See Château Mouton Rothschild), Graves 1953 and 1959, Saint-Émilion 1955 (revised at regular 10 year intervals), Sauternes 1855.

Cru Claverie (Fr). A vineyard in the commune of Sauternes. A.C. Sauternes, Bordeaux. 2 ha.

Cru Cleyrac (Fr). A vineyard in the commune of Cérons. A.C. Cérons, Bordeaux. 5 ha.

Cru Cluziot (Fr). A vineyard in the commune of Barsac. A.C. Barsac (or Sauternes), Bordeaux. 1 ha.

Crucoli (It). A wine-producing commune in the Calabria district. Is noted for its red, rosé and white Ciró wines.

Cru Commarque (Fr). A vineyard in the commune of Bommes. A.C. Sauternes, Bordeaux. 1 ha.

Cru Commarque (Fr). A vineyard in the commune of Sauternes. A.C. Sauternes, Bordeaux. 6 ha.

Cru Commet-Magey (Fr). A vineyard in the commune of Preignac. A.C. Sauternes, Bordeaux. 4 ha.

Cru Commet-Magey-Briatte (Fr). A vineyard in the commune of Preignac. A.C. Sauternes, Bordeaux. 4 ha.

Cru Côtes-du-Fayan (Fr). A vineyard in the commune of Puisseguin-Saint-Émilion. A.C. Puisseguin-Saint-Émilion, Bordeaux. 8 ha.

Cru Côtes-Pressac (Fr). A vineyard in the A.C. Saint-Émilion, Bordeaux. 2 ha.

Cru Côtes-Roland (Fr). A vineyard in the A.C. Saint-Émilion, Bordeaux. 2 ha.

Cru Côtes-Veyrac (Fr). A vineyard in the A.C. Saint-Émilion, Bordeaux. 2 ha.

Cru Coussères (Fr). A vineyard in the commune of Fargues. A.C. Sauternes, Bordeaux. 1 ha.

Cru Coustet (Fr). A vineyard in the commune of Barsac. A.C. Barsac (or Sauternes), Bordeaux. 1 ha.

Cru d'Arche-Pugnau (Fr). A vineyard in the Commune of Preignac. A.C. Sauternes. Address = 33210 Langon, Bordeaux. 15 ha. Also Château Peyraguey-la-Rousset.

Cru d'Arrançon (Fr). A vineyard in the commune of Preignac. A.C. Sauternes, Bordeaux. 5 ha.

Cru de Barboye (Fr). A vineyard in the commune of Bommes. A.C. Sauternes, Bordeaux. 2 ha.

Cru de Bérot (Fr). A vineyard in the commune of Arbanats. A.C. Graves, Bordeaux. 2 ha. (white).

Cru de Bizeaudon (Fr). A vineyard in the commune of Ludon. A.C. Médoc, Bordeaux. Cru Bourgeois.

Cru de Borderie (Fr). A vineyard in the commune of Portets. A.C. Graves, Bordeaux. 5 ha. (red and white).

Cru de Bouley (Fr). A vineyard in the commune of Illats. A.C. Cérons, Bordeaux. 4 ha.

Cru de Boutec (Fr). A vineyard in the commune of Illats. A.C. Cérons, Bordeaux. 5 ha.

Cru de Braze (Fr). A vineyard in the commune of Illats. A.C. Cérons, Bordeaux. 7 ha.

Cru de Cabiro (Fr). A vineyard in the commune of Illats. A.C. Cérons, Bordeaux. 3 ha.

Cru de Cadenne (Fr). A vineyard in the commune of Pujols. A.C. Graves, Bordeaux. 5 ha. (white).

Cru de Cap-de-Hé (Fr). A vineyard in the commune of Pujols. A.C. Graves, Bordeaux. 2 ha. (white).

Cru de Gaillardet (Fr). A vineyard in the

C

commune of Sainte-Croix-du-Mont.
A.C. Sainte-Croix-du-Mont, Bordeaux.
1 ha.

Cru de Gonthier (Fr). A vineyard in the
commune of Portets. A.C. Graves,
Bordeaux. 3 ha. (red and white).

Cru de Guerisson (Fr). A vineyard in the
commune of Sainte-Croix-du-Mont.
A.C. Sainte-Croix-du-Mont, Bordeaux.
3 ha.

Cru de Haut-Blanc (Fr). A vineyard in the
commune of Pujols. A.C. Graves,
Bordeaux. 1 ha. (white).

Cru de Haute-Mayne (Fr). A vineyard in
the commune of Cérons. A.C. Cérons,
Bordeaux. 3 ha.

Cru de la Cave (Fr). A vineyard in the
commune of Preignac. A.C. Sauternes,
Bordeaux. 2 ha.

Cru de la Chatolle (Fr). A vineyard in the
commune of St. Laurent. A.C. Médoc,
Bordeaux. Cru Bourgeois.

Cru de la Colonie (Fr). The second wine of
Château   Malescot-Saint-Exupéry.
Grand Cru Classé (3rd). A.C. Margaux,
Bordeaux.

Cru de la Côte Dorée (Fr). A vineyard in
the commune of Sainte-Croix-du-Mont.
A.C. Sainte-Croix-du-Mont, Bordeaux.
2 ha.

Cru de la Girouette (Fr). A vineyard in the
commune of Fours. A.C. Côtes de
Blaye, Bordeaux.

Cru de Lamoigon (Fr). A vineyard in the
commune of Pujols. A.C. Graves,
Bordeaux. 3 ha. (white).

Cru de la Nouvelle-Église (Fr). A vineyard
in the commune of Pomerol. A.C.
Pomerol, Bordeaux. 2 ha.

Cru de la Poste (Fr). A vineyard in the
commune of Virelade. A.C. Graves,
Bordeaux. 4 ha. (white).

Cru de la Sablière (Fr). A vineyard in the
commune of Loupiac. A.C. Loupiac,
Bordeaux. 4 ha.

Cru de la Vigne du Diable (Switz). A
vineyard based in Cortaillod, Neuchâtel. (white).

Cru de l'Église (Fr). A vineyard in the
commune of Virelade. A.C. Graves,
Bordeaux. 2 ha. (white).

Cru de l'Hermitage (Fr). A vineyard in the
commune of Budos. A.C. Graves,
Bordeaux. 8 ha. (red).

Cru de Lionne (Fr). A vineyard in the
commune of Illats. A.C. Cérons,
Bordeaux. 7 ha.

Cru de Lubat (Fr). A vineyard in the
commune of St-Pierre-de-Mons. A.C.
Graves, Bordeaux. 8 ha. (white).

Cru de Mahon (Fr). A vineyard in the
commune of Preignac. A.C. Sauternes,
Bordeaux. 2 ha.

Cru de Menjon (Fr). A vineyard in the
commune of Illats. A.C. Cérons,
Bordeaux. 3 ha.

Cru de Montagne (Fr). A vineyard in the
commune of Sainte-Croix-du-Mont. A.C.
Sainte-Croix-du-Mont, Bordeaux. 5 ha.

Cru de Montalivet (Fr). A vineyard in the
commune of Barsac. A.C. Barsac (or
Sauternes), Bordeaux.

Cru de Perret (Fr). A vineyard in the
commune of Bommes. A.C. Sauternes,
Bordeaux. 2 ha.

Cru de Peyre (Fr). A vineyard in the
commune of Fargues. A.C. Sauternes,
Bordeaux. 1 ha.

Cru de Pistoulet-Peyraguey (Fr). A vineyard in the commune of Bommes. A.C.
Sauternes, Bordeaux. 2 ha.

Cru de Portails (Fr). A vineyard in the
commune of Landiras. A.C. Graves,
Bordeaux. 2 ha. (white).

Cru de Rouquette (Fr). A vineyard in the
commune of Loupiac. A.C. Loupiac,
Bordeaux. 8 ha.

Cru des Deux Moulins (Fr). A vineyard in
the commune of Illats. A.C. Cérons,
Bordeaux. 4 ha.

Cru des Deux-Moulins (Fr). A vineyard in
the commune of St-Christoly. A.C.
Médoc, Bordeaux. 13 ha.

Cru des Graves (Fr). A vineyard in the
commune of Portets. A.C. Graves,
Bordeaux. 4 ha. (red and white).

Cru des Graves (Fr). A vineyard in the A.C.
Saint-Émilion, Bordeaux. 2 ha.

Cru des Guizats (Fr). A vineyard in the
commune of Pujols. A.C. Graves,
Bordeaux. 2 ha. (white).

Cru des Moulins-à-Vent (Fr). A vineyard in
the commune of Cérons. A.C. Cérons,
Bordeaux. 12 ha. Has 2 owners – 3 ha.
and 9 ha.

Cru des Parrajots (Fr). A vineyard in the
commune of Illats. A.C. Graves,
Bordeaux. 3 ha.

Cru des Plantes (Fr). A vineyard in the
commune of Landiras. A.C. Graves,
Bordeaux. 14 ha. (white).

Cru des Ptolemées (Egy). A brand of white
wine produced by Gianaclis Vineyards
at Abú-Hummus.

Cru des Terrefort (Fr). A vineyard in the
commune of Loupiac. A.C. Loupiac,
Bordeaux. 4 ha.

Cru des Terrefort Pierre Noire (Fr). A
vineyard in the commune of Loupiac.
A.C. Loupiac, Bordeaux. 3 ha.

Cru des Terres Rouges (Fr). A vineyard in
the commune of Barsac. A.C. Barsac (or
Sauternes), Bordeaux. 2 ha.

Cru des Tonnelles (Fr). A vineyard in the
commune of St-Aignan. A.C. Côtes de
Fronsac, Bordeaux. 3 ha.

C

Cru de Troupian (Fr). A vineyard in the commune of Saint-Estèphe. A.C. Saint-Estèphe, Bordeaux. 2 ha.

Cru de Vieux-Château Landon (Fr). A vineyard in the commune of Bégadan. A.C. Médoc, Bordeaux. 20 ha.

Cru Druenn (Fr). A vineyard in the commune of Barsac. A.C. Barsac (or Sauternes), Bordeaux. 2 ha.

Cru du Caladis (Fr). A vineyard in the commune of Portets. A.C. Graves, Bordeaux. 7 ha. (red and white).

Cru du Canet (Fr). A vineyard in the commune of Sainte-Croix-du-Mont. A.C. Sainte-Croix-du-Mont, Bordeaux. 3 ha.

Cru du Carrefour (Fr). A vineyard in the commune of Sauternes. A.C. Sauternes, Bordeaux. 1 ha.

Cru Ducas (Fr). A vineyard in the commune of Illats. A.C. Cérons, Bordeaux. 2 ha.

Cru Ducasse (Fr). A vineyard in the commune of Fargues. A.C. Sauternes, Bordeaux. 2 ha.

Cru du Chalet (Fr). A vineyard in the commune of Barsac. A.C. Barsac (or Sauternes), Bordeaux. 2 ha.

Cru du Chalet (Fr). A vineyard in the commune of Preignac. A.C. Sauternes, Bordeaux. 1 ha.

Cru du Clocher (Fr). A red wine produced by Château Caillou. Grand Cru Classé (2nd). A.C. Barsac, Bordeaux.

Cru du Couet (Fr). A vineyard in the commune of St-Pierre-de-Mons. A.C. Graves, Bordeaux. 2 ha. (white).

Cru du Grand Chêne (Fr). A vineyard in the commune of Cérons. A.C. Cérons, Bordeaux. 3 ha.

Cru du Haire (Fr). A vineyard in the commune of Preignac. A.C. Sauternes, Bordeaux. 6 ha.

Cru du Haut-Claron (Fr). A vineyard in the commune of St-Morillon. A.C. Graves, Bordeaux. 3 ha. (white).

Cru du Hère (Fr). A vineyard in the commune of Preignac. A.C. Sauternes, Bordeaux. 2 ha.

Cru du Moulin-à-Vent (Fr). A vineyard in the commune of Illats. A.C. Cérons, Bordeaux. 2 ha.

Cru du Moulin-à-Vent (Fr). A vineyard in the commune of Landiras. A.C. Graves, Bordeaux. 3 ha. (white).

Cru du Moulin de Laborde (Fr). A vineyard in the commune of Listrac. A.C. Listrac, Bordeaux. 7 ha.

Cru du Moulin Neuf (Fr). A vineyard in the commune of Preignac. A.C. Sauternes, Bordeaux. 1 ha.

Cru du Moulin-à-Vent (Fr). A vineyard in the commune of Cérons. A.C. Graves, Bordeaux. 3 ha. (white).

Cru du Moulin Vieux (Fr). A vineyard in the commune of Loupiac. A.C. Loupiac, Bordeaux. 5 ha.

Cru du Noulin (Fr). A vineyard in the commune of Cérons. A.C. Cérons, Bordeaux. 3 ha.

Cru du Pageot (Fr). A vineyard in the commune of Bommes. A.C. Sauternes, Bordeaux. 4 ha.

Cru du Perliques (Fr). A vineyard in the commune of Illats. A.C. Cérons, Bordeaux. 3 ha.

Cru du Pin (Fr). A vineyard in the commune of Sainte-Croix-du-Mont. A.C. Sainte-Croix-du-Mont, Bordeaux. 2 ha.

Cru du Placey (Fr). A vineyard in the commune of Barsac. A.C. Barsac (or Sauternes), Bordeaux. 1 ha.

Cru du Roc (Fr). A vineyard in the commune of Couquèques. A.C. Médoc, Bordeaux. 2 ha.

Cru du Terrefort (Fr). A vineyard in the commune of Sainte-Croix-du-Mont. A.C. Sainte-Croix-du-Mont, Bordeaux. 2 ha.

Cru du Violet (Fr). A vineyard in the commune of Preignac. A.C. Sauternes, Bordeaux. 1 ha.

Cru du Violet-et-Lamothe (Fr). A vineyard in the commune of Preignac. A.C. Sauternes, Bordeaux. 5 ha.

Cru Duzan (Fr). A vineyard in the commune of Barsac. A.C. Barsac (or Sauternes), Bordeaux. 1 ha.

Crue (Fr). The old word for a flask or bottle.

Cruet (Fr). A mediaeval name for a flask used for the wine or water for the Eucharist.

Cruet (Fr). A V.D.Q.S. vineyard based on the right bank of the river Isère in the Savoie region, south-eastern France.

Cru Exceptionnel (Fr). A grading used in the Graves for certain wines not quite of Grand Cru standard. See also Cru Bourgeois Exceptionnel.

Cru Eyquem (Fr). A vineyard in the commune of La Brède. A.C. Graves, Bordeaux. 5 ha. (white).

Cru Ferrandat (Fr). A vineyard in the A.C. Saint-Émilion, Bordeaux. 1 ha.

Cru Fillau (Fr). A vineyard in the commune of Fargues. A.C. Sauternes, Bordeaux. 4 ha.

Cru Fort Médoc (Fr). A vineyard in the commune of Cussac-Fort-Médoc. A.C. Haut-Médoc, Bordeaux. 50 ha. Grape varieties – Cabernet 50% and Merlot 50%.

Cru Franc-Mazerat (Fr). A vineyard in the A.C. Saint-Émilion, Bordeaux. 2 ha.

Cru Franc-Roxier (Fr). A vineyard in the A.C. Saint-Émilion, Bordeaux. 3 ha.

Cru Galad (Fr). A vineyard in the commune of Cérons. A.C. Graves, Bordeaux. 1 ha. (white).

Cru Gavach (Fr). A vineyard in the commune of Fargues. A.C. Sauternes, Bordeaux. 3 ha.

Cru Gavailles (Fr). A vineyard in the commune of Preignac. A.C. Sauternes, Bordeaux. 2 ha.

Crugny (Fr). A Cru Champagne village in the Canton de Fismes. District = Reims.

Cru Grand Bourgeois (Fr). A 1978 classification for certain properties which includes the rules of Cru Bourgeois plus the requirement to age young wine in oak casks. Nine properties were classified those of – Châteaux Greysac, La Cardonne, La Tour de By, Laujac, Les Ormes Sorbet, Loudenne, Patache d'Aux, Potensac and Sigognac. See also Cru Grand Bourgeois Exceptionnel.

Cru Grand Bourgeois Exceptionnel (Fr). A 1978 classification. As for Cru Grand Bourgeois but Châteaux must be sited in communes that contain Grand Cru Classé (1855) vineyards in the Haut-Médoc.

Cru Grand-Carretey (Fr). A vineyard in the commune of Barsac. A.C. Barsac (or Sauternes), Bordeaux. 6 ha.

Cru Grand Champ (Fr). A vineyard in the commune of Pomerol. A.C. Pomerol, Bordeaux.

Cru Grand-Jauga (Fr). A vineyard in the commune of Barsac. A.C. Barsac (or Sauternes), Bordeaux. 2 ha.

Cru Grand-Mazeyres (Fr). A vineyard in the commune of Pomerol. A.C. Pomerol, Bordeaux. 2 ha.

Cru Grotte-d'Arcis (Fr). A vineyard in the A.C. Saint-Émilion, Bordeaux. 3 ha.

Cru Guillem-du-Rey (Fr). A vineyard in the commune of Preignac. A.C. Sauternes, Bordeaux. 7 ha.

Cru Gutteronde (Fr). A vineyard in the commune in Barsac. A.C. Barsac (or Sauternes), Bordeaux. 1 ha.

Cru Haut-Buhan (Fr). A vineyard in the commune of Illats. A.C. Cérons, Bordeaux. 7 ha.

Cru Hautes Plantes (Fr). A vineyard in the commune of Landiras. A.C. Graves, Bordeaux. 3 ha. (white).

Cru Haut-Grand-Faurie (Fr). A vineyard in the A.C. Saint-Émilion, Bordeaux. 1 ha.

Cru Haut-Gravette (Fr). A vineyard in the commune of St-Morillon. A.C. Graves, Bordeaux. 3 ha. (white).

Cru Haut-Groupey (Fr). A vineyard in the commune of Pomerol. A.C. Pomerol, Bordeaux. 2 ha.

Cru Haut-Lagueritte (Fr). A vineyard in the commune of Bommes. A.C. Sauternes, Bordeaux. 2 ha.

Cru Haut la Hountasse (Fr). A vineyard in the commune of Illats. A.C. Cérons, Bordeaux. 8 ha.

Cru Haut-Larrivat (Fr). A vineyard in the commune of Sainte-Croix-du-Mont. A.C. Sainte-Croix-du-Mont, Bordeaux. 3 ha.

Cru Haut-Mayne (Fr). A vineyard in the commune of Cérons. A.C. Cérons, Bordeaux. 2 ha.

Cru Haut-Medouc (Fr). A vineyard in the commune of Sainte-Croix-du-Mont. A.C. Sainte-Croix-du-Mont, Bordeaux. 3 ha.

Cru Haut-Piquan (Fr). A vineyard in the commune of Sauternes. A.C. Sauternes, Bordeaux. 1 ha.

Cru Haut-Reys (Fr). A vineyard in the commune of La Brède. A.C. Graves, Bordeaux. 3 ha. (red and white).

Cru Hontane (Fr). See Château Côtes de Blaignan, A.C. Médoc, Bordeaux.

Cru Hourmalas (Fr). A vineyard in the commune of Barsac. A.C. Barsac (or Sauternes), Bordeaux. 2 ha.

Cru Janot-Bayle (Fr). A vineyard in the commune of Budos. A.C. Graves, Bordeaux. 8 ha. (red).

Cru Jauguet (Fr). A vineyard in the commune of Barsac. A.C. Barsac (or Sauternes), Bordeaux. 5 ha.

Cru Jeanguillot (Fr). A vineyard in the A.C. Saint-Émilion, Bordeaux. 2 ha.

Cru Jeannonier (Fr). A vineyard in the commune of Bommes. A.C. Sauternes, Bordeaux. 3 ha.

Crujidera (Sp). A red grape variety grown in southern Spain.

Crujillón (Sp). A black grape variety related to the Carignan and Mazuelo.

Cru Jubilé (Fr). A vineyard in the A.C. Saint-Émilion, Bordeaux. 2 ha.

Cru Junka (Fr). A vineyard in the commune of Preignac. A.C. Sauternes, Bordeaux. 8 ha.

Cru la Bernisse (Fr). A vineyard in the commune of Barsac. A.C. Barsac (or Sauternes), Bordeaux. 3 ha.

Cru la Bouchette (Fr). A vineyard in the commune of Bommes. A.C. Sauternes, Bordeaux. 1 ha.

Cru la Bouchette (Fr). A vineyard in the commune of Preignac. A.C. Sauternes, Bordeaux. 2 ha.

Cru Labrousse (Fr). A vineyard in the commune of Barsac. A.C. Barsac (or Sauternes), Bordeaux. 2 ha.

Cru la Cabane (Fr). A vineyard in the commune of Pujols. A.C. Graves, Bordeaux. 4 ha. (white).

Cru la Capère (Fr). A vineyard in the commune of Landiras. A.C. Graves, Bordeaux. 4 ha. (white).

Cru la Chapelle (Fr). A vineyard in the

C

commune of Parsac-Saint-Émilion. A.C. Parsac-Saint-Émilion, Bordeaux. 7 ha.

Cru la Côte (Fr). A vineyard in the commune of Fargues. A.C. Sauternes, Bordeaux. 5 ha.

Cru la Croix-Blanche (Fr). A vineyard in the commune of Montagne-Saint-Émilion. A.C. Saint-Émilion, Bordeaux. 2 ha.

Cru Lafon (Fr). A vineyard in the commune of St-Pierre-de-Mons. A.C. Graves, Bordeaux. 2 ha. (white).

Cru Lagardan (Fr). A vineyard in the commune of Pomerol. A.C. Pomerol, Bordeaux.

Cru la Garelle (Fr). A vineyard in the A.C. Saint-Émilion, Bordeaux. 1 ha.

Cru la Girouette (Fr). A vineyard in the commune of Cantelègue. A.C. Côtes de Blaye, Bordeaux.

Cru l'Agnet (Fr). A vineyard in the commune of Bommes. A.C. Sauternes, Bordeaux. 2 ha.

Cru Lagrange (Fr). A vineyard in the commune of Pomerol. A.C. Pomerol, Bordeaux.

Cru la Grave (Fr). A vineyard in the commune of Sainte-Croix-du-Mont. A.C. Sainte-Croix-du-Mont, Bordeaux. 2 ha.

Cru la Gravière (Fr). A vineyard in the commune of Preignac. A.C. Sauternes, Bordeaux. 2 ha.

Cru Lahonade-Peyraguey (Fr). A vineyard in the commune of Bommes. A.C. Sauternes, Bordeaux. 2 ha.

Cru la Hounade (Fr). A vineyard in the commune of Pujols. A.C. Graves, Bordeaux. 2 ha. (white).

Cru Lalot (Fr). A vineyard in the commune of Preignac. A.C. Sauternes, Bordeaux. 6 ha.

Cru la Mainionce (Fr). A vineyard in the commune of Pujols. A.C. Graves, Bordeaux. 3 ha. (white).

Cru la Médicine (Fr). A vineyard in the commune of St-Pierre-de-Mons. A.C. Graves, Bordeaux. 2 ha. (white).

Cru Lamothe (Fr). A vineyard in the commune of Sauternes. A.C. Sauternes, Bordeaux. 6 ha.

Cru la Mouleyre (Fr). A vineyard in the commune of Sainte-Croix-du-Mont. A.C. Sainte-Croix-du-Mont, Bordeaux. 3 ha.

Cru Landarey (Fr). Part of Cru Hennebelle, A.C. Haut-Médoc, Bordeaux.

Cru Lanère (Fr). A vineyard in the commune of Sauternes. A.C. Sauternes, Bordeaux. 11 ha.

Cru Langa (Fr). A vineyard in the commune of Cussac. A.C. Haut-Médoc, Bordeaux. 3 ha.

Cru Lanusquet (Fr). A vineyard in the commune of Fargues. A.C. Sauternes, Bordeaux. 2 ha.

Cru Lapinesse (Fr). A vineyard in the commune of Barsac. A.C. Barsac (or Sauternes), Bordeaux. 7 ha.

Cru la Pinesse (Fr). A vineyard in the commune of Barsac. A.C. Barsac (or Sauternes), Bordeaux. 2 ha.

Cru la Rame (Fr). A vineyard in the commune of Sainte-Croix-du-Mont. A.C. Sainte-Croix-du-Mont, Bordeaux. 6 ha.

Cru Lardite (Fr). A vineyard in the commune of Arbanats. A.C. Graves, Bordeaux. 4 ha. (white).

Cru Larode (Fr). A vineyard in the commune of Sauternes. A.C. Sauternes, Bordeaux. 1 ha.

Cru la Rose (Fr). A vineyard in the commune of Puisseguin-Saint-Émilion. A.C. Puisseguin-Saint-Émilion, Bordeaux. 5 ha.

Cru Larragay (Fr). A vineyard in the commune of Listrac. A.C. Haut-Médoc, Bordeaux. 2 ha.

Cru Larroucat (Fr). A vineyard in the commune of Pujols. A.C. Graves, Bordeaux. 2 ha. (white).

Cru Larrouquey (Fr). A vineyard in the commune of Cérons. A.C. Cérons, Bordeaux. 7 ha.

Cru la Terce (Fr). A vineyard in the commune of Budos. A.C. Graves, Bordeaux. 2 ha. (red).

Cru la Tour-Fonrazade (Fr). Part of Château Haut-Fonrazade, A.C. Saint-Émilion, Bordeaux.

Cru la Tuilerie (Fr). A vineyard in the commune of Landiras. A.C. Graves, Bordeaux. 2 ha. (white).

Cru l'Aubépin (Fr). A vineyard in the commune of Bommes. A.C. Sauternes, Bordeaux. 10 ha.

Cru l'Aubépine (Fr). A vineyard in the commune of Bommes. A.C. Sauternes, Bordeaux. 3 ha.

Cru l'Aubépins (Fr). A vineyard in the commune of Sauternes. A.C. Sauternes, Bordeaux. 3 ha.

Cru le Bécasse du Ferrey (Fr). Part of Château Ferrey Gros Caillou, A.C. Haut-Médoc, Bordeaux.

Cru le Bourut (Fr). A vineyard in the commune of Pujols. A.C. Graves, Bordeaux. 2 ha. (white).

Cru le Franc-Rival (Fr). A vineyard in the commune of Lussac-Saint-Émilion. A.C. Saint-Émilion, Bordeaux. 2 ha.

Cru le Haut Bommes (Fr). A vineyard in the commune of Bommes. A.C. Sauternes, Bordeaux. 0.5 ha.

Cru le Monteil (Fr). A vineyard in the

C

commune of Arsac. A.C. Médoc, Bordeaux. Cru Bourgeois Supérieur.

Cru le Pageot (Fr). A vineyard in the commune of Bommes. A.C. Sauternes, Bordeaux. 2 ha.

Cru le Roc (Fr). A vineyard in the commune of Preignac. A.C. Sauternes, Bordeaux. 1 ha.

Cru le Rousseau (Fr). A vineyard in the commune of Bommes. A.C. Sauternes, Bordeaux. 2 ha.

Cru les Arroucats (Fr). A vineyard in the commune of Sainte-Croix-du-Mont. A.C. Sainte-Croix-du-Mont, Bordeaux. 2 ha.

Cru les Cailloux (Fr). A vineyard in the commune of Bommes. A.C. Sauternes, Bordeaux. 2 ha.

Cru Lescourt (Fr). A vineyard in the commune of Listrac. A.C. Haut-Médoc, Bordeaux. 2 ha.

Cru les Graves (Fr). A vineyard in the commune of Toulenne. A.C. Graves, Bordeaux. 4 ha.

Cru les Graves (Fr). A vineyard in the commune of Barsac. A.C. Barsac (or Sauternes), Bordeaux. 1 ha.

Cru les Guizats (Fr). A vineyard in the commune of Pujols. A.C. Graves, Bordeaux. 2 ha. (white).

Cru les Mengets (Fr). A vineyard in the commune of Pujols. A.C. Graves, Bordeaux. 2 ha. (white).

Cru les Pinsas (Fr). A vineyard in the commune of Pujols. A.C. Graves, Bordeaux. 2 ha. (white).

Cru les Quints (Fr). A vineyard in the commune of Barsac. A.C. Barsac (or Sauternes), Bordeaux. 1 ha.

Cru les Rochers (Fr). A vineyard in the commune of Preignac. A.C. Sauternes, Bordeaux. 2 ha.

Cru les Rocs (Fr). A vineyard in the commune of Pujols. A.C. Graves, Bordeaux. 2 ha. (white).

Cru Lestage (Fr). A vineyard in the commune of Landiras. A.C. Graves, Bordeaux. 4 ha. (white).

Cru les Tourelles (Fr). A vineyard in the commune of Blaignan. A.C. Médoc, Bordeaux. 15 ha.

Cru les Tuileries (Fr). A vineyard in the commune of Fargues. A.C. Sauternes, Bordeaux. 1 ha.

Cru le Tarey (Fr). A vineyard in the commune of Sainte-Croix-du-Mont. A.C. Sainte-Croix-du-Mont, Bordeaux. 5 ha.

Cru le Tinan (Fr). A vineyard in the commune of Illats. A.C. Cérons, Bordeaux. 3 ha.

Cru Lioy (Fr). A vineyard in the commune of Budos. A.C. Graves, Bordeaux. 3 ha. (red).

Cru Madérot (Fr). A vineyard in the

commune of Podensac. A.C. Cérons, Bordeaux. 11 ha. (has 2 owners).

Cru Magnaud (Fr). A vineyard in the commune of La Brède. A.C. Graves, Bordeaux. 5 ha. (red and white).

Cru Mahon (Fr). A vineyard in the commune of Bommes. A.C. Sauternes, Bordeaux. 1 ha.

Cru Mahon (Fr). A vineyard in the commune of Preignac. A.C. Sauternes, Bordeaux. 2 ha.

Cru Majans (Fr). A vineyard in the commune of Cérons. A.C. Cérons, Bordeaux. 3 ha.

Cru Marc (Fr). A vineyard in the commune of Illats. A.C. Cérons, Bordeaux. 5 ha.

Cru Marges Dusseau (Fr). A vineyard in the commune of Loupiac. A.C. Loupiac, Bordeaux. 4 ha.

Cru Massiot (Fr). A vineyard in the commune of Martillac. A.C. Graves, Bordeaux. 2 ha. (white).

Cru Mauras (Fr). A vineyard in the commune of Bommes. A.C. Sauternes, Bordeaux. 3 ha.

Cru Mauvin (Fr). A vineyard in the commune of Preignac. A.C. Sauternes, Bordeaux. 6 ha.

Cru Mayne d'Eyquem (Fr). A vineyard in the commune of La Brède. A.C. Graves, Bordeaux. 5 ha. (red and white).

Cru Maynine (Fr). A vineyard in the commune of Illats. A.C. Cérons, Bordeaux. 3 ha.

Cru Medouc (Fr). A vineyard in the commune of Sainte-Croix-du-Mont. A.C. Sainte-Croix-du-Mont, Bordeaux. 4 ha.

Cru Medouc la Grave (Fr). A vineyard in the commune of Sainte-Croix-du-Mont. A.C. Sainte-Croix-du-Mont, Bordeaux. 2 ha.

Cru Menate (Fr). A vineyard in the commune of Barsac. A.C. Barsac (or Sauternes), Bordeaux. 1 ha.

Cru Mercier (Fr). A vineyard in the commune of Barsac. A.C. Barsac (or Sauternes), Bordeaux. 1 ha.

Cru Miaille (Fr). A vineyard in the commune of Barsac. A.C. Barsac (or Sauternes), Bordeaux. 1 ha.

Cru Miselle (Fr). A vineyard in the commune of Preignac. A.C. Sauternes, Bordeaux. 3 ha.

Cru Monteil (Fr). A vineyard in the commune of Bommes. A.C. Sauternes, Bordeaux. 3 ha.

Cru Monteils (Fr). A vineyard in the commune of Preignac. A.C. Sauternes, Bordeaux. 1 ha.

Cru Montjoie (Fr). A vineyard in the commune of Preignac. A.C. Sauternes, Bordeaux. 2 ha.

Cru Morange (Fr). A vineyard in the

commune of Virelade. A.C. Graves, Bordeaux. 2 ha. (red and white).

Cru Mothes (Fr). A vineyard in the commune of Fargues. A.C. Sauternes, Bordeaux. 8 ha.

Cru Moulie de la Glorie (Fr). A vineyard in the commune of Illats. A.C. Cérons, Bordeaux. 2 ha.

Cru Moulin-à-Vent (Fr). A vineyard in the commune of Illats. A.C. Cérons, Bordeaux. 16 ha.

Cru Mourens (Fr). A vineyard in the A.C. Saint-Émilion, Bordeaux. 2 ha.

Cru Mouret (Fr). A vineyard in the commune of Fargues. A.C. Sauternes, Bordeaux. 3 ha.

Cru Mussotte (Fr). A vineyard in the commune of Fargues. A.C. Sauternes, Bordeaux. 1 ha.

Cru Napoléon (Fr). A vineyard in the A.C. Saint-Émilion, Bordeaux. 2 ha.

Cru Nodoy (Fr). A vineyard in the commune of Virelade. A.C. Graves, Bordeaux. 5 ha. (red and white).

Cruover (Fr). A unit invented by Jacques Fourès in 1979. Is a dispenser where fine wines are decanted into the multi-units and kept fresh using nitrogen even though some of the wines have been dispensed. Enables fine wines to be sold 'by the glass' without deteriorating. Has 15 separate units. (Fr) = Cru au Verre, (USA) = Cruvinet.

Cru Passérieux (Fr). A vineyard in the commune of Barsac. A.C. Barsac (or Sauternes), Bordeaux. 3 ha.

Cru Patarabet (Fr). A vineyard in the A.C. Saint-Émilion, Bordeaux. 1 ha.

Cru Patiras (Fr). A vineyard in the commune of Toulenne. A.C. Graves, Bordeaux. 2 ha. (white).

Cru Paysan (Fr). An old Cru grading rank below Cru Artisan. Now no longer used.

Cru Peillot (Fr). A vineyard in the commune of Sainte-Croix-du-Mont. A.C. Sainte-Croix-du-Mont, Bordeaux. 2 ha.

Cru Perran (Fr). A vineyard in the commune of Landiras. A.C. Graves, Bordeaux. 3 ha. (white).

Cru Petit-Gontey (Fr). A vineyard in the A.C. Saint-Émilion, Bordeaux. 2 ha.

Cru Petit-Grillon (Fr). A vineyard in the commune of Barsac. A.C. Barsac (or Sauternes), Bordeaux. 2 ha.

Cru Peyraguey (Fr). A vineyard in the commune of Preignac. A.C. Sauternes, Bordeaux. 8 ha.

Cru Peyroutene (Fr). A vineyard in the commune of Cérons. A.C. Cérons, Bordeaux. 4 ha.

Cru Pezeau (Fr). A vineyard in the

commune of Beautiran. A.C. Graves, Bordeaux. 3 ha. (red).

Cru Pian (Fr). A vineyard in the commune of Barsac. A.C. Barsac (or Sauternes), Bordeaux. 2 ha.

Cru Pilote (Fr). A vineyard in the commune of Fargues. A.C. Sauternes, Bordeaux. 3 ha.

Cru Pinaud (Fr). A vineyard in the commune of Cérons. A.C. Cérons, Bordeaux. 4 ha.

Cru Pinaud (Fr). A vineyard in the commune of Cérons. A.C. Graves, Bordeaux. 2 ha. (white).

Cru Piney (Fr). A vineyard in the A.C. Saint-Émilion, Bordeaux. 1 ha.

Cru Piquey (Fr). A vineyard in the commune of Bommes. A.C. Sauternes, Bordeaux. 1 ha.

Cru Plaisance (Fr). A vineyard in the A.C. Saint-Émilion, Bordeaux. 6 ha.

Cru Planton (Fr). A vineyard in the commune of Barsac. A.C. Barsac (or Sauternes), Bordeaux. 1 ha.

Cru Plateau-Jappeloup (Fr). A vineyard in the A.C. Saint-Émilion, Bordeaux. 3 ha.

Cru Pontet-Chappez (Fr). A vineyard in the commune of Arsac. A.C. Haut-Médoc, Bordeaux. 4 ha.

Cru Pouteau (Fr). A vineyard in the commune of Fargues. A.C. Sauternes, Bordeaux. 2 ha.

Cru Pouton (Fr). A vineyard in the commune of Preignac. A.C. Sauternes, Bordeaux. 2 ha.

Cru Puydomine (Fr). A vineyard in the commune of Bommes. A.C. Sauternes, Bordeaux. 2 ha.

Cru Richard Barbe (Fr). A vineyard in the commune Bommes. A.C. Sauternes, Bordeaux. 2 ha.

Cru Ripaille (Fr). A vineyard in the commune of Preignac. A.C. Sauternes, Bordeaux. 1 ha.

Cru Rol-de-Frombrauge (Fr). A vineyard in the A.C. Saint-Émilion, Bordeaux. 4 ha.

Cru Roudet (Fr). A vineyard in the commune of Pujols. A.C. Graves, Bordeaux. 5 ha. (white).

Crus (Fr). Growths. When applied to vineyards denotes the production of the vineyard. The wines produced are usually classified into Crus. e.g. Grand Cru, Premier Cru, Grand Cru Classé etc. See Croître.

Cru Sabade-Terrefort (Fr). A vineyard in the commune of Sauternes. A.C. Sauternes, Bordeaux. 2 ha.

Cru Sadout (Fr). A vineyard in the commune of Virelade. A.C. Graves, Bordeaux. 6 ha. (red and white).

Cru Sarraguey (Fr). A vineyard in the commune of Virelade. A.C. Graves, Bordeaux. 5 ha. (red and white).

Crus Artisans (Fr). See Cru Artisan.

Crus Bourgeois (Fr). See Cru Bourgeois.

Crus Bourgeois Supérieures (Fr). An old Médoc grading now no longer used.

Crus Classés (Fr). See Cru Classé.

Cruse (Eng). The name for a water jug in the middle ages.

Cruse et Fils Frères (Fr). Négociants-éleveurs based in Bordeaux and in Nuits-Saint-Georges, Burgundy.

Crus Exceptionnels (Fr). See Cru Exceptionnel.

Crush Bar (Fr). The nickname given to a theatre bar used for serving drinks during the interval at a performance.

Crusher (Eng). A machine that bursts or crushes the grapes to allow the juice to run freely. Replaces the practice of treading the grapes.

Crushing (Eng). The method of extracting the juice from fruit as opposed to pressing which squeezes out the juice. The crushing only breaks the skins and allows the free run juice to be removed. See Pressing.

Crushing Station (USA). A press-house.

Crus Non Côtes (Fr). A term used in the Champagne region to describe the lower-priced growths from vineyards in the Marne.

Cru Soula (Fr). A vineyard in the commune of Fargues. A.C. Sauternes, Bordeaux. 4 ha.

Crus Paysans (Fr). See Cru Paysan.

Crust (Eng). In fermentation the name given to the cap of skins etc. on top of the fementing must.

Crust (Port). The sediment in a bottle of Vintage or Crusted Port.

Crusta (Cktl). A mixed drink with the glass rim rubbed with either orange or lemon peel and dipped in powdered sugar.

Crusta Glass (USA). Similar to a small wine glass used for serving Crustas.

Crustas (Cktl). ½ gill Spirit, juice ½ lemon or orange, 2 dashes Maraschino, 2 dashes Angostura. Shake over ice, strain into a crusta glass which has been rubbed with lemon or orange peel and dipped on sugar.

Crusted Port (Port). A blended Port wine bottled after two years, has almost the same qualities as a Vintage Port and needs laying down to mature when it will 'throw' a crust (sediment). Is a blend of different years' wines.

Cru St-Louis (Fr). A vineyard in the commune of Couquèques. A.C. Médoc, Bordeaux. 3 ha.

Cru St-Michel (Fr). A vineyard in the commune of Barsac. A.C. Barsac (or Sauternes), Bordeaux. 1 ha.

Cru St-Roch (Fr). A vineyard in the commune of Illats. A.C. Cérons, Bordeaux. 2 ha.

Cru St-Romain (Fr). A vineyard in the commune of Loupiac. A.C. Loupiac, Bordeaux. 4 ha.

Cru St-Sardeau (Fr). A vineyard in the commune of Fargues. A.C. Sauternes, Bordeaux. 2 ha.

Crust Test (Eng). See Wet Smell.

Cru Terrefort (Fr). A vineyard in the commune of Bommes. A.C. Sauternes, Bordeaux. 4 ha.

Cru Terrefort (Fr). A vineyard in the commune of Pujols. A.C. Graves, Bordeaux. 3 ha. (white).

Cru Thibaut (Fr). A vineyard in the commune of Fargues. A.C. Sauternes, Bordeaux. 7 ha.

Crutin (It). See Infernotti.

Cru Toumilon (Fr). A vineyard in the commune of St-Pierre-de-Mons. A.C. Graves, Bordeaux. 2 ha. (white).

Cru Tucan (Fr). A vineyard in the commune of Barsac. A.C. Barsac (or Sauternes), Bordeaux. 2 ha.

Cru Tucou (Fr). A vineyard in the commune of Preignac. A.C. Sauternes, Bordeaux. 1 ha.

Cru Verdon (Fr). A vineyard in the commune of Valeyrac. A.C. Médoc, Bordeaux. 3 ha.

Cru Videau (Fr). A vineyard in the commune of Pujols. A.C. Graves, Bordeaux. 6 ha. (white).

Cru Vigne-Vieille (Fr). A vineyard in the commune of Barsac. A.C. Barsac (or Sauternes), Bordeaux. 3 ha.

Cruvinet (USA). See Cruover.

Cru Voltaire (Fr) A vineyard in the commune of Cérons. A.C. Cérons, Bordeaux. 4 ha.

Cruzan (W.Ind). The brand-name used on all Rum labels produced by the government-run distillery (Virgin Islands Rum Industries Ltd) in the Virgin Islands.

Cruzan Rum (W.Ind). See Cruzan.

Cruzeta (Port). A system of growing vines, the first Ergonomic system. The grapes grow at the ideal height for gathering.

C.R.V.C. (Fr) (abbr). Coopérative Régionale de Vins de Champagne.

Cryptococcus (Lat). A slime yeast that can attack and spoil wine. Caused through poor hygiene.

Cryptogamic (Eng). Non-flowering plant e.g. Fungi.

Crystal (Eng). See Lead Crystal.

Crystal (USA). The name used in America for the Budvar beer of Czec.

C

Crystal Ale (Eng). An Export IPA 1038 O.G. brewed by Matthew Brown Brewery in Blackburn, Lancashire.

Crystal Ale (Eng). A keg and bottled Ale 1030 O.G. brewed by Eldridge Pope Brewery in Dorset.

Crystal Beach (Can). A wine region.

Crystal Beer (Can). A dry (bitter) beer brewed by the Labatt Brewery.

Crystal Clear Oke (USA). A pure, clear style of Okolehao.

Crystal Dry (Fr). Cognac producer. Address = Castel Sablons, Saint Maigrin, 17520 Archiac. 80 ha. in the Fins Bois.

Crystal Gin (Can). A brand of dry Gin produced by Hiram Walker.

Crystal (Le) (Fr). The brand-name used by Berger for their clear Anis.

Crystallisation (Eng). The precipitation of tartaric acid. See Crystals.

Crystal Malt (Eng). A barley malt for brewing. Is placed in a pre-heated kiln at a high temperature to produce a glossy finish. It enhances the body of the finished beer.

Crystals (Eng). Found in white and red wines. Caused by the precipitation of tartaric acid and others due to long storage at cold temperatures. Disappears if wine is brought to room temperature for a short while. Harmless.

Crystal Slipper (Cktl). ¾ measure dry Gin, ¼ measure Crème Yvette, 2 dashes Orange bitters. Stir over ice, strain into a cocktail glass.

Crystal Spring (USA). A brand of Rum produced by Felton and Son in New England.

Crystal Spring Mineral Water (Wales). A natural mineral water bottled by the Carmarthen Water Co. in south-western Wales.

Csàszarkörte (Hun). A fruit Brandy made from pears.

Csopaki Furmint (Hun). A full-bodied dry white wine similar to Tokay.

C.S.R. (Austr) (abbr). Colonial Sugar Refining Co.

C.T.C. (E.Asia) (abbr). Crushing, Tearing and Curling. Name for a machine which cuts the tea leaf up after it has been withered (dried).

C.T.G.S. (Eng) (abbr). Catering Tea Grading Scheme.

Cuach (Scot). See Quaich.

Cuadrilla Forestera (Sp). The name given to a group of grape pickers.

Cuarenta-y-Tres (Sp). A yellow herb liqueur made from 43 different herbs in Cartagena. 31.5% alc. by vol. Also known as Licor 43.

Cuartillo (Sp). A specific amount of wine, measured by volume ⅟₃₂ arroba.

Cuatrao Rayas (Sp). A superior wine. Made from over 60% Verdejo grapes by Cooperativa La Seca in La Rueda.

Cuatro Año (Sp). Denotes 4 years in cask before bottling.

Cuatro Palmas (Sp). A mark on a Sherry cask. Shaped like a palm, it denotes an old Fino sherry.

Cuatro Rayas (Sp). Lit – 'Four stokes'. The marks on a sherry butt used to denote the destiny of wine. Here it is destined to be distilled.

Cuauhtémoc Brewery (Mex). A brewery which also has a third share in the Yucateca Brewery.

C.U.B. (Austr). Brewing Company with breweries based in Ballarat, Brisbane, Cairns, Darwin, Geelong and Melbourne.

Cuba (W.Ind). A white Rum-producing island in the Caribbean.

Cuba (Chile) (Port). Cask, barrel. Also a vat.

Cuba (Port) (Sp). Stainless steel or concrete vats used in the production of Port (and still) wines.

Cubaexport (W.Ind). A light Rum distillery based on the island of Cuba.

Cuba Libre (Cktl). Place 1½ ozs. white Rum, 1 bottle Cola in a small highball glass, add ice, stir lightly and top with a squeeze of a ¼ fresh lime.

Cuba Libre Supreme (Cktl). In an ice-filled collins glass place a measure of Southern Comfort, juice of ½ lime, and spent lime shell. Stir, top with Coca Cola.

Cuban Cocktail (Cktl). ½ measure Brandy, ¼ measure Apricot brandy, ¼ measure lime juice. Shake over ice, strain into a cocktail glass.

Cuban Coffee (W.Ind). A smooth, mellow and somewhat spicy coffee with a smoky taste and aroma from Cuba.

Cuban Ron (W.Ind). The nickname for white Rum from the island of Cuba.

Cuban Special (Cktl). ⅓ gill white Rum, ½ gill pineapple juice, juice ½ lime, 2 dashes Cointreau. Shake over ice, strain into a cocktail glass. Top with a pineapple cube and cherry.

Cubero (Sp). Cooper, Cask maker.

Cucamonga (USA). Californian wine region which contains the districts of Los Angeles, San Bernardino and Riverside. Produces table and dessert wines.

Cucamonga Winery (USA). A large winery based in Cucamonga, California. Grape varieties – Cabernet sauvignon, Johannisberg riesling, Petit

C

syrah and Zinfandel. Produces varietal wines.

Cuchery (Fr). A Cru Champagne village in the Canton de Châtillon-sur-Marne. District = Reims.

Cuckmere (Eng). A vineyard based at the English Wine Centre, Drusillas Corner, Alfriston, East Sussex. Was first planted in 1973. 0.33 ha. Grape varieties – Huxelrebe, Müller-Thurgau, Seyval blanc plus others.

Cucugnan (Fr). A Vins de Pays area within the Aude Département in central-southern France. Produces red and rosé wines.

Cuenca (Sp). A wine-producing area in the La Mancha region.

Cuero (Sp). A pigskin used to hold wine.

Cueros (Sp). See Cuero.

Cuers (Fr). A wine-producing village in the Côtes de Provence, south-eastern France. Produces rosé wines.

Cuervo (José) (Mex). A noted producer of Tequila sold under the same name.

Cues (Ger). An old English spelling of Kues, Mosel-Saar-Ruwer.

Cuesta (Sp). A brand of Sherry shipped by Saccone and Speed. Produced in Puerto de Santa Maria. Brands include Troubador. (part of Caballero).

Cuevo (Mex). The brand-name for Tequila. 38% alc. by vol.

Cuff and Buttons (USA). The name given to Southern Comfort liqueur whiskey in the 1870s. Meant – 'White tie and tails'.

Cufic Vines (Eng). A vineyard based at Tuttors Hill, Cheddar, Somerset. Was first planted in 1973. 0.20 ha. Grape varieties – Gewürztraminer, Huxelrebe, Madeleine angevine, Müller-Thurgau 90%, Reichensteiner, Seyval blanc and others.

Cugat (Sp). A noted white-wine-producing area based in Cataluña.

Cuiller à Thé (Fr). Teaspoon.

Cuis (Fr). A Premier Cru Champagne village in the Canton d'Avize. District = Épernay.

Cuisles (Fr). A Cru Champagne village in the Canton de Châtillon-sur-Marne. District = Reims.

Cuit (Fr). A wine that has been heated or cooked. e.g. Marsala.

Culaton (It). A word used in the Piemonte region for the lees in the bottom of a bottle of wine.

Culbertson (USA). A winery based in San Diego, California. Produces varietal wines.

Culemborg Wines (S.Afr). Varietal wines produced by Union Wines in Wellington.

Cul en l'Air (Fr). Lit – 'Bottom up'. How Champagne used to be sold (before remuage). The sediment was found in the neck of the bottle resting on the cork.

Culha (Bra). See Yerba Maté.

Cullens Willybrup (Austr). Vineyard. Address = P.O. Box 17. Cowaramup, Western Australia. 20 ha. Grape varieties – Cabernet franc, Cabernet sauvignon, Chardonnay, Merlot, Pinot noir, Rhine riesling, Sauvignon blanc and Sémillon.

Culleus (Lat). A leather pouch used for carrying beverages (wine, water, etc).

Cully (Switz). A noted vineyard based in Lavaux.

Culm (Scot). The dried sprouts of the malted barley which are removed before being milled into grist.

Cul-Net (Fr). A term used in the Champagne region. Denotes 'in one gulp'.

Cul Sec (Fr). Denotes extremely dry.

Cultivar (Eng). A variety of plant that was produced from natural species and is maintained by cultivation.

Cultivars (S.Afr). Vine varieties. See Cultivar.

Cultivation d'Grappes (Fr). Viniculture.

Cultivé à l'Ancienne (Fr). A term which denotes that traditional viticultural methods are used.

Culture Large (Eng). Denotes a method of training the vines high and planted wide apart.

Culullus (Lat). A goblet. See also Poterium.

Cumbrero (Sp). A red Rioja from the Bodegas Montecillo.

Cumières (Fr). A Premier Cru Champagne village in the Canton d'Ay. District = Reims.

Cumin Liquidum Optimum Castelli (Den). See C.L.O.C.

Cunachos (Sp). The name used in the Rioja region for 22 kilogramme wicker baskets used for grape harvesting.

Cune (Sp). A red Rioja table wine produced by C.V.N.E. in the Alta region. Produced from the Garnacha 20%, Mazuelo 5%, Tempranillo 60% and Viura 15%.

Cunningham (Mad). A red grape variety. Also known as the Canica.

Cup (Eng). Alternative name for the Chalice used to hold the wine for the Eucharist.

Cup (Eng). A bar measure which equals 8 fl.ozs.

Cup (Eng). A china drinking vessel with a handle for holding hot liquids such as tea, coffee, cocoa. Capacities of ⅙, ⅓ and ½ pint.

Cup (USA). A long refreshing drink used as an apéritif. Made of either Champagne, cider, wine or fortified wines. See Champagne Cup, Dancer's Cup, Pearce Cup, Cider Cup etc.

Cup (USA). A measure of 8 U.S. fl.ozs.

Cupaje (Sp). Vatting or blending. (Fr) = Coupage.

Cup Bearer (Eng). A servant who fills the wine cups and serves them in a Royal household. See also Échanson.

Cup Crillon Cocktail (Cktl). 1 fl.oz. white Rum, ¼ fl.oz. Crème de Cassis, ¼ fl.oz. Grand Marnier, dash lemon juice. Shake over ice. Strain into a highball glass. Top with ginger ale, cherry and spiral of lemon peel.

Cuperly (Fr). Champagne producer. Address = 2 Rue Ancienne Église, 51380 Verzy. Récoltants-manipulants. Produces vintage and non-vintage wines.

Cuper's Gardens (Eng). Eighteenth-century tea gardens.

Cupertino (USA). A small wine-producing area in Santa Clara County, California.

Cupid's Bow (Cktl). ¼ measure Gin, ¼ measure Aurum, ¼ measure Forbidden Fruit liqueur, ¼ measure Passion fruit juice. Shake over ice, strain into a cocktail glass.

Cup of Cha (Eng) (slang). Cup of tea.

Cups (USA). See Cup.

Curaçao (W.Ind) A liqueur made from bitter oranges from the island of Curaçao. Now made in many styles and colours mainly in France and Holland. 40% alc. by vol.

Curaçao Cocktail (Cktl). ¾ measure Scotch whisky, ½ measure lemon juice, ¼ measure white Curaçao. Shake over ice, strain into a cocktail glass.

Curaçao Triple Sec (Hol). A clear orange liqueur. Drier and stronger than Curaçao. Produced by many companies including Bols.

Cure d'Attalens (Switz). A white wine produced in Lavaux.

Curicó (Chile). A wine-producing region in southern Chile.

Curieux et Courtois des Chevaliers de Saint-Bacchus (Fr). A noted wine brotherhood based in Paris.

Curing (Eng). See Kilning.

Curing (Eng). The word used to denote the preparation of the coffee beans. One of two methods are used. Wet or Dry method.

Curler Blend (Scot). A brand of Scotch whisky once produced by Arthur Bell and Sons.

Curtis Distillery (Eng). Address =

London EC1P 1BJ. Distillers of Curtis Gin 43% alc. by vol. Part of Stewart and Son.

Curtis Distillery (Scot). Based in Dundee. Distillers of Curtis blended Scotch whisky 40% alc. by vol. Part of Stewart and Son.

Curtis Gin (Eng). A London Dry Gin 43% alc. by vol. produced by the Curtis Distillery, London. Part of Stewart and Son.

Cusanushaus (Ger). See Cusanusstift.

Cusanusstift (Ger). A charitable foundation established at the town opposite Bernkastel on the river Mosel. Depends on the produce of the Bernkasteler vineyard.

Cusenier (Fr). A famous French liqueur company producing most types of popular liqueurs.

Cushman (Cktl). ¼ measure dry Vermouth, ¾ measure dry Gin. Shake over ice, strain into an ice-filled goblet.

Cussac (Fr). A small commune in the Haut-Médoc. Wines may be sold under the A.C. Saint-Julien (adjoining commune) or A.C. Haut-Médoc, Bordeaux. See Cussac-Fort-Médoc.

Cussac-Fort-Médoc (Fr). The full title for the commune of Cussac, Médoc, Bordeaux.

Customs (Eng). A charge made on alcohol and other goods imported into any country. (Fr) = Douane.

Cut (Eng). The adulteration of a better quality wine with an inferior one (or water) to increase its bulk.

Cut Kümmel (Cktl). Into a small 5 oz. wine glass place some shaved ice and slice of lemon. Pour ⅕ gill Kümmel on top then a dash of Scotch whisky.

Cutting (Port). A term used in the Douro region to describe the treading of the grapes for Port wine. i.e. 40 men to 'cut' a 20 pipe lagar.

Cutting Wine (USA). Poor quality wines used to lower the quality of better wines to make both saleable at a lower price.

Cutty Sark (Scot). A blended Scotch whisky produced in Glasgow by Berry Brothers and Rudd. 43% alc. by vol.

Cutty Twelve (Scot). A De luxe version of Cutty Sark Scotch whisky produced in Glasgow by Berry Brothers and Rudd. 43% alc. by vol.

Cuva (Sp). Large cask used in the Rioja region. Contains 25,000 litres (5,500 gallons).

Cuvaison (Fr). The period of the first violent fermentation during which the must remains in contact with the grape skins to obtain colour and tannin. An aerobic fermentation. Applies only to red wines.

Cuvaison, Inc (USA). A large winery based near Calistoga, Napa Valley, California.

C

166 ha. Grape varieties – Cabernet sauvignon, Chardonnay and Merlot. Produces varietal wines.

Cuve (Fr). Vat, tun or cask.

Cuveau (Fr). A small vat.

Cuve Close (Fr). Method of making sparkling wines by having the second fermentation in pressurised tanks. The wine is then filtered under pressure and bottled. (Sp) = Gran Vas.

Cuvedor Riserva (It). A brandy produced by Fabbri.

Cuvée (Fr). Lit – 'Vatful' A specific blend of wines from more than one vat of a similar style, usually the best. Premier cuvée means the best of a commune. Tête de cuvée means the best batch of a vintage.

Cuvée Amazone (Fr). A De Luxe cuvée Champagne produced by Palmer & Co. from 50% Chardonnay and 50% Pinot noir grapes.

Cuvée Anniversaire (Fr). An Armagnac produced by Samalens from brandies of the Bas Armagnac up to 100 years old.

Cuvée Bévy (Fr). The name applied to wines made at Bévy in the Hautes Côtes de Nuits, Burgundy.

Cuvée Centenaire (Fr). The bottom grade of wine from Salins du Midi.

Cuvée Commodore (Fr). A vintage De Luxe cuvée Champagne produced by De Castellane from 25% Chardonnay and 75% Pinot noir grapes.

Cuvée de Centenaire (Fr). A vintage De Luxe cuvée Champagne produced by George Goulet from 60% Chardonnay and 40% Pinot noir grapes.

Cuvée de la Reine (Fr). A De Luxe cuvée Champagne produced by Marie Stuart from a blend of vintages.

Cuvée de l'Ermitage (Bel). A strong, amber-coloured Ale 8° brewed by the Union Brasserie in Heinaut.

Cuvée de Prestige (Fr). A vintage De Luxe cuvée Champagne produced by De Courcy.

Cuvée des Celtes (Fr). A.C. Muscadet de Sèvre et Maine. Address = La Chapelle-Heulin, Loire Atlantique. Sur Lie.

Cuvée des Echansons (Fr). A De Luxe cuvée Champagne produced by Champagne Société de Producteurs, Mailly-Champagne from a blend of vintages. 25% Chardonnay and 75% Pinot noir grapes.

Cuvée des Roys (Fr). A vintage De Luxe cuvée Champagne produced by Duval Leroy from 80% Chardonnay and 20% Pinot noir grapes.

Cuvée des Seigneurs de Ribeaupierre (Fr). A Gewürztraminer-based wine produced by Trimbach in Ribeauville, Alsace.

Cuvée Elysée (Fr). A vintage De Luxe cuvée Champagne produced by Oudinot-Jeanmarie from 100% Chardonnay grapes.

Cuvée Frederic Ejile (Fr). A Riesling wine produced by Trimbach in Ribeauville, Alace.

Cuvée Gastronomique (Fr). A middle grade of wine from Salins du Midi.

Cuvée Grand Couronnement Brut (Fr). A vintage De Luxe cuvée Champagne produced by De Telmont from 100% Chardonnay grapes.

Cuvée Grand Siècle (Fr). A De Luxe cuvée Champagne produced by Laurent-Perrier from a blend of vintages of 55% Chardonnay and 45% Pinot noir grapes.

Cuvée Irene (Fr). A.C. Muscadet de Sèvre et Maine.

Cuvée Jean d'Alibert (Fr). A V.D.Q.S. red wine from Minervois, southern France.

Cuvée Liesse d'Harbonville (Fr). A vintage cuvée produced by Ployez-Jacquemart from 100% Pinot noir grapes.

Cuvée Lila (Ger). The brand-name sparkling dry sekt from the Riesling grape made by Deinhard and Co.

Cuvée Madelaine (Fr). A.C. Muscadet de Sèvre et Maine. Produced by the Compagnie de la Vallée de la Loire.

Cuvée Marquise de la Tourette (Fr). A Rhône wine produced by Delas at Tournon.

Cuvée Napoléon (Fr). A red wine from Buzet. Aged in new oak barrels for 6–9 months.

Cuvée Prestige (Fr). A non-vintage De Luxe cuvée produced by A. Desmoulins from 50% Chardonnay and 50% Pinot noir grapes.

Cuvée Privée (Fr). Private selection. Non-vintage wine sold by the proprietor.

Cuvée Régence (Fr). The top grade of wine from Salins du Midi.

Cuvée Renaissance (Fr). A classification of Château Grillet in northern Rhône.

Cuvée Rubis (Fr). A non-vintage rosé Champagne produced by Palmer and Company.

Cuvée S (Fr). A vintage De Luxe cuvée Champagne produced by Salon from 100% Chardonnay grapes.

Cuvée Signée Chatellier (Fr). A De Luxe vintage cuvée Champagne produced by De St. Marceaux & Co. from 87% Chardonnay and 13% Pinot noir grapes.

Cuvée Sir Winston Churchill (Fr). A De Luxe cuvée vintage Champagne produced by Pol Roger in a black (magnum) bottle to commemorate Sir Winston Churchill. Vintages – 1975, 1979, 1985.

Cuvée St. Amands (Bel). A dark, strong Ale brewed in Bavikhove, western Flanders.

C

Cuvée III (Fr). A De Luxe cuvée Champagne produced by Lang-Biemont from a blend of vintages.
Cuvée William Deutz (Fr). A vintage cuvée Champagne produced by Deutz from 30% Chardonnay, 60% Pinot noir and 10% Pinot meunier grapes.
Cuve Nature (Eng). The English name for Cuve Close.
Čuveno Vino (Yug). Selected wine.
Cuverie (Fr). Fermentation cellar.
Cuvette (Eng). A small shallow drinking vessel (cup) used in the seventeenth century.
Cuvier (Fr). Fermentation rooms. Misspelling of Cuverie.
Cuviller (Fr). An alternative name for the Cinsault grape.
Cuvillo (Sp). A Sherry bodega based at Puerto de Santa Maria. Noted for a wide range of sherries.
Cuytes (Sp). An alternative name for Vino de Color.
Cuzco (S.Am). The name for an ancient Inca village in Peru where old vineyards are situated.
Cuzcurrita (Sp). A noted wine-producing village based in the Rioja Alta, northeastern Spain.
CVBG. (Fr). Noted négociants whose brands include Dourthe Frères. Have over 20 exclusive Châteaux.
C.V.C. (Fr) (abbr). Club de Viticulteurs Champenois. An organisation devoted to maintaining quality standards amongst Champagne growers.
Cviček (Yug). Slovenia dark rosé wine.
C.V.M. (Afr) (abbr). Comptoir des Vins du Maroc (Morocco).
C.V.N.E. (Sp) (abbr). Compañía Vinícola del Norte de España. Wine producer in the Alta region of Rioja.
CVPV Maiolati (It) (abbr). See Cooperativa Vinicola Produttori Verdicchio Monte Schiavo.
C.V.R.V.V. (Port) (abbr). Comissão de Viticultura da Região dos Vinhos Verdes. Viticultural Commission for the region of Vinhos Verdes.
CWA. (USA) (abbr). California Wine Association.
CW & D. (S.Afr) (abbr). Cape Wines and Distillers. Part of SFW.
Cwm Dale (Wales). A carbonated mineral water with a natural lemon flavour from South Wales.
Cwpan (Wales). Cup (tea).
Cwrw (Wales). Ale, beer.
Cyathus (Lat). Wine ladle.
Cyclades Islands (Gre). Southern islands of Greece. Produce highly alcoholic white wines. Isles of Paros and Thira are main wine producers.

Cyder (Eng). Old way of spelling cider. From Hebrew Schekar. See also Sicera.
Cyder Fizz (Cktl). ⅙ gill Calvados placed into an ice-filled highball glass. Top with ½ sparkling sweet Cider and ½ dry Champagne.
Cyder Royal (Eng). A medium-dry, extra strength Cider produced by the Whiteways Co. Exeter, Devon.
Cyder Soup (Punch). Place into a punch bowl 1 pint Calvados, 1 quart dry sparkling Cider, juice of 3 oranges, 1 syphon soda water. Add ice cubes, stir and decorate with slices of apple and orange.
Cyder with Rose (Cktl). 1 measure Calvados, ¼ measure Grenadine. Stir together in an ice-filled highball glass. Top with dry sparkling Cider. Serve with an apple slice and straws.
Cydrax (Eng). A non-alcoholic, apple-based, sparkling drink from the Whiteways Co. Exeter, Devon.
Cydweithredol (Wales). Co-operative.
Cygnet Cellars (USA). A small winery based in San Benito County, California. Grape varieties – Carignane and Zinfandel. Produces varietal wines.
Cymbium (Lat). Cup. See also Pocullum.
Cynar (It). Quinine-flavoured apéritif made from artichokes. 18% alc. by vol.
Cynhaeaf Gwin (Wales). Vintage (wine).
Cyprus (Cyp). A large wine-producing island in the eastern Mediterranean. Noted for its highly alcoholic wines and Commanderia. Regions – Paphos and Troodos produce most of the countries finest wines. Limassol is main wine centre.
Cyprus Sherry (Cyp). Sherry type wines which include Fino, Medium and Cream styles. Producers are Etko, Haggipavlo, Keo, Loel and Sodap.
Cyprus Trade Centre (Eng). Address = 213, Regent Street, London W1R 8DA. Wine information.
Cyriakusberg (Ger). Vineyard. (Anb) = Franken. (Ber) = Maindreieck. (Gro) = Hofrat. (Vil) = Sulzfeld.
Cyser (Eng). An apple juice and honey-based mead. Similar to Sherry. Dry and sweet styles produced.
Cystine (Eng). An amino acid found in wines. Is formed by yeasts.
Cytnówka (Pol). A lemon-flavoured Vodka produced by Polmos 40% alc. by vol.
Czarine (Cktl). ½ measure Vodka, ¼ measure Apricot brandy, ¼ measure dry Vermouth, dash Angostura. Stir over ice, strain into a cocktail glass.
Czaroff (Eng). A proprietary brand of Vodka. 40% alc. by vol.

C

Czec (abbr). Czechoslovakia.

Czechoslovakia (Czec). Country of the Eastern Bloc. Noted mainly for its Pilsener beer (and other styles). Has three main wine-producing regions of Bohemia (west), Moravia (central) and Slovakia (east). Wines produced from Vitis vinifera stock are mainly consumed in the country.

Czopowe (Pol). A 'Tap tax' imposed on the sale of beer, mead and spirits in the sixteenth century.

D

D.A. (Austr) (abbr). Dinner Ale.

D.A.B. (Ger) (abbr). Dortmunder Actien Brauerei. Large brewery in Dortmund Westphalia, Germany. Largest brewery in Germany.

D.A.B. (Ger) (abbr). Dortmunder Actien Bier. A light beer brewed at the Dortmunder Actien Brauerei in Dortmund Westphalia, Germany.

D.A.B. Altbier (Ger). A famous Altbier brewed by D.A.B. although it is milder than the Düsseldorf variety.

D.A.B. Export (Ger). A fine Dortmunder export beer brewed by D.A.B.

Dabug (Ger). Vineyard. (Anb) = Franken. (Ber) = Maindreieck. (Gro) = Not yet assigned. (Vil) = Randersacker.

Dabuki (Isr). A local red grape variety.

Dachgewann (Ger). Vineyard. (Anb) = Rheinhessen. (Ber) = Nierstein. (Gro) = Gutes Domtal. (Vil) = Zornheim.

Dachsberg (Ger). Vineyard. (Anb) = Rheingau. (Ber) = Johannisberg. (Gro) = Erntebringer. (Vil) = Winkel.

Dachsberg (Ger). Vineyard. (Anb) = Rheingau. (Ber) = Johannisberg. (Gro) = Steinmacher. (Vil) = Schierstein.

Dachsberg (Ger). Vineyard. (Anb) = Württemberg. (Ber) = Württembergisch Unterland. (Gro) = Heuchelberg. (Vil) = Brackenheim.

Dachsberg (Ger). Vineyard. (Anb) = Württemberg. (Ber) = Württembergisch Unterland. (Gro) = Heuchelberg. (Vil) = Haberschlacht.

Dachsbuckel (Ger). Vineyard. (Anb) = Baden. (Ber) = Badische Bergstrasse/ Kraichgau. (Gro) = Mannaberg. (Vil) = Heidelberg.

Dachsteiger (Ger). Vineyard. (Anb) = Württemberg. (Ber) = Württembergisch Unterland. (Gro) = Lindelberg. (Vil) = Harsberg (ortsteil Neuholz)

Dachsteiger (Ger). Vineyard. (Anb) = Württemberg. (Ber) = Württembergisch Unterland. (Gro) = Lindelberg. (Vil) = Michelbach a. W.

Dachsteiger (Ger). Vineyard. (Anb) = Württemberg. (Ber) = Württembergisch Unterland. (Gro) = Lindelberg. (Vil) = Untersteinbach.

Dackenheim (Ger). Village. (Anb) = Rheinpfalz. (Ber) = Mittelhaardt-Deutsche Weinstrasse. (Gro) = Kobnert. (Vins) = Kapellgarten, Liebesbrunnen, Mandelröth.

Daffy's Elixir (Eng). The nickname for Gin in the eighteenth century.

Dafnes (Gre). A dessert wine from the isle of Crete. Made with the red Liatiko grape.

Da Fonseca (Port). The main producer of wine in Setúbal and Dāo. Founded in Azeitāo in 1834.

Dagen Lager (Eng). A continental-style Lager brewed by the Burtonwood Brewery, Warrington, Cheshire.

Daghestan (USSR). A fine wine-producing area in Armenia.

Daglig Snaps (Den). The brand-name of an Akvavit.

D'Agostini (USA). A winery based in the Shenandoah Valley, Amador, California. 52 ha. Grape variety – Zinfandel.

Dags (Eng). Leather bottles in the shape of old pistols. Used as an imitation pistol to ward off highwaymen, especially at night. Carried spirits or ale. Could also be used as a club.

Daguin (Fr). An Armagnac producer. Address = Rue Guynemer, 32000 Auch.

Dahdi (Ind). A style of fermented milk.

Daheuiller (Claude) (Fr). A noted wine-producer based at Varrains, Saumur, Anjou-Saumur, Loire. Is noted for his Saumur Mousseux.

Dahls Brewery (Nor). A brewery based in Trondheim. Brews Tuborg under licence.

Dahra (Alg). A noted wine-producing area based in the Oran Département.

Dailuaine (Scot). A single Malt whisky distillery at Carron Burn. Owned by Dailuaine-Talisker Ltd. A Highland malt whisky. 40% alc. by vol.

Daily Mail (Cktl). ⅓ measure Rye whiskey, ⅓ measure Amer Picon, ⅓ measure orange squash, 3 dashes orange bitters. Shake over ice, strain into cocktail glass.

Daimiel (Sp). Important wine centre of La Mancha region of central Spain.

Daimieleña (La) (Sp). A noted wine cooperative based in La Mancha. Produces

D

Clavileño (a dry white wine).

Daiquiri (Cktl).(1). 1½ ozs. Bacardi White Label, juice of ½ lime, ½ teaspoon sugar. Combine sugar with lime juice, put in shaker with ice and Rum. Shake well, strain into a cocktail glass.

Daiquiri (Cktl).(2). 2 ozs. Bacardi White Label, ½ oz. lime juice, 1 teaspoon grapefruit juice, 1 teaspoon sugar, 1 teaspoon Maraschino. Combine sugar with lime and grapefruit juice, add ice, Maraschino and Rum, shake well, strain into a cocktail glass.

Daiquiri (Cktl).(3). 2 ozs. Bacardi White Label, 2 dashes Curaçao, juice ½ lime, 1 teaspoon sugar, 1 teaspoon grapefruit juice. Combine sugar and juices, add other ingredients, shake over ice, strain into a cocktail glass.

Daiquiri (Cktl).(4). ¾ measure white Rum, ¾ measure lemon juice, 3 dashes Gomme syrup. Shake well over ice, strain into a cocktail glass.

Daïquiri (W.Ind). A Demerara white (non-matured) Rum.

Daiquiri Blossom (Cktl). ½ measure white Rum, ½ measure fresh orange juice, dash Maraschino. Shake over ice, strain into a cocktail glass.

Daiquiri Liberal (Cktl). ⅔ measure white Rum, ⅓ measure sweet Vermouth, dash Amer Picon. Stir over ice, strain into a cocktail glass.

Daiquiri Mambi (Cktl). 1½ ozs. Bacardi White Label, juice ½ lime, 1 teaspoon sugar. Place all in a jug with plenty of ice, stir until cold, serve in a 5 oz. goblet.

Dairen (China). Branch of the China National Cereals, Oils and Foodstuffs Import and Export Corporation. Uses Hung Mei brand. Produces a Cider.

Dairy (Eng). A place where cows are milked, where milk is stored, or where milk products are produced.

Daisies (Cktl). An American drink from spirit, raspberry syrup, lemon juice, soda and fruit. Serve over crushed ice in highball glasses.

Daisy Fizz (Cktl). 1 measure Brandy, ½ measure orange juice, juice ½ lime and lemon. Shake over ice, strain into a highball glass. Top with soda water.

Dajeeling Tea (Ind). The mis-spelling of Darjeeling Tea.

Daktari (Hol). Banana and white Rum liqueur. Made for Matthew Clark by De Kuyper. Also known as Banana Daktari.

Dalberg (Ger). Village. (Anb) = Nahe. (Ber) = Kreuznach. (Gro) = Pfarrgarten. (Vins) = Schlossberg, Sonnenberg, Ritterhölle.

Dalesice Brewery (Czec). A brewery

based in southern Czec.

Dalheim (Ger). Village. (Anb) = Rheinhessen. (Ber) = Nierstein. (Gro) = Gutes Domtal. (Vins) = Altdörr, Kranzberg, Steinberg.

Dalila (Cezc). A medium-dark Lager beer brewed at the Samson Brewery in České Budějovice.

Dalintober (Scot). A single Highland malt whisky that was bottled in 1905.

Dallas Dhu (Scot). A single Malt whisky distillery on the outskirts of Forres in Morayshire. A Highland malt whisky. Part of the DCL group. 43% alc. by vol.

Dalmaciajavino (Yug). A co-operative at Split. Produces a wide range of wines.

Dalmatia (Yug). A wine region which produces red wines from the Cabernet, Gamay, Merlot and Pinot noir grapes. Also noted for its' Opolo, a rosé from the Plavac grape.

Dalmatia Maraschino (Yug). A cherry-flavoured liqueur.

Dalmatian Islands (Yug). See Dalmatia.

Dalmatian Oak (Sp). An oak used for wine vats in the Rioja region.

Dalmore (Scot). A single Malt whisky distillery at Alness, Ross-shire. A Highland malt whisky. Owned by Whyte and Mackay Ltd. Produces 8, 12 and 20 year old varieties. 40% alc. by vol.

Dalsheim (Ger). Village. (Anb) = Rheinhessen. (Ber) = Wonnegau. (Gro) = Burg Rodenstein. See Flörsheim-Dalsheim.

Dalva (Port). A Grande Reserve sparkling (méthode champenoise) wine produced by Caves da Silva). Also the name for their Dão wines.

Dalwhinnie (Scot). A single malt whisky distillery from town of same name. A Highland malt whisky. Part of the DCL group. 40% alc. by vol.

Dalwood Vineyard (Austr). Vineyard based in New South Wales. Part of the Penfolds Vineyards.

Damacana (Tur). A demi-john.

Damalatmak (Tur). A word to denote 'to pour slowly'.

Damas (Iran). A red grape variety.

Damaschino (It). A white grape variety grown in Sicily.

Damascus (Arab). A hilly wine-producing region of northern Syria.

Damas do Campo (Cktl). ⅓ measure Bacardi White Label, ⅓ measure Campari, ⅓ measure Anis, 2 dashes Grenadine. Stir over ice, strain, add a slice of orange and a cherry.

Damblat (Fr). Armagnac producer. Address = Rue République, Castelnau d'Auzan, 32800 Eauze. 40% alc. by vol.

Dame-Jeanne (Fr). A wide-waisted

D

covered glass wicker jar which holds 2.5 – 45.5 litres. Used for storing Madeira. A demi-john.

Dame Noir (Fr). The local name in Cahors for the Jurançon grape.

Damenwein (Aus). A Zuckerhütl wine. Is medium-sweet.

Damery (Fr). A Cru Champagne village in the Canton d'Épernay. District = Reims.

Dames de la Charité (Fr). A cuvée in the A.C. commune of Pommard, Côte de Beaune, Burgundy. Is owned by the Hospices de Beaune.

Dames Hautes (Fr). An exclusive estate of Geisweiler in the A.C. commune of Nuits-Saint-Georges, Côte de Nuits, Burgundy.

Dames Hospitalières (Fr). A cuvée in the A.C. commune of Pommard, Côte de Beaune, Burgundy. Is owned by the Hospices de Beaune.

Damien Distillery (W.Ind). A distillery on the isle of Haiti that produces Barbancourt.

Damitmak (Tur). To distill.

Dämmerschoppen (Ger). Denotes an evening drink, cocktails.

Dammheim (Ger). Village. (Anb) = Rheinpfalz. (Ber) = Südliche Weinstrasse. (Gro) = Bischofskreuz. (Vin) = Höhe.

Damn Brewery (Sp). A brewery based in Barcelona.

Damn-the-Weather (Cktl). ⅓ measure dry Gin, ⅙ measure sweet Vermouth, ⅙ measure orange juice, 4 dashes Cointreau. Shake over ice, strain into a cocktail glass.

Damoisel V.S.O.P (Fr). A 15 year old Cognac produced by Rouyer. 40% alc. by vol.

Damoy (Julien) (Fr). A Rhône négociant based at 1, Rue des Oliviers, 94320 Thiais.

Dampierre (Fr). A commune of Coteaux de Saumur. Produces mainly white wines with some red.

Dampierre (Comte de) (Fr). Cognac producer. Address = Château de Plassac, 17240 Plassac. 30 ha. in the Bons Bois.

Damscheid (Ger). Village. (Anb) = Mittelrhein. (Ber) = Rheinburgengau. (Gro) = Schloss Schönburg. (Vins) = Frankenhell, Goldemund, Sonnenstock.

Damson Cream (Eng). An egg-based drink produced by Townend of Hull.

Dancer's Cup (Cktl). Place ice into a large jug, add a measure of Orgeat, and a wine glass of brandy. Fill jug with Cider and soda water. Stir well and decorate with lemon slices.

Dandelion (Eng). A weed. Taraxacum Officinale. Family – Compositae. Used to produce Dandelion and Burdock. Leaves only used.

Dandelion and Burdock (Eng). A non-alcoholic carbonated drink.

Dandelion Coffee (Eng). A coffee made from the dried and roasted roots of young dandelions that are ground and infused for 10 minutes in boiling water. Use same amount as for normal coffee.

Dandy (Cktl). ½ measure Dubonnet, ½ measure Rye whiskey, dash Angostura, 3 dashes Cointreau. Stir over ice, strain into a cocktail glass, add a piece of orange and lemon peel.

D'Angelo (It). A winery based at Rionero in Basilicata.

Danglade, [L. et Fils] (Fr). Bordeaux négociant, well known for Saint-Émilion and Pomerol wines.

Danielis (Gre). A red wine produced by Achaia Clauss.

Danielli (Cktl). ⅗ measure Vodka, ³⁄₁₀ measure dry Vermouth, ¹⁄₁₀ measure Campari, Stir over ice, strain into a cocktail glass.

Danish Distilleries (Den). D.D.S. De Danske Spritfabrikker. Main producer of Akvavit. Based at Aalborg.

Danish Gin Fizz (Cktl). ¾ measure dry Gin, ¼ measure Cherry Heering, 3 dashes Kirsch, juice ½ lime, barspoon Gomme syrup. Shake well over ice, strain into an ice-filled highball glass. Top with soda water.

Danish Light Lager (Den). A low alcohol Lager 0.6% by vol. brewed in Copenhagen. Imported into U.K. by Allied Breweries.

Danish Mary (Cktl). 3 fl.ozs. tomato juice, 1 fl.oz. Akvavit, 2 dashes Worcestershire sauce, 2 dashes lemon juice, dash celery salt. Shake over ice, strain into an ice-filled highball glass.

Danish Whiskey (Den). A Whiskey distilled in a patent still.

Dank Cellar (Eng). A description of a cellar that is unfit for wine storage. Denotes that it is damp, cold and musty.

Danny Brown Ale (Eng). Brown ale 1034 O.G. brewed by Daniel Thwaites.

Danny's Special Cocktail (Cktl). ⅓ gill Jack Daniels Bourbon, ⅛ gill Triple Sec, 2 dashes orange Curaçao, juice ½ lemon. Stir over ice, strain into a 5 oz. goblet.

Dansk Bartender Laug (Den). D.B.L. The Danish Bartenders' Association. Address = Postbox 230 D.K. 1502 Copenhagen.

Dansk LA (Den). A low alcohol Lager 0.9% alc. by vol. brewed by Carlsberg-Tuborg at their Wiibroes Brewery, Elsinore.

Dantzig (Fr). A herb liqueur with gold leaf. Is similar to Goldwasser. 45% alc. by vol.

D

Danziger Goldwasser (Den). A herb-flavoured liqueur, clear, with fine cut gold leaf added. Aniseed and caraway. Also made in West Berlin. See also Bruidstranen.

Danzig Silverwasser (Den). Has not been produced since the second world war. Similar to Danziger goldwasser but contains silver flakes.

Dão (Port). A demarcated wine-producing district in northern Portugal. Produces red and white wines.

Dão Adegas Cooperativas (Port). The name used by the União das Adegas Cooperativas do Dão for their Dão wines.

Dão Aliança (Port). A Dão wine produced by Caves Aliança.

Dão Caves Velhas (Port). The brand-name used by Caves Velhas for their Dão wines.

Dão Ferreira Malaquias (Port). A Dão wine produced by Ferreira Malaquias.

Dão Fundação (Port). Dão wines produced by Caves Fundação.

Dão Primavera (Port). Dão wines produced by the Caves Primavera.

Dão S. Domingos (Port). Dão wines produced by Caves de Solar de S. Domingos.

Daose (Ch.Isles). A drinking bout. Also spelt Dosaïe.

Dão Serra (Port). A Dão wine produced by J. Serra and Sons.

Daphnes (Gre). The name given to red and rosé wines produced on the isle of Crete made from the Liatiko grape.

Dapple Sparkler (Cktl). 2 parts Dubonnet, 1 part Cider, 1 part lemonade. Stir on ice in a highball glass, decorate with a slice of apple.

Darb Cocktail (Cktl). ⅓ measure dry Gin, ⅓ measure Apricot brandy, ⅓ measure French vermouth, juice ¼ lemon. Shake over ice, strain into a cocktail glass.

Dar Bel Amri (Afr). A noted red-wine-producing area near Rabat in Morocco. See also Dar Bel Hamri.

Dar Bel Hamri (Afr). The alternative spelling of Dar Bel Amri.

D'Arbis (Fr). A commune in the Haut-Benauge, central Bordeaux.

D'Arenberg (Austr). Vineyard. Address = Osbourne Road, McLaren Vale, South Australia 5171. 78 ha. Grape varieties – Cabernet sauvignon, Chardonnay, Grenache, Palomino, Riesling and Shiraz.

Darjeeling (Ind). Famous tea-producing area of northern India. Produces high quality teas with a 'Muscatel' flavour. Broken orange pekoe grade.

Dark (Wales). Name given to the mild beers of South Wales.

Dark Golden (Sp). D.G. An old classification of Sherry. (Raya).

Dark Star Ale (Eng). A bottled Sediment ale 1050 O.G. brewed by Pitfield's Brewery, London.

Darley Brewery (Eng). A brewery now owned by Vaux of Sunderland. Noted for its' cask conditioned Thorne Best Bitter 1038 O.G. Based at Thorne in south Yorkshire.

Darlington Wines (Eng). Specialist Bag-in-box wines. Designed for Pubs, Hotels, etc. Wines dispensed from patented equipment installed in the premises.

Darllaw (Wales). To brew (beer).

Darllawdy (Wales). Brewery.

Darllawydd (Wales). Brewer.

Daroca (Sp). A wine-producing region of Aragón. Produces red wines that are high in alcohol. 13 – 16% by vol.

Darona (Pierre) (Fr). A noted producer of A.C. Saint-Peray Mousseux in the Côtes du Rhône.

Dart (Swe). A dark, malty Beer 5.6% alc. by vol. brewed by the Pripps Brewery.

D'Artagnan (Fr). The Patron Saint of Armagnac. Also known as Charles de Batz de Montesquiou Fezenzac.

Dartigalongue et Fils (Fr). An Armagnac producer. Address = 32110 Nogaro.

Dartmoor (Eng). The brand-name of a keg Bitter 1037 O.G. and a Lager 1036 O.G. brewed by Thompson's Brewery of Ashburton in Devon.

Daru Spirit (Sri.L). See Madhvi.

Darwin Stubby (Austr). A 2.25 litre bottle of Northern Territory. Draught produced in Darwin by C.U.B. and Swan. (Also colloquial name for a 37 cl. bottle).

Dash (Wales). A nickname given to the Worthington dark Mild 1034 O.G. in Swansea, South Wales.

Dash (USA). A measure for a cocktail. Approx. ⅙ teaspoon.

Dasher (USA). A special type of stopper which is used for making cocktails. Only allows small amounts out of the bottle.

Dashers Beer (Eng). A cask conditioned Beer 1040 O.G. brewed by the Fox and Hounds public house in Stottesdon, Shropshire.

Dasher Stopper (USA). See Dasher.

Dash of Bitters (Cktl). Adding a 'dash' of bitters (Angostura, Amer Picon etc) to a cocktail.

Dated Ports (Port). Denotes Ports of an indicated age, bottled in Oporto and sold as 10, 20, 30 or over 40 years only. The 10 year old Ports may not necessarily contain 10 year old Ports but as long as they pass an Instituto do Vinho do Porto blind tasting and conform to the character of a 10 year old then may be labelled as such.

Dated Solera System (Mad). Used since the Phylloxera outbreak where the oldest wine (date) in the system is used on the label.

Date of Harvest (Port). Refers to Port that has been in wood for at least 7 years, then bottled. Must bear vintage date, year of bottling, and indication that it has been aged in cask.

Dattenberg (Ger). Village. (Anb) = Mittelrhein. (Ber) = Rheinburgengau. (Gro) = Burg Hammerstein. (Vin) = Gertrudenberg.

Dattingen (Ger). Village in the Anbaugebiet of Baden. See Britzingen.

Daubhaus (Ger). Vineyard. (Anb) = Ahr. (Ber) = Walporzheim/Arhtal. (Gro) = Klosterberg. (Vin) = Ahrweiler. (red wine).

Daubhaus (Ger). Grosslage. (Anb) = Rheingau. (Ber) = Johannisberg. (Vils) = Flörsheim, Hochheim, Kostheim, Wicker.

Daubhaus (Ger). Vineyard. (Anb) = Rheinhessen. (Ber) = Bingen. (Gro) = Abtey. (Vil) = Appenheim.

Daubhaus (Ger). Vineyard. (Anb) = Rheinhessen. (Ber) = Nierstein. (Gro) = Güldenmorgen. (Vil) = Oppenheim.

Daubrion (Fr). Ancient spelling of Château Haut-Brion, Graves, Bordeaux.

Dausenau (Ger). Village. (Anb) = Mittelrhein. (Ber) = Rheinburgengau. (Gro) = Lahntal. (Vin) = Hasenberg.

Dautenheim (Ger). Village. (Anb) = Rheinhessen. (Ber) = Wonnegau. (Gro) = Sybillenstein. (Vin) = Himmelacker.

Dautenpflänzer (Ger). Vineyard. (Anb) = Nahe. (Ber) = Kreuznach. (Gro) = Schlosskapelle. (Vil) = Münster-Sarmsheim.

Davenports Brewery (Eng). A famous brewery noted for its' 'Beer at home' service, (now no longer in operation). Based in Birmingham, produces many noted beers including – Brummie Brown 1032 O.G. Chequer Bitter 1036.5 O.G. Continental Lager 1033.9 O.G. Drum Bitter 1036.5 O.G. Top Brew De Luxe 1074 O.G. and Jager Lager 1032 O.G.

Dave's Lager (Eng). A Lager 1048 O.G. brewed by the Brewhouse Brewery in Dorset.

David et Foillard (Fr). A négociant based at Saint Georges de Reneins in the Burgundy region.

David's Old Crofter's Bitter (Eng). A Bitter beer brewed by the home-brew

public house 'First in Last out' in Hastings, Sussex.

Davisons (Eng). The trading name used for over 85 specialist wine Off-licences that belong to J.T. Davies and Sons.

Dawes Soft Drinks (Eng). A family-run soft drinks manufacturer based in Paignton, Devon.

Day by Day (Cktl). ⅓ measure Mandarine Napoléon, ⅓ measure Scotch whisky, ⅓ measure sweet Vermouth. Shake well over ice, strain into a cocktail glass.

Daydream Cocktail (Cktl). ⅓ gill Brandy, 1 teaspoon Maraschino, 1 teaspoon brown Curaçao, 1 teaspoon Angostura. Stir over ice, strain into a cocktail glass, serve with dash of Champagne, a cherry and a dash of lemon peel juice.

D.B.L. (Den) (abbr). Dansk Bartender Laug. Danish Bartenders' Association. Address = Postbox 230, D.K. 1502 Copenhagen.

D.B.S. (Yug) (abbr). Drustvo Barmanov Slovenije. Yugoslavian Bartenders' Association. Address = Hotel Lev-Vosnjakova, 1–6100, Ljubljana.

D.B.U. (Ger) (abbr). Deutsche Barkeeper Union e. V. German Bartenders' Association. Address = Rentzelstrasse 36–40, 2000 Hamburg 13.

D.C.L. (Eng) (abbr). Distillers Company Limited. Large company owning many of the Scotch whisky distilleries.

D.D. (Eng) (abbr). Double Diamond. Famous for Ind Coope Pale ale.

DDS (Den) (abbr). See Danish Distilleries.

De-Acidification (Eng). The removal of excess acid in wine by the addition of calcium carbonate or other calcium compounds to neutralise the acids.

Dead Arm Disease (Eng). English vine disease.

Dead Stock (Eng). A term used to describe wine maturing in a restaurant's cellar.

Dead Wash (W.Ind). The name given to the distilling mash in the production to Rum that is made up of Limings and Dunder.

Dealul-Mare (Rum). A wine region producing good red and white wines from the Cabernet sauvignon, Pinot noir and Welschriesling grapes.

De-amination (Eng). The break down of protein into amino acids and the removal of the nitrogen-containing group of atoms. Poisonous Amyl alcohol is produced during this process.

Dean's Gate (Cktl). ½ measure Drambuie, ½ measure white Rum, ¼ measure lime juice cordial. Stir over ice, strain into a cocktail glass, add a twist of orange.

Deanston Mill (Scot). A single Malt whisky distillery based at Deanston in

Perthshire. Matured and bottled by Longman Distillers, Glasgow. A Highland malt whisky. 40% alc. by vol. Part of the Invergordon Distillers.

Deauville Cocktail (Cktl).(1). ½ gill dry Gin, 2 dashes lime juice, 2 dashes plain syrup. Shake over ice, strain into a cocktail glass, serve with a dash of lemon peel juice.

Deauville Cocktail (Cktl).(2). ¼ gill Cointreau, ¼ gill Brandy, ¼ gill Calvados, ¼ gill lemon juice, Shake well over ice, strain into a cocktail glass.

Deaver Ranch (USA). A vineyard based in the Shenandoah Valley, Amador County, California. 41.5 ha. Grape varieties – mainly Zinfandel.

De Azevado (Maria Pinto) (Port). A producer of Casal de Vale Pradinhos (an Aguardente).

De Bahèzre de Lanlay (Fr). A cuvée in the Premier Cru vineyard of Les Charmes-Dessus in the A.C. commune of Meursault-Charmes, Côte de Beaune, Burgundy. Is owned by the Hospices de Beaune. 0.5 ha.

De Bakker Brewery (USA). A brewery based in Marin County, California. Noted for its' De Bakker Pale Ale 5.2% alc. by vol. and Dry Porter 5.2% alc. by vol.

De Bartoli (It). A winery based at Samperi, near Marsala in Sicily.

De Beauceyrac (Philippe) (Fr). Cognac producer. Address = La Bergerie, N. 137, 17150 Mirambeau. 160 ha. mainly in the Fins Bois. Produces a range of Cognacs.

De Bersac (Guy) (Fr). Cognac producer. Address = Domaine du Chillot, Saint-Preuil, 16130 Segonzac. Produces – Grande Fine Champagne 10 year old and Très Vielle Fine Cognac 25 years old.

De Bêthe d'Jus Fruit (Ch.Isles). A drink made with pomegranates. Non-alcoholic.

De Beukelaer (Bel). Producers of Élixir d'Anvers in Antwerp. Owns the rights to Élixir de Spa liqueur from Spa town in Walloon Hills.

Debina (Gre). A white grape variety grown in Epirus. Produces Zitsa (a natural sparkling dry, medium and sweet white wine).

De Bortoli Winery (Austr). Address = De Bortoli Road, Bilbul, New South Wales. 60 ha. Grape varieties – Colombard, Grenache, Muscat gordo blanco, Muscat Hamburg, Sémillon and Shiraz.

Débouchier (Fr). Uncork, open.

Débouchier (Ch.Isles). To uncork, remove a cork.

Débourbage (Fr). A term used in the making of white wines to denote the delaying of the fermentation for 24 hours after pressing. This allows time for the juice to clear so that it can be drawn off leaving the coarse sediment behind. (Ger) = Entschleimen, (Sp) = Desfangado.

Débourrement (Fr). The term used to describe the buds of the vine which form after the leaves, allows growth before the flowering parts develop.

Debrö (Hun). A wine region in Eger. Produces Debröi Hàrslevelü.

Debröi Hàrslevelü (Hun). A medium sweet white wine with a good bouquet produced in the Eger district from the Hàrslevelü grape.

Deb's Delight (Cup). 1 bottle Lutomer riesling, ⅓ gill Maraschino, ⅙ gill Cointreau, ⅙ gill Gomme syrup. Stir together over ice, top with soda water, sliced orange, pineapple cubes and a mint sprig.

Débuttage (Fr). The removal of soil away from the roots of the vine to form a basin to absorb the spring rainfall.

Decaff (Eng) (slang). For decaffeinated coffee.

Decaffeinated Coffee (Eng). See Decaffeinised Coffee. The caffeine is extracted using Dichloroethylene or Trichloroethylene chlorinated solutions and used before being roasted (green coffee). See also Secoffex Water Process.

Decaffeinised Coffee (Eng). Coffee which has had the caffeine removed. Brands H.A.G. (Hol), Maxima (Ger) and Sanka (USA). See also Decaffeinated Coffee.

Decant (Eng). The removal of wine from the bottle leaving the sediment behind. Port and old red wines especially need decanting. Also allows the wine to 'breath' before drinking. White wine may need decanting if tartrates are present. Wines are decanted into a decanter or other suitable receptacle.

Decantae (Wales). A still and sparkling mineral water from source near mount Snowdon, North Wales. Produced by Trofarth Industries.

Decantare (It). To decant.

Decanter (Eng). A glass container usually of lead crystal for decanting wines into. Also can be used for spirits and fortified wines. Differs from a carafe in that it has a stopper.

Décanter (Fr). To decant.

Decanter Label (Eng). Bottle tickets. Early ones made of parchment, bone, wood, ivory etc. Are used to indicate the contents of the decanter. Also used in the eighteenth century to indicate the

D

contents of dark-coloured wine bottles that were used as decanters. When glass decanters became the vogue then labels were made of precious metals, porcelain, enamel and silk.

Decanter Magazine (Eng). A monthly magazine first published in 1975 for both the public and trade. Deals with wines and spirits, also specialises in vintage and auction reports. Has many M.W's contributing articles. Address = St. John's Chambers, 2–10, St. John's Road, London SW11 1PN.

Decanter Wagon (Eng). A small, wheeled unit with 2–3 fixed coasters. Used for passing wine decanters around the dining table. Eighteenth and nineteenth centuries.

Décànteur (Ch.Isles). Decanter.

Decantevin (the) (Eng). A patented mechanical decanting machine from Yeo Ratcliffe & Dawe, Sheepcote Farm, Wooburn Common, Bucks.

Decanting (Eng). See Decant.

Decanting Cradle (Eng). A mechanical cradle for decanting wines. Is also known as a Port tilter.

De Carabantes (Francisco) (Chile). A missionary who was supposedly one of the first to introduce vines into Chile in the sixteenth century.

De Carli (It). A Chianti Classico producer based in Tuscany.

De Castaigne and Co (Philippe) (Fr). Cognac producer. Address = Domaine de Lafont, 16200 Jarnac. 40 ha. in the Fins Bois. Produces a range of Cognacs.

De Casta Rosado (Sp). A rosé wine produced by Torres in Penedés. Made from 40% Carinena and 60% Garnacha grapes.

De Castellane (Fr). Champagne producer. Address = 57 Rue de Verdun, 51200 Épernay. Produces – Vintage and non-vintage wines. Vintages – 1971, 1973, 1975, 1976, 1979, 1980, 1981. Top cuvée – Cuvée Commodore.

De Cazanove (Fr). Champagne producer. Address = 1, Rue des Cotelles, BP 118, 51204 Épernay. Produces – Vintage and non-vintage wines. Vintages – 1981, 1985.

Deceitful Cocktail (Cktl). ½ measure Gin, ¼ measure Apricot brandy, ⅛ measure green Curaçao, ⅛ measure lemon juice. Shake over ice, strain into a cocktail glass. Top with a cherry.

Dechantsberg (Ger). Vineyard. (Anb) = Mosel-Saar-Ruwer. (Ber) = Zell/Mosel. (Gro) = Goldbäumchen. (Vil) = Treis-Karden.

De Chassey (Guy) (Fr). Champagne producer. Address = Louvois, Marne. Produces vintage and non-vintage wines.

De Chaunac (USA). A hybrid red grape variety used to make dark red wines.

Deci (Switz). A standard ¹⁄₁₀ litre glass used for wine in Switzerland.

Děčín Brewery (Czec). A brewery based in north-western Czec.

Deckrot (Ger). A red grape variety. A cross between the Rülander and the Teinturier grapes. Makes an excellent colour blending wine.

Déclaration de Récolte (Fr). The declaration of the vintage in Burgundy.

De Clieu (W.Ind). A young French naval officer who transported the first coffee seedling to the Caribbean (Island of Martinique) from France in 1723.

Decocta (Lat). A cold drink.

Decoction (Eng). The extraction of water soluble substances from botanicals by boiling.

Decoction (Eng). The name for the essence or liquor that results from decoction.

Decoction (Euro). A method of mashing used for Lager beers. (In the U.K. the infusion method is used). Usually done in 3 steps with staged temperature rises.

De Couleur Oeil de Perdrix (Fr). A grade of rosé wine. Partridges' eye colour.

De Courcy Père et Fils (Fr). A Champagne producer based in Épernay. Produces – Vintage and non-vintage wines and Coteaux Champenois N.V. Vintages – 1971, 1973, 1976, 1979. See also Mary Rose.

Décuvage (Fr). The drawing off of the fermenting must from the skins after the first violent fermentation.

Décuvage (Fr). The racking of the fermenting (red) wine from the pomace so that the pomace can be pressed and used for Piquette.

De Doorns Co-operative (S.Afr). Winery based in Worcester. Address = De Doorns Wine Cellars, Box 129, De Doorns 6857. Produces varietal wines.

Deep (Eng). Term used to describe a wine that is either deep in colour, bouquet or flavour. i.e. has layers of flavour underlying each other. A fine wine.

Deep Sea Cocktail (Cktl). ¼ gill Old Tom Gin, ¼ gill French vermouth, dash Orange bitters, dash Absinthe. Shake well over ice, strain into a cocktail glass, add olive and squeeze of lemon peel juice.

Deep Valley Cocktail (Cktl). 1 fl.oz. blue Curaçao, 1 fl.oz. dry Gin, 1½ fl.ozs. pineapple juice, 2 dashes lemon juice. Stir over ice in a collins glass. Top with soda water, lemon peel spiral and cherry.

Deerfield Wine Cellars (USA). A winery based in Edenton, North Carolina. Produces Scuppernong wines.

D

Defence of the Realm Act (Eng). See D.O.R.A.

De Fère (Charles) (Fr). A producer of sparkling wines. Uses grapes from just outside the Champagne and Loire regions.

Defrutum (Lat). The name given to a new wine (or must) that has been boiled down.

Degerloch (Ger). Village. (Anb) = Württemberg. (Ber) = Remstal-Stuttgart. (Gro) = Weinsteige. See Stuttgart.

Degorjat (Sp). Disgorging. The removal of the sediment from a bottle of Cava wine. See also Degüelle. (Fr) = Dégorgement.

Dégorgement (Fr). The release of the sediment from Champagne bottles either by hand and a keen eye or by firstly freezing the neck in dry ice and then releasing the plug of frozen wine with the sediment embodied in the ice. Invented by the Widow Clicquot in the nineteenth century. (Sp) = Degorjat.

Dégorgement à la Volée (Fr). Denotes hand extraction of the sediment. See Dégorgement.

Dégorgement Automatique (Fr). The extraction by machine of the sediment in Champagne after it has been frozen. See Dégorgement.

Dégorgeur (Fr). A skilled worker who releases the crown cork or unclips the first cork of a Champagne bottle to remove the deposit or frozen plug. See Dégorgement.

De Gouberville (Gilles) (Fr). A nobleman who, in 1553 made the first Calvados.

Degré Alcoolique (Fr). A term to express the degrees of alcohol as a percentage of volume.

Degree Days (USA). University of Davis devised this climate zone (5 zones) system, based on heat summation (a measure of degree days during the vine's annual period of growth) from April 1st to October 31st. Each days temperature is averaged, 50°F is subtracted and the total averaged over a number of years.

Degüelle (Sp). Bottling and corking. See also Desgüelle.

Degustacao (Bra). Easy drinking wine.

Degustación (Sp). Enjoyment of wine etc.

Degustar (Port). To taste wine (a liquid).

Dégustation (Fr). Wine tasting.

De Helderberg Koöperatiewe Wijnmakeriji Beperkt (S.Afr). See Helderberg Co-operative.

Dehlinger Vineyard (USA). A winery based in the Russian River Valley, Sonoma, California. 6 ha. Grape varieties – Cabernet sauvignon, Chardonnay and Zinfandel. Produces varietal wines.

Deidesheim (Ger). Village. (Anb) = Rheinpfalz. (Ber) = Mittelhaardt-Deutsche Weinstrasse. (Gro) = Hofstück. (Vin) = Nonnenstück.

Deidesheim (Ger). Village. (Anb) = Rheinpfalz. (Ber) = Mittelhaardt-Deutsche Weinstrasse. (Gro) = Mariengarten. (Vins) = Grainhübel, Herrgottsacker, Hohenmorgen, Kalkofen, Kieslberg, Langenmorgen, Leinhöhle, Mäushöhle, Paradiesgarten.

Deidesheim (Ger). Village. (Anb) = Rheinpfalz. (Ber) = Mittelhaardt-Deutsche Weinstrasse. (Gro) = Schnepfenflug an der Weinstrasse. (Vin) = Letten.

Deinhard (Ger). Famous wine merchants that produce Green Label, Hanns Christof and Docktor wines. Based in Koblenz.

Deinhock (Ger). A medium-dry red tafelwein from Deinhard of Koblenz.

Deinmoselle (Ger). A light white Qba. wine from Deinhard of Koblenz.

Deipnosophistae (Egy). A major written work on food and wine in ancient Egypt written in the third century by Athenaeus.

De-Juicing (USA). The removal of the free-run juice before the grapes are pressed. (Fr) = Égouttage.

De Keersmaecker Brasserie (Bel). A brewery based in Brussegem, northern Belgium.

Dekeleia (Gre). The name given to the red and white wines produced near Marathon.

De Kluis Brasserie (Bel). A brewery based in Hoegaarden. Noted for its' White beers – Hoegaards Wit, Peeterman and Bénédict (an Abbaye-style beer). Also known as Hoegaards Brasserie.

De Koninck (Bel). An unpasteurised allmalt Ale 5.2% alc. by vol. which is made by top-fermentation. Similar in style to German Altbier. Served on draught.

De Koninck Brasserie (Bel). A brewery based in Antwerp. Noted for its' topfermented beers. See De Koninck.

De Koninck-Proost (Bel). A small Lambic brewery based in Dworp. Noted for its' Cherry beer.

De Kroon Brouwerij (Hol). The 'Crown' Brewery of Oirschot, North Brabant. Beers are pasteurised. Noted for Briljant.

De Kuyper (Hol). A large distillery producing Genever and a wide range of liqueurs in Schiedam.

De la Boe (Dr Franciscus) (Hol). Is purported to have invented Gin in Leiden in the sixteenth century.

D

De la Calle (Manuel) (Sp). A noted Sherry producer based in Jerez de la Frontera.

Delacote (Henry) (Fr). A Cognac producer based at Saint-Hilaire. Produces a variety of Cognacs.

De la Cuesta (José) (Sp). A fine Sherry producer based in Jerez de la Frontera. Is noted for Troubadour (a pale, dry Fino sherry).

Delaforce (Port). Vintage Port shippers. Vintages – 1870, 1873, 1875, 1878, 1881, 1884, 1887, 1890, 1894, 1896, 1900, 1904, 1908, 1912, 1917, 1919, 1920, 1927, 1935, 1945, 1947, 1950, 1955, 1958, 1960, 1963, 1966, 1970, 1975, 1977, 1980. See Quinta da Corte.

De Lagrange (Gaston) (Fr). Cognac producer. Address = Rue de la Pierre Levée, Château Bernard, 16100 Cognac. 60 ha. in Fins Bois 75% and Bois Ordinaires 25%. Formed in 1949 by union of Antier and Pomerol Cognac houses.

De Lahaye (Fr). Champagne producer based in Épernay. Produces – Vintage and non-vintage wines including Jacqueline (a non-vintage brut rosé).

Delaire Vineyards (S.Afr). Based in Stellenbosch. Address = Box 3058, Stellenbosch 7602. Produces varietal wines.

Delamain (Fr). Cognac producers. Address = Delamain & Co. BP 16, 16200, Jarnac. Produces – Vesper Grande Champagne, Pale and Dry Grande Champagne. Owns no vineyards. All Cognacs bought in are from the Grande Champagne.

Delano (USA). A vine-growing town in Kern, San Joaquin Valley, California.

Delas Frères (Fr). Wine négociant-éleveurs based in the Rhône at Tournon. Address = Saint-Jean-de-Muzols, 07300 Tournon-sur-Rhône.

De la Torre y Lapuerta (Sp). A principal wine-producer based in Rioja, north-eastern Spain.

Delaware (USA). Native white grape variety. (Vitis labrusca). Has a pale yellow juice and soft skin. Considered the best north American species. Used for dry, semi-dry and sparkling wines. Gives juice with high sugar content.

Délayer (Fr). Diluting.

Delbeck (Fr). A Champagne producer based in Reims. Was a Grande Marque. Now owned by Piper Heidsieck.

Del Duque (Sp). The brand-name of a Sherry produced by Gonzalez Byass.

De l'Eau d'Cannelle (Ch.Isles). Cinnamon water. 2 parts Brandy, 1 part water, sugar to taste and cinnamon. Heat together. Serve hot or cold.

De Leeuw Brouwerij (Hol). A brewery based in Valkenburg, Limburg. Noted for its' unpasteurised beers – Super Leeuw and Donker.

Delegats Winery (N.Z.). Address = Hepburn Road, Henderson. Grape varieties – Cabernet sauvignon, Chardonnay, Gewürztraminer, Sauvignon blanc and Sémillon.

Delgado (Sp). The term used to describe a thin Sherry.

Delgado Zuleta (Sp). Address = Carmen 32, Sanlúcar de Barrameda. A noted Sherry and Brandy producer. Names include La Goya (sherry) and Monteagudo (brandy).

Delheim Wines (S.Afr). A winery based in Stellenbosch and Simonsberg. Address = P.O. Box 10, Koelenhof 7605. 120 ha. Produces varietal wines. Labels are Spatzendreck and Heeren Wijn.

Delicado (Sp). A Fino sherry produced by Crofts.

Délicat (Fr). Delicate. An elegant, well-balanced wine that is not harsh or coarse. Usually low in alcohol.

Delicate (Eng). A wine taster's term for a light, rather thin, full wine that is not great but fine and elegant.

Délicatesse (Fr). Delicacy. See Délicat.

Delicatessen (USA). A hybrid red grape variety developed in Texas.

Delicator (Ger). A Doppelbock beer produced by the Hofbräuhaus Brauerei of Munich.

Delicato Vineyards (USA). A large winery based near Manteca, San Joaquin, California. Produces varietal and dessert wines.

Delicato Winery (Euro). A large noted winery based in Malta.

Delicías (Mex). A noted wine-producing area in the Chihuahua district.

Delikat (Ger). A delicate wine.

Delimited Areas (Eng). Certain areas whose regional name is given to the wine or spirit produced within the geographical limits of the region.

Delirium Tremens (Eng). See D.T.'s.

Delisle (W.Ind). A noted Rum Distillery based on the island of Guadeloupe.

Della Valle (Pietro) (It). The man who introduced coffee into Italy in the seventeenth century.

Dellchen (Ger). Vineyard. (Anb) = Nahe. (Ber) = Schloss Böckelheim. (Gro) = Burgweg. (Vil) = Norheim.

Dellchen (Ger). Vineyard. (Anb) = Nahe. (Ber) = Schloss Böckelheim. (Gro) = Rosengarten. (Vil) = Mandel.

Dellhofen (Ger). Village. (Anb) = Mittelrhein. (Ber) = Rheinburgengau. (Gro) = Schloss Schönburg. (Vins) = Römerkrug, St. Wernerberg.

Dell'Ugo (It). A Chianti Putto producer based in Tuscany.
Del Mar Ranch (USA). A brand of dry white wine produced by the Monterey Vineyard in Monterey County, California.
Delmonico (Cktl).(1). ⅖ measure dry Gin, ⅕ measure dry Vermouth, ⅕ measure sweet Vermouth, ⅕ measure Brandy. Stir over ice, strain into a delmonico glass. Add a twist of lemon peel.
Delmonico (Cktl).(2). ⅗ measure dry Gin, ⅖ measure dry Vermouth, dash Orange bitters. Stir over ice, strain into a delmonico glass. Add a twist of lemon peel.
Delmonico (USA). A type of cocktail glass. 4–5 ozs. capacity that is short and stubby (a small version of a highball glass). Also known as a 'juice' glass.
Del Monte (Eng). A firm that produces a range of canned and Tetra-pack fruit juices.
Deloach Vineyards (USA). A winery based in the Russian River Valley, Sonoma, California. 51 ha. Grape varieties – Chardonnay, Gewürztraminer, Pinot noir and Zinfandel. Produces varietal wines.
Délor (A. et Cie) (Fr). A wine négociant of Bordeaux. Holds some of the largest stocks of classic growth wines in Bordeaux.
Delorme (Ándre) (Fr). A Burgundy négociant based at Rully, Côte Chalonnaise. Produces fine wines and Crémant de Bourgogne.
Delorme-Meulien (Fr). See Delorme (André).
Delord (Fr). Armagnac producer. Address = Delord Frères, Lannepax 32190 Vic-Fezensac. 20 ha. in Bas Armagnac. Produces – Delord vintage 1942 and Delord 20 Ans d'Âge.
Del Pedro (Austr). The brand-name of a Sherry produced by Reynella.
Delphinette (Switz). A green-coloured, multi-herb liqueur.
Delph Strong Ale (Eng). A Beer 1054 O.G. brewed by Bathams at their Delph Brewery in Brierly Hill, Staffs.
Del Produttore all'Origine (It). Estate bottled.
Delta Domaines (Fr). A group based in southern France. Is made up of ten Master Growers. A marketing company and office of oenology from L'Aude, L'Hérault, Roussillon and Corbiéres region.
De Luxe (Can). A blended Canadian whisky produced by Jas Barclay and Co. Part of Hiram Walker.
De Luxe (Fr). First class.
De Luxe Scotch Whisky (Scot). A blended Scotch whisky with a high proportion of Malt whiskies in the blend.
De Luze [A. et Fils] (Fr). Négociants and growers in Bordeaux.
Dema Glass (Eng). One of the largest British producers of drinking glasses Address = Pottery Lane, Chesterfield, Derbyshire S41 9BH.
De Malliac (J.) (Fr). Armagnac producer. Address = Ste Fermière du Château de Malliac, Montreal du Gers 32250.5 ha. in Ténarèze.
Demand Valve (Eng). See Aspirating Valve or Cask Breather.
De Marcilly Frères (P.) (Fr). Burgundy négociants based in Beaune, Côte de Beaune, Burgundy.
De Martinez (Mex). A brand-name for a Tequila.
Demay Wine Cellars (USA). A winery based in Hammondsport, Finger Lakes, New York. Produces native and hybrid wines.
Demels (Aus). A famous coffee house in Vienna.
Demerara Distillers (S.Am). A subsidiary of the Guyana Distilleries, Guyana.
Demerara Rum (S.Am). The name given to the dark, pungent Rum from British Guyana.
Demestica (Gre). A light, dry, red or white wine made in Patras. Produced by Achaia-Clauss.
Demi (Fr). Half. e.g. demi-tasse = half cup, demi sec = half dry. When applied to beer is for a 30 centilitre glass of beer.
Demi-Barrique (Fr). Half a Bordeaux barrique. 112 litres.
Demi John (Fr). A wide-waisted, covered glass jar for storing wines. Holds from ½ a gallon to 10 gallons depending on area.
Demi-Mesure (Fr). Half measure.
Demi-Muids (Fr). Oak vats used for storing Vermouth. 130 gallons.
Demineralized Water (Eng). Used to reduce spirits to correct strength.
Demi-Queue (Fr). A half queue, a Burgundy cask of 228 litres.
Demir Kapija (Yug). A noted wine-producing district based in Macedonia.
De Misa (Sp). A Brandy and Sherry producer based in Jerez.
Demi-Sec (Fr). Half dry, fairly sweet.
Demi-Tasse (Fr). Lit – 'half cup'. A small china cup used for serving coffee after a dinner meal. Capacity ⅙ pint. Derived from the small cups used in the Middle-east for Turkish-style coffee.
Demockaat (Hol). A coffee and Advocaat-flavoured liqueur produced by Bols.
Demoiselle (Fr). A term used for a measure of spirits in western France.

D

Demoiselles (Les) (Fr). A vineyard in Sancerre-Chavignol, Central Vineyards district in the Loire.

Demolombe (Jean) (Fr). A producer of A.C. Blanquette de Limoux under the Colombe Cathare label.

De Montal (Fr). A brand of Armagnac produced by Compagnie des Produits de Gascogne, Auch, Gers. Produces – V.S.O.P. and Armagnac de Montal. 40% alc. by vol.

Dempsey Brewery (Ire). Opened in 1983 in Dublin. Noted for its' Cask conditioned Dempsey's Real Ale 1037 O.G. and Dublin Pride 1040 O.G.

Dempsey Cocktail (Cktl). ½ gill Gin, ⅓ gill Calvados, 1 teaspoon Grenadine, 2 dashes Absinthe. Shake over ice, strain into a cocktail glass.

De Muller (Sp). A noted wine-producer based in Scala Dei, Tarragona. Uses the label name of Solimar for his red and white wines.

Denaka Danish Vodka (USA). A Vodka launched by Whitbread in North America. Is sold in a triangular-shaped bottle. 40% alc. by vol.

Denaturant (Eng). Added to alcohol to ensure it is unfit to drink so avoiding the excise duty that would otherwise be payable.

Denée (Fr). A commune in the A.C. Coteaux de l'Aubance, Anjou-Saumur, Loire.

De Neuville (Fr). A wine-producer based at St-Hilaire-St-Florent, Anjou-Saumur, Loire. Noted for Saumur Mousseux.

De Nève Brewery (Bel). A brewery based in Schepdaal, central Belgium. Taken over by the Belle-Vue Brewery. Produces filtered beers.

Denice (Fr). A commune in the Beaujolais. Has A.C. Beaujolais-Villages or A.C. Beaujolais-Denice status.

Denisa (Cktl). 1½ fl.ozs. Lemon vodka, ¾ fl.oz. Galliano, ¾ fl.oz. fresh cream, scoop lemon ice cream. Blend all together, serve in a large goblet.

Denizli (Tur). A noted wine-producing vineyard in the Aegean. Produces white wines.

Denman Winery (Austr). A winery based in the Hunter Valley, New South Wales.

Denoix (Fr). A liqueur producer based in Brive in the Périgord-Quercy region. Produces Liqueur de Jus de Noix Vertes, Fenouillette and Roc Amadour.

Denominação de Origem (Port). Government quality control of wines by the Junta Nacional do Vinho.

Denominación de Origen Controlada (Sp). Run on similar lines to France's Appellation Contrôlée laws governing wine production.

Denominazione d'Origine Controllata (It). D.O.C. The Italian equivalent of France's Appellation Contrôlée. Laws include specific grapes, traditional methods, limited yields, proper ageing, adequate records, tasting panels etc. Formed in 1963.

Denominazione d'Origine Controllata e Garantita (It). D.O.C.G. Top award given to certain wines only within the D.O.C. zones. Must be of a very high standard and pass stringent tests. Bottles sealed with government seal. The highest grade in Italy. Only a few wines have this seal. e.g. Barolo and Chianti.

Denominazione d'Origine Semplice (It). An old wine control standard which was below D.O.C. Now no longer used.

Densimeter (Eng). Also referred to as a Mustimeter or Saccharometer. Used to test the grape must density. A hollow, cylindrical float that has a ball beneath it and above it. A graduated rod.

Densimètre (Fr). Densimeter.

Density (Eng). The specific gravity of a liquid when compounded with an equal amount of distilled water.

Denzlingen (Ger). Village. (Anb) = Baden. (Ber) = Breisgau. (Gro) = Burg Zähringen. (Vins) = Eichberg, Sonnhalde.

Deoch (Ire). A small amount of Poteen offered to a possible business dealer to encourage him to quote a fair price.

Deoch-an-Dorius (Scot). Expression used for a drink offered to a departing guest.

De Oegstgeester Wijnkooperij (Hol). A noted, old established firm of wine merchants. Address = De Kempenoerstraat 77 Oegstgeest, Netherland 2341 GJ.

Deo Optimo Maximo (Fr). See D.O.M.

Départ de la Végétation (Le) (Fr). The first signs that the growers have of the condition of the vines after the Winter and Spring frosts. See Austried.

Département (Fr). Department. An administrative subdivision. Equivalent of an English county.

Department of Scientific and Industrial Research (N.Z.). D.S.I.R. Conducts tests and analysis on wines.

Deposit (Eng). The sediment which many red and some white wines throw whilst in bottle. In white wine it is usually tartrate crystals which are harmless but in red wines it is the tannin and colouring matter which tastes bitter and unpleasant. Wines are decanted to remove the sediment.

Deposito (Port). A large vat or tank for

blending and storing wines.
Depositos (Sp). The name for large, resin-lined, cement fermentation vats placed underground to assist cold fermentation. Approximately 1,000 hectolitres capacity. Used mainly in the Cataluña region.
Dépôt (Fr). Sediment.
Dépouillé (Fr). A term used to describe a wine of some age that has no body or colour left.
Dépourissage (Fr). The term used for the gathering of the botrytised grapes off the bunches on the vines over a period of weeks.
De Primer Año (Sp). Rioja wines sold in the year of production.
Depth (Eng). The term to describe the depth of flavour a wine has and so its depth of interest.
Depth Bomb Cocktail (Cktl). ¼ gill Brandy, ¼ gill Calvados, 1 teaspoon Grenadine, 2 teaspoons lemon juice. Shake well over ice, strain into a cocktail glass.
Derby Cocktail (Cktl).(1). ½ gill Brandy, 2 dashes Curaçao, 2 dashes Maraschino, 2 dashes Angostura. Stir over ice, strain into a cocktail glass, top with iced Champagne, cherry and squeeze of lemon peel juice.
Derby Cocktail (Cktl).(2). 2 fl.ozs. Gin, 2 dashes peach juice, 2 sprigs mint. Shake over ice, strain into a cocktail glass.
Derby Daiquiri (Cktl). ⅓ gill white Rum, ⅕ gill orange juice, juice ¼ lime, 1 teaspoon sugar. Blend with a scoop of crushed ice. Pour into a Champagne flute.
Derby Day (Sp). A brand of Fino sherry produced by Romate in Jerez de la Frontera.
Derby Fizz (Cktl). 1 measure Scotch whisky, 1 egg, 1 teaspoon powdered sugar, 4 dashes Cointreau, juice ½ lemon. Shake over ice, strain into an ice-filled highball glass. Top with soda water.
Derby Winner (Cktl). ⅓ measure Vodka, ⅓ measure Eau-de-vie-de-poire, ⅓ measure Triple Sec, dash lime juice. Shake over ice, strain into a cocktail glass. Dress with a slice of lime and a cherry.
De Redcliffe (N.Z.). A winery near Te Kauwhata. 9 ha.
De Ridder Brasserie (Bel). A brewery based in Maastricht, South Limburg. Brews Maltezer 6.25% alc. by vol.
Dermatophora Necatrix (Lat). Fungus. (Family – Pourridié) that attacks the vine roots. See Armillaria Root-rot.
Dermond (Paul-Louis) (Fr). A sparkling wine-producer based in Saumur, Anjou-Saumur, Loire.
Dernau (Ger). Village. (Anb) = Ahr. (Ber) = Walporzheim/Ahrtal. (Gro) = Klosterberg. (Vins) = Burggarten, Goldkaul, Hardtberg, Pfarrwingert, Schieferlay.
Deroldego (It). A red grape variety grown in the Trentino-Alto Adige.
Derrière-la-Grange (Fr). A Premier Cru vineyard in the A.C. commune of Chambolle-Musigny, Côte de Nuits, Burgundy. 0.73 ha.
Derrière Saint-Jean (Fr). A Premier Cru vineyard in the A.C. commune of Pommard, Côte de Beaune, Burgundy. 1.2 ha.
Dertig (Hol). Thirsty. Dorst = Thirst.
Dertingen (Ger). Village. (Anb) = Baden. (Ber) = Badische Frankenland. (Gro) = Tauberklinge Mandelberg. (Vin) = Sonnenberg.
De Rust Wines (S.Afr). Wines made by the Mooiuitsig Wynkelders.
Derwen (Wales). Oak.
Desavinho (Port). A vine malady. Also known as Coulure.
Descampe (Bel). A large distillery in Gembloux.
Descamps Brasserie (Fr). A brewery based at Monceau St. Waast in the Nord Département. Produces top-fermented beers.
Des Chais des Grands Armagnacs [Castagnon] (Fr). An Armagnac producer. Address = Route de Toulouse, 32110 Nogaro.
Desclieux (Fr). A Frenchman who introduced the coffee plant to the West Indies (Martinique) in the eighteenth century. The alternative spelling of De Clieu.
Descorchar (Sp). To uncork a bottle.
Deserpia (Sp). A method of ensuring that the heavy rains of October and November are conserved by making a ridge around the vines to ensure the vines get water. Mainly applicable to the Sherry region. See also Serpia (La).
Desert Healer (Cktl). ⅓ measure Gin, ½ measure Cherry brandy, juice of an orange. Shake over ice, strain into an ice-filled highball glass. Top with ginger beer.
Desertnoe Vino (USSR). Dessert wine.
Desertno Vino (Yug). Dessert wine.
Desfangado (Sp). Clarification. (Fr) = Débourbage. (Ger) = Entschleimen.
Desgalhar (Port). To prune.
Desgüelle (Sp). The disgorging of Cava wines. (Fr) = Dégorgement. See also Degüelle.

D

Desiree (Cktl). 1 measure Gin, ½ measure Crème de Noyau, ½ measure lemon juice, 3 dashes Maraschino. Shake over ice, strain into a cocktail glass.

De Sleutel (Hol). A hoppy Beer 6% alc. by vol. brewed by the Heineken Brouwerij.

Desliar (Sp). Racking.

Desloch (Ger). Village. (Anb) = Nahe. (Ber) = Schloss Böckelheim. (Gro) = Paradiesgarten. (Vins) = Hengstberg, Vor der Hölle.

Desmond and Duff (Scot). Blended Scotch whisky distillers based in Edinburgh. Produce a blend and a 12 year old De Luxe blend mainly for the U.S.A. market.

Desmoulins (A). (Fr). Champagne producer. Address = 44 Avenue Foch, 51201 Épernay. Produces – Nonvintage wines. Label = Cuvée Prestige.

Desnoes and Geddes Brewery (W.Ind). A brewery based in Jamaica which brews Dragon (a strong Stout) and Red Stripe lager.

De Soto (Sp). A famous Sherry producer based in Jerez de la Frontera. Produces fine sherries of all styles. Labels include – Fino Soto, Soto and Poncho Soto brandy.

Desperate Dan (Cktl). ⅓ gill Campari and 1 gill pineapple juice. Stir over ice in a highball glass. Dress with a slice of orange.

Des Seigneurs (Fr). A 3 year old Armagnac produced by Paluel-Marmont.

Dessert Wines (Eng). Usually applied to fortified sweet wines such as Port, Sherry, Madeira etc. as opposed to table wines. Can also be applied to such sweet wines as Sauternes, Trokenbeerenauslese etc. which are unfortified.

Dessilani (It). One of the top producers of Gattinara D.O.C. wines in the Piemonte region.

Dessous (Fr). Coaster.

Dessous de Bouteille (Fr). A bottle coaster.

Dessous de Verre (Fr). A drinking glass coaster.

Destalking (Eng). The removal of the grapes from the stalks to prevent an accumulation of tannin in the must. (Fr) = Égrappage. (Ger) = Gerbelt.

De Stel (Hol). A Dutch governor who planted the Constantia vineyard and gave his name to Stellenbosch in South Africa.

Destileria Huasteca (Mex). A Rum Distillery that produces Potosi (a range of Rums including Oro, Anejo and Blanco).

Destille (Ger). A Berlin expression for a hard-drinking bar that specialises in spirits.

De St. Mardeaux & Co (Fr). Champagne producer. Address = 2–4 Ave du Général Giraud, 51100 Reims. Produces – Vintage and non-vintage wines. Top vintage cuvée = La Cuvée Signée Chatellier.

Destreilles (Fr). Cognac producer. Address = Vignobles des Treilles, Le Taire, 16360 Baignes. 60 ha. 25% in Petite Champagne, 50% in Fins Bois, and 25% in Bon Bois. Produces – 3* Destreilles (3–4 old), Napoléon Destreilles (10–15 years old) and Vieux Réserve du Vignerons (30+ years old).

Desvignes Aîné (Fr). A négociant based in La Chapelle Pontanevaux, Burgundy.

Desvinador (Sp). De-juicer (used to crush the grapes).

De Telmont (Fr). A Champagne producer. Address = 1, Avenue de Cham–BP 17, Damery, 51316 Épernay. Produces – Vintage and non-vintage wines. Top vintage De Luxe cuvée = Cuvée Grand Couronnement.

De Terrazas (Bartoloméo) (Chile). A missionary who was supposedly one of the first to introduce vines into Chile in the sixteenth century.

De Terry (Sp). See Terry.

De Torens (Bel). Lit – 'The towers'. Old name for Geens Distillery.

De Troch Brasserie (Bel). A brewery based in Wambeek, north Belgium.

Dettelbach (Ger). Village. (Anb) = Franken. (Ber) = Maindreieck. (Gro) = Honigberg. (Vils) = Berg-Rondell, Sonnenleite.

Dettling (Switz). A liqueur producer based in Brunnen. Is noted for a Kirsch produced from black cherries. 40% alc. by vol.

Detzem (Ger). Village. (Anb) = Mosel-Saar-Ruwer. (Ber) = Bernkastel. (Gro) = Sankt Michael. (Vins) = Maximiner Klosterlay, Würzgarten.

De Urdiñola (Francisco) (Mex). A Spanish captain who planted the first vineyard at Parras de la Fuente.

Deuslay (Ger). Vineyard. (Anb) = Mosel-Saar-Ruwer. (Ber) = Zell/Mosel. (Gro) = Rosenhang. (Vil) = Mesenich.

Deutelsberg (Ger). Grosslage. (Anb) = Rheingau. (Ber) = Johannisberg. (Vils) = Erbach, Hattenheim, Estate.

Deutsche Barkeeper Union e. V. (Ger). D.B.U. German Bartenders' Association. Address = Rentzelstrasse 36–40, 2000 Hamburg 13.

Deutsche Landwirtschafts-Gesellschaft (Ger). DLG. Founded in 1885. Grants awards to wines. A Federal organisation, recognised by the EEC. Given only to quality wines.

Deutscher Devil (Cktl). ⅓ measure Schnapps, ⅓ measure Brandy, ⅓ measure orange juice, dash Gomme syrup. Shake over ice, strain into a cocktail glass. Top with an orange slice.

Deutscher Rum (Ger). A Rum distilled from German-grown sugar beet, molasses and sugar beet juice.

Deutscher Sekt (Ger). A sparkling wine made from at least 80% of German wine.

Deutscher Tafelwein (Ger). Table wine. (Not to be confused with the EEC Aus Ländern der E.W.G.). Produced from the regions of Rhein, Mosel, Main, Neckar and Oberrhein. See Untergebiete.

Deutsches Erzeugnis (Ger). On a label denotes 'Product of Germany'.

Deutsches Weinlesefest (Ger). A Rheinpfalz wine festival held in Neustadt in October.

Deutsches Weinsiegel (Ger). A quality seal that appears on the neck label of those wines that have obtained a certain standard in test.

Deutsches Weintor (Ger). German wine gate. Start of the Deutsche Weinstrasse. On the border of Alsace at Schweigen, Rheinpfalz.

Deutsche Weinstrasse (Ger). German wine route. Wine walk from Bockenheim to Schweigen. 80 kilometres long.

Deutschherrenberg (Ger). Vineyard. (Anb) = Mosel-Saar-Ruwer. (Ber) = Bernkastel. (Gro) = Münzlay. (Vil) = Zeltingen-Rachtig.

Deutschherrenberg (Ger). Vineyard. (Anb) = Mosel-Saar-Ruwer. (Ber) = Saar-Ruwer. (Gro) = Römerlay. (Vil) = Trier.

Deutschherrenköpfchen (Ger). Vineyard. (Anb) = Mosel-Saar-Ruwer. (Ber) = Saar-Ruwer. (Gro) = Römerlay. (Vil) = Trier.

Deutsch-Kreutz (Aus). A wine-producing area in the Mattersburg district.

Deutz & Geldermann (Fr). Champagne producer. Address = 16 Rue Jeanson, 51160, Ay. A Grande Marque. 42 ha. Produces – Vintage and non-vintage wines. Vintages – 1919, 1920, 1921, 1924, 1925, 1926, 1928, 1929, 1931, 1934, 1936, 1938, 1945, 1947, 1948, 1949, 1953, 1955, 1959, 1961, 1962, 1964, 1966, 1969, 1970, 1973, 1976, 1976, 1979, 1981, 1982. De Luxe vintage Cuvée William Deutz. Cuvée is Cuvée William Deutz.

Deuxièmes Crus (Fr). The second growths in Bordeaux. See Cru.

Deuxièmes Premiers Crus (Fr). A Bordeaux classification. See Deuxièmes Crus.

Deuxième Taille (Fr). The third pressing of the Champagne grapes.

De Vaca (Alvar Nuñez Cabeza) (Sp). Man who discovered Florida and introduced Sherry to the USA.

Devanha Brewery (Scot). Opened in 1982 in north-eastern Scotland, produces cask conditioned Pale Eighty 1042 O.G. XB 1036 O.G. and XXX 1042 O.G.

Deveaux (Fr). A liqueur made from brandy, cream, hazelnuts, herbs and cocoa. 17% alc. by vol.

Devenish Brewery (Eng). Breweries in Weymouth, Dorset and Redruth in Cornwall. Produce many fine beers including – cask conditioned John Devenish 1032 O.G. Cornish 1042 O.G. Wessex 1042 O.G. Newton's Ale 1032 O.G. Saxon 1033 O.G. Falmouth Bitter 1038 O.G. and John Groves 1034 O.G. Also Grünhalle Lager 1036 O.G. and Great British Henry.

De Venoge (Fr). A Champagne producer. Address = 30 Avenue de Champagne 51204 Épernay. Produces – Vintage and non-vintage wines. Vintages – 1971, 1973, 1975, 1979 1980. Top De Luxe vintage cuvée = Cuvée des Princes and Cordon Bleu (a non-vintage Champagne). Also specialises in B.O.B. Champagnes.

Deversorium (Lat). Inn, public house.

De Villamont (Henry) (Fr). A Burgundy négociant based at Savigny-lès-Beaune, Côte de Beaune, Burgundy. Part of the Schenk group of Switzerland.

De Vilanova (Arnaud) (Fr). Fourteenth-century professor in the University of Montpellier who is believed to have rediscovered the art of distillation.

De Vilanova (Arnàu) (Sp). A Catalan chemist born c. 1240. Invented herb tinctures (similar to liqueurs).

Devil's Cauldron (Eng). A vineyard based at Ransley Farm, High Halden, Kent. First planted 1977. 1.5 ha. Grape variety – Gutedel.

Devil's Cocktail (Cktl).(1). ½ measure dry Vermouth, ½ measure Port, 2 dashes lemon juice. Shake with ice, strain into a cocktail glass.

Devil's Cocktail (Cktl).(2). ¼ gill Cognac, ¼ gill Crème de Menthe (green). Shake over ice, strain into a cocktail glass, add pinch of cayenne pepper on top.

Devil's Disciple (Cktl). Place some ice into an old-fashioned glass, add 1 oz. Crème de Menthe, 1 oz. Dubonnet, 2 ozs. tonic water. Stir, finish with a slice of orange.

Devil's Tail (Cktl). 1 measure dark Rum, ½ measure Vodka, ⅛ measure Grenadine, ⅛ measure Apricot brandy, juice ¼ lime. Blend altogether with a scoop of crushed ice. Pour into a flute glass. Top with iced Champagne and a twist of lime peel.

De Vin Seu (Ch.Isles). Elderflower Champagne.

De Vit Brasserie (René) (Bell). A brewery based in Lembeek, central Belgium.

Devizes Bitter (Eng). A cask conditioned Bitter 1030 O.G. brewed by the Wadworth's Brewery in Wiltshire.

Devlin Wine Cellars (USA). A small winery based in Santa Cruz, California. Grape varieties – Cabernet sauvignon, Chardonnay, Pinot blanc and Zinfandel. Produces varietal wines.

Devoir Parisien des Compagnons du Beaujolais (Fr). Formed by exiled Beaujolais compatriots in Paris. Promotes the region and its' wines.

Devon Best (Eng). A keg Bitter 1036 O.G. brewed by the Blackawton Brewery in Devon.

Devon Gold Cider (Eng). A medium-dry or medium-sweet Cider produced by Countryman in Devon.

Devonia Cocktail (Cktl). 4 ozs. sparkling Cider, 2 ozs. Gin, 2 dashes Orange bitters. Stir lightly over ice, strain into a highball glass.

Devonshire Cream (Eng). Clotted cream. Full cream milk (from Guernsey or Jersey cattle) that has been heated gently so that the cream thickens. It is then skimmed off the top of the milk.

Devonshire Cyder (Eng). A Cider produced by the Whiteways Co. Has no additives, artificial colouring or flavourings.

Devonshire Royal Cream (Eng). A brandy- and whisky-based cream liqueur produced in Plymouth, Devon.

Devon Special (Eng). A cask conditioned Bitter 1043 O.G. brewed by the Mill Brewery in Newton Abbot.

Devon Valley Estate (S.Afr). Vineyards of Bertrams Wines in the Stellenbosch region.

Dewar (John) (Scot). A Perth man who is supposed to have introduced the blending of whisky by adding all the remnants of his casks together. See Dewar's.

Dewar's (Scot). A Vatted malt. Produced by John Dewar and Sons Ltd., Perth. 40% alc. by vol. Part of DCL.

Dewar's Ancestor de Luxe Scotch Whisky (Scot). A De Luxe blended Scotch whisky produced by Dewar's of Perth. Is known as Dewar's Ne Plus Ultra in Canada.

Dewar's Ne Plus Ultra (Can). See Dewar's Ancestor De Luxe Scotch Whisky.

Dewar's White Label (Scot). A famous blended Scotch whisky from Dewar's of Perth.

De Wet Co-operative (S.Afr). A winery based in the Breede River Valley. Address = Box 16, De Wet 6853. Produces varietal wines sold under the Breërivervallei Wines.

De Wetshof Estate (S.Afr). Wine estate based in Robertson. Address = Dewetshof Box 31, Robertson 6705. Produces varietal wines.

Dewmiel (Scot). A herb and whisky-based liqueur. 40% alc. by vol.

Dexheim (Ger). Village. (Anb) = Rheinhessen. (Ber) = Nierstein. (Gro) = Gutes Domtal. (Vin) = Doktor.

Dextrin (Eng). Fermentable sugar in malted barley for beer and whisky production.

Dextrocheck (Eng). A tablet used for testing the residual sugar in still wine before dosage occurs. Applied mainly in home-made wine production.

Dextrose (Eng). $C_6H_{12}O_6$. Fruit sugar. Also known as grape sugar. See Glucose.

De Yuma (Sp). The name given to the must obtained from the first light pressing of the grapes.

Dézaley (Switz). A top quality dry white wine made from the Chasselas grape in the Canton of Vaud.

Dezberg (Ger). Vineyard. (Anb) = Württemberg. (Ber) = Württembergisch Unterland. (Gro) = Salzberg. (Vil) = Eberstadt.

Dezberg (Ger). Vineyard. (Anb) = Württemberg. (Ber) = Württembergisch Unterland. (Gro) = Salzberg. (Vil) = Gellmersbach.

Dezize-les-Maranges (Fr). A village within the commune of Santenay, Côte de Beaune, Burgundy.

De Zoete Inval Estate (S.Afr). A wine estate based in Paarl. Address = P.O. Box Suider Paarl 7625. Produces varietal wines.

D-Fructose (Eng). A monosaccharide found in grape must.

D.G. (Sp) (abbr). Dark Golden (colour grade for Raya sherries).

D.G.I. (Fr) (abbr). Direction Générale des Impôts.

Dgin (Ch.Isles). Gin.

Dgin dé Prunelles (Ch.Isles). Sloe gin.

Dharmapuri (Ind). A wine-producing area.

Dhoros (Cyp). A village on the south-eastern side of the island that produces grapes for Commanderia.

Diabetiker Wein (Ger). A very dry white wine, low in residual sugar, suitable for diabetics.

Diablo Cocktail (Cktl). ⅗ measure white Apéritif Port, ⅖ measure Italian vermouth, 3 dashes lemon juice. Shake over ice, strain into a cocktail glass.
Diablo Vista (USA). A winery based in Solano, California. Grape varieties – Cabernet sauvignon, Chardonnay and Zinfandel. Produces varietal wines.
Diabolo Cocktail (Cktl).(1). ¼ gill Brandy, ¼ gill French vermouth, 3 dashes orange Curaçao, 2 dashes Angostura. Stir over ice, strain into a cocktail glass, top with squeeze lemon juice and add cherry and an olive. Also known as Youngman.
Diabolo Cocktail (Cktl).(2). As for Diabolo Cocktail but omit the orange Curaçao and use brown Curaçao instead.
Diabolo Cocktail (Cktl).(3). ⅔ measure white Rum, ⅙ measure French vermouth, ⅙ measure Cointreau, 2 dashes Angostura. Shake over ice, strain into a cocktail glass with a little crushed ice. Squeeze of orange peel juice on top.
Diacetyl (Eng). A glycerin-related compound found in wine in small quantities.
Diactyl (Eng). Is produced by Lactobacilli. Gives the wine a bitter taste.
Diamant Bleu (Fr). A De Luxe vintage cuvée Champagne produced by Heidsieck Monopole from an equal blend of black and white grapes.
Diamante (Sp). A red wine from the Bodegas Franco-Españolas. Made from the Garnacha 25%, Mazuelo 15% and Tempranillo 60%. Matured in oak for 1½ years and in bottle ½-1 year.
Diamiat (Bul). A dry white wine.
Diamond (USA). A white hybrid grape variety.
Diamond (S.Am). A Rum distillery based in Guyana.
Diamond Bitter (Eng). A keg Bitter 1033 O.G. brewed by the Ind Coope Brewery in Burton-on-Trent.
Diamond Cocktail (Cktl). ⅙ gill dry Gin, ⅙ gill brown Curaçao, ⅙ gill Rum. Shake over ice, strain into a cocktail glass. Serve with a dash lemon peel juice.
Diamond Creek (USA). A winery based near Calistoga, Napa Valley, California. 8.25 ha. Grape variety – Cabernet sauvignon. Wines sold under Gravelly Meadow, Red Rock Terrace and Volcano Hill labels.
Diamond Dipper (Punch). ½ pint dry Cinzano, ½ pint Vodka. Stir in a punch bowl, add 3 bottles Perrier water. Dress with lemon and lime slices.
Diamond Export (Scot). A bottled Ale 1042 O.G. brewed by the Alloa Brewery. If on draught then called Alloa Export.
Diamond Fizz (Cktl). ⅓ gill Gin, juice ½ lemon, teaspoon powdered sugar. Shake over ice, strain into an ice-filled highball glass. Top with iced Champagne.
Diamond Heavy (Scot). A keg Ale 1036 O.G. brewed by the Alloa Brewery.
Diamond Liquors (S.Am). A noted Rum Distillery based in Guyana.
Diamond White (Eng). A strong, bottled white Cider produced by the Taunton Cider Co. Taunton, Somerset. 8.2% Alc. by vol.
Diana (USA). A native red grape variety (Vitis Labrusca) used for making varietal wines.
Diana Cocktail (Cktl).(1). Fill a cocktail glass with crushed ice. Place ⅕ gill white Crème de Menthe into the glass, then float liqueur Cognac on top.
Diana Cocktail (Cktl).(2). As for (1) but substitute Schnapps for the Crème de Menthe.
Diane de Poitiers (Fr). A non A.C. sparkling (méthode champenoise) wine produced at a Haut-Poitou Co-operative from 100% white Chardonnay grapes.
Diastase (Eng). The enzyme complex which causes the starch in malted barley to be converted into invert sugar. Hydrolises the starch. See Diastasis.
Diastasis (Eng). See Diastase.
Diatomaceous Earth (Eng). Made up of minute animals which is used in fining wines. Known as Bentonite. See also Kieselguhr and Tierra de Vino.
Diät Pils (Ger). A low carbohydrate, high-alcohol beer 6% by vol. Brewed in west Germany. e.g. Holsten from Hamburg.
Di Castacciaro (Tommaso) (It). The Calmaldolese monk who is reputed to have turned water into wine in the thirteenth century.
Dickel (George) Cascade Distillery (USA). A distillery based near Tullahoma, Coffee County, Tennessee. Produces Tennessee whiskey (a Sour mash whiskey filtered through charcoal).
Dickens Own (Eng). A cask conditioned Bitter 1042 O.G. brewed by the Tooley Street Brewery in Central London. See also Dickens Own Special.
Dickens Own Special (Eng). A cask conditioned Bitter 1050 O.G. brewed by the Tooley Street Brewery in Central London. See also Dickens Own.
Dickkopp (Ger). Vineyard. (Anb) = Rheinpfalz. (Ber) = Mittelhaardt-Deutsche Weinstrasse. (Gro) = Feuerberg. (Vil) = Ellerstadt.
Didiers (Les) (Fr). A Premier Cru vineyard of the village of Prémeaux in the southern end of the A.C. commune of Nuits-Saint-Georges, Côte de Nuits, Burgundy. 2.8 ha.
Die (Fr). See Clairette de Die.

D

Diebels Alt (Ger). An Altbier from Düsseldorf. Well-made and full-flavoured. See Diebels Brauerei.

Diebels Brauerei (Ger). A famous Alt brewery based at Issum, near Düsseldorf.

Die Bergkelder (S.Afr). Famous wine cellars based in Stellenbosch. Stocks most of the top South African wines. Address = P.O. Box 5001, Stellenbosch 7600. See Fleur du Cap.

Dieblesberg (Ger). Vineyard. (Anb) = Württemberg. (Ber) = Württembergisch Unterland. (Gro) = Salzberg. (Vil) = Affaltrach.

Dieblesberg (Ger). Vineyard. (Anb) = Württemberg. (Ber) = Württembergisch Unterland. (Gro) = Salzberg. (Vil) = Löwenstein (ortsteil Hösslinsülz).

Dieblesberg (Ger). Vineyard. (Anb) = Württemberg. (Ber) = Württembergisch Unterland. (Gro) = Salzberg. (Vil) = Willsbach.

Dieblich (Ger). Village. (Anb) = Mosel-Saar-Ruwer. (Ber) = Zell/Mosel. (Gro) = Weinhex. (Vin) = Heilgraben.

Dieboldshausen (Fr). German name for the Alsace town of Le Bonhomme.

Diedesfeld (Ger). Village. (Anb) = Rheinpfalz. (Ber) = Mittelhaardt-Deutsche Weinstrasse. (Gro) = Pfaffengrund. (Vin) = Berg.

Diedesfeld (Ger). Village. (Anb) = Rheinpfalz. (Ber) = Mittelhaardt-Deutsche Weinstrasse. (Gro) = Rebstöckel. (Vins) = Johanniskirchel, Ölgässel, Paradies.

Diedesheim (Ger). Village. (Anb) = Baden. (Ber) = Badische Bergstrasse/Kraichgau. (Gro) = Stiftsberg. (Vin) = Herzogsberg.

Diefenbach (Ger). Village. (Anb) = Württemberg. (Ber) = Württembergisch Unterland. (Gro) = Stromberg. (Vin) = König.

Dieffert (Lux). A vineyard site in the village of Stadtbredimus.

Diekirch Brewery (Lux). The largest brewery based in Diekirch.

Dielheim (Ger). Village. (Anb) = Baden. (Ber) = Badische Bergstrasse/Kraichgau. (Gro) = Mannaberg. (Vins) = Rosenberg, Teufelskopf.

Diemersdal Vineyard (S.Afr). A wine estate based in Durbanville. Address = P.O. Durbanville 7550. Produces varietal wines bottled by KWV.

Dienheim (Ger). Village. (Anb) = Rheinhessen. (Ber) = Nierstein. (Gro) = Güldenmorgen. (Vins) = Falkenberg, Herrenberg, Höhlchen, Kreuz-Siliusbrunnen, Tafelstein.

Dienheim (Ger). Village. (Anb) = Rhein-hessen. (Ber) = Nierstein. (Gro) = Krötenbrunnen. (Vins) = Herrengarten, Paterhof, Schloss.

Dierbach (Ger). Village. (Anb) = Rheinpfalz. (Ber) = Südliche Weinstrasse. (Gro) = Guttenberg. (Vin) = Kirchhöh.

Diersburg (Ger). Village. (Anb) = Baden. (Ber) = Ortenau. (Gro) = Fürsteneck. (Vins) = Kinzigtäler, Schlossberg.

Diestro (Sp). A Jerez Brandy producer. Produces Ponche.

Diesus (It). A bitter apéritif made by Barbero.

Dietale (Austr). A dry, diet Beer brewed by C.U.B. in Victoria.

Diet Coke (USA). A low-calorie version of the famous Coca Cola.

Diet Fresca (Eng). See Fresca.

Diethylene Glycol (Eng). A sweet syrupy liquid used as an anti-freeze in motor vehicles. Has a high S.G. An illegal additive in wines (used to sweeten them). Is poisonous. Caused a scandal in Austria in 1985.

Diethylpyrocarbonate (Eng). A wine preservative. See Baycovin.

Dietlingen (Ger). Village. (Anb) = Baden. (Ber) = Badische Bergstrasse/Kraichgau. (Gro) = Hohenberg. (Vins) = Keulebuckel, Klepberg.

Diet Pepper (USA). A low-calorie version of the Dr. Pepper drink.

Diet Pepsi (USA). A low-calorie version of the famous Pepsi Cola.

Diet Pils (Ger). See Diät Pils.

Dietzenbach (Ger). Village. (Anb) = Hessische Bergstrasse. (Ber) = Umstadt. (Gro) = Not yet assigned. (Vin) = Wingertsberg.

Dieu Donne et de Lucque Estates (S.Afr). A winery based in the municiple area of Franschhoek. Produces varietal wines.

Diez Hermanos (Port). Vintage Port shippers. Vintage – 1975. Also produces sherries.

Diez Hermanos (Sp). A noted Sherry producer based in Jerez de la Frontera. Brand of Sherry from Diez Merito. Range = Favorito Palma, Figaro, Imperial Fino, La Torera, Oloroso, Realengo and Victoria Regina.

Diez Merito (Sp). Produces a range of sherries under the labels of Don Zolio, Diez Hermanos and Duque d'Alba brandy.

Digby (Sir Kenelm) (Eng). Said to have invented the glass bottle in the year 1600.

Digestif (Eng). An aid to digestion. Applied to herb liqueurs.

Digestive (Eng). See Digestif.

Dignac et Loirac (Fr). A commune in the Bas Médoc, north-western Bordeaux.

Diki-Diki (Cktl). ¼ gill Calvados, ⅛ gill Caloric Punsch, ⅛ gill grapefruit juice. Shake over ice, strain into a cocktail glass.
Dikoya (Sri.L). A tea-producing region in the High region.
Diktiner (Ger). A rich herb liqueur similar to Bénédictine. Green, red and yellow versions are produced.
Dillatini (Cktl). As for a Dry Martini but adding a dilly bean instead of an olive.
Diluer (Fr). To dilute, water down.
Dilute (Eng). To make weaker in strength (flavour or alcohol) by the addition of water or other weaker substance.
Dilution (Eng). The act of diluting (the thinning or weakening of a solution).
Di Mauro (Paolo) (It). A wine-producer based in Latium who specialises in red wines.
Dimbach (Ger). Vineyard. (Anb) = Württemberg. (Ber) = Württembergisch Unterland. (Gro) = Lindelberg. (Vin) = Schlossberg.
Dimbula (Sri.L). A tea-producing region in the High region.
Dimiat (Bul). A white grape variety which produces dry fruity wines with a green tinge. Also spelt Dimyat.
Di Montezemolo (Paolo Codero) (It). A noted wine-producer based in the La Morra district of Barolo, Piemonte.
Dimple Haig (Scot). A 12 year old De Luxe Scotch whisky produced by John Haig and Co. at Markinch. See also Pinch-bottle.
Dimples (Cktl). ½ measure Dimple Haig Scotch whisky, ½ measure apple juice, dash green Chartreuse. Shake over ice, strain into an ice-filled highball glass. Top with a dash of soda and sprig of mint.
Dimrit (Tur). A white grape variety grown in central Anatolia.
Dimyat (Bul). See Dimiat.
Dinah Cocktail (Cktl). ⅕ Bourbon whiskey, juice ¼ lemon, 2 dashes Gomme syrup. Shake well over ice, strain into a cocktail glass. Top with a mint leaf.
Dinant Brasserie (Bel). A brewery based in Dinant. Produces the top-fermented beer Copère.
Dingač (Yug). A strong red wine made from the Plavac grape in Croatia. Full bodied and high in alcohol.
Ding-a-ling (Scot) (slang). A request for a tot of Bell's Scotch whisky.
Dinkarebe (Aus). An old red grape variety that is little used nowadays.
Dinkel Acker (Ger). A Bier produced by the Dinkelacker Brauerei in Stuttgart.
Dinkelacker Brauerei (Ger). A noted brewery of Stuttgart in southern West Germany. Noted for its' Sanwald brand and C.D. beers.
Dinner Ale (Austr). D.A. A pale, hoppy Lager brewed by the Tooth's Brewery in New South Wales.
Dinner Ale (Austr). A low-gravity Ale 4.75% alc. by vol. produced by the Cooper Brewery in Adelaide. Is wood-fermented and bottle-conditioned.
Dinner Ale (Eng). A rare low-gravity bottled Beer made by a second mash of malt.
Diod (Wales). A drink.
Diod Fain (Wales). A small beer.
Diod Feddwol (Wales). Alcoholic drink, liquor.
Diod Gadarn (Wales). Strong drink.
Diodi (Wales). To give a drink.
Diod Lemon (Wales). Lemonade.
Diodlestr (Wales). Tankard (beer).
Diognières (Les) (Fr). A vineyard in the A.C. Hermitage, northern Rhône.
Dionysia (Gre). Ancient Greek festivals to the God Dionysos.
Dionysius (Gre). Alternative spelling of Dionysos.
Dionysos Cocktail (Cktl). ⅕ gill Metaxa brandy, 1 teaspoon honey. Shake well over ice, strain into a large liqueur glass. Float ⅙ gill cream on top.
Dionysos (Gre). Ancient Greek God of wine. See also Bacchus.
Dionysus (Gre). Alternative spelling of Dionysos.
Diosig (Rum). A noted white wine-producing vineyard.
Dioxymalic Acid (Eng). A wine acid formed due to the oxidation of tartaric acid.
Dioxytartaric Acid (Eng). A wine acid formed due to the oxidation of tartaric acid.
Diploma Beer (N.Z.). A Beer brewed by the Dominion Brewery.
Diplomat (Czec). A dark, hoppy, full, strong Lager 18°. Brewed by the Gambrinus Brewery in Pilsen.
Diplomat Cocktail (Cktl). ⅛ gill pineapple syrup, ⅛ gill Italian vermouth, ⅛ gill French vermouth. Stir over ice, strain into a cocktail glass, serve with dash of lemon peel juice and a cherry.
Diplomate Cocktail (Cktl). ⅓ gill French vermouth, ⅓ gill Italian vermouth, 2 dashes Maraschino. Stir over ice, strain into a cocktail glass, add cherry and squeeze of lemon peel on top.
Dipping Rod (Eng). Alternative name for a Dipstick.
Dipso (Eng) (slang). Expression to describe a person who is suffering from dipsomania.
Dipsomania (Eng). Uncontrollable crav-

ing for alcohol.

Dipsomaniac (Eng). A victim of dipso-mania.

Dipstick (Eng). A thin calibrated rod dipped into a cask of ale through the spile hole to measure the contents. Also known as a Dipping rod.

Direct Distillation (USA). A method of producing flavoured spirits such as Gin by putting the botanicals above the still so that the alcoholic vapours percolate through the botanicals, extracting their flavour.

Direction Générale des Impôts (Fr). D.G.I. Group which maintains the control and marketing of wines.

Director's Bitter (Eng). A strong Bitter 1046 O.G. brewed by Courage in Bristol.

Director's Choice (USA). A dry red wine produced by the Golden Rain Tree Winery in Wadesville, Indiana.

Dirkzwager (Hol). A distillery noted for its' Genever.

Dirmstein (Ger). Village. (Anb) = Rheinpfalz. (Ber) = Mittelhaardt-Deutsche Weinstrasse. (Gro) = Schwarzerde. (Vins) = Herrgottsacker, Jesuitenhofgarten, Mandelpfad.

Dirty (Eng). A term applied to a wine that has an unpleasant off-smell or off-taste. Usually due to poor vinification or bad bottling.

Dirty Habit (Cktl). 1 measure Southern Comfort, 1 measure Amaretto. Stir over ice in an old-fashioned glass.

Dirwest (Wales). Abstinence.

Disappointed Lady (Cktl). ½ measure Crème de Noyau, ½ measure Tia Maria, ½ measure Brandy, ½ measure orange juice, dash egg white. Shake over ice, strain into a cocktail glass. Add a dash of Grenadine and a little grated nutmeg on top.

Disbor (Fr). A liqueur producing Co. based in Bordeaux. Address = 17, Cours de Luze, Bordeaux. Produces a large range of liqueurs and Eau-de-Vie.

Disc (The) (Eng). The wine-taster's name for the Meniscus.

Disco Dancer (Cktl). 2 parts Johnnie Walker Red Label, 2 parts Peach brandy, 6 parts orange juice, dash Grenadine, dash egg white. Shake over ice, strain into a highball filled with ice, dress with a slice of orange.

Disgorgement (Eng). See Dégorgement.

Disibodenberg (Ger). Vineyard. (Anb) = Nahe. (Ber) = Schloss Böckelheim. (Gro) = Paradiesgarten. (Vil) = Odernheim.

Distill (USA). See Distillation.

Distillate (Eng). The product of distill-ation.

Distillateur (Fr). Distiller.

Distillation (Eng). The application of heat which extracts alcohol from fermented liquids.

Distillation (Fr). Distillation.

Distillato di Vennacia (It). Is similar to Marc de Bourgogne.

Distilled Beverages (Eng) (USA). The name given to spirits which result from pure distillation of fermented beverages.

Distilled Gin (USA). A Gin which has been flavoured by passing the vapours through the 'Gin head' to extract the flavours. See Direct Distillation.

Distiller (Fr). To distil.

Distillerie (Fr). Distillery.

Distillerie Ambulante (Fr). Mobile distill-ery. Looks similar to a steam tractor engine.

Distillerie Camel (It). Producer of Fogolar (Brandy and Grappa).

Distillerie Carrère (Fr). Armagnac pro-ducer. Address = 36, Rue des Alliés, 32500 Fleurance.

Distillerie de la Côte Basque (Fr). A distillery based in the Pyrénées. Pro-duces Izarra.

Distillerie de la Métairie (Fr). A Cognac producer. Address = Mazière Guimps, 16300 Barbezieux. 14 ha. in the Petite Champagne.

Distillerie des Moisans (Fr). Cognac pro-ducers. Address = Les Moisans-Sireuil, 16440 Roullet Saint-Estèphe. 20 ha. in the Grande Champagne and 40 ha in the Fins Bois. Produces a wide range of Cognacs.

Distillerie des Rhums Agricoles (W.Ind). See D.R.A.

Distillerie Montmorency Ltee (Can). A producer of a range of Canadian whis-kies. (A subsidiary of Seagram).

Distillerie Riunite (It). A liqueur pro-ducer based in Milan. Noted for its' Galliano.

Distillerie Rougé Sumagne (Fr). Cognac producer. Address = 17770 Bri-zambourg. 56 ha. in the Fins Bois. Produces wide range of Codnacs including V.S.O.P, Napoléon and X.O.

Distilleries Associées Belges (Bel). Address = Jumet, Nr. Charleroi. Pro-duces Liqueur aux Fraises and Sève de Sapin.

Distillerie Stock (It). Large Brandy pro-ducer. Address = Distillerie Stock Sp.A., Trieste. Produces a V.S.O.P. oak-aged Brandy.

Distillers Agency Limited (Scot). The export branch of DCL based near Edinburgh. Has the licence for Rose-bank and King George IV.

D

Distillers Company Limited (Scot). DCL. Major Whisky distillers. Owns many famous brand-names including White Horse, VAT 69, Johnnie Walker, Haig. Taken over by Guinness in 1986.

Distillers Corporation (S.Afr). Producers of Oude Meester liqueur brandy. See Oude Meester Group.

Distiller's Safe (Scot). See Whisky Safe.

Distinctive (Eng). A term to describe a wine that has a positive character.

Distingué (Fr). A term used to denote a fine wine that has finesse and quality.

Distinguished (Eng). A term used by the wine experts to describe the finest wines of superb quality.

Ditchling Vineyard (Eng). Address = Claycroft, Beacon Road, Ditchling, Sussex. Planted 1979. 3 ha. Grape varieties – Müller-Thurgau, Ortega and Reichensteiner.

Dittelsheim-Hessloch (Ger). Village. (Anb) = Rheinhessen. (Ber) = Wonnegau. (Gro) = Pilgerpfad. (Vins) = Edle Weingärten, Geiersberg, Kloppberg, Leckerberg, Liebfrauenberg, Mönchhube, Mondschien, Pfaffenmütze.

Dividend (USA). The part of the cocktail after it has been poured out that is left in the shaker or jug.

Dixie (Cktl). 1 measure dry Gin, ½ measure dry Vermouth, juice ¼ orange, ¼ measure Absinthe. Shake over ice, strain into a cocktail glass.

Dixie Brewery (USA). Based in New Orleans. Produces a beer of the same name.

Dixie Julep (Cktl). ⅓ gill Bourbon whiskey, 1 teaspoon powdered sugar. Place into an ice-filled collins glass and stir until frosted on the outside. Dress with mint sprigs and serve with straws.

Dixie Whiskey (Cktl). ⅕ gill Bourbon whiskey, 2 dashes Crème de menthe (white), 2 dashes Curaçao (white), 1 dash Angostura, dash Gomme syrup. Shake over ice, strain into cocktail glass.

Dixon (Port). Vintage Port shippers. Vintages – 1884, 1887, 1890.

Dizy (Fr). A Premier Cru Champagne village in the Canton d'Ay. District = Reims.

Djakoro (Yug). A northern wine-producing town in Croatia.

Djaousse (USSR). A white grape variety grown in Tadzhikistan. Used to produce dessert wines.

Djemsheed (Shah) (M.East). The old Persian (Iran) version of who first discovered wine.

Djeudyjelÿa (Yug). A noted wine-producing area in Macedonia.

Djimma (Afr). An important coffee-producing region of Ethiopia.

Djougue (Ch.Isles). Pitcher, jug. See also Ecueul.

D'la Bièthe Gengivre (Ch.Isles). Ginger beer.

D'Lemonade (Ch.Isles). Fresh lemonade.

D.L.G. (Ger) (abbr). Deutsche Landwirtschaft Gesellschaft. German agricultural society.

Dniepropetrovsk (USSR). A wine-producing centre on the river Dnieper in the Ukraine.

Dobbelen Bruinen (Bel). A double-brown Ale brewed by the Roman Brasserie in Mater near Oudenaarde.

Doble Pasto (Sp). A heavy blending wine sold for blending with thin, weak wines. Produced in central and southern Spain, it is often exported to eastern Europe.

Dobo (Captain Istvan) (Hun). 1552. Leader of the Magyar defenders of Eger. Bull's Blood was named after the red wine his troops were seen drinking.

D'Obrion (Fr). The ancient spelling of Château Haut-Brion in the Graves, Bordeaux.

Dobruska Brewery (Czec). A brewery based in northern Czec.

D.O.C. (It) (abbr). Denominazione d'Origine Controllata.

D.O.C. (Sp) (abbr). Denominación de Origen Controlada.

Doçar (Port). A red grape variety grown in Monçao (a sub-region of the Vinhos Verdes).

Doce (Port). Sweet.

D.O.C.G. (It) (abbr). Denominazione d'Origine Controllata e Garantita.

Dock Glass (Eng). A glass used for drinking Port in the nineteenth century.

Docktor (Ger). See Doctor and Bernkasteler Docktor.

Docteur Peste (Fr). A vineyard based in the commune of the A.C. Corton in the Côte de Beaune, Burgundy. Is owned by the Hospices de Beaune 1 ha. Corton Bressandes, 0.5 ha. Clos du Roi, 0.4 ha. Fiètre, 0.1 ha. Les Grèves, 1 ha. Les Chaumes and 1 ha. Voirosses.

Doctor (Ger). Vineyard. (Anb) = Mosel-Saar-Ruwer. (Ber) = Bernkastel. (Gro) = Badstube. (Vil) = Bernkastel-Kues.

Doctor Pepper (USA). See Dr. Pepper.

Doctor's Cocktail (Cktl). ⅙ gill lemon juice, ⅙ gill orange juice, ⅙ gill Swedish Punsch. Shake over ice, strain into a cocktail glass.

Dodecanese Islands (Gre). A group of islands of which Rhodes is the chief wine producer in S.E. Greece near the Turkish coast.

Dodoma (Afr). A region in Tanzania that

produces full-bodied red wines. Especially noted are those from the Holy Ghost Fathers.

Doeppel Kümmel (Ger). High strength Kümmel.

Doerflinger Wine Cellars (USA). A winery based in Bloomsburg, central Pennsylvania.

Doga (It). A cask stave.

Dog and Parrot (Eng). A public house in Newcastle-on-Tyne which brews its' own beer. Owned by Whitbreads. Produces a cask conditioned Scotswood Ale 1036 O.G. and Wallop 1046 O.G.

Dog Bolter Ale (Eng). A cask conditioned Ale 1060 O.G. brewed by the Ferret and Firkin, a Bruce home-brew public house in London.

Dog's Nose (Eng). A glass of beer with a dash of Gin in it. An old naval drink.

Do Hospital (El) (Port). A commune in the Dão region.

Dojon (Fr). An almond and Cognac flavoured liqueur produced by Serres in Toulouse.

Doktor (Ger). Vineyard. (Anb) = Rheinhessen. (Ber) = Nierstein. (Gro) = Gutes Domtal. (Vil) = Dexheim.

Doktor (Ger). Vineyard. (Anb) = Rheinpfalz. (Ber) = Südliche Weinstrasse. (Gro) = Trappenberg. (Vil) = Venningen.

Doktorberg (Ger). Vineyard. (Anb) = Mosel-Saar-Ruwer. (Ber) = Saar-Ruwer (Gro) = Romerlay. (Vil) = Waldrach.

Doktorgarten (Ger). Vineyard. (Anb) = Baden. (Ber) = Kaiserstuhl-Tuniberg. (Gro) = Vulkanfelsen. (Vil) = Ihringen (ortsteil Blankenhornsberg).

Dökülgen (Tur). A red grape variety grown in southern Turkey.

Dolamore Ltd (Eng). A college wine merchant. Branches in Oxford (1) and Cambridge (2). Also a shop in Craven Road, London W2.

Dolce (It). Very sweet.

Dolceacqua (It). A red wine from Ligurian region. Lit – 'Sweet water'. Made from the Dolcetto, Rossese and Vermentino grapes. Also gives its' name to wines. See Rossese di Dolceacqua.

Dolce Amaro (It). A wine apéritif with a bitter-sweet almond taste. 10.5% alc. by vol. Made from old family recipes of D'Elia family in Naples.

Dolce Naturale (It). Naturally sweet wine.

Dolcetto (It). A red grape variety.

Dolcetto (It). D.O.C. red wine from the Piemonte region. Named after grape variety.

Dolcetto d'Acqui (It). D.O.C. red wine from Piemonte. Made in the commune of Acqui Terme from the Dolcetto

grape. If 12.5% alc. by vol. and aged for at least 1 year then classed Superiore.

Dolcetto d'Alba (It). D.O.C. red wine from Piemonte. Made in the communes of Alba and Barolo and 23 others in province of Cuneo from the Dolcetto grape. If 12.5% alc. by vol. and aged for 1 year then classed Superiore.

Dolcetto d'Asti (It). D.O.C. red wine from Piemonte in the commune of Asti. Made from the Dolcetto grape. If 12.5% alc. by vol. and aged 1 year then classed Superiore.

Dolcetto delle Langhe Monregalesi (It). D.O.C. red wine from Piemonte. Made from the Dolcetto grape. If 12.5% alc. by vol. and aged for 1 year then classed Superiore.

Dolcetto di Diano d'Alba (It). D.O.C. red wine from Piemonte. Made from the Dolcetto grape. If 12.5% alc. by vol. and aged for minimum 1 year then classed Superiore.

Dolcetto di Dogliani (It). D.O.C. red wine from Piemonte. Made from the Dolcetto grape. If 12.5% alc. by vol. and aged for 1 year or more then classed Superiore.

Dolcetto di Ovado (It). D.O.C. red wine from Piemonte. Made from the Dolcetto grape. If 12.5% alc. by vol. and aged for minimum 1 year then classed Superiore.

Dôle (Switz). A red wine made from the Pinot noir and Gamay grape varieties. Light and soft. Made in the Valais region.

Dolfi (Fr). A famous Eau-de-Vie liqueur producer.

Dolgesheim (Ger). Village. (Anb) = Rheinhessen. (Ber) = Nierstein. (Gro) = Krötenbrunnen. (Vins) = Kreuzberg, Schützenhütte.

Dolia (Lat). The name given to ancient fermenting jars.

Dolias (Gre). An ancient Greek container lined with pitch to store and carry wines.

Dolin (Fr). Company in the Haute-Savoie, that produces dry, aromatic apéritif wines. e.g. Chambéry and Chambéryzette.

Dolores Cocktail (Cktl). ⅓ measure Spanish brandy, ⅓ measure Cherry brandy, ⅓ measure Crème de Cacao. Shake over ice, strain into a cocktail glass. Top with a cherry.

Dolphi (Fr). A fruit liqueur producer based in Strasbourg, Alsace.

Dolphin Bitter (Eng). A cask conditioned Bitter 1038 O.G. brewed by the Poole Brewery in Dorset.

Doluca (Tur). Private wine-producing firms.

D

D.O.M. (Fr) (abbr). Deo Optimo Maximo. On the Bénédictine liqueur label means 'To God, most good, most great'.

Domain Chandon (USA). A winery in Yountville, Napa Valley, California, belonging to Möet and Chandon of France. Produces sparkling wines from the Chardonnay, Pinot blanc and Pinot noir grapes by the méthode champenoise.

Domain Durban (Fr). A noted producer of Muscat de Beaumes de Venise in the Côtes du Rhône-Villages, south-eastern France.

Domaine (Fr). Privately owned vineyard, estate, field.

Domaine Abelanet (Fr). A vineyard in the A.C. Fitou, south-western France.

Domaine Allée-de-Lescours (Fr). A vineyard in the A.C. Saint-Émilion, Bordeaux. 4 ha.

Domaine Andron (Fr). A vineyard in the commune of St-Selve. A.C. Graves, Bordeaux. 3 ha. (white).

Domaine Arzac (Fr). A vineyard in the commune of St-Selve. A.C. Graves, Bordeaux. 2 ha. (white).

Domaine Bastide Blanche (Fr). A V.D.Q.S. wine from the Côtes-de-Provence, south-eastern France.

Domaine Bellevue (Fr). A vineyard in the commune of Toulenne. A.C. Graves, Bordeaux. 1 ha. (white).

Domaine Boingnères (Fr). Armagnac producers. Address = M. et Mme Léon Lafitte, Le Freche, 40190 Villeneuve de Marsan. 19 ha.

Domaine Bonneau de Martray (Fr). Producer of A.C. Corton and Corton-Charlemagne in the Côte de Beaune, Burgundy.

Domaine Bottled (Fr). The Burgundy equivalent of the Bordeaux Château bottled. Lit – 'bottled in the vineyards cellars'.

Domaine Caillol (Fr). A vineyard in the A.C. Cassis. Côtes-de-Provence, south-eastern France.

Domaine Caillou Rouley (Fr). A vineyard in the commune of Podensac. A.C. Cérons, Bordeaux. 8 ha.

Domaine Carros (Fr). A vineyard in the commune of St-Selve. A.C. Graves, Bordeaux. 2 ha. (white).

Domaine Castelnaud (Fr). A vineyard in the commune of St-Pierre-de-Mons. A.C. Graves, Bordeaux. 2 ha. (white).

Domaine Cauhapé (Fr). A vineyard in the A.C. Jurançon, south-western France.

Domaine Chandon (USA). See Domain Chandon.

Domaine Chante-Alouette-Cormeil (Fr). Address = Château Gueyrosse, Libourne 33500. Grand Cru. A.C. Saint-Émilion. Commune = Saint-Émilion. 18 ha. Grape varieties – Cabernet franc 20%, Cabernet sauvignon 20% and Merlot 60%.

Domaine Chante Cigale (Fr). A vineyard in the A.C. Châteauneuf-du-Pape, southern Rhône. Grape varieties – Cinsault 5%, Grenache 80%, Mourvèdre 5% and Syrah 10%.

Domaine Château Lichten (Switz). A Loèche Ville vineyard that produces Valais-style wines.

Domaine Clair-Daü (Fr). A large estate in the Côte d'Or of which 27 ha. is in the commune of Marsannay. Produces the famous Rosé de Marsannay.

Domaine Comte de Vogüé (Fr). A wine-producer based in the commune of Chambolle-Musigny who owns part of the vineyards of Musigny (7.5 ha.) and others.

Domaine Cosse (Fr). A vineyard in the commune of Fargues. A.C. Sauternes, Bordeaux. 6 ha.

Domaine Croix-de-Grézard (Fr). A vineyard in the commune of Lussac-Saint-Émilion. A.C. Saint-Émilion, Bordeaux. 2 ha.

Domaine d'Ahera (Cyp). The name given to a light, red wine produced by the Keo Co. in Limassol.

Domaine Damanieu (Fr). A vineyard in the commune of Sainte-Croix-du-Mont. A.C. Sainte-Croix-du-Mont, Bordeaux. 3 ha.

Domaine d'Arriailh (Fr). A vineyard in the commune of Montagne-Saint-Émilion. A.C. Saint-Émilion, Bordeaux. 4 ha.

Domaine d'Artois (Fr). A vineyard in the A.C. Amboise Touraine-Mesland, Loire. A red wine produced from the Gamay grape. Address = 7, Quai des Violettes, Amboise, Touraine, Loire.

Domaine de Augiers (Fr). A vineyard in the commune of Comps. A.C. Côtes de Bourg, Bordeaux.

Domaine de Badon-Patarbet (Fr). A vineyard in the A.C. Saint-Émilion, Bordeaux. 2 ha.

Domaine de Bardoulet (Fr). A vineyard in the A.C. Saint-Émilion, Bordeaux. 3 ha.

Domaine de Barraud (Fr). A vineyard in the commune of Montagne-Saint-Émilion. A.C. Saint-Émilion, Bordeaux. 4 ha.

Domaine de Bayard (Fr). A vineyard in the commune of Montagne-Saint-Émilion. A.C. Saint-Émilion, Bordeaux. 8 ha.

Domaine de Beaucastel (Fr). A vineyard estate in the A.C. Châteauneuf-du-Pape, southern Rhône. 85 ha.

Domaine de Beaurenard (Fr). A vineyard estate in the A.C. Châteauneuf-du-Pape.

D

Address = 84320 Rhône. 31 ha. Grape varieties – Cinsault 10%, Grenache 70%, Mourvèdre 10% and Syrah 10%.

Domaine de Bel-Air (Fr). A vineyard in the commune of Samonsac. A.C. Côtes de Bourg, Bordeaux.

Domaine de Belair (Fr). A.C. Bordeaux Rouge.

Domaine de Bellevue (Fr). A vineyard in the commune of St-Selve. A.C. Graves, Bordeaux. 4 ha. (white).

Domaine de Ben Naceaur (Afr). A brand of red wine produced in Morocco by the Société Socovin, Casablanca.

Domaine de Bequin (Fr). A vineyard in the commune of Portets. A.C. Graves, Bordeaux. 8 ha. (red and white).

Domaine de Berlière (Fr). A vineyard in the commune of Parsac-Saint-Émilion. A.C. Saint-Émilion, Bordeaux. 3 ha.

Domaine de Bévy (Fr). A large vineyard in the Hautes-Côtes-de-Nuits. Owned by Maison Geisweiler. 76.5 ha. It produces fine light wines. The slopes of Bévy have a fine micro-climate and it is often known as the Côte d'Azur de la Côte d'Or.

Domaine de Biot (Fr). A vineyard in the commune of Arbanats. A.C. Graves, Bordeaux. 4 ha. (red and white).

Domaine de Bonne (Fr). A vineyard in the commune of Gauriac. A.C. Côtes de Bourg, Bordeaux.

Domaine de Bonneau (Fr). A vineyard in the commune of Montagne-Saint-Émilion. A.C. Saint-Émilion, Bordeaux. 4 ha.

Domaine de Bosquet (Fr). A light white wine produced in the Salins du Midi from Cabernet sauvignon grapes.

Domaine de Bouche (Fr). A vineyard in the commune of Samonac. A.C. Côtes de Bourg, Bordeaux.

Domaine de Bourdac (Fr). A vineyard in the commune of Illats. A.C. Cérons, Bordeaux. 7 ha.

Domaine de Bourg-Neuf (Fr). A vineyard in the commune of Pomerol. A.C. Pomerol, Bordeaux. 1 ha.

Domaine de Breton (Fr). A vineyard in the commune of Saint Martial. A.C. Côtes de Bordeaux Saint Macaire.

Domaine de Brochon (Fr). A vineyard in the commune of Arbanats. A.C. Graves, Bordeaux. 5 ha. (red and white).

Domaine de Brondelle (Fr). A vineyard in the commune of Langon. A.C. Graves, Bordeaux. 2 ha. (white).

Domaine de Brouillaud (Fr). A vineyard in the commune of St-Médard-d'Eyrans. A.C. Graves, Bordeaux. 7 ha. (white).

Domaine de Bujan (Fr). A vineyard in the

commune of Gauriac. A.C. Côtes de Bourg, Bordeaux.

Domaine de By (Fr). A vineyard in the commune of Bégadan. A.C. Médoc, Bordeaux. 31 ha.

Domaine de Cantereau (Fr). A vineyard in the commune of Pomerol. A.C. Pomerol, Bordeaux. 1 ha.

Domaine de Caplane (Fr). A vineyard in the commune of Sauternes. A.C. Sauternes, Bordeaux. 5 ha.

Domaine de Cassah (Fr). A vineyard in the commune of Pusseguin-Saint-Émilion. A.C. Saint-Émilion, Bordeaux. 6 ha.

Domaine de Cassanel (Fr). An Armagnac producer. See Pallas S.A. (San Gil).

Domaine de Casseuil (Fr). A vineyard in the commune of Langon. A.C. Graves, Bordeaux. 4 ha. (white).

Domaine de Castel Oualou (Fr). A vineyard in the A.C. Lirac, Rhône. Address = 30150 Roquemaure, Gard.

Domaine de Chante-Perdix (Fr). A vineyard estate in the A.C. Châteauneuf-du-Pape, southern Rhône.

Domaine de Chevalier (Fr). Address = 33850 Léognan. Grand Cru Classé. A.C. Graves. Commune = Léognan. 18 ha. Grape varieties – Cabernet franc 5%, Cabernet sauvignon 65% and Merlot 30%.

Domaine de Christoly (Fr). A vineyard in the commune of Prignac Marcamps. A.C. Côtes de Bourg, Bordeaux.

Domaine de Ciron (Fr). A vineyard in the commune of Pujols. A.C. Graves, Bordeaux. 5 ha. (white).

Domaine de Clare (Fr). A vineyard in the commune of Landiras. A.C. Graves, Bordeaux. 3 ha. (white).

Domaine de Clastron (Fr). A vineyard in the A.C. Côtes-de-Provence. 28 ha. Address = 83920 La Motte. Grape varieties – Cabernet sauvignon, Cinsault, Grenache and Syrah.

Domaine de Clostel (Fr). A vineyard in the A.C. Savennières, Anjou-Saumur, Loire.

Domaine de Couitte (Fr). A vineyard in the commune of Prignac. A.C. Sauternes, Bordeaux. 3 ha.

Domaine de Coullander (Fr). A vineyard in the commune of Sainte-Croix-du-Mont. A.C. Sainte-Croix-du-Mont, Bordeaux. 1 ha.

Domaine de Courbon (Fr). A vineyard in the commune of Toulenne. A.C. Graves, Bordeaux. 4 ha. (white).

Domaine de Courniaud (Fr). A vineyard in the commune of Montagne-Saint-Émilion. A.C. Saint-Émilion, Bordeaux. 5 ha.

D

Domaine de Courniaud-Lussac (Fr). A vineyard in the commune of Lussac-Saint-Émilion. A.C. Saint-Émilion, Bordeaux. 3 ha.

Domaine de Curebourse (Fr). The second wine of Château Dufort-Vivens, Grand Cru Classé (2nd) A.C. Margaux.

Domaine de Darrouban (Fr). A vineyard in the commune of Portets. A.C. Graves, Bordeaux. 5 ha. (red and white).

Domaine de Durban (Fr). Address = 84190 Beaumes-de-Venise, Vaucluse. A vineyard in the A.C. Beaumes-de-Venise, Côtes du Rhône-Villages, south-eastern France.

Domaine de Durce (Fr). A vineyard in the commune of Portets. A.C. Graves, Bordeaux. 3 ha. (red and white). Also Domaine de Papoula.

Domaine de Faye (Fr). A vineyard in the commune of Portets. A.C. Graves, Bordeaux. 3 ha. (red and white).

Domaine de Fief Guerin (Fr). A vineyard in the A.C. Muscadet de Sèvre et Maine, Pays Nantais, Loire.

Domaine de Fonbonne (Fr). A vineyard in the commune of Teuillac. A.C. Côtes de Bourg, Bordeaux.

Domaine de Fonbonne-Agassac (Fr). A vineyard in the commune of Ludon. A.C. Médoc, Bordeaux. Cru Bourgeois.

Domaine de Fontarney (Fr). The second wine of Château Brane-Cantenac. Grand Cru Classé (2nd). Margaux.

Domaine de Fontmurée (Fr). A vineyard in the commune of Montagne-Saint-Émilion. A.C. Saint-Émilion, Bordeaux. 10 ha.

Domaine de Fouquet (Fr). A vineyard in the commune of Saint-Émilion. A.C. Saint-Émilion, Bordeaux. 6 ha.

Domaine de Fourn (Fr). An A.C. Blanquette de Limoux, Languedoc, south-western France.

Domaine de Freigate (Fr). A vineyard in the A.C. Bandol, Provence, south-eastern France.

Domaine de Fussignac (Fr). A.C. Bordeaux Supérieur, Bordeaux Blanc and Bordeaux Mousseux.

Domaine de Gaillat (Fr). A vineyard in the commune of Langon. A.C. Médoc, Bordeaux.

Domaine de Gamage (Fr). A vineyard in the commune of Saint-Pey-de-Castets. A.C. Bordeaux Supérieur. Address = Saint-Pey-de-Castets, 33350 Castillon la Bataille.

Domaine de Gardennes (Fr). A vineyard in the commune of Illats. A.C. Cérons, Bordeaux. 3 ha.

Domaine de Godons (Fr). Address = Route de Sancerre, 18300 Sury-en-Vaux. A vineyard in the A.C. Sancerre, Central Vineyards, Loire.

Domaine de Grand Moine (Fr). A vineyard in the commune of Lalande de Pomerol. A.C. Lalande de Pomerol, Bordeaux.

Domaine de Grangeneuve (Fr). A vineyard in the A.C. Coteaux du Tricastin. Grape varieties – Cinsault, Grenache and Syrah.

Domaine de Graulet (Fr). A vineyard in the commune of Plassac. A.C. Côtes de Blaye, Bordeaux.

Domaine de Gravette (Fr). A vineyard in the commune of St-Morillon. A.C. Graves, Bordeaux. 15 ha. (white).

Domaine de Grimon (Fr). A vineyard in the commune of Saint-Georges-Saint-Émilion. A.C. Saint-Émilion, Bordeaux. 5 ha.

Domaine de Guérin (Fr). A vineyard in the commune of Castres. A.C. Graves, Bordeaux. 4 ha. (red).

Domaine de Guerrit (Fr). A vineyard in the commune of Tauriac. A.C. Côtes de Bourg, Bordeaux.

Domaine de Guirauton (Fr). A vineyard in the commune of St-Morillon. A.C. Graves, Bordeaux. 6 ha. (red and white).

Domaine de Haut-Barbey (Fr). A vineyard in the A.C. Saint-Émilion, Bordeaux. 2 ha.

Domaine de Haut-Blanc (Fr). A vineyard in the commune of Pujols. A.C. Graves, Bordeaux. (white).

Domaine de Haut-Courneau (Fr). A vineyard in the commune of Portets. A.C. Graves, Bordeaux. 10 ha. (red and white).

Domaine de Haut-Marchand (Fr). A vineyard in the commune of Montagne-Saint-Émilion. A.C. Saint-Émilion, Bordeaux. 4 ha.

Domaine de Haut-Pignin (Fr). A vineyard in the commune of Pomerol. A.C. Pomerol, Bordeaux. 2 ha.

Domaine de Haut-Tropchaud (Fr). A vineyard in the commune of Pomerol. A.C. Pomerol, Bordeaux. 1 ha.

Domaine de Hourbanon (Fr). Cru Bourgeois. A.C. Médoc. 15 ha. Grape varieties – Cabernet franc, Cabernet sauvignon and Merlot.

Domaine de Hyvernière (Fr). A vineyard in the A.C. Muscadet de Sèvre et Maine, Pays Nantais, Loire.

Domaine de Jarras (Fr). An A.C. rosé wine produced by Listel in the Midi, southern France.

Domaine de Jaussans (Fr). A vineyard in the commune of Illats. A.C. Cérons, Bordeaux. 8 ha.

Domaine de Jean-Marie (Fr). A vineyard in the A.C. Saint-Émilion, Bordeaux. 2 ha.

Domaine de l'Abbaye-Skinner (Fr). A vineyard in the commune of Verteuil. A.C. Médoc, Bordeaux. Cru Bourgeois.

D

Domaine de Labeillon (Fr). A vineyard in the commune of St-Pierre-de-Mons. A.C. Graves, Bordeaux. 2 ha. (white).

Domaine de la Blancherie (Fr). A vineyard in the commune of La Brède. A.C. Graves, Bordeaux. 10 ha. (white).

Domaine de la Bodinière (Fr). A.C. Muscadet de Sèvre et Maine. Domaine bottled. Address = La Bodinière, Vallet, Loire Atlantique.

Domaine de Labouade-Rambaud (Fr). A vineyard in the commune of Barsac. A C. Barsac (or Sauternes), Bordeaux. 1 ha.

Domaine de la Bretonnière (Fr). A vineyard in the A.C. Muscadet de Sèvre et Maine, Pays Nantais, Loire. Domaine bottled.

Domaine de Lacapère (Fr). A vineyard in the commune of Landiras. A.C. Graves, Bordeaux. 2 ha. (white).

Domaine de la Cassemichère (Fr). A vineyard in the A.C. Muscadet de Sèvre et Maine, Pays Nantais, Loire. Domaine bottled.

Domaine de la Cateau (Fr). A vineyard in the A.C. Saint-Émilion, Bordeaux. 3 ha.

Domaine de la Chapelle (Fr). A vineyard in the commune of Preignac. A.C. Sauternes, Bordeaux. 3 ha.

Domaine de la Chapelle (Fr). A vineyard in the A.C. Saint-Émilion, Bordeaux. 3 ha.

Domaine de la Chartreuse (Fr). A vineyard in the A.C. Côtes du Rhône, southern France.

Domaine de la Chauvillière (Fr). A noted Pineau des Charentes producer in Cognac.

Domaine de la Chevalerie (Fr). A vineyard in the A.C. Bourgueil, Touraine, Loire. Address = Restigné 37140.

Domaine de la Citadelle (Fr). A vineyard in the commune of Illats. A.C. Cérons, Bordeaux. 4 ha.

Domaine de la Clotte (Fr). A vineyard in the commune of Montagne-Saint-Émilion. A.C. Saint-Émilion, Bordeaux. 5 ha.

Domaine de Lacoste (Fr). A vineyard in the commune of Sainte-Croix-du-Mont. A.C. Sainte-Croix-du-Mont, Bordeaux. 2 ha.

Domaine de la Cour (Fr). A vineyard in the A.C. Muscadet de Sèvre et Maine. Domaine bottled. Address = 44 Chapelle-Heulin, Loire Atlantique.

Domaine de la Courrège (Fr). A vineyard in the commune of Illats. A.C. Graves, Bordeaux. Grape varieties – Cabernet sauvignon and Merlot. (red and white).

Domaine de la Coustarelle (Fr). Address = 46220 Frayssac. A vineyard in the A.C. Cahors, south-western France.

Domaine de la Croix (Fr). A vineyard in the commune of Langon. A.C. Graves, Bordeaux. 4 ha. (white).

Domaine de la Croix (Fr). A vineyard in the commune of Ordonnac. A.C. Médoc, Bordeaux. 16 ha.

Domaine de la Croix-Mazerat (Fr). A vineyard in the A.C. Saint-Émilion, Bordeaux. 2 ha.

Domaine de la Dimerie (Fr). A vineyard in the A.C. Muscadet de Sèvre et Maine, Pays Nantais, Loire.

Domaine de la Faubretière (Fr). A vineyard in the A.C. Muscadet de Sèrve et Maine, Pays Nantais, Loire.

Domaine de la Fèvrie (Fr). A vineyard in the A.C. Muscadet de Sèvre et Maine, Pays Nantais, Loire. Sur Lie.

Domaine de Lafon (Fr). A vineyard in the commune of Prignac. A.C. Médoc, Bordeaux. 3 ha.

Domaine de la Font-du-Loup (Fr). A vineyard in the A.C. Châteauneuf-du-Pape, Rhône, southern France. 12.5 ha.

Domaine de la Forêt (Fr). A vineyard in the commune of Preignac. A.C. Sauternes, Bordeaux. 21 ha.

Domaine de la Fruitière (Fr). A vineyard in the A.C. Muscadet de Sèvre et Maine, Pays Nantais, Loire.

Domaine de la Gaffelière (Fr). A vineyard in the A.C. Saint-Émilion, Bordeaux. 2 ha.

Domaine de la Genetière (Fr). A vineyard in the A.C. Tavel, southern Rhône.

Domaine de la Girafe (Fr). A vineyard in the commune of Portets. A.C. Graves, Bordeaux. 7 ha. (red and white).

Domaine de la Gleyre (Fr). A vineyard in the commune of Pujols. A.C. Graves, Bordeaux. 2 ha. (white).

Domaine de Lagraulet (Fr). An Armagnac produced by the Domaine de Lasgraves.

Domaine de la Grave (Fr). A vineyard in the commune of St-Selve. A.C. Graves, Bordeaux. 3 ha. (white).

Domaine de la Haute-Faucherie (Fr). A vineyard in the commune of Montagne-Saint-Émilion. A.C. Saint-Émilion, Bordeaux. 3 ha.

Domaine de la Hautière (Fr). A vineyard in the A.C. Muscadet de Sèvre et Maine, Pays Nantais, Loire.

Domaine de Lajorty (Fr). A.C. Graves. Commune = Langon. See Château Balouet-Roailloy.

Domaine de la Lagune (Fr). A vineyard in the commune of Bégadan. A.C. Médoc, Bordeaux. 5 ha.

Domaine de Lalibarde (Fr). A vineyard in the commune of Bourg. A.C. Côtes de Bourg, Bordeaux.

Domaine de la Loge (Fr). A vineyard in the A.C. Muscadet de Sèvre et Maine. Address = 44330 Vallet, Loire Atlantique.

Domaine de Lamaçonne (Fr). A vineyard in the commune of Montagne-Saint-Émilion. A.C. Saint-Émilion, Bordeaux. 3 ha.

Domaine de la Maladière (Fr). The brand label used by William Fèvre in Chablis, Burgundy.

Domaine de Lamothe (Fr). Fine distillers of Armagnac based in Canon-Bordeaux. Noted for Gauvin 40% alc. by vol.

Domaine de la Motte (Fr). A vineyard in the A.C. Coteaux du Layon, Anjou-Saumur, Loire.

Domaine de la Mouchetière (Fr). A vineyard in the A.C. Muscadet de Sèvre et Maine. Address = 44430 Laraux-Battereau, Vallet, Loire Atlantique.

Domaine de la Mouleyre (Fr). A vineyard in the A.C. Saint-Émilion, Bordeaux. 5 ha.

Domaine de l'Angebert (Fr). A vineyard in the A.C. Muscadet de Sèvre et Maine, Pays Nantais, Loire.

Domaine de la Noirie (Fr). A vineyard in the commune of Morgon. A.C. Morgon Cru Beaujolais-Villages, Burgundy.

Domaine de la Perrière (Fr). Address = La Perrière, 37500 Cravant-les-Coteaux. A vineyard in the A.C. Chinon, Anjou-Saumur, Loire.

Domaine de Laplaigne (Fr). A vineyard in the commune of Puisseguin-Saint-Émilion. A.C. Saint-Émilion, Bordeaux. 7 ha.

Domaine de Laraude (Fr). A vineyard in the commune Sauternes. A.C. Sauternes, Bordeaux. 2 ha.

Domaine de l'Ardennerie (Fr). A vineyard in the A.C. Muscadet de Sèvre et Maine. Address = 44450 La Chapelle, Basse-Mer, Loire.

Domaine de la Renjardière (Fr). A vineyard in the A.C. Côtes du Rhône, southern France.

Domaine de l'Arieste (Fr). A vineyard in the commune of Preignac. A.C. Sauternes, Bordeaux. 8 ha.

Domaine de Larnavey (Fr). A vineyard in the commune of St-Selve. A.C. Graves, Bordeaux. 2 ha. (red).

Domaine de la Roche-Marot (Fr). A vineyard in the A.C. Bergerac, south-western France.

Domaine de la Rocher (Fr). A vineyard in the A.C. Muscadet de Sèvre et Maine, Pays Nantais, Loire.

Domaine de la Rose (Fr). A vineyard in the A.C. Saint-Émilion, Bordeaux. 2 ha.

Domaine de la Roudette (Fr). A vineyard in the commune of Sauternes. A.C. Sauternes, Bordeaux. 2 ha.

Domaine de la Rouillère (Fr). A vineyard in the A.C. Côtes-de-Provence, south-eastern France. Address = St-Tropel, Gassin-Var.

Domaine de la Salle (Fr). Address = Château Sansonnet, 33330 Saint-Émilion. A.C. Saint-Émilion. Commune = Saint-Émilion.

Domaine de Lasgraves (Fr). Armagnac producer. Address = 10 Impasse Andrée Cherier, 40000 Mont de Marsan. 8 ha. in Bas Armagnac. Produces – Domaine de Lagraulet and Domaine de Martiques.

Domaine de la Solitude (Fr). A vineyard estate in the A.C. Châteauneuf-du-Pape, southern Rhône. 33.5 ha.

Domaine de la Solitude (Fr). Address = 33650 Martillac. A.C. Graves. Commune = Léognan. 23 ha. Grape varieties – Cabernet franc, Cabernet sauvignon, Merlot, Sauvignon 50% and Sémillon 50%.

Domaine de la Soucherie (Fr). A vineyard in the A.C. Coteaux du Layon, Anjou-Saumur, Loire.

Domaine de Lassalle (Fr). A vineyard in the commune of La Brède. A.C. Graves, Bordeaux. 6 ha. (red and white).

Domaine de la Trappe (Alg). A red wine produced in the south-eastern region of Algeria.

Domaine de la Treille (Fr). A.C. Fleurie. Cru Beaujolais-Villages, Burgundy.

Domaine de la Tuilière (Fr). Address = Pourcieux, 83470 Maximin. A vineyard in the A.C. Côtes-de-Provence. (red and rosé).

Domaine Latuque Bel Air (Fr). A vineyard in the A.C. Côtes de Castillon, Bordeaux.

Domaine de l'Aurière (Fr). A vineyard in the A.C. Muscadet de Sèvre et Maine. Address = Vallet, Loire Atlantique.

Domaine de la Vialle (Fr). A vineyard in the A.C. Côtes du Rhône, southern France.

Domaine de la Vieille-Cloche (Fr). A vineyard in the A.C. Saint-Émilion, Bordeaux. 4 ha.

Domaine de la Vieille-École (Fr). A vineyard in the commune of Pomerol. A.C. Pomerol, Bordeaux. 1 ha.

Domaine de la Voulte (Fr). A vineyard in the A.C. Corbières, Languedoc, south-western France.

Domaine de l'Écu (Fr). A vineyard in the A.C. Muscadet de Sèvre et Maine, Pays Nantais, Loire. Sur Lie.

Domaine de l'Église (Fr). A vineyard in the commune of Pomerol. A.C. Pomerol, Bordeaux. The oldest estate in Pomerol. 7 ha.

D

Domaine de l'Épenay (Fr). A vineyard in the A.C. Vouvray, Touraine, Loire. Produces sparkling (méthode champenoise) wines. Address = 37210 Vouvray.

Domaine de l'Escaley (Fr). A vineyard in the commune of Sainte-Croix-du-Mont. A.C. Sainte-Croix-du-Mont, Bordeaux. 2 ha.

Domaine de l'Hôpital (Fr). A vineyard in the commune of Castres. A.C. Graves, Bordeaux. 3 ha. (red).

Domaine de l'Hyvernière (Fr). A vineyard in the A.C. Muscadet de Sèvre et Maine, Pays Nantais, Loire. Sur Lie.

Domaine de l'If (Fr). A vineyard in the commune of Sainte-Croix-du-Mont. A.C. Sainte-Croix-du-Mont, Bordeaux. 3 ha.

Domaine de l'Île Margaux (Fr). A vineyard in the Île de la Tour de Mons, Gironde. A.C. Bordeaux Supérieur. 16 ha.

Domaine de Louisot (Fr). A vineyard in the commune of Virelade. A.C. Graves, Bordeaux. 4 ha. (white).

Domaine de Louqsor (Fr). A vineyard in the commune of Sainte-Croix-du-Mont. A.C. Sainte-Croix-du-Mont, Bordeaux. 1 ha.

Domaine de Magnol (Fr). A vineyard in the commune of Blanquefort. A.C. Haut-Médoc, Bordeaux. 9 ha.

Domaine de Maisonneuve (Fr). A vineyard in the commune of Saint-Georges-Saint-Émilion. A.C. Saint-Émilion, Bordeaux. 17 ha.

Domaine de Marchandise (Fr). Address = 83520 Roquebrune-sur-Argens. A vineyard in the A.C. Côtes-de-Provence. (red and rosé).

Domaine de Maron (Fr). A vineyard in the commune of Landiras. A.C. Graves, Bordeaux. 2 ha. (red).

Domaine de Marquisat (Fr). A vineyard in the commune of Lansac. A.C. Côtes de Bourg, Bordeaux.

Domaine de Martinoles (Fr). A winery based in St. Hilaire, southern France. Produces a sparkling (méthode champenoise) wine.

Domaine de Martiques (Fr). Armagnac produced by Domaine de Lasgraves.

Domaine de Mathalin (Fr). A vineyard in the commune of Barsac. A.C. Barsac (or Sauternes), Bordeaux. 1 ha.

Domaine de Matourne (Fr). A vineyard in the A.C. Côtes-de-Provence. Address = 83780 Flayosc.

Domaine de Mayrac (Fr). A vineyard in the Vins de Pays de Haute Vallée de l'Aude. Grape varieties – Cabernet franc, Cabernet sauvignon and Merlot.

Domaine de Menaut Larrouquey (Fr). A vineyard in the commune of Cérons. A.C. Cérons, Bordeaux. 12 ha.

Domaine de Meriguet (Fr). A vineyard in the A.C. Cahors, south-western France.

Domaine de Metivier (Fr). A vineyard in the commune of Ayguemortes. A.C. Graves, Bordeaux. 3 ha. (white).

Domaine de Mongenan (Fr). A vineyard in the commune of Portets. A.C. Graves, Bordeaux. 5 ha. (red and white).

Domaine de Monteils (Fr). A vineyard in the commune of Preignac. A.C. Sauternes, Bordeaux. 7 ha.

Domaine de Montifaud (Fr). Cognac producer. Address = Jarnac, Champagne 17520 Archaic. 50 ha. in the Petite Champagne.

Domaine de Mont-Redon (Fr). A vineyard estate in the A.C. Châteauneuf-du-Pape, Rhône. 95 ha. Address = 84230 Châteauneuf-du-Pape. (red and white).

Domaine de Montremblant (Fr). A vineyard in the A.C. Saint-Émilion, Bordeaux. 5 ha.

Domaine de Mortiers Gobin (Fr). A vineyard in the A.C. Muscadet de Sèvre et Maine, Pays Nantais, Loire. Address = Robert Brosseau, La Haie Fouassière.

Domaine de Mouchac (Fr). A single vineyard in the Bas Armagnac. The grapes grown are produced into Armagnac by Janneau.

Domaine de Mounic (Fr). A vineyard in the commune of Fargues. A.C. Sauternes, Bordeaux. 1 ha.

Domaine de Musset (Fr). A vineyard in the commune of Lalande-de-Pomerol. A.C. Lalande-de-Pomerol, Bordeaux.

Domaine de Nalys (Fr). A vineyard estate in the A.C. Châteauneuf-du-Pape, Rhône. 52 ha. (red and white). See Dufays (Doctor).

Domaine de Noriou-Lalibarde (Fr). A vineyard in the commune of Bourg. Côtes de Bourg, Bordeaux.

Domaine de Pallus Beauséjour (Fr). A vineyard in the A.C. Chinon, Touraine, Loire. Address = 37500 Cravant-les-Coteaux, Loire.

Domaine de Pampelune (Fr). A vineyard in commune of Sainte-Croix-du-Mont. A.C. Sainte-Croix-du-Mont, Bordeaux. 3 ha.

Domaine de Panisse (Fr). A vineyard estate in the A.C. Châteauneuf-du-Pape, Rhône.

Domaine de Paousset (Fr). A.C. Chiroubles. Cru Beaujolais-Villages, Burgundy.

Domaine de Papoula (Fr). A vineyard in the commune of Portets. A.C. Graves, Bordeaux. 3 ha. (red and white). Also Domaine de Durce.

Domaine de Parenteau (Fr). A vineyard in

the commune of Sainte-Croix-du-Mont.
A.C. Sainte-Coix-du-Mont, Bordeaux. 4
ha.

Domaine de Pasquette (Fr). A vineyard in
the A.C. Saint-Émilion, Bordeaux. 5 ha.

Domaine de Patache (Fr). A vineyard in
the commune of Bégadan. A.C. Médoc,
Bordeaux. 36 ha.

Domaine de Pérey (Fr). A vineyard in the
A.C. Saint-Émilion, Bordeaux. 2 ha.

Domaine de Petror (Fr). A vineyard in the
commune of Gauriac. A.C. Côtes de
Bourg, Bordeaux.

Domaine de Plantat (Fr). A vineyard in
the commune of St-Morillon. A.C.
Graves, Bordeaux. 9 ha. (red and white).

Domaine de Plantes (Fr). A vineyard in
the commune of Landiras. A.C. Graves,
Bordeaux. 4 ha. (white).

Domaine de Prouzet (Fr). A vineyard in
the commune of Illats. A.C. Cérons,
Bordeaux. 7 ha.

Domaine de Rambaud (Fr). A vineyard in
the commune of Lussac-Saint-Émilion.
A.C. Saint-Émilion, Bordeaux. 3 ha.

Domaine de René (Fr). A vineyard in the
commune of Pomerol. A.C. Pomerol,
Bordeaux. 3 ha.

Domaine de Rey (Fr). A vineyard in the
A.C. Saint-Émilion, Bordeaux. 4 ha.

Domaine de Ribereau (Fr). A vineyard in
the commune of Pugnac. A.C. Côtes de
Bourg, Bordeaux.

Domaine de Rimauresq (Fr). A vineyard
in the commune of Pignans. A.C. Côtes-
de-Provence, south-eastern France.
Address = 83790, Pignans. (red and
white).

Domaine de Rivière (Fr). A vineyard in
the A.C. Saint-Émilion, Bordeaux. 5 ha.

Domaine de Robert (Fr). A vineyard in the
commune of Pomerol. A.C. Pomerol,
Bordeaux. 4 ha.

Domaine de Roby (Fr). A vineyard in the
commune of Loupiac. A.C. Loupiac,
Bordeaux. 5 ha.

Domaine de Rol (Fr). A vineyard in the
A.C. Saint-Émilion, Bordeaux. 3 ha.

Domaine de Roudier (Fr). A vineyard in
the commune of Montagne-Saint-
Émilion. A.C. Saint-Émilion, Bordeaux.
7 ha.

Domaine de Saint Baillon (Fr). A vineyard in the A.C. Côtes-de-Provence,
south-eastern France. Address = Flass-
ans 83340 Le Luc.

Domaine des Anguilleys (Fr). A vineyard
in the commune of Bégadan. A.C.
Médoc, Bordeaux. 8 ha. Part of Château
Vieux Robin.

Domaine des Arcades (Fr). A vineyard in
the commune of Morgon. A.C. Morgon.
Cru Beaujolais-Villages, Burgundy.

Domaine des Aspras (Fr). A vineyard in the
A.C. Côtes-de-Provence, south-eastern
France.

Domaine des Bateliers (Fr). A vineyard in
the A.C. Cahors, south-western France.
Address = Courbenac, 46700 Puy
l'Évêque.

Domaine des Baumard (Fr). A vineyard in
the A.C. Savennières, Anjou-Saumur,
Loire.

Domaine des Beaumard (Fr). A Crémant de
Loire producer based at Rochefort-sur-
Loire.

Domaine des Brissons de Laage (Fr). A
Cognac producer. Address = Reaux,
175000 Jarnac. 72 ha. in the Petite Champagne. Produces and sells its' own
Cognacs.

Domaine des Causses et Saint-Eynes (Fr).
A vineyard in the commune of St-
Laurent-des-Arbes and Saint Victor-la-
Coste. A.C. Lirac, Gard, southern France.

Domaine des Clones (Fr). A vineyard in the
commune of Pomerol. A.C. Pomerol,
Bordeaux. 2 ha.

Domaine des Comtes de Lupfen (Fr). A
noted wine-producer based at Kientzheim, Kaysersberg, Haut-Rhin, Alsace.

Domaine des Cotelins (Fr). A vineyard in
A.C. Sancerre, Central Vineyards, Loire.

**Domaine des Dépendances Cru Jaugue-
blanc** (Fr). A vineyard in the A.C. Saint-
Émilion, Bordeaux. 3 ha.

Domaine des Dorices (Fr). A vineyard in
the A.C. Muscadet de Sèvre et Maine,
Pays Nantais, Loire.

Domaine de Sème (Fr). A vineyard in the
A.C. Saint-Émilion, Bordeaux. 4 ha.

Domaine de Serres (Fr). A vineyard in the
A.C. Châteauneuf-du-Pape, Rhône.

Domaine des Escardos (Fr). A vineyard in
the A.C. Saint-Émilion, Bordeaux. 7 ha.

Domaine des Fontaines (Fr). A.C. Moulin-
à-Vent. Cru Beaujolais-Villages,
Burgundy.

Domaine des Gaillardins (Fr). A vineyard
in the commune of St-Selve. A.C. Graves,
Bordeaux. 4 ha. (white).

Domaine des Gautronnières (Fr). A vineyard in the A.C. Muscadet de Sèvre et
Maine, Pays Nantais, Loire.

Domaine des Grands Bois Chagneau (Fr).
A vineyard in the commune of Néac.
A.C. Lalande de Pomerol, Bordeaux.

Domaine des Grands-Champs (Fr). A vineyard in the commune of Montagne-Saint-
Émilion. A.C. Saint-Émilion, Bordeaux.
4 ha.

Domaine des Grands-Pairs (Fr). A vineyard in the commune of Lussac-Saint-
Émilion. A.C. Saint-Émilion, Bordeaux.
2 ha.

Domaine des Gravières (Fr). A vineyard in

the commune of Portets. A.C. Graves, Bordeaux. 2 ha. (red).

Domaine des Hautes-Pémions (Fr). A vineyard in the A.C. Muscadet de Sèvre et Maine, Pays Nantais, Loire.

Domaine des Hautes Perrières (Fr). A vineyard in the A.C. Muscadet de Sèvre et Maine, Pays Nantais, Loire.

Domaine des Hoscottières (Fr). A vineyard in the A.C. Muscadet de Sèvre et Maine, Pays Nantais, Loire.

Domaine des Justices (Fr). A vineyard in the commune of Preignac. A.C. Sauternes, Bordeaux. 14 ha. Also Châteaux Gilette, Lamothe, Remparts and les Rochers.

Domaine des Lambertins (Fr). A vineyard in the commune of Vacqueyras. A.C. Côtes du Rhône Villages, Rhône.

Domaine des Lauzières (Fr). Address = 13890 Mouries. V.D.Q.S. Coteaux-de-Baux-en-Provence. (red and rosé).

Domaine des Lucques (Fr). A vineyard in the commune of Portets. A.C. Graves, Bordeaux. 7 ha. (red and white).

Domaine des Morines (Fr). A vineyard in the A.C. Muscadet de Sèvre et Maine, Pays Nantais, Loire.

Domaine des Mouilles (Fr). A vineyard in the commune of Juliénas. A.C. Juliénas Cru Beaujolais-Villages, Burgundy.

Domaine des Moulins-à-Vent (Fr). A vineyard in the commune of Illats. A.C. Cérons, Bordeaux. 9 ha.

Domaine des Noyers (Fr). A vineyard in the commune of Sainte-Croix-du-Mont. A.C. Sainte-Croix-du-Mont, Bordeaux. 7 ha.

Domaine des Ollieux (Fr). A vineyard in the A.C. Corbières, Languedoc, southwestern France.

Domaine Despagnet (Fr). A vineyard in the A.C. Saint-Émilion, Bordeaux. 3 ha.

Domaine des Pierres Noires (Fr). A vineyard in the A.C. Muscadet de Sèvre et Maine, Pays Nantais, Loire.

Domaine des Places (Fr). A vineyard in the commune of Arbanats. A.C. Graves, Bordeaux. 3 ha. (red and white).

Domaine des Pontifes (Fr). A vineyard in the A.C. Châteauneuf-du-Pape, southern Rhône.

Domaine des Rochers (Fr). A vineyard in the commune of Côtes de Castillon. A.C. Bordeaux Supérieur, Bordeaux.

Domaine des Rochers (Fr). A vineyard in the A.C. Muscadet de Sèvre et Maine, Pays Nantais, Loire. Address = Moutillon, 44330, Vallet.

Domaine des Rochettes (Fr). A vineyard in the A.C. Anjou, Anjou-Saumur, Loire. Grape variety – Cabernet franc. (red).

Domaine des Rocs (Fr). A vineyard in the commune of Lussac-Saint-Émilion. A.C. Saint-Émilion, Bordeaux. 8 ha.

Domaine des Sarrots (Fr). A vineyard in the commune of St-Pierre-de-Mons. A.C. Graves, Bordeaux. 2 ha. (white).

Domaine des Sénéchaux (Fr). A vineyard in the A.C. Châteauneuf-du-Pape, southern Rhône. Address = 1, Rue de la Nouvelle Poste, B.P. 27, 84230 Châteauneuf-du-Pape.

Domaine d'Esteau (Fr). A part of Château Fontesteau in the A.C. Haut-Médoc, Bordeaux.

Domaine des Templières (Fr). A vineyard in the commune of Lalande de Pomerol. A.C. Lalande de Pomerol, Bordeaux.

Domaine des Terres Blanches (Fr). Address = 13210 Saint-Rémy-de-Provence. V.D.Q.S. Coteaux-des-Baux-en-Provence. (white).

Domaine des Trois Chènes (Fr). A vineyard in the A.C. Muscadet de Sèvre et Maine, Pays Nantais, Loire.

Domaine des Trois Noyers (Fr). A vineyard in the A.C. Sancerre, Central Vineyards, Loire. Address = Verdigny-en-Sancerre.

Domaine de Surget (Fr). A vineyard in the commune of Néac. A.C. Lalande de Pomerol, Bordeaux.

Domaine des Vergnes (Fr). A vineyard in the commune of Portets. A.C. Graves, Bordeaux. 3 ha. (red and white).

Domaine des Villots (Fr). A vineyard in the A.C. Sancerre, Central Vineyards, Loire.

Domaine de Terrefort (Fr). A.C. Bordeaux Supérieur.

Domaine de Terrefort (Fr). A vineyard in the commune of Sauternes. A.C. Sauternes, Bordeaux 3 ha.

Domaine de Teycheney (Fr). A vineyard in the commune of Virelade. A.C. Graves, Bordeaux. 2 ha. (white).

Domaine de Teychon (Fr). A vineyard in the commune of Arbanats. A.C. Graves, Bordeaux. 4 ha. (white).

Domaine de Thalabet (Fr). An A.C. Crozes-Hermitage, Rhône. Produced by Jaboulet Aîné et Fils.

Domaine de Thibar (Afr). A vineyard in Tunisia. Produces wines under Thibar label.

Domaine de Toumalin (Fr). A vineyard in the commune of Fronsac. A.C. Côtes de Canon-Fronsac, Bordeaux. 2 ha.

Domaine de Tourtouil (Fr). A vineyard in the A.C. Tavel, Rhône, Gard. Address = 30126, Tavel, Gard.

Domaine de Trapeau (Fr). A vineyard in the A.C. Saint-Émilion, Bordeaux. 3 ha.

Domaine de Treilhes (Fr). A vineyard in

D

the Languedoc. Produces A.C. Blanquette de Limoux.

Domaine de Trepesson (Fr). A vineyard in the commune of St-Michel. A.C. Côtes de Canon-Fronsac, Bordeaux. 2 ha.

Domaine de Trévallon (Fr). Address = 13150 Saint-Étienne-du-Gris. V.D.Q.S. Coteaux-des-Baux-en-Provence. (red).

Domaine de Valmont (Switz). A red wine produced by Schenk in Salvagnin, Vaud from the Gamay and Pinot noir grapes.

Domaine de Valori (Fr). A vineyard in the A.C. Châteauneuf-du-Pape, Rhône. (red and white).

Domaine de Viaud (Fr). A vineyard in the commune of Lalande de Pomerol. A.C. Lalande de Pomerol, Bordeaux.

Domaine de Viaud (Fr). A vineyard in the commune of Pugnac. A.C. Côtes de Bourg, Bordeaux.

Domaine de Vincent (Fr). A vineyard in the commune of St-Aignan. A.C. Côtes de Fronsac, Bordeaux. 4 ha.

Domaine du Barque (Fr). A vineyard in the commune of St-Selve. A.C. Graves, Bordeaux. 6 ha. (red).

Domaine du Basque (Fr). A vineyard in the commune of Pujols. A.C. Graves, Bordeaux. 3 ha. (white).

Domaine du Beau-Site (Fr). A vineyard in the commune of Portets. A.C. Graves, Bordeaux. 3.5 ha. (red and white).

Domaine du Bois Bruley (Fr). A vineyard in the A.C. Muscadet de Sèvre et Maine, Pays Nantais, Loire. Address = Saint Fiacre sur Maine, Loire Atlantique.

Domaine du Bonat (Fr). A vineyard in the commune of St-Selve. A.C. Graves, Bordeaux. 5 ha. (white).

Domaine du Born (Fr). A vineyard in the commune of Sainte-Croix-du-Mont. A.C. Sainte-Croix-du-Mont, Bordeaux.

Domaine du Bosc (Fr). A vineyard in the Hérault Département. Produces Vins de Pays (red and white) from Cabernet sauvignon, Cinsault, Merlot, Sauvignon blanc and Syrah grapes.

Domaine du Boscq (Fr). A vineyard in the commune of St-Morillon. A.C. Graves, Bordeaux. 2 ha. (white).

Domaine du Bougan (Fr). A vineyard in the commune of Sainte-Croix-du-Mont. A.C. Sainte-Croix-du-Mont, Bordeaux. 3 ha.

Domaine du Bourg (Fr). A vineyard in the commune of Néac. A.C. Lalande de Pomerol, Bordeaux.

Domaine du Bourg (Fr). A vineyard in the A.C. Saint-Émilion, Bordeaux. 2 ha.

Domaine du Bugat (Fr). A vineyard in the commune of Sainte-Croix-du-Mont.

A.C. Sainte-Croix-du-Mont, Bordeaux. 3 ha.

Domaine du Caillou (Fr). A vineyard in the commune of Cérons. A.C. Cérons, Bordeaux. 5 ha.

Domaine du Cardneau (Fr). A vineyard in the commune of Saillans. A.C. Côtes de Fronsac, Bordeaux. 6 ha.

Domaine du Chai (Fr). A vineyard in the commune of Fours. A.C. Côtes de Blaye, Bordeaux.

Domaine du Chasseloir (Fr). A vineyard in the A.C. Muscadet de Sèvre et Maine, Pays Nantais, Loire.

Domaine du Chatain (Fr). A vineyard in the commune of Montagne-Saint-Émilion. A.C. Saint-Émilion, Bordeaux. 3 ha.

Domaine du Chatain (Fr). A vineyard in the commune of Néac. A.C. Lalande de Pomerol, Bordeaux.

Domaine du Chay (Fr). A vineyard in the commune of Loupiac. A.C. Loupiac, Bordeaux. 12 ha.

Domaine du Cléray (Fr). A vineyard in the A.C. Muscadet de Sèvre et Maine, Pays Nantais, Loire.

Domaine du Couprat (Fr). A vineyard in the commune of Saillans. A.C. Côtes de Fronsac, Bordeaux. 5 ha.

Domaine du Courreau (Fr). A vineyard in the commune of St-Médard-d'Eyrans. A.C. Graves, Bordeaux. 3 ha. (red and white).

Domaine du Courreau (Fr). A vineyard in the commune of St-Morillon. A.C. Graves, Bordeaux. 3 ha. (white).

Domaine du Coy (Fr). A vineyard in the commune of Sauternes. A.C. Sauternes, Bordeaux. 3 ha.

Domaine du Crampilh (Fr). A vineyard in the A.C. Madiran, south-western France. (red).

Domaine du Devoy (Fr). Address = St-Laurent-des-Arbes, 30126 Tavel, Gard. A.C. Lirac.

Domaine du Druc (Fr). A vineyard in the commune of Landiras. A.C. Graves, Bordeaux. 2 ha. (white).

Domaine du Faucaudat (Fr). Cognac producer. Address = Gilbert Ricard, 16130 Juillac le Coq. 12 ha. in Grande Champagne.

Domaine du Freyron (Fr). A vineyard in the commune of Cérons. A.C. Cérons, Bordeaux. 3 ha.

Domaine du Gaël (Fr). A vineyard in the commune of Sainte-Croix-du-Mont. A.C. Sainte-Croix-du-Mont, Bordeaux. 2 ha.

Domaine du Gourdins (Fr). A vineyard in the commune of Sables-Saint-Émilion. A.C. Saint-Émilion, Bordeaux. 1 ha.

Domaine du Grand-Abord (Fr). A vineyard in the commune of Portets. A.C. Graves, Bordeaux. 5 ha. (white).

Domaine du Grand-Bigaroux (Fr). A vineyard in the A.C. Saint-Émilion, Bordeaux. 2 ha.

Domaine du Grand Clos (Fr). A vineyard in the A.C. Bourgueil, Touraine, Loire. Address = 37140 Bourgueil, Touraine, Loire.

Domaine du Grand-Faurie (Fr). A commune in the A.C. Saint-Émilion, Bordeaux. 4 ha.

Domaine du Grand-Gontey (Fr). A vineyard in the A.C. Saint-Émilion, Bordeaux. 2 ha.

Domaine du Grand Ormeau (Fr). A vineyard in the commune of Néac. A.C. Lalande de Pomerol, Bordeaux.

Domaine du Grand Tinel (Fr). A vineyard in the A.C. Châteauneuf-du-Pape, southern Rhône. Address = Route de Bédarrides, 84270 Châteauneuf-du-Pape.

Domaine du Haut-Badon (Fr). A vineyard in the A.C. Saint-Émilion, Bordeaux. 3 ha.

Domaine du Haut-Cloquet (Fr). A vineyard in the commune of Pomerol. A.C. Pomerol, Bordeaux. 1 ha.

Domaine Dujac (Fr). Owners and producers of many great wines. Sited at Morey-Saint-Denis. Wines such as Clos de la Roche, Clos Saint-Denis etc.

Domaine du Jau (Fr). A vineyard in the commune of St-Morillon. A.C. Graves, Bordeaux. 3 ha. (white).

Domaine du Labrande (Fr). A vineyard in the commune of Saillans. A.C. Côtes de Fronsac, Bordeaux. 5 ha.

Domaine du Léonard (Fr). A vineyard in the commune of Puisseguin-Saint-Émilion. A.C. Saint-Émilion, Bordeaux. 9 ha.

Domaine du Lucrabey (Fr). A vineyard in the commune of Cussac. A.C. Haut-Médoc, Bordeaux. 5 ha.

Domaine du Mas Blanc (Fr). Address = 66650 Banyuls-sur-Mer. A.C. Banyuls, south-western France. Vin-Doux-Naturel.

Domaine du May (Fr). A vineyard in the commune of Portets. A.C. Graves, Bordeaux. 5 ha. (red and white).

Domaine du Mayne (Fr). A vineyard in the commune of Langon. A.C. Graves, Bordeaux. 3 ha. (white).

Domaine du Mouchez (Fr). A vineyard in the commune of Fronsac. A.C. Côtes de Canon-Fronsac, Bordeaux. 7 ha.

Domaine du Nalys (Fr). A vineyard in the A.C. Châteauneuf-du-Pape, southern Rhône.

Domaine du Pasquet (Fr). A vineyard in the commune of Loupiac. A.C. Loupiac, Bordeaux.

Domaine du Père Caboche (Fr). A vineyard in the A.C. Châteauneuf-du-Pape, southern Rhône. (red and white).

Domaine Duperneau (Fr). A vineyard in the commune of Bommes. A.C. Sauternes, Bordeaux. 3 ha.

Domaine du Petit Clos (Fr). A vineyard in the A.C. Saint-Émilion, Bordeaux. 4 ha.

Domaine du Petit-Gontey (Fr). A vineyard in the A.C. Saint-Émilion, Bordeaux. 3 ha.

Domaine du Petit-Gueyrot (Fr). A vineyard in the A.C. Saint-Émilion, Bordeaux. 2 ha.

Domaine du Petit Metris (Fr). A.C. Coteaux du Layon. Quarts de Chaume. Anjou-Saumur, Loire.

Domaine du Plantey (Fr). A vineyard in the commune of Castres. A.C. Graves, Bordeaux. 3 ha. (red and white).

Domaine du Puynormond (Fr). A vineyard in the commune of Parsac-Saint-Émilion. A.C. Saint-Émilion, Bordeaux. 5 ha.

Domaine du Reys (Fr). A vineyard in the commune of La Brède. A.C. Graves, Bordeaux. 3 ha. Grape varieties – Cabernet 35%, Merlot 65%, Sauvignon 35% and Sémillon 65%. (red and white).

Domaine Durieu (Fr). A vineyard in the A.C. Châteauneuf-du-Pape, southern Rhône. 20 ha.

Domaine du Roudier (Fr). Address = Montagne-Saint-Émilion, 33330 Saint-Émilion. A.C. Montagne-Saint-Émilion. Commune = Montagne-Saint-Émilion.

Domaine du Roux (Fr). A vineyard in the A.C. Saint-Émilion, Bordeaux. 2 ha.

Domaine du Salut (Fr). Name for the wine of Château Huradin. A.C. Cérons, Bordeaux.

Domaine du Sapeur (Fr). A vineyard in the commune of Portets. A.C. Graves, Bordeaux. 4 ha. (red and white).

Domaine du Single (Fr). A vineyard in the A.C. Cahors, south-western France.

Domaine du Ventois (Fr). A vineyard in the A.C. Muscadet de Sèvre et Maine, Pays Nantais, Loire. Address = Place de la Maine, 44 Saint Fiacre, Loire.

Domaine du Vieux Lazaret (Fr). A vineyard in the A.C. Châteauneuf-du-Pape, southern Rhône. Address = 84230 Châteauneuf-du-Pape.

Domaine du Vieux-Moulin-de-Calon (Fr). A vineyard in the commune of Montagne-Saint-Émilion. A.C. Saint-Émilion, Bordeaux. 1 ha.

Domaine du Vieux Télégraphe (Fr). A

vineyard in the A.C. Châteauneuf-du-Pape, southern Rhône. 52 ha. Address = 84370 Bédarrides.

Domaine du Vignots (Fr). A vineyard in the commune of Sainte-Croix-du-Mont. A.C. Sainte-Croix-du-Mont, Bordeaux. 2 ha.

Domaine Étienne (Fr). A vineyard in the commune of St-Morillon. A.C. Graves, Bordeaux. 2 ha. (white).

Domaine Florimond (Fr). A vineyard in the commune of Berson. A.C. Côtes de Blaye, Bordeaux. Address = 33390 Berson, Blaye.

Domaine Font de Michele (Fr). A vineyard in the A.C. Châteauneuf-du-Pape, southern Rhône. 29.5 ha. Address = 84370 Bédarrides. Grape varieties – Bourboulenc, Cinsault, Clairette, Grenache blanc, Mourvèdre and Syrah.

Domaine Franc-Baudron (Fr). A vineyard in the commune of Montagne-Saint-Émilion. A.C. Saint-Émilion, Bordeaux. 6 ha.

Domaine Frapin Grande Fine Champagne (Fr). A fine Cognac produced by Frapin et Cie.

Domaine Geisweiler (Fr). See Geisweiler et Fils.

Domaine Gresser (André et Rémy) (Fr). An Alsace wine producer. Address = 2, Rue de l'Ecole, Andlau 67140 Barr.

Domaine Haut-Caillate (Fr). A vineyard in the commune of Saint-Georges-Saint-Émilion. A.C. Saint-Émilion, Bordeaux. 2 ha.

Domaine Haut-Callens (Fr). A vineyard in the commune of Beautiran. A.C. Graves, Bordeaux. 3 ha. (red).

Domaine Haut-Corbière (Fr). A vineyard in the commune of Sables-Saint-Émilion. A.C. Saint-Émilion, Bordeaux. 2 ha.

Domaine Haute-Rouchonne (Fr). A vineyard in the A.C. Saint-Émilion, Bordeaux. 4 ha.

Domaine Haut-Guillennay (Fr). A vineyard in the commune of Sables-Saint-Émilion. A.C. Saint-Émilion, Bordeaux. 2 ha.

Domaine Haut-Patarabet (Fr). A part of Clos Chante-l'Alouette, A.C. Saint-Émilion, Bordeaux.

Domaine Haut-Trimoulet (Fr). A vineyard in the A.C. Saint-Émilion, Bordeaux. 5 ha.

Domaine Haut-Vachon (Fr). A vineyard in the A.C. Saint-Émilion, Bordeaux. 4 ha.

Domaine Jean-Robert (Fr). A vineyard in the commune of Preignac. A.C. Sauternes, Bordeaux. 1 ha.

Domaine Klipfel (Fr). A vineyard in Alsace. 34 ha. Address = 67140, Barr.

Domaine la Beillonne (Fr). A vineyard in the A.C. Saint-Émilion, Bordeaux. 2 ha.

Domaine la Borie (Fr). A vineyard in the commune of Saillans. A.C. Côtes de Fronsac, Bordeaux. 6 ha.

Domaine la Grave (Fr). Address = 33460 Portets. A.C. Graves. Commune = Portets. 7 ha. Grape varieties – Cabernet sauvignon 50%, Merlot 50% and Sémillon 100%.

Domaine Lagrave de Bertin (Fr). A.C. Bordeaux Supérieur.

Domaine la Jouchère (Fr). A Premier Cru vineyard in the A.C. Chablis, Burgundy.

Domaine la Moussière (Fr). A vineyard in the A.C. Sancerre, Central Vineyards, Loire. Address = B.P. 18, 18300 Sancerre. Loire.

Domaine la Payrère (Fr). A vineyard in the commune of St-Selve. A.C. Graves, Bordeaux. 5 ha. (red and white).

Domaine la Place (Fr). A vineyard in the A.C. Madiran, south-western France.

Domaine la Pointe (Fr). A vineyard in the commune of Pomerol. A.C. Pomerol, Bordeaux. 4 ha.

Domaine la Raze (Fr). A vineyard in the A.C. Bergerac, south-western France. (red).

Domaine Laroche (Fr). Address = 89800 Chablis. Grand Cru Chablis. 'Les Clos'

Domaine Larrouquey (Fr). A vineyard in the commune of Cérons. A.C. Cérons, Bordeaux. 5 ha.

Domaine la Solitude (Fr). A vineyard in the commune of Martillac. A.C. Graves, Bordeaux. 6 ha. (red and white).

Domaine Laurier (USA). A winery based in the Russian River Valley, Sonoma, California. Grape varieties – Cabernet sauvignon, Chardonnay, Johannisberg riesling, Pinot noir and Sauvignon blanc. Produces varietal wines.

Domaine le Breton (Fr). A vineyard in the commune of Massugas. A.C. Saint-Foy-Bordeaux, Bordeaux.

Domaine le Cossu (Fr). A vineyard in the commune of Podensac. A.C. Cérons, Bordeaux. 5 ha.

Domaine le Fief Joyeux (Fr). A.C. Muscadet de Sèvre et Maine. Produced by Donatien Bahuaud.

Domaine les Bernard (Fr). A vineyard in the commune of Saillans. A.C. Côtes de Fronsac, Bordeaux. 4 ha.

Domaine les Cluchets (Fr). A vineyard in the commune of Langon. A.C. Graves, Bordeaux. 4 ha. (white).

Domaine les Genêts (Fr). A vineyard in the commune of Montagne-Saint-Émilion. A.C. Saint-Émilion, Bordeaux. 3 ha.

Domaine les Jays (Fr). A.C. Bordeaux Supérieur.

Domaine les Marcottes (Fr). A vineyard in the commune of Sainte-Croix-du-Mont.

A.C. Sainte-Croix-du-Mont, Bordeaux. 4 ha.

Domaine les Pallières (Fr). A vineyard in the A.C. Gigondas. Côtes du Rhône-Villages, south-eastern France. 25 ha. Grape varieties – Cinsault 10%, Grenache 65%, Mourvèdre 10% and Syrah 10%.

Domaine Lestang (Fr). A vineyard in the commune of St-Selve. A.C. Graves, Bordeaux. 5 ha. (red and white).

Domaine Long-Depaquit (Fr). A vineyard in the A.C. Chablis, Burgundy. (Domaine bottled).

Domaine Marey-Monse (Fr). A négociant-éleveur based in the Côte d'Or, Burgundy.

Domaine Martin (Fr). A vineyard in the commune of Roaillan. A.C. Graves, Bordeaux. 2 ha. (white).

Domaine Montjoie (Fr). A vineyard in the A.C. Corbières, Languedoc, south-western France.

Domaine Mumm (USA). The name given to the Californian branch of G.H. Mumm (Californian Champagne). Produced from 40% Chardonnay and 60% Pinot noir.

Domaine Normand (Fr). A vineyard in the commune of Saillans. A.C. Côtes de Fronsac, Bordeaux. 13 ha.

Domaine Palga Raffault (Fr). A vineyard in the A.C. Chinon, Anjou-Saumur, Loire. Address = Roguinet, 37420 Savigny-en-Veron, Loire.

Domaine Pasquet (Fr). A vineyard in the commune of Escoussans. A.C. Entre-Deux-Mers, Bordeaux.

Domaine Patarabet-la-Gaffelière (Fr). A vineyard in the A.C. Saint-Émilion, Bordeaux. 2 ha.

Domaine Perin de Naudine (Fr). Address = 33640 Portets, Castres-Gironde. A.C. Graves. Commune = Castres. 4.52 ha. Grape varieties – Cabernet 50% and Merlot 50%. (red). See also Château Perin de Naudine.

Domaine Petit-Basque (Fr). A vineyard in the A.C. Saint-Émilion, Bordeaux. 2 ha.

Domaine Pillebourse (Fr). A vineyard in the commune of Saillans. A.C. Côtes de Fronsac, Bordeaux. 3 ha.

Domaine Porto Carras (Gre). A large winery based at Halkidiki, northern Greece. 350 ha. Grape varieties – Cabernet franc, Cabernet sauvignon, Cinsault, Grenache, Merlot, Petite syrah, Sauvignon blanc and Ugni blanc. See also Château Carras and Carras (John).

Domaine Rabion-Pailhas (Fr). A vineyard in the A.C. Saint-Émilion, Bordeaux. 4 ha.

Domaine Ribet (Fr). See Château Guerry.

Domaine Roc de Cailloux (Fr). A vineyard in the A.C. Buzet, south-western France.

Domaine Roland (Fr). A vineyard in the commune of Langon. A.C. Graves, Bordeaux. 3 ha. (white).

Domaine Saint-Jean (Fr). A vineyard in the A.C. Côtes de Provence, south-eastern France. Address = Vignobles Maille, 83570 Carcès.

Domaine Saint Joseph (Fr). A vineyard in the A.C. Corbières, Languedoc, south-western France.

Domaine Saint-Maurice (Fr). A vineyard in the A.C. Corbières, Languedoc, south-western France.

Domaine Saupiquet (Fr). A vineyard in the A.C. Saint-Émilion, Bordeaux. 2 ha.

Domaine Saurrute (Fr). The dry white wine from Château Caillou Grand Cru Classé (2nd), Barsac.

Domaines de Villemajou (Fr). Vineyards in the A.C. Corbières, Languedoc, south-western France.

Domaines du Château de Riquewihr (Fr). Only allocated to Dopff and Irions wines of Château Riquewihr in Alsace of the vineyards Les Sorcières, Amandiers, Maguisards and Murailles.

Domaines Font-Sainte (Fr). Vineyards in the A.C. Corbières, Languedoc, south-western France.

Domaines Ott (Fr). A family-owned winery based in the Côtes de Provence. Produces – Château de Selle, Château Romassan and Clos Mireille. Sold in special shaped bottles.

Domaines Robert Guiraud (Fr). A Bordeaux négociant. Address = B.P. 31, 33240 St. André-de-Cubzac, Gironde. Distributes Château Moulin de Bel-Air exclusively.

Domaine St. Demetrios (USA). A winery based near St. Helena, Napa Valley, California. Grape varieties – Cabernet sauvignon, Chardonnay, Chenin blanc, Gamay, Johannisberg riesling and Sauvignon blanc. Produces varietal wines.

Domaine St. Eulalie (Fr). A vineyard in the V.D.Q.S. Minervois, south-western France.

Domaine St. Gayan (Fr). A vineyard in the A.C. Gigondas, Côtes du Rhône-Villages, south-eastern France.

Domaine St-Jean-de-Béard (Fr). A vineyard in the A.C. Saint-Émilion, Bordeaux. 4 ha.

Domaine St. Roman d'Esclans (Fr). A vineyard in the A.C. Côtes de Provence, south-eastern France.

Domaine Suteau (Fr). A vineyard in the A.C. Muscadet de Sèvre et Maine, Pays Nantais, Loire.

Domaine Tauzinat (Fr). A vineyard in the A.C. Saint-Émilion, Bordeaux. 3 ha.

Domaine Tchit (Fr). A vineyard in the

commune of Fargues. A.C. Sauternes, Bordeaux. 1 ha.

Domaine Templar (Fr). A vineyard in the A.C. Bandol, Provence, south-eastern France. (red).

Domaine Vachon (Fr). A vineyard in the A.C. Saint-Émilion, Bordeaux. 3 ha.

Domaine Viticoles (Fr). A large co-operative winery based in Salins du Midi, south-western France. 1,700 ha.

Domaine Viticole Schlumberger (Fr). Alsace wine producer. Address = 100, Rue Theodore Deck, 68500 Guebwiller.

Domaine Weinbach (Fr). A Grand Cru vineyard in A.C. Alsace. Owned by Théo Faller. Grape variety – Riesling.

Domaine Zind-Humbrecht (Fr). A vineyard in the A.C. Alsace. 26.5 ha. Address = Wintzenheim, 68000 Colmar.

Domäne (Ger). Usually a state-owned or state-managed vineyard or property.

Domänerat (Ger). State-managed vineyards.

Domange (Christian) (Fr). Armagnac producer. Address = Domaine de la Las Lannes, Bezolles 32310 Valence-sur-Baise. Produces Hors d'Âge 10 year old.

Domažlice Brewery (Czec). An old brewery based in western Czec. c1341.

Domberg (Ger). Vineyard. (Anb) = Nahe. (Ber) = Kreuznach. (Gro) = Schlosskapelle. (Vil) = Waldlaubersheim.

Domberg (Ger). Vineyard. (Anb) = Nahe. (Ber) = Schloss Böckelheim. (Gro) = Paradiesgarten. (Vil) = Sobernheim.

Domblick (Ger). Grosslage. (Anb) = Rheinhessen. (Ber) = Wonnegau. (Vils) =. Hohen-Sülzen, Mölsheim, Monsheim, Offstein, Wachenheim

D.O.M. Cocktail (Cktl). ⅓ gill Gin, ⅙ gill orange juice, ⅛ gill Bénédictine. Shake over ice, strain into a goblet.

Domdechaney (Ger). Vineyard. (Anb) = Rheingau. (Ber) = Johannisberg. (Gro) = Daubhaus. (Vil) = Hochheim. Lit – 'Deanery'.

Domecq (Sp). Brandy producer. Address = Pedro Domecq SA, San Ildefonso N° 3, Jerez 30. Wines from Estremadura, Huelva and La Mancha. Produces – Tres Cepas 2 year old, Fundador 3 year old, Carlos 111 6 year old, and Carlos 1 12 year old. Also produce a well known range of Sherries (see Double Century).

Domecq (Sp). A great Sherry family. Own 2,600 ha. of vineyards in Jerez de la Frontera. Noted Sherry-brands include Bolivar, Celebration, Double Century, Imperial 1914, La Ina, MDV, Napoleon, Nelson, Rio Viejo and Sibarita. Also a noted Brandy producer.

Domecq Domain (Sp). The brand-name

for red and white wines produced by the Bodegas Domecq S.A., Rioja.

Domecq Double Century (Sp). The brand-name for a light dry sherry produced by Domecq in Jerez.

Dömek (Tur). To pour a drink.

Domestic Spumante (USA). An American type of sparkling wine. Carbon-dioxide is added artificially.

Domgarten (Ger). Vineyard. (Anb) = Mosel-Saar-Ruwer. (Ber) = Zell/Mosel. (Gro) = Weinhex. (Vil) = Winningen.

Dom Henriques (Mad). The label used by Tarquinio Lomelino for their range of Madeiras.

Domherr (Ger). Vineyard. (Anb) = Mosel-Saar-Ruwer. (Ber) = Bernkastel. (Gro) = Michelsberg. (Vil) = Piesport.

Domherr (Ger). Grosslage. (Anb) = Rheinhessen. (Ber) = Nierstein. (Vils) = Budenheim, Essenheim, Gabsheim, Klein-Winternheim, Mainz-Drais, Mainz-Finthen, Ober-Olm, Saulheim, Schornsheim, Stadecken-Elsheim, Udenheim.

Domherrenberg (Ger). Vineyard. (Anb) = Mosel-Saar-Ruwer. (Ber) = Saar-Ruwer. (Gro) = Römerlay. (Vil) = Trier.

Domherrenberg (Ger). Vineyard. (Anb) = Mosel-Saar-Ruwer. (Ber) = Zell/ Mosel. (Gro) = Schwarze Katz. (Vil) = Zell.

Domina (Ger). A red grape variety. A cross between the Portugieser and the Spätburgunder. Produces sound wines.

Domingas Ranch (USA). The former name used for the Beatty Ranch Vineyard in the Napa Valley, Sonoma, California.

Dominica (W.Ind). A coffee-producing island. Produces strong-flavoured and full-bodied coffees.

Dominicus Fino (Eng). A fine, dry, Fino sherry from the Peter Dominic wine shops.

Dominikanerberg (Ger). Vineyard. (Anb) = Mosel-Saar-Ruwer. (Ber) = Saar-Ruwer. (Gro) = Römerlay. (Vil) = Kasel.

Dominikanerberg (Ger). Vineyard. (Anb) = Mosel-Saar-Ruwer. (Ber) = Saar-Ruwer. (Gro) = Römerlay. (Vil) = Morscheid.

Dominion (N.Z.). A company in Auckland which invented continuous fermentation. Is the second largest brewing group in the country.

Dominion Ale (Can). A bottom-fermented Beer brewed in Newfoundland by the Dominion Brewery.

Dominode (La) (Fr). A Premier Cru vineyard in the A.C. commune of Savigny-lès-Beaune, Côte de Beaune, Burgundy.

Domlay (Ger). Vineyard. (Anb) = Ahr.

(Ber) = Walporzheim/Ahrtal. (Gro) = Klosterberg. (Vil) = Walporzheim.

Dommels Brouwerij (Hol). A brewery owned by the Stella Artois Co.

Dommels Pils (Hol). A Pilsener Beer brewed by the Dommels Brouwerij.

Domoshni (USSR). Home-made (wine).

Dom Pérignon (Fr). 1668–1715. A Bénédictine monk who, as cellar master of the cellars at Hautvillers Abbey, invented the process of second fermen tation in the bottle which put the bubbles in Champagne. See also Ondart and Pérignon (Pierre).

Dom Pérignon (Fr). A De Luxe vintage cuvée Champagne from Moët et Chandon. Sold in a distinctive old-style Champagne bottle.

Domprobst (Ger). Vineyard. (Anb) = Mosel-Saar-Ruwer. (Ber) = Bernkastel. (Gro) = Münzlay. (Vil) = Graach.

Domski (USSR). A white wine produced in the Crimea.

Dom Yago Rosado (Sp). A naturally sparkling, medium-dry, rosé wine produced by Dom Yago using the cuve close method. Is sold under the Gran-Vas label.

Doña Antonia Personel Reserve (Port). A fine old Tawny Port from Ferreira shippers.

Doña Branca (Port). A white grape variety grown in the Dão region.

Dona Juana (Sp). A brand of Sherry produced by Sanchez Romate.

Donau (Ger). An Untergebiet of the Bayern district.

Donau Perle (Bul). Lit – 'Pearl of the Danube'. A full white wine made in the Danube basin from the Fetiaska grape.

Don Cortez (Eng). The brand name for Grants of St. James Spanish wines. Famous in the 1960's for their advertising slogan 'Ten bob the bottle'.

Donetskaya Vodka (USSR). A Vodka produced in Donetsk, Ukraine.

Don Felipe (Sp). A noted Sherry producer of Jerez de la Frontera.

Don Fino (Sp). A dry, Fino sherry produced by Sandeman.

Don García (Sp). The brand-name used by Bodegas García Carrión in Jumilla for a range of red, rosé and white wines.

Dongermain (Fr). A commune in the Côtes de Toul. Lorraine. Produces Vins gris.

Dongine (Fr). The local name used in Bugey for the Mondeuse grape.

Don Guisa (Sp). A brand of Fino sherry produced by Caballero.

Don Jacobo (Sp). The brand-name for wines produced by Bodegas Corral S.A., Alta region, Rioja.

Donjon (Fr). A Brandy- and almond-flavoured liqueur produced by Benoit Serres in Toulouse.

Don Jose (Sp). A soft Oloroso sherry produced by Romate.

Donker (Hol). A sweet, full-bodied, 'old brown' Beer brewed by the De Leeuw Brouwerij in Valkenburg, Limburg.

Donkey Box (Eng). Part of a public house. A snug that seats less than 12 people.

Don Luis (Chile). A light, red, Cabernet-based wine produced by Cousiño Macul.

Don Luis (Sp). A wine produced by the Bodegas Bardón in Ribera Baja from Tempranillo 60% and other grapes.

Don Matias (Chile). A tannic, dark, Cabernet-based red wine produced by Cousiño Macul.

Don Miguel (Chile). A brand of white wine produced by Torres from Gewürztraminer and Riesling grapes.

Donna Antonia (Port). A Vintage character Port produced by Ferreira shippers.

Donna Maria Vineyards (USA). A winery based near Windsor, Sonoma, California. 63 ha. Grape varieties – Gewürztraminer, Pinot noir and Zinfandel. Produces varietal wines.

Don Narciso (Sp). A Brandy produced by Mascaró.

Donnaz (It). D.O.C. red wine from the Val d'Aosta region. Made from the Nebbiolo plus 15% of Freisa, Neyret and Viende nus. From the communes of Bard, Donnaz, Perloz and Pont St. Martin. Must be aged for 3 years (2 in oak or chestnut).

Don Nazario Ortiz Garza (Mex). A Brandy and wine producer based at Soltillo, Coahuila. Also has vineyards in Aguascalientes.

Donnici (It). D.O.C. red or rosé wine from Calabria. Made from the Gaglioppa 50%, Greco nero, Malvasia bianca, Montonico bianco and Pecorella grapes.

Donnington Brewery (Eng). Based at Stow-in-the-Wold, Gloucestershire. Produces – cask conditioned XXX Dark Mild and Double Dunn 1042 O.G.

Donnybrook (Ire). A drunken, rowdy brawl. So named after the nineteenth century Donnybrook fair, an annual event until 1855. Based near Dublin.

Don Pablo Cocktail (Cktl). ⅙ gill golden Rum, juice ¼ lime, ⅓ gill tomato juice, dash Tobasco sauce, celery salt and pepper. Stir well over ice, strain into an ice-filled collins glass. Dress with a stick of celery.

Don Q (W.Ind). The brand-name of a

Puerto Rican Rum distilled by Serralles at Ponce.

Don Ramon (Sp). A full-bodied red wine made with the Garnacha grape by Vincente Suso y Perez in Cariñena, north-eastern Spain.

Don Ramos (Sp). A brand of Fino sherry produced by Bodegas Don Ramos, Jerez de la Frontera.

Don River Valley (USSR). A wine region that produces red, white and sparkling wines. See Donski.

Donski (USSR). A sparkling wine exported to USA. Produced near Rostov in the Don River Valley region.

Don Suero (Sp). A fruity, red, oak-aged wine produced by VILE in León.

Don Thomas (Sp). The brand-name of a Sherry produced by Valdespino.

Donzelinho (Port). A white grape variety used in the making of Port.

Donzelinho Tinto (Port). A red grape variety used in the making of Port.

Don Zoilo (Sp). The world's most expensive range of Sherries produced by Diez-Merito, Diego-Fernandez Herrera, 16, Jerez de la Frontera. Also produce brandies. (Gran Duque d'Alba is a brand).

Dooars (Ind). A tea plantation area in northern India.

Doomsday English Wine (Eng). Produced by St. George's English Wines, Waldron Vineyards, near Heathfield. Produced to commemorate the 900th anniversary of the Doomsday Book.

Doornkaat (Ger). A brand of Kornbranntwein from Norden in north-west Germany. Also called Frisian country wine.

Doornkraal (S.Afr). A vineyard based in Klein Karoo. Produces varietal and dessert wines.

Doosberg (Ger). Vineyard. (Anb) = Rheingau. (Ber) = Johannisberg. (Gro) = Gottesthal. (Vil) = Östrich.

Dop-Brandy (S.Afr). A brandy made by distilling the residue grape pulp from the wine process. (Fr) = Marc. (It) = Grappa.

Dopff-au-Moulin (Fr). Producers of sparkling Alsace wines based at Riquewihr, Alsace. Address = 68340 Riquewihr. 77 ha.

Dopff et Irion (Fr). Noted viticulturalists of Alsace. Address = Château de Riquewihr, 68340 Riquewihr. 37 ha.

Doppelbock (Ger). An extra-strong beer 7.5% alc. by vol. Lit – 'Double bock'. See Eisbock and Salvator.

Doppelbock Dunkel (Ger). A dark double Bock beer from the Andechs Brauerei in Erling-Andechs, Bavaria. Has a rich malty aroma and flavour.

Doppelbock Hell (Ger). A double bock beer from the Andechs Brauerei in Bavaria. A rich malty brew.

Doppelbogen (Ger). The 'Double Guyot' method of vine training. See also Einzelbogen.

Doppelkaramelbier (Ger). A malty Bier enriched with sugar.

Doppelkorn (Ger). A spirit derived from mashed corn, sometimes it is flavoured with herbs. 38% alc. by vol.

Doppelohm (Ger). A cask of the Rhine and Mosel holding 300 litres. (66 gallons).

Doppelstück (Ger). A large oak fermenting cask.

Doppelweizen (Ger). A spirit derived from mashed wheat.

Doppo Cedro (It). A lemon-flavoured liqueur.

Doquet-Jeanmarie (Fr). Champagne producers. Récoltants-manipulants. Address = Route de Voipreux, 51130 Vertus. Produces – Vintage and non-vintage wines.

Dor (A.E.) (Fr). Cognac producer. Address = 14 Bis Rue J. Moreau, 16200 Jarnac. Vineyards 22 ha. in Petite Champagne. Produces – Hors d'Age (35–60 y.o) and Trés Vielle Grande Champagne (a 30 to 60 y.o. the oldest), Roi de Rome, Louis Philippe, Prince Albert, Prince Impérial and Excellence.

D.O.R.A. (Eng) (abbr). Defence of the Realm Act. Restricted pub opening hours during wartime.

Dorada (Sp). A flor-attacked, tawny-gold wine produced by Cooperativa La Seca in La Rueda.

Doradillo (Austr). A white grape variety grown in Riverland in South Australia. One of the varieties used to make brandy.

Doran Lager (Can). A Lager beer brewed by the Doran Brewery.

Dorchester Bitter (Eng). A cask conditioned Ale 1033 O.G. brewed by Eldridge Pope Brewery in Dorchester, Dorset.

Dordogne [River] (Fr). River running to the west coast of France in Bordeaux. Joins the river Garonne to form the river Gironde.

Doreen's Delight (Punch) (Non-alc). 1 bottle Eisberg (alcohol-free) wine, 1 pint Cydrax (alcohol-free) Cider, ½ pint lemonade, ⅓ pint dry ginger, 2 teaspoons Rum essence. Stir with ice, Dress with sliced apples and lemons.

D'Orfin (Fr). A sparkling wine producer based in Aigre. All styles produced.

Dorfprozelten (Ger). Village. (Anb) = Franken. (Ber) = Mainviereck. (Gro) = Not yet assigned. (Vin) = Predigtstuhl.

D

Doria (It). A wine producer based in Oltrepo Pavese in the Lombardy region. Produces sparkling wines by the Tank method.

Dorin (Switz). The local name for the white Chasselas grape in the Vaud region. See Dorin Epesses, Lutry and Vaud.

Dorin (Switz). The generic name for all white wines from the canton of Vaud.

Dorin Epesses (Switz). The local name for the white Chasselas grape in the Vaud region. See also Dorin Lutry and Dorin Vaud.

Dorin Lutry (Switz). The local name for the white Chasselas grape in the Vaud region. See also Dorin Epesses and Dorin Vaud.

Dorin Vaud (Switz). Local name for the white Chasselas grape in the Vaud region. See also Dorin Epesses and Dorin Lutry.

Dörlers Kiwi-Fruit Winery (N.Z.). A winery based at Tawa Road, Kumeu, Ph 412–9723. Produces a medium-dry Kiwi-fruit wine. 10.2% alc. by vol.

Dormalt (Eng). A method of malting using a continuous conveyor.

Dormans (Fr). Champagne Canton. District of Épernay. Contains the Cru villages of – Boursault, Champvoisy, Comblizy, Dormans (Chavenay, Try, Vassy and Vassieux), Festigny, Le Breuil, Le Mesnil-le-Hutier, Leuvrigny, Mareuil-le-Port, Nesle-le-Repons, Oeuilly, Port à Binson, Soilly, Troissy-Bouquigny, Verneuil and Vincelles.

Dormans (Fr). A Cru Champagne village in the Canton de Dormans. District = Épernay.

Dorn-Dürkheim (Ger). Village. (Anb) = Rheinhessen. (Ber) = Nierstein. (Gro) = Rheinblick. (Vins) = Hasensprung, Römerberg.

Dornot (Fr). A white wine produced in Lorraine.

Dornpfad (Ger). Vineyard. (Anb) = Rheinhessen. (Ber) = Nierstein. (Gro) =Domherr. (Vil) = Gabsheim.

Doron (Isr). A dry white table wine.

Dörrenbach (Ger). Village. (Anb) = Rheinpfalz. (Ber) = Südliche Weinstrasse. (Gro) = Guttenberg. (Vin) = Wonneberg.

Dörscheid (Ger). Village. (Anb) = Mittelrhein. (Ber) = Rheinburgengau. (Gro) = Herrenberg. (Vins) = Kupferflöz, Wolfsnack.

Dorset Original IPA (Eng). A cask conditioned Bitter 1041 O.G. brewed by the Eldridge Pope Brewery in Dorchester, Dorset.

Dorsheim (Ger). Village. (Anb) = Nahe.

(Ber) = Kreuznach. (Gro) = Schlosskapelle. (Vins) = Burgberg, Goldloch, Honigberg, Jungbrunnen, Klosterpfad, Laurenziweg, Nixenberg, Pittermännchen, Trollberg.

Dorst (Hol). Thirst. Dertig = thirsty.

Dort (Bel). A style of malty Beer with a density of more than 5.0. Is less hopped than a Dortmunder and produced without the use of maize.

Dort (Hol). A malty Beer 6.5% alc. by vol. brewed by the Gulpen Brouwerij in Gulpen, Limburg.

Dortmund Actien Bier (Ger). D.A.B. A Beer made by the Dortmund Actien Brauerei in Dortmund Westphalia. A light beer with a fine hop flavour.

Dortmunder (Ger). A golden beer between a Pilsener and Munchener in flavour. 5.2% alc. by vol. Brewed in Dortmund.

Dortmunder Actien Brauerei (Ger). Also known as D.A.B. A brewery based at Dortmund Westphalia. The biggest in Germany, it produces most styles of German beers and is noted for Altbier and Export.

Dortmunder Export (Ger). A famous beer from the breweries of Dortmund in West Germany. See D.A.B. Export, Hansa Export, Ritter Export, Stifts Export, Thier Export, Dortmunder Kronen Export and D.U.B. Export.

Dortmunder Hansa (Ger). A brewery of Dortmund in Westphalia. Part of the D.A.B. Produces fine Export and light Pilsener beers.

Dortmunder Kronen (Ger). The oldest brewery in Dortmund, Westphalia. Noted for its' fine beers. See Pilskrone, Classic and Dortmunder Kronen Export.

Dortmunder Kronen Export (Ger). A very fine Dortmunder Export beer brewed by the Dortmunder Kronen Brauerei in Dortmund, Westphalia. 5% alc. by vol.

Dortmunder Ritter (Ger). A brewery in Dortmund Westphalia owned by the D.U.B. Schultheiss. It produces average beers. See Ritter Export.

Dortmunder Stifts (Ger). A small brewery in Dortmund Westphalia owned by Watney Mann of G.B. Produces sweetish beers of good quality. See Stifts Export.

Dortmunder Thier (Ger). A small brewery in Dortmund Westphalia. Produces full-bodied malty beers. See Thier Export.

Dortmunder Union (Ger). A medium strength Bier brewed by the D.U.B.

Dortmunder Union Brauerei (Ger). D.U.B. A large brewery in Rheinische

Street, Dortmund, Westphalia. Produces a fine range of beers. See D.U.B. Export, Siegel Pils and Brinckhoffs N°.1.

Dörzbach (Ger). Village. (Anb) = Württemberg. (Ber) = Kocher-Jagst-Tauber. (Gro) = Kocherberg. (Vin) = Altenberg.

D.O.S. (It) (abbr). Denominazione d'Origine Semplice. A plain denomination no longer used since the D.O.C. laws.

Dosage (Fr). After Champagne has been disgorged (dégorgement) it is quite dry so a dosage, which consists of a varying amount of syrup (fortified grape must) is added. The amount of dosage will decide on the class of Champagne e.g. Brut, Extra dry, Sec, Doux.

Dosaïe (Ch.Isles). A drinking bout. See also Daose.

Dos Cortados (Sp). A brand of dry Oloroso sherry from Williams and Humbert, Jerez de la Frontera.

Dos Equis (Mex). Lit – 'Two crosses'. A Vienna-style amber beer.

Dosio (It). Producer of sparkling (méthode champenoise) wines in Piemonte.

Dos Rayas (Sp). Lit – 'Two strokes'. When applied to a sherry butt denotes wines destined to become Olorosos. See Raya.

Dossenheim (Ger). Village. (Anb) = Baden. (Ber) = Badische Bergstrasse/Kraichgau. (Gro) = Rittersberg. (Vin) = Ölberg.

Dotzheim (Ger). Village. (Anb) = Rheingau. (Ber) = Johannisberg. (Gro) = Steinmächer. (Vin) = Judenkirch.

Double (Eng). A double measure of spirits. 2 tots.

Double Ale (Eng). A term for a stronger brewed beer than an ordinary beer.

Double Aum (Ger). A wine cask of 300 litres. See Doppelohm.

Double Brown Ale (Eng). A Brown ale 1037 O.G. brewed by the Bateman's Brewery in Lincolnshire.

Double Brown Beer (Eng). A keg Bitter 1041 O.G. brewed by the John Smith Brewery.

Double Century (Sp). A famous range of sherries produced by Domecq in Jerez de la Frontera.

Double Century Ale (Scot). A bottled Ale 1054 O.G. brewed by the William Younger Brewery in Edinburgh to celebrate their bi-centenary of brewing in 1949.

Double Chance Bitter (Eng). A cask conditioned Ale 1039 O.G. brewed by the Malton's Brewery in North Yorkshire.

Double D (Eng). The nickname for Double Diamond.

Double Dagger Ale (Eng). A Pale ale 1050 O.G. brewed by the Oak Brewery in Cheshire.

Double Diamond (Eng). A famous old Pale ale 1043 O.G. brewed by Ind Coope in Burton-on-Trent. Originates from an old cask-conditioned Burton ale recipe. See D.D.

Double Donn Bitter (Eng). A bottled special Bitter 1042 O.G. brewed by the Donnington Brewery in the Cotswolds.

Double Dragon (Wales). A cask conditioned Bitter 1042 O.G. brewed by the Felinfoel Brewery in Llanelli. First beer to be canned.

Double Enghien (Bel). A dry, full-bodied Ale brewed by the Dupont Brewery in Tourpes.

Double Magnum (Fr). A four-bottle capacity bottle of red wine from the Bordeaux region. See also Jereboam.

Double Maxim Ale (Eng). A Brown ale 1044 O.G. brewed by Vaux Brewery in Sunderland.

Double Q [QQ] (Scot). A blended 12 year old Scotch whisky distributed by the Montrose Whisky Company.

Double Springs (USA). A Bourbon whiskey distillery based in Louisville, Kentucky.

Double Standard Sour (Cktl). ½ measure Gin, ½ measure Bourbon whiskey, juice ½ lemon, 2 dashes Grenadine, 2 dashes Gomme syrup. Shake over ice, strain into a sour glass. Top with a cherry and a slice of lemon.

Double Star Ale (Eng). A Pale ale 1040 O.G. brewed by the Charles Wells Brewery in Bedford.

Double Strong Ale (Wales). A bottled strong Ale 1075 O.G. brewed by the Felinfoel Brewery in Llanelli, South Wales. Sold as Hercules in the USA.

Doublet (Fr). A species of barley malt of the Triumph variety. Gives good sugar yields.

Double Top Ale (Eng). A Brown ale 1033 O.G. brewed by the Higson's Brewery in Liverpool, Lancashire.

Double Whisky (Scot). A mark found on a hydrostatical bubble used to measure alcoholic strengths.

Double Whisky (Eng). See Double.

Double Zero Seven [007] (Cktl). ⅓ gill Bacardi White Label, juice of ¼ lemon and ½ lime, ⅙ gill sweet Vermouth, dash Gomme syrup. Shake over ice, strain into a cocktail glass. Dress with a slice of orange and mint sprig.

Double Zero Seven [007] (Eng). A cask conditioned Bitter 1055 O.G. brewed by the Bridge House home-brew public house in London.

D

Doubling (USA). The name given to the process of re-distilling after the first distillation in Whiskey production.

Doucillon (Fr). A white grape variety grown in the Bandol district of Provence.

Doudet Naudin (Fr). A Burgundy négociant based at Savigny-lès-Beaune, Burgundy.

Dou Dou Fizz (Cktl).(Non-alc). 1 measure coconut cream, 1 measure lemon juice, 1 egg white, ½ measure Gomme syrup. Blend with a scoop of ice in a blender. Pour into a goblet, top with soda and a slice of lemon.

Douglas Co-operative (S.Afr). Vineyards based at Douglas. Address = Douglas Koöperatiewe Wynmakery, Box 47, Douglas 8730. Produces varietal wines.

Douglas Green (S.Afr). Wine merchants of Paarl. Sell many wines under own label, plus many top South African and European wines. Address = Box 3337, Cape Town. See St. Agustine (a wood-aged red wine).

Douglas Koöperatiewe Wynmakery (S.Afr). See Douglas Co-operative.

Douglas Scotch (Fr). The name given to Gordon's Scotch whisky (Belgium) when it crosses the border into France.

Douil (Fr). Large tubs used in the Médoc which are filled with grapes to take them from the vineyards to the winery by cart.

Doukkala (Afr). An A.O.G. wine-producing area in the region of Casablanca, Morocco.

Doura Branca (Port). A white grape variety grown in the Dão region. Is derived from the Riesling. Produces light, fruity, young wine.

Douradinha (Port). A white grape variety grown in Peñafiel (a sub-region of Vinho Verde).

Dourado (Port). A white grape variety grown in the Entre Minho e Douro. Used in the making of Vinhos Verdes.

Douro Bake (Port). A hot taste that is associated with some Port wines produced in very hot summers.

Douro e Tras os Montes (Port). Demarcated regions of Portugal. See Tras os Montes.

Douro Cask (Port). See Douro Pipe.

Douro Pipe (Port). Holds 550 litres. 450 of Wine and 100 of Brandy. See also Pipe.

Douro [River] (Port). A river on whose banks are grown the grapes that go to make Port wine. Northern Portugal. See Duero.

Dourthe Frères (Fr). The principal brand of CVBG in Bordeaux.

Dousico (Gre). An alternative spelling of Douzico.

Douwe Egberts (Hol). Famous coffee producers based at Royal Factories, Utrecht,

Holland. Is noted for its' Moccona (an instant coffee brand).

Doux (Fr). Sweet.

Douzanelle (Fr). An alternative name for the Muscadelle grape in south-western France.

Douzico (Tur). An aniseed-flavoured spirit. Clear, similar to Ouzo. See also Dousico.

Dover Vineyards (USA). A winery based in Westlake, Ohio. Produces mainly Concord wines.

Dow (Hun). The grape pulp (paste) from the grape of Tokay Aszú. The dow goes into the puttonyos.

Dow (Port). Vintage Port shippers. Vintages – 1870, 1872, 1873, 1875, 1878, 1881, 1884, 1887, 1890, 1892, 1896, 1899, 1904, 1908, 1912, 1917, 1919, 1920, 1924, 1927, 1931, 1934, 1935, 1945, 1947, 1950, 1955, 1960, 1963, 1966, 1970, 1972, 1975, 1977, 1980, 1983.

Dow Brewery (Can). See Dow's Ale.

Down Cocktail (Cktl). ⅔ measure dry Gin, ⅓ measure sweet Vermouth, dash Orange bitters. Shake over ice, strain into a cocktail glass. Top with an olive.

Downers Vineyard (Eng). A vineyard based at Fulking, Henfield, Sussex. 2.2 ha. Grape variety – Müller-Thurgau.

Downham Bitter (Eng). See Downham Brewery.

Downham Brewery (Eng). A home-brewery at the Castle hotel, Downham market, Norfolk. Brews Downham Bitter 1036 O.G. and Old 1048 O.G. Uses malt extract.

Down Moore Ale (Eng). A cask conditioned premium Ale 1042 O.G. brewed by the Cirencester Brewery in Gloucestershire.

Down Royal (Ire). A public house brewery in Lisburn, County Antrim, Northern Ireland. Produces a cask conditioned Export 1043 O.G.

Downy Mildew (Eng). Peronosporaceae.

Dow Porter (Can). A creamy-style Porter brewed by Carling in Toronto.

Dow's Ale (Can). An Export Ale brewed by the Dow's brewery. Exported to the USA.

Dowsing Rod (Eng). See Divining Rod.

Doyen d'Age (Fr). A 20–30 year old Armagnac produced by Lafontan.

DPA (Eng) (abbr). Derby Pale Ale. A keg Mild 1033 O.G. brewed by the Mitchells and Butlers Brewery.

D.R.A. (W.Ind) (abbr). Distillerie des Rhums Agricoles in Martinique. Produces – La Favorite (a popular brand of Rum).

Draaihoogte Vineyard (S.Afr). A vineyard based in Paarl. Grapes are sold to wineries.

Drab (Hol). The sediment or lees. See also Droesem.

D

Drachenblut (Ger). Lit – 'Dragon's blood'. A red wine made from the Spätburgunder grape in Siebengebirge, Mittelrhein.

Drachenbrunnen (Ger). Vineyard. (Anb) = Nahe. (Ber) = Schloss Böckelheim (Gro) = Burgweg. (Vil) = Waldböckelheim.

Drachenfels (Ger). Vineyard. (Anb) = Mittelrhein. (Ber) = Siebengebirge. (Gro) = Petersberg. (Vil) = Königswinter.

Drachenfels (Ger). Vineyard. (Anb) = Mittelrhein. (Ber) = Siebengebirge. (Gro) = Petersberg. (Vil) = Rhöndorf.

Drachenstein (Ger). Vineyard. (Anb) = Rheingau. (Ber) = Johannisberg. (Gro) = Burgweg. (Vil) = Rüdesheim.

Drachm (Eng). ⅛ fl.oz. Also known as a fluid dram.

Dracs (Eng). The middle ages name for a mixed drink of coarse spirit and other ingredients in the taverns. Usually amongst sailors.

Draff (Scot). The residue from the wort in whisky production, used as cattle food.

Draft (Eng). The name for the spent barley after brewing in the brewery.

Draft Beer (Eng). Denotes Beer drawn from a barrel or keg by tap or suction.

Draft Brewed (USA). On a beer bottle label denotes the contents have been brewed by traditional cask beer methods.

Drăgăşăni (Rum). A region south of the Carpathian mountains. Noted for its' Muskat-Ottonel.

Dragon (W.Ind). A strong, medium-sweet Stout 1070 O.G. brewed by the Desnoes and Geddes Brewery in Jamaica.

Dragon Cider Company (Wales). A Cider producing factory based at Hirwaun, West Glamorgan. Produces Thatcher's Ruin.

Dragon in the Clouds (Cktl). ⅕ measure Mandarine Napoléon, ⅕ measure lime juice, ³⁄₁₀ measure fresh orange juice, ³⁄₁₀ measure Gin. Shake well over ice, strain into a Champagne flute.

Dragon Lady Cocktail (Cktl). 1 measure orange juice, ¾ measure white Rum, dash Curaçao, dash Grenadine. Stir well over ice, strain into an ice-filled highball glass. Dress with a cherry and a slice of orange.

Dragon Punch (Cktl). ½ gill Brandy, ½ gill dry Sherry, ½ pint Stout, ½ pint Lager, 1 bottle dry Champagne (iced). Mix well together over ice, decorate with slices of lemon.

Dragon's Blood (Eng). A barley wine brewed by the Flowers Brewery.

Dragon's Blood (Ger). The name given to the wine from the vineyards around Königswinter called Drachenfels where, according to legend, Siegfried slew the dragon then bathed in its' blood.

Dragon's Eye (China). A white grape variety grown in the Tianjin and Hebei regions. See Loong Yan.

Dragon's Well (China). A green tea from the Hangchow area. Has a thick curled leaf which is still curled by hand.

Drahtrahmenerziehung (Ger). A method of vine training using wire frames.

Drainers (Eng). Stainless steel vats with sieves to allow the juice to drain out before pressing.

Drakenstein Co-operative (S.Afr). Vineyards based in Paarl. Address = Box 19, Simondium, 7670. Produces varietal wines. Winery founded in 1906.

Drake Port (Eng). The brand-name of Port bottled by Avery's of Bristol. Old Tawny style.

Drakes Cocktail (Cktl). ⅔ measure Plymouth Gin, ½ fl.oz. Crème de Framboise, dash egg white, 2 dashes lemon juice. Shake over ice, strain into a cocktail glass. Dress with a slice of lemon.

Dram (Scot) (slang). A term for a measure of spirits (usually whisky). e.g. "A wee dram" (a small measure).

Dramblat (Fr). Armagnac producer. Address = Maison Dramblat, Castelnau d'Auzan 32240. 15 ha. Produces – Millesimes.

Drambuie (Scot). The oldest whisky liqueur. Made from whisky, heather, honey and herbs. 40% alc. by vol.

Drambuie Eggnog (Cktl). 3 egg yolks creamed together with a teaspoon of sugar until smooth. Stir in ⅓ gill Sherry, ⅔ gill Drambuie, ⅓ pint vanilla ice cream, 1 pint milk. Mix well, add whipped egg whites, and grated nutmeg.

Drambuie Swizzle (Cktl). ⅕ gill Drambuie, juice ½ lime, 1 teaspoon sugar. Stir over crushed ice in a highball glass. Top with soda water and mint sprig.

Drank (Hol). Beverage. Drink. Also spirits.

Dranken (Hol). Drinks.

Drankkwast (Hol). Lemon squash.

Drankwinkel (S.Afr). Wine shop, store.

Drankzuchtig (Hol). Dipsomaniac.

Drapeau (Fr). Pipes used for cooling (or heating) the fermenting must.

Drappier (André) (Fr). Champagne producer. Address = Urville, 10200 Bar-sur-Aube. 24 ha. Produces – Vintage and non-vintage wines. Vintages – 1973, 1976, 1979, 1981, 1982, 1983.

Labels – Grande Sendrée (De Luxe Cuvée) and Valdes Desmoiselles (a vintage rosé).

Draught (Eng). The term used to denote a portion of liquid to be drunk. May be used as a slang term e.g. "Draught of ale".

Draught (Scot). See Draught. "A wee draught". A small measure of Whisky.

Draught Beer (Eng). Either cask conditioned or brewery conditioned beers. Beers that are drawn from a cask or keg.

Draught Excluder (Eng). A high gravity Winter ale 1070. O.G. brewed by the Chudley Brewery in London.

Draw Off (Eng). Denotes the removal of liquid from a cask. Usually off the lees. e.g. Racking, decanting, syphoning.

Dray (Eng). Originally a horse-drawn cart but now a motorised vehicle used for transporting and delivering ales.

Drayman's Choice (Eng). A low-gravity Bitter beer brewed by the Mansfield Brewery, Nottinghamshire.

Draytons (Austr). An estate winery in the Hunter Valley, New South Wales. Grape varieties – Chardonnay, Hermitage and Sémillon.

Dr. Cameron's (Eng). A British wine and whisky drink produced by the Wham Co.

Dr. Cook Cocktail (Cktl). ⅓ measure dry Gin, juice ¼ lemon, dash Maraschino, 1 egg white. Shake over ice, strain into a 5 oz. goblet.

Dream Cocktail (Cktl). 1 measure Brandy, ½ measure Cointreau, 2 dashes Anisette. Shake over ice, strain into a cocktail glass.

Drèche (Fr). See Draft.

Dregs (Eng). Lees. Particles remaining in the bottom of a drink. e.g. coffee grounds, tea leaves, tannin, tartrate crystals etc.

Dreher (It). Anton Dreher. Name appears only on a brewing group jointly controlled by Whitbreads and Heineken.

Dreher Brauerei (Aus). Founded by Anton Dreher. Produced the first modern Lager beer. Breweries in – Vienna (Schwechat), Czec. (Michelob, Bohemia), Hungary (Budapest) and Italy (Trieste).

Dreher Neto (Carlos) (Bra). A leading wine producer in the country.

Dreikönigs Bier (Switz). Lit – 'Three King Beer'. A beer brewed by the Hürlimann Brewery in Zürich. A Starkbier.

Dreikönigswein (Ger). Name given to wines made from grapes picked on the 6th January. (12th night).

Dreimanner (Czec). A white grape variety.

Dreimännerwein (Ger). Lit – 'Three man wine'. Name given to wine produced in the Saar-Ruwer from the Elbling grape. In good years the wine is austere but in poor years it takes 2 men to hold the third down to make him drink it. Hence the name.

Dreis (Ger). Village. (Anb) = Mosel-Saar-Ruwer. (Ber) = Bernkastel. (Gro) = Schwarzlay. (Vin) = Johannisberg.

Dressing (Eng). Term used to denote the labelling and foiling of wine and beer bottles.

Dressler Brauerei (Ger). A subsidiary brewery of the Holstein Brauerei Hamburg, situated in Bremen. Noted for its' Lager beers.

Dr. Hogg Muscat (N.Z.). A white dessert wine grape.

Dried Milk (Eng). Skimmed milk (of its' cream) that is evaporated by the use of heated cylinders, freeze-drying, etc.

Drie Fonteiner Brasserie (Bel). A brewery based in Beersel, central Belgium.

Drie Hoefijzers Brasserie (Bel). Lit – 'Three horseshoes'. A brewery based in Breda. Brews Dutch Skol Lager.

Driesprong (S.Afr). Wine estate.

Drigo (Ch.Isles). Drink, Grog.

Drikke en Rus (Den). To become drunk, intoxicated.

Drink (Eng). To swallow liquid, absorb, to take intoxicating liquor.

Drink a Person Under the Table (Eng). A term used to denote that one person can consume more alcoholic drink than another.

Drinkbaar (Hol). Potable.

Drinkebroer (Hol). Drinker, tippler.

Drinken (Hol). To drink.

Drinkgelag (Hol). A drinking bout.

Drinking Chocolate (Eng). A drink made with milk/water and chocolate. Usually a commercially produced preparation in powder form.

Drinking Straw (Eng). A thin tube of metal, straw, paper, wood, glass, plastic, etc. used for drinking liquids from a vessel. They are especially used for many cocktails that have ice or fruit in them.

Drinking Table (Eng). A kidney-shaped table produced in Georgian times for drinking and serving wines, spirits, etc.

Drinking Up Time (Eng). The time permitted by law for the consumption on licensed premises of those drinks purchased during permitted hours. 10 minutes in England and Wales, 15 minutes in Scotland and Isle of Man, 30 minutes in Northern Ireland. In restaurants it is 30 minutes.

Drinking Vouchers (Eng) (slang). A term

used in the north of England for sterling paper money (£5, £10, £20 and £50). Usually are referred to by the note's colour. e.g. A £5 note would be described as a "Blue drinking voucher".

Drink Mixer (Eng). See Blender.

Drink With the Flies (Austr). A term to denote a person drinking on their own. Alone.

Drioli (It). A liqueur producer based in Venice. Noted for Maraschino.

Drip Mat (Eng). See Beer Mat. Another name for a beer mat.

Dripolator (USA). A method of coffee making in which very hot water is percolated through coffee grounds.

Drip Tray (Eng). A plastic or metal tray fitted under draught beer taps to catch the ullages (overflow).

Drivers (Eng). Non-alcoholic, 6 fl.oz. bottles of simulated drinks e.g. Gin and tonic, Whisky and ginger, Rum and coke. Distributed by Britvic Canada Dry.

Dr. Milton's (Eng). Eighteenth century tea blend.

Droë Rooi (S.Afr). Dry red.

Droesem (Hol). Lees, sediment. See also Drab.

Droë Wit (S.Afr). Dry white.

Droë Wit (S.Afr). A dry, white, fruity wine made from Colombard and Steen grapes by the Opstal estate.

Droit de Banvin (Fr). The start of the harvest.

Drôme (Fr). Département of the Côtes du Rhône.

Dromersheim (Ger). Village. (Anb) = Rheinhessen. (Ber) = Bingen. (Gro) = Sankt Rochuskapelle. (Vins) = Honigberg, Kapellenberg, Klosterweg, Mainzerweg. Bergkelder.

Dronck (Eng). A seventeenth century spelling of drunk, intoxicated.

Dronkaard (Hol). Drunkard.

Dronken (Hol). Drunken, tipsy.

Dronkenschap (Hol). Drunkenness.

Droog (S.Afr). Dry.

Drop Inn (S.Afr). See Drop in Wines.

Drop in Wines (S.Afr). A large stores group that sells wines under the Drop Inn, Springlands and Vintner's Choice labels.

Drosophila Melanogaster (Lat). Vinegar fly.

Drosselborn (Ger). Vineyard. (Anb) = Rheinhessen. (Ber) = Bingen. (Gro) = Abtey. (Vil) = Appenheim.

Drostdy (S.Afr). The name for a range of South African sherries from the Drostdy Co-operative.

Drostdy Co-operative (S.Afr). Winery based at Tulbagh. (The oldest South African Co-op). Address = Die Drostdyse Koöperatiewe Wynkelders, Box 85, Tulbagh 6820. Produces varietal wines under Drostdy-Hof Wines and Witzenberg Wines labels.

Drostdy-Hof Wines (S.Afr). See Drostdy Co-operative.

Drostdy Pale Dry (S.Afr). A pale, dry Fino South African sherry. Made by the Drostdy Co-operative.

Drostdyse Koöperatiewe Wynkelder (Die) (S.Afr). See Drostdy Co-operative.

Drouhin, [J. et Cie] (Fr). A négociant-éleveur based in Beaune, Burgundy.

Drown One's Sorrows (To) (Eng). A term used to denote a person drinking alcohol to forget their troubles.

Dr. Pepper (USA). A famous soft drink Company.

Druid's Ale (Wales). A cask conditioned strong ale brewed by the Silverthorne Brewery in South Wales.

Druid's Delight (Cktl). 1 gill Mead, ⅓ gill French vermouth. Stir over ice, strain into a highball glass. Dress with a mint leaf and a lemon slice.

Druids Special (Eng). See Ancient Druids.

Druif (Hol). Grape.

Druivennat (Hol). Grape juice. See also Druivesap.

Druivenpers (Hol). Wine-press.

Druivesap (Hol). Grape juice. See also Druivennat.

Drum Bitter (Eng). A keg Bitter 1036.5 O.G. brewed by the Davenport's Brewery in Birmingham.

Drum Bitter (Eng). A keg Bitter 1034 O.G. brewed by the Tetley Brewery in Leeds.

Drum Malting (Eng). A malting system developed in the 1950's using revolving drums to germinate and heat the barley.

Drunk (Eng) (slang). Term to describe a person who is under the influence of alcohol.

Drunkometer (USA). The equivalent of the U.K. Breathaliser in America.

Drupe (Lat). The botanical name for the coffee-tree cherry (fruit).

Drupeggio (It). A white grape variety grown in Umbria.

Drustvo Barmanov Slovenije (Yug). D.B.S. Yugoslavian Bartenders' Association. Address = Hotel Lev-Vosnjakova, 1–6100, Ljubljana.

Dr. Willkomm Liebfraumilch (Ger). A noted Liebfraumilch Qba. white wine from the Rheinpfalz. Bottled in Bernkastel-Kues, Mosel-Saar-Ruwer.

Dry (Eng). When applied to wines it denotes one which has been fermented out. A wine that has no unfermented sugar remaining in the wine.

Dry (S.Afr). A classification of wine. Has 4 grams per litre of sugar or less.

Dry Americano Cocktail (Cktl). ⅓ gill Noilly Prat, ⅓ gill Campari. Stir over ice, strain into a cocktail glass. Add ice and a slice of orange.

Dry Blackthorn Cider (Eng). The brand-name of a noted dry Cider from Taunton, Somerset.

Drybrough (Scot). A brewery in Edinburgh owned by Watneys. Produces – cask conditioned Pentland 1036 O.G. Eighty 1042 O.G. Scotch 1034 O.G. Burn's Special 1036 O.G. Original 1042 O.G. and Scottish Pride Lager 1032 O.G.

Dry Buccaneer (Cktl). 1 measure white Rum, 1 measure dry Dubonnet, 1 measure dry ginger. Fill a highball with ice, add all the ingredients, stir and decorate with a slice of orange.

Dry Cane (W.Ind). The brand-name of a white Rum matured by Courage Breweries. 40% alc. by vol.

Dry Cherry Vodka (Pol). A semi-sweet cherry-flavoured Vodka produced by Polmos. 40% alc. by vol.

Dry Co-operative Cellar (Euro). Denotes a collecting station for the grower's grapes which are sorted (and often pressed), then distributed for vinification at other cellars. Is popular in Germany.

Dry Creek (USA). A winery in Healdsburg, Sonoma, California. 21 ha. Grape varieties – Cabernet sauvignon, Chardonnay, Chenin blanc, Petit syrah and Zinfandel. Produces varietal wines.

Dry Creek Valley (USA). A wine-producing region in Sonoma County, California.

Dry Don (Sp). A brand of Amontillado sherry produced by Sandeman.

Dry Farming (USA). No artificial irrigation. Only natural rainfall.

Dry Fly (Eng). A brand of Amontillado sherry shipped by Findlater's of London.

Dry Gin (Eng). Produced in England and America it is light in flavour and body but has a good aromatic aroma and taste.

Dry Hopping (Eng). The addition of a handful of dry hops to a finished brew when in cask to give the beer a hop aroma.

Drying Up (Eng). A term applied to wines that have lost their freshness and fruit through age in the bottle.

Dry Lustau (Sp). The brand-name for a range of dry Sherries produced by Lustau in Jerez.

Dry Martini (Cktl). 2½ fl.ozs. dry Gin, 2 dashes dry Vermouth. Stir over ice, serve straight or 'on the rocks'. Add a twist of lemon or an olive. See Martini.

Dry Martini (It). The brand-name of a dry Vermouth from Martini and Rossi.

Dry Martini Cocktail (Eng). A ready-mixed drink produced by Gordon's in London.

Dry Melody (Cktl). ⅘ measure Vodka, ¹⁄₁₀ measure Fraises des Bois, ¹⁄₁₀ measure Mandarine liqueur. Shake over ice, strain into a cocktail glass.

Dry Method (Eng). A method of removing the coffee beans from the fruit by drying the fruit in the sun then removing the beans with a hulling machine. See also Wet Method.

Dry Millenary (Cktl). ⅗ measure Gilbey's Gin, ⅕ measure Cinzano Americano, ⅕ measure Rosé Cinzano, dash Cinzano dry. Stir over ice, strain into a cocktail glass.

Dry Monopole (Fr). The brand-name for Heidsieck and Co. non-vintage Champagne.

Drynke (Eng). Old English spelling of drink in the sixteenth century.

Dry Presidente (Cktl). 1½ ozs. Bacardi white label, 1½ ozs. dry Vermouth. Stir with ice, strain into a cocktail glass. Twist a slice of orange over glass. Dress with an olive.

Dry Sack (Sp). A registered trade mark of Sherry shippers Williams and Humbert. A medium sherry.

Dry Sauterne (USA). See California Sauterne.

Drystone Cider (Eng). A Cider produced by the Symonds Cider Co. in Hereford. Also known as Symonds Drystone Cider.

Dry Tang (Port). A white Port produced by Cockburns.

Dry Vermouth (Fr). Colour varies from clear to light gold. Now also made in Italy.

Dry Wit Sherry (USA). The brand-name used by the Llords and Elwood Winery in California for a range of their sherries.

D.S.I.R. (N.Z.) (abbr). See Department of Scientific and Industrial Research.

D.T.s (Eng) (abbr). Dilirium Tremens. The shakes from over indulgence in alcohol.

D.U.B. (Ger) (abbr). Dortmunder Union Brauerei. See.

Dubac (Fr). A Brandy produced by Landy Frères.

Du Baril (Switz). A red wine produced in

Salvagnin from the Gamay and Pinot noir grapes.

Du Barry (Cktl). ⅗ measure Gin, ⅖ measure dry Vermouth, 2 dashes Angostura. Shake over ice, strain into a cocktail glass. Dress with a slice of orange.

Dubbel (Bel). A dark-brown Beer 7% alc. by vol. brewed by the Westmalle Brasserie.

Dubbele Graan (Hol). Term used for a Genever distilled with juniper. See also Gebeide and Dubbel Gebeide.

Dubbel Gebeide (Hol). See Gebeide and Dubbele Graan.

D.U.B. Export (Ger). An Export beer brewed by the D.U.B. in Westphalia.

Dublin Distillers (Ire). Formerly William Jameson and Co. Now closed down.

Dublin Pride Ale (Ire). A bottled Export ale 1040 O.G. brewed by the Dempsey Brewery in Dublin. Brewed for the USA market.

Du Bocq Brasserie Centrale (Bel). A brewery based in Purnode and Marbaix. Noted for their Saison beer, Winston (pale styled beer) and Gauloise (a malty copper-coloured Ale).

Duboeuf (Fr). A Beaujolais négociant based at Romanèche-Thorins, Beaujolais, Burgundy.

Du Bon (Cktl). ⅓ gill Dubonnet, ⅙ gill dry Gin, juice of ½ lemon. Stir over ice in a highball glass. Top with lemonade and a lemon slice.

Dubonnet (Fr). A bitter Vermouth made from the Carignan, Grenache and Malvoise muscat grapes and flavoured with quinine and bitter bark. Also produce a red and blonde version. 17% alc. by vol.

Dubonnet Blonde (Fr). A white version of the famous Dubonnet vermouth.

Dubonnet Cassis (Cktl). ⅔ measure red Dubonnet, ⅓ measure Crème de Cassis. Stir over ice in a highball glass. Top with Perrier water.

Dubonnet-Citron (Cktl). ½ gill Dubonnet, ⅙ gill Sirop de Citron, soda water and ice. Stir over ice, strain into a highball glass over ice.

Dubonnet Cocktail (Cktl).(1). ½ oz. dry Gin, 1 oz. Dubonnet. Stir over ice, strain into a cocktail glass. Squeeze lemon peel juice on top.

Dubonnet Cocktail (Cktl).(2). ⅓ gill Dubonnet, ⅙ gill dry Sherry, 3 dashes Orange bitters. Shake well over ice, strain into a cocktail glass.

Dubonnet Fizz (Cktl). 1 measure Dubonnet, ½ measure Cherry brandy, 1 fl.oz. lemon juice, 1 fl.oz. orange juice, 1 egg white. Shake well together over ice, strain into a highball glass with ice. Top with soda water, serve with straws and muddler.

Dubonnet Mint Julep (Cktl). Crush some mint leaves with ice in a highball glass. Add ⅕ gill Crème de Menthe. Top with Dubonnet Blonde. Serve with straws.

Dubonnet Royal (Cktl). ⅓ measure dry Gin, ⅔ measure Dubonnet, 2 dashes Angostura, 2 dashes Orange bitters, 1 dash Pastis. Stir together over ice except Pastis. Strain into a cocktail glass, add Pastis and dress with a cherry.

Dubor and Co (Fr). Brandy producers.

Dubravka(Yug). A red wine produced in eastern Serbia.

Dubroca (Louis) (Fr). A Bordeaux négociant-éleveur. Address = Domaine de Ribet, St. Loubes 33450. Has properties in the Médoc.

Dubuisson Brasserie (Bel). A brewery based near Tournai. Noted for its' Bush Beer.

Dubuque Star (USA). A Beer 4.8% alc. by vol. brewed by the Pickett Brewery in Dubuque, Iowa.

Duc (Le) (Fr). A popular brand of Normandy cider from the Duché de Longueville Ciderie.

Duca d'Asti (It). A producer of sparkling (méthode champenoise) wines based in Calamandrana Asti, Piemonte. The labels include Granduca Brut.

Ducastaing (Fr). Armagnac producer. Address = 32190 Vic-Fezensac. Ténarèze. Produces – Bernard VII X.O. 10 year old, Duc d'Aquitaine 10 year old and B.B. Martine V.S.O.P. 5 year old.

Duc d'Aquitaine (Fr). A 10 year old Armagnac produced by Ducastaing.

Duc de Berry Rouge (S.Afr). A blended red wine made with the Cinsault 40% and Shiraz 60% grapes by the Eikendal vineyards in Stellenbosch.

Duc de Niçoise (Cyp). A sparkling dry wine produced by the Keo Co.

Du Chadé (Ch.Isles). A hot cider drink from Jersey, made from equal quantities of milk and cider (½ pint) plus 2 eggs. Heated but not boiled.

Duché de Longueville Cidery (Fr). A fine Cider-producing company based near Dieppe on the river Scie in Normandy, northern France. Produces Le Duc brand ciders.

Duchess (USA). A native white grape variety suitable for late picking because of its' thick skin.

Duchess Cocktail (Cktl). ⅓ measure Pastis, ⅓ measure dry Vermouth, ⅓ measure sweet Vermouth. Stir over ice, strain into a cocktail glass.

Duchesse (Bra). A white grape variety also known as the Riesling de Caldas.

Duchroth (Ger). Village. (Anb) = Nahe. (Ber) = Schloss Böckelheim. (Gro) =

D

Burgweg. (Vins) = Felsenberg, Feuerberg, Kaiserberg, Königsfels, Rothenberg, Vogelschlag.

Duchy Beer (Eng). A bottled Ale 1037 O.G. brewed in St. Austell, Cornwall.

Duck Decanter (Eng). A style of decanter that is shaped like a sitting duck. Has an oval body and wide neck at a 45° angle from the body. Also has a looped handle.

Duckhorn Vineyards (USA). A small winery based near St. Helena, Napa Valley, California. Grape varieties – Cabernet sauvignon, Merlot and Sauvignon blanc. Produces varietal wines.

Ducs d'Esmé, Prinal, Guy Labarde (Fr). Cognac producer. Address = Ste Brugerolle S.A. 17160 Matha.

Dudognon (Raymond) (Fr). Cognac producer. Address = Lignières-Sonneville, 16130 Segonzac. 29 ha. in Grande Champagne. Produces a range of Cognacs including Réserve des Ancestres.

Duenn (Ger). Denotes ordinary thin wine.

Duero (Port). River Douro. Portuguese spelling.

Dufays (Doctor) (Fr). A pioneer of the maceration carbonique method of fermentation who died in 1978. Was the owner of Domaine de Nalys in Châteauneuf-du-Pape in the southern Rhône.

Dufftown-Glenlivet (Scot). A single Malt whisky distillery near Dufftown in Banffshire. Owned by Arthur Bell and Sons. A Highland malt whisky. 43% alc. by vol.

Dufouleur Pères et Fils (Fr). A Burgundy négociant based at Nuits-Saint-Georges, Burgundy.

Duft (Ger). Fragrant.

Duftig (Ger). Fine bouquet. Fragrance.

Du Gin de Prunelles (Ch.Isles). Sloe Gin.

Du Gin d'Orange (Ch.Isles). Orange cordial.

Duhat (E.Ind). Known as the Java plum. Used for making fruit wines in the Philippines.

Duivelsbier (Bel). Lit – 'Devil's beer'. A dark Gueuze-type beer brewed by the Vanderlinden Brasserie in Halle, central Belgium.

Dujardin Fine (Ger). A Weinbrand that has been matured for 8 years. Distilled at Urdingen on the lower Rhine.

Dujardin Imperial (Ger). A Weinbrand distilled at Urdingen on the lower Rhine.

Dujardin Scale (Fr). A hydrometer. Approximately ½ reading of the Balling scale. e.g. 1.039 O.G. equals 10° Balling and 4.5° Dujardin.

Duke (Eng). The domestic servant's nickname for Gin.

Duke (Cktl). ½ measure Drambuie, ¼ measure orange juice, ¼ measure lemon juice. Shake well together, strain into a wine glass, add a dash of Champagne.

Duke Cocktail (Cktl). 1 egg, ⅙ gill Cointreau, ⅛ gill lemon juice, 4 dashes orange juice, 2 dashes Maraschino. Shake over ice, strain into a flute glass. Top with chilled Champagne.

Duke of Cambridge Verdelho (Mad). A medium to dry Madeira produced by the Blandy brothers.

Duke of Clarence (Mad). A brand of Malmsey produced by Blandy in Funchal.

Duke of Cumberland Bual (Mad). A medium to sweet Madeira produced by the Blandy Brothers.

Duke of Sussex Sercial (Mad). A medium dry Madeira produced by the Blandy Brothers.

Duke of Wellington (Sp). A top class range of Sherries produced by Bodegas Internacionales.

Dulce (It). Sweet.

Dulce (Sp). Sweet.

Dulce Apagado (Sp). See Mistelle. Grape must arrested from fermentation by the addition of alcohol.

Dulce de Alimbar (Sp). A solution of wine and invert sugar used for sweetening pale sherries.

Dulce Negro (Sp). A sweet style of Málaga.

Dulce Pasa (Sp). A sweetening wine used in the making of Sherry. Is made from the Palomino grape.

Dullgärten (Ger). Vineyard. (Anb) = Mosel-Saar-Ruwer. (Ber) = Obermosel. (Gro) = Königsberg. (Vil) = Igel.

Dumb (Eng). A term used to describe a wine that is under-developed.

Dumbarton Distillery (Scot). A Grain whisky distillery based north-west of Glasgow.

Dumbuck (Scot). A heavily peated Malt whisky that was produced by the Littlemill Distillery. Now no longer available.

Dumfries Octocentenary Ale (Scot). An Ale brewed by the Scottish Brewers to commemorate the 800th birthday celebrations of the town of Dumfries.

Dummy Daisy (Cktl).(Non-alc). 1 measure raspberry syrup, ½ measure lime juice, 1 teaspoon sugar. Shake over crushed ice. Pour into a cocktail glass.

Du Moulin (Fr). A Bière brewed by the Ricour Brasserie.

Dunbar (Jap). A brand of Whiskey produced by Kiran Seagram.

Dunbar Sweet Stout (Scot). A sweet Stout brewed and bottled by the Belhaven Brewery Co. Ltd. in Dunbar.

Duncan Brewery (USA). A small brewery based in Auburndale, Florida.

Dunder (W.Ind). The skimmings from the sugar boilers which is added to the molasses in the fermentation vats for Rum. Also known as Burnt ale.

Dunderhead (Eng). An old English nickname for an alcoholic who gets drunk on Rum.

Dunglass (Scot). A lightly peated Malt whisky that was produced by the Littlemill distillery. Now no longer available.

Dunhill Old Master Finest Scotch Whisky (Scot). A de Luxe Scotch whisky produced for Alfred Dunhill of London by the International Distillers and Vintners.

Dunhill '71 (Cktl). ⅓ measure Brandy, ⅓ measure Crème de Banane, ⅓ measure Royal Orange Liqueur. Shake over ice, strain into a cocktail glass, float cream on top.

Dunhill '74 (Cktl). ½ measure dry Gin, ¹⁄₁₀ measure Peach brandy, ²⁄₁₀ measure Apricot brandy, ¹⁄₁₀ measure orange squash, ¹⁄₁₀ measure Lemon barley water, 1 egg white. Shake over ice, strain into cocktail glass. Add ½ slice of orange and lemon.

Dunkel (Ger). Dark. Refers to the colour of beers. Usually Münchener beers.

Dunkel Spezial (Ger). A dark, mature, Münchner-style Beer 5.6% alc. by vol. brewed by the Riegele Brauerei in Augsburg.

Dunny Cocktail (Cktl). ½ measure Drambuie, ½ measure Islay malt whisky, 2 dashes lime juice. Shake over ice, strain into a cocktail glass. Dress with a slice of lime.

Dunphy's (Ire). A blend of light pot still whiskey and Middleton grain. Matured in charred American oak casks.

Dun's Surprise (Cktl). ½ measure Cointreau, ½ measure (green) Crème de Menthe. Shake over ice, strain into a large Sherry Elgin glass. Float double cream on top.

Dun Tumas (Euro). A white grape variety grown on the island of Malta.

Dupeyron (Fr). A brand of Armagnac brandy produced by Ryst-Dupeyron, Armagnac.

Dupeyron (J.) (Fr). Armagnac producer. Address = Ryst-Dupeyron, BP 58, 32100 Condom, Ténarèze.

Duplin Wine Cellars (USA). A winery based at Rose Hill, North Carolina. Produces French-American hybrid wines.

Dupont Brasserie (Bel). A brewery based in Tourpes. Noted for its' top-fermented Saison Dupont and Abbaye de la Moinette (an Abbaye-style beer).

Dupratt Vineyard (USA). A vineyard based on the west side of the Anderson Valley, California. 3 ha. Grape variety – Zinfandel.

Dupuy (Fr). Cognac producer. Address = 32 Rue de Boston, P.O. Box 62, 16102, Cognac.

Duque Braganca (Port). A 20 year old Tawny Port from A.A. Ferreira Port shippers.

Duque d'Alba (Sp). The name given to a range of brandies from Diez Merito.

Duque de Sevilla (Sp). A full-bodied, cask-aged, red wine from the Vincente Suso y Perez vineyards in Carinena, north-eastern Spain.

Duquesne (USA). A brewing Co. in Cleveland, Ohio.

Duquesne (W.Ind). A distillery producing a white Rum called Genippa on Martinique. Also Grand Case and Val d'Or (both dark Rums).

Dur (Fr). Hard.

Durango Cocktail (Cktl). ½ measure Tequila, ½ measure grapefruit juice, 2 dashes Orgeat. Shake over ice, strain into an ice-filled highball glass. Top with Perrier water and mint sprig.

Duras (Fr). Region of south-eastern Bordeaux.

Durbach (Ger). Village. (Anb) = Baden. (Ber) = Ortenau. (Gro) = Fürsteneck. (Vins) = Berghaupten, Bermersbach, Bottenau, Diersburg, Durbach, Erlach, Gengenbach, Hofweier, Lautenbach, Nesselried, Niederschopfheim, Nussbach, Offenburg (ortsteil Zell-Weierbach), Offenburg (ortsteil Fessenbach), Oberkirch, Oberkirch (ortsteil Haslach), Ödsbach, Ohlsbach, Ortenberg, Rammersweier, Reichenbach, Ringelbach, Stadelhofen, Tiergarten, Ulm, Zunsweier.

Durbanville (S.Afr). A district north-east of Cape Town. Has two wine estates – Meerendal and Diemersdal.

Durchgegoren (Ger). Fully fermented. Term now no longer allowed on a wine label.

Durchriesling (Aus). Coulure.

Durello Spumante Brut (It). A sparkling (méthode champenoise) wine produced by A.G. Santi in Veneto.

Durendal Wines (S.Afr). The brand-name of wines from the Spier Estate in Stellenbosch.

Duresse (Fr). A Premier Cru vineyard in the A.C. commune of Monthélie, Côte de Beaune, Burgundy. 10.3 ha.

Duresses (Les) (Fr). A Premier Cru vineyard in the A.C. commune of Auxey-Duresses, Côte de Beaune, Burgundy. 10.6 ha.

Durette (Fr). A commune in the Beaujolais. Has A.C. Beaujolais-Villages or Beaujolais-Durette status.

D

Durham Ale (Eng). A cask conditioned Bitter 1036 O.G. brewed by the Whitbread Brewery at Castle Eden.

Durif (Austr). A red grape variety. Also known as the Petit syrah. Is high in tannin.

Duriff (USA). A red grape variety of California. Known as the Petit syrah in France.

Dürkheimer Wurstmarkt (Ger). A Rheinpfalz wine festival held at Bad Dürkheim in September.

Durney Vineyard (USA). A winery based in the Carmel Valley, Monterey, California. 29 ha. Grape varieties – Cabernet sauvignon, Chenin blanc, Gamay beaujolais, Johannisberg riesling, Rosé of Cabernet. Produces varietal wines.

Durnstein (Aus). A village of the Wachau, known for its' white wines of the same name.

Duro (Sp). Term used to describe a hard Sherry.

Duroc (Fr). Brandy négociants.

Dürrenberg (Ger). Vineyard. (Anb) = Baden. (Ber) = Markgräflerland. (Gro) = Lorettoberg. (Vil) = Schallstadt-Wolfenweile.

Dürrenzimmern (Ger). Village. (Anb) = Württemberg. (Ber) = Württembergisch Unterland. (Gro) = Heuchelberg. (Vin) = Mönchsberg.

Dürrn (Ger). Village. (Anb) = Baden. (Ber) = Badische Bergstrasse/Kraichgau. (Gro) = Hohenberg. (Vin) = Eichelberg.

Durst (Ger). Thirst.

Dürsten (Ger). To be thirsty.

Durstig (Ger). Thirsty.

Durup (Jean (Fr). A major négorciant-éleveur based at domaine de l'Eglantière Maligny, Chablils. Has cuvées in many of the Côte d'Or vineyards.

Dusi Ranch (USA). A vineyard based near Templeton, San Luis Obispo, California. 16.5 ha. Grape variety – Zinfandel.

Dusi Vineyard (USA). On a label denotes the source of Mastantuono Winery Zinfandel as from the Dusi Ranch in San Luis Obispo, California.

Düssel Alt (Ger). A full-flavoured Alt bier from Düsseldorf, West Germany.

Dust (Eng). Type of broken tea leaf grade used in the making of tea bags. Part usually broken off during manufacture, gives a good thick liquor.

Dusty (Eng). A term used to describe a wine that has a cellar-like smell with a high tannin content.

Dusty Miller (Austr). An alternative name used for the Pinot meunier grape.

Dutch Coffee (Liq.Coffee). Using a measure of Genever Gin.

Dutch County Wine Cellars (USA). A winery based in Lenhartsville, Pennnsylvania.

Dutch Courage (Eng). Name given to Gin by the soldiers of James 1st.

Dutch Courage Cocktail (Cktl). 1 measure dry Gin, dash Orange bitters. Shake over ice, strain into a large liqueur glass. Float a ½ measure of double cream on top.

Dutchess (USA). A white, hybrid grape variety developed at Dutchess County in New York.

Dutch Gin (Hol). Hollands, Genever or Shiedam Gin. Are full-flavoured, full-bodied and possess a clean malty aroma and taste.

Dutch-Norman Bottle (Fr). A bottle-shape which is used for Calvados. Of 70 cls. capacity.

Dutch Trade Winds Cocktail (Cktl). ⅓ measure dry Gin, ⅛ measure Curaçao, ⅛ measure lemon juice, 2 dashes Gomme syrup. Shake over ice, strain into a cocktail glass.

Dutch Whiskey (Hol). A whiskey made by the Patent still method.

Duties (Eng). Taxes on goods.

Du Toitskloof Co-operative (S.Afr). Vineyards based in Worcester. Address = Du Toitskloof Koöperatiewe Wynkelder, Box 55, Rawsonville 6854. Produces varietal wines.

Du Toitskloof Koöperatiere Wynkelder (S.Afr). See Du Toitskloof Cooperative.

Duttenberg (Ger). Village. (Anb) = Württemberg. (Ber) = Württembergisch Unterland. (Gro) = Staufenberg. (Vin) = Schön.

Duttons (Eng). A cask conditioned Bitter 1034 O.G. brewed by the Chester Brewery in the north of England.

Dutton Vineyard (USA). A vineyard based in the lower Russian River Valley. 21 ha. Grape variety – Chardonnay used for the Burgess Cellars Chardonnay.

Duttweiler (Ger). Village. (Anb) = Rheinpfalz. (Ber) = Mittelhaardt-Deutsche Weinstrasse. (Gro) = Pfaffengrund. (Vins) = Kalkberg, Kreuzberg, Mandelberg.

Duty (Eng). Taxes levied by Customs and Excise.

Duty Free (Eng). Denotes goods bought on an outward journey which are free of duties.

Duty Free Shop (Eng). A shop sited on board a ship etc. or at an Airport or Port. Sells alcoholic drinks etc. free of duties (taxes).

Duval (Eng). A Vermouth made by the British wine method and flavoured with herbs and quinine.

Duval (It). A subsidiary of Martini & Rossi that produces Pastis under the Duval label.

Duval Leroy (Fr). Champagne producer. Address = B.P. 37, 51130 Vertus. 80 ha. Produces – Vintage and non-vintage wines. Vintages – 1973, 1975, 1976, 1978, 1981, 1982. De Luxe cuvée is Cuvée des Roys.

Duvel (Bel). A bottle conditioned Ale 8.5% alc. by vol. brewed by the Moortgate Brewery near Antwerp.

Duvel Brasserie (Bel). A brewery based in Breendonk. Is noted for its' top-fermented beers – Duvel and Maredsous brewed for the Maredsous monastry.

Du Veron (D.) (Fr). Cognac producer. Address = Mesnac, 16370, Cherves Richemont, Cognac. 20 ha. in Fins Bois.

Du Vin Brulaï (Ch.Isles). Mulled wine.

Du Vin Pimentaï (Ch.Isles). Spiced wine.

Duyck Brasserie (Fr). A brewery based near Valenciennes. Brews top-fermented beers – Jenlain Bière de Luxe

20°, a deep bronze-coloured beer which is filtered but not pasteurised.

Dvine (USSR). A white grape variety grown in Armenia. Used in the production of brandy.

Dvur Kràlové Nad Labem (Czec). A brewery based in northern Czec.

Dwarsrivier Kelders (S.Afr). The other name for the Cederberg Kelders.

Dwr (Wales). Water.

Dynamite Cocktail (Cktl). ½ measure Cognac, ½ measure Grand Marnier, 1 measure orange juice. Shake over ice, strain into a flute glass. Top with iced Champagne and dress with an orange slice on the rim of glass. Add a cherry.

Dynasty (China). A medium-dry, white wine from the Kian Diam Cong Lu wine farm in Tianju. Made from the Dimlat, Muscat de Hamburg, Homique and Dragon's eye grapes. A joint venture between the Chinese government and Rémy Martin.

E

E. (Eng) (abbr). Worthington 'E'. A keg Bitter 1041 O.G. brewed by the Bass Breweries.

E.A. (Ger) (abbr). Erzeuger-Abfullung. Estate bottled.

Eagle (Cktl). 8 parts Gin, 1 part Parfait Amour, 2 parts lemon juice, dash egg white. Shake well with ice, strain into a wine goblet

Eagle Bitter (Eng). A cask conditioned Bitter 1035 O.G. brewed by the Charles Wells Brewery of Bedford.

Eagle Brewery (Wales). A wholesale company who have recently taken over the Powys Brewery to brew Samuel Powell Traditional Bitter 1040 O.G. in central Wales. See Powell.

Eagle Point Vineyard (USA). A small vineyard based at Talmage, Mendocino County, California. Grape variety – Zinfandel.

Eagle Rare (USA). The brand-name of a 10 year old Kentucky Bourbon whiskey distilled by the Old Prentice Distillery, Lawrenceburg, Kentucky.

Eagle's Dream (Cktl). ¾ measure dry Gin, ¼ measure Crème Yvette, ¼ measure lemon juice, 1 egg white, 2 dashes Gomme syrup. Shake over ice, strain into a goblet. Top with a cherry.

Eagle Stout (Afr). A bitter Stout 1068 O.G. brewed by the Golden Guinea Breweries in Nigeria.

Eaglet Cocktail (Cktl). 1 measure Mandarine Napoléon in a flute glass. Top with iced, dry Champagne.

Ealu (Eng). A mediaeval word for ale, beer. See also Alu, Alofat.

E and K Wine Company (USA). A winery based in Sandusky, Ohio. Produces vinifera and French-American hybrid wines.

Earl Grey (Eng). A blend of China and Darjeeling teas. Has a large leaf and is delicately scented with oil of Bergamot. Very fragrant. Jacksons still make the original blend given to Earl Grey by a Chinese Mandarin.

Earl's Bitter (Eng). A cask conditioned Bitter 1048 O.G. brewed by the Bridgewater Arms, Herts.

Early Burgundy (USA). A black grape variety grown in California. Is slowly being phased out.

Early Doors (Eng). A term used for early opening time in the north of England especially in Lancashire.

Early-Landed Cognac (Eng). Refers to Cognac brandies that have been sold to British wine merchants who then age and bottle them after 15–20 years in cask.

Early Times (USA). The brand-name of a Bourbon whiskey.

Earthquake (Cktl). ⅛ gill Tequila, 2 dashes Campari, 4 dashes Grenadine, scoop crushed ice. Blend altogether, strain into a flute glass. Decorate with fresh strawberries and orange segments.

Earthquake Cocktail (Cktl). ⅔ measure Pernod, ⅔ measure dry Gin, ⅔ measure Whisky. Shake over ice, strain into a cocktail glass.

Earthy (Eng). A term applied to wines which have a special flavour due to the kind of soil on which the grapes grow. It can apply to fine wines such as red Graves.

Easley Winery (USA). A winery based in Indianapolis, Indiana. Produces French hybrid wines.

East (Afr). A wine-producing region in Morocco. Contains the A.O.G. areas of Angad and Berkane. Has alluvial soil.

East African Breweries (Afr). One of the largest breweries in Kenya. Also has shares in the Tanzania Breweries.

East and West Cocktail (Cktl). ½ measure medium Sherry, ½ measure Vodka. Shake over ice, strain into a cocktail glass. Decorate with an olive.

East Anglian English Wine Fair (Eng). A wine festival held each year in August at Ipswich, Suffolk.

East Anglian Wine Growers' Association (Eng). A body that conducts research and education to help improve English wine standards.

Eastcote Ale (Eng). A cask conditioned bitter 1041 O.G. brewed by the Banks and Taylor Brewery in Bedfordshire.

Eastern Brewing (USA). A brewery based in Hammonton.

E

Eastern Promise (Punch) (Non-alc). ½ pint cold Jasmine tea, ¼ pint bitter lemon, ⅓ gill pineapple juice, ⅛ gill orange squash. Stir over crushed ice in a large jug. Dress with slices of orange and pineapple.

Eastern Vineyards (N.Z.). A vineyard that used to produce grapes in the Waitakere Ranges. Now has closed down.

East India (Mad). The quality name sometimes seen on the label of a Madeira bottle. This is a 'lot' name.

East India Cocktail (Cktl).(1). ½ gill Brandy, 2 dashes Curaçao, 2 dashes Maraschino, 2 dashes Angostura. Stir over ice, strain into a cocktail glass, add a cherry and squeeze of lemon peel juice. Pineapple juice can be added instead of Maraschino.

East India Cocktail (Cktl).(2). ½ measure dry Vermouth, ½ measure dry Sherry, 1 dash Orange bitters. Shake over ice, strain into a cocktail glass.

East India Sherry (Eng). A Brown sherry shipped from home to the Far East and back. Journey allows the sherry to mature during the long voyage.

East Lancs (Eng). A Pale ale 1036 O.G. brewed by the Thwaites Brewery in Blackburn.

East-Side Winery (USA). A grower's co-operative based near Lodi, California. Grape varieties – Emerald riesling, Sémillon and Zinfandel. Produces table and dessert wines under the Angelica Antigua, Conti Royale, Gold Bell and Royal Host labels.

Eau d'Arque Busade (Fr). The alternative spelling of Eau d'Arquebuse.

Eau d'Arquebuse (Fr). A medicinal liqueur once produced in Lyons. See also Eau d'Arque Busade.

Eau de Gruau (Fr). Oatmeal water. A nutritional beverage similar in style to barley water.

Eau de la Barbade (Fr). A Bordeaux-produced herb liqueur similar in style to Chartreuse.

Eau de Ma Tante (Hol). Lit – 'Water of my aunt'. An orange-based Dutch liqueur.

Eau de Mélisse (Fr). Melissa (lemon balm) cordial. A spirit distilled from melissa.

Eau de Mélisse des Carmes Boyer (Fr). An Élixer of alcohol, angelica, melissa, cloves, lemon, spices and cress. Sold in medicine bottles by Renouard Larivière, Paris. Drunk diluted with water or on a sugar cube it relieves nervous tension, fatigue and travel sickness.

Eau de Noix Serres (Fr). A liqueur made from the extract of walnuts (harvested in June). Produced by Serres in Toulouse.

Eau de Seltz (Fr). Soda water.

Eau de Table (Fr). Table water.

Eau-de-Vie (Fr). Lit – 'Water of life'. Name given to spirits. Distillates.

Eau-de-Vie-Blanche (Fr). White spirits, non cask matured. e.g. Kirsch.

Eau-de-Vie-d'Alisier (Fr). A fruit Brandy made from rowanberries.

Eau-de-Vie-d'Andaye (Fr). A type of Marc made in the Basque area near Hendaye, southern France.

Eau-de-Vie-de-Baie-d'Alisier (Fr). A rowanberry Eau-de-Vie.

Eau-de-Vie-de-Baie-de-Houx (Fr). An Eau-de-Vie made from the holly berry.

Eau-de-Vie-de-Baie-de-Sureau (Fr). An elderberry-based Eau-de-Vie.

Eau-de-Vie-de-Charente (Fr). Cognac brandy.

Eau-de-Vie-de-Cidre (Fr). Calvados. Distillate of cider.

Eau-de-Vie-de-Coing (Fr). A fruit brandy made from quinces.

Eau-de-Vie-de-Danzig (Fr). The French version of the German Danziger Goldwasser.

Eau-de-Vie-de-Fraise (Fr). Strawberry brandy. A distillate from strawberries. 44.5% alc. by vol.

Eau-de-Vie-de-Framboise (Fr). A raspberry-flavoured liqueur.

Eau-de-Vie-de-Genévrier (Fr). A juniper-based Eau-de-Vie (similar to Gin).

Eau-de-Vie-de-Gentiane (Fr). An Eau-de-Vie made from gentian root.

Eau-de-Vie-d'Eglantine (Fr). An Eau-de-Vie flavoured with the dog rose.

Eau-de-Vie-de-Grain (Fr). A term applied to spirits distilled from grain. e.g. Whisky.

Eau-de-Vie-de-Groseille (Fr). A fruit Brandy made from white or red currants.

Eau-de-Vie-de-Houx (Fr). A fruit Brandy made from hollyberries.

Eau-de-Vie-de-Kirsch (Fr). A fruit brandy made from fermented cherry juice and kernels. 40% alc. by vol.

Eau-de-Vie-de-Lie (Switz). A liqueur made from the lees of wine casks.

Eau-de-Vie-de-Marc (Fr). A Brandy produced from the pomace of wine. It is produced in most wine regions.

Eau-de-Vie-de-Marc-de-Champagne (Fr). A Brandy made from the wine produced by the pressing of the pomace in Champagne.

Eau-de-Vie-de-Mirabelle (Fr). A fruit brandy made from Mirabelle plums. 44.5% alc. by vol.

E

Eau-de-Vie-de-Mûre (Fr). A fruit Brandy made from blackberries.

Eau-de-Vie-de-Mûre Sauvage (Fr). A fruit Brandy made from wild blackberries.

Eau-de-Vie-de-Myrtille (Fr). A fruit Brandy made from bilberries.

Eau-de-Vie-de-Nèfle (Fr). A medlar-based Eau-de-Vie.

Eau-de-Vie-de-Pêche (Fr). A fruit Brandy made from peaches.

Eau-de-Vie-de-Poire (Fr). A liqueur distilled from fermented pear juice. William or Bartlett variety used.

Eau-de-Vie-de-Prune (Fr). A fruit brandy distilled from plum juice. 40% alc. by vol.

Eau-de-Vie-de-Prunelle (Fr). A fruit Brandy made from sloes.

Eau-de-Vie-de-Quetsch (Fr). A fruit brandy made from Switzen plums. 44.5% alc. by vol.

Eau-de-Vie-de-Reineclaude (Fr). A fruit Brandy made from greengages.

Eau-de-Vie-de-Sapin (Fr). An Eau-de-Vie made from pine needles.

Eau-de-Vie-de-Sorbier (Fr). A fruit Brandy made from sorb apples.

Eau-de-Vie-de-Sureau (Fr). A fruit Brandy made from elderberries.

Eau-de-Vie-de-Vin (Fr). The name given to any spirit distilled from wine.

Eau-de-Vie-de-Vin-de-Champagne (Fr). Fine de Marne. Brandy made from the last pressing of grapes (rebêche) in Champagne.

Eau d'Orge (Fr). Barley water.

Eau Fraîche (Fr). Cold water.

Eau Miellée (Fr). A drink made from honey, spirits and water.

Eau Minérale Naturelle (Fr). The A.C. of mineral waters. Given by the Government to waters with therapeutic qualities. e.g. Evian, Vichy, Volvic etc.

Eau Nuptile (Fr). A popular eighteenth century Eau-de-vie.

Eau Plate (Fr). Tap water.

Eaux de Source (Fr). A government grading of mineral waters that are not quite as high in therapeutic qualities as Eau minérale naturelle. V.D.Q.S. type.

Eaux-de-Vie (Fr). Alsace name for Alcools blancs or Eau-de-Vie.

Eaux Minéralés de Carbonnieux (Fr). A label term used by the Bénédictine owners of Château Carbonnieux in the Graves district of Bordeaux so as to sell their wines in Moslem Turkey in the eighteenth century.

Eauze (Fr). An important town in the Gers département where Armagnac is produced.

E.B. (Eng) (abbr). Estate Bottled (on a French wine label).

Ebbrezza (It). Drunkenness, intoxication.

Ebbro (It). Drunk.

Ebenrain (Ger). Vineyard. (Anb) = Baden. (Ber) = Badische Frankenland. (Gro) = Tauberklinge. (Vil) = Lindelbach.

Eberbach (Ger). Village. (Anb) = Baden. (Ber) = Badische Bergstrasse/Kraichgau. (Gro) = Stiftsberg. (Vin) = Schollerbuckel.

Ebereschen-Branntwein (Ger). A Brandy made from rowanberries, red in colour.

Eberfürst (Ger). Vineyard. (Anb) = Württemberg. (Ber) = Württembergisch Unterland. (Gro) = Salzberg. (Vil) = Eberstadt.

Ebersberg (Ger). Vineyard. (Anb) = Rheinhessen. (Ber) = Nierstein. (Gro) = Sankt Alban. (Vil) = Bodenheim.

Ebersberg (Ger). Vineyard. (Anb) = Rheinhessen. (Ber) = Nierstein. (Gro) = Spiegelberg. (Vil) = Nierstein.

Eberstadt (Ger). Village. (Anb) = Württemberg. (Ber) = Württembergisch Unterland. (Gro) = Salzberg. (Vins) = Dezberg, Eberfürst, Sommerhalde.

Ebibo (Lat). I drink up, I drain my glass.

Ebony (Eng). A bottled dark Ale 1067 O.G. brewed by the Greenhall Whitley Brewery. See Old Chester.

Ebony (W.Ind). A dark Lager beer 9% alc. by vol. brewed by the Bank's Brewery in Barbados.

Ebrietas (Lat). Drunkenness.

Ebringen (Ger). Village. (Anb) = Baden. (Ber) = Markgräflerland. (Gro) = Lorettoberg. (Vin) = Sommerberg.

Ébrio (Port). Drunk, intoxicated.

Ebriolus (Lat). Tipsy.

Ebriositas (Lat). Alcoholism. Addiction to drink.

Ebriosus (Lat). Drunkard.

Ebrius (Lat). Intoxicated, drunk. See also Potus, Vinolentus.

Ebro [River] (Sp). A river of northern Spain in the Rioja region.

Ebulam (Eng). A strong Ale flavoured with juniper and elderberries produced in the middle-ages.

Ebulliscope (Eng). An instrument used to measure the quantity of alcohol present in a liquid by noting the boiling point of the liquid. (Alcohol boils at a lower temperature [78°C] than water [100°C]). Is measured using a set quantity at a set atmospheric pressure.

Ébullition (Fr). Lit – 'boiling'. Term often used for the first violent fermentation when it has the appearance of boiling.

Ebulum (Eng). See Ebulam.

Échanson (Fr). Lit – 'Cup bearer'. A person who pours the wine for a dignitary.

E

Échansonnerie des Papes (Fr). A wine brotherhood of Châteauneuf-du-Pape, southern Rhône.

Échebrune (Fr). A commune in the Charente-Maritime Département whose grapes are classed Petite Champagne (Cognac).

Échelle des Crus (Fr). The Champagne regions' classification of grapes (vineyard areas). Grand Cru = 100%, Premier Cru = 90–99% and Cru 80–89%.

Echézeaux (Fr). A top Grand Cru vineyard in the A.C. commune Vosne-Romanée, Côte de Nuits, Burgundy. 30 ha.

Echmiadzin (USSR). A wine-producing centre in Armenia.

Echt (Aus) (Ger). Genuine or right. Often seen on a beverage label. See also Echte.

Echt (Pol) (USSR). A style of Kümmel Crystallise (sugar has been added and has crystallised).

Echte (Hol). Genuine. Often seen on a Genever label.

Echter-Rum (Ger). A high-proof imported rum.

Echt Stonsdorfer (Ger). A herb liqueur.

Echunga Hock (Austr). The first wine made in the colonies of Australia, sent to H.M. Queen Victoria via Lord Stanley the then Secretary of State for the Colonies. The wine was first sent in 1845.

Eck (Ger). Vineyard. (Anb) = Ahr. (Ber) = Walporzheim/Ahetal. (Gro) = Klosterberg. (Vil) = Altenahr.

Eckartsberg (Ger). Vineyard. (Anb) = Baden. (Ber) = Kaiserstuhl-Tuniberg (Gro) = Vulkanfelsen. (Vil) = Breisach.a.Rh.

Eckberg (Ger). Vineyard. (Anb) = Baden. (Ber) = Kaiserstuhl-Tuniberg. (Gro) = Vulkanfelsen. (Vil) = Bötzingen.

Eckberg (Ger). Vineyard. (Anb) = Baden. (Ber) = Ortenau. (Gro) = Schloss Rodeck. (Vil) = Baden-Baden.

Eckelsheim (Ger). Village. (Anb) = Rheinhessen. (Ber) = Bingen. (Gro) = Rheingrafenstein. (Vins) = Eselstreiber, Kirchberg, Sonnenkopfchen.

Eckes (Ger). Distillers based at Neider-Olm. Producers of Chantre (a Weinbrand), Edelkirsch, Klosterberg and Sechsamtertropfen.

Eckte (Ger). See Echt.

Eckweg (Ger). Vineyard. (Anb) = Hessische Bergstrasse. (Ber) = Starkenburg. (Gro) = Schlossberg. (Vil) = Heppenheim (including Erbach and Hambach).

Eclipse (Cktl). ⅔ measure Sloe gin, ⅓ measure dry Gin, 2 dashes lemon juice. Shake over ice, strain into a cocktail glass that has an olive and 2 teaspoons of Grenadine in. Do not stir.

Écloseaux (Fr). A vineyard in the A.C. commune of Rully, Côte Chalonnaise, Burgundy.

École du Vin (Fr). Wine school, wine academy.

Economiser (Eng). See Autovac.

Écossais (Fr). Scotch. (Either Scotch whisky or Scotsman).

Écoulage (Fr). Racking.

Écouvres (Fr). A commune in the Côtes de Toul, Lorraine. Produces Vins gris.

Ecoyen Tinto (Sp). A brand of red wine that is aged for 2 years in cask and 1 year in bottle. Produced by Señorio de Sarría in Navarra.

Ecu (À l') (Fr). A Premier Cru vineyard in the A.C. commune of Beaune, Côte de Beaune, Burgundy. 5 ha.

Ecuador (S.Am). A coffee-producing country that grows Arabica and Robusta coffees. Produces acidic coffees for blending.

Écueil (Fr). A Cru Champagne village in the Canton de Ville-en-Tardenois. District = Reims.

Écueul (Ch.Isles). Jug, pitcher. See also Djougue.

Écusson Rouge Three Star (Fr). A Cognac produced by Château Paulet.

Edaphology (Eng). The study of the relationship between the plants and the soil.

Edel (Ger). Noble.

Edelauslese (Ger). An old designation for 'Noble select wine'. Now no longer used.

Edelbeerenauslese (Ger). An old designation for wine made from extraordinary individual grapes which have not dried out thus preventing classification as a Trokenbeerenauslese. Now no longer used.

Edelberg (Ger). Vineyard. (Anb) = Baden. (Ber) = Badische Frankenland. (Gro) = Tauberklinge. (Vil) = Tauberbischofsheim.

Edelberg (Ger). Vineyard. (Anb) = Mosel-Saar-Ruwer. (Ber) = Bernkastel. (Gro) = Schwarzlay. (Vil) = Enkirch.

Edelberg (Ger). Vineyard. (Anb) = Nahe. (Ber) = Schloss Böckelheim. (Gro) = Paradiesgarten. (Vil) = Lauschied.

Edelberg (Ger). Vineyard. (Anb) = Nahe. (Ber) = Schloss Böckelheim. (Gro) = Paradiesgarten. (Vil) = Meddersheim.

Edel Bier (Ger). See Feuerfest Edel Bier.

Edelbrau Lager (Eng). A Lager beer 1052 O.G. from Lees Brewery, Manchester.

Edelfäule (Ger). Botrytis cinerea. Noble rot. Also known as Eingeschrumpften. See Trokenbeerenauslese.

E

Edelfrau (Ger). Vineyard. (Anb) = Franken. (Ber) = Maindreieck. (Gro) = Not yet assigned. (Vil) = Homburg.

Edelfraulein (Aus). A sweet estate-bottled white wine from Wachau district. Made from the Muscat ottonel grape.

Edelgewächs (Ger). An old term for 'Noble growths'. Best vintages.

Edelkeur (S.Afr). Botrytis cinerea. Noble rot.

Edelkeur (S.Afr). A sweet, white, dessert wine made from botrytis-attacked grapes produced by the Nederburg Estate in Paarl.

Edelkirsch (Ger). A liqueur produced by Ekes distillery from mascara cherries.

Edel Laat oes Superior (S.Afr). A rich, dessert wine made from Steen grapes which have been botrytis-attacked. Produced by the McGregor Co-operative.

Edelmann (Ger). Vineyard. (Anb) = Rheingau. (Ber) = Johannisberg. (Gro) = Erntebringer. (Vil) = Mittelheim.

Edelmann (Ger). Vineyard. (Anb) = Rheingau. (Ber) = Johannisberg. (Gro) = Honigberg. (Vil) = Mittelheim.

Edelmann (Ger). Vineyard. (Anb) = Rheinhessen. (Ber) = Nierstein. (Gro) = Sankt Alban. (Vil) = Mainz.

Edeloes (S.Afr). A sweet, white, dessert wine produced from botrytis-attacked grapes by the De Wetshof Estate in Robertson.

Edelreife (Ger). Over-ripe. Associated with Edelfäule.

Edelrood (S.Afr). A red wine made with the Cabernet and Shiraz grapes by the Nederburg Estate in Paarl.

Edelsuesse (Ger). Great, natural, noble sweetness.

Edeltropfen (S.Afr). A medium-sweet, white wine made from a blend of Riesling and Steen grapes by the Nederburg Estate in Paarl.

Edelwein (Ger). An old designation. 'Noble wine'. Now no longer used.

Edelweiss (It). A pale gold liqueur, herb flavoured and sweetened with crystallised sugar on a twig standing in the bottle. Is similar in style to Fior d'Alpi.

Edelweiss (USA). A Beer 4.8% alc. by vol. brewed by the Pickett Brewery in Dubuque, Iowa.

Edelzwicker (Fr). Noble blend. In Alsace denotes a blend of noble grape varieties to make a wine.

Edenkoben (Ger). Village. (Anb) = Rheinpfalz. (Ber) = Südliche Weinstrasse. (Gro) = Schloss Ludwigshöhe. (Vins) = Bergel, Blücherhöhe, Heidegarten, Heilig Kreuz, Kastaniengarten, Kirchberg, Klostergarten, Mühlberg, Schwarzer Letten.

Eden Pure Fruit Juices (Ger). The brandname used for a range of unfermented water and sugar-free fruit juices. Serve diluted or straight. Imported into U.K. by Leisure Drinks, Derby.

Eden Valley Road (Austr). A winery in South Australia in the Hill-Smith Estate. Address = Angastron, South Australia 5353.

Eden Valley Shiraz (Austr). A white wine from the Château Leonay vineyard in South Australia.

Ederra Rioja (Sp). The brand wines of the Bodegas Bilbainas S.A., Alta region, Rioja.

Édes (Hun). Sweet.

Edesheim (Ger). Village. (Anb) = Rheinpfalz. (Ber) = Südliche Weinstrasse. (Gro) = Ordensgut. (Vins) = Forst, Mandelhang, Rosengarten, Schloss.

Edes Szamorodni (Hun). A sweet style of Szamorodni wines that can be matched to a Tokay aszú.

Ediger-Eller (Ger). Village. (Anb) = Mosel-Saar-Ruwer. (Ber) = Zell/ Mosel. (Gro) = Grafschaft. (Vins) = Bienenlay, Calmont, Elzogberg, Engelströpfchen, Feuerberg, Höll, Osterlämmchen, Pfaffenberg, Pfirsichgarten, Schützenlay.

Edingen (Ger). Village. (Anb) = Mosel-Saar-Ruwer. (Ber) = Obermosel. (Gro) = Königsberg. (Vins) = Not yet choosen.

Edirne-Kirklareli (Tur). A vineyard based in the Thrace and Marmara region. Produces white wines.

Edle Weingärten (Ger). Vineyard. (Anb) = Rheinhessen. (Ber) = Wonnegau. (Gro) = Pilgerpfad. (Vil) = Dittelsheim-Hessloch.

Edmeades Vineyard (USA). A winery based in the Anderson Valley, Mendocino County, California. 14.5 ha. Grape varieties – Cabernet sauvignon, Chardonnay, French colombard, Gewürztraminer, White riesling and Zinfandel. Produces varietal wines and Icewine.

Edna Valley (USA). A fine vine-growing district in San Luis Obispo, California.

Edna Valley Vineyards (USA). A winery in San Luis Obispo, California. Grape varieties – Chardonnay and Pinot noir. Produces varietal wines.

Edourd Robinson (Eng). A honey-flavoured drink produced by the Cornish Mead Co.

Edradour (Scot). A single Malt whisky distillery based at Pitlochry, Perthshire. A Highland malt whisky. Produced by S. Campbell & Sons Ltd. (Part of Pernod-Ricard).

Ed's Baby (Cktl). 1/10 measure Banana

E

liqueur, ⁵⁄₁₀ measure white Rum, ²⁄₁₀ measure Curaçao, ³⁄₁₀ measure Cherry brandy, juice of a lime. Shake over ice, strain into a cocktail glass.

Educación (Sp). The blending and maturing of new wines.

Edward Lloyd's Coffee House (Eng). A coffee house based in London in the eighteenth century in Lombard Street. Was visited by ship owners and marine insurance brokers. Led to the formation of the headquarters of Lloyd's of London.

Eesterivier Valleise Co-operative (S.Afr). Vineyards based in Stellenbosch. Address = Eesterivier Valleise Koöperatiewe Wynkelder, Box 2, Vlottenburg 7604. Produces varietal wines. Also makes Hanseret Wines.

Eesterivier Valleise Koöperatiewe Wynkelder (S.Afr). See Eesterivier Valleise Co-operative.

Efes Brewery (Tur). Breweries based in Izmir and İstanbul which are noted for Pilsener and dark beers.

Effervescence (Eng). The bubbling effect which occurs when a gas (CO_2) is released from a liquid. To give off bubbles.

Efringen-Kirchen (Ger). Village. (Anb) = Baden. (Ber) = Markgräflerland (Gro) = Vogtei Rötteln. (Vins) = Kirchberg, Oelberg, Sonnhohle, Steingässle.

E.G. (Eng) (abbr). A draught Ale 1047 O.G. brewed by Paines and Co. in St. Neots, Cambridgeshire. Named after the Eynesbury Grant.

Égalisage (Fr). The blending of wines from different vats in Bordeaux.

Eger (Hun). A town 137 kms north-east of Budapest. Is the centre of the vineyards that produces the reknowned Egri Bikavér wine. See Bull's Blood. Grape varieties – Kardarka, Kékfrankos, Leànyka and Médoc noir.

Eggenberg (Aus). A Weinviertel that produces light red and white wines.

Eggenberg Brauerei (Aus). A small brewery based between Salzburg and Linz.

Egger (Eng). A Pilsener Lager from H. Augustin, an Austrian drink importer based in Kensington.

Egger Brauerei (Switz). A brewery based in Worb.

Eggert (Ger). A liqueur producer. Address = 3116 Bevensen, Luneburger Heide.

Egg Flip (Cktl). An alternative name for Egg nog.

Egg Harbor (USA). A wine region near Atlantic City in the district of New Jersey.

Egg Lemonade (Cktl).(Non-alc). Juice of a lemon, 2 teaspoons powdered sugar, 1 egg. Shake over ice, strain into an ice-filled highball glass, top with soda water. Serve with straws.

Eggnog (Cktl). ²⁄₃ gill Brandy, 1 dash Rum, ³⁄₄ gill milk, 1 egg, 1 teaspoon sugar. Shake over ice, strain into a tumbler, add a dash of nutmeg on top. Can use Gin, Rum, Whisky in place of Brandy.

Egg Nogg (USA). An alternative spelling of Eggnog.

Egg Noggin (Eng). An old name for an Eggnog.

Eggnog Glass (USA). A straight-sided glass of 8 fl.oz. capacity.

Egg Sour (Cktl). 1 measure Brandy, 1 measure orange juice, 1 egg, lemon juice, teaspoon Gomme syrup. Shake over ice, strain into a goblet.

Egg Sour (Cktl).(Non-alc). Juice ½ lemon, 1 egg, sugar syrup to taste. Shake well over ice, strain into a wine glass. Add a splash of soda.

Egg White (Eng). Used as a fining agent. A little wine is whisked with the whites and this is added to the wine, which, as it sinks to the bottom takes impurities with it.

Eglantine Vineyard (Eng). A vineyard based at Eglantine House, Ash Lane, Costock, Near Loughborough, Leicestershire. Was first planted in 1980. 1.5 ha. Grape varieties – Madeleine angevine 65%, Müller-Thurgau and Seyval blanc.

Egli (Augusto) (Sp). A wine-producer based in Valencia. Produces red and white wines.

Égouttage (Fr). The removal of the free-run juice before the grapes are pressed. (USA) = De-juicing.

Égrappage (Fr). The process of removing the stalks from the grapes before fermentation. Used especially for white wines.

Égrappé (Fr). A mixture of grapes (red) with some of the stalks left in to increase the tannin content of the must.

Égrappoir (Fr). A machine used to de-stalk grapes before pressing. Also name for a person in pre-machine days who performed the same task.

Egri Bikavér (Hun). A reknowned, robust red wine of the Eger district, known as Bull's Blood. Made from a combination of Kardarka, Kékfrankos and Médoc noir grapes. See Bull's Blood and Dobo (Captain Istvan).

Egri Kadarka (Hun). A red grape and wine from the vineyards of Eger.

Egri Leànyka (Hun). A light, soft white wine from the local grape variety of same name.

E

Egri Leànyka (Hun). A white grape variety also known as the Luglianca bianca in Italy.

Egringen (Ger). Village. (Anb) = Baden. (Ber) = Markgräflerland. (Gro) = Vogtei Rötteln. (Vin) = Sonnhohle.

Eguisheim (Fr). A wine commune of the Haut-Rhin in Alsace.

Egyptian Vineyards and Distillers Company (Egy). A state-run cooperative that has vineyards near Alexandria. Noted for its Omar Khayyam (a red wine) and range of Brandies.

Ehnen (Lux). A wine village on the river Moselle. Vineyards – Kelterberg, Broomelt, Wousselt.

Ehrenberg (Ger). Vineyard. (Anb) = Mosel-Saar-Ruwer. (Ber) = Saar-Ruwer. (Gro) = Römerlay. (Vil) = Waldrach.

Ehrenfelser (Ger). A white, late-ripening grape variety, a cross between the Riesling and Sylvaner. Gives fruity acid wines.

Ehrenhausen (Aus). A wine-producing area in Südsteiermarken.

Ehrenstetten (Ger). Village. (Anb) = Baden. (Ber) = Markgräflerland. (Gro) = Lorettoberg. (Vins) = Oelberg, Rosenberg.

Ehrentrudis Spätburgunder Weissherbst (Ger). Must be, according to a Baden-Württemberg decree of the 4–7–1973 for Badener rosé wines of quality or Prädikat, made from Blauer Spätburgunder, grown in the Bereich of Kaiserstühl-Tuniberg.

Ehrle Brothers Winery (USA). A winery based in Iowa. Produces mainly French hybrid wines.

Ehrwein (Ger). Very fine wine.

Eibelstadt (Ger). Village. (Anb) = Franken. (Ber) = Maindreieck. (Gro) = Not yet assigned. (Vins) = Kapellenberg, Mönchsleite.

Eibensbach (Ger). Village. (Anb) = Württemberg. (Ber) = Württembergisch Unterland. (Gro) = Heuchelberg. (Vin) = Michaelsberg.

Eich (Ger). Village. (Anb) = Rheinhessen. (Ber) = Nierstein. (Gro) = Krötenbrunnen. (Vin) = Goldberg.

Eichberg (Ger). Vineyard. (Anb) = Baden. (Ber) = Breisgau. (Gro) = Burg Zähringen. (Vil) = Denzlingen.

Eichberg (Ger). Vineyard. (Anb) = Baden. (Ber) = Breisgau. (Gro) = Burg Zähringen. (Vil) = Glottertal.

Eichberg (Ger). Vineyard. (Anb) = Baden. (Ber) = Breisgau. (Gro) = Burg Zähringen. (Vil) = Heuweiler.

Eichberg (Ger). Vineyard. (Anb) = Baden. (Ber) = Kaiserstuhl-Tuniberg. (Gro) = Vulkanfelsen. (Vil) = Oberrotweil.

Eiche (Ger). Oak (tree).

Eichelberg (Ger). Lit – 'Acorn hill'. Name used for seven vineyards in Germany.

Eichelberg (Ger). Vineyard. (Anb) = Baden. (Ber) = Badische Bergstrasse/ Kraichgau. (Gro) = Hohenberg. (Vil) = Dürrn.

Eichelberg (Ger). Village. (Anb) = Baden. (Ber) = Badische Bergstrasse/Kraichgau. (Gro) = Stiftsberg. (Vin) = Kapellenberg.

Eichelberg (Ger). Vineyard. (Anb) = Baden. (Ber) = Badische Bergstrasse/ Kraichgau. (Gro) = Stiftsberg. (Vil) = Sinsheim (stadtteil Hilsbach).

Eichelberg (Ger). Vineyard. (Anb) = Rheinhessen. (Ber) = Bingen. (Gro) = Rheingrafenstein. (Vil) = Fürfeld.

Eichelberg (Ger). Vineyard. (Anb) = Rheinhessen. (Ber) = Bingen. (Gro) = Rheingrafenstein. (Vil) = Neu-Bamberg.

Eichelberg (Ger). Village. (Anb) = Württemberg. (Ber) = Württembergisch Unterland. (Gro) = Salzberg. (Vin) = Hundsberg.

Eichelberg (Ger). Vineyard. (Anb) = Württemberg. (Ber) = Württembergisch Unterland. (Gro) = Stromberg. (Vil) = Lienzingen.

Eichert (Ger). Vineyard. (Anb) = Baden. (Ber) = Kaiserstuhl-Tuniberg. (Gro) = Vulkanfelsen. (Vil) = Jechtingen.

Eichhof Brauerei (Switz). A brewery based in Lucerne.

Eichstetten (Ger). Village. (Anb) = Baden. (Ber) = Kaiserstuhl-Tuniberg (Gro) = Vulkanfelsen. (Vins) = Herrenbuck, Lerchenberg.

Eichtersheim (Ger). Village. (Anb) = Baden. (Ber) = Badische-Bergstrasse/ Kraichgau. (Gro) = Stiftsberg. (Vin) = Sonnenberg.

Eichwäldele (Ger). Vineyard. (Anb) = Baden. (Ber) = Ortenau. (Gro) = Schloss Rodeck. (Vil) = Obersasbach.

Eiderdown (Cktl). 1 part dry Gin, 4 parts apple wine. Stir together with ice, strain into a goblet, garnish with a twist of lemon peel.

Eierlikoer (Ger). Egg flip. The best known type in which the alcohol is only Brandy is called Eiweinbrand.

Eigenbaugewächs (Aus). From the maker's own vineyards.

Eigenbauwein (Aus). Describes a producer who sells his own wines.

Eigene Abfüllung (Ger). Bottled by the producer.

Eigengewächs (Ger). Growth.

Eight Bells (Cktl). ½ measure dark Rum, ⅙ measure dry Vermouth, ⅙ measure Van der Hum, ⅙ measure orange and lemon squash. Shake over ice, strain into a cocktail glass, top with grated nutmeg.

Eighteen Forty Three [1843] (Eng). A Lager 1042 O.G. brewed by the Arkell Brewery

E

in Swindon, Wiltshire. Name comes from the year the brewery was founded.

Eighteenth Amendment (USA). A law passed in June 1919 to introduce Prohibition.

Eighteen Twelve [1812] Vodka (Eng). A Vodka produced by Nicholson and Co. Ltd., London. (A subsidiary of Stewart and Son).

Eighty Shilling [80/-] Ale (Scot). A premium Beer brewed in Scotland. Sometimes called Export.

Eighty Shilling [80/-] Ale (Scot). Brewed by the Drybrough Brewery in Edinburgh.

Eighty Shilling [80/-] Export (Scot). A Beer brewed by the Belhaven Brewery in Dunbar, East Lothian. See Eighty Shilling [80/-] Ale.

Eightythree [83] (Can). A blended Canadian whisky produced by Seagram to commemorate Joseph Seagram's acquisition of his distillery in 1983.

Eikendal Vineyards (S.Afr). Vineyards based in Stellenbosch. Produces varietal wines.

Eilfingerberg (Ger). Lit – 'Eleven finger hill'. Name derived from the time during Lent when the abbot allowed the testing of the wine with the fingers only. A monk was purported to have said "One needs eleven fingers!". See Eilfingerberg Klosterstück.

Eilfingerberg Klosterstück (Ger). Vineyard. (Anb) = Württemberg. (Ber) = Württembergisch Unterland. (Gro) = Stromberg. (Vil) = Maulbronn

Eimeldingen (Ger). Village. (Anb) = Baden. (Ber) = Markgräflerland. (Gro) = Vogtei Rötteln. (Vin) = Sonnhohle.

Eimer (Aus). Bucket of wine.

Eimsheim (Ger). Village. (Anb) = Rheinhessen. (Ber) = Nierstein. (Gro) = Krötenbrunnen. (Vins) = Hexelberg, Römerschanze, Sonnenhang.

Einbeck (Ger). A city where the beer 'Bock' was first brewed. A corruption of 'Beck' by the people of Munich.

Einbecker Brauerei (Ger). A brewery of Einbeck in lower Saxony. Produces Bock beer and Einbecker Ur-Bock.

Einbecker Ur-Bock (Ger). A Bock beer produced by the Einbecker Brauerei in lower Saxony.

Einfachbieres (Ger). Weak German beers with an alcoholic strength of between 4.5% and 5.5% by vol.

Eingeschrumpften (Ger). An alternative name for Edelfäule.

Einhorn Lager (Eng). A keg Lager 1035 O.G. brewed by the Robinson Brewery in Stockport.

Einselthum (Ger). Village. (Anb) =

Rheinpfalz. (Ber) = Mittelhaardt-Deutsche Weinstrasse. (Gro) = Schnepfenflug vom Zellertal. (Vins) = Klosterstüch, Kreuzberg.

Einzelbogen (Ger). The single Guyot vine-training system. See also Doppelbogen.

Einzellage (Ger). Site. One individual vineyard. Divided up between different owners but must use the vineyard name.

Eisacktaler (It). A German term which means D.O.C. of Valle Isarco in Trentino-Alto Adige. White wine.

Eisack Valley (It). A principal wine-producing district in the Südtirol (known in Italian as the Valle d'Isarco).

Eisberg (Ger). An alcohol-free 0.05% alc. by vol. white wine. Low in calories and slightly sparkling.

Eisbock (Ger). A style of Doppelbock. The beer is frozen to remove some of the water to produce a strong beer 13.2% alc. by vol. Produces a rich flavour. See Kulminator.

Eisele Vineyard (USA). A vineyard based near Calistoga, Napa Valley, California. 8.5 ha. Grape variety – Cabernet sauvignon.

Eisele Vineyard [Volker] (USA). A small vineyard based in Chiles Valley, Napa Valley, California. Grape variety – Zinfandel. Wine sold under Page Mill label.

Eisenberg (Aus). A wine district within the region of South Burgenland. Produces mainly white wines with some reds.

Eisenstadt (Aus). A wine-producing district in Burgenland near the Leitha mountains. Produces mainly white wines.

Eisental (Ger). Village. (Anb) = Baden. (Ber) = Ortenau. (Gro) = Schloss Rodeck. (Vins) = Betschgräbler, Sommerhalde.

Eiserne Hand (Ger). Vineyard. (Anb) = Rheinhessen. (Ber) = Nierstein. (Gro) = Krötenbrunnen. (Vil) = Guntersblum.

Eisingen (Ger). Village. (Anb) = Baden. (Ber) = Badische Bergstrasse/Kraichgau. (Gro) = Hohenberg. (Vins) = Klepperg, Steig.

Eiskorn (Ger). A flavoured Kornbranntwein.

Eis-Liköre (Ger). When found on a liqueur bottle label, denotes that the contents are best drunk iced. 'On the rocks'.

Eiswein (Aus). Must be made exclusively from frozen grapes (both during harvest and pressing). Minimum must weight 25° KMW. The use of additional Prädikats such as Spätlese, Auslese etc. is forbidden. See also Schneewein.

Eiswein (Ger). Ripe grapes which have been frozen whilst on the vine. The water freezes but the juice doesn't. Rarely

E

occurs, but when it does produces luscious sweet wines. Gathered at below 8° C and crushed whilst still frozen. Used to have Prädikat gradings added, e.g. Auslese Eiswein, but now must be sold as a single Prädikat. Since 1982 a minimum of 110° Oescle.

Eitcheld Process (Fr). A method of fermentation.

Eitelsbach (Ger). A wine village on the River Ruwer.

Eitelsbacher Karthäuserhofberer (Ger). A wine that is noted for having the smallest label in Germany.

Ejarque Rebollar (Sp). A private bodega based in Utiel-Requena area in the Levante.

Éjetonnement (Fr). See Évasivage.

Ekenroth (Ger). Village. (Anb) = Nahe. (Ber) = Kreuznach. (Gro) = Schlosskapelle. (Vins) = Felsenberg, Hölle.

Ekko (Cktl). ½ oz. Mandarine Napoléon, ½ oz. Vodka, juice of ½ lemon, 1 dash Grenadine. Shake well over ice, strain into a cocktail glass. Add a cherry and a twist lemon peel.

Ekşi (Tur). Sour, very acidic. See also Kekre.

E.K.U. Brauerei (Ger) (abbr). Erste Kulmbacher Actienbrauerei. A brewery in Kulmbach. Makes one of the worlds' strongest beers. See Kulminator.

Elaberet Estate (Afr). A winery based in northern Ethiopia.

Elaboración (Sp). The initial blending of Brandy.

Elaborado (Sp). See Montilla-Moriles.

Eladorado y Añejado Por (Sp). Made and aged by.

Elba (It). An island between Tuscany on the mainland and Corsica. Produces both red and white wines. Wines sometimes taste of the tang of the sea.

Elba Bianco (It). D.O.C. white from the island of Elba. Made from the Trebbiano toscano grapes. D.O.C. also applies to the naturally sparkling wines made according to regulations.

Elba Rosso (It). D.O.C. red wine from the island of Elba. Made from the Canaiolo, Sangiovese and Trebbiano toscano bianco grapes.

Elbling (Ger). A white grape variety which is used in some of the wine regions. Gives a high yield. Also known as the Knipperlé. See also Albling, Alben, Grober, Grobriesling, Kleinberger, Kleinelbling and Kleinpereich.

El Calvador (Fr). The name of a Spanish galleon of the Armada which was shipwrecked on the Normandy coast from which Calvados takes its name.

El Cerro (Cktl). ½ fl.oz. Galliano, 1 fl.oz.

light Rum, 1 fl.oz. dark Rum, ½ fl.oz. Curaçao, 2 fl.ozs. pineapple juice, dash Grenadine. Shake over ice, strain into an ice-filled highball glass. Decorate with a pineapple ring, fresh strawberry and straws.

El Cesar (Sp). A 5 year old brandy produced by Romate.

El Cíd (Sp). A brand of Amontillado sherry produced by Duff Gordon.

Elciego (Sp). A noted wine-producing village based in the Alavesa district of Rioja, north-eastern Spain.

El Coto (Sp). The name for red and white wines produced by the Bodegas El Coto, S.A. Rioja.

El Değirmeni (Tur). Coffee grinder.

Elderberry (Eng). A wild fruit that produces fruit wines which are similar to heavy red wines. (Juice was sometimes used to improve the body of grape wines though now no longer practised). The flowers are used to produce home-made wines. (Produces a Gewürztraminer-style wine).

Elderflower (Eng). A popular flower (of the Elderberry tree) used in the making of dry home-made wines. Produces a wine similar in bouquet to the Gewürztraminer.

Elderflower Tea (Eng). A fragrant herbal tea that aids cold cures.

El Diablo Cocktail (Cktl). 1½ measures Tequila, ¾ measure Crème de Cassis, juice of ½ lime. Stir over ice in a highball glass together with the spent lime shell. Top with ginger ale and serve with straws.

Eldorado (USA). A vinegrowing county in the Sierra Foothills in California.

Eldorado Cocktail (Cktl). ⅓ gill Tequila, ⅕ gill lemon juice, teaspoon honey. Shake well over ice, strain into a collins glass with ice. Add a slice of orange.

Eldridge Pope Brewery (Eng). Based in Dorset, produces many fine beers including Thomas Hardy Ale 1125 O.G. Britain's strongest beer. Also produced are – cask conditioned Royal Oak 1048 O.G. Dorset Original IPA 1041 O.G. Pope's 1880 1041 O.G. Green top 1042 O.G. Crystal Bitter 1034 O.G. Faust Pilsener 1035 O.G. Sold under the Huntsman Ales name. Also owns 12 retail wine outlets in the Dorset area and J.B. Reynier in London.

Eleanor of Aquitaine (Fr). Queen. Married Henry 2nd of England in A.D. 1152 and so brought the vineyards of Bordeaux and Gascony under English control and introduced French wines in quantity into England.

Electric Pump (Eng). Beer dispenser. Two

types – Free flow pumps which switch on by a pressure switch that senses when the tap is opened and the displacement-type pump which has a calibrated half pint container where the beer is displaced when a button is pressed. (Latter is sealed by Customs and Excise).

Élégance (Fr). A term to describe a wine of good vintage having delicacy and lightness, but does not promise longevity.

Elegant (Eng). A term used by a wine taster to describe a wine of breeding but not with such high praise as to be distinguished.

Elegante Dry Fino (Sp). A brand of Fino sherry produced by Gonzalez Byass in Jerez.

Elephantenwein (Ger). A wine made from grapes that are so hard that an elephant would be required to crush them. Made in Tübingen and Reutlingen.

Elephant Lager (Den). Export lager 1062 O.G. brewed by the Carlsberg Brewery in Copenhagen, Denmark. Imported into England as Carlsberg 68.

Elephants (Eng). A grade of coffee bean. Those that are too large or have grown together in the coffee cherry.

Eleus (Lat). Word used for Bacchus. See also – Bassareus, Bromius, Dionysos, Dionysus, Euhan, Euan, Euhius, Euius, Lacchus, Lyaeus and Thyoneus.

Élevage (Fr). A term for the time between completion of fermentation and bottling when the wine is 'looked after'. An important time in viniculture.

Élevé (Fr). A label term which denotes 'grown'.

Eleven (Eng). A light, medium-sweet Sherry designed as a mixer from Harveys of Bristol.

Elevenses (Eng). An informal slang term for Morning coffee. Usually served at 11 am, but can be any time around that hour.

Éleveur (Fr). Grower. See Négociant-Éleveur.

Elfenlay (Ger). Vineyard. (Anb) = Mittelrhein. (Ber) = Rheinburgengau. (Gro) = Gedeonseck. (Vil) = Boppard.

El Gaitero (Sp). A noted brand of Cider produced in Chacolí, north-eastern Spain.

Elgin Glass (Eng). A small slim-waisted glass used for fortified wines and liqueurs.

Elgood Brewery (Eng). Based in Wisbech, Cambs. Produces – cask conditioned Fenman Bitter 1033 O.G. Russet Ale 1032 O.G. See Centenary Ale.

Elham Park (Eng). Vineyard. Address = North Elham, Dereham, Norfolk. 3 ha.

Soil – gravelly loam. Grape varieties – Müller-Thurgau 60% plus a variety of others. Produces – Elham Parker Müller-Thurgau.

Elham Parker Müller-Thurgau (Eng). See Elham Park.

Elham Valley Vineyards (Eng). A vineyard based at Breach, Barham, Kent. Was first planted in 1981. 0.75 ha. Grape varieties – Chasselas, Kerner, Madeleine angevine, Müller-Thurgau and Seyval blanc. Produces Pendant (a blended wine).

Elias Wineries (Isr). See Eliaz Wineries (alternative spelling).

Eliaz Wineries (Isr). A group of wineries, the best based in Binyamina.

Elisa (Cktl). ⅛ measure sweet Vermouth, ½ measure light Rum, ⅛ measure Apricot brandy, ⅛ measure Amaro. Stir over ice, strain into a Champagne flute, top with iced Asti Spumante. Add the zest of an orange and a cherry.

Elisabethanberg (Ger). Vineyard. (Anb) = Baden. (Ber) = Bodensee. (Gro) = Sonnenufer. (Vil) = Hilzingen.

Elisabethenberg (Ger). Vineyard. (Anb) = Baden. (Ber) = Bodensee. (Gro) = Sonnenufer. (Vil) = Singen.

Elisenberg (Ger). Vineyard. (Anb) = Mosel-Saar-Ruwer. (Ber) = Bernkastel. (Gro) = Kurfürstlay. (Vil) = Mülheim.

Elisenberg (Ger). Vineyard. (Anb) = Mosel-Saar-Ruwer. (Ber) = Bernkastel. (Gro) = Kurfürstlay. (Vil) = Veldenz.

Élixer (Fr). The old term used to describe liqueurs. Liqueurs made from the finest distillates.

Élixer d'Amorique (Fr). A herb liqueur produced near Lannion in north-western France.

Élixer d'Anvers (Bel). A yellow-green, bitter-sweet liqueur made from herbs by De Beuckelaer. 34.5% alc. by vol.

Élixer de Garrus (Fr). A brand of elixir produced by Picard et Cazot Fils, Lyons. Made from spirits, vanilla, saffron, maidenhead fern and orange flower water.

Élixer de la Chartreuse (Fr). A brand of elixir produced by Picard et Cazot Fils, Lyons.

Élixer de la Maréchale d'Estrées (Fr). Considered to be the original recipe for Chartreuse (green). Produced in the eighteenth century. See Élixer de Santé.

Elixer dell'Eremita (It). A herb-flavoured liqueur made by the Camaldoli order.

Élixer de Monbazillac (Fr). A nickname for the sweet wine of Bergerac.

Elixer de Mondorf (Lux). A liqueur which originates from the nineteenth century.

Élixer de Santé (Fr). 'Elixir of health'.

E

1764, forerunner of Green Chartreuse. See Élixer de la Maréchale d'Estrées.

Élixer des Braves (Fr). A brand of elixir produced by Picard et Cazot Fils, Lyons.

Élixer de Spa (Bel). A pale green-yellow herb liqueur produced by the Capuchin monks in the town of Spa.

Élixer de Table (Fr). An old name for liqueurs used as digestifs.

Elixer di China (It). A sweet colourless liqueur made from aniseed.

Élixer du Mont Ventoux (Fr). A herb liqueur produced in Avignon.

Elixer Longae Vitae (Ger) (Hol). An alternative name for Pommeranzen bitters.

Élixer Végétal (Fr). An 80% alc. by vol. version of the Élixer de Santé. Sold in a small bottle. Used as a medicinal liqueur.

Élixer Vital (Fr). A brand of elixir produced by Picard et Cazot Fils, Lyons, southern France.

Elixir (Eng). The English spelling of Elixer.

Elizabethan (Eng). A pale, dry, Fino sherry from Avery's of Bristol.

Elizabethan Barley Wine (Eng). A strong Pale ale 1090 O.G. brewed by the Harvey's Brewery in Lewes, Sussex. Occasionally sold in draught form.

Elizabethan Mead (Eng). The brand-name of a Mead produced by Lamb and Watt of Liverpool.

El Jardinero Cocktail (Cktl). ¾ measure white Rum, ½ measure Sambuca, ¼ measure lime juice. Shake well over ice, strain into a scooped out marrow shell. Serve with straws.

Elk (Hol). Oak.

Elk Cove Vineyards (USA). A small winery based in Gaston, Oregon. 8 ha. Produces vinifera wines.

Elkersberg (Ger). Vineyard. (Anb) = Nahe. (Ber) = Schloss Böckelheim (Gro) = Paradiesgarten. (Vil) = Alsenz.

Elk's Own (Cktl). 1 measure Bourbon whiskey, ½ measure Port, juice ¼ lemon, 1 egg white, dash Gomme syrup. Shake over ice, strain into a cocktail glass. Decorate with piece of pineapple.

Ellagic Acid (Eng). Is obtained from the wooden casks. Absorbed by the wines that are matured in them. A simple tannin that causes astringency in the wine.

Ellenz-Poltersdorf (Ger). Village. (Anb) = Mosel-Saar-Ruwer. (Ber) = Zell/Mosel. (Gro) = Goldbäumchen. (Vins) = Alterberg, Kurfürst, Ruberberger Domherrenberg.

Ellenz-Poltersdorf (Ger). Village. (Anb) = Mosel-Saar-Ruwer. (Ber) = Zell/Mosel.

(Gro) = Rosenhang. (Vins) = Silberberg, Woogberg.

Ellergrub (Ger). Vineyard. (Anb) = Mosel-Saar-Ruwer. (Ber) = Bernkastel. (Gro) = Schwarzlay. (Vil) = Enkirch.

Ellerstadt (Ger). Village. (Anb) = Rheinpfalz. (Ber) = Mittelhaardt-Deutsche Weinstrasse. (Gro) = Feuerberg. (Vins) = Bubeneck, Dickkopp, Sonnenberg.

Ellerstadt (Ger). Village. (Anb) = Rheinpfalz. (Ber) = Mittelhaardt-Deutsche Weinstrasse. (Gro) = Hofstück. (Vin) = Kirchenstück.

Ellhofen (Ger). Village. (Anb) = Württemberg. (Ber) = Württembergisch Unterland. (Gro) = Salzberg. (Vins) = Altenberg, Althälde, Rauzenberg.

Elliot Winery (Austr). A winery based in Hunter Valley, New South Wales. Their vineyard is called Oakville.

Ellisse Cocktail (Cktl). 1 measure Cognac, dash Angostura, dash Strega. Stir over ice, strain into an ice-filled highball glass. Top with ginger ale and lemon peel spiral.

Ellis Vineyard (USA). The label used by the Mark West vineyards, Russian River Valley, California.

Ellmendingen (Ger). Village. (Anb) = Baden. (Ber) = Badische Bergstrasse/Kraichgau. (Gro) = Hohenberg. (Vin) = Keulebuckel.

Ellner et Fils (Fr). A Champagne producer based in Épernay.

El Metraya (Cktl). 1 fl.oz. Tia Maria, ½ fl.oz. dark Rum, 3 fl.ozs. cane syrup. Shake well over ice. Pour into a goblet.

El Mezcal (Mex). The brand-name of a Tequila.

Elmham Park Vineyard (Eng). Situated in Norfolk. 3 ha. First planted 1971. Grape varieties – Madeleine angevine 20% and Müller-Thurgau 80%.

El Montecillo (Sp). See Bodegas El Montecillo.

Elongated Wine (Eng). A term used to describe a wine that has been increased by the addition of water to reduce the alcoholic strength for purposes of Excise duty.

Eloro (It). The name for red and white wines produced in Sicily near Noto and Ragusa.

El Paso Winery (USA). A winery based in Ulster Park, Hudson Valley, New York.

El Pepino Cocktail (Cktl). 1 fl.oz. golden Rum, ½ fl.oz. Triple Sec, 1½ fl.ozs. pineapple juice, 1½ fl.ozs. orange juice, dash Grenadine. Stir well over ice, strain into a scooped-out marrow shell. Serve with straws.

Elpersheim (Ger). Village. (Anb) =

Württemberg. (Ber) = Kocher-Jagst-Tauber. (Gro) = Tauberberg. (Vins) = Mönchsberg, Probstberg.

El Presidente (Cktl). 1/3 gill Rum, 1/8 gill pineapple juice, 1/8 gill Grenadine, juice of a lime. Shake over ice, strain into a cocktail glass.

El Presidente Cocktail (Cktl). 3/5 measure Rum, 1/5 measure Curaçao, 1/5 measure dry Vermouth, dash Grenadine. Shake over ice, strain into a cocktail glass. Decorate with a twist orange peel.

Elqui (Chile). A principal wine region in the north, producing fine wines.

Els (Ger). A Bitters made by the Hennekens Distillery at Beck.

El Salvador (C.Am). A coffee-producing country that produces mainly Arabica beans.

Elsäss (Ger). The name for the Alsace region in the nineteenth century. See also Ilsace.

Elsässer Wein (Ger). The name for the wines of Alsace to distinguish them from the Rhine wines.

Elsäss-Lothringen (Ger). Alsace-Lorraine.

Elsenz (Ger). Village. (Anb) = Baden. (Ber) = Badische Bergstrasse/Kraichgau. (Gro) = Stiftsberg. (Vin) = Spiegelberg.

Elsinore (Austr). A winery based in Granite Belt, Queensland.

Elskebitter (Hol). A bitter beer.

Elster (Ger). Vineyard. (Anb) = Rheinpfalz. (Ber) = Mittelhaardt-Deutsche Weinstrasse. (Gro) = Mariengarten. (Vil) = Forst.

Elterberg (Lux). A vineyard site in the village of Wormeldange.

Eltville (Ger). Village. (Anb) = Rheingau. (Ber) = Johannisberg. (Gro) = Heiligenstock. (Vin) = Sandgrub.

Eltville (Ger). Village. (Anb) = Rheingau. (Ber) = Johannisberg. (Gro) = Steinmächer. (Vins) = Langenstück, Rheinberg, Sandgrub, Sonnenberg, Taubenberg.

El Viejito (Mex). A producer of Tequila of same name. 47% alc. by vol.

Elvira (USA). A white grape variety produced from Vitis Riparia and Vitis Labrusca cross. Is slowly being replaced.

Elvot (Eng). An old English cider-making apple.

Elzogberg (Ger). Vineyard. (Anb) = Mosel-Saar-Ruwer. (Ber) = Zell/Mosel. (Gro) = Grafschaft. (Vil) = Ediger-Eller.

El Zorzal Cocktail (Cktl). 1/2 measure Anisette, 1/2 measure white Rum, 1 measure orange juice, dash Grenadine. Shake well over ice, strain into an ice-filled old-fashioned glass. Dress with a pineapple slice, orange slice and cherry.

Embassy Royal (Cktl). 1/2 measure Bourbon whiskey, 1/4 measure Drambuie, 1/4 measure sweet Vermouth, 2 dashes orange squash. Shake over ice, strain into a cocktail glass.

Embolicaire (Sp). A black grape variety grown in central Spain.

Embotellado (Sp). Bottled.

Embres-et-Castelmaure (Fr). A noted wine-producing village based in the A.C. Corbières district of Languedoc, south-western France.

Embriaguaz (Port). Intoxication, drunken.

Emerald Cocktail (Cktl). 1/3 gill Gin, 1/8 gill (green) Crème de Menthe, dash Angostura, dash lemon juice, 1/2 egg white. Shake over ice, strain into a cocktail glass. Top with a green cherry.

Emerald Dry (USA). A white grape variety developed by the University of California and grown in the Paul Masson Vineyards.

Emerald Isle Cocktail (Cktl). 1/5 measure dry Gin, 4 dashes green Crème de Menthe, 3 dashes Angostura. Stir over ice, strain into a cocktail glass.

Emerald Riesling (USA). A hybrid grape variety grown in California. High yielding it produces dry white wines. Cross between the White riesling and the Muscatelle (Muscat).

Emerald Sparkler (Cktl). 1 part Midori liqueur, 3 parts Champagne. Pour Midori and Champagne in a saucer glass. Decorate with a green cherry.

Emerald Swizzle (Cktl). Into an ice-filled highball glass place 1 measure Midori, 2 measures dry Cinzano. Stir, top with lemonade. Serve with straws.

Emeringes (Fr). A commune in the Beaujolais. Has the A.C. Beaujolais-Villages of Beaujolais-Emeringes status.

Emerson Cocktail (Cktl). 3/4 measure Gin, 1/4 measure sweet Vermouth, juice 1/2 lemon, 4 dashes Maraschino. Shake over ice, strain into a cocktail glass.

Emeryville (USA). A vine-growing city in Almeda County, California.

Émet (Ch.Isles). Cider press.

Emilia (Cktl). 1/2 measure Bacardi Rum, 1/4 measure Apricot brandy, 1/4 measure Grand Marnier, dash Orange bitters. Stir over ice, strain into a cocktail glass.

Emilia Romagna (It). A wine region around Bologna. Red wines being the main production. Lambrusco, Sangiovese, etc.

Eminencia (Sp). A 6 year old Brandy produced by Palomino y Vergara S.A., Colon 1–25, Jerez de la Frontera, Cadiz.

Emir (Tur). A red grape variety grown in Middle Anatolia.

Emita d'Espiells (Sp). An estate-bottled white wine produced by Juvé y Camps in San Sadurní de Noya, Cataluña, south-eastern Spain.

E

Emma Green (Cktl). 2/10 measure dry Gin, 1/10 measure Amaretto di Saronno, 1/10 measure blue Curaçao, 1/10 measure orange juice, 5/10 measure sparkling wine, dash egg white. Shake well over ice, strain, add sparkling wine and a slice of lime.

Emmendingen [ortsteil Hochberg] (Ger). Village. (Anb) = Baden. (Ber) = Briesgau. (Gro) = Burg Zähringen. (Vin) = Halde.

Emmets (Ire). A brand of cream liqueur produced by Emmet & Company. 17% alc. by vol.

Empéreur (Fr). A brand of Grande Champagne Cognac produced by Lafont de Saint-Preuil.

Emperor (USA). A white grape variety used in small quantities for Brandy production.

Emperor's Brandy (The) (Eng). A name given to Courvoisier Cognac after casks of it were found on his ship in 1815 when he was fleeing to America.

Empilage (Fr). The rest period for Champagne. Gives the wine a chance to settle down after the disturbance of dégorgement which cannot be skimped if quality is the aim.

Empire Cocktail (Cktl). 1/4 measure Gin, 1/4 measure Calvados, 1/4 measure Apricot brandy. Shake well over ice, strain into a cocktail glass.

Empire Glory (Cktl). 1/2 measure Rye whiskey, 1/4 measure lemon juice, 1/4 measure Ginger wine, 3 dashes Grenadine. Shake well over ice, strain into a cocktail glass.

Emu (Austr). A brand-name used by the Swan Brewery for their Emu Export Lager and Emu Bitter (a Lager beer).

Emu (Austr). A bulk shipper in South Australia.

Emu Bitter (Austr). See Emu.

Emu Export Lager (Austr). See Emu.

Emu Winery (Austr). A winery based in Reynella in Southern Vales, South Australia.

Emva Cream (Cyp). A famous brand of Cyprus sweet sherry produced by the Etko Co. (A subsidiary of Haggipavlu in Limassol).

En Cailleret (Fr). A Premier Cru vineyard [part] in the A.C. commune of Chassagne-Montrachet, Côte de Beaune, Burgundy. 5.49 ha. Also known as Les Cailleret.

En Caradeux (Fr). A Premier Cru vineyard [part] in the A.C. commune of Pernand-Vergelesses, Côte de Beaune, Burgundy. 20 ha.

Encépagement (Fr). Vine varieties planted in a particular vineyard.

Enchada (Mad). A tool which is a cross between a hoe and a pick for tending the vineyard soil.

En Champans (Fr). A Premier Cru vineyard in the A.C. commune of Volnay, Côte de Beaune, Burgundy. 11.3 ha. Also known as Les Champans.

Encruzado (Port). A white grape variety grown in the Dão region.

Endeavour (Austr). The brand-name of a Rum produced by Bundaberg in Queensland.

En de l'El (L') (Fr). A white grape variety grown in the Gaillac region of southwestern France.

Endersbach (Ger). Village. (Anb) = Württemberg. (Ber) = Remstal-Stuttgart. (Gro) = Wartbühl. (Vins) = Happenhalde, Wetzstein.

Endersbach (Ger). Village. (Anb) = Württemberg. (Ber) = Remstal-Stuttgart. See Weinstadt.

Endikos Diateremenon (Gre). On the bottle label means 'Mature quality wine'. See also Endikos Diatirimenon.

Endikos Diatirimenon (Gre). The alternative spelling of Endikos Diateremenon.

Endingen (Ger). Village. (Anb) = Baden. (Ber) = Kaiserstuhl-Tuniberg. (Gro) = Vulkanfelsen. (Vins) = Engelsberg, Steingrube, Tannacker.

Endocarp (Eng). The alternative name for the Parchment in a coffee cherry.

Energiser (Eng). A compound added to slow or reluctant fermentations to reactivate the yeast.

En Ergots (Fr). See Ergots.

Enfant-Jésus (Fr). Part of the Premier Cru vineyards of Les Grèves, in the Côte de Beaune. Owned by Bouchard Père.

Enfer d'Arvier (It). A red wine from the Val d'Aosta. Made from the Dolcetto, Neyret, Petit-rouge and Viendenus grapes. Must age for minimum 1 year in wooden casks holding no more than 3 hl.

Enforcado (Port). A method of lacing vines through the branches of trees.

Engadi (Cyp). An ancient vineyard based in southern Cyprus. Was written about in the Bible (Solomon's Song of songs Chapter 1 verse 14).

Engageat Blanc (Fr). An alternative name for the Folle blanche grape.

Engarrafado na Origem (Port). Estate bottled.

Engelgrube (Ger). Vineyard. (Anb) = Mosel-Saar-Ruwer. (Ber) = Bernkastel. (Gro) = Michelsberg. (Vil) = Neumagen-Dhron.

Engelmannsberg (Ger). Vineyard. (Anb) = Rheingau. (Ber) = Johannisberg. (Gro) = Deutelsberg. (Vil) = Hattenheim.

Engelsberg (Ger). Vineyard. (Anb) =

E

Baden. (Ber) = Kaiserstuhl-Tuniberg. (Gro) = Vulkanfelsen. (Vil) = Endingen.

Engelsberg (Ger). Village. (Anb) = Franken. (Ber) = Mainviereck. (Gro) = Not yet assigned. (Vin) = Klostergarten.

Engelsberg (Ger). Vineyard. (Anb) = Rheinhessen. (Ber) = Nierstein. (Gro) = Spiegelberg. (Vil) = Nackenheim.

Engelsberg (Ger). Vineyard. (Anb) = Rheinhessen. (Ber) = Wonnegau. (Gro) = Domblick. (Vil) = Offstein.

Engelsberg (Ger). Vineyard. (Anb) = Rheinpfalz. (Ber) = Südliche Weinstrasse. (Gro) = Herrlich. (Vil) = Herxheim bei Landau.

Engelsfelsen (Ger). Vineyard. (Anb) = Baden. (Ber) = Ortenau. (Gro) = Schloss Rodeck. (Vil) = Bühlertal.

Engelstadt (Ger). Village. (Anb) = Rheinhessen. (Ber) = Bingen. (Gro) = Kaiserpfalz. (Vins) = Adelpfad, Römerberg.

Engelstein (Ger). Vineyard. (Anb) = Mittelrhein. (Ber) = Rheinburgengau. (Gro) = Gedeonseck. (Vil) = Boppard.

Engelstein (Ger). Vineyard. (Anb) = Mittelrhein. (Ber) = Rheinburgengau. (Gro) = Gedeonseck. (Vil) = Spay.

Engelströpfchen (Ger). Vineyard. (Anb) = Mosel-Saar-Ruwer. (Ber) = Zell/Mosel. (Gro) = Grafschaft. (Vil) = Ediger-Eller.

En Genêt (Fr). A Premier Cru vineyard in the A.C. commune of Beaune, Côte de Beaune, Burgundy. 4.32 ha.

Enggass (Ger). Vineyard. (Anb) = Mosel-Saar-Ruwer. (Ber) = Bernkastel. (Gro) = Sankt Michael. (Vil) = Thörnich.

England (Eng). A country which produces wines, mainly white in style, fairly acidic and light in body. Relies heavily on the weather which in most years is insufficient to produce wines of quality. See also British Wines.

English Ale (Eng). A bottled beer 1042 O.G. brewed by Whitbreads Brewery. Is low in carbohydrates, so suitable for diabetics.

English Bishop (Cktl). Bake an orange with 12 cloves, cut into quarters. Place in bowl and top with a bottle of heated Port. Add sugar, return to heat, cover for ½ hour. Add 1 gill Rum, ground ginger and cinnamon to taste.

English Bolo (Cktl). 1 gill Manzanilla, juice ½ lemon, ¼ teaspoon sugar ¼ teaspoon ground cinnamon. Mix sugar, cinnamon and lemon juice together in an old-fashioned glass. Add ice and Sherry, stir and serve.

English Breakfast Tea (Eng). A blend of Ceylon (Sri Lanka) and Indian small leaf teas. Gives a full-bodied tea.

English Coffee (Liq.Coffee). Using a measure of London dry Gin.

English Factory House (Port). See Feitoria Inglesa.

English Highball (Cktl). ⅓ measure Brandy, ⅓ measure Italian vermouth, ⅓ measure Gin. Shake over ice, strain into an ice-filled highball glass. Top with soda water and a twist of lemon peel juice.

English London Dry (USA). A style of dry Gin.

English Market (USA). A dry Gin. Brand-name of the Old Mr. Boston Distillers of Boston, Massachusetts.

English Rose (Cktl). ½ measure dry Gin, ¼ measure Apricot brandy, ¼ measure French vermouth, 4 dashes Grenadine, 2 dashes lemon juice. Shake over ice, strain into a sugar-rimmed cocktail glass. Top with a cherry.

English Vineyards Association Limited (Eng). Address = 38, West Park London SE9 4RH.

English Vineyards Certification Trade Mark (Eng). The A.C. equivalent for the wines of England.

English Wine (Eng). A wine made from freshly gathered grapes grown in England and vinified without any preservative. See British Wine.

Engweg (Ger). Vineyard. (Anb) = Württemberg. (Ber) = Kocher-Jagst-Tauber. (Gro) = Kocherberg. (Vil) = Niedernhall.

Engweg (Ger). Vineyard. (Anb) = Württemberg. (Ber) = Kocher-Jagst-Tauber. (Gro) = Kocherberg. (Vil) = Weissbach.

Eniséli (USSR). A white grape variety grown in the Georgia region. Is used in the production of Brandy.

Enivrer (Fr). Intoxicate.

Enkirch (Ger). Village. (Anb) = Mosel-Saar-Ruwer. (Ber) = Bernkastel. (Gro) = Schwarzlay. (Vins) = Batterieberg, Edelberg, Ellergrub, Herrenberg, Monteneubel, Steffensberg, Weinkammer, Zeppwingert.

En la Chaîne-Carteau (Fr). A Premier Cru vineyard [part] in the A.C. commune of Nuits-Saint-Georges, Côte de Nuits, Burgundy. 2.6 ha.

En l'Orme (Fr). A Premier Cru vineyard in the A.C. commune of Beaune, Côte de Beaune, Burgundy. 2.02 ha.

En l'Ormeau (Fr). A Premier Cru vineyard in the A.C. commune of Volnay, Côte de Beaune, Burgundy. 4.3 ha. Also known as L'Ormeau.

Enmore (S.Am). A Rum distillery based in Guyana.

Enocarboj (It). A noted wine co-operative based in Sciassa, Sicily.

Enoch's Hammer (Eng). A cask condi-

E

tioned Bitter 1080 O.G. from Sair, a home-brew public house in Linthwaite, Huddersfield.
Enologia (Sp). The study of wine.
Enologica Valtellinese (It). A wine producer in the Valtellina region noted for their Valtellina, Grumello and Inferno wines.
Enology (Eng). An alternative spelling of Oenology. The study of wine.
Enoteca (It). A wine library where wines are shown, tasted and sold.
Enoteca Permanente (It). A wine library in the Grinzano Castle near Alba. Wines of the region are on show and for tasting.
Enotecnio (It). Oenological consultant.
En Pauland (Fr). A Premier Cru vineyard [part] in the A.C. commune of Aloxe-Corton, Côte de Beaune, Burgundy.
En Remilly (Fr). A Premier Cru vineyard in the A.C. commune of Saint-Aubin, Côte de Beaune, Burgundy. 2 ha.
Enrichment (Eng). The sugaring of the grape must. (Fr) = Chaptalisation. (Ger) = Anreichern.
En Saussilles (Fr). A Premier Cru vineyard in the A.C. commune of Pommard. Côte de Beaune, Burgundy. 3.8 ha. Is also known as Les Saussilles.
Ensch (Ger). Village. (Anb) = Mosel-Saar-Ruwer. (Ber) = Bernkastel. (Gro) = Sankt Michael. (Vins) = Mühlenberg, St. Martin, Sonnenlay.
Enselberg (Ger). Vineyard. (Anb) = Baden. (Ber) = Kaiserstuhl-Tuniberg. (Gro) = Vulkanfelsen. (Vil) = Bischoffingen.
Enselberg (Ger). Vineyard. (Anb) = Baden. (Ber) = Kaiserstuhl-Tuniberg. (Gro) = Vulkenfelsen. (Vil) = Jechtingen.
Ensheim (Ger). Village. (Anb) = Rheinhessen. (Ber) = Bingen. (Gro) = Adelberg. (Vin) = Kachelberg.
Ensingen (Ger). Village. (Anb) = Württemberg. (Ber) = Württembergisch Unterland. (Gro) = Stromberg. (Vin) = Schanzreiter.
Enterprise Wines (Austr). A winery based in the Clare Valley, South Australia. Grape varieties – Cabernet sauvignon, Fumé blanc and Rhine riesling. Produces varietal wines.
Entire (Eng). A form of Porter called Entire butts. Brewed to incorporate three separate beers in one butt or cask a Pale, a Brown and a Stock ale. In the early eighteenth century sold as three thirds or three threads.
Entire Bitter (Eng). A cask conditioned Bitter 1043 O.G. brewed by the Holt, Plant and Deakin Brewery.

Entire Butts (Eng). See Entire.
Entonneurs Rabelaisiens (Fr). A wine society based in Chinon, Loire.
Entonnoir à Porto (Fr). Wine funnel. A device used for decanting Port. The end of the funnel is rested against the side of the decanter so that the wine does not gather air as it is decanted.
Entournerier (Fr). An alternative name for the Syrah grape.
Entre Blanc et Rouge (Fr). A grade of rosé wine made from a blend of red and white wine.
Entre-Deux-Mers (Fr). A large wine area within the Bordeaux region. Lit – 'Between two seas'. Lies between the rivers Garonne and Dordogne. Produces A.C. white wines and A.C. Bordeaux reds.
Entre-Deux-Mers Haut Benauge (Fr). A white wine A.C. See Haut Benauge.
Entre Fino (Sp). A term used to describe a Fino sherry that is lacking in distinction.
Entre Minho e Douro (Port). A demarcated region of Portugal. Vinho Verde is the main wine produced.
Entre Ríos (Arg). A wine-producing area west of Santa Fe.
Entschleimen (Ger). The process of letting the freshly pressed must stand to let the solids settle to the bottom. (Fr) = Débourbage, (Sp) = Desfangado.
Envase (Sp). Bottling.
Enveloppe (Fr). A straw case that was used to protect bottles. Cardboard has now mainly replaced the straw. (Is banned in USA).
En Verseuil (Fr). A Premier Cru vineyard in the A.C. commune of Volnay, Côte de Beaune, Burgundy. 18 ha.
Envites (Lat). A sub-genus of the Vitis species of Ampelidaceae of which grapes for wine production are members.
Enzian (Ger). A term used to signify Gentian-flavoured liqueurs. Enzian means Gentian. Also used in Austria and Bavaria.
Enzian Calisay (Sp). Sweet, pale gold liqueur based on gentian and other herbs.
Enz [River] (Ger). A tributary of the river Neckar in Württemberg. Soil is shell limestone.
Enz Vineyards (USA). A winery based in San Benito, California. 12.5 ha. Grape varieties – Chasselas, Pinot St. Georges and Zinfandel. Produces varietal wines and Limestone (a flavoured apéritif wine).
Enzymes (Eng). A group of substances found in animals and plants which decompose carbon compounds.
Eocene (It). Clay schist soils.
Epee (Cktl). ¾ measure Cognac, ¼ measure

sweet Vermouth. Stir well with ice, strain into a cocktail glass.

Épenots (Fr). A Premier Cru vineyard of the A.C. commune of Pommard, Côte de Beaune, Burgundy. 8.06 ha. Also spelt Les Epenottes.

Epenottes (Les) (Fr). A Premier Cru vineyard [part] in the A.C. commune of Beaune, Côte de Beaune, Burgundy. 8.06 ha.

Épernay (Fr). An important Champagne centre. Headquarters of many of the Grandes Marques. Canton d'Épernay has the Grand Cru village of Chouilly [white], Premier Cru villages of Chouilly [red] and Pierry, and Cru villages of Damery, Épernay, Fleur-la-Rivière, Mardeuil, Moussy, Saint-Martin-d'Ablois, Vaucienne, Venteuil and Vinay.

Épernay (Fr). A Cru Champagne town in the Canton d'Épernay. District = Épernay.

Épesses (Switz). A dry white wine-producing village in the Vaud canton.

Épieds (Fr). A region in the A.C. Saumur, Anjou-Saumur, Loire. Produces red and white wines.

Epinette Blanche (Fr). An alternative name for the Chardonnay grape.

Epinettes (Fr). The scissor-like cutters used to cut off the bunches of grapes in Champagne.

Épineuil (Fr). A village in the Yonne, noted for its' Vin gris.

Epinottes (Les) (Fr). A Premier Cru vineyard of A.C. Chablis. Often is reclassified as the Premier Cru Mélinots.

Epirus (Gre). A red and white wine-producing region in north-western Greece. Grapes – Debina (white) and Cabernet sauvignon (red).

Epirus (Gre). A white grape variety grown in Attica.

Episcopal (Cktl). ½ measure yellow Izarra, ½ measure green Izarra. Pour over crushed ice, serve in a goblet with straws.

Epitrapezio Krasi (Gre). Table wine.

Épluchage (Fr). The picking out of rotten and broken black grapes from the picked bunches especially in the Champagne region.

Épondage (Fr). The pruning of dead twigs and suckers off the vine. Is usually done in November.

Epotare (Lat). To drink up, booze.

Eppelsheim (Ger). Village. (Anb) = Rheinhessen. (Ber) = Wonnegau. (Gro) = Bergkloster. (Vin) = Felsen.

Eppingen (Ger). Village. (Anb) = Baden. (Ber) = Badische Bergstrasse/Kraichgau. (Gro) = Stiftsberg. (Vin) = Lerchenberg.

Équilibré (Fr). Harmonious, a well-balanced wine.

Equipe 5 (It). A group formed by five independent producers. Noted for a wide range of sparkling (méthode champenoise) wines.

Eral (Sp). A red wine produced by Bodegas José Palacios, Alta region in Rioja. Made from Garnacha 60% and Tempranillo 40%. Reservas and Gran Reservas are oak matured and then bottle matured.

Éraville (Fr). A commune in the Charente Département whose grapes are classed Grande Champagne (Cognac).

Erbach (Ger). Village. (Anb) = Rheingau. (Ber) = Johannisberg. (Gro) = Deutelsberg. (Vins) = Hohenrain, Honigberg, Marcobrunn, Michelmark, Schlossberg, Siegelsberg, Steinmorgen.

Erbacher Vineyards (USA). A winery based in Roxburg, Connecticut. Produces mainly French hybrid grapes.

Erbaluce (It). A white wine grape variety.

Erbaluce di Caluso (It). D.O.C. white wine from Piemonte. Made from the Erbaluce grape grown in the commune of Caluso and others.

Erbalus di Caluso (USA). White grape variety grown in California to make dessert wines.

Erbarola (It). A Ligurian name for the white Albarola grape.

Erben (Ger). Estate of, Heirs of.

Erbes-Bürdesheim (Ger). Village. (Anb) = Rheinhessen. (Ber) = Bingen. (Gro) = Adelberg. (Vins) = Geisterberg, Vogelsang.

Erdbeergeist (Ger) (Switz). Strawberry brandy. Soft fruit brandy.

Erdeck (Tur). A wine-producing area in north-western Turkey. Produces red and white wines.

Erdelega (Eng). Vineyard at Ardleigh, Essex.

Erden (Ger). Village. (Anb) = Mosel-Saar-Ruwer. (Ber) = Bernkastel. (Gro) = Schwarzlay. (Vins) = Busslay, Herrenberg, Prälat, Treppchen.

Erdevik (Yug). A wine-producing area in Fruška Gora, Vojvodina.

Erdig (Ger). Earthy.

Erdmannhausen (Ger). Village. (Anb) = Württemberg. (Ber) = Württembergisch Unterland. (Gro) = Schalkstein. (Vin) = Neckarhälde.

Erdöbénye (Hun). A wine-producing village based in the southern foothills.

Erdut (Yug). A wine-producing town based in northern Croatia.

Erévan (USSR). A white grape variety grown in Armenia. Used in Brandy production.

Ergersheim (Ger). Village. (Anb) = Franken. (Ber) = Steigerwald. (Gro) = Schlosstück. (Vin) = Altenberg.

Ergonomic System (Eng). Vine growing. Bio-Technological.

Ergots (Fr). A Premier Cru vineyard in the A.C. commune of Gevrey-Chambertin, Côte de Nuits, Burgundy. 1.17 ha. Also known as En Ergots.

Erie Brewery (USA). A brewery based in Erie.

Erikois (Fin). A term denoting 'Special' (in relation to beer).

Erinose (Eng). A tiny mite that forms blisters on flower clusters, leaves and grapes. Many vines are now resistant to it.

Eriophyes Vitis (Lat). The name given to the grape bud mite. See also Acariosis.

Eriosoma Lanigera (Lat). See Apple Blight.

Eritire (Afr). One of three main wine-producing regions in Ethiopia. See also Abadir-Dukem and Guder.

Erkenbrecht (Ger). Vineyard. (Anb) = Rheinpfalz. (Ber) = Mittelhaardt-Deutsche Weinstrasse. (Gro) = Rebstöckel. (Vil) = Neustadt an der Weinstrasse.

Erlabrunn (Ger). Village. (Anb) = Franken. (Ber) = Maindreieck. (Gro) = Ravensburg. (Vin) = Weinsteig.

Erlach (Ger). Village. (Anb) = Baden. (Ber) = Ortenau. (Gro) = Fürsteneck. (Vin) = Renchtäler.

Erlach (Switz). A red wine produced from the Bienne vineyards in Berne.

Erlau (Hun). A wine district that produces red and white wines.

Erlenbach (Ger). Village. (Anb) = Württemberg. (Ber) = Württembergisch Unterland. (Gro) = Staufenberg. (Vin) = Kazberg.

Erlenbach (Switz). A principal vineyard based in Zurich.

Erlenbach a. Main (Ger). Village. (Anb) = Franken. (Ber) = Mainviereck. (Gro) = Not yet assigned. (Vin) = Hochberg.

Erlenbach bei Marktheidenfeld (Ger). Village. (Anb) = Franken. (Ber) = Maindreieck. (Gro) = Not yet assigned. (Vin) = Krähenschnabel.

Erlen Brauerei (Switz). An independent brewery based in Glarus.

Erligheim (Ger). Village. (Anb) = Württemberg. (Ber) = Württembergisch Unterland. (Gro) = Stromberg. (Vin) = Lerchenberg.

Ermida (Port). A red wine produced by Real Companhía Vinícola do Norte de Portugal.

Ermitage (Fr). A light, rosé wine produced in the eighteenth century. A blend of Auvernat red wine and light wines from the eastern Loire and Orléans. Now no longer produced.

Ermitage (Fr). The French spelling of Hermitage in the Côtes du Rhône, southern France.

Ermitage (Switz). The name for the white French grape variety Marsanne.

Ermitage (Switz). A speciality of the Valais canton. A dry generous wine.

Ernsbach (Ger). Village. (Anb) = Württemberg. (Ber) = Kocher-Jagst-Tauber. (Gro) = Kocherberg. (Vin) = Flatterberg.

Ernst (Ger). Village. (Anb) = Mosel-Saar-Ruwer. (Ber) = Zell/Mosel. (Gro) = Goldbäumchen. (Vins) = Feuerberg, Kirchlay.

Erntebringer (Ger). Grosslage. (Anb) = Rheingau. (Ber) = Johannisberg. (Vils) = Geisenheim, Johannisberg, Estate, Mittelheim, Winkel.

Erolzthaler (Switz). The name of a Brandy-producing company based in Ormalingen. Produces apple-based brandies.

Eros Cocktail (Cktl). ⅓ measure Cointreau, ⅓ measure Calvados, ⅓ measure sweet Vermouth, dash Grenadine, dash lemon juice. Shake well over ice, strain into a cocktail glass.

Erpolzheim (Ger). Village. (Anb) = Rheinpfalz. (Ber) = Mittelhaardt-Deutsche Weinstrasse. (Gro) = Kobnert. (Vin) = Kirschgarten.

Erpolzheim (Ger). Village. (Anb) = Rheinpfalz. (Ber) = Mittelhaardt-Deutsche Weinstrasse. (Gro) = Rosenbühl. (Vins) = Goldberg, Keiselberg.

Ersatz Genever (Hol). A rare type of Gin.

Ersingen (Ger). Village. (Anb) = Baden. (Ber) = Badische Bergstrasse/ Kraichgau. (Gro) = Hohenberg. (Vin) = Klepberg.

Erste Kulmbacher Actienbrauerei (Ger). A brewery based in Kulmbach, West Germany. Brews Kulminator, one of the strongest beers in the world. See E.K.U.

Erven Lucas Bols (Hol). Dutch distiller of the sixteenth century who invented Kümmel. See Bols.

Erzeugerabfüllung (Ger). From the producer's own estate. Produced and bottled by the producer. May blend 25% of another vineyard and 15% of another grape or vintage with his own.

Erzgrupe (Ger). Vineyard. (Anb) = Nahe. (Ber) = Schloss Böckelheim. (Gro) = Burgweg. (Vil) = Bad Münster a. St.-Ebernburg.

Erzingen (Ger). Village. (Anb) = Baden. (Ber) = Bodensee. See Klettgau.

Esa (Swe). Yeast.

E.S.B. (Eng) (abbr). Extra Special Bitter. 1055.75 O.G. Brewed by the Fullers Brewery in London. Export version 1060 O.G.

E.S.B. (Eng) (abbr). Extra Special Bitter. 1044.8 O.G. Brewed by the Mitchells

E

Brewery of Lancaster.

Escalas (Sp). Scales of the Solera system.

Escalon (USA). The central region of the Central Valley in California. Produces dessert and table wines.

Escande (Fr). Cognac producer. Address = Domaine de Courpe, 17150-Mirambeau, Près Cognac. 22 ha. in Fins bois. Produces – Hors d'Âge XO 25 years old.

Escanyavella (Sp). An alternative name for the Merseguera grape.

Escarchardo (Port). An aniseed-flavoured liqueur containing sugar crystals in the bottle.

Escava (Port). A depression made around the base of the vine in the Douro region. Fertiliser is put in and then covered over.

Escharchado (Port). See Escarchardo. Alternative spelling.

Eschbach (Ger). Village. (Anb) = Baden. (Ber) = Markgräflerland. (Gro) = Lorettoberg. (Vin) = Maltesergarten.

Eschbach (Ger). Village. (Anb) = Rheinpfalz. (Ber) = Südliche Weinstrasse. (Gro) = Herrlich. (Vin) = Hasen.

Eschelbach (Ger). Village. (Anb) = Baden. (Ber) = Badische Bergstrasse/Kraichgau. (Gro) = Stiftsberg. (Vin) = Sonnenberg.

Eschelbach (Ger). Village. (Anb) = Württemberg. (Ber) = Württembergisch Unterland. (Gro) = Lindelberg. (Vin) = Schwobajörgle.

Eschenau (Ger). Village. (Anb) = Württemberg. (Ber) = Württembergisch Unterland. (Gro) = Salzberg. (Vin) = Paradies.

Eschenauer (Fr). A Bordeaux négociant-éleveur and owner of Châteaux Smith Haut-Lafitte and Rausan-Ségla. Based in Martillac, Gironde.

Eschen Vineyard (USA). A vineyard based in Shenandoah Valley, Amador, California. 8.5 ha. Grape variety – Zinfandel.

Escherndorf (Ger). Village. (Anb) = Franken. (Ber) = Maindreieck. (Gro) = Kirchberg. (Vins) = Berg, Fürstenberg, Lump.

Escondido (USA). A wine district in San Diego, southern California which produces sparkling, table and dessert wines.

Escorial (Ger). A yellow or green herb liqueur similar to Chartreuse.

Escoussans (Fr). A commune in the Haut-Benauge, Bordeaux.

Escritório Comercial de Portugal (Bra). Information bureau on Portuguese wines. Address = Avenida Paulista, 2001–6°. Andar-Salus 1604/7 Caixa

Postal 22045-(CEP-01311)-S.Paulo.

Escrivains (Fr). A vine pest in mediaeval times.

Escubac (Sp). A Brandy-based cordial which contains sugar, liquorice, cinnamon, raisins and sugar. Also known as Ratafia.

Escudo Rosé (Port). A still, dry, pale rosé wine.

Escusseaux (Les) (Fr). A Premier Cru vineyard in the A.C. commune of Auxey-Duresses, Côte de Beaune, Burgundy. 6.43 ha.

Eselsberg (Ger). Vineyard. (Anb) = Franken. (Ber) = Maindreieck. (Gro) = Kirchberg. (Vil) = Stammheim.

Eselsberg (Ger). Vineyard. (Anb) = Württemberg. (Ber) = Württembergisch Unterland. (Gro) = Kirchenweinberg. (Vil) = Flein.

Eselsbuckel (Ger). Vineyard. (Anb) = Rheinpfalz. (Ber) = Südliche Weinstrasse. (Gro) = Guttenberg. (Vil) = Nierderotterbach.

Eselshaut (Ger). Vineyard. (Anb) = Rheinpfalz. (Ber) = Mittelhaardt-Deutsche Weinstrasse. (Gro) = Meerspinne. (Vil) = Mussbach.

Eselspfad (Ger). Vineyard. (Anb) = Rheinhessen. (Ber) = Bingen. (Gro) = Abtey. (Vil) = Appenheim.

Eselstreiber (Ger). Vineyard. (Anb) = Rheinhessen. (Ber) = Bingen. (Gro) = Rheingrafenstein. (Vil) = Eckelsheim.

Esgano-Cão (Port). A white grape variety used in Bucelas.

Esganose (Port). A white grape variety grown in the Vinho Verde region. Is also spelt Esganoso.

Esganoso (Port). A white grape variety grown in Peñafiel (a sub-region of the Vinho Verde). Is also spelt Esganose.

Eskie (Austr). A nickname given to a portable Thermos flask used to keep beer cool.

Eskisehir-Nevsehir (Tur). A vineyard based in Middle Anatolia. Produces white wines.

Esk Valley (N.Z.). A vineyard. 5.5 ha. planted for the Glenvale Winery. The wines for Glenvale sold under Esk Valley label.

Esmagamento (Port). The crushing of the grapes.

Esmeralda (Arg)l A wine producer based at Córdoba. Noted for St. Felician (a Cabernet-based wine).

Esola Vineyard (USA). A vineyard based in the Shenandoah Valley, Amador, California. 8.5 ha. Grape variety – Zinfandel.

Espada (Sp). A method of vine training used in the Sherry region. See Spade.

E

Espadeiro (Port). A black grape variety used to make deep red wines in the Entre e Douro region.

Espadeiro de Basto (Port). A black grape variety grown in the Basto (a sub-region of Vinho Verde).

Espagna (Fr). An alternative name for the Cinsault grape.

Espalier (Fr). A method of vine training using a firm base with vertical shoots rising upwards from 2 horizontal arms.

Espar (Fr). A red grape variety also known as the Mourvèdre.

Esparto Grass (Sp). Grass used to make mats to lay out the grapes to dry in the sun in the Almijar in Andalusia.

Esparto Mats (Sp). See Esparto Grass.

Esper (Ger). Vineyard. (Anb) = Rheinpfalz. (Ber) = Mittelhaardt-Deutsche Weinstrasse. (Gro) = Schnepfenflug vom Kellertal. (Vil) = Kerzenheim.

Espirito (Port). A brand of Brandy from Fonseca.

Espirituoso (Port). A term used to denote a beverage that is high in alcohol (beer, wine, etc).

Espirraque (Sp). The name used to denote the third pressing that occurs in the small Jerez vineyards. See also Prensa.

Espresso (USA). An Italian coffee liqueur made in Ancona. See Illy Coffee Liqueur. 30% alc. by vol.

Espresso Coffee (It). A coffee drink made by forcing steam under pressure through the coffee grounds then topping with frothy hot milk. See also Cappuccino Coffee. Is often wrongly spelt Expresso. See Gaggia.

Espresso Coffee Liqueur (It). A coffee flavoured liqueur made with espresso brewed coffee.

Esprit (Fr). The name given to a Cognac that is above 84%.

Esprit Cocktail (Cktl). ⅓ gill Armagnac brandy, ⅙ gill Crème de Noyau, 2 dashes (white) Crème de Cacao. Stir over ice, strain into an ice-filled old-fashioned glass.

Espirit d'Amour (W.Ind). The local name for 'Moonshine' on the island of St. Lucia.

Esprit de France (Fr). An Armagnac producer. Is noted for Palvel Marmont and Des Seigneurs (a 3 year old).

Espumante (Port). Sparkling.

Espumantes Naturais (Port). The méthode champenois.

Espumoso (Sp). Sparkling.

Esquerre-Bounoure (Fr). An Armagnac producer. Address = Place des Maures, 32000 Auch. Based in the Haut Armagnac.

Essais (Fr). Cups used in the middle-ages for tasting the Royal wine to check if free from poisoning. Used by the Royal taster.

Esselborn (Ger). Village. (Anb) = Rheinhessen. (Ber) = Wonnegau. (Gro) = Bergkloster. (Vin) = Goldberg.

Essence (Eng). Describes brewed coffee that has most of the moisture removed by evaporation. Often sold slightly sweetened. See Camp.

Essence of Lockjaw (USA) (slang). A term used in the eastern States for Applejack brandy.

Essenheim (Ger). Village. (Anb) = Rheinhessen. (Ber) = Nierstein. (Gro) = Domherr. (Vins) = Römerberg, Teufelspfad.

Essenz (Hun). Essence. See Tokay Essēnz.

Essex Ale (Eng). A bottled Light ale 1030 O.G. brewed by the Ridley Brewery in Essex.

Essigstich (Ger). Denotes a wine with a flavour of vinegar.

Essingen (Ger). Village. (Anb) = Rheinpfalz. (Ber) = Südliche Weinstrasse. (Gro) = Trappenberg. (Vins) = Osterberg, Rossberg, Sonnenberg.

Esslingen (Ger). Village. (Anb) = Württemberg. (Ber) = Remstal-Stuttgart. (Gro) = Weinsteige. (Vins) = Ailenberg, Kirchberg, Lerchenberg, Schenkenberg.

Estação Vitivinícola de Beira Litoral (Port). The research station based in Anadia, Bairrada that advises wine growers and helps to improve techniques.

Estación de Viticultura y Enología (Sp). A body that administers the Consejo Regulador quality control of Spanish wines.

Estación de Viticultura y Enología de Navarra (Sp). EVENSA. Checks wines before D.O. seal is awarded. Research station. Viticultural research and research into rootstock. Owns 5 vineyards.

Estagel (Fr). A red wine from the A.C. Côtes du Roussillon-Villages in south-eastern France.

Estàgio (Mad). The name given to the rest period that Madeira wine goes through after it leaves the Estufa.

Estàgio (Port). Lit – 'Wine in the making'. Vinification.

Estalagem (Port). A small hotel or country inn.

Estaminet (Fr). A small bar or café usually of a shabby nature that was popular in the nineteenth century.

Estancia Vineyard (La) (USA). A small vineyard based in Salinas Valley, Monterey, California, Grape varieties –

E

Chardonnay and Pinot noir. Produces varietal wines.

Estanciero (Arg). A red wine from the Mendosa region.

Estate (Ger). Village. (Anb) = Mosel-Saar-Ruwer. (Ber) = Saar-Ruwer. (Gro) = Scharzberg. (Vins) = Scharzhofberger, Schlagengraben, Schlossberg.

Estate (Ger). Village. (Anb) = Rheingau. (Ber) = Johannisberg. (Gro) = Deutelsberg. (Vin) = Steinberg.

Estate (Ger). Village. (Anb) = Rheingau. (Ber) = Johannisberg. (Gro) = Erntebringer. (Vins) = Schloss Johannisberg, Schwartzenstein, Vogelsang.

Estate (Ger). Village. (Anb) = Rheingau. (Ber) = Johannisberg. (Gro) = Honigberg. (Vin) = Schloss Vollrads.

Estate Bottled (Eng). Wine bottled by the vineyard owner, producer. See (Fr) = Mis-en-bouteille-au-Château, Mis-en-bouteille-au-Domaine, (Ger) = Erzeugerabfüllung, (It) = Nel'Origine.

Estates (W.Ind). A term applied to Jamaican and British West Indies sugar plantations where the best materials for distilling rum are obtained.

Estatuto de la Viña, del Vino y de Los Alcoholes (Sp). 1970 regulations that apply to the whole of Spain. All wine produced must conform to these.

Esterhazy (Aus). A family-owned vineyard in Ausbruch and Burgenland. Produces white wines of fine quality..

Esterification (Eng). Production of wine esters. Helps soften old wines by reducing the acidity during the process of esterification.

Esternay (Fr). A canton based in the Champagne district of Épernay. Cru villages of Bethon and Chantemerle.

Esters (Eng). A combination of acids and alcohol which gives wines its bouquet.

Est! Est!! Est!!! (It). D.O.C. white wine from the Latium region. Made from Trebbiano toscano 65%, Malvasia bianco toscana and Rossetto grapes. Vinification can take place within the production area and commune of Viterbo. See Montefiascone and Fugger (Bishop).

Esteva (Port). A red wine from the Douro produced by Ferreira (Port house). Cold fermented.

Estonian Viru Valge (USSR). A brand of Vodka. 40% alc. by vol.

Estoril (Cktl). ⅕ gill Bacardi White Label Rum, 2 dashes Orgeat syrup, 2 dashes lemon juice, dash Amaretto. Shake well over ice, strain into a highball glass. Top with soda water. Dress with a slice of lemon and serve with straws.

Estoril (Port). A district in Carcavelhos. Allowed to use that designation.

Estrada Winery (USA). A small winery based in the Mesilla Valley, New Mexico. Produces table wines.

Estrangey (Fr). An alternative name for the Malbec grape.

Estrangle-Chien (Fr). An obscure name for the Mourvèdre grape in southern France. Lit – 'Dog strangler'.

Estrella River (USA). A large winery based in Shandon, San Luis Obispo, California. 291 ha. Grape varieties – Cabernet sauvignon, Chardonnay, Johannisberg riesling, Muscat blanc and Syrah. Produces varietal wines.

Estremadura (Port). A Denominação de Origem wine-producing region based north-west of Lisbon. Produces red and full-bodied white wines.

Estufa (Mad). The name for a room where Madeira wine is held at a high temperature when it is made to give it the special 'cooked' flavour. Lit – 'stove'.

Estufado (Mad). Lit – 'To stew'. The process of heating Madeira wine in an Estufa.

Estufa do Sol (Mad). Houses where the Madeira is stored and heated by the sun only.

Estufagem (Mad). Invented by a monk, it is a method of heating the wine of Madeira (see Estufa) to compensate for the loss of travelling that the wine obtained passing over the Equator many times giving the original wine its 'cooked' flavour.

Eszencia (Hun). See Tokay Eszencia.

Étampé (Fr). Lit – 'Stamped' or 'branded', associated with the marking of corks as a guarantee of the bottles contents.

Etaulier (Fr). An alternative name for the Malbec grape.

Etchmiadzine (USSR). A white grape variety grown in Armenia.

Ethanal (Eng). An Aldehyde. Produced from oxidation of Ethanol. CH_3CHO. Molecular weight of 44 and S.G. of 0.78.

Ethanoic Acid (Eng). A volatile acid found in wine. CH_3COOH.

Ethanol (Eng). The main alcohol produced by the yeast Sacchromyces Ellipsoideus, converting grape sugar into Ethyl alcohol and CO_2. C_2H_5OH. Molecular weight of 46, freezing point -133°C. boiling point 78.3°C. S.G. 0.79044 at 20°C.

Ethel Duffy Cocktail (Cktl). ⅓ measure Cointreau, ⅓ measure Brandy, ⅓ measure white Crème de Menthe. Shake over ice, strain into a cocktail glass.

Ethelene (Eng). The hormone that makes fruit ripen.

Ethereal Oils (Eng). Important for coffee aroma. Are released during the roasting process.

Etherel (Eng). A term only applied to a

superb wine with an excellent bouquet and character.

Etherium (Eng). A Victorian registered trade-mark. Lead-free vitrious enamel glazed earthenware used for holding drinking water.

Ethers (Eng). The minute etheral qualities which form the bouquet of a wine or spirit together with the esters.

Ethiopian Coffee (Afr). Home of Arabica coffee. Produces robust, tangy and winy coffee. The coffee is often roasted with cloves or cinnamon and stirred with a Tena-adam branch to add flavour. Drink with rock salt. e.g. Longberry Harar – resembles Mocha and Ethiopian Mocha. (3 regions – Djimma, Kaffa and Sidamo). See also Abyssinian Coffee.

Ethiopian Mocha (Afr). A style of coffee that resembles Mocha.

Ethyl Acetate (Eng). $CH_3COOC_2H_5$. An ester of ethyl alcohol and acetaldehyde. Has a smell similar to nail varnish. In strong concentrations is unpleasant and indicates that the wine is turning to vinegar. Apple, pear, peach and strawberry aromas.

Ethyl Alcohol (Eng). See Ethanol. Alcohol produced by the fermentation of yeast on sugar. C_2H_5OH.

Ethyl Ethanoate (Eng). Caused by Acetic fermentation. Gives a sweet vinegary aroma to the wine.

Ethyl Pyrocarbonate (Eng). The result of a combination of ethyl alcohol and CO_2 during bottle fermentation and storage of sparkling wines. The more pyrocarbonate is formed the longer the bead (bubbles) will rise.

Etiqueta (Sp). Label.

Etiqueta Blanca (Sp). A 4 year old white wine produced by Marqués de Murrieta S.A. in the Rioja Alta.

Etiquetta Blanca (Arg). A white wine produced by Bodegas Suter.

Etiquetta Marron (Arg). A red wine produced by Bodegas Suter.

Etiquette (Fr). Bottle label.

Etko (Cyp). A subsidiary wine producing company of Haggipavlu. Based in Limassol, south-eastern Cyprus.

Etna (It). Red and white wines produced in the vineyards around Mount Etna in Sicily.

Etna Bianco (It). D.O.C. white wine from Sicily. Made from the Carricante, Catarratto bianco comune, Minella bianca and Trebbiano grapes. Produced in 20 communes in the province of Catania. If has a minimum of 11.5% alc. by vol. and produced from 80% Carricante grapes in the Milo commune then classed Superiore.

Etna Rosato (It). D.O.C. rosé wine from Sicily. Made from Nerello mantellato and Nerello mascalese grapes. Produced in 20 communes in the province of Catania.

Etna Rosso (It). D.O.C. red wine from Sicily. Made from Nerello mantellato and Nerello mascalese grapes. Produced in 20 communes in the province of Catania.

Étoffé (Fr). Describes a well conserved wine with fine qualities.

Étoges (Fr). A Cru Champagne villages in the Canton de Montmort. District = Épernay.

Étoile (Fr). A vineyard district in the Jura. Noted for vin jaune and vin de paille wines. A.C. Grape varieties – Chardonnay and the Savagnin.

Étoile Mousseux (L') (Fr). A sparkling (Charmat method). A.C. wine produced in Étoile, Savoie.

Eton Blazer (Cktl). ⅖ measure dry Gin, ⅕ measure Kirsch, juice of ½ lemon, 4 dashes Gomme syrup. Shake well over ice, strain into an ice-filled highball glass. Top with soda water.

Étonner (Fr). Casking. The pouring of liquids into a cask.

Étournelles (Fr). A Premier Cru vineyard in the A.C. commune of Gevrey-Chambertin, Côte de Nuits, Burgundy. 2 ha.

Étranger (Fr). An alternative name for the Malbec grape.

Et Rates (Eng). Evapotranspiration rates that measure the vines' water uptake.

Étrechy (Fr). A Premier Cru Champagne village in the Canton de Vertus. District = Châlons. Red grapes (Premier Cru) and white grapes (Cru).

Etrigny (Fr). A commune in the Mâconnais region where Mâcon Supérieur may be produced.

Etschtaler (It). A German name used in the Südtirol region. See Valdadige Bianco or Valdadige Rosso.

Ettalier (Ger). A herb liqueur made at Kloster Ettal. Made in a green (dry) or yellow (sweet) style.

Ettenheim (Ger). Village. (Anb) = Baden. (Ber) = Breisgau. (Gro) = Burg Lichteneck. (Vin) = Kaiserberg.

Ettenheim [ortsteil Wallburg] (Ger). Village. (Anb) = Baden. (Ber) = Breisgau. (Gro) = Schutterlindenberg. (Vin) = Kirchberg.

Etter (Switz). A noted Eau-de-vie producer based in Zoug.

Euan (Lat). A word used for Bacchus. See also Dionysos, Dionysus, Bassareus, Bromius, Euhan, Euhius, Euius, Lacchus, Lyaeus and Thyoneus.

Euboea (Gre). An island of central Greece. Produces red and white wines mainly for home consumption.

Eucharist (Lat). A Christian religious ceremony (The last supper) during which wine is offered together with bread.

Euchariusberg (Ger). Vineyard. (Anb) = Mosel-Saar-Ruwer. (Ber) = Saar-Ruwer. (Gro) = Scharzberg. (Vil) = Konz.

Euchariusberg (Ger). Vineyard. (Anb) = Mosel-Saar-Ruwer. (Ber) = Saar-Ruwer. (Gro) = Scharzberg. (Vil) = Mennig.

Eudemis (Fr). Grape-berry moth. Similar to the Cochylis.

Eugenio Bustos (Arg). A wine-producing area in central Argentina.

Euhan (Lat). Word used for Bacchus. See also Dionysos, Dionysus, Bassareus, Bromius, Euan, Euhius, Lacchus, Lyaeus and Thyoneus.

Euhius (Lat). A word used for Bacchus. See also Dionysos, Dionysus, Bassareus, Bromius, Euhan, Euan, Euius, Lacchus, Lyaeus and Thyoneus.

Euius (Lat). A word used for Bacchus. See also Dionysos, Dionysus, Bassareus, Bromius, Euhan, Euan, Euhius, Lacchus, Lyaeus and Thyoneus.

Eulengrund (Ger). Vineyard. (Anb) = Franken. (Ber) = Steigerwald. (Gro) = Kapellenberg. (Vil) = Schmachtenberg.

Euler Landpils (Ger). Lager beer.

Eumelan (USA). A red grape variety grown in the eastern states.

Eurageot (Fr). The Bordeaux name for the Folle blanche grape.

Euroblend (Euro). Table wines (Vins de table and Tafelwein) produced from a blend of EEC wines. Usually blended and bottled in Germany.

Europadorf (Aus). See Alberndorf.

European Cellars (Eng). An Allied-Lyons and Whitbread-owned company. Own Black Tower, Calvet, Don Cortez, Langenbach and Piemontello.

Eussenheim (Ger). Village. (Anb) = Franken. (Ber) = Maindreieck. (Gro) = Rosstal. (Vin) = First.

Eva (Cktl). ¼ measure Crème de Violettes, ⅜ measure Caperatif, ⅛ measure orange juice, ⅛ measure lemon juice, ⅛ measure Grenadine, dash Pernod. Shake over ice, strain into a cocktail glass.

E.V.A. (Eng) (abbr). English Vineyards Association. Offers a seal of quality to English wines.

Evans (Cktl). 2 fl.ozs. Rye whiskey, dash Curaçao, dash Apricot brandy. Stir over ice, strain into a cocktail glass.

Evans and Tate (Austr). Vineyard. Address = Swan St. West Swan, Western Australia 6055. 24 ha. Grape varieties – Cabernet sauvignon, Chardonnay, Merlot, Sauvignon blanc, Shiraz, Traminer.

Evaporated Milk (Eng). A tinned (canned) milk, unsweetened, from which some of the water has been removed (evaporated).

Evaporation (Eng). Occurs during maturation of a wine in cask. The ullage must be filled frequently to help reduce evaporation of wine (or spirits) and alcohol. Also prevents spoilage.

Évasivage (Fr). The de-suckering of the vine and general tidying up. Usually done in May. Also known as Éjotonnement.

Evel (Port). A red wine produced by Real Companhía Vinícola do Norte de Portugal near Vila Real, Trás-Os-Montes.

Evelita (Port). A wine produced in Lafões.

Evenos (Fr). A commune of which part is in the A.C. Bandol, south-eastern France.

EVENSA (Sp) (abbr). Estación de Viticultura y Enología de Navarra.

Evensen Winery (USA). A small winery based in the Napa Valley, California. 8.5 ha. Grape variety – Gewürztraminer.

Éventé (Fr). Describes a wine that is over-oxidised (either in cask or bottle).

Everards (Eng). A small brewery in Leicester. Produces – Old Original 1050 O.G. Red Crown 1034.5 O.G. See Old Burton Brewery.

Everards Beacon Bitter (Eng). A cask conditioned Bitter from Everards Brewery, Leicester.

Evergreen Cocktail (Cktl). 1 fl.oz. Tequila, ½ fl.oz. (green) Crème de Menthe, ¼ fl.oz. Galliano, 3 fl.ozs. pineapple juice. Stir over ice, strain into a goblet. Dress with a sprig of mint.

Everybody's Irish (Cktl). ⅓ gill Irish whiskey, 1 barspoon green Chartreuse, 1 barspoon green Crème de Menthe. Stir over ice, strain into a cocktail glass. Dress with an olive.

Evian (Fr). A still mineral water (Eau minérale naturelle) from Evian-les-Bains at the foot of Mont Blanc. Bottled at Cachat Spring.

Évier (Fr). A fourteenth century large jug or pitcher.

Ewer (Eng). A decanter with a handle. Jug shaped.

Ewig Leben (Ger). Grosslage. (Anb) = Franken. (Ber) = Maindreieck. (Vil) = Randersacker. (Vins). Marsberg, Pfülben, Sonnenstuhl, Teufelskeller.

Ex-Bier (Switz). An alcohol-free lager brewed by the Feldschlösschen Brewery.

Ex-Cellars (Eng). Means that duty and VAT do not become payable until wine etc has been cleared from bond.

Excellence (Fr). An 1889 distilled Cognac produced by A.E. Dor in Jarnac. 35% alc. by vol.

Excellence (Jap). A brand of Whiskey produced by Suntory.

Excellent (Austr). The brand-name of a locally produced Brandy.

Excelsior (S.Am). A grade of coffee. Produces a rich, strong, smooth brew. Grown in Colombia.

Excelsior Estate (S.Afr). A wine estate based in Aston, Robertson. Owned by the De Wet Brothers. Wines sold in bulk to merchants. Address P.O. Aston, 6715, Robertson. Produces varietal wines.

Excise (Eng). A tax on liquor produced in the country of production. See Duty, and Customs and Excise.

Exclusiv (Ger). The name given to describe a premium beer of the Astra brand produced by the Bavaria-St-Pauli Brauerei in Hamburg.

Excoriose (Lat). A fungal disease that attacks the branches of the vine. Treated using copper suphate.

Exhibition (Eng). A bottled Brown ale 1042 O.G. Brewed by the Harvey Brewery in Sussex.

Exhibition (Eng). A cask conditioned/keg Bitter 1042 O.G. Brewed in Newcastle.

Exhibition (Eng). A cask conditioned Ale 1051 O.G. brewed by the Smiles Brewery in Bristol.

Exhibition (Wales). A cask conditioned Ale 1054 O.G. brewed by the Silverthorne Brewery, South Wales.

Exhibition (Wales). A Light mild 1034 O.G. brewed by the Border Brewery in North Wales.

Exmoor Ale (Eng). A cask conditioned Bitter 1039 O.G. brewed by the Golden Hill Brewery in Somerset.

Expédier en Fût (Fr). A term used to describe a wine being despatched into the wood (cask).

Explorer Vodka (Swe). A Vodka brand-name used by Aktiebolaget Vin and Spritcentralem.

Exportación (Sp). Exporting.

Exportador (Sp). An exporter.

Export Akvavit (Den). A Madeira-flavoured akvavit.

Export Beer (Eng). The term used for premium beers that may or may not be exported. Usually bottled beers. See Export Beer (Scot)

Export Beer (Ger). Nothing to do with the export trade. It refers to the strength of the beer. O.G. = 12.5–14%

Export Beer (Scot). Either bottled or cask conditioned Ales which may be exported. See Eighty Shilling Export [80/-].

Export Cassis (Fr). Another name for the apéritif Vermouth-Cassis.

Export Gold (Eng). A Barley wine 1070 O.G. brewed by Watney Mann, London.

Express Cocktail (Cktl). 1 fl.oz. Scotch whisky, 1 fl.oz. sweet Vermouth, dash Orange bitters. Stir over ice, strain into a cocktail glass.

Expressed Juice (Eng). The must after pressing the juice.

Expresso Coffee (USA). The American way of spelling of Espresso coffee.

Exquitxagos (Sp). An alternative name for the Merseguera grape.

Exshaw (Fr). Cognac producer. Address = Exshaw S.A., 127 Boulevard-Denfert-Rochereau 16100 Cognac. Produces – Cognac Exshaw N° 1. and Cognac Exshaw Age d'Or. Is part of Otard.

Extra (Fr). On an Armagnac label denotes a minimum of 5 years of age.

Extra (Fr). A Cognac term found on a brandy label. Denotes that the brandy has been at least 75 years in cask.

Extra (Scot). The name given to a keg Lager 1044 O.G. brewed by Tennent's Brewery.

Extra Ale (Scot). A strong Ale 1085 O.G. brewed by Borve House in the Isle of Lewis.

Extra Belle Réserve (Fr). A Cognac produced by Monnet.

Extra Bitter (Eng). The former name of the Dutchy keg Bitter 1044 O.G. brewed by the St. Austell Brewery in Cornwall.

Extra Choice Old Tawny (Port). A fine old Tawny Port from Cockburn, Martinez and Mackenzie.

Extract (Eng). In wine the sugar-free extract matter left after the wine has been fined. Also called Total Extract.

Extracteur à Bouchon (Fr). Cork extractor.

Extra Droog (S.Afr). Extra dry.

Extra Dry (S.Afr). A wine classification. Must contain 2.5 grams per litre of sugar or less. See also Extra-Sec and Extra Droog.

Extra Dry Gin (USA). Denotes a Gin that has drier-tasting flavourings (botanicals) than dry Gin.

Extra Gammal (Swe). Swedish Punsch 55.5% alc. by vol. Produced by Aktiebolaget Vin and Spritcentralem.

Extrait de Malt (Fr). Malt extract.

Extrait des Pins (Fr). A pine needle-flavoured liqueur produced by Clacquesin. Also known as Sapindor or Liqueur des Pins.

Extra Light Beer (Eng). A cask conditioned/keg bitter 1031 O.G. brewed by Bass Breweries for the north of England.

Extra Light Beer (USA). A very low alcohol beer (see Light Beer). Has a strong hop flavour.

Extralite (Eng). A low carbohydrate Ale 1030 O.G. brewed by the Wadworth Brewery in Wiltshire.

Extra N° 9 (Fr). A 1914 distilled Cognac produced by A.E. Dor. Stored in demijohns after 50 years of ageing.

Extra Parés Baltá (Sp). A méthode champenois sparkling (Cava) wine from the Cavas Parés Baltá, Pachs de Penedés.

Extra Reserve Madeira (Mad). Blended, youngest wine. Must be a minimum of 15 years old after Estufagem. If grape variety stated must contain 85% of named variety.

Extra Sec (Fr). Denotes less dry than Brut.

Extra-Sec (S.Afr). A wine classification. Must contain 2.5 grams of sugar per litre or less. Also Extra dry.

Extra Special Bitter (Eng). A bottled Bitter 1038 O.G. brewed by the Simpkiss Brewery, Brierley Hill in Staffordshire.

Extra Special Bitter (Eng). See E.S.B.

Extra Viejo (Arg). Extra old.

Extremadura (Sp). A region of central Spain on the Portuguese border. Covers Cáceres and Badajoz. Makes up part of the Meseta Central.

Extrísimo (Sp). A sweet white wine from Masía Bach in the Penedés, Catalan.

Eyelids of Buddha (China). An old Chinese name for tea. (Leaves are shaped like eyelids).

Eye-Opener (Cktl). ⅙ gill Liqueur brandy, ⅙ gill Crème de Menthe, ⅙ gill Absinthe, 1 whole egg. Shake well over ice, strain into a cocktail glass. Top with a pinch of cayenne pepper.

Eye Opener Cocktail (Cktl). 1 measure white Rum, 1 egg yolk, 1 barspoon each of Pernod, Cointreau and Crème de Cacao (white), ½ teaspoon Gomme syrup. Shake over ice, strain into a flip glass.

Eye Openers (USA). An early slang term for cider and beer. Also for an alcoholic drink taken early in the morning.

Eye Water (Eng). The nickname for Gin from the London printers.

Eylenbosch Brasserie (Bel). A brewery based in Schepdaal in northern Belgium. Noted for its' dry Lambic-style beers.

Eynesbury Giant (Eng). A strong Bitter ale brewed by the Paines Brewery in St.Neots, Cambridgeshire. Named after a local giant caller James Toller who was 8 foot 6 inches tall.

Eyre Vineyards (USA). A wine producer in Willamette Valley, Oregon in the Pacific North-West. Grape varieties – Chardonnay, Pinot gris, Pinot meunier and Pinot noir. Produces varietal wines.

Eyrons (Fr). A commune in the A.C. Côtes de Blaye in north-eastern Bordeaux.

Eyzines (Fr). A commune in the A.C. Graves district of south-western Bordeaux.

Ezerja (Hun). An alternative spelling of the Ezerjó grape.

Ezerjó (Hun). The principal white grape of the Mór region. Produces dry golden wines. e.g. Móri ezerjó.

F

Fabbrica [di Birra] (It). Brewery.
Faber (Ger). A white grape variety. A cross between the Weissburgunder and the Müller-Thurgau. Is early ripening and gives a fruity muscat-type bouquet. Also known as the Faberrebe.
Faber (Ger). A noted producer of Sekt made by the cuve close method.
Faberrebe (Ger). See Faber.
Fabrini (It). A producer of sparkling (méthode champenoise) wines – Verdicchio-Vernaccia di Serrapetrona and sparkling red wine in the Marche region.
Fabuloso (Sp). A 3 year old brandy produced by Palomino y Vergara S.A.
Facama Vineyard (S.Am). A vineyard based in Ica, Peru. Produces everyday table wines.
Fachbach (Ger). Village. (Anb) = Mittelrhein. (Ber) = Rheinburgengau. (Gro) = Lahntal. (Vin) = Sites not yet choosen.
Fächern (Ger). Vineyard. (Anb) = Mosel-Saar-Ruwer. (Ber) = Zell/Mosel. (Gro) = Weinhex. (Vil) = Niederfell.
Façon de Venise (Fr). In the fashion of Venice. Name for glass made in France, Holland, England, etc. (around 1500–1700 A.D).
Façonnières (Les) (Fr). A Premier Cru vineyard in the A.C. commune of Morey-Saint-Denis, Côte de Nuits, Burgundy. 1.7 ha.
Factory House (The) (Port). Based in Oporto. The building was built in 1870s for the Port Factors – British who were shipping Port to U.K. Now used for the meeting of Port shippers. Male only. See Feitoria Inglesa. Members are – Cockburn Smithes & Cia Lda., Croft & Cia Lda., Delaforce Sons & Cia Vinhos S.A.R.L., Graham W & J. & Co., Guimaraens (Vinhos) S.A.R.L. (Fonseca's Port), Martinez Gassiot & Co. Ltd., Robertson Brothers & Cia Lda., Sandeman & Cia Lda., Silva & Cosens Ltd (Dow's Port), Taylors, Fladgate & Yeatman, Vinhos S.A.R.L. and Warres & Cia Lda.
Fad (Den). In association with beer and lager denotes draught.
Fad (Ger). Insipid.

Fahr (Ger). Village. (Anb) = Franken. (Ber) = Maindreieck. (Gro) = Kirchberg. (Vins) = Assorted parts of vineyards.
Fahrberg (Ger). Vineyard. (Anb) = Mosel-Saar-Ruwer. (Ber) = Zell/Mosel. (Gro) = Weinhex. (Vil) = Kattenes.
Fahrberg (Ger). Vineyard. (Anb) = Mosel-Saar-Ruwer. (Ber) = Zell/Mosel. (Gro) = Weinhex. (Vil) = Kobern-Gondorf.
Fahrberg (Ger). Vineyard. (Anb) = Mosel-Saar-Ruwer. (Ber) = Zell/Mosel. (Gro) = Weinhex. (Vil) = Moselsürsch.
Faible (Fr). Thin wine. In Cognac refers to a weak brandy added to new Cognac to help 'reduce' it down.
Faillac Mousseux (Fr). Sparkling wines produced in south-eastern France by either méthode champenoise or méthode gaillaçoise.
Failsworth Brewery (Eng). Opened in 1982 in Manchester, Lancs. Produces cask conditioned Failsworth Original 1037 O.G. and cask conditioned Failsworth Strong 1044 O.G.
Fair and Warmer (Cktl). 1/3 measure dark Rum, 1/5 measure Italian vermouth, 1/6 measure Curaçao. Stir over ice, strain into a cocktail glass.
Fairbank Cocktail (Cktl). 1/4 gill dry Gin, 1/4 gill French vermouth, 2 dashes Noyau Rose, 2 dashes Orange bitters. Stir over ice, strain into a cocktail glass, add a squeeze of lemon peel juice on top.
Fairbank's Cocktail (Cktl). 1 fl.oz. Rye whiskey, 1/4 fl.oz. Apricot brandy, dash Angostura. Stir over ice, strain into an old-fashioned glass.
Faire Champoreau (Fr) (slang). Denotes a Cognac added to a Café au lait (coffee with milk).
Fairhall Dry Red (N.Z.). Produced by Montana Wines, the country's most popular red wine. Made from a blend of Cabernet sauvignon and Pinotage grapes. Has a dry aroma and full, fruity sweetness.
Fairview (S.Afr). A wine estate based in Paarl. Address = Box 583, Suider-Paarl 7625. Produces varietal wines including Charles Gerard.

F

Fairy Belle (Cktl). ¾ measure dry Gin, ¼ measure Apricot brandy, 1 barspoon Grenadine. 1 egg white. Shake over ice, strain into a cocktail glass.

Faisca (Port). The brand-name of a carbonated rosé wine produced by J.M. da Fonseca.

Faiveley (J.) (Fr). A Burgundy négociant-éleveur based at Nuits-Saint-Georges. Has vineyards on the Côte d'Or and in Mercurey.

Fajouet Jean Voisin (Fr). The second wine of Château Voisin. Grand Cru Saint-Émilion. See also Jean Voisin.

Falanda (Sp). The name given to an Oloroso sherry produced by Harveys of Bristol.

Falandy-Liandry (Fr). A Cognac producer. Address 6, Rue Barbezieux, 16100 Cognac.

Falanghino (It). A white grape variety used in the production of white Falerno made in Campi Flegrei, Mondragone, Capua or Sessa Aurunca in Campania.

Falchini (Roberto) (It). A noted sparkling (méthode champenoise) wine producer based in Tuscany.

Falcon (It). A beer brewed by the Falcon Brewery in Sicily.

Falcon Ales (Eng). The brand-name for the Okell Brewery's beers in the Isle of Man.

Falcon Lager (Eng). A canned Lager 1032 O.G. brewed by the Allied Breweries solely for Victoria wine shops.

Falerio dei Colli Ascolani (It). D.O.C. white wine from The Marches. Made from 80% Trebbiano toscano with Malvasia toscano, Passerina, Pecorino, Pinot bianco and Verdicchio grapes.

Falerno (It). A modern product of the ancient Falernum. Red or white produced (red) = Aglianico grape, (white) = Falanghino grape.

Falernum (Lat). A favourite wine of ancient Rome. Produced between Rome and Naples. Was a heavy yellow wine. See also Falerno.

Falernum (W.Ind). A flavouring syrup of 3% alc. by vol. made of syrup, ginger, spices and limes. Clear, it is used on the Isle of Barbados in the British West Indies.

Falkenberg (Ger). Vineyard. (Anb) = Mosel-Saar-Ruwer. (Ber) = Bernkastel. (Gro) = Michelsberg. (Vil) = Piesport.

Falkenberg (Ger). Vineyard. (Anb) = Nahe. (Ber) = Schloss Böckelheim. (Gro) = Paradiesgarten. (Vil) = Alsenz.

Falkenberg (Ger). Vineyard. (Anb) = Rheinhessen. (Ber) = Nierstein. (Gro) = Güldenmorgen. (Vil) = Dienheim.

Falken Brauerei (Switz). A brewery based in Schaffhausen. Part of the Interbera group.

Falken Brewery (Swe). A brewery based in Falkenberg in south-western Sweden. Is the second largest brewery in the country.

Falkenstein (Aus). A wine district in the region of Niederösterreich. Produces mainly white wines. See also Weinviertel.

Falkensteiner Hofberg (Ger). Vineyard. (Anb) = Mosel-Saar-Ruwer. (Ber) = Saar-Ruwer. (Gro) = Scharzberg. (Vil) = Konz.

Falklay (Ger). Vineyard. (Anb) = Mosel-Saar-Ruwer. (Ber) = Bernkastel. (Gro) = Schwarzlay. (Vil) = Burg.

Falklay (Ger). Vineyard. (Anb) = Mosel-Saar-Ruwer. (Ber) = Bernkastel. (Gro) = Vom Heissen Stein. (Vil) = Reil.

Fall Bright (Eng). The term given to a wine or beer that becomes clear on its' own. Usually after a long period in cask. Doesn't need any finings.

Fall Creek Vineyards (USA). A winery based in Tow, south-western Texas.

Fallen Angel (Cktl). ¾ measure Gin, 2 dashes Crème de Menthe, juice of ¼ lemon or lime juice, dash Angostura. Shake over ice, strain into a cocktail glass.

Faller (Robert et Fils) (Fr). A wine-producer and shipper based in Ribeauville, Alsace.

Faller Frères (Fr). A noted Alsatian wine shipper based in Kayserberg.

Falling Down Water (Eng) (slang). A term used in northern England for beer (or other alcoholic drinks).

Falloux (Denis) (Fr). A wine-producer based at Le Puy-Notre-Dame in the Saumur district of Anjou-Saumur, Loire. Is noted for Saumur Mousseux.

Falls City Brewery (USA). A noted brewery based in Louisville.

Falmouth Bitter (Eng), A keg Bitter 1038 O.G. brewed by the Cornish Brewery Company in Dorset.

Falsete (Sp). The tight-bunged hole near the bottom of the cask at the front. A canuto is driven into this prior to racking.

Falstaff Mild (Eng). A cask conditioned (and keg) light Mild 1032 O.G. brewed by the Tetley Brewery. Also known as Best or Scotch depending on the region. See Best Mild and Scotch Mild.

Family Ale (Eng). An old name for bottled pale bitter beers.

Famous Grouse (Scot). A blended Scotch whisky produced by Matthew Gloag and Sons Ltd., Perth. 40% alc. by vol.

Famous Taddy Porter (Eng). A bottled

Porter 1050 O.G. brewed by the Sam Smith Brewery in Tadcaster, Yorkshire.

Fancy Brandy Cocktail (Cktl). Another name for a Chicago Cocktail.

Fancy Free Cocktail (Cktl). 1½ ozs. Rye whiskey, dash orange bitters, 2 dashes Maraschino, dash Angostura. Shake over ice, strain into cocktail glass rimmed with powdered sugar.

Fancy Gin Cocktail (Cktl). ⅕ measure Gin, dash Angostura, 2 dashes Cointreau, 2 dashes Gomme syrup. Shake over ice, strain into a cocktail glass. Top with a twist of lemon peel juice.

Fancy Gin Smash (Cktl). As for Gin Smash but the glass is filled with shaved ice and decorated with fruits and a sprig of mint. Serve with straws and a spoon.

Fancy Whiskey Cocktail (Cktl). ⅕ measure Bourbon whiskey, 1 dash Angostura, 2 dashes Cointreau, 2 dashes Gomme syrup. Shake over ice, strain into a cocktail glass. Top with a twist of lemon peel juice.

Fanega (Sp). A measurement used in Málaga. 1 acre equals 1.5 Fanegas.

Fangos (Austr). A principal liqueur producer. Produces many styles of liqueurs.

Fanleaf (Eng). Disease (virus) of the vine. See Court Noué.

Fannings (Eng). A type of broken tea leaf grade. Small leaf between B.P. and Dust in size. Usually used in teabags. Name derived from the way the 'fannings' that were on the floor were 'fanned' into piles.

Fanta (USA). A non-alcoholic, still or sparkling, orange drink produced by the Coca Cola Co.

Fantaisie (Fr). If found on a label denotes synthetic products have been used.

Fantaisie (Fr). A term applied to Kirsch made from neutral alcohol, natural Kirsch and other ingredients.

Fantasia Cocktail (Cktl). ⅕ gill Green Chartreuse, ⅙ gill Vodka, ⅛ gill grapefruit juice, 4 dashes Cherry brandy. Stir over ice, strain into a frosted cocktail glass. Dress with an orange slice and a cherry.

Fantasia Ramazzotti (It). A banana-flavoured liqueur.

Fantasio Cocktail (Cktl). ⅓ gill Brandy, ⅛ gill Maraschino, ⅛ gill (white) Crème de Menthe, ⅛ gill dry Vermouth. Stir over ice, strain into a cocktail glass.

F.A.Q. (Austr) (abbr). Fair Average Quality.

Fara (It). D.O.C. red wine from Piemonte. Produced in the commune of Novara from 40% Bonarda, 30–50% Nebbiolo and 10–30% Vespolina grape varieties. Must be aged for 3 years (at least 2 years in oak/chestnut casks).

Fare la Birra (It). Brew.

Fares (Fr). A vineyard based in Vienne, Isère Département. Produces red wines.

Fare Thee Well Cocktail (Cktl). ⅓ measure dry Gin, ⅛ measure dry Vermouth, dash sweet Vermouth, dash Cointreau. Shake over ice, strain into a cocktail glass.

Farewell (Eng). An alternative term sometimes used in place of aftertaste.

Farfelu Vineyard (USA). A small vineyard based in Flint Hill, Virginia. 5 ha. Produces French hybrid and vinifera wines.

Fargo Ale (Eng). A bottled strong Ale 1046 O.G. brewed by the Charles Wells Brewery in Bedford.

Fargues (Fr). A commune in the Sauternes district of Bordeaux. Wines are sold under the A.C. Sauternes..

Farmer's Ale (Eng). A bottled Bitter ale 1036 O.G. brewed by the McMullen Brewery in Hertford.

Farmer's Ale (Eng). A cask conditioned Bitter 1038 O.G. brewed by the Oakhill Brewery, Bath, Wiltshire.

Farmer's Glory (Eng). A cask conditioned Bitter 1046 O.G. brewed by the Wadworth Brewery in Devizes, Wiltshire.

Farmer's Joy (Cktl).(Non-alc). 3 fl.ozs. tomato juice, 1 egg yolk, dash lemon juice, celery salt, milled pepper, Worcestershire sauce. Shake well over ice, strain into an old-fashioned glass. Serve with a stick of celery.

Farm Stout (Eng). A sweet Stout 1035 O.G. brewed by the Greene King Brewery in East Anglia.

Farm Winery Bill (USA). A law passed in 1968 in Pennsylvania that prevents wineries producing in excess of 100,000 U.S. gallons of wine per year.

Faro (Bel). A Lambic beer. Sweetened version.

Faro (Fr). A low-alcohol, sour beer. Is often sweetened.

Faro (It). Red and rosé wines made from the Nerello, Nocnera and Cintana grapes in Sicily.

Faros (Yug). A smooth red wine from Hvar Island.

Farse (Iran). A wine-producing province in northern Iran.

Farsons Brewery (Euro). Full name is Simonds Farsons Cisk on the island of Malta. Brews top-fermented and pasteurised beers. See Blue label, Brewer's Choice and Hop Leaf.

Fartó (Sp). A white grape variety grown in Alicante.

Fass (Ger). Cask.

F

Fässerlay (Ger). Vineyard. (Anb) = Mittelrhein. (Ber) = Rheinburgengau. (Gro) = Gedeonseck. (Vil) = Boppard.

Fassle (Ger). A small cask of 5 litres in capacity. Is similar to a Spanish Porrón. Requires a steady hand to drink from.

Fass N° (Ger). Cask number.

Fat (Eng). A term usually applied to dry white wines that lack acidity but have plenty of fruit.

Father of Californian Viticulture (USA). Count Agoston Haraszthy.

Fattigmands Snaps (Den). A noted brand of Akvavit.

Fattoria (It). Farm, vineyard.

Fattoria dei Pagliaresi (It). A Chianti Classico producer based in Siena, Tuscany.

Fattoria delle Lodoline (It). A Chianti Classico producer based in Vagliagli, Tuscany.

Fattoria dell'Ugo (It). A Chianti Putto producer based in Tuscany.

Fattoria le Pici (It). A Chianti Classico producer based in San Gusine, Tuscany.

Fattoria Montellori (It). A Chianti Putto producer based in Tuscany.

Fattoria Nico (It). See Illuminati.

Fattoria Paradiso (It). A winery based at Bertinoro in the Emilia Romagna region. 30 ha.

Fattoria Saulina (It). A Chianti Putto producer based in Tuscany.

Fauconberg Wine Stores (Eng). The trading name for one of J.T. Davies retail wine and spirit outlets in Chiswick, London.

Faugères (Fr). An A.C. commune in the Coteaux du Languedoc, Midi. Produces red and white wines. Minimum alc. by vol. 11%.

Fäul (Ger). Mouldy or foul.

Faure (Michel) (Fr). A V.S.O.P. Armagnac produced in the Bas Armagnac by Michel Faure. 40% alc. by vol.

Faust Brauerei (Ger). A famous brewery based in Bavaria. Is noted for Pilsener lagers. See Faust Lager.

Faustianum (Lat). A red wine produced in central-western Italy during Roman times.

Faustino (Sp). A brand-name for the Bodegas Faustino Martinez S.A., Oyón, Rioja. Many grades are produced.

Faustino I (Sp). A Tinto Gran Reserva produced by Bodegas Faustino Martinez S.A. 12.5% alc. by vol. Produced from Graciano 15%, Mazuelo 15% and Tempranillo 70%.

Faustino IV (Sp). A red Reserva wine produced by Bodegas Faustino Martinez S.A.

Faustino Rivero Ulecia, S.A (Sp). Address = Ctra Garray, Km 73, Arnedo La Rioja. 30 ha. Grape varieties – Garnacha 50%, Tempranillo 30% and Viura 20%. Wines – Red 70%, Rosé 20% and White 10%.

Faustino V (Sp). The brand-label for red and white wines produced by the Bodegas Faustino Martinez, Rioja. (red) = 20% Garnacha, 80% Tempranillo, (white) = Viura 100%. Also a rosé version.

Faust Lager (Eng). A Pilsener Lager 1035 O.G. brewed by the Eldridge Pope Brewery in Dorchester, Dorset. Also an Export version 1042 O.G. and a Diät Pils 1035 O.G. All brewed under licence from the Faust Brauerei in Bavaria.

Fauvelots (Fr). A grade of rosé to red wine.

Fauvet (Fr). An alternative name for the Pinot gris grape.

Faventinum (Lat). A white wine produced in north-eastern Italy during Roman times.

Faverolles (Fr). A Cru Champagne village in the Canton de Ville-en-Tardenois. District = Reims.

Favorita (It). A red grape variety grown in Alba. Is also used to lighten Barbera wines.

Favorite (La) (W.Ind). A popular brand of Rum produced on the island of Martinique by D.R.A.

Favorito (Port). A fine old Tawny Port from Smith Woodhouse Port shippers.

Favorito (Sp). A brand of Oloroso cream sherry from the Diez Hermanos range produced by Diez Merito.

Favourite Cocktail (Cktl).(1). ⅓ measure Gin, ⅓ measure Apricot brandy, ⅓ measure dry Vermouth, 2 dashes lemon juice. Shake over ice, strain into a cocktail glass.

Favourite Cocktail (Cktl).(2). ½ measure Gin, ½ measure Cognac, 3 dashes Grenadine, 2 dashes lemon juice. Shake well over ice, strain into a cocktail glass. Dress with a slice of lemon.

Faxe Brewery (Den). Produces an unpasteurised beer called Faxe Fad, a bottled Lager 4.5% alc. by vol. See Fad.

Faxe Fad (Den). A bottled Lager 4.5% alc. by vol. brewed by the Faxe Brewery in Denmark. See Fad.

Fayal (Port). A vineyard in the Azores that produced wines under label of same name. Now no longer in operation.

Faye d'Anjou (Fr). A.C. commune in the Coteaux du Layon, Anjou-Saumur, Loire.

Fayre Ladye (Cktl). 1 measure dry Gin, ⅙

F

measure Crème de Violette, ⅓ measure Grand Marnier, ⅙ measure pink Crème de Noyau, ⅓ measure lemon juice, dash egg white. Shake over ice, strain into a cocktail glass.

Fay Vineyard (USA). A vineyard based near Yountville, Napa Valley, California. 50 ha. Grape variety – Cabernet sauvignon.

Fazendas (Bra). The coffee farms.

Fazi-Battaglia (It). A noted producer of Verdicchio in the Marche region. The main winery is based at Castelplanio.

F.B. (Eng) (abbr). French bottled.

F.B.S.K. (Fin) (abbr). Finland Bartenders' och Supporters' Klubb. Finnish Bartenders' Association. Address = Box 150–131 Helsinki 13.

Feather Cocktail (Cktl). ¾ measure sweet Vermouth, ¼ measure dry Vermouth, ½ measure Pernod. Shake over ice, strain into a cocktail glass.

Fécamp (Fr). Home of the Bénédictine monastery where the drink of the same name is made. See Bénédictine.

Federação dos Vinicultores do Dão (Port). Founded in 1942 to improve the standards of quality and labelling of Dão wines.

Federal Institute for Viticulture (Ger). Sited at Siebeldingen in the Rheinpfalz.

Federation (Eng). A specialist Club Brewery (The Northern Clubs Federation Brewery). Brewery sited in Dunston, Newcastle. Produces only processed beers. Noted for Ace Lager 1032 O.G. LCL Pils 1036 O.G. Medallion Lager 1036 O.G. and a bottled sweet Federation Stout 1043 O.G.

Fédération Nationale de Producteurs de Rhum (Fr). FENARUM. The French equivalent of CODERUM in Martinique, West Indies.

Federation of Sherry and Spirit Producers (Sp). F.E.V.Y.B.A. Body for industrial and home market affairs.

Federico Paternina (Sp). Address = Avd. Santo Domingo, N° 11, Haro (La Rioja). Has no vineyards, buys in wines – 71.3% red, 11.3% rosé and 16.9% white. Labels – Banda Dorada (white), Banda Azul (red), Conde de los Andes (red), Rinsol (white) and Viña Vial (red).

Federweissen Festival (Ger). See Fest des Federweissen.

Federweisser (Aus). Fermenting must.

Federweisser (Ger). A milky-white, still-fermenting, strong, young wine drunk in Germany by the local residents.

Fefiñanes Palacio (Sp). An oak-aged, white wine produced by Marqués de Figueroa in Zona del Albariño, Galicia, north-western Spain.

Fehér (Hun). White.

Féherbór (Hun). White wine.

Fehérburgundi (Hun). A white grape variety grown in south-western Hungary. Known as the Pinot blanc in France.

Feher Szagos (USA). A white grape variety used in the making of dessert wines in California.

Feilbingert (Ger). Village. (Anb) = Nahe. (Ber) = Schloss Böckelheim. (Gro) = Paradiesgarten. (Vins) = Bocksberg, Feuerberg, Höchstes Kreuz, Kahlenberg, Königsgarten.

Fein (Ger). Fine. Pre 1971 designation on wine labels.

Feiner Weisser Burgunder (Ger). The local name for the Chardonnay grape.

Feinste (Ger). Finest.

Feints (Scot). The 'lasts' from a pot still used for Whisky and grain spirits. The 'firsts' are called 'Foreshots' and between the two is called 'the Heart'.

Feis (Ch.Isles). A tot or dram of drink. See also Lache.

Feist (Port). Vintage Port shippers. Vintage – 1922.

Feitoria Inglesa (Port). A club building based in Oporto. Originally was a factory system. British had extra-territorial rights. Members are partners in British Port firms (Oporto-based). See The Factory House. Males only.

Felanitx (Sp). A major wine-producing area on Majorca, Balearic Isles.

Feldbach (Aus). A wine-producing area in southern Austria.

Feldberg (Ger). Village. (Anb) = Baden. (Ber) = Markgräflerland. (Gro) = Burg Neuenfels. (Vin) = Paradies.

Feldebro (Hun). A wine-producing village in Debrö that produces sweet white Hàr-slevelü wine.

Feldschlösschen Brauerei (Switz). A large brewery based in Rheinfelden. Is noted for its' Castello.

Feliciano (Sp). A deep straw-coloured Cream sherry produced by Wisdom and Warter in Jerez de la Frontera.

Felicitation Cocktail (Cktl).(Non-alc). ⅓ measure tomato juice, ⅓ measure orange juice, ⅓ measure blackcurrant juice, 1 egg yolk. Blend together with a scoop of crushed ice in a blender. Serve in a flute glass with an orange slice on rim.

Felinfoel Brewery (Wales). Based in Llanelli in South Wales. Noted for its' cask conditioned/keg Double Dragon 1041 O.G. (The first beer to be canned), Cream Stout 1040 O.G. Nut Brown 1032 O.G. John Brown 1032 O.G. and St. David's Porter 1036 O.G

Felipe II (Sp). A noted Brandy produced by Agustín Blázquez.

Fell (Ger). Village. (Anb) = Mosel-Saar-Ruwer. (Ber) = Bernkastel. (Gro) = Probsterg. (Vin) = Maximiner Burgberg.

Fellbach (Ger). Village. (Anb) = Württemberg. (Ber) = Remstal-Stuttgart. (Gro) = Weinsteige. (Vins) = Gips, Goldberg, Herzogenberg, Hinterer, Berg, Lämmler, Mönchberg, Wetzstein.

Fellbacher Herbst (Ger). A Württemberg wine festival held at Fellbach in October.

Fellerich (Ger). Village. (Anb) = Mosel-Saar-Ruwer. (Ber) = Obermosel. (Gro) = Gipfel. (Vin) = Schleidberg.

Fellini Cocktail (Cktl). 2 fl.ozs. Eisberg alcohol-free wine, 2 fl.ozs Peach liqueur. Stir over crushed ice, strain into a paris wine goblet.

Fellini Cocktail (Cktl).(Non-alc). 2 fl.ozs. Eisberg alcohol-free wine, 2 fl.ozs. peach juice. Stir over crushed ice, strain into a paris goblet.

Fellow's Bitter (Eng). A cask conditioned Bitter 1040 O.G. brewed by the Whitbread's home-brew public house Fellows, Morton and Clayton in Nottingham. Made with malt extract.

Fellows, Morton and Clayton (Eng). A home-brew public house owned by Whitbread's, based in Nottingham. Produces a cask conditioned Clayton's Original 1048 O.G. and Fellow's Bitter 1040 O.G.

Fells Manzanilla (Sp). The brand-name for a Manzanilla sherry produced by Rafael O'Neaule of Jerez de la Frontera.

Fels (Ger). Vineyard. (Anb) = Mosel-Saar-Ruwer. (Ber) = Saar-Ruwer. (Gro) = Scharzberg. (Vil) = Könen.

Fels (Ger). Vineyard. (Anb) = Nahe. (Ber) = Kreuznach. (Gro) = Schlosskapelle. (Vil) = Windesheim.

Fels (Ger). Vineyard. (Anb) = Nahe. (Ber) = Schloss Böckelheim. (Gro) = Rosengarten. (Vil) = St. Katharinen.

Fels (Ger). Vineyard. (Anb) = Rheinhessen. (Ber) = Bingen. (Gro) = Rheingrafenstein. (Vil) = Frei-Laubersheim.

Fels (Lux). A vineyard site in the village of Grevenmacher.

Felsberg (Lux). A vineyard site in the village of Wintrange.

Felsen (Ger). Vineyard. (Anb) = Rheinhessen. (Ber) = Wonnegau. (Gro) = Bergkloster. (Vil) = Eppelsheim.

Felsenau Brauerei (Switz). A small brewery based in Bern.

Felsenberg (Ger). Vineyard. (Anb) = Nahe. (Ber) = Kreuznach. (Gro) = Schlosskapelle. (Vil) = Eckenroth.

Felsenberg (Ger). Vineyard. (Anb) = Nahe. (Ber) = Schloss Böckelheim. (Gro) = Burgweg. (Vil) = Duchroth.

Felsenberg (Ger). Vineyard. (Anb) = Nahe.

(Ber) = Schloss Böckelheim. (Gro) = Burgweg. (Vil) = Oberhausen an der Nahe.

Felsenberg (Ger). Vineyard. (Anb) = Nahe. (Ber) = Schloss Böckelheim. (Gro) = Burgweg. (Vil) = Schlossböckelheim.

Felseneck (Ger). Vineyard. (Anb) = Nahe. (Ber) = Kreuznach. (Gro) = Pfarrgarten. (Vil) = Gutenberg.

Felseneck (Ger). Vineyard. (Anb) = Nahe. (Ber) = Kreuznach. (Gro) = Pfarrgarten. (Vil) = Wallhausen.

Felseneck (Ger). Vineyard. (Anb) = Nahe. (Ber) = Schloss Böckelheim. (Gro) = Burgweg. (Vil) = Bad Münster a. St-Ebernburg.

Felsen Export (Ger). A fine beer produced by the Felsenkeller Brauerei of Beerfelden in Hesse.

Felsengarten (Ger). Vineyard. (Anb) = Baden. (Ber) = Bodensee. (Gro) = Sonnenufer. (Vil) = Überlingen.

Felsengarten (Ger). Vineyard. (Anb) = Württemberg. (Ber) = Württembergisch Unterland. (Gro) = Schalkstein. (Vil) = Besigheim.

Felsengarten (Ger). Vineyard. (Anb) = Württemberg. (Ber) = Württembergisch Unterland. (Gro) = Schalkstein. (Vil) = Hessigheim.

Felsenkeller Brauerei (Ger). A small brewery of Beerfelden in Hesse. Produces fine beers, including Pilseners and Bocks.

Felsenkopf (Ger). Vineyard. (Anb) = Mosel-Saar-Ruwer. (Ber) = Bernkastel. (Gro) = Michelsberg. (Vil) = Trittenheim.

Felsenköpfchen (Ger). Vineyard. (Anb) = Nahe. (Ber) = Kreuznach. (Gro) = Kronenberg. (Vil) = Bretzenheim.

Felsensteyer (Ger). Vineyard. (Anb) = Nahe. (Ber) = Schloss Böckelheim. (Gro) = Burgweg. (Vil) = Niederhausen an der Nahe.

Felsentreppche (Ger). Vineyard. (Anb) = Mosel-Saar-Ruwer. (Ber) = Bernkastel. (Gro) = Schwarzlay. (Vil) = Wittlich.

Felslay (Ger). Vineyard. (Anb) = Mosel-Saar-Ruwer. (Ber) = Saar-Ruwer. (Gro) = Römerlay. (Vil) = Mertesdorf.

Felstar (Eng). The brand-name for wine from the vineyards at Crick's Green, Felstead, Essex. First planted in 1966 of 4.35 ha. Grape varieties – Chardonnay, Madeleine angevine, Müller-Thurgau, Pinot noir and Seyval blanc.

Felton and Son (USA). A distillery of New England Rum including Crystal Spring and Pilgrim brands.

Felton-Empire (USA). Vineyards based at Santa Cruz, California. Has vineyards at Beauregard, Hallcrest and Vine Hill.

F

Grape varieties – Gewürztraminer and White riesling. Produces table and dessert (botrytis) wines.

Femage (Fr). The renting out of a domaine or vineyard in Burgundy.

FENARUM (Fr) (abbr). Fédération Nationale de Producteurs de Rhum.

Fen Chiu (China). A Grain spirit produced from wheat and millet in Sing Hua village, Shansi province.

Fendant (Switz). A white wine grape known as the Chasselas in France and the Gutedel in Germany. See also Bon Blanc.

Fendant de Sion (Switz). A local name for the Chasselas grape in the Valais region. See also Fendant du Valais and Fendant Vert.

Fendant du Valais (Switz). A local name for the Chasselas grape in the Valais region. See also Fendant de Sion and Fendant Vert.

Fendant Vert (Switz). A local name for the Chasselas grape in the Valais region. See also Fendant de Sion and Fendant du Valais.

Fendant Wine (Switz). A white wine, best known in the Valais region, made from the Fendant (Chasselas) grape.

Fenland Fizzer (Cktl). 1 oz. Tia Maria, 1 oz. Vodka. Stir over ice, strain into a highball glass with ice, top up with cola and add a slice of lemon.

Fenman Bitter (Eng). A keg Bitter 1033 O.G. brewed by the Elgood Brewery in Wisbech, Cambridgeshire.

Fennel Water (Eng). See Fenouillette (a fennel-flavoured liqueur).

Fenn Valley Vineyards (USA). A winery based in Fennsville, Michigan. Noted for its' Riesling wines.

Fenouillette (Fr). A fennel-based liqueur produced by Denoix of Brive.

Fenton Acres (USA). A winery based in the Russian River Valley, Sonoma County, California. Grape variety – Chardonnay.

Fer (Fr). A red grape variety grown in the Bergerac region.

Fer Dervadou (Fr). A white grape variety grown in the Côtes du Marmandais.

Ferdinand Schumacher Brauerei (Ger). A brewery of Düsseldorf, West Germany in the Oststrasse. Produces fine Altbier. See Schumacker Altbier.

Fèrebrianges (Fr). A Cru Champagne village in the Canton de Montmort. District = Épernay.

Fergie's Fizz (Cktl). ½ measure Cointreau, ½ measure Cherry brandy. Shake over ice, strain into a flute glass. Top with Champagne.

Fergusson's Winery (Austr). Address = Wills Road, Yarra Glen, Victoria, 3775, Australia. 6 ha. Grape varieties – Cabernet franc, Cabernet sauvignon, Chardonnay, Marsanne, Pinot noir, Rhine riesling, Shiraz.

Feria (Sp). A spectacular celebration of Jerez to start the harvest of the grapes.

Fermage (En) (Fr). The term used when a Négociant dictates to a Château wine-producer how they require the wine to be produced (grapes grown, cépage, viniculture, etc).

Fermé (Fr). A firm, full wine which possesses a hardness when mature that it should have lost. See also Fermenté.

Ferment (Eng). From the Latin Fervere = to boil. Denotes the process of yeasts on sugars to produce alcohol and CO_2.

Fermentare (It). To ferment.

Fermentation (Eng). The action of a ferment.

Fermentation Lock (Eng). Also known as an Airlock. A valve used in the fermentation of home-made wines which allows CO_2 gas to escape but prevents the entry of any contamination (air or bacterial). Uses a water seal as the airlock.

Fermentazione (It). The fermentation process.

Fermentazione in Bianco (It). Removing the skins from the must for white wines.

Fermentazione Naturale (It). Natural fermentation. Either in tank or méthode champenoise, but the former is most likely.

Fermenté (Fr). A firm full wine which possesses a hardness when mature that it should have lost. See also Fermé.

Fermented Beverages (USA). The name given to beverages made from grain or fruits with alcoholic strengths that range from 7–14% alc. by vol.

Fermented Milk (Eng). A method of preserving milk. Alters the flavour and appearance. See also Dahdi, Huslanka, Lad Anzebadi, Mazyn and Taetta.

Fermenting (Eng). The action of fermentation.

Fermentor (USA). A vessel in which the fermentation takes place in the production of whiskey.

Fermentum (Lat). Yeast.

Fernandez Distillery (W.Ind). Rum distilleries based on the islands of Puerto Rico and Trinidad.

Fernandez Vat 19 (W.Ind). A golden Rum produced by the Fernandez Distillery on the island of Puerto Rico.

Fernand Pernot (Fr). A négociant-éleveur based in the Côte d'Or, Burgundy.

Fernaô Pires (USA). A white grape

417

variety used in the making of dessert wines in California.

Fernet (It). A herbal bitters digestif made by Martini & Rossi in Turin. 45% alc. by vol.

Fernet Branca (Fr). A producer in St-Louis, Haut-Rhin, Alsace of a liqueur of same name (Fleurs des Alpes and Branca Menthe).

Fernet Branca (It). A Bitters. Has a medicinal flavour and aroma. Produced in Turin. 40% alc. by vol.

Fernet Branca Cocktail (Cktl). ½ measure Fernet Branca, ½ measure sweet Vermouth, 1 measure Brandy. Shake over ice, strain into a cocktail glass.

Fernet Branca Menta (It). A mint-flavoured Bitters from the Fratelli Branca Distilleries S.p.A.

Fernet Cocktail (Cktl). ¼ gill Fernet Branca, ¼ gill Cognac, 1 dash Angostura, 2 dashes Gomme syrup. Stir over ice, strain into a cocktail glass, top with a squeeze of lemon peel juice.

Fernet Gambarotti (It). A herb-flavoured liqueur produced by the Gambarotta di Inga & C. S.p.A., Serravalle Scrivia.

Fernet Menthe (Cktl). ⅔ measure Fernet Branca, ⅓ measure (green) Crème de Menthe. Stir together over ice, strain into a cocktail glass. A Pick-me-up.

Fernets (Cktl). The name given to cocktails which have Fernet Branca in the recipe.

Fernhill (N.Z.). Part of the Cooks Winery.

Ferral (Mad). A white grape variety used in the making of Madeira.

Ferrana (Alg). A white grape variety.

Ferrand (Pierre) (Fr). Cognac producer. Address = La Nerolle, 16130 Segonzac. 27 ha. in the Grande Champagne. Produces – Réserve Ancestrale and Sélection des Anges.

Ferrara Winery (USA). A small winery based in Escondido, San Diego, California. Produces varietal and dessert wines.

Ferrarelle (It). A mineral water bottled and carbonated at Ferrarelle spring in Caserta.

Ferrari (It). Producers of sparkling (méthode champenoise) wines from the Trentino area of the Venetian region in north-eastern Italy. All estate-bottled. Also produce still wines.

Ferrari Cocktail (Cktl). ⅔ measure French vermouth, ⅓ measure Amaretto. Stir over ice in a highball glass. Dress with a lemon slice.

Ferratum (Lat). A mediaeval wine produced in southern England. Was classed as a Tonic wine because of its iron content.

Ferraud (Pierre) (Fr). A négociant-éleveur based in Beaujolais and Mâconnais wines. Address = 31, Rue Maréchale Foch, 69823 Belleville.

Ferraz Lda (Mad). A noted producer of Madeira wines.

Ferreira [A.A] (Port). Vintage Port shippers. Vintages – 1894, 1896, 1897, 1900, 1904, 1908, 1912, 1917, 1920, 1924, 1927, 1935, 1937.

Ferreira [A.A. Sucrs] (Port). Vintage Port shippers. Vintages – 1945, 1955, 1960, 1963, 1966, 1970, 1975, 1977, 1980, 1982, 1983, 1985.

Ferreira (Raul & Filho) Lda (Port). Own Quinta do Barão, the only remaining vineyard in Carcalvelos.

Ferreira dos Santos (Port). Producer of Dão wines based in Povolide and Viseu.

Ferreira Malaquias (Port). Producers of Dão wines under the Dão Ferreira Malaquias label.

Ferren (Sp). A red grape variety grown in the Galicia region.

Ferrer (Sp). A wine-producer based in Mallorca. Produces mainly red wines.

Ferrerinha (Port). The brand-name of a light red wine produced by Ferreira.

Ferrero Vineyard (USA). A small winery based in Shenandoah Valley, Amador, California. 8.5 ha. Grape variety – Zinfandel.

Ferret Ale (Eng). A cask conditioned Bitter 1045 O.G. brewed by the Bruce's Ferret and Firkin home-brew public house in London.

Ferret and Firkin (Eng). A home-brew public house owned by Bruce's in London. Produces – Dogbolter 1060 O.G. Ferret Ale 1045 O.G. and a Stout 1036 O.G.

Ferret y Mateu (Sp). A noted wine-producer based in the Penedés. Produces Viña Laranda Blanco.

Ferric Casse (Eng). Caused by a high iron content in the wine resulting in cloudiness and a deposit forming. Is cured by adding blue finings (forbidden in some countries).

Ferro China (It). An aromatic Bitters similar to Fernet Branca produced in Milan. 21% alc. by vol.

Ferro-China Bisteri (It). See Ferro-China.

Ferrón (Sp). A black grape variety grown in Ribeiro.

Ferruginous Clay (Sp). Iron-rich clay soil found in the Rioja region of north-western Spain.

Fervere (Lat). To boil. Word from which ferment derives.

F.E.S. (Eng) (abbr). See Foreign Extra

F

Stout.

Fesq (Austr). A principal liqueur producer.

Fessenbach (Ger). Village. (Anb) = Baden. See Offenburg.

Festa de la Verena (Sp). A 'Vintage festival'. Occurs in Sitges, Barcelona.

Fest des Federweissen (Ger). Federweissen festival. A wine festival held in Landau in the Rheinpfalz in the Autumn.

Festigny (Fr). A Cru Champagne village in the Canton de Dormans. District = Épernay.

Festival Ale (Eng). A cask conditioned Bitter 1055 O.G. brewed by the Burton Bridge Brewery in Burton-on-Trent.

Festival Ale (Eng). A keg Bitter 1039 O.G. brewed by the Greenall Whitley Brewery in Warrington, Cheshire. Also sold in bottle 1042 O.G.

Festival Ale (Eng). A Pale ale 1050 O.G. brewed by the King and Barnes Brewery in Sussex.

Festival Ale (Eng). A cask conditioned Ale 1052 O.G. brewed by the Woodeforde Brewery in Norfolk.

Festivale (Eng). A special beer brewed by the Courage Brewery for the 1986 Great Western Beer Festival.

Festival Wines (S.Afr). The brand-name of Gilbeys Ltd. Varietal wines.

Festive Wines (USA). The name given to sparkling wines.

Fest Rund um die Naheweinstrasse (Ger). Held in each of the greater communities of the Nahewein route during the end of August.

Festrus (Cktl). ⅓ measure Grand Marnier, ⅓ measure Smirnoff vodka, ⅓ measure bitter Cinzano. Stir over ice, strain into a cocktail glass, add a twist of orange peel and a cherry.

Fetească (Rum). A white grape variety which produces full-bodied wines. Also grown in Bulgaria = (Fetiaska). Hungary = (Leànyka).

Fetească Albă (Rum). A white grape variety grown in central and eastern Rumania.

Fetească de Tîrnave (Rum). A white wine from the Tîrnave region.

Fetească Neagră (Rum). A red grape variety grown in Husi near the Russian border in eastern Rumania.

Fetească Regală (Rum). A white grape variety.

Fête de la Fleur (Fr). A festival held in June of each year in Bordeaux to celebrate the appearance of the flowers on the vines.

Fête des Vignerons (Switz). See Vevey Festival.

Fête du Biou (Fr). Held on the first Sunday of September annually. The great vintage celebration of Arbois.

Fetiaska (Bul). A white grape variety which produces medium-dry white wines. (Hun) = Leànyka. (Rum) = Fetească.

Fetiaska (USSR). A dry white wine from Moldavia.

Fetjaska (USSR). See Fetiaska. Another spelling.

Fett (Ger). Lit – 'Fat'. A full, big wine.

Fettercairn (Scot). A single Malt whisky distillery based on the east coast of Scotland. A Highland malt whisky. 43% alc. by vol.

Fettgarten (Ger). Vineyard. (Anb) = Mosel-Saar-Ruwer. (Ber) = Zell/Mosel. (Gro) = Schwarze Katz. (Vil) = Zell-Merl.

Fetzer Vineyards (USA). A winery based at Redwood Valley, Mendocino, California. 83 ha. Grape varieties – Cabernet sauvignon, Carignane, Johannisberg riesling, Petit syrah and Zinfandel. Varietal and table wines sold under the Bel Arbes label.

Feuer (Ger). Vineyard. (Anb) = Rheinpfalz. (Ber) = Mittelhaardt-Deutsche Weinstrasse. (Gro) = Rebstöckel. (Vil) = Hambach.

Feuerbach (Ger). Village. (Anb) = Baden. (Ber) = Markgräflerland. (Gro) = Vogtei Rötteln. (Vin) = Steingässle.

Feuerbach (Ger). Vineyard. (Anb) = Franken. (Ber) = Steigerwald. (Gro) = Herrenberg. (Vil) = Castell.

Feuerbach (Ger). Village. (Anb) = Württemberg. (Ber) = Remstal – Stuttgart. (Gro) = Weinsteige. See Stuttgart.

Feuerbach (Ger). Vineyard. (Anb) = Baden. (Ber) = Kaiserstuhl-Tuniberg. (Gro) = Vulkanfelsen. (Vil) = Burkheim.

Feuerberg (Ger). Vineyard. (Anb) = Mosel-Saar-Ruwer. (Ber) = Zell/Mosel. (Gro) = Goldbäumchen. (Vil) = Ernst.

Feuerberg (Ger). Vineyard. (Anb) = Mosel-Saar-Ruwer. (Ber) = Zell/Mosel. (Gro) = Grafschaft. (Vil) = Ediger-Eller.

Feuerberg (Ger). Vineyard. (Anb) = Nahe. (Ber) = Schloss Böckelheim. (Gro) = Burgweg. (Vil) = Bad Münster a. St-Ebernburg.

Feuerberg (Ger). Vineyard. (Anb) = Nahe. (Ber) = Schloss Böckelheim. (Gro) = Burgweg. (Vil) = Duchroth.

Feuerberg (Ger). Vineyard. (Anb) = Nahe. (Ber) = Schloss Böckelheim. (Gro) = Paradiesgarten. (Vil) = Feilbingert.

Feuerberg (Ger). Vineyard. (Anb) = Rheinhessen. (Ber) = Wonnegau. (Gro) = Bergkloster. (Vil) = Flomborn.

Feuerberg (Ger). Grosslage. (Anb) =

F

Rheinpfalz. (Ber) = Mittelhaardt-Deutsche Weinstrasse. (Vils) = Bad Dürkheim, Bobenheim am Berg, Ellerstadt, Gönnheim, Kallstadt, Weisenheim am Berg.

Feuerfest Brauerei (Ger). Based in Treuchtlingen, Bavaria. Is noted for its strong beers e.g. Edel Bier. Also known as Schäffbräu.

Feuerfest Edel Bier (Ger). A strong long-lagered beer 11% alc. by vol. Sold in numbered and sealed bottles. Brewed by the Feuerfest Brauerei in Treuchtlingen, Bavaria.

Feuerheerd (Port). Vintage Port shippers. Vintages – 1870, 1872, 1873, 1875, 1878, 1881, 1884, 1887, 1890, 1894, 1896, 1900, 1904, 1908, 1912, 1917, 1920, 1924, 1927, 1942, 1943, 1944, 1945, 1951, 1955, 1957, 1960, 1963, 1966, 1970.

Feuerlay (Ger). Vineyard. (Anb) = Mittelrhein. (Ber) = Rheinburgengau. (Gro) = Gedeonseck. (Vil) = Boppard.

Feuermännchen (Ger). Vineyard. (Anb) = Rheinpfalz. (Ber) = Mittelhaardt-Deutsche Weinstrasse. (Gro) = Höllenpfad. (Vil) = Neuleiningen.

Feuerstein (Ger). Vineyard. (Anb) = Franken. (Ber) = Maindreieck. (Gro) = Not yet assigned. (Vil) = Röttingen.

Feuersteinrossel (Ger). Vineyard. (Anb) = Nahe. (Ber) = Schloss Böckelheim. (Gro) = Paradiesgarten. (Vil) = Oberndorf.

Feuerwant (Ger). A local name for the wine of Beutelsbach in Württemberg, West Germany. Lit – 'Fire wall'.

Feuillaison (Fr). When the leaves begin to appear on the vines.

Feuillatte (Nicolas) (Fr). Champagne producer. Address = B.P. 210, Chouilly, 51206 Épernay. 6,000 ha. owned by co-operative members. Founded in 1972. Produces – Vintage and non-vintage wines.

Feuilles Mortes (Fr). The local name for the yellow-green Burgundy bottles.

Feuillette (Fr). A capacity measure of a barrel of Chablis. 112–140 litres. (175 bottles average). Various sizes, Burgundy 114 litres, Chablis 132 litres.

Feuillette Bourgogne (Fr). A Burgundy cask holding 114 litres.

Feuillette Chablais (Fr). A Chablis cask holding 132 litres.

Feurig (Ger). Lit – 'Fiery'. Denotes a red wine with a high alcohol content.

Fever Thermometer (USA). The nickname for the signs that acetobacteria are present in a wine and it is turning to vinegar. See also Pulse.

Fèves (Les) (Fr). A Premier Cru vineyard in the A.C. commune of Beaune, Côte de Beaune, Burgundy. 4.4 ha.

Fichots (Les) (Fr). A Premier Cru vineyard in the A.C. commune of Permand-Vergelesses, Côte de Beaune, Burgundy. 11 ha.

F.E.V.Y.B.A. (Sp). See Federation of Sherry and Spirit Producers.

Fez (Afr). A wine-producing region in Morocco.

F.F. (Den) (abbr). Fine Festival. A Beer 7.75% alc. by vol. brewed by the Tuborg Brewery. Also known as Royal Denmark.

F.F. Ferraz Lda (Mad). A company that ships Madeira wines to the U.K.

F.I. (USA) (abbr). Fratt Industries. The brand-name of a Brandy bottled by a company of same name.

Fiano (It). A white grape variety grown in the Puglia region.

Fiaschetteria (It). A shop that sells wines.

Fiaschi (It). Straw-encased flasks.

Fiasco (It). A wicker-wrapped bottle used for Italian wines. 2 litres in size, usually smaller versions are called Mezzofiasco (they hold 1 litre). Generic Chianti is sold in this style of bottle.

Fiasque (Fr). Wine flask.

Fibber McGee (Cktl). 1½ ozs. dry Gin, ½ oz. sweet Vermouth, ½ oz. grapefruit juice, 2 dashes Angostura. Stir with ice, strain into a cocktail glass, add a twist of lemon peel.

Fichots (Le) (Fr). A Premier Cru vineyard in the A.C. commune of Pernand-Vergelesses, Côte de Beaune, Burgundy. 11 ha.

Fiçi (Tur). Cask, barrel.

Ficklin Vineyard (USA). A winery of San Joaquin in California. Produces dessert wines and Tinta Port-style wine.

Fiddletown (USA). A wine-producing area of vineyards in the Sacramento Valley, California.

Fiefs Vendéens (Fr). A Vins de Pays area in the Vendée Département in western France.

Fieille dé Thée (Ch.Isles). Tealeaf.

Field Grafting (Eng). The grafting of European vine-stock onto the roots of American vine-stock in the vineyard as opposed to the method of Bench-grafting.

Fierce Bull (Punch). Heat gently until very hot 1 bottle red Castle d'Almain and sugar to taste. Add 1 gill Brandy and grated nutmeg. Remove from heat and stir in a beaten egg.

Fiesta (Sp). The brand-name used by Bodegas García Carrión in the Jumilla region for a Sangría.

Fiesta Cocktail (Cktl).(1). ⅓ gill white Rum, ⅛ gill lemon juice, 3 dashes Cointreau, dash Grenadine, dash

Gomme syrup. Stir well over crushed ice. Strain into a flute glass, top with soda water. Dress with a lemon peel spiral.

Fiesta Cocktail (Cktl).(2). ½ measure white Rum, ¼ measure dry Vermouth, ¼ measure Calvados. Shake well over ice, strain into a cocktail glass.

Fiesta de la Vendimia (Sp). Vintage fête for sherry. The celebration for the start of the harvest. Lasts 4 days. See Saint Ginés de la Jara.

Fiesta Punch (Punch). 1 bottle sweet white wine, 1 bottle soda water, 1 can unsweetened pineapple juice, 3 fl.ozs. lemon juice, sugar to taste. Dissolve sugar in fruit juices, add wine, chill. Add mix to bowl containing ice, add soda, float sliced fruit on top.

Fiétres (Les) (Fr). A vineyard within the Grand Cru A.C. Corton, Côte de Beaune, Burgundy. Also known as Clos des Fiétres.

Fifth (USA). A bottle size 25.36 U.S. fl.ozs. (⅘ quart).

Fifth Avenue (USA). A type of tall, thin cocktail glass.

Fifth Avenue Cocktail (Pousse Café). Pour in order ½ measure Crème de Cacao, ½ measure Apricot brandy, ⅙ measure cream.

Fifty Eight [58] (Can). A blended Canadian whisky produced by Hiram Walker.

Fifty-Fifty (Cktl). 1 measure dry Gin, 1 measure French vermouth. Stir together with ice, strain into a cocktail glass.

Figarella (Fr). Large wine-producers of Corsica. 192 ha. A.C. Corse-Calvi. Grape varieties – Carignan, Cinsault, Nielluccio and Sciacarello (red, rosé and white).

Figari (Fr). An A.C. sub-region of Corsica.

Figaro (Sp). A brand of medium-dry Sherry from the Diez Hermanos range produced by Diez Merito.

Fighting Cocks Brewery (Eng). A small brewery based at Grantham, Lincolnshire.

Figs (Eng). A blended coffee additive. They are roasted. Makes the coffee stronger, more bitter with an underlying sweetness. See Viennese Coffee.

Filby [The] (Cktl). ⅖ measure dry Gin, ⅕ measure dry Vermouth, ⅕ measure Amaretto di Saronno, ⅕ measure Campari. Stir with ice, add a twist of orange.

Filfar (Cyp). A bitter orange liqueur usually bottled in stone jugs.

Filipetti (It). A producer of sparkling (cuve close) wines in the Piemonte region.

Filippi Winery (USA). A winery based in Cucamonga, California. 133 ha. Produces a wide range of varietal, sparkling and dessert wines.

Fillette (Fr) (slang). For a half-bottle of wine. See Anjou Fillette.

Fillette d'Anjou (Fr). See Anjou Fillette.

Fillette de Touraine (Fr). See Anjou Fillette.

Filliers (Bel). Jenever and liqueur producers. Address = Bachte-Maria-Leerne, near Saint-Martens-Latem.

Fillioux (Jean) (Fr). Cognac producer. Address = Fillioux Fils, La Pouyade, Juillac-le-Coq, 16130, Segonzac. 16 ha. in Grande Champagne. Produces – Coq = 3–4 year old, Cep d'Or = 15 year old and Réserve Familiale = over 45 years old. Also noted for receiving the Cep d'Or award for quality. (The only Cognac ever to do so).

Film Yeast (Eng). The alternative name for Flor.

Fils (Fr). Sons.

Filsen (Ger). Village. (Anb) = Mittelrhein. (Ber) = Rheinburgengau. (Gro) = Marksburg. (Vin) = Pfarrgarten.

Filsinger Vineyards (USA). A winery based in Temecula, California. 25 ha. Grape varieties – Chardonnay, Petit syrah, Sauvignon blanc, White riesling and Zinfandel. Produces varietal wines.

Filter (Eng). A paper or metal unit used to restrain the solid matter from the liquid (coffee, wine, beer, etc) after infusion, brewing, fermenting, etc. See also Membrane Filter.

Filter Coffee (Eng). A method of making coffee where the grounds are placed in a filter and water at 96°C is poured or sprayed (automatic) over them to percolate through to produce coffee on the other side of filter.

Filtering (Eng). To remove the unwanted particles in wine or beer to leave it bright. See also Hippocrate's Sleeve.

Filter Tubes (Eng). Fine, medium or coarse fibre tubes fitted with a plastic cap at one end to stop the wine from by-passing the filter medium. Is used to give a final 'polish' to the wine.

Filtrage (Fr). Percolation.

Filtrato Dolce (It). Lit – 'Sweet filtrate'. Grape must filtered and chilled in southern Italy then shipped to northern Italy for making Vermouth and Vino da Tavola wines. Made from the Moscato grape on the island of Pantelleria.

Filtre (Fr). Filter. See Café Filtre.

Filtrer (Fr). Percolate.

Filtrier-Geschmack (Ger). Lit – 'Filter-taste'. Describes a wine with an asbestos taste.

F

Filzen (Ger). Village. (Anb) = Mosel-Saar-Ruwer. (Ber) = Saar-Ruwer. (Gro) = Scharzberg. (Vins) = Altenberg, Herrenberg, Liebfrauenberg, Pulchen, Steinberger, Unterberg, Urbelt.

Fin (Fr). Fine, delicate.

Fina (Port). A white grape variety of the Malvasia strain. Used in the making of white Port.

Final Gravity (Eng). Normally about 1008–1015 S.G. The higher the amount then the sweeter the beer. The term applies to the end of fermentation.

Fincas (S.Am). The name given to the coffee farms in the Spanish speaking, Latin-American countries. Also known as Haciendas.

Fin de Bouche (Fr). A term associated with wine tasting. Final taste (after-taste).

Findlater, Mackie Todd and Co. Ltd (Scot). A company which produces Marlodge (a Vatted malt whisky) and Findlater's range of sherries.

Findlater's (Eng). Noted London wine merchants. Ship Dry Fly Amontillado, Tia Lola, River Fly, May Fly and Lake Fly sherries.

Findling (Ger). A white grape variety. A mutation of the Müller-Thurgau.

Findling (Ger). Vineyard. (Anb) = Rheinhessen. (Ber) = Nierstein. (Gro) =Spiegelberg. (Vil) = Nierstein.

Fine (Eng). To add finings to a cask of beer or wine. See Fining.

Fine (Fr). Denotes a brandy of no great distinction.

Fine à l'Eau (Bel). A Brandy and mineral water.

Fine and Dandy (Cktl). ¾ measure dry Gin, ¼ measure Cointreau, juice ¼ lemon, dash Angostura. Shake over ice, strain into a cocktail glass. Top with a cherry.

Fine Bourgogne (Fr). A fine mark brandy made from the lees and sediment of Burgundy wines. Matured in oak casks.

Fine Champagne (Fr). The finest Cognac brandy. A blend of Grande and Petite Champagne Cognacs. Minimum of 50% Grande Champagne.

Fine de Bordeaux (Fr). An Eau-de-vie distilled from Bordeaux wine.

Fine de la Maison (Fr). 'House brandy' or 'Bar brandy'.

Fine de Marne (Fr). Eau-de-Vie-de-Vin-de-Champagne. Marc brandy produced in Champagne from last (rebêche) pressings.

Fine Festival (Den). The local name for Royal Denmark (a Lager beer 7.75% alc. by vol) brewed by the Tuborg Brewery in Copenhagen.

Finegr (Wales). Vinegar.

Fine Lachamp (Fr). A prune and nut liqueur produced by the Germain Company in southern France.

Fine Maison (Fr). Brandy of the 'House' or 'Restaurant'.

Finenc (Fr). A red grape variety grown in Madiran.

Fine Old Malmsey (Mad). A Madeira produced by Rutherford and Miles.

Fine Pyrénées (Fr). An angelica-based liqueur produced by Serres in Toulouse.

Fines Roches (Les) (Fr). Part of the Châteauneuf-du-Pape area in southern Rhône.

Finesse (Eng). A wine taster's term for a wine which has breed or class. A wine which is more than ordinary in quality. An elegant wine.

Finesse (Sp). A pale Cream sherry produced by Harvey in Jerez de la Frontera.

Finest Madeira (Mad). May use a brandname or word 'Madeira' and a description e.g. dry, medium, but not the name of the grape. Must be of minimum age of 3 years after Estufagem.

Fine Wine (Eng). A top quality wine. One with breeding and all the right characteristics.

Finger Lakes (USA). A wine district of the New York region. Also known as the Five Finger Lakes.

Fingers (USA). A term for a measure of spirits. e.g. 3 fingers is the span of 3 fingers up the glass which will be the measure.

Finggan (Egy). An Egyptian coffee cup.

Fining (Eng). The clarifying of a wine or beer in a cask or tank. Egg white, Islinglass, Oxblood, Gelatine and some clays (Bentonite) are used for the purpose. See Colloids.

Finish (Eng). The after-taste a wine leaves in the mouth. Describes the length of the taste after the wine has been swallowed (or spat out into a spittoon).

Finish (Eng). A term used to describe the appearance of wine or beer. See also Polish.

Finishing Yeast (Eng). Saccharomyces oviformis used in sparkling (méthode champenoise) wine production.

Finkel (Nor). A type of Gin spirit.

Fink Winery (USA). A winery based in Dundee, Michigan. Produces hybrid wines.

Finland Bartenders' Och Supporters' Klubb (Fin). F.B.S.K. Finnish-Bartenders' Association. Address = Box 150–131, Helsinki 13.

Finlandia (Fin). A clean, neutral Vodka 47% alc. by vol. sold in a frosted, 'rippled' bottle.

Finnor (Cktl). 1 fl.oz. Cointreau, 1 fl.oz. Rye whiskey, juice of half a lemon, orange tonic, dash Grenadine. Blend the whiskey, Cointreau and lemon juice into an ice-filled highball glass. Stir in orange tonic, add Grenadine and garnish with a slice of orange and cherry.

Finn Valley (Eng). Vineyard. Address = Cherrybank Estates, Otley, Ipswich, Suffolk. Planted 1972. 4.2 ha. Soil – heavy boulder clay. Grape variety – Müller-Thurgau.

Fino (Sp). The driest sherry, Oloroso, attacked by flor. 17% alc. by vol. See Saccharomyces Beticus.

Fino Apitivi (Sp). An extra-dry Fino sherry produced by the Sandeman Company.

Fino Camborio (Sp). A Fino sherry produced by De Terry, Jerez de la Frontera.

Fino Campero (Sp). The Spanish name given to a Fino sherry known as Fino Soto in Great Britain.

Fino Chiquilla (Sp). The brand-name of a Fino sherry produced by Marqués de Misa.

Fino Cristal (Sp). A brand of Fino sherry produced by Sanchez Romate.

Fino Feria (Sp). A pale Fino Sherry produced by Duff Gordon in Puerto de Santa Maria.

Fino Mac (Cktl). 1 fl.oz. Ginger wine, 2 fl.ozs dry Sherry. Stir over ice, strain into a cocktail glass.

Fino Marismeño (Sp). A brand of Fino sherry produced by Romate in Jerez de la Frontera.

Fino Martini (Cktl). ½ measure dry Gin, ¼ measure Fino sherry. Stir over ice, strain into a cocktail glass, add a twist of lemon peel juice on top.

Fino Pavon (Sp). A brand of Fino sherry produced by Luis Caballero, Jerez de la Frontera.

Fino Quinta (Sp). A fine old Fino sherry from Osborne and Co.

Fino San Patricio (Sp). A brand of Fino sherry produced by Garvey's in Jerez de la Frontera.

Fino Soto (Eng). The name used in Great Britain for a light Fino sherry from Sandeman known as Fino Campero in Spain.

Fino Soto (Fr). A fine Fino sherry produced by José de Soto, Jerez de la Frontera.

Fino Valley (N.Z.). A winery based in Henderson, North Island. 3 ha. Is noted for its' Alphonse Lavalee (a sweet red, high-alcohol wine).

Fin Bec (Fr). Denotes a person with a finely tuned nose (smell).

Fins Bois (Fr). The fourth Cru of Cognac. Covers 35.5% of region.

Finsbury Distillery (Eng). Home of Stone's Original Green Ginger Wine in north London.

Finsprit (Den). The brand-name of an Akvavit produced by D.D.S.

Fiorano (It). A red wine produced by Boncampagni Ludovisi in Latium.

Fior d'Alpe (It). A very sweet, spicy liqueur. Made from such herbs as mint, thyme, majoram, hyssop, juniper etc. Has a sprig of herb inside bottle on which the sugar crystallises. 46% alc. by vol. Also called Fior d'Alpi.

Fior d'Alpi (It). See Fior d'Alpe. 40% alc. by vol.

Fior di Mandorla (Cktl). ⁵⁄₁₀ measure white Rum, ³⁄₁₀ measure sweet Vermouth, ¹⁄₁₀ measure Apricot brandy, ¹⁄₁₀ measure Amaretto. Shake over ice, strain into a cocktail glass.

Fiore (It). A high quality grape must.

Fioupe Cocktail (Cktl). ¼ gill Cognac, ¼ gill Italian vermouth, 1 teaspoon Bénédictine. Stir over ice, strain into a cocktail glass. Add a cherry, and a squeeze of lemon peel juice on top.

Fire Cracker (Punch). 1 bottle red wine, 1 pint water, ½ lb. sugar, 2 lemons, 4 sticks cinnamon, 4 cloves. Boil the water with sugar, lemon juice, cloves and cinnamon for 5 minutes. Add wine, heat slowly to boiling point, serve.

Fire Devil Cocktail (Cktl). ¼ gill Sloe gin, ¼ gill French vermouth, ¼ gill Italian vermouth, 2 dashes Angostura. Stir over ice, strain into a cocktail glass, serve with a dash of lemon peel juice.

Fireman's Sour (Cktl). 1½ fl.ozs. golden Rum, ½ fl.oz. Grenadine, 1 fl.oz. lime juice, 2 dashes Gomme syrup. Shake over ice, strain into a large cocktail glass. Top with a splash of soda water. Decorate with a slice of orange and a cherry.

Firenze (It). Florence.

Fireside Port (Austr). A Port-style wine produced by Miranda Wines in New South Wales.

Firestone Vineyard (USA). A large winery on the Solvang Plateau in the Santa Ynez Valley, Santa Barbara, California. 125 ha. Grape varieties – Cabernet sauvignon, Chardonnay, Gewürztraminer, Johannisberg riesling, Merlot and Pinot noir. Produces varietal and table wines.

Firewater (USA). The old American Indian name for Whiskey (as it gave a burning sensation as they swallowed it).

Firkin (Eng). A nine gallon beer cask.

Firkin (Eng). The name given to a chain of Public houses that brew their own beers in London under the Bruce name.

Firkin Special Brew (Eng). See F.S.B.

Firm (Eng). A term used to describe wines

that have a good constitution, held up with a certain amount of acidity and tannin.

Firme (Sp). A word used to describe a stable Sherry.

Firn (Ger). A tired, woody, madeirised wine.

Firnriesling (USA). A white grape variety. A cross between the White riesling and the Muscat St. Laurent.

First (Ger). Vineyard. (Anb) = Baden. (Ber) = Badische Frankenland. (Gro) = Tauberklinge. (Vil) = Reicholzheim.

First (Ger). Vineyard. (Anb) = Franken. (Ber) = Maindreieck. (Gro) = Rosstal. (Vil) = Eussenheim.

First Aid Cocktail ((Eng) (Slang). For a 'double brandy'.

First Chop (China). The name given to finest quality tea which is gathered in April and May.

First Marriage (Scot). The term used during Whisky production for the marrying of the malt whiskies. See also Marriage.

First Night (Cktl). ¼ measure Tia Maria, ¼ measure Van der Hum, ½ measure Brandy, 1 barspoon cream. Shake over ice, strain into a cocktail glass.

First Season Vine (Fr). A name given to the vines like the Pinots that ripen early, are young maturing and degenerate quickly.

Fiscanensis (Fr). An Élixer made by the monks of Fécamp. Now called Bénédictine.

Fisch (Ger). Village. (Anb) = Mosel-Saar-Ruwer. (Ber) = Obermosel. (Gro) = Gipfel. (Vins) = Sites not yet choosen.

Fischer (Ger). Vineyard. (Anb) = Franken. (Ber) = Maidreieck. (Gro) = Not yet assigned. (Vil) = Frickenhausen am Main.

Fischerpfad (Ger). Vineyard. (Anb) = Rheinhessen. (Ber) = Nierstein. (Gro) = Rheinblick. (Vil) = Alsheim.

Fischingen (Ger). Village. (Anb) = Baden. (Ber) = Markgräflerland. (Gro) = Vogtei Rötteln. (Vin) = Sonnhohle.

Fisherman Ale (Eng). A Brown ale 1042 O.G. brewed by the Adnams Brewery in Suffolk.

Fisher Vineyards (USA). A winery based near Santa Rosa, Sonoma County, California. 8 ha. Grape varieties – Cabernet sauvignon, Chardonnay and Sauvignon blanc. Produces varietal wines.

Fish Glue (USA) (slang). For Isinglass.

Fish House Punch (Punch). 2 quarts Jamaican Rum, 1 quart Cognac, 2 quarts water, ¾ lb. loaf sugar, juice 2 lemons, 1 wine-glass Peach brandy. Heat all together, serve.

Fish T'Ale (Eng). A cask conditioned Ale 1036 O.G. brewed by the homebrew public house the Flounder and Firkin based in London. Owned by Bruce's.

Fismes (Fr). A Canton in the Champagne region. Has the Cru villages of Châlons-sur-Vesle, Chenay, Crugny, Hermonville, Hourges, Pévy, Prouilly, Trigny, Unchair and Vandeuil.

Fita Azul (Port). A brand-name for a sparkling wine.

Fitger (USA). The brand-name used by Schell in New Ulm, Minnesota for their range of Light beers.

Fitou (Fr). A commune within the A.C. Fitou region, Languedoc, south-western France. Produces red wines.

Fitou (Fr). An A.C. wine region near Corbières, Languedoc-Roussillon. Produces red and white wines. Communes are = Cascastel, Caves-de-Treilles, Fitou, Lapalme, Leucate, Paziols, Treilles, Tuchan and Villeneuve-les-Corbières. Minimum alc. 12% by vol.

Fitusberg (Ger). Vineyard. (Anb) = Rheingau. (Ber) = Johannisberg. (Gro) = Steinmacher. (Vil) = Oberwalluf.

Five Alive Lite (Eng). A mixed citrus drink containing an artificial sweetener (no added sugar) produced by Refreshment Spectrum.

Five Crowns (Port). A brand of Tawny Port produced by Graham Port shippers, Oporto.

Five Finger Lakes (USA). See Finger Lakes.

Five Hundred [500] (Eng). A special Ale 1090–1100 O.G. brewed by the Watney Coombe Reid Brewery to celebrate 500 years of brewing in 1987.

Five Kings (Eng). The kings of Cyprus, Denmark, England, France and Scotland who, in 1363, were invited to a banquet by the mayor of London (Sir Henry Picard) to discuss and help improve the English wine trade.

Five-O-One [501] (Sp). A brand of Fino sherry produced by De Terry in Puerto de Santa Maria.

Five Star (Switz). A De Luxe beer brewed by the Hurlimann Brauerei in Zurich.

Five Star Bitter (Eng). A keg Bitter 1043 O.G. brewed by the Home Brewery in Nottingham.

Five Star Rhum (W.Ind). A straight unblended 7 year old vintage spirit from Haiti.

Five Thirty (Can). A Canadian whisky produced by the Canadian Schenley Distilleries Ltd. 40% alc. by vol.

Five Towns Brewery (Eng). A brewery based at Hanley in Staffordshire. Opened in 1983. Noted for its cask conditioned Bursley Bitter 1040 O.G. and Bennet's Strong Ale 1057 O.G.

Five X (Eng). A cask conditioned Ale 1044 O.G. brewed by the Shepherd Neame Brewery in Kent.

F.I.V.S. (Fr) (abbr). The International Federation of Wine and Spirit Merchants.

Fix (Gre). A well-known brand of Lager beer.

Fixed Acids (Eng). The principal fixed acids (non-volatile) to be found in wine are Tartaric, Malic, Succinic and Lactic.

Fixer (Cktl). ¼ measure Brandy, ¼ measure Prunelle, ¼ measure Crème de Noyau, ⅛ measure cream. Shake over ice, strain into a cocktail glass.

Fixes (Cktl). Spirit, lemon, sugar, water and fruit. Served in a highball glass with shaved ice.

Fixin (Fr). A commune in the north of the Côte de Nuits, sited around the hamlet of Fixey. Has its' own A.C. and also part of the A.C. Côte de Nuits. Has 6 Premiers Crus – Aux Cheusots, Clos de la Perrière, Clos du Chapitre, Les Arvelets, Les Hervelets and Les Meix-Bas. 22.14 ha. Has a good micro-climate and 131 ha. vineyards. Also sells part of the wine under the A.C. Côte de Beaune-Villages.

Fizz (Cktl). 5 parts iced sparkling wine to 1 part Grenadine served in a flute (or tall) glass.

Fizz (Eng) (slang). A term for sparkling wine.

Fizzes (Cktl). Spirit, lemon, sugar and soda water served in a tall glass with ice cubes. Usually consumed in the mornings.

Fizz Glass (USA). A tumbler-shaped glass 6–8 fl.oz. capacity.

Fjord Cocktail (Cktl). ⅓ gill Cognac, ⅛ gill Akvavit, ⅛ gill orange juice, ⅛ gill lime juice, 4 dashes Grenadine. Shake well over ice, strain into an ice-filled old-fashioned glass.

Flabby (Eng). A term to describe a wine that lacks acidity.

Flach (Ger). Lit – 'Flat'. Describes a wine that possesses no outstanding characteristics.

Fläche (Ger). Vineyard. (Anb) = Nahe. (Ber) = Kreuznach. (Gro) = Kronenberg. (Vil) = Bad Kreuznach. (n.b. is not an Einzellagen).

Flacon (Fr). Bottle, flask or flagon.

Fladderack (Hol). A citrus-flavoured Brandewijn.

Flag Ale (Austr). A dark Ale brewed by the Toohey's Brewery in New South Wales.

Flagey-Échezeaux (Fr). A noted wine town within the Côte de Nuits, Burgundy. See Échezeaux and Grand-Échezeaux.

Flagon (Eng). A quarter bottle. 39 fl.ozs. used for beers and cider.

Flag Speciale (Afr). A Beer 12.5° Plato brewed in Benin.

Flambeau d'Alsace (Fr). A white wine of Alsace from noble grapes, gathered after a certain prescribed date. Also Chevalier d'Alsace.

Flambé Cocktail (Cktl). 1 measure dry Vermouth, 1 measure lemon juice. Stir over ice, strain into a saucer glass with crushed ice. Place a small slice of lemon on top and coat with a teaspoon of flaming Galliano.

Flamboyant Cocktail (Cktl). 1 measure golden Rum, 1 measure Crème de Cacao, juice ¼ orange, 1½ measures pineapple juice, dash Grenadine, 2 dashes lime juice. Shake over ice, strain into an ice-filled highball glass. Top with a slice of lime and a pineapple cube. Serve with straws.

Flame Muscat (USA). A relation of the Muscat true grape. See also Red Hanepoot.

Flames Over New Jersey Punch (Punch). Heat a bottle of Applejack brandy with ½ lb. sugar. Add 1 barspoon Angostura and ignite. Finally add 1 pint barley water, stir, serve in toddy mugs.

Flame Tokay (USA). A white grape variety used for making dessert wines in California.

Flaming Cocktail (Cktl). Another name for a traditionally-served Sambuca.

Flaming Glögg (Punch). Stir well together 1 bottle Akvavit, 1 bottle Claret, ½ pint orange juice, ginger root, 6 cloves, stick of cinnamon and the rind of an orange and lemon. Into a scooped-out ½ orange shell (the rim having been dipped in sugar) put some Akvavit and set alight. Float on top of the mixture for 2 minutes then overturn the orange shell and serve.

Flamingo (Cktl). 1 fl.oz. Bourbon whiskey, ¾ fl.oz. Crème de Banane, 2 fl.ozs. orange juice, ¾ fl.oz. lemon juice, 2 dashes Grenadine, dash egg white. Shake over ice, strain into old-fashioned glass, decorate with a slice of orange and a cherry.

Flamingo Cocktail (Cktl).(1). ¾ measure Gin, ¼ measure Apricot brandy, juice ½ lime, 4 dashes Grenadine. Shake well over ice, strain into a cocktail glass.

Flamingo Cocktail (Cktl).(2). ¾ fl.oz. Vodka, ¾ fl.oz. Campari. Shake over ice, strain into a flute glass. Top with iced Champagne. Dress with a slice of orange.

Flanagan (Betsy) (USA). An Irish lady who is purported to have invented the cocktail.

Flap (Cktl). 1 measure of Brandy topped with soda water.

Flasca (Lat). Flask, bottle.

Flasce (Eng). The mediaeval word for flask, bottle.

Flasche (Aus) (Ger). Bottle.

Flasche Bordeaux (Ger). A Bordeaux bottle.

Flaschenkrank (Ger). Bottle-sickness.

Flaschenschild (Ger). Label.

Flash Cocktail (Cktl). ½ gill Gin, 1 teaspoon Absinthe, 1 teaspoon Angostura. Shake over ice, strain into a cocktail glass. Serve with a cherry and a dash of lemon peel juice.

Flash Cooler (Eng). A refrigerated unit connected to the drink supply line near to the dispense tap. Serves the drink in the line at a pre-determined temperature. Usually applied to beer, lager and cider.

Flash of Lightning (Eng) (slang). An old term for Gin.

Flash Pasteurisation (Eng). A reliable method of passing wine through a heat exchanger where it is rapidly heated to 95°C for 1–2 seconds and then rapidly cooled.

Flask (Eng). A style of jug or bottle. (Fr) = Gourde, (Ger) = Flasche, (Hol) = Fles, (Lat) = Flasca.

Flask (Eng). A vacuum container for keeping drinks either hot or cold. See Thermos.

Flaske (Fr). A fourteenth century word for flask, bottle. See also Flasket, Flasque, Flasquet and Flaxe.

Flasket (Fr). A small flask or bottle. Name often given to a hip flask. See also Flaske, Flasque, Flasquet and Flaxe.

Flasque (Fr). An old mediaeval word for flask or bottle. See also Flaske, Flasket, Flasquet and Flaxe.

Flasquet (Fr). An old mediaeval word for a flask or bottle. See also Flaske, Flasket, Flasque and Flaxe.

Flat (Eng). A term applied to sparkling wines that have lost their mousse. Also applied to wines that have a lack of acidity on the finish. Lifeless.

Flat Bean Santos (Bra). A variety of Santos pure coffee.

Flat Beer (Eng). A description of a beer that has lost its' carbonation. (Draught or bottled).

Flatterberg (Ger). Vineyard. (Anb) = Württemberg. (Ber) = Kocher-Jagst-Tauber. (Gro) = Kocherberg. (Vil) = Ernsbach.

Flatterberg (Ger). Vineyard. (Anb) = Württemberg. (Ber) = Kocher-Jagst-Tauber. (Gro) = Kocherberg. (Vil) = Forchtenberg.

Flavanol (Eng). A group of pigments which give the yellow colour to white wines.

Flavenoids (USA). The name given to the flavouring compounds found in wines by Dr. Len McCloskey Ph.D. who owns the Felton-Empire Winery in Santa Cruz, mid-California. See Oenin.

Flavones (Eng). The alternative name for Anthoxanthins.

Flavor (USA). Spelling of Flavour.

Flavored Brandy (USA). A Brandy-based liqueur which has an infusion of named fruit as flavouring.

Flavored Gin (USA). A sweet Gin usually flavoured with either citrus or botanicals. e.g. orange, lemon, lime or mint.

Flavored Rums (USA). Spirits which have a mixture of flavourings added after fermentation and before distillation to give the finished spirit such flavours as Sherry, Madeira, Almond etc.

Flavored Vodka (USA). A sweetened and flavoured Vodka. Is usually flavoured with citrus fruits, mint or grape juice.

Flavored Wines (USA). See Pop Wines.

Flavour (Eng). The taste experienced in the mouth from drink, food, etc. Can be pleasant or unpleasant. See Finish and also After taste.

Flaxe (Fr). A mediaeval word for flask. See also Flaske, Flasket, Flasque and Flasquet.

Fleece and Firkin (Eng). A home-brew public house based in Bristol. Owned by Halls. Noted for its' cask conditioned Coal Porter 1048 O.G. Best Bristol 1045 O.G. Bootlace 1038 O.G. and Dogbolter 1060 O.G.

Flehingen (Ger). Village. (Anb) = Baden. (Ber) = Badische Bergstrasse/Kraichgau. (Gro) = Stiftsberg. (Vin) = Lerchenberg.

Flein (Ger). Village. (Anb) = Württemberg. (Ber) = Württembergisch Unterland. (Gro) = Kirchenweinberg. (Vins) = Altenberg, Eselsberg, Sonnenberg.

Fleischmann (USA). A Bourbon whiskey distillery based on the Indiana border in Kentucky.

Fleischmann Preferred (USA). The brand-name of a blended Whiskey. 40% alc. by vol.

Fleischtraube (Ger). Lit – 'Fleshy or pulpy'. The name for the red grape variety Trollinger.

Flemlingen (Ger). Village. (Anb) = Rheinpfalz. (Ber) = Südliche Weinstrasse. (Gro) = Bischofskreuz. (Vins) = Herrenbuckel, Vogelsprung, Zechpeter.

Fles (Hol). Bottle.

Fleshy (Eng). A term used to describe wines with plenty of fruit and body.

Flessebakje (Hol). Coaster.

Fletcherism (USA). The practice of drinking in small sips to aid the digestion (this together with chewing food thoroughly). Was invented by Horace Fletcher (1840–1919) an American nutritionalist.

Flétri (Switz). A term for withered botrytis cinerea attacked grapes used to make sweet wines.

Fleur (Eng). An alternative name for Mycodermae.

Fleuraison (Fr). The flowering of the vine. (May-June). (Eng) = Floraison.

Fleur de Cap Wines (S.Afr). The brandname for the Die Bergkelder Estate varietal wines.

Fleur du Lys (Fr). The name of an A.C. Blanquette de Limoux produced by Producteurs de Blanquette de Limoux.

Fleurie (Fr). An A.C. Cru Beaujolais-Villages, Burgundy. Has 780 ha. under vines.

Fleuron (Le) (USA). The brand-name label used by the Joseph Phalps Vineyards for a range of varietal and table wines.

Fleurs de Vin (Fr). A fungus which develops on low-alcoholic wines. Appears as a whitish film on ullaged wines. Mycodermae vini.

Fleury-la-Rivière (Fr). A Cru Champagne village in the Canton d'Épernay. District = Épernay.

Flexerne Fruit Farm (Eng). Vineyard. Address = Fletching Common, Newick, Sussex. Planted 1965. 1.2 ha. Soil – Sand. Grape variety – Müller-Thurgau. Vinification by Merrydown Wine Co.

Fleys (Fr). A commune in the A.C. Chablis, Burgundy.

Fliers (Eng). The name given to the dead yeasts (lees) on unracked wine that lift from the bees occasionally, especially if an un-dégorged bottle of Champagne is opened. See Beeswine.

Flietre (Fr). The name for the Syrah grape in the Drôme, Rhône.

Fliniaux (Roland) (Fr). Champagne producer. Address = 1 Rue Leon Bourgeois 51160 Ay. Produces = Vintage and non-vintage wines. 4 ha. Vintages – 1973, 1976.

Flint Glasses (Eng). An old nickname for cut-glass.

Flinty (Eng). A term describing a dry, clean white wine which has a special bouquet, and a particular finish on the palate. e.g. Pouilly Fumé.

Flip Pot (USA). The American name for the Neapolitan Pot (coffee-making method). See also Machinetta.

Flips (Cktl). Spirit, sugar, egg yolk and nutmeg, shaken over ice, strained and served in a small glass.

Flives (Fr). A grade of rosé wine produced in the seventeenth century in northern France.

Floated Liqueurs (USA). The name for Pousse-cafés.

Floater (USA). A long drink consisting of soda covered with a measure of liqueur or Brandy poured in carefully over a spoon.

Floaters (Eng). The term used for odd 'bits' seen suspended in the wine. Results from fruit pulp, filtering medium, casks or corks.

Floaters (Eng) (slang). A term used for the tea leaves that float on top of the brewed tea. Usually caused through poor brewing (water not boiling, insufficient infusion) or poor quality tea (the stem of the tea leaf).

Floats (Eng). Used on wines in tanks to stop air contaminating the wine.

Floc (Fr). A fortified, unfermented grape juice apéritif wine from the Gers Département in southern France. 16–18% alc. by vol.

Flocculate (Eng). See Flocculent.

Flocculation (Eng). See Flocculent.

Flocculent (Eng). A term used to describe the deposit after fermentation that is easily disturbed. Also referred to as Flocculate and Flocculation.

Floc de Gascogne (Fr). See Floc.

Flogger (Eng). A wooden implement for corking bottles. See Boot and Flogger.

Flöhpeter (Ger). A term used for very sour (acidic) wines. Are so sour that any fleas that bit the drinker would die due to the acid in the blood. Flöh = 'flea'.

Flomborn (Ger). Village. (Anb) = Rheinhessen. (Ber) = Wonnegau. (Gro) = Bergkloster. (Vins) = Feuerberg, Goldberg.

Flonheim (Ger). Village. (Anb) = Rheinhessen. (Ber) = Bingen. (Gro) = Adelberg. (Vins) = Bingerberg, Klostergarten, La Roche, Pfaffenberg, Rotenpfad.

Floor Malting (Eng). The traditional method of germinating the Barley (malting) on wooden floors. Barley is turned with wooden spades and forks to dispel excess heat. See also Saladin Box.

Flor (Sp). Lit – 'Flower'. A yeast growth on Oloroso sherries which gives a white film and produces Fino sherry. The yeast is Saccharomyces Ellipsoideus Beticus which feeds at alcohol levels of 15.2–15.4% by vol. on air, glycerine, alcohol and fusel oils. Killed at 16.3–16.4% alc. by vol. See Voile.

Flor (N.Z.). A white grape variety.

Flora (Austr). A rich, golden-coloured wine produced from late-picked grapes (cross between Gewürztraminer and Sémillon) by Brown Brothers Winery.

Flora (USA). A white grape variety grown in California to make white wines.

Flora Blanche (La) (Eng). A brand-name used by J.R. Parkington's to describe a sweet (and a medium-sweet) white wine from the A.C. Premières Côtes de Bordeaux.

Flora di Alpi (It). See Fior d'Alpi. Misspelling of.

Flora di Monteuliveto (It). A herb liqueur produced in the monastery in Monteuliveto.

Floradora Cooler (Cktl). Into a highball glass place the juice of a lime, 1 teaspoon powdered sugar, ⅛ gill Grenadine, 2 fl.ozs. soda water. Stir, fill with ice and add ⅓ gill dry Gin. Top with ginger ale.

Floraison (Eng). See Fleuraison.

Flora Spring Wine Co (USA). A winery based near St. Helena, Napa Valley, California. 91 ha. Grape varieties – Johannisberg riesling and Sauvignon blanc. Produces varietal wines.

Flor do Douro (Port). A red grape variety used in the making of Port to give fruit and body.

Floreffe (Bel). An Abbaye-style beer, bottle-conditioned, brewed by the Anker Brasserie.

Flores Hermanos (Sp). A producer and exporter of Málaga wines.

Florida (Cktl). 1 fl.oz. Galliano, 1½ fl.ozs. dry Gin, ½ fl.oz. Campari, 4 fl.ozs. grapefruit juice. Shake well over ice, strain into an ice-filled highball glass. Top with soda and a slice of orange.

Florida (USA). A wine-producing state in south-eastern America. Produces mainly Muscadine wines.

Florida Cocktail (Cktl).(1). 1 part dry Gin, 1 part pineapple juice, 1 part sweet Vermouth. Shake well over ice, strain into a cocktail glass.

Florida Cocktail (Cktl).(2) (Non-alc). Juice of ½ lemon, juice of ½ orange, 3 dashes Angostura, 2 dashes Gomme syrup. Shake well over ice, strain into a cocktail glass.

Florida Cocktail (Cktl).(3) (Non-alc). 2 fl.ozs. Gomme syrup, 3½ fl.ozs. grapefruit juice, 1½ fl.ozs. orange juice, 2 dashes lemon juice, pinch salt. Shake together with ice, strain into a highball glass filled with crushed ice, top with soda water and decorate with sprig of mint.

Florida Cocktail (Cktl).(4). ¼ measure dry Gin, ⅛ measure Kirsch, ¼ measure Cointreau, ½ measure orange juice, 4 dashes lemon juice. Shake over ice, strain into a cocktail glass.

Florida Daiquiri (Cktl). ⅓ gill white Rum, juice of a lime, dash Maraschino. Blend together with a scoop of crushed ice in a blender. Pour into a flute glass, top with a cherry.

Florio (It). A noted Brandy and wine producer.

Florita (Austr). A vineyard in Watervale, South Australia. Owned by the Leo Buring Co.

Flörsheim (Ger). Village. (Anb) = Rheingau. (Ber) = Johannisberg. (Gro) = Daubhaus. (Vin) = Herrnberg.

Flörsheim-Dalsheim (Ger). Village. (Anb) = Rheinhessen. (Ber) = Wonnegau. (Gro) = Burg Rodenstein. (Vins) = Bürgel, Frauenberg, Goldberg, Hubacker, Sauloch, Steig.

Flor Sherry (Sp). A Sherry-style, dry wine made from the Palomino grape that has been attacked by Flor.

Flounder and Firkin (Eng). A homebrew public house owned by Bruce Co. in London. Produces – cask conditioned Dogbolter 1060 O.G. Fish T'Ale 1036 O.G. and Whale Ale 1045 O.G.

Flower-Honey (Eng). A tasting term often used to describe the sweet taste of old Vouvray or other sweet honeyed wines.

Flowering (Sp). The term used to describe the growth of Flor on Sherry.

Flower Liqueurs (Jap). Made from tea and rose petal, blue gentian, cherry blossom etc.

Flowers (Eng). The name used by Whitbreads for some of their southern beers and their West Midlands trading company. Noted for their cask conditioned Flowers IPA 1036 O.G.

Flowers of Wine (Eng). The alternative name for Flor.

Flowery (Eng). The term used to describe the bouquet of certain wines. It is likened to the scent of flowers. Fine Mosels have this particular quality as also some rieslings.

Flowery Orange Pekoe (Eng). A grade of unbroken tea leaf. The youngest leaf with tips.

Fl.oz. (Eng). ¹⁄₂₀ᵗʰ of an Imperial pint. 20 fl.ozs. = 1 pint.

Fl.oz. (USA). ¹⁄₁₆ᵗʰ of a U.S. pint. 16 fl.ozs. = 1 U.S. pint.

Fluchtig (Ger). Light, empty.

Fluffy Duck (Cktl). 1 fl.oz. dry Gin, 1 fl.oz. Advocaat, ½ fl.oz. Cointreau, ¾ fl.oz. orange juice. Build into an ice-filled highball glass. Stir in soda water, add straws and a stirrer.

Fluid Dram (Eng). ⅛ fl.oz. See also Drachm.

Fluidised Bed Roaster (Eng). Used in coffee production in the roasting process. Lifts the coffee beans into a jet of hot air which roasts them for 3–10 minutes.

Fluoridation (Eng). The addition of Fluoride to the drinking water supply to help prevent tooth decay.

Flurbereinigung (Ger). Involves the pulling together of small vineyards and their reconstruction into larger units. The costs of this operation are shared between the state and the owners and are funded by a 'per litre tax' called the Stabilisierungsfonds. Used to increase the root-stock after Phylloxera.

Flushes (Eng). A tip of 2 tea bush leaves and open bud. (The portion of the bush which is used in tea making).

Flussbach (Ger). Village. (Anb) = Mosel-Saar-Ruwer. (Ber) = Bernkastel. (Gro) = Schwarzlay. (Vin) = Reichelberg.

Flute (Fr). A tall Champagne glass. See also Flûte d'Alsace.

Flûte d'Alsace (Fr). The bottle used for Alsatian wines. Is the same shape and colour as the Mosel wine bottle but is 2 centimetres taller. See also Flute.

Flyer (Eng). A term for a particle floating in wine.

Flying Dutchman (Cktl). 1 measure dry Gin, dash Cointreau. Shake well over ice, strain into an ice-filled old-fashioned glass.

Flying Grasshopper (Cktl). ⅓ measure Vodka, ⅓ measure (green) Crème de Menthe, ⅓ measure (white) Crème de Cacao. Stir over ice, strain into a cocktail glass.

Flying High (Cktl). 1½ fl.ozs. High & Dry Gin, 1 fl.oz. orange juice, 1 fl.oz. Cherry brandy, 4 dashes lemon juice, dash Angostura, 1 egg white. Shake over ice, strain into a wine glass.

Flying Horse (Ind). A premium Lager beer 1052 O.G. brewed by the United Breweries in Bangalore.

Flying Scotsman (Cktl). ½ measure Scotch whisky, ½ measure Italian vermouth, dash Angostura, 2 dashes Gomme syrup. Stir over ice, strain into a cocktail glass.

Flying Tiger (Cktl). 1½ ozs. Bacardi Gold Label, ½ oz. Gin, 1 teaspoon Grenadine, 2 dashes Angostura. Shake well with ice, strain into a cocktail glass.

Foam (Eng). The name given to the formation of bubbles which collect briefly at the top of a glass of sparkling wine. Also known as the Mousse.

Foam (USA). See Foam Collar.

Foam Collar (USA). A name given to the frothy head on a glass of beer.

Foaming Cocktail (USA). Any cocktail that has had egg white added so that when shaken over ice produces a 'head' of foam.

Fob (Eng). The excessive froth seen when serving keg beer or lager beer. Occurs from over carbonation or if there is an air leak in the connections especially in cask conditioned ales.

F.O.B. (Eng) (abbr). Freight On Board.

Foch (USA). A red grape variety hybrid developed in Alsace, France.

Fockink (Ger). The producers of a noted brand of Kümmel liqueur.

Focsani (Rum). A wine region noted for its' white wines from the riesling grape, and also its' dessert wines from the Murfatler Hills. Includes the areas of Cotesti, Nicoresti and Odobesti.

Foehn (Ger). See Föhn.

Fog Cutter Cocktail (Cktl). ⅓ measure dark Rum, ⅓ measure lemon juice, ⅙ measure dry Gin, ⅙ measure Brandy, juice of ½ an orange, 2 barspoons Orgeat syrup. Shake over ice, strain into an ice-filled highball glass. Top with a dash of sweet Sherry.

Fog Cutters (USA) (slang). Early American for cider and beer.

Fog Horn Cocktail (Cktl). ⅕ gill dry Gin, juice ½ lime. Shake well over ice, strain into an ice-filled highball glass. Top with ginger ale and a slice of lime.

Fogolar (It). A Brandy produced by Distillerie Camel.

Fogoneu (Sp). A red grape variety grown on the Balearic islands.

Föhn (Ger). A warm wind that blows across Lake Constance in Baden.

Fohrenberg (Ger). Vineyard. (Anb) = Baden. (Ber) = Bodensee. (Gro) = Sonnenufer. (Vil) = Meersburg.

Fohrenberg (Ger). Vineyard. (Anb) = Baden. (Ber) = Bodensee. (Gro) = Sonnenufer. (Vil) = Stetten.

Fohrenberg (Ger). Vineyard. (Anb) = Baden. (Ber) = Kaiserstuhl-Tuniberg. (Gro) = Vulkanfelsen. (Vil) = Ihringen.

Foils (USA). The metal or tinfoil capsules on Champagne and sparkling wine bottles.

Foire aux Vins d'Orange (Fr). Orange wine fair. Held on the Saturday closest to the middle of January in Orange. Shows off and judges the new wines of the region.

Fol (It). A noted producer of sparkling (cuve close) wines in Veneto.

Folatières (Les) (Fr). A Premier Cru vineyard in the A.C. commune of Puligny-Montrachet, Cô te de Beaune, Burgundy. 3.4 ha.

Folded Edge (Eng). A name given to the

F

base of drinking glasses made in the seventeenth century which is turned under at the base.

Folgosão (Port). A white grape variety used in the production of Port.

Folha de Figo (Bra). A red grape variety. Lit – 'Fig leaf'.

Folk Hero (Yug). A sparkling mineral water bottled in Serbia.

Folle Blanche (Fr). A white grape variety which gives a pale acid wine that is low in alcohol. It is grown in France under many names. Picpoul in Cognac and Armagnac and Gros plant in the Loire. Also Avillo, Engageat blanc, Euragest and Picapoll blanc.

Folle Blanche (USA). See California Folle Blanche.

Folle Noire (Fr). A red grape variety grown in Bellet, Provence. Is also known as the Fuella nera.

Fond (Ger). A stabilization fund formed by Weinwirtschaftsgesetz to increase wine quality, help guarantee the grower a realistic price, increase wine publicity and to store wine.

Fonda (Sp). Inn, Tavern.

Fond de Culotte (Cktl). 1½ fl.ozs. Suze, ½ fl.oz. Crème de Cassis. Add to ice in a Paris goblet. Top with a little water if required.

Fondé (Fr). Founded.

Fondillón (Sp). A red wine produced in Santonja, Valencia by Vincente Sinó.

Fonsana Somosierra (Sp). A still Mineral water from La Cabrera.

Fonseca (Port). Vintage Port shippers. Vintages – 1870, 1873, 1878, 1881, 1884, 1887, 1890, 1896, 1900, 1904, 1908, 1912, 1920, 1922, 1924, 1927, 1934, 1945, 1948, 1955, 1960, 1963, 1966, 1970, 1975, 1977, 1980, 1983. See also Guimaraens.

Fonseca, [J.M.Da] (Port). A family firm based in Estremadura. Produces a wide range of wines.

Fontainbleu (Fr). An alternative name for the Golden chasselas grape.

Fontainbleu Special (Cktl). ⅖ measure Cognac, ⅖ measure Anisette, ⅕ measure French vermouth. Shake over ice, strain into a cocktail glass.

Fontana Candida (It). A noted Frascati Classico producer.

Fontanafredda (It). A famous winery in Alba, Piemonte in north-western Italy. Produces a wide range of fine quality still and sparkling wines.

Fontanaro (Ger). A white grape variety cross between the Rieslaner and the Müller-Thurgau.

Fontanella (N.Z.). A sparkling (méthode champenoise) wine made from the Pinot meunier grape. Made by the Mission Vineyards near Napier in the Hawkes Bay region.

Fontegal (Port). A white grape variety grown in Beiras.

Fontenac (Sp). A 12 year old brandy produced by Torres in the Penedés region, Cataluña.

Fontenay (Fr). A commune in the A.C. Chablis, Burgundy.

Fonteny (Le) (Fr). A Premier Cru vineyard in the A.C. commune of Gevrey-Chambertin, Côte de Nuits, Burgundy. 3.80 ha.

Fonternel (S.Afr). A spicy, white, medium-sweet wine made from a blend of Muscat d'Alexandrie, Muscadelle and Steen grapes by the Nederburg Estate in Paarl.

Fontès (Fr). A wine-producing commune in the A.C. Clairette du Languedoc, south-western France.

Fonti di Crodo (It). A sparkling mineral water bottled and carbonated at Crodo Springs, Formazzo.

Fonti San Bernardo (It). A still mineral water from the springs of Garessio. There is also a sparkling style bottled.

Fontovova (Sp). A naturally sparkling mineral water from the Verin Valley.

Food and Beverage Managers' Association (Eng). Address = c/o Goring Hotel, 15, Beeston Place, London SW1W 0JW.

Food and Drink Federation (Eng). Address = 6, Catherine Street, London WC2B 5JJ.

Food and Wine From France Ltd (Eng). Address = Nuffield House, 41–46, Piccadilly, London W1.

Footed Glass (USA). The name given to a glass that has a wide base and stem.

F.O.P. (Eng) (abbr). Flowery Orange Pekoe. A tea grade.

Foppiano (USA). A winery in the Sonoma County, California. 83 ha. Grape varieties – Cabernet sauvignon, Chardonnay, Chenin blanc, French colombard, Petit syrah and Zinfandel. Produces varietal wines.

Foral (Port). The brand-name of a red wine produced by Caves Aliança.

Forastera (It). A white grape variety and white wine from the island of Ischia in southern Italy.

Forastero (S.Am). A grade of coffee bean which is classed as a common grade and is fermented longer with its' pulp from the pod to give average flavour. See also Criollo.

Forbidden Fruit (USA). A liqueur made from a type of grapefruit called a Shaddock. Made with brandy and honey.

F

32% alc. by vol. Sold in a round (spherical) bottle.

Forcayat (Sp). A red grape variety grown in the Valencia region.

Forceful (Eng). A term used to describe a wine that is assertive and has tannin and acidity.

Forchtenberg (Ger). Village. (Anb) = Württemberg. (Ber) = Kocher-Jagst-Tauber. (Gro) = Kocherberg. (Vin) = Flatterberg.

Forditàs (Hun). See Tokay Forditàs.

Foreign Extra Stout (E.Asia). A Guinness Stout brewed under contract by the Amarit Brewery in Thailand.

Foreign Extra Stout (W.Ind). F.E.S. A Guinness-type brew 1073 O.G. Is higher than regular Guinness, has a sharp acidity due to the introduction of some older Guinness into the brew to create lactic acid by fermentation. Is then pasteurised.

Forellenwein (Ger). A brand of white table wine produced by Deinhard in Koblenz.

Foreshots (Scot). The first part of the distillation which is returned because it contains impurities. Only the 'heart' is kept. The end of the distillation is called the 'Feints'.

Forest Brown (Eng). A Brown ale 1032 O.G. brewed by the Whitbread Brewery.

Forest Crimmins Ranch (USA). See Crimmins Ranch.

Forester (Eng). The brand-name of a Cider from Linfood Cash & Carry, Northamptonshire.

Forester's Delight (Cktl). 1½ fl.ozs. Cointreau, 1½ fl.ozs. Bourbon whiskey, 2 dashes lemon juice, 2 dashes blue Curaçao. Shake over ice, strain into a sugar-rimmed flute glass. Top with a cherry.

Forest Hill (Austr). A winery based in the Great Southern region of Western Australia.

Forest Lager (Eng). A Lager beer 1038 O.G. brewed in the New Forest Brewery, Cadnam, Hampshire.

Forestville (USA). A wine-producing town in the Russian River Valley, California.

Foret (Fr). See Gimlet.

Foretaste (Eng). The experience, albeit limited, that a person has of a wine before it is taken in the mouth. Is created by the senses of sight, smell and knowledge of the wine.

Forêts (Fr). An A.C. Premier Cru Chablis. Often reclassified as the Premier Cru Montmains.

Forgeron (Michel) (Fr). A Cognac producer. Address = Chez Richon, 16130 Segonzac. Owns 11 ha. in the Grande Champagne.

Forgeron Winery (USA). A winery based in Elmira, Willamette Valley, Oregon. Produces vinifera wines.

Forges (Fr). A Chalybeate mineral water.

Formaldehyde (Eng). An aldehyde found in wine that contributes to the bouquet and flavour of the wine.

Forman Winery (USA). A winery based near Saint Helena, Napa Valley, California. 21 ha. Grape varieties – Merlot and Sauvignon blanc. Produces varietal wines.

Formianum (Lat). A red wine produced in central western Italy during Roman times.

Formic Acid (Eng). H.COOH. An acid found in wines in minute traces.

Formosa Dourada (Port). A white grape variety grown in Alentejo.

Formosa Oolong (E.Asia). A tea that has a large leaf and a unique peach fragrance. Produced in Taiwan.

Formula 1 (Cktl). ⅕ gill Bell's Scotch whisky, ⅛ gill Galliano, ⅓ gill orange juice, 2 dashes lime juice. Shake well over ice, strain into an ice-filled highball glass. Top with soda water and an orange slice. Serve with straws.

Formula 2 (Cktl). ⅔ measure sweet Martini, ⅓ measure dry Martini, juice of ½ grapefruit, dash tonic water. Mix in a highball glass. Decorate with slices of orange, lemon, grapefruit and cherry.

Forneret (Fr). Cuvées in the vineyards of Les Marconnets [0.8 ha] and Les Peuillets [1 ha] of A.C. Savigny-lès-Beaune, Burgundy. Are owned by the Hospices de Beaune.

Fornterutoli (It). A Chianti Classico producer based in Tuscany.

For Planter's Punch (USA). A label statement on dark Rum bottles to denote a suitable drink that particular Rum can be used for.

Forshaw (Eng). Owners of Burtonwood Regional Brewery. See Burtonwood.

Forst (Ger). Vineyard. (Anb) = Nahe. (Ber) = Kreuznach. (Gro) = Kronenberg. (Vil) = Bad Kreuznach.

Forst (Ger). Village. (Anb) = Rheinpfalz. (Ber) = Mittelhaardt-Deutsche Weinstrasse. (Gro) = Mariengarten. (Vins) = Elster, Freundstück, Jesuitengarten, Kirchenstück, Musenhang, Pechstein, Ungerheuer

Forst (Ger). Village. (Anb) = Rheinpfalz. (Ber) = Mittelhaardt-Deutsche Weinstrasse. (Gro) = Schnepfenflug an der Weinstrasse. (Vins) = Bischofsgarten, Stift, Süsskopf.

F

Forst (Ger). Vineyard. (Anb) = Rheinpfalz. (Ber) = Südliche Weinstrasse. (Gro) = Ordensgut. (Vil) = Edesheim.

Forstberg (Ger). Vineyard. (Anb) = Ahr. (Ber) = Walporzheim/Ahrtal. (Gro) = Klosterberg. (Vil) = Ahrweiler.

Forstberg (Ger). Vineyard. (Anb) = Mittelrhein. (Ber) = Rheinburgengau. (Gro) = Burg Hammerstein. (Vil) = Leutesdorf.

Forstberg (Ger). Vineyard. (Anb) = Württemberg. (Ber) = Württembergisch Unterland. (Gro) = Wunnenstein. (Vil) = Gronau.

Forstberg (Ger). Vineyard. (Anb) = Württemberg. (Ber) = Württembergisch Unterland. (Gro) = Wunnenstein. (Vil) = Oberstenfeld.

Försterlay (Ger). Vineyard. (Anb) = Mosel-Saar-Ruwer. (Ber) = Bernkastel (Gro) = Schwarzlay. (Vil) = Lösnich.

Forstgrube (Ger). Vineyard. (Anb) = Württemberg. (Ber) = Württembergisch Unterland. (Gro) = Stromberg. (Vil) = Illingen.

Forstgrube (Ger). Vineyard. (Anb) = Württemberg. (Ber) = Württembergisch Unterland. (Gro) = Stromberg. (Vil) = Rosswag.

Forstweg (Ger). Vineyard. (Anb) = Rheinpfalz. (Ber) = Südliche Weinstrasse. (Gro) = Bischofskreuz. (Vil) = Walsheim.

Fort (Fr). Strong.

Forta (Ger). A white grape variety. A cross between the Madeleine angevine and the Silvaner. Gives high sugar.

Forte's Fizz (Cktl). 1 oz. Vodka, 1 oz. Cassis. Place in a highball with ice, top with iced Champagne, stir, decorate with a slice of lemon.

Fort Garry Ltd (Can). A subsidiary of Seagram. Produces a fine range of Canadian whiskies.

Forth Flyer (Cktl). 1 fl.oz. Glayva, ½ fl.oz. blue Curaçao, ½ fl. oz. Galliano, 4 fl.ozs. ginger ale. Stir over ice in a Slim Jim glass. Dress with a lemon and orange slice. Serve with straws.

Fortia (La) (Fr). Part of the Châteauneuf-du-Pape area in the southern Rhône.

Fortification (Eng). The addition of brandy to wine. See Fortified.

Fortified (Eng). A wine that has had its' alcohol level raised by the addition of brandy. The spirit may be added before, during or after natural fermentation and is added to raise the alcohol level above that which yeast can work. 18% by vol.

Fortified (S.Afr). Denotes wines which have had their alcohol content increased to 16% alc. by vol. with spirits.

Fortifying (Eng). The adding of brandy to wine. See Fortified.

Fort Ile (W.Ind). A Rum distillery based in Guadeloupe.

Fortino Winery (USA). A winery based in southern Santa Clara, California. Grape varieties – Barbera, Cabernet sauvignon, Charbono, Carignane, Petit syrah and Ruby cabernet. Produces fine varietal wines.

Fort Lauderdale (Cktl). ⅕ measure dark Rum, ⅛ measure sweet Vermouth, juice ¼ lemon and lime. Shake well over ice, strain into an ice-filled old-fashioned glass. Top with a slice of orange.

Fort Schuyler (USA). A top and bottom-fermented beer brewed by the West End Brewing Co. in Utica, New York.

Forts de Latour (Les) (Fr). The second wine of Château Latour in the commune of Pauillac, Haut-Médoc, Bordeaux.

Forty Eight (Cktl). ⅕ measure Apricot brandy, ⅕ measure orange Curaçao, ⅕ measure dry Vermouth, ⅖ measure dry Gin, dash lemon juice. Shake over ice, strain into a cocktail glass.

Forty-Five South [45] (N.Z.). The brand-name of a Whiskey produced by Wilson's Distillery in Dunedin.

Fortyniner (Eng). A Bitter 1049 O.G. brewed by the Ringwood Brewery in Hampshire.

Forty Seven (Den). An amber-coloured Beer brewed by Carlsberg C47. Commemorates when Carlsberg was founded in 1947. 5.5% alc. by vol.

Forum Humuli (Ger). A famous hop market in Hamburg.

Forward (Eng). A term used to describe a wine with a well-marked aroma and taste.

Forzato (It). A term used to describe a wine produced from over-ripe grapes.

Fossanova (It). A Cistercian liqueur made from herbs.

Fosse (La) (Fr). A vineyard in the A.C. commune of Rully, Côte Chalonnaise, Burgundy.

Fossi (It). A Chianti Classico producer based in Tuscany.

Foster Burgess Winery (USA). A winery based in Freeport, Florida. Produces Muscadine wines.

Fosters (Austr). A canned Lager 4.8% alc. by vol. brewed by the Carlton United Brewery in Melbourne.

Fosters Draught (Eng). A Lager beer 1035 O.G. brewed by Watney's Mortlake Brewery in London.

Foudre (Fr). Huge cask for storing wine.

Fouesnant (Fr). A noted growth of Cider from Brittany, north-western France.

Fougères (Fr). A V.D.Q.S. red wine-producing region of the Languedoc-Roussillon, south-western France.

Foulage (Fr). The pressing of the grapes through grooved rollers.

Foulage au Pied (Fr). The crushing of the grapes by foot.

Foulage Méchanique (Fr). The mechanical pressing of the grapes.

Foulage Méchanique à Cylindres (Fr). Cylinder pressing. Press known as Égrappoir à Tambour.

Foulage Méchanique Centrifuge (Fr). Centrifugal pressing. Press known as Égrappoir Centrifuge.

Foule (Èn) (Fr). The term to denote the practice of planting vines haphazardly.

Foulograppe (Fr). The alternative name for an Egrappoir.

Fouloir (Fr). A long revolving tube that extracts the juice out of the grapes. Used in the Sauternes district of Bordeaux.

Foul-Pipe (Ire). In a Whiskey distillery the pipe that returns the condensate from the Lyne arm to the still.

Founder's Ale (Eng). A cask conditioned Ale 1045 O.G. brewed by the Usher Brewery in Wiltshire.

Fountaingrove (USA). A former winery of a religious sect before Prohibition. Today is a brand of Martini & Prati.

Fouquerand (Fr). A vineyard in the A.C. commune of Savigny-lès-Beaune, Burgundy. Is owned by the Hospices de Beaune.

Fouquet (André) (Fr). A viticulteur-récoltant based in Vouvray, Touraine, Loire. Address = 47, Rue Gambetta, 37210. Produces fine A.C. Vouvray wines.

Four Ale Bar (Eng). A public bar from the days when ale was sold at 4 old pennies a quart. Hence the name.

Four Bells Navy Rum (Eng). A dark Rum produced by Charles Lamb of London. 40% alc. by vol.

Fourchaume (Fr). An A.C. Premier Cru Chablis. Often has the Premier Cru vineyards of Vaupulent, Côte de Fontenay, Valorent and l'Homme-Mort reclassified to this vineyard name.

Fourderaine (Fr). A sloe-flavoured, home-made liqueur produced by soaking sloes (which have been pricked many times) in Marc. See also Sloe Gin.

Four K Bitter [4K] (Eng). See Four Keys.

Four Keys (Eng). A home-brew public house in Sussex that produces – 4K Bitter 1036 O.G. and Stallion 1045 O.G.

Fourneaux (Les) (Fr). A Premier Cru A.C. Chablis. Often has the Premier Crus of Morein and Côte des Prés-Girots reclassified as its vintages.

Fournier (Charles) (USA). Runs the Gold Seal Vineyards at Hammondsport in New York State. Was chief wine-maker of Veuve-Clicquot until 1934.

Fournières (Les) (Fr). A Premier Cru vineyard in the A.C. commune of Aloxe-Corton, Côte de Beaune, Burgundy.

Fournier Père et Fils (Fr). Address = B.P. 7, Chaudoux, 18300 Verdigny-en-Sancerre. Produces A.C. Sancerre wines.

Four Pack (USA) (slang). A term for a pack of cans or bottles of beer containing 4 cans. See also 'Six Pack'.

Four Roses (USA). A brand-name of a blended Bourbon whiskey produced by the Four Roses Distilling Co. in Baltimore, Lawrenceburg. 40% alc. by vol.

Four Row Barley (Eng). The poorest of the barleys for the brewing of beer. Refers to the number of rows of grain per ear. See also Two Row and Six Row.

Four Seasons (Austr). The brand-name of a Whiskey produced by United Distillers.

Four Sheets to the Wind (Eng) (slang). An old naval description used to describe someone under the influence of alcohol who is 'All over the place' as sails are on a ship in a strong wind.

Foursome (Eng). The local name given to large cans of beer from the Bank's Brewery in Wolverhampton.

Fourth Degree (Cktl). A Martinez cocktail with a dash of Absinthe and a cherry (less ¼ gill Gin and ⅛ gill French vermouth).

Fourth of July (Cktl). ⅕ measure Kahlúa, ⅕ measure Bourbon whiskey, ⅕ measure Galliano, ⅕ measure orange juice, ⅕ measure cream. Place the Whiskey and Galliano into a warm cocktail glass, flame, shake in some ground cinnamon, whilst still flaming. Strain, mix in remaining ingredients and add a cherry.

Four X (Eng). An Old ale 1040 O.G. brewed by the Burt Brewery in the Isle of Wight. Bottled as a 4X Brown.

Four X (Wales). A cask conditioned Mild 1036 O.G. brewed by the Crown Brewery in Pontyclun, Mid Glamorgan.

Four X (Wales). A cask conditioned Mild 1030 O.G. brewed by the Border Brewery, Wrexham.

Four X (Eng). See XXXX.

Four XXXX (Eng). A cask conditioned Bitter 1045 O.G. brewed by the Mansfield Brewery in the East Midlands.

Fousselottes (Les) (Fr). A Premier Cru vineyard in the A.C. commune of Chambolle-Musigny, Côte de Nuits, Burgundy. 4 ha.

Fousslach (Lux). A vineyard site in the village of Bech-Kleinmacher.

Fowler's Wee Heavy Ale (Scot). A strong bottled Ale 1070 O.G. brewed by the

Belhaven Brewery of Dunbar for Tennent-Caledonian.

Fox and Firkin (Eng). A home-brew public house owned by Bruce in London. Produces – cask conditioned Bruce's Bitter 1045 O.G. Dogbolter 1060 O.G. and Vixen 1036 O.G.

Fox and Hounds (Eng). A home-brew public house near Royston in Hertfordshire. Noted for its' Hogshead Bitter 1043 O.G. Nog 1040 O.G. and Nathaniel's Special 1034 O.G.

Fox and Hounds (Eng). A home-brew public house in Stottesdon, Shropshire. Produces – cask conditioned Dasher's Draught 1040 O.G.

Fox and Newt (Eng). A home-brew public house owned by Whitbread in Leeds. Noted for its' cask conditioned Old Willow 1046 O.G. and Burley 1036 O.G.

Fox Grape (USA). The name given to the American native grape variety Vitis Riparia in the nineteenth century when domesticated. Hence the term 'Foxy wines'.

Foxiness (USA). A term used to describe the very pronounced grapy flavour to be found in wines produced from American native grape varieties in the Eastern States. Especially from the Vitis Riparia.

Fox River Cocktail (Cktl). 1 measure Bourbon whiskey, ¼ measure Crème de Cacao, 4 dashes Angostura. Stir over ice, strain into a cocktail glass.

Foxwhelp (Eng). An excellent variety of cider apple. Is very sweet with little acidity.

Foxy (USA). A taste description of wines made from the Vitis Riparia grape. See Fox Grape.

Fracia (It). A D.O.C. red wine from Valtellina in Lombardy. Produced from the Nebbiolo grape.

Fractional Blending (Eng). A term used for the Solera system where a proportion of each year's wine is taken from casks in a tier system so that a portion is drawn off each year and replaced by wine from the following year.

Fragny (Fr). A wine-producing village of the Roussette de Savoie, south-eastern France.

Fragrant (Eng). A term used to describe a very pronounced and pleasing aroma in a wine.

Frais (Fr). Fresh or cool. When applied to wine is seen on the label as 'Servir très frais'. Means 'Serve well chilled'.

Fraise (Fr). A strawberry spirit liqueur. 43% alc. by vol.

Fraise d'Anjou (Fr). A Strawberry brandy produced in western France.

Fraise de Bois (Fr). A liqueur flavoured with wild strawberries.

Fraise de Bois Dolfi (Hol). A Dutch strawberry liqueur produced from wild strawberries.

Fraise Royale (Cktl). 2 fresh strawberries, dash Fraise liqueur, iced Champagne. Blend strawberries with liqueur, pour into a flute, top with iced Champagne.

Fraises Fizz (Cktl). ⅗ measure Gin, ⅔ measure Crème de Fraises, juice ¼ lemon, 2 dashes Gomme syrup. Shake over ice, strain into an ice-filled highball glass. Top with soda water, slice of strawberry and squeeze of lemon peel juice.

Fraisette Cornu (Fr). A non-alcoholic strawberry syrup.

Framboise (Fr). A raspberry spirit liqueur. 43% alc. by vol.

Framboise (Bel). A Lambic beer which has raspberries added to start a new fermentation. 6% alc. by vol.

Framboise de Bordeaux (Fr). A raspberry liqueur produced by Marie Brizzard. Made by maceration and distillation. 20% alc. by vol.

Frambozenbrandewijn (Hol). A raspberry-flavoured Brandy.

Framersheim (Ger). Village. (Anb) = Rheinhessen. (Ber) = Niersteim. (Gro) = Petersberg. (Vins) = Hornberg, Kreuzweg, Zechberg.

Framework of Hospitality (The) (Eng) (slang). An old English saying that advocated three sips of a drink instead of one gulp especially for spirits (brandy and rum) when offered at a host's house.

Frampton Village (Eng). A dry (and medium-sweet) Cider produced by the Frampton Village Cider Company, Gloucestershire.

Frampton Village Cider Company (Eng). Cider producers based on the banks of the Gloucester and Sharpness Canal in Frampton-on-Severn, Gloucestershire. Produces – Cotswold Cottage and Frampton Village Ciders.

Franc (Fr). Clean tasting.

Francavilla (It). A white grape variety grown in the Puglia region.

Franc de Goût (Fr). A term for the refreshing, clean taste of a wine.

France (Fr). The country that produces the top wines of the world. Has many regions which lead with their style and are copied by most other countries. See Alsace, Armagnac, Bordeaux, Burgundy, Champagne, Cognac, Jura, Loire, Midi, Rhône, Roussillon. See Appellation Contrôlée, V.D.Q.S, Vins de Pays and Vin de Table.

Francerre (Eng). A range of sparkling non-alcoholic fruit juices with no artificial additives from Copak Drinks. (Apple, apple and blackcurrant, red and white grape juices).

Franche-Comté (Fr). A Vins de Pays area in the Jura Département in eastern France. Produces red, rosé and dry white wines.

Franchette (Arg). A full red table wine produced by the Andean Vineyards in Mendoza.

Franciacorta (It). D.O.C. red wine of good flavour produced in the Garda district of Lombardy. D.O.C.

Franciacorta Pinot (It). D.O.C. white wine made in the Garda district of Lombardy from the Pinot bianco grape. The D.O.C. can be applied to a sparkling wine made from musts and wines according to regulations.

Franciacorta Rosso (It). D.O.C. red wine from the Garda district of Lombardy. Made from 20–30% Barbera, 40–50% Cabernet franc, 10–15% Merlot and 15–20% Nebbiolo.

Franciscan Vineyard (USA). A large winery based near Rutherford, Napa Valley, California. 250 ha. Grape varieties – Cabernet sauvignon, Chardonnay and White riesling. Produces varietal wines.

Franco-British Basin of Chalk (Eng). Caused by a drying up of the sea 69 million years ago over northern France and southern England in places over 1,000 feet deep. The Champagne district lies on it.

Franco-Españolas S.A. (Sp). See Bodegas Franco-Españolas S.A.

Franco-Fiorina (It). A winery based in Alba, Piemonte. Produces wines from bought-in grapes.

François de Salins (Fr). A cuvée in the Grand Cru vineyard of A.C. Corton-Charlemagne, Côte de Beaune, Burgundy. Is owned by the Hospices de Beaune.

Francoli (It). A liqueur producer based in Gattinara.

Franconia (Ger). A wine region. Most easterly of all regions, lies on the river Main. See Anbaugebiet and Franken.

Francorvm (Fr). The old Latin name for Fronsac and name for A.C. Fronsac. Fronsac wines from the Société du Château de la Rivière, 33145 Saint Michel de Fronsac.

Frangelico (It). A liqueur made with berries, herbs and hazelnuts. 23% alc. by vol.

Frank (Dr Konstantin) (USA). Founder of the New York State Vinifera Winery.

Franken (Ger). The most easterly of the Anbaugebiete. See Franconia.

Franken (Ger). Anbaugebiet. (Bers) = Bayer, Bodensee, Maindreieck, Mainviereck, Steigerwald. Produces 98% white and 2% red wines. Main grapes are Müller-Thurgau 47% and Silvaner 28%.

Frankenberg (Ger). Vineyard. (Anb) = Baden. (Ber) = Badische Frankenland. (Gro) = Tauberklinge. (Vil) = Lauda.

Frankenberg (Ger). Vineyard. (Anb) = Baden. (Ber) = Badische Frankenland. (Gro) = Tauberklinge. (Vil) = Marbach.

Frankenberg (Ger). Village. (Anb) = Franken. (Ber) = Steigerwald. (Gro) = Schlosstück. (Vin) = Herrschaftsberg.

Frankenheim Alt (Ger). An Altbier brewed in Düsseldorf, West Germany. Has a full hop flavour but is thin in body.

Frankenhell (Ger). Vineyard. (Anb) = Mittelrhein. (Ber) = Rheinburgengau. (Gro) = Schloss Schönburg. (Vil) = Damscheid.

Franken Information Service (Ger). Frankenwein-Frankenland e V. Postfach 764, 8700 Würzburg Z., West Germany.

Frankenjack (Cktl). $\frac{1}{10}$ measure dry Gin, $\frac{3}{10}$ measure dry Vermouth, $\frac{2}{10}$ measure Apricot brandy, $\frac{1}{10}$ measure Cointreau. Stir over ice, strain into a cocktail glass. Top with a cherry.

Frankenland (Ger). An alternative name for Franken (Franconia).

Frankenriesling (Ger). The erroneous varietal name for the white grape Green silvaner.

Frankenstein (Ger). Vineyard. (Anb) = Rheinhessen. (Ber) = Wonnegau. (Gro) = Sybillenstein. (Vil) = Freimersheim.

Frankental (Fr). A black grape variety also known as the Black Hamburg.

Frankentha (Ger). Vineyard. (Anb) = Rheingau. (Ber) = Johannisberg. (Gro) = Steil. (Vil) = Assmannshausen.

Frankenthal (Fr). A black grape variety also known as the Trollinger.

Frankenthaler (Ger). An erroneous varietal name for the red grape Trollinger.

Franken Traube (Ger). Another name for the Sylvaner grape.

Frankenwein (Ger). The wine of Franken (Franconia). Also called Steinwein. From the Stein vineyards.

Franken Wine Festivals (Ger). See Fränkisches Weinfest-Volkach, Fränkisches Weinfest Sulzfeld, Winzerfest-Klingenberg, Winzerfest Würzburg.

Franken Wine Route (Ger). Known as the Bocksbeutelstrasse.

Frankenwinheim (Ger). Village. (Anb) =

F

Franken. (Ber) = Maindreieck. (Gro) = Not yet assigned. (Vin) = Rosenberg.

Frankfort (USA). A town based in north Kentucky. Is the home to many famous Bourbon whiskey distilleries.

Frankfort Distilling Co (USA). A distillery based in Athertonville, Kentucky. Produces Antique (a Kentucky Bourbon whiskey 40% alc. by vol). Part of Seagram.

Frankfurt Diät Pils (Ger). A Lager beer brewed by the Henninger-Brauerei in Frankfurt for the Courage Brewery in London.

Frankfurt/Main (Ger). Village. (Anb) = Rheingau. (Ber) = Johannisberg. (Gro) = Not yet assigned. (Vin) = Lohberger Hang.

Frank Hill Cocktail (Cktl). ½ measure Brandy, ½ measure Cherry brandy. Shake over ice, strain into a cocktail glass. Top with a cherry and a twist of lemon peel juice.

Frankinja Crna (Yug). A local name for the Gamay noir à jus blanc.

Frankinja Modra (Yug). A local name for the Gamay noir à jus blanc.

Frankischer Landwein (Ger). A new Deutsche Tafelwein zone.

Fränkisches Weinfest-Sulzfeld (Ger). A Franken wine festival held at Sulzfeld in August.

Fränkisches Weinfest-Volkach (Ger). A Franken wine festival held at Volkach in the middle of August.

Frankland (Austr). A wine region in the province of Western Australia.

Frankland River (Austr). A vineyard of 94 ha. belonging to the Houghton Vineyards, Western Australia.

Franklin County (USA). A wine-producing region of Arkansas.

Frankovka (Yug). A white wine produced in north-eastern Yugoslavia near the Hungarian border.

Frankweiler (Ger). Village. (Anb) = Rheinpfalz. (Ber) = Südliche Weinstrasse. (Gro) = Königsgarten. (Vins) = Biengarten, Kalkgrube.

Franschhoek Co-operative (S.Afr). A winery based in Franschhoek. Address = Franschhoek Koöpatief Bpk. Box 52, Franschhoek 7690. Produces varietal wines.

Franschhoek Koöpatief (S.Afr). See Frankschhoek Co-operative.

Franschhoek Valley (S.Afr). A wine-producing area situated east of the Stellenbosch region. See Vignerons de Franschhoek.

Fransdruif (S.Afr). The name for the Palomino grape used in the making of South African sherry.

Franta's Rules (Czec). A Falstaffian code of taverns. Named after a taproom in Pilsen.

Franzenheim (Ger). Village. (Anb) = Mosel-Saar-Ruwer. (Ber) = Saar-Ruwer. (Gro) = Römerlay. (Vin) = Johannisberg.

Franzensberger (Ger). Vineyard. (Anb) = Baden. (Ber) = Ortenau. (Gro) = Fürsteneck. (Vil) = Offenburg (ortsteil Fessenbach).

Franzensberger (Ger). Vineyard. (Anb) = Baden. (Ber) = Ortenau. (Gro) = Fürsteneck. (Vil) = Ortenberg.

Franzia Brandy (USA). The brand-name for a Brandy produced by the Franzia Brothers Winery, Ripon, San Joaquin Valley, California. 40% alc. by vol.

Franzia Brothers Winery (USA). A family winery in Ripon, San Joaquin Valley, California. Produces varietal and sparkling wines, also brandies. Owned by Coca Cola Co.

Franziskaner (Ger). Vineyard. (Anb) = Baden. (Ber) = Kaiserstuhl-Tuniberg. (Gro) = Attilafelsen. (Vil) = Oberimsingen.

Franziskus (Ger). A pale Bock bier 6.7% alc. by vol. brewed by the Spätenbrau Brauerei in Munich.

Französicher Landwein (Ger). French Vin de Pays.

Frapin (Fr). A famous Cognac producer based in Segonzac. 137 ha. in the Grande Champagne. Produces Château de Fontpinot Grande Champagne and Domaine Frapin Grande Fine Champagne.

Frappato (It). A red grape variety used in Sicily.

Frappato di Vittoria (It). A sweet, dessert, red wine produced near Ragusa in Sicily from the Frappato grape.

Frappé (Fr). Iced or very cold. A term used for serving sparkling wines or for liqueurs that are served with crushed ice.

Frappés (Cktl). Well-iced liqueurs or spirits which are served with finely crushed ice and straws.

Frascati (It). D.O.C. white wine from Latium. Made from the Bellone, Bonvino, Greco, Malvasia bianca di candia, Malvasia del Lazio and Trebbiano toscano grapes. Produced in the commune of Frascati and others. Secco, Amabile and Dolce styles produced. For the latter, 2 varieties of botrytis cinerea (muffa nobile) attacked grapes are used. If alc. content is 12% by vol. minimum then classed Superiore. The D.O.C. also applies to sparkling wines. See Classico. Also known as Vini dei Castelli Romani.

Frasco (Sp). A small bottle, flask.

F

Frasinetti and Sons (USA). A winery based in Sacramento, California. Produces table and dessert wines.

Frasqueira (Port). A bottle case, crate.

Fratelli (It). Brothers.

Fratelli Barale (It). A long-standing Barolo producing winery in the Piemonte region.

Fratelli Branca (USA). A version of the Italian bitters (Fernet Branca) produced for the American market.

Fratelli Cora (G and L) (It). A sparkling (méthode champenoise) white producer based in the Piemonte region. Labels include Royal Ambassador Brut.

Fratelli d'Angelo (It). See d'Angelo.

Fratelli Oddero (It). Noted vineyard owners and producers of Barolo based at La Morra, Barolo, Piemonte.

Fratelli Pasqua (It). Sparkling wine producers based in Verona.

Fratelli Pedrotti (It). Producers of sparkling (méthode champenoise) wines in the Trentino-Alto Adige region.

Fratelli Pisoni (It). Producers of sparkling (méthode champenoise) wines in the Trentino-Alto Adige region.

Fratt Industries Ltd (USA). A distillery based in Delano, California. Producers of F1 Brandy.

Frauenberg (Ger). Vineyard. (Anb) = Baden. (Ber) = Markgräflerland. (Gro) = Burg Neuenfels. (Vil) = Mauchen.

Frauenberg (Ger). Vineyard. (Anb) = Mosel-Saar-Ruwer. (Ber) = Zell/Mosel. (Gro) = Grafschaft. (Vil) = Bremm.

Frauenberg (Ger). Vineyard. (Anb) = Mosel-Saar-Ruwer. (Ber) = Zell/Mosel. (Gro) = Grafschaft. (Vil) = Neef.

Frauenberg (Ger). Vineyard. (Anb) = Rheinhessen. (Ber) = Wonnegau. (Gro) = Burg Rodenstein. (Vil) = Flörsheim-Dalsheim.

Frauenfeld Brauerei (Switz). A noted brewery based in Frauenfeld, eastern Switzerland.

Frauengarten (Ger). Vineyard. (Anb) = Rheinhessen. (Ber) = Nierstein. (Gro) = Krötenbrunnen. (Vil) = Wintersheim.

Frauenländchen (Ger). Vineyard. (Anb) = Rheinpfalz. (Ber) = Mittelhaardt-Deutsche Weinstrasse. (Gro) = Höllenpfad. (Vil) = Kleinkarlbach.

Frauenstein (Ger). Village. (Anb) = Rheingau. (Ber) = Johannisberg. (Gro) = Steinmacher. (Vins) = Herrenberg, Homberg, Marschall.

Frauenzimmer (Ger). Vineyard. (Anb) = Württemberg. (Ber) = Württembergisch Unterland. (Gro) = Salzberg. (Vil) = Lehrensteinsfeld.

Frauenzimmern (Ger). Village. (Anb) = Württemberg. (Ber) = Württembergisch

Unterland. (Gro) = Heuchelberg. (Vins) = Kaiserberg, Michaelsberg.

Fräulein Frankfurt (Cktl). 1 measure Gin, $\frac{1}{3}$ measure Cherry brandy, $\frac{1}{3}$ measure Crème de Noyau, $\frac{1}{3}$ measure lemon juice. Shake well over ice, strain into a cocktail glass.

Fray Junipéro (USA). See Serra (Friar Junipéro).

Frecciarossa (It). Wines made by a single family (the Odero family). Produce red, rosé and slightly sweet white wines around a village near Casteggio in Lombardy.

Freckenfeld (Ger). Village. (Anb) = Rheinpfalz. (Ber) = Südliche Weinstrasse. (Gro) = Guttenberg. (Vin) = Gräfenberg.

Freddie Fudpucker Cocktail (Cktl). $\frac{1}{3}$ gill Tequila gold, 1 gill orange juice. Pour over ice in a highball glass. Add 1 teaspoon of Galliano on top and a cherry.

Frederick Johnson Winery (USA). A winery based in Westfield, Chautauqua, New York. Produce wines mainly from the Concord grape.

Fredonia (USA). A black grape variety, the juice used for blending with Concord must.

Fredrikstad Brewery (Nor). A brewery based in Fredrikstad, south-eastern Norway.

Free Flow (Eng). A pressurised keg which is connected to a small on/off tap. Beer flows when the tap is opened. Used to serve keg or top pressure beer.

Free House (Eng). A public house which is not connected (tied) to a brewery and which can offer beers etc. from different breweries and outlets. See Tied House.

Freemark Abbey Winery (USA). A winery based near Saint Helena, Napa Valley, California. Grape varieties – Chardonnay, Johannisberg riesling and Petit syrah. Produces varietal wines.

Free Run Wine (Fr). The juice from partially crushed and destalked grapes which is fermented out. Produces fine wine.

Free Silver Cocktail (Cktl). $\frac{2}{5}$ measure dry Gin, $\frac{1}{5}$ measure dark Rum, $\frac{1}{5}$ measure lemon juice, dash Gomme syrup, 2 teaspoons milk. Shake over ice, strain into an ice-filled highball glass. Top with soda water.

Free SO$_2$ (Eng). Unbound Sulphurdioxide active in wine as a bactericide.

Freeze Dried Coffee (Eng). An instant coffee made from fresh brewed coffee and dried freezing in a vacuum (Lyophilization).

Freezomint (Fr). A mint digestive liqueur.

F

27% alc. by vol. Produced by the Cusenier Co.

Freiburg (Ger). Village. (Anb) = Baden. (Ber) = Markgräflerland. (Gro) = Lorettoberg. (Vins) = Jesuitenschloss, Steinler.

Freiburger Weintage (Ger). A Baden wine festival held at Freiburg in June annually.

Freiburg i. Br. (Ger). Village. (Anb) = Baden. (Ber) = Breisgau. (Gro) = Burg Zähringen. (Vin) = Schlossberg.

Freiburg i. Br. (Ger). Village. (Anb) = Baden. See Freiburg.

Freihand (Ger). A term used for those wines that are sold from the cellars directly to the purchasers through brokers.

Freiherr (Ger). Baron.

Freiherr von Brentano (Ger). A family estate in Winkel, Rheingau.

Frei-Laubersheim (Ger). Village. (Anb) = Rheinhessen. (Ber) = Bingen. (Gro) = Rheingrafenstein. (Vins) = Fels, Kirchberg, Reichskeller, Rheingrafenberg.

Freimersheim (Ger). Village. (Anb) = Rheinhessen. (Ber) = Wonnegau. (Gro) = Sybillenstein. (Vin) = Frankenstein.

Freimersheim (Ger). Village. (Anb) = Rheinpfalz. (Ber) = Südliche Weinstrasse. (Gro) = Trappenberg. (Vin) = Bildberg.

Freinsheim (Ger). Village. (Anb) = Rheinpfalz. (Ber) = Mittelhaardt-Deutsche Weinstrasse. (Gro) = Rosenbühl. (Vin) = Goldberg.

Freisa (It). A red wine grape variety grown in the Piemonte. Produces a sparkling red wine called Freisa.

Freisa (It). A sparkling red wine made from the Freisa grape in the Piemonte.

Freisa d'Asti (It). D.O.C. red wine from Piemonte. Made from the Freisa grape. If alc. 11.5% by vol. and aged for minimum 10–11 months then classed Superiore. D.O.C. also applies to the naturally sparkling wines produced in the specific region. Spumante or Frizzante.

Freisa di Chieri (It). D.O.C. red wine from Piemonte. Made from the Freisa grape throughout the commune of Chieri and others. Either dry or semi-sweet. Freisa Secco or Amabile. If aged for 10–11 months and alc. content 11.5% by vol. then classed Superiore.

Freisa di Chieri (It). D.O.C. which can be applied to sparkling and semi-sparkling wines obtained by re-fermenting the natural sugar left in the sweet wine kept by filtration or refrigeration.

Freisamer (Ger). A white grape variety. A cross between the Sylvaner and the Ruländer. Gives full neutral wines.

Freisheim (Ger). Village. (Anb) = Rheinpfalz. (Ber) = Mittelhaardt-Deutsche Weinstrasse. (Gro) = Kobnert. (Vins) = Musikantenbuckel, Oschelskopf, Schwarzes Kreuz.

Freitas Martins Caldeira Lda (Mad). A noted shipper of Madeira wines to the United Kingdom.

Freixedas (José) (Sp). A producer of sparkling (cuve close) wines including Castillo la Torre.

Freixenet (Sp). A major sparkling wine producer. Wines made by the Cava method in Catalonia, San Sadurní de Noya, Barcelona. Noted for Cordon Negro, Brut Nature, Brut Rosé and Carta Nevada Extra.

Fremersberger Feigenwäldchen (Ger). Vineyard. (Anb) = Baden. (Ber) = Ortenau. (Gro) = Schloss Rodeck. (Vil) = Sinzheim.

Fremières (Les) (Fr). A Premier Cru vineyard in the A.C. commune of Morey-Saint-Denis, Côte de Nuits, Burgundy. 2.4 ha.

Fremiers (Les) (Fr). A Premier Cru vineyard in the A.C. commune of Pommard, Côte de Beaune, Burgundy. 4.9 ha.

Fremiets (Fr). A Premier Cru vineyard in the A.C. commune of Volnay, Côte de Beaune, Burgundy. 6.5 ha. Also known as Les Fremiets.

Fremlins Brewery (Eng). Whitbread's Kent Brewery in Faversham. Noted for its' keg AK 1032 O.G. and Trophy Bitter 1035 O.G.

French (Eng). When applied to drinks usually denotes a dry, white Vermouth such as Noilly Prat, Dubonnet, etc.

French Apéritifs (Fr). Appetizers. Long drinks usually served with cold water. See – Dubonnet-Citron, Picon Grenadine, Polichinelle, Curaçao etc.

French Coffee (Eng). A coffee blend that usually has roasted chicory added which gives it a bitter taste.

French Colombard (USA). A white grape variety grown in California to produce dry white wines.

French Connection (Cktl).(1). 1½ fl.ozs. Amaretto, 1½ fl.ozs. Brandy. Build into an ice-filled old-fashioned glass.

French Connection (Cktl).(2). Build 1 fl.oz. Glayva into an ice-filled Slim Jim glass. Stir in Perrier water.

French Egg Nogg (Fr). See Lait de Poule.

French Emperor (Cktl). ⅔ measure Mandarine Napoléon, ⅓ measure (green) Crème de Menthe, dash egg white. Stir then add ice and top up with soda water.

438

French Fruit (Cktl). ¼ oz. Mandarine Napoléon, ¼ oz. Southern Comfort, orange juice. Fill a highball glass with ice. Add ingredients, stir.

French Grape (S.Afr). The local name for the Palomino vine.

French Green Dragon Cocktail (Cktl). ½ measure Cognac, ½ measure Green Chartreuse. Shake well over ice, strain into a cocktail glass.

French Oak (Fr). Oak used in the making of wine and spirit casks usually from the forests of Limousin, Monlezun, Nevers and Tronçais. Imparts a vanillin flavour to the wine or spirit.

French Pousse Café (Pousse Café). In a liqueur glass pour in order ¼ measure green Chartreuse, ¼ measure Maraschino, ¼ measure Cherry brandy, ¼ measure Kümmel. Do not stir.

French Rose (Cktl). ⅗ measure dry Gin, ⅕ measure Cherry brandy, ⅕ measure dry Vermouth. Stir over ice, strain into a cocktail glass.

French Seventyfive [75] (Cktl).(1). 1 jigger Brandy, juice 1 lemon, 1 teaspoon sugar. Shake over ice, strain into a highball glass and top with iced Champagne.

French Seventyfive [75] (Cktl).(2). 2 ozs. dry Gin, juice of ½ lemon, 1 teaspoon sugar. Shake well with ice, strain into a highball glass, top with iced Champagne.

French Sherbert (Cktl). Place into a flute glass 3 dashes Cognac, 3 dashes Kirsch, dash Angostura. Stir, add a scoop of water ice and top with iced Champagne.

French Sherbert (USA). The nickname for Champagne.

French Smellers (Fr). Government agents who smelt out coffee smugglers in the seventeenth century travelling to Germany.

French Vermouth (Fr). Drier than Italian vermouth. White and dry. Base wine is stored in thick oak casks, then allowed to spend some time outside to allow exposure to sea air. Has a spicy aroma.

Frénette (Fr). A low-alcohol fermented beverage made from ash leaves, sugar and roasted chicory. A second fermentation takes place in the bottle to give a sparkle similar to lemonade. See also Ash Drink.

Frères du Cênes (Fr). Cognac producer. Address = Distillerie Merlet, St. Sauvant, 17610 Chaniers. 40 ha. Situated in the Borderies 50% and Fins Bois 50%.

Fresca (Eng). A low-calorie diet grapefruit-flavoured drink from the Coca Cola Co.

Frescobaldi (It). Wine producers in Florence, Tuscany. Noted for Chianti Ruffina. 540 ha. Also produces sparkling (méthode champenoise) wines.

Frescobaldi [Marchese Vittorio] (It). See Frescobaldi.

Fresh (Eng). The term that describes a young wine which has not lost its charm.

Freslier (André) (Fr). A noted producer of pétillant wines based in the A.C. Vouvray area, Touraine, Loire.

Fresno (USA). The Fresno-San Joaquin Valley, California. Southern part of the Great Valley. Produces most of Californias' dessert wines with some table and sparkling wines.

Fresno State (USA) (abbr). California State University based at Fresno where practical training in viticulture and oenology occurs.

Fret (Eng). To undergo a secondary fermentation after the wine has been fermented and racked. A small ring of bubbles appears and the wine slowly ferments. Caused through sugar still remaining or a malo-lactic fermentation.

Frettenheim (Ger). Village. (Anb) = Rheinhessen. (Ber) = Wonnegau. (Gro) = Pilgerpfad. (Vin) = Heil.

Freudenlese (S.Afr). A special late harvest wine produced by Hazendal.

Freudenstein (Ger). Village. (Anb) = Württemberg. (Ber) = Württembergisch Unterland. (Gro) = Stromberg. (Vin) = Reichshalde.

Freudental (Ger). Vineyard. (Anb) = Baden. (Ber) = Ortenau. (Gro) = Fürsteneck. (Vil) = Ortenberg.

Freudental (Ger). Village. (Anb) = Württemberg. (Ber) = Württembergisch Unterland. (Gro) = Stromberg. (Vin) = Kirchberg.

Freundstück (Ger). Vineyard. (Anb) = Rheinpfalz. (Ber) = Mittelhaardt-Deutsche Weinstrasse. (Gro) = Mariengarten. (Vil) = Forst.

Freycinet Estate (Austr). Vineyard. Address = Lot 1, Gnaraway Road, Margaret River, Western Australia. 8 ha. Grape varieties – Cabernet franc, Cabernet sauvignon, Chardonnay, Chenin blanc, Merlot, Sauvignon blanc and Sémillon.

Freyung (Aus). Lit – 'Without water'. Name given to 1968 Eiswein (one of the first produced for a long while).

Friand (Fr). Applies to a young wine that is fresh, fruity and has a good flavour.

Friar's Ale (Eng). A keg Bitter 1036 O.G. brewed by the Morrell Brewery in Oxford.

F

Friary Meux Brewery (Eng). A brewery based in Goldaming, Surrey. Part of the Ind Coope Breweries. Noted for its' Treble Gold 1052 O.G.

Frick (Pierre et Fils) (Fr). Alsace wine producer. Address = 5, Rue de Baer, 68250 Pfaffenheim.

Frickenhausen (Ger). Village. (Anb) = Württemberg. (Ber) = Remstal-Stuttgart. (Gro) = Hohenneuffen. (Vin) = Schlossteige.

Frickenhausen am Main (Ger). Village. (Anb) = Franken. (Ber) = Maindreieck. (Gro) = Not yet assigned. (Vins) = Fischer, Kapellenberg, Markgraf, Babenberg.

Friedelsheim (Ger). Village. (Anb) = Rheinpfalz. (Ber) = Mittelhaardt-Deutsche Weinstrasse. (Gro) = Hofstück. (Vins) = Gerümpel, Rosengarten.

Friedelsheim (Ger). Village. (Anb) = Rheinpfalz. (Ber) = Mittelhaardt-Deutsche Weinstrasse. (Gro) = Schnepfenflug an der Weinstrasse. (Vins) = Bischofsgarten, Kreuz, Schlossgarten.

Friedman-Tnuva (Isr). A noted winery. Produces red, rosé and white wines.

Friedrich Wilheim Gymnasium (Ger). A charitable estate in the Rheingau. 46 ha. (Gro) = Burgweg. (Vins) = Rothenberg and Kläuserweg.

Friendship Cocktail (Cktl). ⅓ measure Gin, ⅓ measure orange Curaçao, ⅓ measure lemon juice. Shake over ice, pour into a cocktail glass. Dress with a slice of orange and lemon.

Friesengeist (Ger). A (herb) mint liqueur from the Frisian part of Germany. 45% alc. by vol. Produced by Johann Eschen.

Friesenheim (Ger). Village. (Anb) = Baden. (Ber) = Breisgau. (Gro) = Schotterlindenberg. (Vin) = Kronenbühl.

Friesenheim (Ger). Village. (Anb) = Rheinhessen. (Ber) = Nierstein. (Gro) = Gutes Domtal. (Vins) = Altdörr, Bergpfad, Knopf.

Frigola (Sp). A thyme-flavoured liqueur from the Balearic Islands.

Frincuşa (Rum). A white grape variety.

Frio (Mex). Chilled. See also Helado.

Frionnes (Les) (Fr). A Premier Cru vineyard in the A.C. commune of Saint-Aubin, Côte de Beaune, Burgundy.

Frisch (Ger). Fresh, sprightly.

Frische (Ger). Freshness.

Frisco Sour (Cktl). ½ fl.oz. Bénédictine, 1½ fl.ozs. Bourbon whiskey, ½ fl.oz. lime juice, ½ fl.oz. lemon juice. Shake over ice, strain into a large cocktail glass. Decorate with slices of lemon and lime.

Frisian Coffee (Liq.Coffee). From Germany made with Friesengeist (which is set alight). Serve black.

Frisian Country Wine (Ger). See Doornkaat.

Frisians (Ger). Early seventh century merchants who navigated the Rhine and took the German wines to western ports in U.K., Iberia and France.

Frisk Lager (Eng). A low-carbohydrate Lager 1033 O.G. brewed by the Vaux Brewery in Sunderland.

Frithsden (Eng). Vineyard. Address = Berkhampsted, Hertfordshire. 1 ha. Soil – heavy loam with flint and chalky subsoil. Grape varieties – Müller-Thurgau, Pinot meunier, Pinot noir, Ruländer and Weissburgunder. Vinification at Gamlingay Vineyards.

Friularo (It). A black grape variety grown in the Veneto region. Also name of red table wine made from same grape.

Friuli-Venezia Giulia (It). One of the smallest regions. Situated between Veneto and Yugoslavia it borders Austria to the north and has the Adriatic sea to the south.

Frizzante (It). Slightly sparkling. (Fr) = Pétillant. (Ger) = Spritzig.

Froccs (Hun). A light white wine mixed with soda water as a thirst quencher.

Frog and Firkin (Eng). A home-brew public house owned by Bruce in London. Noted for its' cask conditioned Bullfrog 1045 O.G. Dogbolter 1060 O.G. and Tavistock 1036 O.G.

Frog and Frigate (Eng). A home-brew public house in Southampton. Noted for its' Croaker 1050 O.G. and Frog's Original 1040 O.G.

Frog and Parrot (Eng). A home-brew public house owned by Whitbread in Sheffield. Noted for its' cask conditioned Old Croak 1035 O.G. Reckless Bitter 1046 O.G. Roger's Special 1065 O.G. all using malt extract.

Froher Weingarten (Ger). Vineyard. (Anb) = Mittelrhein. (Ber) = Bacharach. (Gro) = Schloss Reichenstein. (Vil) = Niederheimbach.

Fröhlich (Ger). Vineyard. (Anb) = Rheinhessen. (Ber) = Wonnegau. (Gro) = Sybillenstein. (Vil) = Bechenheim.

Fröhliche Weinberg (Der) (Ger). Play by Carl Zuckemeyer. 'The Merry Vineyard'.

Frohnwingert (Ger). Vineyard. (Anb) = Rheinpfalz. (Ber) = Südliche Weinstrasse. (Gro) = Kloster Liebfrauenberg. (Vil) = Oberhausen.

Frohnwingert (Ger). Vineyard. (Anb) = Mittelrhein. (Ber) = Rheinburgengau. (Gro) = Burg Rheinfels. (Vil) = St. Goar-Werlau.

Froichots (Les) (Fr). A Premier Cru vineyard in the A.C. commune of Morey-Saint-Denis, Côte de Nuits, Burgundy.

Fromenteau (Fr). A white table grape sometimes used to produce wine. Produces flat, sweet wines.
Fromentot (Fr). An alternative name for the Pinot gris grape.
Frondator (Lat). Vine-pruner.
Fronhof (Ger). Vineyard. (Anb) = Rheinpfalz. (Ber) = Mittelhaardt-Deutsche Weinstrasse. (Gro) = Schenkenböhl. (Vil) = Bad Dürkheim.
Fronsac (Fr). A.C. red wine commune in eastern Bordeaux.
Fronsadais (Fr). Wines of the Fronsac commune in Bordeaux. Heavy, meaty wines.
Frontenac Vineyard (USA). A winery based in Paw Paw, Michigan. Produces a variety of alcoholic beverages including wines.
Frontignac (Fr). A Vin doux naturel produced from the Frontignan grape. From north of the Pyrénées in southern France.
Frontignan (Fr). See Muscat de Frontignan.
Frontignan (Fr). A type of bottle used in Bordeaux. Especially Pauillac and Sauternes.
Fronton (Fr). A wine-producing area in the Haute-Garonne, south-western France. Produces V.D.Q.S. red, rosé and white wines.
Frost (Eng). A weather condition that is feared by the wine producers especially when the vines start to bud. Combatted by such methods as spraying vines with water or heating the vineyards with fire or smudge pots. In Germany can help produce Eiswein.
Frostbite Cocktail (Cktl). ⅓ measure Tequila, ⅓ measure (white) Crème de Cacao, ⅓ measure cream. Shake over ice, strain into a cocktail glass. Top with grated nutmeg.
Frostbiter (Eng). A cask conditioned Ale 1055 O.G. brewed by the homebrew Ancient Druids public house in Cambridge.
Frosted Coffee Hawaii (USA). 1 pint cold strong black coffee, ½ pint pineapple juice, 1 block vanilla ice cream. Blend together in a blender until smooth and foamy. Serve with straws.
Frosted Glass (Cktl). A glass in which the rim has been dipped in egg white, lemon juice or other and then in sugar to give a frosted appearance. Also can apply to a glass which has been chilled in a refrigerator to chill cocktails down without the aid of ice.
Frostgeschmack (Ger). Lit – 'Frosty flavour'. A wine that has been made from frost-affected grapes.
Frosty Amour (Cktl). ⅓ measure Smirnoff Vodka, ⅓ measure Southern Comfort, ⅓ measure Apricot brandy, dash Parfait Amour, dash Crème de Banane. Shake over ice, strain into a highball glass, fill with 7-Up. Serve with straws.
Frosty Dawn (Cktl). ⅓ measure white Rum, ⅙ measure Maraschino, ⅙ measure Falernum syrup, ⅓ measure orange juice. Shake over ice, strain into a cocktail glass.
Frosty Lime Cocktail (Cktl).(Non-alc). ¾ measure grapefruit juice, ¾ measure mint syrup, scoop of lime sorbet. Blend altogether in a blender. Pour into a saucer glass, dress with a lemon slice and mint leaf. Serve with straws.
Froth (Eng). Also known as the 'head'. The foamy bubbles seen on the top of a glass of beer.
Froth Blower (Cktl). ⅕ gill dry Gin, 4 dashes Grenadine, 1 egg white. Shake well over ice, strain into a cocktail glass.
Frothing (Eng). An upsurge of bubbles and debris at the start of fermentation. Causes tiny particles to be lifted up by CO_2 gas bubbles and to froth over.
Froupe Cocktail (Cktl). ½ measure Brandy, ½ measure Italian vermouth, 4 dashes Bénédictine. Stir well over ice, strain into a cocktail glass.
Frozen Apple Cocktail (Cktl). ⅕ measure Calvados, ⅛ measure lime juice, 2 dashes Gomme syrup, ½ egg white. Blend together with a scoop of crushed ice, serve in a flute glass.
Frozen Berkeley (Cktl). ¾ measure white Rum, ¼ measure Brandy, 2 barspoons passion fruit juice, juice ¼ lemon. Blend with a scoop of crushed ice in a blender. Pour into a flute glass.
Frozen Daiquiri (Cktl). 1½ fl.ozs. white Rum, juice ½ lime, dash Maraschino, dash Gomme syrup. Blend on high speed in a blender with a scoop of crushed ice. Pour into a highball glass, serve with straws.
Frozen Matador (Cktl). ⅖ measure Tequila, ⅗ measure pineapple juice, juice ¼ lime. Blend together with a scoop of crushed ice. Pour into an old-fashioned glass. Dress with a pineapple cube.
Frozen Mint Daiquiri (Cktl).(1). ⅕ measure white Rum, juice ¼ lime, 6 mint leaves, 1 barspoon Gomme syrup. Blend together with a scoop of crushed ice. Pour into an old-fashioned glass.
Frozen Mint Daiquiri (Cktl).(2). 1 fl.oz. white Rum, ½ fl.oz. (white) Crème de Menthe, ½ fl.oz. lime juice. Blend

together with a scoop of crushed ice in a blender. Pour into a saucer glass. Dress with mint leaves.

Frozen Pineapple Daiquiri (Cktl) (1). ⅕ measure Bacardi White Label, juice ¼ lemon, 2 dashes Gomme syrup, 4 pineapple cubes. Blend together in a blender with a scoop of crushed ice, pour into a flute glass.

Frozen Pineapple Daiquiri (Cktl) (2). 1 fl.oz. white Rum, ½ fl.oz. lime juice, 3 dashes Cointreau, 2 pineapple slices. Blend together in a blender with a scoop of crushed ice. Pour into a saucer glass, dress with a pineapple cube and a cherry.

Frozen Scotch Cocktail (Cktl). ⅕ gill Scotch whisky, ⅕ gill lemon juice, dash Angostura, dash Cointreau, 4 dashes Gomme syrup, 3 pineapple cubes. Blend together with a scoop of crushed ice in a blender. Pour into an old-fashioned glass. Dress with a pineapple cube.

Frozen Southern Comfort (Cktl). ⅕ gill Southern Comfort, juice ½ lime, ½ teaspoon sugar. Blend together with a scoop of crushed ice in a blender. Pour into a saucer glass. Serve with straws.

Frozen Spirits Cocktail (Cktl). ¾ measure Brandy, ¼ measure white Rum, 1 egg yolk, teaspoon Gomme syrup, 2 dashes lemon juice. Blend together with a scoop of crushed ice in a blender. Pour into a flute glass.

Frozen Steppes (Cktl). 1 fl.oz. Vodka, ½ fl.oz. Crème de Cacao, scoop vanilla ice cream. Blend well together, serve in a small goblet with straws.

Frozen Strawberry Cocktail (Cktl). ⅙ gill Crème de Fraises, ⅙ gill Tequila, dash lemon juice, 4 strawberries. Blend together in a blender with a scoop of crushed ice. Pour into a saucer glass. Dress with a strawberry and lemon slice.

Fruchsftlikors (Ger). A spirit that is flavoured with a single fruit extract.

Fruchtig (Ger). Fruity.

Fruchtaromalikors (Ger). On a label denotes that there are no additives used.

Fruchtschaumwein (Ger). A sparkling lemonade flavoured with fruit juice.

Fructexport (Rum). The government exporting agency.

Fructose (Eng). $C_6H_{12}O_6$. Fruit sugar. Is easily fermentable by yeast into alcohol and CO_2.

Früh Brauerei (Ger). A home-brew house in Cologne which brews Colner Hofbräu.

Frühburgunder (Ger). A red grape variety

used in the Ahr region and the Rheinhessen.

Frühjahrsbierfest (Ger). A springtime beer festival held in Munich. Begins on Saint Joseph's day.

Frühlingsplätzchen (Ger). Vineyard. (Anb) = Nahe. (Ber) = Schloss Böckelheim. (Gro) = Paradiesgarten. (Vil) = Monzingen.

Frühmess (Ger). Vineyard. (Anb) = Rheinpfalz. (Ber) = Südliche Weinstrasse. (Gro) = Kloster Liebfrauenberg. (Vil) = Glieszellen-Gleishorbach.

Frühmesse (Ger). Vineyard. (Anb) = Rheinhessen. (Ber) = Nierstein. (Gro) = Rheinblick. (Vil) = Alsheim.

Frühmessler (Ger). Vineyard. (Anb) = Baden. (Ber) = Ortenau. (Gro) = Schloss Rodeck. (Vil) = Sinzheim.

Frühroter Veltliner (Aus). A white grape variety.

Fruit Brandies (Euro). Spirits distilled from fermented fruit juices and fruit kernels. 40–44.5% alc. by vol.

Fruit Cups (Cktl). Non-alcoholic fruit drinks based on fruit juices, diluted squashes or cordials. Usually served chilled in a large bowl and put in tumblers. Dressed with sliced fruit.

Fruité (Fr). Fruity.

Fruit Lemonade (Cktl).(Non-alc). ½ gill lemon juice and ½ gill orange juice, Grenadine to taste. Mix well together, top with non-alcoholic cider and garnish with mint. Serve chilled.

Fruit Punch (Cktl).(Non-alc). 2 fl.ozs. orange juice, 1½ fl.ozs. lemon juice, 1½ fl.ozs. pineapple juice, 2 dashes Grenadine. Stir over ice, strain into a goblet with ice. Dress with fruit in season.

Fruit Spirits (Eng). Alcohols made from fruit-based wines. e.g. strawberry, cherry, raspberry etc.

Fruit Squashes (Eng). A sweetened liquid fruit concentrate, usually diluted before drinking.

Fruit Wines (Eng). Wines produced from any fruit other than grapes. Usually sugar and yeast have to be added before fermentation.

Fruity (Eng). A term for a wine which has a definite flavour and aroma of fresh fruit. Most fine young wines are 'fruity'.

Fruška Gora (Yug). A wine district in Vojvodina. Has many noted wineries based within its' boundaries.

Fruškogoraki Biser (Yug). A light sparkling white wine from Serbia. Demi-sec, it has a light sparkle.

Frydenlunds Brewery (Nor). A famous Norwegian brewery based in Oslo. Produces Bock biers and Tuborg Lager under licence.

F

Fryns (Bel). A company that produces a wide range of fruit liqueurs and Jenever.

FSB. (Eng) (abbr). Firkin Special Brew 1058 O.G. Beer brewed by the Bosham Brewery in West Sussex.

Fuchs (Ger). Vineyard. (Anb) = Mosel-Saar-Ruwer. (Ber) = Saar-Ruwer. (Gro) = Scharzberg. (Vil) = Saarburg.

Fuchsberg (Ger). Vineyard. (Anb) = Rheingau. (Ber) = Johannisberg. (Gro) = Burgweg. (Vil) = Geisenheim.

Fuchsen (Ger). Vineyard. (Anb) = Nahe. (Ber) = Kreuznach. (Gro) = Schlosskapelle. (Vil) = Laubenheim.

Fuchsgeschmack (Aus). A term for a wine with a 'foxy' taste produced from hybrid grapes.

Fuchshöhle (Ger). Vineyard. (Anb) = Mosel-Saar-Ruwer. (Ber) = Zell/Mosel. (Gro) = Weinhex. (Vil) = Kobern-Gondorf.

Fuchsloch (Ger). Vineyard. (Anb) = Mosel-Saar-Ruwer. (Ber) = Obermosel. (Gro) = Gipfel. (Vil) = Wincheringen.

Fuchsloch (Ger). Vineyard. (Anb) = Rheinhessen. (Ber) = Nierstein. (Gro) = Petersberg. (Vil) = Gau-Odernheim.

Fuchsloch (Ger). Vineyard. (Anb) = Rheinpfalz. (Ber) = Mittelhaardt-Deutsche Weinstrasse. (Gro) = Hofstück. (Vil) = Hochdorf-Assenheim.

Fuchsloch (Ger). Vineyard. (Anb) = Rheinpfalz. (Ber) = Mittelhaardt-Deutsche Weinstrasse. (Gro) = Hofstück. (Vil) = Rödersheim-Gronau.

Fuchsmantel (Ger). Vineyard. (Anb) = Rheinpfalz. (Ber) = Mittelhaardt-Deutsche Weinstrasse. (Gro) = Schenkrenböhl. (Vil) = Bad Dürkheim.

Fuchsmantel (Ger). Vineyard. (Anb) = Rheinpfalz. (Ber) = Mittelhaardt-Deutsche Weinstrasse. (Gro) = Schenkenböhl. (Vil) = Wachenheim.

Füder (Ger). A cask for storing wine. 250 gallons.

Füder N° (Ger). Cask number.

Fuées (Les) (Fr). A Premier Cru vineyard in the A.C. commune of Chambolle-Musigny, Côte de Nuits, Burgundy. 6.2 ha.

Fuella (Fr). An alternative name for the Folle blanche grape grown in the Bellet district of Provence, south-eastern France.

Fuella Nera (Fr). A red grape variety grown in the Bellet district of Provence, south-eastern France. Also known as the Folle noire.

Fuelle (Ger). Denotes a rich, fine wine.

Fuencaliente (Sp). A light red wine produced on the Canary Islands. Has 12–15% alc. by vol.

Fuenmayor (Sp). A noted wine-producing village of the Rioja region in north-eastern Spain.

Fuenzalida Eyzaguirre (Chile). A noted wine exporter based in Santiago.

Fufluns (It). The Etruscans' God of wine.

Fugari (Fr). A white wine from Sartene in Corsica.

Fugger (Bishop) (Ger). Bishop John Fugger of Ausburg, Swabia who, in 1110 on a visit to Rome, had sent his servant ahead to test the wines of the Inns on route and chalk either Est! (good) or Non Est (is not good) on the wall. At Montefiascone the wine was so good he chalked Est! Est!! Est!!! The Bishop arrived there in early 1111 and stayed for the rest of his life, never reaching Rome. See Est! Est!! Est!!!

Fuggles (Eng). A popular traditional variety of hop. Gives good bitterness to beers.

Fuglsang Brewery (Den). A brewery based in Haderslev that is noted for its' draught, unpasteurised beers.

Fuissé (Fr). A commune in the A.C. Pouilly-Fuissé district of the Mâconnais in the Burgundy region. Top vineyards are – Château Fuissé, Clos de la Chapelle, Clos de Varabond, Le Clos, Les Brûlets, Les Châtenets, Les Perrières, Les Vignes-Blanches, Menetrières and Versarmières.

Fukien Loh Chiu (China). A noted brand of rice wine produced in Shantung province from yellow rice. See also Shaoh-Hsing Rice Wine.

Fulda (Bishop of) (Ger). A German Bishop who is purported to have let his grapes rot on the vine because he was so lazy. He then gave the rotten grapes to the peasants who made wine with them. The elixer that was produced was the forerunner of Sauternes and Trokenbeerenauslese.

Full (Austr) (slang). A drunken person.

Full (Eng). A term used for a wine that is big in taste and not light or watery.

Full-Bodied (Eng). A term applied to wines with a rich bouquet that are high in fruit and alcohol.

Fülle (Ger). Plenty of richness in great wines.

Fullers (Eng). The trading name for a 56-strong group of Off-Licences used by Fuller Smith and Turner PLC.

Fullers Brewery (Eng). Based in London, is noted for its' cask conditioned Chiswick Bitter 1035.7 O.G. London Pride 1041.5 O.G. and Golden Pride 1090 O.G.

Füllig (Ger). Full-bodied.

Full Roast (Eng). A dark roasted coffee

that has a slightly bitter taste. Is popular in Italy.

Füllwein (Ger). Topping up with wine. Wine used to top up casks after racking or through evaporation.

Full Wine (Eng). Denotes a wine of good body.

Fulschette (Lux). A vineyard site in the village of Wellenstein.

Fumarium (Lat). An ancient hot room used for wines that were exposed to smoke in order to improve them.

Fumé (Fr). Smoked. Refers to the 'bloom' on the grape which gives it a smoky appearance. e.g. Blanc fumé.

Fumé Blanc (USA). The alternative name for the Sauvignon blanc.

Fumet (Fr). A definite bouquet.

Fumeux (Fr). A spirity or heady wine.

Fumé Vert (N.Z.). A wine from the Babich vineyard in Auckland. Has a herb flavour and aroma with a smoky touch.

Fumigation (Eng). The burning of a sulphur wick in a wine barrel to destroy bacteria. (Fr) = Méchage.

Fumosity (Eng). A term used to describe the heady vapours that are given off by some wines when they are poured out.

Fun and Games (Cktl). ½ measure Gin, ¼ measure blackcurrant cordial, ¼ measure lemon juice, dash Angostura. Shake over ice, strain into a cocktail glass. Serve with a small segment of lemon.

Funapple (Cktl).(Non-alc). Place 2 dashes Angostura and 2 dashes Rum essence into a large ice-filled highball glass. Top with non-alcoholic Cider or sparkling apple juice. Dress with an apple slice.

Funchal (Mad). The principal wine town where Madeira wine is aged and stored.

Funck-Bricher Brasserie (Lux). See Brasserie Nationale. Brews Bricher Meisterbock.

Fundador (Sp). A 3 year old brandy produced by Domecq. 40% alc. by vol.

Fundanum (Lat). A red wine produced in central-western Italy in Roman times.

Fund d'Bôta (It). The wine left in the bottle. Not drunk the same day.

Fundillón (Sp). A red wine produced from 100% Monastrell grapes. Is wood aged for 15 years. Produced only in good years.

Fungicide (Eng). A fungus destroyer.

Fungus (Eng). A mushroom or allied plant, spongy or morbid growth.

Funkenberg (Ger). Vineyard. (Anb) = Mosel-Saar-Ruwer. (Ber) = Zell/Mosel. (Gro) = Goldbäumchen. (Vil) = Münden.

Fun Pub (Eng). A term used in the 1980's to describe a public house with bright lights, loud music and catering for young customers.

Fürfeld (Ger). Village. (Anb) = Rheinhessen. (Ber) = Bingen. (Gro) = Rheingrafenstein. (Vins) = Eichelberg, Kapellenberg, Steige.

Furfural (Eng). An aldehyde obtained from oak casks. Part of the congeners in cask matured spirits.

Furlotti (Arg). A fine winery based in Mendoza.

Furmint (Hun). The famous white grape used mainly in the making of Tokay. There are other Hungarian wines made with the Furmint grape and it usually appears on the label following the name of the district. (Yug) = Šipon.

Furmint (N.Z.). A spicy, fruity white wine made by the Te Mata vineyards.

Furore (Cktl). ³⁄₁₀ measure Brandy, ²⁄₁₀ measure Lillet, ⅖ measure Aurum, ¹⁄₁₀ measure orange juice. Shake over ice, strain into a cocktail glass.

Fürst Bismark (Ger). A Kornbranntwein made from Rye and wheat only by Fürstlich von Bismark 'sche, Brennerei GmBh, Friedrichsruh.

Fürstenberg (Ger). Vineyard. (Anb) = Franken. (Ber) = Maindreieck. (Gro) = Kirchberg. (Vil) = Escherndorf.

Fürstenberg (Ger). Vineyard. (Anb) = Mittelrhein. (Ber) = Bacharach. (Gro) = Schloss Stahleck. (Vil) = Oberdiebach.

Fürstenberg Brauerei (Ger). A noted brewery from Donaueschingen in Baden. Produces a full-bodied beer of same name 5% alc. by vol.

Fürsteneck (Ger). Grosslage. (Anb) = Baden (Vils) = Berghaupten, Bermersbach, Bottenau, Diersburg, Durbach, Erlach, Gengenbach, Hofweier, Lautenbach, Nesselried, Niederschopfheim, Offenburg, (ortsteil Zell-Weierbach), Offenbach (ortsteil Fessenbach), Oberkirch, Oberkirch (ortsteil Haslach), Ödsbach, Ohlsbach, Ortenberg, Rammersweier, Reichenbach, Ringelbach, Stadelhofen, Tiergarten, Ulm, Zunsweier.

Fürstenlager (Ger). Vineyard. (Anb) = Hessische Bergstrasse. (Ber) = Starkenburg. (Gro) = Rott. (Vil) = Bensheim-Auerbach.

Fusel Oils (Eng). Higher alcohols. Alcohol (not Ethyl) found in spirits and in minute traces in some wines. Propyl, Butyl, Amyl, Hexyl and Heptyl.

Fussell's Bitter (Wales). A cask conditioned Bitter 1038 O.G. brewed by the Bass Brewery in Cardiff.

Fuste (Ch.Isles). Keg. See also P'tit Barri.

Fusto (It). A wooden barrel.

Fusty (Eng). Denotes musty, damp or mouldy smelling.

F

Fût (Fr). A hogshead cask holding 225 litres. Also known as a Pièce.

Fûts Roux (Fr). Casks that are between 5 and 10 years old. Neither new or old. Used for Cognac maturation.

Futurity Cocktail (Cktl). ½ measure sweet Vermouth, ½ measure Sloe gin, 2 dashes Angostura. Stir over ice, strain into a cocktail glass.

Fuzzy Navel (Cktl). Place 1 measure of Peach County Schnapps into an ice-filled highball glass. Top with 2 measures orange juice and a slice of orange.

Fyfield Hall Vineyard (Eng). First planted in 1976 in Essex. 2.25 ha. Grape variety – Müller-Thurgau.

G

G. (Sp) (abbr). Golden. Colour grade for Oloroso and Palo Cortado sherries.

Gaamez (Sp). An alternative name for the Gamay noir à jus blanc.

Gabarnac (Fr). A commune in the Premières Côtes de Bordeaux, central Bordeaux.

Gables Collins (Cktl). ⅗ measure Vodka, ⅖ measure Crème de Noyau, juice ¼ lemon, ⅛ gill pineapple juice. Shake over ice, strain into an ice-filled collins glass. Top with soda, a slice of lemon and a pineapple chunk.

Gablinger (USA) The brand-name used by Rheingold for their 'Light' beers.

Gabriela (Sp). The alternative name for Mantúo de Pila.

Gabriel Boudier (Fr). A distillery and liqueur producer based in Dijon, Burgundy.

Gabsheim (Ger). Village. (Anb) = Rheinhessen. (Ber) = Nierstein. (Gro) = Domherr. (Vins) = Dornpfad, Kirchberg, Rosengarten.

Gaeiras (Port). A full-bodied, dry, red wine produced in Óbidos, Estremadura.

Gaelic Coffee (Liq.Coffee). See Irish Coffee.

Gaelic Cow (Cktl). Place 1½ fl.ozs. Glayva into a highball containing hot milk. Top with a teaspoon of honey if required.

Gafé (S.Asia). The word for coffee in Thailand.

Gagarin Blue (Eng). A red grape variety of Russian origin named by Barrington Brock in 1965.

Gaggia (Achille) (It). The inventor of the Espresso coffee machine in 1946

Gaglioppo (It). A red grape variety in Calabria. Known locally as Mantonico nero.

Gaia Entrepot (Port). The district in Vila Nova de Gaia where the wine lodges are situated.

Gaia Pipe (Port). Storage casks in Vila Nova de Gaia for Port. 550 litres in capacity.

Gaillac (Fr). A red grape variety grown in Gaillac, south-western France.

Gaillac (Fr). A region near Bordeaux.

Produces – red, rosé, sparkling, pétillant and white wines. Grape varieties – Gaillac, Negrette, Ouras and Syrah (red). L'En de l'El, Maizac, Muscadelle, Ordenc, Sauvignon and Sémillon (white). If wine has 10.5% alc. by vol. then Gaillac. If 12% alc. by vol. then Premières Côtes de Gaillac.

Gaillac Mousseux (Fr). An A.C. sparkling (méthode gaillaçoise) wine produced in Gaillac, western France.

Gaillaçoise (Fr). A sparkling wine method where no sugar or Liqueur de Tirage is added. Fermentation is stopped by filtration.

Gaillac Perlé (Fr). A slightly sparkling white wine produced in the Gaillac region of western France.

Gaillard (N.Z.). A white hybrid grape variety.

Gain d'Espace (Fr). An ice-bucket stand. A holder that attaches itself to the table to avoid a free-standing ice-bucket at the table. For Champagne, white wine etc.

Gairé (Fr). A nineteenth century Cognac producer.

Gaisböhl (Ger). Vineyard. (Anb) = Rheinpfalz. (Ber) = Mittelhaardt-Deutsche Weinstrasse. (Gro) = Hofstück. (Vil) = Ruppertsberg.

Gaisburg (Ger). Village. (Anb) = Württemberg. (Ber) = Remstal-Stuttgart See Stuttgart.

Gaispfad (Ger). Vineyard. (Anb) = Mosel-Saar-Ruwer. (Ber) = Bernkastel. (Gro) = Schwarzlay. (Vil) = Traben-Trarbach.

Gaja (It). A producer based in Barbaresco, Piemonte. See Azienda Agricola di Angelo Gaja.

Gala (Gre). Milk.

Gala Caffé (It). A coffee liqueur produced by the Stock Co.,Trieste. 26% alc. by vol.

Galactic (Eng). Relating to milk.

Galactometer (Eng). An instrument similar to a hydrometer used for measuring the relative density of milk. Used to determine fat content.

Galactozyme (Fr). See Galazyme.

G

Gala Export Beer (Afr). A light Beer brewed by the Brasseries du Logone, Chad.

Galamus (Fr). A tawny-coloured, sweet dessert wine from the Roussillon region, southern France.

Galati (Rum). A wine-producing (white) area.

Galaxy (USA). A brand of Whiskey produced by Seagram.

Galazyme (Fr). Lightly fermented milk, frothy in appearance. Is also known as Galactozyme.

Galbenă (Rum). A white grape variety grown near Foscani in eastern Rumania.

Galego Dourado (Port). A white grape variety used in the production of Carcavelos.

Galerie (Fr). Coaster.

Galerie de Vin (Fr). Wine coaster.

Galeries (Fr). Part of the Chalk caves in Champagne used for the storage of maturing wines.

Gales Brewery (Eng). Based at Horndean in Hampshire. Noted for its' Prize Old Ale 1095 O.G. (Britain's only bottle conditioned beer). Treble Seven 1034 O.G. Southdown Bitter 1040 O.G. Nourishing Stout 1034 O.G. Champion Ale 1040 O.G. and Tudor Ale 1051 O.G.

Galestrino (It). A local Tuscany name for the small silica pebbles found in the schistous clay soil in the Chianti district. Is also known as Galestro.

Galestro (It). See Galestrino.

Galestro (It). A white Vino da Tavola made from the Malvasia, Sauvignon blanc and Trebbiano grapes in Tuscany.

Galgenberg (Ger). Vineyard. (Anb) = Nahe. (Ber) = Kreuznach. (Gro) = Kronenberg. (Vil) = Bad Kreuznach (ortsteil Bosenheim).

Galgenberg (Ger). Vineyard. (Anb) = Rheinhessen. (Ber) = Bingen. (Gro) = Rheingrafenstein. (Vil) = Hackenheim.

Galgenberg (Ger). Vineyard. (Anb) = Rheinhessen. (Ber) = Bingen. (Gro) = Sankt Rochuskapelle. (Vil) = Badenheim.

Galgenberg (Ger). Vineyard. (Anb) = Rheinpfalz. (Ber) = Südliche Weinstrasse. (Gro) = Guttenberg. (Vil) = Kandel.

Galgenwein (Ger). Lit – 'Gallows wine'. Refers to a strong, harsh, fiery wine, which, it is said, "Can choke a drinker and so the gallows rope is not needed!"

Galgon (Fr). A commune in the A.C. Côtes de Fronsac, Bordeaux.

Galibert (Fr). A famous French hybridiser.

Galicia (Sp). District in north-western Spain. Produces Vinhos Verdes similar to those in Portugal. Has two Denominaciónes de Origen – Ribeiro and Valdeorras.

Galil (Isr). A dry white wine produced in the Galilee region.

Galilee (Isr). A wine-producing region. Noted for its' red and white wines.

Galion Brewery (E.Ind). A brewery based in Medan, Sumatra. Brews Galion (a Pilsener-style beer).

Gall (Ger). A chemist who pioneered the addition of sugar (non-grape) to grape must.

Gallagher and Burton (USA). The brand-name for a blended Bourbon whiskey bottled by Gallagher and Burton Co. Baltimore. 40% alc. by vol.

Galland (Aus). A liqueur producer based in Vienna. Produces a fine range of liqueurs.

Galleano Winery (USA). A winery based in Cucamonga, California. Grape variety – Zinfandel.

Galleon Wine (Eng). A large Off-Licence chain (298) owned by the Bass group.

Galliano (It). A spicy, herb-flavoured liqueur from Livorno. Also known as Liquore Galliano. 35% alc. by vol. Produced by the Distillerie Riuniti, Solano.

Galliano's Golden Cup (Punch). 2 pints hot tea, 2¼ pints orange juice, ⅓ pint Galliano, cinnamon stick, sugar syrup. Heat together, strain, garnish with mint leaves and orange slices. Serve hot.

Gallic Acid" (Eng). An acid obtained during storage in wooden casks.

Gallic Coffee (Liq.Coffee). See Gaelic Coffee. (Alternative spelling of in USA).

Gallice (Lat). See Spiritus Vini de Gallice.

Gallization (Ger). For Chaptalisation. Named after the German chemist Gall. Adding sugar to grape must to raise the alcohol level. See (Ger) = Verbesserung and (Fr) = Chaptalisation.

Gallo (USA). A large winery in San Joaquin Valley, California. Est. 1933. Produces nearly 40% of total Californian wine output. Produce table, sparkling and dessert wines from a large variety of grapes. Has contracts with wineries in Sonoma and Napa Valley. See also Livingstone Cream.

Gallo d'Oro (It). A wine-producer based in Piemonte. Is noted for Verbeso (white wine) and Barbaresco.

Gallon (Eng). Imperial measure. Equals 8 pints or 4 quarts, 1.2 US gallons, 4.54 Litres. 277.42 Cubic inches.

Gallon (USA). US Gallon. Equals 0.83

Imperial gallons. 3.79 Litres. 231 Cubic inches.

Gallonage (Eng). The total amount in gallons.

Gallo Nero (It). Lit – 'Black cockerel'. The Seal for Chianti Classico wines.

Gallo's Thunderbird (USA). A popular flavoured and fortified 'Pop' wine at about 10% alc. by vol.

Gallweys (Ire). A liqueur based on whiskey, honey, herbs and coffee. 31% alc. by vol.

Galon (Fr). The mediaeval word for gallon. See also Jalon.

Galvez Fizz (Cktl). 1½ fl.ozs. dry Gin, 1½ fl.ozs. cream, 1 egg white, 3 dashes Grenadine, dash orange flower water, juice of a lemon, barspoon sugar. Shake well over ice, strain into a highball glass. Top with lemonade.

Galway Grey (Cktl). ⅓ measure Vodka, ⅙ measure Cointreau, ⅙ measure Crème de Cacao, ⅓ measure lime juice. Stir, float cream on top. Add a twist of orange.

Galwyn (Wales). Gallon, 8 pints.

Gamay (Fr). A red grape variety grown mainly in the Beaujolais, Rhône and the Loire. See Gamay Noir à Jus Blanc. (Aus) = Blaufränkisch, (Hun) = Kékfrankos.

Gamay (USA). See California Gamay and Napa Gamay.

Gamay à Jus Coloré (Fr). Lit – 'Gamay with coloured juice'. A red grape variety grown in southern Burgundy. Known also as the Gamay-Teinturier. Also spelt Gamay au Jus Coloré.

Gamay au Jus Blanc (Fr). See Gamay Noir à Jus Blanc.

Gamay au Jus Coloré (Fr). See Gamay à Jus Coloré.

Gamay Beaujolais (USA). A red grape variety grown in California. Name for the Vitis vinifera Gamay.

Gamay Blanc à Feuilles Rondes (Fr). An alternative name for the Muscadet grape.

Gamay Crni (Yug). A red grape variety grown in Istria, Croatia.

Gamay de Liverdun (Fr). A red grape variety grown in the Côtes de Toul, Lorraine.

Gamay de Toul (Fr). A red grape variety grown in the Côtes de Toul, Lorraine.

Gamay Noir à Jus Blanc (Fr). Lit – 'Black Gamay with white juice'. A red grape variety grown in the Beaujolais, Loire and Rhône. See Gamay. Also known as Blaufränkischer, Borgogna Crna, Bourgignon noir, Frankinja Crna, Frankinja Modra, Gaamez, Gamay au Jus Blanc, Gamay beaujolais, Gamay rond, Kékfrankos, Limberger, Napa gamay and Petit gamai.

Gamay Rond (Fr). An alternative name for the Gamay noir à jus blanc.

Gamay Rosé (USA). A rosé wine produced in California from the Gamay Beaujolais grape.

Gamay St. Romain à Jus Blanc (Fr). A red grape variety grown in the Côtes Roannaises, Loire.

Gamay Teinturier (Fr). See Gamay à Jus Coloré.

Gamba (Port). The brand-name of a Vinho Verde from Borges & Irmão. Is sold in flasks.

Gambach (Ger). Village. (Anb) = Franken. (Ber) = Maindreieck. (Gro) = Rosstal. (Vin) = Kalbenstein.

Gambarotta (Fr). Producers of Brandy del Bourgogne.

Gambarotta di Inga (It). Liqueur producers based in Serravalle, Scrivia. Produce Fernet Gambarotta (a herb liqueur 43% alc. by vol).

Gambellara (It). A small town half-way between Verona and Vicenza. Also the name of a white wine.

Gambellara (It). A D.O.C. white wine from Veneto. Made from the Garganega and Trebbiano nostrano grapes. If total alc. content is 11.5% by vol. then classed Superiore.

Gambia Distillers Ltd (Afr). Distillers of a range of spirits based in Kanifing, Gambia.

Gambrinus (Czec). A brewery in Pilsen which is noted for its' Pilsener Lager called Světovar. Also Diplomat, a strong, dark Lager beer with a good hop flavour.

Gamebird (Port). A brand of both Tawny and Ruby Ports from Robertson.

Gamel (Nor). A brand of Aquavit.

Gamet (Fr). The name used for the Gamay grape in the seventeenth and eighteenth centuries.

Gamla (Isr). The name given to a range of Israeli wines which are imported into the U.K. by the House of Hallgarten, London.

Gamle Carlsberg (Den). 'Old Carlsberg'. A Münchener-style Lager beer.

Gamlingay (Eng). Vineyard. Address = Near Sandy, Bedfordshire. 4.5 ha. Soil – Greensand. Grape varieties – Faber, Müller-Thurgau, Reichensteiner, Rieslaner, Scheurebe.

Gammel Dansk (Den). A style of alcoholic Bitters distilled from a variety of berries, herbs and spices. 38% alc. by vol.

Gammelholm Snaps (Den). The brand-name of an Akvavit.

Gammel Porter (Den). A medium-sweet Imperial Stout 6.1% alc. by weight brewed by Carlsberg.

G

Gampal (Port). A white grape variety grown in Torres Vedras.

Gamza (Bul). A red grape variety which produces a full rich red Beaujolais style of wine. (Hun) = Kadarka.

Gamza (Bul). A red wine produced near northern Sofia from the grape of same name.

Gancia (It). Major wine producers near Asti in the Piemonte region. Noted for their Asti spumante and Vermouths.

Gancia (Carlo) (It). Creator of Asti Spumante in the nineteenth century.

Gandesa Terralta (Sp). A Denominación de Origen region near Priorato, Catalonia. Produces red wines from the Cariñena, Garnacha and Macabéo grapes.

G and G (Jap). A brand of Whiskey produced by the Nikka Distilleries.

Gangadine Cocktail (Cktl). ⅓ measure Gin, ⅓ measure (white) Crème de Menthe, ⅓ measure Oxygénée Cusenier, 2 dashes Framboise syrup. Shake over ice, strain into a cocktail glass.

Gangster Cocktail (Cktl). ¼ gill brown Curaçao, ¼ gill Brandy. Shake over ice, strain into a cocktail glass. Serve with a cherry and a dash of lemon peel juice.

Gannaru (Euro). A red grape variety grown on the island of Malta.

Gäns (Ger). Vineyard. (Anb) = Mosel-Saar-Ruwer. (Ber) = Zell/Mosel. (Gro) = Weinhex. (Vil) = Kobern-Gondorf.

Gänsberg (Ger). Vineyard. (Anb) = Baden. (Ber) = Ortenau. (Gro) = Schloss Rodeck. (Vil) = Neuweier.

Garabana (Iran). A large flagon used during early Persian times.

Garance (Fr). A type of plant (also known as the Madder wort) from which can be brewed a style of beer.

Garaway's Coffee House (Eng). 1615. Purported to have been the first coffee house to serve tea.

Garbi (Sp). See Llebeig.

Garboon (Eng). The name given to the spittoon used by professional coffee tasters to deposit the coffee they are assessing.

Garceta (Sp). A finely woven sack that is used to slow down wine that is being transferred into a cask.

Garchères (Les) (Fr). A vineyard in the A.C. commune of Montagny, Côte Chalonnaise, Burgundy.

Garcia Caribbean Cream (Hol). A Jamaican rum and cream liqueur from Cooymans. 14.9% alc. by vol.

García Poveda (Sp). A large bodega based in Alicante. Produces wines under the Costa Blanc label.

Garçon de Comptoir (Fr). Barman.

Garco Wine Company (USA). A winery based in St. Louis, Missouri.

Garcy (Fr). A commune in the Central Vineyards region of the Loire. Produces Pouilly Fumé.

Gard (Fr). A département of the Languedoc-Roussillon. Including the Plaine du Vistre and the Plaine du Vidourle. Noted for its' Costières and Clairette de Bellegarde. See also Costières-du-Gard.

Garda (It). The name given to wines that are grown near Lake Garda in northern Italy. Moniga-del-Garda and Chiaretto-del-Garda.

Garden Creek Ranch (USA). A vineyard based in Alexander Valley, Sonoma County, California. 17 ha. Grape varieties – Cabernet sauvignon and Gewürztraminer. Produces varietal wines.

Garden Party (Cktl). ½ fl.oz. Vaapukka liqueur, Champagne. Pour liqueur into Champagne flute and top with iced Champagne.

Gardet and Co (Fr). Champagne producer. Address = 13 Rue Georges Legros, Chigny les Roses, 51500 Rilly La Montagne. Produces – Vintage and non-vintage wines. Vintages – 1973, 1975, 1976, 1979, 1982.

Garenne (Fr). A Premier Cru vineyard in the A.C. commune of Puligny-Montrachet, Côte de Beaune, Burgundy. 0.4 ha.

Garfoli (It). A noted Verdicchio dei Castelli di Jesi producer based at Loreto.

Garganega (It). A white grape variety grown around Lake Garda in northern Italy.

Garganega di Gambelare (It). A dry white wine from the province of Vicenza in the Venetia (Verona).

Gargle (Eng) (slang). For a drink in the north of England. Lit – 'To rinse out the mouth with liquid'.

Gargoyle Cocktail (Cktl). ⅓ measure dry Gin, ⅓ measure Cointreau, ⅓ measure Cognac. Stir well over ice, strain into a cocktail glass.

Garibaldi Dolce (It). See G.D.

Gärkammer (Ger). Vineyard. (Anb) = Ahr. (Ber) = Walporzheim/Ahrtal. (Gro) = Klosterberg. (Vil) = Walporzheim.

Garlic (Eng). If present on the bouquet of a wine then denotes the presence of Sorbic acid.

Garnacha (Sp). A black grape variety used in the Rioja and Penedés. See also Garnacho and Grenache.

Garnacha Blanca (Sp). A white grape variety grown in Cataluña, south-eastern Spain. Also known as the Garnacho blanco.

G

Garnacha de Alicante (Sp). A red grape variety grown in the Galicia region.

Garnacha Negra (Sp). A red grape variety grown in the Penedés region.

Garnacha Paluda (Sp). A red grape variety grown in Alella, near Barcelona, south-eastern Spain. A variant of the Garnacha tinta. Also spelt Garnacha peluda. The grapes are darker and thicker skinned than Garnacha tinta.

Garnacha Peluda (Sp). An alternative spelling of the Garnacha paluda.

Garnacha Tinta (Sp). A red grape variety grown in the Rioja region. See Garnacho.

Garnacha Tintorera (Sp). A red grape variety grown in the southern regions of Spain.

Garnache (Sp). An alternative name for the Grenache.

Garnacho (Sp). A black grape variety grown in the Rioja region. It ripens late and is resistant to Oïidium. Also produces white grapes depending on method of cultivation. Also known as the Alicante, Garnacha tinta, Grenache, Granaccia, Llandoner, Roussillón tinto, Tinta aragonés and Uva di spagna.

Garnacho Blanco (Sp). A white grape variety grown in the Rioja region of north-eastern Spain. Also known as the Garnacha blanco.

Garnacho Paluda (Sp). An alternative spelling of the Garnacha paluda.

Garnet (It). A desirable colour in the red wines of northern Italy.

Garnheath (Scot). A Grain spirit once produced by Inver House Distillers at Airdrie, West Lothian.

Garnier (Fr). A famous liqueur firm owned by Bénédictine. Produces a range of fruit liqueurs including Abricotine.

Garoa (Sp). A red Riojan wine from the Bodegas Velazquez.

Garofoli (It). A winery based at Loreto in the Marches. Owns 60 ha. of vineyards. Noted for its' Verdicchio wines.

Garolla (Fr). An alternative name for the Égrappoir.

Garollières (Les) (Fr). See Les Jarolières.

Garonne (S.Afr). A dessert wine made from the Rhine riesling and Steen grapes by the Villiera Estate in Paarl.

Garonne [River] (Fr). A river that runs to the west coast of France in Bordeaux. Joins with the river Dordogne to form the river Gironde.

Garoto (Port). A small black coffee (Portuguese espresso) served with milk.

Garrafa (Sp). Carafe, bottle.

Garrafào (Port). A large bottle.

Garrafeira (Port). If found on a wine label denotes best wine of that year. Sometimes a little wine of another year is blended in to add body. Top quality.

Garreau (Fr). Armagnac producer. Address = Charles Garreau et ses Enfants, SARL, Château Garreau, 40240 Labastide d'Armagnac. 21 ha. in Bas Armagnac.

Garrido Fino (Sp). A white grape variety grown in south-western Spain (Huelva).

Garrigos (Sp). Wine-producers and bottlers based in Valencia.

Garrigues (Fr). The name given to moorland in the Languedoc et Roussillon region of south-western France.

Gärtchen (Ger). Vineyard. (Anb) = Mosel-Saar-Ruwer. (Ber) = Bernkastel. (Gro) = Michelsberg. (Vil) = Piesport.

Gartenlay (Ger). Vineyard. (Anb) = Mittelrhein. (Ber) = Rheinburgengau. (Gro) = Burg Hammerstein. (Vil) = Leutesdorf.

Garvey (Sp). A noted Sherry and Brandy producer based in Jerez de la Frontera. Was owned by Rumasa. Sherry-range includes Tio Guillermo, La Lidia, San Patricio and Ochavico.

G.A.S. (Rum) (abbr). Gaspodaniile Agricole de Stat. State agricultural enterprise.

Gas Blanketing (Eng). A treatment of wine in which air in an ullaged vat is replaced with CO_2 or Nitrogen. Prevents attack by acetobacter and oxidation.

Gas Chromatography (Eng). A process which measures the chemical content of substances by turning them into gases (by heating). Used to measure the blood alcohol level in drunken drivers.

Gascosa (Port). Mineral water, fizzy drink, pop.

Gaseosa (Sp). Mineral water.

Gaseoso (Sp). The name given to a sparkling wine produced by an injection of CO_2 gas.

Gasificado (Sp). CO_2 injected sparkling wines.

Gas Light (The) (Cktl). 1½ fl. ozs. Scotch whisky, ½ fl. oz. Italian vermouth, dash orange Curaçao. Shake well over ice, strain into an ice-filled goblet. Add ¼ fl.oz. Drambuie, garnish with a twist of orange.

Gaspo (Fr). A buttermilk drink which is popular in Auvergne.

Gässel (Ger). Vineyard. (Anb) = Rheinpfalz. (Ber) = Mittelhaardt-Deutsche Weinstrasse. (Gro) = Pfaffengrund. (Vil) = Geinsheim.

Gassificato (It). Artificially gas injected with CO_2.

Gassosa (It). The general term for sparkling drinks.

Gastenklinge (Ger). Vineyard. (Anb) = Württemberg. (Ber) = Remstal-Stuttgart. (Gro) = Wartbühl. (Vil) = Strümpfelbach.

Gasthaus (Ger). Guesthouse, Inn.

G

Gastritis (Eng). A disease of the stomach caused through chronic alcoholism.

Gatão (Port). The brand-name of a Vinho Verde produced by Soc. Vinhos Borges & Irmao, Porto-Portugal.

Gate (Eng). The name for the home-brew public house The Lee, Buckinghamshire. Produces Carr's Best Bitter 1041 O.G.

Gate (Eng). A home-brew public house owned by Whitbread in Southampton noted for its' cask conditioned Three Bar 1035 O.G. and Five Bar 1050 O.G.

Gato Cocktail (Cktl). ⅓ gill Gin, 4 dashes Gomme syrup, 6 strawberries. Blend together with a scoop of crushed ice in a blender, strain into a saucer glass. Dress with a strawberry.

Gattinara (It). A commune in the provence of Vercelli, Piemonte.

Gattinara (It). D.O.C. red wine from Piemonte. Made from the Nebbiolo grape. Has to age 4 years (2 years in oak/chestnut casks). Is a dry wine with slight bitter taste.

Gatzweiler (Ger). A brewery in Düsseldorf. Owned by Zum Schlüssel. Produces a fine Altbier.

Gatzweiler Alt (Ger). A fine Altbier brewed by the Gatzweiler Brauerei in Düsseldorf. Is a bitter, light, slightly acid brew.

Gau-Algesheim (Ger). Village. (Anb) = Rheinhessen. (Ber) = Bingen. (Gro) = Abtey. (Vins) = Goldberg, Johannisberg, Rothenberg, St. Laurenzikapelle, Steinert.

Gau-Bickelheim (Ger). Village. (Anb) = Rheinhessen. (Ber) = Bingen. (Gro) = Kurfürstenstück. (Vins) = Bockshaut, Kapelle, Sankopf.

Gau-Bischofsheim (Ger). Village. (Anb) = Rheinhessen. (Ber) = Nierstein. (Gro) = Sankt Alban, (Vins) = Glockenberg, Herrnberg, Pfaffenweg.

Gaucho (Cktl). ½ measure Dutch Gin, ½ measure Hesperidina, dash Angostura. Shake over ice, strain into an ice-filled old-fashioned glass. Decorate with a slice of orange.

Gaudenzio (It). A producer of Moscato d'Asti Spumante in the Piemonte region.

Gaudi (Ind). The name given to a drink produced from the crystallised residue left from Sidhu by Ancient Indians.

Gaudichots (Les) (Fr). A Premier Cru vineyard in the A.C. commune of Vosne-Romanée, Côte de Nuits, Burgundy. 5.8 ha.

Gaudin (Fr). A company based in the Haute-Savoie, eastern France that produces dry, aromatic Apéritif wines e.g. Chambéry and Chambéryzette.

Gauersheim (Ger). Village. (Anb) = Rheinpfalz. (Ber) = Mittelhaardt-

Deutsche Weinstrasse. (Gro) = Schnepfenflug vom Zellertal. (Vin) = Goldloch.

Gaugrehweiler (Ger). Village. (Anb) = Nahe. (Ber) = Schloss Böckelheim. (Gro) = Paradiesgarten. (Vin) = Graukatz.

Gauguin Cocktail (Cktl). ⅙ measure white Rum, ⅙ measure Passion fruit syrup, ⅙ measure lemon juice, ⅙ measure lime juice. Blend together with a scoop of crushed ice. Pour into an old-fashioned glass, top with a cherry.

Gau-Heppenheim (Ger). Village. (Anb) = Rheinhessen. (Ber) = Nierstein. (Gro) = Petersberg. (Vins) = Pfarrgarten, Schlossberg.

Gauloise (Fr). Very old Apéritif. Made in three styles – dry, medium and sweet.

Gau-Odernheim (Ger). Village. (Anb) = Rheinhessen. (Ber) = Nierstein. (Gro) = Petersberg. (Vins) = Fuchsloch, Herrgottspfad, Olberg, Vogelsang.

Gauranum (Lat). A red wine produced in central Italy during Roman times.

Gauriac (Fr). A commune in the A.C. Côtes de Bourg in north-eastern Bordeaux.

Gautier (Fr). Cognac producer. Address = 28 Rue des Ponts, 16140 Aigre.

Gautier (Laurent) (Fr). A négociant-éleveur based at Savigny-lès-Beaune, Côte de Beaune, Burgundy.

Gauvin (Fr). A vineyard based in the A.C. Volnay-Santenots. Is owned by the Hospices de Beaune. (Based in the Santenots vineyard).

Gauvin (Fr). The brand-name of an Armagnac produced by Domaine de Lamothe.

Gau-Weinheim (Ger). Village. (Anb) = Rheinhessen. (Ber) = Bingen. (Gro) = Kuefürstenstück. (Vins) = Geyersberg, Kaisergarten, Wissberg.

Gavi (It). See Cortese di Gavi.

Gavilan (Mex). A noted distillery based in Jalisco. Produces Tequila Especial. 40% alc. by vol.

Gavine (S.Afr). A leading brand of double-distilled cane spirit.

Gavotte (S.Afr). A red wine blend of Cabernet and Shiraz grapes which is produced by the Villiera Estate, Paarl. Also a white (Blanc de noir) version produced.

Gay Lussac (Fr). Inventor of a Hydrometer named after him. Measures the volume of alcohol on a scale of 0° water – 100° pure alcohol.

Gaymers Olde English Cyder (Eng). A brand of Cider produced by the Showerings Co. (part of Allied Lyons).

Gaza (Isr). A Palestine wine written about in Roman times.

Gaz Carbonique (Fr). Carbon-dioxide, CO_2.

G

Gazéifié (Fr). A term for artificially carbonated sparkling wines.

Gazela (Port). The brand-name of a Vinho Verde wine.

Gazeux (Fr). Aerated.

Gaziantep (Tur). A vineyard noted for its' red and white wines based in eastern Turkey.

Gazino (Tur). Beer house, pub (usually with entertainment).

Gazoz (Tur). Denotes a sparkling soft drink (non-alcoholic) e.g. pop, ginger beer, lemonade, etc.

G.B. (Eng) (abbr). The initials of the Greengate Brewery in Manchester. See G.B. Lees Mild.

G.B. Lees Mild (Eng). A Mild beer 1032 O.G. brewed by the Greengate Brewery in Manchester.

G.D. (It) (abbr). Garibaldi Dolce. The old-style name given to Marsala. Denotes 2 years ageing and 18% alc. by vol.

G.D.C. (Eng) (abbr). Geneva Double Curtain.

Gean Whisky (Scot). A black cherry Whisky. Is also spelt Geen whisky. See also Cherry Whisky.

Geb de Koninck Brasserei (Bel). A brewery based in Dwarp, central Belgium.

Geb de Vit Brasserei (Bel). A brewery based in Asse, north Belgium.

Gebeide (Hol). A term used for a Jenever distilled from juniper. See also Dubbele Graan and Dubbel Gebeide.

Gebiet (Ger). A vine-growing region. e.g. Rheinhessen. See Anbaugebiet.

Gebietsweinmarkt der Ahr (Ger). A wine festival held at Ahrweiler each May.

Gebirgsbitter (Ger). A Brandy with additional aromatic and bitter ingredients. Brown or green in colour.

Gebweiler (Fr). The German name for the Alsace town of Guebwiller.

Gecht (A.) de Luxe Brandy (USA). The brand-name of brandy bottled by Liquors Co. of America. 40% alc. by vol.

Geddelsbach (Ger). Village. (Anb) = Württemberg. (Ber) = Württembergisch Unterland. (Gro) = Lindelberg. (Vin) = Schneckenhof.

Gedeonseck (Ger). Grosslage. (Anb) = Mittelrhein. (Ber) = Rheinburgengau. (Vils) = Boppard, Brez, Rhens, Spay.

Gedera (Isr). The viticultural centre of Israel which produces most types of wines.

Geelong (Austr). A wine-producing area in Victoria.

Geens (Bel). A distillery based in Aarschot. Produces a large range of liqueurs and a Genever. Also owns French vineyards and produces French table wines.

Geen Whisky (Scot). See Gean Whisky.

Gefällig (Ger). Pleasing, harmonious wine.

Geffard (Henri) (Fr). A Cognac producer.

Address = Verriers, 16130, Segonzac. 25 ha. in the Grande Champagne. Produces a wide range of fine Cognacs.

Gefüllt (Ger). Full, rich wine.

Geheelonthouder (Hol). Teetotaler.

Gehrig Brothers (Austr). A winery based in north-east Victoria.

Gehrn (Ger). Vineyard. (Anb) = Rheingau. (Ber) = Johannisberg. (Gro) = Steinmacher. (Vil) = Rauenthal.

Gehvé (Iran). Coffee.

Geiersberg (Ger). Vineyard. (Anb) = Rheinhessen. (Ber) = Bingen. (Gro) = Adelberg. (Vil) = Armsheim.

Geiersberg (Ger). Vineyard. (Anb) = Rheinhessen. (Ber) = Wonnegau. (Gro) = Pilgerpfad. (Vil) = Dittelsheim-Hessloch.

Geiershöll (Ger). Vineyard. (Anb) = Rheinhessen. (Ber) = Nierstein. (Gro) = Domherr. (Vil) = Klein-Winternheim.

Geinsheim (Ger). Village. (Anb) = Rheinpfalz. (Ber) = Mittelhaardt-Deutsche Weinstrasse. (Gro) = Pfaffengrund. (Vin) = Gässel.

Geisberg (Ger). Vineyard. (Anb) = Mosel-Saar-Ruwer. (Ber) = Bernkastel. (Gro) = Michelsberg. (Vil) = Rivenich.

Geisberg (Ger). Vineyard. (Anb) = Mosel-Saar-Ruwer. (Ber) = Saar-Ruwer. (Gro) = Scharzberg. (Vil) = Ockfen.

Geisberg (Ger). Vineyard. (Anb) = Mosel-Saar-Ruwer. (Ber) = Saar-Ruwer. (Gro) = Scharzberg. (Vil) = Schoden.

Geisberg (Ger). Vineyard. (Anb) = Mosel-Saar-Ruwer. (Ber) = Zell/Mosel. (Gro) = Schwarze Katz. (Vil) = Zell.

Geisberg (Ger). Vineyard. (Anb) = Nahe. (Ber) = Schloss Böckelheim. (Gro) = Rosengarten. (Vil) = Bockenau.

Geisburger (Fr). A lesser white grape variety grown in Alsace.

Geisenheim (Ger). Village. (Anb) = Rheingau. (Ber) = Johannisberg. (Gro) = Burgweg. (Vins) = Fuchsberg, Mäuerchen, Mönchspfad, Rothenberg.

Geisenheim (Ger). Village. (Anb) = Rheingau. (Ber) = Johannisberg. (Gro) = Erntebringer. (Vins) = Kilzberg, Klaus, Klauserweg, Schlossgarten.

Geisenheim Institute (Ger). A noted institute for vine breeding and grafting. See Omega Graft.

Geissberg (Ger). Vineyard. (Anb) = Rheinhessen. (Ber) = Bingen. (Gro) = Kaiserpfalz. (Vil) = Heidesheim.

Geissenkopf (Ger). Vineyard. (Anb) = Nahe. (Ber) = Schloss Böckelheim. (Gro) = Paradiesgarten. (Vil) = Niedermoschel.

Geissenkopf (Ger). Vineyard. (Anb) = Nahe. (Ber) = Schloss Böckelheim. (Gro) = Paradiesgarten. (Vil) = Obermoschel.

Geisskopf (Ger). Vineyard. (Anb) =

G

Rheinpfalz. (Ber) = Mittelhaardt-Deutsche Weinstrasse. (Gro) = Schwarzerde. (Vil) = Kirchheim.

Geist (Ger). The term to describe types of fruit liqueurs, distilled from unfermented berries, apricots, peaches plus the addition of alcohol.

Geisterberg (Ger). Vineyard. (Anb) = Rheinhessen. (Ber) = Bingen. (Gro) = Adelberg. (Vil) = Erbes-Bürdesheim.

Geisweiler et Fils (Fr). Burgundy shippers based at Nuits-Saint-Georges. Owns 70% of the vineyards in the Hautes Côtes de Nuits. See Domaine Geisweiler.

Gekkeikan (Jap). A liqueur made from a special kind of plum which gives a luscious flavour.

Gekkeikan (Jap). A popular brand of Saké.

Gélas et Fils (Ets) (Fr). Armagnac producer based in Ténarèze. Address = Avenue Bergès, 32190 Vic-Fezensac.

Gelatine (Eng). Used as a finings for wines. A little wine is mixed with the dissolved gelatine and then poured in the wine. As it sinks impurities in the wine are taken to the bottom.

Gelber Moseler (Aus). Another name for the Furmint grape used in Germany and Austria.

Gelber Ortlieber (Aus). Another name for the Knipperlé grape.

Gelendshik (USSR). A wine region of the Crimean peninsula.

Gelin (Pierre) (Fr). A négociant-éleveur based in the Côte d'Or. Address = 62, Route des Grands Crus, 21220 Gevrey-Chambertin, Burgundy.

Gellewza (Euro). A white grape variety grown on the island of Malta. Also known as the Mammolo.

Gellmersbach (Ger). Village. (Anb) = Württemberg. (Ber) = Württembergisch Unterland. (Gro) = Salzberg. (Vin) = Dezberg.

Gemarkung (Ger). Wine town or village. See also Weinbauort and Gemeinde.

Gemberbier (Hol). Ginger beer.

Gem City Vineland Compagny (USA). A winery based in Nauvoo, Illinois. Produces Labrusca wines.

Gemeaux Cherbaudes (Les) (Fr). A Premier Cru vineyard in the A.C. commune of Gevrey-Chambertin, Côte de Nuits, Burgundy.

Gemeinde (Ger). Another name for a wine-producing village. See also Weinbauort and Gemarkung.

Gemeinde (USA). A Mild beer brewed by the Cold Spring Brewery based in Cold Spring, Minnesota.

Gemello Winery (USA). A winery based in Santa Clara, California. Grape varieties – Barbera, Petit syrah and Zinfandel. Produces varietal wines.

Geminianum (Lat). A red wine produced in south-western Italy during Roman times.

Gemma d'Abeto (It). A pine-needle-flavoured liqueur produced by the Servite friars near Florence.

Gemmingen (Ger). Village. (Anb) = Baden. (Ber) = Badische Bergstrasse/Kraichgau. (Gro) = Stiftsberg. (Vin) = Vogelsang.

Gemmrigheim (Ger). Village. (Anb) = Württemberg. (Ber) = Württembergisch Unterland. (Gro) = Schalkstein. (Vins) = Neckarberg, Wurmberg.

Genalpy (Fr). A herb-flavoured liqueur produced in Paris.

Genders Winery (Austr). A winery based in McLaren Vale, South Australia.

Génépi des Alpes (Switz). An orange-flavoured liqueur.

Générac (Fr). An area of vinification for V.D.Q.S. wines of the Costières du Gard, Languedoc, south-western France.

General Alvear (Arg). A wine-producing area in southern Argentina.

General Brewing (Can). A brewery based in Vancouver.

General Brewing Anchor Steam Beer (USA). A brewery based in San Francisco.

General Foods (Eng). A large company based at Ruscote Avenue, Banbury, Oxon. OX16 7QU. Produces a wide range of ground and instant coffes including Master Blend, Maxwell House and Mellow Bird's.

General Harrison's Egg Nogg (Cktl). 1 egg, sugar syrup to taste, juice of a lemon, fresh milk. Shake well over ice, strain into a highball glass, top with grated nutmeg.

Général Muteau (Fr). A cuvée in the vineyard of Volnay le Village, A.C. Volnay, Côte de Beaune, Burgundy. Is owned by the Hospices de Beaune. 0.8 ha.

General Sutter Kirsch (Switz). The brand-name used by the Nebiker Distillery based in Sissach.

Généreux (Fr). A generous wine. One with plenty of alcohol. A fortified sweet wine.

Generic (Eng). A wine name which is not related to the wine's origin. e.g. Vin rosé, sparkling wine. This term is also used to denote a district wine such as Saint-Émilion, Médoc etc. (Fr) = Générique.

Generic Bottling (Eng). A term that refers

G

to the bottling of wines from a specific area. e.g. Sauternes, Saint-Émilion, Graves, Médoc, etc.

Generic Wine (Eng). Wine sold under a commune name of an Appellation. e.g. Saint-Émilion, Sauternes, Graves etc.

Générique (Fr). Describes a regional A.O.C. wine that has no communal appellation or cru. (Eng) = Generic.

Generosos (Port). Strong, sweet wines such as Port, Madeira, Moscatel, Setúbal etc.

Generous (Eng). Denotes a wine that is rich and warm in vitality and alcohol.

Genesee (USA). A brewery in Rochester, New York. Produces American Cream Ale 4.7% alc. by vol. and Twelve Horse 5% alc. by vol.

Genesis Green (Eng). A vineyard based at Wickhambrook in Suffolk.

Geneva (Hol). The Dutch name for juniper and for Gin. See Jenever.

Geneva (Switz). The local name for the Chasselas grape which produces light and slightly sparkling wines.

Geneva (Switz). The smallest Canton. Produces mainly light, dry and slightly pétillant wines. Red wines are produced from the Gamay grape.

Geneva Double Curtain (Eng). A method of vine cultivation. High wire trellis system (vines are trained to height of 5 feet, allows optimum photosynthesis). G.D.C.

Genever (Hol). Juniper. The old name for Gin. See Geneva and Jenever.

Genever Coffee (Liq.Coffee). Melt a knob of butter in a pan and add ½ oz. castor sugar. Dissolve, then add 12 juniper berries. Flame with ⅕ gill Hollands gin and douse with ⅓ pint hot black coffee. Pour into mug and top with whipped cream.

Genevières (Les) (Fr). A Premier Cru vineyard of the A.C. commune of Morey-Saint-Denis, Côte de Nuits, Burgundy. 0.9 ha.

Genevrette (Fr). A wine made from juniper berries, drunk for medicinal purposes.

Genevrières-Dessous (Fr). A Premier Cru vineyard in the A.C. commune of Meursault, Côte de Beaune, Burgundy. 5.25 ha.

Genevrières-Dessus (Les) (Fr). A Premier Cru vineyard in the A.C. commune of Meursault, Côte de Beaune, Burgundy. 7.7 ha.

Gengenbach (Ger). Village. (Anb) = Baden. (Ber) = Ortenau. (Gro) = Fürsteneck. (Vins) = Kinzigtäler, Nollenköpfle.

Genheim (Ger). Village. (Anb) = Nahe.

(Ber) = Kreuznach. (Gro) = Schlosskapelle. (Vin) = Rossel.

Genièvre (Fr). Juniper. Old name for Gin.

Genippa (W.Ind). The brand-name of a white Rum sold by Duquesne in Martinique.

Genoa Cocktail (Cktl). ⅓ gill Grappa, ⅛ gill Sambuca, ⅛ gill dry Vermouth. Shake over ice, strain into an ice-filled balloon glass.

Genopy des Alpes (Fr). A digestive liqueur produced in Grenoble, eastern France.

Gensac-la-Pallue (Fr). A commune in the Charente Département whose grapes are classed Grande Champagne (Cognac).

Gensingen (Ger). Village. (Anb) = Rheinhessen. (Ber) = Bingen. (Gro) = Sankt Rochuskapelle. (Vin) = Goldberg.

Genté (Fr). A commune in the Grande Champagne district of Cognac, Charente.

Gentian (Eng). An ingredient in many herb liqueurs and apéritifs. Bitter in flavour, it possesses digestive properties.

Gentiane (Fr) (Switz). A bitter liqueur digestif made from gentian and spirits.

Gentil (Fr). A lesser white grape variety of the Pinot family grown in Alsace.

Gentil (Fr). No real legal definition. Old Alsace name for noble. Used for wines made with the Traminer and Gewürztraminer. Gentil Aromatique is the term now used for spicy wines.

Gentil Aromatique (Fr). An old name for the grape variety Gewürztraminer in Alsace.

Gentile-Groppellone (It). A variety of the red grape Groppello.

Gentilshommes de Fronsac (Fr). A wine brotherhood for the promotion of the wines of Fronsac, eastern Bordeaux.

Gentle (Eng). A term used to describe a wine as being unassertive and mild. Pleasant to drink.

Gentle Ben Cocktail (Cktl). ⅓ measure Vodka, ⅓ measure dry Gin, ⅓ measure Tequila. Shake over ice, strain into an ice-filled highball glass. Top with fresh orange juice, a slice of orange and a cherry.

Gentleman (USA). The brand-name of a Bourbon whiskey. 40% alc. by vol.

Gentling (Eng). A term to describe the maturing of wines in casks. Especially the hard tannic red wines of Spain.

Genuense (Lat). A white wine produced in north-western Italy during Roman times.

Geokchai (USSR). A major wine-producing centre in Azerbaijan.

G

George and Chestnut Teal (Austr). The brand-name of an Australian sherry.

George Dickel Tennessee Sour Mash (USA). A sour mash Whiskey produced by the George Dickel Cascade Distillery in Coffee County, Tennessee. Is filtered through activated charcoal, made from sugar maple wood.

George IV (Scot). A blended Scotch whisky produced by the DCL group. 43% alc. by vol.

George's (Wales). A large west Wales wholesaler who deals with Ansells Brewery. Has its' own keg bitter George's Best 1037 O.G. which is brewed in Burton-on-Trent.

Georges de Latour (USA). A private réserve Cabernet sauvignon wine produced by the Beaulieu Vineyards.

George's Home Brewed Ale (Eng). A Pale ale (bottled) 1042 O.G. brewed by Courage. Named after the Bristol Brewery that makes it.

Georgia (USA). A wine-producing state in south-eastern America. Produces mainly Concord and Muscadine wines.

Georgia (USSR). The main wine region between the Black and Caspian seas. Produces most styles of wines especially sparkling.

Georgia Mint Julep (Cktl). ⅓ measure Brandy, ⅔ measure Peach brandy, 1 teaspoon sugar, 2 sprigs mint. Crush mint and sugar together with a drop of water in a highball glass. Add ice and spirits, stir and dress with mint leaves. Serve with straws.

Georgian Rczaziteli (USSR). A white grape variety. See also Rcakzitelli.

Georg Scheu (Ger). A hybridiser who produced the Huxelrebe 1927 and the Scheurebe 1916.

Geradstetten (Ger). Village. (Anb) = Württemberg. (Ber) = Württembergisch Unterland. (Gro) = Wartbühl. (Vins) = Litchenberg, Sonnenberg.

Geranium Odour (Eng). A wine malady. Caused by the attack of Lactobacillus on sorbic acid. Occurs due to a lack of hygiene. Has a smell of Pelargonium.

Gérant (Fr). An agent in Bordeaux who is responsible for the sale of wine from a Château.

Gerard 157 (N.Z.). A white hybrid grape variety.

Gerebelt (Ger). Destalking of grapes.

Gerente (Sp). The name given to a Bodega manager.

Gerhardt (Jakob) (Ger). A wine grower and merchant based in Nierstein. Market wines of Staatliche Weinbaudomäne Rheinhessia (State-owned vineyard of Rheinhessia) plus many from northern Germany, France and other countries.

Gering (Ger). Rather poor wine.

Gerk (Yug). The alternative spelling of Grk.

Gerlachsheim (Ger). Village. (Anb) = Baden. (Ber) = Badische Frankenland. (Gro) = Tauberklinge. (Vin) = Herrenberg.

Gerlingen (Ger). Village. (Anb) = Württemberg. (Ber) = Remstal-Stuttgart. (Gro) = Weinsteige. (Vin) = Bopser.

Germain (Fr). A liqueur producer based in St. Florent sur Auzonnet, southern France. Famous for its' Auzonnet, Fine Lachamp, Gorges du Tarn, Ravanello and Vervine du Rouvergue liqueurs.

Germain (François) (Fr). A Burgundy négociant-éleveur based in Beaune, Côte de Beaune, Burgundy.

Germain (H. et Fils) (Fr). Champagne producer. Address = 36 Rue de Reims, 51500 Rilly La Montagne. 23 ha. Produces – Vintage and non-vintage wines. Vintages – 1971, 1973, 1975, 1976, 1979, 1981, 1982, 1983. De Luxe vintage cuvée Grande Cuvée Venus Brut.

Germain (Jean) (Fr). A négociant-éleveur based in Meursault, Côte d'Or, Burgundy. Address = 9, Rue la Barre, 21190 Meursault.

German Band Cocktail (Cktl). ⅓ gill Schnapps (Steinhäger), ⅙ gill Blackberry liqueur, dash bitters. Stir over ice, strain into a chilled cocktail glass.

German Coffee (Liq.Coffee). Using a measure of Kirsch.

German Gin (Ger). A light-flavoured Gin with a hint of sweetness.

German Purity Law (Ger). A 1516 law to control the production of beer. The Reinheitsgebot.

German Whiskey (Ger). A medium-flavoured Whiskey made from a variety of grains. Continuous stilled.

German Wine Academy (Ger). Kloster Eberbach. Address = 65 Mainz, Gutenbergplatz 3–5 P.O. Box 3860 Western Germany.

German Wine Academy (Ger). Kloster Eberbach. Address = c/o Riesburo A. Bartholomae, D-6200 Wiesbaden, Withelmstr 8. Germany.

German Wine Gate (Ger). See Deutsches Weintor.

German Wine Information Bureau (USA). Address = 99 Park Avenue-Third Floor, New York, N.Y. 10016.

German Wine Information Service (Can). Address = 20, Eglinton Ave East, Toronto, Ontario.

G

German Wine Information Service (Den). See Informations-Service for Tyske Vine.

German Wine Information Service (Eng). 121 Gloucester place, London W1H 3PJ.

German Wine Information Service (Ger). Deutsches Weininstitut. Address = Gutenbergplatz 3–5, 6500 Mainz, Western Germany.

German Wine Information Service (Jap). K.S. Building, 5, Kojimachi 4-Chome Chiyoda-ku, Tokyo 102.

German Wine Information Service (Swe). See Tysk Vin Information.

German Wine Law (Ger). Passed in 1971. Gave strict controls on the production and labelling of German wines.

German Wine Route (Ger). See Deutsche Weinstrasse.

Germany (Ger). The most northerly European wine-producing country. Produces mainly white wines which are, in the main, sweet in style. Some red wine is produced but this tends to be austere and is consumed locally. A sparkling wine called Sekt is also produced. See Anbaugebiet for regions.

Germignac (Fr). A commune in the Charente-Maritime Département whose grapes are classed Petite Champagne (Cognac).

Germigny (Fr). A Cru Champagne village in the Canton de Ville-en-Tardenois. District = Reims.

Germination (Eng). A term for barley as it sprouts shoots to convert the starch into fermentable sugars.

Gerolsheim (Ger). Village. (Anb) = Rheinpfalz. (Ber) = Mittelhaardt-Deutsche Weinstrasse. (Gro) = Schwarzerde. (Vins) = Klosterweg, Lerchenspiel.

Gerolsteiner (Ger). A naturally sparkling mineral water bottled at source.

Gerona (Sp). An area in the northern province which produces a variety of wine styles.

Geronimo (Cktl). 1 fl.oz. white Rum, 1 fl.oz. orange juice, 1 fl.oz. pineapple juice, ½ fl.oz. lime juice, dash Angostura, dash Grenadine. Shake well over ice. Strain into an ice-filled Collins glass. Dress with a slice of pineapple and orange.

Geropiga (Port). A natural Port or special liquid made to sweeten other Portuguese wines. Also spelt Jeropiga.

Gers (Fr). A département in south-western France. Most of the wine is used in the production of Armagnac or in blending.

Gerst (Hol). Barley.

Gerstel Lager (Hol). A low-alcohol Lager 0.8% alc. by vol. brewed by the Henninger Brauerei and imported into Britain by Courage.

Gertrudenberg (Ger). Vineyard. (Anb) = Mittelrhein. (Ber) = Rheinburgengau. (Gro) = Burg Hammerstein. (Vil) = Dattenberg.

Gerümpel (Ger). Vineyard. (Anb) = Rheinpfalz. (Ber) = Mittelhaardt-Deutsche Weinstrasse. (Gro) = Hofstück. (Vil) = Freidelsheim.

Gerümpel (Ger). Vineyard. (Anb) = Rheinpfalz. (Ber) = Mittelhaardt-Deutsche Weinstrasse. (Gro) = Mariengarten. (Vil) = Wachenheim.

Geschmack (Ger). A term meaning taste. e.g. Nachgeschmach = aftertaste.

Gesellschaft mit beschränkter Haftung (Ger). See GmbH.

Gesetz über Massnahmen auf dem Gebiete der Weinwirtschaft (Ger). Formed the Fond – law and regulations that govern German viticulture. Rules about setting up new plantations. (abbr) = Weinwirtschaftsgesetz.

Gestühl (Ger). Vineyard. (Anb) = Baden. (Ber) = Kaiserstuhl-Tuniberg. (Gro) = Vulkanfelsen. (Vil) = Jechtingen.

Gestühl (Ger). Village. (Anb) = Baden. (Ber) = Kaiserstuhl-Tuniberg. (Gro) = Vulkanfelsen. (Vin) = Leiselheim.

Getashan (USSR). A dessert wine produced in Armenia.

Getaufer (Ger). Watered wine.

Getränke (Ger). Drinks.

Geur (Hol). Aroma.

Gevrey-Chambertin (Fr). A top A.C. commune in the Côte de Nuits, Burgundy. Has 8 Grand Crus [Chambertin, Chambertin-Clos de Bèze, Chapelle-Chambertin, Charmes-Chambertin, Griotte-Chambertin, Latricières-Chambertin, Mazoyères-Chambertin and Mazys (Mazis)-Chambertin] 96.37 ha. plus 23 Premier Cru vineyards [Au Closeau, Aux Combottes, Bel-Air, Champeaux, Champitennois (or Petite Chapelle), Champonnet, Cherbaudes, Clos du Chapitre, Clos-Prieur, Clos Saint-Jacques, Combeau-Moine, Craipillot, En Ergot, Étournelles, Issarts (or Plantigone), La Perrière, Lavaut, Le Fonteny, Les Cazetiers, Les Corbeaux, Les Goulots, Poissenot and Varoilles] 83.61 ha.

Gewächs (Ger). Vineyard of.

Geweerloop (Hol). Barrel, or vat.

Gewoon (Hol). Lit – 'Normal'. A term used to denote a 25 cls. glass.

Gewürz (Ger). Means spicy. Applied to a variety of the Traminer grape called the Gewürztraminer.

G

Gewürzgartchen (Ger). Vineyard. (Anb) = Rheinhessen. (Ber) = Bingen. (Gro) = Sankt Rochuskapelle. (Vil) = Horrweiler.

Gewürzgarten (Ger). Vineyard. (Anb) = Rheinhessen. (Ber) = Bingen. (Gro) = Rheingrafenstein. (Vil) = Hackenheim.

Gewürztraminer (Ger). A white grape variety that produces spicy wines. First produced in the Trentino-Alto Adige and now used in the Rhine, Alsace, Austria and New World.

Geyer Brewery (USA). A brewery based in Frankenmuth, Michigan. Is noted for its' Krausened beers that are fermented in open iron tanks.

Geyersberg (Ger). Vineyard. (Anb) = Rheinhessen. (Ber) = Bingen. (Gro) = Abtey. (Vil) = Sankt Johann.

Geyersberg (Ger). Vineyard. (Anb) = Rheinhessen. (Ber) = Bingen. (Gro) = Kurfürstenstück. (Vil) = Gau-Weinheim.

Geyersberg (Ger). Vineyard. (Anb) = Rheinhessen. (Ber) = Wonnenegau. (Gro) = Gotteshilfe. (Vil) = Bechtheim.

Geyser Peak (USA). A large winery based in Sonoma County, California. 166 ha. Produces a range of wine styles from a large variety of grapes. Also owns vineyards in the Russian River Valley.

Geyserville (USA). A noted wine town in the Alexander Valley, Sonoma County, California.

Gezuckert (Ger). Sugared. i.e. Verbessert, or improved.

Gharb (Afr). A wine-producing region in Morocco. Contains the A.O.G. areas of Chellah, Gharb, Zaer and Zemmour. Soil – sandy.

Gharb (Afr). A.O.G. area within the region of Gharb in Morocco.

Ghemme (It). D.O.C. red wine from Piemonte. Made from the Bonardo novarese 15%, Nebbiolo 60–80% and Vespolina 10–30%. Has to age 4 years (3 years in oak/chestnut cask).

Gherardi (Austr). A winery based in the Margaret River region of Western Australia.

Ghezala (Afr). A noted co-operative based in Tunisia. One of 14 that belongs to the UCCVT.

Ghioroc (Rum). A wine-producing area, part of the Banat Vineyard.

Ghirgentina (Euro). A white grape variety grown on the island of Malta. Known as the Inzolia in Sicily.

Ghurdjurni (USSR). A white table wine produced in the region of Georgia.

Gianaclis Vineyard (Egy). A noted winery based at Abú-Hummus, northwest of the Nile Delta. Produces mainly white wines with a little red. See Cru des Ptolemées and Reine Cléopatre (both white wines).

Giascosa Bruno (It). A large winery based in Piemonte. Noted for its' Barbaresco, Barbera d'Alba, Barolo and Nebbiolo d'Alba wines.

Gibberellic Acid (Eng). A sugar-based natural acid which is added to barley that has been steeped in water to encourage embryo development in the malting process.

Gibbons (USA). The brand-name used by the Lion Brewery in Wilkes-Barre, Pennsylvania for a range of their beers.

Gibbs Mew (Eng). A brewery based in Salisbury, Wiltshire. Also owns Seymour soft drinks in Sherbourne, Dorset. Noted for its' cask conditioned Wiltshire Bitter 1036 O.G. Salisbury Best 1042 O.G. Bishop's Tipple 1066 O.G. Chairman's Choice 1039 O.G. Moonraker Brown 1032 O.G. and Sarum Special 1048 O.G.

Gibier (Fr). Lit – 'Game'. A term used to denote old red wines that have oxidised slightly, 'ripe or well hung'.

Gibó (It). The name used by Giovanni Bosca for a range of Vermouths, Marsalas and sparkling wines.

Giboudot Blanc (Fr). A lesser name for the Aligoté grape in southern France.

Gibson (Cktl). ⅔ measure dry Gin, ⅓ measure dry Vermouth. Stir together with ice, strain into a cocktail glass. Add a pearl onion. Another version has a piece of garlic in place of the onion!

Gibson Vineyards (USA). A winery based in Fresno, California. Produces generic table and dessert wines which are sold under the Château Moreau, Cresta Bella and Gibson Vineyards labels.

Giebelhöll (Ger). Vineyard. (Anb) = Mittelrhein. (Ber) = Rheinburgengau. (Gro) = Lahntal. (Vil) = Weinähr.

Giesler (Fr). Champagne producer. Produces – Vintage and non-vintage wines. Vintages – 1900, 1904, 1906, 1911, 1914, 1921, 1926, 1928, 1934, 1937, 1941, 1943, 1945, 1947, 1949, 1952, 1953, 1955, 1959, 1961, 1962, 1964, 1966, 1969, 1970, 1971, 1973, 1975, 1978, 1982.

Gieten (Hol). Pour.

Giffard (Fr). A distillery based in Anjou-Saumur, Loire. Produces liqueurs. Noted for its' Menthe Pastille and Peppermint Pastille.

Giggle Water (USA) (slang). A term used for Champagne or other sparkling wines. Especially in the 1920's-1930's.

Gigondas (Fr). A.C. district of the Rhône. Produces red, rosé and white wines. Reds are full-bodied.

457

Gilbey Canada Ltd (Can). A large distillery which produces a range of Canadian whiskies etc. Pallister Distillers is a subsidiary company.

Gilbey Distillers and Vintners (S.Afr). See Gilbeys Ltd.

Gilbey [S.A.] (Fr). Bordeaux négociant-éleveurs and owners of Château Loudenne.

Gilbeys Ltd (S.Afr). A large wine merchant based in Stellenbosch. Address = Gilbeys Distillers and Vintners, Box 137, Stellenbosch 7600. Wines sold under a large variety of labels such as Alphen, Bertrams, Klein Zalze, Montagne, etc. A subsidiary of W & A Gilbey, London.

Gilbey Vintners (Eng). A distillery based in Harlow, Essex. Produces a range of spirits including Gin and Smirnoff Vodka (under licence from the USA). See also Gilbey [W.A].

Gilbey [W.A.] (Eng). A large wines and spirits merchants. Address = Gilbey House, Fourth Avenue, Harlow Essex. CM20 1DX. (Part of IDV).

Gilde de Saint-Vincent de Belgique (Bel). A wine brotherhood.

Gildenbier (Bel). A Münchener-style dark beer brewed at the Diest Brasserei. Is matured for 9 months.

Gilde Taffel (Nor). The brand-name of an Akvavit produced by the A/S Vinmonopolet.

Giles Vineyard (USA). A small independent vineyard based in Sonoma County, California. 2.5 ha. Grape variety – Chardonnay.

Gilka Kümmel (Ger). A caraway and cumin-flavoured liqueur made in Berlin. 40% alc. by vol.

Gill (Eng). 5 fl.ozs. ¼ imperial pint.

Gill (Eng) (slang). "Let's go for a gill". A term used in the north for "Let's go for a drink". Used to mean '½ pint of beer'.

Gille (Fr). A mediaeval word for vat, tub.

Gillenza (Euro). A black grape variety grown on the island of Malta. Is known as the Mammolo in Italy.

Gillet (Jean-Pierre) (Fr). A producer of sparkling Vouvray based at Parcay-Meslay, Loire.

Gillies and Co (Scot). A company based in Glasgow. Produces Royal Culross (a Vatted malt whisky).

Gill Measure (Eng). Graded to allow the measuring of such fractions as ½ gill, ⅓ gill, ¼ gill, ⅕ gill and ⅙ gill.

Gilon (Isr). A sweet, dark, dessert wine which is similar in style to Málaga.

Gilroy (USA). A vine-growing district in southern Santa Clara, California.

Gilroy Cocktail (Cktl). ½ measure Gin, ½ measure Cherry brandy, juice ¼ lemon, dash Orange bitters, 4 dashes dry Vermouth. Shake well over ice, strain into a cocktail glass.

Gilt Edge (Austr). The brand-name of a Whiskey produced by Gilbeys.

Gimbsheim (Ger). Village. (Anb) = Rheinhessen. (Ber) = Nierstein. (Gro) = Krötenbrunnen. (Vins) = Liebfrauenthal, Sonnenweg.

Gimeux (Fr). A commune based in the Charente-Maritime Département whose grapes are classed Grande Champagne (Cognac).

Gimileo (Sp). A wine-producing village in the Rioja Alta, north-eastern Spain.

Gimlet (Cktl). ⅔ measure dry Gin, ⅓ measure lime juice cordial. Shake over ice, strain into an ice-filled highball glass, add a good splash of soda.

Gimlet (Eng). A sharp, pointed metal implement used to penetrate casks and often used to remove corks from bottles. (Fr) = Foret.

Gimmeldingen (Ger). Village. (Anb) = Rheinpfalz. (Ber) = Mittelhaardt-Deutsche Weinstrasse. (Gro) = Meerspinne. (Vins) = Biengarten, Kapellenberg, Mandelgarten, Schlössel.

Gimonnet (Pierre et Fils) (Fr). Champagne producer. Address = 1 Rue de la République, 51200 Épernay. Récoltants-manipulants. Produces – Vintage and non-vintage wines. A member of the C.V.C.

Gin (Eng). The rectified neutral spirit distilled from any grain, potato or beet. Flavoured with Juniper. See London Dry, Plymouth Dry and Old Tom. (Fr) = Genièvre, (Ger) = Wacholder-Schnaps, (Hol) = Jenever, (It) = Ginepro, (Port) = Genebra, (Sp) = Ginebra, (Wales) = Jin.

Gin Acts (Eng). First passed in 1736. Was designed to help reduce the amount of Gin shops and to make the spirit too expensive for the working classes to drink. It put a tax on Gin and introduced the need for a licence to sell spirits.

Gin Alexander (Cktl). Also known as Princess Mary. See Alexander.

Gin Aloha (Cktl). ½ measure dry Gin, ½ measure Cointreau, ⅛ gill pineapple juice, dash Orange bitters. Shake well over ice, strain into a cocktail glass.

Gin and Bitters (Cktl). See Pink Gin.

Gin and French (Cktl). ½ measure of dry Gin and ½ measure of French (dry white) vermouth. Stir over ice, strain into a cocktail glass.

Gin and It (Cktl). ½ measure dry Gin and ½ measure Italian (sweet red) vermouth. Stir over ice, strain into a cocktail glass. Top with a cocktail cherry.

Gin and Sin (Cktl). ⅕ gill dry Gin, ⅕ gill lemon juice, ⅛ gill orange juice, dash Grenadine. Shake over ice, strain into a cocktail glass.

Gin and Tansy (Eng). Is produced by macerating a bunch of tansy in a bottle of Gin for 3–4 weeks. Serve 'On the rocks'.

Gin and Tonic (Cktl). 1 measure of dry Gin placed into an ice-filled highball glass. Top with soda water and a slice of lemon.

Gin Aurum (Cktl). ³⁄₁₀ measure Aurum, ⁴⁄₁₀ measure Gin, ³⁄₁₀ measure lemon juice, dash Grenadine. Shake over ice, strain into a cocktail glass.

Gin Buck (Cktl). ⅕ gill dry Gin, juice ½ lemon. Place into an ice-filled highball glass, stir, top with ginger ale.

Gin Cobbler (Cktl). Gin, barspoon sugar, 4 dashes orange Curaçao. Fill a medium sized wine glass with ice. Add a measure of Gin, sugar and Curaçao, stir, decorate with fruit. Add a sprig of mint. Serve with straws.

Gin Cocktail (Cktl).(1). ⅓ gill Gin, 2 dashes brown Curaçao, 1 dash Angostura bitters. Stir over ice, strain into a cocktail glass, decorate with a cherry and a dash of lemon peel juice.

Gin Cocktail (Cktl).(2). 2 measures Gin, 3 dashes Orange bitters. Shake over ice, strain into a cocktail glass. Add a twist of orange peel.

Gin Cooler (Cktl). Place ½ teaspoon powdered sugar and 2 fl.ozs. soda water into a collins glass, stir, add ice and ⅓ gill dry Gin. Top with soda water and decorate with a spiral of orange peel and lemon peel.

Gin Crusta (Cktl). ⅓ gill dry Gin, 1 teaspoon Maraschino, 1 dash Angostura, 1 dash orange bitters, 1 teaspoon syrup. Shake over ice, strain, moisten inside of wine glass with lemon juice and with ½ teaspoon of sugar, serve with spiral of lemon peel and slices of fresh fruit.

Gin Daisy (Cktl). ½ gill dry Gin, ⅛ gill lemon juice, ⅛ gill Grenadine. Shake over ice, strain into a highball glass and fill with soda water. Serve with slices of fresh fruit.

Gin de Prunelles (Ch.Isles). Sloe Gin. See also Du Gin de Prunelles.

Ginder (Bel). A beer (Abbaye-style) brewed by the Artois Brasserei in Louvain.

Ginebra (Sp). Gin.

Ginepro (It). Gin (juniper).

Ginepy (It). A green or white liqueur with an anise flavour.

Ginestet (Fr). Bordeaux négociants.

Gin Fix (Cktl). 2½ fl.ozs. Gin, 1 fl.oz. lemon juice, teaspoon Gomme syrup. Build into a wine goblet filled with crushed ice. Stir lightly. Add a slice of lemon, serve with straws.

Gin Fizz (Cktl). 1½ ozs. dry Gin, 1 teaspoon sugar. Stir together with ice until sugar has dissolved. Top up with soda water in a highball glass.

Ginger Ale (Eng). Carbonated water, ginger extract and sugar. Is non-alcoholic. e.g. American Dry, Canada Dry, Dry ginger, etc.

Ginger Ale Cup (Cktl). 1 quart ginger ale, 1 tablespoon sugar, ½ gill Brandy, ¼ gill lime juice, ¼ gill Maraschino, 2–3 dashes Bénédictine. Stir over ice, strain. Serve in a highball glass with lemon/orange slices and sprigs of mint.

Ginger Beer (Eng). Ginger, sugar, water and yeast. Fermented. Cream of tartar, tataric acid or lemon essence may be included. Alcohol content is below 2% by vol.

Ginger Brandy (Eng). A ginger-flavoured Brandy. Has a deep, tawny colour.

Ginger Fizz (Cktl).(Non-alc). ½ pint cold tea, juice of an orange and ½ a lemon, sugar to taste, ginger ale. Stir together over ice. Decorate with a slice of orange.

Ginger Flavoured Brandy (USA). A brandy based liqueur infused with ginger root.

Ginger Highball (Cktl). ⅓ gill Bourbon whiskey stirred over ice in a highball glass, top with ginger ale and a piece of ginger root.

Ginger Liqueur (Hol). Made from ginger roots steeped in spirit.

Ginger Mist Cocktail (Cktl). 2 measures Irish Mist in an ice-filled highball glass. Top with ginger ale and a squeeze of lemon peel juice.

Ginger Rum Tea (Cktl). Pour ⅕ gill dark Rum into a cup of black tea. Top with a piece of preserved ginger. Can be served hot or cold.

Ginger Square (Cktl). 1 fl.oz. Ginger brandy, 1 fl.oz. ginger ale. Stir both together, build into an ice-filled highball glass.

Ginger Tea (Eng). See Cold Ginger Tea.

Ginger Wine (Eng). A grape wine base with ginger and spices, herbs and fruits added. See Crabbie's and Stones.

Gin Gin (Cktl). Equal measures of Booth's Gin, Crabbie's Green Ginger Wine and orange squash. Shake over ice, strain into a large cocktail glass.

Ginginha (Port). Fruit wines.

Gin Head (Eng). A unit at the point where freshly distilled vapours have to pass through. Is packed with juniper and botanicals, the flavour of which is extracted by the vapour as it passes through.

Gin Highball (Cktl). ⅙ gill Gin, ⅙ gill soda water. Place a lump of ice into a highball, add Gin and soda, serve with slice of lemon.

Gini (Bel). A lemon and tonic drink produced by Boire Citron Français in 20 cls. cans.

Ginjinha (Port). Cherry brandy.

Gin Julep (Cktl). As for Mint Julep but substituting Gin for Brandy.

Gin Lane (Eng). The name of Hogarth's famous eighteenth century painting depicting the degradation of gin drinking of the age.

Gin Long Drink (Fin). A Gin and grapefruit drink.

Gin Milk Punch (Cktl). 2 fl.ozs. dry Gin, ⅓ pint milk, 1 teaspoon powdered sugar. Shake over ice, strain into a collins glass. Top with grated nutmeg.

Gin Palace (Eng). An eighteenth and early nineteenth century name given to the more respectable public houses of the time.

Gin Punch (Punch). ½ pint Gin, ¼ pint Maraschino, juice of 3 lemons, Blend together, chill, serve in chilled highball glasses with ice and top with soda water. Dress with a lemon peel spiral.

Gin Ricky (Cktl).(1). 1 measure dry Gin, juice of 1 lime. Build into an ice-filled old-fashioned glass. Add spent lime shell. Stir in soda water.

Gin Ricky (Cktl).(2). 2 ozs. dry Gin, juice ½ lemon. Place ice into a small tumbler, stir in ingredients. Add rind of lemon, top with soda water.

Gin Sangaree (Cktl). Dissolve a ½ teaspoon of powdered sugar in a teaspoon of water in a highball glass. Add ice and 2 fl.ozs. Gin. Top with soda water and float ⅛ gill Port on top. Dress with grated nutmeg.

Ginseng Ju (E.Asia). A liqueur produced by Jinro of Seoul, South Korea. Has a large piece of ginseng root in each bottle.

Ginseng Piu Chiew (E.Asia). A type of Choum. Infused with a root native to North Vietnam. Various types – Ruou Cuc (chrysanthemum), Ruou Tam (slightly sparkling) and Ruou Tiêt dê (alcohol and goat's blood).

Ginseng Ruou Cuc (E.Asia). See Ginseng Piu Chiew.

Ginseng Ruou Tam (E.Asia). See Ginseng Piu Chiew.

Ginseng Ruou Tiêt Dê (E.Asia). See Ginseng Piu Chiew.

Ginseng Tea (E.Asia). A tisane produced from the Ginseng root. Is drunk for its aphrodisiac properties.

Gin Sling (Cktl). Add to a large tumbler containing a large piece of ice, juice ¾ lemon, ½ tablespoon powdered sugar, 1 measure Gin. Top with water, float a dash of Angostura on top. Decorate with a slice of lemon.

Gin Sling [Hot] (Cktl). Dissolve a sugar cube in ¼ pint hot water in an old-fashioned glass. Add 1 measure dry Gin, stir, top with grated nutmeg and a lemon slice.

Gin Smash (Cktl). Dissolve a little sugar in 1 measure of water, 1 measure Gin, 3 sprigs of mint and ice. Shake well together, strain into a wine glass, dress with fruit in season and serve with a spoon.

Gin Sour (Cktl). 2 ozs. Gin, juice ½ lemon, ½ teaspoon sugar, dash egg white. Shake well with ice, strain into a cocktail glass.

Gin Squirt (Cktl). 1 measure dry Gin, 1 teaspoon Grenadine, 1 teaspoon Gomme syrup. Stir over ice, strain into an ice-filled highball glass. Top with soda water and dress with a pineapple cube and a fresh strawberry.

Gin Swizzle (Cktl). 1 fl.oz. Gin, ½ fl.oz. lime juice, 2 dashes Gomme syrup, 2 dashes Angostura. Build into a 12 oz. glass filled with crushed ice. Fill glass with soda water, serve with a small swizzle stick.

Gin Thing (Cktl). 1 measure dry Gin, juice ½ lime. Pour into an ice-filled highball glass, stir, top with ginger ale.

Gin Toddy (Cktl). Place ½ teaspoon sugar and 2 teaspoons water into a highball glass. Stir, add 2 fl.ozs. dry Gin and ice cubes. Stir, add a twist of lemon peel juice.

Gin Toddy [Hot] (Cktl). Place a sugar cube into an old-fashioned glass, fill ⅔ with boiling water. Add 2 fl.ozs. dry Gin, slice of lemon and top with grated nutmeg.

Gin Tropical (Cktl). ¾ measure Gin, ½ measure passion fruit juice, juice ¼ orange and lemon. Shake over ice, strain into an ice-filled highball glass. Top with soda water, stir, add a dash of blue Curaçao. Dress with a cherry and serve with straws.

Giol (Arg). A large state-owned co-operative in the province of Maipú. Deals with bulk wines and has a premium range under the Canciller label.

Gipfel (Ger). Grosslage. (Anb) = Mosel-Saar-Ruwer. (Ber) = Obermosel. (Vils) = Bitzengen, Fellerich, Fisch, Helfant-Esingen, Kirf, Köllig, Kreuzweiler, Meurich, Nittel, Oberbillig, Onsdorf, Palzem, Portz, Rehlingen, Soest, Tawern, Tammels, Wasserliesch, Wehr, Wellen, Wincheringen.

Gips (Ger). Vineyard. (Anb) = Württem-

G

berg. (Ber) = Remstal-Stuttgart. (Gro) = Weinsteige. (Vil) = Fellbach.

Gips (Ger). Vineyard. (Anb) = Württemberg. (Ber) = Remstal-Stuttgart. (Gro) = Weinsteige. (Vil) = Stuttgart (ortsteil Untertürkheim).

Gipsy (Cktl).(1). ⅓ measure Bénédictine, ⅔ measure Vodka, dash Angostura. Shake over ice, strain into a cocktail glass.

Gipsy (Cktl).(2). ¼ measure Mandarine Napoléon, ¾ measure Cognac, ¾ measure dry Gin, ¾ measure Cherry brandy. Shake together with ice in a highball glass. Top with tonic water and garnish with a slice of orange and a cherry.

Gipsy's Brew (Punch). 1 pint Gin, 1 quart Ale, 2 x 6 inch roots horseradish. Mix Gin and Ale, grate in horseradish. Stand for 3 days. Strain and bottle. Good for arthritis.

Girardin Brasserei (Bel). A brewery based in St-Ulricks-Kapelle in northern Belgium. Noted for its' fruity Lambic beers.

Girasols (Sp). Metal racks which are mechanical and replace the old pupîtres which were operated by hand (remuage). Used for all méthode champenoise in Spain. See Crécelle, Giro-Palettes and Gyropalettes. Holds 540 bottles. Lit − 'Sunflower'.

Giraud (Paul) (Fr). Cognac producer. Address = Bouteville, 16120 Châteauneuf. 28 ha. in the Grande Champagne. Produces a wide range of Cognacs.

Girault-Artois (Fr). A Crémant de Loire producer based at Amboise, Loire.

Girelli (It). A producer of sparkling (méthode champenoise) wines based in Veneto.

Girgentina (Euro). A white grape variety grown on the island of Malta. Also known as the Insolia.

Girl's Wines (Eng). Usually applied to the sweet white wines such as Sauternes and Barsac. See Lady's Wine.

Girò (It). A red grape variety grown in Sardinia, produces sweet, soft, velvety still and dessert wines.

Girò di Cagliari (It). D.O.C. red wine from Sardinia. Made from the Girò grape in the province of Cagliari. Vinification and ageing must occur in the region. 4 types produced − Dolce naturale, Secco, Liquoroso dolce naturale and Liquoroso secco. The last two are fortified and if aged for 2 years (1 year in wood) then classed Riserva. Grapes can dry on vines or on frames.

Girò di Sardegna (It). A red dessert wine of Sardinia.

Gironde [River] (Fr). A river in western France in the Bordeaux region. Is made up of the rivers Dordogne and Garonne and runs to the Bay of Biscay. Has the Médoc along its' west bank.

Girone (It). A name used in Sardinia for the Bovale grande red grape.

Giro-Pallets (Eng). The name for the automatic remueurs. See also Crécelle and Gyropalettes.

Giro-Palettes (Fr). The name for the Crécelle (automatic remueur). See also Girasols and Gyropalettes.

Girrawheen (Austr). A winery based in the Granite Belt, Queensland.

Girvan Distillery (Scot). A Grain whisky distillery based in south-west Scotland.

Gisborne (N.Z.). An area on the east coast of the North Island.

Gisselbrecht (Louis) (Fr). An Alsace wine producer. Address = Dambach-la-Ville. 5 ha.

Gist (Hol). Yeast.

Gisten (Hol). Ferment.

Gisting (Hol). Fermentation.

Gitana (La) (Sp). A brand of Manzanilla sherry produced by Vinícola Hidalgo in Sanlúcar de Barrameda.

Giumarra Vineyards (USA). A winery based near Bakersfield, Kern County, California. 1,660 ha. Grape varieties − Cabernet sauvignon, Chardonnay and Zinfandel. Produces varietal wines.

Giustina-Leitac (It). See Leitacher.

G.I.V. (It) (abbr). Gruppo Italiano Vini.

G.I.VI.S.O. (Fr) (abbr). Groupement d'Intérêt Économique des Vignerons du Sud-Ouest.

Givreur (Le) (Bel). An automatic 'glass froster'. Frosts drinking glasses so enhancing presentation. Imported by Nimrod International Ltd. 124, Mount Street, Berkeley Square, London W1Y 5HA.

Givry (Fr). A district within the Côte Chalonnaise in southern Burgundy. Produces A.C. red wines from the Pinot noir grape and some white wines.

Givry-les-Loisy (Fr). A Cru Champagne village in the Canton de Vertus. District = Reims.

G.L. (Fr) (abbr). Gay Lussac.

G.L.A.A.S. (Eng) (abbr). Greater London Alcohol Advisory Service. With Alcohol Concern ran a campaign of 'Think before you drink' to promote moderate drinking in the early 1980's.

Glace (A la) (Fr). A method of dégorgement using dry ice to freeze the wine in the neck of the bottle. See also Volée (À la).

Glacé (Fr). Chilled.

Glacial Moraine (Eng). A soil containing medium and large boulders which were deposited during the Ice Age.

Glacier Mint (Cktl). 1 dash P.L.J., 1 fl.oz. Vodka, ½ fl.oz. (green) Crème de Menthe. Stir with ice, strain into a sugar-rimmed glass, decorate with a sprig of mint.

Glad Eye (Cktl). ⅓ gill Absinthe Pernod, ¼ gill Peppermint Get. Shake well over ice, strain into a cocktail glass.

Glamour Cocktails (Eng). The name given to colourful cocktails designed for female and young drinkers that are usually decorated with toys and trimmings as part of the garnish.

Glan Usk (Wales). A dry Gin produced in south Powys.

Glasgow Flip (Cktl). See Lover's Dream.

Glass (Ire). A term used for a half pint of beer.

Glass (Eng). A clear vessel used for holding cold beverages for drinking. The clearness of the glass allows the full appreciation of the drink's colours and its shape will help in the appreciation of the bouquet. See Crystal Glass.

Glass Balloon (USA). The American name for the vacuum method of coffee brewing.

Glass Cloth (Eng). A soft cloth made of linen used for the drying and polishing of drinking glasses.

Glass Excise Acts (Eng). 1745. A tax levied on glass according to the weight of materials used in manufacture. Glass became light and elegant. See Rococo.

Glassing (Eng) (slang). A term used for the action of pushing a beer glass into the face of an opponent in a public house brawl.

Glass of Beer (Eng). A request for a ½ pint of Draught ale (Mild or Bitter).

Glass Ring (Eng). Found on the neck of early flasks or decanters so that the cork could be secured with string.

Glastwr (Wales). Milk and water.

Glatt (Ger). Smooth.

Glatzen (Ger). Vineyard. (Anb) = Franken. (Ber) = Maindreieck. (Gro) = Kirchberg. (Vil) = Neuses.

Glayva (Scot). A Whisky-based liqueur flavoured with herbs and spices. 40% alc. by vol.

Glayva Belgravia Special (Cktl). 1 measure Glayva, 1 measure dry Vermouth. Stir with ice in a highball glass. Top up with Cola, finish with a slice of lemon.

Glayva Celebration (Cktl). 1 oz. Glayva, 1 oz. Passion fruit juice. Stir together with ice, strain into a flute glass. Top with iced Champagne.

Glayva Champagne Cocktail (Cktl). Soak a cube of sugar with Angostura in a highball glass. Add ½ fl.oz. Glayva and top with iced, dry Champagne.

Glayva Champagne Punch (Punch). ⅕ pint Glayva, ⅕ pint Cognac, ⅕ pint Maraschino, ½ lb. sugar, 2 pints Perrier water, 2 pints Champagne. Mix together in a punch bowl over ice. Add fruits in season.

Glayva Ciderific (Cktl). Bring 2 pints Cider to the boil, remove from the heat and add ⅖ gill Glayva. Pour into mugs, add a knob of butter, lemon slice, cinnamon stick and clove to each mug.

Glayva Cider Punch (Punch). 3 fl.ozs. Glayva, 2 pints chilled sweet Cider, ⅓ pint soda water, 3 fl.ozs. dry Sherry, 1 fl.oz. lemon juice. Mix together in a punch bowl over ice. Flavour with nutmeg and sugar and decorate with apple slices and borage.

Glayva Collins (Cktl). 1 oz. Glayva, 4 ozs. soda water, 2 ozs. lemon juice, ½ oz. Gomme syrup. Place ingredients into an ice-filled 10 oz. highball glass. Stir, top with soda water, lemon slice. Serve with straws.

Glayva Gleam (Cktl). ⅕ gill Glayva, ⅛ gill orange Curaçao, ½ egg white, dash lemon juice. Shake well over ice, strain into a cocktail glass.

Glayva Highball (Cktl). Pour 1 fl.oz. Glayva into an ice-filled highball glass. Stir in 4 fl.ozs. dry ginger ale. Top with a twist of lemon.

Glayva Horse's Neck (Cktl). Place 1 fl.oz. Glayva in a 10 oz. Slim Jim glass with a lemon peel spiral inside. Top with ginger ale and a dash of Angostura.

Glayva Hot Toddy (Cktl). Place a teaspoon of brown sugar and 1 measure of Glayva into a ½ pint mug. Top with boiling water, stir, add a lemon slice and a teaspoonful of honey.

Glayva Iceberg (Cktl). In a 10 oz. Slim Jim glass place some ice and 1½ fl.ozs. Glayva. Stir in chilled milk, top with grated nutmeg.

Glayva Mai Tai (Cktl). 1 oz. golden Rum, 1 oz. white Rum, ½ oz. Glayva, ¼ oz. lime juice, dash Grenadine. Build into a large, ice-filled old-fashioned glass. Decorate with a cherry and mint. Serve with straws.

Glayva Old Fashioned (Cktl). Place a sugar cube in an old-fashioned glass. Soak with Angostura, add enough water to dissolve the sugar. Fill with ice, add ⅕ gill Glayva, dress with an orange slice and a cherry.

Glayva Passion (Cktl). ⅓ measure Glayva, ⅓ measure Scotch whisky, ⅓ measure Passion fruit juice. Shake over ice, strain into a large cocktail glass.

Glayva Sour (Cktl). 1½ fl.ozs. Glayva, 2 fl.ozs. lemon juice, ½ oz. sugar, dash egg white. Shake over ice, strain into an ice-filled large goblet.

Glayva Sunset (Cktl). 1 oz. Glayva, 1 oz. Amaretto, 4 ozs. orange juice. Shake together over ice, strain into a 10 oz. Slim Jim glass. Add a dash Grenadine and an orange slice. Serve with straws.

Glayva Tammy (Cktl). ½ measure Glayva, ½ measure Glenlivet malt whisky. Stir with ice in an old-fashioned glass. Dress with a twist of lemon peel juice.

Glayva Tropical Punch (Punch). 2 bottles Glayva, 1¼ pints Passion fruit juice, 1¼ pints orange juice, ¼ pint lemon squash. Mix together and chill for 2 hours. Pour into a punch bowl with ice, add 2 pints Perrier water and fruit in season.

Gleisweiler (Ger). Village. (Anb) = Rheinpfalz. (Ber) = Südliche Weinstrasse. (Gro) = Bischofskreuz. (Vin) = Hölle.

Gleiszellen-Gleishorbach (Ger). Village. (Anb) = Rheinpfalz. (Ber) = Südliche Weinstrasse. (Gro) = Kloster Liebfrauenberg. (Vins) = Frühmess, Kirchberg.

Glen Albyn (Scot). A single Malt whisky distillery on the banks of the Caledonian canal basin. Owned by MacKinleys and Birnie Ltd. Produce a 15 year old whisky at 45% alc. by vol. A Highland malt.

Glenallachie (Scot). A single Malt whisky distillery based north-west of Dufftown. A Highland malt whisky 12 years old. 43% alc. by vol. Part of Charles MacKinlay & Co.

Glenalwyn (Austr). A winery based in the Swan Valley, Western Australia.

Glenburgie-Glenlivet (Scot). A single Malt whisky distillery. Owned by J.and C. Stodart Ltd. Produce a 16 year old whisky at 45% alc. by vol. A Highland malt. (Part of Hiram Walker).

Glenburn (N.Z.). A small winery in the Kumeu area of Riverhead.

Glencadam (Scot). A single Malt whisky distillery based near to the river Esk, half a mile out of Brechen. Owned by Hiram Walker Group. Produces a 14 year old whisky. 45% alc. by vol. A Highland malt.

Glen Calder Fine Old Scotch Whisky (Scot). A De Luxe Scotch Whisky which is blended by Gordon and MacPhail of Elgin.

Glencoe (Scot). A Vatted malt whisky. Produced by R.N. MacDonald & Co. 8 year old. 56% alc. by vol.

Glen Deveron (Scot). A single Malt whisky distillery owned by William Lawson. A Highland malt whisky. Produce a 5 and 10 year old malt Whisky. 43% alc. by vol.

Glendeveron (Scot). Another name for the malt whisky MacDuff.

Glen Distilleries of Cork (Ire). A distilling company based in Cork, Eire that closed in 1925.

Glendronach (Scot). A single Malt whisky distillery based in the valley of Forgue, 9 miles from Huntley in Aberdeenshire. Owned by William Teacher and Sons Ltd. 8 year old. A Highland malt.

Glen Drummond (Scot). A Vatted malt whisky. Blended Speyside malts. Produced by Melrose-Drover of Leith.

Glendullan (Scot). A single Malt whisky distillery based at Dufftown. A Highland malt whisky. Part of MacDonald Greenlees,

Glen Elgin (Austr). An estate belonging to Tulloch Vineyards based near Polkobin, New South Wales.

Glen Elgin (Scot). A single Malt whisky distillery near Longmorn, Elgin in Morayshire. Owned by White Horse Distilleries. Produce an 8 year and 12 year old malt whisky 43% alc. by vol. A Highland malt. (Part of the DCL group).

Glen Ellen (USA). A noted wine town in the Sonoma Valley, California.

Glen Ellen Winery (USA). A small winery based in the Sonoma Valley, California. 13.5 ha. Grape variety – Cabernet sauvignon.

Glenesk (Scot). A single Malt whisky distillery from the Hillside Distillery, near Montrose, Angus. Produce a 12 year old whisky. A Highland malt. Licence held by William Sanderson & Son.

Glenfarclas (Scot). A single Malt whisky distillery based near Marypark, Ballindalloch in Banffshire. Owned by J. and G. Grant. Produces – 8 year old, 12 year old, 15 year old, 21 year old and a 25 year old – all at 40% alc. by vol. A Highland malt. Also known as Glenfarclas-Glenlivet.

Glenfarclas-Glenlivet (Scot). See Glenfarclas.

Glenfiddich (Scot). A single Malt whisky distillery based at Dufftown in Banffshire. Owned by the Grant family. Produce an 8 year old and 12 year old whisky. 40% alc. by vol. A Highland malt.

Glen Flagler (Scot). A single Malt whisky distillery once produced by Moffat. Now owned by Inver House Distillers. Based at Airdrie. A Lowland malt whisky.

Glenforres (Scot). A Vatted malt whisky. Is blended from the output of the Edradour Distillery owned by the Glenforres

Glenlivet Distillery Co. Is distributed by William Whiteley and Co. 43% alc. by vol.

Glen Foyle (Scot). A single Malt whisky distillery. A Highland malt whisky.

Glenfyne (Scot). A single Malt whisky distillery based near Loch Fyne. A Highland malt whisky.

Glen Garioch (Scot). A single Malt whisky distillery based in Meldrum. A Highland malt whisky.

Glengarry Winery (Austr). A winery based in Tasmania.

Glenglassaugh (Scot). A single Malt whisky distillery based in north-eastern Scotland near the river Deveron. A Highland malt whisky.

Glen Goyne (Scot). A single Malt whisky distillery based near Dumgoyne in Stirlingshire. Owned by the Lang Brothers. Produce an 8 year old whisky 40% alc. by vol. A Highland malt.

Glen Grant (Scot). A single Malt whisky distillery near the village of Rothes in Morayshire. Owned by The Glenlivet Distillers, a part of the Seagram empire. Produce an 8 year old at 56% alc. by vol. 15 year old at 40% and 56% alc. by vol. 21 year old at 40% alc. by vol. and a 25 year old at 40% alc. by vol. A Highland malt. Known as Glen Grant-Glenlivet.

Glen Grant-Glenlivet (Scot). See Glen Grant.

Glenkeith-Glenlivet (Scot). A single Malt whisky distillery in Keith. Owned by the Chivas Brothers. Produce a 12 year old malt. 45% alc. by vol. A Highland malt. (Part of Seagram).

Glenkinchie (Scot). A single Malt whisky distillery in the Glen of Kinchie. Owned by John Haig and Co. Produces a 13 year old whisky 45% alc. by vol. A Lowland malt. (Part of DCL group).

Glenleven (Scot). A Vatted malt whisky. 12 year old, 6 different malts. Produced by John Haig and Co. Ltd.

Glenlivet (Scot). The most famous glen in Scotland on the Speyside. Produces the finest Highland malt whiskies.

Glenlivet (The) (Scot). A single Malt whisky distillery in the Livet valley. Banffshire. Operated by J.G. Smith Ltd. (Part of The Glenlivet Distilleries Ltd [Seagram]). A Highland malt. Produces a 12 year old Malt and a 21 year old Malt. 45% alc. by vol.

Glenlivet and Glen Grant Distillers Limited (Scot). An amalgamation of Glen Grant and George and J.G. Smith. Later on they became known as the Glenlivet Distillers Limited.

Glenlivet Distillers Limited (Scot). Originally known as Glenlivet and Glen Grant Distillers Limited. Owned by Seagram.

Glenlochy (Scot). A single Malt whisky distillery. A rare Highland malt.

Glenlossie-Glenlivet (Scot). A single Malt whisky distillery based 4 miles outside Elgin in Morayshire. Owned by the D.C.L. Group. Produce a 21 year old whisky at 45% alc. by vol. A Highland malt.

Glenloth Winery (Austr). A vineyard based in Reynella, Southern Vales, New South Wales.

Glen Mhor (Scot). A single Malt whisky distillery based in Inverness. Produce an 8 year old whisky. A Highland malt. (Part of the DCL group). 40% alc. by vol.

Glen Mist (Scot). A whisky-based liqueur flavoured with herbs, spices and honey. Matured in whisky casks. 2 styles – Red seal 40% alc. by vol. and dry in taste and Gold seal 23% alc. by vol. and sweet in taste.

Glen Mister (Cktl). 1 measure Glen Mist, 1 measure Rose's lime juice. Shake together over ice, strain into a highball glass and add tonic or bitter lemon to taste.

Glenmorangie (Scot). A single Malt whisky distillery based in Coy, Tain, Ross-shire. Owned by MacDonald and Muir. Produce a 10 year old whisky. A Highland malt. 43% alc. by vol.

Glen Moray (Scot). A single Malt whisky distillery based near Elgin in Morayshire. Owned by MacDonald and Muir. Produce a 10 year old whisky. A Highland malt. 43% alc. by vol.

Glenmore (USA). A Bourbon whiskey distillery based in Louisville and on the Indiana border in Kentucky. Produce a Bourbon whiskey of same name. 40% alc. by vol.

Glen Moriston Estates (Scot). Whisky distillers based in Glenmoriston, Invermoriston, Loch Ness. See Old Farm.

Glenny Brewery (Eng). Opened in 1983 in Witney, Oxfordshire. Produce a cask conditioned Witney Bitter 1037 O.G. and Wychwood Best Bitter 1044 O.G. See Clinch's Brewery.

Glen Oran (Scot). The old name used for Glenordie Malt whisky distillery.

Glen Ordie (Scot). A single Malt whisky distillery (formerly known Glen Oran). A Highland malt whisky. Produced by Dewar's. 12 years old, 43% alc. by vol.

Glen Rossie (Scot). A blended Scotch whisky produced by Laing. 37.5% alc. by vol.

Glen Rothes (Scot). A single Malt whisky distillery based near Rothes in Morayshire. Owned by the Highland Distillers

Ltd. Produce an 8 year old whisky. A Highland malt. Known as the Glen Rothes-Glenlivet. 43% alc. by vol.

Glen Rothes-Glenlivet (Scot). See Glen Rothes.

Glenrowan (Austr). A wine-producing area in north-eastern Victoria.

Glen Scotia (Scot). A single Malt whisky distillery based at Campbeltown, Mull of Kintyre. Produce a 5 and 8 year old whisky. 43% alc. by vol. A Campbeltown malt. Produced by Amalgamated Distilled Products.

Glenside (Scot). A blended Scotch whisky produced by Laing. 37.5% alc. by vol.

Glen Spey (Scot). A single Malt whisky distillery based north of Inverness. An 8 year old Highland malt whisky. 43% alc. by vol. Part of International Distillers and Vintners.

Glen Talloch (Scot). An 8 year old single Highland malt whisky distilled in Scotland and bottled in Holland from Carmichael and Sons, Aidrie. 43% alc. by vol.

Glentauchers (Scot). A single Malt whisky distillery based north of Dufftown. A Highland malt whisky.

Glenturret (Scot). A single Malt whisky distillery. A Highland malt whisky. Produce 8, 12 and 15 year old Malt whiskies. 43% alc. by vol.

Glenugie (Scot). A single Malt whisky distillery based near Peterhead. Produces a 14 year old 45% alc. by vol. whisky and a vintage 1966. A Highland malt whisky.

Glenury-Royal (Scot). A single Malt whisky distillery based south of Aberdeen. A Highland malt whisky.

Glenvale Winery (N.Z.). Address = Main Road, Bay View, Hawkes Bay. 75 ha of which 20 are at Bay View and 50 at Esk Valley.

Glimmerschiefer (Ger). Slate soil mainly found in Franken.

Globe (Wales). A home-brew public house based in Fishguard, Dyfed. Noted for its' cask conditioned Black Fox 1038 O.G. (using malt extract).

Glöck (Ger). Vineyard. (Anb) = Rheinhessen. (Ber) = Nierstein. (Gro) = Auflangen. (Vil) = Nierstein.

Glockenberg (Ger). Vineyard. (Anb) = Rheinhessen. (Ber) = Nierstein. (Gro) = Sankt Alban. (Vil) = Gau-Bischofsheim.

Glockenzehnt (Ger). Vineyard. (Anb) = Rheinpfalz. (Ber) = Mittelhaardt-Deutsche Weinstrasse. (Gro) = Meerspinne. (Vil) = Mussbach.

Glögg (Punch). 1 bottle red wine, 1 bottle medium sherry, 3 oz. powdered sugar, ½ bottle Brandy, 8 dashes Angostura. Heat, pour into mugs containing raisins and unsalted almonds.

Gloire de Montpellier (Fr). USA root stock used for grafting in the Rhône.

Gloom Chaser (Cktl).(1). ¼ measure Grenadine, ¼ measure Grand Marnier, ¼ measure white Curaçao, ¼ measure lemon juice. Shake over ice, strain into a cocktail glass.

Gloom Chaser (Cktl).(2). 1 oz. dry Vermouth, 1½ ozs. Gin, ½ teaspoon Grenadine, 2 dashes Pernod. Shake over ice, strain into a cocktail glass.

Gloom Lifter (Cktl).(1). ⅔ measure Scotch whisky, ⅓ measure Brandy, juice ½ lemon, 2 dashes Gomme syrup, 4 dashes Raspberry syrup, ½ egg white. Shake over ice, strain into an ice-filled highball glass.

Gloom Lifter (Cktl).(2). ⅕ gill Irish whiskey, juice of ½ lemon, 2 dashes Gomme syrup, 1 egg white. Shake over ice, strain into a cocktail glass.

Gloom Raiser (Cktl). ⅙ gill dry Gin, ⅙ gill Noilly Prat, 2 dashes Grenadine, 2 dashes Absinthe. Stir over ice, strain into a cocktail glass, add a squeeze lemon peel juice on top.

Gloria (Ger). A white grape variety. A cross between the Sylvaner and the Müller-Thurgau. An early ripener which gives good sugar but has a neutral flavour.

Gloria Mundi (Mad). A popular bone-dry Sercial produced by Leacocks and Co. for the USA market.

Glorioso (Sp). A red wine produced by Bodegas Palacio in the Rioja Alavasa, north-eastern Spain.

Glorious Twelfth (Scot). A De luxe blended Scotch Whisky of 12 years old minimum. Produced by John Buckmaster and Sons. 43% alc. by vol.

Glottertal (Ger). Village. (Anb) = Baden. (Ber) = Breisgau. (Gro) = Burg Zähringen. (Vins) = Eichberg, Roter Bur.

Glucometer (Eng). A scaled hydrometer for measuring the sugar content in liquids. e.g. in grape must. (Fr) = Glucomètre.

Glucomètre (Fr). Glucometer.

Gluconic Acid (Eng). A wine acid formed from Eudemized grapes.

Gluco-Oenometer (Port). An instrument used in Port production to test the sugar levels in the Musts. See also Glucometer.

Glucose (Eng). $C_6H_{12}O_6$. Simple grape sugar. Combines with fructose to form sucrose. Enzymes secreted by the wine yeasts convert it into alcohol and CO_2.

G

Glühwein (Ger). A mulled wine, spiced and sweetened. Uses lemon zest, ginger, cinnamon, cloves, sugar and a little water. Heat together and infuse 5 minutes, strain and serve as hot as possible.

Glun (Fr). A commune of the A.C. Saint-Joseph in the northern Rhône.

Glutamic Acid (Eng). An Amino acid found in wine. Is formed by the yeasts.

Glutinous Rice Chiew (China). A style of rice wine.

Glycerine (Eng). An oil residue used as a non-fermentable sweetener. Is found naturally in wines and spirits as a by-product of plant oils. See also Glycerol.

Glycerol (Eng). A by-product of fermentation which develops in early stages. S.G. 1.2613 at 20°C. Molecular weight 92. $C_2H_5(OH)_3$. See also Glycerine.

Glycine (Eng). An Amino acid found in wine. Is formed by the yeasts.

Glycolysis (Eng). The decomposition of glucose or glycogen into simpler compounds.

Glycuronic Acid (Eng). A wine acid formed from Eudemized grapes.

GMA. (Fr) (abbr). Grandes Maisons d'Alsace.

G.m.b.H. (Ger) (abbr). Gesellschaft mit beschränkter Haftung. Denotes a limited liability company. (Eng) = Ltd.

Gnangara Vineyards (Austr). Part of the Evans and Tate Winery, Western Australia.

Goacher Brewery (Eng). Opened in 1983 in Kent. Noted for its' cask conditioned Maidstone Light 1036 O.G. Maidstone Ale 1040 O.G. and Goacher's-1066 1066 O.G.

Goaty (Eng). A term used to describe some wines made from the Traminer grape. Has a rich animal-like flavour.

Gobelet (Fr). A method of cultivating vines on a vertical trunk, with branches rising and spreading to form the shape of a goblet, hence the name. Bush formation. (Sp) = En Cabeza.

Gobelet (Fr). Goblet. A wide-rimmed drinking vessel. See also Tastevin.

Gobelet (Dom) (Fr). The cellar master of Clos de Vougeot at the time of the French revolution.

Goblet (Eng). A drinking vessel either of metal or glass with a large bowl and stem. (Fr) = Gobelet.

Gochsheim (Ger). Village. (Anb) = Baden. See Kraichtal.

Göcklingen (Ger). Village. (Anb) = Rheinpfalz. (Ber) = Südliche Weinstrasse. (Gro) = Herrlich. (Vin) = Kaiserberg.

Göcklingen (Ger). Village. (Anb) = Rheinpfalz. (Ber) = Südliche Weinstrasse. (Gro) = Kloster Liebfrauenberg. (Vin) = Herrenpfad.

Göcseji Barna (Hun). The brand-name of a beer brewed by the Nagykanizsa Brewery.

Godailler (Fr). A term used in the Champagne region to denote the visit to a café (pub).

Godello (Sp). A white grape variety grown in Galicia. Produces fragrant, fresh wines.

Godendorf (Ger). Village. (Anb) = Mosel-Saar-Ruwer. (Ber) = Obermosel. (Gro) = Königsberg. (Vin) = Sites not yet chosen.

Godet (Fr). Cognac producer. Address = Godet Frères, 1 Rue du Duc, La Rochelle 17003. Produces – V.S.O.P. Fine Champagne Gastronome 7–9 year old Cognac.

Godfather (Cktl). ¾ fl.oz. Amaretto, 1½ fl.ozs. Scotch whisky. Build into an ice-filled old-fashioned glass.

Godmother (Cktl). 1 part Amaretto, 1 part Vodka. Build into an ice-filled old-fashioned glass.

Godo Shusei (Jap). A Whiskey producer.

Godoy Cruz (Arg). A wine-producing area in the Mendoza region.

Godramstein (Ger). Village. (Anb) = Rheinpfalz. (Ber) = Südliche Weinstrasse. (Gro) = Königsgarten. (Vins) = Klostergarten, Münzberg.

Godrich and Petman (Eng). A retail Off-licence owned by Eldridge Pope.

God's Garden (Ger). German nickname for the Rheinhessen because of its' fertility and wealth.

Godsun Chudley (Eng). Two breweries that merged in 1984. Based in London. Produce – cask conditioned Godson's Black Horse 1048 O.G. Stock Ale 1085 O.G. Chudley's Local Line 1038 O.G. Wilmot's Hop Cone 1042 O.G. Lord's Strong 1048 O.G. and Draught Excluder 1070 O.G.

Goede Hoop Estate (S.Afr). A wine estate based in Stellenbosch. Address = P.O. Kuils River, 7580. Produces varietal wines.

Goedgeloof Vineyards (S.Afr). A part of the Spier Estate.

Goedverwacht Vineyards (S.Afr). A wine estate based in Robertson. Wines are sold to be bottled by merchants.

Goetheberg (Ger). Vineyard. (Anb) = Mittelrhein. (Ber) = Rheinburgengau. (Gro) = Lahntal. (Vil) = Obernhof.

Goglet (Ind). A large, long-necked, porous, earthenware bottle used for cooling drinking water. Also spelt Gurglet and Guglet.

Golcuv Jeníkov Brewery (Czec). A brewery based in central Czec.

G

Gold Acquette (Eng). See Acquette d'Or.
Goldatzel (Ger). Vineyard. (Anb) = Rheingau. (Ber) = Johannisberg. (Gro) = Erntebringer. (Vil) = Johannisberg.
Goldbächel (Ger). Vineyard. (Anb) = Rheinpfalz. (Ber) = Mittelhaardt-Deutsche Weinstrasse. (Gro) = Mariengarten. (Vil) = Wachenheim.
Goldbäumchen (Ger). Grosslage. (Anb) = Mosel-Saar-Ruwer. (Ber) = Zell/ Mosel. (Vils) = Briedern, Bruttig-Fankel, Cochem, Ellenz-Poltersdorf, Ernst, Klottern, Moselkern, Münden, Pommern, Senheim, Treis-Karden.
Goldbeerenauslese (Ger). An old term for a wine between Beerenauslese and Trokenbeerenauslese, the wine being not quite up to Trokenbeerenauslese quality. Now no longer used.
Gold Bell (USA). A brand-label used by the East-Side Winery, California for their generic wines.
Goldberg (Ger). Lit – 'Golden hill'. The name used for a vineyard usually in a south facing position. There are 32 vineyards in Germany with this name.
Goldberg (Ger). Vineyard. (Anb) = Baden. (Ber) = Badische Bergstrasse/ Kraichgau. (Gro) = Mannaberg. (Vil) = Mingolsheim und Langenbrücken.
Goldberg (Ger). Vineyard. (Anb) = Baden. (Ber) = Badische Bergstrasse/ Kraichgau. (Gro) = Stiftsberg. (Vil) = Sinsheim (stadtteil Weiler)
Goldberg (Ger). Vineyard. (Anb) = Mosel-Saar-Ruwer. (Ber) = Saar-Ruwer. (Gro) = Scharzberg. (Vil) = Wawern.
Goldberg (Ger). Vineyard. (Anb) = Mosel-Saar-Ruwer. (Ber) = Zell/Mosel. (Gro) = Goldbäumchen. (Vil) = Pommern.
Goldberg (Ger). Vineyard. (Anb) = Rheingau. (Ber) = Johannisberg. (Gro) = Erntebringer. (Vil) = Mittelheim.
Goldberg (Ger). Vineyard. (Anb) = Rheinhessen. (Ber) = Bingen. (Gro) = Abtey. (Vil) = Gau-Algesheim.
Goldberg (Ger). Vineyard. (Anb) = Rheinhessen. (Ber) = Bingen. (Gro) = Kaiserpfalz. (Vil) = Jugenheim.
Goldberg (Ger). Vineyard. (Anb) = Rheinhessen. (Ber) = Bingen. (Gro) = Kurfürstenstück. (Vil) = Vendersheim.
Goldberg (Ger). Vineyard. (Anb) = Rheinhessen. (Ber) = Bingen. (Gro) = Sankt Rochuskapelle. (Vil) = Gensingen.
Goldberg (Ger). Vineyard. (Anb) = Rheinhessen. (Ber) = Bingen. (Gro) = Sankt Rochuskapelle. (Vil) = Horrweiler.
Goldberg (Ger). Vineyard. (Anb) = Rheinhessen. (Ber) = Nierstein. (Gro) = Domherr. (Vil) = Udenheim.
Goldberg (Ger). Vineyard. (Anb) = Rheinhessen. (Ber) = Nierstein. (Gro) = Gutes

Domtal. (Vil) = Nieder-Olm.
Goldberg (Ger). Vineyard. (Anb) = Rheinhessen. (Ber) = Nierstein. (Gro) = Gutes Domtal. (Vil) = Undenheim.
Goldberg (Ger). Vineyard. (Anb) = Rheinhessen. (Ber) = Nierstein. (Gro) = Krötenbrunnen. (Vil) = Alsheim.
Goldberg (Ger). Vineyard. (Anb) = Rheinhessen. (Ber) = Nierstein. (Gro) = Krötenbrunnen. (Vil) = Eich.
Goldberg (Ger). Vineyard. (Anb) = Rheinhessen. (Ber) = Nierstein. (Gro) = Krötenbrunnen. (Vil) = Mettenheim.
Goldberg (Ger). Vineyard. (Anb) = Rheinhessen. (Ber) = Wonnegau. (Gro) = Bergkloster. (Vil) = Esselborn.
Goldberg (Ger). Vineyard. (Anb) = Rheinhessen. (Ber) = Wonnegau. (Gro) = Bergkloster. (Vil) = Flomborn.
Goldberg (Ger). Vineyard. (Anb) = Rheinhessen. (Ber) = Wonnegau. (Gro) = Burg Rodenstein. (Vil) = Flörsheim-Dalsheim.
Goldberg (Ger). Vineyard. (Anb) = Rheinhessen. (Ber) = Wonnegau. (Gro) = Gotteshilfe. (Vil) = Osthofen.
Goldberg (Ger). Vineyard. (Anb) = Rheinhessen. (Ber) = Wonnegau. (Gro) = Liebfrauenmorgen. (Vil) = Worms.
Goldberg (Ger). Vineyard. (Anb) = Rheinhessen. (Ber) = Wonnegau. (Gro) = Pilgerpfad. (Vil) = Monzernheim.
Goldberg (Ger). Vineyard. (Anb) = Rheinpfalz. (Ber) = Mittelhaardt-Deutsche Weinstrasse. (Gro) = Höllenpfad. (Vil) = Grünstadt.
Goldberg (Ger). Vineyard. (Anb) = Rheinpfalz. (Ber) = Mittelhaardt- Deutsche Weinstrasse. (Gro) = Rosenbühl. (Vil) = Erpolzheim.
Goldberg (Ger). Vineyard. (Anb) = Rheinpfalz. (Ber) = Mittelhaardt-Deutsche Weinstrasse. (Gro) = Rosenbühl. (Vil) = Freinsheim.
Goldberg (Ger). Vineyard. (Anb) = Rheinpfalz. (Ber) = Mittelhaardt-Deutsche Weinstrasse. (Gro) = Rosenbühl. (Vil) = Weisenheim/Sand.
Goldberg (Ger). Vineyard. (Anb) = Rheinpfalz. (Ber) = Mittelhaardt-Deutsche Weinstrasse. (Gro) = Schwarzerde. (Vil) = Bisserheim.
Goldberg (Ger). Vineyard. (Anb) = Württemberg. (Ber) = Remstal-Stuttgart. (Gro) = Weinsteige. (Vil) = Fellbach.
Goldberg (Ger). Vineyard. (Anb) = Württemberg. (Ber) = Württembergisch Unterland. (Gro) = Lindelberg. (Vil) = Bretzfeld.
Goldberg (Ger). Vineyard. (Anb) = Württemberg. (Ber) = Württembergisch Unterland. (Gro) = Lindelberg. (Vil) = Pfedelbach.

Goldberg (Ger). Vineyard. (Anb) = Württemberg. (Ber) = Württembergisch Unterland. (Gro) = Lindelberg. (Vil) = Verrenberg.

Goldberg (Ger). Vineyard. (Anb) = Württemberg. (Ber) = Württembergisch Unterland. (Gro) = Lindelberg. (Vil) = Windischenbach.

Gold Bitter (Wales). A keg Bitter 1043 O.G. brewed by the Buckley Brewery in South Wales.

Gold Blend (Eng). The brand-name of an instant coffee produced by Nestlé. A decaffeinated version is also available.

Goldblume (Ger). Vineyard. (Anb) = Mosel-Saar-Ruwer. (Ber) = Zell/Mosel. (Gro) = Weinhex. (Vil) = Löf.

Goldbräu (Aus). A Beer 5% alc. by vol. brewed by the Stiegl Brauerei in Salzburg.

Gold Cadillac (Cktl). ¾ oz. Galliano, ¾ oz. Crème de Cacao (white), 2 ozs. Cream. Shake well over ice, strain into a cocktail glass.

Gold Cap (Eng). A fine, old, Tawny Port from Balls Brothers of London.

Gold Coconut Cocktail (Cktl).(1). ½ measure Maraschino, ½ measure Cognac, 1 measure orange juice, dash egg white. Shake well over ice, strain into a cocktail glass. Top with a cherry.

Gold Coconut Cocktail (Cktl).(2). ½ measure Maraschino, ½ measure Malibu, 1 measure orange juice, dash egg white. Shake well over ice, strain into a cocktail glass. Top with a dash of Grenadine. Do not stir.

Gold Crest (Can). A blended Canadian whisky produced by Hiram Walker.

Gold Eagle Bitter (Eng). A keg Bitter 1034 O.G. brewed by the Charles Wells Brewery in Bedford.

Goldeck (Aus). A brand of sparkling wine produced by Schlumberger in Vöslau.

Goldemund (Ger). Vineyard. (Anb) = Mittelrhein. (Ber) = Rheinburgengau. (Gro) = Schloss Schönburg. (Vil) = Damscheid.

Goldemund (Ger). Vineyard. (Anb) = Mittelrhein. (Ber) = Rheinburgengau. (Gro) = Schloss Schönburg. (Vil) = Oberwessel.

Golden (Sp). See 'G'. A colour grade for Oloroso and Palo Cortado sherry.

Golden Age (Scot). A De Luxe blended Scotch whisky produced by Haig. 43% alc. by vol.

Golden Ale (Eng). A cask conditioned Ale 1050 O.G. brewed by the Archers Brewery in Swindon, Wiltshire.

Golden Ale (Eng). A keg Pale ale 1039 O.G. brewed by the Holden Brewery in the Black Country.

Golden Ale (Eng). A Light ale 1030 O.G. brewed by the Ridley Brewery in Essex.

Golden Bahaï (Cktl). Into a highball glass place 2 measures dry Gin, 2 measures Cinzano, juice ½ lemon, dash Gomme syrup. Stir in an egg yolk and top with pineapple juice. Dress with fruit.

Golden Barret (Scot). The brand-name of a 5 year old blended Scotch whisky. 43% alc. by vol.

Golden Beneagles (Scot). A blended Scotch whisky from Peter Thomson (Perth) Ltd. 43% alc. by vol.

Golden Best Mild (Eng). A Light mild 1033 O.G. brewed by the Timothy Taylor Brewery in Keighley, Yorkshire. Also known as Bitter ale.

Golden Cadillac (Cktl). See Gold Cadillac.

Golden Cadillac (Cktl). 1 fl.oz. (white) Crème de Cacao, 1 fl.oz. cream, 1 fl.oz. Galliano. Shake over ice, strain into a saucer-type glass.

Golden Cap (Eng). A blended Whisky produced by the Palmer Brewery in Bridport, Dorset from a 50–50 blend of North British and Glen Grant.

Golden Chasselas (USA). See Chasselas Doré.

Golden Cock Gin (Nor). A smooth locally produced Gin.

Golden Dawn Cocktail (Cktl). ¼ measure Calvados, ¼ measure Apricot brandy, ¼ measure Gin, ¼ measure orange juice, dash Grenadine. Shake together (except the Grenadine). Strain into a cocktail glass. Add Grenadine.

Golden Daze (Cktl). ¾ measure Gin, ¼ measure Peach brandy, juice ½ orange. Shake over ice, strain into a cocktail glass.

Golden Delicious (Gre). The name given to a sweet white liqueur wine produced by Tsantali. A red version is known as Red Delicious.

Golden Dream (Cktl). ¼ measure Cointreau, ¼ measure Galliano, ¼ measure orange juice, ¼ measure cream. Shake over ice, strain into a cocktail glass.

Golden Eagle (Cup). 1 bottle Tiger Milk, ⅙ gill Curaçao, ⅙ gill Cognac, 3 dashes Maraschino, juice of a lemon and the juice of 2 oranges. Chill well, pour into an ice-filled jug. Top with a ¾ pint of soda water and serve.

Golden Eagle (Ind). A Lager beer 1050 O.G. brewed by the Mohan Meakin Brewery in Simla Hills, Solan.

Goldene Luft (Ger). Vineyard. (Anb) = Rheingau. (Ber) = Johannisberg. (Gro) = Daubhaus. (Vil) = Wicker.

Goldene Luft (Ger). Vineyard. (Anb) = Rheinhessen. (Ber) = Nierstein. (Gro) = Rehbach. (Vil) = Nierstein.

G

Goldener Oktober (Ger). A Rhine wine produced by St. Ursula. (Brand).

Goldenes Horn (Ger). Vineyard. (Anb) = Rheinhessen. (Ber) = Bingen. (Gro) = Rheingrafenstein. (Vil) = Siefersheim.

Golden Fizz (Cktl). 1 egg yolk, ¾ gill Gin, 1 teaspoon sugar syrup, juice of lemon. Shake well over ice, strain into a highball, top with soda water.

Golden Fling Cocktail (Cktl). ⅓ measure Galliano, ⅓ measure golden Rum, ⅓ measure pineapple juice. Shake well over ice, strain into a highball glass. Top with bitter lemon and dress with fruit in season.

Golden Frappé (Cktl). 1 gill Port wine, juice 2 oranges, juice ¼ lemon, 1 teaspoon sugar. Stir juices and sugar together in a collins glass, add crushed ice and Port.

Golden Gate Cocktail (Cktl). ⅕ gill white Rum, 4 dashes dry Sherry. Stir over ice, strain into cocktail glass. Dress with a lemon peel spiral.

Golden Gin (USA). A Gin that has been aged in wood and has a golden hue colour.

Golden Gleam (Cktl). ⅓ measure Grand Marnier, ⅓ measure Brandy, ⅙ measure lemon juice, ⅙ measure orange juice. Shake over ice, strain into a cocktail glass.

Golden Glory Cocktail (Cktl). ⅓ measure dry Martini, ⅓ measure Scotch whisky, ⅓ measure medium Sherry. Stir over ice, strain into a cocktail glass. Top with a squeeze of orange peel juice.

Golden Guinea (Fr). A sparkling wine from the Saumur in the Anjou-Saumur district of the Loire. Made by the cuve close method using the Chenin blanc and Muscatel dosage. Brut or Demi-sec.

Golden Guinea Breweries (Afr). A brewery based in Nigeria. Produce Eagle Stout and Eagle Lager.

Golden Heart (Hol). A sweet, herb-flavoured liqueur with pieces of gold flake added. Produced by De Kuyper. A type of Goldwasser. 30% alc. by vol.

Golden Hill Brewery (Eng). Set up in 1980 in Wiveliscombe, Somerset. Noted for its' cask conditioned Exmoor Ale 1039 O.G.

Golden IPA (Eng). A bottled Pale ale 1040 O.G. brewed by the Burt Brewery in Ventnor on the Isle of Wight.

Golden Lady Cocktail (Cktl). ⅓ measure Brandy, ⅓ measure Orange gin, ⅙ measure lemon juice, ⅙ measure grapefruit juice. Shake over ice, strain into a cocktail glass.

Golden Lager (Iraq). A Lager beer brewed by the Government-owned Brewery based in Baghdad. 11.5° Balling.

Golden Lemonade (Cktl).(Non-alc). Juice 1 lemon, 2 teaspoons of powdered sugar, 1 egg yolk. Shake over ice, strain into an ice-filled highball glass. Top with Perrier water and slices of orange, lemon and a cherry.

Golden Medallion (Cktl). ⅓ measure old Cognac, ⅓ measure Galliano, ⅓ measure orange juice, dash egg white. Shake over ice, strain into a cocktail glass, add zest of orange.

Goldenmuskateller (It). The German name for the Moscato giallo grape variety in the Südtirol. (Trentino-Alto Adige).

Golden Mustang (S.Afr). A medium-sweet wine produced by the SFW from the Muscat d'Alexandrie and White cinsault grapes.

Golden Oke (USA). A golden type of Okolehao.

Golden Pippins (Eng). An old English cider-making apple.

Golden Pride Ale (Eng). A Pale ale (bottled) 1090 O.G. brewed by the Fullers Brewery in London.

Golden Promise (Scot). A top Scottish barley considered perfect for brewing. Gives medium sugar yields. Includes varieties – Halcyon, Kaskade, Kym, Magie, Pipkin and Tweed.

Golden Rain Tree Winery (USA). A winery based in Wadesville, Indiana. Produces hybrid blends. Noted for its' Director's Choice (a dry red wine).

Golden Rum (W.Ind). A style of Rum from Cuba, Puerto Rico and the Virgin Islands. Is aged for 3 years and coloured with caramel. Light-bodied. 40% alc. by vol.

Golden Screw (Cktl). ⅕ gill dry Gin, ⅖ gill orange juice, dash Angostura. Stir together in an ice-filled old-fashioned glass. Dress with an orange slice.

Golden Slipper ⅓ measure Advocaat, ⅓ measure Gin, ⅓ measure orange juice, dash Gomme syrup, dash egg white. Shake well over ice, strain into a cocktail glass.

Golden Slipper (Cktl).(Pousse Café). Place in a liqueur glass in order 1 egg yolk, ⅙ gill yellow Charteuse, ⅙ gill Goldwasser.

Golden Slipper Cocktail (Cktl). ⅘ measure Apricot brandy, ⅕ measure yellow Chartreuse. Stir over ice, strain into a cocktail glass, float an unbroken egg yolk on top.

Golden Star (China). The brand-name used by T'ien-chin.

Golden Tang (Cktl). ¼ measure Strega, ½ measure Vodka, ⅛ measure Crème de Banane, ⅛ measure orange squash. Shake over ice, strain into a cocktail glass. Add a cherry.

Golden Tea (Cktl). Heat gently 3 fl.ozs. strong tea with 1 fl.oz. Arak and 3 fl.ozs.

G

cream. Stir continuously. Add 2 egg yolks that have been beaten with 3 teaspoons of sugar. Stir, pour into a heatproof glass and serve with a cinnamon stick.

Golden Tequila (Mex). A wood-aged silver Tequila that has taken on a golden hue. Known as Tequila Anejo.

Golden Tip (Eng). A grade (quality) of tea from the Assam tea bush (dark leaves) which is produced in its second flush.

Golden Valley (S.Afr). The brand label of the Jonkheer Farmer's Winery.

Golden Velvet (Can). A straight rye Canadian whisky produced by Gilbey Canada Ltd.

Golden West Beer (Can). A beer brewed by the Carling O'Keefe Brewery.

Goldfassl (Aus). The brand-name used by Ottakringer Harmer Brauerei in Vienna for their beers.

Goldfüsschen (Ger). Vineyard. (Anb) = Mittelrhein. (Ber) = Siebengebirge. (Gro) = Petersberg. (Vil) = Niederdollendorf.

Goldgrübchen (Ger). Vineyard. (Anb) = Mosel-Saar-Ruwer. (Ber) = Zell/Mosel. (Gro) = Rosenhang. (Vil) = Mesenich.

Goldgrube (Ger). Vineyard. (Anb) = Mosel-Saar-Ruwer. (Ber) = Bernkastel. (Gro) = Schwarzlay. (Vil) = Traben-Trarbach (ortsteil Wolf).

Goldgrube (Ger). Vineyard. (Anb) = Nahe. (Ber) = Schloss Böckelheim. (Gro) = Rosengarten. (Vil) = Rüdesheim.

Goldgrube (Ger). Vineyard. (Anb) = Nahe. (Ber) = Schloss Böckelheim. (Gro) = Paradiesgarten. (Vil) = Staudernheim.

Goldgrube (Ger). Vineyard. (Anb) = Rheinhessen. (Ber) = Nierstein. (Gro) = Gutes Domtal. (Vil) = Köngernheim.

Goldgrube (Ger). Vineyard. (Anb) = Rheinpfalz. (Ber) = Mittelhaardt-Deutsche Weinstrasse. (Gro) = Grafenstück. (Vil) = Bockenheim.

Gold Harp Light Special (S.E.Asia). An all-malt brew launched in 1975. Brewed by an associate company of Guinness. Brewed in Malaya.

Goldie (Eng). A Barley wine 1085 O.G. brewed by the Eldridge Pope Brewery in Dorset.

Goldie Cocktail (Cktl). ⅓ measure white Rum, ⅓ measure orange juice, ¼ measure Cointreau, ¼ measure Cherry Heering. Shake over ice. Strain into a highball glass. Top with orangeade and dress with a spiral of orange peel.

Golding Ale (Eng). A Barley wine 1075 O.G. brewed by the King and Barnes Brewery in Sussex. Named after the Goldings hop used in its' making.

Goldings (Eng). A traditional hop variety which gives good bitterness to beers.

Goldkaul (Ger). Vineyard. (Anb) = Ahr. (Ber) = Walporzheim/Ahrtal. (Gro) = Klosterberg. (Vil) = Dernau.

Gold Keg (Can). A malty Lager beer brewed by the Labatt Brewery.

Goldkupp (Ger). Vineyard. (Anb) = Mosel-Saar-Ruwer. (Ber) = Bernkastel. (Gro) = Sankt Michael. (Vil) = Mehring.

Goldkupp (Ger). Vineyard. (Anb) = Mosel-Saar-Ruwer. (Ber) = Bernkastel. (Gro) = Sankt Michael. (Vil) = Longen.

Goldkupp (Ger). Vineyard. (Anb) = Mosel-Saar-Ruwer. (Ber) = Bernkastel. (Gro) = Sankt Michael. (Vil) = Lörsch.

Gold Label (Can). A blended Canadian whisky produced by Jas Barclay and Co. (A subsidiary of Hiram Walker).

Gold Label (Ch.Isles). A brand of blended Scotch whisky bottled by Bucktrout & Co. Ltd, St. Peter Port, Guernsey. 43% alc. by vol.

Gold Label (Eng). A Barley wine 1098 O.G. brewed by the Whitbread Brewery in Sheffield, Yorkshire.

Gold Label (Eng). A Lager beer 1045 O.G. from Grünhalle.

Gold Label (Hol). A Lager beer brewed by Amstel.

Gold Label Lager (Eng). A keg Lager 1036 O.G. brewed by the Whitbread Brewery in Sheffield, Yorkshire.

Gold Label Rum (W.Ind). A deeper coloured Rum than the Silver label variety. Has a slightly sweet taste with a strong 'Rum' flavour.

Goldlack (Ger). A Spätlese wine from the Herrgottströpfchen range of wines from Jakob Gerhardt, Nierstein.

Gold Lager (Den). A Lager beer 1045 O.G. brewed by Tuborg.

Goldlay (Ger). Vineyard. (Anb) = Mosel-Saar-Ruwer. (Ber) = Bernkastel. (Gro) = Vom Heissen Stein. (Vil) = Pünderich.

Goldlay (Ger). Vineyard. (Anb) = Mosel-Saar-Ruwer. (Ber) = Bernkastel. (Gro) = Vom Heissen Stein. (Vil) = Reil.

Goldlay (Ger). Vineyard. (Anb) = Mosel-Saar-Ruwer. (Ber) = Zell/Mosel. (Gro) = Weinhex. (Vil) = Niederfell.

Goldlay (Ger). Vineyard. (Anb) = Mosel-Saar-Ruwer. (Ber) = Zell/Mosel. (Gro) = Weinhex. (Vil) = Oberfell.

Gold Lion (Cktl). ⅔ measure Nassau Orange Liqueur, ⅙ measure orange juice, ⅙ measure lemon juice. Shake well with ice, strain into a cocktail glass, decorate with a slice of orange and lemon.

Goldloch (Ger). Vineyard. (Anb) = Nahe.

G

(Ber) = Kreuznach. (Gro) = Schlosskapelle. (Vil) = Dorsheim.
Goldloch (Ger). Vineyard. (Anb) = Rheinpfalz. (Ber) = Mittelhaardt-Deutsche Weinstrasse. (Gro) = Schnepfenflug vom Kellertal. (Vil) = Gauersheim.
Gold Medal (S.Am). A brand of Demerara rum produced by Banks DIH Ltd. in Guyana. Is aged for 2½ years in cask.
Gold Peak (USA). The label used by the Lamont Winery, California for their range of low-priced wines.
Goldpfad (Ger). Vineyard. (Anb) = Rheinhessen. (Ber) = Wonnegau. (Gro) = Liebfrauenmorgen. (Vil) = Worms.
Goldriesling (Ger). A white grape variety. A cross between the White riesling and the Muscat précoce de Courtiller. Also known as the Riesling doré and the Knipperlé.
Gold Seal (USA). A large New York state winery owned by Seagram. Is sited on the west shore of Lake Keuka. (Formerly known as the Urbana Wine Co).
Gold Seal Vineyards (USA). A leading vineyard of the Fingers Lakes region in the New York district.
Gold Standard (Eng). The label of a Lager beer 8% alc. by vol. used by the Nurdin and Peacock Cash & Carry.
Gold Star (Isr). An Ale-type beer brewed by a Canadian backed brewery. 12° Balling.
Gold Star Ale (Eng). A Light ale 1034 O.G. brewed by the Shipstone Brewery in Nottingham.
Goldstückchen (Ger). Vineyard. (Anb) = Rheinhessen. (Ber) = Bingen. (Gro) =Adelberg. (Vil) = Armsheim.
Gold Time Cocktail (Cktl). ⅓ measure golden Rum, ⅓ measure egg yolk, ⅓ measure pineapple juice, dash lemon juice. Shake well over ice, strain into a cocktail glass. Top with a cherry, lemon slice and serve with straws.
Goldtröpfchen (Ger). Vineyard. (Anb) = Mosel-Saar-Ruwer. (Ber) = Bernkastel. (Gro) = Michelsberg. (Vil) = Piesport.
Gold Vodka (Pol). A cask matured Vodka, may be matured for up to 10 years.
Goldwasser (Den). See Danziger Goldwasser.
Goldwell (Eng). A Kent-based firm that produces – Beachcomber Cream Liqueur, Calypso, Country Manor English Perry and Country Satin.
Golf (Cktl). 1 oz. Gin, ½ oz. dry Vermouth, dash Angostura. Stir over ice, strain into a cocktail glass, serve with an olive.
Golfan (Fr). A wine-producing district in Bellet, Provence.

Gollebour (Lux). A vineyard site in the village of Machtum.
Gollenberg (Ger). Vineyard. (Anb) = Rheinpfalz. (Ber) = Südliche Weinstrasse. (Gro) = Trappenberg. (Vil) = Bellheim.
Gollenberg (Ger). Vineyard. (Anb) = Rheinpfalz. (Ber) = Südliche Weinstrasse. (Gro) = Trappenberg. (Vil) = Knittelsheim.
Gollop (Eng). Nineteenth century term for eating or drinking quickly.
Golubok (Sp). The brand-name of a Vodka produced by Palomino y Vergara S.A. in Jerez.
Gómez (Felix Garcia) (Sp). A producer and exporter of Málaga wines.
Gomes (Luís) [Vinhos] Lda (Mad). A noted firm of Madeira shippers.
Gomes (Marcelo) & Cia Lda (Mad). A noted shipper of Madeira to the U.K.
Gomme Exir (Fr). A barley sugar-flavoured sirop.
Gomme Syrup (Fr). A non-alcoholic syrup used for sweetening cocktails.
Gönci (Hun). Small tokay casks. See Gonczi, Gyöncz and Gönz.
Gonczi (Hun). Small casks into which the juice for Tokay is run. See Gönci, Gyöncz and Gönz.
Gondeville (Fr). A commune in the Charente-Maritime Département whose grapes are classed Grande Champagne (Cognac).
Gonet (François) (Fr). Champagne producer. Address = Rue du Stade, 51190 Mesnil sur Oger. Récoltants-manipulants. Produces – Vintage and non-vintage wines. Member of C.V.C.
Gonet (Michel) (Fr). Champagne producer. Address = Avenue Jean Jaurès, 51190 Avize. Récoltants-manipulants. Produces – Vintage and non-vintage wines. A member of the C.V.C.
Gönnheim (Ger). Village. (Anb) = Rheinpfalz. (Ber) = Mittelhaardt-Deutsche Weinstrasse. (Gro) = Feuerberg. (Vin) = Martinshöhe.
Gönnheim (Ger). Village. (Anb) = Rheinpfalz. (Ber) = Mittelhaardt-Deutsche Weinstrasse. (Gro) = Hofstück. (Vins) = Klostergarten, Mandelgarten, Sonnenberg.
Gontchi (USSR). A red dessert wine grape grown in Tadzhikistan.
Gönz (Hun). See Gönz, Gonczi and Gyöncz.
Gonzales (USA). A town in Salina Valley, Monterey, California. Is home to one small winery.
Gonzales (Miguel) (USA). A winery based in New Mexico. Produces table wines.
Gonzalez (Eucario) (Mex). A producer of Tequila of same name.

G

Gonzalez Byass (Sp). A brandy and sherry producer. Address = Manuel M. Gonzalez 12, Jerez de la Frontera, Cadiz. Source of base wine is in La Mancha and Jerez de la Frontera. Produce – Soberano 2 year old, Insuperable a 5 year old, Conde Duque 8 year old and Lepanto 15 year old plus (brandies), La Concha, Nectar Cream, San Domingo and Tio Pepe (sherries). Also own Wisdom and Warter in Jerez de la Frontera. See also Gonzalez y Dubosc.

Gonzalez Byass (Sp). Vintage Port shippers. Vintages – 1896, 1900, 1904, 1908, 1912, 1917, 1920, 1945, 1955, 1960, 1963, 1967, 1970, 1975. Also produces fine brandies and sherries.

Gonzalez y Dubosc (Sp). A wineproducer based in Catalonia. Produce Cava sparkling wines in cavas of Segura Viudas. Sold in U.K. under the Jean Perico label. A marque owned by Gonzalez Byass.

Good Company (Mad). The brand-name for Madeira wines produced by Cossart Gordon.

Goodnight Cocktail (Cktl). ⅓ measure Gin, ⅓ measure Vodka, ⅓ measure Rye whiskey, dash Crème de Noyau. Stir over ice, strain into a cocktail glass.

Goodnight Kiss (Cktl). Cherry 'B' and cider.

Goods (Eng). A term used to describe the contents of the mash tun.

Goorjuani (USSR). A dry white wine from the Rion Valley district of the Georgia region.

Goose Ale (Eng). A cask conditioned Beer 1036 O.G. brewed by the Goose and Firkin home-brew public house in London.

Goose and Firkin (Eng). A Bruce home-brew public house in London. Produces – Borough 1045 O.G. Dogbolter 1060 O.G. and Goose Ale 1036 O.G. All brewed with malt extract.

Goose Eye Brewery (Eng). A small brewery near Keighley in Yorkshire. Noted for its Special (or Wharfedale) Ale 1045 O.G. and Pommie's Revenge 1060 O.G.

Gordo (Austr). A white grape variety that produces delicate, aromatic wines.

Gordo (Sp). A term used to describe a fat Sherry (depends on strength). See also Gordura.

Gordon (Duff) (Sp). Shippers of Sherry. Owned by Osborne and based at Puerto de Santa Maria. Produces El Cid, Fino Feria and Santa Maria.

Gordon's (Eng). A range of Gins and Vodkas produced by Gordon & Co. Ltd. Distillery. Part of DCL Co. Ltd.

Gordons Ale (Scot). A strong bottled Ale 9.5% alc. by vol. brewed by the Scottish and Newcastle Brewery for Belgium.

Gordon's Cup (Cktl). In a large glass filled with ice add ½ glass of Gordon's Gin, ½ glass Port. Top with tonic water or lemonade. Garnish with a slice of cucumber, slice of lemon and crushed mint leaves.

Gordura (Sp). Describes 'fatness' in an Oloroso sherry. Has rich vinosity. See also Gordo.

Gore-Browne (Eng). A pioneer of English wine-making. Started the Beaulieu Abbey Vineyard.

Gorgée (Fr). Sup.

Gorges (Fr). A noted village in the Sèvre et Maine, Loire Atlantique. Produces fine Muscadet de Sèvre et Maine wines.

Gorges de l'Hérault (Fr). A Vins de Pays area in the Hérault Département in southern France.

Gorges du Tarn (Fr). A herb liqueur produced by Germain Distillery in southern France.

Gornac (Fr). A commune in the Haut Benauge, central Bordeaux.

Gornie Radgona (Yug). A white wine produced in the Slovenia region.

Gorny Doubnyak (USSR). A bitter liqueur made from ginger, galingale, angelica, clove, acorns and oak shavings.

Goron (Switz). A red Valais wine that has not passed the stringent tests to enable it to be called Dôle.

Gorzaika (Pol). Low-alcohol Vodkas produced in the eleventh and twelfth centuries as medicines.

Gospodaniile Agricole de Stat (Rum). G.A.S. State Agricultural Enterprise.

Gössenheim (Ger). Village. (Anb) = Franken. (Ber) = Maindreieck. (Gro) = Rosstal. (Vin) = Arnberg.

Gösser Brauerei (Aus). A brewery based at Leoben. The headquarters are opposite to the Renaissance Bénédictine Abbey. Is noted for its' Steirisch Pils and Stiftsbräu beers.

Gosset (Fr). Champagne producer. Address = 69 Rue Jules Blondeau, 51160 Ay. Produce – Vintage and non-vintage wines. Vintages – 1914, 1919, 1921, 1923, 1926, 1928, 1929, 1934, 1939, 1947, 1952, 1953, 1955, 1959, 1961, 1964, 1966, 1969, 1970, 1971, 1973, 1975, 1976, 1979, 1981. Hand remuage only. The De Luxe vintage cuvée is Grande Millésime.

Gota (Sp). Virgin wine. The alternative name for Vino de Yema.

Gothe (Bra). A white grape variety.

Gottenheim (Ger). Village. (Anb) = Baden. (Ber) = Kaiserstuhl-Tuniberg. (Gro) = Attilafelsen. (Vin) = Kirchberg.

Götterlay (Ger). Vineyard. (Anb) = Mosel-Saar-Ruwer. (Ber) = Zell/Mosel. (Gro) = Goldbäumchen. (Vil) = Bruttig-Fankel.

Gottesacker (Ger). Vineyard. (Anb) = Baden. (Ber) = Markgräflerland. (Gro) = Burg Neuenfels. (Vil) = Hügelheim.

Gottesacker (Ger). Vineyard. (Anb) = Rheinpfalz. (Ber) = Südliche Weinstrasse. (Gro) = Trappenberg. (Vil) = Altdorf.

Gottesfuss (Ger). Vineyard. (Anb) = Mosel-Saar-Ruwer. (Ber) = Saar-Ruwer. (Gro) = Scharzberg. (Vil) = Wiltingen.

Gottesgarten (Ger). Vineyard. (Anb) = Rheinhessen. (Ber) = Nierstein. (Gro) = Gutes Domtal. (Vil) = Selzen.

Gotteshilfe (Ger). Grosslage. (Anb) = Rheinhessen. (Ber) = Wonnegau. (Vils) = Bechtheim, Osthofen.

Gottesthal (Ger). Grosslage. (Anb) = Rheingau. (Ber) = Johannisberg. (Vils) = Estate, Östrich.

Gotto d'Oro (It). A modern winery based in Latium. Is noted for its' Marino (a dry white wine).

Gott's Vineyard (USA). A vineyard which sells its' grapes (Zinfandel) to the Monteviña Winery in the Shenandoah Valley, California.

Göttweig (Aus). A wine-producing abbey based near Krems.

Götzenberg (Ger). Vineyard. (Anb) = Württemberg. (Ber) = Remstal-Stuttgart. (Gro) = Weinsteige. (Vil) = Stuttgart (ortsteil Uhlbach).

Götzenberg (Ger). Vineyard. (Anb) = Württemberg. (Ber) = Württembergisch Unterland. (Gro) = Wunnenstein. (Vil) = Kleinbottwar.

Götzenborn (Ger). Vineyard. (Anb) = Rheinhessen. (Ber) = Bingen. (Gro) = Abtey. (Vil) = Wolfsheim.

Götzenfels (Ger). Vineyard. (Anb) = Nahe. (Ber) = Schloss Böckelburg. (Gro) = Burgweg. (Vil) = Bad Münster a. St-Ebernburg.

Götzenfels (Ger). Vineyard. (Anb) = Nahe. (Ber) = Schloss Böckelheim. (Gro) = Burgweg. (Vil) = Norheim.

Götzhalde (Ger). Vineyard. (Anb) = Baden. (Ber) = Badische Bergstrasse/Kraichgau. (Gro) = Stiftsberg. (Vil) = Neckarzimmern.

Gouais (Fr). A white grape popular in the seventeenth and eighteenth centuries used in the production of verjuice.

Goudallier (Ch.Isles). To drink alcoholic beverages. See also Goudélair.

Goudélair (Ch.Isles). To drink alcoholic beverages. See also Goudallier.

Goudenband Special Provisie (Bel). A bottle conditioned Brown ale 6.5% alc. by vol. brewed by Liefmans Brasserei in Oudenaarde. Is matured for 8–12 months and bottled before the fermentation is completed.

Gouden Carolus (Bel). A strong, dark Ale brewed by the Anker Brasserie.

Goudge (Arg). A wine-producing area in the south of Argentina.

Goudini Co-operative (S.Afr). Vineyards based in Goudini. Address = Box 132, Rawsonville 6845. Produces varietal wines.

Goudoulin (Fr). A brand of Armagnac produced by Veuve J. Goudoulin in the Bas Armagnac.

Goudron (It). Tar. Applies to the bouquet and taste in Barolo wines.

Goue Vallei (S.Afr). The alternative name for the Citrusdal Cooperative.

Gough Brothers (Eng). A large chain of retail Off-Licences owned by the Seagram Distillers PLC.

Goujan (Fr). An alternative name for the Pinot meunier grape.

Goulburn Valley (Austr). An area of Victoria around the town of Nagambia. Produces quality red and white table wines.

Gould Campbell (Port). Vintage Port shippers. Vintages – 1870, 1872, 1873, 1875, 1878, 1881, 1884, 1885, 1887, 1890, 1892, 1896, 1900, 1904, 1908, 1912, 1917, 1920, 1922, 1924, 1927, 1934, 1942, 1945, 1947, 1955, 1960, 1963, 1966, 1970, 1975, 1977, 1980, 1983.

Goulet (George) (Fr). Champagne producer. Address = 2–4 Avenue du Général Giraud, 51100 Reims. Produces vintage and non-vintage wines. Vintages – 1921, 1926, 1928, 1934, 1937, 1941, 1943, 1945, 1947, 1949, 1952, 1953, 1955, 1959, 1961, 1962, 1964, 1966, 1969, 1970, 1971, 1973, 1975, 1976, 1979, 1981. De Luxe vintage cuvée is Cuvée de Centenaire.

Gouleyance (Fr). Denotes a quaffing wine. An easy drinking wine.

Goulistane (USSR). A white grape variety grown in Turkmenistan. Used in the production of fortified wines.

Goulot (Fr). The name given to the bottle neck.

Goulots (Les) (Fr). A Premier Cru vineyard in the A.C. commune of Gevrey-Chambertin, Côte de Nuits, Burgundy.

Goumenissa (Gre). A dry, light-bodied, red wine produced by Boutari from the Negoska and Xinomavro grapes. Has some wood-ageing.

Goundrey (Austr). A winery based in the Great Southern Region, Western Australia.

G

Gouron (René) (Fr). A noted producer of Touraine rosé pétillant wine based in Chinon, Loire.

Gourd (Afr). A bottle or flask made from the dried shell of the bottle gourd.

Gourdjaani (USSR). A white wine produced in Takhetia region in Georgia.

Gourdoux (Fr). An alternative name for the Malbec grape.

Goureau (Fr). A cuvée in the Poruzots vineyard, A.C. Meursault, Côte de Beaune, Burgundy. Is owned by the Hospices de Beaune.

Gouresses (Les) (Fr). A vineyard in the A.C. commune of Montagny, Côte Chalonnaise, Burgundy.

Gourmand (Fr). A person who is devoted to food and drink. Eats to excess. See Gourmet (Opposite).

Gourmel (L.) (Fr). Cognac producer. Address = B.P. 194, 16106 Cognac. 75 ha. in Grande Champagne and 13 ha in Fins Bois. Produces – L'Âge des Fleurs 12 year old, L'Âge des Épices 15 year old and Quintessence 21 year old.

Gourmet (Fr). A person who enjoys good food and drink. One who has a cultured palate. See also Gourmand (opposite).

Gourmet (Fr). A winebroker. See also Courtier.

Gourry de Chadeville (Fr). Cognac producer. Address = SARL Gourry de Chadeville, 16130 Segonzac. 16 ha. in the Grande Champagne. Produces – Très Vieux 18–20 year old.

Gourzouf (USSR). A pink dessert wine from the southern Crimea.

Gout (Eng). A disease of the eighteenth and nineteenth centuries which was attributed to alcohol.

Goût (Fr). Taste.

Goût Américan (Fr). Fairly sweet. Sparkling wines which are sweeter than French dosage.

Goût Anglais (Fr). Dry taste.

Goût de Bois (Fr). Woody taste.

Goût de Bouchon (Fr). Corky tasting wine.

Goût de Capsule (Fr). Taste and smell of the lead capsule.

Goût de Chêne (Fr). Oaky taste.

Goût de Cuivre (Fr). Taste of copper. Applicable to brandy (Cognac) after distillation but passes after a year or so in oak.

Goût de Ferment (Fr). Denotes that the wine is not ready to drink as it is still in the process of fermentation.

Goût de Fox (Fr). See Goût de Renard.

Goût de Grèle (Fr). Lit – 'Taste of hail'. Applied to wines that have been made from grapes damaged by hailstones before the harvest. Applies especially to Burgundy wines. The hail bruises the skins and mildew forms which gives a curious objectionable flavour.

Goût de Moisi (Fr). Musty taste.

Goût de Paille (Fr). Straw taste.

Goût de Pierre à Fusil (Fr). A flinty taste to be found in Chablis.

Goût de Piqué (Fr). Wine going towards vinegar.

Goût de Rancio (Fr). Bottle-stink.

Goût de Renard (Fr). Foxiness. The taste obtained from the Vitis Labrusca grape in America. Also known as Goût de Fox.

Goût de Souris (Fr). Mousiness.

Goût de Taille (Fr). Uncouth taste. Made from the final pressing of the grapes.

Goût de Terroir (Fr). Earthy taste.

Goût d'Éventé (Fr). Flat taste. A taste wine obtains from old casks or badly cleaned casks. See Éventé.

Goute (Ch.Isles). A small sip of a drink.

Goût Français (Fr). Sweet taste.

Goutorbe (Henri) (Fr). Champagne producer. Address = 11, Rue Léon Bourgeois, 51160 Ay. Récoltants-manipulants. 15 ha. Produces vintage and non-vintage wines. Member of C.V.C. Vintages – 1971, 1973, 1974, 1975, 1976, 1978, 1979, 1980, 1982. De Luxe vintage cuvée is Special Club. Also produces Cuvées – Traditionelle, Prestige and Rosé.

Goût Parisien (Fr). A description of the style of wine preferred by the inhabitants of Paris. Wines which are usually high in alcohol.

Goutte d'Or (Fr). A fine quality Meursault wine produced in the late eighteenth century.

Goutte d'Or (La) (Fr). A vineyard in the A.C. commune of Meursault, Côte de Beaune, Burgundy. 5.3 ha.

Gouveio (Port). A white grape variety used in the making of white Port.

Gouveiro (Mad). An alternative name for the Verdelho grape.

Government Stamped (Eng). The crown and a number issued by H.M. Customs and Excise when they have tested glasses used for beers, ciders and for spirit measures.

Governo all'Uso Toscano (It). Tuscan oenological procedure. Bunches of grapes are dried indoors, then crushed, heated and added to the fermenting must in November, December and January after the harvest. 3% of total grapes (Canaiolo, Colorino and Sangiovese).

Governo Method (It). See Governo all'Uso Toscano.

Goya (La) (Sp). A Manzanilla Pasada sherry produced by Delgado Zuleta.

G

Graach (Ger). Village. (Anb) = Mosel-Saar-Ruwer. (Ber) = Bernkastel. (Gro) = Münzlay. (Vins) = Abtsberg, Domprobst, Himmelreich, Josephshöfer.

Graan (Hol). Denotes a Jenever made from grain only.

Graben (Ger). Vineyard. (Anb) = Mosel-Saar-Ruwer. (Ber) = Bernkastel. (Gro) = Badstube. (Vil) = Bernkastel-Kues.

Graca (S.Afr). A dry white wine made from the Cape riesling and Sémillon grapes produced by the SFW. Is slightly pétillant.

Gra-Car (It). A liqueur which is similar in style to Chartreuse. Produced by the monks at Grand Chartreuse, Grenoble.

Grace Cup (Eng). A cup of wine passed around the table at the end of a meal in the eighteenth century.

Graceful (Eng). A term that describes a wine as being stylish and elegant in character.

Graceful Cocktail (Cktl). 1 measure (green) Crème de Menthe. Stir over ice, strain into a cocktail glass. Top with cream and sprinkle with grated chocolate.

Gracerry Vineyards (Austr). See Stanton and Killeen.

Gracia Hermanos S.A. (Sp). A winery based in Montilla. Produces fine Montilla-Moriles wines.

Graciano (Sp). A red grape variety used in the Rioja.

Gradazione Alcoolica Complessiva (It). A term meaning 'total alcohol content'.

Gradi (It). Grade. See Gradi Alcool.

Gradi Alcool (It). Percentage of alcohol by volume in a beverage. (100% as pure alcohol).

Gradi Alcoolico (It). Lit – 'Alcoholic grade'. See Gradi Alcool.

Gradignan (Fr). A commune in the A.C. Graves region in south-western Bordeaux.

Graf (Ger). Count.

Graf Beyssel-Herrenberg (Ger). Vineyard. (Anb) = Mosel-Saar-Ruwer. (Ber) =Zell/Mosel. (Gro) = Grafschaft. (Vil) = Bullay.

Graf Eberhard Kuenberg (It). A winery based in Schloss Sallegg, Kaltern, Trentino-Alto Adige. 25 ha.

Grafenberg (Ger). Vineyard. (Anb) = Mosel-Saar-Ruwer. (Ber) = Bernkastel. (Gro) = Michelsberg. (Vil) = Neumagen-Dhron.

Grafenberg (Ger). Vineyard. (Anb) = Nahe. (Ber) = Schloss Böckelheim. (Gro) = Rosengarten. (Vil) = Sponheim.

Gräfenberg (Ger). Vineyard. (Anb) =

Rheingau. (Ber) = Johannisberg. (Gro) = Geiligenstock. (Vil) = Kiedrich.

Gräfenberg (Ger). Vineyard. (Anb) = Rheinpfalz. (Ber) = Südliche Weinstrasse. (Gro) = Guttenberg. (Vil) = Freckenfeld.

Grafenberg (Ger). Vineyard. (Anb) = Württemberg. (Ber) = Remstal-Stuttgart. (Gro) = Kopf. (Vil) = Schorndorf.

Grafenberg (Ger). Vineyard. (Anb) = Württemberg. (Ber) = Württembergisch-Unterland. (Gro) = Heuchelberg. (Vil) = Kleingartach.

Grafenberg (Ger). Vineyard. (Anb) = Württemberg. (Ber) = Württembergisch Unterland. (Gro) = Heuchelberg. (Vil) = Leingarten.

Grafenberg (Ger). Vineyard. (Anb) = Württemberg. (Ber) = Württembergisch Unterland. (Gro) = Heuchelberg. (Vil) = Neipperg.

Grafenberg (Ger). Vineyard. (Anb) = Württemberg. (Ber) = Württembergisch Unterland. (Gro) = Heuchelberg. (Vil) = Niederhofen.

Grafenberg (Ger). Vineyard. (Anb) = Württemberg. (Ber) = Württembergisch Unterland. (Gro) = Heuchelberg. (Vil) = Nordheim.

Gräfenberg (Ger). Vineyard. (Anb) = Württemberg. (Ber) = Württembergisch Unterland. (Gro) = Heuchelberg. (Vil) = Nordheim.

Grafenberg (Ger). Vineyard. (Anb) = Württemberg. (Ber) = Württembergisch Unterland. (Gro) = Heuchelberg. (Vil) = Schwaigern.

Grafensprung (Ger). Vineyard. (Anb) = Baden. (Ber) = Ortenau. (Gro) = Schloss Rodeck. (Vil) = Obersrot.

Grafenstück (Ger). Grosslage. (Anb) = Rheinpfalz. (Ber) = Mittelhaardt-Deutsche Weinstrasse. (Vils) = Bockenheim, Kindenheim, Obrigheim.

Grafschaft (Ger). Grosslage. (Anb) = Mosel-Saar-Ruwer. (Ber) = Zell/Mosel. (Vils) = Alf, Beuren, Bremm, Bullay, Ediger-Eller, Neef, Nehren, St. Aldegund, Zell-Merl.

Grafschafter Sonnenberg (Ger). Vineyard. (Anb) = Mosel-Saar-Ruwer. (Ber) = Bernkastel. (Gro) = Kurfürstlay. (Vil) = Veldenz.

Grafting (Eng). A method used to attach young vine stems (Scions) onto disease-resistant root stocks to help combat Phylloxera. See Bench Grafting, Cleft Grafting, Crown Graft, Field Grafting, Greffe, Greffe Anglaise and Omega Grafting.

Gragnano (It). A dark, rich, red, fruity wine from the Campania region.

G

Graham (Port). Vintage Port shippers. Vintages – 1870, 1872, 1873, 1875, 1878, 1880, 1881, 1884, 1885, 1887, 1890, 1892, 1894, 1886, 1887, 1900, 1901, 1904, 1908, 1912, 1917, 1920, 1924, 1927, 1935, 1942, 1945, 1948, 1955, 1963, 1960, 1966, 1970, 1975, 1977, 1980, 1982, 1983, 1985.

Graham Cocktail (Cktl). ¾ measure sweet Vermouth, ¼ measure dry Vermouth. Stir well over ice, strain into a cocktail glass.

Graham's Emperor (Port). A fine, old, Tawny Port from Graham Port Shippers.

Grain (Ger). Vineyard. (Anb) = Rheinpfalz. (Ber) = Mittelhaardt-Deutsche Weinstrasse. (Gro) = Rebstöckel. (Vil) = Neustadt an der Weinstrasse.

Grain Alcohol (Eng). Ethanol, containing approximately 10% of water. Made from a distillation of fermented grains.

Grain Alcohol (USA). The name used for Gin, Vodka, etc.

Grain de Café (Fr). Coffee bean.

Grainer (Ger). Local name for red wine from the town of Kleinheppach in Württemberg.

Grainhübel (Ger). Vineyard. (Anb) = Rheinpfalz. (Ber) = Mittelhaardt-Deutsche Weinstrasse. (Gro) = Mariengarten. (Vil) = Deidesheim.

Grain Neutral Spirits (USA). Pure spirits. The name for any of the distillates which are distilled to over 190°U.S. Proof (95% alc. by vol). e.g. Gin and Vodka.

Grain Spirits (USA). Neutral spirits distilled from a fermented mash of grain and stored in oak containers.

Grain Whisky (Scot). A Whisky made from grains (mainly wheat) other than barley. Not malted. Used for blending with malt whiskies to produce Blended Scotch Whisky. See also Old Cameron Brig.

Graisse (Fr). A flat, oily, faded wine. A diseased wine. Often occurs in Champagne in the wine from the last pressing. Wines lose some of their sugar and increase in acidity. (Sp) = Hilo.

Graisse Blanc (Fr). An alternative name used for the Ugni blanc white grape.

Graisse des Vins (Fr). Occurs in white wines as a result of harsh pressing of the grapes. Wine is left cloudy. Necessary to add tannin to clear the sediment. Also known as ropiness.

Gramp Winery (Austr). A winery owned by Orlando, Reckitt and Colman in the Barossa Valley.

Granaccia (Sp). An alternative name for the Garnacho grape.

Granada (Cktl).(1). 1 oz. Mandarine Napoléon, 1 oz. Campari, 1 oz. dry Gin, 2 ozs. lemon juice. Shake well over ice, strain into a cocktail glass.

Granada (Cktl).(2). 1 oz. Mandarine Napoléon, 1 oz. Campari, 1 oz. dry Gin, 2 ozs. lime juice cordial. Shake well with ice, strain into a highball glass, add ice, top with lemonade, a slice of lemon. Serve with straws.

Granado (W.Ind). The brand-name of a distilled white Rum from a distillery of same name in Puerto Rico.

Granary Bitter (Eng). A cask conditioned Bitter 1038 O.G. brewed by the Reepham Brewery in Norfolk.

Granàt (Czec). Lit – 'Garnet'. A beer brewed by the Hora Brewery based in South Morana, Cerna.

Granato (It). A term used to describe the colour of red wines. Deep ruby with golden tinges around the edges.

Gran Canciller (Sp). A 10 year old Brandy produced by Palomino y Vergara S.A., Calon 1–25, Jerez de la Frontera, Cadiz.

Gran Capitán (Sp). See Bobadilla.

Gran Claustro (Sp). A top of the range sparkling wine of the Perlada Co.

Gran Coronas (Sp). A fine red wine from Torres, Penedés. Produced from Cabernet sauvignon 45%, Monastrell 5% and Ull de llebre 50%. Is aged 20 months in oak and 3 months in bottle.

Gran Coronas Black Label (Sp). A fine red wine from Torres, Penedés. Produced from Cabernet sauvignon 70%, Cabernet franc 10% and Ull de llebre 20%. Is oak aged.

Gran Crémant Semi Seco (Sp). A slightly sweet-tasting, sparkling white wine that has a dry finish. Produced by the Marqués de Monistrol.

Grand Armagnac Janneau (Fr). Armagnac producer. Address = Janneau Fils SA, 50 Avenue d'Acquitaine, 32100 Condom. Produces – Janneau Tradition 4–5 years old.

Grand Arôme (W.Ind). The name given to those Rums that are produced from molasses, fermented with dunder, coloured with caramel and slow fermented for 8–12 days. Known as Plummer or Wedderburn on the island of Jamaica.

Grand-Bois (Le) (Fr). A wine-producing district in A.C. Bellet, Provence.

Grand Casse (W.Ind). A 'Silver Label' Rum that has been aged for three years. (Derived from Rhum Duquesne production) in Martinique.

Grand Chasseur Estate (Le) (S.Afr). A vineyard based in Robertson. Address = P.O. Box 439, Robertson 6705. Produces varietal wines.

G

Grand Chemarin (Le) (Fr). A vineyard in the commune of Bué, A.C. Sancerre, Central Vineyards, Loire.

Grand Cidre Bouché (Fr). Stoppered cider.

Grand Clos (Fr). An A.C. Bourgueil red wine vineyard.

Grand Conseil de Bordeaux (Fr). A wine society based in Bordeaux.

Grand Cour (Fr). A vineyard in A.C. Fleurie Cru Beaujolais-Villages, Burgundy.

Grand Cru (Bel). A White beer brewed from wheat and oats from the De Kluis Brasserie. 7.5% alc. by vol.

Grand Cru (Fr). In Alsace denotes a specific vineyard site. Once it has been designated any producer wishing to use the 'Grand Cru' on his/her label may do so if the grapes come only from that vineyard with a minimum specified natural sugar content and they are restricted to 70 hl/ha. maximum yield. Produced from noble grapes (Gewürztraminer, Muscat, Pinot gris, Pinot noir and Riesling) and be tested in bottle by a tasting panel. Also known as Grand Vin.

Grand Cru (Fr). The top grading of Burgundy wines. The Tête de Cuvée.

Grand Cru (S.Afr). Great Growth. Makers own rating.

Grand Cru Classé (Fr). Top classification of vineyards in Bordeaux. Barsac 1855, Graves 1953 and 1959, Médoc 1855, Saint-Émilion 1955 (reviewed every 10 years) and Sauternes 1855.

Grand Cru Vineyards (USA). A winery in the Alexander Valley, Sonoma County, California. Grape varieties – Cabernet sauvignon, Chenin blanc, Gewürztraminer and Sauvignon blanc. Produces varietal wines.

Grand Cumberland (Austr). A sweet liqueur made with Passion fruit, golden in colour.

Grand Deluge (Le) (S.Afr). See Roodezandt Co-operative.

Grand Domaine Jean-Voisin (Fr). A vineyard in the commune of Saint-Émilion. A.C. Saint-Émilion, Bordeaux. 2 ha.

Grand Duque de Alba (Sp). Address = Bodegas Zolio Ruiz-Mateos S.A. C/ Porvera 48, Jerez de la Frontera. Source of base wine – Jerez. Produces – Gran Duque de Alba 25–30 year old.

Grande Champagne (Fr). The classical area of Cognac. The ultimate in quality of brandy together with Fine Champagne. Covers 14.4% of the Cognac region. Communes – Ableville, Angeac-Champagne, Bonneuil, Bourg-Charente, Bouteville, Château-Bernard, Cognac, Criteuil-la-Magdeleine, Eraville, Gensac-la-Pallue, Genté, Gimeux, Gondeville, Juillac-le-Coq, Lignières-Sonneville, Mainxe, Malaville, Merpins, Salles-d'Angles, Saint-Brice, Saint-Fort-sur-le-Né, Saint-Même, Saint-Preuil, Segonzac, Touzac, Verrières and Viville.

Grande Cuvée Venus Brut (Fr). A De Luxe cuvée vintage Champagne produced by Germain et Fils from 50% Chardonnay and 50% Pinot noir grapes.

Grande Dame (La) (Fr). A De Luxe vintage cuvée Champagne produced by Veuve Clicquot Ponsardin from 33% Chardonnay and 66% Pinot noir grapes.

Grande Fine Ancestrale (Fr). A 4–5 year old Cognac produced by Menard.

Grande Liqueur (Fr). A green (or yellow) herb liqueur, Green is dry, yellow is sweet.

Grandelite (Port). A wine produced by Ca-Gera Agricola Vinhos Alto Douro.

Grande Marque Impériale (Fr). A vintage cuvée Champagne produced by Abele.

Grande Millésime (Fr). A De Luxe vintage cuvée Champagne produced by Gosset from 66% Chardonnay and 33% Pinot noir grapes.

Grand Empereur (Fr). A well-known brand of Brandy.

Grand Enclos du Château de Cérons (Fr). A vineyard in the commune of Cérons. A.C. Cérons, Bordeaux. 11 ha.

Grande Pièce (La) (Fr). A vineyard in the A.C. commune of Montagny, Côte Chalonnaise, Burgundy.

Grande Pompée (La) (Fr). A vineyard in the A.C. Saint-Joseph, Rhône, southern France.

Grande Réserve (Fr). An old designation in Alsace for 'Late picked'. Same grade as Spätlese in Germany. See also Réserve Spéciale.

Grande Réserve (Lux). The top grading of wines.

Grandes Appellations (Fr). Famous, well-known and consistent A.C. wines. e.g. Médoc, Graves, Sauternes.

Grande Sendrée (Fr). A De Luxe cuvée Champagne produced by André Drappier.

Grandes-Lolières (Les) (Fr). A Premier Cru vineyard in the commune of Ladoix-Serrigny, A.C. Aloxe-Corton, Côte de Beaune, Burgundy.

Grandes Maisons d'Alsace (Fr). G.M.A. Formed by association of eight top quality wine-producing houses of Alsace to promote their wines.

Grandes Marques (Fr). The top 27 Champagne houses. Lit – 'Great brand' or 'Famous name'. Houses are – A. Salon,

Ayala, Bollinger, Billecart Salmon, Canard Duchêne, Charles Heidsieck-Henriot, Ch. et A. Prieur, Geldermann, G.H. Mumm, Heidsieck Monopole, Irroy, Joseph Perrier Fils, Krug, Lanson Père et Fils, Laurent Perrier, Louis Roederer, Massé Père et Fils, Mercier, Moët et Chandon, Montebello, Perrier Jouët, Piper Heidsieck, Pol Roger, Pomméry et Greno, Ruinart Père et Fils, Taittinger and Veuve Clicquot-Ponsardin.

Grandes-Ruchottes (Fr). A Premier Cru vineyard [part] in the A.C. commune of Chassagne-Montrachet, Côte de Beaune, Burgundy. 0.64 ha. Also known as Les Grandes-Ruchottes.

Grandes Terra Alta (Sp). See Terra Alta.

Grandes Versannes (Les) (Fr). The second wine of Château Gravet-Renaissance, Grand Cru A.C. Saint-Émilion.

Grand-Formats (Fr). Large bottle sizes.

Grandjo (Port). A wine produced in Lafões by Real Companhía Vinícola do Norte de Portugal.

Grandma (Eng). Old ale and Mild ale mixed, half and half.

Grandma (Eng). A sweet Stout and Old ale mix in the Midlands.

Grand Marnier (Fr). A Curaçao with a Cognac base. Two versions produced, Cordon Rouge – Fine Champagne Cognac, red brown in colour and Cordon Jaune – lower quality brandy, lower in alcohol and pale yellow. Also a Crème de Grand Marnier.

Grand Marnier-Lapostolle (Fr). A famous liqueur producer. Produces Grand Marnier.

Grand Mousseux (Fr). A term used when a Champagne has the highest pressure in bottle producing a lot of sparkle on pouring.

Grand Mousseux Wines (S.Afr). A brand of sparkling wines produced by the SFW.

Grand Musigny (Fr). An old division of the Grand Cru vineyard of Musigny. The other division was Petit Musigny.

Grand Noir (USA). A white grape variety used in the making of dessert wines in California.

Grand Nord Cocktail (Cktl). ½ measure green Chartreuse, ½ measure Vodka. Stir over ice in an old-fashioned glass.

Grand Old Parr (Scot). See Old Parr.

Grand Pacific Vineyards (USA). A winery based in Marin, near San Francisco, California. Grape varieties – Chardonnay, Merlot and Sauvignon blanc. Produces varietal wines.

Grand Passion Cocktail (Cktl). ⅗ measure dry Gin, ⅖ measure Passion fruit juice, 2 dashes Angostura. Shake over ice, strain into a cocktail glass.

Grand Pompé (Le) (Fr). An A.C. St. Joseph red wine from Jaboulet Aîné in the Côtes du Rhône.

Grand Premier Cru (Lux). Classification of wines. See also Marque Nationale.

Grand Prix Cocktail (Cktl). 1 fl.oz. Vodka, ¾ fl.oz. dry Vermouth, ¼ fl.oz. Curaçao, dash lemon juice, dash Grenadine. Shake well over ice, strain into a goblet. Serve with straws.

Grand Quetsch Cocktail (Cktl). ⅕ gill Grand Marnier, ⅛ gill Quetsch, ⅛ gill orange juice. Stir together over ice, strain into a flute glass filled with crushed ice. Top with a squeeze of orange peel juice.

Grand Réserve (Fr). A wine with over 11% alc. by vol.

Grand River Winery (USA). A winery based in Madison, Ohio. 8 ha. Is planted with Vitis Vinifera and hybrid vines.

Grand Roussillon (Fr). A region in southern France. Famous for sweet and fortified wines. e.g. Banyuls, Rivésaltes, Maury, Côtes du Roussillon.

Grand Royal Fizz (Cktl). 2 fl.ozs. dry Gin, juice ½ lemon, juice ½ orange, 3 dashes Gomme syrup, 2 dashes Maraschino, ½ fl.oz. cream. Shake over ice, strain into an ice-filled highball glass. Top with soda water, stir.

Grands-Champs (Les) (Fr). A Premier Cru vineyard in the A.C. commune of Auxey-Duresses, Côte de Beaune, Burgundy. 4.86 ha.

Grands Crus (Fr). A classification of Bordeaux wines. See Classification of Bordeaux.

Grands Crus Classés (Fr). See Classification of Bordeaux.

Grands-Échezeaux (Fr). A Grand Cru vineyard in the A.C. commune Vosne-Romanée, Côte de Nuits, Burgundy. 9.2 ha.

Grand Slam (Cktl). ¼ measure sweet Vermouth, ¼ measure dry Vermouth, ½ measure Swedish Punsch. Stir over ice, strain into a cocktail glass.

Grand Slam Cocktail (Cktl). ¼ measure Irish whiskey, ¼ measure Glayva, ¼ measure dry Gin, ¼ measure Cointreau, ½ measure orange juice, dash Grenadine. Shake well over ice, pour into a large goblet. Dress with an orange slice, blue cherry and serve with straws.

Grandson (Switz). A red and white wine-producing area in northern Vaud.

Granduca Brut (It). A sparkling (méthode

champenoise) wine produced by Duca d'Asti, Piemonte.

Granducato (It). A Chianti Classico producer based in Siena, Tuscany.

Gran Duque d'Alba (Sp). An amber-coloured, Gran Reserva brandy produced by Don Zolio in Jerez de la Frontera. (Part of Diez-Merito).

Grand Val (USA). The second wine of Clos du Val, Napa Valley, California.

Grand Vin (Fr). An Alsace grading which can only be used on wines coming from superior grape varieties and containing 11% alc. by vol. Also referred to as Grand Cru.

Granel (Sp). The name given to a white wine produced in bulk by Bodega Cooperativa de Ribeiro.

Gran Enologica (Sp). A fine red wine produced by Rioja Santiago S.A., Rioja.

Granfiesta (Austr). A brand of Australian sherry produced by Quelltaler in Clare Watervale, South Australia.

Gran Fuedo (Sp). The brand-name of a 4 year old red wine produced by Julián Chivite in Navarra. Also the name of a rosé wine.

Grange Hermitage (Austr). A red wine from the Penfold Co. vineyards in South Australia. Shiraz grape.

Grängesbergs Brewery (Swe). A brewery based in Grängesberg, central Sweden. Produces fine Lager beers.

Granila al Caffé (It). An iced coffee with 'frozen' egg white, it is eaten with Rum.

Granite (Fr). Soil composition suitable for grape cultivation. Consists of Granitic sand. e.g. Northern Rhône and Beaujolais.

Granite Belt (Austr). A wine region in Queensland.

Granja Nuestra Señora de Remelluri (La) (Sp). Vineyard. Address = Labastida, Alava, Rioja. 40 ha. in the Rioja Alavesta. Produces Remelluri (a red estate wine from 10% Mazuela, 80% Tempranillo and 10% Viura).

Granja Remelluri (La) (Sp). See Granja Nuestra Señora de Remelluri (La).

Granja União (Bra). A label used by Indústria Comércio e Navegação, Sociedade Vinícola Rio Grandense, Ltda. for its' red and white wines.

Granjo (Port). A naturally sweet white wine.

Gran Manzeda (Eng). A fine Manzanilla sherry from Balls Brothers of London.

Gran Negro (Sp). A red grape variety grown in Galicia.

Grano (Sp). The berry of the grape. A single grape.

Gran Orden de Caballeros del Vino (Sp). A wine fellowship created by Vino de

España in 1985. Created to honour people in the wine trade who have given outstanding personal service to the furtherance of Spanish wines.

Gran Provence (S.Afr). A sparkling, medium-sweet, white wine made from Clairette blanche and Steen grapes by Union Wines.

Gran Reservas (Sp). Wines that have been matured for more than 6 years in cask.

Gran Sangre de Toro (Sp). A fine red wine from Torres, Penedés. Produced from Cariñena 40% and Garnacha 60%. Is oak aged.

Grans Brewery (Nor). A brewery based in Sandefjord in south-eastern Norway.

Gran Señor Choice Old Cream (Sp). A brand of Cream sherry produced by Caballero.

Gran Spumante (It). A dry sparkling wine from the Pinot grape made by the méthode champenoise.

Grant and Sons (Scot). See William Grant.

Gran Torres (Sp). A Brandy and orange liqueur produced by the Torres Co. in Penedés.

Grant (William and Sons) (Scot). A famous Scotch whisky distillery based at Dufftown, Banffshire. Produces Highland and Lowland Malt whiskies and blended Scotch whiskies. See Glenfiddich, Grants Royal, Standfast, The Balvenie.

Grant's (Scot). A 12 year old De Luxe Scotch whisky. Is a re-designed and re-named version of Grant's Royal from William Grant and Sons. 43% alc. by vol.

Grantschen (Ger). Village. (Anb) = Württemberg. (Ber) = Württembergisch Unterland. (Gro) = Salzberg. (Vin) = Wildenberg.

Grant's Morello Cherry Brandy (Eng). A Kent-made liqueur 25% alc. by vol.

Grants of St. James (Eng). London based wine merchants famous for their 'Don Cortez' Spanish wines. See also Le Soir.

Grant's Royal (Scot). See Grant's.

Grant's Standfast (Scot). A blended Scotch Whisky from William Grant and Sons, Banffshire.

Granules (Eng). A style of instant coffee produced by freeze drying. The resulting powder is shaped into granules to imitate ground coffee.

Gran Val (USA). The label used by the Clos du Val Wine Co. for their range of varietal wines.

Gran Vas (Sp). The cuve close sparkling wine method (the second fermentation carried out in a sealed container and not in the bottle). Also written Granvas.

Granvas (Sp). See Gran Vas.

Gran-Vas (Sp). See Dom Yago Rosado.

Gran Viña Sol (Sp). A fine white wine from

G

Torres, Penedés. Produced from Chardonnay 20% and Parellada 80%.

Gran Viña Sol Green Label (Sp). A fine white wine from Torres, Penedés. Produced from Parellada 70% and Sauvignon blanc 30%.

Gran Vino (Chile). A wine older than six years before bottling.

Gran Vino Godello (Sp). A very dry, white varietal wine produced by the Cooperativa Jesus Nazareno 13.5% alc. by vol.

Gran Vino Para Banquetes (Chile). Label term 'Great wine for banquets'.

Gran Vino Tinto (Chile). A red wine produced by Undurraga.

Grão Vasco (Port). The brand-name for red and white Dão wines blended and matured by SOGRAPE at Viseu.

Grapa (Sp). The name given to a metal hook that retains the temporary corks during sparkling (cava) wine manufacture. (Fr) = Agrafe.

Grape (Eng). The fruit of the Vitis Vinifera that produces the raw material for wine making. A wide variety of species is grown around the world. (Fr) = Raisin, (Ger) = Traube, (Hol) = Druif, (It) (Lat) (Port) (Sp) = Uva, (Tur) = Üzüm, (Wales) = Grawnwin.

Grape (The) (Eng) (slang). A term for wine. See Juice of the Grape.

Grape Brandy (Eng). Any other brandy produced from the distillation of wine other than Cognac or Armagnac. See Aguardiente, Bagaceira, Grappa and Marc.

Grape Bud Mite (Eng). Eriophyes Vitis. See Acariosis.

Grape Certificate Program (USA). Formed by the University of California in 1952 to certify authentic grape varieties.

Grape Cocktail (Cktl).(Non-alc). ¼ gill grape juice, ¼ gill plain syrup, 2 slices fresh fruit, dash Angostura. Stir over ice, strain into a highball glass. Fill with soda water.

Grape Crusher (Eng). The general term for a unit which presses the whole grape to extract the juice. See Grape Mill.

Grapefruit Champagne (Cktl).(Non-alc). ⅓ gill grapefruit juice, 3 dashes lemon juice, dash Gomme syrup. Shake well over ice, strain into a flute glass. Top with iced lemonade.

Grapefruit Cocktail (Cktl). ½ measure grapefruit juice, ½ measure Gin, dash Gomme syrup. Shake over ice, strain into a cocktail glass.

Grapefruit Nog (Cktl). 3 fl.ozs. grapefruit juice, 1½ fl.ozs. Brandy, 1 fl.oz. lemon juice, 1 egg, 2 teaspoons honey. Blend altogether with a scoop of crushed ice. Pour into an ice-filled highball glass.

Grape Leafhoppers (USA). Insects that attack the cell structure of the leaf. Causes defoliation and turns grapes to raisins through too much sunshine.

Grape Mash (USA). Grape juice, skins and pips used for red wines so that at the start of fermentation, the tannin and colour are extracted.

Grape-Mill (USA). Another name for the grape crusher.

Grape of the Estruscans (It). See Canaiolo Nero.

Grape Pie (USA). The grape pulp after juice extraction.

Grape Rust Mite (Eng). Calepitrimerus Vitis, Phyllocoptes Vitis. See Acariosis.

Grape Spirit (Eng). Brandy.

Grape Sugar (Eng). Glucose $C_6H_{12}O_6$ and Dextrose are grape sugars.

Grape Vodka Froth (Cktl). ⅗ measure Vodka, ⅕ measure grape juice, ⅕ measure lemon juice, 1 egg white. Shake well over ice, strain into a 5 oz. goblet.

Grapey (Eng). The term used to describe the flavour and bouquet given off by certain grape varieties. If the flavour is too pronounced the wines usually lack subtlety.

Grappa (It). The Italian equivalent of French Marc. After grape juice has been removed, residue is fermented and distilled to produce a harsh brandy. Also made from distilled wine. Can be both Pot or Patent stilled. Flavoured with a sprig of Rue as an infusion.

Grappa (S.Am). A spirit flavoured with aniseed, distilled from cane sugar. 45% alc. by vol. Produced in Colombia and Ecuador.

Grappa (USA). See California Grappa.

Grappa Blanche (W.Ind). The name given to a Rum produced in Martinique that has no cask ageing.

Grappa Bochino (It). An oak-aged Grappa produced in Friuli. Is pale-gold in colour.

Grappa d'Or (Switz). Golden grape.

Grappa Julia (Eng). The brand-name of a Grappa produced by Stocks Distilleries in Trieste, Piemonte. 40% alc. by vol.

Grappa Strega (Cktl). ½ measure Grappa, ½ measure Strega, 3 dashes lemon juice, 3 dashes orange juice. Shake well over ice, strain into a cocktail glass.

Grappe (Fr). A bunch of grapes.

Grappes d'Or (Fr). A three star Cognac produced by Dupuy.

Grapple (Eng). The name used by Chilsdown for a ½ apple and ½ Chilsdown wine.

Grappling Hook (Cktl). Equal quantities of red wine, Port wine and Brandy shaken over ice, strained into a cocktail glass.

Grappolo (It). A bunch of grapes.

Grapy (Eng). See Grapey. (Alternative spelling).

Gras (Fr). Ropey. See Rope. A condition (malady) of the wine. Is also used to describe a rich, round, robust wine.

Gras (Les) (Fr). See Cras (Les).

Grasă (Rum). The local name for the Furmint grape.

Grasă di Cotnari (Rum). Equivalent of the Hungarian Furmint. Produced from the Grasă grape.

Graşevina (Yug). A fine medium white wine from Croatia. Made from the Welschriesling grape. See also Grassevina.

Grasgeschmack (Aus). Denotes a taste of green plants, usually derived from unripe grapes or those that have been overpressed.

Grasica (Yug). A local name for the white grape variety Welschriesling. See also Grassevina.

Graspa (It). The Venetian spelling of Grappa.

Grassevina (Yug). A local name for the Welschriesling. See also Grasica and Graşevina.

Grasshopper (Cktl).(1). ¾ fl.oz. (green) Crème de Menthe, ¾ fl.oz. (white) Crème de Cacao, ¾ fl.oz. light cream. Shake well with ice, strain into a cocktail glass.

Grasshopper (Cktl).(2). In a liqueur glass pour in ½ measure Crème de Menthe then ½ measure Crème de Cacao. Do not stir.

Grassy (Eng). A term used mainly for wines made from the Gewürztraminer, Sauvignon blanc and Scheurebe grapes which have a grassy type of fruitiness.

Graticci (It). Straw mats used for drying the grapes for Passito wines.

Gratien (Alfred) (Fr). Champagne producer. Address = 30 Rue Maurice Cervaux, 51201 Épernay. Produces Vintage and non-vintage wines. Vintages – 1904, 1906, 1926, 1928, 1929, 1933, 1934, 1937, 1938, 1942, 1943, 1945, 1947, 1949, 1952, 1953, 1955, 1959, 1961, 1962, 1964, 1966, 1969, 1970, 1971, 1973, 1976, 1979, 1982, 1983.

Gratien et Meyer (Fr). Négociants in Anjou-Saumur. Produce fine sparkling wines by the méthode champenoise. Address = Route de Montsoreau, B.P. 22–16135 Saumur-Cedex. See Royal Framboise.

Gratiesti (USSR). A dessert wine produced from the Rcakzitelli grape in the Moldavia region.

Gratitude (La) (S.Afr). A dry white wine from the Steen and Clairette blanche grapes produced by the SFW at their Libertas Winery.

Gratte-Cul (Fr). A flavoured spirit made from the dog rose.

Grauburgunder (Ger). See Grauerburgunder.

Grau Clevner (Fr). A local name for the Pinot blanc grape.

Grauerburgunder (Ger). A local name for the Pinot gris grape.

Grauer Riesling (Ger). An eroneous varietal name for the red Ruländer.

Graukatz (Ger). Vineyard. (Anb) = Nahe. (Ber) = Schloss Böckelheim. (Gro) = Paradiesgarten. (Vil) = Gaugrehweiler.

Graukatz (Ger). Vineyard. (Anb) = Nahe. (Ber) = Schloss Böckelheim. (Gro) = Paradiesgarten. (Vil) = Kalkofen.

Graukatz (Ger). Vineyard. (Anb) = Nahe. (Ber) = Schloss Böckelheim. (Gro) = Paradiesgarten. (Vil) = Münsterappel.

Graukatz (Ger). Vineyard. (Anb) = Nahe. (Ber) = Schloss Böckelheim. (Gro) = Paradiesgarten. (Vil) = Niederhausen an der Nahe.

Graukatz (Ger). Vineyard. (Anb) = Nahe. (Ber) = Schloss Böckelheim. (Gro) = Paradiesgarten. (Vil) = Oberhausen an der Nahe.

Graukatz (Ger). Vineyard. (Anb) = Nahe. (Ber) = Schloss Böckelheim. (Gro) = Paradiesgarten. (Vil) = Winterborn.

Graukatz (Ger). Vineyard. (Anb) = Rheinhessen. (Ber) = Bingen. (Gro) = Rheingrafenstein. (Vil) = Tiefenthal.

Graumönch (Ger). Lit – 'Grey monk'. The German name for the Pinot gris. Also known as the Grey Friar in Hungary.

Grauvernatsch (It). The German name for a red wine from the Südtirol region. Known as Schiava grigia in Italy.

Grauves (Fr). A Premier Cru Champagne village in the Canton d'Avize. District = Épernay. (Red and white grapes).

Grave del Friuli (It). D.O.C. red wines from Friuli-Venezia Giulia. The name is followed by the grape variety. Grave del Friuli Cabernet, Grave del Friuli Merlot and Grave del Friuli Reposco. Also name for white wines Grave del Friuli Pinot bianco, Grave del Fruili Pinot grigio, Grave del Friuli Tocai and Grave del Fruili Verduzzo. Vinification can take place in the Udine and Pordenone provinces and several communes.

Gravedigger Beer (Eng). A cask conditioned Bitter 1050 O.G. brewed by the home-brew public houses Pier Hotel in Gravesend and the South-eastern in Strood.

Gravel (Fr). See Graves. A wide area of

G

Bordeaux, has soil of a gravelly nature.

Gravel (USA). A term used for the tartrate crystals which appear in wines that have been chilled and precipitated out.

Gravelly Meadow (USA). The brandname used by the Diamond Creek Winery for one of their styles of wines from the vineyard of that name.

Graves (Fr). A commune in the Charente Département whose grapes are classed Petite Champagne (Cognac).

Graves (Fr). A large wine district in Bordeaux on the S.E. bank of the river Garonne around and to the south of Bordeaux town. Named after its' gravel soil. Produces fine red and white wines. Communes = Arbanats, Ayguemortes, Beautiran, Budos, Castres, Cadaujac, Canéjean, Cérons, Eyzines, Gradignan, La Brède, Landiras, Langon, Léognan, Martillac, Mazères, Mérignac, Pessac, Podensac, Portets, Pujols, Ropaillan, St-Médard d'Eyrans, St-Morillon, St-Pardons-de-Conques, St-Pierre-de-Mons, St-Selve, Toulenne, Villenave-d'Ornon and Virelade.

Graves Bonne Terre (Fr). The brandname for a dry white wine from Sichels.

Graves de Saint-Émilion (Fr). A small Saint-Émilion district. Name derives from the soil (gravel).

Graves de Vayres (Fr). A district south of the Côtes de Fronsac in the Bordeaux region. Produces red and white wines.

Graves et Sables Anciens (Fr). Lit – 'Gravel with old sand'. A production zone in Saint-Émilion, south-eastern Bordeaux.

Graves Saint-Émilion (Fr). See Graves de Saint-Émilion.

Graves Supérieures (Fr). Denotes a white wine from the A.C. Graves that has attained 12% alc. by vol. by natural fermentation.

Gravier (Fr). Gravelly soil.

Gravières (Les) (Fr). A Premier Cru vineyard [part] in the A.C. commune of Santenay, Côte de Beaune, Burgundy.

Gravillons (Fr). A coarse gravel soil in the commune of Margaux in Bordeaux. Is grittier than the sandy topsoil. Found underneath.

Gravina (It). The brand-name of a well-known Grappa.

Graviscanum (Lat). A red wine produced in central-western Italy during Roman times.

Gravitas (Fr). A wine with weight, body.

Gravity (Eng). A measure of the beer's density. See Original Gravity.

Gravity (Eng). The name given to method of dispensing beer direct from the cask behind the bar.

Grawnwin (Wales). Grapes.

Gray Dutchess (USA). See Grey Riesling.

Graylyn (Austr). A winery based in the Margaret River, Western Australia.

Gray Riesling (USA). The alternative name for the Chauche gris. See also Trousseau, Grey Riesling.

Gräzer (Aus). A white grape variety which is little used nowadays. Is also known as the Banater riesling.

Graziola (It). A Moscato d'Asti Spumante producer based in the Piemonte region.

Great (Eng). A term used to describe a wine which has no flaws and has real distinction.

Great British Beer Festival (Eng). Annual celebration run by the CAMRA organisation which has up to 250 different beers for tasting.

Great British Heavy (Eng). A strong Bitter beer brewed by the Cornish Brewery Co, Devon.

Great Cask (Ger). Sited in the castle at Heidelberg in Baden. Holds 220,000 litres.

Great Central Valley (USA). A wine area of California. Produces mainly sweet dessert wines.

Greater London Alcohol Advisory Service (Eng). See G.L.A.A.S.

Greatest Reform Act (USA). The name given to the Prohibition of the USA in 1919–1933. See also Noble Experiment.

Great Growth (Fr). A term used to describe the top classified wines from Bordeaux and Burgundy.

Great Guns Cocktail (Cktl).(1). ⅙ gill Dubonnet, ⅛ gill dry Vermouth, ⅛ gill pale Sherry, 2 dashes Angostura. Stir over ice, strain into a cocktail glass. Serve with a cherry and a dash of lemon peel juice on top.

Great Guns Cocktail (Cktl).(2). As for (1) using Orange bitters and orange peel juice instead of Angostura and lemon peel juice.

Great Northern Bitter (Eng). A keg/canned Bitter 1036 O.G. brewed by the Watney Mann, Truman breweries.

Great Plain (Hun). The largest wine-producing area. Stretches from the Rumanian border to the river Danube.

Great River Winery (USA). A winery based in the Hudson Valley, New York. Is noted for its' French hybrid and Marlboro sparkling wines.

Great Thirst (The) (USA). The years of the Prohibition 1919–1933 were often called this mainly for the lack of beer.

Great Wall Chinese Vodka (China). The

brand-name of the first Vodka produced in China. (1976). Made from mineral water and golden wheat. 40% alc. by vol.

Great Wall White Wine (China). A white wine produced from the Loong Yan (Dragon's Eye) grape by the Great Wall Wineries in Hebei.

Great Wall Wineries (China). A large winery based in Hebei. Produces dry fragrant white wines from the Loong Yan grape. See also Dragon's Eye.

Great Western (Austr). An area in Victoria noted for its' fine sparkling wines.

Great Western (USA). The brand-name used by the Pleasant Valley Wine Co. for their California Champagne range.

Great Western Beer Festival (Eng). The name for a commercial beer festival held annually in Bristol for beers and lagers.

Great Western Bitter (Wales). A keg Bitter 1041 O.G. brewed by the Crown Brewery in South Wales.

Great Western Winery (Austr). Winery in Seppelts. Address = Western Highway, Great Western, Victoria.

Grecanico (It). A white grape variety grown in Sicily.

Grechetto Bianco (It). A white grape variety grown in Umbria.

Grechetto di Todi (It). A white Vino da Tavola from the Grechetto grape produced in Todi, Umbria.

Grecian Urn (Gre). The name given to a dry red and a dry white table wine from Tsantali.

Greco (It). A white grape variety grown mainly in central Italy. Known as the Grechetto in Tuscany.

Greco Bianco (It). A white grape variety grown in Calabria.

Greco di Gerace (It). A white grape variety used in the making of fine dessert wines of the same name in Calabria.

Greco di Gerace (It). A golden amber dessert wine from Calabria. It has an orange blossom nose, and is high in sugar and alcohol 16–17% by vol.

Greco di Tufo (It). A white grape variety grown in the Campania region.

Greco di Tufo (It). D.O.C. white wine from Campania. Made from the Coda di Volpe bianco and Greco di tufo grapes. Vinification can take place throughout the province of Avellino. D.O.C. also applies to the sparkling wines obtained according to the regulations.

Greco Giallo (It). The Latium region name for the white Trebbiano giallo grape variety.

Greco Hermanos (Arg). Wine-producers based in Mendoza. Produces Oro del Rhin (a dry white wine).

Greco Nero (It). A red grape variety grown in Calabria.

Greece (Gre). Country on the north eastern Mediterranean. A very old wine producing country. Noted for its dessert wines and for resin-flavoured 'Retsina'. See also Demestica.

Greek Wine Information Bureau (Eng). Address = The Old Vicarage, Newstead Abbey Park, Nottingham. NG15 8GE.

Green (Eng). The term applied to wines that are young and tart. e.g. Vinhos Verdes.

Greenall Whitley (Eng). A large brewery based in Warrington. Also owns the Wem Brewery in Shropshire and the Shipstone Brewery in Nottingham. Noted for its' bottled Bulls Eye Brown 1035 O.G. Champion Ale 1038 O.G. Grünhalle Lager 1035 O.G. keg Festival 1039 O.G. Old Chester 1067 O.G. Old Glory 1074 O.G. Red Rose Stout 1074 O.G. and D.B. Pils 1038 O.G.

Green and Red Vineyard (USA). A winery based in the Napa Valley, California. 3 ha. Grape variety – Zinfandel.

Greenback Cocktail (Cktl). ⅗ measure Gin, ⅕ measure (green) Crème de Menthe, ⅕ measure lemon juice. Shake over ice, strain into an ice-filled old-fashioned glass.

Green Bean (Eng). The name given to the unroasted coffee beans.

Green Beer (Eng). Unmatured raw materials used in the brewing process which have been converted to a liquid. Produce 'green beer' which is then matured for a further period.

Greenbriar (Cktl). ⅓ measure dry Vermouth, ⅔ measure dry Sherry, dash Peach bitters. Stir over ice, strain into a cocktail glass. Add a sprig of mint.

Green Buck Cocktail (Cktl). ⅕ gill Metaxa brandy, juice ½ lemon. Shake over ice, strain into an ice-filled highball glass. Top with ginger ale and float a teaspoonful of Ouzo on top.

Green Chartreuse (Fr) (Sp). A potent herb-flavoured liqueur originally made to treat Cholera victims in 1832.

Green Coffee (Eng). Coffee beans before they are dried and roasted.

Green Death (USA). A Beer brewed by the Rainier Brewery in Seattle, Washington. Has a green label, hence the name. 7.25% alc. by vol.

Green Devil Cocktail (Cktl). ⅓ gill dry Gin, ⅛ gill (green) Crème de Menthe, juice of ¼ orange. Shake over ice, strain into an ice-filled highball glass. Top with mint leaves.

Green Dragon (Cktl). ½ measure dry Gin, ¼ measure (green) Crème de Menthe, ⅛ measure Kümmel, ⅛ measure lemon juice. Shake over ice, strain into a cocktail glass.

Green Dragon Cocktail (Cktl). ⅓ gill Pernod, ⅓ gill Milk, ⅙ gill Gomme syrup. Shake over ice, strain into an ice-filled highball glass.

Greenfield (USA). A wine town in the Salinas Valley, Monterey, California.

Green Fizz (Cktl).(1). 2 fl.ozs. Gin, juice ½ lemon, 4 dashes (green) Crème de Menthe, 4 dashes Gomme syrup, 1 egg white. Shake over ice, strain into an ice-filled highball glass. Top with soda.

Green Fizz (Cktl).(2). 1 part lime juice, 2 parts white wine. Stir together in an ice-filled highball glass. Top with sparkling Ashbourne water.

Green Ginger Wine (Eng). Produced by the Finsbury Distillery. Brand-name is Stone's. Made from dried grapes, fortified and powdered pure root ginger is added. Matured for 9 months in oak vats.

Green Ginger Wine (Scot). Produced by Crabbie's since 1801.

Green Goddess (Eng). An egg-based drink produced by Townend of Hull.

Green Goddess (Fr). A nickname given to Pernod because of its' colour.

Green Goddess (Fr). The old nickname for Absinthe.

Green Grape (S.Afr). A white grape variety also known as the Groendruif.

Green Gunpowder (Eng). A tea from China and Formosa. The leaf has the appearance of gunpowder (curled leaf). See Pin Head. Called Pearl Tea in China. Low in caffeine.

Greenhall Ltd (Eng). Distillers based in Warrington, Lancashire. Produces 1761 and Bombay London Dry Gins and Vladivar Vodka.

Green Hope (Cktl). ½ measure Vodka, ⅛ measure Crème de Banane, ¼ measure Bols green Curaçao, ⅛ measure grape juice, dash lemon juice. Shake over ice, strain into a cocktail glass. Add a cherry.

Green Hornet (Cktl). 2 fl.ozs. Vodka, juice of a lime. Shake over ice, strain into an ice-filled highball glass. Top with soda water and a slice of lime.

Green Hungarian (USA). A white grape variety grown in California to make dessert and white table wines.

Green Island (Afr). A brand of cane spirit from Mauritius.

Greene King (Eng). Has breweries in Bury St. Edmunds, Biggleswade and Furneux Pelham. Noted for its' cask conditioned Abbot Ale 1048 O.G. Farm Stout 1035 O.G. Harvest Brown 1031 O.G. King Keg 1038 O.G. St.Edmund 1060 O.G. Strong Suffolk 1056 O.G. and Yeoman 1038 O.G.

Green Label (Austr). A strong Bitter beer 4.56% alc. by vol. brewed by the Cascade Brewery in Tasmania.

Green Label (Eng). A bottled XXXXXX Ale 1040 O.G. brewed by the Wadworth Brewery in Wiltshire.

Green Label (Eng). A keg/tank Mild 1034 O.G. brewed by the Webster Brewery in Halifax, Yorkshire. Bottled/canned version 1038 O.G.

Green Label (Ger). A well-known brand of Bereich Bernkastel Qmp. produced by Deinhard in Koblenz.

Green Lady (Cktl). ½ measure dry Gin, ⅓ measure green Chartreuse, ⅓ measure yellow Chartreuse. Shake over ice, strain into a cocktail glass. Top with a slice of lime.

Green Malt (Eng). Germinated barley before it is transferred to the kiln for drying.

Greenmantle (Scot). A cask conditioned Ale 1038 O.G. brewed by the Broughton Brewery.

Greenmeadows (N.Z.). Vineyards based in the Hawke's Bay region. Are owned by Marist Fathers who produce red and white wines and liqueurs.

Green Mist (Cktl). ¼ measure Italian vermouth, ¼ measure French vermouth, ¼ measure Galliano, ¼ measure green Chartreuse. Stir over ice, strain into a cocktail glass.

Green Muse (USA). The name given for Absinthe. 'The water of the star Wormwood'.

Greenness (Eng). A term applied to wines that are young and not ready for drinking.

Green Opal (Cktl). ½ measure Pernod, ½ measure dry Gin, ½ measure Anisette. Shake over ice, strain into a cocktail glass.

Green Room (Cktl). ⅔ measure dry Vermouth, ⅓ measure Brandy, 2 dashes orange Curaçao. Stir over ice, strain into a cocktail glass.

Green's (Port). Vintage Port shippers.

Green Seal (W.Ind). A brand of dark Rum produced by Wray and Nephew on the island of Jamaica.

Green Silvaner (Ger). A white grape variety also known as Franken riesling, Monterey riesling and Sonoma riesling.

Greensleeves (Eng). A green liqueur made from brandy and flavoured with peppermint.

Green Snake (The) (USSR). A nickname

given to alcohol in Russia.

Green's Vineyard (Eng). Address = Ongar Farms Ltd., Green's Moreton, Essex. 1.75 ha. Grape varieties – Huxelrebe, Kerner, Müller-Thurgau, Scheurebe, Schönburger and Wurzer.

Green Swizzle (Cktl). As for Gin Swizzle but with 2 barspoons of green Crème de Menthe. (Other spirits may be used instead of Gin).

Green Sylvaner (Ger). See Green Silvaner.

Green Tea (Eng). The designation for unfermented tea from China, Japan and Taiwan.

Green Tea Liqueur (Jap). A liqueur made from Matcha powdered tea essence and Gyokuro rolled tea. Also called O-Cha.

Green Tea Powder (Jap). The original instant tea! Made from tea extracts. Also known as soluble tea.

Green Top Ale (Eng). A bottled Export Ale 1042 O.G. brewed by the Eldridge Pope Brewery in Dorchester, Dorset.

Green Valley Vineyards (USA). A winery based in Hermann, Missouri. Produces mainly hybrid wines.

Green Vodka (Pol). Made by steeping Zubrowka grass in Polish vodka. Has a delicate aromatic bouquet. Bottle often contains a stem of the grass.

Green Whiskey (USA). The name given to the spirit after it has been distilled and before it is matured. Is colourless.

Green Wine (Eng). Young wines. e.g. Portuguese Vinhos Verdes.

Greenwood's (Eng). The West Crown Brewery in Newark, Nottingham. Brews Greenwood's N° 8 and N° 10 beers.

Greffe (Fr). Graft.

Greffe Anglaise (Fr). Lit – 'English graft'. A whip and tongue graft. See Graft.

Greffieux (Les) (Fr). A vineyard in the A.C. Hermitage, northern Rhône.

Grégoire (Henri-Lucius) (Fr). A producer of Crémant de Bourgogne based at Davaye, Burgundy.

Greguniedda (It). A sweet dessert wine produced in Oristano, Sardinia.

Greifenberg (Ger). Vineyard. (Anb) = Rheinhessen. (Ber) = Bingen. (Gro) = Adelberg. (Vil) = Sulzheim.

Greifenlau Brauerei (Ger). A brewery based in Bamburg. Produces Rauchbiers.

Greiner (Ger). Vineyard. (Anb) = Württemberg. (Ber) = Remstal-Stuttgart. (Gro) = Kopf. (Vil) = Kleinheppach.

Greiveldange (Lux). A wine village on the river Moselle. Vineyard sites – Huette, Herrenberg.

Greiveldange (Lux). One of six co-

operatives belonging to Vinsmoselle.

Greke Wyne (Eng). The sixteenth century spelling of Greek Wine (the fortified and sweet wines of Greece).

Gremi (USSR). A white grape variety grown in Georgia. Is used in the production of Brandy.

Gremio dos Exportadores (Port). The Portuguese official body which controls quality and production of wines for export.

Grenache (Fr). A good quality red grape grown in the southern Rhône and other regions of southern France plus the Rioja in Spain (See Garnacho). Also grown in North Africa and California. Also known as the Alicante, Alicante Grenache, Aragón, Garnacha, Garnache, Granaccia, Grenache nera, Roussillon tinto, Tinto aragonés and Uva di spagna.

Grenache Nera (Sp). An alternative name for the Grenache grape.

Grenache Rosé (USA). A rosé wine produced in California from the Grenache grape.

Grenadier (Cktl).(1). 1 oz. Cognac, 1 oz. ginger wine, teaspoon powdered sugar. Shake well with ice, strain into a cocktail glass.

Grenadier (Cktl).(2) (Non-alc). ⅙ gill Grenadine, juice ½ orange. Shake over ice, strain into an ice-filled highball glass. Top with tonic water and an orange slice.

Grenadine (Fr). A non-alcoholic red syrup made from Pomegranates.

Grenadine Cocktail (Cktl). 3 parts Grenadine, 6 parts Gin, 1 part lemon juice, 3 dashes Orange bitters. Shake well with ice, strain into a cocktail glass.

Grenadine Rickey (Cktl).(Non-alc). 1½ fl.ozs. Grenadine, juice ½ lime. Stir over ice in a highball glass. Top with soda water and a slice of lime.

Grenadine Shake Cocktail (Cktl).(Non-alc). 1 measure pineapple juice, 1 measure Grenadine, ½ measure lemon juice, 1 egg white. Blend with a scoop of crushed ice in a blender. Pour into a club goblet, top with lemonade. Dress with a cherry and sprig of mint.

Grenenmacher (Lux). One of six co-operatives. Part of Vinsmoselle.

Grenon (Fr). Cognac producer. Address = Dom-Pierre-sur-Charente, 17610 Chaniers. 32 ha. in the Petite Champagne and Borderies.

Grenouilles (Fr). An A.C. Grand Cru Chablis, Burgundy.

Gren Vino Sanson (Sp). A dark, sweet Málaga Lágrima made with the Lágrima (tear) must by Hijos de Antonio Barceló. Sold under the Barcarles label.

G

Grenzach (Ger). Village. (Anb) = Baden. (Ber) = Markgräflerland. (Gro) = Vogtei Rötteln. (Vin) = Hornfelsen.

Grenzquell (Ger). A dry malt beer from the Bavaria-St. Pauli in Hamburg. Is marketed in the USA by Olympia.

Grésigny (Fr). Vineyard based in the A.C. commune of Rully, Côte Chalonnaise, Burgundy.

Gressier Grand Poujeaux (Fr). A vineyard in the commune of Moulis. A.C. Haut-Médoc, Bordeaux. Cru Bourgeois.

Greth (Ger). Vineyard. (Anb) = Mosel-Saar-Ruwer. (Ber) = Zell/Mosel. (Gro) = Rosenhang. (Vil) = Treis-Karden.

Greuth (Ger). Village. (Anb) = Franken. (Ber) = Steigerwald. (Gro) = Schild. (Vin) = Bastel.

Grevenmacher (Lux). A wine village on the river Moselle in the north. Vineyard sites – Fels, Groerd, Rosenberg. Soil – Marl and Mussellime (chalk).

Grèves (Les) (Fr). A Premier Cru vineyard (including La Vigne de l'Enfant Jesus) in the A.C. commune of Beaune, Côte de Beaune, Burgundy, 31.68 ha.

Grewenich (Ger). Village. (Anb) = Mosel-Saar-Ruwer. (Ber) = Obermosel. (Gro) = Königsberg. (Vin) = Sites not yet chosen.

Grey Champagne (Fr). The old name for still Champagne that had a light rosé colour.

Grey Friar (Fr). An alternative name for the Pinot gris.

Greyhound (Eng). A home-brew public house of the Clifton Inns Co. Noted for its' cask conditioned Streatham Strong 1047 O.G. and the Greyhound Special 1037 O.G.

Greyhound Special (Eng). See Greyhound.

Grey Mould (Fr). A botrytis attack on red grapes. See Pourriture Gris.

Grey Pinot (USA). An American name for the Pinot gris.

Grey Riesling (USA). A white grape variety grown in California to make average white wines. See also Chauche Gris, Gray Riesling and Grey Dutchess.

Grey Rot (Fr). Pourriture gris. The rot which is found in damp conditions and lowers the quality of the grape must. Cure is good climatic conditions. See Grey Mould.

Greystone (USA). The label name used by the Perelli-Minetti Winery.

Grgich Hills (USA). A large winery based near Rutherford, Napa Valley, California. 58 ha. Grape varieties – Chardonnay, Johannisberg Zinfandel. Produces varietal wines.

Gries (Fr). A lesser white grape variety grown in Alsace.

Griffi (It). A red Vino da Tavola made from the Cabernet 10–30% and Sangiovese 80–90% in central-western Italy.

Griffin Vineyards (USA). See Hop Kiln Winery. 21 ha.

Grifforin (Fr). An alternative name for the Malbec grape.

Grigia (It). A variety of the Schiave gentile red grape.

Grigio-Verde (Cktl). ½ measure Grappa, ½ measure Crème de Menthe. Stir together over ice. strain into a cocktail glass.

Grignan (Fr). A herb liqueur made by Trappist monks, similar to Chartreuse. 45% alc. by vol.

Grignolino (It). A red wine grape variety of excellent quality grown in the Piemonte region. Produces a wine of unmistakable bouquet.

Grignolino (It). A red wine from the Piemonte region named after the red grape variety of same name.

Grignolino (USA). See California Grignolino.

Grignolino d'Asti (It). D.O.C. red wine from Piemonte. Made from the Grignolino grape. Produced throughout the 35 communes in the province of Asti.

Grignolino del Monferrato Casalese (It). D.O.C. red wine from Piemonte. Made from the Grignolino grape, grown within the 35 communes in Monteferrato Casalese.

Grignolino Rosé (USA). A rosé wine produced from the Grignolino grape in California.

Grillo (It). A white grape variety grown in Sicily. Used in the making of Marsala.

Grimbergen (Bel). An Abbaye-style beer brewed by the Maes Brewery which is owned by Watneys.

Grimbergen Brasserie (Bel). See Grimbergen.

Grimsby (Can). A wine district between Niagara and Crystal Beach.

Grinds (Eng). The name given to ground coffee after the beans have been roasted and cut (ground) up. Size can vary from coarse to very fine.

Grinzing (Aus). A famous white wine produced outside Vienna from a region of same name.

Griotte-Chambertin (Fr). A Grand Cru vineyard in the A.C. commune of Gevrey-Chambertin, Côte de Nuits, Burgundy. 5.6 ha.

Griottes (Les) (Fr). A vineyard in the A.C. Pouilly Fumé, Central Vineyards, Loire. Address = 18, Rue F. Gambon, 58150 Pouilly-sur-Loire.

Grip (Eng). A term that is applied to a wine that has a good finish and if red has tannin and acidity.

Gripe Water (Eng). A liquid used for 'winding' babies. Contains 4½% alc. by vol. Caraway-flavoured. Relieves colic.

Gris Cordelier (Fr). An alternative name for the Pinot gris.

Gris de Boulaouane (Afr). A 'grey wine' produced in Morocco. Bottled by CVM.

Gris de Gris (Fr). An A.C. rosé wine from Provence produced by Listel.

Gris de Guerrouane (Afr). A brand of pale, dry rosé wine from Morocco. Grape varieties – Carignan and Cinsault. A 'Grey wine'. Carries the A.O.G. Guerrouane. Bottled by CVM.

Gris-Meunier (Fr). A red grape variety grown in the Touraine district of the Loire. Related to the Pinot meunier.

Grist (Eng). Milled malted barley used for brewing and Whisky making.

Grist Case (Eng). A hopper that holds the ground malt (Grist).

Grist Hopper (Scot). Another name for the Grist case.

Grist Mill (Eng). A unit for grinding grain (especially barley) into grist.

Grk (Yug). A strong white wine which is very dry. Not unlike a natural sherry. Made from a grape of same name on the island of Korcula. Also spelt Gerk.

Grober (Ger). An alternative name for the Elbling grape.

Grobriesling (Ger). An alternative name for the Elbling grape.

Groendruif (S.Afr). An alternative name for the Green grape.

Groenkloof Drankhandelaars Dry Red (S.Afr). A blended red wine made from 25% Cinsault, 50% Pinotage and 25% Tinta barocca produced by the Mamreweg Co-operative.

Groenkloof Drankhandelaars Wines (S.Afr). A brand label name used by the Mamreweg Co-operative.

Groerd (Lux). A vineyard site in the village of Grevenmacher.

Grog (Austr) (slang). A term for any alcoholic beverage.

Grog (Cktl). 1 measure dark Rum, 2 cloves, lump of sugar, lemon juice, stick of cinnamon. Place all in an old-fashioned glass, top with boiling water, stir.

Grog (Eng). A British navy term for Rum. Derived from Grogram (cloak) which was worn by its' officer Edward Vernon (1684–1757).

Grog (Fr). Toddy.

Grog Blossom (Austr) (slang). A name for the red nose of a heavy drinker.

Groggy (Eng). Unsteady. Comes from the old naval word meaning under the influence of alcohol (grog).

Grogier (Ch.Isles). Tipple. See also Bevounnair.

Grognard (Le) (Liq. Coffee). Put a teaspoonful of castor sugar in a Paris goblet. Add ⅔ oz. Mandarine Napoléon, flambé. Add hot coffee. Top with fresh cream and garnish with tangerine peel.

Grokje (Hol). Toddy.

Grolla (Aus). A wooden drinking vessel. A hollowed out log which is filled with assorted beverages that are drunk through holes in the side of the vessel with the aid of straws. Can be served hot or cold. Used by one or more persons together. Aids friendship.

Grolle (It). A round, decorated wooden vessel used for serving and drinking hot Alpine punch. (Aus) = Grolla.

Grolleau (Fr). A red grape variety used in the making of rosé wines in the Anjou district of the Loire.

Grolsch (Hol). An unpasteurised bottled beer sold in a pot-stoppered bottle. A Pilsener beer brewed by the Grolsch Brouwerij in Groenlo.

Grolsch Brouwerij (Hol). A brewery based in Groenlo, Gelderland. Noted for its' pot-stoppered Grolsch Pilsener Lager.

Grolsheim (Ger). Village. (Anb) = Rheinhessen. (Ber) = Bingen. (Gro) = Sankt Rochuskapelle. (Vin) = Ölberg.

Grom (Yug). A red wine produced in southern Serbia.

Grombalia (Afr). A co-operative winery owned by the UCCVT.

Grombalia (Afr). A major wine-producing district in Tunisia.

Gronau (Ger). Village. (Anb) = Württemberg. (Ber) = Württembergisch Unterland. (Gro) = Wunnenstein. (Vin) = Forstberg.

Grön Curaçao (Nor). A green-coloured Curaçao.

Grøn Tuborg (Den). Lit – 'Green Tuborg'. A Pilsener-style Lager 3.7% alc. by vol. brewed by Carlsberg.

Groot (Hol). Lit – 'Large'. A term used to describe a 30 cl. glass.

Groot Constantia Estate (S.Afr). Vineyards based in Constantia. Address = Groot Constantia State Estate, Private Bag, Constantia 7848. Produces varietal wines. Owned by the South African Government.

Groot Constantia State Estate (S.Afr). See Groot Constantia Estate.

Groot Eiland Co-operative (S.Afr). Vineyards based in Goudini. Address = Groot Eiland Koöperatiewe Wynkelder, Box 93, Rawsonville 6845. Produces varietal wines.

Groot Eiland Koöperatiewe Wynkelder (S.Afr). See Groot Eiland Cooperative.

Groot Toren (S.Afr). A dry, white wine made from a blend of Colombard, Steen and Weisser riesling grapes by the McGregor Co-operative. Is matured in wood.

Groppello (It). A red wine grape variety also known as the Rossignola. Used in the making of Valpolicella in Veneto.

Groppellone (It). See Groppello.

Gros Auxerrois (Fr). An alternative name for the Muscadet grape.

Gros Bouchet (Fr). A name used in the Saint-Émilion district of Bordeaux for the Cabernet sauvignon grape.

Gros Cabernet (Fr). The local name in Bordeaux for the Cabernet franc.

Groseille (Fr). Redcurrant syrup.

Groseilles (Les) (Fr). A Premier Cru vineyard in the A.C. commune of Chambolle-Musigny, Côte de Nuits, Burgundy. 1.5 ha.

Groslot (Fr). A red grape variety grown in the Anjou district of the Loire used in the making Rosé d'Anjou.

Gros Manseng (Fr). A noble white grape variety grown in the Jurançon.

Gros Manzenc (USA). A red grape variety grown in California.

Gros Noir (Fr). An alternative name for the Malbec grape.

Gros Noiren (Fr). The local name for the Pinot noir in the Arbois, Jura.

Gros-Pin (Fr). A wine-producing district in Bellet, Provence.

Gros Plant (Fr). A white acidic grape variety grown in the Pays Nantais district of the Loire. Produces an acidic V.D.Q.S. wine. Also known as the Folle blanche in Cognac and elsewhere in France.

Gros Plant Doré d'Ay (Fr). A variety of the Pinot noir grape grown in the Champagne region.

Gros Plant du Pays Nantais (Fr). A V.D.Q.S. dry, white, acidic wine made from the Gros plant grape in the Pays Nantais district of the Loire.

Gros Producteurs (Fr). Vine varieties which produce large quantities, but not fine quality wines.

Gros Rhin (Fr). The local Alsace name for the Sylvaner grape.

Gross (Ger). Lit – 'great'. Denotes a wine that is of fine quality.

Grossa (It). A red grape variety grown in the Trentino-Alto Adige region for making Lago di Caldaro.

Grossachsen (Ger). Village. (Anb) = Baden. (Ber) = Badische Bergstrasse/Kraichgau. (Gro) = Rittersberg. (Vin) = Sandrocken.

Grossbottwar (Ger). Village. (Anb) = Württemberg. (Ber) = Württembergisch Unterland. (Gro) = Wunnenstein. (Vins) = Harzberg, Lichtenberg.

Grosse Montagne (W.Ind). A very popular brand of Rum produced on the island of Guadeloupe by Simonnet.

Grosser Hengelberg (Ger). Vineyard. (Anb) = Mosel-Saar-Ruwer. (Ber) = Bernkastel. (Gro) = Michelsberg. (Vil) = Neumagen-Dhron.

Grosser Herrgott (Ger). Vineyard. (Anb) = Mosel-Saar-Ruwer. (Ber) = Bernkastel. (Gro) = Kurfürstlay. (Vil) = Wintrich.

Grosses Terres (Fr). The very best soil of the Sancerre in the Central Vineyards, Loire. Almost brown with some yellow brown (clay).

Grossheppach (Ger). Village. (Anb) = Württemberg. (Ber) = Remstal-Stuttgart. (Gro) = Kopf. (Vin) = Wanne.

Grossheppach (Ger). Village. (Anb) = Württemberg. (Ber) = Remstal-Stuttgart. (Gro) = Wartbühl. (Vins) = Steingrüble, Zügernberg.

Grossheubach (Ger). Village. (Anb) = Franken. (Ber) = Mainviereck. (Gro) = Not yet assigned. (Vin) = Bischofsberg.

Gross Highland Winery (USA). A winery based in Absecon, New Jersey. Is noted for its' sparkling (Charmat method) wines.

Gross-Höflein (Aus). A wine-producing area in the Eisenstadt district.

Grossier (Fr). A big but hard, coarse wine.

Grossingersheim (Ger). Village. (Anb) = Württemberg. (Ber) = Württembergisch Unterland. (Gro) = Schalkstein. (Vin) = Schlossberg

Gros Sirops (Fr). Molasses.

Grosskarlbach (Ger). Village. (Anb) = Rheinpfalz. (Ber) = Mittelhaardt-Deutsche Weinstrasse. (Gro) = Schwarzerde. (Vins) = Burgweg, Osterberg.

Grosslage (Ger). An area formed by a number of vineyards. May be a village or not. A number of Grosslagen make up a Bereich.

Grosslagenfrei (Ger). No Grosslagen. Not yet assigned to a Grosslage. (associated with a Weinbaort).

Grosslangheim (Ger). Village. (Anb) = Franken. (Ber) = Steigerwald. (Gro) = Schlossberg. (Vin) = Kiliansberg.

Grosslay (Ger). Vineyard. (Anb) = Mosel-Saar-Ruwer. (Ber) = Zell/Mosel. (Gro) = Goldbäumchen. (Vil) = Müden.

Gross Lees (Fr). The sediment in the wine before bottling.

Grossman [The] (USA). An all purpose lead crystal glass which has a fill-line at 4 fl.ozs.

Grossmulde (Ger). Vineyard. (Anb) = Württemberg. (Ber) = Remstal-Stuttgart. (Gro) = Kopf. (Vil) = Beinstein.

G

Grossniedesheim (Ger). Village. (Anb) = Rheinpfalz. (Ber) = Mittelhaardt-Deutsche Weinstrasse. (Gro) = Schwarzerde. (Vin) = Schafberg.

Grosso Nero (It). A red grape variety grown in Sicily.

Grossostheim (Ger). Village. (Anb) = Franken. (Ber) = Mainviereck. (Gro) = Heiligenthal. (Vins) = Reischklingeberg, Harstell.

Grossrinderfeld (Ger). Village. (Anb) = Baden. (Ber) = Badische Frankenland. (Gro) = Tauberklinge. (Vin) = Beilberg.

Gross-Umstadt (Ger). Village. (Anb) = Hessische Bergstrasse. (Ber) = Umstadt. (Gro) = no Grosslagen. (Vins) = Steingerück, Herrnberg.

Gross Und Kleinfischlingen (Ger). Village. (Anb) = Rheinpfalz. (Ber) = Südliche Weinstrasse. (Gro) = Trappenberg. (Vin) = Kirchberg.

Grossvernatsch (It). A German name for the red wine grape known as the Schiava grossa in the Südtirol. Also known as the Trollinger.

Grosswallstadt (Ger). Village. (Anb) = Franken. (Ber) = Mainviereck. (Gro) = Not yet assigned. (Vin) = Lützeltalerberg.

Gross-Winternheim (Ger). Village. (Anb) = Rheinhessen. (Ber) = Bingen. (Gro) = Kaiserpfalz. (Vins) = Bockstein, Heilighäuschen, Klosterbruder, Schlossberg.

Gros Vidure (Fr). The alternative name for the Cabernet franc.

Grottaferrata (It). A wine town based south of Frascati in the Latium region noted for its' white wines.

Grötzingen (Ger). Village. (Anb) = Baden. (Ber) = Badische Bergstrasse/Kraichgau. (Gro) = Hohenberg. (Vins) = Lichtenberg, Turmberg.

Grounds (Eng). The alternative name for the (coffee) grinds.

Groupement des Grandes Liqueurs de France (Fr). An inner court of the Syndicat National des Fabricants de Liqueurs which consists of 13 of Frances' biggest liqueur producers producing internationally-known brands of liqueurs.

Groupement d'Intérêt Économique des Vignerons du Sud-Ouest (Fr). G.I.VI.S.O. Group of co-operatives from the A.C. districts of south-western France (Buzet, Cahors, Gaillac, Jurançon and Madiran).

Groupement Interprofessionnel des Vins de Île de Corse (Fr). Address = 6, Rue Gabriel-Péri 20000 Bastia, Corsica.

Grouts (USA). The name for the tea leaves after brewing.

Grover Gulcg Winery (USA). A winery based in Soquel, Santa Cruz, California. Produces varietal wines.

Grower's Old Reserve (USA). The brandname of a Brandy produced by the California Grower's Winery in Cutler, California.

Growth (Fr). Can mean a vineyard normally classed as a Great Growth. Produces the best wines.

Gruber (Ger). An alternative name for the Sylvaner grape.

Gruel (Eng). A drink of thin porridge made by boiling oatmeal in water or milk.

Gruener Veltliner (Aus). The main white grape variety grown in Burgenland 20% plus. Produces fresh, spicy, fruity wines with a high acidity.

Gruit (Eng). A mixture of aromatic herbs used for flavouring beer.

Grume (Fr). The name used in Burgundy for the grape berry (single grape).

Grumello (It). A sub-district of Lombardy, in the foothills of the Alps, in the Valtellina Valley. Produces red wines of the same name from the Nebbiolo grape.

Grün (Ger). Young, green, immature.

Grunbach (Ger). Village. (Anb) = Württemberg. (Ber) = Remstal-Stuttgart. (Gro) = Kopf. (Vin) = Berghalde.

Grunbach (Ger). Village. (Anb) = Württemberg. (Ber) = Remstal-Stuttgart. (Gro) = Wartbühl. (Vin) = Klingle.

Grünberger Stein (S.Afr). A white wine sold in the familiar German Stein bottle from Die Bergkelder Ltd, Stellenbosch.

Grünberger Wines (S.Afr). Wines made by the Die Bergkelder in Stellenbosch. Varietal wines.

Gründelbach (Ger). Village. (Anb) = Württemberg. (Ber) = Württembergisch Unterland. (Gro) = Stromberg. (Vins) = Steinbachhof, Wachtkopf.

Grundersbacher Schlosskellerei Thun (Switz). Noted producers of sparkling wines.

Grundkataster (Aus). The land register.

Gruenchers (Les) (Fr). A Premier Cru vineyard (part) in the A.C. commune of Chambolle-Musigny, Côte de Nuits, Burgundy. 3 ha.

Gruenchers (Les) (Fr). A Premier Cru vineyard (part) in the A.C. commune of Morey-Saint-Denis, Côte de Nuits, Burgundy. 0.6 ha.

Grüner Husar (Aus). A medium-dry, white wine produced from the Grüner veltliner by Sepp Hold in St. Georgen.

Grunern (Ger). Village. (Anb) = Baden. (Ber) = Markgräflerland. (Gro) = Loretoberg. (Vins) = Altenberg, Schlossberg.

Grüner Veltliner (Aus). See Gruener Veltliner.

Grünhalle Lager (Ch.Isles). A Lager beer

G

brewed by Randall's Brewery in Jersey. Now brewed under licence by Greenall Whitley Brewery in Warrington and Devenish Brewery. Bottled/keg and Export Gold. See also Gold Label.

Grünhaus (Ger). A Ruwer estate in the Mosel-Saar-Ruwer. Wines are known as Maximin Grünhauser because the vineyard was once the property of St. Maximin Abbey in Trier.

Grünling (Ger). An alternative name for the Sylvaner grape.

Grunnengold (Ger). The brand-name of an EEC blended table wine. 9.3% alc. by vol.

Grünsilvaner (Rum). A white wine.

Grünstadt (Ger). Village. (Anb) = Rheinpfalz. (Ber) = Mittelhaardt-Deutsche Weinstrasse. (Gro) = Höllenpfad. (Vins) = Bergel, Goldberg, Honigsack, Hütt, Klostergarten, Röth, St. Stephan, Schloss.

Grupo de Exportadores (Sp). A group that was based in Jerez de la Frontera. Now disbanded. Has been replaced by the Asociación de Criadores Exportadores de Vino de Jerez.

Grupo de Exportadores de Vinos de Navarra (Sp). Address = Yanguas Miranda 27, Pamplona. A body for the promotion of Navarra wines.

Gruppo Italiano Vini (It). GIV. Help promote Italian wine drinking.

Gruta (Sp). Cavern.

Gruzinskoe Vino (USSR). A wine produced in the Georgia region.

Guadaloupe Valley Winery (USA). A winery based in New Braunfels, southwest Texas.

Guadalquivir [River] (Sp). Mouth of which Sanlúcar de Barrameda is situated. Here Manzanilla sherries are matured.

Guadalupe (Mex). A wine-producing region in Baja California. Has the wineries of Luis Cetto Vineyards and Productos Vinícola.

Guadalupe (Sp). An Amontillado sherry produced by La Riva in Jerez de la Frontera.

Guadelete [River] (Sp). A river in the Andalusia (sherry) region.

Guadeloupe (Cktl). 1 measure Mardi Gras, dash lime cordial. Shake over ice, strain into an ice-filled highball glass. Top with soda water.

Guadeloupe Rum (W.Ind). A dark, full-bodied dry Rum with a burnt flavour.

Guadiana [River] (Sp) (Port). A river that runs through both Spain and Portugal.

Guarapita (S.Am). The local name given to Rum mixed with fruit juice in Venezuela.

Guarapo (W.Ind). A fermented sugarcane drink similar to beer.

Guards (Cktl). ⅓ measure sweet Vermouth, ⅔ measure dry Gin, 3 dashes orange Curaçao. Stir over ice, strain into a cocktail glass.

Guarnaccia (It). A red grape variety grown in Campania.

Guarnaccia Bianca (It). A white grape variety grown in Pollino, Calabria.

Guaruzo (Chile). A beer produced from fermented rice.

Guasti (USA). The label used by Perelli-Minetti Winery for a range of their wines.

Guatemala Coffee (C.Am). A fairly smooth, mellow coffee which has a tangy after-taste. Has good acidity and bouquet.

Guder (Afr). One of three wine-producing regions in Ethiopia. See also Eritire and Abadir-Dukem.

Guebwiller (Fr). A town in the Haut-Rhin region of Alsace. (Gr) = Gebweiler.

Guenoc Vineyards (USA). A winery based in Lake County, Napa Valley, California.

Guépie (Fr). An alternative name for the Muscadelle grape.

Guerbé (Jean) (Fr). Cognac producer. Address = Maison Guerbé et Cie, Hameau de L'Echalotte, Juillac le Coq, 16130 Segonzac. 34 ha. in Grande Champagne. Produces – Logis 5 year old.

Guérets (Les) (Fr). A Premier Cru vineyard in the A.C. commune of Aloxe-Corton, Côte de Beaune, Burgundy.

Guernsey Brewery 1920 Ltd (Ch.Isles). Based in St. Peter Port, Guernsey. Noted for its' Pony Ale 1037.7 O.G. Milk Stout 1042 O.G. Stein Lager 1048 O.G. and LBA Mild 1037.7 O.G.

Guernsey Cream Liqueur (Ch.Isles). A cream-based, Brandy and Amaretto-flavoured liqueur produced in Guernsey. 17% alc. by vol.

Guerrieri-Rizzardi (It). A large Veneto wine producer. Produces most wine styles of the region. Address = 37011 Bardolino, Verona.

Gueule de Bois (Fr). Lit – 'Wooden throat'. A term used for a hangover.

Gueutrange (Fr). A name given to red and white wines from Lorraine.

Gueux (Fr). A Cru Champagne village in the Canton de Ville-en-Tardenois. District = Reims.

Gueze (Bel). A blend of 2 Lambic beers which re-ferment to produce a good CO_2 bead. Is a fruity beer 5.5% alc. by vol.

Gueze Lambic (Bel). A local Brussels beer

G

often sweetened by adding a lump of sugar and dash of Grenadine.

Guggenheim (Cktl). 1 measure dry Vermouth, dash Orange bitters, 2 dashes Fernet Branca. Shake over ice, strain into a cocktail glass.

Guglet (Ind). See Goglet.

Guglielmo Winery (USA). A winery based in Santa Clara, California. 34 ha. Grape varieties – Barbera, Burgundy, Petite sirah, Ruby cabernet and Zinfandel. Also has vineyards in Morgan Hill. Produces varietal wines.

Güglingen (Ger). Village. (Anb) = Württemberg. (Ber) = Württembergisch-Unterland. (Gro) = Heuchelberg. (Vins) = Kaiserberg, Michaelsberg.

Guido Berlucchi (It). A producer of sparkling (méthode champenoise) wines based in Lombardy. Labels include Max Rosé and Pas Dosé.

Guignolet (Fr). A Cherry brandy produced in Angers from the Guigne (a small black cherry). An Eau-de-vie.

Guignolet d'Anger (Fr). A cherry-flavoured liqueur from the Anjou-Saumur district of the Loire.

Guignolet d'Anjou (Fr). A cherry-flavoured liqueur made in the Loire. 16% alc. by vol.

Guignolet de Bourguignon (Fr). A cherry brandy produced in Dijon in Burgundy.

Guigone de Salins (Fr). A cuvée in the A.C. Beaune, Côte de Beaune, Burgundy. Is owned by the Hospices de Beaune.

Guilbaud Frères (Fr). A noted producer of Muscadet wines. Address = Mouzillon 44300 Vallet, Loire Atlantique.

Guild Blue Ribbon Brandy (USA). The brand-name of a Brandy bottled by the Guild of Wineries and Distillers in Lodi, California.

Guildhive (Fr) (slang). The term used for Kill-devil in the early twentieth century.

Guildhive (W.Ind). The name given to a sugar cane distillery.

Guild of Cellarmasters (Eng). Address = 107, Carterhatch Lane, Enfield, Middlesex.

Guild of Professional Toastmasters (Eng). 12, Little Bornes, Alleyn Park, Dulwich, London SE21 8SE.

Guild of Sommeliers (Eng). Standish, Rockshaw Road, Merstham, Surrey.

Guild of Wineries and Distilleries (USA). A San Joaquin co-operative producing Brandy, table, dessert and sparkling wines in California. Also owns the Cresta Blanca in Mendocino, California. Uses the Cribari and Sons, Roma, Tavola and Winemaster labels.

Guilford Farm Vineyard (USA). A winery based in Stanley, Virginia. Produces French hybrid and vinifera wines.

Guillan (Fr). An alternative name for the Muscadelle grape.

Guillan Musqué (Fr). An alternative name for the Muscadelle grape.

Guillan Rouge (Fr). An alternative name for the Malbec grape.

Guimaraens (Port). Vintage Port. Vintages – 1952, 1957, 1958, 1961, 1962, 1964, 1965, 1967, 1968. Not a single Quinta Port. The second wine of the Fonseca Port shippers.

Guimps (Fr). A commune in the Charente Département whose grapes are classed Petite Champagne (Cognac).

Guindado (S.Am). A fermented cherry liqueur produced in Uruguay.

Guinea Gold Ale (Eng). A bottled Light ale 1032 O.G. brewed by the Hardy's and Hanson's Brewery in Nottingham.

Guinevere's Champion (Cktl). 2 parts Merrydown mead, 2 parts Vodka, splash Curaçao. Pour into a frosted highball glass. Add ice and slice of orange.

Guingette (Ch.Isles). A small Inn.

Guinness (Ire). Breweries in Dublin and in Park Royal, London. Brews a naturally conditioned Stout. 14 other breweries around the world. Also produces Harp Lager and controls Irish Ale Breweries. Took over DCL in 1986.

Guinness Cooler (Cktl). In a large tumbler containing a piece of ice add ⅙ measure Dubonnet, ⅓ liqueur glass each of Curaçao and Crème de Cacao. Fill glass with Baby Guinness, decorate with a spiral of lemon peel.

Guinness Tan (Eng). Guinness and draught Bitter ale. Half and half.

Guissare (USSR). A red grape variety used for dessert wine production in Tadzhikistan.

Guita (La) (Sp). The brand-name of a Manzanilla sherry produced by Sanchez de Alba.

Guitar (Sp). A pale Cream sherry produced by Domecq in Jerez.

Guitton-Figerou and Co (Fr). A nineteenth century Cognac producer.

Gulden Anker (Hol). A Jenever produced by Allied Breweries.

Güldenkern (Ger). Vineyard. (Anb) = Württemberg. (Ber) = Württembergisch Unterland. (Gro) = Schalkstein. (Vil) = Rietenau.

Güldenmorgen (Ger). Grosslage. (Anb) = Rheinhessen. (Ber) = Nierstein. (Vils) = Dienheim, Oppenheim.

Güldenmorgen (Ger). Vineyard. (Anb) =

G

Rheinhessen. (Ber) = Nierstein. (Gro) = Gutes Domtal. (Vil) = Zornheim.

Guldental (Ger). Village. (Anb) = Nahe. (Ber) = Kreuznach. (Gro) = Schlosskapelle. (Vins) = Apostelberg, Hipperich, Hölle, Honigberg, Rosenteich, St. Martin, Sonnenberg, Teufelsküche.

Guldenzoll (Ger). Vineyard. (Anb) = Hessische Bergstrasse. (Ber) = Starkenburg. (Gro) = Schlossberg. (Vil) = Heppenheim including Erbach and Heimbach.

Gulder Lager (Afr). A Lager beer 1047 O.G. brewed by the Kumasi Brewery in Ghana.

Gulder Lager (Afr). A Lager beer 1047 O.G. brewed by the Nigerian Breweries Ltd in Nigeria.

Guld Export (Den). Carlsberg Gold Export. A Pilsener-style beer 4% alc. by weight.

Gulp (Eng). To swallow quickly. Drink fast.

Gulpen Brouwerij (Hol). A brewery based in Gulpen, south Limburg. Produces Dort 6.5% alc. by vol. and X-pert 5% alc. by vol. Both are unpasteurised beers.

Gulpers (Eng) (slang). A term used in the Navy to obtain one large mouthful of a shipmate's Rum issue.

Gul Rose Liqueur (Tur). The brand-name of a Rose liqueur.

Güls (Ger). Village. (Anb) = Mosel-Saar-Ruwer. (Ber) = Zell/Mosel. (Gro) = Weinhex. (Vins) = Bienengarten, Im Röttgen, Königsfels, Marienberg.

Gumbsheim (Ger). Village. (Anb) = Rheinhessen. (Ber) = Bingen. (Gro) = Kurfürstenstück. (Vin) = Schlosshölle.

Gümmel (Cktl). 1 measure High and Dry Gin, 1 measure Kümmel. Shake over ice, strain into a cocktail glass.

Gumpoldskirchen (Aus). A wine-producing district within the region of Niederosterreich. Produces both red and white wines.

Gumpoldskirchner (Aus). A fruity white wine of the Baden district.

Gumpoldskirchner Königssekt (Aus). A brand of Sekt produced by Inführ.

Gum Syrup (Eng). A plain syrup used for sweetening cocktails.

Gumza (Bul). The alternative spelling of Gamza.

Gundelsheim (Ger). Village. (Anb) = Württemberg. (Ber) = Württembergisch Unterland. (Gro) = Staufenberg. (Vin) = Himmelreich.

Gundersheim (Ger). Village. (Anb) = Rheinhessen. (Ber) = Wonnegau. (Gro) = Bergkloster. (Vins) = Höllenbrand, Konigstuhl.

Gundheim (Ger). Village. (Anb) = Rheinhessen. (Ber) = Wonnegau. (Gro) = Bergkloster. (Vins) = Hungerbiene, Mandelbrunnen, Sonnenberg.

Gundlach-Bundschu Vineyard Co (USA). A winery based in the Sonoma Valley, California. 46 ha. Grape varieties – Cabernet sauvignon, Gewürztraminer, Johannisberg riesling, Kleinberger riesling, Merlot and Zinfandel. Produces varietal wines.

Gun-Flint (Fr). A taste of the wines of the Loire, especially of the wines from the Central Vineyards. (Pouilly fumé and Sancerre).

Gunpowder (China). A grade of tea. Young teas. See Green Gunpowder.

Guntersblum (Ger). Village. (Anb) = Rheinhessen. (Ber) = Nierstein. (Gro) = Krötenbrunnen. (Vins) = Eiserne Hand, Sankt Julianenbrunnen, Sonnenberg, Sonnenhang, Steinberg.

Guntersblum (Ger). Village. (Anb) = Rheinhessen. (Ber) = Nierstein. (Gro) = Vogelsgärten. (Vins) = Authental, Bornpfad, Himmelthal, Kreuzkapelle, Steig-Terrassen.

Günterslay (Ger). Vineyard. (Anb) = Mosel-Saar-Ruwer. (Ber) = Bernkastel. (Gro) = Michelsberg. (Vil) = Minheim.

Günterslay (Ger). Vineyard. (Anb) = Mosel-Saar-Ruwer. (Ber) = Bernkastel. (Gro) = Michelsberg. (Vil) = Piesport.

Güntersleben (Ger). Village. (Anb) = Franken. (Ber) = Maindreieck. (Gro) = Ravensburg. (Vin) = Sommerstuhl.

Guntrum (Ger). Louis Guntrum. Family wine-producer based in Nierstein, Rheinhessen.

Gurdzhaani (USSR). A white wine from the Georgia region.

Gurglet (Ind). See Goglet.

Gurgling Jug (Eng). A solid silver fish-shaped jug donated by Plymouth Gin. Is used as a perpetual trophy for the field gunners competition at the Royal Tournement.

Gurpegui (Sp). See Bodegas Gurpegui.

Gurten Brauerei (Switz). A brewery based in Bern. Is part of the Feldschlösschen group.

Gush (Eng). A term meaning 'to Fob'.

Gustation (Eng). The art (skill) of tasting. Faculty of taste.

Gustatory (Eng). Denotes the enjoyment of wine.

Gustillo (Sp). Vineyard. Address = Avda Cenicéro N°.50, Fuenmayor (La Rioja). 50 ha. Grape varieties – Garnacha 10%, Tempranillo 80% and Viura 10%. Produces 100% red wine.

Gut (Ger). Good.

Gut Alsenhof (Ger). Vineyard. (Anb) = Baden. (Ber) = Ortenau. (Gro) = Schloss Rodeck. (Vil) = Lauf.

Gutedel (Ger). A white grape variety grown in the Baden Anbaugebiet. Known as the

Chasselas in France and the Fendant in Switzerland. Also called the Markgräfler.

Gutedelrebe (Ger). A white grape variety grown mainly in the Baden Anbaugebiet.

Gutenberg (Ger). Village. (Anb) = Nahe. (Ber) = Kreuznach. (Gro) = Pfarrgarten. (Vins) = Felseneck, Römerberg, St. Ruppertsberg, Schlossberg, Schloss Gutenberg, Sonnenlauf.

Gutenberg (Ger). Vineyard. (Anb) = Rheingau. (Ber) = Johannisberg. (Gro) = Honigberg. (Vil) = Winkel.

Gutenborner (Ger). A white grape variety. A cross between the Müller-Thurgau and the Chasselas.

Gutenhölle (Ger). Vineyard. (Anb) = Nahe. (Ber) = Schloss Böckelheim. (Gro) = Rosengarten. (Vil) = Hüffelsheim.

Gutental (Ger). Vineyard. (Anb) = Nahe. (Ber) = Kreuznach. (Gro) = Kronenberg. (Vil) = Bad Kreuznach.

Gutes Domtal (Ger). Grosslage. (Anb) = Rheinhessen. (Ber) = Nierstein. (Vils) = Dalheim, Dexheim, Friesenheim, Hahnheim, Köngernheim, Lörzweiler, Mommenheim, Nackenheim, Nieder-Olm, Nierstein, Selzen, Sörgenloch, Undenheim, Weinolsheim, Zornheim.

Gutleuthaus (Ger). Vineyard. (Anb) = Rheinhessen. (Ber) = Nierstein. (Gro) = Güldenmorgen. (Vil) = Oppenheim.

Gutsy (Eng). A term applied to wines that are full in body, fruit and alcohol.

Guttenberg (Ger). Grosslage. (Anb) = Rheinpfalz. (Ber) = Südliche Weinstrasse. (Vils) = Bad Bergzabern, Dierbach, Dörrenbach, Freckenfeld, Kandel, Kapsweyher, Minfeld, Niederotterbach, Oberotterbach, Schweigen-Rechtenbach, Schweighofen, Steinfeld, Vollmersweiler.

Gutturnio dei Colli Piacentini (It). D.O.C. red wine from the Emilia-Romagna. Made from the Barbera and Bonarda grapes in the defined area in the province of Piacenza.

Gutturnium (It). A large cup. Gutturnio is named after this cup.

Guyana Distilleries (S.Am). A distillery based at Uitvlugt, Guyana. Demerara Distillers is its' subsidiary company. Is noted for the Rum brands – Blue Seal, High and Dry, High Wine Bonded and Ordinary El Dorado.

Guyana Liquor Corporation (S.Am). Formed in 1976 as a holding company for Demerara Distillers, Diamond Liquors and Guyana Distilleries in Guyana.

Guyne (Fr). See Cherry Whisky.

Guyon (Comte de) (Fr). Armagnac producer. Address = Guyon de Pampetonne, Château de Lassalle, Maupas en Armagnac, 32240 Estang. 20 ha. in Bas Armagnac. Produces – Comte de Guyon Hors d'Âge 10 and 15 year old Armagnac.

Guyot (Dr.) (Fr). Inventor of the method of growing vines to best advantage to produce the best crops. See Guyot Simple, Guyot Double and Bogen.

Guyot à Queue (Fr). A vine training method.

Guyot Double (Fr). A method of vine pruning and growing. Consists of 2 branches with 6 buds on each. (Ger) = Doppelbogen.

Guyot Double Médocaine (Fr). The style of vine pruning (Guyot double) used in the Médoc, Bordeaux.

Guyot Poussard (Fr). The style of vine pruning used in Saint-Émilion, Bordeaux.

Guyot Simple (Fr). A method of vine pruning and growing. Consists of 1 branch with 3–4 buds and a reserve bud for the following year. (Ger) = Einzelbogen.

Guy Testaud (Fr). Cognac producer. Address = Plaisance, NW Lamerac, 16300 Barbezieux-St-Hilaire. 20 ha. 20% Grande Champagne and 80% Petite Champagne. Produces – V.S.O.P. 7 year old, Napoléon X.O. 12 year old, Hors d'Âge 20 year old.

Guzbag (Tur). The state monopoly approved name for rosé wines produced in Trakya.

Güzel Koku (Tur). Bouquet, aroma (of a wine).

Guzzle (Eng). To consume (drink or food) excessively and quickly.

Gweinydd Gwin (Wales). Wine waiter, sommelier.

Gwent Ales (Wales). Now known as the Silverstone Brewery.

Gwin (Wales). Wine.

Gwinllan (Wales). Vineyard.

Gwin o Cymru (Wales). Welsh wine.

Gwinwryf (Wales). Grape press.

Gwinwydden (Wales). Grape vine.

Gwirod (Wales). Liquor.

Gwydr Gwin (Wales). Wineglass.

Gwyn (Wales). White.

Gwyn Gwin (Wales). White wine.

Gye-sur-Seine (Fr). A Cru Champagne village in the Canton de l'Aube. District = Château Thierry.

Gyle (Eng). A term to describe a batch of beer from one brewing.

Gymkhana (Ind). A Lager beer 1045 O.G. brewed by the Mohan Meakin Brewery in Simla Hills, Solan.

Gyokuro Rikyu (Jap). A low-alcohol liqueur based on green tea and brandy.

Gyöncz (Hun). A cask used in the Hegyalja region which produces Tokay. Holds approx. 35 gallons. See also Gönz.

Gyöngyös (Hun). A sparkling red and white table wine produced in the region of same name.

Gypsies' Kiss (Liq.Coffee). Made with a measure of Galliano.

Gypsum (Eng). Calcium sulphate. Added to the grape must (especially to increase acidity). CASO$_4$.

Gypsy Cocktail (Cktl).(1). ⅓ measure Bénédictine, ⅔ measure Vodka, dash Angostura. Stir with ice, strain into a cocktail glass.

Gypsy Cocktail (Cktl).(2). ½ measure sweet Vermouth, ½ measure Gin. Stir over ice, strain into a cocktail glass.

Gypsy's Kiss (Cktl). 1 measure Irish Mist, ½ measure Vodka, 2 measures orange juice, 2 dashes lemon juice, dash Gomme syrup, dash egg white. Shake well over ice. Strain into a cocktail glass, top with a slice of orange and lemon.

Gyropalettes (Fr). The alternative name for Crécelles (auto remuage).

Gyrovagues (Eng). The mediaeval name for monks who used their guises to travel begging food and drink. They were heavy drinkers.

H

Ha. (Fr) (abbr). Hectare.

Haacht (Bel). The brand-name of a Pilsener beer.

Haagen (Ger). Village. (Anb) = Württemberg. (Ber) = Kocher-Jagst-Tauber. (Gro) = Tauberberg. (Vin) = Schafsteige.

Haagen Lager (Eng). A keg Lager beer 1032 O.G. brewed by the Greenall Whitley Brewery in Warrington, Cheshire.

Haake-Beck Brauerei (Ger). An associate company of the Beck's Brauerei in Bremen. Produces Kreusenbier (a sediment beer) and Seefartbier.

Haarberg-Katzensteg (Ger). Vineyard. (Anb) = Rheinhessen. (Ber) = Bingen. (Gro) = Rheingrafenstein. (Vil) = Wöllstein.

Haardt (Ger). The continuation of the French Vosges mountains. They shelter the Palatinate area of Western Germany.

Haardt (Ger). Village. (Anb) = Rheinpfalz. (Ber) = Mittelhaardt-Deutsche Weinstrasse. (Gro) = Meerspinne. (Vins) = Bürgergarten, Herrenletten, Herzog, Mandelring.

Haberschlacht (Ger). Village. (Anb) = Württemberg. (Ber) = Württembergisch Unterland. (Gro) = Heuchelberg. (Vin) = Dachsberg.

Habillage (Fr). The term used to describe the capsuling of Champagne bottles.

Habsburg-Husar (Aus). A white wine produced from the Grüner veltliner grape by Sepp Höld based at St. Georgen.

Habzö (Hun). Sparkling.

Haciendas (S.Am). The alternative name for the Fincas.

Hacienda Vineyard (USA). A winery based in Sonoma County, California. Grape varieties – Cabernet sauvignon, Chardonnay, Gewürztraminer, Pinot noir and Zinfandel. Also has vineyards in Russian River Valley.

Hackenheim (Ger). Village. (Anb) = Rheinhessen. (Ber) = Bingen. (Gro) = Rheingrafenstein. (Vins) = Galgenberg, Gewürzgarten, Kirchberg, Klostergarten, Sonnenberg.

Hacker Marzen (Ger). A specially brewed dark Bier from the Hacker-Pschorr Brauerei.

Hacker-Pschorr Brauerei (Ger). A famous brewery based in Munich that is noted for its' Hacker Marzen.

Häder (Ger). Vineyard. (Anb) = Württemberg. (Ber) = Remstal-Stuttgart. (Gro) = Wartbühl. (Vil) = Rommelshausen.

Häder (Ger). Vineyard. (Anb) = Württemberg. (Ber) = Remstal-Stuttgart. (Gro) = Wartbühl. (Vil) = Stetten i R.

Haderburg (It). A sparkling (méthode champenoise) wine producer based in Piemonte.

Hafle Vineyards (USA). Large vineyards and wineries based in Columbus and Springfield. Produces French-American hybrid wines.

Häfnerhaslach (Ger). Village. (Anb) = Württemberg. (Ber) = Württembergisch Unterland. (Gro) = Stromberg. (Vin) = Heiligenberg.

HAG (Ger). A brand of de-caffeinised coffee from Hag of AG Bremen.

Hagebuttenlikoer (Ger). A liqueur made from rosehips. Yellow in colour.

Hagel en Donder (Hol). Lit – 'Hail and thunder'. A Frisian sweet brandewijn that is flavoured with anis.

Hägenich (Ger). Vineyard. (Anb) = Baden. (Ber) = Badische Bergstrasse/Kraichgau. (Gro) = Mannaberg. (Vil) = Wiesloch.

Haggipavlu (Cyp). A large winery based in Limassol, south-eastern Cyprus. Trades under the Etko label. Produces wines and spirits.

Hagnau (Ger). Village. (Anb) = Baden. (Ber) = Bodensee. (Gro) = Sonnenufer. (Vin) = Burgstall.

Hahn (Ger). Vineyard. (Anb) = Mittelrhein. (Ber) = Bacharach. (Gro) = Schloss Stahlech. (Vil) = Bacharach.

Hahn (Ger). Vineyard. (Anb) = Nahe. (Ber) = Schloss Böckelheim. (Gro) = Paradiesgarten. (Vil) = Rehborn.

Hähnchen (Ger). Vineyard. (Anb) = Rheinhessen. (Ber) = Bingen. (Gro) = Adelberg. (Vil) = Bornheim.

Hahnen (Ger). Vineyard. (Anb) =

Rheinpfalz. (Ber) = Mittelhaardt-Deutsche Weinstrasse. (Gro) = Rosenbühl. (Vil) = Weisenheim/Sand.

Hahnenberg (Ger). Vineyard. (Anb) = Württemberg. (Ber) = Württembergisch Unterland. (Gro) = Heuchelberg. (Vil) = Burgbronn.

Hahnenkamm (Ger). Vineyard. (Anb) = Rheinpfalz. (Ber) = Mittelhaardt-Deutsche Weinstrasse. (Gro) = Schnepfenflug vom Zellertal. (Vil) = Bubenheim.

Hahnenschrittchen (Ger). Vineyard. (Anb) = Mosel-Saar-Ruwer. (Ber) = Bernkastel. (Gro) = Schwarzlay. (Vil) = Burg.

Hahnheim (Ger). Village. (Anb) = Rheinhessen. (Ber) = Nierstein. (Gro) = Gutes Domtal. (Vins) = Knopf, Moosberg.

Hahnhölle (Ger). Vineyard. (Anb) = Nahe. (Ber) = Schloss Böckelheim. (Gro) = Paradiesgarten. (Vil) = Niedermoschel.

Haie Fouassière (La) (Fr). A village in the central A.C. Muscadet de Sèvre et Maine district in the Pays Nantais, Loire. Produces some of the finest wines.

Haig (Scot). John Haig and Co. Ltd. Markinch. Large Scotch whisky blenders. See Dimple Haig, Glenleven, Golden Age and Old Cameron Brig. Part of DCL.

Haight Wineries (USA). A small winery based in Liotchfield, north-western Connecticut. 8 ha. Grape varieties – Chardonnay, Foch and Riesling.

Hainburg (Aus). A wine-producing area based on the right-bank of the river Danube. Produces mainly white wines.

Hainfeld (Ger). Village. (Anb) = Rheinpfalz. (Ber) = Südliche Weinstrasse. (Gro) = Ordensgut. (Vins) = Kapelle, Kirchenstück, Letten.

Hainhölzer (Ger). The brand-name used by August Schmidt for a range of Kornbranntwein.

Hair of the Dog (Eng) (slang). The term for a drink of the same that caused the hangover of person requesting it. i.e. if they had been drinking brandy all night then they would have a brandy as 'the hair of the dog'.

Hair of the Dog Cocktail (Cktl). 1 oz. Scotch whisky, 1½ ozs cream, ½ oz. honey. Shake together with ice, strain into a cocktail glass.

Hair Raiser (Cktl). 1 oz. Vodka, 1 oz Dubonnet. Fill a highball glass with ice, stir in ingredients. Top up with tonic to taste. Serve with a slice of lemon.

Haiti Coffee (W.Ind). Often a harsh, earthy coffee with a strong aroma and good acidity. Is a good blender with the softer coffee of South America.

Haiti Rum (W.Ind). A medium dark Rum. Not as pungent as the Jamaican rums.

Sometimes called Brandy rums. Pot stilled. 40% alc. by vol.

Hajos (Hun). A noted wine-producing town in Mecsek, southern Hungary. Its' Cabernet sauvignon wines are of sound quality.

Hakovo (Bul). A wine-producing region in southern Bulgaria. Main grape varieties are Dimiat, Mavrud, Merlot and Tamianka.

Hakushu Distillery (Jap). One of the largest distilleries in the world. Is owned by Suntory.

Hakutsuru (Jap). A famous brand of Saké.

Halb Extra Liqueur (Ger). A less bitter version of the liqueur Halb Schimmegespann.

Halbfuder (Ger). A Mosel cask holding 500 litres (110 gallons).

Halbrot (Switz). A rosé wine made from black and white grapes.

Halb Schimmegespann (Ger). A liqueur which gets its' name from a half bitter and half sweet taste. Herb-flavoured. See also Halb Extra Liqueur.

Halbstück (Ger). A round barrel that holds 600 litres. Used in the Palatinate region.

Halb Troken (Ger). Medium dry. Lit – 'Half dry'.

Halb und Drittel Bau (Aus). Lit – 'Half and one third cultivation'. A Tenant of a leased vineyard would give the landlord ⅓ or ½ of his crop instead of payment for rent.

Halb und Halb (Ger). A liqueur. A blend of Curaçao and Orange bitters.

Halcyon (Eng). A species of barley malt of the Golden promise variety. Gives medium sugar yields.

Halde (Ger). The local name for the wine of Schait in Württemberg. Made from the Sylvaner grape.

Halde (Ger). Vineyard. (Anb) = Baden. (Ber) = Breisgau. (Gro) = Burg Zähringen. (Vil) = Emmendingen (ortsteil Hochburg).

Halde (Ger). Vineyard. (Anb) = Rheinpfalz. (Ber) = Mittelhaardt-Deutsche Weinstrasse. (Gro) = Rosenbühl. (Vil) = Weisenheim/Sand.

Halde (Ger). Vineyard. (Anb) = Württemberg. (Ber) = Remstal-Stuttgart. (Gro) = Weinsteige. (Vil) = Stuttgart (ortsteil Cannstatt).

Halde (Ger). Vineyard. (Anb) = Württemberg. (Ber) = Württembergisch Unterland. (Gro) = Stromberg. (Vil) = Illingen.

Halde (Ger). Vineyard. (Anb) = Württemberg. (Ber) = Württembergisch Unterland. (Gro) = Stromberg. (Vil) = Mühlhausen.

Halde (Ger). Vineyard. (Anb) = Württemberg. (Ber) = Württembergisch Unterland. (Gro) = Stromberg. (Vil) = Rosswag.

H

Haldengut Brauerei (Switz). A brewery based in Winterthur. Is noted for its' Albanibräu.

Hale Cellars (USA). A winery based in Los Alamos Valley, Santa Barbara, California. 142 ha. Produces varietal wines.

Halenberg (Ger). Vineyard. (Anb) = Nahe. (Ber) = Schloss Böckelheim. (Gro) = Paradiesgarten. (Vil) = Monzingen.

Half (Scot) (Ire). A request for a measure of Malt whisky and Grain (blended) whisky.

Half and Half (Cktl). 2 ozs. sweet Vermouth, 2 ozs. dry Vermouth. Pour into an old-fashioned glass with ice and a twist of lemon.

Half-and-Half (Eng). An equal quantity of two beers in a pint. Usually Mild and Bitter.

Half and Half (Ger). A liqueur. A blend of Curaçao and Orange bitters.

Half-Bocoy (Sp). See Media Bocoy.

Half-Bota (Sp). See Media Bota.

Half-Bottle (Eng). Contains half the amount of a standard bottle. (U.K) = 12 fl.ozs. [35 cls], (USA) = 15.5 fl.ozs.

Half Gassed (USA) (slang). A term for intoxicated.

Half-Jack (S.Afr). A flat, pocket-sized bottle of alcoholic beverage. See also Hip Flask.

Half-om-Half (Hol). A liqueur. A blend of Curaçao and Orange bitters. Produced by De Kuyper. 30% alc. by vol.

Half-Pint (USA). Cocktail measure. 8 fl.ozs. Cup. (¼ quart).

Halfsoet Hanepoot (S.Afr). An amber-coloured, dessert wine made from the Muscadelle grape by the Klawer co-operative.

Halfsoet Wyn (S.Afr). Semi-sweet wine.

Halifax Harlot (Cktl). 1 measure Mandarine Napoléon, ¼ measure Galliano, dash orange juice. Shake well over ice, strain into a flute glass. Top with iced Champagne.

Halkidas (Gre). A red wine produced on the island of Euboea.

Halkidiki Peninsula (Gre). A wine-producing island in Macedonia. Grows the Limnio grape.

Hall and Woodhouse Brewery (Eng). Based in Blandford Forum, Dorset. It specialises in canned beers and soft drinks using the Panda name. Noted for its' cask conditioned Hector's Bitter 1034 O.G. Badger Best 1041 O.G. Tanglefoot 1048 O.G. Malthouse Keg 1033 O.G. Brock Lager 1033 O.G. and bottled Stingo 1066 O.G. Also canned Skona Lager 1032 O.G.

Hallau (Switz). A village in the Schaffhausen canton, eastern Switz.

Hallburg (Ger). Village. (Anb) = Franken.

(Ber) = Maindreieck. (Gro) = Not yet assigned. (Vin) = Schlossberg.

Hallcrest Vineyard (USA). See Felton-Empire.

Hall Cross (Eng). See Stocks Brewery.

Hallelujah Brandy (USSR). An orange-flavoured, brandy-based liqueur.

Hallerbrau Lager (Eng). An unpasteurised, filtered Lager beer 1042 O.G. brewed by the Phillips Brewery in Buckinghamshire.

Haller's County Fair (USA). The brand-name of a Bourbon whiskey.

Hallertaus (Ger). A species of hops grown in Bavaria. Has a spicy, full flavour and aroma. Often used for dry-hopping beers.

Hallgarten (Eng). A famous wine and liqueur producer based in north London. Noted for Royal Mint Chocolate series of liqueurs.

Hallgarten (Ger). Village. (Anb) = Rheingau. (Ber) = Johannisberg. (Gro) = Mehrhölzchen. (Vins) = Hendelberg, Jungfer, Schönhell, Würzgarten.

Hallmint Cocktail (Cktl). ½ measure Cognac, ½ measure Royal Mint Chocolate liqueur, 2 dashes Cointreau. Stir with ice, strain into a cocktail glass.

Hall's Brewery (Eng). A brewery originally based in Oxford which ceased brewing in 1952. Now owned by Allied Breweries who use its' name for their West country public houses. Produce in Burton-on-Trent a cask conditioned Harvest Bitter 1037 O.G. and Barleycorn 1033 O.G. for sale in the public houses.

Hall's Bristol Brewery (Eng). Part of the Allied Breweries' Hall's set up. Brews cask conditioned Jacob's Pride 1038 O.G. and Bristol Pride 1045 O.G.

Hall's Plympton Brewery (Eng). Part of the Allied Breweries' Hall's set up. Brews cask conditioned Plympton Best 1039 O.G. and Plympton Pride 1039 O.G.

Halmei (Rum). A wine-producing region in the district of Siebenbürgen.

Haltingen (Ger). Village. (Anb) = Baden. (Ber) = Markgräflerland. (Gro) = Vogtei Rötteln. (Vin) = Steige.

Haltnau (Ger). Vineyard. (Anb) = Baden. (Ber) = Bodensee. (Gro) = Sonnenufer. (Vil) = Meersburg.

Hamar Brewery (Nor). A brewery based in Hamar, eastern Norway.

Hamarteff (Isr). A large winery based in southern Israel.

Hambach (Ger). Village. (Anb) = Rheinpfalz. (Ber) = Mittelhaardt-Deutsche Weinstrasse. (Gro) = Pfaffengrund. (Vin) = Römerbrunnen.

Hambach (Ger). Village. (Anb) = Rheinpfalz. (Ber) = Mittelhaardt-Deutsche Weinstrasse. (Gro) = Rebstöckel. (Vins) = Feuer, Kaiserstuhl, Kirchberg, Schlossberg.

Hambledon (Eng). A wine from the Mill Down vineyards, Hambledon, Portsmouth, Hampshire. 3.25 ha. Grape varieties – Auxerrois, Chardonnay, Pinot noir and Seyval blanc.

Hambusch (Ger). Vineyard. (Anb) = Mittelrhein. (Ber) = Bacharach. (Gro) = Schloss Stahleck. (Vil) = Bacharach/Steeg.

Hameau de Blagny (Fr). A Premier Cru vineyard in the A.C. commune of Puligny-Montrachet, Côte de Beaune, Burgundy. 4 ha.

Hamedan (Iran). A wine-producing region in the north of the country.

Hamilton Russell Vineyards (S.Afr). A winery based in Overberg. Address = Oude Hemel en Aarde, P.O. Box 158, Hermanus 7200. Produces varietal wines. Is the most southerly of South Africa's vineyards.

Hamilton's (Austr). A family winery at Barossa and Adelaide, South Australia.

Hamilton (Richard) Winery (Austr). A winery based in Clare-Watervale, Southern Vales, South Australia.

Hamlet Glasses (Eng). A brand-name for a range of glasses produced by the Dema glass company.

Hamlet Hill Vineyard (USA). A vineyard based in Pomfret, Connecticut. Produces mainly French hybrid grapes.

Hamlet [The] (Cktl). ½ measure Aalborg Akvavit, ½ measure Peter Heering. Stir over ice, strain into a cocktail glass.

Hamm (Ger). Village. (Anb) = Mosel-Saar-Ruwer. (Ber) = Saar-Ruwer. (Gro) = Scharzberg. (Vin) = Altenberg.

Hamm (Ger). Vineyard. (Anb) = Mosel-Saar-Ruwer. (Ber) = Zell/Mosel. (Gro) = Weinhex. (Vil) = Koblenz (ortsteil Moselweiss).

Hamm (Ger). Vineyard. (Anb) = Mosel-Saar-Ruwer. (Ber) = Zell/Mosel. (Gro) = Weinhex. (Vil) = Winningen.

Hamm (Ger). Vineyard. (Anb) = Nahe. (Ber) = Schloss Böckelheim. (Gro) = Burgweg. (Vil) = Waldböckelheim.

Hämmchen (Ger). Vineyard. (Anb) = Mittelrhein. (Ber) = Rheinburgengau. (Gro) = Gedeonseck. (Vil) = Brey.

Hammel (Switz). A vine grower and merchant based at Rolle, La Côte.

Hammelburg (Ger). Village. (Anb) = Franken. (Ber) = Maindreieck. (Gro) = Burg. (Vins) = Heroldsberg, Trautlestal.

Hammelhoden (Ger). An erroneous varietal name for the red grape variety Trollinger. Hammel = 'castrated ram', Hoden = 'testicles'.

Hammerhead Ale (Eng). A strong Ale 1050 O.G. brewed by the Clark Brewery in Wakefield, Yorkshire.

Hammerstein (Ger). Village. (Anb) = Mittelrhein. (Ber) = Rheinburgengau. (Gro) = Burg Hammerstein. (Vins) = Hölle, In den Layfelsen, Schlossberg.

Hammerstein (Ger). Vineyard. (Anb) = Mosel-Saar-Ruwer. (Ber) = Saar-Ruwer. (Gro) = Römerlay. (Vil) = Trier.

Hammerton's Porter (Eng). A highly-hopped Porter 1038 O.G. brewed by the Watney Combe Reid Brewery in London.

Hammond (W.Ind). The local name for 'Moonshine rum' on St. Kitts.

Hammondsport Wine Company (USA). A winery based in the Finger Lakes district, New York. Noted for bottle-fermented, sparkling wines.

Hammurabi (M.East). King of Babylon. See Laws of Hammurabi.

Hampden Distillery (W.Ind). A Rum distillery based in north-western Jamaica. Produces Rum which is usually used for blending.

Hancock Brewery (Den). A brewery based in Viborg, north Jutland.

Hancock's Brewery (Wales). A Cardiff brewery now owned by Bass Worthington which operates as Welsh Brewers.

Hancock's HB (Wales). A Bitter 1037 O.G. brewed by the Welsh Brewers.

Hancock Sour (Cktl). 1½ fl.ozs. Bourbon whiskey, 4 dashes Gomme syrup, 2 dashes Jamaican rum, juice of a small lime. Stir well over ice, strain into a highball glass. Top with soda water and decorate with fruit in season.

Hancock's PA (Wales). A Light mild ale 1033 O.G. brewed by the Welsh Brewers.

Handicap Cocktail (Cktl). ¼ gill Grand Marnier, 1 wine-glass Fruchtschaumwein. Stir well over ice, strain into a large wine glass, add a slice of lemon.

Hand (Peter) Brewery (USA). A noted brewery based in Chicago. Brews Van Meritt beers.

Handle (Eng). A customer's request for a glass mug with a handle.

Handpull (Eng). See Handpump.

Handpump (Eng). Also known as the Handpull or the Beer engine. Used for the dispensing of beer in the bar.

Handthal (Ger). Village. (Anb) = Franken. (Ber) = Steigerwald. (Gro) = Not yet assigned. (Vin) = Stollberg.

Hanepoot (S.Afr). A white grape variety which has a high sugar content and good body. Used for making dessert wines in Klein Karoo. Is also known as the Muscat Alexandria.

Hangen-Weisheim (Ger). Village. (Anb) = Rheinhessen. (Ber) = Wonnegau. (Gro) = Bergkloster. (Vin) = Sommerwende.

Hangover (Eng). Indisposition due to a heavy drinking bout.

Hangtown (USA). The brand-name used for a range of red and white wines produced by the Boeger Winery in Eldorado, California.

Hanky Bannister (Scot). The producers of a blended Scotch whisky of the same name based in Leith, Edinburgh, Midlothian.

Hanky-Panky (Cktl). ½ measure Gin, ½ measure Italian vermouth, 2 dashes Fernet Branca. Stir over ice, strain into a cocktail glass. Squeeze of lemon peel juice on top.

Hannan's (Austr). The brand-name used by the Swan Brewery for Lager and Stout brewed at their Kalgoorlie plant.

Hannan's Lager (Austr). See Hannan's.

Hannan's Stout (Austr). See Hannan's.

Hannen Alt (Ger). An Alt bier from Düsseldorf. Soft, dark and delicate. 4.5% alc. by vol.

Hannesen (Ger). Noted producers of Perlwein.

Hanneton (Eng). A beetle that attacks the roots of the vine and slows down its' growth. Cured with the treatment of Sulphur around the roots. Is similar to the Vespere beetle.

Hannetot Grand Maison (Fr). A vineyard in the commune of Léognan. A.C. Graves, Bordeaux. 5 ha. (red).

Hanns Christof (Ger). The brand-name of a Liebfraumilch from the shippers Deinhard and Co. Koblenz.

Hanns Kornell Champagne Cellars (USA). See Kornell Champagne Cellars.

Hansa Brauerei (Ger). A brewery based in Dortmund, Westphalia.

Hansa Brewery (Afr). A brewery based in Namibia. Noted for its' Pilsener lager beer.

Hansa Brewery (Nor). A brewery based in Bergen, western Norway. Brews Heineken under licence.

Hansa Export (Ger). A Dortmunder Export beer brewed by the Dortmunder Hansa Brauerei in Dortmund, Westphalia.

Hansa Lager (Eng). A Lager beer 1036 O.G. brewed under licence by the Cameron's Brewery in Hartlepool, County Durham.

Hansa Pils (Ger). A Pilsener lager beer brewed by the Dortmunder Hansa Brauerei in Dortmund, Westphalia.

Hansa Pilsener (Afr). A Lager beer brewed by the Hansa Brewery in Namibia.

Hansa Pilsener (S.Afr). A Lager beer brewed by the South African Breweries.

Hansa Urbock (Afr). A dark Bock beer 1080 O.G. brewed by the Hansa Brewery in Namibia.

Hansenberg (Ger). Vineyard. (Anb) = Rheingau. (Ber) = Johannisberg. (Gro) = Erntebringer. (Vil) = Johannisberg.

Hansen Caribbean Rum Co (W.Ind). A Rum producer based on Ariba. Produces White Cap 38% alc. by vol.

Hansen GmbH & Co (Ger). A large Rum producer based in Flensburg. Produces Rums under the labels of Balle, Colding, Hansen, Nissen, Old Schmidt and Präsident.

Hanseret Wines (S.Afr). The brand-name for table wines produced by the Eesterivier Valleise Co-operative in Stellenbosch.

Hansjakob (Heinrich) (Ger). A priest who in 1881 founded the Baden wine co-operative.

Hansje in de Kelder (Hol). Lit – 'Hans in the cellar' (or Jack in the box). An old Dutch liqueur served as a discreet method used to announce a pregnancy in the family. The mother-to-be would blush when her turn came to sip the wine.

Hanson's Brewery (Eng). Part of the Wolverhampton and Dudley Breweries. Produces cask conditioned beers.

Hanssen's Brasserie (Bel). A brewery based in Dworp, central Belgium.

Hanušovice Brewery (Czec). A brewery based in northern Czec.

Hanweiler (Ger). Village. (Anb) = Württemberg. (Ber) = Remstal-Stuttgart. (Gro) = Kopf. (Vin) = Berg.

Hanweiler (Ger). Village. (Anb) = Württemberg. (Ber) = Remstal-Stuttgart. (Gro) = Wartbühl. (Vin) = Maien.

Hanwood Winery (Austr). A part of the McWilliams Vineyards in Riverina, New South Wales. 87 ha. Grape varieties – Cabernet sauvignon, Chardonnay, Malbec, Pinot noir, Rhine riesling and Shiraz.

Hanzell Winery (USA). A winery based in Sonoma County, California. Grape varieties – Chardonnay and Pinot noir. Produces varietal wines.

Happenhalde (Ger). Vineyard. (Anb) = Württemberg. (Ber) = Remstal-Stuttgart. (Gro) = Wartbühl. (Vil) = Endersbach.

Happs Winery (Austr). Vineyard.

H

Address = P.O. Dunsborough, Western Australia 6281. Grape varieties – Cabernet sauvignon, Chardonnay, Merlot, Shiraz and Verdelho. Winery at Commonage Road, Yallingup, Margaret River, Western Australia.

Happy 'B' Farm Winery (USA). A winery based in Forsyth, Georgia. Produces wines mainly from the Concord and Muscadine grapes.

Happy Birthday (Cktl). ¼ fl.oz. Bacardi Rum, ¾ fl.oz. Bols Johannisbeerlikoer, 2 dashes peach juice, 2 dashes pineapple juice. Build into a highball glass. Top with Champagne, add a slice of lemon and cherry.

Happy Day (Scot). A term for a pint of beer made up using ⅔ pint of Light ale with a nip-sized bottle of strong Ale (a Wee heavy).

Happy Horse (Cktl). 1 oz. White Horse Scotch Whisky, 2 ozs. grapefruit juice, dash Grenadine, dash egg white. Shake with ice, strain into a 6 oz. goblet, add a slice of orange.

Happy Hour (Eng). A term used for the early part of the evening during licensed hours when drinks are offered at a reduced price to attract customers and hopefully keep them when the hour ends and normal prices return.

Happy Medium (Cktl). ⅛ measure Lillet, ⅛ measure orange squash, ¼ measure Pimm's N°1, ¼ measure Gin, ¼ measure Cointreau. Shake over ice, strain into a cocktail glass

Happy Valley (Austr). An estate based in Hunter Valley, New South Wales. Owned by Drayton.

Happy Youth (Cktl). ½ fl.oz. Cherry brandy, 1½ fl.oz. fresh orange juice, 1 lump sugar, Champagne. Place sugar in a Champagne flute with the orange juice and cherry brandy. Stir, top up with iced Champagne.

Harald Jensen Taffel Akvavit (Den). The brand-name of a famous Akvavit. 45% alc. by vol.

Haraszthy (Count Agoston) (USA). An early (1849) pioneer of Vitis vinifera vineyards in California. Considered by many as the father of Californian viticulture.

Haraszthy and Sons (USA). A winery based in Sonoma Valley, California. Grape varieties – Johannisberg riesling, Pinot noir and Zinfandel. Produces varietal wines.

Harboes Brewery (Den). A brewery based in Fakse.

Harbor Winery (USA). A winery based in Sacramento, California. Grape varieties – Chardonnay and Zinfandel. Produces varietal wines.

Harbourne Vineyard (Eng). A vineyard based at Harbourne Lane, High Halden, Ashford, Kent. Was first planted 1980. 1.2 ha. Grape varieties – Madeleine angevine, Müller-Thurgau, Reichensteiner and Seyval blanc.

Harcourt Valley (Austr). Vineyard. Address = Calder Highway, Harcourt, Victoria 3453. 6 ha. Grape varieties – Cabernet sauvignon, Chardonnay, Pinot noir, Rhine riesling, Shiraz.

Hard (Eng). A term used by wine tasters for a wine without much charm. Many wines which are 'hard' when young develop suppleness in time. Hardness is due to the tannin in the wine.

Hard Bean (Eng). Denotes the best type of coffee bean (top quality). Has good body and acidity.

Hard Cider (USA). A term for rough, alcoholic cider.

Hardie (Scot). A Higland malt and Scotch whisky distiller. Part of DCL. Noted for The Antiquary.

Hardington Brewery (Eng). Based in the Brewers Arms, South Petherton, Somerset. Noted for its' cask conditioned Somerset Special 1043 O.G. and keg Landsdorf Lager 1034 O.G.

Hardt (Ger). Vineyard. (Anb) = Württemberg. (Ber) = Kocher-Jagst-Tauber. (Gro) = Tauberberg. (Vil) = Weikersheim.

Hardtberg (Ger). Vineyard. (Anb) = Ahr. (Ber) = Walporzheim/Ahrtal. (Gro) = Klosterberg. (Vil) = Dernau.

Hardtberg (Ger). Vineyard. (Anb) = Ahr. (Ber) = Walporzheim/Ahrtal. (Gro) = Klosterberg. (Vil) = Rech.

Hard Water (Eng). Denotes water that has a high dissolved mineral content and is very alkaline. Tea and coffee takes much longer to brew in hard waters. See also Soft Water.

Hardy A (Fr). Cognac producer. Address = BP 27, 147 Rue Basse, de Croun, 16100 Cognac. Noted for Noces d'Or, a 50 y.o. Cognac and *** Red Corner.

Hardy's Ale (Eng). See Thomas Hardy's Ale.

Hardy's and Hanson's (Eng). A brewery based in Kimberly, Nottinghamshire. Noted for its' Blackamoor Stout 1044 O.G. Guinea Gold 1032 O.G. Special Brown 1036 O.G. and Starbright IPA 1039 O.G.

Hardy's Coronet Tawny (Austr). A well-matured old tawny Port style wine.

Hardy's Winery (Austr). A winery based in South Australia. Has vineyards in the Barossa Valley, Clare-Watervale, Riverland and Southern Vales. Produces a wide range of wines and Port-style wines.

Hargesheim (Ger). Village. (Anb) = Nahe. (Ber) = Kreuznach. (Gro) = Kronnenberg. (Vins) = Mollenbrunnen, Straussberg.

Hargrave Vineyard (USA). Winery based at North Fork, Long Island. Grape varieties – Chardonnay and Pinot noir. Produces varietal wines.

Hari-Kiri Cooler (Cktl). Into a large tumbler place ½ gill whisky and the juice of ½ a lemon with a little sugar syrup. Add ½ soda and ½ Vichy water. Stir, decorate with seasonal fruits. Serve with a spoon.

Harlem Cocktail (Cktl). ⅗ measure dry Gin, ⅖ measure pineapple juice, 2 dashes Maraschino. Shake well over ice, strain into a cocktail glass. Decorate with pineapple chunks.

Harling (Eng). A vineyard at East Harling in Norfolk.

Harmanlamak (Tur). Tea blending, to blend teas.

Harmonisch (Ger). Denotes a harmonious, well-balanced wine.

Haro (Sp). A town in the centre of the Rioja Alta.

Harper Distillery (USA). A Bourbon whiskey distillery based in Louisville, Kentucky.

Harp Lager (Ire). A Lager beer brewed by the Guinness Brewery in Dublin. Brewed under licence by Scottish and Newcastle Brewery and the Courage Brewery.

Harpoon (Cktl). 1 measure Scotch whisky, ½ measure Mandarine Napoléon, juice of 2 tangerines, 1 teaspoon castor sugar. Stir with ice, strain into a highball glass and top with soda. Add a twist of tangerine peel and ice.

Harriague (S.Am). A red grape variety grown in Uruguay. Known as the Tannat in France.

Harrison Cocktail (Cktl). ⅓ gill Gin, ⅙ gill lemon or lime juice, ½ teaspoon powdered sugar, 1 teaspoon Angostura. Shake over ice, strain into a cocktail glass.

Harrity (Cktl). 1 oz. Canadian whisky, dash Gin, dash Angostura. Stir over ice, strain into a cocktail glass.

Harrod's Guides (Eng). Information guides published through the Decanter Magazine on subjects such as Brandy, Champagne, Liqueurs, Sherry, Whisky, etc.

Harrogate (Eng). A still sulphurous mineral water from northern England.

Harry Lauder Cocktail (Cktl). ½ measure Scotch whisky, ½ measure sweet Vermouth, 2 dashes Gomme syrup. Stir over ice, strain into a cocktail glass.

Harry Mahlo Signature Series Cabernet Shiraz (Austr). A wine from the Yalumba vineyard in South Australia. Named after the master cooper at Yalumba.

Harry's Cocktail (Cktl). ⅔ measure Gin, ⅓ measure Italian vermouth, dash Pernod. Shake well over ice, strain into a cocktail glass. Decorate with mint sprigs and a stuffed olive.

Harsberg [ortsteil Neuholz] (Ger). Village. (Anb) = Württemberg. (Ber) = Württembergisch Unterland. (Gro) = Lindelberg. (Vins) = Dachsteiger, Spielbühl.

Harsh (Eng). This is the term used for extreme hardness in a wine when it is very astringent. Some wines lose this quality in time.

Hárslevelü (Hun). A species of grape used to a small degree in Tokay with the Muskotàly and the main grape the Furmint.

Harstell (Ger). Vineyard. (Anb) = Franken. (Ber) = Mainviereck. (Gro) = Heiligenthal. (Vil) = Grossostheim.

Hart (Ger). Hard, acid, even vinegary.

Hartberg (Aus). A wine-producing area in southern Austria.

Hartenberg Vineyard (S.Afr). A winery based in Stellenbosch. Address = Box 69, Koelenhof 7605. Produces varietal wines. Is owned by Gilbeys Ltd.

Hartley Brandy (USA). The brand-name of a Brandy produced by the United Vintners, Lodi, California.

Hartley's Brewery (Eng). A brewery based in Ulverston, Cumbria. Produces XB Bitter 1040 O.G.

Hartmann (André et Fils) (Fr). Alsace wine producer. Address = 11, Rue Roger-Frémaux, 68420 Voegtlinshoffen.

Hartridge (Austr). A winery based in the south-west coastal plain, Western Australia.

Hartsman Lager (Eng). A Lager beer 1035 O.G. brewed by the McMullen's Brewery in Hertford, Hertfordshire.

Hart Vineyards (USA). A winery based in Temecula, California. Grape varieties – Cabernet sauvignon, Chardonnay, Sauvignon blanc and Zinfandel. Produces varietal wines.

Hartwall Brewery (Fin). Breweries based in Lappeenranta, south-eastern Finland, Turku, south-western Finland and Vaasa, western Finland.

Harty Brewery (Ire). Based in Blessington, Co. Kildare. Produces Harty's Lager 1039 O.G.

Harvard Cocktail (Cktl).(1). ¼ gill Brandy, ¼ gill Italian vermouth, dash

Gum syrup, 2 dashes Angostura. Stir well over ice, strain into a cocktail glass, add a squeeze of lemon peel on top.

Harvard Cocktail (Cktl).(2). ⅔ measure dry Gin, ⅓ measure French vermouth, dash Pernod, 2 dashes Grenadine. Shake well over ice, strain into a cocktail glass.

Harvard Cooler (Cktl). 1 measure Applejack brandy, barspoon Gomme syrup, juice of lemon or lime. Shake well together over ice, strain into a highball glass. Top up with soda water.

Harvest (Eng). The gathering of the grapes. (Fr) = Vendange. (Ger) = Ernte. (Hol) = Oogst. (It) = Raccolto. (Lat) = Messis. (Port) = Colheita. (Sp) = Vendimiar. (Wales) = Cynhaeaf.

Harvest Ale (Eng). A bottled Brown ale 1031 O.G. brewed by the Greene King Brewery, Bedford, Bedfordshire.

Harvest Ale (Eng). A bottled Pale ale brewed by the Lees Brewery, Middleton, Manchester.

Harvest Banns (Fr). A famous ceremony held during the official declaration of the harvest.

Harvest Bitter (Eng). A cask conditioned Bitter 1037 O.G. brewed by the Hall's Brewery in Burton-on-Trent.

Harvey (Scot). Part of DCL. Hold the licence for the Aultmore Distillery near Keith. A Highland malt.

Harvey Brewery (Eng). Based in Lewes in Sussex. Brews for Beards of Lewes. Noted for its' Blue Label 1038 O.G. Elizabethan 1090 O.G. Exhibition Brown 1042 O.G. and Sussex Stout 1030 O.G. Also a Jubilee Ale.

Harvey Cowpuncher (Cktl). 1½ measures Galliano, milk. Pour Galliano into an ice-filled highball glass, top up with iced milk.

Harveys (Sp). A noted Sherry producer. Address = Arcos 53, Apartado 494, Jerez de la Frontera. Owns the De Terry and Palomino y Vergara bodegas. Sherry brands include Bristol Cream, Club Amontillado, Finesse, Luncheon Dry, Merienda and Tico. See Harveys of Bristol (U.K. agents).

Harveys Bristol Cream (Sp). A famous Cream sherry shipped by Harveys of Bristol.

Harveys Bristol Milk (Sp). A very sweet Sherry shipped by Harveys of Bristol.

Harveys Brunel Blend (Sp). A fine, old, Oloroso sherry produced by Harveys to celebrate the Great Western Railway's 150ᵗʰ anniversary in 1985.

Harveys of Bristol (Eng). A noted wine importers and bottlers based in Bristol.

Address = 12, Denmark Street, Bristol BS1 5DQ. Produce Sherries, Ports and Madeiras. The U.K. agents for Harveys in Jerez de la Frontera. Owned by Allied Lyons.

Harvey's Vintage Port (Port). Vintage Port shippers. Vintages – 1958, 1962.

Harvey Wallbanger (Cktl). 2 ozs. Vodka, 4 ozs. orange juice. Shake over ice, strain into an ice-filled highball glass, float 2 teaspoons of Galliano on top. Serve with straws.

Harwood Distilleries Ltd (Can). A distillery based in Vancouver. Produces Harwood Canadian whisky. 45% alc. by vol.

Harxheim (Ger). Village. (Anb) = Rheinhessen. (Ber) = Nierstein. (Gro) = Sankt Alban. (Vins) = Börnchen, Lieth, Schlossberg.

Harzberg (Ger). Vineyard. (Anb) = Württemberg. (Ber) = Württembergisch Unterland. (Gro) = Wunnenstein. (Vil) = Grossbottwar.

Harzberg (Ger). Vineyard. (Anb) = Württemberg. (Ber) = Württembergisch Unterland. (Gro) = Wunnenstein. (Vil) = Hof und Lembach.

Harzberg (Ger). Vineyard. (Anb) = Württemberg. (Ber) = Württembergisch Unterland. (Gro) = Wunnenstein. (Vil) = Oberstenfeld.

Harzberg (Ger). Vineyard. (Anb) = Württemberg. (Ber) = Württembergisch Unterland. (Gro) = Wunnenstein. (Vil) = Winzerhausen.

Hasandede (Tur). A red grape variety.

Hascombe Vineyard (Eng). Address = Goldalming, Surrey. 2½ ha. Soil – green sand on bargate. Grapes – Müller-Thurgau 60% and Seyval blanc 40%.

Hasekamp (Hol). A major distiller of Jenever.

Haselstaude (Ger). Vineyard. (Anb) = Baden. (Ber) = Breisgau. (Gro) = Schutterlindenberg. (Vil) = Kippenheim.

Haselstaude (Ger). Vineyard. (Anb) = Baden. (Ber) = Breisgau. (Gro) = Schutterlindenberg. (Vil) = Mahlberg.

Haselstaude (Ger). Vineyard. (Anb) = Baden. (Ber) = Breisgau. (Gro) = Schutterlindenberg. (Vil) = Sulz.

Haselstein (Ger). Vineyard. (Anb) = Württemberg. (Ber) = Remstal-Stuttgart. (Gro) = Wartbühl. (Vil) = Breuningsweiler.

Haselstein (Ger). Vineyard. (Anb) = Württemberg. (Ber) = Remstal-Stuttgart. (Gro) = Wartbühl. (Vil) = Winnenden.

Hasen (Ger). Vineyard. (Anb) = Rheinpfalz. (Ber) = Südliche Weinstrasse. (Gro) = Herrlick. (Vil) = Eschbach.

H

Hasenberg (Ger). Vineyard. (Anb) = Baden. (Ber) = Kaiserstuhl-Tuniberg. (Gro) = Vulkanfelsen. (Vil) = Königschaffhausen.

Hasenberg (Ger). Vineyard. (Anb) = Mittelrhein. (Ber) = Rheinburgengau. (Gro) = Lahntal. (Vil) = Bad Ems.

Hasenberg (Ger). Vineyard. (Anb) = Mittelrhein. (Ber) = Rheinburgengau. (Gro) = Lahntal. (Vil) = Dausenau.

Hasenbiss (Ger). Vineyard. (Anb) = Rheinhessen. (Ber) = Wonnegau. (Gro) = Gotteshilfe. (Vil) = Osthofen.

Hasenlauf (Ger). Vineyard. (Anb) = Rheinhessen. (Ber) = Wonnegau. (Gro) = Bergkloster. (Vil) = Bermersheim.

Hasenläufer (Ger). Vineyard. (Anb) = Mosel-Saar-Ruwer. (Ber) = Bernkastel. (Gro) = Kurfurstlay. (Vil) = Brauneberg.

Hasenläufer (Ger). Vineyard. (Anb) = Mosel-Saar-Ruwer. (Ber) = Bernkastel. (Gro) = Kurfurstlay. (Vil) = Burgen.

Hasensprung (Ger). Vineyard. (Anb) = Baden. (Ber) = Badische Bergstrasse/ Kraichgau. (Gro) = Hohenberg. (Vil) = Walzbachtal (ortsteil Jöhlingen).

Hasensprung (Ger). Vineyard. (Anb) = Rheingau. (Ber) = Johannisberg. (Gro) = Honigberg. (Vil) = Winkel.

Hasensprung (Ger). Vineyard. (Anb) = Nahe. (Ber) = Kreuznach. (Gro) = Pfarrgarten. (Vil) = Wallhausen.

Hasensprung (Ger). Vineyard. (Anb) = Rheinhessen. (Ber) = Bingen. (Gro) = Kaiserpfalz. (Vil) = Jugenheim.

Hasensprung (Ger). Vineyard. (Anb) = Rheinhessen. (Ber) = Nierstein. (Gro) = Rheinblick. (Vil) = Dorn-Dürkheim.

Hasensprung (Ger). Vineyard. (Anb) = Rheinhessen. (Ber) = Wonnegau. (Gro) = Pilgerpfad. (Vil) = Bechtheim.

Hasenzeile (Ger). Vineyard. (Anb) = Rheinpfalz. (Ber) = Mittelhaardt-Deutsche Weinstrasse. (Gro) = Rosenbühl. (Vil) = Weisenheim/Sand.

Haskovo (Bul). A delimited wine-producing area in the southern region.

Haslach (Ger). Village. (Anb) = Baden. See Oberkirch.

Hassel (Ger). Vineyard. (Anb) = Rheingau. (Ber) = Johannisberg. (Gro) = Deutelsberg. (Vil) = Hattenheim.

Hasseltse Koffie (Bel). A variation of Irish coffee.

Hassendean (N.Z.). A medium-dry, white wine produced by the Ormond Vineyard, North Island.

Hassmannsberg (Ger). Vineyard. (Anb) = Rheinpfalz. (Ber) = Mittelhaardt-Deutsche Weinstrasse. (Gro) = Grafenstück. (Vil) = Bockenheim.

Hassmersheim (Ger). Village. (Anb) =

Baden. (Ber) = Badische Bergstrasse/ Kraichgau. (Gro) = Stiftsberg. (Vin) = Kirchweinberg.

Hastings (N.Z.). A wine area on the east coast of the North Island.

Hastings Glasses (Eng). The brand-name for a range of glasses produced by the Dema glass company.

Hasty Cocktail (Cktl). ½ measure dry Gin, ¼ measure dry Vermouth, ⅙ measure Pernod, 4 dashes Grenadine. Stir over ice, strain into a cocktail glass.

Hatay (Tur). A vineyard based in southern Turkey. Produces good quality red wines.

Hatswell (Eng). A vineyard in Washfield, Tiverton, Devon.

Hattenheim (Ger). Village. (Anb) = Rheingau. (Ber) = Johannisberg. (Gro) = Deutelsberg. (Vins) = Engelmannsberg, Hassel, Heiligenberg, Mannberg, Nussbrunnen, Pfaffenberg, Schützenhaus, Wisselbrunnen.

Hatzenport (Ger). Village. (Anb) = Mosel-Saar-Ruwer. (Ber) = Zell/Mosel. (Gro) = Weinhex. (Vins) = Burg Bischofsteiner, Kirchberg, Stolzenberg.

Haubenberg (Ger). Vineyard. (Anb) = Rheinhessen. (Ber) = Nierstein. (Gro) = Domherr. (Vil) = Saulheim.

Hauerinnung (Aus). A wine co-operative based at Traismauer.

Hauerzeche (Aus). Wine growers' guild.

Haugsdorf (Aus). A district in the Weinviertel. Produces light-styled wines.

Hauptlese (Ger). The name given to the general harvest that takes place between the Vorslese and the Spätlese.

Hausen/Z (Ger). Village. (Anb) = Württemberg. (Ber) = Württembergisch Unterland. (Gro) = Heuchelberg, (Vins) = Jupiterberg, Staig, Vogelsang.

Hausgiebel (Ger). Vineyard. (Anb) = Nahe. (Ber) = Kreuznach. (Gro) = Schlosskapelle. (Vil) = Windesheim.

Haus Österreich Troken Sekt (Aus). A dry, sparkling wine made by the cuve close method by the Kremser Winzergenossenschaft at Krems.

Haustrunk (Ger). A family drink. Made from grapes with a very low sugar content. Cannot be made into wine or sold.

Haut (Fr). A term meaning a superior quality wine or growth at a high altitude. Lit – 'High'.

Hautains (En) (Fr). A method of vine training used in south-western France. Vines are grown up on wooden or metal stakes, supported by a cross-piece 6 foot from the ground.

Haut-Armagnac (Fr). A sub-region of Armagnac in the Gers Département.

Haut-Bages-Avéros (Fr). See Château Haut-Bages-Avéros.

Haut-Bailly (Fr). See Château Haut-Bailly.

Haut Batailley (Fr). See Château Haut Batailley.

Haut-Beaujolais (Fr). The northern half of the Beaujolais region from the river Nizerand to the Mâconnais. Has granite soil and the Cru Beaujolais-Villages within its' boundaries.

Haut-Benauge (Fr). A wine-producing district in the A.C. Entre-Deux-Mers. Communes – Cantois, D'Arbis, Escoussans, Gornac, Ladaux, Mourens, Soulignac, St. Pierre-de-Bat, Targon.

Haut-Comtat (Fr). An A.C. for 6 villages in a hilly area known as Les Baronnies in the Côtes du Rhône. Produces red and rosé wines.

Haut-Dahra (Alg). A wine-producing area in the Alger Département. Mostly red wines.

Haut de Sève (Le) (Fr). A vineyard in the A.C. Muscadet de Sèvre et Maine. Address = 44190 Clisson, Loire Atlantique.

Haut-Lieu (Le) (Fr.) A vineyard in the A.C. Vouvray. Address = Huet Viticulteur, Le Haut-Lieu, Vouvray, I & L. France.

Haute Normande (Fr). The name for a bottle which is similar in style to the Bordeaux bottle. Used for Roussillon wines and Calvados.

Hauterive en Pays d'Aude (Fr). A Vins de Pays area of the Aude Département in southern France.

Hautes Bretonnières (Les) (Fr). A vineyard in the A.C. Muscadet de Sèvre et Maine, Pays Nantais, Loire.

Hautes Côtes (Fr). Part of the Côte d'Or on the upper part of the Côte. Comprises of the Hautes Côtes de Nuits and the Hautes Côtes de Beaune. Comprises 28 communes.

Hautes Côtes de Beaune (Fr). On the S. Western part of the Côte d'Or. Produces some fine wines under the A.C. Bourgogne Hautes Côtes de Beaune.

Hautes Côtes de Nuits (Fr). On the N. Western part of the Côte d'Or. Produces fine wines under the A.C. Bourgogne Hautes Côtes de Nuits. See Geisweiler.

Haute Vallée de l'Aude (Fr). A Vins de Pays area of the Aude Département in southern France. Produces red, rosé and dry white wines.

Haute Vallée de l'Orb (Fr). A Vins de Pays area of the Hérault Département in southern France.

Haut-Médoc (Fr). The finest area within the Bordeaux region. Produces the finest red wines. A.C. communes of Listrac, Margaux, Moulis, Pauillac, Saint-Estèphe, Saint-Julien and the Haut-Médoc itself.

Haut Montravel (Fr). An A.C. commune in the Côtes de Bergerac. Produces medium-sweet white wines.

Haut Mornag (Afr). The brand-name for red and rosé wines from the UCCVT in Tunisia.

Haut Pays (Fr). S.W. France. See Languedoc.

Haut Poitou (Fr). A V.D.Q.S. area near Anjou, Anjou-Saumur, Loire. Produces mainly white wines from the Chardonnay and Sauvignon blanc grapes. Also produces a little red and rosé wine.

Haut Provence Vineyard (S.Afr). A vineyard based in Franschhoek. Address = P.O. Franschhoek 7690. Produces varietal wines.

Haut-Pruliers (Les) (Fr). A Premier Cru vineyard in the A.C. commune of Nuits-Saint-Georges, Côte de Nuits, Burgundy. 4.5 ha.

Haut-Rhin (Fr). Lit – 'High Rhine'. A region of southern Alsace. See Bas Rhin.

Hautrive en Pays de l'Aude (Fr). A Vins de Pays area in the Aude Département, southern France. Produces red, rosé and dry white wines.

Haut Roche (Fr). A vineyard based in the Petite Champagne district of Cognac, Charente-Maritime.

Haut Sauterne (USA). A Californian sweet white wine made from the Sauvignon blanc, Sémillon and Muscadelle grapes.

Hauts de Badens (Fr). A Vins de Pays area in Badens, Aude Département, southern France. Produces red and rosé wines.

Hauts-Doix (Les) (Fr). A Premier Cru vineyard in the A.C. commune of Chambolle-Musigny, Côte de Nuits, Burgundy. 1.75 ha.

Hauts-Jarrons (Les) (Fr). A Premier Cru vineyard in the A.C. commune of Savigny-lès-Beaune, Côte de Beaune, Burgundy.

Hauts-Marconnets (Les) (Fr). A Premier Cru vineyard in the A.C. commune of Savigny-lès-Beaune, Côte de Beaune, Burgundy.

Hautvillers (Fr). The Abbey in Champagne where Dom Pérignon is supposed to have developed the second fermentation in bottle when he was cellar master there in 1670's. A Bénédictine Abbey.

Hautvillers (Fr). A Premier Cru Champagne village in the Canton d'Ay.

H

District = Reims.

Havana (Cktl). ½ measure Apricot brandy, ¼ measure Gin, ¼ measure Swedish Punsch, dash lemon juice. Shake over ice, strain into a cocktail glass.

Havana Beach (Cktl). 1 measure white Rum, 1 measure pineapple juice, 2 dashes Gomme syrup. Shake over ice, strain into a sugar-rimmed cocktail glass.

Havana Cocktail (Cktl). See Havana Special.

Havana Special (Cktl). 1½ ozs. Bacardi White Label. 1 oz. pineapple juice, ½ teaspoon sugar. Shake well together over ice, strain into a highball glass filled with ice.

Havelock (Cktl). ½ gill Brandy, 1 gill ginger ale in a goblet with a lump of ice.

Havlíckuv Brod (Czec). A brewery based in central Czec.

Havstryger Aalborg (Den). The brand-name of an Akvavit produced by DDS.

Hawaiian Brandy (Cktl). ⅓ gill Calvados, ⅙ gill pineapple juice, dash Maraschino, dash lemon juice, ½ teaspoon sugar. Shake well over ice, strain into a cocktail glass.

Hawaiian Cocktail (Cktl). ½ measure Gin, ½ measure orange juice, dash orange Curaçao. Shake over ice, strain into a cocktail glass.

Hawaiian Coffee (Cktl). Blend with a scoop of crushed ice in a blender ⅓ gill white Rum, ⅔ gill pineapple juice and 1 gill cold black coffee. Pour into a high-ball glass. Serve with straws.

Hawaiian Coffee (USA). Fresh brewed coffee to which is added ⅓ part hot coconut. Topped with whipped cream and dressed with toasted desiccated coconut on top.

Hawaii Cocktail (Cktl). 1 measure dry Gin, ¾ measure pineapple juice, ¼ measure Grenadine, dash egg white. Shake well over ice, strain into a cocktail glass.

Hawaii Coffee (USA). A coffee with a mild, smooth butter taste and a good aroma. Not usually blended. The best is Kona coffee.

Hawk Crest (USA). The label used by the Stag's Leap Wine Cellars, Napa Valley, California for a range of their varietal wines.

Hawker (Eng). A noted producer of Sloe gin based in Plymouth, Devon.

Hawkes Bay (N.Z). A wine-producing area on the east coast of the North Island.

Hawkins and Nurick (Eng). Fine wine merchants. Addresses = 147, Bishop

Mansions, Bishop's Park Road, London SW6 6DX. and 31F, High Street, Oakham, Rutland, Leicestershire. LE15 6AH.

Hawthorne Strainer (Eng). A wire-rimmed strainer for cocktails. Fits over or inside the mouth of mixing jugs.

Häxli (Switz). The term for a small bottle of beer.

Haynes Vineyard (USA). A small vine-yard based in the Wild Horse Valley, Napa Valley, California. Grape variety – Chardonnay.

Haywood Vineyard (USA). A small vine-yard based near Sebastiani, Sonoma County, California. Grape varieties – Chardonnay and Riesling. Produces varietal wines.

Haze (Eng). See Chill Haze.

Hazelburn Distillery (Scot). An old Campbeltown malt whisky distillery now no longer in production.

Hazelmere (Austr). A winery based in Clare-Watervale, Southern Vales, South Australia.

Hazendal Estate (S.Afr). Vineyards based in Stellenbosch. Address = Hazendal Langoed, Kuils River 7580. Produces varietal wines including Freudenese.

Hazendal Langoed (S.Afr). See Hazendal Estate.

Hazes (Eng). In a wine can be caused by metal contamination, suspended starch, micro-organisms, pectin part-icles, hydro-colloids or protein/ cellulose tissue particles. Are cleared by various methods.

HB (Ger) (abbr). Hofbrauhaus Brauerei. A State-owned former brewery of Bavaria which developed German Bock beer. Also made popular the Weizenbier in southern Germany.

HB. (Nor) (abbr). See Homebum.

HB. (Wales) (abbr). Hancock's Bitter. A Bitter beer 1037 O.G. brewed by the Welsh Brewers in Cardiff.

HE. (Eng) (abbr). Hartford End. A cask conditioned Bitter 1045 O.G. brewed by the Ridley Brewery in Essex.

Head (Eng). The frothy, foamy top to a glass of beer. (USA) = 'collar'.

Headache Makers (Austr) (slang). A term for red wines that are high in alcohol.

Head and Cold Mixing System (USA). A method used to flavour Gin with botanicals.

Headbanger (Eng). A cask conditioned Ale 1065 O.G. brewed by the Archers Brewery in Swindon, Wiltshire.

Header Tank (Eng). The storage tank for water (liquor) in a brewery.

Headings (Fr). The beginning of distill-ation of Cognac. They are removed by the distiller and only the 'Heart' is retained. The latter part is called 'Tailings'.

Headless Horseman (Cktl). 2 fl.ozs. Vodka, 3 dashes Angostura. Pour into an ice-filled Collins glass. Top with ginger ale, stir, add a slice of orange.

Head Method (USA). A method of Gin production. The alcoholic vapours pass through the still head which contains the botanicals.

Head of the Bourbon Family (USA). The name given to the Bourbon whiskey 'Old Grandad'.

Heads (Fr). See Headings.

Headstrong (Eng). A Bitter beer 1048 O.G. brewed by the Blackawton Brewery, Devon.

Head Tank (Eng). See Header Tank.

Heady (Eng). A term for a wine that is high in alcohol.

Healdsburg (USA). A town based between the Dry Creek and Alexander Valleys in the Russian River Valley, Sonoma County, California. Has many of the region's wineries there.

Heart's Desire (Cktl). ⅓ measure Bacardi, ⅓ measure Swedish Punsch, ⅓ measure grapefruit juice, 2 dashes Grand Marnier. Shake over ice, strain into a cocktail glass.

Heart Starter (Cktl). 1 measure Gin in a highball glass of iced water. Add 1 teaspoon Andrews liver salts. Drink quickly.

Hearty (Eng). A term that describes a red wine as being warm, high in alcohol and robust.

Heather Ale (Scot). A traditional Scottish drink.

Heather Cream Scotch Whisky Liqueur (Scot). A Malt whisky and cream liqueur produced by R. Carmichael & Sons Ltd. (Part of the Inver House Distillers Ltd), Airdrie, Lanarkshire. 17% alc. by vol.

Heather Mist Cocktail (Cktl). 2 fl.ozs Lemon mix, 1 fl.oz. Scotch whisky, ¼ fl.oz. Cointreau, dash Grenadine. Shake over ice, strain into a cocktail glass. Add a twist of lemon.

Heat Summation (USA). The alternative name for Degree Days.

Heat Treatment (Eng). A treatment to wines to de-nature proteins. 15 minutes at 75°C. Can alter the flavour of the wines so it should be used with caution.

Heaven, Hell and Purgatory (Eng). The name given to the taverns outside of Westminister Hall in mediaeval times.

Heavy (Eng). A term applied to a full-bodied wine without much distinction.

The heaviness is usually due to an excess of alcohol.

Heavy Beer (Scot). A term used for a medium gravity beer 1034–1039 O.G. which is light in colour.

Heavy Bodied Rums (USA). The name given to Rums from Barbados, British Guyana, Jamaica, Martinique, New England and Trinidad.

Heavy Dark Rum (W.Ind). A full-bodied Puerto Rican Rum which is dark and pungent.

Hebei (China). A noted wine-producing region.

Hebsack (Ger). Village. (Anb) = Württemberg. (Ber) = Remstal-Stuttgart. (Gro) = Wartbühl. (Vin) = Litchenberg.

Hecho (Sp). Made. A complete wine ready for bottling and shipping.

Hecker Pass Winery (USA). A winery based near Gilroy, Santa Clara, California. 6 ha. Grape varieties – Carignan, Ruby cabernet and Zinfandel. Produces table and dessert wines.

Hecklingen (Ger). Village. (Anb) = Baden. (Ber) = Breisgau. (Gro) = Burg Lichteneck. (Vin) = Schlossberg.

Hectare (Fr). 2.471 acres. 10,000 square metres.

Hecto (Euro) (abbr). Hectolitre.

Hectolitre (Fr). Equals 100 litres (22 gallons). (abbr) = Hl.

Hectolitres of Pure Alcohol (Euro). HLPA. An expression used for measuring a given quantity of alcohol in a given quantity of spirit. See also LPA.

Hector's Bitter (Eng). A cask conditioned Bitter 1034 O.G. brewed by Hall and Woodhouse Brewery in Dorset.

Hedelfingen (Ger). Village. (Anb) = Württemberg. (Ber) = Remstal-Stuttgart. (Gro) = Weinsteige. (Vin) = See Stuttgart.

Hedges and Butler (Eng). Major importers and distributors of fine wines and spirits in the U.K. Address = Three Mill Lane, Bromley-by-Bow, London E3 3DU. See Hirondelle.

Hedging (Sp). A method of planting vines in the sherry region. Vines are planted 1 metre apart and 2 metres between rows so that the tractors can pass along. Vines are trained on wires.

Hedonic Scale (USA). A scoring system developed by the BTI in New York for scoring on a wine tasting. 0–1 [dislike extremely], 2–3 [dislike strongly], 4–5 [dislike slightly], 6–7 [neutral], 8–9 [like slightly], 10–11 [like strongly] and 12–13 [like extremely].

Heeley (James and Sons) (Eng). A nineteenth-century corkscrew producer based in Birmingham. Patented many fine example.

Heeltap (Eng). Derived from the lift or wedge of leather used to increase the height of shoe heel in the eighteenth century. Used for the draining of wine or spirits at the bottom of the glass. A heeltap glass has no foot. 'No heeltaps' means that glasses have to be drained before putting down.

Heeltap (Eng). A nineteenth century term for the dregs left in the bottom of a glass after drinking. Usually has sediment in.

Heeltap Glass (Eng). See Heeltap.

Heemskerk Vineyard (Austr). Address = Pipers Brook, Tasmania 7254. Office – P.O. Box 1408, Launcestron, Tasmania 7250. 25 ha, Grape varieties – Cabernet sauvignon, Chardonnay, Pinot noir and Rhine riesling.

Heerenrood (S.Afr). A red wine blend of Shiraz and Cabernet grapes produced by the Groot Constantia Estate.

Heerenwijn (S.Afr). A light, dry, white wine made from a blend of Colombard and Steen grapes by Delheim Wines.

Heering (Peter) (Den). Producer of Cherry Heering and Akvavit (under the Christianshavner label). Also Cloc and San Michele liqueurs.

Heering's Cherry Brandy (Den). Originally known as Cherry Heering. Cherry brandy 24.5% alc. by vol. See Heering (Peter).

Heerkretz (Ger). Vineyard. (Anb) = Rhein-hessen. (Ber) = Bingen. (Gro) = Rhein-grafenstein. (Vil) = Neu-Bamberg.

Heerkretz (Ger). Vineyard. (Anb) = Rhein-hessen. (Ber) = Bingen. (Gro) = Rhein-grafenstein. (Vil) = Siefersheim.

Hefe (Ger). Yeast.

Hefebranntwein (Ger). A Brandy which has been distilled from the residue left after wine production.

Hefefrei (Ger). A filtered Weizen beer (wheat) that is free of yeast. Lit – 'Yeast free'.

Hefegeschmack (Ger). Yeasty tasting. Not a fashionable term.

Hefeweizen (Ger). A Weizenbeer (wheat) with a sediment. 5% alc. by vol. Produced by the Riegele Brauerei in Augsburg.

Heide (Ger). Vineyard. (Anb) = Rheinpfalz. (Ber) = Südliche Weinstrasse. (Gro) = Ordensgut. (Vil) = Weyher.

Heidegarten (Ger). Vineyard. (Anb) = Rheinpfalz. (Ber) = Südliche Wein-strasse. (Gro) = Schloss Ludwigshöhe. (Vil) = Edenkoben.

Heidelbeergeist (Ger). A liqueur made from bilberries, either by distilling the fermented juice or by mixing the berries with alcohol.

Heidelberg (Ger). Village. (Anb) = Baden. (Ber) = Badische Bergstrasse/Kraichbau.

Heidelberg (Ger). Village. (Anb) = Baden. (Ber) = Badische Bergstrasse/Kraichgau. (Gro) = Mannaberg. (Vins) = Burg, Dachsbuckel, Herrenberg.

Heidelberg (Ger). Village. (Anb) = Baden. (Ber) = Badische Bergstrasse/Kraichgau. (Gro) = Rittersberg. (Vins) = Heiligen-berg, Sonnenseite ob der Bruck.

Heidelberg Lager (Afr). A dark, sweet Lager beer brewed by the Intercontinental Breweries.

Heidelsheim (Ger). Village. (Anb) = Baden. (Ber) = Badische Bergstrasse/ Kraichgau. (Gro) = Mannaberg. (Vin) = Altenberg.

Heidesheim (Ger). Village. (Anb) = Rhein-hessen. (Ber) = Bingen. (Gro) = Kaiserpfalz. (Vins) = Geissberg, Höllen-berg, Steinacker.

Heid Heezy (Cktl). ⅓ measure MacKinlays Original, ⅓ measure orange juice, ⅓ measure sparkling wine. Build together in an ice-filled old-fashioned glass. Dress with a slice of orange.

Heidsieck (Fr). Three separate Champagne houses. See Heidsieck-Henriot (Charles), Heidsieck Monopole and Piper Heid-sieck.

Heidsieck-Heriot (Charles) (Fr). Cham-pagne producer. Address = 3, Place Droits de l'Homme, Reims. A Grande Marque. 120 ha. Produces – Vintage and non-vintage wines. Vintages – 1900, 1904, 1906, 1911, 1914, 1917, 1921, 1923, 1926, 1928, 1929, 1933, 1934, 1937, 1943, 1945, 1947, 1949, 1952, 1953, 1955, 1959, 1961, 1962, 1964, 1966, 1969, 1979, 1971, 1973, 1975, 1976, 1979, 1981. Owned by Rémy Martin. See Champagne Charlie (De Luxe vintage cuvée).

Heidsieck Monopole (Fr). Champagne pro-ducer. Address = 83 Rue Cocquebert, 51100 Reims. Grande Marque. 110 ha. Produces – Vintage and non-vintage wines. Vintages – 1900, 1904, 1906, 1911, 1913, 1920, 1921, 1923, 1926, 1928, 1929, 1933, 1934, 1937, 1941, 1943, 1945, 1947, 1949, 1952, 1953, 1955, 1958, 1959, 1961, 1962, 1964, 1966, 1969, 1971, 1973, 1975, 1976, 1979, 1982, 1985. De Luxe vintage cuvée is Diamant Bleu.

Heil (Ger). Vineyard. (Anb) = Rheinhessen. (Ber) = Bingen. (Gro) = Kurfürstenstück. (Vil) = Wallertheim.

Heil (Ger). Vineyard. (Anb) = Rheinhessen. (Ber) = Wonnegau. (Gro) = Pilgerpfad. (Vil) = Frettenheim.

Heilbronn (Ger). Village. (Anb) = Württem-berg. (Ber) = Württembergisch Unter-land. (Gro) = Kirchenweinberg. (Vins) = Altenberg, Sonnenberg.

Heilbronn (Ger). Village. (Anb) = Württem-berg. (Ber) = Württembergisch Unter-land. (Gro) = Staufenberg. (Vins) = Stahbühl, Stiftsberg, Wartberg.

Heilbronner Herbst (Ger). A Württemberg

H

wine festival held at Heilbronn in September.

Heilbronn [ortsteil Klingenberg] (Ger). Village. (Anb) = Württemberg. (Ber) = Württembergisch Unterland. (Gro) = Heuchelberg. (Vins) = Schlossberg, Sonntagsberg.

Heileman Brewery (USA). Breweries based in La Crosse and St. Paul. Noted for its' Old Style and Special Export (a krausened beer).

Heilgarten (Ger). Vineyard. (Anb) = Mittelrhein. (Ber) = Bacharach. (Gro) = Schloss Stahleck. (Vil) = Manubach.

Heilgraben (Ger). Vineyard. (Anb) = Mosel-Saar-Ruwer. (Ber) = Zell/Mosel. (Gro) = Weinhex. (Vil) = Dieblich.

Heiligenbaum (Ger). Vineyard. (Anb) = Rheinhessen. (Ber) = Nierstein. (Gro) = Auflagen. (Vil) = Nierstein.

Heiligenberg (Ger). Vineyard. (Anb) = Baden. (Ber) = Badische Bergstrasse/ Kraichgau. (Gro) = Rittersberg. (Vil) = Heidelberg.

Heiligenberg (Ger). Vineyard. (Anb) = Baden. (Ber) = Badische Frankenland. (Gro) = Tauberklinge. (Vil) = Krautheim.

Heiligenberg (Ger). Vineyard. (Anb) = Baden. (Ber) = Badische Frankenland. (Gro) = Tauberklinge. (Vil) = Krautheim (ortsteil Klepsau).

Heiligenberg (Ger). Vineyard. (Anb) = Nahe. (Ber) = Schloss Böckelheim. (Gro) = Paradiesgarten. (Vil) = Weiler bei Monzingen.

Heiligenberg (Ger). Vineyard. (Anb) = Rheingau. (Ber) = Johannisberg. (Gro) = Deutelsberg. (Vil) = Hattenheim.

Heiligenberg (Ger). Vineyard. (Anb) = Rheinpfalz. (Ber) = Südliche Weinstrasse. (Gro) = Mandelhöhe. (Vil) = Maikammer.

Heiligenberg (Ger). Vineyard. (Anb) = Württemberg. (Ber) = Württembergisch Unterland. (Gro) = Stromberg. (Vil) = Häfnerhaslach.

Heiligenberg (Ger). Vineyard. (Anb) = Württemberg. (Ber) = Württembergisch Unterland. (Gro) = Stromberg. (Vil) = Schützingen.

Heiligenborn (Ger). Vineyard. (Anb) = Rheinpfalz. (Ber) = Mittelhaardt-Deutsche Weinstrasse. (Gro) = Schnepfenflug vom Zellertal. (Vil) = Albisheim.

Heiligenhaus (Ger). Vineyard. (Anb) = Rheinhessen. (Ber) = Nierstein. (Gro) = Domherr. (Vil) = Saulheim.

Heiligenhäuschen (Ger). Vineyard. (Anb) = Mosel-Saar-Ruwer. (Ber) = Saar-Ruwer. (Gro) = Römerlay. (Vil) = Morscheid.

Heiligenhäuschen (Ger). Vineyard. (Anb) = Mosel-Saar-Ruwer. (Ber) = Saar-Ruwer. (Gro) = Römerlay. (Vil) = Riveris.

Heiligenhäuschen (Ger). Vineyard. (Anb) = Mosel-Saar-Ruwer. (Ber) = Saar-Ruwer. (Gro) = Römerlay. (Vil) = Waldrach.

Heiligenhäuschen (Ger). Vineyard. (Anb) = Rheinhessen. (Ber) = Bingen. (Gro) = Kaiserpfalz. (Vil) = Jugenheim.

Heiligenkirche (Ger). Vineyard. (Anb) = Rheinpfalz. (Ber) = Mittelhaardt-Deutsche Weinstrasse. (Gro) = Grafenstück. (Vil) = Bockenheim.

Heiligenkreuz (Aus). See Stift Heiligenkreuz.

Heiligenpfad (Ger). Vineyard. (Anb) = Rheinhessen. (Ber) = Bingen. (Gro) = Adelberg. (Vil) = Wendelsheim.

Heiligenstein (Ger). Vineyard. (Anb) = Baden. (Ber) = Badische Bergstrasse/ Kraichgau. (Gro) = Mannaberg. (Vil) = Mühlhausen.

Heiligenstein (Ger). Vineyard. (Anb) = Baden. (Ber) = Ortenau. (Gro) = Schloss Rodeck. (Vil) = Neuweier.

Heiligenstock (Ger). Grosslage. (Anb) = Rheingau. (Ber) = Johannisberg. (Vils) = Eltville, Kiedrich.

Heiligenthal (Ger). Grosslage. (Anb) = Franken. (Ber) = Mainviereck. (Vils) = Grossostheim, Wenigumstadt.

Heiligenzell (Ger). Village. (Anb) = Baden. (Ber) = Breisgau. (Gro) = Schutterlindenberg. (Vin) = Kronenbühl.

Heiliger Blutberg (Ger). Vineyard. (Anb) = Rheinhessen. (Ber) = Wonnegau. (Gro) = Sybillenstein. (Vil) = Weinheim.

Heiliger Dreikönigswein (Ger). The name given to wine made from grapes picked on the same day that the Three Wise Men visited the infant Jesus.

Heilighäuschen (Ger). Vineyard. (Anb) = Rheinhessen. (Ber) = Bingen. (Gro) = Kaiserpfalz. (Vil) = Gross-Winternheim.

Heilighäuschen (Ger). Vineyard. (Anb) = Rheinpfalz. (Ber) = Mittelhaardt-Deutsche Weinstrasse. (Gro) = Schnepfenflug vom Zellertal. (Vil) = Stetten.

Heiligkreuz (Ger). Vineyard. (Anb) = Rheinhessen. (Ber) = Wonnegau. (Gro) = Pilgerpfad. (Vil) = Bechtheim.

Heilig Kreuz (Ger). Vineyard. (Anb) = Rheinpfalz. (Ber) = Südliche Weinstrasse. (Gro) = Schloss Ludwigshöhe. (Vil) = Edenkoben.

Heilig Kreuz (Ger). Vineyard. (Anb) = Württemberg. (Ber) = Kocher-Jagst-Tauber. (Gro) = Kocherberg. (Vil) = Belsenberg.

Heim (Fr). An Alsace producer. Address = 68111 Westhaltau. Combined growers' vineyards total 92 ha.

Heimbach (Ger). Village. (Anb) = Baden.

H

(Ber) = Breisgau. (Gro) = Burg Lichteneck. (Vin) = Bieninberg.

Heimberg (Ger). Vineyard. (Anb) = Nahe. (Ber) = Schloss Böckelheim. (Gro) = Burgweg. (Vil) = Schlossböckelheim.

Heimersheim (Ger). Village. (Anb) = Ahr. (Ber) = Walporzheim/Ahrtal. (Gro) = Klosterberg. (Vins) = Burgarten, Kapellenberg, Landskrone.

Heimersheim (Ger). Village. (Anb) = Rheinhessen. (Ber) = Wonnegau. (Gro) = Sybillenstein. (Vin) = Sonnenberg.

Heineken (Hol). A famous Dutch (Amsterdam) Lager brewed under licence in 20 countries. Brewed in the U.K. by Whitbread Brewery. 1033 O.G. Also an imported bottled Export 1048 O.G.

Heineken Brouwerij (Hol). Famous breweries based at Zoueterwoude and s'Hertogenbosch. Lager beers brewed under licence in most countries. See Heineken.

Heineman (USA). A winery based in Put-in-Bay, Ohio. Produces wines made from American vines.

Heinrichhaus (USA). A winery based in St. James, Missouri. Produces wines from American vines.

Heinsheim (Ger). Village. (Anb) = Baden. (Ber) = Badische Bergstrasse/ Kraichgau. (Gro) = Stiftsberg. (Vin) = Burg Ehrenberg.

Heisser Stein (Ger). Vineyard. (Anb) = Franken. (Ber) = Maindreieck. (Gro) = Hofrat. (Vil) = Buchbrunn.

Heisterberg (Ger). Vineyard. (Anb) = Mittelrhein. (Ber) = Siebengebirge. (Gro) = Petersberg. (Vil) = Niederdollendorf.

Heitersbrünnchen (Ger). Vineyard. (Anb) = Rheinhessen. (Ber) = Nierstein. (Gro) = Sankt Alban. (Vil) = Bodenheim.

Heitersheim (Ger). Village. (Anb) = Baden. (Ber) = Markgräflerland. (Gro) = Lorettoberg. (Vins) = Maltesergarten, Sonnhohle.

Heitz Vineyards (USA). Fine vineyards sited in St. Helena, Napa Valley, California. Also known as Martha May's vineyard. 17 ha. Grape varieties – Cabernet sauvignon and Chardonnay. Produces varietal, sparkling and dessert wines.

Helado (Mex). Chilled. See also Frio.

Helbon (Gre). A sweet white wine drunk in ancient Greece. Was produced near Damascus. Also known as Chalybon.

Held (Ger). Vineyard. (Anb) = Mosel-Saar-Ruwer. (Ber) = Bernkastel. (Gro) = Probstberg. (Vil) = Kenn.

Held (Ger). Vineyard. (Anb) = Mosel-Saar-Ruwer. (Ber) = Bernkastel. (Gro) = Sankt Michael. (Vil) = Köwerich.

Held (Ger). Vineyard. (Anb) = Mosel-Saar-Ruwer. (Ber) = Bernkastel. (Gro) = Sankt Michael. (Vil) = Pölich.

Held (Ger). Vineyard. (Anb) = Mosel-Saar-Ruwer. (Ber) = Obermosel. (Gro) = Konigsberg. (Vil) = Mesenich.

Held (Ger). Vineyard. (Anb) = Rheinpfalz. (Ber) = Mittelhaardt-Deutsche Weinstrasse. (Gro) = Schwarzerde. (Vil) = Bisserheim.

Heldenbrau Lager (Eng). A Lager beer 1032 O.G. brewed by Whitbread for the north west of England.

Helderberg Co-operative (S.Afr). Vineyards based in Stellenbosch. Address = De Helderberg Koöperatiewe Wijnmakerij Beperkt, P.O. Firgrove 7110. Produces varietal wines.

Helenenkloster (Ger). Vineyard. (Anb) = Mosel-Saar-Ruwer. (Ber) = Bernkastel. (Gro) = Kurfürstlay. (Vil) = Mülheim.

Helfant-Esingen (Ger). Village. (Anb) = Mosel-Saar-Ruwer. (Ber) = Obermosel. (Gro) = Gipfel. (Vin) = Kapellenberg.

Helfensteiner (Ger). A white grape variety. A cross between the Frühburgunder and the Trollinger. Ripens early and has a neutral flavour.

Helions Vineyard (Eng). Address = Helions, Bumpstead, Haver Hill, Suffolk. 0.5 ha. First planted 1979. Grape varieties – Müller-Thurgau, Reichensteiner.

Hell (Cktl). 1 oz. Brandy, 1 oz. Crème de Menthe. Shake over ice, strain into a cocktail glass. Top with cayenne pepper.

Hell (Ger). Pale. A word sometimes used when ordering a pale Münchner bier.

Hellenic Brewery (Gre). A noted brewery based in Athens.

Hellenpfad (Ger). Vineyard. (Anb) = Nahe. (Ber) = Schloss Böckelheim. (Gro) = Rosengarten. (Vil) = Braunweiler.

Heller Beer (Eng). A cask conditioned Bitter 1060 O.G. brewed by the homebrew public house Royal Inn at Horsebridge.

Hellfire (Eng). A cask conditioned Ale 1063 O.G. brewed by the Victoria Brewery, Ware, Hertfordshire.

Helligenborn (Ger). Vineyard. (Anb) = Mosel-Saar-Ruwer. (Ber) = Saar-Ruwer. (Gro) = Scharzberg. (Vil) = Serrig.

Helmholz Vineyard (USA). A vineyard based in Alexander Valley, California. Grape variety – Cabernet sauvignon. Grapes are vinified at the Veedercrest Winery.

Helmsheim (Ger). Village. (Anb) = Baden. (Ber) = Badische Bergstrasse/Kraichgau. (Gro) = Mannaberg. (Vin) = Burgwingert.

Helopeltis Theivora (Lat). The Tea mosquito. A serious pest on the African

H

continent and other tea producing countries.

Helvita Sangría [U.K] (Eng). A subsidiary of the Swiss company Helvita corporation. Set up in June 1985. Markets Wins Sangría.

Hemel-en-Aarde Valley Wines (S.Afr). The brand-name for the Hamilton Russell Vineyards.

Hemeling Lager (Eng). A light Lager beer 1030.7 O.G. brewed by Bass.

Hemileia Vastatrix (Lat). Leaf rust. A fungus that attacks the leaves of the coffee bush (especially the Arabica variety). See also Coffee Leaf Rust.

Hemingway (Cktl). ⅕ gill Pernod placed into a flute glass. Top with iced Champagne.

Hemisphere (Eng). Latitudes 35°N to 50°N and 23°S to 40°S. Ideal for the growing of grapes suitable for wine making.

Hemling Lite (Eng). See Hemeling Lager.

Hempje Licht Op (Hol). Lit – 'Lift up your petticoat'. A liqueur produced by Van Zuylekom of Amsterdam.

Hemsbach (Ger). Village. (Anb) = Baden. (Ber) = Badische Bergstrasse/Kraichgau. (Gro) = Rittersberg. (Vin) = Herrnwingert.

Hemus (Bul). A medium-sweet white wine. From Karlovo.

Henan (China). A noted wine-producing region.

Henchard Bitter (Eng). A cask conditioned Bitter 1045 O.G. brewed by the Bourne Valley Brewery in Hampshire.

Hendelberg (Ger). Vineyard. (Anb) = Rheingau. (Ber) = Johannisberg. (Gro) = Mehrholzchen. (Vil) = Hallgarten.

Hendred Vineyard (Eng). A vineyard based at East Hendred, Wantage, Oxon, Oxfordshire. 1.4 ha. Was first planted in 1973. Grape variety – Reichensteiner.

Hengelo Brouwerij (Hol). A brewery based in eastern Holland. Noted for its' Hengelo Pilsener.

Hengelo Pilsener (Hol). The name used by the Artois Brasserie of Belgium for their beer brewed in the Hengelo Brouwerij, eastern Holland.

Hengelweine (Aus). The name given to wines that were sold by the growers that produced them. Derived from the branches that were hung outside their houses to show that they had wines to sell.

Hengstberg (Ger). Vineyard. (Anb) = Nahe. (Ber) = Schloss Böckelheim. (Gro) = Paradiesgarten. (Vil) = Desloch.

Henkell (Ger). A noted producer of Sekt by the cuve close method.

Henkenberg (Ger). Vineyard. (Anb) = Baden. (Ber) = Kaiserstuhl-Tuniberg.

(Gro) = Vulkanfelsen. (Vil) = Oberrotweil.

Henkes (Can). A brand-name used by the Canadian Schenley Distilleries Ltd. for a range of liqueurs.

Henkes (Hol). A distiller of Jenever.

Henley Brewery (Eng). See Brakspear's.

Hennekens (Ger). A distillery based at Beck. Produces Els (a bitters).

Hennessy (Fr). Cognac producer. Address = Société Jas Hennessy and Co., 1 Rue de la Richonne, 16101 Cognac. Produces – Paradis. See Hennessy (Richard).

Hennessy (Maurice) (Fr). An Irishman who introduced the Star rating system for quality in Cognac brandies in 1865.

Hennessy (Richard) (Fr). An Irishman who, at the age of 26, settled in France. He discovered the Charente region, left the army and became an Eau-de-Vie dealer. Settled in Cognac and exported to Ireland and G.B. Founder of the Hennessy firm.

Henniger Brauerei (Ger). A well-known Frankfurt brewery noted for its' Kaiser Pilsener and long lagered Export beer.

Henniger Export (Ger). See Henniger Brauerei.

Henniger Pils (Ger). A Pilsener lager 1044 O.G. brewed by Henniger Brauerei in Frankfurt. Imported into Britain by Courage.

Henri Marchant (USA). The brand-name used by the Gold Seal Winery in the Finger Lakes for their range of American-grape wines.

Henriot (Fr). Champagne producer based in Reims. Owned by Charles Heidsieck. Produces – Vintage and non-vintage wines. Vintages – 1973, 1975, 1976, 1979, 1982, 1983.

Henriot 'Réserve Baron Philippe de Rothschild' (Fr). A vintage Champagne produced by Henriot. Vintages – 1903, 1905, 1911, 1921, 1928, 1929, 1934, 1937, 1939, 1941, 1943, 1945, 1947, 1949, 1952, 1953, 1955, 1959, 1961, 1964, 1966, 1969, 1971, 1973, 1975, 1976, 1979, 1982, 1983.

Henriot Royal Wedding Cuvée (Fr). A non-vintage brut Champagne produced by Henriot of Reims for the Royal wedding in 1986.

Henriques and Henriques (Mad). A Funchal-based Madeira shipper.

Henry II (Eng). A King of England who, in 1152, married Queen Eleanor of Aquitaine and inherited the vineyards of Bordeaux and Gascony.

Henry Boon Ale (Eng). A Beer 1038.5. O.G. brewed by the Clark's Wakefield Brewery. Named after the brewery founder.

Henry McKenna (USA). A brand of Bourbon whisky produced by Seagram.

H

Henry Weinhard's Private Reserve
(USA). A premium Lager brewed by the
Blitz-Weinhard Brewery in Portland,
Oregon.

Henschke (Austr). A Barossa Valley family
noted for their red table wines.

Hen's Dream (Cktl).(Non-alc). 1 egg, juice
of ½ lemon, juice of ½ orange, 2 dashes
Grenadine. Shake over ice, strain into a
cocktail glass, decorate with a twist of
lemon zest.

Henshall Disk (Eng). A patented corkscrew
c1795 invented by the Rev. Samuel Henshall. It had a disk at the top of the screw
to prevent the tip of the screw passing
through the base of the cork.

**Heppenheim [including Erbach and Ham-
bach]** (Ger). Village. (Anb) = Hessische
Bergstrasse. (Ber) = Starkenberg. (Gro) =
Schlossberg (Vins) = Eckweg, Gul-
denzoll, Maiberg, Stemmler, Steinkopf,
Zentgereich.

Heppenstein (Ger). Vineyard. (Anb) =
Mosel-Saar-Ruwer. (Ber) = Saar-Ruwer.
(Gro) = Scharzberg. (Vil) = Ockfen.

Heppingen (Ger). Village. (Anb) = Ahr.
(Ber) = Walporzheim/Ahrtal. (Gro) =
Klosterberg. (Vin) = Berg.

Hepplethwaite Cocktail (Cktl). ⅓ gill white
Rum, ⅙ gill Crème de Fraises, dash lemon
juice. Shake over ice, strain into a
cocktail glass. Top with a strawberry
slice.

Heptyl (Eng). A higher alcohol. Part of the
Fusel oils.

Herald Ale (Ire). See Herald Brewery.

Herald Brewery (Ire). A small free trade
brewery based in Northern Ireland.
Opened in 1983. Noted for its' Herald
Ale 1036 O.G. which is sold under
blanket pressure.

Herard (Paul) (Fr). Champagne producer.
Address = Neuville-sur-Seine, 10250,
Mussy-sur-Seine. Récoltants-manipulants. Produces – Vintage and non-
vintage wines. Vintages – 1971, 1975,
1976, 1979, 1982, 1983.

Heras (Las) (Arg). A wine-producing area
in the Mendoza region.

Heraud (Ets) (Fr). Cognac producer.
Address = Saint-André-de-Lidon, 17260
Gemonzac. 15 ha. in the Bons Bois.
Produces a wide range of Cognacs.

Héraud (L') (Fr). Cognac producer. Address
= Domaine de Lasdoux, Angeac-Charente, 16120 Châteauneuf-sur-Charente.
62 ha. in the Petite Champagne. Produces a wide range of Cognacs by natural
production methods. (A single
vineyard).

Hérault (Fr). A département of the
Languedoc-Roussillon, in the low plain
of Hérault and Orb. Most wine produced

is used for the making of Vermouth.

Herb (Ger). Bitter. Found on a beer label or
on Mosel wines but here more akin to
'dry'.

Herbal (Eng). A term used to describe
wines that have been matured in a cask.

Herbal Tea (Eng). Teas made from leaves
other than tea leaves. Also known as
Tisanes.

Herbe aux Vers (Fr). Lit – 'Worm herb'. See
Mugwort.

Herbemont (Mad). A hybrid grape variety
which is now banned from use in Madeira production.

Herberg (Hol). Public house, Inn, Tavern.

Herbergier (Hol). Innkeeper.

Herb Liqueurs (Eng). One or more varieties
of herbs steeped in spirit. There are many
combinations. See Elixers.

Herb Maté (S.Am). The mis-spelling of
Yerba maté.

Herbolzheim (Ger). Village. (Anb) =
Baden. (Ber) = Badische Bergstrasse/
Kraichgau. (Gro) = Stiftsberg. (Vin) =
Berg.

Herbolzheim (Ger). Village. (Anb) =
Baden. (Ber) = Breisgau. (Gro) = Burg
Lichteneck. (Vin) = Kaiserberg.

Herbsaint (Fr). An aniseed-flavoured spirit.

Hercegovina (Yug). A large wine-
producing region in central Yugoslavia.

Hercules (Wales). An American export
name for a bottled Double Strong Ale
1075 O.G. brewed by the Felinfoel
Brewery, Llanelli.

Hercules Cocktail (Cktl). ½ measure
Cognac, ½ measure Amaretto, 1 measure
orange juice, 3 dashes Grenadine. Stir
well over ice in a highball glass. Dress
with orange and lemon peel spirals.

Heredad Montsarra (Sp). A bodega based
in the Penedés region. Produces varietal
white wines.

**Heredos de Enrique Bilbao-Bodegas
Ramón Bilbao** (Sp). One of the main
wine-producers based in Rioja. See
Bodegas Ramón Bilbao.

Hereford Bitter (Eng). See Herefordshire
Ales.

Hereford Cows (USA). A cream liqueur.

Herefordshire Ales (Eng). A new brewery
opened in 1985 in Hereford. Noted for its
cask conditioned Hereford Bitter 1038
O.G.

Herencia Remondo (Sp). A white wine
made from mainly Viura grapes. Produced by the Bodegas José Palacios. Also
available as red or rosé.

Here Tonight (Cktl). ½ measure Parfait
Amour, ½ measure blue Curaçao, 1
measure cream. Shake well over ice,
strain into a cocktail glass.

Hereward Brewery (Eng). A brewery based

in Market Deeping, Lincolnshire. Founded in 1983. Brews a Bitter beer 1038 O.G. and Hereward Warrior 1055 O.G.

Hereward Warrior (Eng). A cask conditioned Ale 1055 O.G. brewed by the Hereward Brewery, Market Deeping, Lincolnshire.

Here XVIII (S.Afr). A sparkling, dry white wine made from the Steen and Sémillon grapes by Die Bergkelder.

Herforder Brauerei (Ger). A well-known brewery from Herford, Westphalia. Noted for its' well-matured Pilsener lagers.

Herforder Pils (Ger). A long-matured Pilsener lager 4.9% alc. by vol. brewed by the Herforder Brauerei in Westphalia.

Hergenfeld (Ger). Village. (Anb) = Nahe. (Ber) = Kreuznach. (Gro) = Pfarrgarten. (Vins) = Herrschaftsgarten, Mönchberg, Sonnenberg.

Hergersweiler (Ger). Village. (Anb) = Rheinpfalz. (Ber) = Südliche Weinstrasse. (Gro) = Kloster Liebfrauenberg. (Vin) = Narrenberg.

Hering (Fr). Alsace wine producer. Address = 6, Rue de Docteur-Sultzer 67140 Barr.

Heriot (Fr). A species of barley malt from the Triumph variety. Gives a good sugar yield.

Heriot Brewery (Scot). A cask conditioned 80/- Ale brewed by Tennent's Brewery. Named after their Edinburgh brewery.

Heritage (Can). A brand of Canadian whisky produced by the Canadian Distillers Ltd. (part of Seagram).

Heritage (Eng). The brand-name of a coffee produced by Lyons. A blend of Arabica beans that are medium-roasted to produce a smooth coffee.

Heritage Ale (Wales). A malt extract Ale 1038 O.G. brewed by the home-brew public house in Cardiff owned by Whitbread.

Heritage Bitter (Eng). A cask conditioned Bitter 1036 O.G. brewed by the Phillips Brewery in Buckinghamshire.

Heritage Gaston Briand la Paradis (Fr). A 90 year old Cognac produced by Ragnaud Sabourin.

Heritage Mme Paul Ragnaud (Fr). A vintage 1903 Cognac produced by Ragnaud Sabourin.

Heritage Vineyards (USA). A winery based in West Milton, Ohio. Produces wines from American and French-American hybrid vines.

Heritier-Guyot (Fr). A Burgundy négociant based at Dijon. Produces Crème de Cassis and fine wines.

Herman Joseph's (USA). A premium Beer with a strong hop flavour brewed by the Coors Brewery in Golden, Colorado.

Hermannhof Winery (USA). A winery based in Hermann, Missouri.

Hermannshöhle (Ger). Vineyard. (Anb) = Nahe. (Ber) = Schloss Böckelheim. (Gro) = Burgweg. (Vil) = Niederhausen an der Nahe.

Hermanos Solera (Sp). A dry Málaga produced by Scholtz.

Hermaphrodite Screw (Eng). A patent method corkscrew which has a central raising screw which is female to the inner shank and male to the outer barrel. Invented by Edward Thomason in 1802.

Hermes (Cyp). A fine dry, red wine produced by Loel in Limassol.

Herm Harrier (Cktl). 2 measures orange juice, 1 measure Sloe gin, ½ measure Grand Marnier. Shake over ice, strain into a flute glass.

Hermitage (Austr). The alternative name for the Syrah grape.

Hermitage (Fr). An A.C. district in the northern Rhône. Noted for its' terraced vineyards. Uses the Syrah grape variety only for red wines and the Viognier for the whites. See also Crozes Hermitage and Ermitage.

Hermitage (S.Afr). The alternative name for the Cinsault grape.

Hermitage (L') (Fr). 120 hectares of vineyards in the commune of Tain in the northern Rhône in the Hermitage region.

Hermitage Brewery (Eng). A small brewery attached to the Sussex Brewery public house in West Sussex. Noted for its' cask conditioned Best Bitter 1048 O.G. Bitter 1040 O.G. Lumley Old Ale 1050 O.G. Mild 1034 O.G. and Triple X 1044 O.G.

Hermonville (Fr). A Cru Champagne village in the Canton de Fismes. District = Reims.

Hermosillo (Mex). A wine-producing area in the Sonora district.

Hernsberg (Ger). Vineyard. (Anb) = Hessische Bergstrasse. (Ber) = Starkenburg. (Gro) = Wolfsmagen. (Vil) = Bensheim.

Heroldrebe (Ger). A red grape variety. A cross between the Portugieser and the Limberger. Produces light neutral wines. Has a low sugar content.

Heroldsberg (Ger). Vineyard. (Anb) = Franken. (Ber) = Maindreieck. (Gro) = Burg. (Vil) = Hammelburg.

Heron and Brearley (I.O.M). Brewers on the island. Breweries in Douglas and Castletown (The Okell Brewery).

Heron Hill Vineyards (USA). A winery based in the Finger Lakes, New York. 12 ha. Grape varieties – Chardonnay and Riesling. Produces varietal wines.

H

Herradura (Mex). A producer of a Tequila of the same name.

Herrenberg (Ger). Lit – 'The lord (or Master's) hill'. A popular vineyard name in Germany (37 individual sites are so named).

Herrenberg (Ger). Grosslage. (Anb) = Franken. (Ber) = Steigerwald. (Vil) = Castell.

Herrenberg (Ger). Grosslage. (Anb) = Mittelrhein. (Ber) = Rheinburgengau. (Vils) = Dörscheid, Kaub.

Herrenberg (Ger). Vineyard. (Anb) = Ahr. (Ber) = Warporzheim/Ahrtal. (Gro) = Klosterberg. (Vil) = Rech.

Herrenberg (Ger). Vineyard. (Anb) = Baden. (Ber) = Badische Bergstrasse/Kraichgau. (Gro) = Mannaberg. (Vil) = Heidelberg.

Herrenberg (Ger). Vineyard. (Anb) = Baden. (Ber) = Badische Bergstrasse/Kraichgau. (Gro) = Mannaberg. (Vil) = Leimen.

Herrenberg (Ger). Vineyard. (Anb) = Baden. (Ber) = Badische Frankenland. (Gro) = Tauberklinge. (Vil) = Gerlachsheim.

Herrenberg (Ger). Vineyard. (Anb) = Baden. (Ber) = Badische Frankenland. (Gro) = Tauberklinge. (Vil) = Oberschüpf.

Herrenberg (Ger). Vineyard. (Anb) = Baden. (Ber) = Breisgau. (Gro) = Burg Lichteneck. (Vil) = Nordweil.

Herrenberg (Ger). Vineyard. (Anb) = Franken. (Ber) = Steigerwald. (Gro) = Not yet assigned. (Vil) = Oberschwarzach.

Herrenberg (Ger). Vineyard. (Anb) = Mosel-Saar-Ruwer. (Ber) = Bernkastel. (Gro) = Kurfürstlay. (Vil) = Kesten.

Herrenberg (Ger). Vineyard. (Anb) = Mosel-Saar-Ruwer. (Ber) = Bernkastel. (Gro) = Nacktarsch. (Vil) = Kröv.

Herrenberg (Ger). Vineyard. (Anb) = Mosel-Saar-Ruwer. (Ber) = Bernkastel. (Gro) = Probstberg. (Vil) = Schweich.

Herrenberg (Ger). Vineyard. (Anb) = Mosel-Saar-Ruwer. (Ber) = Bernkastel. (Gro) = Schwarzlay. (Vil) = Enkirch.

Herrenberg (Ger). Vineyard. (Anb) = Mosel-Saar-Ruwer. (Ber) = Bernkastel. (Gro) = Schwarzlay. (Vil) = Erden.

Herrenberg (Ger). Vineyard. (Anb) = Mosel-Saar-Ruwer. (Ber) = Saar-Ruwer. (Gro) = Römerlay. (Vil) = Kasel.

Herrenberg (Ger). Vineyard. (Anb) = Mosel-Saar-Ruwer. (Ber) = Saar-Ruwer. (Gro) = Römerlay. (Vil) = Mertesdoef (ortsteil Maximin Grünhaus)

Herrenberg (Ger). Vineyard. (Anb) = Mosel-Saar-Ruwer. (Ber) = Saar-Ruwer. (Gro) = Römerlay. (Vil) = Trier.

Herrenberg (Ger). Vineyard. (Anb) = Mosel-Saar-Ruwer. (Ber) = Saar-Ruwer. (Gro) = Scharzberg. (Vil) = Filzen.

Herrenberg (Ger). Vineyard. (Anb) = Mosel-Saar-Ruwer. (Ber) = Saar-Ruwer. (Gro) = Scharzberg. (Vil) = Mennig.

Herrenberg (Ger). Vineyard. (Anb) = Mosel-Saar-Ruwer. (Ber) = Saar-Ruwer. (Gro) = Scharzberg. (Vil) = Ockfen.

Herrenberg (Ger). Vineyard. (Anb) = Mosel-Saar-Ruwer. (Ber) = Saar-Ruwer. (Gro) = Scharzberg. (Vil) = Schoden.

Herrenberg (Ger). Vineyard. (Anb) = Mosel-Saar-Ruwer. (Ber) = Saar-Ruwer. (Gro) = Scharzberg. (Vil) = Serrig.

Herrenberg (Ger). Vineyard. (Anb) = Mosel-Saar-Ruwer. (Ber) = Zell/Mosel. (Gro) = Goldbäumchen. (Vil) = Cochem.

Herrenberg (Ger). Vineyard. (Anb) = Mosel-Saar-Ruwer. (Ber) = Zell/Mosel. (Gro) = Grafschaft. (Vil) = Alf.

Herrenberg (Ger). Vineyard. (Anb) = Mosel-Saar-Ruwer. (Ber) = Zell/Mosel. (Gro) = Rosenhang. (Vil) = Briedern.

Herrenberg (Ger). Vineyard. (Anb) = Mosel-Saar-Ruwer. (Ber) = Zell/Mosel. (Gro) = Rosenhang. (Vil) = Valwig.

Herrenberg (Ger). Vineyard. (Anb) = Nahe. (Ber) = Schloss Böckelheim. (Gro) = Paradiesgarten. (Vil) = Boos.

Herrenberg (Ger). Vineyard. (Anb) = Nahe. (Ber) = Schloss Böckelheim. (Gro) = Paradiesgarten. (Vil) = Rehborn.

Herrenberg (Ger). Vineyard. (Anb) = Nahe. (Ber) = Schloss Böckelheim. (Gro) = Paradiesgarten. (Vil) = Staudernheim.

Herrenberg (Ger). Vineyard. (Anb) = Rheingau. (Ber) = Johannisberg. (Gro) = Steinmacher. (Vil) = Frauenstein.

Herrenberg (Ger). Vineyard. (Anb) = Rheinhessen. (Ber) = Nierstein. (Gro) = Güldenmorgen. (Vil) = Dienheim.

Herrenberg (Ger). Vineyard. (Anb) = Rheinhessen. (Ber) = Nierstein. (Gro) = Güldenmorgen. (Vil) = Oppenheim.

Herrenberg (Ger). Vineyard. (Anb) = Rheinhessen. (Ber) = Wonnegau. (Gro) = Burg Rodenstein. (Vil) = Ober-Flörsheim.

Herrenberg (Ger). Vineyard. (Anb) = Rheinpfalz. (Ber) = Mittelhaardt-Deutsche Weinstrasse. (Gro) = Höllenpfad. (Vil) = Kleinkarlbach.

Herrenberg (Ger). Vineyard. (Anb) = Rheinpfalz. (Ber) = Mittelhaardt-Deutsche Weinstrasse. (Gro) = Honigsäckel. (Vil) = Ungstein.

Herrenberg (Ger). Vineyard. (Anb) = Rheinpfalz. (Ber) = Südliche Weinstrasse. (Gro) = Bischofskreuz. (Vil) = Nussdorf.

Herrenberg (Ger). Vineyard. (Anb) = Rheinpfalz. (Ber) = Südliche Weinstrasse. (Gro) = Guttenberg. (Vil) = Minfeld.

H

Herrenberg (Lux). A vineyard site in the village of Greiveldange.
Herrenberg (Lux). A vineyard site in the village of Nertert.
Herrenberger (Ger). Vineyard. (Anb) = Mosel-Saar-Ruwer. (Ber) = Saar-Ruwer. (Gro) = Scharzberg. (Vil) = Ayl.
Herrenberger (Ger). Vineyard. (Anb) = Mosel-Saar-Ruwer. (Ber) = Saar-Ruwer. (Gro) = Scharzberg. (Vil) = Wawern.
Herrenbuck (Ger). Vineyard. (Anb) = Baden. (Ber) = Kaiserstuhl-Tuniberg (Gro) = Vulkanfelsen. (Vil) = Eichstetten.
Herrenbuckel (Ger). Vineyard. (Anb) = Rheinpfalz. (Ber) = Südliche Weinstrasse. (Gro) = Bischofskreuz. (Vil) = Flemlingen.
Herrengarten (Ger). Vineyard. (Anb) = Rheinhessen. (Ber) = Nierstein. (Gro) = Krötenbrunnen. (Vil) = Dienheim.
Herrengarten (Ger). Vineyard. (Anb) = Rheinhessen. (Ber) = Nierstein. (Gro) = Krötenbrunnen. (Vil) = Oppenheim.
Herrenhäusen Brauerei (Ger). A brewery of Hanover in Western Germany. Noted for its' mature Pilsener lagers.
Herrenhäuser Pilsener (Ger). A Pilsener lager brewed by the Herrenhäusen Brauerei in Hanover. A long lagered beer 5.2% alc. by vol.
Herrenletten (Ger). Vineyard. (Anb) = Rheinpfalz. (Ber) = Mittelhaardt-Deutsche Weinstrasse. (Gro) = Meerspinne. (Vil) = Haardt.
Herrenmorgen (Ger). Vineyard. (Anb) = Rheinpfalz. (Ber) = Mittelhaardt-Deutsche Weinstrasse. (Gro) = Feuerberg. (Vil) = Bad Dürkheim.
Herrenpfad (Ger). Vineyard. (Anb) = Rheinpfalz. (Ber) = Südliche Weinstrasse. (Gro) = Kloster Liebfrauenberg. (Vil) = Göcklingen.
Herrenpfad (Ger). Vineyard. (Anb) = Rheinpfalz. (Ber) = Südliche Weinstrasse. (Gro) = Kloster Liebfrauenberg. (Vil) = Heuchelheim-Klingen.
Herrenrood (S.Afr). A red wine produced by Groot Constantia.
Herrenstubengesellschaft (Fr). The Guild of Burgesses in Alsace. The original name of the Confrérie Saint-Étienne.
Herrenstück (Ger). Vineyard. (Anb) = Baden. (Ber) = Kaiserstuhl-Tuniberg (Gro) = Vulkanfelsen. (Vil) = Bickensohl.
Herrentisch (Ger). Vineyard. (Anb) = Baden. (Ber) = Breisgau. (Gro) = Schutterlindenberg. (Vil) = Lahr.
Herrenwingert (Ger). Vineyard. (Anb) = Rheinpfalz. (Ber) = Südliche Weinstrasse. (Gro) = Guttenberg. (Vil) = Steinfeld.

Herrenzehntel (Ger). Vineyard. (Anb) = Nahe. (Ber) = Schloss Böckelheim (Gro) = Paradiesgarten. (Vil) = Weiler bei Monzingen.
Herrgards (Swe). A whisky, sherry and caraway-flavoured Aquavit. Is matured in Sherry casks.
Herrgottsacker (Ger). Vineyard. (Anb) = Rheinpfalz. (Ber) = Mittelhaardt-Deutsche Weinstrasse. (Gro) = Höllenpfad. (Vil) = Kleinkarlbach.
Herrgottsacker (Ger). Vineyard. (Anb) = Rheinpfalz. (Ber) = Mittelhaardt-Deutsche Weinstrasse. (Gro) = Mariengarten. (Vil) = Diedesheim.
Herrgottsacker (Ger). Vineyard. (Anb) = Rheinpfalz. (Ber) = Mittelhaardt-Deutsche Weinstrasse. (Gro) = Schwarzerde. (Vil) = Dirmstein.
Herrgottshaus (Ger). Vineyard. (Anb) = Rheinhessen. (Ber) = Nierstein. (Gro) = Domherr. (Vil) = Klein-Winternhaus.
Herrgottspfad (Ger). Vineyard. (Anb) = Rheinhessen. (Ber) = Nierstein. (Gro) = Petersberg. (Vil) = Gau-Odernheim.
Herrgottsrock (Ger). Vineyard. (Anb) = Mosel-Saar-Ruwer. (Ber) = Saar-Ruwer. (Gro) = Scharzberg. (Vil) = Pellingen.
Herrgottströpfchen (Ger). Lit – 'Drops of heaven'. The name of a range of wines produced by Jakob Gerhardt. See Blaulack, Goldlack, Lilalack and Weisslack.
Herrlesberg (Ger). Vineyard. (Anb) = Württemberg. (Ber) = Württembergisch Unterland. (Gro) = Kirchenweinberg. (Vil) = Neckarwestheim.
Herrliberg (Switz). One of the principal vineyards in Zürich.
Herrlich (Ger). Grosslage. (Anb) = Rheinpfalz. (Ber) = Südliche Weinstrasse. (Vils) = Eschbach, Göcklingen, Herxheim bei Landau, Herxheimweyher, Ilbesheim, Impflingen, Insheim, Leinsweiler, Mörzheim, Rohrbach, Wollmesheim.
Herrmannsberg (Ger). Vineyard. (Anb) = Nahe. (Ber) = Schloss Böckelheim. (Gro) = Burgweg. (Vil) = Niederhausen an der Nahe.
Herrnberg (Ger). Vineyard. (Anb) = Hessische Bergstrasse. (Ber) = Umstadt. (Gro) = Not yet assigned. (Vil) = Gross-Umstadt.
Herrnberg (Ger). Vineyard. (Anb) = Rheingau. (Ber) = Johannisberg. (Gro) = Daubhaus. (Vil) = Flörsheim.
Herrnberg (Ger). Vineyard. (Anb) = Rheingau. (Ber) = Johannisberg. (Gro) = Daubhaus. (Vil) = Hochheim.
Herrnberg (Ger). Vineyard. (Anb) = Rheinhessen. (Ber) = Nierstein. (Gro) = Sankt Alban. (Vil) = Gau-Bischofsheim.
Herrnwingert (Ger). Vineyard. (Anb) =

H

Baden. (Ber) = Badische Bergstrasse/ Kraichgau. (Gro) = Rittersberg. (Vil) = Hemsbach.

Herrnwingert (Ger). Vineyard. (Anb) = Baden. (Ber) = Badische Bergstrasse/ Kraichgau. (Gro) = Rittersberg. (Vil) = Sulzbach.

Herrnwingert (Ger). Vineyard. (Anb) = Hessische Bergstrasse. (Ber) = Starkenburg. (Gro) = Rott. (Vil) = Bensheim-Schönberg.

Herrschaft (Switz). A small wine-producing district bordering Austria and Liechtenstein. Produces Blauburgunder and Completer vines.

Herrschaftsberg (Ger). Vineyard. (Anb) = Franken. (Ber) = Steigerwald. (Gro) = Schlosstück. (Vil) = Frankenberg.

Herrschaftsberg (Ger). Vineyard. (Anb) = Franken. (Ber) = Steigerwald. (Gro) = Schlosstück.'(Vil) = Ippesheim.

Herrschaftsgarten (Ger). Vineyard. (Anb) = Nahe. (Ber) = Kreuznach. (Gro) = Pfarrgarten. (Vil) = Hergenfeld.

Herte Kamp Jenever (Bel). The brandname for a Jenever produced by Bruggeman.

Herten (Ger). Village. (Anb) = Baden. (Ber) = Markgräflerland. (Gro) = Vogtei Rötteln. (Vin) = Steinacker.

Hertingen (Ger). Village. (Anb) = Baden. (Ber) = Markgräflerland. (Gro) = Vogtei Rötteln. (Vin) = Sonnhohle.

Hertmannsweiler (Ger). Village. (Anb) = Württemberg. (Ber) = Remstal-Stuttgart. (Gro) = Wartbühl. (Vin) = Himmelreich.

Herukka (Fin). A blackcurrant liqueur.

Hervelets (Les) (Fr). A Premier Cru vineyard in the A.C. commune of Fixin, Côte de Nuits, Burgundy, 3.83 ha.

Hervós (Sp). A wine-growing area in Cáceres, south-western Spain.

Herxheim/Berg (Ger). Village. (Anb) = Rheinpfalz. (Ber) = Mittelhaardt-Deutsche Weinstrasse. (Gro) = Kobnert. (Vins) = Himmelreich, Honigsack, Kirchenstück.

Herxheim ber Landau (Ger). Village. (Anb) = Rheinpfalz. (Ber) = Südliche Weinstrasse. (Gro) = Herrlich. (Vin) = Engelsberg.

Herxheimweyher (Ger). Village. (Anb) = Rheinpfalz. (Ber) = Südliche Weinstrasse. (Gro) = Herrlich. (Vin) = Am Gaisberg.

Herzchen (Ger). Vineyard. (Anb) = Mosel-Saar-Ruwer. (Ber) = Bernkastel. (Gro) = Vom Heissen Stein. (Vil) = Briedel.

Herzegovina (Yug). A small region which produces good white wines including Mostarska Zilavka.

Herzfeld (Ger). Vineyard. (Anb) = Rheinpfalz. (Ber) = Mittelhaardt-Deutsche Weinstrasse. (Gro) = Kobnert. (Vil) = Leistadt.

Herzhaft (Ger). Hearty.

Herzlay (Ger). Vineyard. (Anb) = Mosel-Saar-Ruwer. (Ber) = Bernkastel. (Gro) = Schwarzlay. (Vil) = Bausendorf.

Herzog (Ger). Vineyard. (Anb) = Rheinpfalz. (Ber) = Mittelhaardt-Deutsche Weinstrasse. (Gro) = Meerspinne. (Vil) = Haardt.

Herzogenberg (Ger). Vineyard. (Anb) = Württemberg. (Ber) = Remstal-Stuttgart. (Gro) = Weinsteige. (Vil) = Fellbach.

Herzogenberg (Ger). Vineyard. (Anb) = Württemberg. (Ber) = Remstal-Stuttgart. (Gro) = Weinsteige. (Vil) = Stuttgart (orsteil Cannstatt).

Herzogenberg (Ger). Vineyard. (Anb) = Württemberg. (Ber) = Remstal-Stuttgart. (Gro) = Weinsteige. (Vil) = Stuttgart (ortsteil Untertürkheim).

Herzogsberg (Ger). Vineyard. (Anb) = Baden. (Ber) = Badische Bergstrasse/ Kraichgau. (Gro) = Stiftsberg. (Vil) = Binau.

Herzogsberg (Ger). Vineyard. (Anb) = Baden. (Ber) = Badische Bergstrasse. (Gro) = Stiftsberg. (Vil) = Diedesheim.

Hesperidina (Sp). A low-alcohol drink made from orange and lemon skins.

Hessern (Ger). Vineyard. (Anb) = Mittelrhein. (Ber) = Rheinburgengau. (Gro) = Loreleyfelsen. (Vil) = St. Goarshausen.

Hesse Wine (Ger). Name given to the wine of the Rheinhessen.

Hessheim (Ger). Village. (Anb) = Rheinpfalz. (Ber) = Mittelhaardt-Deutsche Weinstrasse. (Gro) = Schwarzerde. (Vin) = Lange Els.

Hessian Fly (Eng). Mayetiola Destructor. A small Dipterous fly whose larvae damage corns (barley, rye, wheat). Family Donyidae.

Hessigheim (Ger). Village. (Anb) = Württemberg. (Ber) = Württembergisch Unterland. (Gro) = Schalkstein. (Vins) = Felsengarten, Käsberg, Katzenöhrle.

Hessische Bergstrasse (Ger). Anbaugebiet. (Bers) = Umstadt, Starkenburg.

Hessische Bergstrasse Information Service (Ger). Weinbauverband Hessische Bergstrasse e. V. Königsberger Strasse 4. 6148 Heppenheim/Bergstrasse, Western Germany.

Hessische Bergstrasse Wine Festivals (Ger). Bergsträsser Weinmarkt. Bergsträsser Winzerfest.

Hessische Forschung-Sanstalt für Wein-Obst und Gartenbau (Ger). A research wine school in Geisenheim, Rheingau.

Hessweg (Ger). Vineyard. (Anb) = Nahe.

(Ber) = Schloss Böckelheim. (Gro) = Paradiesgarten. (Vil) = Odernheim.

Het Pint (Scot). A traditional New Year drink, made of ale, whisky, eggs, nutmeg and sugar.

Hetzerath (Ger). Village. (Anb) = Mosel-Saar-Ruwer. (Ber) = Bernkastel. (Gro) = Michelsberg. (Vin) = Brauneberg.

Heublein Inc (USA). A liqueur producer based in Connecticut. Owner's of the Smirnoff trade name.

Heublein's (USA). A wine company who through Christie's of London, organise wine auctions in the USA. See Heublein Inc.

Heuchelberg (Ger). Grosslage. (Anb) = Württemberg. (Ber) = Württembergisch Unterland. (Vils) = Brackenheim, Brackenheim (ortsteil Botenheim), Burg-bronn, Cleebronn, Dürrenzimmern, Eibensbach, Frauenzimmern, Güglingen, Haberschlacht, Hausen/Z, Heilbronn (ortsteil Klingenberg), Kleingartach, Leingarten, Hassenbach-hausen, Meimsheim, Neipperg, Nieder-hofen, Nordhausen, Nordheim, Pfaffenhofen, Schwaigern, Stetton a. H., Stockheim, Weiler/Z, Zaberfeld.

Heuchelheim/Frankenthal (Ger). Village. (Anb) = Rheinpfalz. (Ber) = Mit-telhaardt-Deutsche Weinstrasse. (Gro) = Schwarzerde. (Vin) = Steinkopf.

Heuchelheim-Klingen (Ger). Village. (Anb) = Rheinpfalz. (Ber) = Südliche Wein-strasse. (Gro) = Kloster Liebfrauenberg. (Vin) = Herrenpfad.

Heunisch (Aus). An ancient red grape variety rarely grown now.

Heurige (Aus). A light white wine, young wine, new wine.

Heurigen (Aus). An inn or tavern where the Heurige (young wines) are consumed. Owner can only sell his own wines. Also known as Heurizes.

Heurizes (Aus). See Heurigen.

Heuweiler (Ger). Village. (Anb) = Baden. (Ber) = Breisgau. (Gro) = Burg Zäh-ringen. (Vin) = Eichberg.

Hewitts (Ire). A blend of Malt and Grain whiskies from Midleton, Cork.

Hexelberg (Ger). Vineyard. (Anb) = Rhein-hessen. (Ber) = Nierstein. (Gro) = Krötenbrunnen. (Vil) = Eimsheim.

Hexenbock (Switz). A ruby-coloured beer brewed by the Hurlimann Brauerei.

Hexose (Eng). The name given to sugars that contain 6 carbon $[C_6]$ atoms. e.g. Fructose and Glucose.

Hex Vom Dasenstein (Ger). Vineyard. (Anb) = Baden. (Ber) = Ortenau. (Gro) = Schloss Rodeck. (Vil) = Kappelrodeck.

Hexyl (Eng). A higher alcohol. Part of the Fusel oils.

Heylzu Herrnsheim (Ger). A famous estate based in Nierstein. 30 ha. Grape variety – Riesling 55%.

Heyvaert Brasserie (Bel). A brewery based in Asse, northern Belgium.

Hhd. (Eng) (abbr). Hogshead.

Hibernian Special (Cktl). ⅓ measure dry Gin, ⅓ measure green Curaçao, ⅓ measure Cointreau, dash lemon juice. Shake over ice, strain into a cocktail glass.

Hi-Brau (Ch.Isles). See Stein Lager.

Hickinbotham Family Vineyard (Austr). Address = Straughton Vale Road, Anakie, Victoria 3221. 15 ha. Grape varie-ties – Cabernet franc, Cabernet sau-vignon, Chardonnay, Dolcetto, Riesling, Shiraz.

Hicks Special (Eng). A strong Bitter beer 1050 O.G. brewed by the St. Austell Brewery in St. Austell, Cornwall.

Hidalgo (Mex). A wine-producing area in northern Mexico.

Hierochloe Odorata (Pol). The name given to the grass used in Zubrowka vodka. Also known as Zubrowka grass or Bison grass.

High (Eng). A term used to denote a state of altered consciousness induced by alco-hol (or drugs).

High and Dry (Eng). A London Dry Gin produced by the Booth's Distilling Co. (part of The Distillers Co. Ltd).

High and Dry (S.Am). A brand of Demerara rum produced in Guyana by the Guyana Distilleries.

Highball (Cktl). Spirit, ginger ale or soda served in a tall glass with ice.

Highball Glass (Eng). A straight-sided glass used for holding Highballs. Of 6 oz. 8 oz. 10 oz. or 12 oz. capacity.

High Culture System (Aus). A system of vine training invented by Professor Lenz Moser. Vines are planted 1.2 metres apart in rows 3 metres apart and trailed on wires 1.2 metres above the ground. Hochkultur. See Lenz-Moser.

High Diver (Cktl). 1 measure Montezuma Silver Tequila in a highball on ice, top with lemonade and a slice of lemon.

Higher Alcohols (Eng). Also known as Fusel Oils. Are more toxic alcohols than Ethyl alcohol. They include Amyl, Propyl, Isobutyl.

Highgate Brewery (Eng). A brewery belonging to Bass, Mitchells and Butlers. Brews Mild beer only. Noted for Highgate Mild.

Highgate Mild (Eng). A Mild beer 1036 O.G. brewed by the Highgate Brewery.

High Gravity Brewing (USA). A method of brewing to a high strength and then diluting to required strength. Used for the making of light beers.

High Hat Cocktail (Cktl). ¾ measure Scotch whisky, ¼ measure Cherry brandy, ½ measure lemon juice. Shake over ice, strain into a cocktail glass. Dress with a cherry.

Highland Coffee (Liq.Coffee). Using a measure of Drambuie.

Highland Command (Scot). A brand of blended Scotch whisky sold through the Victoria Wines Off-Licences. 37.2% alc. by vol.

Highland Cooler (Cktl). Into a collins glass place ½ teaspoon of powdered sugar and a little water. Stir, add ice and ⅓ gill Scotch whisky. Top with ginger ale and decorate with a spiral of orange peel over the rim of the glass.

Highland Cream (Scot). A limited edition, 18 year old, blended Scotch whisky (at least 45% Malt whisky) produced by Teacher's.

Highland Daisy (Cktl). ⅔ measure Scotch whisky, 1 measure Gomme syrup, juice ½ lime, lemon and an orange. Serve over crushed ice in a goblet. Decorate with strips of lime, lemon and orange zest.

Highland Distilleries Co (Scot). A company that through other subsidiaries owns Scottish Cream blends, Red Hackle and Langs. Brands include Bunnahabhain, Highland Park, Tamdhu, The Famous Grouse.

Highland Fling (Cktl).(1). ⅔ measure Scotch whisky, ⅓ measure sweet Vermouth, 2 dashes Orange bitters. Stir over ice, strain into a cocktail glass. Top with an olive.

Highland Fling (Cktl).(2). 1 measure Scotch whisky, 1 measure strong Assam tea (cold), ½ measure lemon juice, dash Gomme syrup. Stir over ice, strain into a highball glass. Top with ginger ale. Serve with straws.

Highland Malts (Scot). Single malt whiskies produced north of a line drawn from Greenock to Dundee. Light and full-flavoured whiskies.

Highland Manor Winery (USA). A winery based in Jamestown, Tennessee. Wines produced from American vines.

Highland Milk Punch (Cktl). ⅓ gill Scotch whisky, 1 gill milk, dash Gomme syrup. Shake well over ice, strain into a large goblet. Top with grated nutmeg.

Highland Park (Scot). A single Malt whisky distillery situated outside Kirkwall in the Isle of Orkney. Owned by James Grant and Co. Produces – 12 year old malt whisky. A Highland malt whisky. 40% alc. by vol. Part of Highland Distilleries Co.

Highland Prince (Eng). A blended Scotch whisky produced by Edward Butler in London. 37.2% alc. by vol.

Highland Queen (Scot). A blended Scotch Whisky produced by MacDonald and Muir. Has a high proportion of Glenmorangie and Glen Moray in the blend. 40% alc. by vol.

Highland Queen Grand Reserve (Scot). A 15 year old De Luxe Scotch Whisky produced by MacDonald and Muir. 40% alc. by vol.

Highland Queen Supreme (Scot). A 21 year old rare De Luxe Scotch Whisky produced by MacDonald and Muir. 40% alc. by vol.

Highland Spring (Scot). A natural or carbonated spring water bottled in Perthshire.

High Life Lager (Eng). A Lager beer 1032 O.G. brewed by the Ind Coope Brewery in Romford, Essex.

High Mountain Supreme (W.Ind). One of the three grades of coffee produced on Jamaica. A Pure coffee of fine body, acidity and aroma. See also Blue Mountain and Red Mountain.

High Proof (USA). Spirits which have alcohol content near absolute alcohol. e.g. Gin, Vodka, Brandy used for fortification of wines.

High Roast (Eng). A dark roasted coffee in which the bitter aspects of the coffee are accentuated. Much of the original flavour is lost.

High Street Mild (Eng). A cask conditioned Mild ale 1035 O.G. brewed by the Brewhouse Brewery in Dorset.

High Tea (Eng). An early evening substantial meal (usually cooked) at which tea is served as the beverage instead of alcohol.

High-Toned (Eng). Describes a wine as having a bouquet with a volatile character.

High Tor (USA). A vineyard based in the Hudson River Valley. Produces red and rosé wines from hybrid grapes and white wine from the Delaware grape.

Highway (Eng). A low-alcohol Ale 1% alc. by vol. brewed by the Elgood Brewery, Wisbech, Cambridgeshire. The alcohol is removed by reverse osmosis.

Highwaymans (Eng). A vineyard estate near Risby, Bury St. Edmunds in Suffolk. 10 ha. Owned by Macrae Farms. Grape varieties – Müller-Thurgau, Pinot noir and others. See Abbey Knight.

High Weald Winery (Eng). The first winery in the U.K. founded by Co. Lindlar to provide a marketing and wine-making consultancy service.

H

High Wine (S.Am). A brand of Demerara rum produced in Guyana by the Guyana Distilleries.

High Wines (Eng). The useful spirits obtained in distillation after the heads and tails have been removed.

Hignin (Fr). An alternative name for the Syrah grape.

Hignin Noir (Fr). An alternative name for the Syrah grape.

Higsons Brewery (Eng). Based in Liverpool, Lancashire. Noted for its' Stingo 1078 O.G. bottled beer and Prost Lager 1031 O.G. Is owned by Boddinton Brewery, Manchester.

Hijos (Sp). Lit – 'Son's of'.

Hijos de A. Barceló (Sp). A producer and exporter of Málaga.

Hijos de Alberta Gutiérrez (Sp). A noted winery based in Serrada, Valladolid, north-western Spain.

Hijos de José Suárez Villalba (Sp). A producer and exporter of Málaga.

Hilchenfest (Ger). A Rheingau wine festival held at Lorch in June.

Hildegardisberg (Ger). Vineyard. (Anb) = Rheinhessen. (Ber) = Bingen. (Gro) = Adelberg. (Vil) = Bermersheim v. d. H.

Hildegardisbrünnchen (Ger). Vineyard. (Anb) = Nahe. (Ber) = Kreuznach. (Gro) = Schlosskapelle. (Vil) = Bingen-Bingerbrück.

Hilden Ale (Ire). See Hilden Brewery.

Hilden Brewery (Ire). Opened in 1981 in Lisburn, near Belfast. Noted for its' cask conditioned Hilden Ale 1040 O.G. (also sold in bottle as a naturally conditioned ale).

Hill Billy Highball (Cktl). 2 fl.ozs. Corn whiskey served over ice in a highball glass, top with sparkling mineral water and a twist of lemon peel juice.

Hillcrest Vineyard (USA). A winery based in Roseburg, Oregon in the Pacific North-West. 12 ha. Produces wines from European vines.

Hillesheim (Ger). Village. (Anb) = Rheinhessen. (Ber) = Nierstein. (Gro) = Krötenbrunnen. (Vins) = Altenberg, Sonnheil.

Hillfoot Vineyard (Eng). A vineyard based at Beenham, near Reading, Berkshire. 3.25 ha. Grape varieties – Müller-Thurgau and Seyval blanc.

Hillgrove Vineyard (Eng). Address = Swanmore, Hampshire. 3.5 ha. Was first planted in 1977. Grape varieties – Madeleine angevine, Müller-Thurgau, Pinot meunier, Seyval blanc, Triomphe d'Alsace and Zweigeltrebe.

Hill of Gold Winery (Austr). Address = Henry Lawson Drive, Mudgee, New South Wales 2850. 12 ha. Grape varieties – Chardonnay and Pinot noir.

Hillside (Scot). A single Malt whisky distillery based on the east coast of Scotland. A Highland malt whisky. 40% alc. by vol.

Hill-Smith Estate (Austr). Address = P.O. Box. 10, Angaston, South Australia. 8 ha. Grape varieties – Cabernet sauvignon, Chardonnay, Malbec, Riesling, Sauvignon blanc, Sémillon, Shiraz and Viognier. Vineyards are – Koomanda, Old Triangle, Old Winery and The Home.

Hill, Thompson and Co (Scot). Scotch whisky distillers. Part of the Glenlivet Distillers. Brand-names include Longman, Queen Anne and Something Special.

Hill Winery (USA). A winery based in the Napa Valley, California. 250 ha. Grape varieties – Cabernet sauvignon, Chardonnay. Produces varietal wines.

Hi-Lo (Austr). A diabetic beer brewed by the Toohey's Brewery under the Miller's label.

Hilo (Sp). A flat, oily, faded wine. A diseased wine. (Fr) = Graisse.

Hilsbach (Ger). See Sinsheim.

Hilton Brewery (Eng). Name of breweries in 2 home-brew public houses in Kent. The Pier Hotel, Gravesend and the Southeastern in Strood. Noted for their cask conditioned Buccaneer 1065 O.G. Clipper 1040 O.G. Gravedigger 1050 O.G. Lifebuoy 1075 O.G. and Pirate Porter 1036 O.G.

Hilton Glasses (Eng). A brand-name for a style of glasses produced by the Dema Company.

Hilzingen (Ger). Village. (Anb) = Baden. (Ber) = Bodensee. (Gro) = Sonnenufer. (Vin) = Elisabethenberg.

Himbeer (USA). A raspberry-flavoured liqueur. 30% alc. by vol.

Himbeergeist (Ger). An Eau-de-Vie made from raspberries. 32% alc. by vol.

Himmelacker (Ger). Vineyard. (Anb) = Rheinhessen. (Ber) = Wonnegau. (Gro) = Sybillenstein. (Vil) = Dantenheim.

Himmelberg (Ger). Vineyard. (Anb) = Baden. (Ber) = Badische Bergstrasse/Kraichgau. (Gro) = Stiftsberg. (Vil) = Michelfeld.

Himmelchen (Ger). Vineyard. (Anb) = Ahr. (Ber) = Walporzheim/Ahrtal. (Gro) = Klosterberg. (Vil) = Walporzheim.

Himmelgarten (Ger). Vineyard. (Anb) = Nahe. (Ber) = Kreuznach. (Gro) = Kronenberg. (Vil) = Bad Kreuznach (ortsteil Ippesheim).

Himmelreich (Ger). Vineyard. (Anb) = Baden. (Ber) = Badische Bergstrasse/Kraichgau. (Gro) = Mannaberg. (Vin) = Ubstadt-Weiher (ortsteil Stettfeld).

Himmelreich (Ger). Vineyard. (Anb) =

H

Baden. (Ber) = Badische Bergstrasse/ Kraichgau. (Gro) = Mannaberg. (Vil) = Zeutern.

Himmelreich (Ger). Vineyard. (Anb) = Mosel-Saar-Ruwer. (Ber) = Bernkastel. (Gro) = Münzlay. (Vil) = Graach.

Himmelreich (Ger). Vineyard. (Anb) = Mosel-Saar-Ruwer. (Ber) = Bernkastel. (Gro) = Münzlay. (Vil) = Zeltingen-Rachtig.

Himmelreich (Ger). Vineyard. (Anb) = Mosel-Saar-Ruwer. (Ber) = Zell/ Mosel. (Gro) = Grafschaft. (Vil) = St. Aldegund.

Himmelreich (Ger). Vineyard. (Anb) = Rheinpfalz. (Ber) = Mittelhaardt-Deutsche Weinstrasse. (Gro) = Kobnert. (Vil) = Herxheim/Berg.

Himmelreich (Ger). Vineyard. (Anb) = Württemberg. (Ber) = Remstal-Stuttgart. (Gro) = Wartbühl. (Vil) = Baach.

Himmelreich (Ger). Vineyard. (Anb) = Württemberg. (Ber) = Remstal-Stuttgart. (Gro) = Wartbühl. (Vil) = Hertmannsweiler.

Himmelreich (Ger). Vineyard. (Anb) = Württemberg. (Ber) = Württembergisch Unterland. (Gro) = Lindelberg. (Vil) = Langenbeutingen.

Himmelreich (Ger). Vineyard. (Anb) = Württemberg. (Ber) = Württembergisch Unterland. (Gro) = Lindelberg. (Vil) = Siebeneich.

Himmelreich (Ger). Vineyard. (Anb) = Württemberg. (Ber) = Württembergisch Unterland. (Gro) = Staufenberg. (Vil) = Gundelsheim.

Himmelstadt (Ger). Village. (Anb) = Franken. (Ber) = Maindreieck. (Gro) = Rosstal. (Vin) = Kelter.

Himmelsteige (Aus). The brand-name of a white wine produced in the Wachau region from Gruener veltliner grapes.

Himmelthal (Ger). Vineyard. (Anb) = Rheinhessen. (Ber) = Nierstein. (Gro) = Vogelsgärten. (Vil) = Guntersblum.

Hine (Fr). Cognac producer. Address = Cognac Hine S.A., 16 Quai de l'Orangerie, 16200, Jarnac. Produces – Antique 25 year old, Old Vintage 30–35 year old, Triomphe 40 year old, Signature and a family vintage Cognac.

Hine Antique (Fr). A famous brand of Cognac (average 20–25 years old) produced by Hine.

Hi Nikka (Jap). A brand of Whiskey produced by the Nikka Distilleries.

Hinkelstein (Ger). Vineyard. (Anb) = Nahe. (Ber) = Kreuznach. (Gro) = Kronenberg. (Vil) = Bad Kreuznach.

Hintere Klinge (Ger). Vineyard. (Anb) = Württemberg. (Ber) = Remstal-Stuttgart. (Gro) = Sonnenbühl. (Vil) = Weinstadt (ortsteil Endersbach).

Hinterer Berg (Ger). Vineyard. (Anb) = Württemberg. (Ber) = Remstal-Stuttgart. (Gro) = Weinsteige. (Vil) = Fellbach.

Hinterkirch (Ger). Vineyard. (Anb) = Rheingau. (Ber) = Johannisberg. (Gro) = Steil. (Vil) = Assmannshausen-Aulhausen.

Hinzerling Vineyards (USA). A winery based in Prosser, Washington. 9 ha. Grape varieties – Cabernet sauvignon, Chardonnay, Gewürztraminer and Riesling. Produces varietal wines.

Hip Flask (Eng). A small, flat bottle of glass or metal used to carry spirits in the pocket. Approximately 6–10 fl.ozs. capacity. See Flasket.

Hipperich (Ger). Vineyard. (Anb) = Nahe. (Ber) = Kreuznach. (Gro) = Schlosskapelle. (Vil) = Guldental.

Hipping (Ger). Vineyard. (Anb) = Rheinhessen. (Ber) = Nierstein. (Gro) = Rehbach. (Vil) = Nierstein.

Hippocras (Eng). The name of a mead produced in Cornwall.

Hippocras (Gre). Ancient Greek wine made by Hippocrates. Was flavoured with cinnamon and honey. 5th century B.C. Often mentioned in poetry. See Hippocrates' Sleeve.

Hippocrates' Sleeve (Gre). The name given to the woollen filter through which the wine Hippocras was passed to clear it of its debris.

Hiram Walker (Can). A large Company that owns many brewing, distilling and wine-making outlets including Ardbeg, Glencadam, Miltonduff-Glenlivet.

Hirondelle (Cyp). A brand-name of wines produced by the Etko Co.

Hirondelle (Eng). The brand-name of Hedges and Butler's Liebfraumilch Qba. (one of the top selling Liebfraumilch in U.K.).

Hirschau (Ger). Village. (Anb) = Württemberg. See Kressbronn am Bodensee Tübingen.

Hirschberg (Ger). Vineyard. (Anb) = Baden. (Ber) = Badische Frankenland. (Gro) = Tauberklinge. (Vil) = Werbach.

Hirschgarten (Ger). A famous 7,000 seater beer garden in Münich. Serves Augustiner beers.

Hirschlay (Ger). Vineyard. (Anb) = Mosel-Saar-Ruwer. (Ber) = Bernkastel. (Gro) = Probstberg. (Vil) = Longuich.

Hirtengarten (Ger). Vineyard. (Anb) = Mosel-Saar-Ruwer. (Ber) = Obermosel. (Gro) = Gipfel. (Vil) = Oberbillig.

Hirtenhain (Ger). Vineyard. (Anb) = Nahe. (Ber) = Kreuznach. (Gro) = Kronnenberg. (Vil) = Bad Kreuznach (ortsteil Bosenheim).

Hirzenach (Ger). Village. (Anb) = Mittelrhein. (Ber) = Rheinburgengau. (Gro) = Not yet assigned. (Vin) = Probsteiberg.

Hisar (Bul). A still mineral water from the Hisar-Momina spring.

His Eminence's Choice (Port). An Old Tawny Port. A brand-name of the Delaforce Company.

Histidine (Eng). An Amino acid found in wines. Is formed by the yeast.

Hitohada (Jap). Body temperature. The temperature that Saké should be drunk.

Hitzendorf (Aus). A wine-producing area in Weststeiermark.

Hitzlay (Ger). Vineyard. (Anb) = Mosel-Saar-Ruwer. (Ber) = Saar-Ruwer. (Gro) = Römerlay. (Vil) = Kasel.

HJT (Austr) (abbr). Harry J. Tinso. A wine-maker at Baileys who's initials are seen on some labels.

Hlinskov Čechàch Brewery (Czec). A brewery based in central Czec.

Hlohovec Brewery (Czec). An old brewery based in south-eastern Czec.

HLPA (Eng) (abbr). Hectolitres of Pure Alcohol.

H.M.R. (USA) (abbr). Hoffman Mountain Ranch. A small winery based near Paso Robles, San Luis Obispo, California. 50 ha. Grape varieties – Cabernet sauvignon, Chardonnay and Zinfandel.

HOB (Eng) (abbr). A cask conditioned Bitter 1041 O.G. brewed by the Hoskins and Oldfield Brewery in Leicester.

Hobec (Hol). A strong Lager beer 1048 O.G. Is sold in embossed green glass bottles of 440 mls.

Ho Bryan (Eng). Samuel Pepys' written name for Château Haut Brion. c1663

Hoch (Ger). Vineyard. (Anb) = Rheinhessen. (Ber) = Nierstein. (Gro) = Sankt Alban. (Vil) = Bodenheim.

Hochbenn (Ger). Vineyard. (Anb) = Rheinpfalz. (Ber) = Mittelhaardt-Deutsche Weinstrasse. (Gro) = Hochmess. (Vil) = Bad Dürkheim.

Hochberg (Ger). Vineyard. (Anb) = Baden. (Ber) = Kaiserstuhl-Tuniberg. (Gro) = Vulkanfelsen. (Vil) = Jechtingen.

Hochberg (Ger). Vineyard. (Anb) = Franken. (Ber) = Mainviereck. (Gro) = Not yet assigned. (Vil) = Erlenbach a. Main.

Hochberg (Ger). Vineyard. (Anb) = Franken. (Ber) = Mainviereck. (Gro) = Not yet assigned. (Vil) = Klingenberg.

Hochberg (Ger). Vineyard. (Anb) = Rheinhessen. (Ber) = Wonnegau. (Gro) = Liebfrauenmorgen. (Vil) = Worms.

Hochburg (Ger). See Emmendingen.

Hochdorf-Assenheim (Ger). Village. (Anb) = Rheinpfalz. (Ber) = Mittelhaardt-Deutsche Weinstrasse. (Gro) = Hofstück. (Vin) = Fuchsloch.

Hochdorf Brauerei (Switz). A small independent brewery based in Hochdorf.

Hochfeinste (Ger). An old term used on wine bottle label to denote 'very finest'. Now illegal.

Hochgericht (Ger). Vineyard. (Anb) = Rheinpfalz. (Ber) = Mittelhaardt-Deutsche Weinstrasse. (Gro) = Grafenstück. (Vil) = Obrigheim.

Hochgericht (Ger). Vineyard. (Anb) = Rheinpfalz. (Ber) = Südliche Weinstrasse. (Gro) = Trappenberg. (Vil) = Altdorf.

Hochgewächs (Ger). Superb, superior vineyard or growth.

Hochheim (Ger). A village in the eastern end of the Rheingau whos' wines gave the name 'Hock' to the Rhine wines. The shortened version of 'Hockamore' was the Victorian name for the wines of the district. See also Hock.

Hochheim (Ger). Village. (Anb) = Rheingau. (Ber) = Johannisberg. (Gro) = Daubhaus. (Vins) = Berg, Domdechaney, Herrnberg, Hofmeister, Hölle, Kirchenstück, Stein, Königin, Viktoriaberg, Reichestal, Sommerheil, Steilweg.

Hochheimer Weinfest (Ger). A Rheingau wine festival held at Hochheim in July.

Hochkultur (Aus). Viticultural system. See High Culture.

Hochlay (Ger). Vineyard. (Anb) = Mosel-Saar-Ruwer. (Ber) = Zell/Mosel. (Gro) = Goldbäumchen. (Vil) = Cochem.

Hochmess (Ger). Grosslage. (Anb) = Rheinpfalz. (Ber) = Mittelhaardt-Deutsche Weinstrasse. (Vils) = Bad Dürkheim, Ungstein.

Hochriegl (Aus). A brand of dry sparkling wine produced by Kattus.

Hochstadt (Ger). Village. (Anb) = Rheinpfalz. (Ber) = Südliche Weinstrasse. (Gro) = Trappenberg. (Vin) = Rotenberg.

Hochstätten (Ger). Village. (Anb) = Nahe. (Ber) = Schloss Böckelheim. (Gro) = Paradiesgarten. (Vin) = Liebesbrunnen.

Höchstes Kreuz (Ger). Vineyard. (Anb) = Nahe. (Ber) = Schloss Böckelheim (Gro) = Paradiesgarten. (Vil) = Feilbingert.

Hochwart (Ger). Vineyard. (Anb) = Baden. (Ber) = Bodensee. (Gro) = Sonnenufer. (Vil) = Reichenau.

H

Hock (Eng). The former name for a malty dark Mild brewed by the Fullers Brewery in London.

Hock (Ger). Mis-spelling of Hochheim. See Hoch.

Hockamore (Eng). Seventeenth and eighteenth century spelling of the word Hochheim from which Hoch derives. See Hochheim.

Hock Cup (Cktl).(1). Into a large jug place some ice, 1 measure of Curaçao, 2 measures Brandy, 1 bottle Hock (Rhine wine), 1 bottle soda water. Stir well and decorate with fruit in season, mint or borage and cucumber peel.

Hock Cup (Cktl).(2). 1 bottle Hock (Rhine wine), ¼ gill Maraschino, ½ gill Brandy, ¼ gill Kümmel, ⅓ gill Yellow Chartreuse, 1 pint soda water. Stir in a bowl with plenty of ice, strain, serve in large tumblers with lemon, orange and fresh fruit slices on top.

Hockenmühle (Ger). Vineyard. (Anb) = Rheinhessen. (Ber) = Bingen. (Gro) = Sankt Rochuskapelle. (Vil) = Ockenheim.

Hockfeine (Ger). Extra fine. Now no longer used.

Hockfeinste (Ger). Lit – 'Best of all'. Old term for Mosel wines, now no longer used.

Hock Sparkler (Cup). 3 bottles Hock (Rhine wine), 1 bottle Sekt, 4 fl.ozs. Brandy, 1 melon or other fresh fruit. Cube the melon or slice the fruit, place in a large bowl with some sugar and the wine. Leave 1 hour. Add Sekt and the rest of the ingredients. Serve with ice and fruit.

Hockweiler (Ger). Village. (Anb) = Mosel-Saar-Ruwer. (Ber) = Saar-Ruwer (Gro) = Römerlay. (Vin) = Sites not yet chosen.

Hoegaarden Brasserie (Bel). A brewery based in Hoegaarden. Noted for its' Hoegaards Wit (wheat beer) and Grand Cru. Also known as the De Kluis Brasserie.

Hoegaards Wit (Bel). A white Beer brewed by the De Kluis Brasserie in Louvain. Brewed from wheat and oats and garnished with Curaçao and corriander.

Hoeilaart (Bel). A town in Belgium that produces wines from grapes grown under glass. Is sold and consumed locally.

Hoë Krans Wynmakery (S.Afr). See Die Krans Estate.

Hoe Langer Hoe Liever (Hol). Lit – 'The longer the better'. A liqueur produced by Van Zuylekom of Amsterdam.

Hoeppslei (Ger). Vineyard. (Anb) =

Mosel-Saar-Ruwer. (Ber) = Saar-Ruwer (Gro) = Scharzberg. (Vil) = Serrig.

Hofberg (Ger). Vineyard. (Anb) = Württemberg. (Ber) = Kocher-Jagst-Tauber. (Gro) = Kocherberg. (Vil) = Möckmühl.

Hofberg (Ger). Vineyard. (Anb) = Württemberg. (Ber) = Kocher-Jagst-Tauber. (Gro) = Kocherberg. (Vil) = Siglingen.

Hofberg (Ger). Vineyard. (Anb) = Württemberg. (Ber) = Kocher-Jagst-Tauber. (Gro) = Kocherberg. (Vil) = Widdern.

Hofberger (Ger). Vineyard. (Anb) = Mosel-Saar-Ruwer. (Ber) = Bernkastel. (Gro) = Michelsberg. (Vil) = Neumagen-Dhron.

Hof Brauerei (Switz). A small brewery based in Wil.

Hofbraühaus (Ger). A brewer of Weizen (wheat) beers. See H.B.

Hofbräuhaus Brauerei (Ger). A brewery based in Münich. Was originally set up in 1589 as the Court Brauerei by Elector William of Bavaria.

Hofen (Ger). Village. (Anb) = Württemberg. (Ber) = Remstal-Stuttgart. (Gro) = Weinsteige. See Stuttgart.

Hofen (Ger). Village. (Anb) = Württemberg. (Ber) = Württembergisch Unterland. (Gro) = Stromberg. (Vin) = Lerchenberg.

Hoffman House Cocktail (Cktl). ⅗ measure dry Gin, ⅖ measure dry Vermouth, 2 dashes Orange bitters. Stir over ice, strain into a cocktail glass. Top with an olive.

Hoffmann Mountain Ranch (USA). See H.M.R.

Hoffmans (Austr). Vineyard. Address = Para road, North Para, (P.O. Box. 37), Tanunda, South Australia. 40 ha. Grape varieties – Cabernet sauvignon, Frontignan, Rhine riesling and Shiraz.

Hofgarten (Ger). Vineyard. (Anb) = Nahe. (Ber) = Kreuznach. (Gro) = Kronenberg. (Vil) = Bad Kreuznach.

Hofgut (Ger). Vineyard. (Anb) = Nahe. (Ber) = Kreuznach. (Gro) = Kronenberg. (Vil) = Bretzenheim.

Hofkellerei (Ger). Wine cellar of a Royal Court.

Hof Lager (Den). A Lager beer 1042 O.G. from Carlsberg brewed in Great Britain.

Hofmeister (Ger). Vineyard. (Anb) = Rheingau. (Ber) = Johannisberg. (Gro) = Daubhaus. (Vil) = Hochheim.

Hofmeister Lager (Eng). A keg Lager beer 1036 O.G. brewed by Courage. Also a canned version 1032 O.G.

Hofrat (Ger). Grosslage. (Anb) = Franken. (Bers) = Maindreieck, Buchbrunn.

H

(Vils) = Kitzingen, Mainstockheim, Marktbreit, Repperndorf, Segnitz, Sulzfeld.

Hofstätter (J.) (It). A fine winery based in Rathausplatz, Südtirol.

Hofsteige (Ger). Vineyard. (Anb) = Württemberg. (Ber) = Remstal-Stuttgart. (Gro) = Hohenneuffen. (Vil) = Metzingen.

Hofstetten Brauerei (Aus). A small brewery based in St. Martin.

Hofstück (Ger). Vineyard. (Anb) = Franken. (Ber) = Maindreieck. (Gro) = Hofrat. (Vil) = Mainstockheim.

Hofstück (Ger). Grosslage. (Anb) = Rheinpfalz. (Ber) = Mittelhaardt-Deutsche Weinstrasse. (Vils) = Deidesheim, Ellerstadt, Friedelsheim, Gönnheim, Hochdorf-Assenheim, Meckenheim, Niederkirchen, Rödersheim-Gronau, Ruppertsberg.

Hof und Lembach (Ger). Village. (Anb) = Württemberg. (Ber) = Württembergisch Unterland. (Gro) = Wunnenstein. (Vins) = Harzberg, Lichtenberg.

Hofweier (Ger). Village. (Anb) = Baden. (Ber) = Ortenau. (Gro) = Fürsteneck. (Vin) = Kinzigtäler.

Hogshead (Eng). Cask. 54 gallons. (abbr) = Hhd.

Hogshead (Fr). Cask. Bordeaux 48 gallons.

Hogshead (Port). Cask. 267 litres. 57 gallons.

Hogshead (Sp). Cask. 56 gallons.

Hogshead (W.Ind). Cask. 56 gallons.

Hohberg (Ger). Vineyard. (Anb) = Baden. (Ber) = Badische Bergstrasse/Kraichgau. (Gro) = Stiftsberg. (Vil) = Neckarmühlbach.

Hohberg (Ger). Vineyard. (Anb) = Rheinhessen. (Ber) = Nierstein. (Gro) = Gutes Domtal. (Vil) = Weinolsheim.

Hohberg (Ger). Vineyard. (Anb) = Rheinhessen. (Ber) = Nierstein. (Gro) = Sankt Alban. (Vil) = Lörzweiler.

Höhe (Ger). Vineyard. (Anb) = Rheinpfalz. (Ber) = Südliche Weinstrasse. (Gro) = Bischofskreuz. (Vil) = Dammheim.

Hoheburg (Ger). Vineyard. (Anb) = Rheinpfalz. (Ber) = Mittelhaardt-Deutsche Weinstrasse. (Gro) = Hofstück. (Vil) = Ruppertsberg.

Hohe Eiche (Ger). Vineyard. (Anb) = Württemberg. (Ber) = Württembergisch Unterland. (Gro) = Kirchenweinberg. (Vil) = Talheim.

Höhefeld (Ger). Village. (Anb) = Baden. (Ber) = Badische Frankenland. (Gro) = Tauberklinge. (Vin) = Kemelrain.

Hohenberg (Ger). Grosslage. (Anb) = Baden. (Ber) = Badische Bergstrasse/

Kraichgau. (Vils) = Berghausen, Bilfingen, Dietlingen, Dürrn, Eisingen, Ellmendingen, Ersingen, Grötzingen, Hohenwettersbach, Karlsruhe-Durlach, Söllingen, Walzbachtal (ortsteil Jöhlingen), Weingarten, Wöschbach.

Hohenberg (Ger). Vineyard. (Anb) = Württemberg. (Ber) = Württembergisch Unterland. (Gro) = Heuchelberg. (Vil) = Pfaffenhofen.

Hohenberg (Ger). Vineyard. (Anb) = Württemberg. (Ber) = Württembergisch Unterland. (Gro) = Heuchelberg. (Vil) = Weiler/Z.

Hohenberg (Ger). Vineyard. (Anb) = Württemberg. (Ber) = Württembergisch Unterland. (Gro) = Heuchelberg. (Vil) = Zaberfeld.

Hohenbühl (Ger). Vineyard. (Anb) = Franken. (Ber) = Steigerwald. (Gro) = Schlosstück. (Vil) = Seinsheim.

Hoheneck (Ger). Village. (Anb) = Württemberg. (Ber) = Württembergisch Unterland. (Gro) = Schalkstein. See Ludwigsburg.

Hoheneck (Ger). Village. (Anb) = Württemberg. (Ber) = Württembergisch Unterland. (Gro) = Wunnenstein. See Ludwigsburg.

Hohenhaslach (Ger). Village. (Anb) = Württemberg. (Ber) = Württembergisch Unterland. (Gro) = Stromberg. (Vins) = Kirchberg, Klosterberg.

Hohenmorgen (Ger). Vineyard. (Anb) = Rheinpfalz. (Ber) = Mittelhaardt-Deutsche Weinstrasse. (Gro) = Mariengarten. (Vil) = Deidesheim.

Hohenneuffen (Ger). Grosslage. (Anb) = Württemberg. (Ber) = Remstal-Stuttgart. (Vils) = Beuren, Frickenhausen, Kappishäusern, Kohlberg, Linsenhofen, Metzingen, Neuffen, Weilheim.

Hohenrain (Ger). Vineyard. (Anb) = Rheingau. (Ber) = Johannisberg. (Gro) = Deutelsberg. (Vil) = Erbach.

Hohenrain (Ger). Vineyard. (Anb) = Rheinpfalz. (Ber) = Südliche Weinstrasse. (Gro) = Bischofskreuz. (Vil) = Knöringen.

Hohensachsen (Ger). Village. (Anb) = Baden. (Ber) = Badische Bergstrasse/Kraichgau. (Gro) = Rittersberg. (Vin) = Stephansberg.

Hohenstein (Ger). Village. (Anb) = Württemberg. (Ber) = Württembergisch Unterland. (Gro) = Stromberg. (Vin) = Kirchberg.

Hohen-Sülzen (Ger). Village. (Anb) = Rheinhessen. (Ber) = Wonnegau. (Gro) = Domblick. (Vins) = Kirchenstück, Sonnenberg.

Hohenwettersbach (Ger). Village. (Anb) = Baden. (Ber) = Badische Bergstrasse/

Kraichgau. (Gro) = Hohenberg. (Vin) = Rosengarten.

Hoher Berg (Ger). Vineyard. (Anb) = Württemberg. (Ber) = Kocher-Jagst-Tauber. (Gro) = Kocherberg. (Vil) = Criesbach.

Hoher Berg (Ger). Vineyard. (Anb) = Württemberg. (Ber) = Kocher-Jagst-Tauber. (Gro) = Kocherberg. (Vil) = Künzelsau.

Hoher Berg (Ger). Vineyard. (Anb) = Württemberg. (Ber) = Kocher-Jagst-Tauber. (Gro) = Kocherberg. (Vil) = Ingelfingen.

Hoher Berg (Ger). Vineyard. (Anb) = Württemberg. (Ber) = Kocher-Jagst Tauber. (Gro) = Kocherberg. (Vil) = Niedernhall.

Hoher Herrgott (Ger). Vineyard. (Anb) = Baden. (Ber) = Badische Frankenland. (Gro) = Tauberklinge. (Vil) = Külsheim.

Höhlchen (Ger). Vineyard. (Anb) = Rheinhessen. (Ber) = Nierstein. (Gro) = Güldenmorgen. (Vil) = Dienheim.

Hohnart (Ger). Vineyard. (Anb) = Franken. (Ber) = Steigerwald. (Gro) = Herrenberg. (Vil) = Castell.

Hokkaido Cocktail (Cktl). 1½ fl.ozs. dry Gin, 1 fl.oz. Saké, ½ fl.oz. Cointreau. Shake well over ice, strain into a cocktail glass.

Holanda (Sp). A raw grape spirit. 65% alc. by vol. See also Holanda Columna.

Holanda Columna (Sp). A spirit made in the Patent (continuous) still at 65–70% alc. by vol. used in Brandy production.

Holden Brewery (Eng). Based in Woodsetton, near Dudley, West Midlands. Noted for its' cask conditioned Black Country Bitter 1039 O.G. Keg Golden 1039 O.G. and bottled Master Ale 1080 O.G.

Holdenried Vineyards (USA). A vineyard based in Kelseyville, Lake County, California. 146 ha. Grape variety – Cabernet sauvignon.

Hole-in-One (Cktl). 2 ozs. Scotch whisky, 1 oz. dry Vermouth, juice ¼ lemon, 2 dashes Orange bitters. Shake over ice, strain into a cocktail glass.

Holešovice Brewery (Czec). A brewery in Prague. Noted for its' pale lagers.

Holiday Lager Beer (Can). A Lager beer brewed by the Carling O'Keefe Brewery, Toronto.

Höll (Ger). Vineyard. (Anb) = Franken. (Ber) = Maindreieck. (Gro) = Kirchberg. (Vil) = Obereisenheim.

Höll (Ger). Vineyard. (Anb) = Mosel-Saar-Ruwer. (Ber) = Zell/Mosel. (Gro) = Grafschaft. (Vil) = Ediger-Eller.

Höll (Ger). Vineyard. (Anb) = Nahe. (Ber)

= Kreuznach. (Gro) = Pfarrgarten. (Vil) = Spabrücken.

Höll (Ger). Vineyard. (Anb) = Nahe. (Ber) = Schloss Böckelheim. (Gro) = Burgweg. (Vil) = Bad Münster a. St. Ebernburg.

Hollabrunn (Aus). A noted wine-producing area in the Weinviertel. Produces light-styled wines.

Hollander Liqueur Cocktail (Cktl). ½ measure Hollands Gin, ⅖ measure grape juice, ⅕ measure Apricot brandy. Shake over ice, strain into a cocktail glass.

Hollands (Eng). Early name for Gin.

Hollands (Sp). The first distillation of Spanish brandy. It is distilled at a temperature below 65° Celcius, then distilled at a higher temperature for the second time.

Hollands Gin (Hol). A clean, malty Gin used mainly in the making of cocktails.

Höllberg (Ger). Vineyard. (Anb) = Baden. (Ber) = Markgräflerland. (Gro) = Burg Neuenfels. (Vil) = Hügelheim.

Höllberg (Ger). Vineyard. (Anb) = Baden. (Ber) = Markgräflerland. (Gro) = Lorettoberg. (Vil) = Buggingen.

Höllberg (Ger). Vineyard. (Anb) = Hessische Bergstrasse. (Ber) = Starkenburg. (Gro) = Rott. (Vil) = Bensheim-Auerbach.

Höllberg (Ger). Vineyard. (Anb) = Rheinhessen. (Ber) = Bingen. (Gro) = Rheingrafenstein. (Vil) = Siefersheim.

Hölle (Ger). Vineyard. (Anb) = Mittelrhein. (Ber) = Rheinburgengau. (Gro) = Burg Hammerstein. (Vil) = Hammerstein.

Hölle (Ger). Vineyard. (Anb) = Mosel-Saar-Ruwer. (Ber) = Saar-Ruwer. (Gro) = Scharzberg. (Vil) = Wiltingen.

Hölle (Ger). Vineyard. (Anb) = Mosel-Saar-Ruwer. (Ber) = Zell/Mosel. (Gro) = Grafschaft. (Vil) = Alf.

Hölle (Ger). Vineyard. (Anb) = Nahe. (Ber) = Kreuznach. (Gro) = Schlosskapelle. (Vil) = Burg Layen.

Hölle (Ger). Vineyard. (Anb) = Nahe. (Ber) = Kreuznach. (Gro) = Schlosskapelle. (Vil) = Eckenroth.

Hölle (Ger). Vineyard. (Anb) = Nahe. (Ber) = Kreuznach. (Gro) = Schlosskapelle. (Vil) = Guldental.

Hölle (Ger). Vineyard. (Anb) = Nahe. (Ber) = Kreuznach. (Gro) = Schlosskapelle. (Vil) = Rümmelsheim.

Hölle (Ger). Vineyard. (Anb) = Nahe. (Ber) = Kreuznach. (Gro) = Schlosskapelle. (Vil) = Windesheim.

Hölle (Ger). Vineyard. (Anb) = Nahe. (Ber) = Schloss Böckelheim. (Gro) = Paradiesgarten. (Vil) = Alsenz.

Hölle (Ger). Vineyard. (Anb) = Rheingau.

H

(Ber) = Johannisberg. (Gro) = Daubhaus. (Vil) = Hochheim.
Hölle (Ger). Vineyard. (Anb) = Rheingau. (Ber) = Johannisberg. (Gro) = Erntebringer. (Vil) = Johannisberg.
Hölle (Ger). Vineyard. (Anb) = Rheingau. (Ber) = Johannisberg. (Gro) = Steinmacher. (Vil) = Schierstein.
Hölle (Ger). Vineyard. (Anb) = Rheinhessen. (Ber) = Bingen. (Gro) = Abtey. (Vil) = Sprendlingen.
Hölle (Ger). Vineyard. (Anb) = Rheinhessen. (Ber) = Bingen. (Gro) = Rheingrafenstein. (Vil) = Wöllstein.
Hölle (Ger). Vineyard. (Anb) = Rheinhessen. (Ber) = Bingen. (Gro) = Rheingrafenstein. (Vil) = Wonsheim.
Hölle (Ger). Vineyard. (Anb) = Rheinhessen. (Ber) = Bingen. (Gro) = Sankt Rochuskapelle. (Vil) = Pfaffen-Schwabenheim.
Hölle (Ger). Vineyard. (Anb) = Rheinhessen. (Ber) = Nierstein. (Gro) = Domherr. (Vil) = Saulheim.
Hölle (Ger). Vineyard. (Anb) = Rheinhessen. (Ber) = Nierstein. (Gro) = Spiegelberg. (Vil) = Nierstein.
Hölle (Ger). Vineyard. (Anb) = Rheinhessen. (Ber) = Wonnegau. (Gro) = Sybillenstein. (Vil) = Weinheim.
Hölle (Ger). Vineyard. (Anb) = Rheinpfalz. (Ber) = Südliche Weinstrasse. (Gro) = Bischofskreuz. (Vil) = Gleisweiler.
Hollejo (Sp). Grapeskin.
Höllenberg (Ger). Lit – 'Hellish hill'.
Höllenberg (Ger). Vineyard. (Anb) = Nahe. (Ber) = Schloss Böckelheim. (Gro) = Paradiesgarten. (Vil) = Nussbaum.
Höllenberg (Ger). Vineyard. (Anb) = Rheingau. (Ber) = Johannisberg. (Gro) = Steil. (Vil) = Assmannshausen-Aulhausen.
Höllenberg (Ger). Vineyard. (Anb) = Rheinhessen. (Ber) = Bingen. (Gro) = Kaiserpfalz. (Vil) = Heidesheim.
Höllenbrand (Ger). Vineyard. (Anb) = Nahe. (Ber) = Kreuznach. (Gro) = Kronenberg. (Vil) = Bad Kreuznach (ortsteil Bosenheim).
Höllenbrand (Ger). Vineyard. (Anb) = Rheinhessen. (Ber) = Wonnegau. (Gro) = Bergkloster. (Vil) = Gundersheim.
Höllenpfad (Ger). Vineyard. (Anb) = Nahe. (Ber) = Kreuznach. (Gro) = Pfarrgarten. (Vil) = Wallhausen.
Höllenpfad (Ger). Vineyard. (Anb) = Nahe. (Ber) = Schloss Böckelheim. (Gro) = Rosengarten. (Vil) = Burgsponheim.
Höllenpfad (Ger). Vineyard. (Anb) = Nahe. (Ber) = Schloss Böckelheim. (Gro) = Rosengarten. (Vil) = Roxheim.
Höllenpfad (Ger). Grosslage. (Anb) =

Rheinpfalz. (Ber) = Mittelhaardt-Deutsche Weinstrasse. (Vils) = Battenberg, Grünstadt, Kleinkarlbach, Mertesheim, Neuleiningen.
Höllenweg (Ger). Vineyard. (Anb) = Rheinhessen. (Ber) = Bingen. (Gro) = Kaiserpfalz. (Vil) = Ingelheim.
Höllhagen (Ger). Vineyard. (Anb) = Baden. (Ber) = Markgräflerland. (Gro) = Lorettoberg. (Vil) = Kirchhofen.
Höllisch Feuer (Ger). Vineyard. (Anb) = Württemberg. (Ber) = Württembergisch Unterland. (Gro) = Stromberg. (Vil) = Vaihingen.
Hollister (USA). A noted wine-producing town based in San Benito County, California.
Hollow (Eng). A term applied to wines which lack flavour after showing promise on the nose.
Holly Bush Vineyard (Eng). A vineyard based at Brockenhurst, Hampshire. Was first planted in 1982. 0.5 ha. Grape variety – Seyval villard.
Holly Spirit (Fr). See Houx.
Hollywood Cocktail (Cktl). ¼ gill dry Gin, ⅛ gill French vermouth, ⅛ gill Italian vermouth, 2 dashes brown Curaçao. Stir over ice, strain into a cocktail glass. Serve with a cherry and a dash of lemon peel juice.
Holoferment (Eng). Denotes the whole fermentation.
Holstein Cocktail (Cktl). ½ measure Cognac, ½ measure Blackberry brandy, dash Amer Picon. Shake over ice, strain into a cocktail glass.
Holsten (Ger). Northern Germany's biggest selling beer. Made in Hamburg. Noted for its' Moravia Pils 4.9% alc. by vol. and Diät Pils 1045 O.G. Also Holsten Export lager 1045 O.G. brewed under licence by Watneys.
Holsten Diät Pils (Ger). A famous Pilsener lager beer 6% alc. by vol. brewed by the Holsten Brauerei in Hamburg.
Holt Brewery (Eng). Based in Manchester. Noted for its' Holtenbrau 1033 O.G. Regal Lager 1039 O.G. and Sixex 1064 O.G.
Holtenbrau Lager (Eng). A light Lager beer 1033 O.G. brewed by the Holt Brewery in Manchester.
Holt, Plant and Deakin (Eng). Opened in 1984, an Ansells Black Country Co. running public houses in the region. Noted for its' cask conditioned Holts Mild 1036.5 O.G. (brewed by Tetley-Walker Brewery in Warrington) and Entire 1043 O.G. (brewed in Oldbury).
Holt Vineyard (The) (Eng). A vineyard based at Woolten Hill, Newbury, Berkshire. 0.5 ha. Grape varieties – Madeleine angevine and Müller-Thurgau.

Produces wines under the Woodhay label.
Holunderbeerlikoer (Ger). A liqueur made from ripe elderberries.
Holy Water (Eng). Water that has been blessed by a priest for use in symbolic rituals of purification.
Holzen (Ger). Village. (Anb) = Baden. (Ber) = Markgräflerland. (Gro) = Vogtei Rötteln. (Vin) = Steingässle.
Holzenberg (Ger). Vineyard. (Anb) = Württemberg. (Ber) = Remstal-Stuttgart. (Gro) = Kopf. (Vil) = Breuningsweiler.
Holzenberg (Ger). Vineyard. (Anb) = Württemberg. (Ber) = Remstal-Stuttgart. (Gro) = Kopf. (Vil) = Winnenden.
Holzgeschmack (Ger). Woody taste.
Homberg (Ger). Vineyard. (Anb) = Rheingau. (Ber) = Johannisberg. (Gro) = Steinmacher. (Vil) = Frauenstein.
Homberg (Ger). Vineyard. (Anb) = Rheinhessen. (Ber) = Nierstein. (Gro) = Petersberg. (Vil) = Albig.
Homberg (Ger). Vineyard. (Anb) = Rheinhessen. (Ber) = Nierstein. (Gro) = Petersberg. (Vil) = Bechtolsheim.
Homburg (Ger). Village. (Anb) = Franken. (Ber) = Maindreieck. (Gro) = Not yet assigned. (Vins) = Edelfrau, Kallmuth.
Home Brew (Eng). A term used for any beer, wine, etc. that is produced in a persons' own home for consumption there. Cannot by law be offered for sale without a licence.
Home Brewed Ale (Eng). A bottled Brown ale 1036 O.G. brewed by the Home Brewery in Nottingham.
Home Brewed Ale (Eng). Ale brewed from a kit (or raw ingredients) at a persons' home. See Home Brew.
Home Brewery (Eng). Based in Nottingham. Noted for its' cask conditioned Five Star 1043 O.G. (also Mild 1036 O.G. and Bitter 1038 O.G). Bottled Centenary 1060 O.G. Little John 1070 O.G. Luncheon Ale 1034 O.G. and Robin Hood 1045 O.G. Bottled Home-brewed Brown Ale 1036 O.G.
Home Brew House (Eng). A term used for a Public house that brews its' own ales.
Home Brew Public House (Eng). See Home Brew House.
Homeburn (Nor). A spirit produced from sugar and yeast. Also known as H.B.
Homer (Isr). Old Hebrew (Bible) name for fresh young unmixed wine.
Homestead Cocktail (Cktl). ⅗ measure Gin, ⅖ measure sweet Vermouth. Stir over ice, strain into a cocktail glass. Top with a slice of orange.
Home Vineyard (The) (Austr). A vineyard based in the Barossa Valley. Is owned by the Hill-Smith Estate. 4 ha.
Hominy (USA). Prepared cereal for brewing beer.
Homique (China). A white grape variety grown in the Tianjin region.
Hommelsberg (Lux). A vineyard site in the village of Wintrange.
Homme-Mort (L.) (Fr). A Premier Cru vineyard of A.C. Chablis. Often is reclassified as the Premier Cru Fourchaume.
Homogenise (Eng). In relation to milk – To break up the fat globules in milk or cream so that they are evenly distributed through the whole and stay in that state throughout. Produced under high pressure. 3,000 lbs. per sq.in. Also spelt Homogenize.
Homogenize (USA). The American spelling of Homogenise.
Homs (Arab). A hilly wine-growing area in northern Syria.
Honegar (Eng). An old fourteenth century medicinal drink made from Vinegar and Honey. Also known as Oxymel or Pharmacopeia.
Honest (Eng). A term used to describe a wine as ordinary, decent and well-made.
Honey and Orange Cream Coffee (Eng). 1 orange (peel and juice), ¾ pint hot coffee, 1 oz. clear Honey, 1 oz. double cream. Add the juice to the hot coffee, sweeten with honey, chill. Pour into glasses, swirl with cream and decorate with peel.
Honey Brandy (Eng). The name given to the spirit obtained from distilled Mead.
Honeyed (Eng). A term used to describe a wine as having some bottle age, fragrance and taste similar to the fine wines of Sauternes.
Honeymoon (Cktl). ⅓ measure Applejack brandy, ⅓ measure Bénédictine, ⅓ measure lemon juice, 3 dashes orange Curaçao. Shake over ice, strain into a cocktail glass.
Honeymoon Cocktail (Cktl).(Non-alc). ⅕ gill apple juice, ⅕ gill orange juice, juice ¼ lime, 2 teaspoons clear honey. Shake well over crushed ice, strain into a flute glass. Dress with a cherry and spiral of orange peel.
Honeysuckle Cocktail (Cktl). ⅕ gill golden Rum, juice of a lime, 1 teaspoon clear honey. Shake well over ice, strain into a cocktail glass.
Honeysweet Coffee (Cktl). Dissolve a teaspoon of clear honey in ⅓ pint of hot, fresh-brewed coffee. Chill down, when cool add a dash of Angostura bitters and a pinch of grated nutmeg. Shake over ice, strain into a highball glass. Top with whipped cream.
Honey Water (Mex). A name for the Aguamiel. The sap of the Agave cactus.
Honig (Ger). Honey.

H

Honigartig (Ger). Honey-like aroma and taste.

Honigberg (Ger). Grosslage. (Anb) = Franken. (Ber) = Maindreieck. (Vil) = Dettelbach.

Honigberg (Ger). Grosslage. (Anb) = Rheingau. (Ber) = Johannisberg. (Vils) = Mittelheim, Estate, Winkel.

Honigberg (Ger). Vineyard. (Anb) = Mosel-Saar-Ruwer. (Ber) = Bernkastel. (Gro) = Kurfürstlay. (Vil) = Maring-Noviand.

Honigberg (Ger). Vineyard. (Anb) = Nahe. (Ber) = Kreuznach. (Gro) = Kronenberg. (Vil) = Bad Kreuznach (ortsteil Winzenheim).

Honigberg (Ger). Vineyard. (Anb) = Nahe. (Ber) = Kreuznach. (Gro) = Schlosskapelle. (Vil) = Dorsheim.

Honigberg (Ger). Vineyard. (Anb) = Nahe. (Ber) = Kreuznach. (Gro) = Schlosskapelle. (Vil) = Guldental.

Honigberg (Ger). Vineyard. (Anb) = Rheingau. (Ber) = Johannisberg. (Gro) = Deutelsberg. (Vil) = Erbach.

Honigberg (Ger). Vineyard. (Anb) = Rheinhessen. (Ber) = Bingen. (Gro) = Abtey. (Vil) = Nieder-Hilbersheim.

Honigberg (Ger). Vineyard. (Anb) = Rheinhessen. (Ber) = Bingen. (Gro) = Abtey. (Vil) = Sprendlingen.

Honigberg (Ger). Vineyard. (Anb) = Rheinhessen. (Ber) = Bingen. (Gro) = Adelberg. (Vil) = Sulzheim.

Honigberg (Ger). Vineyard. (Anb) = Rheinhessen. (Ber) = Bingen. (Gro) = Kaiserstpfalz. (Vil) = Bubenheim.

Honigberg (Ger). Vineyard. (Anb) = Rheinhessen. (Ber) = Nierstein. (Gro) = Krotenbrunnen. (Vil) = Ludwigshöhe.

Honigberg (Ger). Vineyard. (Anb) = Rheinhessen. (Ber) = Bingen. (Gro) = Sankt Rochuskapelle. (Vil) = Biebelsheim.

Honigberg (Ger). Vineyard. (Anb) = Rheinhessen. (Ber) = Bingen. (Gro) = Sankt Rochuskapelle. (Vil) = Dromersheim.

Honiggoscherl (Aus). The local name for a lesser white grape variety.

Honiglerrebe (Aus). An ancient white grape variety which is little used nowadays.

Honiglikoer (Ger). Honey-based liqueur.

Honigsack (Ger). Vineyard. (Anb) = Rheinpfalz. (Ber) = Mittelhaardt-Deutsche Weinstrasse. (Gro) = Höllenpfad. (Vil) = Grünstadt.

Honigsack (Ger). Vineyard. (Anb) = Rheinpfalz. (Ber) = Mittelhaardt-Deutsche Weinstrasse. (Gro) = Kobnert. (Vil) = Herxheim/Berg.

Honigsäckel (Ger). Grosslage. (Anb) =

Rheinpfalz. (Ber) = Mittelhaardt-Deutsche Weinstrasse. (Vil) = Ungstein.

Honolulea (Cktl). ½ measure Irish whiskey, ¼ measure orange Curaçao, ¼ measure lemon juice, dash Gomme syrup. Shake over ice, strain. Decorate with a slice of orange and cherry.

Honolulu Cocktail (Cktl).(1). 2 measures Gin, 1 measure orange juice, 1 measure pineapple juice, dash Orange blossom, dash sugar, Shake over crushed ice, strain into a cocktail glass.

Honolulu Cocktail (Cktl).(2). ⅓ measure Bénédictine, ⅓ measure dry Gin, ⅓ measure Maraschino. Stir over ice, strain into a cocktail glass.

Hooch (Eng) (slang). Word for drink.

Hooch (USA) (slang). Word for Gin.

Hooijberg (Hol). A Bock-style beer 6% alc. by vol. brewed by the Heineken Brouwerij.

Hook Ale (Eng). A bottled Mild ale 1032 O.G. brewed by the Hook Norton Brewery, Banbury, Oxfordshire.

Hooker (USA) (slang). A draught of alcoholic drink, especially spirits.

Hook Norton Brewery (Eng). Based near Banbury in Oxfordshire. Noted for its' cask conditioned Old Hookey 1049 O.G. and bottled Hook Ale 1032 O.G. Jack Pot 1036 O.G. Jubilee 1049 O.G.

Hookway Vineyard (Eng). A vineyard based in Hookway, Surrey. 1.2 ha.

Hooper (Eng). An alternative name for a Cooper (cask maker). Derived from the metal hoops that hold the staves together.

Hoopla (Cktl). ¼ measure Brandy, ¼ measure Lillet, ¼ measure Cointreau, ¼ measure lemon juice. Shake over ice, strain into a cocktail glass.

Hootch (USA) (slang). Illicitly distilled spirits. Also for alcoholic drink. Word derived from the Tlingit Hootchinoo Indian tribe that distilled a type of liquor. See also Hooch.

Hoots Mon (Cktl). ½ measure Scotch whisky, ¼ measure sweet Vermouth, ¼ measure Lillet. Stir over ice, strain into a cocktail glass.

Hoots Mon Cocktail (Cktl). ⅗ measure Scotch whisky, ¼ measure sweet Vermouth, ¼ measure Bénédictine. Stir over ice, strain into an ice-filled cocktail glass. Top with a twist of lemon peel juice.

Hop (Eng). Humulus Lupulus. Flowering vine. Plant used in beer making to give bitterness and help preserve the beer. Female plant only is used in Germany and Czec. Fuggles, Goldings and Salz are some examples. (Fr) = Houblon.

H

(Ger) = Hopfo. (Den) = Hop. (It) = Luppolo. (Port) = Lúpulo. (Sp) = Lúpulo.

Hop Back (Eng). In brewing, equipment that separates the spent hops from the wort. Hop strainer.

Hop Bine (Eng). A hop grower's name for the hop plant.

Hop Character (Eng). The aroma and flavour given to a beer from certain types of hops.

Hop Cone (Eng). A term for the hop flower head.

Hôpertsbour (Lux). A vineyard site in the village of Remich.

Hop Extract (Eng). The flavouring obtained from hops, including oils, sold in pellet form. Added to the wort during brewing. Replaces the dried hops.

Hopfenbitter (Ger). A Brandy made slightly bitter by the addition of hop cones.

Hopfenperle (Aus). A dark, full-bodied Beer 13°. brewed by the Schwechat Brauerei.

Hopfenperle (Switz). A Lager beer brewed by the Feldschlösschen Group Brauerei. Also brewed under licence in the U.K. by the North Country Breweries, Hull, Yorkshire.

Hop Field (Eng). See Hop Garden and Hop Yard.

Höpfigheim (Ger). Village. (Anb) = Württemberg. (Ber) = Württembergisch Unterland. (Gro) = Schalkstein. (Vin) = Königsberg.

Hopfo (Ger). Hop.

Hop Garden (Eng). The name given to the hop field in Kent.

Hôpital Saint-Jean (Fr). A museum based at Angers in the Loire. Has a display of bottles and glasses and a twelfth century cellar which is now a wine museum.

Hop Jack (USA). An American name for the hop back.

Hop Kiln (Eng). Also known as the Oast house. Used for drying the hop cones.

Hop Kiln Winery (USA). A winery based at the Griffin Vineyards, Russian River Valley, Sonoma County, California. Grape varieties – French colombard, Gewürztraminer, Petite syrah and Zinfandel.

Hopkins and Company (Scot). A Highland malt and Scotch whisky distillery. Part of DCL. Brands include Oban and Old Mull.

Hopland (USA). A wine town in Ukiah, Mendocino County, California. Has two large wineries based there.

Hop Leaf Ale (Euro). A Pale ale 1040 O.G.

brewed by the Farsons Brewery on the island of Malta.

Hop'n'Gator (USA). A beer flavoured with lime. Was launched in 1970 by the Pittsburgh Brewery.

Hop Oil (Eng). The chemical extract from the female hop flower.

Hoppe (Hol). A distillery based in Schiedam (part of Heineken). Produces Jenever and a range of liqueurs.

Hopped-Wort (Eng). The name given to the wort after the hops have been strained through the hop back.

Hop Pellets (Eng). Compacted from natural hops. Used in brewing with the same results as natural hops. Makes transportation easier.

Hop Pillow (Eng). A sleep-inducing pillow stuffed with fresh hops. The oil of the flowers have narcotic effects.

Hopping (Eng). The adding of hops to the wort.

Hop Pocket (Eng). A sack containing fresh hops. 1½ hundredweight.

Hop Strainer (Eng). See Hop Back and Hop Jack.

Hop Toad (Cktl). ½ measure Bacardi White Label, ½ measure Apricot brandy, juice ½ lime. Stir over ice, strain into a cocktail glass.

Hop Up (USA) (slang). For a heavy drinking bout or party (especially of beer drinking).

Höpürdetmek (Tur). To slurp, to drink noisily and heavily.

Hop Yard (Eng). The south-west Midlands name for a hop field.

Horam Manor (Eng). Vineyard. Address = Horam, Heathfield, East Sussex. Planted 1963–66. 1.2 ha. Soil – Clay, sandy loam over sandstone. Grape varieties – Huxelrebe 8%, Müller-Thurgau 90% and 2% others.

Horchata (Sp). Orgeat, iced drink.

Horchata de Chufas (Sp). 'Tiger nut' drink.

Hordeum Vulgar (Lat). Barley.

Hörecker (Ger). Vineyard. (Anb) = Mosel-Saar-Ruwer. (Ber) = Saar-Ruwer. (Gro) = Scharzberg. (Vil) = Kanzem.

Horgazuela (Sp). The alternative name used for the Palomino grape grown in Puerto de Santa Maria, Jerez.

Hořice Brewery (Czec). A brewery based in northern Czec.

Horizontal Cylindrical Press (Eng). A type of grape press. Consists of a cylinder with a plate at each end which are linked by chains. As the drum rotates the chains are shortened, drawing the plates together so crushing the grapes. The must passes through

H

slits in the sides of the drum while the chains keep the pulp loose.

Horizontal Tasting (Eng). A tasting of wines of different origins but of the same age.

Horizon Winery (USA). A small winery based near Santa Rosa, Sonoma County, California. Grape variety – Zinfandel.

Horkheim (Ger). Village. (Anb) = Württemberg. (Ber) = Württembergisch Unterland. (Gro) = Staufenberg. (Vin) = Stiftsberg.

Horlicks (Eng). A famous brand-name of a malted milk drink. Sold in powder form, it is diluted with hot milk.

Horn (Ger). Vineyard. (Anb) = Rheinhessen. (Ber) = Bingen. (Gro) = Kaiserpfalz. (Vil) = Ingelheim.

Horn (Ger). Vineyard. (Anb) = Rheinhessen. (Ber) = Wonnegau. (Gro) = Domblick. (Vil) = Wachenheim.

Horn (Ger). Vineyard. (Anb) = Rheinpfalz. (Ber) = Mittelhaardt-Deutsche Weinstrasse. (Gro) = Saumagen. (Vil) = Kallstadt.

Hornberg (Ger). Vineyard. (Anb) = Rheinhessen. (Ber) = Nierstein. (Gro) = Petersberg. (Vil) = Framersheim.

Hörnchen (Ger). Vineyard. (Anb) = Nahe. (Ber) = Kreuznach. (Gro) = Pfarrgarten. (Vil) = Wallhausen.

Hörnchen (Ger). Vineyard. (Anb) = Nahe. (Ber) = Kreuznach. (Gro) = Schlosskapelle. (Vil) = Laubenheim.

Hörnchen (Ger). Vineyard. (Anb) = Nahe. (Ber) = Kreuznach. (Gro) = Schlosskapelle. (Vil) = Waldlaubersheim.

Horndale Winery (Austr). A winery based near Reynella, Southern Vales, South Australia. Produces varietal, table and dessert wines.

Horndean Special Bitter (Eng). See HSB.

Hornfelsen (Ger). Vineyard. (Anb) = Baden. (Ber) = Markgräflerland. (Gro) = Vogtei Rötteln. (Vil) = Greuzach.

Hornimans and Co. Ltd (Eng). Noted producers of a wide range of fine teas. Address = 325, Oldfield Lane, Greenford, Middlesex.

Hörnle (Ger). Vineyard. (Anb) = Württemberg. (Ber) = Remstal-Stuttgart. (Gro) = Kopf. (Vil) = Korb.

Hörnle (Ger). Vineyard. (Anb) = Württemberg. (Ber) = Remstal-Stuttgart. (Gro) = Kopf. (Vil) = Waiblingen.

Horrenberg (Ger). Village. (Anb) = Baden. (Ber) = Badische Bergstrasse/ Kraichgau. (Gro) = Mannaberg. (Vin) = Osterberg.

Horrheim (Ger). Village. (Anb) = Württemberg. (Ber) = Württembergisch

Unterland. (Gro) = Stromberg. (Vin) = Klosterberg.

Horrweiler (Ger). Village. (Anb) = Rheinhessen. (Ber) = Bingen. (Gro) = Sankt Rochuskapelle. (Vins) = Gewürzgärtchen, Goldberg.

Hors Classe (Fr). Unclassified.

Hors d'Âge (Fr). 'Beyond recorded age'. Applied to Cognac brandies.

Hors d'Âge (Fr). On an Armagnac label indicates a minimum age of 5 years.

Horsebridge Best (Eng). A cask conditioned Bitter 1045 O.G. brewed by the Royal Inn Brewery (a home-brew public house) in Horsebridge.

Horse's Collar (Cktl). Spiral of orange peel moistened in rum, dusted with brown sugar. Place in a mug, add 6 cloves (prepared in the same way). Place mug on stove, when hot, flame. Allow to burn until the edges of peel brown. Add 2 measures rum, top with boiling water. Float butter on top.

Horse's Neck (Cktl). ½ gill of spirit, spiral of lemon placed in a highball glass, add ice, top with ginger ale.

Horsing (Eng). See Stillage.

Hörstein (Ger). Village. (Anb) = Franken. (Ber) = Mainviereck. (Gro) = Reuschberg. (Vin) = Abtsberg.

Hosbag (Tur). A state monopoly-approved name for red and white wines produced in Trakya.

Hoskins and Oldfield Brewery (Eng). Opened in 1984 in Leicester. Noted for its' HOB Bitter 1041 O.G.

Hoskins Brewery (Eng). Based in Leicester. Noted for its' cask conditioned Penn's Ale 1045 O.G. and Old Nigel 1060 O.G.

Hospices de Beaujeu (Fr). The name given to the red wines from the Beaujolais hills sold to benefit the Beaujeu hospital.

Hospices de Beaune (Fr). Built in 1443 by Nicholas Rolin as a charitable hospital for the poor. Based in the town of Beaune in the Côte de Beaune. Owns many pieces of fine vineyards in the Côte de Beaune which are auctioned on the 3rd Sunday in November in Beaune and the proceeds used for the running of the hospital. Also known as the Hôtel-Dieu. See Paulée (La).

Hospices de Nuits (Fr). Similar to the Hospices de Beaune but situated in the Côte de Nuits in Nuits-Saint-Georges. Has many plots of fine vineyards in the Côte de Nuits. Auction takes place on Palm Sunday.

Hospitaliers de Pomerol (Fr). A brotherhood of the wine producers of Pomerol in Bordeaux.

H

Hösslinsülz (Ger). Village. (Anb) = Württemberg. (Ber) = Württembergisch Unterland. (Gro) = Salzberg. See Löwenstein.

Host (Eng). A term used to describe the licensees and their spouses. Usually used by the trade press.

Hostan (Czec). A light beer brewed by the Znojmo Brewery.

Hostelry (Eng). A nickname for a public house. Old name for public house with accomodation..

Hot (Eng). A term used to describe a 'baked' wine. A wine made in a hot climate. Has a cooked taste.

Hot Applejack Sling (Cktl). Fill a tumbler ½ full with barley water and sugar syrup. Add ¾ gill Applejack brandy or Calvados, squeeze of lemon peel on top. Stir, top with grated nutmeg.

Hot Apple Toddy (Cktl). Strain juice of a baked apple, add a little sugar syrup and hot water, ¾ gill Calvados. Top with boiling water and grated nutmeg.

Hot Bottling (Eng). Denotes a wine that is bottled immediately after pasteurisation whilst it is still hot. Is decreasing in popularity as it affects the freshness and delicacy of the wine.

Hot Brandy Flip (Cktl).(1). Beat a whole egg with 1 teaspoon of sugar and ⅕ gill Brandy. Pour into a mug, top with hot milk, stir and dust with grated nutmeg.

Hot Brandy Flip (Cktl).(2). Place 1 gill black coffee, ⅕ gill Cognac, ⅓ gill Port into a saucepan and heat. Pour over an egg yolk beaten with a teaspoon of sugar (stirring well). Serve in a heat-proof glass topped with grated nutmeg.

Hot Break (USA). The brewer's name for substances in the wort that when boiled coagulate into insoluble materials.

Hot Brick Toddy (Cktl). Pour ⅕ gill Scotch whisky with sugar to taste into a mug. Add a pat of butter, cinnamon stick and top up with boiling water. Stir, serve hot.

Hot Bullshot (Cktl). ⅕ gill Vodka, juice of ¼ lemon, dash Tabasco, 1 teaspoon Worcestershire sauce. Add to a cup of hot consommé, stir and serve.

Hot Bush (Cktl). An ideal nightcap. 1 measure Scotch whisky mixed with sugar to taste, cloves and boiling water. Place in a mug, stir, drink hot.

Hot Buttered Rum (Cktl). 1 measure dark Rum, lump sugar, ½ oz butter, cloves. Place in old-fashioned glass, top with boiling water.

Hot Buttered Wine (Cktl). Heat 3 fl.ozs. Muscatel wine with 3 fl.ozs. water. Pour into a mug, add 1 oz. butter and teaspoon of maple syrup. Stir, top with grated nutmeg.

Hot Egg Nogg (Cktl). 1 egg, 1 measure Brandy, 1 measure Rum, 1 teaspoon sugar. Place in a highball glass, top with hot milk. Stir, grate nutmeg on top.

Hotel (Austr). Public house.

Hotel (Eng). A licensed or unlicensed establishment with a full meal service plus accomodation.

Hôtel-Dieu (Fr). See Hospices de Beaune.

Hotel Plaza (Cktl). ⅓ measure dry Gin, ⅓ measure French vermouth, ⅓ measure Italian vermouth. Stir over ice, strain into a cocktail glass. Decorate with a crushed slice of pineapple.

Hot Jamaican Cow (Cktl). Pour ⅓ pint heated milk into a warmed mug. Add ⅕ gill coffee liqueur. Stir and serve.

Hot Jamaica Punch (Cktl). Into a highball pour 1 measure Jamaican Rum, ½ tablespoon sugar, dash Angostura, ¾ measure lemon juice, 3 cloves, slice of lemon. Top up with boiling water. Stir and serve.

Hot Liquor (Eng). During the brewing process the hot liquor (water) is sparged onto the grist in the mash tun.

Hot Maceration (Eng). Grapes are heated to 80°C. for ½ hour. This dissolves the colour from skins but not the tannin. They are then cooled and pressed. Can lose colour later, so often blended with traditional red wines.

Hot Orange Tea (Cktl). Heat ½ pint of Mandarin Orange Tea with ⅓ gill Jamaican rum, ⅓ pint orange juice. Stir, pour into heat-proof glasses. Serve with orange slices.

Hot Pants (Cktl). ¾ measure Tequila, ¼ measure Peppermint Schnapps, ⅛ measure grapefruit juice, 2 dashes Gomme syrup. Shake over ice, strain into a salt-rimmed, ice-filled old-fashioned glass.

Hot Press Wine (USA). A method of heating grapes, the grape must and cap to speed up the extraction of colour without tannin. Has a slightly 'cooked' flavour.

Hot Rum Cow (Cktl). Blend together ⅕ gill light Rum, dash Angostura, dash vanilla essence, teaspoon powdered sugar, ½ pint hot milk. Pour into a mug, top with grated nutmeg.

Hot Rum Grog (Cktl). In a goblet place a little boiling water and dissolve 2 barspoons of demerara sugar. Add ½ oz. lemon juice, 2 cloves, 1½ ozs. dark Rum, grated nutmeg and stir. Top up with boiling water. Serve with a cinnamon stick.

Hot Scotch Toddy (Cktl). 2 fl.ozs. Scotch whisky, ½ fl.oz. lemon juice, dash Angostura, teaspoon honey, teaspoon powdered sugar, 3 fl.ozs. boiling water. Mix ingredients in a silver tankard. Pour into a 6 oz. stemmed glass. Add a slice of lemon. Serve with a napkin.

Hot Spiced Rum (Cktl). 1 gill Old Jamaican Rum, 3 lumps sugar, boiling water. Stir together. Top with ½ oz butter and a teaspoon of mixed spices. Stir well and serve.

Hot Springs (Cktl). 2 fl.ozs. dry white wine, ½ fl.oz. pineapple juice, 2 dashes Maraschino, dash Orange bitters. Shake over ice, strain into a cocktail glass.

Hotte (Fr). A wooden hod-like receptacle for the carrying of picked grapes in Bordeaux. Truncated cone shape.

Hottiches (Fr). A type of Hotte used in Alsace.

Hot Toddy (Cktl). 1 measure of desired spirit, 1 teaspoon sugar. Fill a medium-sized goblet with boiling water together with spirit and sugar. Stir, add a slice of lemon. Dust with grated nutmeg.

Hotx Hotxa Edan (Fr). Lit – 'Chill before serving'. Found on a rosé Basque wine label (usually from Irouléguy).

Houblon (Fr). Hop.

Houghton's Verdell (Austr). A dry white wine made from the Verdelho grape by Houghtons.

Houghton Vineyard (Austr). Address = Dale road, Middle Swan, Western Australia 6056. 264 ha. in Swan Valley, Frankland River and Moondah Brook. Grape varieties – Cabernet sauvignon, Chardonnay, Chenin blanc, Rhine riesling, Shiraz and Verdelho.

Houla Houla (Cktl). ⅔ measure dry Gin, ⅓ measure orange juice, 3 dashes orange Curaçao. Shake over ice, strain into a cocktail glass.

Hourges (Fr). A Cru Champagne village in the Canton de Fismes. District = Reims.

Houringue (La) A vineyard in the commune of Margaux. A.C. Haut-Médoc, Bordeaux. Part of Château Giscours. 18 ha.

Hour of the Wolf (USSR). The nickname for opening time in Russia.

House of Commons N°1 (Scot). A 12 year old blended Scotch whisky produced by Buchanan & Co. for the House of Commons. 43% alc. by vol.

House of Horrors (Eng). A nineteenth century gimmick Public house in London owned by Whitbread.

House of Lords (Scot). An 8 year old blended Scotch whisky produced by Glenforres Glenlivit Distillery Co., William Whitelay and Co, Pitlochry. 40% alc. by vol. (Now owned by Pernod Ricard).

House of Stuart (Scot). A brand of Scotch whisky 40% alc. by vol. Produced by the House of Stuart Bonding Co. Ltd., Alexandria, Dunbartonshire.

House Wine (Eng). The wine of the establishment. Usually of Vin de table quality served by the glass or carafe.

Houx (Fr). An alcool-blanc white alcohol made from the holly-berry in the Alsace region. Also known as Holly Spirit.

Howf (Scot). The name for a public house in the sixteenth century.

Hoxton Heavy Bitter (Eng). A cask conditioned Bitter 1048 O.G. brewed by the Pitfield Brewery in London.

H.P.W. (Cktl).(abbr). Stands for Harry Payne Whitney. ¼ gill dry Gin, ⅓ gill Italian vermouth, slice of orange. Shake well over ice, strain into a cocktail glass.

Hrad (Czec). The name for a white wine from Bzenee.

Hradec Kràlové Brewery (Czec). A brewery based in northern Czec.

HSB (Eng) (abbr). Horndean Special Bitter 1051 O.G. brewed by Gales Brewery in Horndean, Hampshire.

Hsiang Hsueh (China). A noted brand of rice wine from Shanghai. See Shao-Hsing Rice Wine.

Huapai Soil (N.Z.). Loam soil.

Huasco (Chile). A principal wine region. Produces all types of wines.

Hua Tiao (China). A noted brand of rice wine from Shanghai. See Shao-Hsing Rice Wine.

Huatusco (Mex). A coffee producing region.

Hubacker (Ger). Vineyard. (Anb) = Rheinhessen. (Ber) = Wonnegau. (Gro) = Burg Rodenstein. (Vil) = Flörsheim-Dalsheim.

Hubberg (Ger). Vineyard. (Anb) = Baden. (Ber) = Badische Bergstrasse/Kraichgau. (Gro) = Rittersberg. (Vil) = Weinheim.

Huber Brewery (USA). A brewery based in Monroe, Wisconsin. Is noted for its' Augsburger, Huber Rheinlander and Regal Bräu.

Huber Rheinlander (USA). A Beer 4.5% alc. by vol. brewed by the Huber Brewery.

Hubertsborn (Ger). Vineyard. (Anb) = Mosel-Saar-Ruwer. (Ber) = Zell/Mosel. (Gro) = Weinhex. (Vil) = Koblenz (ortsteil Lay).

Hubertus (Hun). A bitter herb-flavoured liqueur.

Hubertusberg (Ger). Vineyard. (Anb) = Mosel-Saar-Ruwer. (Ber) = Obermosel. (Gro) = Gipfel. (Vil) = Nittel.

Hubertusberg (Ger). Vineyard. (Anb) =

H

Mosel-Saar-Ruwer. (Ber) = Obermosel. (Gro) = Gipfel. (Vil) = Onsdorf.

Hubertusberg (Ger). Vineyard. (Anb) = Mosel-Saar-Ruwer. (Ber) = Saar-Ruwer. (Gro) = Römerlay. (Vil) = Waldrach.

Hubertusberg (Ger). Vineyard. (Anb) = Mosel-Saar-Ruwer. (Ber) = Saar-Ruwer. (Gro) = Scharzberg. (Vil) = Irsch.

Hubertusbräu (Aus). A noted beer brewed by the Hubertus Brauerei.

Hubertus Brauerei (Aus). A small independent brewery based at Laa, near the Czec border. Brews Hubertusbräu.

Hubertuslay (Ger). Vineyard. (Anb) = Mosel-Saar-Ruwer. (Ber) = Bernkastel. (Gro) = Schwarzlay. (Vil) = Bausendorf.

Hubertuslay (Ger). Vineyard. (Anb) = Mosel-Saar-Ruwer. (Ber) = Bernkastel. (Gro) = Schwarzlay. (Vil) = Kinheim.

Hübsch (Ger). Used to refer to a nice delicate wine.

Huckle My Buff (Eng). A hot drink made of Brandy, beer and egg that is favoured in Sussex.

Hudepohl Brewery (USA). A brewey based in Cincinnati, Ohio. Noted for its' Burger, Hofbrau and Tap.

Hudor (Gre). Water.

Hudson (Arg). A winery near Buenos Aires. Owns vineyards in San Rafael, Mendoza. See Bianchi.

Hudson and Cooper (Eng). A brand-name used by Vine Products Ltd. for British Sherry.

Hudson Bay Cocktail (Cktl). ⅙ gill dry Gin, ⅛ gill Cherry brandy, ⅛ gill Jamaican rum, ⅛ gill orange juice, juice ¼ lime. Shake over ice, strain into a cocktail glass.

Hudson River Valley (USA). A wine region of Eastern America. 15 miles out of Newburgh, New York. Concord, Delaware and Catawba grape varieties are grown. Produces red, rosé and sweet white wines.

Hudson's Bay (S.Am). The brand-name of a Demerara Rum from Guyana. Is bottled in the U.K.

Hudson's Bay Co (Can). A distillery based in Winnipeg. Produces a range of Canadian whiskies. (A subsidiary of Seagram).

Hudson Valley Wine Company (USA). A major winery based in the Hudson River Valley.

Huelva (Sp). A wine province of south west Spain on the border with Portugal. See Condado de Huelva.

Huesgen (Adolf) GmbH (Ger). A noted wine company based at D-5580, Traben-Trarbach, Mosel. Produces wines of all qualities.

Huet (Gaston) (Fr). A noted producer of sparkling Vouvray in Touraine, Loire.

Huet (S.A.) (Fr). A viticulteur based in Le Haut-Lieu, Vouvray. Loire. Produces A.C. Vouvray wines.

Huette (Lux). A vineyard site in the village of Greiveldange.

Hufen (Wales). Cream.

Hüffelsheim (Ger). Village. (Anb) = Nahe. (Ber) = Schloss Böckelheim. (Gro) = Rosengarten. (Vins) = Gutenhölle, Monchberg, Steyer.

Hugel (Fr). A wine négociant-éleveur of Alsace. (Hugel Père et Fils). Based at 68340 Riquewihr. 26 ha. One of the region's top producers.

Hügelheim (Ger). Village. (Anb) = Baden. (Ber) = Markgräflerland. (Gro) = Burg Neuenfels. (Vins) = Gottesacker, Höllberg, Schlossgarten.

Hugel Père et Fils (Fr). See Hugel.

Hugget (Scot). A term for Hogshead.

Hugsweier (Ger). Village. (Anb) = Baden. (Ber) = Breisgau. (Gro) = Schutterlindenberg. (Vin) = Kronenbühl.

Huguenac (S.Afr). A brand of Brandy produced by the Huguenot Wine Farmers.

Huguenot Wine Farmers (S.Afr). A wine and Brandy producing Co-operative.

Hugues and Louis Bétault (Fr). A cuvée in the Les Grèves vineyard, A.C. Beaune, Côte de Beaune, Burgundy. Is owned by the Hospices de Beaune.

Hühnerberg (Ger). Vineyard. (Anb) = Mosel-Saar-Ruwer. (Ber) = Bernkastel. (Gro) = Schwarzlay. (Vil) = Traben-Trarbach.

Huile de Vénus (Fr). A popular Eau-de-vie in the eighteenth century. Now no longer produced.

Huisbaas (Hol). Landlord.

Huiswyn (S.Afr). A dry, white wine made from a blend of Kerner and Steen grapes. Is produced by the Lievland Estate.

Hula-Hula (Cktl). ⅓ gill dry Gin, ⅙ gill orange juice, dash Gomme syrup. Shake over ice, strain into a cocktail glass.

Hull (Charles) (Eng). A noted corkscrew maker of the nineteenth century. Made many new inventions for extracting corks which are now highly collectable.

Hull Brewery (Eng). Based at Kingston-upon-Hull. Renamed the North Country Breweries in 1972.

Hull Brewery (USA). A brewery based in New Haven.

Hulstkamp (Hol). A producer of old Jenever.

H

Hultgren and Stamperton (USA). A winery based in the Russian River Valley, Sonoma County, California. Grape varieties – Cabernet sauvignon, and Chardonnay. Produces varietal wines.

Humange (Switz). A white grape variety grown in Valais and Vaud.

Humange (Switz). A red or white wine produced from the grape of the same name in Valais and Vaud. Has the full tang of its' native vineyard.

Humblot (Fr). A vineyard in the A.C. Meursault, Côte de Beaune, Burgundy. Is owned by the Hospices de Beaune.

Hummelberg (Ger). Vineyard. (Anb) = Baden. (Ber) = Badische Bergstrasse/ Kraichgau. (Gro) = Mannaberg. (Vil) = Ostringen.

Hummelberg (Ger). Vineyard. (Anb) = Baden. (Ber) = Breisgau. (Gro) = Burg Lichteneck. (Vil) = Keuzingen.

Hummelberg (Ger). Vineyard. (Anb) = Baden. (Ber) = Breisgau. (Gro) = Burg Lichteneck. (Vil) = Wagenstadt.

Humper (Ger). A glass from Bavaria. Is shaped like a concave barrel without a stem.

Humpolec Brewery (Czec). An old brewery based in central Czec.

Hundert (Ger). Vineyard. (Anb) = Mittelrhein. (Ber) = Rheinburgengau. (Gro) = Schloss Schonburg. (Vil) = Langscheid.

Hundertgulden (Ger). Vineyard. (Anb) = Rheinhessen. (Ber) = Bingen. (Gro) = Abtey. (Vil) = Appenheim.

Hundred Pipers (Scot). A blended Scotch whisky produced by the Chivas Brothers. 40% alc. by vol.

Hundsberg (Ger). Vineyard. (Anb) = Württemberg. (Ber) = Württembergisch Unterland. (Gro) = Salzberg. (Vil) = Eichelberg.

Hundsberg (Ger). Vineyard. (Anb) = Württemberg. (Ber) = Württembergisch Unterland. (Gro) = Salzberg. (Vil) = Weiler.

Hundskopf (Ger). Vineyard. (Anb) = Rheinhessen. (Ber) = Nierstein. (Gro) = Petersberg. (Vil) = Albig.

Hungària (Hun). A non-vintage sparkling wine. Demi-sec, extra-dry and rosé styles are produced.

Hungària (Hun). A strong pale Lager-style beer brewed by the Köbànya Brewery.

Hungarovin (Hun). A state-owned wine trust based near Budapest. Its' main function is to cellar and bottle the wines from co-operatives and farms.

Hungary (Hun). A large East European wine-producing country that produces most styles of wines. Famous for its

Tokay and Bull's Blood. Regions – Northern Hungary [Bükkalja, Eger, Màtraalja and Tokajhegyalja], Northern Transdanubia [Aszar-Neszmely, Badacsony, Balatonfüred-Csopak, Balatonmellek, Mór, Somló and Sopron], Southern Transdanubia [Mecsekalja, Szekszàrd and Villàny-Siklós] and The Great Plain [Alföld].

Hungerberg (Ger). Vineyard. (Anb) = Württemberg. (Ber) = Remstal-Stuttgart. (Gro) = Kopf. (Vil) = Winterbach.

Hungerbiene (Ger). Vineyard. (Anb) = Rheinhessen. (Ber) = Wonnegau. (Gro) = Bergkloster. (Vil) = Gundheim.

Hungerford Hill (Austr). A Hunter Valley Estate and Coonawarra Winery.

Hung Mei (China). The brand-name used by Dairen.

Hung Mei Chinese Port Wine (China). A tonic and digestive wine produced by Dairen.

Hungriger Wolf (Ger). Vineyard. (Anb) = Nahe. (Ber) = Kreuznach. (Gro) = Kronenberg. (Vil) = Bad Kreuznach.

Hunnenstein (Ger). Vineyard. (Anb) = Mosel-Saar-Ruwer. (Ber) = Zell/Mosel. (Gro) = Weinhex. (Vil) = Alken.

Hunolsteiner (Ger). Vineyard. (Anb) = Nahe. (Ber) = Schloss Böckelheim. (Gro) = Paradiesgarten. (Vil) = Merxheim.

Hünsrück (Ger). Lit – 'Dog's-back'. A mountain range in the Nahe district. The river Nahe rises in the Hünsrück. It separates the river Nahe from the river Mosel.

Hunter Ale (Austr). A light, fruity Beer 3.41% alc. by vol. brewed by the Castlemaine Toohey Brewery in New South Wales.

Hunter Brewery (Austr). A brewery based in Newcastle. Is owned by Toohey's of Sydney.

Hunter Cocktail (Cktl). $\frac{1}{3}$ measure Cherry brandy, $\frac{2}{3}$ measure Rye whiskey. Stir over ice, strain into a cocktail glass.

Hunter Estate Winery (Austr). Vineyard. Address = Hermitage road, Pokolbin, New South Wales 2321. 91.1 ha. Grape varieties – Cabernet sauvignon, Chardonnay, Pinot noir, Rhine riesling, Sémillon, Shiraz and Traminer.

Hunter Riesling (Austr). An erroneous varietal name for the Sémillon.

Hunter River (Austr). A top wine region in New South Wales. Not affected by Phylloxera. Produces fortified and table wines.

Hunter River White Burgundy (Austr). A full-bodied white wine produced by the Lindemans Winery in Hunter River, New South Wales.

Hunters (N.Z.). A small winery based in Rapura Road, Marlborough (25 ha) and Belfast, Christchurch (4 ha).

Hunters Farms (USA). A small vineyard based in the Sonoma Valley, California. 16.5 ha. Grape variety – Chardonnay. Grapes are vinified at Château St. Jean.

Hunter Valley (Austr). A wine region situated north of Sydney. Estates include – Brokenwood, Drayton's, Lake's Folly, Rothbury and Tyrrells.

Hunter Valley Hermitage (Austr). A full-bodied red wine from the Wyndham Estate in New South Wales.

Hunter Valley Riesling (Austr). An erroneous name for the Sémillon grape.

Hunter Vodka (Pol). Mysliwska. 43% alc. by vol. A Vodka flavoured with herbs, rectified juniper distillates. Produced by Polmos.

Hunting Lodge (Eng). The brand-name of a British Sherry from Linfood Cash and Carry, Northamptonshire.

Hunting Port (Port). A Tawny Port produced by Harveys of Bristol.

Huntington Estate (Austr). Vineyard. Address = Cassilis Road, Mudgee, New South Wales 2850. 42 ha. Grape varieties – Cabernet sauvignon, Chardonnay, Merlot, Pinot noir, Sémillon and Shiraz.

Hunt [Roope] (Port). A vintage Port shipper.

Hunts (Eng). The brand-name used for a range of soft drinks by Beecham Products of Brentford, Middlesex.

Huntsman (Cktl). ¾ measure Vodka, ¼ measure Jamaican rum, juice ½ lime, dash Gomme syrup. Shake over ice, strain into a cocktail glass.

Huntsman Ales (Eng). See Eldridge Pope Brewery.

Huntsman Ales (Eng). A design used by Tetleys Brewery in the north of England.

Hunyadi Janos (Hun). A brand of mineral water.

Hupeh (China). A branch of Dairen.

Hupperath (Ger). Village. (Anb) = Mosel-Saar-Ruwer. (Ber) = Bernkastel. (Gro) = Schwarzlay. (Vin) = Klosterweg.

Hurbanovo Brewery (Czec). A brewery based in south-eastern Czec. Opened in 1967.

Hurdle Creek Vineyard (Austr). A part of the Brown Brothers in Victoria.

Hurlimann Brauerei (Switz). A brewery based in Zurich. Brews the World's strongest beer Samichlaus 14% alc. by vol. See Hurlimann Sternbrau and Five Star.

Hurlimann Sternbrau (Eng). A strong Lager brewed by the Shepherd Neame Brewery under licence from Hurlimann in Switzerland.

Hurricane Punch (Cktl). 1½ fl.ozs. dark Rum, 1½ fl.ozs. lemon juice, 2 fl.ozs. Passion fruit juice, ¼ fl.oz. Gomme syrup. Shake over ice, strain into an ice-filled highball glass. Add a splash of soda water. Decorate with a slice of lemon. Serve with straws.

Husch Vineyards (USA). A small winery based in the Anderson Valley, Mendocino County, California. 14.5 ha. Grape varieties – Cabernet sauvignon, Chardonnay, Gewürztraminer and Pinot noir. Produces varietal wines.

Huşi (Rum). A wine-producing area based near the Russian border. Produces white wines of the same name.

Huslanka (USSR). A style of fermented milk from southern Russia.

Hütt (Ger). Vineyard. (Anb) = Rheinpfalz. (Ber) = Mittelhaardt-Deutsche Weinstrasse. (Gro) = Höllenpfad. (Vil) = Grünstadt.

Hüttberg (Ger). Vineyard. (Anb) = Rheinhessen. (Ber) = Nierstein. (Gro) = Sankt Alban. (Vil) = Mainz.

Hütte (Ger). Vineyard. (Anb) = Mosel-Saar-Ruwer. (Ber) = Saar-Ruwer. (Gro) = Scharzberg. (Vil) = Oberemmel.

Hüttenberg (Ger). Vineyard. (Anb) = Nahe. (Ber) = Schloss Böckelheim. (Gro) = Rosengarten. (Vil) = Roxheim.

Hüttenheim (Ger). Village. (Anb) = Franken. (Ber) = Steigerwald. (Gro) = Schlosstück. (Vin) = Tannenberg.

Hüttenviertel (Aus). A dry, white wine from the Grüner veltliner grape. Is produced by the Augustine monks at Klosterneuburg, Vienna. Is often recommended as a diabetic wine.

Hütte-Terrassen (Ger). Vineyard. (Anb) = Rheinhessen. (Ber) = Bingen. (Gro) = Adelberg. (Vil) = Bornheim.

Huttingen (Ger). Village. (Anb) = Baden. (Ber) = Markgräflerland. (Gro) = Vogtei Rötteln. (Vin) = Kirchberg.

Huxelrebe (Ger). A white grape variety. A hybrid cross between the Weisser gutedel and the Courtillier musqué. First produced in 1927 by Georg Schen at the Landesanstalt für Rebenzüchtung in Alzey.

Huzzar (Ire). A brand of Vodka produced by the Irish Distillers Group.

Hvantchkara (USSR). A red grape variety grown in Georgia to produce fine dessert wines.

Hvar (Yug). A wine-producing island off the Dalmatian coast.

Hvidtøl (Den). A tax-free beer, medium

density, low in alcohol 1.3% alc. by vol. brewed by the United Breweries. Also called a dark white ale (Mørkt brew).

Hybrid (Eng). A cross vine. A cross between European and American vines.

Hydes Brewery (Eng). A brewery based in Manchester, Lancashire. Noted for its' cask conditioned Anvil Strong 1080 O.G. and Amboss Lager 1036 O.G.

Hydraulic Press (Eng). A grape press. Consists of a slatted wooden vat with a plate on top. Grapes are placed in the vat and the plate is forced upon them. The must is collected beneath the slats.

Hydria (Gre). A large water jug used in ancient Greece (and Rome).

Hydro-Colloids (Eng). Colloidal particles in wine which are surrounded by a film of absorbed water. If they all have the same electrical charge in a wine, they remain suspended and cause hazing.

Hydrogen Sulphide (Eng). H_2S. The 'rotten egg' odour that wine sometimes obtains after fermentation. Often found on opening the bottle.

Hydrolysis (Eng). A reaction caused by an enzyme. Involves a chemical compound and water, resulting in other compounds. e.g. the conversion of sucrose to glucose and fructose caused by the enzyme invertase.

Hydrolyzable Tannins (Eng). Obtained from wooden casks.

Hydromel (Eng). The old English word for Mead.

Hydromella (Eng). A Mead produced in Anglo-Saxon times.

Hydrometer (Eng). An instrument to measure the density of alcohol or sugar in wine, beer, spirit or must. See Balling, Brix, Clarkes, Dujardin Scale, Gay Lussac, OIML, Oechsle, Sykes.

Hydrometer Act (Eng). 1818. Adopted Bartholomew Sykes' hydrometer as the unit for measuring the alcoholic content of all alcoholic beverages.

Hydrostatical Bubbles (Eng). Glass bubbles engraved with different numbers to measure the strength of spirits. Used as a rough measure to see if spirits have been tampered with during transit.

Hydroxymethylfurfural (Eng). Is found in small traces in Madeira and Sherry-style wines.

Hymettus (Gre). A honey-scented, delicate, dry white wine and red wine.

Hypocras (Fr). A spiced wine of cloves, cinnamon, aniseed, saffron, pepper, ginger and sugar. Dates back to Louis XIV.

Hyson (China). A grade of China tea.

I

Iaoue (Ch.Isles). Water. See also Iaue.
Iaoue d'Orge (Ch.Isles). Barley water.
I.A.S (Rum) (abbr). Interprinderile Agricole de Stat. The State Agricultural Enterprise. See also G.A.S. (The old-style name for I.A.S).
Iaue (Ch.Isles). Water. See also Iaoue.
I.B.A. (Eng) (abbr). International Bartenders' Association. Est. 1951.
Iberia (Euro). Spain and Portugal.
Iberia Cream (Sp). A blend of fine Pedro Ximénez and Oloroso sherries produced by Romate.
Ibiza (Sp). A wine-producing island. Produces highly alcoholic wines mainly from co-operative vineyards.
Ibrik (Tur). Small brass or tin lined copper pots for making Turkish coffee. Also known as Briki in Greece and Kanaka in Arabic.
Ica (S.Am). A wine-producing area in Peru. The noted Facama vineyard is in the region.
I.C.C.A. (USA) (abbr). The International Correspondence of Corkscrew Addicts. Guild of corkscrew collectors formed by the Christian Brothers of California.
Iceberg (Cktl). In a highball place some ice cubes, 2 ozs. Vodka, add a dash of Pernod and stir.
Iceberg Cocktail (Cktl). ⅓ gill Galliano, ⅙ gill Triple Sec, scoop orange water ice. Blend together in a blender. Serve in a Champagne flute with straws.
Ice-Bock (Ger). A strong beer with an O.G. of 25%.
Icebreaker Cocktail (Cktl). 1½ measures Tequila, ½ measure grapefruit juice, ½ oz. Cointreau, ¼ oz. Grenadine, scoop of crushed ice. Blend together in a blender, serve with crushed ice in a Champagne flute.
Ice Bucket (Eng). A container which is usually insulated and is used for holding ice in the bar.
Ice Cap (Cktl). 1 oz. Brandy, ¾ oz. Crème de Cacao, 1 teaspoon of cream. Shake over ice, strain into 5 oz. wine glass.
Içecek (Tur). Berverage, drink.
Ice Cold (Austr). A term for a glass of Lager.

Ice Cream Flip (Cktl). 1 oz. Cointreau, 1 oz. Maraschino, 1 egg, 1 scoop vanilla ice cream. Blend together in a blender. Serve in a large goblet.
Ice Cream Soda (USA). Soda water, milk and ice cream served together in a tall glass.
Iced Bishop (Punch). 1 bottle Champagne, 1 gill tea (lime blossom), 1 gill Gomme syrup, slice of orange and lemon. Mix together, chill down, add 1 gill Brandy. Serve over crushed ice in old-fashioned glasses.
Iced Coffee (Eng). Fresh brewed coffee. Cooled, sweetened with sugar syrup, served over ice. Top with whipped cream.
Iced Coffee Fillip (Cktl). ⅓ pint strong black coffee, ⅛ gill Tia Maria. Stir over ice, strain into a highball glass.
Iced Mint Tea (Eng). Steep 12 mint sprigs in 2 cups of boiling water for 30 minutes. Strain, cool. Combine with 2 pints cold water in a large jug. Add sugar to taste. Serve in tall glasses with ice and garnish with a spiral of lemon peel and mint sprigs.
Iced Tea (Eng). Freshly brewed tea. Cooled, sweetened with sugar syrup. Served over ice with a slice of lemon.
Ice Machine (Eng). A machine (refrigerated) which automatically produces ice cubes (in various shapes depending on the make of the machine) suitable for drinks.
Ice Pick (Eng). An implement used to chip pieces of ice from large blocks for drinks, especially cocktails.
Ice Saints (Fr). Sometimes referred to by growers. Are Servatius, Boniface and Sophid whose days occur in mid-May, the time when late frosts can seriously damage the vine. See Saints.
Ice Scoop (Eng). An implement for picking up and transferring crushed and shaved ice from container to glass.
Ice Shaver (Eng). A special implement for taking off slivers of ice from a large block so that they can be used to cool down drinks quickly.
Ice Tongs (Eng). An implement for hand-

ling ice from the ice bucket to the glass or cocktail shaker etc.

Ice Water (USA). Drinking water cooled by refrigeration (or by the addition of ice cubes).

Ice Wine (Ger). See Eiswein.

Ichbien (Cktl). ¾ measure Cognac, ¼ measure Grand Marnier, yolk of egg, 3 measures milk. Shake well over ice, strain into a 5 oz. goblet. Grate nutmeg on top.

Içilen Şey (Tur). Beverage, drink.

Içki (Tur). Drink.

Içkili (Tur). A licensed restaurant. Also denotes 'a drink'.

Içme (Tur). Mineral water, spring drinking water.

Icod (Sp). A white wine 11–13% alc. by vol. produced on the Canary Islands.

Idaho (USA). A lesser wine-producing region in the Pacific North-West.

Ideal (Cktl). 1 oz. Gin, ½ oz. grapefruit juice, ½ oz. dry Vermouth, 1 teaspoon powdered sugar, 2 dashes Angostura. Shake over ice, strain into a cocktail glass. Add a cherry.

Idig (Ger). Vineyard. (Anb) = Rheinpfalz. (Ber) = Mittelhaardt-Deutsche Weinstrasse. (Gro) = Meerspinne. (Vil) = Königsbach.

IDV (Eng) (abbr). International Distillers and Vintners Co.

Idyll Blush (Austr). A rosé wine made from the Shiraz grape from the Idyll vineyard in Victoria.

Idyll Vineyard (Austr). Address = Ballan road, Moorabool, Victoria, 3221. 20 ha. Grape varieties – Cabernet sauvignon, Chardonnay, Gewürztraminer and Shiraz.

Igel (Ger). Village. (Anb) = Mosel-Saar-Ruwer. (Ber) = Obermosel. (Gro) = Königsberg. (Vin) = Dullgärten.

Ightham Vineyard (Eng). Address = Ivy Hatch, Kent. 1¼ ha. Planted 1972. Grape variety – Müller-Thurgau.

Igloos (Port). The name given to the large concrete domes that are used to store wines for short periods. See Baloes.

Ihringen (Ger). Village. (Anb) = Baden. (Ber) = Kaiserstuhl-Tuniberg. (Gro) = Vulkanfelsen. (Vins) = Castellberg, Fohrenberg, Kreuzhalde, Schlossberg, Steinfelsen, Winklerberg.

Ihringen [ortsteil Blankenhornsberg] (Ger). Village. (Anb) = Baden. (Ber) = Kaiserstuhl-Tuniberg. (Gro) = Vulkanfelsen. (Vin) = Doktorgarten.

Ijs (Hol). Ice.

Ika Cocktail (Cktl). ⅓ gill Gin, ⅙ gill Grenadine. Stir over ice, strain into a cocktail glass. Serve with a dash of lemon peel juice on top.

Iksir (Tur). Elixir, liqueur.

Ilbesheim (Ger). Village. (Anb) = Rheinpfalz. (Ber) = Südliche Weinstrasse. (Gro) = Herrlich. (Vin) = Rittersberg.

Île Bouchard (Fr). An island in the river Gironde, Bordeaux. Produces red and white wines.

Île de Beauté (Fr). A Vins de Pays area on Corsica. Produces red, rosé and white wines.

Île-de-France (Fr). Caused by an earthquake 20 million years ago. Raised the level of the chalk ground approx. 300 feet. The Franco-British basin of chalk was split and tertiary deposits settled on the surface 11 million years ago. Champagne region is situated on this.

Île de Ré (Fr). Part of the Bois Ordinaires in the Cognac district of the Charente-Maritime Département, western France.

Île-des-Vergelesses (Fr). An area of 97 ha. in the parish of Pernand in the Côte d'Or, Burgundy. Produces white wines of finesse and distinction. Has a Premier Cru vineyard in the A.C. Pernand-Vergelesses.

Île-des-Vergelesses (Fr). A Premier Cru vineyard in the A.C. commune of Pernand-Vergelesses, Côte de Beaune, Burgundy. 9.2 ha.

Île des Vignes (Eng). The old Norman name for the Isle of Ely in Cambridgeshire.

Île d'Oléron (Fr). Part of the Bois Ordinaires in the Cognac district of the Charente-Maritime Département, western France.

Île du Nord (Fr). An island in the river Gironde, Bordeaux. Produces mainly red wines.

Île Fumadelle (Fr). An island in the river Gironde, Bordeaux. Red wines under commune of Soussans, A.C. Haut-Médoc, Bordeaux.

Île Margaux (Fr). An island in the river Gironde, Bordeaux. Produces mainly red wines.

Île Nouvelle (Fr). An island in the river Gironde, Bordeaux. Produces red and white wines. Also known as the Île Sanspain.

Île Patiras (Fr). An island in the river Gironde, Bordeaux. Produces red and white wines.

Île Sanspain (Fr). See Île Nouvelle.

Îles de la Gironde (Fr). The collective name for the group of islands off the Haut-Médoc on the river Gironde, Bordeaux. See Îles Bouchard, du Nord, Fumadelle, Margaux, Nouvelle (Sanspain), Patiras and Verte. Produces red and white wines.

Île Verte (Fr). An island in the river Gironde, Bordeaux. Produces red and white wines.

Illats (Fr). A commune within the district of A.C. Cérons in south-western Bordeaux. Produces sweet white wines.

Illicium Anisatum (Lat). The botanical name for Badiane, a form of Anise from China used in the making of Pastis.

Illingen (Ger). Village. (Anb) = Württemberg. (Ber) = Württembergisch Unterland. (Gro) = Stromberg. (Vins) = Forstgrube, Halde, Lichtenberg, Schanzreiter.

Illinois (USA). A large wine-producing State. Has many wineries producing most styles of wines from French hybrid and Vitis vinifera vines.

Illmitz (Aus). A wine-producing area in the Eisenstadt district.

Ill [River] (Fr). The river that runs through the Alsace region. A tributary of the river Rhine. See Ilsace.

Illuminati (It). A 50 ha. winery based at Controguerra in Abruzzo. Controls Fattoria Nico. Is noted for its' Montepulciano d'Abruzzo.

Illustre Cour des Seigneurs de la Corbière (Fr). A wine society based in the Midi.

Illva (It). A famous Amaretto di Saronno producer.

Illy Coffee (It). A popular brand of Italian coffee.

Illy Coffee Liqueur (It). A coffee liqueur produced in Ancona from the famous Illy coffee. 30% alc. by vol.

Ilok (Yug). A major wine town in northern Croatia.

Ilsace (Fr). The original name from which Alsace derives. From the river Ill (a tributary of the Rhine). See also Elsass.

Ilsfeld (Ger). Village. (Anb) = Württemberg. (Ber) = Württembergisch Unterland. (Gro) = Schozachtal. (Vin) = Rappen.

Ilsfeld (Ger). Village. (Anb) = Württemberg. (Ber) = Württembergisch Unterland. (Gro) = Wunnenstein. (Vin) = Lichtenberg.

Ilsfeld [ortsteil Schozach] (Ger). Village. (Anb) = Württemberg. (Ber) = Württembergisch Unterland. (Gro) = Kirchenweinberg. (Vins) = Mühlberg, Roter Berg, Schelmenklinge.

Imbibe (Eng). To drink.

Imbik (Tur). Pot still.

Imbottare (It). Put in barrels.

Imbottigliare (It). To bottle.

Imbottigliato (It). Bottled.

Imbottigliato all'Origine (It). Bottled in the region of origin.

Imbottigliato Nello Stabilimento Della Ditta (It). Bottled on the premises of the firm.

Imbuteliat (Rum). Bottled.

Imbuvable (Fr). Undrinkable.

Imesch (Switz). A red wine produced in Sion, Valais canton. Produced from the Pinot noir grape.

Im Felseneck (Ger). Vineyard. (Anb) = Nahe. (Ber) = Schloss Böckelheim. (Gro) = Rosengarten. (Vil) = Bockenau.

Im Füchschen (Ger). A brewery at 28, Ratingerstrasse, Düsseldorf. Noted for its' Altbier. See Im Füchschen Altbier.

Im Füchschen Altbier (Ger). A fine hoppy Altbier brewed by the Im Füchschen Brauerei in Düsseldorf.

Im Heubusch (Ger). Vineyard. (Anb) = Rheinpfalz. (Ber) = Mittelhaardt-Deutsche Weinstrasse. (Gro) = Schnepfenflug vom Kellertal. (Vil) = Morschheim.

Imiglykos (Gre). A range of red and white, medium-sweet table wines produced by Tsantali.

Immature Spirits Act (Eng). States that no spirits may be sold in Great Britain under 3 years old.

Immengarten (Ger). Vineyard. (Anb) = Rheinpfalz. (Ber) = Südliche Weinstrasse. (Gro) = Mandelhöhle. (Vil) = Maikammer.

Immenstaad (Ger). Village. (Anb) = Baden. (Ber) = Bodensee. (Gro) = Sonnenufer. (Vin) = Burgstall.

Immesheim (Ger). Village. (Anb) = Rheinpfalz. (Ber) = Mittelhaardt-Deutsche Weinstrasse. (Gro) = Schnepfenflug vom Kellertal. (Vin) = Sonnenstück.

Immiscible (Eng). Unmixable. Denotes two or more liquids that are incapable of being mixed to a homogeneous substance. e.g. oil and water.

Im Neuberg (Ger). Vineyard. (Anb) = Nahe. (Ber) = Schloss Böckelheim. (Gro) = Rosengarten. (Vil) = Bockenau.

Imperator (Hol). An all-malt, lightly hopped, unpasteurised Beer 6.3% alc. by vol. Brewed by the Brand Brouwerij in Wijlre, Limburg.

Imperial (Can). A blended Canadian whiskey produced by Hiram Walker.

Imperial (China). A grade of medium aged tea.

Imperial (Cktl). ⅓ measure Mandarine Napoléon, ⅓ measure dry Gin, ⅙ measure Amaretto, ⅙ measure Sambuca, 1 dash lemon juice. Shake well over ice, strain into a cocktail glass.

Imperial (Eng). See Impériale. 8 bottle capacity.

Imperial (Iran). A white grape variety from the Tauris region.

Imperial (Jap). A brand of Whiskey produced by the Suntory Co.

Impérial (Port). A red wine produced by the Caves Império.

Imperial (Scot). A single Malt whisky distillery operated by the Dailuaine-Talisker distilleries Ltd. Part of the DCL Group. Produces an 18 year old malt 43% alc. by vol. A Highland malt.

Imperial (Sp). A brand of fine old matured red wine from the Rioja of Reserva and Gran Reserva classification. Produced by C.V.N.E.

Imperial Bitter (Eng). A keg Bitter 1042 O.G. brewed by the Tetley Brewery for north-eastern England.

Imperial Blend (Eng). A brand of fine teas produced by Ridgways Co.

Imperial Bounty (Austr). The brand-name for red and white dessert wines.

Imperial Cocktail (Cktl). 1 part dry Vermouth, 1 part Gin, 2 dashes Maraschino, 1 dash Angostura. Stir over ice, strain into a cocktail glass. Decorate with a cherry.

Impériale (Fr). A large bottle that holds between 6–9 bottles. Claret is sometimes matured in them. 1½ gallons.

Imperial Fino (Sp). A brand of Fino sherry from the Diez Hermanos produced by Diez Merito.

Imperial Fizz (Cktl). ¾ measure Scotch whisky, ¼ measure Bacardi White Label, juice ½ lemon. Shake over ice, strain into an ice-filled highball glass. Top with a dash of soda water.

Imperial 1914 (Sp). An old Oloroso sherry produced by Domecq.

Imperial Old Ale (Eng). A dark Barley wine 1096 O.G. brewed by the Banks Brewery in Wolverhampton, Staffordshire.

Imperial Pale (Scot). A bottled Pale ale 1030 O.G. brewed by the Maclays Brewery in Alloa, Clackmannanshire.

Imperial Pop (Eng). A drink made from ginger, lemon juice, sugar and cream of tartar. Fermented with yeast.

Imperial Scotch Whisky (The) (Ch.Isles). The brand-name for a Scotch whisky imported and bottled by Le Riches Stores of Jersey and Guernsey. 43% alc. by vol.

Imperial Stout (Eng). A high gravity Stout exported in the nineteenth century to Russia. Also produced in Denmark and Finland. Brewed by Courage.

Imperial Tawny (Port). A full-bodied Tawny Port from Sandeman shippers. 20 year old.

Imperial Vinícola Limitada (Port). A noted shipper of Dão wines.

Imperio Grand Reserve (Sp). A 5 year old brandy produced by Terry.

Impesa (Mad). First pressing.

Impflingen (Ger). Village. (Anb) =

Rheinpfalz. (Ber) = Südliche Weinstrasse. (Gro) = Herrlich. (Vin) = Abtsberg.

Imp. Gal. (Eng) (abbr). Imperial gallon. Also Imp. Gall.

Imp. Gall. (Eng) (abbr). Imperial gallon. Also Imp. Gal.

Impigno (It). A white grape variety grown in Puglia.

Impotable (Fr). Undrinkable.

Impregnation Method (Eng). A method of making sparkling wines by putting the wine into a pressurised tank then injecting CO_2 gas into it. It is then bottled under pressure. When opened, gives off large bubbles and goes 'flat' quickly.

Improvement of Musts (Eng). See Chaptalisation.

Im Röttgen (Ger). Vineyard. (Anb) = Mosel-Saar-Ruwer. (Ber) = Zell/ Mosel. (Gro) = Weinhex. (Vil) = Güls.

Im Röttgen (Ger). Vineyard. (Anb) = Mosel-Saar-Ruwer. (Ber) = Zell/ Mosel. (Gro) = Weinhex. (Vil) = Winningen.

Im Sonnenschein (Ger). Vineyard. (Anb) = Rheinpfalz. (Ber) = Südliche Weinstrasse. (Gro) = Konigsgarten. (Vil) = Siebeldingen.

Im Stein (Ger). Vineyard. (Anb) = Franken. (Ber) = Maindreieck. (Gro) = Rosstal. (Vil) = Karlstadt.

Ina (La) (Sp). A pale dry Sherry produced and bottled by Pedro Domecq S.A. Shipped by Domecq, Hereford.

I.N.A.O. (Fr) (abbr). Institut National des Appellations d'Origine des Vins et Eaux-de-Vie.

In Bond (Eng). See Bond.

In Bond Shop (W.Ind). Duty free shop.

Inca Cocktail (Cktl) (1). ⅙ measure Plymouth Gin, ⅙ measure French vermouth, ⅙ measure dry Sherry, 2 dashes Orange bitters, 2 dashes Orgeat syrup. Stir well over ice, strain into a cocktail glass, add a piece of pineapple, squeeze of orange peel juice on top.

Inca Cocktail (Cktl) (2). ⅛ gill dry Sherry, ⅛ gill French vermouth, ⅛ gill Gin, 1 teaspoon plain syrup, 1 teaspoon Orange bitters. Stir over ice, strain into a cocktail glass. Serve with a dash of orange peel juice and a cherry.

Inca Cocktail (Cktl) (3). ¼ measure dry Sherry, ¼ measure dry Gin, ¼ measure French vermouth, ¼ measure Italian vermouth, dash Orgeat, dash Campari. Shake over ice, strain into a cocktail glass.

Inca Pisco (Peru). A well-known brand of Pisco sold in black bottles moulded in the shape of an Indian head. Produced by Casa Ranuzzi.

INCAVI (Sp) (abbr). Instituto Catalán de

Vino. Also spelt Institut Catala de la Vinya i del Vi.

Inchgower (Scot). A single Malt whisky distillery near Buckie in Banffshire. Owned by Arthur Bell and Sons Ltd. Produces a 12 year old Malt. 40% alc. by vol. A Highland malt.

Incider Cocktail (Cktl). Pour ⅕ gill Bourbon whiskey into an ice-filled old-fashioned glass. Top with dry sparkling cider and a slice of apple.

Inciuccarsi (It). To become intoxicated (drunk).

Incognito (Cktl). 3/10 measure Cognac brandy, 6/10 measure Lillet, 1/10 measure Apricot brandy, dash Angostura. Stir over ice, strain into a cocktail glass.

Income Tax (Cktl). ⅖ measure sweet Vermouth, ⅖ measure dry Vermouth, ⅕ measure dry Gin, juice ¼ lemon, dash of Angostura. Shake over ice, strain into a cocktail glass.

Incorporated Brewers Guild (Eng). Address = 8, Ely Place, London EC1N 6SD.

Incorruptible Champagne Cocktail (Cktl).(Non-alc). ½ fl.oz. orange juice, 1 fl.oz. grapefruit juice. Shake over ice, strain into a Champagne flute. Top with chilled lemonade.

Incrocio Terzi N.I (It). A red grape variety. A cross between the Barbera and Cabernet franc.

Incrustation (Eng). A term used to describe the forming of a 'crust' sediment in red wines. e.g. Port, Claret, etc.

Ind Coope Brewery (Eng). A part of Allied Breweries. Originally two breweries based at Burton and Romford in Essex. Merged in 1961 with Ansells and Tetley Walker. Produce many fine cask conditioned, keg and bottled beers. See Double Diamond, Skol.

In Den Felsen (Ger). Vineyard. (Anb) = Nahe. (Ber) = Schloss Böckelheim. (Gro) = Burgweg. (Vil) = Schlossböckelheim.

In Den Layfelsen (Ger). Vineyard. (Anb) = Mittelrhein. (Ber) = Rheinburgengau. (Gro) = Burg Hammerstein. (Vil) = Hammerstein.

In Den Siebzehn Morgen (Ger). Vineyard. (Anb) = Nahe. (Ber) = Kreuznach. (Gro) = Kronenberg. (Vil) = Bad Kreuznach (ortsteil Winzenheim).

Independence Day Punch (Punch). Blend together in a large punch-bowl 2 lbs. powdered sugar, 1 pint lemon juice. Add 3 bottles Claret, 1 bottle Cognac, 1 bottle Champagne, stir, add 6 sliced lemons, ice cubes and serve.

Independencia (Sp). A 10 year old Brandy produced by Osborne.

India (Ind). A large tea, coffee, wine and spirit producing country in central southern Asia. Wines produced for over 2,000 years. Regions of Dharmapuri, Kodaikanal, Madras and Penukanda. Vines of Vitis vinifera on American root stock.

Indiana (USA). A wine-producing State. Produces mainly French hybrid wines.

Indian Breakfast (Ind). A blend of tea from the Assam province. Has a distinct malty flavour.

Indian Cocktail (Cktl). ⅛ gill Whisky, ⅛ gill Italian vermouth, ⅛ gill Gin, ½ teaspoon each of brown Curaçao, orange bitters and Cointreau. Stir over ice, strain into a cocktail glass, serve with a dash of lemon peel juice.

Indian Coffee (Ind). Mainly from the southern regions – Mysore, Tamil Nadu, Kerala Niligri, Coorg and Malabar. Gives a full-bodied taste and acidity.

Indian Market (Mad). An old-style name for Madeira wine (sweet). Now no longer used.

Indian Quinine Water (Eng). The original name for tonic water.

Indian Summer Cocktail (Cktl). 1 measure white Rum, 1 measure dry Gin, 1½ measures coconut milk, 1 measure Malibu, 1 measure cream, scoop crushed ice. Blend together in a blender. Pour into a highball glass. Dress with a cherry, coconut slice and serve with straws.

Indian Teas (Ind). Main production regions are Assam, Dooars, Cacher, Darjeeling, Kerala, Niligiri and Mysore.

Indian Tonic Water (Eng). See Indian Quinine Water.

India Pale Ale (Eng). Originally applied to strong Pale ales brewed to mature on the long sea voyage to India. Shipwrecked casks were retrieved and drunk, creating a home demand for more. Term now applies to draught bitters of ordinary quality and also for bottled beers of same strength.

Indicacão de Proveniencia Regulamentado (Port). IPR. Denotes quality wines from named regions. Is equivalent to V.D.Q.S. in France.

Indication of Age (Port). Tawny Ports that have been aged for 10, 20, 30 or over 40 years. Label must carry indication of age, year of bottling and state that it has been aged in cask.

Indio Oscura (Mex). A Viennese-style Lager beer.

Individual Berry Selected (USA). The American equivalent to the German Trokenbeerenauslese. Sugar range of 32°-45° Balling.

Individual Bunch Selected (USA). The American equivalent to the German

I

Auslese or Beerenauslese. Sugar range of 26°-32° Balling.

Individual Paddock (Austr). The brand-name of the Rothburg Estate vineyards in the Hunter Valley.

I.N.D.O. (Sp) (abbr). Instituto Nacional de Denominaciónes de Origen.

Indonesian Coffee (E.Ind). The best is from Java, the Celebes Islands and Sumatra, with Bali and Timor producing good Arabica coffee. They have a mellow flavour with a strong aroma.

Indonesian Teas (E.Ind). Teas used mainly for blending.

Indre-et-Loire (Fr). A Vins de Pays area in Touraine in the Jardin de la France (Garden of France). Produces red, rosé and dry white wines.

Indústria Comércio e Navegação, Sociedade Vinícola Rio Grandense, Ltda (Bra). The largest wine producer in Brazil. Produces both red and white wines under the Granja União label.

Industria Licorera de Bolivar (Col). A State-owned distillery based at Cartagena. Produces Ron Popular and Très Esquinas, Gins and Aguardiente.

Industrias de la Fermentacíon (Mex). A large winery based in Saltillo, Coahuila.

Inebriate (Eng). To make drunk. Intoxicate.

Inebriated Person (Eng). Drunken person. Usually defines a habitually drunken person.

Inebriety (Eng). Drunkenness.

Infanta Isabela (Port). A 10 year old dated Tawny Port from Rozes.

Infants Vintage Seco (Port). A wine produced by Caves São João.

INFE (Sp) (abbr). Instituto Nacional de Fomento de la Exportación.

Infectious Degeneration (Eng). A virus-like disease that attacks the vines. See Court Noué and Fanleaf.

Inferno (It). A sub district of the Lombardy in the foothills of the Alps in the Valtellina Valley. Produces red wines of the same name from the Nebbiolo grape.

Infernotti (It). Secret cellars in the Piemonte region. Also known as Crutin.

Infiascato (It). Put in flasks.

Infiascato alla Fattoria (It). Bottled in flasks at the winery.

Informations-Service for Tyske Vine (Den). German Wine Information Service. Address = Hovedvagtsgade 6 DK-1006 Kopenhagen K.

Inführ (Aus). One of the country's leading sparkling wine producers. Produces Gumpoldskirchener Königssekt, Ritter von Dürnstein trocken sekt.

Infuse (Eng). The action of steeping a solid in a liquid to extract the colour and flavour. e.g. Coffee, tea, liqueurs, etc.

Infuser (Eng). A technical description of a tea maker. e.g. Tea pot. See Tea Maker.

Infuser (Fr). To infuse. See also Tisane.

Infusion (Eng). The action of extracting the flavour and colour from a solid into a liquid. e.g. Tea, liqueurs etc. Also during brewing applies to the extraction of the fermentable materials from the grist. See Decoction.

Infusionar (Sp). Lit – 'To brew a cup of tea'.

Ing (Aus) (abbr). Ingenieur.

Ingelfingen (Ger). Village. (Anb) = Württemberg. (Ber) = Kocher-Jagst-Tauber. (Gro) = Kocherberg. (Vin) = Hoher Berg.

Ingelheim (Ger). Village. (Anb) = Rheinhessen. (Ber) = Bingen. (Gro) = Kaiserpfalz. (Vins) = Burgweg, Höllenweg, Horn, Kirchenstück, Lottenstück, Pares, Rabenkopf, Rheinhöhe, Rotes Kreuz, Schlossberg, Schloss Westerhaus, Sonnenberg, Sonnenhang, Steinacker, Täuscherspfad.

Ingenieur (Aus). A wine qualification awarded to graduates from viticultural colleges. See Ing.

Ingieten (Hol). To infuse.

Ingieting (Hol). Infusion.

Inglenook (USA). A vineyard in the Napa Valley, California. Grape varieties – Cabernet sauvignon, Charbono, Chardonnay, Chenin blanc, French colombard, Gewürztraminer, Johannisberg riesling, Pinot noir and Zinfandel. Produces quality still, sparkling and dessert wines.

Ingrandes (Fr). A commune in the A.C. Savennières, Anjou-Saumur, Loire.

Ingwerlikoer (Ger). A ginger liqueur.

Injection Method (Eng). Lit – The pumping of CO_2 gas into wine to make it sparkle.

Injerto (Sp). Vine graft.

Inkelhöll (Ger). Vineyard. (Anb) = Nahe. (Ber) = Schloss Böckelheim. (Gro) = Paradiesgarten. (Vil) = Lettweiler.

Ink Street (Cktl). ⅓ measure Rye whiskey, ⅓ measure orange juice, ⅓ measure lemon juice. Shake over ice, strain into a cocktail glass.

Inky (Eng). A term used to describe the deep red wines of Bordeaux, northern Rhône, Rioja etc. Especially when they are young.

Inky Cocktail (Cktl). ⅓ gill Port wine, ⅙ gill Brandy, ⅙ gill blackcurrant cordial, dash lemon juice. Shake over ice, strain into an ice-filled highball glass. Top with soda water.

Inländerrum (Aus). The name given in the 1930's to Kunstrum. Contained between

1–2% Rum only (less than Rumverschnitt).

Inländischem Schaumwein (Ger). A wine produced in Germany from any red, rosé or white wine from any part of the world.

Inn (Eng). A licensed hostelry that caters for travellers giving them refreshment and accomodation.

Innere Leiste (Ger). Vineyard. (Anb) = Franken. (Ber) = Maindreieck. (Gro) = Not yet assigned. (Vil) = Würzburg.

Inniskillin (Can). A small winery based at Niagara. Produces both hybrid and Vitis vinifera wines.

Inn Sign (Eng). A signboard positioned outside a public house or Inn showing its' name (often drawn/painted from the days when most people could not read) with the name of the brewery which owns it (or Free House).

Innswood (W.Ind). A Rum distillery based on the island of Jamaica. Produces dark Rums.

Inocente (Sp). A brand of Fino sherry produced by Valdespino at Jerez.

Inositol (Eng). A vitamin found in most wines.

Insel Heylesern Wert (Ger). Vineyard. (Anb) = Mittelrhein. (Ber) = Bacharach. (Gro) = Schloss Stahleck. (Vil) = Bacharach.

Insensible Ferment (Eng). The name given to the slight fermentation that takes place after the first fermentation. Also known as the Malo-lactic fermentation.

Insheim (Ger). Village. (Anb) = Rheinpfalz. (Ber) = Südliche Weinstrasse. (Gro) = Herrlich. (Vin) = Schäfergarten.

Insolia (It). A white grape variety grown in Sicily to make Marsala.

Insosso (Port). A term which denotes a tasteless, insipid wine.

Inspecteurs de la Repression des Fraudes (Fr). Inspectors for the A.C. to see that the rules are conformed to. They issue Acquits verts.

Inspiration (Cktl). ¼ measure Calvados, ¼ measure Gin, ¼ measure Grand Marnier, ¼ measure dry Vermouth. Stir over ice, strain into a cocktail glass, add a cherry.

Inspissated Wine (Eng). A flavouring or colouring wine. Can be either unfermented grape juice or boiled down must.

Instant Coffee (Eng). Fresh brewed coffee which is either freeze dried, roller dried or vacuum dried. See Washington, (G.) Sartori Kato and Lyophilization. Also known as Soluble coffee.

Institue Nazionale per la Tutela del Brandy Italiano (It). The body that has set standards for the wine used as the distillate, the distillation process and the amount of ageing required for Brandy in Italy.

Institut Catala de la Vinya i el Vi (Sp). See INCAVI.

Institute of Brewing (Eng). Address = 33, Clarges Street, London W1Y 8EE.

Institute of Masters of Wine Limited (Eng). Address = Black Swan House, Kennet Wharf Lane, London EC4V 3BE.

Institut Für Schnittreben (Aus). An institute of vine cuttings based in Vöslau.

Institut National des Appellations d'Origine des Vins et Eaux-de-Vie (Fr). Authority who set and monitor the French wine and spirit laws and classifications. I.N.A.O. See also Appellation Contrôlée.

Instituto Catalán de Vino (Sp). INCAVI. Responsible to INDO and the Departement of Agriculture in Cataluña. Experiment in drip irrigation, soils and vine training with wires.

Instituto Commercio Estero (It). Institute of Foreign Commerce. Gives a seal to all Italian wines exported to the USA and Canada which indicates that the wine has met the Italian regulations.

Instituto do Vinho da Madeira (Mad). I.V.M. See Madeira Wine Insitute.

Instituto do Vinho do Porto (Port). Institute that follows Port production and tests quality under government directions. I.V.P. Formed 1933.

Instituto Nacional de Denominaciónes de Origin (Sp). Legislative body for the control of vine cultivation and wine production attached to the Ministry of Agriculture. See Consejo Regulador de la Denominación de Origin. (abbr) = I.N.D.O.

Instituto Nacional de Fomento de la Exportación (Sp). I.N.F.E. Address = Paseo de la Castellana, 14, Madrid 28046. A body for the promotion of Spanish wines.

Instituto Nacional de Vitivinicultura (Arg). INV. A body set up in 1959 to control all commercial practices and production methods, analyses wine and grape samples.

Instituto Regionale della Vita e del Vino (It). A Sicilian organisation designed to assist the vine growers with every aspect of wine production from vine to bottle. Also for the promotion of Sicilian wines.

Instituto Valenciano de Viticultura y Enología (Sp). I.V.V.E. Founded in 1910. Supervised vineyards after phylloxera. Tests new products and analyses samples for export certification.

I

Insuperable (Sp). A 5 year old Brandy produced by Gonzalez Byass.

Intercellular Fermentation (Fr). A style of fermentation where the whole grape is fermented without oxygen and fermentation takes place within the grape. Is also known as macération semi-carbonique.

Intercontinental Breweries (S.Afr). A brewery set up in 1973. Noted for its Lager beers (1040–1050 O.G.) Heidelberg Lager and Sportsman Lager.

International Beer Convention (Ger). A Munich-based group who hold competitions and research projects with a view of upgrading beer-drinking. Members call themselves 'The Notables'.

International Coffee Agreement (Eng). Inaugurated in 1962 at the United Nations in New York, is now reviewed and updated by the International Coffee Organisation at their headquarters in London. Agreement includes the limitation of production, supply, importation and exportation of coffee and to promote the consumption of coffee of both producing and non-producing members.

International Coffee Organisation (Eng). Formed in 1963 and based in London at 32, Berner's Street, W1. Formed to organise and administer the International Coffee Agreement and to promote and research coffee production and drinking.

International Correspondence of Corkscrew Addicts (USA). See I.C.C.A.

International Distillers and Vintners Ltd (Eng). Address = York Gate, Regents Park, London. NW1. Produces Chelsea Gin and many brands of Scotch whisky including Justerini and Brooks, Dunhill, Catto's and Gilbey.

International Food and Wine Society (Eng). A society founded by André Simon that meets regularly for the appreciation of good food and wine. Address = 108, Old Brompton Road, London SW7 3RA.

International Standards Organisation (Euro). See I.S.O. and ISO glass.

Interprinderile Agricole de Stat (Rum). See I.A.S.

Intoxicate (Eng). Causes a person to be in a state of euphoria, to stupor from alcoholic drink with loss of control of motion and inhibitions. See Inebriate.

Intoxicated (Eng). A person who is drunk, inebriated.

INV (Arg) (abbr). Instituto Nacional de Vitivinicultura.

Invalid Port (S.Afr). A soft, ruby red Port-style wine with a fine grapey flavour.

Invechiata (It). Refers to aged Grappa.

Invergordon (Scot). A Grain whisky distillery based north of Inverness.

Inver House (Scot). A major brand-name of a blended Scotch whisky Produced by Inver House Distilleries, Airdrie. See William Davidson and Co. 43% alc. by vol.

Inverleven (Scot). A Malt whisky distillery based on the mouth of the river Clyde near Glasgow. 40% alc. by vol. A Lowland malt whisky. (Part of Hiram Walker).

Invertase (Eng). An enzyme in yeast that converts (inverts) the unfermentable sugars Sucrose and Sacchrose into fermentable (invert) sugar.

Invert Sugar (Eng). Sugar which has been treated with acids to make it fermentable by yeast. See also Invertase.

Investment (Eng). The process of laying down Port and fine red wines bought young to mature in quality and value for later sale or drinking. Can also apply to fine white wines and Champagne.

Invicta Bitter (Eng). A cask conditioned Bitter 1044 O.G. brewed by the Shepherd Neame Brewery.

In Vino Veritas (Lat). Lit – 'In wine there is truth'. Denotes that people who are drunk usually speak the truth!

Inzolia (It). A white grape variety grown in Sicily for the making of Marsala and other wines.

Inzolia Bianca (USA). A white grape variety grown in California to make dessert wines.

Iodine (Eng). Used in wine-making to detect the presence of starch in hazy wines.

Io Furmint (Hun). A white grape variety used exclusively in the making of Tocjai aszú.

Iona (USA). A lesser red grape (native) variety used in the making of varietals. Vitis Labrusca.

Ion Exchange (Eng). Treatment of wines used for tartrate stabilisation by removing potassium and calcium ions and replacing with sodium. This is now banned by the EEC.

Ionian Islands (Gre). The islands of western Greece – Corfu, Zante, Levakas, Cephalonia. Produce mainly country-style wines.

Iowa (USA). A wine-producing State that produces wines mainly from French hybrid varieties.

I.P. (It) (abbr). Italia Particolare.

I.P.A. (Eng) (abbr). India Pale Ale.

I.P.1. (Ger) (abbr). A table grape used in German crossings. Is a cross between the Chasselas and Muscat Hamburg.

Iphofen (Ger). Village. (Anb) = Franken. (Ber) = Steigerwald. (Gro) = Burgweg. (Vins) = Julius-Eckter-Berg, Kalb, Kronsberg.

I

I Piani (It). A dry, cherry-red wine named after the area in the Nurra region of Sardinia.

Ipiros (Gre). A region that produces red and white pétillant wines.

Ipocras (Eng). Chaucer's way of spelling Hypocras in his book of The Canterbury Tales.

Ippesheim (Ger). Village. (Anb) = Franken. (Ber) = Steigerwald. (Gro) = Schlontück. (Vin) = Herrschaftsberg.

IPR (Port) (abbr). Indicacão de Proveniencia Regulamentado.

Ipswich Special Bitter (Eng). A Bitter beer brewed by the Tolly Cobbold Brewery in Ipswich.

Iran (M.East). One of the earliest places where viticulture occurred. Then known as Persia. Vineyards in the northern provinces of East Azerbaijan, Farse, Hamedan, Khorasan, Lorestan, Teheran, West Azerbaijan and Zanjan. A wide variety of medium-sweet and dessert wines are produced for the home market mainly from the Thompson seedless grape.

Irancy (Fr). A village near Chablis in northern Burgundy. Produces red and rosé wines from the César grape.

Ireland (Ire). Wines are produced near Cork. See Mayville.

Iris Cocktail (Cktl). ⅔ measure Gin, ⅓ measure lemon juice, 1 teaspoon powdered sugar. Shake well over ice, strain into a cocktail glass. Decorate with a mint sprig.

Irish Ale Breweries (Ire). A Guinness-controlled group of which Allied Breweries own a third. Runs 3 breweries in Ireland – Cherrys, Macardles and Smithwicks.

Irish Breakfast (Ind). A blend of teas from the Assam province. Produces a strong, thick, rich tea.

Irish Cheer Cocktail (Cktl). 1 fl.oz. Irish whiskey, ¼ fl.oz. sweet Vermouth. Stir over ice, strain into a cocktail glass.

Irish Coffee (USA). 1½ ozs. Irish whiskey, 5 ozs. strong hot black coffee, 1 teaspoon sugar, 1 spoonful whipped cream. Into a warmed glass place the sugar and coffee, stir, add whiskey and top with the cream.

Irish Cow (Ire). A liqueur made from Irish whiskey, double cream and chocolate by Baileys in Dublin.

Irish Distillers Group Ltd (Ire). Controls the Irish whiskey industry by an amalgamation of John Power and Son, John Jameson and Son and the Cork Distillery Co.

Irish Handshake (Cock), 2 parts Irish whiskey, 1 part green Curaçao, 1 part

fresh cream. Shake well over ice, strain into a cocktail glass.

Irish Mist (Ire). A whiskey-based liqueur flavoured with herbs and honey, 35% alc. by vol. Produced in Tulach Mhor.

Irish Moss (Eng). A mixture of 2 marine algae used to clarify beer during brewing.

Irish Moss (USA). A liqueur similar to Rock and Rye, but flavoured with Irish moss. Is produced by Leroux.

Irish Nigger (Pousse Café). Into a liqueur glass pour in order – ½ measure Crème de Cacao, ½ measure (green) Crème de Menthe.

Irish Punch (Cktl). ½ lemon studded with 12 cloves, 1 measure Irish whiskey, 1 teaspoon sugar, hot water. Heat together, strain into a wine glass.

Irish Red Ale (Ire). See Killian.

Irish Rickey (Cktl) 2 fl. ozs. Irish whiskey, juice ½ lime. Pour into an ice-filled highball glass. Top with soda water and a slice of lime.

Irish Russet Ale (Fr). A highly carbonated Ale produced in France.

Irish Shillelagh (Cktl). ⅓ measure Irish whiskey, ⅛ measure Sloe gin, ⅛ measure dark Rum, juice ½ lemon, dash Gomme syrup. Shake over ice, strain into an old-fashioned glass. Decorate with fruits in season.

Irish Velvet (Ire). A liqueur based on Irish whiskey, strong black coffee and sugar.

Irish Velvet (Ire). A package to make Irish Coffee. Contains freeze-dried coffee, Irish whiskey, sugar and sweeteners. Produced by Irish Distillers. Need to add water and cream.

Irish Whiskey (Ire). A Whiskey produced from malted barley, cereals, water and yeast. Triple pot-stilled, blended and matured in used Sherry butts. The oldest pot-stilled whisk(e)y .

Irish Whiskey Cocktail (Cktl). ⅘ measure Irish whiskey, ¹⁄₁₀ measure Pernod, ¹⁄₁₀ measure Cointreau, 2 dashes Maraschino, dash Angostura. Stir well over ice, strain into a cocktail glass. Decorate with an olive.

Irish Whiskey Sour (Cktl). 2 ozs. Irish whiskey, juice of small lemon, teaspoon sugar, white of egg. Shake juice, sugar and egg white well over ice, pour into a highball glass, add the whiskey and a little soda.

Irmos Unidos (Port). An Aguardente produced by the Caves São João.

Irn Bru (Eng). A soft drink produced in the north of England. A.G. Barr.

Iron Casse (Eng). A wine malady. A fine greyish-white deposit looking like yeast. Caused by a high iron content in the wine. Citric acid or blue fining will rectify. Also known as Casse Bleu and Casse Ferrique.

Iron City (USA). A beer brewed by the Pittsburgh Brewery, Pittsburgh, Pennsylvania.

Iron Horse Ranch and Vineyard (USA). A winery based in the Russian River Valley, Sonoma County California, 46 ha. Grape varieties – Cabernet sauvignon, Chardonnay, Pinot noir, Sauvignon blanc and Zinfandel. Produces varietal wines.

Iron Lady (Cktl). 1 measure vodka, ½ measure Sambuca, 1 measure orange juice. Frost the top of a highball glass with castor sugar, add spirals of lemon and orange peel and ice. Add ingredients, stir and top up with Iron-bru or Lucozade.

Irouléguy (Fr). A.C. white, rosé and red wines of the Basses Pyrénées region. See Béarn. The production is controlled by one co-operative. Minimum alc. by vol. 10%, maximum 14%.

Irrache (Sp). A major wine-producer of north-eastern Navarra.

Irrigazione a Zampillo (It). A method of irrigation of vineyards where the soil between the vines is sprayed with water from above.

Irroy (Eng). The brand-name of a Champagne that was popular in Victorian times. Based at Reims. A Grande Marque. Second label of the Taittinger Champagne house.

Irsch (Ger). Village. (Anb) = Mosel-Saar-Ruwer. (Ber) = Saar-Ruwer. (Gro) = Scharzberg. (Vins) = Hubertusberg, Sonnenberg, Vogelsang.

Irshavskoje (USSR). A white table wine produced near Cherson in the Ukraine.

Irvine's White (Austr). A white grape variety used in the making of sparkling wines. A distant cousin of the Folle blanche.

Irving Cocktail (Cktl). ½ measure dry Gin, ¼ measure Calisaya, ¼ measure dry Vermouth. Shake over ice, strain into a cocktail glass. Top with a slice of orange.

Isabel (Port). A rosé wine produced by the Caves da Silva.

Isabelita (Eng). A fine, dry, Fino sherry from Harvey's of Bristol.

Isabella (Mad). A hybrid grape variety which was used in the production of Madeira wines but has now been banned.

Isabella (USA). A black grape variety grown in the north.

Isabellita (Cktl). 1½ ozs. Amontillado, ½ oz. Peach brandy, ½ oz. Vodka. Stir with ice, strain onto ice in a highball, top up with lemonade. Decorate with zest of large lemon and orange.

I.S.C. (USA) (abbr). Italian Swiss Colony.

Ischia (It). Southern island in the Campania region. Known as the 'Green Island' because of its' numerous pinewoods. It is the longest island in the Bay of Naples. D.O.C. is applicable to red and white wines. See Forastera and Biancolella.

Ischia Bianco (It). D.O.C. white wine from Campania. Made from the Biancolella and Forastera grapes.

Ischia Bianco Superiore (It). D.O.C. white wine from Campania. Made from the Biancolella, Forastera and Sanlunardo grapes. Has a higher alcoholic content that Ischia Bianco.

Ischia Rosso (It). D.O.C. red wine from Campania. Made from the Barbera, Garnaccio and Piedirosso grapes.

Isimljanskoje Ygristoje (USSR). A dry sparkling wine produced in the Krasnodar region.

Isinglass (Eng). Fish gelatine often made from the swimbladder of the Sturgeon. Used as a fining agent for wines and beers.

Iskendiriye (Bul). An alternative name for the Muscat of Alexandria grape.

Iskra (Bul). The brand-name of a méthode champenoise sparkling wine. Red, rosé and white varieties are produced.

Iskriashto Vino (Bul). Sparkling wine.

Islamic Wine (Eng). Old nineteenth century nickname for coffee.

Island Cask (Eng). A blackcurrant-flavoured Rum produced by Lamb and Watt of Liverpool, Lancashire.

Island Cream Grog (Punch). 3 fl.ozs. Jamaican rum, 7 fl. ozs. boiling water. Mix together in a mug, sweeten to taste, top with whipped cream and grated nutmeg.

Island Fruits (Eng). A range of non-alcoholic, carbonated fruit drinks produced by Schweppes.

Island Malts (Scot). The name given to Malt whiskies produced in the Scottish Islands. Those from Islay, Scapa, Orkney (Highland Park), Jura and Skye (Talisker).

Islay (Scot). An island in the Hebrides which produces classic malt whiskies which have a pronounced Peat Reek. See – Ardbeg, Bowmore, Bruichladdich, Bunnahabhain, Caol Ila, Lagavulin, Laphroaig and Port Ellen.

Islay Mist (Scot). A Vatted Malt produced by Long John International. First produced by D. Johnson and Co. Has a high proportion of Laphroaig. 8 year old. 40% alc. by vol.

I

Isle of Ely Vineyard (Eng). Address = Wilburton, Ely, Cambridgeshire. Soil – Sandy clay loam. First planted 1972. 1.1 ha Grape varieties – Chardonnay, Müller-Thurgau and Wrotham pinot, Produces – St. Etheldreda white.

Isle of Jura (Scot). An island in the Hebrides from which the famous Isle of Jura male whisky is produced. Is classed as a Highland Malt but has the characteristics of an Islay malt.

Isle of Jura (Scot). A single Malt whisky distillery on the Isle of Jura. Owned by Charles Mackinlay and Co. 8 year old and a 10 year old. A Highland malt. 43% alc. by vol.

Isle of Pines (Cktl). 2 ozs. Bacardi White Label, ½ oz. grapefruit juice, ½ teaspoonful sugar. Combine juice with sugar, add Rum, shake well with ice, strain into a cocktail glass.

I.S.O. (Euro) (abbr). International Standards Organisation.

Iso-Amyl Alcohol (Eng). A high alcohol. (Part of the Fusel oils).

Isobutyl Alcohol (Eng). C_4H_9OH. A higher alcohol. (Part of the Fusel oils).

I.S.O. Glass (Eng). A wine glass designed by the I.S.O. which best suits wine drinking. (It is deep-bowled and tulip-shaped to allow all the characteristics of the wine to be best shown).

Isolabella (It). A liqueur of the same style as Fior d'Alpi.

Isoleucine (Eng). An Amino acid found in wines. Is formed by the yeasts.

Isonzo (It). D.O.C. red (2) and white (8) wines from Fruili-Venezia region. Name is followed by grape. Reds – Cabernet and Merlot. Whites – Fruilano, Istriana, Pinot bianco, Pinot grigio, Renanno, Sauvignon, Tocai and Traminer aromatico. Vinification can occur in Gorizia and Cervignano.

I.S.O. Tank Container (Eng). 20,000 litre contained for the transportation of wine, usually of stainless steel. Can be a single container or of multiple compartments.

Ispanyol Şarabi (Tur). Spanish sherry.

Isparta (Tur). A wine-producing region in south-western Turkey. Produces red and white wines.

Isparta-Icel-Burdur (Tur). A noted vineyard based in the Isparta region. Produces medium-dry white wines.

Ispirato (Tur). Alcohol, spirit.

Israel (Isr). An ancient wine-producing country in the Middle-East. Wine-making recorded 3,000 years B.C. Most styles of wines are produced, mainly in co-operatives. Regions are – Gallilee, Jerusalem Environs, Negev, Sydoo-Gezer and Zikhron-Yaacov.

Israel Gin (Isr) A light-style, medium-sweet Gin. Patent-stilled.

Israeli Distillers (Isr). A leading spirit and wine-producing company.

Israeli Wine Institute (Isr). Formed in 1957 and based at Rehovat. Experiments with vines, conducts quality tests on wines and research into viticulture and viniculture.

Issarts (Fr). A Premier Cru vineyard of the A.C. commune Gevrey-Chambertin in the Côte de Nuits, Burgundy. 1.82 ha. Is also known as Plantigone.

Istein (Ger). Village. (Anb) = Baden. (Ber) = Markgräflerland. (Gro = Vogtei Rötteln. (Vin) = Kirchberg.

Istituzione del Comitato Nazionale Per la Tutela delle Denominazioni di Origine (It). The national institute for the protection of the denomination of origin. Body of 28 members and a President. Promotes and checks guaranteed and controlled wines.

Istra Bitters (Yug). An orange bitters which is similar in style to Campari. Drunk as an apéritif with ice and soda water.

Istria (Yugo). A wine region. Produces red wines from the Cabernet, Gamay, Merlot and Pinot noir grapes.

Istrita (Rum). A wine-producing area. Part of Dealul-Mare Vineyards.

Italian Bottle Grades: (It). Letters embossed on Italian bottles and flasks, i.e. A., D., S.P., etc. which indicate the minimum contents at 20 degrees Celcius.

Italian Coffee (Eng). A liqueur coffee containing Strega.

Italian Gin (It). A light, dry Gin produced by the Patent-still method.

Italian Institute for Foreign Trade (Eng). Italian wine information centre. Address = Heathcoat House, 20, Saville Row, London, W1X 2DQ,

Italianski Rizling (Yug). A regional name for the white Welschriesling grape variety.

Italiansky Rizling (Bul). The name given to the white Welschriesling grape variety.

Italian Sombrero (Cktl). ⅛ gill Amaretto, ⅓ gill cream. Blend together with a scoop of crushed ice. Serve in a Champagne flute.

Italian Swiss Colony (USA). An old established winery in the Russian River Valley, Sonoma County, California. Now owned by Heublein (United Vintners). Name now transferred to their winery in Madera Town. Grape varieties – Cabernet sauvignon, Chenin blanc, Colombard and Zinfandel. Produces dessert and varietal wines under the 'Colony' label.

Italian Swiss Colony Brandy (USA). The brand-name for a Brandy produced by the United Vintners, Lodi, California.

Italian Vermouth (It). Produced in Turin, Piemonte. Sweeter than the French variety and red in colour.

Italia Particolare (It). I.P. The old name for the lowest grade of Marsala wine.

Italijanski Rizling (Yug). A white grape variety. Also known as the Italianski rizling.

Italvini (It). A Moscato Spumante producer based in the Piemonte region, north-western Italy.

Italy (It). Largest wine producing country in the world. Produces all styles of wines. Regions – Abruzzi, Apulia (Puglia), Basilicata (Lucania), Calabria, Campania, Emilia-Romagna, Friuli-Venezia Giulia, Latium (Lazio), Liguria, Lombardy, Molise, Piemonte, Sardinia, Sicily, Trentino-Alto Adige, The Marches, Tuscany, Umbria, Valle d'Aosta and Veneto.

Itata (Chile). A wine region of southern Chile. Produces sound table wines.

Itchiban (Cktl). Chinese egg nogg. 1 fresh egg, 1 teaspoon Crème de Cacao, 1 teaspoon Bénédictine, ½ gill Brandy. Shake well over ice, strain into a highball glass, top with full-cream milk and grated nutmeg.

I Ti (China). See I-Ty.

Ituri (Afr). A coffee-producing region in Zaire.

I-Ty (China). A Chinese gentleman who discovered wine. He is reputed to have discovered it 2,200 years B.C. Also spelt I Ti.

Itza Paramount (Cktl). ½ measure dry Gin, ¼ measure Drambuie, ¼ measure Cointreau. Stir over ice, strain into a cocktail glass. Top with a cherry.

Iuvarella (It). The Pollino, Calabria name for the white Malvasia bianco grape variety.

Ivernel (Fr). Champagne producer. Address = 4 Rue Jules Lobet, 51160, Ay. 2 ha. Produces – Vintage and non-vintage wines. Vintages – 1971, 1973, 1976, 1979, 1982.

Ivérouogn (Ch. Isles). A drunkard (alcoholic). Also spelt Ivraon.

Ivérouognise (Ch. Isles). Drunkness (alcoholism).

Ives (USA). A black grape variety used in the northern states.

I.V.M. (Mad) (abbr). Instituto do Vinho da Madeira.

I.V.P. (Port) (abbr). Instituto do Vinho do Porto.

Ivraon (Ch. Isles). A drunkard (alcoholic).

Ivre (Fr). Drunk, tipsy, intoxicated.

Ivresse (Fr). Intoxication.

Ivrogne (Fr). Drunken, drunkard.

Ivrognerie (Fr). Drunkeness.

I.V.V.E. (Sp) (abbr). Instituto Valenciano de Viticultura y Enología.

I.W. Harper (USA). The brand-name of a Bourbon whiskey.

Izaak Walton (Port). A pale, Tawny Port produced by Robertsons Port shippers.

Izarra (Fr). A Basque liqueur made from Eau-de-Vie, Armagnac, grain fruits, honey, flowers and white sugar. Green = 50% by vol. Yellow = 40% by vol.

Iziun (USSR). A red grape variety grown in Uzbekistan.

Izmir (Tur). A wine-producing area in western Turkey. Produces both red and white wines.

Izzara (Fr). A mis-spelling of Izarra.

Jaargang (Hol). Vintage. See also Wijnoogst.

Jablonec (Czec). A brewery based in northern Czec. Produces full-bodied, lager beers.

Jaboulet Aîné et Fils (Fr). A family wine-merchant of the Rhône based at Tain. Also producers of A.C. Hermitage.

Jaboulet-Vercherre (Fr). A Burgundy négociant-éleveur based at 5, Rue Colbert, 21200 Beaune.

Jac-Jan Vineyard (USA). A winery based in Ohio. Produces wines from French hybrid wines.

Jack (Eng). A style of leather-covered bottles used for beers and cider in the sixteenth century.

Jack Daniel (USA). A sour mash whiskey. The oldest registered distillery in the USA based in Lynchburg, Tennessee. 45% alc. by vol.

Jackie O's Rose (Cktl). ⅓ gill Bacardi, juice ½ lime, dash Triple Sec. Shake over ice, strain into a cocktail glass.

Jack-in-the-Box (Cktl). ½ measure pineapple juice, ½ measure Applejack brandy, dash Angostura. Shake over ice, strain into a cocktail glass.

Jack London Vineyard (USA). See London Vineyard.

Jack Pot Bitter (Eng). A bottled Best Bitter 1036 O.G. brewed by the Hook Norton Brewery, Oxfordshire.

Jack Rabbit Cocktail (Cktl). ⅓ gill Calvados, ⅙ gill maple syrup, ⅙ gill orange juice, ⅙ gill lemon juice. Shake over ice, strain into a cocktail glass.

Jack Rose (Cktl).(1). Juice of ½ large lime, 1 teaspoon Grenadine, 1½ ozs. Applejack or Calvados. Shake over ice, strain into a cocktail glass.

Jack Rose (Cktl).(2). ⅓ gill Calvados, ⅙ gill lemon juice, 6 dashes Grenadine. Shake over ice, strain into a cocktail glass, serve with a dash-lemon peel juice.

Jacksons of Piccadilly (Eng). A noted tea producer of a wide range of teas. Address = 1, West Smithfield, London.

Jacksonville Winery (USA). A winery based in south-western Oregon. Produces wines from the Valley View Vineyard.

Jack's Special (Cktl).(Non-alc). 7 fl.ozs. pineapple juice, 1 dash lemon juice, 12 strawberries. Blend well together with 1 scoop of crushed ice in a blender. Pour into a large goblet. Dress with a sliced strawberry.

Jack Zeller (Cktl). ½ measure Dubonnet, ½ measure Old Tom Gin. Stir over ice, strain into a cocktail glass.

Jacobain (Fr). An alternative name for the Malbec grape.

Jacob Brewery (USA). A brewery based in New Bedford.

Jacobert (Fr). A noted Eau-de-Vie producer based in Colmar, Alsace.

Jacobi 1880 (Ger). A Weinbrand produced in Stuttgart, Western Germany.

Jacob Lee Winery (USA). A small winery based in Bordentown, New Jersey. Produces wines from American vines.

Jacobs Best Bitter (Eng). A Bitter beer 1038 O.G. brewed by the Jacobs Brewery in Nailsea, near Bristol, Avon.

Jacobs Brewery (Eng). Opened in 1980 at Nailsea near Bristol, Avon. Taken over by Halls Brewery in 1984. Produces Jacobs Best Bitter.

Jacob's Creek (Austr). A brand-name used by the Orlando Winery for a range of their wines.

Jacobsdal Co-operative (S.Afr). A winery based near Kimberley. Address = Jacobsdal Wynkelder, Box 94, Jacobsdal 8710. Produces varietal wines.

Jacobsdal Estate (S.Afr). A wine estate based in Stellenbosch. Address = Kuils River 7580. Produces varietal wines.

Jacobsdal Wynkelder (S.Afr). See Jacobsdal Co-operative.

Jacquart (Fr). Champagne co-operative. Address = 5 Rue Gosset, BP 467, 51066 Reims. Wines made from members' grapes. Produces – Vintage and non-vintage wines. Vintages – 1970, 1973, 1975, 1976, 1978, 1979, 1980, 1981, 1982, 1983. (abbr) = C.R.V.C. Has 680 members.

Jacquart André (Fr). Champagne pro-

J

ducer. Address = 5 Avenue de la République, Mesnil sur Oger, 51190 Avize. Récoltant-manipulant. Member of C.V.C. Produces – Vintage and non-vintage wines. Vintages – 1973, 1975, 1976, 1979, 1982, 1983.

Jacqueline (Fr). A rosé, non-vintage Champagne produced by De Lahaye in Épernay.

Jacquère (Fr). A white grape variety grown in the Savoie region.

Jacquère Chardonnay (Fr). A white grape variety grown in the Savoie region.

Jacques Bonet Brandy (USA). The brand-name of a Brandy produced by the United Vintners, Lodi, California.

Jacques Gaillard (Bra). A white grape variety.

Jacquesson et Fils (Fr). Champagne producer. Address = 68 Rue du Colonel Fablien, 51200 Épernay. 22 ha. Produces – Vintage and non-vintage wines. Vintages – 1970, 1971, 1973, 1975, 1976, 1979, 1982, 1983. De Luxe vintage cuvée is Signature.

Jacquet (Mad). An alternative spelling of Jacquez.

Jacquez (Mad). A white grape variety used in the making of Madeira. Now banned from use. Also used as grafting stock in USA. Is also spelt Jacquet.

Jaculillo (It). A red grape variety grown in Gragnano, Campania. Produces light red wines of the same name.

Jade Cocktail (Cktl). ⅕ gill Jamaican rum, 2 dashes green Crème de Menthe, 2 dashes Cointreau, juice ¼ lime, 2 dashes Gomme syrup. Shake over ice, strain into a cocktail glass. Dress with a slice of lime.

Jade Mountain (USA). A winery based in Cloverdale, Sonoma County, California. 13 ha. Grape varieties – Cabernet sauvignon and Johannisberg riesling. Produces varietal wines.

Jadot [Louis] (Fr). A noted Burgundy négociant-éleveur. Address = 5, Rue Samuel Legay, 21200 Beaune. Owns approximately 22 ha. of vineyards in the Côte d'Or, Burgundy all of which is of Grand Cru status.

Jaegermeister (Ger). A dark red liqueur with digestive and tonic characteristics. See also Jägermeister. Produced by Mast.

Jaén (Sp). A white grape variety grown in Rioja. Also known as the Cagazal, Calagraño, Jairia and the Navés. No relation to the Jaén varieties grown in the rest of Spain.

Jaén Blanco (Sp). A white grape variety once used to produce Málaga.

Jaén Doradillo (Sp). A white grape variety once used to produce Málaga.

Jaén Tinto (Sp). A red grape variety once used to produce Málaga.

Jaffelin Frères (Fr). A négociant-éleveur. Address = Caves du Chapitre, 2 Rue de Japitre, Beaune, Côte de Beaune, Burgundy.

Jagd Kümmel (Ger). A caraway-flavoured liqueur sold in stone jars. 50% alc. by vol.

Jager Lager (Eng). A bottled and canned Lager 1032 O.G. brewed by the Davenports Brewery, Birmingham.

Jägermeister (Ger). A dark-red herb liqueur. See Jaegermeister.

Jaggery (Ind). Palm juice from the Palmyra tree which is left to evaporate, leaving a sugary brown syrup. See Jaggery Coffee.

Jaggery Coffee (Ind). Made from unrefined palm sugar (Jaggery) boiled with coffee and water. Is drunk black or with milk. The only food before morning prayers.

Jagst [River] (Ger). A tributary of the river Neckar in Württemberg. Soil of shell limestone.

Jahrgang (Ger). Vintage, year.

Jahrgangsjuwel (It). Lit – 'Jewel of the year'. A wine made in the Trentino-Alto Adige from old vines (over 70 years) of the Vernatsch grape.

Jailleu (Fr). A vineyard based in the Grésivaudan Valley, Vienne Département. Produces red wines.

Jaina (Sp). A white grape variety grown in the Rioja. Also known as the Cagazal, Calagraño, Jaén and Navés.

Jalon (Fr). The old sixteenth century word for gallon. See also Galon.

Jamaica Babie (Cktl). 1 measure dark Rum, ½ measure Tia Maria, ½ measure Crème de Noyau, ½ measure orange juice. Shake over ice, strain into a cocktail glass. Add a dash of Grenadine and a little grated nutmeg.

Jamaica Coffee (Eng). Black coffee topped with whipped cream and grated nutmeg. See also Jamaican Coffee.

Jamaica Collins (Cktl). Add to a highball glass containing a large piece of ice – dash Angostura, juice ¾ lemon or lime, teaspoon powdered sugar, 1 measure Jamaican rum. Top with soda water, stir and serve with straws.

Jamaica Hop (Cktl). ⅓ measure Tia Maria, ⅓ measure Crème de Cacao (white), ⅓ measure cream. Shake over ice, strain into a cocktail glass.

Jamaica Jake (Cktl). ½ measure dark Rum, ½ measure Tia Maria, ½ measure Apricot brandy, ½ measure pineapple juice. Shake over ice, strain into a cocktail glass. Add a dash of Grenadine and a little grated nutmeg.

Jamaica Joe (Cktl). ⅓ measure Tia Maria, ⅓ measure Advocaat, ⅓ measure Jamaican rum, dash Grenadine. Shake together over ice except Grenadine. Strain into a cocktail glass, add Grenadine and sprinkle with grated nutmeg.

Jamaica Mountain Cooler (Cktl). ½ pint cold black coffee, 2 tots dark Rum, 1 tot lime cordial, sugar to taste, orange soda, 1 banana, 1 orange. Chill all liquid ingredients, mix well over ice, strain into a highball glass, decorate with sliced banana and an orange slice.

Jamaican Coffee (W.Ind). Considered to be some of the worlds' finest coffee. The best being Blue Mountain from the parishes of St. Andrew, St. Thomas and Portland. Other noted coffees are High Mountain Supreme and Prime Jamaica Washed. Produce a full-flavoured, good acidity, smooth and full-bodied coffee with a nutty flavour. See also Red Mountain and High Mountain.

Jamaican Coffee (Liq.Coffee). Produced with a measure of dark Rum.

Jamaican Cow (Cktl). 1 egg, 7 fl.ozs. cold milk, ⅕ gill Tia Maria. Shake well over ice, strain into an ice-filled highball glass. Serve with straws.

Jamaican Glow (Cktl). ⅕ gill Gin, ⅛ gill red Bordeaux, ⅛ gill orange juice, 3 dashes Jamaican rum. Shake over ice, strain into a cocktail glass.

Jamaican Granito (Cktl). 1 measure Brandy, ½ measure Cointreau, ½ scoop orange water ice, ½ scoop lemon water ice. Blend together, pour into a highball glass. Top with soda and grated nutmeg.

Jamaican Wonder Highball (Cktl). 1 oz. Lemon Hart Rum, 1 oz. Tia Maria, 1 oz. lime juice, dash bitters. Place some ice in a highball glass with a twist and slice of lemon. Add ingredients, stir, top up with ginger ale.

Jamaica Old Fashioned (Cktl). Place 1 lump sugar (which has 3 drops of Angostura soaked in) into an old-fashioned glass. Crush, add a lump of ice, a thick slice of orange and add 1½ measures of Jamaica rum.

Jamaica Orange Cocktail (Cktl). ½ measure Jamaica rum, ¼ measure dry Vermouth, ¼ measure orange juice. Shake well with ice, strain into a cocktail glass.

Jamaica Punch (Punch). 2½ fl.ozs. Jamaican rum, 2½ fl.ozs. water, ½ pint sweet Cider, juice of 2 lemons, 1 finely-chopped and peeled apple, 2½ ozs. dried fruit. Heat fruit and water for 15 minutes. Add remaining ingredients and reheat. Stir, strain and serve.

Jamaica Rum (W.Ind). A rich, dark, full-bodied, pungent Rum made from molasses, Pot-stilled and cask matured.

Jamaica Rum Cocktail (Cktl). ⅚ measure Jamaica rum, ⅙ measure Gomme syrup, dash Angostura. Stir over ice, strain into a cocktail glass.

Jamaica Rum Verschnitt (Ger). A Verschnitt produced from Jamaican rum and spirit by the Schönauer Co.

James (USA). A wild black grape variety, known as Muscadines of the Vitis Rotundifolia.

James Beam Distilling Co (USA). Address = Clermont-Beam, Kentucky. Distillers of Jim Beam Sour Mash Kentucky Bourbon Whiskey.

James Bond Cocktail (Cktl). Into a Champagne flute place a cube of sugar soaked with Angostura bitters. Add a spoon of crushed ice, ⅕ gill Vodka and top with iced Champagne and a spiral of lemon peel.

James E Pepper (USA). The brand-name of a well-known Bourbon whiskey from Kentucky.

James Foxe (Can). The brand-name for a Canadian whisky produced by Seagram.

James Haselgrove (Austr). A noted winery based in Coonawarra, South Australia.

Jameson (Ire). A Whiskey distiller who produces a blend of Pot-still whiskies matured in American oak.

Jameson Crested Ten (Ire). A blend of older Pot-still whiskies which are matured in sherry casks. Produced by Jameson.

Jameson Fifteen (Ire). A blend of Pot-stilled whiskies. Produced by Jameson.

Jameson 1780 (Ire). A 12 year old single Malt Irish whiskey produced by John Jameson. 40% alc. by vol.

Jameson's Irish Velvet (Ire). A liqueur produced from Jameson's Irish whiskey, coffee and sugar. Designed as a base for Irish coffee (boiling water and cream only needed). 20% alc. by vol.

James Paine (Eng). See Paine.

Jamestown Julep (Cktl). A cocktail made with very dry Rum over ice in an old-fashioned glass.

Jammy (Eng). A term used to describe a fat, rich, fruity red wine.

Jampal (Port). A white grape variety grown in the Alenquer region.

J and B Rare (Scot). A blended Scotch whisky produced by Justerini and Brooks Ltd. (part of International Distillers and Vintners group). 40% alc. by vol.

Jane Brook Estate (Austr). Vineyard. Address = Lot 19, Toodyay Road, Middle Swan, Western Australia, 6056.

J

15 ha. Grape varieties – Cabernet franc, Cabernet sauvignon, Chardonnay, Grenache, Muscadelle, Pedro ximénez, Sauvignon blanc, Sémillon and Shiraz.

Janneau Fils et Cie (Fr). Armagnac producer. Address = 50, Avenue d'Aquitaine, 32100 Condom, Ténarèze.

Janneau Tradition (Fr). A 4–5 year old Armagnac produced by Grand Armagnac Janneau.

Janner's Bitter (Eng). A cask conditioned Bitter 1038 O.G. brewed by the Mill Brewery in Newton Abbot, Devon.

Jansen (Hol). A liqueur producer based in Schiedam.

Janvry (Fr). A Cru Champagne village in the Canton de Ville-en-Tardenois. District = Reims.

Japan (Jap). A country that produces many styles of alcoholic beverages – Saké, Lager-style beers and Spirits are the main types with a small wine industry. Wine regions of Nagano, Okayama, Osaka, Yamagata and Yamanashi are the main producers of wines for the domestic market (made from American and European vines). See Suntory.

Japanese Beetles (USA). A vine pest that attacks American vine stock especially in the southern States.

Japanese Cocktail (Cktl). An alternative name for Mikado Cocktail.

Japanese Fizz (Cktl). ⅕ gill Whisky, juice ½ lemon, ⅛ gill Port wine, 1 teaspoon powdered sugar, 1 egg white. Shake over ice, strain into an ice-filled highball glass. Top with soda and a cube of pineapple.

Japanese Green Tea Liqueur (Jap). A liqueur based on tea and grape brandy. Fairly rare outside Japan.

Japanese Rice Wine (Jap). Saké.

Japanese Whiskey (Jap). Pot distilled and blended with Scottish malt whisky. See Suntory.

Jar (Eng) (slang). Used in the north of England for a glass of beer.

Jarana (Cktl). 2 ozs. Tequila, 2 ozs. powdered sugar. Mix together and place in a highball with ice, top with pineapple juice.

Jarandilla (Sp). A wine-producing area in the Extremadura.

Jardinage (Fr). A method of allowing vines to live to their maximum age and then replacing them individually.

Jardin de la France (Fr). A Vins de Pays area in the Cher Département in central France. Regions of Cher, Deux-Sèvres, Haute Vienne, Indre, Indre-et-Loire, Loire-Atlantique, Loiret, Loire-et-Cher, Maine-et-Loire, Vendée and Vienne.

Jardins (Les) (Fr). A vineyard in the A.C.

commune of Montagny, Côte Chalonnaise, Burgundy.

Jarnac (Fr). A town within the Charente Département where Cognac is made.

Jarnac-Champagne (Fr). A commune in the Charente-Maritime Département whose grapes are used in the production of Cognac brandy.

Jarolières (Les) (Fr). A Premier Cru vineyard in the A.C. commune of Pommard, Côte de Beaune, Burgundy. 3.2 ha. Also spelt Les Garollières and Les Jarollières.

Jarollières (Les) (Fr). See Jarolières (Les).

Jarosov (Czec). An old established Brewery based in central-southern Czec.

Jarra (Sp). A jar of varying sizes. 11½-12½ litres used in Sherry blending.

Jarro (Sp). Water jug, pitcher.

Jarrons (Les) (Fr). A Premier Cru vineyard in the A.C. commune of Savigny-lès-Beaune, Côte de Beaune, Burgundy.

Jarry (Daniel) (Fr). A propriétaire-récoltant based in Vouvray, Touraine, Loire. Produces fine Vouvray wines. Address = La Vallée Coquette 37210 Vouvray.

Jarzębiak (Pol). A dry Vodka flavoured with Rowan berries picked in the Autumn. 40% alc. by vol. See Polmos.

Jasi (Rum). A wine-producing area. Noted for its' white wines.

Jasmine Tea (China). A blend of teas from the Kwangtung Province. A large leaf, exotic tea, scented with Jasmine flowers.

Jasne (Pol). A low-alcohol Lager beer with a good bitter flavour.

Jasnières (Fr). An A.C. medium-dry, white wine from the Touraine district, Sarthe Département in the Loire. Minimum alc. by vol. 10%.

Jasper Long Vineyards (USA). See Long Vineyards.

Jàszberényi Rizling (Hun). A light, medium-dry, white wine produced in the Jàszberény region.

Jau (Fr). A commune in the Bas Médoc, north-western Bordeaux.

Jaune (Fr). A malady of white wines when they turn yellow. Treated either with sulphuric acid or fining agents. Not to be confused with Vin Jaune.

Java Coffee (E.Ind). An Indonesian coffee. Produces a mellow but full aroma. Regions – Batavia, Buitenzorg, Cheribon and Preanger.

Java Rum (E.Ind). A medium dark Rum which is popular in Scandinavia.

Javrezac (Fr). A commune in the Borderies area of the Charente-Maritime Département, Cognac.

Jawhara (Iraq). A Lager beer 12.5° Balling produced by the state-owned brewery based in Baghdad.

Jax (USA). A malt Beer brewed by the Pearl

Brewery in San Antonio, Texas.

J.B.A. (Eng). A Bitter beer originally brewed in Wigan, Lancashire but now brewed by the Burtonwood Brewery in Staffordshire.

J. Bavet Fine Brandy (USA). The brand-name of a Brandy produced by the Schenley Distillers, California.

J.C. le Roux (S.Afr). A dry, sparkling wine made from the Sauvignon blanc grape by Die Bergkelder.

J.D. Dry Hop (Eng). A beer brewed by the Cornish Brewery Co. Devon.

Jean (Sp). A white grape variety grown in the Central Spanish regions

Jean Lafitte (Cktl). ½ measure dry Gin, ¼ measure Cointreau, ¼ measure Pernod, 1 egg yolk, 2 dashes Gomme syrup. Shake over ice, strain into a cocktail glass.

Jeannot (Fr). A noted brand of Pastis.

Jean Perico (Sp). A dry sparkling wine made by the cava (méthode champenoise) method by Gonzalez Byass (Gonzalez y Dubosc) in Penedés.

Jean Robert (USA). The brand-name of a Brandy produced by the Schenley Distillers at the Number One Distilling Co., California.

Jean Voisin (Fr). The second wine of Château Jean Voisin, Grand Cru A.C. Saint-Émilion, Saint-Émilion, eastern Bordeaux.

Jechtingen (Ger). Village. (Anb) = Baden. (Ber) = Kaiserstuhl-Tuniberg. (Gro) = Vulkanfelsen. (Vins) = Eichert, Enselberg, Gestühl, Hochberg, Steingrube.

Jefferson and Wine (USA). The Vinifera Wine Growers Association, The Plains, Virginia. Formed 1976.

Jehan de Massol (Fr). A vineyard in part of Santenots, A.C. Volnay, Côte de Beaune, Burgundy. Owned by the Hospices de Beaune.

Jehan Humblot (Fr). A cuvée in the vineyard of Poruzots, A.C. Meursault, Côte de Beaune, Burgundy. Owned by the Hospices de Beaune.

Jekel Vineyard (USA). A winery based in Salinas Valley, Monterey, California. 58 ha. Grape varieties – Cabernet sauvignon, Chardonnay, Gamay and Johannisberg riesling. Produces varietal wines.

Jelly Bag (Eng). A fine cloth bag used for separating the fruit pulp from the juice in home wine-making.

Jenever (Hol). Gin. Also spelt Genever.

Jenks Cocktail (Cktl). ½ measure dry Gin, ½ measure dry Vermouth, dash Bénédictine. Shake over ice, strain into a cocktail glass.

Jenlain (Fr). A Bière de Garde brewed in

Jenlain near Valenciennes in northern France. Top fermented and unpasteurised. 6.5% alc. by vol.

Jenlain Bière de Luxe (Fr). A beer brewed by the Duyck Brasserie. Is presented in a wire-top bottle. Deep bronze in colour, it is matured for 1 month, filtered and unpasteurised.

Jennelotte (La) (Fr). A Premier Cru vineyard in the commune of Blagny, A.C. Meursault, Côte de Beaune, Burgundy. 4.5 ha.

Jennings Brewery (Eng). Based in Cockermouth, Cumbria. Noted for its' sharp cask conditioned Bitter and Castle Keg Mild 1033 O.G.

Jerepigo (S.Afr). A wine fortified with Brandy (grape spirit).

Jerevan (USSR). A wine-producing region in Armenia.

Jerez (Sp). See Jerez de la Frontera.

Jerezaños (Sp). The name given to a Coñac (Spanish brandy). Also known as Jerinacs.

Jerezaños (Sp). A person who lives in Jerez, Andalusia.

Jerez Cocktail (Cktl). 2 fl.ozs. dry Sherry, dash Orange bitters, dash Peach bitters. Stir well together over ice, strain into a cocktail glass.

Jerez Cortado Hidalgo (Sp). A brand of Sherry produced by Vinícola Hildalgo in Sanlúcar de Barrameda.

Jerez de la Frontera (Sp). A town in Andalusia which gives its' name to sherry. The main Sherry port.

Jerez Lustau (Sp). The brand-name of a range of Sherries produced by Lustau in Jerez.

Jerez-Quina (Sp). A quinine-based white wine or Sherry blended with the bitter skins from Seville oranges and macerated Cinchona bark.

Jerez Supérieur (Sp). Consists of the districts Chiclana, Chipiona, Labrija, Puerto de Santa Maria, Puerto Real, Sanlúcar de Barrameda, Trebujena and town of Jerez de la Frontera.

Jerez-Xérès-Sherry y Manzanilla Sanlúcar de Barrameda (Sp). Official D.O. wines produced in Jerez de la Frontera.

Jeriñac (Sp). The brand-name for the Brandies produced in Jerez de la Frontera, Andalusia. Also spelt Cherinac, Xereñac. See also Jerezanos and Coñac.

Jeripegos (S.Afr). The name given to the fortified grape juice at about 32° proof (17% alc. by vol). Used for dessert wines.

Jeroboam (Fr). A large bottle. Holds 4 standard bottles. Used mainly in Champagne.

Jeroboam (USA). A bottle holding 101.44 US fl.ozs. (3 litres).

J

Jeropiga (Port). Boiled down grape juice used to sweeten wines. See Geropiga.

Jerry's Joy (Cktl). ⅓ measure Cointreau, ⅓ measure Vodka, ⅓ measure Lillet, dash Orange bitters, dash egg white. Shake over ice, strain into a cocktail glass. Add a cherry.

Jersey (Ch.Isles). Largest of the Channel Islands. Has one commercial vineyard. See Clos de la Mare and Les Perquages.

Jersey Cocktail (Cktl). ½ pint dry still Cider, 1 teaspoon sugar, 3 dashes Angostura. Shake over ice, strain into a cocktail glass. Decorate with a strip of lemon peel.

Jersey Cocktail (Cktl). (Non-alc). 5 fl.ozs. non-alcoholic Cider, 2 dashes Angostura, 2 dashes Gomme syrup. Stir well over ice, strain into a wine glass, add a cherry and squeeze of lemon juice on top.

Jersey Cream Liqueur (Ch.Isles). Also known as Tipple. A blend of Jersey cream, French brandy with a dash of Amaretto. See also Guernsey Cream Liqueur.

Jersey Lightning (USA). Another name for Apple Jack Brandy.

Jersey Lightning Cocktail (Cktl). ¾ measure Applejack brandy, ¼ measure sweet Vermouth, juice of a small lime. Shake over ice, strain into a cocktail glass.

Jersey Lily (Pousse Café). Equal parts of yellow Chartreuse and old Cognac in that order.

Jerte (Sp). A wine-producing area in Cáceres, south-western Spain.

Jerusalem (Yug). A Lutomer vineyard noted for its' aromatic white wines.

Jerusalem Environs (Isr). A new wine-producing region which produces both red and white wines.

Jerzynowka (Pol). A liqueur made from the maceration of blackberries. 30% alc. by vol. Also spelt Jerzyowka. Known in Germany as Kroatzbeerlikoer.

Jesses Vineyard A vineyard based at Snow Hill, Dinton, near Salisbury, Wiltshire. Was first planted 1977. 0.25 ha. Grape varieties – Madeleine angevine, Müller-Thurgau and Triumphe d'Alsace.

Jesuitenberg (Ger). Vineyard. (Anb) = Franken. (Ber) = Mainviereck. (Gro) = Not yet assigned. (Vil) = Rück.

Jesuitenberg (Ger). Vineyard. (Anb) = Mosel-Saar-Ruwer. (Ber) = Saar-Ruwer. (Gro) = Scharzberg. (Vil) = Wawern.

Jesuitengarten (Ger). Vineyard. (Anb) = Ahr. (Ber) = Walporzheim/Ahrtal. (Gro) = Klosterberg. (Vil) = Marienthal.

Jesuitengarten (Ger). Vineyard. (Anb) = Mosel-Saar-Ruwer. (Ber) = Saar-Ruwer. (Gro) = Römerlay. (Vil) = Waldrach.

Jesuitengarten (Ger). Vineyard. (Anb) = Mosel-Saar-Ruwer. (Ber) = Saar-Ruwer. (Gro) = Scharzberg. (Vil) = Pellingen.

Jesuitengarten (Ger). Vineyard. (Anb) = Rheingau. (Ber) = Johannisberg. (Gro) = Honigberg. (Vil) = Winkel.

Jesuitengarten (Ger). Vineyard. (Anb) = Rheinpfalz. (Ber) = Mittelhaardt-Deutsche Weinstrasse. (Gro) = Mariengarten. (Vil) = Forst.

Jesuitengarten (Ger). Vineyard. (Anb) = Rheinpfalz. (Ber) = Mittelhaardt-Deutsche Weinstrasse. (Gro) = Meerspinne. (Vil) = Königsbach.

Jesuitenhofgarten (Ger). Vineyard. (Anb) = Rheinpfalz. (Ber) = Mittelhaardt-Deutsche Weinstrasse. (Gro) = Schwarzerde. (Vil) = Dirmstein.

Jesuitenschloss (Ger). Vineyard. (Anb) = Baden. (Ber) = Markgräflerland. (Gro) = Lorettoberg. (Vil) = Freiburg.

Jesuitenschloss (Ger). Vineyard. (Anb) = Baden. (Ber) = Markgräflerland. (Gro) = Lorettoberg. (Vil) = Merzhausen.

Jesuitenwingert (Ger). Vineyard. (Anb) = Mosel-Saar-Ruwer. (Ber) = Saar-Ruwer. (Gro) = Römerlay. (Vil) = Trier.

Jever Pilsener (Ger). A very bitter Lager beer brewed by a subsidiary brewery (Oldenburg) of Bavaria – St. Pauli Brauerei in Hamburg. This brewery is based in Friesland. Is imported into U.K. by the Ruddles Brewery. 1046 O.G.

Jevíčko Brewery (Czec). A brewery based in central Czec. Noted for its' Pilsener-style beers.

Jewel Cocktail (Cktl). ⅓ measure dry Gin, ⅓ measure green Chartreuse, ⅓ measure Italian vermouth, dash Orange bitters. Shake over ice, strain into a cocktail glass. Top with a cherry.

Jeyplak (Cktl). ⅔ measure dry Gin, ⅓ measure Italian vermouth, 2 dashes Pernod. Stir over ice, strain into a cocktail glass. Top with a cherry.

Ježek (Czec). Lit – 'Hedgehog'. A noted Lager beer from the Jihlava Brewery.

JFJ Bronco Winery (USA). A large winery based near Modesto, Stanislaus, California. Wines sold under many labels (mainly ordinary table wines), best known are CC and JFJ.

Jiangsu (China). A noted wine-producing province in northern China.

Jicara (Sp). A cup for chocolate.

Jidvei (Rum). An important wine-producing area. Part of the Tirnave Vineyard.

Jigger (USA). A spirit measure mainly

used for cocktails. Size 1½ ozs. (42.6 ccs). Also a 1 oz. and 2 ozs. version.

Jihlava Brewery (Czec). A brewery based in Central Czec. Noted for its Jezek Lager beer.

Jim Beam (USA). The brand-name of a Sour Mash Kentucky Bourbon whiskey distilled by the James Beam Distilling Co., Clermont-Beam, Kentucky. 40% alc. by vol.

Jimmy Woodser (Austr) (slang). A term for a man who drinks by himself.

Jin (Wales). Gin.

Jinro (E.Asia). Noted producers of Gingseng Ju in Seoul, South Korea.

Jirkov Brewery (Czec). An old established brewery based at Jirkov in north-west Czec.

Jiskra (Czec). Lit – 'The Spark'. A full-flavoured Lager beer brewed by the Hradec Kràlové Brewery in eastern Bohemia.

Jiu (China). The general description of wine. Includes both distilled and fermented beverages (alcoholic beverages).

J.J. and S. Liqueur (Ire). An Irish whiskey and John Jameson blend. 50% alc. by vol. Distilled and bottled by Jameson.

J.J. Murphy Cocktail (Cktl). ⅛ gill Gin, ⅛ gill Italian vermouth, ⅛ gill French vermouth, dash Bénédictine, dash lemon peel juice. Stir over ice, strain into a cocktail glass, serve with a cherry.

J.K. (Eng) (abbr). A sweet bottled Stout 1034 O.G. brewed by the King and Barnes Brewery in Sussex. Stands for James King the Brewery founder. Uses German bottom-fermented yeasts.

J. Lohr (USA). The label used by Turgeon and Lohr for their range of table wines.

J.N.V. (Port) (abbr). Junta Nacional do Vinho.

João de Santarém (Port). A red grape variety used in Ribatejo and Bairrada.

Jo'burg (S.Afr). The brand-name of an apéritif similar in style to vermouth.

Jockey Club (Cktl). 1 measure dry Gin, juice ¼ lemon, 2 dashes (white) Crème de Menthe, dash Angostura. Shake over ice, strain into a cocktail glass.

Jockey Club Cocktail (Cktl). ⅕ gill Gin, ⅛ gill (white) Crème de Noyau, juice ½ lemon, 2 dashes Orange bitters, 2 dashes Angostura. Shake over ice, strain into a cocktail glass.

Jocose Julep (Cktl). ⅚ measure Bourbon whiskey, ⅙ measure (green) Crème de Menthe, juice ¼ lime, 3 dashes Gomme syrup, 6 mint leaves. Blend together with a scoop of crushed ice. Pour into a highball glass. Top with soda and a sprig of mint.

Jogger (The) (Ckl). 2 parts Johnny Walker Red Label, 1 part Cointreau, 1 part Amaretto, 6 parts lemonade. Stir together, strain into an ice-filled highball. Decorate with a slice of orange and cucumber peel.

Johannesberg (Ger). Vineyard. (Anb) = Nahe. (Ber) = Schloss Böckelheim. (Gro) = Paradiesgarten. (Vil) = Sobernheim-Steinhardt.

Johannesberg (Ger). Vineyard. (Anb) = Nahe. (Ber) = Schloss Böckelheim. (Gro) = Paradiesgarten. (Vil) = Waldböckelheim.

Johannesberg (Ger). Vineyard. (Anb) = Rheinhessen. (Ber) = Bingen. (Gro) = Abtey. (Vil) = Gau-Augesheim.

Johann Graue (S.Afr). A wine estate based in Paarl.

Johannis (Ger). A still mineral water of the Johannis spring in the Ahrweiler/Rhineland.

Johannisbeerlikoer (Ger). A blackcurrant liqueur.

Johannisberg (Ger). Bereich. (Anb) = Rheingau. (Gros) = Burgweg, Daubhaus, Deutelsberg, Erntebringer, Gottesthal, Heiligenstock, Honigberg, Mehrhölzchen, Landkreis Melsungen, Steil, Steinmächer.

Johannisberg (Ger). Village. (Anb) = Rheingau. (Ber) = Johannisberg. (Gro) = Erntebringer. (Vins) = Goldatzel, Hansenberg, Hölle, Mittelhölle.

Johannisberg (Ger). Vineyard. (Anb) = Franken. (Ber) = Maindreieck. (Gro) = Ravensburg. (Vil) = Thüngersheim.

Johannisberg (Ger). Vineyard. (Anb) = Franken. (Ber) = Mainviereck. (Gro) = Not yet assigned. (Vil) = Rück.

Johannisberg (Ger). Vineyard. (Anb) = Mosel-Saar-Ruwer. (Ber) = Bernkastel. (Gro) = Schwarzlay. (Vil) = Dreis.

Johannisberg (Ger). Vineyard. (Anb) = Mosel-Saar-Ruwer. (Ber) = Saar-Ruwer. (Gro) = Römerlay. (Vil) = Franzenheim.

Johannisberg (Ger). Vineyard. (Anb) = Mosel-Saar-Ruwer. (Ber) = Saar-Ruwer. (Gro) = Römerlay. (Vil) = Mertesdorf.

Johannisberg (Ger). Vineyard. (Anb) = Nahe. (Ber) = Kreuznach. (Gro) = Pfarrgarten. (Vil) = Wallhausen.

Johannisberg (Ger). Vineyard. (Anb) = Nahe. (Ber) = Kreuznach. (Gro) = Schlosskapelle. (Vil) = Burg Layen.

Johannisberg (Ger). Vineyard. (Anb) = Nahe. (Ber) = Kreuznach. (Gro) = Schlosskapelle. (Vil) = Rümmelsheim.

Johannisberg (Ger). Vineyard. (Anb) = Rheinhessen. (Ber) = Bingen. (Gro) = Sankt Rochuskapelle. (Vil) = Aspisheim.

Johannisberg (Ger). Vineyard. (Anb) = Rheinhessen. (Ber) = Bingen. (Gro) = Sankt Rochuskapelle. (Vil) = Zotzenheim.

J

Johannisberg (Ger). Vineyard. (Anb) = Rheinhessen. (Ber) = Nierstein. (Gro) = Sankt Alban. (Vil) = Mainz.

Johannisberg (Switz). A name for the Sylvaner grape.

Johannisberg (Switz). A white wine made from the Johannisberg grape (Sylvaner). Is similar in style to a Rhine wine.

Johannisberger (Ger). A dry white wine from the Johannisberg vineyards in the Rheingau.

Johannisberg Feuergold (Switz). A white wine produced from the Sylvaner grape by Les Fils Maye in Riddes, Valais.

Johannisberg Riesling (USA). A name for the true Riesling grape. Named after the great Schloss Johannisberg in Germany.

Johannisbrünnchen (Ger). Vineyard. (Anb) = Mosel-Saar-Ruwer. (Ber) = Bernkastel. (Gro) = Kurfürstlay. (Vil) = Bernkastel-Kues.

Johanniskirchel (Ger). Vineyard. (Anb) = Rheinpfalz. (Ber) = Mittelhaardt-Deutsche Weinstrasse. (Gro) = Rebstöckel. (Vil) = Diedesfeld.

Johanniswein (Ger). Lit – 'St.John's Wine'. Was drunk by St.John at the Last Supper – said to be poisoned but he suffered no affects. Is often drunk as a Loving Cup as considered to bring peace and to benefit health.

Johannitergarten (Ger). Vineyard. (Anb) = Rheinpfalz. (Ber) = Mittelhaardt-Deutsche Weinstrasse. (Gro) = Meerspinne. (Vil) = Mussbach.

John Arkell Bitter (Eng). See Arkell Bitter 1033 O.G.

John Baker's Private Blend (Austr). A fine red wine from the John Baker vineyards in Coolawin, South Australia. Grape varieties used – Cabernet 20%, Malbec 60% and Shiraz 20%.

John Barleycorn (Eng). An old eighteenth and nineteenth century nickname for beer.

John Barleycorn Bitter (Eng). A Bitter beer brewed by the Pollards Brewery in Stockport.

John Barr (Scot). A blended Scotch Whisky produced by George Cowie and Sons Ltd., Mortlach, Dufftown.

John Baxter's Bitter (Eng). A Bitter beer 1030–1034 O.G. brewed by the Watney Mann Brewery.

John Begg's Bluecap (Scot). A blended Scotch whisky produced by John Begg Distillery. Part of DCL. 40% alc. by vol.

John Brown Ale (Eng). A bottled Brown ale 1031 O.G. brewed by the Hall and Woodhouse Brewery in Dorset.

John Brown Ale (Wales). A bottled Brown ale 1032 O.G. brewed by the Felinfoel Brewery in Llanelli, South Wales.

John Brown's Special (Scot). The brandname of a blended Scotch whisky. 40% alc. by vol.

John Bull Bitter (Eng). A keg Bitter beer 1036 O.G. brewed by the Ind Coope Brewery in Romford, Essex.

John Bull Export Bitter (Eng). An Export bitter 1053 O.G. brewed by the Ind Coope Brewery in Burton-on-Trent, Staffordshire.

John Christ Winery (USA). A winery based in Avon Lake, Ohio. Produces mainly varietal wines from the Concord grape.

John Collins (Cktl). 2 ozs. Hollands Gin, juice ½ lemon, 1 teaspoon sugar. Shake together with ice, strain into an ice-filled highball glass. Top with soda water and a slice of lemon.

John Courage Ale (Eng). A keg and bottled Pale ale 1042 O.G. brewed by Courage Breweries.

John Devenish Bitter (Eng). A cask conditioned Bitter 1032 O.G. brewed by the Cornish Brewery Co. in Dorchester, Dorset.

John Dockery's Winery (USA). A small winery based in Rockingham, North Carolina. Produces Scuppernong wines.

John Dowland's Greensleeves (Eng). A mint-flavoured Brandy and cream liqueur produced in London by John Dowland. 17% alc. by vol.

John Groves Bitter (Eng). A keg Bitter 1034 O.G. brewed by the Cornish Brewery Co. in Dorchester, Dorset.

John Jameson Special Irish Whiskey (Ire). A 12 year old pure pot-still whiskey aged at least 12 years in Sherry casks. Also a Very special old whiskey aged for a minimum of 15 years in Sherry casks.

John Marston (Eng). A keg version 1043 O.G. of the Marston Brewery's Pedigree Bitter.

Johnnie Cocktail (Cktl). ¾ measure Sloe gin, ¼ measure Curaçao, 2 dashes Anisette. Shake over ice, strain into a cocktail glass.

Johnnie Walker Black Label (Scot). A De Luxe blended Scotch Whisky produced by John Walker and Sons Ltd., Kilmarnock, Ayrshire. 43% alc. by vol.

Johnnie Walker 150 (Scot). A special blend of Scotch whiskies produced during Walker's 150th anniversary year (1970). Laid down to mature for 15 years. Packaged in an oak travelling case and presented with its' own crystal decanter.

Johnnie Walker Red Label (Scot). A blended Scotch Whisky produced by

John Walker and Sons Ltd, Kilmarnock, Ayrshire.

Johnnie Walker Swing (Scot). A De Luxe blended Scotch whisky produced by John Walker and Sons Ltd, Kilmarnock, Ayrshire. 43% alc. by vol.

John Peel Bitter (Eng). A cask conditioned Bitter 1040 O.G. brewed by the Matthew Brown Brewery in Blackburn, Lancashire. Also a keg version.

John Peel Lager (Eng). A Lager beer 1060 O.G. Exported to the USA.

John Simon (Cktl). ¼ measure dry Gin, ¼ measure Grand Marnier, ¼ measure Crème de Noyeau, ¼ measure orange squash, dash Angostura. Shake well over ice, strain into a cocktail glass.

Johnson County (USA). A wine-producing region in Arkansas. French and hybrid wines produced.

Johnson Estate Winery (USA). See Frederick Johnson Winery, Westfield.

Johnson's of Alexander Valley (USA). A small winery based in Alexander Valley, Sonoma County, California. 19 ha. Grape varieties – Cabernet sauvignon, Chenin blanc, Johannisberg riesling, Pinot blanc and Zinfandel. Produces varietal wines.

Johnson-Turnbull Vineyards (USA). A small winery based in Rutherford, Napa Valley, California. 8.5 ha. Grape variety – Cabernet sauvignon. Produces varietal wines.

John Thompson Pub (Eng). A home-brew public house in Ingleby, Derbyshire. Produces JTS XXXX bitter. See Lloyd's Country Bitter.

John Young London Lager (Eng). A Lager beer 1037 O.G. brewed by the Youngs Brewery in London. Named after the Chairman of the Brewery.

Joigny (Fr). An old town in the Yonne département, producing Chablis-style white wines.

Jolla (La) (Cktl). ¾ measure Grappa, ¼ measure Crème de Banane, juice ¼ lemon, 2 dashes orange juice. Shake over ice, strain into a cocktail glass.

Jolly Fenman (Eng). A home-brew public house based in Sidcup, Devon. Is owned by Clifton Inns. Noted for its cask conditioned Blackfen Bitter 1037 O.G. and Fenman Fortune 1047 O.G.

Jolly Roger Bitter (Eng). See Jolly Roger Brewery.

Jolly Roger Brewery (Eng). Based at the Old Anchor, Upton-on-Severn, Worcestershire. Is noted for its cask conditioned Severn Bore 1045 O.G. Old Anchor Ale 1060 O.G. Jolly Roger Bitter 1035 O.G. and Old Lowesmore Bitter.

Jonathan's Coffee House (Eng). A seventeenth century coffee house based in

Change Alley, London. Was a meeting place for stockbrokers. Led to the formation of the London Stock Exchange.

Jones Brewery (USA). A brewery based in Smithton, Pennsylvania. Is noted for its' Stoney's beer.

Jones's Ale (Eng). A cask conditioned Bitter brewed by the Penhros Court Brewery in Kingston, Herefordshire.

Jongeberg (Lux). A vineyard site in the village of Remerschen.

Jonge Genever (Hol). Young Dutch Gin.

Jonicole Vineyards (USA). A vineyard based in Umpqua River Valley, Oregon. Produce Vinifera wines at their Roseburg Winery.

Jonkheer Farmers' Winery (S.Afr). A winery based in the Breede River. Address = Box 13, Bonnivale 6730. Produces varietal wines.

Jonquery (Fr). A Cru Champagne village in the Canton de Châtillon-sur-Marne. District = Reims.

Jonzac (Fr). A commune in the Charente-Maritime Département. Grapes are used in the making of Cognac brandy.

Jordan (M.East). A country that now produces only a little wine. Most grapes grown are used for the table. Arrack is now the main alcoholic beverage.

Jordan Vineyard and Winery (USA). A large winery based in the Alexander Valley, Sonoma County, California. 125 ha. Grape varieties – Cabernet sauvignon, Chardonnay and Merlot. Produces varietal wines.

Jordan Winery (Can). A winery based at Twenty Mile Creek, Niagara. Has an adjoining wine museum.

Jørgen B. Lysholm Distillery (Nor). A large distillery based in Trondheim. Is under the control of the A/S Vinmonopolet.

Jorum (Eng). A drinking vessel of ½ pint capacity or more usually used for Punch. i.e. "A Jorum of punch".

Joseph Phelps Vineyard (USA). A leading Napa Valley vineyard in California. See Phelps Vineyards.

Josephsberg (Ger). Village. (Anb) = Baden. (Ber) = Ortenau. (Gro) = Fürsteneck. (Vil) = Durbach.

Josephshöfer (Ger). Vineyard. (Anb) = Mosel-Saar-Ruwer. (Ber) = Bernkastel. (Gro) = Münzlay. (Vil) = Graach.

Joseph Swan Vineyard (USA). See Swan Vineyards.

Joshua Privett (Eng). A cask conditioned Bitter 1043 O.G. brewed by the Pig and Whistle home-brew public house in London.

Jostr (Scan). The old Norse name for yeast.

Joubert (Claude et Michelle) (Fr). Beaujolais producer. Address = Landignié,

69430 Beaujeau. Produces Juliénas and Beaujolais-Villages wines.

Jouffreau et Fils (Fr). A négociant-éleveur based in A.C. Cahors.

Joules Bitter (Eng). A Bitter beer brewed by the Bass Worthington Brewery in Burton-on-Trent.

Joulouville Cocktail (Cktl). ⅕ gill Gin, ⅛ gill sweet Vermouth, juice ¼ lemon, 2 dashes Calvados, 2 dashes Grenadine. Shake over ice, strain into a cocktail glass.

Journal (Fr). A land measure used in Burgundy. ⅓ ha. (⅚ acre).

Journalist Cocktail (Cktl). ⅔ measure dry Gin, ⅙ gill Italian vermouth, ⅙ gill French vermouth, 2 dashes lemon juice, 2 dashes Triple Sec, dash Angostura. Shake over ice, strain into a cocktail glass.

Journaux (Fr). Plural of Journal.

Jouy-lès-Reims (Fr). A Cru Champagne village in the Canton de Ville-en-Tardenois. District = Reims.

Joven (Mex). A brand-name for a Tequila.

Joyau de France (Fr). A vintage De Luxe cuvée Champagne produced by Boizel from 35% Chardonnay and 65% Pinot noir grapes.

Joyous Garde Vineyard (Eng). Address = Crazies Hill, Wargrove, Berkshire. 1¼ ha. First planted 1977. Produces – Crazies white wine. Grapes – Bacchus 50%, Huxelrebe 1%, Müller-Thurgau 49%.

J. Tiefenbrunner-Schlosskellerei Turmhof (It). A noted winery based at Entiklar, Südtirol.

JTS XXX Special Bitter (Eng). A Bitter beer 1045 O.G. brewed by the John Thompsom Pub, Ingleby, Derbyshire.

Juan Ibañez (Sp). A red grape variety used for the production of heavy red wines.

Juanito Cocktail (Cktl). ⅓ measure Pernod, ⅓ measure lime juice, ⅓ measure soda water. Stir over ice, strain into a Champagne saucer, add a cherry.

Juan's Grasshopper Cocktail (Cktl). ⅕ measure Brandy, ⅕ measure white Curaçao, ⅕ measure Crème de Menthe, ⅖ measure cream. Shake with ice, strain into a cocktail glass. Sprinkle with cinnamon.

Jubiläumsrebe (Aus). A white grape variety cross between the black Portugieser and the black Blaufränkischer.

Jubilee (Sri.L). A top-fermented Ale 1060 O.G. brewed by the Ceylon Breweries.

Jubilee Ale (Eng). A bottled Ale brewed by the Harvey's Brewery in Lewes, Sussex to commemorate the Silver Jubilee of Sussex University.

Jubilee Bitter (Eng). A bottled strong Ale 1049 O.G. brewed by the Hook Norton Brewery.

Jubilee Bitter (Eng). A full-flavoured Bitter beer brewed by the Gibbs Mew Brewery in Salisbury.

Jubilee Cocktail (Cktl). ¼ measure Van der Hum, ½ measure dry Gin, ¼ measure lime juice, dash Gomme syrup. Shake with ice, strain into a cocktail glass.

Jubilee Guinness (Eng). A special Guinness 1050 O.G. brewed at the Park Royal Brewery in London in 1986 (to the 1936 gravity) to commemorate the 50th anniversary of the Brewery. 6,000 bottles only were produced.

Jubilee Juggin (The) (Wales). The name given to a Whiskey produced in Bala. Montgomeryshire (now Powys) in the nineteenth century. No longer produced.

Jubilee Lager (Ch.Isles). A bottled strong Lager beer 1064 O.G. brewed by the Mary Ann Brewery in St. Helier, Jersey.

Jubilee Lager (Ind). A Premium Lager beer 1052 O.G. brewed by the United Breweries in Bangalore.

Jubilee Stout (Eng). A bottled sweet Stout 1040 O.G. brewed by the Bass Breweries.

Jubileums Akvavit (Den). A dill-flavoured Akvavit.

Jucalette (Eng). Samuel Pepys spelling of chocolate (drink) in the eighteenth century.

Jückemöller (Ger). A Steinhäger producer, sold under the same name.

Judaczar (Eng). A Vodka distilled from Jamaican molasses. Distilled and bottled in Hull.

Judenkirch (Ger). Vineyard. (Anb) = Rheingau. (Ber) = Johannisberg. (Gro) = Steinmäcker. (Vil) = Dotzheim.

Judge Jr (Cktl). ½ measure dry Gin, ½ measure Bacardi, dash Gomme syrup, dash Grenadine, juice ¼ lemon. Shake over ice, strain into a cocktail glass.

Judgette Cocktail (Cktl). ⅓ measure dry Gin, ⅓ measure Peach brandy, ⅓ measure French vermouth, juice ½ lime. Shake over ice, strain into a cocktail glass. Top with a cherry.

Juffer (Ger). Vineyard. (Anb) = Mosel-Saar-Ruwer. (Ber) = Bernkastel. (Gro) = Kurfürstlay. (Vil) = Brauneberg.

Juffermauer (Ger). Vineyard. (Anb) = Mosel-Saar-Ruwer. (Ber) = Zell/Mosel. (Gro) = Goldbäumchen. (Vil) = Treis-Karden.

Juffer-Sonnenuhr (Ger). Vineyard. (Anb) = Mosel-Saar-Ruwer. (Ber) = Bernkastel. (Gro) = Kurfürstlay. (Vil) =

Braneberg.

Jug (Austr). Kettle.

Jug (USA). Pitcher, urn.

Jug and Bottle (Eng). A name from the times when draught beer was served in jugs or bottles to take home. 'Off-sales'.

Jugenheim (Ger). Village. (Anb) = Rheinhessen. (Ber) = Bingen. (Gro) = Kaiserpfalz. (Vins) = Goldberg, Hasensprung, Heiligenhäuschen, St. Georgenberg.

Jug of Beer (Eng) (slang). The term used for a glass of beer in the north of England.

Jug Method (Eng). A method of brewing coffee. The grinds are placed into a jug, boiling water poured onto them, allowed to infuse to required strength, strained and served.

Jug Wine (USA). Wine slang for Housewine or ordinary table wines.

Jugy (Fr). A commune in the Mâconnais whose grapes can be used in the production of Mâcon Supérieur.

Juhfark (Hun). The name for the Furmint grape in the Somoló region. Lit – 'Lamb's (or sheep's tail).

Juhfark (Hun). Lit – 'Lamb's tail'. A medium white wine from Somoló region near Lake Balatòn. Made from the Furmint grape.

Juice (Eng). The liquid content of the grape. See Must.

Juiced (USA) (slang). Drunk.

Juiced Up (Eng) (slang). A term to denote a drunken person.

Juice Extractor (Eng). An implement used to extract the juice from fruits either mechanically or by hand. Also called a Juicer.

Juice Glass (USA). Another name for the Delmonico glass.

Juice of the Barley (Ire) (Scot). The nickname for whisky, whiskey. Also for beer.

Juice of the Fruit (Eng). The nickname often used for Wine or Brandy.

Juice of the Grape (Eng). The nickname for Brandy (or sometimes Wine).

Juicer (Eng). An alternative name for a Juice extractor.

Juice Up (USA) (slang). For a drinks party.

Juigné-sur-Loire (Fr). A commune in the A.C. Coteaux de l'Aubance in Anjou-Saumur, Loire.

Juillac-le-Coq (Fr). A commune in the Grande Champagne district, Charente-Maritime. Grapes used for the finest Cognac brandies.

Julebryg (Den). A Christmas beer 5.3% alc. by vol. brewed by the Albani Brewery in Odense.

Jule Øl (Den). A low-alcohol, tax-free beer

brewed by the Albani Brewery in Odense.

Jule Øl (Nor). A Christmas beer 6% alc. by vol. brewed by the Aass Brewery in Drammen.

Julep (Cktl). A long drink of spirit, sugar and mint served in a tankard or frosted glass with shaved ice.

Jules Planquette Cognac (Fr). The brand-name of a Cognac 40% alc. by vol. selected for B. Grant & Co. Ltd., Burton-on-Trent, Staffordshire.

Julia (It). The brand-name of a Grappa.

Juliana Blue Cocktail (Cktl). ½ measure dry Gin, 1 measure coconut cream, 1 measure pineapple juice, ¼ measure blue Curaçao, 2 dashes lime juice. Blend together with a scoop of crushed ice. Strain into an ice-filled highball glass, decorate with a cherry, slice of pineapple and serve with straws.

Julie Marie (Cktl). ⅓ measure Bacardi, ⅙ measure Arum, ⅙ measure Brontë Liqueur, ⅓ measure orange squash, 1 egg white. Shake over ice, strain into a cocktail glass.

Juliénas (Fr). An A.C. Cru Beaujolais-Villages, Burgundy. 510 ha. under vines.

Julius-Echter-Berg (Ger). Vineyard. (Anb) = Franken. (Ber) = Steigerwald. (Gro) = Burgweg. (Vil) = Iphofen.

Juliusspital (Ger). Julius Hospice founded in the sixteenth century at Würzberg in Franconia. Wines are dry and bottled in Bocksbeutels. Owns its own vineyards. Proceeds from wine sales are held for the upkeep of the hospital.

Jullié (Fr). A commune in the Beaujolais. Has A.C. Beaujolais-Villages or Beaujolais-Jullié status.

Jully-lès-Buxy (Fr). A wine-producing town in the commune of A.C. Montagny, Côte Chalonnaise, Burgundy.

Julöl (Swe). A Christmas beer 3.5% alc. by vol. brewed by the Pripps Brewery.

Jumbo Cocktail (Cktl). ¼ measure Cognac, ¼ measure Caperitif, ¼ measure French vermouth, ¼ measure Italian vermouth, dash Pastis, dash Campari. Shake over ice, strain into a cocktail glass.

Jumelles (Les) (Fr). A vineyard in the A.C. Côte Rôtie, northern Rhône.

Jumilla (Sp). A Denominación de Origen wine region of southern Spain. D.O. covers red, pale and sweet Mistela white wines. Grapes are Airen, Cencibel, Garnacha, Merseguera, Monastrell, Pedro ximénez and Tintorera.

Jung (Ger). Young, immature wine.

Jung (Carl) (Ger). A winery based in

J

Rudesheim. Noted for its alcohol-free wines. De-alcoholised in a special still. Rotlack = red, Roselack = rosé and Weisslack = white. Low in calories. Also produces Schloss Boosenburg (a sparkling variety).

Jungbrunnen (Ger). Vineyard. (Anb) = Nahe. (Ber) = Kreuznach. (Gro) = Schlosskapelle. (Vil) = Dorsheim.

Jungfer (Ger). Vineyard. (Anb) = Rheingau. (Ber) = Johannisberg. (Gro) = Mehrhölzchen. (Vil) = Hallgarten.

Jungfer (Ger). Vineyard. (Anb) = Württemberg. (Ber) = Württembergisch Unterland. (Gro) = Kirchenweinberg. (Vil) = Lauffen.

Jungfernberg (Ger). Vineyard. (Anb) = Mosel-Saar-Ruwer. (Ber) = Saar-Ruwer. (Gro) = Römerlay. (Vil) = Waldrach.

Jungfernwein (Ger). Lit – 'Virgin wine'. Applies to the first wine made from new vineyards (usually in its' 3rd year).

Jungferstieg (Ger). Vineyard. (Anb) = Baden. (Ber) = Bodensee. (Gro) = Sonnenufer. (Vil) = Meersburg.

Jungle Juice (Cktl).(1). ½ fl.oz. Mandarine liqueur, 1½ fl.ozs. Pisang Ambon Henkes, ¾ fl.oz. Gin, 3 dashes lemon juice, 3 fl.ozs. orange juice. Stir over ice, strain into a highball glass. Dress with a slice of pineapple and a cherry.

Jungle Juice (Cktl).(2). ½ measure Gin, ½ measure lime juice. Shake over ice, strain into a highball glass. Top with ginger beer.

Jungle Juice (Eng) (slang). A term for alcoholic liquor.

Jung's Non-Alcoholic Wines (Ger). See Jung (Carl).

Jung's Roselack (Ger). A low-alcohol rosé wine from Carl Jung, Rudesheim, Western Germany.

Jung's Rotlack (Ger). A low-alcohol red wine from Carl Jung, Rudesheim, Western Germany.

Jung's Weisslack (Ger). A low-alcohol white wine from Carl Jung, Rudesheim, Western Germany.

Junin (Arg). A wine-producing area in the Mendoza region.

Juniper (Eng). Berries used to flavour Gin. From where Gin gets its' name. See Genièvre.

Juniper Wine (Fr). A mediaeval drink of wine flavoured with Juniper berries to hide the off-flavours of the wine.

Junker (Ger). Vineyard. (Anb) = Nahe. (Ber) = Kreuznach. (Gro) = Kronenberg. (Vil) = Bad Kreuznach (ortsteil Ippesheim).

Junker (Ger). Vineyard. (Anb) = Nahe. (Ber) = Kreuznach. (Gro) = Schlosskapelle. (Vil) = Laubenheim.

Junot (Sp). A delicate, fruit-flavoured, white wine produced by Jaime Lluch Casenallas.

Junta Nacional do Vinho (Port). A government sponsored body for brandy distillers of Portugal. Also has control of Madeira. Formed in 1937.

Junta Provincial de Bodegas Cooperativas del Campo (Sp). One of the main wine-producers in Rioja.

Jupiter (Gre). A noted Brandy producer.

Jupiterberg (Ger). Vineyard. (Anb) = Württemberg. (Ber) = Württembergisch Unterland. (Gro) = Heuchelberg. (Vil) = Hausen/Z

Jupiter Brasserie (Bel). A brewery based near Liège. Is noted for its' Pilsener-style Lager beers. Produces Jupiter and Lamot.

Jura (Fr). A.C. wine area of central eastern France. Noted for its' Vins de Paille. See Château Chalon. Also produces red, rosé, and Vin Jaune white wines. See also Arbois and L'Etoile. Grapes – Gros noiren, Melon d'Arbois, Pinot blanc, Poulsard and Trousseau.

Jurade de Saint-Émilion (Fr). A wine brotherhood for the producers of Saint-Émilion in Bordeaux. Promotes the wines of Saint-Émilion.

Jurançon (Fr). An amber-coloured dessert wine produced from vines grown near Pau. Minimum alc. by vol. of 11%. Vines are trained by 'en Hautains' system.

Jurançon (Fr). A grape variety used in the making of Armagnac.

Jurançon (Fr). A.C. wine region of south-west France. Produces mainly dry and sweet white wines. Minimum alc. by vol. of 12.5%.

Jurançon Blanc (Fr). A white grape variety used in the making of Cognac.

Jurignac (Fr). A commune in the Charente-Maritime Département whose grapes are classed Petite Champagne (Cognac).

Jus (Fr). Juice.

Jus de Chapeau (Fr). A term used in northern France for poorly-made coffee.

Jus de Goutte (Fr). The name used in the Beaujolais region for the partially fermented juice obtained from the macération carbonique fermentaion.

Jus de Raisins (Fr). Grape juice.

Justerini and Brooks (Scot). Wine merchants and Scotch whisky producers. Part of International Distillers and Vintners. Brands include Knockando, J & B Rare, J & B Reserve (15 year old).

Justice's Licences (Eng). A licence

issued by the Courts to enable a person to sell alcoholic beverages to the public. See the Brewster Sessions.

Just Juice (Eng). A brand of pure fruit juices from Adams Foods, Leek, Staffordshire.

Juteaux (Fr). Juicy.

Juvé y Camps (Sp). A wine-producer based in San Sadurní de Noya, Barcelona. Produces Ermita d'Espiells.

J.W. Dant (USA). The brand-name of a noted Bourbon whiskey.

K

Kaapse Smaak (S.Afr). Lit – 'Cape taste'. An early version of Marc brandy. Also spelt Cape Smaak.

Kaapse Vonkel (S.Afr). An extraordinary wine made by the méthode champenoise with the Steen grape (plus other varieties) by the Simonsig Estate in Stellenbosch.

Kaapzicht Estate (S.Afr). A vineyard in Bottelay area of Stellenbosch. Address = Steytdal Farm, (Pty) Ltd., Box 5, Sanlamhof 7532. Produces – Kaapzicht Weisser Riesling.

Kaapzicht Weisser Riesling (S.Afr). A white wine from the Rhine riesling grape produced by the Kaapzicht Estate.

Kab (Isr). An old Hebrew measure of approximately 4 pints (2.3 litres) See also Cab.

Kabänes (Ger). A medium-bitter herb liqueur produced in Cologne. 26% alc. by vol.

Kabarcik (Tur). A red grape variety.

Kaberne (USSR). A red wine (Cabernet) from the Moldavia region.

Kabernett (Yug). The Yugoslavian spelling of the Cabernet grape.

Kabinett (Ger). The label description of a wine which is of Qmp quality and one grade up. Has no added sugar, an Oechsle reading of 72° (15° KMW) and is estate bottled. See Cabinet.

Kabinettwein (Ger). An old term used to identify selected barrels of the vineyard owner or special reserve.

Kachelberg (Ger). Vineyard. (Anb) = Rheinhessen. (Ber) = Bingen. (Gro) =Adelberg. (Vil) = Ensheim.

Kachelberg (Ger). Vineyard. (Anb) = Rheinhessen. (Ber) = Bingen. (Gro) = Adelberg. (Vil) = Wörrstadt.

Kadarka (Hun). A red grape variety used in the making of Bull's Blood (Egri Bikavér) together with the Kékfrankos and Médoc noir grapes. Also grown in the Banat region of Rumania. In Bulgaria is known as the Gamza.

Kadarka de Banat (Rum). A red wine produced in the Banat region from the Kadarka grape.

Kadeh (Tur). A glass. Also word for a goblet, cup or any other drinking receptacle.

Kaefferkopf (Fr). A well-known vineyard of Ammerschwihr in Alsace.

Kafa (Asia). The Serbo-Croatian word for coffee.

Kafe (E.Asia). The name for coffee in Laos.

Kafé (E.Asia). The Thai word for coffee.

Kafe (Fr). The Breton word for coffee.

Kafei (China). Coffee.

Kafels (Ger). Vineyard. (Anb) = Nahe. (Ber) = Schloss Böckelheim. (Gro) = Burgweg. (Vil) = Norheim.

Kafenion (Gre). A café serving coffee or alcoholic beverages which is used by males only.

Kafeo (Gre). Coffee.

Kafe Yen (E.Asia). The name in Laos for iced coffee.

Kaffa (Afr). Part of Ethiopia from which coffee is supposed to have originated and from which the name derives.

Kaffa (Arab). Word for wine. See Wine of Araby.

Kaffe (Den). Coffee.

Kaffé (Nor). Coffee.

Kaffee (Isr). Coffee. Also spelt Kavah.

Kaffee Hafooch (Isr). Lit – 'Upside down coffee'. ½ fill a cup with milk and top with coffee.

Kaffeeklatsch (Ger). Lit – 'Coffee and gossip'. Afternoon coffee.

Kaffelstein (Ger). Vineyard. (Anb) = Franken. (Ber) = Mainviereck. (Gro) = Not yet assigned. (Vil) = Kreuzwertheim.

Kaffia (Sp). The Basque word for coffee.

Kaffia (USSR). A sparkling wine from the Crimea.

Kaffir Beer (Afr). A Beer made from Sorghum (Kaffir corn) or from Millet grain.

Kafir (USSR). An alcoholic beverage produced in the Caucasian mountains from fermented cows' milk and Kafir grain. Also spelt Kefir. See also Koumiss.

Kafo (Esp). The Esperanto word for coffee.

K

Kaggi (Scan). The old Norse name for a cask.

Kagor (Alb). A sweet, red dessert wine produced in the Sarandë region of southern Albania.

Kahawa (Afr). The Swahili word for coffee.

Kahisakan (Jap). The name given to tea/coffee houses.

Kahlberg (Ger). Vineyard. (Anb) = Baden. (Ber) = Badische Bergstrasse/Kraichgau. (Gro) = Rittersberg. (Vil) = Leutershausen.

Kahlenberg (Aus). A wine village near Vienna that is noted for its' white 'Heurige' wines.

Kahlenberg (Ger). Vineyard. (Anb) = Nahe. (Ber) = Kreuznach. (Gro) = Kronenberg. (Vil) = Bad Kreuznach.

Kahlenberg (Ger). Vineyard. (Anb) = Nahe. (Ber) = Schloss Böckelheim. (Gro) = Paradiesgarten. (Vil) = Feilbingert.

Kahlenberg (Ger). Vineyard. (Anb) = Rheinpfalz. (Ber) = Südliche Weinstrasse. (Gro) = Trappenberg. (Vil) = Ottersheim.

Kahlenberger Jungherrn (Aus). A white wine made from the Müller-Thurgau grape produced by the Augustine Monks at Klosterneuburg, Vienna.

Kahlenberger Weisse (Aus). An old white grape variety that is little used nowadays.

Kahllay (Ger). Vineyard. (Anb) = Mosel-Saar-Ruwer. (Ber) = Zell/Mosel. (Gro) = Weinhex. (Vil) = Niederfell.

Kahlúa (Mex). A coffee-flavoured liqueur. 26% alc. by vol.

Kahlúa Alexander (Cktl). 1 fl.oz. Kahlúa, 1 fl.oz. Gin, 1 fl.oz. cream. Shake over ice, strain into a cocktail glass.

Kahlúa Cocktail (Cktl). ½ measure Kahlúa liqueur, ½ measure Cognac. Stir gently over ice, strain into a cocktail glass.

Kahlúa Java (Punch). 2 pints hot strong coffee, 2 pints hot cocoa, 1 gill Kahlúa. Heat together and serve in toddy glasses with a marshmallow on top.

Kahmig (Ger). Ropy. A wine that has been attacked by bacteria. See Rope.

Kahouri (USSR). A white grape variety grown in Georgia. Produces dry white wines.

Kahuah (Tur). The old name for coffee.

Kahve (Tur). Coffee.

Kahveci (Tur). A coffee house owner.

Kahvehane (Tur). A coffee-shop (bar) café.

Kahvi (Fin). Coffee.

Kahwa (Afr). See Kahweh.

Kahweh (Afr). The old Arab name for coffee. Means invigorating or stimulating. Also spelt Kahwa, Quawah.

Kaifei (China). Coffee.

Kailberg (Ger). Vineyard. (Anb) = Baden. (Ber) = Badische Frankenland. (Gro) = Tauberklinge. (Vil) = Sachsenflur.

Kairi (W.Ind). A brand of dark Rum produced by the Trinidad Distillers Ltd. Trinidad.

Kaiserberg (Ger). Lit – 'Emperor's hill'. A popular name for vineyards in Germany. There are 12 separate vineyards holding this name.

Kaiserberg (Ger). Vineyard. (Anb) = Baden. (Ber) = Breisgau. (Gro) = Burg Lichteneck. (Vil) = Altdorf.

Kaiserberg (Ger). Vineyard. (Anb) = Baden. (Ber) = Breisgau. (Gro) = Burg Lichteneck. (Vil) = Bleichheim.

Kaiserberg (Ger). Vineyard. (Anb) = Baden. (Ber) = Breisgau. (Gro) = Burg Lichteneck. (Vil) = Broggingen.

Kaiserberg (Ger). Vineyard. (Anb) = Baden. (Ber) = Breisgau. (Gro) = Burg Lichteneck. (Vil) = Ettenheim.

Kaiserberg (Ger). Vineyard. (Anb) = Baden. (Ber) = Breisgau. (Gro) = Burg Lichteneck. (Vil) = Herbolzheim.

Kaiserberg (Ger). Vineyard. (Anb) = Baden. (Ber) = Breisgau. (Gro) = Burg Lichteneck. (Vil) = Ringsheim.

Kaiserberg (Ger). Vineyard. (Anb) = Baden. (Ber) = Breisgau. (Gro) = Burg Lichteneck. (Vil) = Tutschfelden.

Kaiserberg (Ger). Vineyard. (Anb) = Nahe. (Ber) = Schloss Böckelheim. (Gro) = Burgweg. (Vil) = Duchroth.

Kaiserberg (Ger). Vineyard. (Anb) = Rheinpfalz. (Ber) = Südliche Weinstrasse. (Gro) = Bischofskreuz. (Vil) = Nussdorf.

Kaiserberg (Ger). Vineyard. (Anb) = Rheinpfalz. (Ber) = Südliche Weinstrasse. (Gro) = Herrlich. (Vil) = Göcklingen.

Kaiserberg (Ger). Vineyard. (Anb) = Württemberg. (Ber) = Württembergisch Unterland. (Gro) = Heuchelberg. (Vil) = Frauenzimmern.

Kaiserberg (Ger). Vineyard. (Anb) = Württemberg. (Ber) = Württembergisch Unterland. (Gro) = Heuchelberg. (Vil) = Güglingen.

Kaiser Bier (Aus). A Lager beer brewed by the Österreichische Bräu.

Kaiser Bill (Cktl). 1 measure Schnapps, juice of a lime. Shake over ice, strain into an ice-filled highball glass. Top with soda water. Dress with a slice of lime and serve with straws.

Kaiserbirnlikor (Aus). A lemon-flavoured liqueur.

Kaiserdom (Ger). Based at Speyer,

Rheinpfalz. A museum which houses 2,000 years of wine-making history, including an Amphora of Roman origin that still holds the original wine.

Kaiserdom Brauerei (Ger). A Bavarian brewery in Ramburg that is noted for its' Rauchbier (smoked beer).

Kaiser Festbock (Aus). A pale Bock bier brewed by Bräu A.G. 6.7% alc. by vol.

Kaisergarten (Ger). Vineyard. (Anb) = Rheinhessen. (Ber) = Bingen. (Gro) = Kurfürstenstück. (Vil) = Gau-Weinheim.

Kaiser Karl (Ger). Vineyard. (Anb) = Franken. (Ber) = Maindreieck. (Gro) = Hofrat. (Vil) = Repperndorf.

Kaiserpfalz (Ger). Grosslage. (Anb) = Rheinhessen. (Ber) = Bingen. (Vils) = Bubenheim, Engelstadt, Gross-Winternheim, Heidesheim, Ingelheim, Jugenheim, Schwabenheim, Wackernheim.

Kaiser Pilsener (Ger). A well-known Pilsener lager 4.8% alc by vol. brewed by the Henninger Brauerei in Frankfurt. Has a long lagering of 6–9 weeks.

Kaiserstuhl (Ger). Vineyard. (Anb) = Rheinpfalz. (Ber) = Mittelhaardt-Deutsche Weinstrasse. (Gro) = Rebstöckel. (Vil) = Hambach.

Kaiserstuhl Rosé (Austr). A rosé wine produced in the Barossa Valley by the co-operative winery of same name. Part of Penfolds.

Kaiserstuhl-Tuniberg (Ger). Bereich. (Gros) = Attilafelsen, Vulkanfelsen.

Kaiserstuhl-Tuniberg Weinfest (Ger). A Baden wine festival held in Breisach in September.

Kajol (S.Afr). A white blend of Colombard, Hanepoot, Raisin blanc and Sultana grapes. A medium-sweet wine.

Kakabeka (Can). A cream Lager beer brewed by the Doran Brewery.

Kakhetia (USSR). A large earthenware wine storage jar used in the Georgia region.

Kakubin (Jap). The brand-name of a blended Whiskey produced by the Suntory Distillery.

Kalavryta (Gre). A red wine produced in Morea.

Kalb (Ger). Vineyard. (Anb) = Franken. (Ber) = Steigerwald. (Gro) = Burgweg. (Vil) = Iphofen.

Kalbenstein (Ger). Vineyard. (Anb) = Franken. (Ber) = Maindreieck. (Gro) = Rosstal. (Vil) = Gambach.

Kaldi (Arab). A ninth century Arabian goatherd who is reputed to have discovered coffee through the antics of his goats after they had eaten the coffee cherries (berries). He told his discovery to the nearby priests who then brewed a beverage from the fruit so as to keep themselves awake through their long prayers.

Kalebag (Tur). The State monopoly-approved name for red and white wines from Ankara.

Kalecik Karasi (Tur). A white grape variety grown in central Anatolla.

Kaliber (Ire). A low-alcohol Lager brewed by the Guinness Brewery. Is less than 1.2% alc. by vol.

Kalimna (Austr). A winery based north of Nuriootpa, South Australia.

Kalin Cellars (USA). A winery based in San Rafael, Marin, California. Grape varieties – Cabernet sauvignon, Chardonnay, Johannisberg riesling, Sémillon and Zinfandel. Produces varietal and some botrytised wines.

Kalkberg (Ger). Vineyard. (Anb) = Rheinpfalz. (Ber) = Mittelhaardt-Deutsche Weinstrasse. (Gro) = Pfaffengrund. (Vil) = Duttweiler.

Kalkgasse (Ger). Vineyard. (Anb) = Hessiche Bergstrasse. (Ber) = Starkenburg. (Gro) = Wolfsmagen. (Vil) = Bernsheim.

Kalkgrube (Ger). Vineyard. (Anb) = Rheinpfalz. (Ber) = Südliche Weinstrasse. (Gro) = Königsgarten. (Vil) = Frankweiler.

Kalkofen (Ger). Village. (Anb) = Nahe. (Ber) = Schloss Böckelheim. (Gro) = Paradiesgarten. (Vin) = Graukatz.

Kalkofen (Ger). Vineyard. (Anb) = Rheinpfalz. (Ber) = Mittelhaardt-Deutsche Weinstrasse. (Gro) = Kobnert. (Vil) = Leistadt.

Kalkofen (Ger). Vineyard. (Anb) = Rheinpfalz. (Ber) = Mittelhaardt-Deutsche Weinstrasse. (Gro) = Mariengarten. (Vil) = Deidesheim.

Kallenberg (Ger). Vineyard. (Anb) = Rheinhessen. (Ber) = Bingen. (Gro) = Kaiserpfalz. (Vil) = Bubenheim.

Kalligas (Gre). A noted wine-merchant who specialises in Kephalonian wines.

Kallmuth (Ger). Vineyard. (Anb) = Franken. (Ber) = Maindreieck. (Gro) = Not yet assigned. (Vil) = Homburg.

Kallstadt (Ger). Village. (Anb) = Rheinpfalz. (Ber) = Mittelhaardt-Deutsche Weinstrasse. (Gro) = Feuerberg. (Vins) = Annaberg, Kreidkeller.

Kallstadt (Ger). Village. (Anb) = Rheinpfalz. (Ber) = Mittelhaardt-Deutsche Weinstrasse. (Gro) = Kobnert. (Vins) = Kronenberg, Steinacker.

Kallstadt (Ger). Village. (Anb) = Rheinpfalz. (Ber) = Mittelhaardt-Deutsche Weinstrasse. (Gro) = Saumagen. (Vil) = Horn, Kirchenstück, Nill.

K

Kalokhorio (Cyp). A village where the grapes for Commandaria are grown. In the south-east of the island.

Kalopanayotis (Cyp). A wine village on the north-western slopes of the Troodos mountain in the Marathassa region.

Kalta Katchka (USA). Kosher Cold Duck. See Cold Duck.

Kalte Ente (Ger). Lit – 'Cold Duck' a sparkling red wine. See Cold Duck.

Kalte Ente (Ger). A white wine mixed half and half with soda water (or cold water).

Kaltenberg (Ger). A bottled Pilsener lager 1047 O.G. brewed under licence by Whitbread.

Kalterberg (Ger). Vineyard. (Anb) = Württemberg. (Ber) = Württembergisch Unterland. (Gro) = Schalkstein. (Vil) = Rielinghausen.

Kalterersee (It). Also known as Lago di Caldaro. Is a wine from the Trentino-Alto Adige, produced on the shore of the little lake Caldaro near Ora.

Kammer (Ger). Vineyard. (Anb) = Mosel-Saar-Ruwer. (Ber) = Bernkastel. (Gro) = Kurfürstlay. (Vil) = Brauneberg.

Kammer Distillery (Ger). A noted liqueur producing company based in Kammer, Western Germany.

Kammerforst (Ger). Village. (Anb) = Franken. (Ber) = Steigerwald. (Gro) = Not yet assigned. (Vin) = Teufel.

Kamok (Fr). A coffee-flavoured liqueur.

Kamp (Aus). A tributary of the river Danube. It gives its' name to the wines produced in its' valley. Noted for wines from the Veltliner and Riesling.

Kampai (China) (Jap). A toast to guests. Denotes 'Good health', 'Cheers'.

Kamp-Bornhofen-Kestert (Ger). Village. (Anb) = Mittelrhein. (Ber) = Rheinburgengau. (Gro) = Loreleyfelsen. (Vins) = Liebenstein-Sterrenberg, Pilgerpfad.

Kamtchatka Watky (Jap). A spirit made from rice.

Kamzík (Czec). A Lager beer brewed by the Poprad Brewery.

Kanaka (Arab). The Arabian name for the Ibrik (Turkish) coffee boiler.

Kandeel (Hol). An old Dutch liqueur. A Cognac, cloves, vanilla and cinnamon liqueur produced only by Van Zuylekom Distillery in Amsterdam.

Kandel (Ger). Village. (Anb) = Rheinpfalz. (Ber) = Südliche Weinstrasse. (Gro) = Guttenberg. (Vin) = Galgenberg.

Kangaroo Cocktail (Cktl). ¾ measure Vodka, ¼ measure French vermouth. Shake over ice, strain into a cocktail glass. Top with a twist of lemon peel juice.

Kangaroo Jump Cocktail (Cktl). ½ fl.oz. dry Gin, 1 fl.oz. lemon juice, ¼ fl.oz.

Maraschino, dash Gomme syrup. Shake over ice, strain into an ice-filled highball glass. Top with soda. Add 2 dashes Crème de Menthe (green), 1 dash blue Curaçao. Decorate with a spiral of lemon peel. Serve with straws.

Kanga Rouge (Austr). A red wine made from 100% Hermitage grapes.

Kango Co-operative (S.Afr). Based in Klein Karoo. Address = Box 46, Oudtshoorn 6620. Produces – Golden Jerepiko, Hanepoot golden dessert wine, Herfsgoud, Premier blanc, Red Jerepiko, Rijckshof claret, Rozelle and many varietals.

Kanneken (Hol). A metal drinking vessel used in the sixteenth and seventeenth centuries.

Kanokomet (Egy). An ancient wine from the vineyards of Rameses III. 1198–1167 B.C.

Kanonkop Estate (S.Afr). A top vineyard based on the Simonsberg foothills in Stellenbosch. Address = P.O. Muldersvlei 7606. Produces – Paul Sayer Fleur and many Varietals.

Kanta (Gre). A dry white wine, elegant in style.

Kantator (Fr). The brand-name of a beer brewed in Alsace.

Kanterbräu (Fr). An Alsatian beer.

Kantharos (Gre). A two-handled ladling cup used in ancient Greece to serve wines from Amphora.

Kanyak (Tur). Brandy. See also Konyak.

Kanzem (Ger). Village. (Anb) = Mosel-Saar-Ruwer. (Ber) = Saar-Ruwer. (Gro) = Scharzberg. (Vins) = Altenberg, Hörecker, Schlossberg, Sonnenberg.

Kanzemer (Ger). A rare red wine from the Mosel-Saar-Ruwer.

Kanzler (Ger). A white grape variety. A cross between the Müller-Thurgau and the Silvaner. Produces good quality, full-bodied wines.

Kaoliang Chiew (China). A medicinal tonic. 12% alc. by vol.

Kaoliang Wine (China). A spirit distilled from the Kaoliang (a Sorghum-like grain).

Kapé (Afr). North-African name for Coffee.

Kapellchen (Ger). Vineyard. (Anb) = Mosel-Saar-Ruwer. (Ber) = Bernkastel. (Gro) = Michelsberg. (Vil) = Minheim.

Kapelle (Ger). Vineyard. (Anb) = Rheinhessen. (Ber) = Bingen. (Gro) = Kurfürstenstück. (Vil) = Gau-Bickelheim.

Kapelle (Ger). Vineyard. (Anb) = Rheinhessen. (Ber) = Nierstein. (Gro) = Sankt Alban. (Vil) = Bodenheim.

Kapelle (Ger). Vineyard. (Anb) = Rheinpfalz. (Ber) = Südliche Weinstrasse. (Gro) = Ordensgut. (Vil) = Hainfeld.

K

Kapellenberg (Ger). Lit ⸗ 'Church hill'. The name used for many vineyards (28 in all) in Germany. Derived from when the vineyards were owned by the Church.

Kapellenberg (Ger). Grosslage. (Anb) = Franken. (Ber) = Steigerwald. (Vils) = Schmachtenberg, Steinbach, Zeil, Ziegelanger.

Kapellenberg (Ger). Vineyard. (Anb) = Ahr. (Ber) = Walporzheim/Ahrtal. (Gro) = Klosterberg. (Vil) = Heimersheim.

Kapellenberg (Ger). Vineyard. (Anb) = Baden. (Ber) = Badische Bergstrasse/Kraichgau. (Gro) = Stiftsberg. (Vil) = Eichelberg.

Kapellenberg (Ger). Vineyard. (Anb) = Baden. (Ber) = Bodensee. (Gro) = Not yet assigned. (Vil) = Klettau (ortsteil Erzingen).

Kapellenberg (Ger). Vineyard. (Anb) = Baden. (Ber) = Bodensee. (Gro) = Not yet assigned. (Vil) = Klettau (ortsteil Rechberg).

Kapellenberg (Ger). Vineyard. (Anb) = Baden. (Ber) = Kaiserstuhl-Tuniberg. (Gro) = Attilafelsen. (Vil) = Munzingen.

Kapellenberg (Ger). Vineyard. (Anb) = Baden. (Ber) = Markgräflerland. (Gro) = Vogtei Rötteln. (Vil) = Bamlach.

Kapellenberg (Ger). Vineyard. (Anb) = Baden. (Ber) = Markgräflerland. (Gro) = Vogtei Rötteln. (Vil) = Rheinweiler.

Kapellenberg (Ger). Vineyard. (Anb) = Baden. (Ber) = Ortenau. (Gro) = Fürsteneck. (Vil) = Durbach.

Kapellenberg (Ger). Vineyard. (Anb) = Franken. (Ber) = Maindreieck. (Gro) = Not yet assigned. (Vil) = Eibelstadt.

Kapellenberg (Ger). Vineyard. (Anb) = Franken. (Ber) = Maindreieck. (Gro) = Not yet assigned. (Vil) = Frickenhausen am Main.

Kapellenberg (Ger). Vineyard. (Anb) = Mosel-Saar-Ruwer. (Ber) = Obermosel. (Gro) = Gipfel. (Vil) = Helfant-Esingen.

Kapellenberg (Ger). Vineyard. (Anb) = Mosel-Saar-Ruwer. (Ber) = Obermosel. (Gro) = Gipfel. (Vil) = Rehlingen.

Kapellenberg (Ger). Vineyard. (Anb) = Mosel-Saar-Ruwer. (Ber) = Zell/Mosel. (Gro) = Grafschaft. (Vil) = Alf.

Kapellenberg (Ger). Vineyard. (Anb) = Mosel-Saar-Ruwer. (Ber) = Zell/Mosel. (Gro) = Rosenhang. (Vil) = Briedern.

Kapellenberg (Ger). Vineyard. (Anb) = Mosel-Saar-Ruwer. (Ber) = Zell/Mosel. (Gro) = Rosenhang. (Vil) = Bruttig-Fankel.

Kapellenberg (Ger). Vineyard. (Anb) = Mosel-Saar-Ruwer. (Ber) = Zell/Mosel.

(Gro) = Rosenhang. (Vil) = Treis-Karden.

Kapellenberg (Ger). Vineyard. (Anb) = Nahe. (Ber) = Kreuznach. (Gro) = Schlosskapelle. (Vil) = Münster-Sarmsheim.

Kapellenberg (Ger). Vineyard. (Anb) = Nahe. (Ber) = Schloss Böckelheim. (Gro) = Paradiesgarten. (Vil) = Odernheim.

Kapellenberg (Ger). Vineyard. (Anb) = Rheingau. (Ber) = Johannisberg. (Gro) = Burgweg. (Vil) = Lorch.

Kapellenberg (Ger). Vineyard. (Anb) = Rheinhessen. (Ber) = Bingen. (Gro) = Rheingrafenstein. (Vil) = Fürfeld.

Kapellenberg (Ger). Vineyard. (Anb) = Rheinhessen. (Ber) = Bingen. (Gro) = Sankt Rochuskapelle. (Vil) = Bingen.

Kapellenberg (Ger). Vineyard. (Anb) = Rheinhessen. (Ber) = Bingen. (Gro) = Sankt Rochuskapelle. (Vil) = Dromersheim.

Kapellenberg (Ger). Vineyard. (Anb) = Rheinhessen. (Ber) = Nierstein. (Gro) = Domherr. (Vil) = Ober-Olm.

Kapellenberg (Ger). Vineyard. (Anb) = Rheinhessen. (Ber) = Wonnegau. (Gro) = Sybillenstein. (Vil) = Alzey.

Kapellenberg (Ger). Vineyard. (Anb) = Rheinhessen. (Ber) = Wonnegau. (Gro) = Sybillenstein. (Vil) = Weinheim.

Kapellenberg (Ger). Vineyard. (Anb) = Rheinpfalz. (Ber) = Mittelhaardt-Deutsche Weinstrasse. (Gro) = Meerspinne. (Vil) = Gimmeldingen.

Kapellenberg (Ger). Vineyard. (Anb) = Rheinpfalz. (Ber) = Südliche Weinstrasse. (Gro) = Mandelhöhe. (Vil) = Maikammer-Alsterweiler.

Kapellen-Drusweiler (Ger). Village. (Anb) = Rheinpfalz. (Ber) = Südliche Weinstrasse. (Gro) = Kloster Liebfrauenberg. (Vin) = Rosengarten

Kapellengarten (Ger). Vineyard. (Anb) = Rheinpfalz. (Ber) = Mittelhaardt-Deutsche Weinstrasse. (Gro) = Kobnert. (Vil) = Dackenheim.

Kapellenpfad (Ger). Vineyard. (Anb) = Nahe. (Ber) = Kreuznach. (Gro) = Kronenberg. (Vil) = Bad Kreuznach.

Kapellenstück (Ger). Vineyard. (Anb) = Rheinhessen. (Ber) = Wonnegau. (Gro) = Liebfrauenmorgen. (Vil) = Worms.

Kapitein Kok (Cktl). ¾ fl.oz. Tequila, 1½ fl.ozs. Fraises de Bois Dolphi. Build into an ice-filled highball glass. Top up with Bitter orange and add a slice of orange.

Käppele (Ger). Vineyard. (Anb) = Württemberg. (Ber) = Remstal-Stuttgart. (Gro) = Wartbühl. (Vil) = Beutelsbach.

K

Kappelrodeck (Ger). Village. (Anb) = Baden. (Ber) = Ortenau. (Gro) = Schloss Rodeck. (Vin) = Hex vom Dasenstein.

Kappishäusern (Ger). Village. (Anb) = Württemberg. (Ber) = Remstal-Stuttgart. (Gro) = Hohenneuffen. (Vin) = Schlossteige.

Kap Sekt (S.Afr). A brut sparkling wine produced by the Nederburg Estate from the Riesling and Rhine riesling grapes.

Kapsreiter (Aus). A Lager beer brewed by the Kapsreiter Brauerei in Schärding near Linz.

Kapsreiter Brauerei (Aus). A brewery based in Schärding near Linz.

Kapsweyher (Ger). Village. (Anb) = Rheinpfalz. (Ber) = Südliche Weinstrasse. (Gro) = Guttenberg. (Vin) = Lerchenberg.

Kaptenlojtnant (Swe). A blend of Bénédictine and Grape brandy produced by Aktiebolaget Vin & Spritcentralem.

Kapucín (Czec). A Lager beer brewed by the Vratislavice Brewery.

Kapuzinerbuck (Ger). Vineyard. (Anb) = Baden. (Ber) = Markgräflerland. (Gro) = Lorettoberg. (Vil) = Wittnau.

Kapuzinerlikoer (Ger). A brown-coloured Capuchin liqueur based on oils of celeriac, cinnamon, sweet oranges, cummin, fennel, mace with Brandy.

Karabounar (Bul). See Karabunar.

Karabunar (Bul). A red grape variety grown in central-western Bulgaria.

Karabunar (Bul). A red wine produced in the town of same name near Plovdiv, central-western Bulgaria.

Karabunar (Bul). A noted wine-producing area in central-western Bulgaria. Is also spelt Karabounar.

Kara Chanakh (USSR). A dessert wine produced in Baku.

Karaf (Hol). Decanter.

Kara-Isium (USSR). A dessert wine produced in Turkmenistan.

Karaláhana (Tur). A white grape variety grown in Thrace and Marmara.

Karamalz (Ger). A Malzbier brewed by the Henninger Brauerei in Frankfurt.

Kara-Tachanakh (USSR). A white grape variety grown in the Azerbaijan region to produce dessert wines.

Karbacher Brauerei (Switz). An independent brewery based in Schönenwerd.

Karbonat (Tur). A drink charged with CO_2 gas (carbonated).

Karchesia Goblet (It). A large Roman drinking vessel, similar in shape to the modern Elgin glass.

Kardinalsberg (Ger). Vineyard. (Anb) =

Mosel-Saar-Ruwer. (Ber) = Bernkastel. (Gro) = Kurfürstlay. (Vil) = Bernkastel-Kues.

Karel Lager (Czec). A Lager beer brewed in the Karlovy Vary Brewery.

Karlburg (Ger). Village. (Anb) = Franken. (Ber) = Maindreieck. (Gro) = Rosstal. (Vins) = Assorted parts of vineyards.

Karloff (Eng). A proprietary brand of Vodka. 40% alc. by vol.

Karlovac (Yug). A Lager-style beer brewed in Croatia from south of the same city.

Karlovo (Bul). A delimited area in the southern region. Is noted for its' white Misket wine.

Karlov White Muscatel (Bul). A straw coloured dry white wine with a bouquet of roses.

Karlovy Vary Brewery (Czec). A noted brewery based in north-western Czec. Noted for its' Karel Lager.

Karlsberg (Austr). A winery based in the Barossa Valley, South Australia.

Karlsberg (Ger). Vineyard. (Anb) = Mosel-Saar-Ruwer. (Ber) = Saar-Ruwer. (Gro) = Scharzberg. (Vil) = Oberemmel.

Karlsberg (Ger). Vineyard. (Anb) = Württemberg. (Ber) = Kocher-Jagst-Tauber. (Gro) = Tauberberg. (Vil) = Weikersheim.

Karlsfelsen (Ger). Vineyard. (Anb) = Mosel-Saar-Ruwer. (Ber) = Obermosel (Gro) = Gipfel. (Vil) = Palzem.

Karlskopf (Ger). Vineyard. (Anb) = Ahr. (Ber) = Walporzheim/Ahrtal. (Gro) = Klosterberg. (Vil) = Bachem.

Karlsruhe-Durlach (Ger). Village. (Anb) = Baden. (Ber) = Badische Bergstrasse/Kraichgau. (Gro) = Hohenberg. (Vin) = Turmberg.

Karlstadt (Ger). Village. (Anb) = Franken. (Ber) = Maindreieck. (Gro) = Rosstal. (Vin) = Im Stein.

Karmeliterlikoer (Ger). A yellow-green herb-based liqueur.

Karnemelk (Hol). Butter-milk.

Karpi (Fin). A liqueur made by Lignell and Piispanen from cranberries and other fruits. 29% alc. by vol.

Karrawirra (Austr). A winery based in the Barossa Valley, South Australia.

Kartaeuserlikoer (Ger). A herb liqueur similar in style to Chartreuse. See also Karthauser.

Karthauser (Ger). Another name for the liqueur Kartaeuserlikoer.

Karthäuser (Ger). Vineyard. (Anb) = Franken. (Ber) = Maindreieck. (Gro) = Kirchberg. (Vil) = Astheim.

Karthäuser (Ger). Vineyard. (Anb) =

K

Nahe. (Ber) = Kreuznach. (Gro) = Schlosskapelle. (Vil) = Laubenheim.

Karthäuserhofberg Burgberg (Ger). Vineyard. (Anb) = Mosel-Saar-Ruwer. (Ber) = Saar-Ruwer. (Gro) = Römerlay. (Vil) = Trier.

Karthäuserhofberg Kronenberg (Ger). Vineyard. (Anb) = Mosel-Saar-Ruwer. (Ber) = Saar-Ruwer. (Gro) = Römerlay. (Vil) = Trier.

Karthäuserhofberg Orthsberg (Ger). Vineyard. (Anb) = Mosel-Saar-Ruwer. (Ber) = Saar-Ruwer. (Gro) = Römerlay. (Vil) = Trier.

Karthäuserhofberg Sang (Ger). Vineyard. (Anb) = Mosel-Saar-Ruwer. (Ber) = Saar Ruwer. (Gro) = Römerlay. (Vil) = Trier.

Karthäuserhofberg Stirn (Ger). Vineyard. (Anb) = Mosel-Saar-Ruwer. (Ber) = Saar-Ruwer. (Gro) = Römerlay. (Vil) = Trier.

Kasbach (Ger). Village. (Anb) = Mittelrhein. (Ber) = Rheinburgengau. (Gro) = Burg Hammerstein. (Vin) = Stehlerberg.

Käsberg (Ger). Vineyard. (Anb) = Württemberg. (Ber) = Württembergisch Unterland. (Gro) = Schalkstein. (Vil) = Hessigheim.

Käsberg (Ger). Vineyard. (Anb) = Württemberg. (Ber) = Württembergisch Unterland. (Gro) = Schalkstein. (Vil) = Mundelsheim.

Kas Bitters De Luxe (Sp). A non-alcoholic Bitters apéritif which is imported into the U.K. by Leisure Drinks of Derby.

Kasel (Ger). Village. (Anb) = Mosel-Saar-Ruwer. (Ber) = Saar-Ruwer. (Gro) = Römerlay. (Vins) = Dominikanerberg, Herrenberg, Hitzlay, Kehrnagel, Nieschen, Paulinsberg, Timpert.

Kashmiri Tea (Ind). A blend of 3 parts green tea to 1 part Darjeeling tea per pint of boiling water. Is then mixed with nuts and spices, strained and served with milk and brown sugar.

Kaskade (Eng). A species of barley malt from the Golden Promise variety. Gives medium sugar yields.

Kasket Karl (Den). A light-coloured Lager beer 10.7% alc. by vol. brewed by the Thor Brewery.

Käsleberg (Ger). Vineyard. (Anb) = Baden. (Ber) = Kaiserstuhl-Tuniberg. (Gro) = Vulkanfelsen. (Vil) = Oberrotweil.

Kasselberg (Ger). Vineyard. (Anb) = Baden. (Ber) = Ortenau. (Gro) = Fürsteneck. (Vil) = Durbach.

Kastanienbusch (Ger). Vineyard. (Anb) = Rheinpfalz. (Ber) = Südliche Weinstrasse. (Gro) = Königsgarten. (Vil) = Birkweiler.

Kastaniengarten (Ger). Vineyard. (Anb) = Rheinpfalz. (Ber) = Südliche Weinstrasse. (Gro) = Schloss Ludwigshöhe. (Vil) = Edenkoben.

Kastel (N.Z.). A former brand-name used by the Penfolds Winery for a selection of their wines.

Kaštel (USSR). A red muscat dessert wine from southern Crimea.

Kastel (Yug). A wine-producing region on the Dalmatian coast.

Kastell (Ger). Vineyard. (Anb) = Nahe. (Ber) = Schloss Böckelheim. (Gro) = Paradiesgarten. (Vil) = Boos.

Kastell (Ger). Vineyard. (Anb) = Nahe. (Ber) = Schloss Böckelheim. (Gro) = Paradiesgarten. (Vil) = Waldböckelheim.

Kastel-Staadt (Ger). Village. (Anb) = Mosel-Saar-Ruwer. (Ber) = Saar-Ruwer. (Gro) = Scharzberg. (Vins) = König Johann Berg, Maximin Staadt.

Kat (Arab). See Qat, also Khat.

Katabatic Winds (Eng). These occur in regions close to mountains holding glacial snows. Heavy cold air flows down the valleys attaining speeds of 60–80 knots. Examples are the Mistral in France, the Bora in Italy and the El Seré in Spain.

Kater (Hol) (slang). Lit – 'Cat'. A term used for a hangover.

Katergrube (Ger). Vineyard. (Anb) = Nahe. (Ber) = Schloss Böckelheim. (Gro) = Rosengarten. (Vil) = Weinsheim.

Katinka (Cktl). 1 measure Vodka, ½ measure Cherry brandy, juice ¼ lemon. Shake over ice, strain into a cocktail glass. Dress with a slice of lemon.

Katnook (Austr). A winery based in Coonawarra, South Australia. Produces varietal wines.

Kato (Sartori) (USA). A Japanese gentleman who is reputed to have invented instant coffee in Chicago in 1801.

Katsunuma Winery (Jap). Vineyards based in the village of Katsunuma, Yamanashi. Sold under Sapporo wine label.

Kattell-Roc (Fr). A range of low-alcohol drinks (Vermouth, Pastis and Bittersweet) with an alcoholic content of 1% or less. Bacarat (a red Vermouth), Aperitivo (bitters and herbs) are distributed by Brooke Bond Co.

Kattenes (Ger). Village. (Anb) = Mosel-Saar-Ruwer. (Ber) = Zell/Mosel. (Gro) = Weinhex. (Vins) = Fahrberg, Steinchen.

Kattus (Aus). A leading producer of Austrian Sekt. The main brand is Hochriegl.

K

Kätzchen (Ger). Vineyard. (Anb) = Mosel-Saar-Ruwer. (Ber) = Bernkastel. (Gro) = Kurfürstlay. (Vil) = Osann-Monzel.

Katzebuckel (Ger). Vineyard. (Anb) = Rheinhessen. (Ber) = Wonnegau. (Gro) = Burg Rodenstein. (Vil) = Mörstadt.

Katzenbeisser (Ger). Vineyard. (Anb) = Württemberg. (Ber) = Württembergisch Unterland. (Gro) = Kirchenweinberg. (Vil) = Lauffen.

Katzenberg (Ger). Vineyard. (Anb) = Baden. (Ber) = Badische Bergstrasse/ Kraichgau. (Gro) = Hohenberg. (Vil) = Weingarten.

Katzenhölle (Ger). Vineyard. (Anb) = Nahe. (Ber) = Kreuznach. (Gro) = Kronenberg. (Vil) = Bad Kreuznach (ortsteil Planig).

Katzenjammer (Ger) (slang). Lit – 'Cats crying'. A term for a hangover.

Katzenkopf (Ger). Vineyard. (Anb) = Franken. (Ber) = Maindreieck. (Gro) = Kirchberg. (Vil) = Sommerach.

Katzenkopf (Ger). Vineyard. (Anb) = Mosel-Saar-Ruwer. (Ber) = Zell/Mosel (Gro) = Grafschaft. (Vil) = Alf.

Katzenöhrle (Ger). Vineyard. (Anb) = Württemberg. (Ber) = Württembergisch Unterland. (Gro) = Heuchelberg. (Vil) = Meimsheim.

Katzenöhrle (Ger). Vineyard. (Anb) = Württemberg. (Ber) = Württembergisch Unterland. (Gro) = Schalkstein. (Vil) = Besigheim.

Katzenöhrle (Ger). Vineyard. (Anb) = Württemberg. (Ber) = Württembergisch Unterland. (Gro) = Schalkstein. (Vil) = Hessigheim.

Katzenöhrle (Ger). Vineyard. (Anb) = Württemberg. (Ber) = Württembergisch Unterland. (Gro) = Schalkstein. (Vil) = Mundelsheim.

Katzenstein (Ger). Vineyard. (Anb) = Rheinpfalz. (Ber) = Mittelhaardt-Deutsche Weinstrasse. (Gro) = Grafenstück. (Vil) = Kindenheim.

Kaub (Ger). Village. (Anb) = Mittelrhein. (Ber) = Rheinburgengau. (Gro) = Herrenberg. (Vins) = Backofen, Blüchertal, Burg Gutenfels, Pfalzgrafenstein, Rauschelay, Rosstein.

Kaufee (Can). The Eskimo word for coffee.

Kaulenberg (Ger). Vineyard. (Anb) = Nahe. (Ber) = Schloss Böckelheim. (Gro) = Paradiesgarten. (Vil) = Auen.

Kauzenberg in der Mauern (Ger). Vineyard. (Anb) = Nahe. (Ber) = Kreuznach. (Gro) = Kronenberg. (Vil) = Bad Kreuznach.

Kauzenberg-Oranienberg (Ger). Vineyard. (Anb) = Nahe. (Ber) = Kreuznach

(Gro) = Kronenberg. (Vil) = Bad Kreuznach.

Kauzenberg-Rosenhügel (Ger). Vineyard. (Anb) = Nahe. (Ber) = Kreuznach. (Gro) = Kronenberg. (Vil) = Bad Kreuznach.

Kava (Czec). The Bohemian name for coffee.

Kava (USA). A drink made from the root of the pepper plant in Hawaii. Can be made by either chewing the root or beating it between stones. Also produced in Polynesia. Also known as Ava-Ava. Shrub botanical name – Piper Methysticum.

Kava Bowl (Punch). ⅓ pint light Rum, ⅙ gill golden Rum, ⅙ gill Gomme syrup, ⅙ gill Grenadine, 1 gill orange juice, 1 gill lemon juice. Blend together with ½ pint of crushed ice, pour into a punch bowl and decorate with lemon and orange slices.

Kavadarka (Yug). A wine-producing region in southern Macedonia.

Kavah (Isr). The old Hebrew word for coffee. See also Kaffee.

Kavaklidere (Tur). A private wine-producing firm.

Kavé (Hun). The Hebrew word for coffee in Hungary.

Kaveh (Tur). The old Turkish word for coffee.

Kaveh Kanes (Afr). The name given to the ancient coffee houses that were first frequented by men only.

Kawa (S.Asia). The Malayan name for coffee. Also Koppi.

Kawa (Pol). Coffee.

Kayberg (Ger). Vineyard. (Anb) = Württemberg. (Ber) = Württembergisch Unterland. (Gro) = Staufenberg. (Vil) = Erlenbach.

Kayberg (Ger). Vineyard. (Anb) = Württemberg. (Ber) = Württembergisch Unterland. (Gro) = Staufenberg. (Vil) = Oedheim.

Kaylined (Eng) (slang). The term for a person being drunk and incapable.

Kaymagh (Arab). The name for the froth on the top of a cup of Turkish coffee. Lit – 'Coffee cream'.

Kaymak (Tur). Cream.

Kayserberg (Fr). A commune in Alsace.

Kazakhstan (USSR). A wine-producing area in Central Asia that runs from Mongolia to the Caspian Sea.

Kazakhstan (USSR). A white grape variety grown in the Kazakhstan area. Is used mainly for Brandy production.

KB (Austr) (abbr). Kent Brewery. A Lager beer 3.76% alc. by vol. brewed by the Tooth's Brewery and named after their Kent Brewery.

K.B.A. (E.Asia) (abbr). Korean Bartenders'

K

Association. Address = 398–1, Jungnung Dong Sungbuk-ku-Seoul.

K.C.B. (Cktl). ⅜ gill dry Gin, ⅛ gill Kirsch, dash Apricot brandy, dash lemon juice. Mix with ice, strain into a cocktail glass. Top with squeeze of lemon peel juice.

KC Bitter (Eng). A cask conditioned Bitter 1038 O.G. brewed by the Royal Clarence home-brew public house at Burnham-on-Sea, Somerset.

Kecskemét (Hun). An ancient wine-producing area at Alföld in the Great Plain. Produces mainly white wines and fruit liqueurs.

Kecskeméti Barack (Hun). An Apricot brandy produced in the Kecskemét region.

Keefersteiner (Switz). A medium-dry, white wine produced in the Stein-am-Rhein area.

Keelplate (Cktl).(Non-alc). 1 fl.oz. Clam juice, 2 fl.ozs. Tomato juice, 2 dashes Worcester sauce, 2 dashes Celery salt. Shake over ice, strain into 5 oz. wine glass.

Keemun (China). A blend of tea. A delicate flavour with a slight scent of orchids. Originally a black tea, is now a green tea.

Keenan Winery (USA). A winery based near St. Helena, Napa Valley, California. Grape varieties – Cabernet sauvignon and Chardonnay. Produces varietal wines.

Keene Dimick Vineyard (USA). A small vineyard based in the Napa Valley, California. Grape variety – Chardonnay.

Keeskemeter Riesling (Ger). A varietal name for the grape cross between the Weisser pressburger and the Langsteiler.

Keeve (Scot). The name for a 36 gallon barrel.

Kefir (USSR). A drink made from fermented cow's milk (in the Caucasus). Is dried into pellets and then reconstituted with a little water and sugar. Also spelt Kafir.

Keg (Eng). A cask of various sizes for holding brewery conditioned beers. Usually of cylindrical shape. See – Pin, Firkin, Kilderkin and Barrel. Also in metric sizes of 25, 50 and 100 litres.

Keg Beer (Eng). Pressurised, processed or brewery-conditioned beer. Normally pasteurised.

Keg Buster (Eng). Created by cartoonist Bill Tidy, is a cartoon character that represents the spirit of the British Beer drinker.

Kegelbrau (USA). A Premium beer 5%

alc. by vol. brewed by the Cold Spring Brewery, Cold Spring, Minnesota.

Kegging (Eng). A brewery term for the placing of beer into kegs.

Kehr (Ger). Vineyard. (Anb) = Rheinhessen. (Ber) = Nierstein. (Gro) = Gutes Domtal. (Vil) = Weinolsheim.

Kehrberg (Ger). Vineyard. (Anb) = Mosel-Saar-Ruwer. (Ber) = Zell/Mosel. (Gro) = Weinhex. (Vil) = Kobern-Gondorf.

Kehrenberg (Ger). Vineyard. (Anb) = Nahe. (Ber) = Schloss Böckelheim. (Gro) = Burgweg. (Vil) = Altenbamberg.

Kehrnagel (Ger). Vineyard. (Anb) = Mosel-Saar-Ruwer. (Ber) = Saar-Ruwer (Gro) = Römerlay. (Vil) = Kasel.

Keizerbitter (Hol). A brand of aromatic Bitters.

Kékfrankos (Hun). The local name for the Gamay grape.

Kéknyelü (Hun). A white grape variety grown around Lake Balatòn, Badacsonyi area. Produces a sweetish wine.

Kekre (Tur). Sour. See also Eksi.

Kelch (Ger). Goblet, Cup or Chalice.

Kelder (Hol). Cellar.

Kelders (S.Afr). Cellars.

Kélibia (Afr). A co-operative based in Tunisia. Belongs to the UCCVT. Produces Muscat and Mistelle wines.

Kelk (Hol). Cup, Chalice.

Kellar Lager (Eng). A light Lager beer 1033 O.G. brewed by the Arkell Brewery in Swindon, Wiltshire.

Keller (Ger). Cellar.

Kellerabfüllung (Ger). Bottled in the Estate's own cellars.

Kellerabzug (Ger). Lit – 'Cellar proof'. Bottled at the cellar of estate/grower/shipper, etc.

Kellerberg (Ger). Vineyard. (Anb) = Nahe. (Ber) = Schloss Böckelheim. (Gro) = Rosengarten. (Vil) = Weinsheim.

Kellerbrau Lager (Eng). A Lager beer 1034 O.G. brewed by the Charles Wells Brewery in Bedford.

Kellerei (Ger). Cellars.

Kellerlokales (Aus). Wine cellars, bars.

Kellermeister (Ger). Cellar master, Butler.

Kellerprinz Wines (S.Afr). Produced by the SFW. Produce – Amorosa, Grand Cru, Kellerprinz Stein, Late Harvest and Rosanne. See SFW.

Kellersberg (Ger). Vineyard. (Anb) = Rheinhessen. (Ber) = Nierstein. (Gro) = Sankt Alban. (Vil) = Gau-Bischofsheim.

Kellerwegfest (Ger). Rheinhessen wine festival held in Guntersblum in August.

Kelley Creek Vineyard (USA). A small vineyard based in Lower Dry Creek,

Sonoma County, California. 2.5 ha. Grape variety – Zinfandel.

Kellner (Ger). Barman, Waiter or Butler.

Kellybrook Winery (Austr). Vineyard. Address = Fulford Road, Wonga Park, Victoria 3115. 7 ha. Grape varieties – Cabernet sauvignon, Chardonnay, Riesling and Shiraz. Also produces a fine Cider.

Kelsale (Eng). Vineyard. Address = Near Saxmundham, Suffolk. 1 ha. Soil = Clay, loam and flint. Grape varieties – Müller-Thurgau 66% and Seyval 33%. Vinified at Pulham Market vineyard.

Kelter (Ger). Vineyard. (Anb) = Franken. (Ber) = Maindreieck. (Gro) = Rosstal. (Vil) = Himmelstadt.

Kelter (Ger). Wine-press.

Kelterberg (Ger). Vineyard. (Anb) = Württemberg. (Ber) = Württembergisch Unterland. (Gro) = Schalkstein. (Vil) = Kirchberg.

Kelterberg (Ger). Vineyard. (Anb) = Württemberg. (Ber) = Württembergisch Unterland. (Gro) = Schalkstein. (Vil) = Kleinaspach.

Kelterberg (Lux). A vineyard site in the village of Ehnen.

Keltern (Ger). To press the grapes.

Kelvin 66 (Cktl). ¼ measure Aquavit, ¼ measure Dubonnet, ¼ measure orange squash, ¼ measure Grand Marnier. Shake over ice, strain into a cocktail glass, add a cherry.

Kembach (Ger). Village. (Anb) = Baden. (Ber) = Badische Frankenland. (Gro) = Tauberklinge. (Vin) = Sonnenberg.

Kemelrain (Ger). Vineyard. (Anb) = Baden. (Ber) = Badische Frankenland. (Gro) = Tauberklinge. (Vil) = Höhefeld.

Kemelrain (Ger). Vineyard. (Anb) = Baden. (Ber) = Badische Frankenland. (Gro) = Tauberklinge. (Vil) = Reicholzheim.

Kenco Coffee (Eng). A noted range of fine coffees from the Kenco Coffee Company Ltd.

Kenco Coffee Company Ltd (Eng). A noted coffee producing company based at Strathville Road, London SW18 4QY. See Kenco-Typhoo.

Kenco-Typhoo (Eng). A company formed by the merger of the Kenco Coffee Co. and Cadbury Typhoo. Address = Catering Services, P.O. Box 171, Franklin House, Bournville, Birmingham B30 2NA. Produces a vast range of fine coffee and tea products.

Kenn (Ger). Village. (Anb) = Mosel-Saar-Ruwer. (Ber) = Bernkastel. (Gro) = Probstberg. (Vins) = Held, Maximiner-Hofgarten.

Kennedy Wine (USA). A small winery based in Saratoga, Santa Clara, California. Grape variety – Cabernet sauvignon. Also known as the Kathryn Kennedy Wine.

Kentish Ales (Eng). A small Kent brewery re-established in 1984. Noted for its' cask conditioned Royal Porter 1050 O.G. Royal Sovereign 1040 O.G. and Royal Pale 1035 O.G.

Kentish Gold Bitter (Eng). A cask conditioned Bitter 1035 O.G. brewed by the Ashford Brewery, Ashford, Kent.

Kentish Sovereign (Eng). A brand-name for wines produced by the Cherry Hill Vineyards, Nettleshead, Kent.

Kentucky (USA). Where Bourbon whiskey was originally made. Now home to approximately 50% of all the Bourbon distilleries in the USA.

Kentucky Cocktail (Cktl). ⅔ measure Bourbon whiskey, ⅓ measure pineapple juice. Shake over ice, strain into a cocktail glass.

Kentucky Coffee (USA). A coffee substitute made from the seeds of the Kentucky Coffee Tree. Botanical name – Gymnocladus dioica. Produced the same way as for coffee beans.

Kentucky Colonel (Cktl). ¾ measure Bourbon whiskey, ¼ measure Bénédictine. Stir over ice, strain into a cocktail glass. Top with a twist of lemon peel.

Kentucky Gentleman Bittersweet (Cktl). 1½ ozs. Kentucky Gentleman Bourbon Whiskey, juice 1 orange, 2 dashes Angostura, ½ teaspoon powdered sugar. Shake over ice, strain, serve onto ice cubes in a stemmed glass.

Kentucky River (USA). A Bourbon whiskey distillery based south-east of Frankfort in Kentucky.

Kentucky River Products Winery (USA). A small winery based near Frankfort, Kentucky. Produces wines mainly from French hybrid vines.

Kentucky Straight (USA). The brand-name for a Bourbon whiskey produced by the Medley Distillery, Kentucky.

Kentucky Straight Bourbon Whiskey (USA). The name given for any Straight Whiskey produced in Bourbon County, Kentucky.

Kentucky Sunset (Cktl). ⅗ measure Bourbon whiskey, ⅕ measure Anisette, ⅕ measure Strega, Stir over ice, strain into a cocktail glass, add a twist of orange.

Kentucky Tavern (USA). A premium Straight Bourbon whiskey 43% alc. by vol. Produced by the Glenmore Distilleries Co. Louisville, Kentucky.

Kentucky Whiskey (USA). The name for a blend of Straight Whiskies that have been distilled in Kentucky.

K

Kentumi Cocktail (Cktl).(Non-alc). ⅕ gill Passion fruit syrup, 3 dashes lime juice, scoop vanilla ice cream. Blend well together in a blender. Pour into a large goblet, top with soda water and a cherry.

Kenwood (USA). A noted wine town, home of many wineries based in northern County, California.

Kenwood Vineyards (USA). A small winery based in Kenwood, Sonoma County, California. 8.5 ha. Grape varieties – Cabernet sauvignon, Chardonnay, Chenin blanc, Johannisberg riesling, Pinot noir and Zinfandel. Produces varietal wines.

Kenworth Vineyards (USA). A small winery based in Shenandoah Valley, Amador, California. Grape varieties – Cabernet sauvignon, Chardonnay and Zinfandel. Produce varietal wines.

Kenyan Coffee (Afr). Some of the finest coffees. A coffee with a high acidity which is smooth and full flavoured. Arabica.

Kenyan Gold (Afr). A light-styled, spirit-based coffee liqueur.

Kenyan Teas (Afr). Teas used mainly in blending.

Kenzingen (Ger). Village. (Anb) = Baden. (Ber) = Breisgau. (Gro) = Burg Lichteneck. (Vins) = Hummelberg, Roter Berg.

Keo (Cyp). The largest wine firm in the island. Produces fine wines, beers and spirits. Based in Limassol and Paphos.

Keo Beer (Cyp). A Pilsener-style beer brewed by Keo Ltd. of Limassol.

Keosoe (Gre). The Central Union of Wine Producing Co-operatives of Greece. The union of wine co-operatives. 95% of all the co-ops in Greece are members.

Kephalonia (Gre). An Ionian island that is noted for its' Mavrodaphne and Robola wines.

Kephesia (Gre). A wine-producing district of Attica. Produces red and white wines.

Keppoch (Austr). An area north of Coonawarra, South Australia. Is noted for its' Chardonnay and Pinot noir sparkling wines.

Kerala (Ind). A tea-producing region of Southern India.

Kermann (Fr). A herb liqueur both green (dry) and yellow (sweet) versions are produced. Produced by Cazanove. 43% alc. by vol.

Kern (USA). A wine district within the Great Central Valley of California. Produces sweet dessert wines.

Kernen [ortsteil Stetten i.R] (Ger). Village. (Anb) = Württemberg. (Ber) =

Remstal-Stuttgart. (Gro) = Sonnenbühl. (Vins) = Mönchberg, Mönchhalde.

Kerner (Ger). A white grape variety used to replace the Riesling in Switzerland. A cross between the Trollinger and the Riesling. Has a high sugar content.

Kerngeschmack (Ger). Describes a white wine with a flavour of grape pips (left in contact with the must too long).

Kernig (Ger). Firm wine.

Kernobstbranntwein (Ger). Collective name for fruit brandies based on apples or pears.

Kerry Cooler (Cktl). ⅓ gill Irish whiskey, ⅙ gill dry Sherry, 3 dashes Gomme syrup, juice ¼ lemon. Shake well over ice, strain into an ice-filled collins glass, top with soda and a slice of lemon.

Kertz (Ger). Vineyard. (Anb) = Nahe. (Ber) = Schloss Böckelheim. (Gro) = Burgweg. (Vil) = Niederhausen an der Nahe.

Kerzenheim (Ger). Village. (Anb) = Rheinpfalz. (Ber) = Mittelhaardt-Deutsche Weinstrasse. (Gro) = Schnepfenflug vom Kellertal. (Vin) = Esper.

Kesselfeld (Ger). Village. (Anb) = Württemberg. (Ber) = Württembergisch Unterland. (Gro) = Lindelberg. (Vin) = Schwobajörgle.

Kessler (Ger). A large, noted producer of Deutscher Sekt.

Kessler (USA). The brand-name of a blended Whiskey bottled by the Kessler Co., Lawrenceburg, Dundalk, San Francisco. 40% alc. by vol.

Kestelberg (Ger). Vineyard. (Anb) = Baden. (Ber) = Ortenau. (Gro) = Schloss Rodeck. (Vil) = Weisenbach.

Kesten (Ger). Village. (Anb) = Mosel-Saar-Ruwer. (Ber) = Bernkastel. (Gro) = Kurfürstlay. (Vins) = Herrenberg, Paulinsberg, Paulinushofberger.

Kestenholz (Fr). The German name for the Alsace town of Chatenois.

Kestrel Lager (Scot). A Lager beer 1032 O.G. brewed by the Younger Brewery (Scottish and Newcastle).

Kestrel Super Strength (Eng). A lager beer 1080–1088 O.G. brewed by the Scottish and Newcastle Breweries (Younger Brewery).

Ketel (Hol). Kettle.

Ketje (Bel). A top-fermented beer brewed by the Artois Brasserie in Louvain.

Kettle (Eng). A vessel used for boiling water to make tea.

Kettle (Eng). The vessel used for boiling the wort into which is added the hops. Also known as the Copper.

K

Kettmeir (It). Noted wine producers based in the Trentino-Alto Adige region. Produces dry white, light red and sparkling (cuve close) wines.

Keuck (Ger). A noted liqueur distillery of Western Germany.

Keulebuckel (Ger). Vineyard. (Anb) = Baden. (Ber) = Badische Bergstrasse/ Kraichgau. (Gro) = Hohenberg. (Vil) = Dietlingen.

Keulebuckel (Ger). Vineyard. (Anb) = Baden. (Ber) = Badische Bergstrasse/ Kraichgau. (Gro) = Hohenberg. (Vil) = Ellmendingen.

Keuper (Ger). A soil of mixed clay, chalk or Gypsum found in Franken.

Kevedinka (Yug). A white grape variety grown in the regions of Subotička Peščara and Vojvodina.

Keystone (Eng). Used when dealing with cask beers. A wooden bung which has the centre partially bored through to enable the tap to be driven through the Keystone into the cask to let the beer be drawn off.

Keystone Burgundy (Austr). The brand-label for the wines of the Tatachilla Vineyard.

Khaheti (USSR). The process of allowing grape skins to lie on the must for a full month before filtering.

Khalokhorio (Cyp). A major wine-producing village for Commandaria (made from the Xynisteri grape).

Khamar (Isr). See Khemer.

Khan Krum (Bul). A noted State winery based in Bulgaria.

Khat (Arab). See Qat also Kat.

Khatura Cooler (Cktl). ½ measure French vermouth, ½ measure Italian vermouth, ½ measure dry Gin, 1 pint soda water, 2 dashes Angostura. Stir gently with ice, serve in highball glasses.

Khemer (Isr). A white wine mentioned in the Bible. Also spelt Khamar.

Kheteteli (USSR). A white grape variety.

Khios (Gre). An island in the Aegean Islands in Eastern Greece. Produces mainly dessert wines.

Khledia (Afr). A large co-operative based in Tunisia. Owned by the UCCVT.

Khometz (Isr). A white wine mentioned in the Bible, described as being similar to vinegar in taste.

Khorasan (Iran). A noted wine region of northern Iran that produces a red wine of the same name from the Shiraz grape.

Khristianssand Brewery (Nor). A noted brewery based in Khristianssand, southern Norway.

Kia-Fey (China). The name for coffee in Cantonese.

Kian Dian Cong Lu (China). A Rémy Martin supervised wine farm in the Tianjin region near Beijing (Peking). Produces Dynasty (a dry white wine).

Kia-Ora (Eng). A brand of low-sugar squashes produced by Schweppes.

Kibo Chagga (Afr). The finest coffee (Arabica) produced in Tanzania on the slopes of Mount Kilimanjaro by the Chagga tribe. Has fine acidity and body. See also Kilimanjaro Coffee.

Kibowi (Hol). A Kiwi fruit liqueur produced in Amsterdam. 20% alc. by vol.

Kick (Eng) (slang). A term given to some spirits with a high alcohol or fierce alcohol taste that 'hits' the stomach.

Kick (Eng). A small indent at the base of early glass bottles. As the bottles became more onion shaped so the 'kicks' became larger.

Kickelskopf (Ger). Vineyard. (Anb) = Nahe. (Ber) = Schloss Böckelheim. (Gro) = Burgweg. (Vil) = Traisen.

Kid (Eng). A small wooden barrel used for spirits in the home in the eighteenth century.

Kidman (Austr). A noted winery based in the Coonawarra district of South Australia.

Kiechlinsbergen (Ger). Village. (Anb) = Baden. (Ber) = Kaiserstuhl-Tuniberg. (Gro) = Vulkanfelsen. (Vins) = Ölberg, Teufelsberg.

Kiedrich (Ger). Village. (Anb) = Rheingau. (Ber) = Johannisberg. (Gro) = Heiligenstock. (Vils) = Gräfenberg, Klosterberg, Sandgrub, Wasseros.

Kientzler (André) (Fr). An Alsace wine producer. Address = 50, Route de Bergheim, 68150 Ribeauville.

Kieselberg (Ger). Vineyard. (Anb) = Nahe. (Ber) = Schloss Böckelheim. (Gro) = Burgweg. (Vil) = Oberhausen an der Nahe.

Kieselberg (Ger). Vineyard. (Anb) = Rheinhessen. (Ber) = Bingen. (Gro) = Sankt Rochuskapelle. (Vil) = Biebelsheim.

Kieselberg (Ger). Vineyard. (Anb) = Rheinpfalz. (Ber) = Mittelhaardt-Deutsche Weinstrasse. (Gro) = Feuerberg. (Vil) = Bobenheim am Berg.

Kieselberg (Ger). Vineyard. (Anb) = Rheinpfalz. (Ber) = Mittelhaardt-Deutsche Weinstrasse. (Gro) = Höllenpfad. (Vil) = Kleinkarlbach.

Kieselberg (Ger). Vineyard. (Anb) = Rheinpfalz. (Ber) = Mittelhaardt-Deutsche Weinstrasse. (Gro) = Mariengarten. (Vil) = Deidesheim.

Kieselberg (Ger). Vineyard. (Anb) = Rheinpfalz. (Ber) = Mittelhaardt-Deutsche Weinstrasse. (Gro) = Rosenbühl. (Vil) = Erpolzheim.

K

Kieselguhr (Ger). A diatomaceous earth used for initial rough filtration of wines and beers. See also Bentonite.

Kiko Masamune Saké (Jap). A popular brand of Saké.

Kilbeggan (Ire). An Irish whiskey distilled by John Locke & Co. Kilbeggan Offaly. Produced a Vintage 1946 (39 dozen) bottled after 34 years in cask.

Kilderkin (Eng). A beer barrel holding 18 gallons.

Kiliansberg (Ger). Vineyard. (Anb) = Franken. (Ber) = Steigerwald. (Gro) = Schlossberg. (Vil) = Grosslangheim.

Kilimanjaro Coffee (Afr). Also known as Kibo Chagga. Produced on the slopes of Mount Kilimanjaro in Tanzania by the Chagga tribe.

Kilimanjaro Lager (Afr). A full-flavoured Lager beer brewed by the Tanzania Breweries Ltd. in Tanzania.

Killawarra (Austr). A noted winery based in the Adelaide Hills, South Australia.

Killawarra Selection Chardonnay (Austr). A fine white wine from the Wynvale Winery, New South Wales.

Kill-Devil (Eng). The Anglo-Saxon name for Aguardiente. Drawn from the distillation of sugar that is extracted from sugar cane after having left it to ferment.

Kill-Devil (W.Ind). One of the first names applied to Rum in the British West Indies.

Killian (Ire). George Killian's Irish Red Ale brewed by Pelford in France as Bière Rousse and by Coors in USA. Under licence from the Letts Brewery.

Kiln (Eng). A building where germinating barley after malting is dried.

Kilning (Scot). The drying of the malted barley for whisky production.

Kilzberg (Ger). Vineyard. (Anb) = Rheingau. (Ber) = Johannisberg. (Gro) = Erntebringer. (Vil) = Geisenheim.

Kimberley Ales (Eng). Beers brewed by the Hardys and Hansons Brewery in Nottingham, Notts.

Kimërt Bor (Hun). Ordinary wine.

Kimmeridge Clay (Eng). The name for a bituminous clay first discovered around the village of Kimmeridge in Devon. Found in many areas e.g. Chablis (Burgundy) and Quincy (Loire).

Kina (Fr). A brand of French apéritif wine.

Kina (Cktl).(1). ¾ measure dry Gin, ¼ measure Campari Reed Onion. Stir over ice, strain into a cocktail glass.

Kina (Cktl).(2). ½ measure Plymouth gin, ¼ measure Lillet, ¼ measure sweet Vermouth. Shake over ice, strain into a cocktail glass.

Kina-Citron (Cktl). ½ gill Kina, ⅙ gill Sirop de Citron, soda water. Stir over ice, strain into a tall glass with ice.

Kinclaith (Scot). A single Malt whisky distillery based on the outskirts of Glasgow. Owned by Long John. A Lowland malt. 40% alc. by vol.

Kindenheim (Ger). Village. (Anb) = Rheinpfalz. (Ber) = Mittelhaardt-Deutsche Weinstrasse. (Gro) = Grafenstück. (Vins) = Burgweg, Katzenstein, Sonnenberg, Vogelsang.

Kindilan (Austr). A 'Nouveau' wine produced by the Quelltaler Springvale Vineyards from Merlot and Shiraz grapes harvested in Clare Watervale, South Australia.

Kindl Brauerei (Ger). A famous brewery based in West Berlin. Noted for its' Weiss Bier.

Kindzma-Aruli (USSR). The alternative spelling of Kindzmaraouli.

Kindzmaraouli (USSR). A red grape variety grown in Georgia to produce red dessert wines. See also Kindzma-Aruli.

King Alfonse (Cktl). ¾ measure Kahlúa, ¼ measure cream. Float cream on top of Kahlúa in a liqueur glass.

King and Barnes Brewery (Eng). Based in Horsham, West Sussex. Noted for its' cask conditioned Sussex Mild 1034 O.G. Draught Festive 1050 O.G. Sussex Bitter 1034 O.G. J.K. Stout 1034 O.G. and Golding 1075 O.G.

King Arthur (USA). A major brand of dry Gin produced by Seagram.

King Cole (Cktl). ⅓ gill Bourbon whiskey, 2 dashes Gomme syrup, ⅙ gill orange juice, slice of pineapple. Blend together with a scoop of ice. Pour into a flute glass.

King Duncan (Eng). The brand-name of a British Wine and Scotch Whisky drink.

King Fergus Mac (Eng). The brand-name of a Ginger Wine and Scotch Whisky drink.

Kingfisher Lager (Ind). A brand of Lager-style beer brewed by the United Breweries in Bangalore.

Kingfisher Stout (Ind). A bitter Stout 1046 O.G. brewed by the United Breweries in Bangalore.

King George (Cktl). ¼ measure Plymouth gin, ¼ measure sweet Vermouth, ¼ measure Bénédictine, ¼ measure Caperatif, dash Pastis. Shake over ice, strain into a cocktail glass.

King George Fourth (Scot). A blended Scotch Whisky produced by the Distillers Agency Ltd. (Part of the DCL group).

King George Fourth Cocktail (Cktl). ¼ measure Gin, ¼ measure Scotch whisky, ¼ measure Cointreau, ¼ measure lemon juice. Shake over ice, strain into a cocktail glass.

King Keg Bitter (Eng). A keg Bitter 1038 O.G. brewed by the Greene King Brewery in East Anglia.

King of Alsace (Fr). An accolade given to the Riesling grape.

King Peter (Cktl). ⅓ measure Peter Heering, ⅓ measure tonic water, dash lemon juice. Build into an ice-filled highball glass.

Kingpin Mild (Eng). A dark keg Mild beer brewed by the Ansells Brewery.

Kings (USA). A wine district within the Great Central Valley of California. Produces sweet dessert wines.

King's Ale (Eng). A strong bottled Ale 1060 O.G. brewed by Matthew Brown of Blackburn, Lancashire.

King's Arms (Eng). A home-brew public house in Bishop Auckland, County Durham. Noted for its' cask conditioned Weardale Bitter 1038 O.G.

Kings County (USA). A small wine-producing county in San Joaquin (between Tular and Fresno counties), California.

Kings Daiquiri (Cktl). 1½ ozs. white Rum, ½ oz. Parfait Armour, ½ oz. lime juice, ¼ teaspoon sugar, 1 dash egg white. Blend together with crushed ice, pour into a Champagne saucer.

Kingsdown Ale (Eng). A Bitter ale 1050 O.G. brewed by the Arkell Brewery in Stratton St. Margaret, near Swindon, Wiltshire.

King's Ginger Liqueur (The) (Hol). A liqueur produced from root of ginger plant. Produced in Amsterdam for Berry Bros and Rudd of London. 40% alc. by vol.

Kings Green Vineyard (Eng). A vineyard based at Bouton, Gillingham, Dorset. 2.3 ha. Grape varieties – Chardonnay, Gamay noir, Gewürztraminer, Müller-Thurgau, Pinot noir and Zweigeltrebe.

Kings Head (Eng). The name used by Vine Products Ltd. for their white British Dessert Wine and British Sherry.

King's Ransom (Scot). A 12 year old blended Scotch Whisky produced by William Whiteley & Co., Pitlochry. 43% alc. by vol. (Now owned by Pernod-Ricard).

King's Royal (Scot). A blended Scotch Whisky produced by Clyde Distillers of Glasgow. 43% alc. by vol.

King's Screw (Eng). A patented 'Rack and Pinion' corkscrew produced in the eighteenth century.

Kingston (Port). Vintage Port shippers. Vintages – 1922, 1924, 1927.

Kingston Black (Eng). A variety of Cider apple of good quality, high in sugar and low in acidity.

Kingston Cocktail (Cktl).(1). 1 measure Jamaican rum, ¼ measure Kümmel, ¼ measure orange juice, dash Pimento liqueur. Shake over ice, strain into a cocktail glass.

Kingston Cocktail (Cktl).(2). ⅓ measure Bacardi rum, ⅓ measure Cointreau, ⅙ measure Crème de Banane, ⅙ measure pineapple juice, dash blue Curaçao. Shake over ice, strain into a cocktail glass. Top with a slice of lime.

King's Vat (Scot). A blended Scotch whisky produced by Sandeman & Son, Dundee, Perthshire. 40% alc. by vol.

King's Wood Bitter (Eng). A keg Bitter 1039 O.G. brewed by the New Forest Brewery in Hampshire.

Kinheim (Ger). Village. (Anb) = Mosel-Saar-Ruwer. (Ber) = Bernkastel. (Gro) = Schwarzlay. (Vins) = Hubertuslay, Rosenberg.

Kinine (Hol). Quinine.

Kinizsi (Hun). A Lager-style beer 3.5% alc. by vol.

Kinnie (Euro). A branded soft drink produced on the island of Malta.

Kinnie Winnie (Cktl). 1 fl.oz. Brandy, 1 fl.oz. Grand Marnier, 1 fl.oz. orange juice. Pour into a ice-filled highball glass. Top with Kinnie.

Kinross Ale (Eng). A bottled Scotch ale 1064 O.G. brewed for export by the Paines Brewery in Cambridgeshire.

Kintyre (Scot). A peninsular on the west coast of Scotland where the Campbeltown whiskies are produced. Also called the Mull of Kintyre.

Kinver House (Eng). A vineyard based at Dunsley House, Kinver, Worcs. Was first planted in 1973. 1 ha. Grape varieties – Auxerrois, Bacchus, Madeleine angevine, Müller-Thurgau, Pinot noir and others.

Kinzigtäler (Ger). Vineyard. (Anb) = Baden. (Ber) = Ortenau. (Gro) = Fürsteneck. (Vil) = Berghaupten.

Kinzigtäler (Ger). Vineyard. (Anb) = Baden. (Ber) = Ortenau. (Gro) = Fürsteneck. (Vil) = Bermersbach.

Kinzigtäler (Ger). Vineyard. (Anb) = Baden. (Ber) = Ortenau. (Gro) = Fürsteneck. (Vil) = Diersburg.

Kinzigtäler (Ger). Vineyard. (Anb) = Baden. (Ber) = Ortenau. (Gro) = Fürsteneck. (Vil) = Gengenbach.

Kinzigtäler (Ger). Vineyard. (Anb) = Baden. (Ber) = Ortenau. (Gro) = Fürsteneck. (Vil) = Hofweier.

Kinzigtäler (Ger). Vineyard. (Anb) = Baden. (Ber) = Ortenau. (Gro) = Fürsteneck. (Vil) = Niederschopfheim.

K

Kinzigtäler (Ger). Vineyard. (Anb) = Baden. (Ber) = Ortenau. (Gro) = Fürsteneck. (Vil) = Ohlsbach.

Kinzigtäler (Ger). Vineyard. (Anb) = Baden. (Ber) = Ortenau. (Gro) = Fürsteneck. (Vil) = Reichenbach.

Kinzigtäler (Ger). Vineyard. (Anb) = Baden. (Ber) = Ortenau. (Gro) = Fürsteneck. (Vil) = Zunsweier.

Kiola (It). Moscato d'Asti producers based in the Piemonte region,

Kippe (Hol). The eighteenth century name for a common Ale house.

Kippenhausen (Ger). Village. (Anb) = Baden. (Ber) = Bodensee. (Gro) = Sonnenufer. (Vin) = Burgstall.

Kippenheim (Ger). Village. (Anb) = Baden. (Ber) = Breisgau. (Gro) = Schutterlindenberg. (Vin) = Haselstaude.

Kipperlé (Fr). The alternative spelling for the white Knipperlé grape.

Kir (Fr). A Burgundian apéritif of dry white Burgundy wine (Aligoté) and a dash of Cassis. Named after Canon Kir the Mayor of Dijon. See also Kir Royale, Cardinal and Communiste.

Kiraathane (Tur). A coffee house, café (eastern-style).

Kirchardt [ortsteil Berwangen] (Ger). Village. (Anb) = Baden. (Ber) = Badische Bergstrasse/Kraichgau. (Gro) = Stiftsberg. (Vin) = Vogelsang.

Kirchberg (Ger). Lit – 'Church hill'. A popular name for vineyards in Germany. No less than 49 have the name plus a Grosslage and 2 villages.

Kirchberg (Ger). Grosslage. (Anb) = Franken. (Ber) = Maindreieck. (Vils) = Astheim, Escherndorf, Fahr, Köhler, Krautheim, Neuses, Neusetz, Nordheim, Obereisenheim, Obervolkach, Sommerach, Stammheim, Untereisenheim, Volkach, Wipfeld.

Kirchberg (Ger). Village. (Anb) = Baden. (Ber) = Bodensee. See Salem.

Kirchberg (Ger). Village. (Anb) = Württemberg. (Ber) = Württembergisch Unterland. (Gro) = Schalkstein. (Vin) = Kelterberg.

Kirchberg (Ger). Vineyard. (Anb) = Baden. (Ber) = Badische Bergstrasse/Kraichgau. (Gro) = Mannaberg. (Vil) = Kraichtal (stadtteil Oberöwisheim, stadtteil Unteröwisheim).

Kirchberg (Ger). Vineyard. (Anb) = Baden. (Ber) = Badische Frankenland. (Gro) = Tauberklinge. (Vil) = Beckstein.

Kirchberg (Ger). Vineyard. (Anb) = Baden. (Ber) = Badische Frankenland. (Gro) = Tauberklinge. (Vil) = Königheim.

Kirchberg (Ger). Vineyard. (Anb) = Baden. (Ber) = Badische Frankenland. (Gro) = Tauberklinge. (Vil) = Königshofen.

Kirchberg (Ger). Vineyard. (Anb) = Baden. (Ber) = Breisgau. (Gro) = Schutterlindenberg. (Vil) = Ettenheim (ortsteil Wallburg).

Kirchberg (Ger). Vineyard. (Anb) = Baden. (Ber) = Breisgau. (Gro) = Schutterlindenberg. (Vil) = Münchweiler.

Kirchberg (Ger). Vineyard. (Anb) = Baden. (Ber) = Breisgau. (Gro) = Schutterlindenberg. (Vil) = Schmieheim.

Kirchberg (Ger). Vineyard. (Anb) = Baden. (Ber) = Kaiserstuhl-Tuniberg. (Gro) = Attilafelsen. (Vil) = Gottenheim.

Kirchberg (Ger). Vineyard. (Anb) = Baden. (Ber) = Kaiserstuhl-Tuniberg. (Gro) = Vulkanfelsen. (Vil) = Oberrotweil.

Kirchberg (Ger). Vineyard. (Anb) = Baden. (Ber) = Kaiserstuhl-Tuniberg. (Gro) = Vulkanfelsen. (Vil) = Schelingen.

Kirchberg (Ger). Vineyard. (Anb) = Baden. (Ber) = Markgräflerland. (Gro) = Burg Neuenfels. (Vil) = Lipburg.

Kirchberg (Ger). Vineyard. (Anb) = Baden. (Ber) = Markgräflerland. (Gro) = Lorettoberg. (Vil) = Kirchhofen.

Kirchberg (Ger). Vineyard. (Anb) = Baden. (Ber) = Markgräflerland. (Gro) = Vogtei Rötteln. (Vil) = Efringen-Kirchen.

Kirchberg (Ger). Vineyard. (Anb) = Baden. (Ber) = Markgräflerland. (Gro) = Vogtei Rötteln. (Vil) = Huttingen.

Kirchberg (Ger). Vineyard. (Anb) = Baden. (Ber) = Markgräflerland. (Gro) = Vogtei Rötteln. (Vil) = Istein.

Kirchberg (Ger). Vineyard. (Anb) = Franken. (Ber) = Maindreieck. (Gro) = Not yet assigned. (Vil) = Würzberg.

Kirchberg (Ger). Vineyard. (Anb) = Franken. (Ber) = Steigerwald. (Gro) = Herrenberg. (Vil) = Castell.

Kirchberg (Ger). Vineyard. (Anb) = Franken. (Ber) = Steigerwald. (Gro) = Schild. (Vil) = Castell.

Kirchberg (Ger). Vineyard. (Anb) = Hessische Bergstrasse. (Ber) = Starkenburg. (Gro) = Wolfsmagen. (Vil) = Bensheim.

Kirchberg (Ger). Vineyard. (Anb) = Mosel-Saar-Ruwer. (Ber) = Bernkastel. (Gro) = Kurfürstlay. (Vil) = Burgen.

Kirchberg (Ger). Vineyard. (Anb) = Mosel-Saar-Ruwer. (Ber) = Bernkastel. (Gro) = Kurfürstlay. (Vil) = Maring-Noviand.

Kirchberg (Ger). Vineyard. (Anb) = Mosel-Saar-Ruwer. (Ber) = Bernkastel. (Gro) = Kurfürstlay. (Vil) = Veldenz.

Kirchberg (Ger). Vineyard. (Anb) = Mosel-Saar-Ruwer. (Ber) = Saar-Ruwer. (Gro) = Scharzberg. (Vil) = Könen.

Kirchberg (Ger). Vineyard. (Anb) = Mosel-Saar-Ruwer. (Ber) = Zell/Mosel. (Gro) =

K

Goldbäumchen. (Vil) = Moselkern.
Kirchberg (Ger). Vineyard. (Anb) = Mosel-Saar-Ruwer. (Ber) = Zell/Mosel. (Gro) = Weinhex. (Vil) = Hatzenport.
Kirchberg (Ger). Vineyard. (Anb) = Nahe. (Ber) = Schloss Böckelheim. (Gro) = Burgweg. (Vil) = Waldböckelheim.
Kirchberg (Ger). Vineyard. (Anb) = Rheinhessen. (Ber) = Bingen. (Gro) = Rheingrafenstein. (Vil) = Eckelsheim.
Kirchberg (Ger). Vineyard. (Anb) = Rheinhessen. (Ber) = Bingen. (Gro) = Rheingrafenstein. (Vil) = Frei-Laubersheim.
Kirchberg (Ger). Vineyard. (Anb) = Rheinhessen. (Ber) = Bingen. (Gro) = Rheingrafenstein. (Vil) = Hackenheim.
Kirchberg (Ger). Vineyard. (Anb) = Rheinhessen. (Ber) = Bingen. (Gro) = Sankt Rochuskapelle. (Vil) = Bingen.
Kirchberg (Ger). Vineyard. (Anb) = Rheinhessen. (Ber) = Nierstein. (Gro) = Domherr. (Vil) = Gabsheim.
Kirchberg (Ger). Vineyard. (Anb) = Rheinhessen. (Ber) = Nierstein. (Gro) = Domherr. (Vil) = Udenheim.
Kirchberg (Ger). Vineyard. (Anb) = Rheinhessen. (Ber) = Wonnegau. (Gro) = Pilgerpfad. (Vil) = Osthofen.
Kirchberg (Ger). Vineyard. (Anb) = Rheinpfalz. (Ber) = Mittelhaardt-Deutsche Weinstrasse. (Gro) = Rebstöckel. (Vil) = Hambach.
Kirchberg (Ger). Vineyard. (Anb) = Rheinpfalz. (Ber) = Südliche Weinstrasse. (Gro) = Kloster Liebfrauenberg. (Vil) = Barbelroth.
Kirchberg (Ger). Vineyard. (Anb) = Rheinpfalz. (Ber) = Südliche Weinstrasse. (Gro) = Kloster Liebfrauenberg. (Vil) = Gleiszellen-Gleishorbach.
Kirchberg (Ger). Vineyard. (Anb) = Rheinpfalz. (Ber) = Südliche Weinstrasse. (Gro) = Königsgarten. (Vil) = Albersweiler.
Kirchberg (Ger). Vineyard. (Anb) = Rheinpfalz. (Ber) = Südliche Weinstrasse. (Gro) = Schloss Ludwigshöhe. (Vil) = Edenkoben.
Kirchberg (Ger). Vineyard. (Anb) = Rheinpfalz. (Ber) = Südliche Weinstrasse. (Gro) = Schloss Ludwigshöhe. (Vil) = St. Martin.
Kirchberg (Ger). Vineyard. (Anb) = Rheinpfalz. (Ber) = Südliche Weinstrasse. (Gro) = Trappenberg. (Vil) = Grossfischlingen, Kleinfischlingen.
Kirchberg (Ger). Vineyard. (Anb) = Württemberg. (Ber) = Remstal-Stuttgart. (Gro) = Weinsteige. (Vil) = Esslingen.
Kirchberg (Ger). Vineyard. (Anb) = Württemberg. (Ber) = Remstal-Stuttgart. (Gro) = Weinsteige. (Vil) = Stuttgart (ortsteil Obertürkheim).

Kirchberg (Ger). Vineyard. (Anb) = Württemberg. (Ber) = Württembergisch Unterland. (Gro) = Stromberg. (Vil) = Bönnigheim.
Kirchberg (Ger). Vineyard. (Anb) = Württemberg. (Ber) = Württembergisch Unterland. (Gro) = Stromberg. (Vil) = Freudental.
Kirchberg (Ger). Vineyard. (Anb) = Württemberg. (Ber) = Württembergisch Unterland. (Gro) = Stromberg. (Vil) = Hohenhaslach.
Kirchberg (Ger). Vineyard. (Anb) = Württemberg. (Ber) = Württembergisch Unterland. (Gro) = Stromberg. (Vil) = Hohenstein.
Kirchberg (Ger). Vineyard. (Anb) = Württemberg. (Ber) = Württembergisch Unterland. (Gro) = Stromberg. (Vil) = Kirchheim.
Kirchberg (Ger). Vineyard. (Anb) = Württemberg. (Ber) = Württembergisch Unterland. (Gro) = Stromberg. (Vil) = Kleinsachsenheim.
Kirchberg (Ger). Vineyard. (Anb) = Württemberg. (Ber) = Württembergisch Unterland. (Gro) = Stromberg. (Vil) = Riet.
Kirche (Ger). Church.
Kirchenpfad (Ger). Vineyard. (Anb) = Rheingau. (Ber) = Johannisberg. (Gro) = Burgweg. (Vil) = Rüdesheim.
Kirchenstück (Ger). Vineyard. (Anb) = Rheingau. (Ber) = Johannisberg. (Gro) = Daubhaus. (Vil) = Hochheim.
Kirchenstück (Ger). Vineyard. (Anb) = Rheinhessen. (Ber) = Bingen. (Gro) = Adelberg. (Vil) = Bornheim.
Kirchenstück (Ger). Vineyard. (Anb) = Rheinhessen. (Ber) = Bingen. (Gro) = Kaiserpfalz. (Vil) = Ingelheim.
Kirchenstück (Ger). Vineyard. (Anb) = Rheinhessen. (Ber) = Nierstein. (Gro) = Sankt Alban. (Vil) = Mainz.
Kirchenstück (Ger). Vineyard. (Anb) = Rheinhessen. (Ber) = Wonnegau. (Gro) = Domblick. (Vil) = Hohen-Sülzen.
Kirchenstück (Ger). Vineyard. (Anb) = Rheinhessen. (Ber) = Wonnegau. (Gro) = Sybillenstein. (Vil) = Weinheim.
Kirchenstück (Ger). Vineyard. (Anb) = Rheinpfalz. (Ber) = Mittelhaardt-Deutsche Weinstrasse. (Gro) = Hofstück. (Vil) = Ellerstadt.
Kirchenstück (Ger). Vineyard. (Anb) = Rheinpfalz. (Ber) = Mittelhaardt-Deutsche Weinstrasse. (Gro) = Kobnert. (Vil) = Herxheim/Berg.
Kirchenstück (Ger). Vineyard. (Anb) = Rheinpfalz. (Ber) = Mittelhaardt-Deutsche Weinstrasse. (Gro) = Kobnert. (Vil) = Leistadt.
Kirchenstück (Ger). Vineyard. (Anb) =

K

Rheinpfalz. (Ber) = Mittelhaardt-Deutsche Weinstrasse. (Gro) = Mariengarten. (Vil) = Forst.

Kirchenstück (Ger). Vineyard. (Anb) = Rheinpfalz. (Ber) = Mittelhaardt-Deutsche Weinstrasse. (Gro) = Saumagen. (Vil) = Kallstadt.

Kirchenstück (Ger). Vineyard. (Anb) = Rheinpfalz. (Ber) = Sudliche Weinstrasse. (Gro) = Bischofskreuz. (Vil) = Nussdorf.

Kirchenstück (Ger). Vineyard. (Anb) = Rheinpfalz. (Ber) = Südliche Weinstrasse. (Gro) = Mandelhöhe. (Vil) = Maikammer.

Kirchenstück (Ger). Vineyard. (Anb) = Rheinpfalz. (Ber) = Südliche Weinstrasse. (Gro) = Ordensgut. (Vil) = Hainfeld.

Kirchenweinberg (Ger). Grosslage. (Anb) = Württemberg. (Ber) = Württembergisch Unterland. (Vils) = Flein, Heilbronn, Ilsfeld (ortsteil Schozach), Lauffen, Neckarwestheim, Talheim, Untergruppenbach.

Kirchgärtchen (Ger). Vineyard. (Anb) = Rheinhessen. (Ber) = Bingen. (Gro) = Sankt Rochuskapelle. (Vil) = Welgesheim.

Kirchgarten (Ger). Vineyard. (Anb) = Rheinpfalz. (Ber) = Mittelhaardt-Deutsche Weinstrasse. (Gro) = Schwarzerde. (Vil) = Laumersheim.

Kirchhalde (Ger). Vineyard. (Anb) = Baden. (Ber) = Bodensee. (Gro) = Sonnenufer. (Vil) = Oberruhldingen.

Kirchheim (Ger). Village. (Anb) = Rheinpfalz. (Ber) = Mittelhaardt-Deutsche Weinstrasse. (Gro) = Schwarzerde. (Vins) = Geisskopf, Kreuz, Römerstrasse, Steinacker.

Kirchheim (Ger). Village. (Anb) = Württemberg. (Ber) = Württembergisch Unterland. (Gro) = Stromberg. (Vin) = Kirchberg.

Kirchheimbolanden (Ger). Village. (Anb) = Rheinpfalz. (Ber) = Mittelhaardt-Deutsche Weinstrasse. (Gro) = Schnepfenflug vom Kellertal. (Vin) = Schlossgarten.

Kirchhofen (Ger). Village. (Anb) = Baden. (Ber) = Markgräflerland. (Gro) = Lorettoberg. (Vins) = Batzenberg, Höllhagen, Kirchberg.

Kirchhöh (Ger). Vineyard. (Anb) = Rheinpfalz. (Ber) = Südliche Weinstrasse. (Gro) = Guttenberg. (Vil) = Dierbach.

Kirchlay (Ger). Vineyard. (Anb) = Mosel-Saar-Ruwer. (Ber) = Bernkastel. (Gro) = Nacktarsch. (Vil) = Kröv.

Kirchlay (Ger). Vineyard. (Anb) = Mosel-Saar-Ruwer. (Ber) = Bernkastel.

(Gro) = Kurfürstlay. (Vil) = Osann-Monzel.

Kirchlay (Ger). Vineyard. (Anb) = Mosel-Saar-Ruwer. (Ber) = Zell/Mosel. (Gro) = Goldbäumchen. (Vil) = Ernst.

Kirchplatte (Ger). Vineyard. (Anb) = Rheinhessen. (Ber) = Nierstein. (Gro) = Spiegelberg. (Vil) = Nierstein.

Kirchspiel (Ger). Vineyard. (Anb) = Rheinhessen. (Ber) = Wonnegau. (Gro) = Bergkloster. (Vil) = Westhofen.

Kirchtürmchen (Ger). Vineyard. (Anb) = Ahr. (Ber) = Walporzheim/Ahrtal. (Gro) = Klosterberg. (Vil) = Bad Neuenahr.

Kirchweih (Ger). A Bier of 13.9° brewed specially for the Bergkirchweih festival.

Kirchweinberg (Ger). Vineyard. (Anb) = Baden. (Ber) = Badische Bergstrasse/Kraichgau. (Gro) = Stiftsberg. (Vil) = Hassmersheim.

Kirchweinberg (Ger). Vineyard. (Anb) = Baden. (Ber) = Badische Bergstrasse/Kraichgau. (Gro) = Stiftsberg. (Vil) = Neckarzimmern.

Kirchweingarten (Ger). Vineyard. (Anb) = Mosel-Saar-Ruwer. (Ber) = Zell/ Mosel. (Gro) = Grafschaft. (Vil) = Bullay.

Kirchwingert (Ger). Vineyard. (Anb) = Rheinhessen. (Ber) = Bingen. (Gro) = Rheingrafenstein. (Vil) = Neu-Bamberg.

Kirf (Ger). Village. (Anb) = Mosel-Saar-Ruwer. (Ber) = Obermosel. (Gro) = Gipfel. (Vins) = Sites not yet chosen.

Kir Gallique (Fr). A brand-name of Kir.

Kirghizia (USSR). A wine-producing region in the southern Soviet Union. Produces red and white dessert wines.

Kiri (Eng). A sparkling non-alcoholic apple juice drink produced by Bulmers of Hereford, Herefordshire.

Kirigin Cellars (USA). A large winery based near the Hecker Pass district, Santa Clara, California. 19 ha. Grape varieties – Pinot noir and Zinfandel. Produces varietal wines.

Kirin Beer (Jap). A brand of beer 4.5% alc. by vol. exported to USA.

Kirin Brewery (Jap). A large brewery based in Tokyo. Produces beers and Stout of same name.

Kirkham Winery (USA). A small winery based near St. Helena, Napa Valley, California. 5 ha. Grape varieties – Chenin blanc and Gray riesling. Produces varietal wines.

Kirovabad (USSR). A major wine-producing centre in Azerbaijan.

Kir Rouge (Fr). A Crème de Cassis and a dry red Burgundy wine such as Passe-Tout-Grains.

Kir Royale (Fr). ⅙ gill Crème de Cassis topped with chilled brut Champagne.

Kirrweiler (Ger). Village. (Anb) =

K

Rheinpfalz. (Ber) = Südliche Wein-strasse. (Gro) = Mandelhöhe. (Vins) = Mandelberg, Oberschloss, Römerweg.

Kirsbaer (Den). A cherry brandy.

Kirsberry (Den). A cherry liqueur.

Kirsch (Ger). A clear cherry-flavoured liqueur made with the cherry kernels. Is matured in earthenware or paraffin-lined casks so absorbs no colour. 43% alc. by vol.

Kirsch and Cassis Cocktail (Cktl). 1/3 measure Kirsch, 2/3 measure Crème de Cassis. Shake over ice, strain into an ice-filled highball glass. Top with soda.

Kirsch de Zoug (Switz). A cherry brandy made in Zug.

Kirschgarten (Ger). Vineyard. (Anb) = Rheinpfalz. (Ber) = Mittelhaardt-Deutsche Weinstrasse. (Gro) = Kobnert. (Vil) = Erpolzheim.

Kirsch-Gewuerzlikoer (Ger). A liqueur made from cherries and herbal essences.

Kirschheck (Ger). Vineyard. (Anb) = Nahe. (Ber) = Kreuznach. (Gro) = Pfarrgarten. (Vil) = Wallhausen.

Kirschheck (Ger). Vineyard. (Anb) = Nahe. (Ber) = Schloss Böckelheim. (Gro) = Burgweg. (Vil) = Norheim.

Kirsch mit Whisky (Ger). A fruit liqueur based on neutral spirits and whisky as opposed to grape brandy. 34.5%-40% alc. by vol. e.g. Aprikose mit Whisky.

Kirsch Peureux (Fr). A colourless cherry liqueur 40% alc. by vol.

Kirschroth (Ger). Village. (Anb) = Nahe. (Ber) = Schloss Böckelheim. (Gro) = Paradiesgarten. (Vins) = Lump, Wild-grafenberg.

Kirschwasser (Ger). A Black Forest clear cherry brandy.

Kirsebaerlikoer (Mex). A fiery spirit produced from cacti.

Kirseboer Liqueur (Den). The name given to Peter Heering's Cherry Liqueur.

Kishbaba (Iran). A seedless white grape variety.

Kishinev (USSR). A dry white table wine produced in the Moldavia region.

Kishmish (Iran). A white grape variety grown in the Ispahan region.

Kiskadee (Ire). A white Rum made by the Irish Distillers Co.

Kis-Kesay (Cktl). 1/2 measure white Rum, 1/4 measure Crème de Cacao, 1/8 measure lime juice, 1/8 measure blackcurrant juice. Stir together over ice, strain into an ice-filled highball glass, top with orange cream and a twist of orange peel.

Kislav (USSR). A spirit made from water melons.

Kissingen Wasser (Ger). A natural sparkling spring saline water from Bavaria. Reputed to have medicinal properties.

Kiss in the Dark (Cktl). 1/3 measure Gin, 1/3 measure French vermouth, 1/3 measure Cherry brandy. Stir over ice, strain into a cocktail glass.

Kiss Me Quick (Cktl). 1 1/2 ozs. Pernod, 4 dashes Cointreau, 2 dashes Angostura. Shake with ice, strain into a highball glass, add ice, top up with soda.

Kiss the Boys Goodbye (Cktl). 1/6 gill Sloe Gin, 1/6 gill Cognac, juice of small lemon, 1/2 egg white. Shake well over ice, strain into a cocktail glass.

Kistler Vineyards (USA). A large winery based between the Napa and Sonoma Valleys. 16 ha. Grape varieties – Cabernet sauvignon, Chardonnay and Pinot noir. Produces varietal wines.

Kite Bitter (Eng). See Ancient Druids.

Kitron (Gre). A liqueur made from the leaves of lemon trees distilled with grape brandy and sweetened.

Kitty Highball (Cktl). 1/2 measure Claret, 1/2 measure ginger ale. Mix well together, serve on ice.

Kitty Love (Cktl). 1/3 measure Kirsch, 1/3 measure Carpano, 1/3 measure Cointreau, 2 dashes orange juice. Shake with ice, strain into a cocktail glass. Garnish with orange zest.

Kitzingen (Ger). Village. (Anb) = Franken. (Ber) = Maindreieck. (Gro) = Hofrat. (Vin) = Wilhelmsberg.

Kivu (Afr). A major-coffee producing region in Zaire.

Kivu Coffee (Afr). A coffee bean with a high acidity used mainly for blending from the Kivu region in Zaire.

Kiwi Liqueur (N.Z.). A golden green, kiwi fruit liqueur 40% alc. by vol.

Kizlarskoye (USSR). A dessert wine produced near Machackala on the Caspian Sea.

KK (Eng) (abbr). King Keg. A cask conditioned light Mild 1031 O.G. brewed by the Greene King Brewery in East Anglia.

K.K.W. (S.Afr) (abbr). Klawer Koöperatiewe Wynkelders. See Klawer Cooperative.

Klabauter Man (Cktl). 2/5 gill Arak, 2 gills Port wine, 1/6 gill lemon juice. Heat together slowly. Pour into mugs adding sugar to taste.

Klamm (Ger). Vineyard. (Anb) = Nahe. (Ber) = Schloss Böckelheim. (Gro) = Burgweg. (Vil) = Niederhausen an der Nahe.

Klapmuts (S.Afr). Vineyards which produce fine red wines.

Klarer (Ger). A term used to denote clear Schnapps (corn), Gin (Steinhäger).

Klassiek Droë (S.Afr). Classic dry. See also Klassiek Droog.

Klassiek Droog (S.Afr). Classic dry. See also Klassiek Droë.

K

Klassisches Ursprungsgebiet (It). A German term used in the Südtirol. See Classico.

Klàster Hradištĕ Brewery (Czec). An old brewery based in north-western Czec. Noted for its' Lager-style beers.

Klaus (Ger). Vineyard. (Anb) = Rheingau. (Ber) = Johannisberg. (Gro) = Erntebringer. (Vil) = Geisenheim.

Klaus (Ger). Vineyard. (Anb) = Rheingau. (Ber) = Johannisberg. (Gro) = Honigberg. (Vil) = Winkel.

Klausenberg (Ger). Vineyard. (Anb) = Rheinhessen. (Ber) = Wonnegau. (Gro) = Liebfrauenmorgen. (Vil) = Worms.

Kläuserweg (Ger). Vineyard. (Anb) = Rheingau. (Ber) = Johannisberg. (Gro) = Erntebringer. (Vil) = Geisenheim.

Klawer Co-operative (S.Afr). A winery based in the Olifants River area. Address = Klawer Koöperatiewe Wynkelders, Box 8 Klawer 8145. Produces varietals and Halfsoet Hanepoot.

Klein (Ger). Small.

Klein (René et Fils) (Fr). A wine-producer based in Alsace. Address = Route du Haut-Koenigsbourg, 68590 St-Hippolyte.

Kleinaspach (Ger). Village. (Anb) = Württemberg. (Ber) = Württembergisch Unterland. (Gro) = Schalkstein. (Vin) = Kelterberg.

Kleinberger (USA). A white grape variety used in California to make white table wines. Known as the Knipperlé and Elbling in Europe.

Kleinbottwar (Ger). Village. (Anb) = Württemberg. (Ber) = Württembergisch Unterland. (Gro) = Wunnenstein. (Vins) = Götzenberg, Lichtenberg, Obererberg, Sussmund.

Klein Constantia (S.Afr). Vineyards in Constantia.

Kleinelbling (Ger). An alternative name for the Elbling grape. See also Knipperlé.

Kleinergelber (Fr). An alternative name for the white Knipperlé grape.

Kleiner Räuschling (Fr). An alternative name for the white Knipperlé grape.

Kleiner Reuschling (Fr). An alternative name for the white Knipperlé grape.

Kleiner Riesling (Ger). An erroneous varietal name for the Ortlieber (Knipperlé). Also Briesgawer riesling.

Kleingartach (Ger). Village. (Anb) = Württemberg. (Ber) = Württembergisch Unterland. (Gro) = Heuchelberg. (Vins) = Grafenberg, Vogelsang.

Kleinheppach (Ger). Village. (Anb) = Württemberg. (Ber) = Remstal-Stuttgart. (Gro) = Kopf. (Vin) = Greiner.

Kleinheppach (Ger). Village. (Anb) = Württemberg. (Ber) = Remstal-Stuttgart. (Gro) = Wartbühl. (Vins) = Sonnenberg, Steingrüble.

Klein-Höflein (Aus). A wine-producing area in the Eisenstadt district.

Kleiningersheim (Ger). Village. (Anb) = Württemberg. (Ber) = Württembergisch Unterland. (Gro) = Schalkstein. (Vin) = Schlossberg.

Kleinkarlbach (Ger). Village. (Anb) = Rheinpfalz. (Ber) = Mittelhaardt-Deutsche Weinstrasse. (Gro) = Höllenpfad. (Vins) = Frauenlandchen, Herrenberg, Herrgottsacker, Kieselberg, Senn.

Klein Karoo (S.Afr). A demarcated wine district east of Montagu in Cape Province. See also Little Karoo.

Kleinkems (Ger). Village. (Anb) = Baden. (Ber) = Markgräflerland. (Gro) = Vogtei Rötteln. (Vin) = Wolfer.

Kleinlangheim (Ger). Village. (Anb) = Franken. (Ber) = Steigerwald. (Gro) = Not yet assigned. (Vin) = Wutschenberg.

Kleinniedesheim (Ger). Village. (Anb) = Rheinpfalz. (Ber) = Mittelhaardt-Deutsche Weinstrasse. (Gro) = Schwarzerde. (Vins) = Schlossgarten, Vorderberg.

Kleinoscheck (Aus). One of the leading sparkling wine producers of Austria.

Kleinpereich (Ger). An alternative name for the Elbling grape.

Kleinsachsenheim (Ger). Village. (Anb) = Württemberg. (Ber) = Württembergisch Unterland. (Gro) = Stromberg. (Vin) = Kirchberg.

Klein Schwechat (Aus). See Schwechat.

Kleintje (Hol). Lit – 'Baby'. A term used to describe a small glass of drink.

Klein-Umstadt (Ger). Village. (Anb) = Hessische Bergstrasse. (Ber) = Umstadt. (Gro) = Not yet assigned. (Vin) = Stachelberg.

Kleinvernatsch (It). The German name for the red Schiava piccola grape in the Südtirol.

Kleinweiss (Ger). A white grape variety also known as the Budaer riesling.

Klein-Winternheim (Ger). Village. (Anb) = Rheinhessen. (Ber) = Nierstein. (Gro) = Domherr. (Vins) = Geershöll, Herrgottshaus, Villenkelter.

Klein Zalze Estate (S.Afr). Vineyards sited in Stellenbosch. Address = c/o Gilbeys, P.O. Box 137, Stellenbosch 7600. Owned by Gilbeys. Produces Rare Late Vintage and varietals.

Klekovaça (Yug). See Klevovka.

Klekowatsch (USSR). A Balkan juniper berry-flavoured Gin. 38% alc. by vol.

K

Klenk (Ger). A method of red wine fermentation which is similar to maceration carbonique. See also Lidy.

Klepberg (Ger). Vineyard. (Anb) = Baden. (Ber) = Badische Bergstrasse/ Kraichgau. (Gro) = Hohenberg. (Vil) = Bilfingen.

Klepberg (Ger). Vineyard. (Anb) = Baden. (Ber) = Badische Bergstrasse/ Kraichgau. (Gro) = Hohenberg. (Vil) = Eisingen.

Klepberg (Ger). Vineyard. (Anb) = Baden. (Ber) = Badische Bergstrasse/ Kraichgau. (Gro) = Hohenberg. (Vil) = Ersingen.

Klepberg (Ger). Vineyard. (Anb) = Baden. (Ber) = Badische Bergstrasse/ Kraichgau. (Gro) = Hohenberg. (Vil) = Dietlingen.

Kletterberg (Ger). Vineyard. (Anb) = Rheinhessen. (Ber) = Bingen. (Gro) = Rheingrafenstein. (Vil) = Neu-Bamberg.

Klettgau [ortsteil Erzingen] (Ger). Village. (Anb) = Baden. (Ber) = Bodensee. (Gro) = Not yet assigned. (Vin) = Kapellenberg.

Klettgau [ortsteil Rechberg] (Ger). Village. (Anb) = Baden. (Ber) = Bodensee. (Gro) = Not yet assigned. (Vin) = Kapellenberg.

Klevener (Switz). A local name for the Pinot noir grape. Also spelt Clevener.

Klevner (Fr). Another name for the Pinot blanc wine of Alsace.

Klevovka (Yug). The distillation of juniper berries or plums. Also called Klekovaça (Slivovitz = juniper berries).

Klingelberger (Ger). The Baden region name for the Riesling grape.

Klingenberg (Ger). Village. (Anb) = Franken. (Ber) = Mainviereck. (Gro) = Not yet assigned. (Vins) = Hochberg, Schlossberg.

Klingenberg (Ger). Village. (Anb) = Württemberg. (Ber) = Württembergisch Unterland. (Gro) = Heuchelberg. See Heilbronn.

Klingenmünster (Ger). Village. (Anb) = Rheinpfalz. (Ber) = Südliche Weinstrasse. (Gro) = Kloster Liebfrauenberg. (Vin) = Maria Magdalena.

Klingle (Ger). Vineyard. (Anb) = Württemberg. (Ber) = Remstal-Stuttgart. (Gro) = Wartbühl. (Vil) = Grunbach.

Klingshirn Winery (USA). A winery based in Avon Lake, Ohio. Produces mainly Concord wines.

Klinto (It). A name given to a strawberry tasting red wine produced in the Treviso region. Vino rosso.

Klipdrift (S.Afr). The brand-name for a Brandy produced by Castle Wine and Green.

Klipfel (Fr). A Crémant d'Alsace producer based at Barr in Alsace.

Kloch-Ost-Steiermark (Aus). A wine district within the region of Steiermark (Styria). Produces mainly white wines.

Kloeckera Apiculata (Lat). One of the prolific 'wild yeasts' found in grape bloom.

Klondyke Cocktail (Cktl). ¼ gill Applejack, ¼ measure French vermouth, 3 dashes Orange bitters. Stir over ice, strain into a cocktail glass, add a small olive and a squeeze of lemon peel juice on top.

Klondyke Cooler (Cktl). As for Gin Cooler using Bourbon whiskey instead of Gin.

Kloppberg (Ger). Vineyard. (Anb) = Rheinhessen. (Ber) = Wonnegau. (Gro) = Pilgerpfad. (Vil) = Dittelsheim-Hessloch.

Kloppenberg (Ger). Vineyard. (Anb) = Rheinhessen. (Ber) = Nierstein. (Gro) = Gutes Domtal. (Vil) = Mommenheim.

Kloster (Ger). Monastery.

Kloster (Ger). Vineyard. (Anb) = Nahe. (Ber) = Schloss Böckelheim. (Gro) = Paradiesgarten. (Vil) = Odernheim.

Kloster Andechs Brauerei (Ger). A large monastery brewery based in Bavaria, Western Germany. Beers brewed by the Monks.

Kloster Beer (E.Asia). A Lager beer brewed in Kuala Lumpar, Malaya.

Klosterberg (Ger). Lit – 'Monastery hill'. A popular name for vineyards in Germany. Named after the days when vineyards were owned by the Church. There are 24 individual sites with this name. Also a Grosslage.

Klosterberg (Ger). Grosslage. (Anb) = Ahr. (Ber) = Walporzheim/Ahrtal. (Vils) = Ahrweiler, Altenahr, Bachem, Bad Neuenahr, Dernau, Heimersheim, Heppingen, Marienthal, Mayschoss, Rech, Walporzheim.

Klosterberg (Ger). Vineyard. (Anb) = Baden. (Ber) = Badische Bergstrasse/ Kraichgau. (Gro) = Mannaberg. (Vil) = Bruchsal.

Klosterberg (Ger). Vineyard. (Anb) = Mittelrhein. (Ber) = Bacharach. (Gro) = Schloss Reichenstein. (Vil) = Oberheimbach.

Klosterberg (Ger). Vineyard. (Anb) = Mosel-Saar-Ruwer. (Ber) = Bernkastel. (Gro) = Kurfürstlay. (Vil) = Maring-Noviand.

Klosterberg (Ger). Vineyard. (Anb) = Mosel-Saar-Ruwer. (Ber) = Bernkastel. (Gro) = Münzlay. (Vil) = Wehlen.

Klosterberg (Ger). Vineyard. (Anb) =

K

Mosel-Saar-Ruwer. (Ber) = Bernkastel. (Gro) = Sankt Michael. (Vil) = Schleich.

Klosterberg (Ger). Vineyard. (Anb) = Mosel-Saar-Ruwer. (Ber) = Bernkastel. (Gro) = Schwarzlay. (Vil) = Platten.

Klosterberg (Ger). Vineyard. (Anb) = Mosel-Saar-Ruwer. (Ber) = Bernkastel. (Gro) = Schwarzlay. (Vil) = Traben-Trarbach (ortsteil Wolf).

Klosterberg (Ger). Vineyard. (Anb) = Mosel-Saar-Ruwer. (Ber) = Saar-Ruwer. (Gro) = Scharzberg. (Vil) = Konz.

Klosterberg (Ger). Vineyard. (Anb) = Mosel-Saar-Ruwer. (Ber) = Saar-Ruwer. (Gro) = Scharzberg. (Vil) = Saarburg.

Klosterberg (Ger). Vineyard. (Anb) = Mosel-Saar-Ruwer. (Ber) = Saar-Ruwer. (Gro) = Scharzberg. (Vil) = Wiltingen.

Klosterberg (Ger). Vineyard. (Anb) = Mosel-Saar-Ruwer. (Ber) = Zell/Mosel. (Gro) = Schwarze Katz. (Vil) = Zell-Merl.

Klosterberg (Ger). Vineyard. (Anb) = Mosel-Saar-Ruwer. (Ber) = Zell/Mosel. (Gro) = Weinhex. (Vil) = Lehmen.

Klosterberg (Ger). Vineyard. (Anb) = Nahe. (Ber) = Schloss Böckelheim. (Gro) = Burgweg. (Vil) = Norheim.

Klosterberg (Ger). Vineyard. (Anb) = Rheingau. (Ber) = Johannisberg. (Gro) = Burgweg. (Vil) = Rüdesheim.

Klosterberg (Ger). Vineyard. (Anb) = Rheingau. (Ber) = Johannisberg. (Gro) = Gottesthal. (Vil) = Östrich.

Klosterberg (Ger). Vineyard. (Anb) = Rheingau. (Ber) = Johannisberg. (Gro) = Heiligenstock. (Vil) = Kiedrich.

Klosterberg (Ger). Vineyard. (Anb) = Rheingau. (Ber) = Johannisberg. (Gro) = Mehrholzchen. (Vil) = Östrich.

Klosterberg (Ger). Vineyard. (Anb) = Rheinhessen. (Ber) = Bingen. (Gro) = Adelberg. (Vil) = Bermersheim v.d.H.

Klosterberg (Ger). Vineyard. (Anb) = Rheinhessen. (Ber) = Nierstein. (Gro) = Gutes Domtal. (Vil) = Nieder-Olm.

Klosterberg (Ger). Vineyard. (Anb) = Rheinhessen. (Ber) = Nierstein. (Gro) = Petersberg. (Vil) = Bechtolsheim.

Klosterberg (Ger). Vineyard. (Anb) = Rheinhessen. (Ber) = Nierstein. (Gro) = Sankt Alban. (Vil) = Mainz.

Klosterberg (Ger). Vineyard. (Anb) = Rheinhessen. (Ber) = Wonnegau. (Gro) = Pilgerpfad. (Vil) = Osthofen.

Klosterberg (Ger). Vineyard. (Anb) = Württemberg. (Ber) = Württembergisch Unterland. (Gro) = Stromberg. (Vil) = Hohenhaslach.

Klosterberg (Ger). Vineyard. (Anb) = Württemberg. (Ber) = Württembergisch Unterland. (Gro) = Stromberg. (Vil) = Horrheim.

Klosterberg (Ger). A herb liqueur produced by the Eckes Distillery.

Klosterbergfelsen (Ger). Vineyard. (Anb) = Baden. (Ber) = Ortenau. (Gro) = Schloss Rodeck. (Vil) = Varnhalt.

Klosterbitter (Ger). A bitter digestive.

Klosterbock Dunkel (Ger). A dark, long-lagered Beer produced by the Külmbacher Mönschof Brauerei in Bavaria.

Klosterbräu (Aus) (Ger). A Trappist-style beer brewed mainly in Austria.

Klosterbruder (Ger). Vineyard. (Anb) = Rheinhessen. (Ber) = Bingen. (Gro) = Kaiserpfalz. (Vil) = Gross-Winternheim.

Kloster Eberbach (Ger). A Cistercian monastery at Steinberg, on the Rhine. Estates became part of the State domain.

Kloster Fürstental (Ger). Vineyard. (Anb) = Mittelrhein. (Ber) = Bacharach. (Gro) = Schloss Stahleck. (Vil) = Bacharach.

Klostergarten (Aus). A red wine made from the St. Laurent grape by the Augustine monks at Klosterneuburg, Vienna.

Klostergarten (Ger). Lit – 'Monastery garden'. The name used for the old monastery vineyards now privately owned. There are 23 individual sites with this name in Germany.

Klostergarten (Ger). Vineyard. (Anb) = Ahr. (Ber) = Warporzheim/Ahrtal. (Gro) = Klosterberg. (Vil) = Marienthal.

Klostergarten (Ger). Vineyard. (Anb) = Franken. (Ber) = Mainviereck. (Gro) = Not yet assigned. (Vil) = Engelsberg.

Klostergarten (Ger). Vineyard. (Anb) = Mosel-Saar-Ruwer. (Ber) = Bernkastel. (Gro) = Kurfürstlay. (Vil) = Brauneberg.

Klostergarten (Ger). Vineyard. (Anb) = Mosel-Saar-Ruwer. (Ber) = Bernkastel. (Gro) = Sankt Michael. (Vil) = Leiwen.

Klostergarten (Ger). Vineyard. (Anb) = Mosel-Saar-Ruwer. (Ber) = Zell/Mosel. (Gro) = Goldbäumchen. (Vil) = Cochem.

Klostergarten (Ger). Vineyard. (Anb) = Nahe. (Ber) = Kreuznach. (Gro) = Schlosskapelle. (Vil) = Bingen-Bingerbrück.

Klostergarten (Ger). Vineyard. (Anb) = Nahe. (Ber) = Kreuznach. (Gro) = Schlosskapelle. (Vil) = Weiler.

Klostergarten (Ger). Vineyard. (Anb) = Nahe. (Ber) = Schloss Böckelheim. (Gro) = Rosengarten. (Vil) = Sponheim.

K

Klostergarten (Ger). Vineyard. (Anb) = Nahe. (Ber) = Schloss Böckelheim. (Gro) = Rosengarten. (Vil) = St. Katharien.

Klostergarten (Ger). Vineyard. (Anb) = Rheinhessen. (Ber) = Bingen. (Gro) = Abtey. (Vil) = Sankt Johann.

Klostergarten (Ger). Vineyard. (Anb) = Rheinhessen. (Ber) = Bingen. (Gro) = Abtey. (Vil) = Sprendlingen.

Klostergarten (Ger). Vineyard. (Anb) = Rheinhessen. (Ber) = Bingen. (Gro) = Adelberg. (Vil) = Flonheim.

Klostergarten (Ger). Vineyard. (Anb) = Rheinhessen. (Ber) = Bingen. (Gro) = Kaiserpfalz. (Vil) = Schwabenheim.

Klostergarten (Ger). Vineyard. (Anb) = Rheinhessen. (Ber) = Bingen. (Gro) = Rheingrafenstein. (Vil) = Hackenheim.

Klostergarten (Ger). Vineyard. (Anb) = Rheinhessen. (Ber) = Bingen. (Gro) = Sankt Rochuskapelle. (Vil) = Zotzenheim.

Klostergarten (Ger). Vineyard. (Anb) = Rheinhessen. (Ber) = Nierstein. (Gro) = Spiegelberg. (Vil) = Nierstein.

Klostergarten (Ger). Vineyard. (Anb) = Rheinpfalz. (Ber) = Mittelhaardt-Deutsche Weinstrasse. (Gro) = Hofstück. (Vil) = Gönnheim.

Klostergarten (Ger). Vineyard. (Anb) = Rheinpfalz. (Ber) = Mittelhaardt-Deutsche Weinstrasse. (Gro) = Hofstück. (Vil) = Niederkirchen.

Klostergarten (Ger). Vineyard. (Anb) = Rheinpfalz. (Ber) = Mittelhaardt-Deutsche Weinstrasse. (Gro) = Höllenpfad. (Vil) = Grünstadt.

Klostergarten (Ger). Vineyard. (Anb) = Rheinpfalz. (Ber) = Südliche Weinstrasse. (Gro) = Königsgarten. (Vil) = Godramstein.

Klostergarten (Ger). Vineyard. (Anb) = Rheinpfalz. (Ber) = Südliche Weinstrasse. (Gro) = Trappenberg. (Vil) = Lustadt.

Klostergarten (Ger). Vineyard. (Anb) = Rheinpfalz. (Ber) = Südliche Weinstrasse. (Gro) = Trappenberg. (Vil) = Zeiskam.

Klostergarten (Ger). Vineyard. (Anb) = Rheinpfalz. (Ber) = Südliche Weinstrasse. (Gro) = Schloss Ludwigshöhe. (Vil) = Edenkoben.

Klostergut (Ger). Vineyard. (Anb) = Baden. (Ber) = Ortenau. (Gro) = Schloss Rodeck. (Vil) = Sinzheim.

Klostergut Schelzberg (Ger). Vineyard. (Anb) = Baden. (Ber) = Ortenau. (Gro) = Schloss Rodeck. (Vil) = Sasbackwalden.

Klosterkammer (Ger). Vineyard. (Anb) = Mosel-Saar-Ruwer. (Ber) = Zell/Mosel.

(Gro) = Grafschaft. (Vil) = St. Aldegund.

Klosterkeller (Bul). A dry, full-bodied white wine made from the Sylvaner grape for the German market.

Klosterkellerei (It). A sparkling (cuve close) wine producer based in the Trentino-Alto Adige region.

Klosterkeller Siegendorf (Aus). A noted wine estate in Burgenland.

Klosterlay (Ger). Vineyard. (Anb) = Rheingau. (Ber) = Johannisberg. (Gro) = Burgweg. (Vil) = Rüdesheim.

Kloster Liebfrauenberg (Ger). Grosslage. (Anb) = Rheinpfalz. (Ber) = Südliche Weinstrasse. (Vils) = Bade Bergzabern, Barbelroth, Billigheim-Ingenheim, Gleiszellen-Gleishorbach, Göcklingen, Hergersweiler, Heuchelheim-Klingen, Kapellen-Drusweiler, Klingenmünster, Niederhorbach. Oberhausen, Pleisweiler-Oberhofen, Rohrbach, Steinweiler, Winden.

Klosterlikoer (Ger). A sweet digestive liqueur.

Klosterneuburg (Aus). A wine district in the region of Niederösterreich. Produces mainly white wines. The Augustine Monastery is the main producer.

Klosterneuburger (Aus). A white wine that comes from the old monastery vineyards on the Danube. A fruity medium sweet wine with a good bouquet.

Klosterneuburger Mostwaage (Aus). KMW. A measurement for Specific Gravity. Approximate conversion to Oechsle by multiplying KMW X 5.

Klosterpfad (Ger). Vineyard. (Anb) = Nahe. (Ber) = Kreuznach. (Gro) = Schlosskapelle. (Vil) = Dorsheim.

Klosterpfad (Ger). Vineyard. (Anb) = Rheinpfalz. (Ber) = Südliche Weinstrasse. (Gro) = Ordensgut. (Vil) = Rhodt.

Klosterschaffnerei (Ger). Vineyard. (Anb) = Rheinpfalz. (Ber) = Mittelhaardt-Deutsche Weinstrasse. (Gro) = Grafenstück. (Vil) = Bockenheim.

Kloster Schwarz (Ger). A dark, full-bodied beer brewed by the Kulmbacher Mönschof Brauerei in Bavaria. 4.9% alc. by vol.

Klostersekt (Aus). A sparkling wine produced by the Augustine monks at Klosterneuburg, Vienna.

Kloster Stuben (Ger). Vineyard. (Anb) = Mosel-Saar-Ruwer. (Ber) = Zell/ Mosel. (Gro) = Rosenhang. (Vil) = Bremm.

Klosterstüch (Ger). Vineyard. (Anb) = Rheinpfalz. (Ber) = Mittelhaardt-Deutsche Weinstrasse. (Gro) = Schnepfenflug vom Kellertal. (Vil) = Einselthum.

Klosterstück (Ger). Vineyard. (Anb) =

K

Rheinpfalz. (Ber) = Mittelhaardt-Deutsche Weinstrasse. (Gro) = Schnepfenflug vom Zellertal. (Vil) = Zell.

Klosterweg (Ger). Vineyard. (Anb) = Mosel-Saar-Ruwer. (Ber) = Bernkastel. (Gro) = Schwarzlay. (Vil) = Hupperath.

Klosterweg (Ger). Vineyard. (Anb) = Mosel-Saar-Ruwer. (Ber) = Bernkastel. (Gro) = Schwarzlay. (Vil) = Wittlich.

Klosterweg (Ger). Vineyard. (Anb) = Rheinhessen. (Ber) = Bingen. (Gro) = Sankt Rochuskapelle. (Vil) = Dromersheim.

Klosterweg (Ger). Vineyard. (Anb) = Rheinhessen. (Ber) = Bingen. (Gro) = Sankt Rochuskapelle. (Vil) = Ockenheim.

Klosterweg (Ger). Vineyard. (Anb) = Rheinpfalz. (Ber) = Mittelhaardt-Deutsche Weinstrasse. (Gro) = Schwarzerde. (Vil) = Gerolsheim.

Klotten (Ger). Village. (Anb) = Mosel-Saar-Ruwer. (Ber) = Zell/Mosel. (Gro) = Goldbäumchen. (Vins) = Branneberg, Burg Coreidelsteiner, Rosenberg, Sonnengold.

Klotzberg (Ger). Vineyard. (Anb) = Baden. (Ber) = Ortenau. (Gro) = Schloss Rodeck. (Vil) = Bühlertal.

Kluflaske (Den). Decanter.

Klüsserath (Ger). Village. (Anb) = Mosel-Saar-Ruwer. (Ber) = Bernkastel. (Gro) = Sankt Michael. (Vins) = Bruderschaft, Königsberg.

KMW (Aus) (abbr). See Klosterneuberger Mostwagge.

Kneipe (Ger). An old student drinking school. Now denotes a friendly meeting place.

Knickerbein (Pousse Café). Pour into a tall glass in order – yolk of egg, ⅙ gill Curaçao, ⅙ gill Kümmel, 2 dashes Angostura.

Knickerbocker (Cktl).(1). 1 measure dark Rum, ½ measure Curaçao, ½ measure orange juice or lemon juice, dash Grenadine. Shake over ice, strain into a cocktail glass. Serve with a chunk of pineapple.

Knickerbocker (Cktl).(2). 1 measure dry Gin, ½ measure French vermouth, dash Italian vermouth. Shake over ice, strain into a cocktail glass. Top with a squeeze of lemon peel juice.

Knickerbocker Special (Cktl). 2 fl.ozs. dark Rum, 2 dashes Cointreau, ⅛ fl.oz. raspberry syrup, ⅛ fl.oz. orange juice and lemon juice. Shake over ice, strain into a cocktail glass. Top with a slice of pineapple.

Knights Valley (USA). A small wine-producing area in Sonoma County, California.

Knights Valley Estates (USA). A small winery based in Knights Valley, Sonoma County, California. Grape variety – Johannisberg riesling. Noted for its' Late Harvest wines.

Knipperlé (Fr). A white grape variety once grown in Alsace (now banned). Also known as the Kleiner rauschling, Kleingelber, Kipperlé, Elbling.

Knittelsheim (Ger). Village. (Anb) = Rheinpfalz. (Ber) = Südliche Weinstrasse. (Gro) = Trappenberg. (Vin) = Gollenberg.

Knittlingen (Ger). Village. (Anb) = Württemberg. (Ber) = Württembergisch Unterland. (Gro) = Stromberg. (Vin) = Reichshalde.

Knockando (Scot). A single Malt whisky distillery on the Spey in Morayshire. Owned by Justerini and Brooks. A Highland malt whisky. 43% alc. by vol.

Knockdhu (Scot). A single Malt whisky distillery based east of Keith, Buchan. A Highland malt whisky. 40% alc. by vol.

Knock it Back (Eng). An informal request to consume a drink quickly (usually to allow for another drink in the glass).

Knockout Cocktail (Cktl). ⅙ gill dry Gin, ⅙ gill dry Vermouth, 2 dashes Pernod, 4 dashes (white) Crème de Menthe. Stir over ice, strain into a cocktail glass. Top with a cherry.

Knopf (Ger). Vineyard. (Anb) = Rheinhessen. (Ber) = Nierstein. (Gro) = Gutes Domtal. (Vil) = Friesenheim.

Knopf (Ger). Vineyard. (Anb) = Rheinhessen. (Ber) = Nierstein. (Gro) = Gutes Domtal. (Vil) = Hahnheim.

Knops (Eng). The name given to the turned elements in the stem of drinking glasses. e.g. Baluster stems.

Knöringen (Ger). Village. (Anb) = Rheinpfalz. (Ber) = Südliche Weinstrasse. (Gro) = Bischofskreuz. (Vin) = Hohenrain.

Knowle Hill (Eng). Vineyard. Address = Knowle Hill Farm, Ulcombe, Maidstone, Kent. Planted 1970. 1 ha. Grape varieties – Müller-Thurgau and Pinot noir.

Knudsen Erath Winery (USA). A large vineyard based in Dundee, Willamette Valley, Oregon. 38 ha. Grape varieties – Chardonnay, Pinot noir and Riesling. Produces varietal wines.

KNW (Aus) (abbr). The alternative initials used for KMW.

Köbànya Brewery (Hun). A brewery based in Budapest. Noted for its' Rocky Cellar, Bak and Hungària (a strong, pale beer).

Kobarn (USSR). A full-bodied red wine produced in the Crimea.

Kobern-Gondorf (Ger). Village. (Anb) = Mosel-Saar-Ruwer. (Ber) = Zell/ Mosel.

K

(Gro) = Weinhex. (Vins) = Fahrberg, Fuchshöhe, Gäns, Kehrberg, Schlossberg, Uhlen, Weissenberg.

Kobersberg (Ger). Vineyard. (Anb) = Franken. (Ber) = Maindreieck. (Gro) = Not yet assigned. (Vil) = Rimpar.

Kobes (Ger). The name given to the waiters in the tavern of Cölner Höfbrau in Cologne. They wear blue pullovers and leather aprons as their uniforms.

Koblenz-Ehrenbreitstein (Ger). Village. (Anb) = Mittelrhein. (Ber) = Rheinburgengau. (Gro) = Marksburg. (Vin) = Kreuzberg.

Koblenz [ortsteil Lay] (Ger). Village. (Anb) = Mosel-Saar-Ruwer. (Ber) = Zell/Mosel. (Gro) = Weinhex. (Vin) = Hubertsborn.

Koblenz [ortsteil Moselweiss] (Ger). Village. (Anb) = Mosel-Saar-Ruwer. (Ber) = Zell/Mosel. (Gro) = Weinhex. (Vin) = Hamm.

Kobnert (Ger). Grosslage. (Anb) = Rheinpfalz. (Ber) = Mittelhaardt-Deutsche Weinstrasse. (Vils) = Dackenheim, Erpolzheim, Freinsheim, Herxheim/Berg, Kallstadt, Leistadt, Ungstein, Weisenheim am Berg.

Kochberg (Ger). Vineyard. (Anb) = Baden. (Ber) = Ortenau. (Gro) = Fürsteneck. (Vil) = Durbach.

Koch Brewery (USA). A brewery based in Dunkirk, New York. Noted for its' Black Horse Ale (a bottom-fermented beer).

Kocherberg (Ger). Grosslage. (Anb) = Württemberg. (Ber) = Kocher-Jagst-Tauber. (Vils) = Belsenberg, Bieringen, Beutelsbach, Schnait i. R, Endersbach, Rommelshausen, Stetten i. R, Strümpfelbach.

Kocher-Jagst-Tauber (Ger). Bereich. (Anb) = Württemberg. (Gros) = Kocherberg, Tauberberg.

Kocher [River] (Ger). Tributary of the river Neckar in Württemberg. Soil is shell limestone.

Kochgeschmack (Ger). Describes a wine that has a 'cooked' flavour from the over-heating of the wine.

Kociokwik (Pol) (slang). Lit – 'Cats crying'. A term for a hangover.

Kodaikanal (Ind). A wine-producing area in northern India.

Koelenhof Co-operative (S.Afr). A co-operative based in Stellenbosch. Address = Koelenhof Koöperatiewe Wynkelder, Box 1, Koelenhof 7605. Produces – Bukettraube, Koelenhofer, Soet Hanepoot and many varietals.

Koelenhofer (S.Afr). A dry white wine made from the Steen grape by the Koelenhof Co-operative.

Koelenhof Koöperatiewe Wynkelder (S.Afr). See Koelenhof Co-operative.

Koepp (Lux). See Koeppechen.

Koeppechen (Lux). A vineyard site in the village of Wormeldange. Also known as Koepp.

Koerner Distillery (Ger). A noted distillery which produces Enzian. Based at Die Stonsdorferei.

Kofé (USSR). Coffee.

Koff Brewery (Fin). Brewery based in Helsinki. Is noted for its' Koff Finnish Beer 5.4% alc. by vol. and Koff Imperial Stout 7% alc. by vol. (a top-fermented beer).

Koffie (Hol). Coffee.

Koffiekan (Hol). Coffeepot.

Koffietavel (Hol). A luncheon of coffee, cold meats, cheeses, bread and cakes.

Kofu Valley (Jap). A top wine-producing district in the Yamanashi region.

Kohala (Ind). A spirit made from barley. Often has a slight whisky taste.

Kohlberg (Ger). Village. (Anb) = Württemberg. (Ber) = Remstal-Stuttgart. (Gro) = Hohenneuffen. (Vin) = Schlossteige.

Köhler (Ger). Village. (Anb) = Franken. (Ber) = Maindreieck. (Gro) = Kirchberg. (Vins) = Assorted parts of vineyards.

Köhler-Köpfchen (Ger). Vineyard. (Anb) = Nahe. (Ber) = Schloss Böckelheim. (Gro) = Burgweg. (Vil) = Bad Münster a. St. Ebernburg.

Koicha (Jap). One of the stages of 'Chanoyu'. The resulting tea is thick in consistency and has a bitter taste. A 'Kneaded' tea.

Koji (Jap). 'Steamed rice' to which is added Koji mould for making Saké.

Koji Mold (USA). The alternative spelling of Koji Mould.

Koji Mould (Jap). A strain of yeast 'Apergillus Aryzae' used in the making of Saké. Converts starch into sugar.

Kokeicha (Jap). Green tea. See also Sencha Genmaicha and Sencha Fukujyu.

Kokkineli (Cyp). A deep rosé, very dry table wine, high in alcohol.

Kokkineli (Gre). A dark rosé, dry, slightly resinated wine.

Kokteyl (Tur). Cocktail.

Kokur Niznegorsky (USSR). A dry white wine from the Crimean peninsula.

Kola (S.Am). Another spelling of Cola.

Kola Liqueurs (Afr). Liqueurs made from lemon and orange peel, kolanuts, vanilla and spices.

Kolin Brewery (Czec). An old brewery based in western Czec. Noted for its Lager-style beers.

K

Kollektsionye (USSR). A term used for wines that are matured in cask and bottle.

Köllig (Ger). Village. (Anb) = Mosel-Saar-Ruwer. (Ber) = Obermosel. (Gro) = Gipfel. (Vin) = Rochusfels.

Kolln Vineyards (USA). Vineyards based in Bellefonte, central Pennsylvania. Produce French hybrid wines.

Kölner (Ger). The name for a person who drinks Kölsch.

Kolor (Ger). A red grape variety. A cross between the Spätburgunder and the Teinturier. Produces a good colour blending wine.

Kolossi (Cyp). The brand-name used by SODAP for their red and white table wines and Sherry. Named after the castle of the Knights Templar of same name on south-eastern coast of island.

Kölsch (Ger). The shortened name for Kölschbier. Lit – 'From Cologne'.

Kölschbier (Ger). A top-fermented light beer 4.6% alc. by vol. brewed in Cologne and Bonn. Name protected by law. Low in carbonation (a digestif beer).

Kolteschberg (Lux). A vineyard site in the village of Schwebsingen.

Kometenwein (Ger). A wine produced to commemorate the appearance of a comet. (e.g. Haley's comet).

Komovica (Yug). A brandy distilled from the residue of grape pressings after wine production.

Kona Coffee (USA). A Hawaiian coffee from the west volcanic slopes of the island. Does not usually need blending. Produces a smooth, mild, buttery taste and aroma.

Köndringen (Ger). Village. (Anb) = Baden. (Ber) = Breisgau. (Gro) = Burg Lichteneck. (Vin) = Alte Burg.

Könen (Ger). Village. (Anb) = Mosel-Saar-Ruwer. (Ber) = Saar-Ruwer. (Gro) = Scharzberg. (Vins) = Fels, Kirchberg.

Köngernheim (Ger). Village. (Anb) = Rheinhessen. (Ber) = Nierstein. (Gro) = Gutes Domtal. (Vin) = Goldgrube.

Kong Hu Te (China). Lit – 'Tea prepared with care'. e.g. Congou Black Tea, an eighteenth century tea drink.

Koniak (Bul). Brandy.

Koniak (Gre). The name for a grape brandy distilled around Piraeus.

König (Ger). Vineyard. (Anb) = Württemberg. (Ber) = Württembergisch Unterland. (Gro) = Stromberg. (Vil) = Diefenbach.

König (Ger). Vineyard. (Anb) = Württemberg. (Ber) = Württembergisch Unterland. (Gro) = Stromberg. (Vil) = Sternenfels.

König (Ger). A producer of Steinhäger. Sold under the same name.

König Brauerei (Ger). A brewery based in Duisburg. Noted for its' Pilsener-style beer.

Königheim (Ger). Village. (Anb) = Baden. (Ber) = Badische Frankenland. (Gro) = Tauberklinge. (Vin) = Kirchberg.

Königin (Ger). Vineyard. (Anb) = Franken. (Ber) = Maindreieck. (Gro) = Not yet assigned. (Vil) = Tauberrettersheim.

Königin Viktoriaberg (Ger). Vineyard. (Anb) = Rheingau. (Ber) = Johannisberg. (Gro) = Daubhaus. (Vil) = Hochheim.

König Johann Berg (Ger). Vineyard. (Anb) = Mosel-Saar-Ruwer. (Ber) = Saar-Ruwer. (Gro) = Scharzberg. (Vil) = Kastel-Staadt.

König Johann Berg (Ger). Vineyard. (Anb) = Mosel-Saar-Ruwer. (Ber) = Saar-Ruwer. (Gro) = Scharzberg. (Vil) = Serrig.

König-Pilsener (Ger). A Pilsener beer brewed by the König Brauerei in Duisburg.

Königsbach (Ger). Village. (Anb) = Rheinpfalz. (Ber) = Mittelhaardt-Deutsche Weinstrasse. (Gro) = Meerspinne. (Vins) = Idig, Jesuitengarten, Ölberg, Reiterpfad.

Königsbecher (Ger). Vineyard. (Anb) = Baden. (Ber) = Badische Bergstrasse/Kraichgau. (Gro) = Stiftsberg. (Vil) = Odenheim.

Königsberg (Ger). Grosslage. (Anb) = Mosel-Saar-Ruwer. (Ber) = Obermosel. (Vils) = Edingen, Godendorf, Grewenich, Igel, Langsur, Liersberg, Mesenich, Metzdorf, Ralingen, Wintersdorf

Königsberg (Ger). Vineyard. (Anb) = Mosel-Saar-Ruwer. (Ber) = Bernkastel. (Gro) = Sankt Michael. (Vil) = Klüsserath.

Königsberg (Ger). Vineyard. (Anb) = Mosel-Saar-Ruwer. (Ber) = Bernkastel. (Gro) = Schwarzlay. (Vil) = Traben-Trarbach.

Königsberg (Ger). Vineyard. (Anb) = Württemberg. (Ber) = Württembergisch Unterland. (Gro) = Schalkstein. (Vil) = Höpfigheim.

Königschaffhausen (Ger). Village. (Anb) = Baden. (Ber) = Kaiserstuhl-Tuniberg. (Gro) = Vulkanfelsen. (Vins) = Hasenberg, Steingrüble.

Königsfels (Ger). Vineyard. (Anb) = Mosel-Saar-Ruwer. (Ber) = Zell/Mosel. (Gro) = Weinhex. (Vil) = Güls.

Königsfels (Ger). Vineyard. (Anb) = Nahe. (Ber) = Schloss Böckelheim. (Gro) = Burgweg. (Vil) = Duchroth.

Königsfels (Ger). Vineyard. (Anb) = Nahe.

K

(Ber) = Schloss Böckelheim. (Gro) = Burgweg. (Vil) = Schlossböckelheim.
Königsgarten (Ger). Grosslage. (Anb) = Rheinpfalz. (Ber) = Südliche Weinstrasse. (Vils) = Albersweiler, Arzheim, Birkweiler, Frankweiler, Godramstein, Landau, Ranschbach, Siebeldingen.
Königsgarten (Ger). Vineyard. (Anb) = Nahe. (Ber) = Schloss Böckelheim. (Gro) = Burgweg. (Vil) = Bad Münster a St-Ebernburg.
Königsgarten (Ger). Vineyard. (Anb) = Nahe. (Ber) = Schloss Böckelheim. (Gro) = Paradiesgarten. (Vil) = Feilbingert.
Königshofen (Ger). Village. (Anb) = Baden. (Ber) = Badische Frankenland. (Gro) = Tauberklinge. (Vins) = Kirchberg, Turmberg, Walterstal.
Königslay-Terrassen (Ger). Vineyard. (Anb) = Mosel-Saar-Ruwer. (Ber) = Zell/Mosel. (Gro) = Schwarze Katz. (Vil) = Zell-Merl.
Königsschild (Ger). Vineyard. (Anb) = Nahe. (Ber) = Kreuznach. (Gro) = Sonnenborn. (Vil) = Langenlonsheim.
Königsschloss (Ger). Vineyard. (Anb) = Nahe. (Ber) = Kreuznach. (Gro) = Schlosskapelle. (Vil) = Münster-Sarmsheim.
Königstuhl (Ger). Vineyard. (Anb) = Rheinhessen. (Ber) = Nierstein. (Gro) = Gutes Domtal. (Vil) = Lörzweiler.
Königstuhl (Ger). Vineyard. (Anb) = Rheinhessen. (Ber) = Wonnegau. (Gro) = Bergkloster. (Vil) = Gundersheim.
Königsweg (Ger). Vineyard. (Anb) = Rheinpfalz. (Ber) = Mittelhaardt-Deutsche Weinstrasse. (Gro) = Schnepfenflug vom Kellertal. (Vil) = Niefernheim.
Königsweg (Ger). Vineyard. (Anb) = Rheinpfalz. (Ber) = Mittelhaardt-Deutsche Weinstrasse. (Gro) = Schnepfenflug vom Zellertal. (Vil) = Zell.
Königswein (Aus). Lit – 'Royal wine'. Is found on the labels of the top wines. Made only from Neuberger, Rotgipfler and Zierfandler and submitted to a tasting committee.
Königsweingarten (Ger). Vineyard. (Anb) = Baden. (Ber) = Bodensee. (Gro) = Sonnenufer. (Vil) = Bodman.
Königswingert (Ger). Vineyard. (Anb) = Rheinpfalt. (Ber) = Mittelhaardt-Deutsche Weinstrasse. (Gro) = Schenkenböhl. (Vil) = Wachenheim.
Königswinter (Ger). Village. (Anb) = Mittelrhein. (Ber) = Siebengebirge. (Gro) = Petersberg. (Vin) = Drachenfels.
König Wenzel (Ger). Vineyard. (Anb) = Mittelrhein. (Ber) = Rheinburgengau. (Gro) = Gedeonseck. (Vil) = Rhens.

König Wilhelmsberg (Ger). Vineyard. (Anb) = Rheingau. (Ber) = Johannisberg. (Gro) = Daubhaus. (Vil) = Wicker.
Koninklijke Nederlandse Gist en Spiritusfabriek (Bel). A large distillery based in Bruges.
Konocti Cellars (USA). A grower-owned winery based near Kelseyville, Lake County, California. Grape varieties – Cabernet sauvignon, Cabernet franc, Gamay, Sauvignon blanc, White riesling and Zinfandel. Produces varietal wines.
Konsel (Czec). A special beer 14° brewed by the Litoměřice Brewery in northern Bohemia.
Konstanz (Ger). Village. (Anb) = Baden. (Ber) = Bodensee. (Gro) = Sonnenufer. (Vin) = Sonnenhalde.
Konsumwein (Ger). The German equivalent of red Vin ordinaire. An everyday drinking wine.
Kontiki (Hol). A tropical citrus liqueur. 19.5% alc. by vol.
Kontuszowka (Pol). A liqueur flavoured with the oil of lavender.
Konya (Tur). A wine-producing region in southern Turkey. Produces mainly dry white wines.
Konyak (Tur). An Armenian name for Brandy. Also the Albanian name for Brandy.
Konz (Ger). Village. (Anb) = Mosel-Saar-Ruwer. (Ber) = Saar-Ruwer. (Gro) = Scharzberg. (Vins) = Auf der Kupp, Brauneberg, Euchariusberg, Falkensteiner, Hofberg, Klosterberg, Sprung.
Koohii (Jap). Coffee.
Koombahla Cabernet Sauvignon (Austr). A full-flavoured red wine from the Brown Brothers Koombahla Estate in Milawa, Victoria. 1.5 ha.
Koonunga Hill (Austr). A red wine produced by the Penfolds Estate from Cabernet sauvignon and Shiraz grapes.
Kooperatif (Tur). Co-operative (winery).
Koöperatiet Wijnbouwers Vereniging (S.Afr). K.W.V.A wine farmer's Association founded in 1916.
Koopmanskloof Estate (S.Afr). Vineyards based in Stellenbosch. Address = Koopmanskloof Landgoed, Kuils River 7580. Produces varietal wines including Blanc de Marbonne.
Koorianda Vineyard (Austr). A vineyard based in the Barossa Valley. Is owned by the Hill-Smith Estates. 10.5 ha. Grape variety – Sémillon.
Kooriander (Austr). Part of the Hill-Smith Estate in South Australia. Grows mainly Sémillon grapes.
Kopé (USA). The name for coffee in Hawaii.

K

Kope (E.Ind). The name for coffee in Indonesia.

Kopetdague (USSR). A white grape variety grown in Turkmenistan. Used to produce fortified wines.

Kopf (Ger). Grosslage. (Anb) = Württemberg. (Ber) = Remstal-Stuttgart. (Vils) = Beinstein, Breuningsweiler, Bürg, Grossheppach, Grunbach, Hanweiler, Kleinheppach, Korb, Neustadt, Schorndorf, Waiblingen, Winnenden, Winterbach.

Kopf (Ger). The name of the local red wine from Korb in Württemberg.

Kopiaste (Cyp). The Turkish Cypriot custom of inviting people in to their house to join them for a cup of coffee.

Kopke (Port). Vintage Port shipper. Vintages – 1870, 1872, 1873, 1875, 1878, 1881, 1884, 1887, 1890, 1892, 1894, 1896, 1897, 1900, 1904, 1908, 1912, 1917, 1919, 1920, 1922, 1927, 1935, 1945, 1948, 1950, 1952, 1955, 1958, 1960, 1963, 1966, 1970, 1974, 1975, 1977, 1980, 1982, 1983. Also produces brandies. See also Quinta St. Luiz (a single quinta vintage Port). Is supposedly the oldest Port house.

Kopparbergs Brewery (Swe). A small brewery based in Kopparberg, central Sweden. Produces top-fermented beers.

Koppelstein (Ger). Vineyard. (Anb) = Mittelrhein. (Ber) = Rheinburgengau. (Gro) = Marksburg. (Vil) = Braubach.

Koppelstein (Ger). Vineyard. (Anb) = Mittelrhein. (Ber) = Rheinburgengau. (Gro) = Marksburg. (Vil) = Lahnstein.

Koppi (E.Ind). The Malayan name for coffee. See also Kawa.

Koppig (Hol). Heady.

Köpük (Tur). Beerhead, frothy foam.

Köpüren (Tur). Effervescent, sparkling, fizzy.

Korb (Ger). Village. (Anb) = Württemberg. (Ber) = Remstal-Stuttgart. (Gro) = Kopf. (Vins) = Berg, Hörnle, Sommerhalde.

Korb (Ger). Village. (Anb) = Württemberg. (Ber) = Remstal-Stuttgart. (Gro) = Wartbühl. (Vin) = Steingrüble.

Korbell Bros (USA). A vineyard and winery in Sonoma, California. Famous for its' sparkling wines from a blend of Chardonnay and Pinot noir grapes.

Korčula (Yug). A wine-producing island off the Dalmatian coast. Noted for Grk, Maraština, Plavina and Pošip wines.

Korean Bartenders' Association (E.Asia). K.B.A. Address = 398–1, Jungnung Dong Sungbuk-Ku-Seoul.

Korenjenever (Hol). A style of Jenever.

Korenwijn (Hol). A Moutwijn distilled without the addition of juniper.

Korepo (N.Z). A small winery near Blenheim at Ruby Bay, Nelson.

Korkbrand (Ger). Branded cork.

Korken-Geschmack (Ger). Denotes a corky, musky, mouldy wine with a taste of tannin.

Korlingen (Ger). Village. (Anb) = Mosel-Saar-Ruwer. (Ber) = Saar-Ruwer. (Gro) = Römerlay. (Vin) = Laykaul.

Korn (Ger) (abbr). Kornbranntwein. A clear grain spirit 35% alc. by vol. Potstilled, and cask-aged. Originally produced in the Harz mountains.

Kornbrannt (Ger). See Kornbranntwein.

Kornbranntwein (Ger). Lit – 'Corn whiskey'. Equivalent for Rye Whiskey.

Kornbrennerei Schönau GmbH (Ger). A noted producer of Kornbranntwein based in Friedrichsruh, Sachsenwald, Western Germany. Sold under the Schönauer label. Also Boonekamp.

Kornell Champagne Cellars (USA). A winery based in the Napa Valley, California. Noted for its' sparkling wines made by méthode champenoise.

Korn-Genever (Ger). A Kornbranntwein flavoured with juniper.

Kornschnapps (Ger). A Schnapps made from corn only.

Korn-Wacholder (Ger). A Kornbranntwein flavoured with juniper essence.

Koroglu (Tur). The brand-name for a white wine.

Körper (Ger). Body.

Körperarm (Ger). Of poor body.

Koruk (Tur). Unripe grapes.

Kos (Gre). An island which produces both red and white wines.

Kosher Cold Duck (USA). See Kalta Katchka.

Kosher Vodka (USA). A neutral spirit produced under Rabbinical supervision which meets all Talmudic stipulations.

Kosher Wine (Isr). Produced under Rabbinical supervision and meets all Talmudic stipulations.

Koshu (Jap). A native white grape variety.

Košice Brewery (Czec). A brewery based in eastern Czec. Noted for its' Cassovar Lager.

Koskenkorva (Fin). A sweet vodka.

Kosmet (Yug). A province of Serbia near Macedonia and Albania. Noted for its' full-bodied red wines.

Kosovo Pilje (Yug). Vineyards in South Serbia. Main wines are from the Spätburgunder. e.g. Yugoslav Amselfelder Spätburgunder.

Kostelec Nad Černými Lesy (Czec). An old established brewery based in western Czec.

K

Kostheim (Ger). Village. (Anb) = Rheingau. (Ber) = Johannisberg. (Gro) = Daubhaus. (Vins) = Berg, Reichesthal, Steig, Weiss Erd.

Köstritz Black Beer (Ger). A non-fermented, malt extract beer served mixed with pale beers or drunk as a tonic in Eastern Germany.

Kotsifali (Gre). A white grape variety used in the production of Peza and Archanes wines.

Kottabos (Gre). A game played in ancient Greece after dinner where a plate was balanced on a pole and the dregs of wine in a glass were thrown at it. In modern times to swirl dregs around a glass or cup and then to fling them out to hit a predetermined spot on the table or floor.

Koumis (Asia). An alternative spelling of Koumiss.

Koumiss (Asia). Fermented sour Camel or Mare's milk. Made by the Tartars. See also Arjan, Kumiss, Koumis and Koumyss.

Koumyss (Asia). An alternative spelling of Koumiss. See also Koumis, Kumiss and Arjan.

Kourschels (Lux). A vineyard site in the village of Wellenstein.

Kövidinka (Hun). A medium dry, white wine produced in south-western Hungary.

Köwerich (Ger). Village. (Anb) = Mosel-Saar-Ruwer. (Ber) = Bernkastel. (Gro) = Sankt Michael. (Vins) = Held, Laurentiuslay.

Kozel (Czec). A dark special beer 14° brewed by the Velké Popovice Brewery.

Kozjak (Yug). A white wine produced in Slovenia.

KPA (Eng) (abbr). A keg Pale ale 1035 O.G. brewed by the Brakspear Brewery, Henley-on-Thames, Berkshire.

Kraamanis (Hol). A liqueur produced by Van Zuylekom of Amsterdam.

Krabask Bitters (Den). An alcoholic bitters.

Krachtig (Hol). Potent, strong.

Kräftig (Ger). Robust, rich in alcohol.

Krähenberg (Ger). Vineyard. (Anb) = Württemberg. (Ber) = Württembergisch Unterland. (Gro) = Heuchelberg. (Vil) = Massenbachhausen.

Krähenschnabel (Ger). Vineyard. (Anb) = Franken. (Ber) = Maindreieck. (Gro) = Not yet assigned. (Vil) = Rerlenbach bei Marktheidenfeld

Krähenwinkler (Ger). The brand-name of a Weizenkorn produced by August Schmidt Gutsbrennerein, Krähenwinkler, Hannover.

Kraichgau (Ger). A district within the Baden region. See Badische Bergstrasse/Kraichgau.

Kraichtal [stadtteil Bahnbrucker, Gochsheim and Oberacker] (Ger). Village. (Anb) = Baden. (Ber) = Badische Bergstrasse/Kraichgau. (Gro) = Stiftsberg. (Vin) = Lerchenberg.

Kraichtal [stadtteil Landshausen and Menzingen] (Ger). Village. (Anb) = Baden. (Ber) = Badische Bergstrasse/Kraichgau. (Gro) = Stiftsberg. (Vin) = Spiegelberg.

Kraichtal [stadtteil Neuenbürg, Menzingen and Münzesheim] (Ger). Village. (Anb) = Baden. (Ber) = Badische Bergstrasse/Kraichgau. (Gro) = Stiftsberg. (Vin) = Silberberg.

Kraichtal [stadtteil Oberöwisheim, stadtteil Unteröwisheim] (Ger). Village. (Anb) = Baden. (Ber) = Badische Bergstrasse/Kraichgau. (Gro) = Mannaberg. (Vin) = Kirchberg.

Kraipale (Gre). Drunkenness.

Krajina (Yug). A wine region that borders Bulgaria and Rumania. Produces mainly red wines from the Prokupac, Skadarka and Začinka grapes. Also noted for Bagrina (a dry white wine from grape of same name).

Krakonoše (Czec). A Beer 14° brewed by the Trotnov Brewery in eastern Bohemia. Has a strong hop flavour and aroma.

Krakus (Pol). Said to be the ladies' favourite vodka. 40% alc. by vol. Produced from rye by Polmos.

Kralupy nad Vltavou Brewery (Czec). A brewery based in northern Czec.

Krambamuli (Ger). An East German liqueur flavoured with angelica and violet extract.

Krampeln (Aus). Denotes an empty, lifeless wine that has a rough, biting flavour.

Krampen (Ger). A section of wineland around Cochem on the lower Mosel. So called because of the shape of the bend (or Cramp) in the river. It produces poor wines because of the hardness of the soil.

Kranawitter (It). A Gin from juniper berries made in the Südtirol. (Trentino-Alto Adige) 38% alc. by vol.

Krans Estate (Die) (S.Afr). A wine estate based in Klein Karoo. Address = Box 28, Calitzdorp 6660. Produces varietal wines. Was originally known as the Hoë Krans Wynmakery.

Kranz (Ger). A liqueur producer based in Zusenhofen, Schwarzwald.

Kranzberg (Ger). Vineyard. (Anb) = Rheinhessen. (Ber) = Nierstein. (Gro) = Auflangen. (Vil) = Nierstein.

K

Kranzberg (Ger). Vineyard. (Anb) = Rheinhessen. (Ber) = Nierstein. (Gro) = Gutes Domtal. (Vil) = Dalheim.

Krapfenberg (Ger). Vineyard. (Anb) = Rheinpfalz. (Ber) = Südliche Weinstrasse. (Gro) = Guttenberg. (Vil) = Vollmersweiler.

Kraškiteran (Yug). A robust red wine (high in iron and tannin) produced in the Slovenia region.

Krasnodar (USSR). 'Crimean Champagne'. Produced between the Anapa and Gelendshik regions. A region and city in own right.

Krasnoe Vino (USSR). A local red wine produced in the river Don area.

Krasnotop (USSR). A white grape variety grown in the river Don area.

Krasnyi Kamenj (USSR). A white table wine produced near Krasnodar in western Russia.

Krassato (Gre). A red grape variety used for making dry red wines in northern Greece.

Krater (Gre). A wide round bowl that was used to combine wine and water in ancient Greece.

Krater (Yug). A red wine produced in south-eastern Macedonia.

Krating (Asia). A Pilsener-style Lager brewed by the Amant Brewery in Thailand.

Kratosija (Yug). A red wine produced in southern Macedonia.

Kratzig (Ger). Denotes a pétillant, bubbly wine.

Krauel (Carlos J.) (Sp). A noted producer and exporter of Malaga.

Krausen (USA). Unfermented wort added to the beer to produce a second fermentation to carbonate the beer.

Krausening (USA). A process of adding Krausen to the beer.

Kräuterberg (Ger). Vineyard. (Anb) = Ahr. (Ber) = Walporzheim/Ahrtal. (Gro) = Klosterberg. (Vil) = Walporzheim.

Kräuterberg (Ger). Vineyard. (Anb) = Mittelrhein. (Ber) = Bacharach. (Gro) = Schloss Stahleck. (Vil) = Oberdiebach.

Kräuterhaus (Ger). Vineyard. (Anb) = Mosel-Saar-Ruwer. (Ber) = Bernkastel. (Gro) = Schwarzlay. (Vil) = Traben-Trarbach.

Krauterlikor (Ger). A herb-flavoured liqueur.

Krautheim (Ger). Village. (Anb) = Baden. (Ber) = Badische Frankenland. (Gro) = Tauberklinge. (Vin) = Heiligenberg.

Krautheim (Ger). Village. (Anb) = Franken. (Ber) = Maindreieck. (Gro) = Kirchberg. (Vin) = Sonnenleite.

Krautheim [stadtteil Klepsau] (Ger). Village. (Anb) = Baden. (Ber) = Badische

Frankenland. (Gro) = Tauberklinge. (Vin) = Heiligenberg.

Kreaca (Rum). A white grape variety, also known as Banater riesling, Zokkelweiss, Kriacza and Creaca.

Kreidkeller (Ger). Vineyard. (Anb) = Rheinpfalz. (Ber) = Mittelhaardt-Deutsche Weinstrasse. (Gro) = Feuerberg. (Vil) = Kallstadt.

Kreigsberg (Ger). Vineyard. (Anb) = Württemberg. (Ber) = Remstal-Stuttgart. (Gro) = Weinsteige. (Vil) = Stuttgart.

Kreitzberg (Lux). A vineyard site in the village of Remerschen.

Kremer (Louis) (Fr). Champagne producer. Address = BP 149, 51200 Épernay. Produces – Vintage and non-vintage wines. Vintages – 1971, 1973, 1975, 1976, 1978, 1979, 1980, 1982, 1983.

Krems (Aus). A wine district within the region of Niederösterriech. Produces both red and white wines.

Kremser (Aus). A white, fruity wine from Krems district.

Krepkaya (USSR). A Vodka of high proof. 56% alc. by vol. Is fined, filtered through charcoal and polished in a bed of quartz.

Kressbronn am Bodensee Tubingen [ortsteil Hirschau, Unterjesingen] (Ger). Village. (Anb) = Württemberg. (Ber) = Kocher-Jagst-Tauber (Gro) = Not yet assigned. (Vin) = Sonnenhalden.

Kressmann (Fr). An Armagnac producer.

Kressmann La Tour (Fr). See Château La Tour Martillac.

Kreszenz (Ger). A word which denotes a wine grower/vineyard owner.

Kretchma (Cktl). ½ measure Vodka, ½ measure (white) Crème de Menthe, juice ¼ lemon, dash Grenadine. Shake over ice, strain into a cocktail glass.

Kretzer (It). A rosato wine produced in the Südtirol (Trentino-Alto Adige) region.

Kreusenbier (Ger). A yeasty sediment Beer produced by the Haake-Beck Brauerei of Bremen.

Kreuz (Ger). Cross.

Kreuz (Ger). Vineyard. (Anb) = Rheinhessen. (Ber) = Bingen. (Gro) = Sankt Rochuskapelle. (Vil) = Ockenheim.

Kreuz (Ger). Vineyard. (Anb) = Rheinhessen. (Ber) = Nierstein. (Gro) = Güldenmorgen. (Vil) = Dienheim.

Kreuz (Ger). Vineyard. (Anb) = Rheinhessen. (Ber) = Nierstein. (Gro) = Güldenmorgen. (Vil) = Oppenheim.

Kreuz (Ger). Vineyard. (Anb) = Rheinpfalz. (Ber) = Mittelhaardt-

K

Deutsche Weinstrasse. (Gro) = Schnepfenflug an der Weinstrasse (Vil) = Friedelsheim.

Kreuz (Ger). Vineyard. (Anb) = Rheinpfalz. (Ber) = Mittelhaardt-Deutsche Weinstrasse. (Gro) = Schwarzerde. (Vil) = Kirchheim.

Kreuzberg (Ger). Vineyard. (Anb) = Baden. (Ber) = Ortenau. (Gro) = Fürsteneck. (Vil) = Rammersweier.

Kreuzberg (Ger). Vineyard. (Anb) = Baden. (Ber) = Ortenau. (Gro) = Schloss Rodeck. (Vil) = Mösbach.

Kreuzberg (Ger). Vineyard. (Anb) = Baden. (Ber) = Ortenau. (Gro) = Schloss Rodeck. (Vil) = Renchen.

Kreuzberg (Ger). Vineyard. (Anb) = Baden. (Ber) = Ortenau. (Gro) = Schloss Rodeck. (Vil) = Waldulm.

Kreuzberg (Ger). Vineyard. (Anb) = Franken. (Ber) = Maindreieck. (Gro) = Kirchberg. (Vil) = Nordheim.

Kreuzberg (Ger). Vineyard. (Anb) = Mittelrhein. (Ber) = Rheinburgengau. (Gro) = Marksberg. (Vil) = Koblenz-Ehrenbreitstein.

Kreuzberg (Ger). Vineyard. (Anb) = Mosel-Saar-Ruwer. (Ber) = Bernkastel. (Gro) = Schwarzlay. (Vil) = Traben-Trarbach.

Kreuzberg (Ger). Vineyard. (Anb) = Rheinhessen. (Ber) = Nierstein. (Gro) = Krötenbrunnen. (Vil) = Dolgesheim.

Kreuzberg (Ger). Vineyard. (Anb) = Rheinhessen. (Ber) = Nierstein. (Gro) = Sankt Alban. (Vil) = Bodenheim.

Kreuzberg (Ger). Vineyard. (Anb) = Rheinpfalz. (Ber) = Mittelhaardt-Deutsche Weinstrasse. (Gro) = Pfaffengrund. (Vil) = Dutweiler.

Kreuzberg (Ger). Vineyard. (Anb) = Rheinpfalz. (Ber) = Mittelhaardt-Deutsche Weinstrasse. (Gro) = Schnepfenflug vom Kellertal. (Vil) = Einselthum.

Kreuzberg (Ger). Vineyard. (Anb) = Rheinpfalz. (Ber) = Mittelhaardt-Deutsche Weinstrasse. (Gro) = Schnepfenflug vom Kellertal. (Vil) = Niefernheim.

Kreuzberg (Ger). Vineyard. (Anb) = Rheinpfalz. (Ber) = Mittelhaardt-Deutsche Weinstrasse. (Gro) = Schnepfenflug vom Zellertal. (Vil) = Zell.

Kreuzblick (Ger). Vineyard. (Anb) = Rheinhessen. (Ber) = Wonnegau. (Gro) = Liebfrauenmorgen. (Vil) = Worms.

Kreuzhalde (Ger). Vineyard. (Anb) = Baden. (Ber) = Kaiserstuhl-Tuniberg. (Gro) = Vulkanfelsen. (Vil) = Ihringen.

Kreuzhalde (Ger). Vineyard. (Anb) = Baden. (Ber) = Kaiserstuhl-Tuniberg. (Gro) = Vulkanfelsen. (Vil) = Wasenweiler.

Kreuzkapelle (Ger). Vineyard. (Anb) = Rheinhessen. (Ber) = Nierstein. (Gro) = Vogelsgärten. (Vil) = Guntersblum.

Kreuzlay (Ger). Vineyard. (Anb) = Mosel-Saar-Ruwer. (Ber) = Zell/Mosel. (Gro) = Schwarze Katz. (Vil) = Zell.

Kreuznach (Ger). Bereich. (Anb) = Nahe. (Gros) = Kronenberg, Schlosskapelle, Sonnenborn, Pfarrgarten.

Kreuzweg (Ger). Vineyard. (Anb) = Baden. (Ber) = Badische Bergstrasse/ Kraichgau. (Gro) = Mannaberg. (Vil) = Leimen.

Kreuzweg (Ger). Vineyard. (Anb) = Rheinhessen. (Ber) = Nierstein. (Gro) = Petersberg. (Vil) = Framersheim.

Kreuzweiler (Ger). Village. (Anb) = Mosel-Saar-Ruwer. (Ber) = Obermosel (Gro) = Gipfel. (Vin) = Schloss Thorner Kupp.

Kreuzwertheim (Ger). Village. (Anb) = Franken. (Ber) = Mainviereck. (Gro) = Not yet assigned. (Vin) = Kaffelstein.

Kriacza (Rum). A white grape variety also known as Banater riesling, Zakkelweiss, Kreaca, Creaca.

Kriek (Bel). A Lambic beer 5–7% alc. by vol. which has cherries added to produce a new fermentation for 4–8 months.

Kriekenbier (Bel). A cherry beer brewed without the use of Lambic beer.

Krieken Lambic (Bel). See Kriek.

Krim-Sekt (USSR). A sparkling (méthode champenoise) wine, the first to be produced in Russia. c1779.

Kriska (Afr). A potent palm wine produced in western Africa.

Kriss Cocktail (Cktl). ⅙ gill Cognac, ⅛ gill dry Vermouth, ⅛ gill Amaretto, juice ¼ lemon, dash Gomme syrup. Stir over ice, strain into an ice-filled highball glass, top with tonic water, a cherry and a lemon slice.

Kristal (USSR). A brand of Vodka 40% alc. by vol. distilled in Riga.

Kristal-Liköre (Ger). Indicates visible sugar crystals in a liqueur.

Kriter (Fr). A sparkling wine made by the Transfer method. Produced from the Aligoté grape by Patriarche Père et Fils, Burgundy.

Kroatenpfad (Ger). Vineyard. (Anb) = Rheinpfalz. (Ber) = Mittelhaardt-Deutsche Weinstrasse. (Gro) = Pfaffengrund. (Vil) = Lachen-Speyerdorf.

Kroatzbeere (Pol). A blackberry Brandy produced from wild blackberries 30% alc. by vol. See also Jerzyrowka.

Kroatzbeerlikoer (Ger). Blackberry brandy. (Pol) = Jerzyrowka.

Kroeg (Hol). Tavern, Public-house, Pub.

Kroegje (Hol). A street-corner local drinking place.

Kroes (Hol). Cup, mug.

Kroměříž Brewery (Czec). One of the

K

country's oldest breweries based in Kroměříž, central Czec.

Kronberg (Ger). Vineyard. (Anb) = Franken. (Ber) = Steigerwald. (Gro) = Kapellenberg. (Vil) = Zeil.

Krondorf (Austr). Vineyard. Address = 19 North Street, Adelaide, South Australia 5000. 91.5 ha. in Barossa Valley, Lyndoch and McLaren Vale. Grape varieties – Cabernet sauvignon, Chardonnay, Frontignan, Rhine riesling, Sémillon.

Krone (Aus). A dry, golden-coloured beer 12.5° brewed by the Schwechat Brauerei.

Krone (Ger). Vineyard. (Anb) = Mosel-Saar-Ruwer. (Ber) = Saar-Ruwer. (Gro) = Römerlay. (Vil) = Waldrach.

Krone (Ger). Vineyard. (Anb) = Nahe. (Ber) = Kreuznach. (Gro) = Schlosskapelle. (Vil) = Laubenheim.

Krone (Ger). Vineyard. (Anb) = Rheingau. (Ber) = Johannisberg. (Gro) = Burgweg. (Vil) = Lorch.

Kroneberg (Ger). Vineyard. (Anb) = Mosel-Saar-Ruwer. (Ber) = Zell/Mosel. (Gro) = Grafschaft. (Vil) = Bullay.

Kronen (Ger). Dortmund's oldest brewery. Produces Kronen Export 5.2% alc. by vol. and Classic.

Kronenberg (Ger). Grosslage. (Anb) = Nahe. (Ber) = Kreuznach. (Vils) = Bad Kreuznach, Winzenheim, Bosenheim, Ippesheim, Planig, Bretzenheim, Hargesheim.

Kronenberg (Ger). Vineyard. (Anb) = Mosel-Saar-Ruwer. (Ber) = Zell/ Mosel. (Gro) = Grafschaft. (Vil) = Alf.

Kronenberg (Ger). Vineyard. (Anb) = Rheinpfalz. (Ber) = Mittelhaardt-Deutsche Weinstrasse. (Gro) = Kobnert. (Vil) = Kallstadt.

Kronenbourg (Fr). A Lager beer 1046 O.G. brewed under licence by Harp and Courage Breweries from the Kronenbourg Brasserie based in Strasbourg, Alsace.

Kronenbrau 1308 (Afr). A Lager beer brewed under licence by the Intercontinental Breweries.

Kronenbühl (Ger). Vineyard. (Anb) = Baden. (Ber) = Breisgau. (Gro) = Schutterlindenberg. (Vil) = Friesenheim.

Kronenbühl (Ger). Vineyard. (Anb) = Baden. (Ber) = Breisgau. (Gro) = Schutterlindenberg. (Vil) = Heiligenzell.

Kronenbühl (Ger). Vineyard. (Anb) = Baden. (Ber) = Breisgau. (Gro) = Schutterlindenberg. (Vil) = Hugsweier.

Kronenbühl (Ger). Vineyard. (Anb) = Baden. (Ber) = Breisgau. (Gro) = Schutterlindenberg. (Vil) = Lahr.

Kronenbühl (Ger). Vineyard. (Anb) = Baden. (Ber) = Breisgau. (Gro) = Schutterlindenberg. (Vil) = Mietersheim.

Kronenbühl (Ger). Vineyard. (Anb) = Baden. (Ber) = Breisgau. (Gro) = Schutterlindenberg. (Vil) = Oberschopfheim.

Kronenbühl (Ger). Vineyard. (Anb) = Baden. (Ber) = Breisgau. (Gro) = Schutterlindenberg. (Vil) = Oberweier.

Kronenfels (Ger). Vineyard. (Anb) = Nahe. (Ber) = Schloss Böckelheim. (Gro) = Burgweg. (Vil) = Waldböckelheim.

Kronsberg (Ger). Vineyard. (Anb) = Franken. (Ber) = Steigerwald. (Gro) = Burgweg. (Vil) = Iphofen.

Kron Vodka (Den). The brand-name of a noted local Vodka.

Kroon Pilsener (Hol). See De Kroon's.

Krötenbrunnen (Ger). Grosslage. (Anb) = Rheinhessen. (Ber) = Nierstein. (Vils) = Alsheim, Dienheim, Dolgesheim, Eich, Eimsheim, Gimsheim, Guntersblum, Hillesheim, Ludwigshöhe, Mettenheim, Oppenheim, Ülversheim, Wintersheim.

Krötenpfuhl (Ger). Vineyard. (Anb) = Nahe. (Ber) = Kreuzbach. (Gro) = Kronenberg. (Vil) = Bad Kreuznach.

Kröv (Ger). Village. (Anb) = Mosel-Saar-Ruwer. (Ber) = Bernkastel. (Gro) = Nacktarsch. (Vins) = Burglay, Herrenberg, Kirchlay, Letterlay, Paradies, Steffensberg.

Krown (Ind). A strong Lager beer 1048 O.G. brewed by the Mohan Meakin Brewery, Simla Hills, Solan.

Krug (Fr). Champagne producer. Address = 5 Rue Coquebert, 51100 Reims. Grande Marque. 15 ha. Produces – Vintage and non-vintage wines. Vintages – 1900, 1904, 1906, 1911, 1914, 1915, 1918, 1920, 1921, 1926, 1928, 1934, 1937, 1941, 1942, 1943, 1945, 1949, 1952, 1953, 1955, 1959, 1961, 1964, 1966, 1969, 1971, 1973, 1975, 1976, 1979, 1981, 1982, 1983.

Krug Clos du Mesnil (Fr). A vintage cuvée produced by Krug from 100% Chardonnay grapes. 1.9 ha. First fermentation is in small oak barrels. A single vineyard Champagne. Vintages – 1979, 1980, 1981, 1982, 1983, 1984, 1985.

Krug Collection (Fr). A cuvée vintage Champagne produced by Krug. Aged in Krug cellars. Vintages – 1947, 1953, 1961, 1964, 1966, 1969.

Kruger (Bel). The brand-name for a full-flavoured, strong-hopped, Pilsener-style Lager beer.

Kruger's Winery (USA). A medium-sized winery based in Nelson, Missouri. Produces French hybrid wines.

Krug Winery [Charles] (USA). A winery based in the Napa Valley, California. 500

K

ha. Grape varieties – Cabernet sauvignon, Chenin blanc, Gewürztraminer and Johannisberg riesling. Produces varietal wines.

Kruik (Hol). Jug, pitcher.

Krupnik (Pol). A honey-flavoured Vodka (liqueur). 40% alc. by vol.

Kruse Winery (USA). A small winery based in the Hecker Pass, Santa Clara, California. Grape varieties – Cabernet sauvignon, Colombard, Sauvignon blanc and Zinfandel. Produces varietal wines.

Kruškovac (Pol). A pear liqueur produced in Maraska. 43% alc. by vol.

Krušovice Brewery (Czec). A noted old established brewery based in Krusovice, north-western Czec. Produces fine Lager beers.

Krystal Lite (Eng). A low-calorie keg and bottled Beer 1030 O.G. brewed by the Burtonwood Brewery in Cheshire.

Ksara (Leb). A noted wine-producer who produces fine red wines from Aramon, Carignan and Cinsault grapes. Also produces Coteaux de Ksara (a dry white wine).

K2 (Eng). A lager beer brewed by the Fullers Brewery in Chiswick, West London to commemorate the climbing of K2 (a Himalayan mountain).

Kubanskaya (USSR). A Vodka flavoured with citrus peel and slightly sweetened. 40% alc. by vol.

Kuban Valley (USSR). A wine-producing area in Krasnodar which is noted for its dessert and fortified wines.

Küchelberger (It). A red table wine produced from the Schiave grape near Merano, Trentino-Alto Adige.

Küchenmeister (Ger). Vineyard. (Anb) = Franken. (Ber) = Steigerwald. (Gro) = Schlossberg. (Vil) = Rödelsee.

Kuchuk-Lambat (USSR). A red Muscat dessert wine from the southern Crimea.

Kuchuk-Uzen (USSR). A red grape variety grown in the Crimea. Produces Madeira-style dessert wines.

Kuehn (Rene) (Fr). A wine-producer based in Ammerschwihr, Alsace.

Kuentz-Bas (Fr). An Alsace wine producer. Address = 68420 Husseren-lès-Châteaux. 12.5 ha.

Kues (Ger). Vineyards facing Bernkastel on the Mosel. Sometimes spelt Cues.

Küf (Tur). Mildew.

Küfelik (Tur). Very drunk. Highly intoxicated.

Kugelspiel (Ger). Vineyard. (Anb) = Franken. (Ber) = Steigerwald. (Gro) = Herrenberg. (Vil) = Castell.

Kuhberg (Ger). Vineyard. (Anb) = Baden. (Ber) = Badische Bergstrasse/Kraichgau. (Gro) = Rittersberg. (Vil) = Schriesheim.

Kuhlman-Oberlin (Fr). A famous French hybridiser.

Kuhnchen (Ger). Vineyard. (Anb) = Mosel-Saar-Ruwer. (Ber) = Saar-Ruwer. (Gro) = Römerlay. (Vil) = Riveris.

Kuhrmana (Iraq). A Lager beer 13.5° Balling brewed by the State-owned Brewery based in Baghdad.

Kuhstall (Ger). Vineyard. (Anb) = Mittelrhein. (Ber) = Rheinburgengau. (Gro) = Burg Rheinfels. (Vil) = St. Goar-Werlau.

Kuip (Hol). Vat, barrel, tub.

Kuipe (S.Afr). Fermentation vat.

Kuiper (Hol). Cooper.

Kuiperij (Hol). Coopery.

Kujundžuša (Yug). A dry white wine produced by Dalmaciajavino at Split on the Dalmatian coast, western Yugoslavia.

Kulgan (USSR). A strong Vodka flavoured with Ginseng root and produced in the Ukraine.

Kulmbacher Mönschof Brauerei (Ger). A brewery based in Kulmbach, Bavaria. Is noted for its' full-bodied Maingold Lager 5.3% alc. by vol. Kloster Schwarz 4.9% alc. by vol. and Klosterbock Dunkel 6.4% alc. by vol.

Kulminator (Ger). A very strong beer with an original gravity of 28%. See EKU.

Kulminator Dunkles Starkbier (Ger). A dark strong Beer from the EKU Brauerei of Kulmbach, Bavaria. 7.6% alc. by vol.

Kulminator 28 Urtyp Hell (Ger). A strong, slow-lagered beer from the EKU Brauerei in Kulmbach, Bavaria. The 28 denotes the O.G., the beer goes through the freezing process (see Eisbock) to raise its' alcoholic strength.

Különleges (Hun). A wine classification which denotes a wine of distinction similar to Qmp in Germany and Austria.

Külsheim (Ger). Village. (Anb) = Baden. (Ber) = Badische Frankenland. (Gro) = Tauberklinge. (Vin) = Höher Herrgott.

Kulturny (USSR). Cultured.

Kumasi Brewery (Afr). A noted brewery based in Ghana which brews Star Lager and Gulder Lager.

Kumeau River Merlot (N.Z.). A red wine from San Marino.

Kumeu-Huapi-Waimauku (N.Z.). A sub-region of Auckland. north-west of the city.

Kumis (China). A fermented mare's milk. Made by the tribesmen in the north-west of China for ceremonial occasions.

Kumiss (Asia). An alternative spelling of Koumiss. See also Koumis, Koumyss,

Kümme (Ger). Kümmel.

Kümmel (Hol). A clear white spirit/liqueur made from grain and flavoured with caraway seeds. Various alcoholic strengths.

Kümmel Crystallizé (USA). Kümmel which has crystallised sugar in it. (In the bottle).

Kummel della Val d'Aosta (It). A noted monastery herb liqueur produced in north-western Italy.

Kumquat (Gre). A liqueur produced from the minature Japanese Kumquat oranges.

Kumys (USSR). The name used in the sixteenth century for Koumiss made in south-eastern Russia.

Kumyz (Asia). The Tartars' spelling of Koumiss in the middle ages.

Kunstrum (Aus). A neutral spirit distilled from potatoes. The flavour of Rum is produced using chemicals.

Kuntra (Tur). A white grape variety grown in Marmara and Thrace.

Künzelsau (Ger). Village. (Anb) = Württemberg. (Ber) = Kocher-Jagst-Tauber. (Gro) = Kocherberg. (Vin) = Hoher Berg.

Kupelwieser (Fritz) (It). An old established winery based in Salurn, Südtirol (Trentino-Alto Adige).

Kuperflöz (Ger). Vineyard. (Anb) = Mittelrhein. (Ber) = Rheinburgengau. (Gro) = Herrenberg. (Vil) = Dörscheid.

Kupferberg (Ger). A famous Sekt producer who uses the Transfer method.

Kupferberger Auslese (S.Afr). An Auslese-style wine made from the Steen grape. 28 grammes per litre of sugar. Produced by the Bergkelder Co.

Kupfergrube (Ger). Vineyard. (Anb) = Nahe. (Ber) = Schloss Böckelheim. (Gro) = Burgweg. (Vil) = Schlossböckelheim.

Kupferhalde (Ger). Vineyard. (Anb) = Württemberg. (Ber) = Württembergisch Unterland. (Gro) = Stromberg. (Vil) = Obererdingen.

Kupferstube (Ger). A malty, bottom-fermented beer brewed by the Mailaender Bergbräu concern of Fürth. Is copper-red in colour.

Kupp (Ger). Vineyard. (Anb) = Mosel-Saar-Ruwer. (Ber) = Bernkastel. (Gro) = Schwarzlay. (Vil) = Wittlich.

Kupp (Ger). Vineyard. (Anb) = Mosel-Saar-Ruwer. (Ber) = Saar-Ruwer. (Gro) = Römerlay. (Vil) = Trier.

Kupp (Ger). Vineyard. (Anb) = Mosel-Saar-Ruwer. (Ber) = Saar-Ruwer. (Gro) = Scharzberg. (Vil) = Ayl.

Kupp (Ger). Vineyard. (Anb) = Mosel-Saar-Ruwer. (Ber) = Saar-Ruwer. (Gro) = Scharzberg. (Vil) = Ockfen.

Kupp (Ger). Vineyard. (Anb) = Mosel-Saar-Ruwer. (Ber) = Saar-Ruwer. (Gro) = Scharzberg. (Vil) = Saarburg.

Kupp (Ger). Vineyard. (Anb) = Mosel-Saar-Ruwer. (Ber) = Saar-Ruwer. (Gro) = Scharzberg. (Vil) = Serrig.

Kupp (Ger). Vineyard. (Anb) = Mosel-Saar-Ruwer. (Ber) = Saar-Ruwer. (Gro) = Scharzberg. (Vil) = Wiltingen.

Küppers (Ger). A Kolschbier which is exported mainly to the USA. 4.5% alc. by vol.

Kup's Indispensable (Cktl). ⅗ measure dry Gin, ⅕ measure sweet Vermouth, ⅕ measure dry Vermouth, dash Angostura. Stir over ice, strain into a cocktail glass.

Kurbag Cocktail (Cktl). Another name for Whip Cocktail.

Kurdamir (USSR). A red grape variety grown in the Kurdamirsk area of Azerbaijan. Produces red dessert wines.

Kurdamirsk (USSR). One of the major wine-producing areas of Azerbaijan. Noted for its dessert wines.

Kurfürst (Ger). Vineyard. (Anb) = Mosel-Saar-Ruwer. (Ber) = Zell/Mosel. (Gro) = Goldbäumchen. (Vil) = Ellenz-Poltersdorf.

Kurfürst (Ger). Vineyard. (Anb) = Rheinpfalz. (Ber) = Mittelhaardt-Deutsche Weinstrasse. (Gro) = Meerspinne. (Vil) = Mussbach.

Kurfürstenberg (Ger). Vineyard. (Anb) = Mosel-Saar-Ruwer. (Ber) = Saar-Ruwer. (Gro) = Römerlay. (Vil) = Waldrach.

Kurfürstenhofberg (Ger). Vineyard. (Anb) = Mosel-Saar-Ruwer. (Ber) = Saar-Ruwer. (Gro) = Römerlay. (Vil) = Trier.

Kurfürstenstück (Ger). Grosslage. (Anb) = Rheinhessen. (Ber) = Bingen. (Vils) = Gau-Bickelheim, Gau-Weinheim, Gumbsheim, Vendersheim, Wallertheim.

Kurfürstlay (Ger). Grosslage. (Anb) = Mosel-Saar-Ruwer. (Ber) = Bernkastel. (Vils) = Andel, Bernkastel-Kues, Brauneberg, Burgen, Kestern, Lieser, Maring-Noviand, Mulheim, Osann-Monzel, Veldenz, Wintrich.

Kurk (Hol). Cork.

Kurketrekker (Hol). Corkscrew.

Kürnbach (Ger). Village. (Anb) = Baden. (Ber) = Badische Bergstrasse/Kraichgau. (Gro) = Stiftsberg. (Vin) = Lerchenberg.

Kurpfälzisches Winzerfest (Ger). A Baden wine festival held at Wiesloch in August-September.

Kursaal Cocktail (Cktl). ¼ gill Brandy, ⅛ gill Cherry brandy, ⅛ gill French vermouth, dash Absinthe, dash Angostura, dash Orange bitters, 1 teaspoon plain syrup. Shake over ice, strain into a 5 oz. wine glass. Serve with a cherry and squeeze lemon peel juice.

Kurz (Ger). Lit – 'Short'. Denotes very little flavour or aroma.

Kuss mit Liebe (Ger). A unique bottle with two separate liqueurs-Kroatzbeere (blackberry brandy) and Kakao (coffee liqueur) produced by Thienelt near

Düsseldorf. The coffee liqueur is poured gently on top of the blackberry brandy.

Kutjevo (Yug). A noted wine-producing town in Croatia.

Kutnà Hora Brewery (Czec). An old brewery based in western Czec.

Kvalitetno Vino (Yug). Quality wine.

Kvasi (USSR). The Slavic name for yeast.

Kvass (USSR). A light, carbonated beer made from rye and barley. Is often flavoured with juniper, mint or cranberries. See Quass.

Kvass (USSR). A low-alcohol, sweet drink made by the fermentation of bread.

Kwangsi (China). A branch of the China National Cereals, Oils and Foodstuffs Import and Export Corporation.

Kwangtung (China). A branch of the China National Cereals, Oils and Foodstuffs Import and Export Corporation. Uses the Pearl River brand-name for their Rum.

Kwartier na Vijven (Hol). Lit – 'Quarter past five'. A liqueur produced by Van Zuylekom of Amsterdam.

Kwas (USSR). A liqueur made from Rye.

Kweichow (China). A province in south-western China that is noted for its' Mao-t'ai (a grain spirit made from wheat and millet).

K.W.V. (S.Afr) (abbr). Koöperatiewe Wijnbouwers Vereniging Van Zuid-Afrika. Based in Paarl. Founded in 1916 (registered 1918). Is the Wine Farmers' Association. Produces most styles of wines, varietal, fortified wines and brandies. These include – Bonne Esperance, Blanc de Noir, Cape Bouquet, Cape Forêt, La Borie, Musanté, Noble Late Harvest and Roodeberg. Address = Box 528, Suider Paarl 7624. Paarl, Laborie, Steen and Mymering are brand-names for their wines.

Kykko (Cyp). The brand-name used by the Loel Co. for a range of their wines.

Kylix (Gre). A two-handled drinking vessel, often decorated with mythological scenes. Similar to a large Champagne saucer.

Kym (Eng). A species of barley from the Golden Promise variety. Gives medium sugar yields.

L

Laacherberg (Ger). Vineyard. (Anb) = Ahr. (Ber) = Walporzheim/Ahrtal. (Gro) = Klosterberg. (Vil) = Mayschoss.

Laatoes (S.Afr). A white wine blend of Hanepoot and Steen grapes from the Nuwehoop Co-operative.

Laatoes (S.Afr). A fruity, medium-sweet, white wine made from the Steen grape by Louwshoek Voorsorg Co-operative.

Laat-oes (S.Afr). Late-harvested.

Laat Oes (S.Afr). A medium-sweet, white, fruity wine made from the Colombard grape by the Lutzville Co-operative.

Laat Oes Steen (S.Afr). A full-bodied, white, medium-sweet wine made from the Steen grape by the McGregor Co-operative.

Labarde (Fr). A commune within the district of Médoc in north-western Bordeaux.

Labastida (Sp). A noted wine village in the Rioja Alavesa district. Produces mainly red wines.

Labatt's Ale (Can). A famous Ale exported from Labatt's Brewery in Ontario.

Labatt's Brewery (Can). A brewery in Ontario. Produces Labatt's Ale and Blue (a sweet Pilsener). Also brews under licence – Budweiser, Guinness and Skol.

Label (Eng). The identification mark on a bottle. Can be made of paper or a simple paint mark (Port). Usually contains the name of wine, shipper, quality, alcohol content, capacity etc. depending on the laws of each country. e.g. EEC. See also Bottle Ticket, Bottle Label and Flash Mark.

Label Normandie (Fr). A label guarantee found on Normandy Cider bottles to guarantee the quality of contents through analysis.

Laberstall (Ger). Vineyard. (Anb) = Rheinhessen. (Ber) = Bingen. (Gro) = Sankt Rochuskapelle. (Vil) = Ockenheim.

Labicanum (Lat). A red wine produced in central-western Italy in Roman times.

Labologist (Eng). A collector of beer bottle labels. Society formed in 1959.

Labottière (Fr). The name given to red and white wines produced by Cordier. A.C. Bordeaux.

Labouré Gontard (Fr). A noted négociant-éleveur based in Nuits-Saint-Georges, Burgundy. Produces many fine Burgundies and Comtesse de Roseval (a Crémant de Bourgogne).

Labouré-Roi (Fr). A Burgundy négociant-éleveur based in Nuits-Saint-Georges, Côte de Nuits, Burgundy. Has many fine cuvées.

Labrija (Sp). An area in the Jerez Supérieur district of south-western Spain.

Labrum (Lat). Vat, tub.

Labrusca (USA). See Vitis Labrusca.

Lac (Lat). Milk.

Lacchus (Lat). One of the words used for Bacchus. See also Bassareus, Bromius, Dionysus, Euan, Euhan, Euhius, Euius, Lyaeus and Thyoneus.

Lac des Roches (Gre). A full-bodied, deep-flavoured, white wine from Boutari in Crete and the Dodecanese Islands.

Lace (Eng). To add a measure of alcohol (usually spirits) to a drink to give it a 'kick'. May be done with or without the consumer's knowledge.

Lachaise (Fr). A commune of the Charente Département whose grapes are classed Petite Champagne (Cognac).

Lache (Ch.Isles). A tot or small measure of drink. See also Feis.

Lachen-Speyerdorf (Ger). Village. (Anb) = Rheinpfalz. (Ber) = Mittelhaardt-Deutsche Weinstrasse. (Gro) = Pfaffengrund. (Vins) = Kroatenpfad, Langenstein, Lerchenböhl.

Lachlan Valley Vineyard (Austr). Based at Cowra, Central New South Wales. Part of the Rothbury Estate.

Lacons (Eng). The brand-name of a Lager and lime drink 3.8% alc. by vol. 1030–1034 O.G. sold in cans only.

L.A.C.O.S. (Eng) (abbr). Liqueur and Cocktail Orientated Seminars.

Lacourtoisie (Claude) (Fr). Armagnac producer. Address = Domaine de la Coste, 40240 Labastide d'Armagnac. 10 ha. in the Bas Armagnac. Produces brandies aged at least 5 years.

Lacre Violeta (Sp). A sweet, golden-coloured, dessert wine produced in Alella, near Barcelona, eastern Spain. 14% alc. by vol. and cask aged.
Lacrima (It). The local name for the red Gaglioppo grape in Pollino, Calabria.
Lacrima (Sp). A class of Málaga. Equals sweet.
Lacrima Christi (It). Lit – 'Tears of Christ'. A delicate, medium dry white wine from the Campania region, produced on the slopes of Vesuvius. Non D.O.C. Also a red and rosé.
Lacrima d'Abeto (It). Lit – 'Tears of the pine'. A green pine-needle flavoured liqueur made by the Camaldolese order of monks in the Castentino mountains.
Lacrima di Castrovillari (It). A red table wine produced in Castrovillari, southern Italy.
Lacryma Christi del Vesuvio (It). See Lacrima Christi. Alternative spelling of.
Lacteo (Port). Milky.
Lactic Acid (Eng). $CH_3CH(OH)COOH$. Found in wine. Produced during malolactic fermentation by Lactobacillus. Also found in milk.
Lactobacillus (Lat). In the absence of air produces Lactic acid and CO_2 from Malic acid.
Lactose (Eng). Milk sugar, not fermentable by wine yeasts.
Lacy Stagger (Eng). A Cider cocktail produced by the Symonds Cider Co. in Hereford, Herefordshire. Made from Cider, English wine, Vodka and orange juice.
Lad Anzebadi (Egy). A style of fermented milk (Koumiss).
Ladaux (Fr). A commune in the Haut-Benauge, Entre-Deux-Mers, central Bordeaux.
Ladies' Cocktail (Cktl).(1). ¾ measure Bourbon whiskey, ¼ measure Anisette, 2 dashes Angostura. Stir over ice, strain into a cocktail glass. Top with a pineapple cube.
Ladies' Cocktail (Cktl).(2). 1 fl.oz. Rye whiskey, 2 dashes Pernod, 2 dashes Anisette, dash Angostura. Stir over ice, strain into a cocktail glass. Top with a grapefruit segment.
Ladiville (Fr). A commune in the Charente Département in Petite Champagne, Cognac.
Ladoix-Serrigny (Fr). An A.C. of the 2 villages near Beaune in the Côte de Beaune. Has the Premier Cru vineyards of Basses-Mourettes, La Contière, La Toppe-au-Vert, Les Grandes-Lolières, Les Maréchaudes and Les Petites-Lolières. Produces red and white wines.
Ladoucette (Baron de) (Fr). The owner of Château de Nozet, who produces a fine Pouilly Fumé under the name of Baron de L'.
Ladroncillo (Sp). The name given to the metal pipe that transfers the wine from one cask to another.
Lady Amber (Cktl). 1 measure Gin, ½ measure passion fruit juice, ½ measure Kirsch, dash egg white. Shake over ice, strain into a cocktail glass. Add a cherry.
Lady Be Good Cocktail (Cktl). ¾ measure Cognac, ¼ measure (white) Crème de Menthe, 2 dashes sweet Vermouth. Shake over ice, strain into a cocktail glass.
Ladyburn (Scot). A single Malt whisky distillery based at Girvan, Ayrshire. Owned by William Grant and Sons. A Lowland malt. Produces a 14 year old Malt whisky 43% alc. by vol.
Lady Finger Cocktail (Cktl). ⅖ measure dry Gin, ⅖ measure Cherry brandy, ⅕ measure Kirsch. Shake over ice, strain into a cocktail glass. Top with a cherry.
Lady Killer (Cktl). ⅙ gill Gin, juice of lime, dash Cherry brandy, 2 dashes Orgeat. Shake over ice, strain into an ice-filled highball glass. Top with tonic water, a cherry and a slice of lime.
Lady Londonderry (Eng). An old eighteenth-century tea blend.
Lady Love Fizz (Cktl). ⅕ gill dry Gin, 1 teaspoon powdered sugar, juice ½ lemon, 1 egg white, ⅙ gill cream. Shake over ice, strain into an ice-filled highball glass. Top with iced Champagne.
Lady Lyssa (Cktl). 1 part Cointreau, 5 parts dry Gin, 1 part Apricot brandy. Shake over ice, strain into a cocktail glass, add orange zest and a cherry.
Lady's Dream (Cktl). ⅓ measure Bourbon whiskey, ⅓ measure Curaçao, ⅓ measure Crème de Fraises, dash cream. Shake over ice, strain into a cocktail glass.
Ladysmith (S.Afr). A Brandy and table wine-producing area in Klein Karoo (Little Karoo).
Ladysmith Co-operative (S.Afr). Based in Klein Karoo. Address = Ladismith Koöperatiewe Wynmakery, Box 56, Ladismith 6885. Produces – Towerkop Cinsault and Swartberg Aristaat.
Ladysmith Koöperatiewe Wynmakery (S.Afr). See Ladismith Co-operative.
Ladysmith-Oudtshoorn (S.Afr). A district in Klein Karoo noted for its sherry-style wines.
Lady Susan (Eng). A style of turntable combined in a tea-service/breakfast-service used with Crown Derbyware in the nineteenth century.
Lady's Wines (Eng). The name given to

L

sweet white wines such as Sauternes, Barsac etc. See also Girl's Wines.

Laetitia (Fr). A medium dry white wine from Ajaccio in Corsica.

Laevulose (Eng). Another name for Fructose.

Lafaurie-Peyraguey (Fr). See Château Lafaurie-Peyraguey.

Lafayette Punch (Cktl). 1 bottle Pimms N°1, 6 sliced oranges, 2 ozs. sugar, 4 bottles sparkling wine. Mix Pimms, oranges and sugar together, stand 1 hour, add wine and plenty of ice. Serve.

Lafitte (Charles) (Fr). Champagne producer Address = 39, Rue de Général Leclerc, 51130 Vertes. Founded in 1976. Owns no vineyards. Produces – Vintage and non-vintage wines.

Lafões (Port). A small wine-producing region between the Dão and Vinho Verde regions. Produces red and white wines.

Lafontan (Fr). Armagnac producer. Address = Société Distillerie des Coteaux de Gascogne, BP3, 32440 Castelnau d'Auzan. 65 ha. in Bas Armagnac. Produces Doyen d'Âge 20–30 years old.

Lafont de Saint-Preuil (Fr). Cognac producer. Address = Daniel Bouju, 16130 Segonzac. Owns 20 ha. in the Grande Champagne. Produces Tradition, Empéreur and V.S.O.P.

Lagarde-sur-le-Né (Fr). A commune in the Charente Département whose grapes are classed Petite Champagne (Cognac).

Lagares (Sp). Used in Jerez. Wooden troughs where grapes are placed to be pressed.

Lagariavini (It). A producer of sparkling (méthode champenoise) wines based in the Trentino-Alto Adige. Labels include Brut di Concilio.

Lagarino Rosato (It). A light red/rosé wine produced from the Lagrein grape. Was formerly known as Lagreinkretzer.

Lagaritanum (Lat). A red wine produced in south-eastern Italy during Roman times.

Lagars (Port). Wooden or concrete troughs used for the treading of the grapes in the production of Port.

Lagavulin (Scot). A single Malt whisky distillery on the eastern side of the Isle of Islay overlooking Port Ellen. Owned by the White Horse Distillers Ltd. An Islay malt. Produce a 12 year old Malt at 43% alc. by vol.

Lagbi (Afr). A non-alcoholic drink made from the juice of grapes in Libya.

Lage (Ger). A specific named vineyard. See Einzellage and Grosslage.

Lageos (Lat). A red grape variety grown in Greece in Roman times.

Lager (Ger). Lit – 'Store or stock'. A name for the beer produced by bottom fermentation during which it is 'Lagered' for long periods to complete fermentation before it is bottled.

Lagerbier (Ger). Lit – 'Beer for storing'. The nineteenth-century term for Lager.

Lagering (Ger). A method of storing new beer (lager) at very low temperatures so that the yeasts and other solids precipitate out naturally. During this period the flavour improves. Up to 3 months.

Lager-Weisse (Ger). A bottom-fermented wheat beer.

Lagery (Fr). A Cru Champagne village in the Canton de Ville-en-Tardenois. District = Reims.

Lager Yeasts (Eng). The name for yeasts that fall through the liquid and work on the sugar at the bottom of fermenting vessel. See Saccharomyces Carlsbergensis.

Lagni (Alg). Palm milk.

Lagoa (Port). One of five co-operatives along the Algarve coast.

Lago di Caldaro (It). D.O.C. red wine from the Trentino-Alto Adige. Made from 85–100% Lagrein and Pinot nero grapes. Classico if grapes grown from specific communes, Superiore if min. alc. content 10.5% by vol. Scelto or Selezionato if from selected grapes and of 11% alc. by vol. minimum. Also known as Kalterer or Kalterersee.

Lagoena (Lat). Decanter.

Lagosta (Port). The brand-name of a Vinho Verde from Real Companhía Vinícola do Norte de Portugal.

Lag Phase (Eng). A term for the period of time taken by active yeast to multiply (Binary Fission) and build a colony concentrated enough to start off visible fermentation in the beer, cider, wine, etc.

Lagrein (It). A red grape variety grown in the Trentino-Alto Adige. (Südtirol).

Lagrein del Trentino (It). D.O.C. red wine produced in the Trentino-Alto Adige from the Lagrein grape. 12% alc. by vol.

Lagrein di Gries (It). Wines – Lagrein rosato and Alto-Adige Lagrein scuro are entitled to specification if produced in commune of Bolzano in the Trentino-Alto Adige.

Lagrein Dunkel (It). A German name for the red grape variety Lagrein scuro in the Südtirol (Trentino-Alto Adige).

Lagrein Kretzer (It). A German name for the red grape variety Lagrein rosato in the Südtirol (Trentino-Alto Adige).

Lagrein Rosato (It). A red grape variety

L

used in the Trentino-Alto Adige region. Also a wine of same name. See Lagrein Kretzer.

Lagrein Scuro (It). A red grape variety used in the Trentino-Alto Adige region. Also a wine of same name. See also Lagrein Dunkel.

Làgrima (Port). The natural grape sugar in must.

Lágrima (Sp). The finest of the Málagas. Not often shipped abroad. Is produced without using mechanical pressing. Made from the free-run must. Is light in colour, aroma and alcohol.

Lag Screw (Eng). A wooden screw with a square head used to fasten cask staves together in the seventeenth and eighteenth centuries.

Laguardim (Sp). A noted wine-producing village in the Rioja Alavesa.

Laguna Cocktail (Cktl). ⅓ gill Grappa, ⅙ gill Vodka, ⅙ gill sweet white (Bianco) Vermouth, 3 dashes Campari. Shake well over ice, strain into a cocktail glass. Top with a cherry.

Laguna-Verde (Cktl). ½ measure Vodka, ¼ measure Galliano, ¼ measure French vermouth, 2 dashes blue Curaçao. Stir over ice, strain into a cocktail glass, add a cherry.

Lagunilla (Sp). A red and white wine produced by Bodegas Lagunilla. Both are oak matured. Valle Tinto is from the Tempranillo grape and Valle Blanco from Viura grape.

Lahnstein (Ger). Village. (Anb) = Mittelrhein. (Ber) = Rheinburgengau. (Gro) = Marksburg. (Vin) = Koppelstein.

Lahntal (Ger). Grosslage. (Anb) = Mittelrhein. (Ber) = Rheinburgengau. (Vils) = Bad Ems, Dausenau, Fachbach, Nassau, Obernhof, Weinähr.

Lahr (Ger). Village. (Anb) = Baden. (Ber) = Breisgau. (Gro) = Schutterlindenberg. (Vins) = Herrentisch, Kronenbühl.

Laid Back (Eng). A term used to describe wines that are easy to drink. e.g. Californian wines.

Laine Vineyards and Winery (USA). A winery based in Fulton, Kentucky. Produces French hybrid wines.

Laira (Austr). Vineyard. Address = Main Pendar, Naracoorte Highway, (P.O. Box 18) Coonawarra, South Australia 5263. 28 ha. Grape varieties – Cabernet sauvignon, Malbec, Merlot and Shiraz.

Laird o' Logan (Scot). See Logan. (The original name for Logan Whisky).

Laireen (Sp). Another spelling of Lairen.

Lairén (Sp). A white grape variety grown in western Spain to produce medium white wines including Montilla-Moriles.

Lait (Fr). Milk.

Lait (Au) (Fr). Lit – 'with milk'. e.g. Café au lait (coffee with milk).

Lait Condensé (Fr). Condensed milk.

Lait de Coco (Fr). Coconut milk. Is used in some cocktail recipes.

Lait de Poule (Cktl). French egg nogg. 2 egg yolks, castor sugar to taste. Beat up with boiling milk, add ½ gill Brandy.

Lait Desséché (Fr). Dried milk.

Lait Écrôimai (Ch.Isles). Skimmed milk.

Laiteux (Fr). Milky.

Lait Fermenté (Fr). Fermented milk.

Laitiat (Fr). A non-alcoholic drink of whey which has had fruit infused in it. Favoured in the Franche-Comté region.

Laives (Fr). A commune in the A.C. Mâcon where the grapes may be used for Mâcon Supérieur.

Lake Balatòn (Hun). A vineyard region in western Hungary. Produces good white wines from the Furmint and Riesling grape.

Lake County (USA). A wine-producing county on the northern coast of California.

Lake District (Aus). A noted wine-producing area in western Austria which is protected by the Leitha mountains. Produces fine white wines.

Lake Erie (USA). Second of the Great Lakes which has the districts of New York, Pennsylvania and Ohio.

Lake Fly (Eng). The name of an Oloroso sherry from Findlater.

Lake Keuka Wine Co (USA). A winery based in the Finger Lakes region. Produces hybrid and American vine wines.

Lake's Folly (Austr). Vineyard. Address = Broke Road, Pokolbin, New South Wales 2321. 13.2 ha. Grape varieties – Cabernet sauvignon, Chardonnay, Hermitage, Malbec and Petit verdot.

Lakeside Winery (USA). A winery based in Harbert, Michigan. Produces French hybrid wines.

Lake Sylvia Vineyard (USA). A bonded winery based in Minnesota. 3 ha. Produces hybrid wines.

Lakka (Fin). A liqueur with a bitter-sweet tang of cloudberries that are grown only in the Arctic. Also known as Suomurrain. Is produced by Chymos. 29% alc. by vol.

Lalande de Pomerol (Fr). An A.C. subdistrict of Pomerol in eastern Bordeaux.

Laligant-Chameroy (Fr). A Burgundy négociant-éleveur based at Beaune, Côte de Beaune, Burgundy.

Lamarque (Fr). A commune of the Haut-Médoc, Bordeaux.

Lamb and Watt (Eng). A producer of a range of spirits and a Sloe Gin under the Mauget label. Also Vine Leaf Sherry.

L

Lambanog (E.Ind). A distilled Tuba wine from the Philippines.

Lamberhurst Priory (Eng). See Ridge Farm, Kent.

Lambert Bridge (USA). A winery based in Dry Creek Valley, Sonoma County, California. 33 ha. Grape varieties – Cabernet sauvignon, Chardonnay and Johannisberg riesling. Produces varietal wines.

Lamberti (It). Wine producers east of Lake Garda. Produce – Bardolino, Soave and Valpolicella.

Lambic Beer (Bel). A wheat beer, top fermented, which uses the natural wild yeasts to ferment the brew. 4.5% alc. by vol. Produced in the river Senne region. See Brettanomyces Bruxelliensis and Brettanomyces Lambicus.

Lambiek Beer (Bel). An alternative spelling of Lambic beer.

Lamblin et Fils (Fr). A small Burgundy négociant-éleveur based at Maligny, Chablis, Burgundy.

Lambrusco (It). A red grape variety grown in the Po valley in north-eastern Italy. Produces classic red and sparkling red wines.

Lambrusco di Salamino (It). A red grape variety used in the Emilia-Romagna region.

Lambrusco di Sorbara (It). A red grape variety used in the Emilia-Romagna region.

Lambrusco di Sorbara (It). D.O.C. red wine made from 60% Lambrusco di sorbara and 40% Lambrusco di salamino grapes. Vinification can take place in Bologna, Modena, Parma and Reggio Emilia subject to Ministry approval. Vinificato fuori zona (vinified outside production area) must be on label.

Lambrusco Grappa Rossa (It). Is similar to Lambrusco di Sorbara but thinner and darker.

Lambrusco Grasparossa (It). A red grape variety used in the Emilia-Romagna region.

Lambrusco Grasparossa di Castelvetro (It). D.O.C. red wine made from 85% Lambrusco grasparossa and 15% Lambrusco varieties/Uva d'oro grapes. Vinification can take place in Modena. Vinificato fuori zona (vinified outside production area) must appear on the label.

Lambrusco Maestri (It). A red grape variety used in the Emilia-Romagna region.

Lambrusco Marani (It). A red grape variety used in the Emilia-Romagna region.

Lambrusco Montericco (It). A red grape variety used in the Emilia-Romagna region.

Lambrusco Reggiano (It). D.O.C. red or rosé wine made from a variety of Lambrusco grapes. Vinification can also take place in Mantova, Modena and Parma. Vinificato fuori zona (vinified outside production area) must appear on the label.

Lambrusco Salamino (It). See Lambrusco di Salamino.

Lambrusco Salamino di Ste. Croce (It). D.O.C. red wine made from Lambrusco di Salamino grapes grown in the province of Moderna. Vinification can take place in Moderna but can be extended with permission. If so then Vinificato fuori zona (vinified outside production area) must appear on the label.

Lambrusco Varietus (It). A red grape variety used in the Emilia-Romagna region.

Lambsheim (Ger). Village. (Anb) = Rheinpfalz. (Ber) = Mittelhaardt-Deutsche Weinstrasse. (Gro) = Rosenbühl. (Vin) = Burgweg.

Lamb's Navy Rum (Eng). The brand-name for a dark Rum from the West Indies matured in England by United Rum Merchants.

Lamb's Wool (Cktl). Into a large saucepan pour 2 bottles old strong Ale, 1 pint white wine, 1 teaspoon nutmeg, 2 teaspoons mixed spices, brown sugar to sweeten. Mix together. Add 6 cored and roasted apples (sugared and spiced before roasting). Simmer, serve in mugs.

Lamb Winery (USA). A small winery based in Santa Clara County, California. Grape varieties – Chardonnay, Chenin blanc, Gamay and Zinfandel. Produce varietal wines.

Lamego (Port). A district in the Douro that produces red, white and sparkling wines.

Lamiable Frères (Fr). Champagne producer. Address = 8 Rue de Condé, 51150 Tours sur Marne. Récoltant-manipulants. Produces – Vintage and non-vintage wines. Member of C.V.C. Vintages 1971, 1975, 1976, 1979, 1982, 1983.

Lämmler (Ger). Vineyard. (Anb) = Württemberg. (Ber) = Remstal-Stuttgart. (Gro) = Weinsteige. (Vil) = Fellbach.

Lamonts Winery (Austr). Address = Bisdee Road, Millendon, Western Australia 6056. 3 ha. Grape varieties – Cabernet sauvignon, Muscadelle, Sémillon, Shiraz and Verdelho.

Lamont Winery (USA). A large winery based in Delano, Kern County, California. Grape varieties – Colombard and Zinfandel. Produces varietal and dessert

L

wines under Gold Peak, Mountain Gold and Lamont labels. Was originally known as Bear Mountain Winery.

Lamot (Bel). A brewery producing a bottled Pilsener lager 1045 O.G. imported by Bass.

Lampia (It). A sub-species of the Nebbiolo grape.

Lamplighter Gin (Eng). See Nicholson.

Lampons (Fr). A term used in the seventeenth century in verse. Lit – 'Let us drink'.

Lancaster County Winery (USA). A winery based in Willow Street, Pennsylvania. Produces French hybrid wines.

Lancer (Ire). A strong bottled Lager brewed by Harp.

Lancers (Port). A sweet carbonated rosé wine, sold in a distinctively shaped bottle from J.M. da Fonseca. Also a red and a white version produced.

Lancié (Fr). A commune in the Beaujolais. Has A.C. Beaujolais-Villages or Beaujolais-Lancié status.

Lancorta (Sp). A red wine produced by Bodegas Landalan, Alta region in Rioja. Oak and bottle matured. Also a white wine under same name from Viura grape.

Landalan (Sp). See Bodegas Landalan.

Landau (Ger). Village. (Anb) = Rheinpfalz. (Ber) = Südliche Weinstrasse. (Gro) = Königsgarten. (Vin) = Altes Löhl.

Landau (S.Afr). See Blaauwklippen.

Landes (Fr). A Vins de Pays area in south-western France.

Landespreismünze (Ger). An award given for quality at a state level to wines.

Landesregierungen (Ger). The governments of the vine growing Federal states, who determine legislation for the new (1971) wine law.

Landesverordnung Rheinland-Pfalz (Ger). A decree for the Federal state of the Rhenish Palatinate. 12-8-1971 article [4] governs the production of Liebfrauenmilch/Liebfraumilch.

Landewein (Ger). See Landwein.

Landing (USA). Applied to Champagne. Denotes the length of time the Champagne has been in the country. e.g. Champagne that has been in the country for 1 year is said to have 1 year's landing.

Landiras (Fr). A commune in the A.C. Graves region of south-western Bordeaux.

Landkreis (Ger). Parish.

Landlord (Eng). The name given to the publican/licensee.

Landlord (Eng). A strong Bitter 1042 O.G.

brewed by the Timothy Taylor Brewery in Keighley, West Yorkshire.

Landmark Vineyards (USA). A winery based in Windsor, Russian River Valley, Sonoma County, California. 33 ha. Grape varieties – Cabernet sauvignon, Chardonnay, Chenin blanc, Gewürztraminer, Johannisberg riesling and Pinot noir. Produces varietal wines. Vineyards also in Sonoma and Alexander Valleys.

Landot (Fr). A famous hybridiser.

Landry (Fr). A Cognac producer. Address = Logis de Beaulieu, 17520 Germignac. Owns 19 ha. in the Petite Champagne. Founded in 1972. Produces Hors d'Age (a 17 year old Cognac).

Landsdorf (Eng). A fine, non-pasteurised, filtered, draught Lager beer 1034 O.G. brewed by the Hardington Brewery, Somerset.

Landshausen (Ger). See Kraichtal.

Landsknecht (Ger). Vineyard. (Anb) = Franken. (Ber) = Mainsdreieck. (Gro) = Kirchberg. (Vil) = Obervolkach.

Landskrone (Ger). Vineyard. (Anb) = Ahr. (Ber) = Walporzheim/Ahrtal. (Gro) = Klosterberg. (Vil) = Heimersheim.

Landskroon Estate (S.Afr). A large vineyard based in Paarl. Address = P.O. Box 519, Suider-Paarl 7624. 300 ha. Produces Blanc de noir, Bouquet blanc, Bouquet rouge, Tinta Barocca and many varietals plus a Port-type wine.

Landwein (Ger). From 1982, a new designation of Deutsche Tafelwein of EEC. (15 zones). See Untergebiet and Zones.

Landwein der Mosel (Ger). One of fifteen Deutsche Tafelwein zones.

Landwein der Saar (Ger). One of fifteen Deutsche Tafelwein zones.

Landy Frères (It). A producer of Dubac brandy.

Langa Ántica (It). The brand-name for a Grappa.

Lang-Biemont (Fr). Champagne producer. Address = Les Ormissets, 51200 Oiry, Épernay. 60 ha. Produces – Vintage and non-vintage wines. Vintages – 1971, 1973, 1974, 1976, 1977, 1979, 1980, 1982, 1983. De Luxe vintage cuvée is Cuvée III.

Lang Brothers (Scot). Distillers of Scotch whisky based at Glengoyne. A subsidiary of Robertson and Baxter. Produces Langs Supreme.

Langdons (Eng). A Cider-producing firm based at Hewish, near Weston-Super-Mare, Avon. Noted for its West Country Cider.

Lange Els (Ger). Vineyard. (Anb) = Rheinpfalz. (Ber) = Mittelhaardt-Deutsche Weinstrasse. (Gro) = Schwarzerde. (Vil) = Hessheim.

L

Langenbach (Ger). A wine merchant and shipper based in Worms in the Rheinhessen. Produces Liebfraumilch under the brand-name of Crown of Crowns.

Langenberg (Ger). Vineyard. (Anb) = Franken. (Ber) = Maindreieck. (Gro) = Rosstal. (Vil) = Retzstadt.

Langenberg (Ger). Vineyard. (Anb) = Rheingau. (Ber) = Johannisberg. (Gro) = Steinmacker. (Vil) = Martinsthal.

Langenbeutingen (Ger). Village. (Anb) = Württemberg. (Ber) = Württembergisch Unterland. (Gro) = Lindelberg. (Vin) = Himmelreich.

Langenlois (Aus). A wine-producing town of same name. Produces mainly white wines.

Langenlonsheim (Ger). Village. (Anb) = Nahe. (Ber) = Kreuznach. (Gro) = Sonnenborn. (Vins) = Bergborn, Königsschild, Lauerweg, Lohrer Berg, Rothenberg, St. Antoniusberg, Steinchen.

Langenmorgen (Ger). Vineyard. (Anb) = Rheinpfalz. (Ber) = Mittelhaardt-Deutsche Weinstrasse. (Gro) = Mariengarten. (Vil) = Deidesheim.

Langenstein (Ger). Vineyard. (Anb) = Franken. (Ber) = Steigerwald. (Gro) = Not yet assigned. (Vil) = Martinsheim.

Langenstein (Ger). Vineyard. (Anb) = Rheinpfalz. (Ber) = Mittelhaardt-Deutsche Weinstrasse. (Gro) = Pfaffengrund. (Vil) = Lachen-Speyerdorf.

Langenstück (Ger). Vineyard. (Anb) = Rheingau. (Ber) = Johannisberg. (Gro) = Steinmäcker. (Vil) = Eltville.

Langenstück (Ger). Vineyard. (Anb) = Rheingau. (Ber) = Johannisberg. (Gro) = Steinmäcker. (Vil) = Oberwalluf.

Langenstück (Ger). Vineyard. (Anb) = Rheingau. (Ber) = Johannisberg. (Gro) = Steinmäcker. (Vil) = Rauenthal.

Langenthal Brauerei (Switz). A brewery based in Langenthal. Part of the Interbera group.

Langeskov Cherries (Den). Used in the making of cherry wine.

Langgarten (Ger). Vineyard. (Anb) = Mittelrhein. (Ber) = Bacharach. (Gro) = Schloss Stahleck. (Vil) = Manubach.

Langham Vineyard (Eng). A vineyard based at Langham, near Colchester, Essex. 1.6 ha. Grape variety – Müller-Thurgau.

Langhe (It). The name for the clay soil in the Barolo district of the Piemonte region.

Langhölle (Ger). Vineyard. (Anb) = Nahe. (Ber) = Schloss Böckelheim. (Gro) = Paradiesgarten. (Vil) = Obermoschel.

Langhorne Creek (Austr). A wine-producing area in South Australia, east of Adelaide. Produces full-bodied red wines.

Langoed (S.Afr). Estate.

Langoiran (Fr). A commune in the A.C. Premières Côtes de Bordeaux, central Bordeaux.

Langon (Fr). A commune in the A.C. Graves region in south-western Bordeaux.

Langscheid (Ger). Village. (Anb) = Mittelrhein. (Ber) = Rheinburgengau. (Gro) = Schloss Schönburg. (Vin) = Hundert.

Langs Supreme (Scot). A blended Scotch whisky produced by the Lang Brothers Ltd. 40% alc. by vol. See Lang Brothers.

Langstieler (Ger). A lesser white grape variety.

Langsur (Ger). Village. (Anb) = Mosel-Saar-Ruwer. (Ber) = Obermosel. (Gro) = Königsberg. (Vin) = Brüderberg.

Languedoc (Fr). A wine area within the Midi in south-western France together with the Roussillon.

Languedoc-Roussillon (Fr). A region of south-western France. Has the Départements of Aude, Gard, Hérault, Lozère and Pyrénées-Orientales in its boundaries. A mountainous region with coastal plains. All styles of wines produced.

Langverwacht Co-operative (S.Afr). Based in the Boesmans River, Bonnievale, Breede River and Robertson areas. Address = Box 87, Bonnievale 6730. Produces varietals wines.

Lania (Cyp). A village on the south-east side of the Island that produces the grapes for Commandaria.

Lanolin (Eng). A description that is often used to describe wines made with the Sémillon grape. e.g. white Bordeaux. Denotes a soft fragrance.

Lanoy (S.Afr). A red wine blend of Shiraz, Merlot and Cabernet grapes from the Boschendal Estate in Paarl.

Lansdowne Lady (Cktl). 1 part Gin, 2 parts dry Sherry, 1 part orange squash. Shake well over ice, strain into a cocktail glass, add a cherry.

Lanškroun Brewery (Czec). A brewery based in northern Czec. Founded in 1700.

Lanson (Fr). Champagne producer. Address = 12, Boulevard Lundy, BP 163, 51056 Reims. Grande Marque. 200 ha. Produces – Vintage and non-vintage wines. Vintages – 1900, 1904, 1906, 1911, 1914, 1915, 1918, 1920, 1921, 1926, 1928, 1934, 1937, 1941, 1942, 1943, 1945, 1949, 1952, 1953, 1955, 1959, 1961, 1964, 1966, 1969, 1971, 1975, 1976, 1979, 1981, 1982, 1983, 1985. De Luxe vintage cuvées are Noble Cuvée Millesimé and 225 Anniversary Cuvée.

Lanvin Fils (H.) (Fr). The label used by

L

Société Anonyme de Magenta for their vintage cuvée.

Lanzerac (S.Afr). The name used for export wines by the Stellenbosch Farmers' Winery. Produce a fine rosé wine under this label.

Laochiu (China). Drink of wine.

Lap (USA). Chorus girls' slang for Gin.

Lapalme (Fr). One of nine wine communes in the Fitou region, southern France.

Laphroaig (Scot). A single Malt whisky distillery on the eastern side of the Isle of Islay. Owned by Long John Distilleries. An Islay malt. Produce a 10 year old malt. 40% alc. by vol.

Lapic Winery (USA). A winery based at New Brighton, south-western Pennsylvania. Produces French hybrid wines.

Lapin Brewery (Fin). A small brewery based in Tornio, northern Finland.

Lap it up (Eng). A term used to denote that a person is enjoying their beverage or food.

Lapponia (Fin). Loganberry liqueur.

Lapsang Souchong (China). A blend of teas from the Fukien Province. Has a pungent, smoky flavour and large leaf.

Lapuebla de Labarca (Sp). A noted wine-producing village in the Rioja Alavesa.

Lar (Sp). The name of a white wine produced by Bodega Co-operative de Ribeiro.

Laranjada (Port). Orangeade.

Larate (S.Am). A well-known brand of Pisco produced in Peru.

Larios (Sp). A producer of Málaga wine, Brandy and other spirits based in Málaga, southern Spain.

Lark (Cktl). ½ measure Nassau orange liqueur, ¼ measure *** Cognac, ¼ measure lemon squash. Shake well with ice, strain into a cocktail glass, serve with a cherry.

Larmandier-Bernier (Fr). Champagne producer. Address = 43 Rue du 28 Août, 51130 Vertus. Récoltant-manipulants. Produces – Vintage and non-vintage wines. A member of the C.V.C. Vintages – 1971, 1975, 1976, 1979, 1982, 1983.

Larressingle (Fr). The brand-name of an Armagnac produced by Ets. Papelorey SA, Rue des Carmes, 32100 Condom. 40% alc. by vol.

Larsen (Fr). Cognac producer. Address = Larsen SA, 54 Boulevard de Paris, 16102 Cognac. Produces – TVFC Fine Champagne 5 year old, Extra 35 year old and Fines Champagnes.

Larums (Sp). A red wine produced by Bodegas Bardón from the Garnacha

grape (plus other varieties) in Ribera Baja.

Las (Les) (Fr). A vineyard in the A.C. commune of Montagny, Côte Chalonnaise, Burgundy.

Las Aberturas (Sp). A wine-producing area north of Valdepeñas, central Spain.

Lasenberg (Ger). Vineyard. (Anb) = Baden. (Ber) = Kaiserstuhl-Tuniberg. (Gro) = Vulkanfelsen. (Vil) = Bötzingen.

Laski Rizling (Yug). A name given to the white grape variety Welschriesling.

Lasky Cocktail (Cktl). ⅓ measure Swedish Punsch, ⅓ measure Gin, ⅓ measure grapefruit juice. Shake over ice, strain into a cocktail glass.

Lassere (W.Ind). A noted Rum distillery on the island of Guadeloupe.

Lasserre (Paul) (Fr). An Armagnac producer. Address = Hontanx, 40190- Villeneuve de Marsan.

Lass O'Gowrie (Eng). A Whitbread home-brew public house in Manchester. Produces cask conditioned beers using malt extract.

Last Order Cocktail (Cktl). 6 fl.ozs. Brown ale, ½ measure Brandy, 12 raisins, piece stemmed ginger. Heat gently until nearly boiling. Serve in mugs with a cinnamon stick.

Last Orders (Eng). A term called on licensed premises by the landlord to announce that customers may purchase one more round of drinks before the licensing hours cease. See also Drinking-Up Time.

Lastovo (Yug). A major wine-producing region in Dalmatia.

Las Vegas (Chile). A wine-producing area in the Aconcagua province.

Latadas (Port). A method of growing the grapes on the lattice-work trellises on tall granite columns high above the ground.

Late Bottled Vintage (Port). A Port wine from a single year (blend) which has been matured in cask 4–5 years then bottled. Has no sediment.

Late Burgundy (Ger). The English name for the Spätburgunder grape.

Late Gathered (Ger). Spätlese.

Late Harvest (S.Afr). Denotes grapes gathered after the commencement of the harvest date to produce a sweeter wine.

Late Night Final (Eng). An egg-based drink produced by Townend of Hull, Humberside.

Lateron (Michel) (Fr). Crémant de Loire producer based at Amboise, Touraine, Loire.

Lates (Eng) (slang). A term for drinks that are sold after the permitted hours of opening.

Late Vintage (S.Afr). Wines made of Spätlese or Auslese style.

Late Vintage (USA). Late picked grapes. Makes Spätlese style wines.

Latex (Lat). The word used to describe water or other liquids.

Latex (S.Am). A milky white sap of certain plants which is fermented into an alcoholic drink.

Lateyron (Fr). A producer of A.C. Bordeaux Mousseux based in the Saint-Émilion region of eastern Bordeaux.

Lathophora Williamsi (Mex). Mezcal cactus used in the making of Mezcal and Tequila.

Latigné (Fr). A commune in the Beaujolais. Has either A.C. Beaujolais-Villages or Beaujolais-Latigné status.

Latin Quarter (Cktl). ⅔ measure Dubonnet, ⅓ measure Amer Picon, dash Cointreau. Shake over ice, strain into a cocktail glass.

Latisana (It). A locality on the river Tagliamento 50 miles north-east of Venice in the Friuli-Venezia Giulia region. Gives its name to wines of that region from certain communes.

Latisana (It). D.O.C. red and white wines of Friuli-Venezia Giulia. Name followed by a specific grape variety. 3 red – Latisana Cabernet, Merlot and Refosco. 4 white – Latisana Friulano, Pinot bianco, Pinot grigio and Verduzzo friulano. Vinification can occur in the province of Udine.

Latium (It). A region in West-central Italy, south-west of Umbria. Famous for Frascati and Est! Est!! Est!!! See Lazio.

Latour (Fr). See Château Latour.

Latour (F and Co) (Fr). Cognac producer. Address = SARL Cognac, Beausdeil, 34 Rue de Segonzac, 16104 Cognac.

Latour (Louis) (Fr). A Burgundy négociant-éleveur based in beaune, Côte de Beaune, Address = 18, Rue des Tonneliers, 21204 Beaune. The best known and respected of all the Burgundy shippers. Has many cuvées in the region.

Latour de France (Fr). An A.C. red wine in the Côtes du Roussillon, south-western France.

Latricières-Chambertin (Fr). A Grand Cru in the A.C. commune of Gevrey-Chambertin, Côte de Nuits, Burgundy. 6.23 ha.

Latrobe Brewery (USA). A brewery in Latrobe, Pennsylvania. Brews Rolling Rock Lager.

Latt (Ger). Vineyard. (Anb) = Rheinpfalz. (Ber) = Südliche Weinstrasse. (Gro) = Königsgarten. (Vil) = Albersweiler.

Lattacinio Glass (It). Venetian glass that is worked with buds of opaque white or with ribbing and stringing.

Latte (Fr). Boards used to separate the bottles in Champagne whilst they are under-going second fermentation. See Sur Lattes.

Latte (It). Milk.

Latteria (It). Dairy.

Lattiera (It). Milk jug.

Lattivéndolo (It). Milkman.

Lattöl (Swe). Lit – 'A small beer'. A mildly-hopped, light-coloured Lager.

Latzenbier (Ger). A name given to a strong version of Altbier of Düsseldorf 7.5% alc. by vol. brewed in March or September. It is also known as Sticke Alt.

Laubenheim (Ger). Village. (Anb) = Nahe. (Ber) = Kreuznach. (Gro) = Schlosskapelle. (Vins) = Fuchsen, Hörnchen, Junker, Karthäuser, Krone, St. Remigiusberg, Vogelsang.

Lauda (Ger). Village. (Anb) = Baden. (Ber) = Badische Frankenland. (Gro) = Tauberklinge. (Vins) = Altenberg, Frankenberg, Nonnenberg.

Laudamusberg (Ger). Vineyard. (Anb) = Mosel-Saar-Ruwer. (Ber) = Bernkastel. (Gro) = Michelsberg. (Vil) = Neumagen-Dhron.

Laudatio (Aus). A Sekt produced by the Kremser Winzergenossenschaft at Krems.

Laudenbach (Ger). Village. (Anb) = Baden. (Ber) = Badische Bergstrasse/Kraichgau. (Gro) = Rittersberg. (Vin) = Sonnberg.

Laudenbach (Ger). Village. (Anb) = Franken. (Ber) = Maindreieck. (Gro) = Rosstal. (Vins) = Assorted parts of vineyards.

Laudenbach (Ger). Village. (Anb) = Württemberg. (Ber) = Kocher-Jagst-Tauber (Gro) = Tauberberg. (Vin) = Schafsteige.

Laudun (Fr). A region within the south-western Rhône. Communes of Laudun, St. Victor, La Coste and Tresques. Red, rosé and white wines are produced. A Côtes du Rhône-Villages.

Lauerweg (Ger). Vineyard. (Anb) = Nahe. (Ber) = Kreuznach. (Gro) = Sonnenborn. (Vil) = Langenlonsheim.

Lauf (Ger). Village. (Anb) = Baden. (Ber) = Ortenau. (Gro) = Schloss Rodeck. (Vins) = Alter Gott, Gut Alsenhof, Schloss Neu-Windeck.

Laufen (Ger). Village. (Anb) = Baden. (Ber) = Markgräflerland. (Gro) = Burg Neuenfels. (Vin) = Altenberg.

Lauffen (Ger). Village. (Anb) = Württemberg. (Ber) = Württembergisch Unterland. (Gro) = Kirchenweinberg. (Vins) = Jungfer, Katzenbeisser, Nonnenberg,

L

Riedersbückele.

Laugel (Fr.). A famous Alsace wine producer. Address = 67520 Marlenheim. One of the largest producers. 5 ha. See Pichet d'Alsace.

Laumersheim (Ger). Village. (Anb) = Rheinpfalz. (Ber) = Mittelhaardt-Deutsche Weinstrasse. (Gro) = Schwarzerde. (Vins) = Kirchgarten, Mandelberg, Sonnengarten.

Launois Père et Fils (Fr). Champagne producer. Address = 3 Avenue de la République, Le Mesnil-sur-Oger. Récoltants-manipulants. Produces – Vintage and non-vintage wines. A member of C.V.C. Vintages – 1971, 1975, 1976, 1979, 1982, 1983.

Laurentiusberg (Ger). Vineyard. (Anb) = Mosel-Saar-Ruwer. (Ber) = Saar-Ruwer. (Gro) = Petersberg. (Vil) = Oberdollendorf.

Laurentiusberg (Ger). Vineyard. (Anb) = Mosel-Saar-Ruwer. (Ber) = Saar-Ruwer. (Gro) = Römerlay. (Vil) = Waldrach.

Laurentiusberg (Ger). Vineyard. (Anb) = Mosel-Saar-Ruwer. (Ber) = Saar-Ruwer. (Gro) = Scharzberg. (Vil) = Saarburg.

Laurentiusberg (Ger). Vineyard. (Anb) = Mosel-Saar-Ruwer. (Ber) = Zell/ Mosel. (Gro) = Grafschaft. (Vil) = Bremm.

Laurentiusberg (Ger). Vineyard. (Anb) = Nahe. (Ber) = Kreuznach. (Gro) = Pfarrgarten. (Vil) = Wallhausen.

Laurentiusberg (Ger). Vineyard. (Anb) = Nahe. (Ber) = Schloss Böckelheim. (Gro) = Burgweg. (Vil) = Altenbamberg.

Laurentiuslay (Ger). Vineyard. (Anb) = Mosel-Saar-Ruwer. (Ber) = Bernkastel. (Gro) = Sankt Michael. (Vil) = Köwerich.

Laurentiuslay (Ger). Vineyard. (Anb) = Mosel-Saar-Ruwer. (Ber) = Bernkastel. (Gro) = Sankt Michael. (Vil) = Leiwen.

Laurent-Perrier (Fr). Champagne producer. Address = BP3, 51150 Tours-sur-Maine. Grande Marque. Produces – Vintage and non-vintage wines. Vintages – 1904, 1906, 1911, 1914, 1919, 1921, 1926, 1928, 1934, 1937, 1941, 1943, 1945, 1947, 1949, 1952, 1953, 1955, 1959, 1961, 1962, 1964, 1966, 1969, 1970, 1973, 1975, 1976, 1978, 1979, 1982, 1983. De Luxe vintage cuvée is Cuvée is Grande Siècle.

Laurent Perrier (USA). A winery based in Almaden, California. Grape variety – Chardonnay. Produces sparkling wines. Is linked to the Champagne firm of same name in France.

Laurenziweg (Ger). Vineyard. (Anb) = Nahe. (Ber) = Kreuznach. (Gro) = Schlosskapelle. (Vil) = Dorsheim.

Lauric Acid (Eng). $C_{11}H_{23}COOH$. An acid found in wine in minute traces.

Lauschied (Ger). Village. (Anb) = Nahe. (Ber) = Schloss Böckelheim. (Gro) = Paradiesgarten. (Vin) = Edelberg.

Lautenbach (Ger). Village. (Anb) = Baden. (Ber) = Ortenau. (Gro) = Fürsteneck. (Vin) = Renchtäler.

Lauter Tub (USA). See Lauter Tun.

Lauter Tun (Eng). A copper or stainless steel vessel containing a false bottom and series of movable rakes. Used to filter the mash and draw off the wort in brewing.

Lauzet (Fr). A white grape variety grown in the Bergerac and Jurançon regions.

Lavan (Isr). A brand of dry red or white table wines produced by Carmel.

Lavaut (Fr). A Premier Cru vineyard in the A.C. commune of Gevrey-Chambertin, Côte de Nuits, Burgundy. 9.43 ha.

Lavaux (Switz). A sub-region of the Canton of Vaud. Produces white wines from the Chasselas grape.

Laverna (It). A bitter apéritif wine produced in Sicily.

Lavières (Les) (Fr). A Premier Cru vineyard in the A.C. commune of Savigny-lès-Beaune, Côte de Beaune, Burgundy.

Laville-Dieu (Fr). A V.D.Q.S. wine-producing area in Tarn-et-Garonne, south-western France. Produces red and rosé wines.

Lavrottes (Les) (Fr). A Premier Cru vineyard in the A.C. commune of Chambolle-Musigny, Côte de Nuits, Burgundy. 1 ha.

Lawhill Cocktail (Cktl). ⅔ measure Bourbon whiskey, ⅓ measure dry Vermouth, 2 dashes Absinthe, 2 dashes Maraschino, 1 dash Angostura. Stir over ice, strain into a cocktail glass.

Lawrence Winery (USA). A large winery based in the Edna Valley, San Luis Obispo, California. Grape varieties – Cabernet sauvignon, Chardonnay, Chenin blanc, Gewürztraminer, Johannisberg riesling, Pinot noir and Zinfandel. Produces varietal wines.

Law's Cocktail (Cktl). See Coffee Cocktail.

Laws of Hammurabi (Arab). The first Licensing Laws. 2,100 B.C. Written by a Babylonian king and mentioned rules for drinking which included loss of liberty for permitting riotous drinking on the premises and methods of viniculture.

Lawson (William) Distillers (Scot). A Scotch whisky producer based at Coatbridge, Glasgow and MacDuff, Banffshire. Owned by Martini and Rossi. Produces Glendeveron (a 12 year old Highland malt) 43% alc. by vol. and blended Scotch whiskies.

Laws Peach Bitters (Eng). A brand of flavouring bitters.

Lay (Ger). Lit – 'Slate or rock'. When placed at the end of a name denotes slaty soil. e.g. Burglay, Fässerlay, etc.

Lay (Ger). Vineyard. (Anb) = Mosel-Saar-Ruwer. (Ber) = Bernkastel. (Gro) = Badstube. (Vil) = Bernkastel-Kues.

Lay (Ger). Vineyard. (Anb) = Mosel-Saar-Ruwer. (Ber) = Bernkastel. (Gro) = Schwarzlay. (Vil) = Wittlich.

Lay (Ger). Vineyard. (Anb) = Mosel-Saar-Ruwer. (Ber) = Obermosel. (Gro) = Gipfel. (Vil) = Palzem.

Lay (Ger). Vineyard. (Anb) = Mosel-Saar-Ruwer. (Ber) = Zell/Mosel. (Gro) = Not yet assigned. (Vil) = Senheim.

Lay (Ger). Vineyard. (Anb) = Mosel-Saar-Ruwer. (Ber) = Zell/Mosel. (Gro) = Weinhex. (Vil) = Lehmen.

Layenberg (Ger). Vineyard. (Anb) = Mosel-Saar-Ruwer. (Ber) = Zell/Mosel. (Gro) = Rosenhang. (Vil) = Bruttig-Fankel.

Layenberg (Ger). Vineyard. (Anb) = Nahe. (Ber) = Schloss Böckelheim. (Gro) = Paradiesgarten. (Vil) = Niedermoschel.

Laying Down (Eng). The action of cellaring bottles of wines on their sides to mature. This applies mainly to red wines and vintage Port but many fine white wines need this period of maturation. See Bin and Investment.

Laykaul (Ger). Vineyard. (Anb) = Mosel-Saar-Ruwer. (Ber) = Saar-Ruwer. (Gro) = Römerlay. (Vil) = Korlingen.

Layon [River] (Fr). A tributary of the river Loire in the Anjou-Saumur district, A.C. Coteaux du Layon. Produces fine sweet, botrytis-attacked wines. See Coteaux du Layon.

Lazarillo (Sp). A medium-dry, white wine produced by Nuestro Padre Jesus del Perdon.

Lazio (It). The other name for the Latium region which includes Rome.

Lazzaroni (It). A noted producer of Amaretto di Saronno in Milan.

LB (Eng) (abbr). A Light Bitter 1030 O.G. brewed by the Burt Brewery in Ventor, Isle of Wight.

L.B. (Eng) (abbr). London Bottled. Found on a wine list.

L.B. (Port) (abbr). Late Bottled. Applies to Port wines.

LBA (Ch.Isles) (abbr). A draught Mild 1037.7 O.G. brewed by the Guernsey Brewery 1920 Ltd. in St. Peter Port. Initials stand for the ex-name of the Channel Isle Co. London Brewery Ale.

L.B.V. (Port) (abbr). Late Bottled Vintage. Applied to Ports of a single year that have been matured in cask 4–5 years then bottled. Has no sediment (crust).

LCL Pils (Eng). A keg Lager processed beer 1036 O.G. produced at the Dunston plant of the Northern Clubs Federation Brewery.

Lda (Port) (abbr). Limitada (Limited).

Leacock (Mad). A producer and shipper of Madeira. Sold under the St. John Reserve label. Sercial, Verdelho, Bual and Special Reserve Malmsey.

Leadboiler (Eng). A cask conditioned Bitter 1063 O.G. brewed by the homebrew Sair public house in Linthwaite, Huddersfield.

Lead Crystal (Eng). A type of glass made from silica, sand and red lead-oxide. Has a maximum of 33.3% lead content. See Waterford Crystal.

Lead-oxide (Eng). Used in glass making.

Leaf Roll (N.Z.). A virus that is recognised by the downward roll of the margins on the vine leaf. The leaves also have premature Autumn colouring.

Leaguer (S.Afr). Cask. Capacity 127 gallons.

Leaker (Eng). A term used to describe a bottle with wine leaking from the cork. This means air has come into contact with the wine which has either started to spoil or soon will. Usually caused by a poor cork or through great age.

Leamington Spa (Eng). An aperient still mineral water from central England.

Leaning Glass (Switz). A specially-designed wine glass for the 'Glacier Express' to allow for the steep gradients the train has to travel along during the journey. The stem is at an angle to keep the contents level.

Leànyka (Hun). A white grape variety which produces dry average wines. (Rum) = Feteascǎ. (Bul) = Fetiaska.

Leànyka Edes (Hun). A sweet white wine from the Eger region made from the Leànyka grape.

Leànyka Szaraz (Hun). A dry white wine from the Eger region made from the Leànyka grape.

Leap Frog Highball (Cktl). 1/3 gill Gin, juice 1/2 lemon. Place in an ice-filled highball glass. Top with ginger ale.

Leap Year (Cktl).(1). 2/3 measure dry Gin, 1/6 measure Grand Marnier, 1/6 measure Italian vermouth. Shake over ice, strain into a cocktail glass, serve with a cherry.

Leap Year (Cktl).(2). 3/5 measure dry Gin, 1/5 measure Orange gin, 1/5 measure sweet Vermouth, 2 dashes lemon juice. Shake over ice, strain into a cocktail glass.

L

Leasingham (Austr). Vineyard. Address = 7 Dominic Street, Clare, South Australia/ P.O. Box. 56, Dandenong 3175, Victoria. 612 ha. in Clare Valley. Grape varieties – Cabernet sauvignon, Malbec, Rhine riesling and Shiraz.

Leave It To Me (Cktl).(1). Juice ½ lemon, teaspoon raspberry syrup, ½ gill dry Gin. Shake well over ice, strain into a 5 oz. wine glass, add dash soda water.

Leave It To Me (Cktl).(2). ⅗ measure dry Gin, ⅕ measure dry Vermouth, ⅕ measure Apricot brandy, 2 dashes lemon juice, 2 dashes Grenadine. Shake over ice, strain into a cocktail glass.

Leavening (Eng). The old name for yeast.

Leban (Afr). The whey left over from cheese production. Used as a non-alcoholic beverage.

Lebelin (Fr). A cuvée in the A.C. Duresses, Monthélie, Côte de Beaune, Burgundy. Is owned by the Hospices de Beaune.

Lebendig (Ger). A wine with a fresh, racy flavour.

Lebensraum Estate (S.Afr). Sited near Worcester on the Breede River. Address = Lebensraum Landgoed, P.O. Box 36, Rawsonville 6845. Produces varietal wines.

Lechinta (Rum). A wine-producing region noted for its medium-dry white wines.

Leckerberg (Ger). Vineyard. (Anb) = Rheinhessen. (Ber) = Bingen. (Gro) = Adelberg. (Vil) = Armsheim.

Leckerberg (Ger). Vineyard. (Anb) = Rheinhessen. (Ber) = Wonnegau. (Gro) = Pilgerpfad. (Vil) = Dittelsheim-Hessloch.

Leckmauer (Ger). Vineyard. (Anb) = Mosel-Saar-Ruwer. (Ber) = Zell/Mosel. (Gro) = Goldbäumchen. (Vil) = Müden.

Leckzapfen (Ger). Vineyard. (Anb) = Rheinhessen. (Ber) = Wonnegau. (Gro) = Gotteshilfe. (Vil) = Otshofen.

Leclerc Briant (Fr). Champagne producer. Address = Cumierès, 51200 Épernay. Récoltants-manipulants. Own 30 ha. Produces – Vintage and non-vintage wines. A member of C.V.C. Vintages – 1971, 1973, 1976, 1979, 1982, 1983. De Luxe vintage cuvée is Special Club Brut.

Leconfield (Austr). A winery based in Coonawarra, South Australia. Produces mainly Cabernet and Riesling-based wines.

Ledaig (Scot). A single Malt whisky from the Tobermory distillery on the Isle of Mull. A Highland malt. 40% alc. by vol.

Lederer Brauerei (Ger). A brewery that is part of the Nürnberg's Patrizer group.

Lee Poo Yee (Fr). A white table wine (Vin de table) produced by the Caves de la Loire for Chinese restaurants.

Leer (Ger). Thin, lacking in character.

Lees (Eng). A heavy sediment which is thrown by young wines in cask after fining and before racking.

Lees (Eng). A brewery based in Middleton, Manchester, Lancashire. Noted for its cask conditioned Moonracker 1074 O.G. and Keg Edelbrau 1052 O.G. bottled Archer Stout 1042 O.G. Tulip Lager 1034 O.G. and Harvest Ale.

Leeuwin Estate (Austr). Address = P.O. Box 7196, Cloisters Square, Perth, Western Australia. 90 ha. Grape varieties – Cabernet sauvignon, Chardonnay, Gewürztraminer, Pinot noir, Rhine riesling, Sauvignon blanc. Produces varietal wines.

Leeuw Pilsener (Bel). See De Leeuw Brasserie.

Leeward Winery (USA). A winery based on the Camarillo coast, Ventura, California. Grape varieties – Cabernet sauvignon, Chardonnay and Zinfandel. Produces varietal wines.

Leffe Brasserie (Bel). An Abbaye brewery based in southern Belgium.

Lefkàs (Gre). A red wine-producing island in the Aegean sea. Also spelt Levkas.

Legacy (Scot). A blended Scotch whisky produced by MacKinlay (now owned by Scottish and Newcastle Breweries). 43% alc. by vol.

Lega di Chianti (It). A dry white wine produced from Malvasia and Trebbiano grapes in Tuscany.

Legend (Eng). A cask conditioned Bitter beer brewed by the Min Pin Inn homebrew public house in Tintagel, north Cornwall.

Legend (Eng). The information on a bottle label.

Léger (Fr). Light wine.

Légèrement Doux (Switz). A label term for wines with a residual sugar.

Legg Cutter Machine (Eng). A machine used in the production of tea. Used for cutting leaves that have not been 'withered'.

Legras (R.L.) (Fr). Champagne producer. Address = Caves de la Madelaine, Chouilly. Produces – Vintage and non-vintage wines.

Legs (Eng). A term used to describe the ethyl alcohol and glycerine lines which run down the glass after the drink has been swirled around the glass. Also known as 'tears'.

Lehen (Ger). Village. (Anb) = Baden. (Ber) = Breisgau. (Gro) = Burg Zähringen. (Vin) = Bergle.

Lehmann (Peter) (Austr). A noted winery based in the Barossa Valley, South Australia. Produces varietal wines.

L

Lehmen (Ger). Village. (Anb) = Mosel-Saar-Ruwer. (Ber) = Zell/Mosel. (Gro) = Weinhex. (Vins) = Ausoniusstein, Klostergarten, Lay, Wurzlay.

Lehrensteinsfeld (Ger). Village. (Anb) = Württemberg. (Ber) = Württembergisch Unterland. (Gro) = Salzberg. (Vins) = Althälde, Frauenzimmer, Steinacker.

Leicester Brewery (Eng). Based in Syston, Leicestershire. Set up in 1983. Produces – Keg Old John 1036 O.G. and Sport Lager 1036 O.G.

Leidhecke (Ger). Vineyard. (Anb) = Rheinhessen. (Ber) = Nierstein. (Gro) = Sankt Alban. (Vil) = Bodenheim.

Leiersberg (Ger). Vineyard. (Anb) = Württemberg. (Ber) = Württembergisch Unterland. (Gro) = Heuchelberg. (Vil) = Leingarten.

Leikaul (Ger). Vineyard. (Anb) = Mosel-Saar-Ruwer. (Ber) = Saar-Ruwer. (Gro) = Römerlay. (Vil) = Trier.

Leilani (USA). A noted Rum produced in Hawaii by Seagram.

Leimen (Ger). Village. (Anb) = Baden. (Ber) = Badische Bergstrasse/Kraichgau. (Gro) = Mannaberg. (Vins) = Herrenberg, Kreuzweg.

Leinenkugel Brewery (USA). A brewery based in Chippewa Falls, Wisconsin. Is noted for its Chippewa Pride and Leinenkugels.

Leingarten (Ger). Village. (Anb) = Württemberg. (Ber) = Württembergisch Unterland. (Gro) = Heuchelberg. (Vins) = Grafenberg, Leiersberg, Vogelsang.

Leinhöhle (Ger). Vineyard. (Anb) = Rheinpfalz. (Ber) = Mittelhaardt-Deutsche Weinstrasse. (Gro) = Mariengarten. (Vil) = Deidesheim.

Leinsweiler (Ger). Village. (Anb) = Rheinpfalz. (Ber) = Südliche Weinstrasse. (Gro) = Herrlich. (Vin) = Sonnenberg.

Leiselheim (Ger). Village. (Anb) = Baden. (Ber) = Kaiserstuhl-Tuniberg. (Gro) = Vulkanfelsen. (Vin) = Gestühl.

Leistadt (Ger). Village. (Anb) = Rheinpfalz. (Ber) = Mittelhaardt-Deutsche Weinstrasse. (Gro) = Kobnert. (Vins) = Herzfeld, Kalkofen, Kirchenstück.

Leistenberg (Ger). Vineyard. (Anb) = Nahe. (Ber) = Schloss Böckelheim. (Gro) = Burgweg. (Vil) = Oberhausen an der Nahe.

Leisure Drinks (Eng). Based in Derby, a company that specialises in non-alcoholic drinks. Address = 24, Willow Road, Trent Lane, Castle Donnington, Derbyshire. See Jung (Carl).

Leitacher (It). Red and white table wines produced in Bolzano, Südtirol (Trentino-Alto Adige). Sold in Italy as Guistina-Leitach or Santa Giustina. Also sold in Austria.

Leitaria (Port). Dairy.

Leite (Port). Milk.

Leiterchen (Ger). Vineyard. (Anb) = Mosel-Saar-Ruwer. (Ber) = Bernkastel. (Gro) = Michelsberg. (Vil) = Trittenheim.

Leiterchen (Ger). Vineyard. (Anb) = Mosel-Saar-Ruwer. (Ber) = Obermosel. (Gro) = Gipfel. (Vil) = Nittel.

Leith Brewery (Scot). See Argyle Brewery.

Leiwen (Ger). Village. (Anb) = Mosel-Saar-Ruwer. (Ber) = Bernkastel. (Gro) = Sankt Michael. (Vins) = Klostergarten, Laurentiuslay.

Lejay-Lagoute (Fr). A large liqueur producer founded in 1841.

Lejon (USA). The label used by United Vintners in California for their Vermouths, Brandies and sparkling wines.

Lemberger (Ger). A lesser used red grape variety.

Lemberg Estate (S.Afr). A vineyard based in Tulbagh. Address = P.O. Box 108, Tulbagh 6820. Produces varietal wines.

Lembo Vineyards (USA). Vineyards based in Lewistown, central Pennsylvania. Produces French hybrid wines.

Lembras (Fr). A commune in the A.C. district of Pécharmant in northern Bergerac. (Red wines).

Lemnos (Gre). A still white wine produced on the island of the same name. Also spelt Limnos.

Lemonade (Eng). Produced at home or commercially. A non-alcoholic, lemon-flavoured soft drink consisting of lemon juice, water and sugar.

Lemonade (Cktl). 2 fl.ozs. lemon juice, 1½ teaspoons sugar. Fill a tumbler ½ full with cracked ice. Stir. Fill up with water. Add a slice of lemon on top. Serve with straws.

Lemon Barley Water (Eng). A commercially produced concentrated non-alcoholic drink made by Robinsons.

Lemon Breeze (S.Afr). A brand of lemon-flavoured Cane spirit.

Lemon Flip (Cktl).(Non-alc). 1 egg yolk, sugar syrup to taste, ½ gill lemon juice. Shake well over ice, strain into 5 oz. goblet, top with grated nutmeg.

Lemon Frosted Iced Tea (Cup). 2 pints cold tea, 1 pint lemon sorbet. Whisk well together until frothy, serve with lemon slices.

Lemon Gin (Eng). A Gin flavoured with lemon (as opposed to juniper). Peel is steeped in Gin for 8–10 weeks.

Lemon Hart Rum (Eng). Rum brand. Company established in 1804 by Mr. Lemon Hart. Now a brand used by United Rum Merchants.

Lemonique (Hol). A lemon-flavoured liqueur from De Kuyper. 35% alc. by vol.

Lemon Liqueurs (USA). Lemon-flavoured and scented liqueurs.

Lemon Ranch (USA). A small vineyard based near St. Helena, Napa Valley, California. 7.5 ha. Grape variety – Cabernet sauvignon. Owned by Beringer Vineyards.

Lemon Shandy (Eng). Beer and lemonade mixed half and half.

Lemon Squash (Eng). A concentrated cordial made with lemon and sugar produced commercially to be diluted with water.

Lemon Squash (USA). Into a tumbler place ice, juice of a lemon (strained) and sugar syrup to taste, top up with soda water. Stir, add a slice of lemon.

Lemon Tea (Eng). An alternative name for Russian tea. Tea with a slice of lemon and no milk.

Lemon Tea (Sri L). A blend of high grown (Ceylon) teas, medium sized leaf. Has a scent of lemon.

Lemon Twist (Eng). A small spiral of lemon peel (zest) which is rubbed on the rim of the glass, twisted to release oils, then placed in the cocktail.

Lemon Verbena (Eng). A herbal tea with strong sedative properties.

Lemps (Fr). A commune in the A.C. Saint-Joseph region of the central Rhône.

Lena (Cktl). ⁵⁄₁₀ measure Bourbon whiskey, ²⁄₁₀ measure sweet Vermouth, ¹⁄₁₀ measure dry Vermouth, ¹⁄₁₀ measure Galliano, ¹⁄₁₀ measure Campari. Shake over ice, strain into a cocktail glass. Add a cherry.

Lenchen (Ger). Vineyard. (Anb) = Rheingau. (Ber) = Johannisberg. (Gro) = Gottesthal. (Vil) = Östrich.

Lenchen (Ger). Vineyard. (Anb) = Rheinhessen. (Ber) = Nierstein. (Gro) = Domhern. (Vil) = Stadecken-Elsheim.

Lendos (Gre). A dry white wine.

Lengfurt (Ger). Village. (Anb) = Franken. (Ber) = Maindreieck. (Gro) = Not yet assigned. (Vins) = Alter Berg, Oberrot.

Length (Eng). The term which describes a wine where the flavour lingers in the mouth for a long time after it has been swallowed.

Leningrad Cocktail (Cktl). 1 measure Vodka, 1 measure Verveine du Vélay. Stir over crushed ice in an old-fashioned glass. Dress with a yellow cherry.

Lennenborn (Ger). Vineyard. (Anb) = Mittelrhein. (Ber) = Bacharach. (Gro)

= Schloss Stahleck. (Vil) = Bacharach/Steeg.

Lenoir (USA). A black grape variety little used now.

Lenora Cocktail (Cktl). 1 measure dry Gin, ½ measure orange juice, ½ measure raspberry syrup. Shake well over ice, strain into a cocktail glass.

Lenta (Sp). The name given to the second fermentation which is much slower than the first.

Lenzenberg (Ger). Vineyard. (Anb) = Württemberg. (Ber) = Remstal-Stuttgart. (Gro) = Weinsteige. (Vil) = Stuttgart (ortsteil Hedelfingen).

Lenzenberg (Ger). Vineyard. (Anb) = Württemberg. (Ber) = Remstal-Stuttgart. (Gro) = Weinsteige. (Vil) = Stuttgart (ortsteil Rohracker).

Lenz-Moser [Dr] (Aus). A wine grower who discovered that there was no drop in yield if the vines were planted wide apart allowing machinery to be used for much of the old manual jobs. e.g. picking. Produces fine wines.

Léognan (Fr). A commune within the A.C. Graves district of south-western Bordeaux.

León (Sp). A wine region in north-western Spain. Rueda is the Denominación de Origen of the region.

Leonitti Cellar (USA). A winery based near Walla Walla Valley, Washington. Produces Cabernet and Riesling varietal wines.

Leon Millot (USA). A red hybrid grape variety.

Leon Negra (Mex). A dark beer brewed by the Yucateca Brewery.

Leonora (Sp). A dry white wine produced by Bodegas La Rioja Alta.

León S.A. (Sp). A small American-owned firm in Catalonia. Produces red and white wines from mainly the Cabernet and Chardonnay grapes.

Leopard (N.Z.). The smallest of 3 brewing groups, jointly owned by the Heineken and Malayan Breweries.

Leopoldsberg (Ger). Vineyard. (Anb) = Baden. (Ber) = Bodensee. (Gro) = Sonnenufer. (Vil) = Bermatingen.

Léoville (Fr). Formerly one of the largest estates in the Médoc. The property was divided during the revolution into Châteaux Las-Cases, Barton and Poyferré.

Lepanto (Sp). A Brandy of more than 15 years old produced by Gonzalez Byass.

Lepe (Sp). A noted wine-producing town on the coast west of Huelva.

Lepitre (Abel) (Fr). Champagne producer. Address = B.P. 124, Avenue du Général Giraud, 51055 Reims, Pro-

L

duces – Vintage and non-vintage wines. Vintages – 1926, 1928, 1934, 1937, 1941, 1943, 1945, 1947, 1949, 1952, 1953, 1955, 1959, 1961, 1962, 1964, 1966, 1969, 1970, 1971, 1973, 1974, 1975, 1976, 1978, 1979, 1980, 1981, 1982, 1983. Label – De luxe cuvée = Prince A. de Bourbon-Parme.

Leprechaun (The) (Cktl). 1 part Irish whiskey, 2 parts tonic water. Mix over ice in a highball glass, add a twist of lemon peel.

Lerchenberg (Ger). Vineyard. (Anb) = Baden. (Ber) = Bodensee. (Gro) = Sonnenufer. (Vil) = Meersburg.

Lerchenberg (Ger). Vineyard. (Anb) = Baden. (Ber) = Bodensee. (Gro) = Sonnenufer. (Vil) = Stetten.

Lerchenberg (Ger). Vineyard. (Anb) = Baden. (Ber) = Badische Bergstrasse/Kraichgau. (Gro) = Stiftsberg. (Vil) = Bauerbach.

Lerchenberg (Ger). Vineyard. (Anb) = Baden. (Ber) = Badische Bergstrasse/Kraichgau. (Gro) = Stiftsberg. (Vil) = Eppingen.

Lerchenberg (Ger). Vineyard. (Anb) = Baden. (Ber) = Badische Bergstrasse/Kraichgau. (Gro) = Stiftsberg. (Vil) = Flehingen.

Lerchenberg (Ger). Vineyard. (Anb) = Baden. (Ber) = Badische Bergstrasse/Kraichgau. (Gro) = Stiftsberg. (Vil) = Kraichtal (stadtteil Bahnbruchen, Gochsheim and Oberacker).

Lerchenberg (Ger). Vineyard. (Anb) = Baden. (Ber) = Badische Bergstrasse/Kraichgau. (Gro) = Stiftsberg. (Vil) = Kürnbach.

Lerchenberg (Ger). Vineyard. (Anb) = Baden. (Ber) = Badische Bergstrasse/Kraichgau. (Gro) = Stiftsberg. (Vil) = Mühlberg.

Lerchenberg (Ger). Vineyard. (Anb) = Baden. (Ber) = Badische Bergstrasse/Kraichgau. (Gro) = Stiftsberg. (Vil) = Rohrbach a. Gr.

Lerchenberg (Ger). Vineyard. (Anb) = Baden. (Ber) = Badische Bergstrasse/Kraichgau. (Gro) = Stiftsberg. (Vil) = Sulzfeld.

Lerchenberg (Ger). Vineyard. (Anb) = Baden. (Ber) = Badische Bergstrasse/Kraichgau. (Gro) = Stiftsberg. (Vil) = Zaisenhausen.

Lerchenberg (Ger). Vineyard. (Anb) = Baden. (Ber) = Kaiserstuhl-Tuniberg. (Gro) = Vulkanfelsen. (Vil) = Eichstetten.

Lerchenberg (Ger). Vineyard. (Anb) = Rheinhessen. (Ber) = Wonnegau. (Gro) = Liebfrauenmorgen. (Vil) = Worms.

Lerchenberg (Ger). Vineyard. (Anb) =

Rheinpfalz. (Ber) = Südliche Weinstrasse. (Gro) = Guttenberg. (Vil) = Kapsweyher.

Lerchenberg (Ger). Vineyard. (Anb) = Württemberg. (Ber) = Remstal-Stuttgart. (Gro) = Weinsteige. (Vil) = Esslingen.

Lerchenberg (Ger). Vineyard. (Anb) = Württemberg. (Ber) = Württembergisch Unterland. (Gro) = Stromberg. (Vil) = Erligheim.

Lerchenberg (Ger). Vineyard. (Anb) = Württemberg. (Ber) = Württembergisch Unterland. (Gro) = Stromberg. (Vil) = Hofen.

Lerchenböhl (Ger). Vineyard. (Anb) = Rheinpfalz. (Ber) = Mittelhaardt-Deutsche Weinstrasse. (Gro) = Pfaffengrund. (Vil) = Lachen-Speyerdorf.

Lerchenspiel (Ger). Vineyard. (Anb) = Rheinpfalz. (Ber) = Mittelhaardt-Deutsche Weinstrasse. (Gro) = Schwarzerde. (Vil) = Gerolsheim.

Lérida (Sp). A province of Catalonia that borders Aragón. Home to the Raimat Bodega.

Lerin (Sp). One of 3 sub-regions in western Ribera-Alta. Is bordered by the Rioja Baja.

Lérina (Fr). A Cistercian liqueur, herb distillation, both green and yellow produced. Produced in the Abbaye de Lérius off the French coast at Marseilles.

Leroux (Aus). A noted liqueur distiller.

Leroux (USA). A famous liqueur producer. (Subsidiary of Seagram).

Leroux (Patrice) (Fr). Champagne producer. Address = 12 Rue Georges, Legros BP2, 51500 Chigny-les-Roses. Récoltants-manipulants. Produces – Vintage and non-vintage wines. Vintages – 1971, 1973, 1975, 1976, 1979, 1982, 1983.

Leroy (Fr). A Burgundy shipper based at Auxey-Duresses in the Côte de Beaune.

Lès (Fr). Near or by. e.g. Chorey-lès-Beaune. Not to be confused with 'les' meaning 'the'.

Lesbian (Gre). A sweet white wine produced in ancient Greece from the isle of Lesbos.

Lesbos (Gre). An island in the Aegean Islands in Eastern Greece. Produces mainly dessert wines. See also Lesbian.

Lesegut-Aufbesserung (Aus). A method of increasing the alcohol content by the addition of sugar to the fermenting must. (Fr) = Chaptalisation, (Ger) = Anreicherung.

Lessona (It). A D.O.C. red wine from the

L

Piemonte region made from the Nebbiolo grape.

Let Pilsener (Den). A 'light' ale.

Letscheberg (Lux). A vineyard site in the village of Schwebsingen.

Letten (Ger). vineyard. (Anb) = Baden. (Ber) = Markgräflerland. (Gro) = Burg Neuenfels. (Vil) = Auggen.

Letten (Ger). vineyard. (Anb) = Rheinpfalz. (Ber) = Mittelhaardt-Deutsche Weinstrasse. (Gro) = Schnepfenflug an der Weinstrasse. (Vil) = Deidesheim.

Letten (Ger). vineyard. (Anb) = Rheinpfalz. (Ber) = Südliche Weinstrasse. (Gro) = Ordensgut. (Vil) = Hainfeld.

Letterlay (Ger). vineyard. (Anb) = Mosel-Saar-Ruwer. (Ber) = Bernkastel. (Gro) = Nacktarsch. (Vil) = Kröv.

Letts Brewery (Ire). A brewery in Enniscorthy, Wexford which stopped production in 1956. Licenses Coors Brewery of the USA and Pelforth Brewery of France to brew its Ruby Ale as Irish Red Ale (USA) and George Killian's Bière (Fr).

Lettweiler (Ger). Village. (Anb) = Nahe. (Ber) = Schloss Böckelheim. (Gro) = Paradiesgarten. (Vins) = Inkelhöll, Rheingasse.

Leubsdorf (Ger). Village. (Anb) = Mittelrhein. (Ber) = Rheinburgengau. (Gro) = Burg Hammerstein. (Vin) = Weisses Kreuz.

Leucate (Fr). One of nine wine-producing communes in the Fitou region in southern France.

Leucine (Eng). An Amino acid found in wines. Is formed by the yeasts.

Leuconostoc (USA). A bacteria that causes Malo-lactic fermentation.

Leutershausen (Ger). Village. (Anb) = Baden. (Ber) = Badische Bergstrasse/ Kraichgau. (Gro) = Rittersberg. (Vins) = Kahlberg, Standenberg.

Leutesdorf (Ger). Village. (Anb) = Mittelrhein. (Ber) = Rheinburgengau. (Gro) = Burg Hammerstein. (Vins) = Forstberg, Gartenlay, Rosenberg.

Leutschach (Aus). A wine-producing region in the Südsteiermark.

Leuvense Wit (Bel). A white wheat beer.

Leuvrigny (Fr). A Cru Champagne village in the Canton de Dormans. District = Épernay.

Levada (Mad). A type of aqueduct used for irrigation in Madeira.

Levadura (Sp). Yeast.

Levanan (Isr). A dry white table wine.

Levante (Sp). The hot winds in the Sherry district which blow from the east in winter. Blows from the Gulf of Lions.

Levante (Sp). A wine-producing area in eastern Spain that contains the Denominación de Origens of Alicante, Jumilla, Utiel-Requena and Valencia-Yecla.

Levedura (Port). Yeast.

Levert (Hol). A small distilling company that produces Jenevers.

Leviathan (Cktl). ½ measure Brandy, ¼ measure sweet Vermouth, ¼ measure orange juice. Shake over ice, strain into a cocktail glass.

Levissima (It). A still mineral water from Sondrio in the Italian Alps

Levkas (Gre). An island in the Ionian Islands of western Greece. Produces mainly country wines for local consumption. Also spelt Lefkàs.

Levogyrous Sugar (Eng). A sugar found in dried grapes.

Levulose (Eng). Fermentable sugar. (Fructose).

Levurage (Fr). In Champagne the addition of Liqueur de Tirage.

Levure (Fr). The introduction of non-natural yeast strains to start fermentation.

Lex Domitiana (It). A Roman wine law A.D.91 relating to modern day Germany.

Lexham Hall (Eng). A vineyard. Address = King's Lynn, Norfolk. 3.5 ha. Planted 1975. Grape varieties – Madeleine angevine, Müller-Thurgau, Reichensteiner and Scheurebe.

Lexia (Austr). A white grape variety grown in Victoria. See also Muscat Gordo Blanco.

Lexia-Gordo Blanco (Austr). A name for the Muscat of Alexandria grape used for the early brandies of Australia.

Lexias (Sp). The name given to raisins that have been steeped in lye in Málaga.

Leygues (Fr). A noted wine-producing area near Puy-l'Évêque in Cahors, south-western France.

Leyland Brewery (Eng). A small brewery based in Leyland, Lancashire. Produces cask conditioned Tiger Ale 1038 O.G. from malt extract.

Leynes (Fr). A commune in the Beaujolais. Has A.C. Beaujolais-Villages or Beaujolais-Leynes status. Also as Mâconnais Blanc.

Leyrat (Edgard) (Fr). Cognac producer. Address = Domaine de Chez Maillard, 16440 Claix-Blanzac. 50 ha. in the Fins Bois. Produces – Brut de Futs Hors d'Âge, Napoléon and Vieille Réserve.

Li (China). The old Chinese word for wine. See also Chang and Chiu.

L

Lias (Sp). Wine lees.

Liason Cocktail (Cktl). ⅙ gill Cognac, ⅛ gill Cointreau, 1 teaspoon Coconut milk, 2 dashes Angostura. Shake well over ice, strain into an ice-filled high-ball glass.

Liatiko (Gre). A red grape variety used for both dry and dessert wines, especially on the Isle of Crete.

Libanos (S.Am). A noted coffee-producing region of Colombia.

Libare (Lat). To pour an offering drink.

Libarna (It). A noted brand-name of Grappa.

Libatio (Lat). A drink poured out to honour a God.

Libation (Eng). An alcoholic beverage poured out as an offering to honour a God.

Libby (Eng). A firm who produce a wide range of fruit juices.

Libby's Moon Shine (Eng). A mixed berry drink from the Libby Co.

Liberal (Cktl). ½ measure Canadian Whisky, ½ measure sweet Vermouth, 3 dashes Amer Picon, dash Orange bitters. Stir over ice, strain into a cocktail glass.

Liberty Bell (Cktl). 1 oz. Southern Comfort, 1 oz. Royal Mint Choc. Liqueur, 4 ozs. fresh orange juice, 1 egg white. Shake over ice, strain into a goblet, dress with an orange segment.

Liberty Cocktail (Cktl). ⅓ measure white Rum, ⅔ measure Applejack brandy, dash Gomme syrup. Stir over ice, strain into a cocktail glass.

Liberty School (USA). The label used by Caymus vineyards for their range of varietal wines.

Libourne (Fr). An old city on the right side bank of the river Dordogne, once an important market for Pomerol and Fronsac wines.

Librandi (It). A large winery based at Ciró Marina in Calabria.

Licensed Vituallers Association (Eng). See LVA.

Licensee (Eng). A person who holds the Justice's licence to sell alcoholic liquor.

Licensing Justices (Eng). A body of Lay Magistrates who deal with all licence applications and renewals for the selling of alcoholic beverages. See Brewster Sessions and Occasional Licences.

Lichee (Cktl). Equal parts of dry Gin, dry Vermouth and Lychee syrup, 3 dashes Angostura. Shake over ice, strain into a cocktail glass. Serve with canned lychees on a cocktail stick.

Lichine (Alexis) (Fr). Wine author, Château

owner, négociant and an esteemed authority on wines.

Lichtenberg (Ger). vineyard. (Anb) = Baden. (Ber) = Badische Bergstrasse/Kraichgau. (Gro) = Hohenberg. (Vil) = Grötzingen.

Lichtenberg (Ger). vineyard. (Anb) = Württemberg. (Ber) = Remstal-Stuttgart. (Gro) = Wartbühl. (Vil) = Geradstetten.

Lichtenberg (Ger). vineyard. (Anb) = Württemberg. (Ber) = Remstal-Stuttgart. (Gro) = Wartbühl. (Vil) = Hebsack.

Lichtenberg (Ger). vineyard. (Anb) = Württemberg. (Ber) = Württembergisch Unterland. (Gro) = Stromberg. (Vil) = Illingen.

Lichtenberg (Ger). vineyard. (Anb) = Württemberg. (Ber) = Württembergisch Unterland. (Gro) = Stromberg. (Vil) = Rosswag.

Lichtenberg (Ger). vineyard. (Anb) = Württemberg. (Ber) = Württembergisch Unterland. (Gro) = Wunnenstein. (Vil) = Hof und Lembach.

Lichtenberg (Ger). vineyard. (Anb) = Württemberg. (Ber) = Württembergisch Unterland. (Gro) = Wunnenstein. (Vil) = Grossbottwar.

Lichtenberg (Ger). vineyard. (Anb) = Württemberg. (Ber) = Württembergisch Unterland. (Gro) = Wunnenstein. (Vil) = Ilsfeld.

Lichtenberg (Ger). vineyard. (Anb) = Württemberg. (Ber) = Württembergisch Unterland. (Gro) = Wunnenstein. (Vil) = Kleinbottwar.

Lichtenberg (Ger). vineyard. (Anb) = Württemberg. (Ber) = Württembergisch Unterland. (Gro) = Wunnenstein. (Vil) = Oberstenfeld.

Lichtenberg (Ger). vineyard. (Anb) = Württemberg. (Ber) = Württembergisch Unterland. (Gro) = Wunnenstein. (Vil) = Steinhelm.

Lichtenberg (Ger). vineyard. (Anb) = Württemberg. (Ber) = Württembergisch Unterland. (Gro) = Wunnenstein. (Vil) = Winzerhausen.

Licor (Port). Liquid, liquor, liqueur.

Licor Cobana (Sp). A banana liqueur produced in the Canary Isles by Cocal S.A. in Telde.

Licor de Expedición (Sp). The dose of old wine (and sugar) after the Cava wines have been disgorged. (Fr) = Liqueur d'Expédition.

Licor de Miel (Sp). A honey liqueur produced in the Canary Isles by Cocal S.A. in Telde.

Licor de Platano (Sp). Banana liqueur.

Licor de Tiraje (Sp). The dosage of yeast and grape sugar to Cava wines prior to the second fermentation in bottle. (Fr) =

L

Liqueur de Tirage.

Licores (Sp). Liqueurs.

Licor 43 (Sp). The alternative name for Cuarenta y Tres.

Licoroso (Port) (Sp). A rich, sweet, fortified wine.

Licoroso Dulce (Sp). A sweet white wine of the Cariñena region.

Liddington (Eng). Beer wholesalers in the East Midlands who, in 1984, took over Litchborough and moved the plant to their Rugby depot. Produces cask conditioned Litchborough Bitter 1036 O.G. and Tudor Ale 1044 O.G.

Lidia (La) (Sp). A fine Manzanilla sherry produced by Garvey in Jerez de la Frontera.

Lido Cocktail (Cktl). ¼ gill Gin, ¼ gill French vermouth, 2 dashes Apricot brandy. Stir over ice, strain into a cocktail glass, top with a cherry.

Lidy (Gre). A method of red wine fermentation that occurs under pressure. See also Klenk.

Lie (Fr). Lees. See also Sur Lie.

Lie (La) (Fr). A distillation produced from the residue of the grapes after the final pressing in the Savoie region, southeastern France.

Liebehöll (Ger). vineyard. (Anb) = Nahe. (Ber) = Kreuznach. (Gro) = Schlosskapelle. (Vil) = Münster-Sarmsheim.

Liebenberg (Ger). vineyard. (Anb) = Rheinhessen. (Ber) = Wonnegau. (Gro) = Pilgerpfad. (Vil) = Osthofen.

Liebenberg (Ger). vineyard. (Anb) = Württemberg. (Ber) = Württembergisch Unterland. (Gro) = Stromberg. (Vil) = Ochsenbach.

Liebenberg (Ger). vineyard. (Anb) = Württemberg. (Ber) = Württembergisch Unterland. (Gro) = Stromberg. (Vil) = Spielberg.

Liebeneck-Sonnenlay (Ger). vineyard. (Anb) = Mittelrhein. (Ber) = Rheinburgengau. (Gro) = Marksburg. (Vil) = Osterpai.

Lieben-Frauen-Milch (Ger). The eighteenth-century spelling of Liebfraumilch.

Lieben Frawenstift (Ger). The midsixteenth-century spelling of Liebfraumilch.

Liebenstein-Sterrenberg (Ger). vineyard. (Anb) = Mittelrhein. (Ber) = Rheinburgengau. (Gro) = Loreleyfelsen. (Vil) = Kamp-Bornhofen-Kestert.

Lieberstein (S.Afr). A semi-sweet white wine made from a blend of Steen and Clairette blanche grape varieties. Made by the SFW.

Liebesbrunnen (Ger). vineyard. (Anb) = Nahe. (Ber) = Schloss Böckelheim. (Gro) = Paradiesgarten. (Vil) = Hochstätten.

Liebesbrunnen (Ger). vineyard. (Anb) = Rheinpfalz. (Ber) = Mittelhaardt-Deutsche Weinstrasse. (Gro) = Kobnert. (Vil) = Dackenheim.

Liebestraum (N.Z.). A dry white wine produced by Corbans in Henderson Valley, North Island.

Liebfrau (Ger). vineyard. (Anb) = Rheinhessen. (Ber) = Bingen. (Gro) = Rheingrafenstein. (Vil) = Volxheim.

Liebfrauenberg (Ger). vineyard. (Anb) = Mosel-Saar-Ruwer. (Ber) = Saar-Ruwer. (Gro) = Scharzberg. (Vil) = Filzen.

Liebfrauenberg (Ger). vineyard. (Anb) = Nahe. (Ber) = Schloss Böckelheim. (Gro) = Paradiesgarten. (Vil) = Meddersheim.

Liebfrauenberg (Ger). vineyard. (Anb) = Rheinhessen. (Ber) = Wonnegau. (Gro) = Pilgerpfad. (Vil) = Dittelsheim-Hessloch.

Liebfrauenkirche (Ger). Lit – 'The church of our lady' in the city of Worms. Has its own vineyard, the Liebfrauenstifte.

Liebfrauenmorgen (Ger). Grosslage. (Anb) = Rheinhessen. (Ber) = Wonnegau. (Vil) = Worms.

Liebfrauenstifte (Ger). The wine of the Liebfrauenkirche vineyards, Worms in the Rheinhessen. In latter days was the original Liebfraumilch. Known as Liebfrauenstiftwein.

Liebfrauenstift-Kirchenstück (Ger). Vineyard. (Anb) = Rheinhessen. (Ber) = Wonnegau. (Gro) = Liebfrauenmorgen. (Vil) = Worms.

Liebfrauenstiftwein (Ger). The original name for Liebfraumilch, now no longer used.

Liebfrauenthal (Ger). vineyard. (Anb) = Rheinhessen. (Ber) = Nierstein. (Gro) = Krötenbrunnen. (Vil) = Gimbsheim.

Liebfraumilch (Ger). Must be Qba wine and come only from one of the following four 'Quality wine' regions – Rheinhessen, Rheingau, Rheinpfalz and Nahe. Minimum 51% of either Silvaner, Riesling or Müller-Thurgau and 49% of any permitted grape variety.

Liebframinch (Ger). An old spelling of Liebfraumilch.

Lieblich (Ger). Pleasant light wine.

Liebling (Ger). A brand of Liebfraumilch produced by Deinhard in Koblenz.

Liebotschaner (USA). The brand-name used by the Lion Brewery in Wilkes-Barre, Pennsylvania for their range of beers.

Liechtenstein (Euro). A tiny country between Austria and Switzerland. Pro-

L

duces wines on a style between German and Austrian in character. 42 sq. miles. Lit – 'Light coloured stone' (limestone).

Liefmans Brasserie (Bel). A brewery based in Oudenaarde owned by Vaux of Sunderland. Produces Goudenband Special Provisie in litre bottles.

Liège (Fr). Cork. See also Bouchon.

Liel (Ger). Village. (Anb) = Baden. (Ber) = Markgräflerland. (Gro) = Burg Neuenfels. (Vin) = Sonnenstück.

Lienzingen (Ger). Village. (Anb) = Württemberg. (Ber) = Württembergisch Unterland. (Gro) = Stromberg. (Vin) = Eichelberg.

Liersberg (Ger). Village. (Anb) = Mosel-Saar-Ruwer. (Ber) = Obermosel. (Gro) = Königsberg. (Vin) = Pilgerberg.

Liesberg (Ger). vineyard. (Anb) = Nahe. (Ber) = Kreuznach. (Gro) = Schlosskapelle. (Vil) = Waldlaubersheim.

Lieser (Ger). Village. (Anb) = Mosel-Saar-Ruwer. (Ber) = Bernkastel. (Gro) = Beerenlay. (Vins) = Niederberg-Helden, Rosenlay, Sussenberg.

Lieser (Ger). Village. (Anb) = Mosel-Saar-Ruwer. (Ber) = Bernkastel. (Gro) = Kurfürstlay. (Vin) = Schlossberg.

Lieth (Ger). vineyard. (Anb) = Rheinhessen. (Ber) = Nierstein. (Gro) = Sankt Alban. (Vil) = Harxheim.

Lievito (It). Yeast.

Lievland (S.Afr). A vineyard based in Stellenbosch-Simonsberg. Address = Box 66, Klapmuts 7625. Produces – Huiswyn, Rood and many varietals.

Lifebuoy Beer (Eng). A cask conditioned Ale 1075 O.G. brewed by the two home-brew public houses of Pier Hotel, Gravesend and the Southeastern in Strood. Both in Kent.

Liger (Fr). The old French name for the Loire.

Ligero (Sp). Denotes a light Sherry.

Light (Eng). A term for wine which lacks body or is low in alcohol.

Light Ale (Eng). A low-gravity bottled Ale, light in body but not in colour.

Light and Bitter (Eng). ½ bottled Light ale and ½ draught Bitter ale.

Light and Dark (Eng). A mixture of half Guinness and half Light ale.

Light Beer (USA). A low calorie-beer 3.5–4% alc. by vol. A Lager-type.

Light Beverage (USA). A name for natural still wine.

Light-Bodied Rums (USA). The name given to white Rums and light-coloured Rums. Has only a light molasses flavour. e.g. Cuban, Dominican Republic, Haitian, Hawaiian, Mexican, Philippine, Puerto Rican, Venezuelan and Virgin Isles.

Light Dinner Ale (Austr). A green-labelled,

low-gravity beer 3.8% by weight brewed by the Cooper's Brewery in South Australia.

Light Hart Rum (Jam). A brand-name Rum. 40% alc. by vol.

Light Muscat (USA). See California Light Muscat.

Light Oxford (Eng). A bottled Light ale 1032 O.G. brewed by the Morrell Brewery of Oxford.

Light Rum (W.Ind). Denotes Rums which are light in body as opposed to colour. May be white to silver/gold and aged 3 years or more. Coloured with caramel and Pot-stilled. e.g. Cuban, Puerto Rican and Virgin Isles.

Light Whiskey (USA). A Whiskey produced in USA of 160–189° US proof on or after 26 January 1968 and stored in used or uncharred new oak containers and also includes mixtures of such whiskies.

Light Wines (Eng). A term which indicates wines of table wine strength not more than 14% alc. by vol. A heavy wine duty does not have to be paid.

Ligist (Aus). A wine-producing area in the Weststeiermark.

Lignell and Piispanen (Fin). A noted distilling company that produces Karpi, Mesimarja, Suomurrain and Tapio liqueurs.

Lignes (Fr). Cork measure. 24 Lignes = 54 centimetres.

Lignières-Sonneville (Fr). A commune in the Charente Département whose grapes are classed Grande Champagne (Cognac).

Lignification (Eng). The name given to the maturing of the wood on the vine.

Lignins (Eng). Obtained from wooden wine barrels, soluble in ethanol.

Lignorelles (Fr). A commune in the A.C. Chablis, Burgundy.

Ligny-le-Châtel (Fr). A commune in the A.C. Chablis, Burgundy.

Ligte Droë (S.Afr). Light dry.

Liguria (It). The smallest region, it borders France, Piemonte, Emilia-Romagna and Tuscany. To south is the Tyrrhenian sea. The Cinque Terre is part of it. Wines are – Cinqueterre, Cinqueterre sciacchetra, Coronata, Dolceaqua, Polcevera, Rossese di Dolceaqua and Vermentino ligure.

Likeur (Hol). Liqueur.

Likier (Pol). Liqueur.

Likier Ziolowy (Pol). A herb liqueur produced by Polmos.

Likör (Tur). Liqueur.

Likor Kohz Bouchinot (Fr). A sweet, grapey, green liqueur, mainly sold and consumed in Brittany.

Likörwein (Ger). A term for dessert wines. e.g. Trokenbeerenauslese.

Lilac Seal (Ger). A brand of Bernkasteler

L

Qba. wine produced by Deinhard in Koblenz.

Lilalack (Ger). An Auslesen wine from the 'Herrgottströpfchen' range of wines of Jakob Gerhardt, Nierstein.

Lilbert (Georges et Fils) (Fr). Champagne producer. Address = 51200 Épernay. Produces vintage and non-vintage wines.

Lillehammer Brewery (Nor). A noted brewery based in central Norway.

Lillet (Fr). An apéritif wine, (red or white) fortified with Armagnac, herbs, fruit and white Bordeaux wine. Produced in Bordeaux. 17% alc. by vol. Matured in Yugoslavian oak.

Lillet-Citron (Cktl). ½ gill Lillet (blanc), ⅙ gill Sirop de Citron, soda water. Stir over ice, strain into a highball glass with ice.

Lillet Cocktail (Cktl). ⅘ measure Lillet (rouge), ⅕ measure Gin. Stir over ice, strain into a cocktail glass, top with a twist of lemon peel juice.

Lillypilly Estate (Austr). A winery based in Riverina, New South Wales.

Lil Naue Cocktail (Cktl). ½ measure Brandy, ¼ measure Port, ¼ measure Apricot brandy, dash Gomme syrup, 1 egg yolk. Shake well over ice, strain into a 5 oz. goblet. Top with powdered cinnamon.

Lilt (Eng). A sparkling non-alcoholic pineapple and grapefruit drink produced by the Coca Cola Co. Also a diet version produced.

Lily Cocktail (Cktl). ½ measure dry Gin, ½ measure Lillet, ⅓ measure Crème de Noyau, dash lemon juice. Shake over ice, strain into a cocktail glass.

Lima (Port). A wine district of the Entre Minho e Douro region. Produces both red and white wines of the Vinho Verde style.

Limassol (Cyp). The main wine town. Situated in the south-east of the island and is Greek-Cypriot controlled. Most of the Island's wineries are based there. Keo, Sodap, Haggipavlo, Etko.

Limberger (Euro). A red grape variety grown in most western European countries. Also known as the Blaufränkisch and Gamay.

Limbo (Cktl). 1 fl.oz. Peach brandy, 4 fl.ozs. pineapple juice. Serve over ice in a highball glass.

Limbo (S.Afr). A brand of Cane spirit flavoured with lemon juice. Is produced under licence from König of Western Germany.

Limbo Cooler (Cktl). 1 fl.oz. dark Rum, ¾ fl.oz. Amer Picon, 2 fl.ozs. lemon juice, 3 dashes Grenadine. Shake over ice with an orange slice. Strain into a goblet filled with crushed ice, Stir in 7-Up. Decorate with an orange slice, cherry and stirrer.

Limbo Drummer (W.Ind). A brand of Rum produced in Trinidad by the Trinidad Distillers Ltd.

Limberger (Ger). An erroneous varietal name for the Portugais rouge red grape variety.

Limburg (Ger). vineyard. (Anb) = Baden. (Ber) = Kaiserstuhl-Tuniberg. (Gro) = Vulkanfelsen. (Vil) = Sasbach.

Lime (Eng). Citrus aurantifolia. A major fruit whose juice is used in many cocktails. Has a green skin (zest).

Limeade (USA). A non-alcoholic drink made from sweetened lime juice and carbonated water.

Limeade (USA). 3 teaspoons sugar, juice of 4 limes. Dissolve in a highball glass, fill with ice and top with soda water. Top with a slice of lime and a cherry. Serve with straws.

Lime Blossom Tea (Eng). A herbal tea which is good for colds.

Lime Cordial (Eng). A preparation of concentrated lime juice and sugar of which the Rose's brand is the most famous.

Lime Giant Cocktail (Cktl). ⅕ gill Vodka, ⅙ gill lime cordial, juice of a lime. Shake over ice, strain into an ice-filled highball glass. Top with soda water and a slice of lime.

Lime Lager (USA). A Lager beer flavoured with lime brewed by the Lone Star Brewery, San Antonio, Texas.

Lime Lite (W.Ind). A lime-flavoured diet Lager 3.5% alc. by vol. brewed in Barbados.

Lime Rose (Cktl).(Non-alc). ⅓ egg white, ½ measure lemon cordial, 1 measure lime juice cordial. Shake well over ice, strain into a cocktail glass.

Limestone (Eng). See Soils.

Limestone (USA). A flavoured apéritif produced by the Enz vineyards in San Benito, California.

Limestone Cocktail (Cktl). 1 measure Bourbon whiskey, ¼ measure dry Gin, 2 dashes Gomme syrup, juice ½ lemon. Shake over ice, strain into an ice-filled highball glass. Top with soda and squeeze of lemon peel juice.

Limestone Ridge vineyard (Austr). A part of the Lindemans vineyards. New South Wales. 22 ha. planted Shiraz, 2 ha planted Cabernet.

Limey (Cktl).(Non-alc). 1 oz. lime juice, ½ oz. lemon juice, ½ egg white. Shake with ice, strain into a cocktail glass.

Limey Cocktail (Cktl). ⅖ measure white Rum, ⅖ measure lime cordial, ⅕ measure Cointreau, juice of a lime. Blend together with scoop of crushed

L

ice. Pour into a flute glass and top with a twist of lime peel juice.

Limings (W.Ind). The name given to the scum that forms on the surface of the molasses during sugar extraction in Rum production.

Limnio (Gre). A white grape variety grown in the Halkidiki Peninsula and Macedonia.

Limnos (Gre). An island in the Aegean Islands of eastern Greece. Produces mainly dessert wines.

Limoensap (Hol). Lime juice.

Limon (Eng). A carbonated, lemon-flavoured, low calorie soft drink produced by Schweppes.

Limonada (Port) (Sp). Lemonade.

Limonade (Fr) (Hol). Lemonade.

Limonade Gazeuse (Fr). Fizzy lemonade.

Limonadier (Fr). A mediaeval seller of non-alcoholic drinks.

Limonata (It) (Tur). Lemonade.

Limone (It). Flavour of lemon.

Limonnaya (USSR). A Vodka infused with lemon peel. 40% alc. by vol.

Limosin (S.Afr). The brand-name of a Brandy produced by Castle Wine and Green.

Limounade (Ch.Isles). Lemonade.

Limousin (Fr). Special oak from the Limousin forests that is used to make the casks for maturing Cognac.

Limoux (Fr). A sparkling wine from the Gaillac region.

Limpid (Eng). A term used to describe a wine with a clear appearance.

Limpidity (Eng). A description of sight in wine tasting, denotes outstanding brightness and clarity.

Limpio (Sp). Describes a clean Sherry.

Lincoln College (N.Z.). A research college based at Canterbury, South Island that produces experimental wines.

Lincoln Winery (N.Z.). A winery based in Lincoln Road, Henderson, North Island. 35 ha. Noted for their dry Sherry-style wine. Also has 18 ha. at Riverlea.

Linda (Cktl). ¼ measure Gin, ¼ measure Crème de Cassis, ¼ measure Crème de Banane, ¼ measure lemon juice. Shake over ice, strain into a cocktail glass.

Lindau (Ger). An Untergebiet of the Bayern district.

Lindauer (N.Z.). The brand-name used by Montana wines for their bottle-fermented, sparkling wines (brut or sec).

Lindeboom Brouwerij (Hol). A brewery based at Neer in Limburg. Brews unpasteurised, dry, Pilsener-style beers.

Lindelbach (Ger). Village. (Anb) = Baden. (Ber) = Badische Frankenland. (Gro) = Tauberklinge. (Vin) = Ebenrain.

Lindelberg (Ger). Grosslage. (Anb) =

Württemberg. (Ber) = Württembergisch Unterland. (Vils) = Adolzfurt, Bretzfeld, Dimbach, Eschelbach, Geddelsbach, Harsberg (ortsteil Neuholz), Kesselfeld, Langenbeutingen, Maienfels, Michelbach a. W., Obersöllbach, Pfedelbach, Siebeneich, Schwabbach, Unterheimbach, Untersteinbach, Verrenberg, Waldbach, Windischenbach.

Lindemans (Austr). vineyard. Address = 31 Nyrang Street, Lidcombe, New South Wales 2141. 900 ha. in Hunter River Valley, Padthaway, Coonawarra and Karadoc areas.

Lindeman's Brasserie (Bel). A farmhouse brewery at Vlezenbeek. Produces wild Lambic beers, usually exported to France and USA.

Lindeman's Cream (Austr). A fortified wine. A sweet Sherry-type made at Corowa on the river Murray.

Lindenblättrige (Aus). An ancient white grape variety that is rarely grown nowadays.

Lindener Gilde-Brau (Ger). A bottled Diät Pils 1050 O.G. brewed by the Lindener-Gilde Brauerei in Hanover and imported into the U.K. by the Thwaites Brewery, Blackburn, Lancashire.

Lindener-Gilde Brauerei (Ger). Brewery in Hanover. Noted for its malty beers, especially Brozhan Alt, a beer named after a famous Hanover brewmaster of the sixteenth century. Also Ratskeller Edel Pils.

Lindenfest (Ger). A Rheingau wine festival held at Geisenheim in July.

Lindisfarne (Eng). A Whisky-based honey liqueur produced in Northumberland, north-eastern England.

Lindos (Gre). A dry white wine from Rhodes.

Line Brandy (USA). A Brandy glass which has a line marked on it to show the amount to pour.

Linfit Mild (Eng). A cask conditioned Ale 1032 O.G. brewed by the Sair home-brew public house in Linthwaite, Huddersfield, Yorkshire.

Linfood Cash and Carry (Eng). A company based in Northamptonshire that produces many own-label brands of wines, vermouths and spirits.

Lingering (Eng). A term used to describe the length of finish of a wine in the mouth.

Lingestière (Fr). A wine-producing district in the A.C. Bellet, Provence, south-eastern France.

Linhälder (Ger). vineyard. (Anb) = Württemberg. (Ber) = Remstal-Stuttgart. (Gro) = Wartbühl. (Vil) = Stetten i. R.

Linie Akvavit (Nor). A brand of Norwegian Akvavit produced by A/S Vinmonopolet.

L

Linkwood (Scot). A single Malt whisky distillery based south of Elgin in Speyside. Owned by John McEwan and Co. Ltd. A Highland malt. Produces a 12 year old Malt 43% alc. by vol. (part of the DCL group).

Linsenbusch (Ger). vineyard. (Anb) = Rheinpfalz. (Ber) = Mittelhaardt-Deutsche Weinstrasse. (Gro) = Hofstück. (Vil) = Ruppertsberg.

Linsenhofen (Ger). Village. (Anb) = Württemberg. (Ber) = Remstal-Stuttgart. (Gro) = Hohenneuffen. (Vin) = Schlossteige.

Linstead (Cktl). ½ measure Scotch Whisky, 1 dash Pastis, ½ measure pineapple juice. Shake over ice, strain into a cocktail glass, add a twist of lemon peel juice.

Linstead Cocktail (Cktl). 1 fl.oz. Scotch whisky, 1 fl.oz. grapefruit juice, dash Absinthe. Shake over ice, strain into a club goblet. Add a dash of lemon peel juice and a spiral of peel.

Linz (Ger). Village. (Anb) = Mittelrhein. (Ber) = Rheinburgengau. (Gro) = Burg Hammerstein. (Vin) = Rheinhöller.

Lion Ale (Afr). A top-fermented, sweet, copper-brown Ale brewed by the South African Breweries.

Lion Ales (Eng). A keg Bitter 1037 O.G. and Mild 1035 O.G. brewed by the Banks Brewery in Wolverhampton, Staffs.

Lion Ales (Eng). Beers brewed by Matthew Brown's Brewery in Blackburn, Lancashire. See Lion Bitter and Lion Mild.

Lion Ales (N.Z.). The name of the biggest brewing group in the country.

Lion Beer (Ind). A Lager beer 1046 O.G. brewed by the Mohan Meakin Brewery in Simla Hills, Solan.

Lion Beer (N.Z.). A Beer brewed by the New Zealand Breweries.

Lion Bitter (Eng). A keg Bitter beer 1037 O.G. brewed by the Banks Brewery, Wolverhampton, Staffs.

Lion Bitter (Eng). A cask conditioned Bitter 1036 O.G. brewed by Camerons Brewery in Hartlepool.

Lion Bitter (Eng). A Bitter ale 1036 O.G. brewed by Matthew Brown's Brewery, Blackburn, Lancashire.

Lion Brewery (USA). A brewery based in Wilkes-Barre, Pennsylvania. Brews under the Bartels, Gibbons and Liebotschaner labels.

Lion Brown/Red Beer (N.Z.). Copper-coloured, sweet beers 1036 O.G. Highly carbonated beers brewed by the New Zealand Breweries.

Lionel Bruck (Fr). A Burgundy négociant based in Nuits-Saint-Georges, Côte de Nuits, Burgundy. Address = 6, Quai Dumorey, 21700 Nuit-Saint-Georges.

Lion Lager (Afr). A sweet Lager beer brewed by the South African Breweries.

Lion Lager (Sri.L). A Lager beer 1042 O.G. brewed by the Ceylon Breweries.

Lion Mild (Eng). A keg Mild beer 1035 O.G. brewed by the Banks Brewery, Wolverhampton, Staffs.

Lion Mild (Eng). A Mild ale 1031 O.G. brewed by Matthew Brown's Brewery, Blackburn, Lancashire.

Lion's Pride (Cktl). 1 measure Advocaat, ½ measure Crème de Banane, ½ measure lemon juice, dash Crème de Cacao, dash egg white. Shake well over ice, strain into a flute glass. Top with iced Champagne.

Lion Super (N.Z.). A strong, hoppy, golden Lager beer 1045 O.G. brewed by the New Zealand Breweries.

Lipari Islands (It). See Aeolian Islands.

Lipburg (Ger). Village. (Anb) = Baden. (Ber) = Markgräflerland. (Gro) = Burg Neuenfels. (Vin) = Kirchberg.

Lipovina (Czec). A white grape variety used in the making of Czec. 'Tokay'.

Liquefacere (It). Latin. 'To make liquid' or 'dissolve'. From which the word 'Liqueur' derives.

Liqueur (Eng). An alcoholic beverage made from either distilled fruit wines, flavoured spirits (herbs, spices, fruits). sweetened and used as a cocktail additive or Digestif.

Liqueur (Eng). A bottled Barley wine 1072 O.G. brewed by the Castletown Brewery, Isle of Man.

Liqueur (Fr). Cordial.

Liqueur and Cocktail Orientated Seminars (Eng). LACOS. Training sessions held by the De Kuyper Co. to promote and improve knowledge of liqueurs and cocktails.

Liqueur aux Fraises (Bel). A liqueur made from Wépion strawberries by Distilleries Associées Belges at Jumet.

Liqueur Coffee (Eng). 1 measure of Spirit or Liqueur, 1 cube of sugar to taste, hot freshly brewed black coffee, cream. Place a teaspoon into a large Paris goblet, add sugar if required. Pour in coffee (¾ full) and stir to dissolve sugar if used. Is best if stirred clockwise 6 times, then once anti-clockwise as this prevents causing a whirl-pool in the glass. Add spirit/liqueur then pour in cream (lightly whipped helps it to float) into the *bowl* of teaspoon placed over the coffee.

Liqueur d'Angélique (Fr). A liqueur made with Cognac and angelica.

Liqueur de Château (Swe). A liqueur that contains some of the élixir made at Grenoble by Chartreuse. Produced by Aktiebolaget Vin & Spritcentralem.

L

Liqueur de Frère Jean (Fr). See Aiguebelle.

Liqueur de Grand Saint Bernard (Switz). A pale green, honey liqueur which is flavoured with local seeds and flowers.

Liqueur de Jus de Noix Vertes (Fr). A green, walnut-based liqueur produced by Denoix of Brive.

Liqueur de Sapins (Fr). A spicy liqueur made in Pontarlier in the Jura flavoured with pine needle extract.

Liqueur des Moines (Fr). Liqueur made from aromatic plants and Cognac. Yellow in colour.

Liqueur des Pins (Fr). See Sapindor.

Liqueur de Tirage (Fr). Another name for Dosage. Is a sugar syrup added to Champagne before it is bottled for its second fermentation in bottle.

Liqueur d'Expédition (Fr). The sugar and old wine that is added to Champagne after dégorgement. See Brut, Demi-Sec, Sec and Doux.

Liqueur d'Hendaye (Fr). A herbal liqueur produced near Bayonne, south-western France.

Liqueur d'Or (Fr). A lemon-flavoured clear liqueur with a slight herb flavour. Has gold flakes floating in it. 43% alc. by vol. See Goldwasser.

Liqueur Frappé (Cktl). A measure of liqueur of choice, poured into a cocktail glass over shaved ice. Served with small straws.

Liqueur Jaune (Fr). A yellow herbal liqueur produced in north-eastern France.

Liqueur Rum (W.Ind). A term given to Rum that has been aged for over six years. See Vieux Rum.

Liqueur Sandalera (Austr). A sweet, white, wood-aged liqueur-style dessert wine produced by Sandalford, Western Australia.

Liqueur Scotch Whisky (Scot). A blended, aged Scotch Whisky with a high proportion of malts in its blend.

Liqueurs Jaunes (Fr). Yellow liqueurs, herb-flavoured and sweet. e.g. Chartreuse. See also Liqueurs Vertes.

Liqueur Stomachique (Fr). A brand of élixir produced by Picard et Cazot Fils in Lyons, southern France.

Liqueurs Vertes (Fr). Green liqueurs, herb-flavoured, usually dry. e.g. Bénédictine, Chartreuse and Vieille Cure. See also Liqueurs Jaunes.

Liqueur Teas (Eng). A tea that is blended with the aroma of a fine liqueur Cognac, Kirsch, Orange brandy, Rum, Whisky or Cream sherry produced by Frametime of London.

Liqueur Verdelho (Austr). An aged Madeira-style fortified wine (approx. 18 years old) from the Jane Brook Estate, Western Australia.

Liqueur Wines (EEC). The name for fortified wines.

Liquid Coffee (Eng). The name given to the water-soluble solids derived from roasted coffee.

Liquidus (Lat). Liquid.

Liquor (Eng). Alcoholic beverages.

Liquor (Eng). The name for water used in the brewing process.

Liquor Beirão (Port). A medicinal (herb) liqueur from J. Carranca Redonda Lda., of Lousan. 29% alc. by vol.

Liquor Bernardinus (Fr). An old herb liqueur produced by the Cistercian monks at Citeaux in the seventeenth century. Now no longer produced.

Liquor Control Board of Ontario (Can). A rare wines and spirits shop. All wines and spirits in Canada are sold by the Government monopoly.

Liquore (It). Liqueur.

Liquore Carthusia (It). A liqueur made in Capri by Carthusian monks that is flavoured with herbs.

Liquore Galliano (It). See Galliano.

Liquore Santa Vittoria (It). A herb liqueur.

Liquoreux (Fr). A term to describe a sweet fortified wine which has retained much of its natural sugar. Such a wine would be 3° Baume or more.

Liquore Vallombrosa (It). A herb liqueur.

Liquoroso Dolce Naturale (It). Fortified, naturally sweet wine.

Liquoroso Secco (It). Fortified dry wine.

Liquors Co. of America (USA). Bottlers of A. Gecht De Luxe Brandy.

Liquor Up (USA) (slang). To be drunk.

Liquoureux (Fr). A wine which is rich and sweet.

Lirac (Fr). An A.C. district in the Rhône. Produces red, rosé and white wines. Communes – St. Laurent des Arbres, St. Genies-de-Comolas, Roquemaure. Minimum alc. by vol. 11%

Lirac Rouge Classique (Fr). A red A.C. Lirac produced on the Garrigues by J.C. Assmat of Roquemaure, Gard. Grape varieties – Cinsault and Grenache.

Lisbon (Port). A region where the vines are ungrafted. Famous for its Setúbal.

Lisbon Port (Port). A Port-style wine produced in Lisbon. Now no longer allowed due to the Portuguese wine laws introduced in the early 1900s.

Lisbon Wine (USA). Portuguese wines that are shipped from Lisbon in Portugal.

Listán (Sp). A white grape variety grown in south-western Spain.

Listán Palomino (Sp). A white grape used in the making of Sherry.

Listel (Fr). A large Camargue estate in the

L

Midi owned by Salins du Midi. Produces red, rosé and dry white wines.

Listofka (USSR). A blackcurrant-flavoured apéritif.

Listrac (Fr). An A.C. commune in the Haut-Médoc, north-western Bordeaux.

Listrão (Mad). A white grape variety used in the making of Madeira.

Litchborough (Eng). See Liddington.

Litcheur (Ch.Isles). Alcoholic liquor. See also Beuv'rie.

Liter (USA). Spelling of litre. 0.26417 US gallon.

Literninum (Lat). A red wine produced in central-western Italy in Roman times.

Lithiated Water (Eng). A water rich in Lithia salts. e.g. Baden-Baden, Carsbad, St. Marco, Salvator.

Litoměřice (Czec). A wine-producing town near Prague on the river Elbe.

Litoměřice Brewery (Czec). An old brewery based in Litoměřice, northern Czec.

Litoral (Arg). A wine region that joins the provinces of Santa Fe and Buenos Aires.

Litovel Brewery (Czec). A brewery based in northern Czec.

Litr (Wales). Litre.

Litre (Euro). Liquid metric measure. 1.76 pints.

Litres of Absolute Alcohol (Eng). LPA. An expression used for measuring a given quantity of alcohol in a given quantity of spirit. Also seen as HLPA.

Litron (Fr). An old measure of approximately 0.8 litre.

Little Devil (Cktl). ⅗ measure Cointreau, ⅓ measure Bacardi White Label, ⅓ measure dry Gin, juice ¼ lemon. Shake over ice, strain into a cocktail glass.

Little John (Eng). A bottled strong Ale 1070 O.G. brewed by the Home Brewery, Nottingham.

Little Karoo (S.Afr). A major wine-producing area which stretches from Drakenstein to the Swartberg mountains. Produces mainly sweet muscatel wines and brandy. Also called Klein Karoo.

Littlemill (Scot). A single Malt whisky distillery near Bowling in Dumbartonshire. Owned by Barton Distilling Co. A Lowland malt. Produces an 8 year old malt. 43% alc. by vol. Part of Amalgamated Distilled Products.

Little Pook Hill (Eng). A vineyard based at Burwash Weald, Sussex. Was first planted in 1971. 1.9 ha. Grape varieties – Müller-Thurgau, Reichensteiner and others.

Little Princess (Cktl). ½ measure white Rum, ½ measure sweet Vermouth. Stir over ice, strain into a cocktail glass.

Little Wine (Ger). Carafe wine.

Littoral Orb-Hérault (Fr). A Vins de Pays area in the Hérault Département, southern France. Produces red, rosé and dry white wines.

Livadia (USSR). A white muscat dessert wine from the southern Crimea. Also the name of a red wine made from the Cabernet grape.

Lively (Eng). The name given to a wine that stimulates the palate with a pleasant acidity and freshness.

Livener Cocktail (Cktl). 1 oz. Brandy, 3 ozs. Champagne, 1 teaspoon raspberry syrup, 2 dashes Angostura or lemon juice. Stir well in a highball glass with ice.

Live Oaks (USA). A winery based at Hecker Pass, Santa Clara, California. Produces table wines.

Livermore Valley (USA). East of San Francisco. Has gravel soil and produces soft red wines and sweet dessert wines.

Livesey (Joseph) (Eng). The founder of the Temperance Seven in Lancashire in the nineteenth century. Original pledge signed in Preston.

Livio Felluga (It). A sparkling (méthode champenoise) wine producer using Pinot grapes based in the Friuli-Venezia Giulia region.

Livre de Cave (Fr). Cellar record (stock) book.

Livres (Fr). Money used in the eighteenth and nineteenth century. Is often mentioned in old books.

Lizas (Gre). A light-coloured, dry Brandy.

Ljutomer (Yug). See Lutomer-Ormoz.

Lladoner (Sp). The alternative name for the Garnacho grape. Also called Grenache and Tinto Aragonés.

Llaeth (Wales). Milk.

Llaethferch (Wales). Milkmaid.

Llaethwr (Wales). Milkman.

Llano del Maipo (Chile). A central region which produces most of Chile's wines.

Llano Estacado (USA). A small vineyard based in Lubbock, western Texas. 6 ha. Produces many grape varieties.

Llanrhystud Vineyard (Wales). A vineyard based at Llanrhystud, Dyfed. Was first planted in 1973. 0.3 ha. Grape varieties – Madeleine angevine 10%, Müller-Thurgau 30%, Reichensteiner 10%, Seyval blanc 10% plus others.

Llava Brewery (Czec). An old brewery based in eastern Czec.

Llebeig (Sp). A south-western wind that blows through the Penedés region in the summer. Also known as the Garbi. Is a warm wind.

Lledoner Pelut (Fr). A red grape variety grown in the Côtes du Roussillon, south-western France.

Lleno (Sp). Describes a Sherry with a

617

L

foul-smelling bouquet.

Llicorella (Sp). Reddish slate soil found in Tarragona which contains small particles of mica.

Llords and Elwood Winery (USA). A winery based in Alameda and Santa Clara, California. (H/Q in Los Angeles). Produces most styles of wine.

Lloyd and Trouncer (Wales). A subsidiary company of Ansells set up in 1981. Named after Lloyd, Newport and Trouncer of Shrewsbury.

Lloyd Light (Austr). A noted winery based in Southern Vales, South Australia.

Lloyd's Country Bitter (Eng). See John Thompson Pub.

Llwydni (Wales). Mildew.

Llymeltiwr (Wales). Drinker of alcoholic beverages, a tippler.

Loam Soil (Eng). Rich, fertile soil consisting of a mixture of sand, clay and decaying organic material.

Lobe (Eng). Part of a leaf. A vine leaf has five lobes or divisions.

Lobster Cocktail (Cktl).(Non-alc). Make a sauce of tomato juice, grape juice and lemon juice. Add salt, paprika and Worcestershire sauce. Stir over ice, strain, decorate with pieces of lobster in a sherbet glass.

Loburg (Bel). A bottled Lager 1051 O.G. brewed by the Stella Artois Brasserie.

Loca Blanca (Chile). A local variety of white grape which produces medium white table wines.

Lo-Cal (N.Z.). A low-calorie Beer 1036 O.G. brewed by the Leopard Brewery.

Local Bitter (Ch.Isles). A Bitter ale 1036 O.G. brewed by the Randall Vautier Brewery in St. Helier, Jersey.

Local Bitter (Eng). A Bitter ale 1038 O.G. brewed by the Greenall Whitley Brewery in Warrington, Lancashire.

Local Bitter (Eng). A Bitter ale 1037 O.G. brewed by the Shipstone Brewery in Nottingham.

Local Bitter (Eng). A Bitter ale 1037 O.G. brewed by the Tisbury Brewery in Wiltshire.

Località (It). The equivalent of the French Cru.

Local Licensing Justices (Eng). See Licensing Justices.

Local Line (Eng). A cask conditioned Ale 1038 O.G. brewed by the Chudley Brewery in London.

Local [The] (Eng) (slang). A term for the nearest public house to a person's home that is used regularly.

Locarnese (Switz). A noted vineyard based in the Sopra Cenevi, Ticino.

Lochan Ora (Scot). A liqueur based on Scotch Whisky and honey. Owned by Seagram.

Loché (Fr). A commune in the Mâconnais, Burgundy.

Locher Brauerei (Switz). An independent brewery based in Appenzell and Buchs.

Löchgau (Ger). Village. (Anb) = Württemberg. (Ber) = Württembergisch Unterland. (Gro) = Schalkstein. (Vin) = Neckarberg.

Loch Lomond (Scot). A single Malt whisky distillery based north-west of Glasgow. A Highland malt whisky. 40% alc. by vol.

Loch Lomond Cocktail (Cktl). 1½ measures Scotch whisky, 1 measure Gomme syrup, 3 dashes Angostura. Shake over ice, strain into an ice-filled old-fashioned glass.

Lochmühlerley (Ger). vineyard. (Anb) = Ahr. (Ber) = Walporzheim/Arhtal. (Gro) = Klosterberg. (Vil) = Mayschoss.

Lochnagar (Scot). A single Malt whisky distillery near Balmoral, west of the Spey in Aberdeenshire. Operated by John Begg Ltd. (part of the DCL group). A Highland malt. Produces a 12 year old malt. 43% alc. by vol.

Lochside (Scot). A Grain whisky distillery based near Montrose.

Lochside (Scot). A single Malt whisky distillery near Montrose. A Highland malt. Produces a vintage 1965 Malt. 43% alc. by vol.

Locke and Company (Ire). A distillery based at Kilbeggan which closed down in 1952. The last Whiskey produced is now sold as Locke's Kilbeggan (a 1946 Irish Whiskey).

Locke's Kilbeggan (Ire). A 'vintage' Irish whiskey from the last production of the Locke distillery. See Locke and Company.

Locorotondo (It). D.O.C. white wine from Puglia. Made from the Bianco d'alessano and Verdeca grapes. Production area is the commune of Locorotondo and Cisterino plus part of commune of Fasano. D.O.C. also applies to naturally sparkling wines.

Locret-Lachaud (Fr). Champagne producer. Address = 40 Rue Saint Vincent, 51160 Hautviliers. Récoltants-manipulants. Produces – Vintage and non-vintage wines. Vintages – 1971, 1976, 1979, 1982, 1983.

Loddiswell vineyard (Eng). Address = Lilwell, Loddiswell, Kingsbridge, South Devon. Was first planted 1977. Grape varieties – Bacchus, Huxelrebe, Müller-Thurgau, Reichensteiner and Siegerrebe.

Lodge (Mad). A building where Madeira is matured.

Lodge (Port). A building in Vila Nova de Gaia where Port is matured.

L

Lodge Lot Cask (Port). A cask for maturing Port. Holds approximately 630 litres.

Lodi (USA). Lodi-Sacramento. A northern region of the Great Central Valley in California. Produces dessert and table wines.

Loel (Cyp). A large wine and spirits producer. Sells under the labels of Amathus, Commandaria and Kykko.

Loess (Eng). A light-coloured granular loam soil. An accumulation of clay and silt particles, wind deposited.

Loevi Cocktail (Cktl). 1 measure dry Gin, ½ measure Orange gin, ½ measure French vermouth. Shake over ice, strain into an ice-filled highball glass. Serve with straws.

Löf (Ger). Village. (Anb) = Mosel-Saar-Ruwer. (Ber) = Zell/Mosel. (Gro) = Weinhex. (Vins) = Goldblume, Sonnenring.

Loft Withering (Asia). An old method of drying tea where the tealeaf was placed on racks to dry. Little used now.

Logado (Gre). A grapey, straw-gold, white wine from Crete. Made with the Sultana and Villane grapes.

Logan De Luxe Scotch Whisky (Scot). A De Luxe blended Scotch Whisky formerly called Laird o'Logan. Premium brand of White Horse Distillers Ltd. 40% alc. by vol.

Loge aux Moines (La) (Fr). An old historical vineyard of Pouilly-sur-Loire. Produces a fine, excellent A.C. Pouilly Fumé.

Loges (Les) (Fr). A vineyard in the A.C. Pouilly Fumé, Central Vineyards, Loire. 8 ha.

Logis (Fr). A 5 year old Cognac produced by Jean Guerbé.

Logis de la Montagne (Fr). Cognac producer. Address = Paul Bonnin, Logis de la Montagne, Challignac, 16300. 30 ha. in the Fins Bois. Produces – Extra Hors d'Âge 20 year old, Pineau de Charente, Le Sauté Montagne and Vicomte Stephane de Castelbajac.

Logroño (Sp). The centre of the Rioja wine region in the Rioja Alta.

Logwood (Mex). See Campeaching Wood.

Lohberger Hang (Ger). vineyard. (Anb) = Rheingau. (Ber) = Johannisberg. (Gro) = Not yet assigned. (Vil) = Frankfurt/Main.

Löhrer Berg (Ger). vineyard. (Anb) = Nahe. (Ber) = Kreuznach. (Gro) = Sonnenborn. (Vil) = Langenlonsheim.

Loiben (Aus). A wine district within the Wachau region, western Austria.

Loibener (Aus). A light dry white wine from the Wachau region.

Loin d'Oeil (Fr). An alternative name for the Muscadelle grape.

Loire-Atlantique (Fr). A Département in western France in the Pays de la Loire. Has the Muscadet wine region (Pays Nantais) in its boundaries.

Loire [River] (Fr). The longest river in France. Runs from south-east to the north-west coast. Has four wine districts within the region. Pays Nantais, Anjou-Saumur, Touraine and the Central vineyards.

Loiret (Fr). A Vins de Pays area in the Loiret Département, central France (part of the Jardin de la France). Produces red, rosé, gris and dry white wines.

Loir-et-Cher (Fr). A Vins de Pays area in the Loir-et-Cher Département of north-western France (part of the Jardin de la France). Produces red, rosé, gris and dry white wines.

Loisy-en-Brie (Fr). A Cru Champagne village in the Canton de Vertus. District = Châlons.

Løiten (Nor). The brand-name of an Aquavit produced by A/S Vinmonopolet.

Løiten Braenderis-Destillation (Nor). A large distilling company based in Kristiania under the control of A/S Vinmonopolet. Produces Aquavit.

Loja (Port). A lodge or warehouse in Vila Nova de Gaia where Port is matured.

Lolland-Falsters Brewery (Den). A small brewery in Nykøbing. Noted for its Pilsener-style Lager beer 4.5% alc. by vol.

Lolle (Sp). A black grape variety grown in the Canary Isles.

Lolly Water (Austr). The nickname given to any coloured soft (non-alcoholic) drink. e.g. cherryade, orangeade, etc.

Lolly-Water (N.Z.). The nickname given to thin rosé wines that have been sweetened with cane sugar.

Lolonis vineyard (USA). A vineyard based in Redwood Valley, Mendocino, California. 41.5 ha. Grape variety – Zinfandel.

Lombardia (It). See Lombardy.

Lombardi Wines (N.Z.). A family-owned vineyard. Address = Te Mata Road, Hawkes Bay, North Island. 3 ha. Specialises in liqueurs, vermouths and sherries.

Lombard's Hanepoot (S.Afr). An average sweet fortified wine.

Lombardy (It). The third largest region in Italy. Borders Switzerland to the north, Veneto to the east, Piemonte to the west and Emilia-Romagna to the south.

Lomelino (Mad). The brand-name of producers – Tarquinio T. da Camara

L

Lomelino. Produces – Lomelino Imperial Sercial, Verdelho, Bual and Rare old Malmsey. Also Tarquino Sercial, Bual and Malmsey.

Lomond (Scot). A single Malt whisky distillery based north of the river Clyde. A Lowland malt whisky. 40% alc. by vol.

London (Can). A wine district between Niagara and Crystal Beach.

London (Cktl). ¾ measure London dry gin, dash Gomme syrup, dash Maraschino, dash Angostura. Stir well over ice, strain into a cocktail glass. Dress with a spiral lemon peel.

London Bitter (Eng). A cask conditioned Bitter ale 1037 O.G. brewed by the Watney Brewery in London.

London Buck Cocktail (Cktl). ⅕ gill dry Gin, juice ½ lemon. Shake over ice, strain into an ice-filled highball glass. Top with ginger ale.

London Cocktail (Cktl). ½ gill London Dry Gin, 2 dashes Absinthe, 2 dashes Orange bitters, 2 dashes Gomme syrup. Stir over ice, strain into a cocktail glass, add an olive, squeeze of lemon peel juice on top.

London Coffee Information Centre (Eng). Address = 21, Berner's Street, London W1P 4DD. Centre run by the International Coffee Organisation to promote the drinking of coffee.

London Dock Rum (Jam). A Jamaican rum bottled in London and stored in bonded warehouses in London's docks.

London Dry Gin (Eng). A Gin originally produced near or in London. Now denotes a very dry Gin produced anywhere.

Londoner (Cktl). 1½ ozs. dry Gin, ½ oz. Rosehip syrup, ½ oz. dry Vermouth, juice ½ lemon. Pour over ice in a highball glass, stir, top with soda water and a slice of lemon.

London Fog (Cktl). ½ measure Anisette, ½ measure white Crème de Menthe, dash Angostura. Shake over ice, strain into a cocktail glass.

London Gin (Eng). See London Dry Gin.

London Lager (Eng). See John Young's London Lager.

London Market (Mad). The quality name sometimes seen on bottles of Madeira. This is a 'Lot' name.

London Particular (Mad). The quality name sometimes seen on bottles of Madeira. This is a 'Lot' name.

London Pilsener Brewery (Ind). A brewery based in Bangalore, India. Produces London Stout and Maharajah Lager. Is India's largest brewery.

London Pride (Eng). A Bitter beer 1041.5 O.G. brewed by the Fuller, Smith and Turner Brewery of Chiswick. Also a bottled version 1045 O.G.

London Special (Cktl). Place a sugar cube soaked in Orange bitters in a flute glass. Top with iced Champagne and a twist of orange peel juice.

London Stout (Can). A sweet Stout brewed by the Moosehead Brewery.

London Stout (Ind). A medium Stout brewed by the London Pilsener Brewery, Bangalore.

London Stout (Ind). A bitter Stout 1046 O.G. brewed by the United Breweries in Bangalore.

London Stout (USA). The name given to stouts produced outside of U.K.

London Tap Water (Eng). Produced by Sodastream. Available as still-filtered, unfiltered and carbonated.

London vineyard (USA). A small vineyard based at Glen Ellen, west of Sonoma Valley, California. Grape varieties – Cabernet sauvignon and Pinot noir.

Lone Star Beer (USA). A Beer brewed by the Lone Star Brewery in San Antonio, Texas.

Lone Star Brewery (USA). A Texas Brewery and beer from San Antonio. Owned by Olympia in Washington.

Lone Tree (Cktl). ⅓ measure dry Gin, ⅓ measure Italian vermouth, ⅓ measure French vermouth, 2 dashes Orange bitters. Shake over ice, strain into a cocktail glass.

Lone Tree Cocktail (Cktl). ⅔ measure dry Gin, ⅓ measure sweet Vermouth. Stir over ice, strain into a cocktail glass.

Long (Eng). A term used to describe a long, lingering flavour (aftertaste) in a wine. Is often a sign of fine quality.

Longae Vitae (Hol). A brand of herb bitters.

Long Anis Cocktail (Cktl). Place ⅕ gill Anisette and a dash lemon juice in an ice-filled highball glass. Stir, top with soda water.

Longberry Harar (Afr). A style of coffee produced in Ethiopia that resembles Mocha.

Long Blonde (Cktl). ⅕ gill Dubonnet Blonde, ⅕ gill dry Gin. Stir over ice in a highball glass. Top with soda water.

Long Drink (Eng). A large drink of non-alcoholic beverage. e.g. water, squash, lemonade, etc.

Longen (Ger). Village. (Anb) = Mosel-Saar-Ruwer. (Ber) = Bernkastel. (Gro) = Sankt Michael. (Vins) = Goldkupp, Zellerberg.

Longenburgerberg (Ger). vineyard.

L

(Anb) = Mittelrhein. (Ber) = Siebengebirge. (Gro) = Petersberg. (Vil) = Niederdollendorf.

Long Flat Red (Austr). A vintage red wine
from the Tyrrell's Winery in New South
Wales.

Long Glen (Cktl). 1 oz. Gin or Vodka, 1 oz.
Cointreau. Pour over ice cubes in a
highball glass. Stir, add bitter lemon to
taste.

Long Green Cocktail (Cktl). Place 3 ice
cubes in a highball glass. Add 1 fl.oz.
(green) Crème de Menthe and top with
soda water. Decorate with a mint sprig
and serve with straws.

Longhi de Carli (It). A wine producer in
Franciacorta, Lombardy.

Long Island Tea (Cktl). ½ oz. light Rum, ½
oz. Vodka, ½ oz. Gin, 1 fl.oz. cold weak
tea. Build into ice-filled highball glass,
stir in cola. Decorate with a lemon slice
and sprig of mint.

Long John (Scot). A blended Scotch
Whisky from the Long John MacDonald
Distilleries, Glasgow. 40% alc. by vol.

Long John (Scot). A De Luxe blended
Scotch Whisky. 12 year old, from the
Long John MacDonald Distilleries, Glas-
gow. 40% alc. by vol.

Long John International (Scot). Highland,
Islay and Scotch whisky distillers (part
of Whitbread). Whiskies include Laphroaig, Long John and Tormore. See also
Long John MacDonald Distilleries.

Long John MacDonald Distilleries (Scot).
Distilleries based in Glasgow. Part of
Long John International.

Long Life (Eng). A keg Bitter 1040 O.G.
brewed by Allied Breweries, Wrexham.
Also an Export version 1046 O.G.

Longman (Scot). A keg Lager beer 1040
O.G. brewed by the Alice Brewery in
Inverness.

Longmorn-Glenlivet (Scot). A single Malt
whisky distillery near Longmorn. Now
part of The Glenlivet Distillers Ltd. (part
of the Seagram group). A Highland malt.
Produce a 12 year old Malt and a vintage
1957 Malt. 43% alc. by vol.

Long Pond (W.Ind). A noted Rum distillery
based in Jamaica.

Long Pull (Eng). An illegal act. Serving over
a prescribed measure. A Licensing Act
offence.

Longrow (Scot). A 12 year old, double-
distilled, Campbeltown malt whisky
produced by Mitchell and Co. 45% alc.
by vol.

Long Tail (Eng). The term used to denote
the finish in the mouth of a wine. A long
after-taste.

Long Thirst (USA). The alternative nickname for the Prohibition.

Longueteau (W.Ind). A noted Rum
distillery based in Guadeloupe.

Longueville House (Ire). A vineyard
based at Mallow, County Cork, Eire.
Was first planted in 1972. 1.6 ha. Grape
varieties – Müller-Thurgau and
Reichensteiner.

Longuich (Ger). Village. (Anb) = Mosel-
Saar-Ruwer. (Ber) = Bernkastel. (Gro)
= Probstberg. (Vins) = Hirschlay,
Maximiner, Herrenberg.

Long vineyards (USA). A small winery
based near Rutherford, Napa Valley,
California. 8.5 ha. Grape varieties –
Chardonnay and Johannisberg riesling. Produce varietal wines.

Long vineyards (USA). Also known as
the Jasper Long vineyards. Based in
Dry Creek Valley, Sonoma County,
California. Grape variety – Merlot.

Long Whistle (Cktl). ¾ gill Brandy or
Whisky, sugar syrup to taste, hot or
cold milk, grated nutmeg on top.

Longyon (China). See Loong Yan.

Lonsheim (Ger). Village. (Anb) = Rheinhessen. (Ber) = Bingen. (Gro) = Adelberg. (Vins) = Mandelberg, Schönberg.

Lontué (Chile). A wine region of Central
Chile. Produces sound table wines.

Lonz (USA). A winery based in Middle
Bass Island, Ohio. Produces French
hybrid wines.

Lonzac (Fr). A commune in the Charente-
Maritime Département. Grapes are
used for Cognac.

Look Out Below (Cktl). 1 measure Puss-
ers 100° Proof Navy Rum, juice ¼ lime,
1 teaspoon Grenadine. Shake over ice,
strain into an ice-filled old-fashioned
glass.

Loong Ching (China). A green tea, rolled
into pellets. Produced in Canton.

Loong Yan (China). The ancient name for
the white grape variety Dragon's Eye.

Looped (USA) (slang). For under the
influence of alcohol.

Loose Head (Eng). See Head.

López de Heredia (Sp). A noted wine-
producer based at Avenida de Vizeaya
3 and 5, Haro, Rioja Alta. 120 ha. in the
Rioja Alta. Produces – Viña Bosconia,
Viña Cubillo, Viña Gravonia and Viña
Tondonia (red and white).

López Hermanos (Sp). A noted producer
and exporter of Málaga.

López Tello (Sp). An old-established
bodega based in Valdepeñas, central
Spain.

Lopo (Hun). A larger version of a pipette/
valenche. A hollow rod with a bulbous
head for drawing wine out of the cask.
Holds the equivalent of one bottle.

Loppin (Fr). A vineyard in the A.C. Meur-

L

sault, Côte de Beaune. Is owned by the Hospices de Beaune.

Lorch (Ger). Village. (Anb) = Rheingau. (Ber) = Johannisberg. (Gro) = Burgweg. (Vins) = Bodental-Steinberg, Kapellenberg, Krone, Pfaffenweis, Schlossberg.

Lorchhausen (Ger). Village. (Anb) = Rheingau. (Ber) = Johannisberg. (Gro) = Burgweg. (Vins) = Rosenberg, Seligmacher.

Lord Calvert Canadian (Can). A blend of Canadian whiskies 40% alc. by vol. produced by Canadian Distillers Ltd (a subsidiary of Seagram).

Lord Chesterfield (USA). A top-fermented, sweet, well-hopped Ale. Brewed by the Yuengling Brewery in Pottsville.

Lord Ducane (Eng). The brand-name used by Vine Products Ltd. for their British Sherry.

Lord George Port (Port). The brand-name of a Port shipped by Taylor, Fladgate and Yeatman.

Lord's Ale (Eng). A strong Ale 1048 O.G. brewed by the Chudley Brewery in London.

Loreley-Edel (Ger). vineyard. (Anb) = Mittelrhein. (Ber) = Rheinburgengau. (Gro) = Loreleyfelsen. (Vil) = St. Goarshausen.

Loreleyfelsen (Ger). Grosslage. (Anb) = Mittelrhein. (Ber) = Rheinburgengau. (Vils) = Bornich, Kamp-Bornhofen-Kestert, Nochern, Patersberg, St. Goarshausen.

Lorentz (Gustave) (Fr). Alsace wine producer. Address = 35, Grand-Rue, 68750 Bergheim. 31 ha.

Lorestan (Iran). A wine-producing province in northern Iran.

Lorettoberg (Ger). Grosslage. (Anb) = Baden. (Ber) = Markgräflerland. (Vils) = Bad Krotzingen, Biengen, Bollschweil, Buggingen, Ebringen, Ehrenstetten, Eschbach, Freiburg i. Br., Grunern, Heitersheim, Kirchhofen, Mengen, Merzhausen, Norsingen, Pfaffenweiler, Schallstadt-Wolfenweile, Scherzingen, Schlatt, Seefelden, Staufen, Staufen (ortsteil Wettelbrunn), Tunsel, Wittnau.

Lorgues (Fr). A wine-producing village in the Côtes de Provence.

Lorimer and Clark Brewery (Scot). A brewery based in Edinburgh taken over by the Vaux Brewery of Sunderland in 1964. Noted for its cask conditioned 70/- Ale 1036 O.G. (known as Best Scotch in Vaux houses) and Caledonian Strong 1077 O.G.

Loron et Fils (Fr). A Burgundy négociant based at Pontanevaux, 71570 La Chapelle-de-Guinchay, Burgundy.

Lörrach (Ger). Village. (Anb) = Baden. (Ber) = Markgräflerland. (Gro) = Vogtei Rötteln. (Vin) = Sonnenbrunnen.

Lorraine (Fr). A wine province of northeastern France. Red, rosé and white plus Vins gris are produced. V.D.Q.S. quality. Two areas – Vins de la Moselle and Côtes de Toul.

Lörsch (Ger). Village. (Anb) = Mosel-Saar-Ruwer. (Ber) = Bernkastel. (Gro) = Sankt Michael. (Vins) = Goldkupp, Zellerberg.

Lörzweiler (Ger). Village. (Anb) = Rheinhessen. (Ber) = Nierstein. (Gro) = Gutes Domtal. (Vin) = Königstuhl.

Lörzweiler (Ger). Village. (Anb) = Rheinhessen. (Ber) = Nierstein. (Gro) = Sankt Alban. (Vins) = Hohberg, Ölgild.

Los Alamos vineyards (USA). A small winery based near Los Alamos, Santa Barbara, California. Grape varieties – Chardonnay and Zinfandel. Produce varietal wines.

Los Angeles (Cktl). ⅕ gill Bourbon whiskey, 1 egg, dash sweet Vermouth, 1 teaspoon powdered sugar. Shake over ice, strain into a flute glass.

Los Angeles (USA). A Californian wine district within the region of Cucamonga. Produces table and dessert wines.

Los Angeles Cocktail (Cktl). ⅔ measure Scotch Whisky, ⅓ measure lemon juice, 1 egg, dash sweet Vermouth. Shake over ice, strain into a large cocktail glass.

Los Gatos (USA). A town in Santa Clara County, California. Is home to three wineries.

Los Hermanos (USA). The label used by Beringer vineyards for a range of their generic and varietal wines.

Los Llanos (Sp). A wine-producing area west of Valdepeñas, central Spain.

Los Monteros (Sp). A full-bodied red wine produced by Schenk in Valencia from 100% Monastrell grapes.

Lösnich (Ger). Village. (Anb) = Mosel-Saar-Ruwer. (Ber) = Bernkastel. (Gro) = Schwarzlay. (Vins) = Burgberg, Försterlay.

Los Niños (USA). A vineyard based near Yountville, Napa Valley, California. Grape variety – Chardonnay. Grapes vinified at the Con Creek Winery.

Los Olivos (USA). A wine-producing town near Santa Ynez Valley, Santa Barbara, California.

Los Olivos vineyard (USA). A winery based in Santa Ynez Valley, Santa Barbara, California. Grape variety – Chardonnay.

Los Ranchos (S.Am). A noted wine-producer in Uruguay based in Rio Negro.

Los Reyes (Mex). The label used by Luis Cetto vineyards in Guadaloupe, Baja California for a range of their wines.

Los Tercios (Sp). An area within Andalusia whose vineyards produce the grapes for Sherry.

Lot (Fr). A département south-east of the Gironde. Famous for its red Cahors wines. Contains the areas of Coteaux de Glanes and Coteaux du Quercy.

Lot (Port). The designation given to a parcel of Port wine before it is blended.

Lota (Port). The process of racking the new Ports and topping up with brandy to bring up to strength at the end of the first year. (November).

Lotberg (Ger). vineyard. (Anb) = Baden. (Ber) = Kaiserstuhl-Tuniberg. (Gro) = Vulkanfelsen. (Vil) = Wasenweiler.

Lote (Mad). A collection of pipes or vats containing wines with different characteristics. It is from these that shippers create their brands.

Lote (Port). An amount of Port used for blending.

Lot-et-Garonne (Fr). A Vins de Pays area in the Lot-et-Garonne Département, south-western France. Consists of the areas L'Agenais, Côtes de Brulhois and Côtes du Tarn.

Lottenstück (Ger). vineyard. (Anb) = Rheinhessen. (Ber) = Bingen. (Gro) = Kaiserpfalz. (Vil) = Ingelheim.

Lottstetten [ortsteil Nack] (Ger). Village. (Anb) = Baden. (Ber) = Bodensee. (Gro) = Not yet assigned. (Vin) = Steinler.

Lotus (Eng). Orange or tropical-flavoured wine produced by Vine Products. Low in alcohol.

Lotus Flower (Eng). A lotus blossom-flavoured tea produced by Whittards of Chelsea Co, London.

Loubère (Fr). Armagnac producer. Address = 40240 Labastide d'Armagnac. 15 ha. in the Bas Armagnac.

Louche (Fr). Cloudy, no longer clear. A term used for wine that has turned cloudy through age or disease.

Louis California Brandy (USA). A Brandy produced by Schenley Distillers at Number One Distilling Co., California.

Louis de Vernier (Sp). A brand of sparkling wine produced by Casa Masachs (white and rosé).

Louise Pommery (Fr). A De Luxe vintage cuvée Champagne produced by Pommery et Gréno from 60% Chardonnay and 40% Pinot noir grapes.

Louis Guntrum (Ger). A well-known estate in the Rheinhessen. vineyards in Dienheim, Nierstein and Oppenheim. Grapes – Bacchus, Kerner and Rieslaner.

Louisiana Clay (USA). Bentonite.

Louisiana Lullaby (Cktl). ⅓ gill Jamaican rum, ⅛ gill red Dubonnet, 3 dashes Grand Marnier. Stir over ice, strain into a cocktail glass. Add a slice of lemon.

Louis Martini (USA). A Californian winery in the Napa Valley, Sonoma.

Louis Philippe (Fr). An 1840 distilled Cognac produced by A.E. Dor in Jarnac. 34% alc. by vol.

Louis V (USA). The brand-name for a Brandy produced by the Franzia Brothers, Ripon, California.

Louis XIII (Fr). A 50 year old Cognac produced by Rémy Martin.

Louis XIV (S.Afr). The brand-name of a Brandy produced by Oude Meester.

Louisville (USA). A town based in north Kentucky on the Indiana border. Is the home to many Bourbon whiskey distilleries.

Lounge (Eng). A comfortably furnished room in a public house where the drinks are at a slightly higher price than in the public bar.

Louny Brewery (Czec). A brewery based in northern Czec.

Loupiac (Fr). An A.C. commune in Bordeaux which produces sweet white wines. 12.5% alc. by vol. minimum.

Lourd (Fr). Denotes a dull, unbalanced wine.

Loureiro (Port). A white grape variety used in the making of Vinhos Verdes.

Louvois (Fr). A Premier Cru Champagne village in the Canton d'Ay. District = Reims.

Louwshoek Voorsorg Co-operative (S.Afr). Based in the Breede River region. Address = P.O. Voorsorg 6860. Produces – Laatoes and varietal wines.

Louzac (Fr). A commune in the Borderies (Charente-Maritime Département) in the Cognac region.

Lovage (Eng). A low-alcohol, herbal beverage used as a digestive.

Lovage (Eng). A flavoured alcoholic cordial produced by Phillips of Bristol.

Love Cocktail (Cktl). 2 fl.ozs. Gin, 2 dashes lemon juice, 2 dashes Grenadine, 1 egg white. Shake over ice, strain into a cocktail glass.

Lovedale (Austr). An estate belonging to McWilliams in Hunter Valley, New South Wales.

Lovelight (Cktl).(Non-alc). ⅓ gill strawberry syrup, ⅓ gill cream, 2 dashes lemon juice. Shake well over ice, strain into a wine goblet. Top with alcohol-free wine and a lemon slice.

Love Potion (Eng). A drink that is supposed to arouse sexual stimulation in the person who drinks it. Some old liqueurs were based on this idea.

L

Löver (Hun). A Lager beer brewed by the Sopron Brewery.

Lover's Dream (Cktl). A lemon flip filled up with ginger ale. Also known as a Glasgow flip.

Loving Cup (Eng). A style of two-handled glass/drinking vessel of which people take turns to drink out of it, especially at banquets. See also Johanniswein.

Loving Cup Cocktail (Cktl). Pour into an ice-filled jug – 2 fl.ozs. Brandy, 1 fl.oz. Curaçao, 4 fl.ozs. Gomme syrup, 1 bottle Claret, 1 small soda water. Stir, decorate with fruit in season, mint and cucumber.

Low C (Eng). A bottled/keg low carbohydrate Ale 1030 O.G. brewed by Marstons Brewery.

Löwenbräu Brauerei (Ger). A Brewery based in Munich. Beers brewed under licence by Allied Breweries in U.K. Produces – Keg 1041 O.G. (brewed by the Wrexham Brewery). Bottled Special Export 1051 O.G. and Pils 1047 O.G. are imported by Allied. In the USA is licensed by Miller.

Löwenbräu Brauerei (Switz). A brewery based in Zürich. Part of the Interbera group.

Löwengarten Brauerei (Switz). A brewery based in Rorschach. Part of the Interbera group.

Löwenstein (Ger). Village. (Anb) = Württemberg. (Ber) = Württembergisch Unterland. (Gro) = Salzberg. (Vins) = Altenberg, Nonnenrain, Wohlfahrtsberg.

Löwenstein (Ger). Village. (Anb) = Württemberg. (Ber) = Württembergisch Unterland. (Gro) = Schozachtal. (Vin) = Sommerberg.

Löwenstein [ortsteil Hösslinsülz] (Ger). Village. (Anb) = Württemberg. (Ber) = Württembergisch Unterland. (Gro) = Salzberg. (Vins) = Dieblesberg, Zeilberg.

Lower Austria (Aus). A wine region. Sub-divided into 8 districts. Wine towns – Retz, Krems and Lanenlois. See Niederösterreich.

Lower Corgo (Port). A district on the Douro river where the grapes are grown for Port. See also Upper Corgo.

Lower Lake Winery (USA). A bonded winery based in Lake County, California. Grape varieties – Cabernet sauvignon and Fumé blanc. Produces varietal wines.

Lowland (Scot). A classification of Scotch Malt Whisky.

Lowland Malt (Scot). See Auchentoschan, Lowland and Rosebank.

Low Wines (Jam). The Rum after the first distillation. Has to go through a second distillation.

Low Wines (Scot). The Malt whisky after its first distillation. Has to go through a second distillation.

Lozère (Fr). A département in Languedoc-Roussillon on the southern slopes of the Massif Central.

Lozia (Bul). vineyards.

Lozova Prachka (Bul). A red grape variety.

LPA (Eng) (abbr). Litres of (Pure) Absolute Alcohol.

Luaka (Sri.L). De-caffeinated.

Lucas Winery (USA). A small winery based west of Lodi, San Joaquin, California. 12.5 ha. Grape variety – Zinfandel.

Lucena (Sp). A wine town based in Montilla-Moriles, home to many wine producers.

Lucey (Fr). A commune in the Côtes de Toul, Lorraine. Produces Vins gris.

Luckens (Fr). An alternative name for the Malbec grape.

Lucky (Cktl). ½ oz. Mandarine Napoléon, 1 oz. Cognac, ½ oz. Irish Liqueur, dash pineapple syrup. Shake well over ice, strain into a highball glass, top up with tonic water, serve with a twist of lemon.

Lucky Dip (Cktl). ½ measure Vodka, ¼ measure Crème de Banane, ¼ measure lemon squash, 1 egg white. Shake over ice, strain into a cocktail glass.

Lucky Jim (Cktl). ⅙ gill Vodka, 4 dashes French vermouth, 1 dash cucumber juice. Shake over ice, strain into a cocktail glass.

Lucky Summer (Cktl). ¾ oz. Grand Marnier, ¾ oz. Scotch whisky, ¾ oz. lemon juice, 2 dashes Grenadine. Shake with ice, strain, decorate with a cherry and slice of orange.

Lucozade (Eng). A sparkling orange-and-barley-flavoured or natural glucose-flavoured sparkling drink produced by Beecham Products in Middlesex.

Ludes (Fr). A Grande Cru Champagne village in the Canton of Verzy. District = Reims.

Ludon (Fr). A commune in the A.C. Haut-Médoc, north-western Bordeaux. Famous for Château La Lagune.

Ludwigsburg [ortsteil Hoheneck] (Ger). Village. (Anb) = Württemberg. (Ber) = Württembergisch Unterland (Gro) = Schalkstein. (Vin) = Neckarhälde.

Ludwigsburg [ortsteil Hoheneck] (Ger). Village. (Anb) = Württemberg. (Ber) = Württembergisch Unterland. (Gro) = Wunnenstein. (Vin) = Oberer Berg.

Ludwigshöhe (Ger). Village. (Anb) = Rheinhessen. (Ber) = Nierstein. (Gro) = Krötenbrunnen. (Vin) = Honigberg.

Ludwigshöhe (Ger). Village. (Anb) =

Rheinhessen. (Ber) = Nierstein. (Gro) = Vogelsgärten. (Vin) = Teufelskopf.

Luftgeschmack (Ger). Denotes wines that have been in contact with the air and have developed an unpleasant taste.

Lugana (It). A small district near the southern end of Lake Garda in the Lombardy region of northern Italy.

Lugana (It). D.O.C. white wine from the Lombardy region. Made from the Trebbiano di Lugana grape. Vinification can take place in Brescia and Verona.

Luganese (Switz). A noted vineyard based in the Sotto Ceneri, Ticino.

Lugger Cocktail (Cktl). ½ measure Cognac, ½ measure Calvados, 1 dash Apricot brandy. Shake over ice, strain into a cocktail glass.

Luginsland (Ger). vineyard. (Anb) = Rheinpfalz. (Ber) = Mittelhaardt-Deutsche Weinstrasse. (Gro) = Schnepfenflug an der Weinstrasse. (Vil) = Wachenheim.

Luginsland (Ger). vineyard. (Anb) = Württemberg. (Ber) = Remstal-Stuttgart. (Gro) = Wartbühl. (Vil) = Aichelberg.

Luglianca Bianca (It). A white grape variety. Also known as the Egri Leànyka in Hungary.

Luigi Cocktail (Cktl). ½ gill Gin, ¼ gill French vermouth, 1 teaspoon Grenadine, 1 dash Cointreau, juice ½ tangerine. Shake over ice, strain into a cocktail glass.

Luins (Switz). A wine-producing village in La Côte.

Luisa (Cktl). ⁹⁄₁₀ measure Bacardi Rum, ³⁄₁₀ measure Parfait Amour, ³⁄₁₀ measure fresh apple juice, dash egg white. Shake over ice, strain into a cocktail glass. Top with a ½ slice of lemon and a cherry on the rim of the glass.

Luis Cetto vineyards (Mex). A large winery based in Guadalupe, Baja California. Produces wines under the Calafia and Los Reyes labels.

Luisengarten (Ger). vineyard. (Anb) = Nahe. (Ber) = Schloss Böckelheim. (Gro) = Burgweg. (Vil) = Bad Münster a. St-Ebernburg.

Lujan (Arg). A wine-producing area in the Mendoza region.

Luksusowa (Pol). A highly refined (in a technical sense) clear Vodka 44.5% alc. by vol. Is rectified 3 times from potatoes. See Polmos.

Lumberjack's Martini (USA). The nickname for Whiskey.

Lumley Old Ale (Eng). A dark Winter ale 1050 O.G. brewed by the Hermitage Brewery of West Sussex.

Lump (Ger). vineyard. (Anb) = Franken. (Ber) = Maindreieck. (Gro) = Kirchberg.

(Vil) = Escherndorf.

Lump (Ger). vineyard. (Anb) = Nahe. (Ber) = Schloss Böckelheim. (Gro) = Paradiesgarten. (Vil) = Kirschroth.

Lumumba (W.Ind). A nightcap made from a hot cocoa drink with a tot of dark Rum added.

Luna (La) (Sp). A pale, dry, Manzanilla sherry from Findlaters.

Luncheon Ale (Eng). A Bitter ale 1034 O.G. brewed by the Home Brewery in Nottingham.

Luncheon Dry (Sp). A very pale, dry, Fino sherry from Harvey in Jerez de la Frontera. See Harvey's of Bristol.

Lundetangen Brewery (Nor). A noted brewery based in Skien, southern Norway.

Lunel (Fr). A Vin doux naturel from the Hérault Département in southern France. Produced from the Muscatel grape. Also produce a VdL from same grape variety.

Lunense (Lat). A white wine produced in north-western Italy in Roman times.

Lungarotti (It). A winery based at Torgiano, Umbria. 260 ha. Noted for Rubesco Torgiano Riserva D.O.C. (A single vineyard cru).

Lungo Coffee (It). A weak version of Espresso coffee. See also Ristretto Coffee.

Lung Yen vineyard (China). A white wine-producing vineyard based in Peking.

Lupé-Cholet et Cie (Fr). A négociant-éleveur based in Nuits-Saint-Georges, Côte de Nuits, Burgundy.

Lupo Brauerei (Switz). A small brewery based in Hochdorf.

Luppolo (It). Hop.

Lupulin (Eng). The name given to the sticky yellow powder in the hop cone. Gives the bittering and preserving power to the hop.

Lúpulo (Port) (Sp). Hop.

Lurets (Les) (Fr). A Premier Cru vineyard [part] in the A.C. commune of Volnay, Côte de Beaune, Burgundy.

Lurton (André) (Fr). A noted négociant-éleveur based in Léognan, A.C. Graves, south-western Bordeaux.

Luscious (Eng). Descibes sweet, very rich and full-flavoured wines.

Lush (USA) (slang). A heavy drinker especially a female one (an alcoholic).

Lush (USA) (slang). The name given to the contraband liquor that was shipped to the USA during the Prohibition.

Lushai (Ind). A hardy variety of the Assam tea bush. Is noted for its large leaves.

Lu Shan Botanic Garden (China). Based

in the Szechwan province, it produces 'Cloud Mist' tea which originally was solely for the Emperor. Now served to Western V.I.P.s.

Lusitania (Cktl). 1 measure dry Vermouth, ½ measure Brandy, dash Pernod, dash Orange bitters. Shake over ice, strain into a cocktail glass.

Lussac-Saint-Émilion (Fr). An A.C. commune in eastern Bordeaux.

Lustadt (Ger). Village. (Anb) = Rheinpfalz. (Ber) = Südliche Weinstrasse (Gro) = Trappenberg. (Vin) = Klostergarten.

Lustau (Sp). A family-owned Sherry house in Jerez. Address = Plaza del Cubo 4, Apartado 193, Jerez de la Frontera. Range includes Oloroso Muy Viejo, Otaolaurruchi and bottled Almacenista sherries. See also Lustau (Emilio).

Lustau (Emilio) (Sp). A Brandy producer. Produces Señor Lustau. Also produces a fine range of sherries on Jerez de la Frontera under the Lustau label.

Lustav (Señor) (Sp). Brandy producer. Address = Plaza de Cubo, Jerez de la Frontera. Base wine from Jerez.

Lustrillo (Sp). A style of Albariza soil in the Jerez region. Is slightly red due to the presence of iron oxide. Is known as Polvillejo in Sanlúcar de Barrameda.

Lusty Brew (Eng). Denotes a strong beer or drink.

Lutèce Brasserie (Fr). A brewery based in Paris that produces an all-malt beer 5.6% alc. by vol. of same name.

Luter (Fr). A term used in the Champenois 'To drink well/To enjoy a drink'.

Lutmannburg (Aus). A wine-producing area in the Mattersburg district.

Lutomer Fruit Cup (Cup). 1 bottle Lutomer Riesling, 1 pint soda water, fruit in season. Place fruit in the wine and chill down. Add soda water prior to service.

Lutomer-Ormoz (Yug). A town and area of the Slovenia region. Welschriesling and Lutjomer riesling are best known wines. Also spelt Ljutomer-Ormoz.

Lutomer Riesling (Yug). A medium-dry, white wine with a delicate bouquet produced in Ljutomer, north-eastern Yugoslavia.

Lutry (Switz). A wine-producing district near Lavaux in central Vaud.

Luttenberger (Ger). The name used for Ljutomer in Yugoslavia before the First World War.

Lüttje Lage (Ger). Lit – 'Little one'. A small beer accompanied by a Korn (Snaps), the customary drink served at Schützenfest (is drunk simultaneously).

Lützelburg (Ger). Vineyard. (Anb) = Baden. (Ber) = Kaiserstuhl-Tuniberg. (Gro) = Vulkanfelsen. (Vil) = Sasbach.

Lützelsachsen (Ger). Village. (Anb) = Baden. (Ber) = Badische Bergstrasse/ Kraichgau. (Gro) = Rittersberg. (Vin) = Stephausberg.

Lützeltalerberg (Ger). vineyard. (Anb) = Franken. (Ber) = Mainviereck. (Gro) = Not yet assigned. (Vil) = Grosswallstadt.

Lutzville Co-operative (S.Afr). Based in Lutzville. Address = Box 50, Lutzville 8165. Produces Laat Oes and varietal wines.

Luxardo (It). A famous liqueur producer based in Padua. Noted for Maraschino.

Luxator (Lux). A dark Beer brewed by the Clausen Brasserie in Mousel.

Luxembourg (Lux). A small country whose small wine region follows the banks of the river Moselle. Produces mainly light, dry white wines. See Appellation Complète and Marque Nationale. Also produce fine Eaux-de-vies.

Luxembourgeois Moselle (Lux). A very light, sharp, often pétillan wine, almost colourless. It is light and has a cider scent.

Luxery Cocktail (Cktl). ⅓ measure Gin, ⅙ measure Banana liqueur, ⅙ measure Vermouth, ⅙ measure Pimm's Nº1, ⅙ measure lime cordial, dash Angostura. Shake over ice, strain into a cocktail glass.

Luxury Cocktail (Cktl). ⅓ gill Cognac, 2 dashes Orange bitters. Pour into a Champagne saucer glass. Top with iced Champagne.

Luxury Wine (Eng). A liqueur wine. e.g. Vin doux naturel and Vin de Liqueur.

Luzech (Fr). A wine-producing area in central Cahors, south-western France.

L.V.A. (Eng) (abbr). Licensed Vituallers Association. Body of Landlords (full On-licence holders) who wish to promote the interests of the 'Licensed trade'.

Lyaeus (Lat). A word used for Bacchus. See also Bassareus, Bromius, Dionysus, Euan, Euhius, Euius, Lacchus and Thyoneus.

Lychee (Cktl). See Lichee.

Lychee Chiew (China). A lychee-flavoured wine. It has a strength and taste similar to sweet Sherry.

Lydda (Isr). A white Palestinian wine written about by the Romans.

Lying-Arm (Ire). See Lyne Arm.

Lymington vineyard (Eng). A vineyard based at Furzay Cottage, Wainsford, Lymington, Hampshire. Grape varieties – Gutenborner, Huxelrebe, Müller-Thurgau and Schönburger.

Lympha (Lat). Water.

Lynch-Bages (Fr). See Château Lynch-Bages. The property gets its name from having once belonged to an Irishman called Lynch, Mayor of Bordeaux. Today it belongs to the Cazes family.

Lynchet (Eng). An old English name for the terrace on which vines were grown to get the best sun in England.

Lynch-Moussas (Fr). See Château Lynch-Moussas. The property gets its name from having once belonged to an Irishman called Lynch, Mayor of Bordeaux.

Lyndale (Austr). A brand of white riesling wine produced by Orlando Winery.

Lyne Arm (Ire). Part of the Pot-still. A long, horizontal portion of the Still-head in which it lies submerged in a shallow trough filled with water, between the Still-head and the Condenser. Also known as the Lying-arm.

Lynfred Winery (USA). A winery based in Roselle, Illinois. Produces French hybrid, vinifera and native grape wines.

Lynx Lager (Eng). An 'own label' canned Lager beer from the Booker Cash and Carry. Address = Malt House, P.O. Box 65, Field End, Eastcote, Ruislip, Middlesex. HA4 9LA.

Lyonnaise Blanche (Fr). An alternative name for the Muscadet grape in south-eastern France.

Lyons Tetley (Eng). A famous firm noted for their wide range of teas and coffees.

Lyophilization (Eng). A method of freeze-drying freshly brewed coffee to make instant coffee.

Lys (Den). Light-coloured beer.

Lys (Les) (Fr). A Premier Cru A.C. Chablis often reclassified as the Premier Cru Vaillons.

Lysander (Cyp). The brand-name of a medium-sweet Cyprus sherry.

Lysholm Aquavit (Nor). A light, delicate brand of Aquavit which is matured in new Sherry casks. Produced by Vinmonopolet.

Lysine (Eng). An Amino acid found in wines. Formed by the yeasts.

Lytton Springs Winery (USA). A winery based near Healdsburg, Sonoma County, California. Grape variety – Zinfandel. Valley Vista is its home vineyard.

M

M.A. (Fr) (abbr). Marque Anonyme, Marque Autorisée, Marque Auxiliaire, Marque d'Acheteur. Denotes any subsidiary name belonging to an establishment responsible for marketing Champagne that has been made by another producer, or made by a grower registered by C.I.V.C.

MA (Wales). A mixture of SA and Dark. Produced by the Brain's Brewery in Cardiff for The Crown public house in Skewen, near Swansea.

Mabille (Fr). The name for the Horizontal press.

Maborange (Fr). An orange liqueur produced by Intermarque.

Macabeo (Fr). A white grape variety grown in the south of Spain. Is also known as Alcañol, Alcanón and Viura. Also spelt Maccabéo.

Macacauba (Port). Brazilian mahogany from which Port vats are made, (together with oak and chestnut).

Macaco (Port). Lit – 'Monkey'. It is a wooden contrivance used to keep the must moving up and down in the Lagares.

Macallan (The) (Scot). A single Malt whisky distillery at Craigellachie in Morayshire. A Highland malt. Produces – 10 year old malt, 15 year old malt, Vintage 1963, 1950 and 1938 at 43% alc. by vol. Also for the Royal Wedding a blend of 1948 and 1961 single malts (birth years) and The Macallan 60 year old (the most expensive Malt whisky).

Macallan (The) [60 Year Old] (Scot). As yet the world's most expensive whisky produced by Macallan. Sold in a specially designed box of glass and brass (spirit safe shaped). Limited quantities.

Macallan-Glenlivet (Scot). A single Malt whisky distillery based west of Rothes, Morayshire. A Highland malt. Produces Macallan 80°, also a 10 year old and a 25 year old. 45% alc. by vol.

Macardles Brewery (Ire). Based in Dundalk. Is part of Guinness-controlled Irish Ale Breweries. Produces keg and bottled ales.

Macaroni Cocktail (Cktl). ⅔ measure Pastis, ⅓ measure sweet Vermouth. Shake over ice, strain into a cocktail glass.

MacArthurs (Scot). A selected blended Scotch whisky from Airdrie, Lanarkshire. 40% alc. by vol. Produced by Inver House Distillers.

Macau (Fr). A commune within the A.C. Haut-Médoc in north-western Bordeaux.

Maccabee (Isr). A Lager beer 12° Balling brewed by a Canadian-financed brewery.

Maccabéo (Fr). The alternative spelling of Macabeo used in south-western France.

Macca Cocktail (Cktl). ⅓ measure dry Gin, ⅓ measure dry Vermouth, ⅓ measure sweet Vermouth, 2 dashes Crème de Cassis. Stir over ice, strain into an ice-filled highball glass. Top with soda water, dash of lemon peel juice and a lemon peel spiral.

Macchinetta da Caffé (It). Coffee mill.

MacDonald and Muir (Scot). Highland malt whisky distillers based near Tain. Own Glenmorangie and Glenmoray-Glenlivet Distilleries. Brands include Highland Queen, Muirheads, Glenmoray and Glenmorangie.

MacDonald Greenlees (Scot). A Scotch whisky distiller based at Leith, Midlothian. Produces Old Parr 43% alc. by vol. Part of DCL. Glendullan Distillery still is licensed to MacDonald Greenlees.

MacDuff (Scot). A single Malt whisky distillery in Banffshire. A Highland malt. Produces a vintage 1963. Sometimes sold under the name of Glendeveron. 40% alc. by vol.

Macedonia (Gre). A wine region of northern Greece.

Macedonia (Yug). A high mountainous region of southern Yugoslavia. Produces white, rosé and red wines, low in acidity and high in alcohol.

Maceratino (It). A white wine grape variety grown in the Marches region.

Maceration (Eng). Used in the making of aromatised wines and liqueurs. Herbs etc. are steeped in the wine/spirit to extract the flavour.

Macération Carbonique (Fr). A method of fermentation where the whole grapes are placed into large sealed vats under a slight pressure and allowed to ferment for 4 days before pressing. (Fermentation is then completed). This method produces light wines with plenty of colour and fruit without the tannin. e.g. Beaujolais Nouveau.

Macération Semi-Carbonique (Fr). See Intercellular Fermentation.

Machackala (USSR). A wine region based on the Caspian Sea that produces mainly dessert wines.

Machanudo Fino Inocente (Sp). A brand of Fino sherry produced by Valdespino in Jerez de la Frontera.

Macharnudo (Sp). Chalk soil. Area of Andalusia. See also Marchanudo.

Machatten (Cktl). 1½ ozs. Scotch Whisky, 1 oz. sweet Martini, ½ oz. Glayva, dash Angostura. Stir over ice, strain into an old-fashioned glass. Add a cherry.

Mâché (Fr). Lit – 'Mashed'. Denotes a disturbed, unsettled wine.

Macherelles (Les) (Fr). A Premier Cru vineyard [part] in the A.C. commune of Chassagne-Montrachet, Côte de Beaune, Burgundy. 8.01 ha. (red and white).

Machinetta (It). The alternative name for the Neapolitain Pot coffee-making method.

Machtum (Lux). A wine village on the river Moselle. Sites are Ongkaf and Gollebour.

Mack Brewery (Nor). A noted brewery based in Tromsø. Is the most northerly brewery in the world.

Mackenson's Stout (Eng). A bottled sweet Stout 1042 O.G. brewed by Whitbread.

Mackenzie (Port). Vintage Port shippers. Vintages – 1870, 1873, 1875, 1878, 1881, 1884, 1887, 1890, 1896, 1900, 1904, 1908, 1912, 1919, 1920, 1922, 1927, 1935, 1945, 1947, 1948, 1950, 1952, 1954, 1955, 1957, 1958, 1960, 1963, 1966.

Mackenzie (Scot). A blended Scotch whisky. 40% alc. by vol.

MacKinlay and Co (Charles) (Scot). A fine Whisky producer now owned by Invergordon Distillers. Produces Highland malts and blended Scotch whiskies. These include Glenallachie, Isle of Jura, Legacy and The Original Mackinley.

Mackinlay-McPherson (W.Ind). A distiller based in Jamaica. Produces Windjammer (a dark, navy Rum).

MacKinlay's (Scot). A blended Scotch Whisky produced by Charles MacKinlay and Co. Now owned by Invergordon Distillers.

MacKinlay's Legacy (Scot). A 12 year old De Luxe blended Scotch Whisky blended by Donald MacKinlay. Produced by Charles MacKinlay and Co. Now owned by Invergordon Distillers. 40% alc. by vol.

Mackinlay's Vatted Old Ben Vorlich (Scot). The first proprietary brand of Scotch whisky produced by Charles Mackinlay and Co. Now owned by Invergordon Distillers.

Mackintosh (The) (Scot). The brand-name for a blended Scotch whisky produced by Hiram Walker. 40% alc. by vol.

Maclay's Brewery (Scot). A brewery based in Alloa. Produces cask conditioned, keg and bottled Ales. Noted for Imperial Pale Ale 1030 O.G.

Mâcon (Fr). A district within the Burgundy region. Produces classic white wines and some red. Communes = Boyer, Bresse-sur-Grosne, Champagny-sous-Uxelles, Champlieu, Etringy, Jugy, Laives, Mancey, Montceaux-Ragny, Nanton, Sennecey-le-Grand (Vers). See also Pouilly Fuissé, Pouilly-Loché, Pouilly-Vinzelles and Saint-Véran.

Mâconnais Blanc (Fr). A.C. white wine from the Mâcon district in the Burgundy region, minimum alc. by vol. 10%.

Mâconnaise (Fr). An 80 cls. bottle (1.825 pints) used in the Mâconnais region.

Mâconnaise (Fr). A wine cask of 212 litres (58 gallons) used in the Mâconnais region.

Mâcon-Rouge (Fr). An A.C. red wine from the Mâconnais region of southern Burgundy. Minimum alc. by vol. 9%.

Mâcon Supérieur (Fr). Red and white A.C. wines from Sâone-et-Loire in the Mâconnais district in Burgundy.

Mâcon Villages (Fr). A.C. commune within the district of Mâconnais in Burgundy. The name of the commune may replace the name of the village.

Mâcon-Viré (Fr). See Viré.

Macphail's (Scot). A Highland malt whisky produced by Gordon Macphail in Elgin. 43% alc. by vol.

Mac's Brown Ale (Eng). A bottled Brown ale 1031 O.G. brewed by the McMullen Brewery of Hertford.

Mac's Folly (Cktl). Pour into a large jug 1 bottle Gin, 1 measure dry Vermouth. Add plenty of ice, stir and serve.

Mac's N°1 (Eng). A keg/bottled Ale 1036 O.G. brewed by the McMullens Brewery in Hertford.

Maculan (It). A winery based at Breganze in Veneto. 11 ha. Also buys in grapes. Wines sold under Breganze label.

Macvin (Fr). A liqueur from the Jura. Newly fermented red wine is mixed with

Marc, cinnamon and corriander. Also spelt Maquevin.

Màd (Hun). A wine-producing village in the southern foothills.

Madame Goupil (Fr). A noted wine-producer based at Dampierre-sur-Loire, Saumur, Anjou-Saumur, Loire. Noted for Saumur Mousseux.

Madargues (Fr). A sub-appellation of V.D.Q.S. Côtes d'Auvergne region.

Mädchentraube (Aus). A red grape variety rarely grown now.

Madder-Wort (Eng). See Garance.

Madeira (Mad). An island in the Atlantic ocean off the north-western coast of Africa. Belonging to Portugal, it is noted for its fine fortified wines. See Estufado and Zarco (João Gonçalves). Lit – 'Wood'. See also Tossed Wines.

Madeira (Mad). A fortified wine from the island of Madeira. Produced by the Estufado method and Solera system of blending. (Fr) = Madère, (Hol) = Madeira.

Madeira (USA). See California Madeira.

Madeira Cake (Eng). A British invention. Cake eaten with Madeira wine. Does not have Madeira wine in the recipe and is not from the island of Madeira.

Madeira Cup (Cup). Into a large jug place some ice, juice of a lemon, ½ gill Mandarine liqueur, 1 bottle Sercial Madeira, 1 bottle soda water. Stir well and decorate with slices of lemon and borage.

Madeira Guinada (Mad). A style of Madeira laced with quinine that was originally sold to the British army in the nineteenth century.

Madeira Mint Flip (Cktl). ⅓ gill Bual Madeira, ⅛ gill Royal Mint Chocolate Liqueur, 3 dashes Gomme syrup, 1 egg. Shake well over ice, strain into a large cocktail glass. Top with grated nutmeg and chocolate.

Madeira Wine Company (Mad). A group of 27 major Madeira producers who joined forces to market Madeira wine. Founded in 1913.

Madeira Wine Institute (Mad). Known as the I.V.M. Formed in 1979. Fixes the dates for start of harvest, banned the use of hybrid direct producer grapes for use in Madeira. Grants 'Selo de Garantia', runs laboratory tests. See Instituto do Vinho da Madeira.

Madeleine Angevine (Ger). A white grape variety. Also known as Angevine.

Madeleine Collignon (Fr). A cuvée in the vineyard of Mazis-Chambertin, Grand Cru A.C. Gevrey-Chambertin, Côte de Nuits, Burgundy. 1.5 ha. Is owned by the Hospices de Beaune.

Madera (Hol). Madeira.

Madera (USA). A wine district within the Great Central Valley that produces sweet dessert wines.

Madère (Fr). Madeira.

Mader et Fils (Fr). An Armagnac producer based in Ténarèze. Address = Chemin de Ronde, 32190-Vic-Fezensac.

Maderisé (Fr). The term for white or rosé wines that have begun to spoil. It is caused by the wines contact with heat, oxygen or air. Makes the wine taste unpleasant, flat and musty. Not to be confused with Madeira.

Maderization (Eng). See Maderisé.

Maderize (Eng). See Maderisé.

Made Wines (USA). Wines made from preserved musts or dried raisins and not from freshly gathered grapes. See also British Wine.

Madhulika (Ind). A spirit made from wheat.

Madhvi (Sri.L). The name given to an Arrack made from Mahua flowers. Also called Daru spirit.

Madilla (W.Ind). The middle part of the distillation of Rum. (The heart of the spirit). See also Aguardiente.

Madiran (Fr). A.C. red wine of the Béarn, Basses Pyrénées Département. A little white Madiran is also made. Grapes – Acheria rouge, Cabernet franc, Cabernet sauvignon, Finenc and Tannat. Minimum alc. by vol. 11%.

Madone (La) (Fr). A fine vineyard in the A.C. Fleurie Cru Beaujolais-Villages.

Madonnenberg (Ger). vineyard. (Anb) = Baden. (Ber) = Badische Bergstrasse/ Kraichgau. (Gro) = Rittersberg. (Vil) = Schriesheim.

Madre (It). The name given to the wine kept in the cask from the previous bottling to which the next Vin Santo is added.

Madre (Sp). Bunch of grapes.

Madrear (Sp). A term denoting the throwing of the complete bunch of grapes into the wine that has fermented to create a second fermentation.

Madre Pulque (Mex). Lit – 'Mother pulque'. The fermentation of pulques after 10 days of slow fermentation.

Madre Vino (It). Used to sweeten dessert wines. New must boiled to a syrup consistency.

Madre Wines (Port). Used to sweeten dessert wines. New must boiled to a syrup consistency.

Madrid Pact (Sp). See Protection of Names.

Madrigal (Ger). Bottle size. 35 cls. (¾ pint).

Madroñales (Sp). An area within Andalusia. vineyards produce the grapes for Sherry.

Madrona vineyards (USA). A vineyard based in the Sierra Foothills, California.

M

Grape varieties – Cabernet sauvignon and Zinfandel. Produce varietal wines.

Madulsa (Lat). Drunkard.

Madura (W.Ind). An orange liqueur made in Martinique.

Maduro (Port). An old or matured wine.

Maduva (W.Ind). An orange-flavoured spirit drink produced on the island of Martinique.

Maes Brasserie (Bel). Owned by Watney, Mann and Truman. Noted for its Pils and Grimbergen (an Abbaye style beer).

Maestro (El) (Sp). The name given to a large cask known in the nineteenth century as El Cristo.

Maestro Vino (Sp). Lit – 'Master wine'. Used for adding colour to Màlaga wine.

Magarach Research Centre (USSR). An experimental station based at Yalta that tries to improve the quality of wines.

Magazzin (It). A noted distiller of Maraschino and other liqueurs.

Magdala (Chile). A soft red wine produced by Torres mainly from the Pinot noir grape.

Magdalen (Eng). A white table wine produced by the Pulham vineyards in Diss, Norfolk.

Magdalenenkreuz (Ger). Vineyard. (Anb) = Rheingau. (Ber) = Johannisberg. (Gro) = Burgweg. (Vil) = Rüdesheim.

Magdelaine (Fr). See Château Magdelaine.

Magdelen Rivaner (Eng). A white wine made from the Müller-Thurgau grape produced by the Pulham vineyards in Norfolk.

Mager (Ger). Thin, lacking in body, an undistinguished wine.

Maggi (It). A sparkling (méthode champenoise) wine producer based in Lombardy. Labels include Cristal Pinot Brut.

Magical (Sp). The brand-name for a range of Sherries produced by the Bodegas Magical in Jerez de la Frontera.

Magic Trace (Cktl). 1/10 measure Bourbon whiskey, 1/10 measure lemon juice, 1/10 measure orange juice, 1/10 measure dry Vermouth, 3/10 measure Drambuie. Shake over ice, strain into a cocktail glass.

Magie (Eng). A species of Barley (malt) from the Golden Promise variety. Gives medium sugar yields.

Maglieri (Austr). A winery based in Clare-Watervale, Southern Vales, South Australia. Produces varietal wines.

Magliocco (It). A red grape variety grown in Calabria. The local name for the Gaglioppo grape.

Magliocco Canino (It). A white grape variety grown in Savuto, Calabria.

Magnet Beer (Eng). The name given to the keg Bitter 1040 O.G. bottled Pale ale 1040 O.G. and the Old Ale 1070 O.G. brewed by the John Smith's Brewery, Tadcaster, Yorkshire.

Magnifico (It). A slightly bulbous-shaped bottle used by Ruffino in the Chianti region which is capable of improving the maturing of the wine.

Magno (Sp). A 5 year old, dark and sweet Brandy produced by Osborne.

Magnolia (Cktl). 1/2 gill Brandy, 1 tablespoon Curaçao, yolk of egg, 1 tablespoon sugar syrup. Shake well over ice, strain into a highball glass, top with iced Champagne.

Magnum (Fr). A double bottle used in Champagne, Burgundy = 52 fl.ozs. Bordeaux = 48 fl.ozs.

Magnum (USA). Bottle 1.5 litres (50.72 US fl.ozs).

Magnus (Hol). A Trappist double-style beer 6.5% alc. by vol. brewed by the Arcen Brouwerij in Arcen, Limburg.

Mago (Afr). A noted ancient Tunisian author who wrote a manual for vine-growers in the fourth century B.C.

Magret (Fr). An alternative name for the Malbec grape.

Magrico (Port). The name for a dry white Vinho Verde from Minho.

Maguey Cactus (Mex). A plant used to make Pulque from which Tequila is distilled.

Magyar Àllami Pincegazdasàg (Hun). Hungarian State Cellars.

Magyar Rosé (Hun). Very light rosé wine from the Pécs-Villàny region.

Mahewu (Afr). A thick fermented mealie-meal (fine ground maize) porridge drink. Is drunk as a stimulant.

Mahia (Afr). An Eau-de-Vie made from figs and served as an apéritif in Tunisia. Also known as Boukha.

Mahlberg (Ger). Village. (Anb) = Baden. (Ber) = Breisgau. (Gro) = Schutterlindenberg. (Vin) = Haselstaude.

Mähler-Besse (Fr). A Dutch wine négociant-éleveur based in Bordeaux. Part owner of Château Palmer. Address = 49, Rue Camille Godard, 33026 Bordeaux.

Mahogany (Cktl). 1 measure Bols Crème de Cacao over ice, top with Coca Cola.

Mahogany (Cktl). 1/3 measure treacle, 1/3 measure dry Gin. Stir until dissolved.

Mahui Fizz (Cktl). 1 1/2 fl.ozs. white Rum, 1 egg, 4 fl.ozs. pineapple juice, 1/2 fl.oz. Gomme syrup. Blend together with a scoop of crushed ice. Pour into a Champagne saucer, dress with a cherry and a pineapple cube. Serve with straws.

Mahzen (Tur). Cellar.

Maia (Bul) (Yug) (Gre). A name given in the

M

Balkans to milk that has been soured by a previous fermentation.

Maiberg (Ger). vineyard. (Anb) = Hessische Bergstrasse. (Ber) = Starkenburg. (Gro) = Schlossberg. (Vil) = Heppenheim including Erbach and Hambach.

Maibock (Ger). A Bavarian Bock beer developed by the Hofbrauhaus. Is brewed to celebrate maytime celebrations.

Maiden Oak Brewery (Ire). A Northern Ireland brewery set up in 1985 in Londonderry.

Maiden's Blush (Cktl).(1). ½ gill Gin, 2 dashes Oxygénée, 1 tablespoon Grenadine. Shake over ice, strain into a 5 oz. wine goblet.

Maiden's Blush (Cktl).(2). ½ measure Pernod, 1 measure dry Gin, ½ measure lemon juice, dash Grenadine, dash Gomme syrup. Shake over ice, strain into a cocktail glass.

Maiden's Prayer (Cktl). ⅜ measure dry Gin, ⅜ measure Cointreau, ⅛ measure orange juice, ⅛ measure lemon juice. Shake over ice, strain into a cocktail glass.

Maid of Erin Cocktail (Cktl). ⅓ measure Brandy, ⅓ measure Royal Mint Chocolate Liqueur, ⅓ measure cream. Shake over ice, strain into a cocktail glass.

Maidstone Ale (Eng). A Best Bitter 1040 O.G. brewed by the Goacher Brewery in Maidstone, Kent.

Maidstone Light Ale (Eng). A Light ale 1036 O.G. brewed by the Goacher Brewery in Maidstone, Kent.

Maie (Fr). A name given to the traditional Champagne press.

Maien (Ger). vineyard. (Anb) = Württemberg. (Ber) = Remstal-Stuttgart. (Gro) = Wartbühl. (Vil) = Hanweiler.

Maienfels (Ger). Village. (Anb) = Württemberg. (Ber) = Württembergisch Unterland. (Gro) = Lindelberg. (Vin) = Schneckenhof.

Maigre (Fr). A term to denote a thin, feeble wine.

Maikammer (Ger). Village. (Anb) = Rheinpfalz. (Ber) = Südliche Weinstrasse. (Gro) = Mandelhöhe. (Vins) = Heiligenberg, Immengarten, Kirchenstück.

Maikammer-Alsterweiler (Ger). Village. (Anb) = Rheinpfalz. (Ber) = Südliche Weinstrasse. (Gro) = Mandelhöhe. (Vin) = Kapellenberg.

Mailaender Bergbräu Brauerei (Ger). A brewery based in Fürth which brews a copper-red beer known as Kupferstube (a malty bottom-fermented beer, coloured with smoky, roasted malts).

Mailberg (Aus). A village which gives its name to a light wine from the district of Weinviertel. Also the home to Malteser, a wine produced by Lenz Moser.

Mailly-Champagne (Fr). A Grand Cru Champagne village in the Canton de Verzy. District = Reims. Has a large co-operative producing wines under the Mailly name. Vintages – 1928, 1929, 1932, 1934, 1936, 1945, 1948, 1950, 1955, 1960, 1961, 1966, 1969, 1970, 1973, 1975, 1976, 1979, 1982, 1983. See Champagne Société de Producteurs Mailly-Champagne.

Mailly Rosé (Fr). A non-vintage rosé Champagne produced by Champagne Société de Producteurs, Mailly-Champagne from 100% Pinot noir grapes.

Main (Ger). An Untergebiet of the Bayern district.

Mainbrace (Cktl). ⅓ measure Gin, ⅓ measure Cointreau, ⅓ measure grapefruit juice. Shake over ice, strain into a cocktail glass.

Mainbrace (W.Ind). The brand-name of a Demerara rum matured by Allied Breweries in England.

Maindreieck (Ger). Lit – 'Main triangle'. A Bereich within the region of Franconia. Soil of coarse limestone with some overlay of Loess.

Maindreieck (Ger). Bereich. (Anb) = Franken. (Gros) = Burg, Ewig Leben, Hofrat, Honigberg, Kirchberg, Ravensberg, Rosstal. With some vineyards that have not yet been assigned Grosslagen.

Maine-et-Loire (Fr). A Vins de Pays area in the Maine-et-Loire Département, western France (part of the Jardin de la France). Produces red, rosé and dry white wines.

Maingold (Ger). A full-bodied Lager beer 5.3% alc. by vol. brewed by the Kulmbacher Mönschof Brauerei in Bavaria.

Mainhölle (Ger). vineyard. (Anb) = Franken. (Ber) = Mainviereck. (Gro) = Not yet assigned. (Vil) = Bürgstadt.

Mainleite (Ger). vineyard. (Anb) = Franken. (Ber) = Maindreieck. (Gro) = Not yet assigned. (Vil) = Schweinfurt.

Main-Riesling (Ger). A white grape variety grown in Franconia. A cross between the Rheinriesling and the Sylvaner. Also known as the Rieslaner.

Mainstay (S.Afr). The brand-name of a leading double-distilled Cane spirit.

Mainstockheim (Ger). Village. (Anb) = Franken. (Ber) = Maindreieck. (Gro) = Hofrat. (Vin) = Hofstück.

Mainviereck (Ger). Lit – 'Main rectangle'. A Bereich within the region of Franconia. Has a sandstone soil.

M

Mainviereck (Ger). Bereich. (Anb) = Franken. (Gros) = Heiligenthal, Reuschberg.

Mainxe (Fr). A commune in the Charente Département whose grapes are classed Grande Champagne (Cognac).

Mainz (Ger). Village. (Anb) = Rheinhessen. (Ber) = Nierstein. (Gro) = Sankt Alban. (Vins) = Edelmann, Hüttberg, Johannisberg, Kirchenstück, Klosterberg, Sand, Weinkeller.

Mainz-Drais (Ger). Village. (Anb) = Rheinhessen. (Ber) = Nierstein. (Gro) = Domherr. (Vins) = Sites not yet chosen.

Mainzerweg (Ger). (Anb) = Rheinhessen. (Ber) = Bingen. (Gro) = Sankt Rochuskapelle. (Vil) = Dromersheim.

Mainzer Weinmarkt (Ger). A Rheinhessen wine festival held in Mainz in August-September.

Mainz-Finthen (Ger). Village. (Anb) = Rheinhessen. (Ber) = Nierstein. (Gro) = Domherr. (Vins) = Sites not yet chosen.

Maipo (Chile). A principal wine region of Central Chile. Produces good, sound table wines.

Maipú (Arg). A wine-producing area in the Mendoza region.

Maïre (Ch.Isles). Lees.

Maire et Fils (Fr). A négociant-éleveur based in Beaune, Côte de Beaune, Burgundy. Owns Domaine de Château de la Tour.

Maire [Henri] (Fr). A négociant-éleveur based in the Jura region of eastern France.

Maische (Ger). Grape pulp.

Maisdon (Fr). A village in the central area of A.C. Muscadet de Sèvre et Maine. Produces some of the finest wines of the region.

Maison Albert Bichot (Fr). See Bichot (Albert et Cie).

Maison-Blanche (Fr). A vineyard in the A.C. Hermitage, northern Rhône.

Maison-Brûlée (Fr). A Premier Cru vineyard in the A.C. commune of Morey-Saint-Denis, Côte de Nuits, Burgundy.

Maison du Vin, Allée Marine (Fr). One of four Maisons du Vin in Bordeaux. Based in Blaye.

Maison du Vin, Château des Ducs d'Epernon (Fr). One of four Maisons du Vin in Bordeaux. Based in Cadillac.

Maison du Vin d'Anjou (Fr). Based at Boulevard Foch, Anger in the Loire and provides a full history of wine production.

Maison du Vin de Bordeaux (Fr). One of four Maisons du Vin in Bordeaux. Based in Bordeaux. Is also the home of the C.I.V.B. Bordeaux.

Maison du Vin, Quai Ferchaud (Fr). One of four Maisons du Vin in Bordeaux. Based at Pauillac.

Maisons (Fr). A Champagne shipper's name for their office-cum-cellars-cum-factory.

Maisons Marques et Domaines (Eng). A new U.K. company created by Louis Roederer (Champagne) and Bouchard Père et Fils (Burgundy).

Mai Tai (Cktl). 1 oz. white Rum, ½ oz. Curaçao, ½ oz. Orgeat, ½ oz. lime juice, ½ teaspoon sugar, 1 oz. Grenadine. Shake over ice, strain into a large cocktail glass 'on the rocks'. Dress with fresh pineapple and a maraschino cherry.

Mai-Tai (Cktl). ½ pint orange juice, 3 dashes Angostura, 2 dashes almond essence, 8 fl.ozs. Gomme syrup. Blended together, it is used as an ingredient for certain cocktails.

Maitina (W.Ind). An orange-flavoured spirit drink produced on the island of Martinique.

Maitrank (Ger). A drink made in the Spring from white wine, Brandy and woodruff.

Maître de Chai (Fr). Cellar-master.

Maître des Échansons (Fr). A wine society based in Reuilly, Loire.

Maître Sommelier (Fr). Head wine-waiter.

Maiwein (Ger). Aromatised wine made with sweet woodruff flowers (Galum Odoratum) in May. It is normally made in German households.

Majaela (Sp). A red grape variety grown in the Navarra region, north-eastern Spain.

Majărcă (Rum). A white grape variety grown in Banat vineyard for production of white wines in Teremia Mare and Tomnatec.

Majestic (Eng). A large retail wine warehouse with nine outlets.

Majnoni-Guicciardini (It). A producer of Chianti Putto in Tuscany.

Major Bailey Cocktail (Cktl). Place 12 mint leaves in an old-fashioned glass with ½ teaspoon sugar, juice ¼ lime and ¼ lemon. Muddle well. Add ice and ⅓ gill Gin. Dress with mint leaves and serve with straws.

Majorca (Sp). An island off the Catalonian coast that produces average drinking wines. Part of the Balearic Islands.

Major P.R. Reid's (Scot). A single Malt whisky distilled at the Glen Mhor Distillery. A Highland malt. 14 year old. 45.8% alc. by vol.

Majuelo (Sp). The name given to wine

M

pressed from grapes grown on young vines.
Makanissa (Afr). A winery based in northern Ethiopia.
Make Believe (Cktl). ½ fl.oz. Marasquin, ¼ fl.oz. white Rum, ⅛ fl.oz. Framboise, ⅛ fl.oz. pineapple juice. Shake over ice, strain into a cocktail glass. Top with a cherry.
Makelaar (Hol). Wine-broker.
Maker's Mark (USA). The brand-name of a Bourbon whiskey 50% alc by by vol. produced by the Star Hill Distillery in Loretta, Kentucky.
Makheras (Cyp). A region on the eastern side of the Troodos mountain range that produces fine wines.
Malabor (Ind). A coffee-producing region in northern India.
Malacate (Sp). An old method of soil preparation using mules which turn a Noria wheel attached to a cable which in turn pulls a large plough. Still used in Jerez.
Maladière (La) (Fr). A Premier Cru vineyard in the A.C. commune of Santenay, Côte de Beaune, Burgundy.
Málaga (Sp). A coastal wine region in southern Spain. Produces sweet, dark, fortified dessert wines from the Pedro Ximénez and Moscatel grapes. See Axarquía, Lágrima, Malligo, Mountain and Zareas-Antequera.
Malaga (USA). A red grape variety used in the making of dessert wines in California. Also known as the Cinsault and related to the Sémillon.
Malaga (USA). See California Malaga.
Málaga Blanco Dulce (Sp). A golden yellow, sweet style of Málaga.
Málaga Blanco Seco (Sp). A pale gold, dry style of Málaga.
Málaga Dulce Color (Sp). An extremely dark, sweet style of Málaga.
Málaga Golden White (Sp). A light-coloured, sweet style of Málaga.
Málaga Làgrima (Sp). A dark gold, very sweet style of Málaga.
Málaga Moscatel (Sp). An amber-coloured, sweet style of Málaga.
Málaga Negro (Sp). A very dark, sweet style of Málaga.
Málaga Pajarete (Sp). A strong, amber-coloured, sweet style of Málaga.
Málaga Rome (Sp). A strong red (or golden white) medium-dry style of Málaga.
Málaga Semi-Dulce (Sp). A yellow (or red) sweet style of Málaga.
Malagasy (Afr). The old name for the island of Madagascar off the south-west coast. Produces average white and red wines.

Malaka (Sp). The Phoenician name for Málaga.
Malamed's Brandy (S.Afr). The brand-name for a Kosher Brandy produced by Gilbey's S.A. under strict Rabbinical supervision of the Cape Beth Din.
Malamed's Wines (S.Afr). Kosher wines made by Gilbey's. Produced under strict Rabbinical supervision of the Cape Beth Din. Are varietal wines.
Malatya (Tur). A red and white wine-producing region in eastern Turkey.
Malaville (Fr). A commune in the Charente Département whose grapes are classed Grande Champagne (Cognac).
Malawi Carlsberg Lager (Afr). A Lager beer 10.9° Plato produced by the Carlsberg Brewery in association with the Malawi Government.
Malawi Teas (Afr). African teas used mainly for blending.
Malayan Breweries (Asia). A brewery based in Singapore which is noted for its Tiger Beers (Lager and Stout).
Malbec (Fr). A red grape variety grown in Bordeaux. A small percentage planted in a vineyard has been found beneficial if blended with Cabernet and Merlot. Known as the Noir de pressac in Pomerol. Is also known as the Cahors, Côt, Malbeck, Magret, Pied noir, Pied rouge, Prèchet and Séme.
Malbeck (It). A red grape variety used in Puglia. (Fr) = Malbec.
Maldano Egg Flip (Eng). An egg-based drink produced by Townend of Hull, Humberside.
Mâles (Les) (Fr). A vineyard in the A.C. commune of Montagny, Côte Chalonnaise, Burgundy.
Malescot-Saint-Exupéry (Fr). See Château Malescot-Saint-Exupéry.
Malessere (It). Hangover.
Malibu (Eng). A Jamaican rum-based coconut-flavoured liqueur produced by the Twelve Islands Shipping Co. Ltd. 28% alc. by vol.
Malibu Beach Cocktail (Cktl). 2 measures orange juice, ½ measure Vodka, dash Grenadine, dash lemon juice, dash egg white. Shake over ice, strain into a cocktail glass. Dress with a slice of lemon and orange.
Malibu Cocktail (Cktl). ⅓ gill Gin, ⅙ gill French vermouth, 1 teaspoon Absinthe, 1 teaspoon Angostura. Stir over ice, strain into cocktail glass. Decorate with olive and dash lemon peel juice.
Malic (Eng). A term used for an apple-flavoured wine.
Malic Acid (Eng). HOOCCH$_2$CH(OH)COOH. An acid found in fruits and

unripe grapes. Is destroyed as the fruit matures. See Malo-Latic Fermentation.

Maligny (Fr). A commune in the A.C. Chablis, northern Burgundy.

Malinda's vineyard (USA). A vineyard based in Ocala, Florida. Produces mainly Muscadine wines.

Maliniak (Pol). A honey and raspberry juice mead. Dark amber in colour, it is sold in bottles and earthenware jars.

Mali Plavać (Yug). A red grape variety.

Mallasjuoma Breweries (Fin). The largest brewers in Finland. Has breweries in Oulu (northern Finland) and in Heinola and Lahti (southern Finland).

Malleret (Fr). A Bordeaux Mousseux producer based in Saint-Émilion, eastern Bordeaux.

Mallersdorfer Klosterbrauerei (Ger). A noted brewery based in Bavaria.

Mallet Decanter (Eng). See Mallet Shape.

Mallet Shape (Eng). A style of decanter. Has six or eight sides and is shaped like a mallet. Popular in the eighteenth century, was used for Port wines.

Malliac (Fr). Armagnac producer. Address = Sté Fermière du Château de Malliac, Montréal du Gers.

Malligo Sack (Sp). An old name for Málaga wine.

Mallorca (Cktl).(1). ½ measure white Rum, ⅙ measure Drambuie, ⅙ measure dry Vermouth, ⅙ measure Crème de Banane. Stir over ice, strain into a cocktail glass

Mallorca (Cktl).(2). ½ measure Vodka, ¼ measure Grand Marnier, ¼ measure pineapple juice. Shake over ice, strain into a cocktail glass. Decorate with pieces of cherry, orange and lemon.

Malmaison Cocktail (Cktl). ⅕ gill white Rum, juice ½ lemon, ⅛ gill sweet Sherry. Shake well over ice, strain into a cocktail glass which is sugar-rimmed with anisette.

Malmesbury (S.Afr). A wine-producing centre of Swartland. Is noted for its dry white wines and distilleries.

Malmesey (Eng). The sixteenth-century spelling of Malmsey.

Malmsey (Mad). The sweetest of the Madeira wines. Is dark brown with a powerful bouquet and a honied, luscious taste. A true dessert wine. Made with the Malvoisie (Pinot gris) grape.

Malmsey (Mad). An alternative name for the Malvoisie (Pinot gris) grape.

Malmslay (Eng). An old seventeenth-century spelling of Malmsey.

Malmsly (Eng). An old seventeenth-century spelling of Malmsey.

Malm Soil (Eng). A soft limestone soil with some clay.

Malo-Lactic Bacteria (Eng). See Leuconostoc.

Malo-Lactic Fermentation (Eng). The conversion of malic acid into lactic acid which takes place after the normal fermentation. Usually takes place before wine is bottled but for some wines e.g. Vinho Verde is allowed to take place in bottle to give wine some pétillance. In most wine though has an adverse effect. Helps to reduce acidity in wine. See Lactobacillus.

Malsch (Ger). Village. (Anb) = Baden. (Ber) = Badische Bergstrasse/Kraichgau. (Gro) = Mannaberg. (Vins) = Ölbaum, Rotsteig.

Malschenberg (Ger). Village. (Anb) = Baden. (Ber) = Badische Bergstrasse/Kraichgau. (Gro) = Mannaberg. (Vin) = Ölbaum.

Malt (Eng). Barley which has been germinated and through enzyme action had the starch converted into Maltose. Used in brewing and whisky production. Gives body, flavour and if roasted adds colour to beer.

Malta (Euro). An island in the central Mediterranean Sea. Has approx. 2,000 ha. under vines. Grape varieties – Dun Tumas, Gannaru, Gellewza and Nigruwa. Produces ordinary wines for mainly home consumption.

Malt Cellar Range (Scot). Six Malt whiskies packaged together. Includes four Highlands (Linkwood, Lochnager, Strathconnan – a Vatted malt – and Talisker), one Lowland (Rosebank) and one Islay (Lagavulin).

Malt Culms (Scot). The alternative name given to the rootlets on the malting barley grains. Spent culms go for cattle food in Whisky production.

Malt Duck (USA). A strong beer flavoured with grape concentrate from the National Brewing Co. of Baltimore. (Owned by Carling).

Malte (Port). Malt.

Malted Barley (Eng). Barley soaked in water, allowed to germinate and convert, through enzyme action, the starch into Maltose. See Malt.

Malted Milk (Eng). A soluble powder made from dehydrated milk and malted cereals. A hot or cold drink is made from this. See Horlicks (most famous brand).

Malted Rice Fungus (Jap). See Aspergillus Oryzae.

Malterdingen (Ger). Village. (Anb) = Baden. (Ber) = Breisgau. (Gro) = Burg Lichteneck. (Vin) = Bienenberg.

Maltese Bartenders' Guild (Euro). M.B.G. Malta's Bartenders' Association. Address = P.O. Box 368, Valletta.

Malteser (Aus). The brand-name of a wine produced by Lenz Moser in Mailberg.

Maltesergarten (Ger). vineyard. (Anb) = Baden. (Ber) = Markgräflerland. (Gro) = Lorettoberg. (Vil) = Biengen.

Maltesergarten (Ger). vineyard. (Anb) = Baden. (Ber) = Markgräflerland. (Gro) = Lorettoberg. (Vil) = Buggingen.

Maltesergarten (Ger). vineyard. (Anb) = Baden. (Ber) = Markgräflerland. (Gro) = Lorettoberg. (Vil) = Eschbach.

Maltesergarten (Ger). vineyard. (Anb) = Baden. (Ber) = Markgräflerland. (Gro) = Lorettoberg. (Vil) = Heitersheim.

Maltesergarten (Ger). vineyard. (Anb) = Baden. (Ber) = Markgräflerland. (Gro) = Lorettoberg. (Vil) = Schlatt.

Maltesergarten (Ger). vineyard. (Anb) = Baden. (Ber) = Markgräflerland. (Gro) = Lorettoberg. (Vil) = Seefelden.

Maltesergarten (Ger). vineyard. (Anb) = Baden. (Ber) = Markgräflerland. (Gro) = Lorettoberg. (Vil) = Staufen (ortsteil Wetttelbrunn).

Maltesergarten (Ger). vineyard. (Anb) = Baden. (Ber) = Markgräflerland. (Gro) = Lorettoberg. (Vil) = Tunsel.

Malteserkreuz (Den). The brand-name for an Akvavit produced by DDS. 43% alc. by vol.

Malt Extract (Eng). Produced when the wort has been boiled under a very low pressure. The water content evaporates leaving a syrup containing the sugars extracted from the malt. Is used in the brewing process in place of Barley malt. (Fr) = Extrait de malt.

Maltezer (Hol). A Dortmunder-style beer 6.25% alc. by vol. brewed by the De Ridder Brouwerij in Maastricht, Limburg.

Malthouse (Eng). A keg/canned Ale 1033 O.G. brewed by the Hall and Woodhouse Brewery of Dorset.

Maltice (Czec). A wine district within the region of Bohemia. Produces some of the best wines of the region.

Malting[s] (Eng). A building where the malting of the barley takes place.

Malt Liquor (USA). An American beer that varies greatly between each producer from light pale beers to dark hoppy beers. Usually high in alcohol. Breaker and Colt are brands sold in G.B.

Malton Brewery (Eng). Opened in 1985 in Malton North Yorkshire. Noted for its cask conditioned Double Chance Bitter 1039 O.G.

Maltose (Eng). A fermentable sugar produced in germinated barley used for beer and whisky production. See Malt.

Maltroie (La) (Fr). A Premier Cru vineyard [part] in the A.C. commune of Chassagne-Montrachet, Côte de Beaune, Burgundy. 8.9 ha. (red and white).

Malts (Scot). A Scotch whisky made entirely from Malted barley.

Malt Shovel (Scot). A wooden shovel used to turn the germinating barley at floor maltings. Also used in England.

Maltster (Eng). An official who oversees the malting process. Also found in Scotland.

Malt Stout (Eng). A bottled Stout 1042 O.G. brewed by the Morrell's Brewery in Oxford.

Malt Syrup (Eng). A concentrated malt extract used in the mash to convert the grain. Called copper syrup when used in the copper to extend brew length or adjust the gravity.

Malt Tax (Eng). A tax collected by the Government until 1880 when Beer duty was introduced.

Malt Vinegar (Eng). Alegar. Produced from a malt brew (less hops) which has been attacked by Acetobacter.

Malt Whisky (Scot). A Whisky made from malted barley only. See Single Malt Whisky.

Malt Wine (Hol). Second distillate of Hollands Gin at a proof between 50–55% alc. by vol.

Malvagia (Euro). Another name for the Pinot gris grape. See also Malmsey, Malvasia and Malvoisie.

Malvar (Sp). A white grape variety grown in the central areas of Spain

Malvasia (Euro). A famous ancient white grape from Greece. Now grown in most other wine-producing countries. Originally known as the Monemvasia. (Fr) = Pinot gris.

Malvasia Babosa (Mad). A white noble grape used in Malmsey production along with Malvasia candida and Malvasiāo.

Malvasia Bianca (USA). A white grape variety used in the making of dessert wines in California.

Malvasia Bianca di Candia (It). A white grape variety grown in the Tuscany region.

Malvasia Bianca Toscana (It). A white grape variety grown in the Tuscany region.

Malvasia Branca (Port). A white grape variety used in the making of Port wine.

Malvasia Candiae (It). The old name for the wines of Crete in the thirteenth century. See Candia.

Malvasia Candida (Mad). A white noble grape variety used in Malmsey production along with Malvasia babosa and Malvasiāo.

Malvasia Corada (Port). An alternative spelling of Malvasia Corado.

Malvasia Corado (Port). A white grape variety used in the making of Port wine. Used because of its high sugar content.

Malvasia del Chianti (It). A white grape variety grown in the Tuscany region.

Malvasia del Lazio (It). A white grape variety used in Latium.

Malvasia delle Lipari (It). D.O.C. white wine from the Aeolian Isles, north of Sicily. Made from the Corinto nero and Malvasia di Lipari grapes. Also a Passito type made which must have a minimum alc. content of 18% and 6° natural sugar.

Malvasia delle Lipari Liquoroso (It). A fortified wine produced on the Aeolian Isles north of Sicily. Produced by partially drying the grapes to produce a maximum of 60% of wine to be fortified. The finished product must have a minimum alc. content of 20% alc. by vol. of which 16% is natural and at least 6% residual sugar. Wine aged for a minimum of 6 months.

Malvasia de Sitges (Sp). A sweet white wine produced around the little port of Sitges in the Penedés district of Cataluña in south-eastern Spain.

Malvasia di Bosa (It). D.O.C. white wine from Sardinia. Made from the Malvasia di sardegna grapes. Cannot be sold to consumer before 2 years old. Four types produced – Secco, Dolce naturale, Liquoroso dolce naturale, Liquoroso secco.

Malvasia di Cagliari (It). D.O.C. white wine from Sardinia. Made from the Malvasia di sardegna grape within the entire province of Cagliari. 4 types – Secco, Dolce naturale, Liquoroso secco and Liquoroso dolce naturale. Last two are entitled to the designation Riserva if aged 2 years (1 year in wooden casks). The ageing period commences from the date of fortification.

Malvasia di Candia (It). A white grape variety grown in the Emilia-Romagna region.

Malvasia di Casorzo (It). A red grape variety grown in the Piemonte region to make a wine of same name.

Malvasia di Casorzo d'Asti (It). D.O.C. red and rosé wines from Piemonte. Made from 10% Barbera, Freisa and Grignolino and 90% Malvasia di Casorzo grapes. The D.O.C. also applies to the sparkling wine made from musts or wines obtained from grapes in the production area.

Malvasia di Castelnuovo Don Bosco (It). D.O.C. red wine from Piemonte region.

Made from the Malvasia di Schierano grape plus 15% of Freisa. D.O.C. also applies to fully sparkling wines with a minimum alc. content of 11% by vol.

Malvasia di Chianti (It). A red grape variety grown in the Tuscany region.

Malvasia di Lipari (It). A white grape variety grown in Sicily.

Malvasia di Lipari (It). A rich fortified dessert wine produced in Sicily from a grape of the same name.

Malvasia di Nus (It). A dry white Alpine wine produced from the Malvasia grape in Valle d'Aosta.

Malvasia di Sardegna (It). A white grape variety grown in Sardinia.

Malvasia di Schierano (It). A red grape variety grown mainly in the Piemonte region.

Malvasia Fina (Port). A white grape variety used in the making of Port wine.

Malvasia Istriana (It). A white grape variety grown in Collio.

Malvasia Nera (It). A red grape variety grown in the Puglia region.

Malvasião (Mad). A rosé noble grape variety used for Malmsey production along with the Malvasia babosa and Malvasia candida grapes.

Malvasia Preta (Port). A black grape variety used in the making of Port wine. Gives good colour, sugar and is resistant to heat.

Malvasia Puntinata (It). A white grape variety grown in the Latium region.

Malvasia Quinada (Cktl). A cocktail of Malmsey and quinine.

Malvasia Rei (Port). A white grape variety used in the production of Port.

Malvasia Riojana (Sp). The name used in the Rioja region for the local Malvasia grape. Also known as the Rojal blanco and Subirat.

Malvasia Rossa (It). A red grape variety grown in the Latium region.

Malvasia Roxa (Mad). A black grape variety used in the production of Madeira wine.

Malvasia Toscana (It). A white grape variety grown in most regions.

Malvasier (It). The German name for the Malvasia grape in the Südtirol.

Malvasier (Ger). An erroneous varietal name for the Trollinger grape.

Malvazia (Mad). Another spelling of Malvoisie.

Malvazija (Yug). The local spelling of the Malvasia grape grown in the north-west of the country.

Malvaza (Yug). An alternative spelling of the Malvazija grape.

Malvedos Port (Port). A vintage Port shipped by Grahams. See Quinta dos Malvedos.

M

Malvern Water (Eng). A still or carbonated mineral water from the Malvern hills in central England.

Malvesia Fina (Port). See Malvasia Fina.

Malvina (Sp). The red colouring matter present in wines that originate from American root stock. Some countries forbid the importation of wines with malvina.

Malvoisie (Fr). Same as Malvasia. Also known as the Auxerrois gris, Fauvet, Pinot beurot, Pinot gris, Malmsey and Ruländer.

Malvoisie (Switz). A white dessert wine produced from late-gathered grapes.

Malvoisie de Corse (Fr). An alternative name for the Vermentino grape.

Malwa (Afr). A beer brewed in Uganda from fermented millet.

Malý Rohozec Brewery (Czec). A brewery based in northern Czec.

Malzbier (Ger). A low alcohol, dark, sweet, malty beer produced from dark-roasted malt.

Mamertine (It). A light, red wine produced near Messina, Calabria and drunk by Caesar in 46 BC. Also spelt Mamertinum.

Mamertino (It). A white wine from Sicily which was favoured by Julius Caesar. Made from the Catarrato and Grillo grapes in Messina. It is still produced today.

Mamertinum (Lat). See Mamertine.

Mamie Gilroy Cocktail (Cktl). 2 fl.ozs. Scotch whisky, juice ½ lime, dash Angostura. Shake over ice, strain into an ice-filled highball. Top with soda water, stir.

Mamie's Sister (Cktl). Place 2 fl.ozs. dry Gin into an ice-filled highball glass with the juice of a small lime. Top with ginger ale, stir, add a twist of lime peel.

Mamie Taylor (Cktl). 2 fl.ozs. Scotch whisky, juice ½ lime. Shake over ice, strain into an ice-filled highball glass. Top with ginger ale, stir.

Mammolo (It). A lesser red grape variety used in Chianti production.

Mampe (Ger). A noted liqueur producer based in Berlin.

Mampe Bitter Drops (Ger). A type of aromatic bitters.

Mampoer (S.Afr). A spirit that was distilled from moepals and maroelas fruits and the berries of the kareeboom tree. Now no longer made.

Mamreweg Co-operative (S.Afr). Based in Groenkloof. Address = Mamreweg Wynkelders Koöperatief Bpk., P.O. Box 114, Darling 7345. Produces varietal wines under the Groenkloof label.

Mamreweg Wynkelders Koöperatief (S.Afr). See Mamreweg Co-operative.

Mana (Cyp). A large earthenware jar used in Commandaria production.

Mana (Cyp). A system developed in the production of Commandaria. Is similar to the Spanish Solera system but using earthenware jars instead of casks. Lit – 'Mother'. A system of fractional blending.

Manacor (Sp). One of the main wine-producing areas on Majorca in the Balearic Islands.

Mancey (Fr). A commune in the Mâcon region, Burgundy. Grapes may be used for Mâcon Supérieur.

Mancha (Sp). A large Denominación de Origen in La Mancha near the Valdepeñas region. Produces red and white wines.

Manchega (A la) (Sp). A term used to denote the 'spur or head' pruning. Is similar to 'en vaso' pruning method. Used in La Mancha.

Manchuela (Sp). A Denominación de Origen region in the La Mancha, central Spain.

Mancy (Fr). A Cru Champagne village in the Canton d'Avize. District = Épernay.

Mandarin (China). A scented rice wine.

Mandarin (Hol). An orange coloured, orange-flavoured apéritif.

Mandarine (USA). A liqueur made from the dried peel of mandarine (tangerine) oranges. 30% alc. by vol.

Mandarine Napoléon (Bel). An orange and Brandy liqueur made from the Commun tangerine (the rarest of tangerines). Dried skins are macerated in grape brandy. 40% alc. by vol.

Mandarine Sour (Cktl).(1). ½ measure Mandarine Napoléon, juice of ½ lemon. Shake together over ice, strain into a tulip glass. Decorate with a cherry and slice of tangerine.

Mandarine Sour (Cktl).(2). 1½ fl.ozs. Mandarine Napoléon, 1½ fl.ozs. lemon juice, 2 dashes Angostura, 1 dash egg white. Shake over ice, strain into a wine glass. Decorate with a slice of orange.

Mandarine Sunrise (Cktl). ½ oz. Mandarine Napoléon, 1 oz. Tequila, dash Grenadine. Shake well over ice, strain into a highball glass, add ice and top up with orange juice.

Mandarine Tonic (Cktl). 1 measure Mandarine Napoléon. Top up with tonic water. Serve 'on the rocks' with a slice of orange.

Mandarinette (Hol). A mandarine-flavoured liqueur produced by De Kuyper. 30% alc. by vol.

Mandarinetto (It). A tangerine liqueur.

Mandarin Imperiale (Fr). A brand of mandarine liqueur made from Brandy and tangerine peel.

M and B (Eng) (abbr). See Mitchells and Butler.
Mandel (Ger). Village. (Anb) = Nahe. (Ber) = Schloss Böckelheim. (Gro) = Rosengarten. (Vins) = Alte Römerstrasse, Becherbrunnen, Dellchan, Palmengarten, Schlossberg.
Mandelbaum (Ger). vineyard. (Anb) = Rheinhessen. (Ber) = Bingen. (Gro) = Sankt Rochuskapelle. (Vil) = Pfaffen-Schwabenheim.
Mandelberg (Ger). vineyard. (Anb) = Baden. (Ber) = Badische Frankenland. (Gro) = Tauberklinge. (Vil) = Dertingen.
Mandelberg (Ger). vineyard. (Anb) = Rheinhessen. (Ber) = Bingen. (Gro) = Adelberg. (Vil) = Lonsheim.
Mandelberg (Ger). vineyard. (Anb) = Rheinhessen. (Ber) = Wonnegau. (Gro) = Sybillenstein. (Vil) = Offenheim.
Mandelberg (Ger). vineyard. (Anb) = Rheinhessen. (Ber) = Wonnegau. (Gro) = Sybillenstein. (Vil) = Weinheim.
Mandelberg (Ger). vineyard. (Anb) = Rheinpfalz. (Ber) = Mittelhaardt-Deutsche Weinstrasse. (Gro) = Pfaffengrund. (Vil) = Duttweiler.
Mandelberg (Ger). vineyard. (Anb) = Rheinpfalz. (Ber) = Mittelhaardt-Deutsche Weinstrasse. (Gro) = Schwarzerde. (Vil) = Laumersheim.
Mandelberg (Ger). vineyard. (Anb) = Rheinpfalz. (Ber) = Südliche Weinstrasse. (Gro) = Konigsgarten. (Vil) = Birkweiler.
Mandelberg (Ger). vineyard. (Anb) = Rheinpfalz. (Ber) = Südliche Weinstrasse. (Gro) = Mandelhöhe. (Vil) = Kirrweiler.
Mandel Bitter (Ger). Wine that has a taste of bitter almonds.
Mandelbrunnen (Ger). vineyard. (Anb) = Rheinhessen. (Ber) = Wonnegau. (Gro) = Bergkloster. (Vil) = Gundheim.
Mandelgarten (Ger). vineyard. (Anb) = Rheinpfalz. (Ber) = Mittelhaardt-Deutsche Weinstrasse. (Gro) = Hofstück. (Vil) = Gönnheim.
Mandelgarten (Ger). vineyard. (Anb) = Rheinpfalz. (Ber) = Mittelhaardt-Deutsche Weinstrasse. (Gro) = Kobnert. (Vil) = Weisenheim am Berg
Mandelgarten (Ger). vineyard. (Anb) = Rheinpfalz. (Ber) = Mittelhaardt-Deutsche Weinstrasse. (Gro) = Meerspinne. (Vil) = Gimmeldingen.
Mandelgraben (Ger). vineyard. (Anb) = Mosel-Saar-Ruwer. (Ber) = Bernkastel. (Gro) = Kurfürstlay. (Vil) = Braunerberg.
Mandelhang (Ger). vineyard. (Anb) = Rheinpfalz. (Ber) = Südliche Weinstrasse. (Gro) = Ordensgut. (Vil) = Edesheim.
Mandelhöhe (Ger). Grosslage. (Anb) = Rheinpfalz. (Ber) = Südliche Weinstrasse. (Vils) = Kirrweiler, Maikammer, Maikammer-Alsterweiler.
Mandelpfad (Ger). vineyard. (Anb) = Rheinpfalz. (Ber) = Mittelhaardt-Deutsche Weinstrasse. (Gro) = Grafenstück. (Vil) = Obrigheim.
Mandelpfad (Ger). vineyard. (Anb) = Rheinpfalz. (Ber) = Mittelhaardt-Deutsche Weinstrasse. (Gro) = Schwarzerde. (Vil) = Dirmstein.
Mandelpfad (Ger). vineyard. (Anb) = Rheinpfalz. (Ber) = Südliche Weinstrasse. (Gro) = Kloster Liebfrauenberg. (Vil) = Billigheim-Ingenheim.
Mandelpfad (Ger). vineyard. (Anb) = Rheinpfalz. (Ber) = Südliche Weinstrasse. (Gro) = Kloster Liebfrauenberg. (Vil) = Rohrbach.
Mandelring (Ger). vineyard. (Anb) = Rheinpfalz. (Ber) = Mittelhaardt-Deutsche Weinstrasse. (Gro) = Meerspinne. (Vil) = Haardt.
Mandelröth (Ger). vineyard. (Anb) = Rheinpfalz. (Ber) = Mittelhaardt-Deutsche Weinstrasse. (Gro) = Kobnert. (Vil) = Dackenheim.
Mandelstein (Ger). vineyard. (Anb) = Mittelrhein. (Ber) = Rheinburgengau. (Gro) = Gedeonseck. (Vil) = Boppard.
Mandement (Switz). A wine region on the west side of Lake Geneva. Produces red and white wines.
Mandeville Cocktail (Cktl). ⅗ measure white Rum, ⅖ measure dark Rum, juice ¼ lemon, ⅛ gill Coca Cola, 3 dashes Pernod, 2 dashes Grenadine. Shake over ice, strain into an ice-filled old-fashioned glass.
Mandheling Coffee (E.Ind). A coffee from Sumatra. Has a mellow flavour with a good strong aroma.
Mandingo (It). A tangerine-flavoured liqueur.
Mandira (Tur). A dairy farm.
Mandis (Chevalier de) (Fr). Armagnac producer. Address = Cazanove S.A. 47600 Nérac.
M and M Punch (Cktl). ⅔ measure dark Rum, ⅙ measure blackcurrant syrup, ⅙ measure lemon syrup. Add boiling water, stir, add slice of lemon.
Mandois (Michel et Claude) (Fr). Champagne producer. Address = Pierry, 51200 Épernay. Récoltants-manipulants. Produces – Vintage and non-vintage wines. Vintages – 1971, 1973, 1976, 1979, 1982, 1983.
Mandora (Eng). The Mansfield Brewery's soft drinks subsidiary. Has the Rimark and St. Clements range of soft drinks.
Mandorla (It). An almond-flavoured liqueur produced by Francoli.

M

Manduria (It). A strong red wine from Puglia. May be fortified.

Manègue (W.Ind). A noted distillery based in Haiti. Produces Rhum Tropical.

Manfred Vierthaler Winery (USA). A winery based in Sumner, Puyallup River Valley, western Washington. 12 ha. Produces dry white, German-style wines.

Manganese (Eng). A mineral found in the pips of grapes, therefore usually found in higher quantities in red wines than white.

Mango Indica (Eng). A mango blossom flavoured tea produced by Whittards of Chelsea.

Mangra (Port). Mildew. See also Mildio.

Mangualde (Port). A noted co-operative (1 of 10) in the Dão region.

Manhasset Cocktail (Cktl). ⅔ measure Bourbon whiskey, ⅙ measure Italian vermouth, ⅙ measure French vermouth, juice ¼ lemon. Shake over ice, strain into a cocktail glass.

Manhattan (Cktl).(1) (Sweet). 1½ measures Rye whiskey, ½ measure Italian vermouth, dash Angostura. Stir over ice, strain into a cocktail glass. Add a cherry.

Manhattan Cocktail (Cktl).(2) (Sweet). ¼ gill Canadian Club whisky, ¼ gill Italian vermouth, 2 dashes brown Curaçao, dash Absinthe, dash Angostura. Stir over ice, strain into a cocktail glass. Add cherry and piece of orange peel on top.

Manhattan Cocktail (Cktl).(3) (Medium). ¼ gill Canadian Club whisky, ⅛ gill French vermouth, ⅛ gill Italian vermouth, dash Angostura. Stir over ice, strain into a cocktail glass. Add a cherry.

Manhattan Cocktail (Cktl).(4) (Dry). ¼ gill Rye whiskey, ¼ gill dry Vermouth, dash Angostura. Stir over ice, strain into a cocktail glass. Add a cherry.

Manhattan Cooler (Cktl). 2 ozs. Claret, 3 dashes dark Rum, juice ½ lemon, 2 tablespoons powdered sugar. Stir well with ice, strain into a medium-sized goblet. Decorate with fruit in season.

Manhattan Perfect (Cktl). ½ measure Rye whiskey, ⅓ measure dry Vermouth, ⅓ measure sweet Vermouth. Stir over ice, strain into a cocktail glass.

Manhattan Skyscraper (Cktl). In a highball glass containing ice pour 2 ozs. Bourbon whiskey, 1 oz. dry Vermouth, dash Angostura. Top with dry ginger ale.

Manicle (Fr). The name for a white grape variety grown in Bugey (near Savoie).

Manila (E.Ind). A leading brand of Rum produced on the Philippine Islands by La Tondeña.

Manila Fizz (Cktl). 2 fl.ozs. dry Gin, 1 teaspoon powdered sugar, 1 egg, 2 fl.ozs. Sarsaparilla, juice of a lime. Shake over ice, strain into an ice-filled highball glass.

Manila Flame (Cktl). 1 measure Manila rum, ½ measure cranberry juice, ¼ measure passion fruit juice, ¼ measure pineapple juice, juice ½ lime. Shake over ice, strain into a flute glass.

Manipuri (Ind). A hardy variety of the Assam tea bush.

Manisa-Izmir (Tur). A vineyard in the Aegean region that produces both red and white wines.

Manitoba Distillery (Can). A noted producer of Canadian whiskies.

Manizales (S.Am). A fine coffee-producing region in Colombia.

Mannaberg (Ger). Grosslage. (Anb) = Baden. (Ber) = Badische Bergstrasse/Kraichgau. (Vils) = Bad Mingolsheim-Langenbrücken (ortsteil Bad Langenbrücken, ortsteil Bad Mingolsheim), Bruchsal (stadtteil Obergrombach), Bruchsal, Bruschal (stadtteil Untergrombach), Dielheim, Heidelberg, Heidelsheim, Helmsheim, Horrenberg, Kraichtal (stadtteil Oberöwisheim, stadtteil Unteröwisheim), Leimen, Malsch, Malschenberg, Mühlhausen, Nussloch, Östringen, Rauenberg, Rettigheim, Rotenberg, Tairnbach, Ubstadt-Weiher (ortsteil Stettfeld), Ubstadt-Weiher (ortsteil Ubstadt), Wiesloch, Zeutern.

Mannberg (Ger). vineyard. (Anb) = Rheingau. (Ber) = Johannisberg. (Gro) = Deutelsberg. (Vil) = Hattenheim.

Mannequines (Fr). The willow baskets used in Champagne to carry grapes. 150–175 lbs. grapes can be held in each. See also Caques.

Mannite (Sp). A Sherry disease. Results in the formation of Mannitol.

Mannitic Fermentation (Eng). Bacteria Mannitopoen attacks, at high temperatures, the fructose in low-acid wines to produce Mannitol, ethanoic acid, lactic acid and CO_2. The wine throws a deposit and has a 'mousy' taste.

Mannitol (Eng). See Mannitic Fermentation. Recognised by its acrid nose and palate. Sugar is produced when low-acid, sweet wines are attacked by lactic acid bacteria which reduces fructose to mannitol. See Mannite.

Mannochmore (Scot). A single Malt whisky distillery based north of Rothes, Morayshire. A Highland malt whisky. 40% alc. by vol.

M

Mann Ranch (USA). A small vineyard based in Anderson Valley, Mendocino, California. Grape variety – Chardonnay.

Manns (Eng). Watney's East Midland Company. Based in Northampton, the beers are brewed in London or Manchester. Produces all types of beers.

Mann's (Jap). One of the countries main wine-producers based in Katsunuma.

Mann's Brown (Eng). A Brown ale 1034–5 O.G. brewed by the Watney Mann Brewery in London.

Mann's Wine et Cie (Jap). See Mann's.

Mannweiler-Coelln (Ger). Village. (Anb) = Nahe. (Ber) = Schloss Böckelheim. (Gro) = Paradiesgarten. (Vins) = Rosenberg, Schloss Randeck, Seidenberg, Weissenstein.

Manoel d'Porcas Jr (Port). Vintage Port shipper. Vintages – 1967, 1975.

Manseng (Fr). A white grape variety grown in south-western France in the regions of Madiran, Jurançon and Tursan.

Mansfield Brewery (Eng). Based in Mansfield, Notts. Noted for its cask conditioned beers and Marksman Lager 1039 O.G. Took over the North Country Breweries in Hull in 1985. See also Drayman's Choice.

Mansfield Winery (Austr). A winery based in Mudgee, New South Wales.

Mansikka (Fin). A strawberry liqueur.

Mansios (Fr). A red grape variety grown in the Côtes de Saint-Mont in the Gers Département.

Mans Wine (Jap). See Mann's.

Manta (Port). A method of pushing down the Crust of the grape pulp in Port production when fermentation begins. Wooden paddles are used.

Mantar (Tur). Cork (mushroom-shaped). i.e. A Champagne cork or stopper cork.

Mantel (Sp). The name used by Bodegas Alavez in La Rueda for a range of their white wines.

Manteudo (Port). A white grape variety grown in Alentejo.

Mantey's vineyard (USA). A winery based in Sandusky, Ohio. Produces vinifera and French-American hybrid wines.

Mantiko (Gre). A deep ruby red wine from the Isle of Crete. Aged for 1 year in cask.

Mantinea (Gre). An alternative spelling of Mantinia.

Mantineia (Gre). A rosé wine produced in Arcadia, Peloponnese.

Mantinia (Gre). A dry white wine from the Peloponnese made with the Moschofilero grape. Produced by Cambas.

Manto Negro (Sp). A red grape variety grown in the Balearic Islands.

Mantonica (It). A dry red fortified wine from the Calabrian region.

Mantonico Bianco (It). A white grape variety grown in Calabria.

Mantonico Nero (It). The Calabrian name for the red grape Gaglioppo.

Mantúa (Sp). A white grape variety grown in the Huelva region, south-western Spain.

Mantúo Castellano (Sp). A lesser white grape variety used in Sherry production.

Mantúo de Pila (Sp). A lesser white grape variety used in sherry production. Also known as the Gabriela and Mantúo de Rey.

Mantúo de Rey (Sp). An alternative name for the Mantúo de Pila.

Mantúo de Sanlúcar (Sp). A white grape variety grown in the south-western regions.

Manubach (Ger). Village. (Anb) = Mittelrhein. (Ber) = Bacharach. (Gro) = Schloss Stahleck. (Vins) = Heilgarten, Langgarten, Mönchwingert, St. Oswald.

Manwood Wines (Eng). A noted wholesale wine and spirit merchant based in Knutsford, Cheshire.

Manx Pure Beer Act (I.O.M). Introduced in 1874 it decreed that only malt, hops and sugar shall be used to brew beer.

Manzanarès (Sp). An important wine vineyard for the wines of Valdepeñas in the La Mancha region of central Spain.

Manzanilla (Sp). A Fino sherry that is matured on the coast at Sanlúcar de Barrameda to take on a salty tang and flavour.

Manzanilla Amontillado (Sp). A very rare, old, matured wine from Sanlúcar de Barrameda.

Manzanilla de Sanlúcar (Sp). A fine, dry, Manzanilla sherry produced by Antonio Barbadillo in Jerez.

Manzanilla Fina (Sp). The Fino version of Manzanilla sherry.

Manzanilla Oloroso (Sp). An Oloroso version of Manzanilla sherry.

Manzanilla Pasada (Sp). A well-aged Manzanilla sherry.

Manzoni (It). A red grape variety. A cross between the Cabernet and the Prosecco. Yields a big dark red wine. Grown in the Treviso region.

Mao-t'ai (China). A grain spirit produced in Mao-t'ai, Kweichow province, south-western China. Made from wheat and millet. 26% alc. by vol.

Ma Pardoes (Eng). A home-brew public house in Netherton, near Dudley.

M

Known also as the Old-Swan. Produces a cask conditioned Bitter 1034 O.G.

Maple Leaf (Cktl). ⅔ measure Bourbon whiskey, ⅓ measure lemon juice, dash maple syrup. Shake over ice, strain into a cocktail glass.

Maple Leaf (Eng). A home-brew public house in Newark, Notts. Owned by Ind Coope. Produces cask conditioned Ales.

Maquevin (Fr). See Macvin.

Maquey Aloe (Mex). Used to make the spirit Aquadiente and Pulque.

Maquisards (Les) (Fr). A vineyard of Dopff & Irion in Alsace. Produces Gewürztraminer.

Maraca (W.Ind). The brand-name of a light Rum produced in Puerto Rico.

Maracibos Coffee (S.Am). A variety of pure coffee produced in Venezuela.

Maracuja (Bra). A passion fruit-flavoured liqueur.

Maragopipe (S.Am). A large mutant variety of the Arabica coffee bean.

Marais (Les) (Fr). A vineyard in the A.C. commune of Montagny, Côte Chalonnaise, Burgundy.

Maranges (Les) (Fr). A Premier Cru vineyard [part] in the commune of Cheilly-lès-Maranges, A.C. Santenay, Côte de Beaune, Burgundy.

Maranges (Les) (Fr). A Premier Cru vineyard [part] in the commune of Dezize-lès-Maranges, A.C. Santenay, Côte de Beaune, Burgundy.

Maranges (Les) (Fr). A Premier Cru vineyard [part] in the commune of Sampigny-lès-Maranges, A.C. Santenay, Côte de Beaune, Burgundy.

Marao (Cktl). ⅓ measure Port, ⅓ measure Anis, ⅓ measure Advocaat. Shake over ice, strain into a cocktail glass.

Maraschino (It). A clear cherry liqueur made from Maraska cherries including the crushed kernels. 30% alc. by vol.

Maraschino Cherries (It). Bright red dyed cherries preserved in Maraschino and used for cocktail decoration.

Maraska (Yug). A Cherry brandy from Zadar.

Maraska Cherries (Euro). A cherry used in the making of Maraschino and Cherry brandy.

Marasquin (Hol). A cherry-flavoured liqueur produced by De Kuyper from the distillation of green cherry kernels. 30% alc. by vol.

Maraština (Yug). A dry white wine from Croatia. Has an extra dry finish, is high in alcohol, not unlike a dry Sherry.

Marathassa (Cyp). The north-west region of the Troodos mountains. Produces fine wines.

Maratheftika (Cyp). A red grape variety named after the region (Marathessa) it is grown in.

Marbach (Ger). Village. (Anb) = Baden. (Ber) = Badische Frankenland. (Gro) = Tauberklinge. (Vin) = Frankenberg.

Marbach (Ger). vineyard. (Anb) = Nahe. (Ber) = Schloss Böckelheim. (Gro) = Paradiesgarten. (Vil) = Sobernheim.

Marbach (Ger). Village. (Anb) = Württemberg. (Ber) = Württembergisch Unterland. (Gro) = Schalkstein. (Vin) = Neckarhälde.

Marbaix Brasserie (Bel). A brewery based in Charleroi. Brews Gauloise and a Christmas Ale.

Marc (Fr). A Brandy from the 3rd and 4th pressing of the grapes. Known as Eau-de-Vie-de-Marc.

Marc (Fr). The grape pulp. From which Marc brandy gets its name. The wine made from the spent pulp (Marc) is watered, repressed and the resulting fermented wine distilled into Marc (brandy).

Marcación (Sp). A method of vine planting in which the rows are separated by 1.2 metres, although now tends to be 2.4 metres to allow for mechanical harvesting, etc.

Marc de Bourgogne (Fr). A Marc brandy made in Burgundy from a distillation of the skins, pips and stems of the grapes left in the bottom of the casks after the wines have been racked off.

Marc de Café (Fr). Coffee grounds.

Marc de Champagne (Fr). One of the lightest available. Made from the residue pulp. See Rebêche.

Marc de Hospices de Beaune (Fr). A Marc brandy reserved and sold for the famous annual charity held in Beaune, Burgundy.

Marc du Valais (Switz). A Marc brandy produced in the Valais Canton.

Marcel Contreras Brasserie (Bel). A brewery based at Gavere in eastern Flanders. Brews golden-coloured, abbaye-style beers.

Marcella (Eng). The old eighteenth-century spelling of Marsala.

Marcel's Cup (Cktl). ⅓ measure Brandy, ⅓ measure rosé wine, ⅓ measure Bénédictine. Stir with ice in a large jug. Add slices of orange, cucumber peel and mint sprigs. Top with soda water.

Marchampt (Fr). A commune in the Beaujolais. Has A.C. Beaujolais-Villages or Beaujolais-Marchampt status.

Marchànd à Vin (Ch.Isles). Wine merchant.

Marchand de Vins (Fr). Vintner.

Marchanudo (Sp). A district within

M

Andalusia where the Sherry vineyards are based. Has chalky soil. See also Macharnudo.

March Brown (Eng). A Brown sherry produced by Findlater's.

Marche (It). A wine region on the Adriatic coast. Noted for Verdicchio.

Marcher Lager (Eng). A Lager beer 1034 O.G. brewed for their Border Brewery subsidiary in North Wales. See Border Brewery.

Marches de Bretagne (Fr). A Vins de Pays area in the Loire Atlantique Département in western France. Produces red, rosé and dry white wines.

Marches (The) (It). A predominantly mountainous region which borders the Adriatic coast to the west of Umbria.

Marchesi di Barolo (It). A noted winery based in Barolo, Piemonte.

Marchier (Fr). The old term for the treading of the grapes.

March vineyard (USA). A vineyard based in Potter Valley, Mendocino, California. Grape variety – Johannisberg riesling.

Marcilla (Sp). One of 3 sub-zones in the Ribera Alta based in the south of the region. Produces mainly rosado wines.

Marcillac (Fr). A V.D.Q.S. red wine from the Côtes de Saint-Mont in the Gers Département. Made from the Mansios grape.

Marcilly Frères (Fr). A négociant-éleveur based in Beaune, Côte de Beaune, Burgundy.

Marciume Nobile (It). The local (Latium) term for botrytis cinerea. See Muffa Nobile.

Marcobrunn (Ger). vineyard. (Anb) = Rheingau. (Ber) = Johannisberg. (Gro) = Deutelsberg. (Vil) = Erbach.

Marco de Bartoli (It). See De Bartoli.

Marconi (Cktl). 2 parts dry Gin, 1 part sweet Vermouth, 2 dashes Angostura. Stir well with ice, strain into a cocktail glass.

Marconi Cocktail (Cktl). ⅓ measure sweet Vermouth, ⅔ measure Calvados. Stir over ice, strain into a cocktail glass.

Marconnets (Les) (Fr). A Premier Cru vineyard in the A.C. commune of Beaune, Côte de Beaune, Burgundy. 8.81 ha.

Marconnets (Les) (Fr). A Premier Cru vineyard in the A.C. commune of Savigny-lès-Beaune, Côte de Beaune, Burgundy.

Marco Polo (Cktl).(1). 1½ measures Brandy, 1½ measures Port, 1 measure fresh lime or lemon juice. Shake over ice, strain into a wine goblet. Top with soda water. Add straws.

Marco Polo (Cktl).(2). 1 bottle Verdelho Madeira, ¼ lb. sugar, 5 ozs. Cognac, 5 cinnamon sticks, 5 slices lemon, 6 cloves. Heat slowly, strain and serve.

Marco Real (Sp). An old way of planting vines in the Sherry region, 1.5 metres apart. Now planted hedge style (see Hedging) at 1 metre apart.

Marcottage (Fr). The traditional layering method used to propagate vines. Permits the shoots to obtain roots of their own before being pruned from the vine.

Marcques (Les) (Fr). A vineyard in the A.C. commune of Montagny, Côte Chalonnaise, Burgundy.

Mar del Plata (Cktl). ½ measure dry Gin, ⅛ measure Bénédictine, ⅜ measure dry Vermouth, dash Grand Marnier. Stir over ice, strain into a cocktail glass, add a twist of lemon peel.

Mardeuil (Fr). A Cru Champagne village in the Canton de Montmort. District = Épernay.

Mardi Gras (Eng). The brand-name of a drink made from Vodka, passion fruit and soda water. 18% alc. by vol.

Maréchal Foch (Can). A red French hybrid grape variety. A cross between the Gamay and Pinot noir. Is grown in Ontario.

Maréchaudes (Les) (Fr). A Premier Cru vineyard [part] in the A.C. commune of Aloxe-Corton, Côte de Beaune, Burgundy.

Maréchaudes (Les) (Fr). A Premier Cru vineyard [part] in the A.C. commune of Ladoix-Serrigny, A.C. Aloxe-Corton, Côte de Beaune, Burgundy.

Maredsous (Bel). A Bière brewed by the Duvel Brasserie in Breendonk for the Maredsous abbaye.

Maredsous Abbaye (Bel). An abbey in southern Belgium whose ruby and amber beers are now brewed by the Duvel and Moorgat Brasseries.

Mareotic (Egy). An ancient light, sweet, white wine with a fragrant aroma produced near Alexandria at Marea on the banks of Lake Mareotis.

Maresme (Sp). A district of Alella.

Marestel (Fr). A V.D.Q.S. vineyard on the bank of the river Rhône in the Savoie region.

Mareuil-le-Port (Fr). A Cru Champagne village in the Canton de Dormans. District = Épernay.

Mareuil-sur-Aÿ (Fr). A Premier Cru Champagne village in the Canton d'Aÿ. District = Reims.

Marfaux (Fr). A Cru Champagne village in the Canton de Ville-en-Tardenois. District = Reims.

Marfil (Sp). A brand-name used by the

Alella Co-operative in Catalonia for a range of their wines.

Marfil (Sp). A white grape variety grown in Cáceres, south-western Spain. Lit – 'Ivory'.

Marfil Blanco (Sp). A white grape variety grown in Alella and Catalonia. Produces soft, fruity wines.

Margarete (Ger). vineyard. (Anb) = Württemberg. (Ber) = Württembergisch Unterland. (Gro) = Lindelberg. (Vil) = Michelbach a. W.

Margarete (Ger). vineyard. (Anb) = Württemberg. (Ber) = Württembergisch Unterland. (Gro) = Lindelberg. (Vil) = Obersöllbach.

Margaret River (Austr). A wine region in the province of Western Australia. Part of Sandalford.

Margaret River Winery (Austr). See Château Xanadu.

Margaret Rose (Cktl). ½ measure Gin, ⅙ measure Calvados, ⅙ measure Cointreau, ⅙ measure lemon juice, dash Grenadine. Shake over ice, strain into a cocktail glass.

Margarita (Cktl). A blend of Tequila, lime juice and Cointreau. Shake over ice, strain and serve in a salt-rimmed glass.

Margaux (Fr). An A.C. commune in the Haut-Médoc, Bordeaux.

Margaux (Fr). See Château Margaux.

Margoo (Eng). The eighteenth-century spelling of Margaux.

Margoty (Fr). A vineyard in the A.C. commune of Montagny, Côte Chalonnaise, Burgundy.

Marguerite Christel (Fr). The label used by the Société Anonyme de Magenta for their non-vintage and rosé Champagnes.

Marguerite Cristal (Fr). A Champagne producer based in Épernay.

Maria Ardoña (Sp). A black grape variety grown in Valdeorras.

Maria Bonita Cocktail (Cktl). 1½ fl.ozs. white Rum, ½ measure Curaçao, 3 fl.ozs. pineapple juice. Stir over ice, strain into a flute glass. Top with a cherry and pineapple cube.

Mariacron (Ger). The brand-name of a Brandy produced by the Peter Eckes Distillery. Sold in frosted bottles.

Maria Gomes (Port). A white grape variety grown in the Bairrada region.

Maria Magdalena (Ger). Vineyard. (Anb) = Rheinpfalz. (Ber) = Südliche Weinstrasse. (Gro) = Kloster Liebfrauenberg. (Vil) = Klingenmünster.

Marianum (Lat). An ancient red wine produced in south-western Italy in Roman times.

Maria Theresa Cocktail (Cktl). 1½ measures Tequila, ¾ measure lime juice, ¾ measure bilberry juice. Shake over ice, strain into a Champagne saucer.

Maribo Brewery (Den). A brewery based in the town of Maribo.

Maribor (Yug). A region of Slovenia. Produces mainly white wines from the Sylvaner, Traminer and Sauvignon grapes.

Marie Antoinette (Cktl). 1½ fl.ozs. dry Gin, ¾ fl.oz. blue Curaçao, 1 fl.oz. lemon juice, ½ fl.oz. Gomme syrup. Shake over ice, strain into a cocktail glass (rim dipped in Grenadine and castor sugar). Top with a cherry.

Marie Jeanne (Fr). A demi-john used in Bordeaux. Holds 2.5 litres.

Marienberg (Austr). vineyard. Address = Black Road, Coromandel Valley, South Australia 5051. 23 ha. Grape varieties – Cabernet sauvignon, Gewürztraminer, Rhine riesling, Sémillon, Shiraz.

Marienberg (Ger). vineyard. (Anb) = Mosel-Saar-Ruwer. (Ber) = Zell/Mosel. (Gro) = Weinhex. (Vil) = Güls.

Marienburg (Ger). vineyard. (Anb) = Mosel-Saar-Ruwer. (Ber) = Bernkastel. (Gro) = Vom Heissen Stein. (Vil) = Pünderich.

Marienburger (Ger). vineyard. (Anb) = Mosel-Saar-Ruwer. (Ber) = Zell/Mosel. (Gro) = Schwarze Katz. (Vil) = Zell-Kaint.

Mariengarten (Ger). Grosslage. (Anb) = Rheinpfalz. (Ber) = Mittelhaardt-Deutsche Weinstrasse. (Vils) = Deidesheim, Forst, Wachenheim.

Marienholz (Ger). vineyard. (Anb) = Mosel-Saar-Ruwer. (Ber) = Saar-Ruwer. (Gro) = Römerlay. (Vil) = Trier.

Marienpforter Klosterberg (Ger). Vineyard. (Anb) = Nahe. (Ber) = Schloss Böckelheim. (Gro) = Burgweg. (Vil) = Waldböckelheim.

Marienriesling (Ger). A white grape variety. A cross between the White riesling and the St. Laurent.

Mariensteiner (Ger). A white grape variety. A cross between the Silvaner and the Rieslaner.

Marienthal (Ger). Village. (Anb) = Ahr. (Ber) = Walporzheim/Ahrtal. (Gro) = Klosterberg. (Vins) = Jesuitengarten, Klostergarten, Rosenberg, Stiftsberg, Trotzenberg.

Marie Stuart (Fr). Champagne producer. Address = 8 Place de la République, 51100 Reims. Produces – Vintage and non-vintage wines. Vintages – 1973, 1975, 1976, 1979, 1981. See Cuvée de la Reine.

Mariette (Cktl). 1 fl.oz. white Rum, ½

fl.oz. Amaretto di Saronno, ½ fl.oz. Cointreau. Build into an ice-filled highball glass. Top with Kinnie. Decorate with a slice of orange, apple and a cherry.

Marignan (Fr). A dry white wine from Sciez in the Savoie region.

Marillenbrand (Ger). An Apricot brandy.

Marillen Likor (Ger). An apricot-flavoured brandy.

Marin (USA). A small wine-producing area across the Golden Gate from San Francisco, California.

Marinella (Fin). A fruit-based bitters produced by Marli.

Maring-Noviand (Ger). Village. (Anb) = Mosel-Saar-Ruwer. (Ber) = Bernkastel. (Gro) = Kurfürstlay. (Vins) = Honigberg, Kirchberg, Klosterberg, Romerpfad, Sonnenuhr.

Marinissmo (Liq.Coffee). Put a teaspoonful of castor sugar in a wine goblet. Add hot coffee, stir, add 1 measure of Grand Marnier, float thick fresh cream on top.

Marino (It). D.O.C. white wine from Latium. (From town of same name). Made from the Bonvino, Cacchione, Giallo, Malvasia del Lazio, Malvasia rosso, Trebbiano toscano and Trebbiano verde grapes, grown in the commune of Marino and part of the communes of Rome and Castelgandolfo. Is classed Superiore if total alc. content is 12.%5. D.O.C. also applies to naturally sparkling wines.

Marionette (Cktl). ¼ measure each of Apricot brandy, Dry Sack sherry, Cherry Heering and white Rum. Shake well over ice, strain into a cocktail glass. Dress with a cherry.

Mariotte Margaux (La) (Fr). The second wine of Château Marquis-de-Terme, Grand Cru Classé Margaux (4th).

Mariposa (Mex). The brand-name of a popular Tequila.

Mariposa Cocktail (Cktl). 1 measure white Rum, ½ measure Brandy, ⅙ measure lemon juice, ⅙ measure orange juice, 1 dash Grenadine. Shake over ice, strain into a cocktail glass.

Mariscal (Eng). The brand-name for a range of Sherries from Tanner's of Shrewsbury, Shropshire.

Marisco Tavern (G.B.). A Lundy Island home-brew public house which is noted for its Puffin Bitter 1040 O.G. using malt extract.

Marismeno (Sp). A light, pale, dry Fino sherry produced by Romate.

Maris Otter (Eng). A strain of Barley grown in England and Wales.

Marisson (Fr). A vineyard in the A.C. commune of Rully, Côte Chalonnaise, Burgundy.

Maritsa Valley (Bul). A vineyard region in the southern half of the country. Produces the red wine Mavrud.

Markdorf (Ger). Village. (Anb) = Baden. (Ber) = Bodensee. (Gro) = Sonnenufer. (Vins) = Burgstall, Sängerhalde.

Markelsheim (Ger). Village. (Anb) = Württemberg. (Ber) = Kocher-Jagst-Tauber. (Gro) = Tauberberg. (Vins) = Mönchsberg, Probstberg.

Market (Eng). The buying and selling of wines and spirits etc.

Market Brewery (Eng). Market Porter home-brew public house in Southwark, London. Noted for its cask conditioned Beach's Borough Bitter 1038 O.G.

Market Extension (Eng). An extension of normal licensing hours made under an order of Special Exemption which allows public houses to open outside of licensing hours on market days.

Markgraeflerland (Ger). District of Baden. Lit – 'Land of Margraves'. Near Loerrach on the German-Swiss border. Produces light, piquant table wines. Also spelt Markgräflerland.

Markgraf Babenberg (Ger). vineyard. (Anb) = Franken. (Ber) = Maindreieck. (Gro) = Not yet assigned. (Vil) = Frickenwinheim am Main.

Markgraf Karl Friedrich (Ger). A person who planted vines in the Bereich Markgräflerland in the late eighteenth century. The Bereich was named after him.

Markgräfler (Ger). An alternative name for the Gutedel grape variety.

Markgräflerland (Ger). Bereich. (Anb) = Baden. (Gros) = Burg Neuenfels, Lorettoberg, Vogtei Rotteln.

Markgräfschaft (Ger). Another name for Markgräflerland.

Markgröningen (Ger). Village. (Anb) = Württemberg. (Ber) = Württembergisch Unterland. (Gro) = Schalkstein. (Vins) = Berg, Sankt Johännser.

Markham Vineyard (USA). A large winery based near St. Helena, Napa Valley, California. 125 ha. Grape varieties – Cabernet sauvignon, Chardonnay, Chenin blanc, Gamay, Gray riesling, Johannisberg riesling and Muscat de frontignan. Produces varietal wines under the Vinmark and Markham labels.

Markko (USA). A small winery based in Conneaut, Ohio. 4 ha. Grape varieties – Cabernet sauvignon, Chardonnay and Riesling. Produces varietal wines.

Marko (Gre). A dry white wine.

Markobrunn (Ger). See Marcobrunn.

Markovina (N.Z.). A small winery based at Old Railway Road, Kumeu area. Has Grk vines.

M

Marksburg (Ger). Grosslage. (Anb) = Mittelrhein. (Ber) = Rheinburgengau. (Vils) = Braubach, Filsen, Koblenz-Ehrenbreitstein, Lahnstein, Osterspai, Urbai, Vallendar.

Marksman Lager (Eng). A keg Lager beer 1039 O.G. brewed by the Mansfield Brewery in Nottinghamshire.

Marktbreit (Ger). Village. (Anb) = Franken. (Ber) = Maindreieck. (Gro) = Hofrat. (Vin) = Sonnenberg.

Markt Einersheim (Ger). Village. (Anb) = Franken. (Ber) = Steigerwald. (Gro) = Burgweg. (Vin) = Vogelsang.

Mark Up (Eng). The price above cost, charged for wines and spirits etc. in hotels, restaurants, public houses.

Mark West Vineyards (USA). A large winery based in the lower Russian River Valley, California. 15 ha. Grape varieties – Chardonnay, Gewürztraminer, Johannisberg riesling, Pinot noir and Zinfandel. Produces varietal wines.

Marlboro Champagne Cellars (USA). A small estate winery based in Hudson Valley, eastern America.

Marlborough (N.Z.). An area on the northern tip of the South Island.

Marli Distillery (Fin). A distillery based in Marli. Produces Liqueurs, fruit bitters and Cider.

Mar Lodge (Scot). A Vatted Malt. Produced by Findlater, Mackie Todd and Co. Ltd. 8 years old. 43% alc. by vol.

Marl Soil (Eng). A sedimentary soil consisting of clay minerals, calcite or aragonite and silt. Is ideal for red wines.

Marmara (Tur). A wine-producing area in eastern Turkey which produces still and sparkling wines.

Marmari (Gre). A dry white wine from Marmarion, south Euboea.

Marmertino (It). A white table wine produced in Sicily.

Marmorberg (Ger). vineyard. (Anb) = Mittelrhein. (Ber) = Rheinburgengau. (Gro) = Marksburg. (Vil) = Braubach.

Marne (Fr). A Cru Champagne village in the Canton de Suippes. District = Châlons.

Marne & Champagne (Fr). A Champagne house based in Reims.

Marne [River] (Fr). A river that runs through the Champagne region. A tributary of the river Seine.

Marnier-Lapostolle (Fr). A Cognac and Armagnac producer. Also produces Grand Marnier.

Marnier Tonic (Cktl). Fill a highball glass with ice. Add a measure of Grand Marnier and a slice of lemon. Stir, top up with tonic.

Marnique (Austr). A liqueur based on Australian brandy and tangerines (quinces). Produced by Beri Estates in South Australia.

Marnissimo (Cktl). See Marinissimo.

Maronean (Gre). A dark coloured wine which was usually drunk watered down in ancient Greece.

Maroto (Mad). A minor grape variety grown in Madeira.

Marque (Fr). A Champagne house's blend of wines. See Grandes Marques.

Marque (La) (S.Afr). See Twee Jonge Gezellen Estate.

Marque Anonyme (Fr). See M.A.

Marque Autorisée (Fr). See M.A.

Marque Auxiliaire (Fr). See M.A.

Marque d'Acheteur (Fr). See M.A.

Marque Déposée (Fr). Trade mark.

Marque Nationale (Lux). The classification of wines. Certified by a small label on bottle-neck. Q.W.P.S.P. as Vin Classé, Premier Cru or Grand Premier Cru.

Marqués de Alella (Sp). A dry white wine produced by Alta Alella from 60% Pansa and 40% Xarello grapes.

Marqués de Casa Concha (Chile). The brand-name of a wine produced by Concha y Toro in the Maipo Valley. The red is produced from Cabernet sauvignon 100% and oak matured 3–4 years with 1–2 years bottle.

Marqués de Ciria (Sp). A winery based in Rioja. Owned by Savin who also own Campo Viejo (share a bodega).

Marqués de Domecq (Sp). The brand-name of a Brandy produced by Domecq.

Marqués de Figueroa (Sp). A bodega based in Zona del Albariño, north-western Spain. Is noted for Fefiñanes Palacio (a white oak-aged wine).

Marqués de Gastanga (Sp). A medium-dry white wine produced from 100% Cencibel grapes by Luis Megía in Valdepeñas.

Marqués de Griñon (Sp). A dry white wine produced by Bodegas de Crianza Castilla la Vieja in Rueda from must from the first pressing.

Marqués del Puerto (Sp). A red wine produced by Bodegas Lopez-Agos. Made from 20% Garnacha and 80% Tempranillo. Oak matured for 2 years and for 4 years in bottle.

Marqués del Real Tesoro (Sp). A Jerez de la Fontera Sherry shipper.

Marqués de Misa (Sp). A Sherry bodega based in Jerez de la Frontera. Was once part of Rumasa. Labels include Amontillado Abolengo, Fino Chiquilla, Misa and Oloroso la Novia.

Marqués de Monistrol (Sp). A white/rosé

646

sparkling wine made by the méthode champenoise (Cava) in San Sadurní de Noya. 11.5% alc. by vol. Owned by Martini and Rossi.

Marqués de Murrieta (Sp). Wines produced by Bodegas Marqués de Murrieta, Rioja. Many grades are produced.

Marqués de Riscal (Sp). A red wine produced by Vinos de Los Herederos del Marqués de Riscal, Rioja. Made from Tempranillo and Viura grapes. Matured in oak for 3 years.

Marqués de Romeral (Sp). A red wine produced by A.G.E. Bodegas Unidas, S.A. Made from 30% Garnacha, 10% Graciano and 60% Tempranillo grapes. Oak matured for 3 years and for 2 years in bottle.

Marqués de Saporta (Fr). A rosé wine from the A.C. Coteaux d'Aix-en-Provence, south-eastern France.

Marqués de Villamagna Gran Reserva (Sp). A red wine produced by Bodegas Campo Viejo, Rioja. Aged in Limousin oak for 5 years and a further 4 years in bottle. Made from 10% Graciano, 5% Mazuelo and 85% Tempranillo.

Marquette (Cktl). 1 measure dry Gin, ½ measure Italian vermouth, dash Crème de Noyau. Shake over ice, strain into a cocktail glass.

Marquis d'Alesme-Becker (Fr). See Château Marquis d'Alesme-Becker.

Marquis d'Angerville (Fr). A négociant-éleveur based in Volnay, Côte de Beaune, Burgundy.

Marquis de Bessac (Fr). A V.S.O.P. Armagnac produced by St. Maure de Peyriac in Ténarèze. 40% alc. by vol.

Marquis de Caussade (Fr). A brand-name for an Armagnac brandy. Sold by UCVA in Gers. Is blended from Aignan, Cazaubon, Eauze and Panjas distilleries.

Marquis de Goulaine (Fr). A vineyard in the A.C. Muscadet de Sèvre et Maine, Pays Nantais, Loire. Sur Lie wines.

Marquis de Maniban (Fr). Cognac brandies – V.S.O.P. 5 year old and Napoléon 9 year old produced by Château du Busca.

Marquis de Montesquiou (Fr). An Armagnac produced by Société des Produits d'Armagnac.

Marquise de Pompadour (Ind). A demi-sec sparkling (méthode champenoise) wine produced by Narayangaon.

Marquises (Les) (Fr). A vineyard in the A.C. Bourgueil, Touraine, Loire.

Marquista (Sp). Describes a merchant who exports wines under his own label but who has no separate bodega.

Marrakech (Afr). A major wine-producing region in Morocco.

Marrebæk Brewery (Den). A brewery based in Væggersløse.

Marriage Hill (Eng). vineyard. Address = Marriage Farm, Wye, Ashford, Kent Was first planted 1972. 0.75 ha. Grape varieties – Müller-Thurgau, Reichensteiner and Scheurebe.

Marriqcron (Ger). A Weinbrand produced at Oppenheim on the upper Rhine.

Marris Otter Pale Ale (Eng). A brand of malted barley used by the Lees Brewery in Manchester.

Marrying (Eng). The blending of Malt whiskies of different years to produce a blend. Also applies to blended Scotch whisky. After blending the Whiskies are allowed to 'marry' in cask before being bottled.

Marsala (It). Invented by an Englishman John Woodhouse in 1773 on the Isle of Sicily. See Marsh el Allah. 15–18% alc. by vol.

Marsala (It). D.O.C. fortified wine from Sicily. Made from Catarratto, Grillo and Inzolia grapes within parts of the provinces of Agrigento, Palermo and Trapani. Heated must, concentrated must and mistella (sifone) have to come from the defined area and mentioned grape varieties. Base wine has a straw yellow colour. Varieties are Fine, Superiore, Vergine and Speciali.

Marsala (USA). See California Marsala.

Marsala all'Uovo (It). Marsala mixed with eggs and bottled.

Marsala Fine (It). Has a minimum alc. content of 17% by vol. and cannot be sold with less than 12 months of age. Tastes vary from dry to sweet.

Marsala Speciali (It). Various flavours – egg, almond. Have the basic characteristics of Superiore. See Marsala all'Uovo.

Marsala Superiore (It). Known also as L.P., S.O.M., G.D. and O.P. Must age for a minimum of 2 years. Minimum alc. content 18% by vol. Taste varies from dry to sweet.

Marsala Vergine (It). Has to age at least 5 years. Minimum alc. content is 18% by vol. Produced without the addition of 'cooked' must, concentrated must or Sifone. Taste is dry.

Marsalla (Eng). An eighteenth-century spelling of Marsala.

Marsannay-la-Côte (Fr). The most northerly commune in the Côte de Nuits and Côte d'Or. Produces Rosé Bourgogne and Rosé de Marsannay which is the only rosé made in the Côte d'Or.

Marsanne (Fr). A white grape variety grown in the Rhône. Used in the making of white Hermitage and sparkling St. Péray.

Marsberg (Ger). vineyard. (Anb) = Franken. (Ber) = Maindreieck. (Gro) = Ewig Leben. (Vil) = Randersacker.

Marschall (Ger). vineyard. (Anb) = Rheingau. (Ber) = Johannisberg. (Gro) = Steinmacher. (Vil) = Frauenstein.

Marsden (Reverend Samuel) (N.Z.) The man who introduced the first vines to New Zealand in 1819.

Marseillan (Fr). The alternative name for Pelure d'Oignon (onion skin wine).

Marsella (Eng). An eighteenth-century spelling of Marsala.

Marsh el Allah (Arab). Lit – 'Port of God'. The name given to a town in Sicily from which Marsala gets its name.

Marshmallow Coffee (Eng). Milk and coffee in a goblet, topped with a pink and a white marshmallow.

Marsovin (Euro). The largest wine-producing firm on the island of Malta. Based at Marsa. Grape varieties include Gellewza and Girgentina.

Marston Brewery (Eng). Based in Burton-on-Trent. Took over the Border Brewery in Wrexham in 1984. Noted for its cask conditioned Capital 1030 O.G. Mercian Mild 1032 O.G. Merrie Monk 1043 O.G. Pedigree 1043 O.G. Owd Rodger 1080 O.G. Albion Keg Mild 1030 O.G. and John Marston 1043 O.G. Also known as Marston, Thompson and Evershed.

Marston Moor Brewery (Eng). Opened in 1984 in York. Noted for its cask conditioned Cromwell Bitter 1037 O.G.

Marston, Thompson and Evershed (Eng). See Marston Brewery.

Marsum (Lat). An ancient red wine produced in central Italy in Roman times.

Martàgua (Port). A red grape variety grown in Lafões.

Martayrol (Fr). A Cognac producer. Address = 137, Avenue du Président Wilson, 93210 Saint-Denis-la-Plaine. Owns no vineyards or distilleries. Produces Chauffe Coeur and Chauffe Coeur Napoléon.

Martell (Fr). Cognac producer. Address = BP 21, 16100 Cognac. 455 ha. in Grande Champagne 20%, Petite Champagne 30%, Borderies 38% and Fins Bois 12%. Produces – Medaillon V.S.O.P. Cordon Bleu, Cordon Argent Extra, Cordon Noir, Cordon Rubis and Réserve du Fondateur.

Martell (Jean) (Fr). Originally from Jersey in the Channel Islands in 1715. Traded in Cognac and made his fortune. Founder of the Martell Cognac house in Cognac.

Martha May's (USA). See Heitz Vineyards.

Martha's vineyard Island (USA). An island that comes under the jurisdiction of Massachusetts. Is the base for several small wineries.

Martian Lady (Cktl). 1 measure Gin, 1 measure lemon juice, ½ measure Cherry brandy, ½ egg white. Shake over ice, strain into a Champagne flute.

Martillac (Fr). A commune in the A.C. Graves district of south-western Bordeaux.

Martin (John) (Bel). An importer based in Antwerp. Imports Courage's Bulldog Ale and sells it as Martin's Pale Ale.

Martin (Ray) Winery (USA). A winery based near Saratoga, Santa Clara, California. Grape varieties – Cabernet sauvignon, Chardonnay and Pinot noir. Produces varietal wines. La Montaña is the second label.

Martin (Rémy) and Co (Fr). A Cognac producer. Address = BP 37, 16102 Cognac. 150 ha. in the Grande Champagne. Produces only Fine Champagne cognacs. Also has interests in many countries. See also Dynasty.

Martina (It). See Martina Franca.

Martina Franca (It). D.O.C. white wine from Puglia. Made from the Bianco d'alessano, Fiano, Bombino, Malvasia toscana and Verdeca grapes. D.O.C. also applies to the naturally sparkling wine produced with wine/must obtained within specific area.

Martin Brewery (Czec). A brewery based in eastern Czec.

Martin Brewery (Eng). Opened near Dover in 1984. Produces cask conditioned Martin Ale 1040 O.G.

Martiner (Fr). The local (Touraine, Loire) term for to have a drink (of wine).

Martiner le Vin (Fr). Denotes the tapping of a cask of wine in the Touraine district of the Loire region.

Martinez (USA). A wine town in Contra Costa County near San Francisco, California. Home to two small wineries.

Martinez Cocktail (Cktl).(1). The original recipe from Prof. Jerry Thomas. 1 dash bitters, 2 dashes Maraschino, 1 pony Old Tom Gin, 1 wine glass dry Vermouth, 2 ice cubes. Shake, strain into a cocktail glass, add a slice of lemon. For sweet Martinez add 2 dashes of Gomme syrup.

Martinez Cocktail (Cktl).(2) (sweet). ¼ gill dry Gin, ¼ gill Italian vermouth, dash Angostura. Stir over ice, strain into a cocktail glass, serve with a cherry and dash lemon peel juice.

Martinez Cocktail (Cktl).(3) (medium). ¼ gill Gin, ⅛ gill Italian vermouth, ⅛ gill French vermouth, dash Angostura. Stir over ice, strain into a cocktail glass, serve with a cherry or olive and dash lemon peel juice.

Martinez Cocktail (Cktl).(4) (dry). ¼ measure dry Gin, ¼ measure French vermouth, dash Angostura. Stir over ice, strain into a cocktail glass, serve with an olive and dash of lemon peel juice.

Martinez [Gassiot] (Port). Vintage Port shippers. Vintages – 1870, 1872, 1873, 1874, 1875, 1878, 1880, 1881, 1884, 1885, 1886, 1887, 1890, 1892, 1894, 1896, 1897, 1900, 1904, 1908, 1911, 1912, 1919, 1922, 1927, 1931, 1934, 1945, 1955, 1958, 1960, 1963, 1967, 1970, 1975, 1977, 1980, 1982.

Martinez Lacuesta (Sp). Address = Calle la Ventilla, N°.71, Haro, Rioja. Holds no vineyards. Buys in wine. 80% red, 5% rosé and 15% white.

Martinez Special Cocktail (Cktl). ¼ gill dry Gin, ⅙ gill French vermouth, 6 dashes Orange bitters, 1½ teaspoons Maraschino, 4 dashes Angostura. Shake over ice, strain into a cocktail glass. Serve with a cherry or olive and a dash of orange peel juice.

Martini (Cktl). See Martini Cocktail.

Martini (Louis) (USA). A family owned winery in Napa Valley, California. 353 ha. Grape varieties – Barbera, Cabernet sauvignon, Gewürztraminer, Pinot noir, Petite sirah and Zinfandel. Produces varietal and dessert wines.

Martini and Prati (USA). A winery based near Santa Rosa, Sonoma County, California. Grape variety mainly Cabernet sauvignon. Varietal wines sold under the Fountaingrove label.

Martini and Rossi (It). A famous company that produces all types of Vermouth based in Turin. Also produces sparkling (méthode champenoise) wines. Labels include Riserva di Montelera Brut and cuve close wines. Also has many holdings in wine and spirit houses world-wide.

Martini Cocktail (Cktl).(1) (sweet). ⅓ gill Gin, ⅙ gill Italian vermouth, dash Orange bitters. Stir over ice, strain into a cocktail glass, add a squeeze of lemon peel juice on top.

Martini Cocktail (Cktl).(2) (medium). ¼ gill dry Gin, ⅛ measure Italian vermouth, ⅛ gill French vermouth. Stir over ice, strain into a cocktail glass, serve with a dash of lemon peel juice on top.

Martini Cocktail (Cktl).(3) (dry). ¼ gill dry Gin, ¼ gill French vermouth. Stir over ice, strain into a cocktail glass, serve with a dash lemon peel juice.

Martini Cocktail (Cktl).(4). 1 measure dry Gin, ¼ measure French vermouth, 2 dashes Pernod. Stir over ice, strain into a cocktail glass. Decorate with an onion.

Martini Medium (Cktl). See Martini Cocktail (2).

Martinique Coffee (W.Ind). The largest grade of coffee seed (bean), green in colour. Grown on the island of Martinique. See De Clieu [Captain].

Martinique Rhum (W.Ind). A dark, full-bodied Rum which has a dry, full, burnt flavour. Pot-stilled cane juice. 40% alc. by vol. See St. James.

Martinique Rum (W.Ind). See Martinique Rhum.

Martini Special Cocktail (Cktl). ⅕ gill dry Gin, ⅛ gill Italian vermouth, ½ teaspoon of Maraschino, Absinthe and raspberry syrup. Shake over ice, strain into a cocktail glass. Serve with a dash of lemon peel juice.

Martino Tea (Punch). ½ pint hot mint tea, 1 teaspoon honey, ½ gill Arak. Stir together in a warmed mug, add sugar to taste.

Martin Ray (USA). A small winery based in Santa Clara, California.

Martinsberg (Ger). vineyard. (Anb) = Rheinhessen. (Ber) = Bingen. (Gro) = Rheingrafenstein. (Vil) = Siefersheim.

Martinsborn (Ger). vineyard. (Anb) = Mosel-Saar-Ruwer. (Ber) = Zell/Mosel. (Gro) = Rosenhang. (Vil) = Bruttig-Fankel.

Martinsheim (Ger). Village. (Anb) = Franken. (Ber) = Steigerwald. (Gro) = Not yet assigned. (Vin) = Langenstein.

Martinshöhe (Ger). vineyard. (Anb) = Rheinpfalz. (Ber) = Mittelhaardt-Deutsche Weinstrasse. (Gro) = Feuerberg. (Vil) = Gönnheim.

Martinský Porter (Czec). The strongest beer in Czechoslovakia, at 20° Balling, from the Michalovce Brewery.

Martin's Pale Ale (Eng). An Ale brewed by Courage 1068 O.G. known as Bulldog in Britain. Is bottled by the John Martin Co. in Antwerp for sale in Belgium.

Martinstein (Ger). Village. (Anb) = Nahe. (Ber) = Schloss Böckelheim. (Gro) = Paradiesgarten. (Vin) = Schlossberg.

Martinsthal (Ger). Village. (Anb) = Rheingau. (Ber) = Johannisberg. (Gro) = Steinmacker. (Vins) = Langenberg, Rödchen, Wildsau.

Marufo (Port). A red grape variety grown in the Beiras region.

Maruja Fino (Sp). A pale, light, Fino sherry produced by Terry in Jerez de la Frontera.

M

Marumba Cocktail (Cktl). 1 measure Jamaican rum, 1 measure Mandarine Napoléon, juice ½ lemon. Shake over ice, strain into a goblet. Dress with an orange slice.

Marvo (USA). An egg and Marsala tradename drink. Similar to Marsala all'Uovo.

Mary Ann (Ch.Isles). The brand-name of the Ann Street Brewery in St. Helier, Jersey.

Mary Ann (Ch.Isles). A cask conditioned Bitter 1042 O.G. brewed by the Ann Street Brewery, St. Helier, Jersey.

Mary Garden Cocktail (Cktl). ⅔ measure Dubonnet, ⅓ measure dry Vermouth. Stir over ice, strain into a cocktail glass.

Maryland (USA). An eastern American wine district in the state of Maryland.

Mary Pickford (Cktl). ½ measure white Rum, ½ measure unsweetened pineapple juice, dash Grenadine, dash Maraschino. Shake over ice, strain into a cocktail glass.

Mary Rose (Cktl). ½ measure Kirsch de Zoug, ¼ measure Manzanilla, ¼ measure Apricot brandy. Stir with ice, strain, add zest of an orange and a cherry.

Mary Rose Champagne (Eng). A non-vintage Champagne produced by De Courcy et Fils for the Mary Rose Trust in Portsmouth to raise funds for the Mary Rose Trust (for the raising and restoration of Henry VIII's flagship – the Mary Rose in Portsmouth). 1983. Made from 25% Chardonnay and 75% Pinot noir.

Maryroy Vineyard (USA). A noted small winery based near Calistoga, California. 4.5 ha. Grape varieties – Chenin blanc and Petite sirah. Produces varietal wines.

Maryville Vineyard (Ire). A vineyard based near Cork. Address = Kilworth, County Cork. Produces dry white wines.

Marzelle (La) (Fr). See Château le Marzelle.

Marzemino (USA). A red grape variety used to make red wines in California. Also in Italy.

Märzenbier (Ger). A specialty beer served at the Oktoberfest. A dark, strong, slightly sour beer.

Mas (Fr). The name used in Roman times for the stone walls that surrounded the small terraced vineyards in Hermitage, Côtes du Rhône.

Masachs (Sp). A brand of sparkling wine produced by Casa Masachs (rosé and white).

Masada Kosher Wines (S.Afr). Kosher wines produced under strict Rabbinical supervision. Varietals made by Charles Back, Fairview Estate, Box 583, Suider Paarl 7625.

Masaglio (Fr). A dry white wine produced in Sicily.

Masaguera (Sp). A white grape variety grown in the southern regions of Spain.

Masberg Mansion (Euro). A vineyard based at Nauvoo, Liechtenstein. Produces white wines.

Masbout (Egy). Coffee.

Mascara (Afr). The centre of wine production in Algeria.

Mascarello (Giuseppe) (It). A winery based in Monchiero, a district of Barolo, Piemonte.

Mascaró (Sp). A brandy and wine producer. Address = Carbonell del Casal 9, Vilafranca del Penedés, Barcelona. Source of base wines – Penedés region. Produces – V.O. Estilo Fine Marivaux, Narciso Etiqueta Azul, Don Narciso and Viña Fresco.

Maschio (It). A sparkling (méthode champenoise) wine producer based in Veneto. Produces Prosecco di Conegliano-Valdobbiadene.

Mas de Bossard (Fr). The name for the granite soil on the slope of l'Hermitage in the northern Rhône.

Mas de Gourgonnier (Fr). A V.D.Q.S. vineyard in the Coteaux-des-Baux-en-Provence. Address = Le Destet, 13890 Mouriès.

Mas de Greffieux (Fr). A clay soil on the slopes of l'Hermitage in the northern Rhône.

Mas de la Dame (Fr). A V.D.Q.S. vineyard in the Coteaux-des-Baux-en-Provence. Address = Les Baux-Route de Saint-Rémy, 13520 Maussane-lès-Alpilles.

Mas de Méal (Fr). The alluvial soil on the slopes of l'Hermitage in the northern Rhône.

Masdeu (Fr). The name given to fortified red wines of the Roussillon, southern France. Originally spelt Masdieu and Masdu.

Masdieu (Fr). An old spelling of Masdeu.

Masdu (Fr). An old spelling of Masdeu.

Mas du Cellier (Fr). A V.D.Q.S. vineyard in the Coteaux-des-Baux-en-Provence. Address = La Haute Craline, 13210 Saint-Rémy-de-Provence.

Mash (Eng). The mixture of barley Grist or other cereal and water (liquor) before fermentation in beer and whisky production.

Mashing (Eng) (slang). A term for brewing tea.

Mashing (Eng). The extraction of the maltose from the grain (Grist) into a fermentable liquid (Wort).

M

Mash the Tea (Eng). A north of England term for making a pot (brew) of tea.

Mash Tub (Scot). See Mash Tun.

Mash Tun (Eng). A squat cylindrical-shaped vessel where the mash infuses. Has a false floor to retain the spent grains as the Wort is run off.

Masi (It). A large producer of Veneto wines, noted for their Soave and Valpolicella.

Masía Bach (Sp). A Catalan estate. Produces Extrísimo, Masía Bach and Tinto.

Màslàs (Hun). See Tokay Màslàs.

Mason Arms (Eng). A home brew public house based at South Leigh, near Witney, Oxfordshire. Produces a dark malty bitter.

Maşrapa (Tur). A metal drinking cup, tankard.

Massadah (Isr). A dry white, table wine.

Mas Sainte Berthe (Fr). A V.D.Q.S. vineyard in the Coteaux-des-Baux-en-Provence. Address = Les Baux, 13520, Maussane-lès-Alpilles.

Massaly (Eng). An eighteenth-century spelling of Marsala.

Massandra (USSR). A white muscat dessert wine from Massandra in the southern Crimea produced from the Massandra muscatel. Also the name for red and dry white wines.

Massandra Muscatel (USSR). A rich, sweet dessert wine from the Crimea.

Massapes (Mad).The name for the clay soil found on Madeira.

Massenbachhausen (Ger). Village. (Anb) = Württemberg. (Ber) = Württembergisch Unterland. (Gro) = Heuchelberg. (Vin) = Krähenberg.

Massenez (G.E.) (Fr). An Eau-de-vie distiller. Address = Dieffenbach-au-Val, 67220 Villé.

Massé Père et Fils (Fr). A Grande Marque Champagne house based in Reims. Part of Lanson.

Massic (It). A dry white wine produced in central Italy during Roman times.

Massif (Fr). A large mountain range running north-south through central-southern France. The river Loire rises in them.

Massif Central (Fr). See Massif.

Masson Light (USA). A medium dry, white, low-alcohol 0.5% by vol. wine from the Paul Masson estate in California.

Masson [Paul] (USA). A large well-known wine producer of California. See Paul Masson vineyards.

Massum (Lat). A red wine produced in central-western Italy in Roman times.

Mastantuono Winery (USA). A winery based in San Luis Obispo, California. Grape variety – Zinfandel.

Master Ale (Eng). A bottled old Ale 1080 O.G. brewed by the Holden Brewery in Dudley, Worcs.

Master Blend (Eng). The brand-name of an instant coffee with added fresh coffee grounds produced by General Foods in Oxon.

Master Brew (Eng). The brand-name for Shepherd Neame's Beers. For a dark cask Mild 1031 O.G. Bitter 1036 O.G. and a keg Light Mild XX 1033 O.G.

Master Cellar Wine Warehouses (The) (Eng). A wine-warehouse operation based in Aberdeen Road, Croydon, London. Launched by Davidsons.

Master of the Malt (Scot). An annual competition run by Invergordon Distillers at their Tamnavulin Distillery in Glenlivet.

Master of Wine (Eng). The highest qualification in the British wine trade. Obtained through a series of blind tastings and written examinations. Holders have M.W. after their names.

Masterpiece (Can). A Canadian whisky produced by Seagram. 43% alc. by vol.

Masterton (Austr). Address = P.O. Box 255, Seven Hills, South Australia. Owns no vineyards. Winery buys in Cabernet sauvignon, Rhine riesling, Sémillon and Shiraz grapes.

Mastic (Gre). The resin from the Lentisk tree (Turpentine tree) used to flavour Raki. See Mastika.

Mastic (USA). Another name for Mastikha. 45–46% alc. by vol.

Masticha (Gre). An alternative spelling of Mastika.

Mastika (Gre). An Arrack brandy with Resin added. Made from the Gum of the Mastikha plant and aniseed. See Mastic, Masticha and Mastikha.

Mastikha (Gre). An alternative spelling of Mastika.

Mastrasa (USSR). A red table wine produced in Baku.

Mastroberardino (It). A winery based at Atripalda in Campania.

Mata-Bicho (Port). Lit – 'A drop'. Denotes a tot of spirit.

Matador (Sp). The brand-label used by Valdespino for a range of their Sherries.

Matador Cocktail (Cktl). 1½ fl.ozs. Tequila, 2 dashes lemon juice. Shake over crushed ice, strain into an ice-filled highball and top with lemonade.

Matanzas (W.Ind). A major Rum producer on the island of Cuba now State owned.

Matanzas Creek (USA). A winery based near Santa Rosa, Sonoma County, California. Grape varieties – Cabernet sau-

M

vignon, Chardonnay, Gewürztraminer, Pinot blanc and Pinot noir. Produce varietal wines.

Matar (Port). To quench one's thirst.

Matara (Tur). Flask. A metal water bottle used by soldiers.

Mataro (Austr) (Sp). A red grape variety. Also known as Carignan.

Matataki (Eng). A soft drink of oriental fruits and carbonated water with a hint of Saké produced by J.N. Nichols in Manchester.

Matawhero Winery (N.Z.). Vineyard. Address = Riverpoint Road, RDI, Gisbourne. 30 ha. Grape varieties – Chardonnay, Chenin blanc, Gewürztraminer, Riesling-sylvaner, Sauvingnon blanc.

Maté (S.Am). Ilex paraguariensis. A herbal tea. See Yerba Maté.

Màté Lacko Sepsi (Hun). Private Secretary to Zsuzsanna Lorantffy, widow of Gyorgy Rakoczi II, Prince of Transylvania who decided to postpone the vintage because of the threat of war so creating Aszú berries that had shrivelled in the warm Autumn weather.

Mateppe vineyards (Afr). A wine estate based near Marandellas, Harare, Zimbabwe. Grape varieties – Cabernet sauvignon, Chenin blanc, Cinsault, Clairette blanche, Hanepoot and Pinotage tinta. (red and white).

Mater (Bel). A Brown ale brewed by the Roman Brasserie in Mater near Oudenaarde.

Mateus Mule (Cktl). 5 fl.ozs. Mateus rosé, ⅙ measure Brandy, dash lemon juice. Place into a large goblet. Stir, add a cube of ice and a twist of orange.

Mateus Rosé (Port). A famous pétillant rosé wine sold in a bocksbeutel bottle in most countries of the world. Produced by SOGRAPE at Vila Real.

Mathäser Bierstadt (Ger). A famous beer-hall in Bayerstrasse. Serves Löwenbrau beer.

Matheisbildchen (Ger). vineyard. (Anb) = Mosel-Saar-Ruwer. (Ber) = Bernkastel. (Gro) = Badstube. (Vil) = Bernkastel-Kues.

Mather (Eng). A wines and spirits group owned mainly by the Matthew Clark Brewery. Produces Black Beer.

Mathews Napa Valley Winery (USA). An old-time winery in Napa City, Napa Valley, California. Still retains a few Port wines.

Mathias Weingarten (Ger). vineyard. (Anb) = Mittelrhein. (Ber) = Bacharach. (Gro) = Schloss Stahleck. (Vil) = Bacharach.

Mathieu (Serge) (Fr). Champagne producer. Address = Avirey-Lingey, 10340 Les Riceys. Récoltants-manipulants. Produces – Vintage and non-vintage wines.

Matho (Fr). The brand-name of a wine-based apéritif.

Màti (S.Am). The old name for Maté from the Quechua Màti gourd (from which the herbal tea Maté is drunk).

Matilde Rosé (Austr). A dry, full-flavoured rosé wine produced by the Sandalford in Western Australia from the Cabernet sauvignon grape.

Matino (It). D.O.C. red or rosé wine from Puglia. Made from the Malvasia, Negro amaro and Sangiovese grapes in the province of Lecce and part of Murge Salentine. 2 types produced – Rosso and Rosato.

Màtraalya (Hun). A wine district in the Màtra Hills, northern Hungary. Includes areas of Debrö and Eger. Is noted for its fine white wines.

Matt (Ger). A flat, insipid wine.

Matt Brewery (USA). A former brewery based in Utica, New York. Noted for its Lager and Ale beers. See West End Brewing Co.

Mattersburg District (Aus). A wine-producing district at the foothills of Rosalien mountains.

Matthew Brown (Eng). See Brown.

Matthew Brown Lancashire Bitter (Eng). A Bitter ale brewed by the Matthew Brown Brewery, Blackburn, Lancashire.

Matthieu (Louis) (Fr). A Champagne producer based at Reims.

Mattingly and Moore (USA). The brand-name of a straight Bourbon whiskey distilled by Calvert Distillers Co., Lawrenceberg. 40% alc. by vol.

Mattock (Fr). A hand tool for tilling the soil in the vineyards. Similar to a pick.

Matt's Premium (USA). An all-malt Lager beer brewed with imported hops by the West End Brewing Co. in Utica, New York.

Matty's Light Beer (Eng). A light keg Beer 1033 O.G. brewed by the Matthew Brown Brewery in Blackburn, Lancashire.

Matua Valley Winery (N.Z.). Address = Waikoukou Road, Waimauku, Auckland. 25 ha. Grape varieties – Breidecker, Cabernet sauvignon, Chardonnay, Flora, Grey riesling, Muscat blanc, Pinot noir, Sauvignon blanc and Sémillon.

Maturana (Sp). A white grape variety grown in the Rioja region of north-east Spain.

M

Maturana Tinta (Sp). A black grape variety grown in Rioja.

Maturation (Eng). The time given to beer, wines or spirits in cask or bottle for improving the quality and allowing the impurities to settle out.

Matusalem (Sp). A Methuselah bottle (equals 8 standard bottles). Used for Cava wines.

Matuschka-Greiffenclau (Ger). Family-owners of Schloss Vollrads.

Matyas Sor (Hun). A Beer brewed by the Kobànya Brewery.

Matzen (Aus). Part of Weinviertel which is divided into Matzen, Retz and Falkenstein.

Mauchamps (Les) (Fr). A Premier Cru vineyard in the A.C. commune of Morey-Saint-Denis, Côte de Nuits, Burgundy.

Mauchen (Ger). Village. (Anb) = Baden. (Ber) = Markgräflerland. (Gro) = Burg Neuenfels. (Vins) = Frauenberg, Sonnenstück.

Mauchenheim (Ger). Village. (Anb) = Rheinhessen. (Ber) = Wonnegau. (Gro) = Sybillenstein. (Vin) = Sioner Klosterberg.

Mauerberg (Ger). vineyard. (Anb) = Baden. (Ber) = Ortenau. (Gro) = Schloss Rodeck. (Vil) = Neuweier.

Mäuerchen (Ger). vineyard. (Anb) = Mosel-Saar-Ruwer. (Ber) = Saar-Ruwer. (Gro) = Römerlay. (Vil) = Mertesdorf.

Mäuerchen (Ger). vineyard. (Anb) = Rheingau. (Ber) = Johannisberg. (Gro) = Burgweg. (Vil) = Geisenheim.

Mauer Wines (Ger). Wines from Baden which are, with certain wines from Franken, allowed to be sold in bocksbeutel.

Maufoux (Fr). Family merchants based in Santenay in Burgundy.

Mauget (Eng). The brand-name for a range of fruit spirits (Sloe gin, Cherry brandy, Cherry whisky, etc.) produced by Lamb and Watt of Liverpool, Lancashire.

Maugham's Brewery (Asia). A noted brewery based in Singapore. Produces fine Lagers.

Maui Blush (USA). A dry rosé wine produced on the island of Maui, Hawaii by the Tedeschi vineyard.

Maui Lager (USA). A Lager beer of German Bock-style brewed on the island Maui, Hawaii by the Pacific Brewing Co. Inc.

Maui Nouveau (USA). A white wine produced by the Tedeschi vineyard on the island of Maui, Hawaii.

Maulbronn (Ger). Village. (Anb) = Württemberg. (Ber) = Württembergisch Unterland. (Gro) = Stromberg. (Vins) = Eilfingerberg, Klosterstück, Reichshalde.

Mauldon Brewery (Eng). Revived in 1982, this family brewery based in Sudbury, Suffolk produces cask conditioned beers including Christmas Reserve 1065 O.G.

Mauny (La) (W.Ind). A very popular brand of Rum produced on the island of Martinique by Bellonie, Bourdillon et Cie.

Maureen (Cktl). 1 measure Brandy, ½ measure Tia Maria, ½ measure cream. Shake over ice, strain into a cocktail glass.

Maures (Fr). A Vins de Pays area in south-western France. Produces red, rosé and dry white wines.

Maures (Les) (Fr). A Vins de Pays area in the Var Département in south-eastern France.

Mauresque Cocktail (Cktl). 1 measure Pernod, ⅓ measure Orgeat. Place in a highball, top with iced water, stir.

Maurice Cocktail (Cktl). ½ measure dry Gin, ¼ measure Italian vermouth, ¼ measure French vermouth, juice ¼ orange, dash Angostura. Shake over ice, strain into a cocktail glass.

Maurice Drouhin (Fr). A cuvée in the Premier Cru vineyard Champs-Pimont, A.C. Beaune, Côte de Beaune, Burgundy. Owned by the Hospices de Beaune.

Mauritius Breweries Limited (Afr). See Mauritius Brewery.

Mauritius Brewery (Afr). A brewery based on the island of Mauritius on the east coast of Africa. Brews local beers plus F.E.S. and Stella Pilsener Lager under licence.

Maury (Fr). The name for a yeast strain found in Maury near the Pyrénées. Is an excellent yeast for fermenting a honey solution into a sweet mead.

Maury (Fr). An A.C. red Vin doux naturel from Roussillon in south-eastern France. Made from the Grenache grape. Minimum age 2 years.

Mausac (Fr). A red grape variety grown in the southern Rhône.

Mausat (Fr). An alternative name for the Malbec grape.

Mauseln (Ger). Denotes a recognisable smell of mice in the wine.

Mäushöhle (Ger). vineyard. (Anb) = Rheinpfalz. (Ber) = Mittelhaardt-Deutsche Weinstrasse. (Gro) = Mariengarten. (Vil) = Deidesheim.

Maustal (Ger). vineyard. (Anb) = Franken. (Ber) = Maindreieck. (Gro) = Hofrat. (Vil) = Sulzfeld.

Mautner Markoff (Aus). One of the leading sparkling wine producers in Austria.
Mauves (Fr). An A.C. commune of Saint-Joseph in the Rhône.
Mauzac (Fr). A white grape variety grown in the Rhône and Languedoc. Used in the making of Blanquette de Limoux (sparkling). Also grown in the Armagnac.
Mavis Delight (Cktl). ⅔ measure Cordial Médoc, ⅓ measure Scotch whisky. Stir together over ice in a highball glass. Top with lemonade.
Mavro (Gre). Lit – 'Black'. Used to describe dark, red wines.
Mavrodaphne (Gre). A red grape variety grown in Greece to produce sweet, fortified, dessert wines.
Mavrodaphne (Gre). A sweet, red, fortified dessert wine similar in taste to Verdelho.
Mavrodaphne de Cephalonia (Gre). A red dessert wine from the Isle of Cephalonia in the Ionian Islands in western Greece.
Mavrodaphne de Patras (Gre). A fine liqueur red dessert (fortified) wine from the Peloponnese.
Mavrodi (Gre). A dark red wine produced in Delphi from the Mavroutis grape.
Mavro Kalpaki (Gre). A red wine produced on the island of Limnos.
Mavron (Cyp). A red grape variety from Cyprus and Greece used in the making of the rosé wine Kokkineli.
Mavro Naoussis (Gre). A dry red wine from the Naoussa district in central Macedonia.
Mavro Romeiko (Gre). A dry red wine made in Crete from grape of the same name.
Mavroutis (Gre). A red mountain grape variety used to produce the robust red wines of rural Greece.
Mavrud (Bul). A red grape variety which produces a full, soft wine on the sweet side with little acidity. From the Maritsa Valley.
Mawby vineyards (USA). A winery based at Sutton's Bay, Michigan. Produces hybrid wines.
Mawmesey (Eng). The Elizabethan spelling of Malmsey.
Maxima (Ger). A brand of de-caffeinated coffee.
Maximator (Ger). A Doppelbock beer, brewed by the Augustiner Brauerei in Munich.
Maxim Cocktail (Cktl). ⅗ measure dry Gin, ⅖ measure dry Vermouth, dash (white) Crème de Menthe. Shake over ice, strain into a cocktail glass.
Maxime (Cktl). ⅗ measure Vodka, ⅖ measure Campari, 3 dashes Cherry brandy, ⅐ measure Bianco Vermouth. Stir with ice, strain into a cocktail glass, add a twist of lemon and a cherry.
Maximes Frères (Fr). A noted producer of Brandy 40% alc. by vol. of same name.
Maximiner (Ger). vineyard. (Anb) = Mosel-Saar-Ruwer. (Ber) = Saar-Ruwer. (Gro) = Römerlay. (Vil) = Trier.
Maximiner Burgberg (Ger). vineyard. (Anb) = Mosel-Saar-Ruwer. (Ber) = Bernkastel. (Gro) = Probstberg. (Vil) = Fell.
Maximiner Herrenberg (Ger). vineyard. (Anb) = Mosel-Saar-Ruwer. (Ber) = Bernkastel. (Gro) = Probstberg. (Vil) = Longuich.
Maximiner Hofgarten (Ger). vineyard. (Anb) = Mosel-Saar-Ruwer. (Ber) = Bernkastel. (Gro) = Probstberg. (Vil) = Kenn.
Maximiner Klosterlay (Ger). vineyard. (Anb) = Mosel-Saar-Ruwer. (Ber) = Bernkastel. (Gro) = Sankt Michael. (Vil) = Detzem.
Maximin Grünhaus (Ger). A famous wine-producer based in the Mosel-Saar-Ruwer region.
Maximin Staadt (Ger). vineyard. (Anb) = Mosel-Saar-Ruwer. (Ber) = Saar-Ruwer. (Gro) = Scharzberg. (Vil) = Kastel-Staadt.
Maxim's Cuvée Réservée (Fr). A dry Champagne produced for Maxim's restaurant in Paris.
Maxim's de Paris (Fr). The name for a range of Cognacs produced by Château de la Grange. Available as V.S.O.P. (10 years old), Napoléon (20–30 years old) and X.O. (over 35 years old).
Maximus Super (USA). A strong beer brewed by the West End Brewing Co. in Utica, New York.
Max Rosé Pas Dosé (It). A sparkling (méthode champenoise) wine produced by Marco Berlucchi in Lombardy.
Maxwell House (Eng). A famous brand of instant coffee produced by General Foods in Oxon.
Maxwell Wines (Austr). Address = 24 Kangarilla Road, McLaren Vale, South Australia 5171. Has no vineyards. Buys in Cabernet sauvignon, Merlot, Sémillon and Shiraz.
Maya (Tur). Yeast.
Mayacamas (USA). A vineyard in the Napa Valley, California. Grape varieties – Cabernet sauvignon and Chardonnay. Produces varietal wines.
Maya Cocktail (Cktl). 1½ fl.ozs. white Rum, ½ fl.oz. golden Rum, 2 fl.ozs.

pineapple juice, 3 dashes Curaçao, 2 dashes Gomme syrup. Blend together with a scoop of crushed ice in a blender. Strain into an old-fashioned glass, dress with a cherry, mint sprig and pineapple cube.

Mayalamak (Tur). Fermentation.

Mayan Whore Cocktail (Cktl). Place ⅕ gill Tequila into a flute glass, add ⅓ gill pineapple juice (do not stir). Top with soda and then layer 1 measure of Kahlúa on top. Serve with straws.

Mayblossom Brandy (Eng). ¾ fill bottles with picked mayblossom (not leaves or stems). Top up with Brandy, cork and seal. Store 4–6 weeks. Strain off Brandy, rebottle, seal then use as required.

May Blossom Fizz (Cktl). 2 fl.ozs. Swedish Punsch, ¾ fl.oz. lemon juice, 2 dashes Grenadine. Shake over ice, strain into a highball glass containing ice. Top with soda water. Serve with a muddler and straws.

Maye (Les Fils) (Switz). Noted wine-producers based in Riddes, Valais. Are noted for their Johannisberg Feuergold.

Mayetiola Destructor (Lat). See Hessian Fly.

Mayfair Cocktail (Cktl). ¼ measure Gin, ¼ measure orange juice, 2 dashes Apricot syrup, 2 dashes Clove syrup. Shake well over ice, strain into a cocktail glass.

Mayfair Vineyards (N.Z.). A winery based in Sturges Road, Henderson, North Island. Noted for its fortified wines and Blackberry Nip.

Mayflower Special (Cktl). 1 oz. Mandarine Napoléon, ⅓ oz. Angostura, ½ teaspoon powdered sugar. Shake well with ice, strain into a highball glass. Top up with soda water.

May Fly (Eng). A light Oloroso sherry produced by Findlater's.

Mayl (Tur). Liquid.

Mayoral (Eng). The term used to describe an experienced grape picker.

Mayor Cuerpo (Sp). Describes a Sherry with a very full body.

Mayschoss (Ger). Village. (Anb) = Ahr. (Ber) = Walporzheim/Ahrtal. (Gro) = Klosterberg. (Vins) = Burgberg, Laacherberg, Lochmuhlerley, Mönchberg, Schieferley, Silberberg.

May Wine (Ger). The traditional preparation of a light Rhine wine into which the aromatic leaves of the herb Waldmeister (Woodruff) have been infused. May wine is served chilled and ladled from a bowl usually with strawberries or other fruit floating in it.

Mazagran (Arab). Describes hot or cold coffee that is served in a glass.

Mazandaran (Iran). A famous red wine of ancient times produced in the then northern Persia.

Mazard (Eng). Mazer. See also Mazzard.

Mazarin (Fr). A light brown liqueur similar to Bénédictine.

Mazato of Pérou (S.Am). A drink made from boiled maize and sugar water in Peru.

Mazbout (Tur). Medium sweet Turkish coffee.

Mazer (Eng). A drinking vessel, usually of wood, bound and mounted with silver or other metal. The Scottish type is also mounted on a stem. Vessels were often covered and used for the drinking of Mead in mediaeval times. Also spelt Mazard and Mazzard.

Mazères (Fr). A commune within the A.C. Graves district of south-western Bordeaux.

Mazion (Fr). A commune within the A.C. Côtes de Blaye district of north-eastern Bordeaux.

Mazis-Chambertin (Fr). A Grand Cru vineyard in the A.C. commune of Gevrey-Chambertin, Côte de Nuits, Burgundy. Also spelt Mazys or Mazy. 12.6 ha.

Mazoyères-Chambertin (Fr). A Grand Cru vineyard in the A.C. commune Gevrey-Chambertin, Côte de Nuits, Burgundy. 19.5 ha. Is often sold as Charmes-Chambertin which it adjoins because of it not being so well-known.

Mazuela (Sp). A red grape variety grown in the Rioja, north-eastern Spain. Also known as the Carignan and Cariñena.

Mazuelo (Sp). See Mazuela. Alternative spelling.

Mazuran Vineyard (N.Z.). A winery based at Lincoln Road, Henderson, North Island. 6 ha. Is noted for Port and Sherry-style wines.

Mazy-Chambertin (Fr). See Mazis-Chambertin.

Mazyn (Tur). A type of fermented milk from Armenia.

Mazys-Chambertin (Fr). See Mazis-Chambertin.

Mazzard (Eng). See Mazer.

Mazza Vineyards (USA). A winery based in Erie County, Pennsylvania. Produces French hybrid, native American and vinifera wines.

Mazzo (It). Bouquet.

M.B.G. (Euro) (abbr). Maltese Bartenders' Guild. Address = P.O. Box 368, Valletta, Malta.

Mbuni (Afr). An east African coffee made from the whole dried coffee cherry (fruit). Has a bitter taste.

M.C. (Eng) (abbr). On a wine-list denotes Mis en bouteille au Château.

M

McAndrews (Scot). A blended Scotch whisky produced by Stewart and Son. 40% alc. by vol.

MCB (Eng) (abbr). Measuring Container Bottle.

McCallum (Duncan and John) (Scot). Scotch whisky distillers.

McCallum Breweries (Sri.L). A brewery based in Meegoda, Colombo. Brews Sando, Three Coins and Pilsener beers.

McClelland Cocktail (Cktl). ⅔ measure Sloe gin, ⅓ measure Cointreau, dash Orange bitters. Shake over ice, strain into a cocktail glass.

McCormick Distilling (USA). A winery based in Kansas City, Missouri.

McCoys (The) (USA). The term given for the 'Real stuff'. Scotch whisky etc. that was brought in by the Rum runners during the Prohibition 1919–1933. See Real McCoy (The).

McCrea Vineyard (USA). A small vineyard based near Healdsburg, Sonoma County, California. Grape variety – Chardonnay.

McDonald (C & J) (Scot). A subsidiary blend of Arthur Bell and Scos. 40% alc. by vol.

McDowell Valley vineyards (USA). A large winery based near Hopland, Mendocino, California. 150 ha. Grape varieties – Cabernet sauvignon, Chardonnay, Chenin blanc, Colombard, Grenache, Petite sirah, Sauvignon blanc and Zinfandel. Produces varietal wines.

McEwan (Scot). See Scottish and Newcastle.

McEwan and Co (Scot). A Highland and Scotch whisky distillery based in Perthshire. Part of DCL. Linkwood Distillery is under licence to McEwan. Brands include Abbot's Choice, Chequeurs and Linkwood.

McEwan's Strong Ale (W.Ind). A Bitter 1086 O.G. brewed by the Guinness Brewery in Jamaica in association with Scottish and Newcastle Breweries.

McEwan-Younger (Eng). Scottish and Newcastle's north-west England, Yorkshire and north Wales marketing company.

McFadden Ranch (USA). A small vineyard based in Potter Valley, Mendocino, California. Grape variety – Sauvignon blanc.

McGregor Co-operative (S.Afr). Based in McGregor. Address = P/Bag X619 Robertson 6705. Produces – Edel Laat Oes Superior, Groot Toren, Laat Oes Steen and many varietals.

McGuinness Distillers (Can). Distillers of Canadian whisky.

McHenry (Cktl). ½ measure dry Gin, ½ measure Italian vermouth, dash Apricot brandy. Shake over ice, strain into a cocktail glass.

McKesson Liquor Co (USA). Major importers of Inca Pisco from Casa Ranuzzi in Lima, Peru.

McLains Whisky (Eng). The brand-name of a Scotch whisky bottled by Linfood Cash and Carry, Northamptonshire.

McLaren Vale (Austr). A fertile valley in South Australia, south of Adelaide. Wineries include – Hardys and Marienberg, Reynella and Seaview.

McManus Winery (Austr). A winery based in Riverina, New South Wales.

McMullen Brewery (Eng). Based in Hertford. Produces cask conditioned Country Bitter 1041 O.G. Christmas Ale 1071 O.G. Mac's N°1 Keg 1036 O.G. Hartsman Lager 1035 O.G. Farmer's Ale 1036 O.G. Olde Time 1070 O.G. Steingold Lager 1042 O.G. and bottled Mac's Brown 1031 O.G.

McNish (Robert and Co Ltd) (Scot). A blended Scotch whisky producer based in Glasgow.

McSorley's (USA). A bottom-fermented Malt beer brewed by the Schmidt Brewery in Philadelphia, Pennsylvania.

McWilliams (Austr). Address = P.O. Box 41, Pyrmont, New South Wales. 2009. vineyards at Mount Pleasant in the Hunter Valley and in the M.I.A. Grapes are also purchased in large quantities from other growers' vineyards at Lovedale, Mount Pleasant and Rosehill.

McWilliams Dry Friar (Austr). A dry Australian sherry produced by the McWilliams Winery in New South Wales.

McWilliams Wines (N.Z.). Address = Church Road, Taradale, Hawkes Bay. 360 ha. Grape varieties – Cabernet sauvignon, Gamay, Müller-Thurgau, Palomino. Noted for its fortified wines.

M.D. (Eng) (abbr). If found on a wine-list denotes Mis en bouteille au Domaine.

MDV (Sp). A dry Oloroso sherry produced by Domecq in Jerez de la Frontera.

Mead (Eng). Fermented honey, water and herbs. Historically the oldest drink known to man. 8% alc. by vol. Roman = Hydromel. Latin = Muslum, Sweden = Mjöd, Wales = Medd. See also Metheglin.

Meadowbrook (USA). The brand-name of a noted Rye whiskey.

Meadow Creek (Austr). Part of the Brown Brothers Estate in Victoria.

Mead Ranch (USA). A winery based in Atlas Peak, Napa Valley, California. 16.5 ha. Grape variety – Zinfandel.

Meagers Distillery (Can). Noted Canadian whisky distillers.

M

Meal (Scot). Another name for the ground malted grain also known as Grist.

Méal (Le) (Fr). A vineyard in the A.C. Hermitage, northern Rhône.

Mealie Beer (Afr). An alcoholic grain-based drink produced in southern Africa.

Meal Moth (Eng). The alternative name for the Pyralis moth.

Mealt (Eng). The mediaeval name for malt.

Meão (Port). A noted wine town based in the upper Douro. Grapes used for Port.

Measure (Eng). An implement for measuring spirits etc.

Measuring Container Bottles (Eng). Enables the contents in a bottle to be measured externally by means of a templet embossed with a reverse epsilon together with the capacity if it is a MCB.

Measuring Jigger (USA). See Jigger.

Meaty (Eng). A term used to describe a wine rich in tannin and body. A chewy wine.

Mecedor (Sp). A spiked pole used to break up the cap (Sombrero) of skins etc. on the fermenting wine. Also known as Basqueador.

Méchage (Fr). Fumigation (of casks, vats, etc.).

Mechín (Sp). A black grape variety grown in Rioja. Also known as the Monastel, Monastrel, Moraster, Ministrel, Negralejo and Valcarcelia. Grown also in Aragón and Catalonia.

Meckenheim (Ger). Village. (Anb) = Rheinpfalz. (Ber) = Mittelhaardt-Deutsche Weinstrasse. (Gro) = Hofstück. (Vins) = Neuberg, Spielberg, Wolfsdarm.

Mecsek (Hun). A district producing white wines. Includes the areas of Pécs and Vilàny.

Mecvini (It). A noted winery based in the Marches. Noted for its Verdicchio dei Castelli di Jesi.

Meda (Port). A wine-producing area north of Beira Alta.

Medaillon (Fr). The brand-name for a V.S.O.P. Liqueur Cognac from Martell.

Medallion Lager (Eng). A keg Lager beer 1036 O.G. brewed by the Federation Brewery in Newcastle, Tyne and Wear.

Medd (Wales). Mead.

Meddersheim (Ger). Village. (Anb) = Nahe. (Ber) = Schloss Böckelheim. (Gro) = Paradiesgarten. (Vins) = Altenberg, Edelberg, Präsent, Liebfrauenberg, Rheingrafenberg.

Meddw (Wales). Drunk, intoxicated.

Meddwdod (Wales). Drunkenness.

Meddwyn (Wales). An alcoholic. A drunkard.

Meddyglyn (Wales). Metheglin (spiced mead).

Médéa (Alg). A wine area in Alger which produces dry rosé, white and full-bodied red wines.

Medellin Excelso (S.Am). A full-bodied, pure coffee from Colombia.

Meder Distillery (Hol). A noted distillery owned by Heineken. Produces many liqueurs and spirits.

Medford Rum (USA). The old general name for Rum produced in colonial America.

Media (It). A variety of the red Schiave gentile grape.

Media (Sp). A hogshead or half-butt. See Media Bota.

Media Bocoy (Sp). A 76 gallon (350 litres) chestnut cask used for shipping wines. Also known as a Half-bocoy.

Media Bota (Sp). A 56 gallon (250 litres) wine cask also known as a Half bota.

Medias (Rum). An important wine-producing area. Part of the Tîrnave Vineyard.

Medicinal (Eng). Applied to wines and spirits etc. that have a taste of medicine. e.g. Islay whiskies, Vermouths, Bitters and herb Liqueurs.

Medicinal Compounds (USA). May contain up to 40% by vol. of alcohol but not classed as alcoholic beverages therefore not taxed.

Medine Distillery (Afr). A Rum distillery based at Bambous on the island of Mauritius.

Mediona (Sp). A red wine from Cataluña.

Medio y Corazón (Sp). The name given to the grape must obtained by treading and further fermentation.

Mediterranean Cocktail (Cktl). 1 fl.oz. Gin, ½ fl.oz. blue Curaçao. Pour Gin and Curaçao over ice in a highball glass. Top up with lemonade.

Medium (Ire). A term for a half-pint of draught Guinness.

Medium-High Culture (Aus). Mittelhoch-kultur. Vine cultivation system.

Medjidieh (Iran). A dark-brown Pilsener Lager 11° Balling brewed in Tehran by a brewery backed by the Board for the Protection of Industries. Now closed since the overthrow of the Shah.

Medjugorica (Yug). A wine-producing area in Croatia.

Medley Distillery (USA). A Bourbon whiskey distillery based near the Indiana border in Kentucky. See also Mellow Corn.

Médoc (Fr). The top wine district of the Bordeaux region on the west bank of the river Gironde. Made up of the Bas Médoc and the Haut-Médoc (finest).

Médoc Maritime (Fr). The old name for the Bas Médoc.

Médoc Noir (Hun). The Hungarian name

M

for the Merlot. (Also used at times for the Cabernet sauvignon).

Meeboulong (Cktl). ¼ gill Sloe gin, ⅛ gill French vermouth, ⅛ gill Italian vermouth, dash Orange bitters. Stir over ice, strain into a cocktail glass, squeeze lemon peel juice on top.

Meerendal Estate (S.Afr). Based in Durbanville. Address = Meerendal Wynlandgoed, Durbanville 7550. Produces varietal wines.

Meerlust Estate (S.Afr). Based in Stellenbosch. Address = P.O. Box 15, Faure 7131. Produces – Rubicon and varietal wines.

Meersburg (Ger). Village. (Anb) = Baden. (Ber) = Bodensee. (Gro) = Sonnenufer. (Vins) = Bengel, Chorherrnhalde, Fohrenberg, Haltnau, Jungfernstieg, Lerchenberg, Rieschen, Sängerhalde.

Meerspinne (Ger). Grosslage. (Anb) = Rheinpfalz. (Ber) = Mittelhaardt-Deutsche Weinstrasse. (Vils) = Gimmeldingen, Haardt, Königsbach, Mussbach, Neustadt an der Weinstrasse.

Meester (S.Afr). The brand-name of a famous Brandy. See also Oude Meester.

Mega Bottle (Fr). The biggest Bordeaux bottle in the World. (1981). Comes from Cruse et Fils Frères. It contains the equivalent of 36 standard bottles, stands 3 feet six inches tall and weighs 6 stones when full.

Megakeggery (Eng). The nickname sometimes used for processed-beer factories built by the large national brewers.

Megía (Luis) (Sp). A large bodega based in the Valdepeñas district of central Spain. Produces Marqués de Gastanga (100% Cencibel).

Mehana (Rum). The brand-name for a range of wines shipped to the U.K.

Mehedinti (Rum). A red and white wine-producing area.

Mehrhölzchen (Ger). Grosslage. (Anb) = Rheingau. (Ber) = Johannisberg. (Vils) = Hallgarten, Ostrich.

Mehring (Ger). Village. (Anb) = Mosel-Saar-Ruwer. (Ber) = Bernkastel. (Gro) = Probstberg. (Vins) = On the right side of the Mosel.

Mehring (Ger). Village. (Anb) = Mosel-Saar-Ruwer. (Ber) = Bernkastel. (Gro) = Sankt Michael. (Vins) = Blattenberg, Goldkupp, Zellerberg.

Meia Encosta (Port). A fruity dry white wine from Borges and Irmão, Dão.

Meiers Wines Cellars (USA). A firm with wineries in Silverton and Sansky, Ohio. Has vineyards at New Richmond.

Meilen (Switz). A principal vineyard near Zürich.

Meimsheim (Ger). Village. (Anb) =

Württemberg. (Ber) = Württembergisch Unterland. (Gro) = Heuchelberg. (Vin) = Katzenöhrle.

Mein Bräu (Jap). A premium Lager beer 6.4% alc. by vol. brewed by the Kirin Brewery in Tokyo.

Meiner (Cktl). 1 fl.oz. Gin, ¾ fl.oz. Campari. Build into an ice-filled highball glass. Stir in orange juice. Decorate with a slice of orange.

Meinl (Aus). A leading producer of sparkling wines in Austria.

Meio Seco (Port). Medium-dry.

Meireles (Port). A brand of Vinho Verde.

Meisenberg (Ger). vineyard. (Anb) = Mosel-Saar-Ruwer. (Ber) = Saar-Ruwer. (Gro) = Römerlay. (Vil) = Waldrach.

Meisenheim (Ger). Village. (Anb) = Nahe. (Ber) = Schloss Böckelheim. (Gro) = Paradiesgarten. (Vin) = Obere Heimbach.

Meister Pils (Ger). A Pilsener Lager brewed by the D.A.B. Brauerei of Dortmund Westphalia. Is a full-bodied beer.

Meix (Les) (Fr). A Premier Cru vineyard [part] in the A.C. commune of Aloxe-Corton, Côte de Beaune, Burgundy.

Meix-Bas (Les) (Fr). A Premier Cru vineyard in the A.C. commune of Fixin, Côte de Nuits, Burgundy. 1.88 ha.

Meix-Bataille (Le) (Fr). A Premier Cru vineyard in the A.C. commune of Monthélie, Côte de Beaune, Burgundy. 2.4 ha.

Meix-Caillet (Fr). A vineyard in the A.C. commune of Rully, Côte Chalonnaise, Burgundy.

Meix-Rentiers (Fr). A Premier Cru vineyard in the A.C. commune of Morey-Saint-Denis, Côte de Nuits, Burgundy. 1.2 ha.

Meknès-Fez (Afr). A noted vineyard planted with imported Vinifera vines in region of same name in Morocco. Contains A.O.G. areas of Beni M'Tir, Beni Sadden, Guerrouane, Saïs and Zerhoun.

Mélange (Eng). A mixture. Often a cocktail, is referred to as 'A mixture of drinks'.

Mélange (Fr). Blend (refers to Champagne).

Melaza (Sp). The name given to the sweet dregs of the residue in the sugar-making process (inverting). (Fr) = Miel.

Melbourne Bitter (Austr). A dry Lager beer brewed by the Carlton and United Brewery in Melbourne.

Melbourne Brewery (Eng). An old Brewery in Stamford, Lincolnshire that now no longer brews beer but is a

M

Museum. Still has some 38 public houses.

Melbourne STA (Eng). A fictional Australian brand of Lager adopted by the BBC TV soap opera 'East Enders' pub 'The Queen Vic'.

Melcan Distillery (Can). A distiller of Canadian whisky.

Melchers (Hol). A noted producer of Advocaat and Jenevers based in Schiedam.

Melesconera (N.Z.). A light, sharp, fruity red wine once produced by Villa Maria in South Auckland.

Meleto (It). A Ricasoli-produced Chianti Classico.

Melette (It). An Anisette produced in Ascoli Pinceno.

Melini (It). A large Chianti Classico producer at Pontassieve.

Mélinots (Fr). A Premier Cru vineyard of A.C. Chablis. Often the Premiers Crus of Roncières and Les Épinottes are reclassified as the wines of this vineyard.

Melior (Ger). The brand-name of a coffee 'plunger' system.

Melipilla (Chile). A wine-producing area near Santiago.

Melissa (It). A noted wine-producing commune in Calabria. Noted for its red, rosé and white Cirò wines.

Melissa Cordial (Fr). See Eau de Mélisse.

Mélisse (Fr). A Carthusian green liqueur made from balm-mint in the nineteenth century.

Melk (Hol). Milk.

Melkinrichting (Hol). Dairy.

Mellow (Eng). A term used to describe a wine which is at its peak of maturity.

Mellow Bird's (Eng). The brand-name of a mild instant coffee produced by General Foods in Oxon.

Mellow Corn (USA). The brand-name of a Corn whiskey produced by the Medley Distillery in Kentucky.

Mellow Mild (Eng). A keg Mild 1032 O.G. brewed by the Elgood Brewery in Wisbech, Cambridgeshire.

Mellowwood (S.Afr). A brand of Brandy produced by Sedgewick Taylor. 40% alc. by vol.

Melnik (Bul). A good quality red wine, dark and heavy, made from the Melnuk grape. Produced in the city of Melnik.

Mělník (Czec). A wine-producing area of Bohemia.

Melnuk (Bul). A red grape variety which produces full-bodied, heavy red wines. One of the country's oldest grape varieties.

Melomel (Eng). A mead produced from fruit juices or fruit and honey.

Melon (USA). A white grape variety used in the making of white wines in California.

Melonball (Cktl). 1 measure Vodka, 1 measure Midori. Stir in an ice-filled highball glass. Top with orange juice.

Melon Blanc (Fr). A lesser name for the Chardonnay grape.

Melon Cocktail (Cktl). ⅓ gill Gin, 2 dashes Maraschino, 2 dashes lemon juice. Shake over ice, strain into a cocktail glass. Top with a cherry.

Melon d'Arbois (Fr). The local name for the Chardonnay grape in the Jura region.

Melon de Bourgogne (Fr). A white grape variety known as the Muscadet in the Loire.

Melon Driver (Cktl). ⅓ gill Midori, ⅓ gill orange juice. Pour into an ice-filled highball glass. Dress with a slice of orange.

Melotti Brewery (Afr). A brewery based in Asmara, Ethiopia. Produces Melotti Lager 11.7° Plato and a sweet Stout 12° Plato.

Melroses (Scot). An Edinburgh-based tea company. Produces a wide range of fine teas.

Melrose Vineyard (USA). A small winery based in Middleburg, Virginia. 18 ha. Produces hybrid wines.

Melsungen (Ger). Landkries. (Anb) = Rheingau. (Ber) = Johannisberg. (Vil) = Böddiger. (Vin) = Berg.

Membrane Filters (Eng). Made from porous plastic sheeting folded into cartridge form. An absolute filter. Used as a final filter for wines that are already filtered to a high standard.

Memel Oak (Port). The best oak used for maturing Port wine.

Menard (Fr). Cognac producer. Address = J-P Menard et Fils, 16720 Saint Merne-lès-Carrieres. 80 ha. in the Grande Champagne. Produce – Traditional Impériale 20–25 year old. Vieille Réserve Extra 35 year old. Grande Fine Ancestrale 45 year old.

Mencía (Sp). A red grape variety grown almost exclusively in the León region. Also known as the Tintorera.

Mendocino County (USA). A north Californian district that produces mainly table and sparkling wines. Contains the sub-districts of Anderson Valley and Ukiah Valley.

Mendosa (Arg). A wine region in central Argentina.

Mendrisiotto (Switz). A vineyard based in the Sotto Ceneri area of Ticino, southern Switzerland.

Menea (Gre). A wine region based southwest of Corinth. Is noted for its red wines produced from the Agiorghitico grape.

Menesi Rozsa (Rum). Rosé of Menes. The

best rosé wine of Rumania. A full, fruity bouquet and body with a deep rose colour.

Ménétou-Salon (Fr). A.C. red, rosé and white wines from the west of Sancerre in the Central vineyards, Loire. Made from the Pinot noir (red & rosé) and Sauvignon (white).

Menetrières (Fr). A vineyard in the commune of Fuissé in A.C. Pouilly-Fuissé, Mâcon, Burgundy.

Mengen (Ger). Village. (Anb) = Baden. (Ber) = Markgräflerland. (Gro) = Lorettoberg. (Vin) = Alemannenbuck.

Meniscus (Eng). The line between the air and the must in the fermenting vat. Also used in wine-tasting – the line where the wine touches the glass.

Meniscus (Eng). In glass production, crescent shaped.

Mennig (Ger). Village. (Anb) = Mosel-Saar-Ruwer. (Ber) = Saar-Ruwer. (Gro) = Scharzberg. (Vins) = Altenberg, Euchariusberg, Herrenberg, Sonnenberg.

Menor Cuerpo (Sp). Describes a Sherry with a lesser body.

Menta (It). An alternative name for the liqueur Mentuccia.

Menthe Pastille (Fr). A white Crème de Menthe liqueur produced in Angers, Loire. 28% alc. by vol.

Méntrida (Sp). A Denominación de Origen north of La Mancha near Madrid. Produce mainly ordinary table wines.

Mentuccia (It). A herb-flavoured liqueur made from 100 different herbs produced in the Abruzzi mountains, central-eastern Italy. Also known as Centerbe, Menta and Silvestro.

Mentzendorf (Hol). A producer of a Kümmel liqueur based in Amsterdam. 39% alc. by vol.

Menzingen (Ger). See Kraichtal.

Meodu (Eng). The mediaeval name for Mead.

Meraner (It). See Meranese di Collina.

Meraner Hugel (It). See Meranese di Collina.

Meranese (It). See Meranese di Collina.

Meranese di Collina (It). D.O.C. red wine from the Trentino-Alto Adige. Made from the Schiava grossa, Schiava grigia, Schiava media, Schiava piccolo and Tschaggele grapes. Additional specifications of Burgravio if wine obtained in land of former County of Tyrol.

Merced (USA). A county within the Great Central Valley. Produce sweet dessert wines. Climate is hot and dry.

Merced (La) (Sp). A brand of deep-brown, Cream sherry produced by Bobadilla in Sanlúcar de Barrameda.

Mercian (Jap). A major wine-producer in southern Japan.

Mercian Mild (Eng). A cask conditioned Mild 1032 O.G. brewed by the Marston Brewery in Burton-on-Trent, Staffordshire.

Mercier (Fr). Champagne producer. Address = 75 Avenue de Champagne, 51200 Épernay. A Grande Marque. Produces – Vintage and non-vintage wines. Vintages – 1900, 1904, 1906, 1911, 1914, 1921, 1923, 1926, 1928, 1929, 1933, 1934, 1937, 1941, 1943, 1945, 1947, 1949, 1952, 1953, 1955, 1959, 1961, 1962, 1964, 1966, 1969, 1970, 1971, 1973, 1975, 1976, 1978, 1980, 1982, 1983. See Réserve de l'Empéreur.

Mercurey (Fr). An A.C. wine commune in the Côte Chalonnaise, Burgundy. Minimum alc. by vol. 10.5%. Produces red and dry white wines.

Mercurol (Fr). A noted village in the Rhône valley.

Merdingen (Ger). Village. (Anb) = Baden. (Ber) = Kaiserstuhl-Tuniberg. (Gro) = Attilafelsen. (Vin) = Bühl.

Mère de Vinaigre (Fr). See Mother of Vinegar.

Meredyth Vineyard (USA). A small vineyard based in Middleburg, Virginia. 18 ha. Produces French hybrid and Vinifera wines.

Mère Goutte (Fr). The name given to a wine produced from first crushing of the grapes prior to pressing.

Merenzao (Sp). A black grape variety grown in Valdeorras.

Merfy (Fr). A Cru Champagne village in the Canton de Bourgogne. District = Reims.

Meridas Coffee (S.Am). A variety of pure coffee produced in Venezuela.

Merienda (Sp). An Amontillado Sherry from Harvey's of Bristol.

Mérignac (Fr). A commune in the A.C. Graves district of south-western Bordeaux.

Merito (W.Ind). The brand-name of a Puerto Rican Rum usually sold for export.

Merlan (Fr). Another name for the Merlot grape in Bordeaux.

Merlin Ale (Wales). A cask conditioned Bitter 1032 O.G. brewed by the Usher Brewery in South Wales.

Merlot (Fr). A prolific early-ripening wine grape of Bordeaux next in importance to the Cabernet. Used extensively in Saint-Émilion. Also known as Bigney, Crabutet noir, Médoc noir, Petite merle and Vitraille.

Merlot Blanc (Fr). A white wine grape used in small quantities in the Sauternes district of Bordeaux.

M

Merlot del Piave Vecchio (It). See Piave Merlot.

Merlot di Aprilia (It). D.O.C. red wine from Latium. Wine named after the main grape variety. See also Sangiovese di Aprilia and Trebbiano di Aprilia.

Merlot di Pramaggiore (It). D.O.C. red wine from Veneto. Made from the Merlot plus 10% Cabernet grapes. If aged for 3 years and has alc. content of 12% by vol. then called Riserva.

Merlyn (Wales). A Welsh cream and Whisky liqueur.

Merpins (Fr). A commune in the Charente Département whose grapes are used for Grande Champagne Cognac.

Merrain (Fr). A split-oak cask used in the Médoc.

Merrie Monk Mild (Eng). The strongest Mild beer 1043 O.G. in the country. Brewed by the Marston's Brewery in Burton-on-Trent, Staffordshire.

Merry (Eng) (slang). A term to denote a person who is partially drunk (not incoherently) and happy.

Merrydown (Eng). A winery that acts as a co-operative. Noted for its Cider, Meads and fruit-based wines.

Merry K (Cktl). ⅔ measure Bourbon whiskey, ⅓ measure orange Curaçao. Stir over ice, strain into a cocktail glass, add a twist of lemon.

Merry Sour (Cktl). 2 measures Brandy, 4 measures dry Cider, juice of a lemon. Stir over ice in a tall glass, dress with a lemon peel spiral.

Merry Widow (Cktl).(1). ½ measure Dubonnet, ½ measure Noilly Prat, dash Amer Picon. Stir over ice, strain into a cocktail glass. Top with twist of lemon peel.

Merry Widow (Cktl).(2). ½ measure Cherry brandy, ½ measure Maraschino. Shake over ice, strain into a cocktail glass. Top with a cherry.

Merry Widow (Cktl).(3). 1 measure Brandy, 4 measures redcurrant wine, dash Crème de Cassis. Stir together over ice in a highball glass. Top with a spiral of lemon peel.

Merry Widow Cocktail (Cktl).(1). 1½ fl.ozs. Byrrh, 1½ fl.ozs. dry Gin. Stir over ice, strain into a cocktail glass.

Merry Widow Cocktail (Cktl).(2). ½ measure Bénédictine, ½ measure dry Gin, 2 dashes Pernod, 2 dashes Campari. Stir over ice, strain into a cocktail glass. Top with a twist of lemon peel.

Merry Widower (Cktl). ½ measure dry Gin, ½ measure French vermouth, 2 dashes Pernod, 2 dashes Bénédictine, dash Angostura. Shake over ice, strain into a cocktail glass. Top with a twist of lemon peel juice.

Merry Widow Fizz (Cktl).(1). 2 measures Dubonnet, 1 measure lemon juice, 1 measure orange juice, 1 egg white. Shake over ice, strain into an ice-filled highball glass. Top up with soda water. Serve with a muddler and straws.

Merry Widow Fizz (Cktl).(2). ⅕ gill Sloe gin, 1 teaspoon powdered sugar, juice ½ orange, juice ½ lemon, 1 egg white. Shake over ice, strain into an ice-filled highball glass. Top with soda water.

Merseguera (Sp). A white grape variety grown in the Penedés region of southeastern Spain. Also known as the Escanyavella, Exquitxagos and Verdosilla.

Mersin (Tur). An orange liqueur similar to Curaçao.

Mertesdorf (Ger). Village. (Anb) = Mosel-Saar-Ruwer. (Ber) = Saar-Ruwer. (Gro) = Römerlay. (Vins) = Felslay, Johannisberg, Mäuerchen.

Mertesdorf [ortsteil Maximin Grünhaus] (Ger). Village. (Anb) = Mosel-Saar-Ruwer. (Ber) = Saar-Ruwer. (Gro) = Römerlay. (Vins) = Abstberg, Bruderberg, Herrenberg.

Mertesheim (Ger). Village. (Anb) = Rheinpfalz. (Ber) = Mittelhaardt-Deutsche Weinstrasse. (Gro) = Höllenpfad. (Vin) = St. Martinskreuz.

Merum (Lat). Wine. See also Vinum.

Merwespont Co-operative (S.Afr). A winery based at Bonnievale. Address = Merwespont Koöperatiewe Wynmakery, Box 68, Bonnievale 6730. Produces varietal wines.

Merwespont Koöperatiewe Wynmakery (S.Afr). See Merwespont Co-operative.

Merwida Co-operative (S.Afr). A winery based at Worcester. Address = Merwida Koöperatiewe Wynkelder, Box 4, Rawsonville 6845. Produces varietal wines.

Merwida Koöperatiewe Wynkelder (S.Afr). See Merwida Co-operative.

Merxheim (Ger). Village. (Anb) = Nahe. (Ber) = Schloss Böckelheim. (Gro) = Paradiesgarten. (Vins) = Hunolsteiner, Römerberg, Vogelsang.

Merz (Christian) Brauerei (Ger). A noted brewery that specialises in bottom-fermentation Rauchbier. Based in Bamberg.

Merzeguera (Sp). A white grape variety grown in Alicante.

Merzhausen (Ger). Village. (Anb) = Baden. (Ber) = Markgräflerland. (Gro) = Lorettoberg. (Vin) = Jesuitenschloss.

Mesa (Port). Table wine.

Mesa Verde Vineyards (USA). A winery

M

based in Temecula, California. 61 ha. Grape varieties – Cabernet sauvignon, Chardonnay, Gamay and Johannisberg riesling. Produces varietal wines.

Mescal (USA). Spelling of Mezcal.

Mescalin (Mex). A rough, potent spirit produced from the Peyote cactus.

Méscita (It). Wine bar, public house.

Meşe (Tur). Oak.

Mesech (Isr). A 'Bible wine'. Word derives from the Hebrew for mixture of water and wine.

Meseg (Isr). Old Hebrew (Bible) word for mixed wines.

Mesenich (Ger). Village. (Anb) = Mosel-Saar-Ruwer. (Ber) = Obermosel. (Gro) = Königsberg. (Vin) = Held.

Mesenich (Ger). Village. (Anb) = Mosel-Saar-Ruwer. (Ber) = Zell/Mosel. (Gro) = Rosenhang. (Vins) = Abteiberg, Deuslay, Goldgrübchen.

Mesimarja (Fin). A liqueur made from Arctic brambles. Produced by Lignell and Piispanen. Ruby red in colour. 29% alc. by vol.

Mesland (Fr). A commune in the A.C. Touraine district of the Loire. Is allowed to use its name in the A.C. Touraine.

Meslier (Fr). A lesser white grape variety used in the making of Champagne and Armagnac.

Mesneux (Les) (Fr). A Premier Cru Champagne village in the Canton de Ville-en-Tardenois. District = Reims.

Mesnil-le-Hutier (Le). A Cru Champagne village in the Canton de Dormans. District = Épernay.

Mesnil-sur-Oger (Le) (Fr). A Grand Cru Champagne village in the Canton d'Avize. District = Epernay. Reclassified in 1985.

Meso-Inistol (Eng). A vitamin needed by yeast which is found in malt. Usually a solution of malt extract is used in yeast starter bottles.

Mesopotamium (Lat). A red wine produced in Sicily in Roman times.

Meşrubat (Tur). Drinks.

Messager (Fr). A producer of A.C. Bordeaux Mousseux based in Saint-Émilion, eastern Bordeaux.

Messamins (USA). The name used for North American native grape varieties in early times. A large and juicy grape, so named by the American Indians.

Messenia (Gre). A red, rosé and dry white wine-producing area.

Messias (Port). A Bairrada wine firm, produce Vinhos Verdes, Brandy and Garrafeiras (red and white). Founded in 1928.

Messias (Port). A vintage Port Shipper. Vintage – 1975.

Messica (W.Ind). An orange-flavoured spirit drink produced on the island of Martinique.

Messina (It). A noted wine-producing district in north-eastern Sicily.

Messina (It). A brand of beer brewed in Sicily.

Messo in Bottiglia (It). Estate bottled.

Mest (Tur). Drunk (consumed).

Mestres (Sp). A sparkling (Cava) wine produced by Cavas Mestres in San Sadurní de Noya, south-eastern Spain.

Mestres Sagues (Antonio) (Sp). A noted Cava wine-producer based in south-western Spain.

Mestres Tastaires du Languedoc (Fr). A wine brotherhood in the Languedoc region for the promotion of wines of the region.

Meta Brewery (Afr). A brewery based in Addis Ababa, Ethiopia. Brews a Lager beer at 11° Plato.

Métaireau (Louis) (Fr). A noted Muscadet négociant. Address = La Févrie, 44690 Maisdon-sur-Sèvre, Loire Atlantique.

Metala (Austr). A wine producer based in Langhorne Creek, South Australia.

Metall-Geschmack (Ger). Denotes a metallic taste caused by the use of poorly cleaned tools.

Metallic (Eng). A taste that some wines gain from fungicidal spraying. Can be treated with Blue finings. (Potassium Ferrocyanide).

Metal Strainer (Cktl). See Hawthorne Strainer.

Metamorphosis (Eng). The term given to the changing of shape or form. Applies to the flowers changing into grapes and to insects in their change from grub to adult.

Metatartaric Acid (Eng). $C_8H_8O_{10}$. A wine additive. Cologel. Prevents tartrate crystallisation for a limited period only.

Metaxa (Gre). A well-known brand of Brandy. Range of star rating which gives a star for every year of ageing. Also produces V.S.O.P. Grade fine 40 year old. and a Grade fine dry 50 year old.

Metaxa Puff (Cktl). 1 measure Metaxa brandy, 1 measure milk. Place ice cubes into a highball glass. Add ingredients, stir gently. Top up with Perrier or other sparkling mineral water.

Métayage (Fr). A feudal practice (which still occurs in Burgundy) where an owner passes his vines to a farmer or tenant when he no longer wishes to tend them.

Metbrew (USA). A Beer which has survived from the days of Prohibition. Is brewed by the Champale Brewery.

Methanoic Acid (Eng). H.COOH. A volatile acid found in wine.

Methanol (Eng). CH_3OH. A higher alcohol

(fusel oil) which can be removed during distillation because of its lower boiling point. Boiling temperature 66° Celsius. See Methyl Alcohol.

Metheglin (Wales). A type of mead. Flavoured with herbs and spices. Derives from the old Welsh word 'Healing liquor' or 'Spiced drink'.

Methionine (Eng). An Amino acid found in wine. Is formed by the yeasts.

Méthode Ancienne (Fr). Old methods of Viticulture and Viniculture which are still used. See Château Simone.

Méthode Champenoise (Fr). The process of producing a second fermentation in the bottle, remuage and dégorgement. (Sp) = Cava. (Port) = Espumantes Naturais. The term will not be allowed to be used on any sparkling wine label (except Champagne) from 1994.

Méthode Champenoise Cider (Austr). A magnificent old gold cider, rich, oak aged using traditional European varieties of apples. Made by the Kellybrook Winery in Victoria.

Méthode Cuve Close (Fr). Denotes producing sparkling wine by the tank method.

Méthode Dioise (Fr). The local name used in Clairette de Die for the production of Clairette de Die Mousseux. Is similar to the Transfer method but no Liqueur de tirage and no Liqueur d'expédition are added. Dégorgement occurs. Also known as Méthode Rurale.

Méthode Gaillaçoise (Fr). A variation of the Méthode Champenoise way of fermentation. Is similar to Méthode Dioise but no filtration or transfer bottling occurs. Used in the Côtes du Jura Mousseux and Faillac Mousseux production.

Méthode Rurale (Fr). A method for making a semi-sparkling wine from the Languedoc-Roussillon called Vin de Blanquette. The wine is filtered before it has completely finished its normal (first) fermentation and is then bottled. The remaining fermentation is sufficient to give a slight sparkle without creating enough sediment to require removal. See also Méthode Dioise.

Methu (Gre). Mead.

Methuein (Gre). An old Greek word to denote making a person drunk, to make intoxicated.

Methuen (John) (Port). The English ambassador to Portugal who drew up the treaty between the 2 countries that was named after him. See Methuen Treaty.

Methuen Treaty (Eng) (Port). A treaty signed in 1703 giving the wines of Portugal preferential taxation over that for French wines.

Methusalem (Fr). See Methuselah.

Methusalem (Sp). The brand-name for a Sherry produced by Gonzalez Byass.

Methuselah (Fr). A bottle size. Equivalent of 8 standard bottles. Used in Champagne. Also called a Methusalem.

Methyl Alcohol (Eng). CH₃OH. A higher alcohol (fusel oil). Highly toxic. The simplest alcohol. When distilled is known as Methanol.

Methylated Spirits (Eng). Alcohol that has been denatured by the addition of Methanol, Naphtha and Pyridine. Used to test for pectin haze in a sample of hazy wine. A purple dye is also added to identify the Methylated spirit.

Methyl Ethylketone (Eng). An aldehyde formed by the oxidation of alcohols which is found in wine in small traces. Contributes to the bouquet.

Métis (Fr). An intraspecific cross red grape variety.

Metodo Champenois (It). The Champagne method.

Metodo Classico (It). A local name in eastern Italy for the méthode champenoise.

Método Industrial (Sp). A term used to describe the commercial method of vinification.

Método Rural o a la Española (Sp). A term used to describe whole-grape fermentation (used only by a few of the smaller growers).

Metodo Tradicional (Sp). Refers to the Cava wines produced by the méthode champenoise in regions of Alava, Barcelona, Gerona, Lérida, Navarra, Rioja, Tarragona and Zaragoya.

Metro Golden (Cktl). 1 part Glayva, top up with English cider in a highball glass over ice. Dress with ½ lemon slice.

Metropole Extra (Sp). A dry white wine produced by Bodegas La Rioja Alta.

Metropolitain (Cktl). ½ measure Brandy, ½ measure Italian vermouth, 2 dashes Gomme, dash Angostura. Shake over ice, strain into a cocktail glass.

Metsovo (Gre). A red table wine made from the Cabernet sauvignon grape produced in the Ipiros (Epirus) region.

Mettenheim (Ger). Village. (Anb) = Rheinhessen. (Ber) = Nierstein. (Gro) = Krötenbrunnen. (Vin) = Goldberg.

Mettenheim (Ger). Village. (Anb) = Rheinhessen. (Ber) = Nierstein. (Gro) = Rheinblick. (Vins) = Michelsberg, Schlossberg.

Metternich'sche Weingüter (Aus). A noted wine-producer based in Krems.

Metu (Ger). The old German word for Mead.

Metz (Fr). A wine-producing area in the

M

Vins de la Moselle, Lorraine. Produces mainly rosé wines – Clairet de Moselle.

Metzdorf (Ger). Village. (Anb) = Mosel-Saar-Ruwer. (Ber) = Obermosel. (Gro) = Konigsberg. (Vins) = Sites not yet chosen.

Metzingen (Ger). Village. (Anb) = Württemberg. (Ber) = Remstal-Stuttgart. (Gro) = Hohennenffen. (Vins) = Hofsteige, Schlossteige.

Meung (Fr). A red wine from Orleans, central France.

Meunier (USA). A white grape variety used in the making of white wine in California.

Meurich (Ger). Village. (Anb) = Mosel-Saar-Ruwer. (Ber) = Obermosel. (Gro) = Gipfel. (Vins) = Sites not yet chosen.

Meursault (Fr). A commune in the Côte de Beaune. Produces Premier Cru white wines from the Chardonnay grape. Premier Cru vineyards are – Clos des Perrières, La Goutte d'Or, Le Porusot, Le Porusot-Dessus, Les Bouchères, Les Caillerets, Les Charmes-Dessous, Les Charmes-Dessus, Les Cras, Les Genevrières-Dessous, Les Genevrières-Dessus, Les Perrières, Les Petures, Les Santenots-Blancs and Les Santenots du Milieu. 99.45 ha. Also Premier Cru vineyards in Blagny of – La Jennelotte, La Pièce-Sous-le-Bois and Sous le Dos d'Âne. 21.3 ha.

Meuse (Fr). A district of the Lorraine in north-eastern France. Produces Vins de Table.

Meuse Brasserie (Fr). A brewery based in Champigneulles, Lorraine.

Meux (Fr). A commune in the Charente-Maritime Département whose grapes are classed Petite Champagne (Cognac).

Mev (USA). The brand-name used by Mt. Eden vineyards for their Chardonnay wines made from Ventana vineyard purchased grapes.

Mexcalli (Mex). The old Indian word for Mezcal.

Mexicana Cocktail (Cktl). ½ measure Tequila Silver, ¼ measure lemon juice, ⅙ measure pineapple juice, 4 dashes Grenadine. Shake over ice, strain into a cocktail glass.

Mexican Century (Mex). The alternative name for the Maguey cactus.

Mexican Coffee (Liq.Coffee). Using a measure of Kahlúa as the liqueur.

Mexican Coffee (Mex). A mild coffee with a dry aftertaste. Can be drunk on its own, but is often blended with other South American coffees. Has good acidity and body. Produced in Coatepec, Huatusco, Orizaba and Pueblo Hills.

Mexican Dream (Cktl). ⅕ gill Tequila Gold, ⅕ gill Malibu, dash Sirop de Fraises, 1 scoop strawberry ice cream. Blend in a blender with a scoop of crushed ice. Serve in a flute glass with a fresh strawberry.

Mexico (C.Am). Country that produces mainly spirits (notably Tequila) with a small number of vineyards planted in the north (The law prevents wineries owning vineyards). Regions – Aguascalientes, Baja California, Chihuahua (Delicías), Coahuila (Parras and Saltillo), Durango, Hidalgo, Laguna, Querétaro, San Juan del Rio, San Luis Potosi, Sonora (Hermosillo), Tlaxcala and Zacatecas.

Mexicola Cocktail (Cktl). 2 fl.ozs. Tequila Silver, juice ½ lime. Place in an ice-filled highball glass, top with Coca Cola.

Mexico y España (Cktl). 1½ fl.ozs. Tequila, 1½ fl.ozs. Amontillado Sherry. Stir over ice, strain into a cocktail glass. Decorate with a green olive.

Meyblum S.A. (Fr). A noted Eau-de-vie producer based in the Bas-Rhin Alsace.

Meyer (Jos et Fils) (Fr). An Alsace wine producer. Address = 72, Rue Clénenceau, Wintzenheim, 68000 Colmar.

Meyre (Fr). A vineyard in the commune of Avensan. A.C. Médoc, Bordeaux. Cru Bourgeois Supérieur.

Meyva Suyu (Tur). Fruit juice. See also Özsu.

Mezcal (Mex). The early distillation from the Blue Maguey cactus from which Tequila originated. 40–44.5% alc. by vol.

Mezcal Azul (Mex). Lathophora Williamsi. The Blue Maguey cactus from which Tequila is made.

Mezcal Con Gusano (Mex). A Tequila produced by Monte Alban. 38% alc. by vol.

Mezcal Wine (USA). The old name for Tequila.

Mezclar (Sp). To mix or blend.

Mézesfehér (Hun). A white grape variety grown in south-western Hungary. Lit – 'Honey white'.

Mezquita (La) (Sp). 'The Mosque'. The largest Brandy bodega in Spain. Belongs to Domecq. Produces – Fundador and Carlos 111, & 1 brandies.

Mezzo (It). Denotes ½ litre of wine.

Mezzofiasco (It). See Fiasco.

M.I.A. (Austr) (abbr). Murrumbidgee Irrigation Area.

Mia Bira (Gre). A request for a beer.

Miajados (Sp). A wine-producing area in Cáceres near Guadalupe, south-western Spain.

Miamba (Austr). A brand of soft red wine produced by Orlando in the Barossa Valley.

Miami (Cktl). ¾ measure white Rum, ¼ measure (white) Crème de Menthe, dash lemon juice. Shake over ice, strain into a cocktail glass.

Mia Mia vineyard (Austr). Address = Rutherglen, Victoria 3685. 80 ha. Grape varieties – Brown muscat, Cabernet sauvignon, Cinsault, Durif, Hermitage, Muscadelle, Palomino, Sémillon and Shiraz.

Miami Beach (Cktl). ⅓ measure Scotch whisky, ⅓ measure grapefruit juice, ⅓ measure French vermouth. Shake over ice, strain into a cocktail glass.

Miami Cocktail (Cktl). 1 part Dubonnet, 1 part dry Sherry, 2 dashes Orange bitters. Shake well over ice, strain into a cocktail glass. Add twist of orange peel and a cherry.

Michael (Cktl). ⅗ measure Scotch Whisky, ⅕ measure Anis, ⅕ measure orange juice. Shake over ice, strain into a cocktail glass, add a cherry.

Michael Cocktail (Cktl). ½ fl.oz. dry Gin, 1 fl.oz. Lime liqueur, dash Crème de Fraises. Stir over ice, strain into a cocktail glass. Top with a spiral of lemon peel.

Michaeliskapelle (Ger). vineyard. (Anb) = Nahe. (Ber) = Schloss Böckelheim. (Gro) = Rosengarten. (Vil) = Braunweiler.

Michael Juillot (Fr). A négociant-éleveur based in the Côte Chalonnaise, Burgundy.

Michaelsberg (Ger). vineyard. (Anb) = Baden. (Ber) = Badische Bergstrasse/Kraichgau. (Gro) = Mannaberg. (Vil) = Bruchsal (ortsteil Untergrombach).

Michaelsberg (Ger). vineyard. (Anb) = Württemberg. (Ber) = Württembergisch Unterland. (Gro) = Heuchelberg. (Vil) = Cleebronn.

Michaelsberg (Ger). vineyard. (Anb) = Württemberg. (Ber) = Württembergisch Unterland. (Gro) = Heuchelberg. (Vil) = Eibensbach.

Michaelsberg (Ger). vineyard. (Anb) = Württemberg. (Ber) = Württembergisch Unterland. (Gro) = Heuchelberg. (Vil) = Frauenzimmern.

Michaelsberg (Ger). vineyard. (Anb) = Württemberg. (Ber) = Württembergisch Unterland. (Gro) = Heuchelberg. (Vil) = Güglingen.

Michalovce (Czec). A brewery in an eastern Czec town of same name that produces fine beers. Noted for its Siravar (a malty dark Lager). Was known as Micholup.

Michel (José) (Fr). Champagne producer. Address = BP 16, Moussy, 51200 Épernay. Récoltants-manipulants. Produces

– Vintage and non-vintage wines. A member of C.V.C. Vintages – 1971, 1973, 1975, 1976, 1979, 1982, 1983.

Michelau i. Steigerwald (Ger). Village. (Anb) = Franken. (Ber) = Steigerwald. (Gro) = Not yet assigned. (Vin) = Vollburg.

Michelbach (Ger). Village. (Anb) = Franken. (Ber) = Mainviereck. (Gro) = Not yet assigned. (Vins) = Apostelgarten, Steinberg.

Michelbach a. W. (Ger). Village. (Anb) = Württemberg. (Ber) = Württembergisch Unterland. (Gro) = Lindelberg. (Vins) = Deuhsteiger, Margarete.

Michelfeld (Ger). Village. (Anb) = Baden. (Ber) = Badische Bergstrasse/Kraichgau. (Gro) = Stiftsberg. (Vins) = Himmelberg, Sonnenberg.

Michelmark (Ger). vineyard. (Anb) = Rheingau. (Ber) = Johannisberg. (Gro) = Deutelsberg. (Vil) = Erbach.

Michelob (USA). Anheuser-Busch's premium American beer. Has a higher gravity than Budweiser.

Michelsberg (Ger). Grosslage. (Anb) = Mosel-Saar-Ruwer. (Ber) = Bernkastel. (Vils) = Hetzerath, Minheim, Neumagen-Dhron, Piesport, Rivenich, Sehlem, Trittenheim.

Michelsberg (Ger). vineyard. (Anb) = Rheinhessen. (Ber) = Nierstein. (Gro) = Rheinblick. (Vil) = Mettenheim.

Michelsberg (Ger). vineyard. (Anb) = Rheinpfalz. (Ber) = Mittelhaardt-Deutsche Weinstrasse. (Gro) = Hochmess. (Vil) = Bad Dürkheim.

Michelsberg (Ger). vineyard. (Anb) = Rheinpfalz. (Ber) = Mittelhaardt-Deutsche Weinstrasse. (Gro) = Hochmess. (Vil) = Ungstein.

Michelsberg (Ger). vineyard. (Anb) = Rheinpfalz. (Ber) = Südliche Weinstrasse. (Gro) = Ordensgut. (Vil) = Weyher.

Michet (It). A sub-species of the Nebbiolo grape.

Michielon (Luiz) S.A. (Bra). One of Brazil's leading wine-producing companies.

Michigan (USA). A wine region on the edge of Lake Michigan. Best parts are Benton Harbor and Paw Paw. Concorde, Catawba and Delaware are most used vines. Cold Duck is produced here.

Micholup (Czec). See Michalovce.

Mickey (USA). See Mickey Finn.

Mickey Finn (USA). A drink into which has been added a drug to render the consumer unconscious.

Micro-Climate (Eng). Individual climatic conditions of areas within a country.

Effects of winds, sun, frosts, mists, fogs etc.

Micro-Flora (Eng). Yeasts, Bacteria and Moulds.

Micro Vinification (Eng). Production of a wine from a single vine to test for the vine's suitability for wine making. Used to improve cloning.

Middelvlei Estate (S.Afr). vineyards based in Stellenbosch. Address = P.O. Stellenbosch 7600. Produces varietal wines.

Middle Rhine (Ger). The Mittelrhein.

Middle Stave (Eng). The centre piece at the end of a cask in which the keystone (tap hole) is sited.

Middy (Austr). The term used in New South Wales for a 10 fl.oz. glass and in Western Australia for a 7 fl.oz. glass.

Midi (Fr). A large wine area of south-west France. Contains the region of Roussillon and Languedoc, and the Départements of Aude, Gard and Hérault. See Midi-Pyrénées.

Midi-Pyrénées (Fr). The full name of the Midi region of south-western France from the Pyrénées to the Massif Central.

Midi vineyards (USA). A winery based in Lone Jack on the western border of Missouri. Produces hybrid wines.

Midlands Mild (Eng). A keg Mild 1036 O.G. brewed by the John Smith Brewery for the West Midlands.

Midleton Distillery (Ire). A distillery based in Southern Ireland, has pot and patent stills.

Midnight (Cktl). ⅔ measure Apricot brandy, ⅓ measure Cointreau, juice ¼ lemon. Shake over ice, strain into a cocktail glass.

Midnight Cocktail (Cktl). ⅙ measure dry Gin, ⅙ measure French vermouth, ⅙ measure Italian vermouth, dash Angostura, juice ¼ orange. Shake well over ice, strain into a cocktail glass. Also known as a Minnehaha cocktail.

Midori (Jap). A musk melon liqueur made by the Suntory Co. 30% alc. by vol. Is bright green in colour.

Midori Dawn (Cktl). 1 part Midori, 1 part Vodka. Stir over ice in a highball glass. Top with tonic water.

Midori Sharp (Cktl). 1 part Midori, 5 parts grapefruit juice. Serve in a highball glass over ice.

Midori Sour (Cktl). 3 parts Midori, 2 parts lemon juice, 1 egg white, ½ teaspoon castor sugar. Shake well over ice, strain into a cocktail glass. Dress with a cherry.

Midulla vineyards (USA). A vineyard based north of Tampa, Florida. Produces American wines.

Miel (Fr). Lit – 'Honey'. The name given to invert sugar. See also Melaza.

Mié-r'lévaie (Ch.Isles). Teabreak.

Mietersheim (Ger), Village. (Anb) = Baden. (Ber) = Breisgau. (Gro) = Schutterlindenberg. (Vin) = Kronenbühl.

Mignard (Fr). The brand-name of a sparkling white grape juice made by Cidréries Mignard, Bellot, 77510.

Mignon (Jules) (Fr). A Champagne producer based at Ay, Reims.

Mignotte (La) (Fr). A Premier Cru vineyard in the A.C. commune of Beaune, Côte de Beaune, Burgundy. 2.41 ha.

Migraine (Fr). The local name used for wine produced in Auxerre, north-central France.

Miguel del Arco (Sp). A black grape variety grown in Aragón, Rioja and Valencia.

Miguel Torres (Sp). A 12 year old Brandy produced by Torres.

Miguel Torres Special Reserve (Sp). A pot-stilled Brandy aged 1 year in new oak then 10 years in cask by Torres in the Penedés.

Mikado Cocktail (Cktl). ½ gill Cognac, 2 dashes each of Angostura, Orgeat, Curaçao and Noyau. Stir well over ice, strain into a cocktail glass, add a cherry and squeeze of lemon peel juice. Also known as Japanese Cocktail.

Mikulov (Czec). A wine district within the region of Bohemia. Produces some of the region's best white wines.

Mikve Israel (Isr). A dry full-bodied wine sold on the USA market.

Mil (USSR). A dessert wine produced in Baku.

Milano Winery (USA). A winery based in Mendocino County, California. Grape varieties – Cabernet sauvignon, Chardonnay, Gamay and Zinfandel. Produce varietal wines.

Milan Wines (USA). A winery based in Detroit, Michigan. Produce hybrid wines.

Mi Lao Chiu (China). A noted brand of Rice wine produced in Shantung province from yellow rice. See also Shao-Hsing Rice Wine.

Milawa Estate (Austr). 60 ha. Part of the Brown Brothers in Milawa, Victoria. Produce varietal wines.

Milch (Ger). Milk.

Mild (Eng). A dark, low-alcohol beer, brewed mainly in the Midlands and North. Usually darker than bitter due to the higher roasting of the malt and to caramel. (Also a light version made).

Mildara Wines (Austr). Address = Main Rd, Coonawarra, South Australia. Vineyards at Coonawarra, Eden Valley and the Murray River in Victoria. Are Sherry and Brandy specialists.

M

Milde (Ger). Pleasantly soft but undistinguished wine.

Mildew (Eng). A fungus which withers the leaves and berries of the vine, particularly in wet weather. Copper sulphate, quicklime and water are used to treat it. See Alforra, Oiidium and Peronespora.

Mildio (Port). Mildew. See also Mangra.

Mildura (Austr). A New South Wales district that produces good quality wines.

Milk (Eng). A white fluid from the mammary glands of animals, high in nutritional substances and minerals. Food for their young. (Fr) = Lait. (Ger) = Milch. (Hol) = Melk. (It) = Latte. (Lat) = Lac. (Port) = Leite. (Sp) = Leche. (Tur) = Sağmak. (Wales) = Llaeth.

Milk-e-Pan'tch (Ch.Isles). A milk punch made either of Rum or Brandy, eggs and milk. Nutmeg or cinnamon sprinkled on top. Some have lime or lemon juice in. See also Milk o' Punch.

Milk of Amnesia (Eng). A nickname for beer in northern England.

Milk of the Aged (Fr). The term given to wine in France.

Milk o'Punch (Ch.Isles). Eggs, sugar, milk and Rum served in the Isle of Alderney on the first Sunday in May. The first drink a customer receives (free) on entering a bar.

Milk Punch (Cktl). ¼ gill Rum, ½ gill Brandy, milk, loaf sugar and lemon juice. Is bottled and will keep for long periods. Served with grated nutmeg.

Milk Shake (Eng). A non-alcoholic cocktail of milk, fruit juices, syrups or cordials and sugar to taste. Usually blended. Ice cream is optional.

Milk Sherry (Eng). A style of Oloroso sherry which has been sweetened and coloured (between Cream and Brown sherries). Now called Bristol Milk (cannot be called Milk sherry because of Trades Description Act).

Milk Stout (Eng). Is now known as sweet Stout due to the Trades Description Act. (No milk in stout). Alternative name for English Stout. Only the Guernsey Brewery bottle Milk Stout 1042 O.G. is allowed to be called such (as outside U.K. legislation).

Millandes (Les) (Fr). A Premier Cru vineyard in the A.C. commune of Morey-Saint-Denis, Côte de Nuits, Burgundy. 4.3 ha.

Millardet de Grasset (Sp). Root stock. A cross of Vitis Chasselas and Vitis Berlandieri. Grown in Valdepeñas, central Spain.

Mill Brewery (Eng). A Devon brewery opened in 1983 in Newton Abbot. Produces cask conditioned Janner's Ale 1038 O.G. and Devon Special 1043 O.G.

Millburn (Scot). A single Malt whisky distillery based near Inverness, Nairnshire. A Highland malt. Produces a vintage 1966 Malt. 43% alc. by vol.

Mill Creek vineyards (USA). A winery based in the Russian River Valley, Sonoma County, California. 27 ha. Grape varieties – Cabernet sauvignon, Chardonnay, Gewürztraminer and Merlot. Produce varietal wines.

Mill Down (Eng). Address = Hambledon, Portsmouth, Hampshire. Planted 1951. 2 ha. Soil – Chalk. Grape varieties – Auxerrois, Chardonnay, Pinot meunier, Pinot noir and Seyval blanc.

Millefiori (It). A herb liqueur on the style of Fior d'Alpi. 40% alc. by vol.

Millennium (Pol). A honey and strawberry juice flavoured mead. Amber in colour, sold in double-handled flasks.

Millerandage (Fr). Grape clusters which do not ripen evenly and which contain some quasi-raisins which remain small, hard and green. Caused by lack of water and poor climatic conditions.

Miller Brewery (USA). A large brewery in Milwaukee. Brews Löwenbräu under licence. Owned by Phillip Morris. See Miller Lite.

Miller Lite (USA). A lightly hopped Lager 1030–34 O.G. brewed under licence by the Courage Brewery in Reading.

Millers Burgundy (Austr). The name used for the Pinot meunier.

Millésime (Fr). Vintage date. Year of manufacture.

Millesimes (Fr). An Armagnac produced by Damblat.

Milliliter (USA). ¹⁄₁₀₀₀ part of a liter (litre).

Millilitre (Euro). ¹⁄₁₀₀₀ part of a litre.

Milling (USA). The first stage of the process of making Whiskey. The breaking up of the grain kernel to release the starch in the mashing and cooking which follows.

Millionaire (Cktl).(1). ⁷⁄₁₀ measure Brandy, ¹⁄₁₀ measure Orgeat, ¹⁄₁₀ measure orange Curaçao, ¹⁄₁₀ measure Crème de Noyeau, 2 dashes Angostura. Shake over ice, strain into a cocktail glass.

Millionaire (Cktl).(2). ⅓ gill Rye whiskey, ⅙ gill Grenadine, 2 dashes Curaçao, egg white. Shake well over ice, strain into a 5 oz. wine glass, add a dash of Pernod.

Millionaire (Cktl).(3). ⅔ measure Apricot brandy, ⅔ measure Sloe Gin, ⅔ measure Jamaican Rum, dash Grenadine, juice of ½ lime or lemon. Shake over ice, strain into a cocktail glass.

Millionaire Cocktail (Cktl). ⅔ measure Bourbon whiskey, ⅓ measure Cointreau, 2 dashes Grenadine, 1 egg white. Shake over ice, strain into a cocktail glass.

Million Dollar Cocktail (Cktl). 1½ measures Gin, ½ measure sweet Vermouth, 2 teaspoons cream, 1 teaspoon lemon juice, 2 teaspoons pineapple juice, ½ egg white. Shake well over ice, strain into a Champagne flute.

Million Dollars (Cktl). ½ measure dry Gin, ¼ measure Cointreau, ¼ measure Calvados. Shake over ice, strain into a cocktail glass.

Millipore Process (Eng). Describes the special process of rinsing and sterilising the empty bottles before being filled and corked.

Millwood Whiskey Cream (Hol). Coco liqueur, Dutch cream and Irish whiskey-based liqueur produced by Cooymans. 14.9% alc. by vol.

Milly (Fr). A commune in the A.C. Chablis, Burgundy.

Milroy's Malt Whisky (Scot). An 8 year old single Malt whisky made by the Tullibardine distillery for Milroy's, Soho Wine Market, Greek Street, London. A Highland malt. 40% alc. by vol.

Milsch Glass Tankard (Ger). A large glass beer tankard produced in the eighteenth century. Was highly decorated with a milk-white coloured background. Often had a lid.

Miltenberg (Ger). Village. (Anb) = Franken. (Ber) = Mainviereck. (Gro) = Not yet assigned. (Vin) = Steingrübler.

Milton-Duff Glenlivet (Scot). A single Malt whisky distillery based west of Elgin in the Speyside. Owned by George Ballantine and Son Ltd. (part of the Hiram Walker group). A Highland malt. Produces a 12 year old Malt. 40% alc. by vol.

Milvea Cocktail (Cktl). 1 fl.oz. dry Gin, ½ fl.oz. Crème de Banane, ½ fl.oz. St. Raphaël, dash cream. Shake over ice, strain into a cocktail glass. Top with a cherry.

Mimosa (Cktl). Dash of orange Curaçao, orange juice and Champagne. Fill a Champagne flute ⅓ full of orange juice, add Curaçao, top up with iced Champagne.

Mimsach (Isr). A 'Bible wine' described as being similar in character to a Port wine or liqueur.

Minas Gerais (Bra). A noted wine-producing estate in southern Brazil.

Minchinbury (Austr). A district in New South Wales. Noted for its sparkling wines made by the méthode champenoise.

Minchinbury Estate (Austr). A non-producing estate owned by Penfolds Winery. Sometimes used on their wine labels.

Minella Bianca (It). A white wine grape grown in Sicily.

Mineraal Water (Hol). Mineral water.

Minera Brewery (Wales). Run by Lloyd and Trouncer in North Wales at the City Arms, Minera, Wrexham. Produces cask conditioned ales

Minéral (Fr). Mineral.

Mineral Finings (USA). Diatomaceous earth. (e.g. Bentonite).

Minerals (Eng). Substances found in the soil, sub-soil and in wine, such as Iron, Magnesium, Calcium etc.

Mineral Water (Eng). Still or sparkling natural spring water. Rich in minerals. Apollinaris, Brecon, Buxton, Malvern Perrier, Vichy, etc.

Miners Arms (Eng). A home-brew public house opened in 1981 in Somerset Produces cask conditioned and bottled beers.

Minervois (Fr). A.C. wine-producing district in the Languedoc, Midi. Produces red, rosé and white wines. A.C. in 1985. Minimum alc. by vol. 11%.

Minfeld (Ger). Village. (Anb) = Rheinpfalz. (Ber) = Südliche Weinstrasse. (Gro) = Guttenberg. (Vin) = Herrenberg.

Mingolsheim und Langenbrücken (Ger). Village. (Anb) = Baden. (Ber) = Badische Bergstrasse/Kraichgau. (Gro) = Mannaberg. (Vin) = Goldberg.

Minhao (Port). See Minho. Alternative spelling.

Minheim (Ger). Village. (Anb) = Mosel-Saar-Ruwer. (Ber) = Bernkastel. (Gro) = Michelsberg. (Vins) = Burglay, Günterslay, Kapellchen, Rosenberg.

Minho (Port). A wine district of north-west Portugal. Produces Vinho Verde wines. These can be red, rosé or white and the 'green' refers to the wine's age. Tend to be pétillant from the Malolactic fermentation that takes place in bottle.

Minho [River] (Port). A river that runs through the Vinho Verde region.

Miniature [Nip] (USA). Small measure 1.6 fl.ozs. (¹⁄₁₀ pint) used as a measure for cocktails.

Minifundio (Sp). A process of land division into small plots given to each peasant to farm. In wine areas the grapes produced on the plots are usually vinified in co-operatives.

Miniş (Rum). A red wine-producing area, part of the Banat vineyard. Grape varieties – Cabernet and Kardarka. See Kardarka de Banat.

M

Ministrel (Sp). A black grape variety grown in the Aragón, Rioja Baja and Catalonia. See Monastel.

Minnehaha Cocktail (Cktl). Same as a Midnight Cocktail.

Minorca (Sp). Part of the Balearic Islands off the south coast of Spain. Two main producers are Alayor and San Luis.

Minos (Gre). The brand-name for a red wine produced on the island of Crete.

Minöségü Bor (Hun). Best quality wine.

Min Pin Inn (Eng). A home-brew public house based in Tintagel, north Cornwall. Brews cask conditioned Legend and Brown Willy.

Minstrel Mac (Eng). The brand-name of a Whisky and ginger wine drink.

Mint Cocktail (Cktl). ½ gill Crème de Menthe, ½ gill lime juice, dash Angostura. Stir in a highball glass with ice, fill up with soda water. Serve with slices of fruit and fresh mint on top.

Mint Coffee (Cktl). 4 parts hot coffee, 1 part Crème de Menthe, 1 part Crème de Cacao. Heat coffee and liqueurs, place in a glass, top with cream.

Mint Collins (Cktl). 1 measure dry Gin, ½ measure Crème de Menthe, juice ½ lemon, 6 mint leaves. Shake over ice, strain into an ice-filled highball glass. Top with soda water, a slice of lemon and a sprig of mint. Serve with straws.

Mint Cooler (Cktl). 1 dash Crème de Menthe, ½ pint ginger ale, 2–3 sprigs of mint. Squash mint in a highball glass. Add other ingredients and ice cubes. Stir well, decorate with mint sprigs.

Mint Highball (Cktl). Place ⅕ gill Crème de Menthe into a highball glass, top with ginger ale. Dress with a sprig of mint.

Mint Julep (Cktl).(1). Dissolve 5 sprigs of mint in sugar and a little hot water until flavour is extracted. Strain into a bar glass. Add ice and ¾ gill old Cognac, stir well, strain into a Julep glass. Top with a dash of Rum. Glass is decorated with mint leaves dipped in icing sugar.

Mint Julep (Cktl).(2). 1 measure Bourbon whiskey, 1 tablespoon hot water, 1 tablespoon castor sugar. Put 4–5 mint leaves into a highball glass. Crush with the sugar and water. Add whiskey and fill with crushed ice. Stir until outside of glass is frosted. Decorate with sprigs of mint and serve with straws.

Mint Julep Glass (USA). A large glass shaped like bowl. Of 10 fl.ozs. capacity.

Mint on the Rocks (Cktl). 1 measure Crème de Menthe served over ice in an old-fashioned glass.

Mint Royal Cocktail (Cktl). ⅓ measure Royal Mint Chocolate Liqueur, ⅓ measure Brandy, ⅓ measure lemon juice, 1 egg white. Shake over ice, strain into a cocktail glass.

Minuet (S.Afr). A medium dry white wine made from the Steen grape with 13% of Muscat d'Alexandria and 5% Gewürztraminer added. Made by the Villiera Estate, Paarl.

Mirabelle (Fr). A plum brandy made from cherry plums. An Alcool blanc. 43–45% alc. by vol.

Mirabelle de Lorraine (Fr). A plum brandy made from cherry plums in Lorraine, north-eastern France.

Mirabelle Fine du Val de Metz (Fr). A fine plum Brandy that is fermented with special yeasts, wood-aged 2 months and double-distilled.

Mirador (Le) (S.Afr). A dry, white wine with a touch of pink made from the Cabernet grape by the Boschendal Estate in Paarl.

Miraflores (Sp). An area within Andalusia near Sanlúcar where vineyards of Sherry grapes are grown.

Mirage (Eng). A citrus fruit, white wine and Vodka-based drink 14.9% alc. by vol. produced by William Grant and Bulmer (joint) subsidiary companies.

Miramar Vineyard (Austr). Address = Henry Lawson Drive, Eurunderee, Via Mudgee, New South Wales 2850. 20 ha. Grape varieties – Cabernet sauvignon, Chardonnay, Rhine riesling, Sémillon and Shiraz.

Miranda Wines (Austr). Address = Irrigation Way, Griffith, New South Wales 2680. Produces – still/sparkling wines, Vermouth, Marsala and Cocktail nips.

Mirande Distillery (S.Am). A noted white Rum distillery based in Guyana.

Mirassou Winery (USA). A winery based in Monterey County, California. 208 ha. Grape varieties – Cabernet sauvignon, Chardonnay, Gewürztraminer and Zinfandel. Produces sparkling and varietal wines.

Mirin (Jap). A sweet Saké, usually used in cooking.

Mirita (Port). A brand of Vinho Verde from Aliança.

Mirlo (Sp). A white wine produced by Bodegas Ayuso in La Mancha.

Miroir (Fr). The name given to the lower half of the Champagne cork that is in contact with the wine. Consists of 2–3 discs of cork. See also Aggloméré.

Misa (Sp). The brand-name for a range of sherries produced by Marqués de Misa in Jerez de la Frontera.

Mis au Domaine (Fr). Bottled at the vineyard.

Misch (USA). A black grape variety of the

wild vine Vitis Rotundifolia known as a Muscadine.

Miscible (Eng). To be capable of mixing. Drinks must be this for use in cocktails (some are not).

Mise dans nos Caves (Fr). Bottled in our cellars. Not necessarily those of the grower.

Mise d'Origine (Fr). Bottled at the place of origin.

Mise du Château (Fr). Bottled at the Château.

Mise du Domaine (Fr). Bottled at the property where it is made in Bordeaux. Bottled by the owner in Burgundy.

Mise en Bouteilles à la Propriété (Fr). Bottled by the proprieter.

Mise en Bouteilles au Domaine (Fr). Domaine bottled.

Mise en Masse (Fr). The stacking of the bottles in Champagne upside down in the cellars with the neck of one resting in the punt of the other (sur point) after remuage. Allows the wine to age.

Mise-en-Place (Fr). Getting everything ready before mixing a cocktail, decanting wines etc.

Mis en Bouteille (Fr). Bottled.

Mis en Bouteille au Château (Fr). Château bottled.

Mis en Bouteille au Gare (Fr). Bottled at the station. (Plant).

Mis en Bouteille aux Reflets (Fr). Bottled by the union of the leading proprietors of Châteauneuf-du-Pape. Only found on the finest wine's labels.

Mis en Bouteille dans nos Caves (Fr). Bottled by ourselves in our cellars.

Mis en Bouteille dans nos Chais (Fr). Bottled by ourselves in our warehouses.

Mis en Bouteille en France (Fr). Bottled in France. French bottled.

Mis en Bouteille par le Propriétaire (Fr). Bottled by the Proprieter.

Mis en Bouteille par les Producteurs Réunis (Fr). On a bottle label denotes 'bottled by a co-operative'.

Mise par le Propriétaire (Fr). Bottled by the growers.

Mise sur Lie (Fr). Bottled off its lees. See Sur Lie.

Mise sur Point (Fr). A term used during Champagne remuage. Refers to the grad-ual turning upside down of the bottles on the pupître.

Misket (Bul). A white grape variety which produces dry, fruity wines.

Misket de Karlovo (Bul). A dry white wine from the Misket grape.

Misket Karlova (Bul). See Misket de Karlovo.

Misleidende Reklame (Hol). Trade Description Act.

Missery et Frère (Fr). A Burgundy négo-ciant based at Nuits-Saint-Georges, Côte de Nuits, Burgundy.

Mission Grape (USA). A name given to an early Spanish variety taken to America by Franciscan friars (1520) into Cali-fornia. So called because it was planted at their missions.

Mission Haut Brion [La] (Fr). See Château la Mission Haut Brion.

Mission San Jose (USA). A wine-producing town near the south boundary of Alameda County, California.

Mission Vineyard (N.Z.). A winery based in Green Meadows, Hawkes Bay, North Island. 43 ha. Grape varieties – Cabernet sauvignon, Chasselas, Gewürztraminer, Merlot, Müller-Thurgau, Pinot gris, Sau-vignon blanc and Sémillon. Produces varietal and table wines.

Mississippi Planter's Punch (Cktl). ½ measure Brandy, ¼ measure white Rum, ¼ measure Bourbon whiskey, juice of a lemon, sugar syrup to taste. Shake over ice, strain into an ice-filled collins glass. Top with soda water and stir.

Missouri (USA). A white grape variety. A cross between the Vitis Labrusca and the Vitis Riparia.

Missouri (USA). A wine region in north-western USA. Produces wine in the Missouri River Valley and Ozark moun-tains in the southern part of the state. It was granted the first appellation of America by the BATF in 1980.

Missouri Riesling (USA). A white grape variety. A cross between the Vitis Riparia and the Vitis Labrusca.

Missouri River Valley (USA). A wine district within the Missouri region of north-western USA.

Miss Prettyman (Scot). The name given to a small whisky flask of salt-glazed stoneware 6 inches high and embossed with a lady. Made in c1846 by Doulton and Watts.

Mis Sur Point (Fr). Turned by the Remueur (in Champagne making). (See Mise Sur Point).

Mistela (Port) (Sp). Grape juice that has been fortified with brandy to prevent fermentation. Used to sweeten fortified wines.

Mistelas (Sp). See Mistela.

Mistelas (Sp). Sweet red, rosé or white 'muté' wines. 14–17% alc. by vol. (Fr) = Vins Doux Naturels.

Mistelas Moscatel (Sp). A sweet, golden-coloured wine 17% alc. by vol.

Mistelas Rosé (Sp). Medium-sweet, for-tified wines 14–17% alc. by vol.

Mistella (It). Fortified grape juice used for sweetening fortified wines and Ver-

M

mouths.

Mistelle (Fr). Fortified grape juice (must and brandy) used for the sweetening of Vermouths and fortified wines.

Mistletoe Mull (Cup). 1 pint water, 1 bottle red Burgundy, 4 cloves, 2 lemons, ½ lb. granulated sugar, 1 stick cinnamon. Boil water with sugar and spices for 5 minutes. Add thinly sliced lemon, infuse 10 minutes, add wine, serve very hot.

Mistra (Fr). An aniseed-flavoured spirit (Pastis).

Mistral (Fr). A violent, cold dry Katabatic wind that blows down the Rhône Valley.

Mistral Special (Cktl). 1½ fl.ozs. Cherry Whisky liqueur, ¾ fl.oz. Scotch Whisky, ¾ fl.oz. Vieille Cure, dash lime juice. Shake over ice, strain into an ice-filled highball glass. Top with bitter orange.

Misty (Cktl). ⅓ measure Cointreau, ⅓ measure Vodka, ⅓ measure Apricot brandy, dash lemon juice, dash Crème de Banane. Shake over ice, strain into a highball glass, decorate with a slice of orange, cherry and straws.

Misty (Hol). A dairy-based, tropical fruit-flavoured liqueur. 14.9% alc. by vol.

Misty Cooler (Cktl). 1 fl.oz. Irish Mist, 2 fl.ozs. lemon juice, dash Grenadine, dash egg white. Shake over ice, strain into a highball glass with ice. Top with soda water.

Mitad y Mitad (Sp). The name given to equal quantities of mature Sherry and alcohol used in the fortification of Sherry. See also Combinado, Mistela, Miteado and Paxarete.

Mitans (Les) (Fr). A Premier Cru vineyard in the A.C. commune of Volnay, Côte de Beaune, Burgundy. 4 ha.

Mitchell and Co (Scot). Campbeltown whisky distillers based at Springbank. Brands include Longrow and Springbank.

Mitchell (Edgar) Distillery (Afr). A distillery owned by Leroy Francis in Liberia. Produces a large range of spirits.

Mitchells and Butlers (Eng). Owned by Bass. Breweries are the Highgate Brewery in Walsall, Staffordshire, and the Springfield Brewery in Wolverhampton, Staffordshire. Noted for their cask conditioned Brew X1 1040 O.G. Keg DPA 1033 O.G. bottled Sam Brown 1035 O.G. and Allbright 1040 O.G.

Mitchells Brewery (Eng). A large brewery based in Lancaster, Lancs. Produces many fine beers.

Mitchells Winery (Austr). A small winery based in the Clare Valley, South Australia. Grape varieties – Cabernet sauvignon and Riesling. Produce varietal wines.

Mitchelton Winery (Austr). Vineyard. Address = Nagambie, Victoria 3608. 100 ha. Grape varieties – Cabernet sauvignon, Chardonnay, Marsanne, Rhine riesling, Sémillon and Trebbiano. Noted for its wood-aged Marsanne and a botrytised Riesling.

Miteado (Sp). The alternative name for Mitad y Mitad.

Mit Hefe (Ger). Lit – 'With yeast'. Refers to the Weizenbiers which have a sediment and the customer requests to have the sediment served with the beer.

Mittelberg (Ger). Vineyard. (Anb) = Nahe. (Ber) = Schloss Böckelheim. (Gro) = Paradiesgarten. (Vil) = Bayerfeld-Steckweiler.

Mittelhaardt (Ger). A vineyard area of the Pfalz in that section of the Weinstrasse which lies between Bad Dürkheim in the north and Rupertsberg in the south.

Mittelheim (Ger). Village. (Anb) = Rheingau. (Ber) = Johannisberg. (Gro) = Erntebringer. (Vins) = Edelmann, Goldberg, St. Nikolaus

Mittelheim (Ger). Village. (Anb) = Rheingau. (Ber) = Johannisberg. (Gro) = Honigberg. (Vins) = Edelmann, St. Nikolaus.

Mittelhochkultur (Aus). Medium-high culture. A method of vine cultivation.

Mittelhölle (Ger). Vineyard. (Anb) = Rheingau. (Ber) = Johannisberg. (Gro) = Erntebringer. (Vil) = Johannisberg.

Mittelmosel (Ger). The middle section of the Mosel.

Mittelrhein (Ger). Anbaugebiet. (Bers) = Bacharach, Rheinburgengau.

Mittelrhein Information Service (Ger). Mittelrhein-Burgen und Wein e. V. Address = Postfach, 5423 Braubach, Western Germany.

Mittelrhein Wine Festivals (Ger). Weinblütenfest, Weinlesefest, Weinwoche and Weinfest.

Mittelwihr (Fr). A commune of the Haut-Rhin in Alsace.

Mittervernatsch (It). The German name for the red grape variety from the Südtirol. Known as the Schiava media in Italian.

Mit Zugestzter Kohlensaeure (Ger). When found on a wine label denotes 'with added carbonic acid'.

Mix (Cktl). Place ingredients in the cone of electric drink blender, add crushed ice, mix, pour or strain into required glass.

Mixed Case (Eng). A wine merchants' term for a case (12 bottles) of wine that is not all of the same kind.

Mixed Drink (Eng). A combination of more than one beverage whether they

671

M

be alcoholic or non-alcoholic. e.g. cocktails.

Mixers (USA). Non-alcoholic drinks that make up the bulk of a long cocktail. e.g. Mineral water, soda, tonic, ginger ale, etc.

Mixing Glass (Eng). A glass jug for the mixing (stirring) of cocktails. Has no handle.

Mixing Spoon (Eng). A spoon holding about the same amount as a teaspoon but with a very long handle for stirring. May also have a muddler disc on base. Also called a Barspoon.

Mixologist (USA). The nickname for a cocktail barman.

Mjöd (Swe). Mead.

M J Special (Cktl). ¼ measure Cognac brandy, ¼ measure Dubonnet, ¼ measure Apricot brandy, ¼ measure orange squash, 1 egg white, dash Grenadine. Shake over ice, strain into a cocktail glass.

M.O. (Eng) (abbr). On a wine-list denotes Mise d'Origine.

Mobbie (W.Ind). A spirit produced from potatoes on the island of Barbados.

Mocasina (It). A variety of the red grape Groppello.

Moc-Baril (Fr). A producer of Touraine Rosé Pétillant based at Saumur, Loire.

Mocca (Eng). A term used to describe the taste of Tokay Azsú.

Mocha Coffee (Arab). A fine coffee from Arabia (now Yemen). Beans are yellowish in colour, often produced as for Ethiopian Coffee. Was named after city first grown in. Has a winey flavour. Also a pure coffee of Ethiopia.

Mocha Ice Cream Soda (Cktl). Place a portion of ice cream into a highball glass. Add tot of liqueur or coffee essence, top up with soda water. Serve with straws.

Mocha Mint (Cktl).(1). ⅓ measure Kahlúa, ⅓ measure Crème de Cacao, ⅓ measure (white) Crème de Menthe. Shake over ice, strain into an ice-filled highball glass.

Mocha Mint (Cktl).(2). ½ measure Tia Maria, ½ measure (white) Crème de Menthe. Shake over ice, strain into an ice-filled (crushed ice) highball glass. Serve with straws.

Mockingbird (Cktl). 1 measure Tequila, 3 fl.ozs. grapefruit juice, dash lime juice. Fill an old-fashioned glass with ice cubes. Add ingredients, stir, garnish with a cherry.

Möckmühl (Ger). Village. (Anb) = Württemberg. (Ber) = Kocher-Jagst-Tauber. (Gro) = Kocherberg. (Vins) = Ammerlauden, Hofberg.

Mock Orange (Cktl). 1 measure Gin, 4 measures Apple wine, 3 measures Orange wine. Stir together with ice, strain into an ice-filled highball glass.

Moco Moresque (Fr). A ready-mixed Pastis with a small amount of fruit flavouring.

Moco Perroquet (Fr). A ready-mixed Pastis with a small amount of fruit flavouring.

Moco Tomate (Fr). A ready-mixed Pastis that has a small amount of tomato flavouring.

Moctezuma Brewery (Mex). A brewery based in Veracruz which brews Nochebuena (Christmas Eve) and Dos Equis.

Modelo Brewery (Mex). A brewery based in Mexico City. Noted for its Victoria beer.

Modena (It). A province of Emilia-Romagna from which Lambrusco di Sorbara is the best known wine.

Modern Cocktail (Cktl). ⅔ measure Scotch whisky, ⅓ measure lemon juice, 2 dashes Pernod, 2 dashes Jamaican rum, dash Campari. Shake over ice, strain into a cocktail glass. Top with a cherry.

Modesto (USA). The central region of the Central River Valley in California. Produces dessert and table wines.

Modification (Eng). In brewing, the germination stage of the malting process, when the barley sprouts shoots and chemical changes occur.

Modolet Brut (It). A sparkling (bottle-fermented) wine produced by Angons in the Friuli-Venezia Giulia region.

Modra (Czec). A noted wine-producing region. Has a high wine output.

Modri (Yug). When found on a wine label denotes 'black'.

Modri Burgundac (Yug). The Pinot noir grape.

Moelleux (Fr). A term used to denote sweet, sparkling wines.

Moelleux (Fr). Velvety, rich and smooth.

Moët et Chandon (Fr). Champagne producer. Address = 20 Avenue de Champagne, 51200 Épernay. Grande Marque. Produces – Vintage and non-vintage wines. Vintages – 1900, 1904, 1906, 1911, 1914, 1921, 1923, 1928, 1929, 1933, 1934, 1937, 1938, 1941, 1943, 1945, 1947, 1949, 1952, 1953, 1955, 1959, 1961, 1962, 1964, 1966, 1969, 1970, 1971, 1973, 1975, 1976, 1978, 1980, 1981, 1982, 1983. The largest Champagne house. See also Dom Pérignon and M. Chandon.

Moezelwijn (Hol). Moselle (Mosel) wine.

Moffat (Scot). A single Malt whisky

M

distillery based to the east of Glasgow. A Lowland malt whisky. 40% alc. by vol. Also produces a Grain whisky.

Moflete (Sp). A name given to the process in the Sherry region where a vine in the last year of its useful life is allowed to grow as many buds as it can to get maximum production and so exhaust the vine.

Mogen David Corporation (USA). Producers of sweet sacramental wines based in Illinois. Owned by the Coca Cola Bottling Co, New York.

Mogue à Iaoue (Ch.Isles). Water jug.

Mogue à Lait (Ch.Isles). Milk jug.

Mohan Meakin Brewery (Ind). A brewery based in the Simla Hills, Solan. Produces Baller Beer 1040 O.G. Golden Eagle 1050 O.G. Gymkhana 1045 O.G. Krown 1048 O.G. and Lion 1046 O.G.

Moho (Sp). Mildew.

Mohoso (Sp). Mildewed.

Moillard-Grivot (Fr). A Burgundy négociant-éleveur based at Nuits-Saint-Georges. Address = 2, Rue F. Mignotte, 21700 Nuits-Saint-Georges, Burgundy.

Moimento da Beira (Port). A white grape variety grown in the Dão region.

Moingeon-Gueneau Frères (Fr). A producer of Crémant de Bourgogne based in Nuits-Saint-Georges, Burgundy.

Moings (Fr). A commune in the Charente-Maritime Département whose grapes are classed Petite Champagne (Cognac).

Mojito (Cktl). 1½ fl.ozs. Golden Rum, juice ½ lime, 2 dashes Gomme syrup, sugar, 6 mint leaves. Squeeze lime juice into a highball glass, add spent lime shell, sugar and mint leaves. Stir, fill glass with shaved ice, add Rum. Stir, add dash soda water and decorate with mint and straws.

Moka Coffee (Arab). Also known as Yemen coffee. A grade of coffee seed (bean). Has small irregular rounded seeds of yellow appearance. See also Mocha Coffee.

Moka Express (USA). The name given to the household Espresso coffee machine.

Moka Helado (Cktl).(Non-alc). ¼ pint iced coffee, 1 scoop vanilla ice cream, 1 teaspoon of chocolate powder slaked down with a little water. Blend together in a blender. Serve in highball glasses with straws.

Mokha (Arab). An alternative spelling of Mocha. See also Moka.

Mokka mit Sahne (Ger). A liqueur made with coffee and cream.

Molasses (W.Ind). The liquid from cane sugar which after fermentation is distilled into Rum.

Molasses Act (W.Ind). Act passed in 1973 which levied duty on Rum and also on molasses if they were bought from anywhere other than the British West Indies.

Moldavia (USSR). A wine region bordering Rumania (once belonging to Rumania) between the rivers Dnieper and Danube. See also Bessarabia.

Moledora (Sp). A process of passing the grapes through rubber rollers in the Sherry region to lightly press them before they go into the Vaslin press.

Moles Brewery (Eng). Opened in 1982 in Melksham, Wiltshire. Produces cask conditioned Mole's Bitter 1040 O.G. Mole's 97 1048 O.G.

Molette (Fr). A white grape variety grown in Bugey and Seyssel to produce sparkling wines.

Molinara (It). A red grape variety grown in the Veneto region. Used in the making of light red wines. See Rosana.

Molinara (It). The Lombardy region name for the red Rossanella grape.

Mollar (Sp). A white grape variety grown in southern Spain. Also known as the Cañocazo.

Mollenbrunnen (Ger). Vineyard. (Anb) = Nahe. (Ber) = Kreuznach. (Gro) = Kronenberg. (Vil) = Bad Kreuznach.

Mollenbrunnen (Ger). Vineyard. (Anb) = Nahe. (Ber) = Kreuznach. (Gro) = Kronenberg. (Vil) = Hargesheim.

Mölsheim (Ger). Village. (Anb) = Rheinhessen. (Ber) = Wonnegau. (Gro) = Domblick. (Vins) = Silberberg, Zellerweg am Schwarzen, Herrgott.

Molson (Can). Largest of the 'Big three' breweries based in Quebec.

Mombrier (Fr). A commune in the A.C. Côtes de Bourg, north-eastern Bordeaux.

Mominette (Fr). The working-class name for an Absinthe-Swiss Style when sweetened with plain syrup.

Mommenheim (Ger). Village. (Anb) = Rheinhessen. (Ber) = Nierstein. (Gro) = Gutes Domtal. (Vins) = Kloppenberg, Osterberg, Silbergrube.

Mommessin (Fr). A négociant-éleveur based at Charnay lès Mâcon, Mâcon, Burgundy. Owns the Grand Cru Clos de Tart vineyard in the Côte de Nuits.

Monagri (Cyp). A village on the south-east side of the Island that produces grapes for Commandaria.

Mona Lisa (Cktl). ⅓ measure Bénédictine, ⅓ measure Amer Picon, ⅓ measure orange Curaçao, barspoon of double cream. Shake over ice, strain into a cocktail glass. Sprinkle cinnamon on top.

Mona Lisa Cocktail (Cktl). Place ½ measure dry Gin, ½ measure Campari, 1¼ measures orange Chartreuse in an ice-filled highball glass, stir. Top with ginger ale, decorate with a slice of orange and a lemon spiral. Serve with straws.

Monarch Ale (Eng). A bottled Bitter 1065 O.G. brewed by the Morland Brewery in Abingdon, Oxfordshire.

Monarch Wine Company (USA). A winery based in Atlanta, Georgia. Produces mainly Brandy and Peach wines.

Monastel (Sp). See Monastrel.

Monastery Brandy (USA). The brandname of a Brandy produced by the Schenley Distillers.

Monastery Types (USA). Modern liqueurs that are produced as copies of old herbal liqueurs which were produced by monks in the Middle Ages.

Monastrel (Sp). A black grape variety grown in the Aragón, Catalonia, Penedés and Rioja regions. Also known as the Alcayata, Mechín, Ministrel, Monastell, Moraster, Negralejo and Valcarcelica.

Monastrell (Sp). See Monastrel.

Monbazillac (Fr). An A.C. sweet white wine from Bergerac. Produced by the same method as Sauternes with the grapes attacked by botrytis cinerea. Communes of Colombier, Monbazillac, Pomport, Rouffignac and Saint-Laurent-des-Vignes. Minimum alc. by vol. of 13%.

Monbrison (Fr). A vineyard in the commune of Arsac. A.C. Médoc, Bordeaux. Cru Bourgeois Supérieur.

Monção (Port). Northern district of the Entre Minho e Douro. Produces both red and white Vinhos Verdes. Reds are dark coloured.

Mönchbäumchen (Ger). Vineyard. (Anb) = Rheinhessen. (Ber) = Nierstein. (Gro) = Gutes Domtal. (Vil) = Zornheim.

Mönchberg (Ger). Vineyard. (Anb) = Ahr. (Ber) = Walporzheim/Arhtal. (Gro) = Klosterberg. (Vil) = Mayschoss.

Mönchberg (Ger). Vineyard. (Anb) = Nahe. (Ber) = Kreuznach. (Gro) = Kronenberg. (Vil) = Bad Kreuznach.

Mönchberg (Ger). Vineyard. (Anb) = Nahe. (Ber) = Kreuznach. (Gro) = Kronenberg. (Vil) = Bad Kreuznach.

Mönchberg (Ger). Vineyard. (Anb) = Nahe. (Ber) = Kreuznach. (Gro) = Pfarrgarten. (Vil) = Hergenfeld.

Mönchberg (Ger). Vineyard. (Anb) = Nahe. (Ber) = Schloss Böckelheim. (Gro) = Rosengarten. (Vil) = Hüffelsheim.

Mönchberg (Ger). Vineyard. (Anb) = Rheinhessen. (Ber) = Bingen. (Gro) = Rheingrafenstein. (Vil) = Volxheim.

Mönchberg (Ger). Vineyard. (Anb) = Württemberg. (Ber) = Remstal-Stuttgart. (Gro) = Sonnenbühl. (Vil) = Weinstadt (ortsteil Rommelshausen), also Mönchhalde.

Mönchberg (Ger). Vineyard. (Anb) = Württemberg. (Ber) = Remstal-Stuttgart. (Gro) = Sonnenbühl. (Vil) = Weinstadt (ortsteil Stetten i. R.), also Mönchhalde.

Mönchberg (Ger). Vineyard. (Anb) = Württemberg. (Ber) = Remstal-Stuttgart. (Gro) = Weinsteige. (Vil) = Fellbach.

Mönchberg (Ger). Vineyard. (Anb) = Württemberg. (Ber) = Remstal-Stuttgart. (Gro) = Weinsteige. (Vil) = Stuttgart.

Mönchberg (Ger). Vineyard. (Anb) = Württemberg. (Ber) = Remstal-Stuttgart. (Gro) = Weinsteige. (Vil) = Stuttgart (ortsteil Cannstatt).

Mönchberg (Ger). Vineyard. (Anb) = Württemberg. (Ber) = Remstal-Stuttgart. (Gro) = Weinsteige. (Vil) = Stuttgart (ortsteil Untertürkheim).

Mönchgarten (Ger). Vineyard. (Anb) = Rheinpfalz. (Ber) = Mittelhaardt-Deutsche Weinstrasse. (Gro) = Meerspinne. (Vil) = Neustadt an der Weinstrasse.

Mönchhalde (Ger). Vineyard. (Anb) = Württemberg. (Ber) = Remstal-Stuttgart. (Gro) = Sonnenbühl. (Vil) = Weinstadt (ortsteil Rommelshausen), also Mönchberg.

Mönchhalde (Ger). Vineyard. (Anb) = Württemberg. (Ber) = Remstal-Stuttgart. (Gro) = Sonnenbühl. (Vil) = Weinstadt (ortsteil Stetten i. R.). Also Mönchberg.

Mönchhalde (Ger). Vineyard. (Anb) = Württemberg. (Ber) = Remstal-Stuttgart. (Gro) = Weinsteige. (Vil) = Stuttgart.

Mönchhalde (Ger). Vineyard. (Anb) = Württemberg. (Ber) = Remstal-Stuttgart. (Gro) = Weinsteige. (Vil) = Stuttgart (ortsteil Bad Cannstatt).

Monchhof (Aus). The name given to a medium-dry white wine from the Burgenland.

Mönchhube (Ger). Vineyard. (Anb) = Rheinhessen. (Ber) = Wonnegau. (Gro) = Pilgerpfad. (Vil) = Dittelsheim-Hessloch.

Mönchpforte (Ger). Vineyard. (Anb) = Rheinhessen. (Ber) = Bingen. (Gro) = Abtey. (Vil) = Ober-Hilbersheim.

Mönchsberg (Ger). Vineyard. (Anb) = Württemberg. (Ber) = Kocher-Jagst-Tauber. (Gro) = Tauberberg. (Vil) = Markelsheim.

Mönchsberg (Ger). Vineyard. (Anb) = Württemberg. (Ber) = Kocher-Jagst-Tauber. (Gro) = Tauberberg. (Vil) = Elpersheim.

M

Mönchsberg (Ger). Vineyard. (Anb) = Württemberg. (Ber) = Württembergisch Unterland. (Gro) = Heuchelberg. (Vil) = Brackenheim.

Mönchsberg (Ger). Vineyard. (Anb) = Württemberg. (Ber) = Württembergisch Unterland. (Gro) = Heuchelberg. (Vil) = Dürrenzimmern.

Mönchshang (Ger). Vineyard. (Anb) = Franken. (Ber) = Steigerwald. (Gro) = Not yet assigned. (Vil) = Zeil a. Main.

Mönchsleite (Ger). Vineyard. (Anb) = Franken. (Ber) = Maindreieck. (Gro) = Not yet assigned. (Vil) = Eibelstadt.

Mönchspfad (Ger). Vineyard. (Anb) = Rheingau. (Ber) = Johannisberg. (Gro) = Burgweg. (Vil) = Geisenheim.

Mönchspfad (Ger). Vineyard. (Anb) = Rheinhessen. (Ber) = Nierstein. (Gro) = Domherr. (Vil) = Schornsheim.

Mönchspfad (Ger). Vineyard. (Anb) = Rheinhessen. (Ber) = Nierstein. (Gro) = Sankt Alban. (Vil) = Bodenheim.

Mönchspfad (Ger). Vineyard. (Anb) = Rheinpfalz. (Ber) = Südliche Weinstrasse. (Gro) = Königsgarten. (Vil) = Siebeldingen.

Mönchwingert (Ger). Vineyard. (Anb) = Mittelrhein. (Ber) = Bacharach. (Gro) = Schloss Stahleck. (Vil) = Manubach.

Moncreiffe (Scot). An 8 year old blended De Luxe Scotch Whisky (Sir Ian Moncreiffe) produced by Moncreiffe and Co. Ltd. of Perth. 43% alc. by vol.

Mondavi (USA). A large winery in the Napa Valley, California. Owned by Robert Mondavi. 260 ha. Grape varieties – Cabernet sauvignon, Chardonnay, Chenin blanc, Johannisberg riesling and Pinot noir. Produce varietal wines.

Mondego [River] (Port). A river of which the river Dão is a tributary.

Mondeuse (USA). A red grape variety used in the making of red wines in California. Also known as the Refosco and Dongine.

Mon Don (S.Afr). A small winery in Robertson making varietal wines.

Mondragone (It). One of the areas of Campania where Falerno wine is produced.

Mondschein (Ger). Vineyard. (Anb) = Rheinhessen. (Ber) = Wonnegau. (Gro) = Pilgerpfad. (Vil) = Dittelsheim-Hessloch.

Monee Thompson Vineyard (USA). A winery based near Chicago, Illinois. Is noted for its sparkling wines made by the méthode champenoise (white and rosé).

Monemvasia (Gre). The Peloponnesian town which is the origination of the Malvasia grape variety.

Monfort (Ger). vineyard. (Anb) = Nahe. (Ber) = Schloss Böckelheim. (Gro) = Paradiesgarten. (Vil) = Odernheim.

Monhard (Ger). vineyard. (Anb) = Nahe. (Ber) = Kreuznach. (Gro) = Kronenberg. (Vil) = Bad Kreuznach.

Monica (It). A red grape variety grown in Sardinia. Produces soft red velvety wines.

Monica di Cagliari (It). D.O.C. red wine from Sardinia. Made from the Monica grape in the province of Cagliari. Grapes can be dried on vine or frames. 4 types – Dolce naturale, Secco, Liquoroso secco and Liquoroso dolce naturale. Liquoroso dolce and Secco if aged 2 years (1 year in oak/chestnut casks) classed Riserva

Monica di Sardegna (It). D.O.C. red wine from Sardinia. Made from the Monica, Carignano, Bovale grande, Bovale sardo and Pascale di caligari grapes. If aged 1 year and minimum alc. content of 13% by vol. then classed Superiore. Made near Cagliari.

Monichino Winery (Austr). A small winery based in central Victoria.

Moniga-del-Garda (It). A red wine produced in the Lombardy region on the southern shores of Lake Garda.

Monilio Javanica (E.Ind). Batavian arak.

Monimpex (Hun). The state export monopoly that has wine cellars near Budapest.

Monin (Fr). The brand-name of a liqueur made from brandy and lemon peel. 33% alc. by vol.

Monis Wines (S.Afr). Dessert and fortified wines from the SFW.

Monitor (Arg). The brand-name of a sparkling wine produced by the cuve close method.

Monk Cocktail (Cktl). ¼ measure Bénédictine, ½ measure dry Gin, ¼ measure lemon juice. Shake over ice, strain into a cocktail glass.

Monk Export (Ire). The name for canned McEwan's Export 1042 O.G. sold in Northern Ireland.

Monkey (Port). See Macaco.

Monkey (Sp). A small bottle on the end of a piece of string used by the Sherry workers to poach Sherry from the casks whilst the foreman isn't looking.

Monkey Back (Scot). A condition of Malt whisky workers who turn the germinating barley over. A back strain.

Monkey Bottle (Ger). See Affenflasche.

Monkey Gland (Cktl).(1). 1½ measures Gin, ½ measure orange juice, 2 dashes Grenadine, 2 dashes Pernod. Shake over ice, strain into a cocktail glass. Dash of orange peel juice on top.

Monkey Gland (Cktl).(2). ⅓ gill Gin, ⅙ gill Bénédictine, ⅙ gill orange juice, 2 dashes Grenadine. Stir over ice, strain into an ice-filled old-fashioned glass.

Monkeys (Port). Long poles with heavy end

pieces which are used to push the skins down into the must.

Monk's Coffee (Liq.Coffee). Using a measure of Bénédictine.

Monk's Comfort (Liq.Coffee). Same as Monks Coffee.

Monkscroft House Ale (Scot). A bottled Ale 1070 O.G. brewed for Export to Italy by the Belhaven Brewery.

Monlezun Oak (Fr). A black oak used for the making of casks for Armagnac brandy. (Lat) = Quercus Pedonculus Albus.

Monlouis (N.Z.). The brand-name used by the Pacific Vineyards in Henderson, North Island for a range of their wines.

Monmousseau (Fr). The name given to the sparkling wines made by the méthode champenoise in Monmousseau, Touraine, Loire. Owned by Taittinger.

Monmouth Brewery (Wales). Based at the Queen's Head in Monmouth. Noted for its cask conditioned Ten Thirty Five 1035 O.G. and Piston 1045 O.G.

Monnet (Fr). Cognac producer. Address = J.G. Monnet and Co. P.O. Box 22, 52 Avenue Paul-Firno, 16101 Cognac. Produces Anniversaire Très Ancienne Selection, Extra Belle Réserve.

Monnières (Fr). A village in the central part of the A.C. Muscadet de Sèvre et Maine. Produces some of the finest wines.

Mono-Cru (Fr). Denotes single wines sold by the growers in Champagne.

Mononga Cobbler (Cktl). 1½ fl.ozs. Bourbon whiskey, 1 teaspoon icing sugar, dash lemon juice. Shake well over ice, strain into an ice-filled (crushed ice) highball glass. Dress with a slice of orange and lemon. Serve with straws.

Monopole (Fr). On an Armagnac brandy label indicates a minimum age of one year.

Monopole (Fr). Denotes that the whole of the vineyard named belongs to the same proprietor.

Monopole (Sp). A dry, white wine produced by the C.V.N.E. in the Rioja Alta.

Monopole Labelling (USA). Brand labelling.

Monosaccharides (Eng). Unfermentable sugars that cannot be converted by yeast enzymes and remain in the wine. Pentose, Arabinose, Xylose, Ribose etc.

Monos'Ló (Hun). A small wine-producing village in Transdanubia near Lake Balatòn. Is noted for its sweet wines.

Monsanto (It). A noted Chianti Classico producer based in Tuscany.

Monsedro (Port). A red grape variety grown in the Algarve.

Monsheim (Ger). Village. (Anb) = Rheinhessen. (Ber) = Wonnegau. (Gro) = Domblick. (Vins) = Rosengarten, Silberberg.

Monsieur Pastis (Fr). The nickname given to Paul Ricard.

Monsoon Coffee (Ind). The name given to coffee produced during the monsoon period. Has a full aroma and flavour.

Monstelo (Sp). A red grape variety grown in the Galicia region.

Monsupello (It). A noted wine-producer based in Oltrepo Pavese, Lombardy.

Mont (Le) (Fr). A vineyard in the A.C. Vouvray, Touraine, Loire.

Montagna (Ger). A cross grape variety between the Rieslaner and Müller-Thurgau.

Montagne de Reims (Fr). A vineyard region of Champagne, grows mainly black grapes.

Montagne Estate (S.Afr). A large vineyard based in Stellenbosch. 133 ha. Grape varieties – Cabernet sauvignon and Shiraz. Produce varietal wines made by the Gilbey Co.

Montagne-Saint-Émilion (Fr). An A.C. commune within the Saint-Émilion district in eastern Bordeaux.

Montagny (Fr). An A.C. commune of the Côte Chalonnaise in southern Burgundy. (white wines).

Montagu (S.Afr). A district in the Klein Karoo noted for its Sherry-type wines.

Montagu Muskadel Boere Co-operative (S.Afr). Based in Klein Karoo. Address = Box 29, Montagu 6720. Produces Volsoet Rooi Muskadel and varietal wines.

Montalbano Spalletti (It). A noted Chianti Classico producer based in Tuscany.

Montana (Cktl). ½ measure Brandy, ½ measure dry Vermouth, 2 dashes Port, 2 dashes Anisette, 2 dashes Angostura. Stir over ice, strain into a cocktail glass.

Montaña (Sp). A district of the Navarra region in north-eastern Spain.

Montana (La) (USA). The brand-label used by the Martin Ray Vineyards, Santa Clara, California.

Montana Wines (N.Z.). Address = 171 Pilkington Road, Glen Innes, Auckland. Vineyards at – Blenheim, Gisborne, Marlborough and Poverty Bay. Grape varieties – Cabernet sauvignon, Chardonnay, Gewürztraminer, Pinotage, Pinot noir, Rhine riesling, Riesling-sylvaner, Sauvignon blanc.

Montánchez (Sp). A wine-producing village near to Mérida in the Extremadura, south-western Spain that produces flor-attacked wines.

M

Montanha (Port). A winery based in Bairrada. Noted for their red wines.

Montara (Austr). A noted winery based in Great Western, Victoria.

Montarcy Vieux (Fr). The brand-name of a Calvados distributed by the Merrydown Co. in the U.K.

Montaudon (Fr). Champagne producer. Address = 6 Rue Ponsardin, 51100 Reims. Produces – Vintage and non-vintage wines. Vintages – 1970, 1971, 1973, 1975, 1976, 1979, 1982, 1983.

Montauzier (Pierre) (Fr). Cognac producer. Address = Bors-de-Montmoreau, 16190 Montmoreau-Saint-Cybard. 5 ha. in the Bons Bois. Produces Vieille Réserve Napoléon (average age 15 year).

Mont Baudile (Fr). A Vins de Pays area of the Hérault Département in southern France.

Montbazillac (Fr). See Monbazillac. Misspelling of.

Mont-Bellet (Fr). A wine-producing district in Bellet, Provence.

Mont Blem (Isr). A brand of dry white wine.

Mont Blois (S.Afr). Wine estate in Robertson. Address = P.O. Robertson 6705. Produce varietal wines.

Mont Bouquet (Fr). A Vins de Pays area of the Gard Département in south-west France.

Montbray Wine Cellars (USA). A small winery based in Maryland that produces hybrid wines.

Montbré (Fr). A Premier Cru Champagne village in the Canton de Verzy. District = Reims.

Mont Caume (Fr). A Vins de Pays area of the Var Département in south-eastern France. Produces red and rosé wines.

Montceaux-Ragny (Fr). A commune in the A.C. Mâcon. The grapes of which may be used for Mâcon Supérieur.

Montchaude (Fr). A commune in the Charente Département whose grapes are used for Petite Champagne Cognac.

Montchern (Fr). A vineyard in the Yonne Département. Produces red and white wines.

Montclair Winery (USA). A small winery based opposite the Bay of San Francisco, Alameda, California. Grape varieties – Cabernet sauvignon, Colombard and Zinfandel. Produces varietal wines.

Montcuchots (Les) (Fr). A vineyard in the A.C. commune of Montagny, Côte Chalonnaise, Burgundy.

Mont de Milieu Beauroy (Fr). A Premier Cru vineyard of A.C. Chablis, Burgundy.

Mont d'Or (Switz). A brand of dry white wine produced in the Sion district of the Valais region.

Monteagudo (Sp). A Brandy produced by Delgado Zuleta.

Monte Aguila (W.Ind). A spicy digestive liqueur based on pimento produced on the island of Jamaica.

Montebello (Fr). A Grande Marque Champagne house.

Montebello Vineyard (USA). A small vineyard in Santa Clara, California. Grape variety – Cabernet sauvignon. Part of the Ridge vineyards.

Montecarlo (It). D.O.C. white wine from Tuscany. Made from the Pinot bianco, Pinot gris, Roussanne, Sauvignon, Sémillon, Trebbiano toscano, Verminto grapes. Vinification can occur in each of the communes of Montecarlo, Maginone and Altopascio.

Monte Carlo Imperial Highball (Cktl). ⅖ measure Gin, ⅕ measure (white) Crème de Menthe, juice ¼ lemon. Shake over ice, strain into an ice-filled highball. Top with iced Champagne.

Montecatini Terme (It). A noted wine-producer based in the north of the Tuscany region. Produces Montecarlo white wine.

Montecillo Rosé (Sp). A red wine produced by the Bodegas El Montecillo Alta Region, Rioja. Made from the Garnacha grape.

Monte Coman (Arg). A wine-producing area in southern Argentina.

Montecompatri-Colonna (It). D.O.C. white wine from Latium. Made from the Bellone, Bonvino, Malvasia and Trebbiano grapes from the commune of Colonna and part of Montecompatri, Roccapriora and Zagarolo communes. If total alc. content is 12.5% by vol. can be classed Riserva.

Monte Crasto (Port). A noted producer of red and white wines based in the Bairrada region.

Montecristo (Sp). A wine-producing company in Montilla-Moriles. Was part of the Rumasa group.

Montée de Tonerre (Fr). A Premier Cru vineyard of Chablis. Often has the Premiers Crus Chapelot and Pied-d'Aloup reclassified as its vintages.

Montée-Rouge (Fr). A vineyard [part] in the A.C. commune of Beaune, Côte de Beaune, Burgundy.

Montefalco Sagrantino (It). A D.O.C. red wine from Montefalco in the Umbria region. Produced from the Sagrantino grape.

Montefaro (Port). A Vinho Verde producer based at the Quinta de Seara, Palmeira, 4740 Esposende.

Montefiascone (It). See Est! Est!! Est!!!
Monteith (Eng). A large ornamental bowl used for cooling wine-glasses which are suspended from a notched rim.
Montejo (Mex). A pale beer brewed by the Yucateca Brewery.
Monte Jup (Ger). vineyard. (Anb) = Mittelrhein. (Ber) = Rheinburgengau. (Gro) = Burg Hammerstein. (Vil) = Rheinbrohl.
Monteliana e dei Colli Ascolani (La) (It). A sparkling (méthode champenoise) wine producer based in the Veneto region.
Monte Llano (Sp). A red wine produced by the Bodegas Ramón Bilbao SA. Matured in oak for 1 year.
Montelle Vineyards (USA). A winery based in Augusta, Missouri. Produces almost 40 styles of American and European hybrid wines.
Montellori (It). A noted Chianti Putto producer based in Tuscany.
Montenegro (Yug). A small wine-producing district in south-eastern Yugoslavia.
Monteneubel (Ger). vineyard. (Anb) = Mosel-Saar-Ruwer. (Ber) = Bernkastel. (Gro) = Schwarzlay. (Vil) = Enkirch.
Montepaldi (It). A noted Chianti Classico producer based in Tuscany.
Montepulciano (It). A red grape variety grown in Apulia to produce both light red and white wines.
Montepulciano d'Abruzzo (It). D.O.C. red wine from Abruzzi. Made from the Montepulciano and Sangiovese grapes. If skins are left in during fermentation to obtain a cherry red colour then the term Cerasuolo can be added to label. If aged 2 years then the term Vecchio can also appear on the label.
Monte Real Tinto (Sp). A red wine from the Bodegas Riojanas SA, Rioja. Made from 10% Graciano, 10% Garnacha and 80% Tempranillo grapes. Oak-matured for 3 years and bottle aged for 2 years.
Monterey Peninsula Winery (USA). A small winery based in Monterey, California. Grape varieties – Cabernet sauvignon, Chardonnay, Petite sirah, Pinot noir and Zinfandel. Produce varietal wines.
Monterey Riesling (USA). An alternative name for the Green sylvaner grape.
Monterey Valley (USA). A wine area situated south of San Francisco, California. Produces table, dessert and sparkling wines. See Almaden.
Monterey Vineyard (USA). A winery based in the Upper Salinas Valley, Monterey, California. Grape varieties – Gewürztraminer, Johannisberg riesling, Sauvignon blanc and Zinfandel. Is owned by the Coca Cola Co. Produces varietal and Noble rot wines.

Monterez (Eng). The brand-name of a drink of brandy, white wine and orange. Can be drunk straight or used as a mixer. Distributed by Harvey's of Bristol in the U.K. Produced by Monterez Co., 28, St. James's Square, London. Also a lemon version called Monterez Citron.
Monterez Citron (Eng). The lemon-flavoured version of Monterez.
Monterminod (Fr). A V.D.Q.S. vineyard on the bank of Lake Bourget in the Savoie region.
Monte Rossa (It). A sparkling (bottle-fermented) wine producer based in Lombardy.
Monterosso (It). One of the five towns in Cinque Terre, Liguria.
Monterosso Val d'Arda (It). D.O.C. white wine from Emilia-Romagna. Made from the Malvasia di candia, Moscato bianco, Ortrugo, Trebbiano romagnolo grapes. The D.O.C. also applies to naturally sparkling wine obtained from musts and wines made according to the current regulations.
Monterrey (Sp). A Denominación de Origen wine-producing region in Galicia. Produces mainly red wines.
Monte Schiavo (It). A sparkling (cuve close) wine producer based in the Marche region.
Montescudaio Rosso (It). A D.O.C. red wine from the Tuscany region. Produced from the Sangiovese grape.
Monte Seco (Sp). A red wine made by Bodegas Ramón Bilbao SA, Rioja. Matured 2–4 years in oak and for 1–10 years in bottle.
Monte Velaz (Sp). The name given to a range of two red wines produced by Bodegas Velazquez.
Monteverdi (It). A low-alcohol white wine produced by European Vintners from mainly the Moscato grape. 3% alc. by vol.
Monteviña Winery (USA). A winery based in the Shenandoah Valley, Amador County, California. Grape varieties – Barbera, Cabernet sauvignon, Sauvignon blanc and Zinfandel. Produces varietal wines.
Montevista Wines (S.Afr). The brand-name used by the Mooiuitsig Wynkelders for a range of their wines.
Montezuma Cocktail (Cktl). ⅔ measure Silver Tequila, ⅔ measure Verdelho Madeira, 1 egg yolk. Blend together with a scoop of crushed ice in a blender. Pour into a flute glass.
Montezuma Silver (Mex). A clear Tequila with a slight herb flavour.
Mont Fleuri (Switz). A dry white produced in the Sion district of the Valais region

M

from the Riesling grape.

Montgros Blanc (Sp). A grapey white wine produced in the Penedés region by Aquila Rossa.

Montgueux (Fr). A Cru Champagne village in the Canton de l'Aube. District = Château Thierry.

Monthélie (Fr). An A.C. wine village (commune) in the Côte de Beaune. Has ten Premier Cru vineyards – Duresse, La Taupine, Le Cas-Rougeot, Le Château-Gaillard, Le Clos-Gauthey, Le Meix-Bataille, Les Champs-Fulliot, Les Riottes, Les Vignes Rondes and Sur la Velle. 100 ha.

Monthélie-Côte de Beaune (Fr). The alternative A.C. classification of Monthélie wines.

Monthélie-Côte de Beaune-Villages (Fr). The alternative A.C. classification of Monthélie wines.

Monthelon (Fr). A Cru Champagne village in the Canton d'Avize. District = Épernay.

Montherminod (Fr). A noted wine-producing village of Roussette in the Savoie region, south-eastern France.

Monthoux (Fr). A V.D.Q.S. vineyard based on the left bank of the river Rhône in the Savoie region.

Montialbero S.A. (Sp). A noted producer of Montilla wines based in Montilla-Moriles.

Monticello Cellars (USA). A winery based near Trefethen, Napa Valley, California. Grape varieties – Cabernet sauvignon, Chardonnay, Gewürztraminer and Sauvignon blanc. Produce varietal wines.

Monticola (USA). An American vine species used for grafting in the Rhône in France.

Montigny-Sous-Châtillon (Fr). A Cru Champagne village in the Canton de Châtillon-sur-Marne. District = Reims.

Montilla (Sp). See Montilla-Moriles.

Montilla-Moriles (Sp). A wine region in southern Spain. Produce wines similar in style to Sherry, but not fortified. Wines are attacked by Flor to produce Finos. Matured in Tinajas. Wines named Fino and Amontillado. 16% alc. by vol. Grapes – Baladí, Lairén, Moscatel and Pedro Ximénez.

Montilla Sierra (Sp). A fine Montilla (of Fino Sherry quality).

Montilleros (Sp). Montilla wines.

Montils (Fr). A commune in the Charente-Maritime Département whose grapes are used in the production of Cognac (grown in the Bois Ordinaires area). Also the local name for a white grape variety.

Montini (Mex). A noted liqueur producer. Produces Camino Real (a coffee-flavoured liqueur) and Xanath (a vanilla-flavoured liqueur).

Montisol S.A. (Sp). A producer of Montilla based in Montilla-Moriles.

Montjean (Fr). A commune in the A.C. Savennières, Anjou-Saumur, Loire.

Mont la Salle (USA). Part of the Napa Valley, California where the vineyards of the Christian Brothers are situated.

Mont-Laurent (Le) (Fr). A vineyard in the A.C. commune of Montagny, Côte Chalonnaise, Burgundy.

Mont 'Les Pierrailles' (Switz). A white wine produced in Rolle, La Côte, western Switzerland by Hammel.

Mont-le-Vignoble (Fr). A commune in the Côtes de Toul, Lorraine. Produces Vins gris.

Montlouis (Fr). An A.C. white wine produced in the Touraine district in the Central Loire. Produced from the Chenin blanc grape.

Montlouis Mousseux (Fr). An A.C. sparkling white wine from the Touraine district in the Loire.

Montlouis Pétillant (Fr). An A.C. white wine from the Touraine distict in the Loire.

Montmains (Fr). A Premier Cru vineyard of Chablis. Often has the Premier Crus of Forêts and Butteaux used as its vintage.

Mont-Marçal (Sp). A fine-wine producer based in the Penedés region. Produces Blanco Añada and Primer Vi Novell.

Montmartre (Cktl). ¾ measure dry Gin, ⅛ measure Italian vermouth, ⅛ measure Curaçao. Stir over ice, strain into a cocktail glass. Top with a cherry.

Montmélas-Saint-Sorlin (Fr). A commune in the A.C. Beaujolais-Villages or Beaujolais-Montmélas-Saint-Sorlin status.

Montmélian (Fr). A red wine from the Savoie in south-eastern France. Made with the Mondeuse grape.

Montmirail (Fr). An Aperient mineral water.

Montmort (Fr). A canton in the district of Épernay, Champagne. Has the Cru villages of Baye, Beaunay, Broyes, Çoizard-Joches, Congy, Courjeonnet, Étoges, Fèrebrianges, Oyes, Talus-Saint-Prix and Villevenard.

Montmurat (Fr). A red wine of the Cantal Département.

Montner (Fr). A red wine produced in the Côtes du Roussillon-Villages.

Montonec (Sp). An alternative name for the Parellada grape.

Montonel (Sp). An alternative name for

M

the Parellada grape.

Mont-Palais (Fr). A vineyard in the A.C. commune of Rully, Côte Chalonnaise, Burgundy.

Montpellier Estate (S.Afr). Based in Tulbagh. Address = Box 24, Tulbagh 6820. Produce varietal wines including Tuinwingerd.

Montpeyroux (Fr). A.C. red wine of the Montpeyroux in the Hérault-Département, southern France.

Mont-Près-Chambord-Cour-Cheverny (Fr). A V.D.Q.S. white wine from the Loire. Is often shortened to Cheverny.

Montrachet (Fr). A Grand Cru vineyard between the communes of Bâtard-Montrachet, Chassagne-Montrachet, Chevalier-Montrachet, Criot-Bâtard-Montrachet and Puligny-Montrachet in the Côtes de Beaune. 7.7 ha. White wine made with the Chardonnay grape.

Montrachets (Les) (Fr). A Grand Cru vineyard in the A.C. commune of Montrachet, Côte de Beaune, Burgundy.

Montravel (Fr). An A.C. district of the Bergerac region. Produces dry, semi-dry and sweet white wines. See also Haut Montravel and Côtes de Montravel. Minimum alc. by vol. 11%.

Montreal Club Bouncer (Cktl). ⅕ gill dry Gin, 2 dashes Pernod. Stir over ice in an old-fashioned glass.

Montreal Gin Sour (Cktl). ½ measure Gin, ½ measure lemon juice, ½ egg white. Shake over ice, strain into a sour glass. Top with a slice of lemon.

Montredon (Fr). Part of the Châteauneuf-du-Pape area of the southern Rhône.

Montrevenots (Les) (Fr). A Premier Cru vineyard [part] in the A.C. commune of Beaune, Côte de Beaune, Burgundy. 8.28 ha.

Montrose Vineyard (Austr). A winery based in Mudgee, New South Wales.

Montrose Whisky Company (Scot). Founded in 1973. Buys in and then blends to its own labels. Labels include – Double Q, Old Montrose and Pipe Major.

Mont Rouge (Isr). A semi-dry red table wine.

Monts Damnes (Les) (Fr). A vineyard in the commune of Chavignol, A.C. Sancerre, Central Vineyards, Loire.

Monts de la Grage (Fr). A Vins de Pays area in the Saint-Chinian region in the Hérault Département, southern France. Produces red, rosé and dry white wines.

Monts de Milieu (Fr). A Premier Cru vineyard of Chablis, Burgundy.

Monts du Tessalah (Alg). A wine-producing area in the Oran Département. Produces red, rosé and white wines.

Montserrat Cocktail (Cktl). ⅓ gill dry Gin, 2 teaspoons lime juice, 1 teaspoon Grenadine, 2 dashes Absinthe. Shake over ice, strain into a cocktail glass. Serve with a cherry.

Monts-Luisants (Fr). A Premier Cru vineyard in the A.C. commune of Morey-Saint-Denis, Côte de Nuits, Burgundy.

Montsoreau (Fr). A white wine of Saumur in the Anjou-Saumur district of the Loire.

Mont St. John Cellars (USA). A winery based in Carneros, Napa Valley, California. Grape varieties – Cabernet sauvignon, Chardonnay, Gewürztraminer, Johannisberg riesling, Pinot noir and Zinfandel. Produce varietal wines.

Mont-sur-Rolle (Switz). A wine-producing village in La Côte. Sometimes abbreviated to Rolle.

Montulia S.A. (Sp). A producer of Montilla based in Montilla-Moriles.

Monvedro (Port). A black grape variety grown in the Alentejo region.

Monymusk Distillery (W.Ind). A Rum distillery based on the island of Jamaica.

Monzernheim (Ger). Village. (Anb) = Rheinhessen, (Ber) = Wonnegau. (Gro) = Pilgerpfad. (Vins) = Goldberg, Steinböhl.

Monzingen (Ger). Village. (Anb) = Nahe. (Ber) = Schloss Böckelheim. (Gro) = Paradiesgarten. (Vins) = Frühlingsplätzchen, Halenberg, Rosenberg.

Moodemere Red (Austr). A red wine from the Gracerray vineyards. Made from the Cabernet sauvignon, Shiraz or Durif grapes.

Mooiplaas Estate (S.Afr). A vineyard based in Stellenbosch that sells its wines in bulk to the SFW.

Mooiuitsig Wynkelders (S.Afr). A large winery based in Bonnievale. Address = Box 15, Bonnievale 6730. Produces a large number of fortified and varietal wines.

Moomba Cocktail (Cktl). ¾ fl.oz. Bacardi Rum, ¾ fl.oz. Grand Marnier, ½ fl.oz. orange juice, ¼ fl.oz. lemon juice, dash Grenadine. Shake over ice, strain into a cocktail glass, add a twist of orange peel on top.

Moondah Brook (Austr). Part of the Houghton vineyards in Western Australia. 84 ha. Grape varieties – Cabernet sauvignon, Chardonnay, Chenin blanc and Verdelho.

Moonlight Cocktail (Cktl). 2 fl.ozs. Calvados, juice of a lemon, 2 dashes Gomme syrup. Shake over ice, strain into an ice-filled old-fashioned glass.

Moonlighter Cocktail (Cktl). ⅖ measure

Mandarine Napoléon, 1/5 measure white Rum, 2/5 measure pineapple juice, dash egg white. Shake over ice, strain into an ice-filled highball glass. Dress with a pineapple cube and cherry.

Moonquake Cocktail (Cktl). 3/5 measure Jamaican rum, 2/5 measure Tia Maria, juice 1/4 lemon. Shake over ice, strain into a cocktail glass.

Moonraker Brown Ale (Eng). A bottled Brown ale 1032 O.G. brewed by the Mew Gibbs Brewery in Salisbury, Wiltshire.

Moonraker Strong Ale (Eng). A rich, dark, sweet Ale 1047 O.G. brewed by the Lees Brewery in Middleton, Greater Manchester.

Moon River (Cktl). 1/4 measure Gin, 1/4 measure Cointreau, 1/4 measure Apricot brandy, 1/8 measure Galliano, 1/8 measure lime juice. Stir over ice, strain into a cocktail glass, add a cherry.

Moon Rocket (Cktl). 1 measure Kirsch, 1/2 measure Apricot brandy, 1/2 measure orange juice. Shake over ice, strain into a cocktail glass. Add 1/3 barspoon Grenadine.

Moonshine (USA). The nickname of illegally distilled whiskey. Came about because of the 1791 Excise Tax of USA. See Whiskey Rebellion. See also Bushie and Poteen.

Moonshiner (USA). A person who makes and deals with Moonshine.

Moore's Diamond (USA). A white American grape variety grown in NewYork State. Produce neutral dry wines.

Moorhouses (Eng). A brewery opened in 1979 in Burnley, Lancashire. Taken over by Apollo Leisure of Oxford. Noted for its cask conditioned Pendle Witches Brew 1050 O.G.

Moorilla Estate (Austr). vineyard. Address = 655 Main Road, Berriedale, Tasmania 7011. 9 ha. Grape varieties – Cabernet sauvignon, Gewürztraminer, Rhine riesling and Pinot noir. Produce varietal wines.

Moorlynch (Eng). The label used by the Spring Farm vineyard in Somerset for their wines.

Moortgat Brasserie (Bel). A brewery based at Breendonk. Brews Duvel.

Moosberg (Ger). vineyard. (Anb) = Rheinhessen. (Ber) = Nierstein. (Gro) = Gutes Domtal. (Vil) = Hahnheim.

Moosberg (Ger). vineyard. (Anb) = Rheinhessen. (Ber) = Nierstein. (Gro) = Gutes Domtal. (Vil) = Sörgenloch.

Moosehead Brewery (Can). A brewery in St. John, New Brunswick. Produces a bottled Export beer of the same name to U.K.

Moot (Ger). Must.

Moquega (S.Am). A vineyard area based in southern Peru.

Mór (Hun). A wine region 80 km. west of Budapest. One of the few European wine regions that did not succumb to Phylloxera. Ezerjó is the main grape variety and Móri Ezerjó the best wine.

Moracia (Sp). A red grape variety grown in the La Mancha region.

Morand (Switz). An Eau-de-vie distillery based in Valais.

Morandell (Aus). Well-known wine merchants based in the Burgenland, Gumpoldskirchen and Vienna.

Morangis (Fr). A Cru Champagne village in the Canton d'Avize. District = Épernay.

Morastell (Sp). A white grape variety used in the south-eastern area of Spain for sparkling wines.

Moraster (Sp). A black grape variety grown in Aragón, Penedés, Rioja and Catalonia. See Monastrel.

Moravia-Pils (Ger). An outstanding Pilsener Lager 4.9% alc. by vol. from the Moravia Brauerei in Lüheburg. A subsidiary of Holsten.

Mörbisch (Aus). A wine-village in the Burgenland. Produces fine sweet white wines plus some dry white and red wines.

Mór-Csàszàr (Hun). A wine-producing district in northern Transdanubia.

Mordant (Eng). A term given to wines with excess tannin/acid so that they taste sharp and astringent.

Morddré (S.Afr). A medium-sweet, dessert wine made from the Hanepoot grape.

Moreau (Fr). A Burgundy négociant-éleveur based at Chablis. The largest shipper of Chablis wines. Address = Route d'Auxerre, 89800 Chablis. Owns Les Clos and Vaillons.

Morein (Fr). A Premier Cru vineyard of A.C. Chablis. Is often reclassified as the Premier Cru vineyard Les Fourneaux.

Morellino (It). A red grape variety. (A clone of the Sangiovese).

Morellino de Scansano (It). A D.O.C. red wine from Tuscany. Produced from the Morellino (Sangiovese) grape plus up to 15% of other varieties.

Moreno S.A. (Sp). A noted producer of Montilla. Based in Montilla-Moriles.

Moreto (Port). A black grape variety grown in the Bairrada region.

Moretti Breweries (It). A brewing company with two breweries.

Morey (Albert) (Fr). A small négociant based in Beaune, Côte de Beaune, Burgundy.

Morey et Fils (Albert) (Fr). A négociant based in Chassagne-Montrachet and Meursault, Côte de Beaune, Burgundy.

M

Morey (André) (Fr). A noted negociant based in Beaune, Côte de Beaune, Burgundy.

Morey-Rocault (Bernard) (Fr). A noted négociant-éleveur based at Meursault, Côte de Beaune, Burgundy.

Morey-Saint-Denis (Fr). A commune within the Côte de Nuits between the communes of Gevrey-Chambertin and Chambolle-Musigny. Has 5 Grand Crus – Bonne Mares, Clos de la Roche, Clos de Tart and Clos Saint-Denis. 31.9 ha. and 26 Premier Crus – Aux Charmes, Aux Cheseaux, Calouères, Chabiots, Clos Baulet, Clos Bussière, Clos des Lambrays, Clos Sorbet, Côte Rôtie, La Riotte, Le Clos des Ormes, Les Blanchards, Les Bouchots, Les Chaffots, Les Charnières, Les Chénevery, Les Faconnières, Les Fremières, Les Genevrières, Les Gruenchers, Les Millandes, Les Ruchots, Les Sorbet, Maison Brûlée, Meix-Rentiers, Monts-Luisants. 60.5 ha.

Morgan (Port). Vintage Port shippers. Vintages – 1870, 1872, 1873,1875, 1878, 1881, 1884, 1887, 1890, 1894, 1896, 1900, 1904, 1908, 1912, 1920, 1922, 1924, 1927, 1942, 1948, 1950, 1955, 1960, 1963, 1966, 1970, 1977, 1982. (A subsidiary of Croft).

Morgan Hill (USA). A wine town in Santa Clara County, California.

Morgarinha-Bagaceira do Minho (Port). An Aguardente produced by Joaquin Miranda Campelo & Filhos. 43% alc. by vol.

Morgen (Ger). A land measure. 0.25 ha. (0.6 acre).

Morgenbachtahler (Ger). Vineyard. (Anb) = Mittelrhein. (Ber) = Bacharach. (Gro) = Schloss Reichenstein. (Vil) = Trechtingshausen.

Morgeot (Fr). A Premier Cru vineyard [part] in the A.C. commune of Chassagne-Montrachet, Côte de Beaune, Burgundy. 3.94 ha.

Morgon (Fr). An A.C. Cru Beaujolais-Villages, Burgundy. 970 ha. under vines.

Moriah (Isr). A sweet dessert wine.

Moriau Brasserie (Bel). A brewery based near Lot in central Belgium.

Moriers (Les) (Fr). A vineyard in the A.C. Fleurie Cru Beaujolais-Village, Burgundy.

Móri Ezerjó (Hun). A dry golden wine from the Mór region. Made with the Ezerjó grape.

Moriles Alto (Sp). Part of the Montilla-Moriles where the finest grapes are grown for Montilla wines.

Morillon (Aus). A white grape variety related to the Weissburgunder.

Morillon Blanc (Fr). A local name for the Chardonnay grape.

Morillon Taconé (Fr). An alternative name for the Pinot meunier grape in eastern France.

Morin (Fr). A producer of fine Calvados based in Ivry-la-Bataille, (Eure Département).

Morio (Herren) (Ger). A German viticulturist who has produced many crossbred grape varieties. e.g. Morio muscat.

Morio-Muscat (Ger). A white grape variety. A cross between the Sylvaner and the Pinot blanc. Has a strong fruity flavour.

Morisca (Sp). A red grape variety grown in western Spain. Produces good red wines.

Moritz Thienelt (Ger). A noted liqueur producer based in Düsseldorf.

Morjuce (Eng). The brand-name for frozen fruit juices (un-sweetened) from the McCain Co.

Mork and Mindy (Cktl). 1 part Royal Irish Chocolate Mint Liqueur, 2 parts Tia Maria, 3 parts Cognac. Shake over ice, strain into a large cocktail glass, float cream on top.

Mørk (Den). Dark brewed beer (bottom-fermented).

Mörkt (Swe). Dark brewed beer (bottom-fermented).

Morland Brewery (Eng). A brewery based in Abingdon, Oxfordshire. Noted for its cask conditioned Artist's Ale 1032 O.G. and bottled Viking Pale 1042 O.G. Old Speckled Hen 1050 O.G. and Monarch 1065 O.G.

Morland Vineyard (USA). A winery based near King George, Virginia. Produces French hybrid and vinifera wines.

Mornag (Afr). A co-operative based in Tunisia. Owned by the UCCVT.

Morning Advertiser (Eng). A daily newspaper (Monday-Saturday) printed for the licensed trade. The L.V.A. journal.

Morning Advertiser Gin (Eng). See City Gin.

Morning Cocktail (Cktl). ¼ gill Brandy, ¼ gill French brandy, 2 dashes Absinthe, Orange bitters, Curaçao and Maraschino. Stir well over ice, strain into a cocktail glass, add a cherry and a twist of lemon peel juice on top.

Morning Dew (Cktl). ½ measure Irish whiskey, ¾ measure grapefruit juice, ¼ measure Crème de Banane, dash blue Curaçao, 1 egg white. Shake over ice, strain into a cocktail glass. Dress with a cherry and orange slice.

Morning Egg Nogg (Cktl). ⅔ gill Brandy, ⅙

gill yellow Chartreuse, 1 egg, 1 teaspoon sugar, ⅔ gill milk. Shake over ice, strain into a highball glass, dash nutmeg on top.

Morning Glory Cocktail (Cktl).(1). ½ measure Brandy, ¼ measure orange Curaçao, ¼ measure lemon juice, 2 dashes Pastis, 2 dashes Angostura. Shake over ice, strain into a cocktail glass, top with a twist of lemon peel.

Morning Glory Cocktail (Cktl).(2). 1½ fl.ozs. Scotch whisky, 1 egg white, 1 teaspoon sugar. Shake over ice, strain into an ice-filled highball glass. Top with soda water.

Morning Glory Daisy (Cktl). ½ gill of Spirit, juice of ½ lemon, 1 egg white, 1 teaspoon sugar syrup, 3 dashes Absinthe. Shake well over ice, strain into a highball glass filled with ice.

Morning Glory Fizz (Cktl). ¾ gill Spirit, juice ½ lemon (or lime), 3 dashes Pernod, white of egg, sugar syrup to taste. Shake well over ice, strain into a highball glass, top with soda water.

Morning Mashie (The) (Cktl). ⅓ measure dry Gin, ½ measure Anisette, ⅓ measure Lemon squash, 1 teaspoon Pernot, dash Angostura, ½ egg white, juice ½ lemon. Shake well over ice, strain into a 5 fl.oz. goblet.

Moroccan Tea (Afr). 1½ pints freshly made tea, few dashes peppermint essence and sugar to taste. Cool quickly, serve on crushed ice with mint leaves.

Morocco (N.Afr). Produces most styles of wines. The red wines which are robust and high in alcohol are the most popular and by law must have a minimum alcohol content of 11% by vol. Main regions are Casablanca, Fez, Marrakech, Meknès, Oujda and Rabat-Rharb.

Morón (Manuel Pacheco) (Sp). A producer and exporter of Málaga.

Morozkaraso (Tur). A red grape variety grown in eastern Turkey.

Morphett Vale (Austr). A region of South Australia which produces good red wines.

Morra (La) (It). A commune in the Barolo district of Piemonte, north-western Italy.

Morrell Brewery (Eng). Based in Oxford. Noted for its cask conditioned Varsity 1041 O.G. and College Ale 1073 O.G. plus keg Friars Ale 1036 O.G. bottled Light Oxford 1032 O.G. Brown Oxford 1032 O.G. and Castle Ale 1041 O.G.

Morre's Diamond (USA). A hybrid white grape variety grown in the New York State region.

Morris of Rutherglen (Austr). See Mia Mia vineyard.

Morrison (Stanley P.) (Scot). A company that owns the Auchentoshan (a Lowland malt), Bowmore (an Islay malt) and Glen Garioch (a Highland malt) distilleries. Brand-name blended whiskies include Rob Roy.

Morris Winery (USA). A winery based at Emeryville, Alameda, California. Grape varieties – Cabernet sauvignon, Chardonnay, Pinot noir, Sauvignon blanc and Zinfandel. Produces varietal and dessert wines.

Morro Cocktail (Cktl). ⅔ measure dry Gin, ⅓ measure light Rum, juice ¼ lemon, ⅛ measure pineapple juice, 2 dashes Gomme syrup. Shake over ice, strain into a sugar-rimmed, ice-filled goblet.

Morscheid (Ger). Village. (Anb) = Mosel-Saar-Ruwer. (Ber) = Saar-Ruwer. (Gro) = Römerlay. (Vins) = Dominikanerberg, Heiligenhäuschen.

Morschheim (Ger). Village. (Anb) = Rheinpfalz. (Ber) = Mittelhaardt-Deutsche Weinstrasse. (Gro) = Schnepfenflug vom Kellertal. (Vin) = Im Heubusch.

Mörstadt (Ger). Village. (Anb) = Rheinhessen. (Ber) = Wonnegau. (Gro) = Burg Rodenstein. (Vins) = Katzebuckel, Nonnengarten.

Morstein (Ger). vineyard. (Anb) = Rheinhessen. (Ber) = Wonnegau. (Gro) = Bergkloster. (Vil) = Westhofen.

Mortàgua (Port). A red grape variety grown in the Bucelas and Dão regions.

Morterille Noire (Fr). The local name in southern France for the Cinsault grape.

Mortlach (Scot). A single Malt whisky distillery sited just outside Dufftown in the Spey. Owned by George Cowie and Son Ltd. A Highland malt. Produce a 12 year old Malt and a 1936 vintage.

Morton (George) Ltd (Scot). A leading Rum producer based in Montrose, Angus. Produces OVD (Old Vatted Demerara) Rum.

Morton Estate (N.Z.). Address = RD2, Kati Kati, Bay of Plenty. 11 ha. Grape varieties – Cabernet sauvignon, Chardonnay, Chénin blanc, Gewürztraminer, Merlot, Müller-Thurgau, Pinot noir. Produces varietal wines.

Mort Subite (Bel). The nickname given to a style of Lambic beer. Lit – 'Sudden death', it is no stronger than other Lambic beers.

Mort Subite Brasserie (Bel). A brewery based in Kobbegem, northern Belgium. Is noted for its Lambic beers.

Mortuaries (Port). A name given to the

old terraces by the vineyard workers in the Douro region because it is easier to plant new terraces than save the old.

Mory (Juan) & Cia (Sp). A producer and exporter of Málaga.

Mörzheim (Ger). Village. (Anb) = Rheinpfalz. (Ber) = Südliche Weinstrasse. (Gro) = Herrlich. (Vin) = Pfaffenberg.

Mosaic (Cyp). A brand of Cream sherry produced by Keo in Limassol.

Mösbach (Ger). Village. (Anb) = Baden. (Ber) = Ortenau. (Gro) = Schloss Rodeck. (Vin) = Kreuzberg.

Mosca (It). Lit – 'Flies'. The name given to the coffee beans that are floated on top of Sambuca.

Mosca (Port). An Aguardente produced by J.M. da Fonseca.

Moscadel (Fr). The old French spelling of the Muscatel grape. See also Muscadel and Muscadelle.

Moscadello (It). A sweet white wine from the Muscat grape.

Moscata Bianca (It). An alternative name for the Muscat blanc à petits grains grape.

Moscatel (Mad). A white grape variety grown on Porto Santo. Produces good sugar. Is used in Madeira production.

Moscatel (Sp). The sweet fortified wine which is used to sweeten sherries. 2 kinds – Jerez and Chipiona, the former being the sweeter.

Moscatel Branco (Port). A white grape variety used in the making of White Port.

Moscatel de Grano Menudo (Sp). A white grape variety grown in the Navarra region.

Moscatel de Málaga (Sp). A light coloured and light bodied wine. Very sweet, is produced in Málaga from grapes dried in the sun. Made from the Muscat grape. Served as a dessert wine.

Moscatel de Setúbal (Port). See Setúbal.

Moscatella (It). A white grape variety grown in Sicily.

Moscatello (It). An alternative name for the Muscat blanc à petits grains.

Moscatello Giallo (It). Name given to the Moscato bianco grape in the commune of Siracusa, Sicily.

Moscatellone (It). Name given to the white grape variety Zibibbo on the island of Pantelleria of the coast of Sicily.

Moscatel Morisco (Sp). A white grape variety once used in the production of Málaga.

Moscatelo (It). The wine of Montefiascone in Latium. Usually known as Est! Est!! Est!!!

Moscatel Romano (It). An alternative name for the Muscat of Alexandria grape.

Moscatel Roxo (Port). A black grape variety grown in Setúbal, also the name of sweet dessert wine.

Moscati di Trani (It). A sweet aromatic white wine made from the Muscat blanc grape in the province of Apulia.

Moscato (It). A white grape variety with many varietals including the Muscat blanc à petits grains.

Moscato Amabile (USA). A white grape variety similar to the Muscat blanc. Produces a light, often pétillant wine.

Moscato Bianco (It). A white grape variety grown in northern Italy.

Moscato d'Asti (It). See Moscato d'Asti Spumante.

Moscato d'Asti Spumante (It). D.O.C. white sparkling wine from Piemonte. Made from the Moscato bianco grape. Natural fermentation with no artificial carbonation allowed. Is a sweet wine, usually known as Asti Spumante. Minimum alc. by vol. 11.5%.

Moscato del Salento (It). A D.O.C. sweet red or white wine produced from the Muscat grape in the Apulia region.

Moscato del Tempio (It). A white dessert wine of grapey character made in Sardinia.

Moscato di Cagliari (It). D.O.C. white wine from the Cagliari region. Made from the Moscato grape from within the Cagliari province. 2 types – Dolce naturale and Liquoroso dolce naturale. If aged 1 year after fortification can be classed Riserva.

Moscato di Calabria (It). A D.O.C. white wine from the Calabria region. Is produced from dried Moscato grapes. Also known as Moscato di Cosenza.

Moscato di Canelli (It). A white grape variety used in the Veneto. The local name for the Moscato bianco.

Moscato di Casteggio (It). A sweet Muscat wine produced in Frecciarossa, Lombardy.

Moscato di Casteggio Spumante (It). A sweet sparkling wine produced from the Muscat grape in Frecciarossa, Lombardy.

Moscato di Cosenza (It). See Moscato di Calabria.

Moscato di Noto (It). D.O.C. white wine from Sicily. Made from the Moscato bianco and a variety of grapes grown in the communes of Noto, Avola, Pachino and Rosolini. D.O.C. also applies to the sparkling wines and to the fortified wines obtained according to regulations.

M

Moscato di Noto Liquoroso (It). D.O.C. fortified wine from Sicily. Made from Moscato bianco and other selected grapes giving a minimum natural total alc. content of 13% by vol. Fermentation continues to October when minimum alc. content is 6.5% by vol. Fortification then follows.

Moscato di Noto Naturale (It). Also known as Moscato di Noto.

Moscato di Noto Spumante (It). D.O.C. sparkling wine of Sicily. Made from the Moscato bianco grapes grown in the communes of Noto, Avola, Pachino and Rosolini.

Moscato di Pantelleria (It). A rich white wine produced on the small island of Pantelleria between Sicily and Africa. See Moscato di Pantelleria Naturale.

Moscato di Pantelleria Naturale (It). D.O.C. white wine from Pantelleria. Made from the Zibibbo (Moscatellone) grape. Can be classified as Vino naturalmente dolce when total alc. content is not less than 17.5% by vol. of which 13% of alc. by vol. obtained by using partially dried grapes. D.O.C. also applies to naturally sparkling and fortified wines. Spumante or Liquoroso follow the D.O.C. on the label.

Moscato di Salento (It). A white, rich, sweet white wine from the Moscato bianco grape made in the Apulia province. Also known as Salento bianco liquoroso.

Moscato di Sardegna (It). D.O.C. white wine from Sardinia. Produced from the Moscato grape.

Moscato di Siracusa (It). D.O.C. white wine from Sicily. Made from the Moscato bianco grapes grown in the commune of Siracusa in south-east Sicily. Of limited production.

Moscato di Sorso-Sennori (It). D.O.C. sweet white wine from Sardinia. Made from Moscato bianco grapes with up to 5% of other varieties in the communes of Sorso and Sennori. A Liquoroso dolce style can be produced with the addition of alcohol from wine.

Moscato di Trani (It). The local name in the Puglia region for the Moscato bianco grape. Used to make wine of same name.

Moscato di Trani (It). D.O.C. white wine from the Puglia. Made from the Moscato bianco and other Muscat varieties. 2 styles – Dolce naturale and Liquoroso.

Moscato d'Oro (USA). A white grape variety similar to the Muscat blanc.

Moscato-Fior d'Arancio (It). A sweet white dessert wine from Calabria in Sicily. Has a scent of orange blossom. (Fior d'Arancio means flowers of orange).

Moscato Giallo (It). The name for the Moscato bianco grape in the Trentino-Alto Adige region. (Goldenmuskateller in German).

Moscato Gordo Blanco (Sp). A white grape variety.

Moscato Naturale d'Asti (It). D.O.C. still white wine from the Piemonte region. Made from the Moscato bianco grape.

Moscato Nero (It). A red grape variety.

Moscato Passito di Pantelleria (It). D.O.C. sweet white wine from the isle of Pantelleria. Made from the Zibibbo grape. D.O.C. also applies to fortified wine -- Liquoroso on the label. Extra on label when aged for a minimum of 1 year and minimum alc. content 23.9% alc. by vol. of which at least 15.5% alc. by vol. natural fermentation.

Moscato Reale (It). A local name in the Puglia region for the Moscato bianco grape. Also known as the Moscato di Trani in the region.

Moscato Rosa (It). A red grape variety grown in the Trentino-Alto Adige region. (Rosenmuskateller in German). Used in the making of rosé wines.

Moscato Semplice di Canelli (It). A white dessert wine produced from the Moscato di Canelli grape in the Asti district of the Piemonte region.

Moscato Zibibbo (It). A name of the Moscato bianco (Moscatellone) in the isle of Pantelleria.

Moscato Zucco (It). A rich, dark, mellow white wine produced from the Zibibbo grape in Palermo on the isle of Sicily.

Moschofilero (Gre). A white grape variety which produces dry white wines in the Peloponnese. See Mantinia.

Moscophilero (Gre). An alternative spelling of Moschofilero.

Moscow (USSR). A Beer 13° Balling made with rice as opposed to corn. Brewed by the Yantar Brewery.

Moscow Mule (Cktl). Ginger beer, lime juice and Vodka, mixed over ice, strained into a cocktail glass with a twist of lime.

Mosel (Ger). An Untergebiete of the Rhein und Mosel district.

Moselblümchen (Ger). The Mosel-Saar-Ruwer equivalent of Liebfraumilch. Lit – 'Little flower of the Mosel'.

Mosele S.A. (Bra). A leading wine-producer based in southern Brazil.

Moselkern (Ger). Village. (Anb) = Mosel-Saar-Ruwer. (Ber) = Zell/Mosel. (Gro) = Goldbäumchen. (Vins) = Kirchberg, Rosenberg, Übereltzer.

Moselle (Fr). The French spelling of the river Mosel (German). Also of Luxembourg. Often used in the U.K. and USA etc. to denote the wines of the Mosel-Saar-Ruwer.

Moselle Cobbler (Cktl). 1 gill Mosel, 1 dash lemon juice, 2 dashes old Brandy, 3–4 dashes plain syrup. Stir over ice, strain into a highball half filled with crushed ice. Serve with a dash of lemon peel juice, 2 slices of lemon and straws.

Moselle Cup (Cktl). 1 bottle Mosel wine, ½ gill Brandy, ⅓ gill yellow Chartreuse, ¼ gill Maraschino, ¼ gill Kümmel, 1 pint soda water. Stir in a bowl with ice. Strain into highball glasses with orange and lemon slices, fruit and mint.

Mosel [River] (Ger). A tributary of the river Rhine. Runs south to north and has the rivers Saar and Ruwer as its tributaries. See Mosel-Saar-Ruwer. Rises in France and flows through Luxembourg before it enters Germany.

Mosel-Saar-Ruwer (Ger). Anbaugebiet. (Bers) = Bernkastel, Obermosel, Saar-Ruwer, Zell/Mosel. Grape varieties – Elbling 9%, Kerner 3%, Müller-Thurgau 21%, Optima 6% and Riesling 61%.

Mosel-Saar-Ruwer Information Service (Ger). Address = Weinwerbung, Mosel-Saar-Ruwer, Neustrasse 86, 5500 Trier, Western Germany.

Mosel-Saar-Ruwer Wine Festivals (Ger). Mosel-Wein-Woche, Saarweinfest and the Weinfest der Mittelmosel.

Moselsürsch (Ger). Village. (Anb) = Mosel-Saar-Ruwer. (Ber) = Zell/Mosel. (Gro) = Weinhex. (Vin) = Fahrberg.

Moselwein (Ger). A wine from the Mosel-Saar-Ruwer.

Mosel-Wein-Woche (Ger). Mosel-Saar-Ruwer wine festival held at Cochem in June.

Mosen Cleto (Sp). A red wine produced by Vincente Suso y Perez in Cariñena, north-eastern Spain. Is aged 4 years in oak. Made from the Garnacha grape.

Moskovskaya (USSR). Russian vodka. Straight, low strength. Made from grain and flavouring herbs. 37.5% alc. by vol.

Moslem Prohibition (Arab). Followers of Islam were forbidden to touch any form of alcoholic beverage.

Mosler (Yug). An alternative name for the Šipon (Furmint) grape.

Möslinger Fining (Ger). An alternative name for Blue finings.

Moslins (Fr). A Cru Champagne village in the Canton d'Avize. District = Épernay.

Mosnac (Fr). A commune in the Charente Département whose grapes are used for Petite Champagne (Cognac).

Moss Brewery (Nor). A small brewery based in Moss, south-eastern Norway.

Mosselman's Brasserie (Bel). A noted brewery based in Dworp, central Belgium.

Moss Wood vineyard (Austr). Address = Merricup Road, Willyabrop, Western Australia. 10 ha. Grape varieties – Cabernet sauvignon, Chardonnay, Pinot noir and Sémillon.

Most (It) (Port) (Sp). Unfermented grape juice.

Mostaganem-Kenenda (Alg). A wine-producing area of the Oran Département. Produces red, rosé and white wines.

Mostarska Žilavka (Yug). A dry white wine from Croatia around the town of Mostar. Made with the Žilavka grape.

Mostgewicht (Ger). The measuring of the sugar content in the must/wine. Measured in degrees Oechsle.

Mosto (It) (Port) (Sp). Grape juice, must.

Mosto Cotto (It). Boiled grape must used as a sweetening agent in the production of Marsala-type wines.

Mosttraube (Aus). The alternative name for the Chasselas grape.

Mostwager (Aus). Must weigher.

Moterist Beer (Swe). A low-alcohol beer brewed for the motorist in Sweden. 2.8% by weight.

Mother Cognac (Fr). The name for old Cognac at Rémy Martin used in fine blends.

Mother-in-Law (Eng). The Cockney slang for a Bitter ale and Stout mix.

Mother is Watching (Cktl).(Non-alc). Juice ½ grapefruit and 1 orange, 2 dashes Angostura. Shake over ice, strain into a highball glass. Top with Perrier water and a slice of orange.

Mother of Vinegar (USA). The nickname for Mycrodermae aceti (Acetobacter). (Fr) = Mère de vinaigre.

Mother of Wine (Sp). A term in the Sherry region when the Flor sinks to the bottom of the cask.

Mother's Cellar Winery (N.Z.). A small winery based in Henderson, North Island. Produces varietal wines and All Black Port (a Port-style wine).

Mother's Ruin (Eng) (slang). For Gin.

Mother Wine (Eng). Boiling a wine to make it concentrated. Used to strengthen young wines.

Moto (Jap). The next stage of the Koji (steamed rice) when it is added to a thin paste of boiled starch in a vat and it is then allowed to ferment.

Motte (La) (S.Afr). A vineyard in Franschhoek opened in 1983 producing varietal wines.

M

Motte Cordonnier Brasserie (Fr). A noted brewery (part of the Artois Brasserie of Belgium).

Mou (Fr). A flabby wine, lacking in character.

Moueix et Fils (Fr). A famous négociant-éleveur of Bordeaux based in Pomerol and Saint-Émilion. Address = Taillefer 33500, Libourne.

Mouillage (Fr). The addition of water to alcoholic drinks to weaken their strength.

Mouillé (Fr). Watered.

Mouillère (La) (Fr). A vineyard in the A.C. commune of Montagny, Côte Chalonnaise, Burgundy.

Mouldy (Eng). A term used to describe a wine that has an off-flavour. May have originated from stale, dirty casks, rotten grapes or from the wine coming into contact with verdigris from the capsule when being decanted.

Moulesne (Fr). A vineyard in the A.C. commune of Rully, Côte Chalonnaise, Burgundy.

Mouleydier (Fr). A commune within the A.C. district of Pécharmant in northern Bergerac. (red wines).

Moulin à Café (Fr). Coffee mill.

Moulin-à-Vent (Fr). An A.C. Cru Villages Beaujolais, Burgundy. 630 ha. under vines.

Moulin de la Gravelle (Fr). An A.C. Muscadet de Sèvre et Maine.

Moulin de la Pitance (Fr). A vineyard in the commune of St-Girons, A.C. Côtes de Blaye, north-eastern Bordeaux.

Moulin des Carruades (Fr). A wine made in certain good years from Château Lafite vineyards and of the second pressings. Entitled to the A.C. Pauillac if reaches the requirements of the appellation. Always Château bottled.

Moulin Desoubeyran (Fr). A vineyard in the commune of Le Pian. A.C. Haut-Médoc, Bordeaux. Cru Bourgeois.

Moulin-du-Cadet (Fr). Grands Crus Classés of Côtes Saint-Émilion.

Moulinneuf Distillerie (Fr). A Cognac distillery based near Jarnac. Owned by Martell.

Moulin Rouge (Cktl). ½ fl.oz. Brandy, 2 fl.ozs. pineapple juice. Stir over ice, strain into a highball glass half-filled with ice. Top up with dry sparkling wine. Decorate with a cherry, slice of pineapple and orange.

Moulin Rouge Cocktail (Cktl). ⅗ measure Sloe gin, ⅖ measure Italian vermouth, dash Angostura. Stir over ice, strain into a cocktail glass.

Moulin Saint-Georges (Fr). vineyard. Address = 33330, Saint-Émilion. A.C. Saint-Émilion. Commune = Saint-Émilion.

Moulis (Fr). An A.C. commune within the southern part of the Haut-Médoc. Some wines are sold under the adjoining A.C. Listrac.

Moullay-Hofberg (Ger). vineyard. (Anb) = Mosel-Saar-Ruwer. (Ber) = Bernkastel. (Gro) = Vom Heissen Stein. (Vil) = Reil.

Mounié (Denis) (Fr). Cognac producer. Address = BP 14, 16200 Jarnac. Produces Edouard VII Grand réserve Fine Champagne. Owns no vineyards. Part of Hine.

Mounier (Fr). A lesser black grape variety grown in the Champagne region.

Mountadam Winery (Austr). A noted winery based in the Barossa Valley, South Australia. Produces varietal wines.

Mountain (Sp). A classification of Málaga. A medium sweet wine.

Mountain Cocktail (Cktl). 1 measure Bourbon whiskey, 2 dashes Italian vermouth, 2 dashes French vermouth, 2 dashes lemon juice, 1 egg white. Shake over ice, strain into a cocktail glass.

Mountain Gold (USA). The label used by the Lamont Winery for their generic wines.

Mountain Oyster (Cktl). Another name for a Prairie oyster.

Mountain Red (USA). The generic name used for inexpensive dry red wines.

Mountainside (USA). The label used by Château Chevalier for their wines produced from purchased grapes.

Mountain Skier (Cktl). 2 parts Johnnie Walker Red Label, 2 parts Drambuie, 5 parts lemon squash, 1 part lemonade, dash Angostura, dash egg white. Shake all over ice except lemonade. Strain into a highball glass. Top with the lemonade and decorate with beaten egg white and a slice of lemon.

Mountain White (USA). The generic name used for inexpensive dry white wines.

Mount Avoca Winery (Austr). Address = Moates Lane, Avoca, Victoria 3467. 20 ha. Grape varieties – Cabernet sauvignon, Chardonnay, Sauvignon blanc and Shiraz.

Mount Barker (Austr). A wine province in Western Australia.

Mount Barker (Austr). A brand-name for the Jane Brook Estate in Western Australia.

Mount Bethel (USA). A winery based in Altus.

Mount Eden vineyards (USA). A small winery based near Saratoga, Santa

Clara, California. 9.5 ha. Grape varieties – Cabernet sauvignon, Chardonnay and Pinot noir. Produce varietal wines.

Mount Elise vineyards (USA). A small vineyard based in Bingen, South Washington. 12 ha. Produces vinifera wines. Originally known as the Bingen Wine Cellars.

Mount Fuji (Cktl). Blend a scoop of crushed ice, ⅙ gill light Rum, ⅙ gill Applejack brandy, ⅛ gill Southern Comfort, 1 oz. castor sugar and the juice of ½ lime. Pour into an old-fashioned glass, top with ½ lime shell filled with 151° US Proof Rum. Ignite and as drink melts, serve (with straws).

Mount Gay Distillery (W.Ind). A noted Rum distillery in Barbados. Address = Prince Wm. Henry Street, Bridgetown. 40% alc. by vol.

Mount Helen (Austr). A red grape variety.

Mount Helen (Austr). Part of the Tisdall estate, 50 ha. in Victoria.

Mount Mary Winery (Austr). Address = Coldstream, West Road, Lilydale, Victoria 3140. 7.5 ha. Grape varieties – Cabernet franc, Cabernet sauvignon, Chardonnay, Malbec, Merlot, Muscadelle, Pinot noir, Sauvignon blanc and Sémillon.

Mount Palomar Winery (USA). A large winery based near Temecula, southern California. 60 ha. Grape varieties – Cabernet sauvignon, Petite sirah and Sauvignon blanc. Produces varietal wines.

Mount Pleasant Hunter vineyards (Austr). Part of the McWilliams Estate in New South Wales. 115 ha. Grape varieties – Chardonnay, Hermitage and Sémillon.

Mount Pleasant vineyards (USA). A small winery based in Augusta, Missouri. Produce native American and French hybrid wines.

Mount Rufus Port (Austr). A vintage Tawny Port-style wine produced by the Seppelts Winery.

Mount Tivy Winery (USA). A winery owned by the Christian Brothers, Napa Valley, California. Produces and ages Brandies.

Mount Veeder vineyard (USA). A winery based in Napa Valley, California. 8.5 ha. Grape varieties – Cabernet sauvignon, Cabernet franc, Malbec, Merlot, Petit verdot and Zinfandel. Produces varietal and table wines.

Moura Basto (Port). A brand of Vinho Verde made from the Azal grape. Produced in Basto or Amarante.

Mourane (Fr). An alternative name for the Malbec grape.

Mouraton (Sp). A red grape variety grown in the Galicia region.

Mourens (Fr). A commune in the Haut-Benauge, Entre-Deux-Mers, central Burgundy.

Mourestel (USA). A red grape variety grown in California, used for making red wines.

Mourisco (Port). A red grape variety used in the making of Port wine. Gives good fruit.

Mourisco Branco (Port). A white grape variety used in the making of white Port.

Mourisco de Semente (Port). A red grape variety used in the making of Port.

Mourisco Preto (USA). A white grape variety used in the making of dessert wines.

Mourisco Semente (Port). See Mourisco de Semente.

Mournier (Aus). A noted sparkling wine producer.

Mourvèdre (Fr). A red grape variety grown in the southern Rhône. Also known as Beni Carlo, Catalan, Espar, Négron, Mataro and Tinto.

Mousel et Clausen Basserie (Lux). A brewery noted for its Luxator 13° Balling and Royal Altmunster 13° Balling.

Mousey (Eng). See Mousy.

Mousquetaires d'Armagnac (Fr). A body of Armagnac lovers.

Mousse (Fr). The foam or sparkle of Champagne or sparkling wines.

Mousseux (Fr). Foaming, sparkling.

Mousseux de Savoie (Fr). Also known as Vin de Savoie Mousseux. An A.C. sparkling (méthode champenoise or méthode gaillaçoise) wine from the Savoie region.

Mousseux de Savoie-Ayze (Fr). Also known as Vin de Savoie-Ayze Mousseux. An A.C. sparkling (méthode champenoise or méthode gaillaçoise) wine from the Savoie region. Grape varieties – Altesse, Gringet and Roussette d'Ayze.

Mousseux du Bugey (Fr). Also known as Vin du Bugey Mousseux. An A.C. sparkling (méthode champenoise or méthode gaillaçoise) wine from the Savoie region.

Mousseux Naturel (Fr). A sweet white sparkling wine. e.g. Clairette de Die, Demi-Sec.

Moussierend (Ger). Sparkling.

Moussy (Fr). A Cru Champagne village in the Canton d'Épernay. District = Épernay.

Moustère (Fr). The alternative name for the Malbec grape.

Moustillants (Switz). Sparkling.

Moustille (Fr). See Semi-Sparkling.

Moustrou (Fr). An alternative name for the Tannat grape.

Mousy (Eng). An offensive odour and taste

in wine due to the presence of an infection caused by lactic acid bacteria. Occurs in wines that are not regularly racked. Also spelt Mousey.

Moût (Fr). Unfermented grape juice.

Mout (Hol). An old Dutch word for Malt.

Mou-Tai Chiew (China). A spirit made from fermented millet and wheat which is stored in cellars before bottling to give it a characteristic taste. Produced by the Mou-Tai Distillery in Kweichow.

Mou-Tai Distillery (China). A noted distillery based in Kweichow.

Moutard Père et Fils (Fr). Champagne producer. Address = Buxeuil 10110 Bar sur Seine. Récoltants-manipulants. Produces – Vintage and non-vintage wines.

Moutardier (Jean) (Fr). Champagne producer. Address = Le Breuil, 51210 Montmirail. Récoltants-manipulants. Produces – Vintage and non-vintage wines. Vintages – 1971, 1973, 1975, 1976, 1979, 1982, 1983.

Moût de Goutte (Fr). Free-run juice.

Moutere Reserve (N.Z.). A medium-dry white wine made from a blend of Gewürztraminer, Rhine riesling, Chenin blanc and Chardonnay grapes. Produced by Weingut Seigfried in Nelson.

Mouterij (Hol). Malting house.

Mouterij-Branderij de Koning BV (Hol). A large Moutwijn producer. (A subsidiary of Bols).

Mouton-Cadet (Fr). Famous red and white blended vintage wines, A.C. Médoc, from the stable of Baron Philippe de Rothschild.

Mouton d'Armailhacq (Fr). Now Château Mouton-Baron Philippe (name changed in 1956).

Mouton Rothschild (Fr). See Château Mouton Rothschild.

Moutwijn (Hol). Lit – 'Malt wine'. A name given to the distillate before rectification and flavouring of Gin.

Moutwijnjenever (Hol). The name given to Jenever that is redistilled twice.

Mouvedre (N.Z.). A red grape variety. See Mourvèdre.

Mou Vin (Fr). Lifeless wine.

Mouzillon (Fr). A wine village in the Muscadet de Sèvre et Maine region, Pays Nantais, Loire Atlantique.

Movimosto (Port). A machine which pumps and sprays the must over the 'cap' in the fermentation vat.

Mow Toy Wine (China). A clear spirit made from Kaoliang, a Sorghum-like grain. 40% alc. by vol.

Moxie (Eng). The trade mark of a soft drink.

Moya (N.Z.). The alternative name for the black hybrid grape variety Seibel 5455.

Moyer Vineyards (USA). A winery based

on the right bank of the Ohio river, Ohio. Produces hybrid and sparkling wines.

Moyey (Ets) (Fr). Cognac producer. Address = 62, Rue de l'Industrie, 16104 Cognac. Owns no vineyards. Produces many styles of Cognacs.

Moyle (Eng). Old English cider-making apple.

Mozambique Teas (Afr). Teas used mainly for blending.

Mozart Liqueur (Aust). A chocolate kirsch and nougat liqueur 20% alc. by vol.

Mozé (Fr). An A.C. commune in the Coteaux de l'Aubance in Anjou-Saumur, Loire.

M.P. (Eng) (abbr). On a wine list denotes Mis en bouteille à la proprétaire.

Mr. and Mrs. Caudle (Scot). A salt-glazed stoneware whisky flask. 7½ ins. high made by Doulton and Watts c1846. Decorated with an embossed man and woman under bedclothes and inscribed.

Mr. Cherrys (Eng). A home-brew public house in St. Leonards, Sussex. Noted for its Mak's Special Beer 1050 O.G.

Mrira (Afr). A co-operative winery in Tunisia. Is owned by the UCCVT.

Mr. Manhattan (Cktl). Muddle 4 sprigs of mint with juice of ¼ orange and 2 dashes lemon juice. Add 2 fl.ozs. Gin, shake over ice, strain into a cocktail glass.

Mrs. McGillvray's Scotch Apple Liqueur (Scot). An apple and Scotch whisky based liqueur. 25% alc. by vol.

MSB (Eng) (abbr). Mark's Special Beer 1050 O.G. brewed by the Pensans Brewery in Penzance, Cornwall.

Mt. Avoca (Austr). A noted winery based in Pyrenees, Victoria.

Mt. Dangar (Austr). A winery based in the Hunter Valley, New South Wales. Produces varietal wines.

Mt. Erin Müller-Thurgau (N.Z.). The brand-name of a fruity, medium-dry, white wine produced by Vidal Wine Products in Hawkes Bay.

Mt. Gay Distilleries (W.Ind). A large Rum distillery based in Barbados.

Mt. Hope Estate (USA). A winery based in Cornwall, Pennsylvania. Produces hybrid wines.

Mt. Rufur Port (Austr). A traditional fortified Port-type wine from the Seppelts vineyard in South Australia.

Mtzvane (USSR). The alternative spelling of Mzvane.

Muaga vineyards (N.Z.). An old established vineyard based at Henderson, North Island.

Mucaro Cocktail (Cktl). 1 fl.oz. golden

M

Rum, 1 fl.oz. Tia Maria, 2 fl.ozs. cream. Shake over ice, strain into a cocktail glass. Dress with powdered cinnamon and a cinnamon stick.

Mucilage (Eng). A substance present in vegetable organisms which help to give body to a wine (in small quantities only).

Muckerhölle (Ger). vineyard. (Anb) = Nahe. (Ber) = Schloss Böckelheim. (Gro) = Burgweg. (Vil) = Waldböckelheim.

Mud (USA) (slang). Lees.

Muddler (USA). A special wooden implement with a flat head used to mix and crush such items as sugar, mint etc. in liquids in the bottom of a glass or jug.

Muddler Spoon (Eng). A barspoon with a flat disc at its base which acts as a Muddler.

Muddy (Eng). A term used to describe cloudy drinks e.g. red wine which has had the sediment (lees) disturbed, or beer (cask conditioned) that has a haze or its sediment (lees) disturbed. Can also be caused by dirty pipes/casks.

Müden (Ger). Village. (Anb) = Mosel-Saar-Ruwer. (Ber) = Zell/Mosel. (Gro) = Goldbäumchen. (Vins) = Funkenberg, Grosslay, Leckmauer, St. Castorhöhle, Sonnenring.

Mudge (Eng). A Midlands term to denote the crushing of the hops to help extract the oil in brewing.

Mudgee (Austr). A wine region in New South Wales. Estate wineries include – Augustine, Craigmoor and Huntington.

Muehlhausen (Fr). The German name for the district of Mulhouse in Alsace.

Mueller-Thurgau (Eng). The English spelling of Müller-Thurgau.

Muerza (Sp). See Bodegas Muerza S.A.

Muffa Nobile (It). Botrytis Cinerea. Noble Rot.

Mufti of Aden (Arab). A fifteenth-century Arab who is purported to have discovered coffee. See also Kaldi.

Mug (Eng). The name for a beer glass with a handle. See Dimple Mug.

Muga (Sp). A red wine produced by the Bodegas Muga, Rioja. Made from Garnacha tinto, Mazuelo and Viura grapes. Matured for 1 year in oak vats of 18,000 litres and for 2 years in oak Barricas. Also produce white wines.

Mugamart (Sp). The brand-name of a fruity sparkling wine produced by the Bodegas Muga, Rioja.

Mugneret (René) (Fr). A négociant-éleveur based in the Côte d'Or. Address = 21670 Vosne-Romanée, Burgundy.

Mugwort (Eng). An aromatic plant also known as Tansy used in the flavouring of ale in mediaeval times. (Fr) = Barbotine (Herbe aux vers).

Mühlbach (Ger). Village. (Anb) = Baden. (Ber) = Badishe Bergstrasse/Kraichgau. (Gro) = Stiftsberg. (Vin) = Lerchenberg.

Mühlbach (Ger). Village. (Anb) = Franken. (Ber) = Maindreieck. (Gro) = Rosstal. (Vins) = Assorted parts of vineyards.

Mühlbacher (Ger). vineyard. (Anb) = Württemberg. (Ber) = Württembergisch Unterland. (Gro) = Schalkstein. (Vil) = Mundelsheim.

Mühlberg (Ger). vineyard. (Anb) = Baden. (Ber) = Badische Frankenland. (Gro) = Tauberklinge. (Vil) = Boxberg (stadtteil Unterschüpf).

Mühlberg (Ger). vineyard. (Anb) = Mittelrhein. (Ber) = Rheinburgengau. (Gro) = Marksburg. (Vil) = Braubach.

Mühlberg (Ger). vineyard. (Anb) = Mosel-Saar-Ruwer. (Ber) = Bernkastel. (Gro) = Kurfürstlay. (Vil) = Veldenz.

Mühlberg (Ger). vineyard. (Anb) = Nahe. (Ber) = Schloss Böckelheim. (Gro) = Burgweg. (Vil) = Schlossböckelheim.

Mühlberg (Ger). vineyard. (Anb) = Nahe. (Ber) = Schloss Böckelheim. (Gro) = Burgweg. (Vil) = Waldböckelheim.

Mühlberg (Ger). vineyard. (Anb) = Nahe. (Ber) = Schloss Böckelheim. (Gro) = Rosengarten. (Vil) = Sponheim.

Mühlberg (Ger). vineyard. (Anb) = Rheinpfalz. (Ber) = Südliche Weinstrasse. (Gro) = Schloss Ludwigshöhe. (Vil) = Edenkob n.

Mühlberg (Ger). vineyard. (Anb) = Württemberg. (Ber) = Württembergisch Unterland. (Gro) = Kirchenweinberg. (Vil) = Ilsfeld (ortsteil Schozach).

Mühlenberg (Ger). vineyard. (Anb) = Mosel-Saar-Ruwer. (Ber) = Bernkastel. (Gro) = Sankt Michael. (Vil) = Ensch.

Mühlenberg (Ger). vineyard. (Anb) = Nahe. (Ber) = Kreuznach. (Gro) = Pfarrgarten. (Vil) = Wallhausen.

Mühlenberg (Ger). vineyard. (Anb) = Nahe. (Ber) = Schloss Böckelheim. (Gro) = Rosengarten. (Vil) = Roxheim.

Mühlhausen (Ger). vineyard. (Anb) = Baden. (Ber) = Badische Bergstrasse/Kraichgau. (Gro) = Mannaberg. (Vil) = Heilgenstein.

Mühlhausen (Ger). Village. (Anb) = Württemberg. (Ber) = Remstal-Stuttgart. (Gro) = Weinsteige. See Stuttgart.

Mühlhausen (Ger). Village. (Anb) = Württemberg. (Ber) = Württembergisch Unterland. (Gro) = Stromberg. (Vin) = Halde.

Mui Kive Lu (China). A clear spirit distilled from Kaoliang, a Sorghum-like grain. 40% alc. by vol.

Muirheads (Scot). A blended Scotch

whisky produced by MacDonald and Muir. 40% alc. by vol.

Mukuzani (USSR). A red grape variety grown in Georgia.

Mukuzani (USSR). A full red wine from the Georgia region (Tiflis district). 14% alc. by vol. Produced from a grape of the same name.

Mulata (Cktl). 1 oz. Bacardi Elixir, juice ½ lime, 1 oz. Bacardi White Label, ½ teaspoon sugar. Shake well over ice, strain into a cocktail glass.

Mülheim (Ger). Village. (Anb) = Mosel-Saar-Ruwer. (Ber) = Bernkastel. (Gro) = Kurfürstlay. (Vins) = Amtsgarten, Elisenberg, Helenenkloster, Sonnenlay.

Mülhoff (Ger). A producer of liqueurs and wheat-based Whiskey. Address = Spirituosenfabrik 418 Goch.

Mulhouse (Fr). A town and district of Alsace. (Ger) = Muehlhausen.

Mull (Eng). A seventeenth-century practice of heating drinks of wine or ale that have been flavoured with spices, lemon and beaten egg. Heating was usually by means of a red hot poker. Never boiled.

Mulled (Eng). Hot drinks, usually served from a silver jug with a lid.

Mulled Cider (Cktl). 2 pints Cider, 3 fl.ozs. Brandy, 1 tablespoon brown sugar, 6 cloves, ¼ teaspoon ginger and cinnamon. Mix spice, sugar and Cider. Heat slowly until nearly boiling, add Brandy. Serve in warmed glasses with a slice of orange.

Mulled Claret (Cktl). 1 bottle Claret, 1 wine glass Port, ¼ pint water, tablespoon sugar, rind of ½ lemon, 12 cloves, pinch nutmeg. Simmer spices with water, strain, add wine, Port and sugar. Heat, serve very hot with thin slices of lemon rind.

Mulled Red Wine (Cktl). 1 bottle Claret or Burgundy, 2 lemons, ⅓ pint water, 4 ozs sugar, 4 cinnamon sticks, 4 cloves. Boil water, sugar and spices for 5 minutes. Add thinly sliced lemons, infuse 10 minutes. Add wine, heat slowly and serve.

Mulled Spiced Ale (Cktl). 1 teaspoon powdered sugar in ½ pint tankard, add pinch cinnamon, top with strong dark beer. Heat by inserting a hot poker.

Müller (Matheus) (Ger). A large producer of fine Deutscher Sekt.

Müller Brauerei (Switz). An independent brewery based in Baden.

Müller Brauerei (Switz). A brewery based in Neuchâtel. Is part of the Feldschlösschen group.

Müllerrebe (Ger). A red grape variety known also as the Schwarzriesling and the Pinot Meunier. Also spelt Müller Rebe.

Müller-Scharzhofberg (Egon) (Ger). A large wine-producing company based in Wiltingen, Mosel-Saar-Ruwer.

Müller-Schwarzriesling (Ger). See Müllerrebe.

Müller-Thurgau (Ger). A white grape variety. A cross between the Riesling and the Sylvaner. Invented by Hermann Müller at the Geisenheim viticultural research station in the 1890s. Named after the Swiss Canton (Thurgau) he came from.

Müllheim (Ger). Village. (Anb) = Baden. (Ber) = Markgräflerland. (Gro) = Burg Neuenfels.·(Vins) = Pfaffenstück, Reggenhag, Sonnhalde.

Mulligan (Ire). An Irish whiskey and fruit-flavoured liqueur produced in Ballinaneashagh, Waterford. 40% alc. by vol.

Mull of Kintyre (Cktl). 1 part Glayva in a highball glass, top up with ice, Cola and a twist of lemon peel. Serve with straws.

Mulsum, Mulsus (Lat). Mead.

Multaner (Ger). A white grape variety. A cross between the Riesling and the Sylvaner. Only good for wine-making if very ripe.

Mum (Eng). A type of beer brewed in the seventeenth century from cereals and beans.

Mumm Cognac (USA). A Cognac brandy produced by Seagram for the USA market.

Mumm Cuvée Présidente René Lalou (Fr). A De Luxe vintage cuvée Champagne produced by G.H. Mumm from 50% Chardonnay and 50% Pinot noir. Is also known as René Lalou.

Mumme (Ger). A non-fermented malt extract beer from Braunschweig. Served as a tonic or mixed with pale beers.

Mumm [G.H.] (Fr). Champagne producer. Address = 29 Rue de Champ de Mars, 51053 Reims. A Grande Marque. Produces vintage and non-vintage wines. Vintages – 1900, 1904, 1906, 1911, 1913, 1920, 1921, 1923, 1926, 1928, 1929, 1933, 1934, 1937, 1941, 1943, 1945, 1947, 1949, 1952, 1953, 1955, 1958, 1959, 1961, 1962, 1964, 1966, 1969, 1971, 1973, 1975, 1976, 1982, 1983. See also René Lalou, Cordon Rouge, Cordon, Rosé, Cordon Verte. De Luxe vintage cuvée is Mumm Cuvée Présidente René Lalou. Controls Heidsieck Monopole and Perrier Jouët.

Münchner (Ger). A dark, brown, malty, bottom-fermented Beer 4.3% alc. by vol. Originates from Munich.

Münchweiler (Ger). Village. (Anb) = Baden. (Ber) = Breisgau. (Gro) = Schutterlindenberg. (Vin) = Kirchberg.

Mundelsheim (Ger). Village. (Anb) = Württemberg. (Ber) = Wurttembergisch Unterland. (Gro) = Schalkstein. (Vins) = Käsberg, Katzenöhrle, Mühlbächer, Rozenberg.

Mundend (Ger). Denotes a tasty, pleasant wine.

Mundenhamer (Aus). A Bock beer brewed by the brewery of same name.

Mundenhamer Brauerei (Aus). A brewery noted for its Bock beers.

Mundingen (Ger). Village. (Anb) = Baden. (Ber) = Breisgau. (Gro) = Burg Lichteneck. (Vin) = Alte Burg.

Mundkeln (Aus). Denotes a wine with the taste of a dirty cask.

Mundklingen (Ger). vineyard. (Anb) = Hessische Bergstrasse. (Ber) = Starkenburg. (Gro) = Not yet assigned. (Vil) = Seeheim.

Munson (USA). A vine hybridiser. Developed the red Delicatessen.

Münster (Ger). Village. (Anb) = Württemberg. (Ber) = Remstal-Stuttgart. (Gro) = Weinsteige. See Stuttgart.

Münsterappel (Ger). Village. (Anb) = Nahe. (Ber) = Schloss Böckelheim. (Gro) = Paradiesgarten. (Vin) = Graukatz.

Münsterberg (Ger). vineyard. (Anb) = Mosel-Saar-Ruwer. (Ber) = Zell/Mosel. (Gro) = Goldbäumchen. (Vil) = Treis-Karden.

Münster-Sarmsheim (Ger). Village. (Anb) = Nahe. (Ber) = Kreuznach. (Gro) = Schlosskapelle. (Vins) = Dautenpflänzer, Kapellenberg, Konigsschloss, Liebenhöll, Pittersberg, Rheinberg, Römerberg, Steinkopf, Trollberg.

Münsterstatt (Ger). vineyard. (Anb) = Mosel-Saar-Ruwer. (Ber) = Obermosel. (Gro) = Gipfel. (Vil) = Temmels.

Münzberg (Ger). vineyard. (Anb) = Rheinpfalz. (Ber) = Südliche Weinstrasse. (Gro) = Königsgarten. (Vil) = Godramstein.

Münzesheim (Ger). See Kraichtal.

Munzingen (Ger). Village. (Anb) = Baden. (Ber) = Kaiserstuhl-Tuniberg. (Gro) = Attilafelsen. (Vin) = Kapellenberg.

Münzlay (Ger). Grosslage. (Anb) = Mosel-Saar-Ruwer. (Ber) = Bernkastel. (Vils) = Graach, Wehlen, Zeltingen-Rachtig.

Mûr (Fr). Ripe.

Murailles (Les) (Fr). A vineyard of Dopff & Irion in Alsace. Produces Riesling wines.

Muratie Wine Farm (S.Afr). vineyard. Address = Box 9, Koelenhof 7605. 46 ha. Produces varietal and Port-style wines.

Mûre (Fr). A blackberry and Mulberry spirit liqueur.

Muré (Fr). An Alsace wine-producer. Address = 68250 Rouffach. 19 ha.

Mureck (Aus). A wine-producing area in Klöch, southern Austria.

Mürefte (Tur). A wine-producing region in southern Turkey.

Müre Sauvage (Fr). A Brandy-based liqueur flavoured with blackberries.

Murets de Sion (Les) (Switz). A white wine from the Valais produced from the Fendant grape.

Murettes (Les) (Fr). A vineyard of Château de l'Hermitage, northern Rhône. (white wine).

Murfatlar (Rum). A fine dessert wine which has a faint bouquet of orange blossoms produced near the region of Focsani from the vineyard of the same name in Dobrudja.

Murfatlar Hills (Rum). An area near the wine region of Focsani. Noted for its dessert wines.

Murgers-des-Dents-de-Chien (Les) (Fr). A Premier Cru vineyard in the A.C. commune of Saint-Aubin, Côte de Beaune, Burgundy.

Murgeys (Fr). Another name for Cheys.

Murillo (Sp). A Zona de Crianza in the Rioja Baja.

Muristellu (It). A name used in Sardinia for the red Bovale sardo grape.

Murmurer Cocktail (Cktl). ¼ gill Sherry, ¼ gill Gin, ¼ teaspoon lime juice, ½ teaspoon Angostura. Stir over ice, strain into a cocktail glass. Serve with a dash of lemon peel juice on top.

Murphy Brewery (Ire). Based in Cork. Owned by Heineken of Holland. Noted for its Stout.

Murphy's (Ire). A second blend of Middleton light pot-still and grain whiskies, matured in charred barrels.

Murphy's Irish Stout (Ire). A keg/bottled beer brewed by the Murphy Brewery in Cork.

Murr (Ger). Village. (Anb) = Württemberg. (Ber) = Württembergisch Unterland. (Gro) = Schalkstein. (Vin) = Neckarhälde.

Murra Coffee (Tur). The name given to unsweetened Turkish coffee.

Murrão (Port). A white grape variety grown in Peñafiel (a sub-region of Vinho Verde).

Murray [River] (Austr). A wine region of South Australia. Main estates are Angoves and Thomas Hardy. Noted for its Port-style wines and brandies.

Murree Brewery (Pak). A brewery based

in Rawalpindi which produces London Lager 10.4° Balling, Export 11.4° Balling and a bottom-fermented, medium Stout 14.2° Balling.

Murrina (Lat). Myrrh wine.

Murr [River] (Ger). A tributary of the river Neckar in Württemberg. Soil is Red marl.

Murrumbidgee (Austr). A wine region of New South Wales. Main estates are Seppelts, McWilliams, Penfolds, Rooty Hill.

Mûrs (Fr). An A.C. commune in the Coteaux de l'Aubance district of the Anjou-Saumur, Loire. Produces light, white wines.

Mus (Tur). A banana liqueur.

Musanté (S.Afr). A sweet, sparkling white wine from the Muscat grape made by the K.W.V.

Muscade (Fr). An alternative name for the Muscadelle grape.

Muscadel (Eng). An old name for Muscatel wine.

Muscadel (USA). The term for a Port-style fortified wine made with the Muscat grape.

Muscadelle (Austr). A white grape variety also known as the Tokay.

Muscadelle (Fr). A white grape variety grown in Bordeaux. Cultivated in small portions with the Sémillon and Sauvignon blanc. It gives a faint Muscat flavour to the wine. Also known as the Angelicant, Auvernat blanc, Catape, Colle-musquette, Douzanelle, Guépie, Guillan, Guillan musqué, Loin d'Oeuil, Muscade, Muscat fou, Musquette and Resinotte.

Muscadelle du Bordelais (USA). A white grape variety grown in California to make white table wines.

Muscadet (Fr). The local Loire name for the white grape variety Melon de Bourgogne.

Muscadet (Fr). An A.C. classification of wines produced south of Nantes in the Pays Nantais. Accounts for only 10% of the Muscadet produced. Minimum alc. by vol. 9.5%.

Muscadet Coteaux de la Loire (Fr). A.C. category of Muscadet wines. From the east of Nantes, produces about 5% of Muscadet A.C. wines. Minimum alc. by vol. 10%.

Muscadet de Dieppe (Fr). A noted Cider apple grown in the Normandy region. Has good acidity and produces dry ciders.

Muscadet des Coteaux de la Loire (Fr). See Muscadet Coteaux de la Loire.

Muscadet de Sèvre et Maine (Fr). Finest of the A.C. Muscadets. Produced in an area south of Nantes around and between the rivers Sèvre and Maine. Often produced Sur Lie.

Muscadet Saint-Clément (Fr). The name that the wines of Château la Berrière are sold under.

Muscadines (USA). Members of the Vitis Rotundifolia American vine species. 3 types – Sappenog (white), James (black) and Misch (black). Also known as the Scuppernong or Bullace grape.

Muscardin (Fr). A red grape variety grown in the southern Rhône for the making of Châteauneuf-du-Pape.

Muscat (Euro). A wine and table grape with varieties ranging from pale yellow to blue-black. In wine it produces a very distinctive bouquet and flavour. Grown in most wine districts that have plenty of sunshine.

Muscat Aigre (Fr). The lesser name for the Ugni blanc.

Muscat Alexandria (USA). See Muscat of Alexandria.

Muscat Baily A (USA). A white American hybrid grape used in Japan.

Muscat Blanc (USA). The alternative name for the Muscat of Canelli and the Muscat of Frontignan.

Muscat Blanc à Petits Grains (Fr). The local Rhône name for the Muscat d'Alexandria grape in the Clairette de Die, also in the Alsace. Black and white varieties. Also known as the Gelber muscateller, Moscato, Moscato bianco, Moscato branco, Muscat d'Alsace, Muscat rosé à petits grains d'Alsace, Muscatel, Muscatel branco, Muskat, Muskataly, Muskateller, Muskuti and the White frontignan.

Muscat Brandy (USA). See California Brandy.

Muscat Courtillier (Fr). A relation of the Muscat grape. Also known as the Coutillier musqué and Muscat précoce de courtillier.

Muscat d'Alexandria (S.Afr). A white grape variety known as the Muscadelle in Europe.

Muscat d'Alsace (Fr). An A.C. dry white, perfumed wine made from the Muscat grape in Alsace. See Muscat Blanc à Petits Grains, Muscat d'ottenel and Muscat Rosé à Petits Grains.

Muscat de Beaumes de Venise (Fr). An A.C. Vin Doux Naturel from the Côtes du Rhône Villages. Made from the Muscat grape it has a powerful muscat 'honied' aroma.

Muscat de Cephalonia (Gre). A dessert wine from the Island of Cephalonia in the Ionian Isles, Western Greece. Made from the Muscat grape.

M

Muscat de Chypre (Cyp). A fine Muscat dessert wine sold on the USA market.

Muscat de Frontignan (Fr). A VdN dessert wine produced in the Midi region.

Muscat de Grain Rouge (Austr). A red grape variety grown in Victoria.

Muscat de Hambourg (China). A white Muscat grape variety grown in the Tianjin region.

Muscat de Kéliba (Afr). The name given to a white wine from Tunisia (dry and sweet versions) produced by UCCVT. AOC.

Muscat de Lemnos (Gre). A sweet dessert wine from the Muscat d'Alexandria made on the island of Lemnos in the Aegean Isles, eastern Greece.

Muscat de Lunel (Fr). VdN from the Hérault Département in the Midi region (white).

Muscat de Miréval (Fr). A VdN dessert wine produced in Montpellier (white).

Muscat de Patras (Gre). A fine white liqueur dessert wine from the Peloponnese.

Muscat de Rhodes (Gre). A naturally sweet dessert wine made from the Muscat and Muscat de Trani grape varieties. Produced on the Rhodes Islands in the Dodecanese Isles, southeastern Greece.

Muscat de Rivesaltes (Fr). A Vin Doux Naturel from near Perpignan in the Roussillon region (white).

Muscat de Saint-Jean-de-Minervois (Fr). A VdN dessert wine produced in the Midi region (white).

Muscat de Samos (Gre). A sweet white dessert wine from the island of Samos in the Aegean Islands, eastern Greece.

Muscat de Setúbal (Port). A sweet fortified wine produced in southern Portugal around the port of Setúbal. When the required balance is achieved during fermentation it is ceased with grape spirit and then Muscatel grape skins are added and allowed to macerate with the wine until the following spring. It is then racked and matured for up to 25 years before sale.

Muscat de Terracina (Tun). A white grape variety that produces medium-sweet perfumed wines.

Muscat de Trani (Gre). A white grape variety grown mainly in southern Greece to produce naturally sweet wines.

Muscat Doré de Frontignan (Fr). An alternative name for the Muscat blanc à petits grains.

Muscat d'Ottenel (Fr). A white grape variety of Muscat grown in the Alsace region.

Muscat du Moulin [Couderc 19] (Fr). A cross grape variety between the Pedro Ximénez and C603.

Muscatel (Austr). See Muscat Gordo Blanco and Muscat blanc à petits grains.

Muscatel (Isr). A sweet, dessert, Port-style wine.

Muscatel Branco (Port). A white grape variety used in the making of White Port. Also known as the Muscat blanc à petits grains.

Muscateller (Euro). An alternative name for the Muscat Blanc à Petits Grains.

Muscateller Ottonel (Aus). An alternative name for the Muscat ottonel.

Muscat Fou (Fr). An alternative name for the Muscadelle grape.

Muscat Frontignan (USA). See Muscat of Frontignan.

Muscat Gamburgski (Euro). An alternative name for the Muscat of Hamburg.

Muscat Gordo Blanco (Austr). A white grape variety of the Muscat family. Also known as the Muscat of Alexandria, Muscatel and Lexia.

Muscat Hamburg (USA). See Muscat of Hamburg.

Muscat-Hamburg (Yug). A red wine produced in southern Macedonia from the grape of same name.

Muscat Italia (It). A relation of the Muscat grape. A cross between the Bicane and the Muscat Hamburg.

Muscat Massandra (USSR). A medium-dry white wine produced near Simferopol in the Crimea (Ukraine).

Muscato di Amburgo (It). An alternative name for the Muscat of Hamburg.

Muscat of Alexandria (Austr). See Muscat Gordo Blanco.

Muscat of Alexandria (S.Afr). White grape variety also known as the Hanepoot, Iskendiriye, Moscatel romano, Muscat d'Alexandrie, Muscat romain, Panse musquée, White hanepoot and Zibibbo.

Muscat of Alexandria (USA). A white grape variety used in the making of dessert wines in California.

Muscat of Canelli (USA). A white grape variety used in the making of dessert wines in California. Also known as the Muscat de Frontignan and Muscat blanc à petits grains.

Muscat of Frontignan (USA). A white grape variety used in the making of white and dessert wines in California.

Muscat of Hamburg (USA). A black grape variety used in the making of dessert wines in California. Also known as the Black Muscat, Black of Alexandria, Muscat gamburgski, Muscato di Amburgo and Tămâioasă Hamburg.

Muscat of Kirghiz (USSR). A white dessert

M

grape variety grown in the Kirghiz region.

Muscat of Lemnos (Gre). A sweet white wine produced on the Aegean Island of Lemnos from the Muscat grape.

Muscat of Rhodes (Gre). A sweet white wine produced on the Aegean Island of Rhodes from the Muscat grape.

Muscat of Samos (Gre). A sweet white wine produced on the Aegean Island of Samos from the Muscat grape.

Muscat of St. Laurent (USA). A red grape variety used in the making of dessert wines in California.

Muscat Ottonel (Fr). A white grape variety related to the Muscat. Also spelt Muscateller ottonel, Muskat ottonel and the Muskateller ottonel.

Muscat Ottonel (Rum). A highly flavoured dessert wine from the Valea Calugărească region.

Muscat Précoce de Courtillier (Fr). A white grape variety grown in the Midi region. Also known as the Muscat courtillier.

Muscat Reine des Vignes (Hun). A Muscat cross which gives strong scented wines.

Muscat Riesling (Ger). A white grape variety. A cross between the White riesling and the Muscat St. Laurent.

Muscat Rion de Patras (Gre). A fine white dessert liqueur wine from Peloponnese.

Muscat Romain (It). An alternative name for the Muscat of Alexandria.

Muscat Rosé à Petite Grains (Fr). A red skinned grape variety also known as the Muscat d'Alsace, Muscat rosé à petits grains d'Alsace, Rotter Muscateller and Rotter Muskateller.

Muscat Rosé à Petits Grains d'Alsace (Fr). See Muscat Rosé à Petits Grains.

Muscat Sàrgamuskotàly (Hun). A white grape variety. A variety of the Muscat family.

Muscat St. Laurent (Fr). A red grape variety.

Muscat-Sylvaner (Fr). A white grape variety known as the Sauvignon in Germany.

Muscat Violet (USSR). A white grape variety used in the production of dessert wines in the regions of Kazakhstan and Kirghizia.

Muscavado (Sp). The name given to the evaporated liquid derived from sugar cane. The Arabs call it Sukkar.

Muscel (Rum). A noted white wine producing vineyard.

Muschekalk (Ger). A name for the soil of shell-lime in Franconia.

Muscovital (Cktl). 1 oz. Campari, 1 oz.

Vodka, 2 ozs. Green Ginger Wine. Mix over ice in a highball, serve with a cherry.

Musée du Vin de Bourgogne (Fr). A museum which has displays of wine and the vine based at the former Hôtel des Ducs de Bourgogne.

Musée du Vin de Champagne (Fr). A museum based at Épernay. Shows the Champagne process including a model of the abbey at Hautvillers.

Muselage (Fr). Lit – 'Muzzling'. The wiring of the clamps onto Champagne bottles.

Muselet (Fr). The wire cage that is placed over the corks on Champagne and sparkling wine bottles.

Muselet de Fil de Fer (Fr). The name for the wire muzzle used to hold the cork down in a bottle of sparkling wine.

Musenhang (Ger). Vineyard. (Anb) = Rheinpfalz. (Ber) = Mittelhaardt-Deutsche Weinstrasse. (Gro) = Mariengarten. (Vil) = Forst.

Musigny (Fr). A Grand Cru vineyard in the A.C. commune of Chambolle-Musigny, Côte de Nuits, Burgundy. 10.7 ha. owned by 6 owners of various-sized plots. Also known as Les Musigny.

Musigny Blanc (Fr). A rare white wine made by the Comte de Vogue from the Chardonnay grape that is produced in the Musigny vineyard in the Chambolle-Musigny commune. In many none is produced so it is expensive. About 2,000 bottles produced annually.

Musikantenbuckel (Ger). vineyard. (Anb) = Rheinpfalz. (Ber) = Mittelhaardt-Deutsche Weinstrasse. (Gro) = Kobnert. (Vil) = Freinsheim.

Muskat (Aus). An alternative name for the Muscat Blanc à Petit Grains.

Muškat Crveni (Yug). A red grape variety grown in Croatia.

Muskateller (Aus). A white grape variety. See Muscat Blanc à Petits Grains.

Muskat-Ottonel (Aus). A white grape variety which produces wines of intense bouquet. Related to the Muscat family. See Muscat Ottonel.

Muskat-Sylvaner (Aus). A white grape variety.

Muskotàly (Hun). A white grape variety. A species of the Moscatel used in the making of Tokay wines. Also the name of a fortified wine with an intense Muscat flavour. See Muscat Blanc à Petits Grains.

Muskuti (Rum). An alternative name for the Muscat blanc à petits grains.

Musky (Eng). A description of the smell of

M

wines made from the Muscat grape. A pronounced smell of musk.

Muslin Madeira (Eng). The nineteenth-century name of Madeira marketed in London.

Musqué (Fr). An alternative name for the Muscadelle grape.

Musquette (Fr). An alternative name for the Muscadelle grape.

Mussbach (Ger). Village. (Anb) = Rheinpfalz. (Ber) = Mittelhaardt-Deutsche Weinstrasse. (Gro) = Meerspinne. (Vins) = Bischofsweg, Eselshaut, Glockenzehnt, Johannitergarten, Kurfürst, Spiegel.

Must (Eng). Unfermented grape juice. (Fr) = Moût. (Ger) = Moot. (It) (Port) (Sp) = Most, Mosto.

Mustimètre (Fr). A device for measuring the Specific Gravity of grape juice (must). Also known as the Oechsle, Babo, Baume and Areometer.

Mustiness (Eng). The odour that occurs in vessels that have been put away damp (carafes, coffee pots, decanters, jugs, tea pots, etc) enabling fungi to develop and produce a musty smell.

Mustoasă (Rum). A white wine produced near Arad in eastern Rumania.

Mustometer (Eng). See Mustimetre.

Must Weight (Eng). The Specific Gravity of the grape must. Measured on the Mustimetre. The amount of natural sugar in the must.

Musty (Eng). A term for a wine that has a mouldy, damp room smell and taste. Usually obtained through bad cellaring.

Muswellbrook (Austr). A wine-producing region based north of Sydney in New South Wales.

Mut (Fr). Balanced.

Mutage (Fr). The arresting of the fermentage by the addition of alcohol.

Muté (Fr). Mistelle or sweet wine whose fermentation has been inhibited by the addition of Brandy.

Muted Wine (Eng). A wine which has had Brandy added during fermentation. A fortified wine e.g. Port, Pineau des Charentes, Ratafia.

Mutigny (Fr). A Premier Cru Champagne village in the Canton d'Ay. District = Reims.

Mutinense (Lat). A red wine produced in northern Italy in Roman times.

Mütterle (Ger). vineyard. (Anb) = Rheinpfalz. (Ber) = Südliche Weinstrasse. (Gro) = Herrlich. (Vil) = Wollmesheim.

Mutterweinberge (Aus). A vine nursery based in Vöslau.

Mutzig (Fr). The brand-name used by the Albra Brauerei in Alsace.

Muzzling (Eng). See Muselage.

M.W. (Eng) (abbr). See Master of Wine. Highest award in the British Wines and Spirits Trade.

Mycodermae Aceti (Lat). Vinegar yeasts.

Mycodermae Vini (Lat). The yeast responsible for vineous fermentation. See Voile, Flor and Fleurs de Vin.

Myer's Rum (W.Ind). The brand-name of a Rum 40% alc. by vol. distilled in Jamaica by Myers Distillery.

My Fair Lady (Cktl). 1 oz. dry Gin, ½ oz. lemon juice, ½ oz. orange juice, 1 teaspoon Fraise liqueur, 1 egg white. Shake well over ice, strain into a cocktail glass.

Mymering (S.Afr). The brand-name for a South African sherry.

Myr (Fr). Chilled dry white wine and Crème de Myrtilles.

Myrtille (Fr). A bilberry-flavoured brandy. See Crème de Myrtilles.

Myshako Riesling (USSR). A white table wine from the Georgia region.

My Shout (Eng). See Shout.

Mysliwska (Pol). Hunter's Vodka. A Vodka flavoured with juniper berries. See Polmos.

Mysore (Ind). A coffee and tea-producing area of southern India.

Mystic Park (Austr). vineyard. 60 ha. on the shores of Lake Kangaroo. Part of the Brown Brothers Estate in Victoria.

Mzvane (USSR). A full-bodied red wine from the Georgia region. Also spelt Mtzvane.

Nabana (Fr). A banana liqueur produced by Cazanove.

Nabeul (Afr). A wine-producing region situated on the tip of Cap Bon in Tunisia. Is noted for its dry and sweet Muscat wines.

Náchod Brewery (Czec). A brewery based in northern Czec.

Nacional (Port). A term used to refer to ungrafted vinestocks in the Douro region.

Nack (Ger). Village. (Anb) = Baden. (Ber) = Bodensee. See Lottstetten.

Nack (Ger). Village. (Anb) = Rheinhessen. (Ber) = Bingen. (Gro) = Adelberg. (Vin) = Ahrenberg.

Nackenheim (Ger). Village. (Anb) = Rheinhessen. (Ber) = Nierstein. (Gro) = Gutes Domtal. (Vin) = Schmittskapellche.

Nackenheim (Ger). Village. (Anb) = Rheinhessen. (Ber) = Nierstein. (Gro) = Rehbach. (Vin) = Rothenberg.

Nackenheim (Ger). Village. (Anb) = Rheinhessen. (Ber) = Nierstein. (Gro) = Spiegelberg. (Vin) = Engelsberg.

Nacktarsch (Ger). Grosslage. (Anb) = Mosel-Saar-Ruwer. (Ber) = Bernkastel. (Vil) = Kröv.

Naddniprjanske (USSR). A white table wine produced near Cherson in the Ukraine.

Nadwiślański (Pol). A cherry and honey mead. Clear, red in colour, it is sold in earthenware jars.

Nagambie (Austr). A vineyard producing fine Cabernet sauvignon wines. Part of the College winery in Victoria.

Nagambie Cabernet Sauvignon (Austr). A varietal red wine from the Redbank Winery in Victoria.

Nagano (Jap). A wine-producing region in southern Japan.

Nàgyburgundi (Hun). A local variety of the Pinot noir grape.

Nagykanizsa Brewery (Hun). A brewery based in south-western Hungary, noted for Göcseji Barna and Siràly beer.

Nahe (Ger). Anbaugebiet. (Bers) = Kreuznach, Schloss Böckelheim. Pro 90% white wine. Grape varieties – Müller-Thurgau 30%, Riesling 22%, Scheurebe 5% and Silvaner 23%.

Nahegau (Ger). Another name used for the Nahe.

Nahegauer Landwein (Ger). One of the fifteen Deutsche Tafelwein zones.

Nahe Information Service (Ger). Address = Weinland e. V., Kornmarkt 6, 6550 Bad Kreuznach, Western Germany.

Nahe [River] (Ger). A tributary of the river Rhine. Its banks make up the Anbaugebiet of same name.

Naheweinstrasse (Ger). The Nahe wine road route.

Nahe Wine Festival (Ger). Rund um die Naheweinstrasse. Held in late August.

Nahli (Afr). A co-operative winery based in Tunisia. Is owned by the UCCVT.

Nairi (USSR). A white grape variety grown in Armenia. Is used in the production of brandy.

Naked Merry Widow (Cktl). See Mary Garden Cocktail.

Nalagenia (Isr). A Málaga-style, sweet, dessert wine.

Nalevka (Pol). The name given to a fine, first infusion Vodka that is usually kept for guests.

NALHM (Eng) (abbr). The National Association of Licensed House Managers. Trade union for public house and club managers.

Nama (Cyp). The ancient name for Commandaria.

Nancy's Fancy (Punch). 1 bottle apple wine, juice 1 lemon and of 3 oranges, 2 teaspoons of sugar. Blend in a punch bowl over ice, add a syphon of soda and orange and lemon slices.

Nandilari (Gre). A white grape variety grown on the island of Crete for the production of Peza and Archanes wines.

Nanok (Den). A Polar beer 6.5% alc. by vol. A strong Lager beer brewed by the Wiibroe Brewery.

Nantaise Bottle (Fr). A long-necked dump bottle used in the Pays Nantais district mainly for Muscadet wines.

Nantes (Fr). The principal town in the Loire region. Sited in the Pays Nantais in the western Loire on the river's estuary. Noted mainly for its Muscadet and Gros plant.

Nanton (Fr). A commune in the A.C. Mâcon whose grapes may be used to produce Mâcon Supérieur.

Nantz (Fr). The name given to a Brandy produced in Nantes, Loire-Atlantique.

Naoussa (Gre). A full-bodied red wine from the mountains near Salonica, Macedonia. Made from the Xynomavro grape.

Napa Gamay (USA). A red grape variety. See California Gamay and Gamay Noir à Jus Blanc.

Napareuli (USSR). A medium-dry, white wine produced in the Caucasian mountains. Also spelt Napuréouli. Also a red variety produced.

Napa Valley (USA). Famous wine district in northern California. Produces many fine table and dessert wines. Has a climate similar to that of Burgundy.

Napa Valley Co-operative Winery (USA). A large winery based near St. Helena, Napa Valley, California. Produces varietal and table wines.

Napa Vintners (USA). A winery based in the Napa Valley, California. Grape varieties – Cabernet sauvignon, Chardonnay and Zinfandel. Produces varietal wines.

Napa Wine Cellars (USA). A winery based north of Yountville in the Napa Valley, California. Grape varieties – Cabernet sauvignon, Chardonnay, Gewürztraminer and Zinfandel. Produces varietal wines.

Nap Frappé (Cktl). ⅓ measure Brandy, ⅓ measure Kümmel, ⅓ measure Green Chartreuse. Mix over ice, strain into a large cocktail glass containing crushed ice, serve with straws.

Napier Vacuum Pump (Scot). The first fully developed filtration system for coffee. Named after inventor Robert Napier c1840.

Napoléon (Cktl). 1 measure V.S.O.P. Armagnac, ¼ measure Noilly Prat, 1 dash Gomme syrup. Stir over ice, strain into a flute glass, top with iced Champagne.

Napoléon (Fr). Champagne producer. Address = 2, Rue de Villers-aux-Bois, 51130 Vertus. Owns no vineyards. Produces – Vintage and non-vintage wines. Vintages – 1970, 1971, 1973, 1975, 1976, 1978, 1979, 1980, 1982, 1983. Carte Verte (non-vintage) and Carte Orange (non-vintage).

Napoléon (Fr). A marque for Cognac to indicates a minimum of six years in barrels. See Napoléon Brandy.

Napoléon (Fr). On an Armagnac label indicates a minimum age of five years.

Napoléon (Fr). The alternative name for the Bicane Chasselas grape.

Napoleon (Sp). An 1830 vintage Sherry produced by Domecq in Jerez de la Frontera. 21% alc. by vol.

Napoléon Aigle d'Or (Fr). A 25–30 year old Cognac produced by Brugerolle.

Napoléon Aigle Rouge (Fr). A 10 year old Cognac produced by Brugerolle.

Napoléon Brandy (Fr). A name which doesn't denote, as is often thought, a Brandy of long age. For most Brandies it is no more than a gimmick. See Napoléon.

Napoléon Cocktail (Cktl). 1/10 measure Fernet Branca, 7/10 measure dry Gin, 1/10 measure orange Curaçao, 1/10 measure Dubonnet. Stir over ice, strain into a cocktail glass. Add a twist of lemon peel.

Napoléon III Empéreur (Fr). A fine, 1858 distilled Cognac produced by A.E. Dor in Jarnac. 37% alc. by vol.

Napolitana Pot (It). A coffee-making unit. Known as the Flip Pot or Machinetta. Two containers separated by a filter. Cold water is placed in lower container, top unit is screwed on. The unit is then placed on heat, brought to the boil then flipped over so that the hot water passes through the coffee to the bottom unit. See also Neapolitan Flip-Over Pot.

Nappo (It). The name given to a goblet, drinking cup or glass.

Napuréouli (USSR). A white, medium-dry table wine from Takhetia in the Georgia region. Also spelt Napareuli.

Naranja (Sp). Orange.

Naranjada (Sp). Orangeade.

Naranjo (El) (Sp). A noted vineyard in the Moriles area of Montilla-Moriles, southern Spain.

Narayangaon (Ind). The town where India's first sparkling wine was made. See Omar Khayyam, Marquise de Pompadour and Royal Mousseux.

Narbag (Tur). A fine white wine produced in the Anatolia region.

Narbantons (Les) (Fr). A Premier Cru vineyard in the A.C. commune of Savigny-lès-Beaune, Côte de Beaune, Burgundy.

Narciso Etiqueta Azul (Sp). A Brandy produced by Mascaró.

Nardi-Dei (It). A Chianti Putto producer based in Tuscany.

Nardini (It). The brand-name of a Grappa.

Narranga Cocktail (Cktl). ¾ measure Bourbon whiskey, ¼ measure Italian vermouth, dash Anisette. Stir over ice, strain into a cocktail glass. Top with a twist of lemon peel juice.

Narrenberg (Ger). Vineyard. (Anb) = Rheinpfalz. (Ber) = Südliche Weinstrasse. (Gro) = Kloster Liebfrauenberg. (Vil) = Winden.

Narrenberg (Ger). Vineyard. (Anb) =

Rheinpfalz. (Ber) = Südliche Weinstrasse. (Gro) = Kloster Liebfrauenberg.
(Vil) = Hergersweiler.

Narrenberg (Ger). Vineyard. (Anb) =
Rheinpfalz. (Ber) = Südliche Wein-
strasse. (Gro) = Trappenberg. (Vil) =
Römerberg.

Narrenkappe (Ger). Vineyard. (Anb) =
Nahe. (Ber) = Kreuznach. (Gro) =
Kronenberg. (Vil) = Bad Kreuznach.

Nasco (It). A white grape variety grown in
Sardinia. Produces both yellow, delicate table wines and fortified dessert
wines.

Nasco di Cagliari (It). D.O.C. white wine
from Sardinia. Made from the Nasco
grape in the province of Cagliari. 4
styles – Dolce naturale, Secco,
Liquoroso dolce naturale and
Liquoroso secco. Liquoroso dolce and
Liquoroso secco with a minimum age of
2 years in wooden casks can be
classified Riserva.

NASDM (Eng) (abbr). National Association of Soft Drink Manufacturers.

Nashoba Valley Winery (USA). A winery
based at Somerville, Massachusetts.
Produces mainly hybrid wines.

Nashville Egg Nogg (Cktl). ½ pint Brandy,
½ pint golden Rum, 1 pint Bourbon
whiskey, 9 eggs, 3 pints double cream,
½ lb. sugar. Blend together over ice,
strain into small wine goblets. Top with
grated nutmeg.

Nash Vineyard (Eng). A vineyard based at
Nash, Stoywing, Sussex. Was first
planted 1974. 0.6 ha. Grape varieties –
Madeleine angevine 10%, Müller-
Thurgau 50%, Seyve villard 20% and
others.

Nassau (Ger). Village. (Anb) = Mittelrhein. (Ber) = Rheinburgengau. (Gro) =
Lahntal. (Vin) = Schlossberg.

Nassau N°1 (Cktl). 5 parts Nassau Orange
liqueur, 1 part Rum, 2 parts lemon
juice, 1 teaspoon sugar. Shake well over
ice, strain into a cocktail glass, add a
slice of lemon.

Nassau Orange (Hol). A pale gold liqueur
with a flavour of bitter oranges. Also
known as Pimpeltjens Liqueur.

Nassau Orange Tonic (Cktl). 3 cls. Nassau
Orange Liqueur, pour over ice cubes in
a highball glass. Fill with tonic water
and garnish with a slice of lemon.

Nässjö Brewery (Swe). A small brewery
based in Nässjö, south-eastern Sweden.

Nastoika (USSR). A term used to describe
heavily-flavoured Vodkas that are
almost like liqueurs.

Nastro Azzurro (It). An Export Lager
brewed by the Peroni Brewery.

Natasha (Fr). A species of barley malt

from the Triumph variety. Gives a good
sugar yield.

Nathaniel Johnston et Fils (Fr). An old
established firm of wine négociants in
Bordeaux. Specialise in the wines of
the Graves and Médoc.

Nation (Carrie) (USA). A Kansas lady
who used to enter saloons and smash
liquor contents up to, and during the
American Prohibition period.

**National Association of Licensed House
Managers** (Eng). NALHM. The trade
union for public house and club managers. Address = 9, Coombe Lane,
London SW20 8NE. Founded in 1969.

**National Association of Soft Drink
Manufacturers** (Eng). NASDM. A body
that monitors the sales of soft drinks.
See also BSDA.

National Coffee Association of the USA
(USA). An American organisation for
the promotion and sale of coffee.
Address = 120 Wall St., New York.
NY1005.

National Distillers (Isr). A leading wine
and spirits producer based in Israel.

National Distillery (USA). A Bourbon
whiskey distillery based in Frankfort
and Louisville, Kentucky.

**National Institute for the Protection of
Denomination of Origin** (It). See the
Istituzione del Comitato Nazionale per
la Tutela delle Denominazioni di
Origine.

National Union of Licensed Vituallers
(Eng). See NULV.

Natur (Fr). A wine with no sugar added. A
natural wine.

Natural (USA). Denotes a sparkling wine
that has been made without the addition of dosage. Also spelt Naturel.

Naturally-Conditioned (Eng). A term
used to describe a beer which continues
to mature in cask or bottle. See Cask
Conditioned.

Naturally Dutch (Cktl). 1 measure Advocaat, ½ measure Cherry brandy, dash
Grenadine. Shake over ice, strain into a
flute glass. Top with Champagne. Serve
with a cherry.

**Natural Mineral Waters and Bottled
Waters Association** (Eng). NMWBWA.
Association formed to represent the
interests of packers and importers who
bottle natural mineral waters. See also
BSDA.

Naturalno (Bul). Natural (wine).

Natural Production (Eng). Denotes viniculture without the addition of
chemical insecticides or fertilizers.

Natural Sediment (Eng). The sediment
that falls from wine without the aid of a
fining agent.

Natural Wine (Eng). An unadulterated wine. Has not had anything added to alter the strength or taste.

Naturbelassen (Aus). Not sweetened (wine).

Nature (Fr). Applied to Champagne. The driest. No sweetness added. See Brut.

Naturel (Fr). When seen on a Kirsch label indicates natural distillation from cherries with no additives.

Naturel (USA). See Natural.

Nature's Wine (Eng). A nickname for water.

Naturrein (Ger). Natural and pure.

Natürsüsse (Aus). On a wine bottle label indicates that the wine has been naturally sweetened.

Naturwein (Ger). A wine with no added sugar. A natural wine.

Naturweinversteigerer (Ger). See Prädikatsweinversteigerer.

Naughty French Wine Coolers (Fr). A range of wine-based drinks (red and white) with fruit juices 5% alc. by vol. Is distributed in the U.K. by Cambrian Soft Drinks.

Nauvoo State Historic Site and Park Vineyard (USA). A winery based in Nauvoo, Illinois on the Mississippi river.

Navalle (USA). The label used by the Inglenook Winery for a range of varietal and generic table wines made from a blend of San Joaquin and Coastal grapes.

Navarra (Sp). A Denominación de Origen wine region of northern Spain, situated north-east of Rioja. Has 5 districts = Montaña, Ribera Alta, Ribera Baja, Tierraestella and Valdizarbe. The D.O. applies to red, rosé and white wines. Grapes – Garnacha, Graciano, Majaela, Malvasia, Palomino and Viura.

Navarre (Sp). An alternative spelling of Navarra.

Navarrete (Sp). A noted wine-producing village in the Rioja Alta.

Navarro Vineyards (USA). A winery based in the Anderson Valley, Mendocino County, California. Grape varieties – Cabernet sauvignon, Gewürztraminer and Johannisberg riesling. Produce varietal wines.

Navazza (Switz). A noted wine and spirit importation company founded in 1856.

Naveltje Bloot (Hol). Lit – 'Bare navel'. A liqueur on the old Dutch style produced by Van Zuylekom.

Navés (Sp). A white grape variety grown in the Rioja. Is also known as the Cagazal, Calagraño, Jaén and Jaina.

Navip (Yug). A growers' co-operative based at Serbia. The headquarters are in Belgrade. Also produces a Slivovitz of same name which is popular in Greece.

Navy Mixture (Cktl). 1 measure Rum, ½ measure lemon juice, ½ measure dry Vermouth, dash Cherry brandy. Shake over ice, strain into a cocktail glass.

Navy Rum (Eng). Old name, also known as Grog. 1 part dark Rum, 3 parts water.

Navy Rum (W.Ind). A style of dark Rum, very pungent.

Naxos (Gre). An island in the southern Aegean sea. The largest of the Cyclades Islands. Was the ancient centre for the worship of Dionysius.

Naylor Wine Cellars (USA). Based in York, Pennsylvania.

Nazionale Brauerei (Switz). An independent brewery based in Locarno-Muralto.

N.B.C. (Hol) (abbr). Nederlandse Bartenders' Club. Dutch Bartenders' Association. Address = Tollenhof 21, 4041 BH, Kestern, Holland.

N.B.F. (Nor) (abbr). Norsk Bartender Forening. Norwegian Bartenders' Association. Address = P.O. Box 2554, Solli, Oslo 2, Norway.

Ndovu Lager (Afr). A Lager beer brewed by the Tanzania Breweries in Tanzania.

Néac (Fr). A region north of Saint-Émilion producing red wines. Has now merged with the A.C. Lalande de Pomerol.

Neapolitan Flip-Over Pot (It). A method of making filter coffee. Has two pots with the coffee grounds placed between. When the water boils, pots are turned over and boiling water passes through coffee into lower pot. Also known as the Machinetta. See also Napolitana Pot.

Near Beer (Switz). A beer-style, alcohol-free Lager. Brands include Ex-Beer and Birell.

Near Beer (USA). A Beer surviving from the Prohibition days, brewed by the Pearl Brewing Co.

Near Wine (USA). Sugar and water added to grape skins and pulp etc. Fermentation is then induced, the acids and other substances remaining in the skins are released and the resulting liquid is marketed usually as Jug wine (sold by the ½ gallon or more)

Neat (Eng). A term to denote having a drink (usually spirits) without anything added.

Nebbiola (USA). A white grape variety used to produce white table wines in California.

Nebbiolo (It). A red grape of outstanding quality at its best in the Piemonte and Lombardy regions where it produces full-bodied, long-lived wines of high

N

alcohol. Name derives from the Italian word Nebbia meaning fog (because the grapes mature late and so are often gathered in foggy conditions). Is also known as Chiavennasca, Nebbiolo lampia, Nebbiolo michet, Nebbiolo rosé, Nebbiolo-spanna, Picoutener, Picutener, Pugnet, Spanna and Spauna.

Nebbiolo (Switz). A smooth, fruity, red wine from the Ticino region.

Nebbiolo d'Alba (It). D.O.C. red wine from the Piemonte region. Made from the Nebbiolo grape grown in the communes of Alba and Cuneo. Must be aged 1 year. D.O.C. also applies to the sparkling wine obtained from grapes grown within the defined area. See Roero.

Nebbiolo Lampia (It). A local name used for the Nebbiolo grape in the Barbaresco district of Piemonte. A sub-variety of the Nebbiolo.

Nebbiolo Michet (It). A local name used for the Nebbiolo grape in the Barbaresco district of Piemonte. A sub-variety of the Nebbiolo grape.

Nebbiolo Rosé (It). A local name for the Nebbiolo grape in the Barbaresco district of Piemonte. A sub-variety of the Nebbiolo grape.

Nebbiolo-Spanna (It). An alternative name for the Nebbiolo grape in the Piemonte region.

Nebbiolo Spumante (It). A red sparkling wine made from the Nebbiolo grape in the Piemonte region.

Nebiker (Switz). An Eau-de-vie distillery based in Sissach, northern Switzerland. Produces a Kirsch under the General Sutter label.

Nebuchadnezzar (Fr). A large bottle used in Champagne. Equivalent of 20 standard bottles. Rarely used now. The largest of the wine bottles. See also the Mega Bottle and Champagne Bottle Sizes.

Neckarberg (Ger). Vineyard. (Anb) = Württemberg. (Ber) = Württembergisch Unterland. (Gro) = Schalkstein. (Vil) = Besigheim.

Neckarberg (Ger). Vineyard. (Anb) = Württemberg. (Ber) = Württembergisch Unterland. (Gro) = Schalkstein. (Vil) = Bietigheim.

Neckarberg (Ger). Vineyard. (Anb) = Württemberg. (Ber) = Württembergisch Unterland. (Gro) = Schalkstein. (Vil) = Bissingen.

Neckarberg (Ger). Vineyard. (Anb) = Württemberg. (Ber) = Württembergisch Unterland. (Gro) = Schalkstein. (Vil) = Gemmrigheim.

Neckarberg (Ger). Vineyard. (Anb) =

Württemberg. (Ber) = Württembergisch Unterland. (Gro) = Schalkstein. (Vil) = Löchgau.

Neckarberg (Ger). Vineyard. (Anb) = Württemberg. (Ber) = Württembergisch Unterland. (Gro) = Schalkstein. (Vil) = Walheim.

Neckarhälde (Ger). Vineyard. (Anb) = Württemberg. (Ber) = Württembergisch Unterland. (Gro) = Schalkstein. (Vil) = Affalterbach.

Neckarhälde (Ger). Vineyard. (Anb) = Württemberg. (Ber) = Württembergisch Unterland. (Gro) = Schalkstein. (Vil) = Bietigheim.

Neckarhälde (Ger). Vineyard. (Anb) = Württemberg. (Ber) = Württembergisch Unterland. (Gro) = Schalkstein. (Vil) = Benningen.

Neckarhälde (Ger). Vineyard. (Anb) = Württemberg. (Ber) = Württembergisch Unterland. (Gro) = Schalkstein. (Vil) = Erdmannhausen.

Neckarhälde (Ger). Vineyard. (Anb) = Württemberg. (Ber) = Württembergisch Unterland. (Gro) = Schalkstein. (Vil) = Ludwigsburg (ortsteil Hoheneck).

Neckarhälde (Ger). Vineyard. (Anb) = Württemberg. (Ber) = Württembergisch Unterland. (Gro) = Schalkstein. (Vil) = Marbach.

Neckarhälde (Ger). Vineyard. (Anb) = Württemberg. (Ber) = Württembergisch Unterland. (Gro) = Schalkstein. (Vil) = Murr.

Neckarhälde (Ger). Vineyard. (Anb) = Württemberg. (Ber) = Württembergisch Unterland. (Gro) = Schalkstein. (Vil) = Neckarweihingen.

Neckarhälde (Ger). Vineyard. (Anb) = Württemberg. (Ber) = Württembergisch Unterland. (Gro) = Schalkstein. (Vil) = Poppenweiler.

Neckarmühlbach (Ger). Village. (Anb) = Baden. (Ber) = Badische Bergstrasse/ Kraichgau. (Gro) = Stiftsberg. (Vin) = Hohberg.

Neckar [River] (Ger). A tributary of the river Rhine. Runs through the Württemberg Anbaugebiet.

Neckarsulm (Ger). Village. (Anb) = Württemberg. (Ber) = Württembergisch Unterland. (Gro) = Staufenberg. (Vin) = Scheuerberg.

Neckarweihingen (Ger). Village. (Anb) = Württemberg. (Ber) = Württembergisch Unterland. (Gro) = Schalkstein. (Vin) = Neckarhälde.

Neckarwein (Ger). The name given to wines produced around the river Neckar in the Württemberg Anbaugebiet.

Neckarwestheim (Ger). Village. (Anb) =

Württemberg. (Ber) = Württembergisch Unterland. (Gro) = Kirchenweinberg. (Vin) = Herrlesberg.

Neckarzimmern (Ger). Village. (Anb) = Baden. (Ber) = Badische Bergstrasse/ Kraichgau. (Gro) = Stiftsberg. (Vins) = Götzhalde, Kirchweinberg, Wallmauer.

Neckenmarkt (Aus). A wine-producing area in the Mattersburg district.

Nectar (Gre). The wine of the Greek Gods on Mount Olympus in Ancient Greece.

Nectar (Gre). A Muscat dessert wine produced by a co-operative winery on the island of Samos.

Nectar Cream (Sp). A full-flavoured, rich Oloroso sherry produced by Gonzalez Byass in Jerez de la Frontera.

Nectar des Dieux (Fr). Lit – 'Nectar of the Gods'. The designation King Louis XIV gave to the wines of Saint-Émilion.

Ned Belcher's Bitter (Eng). A Bitter beer 1040 O.G. brewed by the Priory Brewery in Nottinghamshire.

Nederburg 'Auction' Wines (S.Afr). Varietal wines sold at the annual Nederburg wine auction of the Nederburg Estate. Instituted by the S.F.W.

Nederburg Estate (S.Afr). A large estate in Paarl. Address = Ernst le Roux, Nederburg, P.O. Box 46, Paarl 7645. Produces a vast range of famous wines including – 'Private bin' and 'Auction' wines, Baronne, Edelrood, Edeltropfen, Fonternel, Kap Sekt and varietals. Operated by the SFW.

Nederburg 'Private Bin' Wines (S.Afr). Specially selected blended wines sold at the annual Nederburg wine auctions of the Nederburg estate. Made by Günter Brözel. e.g. Private Bin S312; the S = sweet, a D = dry and an R = red.

Nederlandse Bartenders Club (Hol). N.B.C. Holland's Bartenders' Association. Address = Tollenhof 21, 4041 BH, Kestern, Holland.

Ned Kelly (Austr). The brand-name of an Australian whiskey.

Neef (Ger). Village. (Anb) = Mosel-Saar-Ruwer. (Ber) = Zell/Mosel. (Gro) = Grafschaft. (Vins) = Frauenberg, Petersberg, Rosenberg.

Neerslag (Hol). Sediment.

Neethlingshof Estate (S.Afr). Based in Stellenbosch. Address = P.O. Box 25, Vlottenburg 7604. Produces mainly varietal wines.

Nefeli (Cyp). A dry white wine produced by the Keo company, Limassol.

Negev (Isr). A newly planted wine-producing region in southern Israel that is noted for its fine white wines.

Négociant (Fr). A wine shipper-merchant. One who buys the wines off the producer and then sells them either in bulk or bottle.

Négociant-Distributeur (Fr). In Burgundy, a négociant who acts as an intermediate for the sale of bottles of wine for a vineyard.

Négociant-Éleveur (Fr). A merchant and grower. One who makes wine and then sells it.

Négociant Manipulant (Fr). Found on a Champagne wine label, denotes the actual maker. See N.M.

Negoska (Gre). A red wine used in the production of Goumenissa wine.

Negoziante (It). Merchant, shipper. (Fr) = Négociant.

Negralejo (Sp). A black Riojan grape variety also known as the Mechín, Monastel, Monastrel, Moraster and Valcarcelia. Also grown in Aragón, Catalonia and Penedés.

Negramaro (It). Another spelling of the red grape Negroamaro.

Negra Mole (Port). A black grape variety grown in the Algarve.

Negrara (It). A red grape variety used in the making of Valpolicella and Bardolino.

Negrara Gattinara (USA). A white grape variety grown in California to make white table wines.

Negrara Trentina (It). A red grape variety.

Negrette (Fr). A red grape variety grown in southern France between the Garonne and Tarn Départements. Produces full-bodied and alcoholic wines.

Negri (It). A wine producer based in Moniga del Garda near Verona.

Negri (It). A fine producer of Valtellina D.O.C. and Sfursat wines in Lombardy.

Negri (USSR). The Russian name for the Malbec grape.

Negri de Purkar (USSR). A light, slightly sweet and scented red wine of Moldavia. Has a taste and scent of blackcurrants. Made from the Cabernet, Rara-Njagra and Sapanis grapes.

Negrita (W.Ind). The brand-name of a dark Rum produced on the island of Martinique. Produced by Bardinet in north-west Martinique.

Negroamaro (It). A red grape variety grown in the Puglia region. Also spelt Negro Amaro and Negramaro. Is the principal black grape of the region.

Négron (Fr). A red grape variety also known as the Mourvèdre.

Negroni (Cktl). ⅓ measure Gin, ⅓ measure sweet Vermouth, ⅓ measure Campari. Shake well with ice, strain into a cocktail glass. Add a twist of lemon.

Negru de Purkar (USSR). A red grape variety.

Negru de Purkar (USSR). A dry, fruity, red

wine from the grape of same name produced in Moldavia.

Negus (Cktl). 1 bottle Sherry, 2 pints boiling water, 2½ fl.ozs. Brandy, sugar, nutmeg, 1 lemon. Warm the wine in a pan, add sliced lemon, water. Finally add Brandy and grated nutmeg. Makes 18 glasses. Port can be used in place of Sherry. The drink is named after Colonel Francis Negus, its inventor in the eighteenth century.

Nehren (Ger). Village. (Anb) = Mosel-Saar-Ruwer. (Ber) = Zell/Mosel. (Gro) = Grafschaft. (Vin) = Römerberg.

Neipperg (Ger). Village. (Anb) = Württemberg. (Ber) = Württembergisch Unterland. (Gro) = Heuchelberg. (Vins) = Grafenberg, Schlossberg, Steingrube, Vogelsang.

Neive (It). A commune in Barbaresco.

Nelas (Port). A noted co-operative based in the Dão region.

Nello Stabilimento (It). On a label denotes – 'at the producer's premises'.

Nel'Origine (It). Estate bottled.

Nelson (N.Z.). A wine-producing area on the north coast of the South Island.

Nelson (Sp). A rare, fine, old, Palo Cortado sherry produced by Domecq in Jerez de la Frontera.

Nelson Decanter (Eng). Similar in style to a Royal decanter but with only one ring around the neck. c1820.

Nelson's Blood (Eng). A term used for dark Rum.

Nemea (Gre). A dry red table wine from Peloponnese. Made from the Agriorgitako grape.

Nemes Kadar (Hun). An unusual rosé wine with a garnet colour made from the Kardarka grape. Has good body and sweetness.

Nepente di Oliena (It). This can appear on the label of Cannonau di Sardegna if grapes used for the wine are produced in Oliena.

Nephritis (Lat). A disease of the kidneys caused through chronic alcoholism.

Neptun Brewery (Den). A brewery based in North Jutland. Owned by the United Breweries.

Nera (It). A fine producer of Valtellina D.O.C. and Sforzato wines in Lombardy.

Nerello (It). A red grape variety grown in Sicily and Calabria. See Nerello Mascalese and Nerello Mantellata.

Nerello Cappuccio (It). The local name (Etna district) for the Nerello Mantellata grape in Sicily.

Nerello Mantellata (It). A red grape variety grown in Sicily.

Nerello Mascalese (It). A red grape variety grown in Sicily.

Nero (It). A black or deep red wine.

Nero Buono di Cori (It). A red grape variety grown in the Latium.

Nero d'Avola (It). A red grape variety grown in Sicily. Also known as the Calabrese.

Néron Distillery (W.Ind). A Rum distillery based in Guadeloupe.

Nertert (Lux). A wine village on the river Moselle. Vineyard sites are Syrberg, Herrenberg.

Nerthe (La) (Fr). Part of the Châteauneuf-du-Pape area in the southern Rhône.

Nerthe (Marquis de) (Fr). A wine maker of the nineteenth century who gave the name to Châteauneuf-du-Pape (originally until 1850 was known as Châteauneuf Calcernier).

Nerveux (Fr). A strong full-bodied wine.

Nervig (Ger). A good, full-bodied wine.

Nervo Winery (USA). A small winery based in the Russian River Valley, California. Produces varietal wines.

Nescafé (Eng). The brand-name used by Nestlé Foodservice for a range of instant coffees. The top-selling U.K. brand.

Nesher Lager (Isr). A Lager beer 10° Balling brewed by a Canadian-financed brewery.

Nesle-le-Repons (Fr). A Cru Champagne village in the Canton de Dormans. District = Épernay.

Nesselried (Ger). Village. (Anb) = Baden. (Ber) = Ortenau. (Gro) = Fürsteneck. (Vins) = Renchtäler, Schlossberg.

Nestlé Foodservice (Eng). Address = St. George's House, Croydon, Surrey CR9 1NR. A famous coffee-producing company. Brands include Blend 37, Gold Blend, Nescafé and Santa Rica. Also markets Ashbourne Mineral Water.

Nes-Ziona (Isr). A viticultural centre of Israel which produces most styles of wines.

Netherlands (Cktl). 1 oz. Brandy, ½ oz. Cointreau, dash Orange bitters. Stir with ice, strain into a cocktail glass.

Netherlands Wijnmuseum (Hol). A wine museum based at Velperweg 23, 6824 BC Arnhem. Has a comprehensive range of wine artefacts from the family firm of Robbers en Van den Hoogen B.V.

Neto Costa (Port). A noted wine-producer in the Bairrada region. Produces fine still and sparkling wines. Also brandies.

Neu-Bamberg (Ger). Village. (Anb) = Rheinhessen. (Ber) = Bingen. (Gro) = Rheingrafenstein. (Vins) = Eichelberg, Heerkretz, Kirschwingert, Kletterberg.

Neuberg (Ger). Vineyard. (Anb) = Rheinhessen. (Ber) = Wonnegau. (Gro) = Gotteshilfe. (Vil) = Osthofen.

Neuberg (Ger). Vineyard. (Anb) =

N

Rheinpfalz. (Ber) = Mittelhaardt-Deutsche Weinstrasse. (Gro) = Hofstück. (Vil) = Meckenheim.

Neuberg (Ger). Vineyard. (Anb) = Rheinpfalz. (Ber) = Südliche Weinstrasse. (Gro) = Trappenberg. (Vil) = Bornheim.

Neuberger (Aus). A white grape variety grown in the Burgenland, Krems and Langenlois.

Neuberger Sylvaner (Czec). A white grape variety.

Neuchâtel (Switz). A wine area which produces good white wines. Also famous for its Cortaillod Oeil de Perdrix (pink wine). Grape varieties – Chasselas and Pinot noir.

Neudenau (Ger). Village. (Anb) = Baden. (Ber) = Badische Bergstrasse/Kraichgau. (Gro) = Stiftsberg. (Vin) = Berg.

Neudorf (N.Z.). Small winery near Blenheim at Upper Moutere, Nelson. 4 ha. Produces varietal wines.

Neuenbürg (Ger). See Kraichtal.

Neuerl (Aus). Denotes a taste of cask. A woody taste. Results from wood resin.

Neuershausen (Ger). Village. (Anb) = Baden. (Ber) = Kaiserstuhl-Tuniberg (Gro) = Vulkanfelsen. (Vin) = Steingrube.

Neuffen (Ger). Village. (Anb) = Württemberg. (Ber) = Remstal-Stuttgart. (Gro) = Hohennenffen. (Vin) = Schlossteige.

Neuholz (Ger). Village. (Anb) = Württemberg. (Ber) = Württembergisch Unterland. (Gro) = Lindelberg. See Harsberg.

Neuillac (Fr). A commune in the Charente-Maritime Département whose grapes are classed Petite Champagne (Cognac).

Neuleiningen (Ger). Village. (Anb) = Rheinpfalz. (Ber) = Mittelhaardt-Deutsche Weinstrasse. (Gro) = Höllenpfad. (Vins) = Feuermännchen, Schlossberg, Sonnenberg.

Neulles (Fr). A commune in the Charente-Maritime Département whose grapes are classed Petite Champagne (Cognac).

Neumagen-Dhron (Ger). Village. (Anb) = Mosel-Saar-Ruwer. (Ber) = Bernkastel. (Gro) = Michelsberg. (Vins) = Engelgrube, Grafenberg, Grosser Hengelberg, Hofberger, Laudamusberg, Rosengärtchen, Roterd, Sonnenuhr.

Neuritis (Eng). A disease of the nervous system caused through chronic alcoholism.

Neusatz (Ger). Village. (Anb) = Baden. See Bühl.

Neuses (Ger). Village. (Anb) = Franken. (Ber) = Maindreieck. (Gro) = Kirchberg. (Vin) = Glatzen.

Neusetz (Ger). Village. (Anb) = Franken.

(Ber) = Maindreieck. (Gro) = Kirchberg. (Vins) = Assorted parts of vineyards.

Neusiedlersee (Aus). A wine region of eastern Burgenland. Is also known as Seewinkel.

Neustadt (Ger). Village. (Anb) = Württemberg. (Ber) = Remstal-Stuttgart. (Gro) = Kopf. (Vin) = Söhrenberg.

Neustadt an der Weinstrasse (Ger). Village. (Anb) = Rheinpfalz. (Ber) = Mittelhaardt-Deutsche Weinstrasse. (Gro) = Meerspinne. (Vin) = Mönchgarten.

Neustadt an der Weinstrasse (Ger). Village. (Anb) = Rheinpfalz. (Ber) = Mittelhaardt-Deutsche Weinstrasse. (Gro) = Rebstöckel. (Vins) = Erkenbrecht, Grain.

Neutral (Eng). A term that describes a wine as having virtually no positive flavour. Often denotes that the wine is blended.

Neutral Brandy (Eng). A Brandy (wine distillate) distilled to 100% alc. by vol. Has no characteristics. Rectified, produced in a Patent still.

Neutral Grain Spirit (Eng). Alcohol produced from cereals, has no flavour. Rectified, produced in a Patent still.

Neutral Spirits (USA). Spirits that are pure and have no flavour. Made from potatoes, grain etc. 190° US proof. (95% alc. by vol).

Neutral Vodka (Eng). Distilled from grain or molasses, rectified, filtered and diluted to required strength.

Neuville (Switz). A wine village in the Berne canton.

Neuville-aux-Larris (La) (Fr). A Cru Champagne village in the Canton de Châtillons-sur-Marne. District = Reims.

Neuville-sur-Seine (Fr). A Cru Champage village in the Canton de l'Aube. District = Château Thierry.

Neuweier (Ger). Village. (Anb) = Baden. (Ber) = Ortenau. (Gro) = Schloss Rodeck. (Vins) = Altenberg, Gänsberg, Heiligenstein, Mauerberg, Schlossberg.

Neuweiler's Cream Ale (USA). A light Malt beer brewed by the Ortlieb Brewery in Philadelphia.

Neuwies (Ger). Vineyard. (Anb) = Mosel-Saar-Ruwer. (Ber) = Saar-Ruwer. (Gro) = Scharzberg. (Vil) = Ockfen.

Nevada Cocktail (Cktl). $\frac{1}{3}$ measure dark Rum, $\frac{1}{3}$ measure lime juice, $\frac{1}{3}$ measure grapefruit juice, $\frac{1}{6}$ measure Gomme syrup. Shake over ice, strain into a cocktail glass.

Nevards Vineyard (Eng). A vineyard

704

N

based at Boxted, Colchester, Essex. Was first planted in 1977. 0.45 ha. Grape varieties – Huxelrebe and Reichensteiner.

Nevers Oak (Fr). French oak used for wine casks in Burgundy.

Nevins Cocktail (Cktl). ½ measure Bourbon whiskey, ½ measure Apricot brandy, ¼ fl.oz. grapefruit juice, ½ fl.oz. lemon juice, dash Angostura. Shake over ice, strain into a cocktail glass.

Nevşehir-Kayseri-Nigde (Tur). A red and white wine-producing vineyard based in the Middle Anatolia region.

New Albion Brewery (USA). A brewery based in Sonoma, California. Is noted for its top-fermented ales at 5.2% alc. by vol.

New Brunswick (Can). A small wine-producing-region based in southeastern Canada.

Newcastle (Eng). A brewery that is part of the Scottish and Newcastle Breweries. Brews cask conditioned/keg Exhibition 1042 O.G. keg IPA 1032 O.G. and bottled Amber 1033 O.G. Brown 1045 O.G.

Newcastle Brown Ale (Eng). A famous Bitter beer 1045 O.G. brewed by the Scottish and Newcastle Breweries. Not a Brown ale. Sold in clear-glass beer bottles. Also canned. First brewed in 1927.

New England Rum (USA). A term given to American Rum of the eighteenth century shipped to Europe and Africa. Made from Indian molasses. Now no longer recognised.

New Fashion Cocktail (Cktl). ⅔ measure dry Sherry, ⅙ measure Grand Marnier, ⅙ measure Cognac, dash Angostura. Shake over ice, strain into a cocktail glass, add a pineapple cube.

New Fashioned Cocktail (Cktl). 1¼ measures Cognac, dash Angostura, sugar cube. Place in an old-fashioned glass with ice. Add a dash of soda, slice of orange and lemon.

New Fermor Arms (Eng). A home-brew public house in Rufford, Lancashire noted for its cask conditioned Blezards Bitter 1039 O.G.

New Forest Brewery (Eng). Opened in 1980 in Cadnam, Hampshire. Brews cask conditioned New Forest Real Ale 1036 O.G. keg Forest Lager 1038 O.G. King's Wood 1039 O.G. Woodsman Mild 1034 O.G. and Old Evel 1048 O.G.

New Hall (Eng). Vineyard. Address = Chelmsford Road, Purleigh, Chelmsford, Essex. 12.5 ha. Soil – heavy London clay. Grape varieties –

Huxelrebe, Müller-Thurgau, Pinot noir, Reichensteiner, Ruländer and Würtzburger perle.

New Inn (Eng). A home-brew public house owned by Tetley in Harrogate, Yorkshire. Noted for its cask conditioned Gate Ale 1045 O.G.

New Jersey (USA). A wine district of the Eastern states. Vines are grown around Egg Harbor near Atlantic City.

Newman Brewery (USA). A brewery opened in 1981 in Albany, New York. Brews a naturally conditioned draught beer called Newman's Pale Ale.

New Orleans Buck (Cktl). ¾ measure white Rum, ¼ measure orange juice, 4 dashes lemon juice. Stir over ice in a highball glass. Top with ginger ale.

New Orleans Fizz (Cktl). 1 large measure Gin, ½ fl.oz. lime juice, ½ fl.oz. lemon juice, 3 dashes Orange flower water, 2 dashes Gomme syrup, 1 dessertspoon cream. Shake well over ice, strain into a highball glass containing ice, top with soda water. Serve with a muddler and straws.

New Orleans Gin Fizz (Cktl). 1½ measures dry Gin, 1½ measures cream, 1 teaspoon sugar, juice ½ lemon, 1 teaspoon Kirsch, ½ egg white. Shake over ice, strain into a highball glass, top with soda water. Serve with straws.

New South Wales (Austr). A wine state. Best areas – Hunter Valley, Mudgee, Murrumbidgee Irrigation Area and Riverina.

New Special Draught (Austr). A golden-coloured, Lager-type beer brewed by Toohey's Brewery in New South Wales.

Newton and Ridley (Eng). A fictitious brewery name used for the television series Coronation Street (Granada T.V.).

Newton's Ale (Eng). A keg Bitter 1032 O.G. brewed by the Devenish Brewery, Weymouth, Dorset.

Newton's Ale (Eng). A keg Bitter 1032 O.G. brewed by the Wilson's Brewery, Manchester.

New Yarmouth Distillery (W.Ind). A Rum distillery based on the island of Jamaica. Produces dark Rums.

New York (USA). A wine region of Eastern America. Contains the Five Finger Lakes, Westfield-Fredonia, Lake Erie, Hudson Valley, Highland in Sullivan County, Chautauqua, Niagara County.

New York Cocktail (Cktl). As for New York Cooler.

New York Cooler (Cktl). ½ gill Canadian Club Whisky, ¼ gill lemon juice, 3 dashes Grenadine. Stir well with ice in a highball glass. Fill up with soda water, stir, serve with a dash of lemon peel juice and a slice of lemon.

New York Market (Mad). The old name given to a style of Madeira that was shipped to the USA.

New York Seltzer (USA). See Original New York Seltzer.

New York Sour (Cktl). 2 fl.ozs. Bourbon whiskey, juice ½ lemon, teaspoon powdered sugar. Shake over ice, strain into a sour glass. Float ½ fl.oz. Claret wine on top, add a cherry and slice of lemon.

New Zealand (N.Z.). Country producing mainly white and fortified wines. Main regions on North Island (Auckland, Gisborne, Hawkes Bay and Waikato). On the South Island, only Marlborough produces any amount of wine. Climate is akin to Germany.

New Zealand Breweries (N.Z.). A large brewing concern that has many plants (based in Wellington). Brews Lion beers and Steinlager.

New Zealand Nouveau (N.Z.). The first wine of the new vintage (March-April) which is shipped to U.K.

New Zealand Viticultural Association (N.Z.). An organisation now no longer in existence.

Neyret (It). A red grape variety.

Nez du Vin (Le) (Fr). A patented cabinet with 54 phials of 'aromas' plus reference cards of the bouquets found in wines.

Nezhinskaya Ryafina (USSR). A liqueur made from rowanberries and spirit.

Ngatarawa Winery (N.Z.). A winery based at Bridge Pa, Hawkes Bay, North Island. 10.5 ha. Grape varieties – Cabernet sauvignon, Chardonnay, Merlot, Rhine riesling and Sauvignon blanc. Produce varietal and table wines.

Niagara (USA). A white grape variety. One of the first hybrids. A cross between Concord and Labrusca. Can withstand very cold winters. Used for still white wines.

Niagara (USA). A wine region of Eastern America between Lake Erie and Ontario on both sides of the river. Produces good quality wines.

Niagara (Le) (Fr). An early nineteenth-century inventor who invented a metallic tower, 70 feet in height, with copper rods on top to try and stop hailstorms.

Niagara Falls (Can). A wine region of Eastern Canada.

Niagara Wine Cellars (USA). A winery based in Lewiston, Niagara, eastern America. Produces American native wines.

Nib (Eng). The edible part of the cocoa

bean after the shell has been removed from which the cocoa is obtained.

Nicaragua (C.Am). A country in central America that produces coffee beans for blending (mainly Robustas).

Nicasio Winery (USA). A winery based in Santa Cruz, California. Produces varietal wines.

Nichelini Vineyards (USA). A winery based near Rutherford, Napa Valley, California. Grape varieties – Cabernet sauvignon and Zinfandel. Produces varietal wines.

Nicholas Cocktail (Cktl). ½ measure Sloe gin, ½ measure Orange gin. Shake over ice, strain into a cocktail glass.

Nicholas [Ets] (Fr). Paris-based wine wholesalers and retailing merchants.

Nicholoff Red Vodka (Eng). A British-made, red-coloured spirit with a base of Dutch vodka. 40% alc. by vol.

Nichols (Austin) Distilling Co (USA). A noted distillery based in Kentucky. Noted for its 8 year old Wild Turkey Bourbon. 53% alc. by vol.

Nicholson Distillery (Eng). A noted distillery based in London. Produces a fine range of Gins and Vodka. Gin sold under the Lamplighter label. J.& W. Nicholson & Co. Ltd.

Nick's Own Cocktail (Cktl). ¼ gill Cognac, ¼ gill Italian vermouth, 1 dash Angostura, 1 dash Absinthe. Stir well over ice, strain into a cocktail glass, add a cherry and lemon peel juice on top.

Nicolasha (Cktl). 1 measure Brandy in a 5 oz. goblet. Place a slice of peeled lemon on rim of glass. Sprinkle liberally with powdered sugar and finely ground coffee. To drink – place lemon with the coating on in mouth and drink brandy through it.

Nicolauswein (Ger). A wine made from grapes gathered on Saint Nicholas day. (6th December).

Nicoreşti (Rum). A wine area which produces good red wines. See Băbeasçă.

Nicotinic Acid (Eng). A vitamin found in wine.

Niebaum-Coppola Estates (USA). A winery based in Rutherford, Napa Valley, California. 67 ha. Grape varieties – Cabernet sauvignon and Chardonnay. Produces varietal wines.

Nieder-Alteich (Aus). A monastery that also owns vineyards near Krems.

Niederberg (Ger). Vineyard. (Anb) = Mosel-Saar-Ruwer. (Ber) = Bernkastel. (Gro) = Michelsberg. (Vil) = Rivenich.

Niederberg-Helden (Ger). Vineyard. (Anb) = Mosel-Saar-Ruwer. (Ber) = Bernkastel. (Gro) = Beerenlay. (Vil) = Lieser.

N

Niederburg (Ger). Village. (Anb) = Mittelrhein. (Ber) = Rheinburgengau. (Gro) = Schloss Schönburg. (Vins) = Bienenberg, Rheingoldberg.

Niederdollendorf (Ger). Village. (Anb) = Mittelrhein. (Ber) = Siebengebirge. (Gro) = Petersberg. (Vins) = Goldfusschen, Longenburgerberg, Heisterberg.

Niedereggenen (Ger). Village. (Anb) = Baden. (Ber) = Markgräflerland. (Gro) = Burg Neuenfels. (Vins) = Röthen, Sonnenstück.

Niederfell (Ger). Village. (Anb) = Mosel-Saar-Ruwer. (Ber) = Zell/Mosel. (Gro) = Weinhex. (Vins) = Fächern, Goldlay, Kahllay.

Niederhausen an der Nahe (Ger). Village. (Anb) = Nahe. (Ber) = Schloss Böckelheim. (Gro) = Burgweg. (Vins) = Felsensteyer, Hermannsberg, Hermannshöhle, Kertz, Klamm, Pfaffenstein, Pflingstweide, Rosenberg, Rosenheck, Steinberg, Steinwingert, Stollenberg.

Niederhausen an der Nahe (Ger). Village. (Anb) = Nahe. (Ber) = Schloss Böckelheim. (Gro) = Paradiesgarten. (Vin) = Graukatz.

Niederheimbach (Ger). Village. (Anb) = Mittelrhein. (Ber) = Bacharach. (Gro) = Schloss Reichenstein. (Vins) = Froher Weingarten, Reiferslay, Schloss Hohneck, Soonecker Schlossberg.

Nieder-Hilbersheim (Ger). Village. (Anb) = Rheinhessen. (Ber) = Bingen. (Gro) = Abtey. (Vins) = Honigberg, Steinacker.

Niederhofen (Ger). Village. (Anb) = Württemberg. (Ber) = Württembergisch Unterland. (Gro) = Heuchelberg. (Vins) = Grafenberg, Vogelsang.

Niederhorbach (Ger). Village. (Anb) = Rheinpfalz. (Ber) = Südliche Weinstrasse. (Gro) = Kloster Liebfrauenberg. (Vin) = Silberberg.

Niederkirchen (Ger). Village. (Anb) = Rheinpfalz. (Ber) = Mittelhaardt-Deutsche Weinstrasse. (Gro) = Hofstück. (Vins) = Klostergarten, Osterbrunnen, Schlossberg.

Niedermayr (Josef) (It). A noted small winery based in Jesuheimstr, Südtirol.

Niedermoschel (Ger). Village. (Anb) = Nahe. (Ber) = Schloss Böckelheim. (Gro) = Paradiesgarten. (Vins) = Geissenkopf, Hahnhölle, Layenberg, Silberberg.

Niedernhall (Ger). Village. (Anb) = Württemberg. (Ber) = Kocher-Jagst-Tauber. (Gro) = Kocherberg. (Vins) = Burgstall, Engweg, Hoher Berg.

Nieder-Olm (Ger). Village. (Anb) = Rheinhessen. (Ber) = Nierstein. (Gro) = Gutes Domtal. (Vins) = Goldberg, Klosterberg, Sonnenberg.

Niederösterreich (Aus). Lower Austria. A wine region in the north of the country that produces most of its wines. Districts of Falkenstein, Gumpoldskirchen, Klosterneuberg, Krems, Langenlois, Retz, Voslau and Wachau.

Niederotterbach (Ger). Village. (Anb) = Rheinpfalz. (Ber) = Südliche Weinstrasse. (Gro) = Guttenberg. (Vin) = Eselsbuckel.

Niederrimsingen (Ger). Village. (Anb) = Baden. (Ber) = Kaiserstuhl-Tuniberg. (Gro) = Attilafelsen. (Vin) = Rotgrund.

Niederschopfheim (Ger). Village. (Anb) = Baden. (Ber) = Ortenau. (Gro) = Fürsteneck. (Vin) = Kinzigtäler.

Niederstetten (Ger). Village. (Anb) = Württemberg. (Ber) = Kocher-Jagst-Tauber. (Gro) = Tauberberg. (Vin) = Schafsteige.

Niederwalluf (Ger). Village. (Anb) = Rheingau. (Ber) = Johannisberg. (Gro) = Steinmacher. (Vins) = Berg Bildstock, Oberberg, Walkenberg.

Niederweiler (Ger). Village. (Anb) = Baden. (Ber) = Markgräflerland. (Gro) = Burg Neuenfels. (Vin) = Römerberg.

Nieder-Weisen (Ger). Village. (Anb) = Rheinhessen. (Ber) = Bingen. (Gro) = Adelberg. (Vin) = Wingertsberg.

Niefernheim (Ger). Village. (Anb) = Rheinpfalz. (Ber) = Mittelhaardt-Deutsche Weinstrasse. (Gro) = Schnepfenflug vom Kellertal. (Vins) = Königsweg, Kreuzberg.

Niehaus (Dr. Charles) (S.Afr). Discovered the indigenous flor yeast in the Cape vineyards in 1935.

Nielka Cocktail (Cktl). ¾ measure Vodka, ¼ measure French vermouth, ½ measure orange juice. Stir over ice, strain into a cocktail glass.

Nielluccio (Fr). A local red grape variety grown in Corsica.

Niepoort (Port). Vintage Port shippers. Vintages – 1927–1945, 1970, 1977, 1980, 1982.

Nierstein (Ger). Bereich. (Anb) = Rheinhessen. (Gros) = Auflangen, Domherr, Güldenmorgen, Gutes Domtal, Krötenbrunnen, Petersberg, Rehbach, Rheinblick, Sankt Alban, Spiegelberg, Vogelgärten.

Nierstein (Ger). Village. (Anb) = Rheinhessen. (Ber) = Nierstein. (Gro) = Auflangen. (Vins) = Bergkirche, Glöck, Heiligenbaum, Kranzberg, Ölberg, Orbel, Schloss Schwabsburg, Zehnmorgen.

Nierstein (Ger). Village. (Anb) = Rheinhessen. (Ber) = Nierstein. (Gro) = Gutes Domtal. (Vin) = Pfaffenkappe.

Nierstein (Ger). Village. (Anb) = Rheinhessen. (Ber) = Nierstein. (Gro) = Rehberg. (Vins) = Brudersberg, Goldene Luft, Hipping, Pettenthal.

Nierstein (Ger). Village. (Anb) = Rheinhessen. (Ber) = Nierstein. (Gro) = Spiegelberg. (Vins) = Bildstock, Brückchen, Ebersberg, Findling, Hölle, Kirchplatte, Klostergarten, Paterberg, Rosenberg, Schloss Hohenrechen.

Niersteiner Domtal (Ger). An old Germanic name now no longer allowed. Now known as Niersteiner Gutes Domtal.

Niersteiner Gutes Domtal (Ger). The name for wine from the Grosslagen of Gutes Domtal in the Bereich of Nierstein.

Nieschen (Ger). Vineyard. (Anb) = Mosel-Saar-Ruwer. (Ber) = Saar-Ruwer. (Gro) = Römerlay. (Vil) = Kasel.

Nietvoorbij (S.Afr). See South African Viticultural and Oenological Research Institute. V.O.R.I.

Nièvre (Fr). A Vins de Pays area in the Nièvre Département, central France. Produces red, rosé and dry white wines.

Nig (Eng). The Victorian name for the metal tag around glass decanter necks. (Bottle ticket).

Nig (USA). Negro slang for Gin.

Nigerian Breweries Limited (Afr). A noted brewery based in Nigeria which produces Star and Gulder Lagers at 1047 O.G.

Night Cap (Eng). A pre-bedtime drink. May be either hot or cold, alcoholic or not.

Night Cap (Cktl).(1). 2 fl.ozs. Jamaican rum, 2 dashes Gomme syrup. Place into a mug, top with warm milk and nutmeg.

Night Cap (Cktl).(2). Heat 1 pint Light Ale, 2 teaspoons cocoa powder and 3 fl.ozs. Scotch whisky slowly until nearly boiling. Pour slowly over 3 egg yolks (beaten with 4 teaspoons sugar). Stir, serve in mugs with a pinch of cinnamon.

Night Cap (Cktl).(3). Heat a bottle of red wine with a thickly-sliced lemon, 3 cloves, cinnamon stick and sugar to taste. Strain and serve very hot in mugs.

Night Cap Cocktail (Cktl). ⅓ measure Cognac, ⅓ measure Grand Marnier, ⅓ measure Anisette, yolk of an egg. Shake well over ice, strain into a cocktail glass.

Night Cap Flip (Cktl). ¼ gill Brandy, ¼ gill Anisette, ¼ gill Curaçao, yolk of egg. Shake well over ice, strain into a cocktail glass.

Night Light (Cktl). ⅓ measure Grand Marnier, ⅔ measure dark Rum, 1 egg yolk. Shake over ice, strain into a large cocktail glass.

Night Light (Punch). Boil the zest of an orange and lemon with a teaspoon of mixed spice and 2 ozs. sugar in ⅓ pint of water for 5 minutes. Add 1 bottle full-bodied red wine, bring almost to the boil, strain and serve.

Nightmare Cocktail (Cktl). ⅗ measure Gin, ⅕ measure Boal Madeira, ⅕ measure Cherry brandy, 4 dashes orange juice. Shake over ice, strain into a cocktail glass. Top with a squeeze of orange peel juice.

Night Shade Cocktail (Cktl). ½ measure Bourbon whiskey, ¼ measure sweet Vermouth, ¼ measure orange juice, dash yellow Chartreuse. Shake over ice, strain into a cocktail glass.

Nigrara (It). A red grape used in the making of Bardolino.

Nigruwa (Euro). A red grape variety grown on the island of Malta in the Mediterranean.

Nikita (Eng). A mild Vodka 20% alc. by vol. produced by Gilbert and John Greenall Ltd., Warrington, Lancashire.

Nikita (Fr). The Beaujolais version of Vin blanc cassis using red wine.

Nikita 20 (Eng). A mild Vodka produced by Vladivar in Warrington, Cheshire.

Nikka Distilleries (Jap). A Whiskey producer. Produces – Black Nikka, G & G, High Nikka and Super Nikka whiskies.

Nikolai (USA). A Vodka 40% alc. by vol. produced by the General Wine and Spirits Co. (a subsidiary of Seagram).

Nikolausberg (Ger). Vineyard. (Anb) = Mosel-Saar-Ruwer. (Ber) = Zell/Mosel. (Gro) = Rosenhang. (Vil) = Cochem.

Nikolayev (USSR). A wine-producing centre in the Ukraine on the Black Sea.

Nikšič (Yug). A full-bodied Beer brewed by the Nikšič Brewery in Montenegro.

Nikšič Brewery (Yug). A brewery based in Montenegro, south-western Yugoslavia.

Nile Breweries (Afr). A noted brewery based in Jinja, Uganda. Noted for its Source of the Nile Ale 1042 O.G. (top-fermented).

Nilgiri (Ind). A coffee and tea-producing region of southern India.

Nill (Ger). Vineyard. (Anb) = Rheinpfalz. (Ber) = Mittelhaardt-Deutsche Weinstrasse. (Gro) = Saumagen. (Vil) = Kallstadt.

Nimburg (Ger). Village. (Anb) = Baden. (Ber) = Kaiserstuhl-Tuniberg. (Gro) = Vulkanfelsen. (Vin) = Steingrube.

Nimrod (Port). The name of a fine Tawny Port produced by the Warre's Port shippers.

Nina (Cktl). 1 fl.oz. each of Bacardi Rum, Vaapukka liqueur, lime juice cordial. Build into an ice-filled highball glass. Stir in ginger ale. Garnish with a cherry and slice of orange.

Nine-O-Nine [909] (Can). A Canadian whisky produced by the Canadian Gibson Distilleries.

Nineteen Hundred [1900] Lefébvre (Bel). A Beer brewed by the Dupont Brasserie in Tourpes.

Nineteenth [19th] Hole (Eng). The nickname for the club bar at a golf club.

Nineteenth Hole (Cktl). ⅓ measure Scotch whisky, ⅓ measure sweet Vermouth, ⅓ measure dry Sherry. Shake over ice, strain into a cocktail glass.

Ninety Seven [97] (Eng). A cask conditioned Bitter 1048 O.G. brewed by the Mole's Brewery in Melksham, Wiltshire. Brews Mole's 97.

Ninety Shilling Ales [90/-] (Scot). A term for Strong ales. See also Shilling System.

Ninotchka (Cktl). ¾ measure Vodka, ¼ measure (white) Crème de Cacao, juice ¼ lemon. Shake over ice, strain into a cocktail glass.

Nip (Eng). A very small bottle of Barley wine, Champagne or Spirits. 6 fl.ozs.

Nip (USA). A cocktail measure. 1.6 fl.ozs.

Nipa (Asia). An alcoholic beverage made in Malaysia from the sap of the Nipa tree (Nipa fructicans).

Nipah (Asia). See Nipa (the alternative spelling).

Nipozzano (It). A Chianti estate near Florence. Outside the Classico area.

Nipperkin (Eng). An eighteenth-century vessel holding approximately ½ pint.

Nissen (Ger). A brand of Rum produced by Hansen in Flensburg.

Nissley Vineyards (USA). A small winery based in Bainbridge, Pennsylvania. 11 ha. Produces French hybrid wines.

Nitra Brewery (Czec). A brewery based in south-eastern Czec. Produces fine Lager-style beers.

Nitrogen (Eng). Found in grape must. The yeasts build the protein they need from the nitrogen. If the grape must is nitrogen deficient the yeast obtains it from dead yeast cells and then produces Fusel oils.

Nittel (Ger). Village. (Anb) = Mosel-Saar-Ruwer. (Ber) = Obermosel. (Gro) = Gipfel. (Vins) = Blümchen, Hubertusberg, Leiterchen, Rochusfels.

Niunai (China). The ancient name for the red grape variety now known as the 'Cow's nipple'.

Nivernaise (Fr). A district in the Central Vineyards (Pouilly-sur-Loire). Mainly dry white wines are produced.

Nix (Cktl). ⅓ measure Brandy, ⅓ measure Port, ⅓ measure lime juice. Shake over ice, strain into an ice-filled highball glass. Top with cola.

Nixenberg (Ger). Vineyard. (Anb) = Nahe. (Ber) = Kreuznach. (Gro) = Schlosskapelle. (Vil) = Dorsheim.

Nizerand [River] (Fr). A small river in the Beaujolais region of Burgundy that separates the Haut-Beaujolais from the Bas-Beaujolais. A tributary of the Saône.

N.M. (Fr) (abbr). Négociant Manipulant on a Champagne wine label that is followed by a number denotes the registered name of the wine by the C.I.V.C.

NMWBWA (Eng) (abbr). See Natural Mineral Waters and Bottled Waters Association.

Noah (Isr). Hebrews say he introduced wine to civilisation.

Noah (USA). A white grape variety now little used.

Nobilo Winery (N.Z.). Address = Station Road, Huapai, Auckland. 60 ha. Grape varieties – Cabernet sauvignon, Merlot, Pinotage, Pinot noir and grapes bought in from Gisborne. (Chardonnay, Gewürztraminer and Müller-Thurgau).

Noble (Fr). A term used for certain grape varieties, certain vineyards and certain wines which are inherently superior to other grapes, vineyards and wines.

Noble (Fr). A red grape variety of the Touraine in the Loire.

Noblé Cuvée Millesimé (Fr). A De Luxe vintage cuvée produced by Lanson from 57% Chardonnay and 43% Pinot noir grapes.

Noble Experiment (USA). The name given to the Prohibition of 1919–1933.

Noblejas (Sp). The name given to the wines originating from Toledo.

Noble Late Harvest (S.Afr). A superior classification for wines with over 50 grammes/litre of residual sugar. Must show botrytis cinerea. A dessert wine.

Noble Mold (USA). Botrytis Cinerea. Also spelt Noble Mould.

Noble Mould (USA). Botrytis Cinerea. Also spelt Noble Mold.

Noble Rot (Eng). Botrytis Cinerea.

Noblessa (Ger). A white grape variety. A cross between the Madeleine angevine and the Sylvaner. Gives very high sugar.

Noblesse (Can). A Canadian whisky produced by the Canadian Gibson Distilleries.

Nobling (Ger). A white grape variety. A cross between the Sylvaner and the Gutedel. Used in Baden. Gives high sugar and balance.

Nocello (It). A walnut-flavoured liqueur produced by Toschi.

Nochebuena (Mex). Lit – 'Christmas Eve'.

A dark beer brewed by the Moctezuma Brewery in Veracruz.

Nochera (It). A red grape variety grown in Sicily.

Nochern (Ger). Village. (Anb) = Mittelrhein. (Ber) = Rheinburgengau. (Gro) = Loreleyfelsen. (Vin) = Brünnchen.

Noches de Maquieta (Cktl). 2 fl.ozs. Golden Rum, 1 teaspoon sugar, dash Angostura, 6 dashes Crème de Cacao, lemon peel. Place sugar, lemon peel, bitters and a dash of soda in an old-fashioned glass. Mix well with ice, add rest of ingredients, decorate with an orange slice, cherry and straws.

Nocino (It). A herb liqueur made from nut husks in spirit by Trappist Monks. 30% alc. by vol.

Nocino (It). A home-made liqueur obtained by steeping hazelnuts or walnuts in sugar and water and letting it ferment in the sun. The fermentation is then arrested by the addition of alcohol.

Noëllat (Charles) (Fr). A négociant-éleveur of fine wines based in Nuit-Saint-Georges, Côte de Nuits, Burgundy.

Nog (Cktl). A filling drink based on eggs served hot or cold in a large bowl or individual mug.

Nogent-l'Abbesse (Fr). A Cru Champagne village in the Canton de Beine. District = Reims.

Nogg (Eng). The East Anglian nickname for strong beer produced locally.

Noggin (Eng). A liquid measure equal to a gill. 5 fl.ozs. See also Quartern.

Noggin (Eng). A keg Best Bitter 1039 O.G. brewed by the Charles Wells Brewery in Bedford, Bedfordshire.

Noggin (Eng). The old English term for a small mug (1 gill capacity).

Noggin (Eng) (slang). A term for a drink (usually of beer). e.g. 'Would you like a noggin?'.

Nogueira do Cravo (Port). A co-operative winery based in the Dão region.

No Heel Taps (Eng). See Heel Tap.

Noilly (Louis) (Fr). Inventor of the dry Vermouth around 1800.

Noilly Prat (Fr). A famous French vermouth made from 40 herbs. 17% alc. by vol. Address = 2BD Anatole de la Forge, Marseille.

Noir de Pressac (Fr). The Pomerol name for the Malbec grape.

Noir Doux (Fr). An alternative name for the Malbec grape.

Noiren (Fr). An alternative name for the Pinot noir grape in the Burgundy region.

Noirots (Les) (Fr). A Premier Cru vineyard in the A.C. commune of Chambolle-Musigny, Côte de Nuits, Burgundy. 2.9 ha.

Noisettia (Fr). A hazelnut liqueur produced by Berger under the Fournier label.

Noizai (Fr). A commune in Vouvray, Touraine district in the Loire.

Nolet (Hol). A small Schiedam company. Produces a Korenjenever called Proosje Van Schiedam.

Nollenköpfle (Ger). Vineyard. (Anb) = Baden. (Ber) = Ortenau. (Gro) = Fürsteneck. (Vil) = Gengenbach.

Nomentane (Gre). A variety of red grape grown in ancient Greece. Had red-tinged stems.

Nomentanum (Lat). A red wine produced in central western Italy in Roman times.

Nominal Volume (EEC). The bottle contents. Amount is shown on label.

Nominé-Renard (Fr). Champagne producer. Address = 51270 Villevenard. Récoltants-manipulants. Produces – Vintage and non-vintage wines. Member of the C.V.C.

Non-Alcoholic Egg Nogg (Cktl). ½ pint milk, 1 egg, teaspoon castor sugar. Shake well over ice, strain into a large tumbler. Top with grated nutmeg.

Nonaville (Fr). A commune in the Charente Département whose grapes are used in Petite Champagne (Cognac).

Non-Combustible Matter (Eng). In vinification the ash residue. Potassium, Sodium, Calcium, Magnesium, Iron, Manganese, Phosphorus, Aluminium, Iodine, Sulphur and Trace elements.

Non Dilué (Fr). Undiluted. Also Pur.

Nonic Glass (Eng). A straight 'Sleeve' glass with an outward protrusion near the lip.

Nonini Winery (USA). A winery based near Fresno City, California. 83 ha. Grape varieties – Barbera, Grenache and Zinfandel. Produces varietal wines.

Nonnberg (Ger). Vineyard. (Anb) = Rheingau. (Ber) = Johannisberg. (Gro) = Daubhaus. (Vil) = Wicker.

Nonnenberg (Ger). Vineyard. (Anb) = Baden. (Ber) = Badische Frankenland. (Gro) = Tauberklinge. (Vil) = Beckstein.

Nonnenberg (Ger). Vineyard. (Anb) = Baden. (Ber) = Badische Frankenland. (Gro) = Tauberklinge. (Vil) = Lauda.

Nonnenberg (Ger). Vineyard. (Anb) = Franken. (Ber) = Steigerwald. (Gro) = Kapellenberg. (Vil) = Steinbach.

Nonnenberg (Ger). Vineyard. (Anb) = Mosel-Saar-Ruwer. (Ber) = Bernkastel. (Gro) = Münzlay. (Vil) = Wehlen.

Nonnenberg (Ger). Vineyard. (Anb) = Rheingau. (Ber) = Johannisberg. (Gro) = Steinmacker. (Vil) = Rauenthal.

Nonnenberg (Ger). Vineyard. (Anb) = Württemberg. (Ber) = Remstal-Stuttgart. (Gro) = Wartbühl. (Vil) = Strümpfelbach.

N

Nonnenberg (Ger). Vineyard. (Anb) = Württemberg. (Ber) = Württembergisch Unterland. (Gro) = Kirchenweinberg. (Vil) = Lauffen.

Nonnengarten (Ger). Vineyard. (Anb) = Mosel-Saar-Ruwer. (Ber) = Bernkastel. (Gro) = Vom Heissen Stein. (Vil) = Breidel.

Nonnengarten (Ger). Vineyard. (Anb) = Mosel-Saar-Ruwer. (Ber) = Bernkastel. (Gro) = Vom Heissen Stein. (Vil) = Pünderich.

Nonnengarten (Ger). Vineyard. (Anb) = Nahe. (Ber) = Kreuznach. (Gro) = Kronenberg. (Vil) = Bad Kreuznach (ortsteil Planig).

Nonnengarten (Ger). Vineyard. (Anb) = Nahe. (Ber) = Schloss Böckelheim. (Gro) = Burgweg. (Vil) = Traisen.

Nonnengarten (Ger). Vineyard. (Anb) = Rheinhessen. (Ber) = Wonnegau. (Gro) = Burg Rodenstein. (Vil) = Mörstadt.

Nonnengarten (Ger). Vineyard. (Anb) = Rheinpfalz. (Ber) = Mittelhaardt-Deutsche Weinstrasse. (Gro) = Feuerberg. (Vil) = Bad Dürkheim.

Nonnenhorn (Ger). Village. (Anb) = Franken. (Ber) = Bayer. Bodensee. (Gro) = Lindauer Seegarten. (Vins) = Seehalde, Sonnenbückel.

Nonnenrain (Ger). Vineyard. (Anb) = Württemberg. (Ber) = Württembergisch Unterland. (Gro) = Salzberg. (Vil) = Löwenstein.

Nonnenstück (Ger). Vineyard. (Anb) = Rheinpfalz. (Ber) = Mittelhaardt-Deutsche Weinstrasse. (Gro) = Hofstück. (Vil) = Deidesheim.

Nonnenwingert (Ger). Vineyard. (Anb) = Rheinhessen. (Ber) = Wonnegau. (Gro) = Liebfrauengarten. (Vil) = Worms.

Non Plus Ultra (Sp). A dry-style sparkling (Cava) wine produced by Codorníu in San Sadurní de Noya, Penedés. The top cuvée of Codorníu.

Non-Returnable (Eng). On a container (bottle, can, etc) denotes that no deposit on the container has been made and it is not needed for recycling (refilling).

Non-Vintage (Eng). A wine blended from wines of two or more years' grapes. Not of a single year. (Fr) = Sans Année

Noppingerbräu (Aus). A beer range brewed by the Noppinger Brauerei.

Noppinger Brauerei (Aus). A brewery based in Oberndorf near Salzburg. Was founded in 1630.

NORA (Eng) (abbr). Northern Real Ale Agency.

Norachéne (USSR). A red grape variety grown in Armenia.

Nordale Co-operative (S.Afr). Based at Bonnievale. Address = Box 105,

Bonnievale 6730. Produces varietal wines.

Nordexpress (Cktl). ⅓ measure Rye whiskey, ⅓ measure Cinzano dry vermouth, ⅓ measure Cordial Médoc. Shake over ice, strain into a cocktail glass.

Nordhausen (Ger). Village. (Anb) = Württemberg. (Ber) = Württembergisch Unterland. (Gro) = Heuchelberg. (Vin) = Sonntagsberg.

Nordheim (Ger). Village. (Anb) = Franken. (Ber) = Maindreieck. (Gro) = Kirchberg. (Vins) = Kreuznach, Vögelein.

Nordheim (Ger). Village. (Anb) = Württemberg. (Ber) = Württembergisch Unterland. (Gro) = Heuchelberg. (Vins) = Grafenberg, Gräfenberg, Ruthe, Sonntagsberg.

Nordic Express (Cktl). 1 part Cordial Médoc, 1 part Rye whiskey, 1 part dry Vermouth. Stir well over ice, strain into a cocktail glass.

Nordoff (Ire). A brand of Vodka 40% alc. by vol. produced by the Irish Distillers Group.

Nordweil (Ger). Village. (Anb) = Baden. (Ber) = Breisgau. (Gro) = Burg Lichteneck. (Vin) = Herrenberg.

Norfolk Dry (Eng). The brand-name of a dry Cider produced by the Showerings Co. (part of Allied Lyons).

Norfolk Porter (Eng). A cask conditioned Ale 1041 O.G. brewed by the Woodforde Brewery in Norfolk.

Norfolk Pride (Eng). A cask conditioned Bitter 1036 O.G. brewed by the Woodforde Brewery in Norfolk.

Norfolk Punch (Eng). A drink made from honey, lemon, herbs, spices and well-water. Made at Welle Manor Hall, Upwell, Norfolk.

Norheim (Ger). Village. (Anb) = Nahe. (Ber) = Schloss Böckelheim. (Gro) = Burgweg. (Vins) = Dellchen, Götzenfels, Kafels, Kirschheck, Klosterberg, Oberberg, Onkelchen, Sonnenberg.

Noria (Sp). The name given to the large wheel in the Malacate method of ploughing the vineyards in the Jerez region.

Normale (It). A non-riserva wine.

Normandin-Mercier (Fr). Cognac producer. Address = Château de la Péraudière, 17139 Dompierre, S.M. Owns no vineyards. Produces a wide range of Cognacs.

Normandy Coffee (Liq.Coffee). Using a measure of Calvados.

Normandy Golden Dawn Cocktail (Cktl). ¼ measure Calvados, ¼ measure Apricot brandy, ¼ measure orange juice, dash Grenadine. Shake over ice, strain into a cocktail glass. Dress with a slice of orange.

Normandy Rose (Cktl). ¼ measure Calvados, ¼ measure Dubonnet, ¼ measure Rye whiskey, ¼ measure Apricot brandy. Shake over ice, strain into a cocktail glass.

Norman's Conquest (Cktl). 1 measure Brandy, 3 measures Mead. Stir well together, strain into a goblet, add ice cube and a cherry.

Norseman Lager (Eng). A Lager that used to be brewed by the Vaux Brewery in Sunderland. No longer produced.

Norsingen (Ger). Village. (Anb) = Baden. (Ber) = Markgräflerland. (Gro) = Lorettoberg. (Vin) = Batzenberg.

Norsk Bartender Forening (Nor). N.B.F. Norway's Bartenders' Association. Address = P.O. Box 2554, Solli, Oslo 2.

Norte (Arg). A wine region that joins Jujvy and Salta.

Northamptonshire Bitter (Eng). A Bitter beer brewed by the Litchborough Brewery in Northamptonshire.

North British (Scot). A Grain whisky distillery based near Edinburgh.

North Carolina (USA). A small wine-producing State. Produces wines made mainly from the Scuppernong grape.

North Coast Counties (USA). Refers to the counties of Mendocino, Napa and Sonoma.

North Country Brewery (Eng). The former name of the Hull Brewery in Yorkshire. Was taken over by the Mansfield Brewery in 1985. Brews cask conditioned Riding Bitter 1038 O.G. and keg Anchor Export 1048 O.G. Hopfenperle Lager 1038 O.G. and Old Tradition mild 1033 O.G.

North Eastern Bitter (Eng). A keg Bitter 1032 O.G. brewed by the Bass Brewery in the north-east of England.

Northeast Vineyards (USA). A winery based in the Hudson Valley, New York. Noted for its hybrid wines.

Northern Brewer (Eng). An intensely flavoured and bitter hop variety.

Northern Clubs (Eng). See Federation.

Northerner Ale (Eng). A bottled dark Ale 1033 O.G. brewed by the Timothy Taylor Brewery in Keighley, Yorkshire.

Northern Lights (Cktl). 2 parts Glayva, 1 part orange juice, 1 part lemon juice. Build into a Slim Jim glass (Glayva, lemon juice and ice). Add orange juice, top with soda water.

Northern Real Ale Agency (Eng). Formed in 1969 as a wholesaler and off-licence to supply polypins and firkins of cask-conditioned ales. (abbr) = NORA.

Northgate Bitter (Eng). A keg Bitter 1036

O.G. brewed by the Wadworth Brewery in Wiltshire.

Northminster Winery (USA). A winery based in Wilmington, Delaware. Produces hybrid wines.

North Para (Austr). A winery based near Seppeltsfield, Barossa Valley, South Australia. Produces varietal wines.

North Pole Cocktail (Cktl). ½ measure dry Gin, ¼ measure lemon juice, ¼ measure Maraschino, 1 egg white. Shake over ice, strain into a cocktail glass. Top with whipped, sweetened cream.

North Port (Scot). A single Malt whisky distillery in Brechin, Angus-shire. Is owned by James Munro and Sons Ltd. A Highland malt. Produces a 15 year old Malt 45% alc. by vol.

North Queensland (Austr). See NQ.

North Salem Vineyards (USA). A winery based in North Salem, Hudson Valley, New York. Produces hybrid wines.

North Star (Eng). A keg Bitter 1036 O.G. brewed by the Arkell Brewery in Swindon, Wiltshire.

Northumbrian Spring (Eng). A recognised mineral water from the north of England.

North Western Wine Merchants' Wines (S.Afr). The name for the Olifantsriver Co-operative.

Norton (Sp). The brand-name for a sparkling wine produced by the Bodegas Norton.

Norton (USA). A black grape variety that is little used now.

Norwegian Fizz (Cktl). 1 measure Kümmel, 1 measure cream, dash lemon juice, dash egg white. Shake well over ice, strain into an ice-filled highball glass. Top with sparkling wine.

Norwegian Gin (Nor). A strong-flavoured dry Gin.

Norwegian Punch (Nor). A sweet liqueur with a Batavian Arrack base. Produced by A/S Vinmonopolet. 27% alc. by vol.

Norwich Brewery (Eng). A Watney's Brewery which has now closed down. Beers are now brewed in London and Manchester. Anchor Bitter 1034 O.G. Anglian Strong Ale 1048 O.G. Bullards Old Ale 1057 O.G. Norwich Bitter 1034 O.G. and cask conditioned S & P Bitter 1038 O.G.

Nose (Eng). The bouquet or aroma of a wine or spirit.

Nose (The) (Sp). The nickname of Don José Ignacio Domecq, a top Sherry maker. See Domecq.

Nosing Glass (Eng). A balloon glass usually used for the drinking of Brandy in U.K. and USA. In France used for testing the bouquet of young wines whilst maturing.

Nosiola (It). A white grape variety grown in the Trentino-Alto Adige.

Nošovice Brewery (Czec). A large modern brewery based in eastern Czec.

Nostrano (Switz). A smooth, fruity red wine from the Ticino region.

Notables (The) (Ger). A name for the members of the International Beer Convention.

Notar Domenico (It). A red grape variety grown in the Puglia region.

Noto (It). A Muscat wine from Sicily.

Notre-Dame du Raisin (Fr). Lit – 'Our lady of the grape'. A religious shrine built in the nineteenth century on the Mont de Brouilly in the hope of ridding the Beaujolais region of Oïdium.

Nottage Hill Claret (Austr). A red wine produced by the Old Mill Winery in South Australia.

Not Tonight (Cktl). ½ measure Bacardi White Label, ⅙ measure blue Curaçao, ⅙ measure Mandarine Napoléon, ⅙ measure Crème de Banane. Stir over ice, strain into a cocktail glass. Top with a cherry and banana slice.

Not Tonight Josephine (Cktl). 1 measure Mandarine Napoléon, 4 drops Malibu Coconut Liqueur, 4 drops Cherry brandy, juice of an orange. Shake with ice, strain into a highball glass filled with ice.

Nourishing Stout (Eng). A bottled Stout 1034 O.G. brewed by the Gales Brewery in Horndean, Hampshire.

Nourishing Stout (Eng). A bottled Stout 1050 O.G. brewed by the Samuel Smith Brewery in Tadcaster, Yorkshire.

Nouveau (Le) (Fr). The French equivalent (Alsace) of Federwisser. A drink of still-fermenting wine.

Nouveau Rouge (S.Afr). A copy of the Beaujolais Nouveau first started by the SFW in 1982.

Nouvel Ordre Hospitalier (Fr). A wine society based in Paris.

Noval (Port). See Quinta do Noval.

Novalja (Yug). A red wine produced on the island of Pag off the north-west Dalmatian coast.

Novà Paka Brewery (Czec). A brewery based in northern Czec.

Nova Scotia (Can). A small wine region.

November 15ᵗʰ (Fr). The old date for the release of Beaujolais Nouveau. Since 1985 changed to the 3ʳᵈ Thursday in November.

Novi Pazar (Bul). A State winery that produces a noted Chardonnay white wine.

Novi Sad (Yug). A wine-producing area in north-eastern Yugoslavia. Produces mainly white wines.

Novitiate Winery (USA). A winery based in Los Gatos, California. Grape varieties – Cabernet sauvignon, Chenin blanc, Johannisberg riesling, Petite sirah and Pinot blanc. Is owned by Jesuit monks and produces Altar wines 18% alc. by vol. See L'Admirable and Vin Doré.

Novocherkassk (USSR). A wine-producing centre in the river Don area. Produces mainly white wines.

Novo Cocktail (Cktl). 1 measure Strega, 1 egg yolk, dash lime juice. Shake over ice, strain into a flute glass. Top with lemonade and a cherry. Serve with straws.

Novo Mundo (Port). A Dão wine produced by the Caves Acàcio.

Novo Selo (Bul). A delimited wine-producing area based in the northern region of Bulgaria. Main grape varieties – Gamza and Pinot noir.

Noyau (Fr). A pale pinkish-yellow liqueur made from peach and apricot kernels. 30% alc. by vol. See also Crème de Noyau.

Noyau Rose (Cktl). See Cocktail Mixer.

Noyaux (Fr). A liqueur produced from a selection of nuts and fruit kernals.

Noyeau (Fr). See Crème de Noyeau.

Nozzole (It). An Estate in the Chianti Classico region.

N.P.U. Amontillado (Sp). A very dry, unblended solera Amontillado sherry produced by Romate.

NQ (Austr) (abbr). North Queensland. A Lager beer brewed by the CUB Brewery.

N.R.B. (Eng) (abbr). Non-Returnable Bottles. Found on a Wine and Beer merchant's list.

Nu (Fr). Bare. Cost of wine without its overheads (cask, bottles etc).

Nuance (Eng). Describes a wine as having a specific smell. e.g. of almonds or flint.

Nube (Fr). Cloudiness.

Nubian Gin (Afr). An east African illegally distilled spirit. Is similar to the USA 'Moonshine'.

Nuchter (Hol). Sober.

Nudes (USA). 1983. Cans of beer that have pictures of near naked women on the sides. The clothes can be removed by rubbing with a coin which reveals the lady naked underneath. Also called Nudies.

Nudies (USA). See Nudes.

Nuestro Padre Jesus del Perdon (Sp). A co-operative winery based in La Mancha. Labels include – Lazarillo and Yuntero.

Nuits-Saint-Georges (Fr). A.C. commune in the Côte de Nuits, Burgundy. Although it has no Grands Crus it has 39 Premier Cru vineyards including those of the village of Prémeaux. Vineyards – Nuits-Saint-Georges = Aux Argillats, Aux Boudots, Aux Bousselots, Aux Chaignots, Aux Champs-Perdrix, Aux Cras, Aux Crots, Aux Damodes, Aux Murgers, Aux Thorey, Aux Vignes-Rondes, En la Chaine-Carteau, En la Perrière-Noblet, La Richemone, La Roncière, La Perrière, Les Argillats, Les Cailles, Les Chaboeufs, Les Hauts-Pruliers, Les Pourrets, Les Poulettes, Les Procès, Les Pruliers, Les Saint-Georges, Les Valleros, Les Vaucrains, Rue-de-Chaux. 129.5 ha. Premeaux = Aux Perdrix, Clos de la Maréchale, Clos des Argillières, Clos des Arlots, Clos des Corvées, Clos des Forêts, Clos des Grandes-Vignes, Les Clos Saint-Marc, Les Corvées-Paget, Les Didiers. 40.3 ha.

N.U.L.V. (Eng) (abbr). National Union of Licensed Vituallers. Union for Public house licensees. Address = Boardman House, 2, Downing Street, Farnham, Surrey GU9 7NX.

Numancia (Sp). The brand-name for a Brandy produced by Pemartin in Jerez.

Numbered Bottles (Eng). Used extensively in Italy but also in many other countries which is used for various reasons. e.g. To tell which cask a particular wine came from, when bottled, amount bottled etc.

Number Eight (Can). A blended Canadian rye whisky produced by Gilbey Canada Ltd. 40% alc. by vol.

Number Nine [N°9] (Eng). A cask conditioned Bitter 1043 O.G. brewed by the Bodicote Brewery in Oxon.

Number One [N°1] (Eng). A keg/bottled Pale ale 1036 O.G. brewed by the McMullen Brewery in Hertford.

Number One [N°1] (I.O.M.). A Barley wine 1070 O.G. brewed by the Okell Brewery in Douglas.

Number One [N°1] (Eng). A naturally conditioned bottled Ale 1039 O.G. brewed by the Selby Brewery in Selby, Yorkshire.

Number One Distilling Company (USA). A distillery belonging to the Schenley Distillers Co.

Number 7 (Eng). A low-carbohydrate, high-alcohol Cider produced by Bulmers of Hereford.

Number Three [N°3] (Scot). A cask conditioned Ale 1043 O.G. brewed by the Youngers Brewery in Edinburgh.

Nuragus (It). A white grape variety grown in Sardinia. Produces the oldest wine in Sardinia (Campidano district). Also known as Campidano bianco.

Nuragus (It). An alternative name for the white wine Campidano bianco in Sardinia.

Nuragus di Cagliari (It). D.O.C. white wine from Sardinia. Made from the Nuragus, Clairette, Semidano, Trebbiano romagnolo, Trebbiano toscano and Vermentino grapes. Area of production is entire province of Cagliari plus other communes.

Nuriootpa (Austr). A wine-producing area in the Barossa Valley, South Australia.

Nuriootpa Winery (Austr). A winery based in Nuriootpa, Barossa Valley, South Australia. Produces varietal wines.

Nursery Vineyard (Austr). Part of the Lindemans winery in New South Wales. 35 ha. Grape variety – Rhine riesling.

Nursing (Eng). The careful care and attention lavished on some wines during their production and maturation. e.g. Clarets.

Nussbach (Ger). Village. (Anb) = Baden. (Ber) = Ortenau. (Gro) = Fürsteneck. (Vin) = Renchtäler.

Nussbaum (Ger). Village. (Anb) = Nahe. (Ber) = Schloss Böckelheim. (Gro) = Paradiesgarten. (Vins) = Höllenberg, Rotfeld, Sonnenberg

Nussbaum (Lux). A vineyard site in the village of Wormeldange.

Nussberg (Ger). Vineyard. (Anb) = Mosel-Saar-Ruwer. (Ber) = Zell/Mosel. (Gro) = Schwarze Katz. (Vil) = Zell.

Nussbien (Ger). Vineyard. (Anb) = Rheinpfalz. (Ber) = Mittelhaardt-Deutsche Weinstrasse. (Gro) = Hofstück. (Vil) = Ruppertsberg.

Nussbrunnen (Ger). Vineyard. (Anb) = Rheingau. (Ber) = Johannisberg. (Gro) = Deutelsberg. (Vil) = Hattenheim.

Nussdorf (Aus). A famous white wine from Vienna.

Nussdorf (Ger). Village. (Anb) = Rheinpfalz. (Ber) = Südliche Weinstrasse. (Gro) = Bischofskreuz. (Vins) = Herrenberg, Kaiserberg, Kirchenstück.

Nussloch (Ger). Village. (Anb) = Baden. (Ber) = Badische Bergstrasse/Kraichgau. (Gro) = Mannaberg. (Vin) = Wilhelmsberg.

Nussriegel (Ger). Vineyard. (Anb) = Rheinpfalz. (Ber) = Mittelhaardt-Deutsche Weinstrasse. (Gro) = Honigsäckel. (Vil) = Ungstein.

Nut Brown (Eng). A name often used by brewers for bottled Brown ales.

Nutcracker (Eng). A cask conditioned Ale 1036 O.G. brewed by the Cotleigh Brewery in Somerset.

Nutty (Eng). Usually applied to Sherries to describe a flavour which is reminiscent of walnuts and hazel nuts.

Nuwara Eliya (Sri.L). A tea producing region in the high region. Teas of the same name have a light, delicate flavour.

Nuwehoop Co-operative (S.Afr). Based in

Goudini. Address = Nuwehoop Wynkelder. Box 100, Rawsonville 6845. Produces Laatoes and varietal wines.

Nuwehoop Wynkelder (S.Afr). See Nuwehoop Co-operative.

Nuy Co-operative (S.Afr). Based in Nuy. Address = Nuy Wynkelder Koöp. Bpk., P.O. Nuy 6700. Produces – Chant de Nuy and varietal wines.

Nuy Wynkelder Koöperatiewe (S.Afr). See Nuy Co-operative.

Nycteri (Gre). A white wine, high in alcohol from Thira Isle in the Cyclades Isles in Southern Greece. From the Assyrtiko grape.

Nyköpings Brannvin (Den). The brand-name of an Akvavit flavoured with aniseed, caraway, fennel and other herbs.

Nylon Powder (USA). Used for fining wines.

Nymburk Brewery (Czec). A brewery based in north-western Czec. Is noted for its Lager-style beers.

Nyon (Switz). A wine-producing area of the Vaud Canton. Produces mainly light red wines from the Gamay grape.

O

Oak (Eng). The best wood for making and maturing wines. American, Argonne, Dalmatian, Limousin, Memel, Monlezun, Nevers and Tronçais are considered to be the best. (Fr) = Chêne. (Ger) = Eiche. (Hol) = Eik. (It) = Quercia. (Lat) = Quercus. (Port) = Carvalho. (Sp) = Roble. (Tur) = Mese. (Wales) = Derwen.

Oak Barrel Winery ((USA). A winery based in Berkley, Alameda, California. Grape varieties – Cabernet sauvignon, Chardonnay, Muscat and Zinfandel. Produces varietal wines.

Oak Cask Chardonnay (Austr). A fruity white wine from the Wyndham estate in New South Wales.

Oak Cheshire (Eng). Opened in 1982 in Ellemere Port, Cheshire. Noted for its cask conditioned Old Oak 1044 O.G. and Double Dagger 1050 O.G.

Oak Chips (Eng). A practice of adding oak chips to wines (usually red) to give a 'cask mature' flavour although wines are in stainless steel vats. Used in Austr, USA, etc.

Oakhill Brewery (Eng). Originally opened as the Beacon Brewery in 1981 in Bath. Changed in 1984 to present name. Brews cask conditioned Farmer's Ale 1038 O.G. and Oakhill Stout 1045 O.G.

Oakhill Stout (Eng). A bottled Stout 1045 O.G. brewed by the Oakhill Brewery in Bath.

Oak Knoll Winery (USA). A winery based in Hillsboro, Oregon. Produces varietal, fruit and berry wines.

Oakleigh Burgundy (N.Z.). A slightly sweet, red wine produced by the Ormond Vineyards.

Oakvale Winery (Austr). A winery based in New South Wales. Part of the Elliot Vineyards.

Oakview Plantations (USA). A large winery based in Woodruff, South Carolina. 148 ha. Grape varieties – Catawba, Concord and Muscadine.

Oakville (USA). A small wine-producing area between Yountville and Rutherford, Napa Valley, California.

Oakville Vineyards (USA). A label used by the Robert Mondavi Winery for varietal and non-vintage wines. Was once the name of a winery.

Oaky (Eng). A taste in wine. Obtained from wines stored in new oak casks.

Oast House (Eng). A kiln where the malted barley is heated to arrest germination.

Oatmeal Stout (Eng). A beer which is made from malted oats as well as malted barley.

OB (Eng) (abbr). Oldham Brewery Lancashire beers have these initials on the side of a bell.

OB (E.Asia) (abbr). Oriental Brewery. A Lager beer brewed in Seoul, South Korea.

Oban (Scot). A single Malt whisky distillery at Argyll on the western coast. Owned by John Hopkins Ltd. (Part of DCL group) A Highland malt. Produces a 12 year old Malt 40% alc. by vol.

OBB (Eng) (abbr). Old Brewery Bitter 1039 O.G. brewed by the Samuel Smith Brewery in Tadcaster, Yorkshire.

Ober (Ger). Lit – 'Upper or higher'. Denotes villages or vineyards that are situated above a town, village, church, etc.

Oberachem (Ger). Village. (Anb) = Baden. See Achern.

Oberacker (Ger). See Kraichtal.

Oberberg (Ger). Vineyard. (Anb) = Nahe. (Ber) = Schloss Böckelheim. (Gro) = Burgweg. (Vil) = Norheim.

Oberberg (Ger). Vineyard. (Anb) = Rheingau. (Ber) = Johannisberg. (Gro) = Steinmacher. (Vil) = Niederwalluf.

Oberbergen (Ger). Village. (Anb) = Baden. (Ber) = Kaiserstuhl-Tuniberg. (Gro) = Vulkanfelsen. (Vins) = Bassgeige, Pulverbuck.

Oberbillig (Ger). Village. (Anb) = Mosel-Saar-Ruwer. (Ber) = Obermosel. (Gro) = Gipfel. (Vins) = Hirtengarten, Römerberg.

Oberdiebach (Ger). Village. (Anb) = Mittelrhein. (Ber) = Bacharach. (Gro) = Schloss Stahleck. (Vins) = Bischofshub, Fürstenberg, Kräuterberg, Rheinberg.

Oberdollendorf (Ger). Village. (Anb) = Mittelrhein. (Ber) = Siebengebirge. (Gro) = Petersberg. (Vins) = Rosenhügel, Laurentiusberg, Sülzenberg.

O

Oberdürrenberg (Ger). Vineyard. (Anb)
= Baden. (Ber) = Markgräflerland. (Gro)
= Lorettoberg. (Vil) = Pfaffenweiler.
Obereggenen (Ger). Village. (Anb) =
Baden. (Ber) = Markgräflerland. (Gro) =
Burg Neuenfels. (Vin) = Röthen.
Obere Heimbach (Ger). Vineyard. (Anb) =
Nahe. (Ber) = Schloss Böckelheim. (Gro)
= Paradiesgarten. (Vil) = Meisenheim.
Oberehnheim (Fr). The German name for
the village of Obernai in Alsace.
Obereisenheim (Ger). Village. (Anb) =
Franken. (Ber) = Maindreieck. (Gro) =
Kirchberg. (Vin) = Höll.
Oberemmel (Ger). Village. (Anb) = Mosel-
Saar-Ruwer. (Ber) = Saar-Ruwer. (Gro) =
Scharzberg. (Vins) = Agritiusberg,
Altenberg, Hütte, Karlsberg, Raul, Rosen-
berg.
Oberer Berg (Ger). Vineyard. (Anb) =
Württemberg. (Ber) = Württembergisch
Unterland. (Gro) = Wunnenstein. (Vil) =
Kleinbottwar.
Oberer Berg (Ger). Vineyard. (Anb) =
Württemberg. (Ber) = Württembergisch
Unterland. (Gro) = Wunnenstein. (Vil) =
Ludwigsburg (ortsteil Hoheneck).
Obererdingen (Ger). Village. (Anb) =
Württemberg. (Ber) = Württembergisch
Unterland. (Gro) = Stromberg. (Vin) =
Kupferhalde.
Oberfell (Ger). Village. (Anb) = Mosel-
Saar-Ruwer. (Ber) = Zell/Mosel. (Gro) =
Weinhex. (Vins) = Brauneberg, Goldlay,
Rosenberg.
Ober-Flörsheim (Ger). Village. (Anb) =
Rheinhessen. (Ber) = Wonnegau. (Gro) =
Burg Rodenstein. (Vins) = Blucherpfad,
Herrenberg.
Oberhausen (Ger). Village. (Anb) =
Rheinpfalz. (Ber) = Südliche Wein-
strasse. (Gro) = Kloster Liebfrauenberg.
(Vin) = Frohnwingert.
Oberhausen an der Nahe (Ger). Village.
(Anb) = Nahe. (Ber) = Schloss Böckel-
heim. (Gro) = Burgweg. (Vins) = Fel-
senberg, Kieselberg, Leistenberg,
Rotenberg.
Oberhausen an der Nahe (Ger). Village.
(Anb) = Nahe. (Ber) = Schloss Böckel-
heim. (Gro) = Paradiesgarten. (Vin) =
Graukatz.
Oberheimbach (Ger). Village. (Anb) = Mit-
telrhein. (Ber) = Bacharach. (Gro) =
Schloss Reichenstein. (Vins) = Kloster-
berg, Römerberg, Sonne, Wahrheit.
Ober-Hilbersheim (Ger). Village. (Anb) =
Rheinhessen. (Ber) = Bingen. (Gro) =
Abtey. (Vin) = Mönchpforte.
Oberkirch (Ger). Village. (Anb) = Baden.
(Ber) = Ortenau. (Gro) = Fürsteneck.
(Vin) = Renchtäler.
Oberkirch [ortsteil Haslach] (Ger). Village.

(Anb) = Baden. (Ber) = Ortenau. (Gro) =
Fürsteneck. (Vin) = Renchtäler.
Oberlauda (Ger). Village. (Anb) = Baden.
(Ber) = Badische Frankenland. (Gro) =
Tauberklinge. (Vins) = Altenberg, Stein-
linge.
Oberlin Wine Research Institute (Fr).
Founded in 1874 in Colmar, Alsace.
Carries out research in clonal selection,
crossing, pest control etc.
Obermoschel (Ger). Village. (Anb) = Nahe.
(Ber) = Schloss Böckelheim. (Gro) =
Paradiesgarten. (Vins) = Geissenkopf,
Langhölle, Schlossberg, Silberberg, Son-
nenplätzchen.
Obermosel (Ger). Bereich. (Anb) = Mosel-
Saar-Ruwer. (Gros) = Gipfel, Konigsberg.
Obernai (Fr). A wine village of the Bas-
Rhin in Alsace. German = Oberehnheim.
Oberndorf (Ger). Village. (Anb) = Nahe.
(Ber) = Schloss Böckelheim. (Gro) =
Paradiesgarten. (Vins) = Aspenberg,
Beutelstein, Feuersteinrossel, Weissen-
stein.
Odernheim (Ger). Village. (Anb) = Nahe.
(Ber) = Schloss Böckelheim. (Gro) =
Paradiesgarten. (Vins) = Disibodenberg,
Hessweg, Kapellenberg, Kloster, Mon-
fort, Weinsack.
Obernhof (Ger). Village. (Anb) = Mittelr-
hein. (Ber) = Rheinburgengau. (Gro) =
Lahntal. (Vin) = Goetheberg.
Ober-Olm (Ger). Village. (Anb) = Rhein-
hessen. (Ber) = Nierstein. (Gro) = Donm-
herr. (Vin) = Kapellenberg.
Oberotterbach (Ger). Village. (Anb) =
Rheinpfalz. (Ber) = Südliche Wein-
strasse. (Gro) = Guttenberg. (Vin) =
Sonnenberg.
Oberöwisheim (Ger). See Kraichtal.
Oberrhein (Ger). A Deutscher Tafelwein
region. Has two Untergebiete–Burgengau
and Romertor.
Oberrimsingen (Ger). Village. (Anb) =
Baden. (Ber) = Kaiserstuhl-Tuniberg.
(Gro) = Attilafelsen. (Vin) = Fran-
ziskaner.
Oberrot (Ger). Vineyard. (Anb) = Franken.
(Ber) = Maindreieck. (Gro) = Not yet
assigned. (Vil) = Lengfust.
Oberrotweil (Ger). Village. (Anb) = Baden.
(Ber) = Kaiserstuhl-Tuniberg. (Gro) =
Vulkanfelsen. (Vins) = Eichberg, Hen-
kenberg, Käsleberg, Kirchberg, Sch-
lossberg.
Obersasbach (Ger). Village. (Anb) =
Baden. (Ber) = Ortenau. (Gro) = Schloss
Rodeck. (Vins) = Alter Gott,
Eichwäldele.
Oberschloss (Ger). Vineyard. (Anb) =
Rheinpfalz. (Ber) = Südliche Wein-
strasse. (Gro) = Mandelhöhe. (Vil) =
Kirrweiler.

O

Oberschopfheim (Ger). Village. (Anb) = Baden. (Ber) = Breisgau. (Gro) = Schutterlindenberg. (Vin) = Kronenbühl.

Oberschüpf (Ger). Village. (Anb) = Baden. (Ber) = Badische Frankenland. (Gro) = Tauberklinge. (Vins) = Altenberg, Herrenberg.

Oberschwarzach (Ger). Village. (Anb) = Franken. (Ber) = Steigerwald. (Gro) = Not yet assigned. (Vin) = Herrenberg.

Obersöllbach (Ger). Village. (Anb) = Württemberg. (Ber) = Württembergisch Unterland. (Gro) = Lindelberg. (Vin) = Margarete.

Oberstenfeld (Ger). Village. (Anb) = Württemberg. (Ber) = Württembergisch Unterland. (Gro) = Wunnenstein. (Vins) = Forstberg, Harzberg, Lichtenberg.

Oberstetten (Ger). Village. (Anb) = Württemberg. (Ber) = Kocher-Jagst-Tauber. (Gro) = Tauberberg. (Vin) = Shafsteige.

Oberstreit (Ger). Village. (Anb) = Nahe. (Ber) = Schloss Böckelheim. (Gro) = Paradiesgarten. (Vin) = Auf dem Zimmerberg.

Obersulm [ortsteil Affaltrach] (Ger). Village. (Anb) = Württemberg. (Ber) = Württembergisch Unterland. (Gro) = Salzberg. (Vins) = Dieblesberg, Zeilberg.

Obersulm [ortsteil Eichelberg] (Ger). Village. (Anb) = Württemberg. (Ber) = Württembergisch Unterland. (Gro) = Salzberg. (Vin) = Hundsberg.

Obersulm [ortsteil Eschenau] (Ger). Village. (Anb) = Württemberg. (Ber) = Württembergisch Unterland. (Gro) = Salzberg. (Vin) = Paradies.

Obersulm [ortsteil Sülzbach] (Ger). Village. (Anb) = Württemberg. (Ber) = Württembergisch Unterland. (Gro) = Salzberg. (Vin) = Altenberg.

Obersulm [ortsteil Weiler] (Ger). Village. (Anb) = Württemberg. (Ber) = Württembergisch Unterland. (Gro) = Salzberg. (Vins) = Hundsberg, Schlierbach.

Obersulm [ortsteil Willsbach] (Ger). Village. (Anb) = Württemberg. (Ber) = Württembergisch Unterland. (Gro) = Salzberg. (Vins) = Dieblesberg, Zeilberg.

Obersülzen (Ger). Village. (Anb) = Rheinpfalz. (Ber) = Mittelhaardt-Deutsche Weinstrasse. (Gro) = Schwarzerde. (Vin) = Schnepp.

Obertsrot (Ger). Village. (Anb) = Baden. (Ber) = Ortenau. (Gro) = Schloss Rodeck. (Vin) = Grafensprung.

Obertürkheim (Ger). Village. (Anb) =

Württemberg. (Ber) = Remstal-Stuttgart. (Gro) = Weinsteige. See Stuttgart.

Oberuhldingen (Ger). Village. (Anb) = Baden. (Ber) = Bodensee. (Gro) = Sonnenufer. (Vin) = Kirchhalde.

Obervolkach (Ger). Village. (Anb) = Franken. (Ber) = Maindreick. (Gro) = Kirchberg. (Vin) = Landsknecht.

Oberwalluf (Ger). Village. (Anb) = Rheingau. (Ber) = Johannisberg. (Gro) = Steinmacher. (Vins) = Fitusberg, Langenstück.

Oberweier (Ger). Village. (Anb) = Baden. (Ber) = Breisgau. (Gro) = Schutterlindenberg. (Vin) = Kronenbühl.

Oberwessel (Ger). Village. (Anb) = Mittelrhein. (Ber) = Rheinburgengau. (Gro) = Schloss Schönburg. (Vins) = Bernstein, Bienenberg, Goldemund, Ölsberg, Römerkrug, St. Martinsberg, Sieben Jungfrauen.

Obester Winery (USA). A small winery based in San Mateo, California. Grape varieties – Cabernet sauvignon, Johannisberg riesling and Sauvignon blanc. Produces varietal wines.

Obrigheim (Ger). Village. (Anb) = Rheinpfalz. (Ber) = Mittelhaardt-Deutsche Weinstrasse. (Gro) = Grafenstück. (Vins) = Benn, Hochgericht, Mandelpfad, Rosengarten, Schloss, Sonnenberg.

Obscuration (Eng). Amount of false reading on a hydrometer caused by impurities. Mainly sugar in the alcohol.

Obstbranntwein (Ger). The term for fruit brandies. Also called Obstwasser. Brandy must be produced without the addition of sweetening, alcohol or colour.

Obstwasser (Aus). Fruit brandies. Most famous is Wacholderbranntwein. See Obstbranntwein.

Obstwasser (Ger). See Obstbranntwein.

O.B.U. (Aus) (abbr). Österreichische Barkeeper Union. Austrian Bartender's Association. Address = Tigergasse 6/2, A-1080, Wien 4.

Occasional Licence (Eng). The licence given to a full-on licence holder to run a licensed bar in an un-licensed premises.

Occasional Permissions (Eng). Licences granted for up to 24 hours to sell alcoholic liquor (usually at an outside bar). 4 licences per year may be granted.

Occhio di Pernice (It). A red grape variety grown in Tuscany.

Occidente (Arg). A wine region that joins Catamarca and La Rioja.

Occitane (Fr). The name for the dumpy bottle used in the Languedoc region of south-western France.

O

OCE (Afr). State body in Morocco responsible for the monitoring and exporting of Moroccan wines. Analyses and tastes the wines and selects wines to be bottled under OCE names.

Ocean [The] (Port). A name given to the area around the estuary of the river Tejo in the Estremadura region. Noted for its wind breaks of reeds to protect the vines from the Atlantic winds.

Ocha (Jap). See O-Cha.

O-Cha (Jap). A liqueur made from essence of Matcha, powdered tea and Gyokuro rolled tea. Also written Ocha.

Ochavico Dry Oloroso (Sp). A brand of Oloroso Sherry produced by Garvey's in Jerez de la Frontera.

Ochoa (Sp). A noted family winery based in the Navarra region. Produces red, rosé and white wines.

Ochsenbach (Ger). Village. (Anb) = Württemberg. (Ber) = Württembergisch Unterland. (Gro) = Stromberg. (Vin) = Liebenberg.

Ochsenberg (Ger). Vineyard. (Anb) = Württemberg. (Ber) = Württembergisch Unterland. (Gro) = Heuchelberg. (Vil) = Brackenheim (ortsteil Botenheim).

Öchsle (Ger). See Oechsle.

Ockenheim (Ger). Village. (Anb) = Rheinhessen. (Ber) = Bingen. (Gro) = Sankt Rochuskapelle. (Vins) = Hockenmühle, Klosterweg, Kreuz, Laberstall, St. Jakobsberg, Schönhölle.

Ockfen (Ger). Village. (Anb) = Mosel-Saar-Ruwer. (Ber) = Saar-Ruwer. (Gro) = Scharzberg, (Vins) = Bockstein, Geisberg, Heppenstein, Herrenberg, Kupp, Neuwies, Zickelgarten.

Ocsidio (Wales). Oxidise.

Octave (Eng). A cask, ⅛ of a Pipe, Butt or Cask. 16½ gallons approx.

Octave (Eng). An old-fashioned term used as a request for Sherry. Eight different Sherries would be presented from very dry to sweet in range.

Octavilla (Sp). An ⅛ of a Sherry cask. 16½ gallons. See Octave.

O'Darby (Ire). A cream liqueur with a chocolate and Irish whiskey base. 17% alc. by vol. Produced in Cork.

Odarka Taffel Aquavit (Swe). A caraway, coriander and fennel-flavoured Aquavit.

Oddbins (Eng). A large retail Wines, Beers and Spirits chain owned by Seagram Distillers PLC.

Odenas (Fr). A commune in the Beaujolais. Has A.C. Beaujolais-Villages or Beaujolais-Odenas status.

Odenheim (Ger). Village. (Anb) = Baden. (Ber) = Badische Bergstrasse/Kraichgau. (Gro) = Stiftsberg. (Vin) = Königsbecher.

Odenwald Mountains (Ger). The slopes on which the vines grow in the Hessische Bergstrasse Anbaugebiet. Also protects the Rheinhessen from easterly winds.

Odessa (USSR). A wine-producing centre on the Black Sea in the Ukraine.

Odeur (Fr). Smell (of wine, yeast, cork, etc).

Odilienberg (Fr). The German name for the village of Sainte-Odile in the Bas-Rhin, Alsace.

Odin Brewery (Den). A noted brewery based in Viborg, North Jutland.

Odinstal (Ger). Vineyard. (Anb) = Rheinpfalz. (Ber) = Mittelhaardt-Deutsche Weinstrasse. (Gro) = Schenkenböhl. (Vil) = Wachenheim.

Odobeşti (Rum). A wine-producing area in central Focsani. Is noted for its white wines produced from the Fetească and Riesling grapes.

Odour (Eng). A pleasant or an unpleasant smell. Also referred to as the bouquet.

Odre (Port). (Sp). A wine bag made from animal skin.

Ödsbach (Ger). Village. (Anb) = Baden. (Ber) = Ortenau. (Gro) = Fürsteneck. (Vin) = Renchtäler.

Oechsle (Ger). Scale of sugar density of grape musts. Recorded as °O. e.g. 82°O = 1082 gravity.

Oechsle (Ferdinand) (Ger). 1774–1852. A chemist of Pforzheim who devised a hydrometer to measure the sugar content of grape must. See Oechsle.

Oechsle [German Wine Ratings] (Ger). Qba = 57–72°O. Qmp = 65–72°O. Kabinett = 70–81°O. Spätlese = 76–90°O. Auslese = 76–91°O. Beerenauslese = 110–125°O. Trokenbeerenauslese = 150°O minimum.

Oedheim (Ger). Village. (Anb) = Württemberg. (Ber) = Württembergisch Unterland. (Gro) = Staufenberg. (Vin) = Kayberg.

Oeil de Perdrix (Fr). Lit – 'Partridge eye'. A tawny pink colour given to certain rosé wines. e.g. sparkling Burgundy. Produced from the Pinot noir.

Oeillade (Fr). A white grape variety from the A.C. Cassis in southern France. Produces high alcohol.

Oeiras (Port). A district in the Carcavelos region which is allowed to use that designation.

Oelberg (Ger). Vineyard. (Anb) = Baden. (Ber) = Markgräflerland. (Gro) = Lorettoberg. (Vil) = Ehrenstetten.

Oelberg (Ger). Vineyard. (Anb) = Baden. (Ber) = Markgräflerland. (Gro) = Vogtei Rötteln. (Vil) = Efringen-Kirchen.

Oelig (Ger). A wine of high consistency that gives the impression of being oily as it is poured. Has viscosity.

Oenin (USA). A newly discovered

compound of wine by Dr. Leo McCluskey PhD. owner of the Felton-Empire Winery in Santa Cruz, Mid-California. Is a secret chemical that has been christened 'Oenin'.

Oenobilia (Eng). Wine artifacts. e.g. Coasters, corkscrews, decanters, wine funnels, glasses, etc.

Oenological Amelioration (N.Z.). The term given to the practice of adding water to wine to help improve the quality.

Oenologist (Eng). A specialist in the study of wine-making.

Oenology (Eng). The study of wine from a scientific point of view.

Oenomel (Eng). An old English drink of wine and honey.

Oenoparagogos (Gre). Wine producer. Also spelt Oinoparagogas.

Oenophile (Eng). A person who enjoys and loves wine and who also wishes to learn more about wine.

Oenopoyeyon (Gre). Winery. Also spelt Oinopoieion.

Oenos (Gre). Wine. Also spelt Oinos.

Oenos Erythros (Gre). Red wine. See also Oenos Mowros and Oinos Erythros.

Oenos Lewkos (Gre). White wine. See also Oinos Lefkos.

Oenos Mowros (Gre). Red wine. See also Oenos Erythros and Oinos Erythros.

Oenotria (Gre). Lit – 'The land of wine'. The ancient Greek name for Italy.

Oenoxidase (Eng). An enzyme found in grape pips which causes a brown stain to occur in white wines if they are not removed before fermentation.

Oerbier Brasserie (Bel). A brewery based in Diksmuide. Is noted for its dark, top-fermented Oerbier 7.5% alc. by vol.

Oesjaar (S.Afr). Vintage.

Oesterreicher (Aus) (Ger). Another name for the white grape variety Sylvaner.

Oesterreichische Weinguetesiegel (Aus). The official seal for Austrian wine. Found on the label.

Oestrich (Ger). Village. See Östrich.

Oeuil de Perdrix (Fr) (Switz). See Oeil de Perdrix. Misspelling of.

Oeuilly (Fr). A Cru Champagne village in the Canton de Dormans. District = Épernay.

OFC (Can). A Canadian rye whisky produced by the Canadian Schenley Distilleries Ltd. 40% alc. by vol.

Off (Eng). A term that when applied to a beverage denotes it is undrinkable through some malady.

Off-Dry (Eng). See Semi-Dry.

Offenau (Ger). Village. (Anb) = Württemberg. (Ber) = Württembergisch Unterland. (Gro) = Staufenberg. (Vin) = Schön.

Offenburg [ortsteil Fessenbach] (Ger). Village. (Anb) = Baden. (Ber) = Ortenau. (Gro) = Fürsteneck. (Vins) = Bergle, Franzensberger.

Offenburg [ortsteil Zell-Weierbach] (Ger). Village. (Anb) = Baden. (Ber) = Ortenau. (Gro) = Fürsteneck. (Vin) = Abtsberg.

Öffener Wein (Aus). Carafe wine.

Öffener Wein (Ger). Wine sold by the glass.

Offenheim (Ger). Village. (Anb) = Rheinhessen. (Ber) = Wonnegau. (Gro) = Sybillenstein. (Vin) = Mandelberg.

Offertory (Eng). A term which refers to the wine etc. which is offered during religious ceremonies. e.g. The Eucharist.

Off-flavour (Eng). Unwanted flavours found in wine. Many causes, the main one being careless or bad wine-making.

Office Commercial du Portugal (Bel). The information centre on Portuguese wines. Address = Rue Joseph II, 5-Boîte 3–1040, Bruxelles.

Office Commercial du Portugal (Fr). The information centre on Portuguese wines. Address = 135, Boulevard Haussmann – 75008 Paris.

Office International du Vin (Fr). A working group of legislators and wine growers who assess other countries' production.

Office National de Comercialisation des Produits Viti-Vinicoles (Alg). ONCV. A state body established in 1968 to supervise the quality, production and distribution of wines.

Office National Interprofessionnel des Vins de Table (Fr). ONIVIT. A body formed in 1973 to help control the quality of Vin de Table wines.

Offley Forrester Boa Vista (Port). Vintage Port shippers. Vintages – 1870, 1872, 1873, 1874, 1875, 1878, 1881, 1884, 1885, 1887, 1888, 1890, 1892, 1894, 1896, 1897, 1900, 1902, 1904, 1908, 1910, 1912, 1919, 1920, 1922, 1924, 1925, 1927, 1929, 1935, 1950, 1954, 1960, 1962, 1963, 1966, 1967, 1970, 1972, 1975, 1977, 1980, 1982, 1983. Grape varieties used are Barroca, Joao de Santarém, Malvasia pieta, Rufete, Tinta amarela, Touriga francesa and Touriga nacional.

Off-Licence (Eng). A special licence issued to a shop, supermarket etc. which permits the sale of alcoholic beverages between 8.30 a.m. and 10.30 p.m. It does not permit alcoholic beverages to be consumed on the premises.

Off Premise (USA). Off licence. i.e. The sale of alcoholic liquor for consumption off the premises.

Offstein (Ger). Village. (Anb) = Rheinhessen. (Ber) = Wonnegau. (Gro) = Domblick. (Vins) = Engelsberg, Schlossgarten.

Off-Vintages (Eng). Denotes great wines in a poor year which are quite drinkable but not great. Other lesser wines of that year would be poor.

Oficina Comercial de Portugal (Switz). The information centre for Portuguese wines. Address = 50, Quai Gustave Ador-1207 Genève.

Ofique (Sp). A type of refrigeration used to prevent the wine from turning cloudy.

O.G. (Eng) (abbr). See Original Gravity.

Oger (Fr). A Grand Cru Champagne village in the Canton d'Avize. District = Épernay. Re-classified in 1985.

Oggau (Aus). A wine region of the Burgenland.

Oh Be Joyful (Eng). A Barley wine brewed by Whitbread's Brewery in Blackburn, Lancashire.

O'Higgins (Chile). A red wine region south of Santiago.

Ohio (USA). A wine region of the eastern states. Vineyards from Cleveland to Sandistay along Lake Erie.

Ohio Cocktail (Cktl). ½ measure sweet Vermouth, ½ measure Scotch whisky, 3 dashes Orange bitters. Shake well with ice, strain into a cocktail glass.

Ohlenberg (Ger). Vineyard. (Anb) = Mittelrhein. (Ber) = Rheinburgengau. (Gro) = Gedeonseck. (Vil) = Boppard.

Ohligpfad (Ger). Vineyard. (Anb) = Rheinpfalz. (Ber) = Mittelhaardt-Deutsche Weinstrasse. (Gro) = Feuerberg. (Vil) = Bobenheim am Berg.

Ohligsberg (Ger). Vineyard. (Anb) = Mosel-Saar-Ruwer. (Ber) = Bernkastel. (Gro) = Kurfürstlay. (Vil) = Wintrich.

Ohlsbach (Ger). Village. (Anb) = Baden. (Ber) = Ortenau. (Gro) = Fürsteneck. (Vin) = Kinzigtäler.

Ohm (Ger). A wine cask of about 160 litres.

Ohrid (Yug). A wine-producing area in Macedonia.

Oïdium Tuckerii (Fr). See Oiidium Tuckerii.

Oiidium Tuckerii (Lat). Uncinula Necator. Powdery mildew. A fungal vine disease. Also spelt Oïdium Tuckerii.

Oiliness (Eng). A wine malady. Should disappear on its own, but if persistent in a wine, treatment by 'airing' (decanting from one cask to another) will help. Then it should be filtered.

O.I.M.L. (Euro) (abbr). Organisation Internationale de Métrologie Légale. A measurement of alcohol by hydrometer at 20° Celcius (pure water 0% and pure alcohol 100%).

Oinoparagogas (Gre). Wine-producer. Also spelt Oenoparagogos.

Oinopoieion (Gre). Winery. Also spelt Oenopoyeyon.

Oinos (Gre). Wine. Also spelt Oenos.

Oinos Erythros (Gre). Red wine. See also Oenos Erythros.

Oinos Lefkos (Gre). White wine. See Oenos Lefkos.

Oiry (Fr). A Grand Cru Champagne village in the Canton d'Avize. District = Épernay. Re-classified in 1985.

O'Jaffa (Isr). A liqueur made from Jaffa oranges, tangerines and grapefruit.

Oja (River) (Sp). River of northern Spain on which the Rioja wine region is situated and from where it gets its name.

Ojen (Sp). A dry high-proof Anis. Made from Star aniseed in the town of Ojen in southern Spain. 42.5% alc. by vol.

Ojo de Gallo (Sp). Lit – 'Partridge eye'. Applied to the rosé wines of Navarra in north-eastern Spain.

Ojo de Liebre (Sp). Lit – 'Eye of the hare'. A red grape variety grown in Cataluña, Penedés. The Cataluñan name for the Tempranillo.

O.K. (Isr). A Pilsener-style beer at 11.5° Balling produced by a Canadian-financed brewery.

Okanagin (Can). A white grape variety grown in the Okanagin Valley, British Columbia.

Okanagin Valley (Can). A wine-producing region in British Columbia.

Okayama (Jap). A wine-producing region.

O.K. Distillery (Afr). A Rum distillery based on the island of Mauritius in the Indian Ocean.

Oke (USA). The Hawaiian name for the spirit drink Okolehao.

O'Keefe (Can). See Carling O'Keefe.

Okell's (I.O.M). Beers of the Falcon Brewery in Douglas. A draught Mild 1035 O.G. a well-hopped Bitter 1036 O.G. and a Barley Wine 1070 O.G.

Okhotnichya (USSR). Hunter's vodka. Flavoured with botanicals, honey, spices, peppers, fruit peel and coffee. 44% alc. by vol.

Oklahoma Cocktail (Cktl). ⅓ measure Jamaican rum, ⅓ measure dry Vermouth, ⅓ measure dry Gin. Shake well with ice, strain into a cocktail glass.

Okoboji Winery (USA). A winery based in Okoboji, Iowa. Produces mainly French hybrid wines.

Okocim (Pol). A major brewing town in Poland.

Okolehao (USA). A spirit made in Hawaii from roots of the Ti plant, molasses and rice lees. Also known as Oke.

Okolehao Cocktail (Cktl). 1 measure Oke,

½ measure lime juice, 1 measure pine-apple juice. Shake well over ice, strain into a cocktail glass.

Okowita (Pol). The old Polish name for Aqua vitae.

Oksamit Ukraine (USSR). A white table wine produced near Cherson in the Ukraine.

Oktemberian (USA). A wine-producing centre in Armenia.

Oktoberfest (Can). A beer festival held by the Mennonites in their county at Niagara.

Oktober Fest (Ger). The Munich beer festival. Held annually for a week in October.

Okura (Jap). A company who, along with Takara Shuzo, have taken over the Scottish distillery of Tomatin in 1986.

Öküz Gözü (Tur). A white grape variety.

Öl (Scan). The old Norse word for ale (beer).

Øl (Nor). Ale, beer.

Olarra (Sp). A red wine produced by the Bodegas Olarra S.A. Made from the Garnacha, Graciano, Mazuelo and Tempranillo grapes.

Olasrisling (Hun). See Olaszriesling. A white grape variety grown in Pécs.

Olaszliszka (Hun). A noted wine-producing village in the southern foothills.

Olaszriesling (Hun). A name for the Welschriesling. See Olasrisling.

Ölbaum (Ger). Vineyard. (Anb) = Baden. (Ber) = Badische Bergstrasse/Kraichgau. (Gro) = Mannaberg. (Vil) = Malsch.

Ölbaum (Ger). Vineyard. (Anb) = Baden. (Ber) = Badische Bergstrasse/Kraichgau. (Gro) = Mannaberg. (Vil) = Malschenberg.

Ölbaum (Ger). Vineyard. (Anb) = Baden. (Ber) = Badische Bergstrasse/Kraichgau. (Gro) = Mannaberg. (Vil) = Rettigheim.

Ölberg (Ger). Vineyard. (Anb) = Baden. (Ber) = Badische Bergstrasse/Kraichgau. (Gro) = Rittersberg. (Vil) = Dossenheim.

Ölberg (Ger). Vineyard. (Anb) = Baden. (Ber) = Kaiserstuhl-Tuniberg. (Gro) = Vulkanfelsen. (Vil) = Kiechlinsbergen.

Ölberg (Ger). Vineyard. (Anb) = Baden. (Ber) = Ortenau. (Gro) = Fürsteneck. (Vil) = Durbach.

Ölberg (Ger). Vineyard. (Anb) = Rheinhessen. (Ber) = Bingen. (Gro) = Rheingrafenstein. (Vil) = Wöllstein.

Ölberg (Ger). Vineyard. (Anb) = Rheinhessen. (Ber) = Bingen. (Gro) = Sankt Rochuskapelle. (Vil) = Grolsheim.

Ölberg (Ger). Vineyard. (Anb) = Rheinhessen. (Ber) = Nierstein. (Gro) = Auflangen. (Vil) = Nierstein.

Ölberg (Ger). Vineyard. (Anb) = Rheinhessen. (Ber) = Nierstein. (Gro) = Petersberg. (Vil) = Gau-Odernheim.

Ölberg (Ger). Vineyard. (Anb) = Rheinpfalz. (Ber) = Mittelhaardt-Deutsche Weinstrasse. (Gro) = Meerspinne. (Vil) = Königsbach.

Old Ale (Eng). A rich, dark, high-gravity draught Ale with good body. Sold usually between November and March. A 'Winter ale'.

Old Anchor Ale (Eng). A strong cask conditioned Ale 1060 O.G. brewed by the Jolly Roger Brewery in Upton-on-Severn, Worcs.

Old Bank Street (Eng). A home-brew public house in Manchester. Noted for its cask conditioned Old Bank Street Bitter 1043 O.G. brewed from malt extract.

Old Bedford (Eng). A bottled Barley wine 1078 O.G. brewed by the Charles Wells Brewery in Bedford.

Old Bill (Eng). A cask conditioned Ale 1065–1071 O.G. brewed by the Everards Brewery, Leicester, Leicestershire.

Old Bismark (Port). A vintage character Port shipped by Yates Bros.

Old Bob Ale (Eng). A bottled strong Pale ale 1050 O.G. brewed by the Ridley Brewery in Chelmsford, Essex.

Old Boone Distillery (USA). A Bourbon whiskey distillery based in Louisville, Kentucky.

Old Borer (Austr). A red wine from the Bonnonee Winery, Victoria.

Old Bosham Bitter (Eng). A cask conditioned Bitter 1044 O.G. brewed by the Bosham Brewery in Bosham, West Sussex.

Old Brewery Bitter (Eng). A cask conditioned and keg Bitter 1039 O.G. brewed by the Samuel Smith Brewery in Tadcaster, Yorkshire.

Old Buck (S.Afr). A brand of medium Sherry.

Old Burton Brewery (Eng). A museum. See Everards.

Old Bushmills (Ire). A single Malt whiskey from the famous distillery of Bushmills. An Irish Whiskey. 43% alc. by vol.

Old Bushmills Black Bush (Ire). A premium blend of Old Bushmills pot-still whiskies matured in Sherry casks for a minimum of 7 years and lightened slightly with a dash of Coleraine grain Whiskey 43% alc. by vol.

Old Buzzard (Eng). A Winter brew 1048 O.G. brewed by the Cotleigh Brewery in Wiveliscombe, Somerset.

Old Cameron Brig (Scot). A straight Grain whisky from the Cameron Brig distillery. The only single Grain whisky sold as a single grain in bottle. 43% alc. by vol. See Cameronbridge.

Old Chalet (S.Afr). A brand of Brandy produced by Uniewyn.

Old Charlie (W.Ind). The brand-name of a dark Rum produced on the island of Jamaica.

Old Charter Distillery Co (USA). A Bourbon whiskey distillery based in Louisville, Kentucky. Produces a Bourbon whiskey of same name. 40% alc. by vol.

Old Chester Ale (Eng). A bottled dark Ale 1067 O.G. brewed by the Greenall Whitley Brewery in Warrington. Exported under the names of Warrington Brown, Ebony and Chester Brown.

Old Colonial Ale (Austr). A full-bodied, well-matured beer brewed by the Courage Brewery in Victoria.

Old Coronation Ruby (Port). A fine Ruby Port (brand-name) from the da Silva Port shippers.

Old Croak Beer (Eng). A cask conditioned Ale 1035 O.G. brewed by the Frog and Parrot home-brew public house, Sheffield, Yorkshire.

Old Crofter (Eng). See David's Old Crofter's Bitter.

Old Crow Bourbon (USA). The oldest Bourbon whiskey brand from the Old Crow distillery started by Dr. James Crow. Now owned by the National Distillers.

Old Crow Distillery (USA). See Old Crow Bourbon.

Old Custom House Extra Special Pale (Mad). A brand of Madeira produced by Rutherford and Miles.

Old Dan Ale (Eng). A bottled Brown Ale 1075 O.G. brewed by the Daniel Thwaites Brewery in Blackburn, Lancashire.

Old Devil (Eng). A strong Ale 1060 O.G. brewed by the Wiltshire Brewery Co. in Tisbury, Wiltshire.

Old Duque de Sevilla (Sp). A cask-aged Brandy produced by Vincente Suso y Perez in Cariñena, north-eastern Spain.

Old Dutch Liqueurs (Hol). These are traditional-styled drinks that are closely associated with domestic life.

Old East India (Eng). An old English grade of Sherry. An old Oloroso with a natural sweet taste. Named by the practice of taking Olorosos on voyages to India. Similar to Madeiras.

Olde English Cyder (Eng). See Gaymers Olde English Cyder.

Olde English 800 (USA). America's strongest beer 7.5% alc. by vol. brewed by the Blitz-Weinhard Brewery in Portland, Oregon.

Old Eli (Eng). A cask conditioned Ale 1050 O.G. brewed by the Sair home-brew public house in Linthwaite, Huddersfield, Yorkshire.

Old England (Eng). The brand-name of a range of British Sherries produced by Mather & Sons.

Old English Advocaat (Eng). An Advocaat produced by J. Townend and Sons of Hull under the name of Keelings. Made from fortified wine and eggs.

Old English Mead (Eng). 2 cups clear honey, 4 quarts spring water, 3 ozs. brown sugar, juice of a lemon, 2 egg whites, 1 oz. yeast. Simmer honey, water, sugar and eggs. Add lemon, cool, add yeast, stand in a warm cupboard, bottle.

Olde Norfolk Punch (Eng). A Monastic herbal drink produced by Welle Manor Hall in Upwell. Contains various herbs.

Oldest (The) (Fr). An 1805 distilled Cognac 30% alc. by vol. produced by A.E. Dor in Jarnac.

Olde Time Ale (Eng). A bottled strong Ale 1070 O.G. brewed by the McMullen's Brewery in Hertford.

Old Etonian (Cktl). ½ measure Lillet, ½ measure Gin, 2 dashes Orange bitters, 2 dashes Crème de Noyau. Stir over ice, strain into a cocktail glass, add a twist of orange peel.

Old Etonian Cocktail (Cktl). ½ measure dry Gin, ½ measure Lillet, 2 dashes Amer Picon, 2 dashes Crème de Noyau. Shake over ice, strain into a cocktail glass.

Old Evel (Eng). A cask conditioned Ale 1048 O.G. brewed by the New Forest Brewery, Hampshire.

Old Expensive Ale (Eng). A strong Winter ale 1065 O.G. brewed by the Burton Bridge Brewery, Burton-on-Trent, Staffs.

Old Farm (Scot). A premium blended Scotch whisky from Glenmoriston Estates, Glenmoriston. 40% alc. by vol.

Old Fashioned (Cktl). Into a heavy tumbler place 1 lump of sugar, moisten with Angostura. Crush, add an ice cube and a slice of orange. Add 2 measures of Bourbon whiskey. Stir and serve with a spoon.

Old Fashioned Cocktail (Cktl). 1 sugar cube, ½ gill Bénédictine, 1 teaspoon Orange bitters, 1 teaspoon Angostura. Place sugar in wine glass, add 1½ tablespoons water and crush. Add an ice cube and rest of ingredients. Stir well. Serve with a dash of lemon peel juice on top.

Old-Fashioned Glass (Eng). A squat, straight-sided tumbler of ⅓ pint capacity used for drinks served 'On the rocks'. Also known as an On-the-rocks glass.

Old Fettercairn (Scot). A single Malt whisky distillery in Kincardineshire.

Owned by Whyte and Mackay Ltd. A Highland malt. Produces an 8 year old Malt. 40% alc. by vol.

Old Fitzgerald Distillery (USA). A Bourbon whiskey distillery based in Louisville, Kentucky. Produces a Bourbon whiskey of same name. 40% alc. by vol.

Old Forester (USA). A brand of Kentucky Bourbon whiskey produced by the Brown-Forman Distillers in Louisville, Kentucky.

Old Fort Brewery (Can). A brewery based in British Columbia. Is noted for its Pacific Gold and Yukon Gold (both Pilsener-style Lager beers).

Old Genie Ale (Eng). A naturally conditioned strong Ale 1070 O.G. brewed by the Big Lamp Brewery in Newcastle-on-Tyne. Is naturally conditioned in the bottle.

Old Georgia Julep (Cktl). Dissolve a little sugar in some water in a tumbler. Add ½ gill Brandy, ½ gill Peach brandy, a few sprigs of mint, ice. Stir and serve. Also known as a Southern Julep.

Old German Beer (USA). A Beer brewed by the Yuengling Brewery in Pottsville.

Old Gloag (Scot). A 60 year old Scotch whisky produced by Mathew Gloag & Sons.

Old Glory (Cktl). 3 parts Zwacks Viennese Apricot, 2 parts lemon juice, 2 parts orange juice, 1 part Barack Palinka, dash egg white. Shake over ice, strain into a cocktail glass.

Old Glory (Eng). A medium strength Bitter produced by the Old Washford Mill home-brew public house at Redditch New Town.

Old Glory Ale (Eng). A bottled Pale ale 1074 O.G. brewed by the Greenall Whitley Brewery in Warrington, Lancashire. Exported as Old Chester Gold or Chester Gold.

Old Gold (Can). A Canadian whisky produced by Gilbey Canada Ltd.

Old Gold (Cktl). Fill a brandy balloon half-full of Golden Tequila, add a few drops of Maggi sauce to give a rich golden colour. Add 8 drops lime juice, stir, top with ice.

Old Gold Beer (Eng). A cask conditioned Ale 1047 O.G. brewed by the Ashford Brewery in Ashford, Kent.

Old Grand-Dad (USA). A famous old Bourbon whiskey from Kentucky. 1880. Commonly known as the 'Head of the Bourbon family'. Produced by a distillery of same name. 40% alc. by vol.

Old Grumble Ale (Eng). A cask conditioned, kegged and bottled Ale 1060 O.G. brewed by the Tisbury Brewery in Wiltshire.

Oldham Brewery (Eng). A brewery that was taken over by the Boddington Brewery in 1982. Brews a variety of beers.

Old Harmany (Scot). A blended Scotch whisky produced exclusively for the Japanese market by John Walker and Son.

Old Hickory (USA). A brand of Bourbon whiskey produced in Illinois. 40% alc. by vol.

Old Highland Blend (Scot). A brand of blended Scotch whisky bottled by Eldridge Pope and Co. Ltd. in Dorset. 40% alc. by vol.

Old Hill Vineyard (USA). A small vineyard based near Glen Ellen, Sonoma Valley, California. Grape variety – Zinfandel.

Old Hock (Eng). An eighteenth-century term found on bottle tickets to define the finer German wines.

Old Hoffman Distillery (USA). A Bourbon whiskey distillery based near Frankfort, Kentucky. Produces a Bourbon whiskey of same name. 40% alc. by vol.

Old Hookey (Eng). A dark Winter ale 1049 O.G. brewed by the Hook Norton Brewery in Oxfordshire.

Old Horizontal Ale (Eng). A strong Ale 1054 O.G. brewed by the Stocks Brewery in Doncaster, Yorkshire.

Old Jack (S.Am). The brand-name of a Demerara Rum from British Guyana.

Old Jock Ale (Scot). A bottled strong Ale 1070 O.G. brewed by the Broughton Brewery near Biggar.

Old John Bitter (Eng). A keg Bitter 1036 O.G. brewed by the Leicester Brewery, Leicester.

Old Kentucky (USA). A brand of Kentucky Bourbon whiskey produced in Louisville, Kentucky.

Old Landed (Eng). The alternative name for British Bonded. Derives from the fact that the Cognac is landed before being put into bottle.

Old Lodge (Port). The brand-name of a fine old Tawny Port produced by the Smith Woodhouse Port shippers.

Old Lowesmoor (Eng). An Ale brewed by the Jolly Roger Brewery in Worcester, Worcestershire.

Old Master Ale (Eng). A strong Ale 1060 O.G. brewed by the Raven Brewery in Brighton.

Old Masters Cream Sherry (The) (N.Z.) A brand of Sherry produced by the Villa Maria Winery in South Auckland.

Old Mill Brewery (Eng). Opened in 1983 in Snaith, Humberside. Brews cask conditioned and keg beers.

Old Mill Special Reserve (Scot). A special reserve Highland malt whisky (vintage

1968) from the Tamnavulin-Glenlivet Distillery. 43% alc. by vol.

Old Mill Winery (The) (Austr). Address = Willunga Road, McLaren Vale, South Australia. Vineyards at Barossa Valley, Tintara in the McLaren Vale and in Waikerie. Winery – Siegersdorf Winery.

Old Montrose (Scot). A De Luxe blended Scotch whisky blended and distributed by the Montrose Whisky Company.

Old Mr. Boston (USA). A large noted distilling Company based in Boston, Massachusetts. Produces most styles of spirits and liqueurs.

Old Mull (Scot). A blended Scotch Whisky from John Hopkins and Co. Ltd. in Glasgow (part of DCL).

Old Navy (W.Ind). The brand-name of a dark Rum sold by Seagram U.K.

Old Nick (Cktl). ¼ measure Drambuie, ½ measure Rye whiskey, ⅛ measure orange juice, ⅛ measure lemon juice, 2 dashes Orange bitters. Shake over ice, strain into a cocktail glass. Top with a cherry.

Old Nick (Eng). A Barley wine 1084 O.G. brewed by the Young Brewery in London.

Old Nick (W.Ind). The brand-name of a white Rum produced by Bardinet on the island of Martinique.

Old Nigel Ale (Eng). A Winter ale 1060 O.G. brewed by the Hoskins Brewery in Leicester.

Old Norfolk Ale (Eng). A Winter ale 1043 O.G. brewed by the Woodforde Brewery in Norfolk.

Old Number 7 (USA). The brand-name of a Sour-mash whiskey produced by the Jack Daniel Distillery, Tennessee. 39% alc. by vol.

Old Oak (W.Ind). A brand of Rum produced on the island of Trinidad by the Trinidad Distillers Ltd.

Old Oak Ale (Eng). A cask conditioned Ale 1044 O.G. brewed by the Oak Brewery in Ellsmere Port, Cheshire.

Old Oporto (Port). The brand-name of a rich old vintage character Port produced by Smith Woodhouse Port shippers. Produced in 1984 to celebrate their centenary.

Old Original (Eng). A strong cask conditioned Bitter 1050 O.G. brewed by the Everards Brewery in Leicester.

Old Overholt (USA). The brand-name of a Rye whiskey. 40% alc. by vol.

Old Pal (Cktl). ⅓ measure Campari, ⅓ measure Rye whiskey, ⅓ measure dry Vermouth. Stir over ice, strain into a cocktail glass.

Old Parr (Scot). A 12 year old De Luxe

blended Scotch whisky produced by MacDonald Greenlees in Leith, Edinburgh. 43% alc. by vol.

Old Particular (It). See O.P.

Old Peculier (Eng). A famous strong Ale 1058.5 O.G. brewed by the Theakstons Brewery in Marsham, Yorkshire. Named after the town's ancient Ecclesiastical court, (Peculier of Marsham) hence the peculiar spelling. Also a variety is exported to Holland at 1066 O.G

Old Pledge (USA). See O.P.

Old Prentice Distillery (USA). A Kentucky Bourbon whiskey distillery based in Lawrenceburg, Kentucky. Produces Eagle Rare.

Old Priory Vintage Character (Port). A full-bodied, ruby Port produced by Smith Woodhouse Port shippers.

Old Pulteney (Scot). A single Malt whisky distillery based in Wick, Caithness. Owned by the Hiram Walker Group. A Highland malt. Produces an 8 year old Malt. 40% alc. by vol.

Old Railway (N.Z). The brand-name used by the Pechar's Vineyards for their wines.

Old Rarity (Scot). A blended Scotch whisky produced by Bulloch, Lade and Co. Ltd. of Glasgow. 40% alc. by vol.

Old Rarity (Scot). A 12 year old De Luxe blended Scotch whisky produced by Bulloch, Lade and Co. Ltd. in Glasgow. 43% alc. by vol.

Old Red Fox (USA). The brand-name of a Kentucky Bourbon whiskey produced by the Old Red Fox Bourbon Whiskey Co. of Louisville, Kentucky. 8 years old, it is aged in charred oak. 40% alc. by vol.

Old Red Fox Kentucky Bourbon Whiskey Co (USA). A distillery based in Louisville, Kentucky. See Old Red Fox.

Old Rio (Cktl). 1 measure Batida de Coco, 1 measure Scotch whisky. Shake well over crushed ice, strain into a cocktail glass. Dress with a cherry.

Old Rummy (Eng). The name given to Admiral Vernon 1745 who used Rum to end scurvy on ships from which the drink gets its name. See Rumbustion and Rumbullion.

Old Santa Beer (Eng). A cask conditioned Bitter 1066 O.G. brewed by the Bridgewater Arms, a home-brew public house in Little Gaddesden, Hertfordshire.

Old Schiedam (Hol). A brand of Dutch Gin. See Schiedam Gin.

Old Schmidt (Ger). A brand of Rum produced by Hansen in Flensburg.

Old Shields Vineyard (Eng). Address =

O

Ardleigh, Essex. 1 ha. planted in 1971. Grape varieties – Müller-Thurgau, Pinot gris.

Old Smuggler (Scot). A blended Scotch whisky from the Hiram Walker group. 40% alc. by vol.

Old Snowy Ale (Eng). A cask conditioned Winter ale 1054 O.G. brewed by the Alexandra Brewery in Brighton.

Old Southside (Eng). The old name for blended Madeira wines in London.

Old South Winery (USA). A small winery based in Natchez, Mississippi. 5.5 ha. Produces Muscadine wines.

Old Speckled Hen (Eng). A bottled strong Ale 1050 O.G. brewed by the Moorland Brewery in Abingdon, Oxfordshire.

Old Spot Prize Ale (Eng). A strong Ale brewed by the Uley Brewery in Gloucestershire.

Old Stagg (USA). The brand-name of a Bourbon whiskey produced in Kentucky. 40% alc. by vol.

Old Stanley Distillery (USA). A Bourbon whiskey distillery based in Kentucky. Produces Bourbon whiskey of same name. 40% alc. by vol.

Old St. Croix (W.Ind). The brand-name of a Rum produced by the Virgin Islands Rum Industries Ltd.

Old Stonehenge Bitter (Eng). A Bitter beer 1041 O.G. brewed by the Wiltshire Brewery Company, Tisbury, Wiltshire.

Old Strong (Eng). A Winter ale 1046 O.G. brewed by the Tolly Cobbold Brewery in Ipswich.

Old Style (USA). A sweet, full-bodied Beer brewed by the Heileman Brewery in La Crosse, Wisconsin.

Old Sunnybrook (USA). The brand-name of a Bourbon whiskey produced in Kentucky. 40% alc. by vol.

Old Suntory (Jap). The brand-name of a mature blended whiskey produced by the Suntory Distilling Co.

Old Swan (Eng). See Ma Pardoes.

Old Swan (Eng). A Whitbread home-brew public house in Cheltenham. Produces cask conditioned beers from malt extract.

Old Tankard (USA). A nationally distributed beer brewed by the Pabst Brewery.

Old Tap (USA). A Lager beer brewed by the Pabst Brewery.

Old Taylor Bourbon (USA). A famous Bourbon whiskey of Kentucky founded in 1880's by Col. E.H. Taylor. 43% alc. by vol.

Old Thumper Beer (Eng). A cask conditioned and bottled Bitter 1060 O.G. brewed by the Ringwood Brewery, Hampshire.

Old Timer Ale (Eng). A draught Bitter 1055 O.G. brewed by the Wadworth Brewery in Wiltshire. Bottled and canned version 1052 O.G.

Old Tom Ale (Eng). A bottled Ale 1065 O.G. brewed by the Oldham Brewery in Lancashire.

Old Tom Ale (Eng). A keg Bitter 1037 O.G. brewed by the John Smith Brewery in East Midlands.

Old Tom Ale (Eng). A strong Ale 1080 O.G. brewed by the Robinson Brewery in Stockport, Greater Manchester.

Old Tom Gin (USA). A sweetened Gin used mainly for cocktails.

Old Tradition (Eng). A Bitter beer 1038 O.G. and a Mild ale 1033 O.G. brewed by the North County Breweries in Hull, Yorkshire.

Old Triangle Vineyard (Austr). Part of the Hill-Smith Estate in the Barossa Valley. 20 ha. of mainly Rhine riesling and Scheurebe grapes.

Old Trinity House Bual (Mad). A medium sweet Madeira produced by Rutherford and Miles.

Old Vienna (Can). A Lager beer brewed by the Carling O'Keefe Brewery.

Old Vintage (Fr). A blend of very old Grande Champagne Cognac (over 30 years) produced by Hine.

Old Washford Mill (Eng). A home-brew public house in Redditch New Town. Brews a medium strength Bitter called Old Glory.

Old Winery Vineyard (Austr). Part of the Hill-Smith Estate in the Barossa Valley. 4 ha.

Oleron's Disease (Eng). A vine bacterial blight. Stains appear on the leaves and flowers and destroy the cell walls. Copper sprays have almost eradicated it from Europe.

Olevano Romano (It). See Cesanese di Olevano Romano.

Olgaberg (Ger). Vineyard. (Anb) = Baden. (Ber) = Bodensee. (Gro) = Sonnenufer. (Vil) = Singen.

Ölgässel (Ger). Vineyard. (Anb) = Rheinpfalz. (Ber) = Mittelhaardt-Deutsche Weinstrasse. (Gro) = Rebstöckel. (Vil) = Diedesfeld.

Ölgild (Ger). Vineyard. (Anb) = Rheinhessen. (Ber) = Nierstein. (Gro) = Sankt Alban. (Vil) = Lörzweiler.

Oliang (Asia). A hot, thick, black coffee served with sugar in glasses with tinned cream in Thailand. If cream is omitted is called Café-Oh.

Oliena (It). The label term for the wine Cannonau di Sardegna if the grapes used for making the wine are produced in this commune.

Oliena (It). A sweet heavy red wine of Sardinia.

Olifant (Hol). A Jenever produced by Allied Breweries.

Olifants River (S.Afr). A wine region based in the north-western Cape province.

Olifantsrivier Co-operative (S.Afr). Based in Olifants River. Address = Olifantsrivier Koöperatiewe Wynkelders, Box 75, Vredendal 8160. North Western Wine Merchants Wines. Produces varietal wines.

Olifantsrivier Koöperatiewe Wynkelders (S.Afr). See Olifantsrivier Cooperative.

Oligocene (It). Sandstone.

Olite (Sp). One of three sub-zones in the Ribera Alta. Based in the north of the region, it produces the best wines. Grapes – Garnacha and Tempranillo.

Olivar (Sp). A straw-coloured Fino sherry produced by Wisdom and Warter in Jerez de la Frontera.

Oliveira Ferrari (Sp). A Cava now owned by Cavas del Ampurdán. Is based in Vilafranca del Penedés.

Olivella (It). A red grape variety grown in Campania.

Olive Oil (Euro). Used in ancient times before the invention of the cork to keep the air from the wine by floating it on top.

Oliver Winery (USA). A winery based in Bloomington, Indiana. Has vineyards in Kentucky.

Olivette Cocktail (Cktl).(1). ½ gill Plymouth Gin, 2 dashes Gomme syrup, 2 dashes Absinthe, 2 dashes Orange bitters. Stir over ice, strain into a cocktail glass, add an olive and squeeze of lemon juice on top.

Olivette Cocktail (Cktl).(2). ¼ gill dry Gin, ¼ gill French vermouth, 2 dashes Absinthe, 2 dashes plain syrup, 2 dashes Angostura, 2 dashes Orange bitters. Stir over ice, strain into a 5 oz. wine glass. Serve with an olive and dash of lemon peel juice on top.

Olivier (Fr). See Château Olivier.

Olizy-Violaine (Fr). A Cru Champagne village in the Canton de Châtillon-sur-Marne. District = Reims.

Ollauri (Sp). A noted wine-producing village in the Rioja Alta.

Olle Cocktail (Cktl). Into a Champagne saucer put an ice cube, 1½ tablespoons dry Gin, 1½ tablespoons Cointreau. Stir and fill up with iced Champagne.

Ollioules (Fr). A commune in the A.C. Bandol, Provence, south-eastern France.

Ollon (Switz). A wine-producing village in the Chablais, Vaud Canton.

Olmeca (Mex). A brand-name of Tequila.

Olmeto (Fr). A wine-producing region of south-western Corsica. Produces full-flavoured wines.

Olomouc Brewery (Czec). A brewery based in north-eastern Czec.

Oloroso (Port). Denotes fragrant, scented.

Oloroso (Sp). Heavy golden Sherries which are dry in their natural state. Are usually sweetened for the U.K. market. See Cream, Milk and Brown Sherries.

Oloroso Dona Juana (Sp). A brand of Oloroso sherry produced by Sanchez Romate in Jerez.

Oloroso la Novia (Sp). A brand of Oloroso sherry produced by Marqués de Misa.

Oloroso Muy Viejo (Sp). An Almacenista sherry bottled by Lustau in Jerez de la Frontera.

Oloroso Sangre y Trabajadero (Sp). A brand of dry Oloroso sherry produced by Cuvillo at Puerto de Santa Maria.

Ölsberg (Ger). Vineyard. (Anb) = Mittelrhein. (Ber) = Rheinburgengau. (Gro) = Schloss Schönburg. (Vil) = Oberwessel.

Ölschnabel (Ger). Vineyard. (Anb) = Franken. (Ber) = Steigerwald. (Gro) = Kapellenberg. (Vil) = Ziegelanger.

Oltrepò Barbera (It). D.O.C. red wine from Lombardy. Made from the Barbera grape 90–100%, Uva rara and Croatina 10% grapes.

Oltrepò Bonarda (It). D.O.C. red wine from Lombardy. Made from the Croatina, Barbera and Uva rara grapes.

Oltrepó Cortese (It). D.O.C. white wine from Lombardy. Made from 100% Cortese grapes.

Oltrepó Moscato (It). D.O.C. white wine from Lombardy. Made from 100% Moscato bianco grapes. The D.O.C. can also be used for the sparkling wines produced in accordance with regulations in the region.

Oltrepó Pavese (It). An area in the province of Pavia in Lombardy. 20 miles south of Milan, south of the bank of the river Pó.

Oltrepó Pavese (It). D.O.C. red wine from Lombardy. Made from the Barbera 65%, Croatina 25% and Uva rara and Ughetta 45% grapes. The D.O.C. can also be used to describe the sparkling wine produced in accordance with regulations in the region.

Oltrepó Pinot (It). A red, rosé or white wine from Lombardy. Style depends on grape variety and vinification method. Pinot grigio and Pinot nero are used. D.O.C. can also be used to describe the sparkling wines produced in accordance with regulations in the region.

Oltrepó Riesling (It). D.O.C. white wine

from Lombardy. Made from the Riesling italico and Renano grapes. D.O.C. can also be used to describe the sparkling wines produced in accordance with the regulations in the region.

Olvi Brewery (Fin). A small brewery based in Iisalmi, central Finland.

Olympia (Gre). A wine-producing region in north-eastern Greece. Produces red, rosé and white wines.

Olympia (USA). A light Beer brewed by the Olympia Brewery in Washington.

Olympia Brewery (USA). A brewery based in St. Paul.

Olympia Brewing (USA). A brewery based in Olympia, Washington.

Olympia Cocktail (Cktl). ⅓ gill dark Rum, juice ½ lime, 2 dashes Cherry brandy. Stir over ice, strain into a cocktail glass.

Olympian (USA). A style of wine glass of various sizes made by the Libbey Company.

Olympic (Cktl). ⅓ measure Brandy, ⅓ measure orange Curaçao, ⅓ measure orange juice. Shake well over ice, strain into a cocktail glass.

Omar Khayyam (Egy). A full red wine with the lightest flavour of dates.

Omar Khayyam (Ind). A dry sparkling (méthode champenoise) wine produced at Narayangaon.

Omega Cut (Ger). A method of bench grafting developed at the Geisenheim Research Institute using a machine which cuts an Omega [Ω] cut into the root-stock with the scion cut so as to slot into the root-cut.

Omnia Cocktail (Cktl). ½ measure Brandy, ½ measure Vodka, 2 dashes each of sweet Vermouth, Maraschino and Grand Marnier. Stir over ice, strain into a cocktail glass. Top with a cherry.

Omphacium (Lat). The juice of unripe grapes.

Onctueux (Fr). A fat, rich, full-bodied wine.

ONCV (Alg) (abbr). See Office National de Commercialisation des Produits Viti-Vinicoles.

Ondaàš (Czec). A dark, Special beer 16° Balling brewed in north Moravia.

Ondarrubi Beltza (Sp). A red grape variety grown in Chacolí.

Ondarrubi Zuria (Sp). A white grape variety grown in Chacolí. Is also known as the Courbut blanc.

Ondenc (Fr). A red grape variety grown in the Bergerac region.

Ondrinkbaar (Hol). Undrinkable.

O'Neale (Sp). A Sherry producer based in Jerez de la Frontera.

One Hundred [100] Pipers (Scot). The

brand-name for a De Luxe blended Scotch whisky from Seagram. 43% alc. by vol.

One Ireland Cocktail (Cktl). ⅕ gill Irish whiskey, 2 dashes (green) Crème de Menthe. Blend with a scoop of vanilla ice cream in a blender. Pour into a Champagne saucer. Dress with a cherry. Serve with straws.

One Yard of Flannel (Cktl). See Ale Flip.

Ongkaf (Lux). A vineyard site in the village of Machtum.

Onion Shape (Eng). A bottle shape of the 1670–1720 era. Made of glass, it was the most associated shape of early glass bottles.

Onion Skin (Eng). A description of the colour of certain rosé wines. e.g. Vin gris of the Jura and Tavel of the Rhône.

ONIVIT (Fr) (abbr). See Office National Interprofessionnel des Vins de Table.

Onkelchen (Ger). Vineyard. (Anb) = Nahe. (Ber) = Schloss Böckelheim. (Gro) = Burgweg. (Vil) = Norheim.

On Licence (Eng). A licence issued by the Licensing Justices for the sale of alcoholic beverages. See Full-On Licence.

On Premise (USA). On licence. i.e. Bar, restaurant, hotel etc. for the consumption of alcohol on the premises of sale.

Onsdorf (Ger). Village. (Anb) = Mosel-Saar-Ruwer. (Ber) = Obermosel. (Gro) = Gipfel. (Vin) = Hubertusberg.

Ontario (USA). A little used white cross grape variety.

Ontario (USA). A wine district of southern California. Produces dessert, table and sparkling wines.

Ontario Department of Agriculture Experimental Station (Can). Based at Vineland, Ontario. A research station that tests vines to establish their wine-making qualities.

On The House (Eng). A term used by the management of a hostelry for free drinks given by them to celebrate an occasion or for some other reason.

On The Nose (Eng). A term given to the art of judging a wine's qualities for blending without tasting, only by smell. Used in Brandy, Port and Sherry production etc.

On The Rocks (USA). Served with ice. Usually straight spirits in a tumbler with plenty of ice.

On-The-Rocks Glass (USA). A name for the 'Old-fashioned' glass.

On The Waggon (Eng). Denotes a person that has 'given up' or is being 'taken off' alcoholic drinks due to ill health or other reasons. e.g. financial, family etc. See also Waggon (Off the).

Onthouding (Hol). Abstinence from

alcohol.

Ontkurken (Hol). Uncork.

Oolitic Chalk (Fr). The chalk soil of Champagne.

Oolong Tea (E.Asia). A designation for semi-fermented tea from Taiwan. See Black Tea and Green Tea.

Oom Tas (S.Afr). A white, dry wine made by the Stellenbosch Farmers' Winery from the white Cinsault and Muscat d'Alexandria grapes.

Oorsprong (S.Afr). Origin.

007 (Eng). See Double Zero Seven [007].

O.P. (Asia) (abbr). Orange Pekoe. A tea grade.

O.P. (It) (abbr). Old Particular. An old style name given to Marsala. Denotes 2 years ageing at 18% alc. by vol.

O.P. (USA) (abbr). Old Pledge. A pledge taken by people in the nineteenth century to drink only moderately.

Opal Cocktail (Cktl).(1). ¾ measure dry Gin, ¼ measure Crème de Banane, dash blue Curaçao, dash lemon juice, teaspoon powdered sugar. Shake well over ice, strain into a cocktail glass (frosted with blue castor sugar). Dress with a slice of lime.

Opal Cocktail (Cktl).(2). 1 measure dry Gin, ½ measure Triple Sec, ½ measure orange juice, 2 dashes Orange flower water, 2 dashes Gomme syrup. Shake over ice, strain into a cocktail glass.

O.P. Anderson (Swe). A brand of aniseed, caraway and fennel-flavoured Akvavit. Is light yellow in colour.

Opava Brewery (Czec). A brewery based in north-eastern Czec.

O.P.B. (It) (abbr). See Opera Pia Barolo.

Open Fermenter (USA). The name given to an open fermentation vat for beer or wine.

Opening Cocktail (Cktl). ½ measure Rye whiskey, ¼ measure sweet Vermouth, ¼ measure Grenadine. Stir over ice, strain into a cocktail glass.

Opening Times (Eng). These are the fixed times that licensed premises are allowed to open. Times vary from region to region.

Openknit (Eng). A term used to describe an open and enjoyable nose or palate on a wine.

Opera (Cktl). ⅔ measure dry Gin, ⅙ measure Dubonnet, ⅙ measure Maraschino. Stir over ice, strain, add a squeeze of orange peel juice on top.

Opera Pia Barolo (It). Stands for the 'Good works of Barolo'. A family named Falletti, the Marchesi of Barolo, were vineyard owners who did much to popularise the wines of Barolo. The last Marchesa, a charitable woman, devoted both time and money to the poor and her activities were known as O.P.B.

Operette (S.Afr). A fresh, dry white wine produced by the Villiera Estate.

Opfingen (Ger). Village. (Anb) = Baden. (Ber) = Kaiserstuhl-Tuniberg. (Gro) = Attilafelsen. (Vin) = Sonnenberg.

Ophélia (Fr). A Bière brewed by the Ricour Brasserie in Cappel.

Opici Winery (USA). A small winery based in Cucamonga, California. Produces varietal wines.

Opimian (Lat). A white wine produced in Falernum in Roman times. Was made from very ripe grapes. Was also known as Falerian Opimian.

Opius One (USA). The name of a rich, red wine produced jointly by Baron Philippe de Rothschild and Robert Mondavi in the Napa Valley, California.

Oplenačka Ružica (Yug). A rosé wine produced in northern Serbia.

Opol (Yug). A dark coloured, medium-dry, rosé made from the Plavac grape in Dalmatia.

Oporto (Hun). A red grape variety grown in central Hungary. Is known as the Bastardo in Portugal.

Oporto (Port). A wine port on the mouth of the river Douro. Is the centre of the Port wine trade.

Oppenheim (Ger). Village. (Anb) = Rheinhessen. (Ber) = Nierstein. (Gro) = Güldenmorgen. (Vins) = Daubhaus, Gutlenthaus, Herrenberg, Kreuz.

Oppenheim (Ger). Village. (Anb) = Rheinhessen. (Ber) = Nierstein. (Gro) = Krötenbrunnen. (Vins) = Herrengarten, Paterhof, Schloss, Schlossberg.

Oppenheimer Goldberg (Ger). An old Germanic name for the wines from around Oppenheim town and vineyards up to 30 kms in area. Now no longer allowed to be used.

Opstal Estate (S.Afr). Based in Slanghoek. Address = Slanghoek, Rawsonville 6845. Produces Droë Wit and varietal wines.

Opthalmo (Cyp). An oval-shaped white grape variety.

Optic (Eng). The name given to the visual measure which is automatic. Gives a pre-set measure. Sizes are ⅓, ¼, ⅕ and ⅙ gill. Sealed by the Government.

Optic Goblet (USA). An alternative name for the Club goblet.

Optima (Ger). A white grape variety. A cross between the Müller-Thurgau and the Sylvaner X Riesling. Gives high sugar.

Optimator (Ger). A Doppelbock beer brewed by the Spatenbräu Brauerei in Munich.

O

Opulent (Eng). A term used to describe a rich, luxurious bouquet and palate. Usually from a recognised grape variety. i.e. Pinot noir, Riesling, Sauvignon, etc.

Oradea (Rum). A wine-producing area of north-western Rumania. Produces mainly medium-dry, white wines.

Oragnac (Hol). A Cognac and Triple Sec flavoured liqueur produced by the Bols company.

Oran (Alg). A mainly red wine-producing region based in western Algeria. The wines are low in acid and strong in alcohol. Principal areas are – Coteaux de Tlemcen, Coteaux du Mascara, Dahra and Monts du Tessalah.

Orange (Eng). A home-brew public house in Pimlico, London. Owned by the Clifton Inns. Brews cask conditioned SW1 1040 O.G. and SW2 1050 O.G.

Orangeade (Eng). A non-alcoholic carbonated orange drink.

Orangeade (USA). Orange juice, sugar syrup, soda water, orange slices. Serve in tall glasses over crushed ice.

Orange Bitters (Euro). Used widely in cocktails, especially Gin based. Has tonic and digestive properties. See Amer Picon.

Orange Bloom (Cktl). ¼ measure Gin, ¼ measure Cointreau, ¼ measure sweet Vermouth. Stir over ice, strain into a cocktail glass. Add a cherry.

Orange Blossom (Cktl). 1 jigger dry Gin, 1 oz. orange juice, 1 teaspoon sugar. shake over ice, strain into a cocktail glass. Top with a squeeze of orange peel juice.

Orange Brandy (Eng). Seville oranges steeped in Brandy with lemons and sugar.

Orange Buck (Cktl). ¾ measure dry Gin, ¼ measure orange juice, juice ¼ lime. Shake over ice, strain into an ice-filled highball glass. Top with ginger ale.

Orange Cadillac (Cktl). 1 fl.oz. Galliano, ¾ fl.oz. white Crème de Cacao, ¼ fl.oz. fresh orange juice, 1 fl.oz. cream, 1 scoop of crushed ice. Blend together in a blender. Serve in a small wine goblet.

Orange Chartreuse (Fr). A new version to the Chartreuse family of fine liqueurs that is flavoured with fresh orange juice.

Orange Cup (Cktl).(Non-alc). Into a large jug place some ice, 1 pint orange juice, juice of a lemon, ½ gill Gomme syrup, ½ gill Apricot syrup. Stir, top with soda water. Decorate with orange slices.

Orange Curaçao (W.Ind). Originally made from oranges from the island of Curaçao. Now made from oranges from most countries and made in many styles.

Orange Daiquiri (Cktl). 1½ fl.ozs. white Rum, 1½ fl.ozs. orange juice, ½ fl.oz. lemon juice, ½ fl.oz. Gomme syrup. Blend together with a scoop of crushed ice. Pour into a Champagne saucer. Dress with a slice of orange.

Orange Fizz (Cktl). ¾ gill dry Gin, juice of an orange, 1 teaspoon Gomme syrup. Shake well over ice, strain into a highball glass. Top with soda water. Sometimes it is then topped with a dash of Cointreau.

Orange Flower Water (Fr). A non-alcoholic, distilled infusion of orange blossoms. Used in some cocktails.

Orange Gin (Eng). Orange peel steeped in Gin for 8–10 weeks. Strained and bottled. May be sweetened.

Orange Liqueurs (Euro). Spirit based, orange-flavoured liqueurs which vary in strength, colour and flavour. See Grand Marnier, Cointreau, Pimpleltjens, Triple Sec, Curaçao etc. Also produced in most other countries.

Orange Lotus Light (Eng). An orange-flavoured Cooler produced from a blend of British wine and sparkling water 4.5% alc. by vol.

Orange Muscat (USA). A white grape variety used in the making of dessert wines in California.

Orange Oasis (Cktl). ¾ measure dry Gin, ¼ measure Cherry brandy, juice 2 oranges. Shake well over ice, strain into an ice-filled highball glass. Top with ginger ale.

Orange Pekoe (Sri.L). A blend of high grown unbroken teas. Made from the youngest leaf, long and wiry in appearance.

Orange-Peppermint Shake (Cktl).(Non-alc). 2 mint sprigs, 2 teaspoons powdered sugar, 1 egg white. Blend with a scoop of crushed ice for two minutes, add ⅓ pint orange juice. Pour into a highball glass. Dress with an orange slice and mint sprig. Serve with straws.

Orange Smile (Cktl).(Non-alc). 1 egg, juice of an orange, ⅙ gill Grenadine. Shake well over ice, strain into a 5 oz. goblet.

Orange Squash (USA). Into a tumbler place juice of orange (strained), add ice, sugar syrup to taste, top with soda water, slice of lemon.

Orange Tea (Eng). Pour a little barley water over a slice of orange in a cup or glass. Top with fresh brewed tea. Stir with a stick of cinnamon.

Orangetraube (Aus). A lesser white grape variety grown in northern Austria.

Orangette (Cktl).(Non-alc). Juice of orange, ½ beaten egg, sugar to taste, water. Shake over ice, strain into a cocktail glass, add a slice of orange.

Orange Wine (Bra). An orange-flavoured wine produced from fermented orange juice.

Orangina (Fr). A non-alcoholic, sparkling orange juice containing natural fruit pulp. Is distributed in the U.K. by Bulmers of Hereford.

Oranjebitter (Hol). A liqueur usually drunk to toast the Dutch Royal family.

Oranjeboom (Hol). Taken over by Allied Breweries in 1967. Lager brewed by Wrexham Breweries at 1033 O.G. Bottled Oranjeboom 1045 O.G. is imported into G.B. by Allied Breweries in Rotterdam.

Oranjegenever (Hol). An orange-flavoured Jenever.

Oranjerivier Wynkelders (S.Afr). Based in the Benede Oranje. Address = Box 544, Upington 800. Produces varietal wines.

O Rayas (Sp). Hieroglyphic-type markings used in the Sherry region to denote a young Oloroso-style wine.

Orbe (Switz). A wine-producing area in the northern Vaud Canton. Produces red and white wines.

Orbel (Ger). Vineyard. (Anb) = Rheinhessen. (Ber) = Nierstein. (Gro) = Auflangen. (Vil) = Nierstein.

Orbey (Fr). A district in Alsace. German = Urbeis.

Orbit (Cktl). ⅖ measure Rye whiskey, ⅕ measure yellow Chartreuse, ⅕ measure Dubonnet, ⅕ measure Cinzano bianco. Stir over ice, strain into a cocktail glass, add a cherry.

Orchata (Sp). A drink made from tiger nuts which are crushed and soaked in water for hours, strained and served sweetened and chilled. Is milky in appearance and popular in Valencia.

Orchid (Cktl). 1 measure dry Gin, ½ measure pink Crème de Noyau, ½ measure lemon juice, dash Crème de Violette. Shake over ice, strain into a sugar frosted cocktail glass.

Orchid Cocktail (Cktl). ⅓ gill dry Gin, dash Crème Yvette, 1 egg white. Shake over ice, strain into a cocktail glass.

Ord (Scot). A single Malt whisky distillery at the Muir of Ord, Inverness-shire. Owned by Peter Dawson Ltd. Glasgow. A Highland malt. Produces a 12 year old Malt. 40% alc. by vol. (Part of the DCL group).

Ordensgut (Ger). Grosslage. (Anb) = Rheinpfalz. (Ber) = Südliche Weinstrasse. (Vils) = Edesheim, Hainfeld, Rhodt, Weyher.

Order of Merit (Can). A Canadian rye whisky produced by the Canadian Schenley Distilleries Ltd.

Ordinaire (Dr. Pierre) (Fr). The creator of the spirit Absinthe in the eighteenth century.

Ordinaire (Fr). A term applied to a beverage wine of no stated origin. Sold in France simply as Vin rouge, Vin blanc or Vin rosé.

Ordinary (Eng). The name used for a standard bitters.

Ordinary el Dorado (S.Am). A brand of Rum produced in Guyana by the Guyana Distilleries Ltd.

Ordonnac (Fr). A commune in the Bas-Médoc, north-western Bordeaux. Wines have A.C. Médoc status. Also known as Ordonnac-et-Potensac.

Ordonnac-et-Potensac (Fr). See Ordonnac.

Ordre de la Boisson de la Stricte Observance des Costières du Gard (Fr). A wine society based in the Midi.

Ordre de la Channe (Switz). A wine society.

Ordre de la Dive Bouteille et Confrérie Albigeoise de Rabelais (Fr). A wine brotherhood based in Gaillac.

Ordre des Chevaliers Bretvins (Fr). See Chevaliers Bretvins.

Ordre des Chevaliers du Cep (Fr). A wine brotherhood based in Montpellier.

Ordre des Compagnons du Beaujolais (Fr). The wine brotherhood of Beaujolais.

Ordre des Coteaux Commanderie de Champagne (Fr). A wine brotherhood of Champagne.

Ordre des Fins Palais de Saint Pourçain et Bourbonnais (Fr). A wine brotherhood based in Côtes d'Auvergne.

Ordre Illustre des Chevaliers de Méduse (Fr). A wine brotherhood based in Côtes de Provence.

Oregon (USA). A wine-producing area in the Pacific North-West. Vineyards cover 800 ha. mainly around the Willamette Valley.

Orendain (Mex). The producers of a Tequila of same name.

Orense (Sp). A principal wine-producing area in Galicia.

Orfila (José) (Arg). A bodega based at St. Martin, Mendoza. Noted for Cautivo (Cabernet and Pinot blanc based wines).

Organic Acids (Eng). Acids produced by plants.

Organic Catalysts (Eng). Enzymes responsible for the fermentation, spoilage and instability of wine. Excreted by micro-organisms.

Organic Wines (Euro). Light table wines made without the use of any chemicals either during viticulture or viniculture.

Organisation Internationale de Métrologie Légale (Euro). O.I.M.L.

Organoleptic Examination (Eng). The only known method of judging the quality of wines, spirits or beers is by the human organs of sight, smell and taste.
Organoleptic Judgment (Eng). See Organoleptic Examination.
Orgeat (Fr). A non-alcoholic, almond-flavoured syrup used in cocktails.
Orgeat Cocktail (Cktl). ½ measure dry Gin, ¼ measure Orgeat syrup, ¼ measure lemon juice, teaspoon sugar. Shake well over ice, strain into a cocktail glass.
Orgle (Fr). Barley.
Orianda (USSR). A dry white wine from the Crimea.
Oridenc (Fr). A white grape variety grown in Gaillac.
Oriental (Cktl). ⅖ measure Rye whiskey, ⅕ measure white Curaçao, ⅕ measure sweet Vermouth, ⅕ measure lime juice. Shake over ice, strain into a cocktail glass.
Oriental Brewery (E.Asia). A brewery based in Seoul, South Korea which produces OB and Crown beers.
Oriental Tea Punch (Cktl). 2 pints fresh tea, 2 tots Brandy or Rum, honey to taste, chopped raisins and almonds. Heat together, strain, top with anise.
Orientation (Sp). In viticulture, the training of the vines on wires. Usually three wires.
Original-Abfüllung (Ger). The term used to indicate that the wine is estate bottled by the producer. Now forbidden. See also Originalabzug.
Originalabzug (Ger). See Original-Abfüllung.
Original Brown (Eng). A bottled Brown ale 1032 O.G. brewed by the Matthew Brown Brewery in Blackburn, Lancashire.
Original Coffee (Eng). A term used to describe unblended coffee. Is also known as Pure coffee.
Original Distillation (USA). After Direct distillation in Gin production the resulting vapours are condensed to complete the Original distillation.
Original Gerstacker Glühwein (Ger). A brand name for a ready-mixed Mulled wine cup. Imported into U.K. by H. Sichel and Sons.
Original Gravity (Eng). O.G. A term used to express beer strength. Pure water is measured as 1000. The density of the Wort is then measured by the Customs and Excise officer to assess Excise duty payable by the brewery. The measurement e.g. 1043 gives the amount of fermentable and unfermentable matter plus water in the Wort.
Original Green Ginger Wine (USA). A ginger-flavoured currant wine, made in the U.K. for the USA market. 19½% alc. by vol.
Original Light Beer (Scot). A dark keg Ale 1032 O.G. brewed by the Alloa Brewery.
Original Mackinlay (The) (Scot). A blended Scotch whisky produced by Charles Mackinlay & Co. 40% alc. by vol.
Original Mackinlay Legacy De Luxe (The) (Scot). A 12 year old blended De Luxe Scotch whisky produced by Charles Mackinlay & Co. 43% alc. by vol.
Original New York Seltzer (USA). A carbonated soft drink available in seven flavours (black cherry, blueberry, concord grape, lemon, lime, raspberry and vanilla). Sold in 250 mls. bottles. Has no added colours or flavours.
Original Norfolk Punch (Eng). A non-alcoholic drink produced in Upwell, Norfolk.
Original Paarl Perlé (S.Afr). A medium-sweet, pétillant wine made from the Steen grape in the Paarl region.
Original Pale Ale (Eng). A keg and canned Light ale 1032 O.G. brewed by the Vaux Brewery in Sunderland.
Original Pale Ale (Scot). A keg and canned Light ale 1032 O.G. brewed by the Alloa Brewery.
Original Peachtree Liqueur (Hol). A clear, peach-flavoured liqueur produced by De Kuyper. 24% alc. by vol.
Original Schlichte (Ger). The oldest brand of Steinhäger produced by Schlichte.
Originalwein (Ger). Original wine. An old term now no longer allowed.
Orinico Flavius Fly (Euro). Cork fly. Insect that lays its eggs on cork and whose grubs eat the cork.
Orion Brewery ((E.Ind). A brewery based in Okinawa. Produces Orion beer.
Oristano (It). A commune in Sardinia in the valley of the Tirso river. Noted for Venaccia.
Orizaba (Mex). A coffee-producing region in southern Mexico.
Orkney Islands (Scot). Noted for two Malt whiskies – Highland Park and Scapa. Both are classed as Highland malts. They are between a Highland malt and an Islay malt in flavour.
Orlando (Austr). Vineyards. Address = Stuart Highway, Rowland Flat, South Australia. 420 ha. at Rowland Flat, Eden Valley and Riverland. Grape varieties – Cabernet sauvignon, Chardonnay and Riesling. Noted for Coolabah, Jacob's Creek and Miamba (label) wines.
Orleance (Eng). An old sixteenth-century name for the wines of Orléans, Central Vineyards, Loire.
Orleanian (Cktl). ⅕ gill Rye whiskey, ⅛ gill Gomme syrup, 3 dashes Absinthe, 2

dashes Angostura. Shake over ice, strain into a cocktail glass. Dress with a lemon peel spiral.

Orlenberg (Ger). Vineyard. (Anb) = Rheinpfalz. (Ber) = Mittelhaardt-Deutsche Weinstrasse. (Gro) = Schwarzerde. (Vil) = Bisserheim.

Orloff (Eng). A British Vodka produced by Seagram.

Ormarins Estate (L') (S.Afr). Based in Franschhoek. Address = P/Bag Suider Paarl 7624. Produces varietal wines.

Ormes (Fr). A Cru Champagne village in the Canton de Reims. District =Reims.

Ormond Vineyard (N.Z.). Part of Montana wines. The name used for their everyday drinking wines. See Waihirere Winery.

Ormož (Yug). A white wine produced in Slovenia.

Oro (It). A style of Marsala from Sicily. See also Ambra and Rubino.

Orobianco (USA). The brand-name of a dry, fragrant, white wine produced by Villa Armando in Alameda, California. 14% alc. by vol.

Oro del Rhin (Arg). A brand of dry white wine produced by Greco Hermanos in Mendoza.

Oro del Rhin (Chile). A medium-dry, white wine blend of Moscatel and Sauvignon blanc. Produced by Concha y Toro.

Oro Penedés (Sp). A white wine produced by Cavas Hill in Moja-Alt, Penedés.

Oro Pilla (It). A noted Brandy producer.

Orotava (Sp). A medium-dry, white wine produced on the Canary Islands.

Orris (It). Root of the Iris. Used in Chianti by putting a piece in the vats of maturing wine to give bouquet. Not now practiced.

Orris Root (It). See Orris.

Ortega (Ger). A white grape variety. A cross between the Müller-Thurgau and the Siegerrebe. Gives good sugar and bouquet.

Ortelberg (Ger). Vineyard. (Anb) = Rheinpfalz. (Ber) = Südliche Weinstrasse (Gro) = Trappenberg. (Vil) = Böbingen.

Ortenau (Ger). A district within the area of Baden, situated in the foothills of the Black Forest. Produces fine wines. Also has the unique right to bottle their product in Bocksbeutels which is, by law, reserved for Franconian wines.

Ortenau (Ger). Bereich. (Anb) = Baden. (Gros) = Fürsteneck, Schloss Rodeck.

Ortenberg (Ger). Village. (Anb) = Baden. (Ber) = Ortenau. (Gro) = Fürsteneck. (Vins) = Andreasberg, Franzensberger,

Freudental, Schlossberg.

Orthophosphoric (Eng). A permitted bacteriacide used in wine-production.

Ortlieb (USA). A Beer brewed by the Schmidt Brewery in Philadelphia, Pennsylvania.

Ortlieber (Ger). A white grape variety also known as the Knipperlé, Briergauer riesling and Kleiner riesling.

Ortman Winery (USA). A winery based in Napa Valley, California. Grapes from St. Clement and Spring Mountain Vineyards.

Ortrugo (It). A white grape variety grown in the Emilia-Romagna region.

Ortsteil (Ger). Lit – 'Suburb of'. (Part of).

Orujo (Sp). The Spanish equivalent of French Marc. The grape pips, skins, etc. which are fermented and distilled into brandy.

Orval (Bel). A triple-fermented Trappist beer 5.7% alc. by vol. from the Abbey of Orval. Sold in skittle-shaped bottles.

Orvieto (It). D.O.C. white wine from Umbria. Made from 50–65% Trebbiano toscano plus Drupeggio, Grechetto, Malvasia toscano and Verdello grapes. Secco and Aboccato produced. Also sold as Orvieto Classico. See Classico.

Orzechowka (Pol). A Vodka flavoured with green walnuts that give it a bitter, nutty taste. Produced by Polmos. 45% alc. by vol.

Orzo (It). Barley.

Osaka (Jap). A small wine-producing province.

Osann-Monzel (Ger). Village. (Anb) = Mosel-Saar-Ruwer. (Ber) = Bernkastel. (Gro) = Kurfürstlay. (Vins) = Kätzchen, Kirchlay, Paulinslay, Rosenberg.

Osborne (Sp). Sherry and Brandy producer. Address = Osborne y Ca, Fernan Caballero S/N, Puerto de Santa Maria, Cadiz. Base wine for brandy from La Mancha. Produces – Conde de Osborne 20 year old. Veterano Brandy. Owns Duff Gordon. Range of sherries includes Coquinero and Fino Quinta.

Oschelkopf (Ger). Vineyard. (Anb) = Rheinpfalz. (Ber) = Mittelhaardt-Deutsche Weinstrasse. (Gro) = Kobnert. (Vil) = Freinsheim.

Oscura (Mex). A Münchner-style beer.

Osey (Eng). The early English word for the wines from around the river Rhine in Alsace. Usually sweet. See Aussay and Osaye. Word also sometimes referred to naturally sweet Iberian wines of that era.

Oshakan (USSR). A dessert wine produced in Armenia.

Osickas (Austr). A noted winery based in Central Victoria. Produces varietal wines.

Osijek (Yug). A beer brewed in Croatia from north of Zagreb.

Osiris (Egy). God of wine.

Osiris (Ger). A white grape variety. A cross between the Riesling and the Rieslaner. Gives good sugar and riesling bouquet.

Osmosis (Eng). The method of perculation of fluids through porous partitions. Used in filtering.

Osmotic Pressure (Eng). Created by high concentrations of sugar. Slows down the yeast activity. e.g. Sauternes, Trokenbeerenauslesen.

Osoye (Eng). See Aussay.

Osterberg (Ger). Vineyard. (Anb) = Baden. (Ber) = Badische Bergstrasse/ Kraichgau. (Gro) = Mannaberg. (Vil) = Horrenberg.

Osterberg (Ger). Vineyard. (Anb) = Rheinhessen. (Ber) = Bingen. (Gro) = Abtey. (Vil) = Wolfsheim.

Osterberg (Ger). Vineyard. (Anb) = Rheinhessen. (Ber) = Bingen. (Gro) = Sankt Rochuskapelle. (Vil) = Bingen.

Osterberg (Ger). Vineyard. (Anb) = Rheinhessen. (Ber) = Nierstein. (Gro) = Gutes Domtal. (Vil) = Mommenheim.

Osterberg (Ger). Vineyard. (Anb) = Rheinhessen. (Ber) = Nierstein. (Gro) = Gutes Domtal. (Vil) = Selzen.

Osterberg (Ger). Vineyard. (Anb) = Rheinhessen. (Ber) = Nierstein. (Gro) = Petersberg. (Vil) = Spiesheim.

Osterberg (Ger). Vineyard. (Anb) = Rheinpfalz. (Ber) = Mittelhaardt-Deutsche Weinstrasse. (Gro) = Kobnert. (Vil) = Ungstein.

Osterberg (Ger). Vineyard. (Anb) = Rheinpfalz. (Ber) = Mittelhaardt-Deutsche Weinstrasse. (Gro) = Schwarzerde. (Vil) = Grosskarlbach.

Osterberg (Ger). Vineyard. (Anb) = Rheinpfalz. (Ber) = Südliche Weinstrasse (Gro) = Trappenberg. (Vil) = Essingen.

Osterbrunnen (Ger). Vineyard. (Anb) = Rheinpfalz. (Ber) = Mittelhaardt-Deutsche Weinstrasse. (Gro) = Hofstück. (Vil) = Niederkirchen.

Osterhöll (Ger). Vineyard. (Anb) = Nahe. (Ber) = Kreuznach. (Gro) = Kronenberg. (Vil) = Bad Kreuznach.

Osteria (It). Inn.

Osterizer (USA). A brand of electric bar mixing machine.

Osterlämmchen (Ger). Vineyard. (Anb) = Mosel-Saar-Ruwer. (Ber) = Zell/Mosel. (Gro) = Grafschaft. (Vil) = Ediger-Eller.

Osterpai (Ger). Village. (Anb) = Mittelrhein. (Ber) = Rheinburgengau. (Gro) = Marksburg. (Vin) = Liebeneck-Sonnenlay.

Österreicher (Ger). Lit – 'Austrian'. A name often used for the Sylvaner grape as it is said to have originated in Austria.

Österreichische Barkeepers Union (Aus). The Austrian Bartenders' Association. Address = Tigergasse 6/2, A-1080, Wein 4.

Österreichische Bräu (Aus). The largest brewery in Austria based in Linz. Has seven breweries based throughout Austria. Brews Kaiser beer.

Oesterreichisches Weingutesiegel (Aus). W.G.S. The Austrian wine quality seal.

Österreichmarke (Aus). The Austrian wine trade-mark. Consists of a wine glass (Roemer) surrounded by a triangle. Is found on all of the Austrian quality wines.

Ostessa (It). The name for an inn's landlady.

Osthofen (Ger). Village. (Anb) = Rheinhessen. (Ber) = Wonnegau. (Gro) = Gotteshilfe. (Vins) = Goldberg, Hasenbiss, Leckzapfen, Neuberg.

Osthofen (Ger). Village. (Anb) = Rheinhessen. (Ber) = Wonnegau. (Gro) = Pilgerpfad. (Vins) = Kirchberg, Klosterberg, Liebenberg, Rheinberg.

Östra Brewery (Swe). A small brewery based in Halmstead, southern Sweden.

Ostrava Brewery (Czec). A brewery based in north-eastern Czec.

Ostreicher (Ger). See Österreicher. Alternative spelling of.

Östrich (Ger). Village. (Anb) = Rheingau. (Ber) = Johannisberg. (Gro) = Gottesthal. (Vins) = Doosberg, Klosterberg, Lenchen.

Östrich (Ger). Village. (Anb) = Rheingau. (Ber) = Johannisberg. (Gro) = Mehrholzchen. (Vin) = Klosterberg.

Östringen (Ger). Village. (Anb) = Baden. (Ber) = Badische Bergstrasse/Kraichgau. (Gro) = Mannaberg. (Vins) = Hummelberg, Rosenkranzweg, Ulrichsberg.

Ostroh Brewery (Czec). An old established brewery based in southern Czec.

Ostuni Ottavianello (It). D.O.C. red wine from Puglia. Made from the Ottavianello, Malvasia nera, Negro amaro, Notar domenico and Sassumariello grapes.

Otaika Vineyards (N.Z.). The name of vineyards belonging to Continental Wines.

Otaolaurruchi (Sp). A mature Manzanilla sherry produced by Lustau in Jerez de la Frontera.

Otard (Fr). Cognac producer. Address = Château de Cognac, BP 3, 16101 Cognac. Produces – Baron Otard V.S.O.P. Fine Champagne 8 year old and Prince de Cognac 15 year old.

Othalmo (Cyp). A black grape variety.

Othello (Cyp). A full-bodied dry red wine made by the Keo Co. in the Limassol region of south-eastern Cyprus.

O

Ötisheim (Ger). Village. (Anb) = Württemberg. (Ber) = Württembergisch Unterland. (Gro) = Stromberg. (Vin) = Sauberg.

Ötlingen (Ger). Village. (Anb) = Baden. (Ber) = Markgräflerland. (Gro) = Vogtei Rötteln. (Vins) = Sonnhohle, Steige.

Ottakringer Harmer Brauerei (Aus). A family-owned brewery based in Vienna. Brews under the Goldfassl label.

Ottavianello (It). A red grape variety grown in the Puglia to make wines of the same name.

Ottavianello di Ostuni (It). See Ostuni Ottavianello.

Otterberg (Ger). Vineyard. (Anb) = Nahe. (Ber) = Kreuznach. (Gro) = Schlosskapelle. (Vil) = Waldlaubersheim.

Ottersheim (Ger). Village. (Anb) = Rheinpfalz. (Ber) = Südliche Weinstrasse. (Gro) = Trappenberg. (Vin) = Kahlenberg.

Ottersheim/Zellerthal (Ger). Village. (Anb) = Rheinpfalz. (Ber) = Mittelhaardt-Deutsche Weinstrasse. (Gro) = Schnepfenflug vom Kellertal. (Vin) = Bräunersberg.

Ottersweier (Ger). Village. (Anb) = Baden. (Ber) = Ortenau. (Gro) = Schloss Rodeck. (Vins) = Althof, Wolfhag.

Ottonese (Lat). A white grape variety grown in Latium. Also known as the Bombino bianco.

Oud and Co (Hol). A noted producer of Advocaat based in Haarlem.

Oudart (Fr). A man who is said to be have been the first to discover the secrets of Champagne wine fermentation near Épernay. See also Dom Pérignon

Oud Bruin (Hol). Old brown beer

Oude Beersel Brasserie (Bel). A fine brewery based in Beersel, central Belgium.

Oude Genever (Hol). Old Gin. Drunk neat from a small glass before dinner, often followed by a beer chaser.

Oude Heerengracht (S.Afr). A selection of fine quality dessert wines by Union Wines Limited of Wellington. Also the name of a ginger liqueur from same company.

Oude Klaren (Hol) (slang). Gin.

Oude Libertas (S.Afr). Varietal wines made by the Stellenbosch Farmers' Winery.

Oude Meester Group (S.Afr). Wine-producers and spirit distillers based in Stellenbosch. Formed in 1970 by a merger of South African Distillers & Wines and some old established wine producers. Is also known as the Distillers Corporation. The wine arm is known as Die Bergkelder.

Oude Molen (S.Afr). A 10–15 year old

Brandy produced by Gilbeys.

Oudenaarde Brasserie (Bel). A brewery based in Oudenaarde, northern Belgium. Noted for its dark brown Ales and Kriek 7% alc. by vol.

Oudenaarde Special (Bel). A bottle-conditioned Ale 5.25% alc. by vol. Brewed by the Oudenaarde Brasserie.

Oude Nektar Estate (S.Afr). Based in Stellenbosch. Address = Box 389, Stellenbosch 7600. Produces varietal wines.

Oude Pruim Brasserie (Bel). A brewery based in Beersel, central Belgium.

Ouderust Wines (S.Afr). See Mooi Uitsig Wynkelders.

Oudinot-Jeanmarie (Fr). Champagne producer. Address = 12 Rue Godart Roger BP 256, 51207 Épernay. Produces – Vintage and non-vintage wines. Vintages – 1971, 1973, 1975, 1976, 1979, 1981. De Luxe vintage cuvée is Cuvée Elysée.

Oud Limburgs (Hol). A copper-coloured Beer 5.5% alc. by vol. brewed by the Arcen Brouwerij in Arcen, Limburg.

Oud Piro (Bel). A Beer brewed by the Bevernagie Brasserie in Lichtervelde, western Flanders. A red beer.

Oudtshoorn (S.Afr). A wine-producing district in Klein Karoo.

Oud-Zottegem (Bel). The brand-name used by the Crombé Brasserie in Zottegem.

Oued-Imbert (Alg). A wine-producing area in the Oran Département. Produces red, rosé and white wines.

Ouillage (Fr). The topping up of the barrels with the same wine to keep out the air.

Oujda (Afr). A wine-producing region of Morocco.

Oujda-Taza (Afr). A noted vineyard in the Oujda region that is planted with vinifera vines.

Ouras (Fr). A red grape variety grown in the Gaillac region of southwest France.

Ourika (Afr). A full-bodied, red wine produced in the Beni Amar Vineyard in Zenatas, Morocco. Grape varieties – Alicante, Cinsault and Grenache.

Our Lady of the Grape (Fr). See Notre Dame du Raisin.

Ousahelohouri (USSR). A white grape variety grown in Georgia to produce white dessert wines.

Oustalet (Afr). A dry white wine produced in Morocco.

Outrigger Cocktail (Cktl). ¼ measure each of Vodka, Peach brandy, lime cordial and pineapple juice. Shake over ice, strain into an ice-filled highball glass.

Ouverture des Vendanges (Fr). In the Champagne region the announcement of the date that the grape harvest may commence.

Ouvrée (Fr). A land measure used in the Burgundy region. ¼₄ ha. (¹⁄₁₀ acre).

Ouzeri (Gre). A small café that specialises in serving ouzo.

Ouzo (Gre). A clear, aniseed-flavoured liqueur distilled from grapes with aromatic herbs. 37–40% alc. by vol. Drunk with water.

OVD (Scot) (abbr). Old Vatted Demerara. A dark Rum bottled by George Montrose.

Ovens Valley Shiraz (Austr). A red wine produced by the Wynns Vineyard, Coonawarra, South Australia.

Overberg (S.Afr). A wine district that surrounds the town of Caledon.

Overberg Co-operative (S.Afr). See Mooi Uitsig Wynkelders.

Over-fining (Eng). The term used for wines that have been excessively fined using too much fining agent. Often have little taste.

Overgaauw Estate (S.Afr). Based in Stellenbosch. Address = P.O. Box 3, Vlottenburg 7604. Produces – Overtinto, Tria Corda and varietal wines.

Overhex Co-operative (S.Afr). Based in Worcester. Address = Overhex Koöperatiewe Wynkelders, Box 139, Worcester 6850. Produces varietal wines.

Overhex Koöpertiewe Wynkelders (S.Afr). See Overhex Co-operative.

Over Proof (Eng). See Proof Testing.

Over Ripe (Ger). A condition of the grapes suitable for the making of sweet white wines. e.g. Auslese.

Överste Brännvin (Swe). A light, spicy brand of Aquavit.

Over the Top (Eng). A wine past its best. Not a clear statement, but is applied to wines that should be drunk young e.g. Beaujolais Nouveau, Vinho Verde or to very old wines that have 'passed it'.

Overtinto (S.Afr). A red wine made from the Tinta Barocca and other Portuguese grape varieties. Made in the Overgaauw Estate.

Overtone (Eng). The term used to describe the dominating element of nose or palate. e.g. oak.

Overval Wines (S.Afr). See Vaalharts Co-operative.

Owd Roger (Eng). A sweet and heavy Barley wine first brewed at the Royal Standard of England at Forty Green in Buckinghamshire. Now brewed by the Marston's Brewery in Burton-on-Trent, Staffordshire.

Own Ale (Eng). A cask conditioned Bitter 1040 O.G. brewed by the Miners Arms home-brew public house in Westbury-sub-Mendip, Somerset.

Oxblood (Eng). Used as a fining agent for wines. A little wine is mixed with the blood and then it is poured on top of the wine. As it sinks through the wine it takes the impurities with it. Used in the Sauternes district.

Oxford Brew House (Eng). A home-brew public house that brews beer and also bakes bread.

Oxhoft (Scan). A liquid measure. 56–58 imperial gallons (67–69 US. galls. 254–264 litres).

Oxidasic Casse (Eng). A wine malady. Caused by the enzyme Polyphenoloxidase which causes the wine to turn cloudy on contact with air and a deposit to form. Occurs in wines made from mouldy or overripe grapes. Is cured by adding Ascorbic acid or SO_2 to wine. Also by heating the musts or adding Bentonite.

Oxidation (Eng). Exposure to air through faulty corking. At worst leads to an unpleasant smell and colour darkening.

Oxidised (Eng). A wine that has started to spoil through too much contact with the air. White wines go flat and brown and smell musty. See Maderised.

Oxidised Wines (Eng). Wines of a style similar to Sherry that have been subjected to oxidation without being spoilt.

Oxjen (Sp). See Ojen.

Oxyder (Fr). Oxidise.

Oxygen (Eng). Needed for wine to mature, also can destroy wine. See Oxidation.

Oxygene (USA). See Oxygénée.

Oxygénée (USA). An aniseed-flavoured absinthe substitute. 40% alc. by vol.

Oxymel (Eng). A British Pharmacopoeia name for the drink of vinegar and honey known as Honegar. An old fourteenth-century remedy.

Oy Alko Ab (Fin). The State monopoly that controls all retailing and domestic spirits production. Has 3 distilling plants at Koskenkorva, Salmivaara and Rajamaki.

Oyes (Fr). A Cru Champagne village in the Canton de Montmort. District = Épernay.

Oyón (Sp). A noted wine-producing village in the Rioja Alavesa.

Oyster Bay Cocktail (Cktl). ½ measure Gin, ½ measure orange Curaçao. Shake over ice, strain into a cocktail glass.

Oyster Stout (I.O.M.). A Stout once produced by the Castletown Brewery, made from real oysters.

Oy Suomen Marjat (Fin). A company that

produces liqueurs sold under the Tyrni brand-name.

Oyzo (Gre). An alternative spelling of Ouzo.

Ozark Mountains (USA). The southern region of the Missouri district in north-western America.

Ozark Vineyards (USA). A winery based in Cuba, Missouri. Produces French-American hybrid wines.

Ozeki (Jap). A popular brand-name of Saké.

Özsu (Tur). Juice. See also Meyva Suyu.

P

PA (Eng) (abbr). Pale Ale. Initials used for a variety of light bitter beers and ales from the West Country.

PA (Eng) (abbr). Pale Ale. A cask conditioned Bitter 1034 O.G. brewed by the Ridley Brewery in Chelmsford, Essex.

Paantsch (Ind). Hindi word for 5 from which 'Punch' derives. See Punch.

Paarl (S.Afr). A wine region which produces fine white and red wines. The KWV headquarters is based in Paarl.

Paarl Cinsault (S.Afr). A red grape variety of the Cinsault strain.

Paarl Perlé (S.Afr). See Union Wines.

Paarl Riesling (S.Afr). An alternative name for the Crouchen grape of France.

Paarl Riesling (S.Afr). A Rhine-style wine from the Paarl vineyards.

Paarl Roodeberg (S.Afr). A Burgundy-style red wine from the Paarl vineyards.

Paarlsack (S.Afr). A South African Sherry range made by the KWV at Paarl.

Paarl Valais Rouge (S.Afr). See Douglas Green.

Paarl Vallei Co-operative (S.Afr). See Bolandse Co-operative. The two have now merged.

Paaske Øl (Den). An Ale brewed by the Wiibroe Brewery in Elsinore.

Pabst Breweries (USA). Breweries based in Los Angeles, Newark, Pabst, Peoria and Milwaukee. Brews Andeker, Blue Ribbon and Old Tap. 4.6% alc. by vol.

Pacaret (Sp). See Paxarete.

Pacheco Ranch Winery (USA). A small winery based in San Rafael, Marin, California. Grape variety – Cabernet sauvignon.

Pachérenc (Fr). A local name for the white Manseng grape in Madiran, south-west France.

Pachérenc du Vic-Bilh (Fr). An A.C. sweet white wine from Pachérenc in the Pyrénées. Adjoins Armagnac. Grapes are Courbu, Manseng, Ruffiac, Sauvignon blanc and Sémillon. Mimimum alc. by vol. 12%. Vines trained in Pachets-en-rang.

Pachets-en-Rang (Fr). The local name used in Pachérenc du Vic-Bilh for Piquets-en-rang (posts in a line used for vines).

Paciencia (Port). The name for the train that carries the Port wine from Pinhão (upper Douro) to Oporto.

Pacific Brewery Co. Inc (USA). A brewery based on the island of Maui in Hawaii. Brews Maui Lager.

Pacific Gold (Can). A Pilsener-style Lager beer brewed by the Old Fort Brewery, British Columbia.

Pacific Vineyards (N.Z.). A winery based in McLeod Road, Henderson, North Island. Produces wines under the Saint Stefan and Montlouis labels. Noted for its fortified wines.

Pacini Vineyard (USA). A small vineyard based near Ukiah, Mendocino County, California. Grape variety – Zinfandel.

Package Store (USA). A store where alcoholic beverages are sold for consumption off the premises. See also Liquor Store. (U.K) = Off-Licence.

Pack o' Cards Pub (Eng). A public house based in Coome Martin, Devon. Is built in the shape of a 'pack of cards house'. Has 52 windows and 4 floors. Was built because of a bet.

Paço d'Anha (Port). A producer of Vinho Verde. Address = Anha, 4900 Vana do Castelo. Grape varieties mainly Loureiro and Trajadura.

Paço Teixeiró (Port). A producer of Vinho Verde. Address = Cidadelhe, 5050 Peso da Regua. Grape variety mainly Avesso.

Paddy (Ire). The second largest selling whiskey in Ireland. Blended from 3 whiskey types – a straight pot-still Malt, a pot-still barley Malt and a Grain whiskey. Distilled in Cork. 40% alc. by vol.

Paddy Cocktail (Cktl). 1½ measures Irish whiskey, ½ measure sweet Vermouth, dash Angostura. Shake over ice, strain into a cocktail glass.

Padeiro (Port). A red grape variety grown in the Vinho Verde region.

Padova (It). A province of the Veneto region. Produces white and red wines, notably Colli Euganei from the Euganean hills.

Padthaway (Austr). A wine from Lindemans in New South Wales.

Paelignum (Lat). A red wine produced in central-easten Italy in Roman times.

P

Päffgen Brauerei (Ger). A small brewery in Cologne (Friesenstrasse). Noted for its Kolschbier.

Pagadebit (It). A white grape variety grown in the Emilia Romagna region.

Pagadebito (USA). A white grape variety grown in California for making dessert wines.

Pagani (Lat). The monastic name for the peasants that worked around the abbeys in early times. This was specially used for those that worked in the abbey's vineyards. They were paid for their labours in grapes, food or wine.

Page Mill Winery (USA). A winery based in the Santa Cruz Mountains, Santa Clara, California. Grape varieties – Cabernet sauvignon, Chardonnay and Chenin blanc. Produces varietal wines.

Pages (Fr). A large liqueur producer based in Le Pay en Vélay in the Auvergne. Produces Verveine du Vélay (a digestif).

Pagliarese (It). A Chianti Classico producer based in San Gusme, Siena, Tuscany.

Paglieri (I) (It). A major wine-producer of Barbaresco in Piemonte.

Pagney-Derrière-Barine (Fr). A commune in the Côtes de Toul, Lorraine. Produces Vins gris.

Pago (Sp). A vineyard area.

Pagodas (Scot). A name given to the kilns of the whisky distilleries.

Pagos (Sp). District.

Pai Chiu (China). A term used to describe grain spirits.

Paicines (USA). A wine-producing region in the central coastal county of San Benito, California.

Paico (S.Am). The brand-name of an Aguardiente from Ecuador.

Païen (Switz). The Valais name for the Traminer grape. See also Savagnin.

Paigny-lès-Reims (Fr). A Cru Champagne village in the Canton de Villen-Tardenois. District = Reims.

Paillard (Rémy) (Fr). A Champagne producer based in Reims. Produces Vintage and non-vintage wines. Vintages – 1976, 1979, 1982.

Paine (Chile). A wine-producing area based near Santiago.

Paine Brewery (Eng). Based in St. Neots, Cambridgeshire. Brews cask conditioned St. Neots Bitter 1041 O.G. EG 1047 O.G. For export – Cambridge Pale Ale 1052 O.G. Kinross 1064 O.G. Royal Stag 1052 O.G. and Special Red 1052 O.G.

Painel (Port). A Dão wine produced by the Caves Império.

Pairie des Grands Vins de France (Fr).

The wine brotherhood of the Jura region.

País (Chile). A white grape variety that originated from Spain.

Paisley Martini (Cktl). ⅗ measure dry Gin, ⅓ measure French vermouth, 3 dashes Scotch whisky. Stir in an ice-filled old-fashioned glass. Top with a twist of lemon peel juice.

Pajarete (Sp). The Andalusian spelling of Paxarette. A wine from Bornos not far from Arcos de la Fronteira. See also Paxerete.

Pajarete (Sp). The term used to describe a semi-sweet Málaga wine.

Pajarete (Sp). A white grape variety grown in southern Spain.

Pajarilla (Sp). A medium white wine produced in the Cariñena region.

Pajuela (Sp). A small insect that weaves a nest around the vine flowers. It eats the shoots and destroys the young branches.

Palace (Eng). The brand-name of a coffee blend of 100% Arabica beans, lightly roasted. The coffee has a low acidity and full body. Produced by the Lyons Co.

Palace Hill Ranch (USA). A vineyard based in Dry Creek Valley, California. Grape variety – Zinfandel.

Palàcio de Brejoeira (Port). A Vinho Verde produced from the Alvarinho grape fermented at 18°C. Address = Pinheiros, 4590 Moncão.

Palacio de Guzmàn (Sp). A light, dry, fruity white wine produced by VILE in León.

Palackozott (Hun). Bottled.

Palaion (Gre). Old wine.

Palate (Eng). The area of the mouth where the wine tastes are pronounced and experienced. Used to describe the taste of a beverage.

Palatinate (Ger). The other name for the Rheinpfalz Anbaugebiet.

Palatinate Cherry Brandy (Eng). A company that also makes other fine liqueurs under this brand name. A British cherry liqueur made by Lamb and Watt of Liverpool, Lancashire.

Pale Ale (Eng). A bottled Ale of medium gravity. A strong Pale ale would be 1045–1050 O.G. In the south-west of England Pale ales are low-gravity draught beers.

Pale Eighty (Scot). An 80/- cask conditioned Ale 1042 O.G. brewed by the Devanha Brewery in north-east Scotland.

Pale Malt (Eng). The term used in brewing for Ale malts.

Palermo (Fr). An alcohol-free Vermouth-style drink (red and white versions) imported into the U.K. by Leisure Drinks of Derby.

Palette d'Aix (Fr). An A.C. wine of the Côtes de Provence. See Château Simone.

Produced from Carignan, Grenache and Mourvèdre grapes.

Palido (Sp). A Flor-attacked wine, rich, honey-coloured with a hint of almonds. Produced by Cooperativa La Seca in La Rueda.

Palisades Cocktail (Cktl). ½ measure dry Gin, ½ measure dry Cider, 2 dashes Angostura. Shake with ice, strain into a cocktail glass.

Palissage (Fr). A method of vine training in Alsace. Vines are trained on high trellises of poles and wires about 2 metres high to afford better elevation above the frosts.

Pallas S.A. [San Gill] (Fr). Armagnac producer. Address = Domaine de Cassanel, 47600 Nérac.

Pallet (Eng). A portable wooden platform used for moving goods i.e. beer crates, wine/spirit boxes, etc. Is slatted and lifted by fork-lift trucks. (A pallet of beer).

Pallet (Le) (Fr). A noted village in the A.C. Muscadet de Sèvre et Maine district in the Pays Nantais, Loire Atlantique Département.

Pallini (Gre). A dry white wine.

Palliser Distillery (Can). A Canadian whisky distillery (part of Gilbey Canada Ltd).

Pall Mall (Cktl). ⅓ measure dry Gin, ⅓ measure French vermouth, ⅓ measure Italian vermouth, 2 dashes Orange bitters, 1 teaspoon (white) Crème de Menthe. Stir over ice, strain into a cocktail glass.

Pallye (Le) (Fr). A vineyard in the A.C. commune of Montagny, Côte Chalonnaise, Burgundy.

Palma (Sp). A classification of young Fino sherries. Marks are placed on casks of original Rayas to denote quality and age of the Sherry. In a style of hieroglyphics.

Palma Cortada (Sp). Denotes a Fino sherry that is almost similar in style to an Amontillado sherry.

Palmarès (Fr). Lit – 'Prize list'. List of Crus Bourgeois of the Bordeaux region.

Palmas (Sp). See Palma.

Palma Sack (Sp). A dry white wine produced in Las Palmas, Gran Canaria.

Palm Beach (Cktl). ⅘ measure dry Gin, ⅙ measure sweet Vermouth, ⅙ measure grapefruit juice. Shake over ice, strain into a cocktail glass.

Palm Beach Coolers (Eng). A range of low-alcohol, sparkling, wine-based drinks (tropical fruit blend of passion fruit and grapes with white wine) and a summer fruit drink with a base of red and white wine. From Bonlouis U.K.

Palmberg (Ger). Vineyard. (Anb) = Mosel-Saar-Ruwer. (Ber) = Zell/Mosel. (Gro) = Rosenhang. (Vil) = Valwig.

Palmberg (Lux). A vineyard site in the village of Ahn.

Palmberg-Terrassen (Ger). Vineyard. (Anb) = Mosel-Saar-Ruwer. (Ber) = Zell/Mosel. (Gro) = Grafschaft. (Vil) = St. Aldegund.

Palm Breeze (Cktl). ⅓ measure yellow Chartreuse, ½ measure dark Rum, ⅙ measure Crème de Cacao, juice ½ lime, dash Grenadine. Shake over ice, strain into a cocktail glass.

Palmela (Port). A demarcated region situated between Lisbon and Setúbal. Produces mainly rosé and red Periquita.

Palmengarten (Ger). Vineyard. (Anb) = Nahe. (Ber) = Schloss Böckelheim. (Gro) = Rosengarten. (Vil) = Mandel.

Palmenstein (Ger). Vineyard. (Anb) = Rheinhessen. (Ber) = Bingen. (Gro) = Sankt Rochuskapelle. (Vil) = Sponsheim.

Palmer and Co (Fr). Champagne producers. Address = 67 Rue Jacquart, 51100 Reims. 200 ha. Founded in 1984 by a group of wine-lovers in Avize. Produces – Vintage and non-vintage wines. De Luxe vintage cuvées are Cuvée Amazone and Cuvée Rubis (rosé).

Palmer Brewery (Eng). Based in Bridport, Dorset. Produces cask conditioned IPA Bitter 1039.5 O.G. and B.B. Bitter 1030.4 O.G. plus Tally Ho 1046 O.G. Also Golden Cap (a blended Scotch whisky).

Palmer Cocktail (Cktl). ⅓ gill Bourbon whiskey, dash Angostura, 2 dashes lemon juice. Stir over ice, strain into a cocktail glass.

Palme 70 (Cktl). ⅓ measure Extra Bitter Badel, ⅓ measure Vinjak Cezar, ⅓ measure Stari Granciar, dash strawberry juice. Stir over ice, strain into a cocktail glass, add a cherry.

Palmetto (Cktl). ½ measure white Rum, ½ measure French vermouth, 2 dashes Angostura. Stir over ice, strain into a cocktail glass.

Palm Wine (Afr). An alcoholic beverage produced from the fermented sap of the palm tree.

Palm Wine (USA). A name used to describe alcoholic drinks made from the sap of tropical palm trees through fermentation. e.g. coconut and date palms.

Palo Cortado (Sp). A classification of Sherry between an Amontillado and Oloroso. Classed as Un Cortado, Dos Cortados, Tres Cortados, Cuatro Cortados, etc.

P

Palomina (Sp). An alternative spelling of the Palomino grape.

Palomino (Sp). The best known and most widely used grape variety in the Jerez region for Sherry production. Also known as the Albán, Chasselas doré, Fransdruif, Horgazuela, Listán, Palomina, Paulo, Perrum and Sweetwater.

Palomino y Vergara (Sp). Sherry shippers based in Jerez. Was part of the Rumasa group. Now owned by Harveys of Bristol. Sherry brands include Tio Mateo and Brandy includes Fabuloso.

Palo Viejo (W.Ind). The brand-name of a Rum produced by Marquis and Co. on the island of Puerto Rico.

Palud (Fr). A lesser district of Bordeaux.

Paluel-Marmont (Fr). Armagnac produced by Esprit de France, Domaine de Taulet, 32330 Gondrin, Ténarèze. Also produce Des Seigneurs (a 3 year old).

Palumbo (It). A white grape variety grown in the Puglia region.

Palus (Fr). Rich alluvial soil, unsuitable to growing those grapes that are to be made into fine wines.

Palwin (Isr). The name given to a range of rich, red, dessert wines produced by Carmel.

Palzem (Ger). Village. (Anb) = Mosel-Saar-Ruwer. (Ber) = Obermosel. (Gro) = Gipfel. (Vins) = Karlsfelsen, Lay.

Pamid (Bul). A red grape variety. Produces sweet, low acid, light coloured wines.

P-Aminobenzoic Acid (Eng). A vitamin that is found in minute traces in wines.

Pampanino (It). A white grape variety grown in the Puglia region. Also known as the Pampanuto.

Pâmpano (Port). A vine-shoot.

Pampanuto (It). See Pampanino.

Pampas (Arg). A white wine from the Mendoza region.

Pampinus (Lat). Vine-shoot.

Panaché (Fr). A Shandy. ½ beer, ½ lemonade.

Panaché Cocktail (Cktl). ½ measure Vodka, ½ measure Noilly Prat, dash Cherry brandy. Stir over ice, strain into a cocktail glass. Top with a cherry.

Panache d'Or (Fr). 3*** and V.S.O.P. Armagnacs produced by Carrère.

Panadés (Sp). See Penedés. Old spelling of.

Panama Cocktail (Cktl). ⁴⁄₁₀ measure Brandy, ³⁄₁₀ measure Crème de Cacao, ³⁄₁₀ measure sweetened cream. Shake well with ice, strain into a cocktail glass.

Pan American Cocktail (Cktl). ⅓ gill Rye whiskey, 2 dashes Gomme syrup, juice ½ lemon. Stir over ice in an old-fashioned glass.

Pan American Coffee Bureau (USA).

Address = 1350 Ave of America, New York. NY 10019.

Panch (Ind). See Paantsch.

Pancho Cocktail (Cktl). 1 measure Pimpeltjens, 1 measure Crème de Café. Stir over ice, strain into a cocktail glass.

Pancho Villa (Cktl). 1 measure Tequila, ½ measure Tia Maria, dash Cointreau. Shake over ice, strain into a cocktail glass. Dress with a lemon slice and coffee bean.

Pancho Villa Cocktail (Cktl). ½ measure Campari, ½ measure Tequila. Shake over ice, strain into a cocktail glass, decorate with a cocktail onion.

Panciu (Rum). White table wines from Focsani.

Pandars (Les) (Fr). A vineyard in the A.C. commune of Montagny, Côte Chalonnaise, Burgundy.

Pandilla (Sp). A white grape variety grown in La Mancha.

Pando (Sp). A full, fine, Fino sherry produced by Williams & Humbert.

Panier (Fr).The name of the basket used for gathering the grapes in the Champagne region.

Panj (Iran). An old Persian word for punch (drink).

Pannier (Fr). Champagne producer. Address = 23 Rue Roger Catillon, B.P.55, 02400 Château Thierry. 250 ha. Produces – Vintage and non-vintage wines. Vintages – 1970, 1975, 1979, 1981, 1983.

Pannier (Rémy) (Fr). Wine merchants based in Saumur in the Anjou-Saumur district of the Loire.

Pannikin (Eng). A small metal cup used in the nineteenth century.

Pannonia Winery (USA). A winery based in the Napa Valley, California. 14 ha. Grape varieties – Chardonnay, Pinot noir and Sauvignon blanc. Produces varietal wines.

Panorama Vineyards (N.Z.). A small winery based at Awaroa Road, Henderson, North Island. 3 ha. Grape varieties – Cabernet sauvignon, Chardonnay, Gewürztraminer, Palomino and Pinotage. Produces varietal wines.

Panquehua (Arg). The brand-name of a white wine produced by Bodegas Gonzales Videla.

Pansa Blanca (Sp). A white grape variety grown in the Alella district. Also known as the Xarel-lo.

Pansa Rosado (Sp). A red grape variety grown in the Alella.

Panse Musquée (Sp). An alternative name for the Muscat of Alexandria.

Pansgue (S.Am). A Rum-based cordial flavoured with cherry juice that is produced in Venezuela.

P

Panstwowy Monopol Spirytusowy (Pol). The Polish State Vodka producer. Polmos (short name). Wyborowa is the principal brand.

Pantelleria (It). An island of volcanic origin, part of the province of Trapani, a town in western Sicily. Better known wines are Moscato and Moscato passito.

Pantelleria (It). The name of a Muscat dessert wine made from sun-dried grapes on the island of same name.

Pantera Cocktail (Cktl). ⅓ measure dry Sherry, ⅓ measure dry Gin, ⅓ measure red Curaçao. Stir with ice, strain into a cocktail glass. Add a sprig of mint.

Panther (Aus). A premium Lager beer 5.4% alc. by vol. brewed by the Reininghaus Brauerei in Graz.

Panther (Fr). A non-alcoholic Bière brewed by the Union de Brasseries, 33 Av. de Wagram, 75017 Paris.

Panther Malta (Fr). A rich, dark, malty, non-alcoholic Bière produced by the Union de Brasseries, Paris.

Pantothenic Acid (Eng). A vitamin that is present in wine in minute traces.

Pany Rum (E.Ind). A leading Rum brand produced in the Philippine Islands.

Papagni Vineyards (USA). A winery based in Madera County, San Joaquin Valley, California. Grape varieties – Alicante bouschet, Barbera, Chenin blanc and Zinfandel. Produce varietal wines.

Papaya Royal Cocktail (Cktl). ⅕ gill white Rum, ⅗ gill milk, 12 ozs. (300 grammes) papaya pulp, 2 dashes Gomme syrup. Blend together with a scoop of crushed ice, pour into the hollowed-out papaya. Serve with straws.

Papaya Sling (Cktl). 1 measure dry Gin, juice of a lime, ½ oz. papaya syrup, dash Angostura. Shake well over ice, strain into an ice-filled highball glass. Top with soda and a pineapple cube.

Papazkarasi (Tur). A white grape variety grown in Marmara and Thrace.

Pape Clément (Fr). See Château Pape Clément.

Papelorey (Ets) (Fr). Armagnac producer based in Ténarèze. Address = Rue des Carmes, 32100 Condom. Noted for Laressingle brand.

Paphos (Cyp). A wine area and town in the south-east of the island.

Papua New Guinea (E.Ind). A coffee-producing country. Produce a soft, full-flavoured coffee.

Paquereau (Fr). Cognac producer. Address = B.P. N°4, Chez Perruchon, 16250 Blanzac. 9.3 ha. in the Fins Bois. Produces a range of fine Cognacs.

Paracelhaus (Aus). A noted Austrian beer.

Paracelsus (Aus). A dark, Münchner-style beer brewed by the Stiegl Brauerei in Salzburg. 4.4% alc. by vol.

Parachute (Eng). A funnel-shaped piece of equipment used in brewing, to draw off excess yeast as it spills over in the fermenting vessel.

Paradella (Sp). A red grape variety which produces rich, red, fruity wines.

Paradies (Ger). Vineyard. (Anb) = Baden. (Ber) = Markgräflerland. (Gro) = Burg Neuenfels. (Vil) = Feldberg.

Paradies (Ger). Vineyard. (Anb) = Franken. (Ber) = Steigerwald. (Gro) = Schlossstück. (Vil) = Bullenheim.

Paradies (Ger). Vineyard. (Anb) = Mosel-Saar-Ruwer. (Ber) = Bernkastel. (Gro) = Nacktarsch. (Vil) = Kröv.

Paradies (Ger). Vineyard. (Anb) = Nahe. (Ber) = Kreuznach. (Gro) = Kronenberg. (Vil) = Bad Kreuznach (ortsteil Bosenheim).

Paradies (Ger). Vineyard. (Anb) = Rheinpfalz. (Ber) = Mittelhaardt-Deutsche Weinstrasse. (Gro) = Rebstöckel. (Vil) = Diedesfeld.

Paradies (Ger). Vineyard. (Anb) = Württemberg. (Ber) = Württembergisch Unterland. (Gro) = Salzberg. (Vil) = Eschenau.

Paradiesgarten (Ger). Grosslage. (Anb) = Nahe. (Ber) = Schloss Böckelheim. (Vils) = Alsenz, Auen, Bayerfeld-Steckweiler, Boos, Desloch, Feilbingert, Gaugrehweiler, Hochstätten, Kalkofen, Kirschroth, Lauschied, Lettweiler, Mannweiler-Coelln, Martinstein, Meddersheim, Meisenheim, Merxheim, Monzingen, Münsterappel, Niederhausen an der Nahe, Niedermoschel, Nussbaum, Oberhausen an der Nahe, Obermoschel, Oberndorf, Oberstreit, Odernheim, Raumbach, Rehborn, Sobernheim, Sobernheim-Steinhardt, Staudernheim, Unkenbach, Waldböckelheim, Weiler bei Monzingen, Winterborn.

Paradiesgarten (Ger). Vineyard. (Anb) = Rheinpfalz. (Ber) = Mittelhaardt-Deutsche Weinstrasse. (Gro) = Mariengarten. (Vil) = Deidesheim.

Paradis (Fr). The name used in the Beaujolais for the juice from the first pressing of the grape pulp after macération carbonique.

Paradis (Fr). A warehouse where old and fine Cognacs are stored. Also the name given to certain fine old Cognacs.

Paradis (USA). A dry white wine produced from the Pinot noir grape by the Alatera Vineyards in the Napa Valley, California.

Paradise (Cktl).(1). ⅔ measure dry Gin, ⅓

measure Apricot brandy, ⅓ measure orange juice or lemon juice. Shake over ice, strain into a cocktail glass.

Paradise (Cktl).(2). 8 parts Bacardi, 1 part Apricot brandy, 2 parts orange juice. Shake over crushed ice, strain into a cocktail glass, add a twist of lemon peel juice.

Paradise Brewery (Eng). Opened in 1981 in Hayle, Cornwall. Noted for its cask conditioned Artists Ale 1055 O.G. and Victory Ale 1070 O.G.

Paradise Lost Cocktail (Cktl).(Non-alc). ½ measure lime juice, ½ measure peppermint cordial, 3 dashes Angostura. Shake over ice, strain into an ice-filled highball glass. Top with soda water.

Paradisi (Hol). A grapefruit-flavoured liqueur 26% alc. by vol.

Paradisiaque (Cktl). 2 fl.ozs. dark Rum, 1 fl.oz. Mandarine Napoléon, ½ fl.oz. syrup of ginger, ½ fl.oz. passion fruit juice, 1 fl.oz. lime juice, 2 fl.ozs. orange juice. Shake over ice, strain into a large highball glass with ice. Decorate with a mint sprig and 2 cherries.

Paradiso Cocktail (Cktl). ¾ measure white Rum, ¼ measure Apricot brandy. Shake over ice, strain into a cocktail glass.

Parador (Sp). The brand-name of a 10 year old, full-bodied red wine produced by Julián Chivite in the Navarra region.

Paraflow (Eng). In the brewing process the heat-exchanger that cools the Wort as it leaves the Copper from near boiling point down to fermenting temperature.

Paragogay ky Euphialosis (Gre). Produced and bottled by. See also Paragogi ke Emfialosis.

Paragogi ke Emfialosis (Gre). Produced and bottled by. See also Paragogay ky Euphialosis.

Paraguay Ta (S.Am). The nickname for Maté.

Para Liqueur Port (Austr). A dark, tawny port-style wine made by Seppelts in South Australia.

Parallèle 45 (Fr). An A.C. Côtes du Rhône from Paul Jaboulet Aîné.

Paralytic (Eng). Lit – 'Paralysed'. i.e. incapable through drink, drunk and incapable.

Paramount Choice (Port). A full, Tawny Port produced by Delaforce Port shippers.

Parcay-Meslay (Fr). A commune in the Loire Valley part of which is in Vouvray in the Touraine district.

Parcel [Land] (Fr). Applied to the vineyards, especially in Burgundy, which were divided amongst the Citoyens after the French Revolution. Lit – 'A piece of land'.

Parcel [Merchant] (Eng). Applies to cases of wine a wine merchant may offer for sale.

Parcel [Wine] (Eng). The name given to bulk wines which are normally blended with other 'parcels' to produce an acceptable wine.

Parchment Skin (Eng). The name given to the thin outer skin on a coffee cherry which covers the seeds. See also Endocarp.

Parde (Fr). An alternative name for the Malbec grape.

Parde de Haut-Bailly (La) (Fr). The second wine of Château Haut-Bailly Grand Cru Classé A.C. Graves.

Pardella (Sp). See Pardillo.

Pardilla (Sp). See Pardillo.

Pardillo (Sp). A white grape variety grown in the central regions. Also known as the Pardella and Pardillo.

Pardubice Brewery (Czec). A brewery based in northern Czec.

Pardubický Porter (Czec). A Porter-style beer 19° Balling brewed by the Pardubice Brewery at Christmas time.

Parducci Wine Cellar (USA). A large winery based in Mendocino, California. 166 ha. Grape varieties – Barbera, Cabernet sauvignon, Chenin blanc, Flora, French colombard, Johannisberg riesling and Petite sirah. Produces varietal and table wines.

Parellada (Sp). A white grape variety grown in the Penedés region. Also known as the Montonel.

Parempuyre (Fr). A commune in the A.C. Haut-Médoc, north-western Bordeaux.

Pares (Ger). Vineyard. (Anb) = Rheinhessen. (Ber) = Bingen. (Gro) = Kaiserpfalz. (Vil) = Ingelheim.

Parfait Amour (Fr). A lilac-coloured Curaçao flavoured with rose petals, vanilla pods and almonds. 30% alc. by vol.

Parfait Amour (USA). A liqueur of purple shade, derived from lemon, citron, coriander, sugar and alcohol. 30% alc. by vol.

Parfum (Fr). The fragrance of perfume in a wine.

Pariah Arrack (Ind). A spirit distilled from Toddy (palm juice).

Parigot et Richard (Fr). A producer of Crémant de Bourgogne based at Savigny-lès-Beaune, Burgundy.

Parilla (Sp). The mark on a Sherry butt. Three lines crossed by another three. Denotes the wine is to be distilled and not used for Sherry.

Pariscot et Cie (Fr). A small négociant based in Beaune, Côte de Beaune, Burgundy.

Paris Goblet (Eng). A round bowled, stemmed glass which is the most common of all glasses used for wines and spirits. Sizes range from ⅙ gill for liqueurs to 12 fl.ozs. for beers. (Fr) = Ballon.

Parish Bitter (Eng). A cask conditioned Bitter 1040 O.G. brewed by the Woods Brewery in Shropshire.

Parisian (Cktl). ⅖ measure Gin, ⅖ measure dry Vermouth, ⅕ measure Crème de Cassis. Stir over ice, strain into a cocktail glass.

Parisian Blonde Cocktail (Cktl). ⅓ measure Jamaican rum, ⅓ measure Curaçao, ⅓ measure cream. Shake over ice, strain into a cocktail glass.

Parisien (Liq.Coffee). Using a measure of Cointreau.

Parisienne (Cktl). 2 parts Warninks Advocaat, 3 parts Bitter lemon. Mix together with ice, decorate with a cherry.

Paris Peacock (Cktl). ½ measure Cognac, ½ measure (green) Crème de Menthe. Shake well over ice, strain into a Champagne flute and top with dry Champagne. Dress with a mint sprig and a cherry.

Park and Tilford Brandy (USA). The brand-name of a Brandy produced by the Schenley Distillers in California.

Park Avenue (Cktl). ⅔ measure dry Gin, ⅓ measure Italian vermouth, ½ fl.oz. pineapple juice. Stir over ice, strain into a cocktail glass.

Park Lane Special (Cktl). ⅗ measure dry Gin, ⅖ measure Apricot brandy, juice ½ orange, dash Grenadine, ½ egg white. Shake over ice, strain into a cocktail glass.

Park Royal (Eng). The Guinness Brewery in London. Opened on Feb. 21st. 1936 it supplies London and southern England.

Parliamentary Brandy (Eng). The name given to poor quality, unflavoured spirit that was sold as it was, outside the scope of the tax put on Gin in 1729. In 1733 an Act was passed forbidding the sale.

Parlour (Eng). A term for the invitation by the public house landlord into his private quarters. Rare now.

Parmelia Moselle (Austr). A fresh, slightly pétillant white wine produced by Sandalford.

Parnay (Fr). A commune in Saumur in the Anjou-Saumur region of the Loire.

Paroisse (La) (Fr). Vineyard. Address = Saint Seurin de Cadourne, Gironde, A.C. Haut-Médoc. Commune = Saint Seurin de Cadourne. 122 ha. Grape varieties – Cabernet franc, Cabernet sauvignon and Merlot.

Paros (Gre). An island in the Cyclades group of islands in southern Greece. Produces Mistelles for the making of Vermouth. Also a red wine of the same name.

Parra (Port). Vine-leaf.

Parra (Sp). Grapevine.

Parral Training (Chile). A method training vines on high trellises.

Parras de la Fuente (Mex). Lit – 'Vine trellises viticulture'. Centre in the Coahuila region where the first vineyard was planted with Don Francisco grapes.

Parreira (Port). Denotes a trellis-grown vine.

Parrina (It). D.O.C. red and white wines from Tuscany. Made from the Ansonica, Malvasia del Chianti and Trebbiano toscano grapes for the white wines and the Canaiolo nero, Colorino, Montepulciano and Sangiovese grapes for the red wines. Produced only in Orbetello (part of the Grosseto province).

Parrina Bianco (It). See Parrina.

Parrina Rosso (It). See Parrina.

Parrot Cocktail (Cktl). ⅕ gill Pernod, 3 dashes mint syrup. Stir over ice in a highball glass, top with water and dress with sliced cucumber and a sprig of mint.

Parsac-Saint-Émilion (Fr). A.C. commune within the Saint-Émilion district of eastern Bordeaux.

Parsons Creek (USA). A winery based near Ukiah, Mendocino County, California. Grape varieties – Chardonnay, Gewürztraminer and Johannisberg riesling. Produces varietal wines.

Parson's Particular (Cktl).(Non-alc). 1 oz. lemon juice, 1 egg yolk, 2 ozs. orange juice, 4 dashes Grenadine. Shake over ice, strain into a large cocktail glass.

Parson's Special (Cktl).(Non-alc). 2 fl.ozs. orange juice, 1 egg yolk, 4 dashes Grenadine. Shake over ice, strain into an ice-filled highball glass, top with soda water.

Parsons Winery (USA). A small winery based in Soquel, Santa Cruz, California. Grape variety – Cabernet sauvignon.

Part des Anges (La) (Fr). The Angel's share. See Angel's Share.

Partenheim (Ger). Village. (Anb) = Rheinhessen. (Ber) = Bingen. (Gro) = Abtey. (Vins) = Sankt Georgen, Steinberg.

Partners (Port). A full Ruby Port produced by Sandeman Port shippers.

Partner's Choice (USA). The brand-name of a single Whiskey.

Partom (Isr). A sweet, full-bodied, Port-style red wine produced for the USA market by Carmel.

Partridge Eye (Eng). See Oeil de Perdrix. The name given to the sparkling Burgundy. Has the colour of a Partridge's eye.

Pasada (Sp). Very old Manzanilla. Also used to describe delicate Fino Sherries.

Pascal Blanc (Fr). A white grape variety grown in southern France. (Rhône and Provence).

Pascale di Cagliari (It). A red grape variety grown in Sardinia.

Pascarete (Sp). Local spelling of Paxarette. Also known as Pacaret.

Pas Dosé (It). Extremely dry (refers to sparkling wines).

Pasha (Tur). A coffee-flavoured liqueur. 25% alc. by vol. Produced by Seagram.

Påske Bryg (Den). An Easter beer 7.75% alc. by vol. brewed by the Albani Brewery in Odense.

Påskebryg (Den). An Easter beer 6.2% alc. by vol. brewed by the Tuborg Brewery.

Pasmados (Port). A red wine produced from a blend of Alentejo grapes by J.M. Fonseca in Azeitão.

Paso Fino (W.Ind). A Rum liqueur produced in Puerto Rico. 31% alc. by vol.

Pasolini (It). A Chianti Putto producer based in Tuscany.

Paso Robles (USA). A noted wine-producing town based in Luis Obispo County, California.

Pasqua (It). A sparkling (cuve close) wine producer based in Veneto.

Pasquiers (Les) (Fr). A vineyard in the A.C. commune of Montagny, Côte Chalonnaise, Burgundy.

Pasquier-Desvignes (Fr). Wine merchants based in Brouilly, Beaujolais in Burgundy. Address = St-Leger, 69220 Belleville.

Passarelle (Fr). The name for dried Muscatel grapes in the Frontignan region. The process is known as Passarillage or Passerillage.

Passarillage (Fr). A method whereby the grape stalks are pinched just above the clusters prior to harvesting. This prevents sap travelling down the stalk. The grapes ripen and dry out since no sap gets through to them. Rich in natural sugar. See Passerelle. Also the name used in the Béarn region for botrytis cinerea attacked grapes used for the wines of Portet.

Passaro (It). A Moscato Spumante producer based in Piemonte.

Passat (Cktl). 1 fl.oz. Peach brandy, 1 fl.oz. Orange Curaçao, 2 fl. ozs. Passion fruit juice, ¼ fl.oz. Gomme syrup, ¼ fl.oz.

lime cordial. Shake over ice, strain into a Champagne flute. Top up with iced Champagne, decorate with a cherry.

Passé (Fr). Applied to wine that is 'over the top'. Past its best.

Passeretta (It). Lit – 'Shrivelled or dried'. A white grape used to add flavour to sweet dessert Moscato wines.

Passerillage (Fr). See Passarelle.

Passerillé (Sp). Pedro Ximénez grapes that are put outside under cover to partially dry out. Produces a very sweet wine which is rich in alcohol.

Passerina (It). A white grape variety grown in the Marches region.

Passes (Fr). The name for a small label carrying information other than the label on the body or neck of the bottle.

Passe-Temps (Le) (Fr). A Premier Cru vineyard in the A.C. commune of Santenay, Côte de Beaune, Burgundy.

Passe-Tout-Grains (Fr). An A.C. red wine of Burgundy. Made from a blend of ⅓ Pinot noir and ⅔ Gamay grapes.

Passing Cloud (Austr). A noted winery based in central Victoria.

Passion Fruit (Austr). A sweet citrus-based liqueur.

Passion Fruit Cocktail (Cktl). ⅓ measure Passion fruit, ⅓ measure Gin, ⅓ measure dry Vermouth. Shake over ice, strain into a cocktail glass.

Passion Fruit Daiquiri (Cktl). ¾ measure white Rum, ¼ measure passion fruit juice, juice of a lime, 2 dashes Gomme syrup. Shake over ice, strain into a cocktail glass.

Passionola (USA). A non-alcoholic cordial produced from passion flowers.

Passion Splitz (USA). A brand of sparkling cooler produced from fruit juices and white wine. 1.2% alc. by vol.

Passionwine (Austr). A sparkling passion-fruit-flavoured wine produced by the Berri Estates in South Australia.

Passiti (It). The Tuscany name for the Vino Passito wines. Grapes have to dry before being made into wine.

Passito (It). A wine made from dried grapes. Once made, the wine has to age until June 1st. following the vintage.

Passito di Pantelleria (It). See Moscato Passito di Pantelleria.

Passover Slivovitz (Pol). A plum-flavoured Vodka, matured in oak casks, bottled at natural strength 75% alc. by vol. Produced by Polmos.

Passover Wine (USA). Jewish wine produced especially for the religious ceremony in the USA. Made from the Concord grape.

Passport (Scot). A blended Scotch whisky 40% alc. by vol. produced by Seagram.

P

Passport Decanter (Eng). A patented Port decanter with a round base and stand, designed so that the decanter cannot be placed on the table but must be passed round all the guests until it is back on its base. Address = Le Talbooth, Dedham, Colchester, Essex.

Passulated Grapes (Eng). Partially dried grapes either on the vine or on the ground. e.g. grapes used for Vin de Paille.

Passum (Lat). Raisin-wine.

Passy (Fr). A Chalybeate mineral water.

Passy-Grigny (Fr). A Cru Champagne village in the Canton de Châtillon-sur-Marne. District = Reims.

Passy-sur-Marne (Fr). A Cru Champagne village in the Canton de Condé-en-Brie. District = Château Thierry.

Pasteurisation (Fr). The process of heating wines and beers to destroy microorganisms which would be harmful to the liquid. Also used to prevent further fermentation. Temperature is strictly controlled 55–60°C (131–140°F) to prevent off-flavours (although it does give beer a biscuity flavour). System was pioneered by Louis Pasteur (82°C for wines).

Pasteurisation Tang (Eng). The term given to some beers that after pasteurisation obtain a stale taste.

Pasteur (Louis) (Fr). A nineteenth-century scientist from the Jura who discovered that yeast causes fermentation and invented the process of Pasteurisation. Also completed many experiments on the effects of oxidation.

Pastiche (Fr). Pastis. True name of Pastis. Introduced when Absinthe was banned because of its poisoning and social effect.

Pastis (Fr). Brandy, aniseed, liquorish and wild herbs. The French name for an aniseed-flavoured apéritif. Means – mixture. See Pastiche. 45% alc. by vol.

Pastis de Marseilles (Fr). An aniseed-flavoured spirit from southern France. See Pastis.

Pastizarra (Cktl). 1 part Yellow Izarra, 1 part Pernod, 3 parts water. Shake over ice, strain into a cocktail glass.

Pastorei (Ger). Vineyard. (Anb) = Nahe. (Ber) = Kreuznach. (Gro) = Kronenberg. (Vil) = Bretzenheim.

Pastorenberg (Ger). Vineyard. (Anb) = Nahe. (Ber) = Kreuznach. (Gro) = Pfarrgarten. (Vil) = Wallhausen.

Pastori Winery (USA). A small winery based in the Russian River Valley, Sonoma County, California. Grape varieties – Cabernet sauvignon and Zinfandel. Produces varietal wines.

Patacas (Mad). Coins of Madeira which were minted for the firm of Cossart Gordon and Co. and paid to their workers for carting the wine. Workers could redeem them at the company shop for goods.

Patamares (Port). Round terraced vineyards (2 metres wide).

Patavinum (Lat). A white wine produced in north-eastern Italy in Roman times.

Patent Apéritifs (Fr). Are similar to Vermouth. Either based on wine or spirits.

Patent Still (Scot). Invented by Robert Stein 1826 and improved by an Irish Excise man called Aeneas Coffey in 1832. A Continuous Still.

Pater (Bel). See Abt.

Paterberg (Ger). Vineyard. (Anb) = Rheinhessen. (Ber) = Nierstein. (Gro) = Spiegelberg. (Vil) = Nierstein.

Paterhof (Ger). Vineyard. (Anb) = Rheinhessen. (Ber) = Nierstein. (Gro) = Krötenbrunnen. (Vil) = Dienheim.

Paterhof (Ger). Vineyard. (Anb) = Rheinhessen. (Ber) = Nierstein. (Gro) = Krötenbrunnen. (Vil) = Oppenheim.

Patersberg (Ger). Village. (Anb) = Mittelrhein. (Ber) = Rheinburgengau. (Gro) = Loreleyfelsen. (Vin) = Teufelstein.

Pâteux (Fr). A term denoting a thick, syrupy consistency.

Patina (Eng). The name given to the hardening process that a cork of a sparkling wine bottle goes through during its time in the bottle under pressure. Goes from a soft, spongy appearance to a hard woody appearance over a period of years.

Pat O'Brian's (USA). America's largest pub based in New Orleans. Open 20 hours per day, has the longest bar in the world. Noted for its Hurricane Cocktail.

Patras (Gre). A still white wine produced in the Peloponnese.

Patriarche Père et Fils (Fr). A Burgundy négociant-éleveur based in Beaune, Côte de Beaune. Produces Kriter sparkling wines.

Patricia (Cktl). ⅓ measure Italian vermouth, ⅓ measure Vodka, ⅓ measure orange Curaçao. Stir over ice, strain into a cocktail glass. Add a twist of lemon.

Patrimoire (Fr). A non-vintage Champagne produced by Canard-Duchêne from 30% Chardonnay, 10% Pinot meunier and 60% Pinot noir grapes.

Patrimonio (Fr). The name given to A.C. red, rosé and white wines produced near the town of Bastia in Corsica.

Patriti Winery (Austr). A winery based near Adelaide, Southern Vales, South Australia. Produces varietal wines.

P

Pattes-de-Lièvre (Fr). Lit – 'Hare's feet'. The local Touraine name given to the Chenin blanc grape (Pineau de la Loire).

Pau Ferro (Port). A red grape variety grown in the Algarve.

Pauillac (Fr). An A.C. commune in the Haut-Médoc. Many rate it the finest of all the communes. Châteaux Lafite, Latour and Mouton Rothschild are all within the commune.

Paulaner Brauerei (Ger). A Münich Brewery which brews the Doppelbock beer known as Salvator. Also Münchner Hell 4.8% alc. by vol. and Urtyp 5.5% alc. by vol. (Lager beers).

Paul-Bara (Fr). Champagne producer. Address = 4 Rue Yvonnet, 51150 Bouzy. Récoltants-manipulants. Produces – Vintage and non-vintage wines. A member of the C.V.C. Vintages – 1970, 1971, 1973, 1975, 1976, 1979, 1982, 1983.

Paul Chanson (Fr). A cuvée based in the Premier Cru vineyard of Corton-Vergennes, Côte de Beaune, Burgundy. Owned by the Hospices de Beaune.

Paulée de Meursault (Fr). A luncheon held on the Monday after the wine sales of the Hospices de Beaune at mid-day. Each guest brings wine to accompany the meal.

Paulhan (Fr). A wine-producing commune in the Clairette du Languedoc, southern France.

Paulinsberg (Ger). Vineyard. (Anb) = Mosel-Saar-Ruwer. (Ber) = Bernkastel. (Gro) = Kurfürstlay. (Vil) = Kesten.

Paulinsberg (Ger). Vineyard. (Anb) = Mosel-Saar-Ruwer. (Ber) = Saar-Ruwer. (Gro) = Römerlay. (Vil) = Kasel.

Paulinslay (Ger). Vineyard. (Anb) = Mosel-Saar-Ruwer. (Ber) = Bernkastel. (Gro) = Kurfürstlay. (Vil) = Osann-Monzel.

Paulinushofberger (Ger). Vineyard. (Anb) = Mosel-Saar-Ruwer. (Ber) = Bernkastel. (Gro) = Kurfürstlay. (Vil) = Kesten.

Paul Jones (USA). The brand-name of a blended Whiskey bottled by the Paul Jones Distilling Co., Louisville, Kentucky. 40% alc. by vol.

Paul Masson Light (USA). A de-alcoholised, slightly sparkling, white wine 0.5% alc. by vol. Produced by Paul Masson from Chenin blanc and Colombard grapes plus wine grape juice. The alcohol is removed by centrifuge.

Paul Masson Vineyards (USA). A large winery based in Monterey County, California and San Joaquin Valley, California. 1872 ha. Grape varieties – Chardonnay, Fumé blanc, Gewürztraminer, Johannisberg riesling and Zinfandel. Produces most styles of wines.

Paulo (Austr). An alternative name for the Palomino grape.

Paul Robert (Alg). A wine-producing area in north-western Algeria. Produces mainly red wines.

Paulsen Vineyard (USA). A vineyard based near Cloverdale, Russian River Valley, Sonoma County, California. Grape variety – Sauvignon blanc. Vinified at Château St. Jean.

Paulus (Ger). Vineyard. (Anb) = Hessische Bergstrasse. (Ber) = Starkenburg. (Gro) = Wolfsmagen. (Vil) = Bensheim.

Pauvre (Fr). Poor, describes a wine without charm.

Pavia (It). A province of Lombardy in northern Italy. Produces mainly red wines, the most famous being Oltrepo Pavese.

Pavillon (Le) (S.Afr). A dry white wine produced by the Boschendal Estate from the Chenin blanc, Clairette blanche and Colombard grapes.

Pavillon Blanc du Château Margaux (Fr). A white wine made in part of Château Margaux (Premier Grand Cru Classé) vineyard in the commune of Margaux, Haut-Médoc, Bordeaux. Sold as Bordeaux Blanc.

Pavillon Cardinal (Fr). A red A.C. Bordeaux wine.

Pavillon de Bellvue (Fr). Address = Ordonnac, 33340 Lesparre Médoc. A.C. Médoc. Commune = Ordonnac. 210 ha. Grape varieties – Cabernet franc, Cabernet sauvignon, Merlot.

Pavillon Rouge du Château Margaux (Fr). A.C. Margaux. A red wine made in part of the Château Margaux (Premier Grand Cru Classé) vineyard in the commune of Margaux, Haut-Médoc, Bordeaux.

Pavlikeni (Bul). A demarcated wine-producing area in northern Bulgaria. Produces Cabernet, Gamza and Pinot noir grapes.

Paw Paw (USA). A wine-producing area in Michigan. Produces Catawba, Concord and Delaware grapes.

Paxarete (Sp). An alternative spelling of Paxarette.

Paxarette (Sp). A sweetening and colouring wine made from the Pedro Ximénez grape. Used also to colour whisky. Also spelt – Pacaret, Pajarete, Paxerette, Paxarete, Paxerete, Paxorotta.

Paxerete (Sp). An alternative spelling of Paxarette.

Paxerette (Sp). An alternative spelling of Paxarette.

Paxorotta (Eng). The spelling of Pax-

P

arette in the eighteenth century when sold as a wine.

Paya (S.Am). A Beer made from sweet potatoes in Guyana.

Paychaud Bitters (USA). An aromatic bitters used for cocktails.

Pays Catalan (Fr). A Vins de Pays area in the Pyrénées-Orientales Département in south-western France.

Pays d'Auge (Fr). An area in which the Appellation Calvados Contrôlée exists, the finest of the Calvados.

Pays de Retz (Fr). A Vins de Pays area in the Loire-Atlantique Département in western France.

Pays Nantais (Fr). A wine area within the Loire region. Situated on the west coast around the mouth of the river. In this area Muscadet and Gros plant are produced.

Pazardjik (Bul). A demarcated area based in the southern region.

Paziols (Fr). A commune in the A.C. Fitou region of southern France.

Pazo (Sp). The brand-name used by Bodegas Cooperativa de Ribeiro for a range of red, rosé and white wines. Produced from selected grapes.

P.D (Fr) (abbr). Producteurs Directs.

Peaberries (Eng). The name given to the individual coffee bean before it is roasted. Also known as Caracol.

Peace Cup (Cup). Crush 4 slices of fresh pineapple, 30 strawberries and 1 oz. castor sugar with a little iced water. Strain into a large jug and add 1 bottle of dry Champagne, ½ gill Maraschino and 1 bottle soda water. Stir, decorate with slices of pineapple and strawberries.

Peaceful Bend Vineyards (USA). A winery based in Steelville near St. James, Missouri. Produces French-American hybrid wines.

Peach Bitters (Eng). Prepared from extract of peach kernels and other flavourings.

Peach Blossom (Cktl). 2 fl.ozs. dry Gin, juice ¼ lemon, 2 dashes Gomme syrup, ½ ripe peach. Blend with a scoop of crushed ice, pour into a highball glass. Top with soda water, dress with a peach slice.

Peach Blow Fizz (Cktl). 2 fl.ozs. Gin, juice ½ lemon, 1 oz. cream, ¼ fresh peach, 2 dashes Gomme. Shake over ice, strain into an ice-filled highball glass. Top with soda.

Peach Brandy (Fr). A liqueur made from ripe peaches and extract of kernels. Medium alc. strength of 30% by vol. May have a small amount of fruit spirit added to improve flavour.

Peach Brandy Mint Julep (Cktl). 1 teaspoon sugar and water to make a smooth paste in a julep glass. Add 2–3 sprigs mint. Rub mint leaves along inside of glass. Add ice, 1½ measures Cognac, 1 measure Peach brandy. Stir, garnish with mint sprigs and a peach slice. Serve with straws.

Peach Bunny (Cktl). ⅓ measure Peach brandy, ⅓ measure (white) Crème de Cacao, ⅓ measure cream. Shake over ice, strain into a cocktail glass.

Peach County Schnapps (Can). A clear peach-flavoured Schnapps from Archers. 23% alc. by vol.

Peach Daiquiri (Cktl). 1½ fl.ozs. white Rum, ½ fl.oz. Peach brandy, juice ½ lime, ⅓ skinned fresh peach. Blend on high speed with 2 scoops crushed ice. Pour into a glass, serve with short straws and wedge of peach.

Peach Fizz (Cktl). Place 2 fl.ozs. Peach County Schnapps into an ice-filled highball glass and top with a dash of soda water.

Peach Flavoured Brandy (USA). A Brandy-based liqueur infused with fresh peaches.

Peach Liqueur (USA). A peach-flavoured liqueur made from fresh and dried peaches. 30% alc. by vol.

Peach Sangaree (Cktl). Place a measure of Peach brandy into an ice-filled highball glass, top with soda water and float 1 fl.oz. Port on top.

Peachtree Liqueur (Eng). See Original Peachtree Liqueur.

Peach West Indies Cocktail (Cktl). ⅕ gill golden Rum, ¼ fresh peach, juice ½ lime, 3 dashes Maraschino. Blend together with scoop of crushed ice. Strain into a flute glass.

Peacock's Tail Character (Eng). Describes a wine whose flavour opens out in the mouth. The explosion of flavour that increases with every second the wine is held in the mouth.

Peak (Eng). The term used to describe the peak in maturity of a wine. (Usually a personal view).

Peardrax (Eng). A sparkling, non-alcoholic pear drink produced by Whiteways.

Pear Drop (Eng). A term used to describe the aroma of wines made using the macération carbonique method. The aroma is due to increased Ethyl acetate produced by this method.

Pearl (Austr). The brand-name of a well-known 'Bag-in-the-box' wine.

Pearl (Eng). A carbonated, non-alcoholic, vanilla and orange drink made with skimmed-milk.

Pearl (N.Z.). A sparkling wine produced by Montana Wines.

P

Pearl Brewery (USA). A brewery based in San Antonio, Texas. Noted for its Jax and Pearl beers.

Pearl of Carmel (Isr). The name given to a sparkling wine made using the méthode champenoise by Carmel.

Pearl of Lake (Cktl). ⅓ measure Scotch whisky, ⅓ measure Bols Gold Liqueur, ⅓ measure lime juice. Shake over ice, strain into a cocktail glass.

Pearl Tea (China). Another name for Green Gunpowder tea in China.

Pearmain (Eng). Old English cider apple.

Pear Soup (Cktl). 4 parts Zwacks Viennese pear, 2 parts Rum, 2 parts lemon juice. Shake well over ice with a sprig of mint and fresh parsley. Strain into a cocktail glass.

Peasant Wine (Eng). The name given to locally produced and consumed wine. Usually sold from the cask.

Peat (Scot). A decomposed vegetable substance found in bogs. Turfs of it are used for fuel to fire malting kilns in Scotch whisky production. See Peat Reek.

Peating (Scot). The use of peat on the kiln fires of the Malt whisky distilleries. The amount of peat used will determine the 'Peat reek' of the finished product.

Peatling and Cawdron (Eng). A chain of 35 wine shops. (Part of Greene King and Son).

Peat Reek (Scot). The aroma from the burning peat used to heat the kiln in the malting of the barley in Scotch 'malt' whisky. The Islay malts have the strongest peat reek.

Peaux (Fr). A commune in the Charente-Maritime Département whose grapes are classed Petite Champagne (Cognac).

Pebbling (Ger). The habit of adding pebbles to the wine casks as the wine evaporates to ensure the casks are always full.

Pec (Fr). A brand Pastis label.

Pécharmant (Fr). An A.C. district of northern Bergerac in south-west France. Communes = Creysse, Lembras, Mouleydier and Saint-Sauveur. Produces medium red wines. Minimum alc. by vol. 11%.

Pechar's Vineyards (N.Z.). A small winery based in Valley Road, Henderson, North Island. 4 ha. Produces hybrid wines under the Old Railway label.

Pêche (Fr). The name for peach liqueurs.

Pechgeschmack (Ger). Taste of tar. Occurs in wines that have come into contact with the aroma of tar. e.g. Freshly tarred roads.

Pechstein (Ger). Vineyard. (Anb) = Rheinpfalz. (Ber) = Mittelhaardt-Deutsche Weinstrasse. (Gro) = Mariengarten. (Vil) = Forst.

Pécket (Bel). A local sparkling Gin made from corn.

Peck Ranch (USA). A small vineyard based in San Luis Obispo County, California. Grape variety – Sauvignon blanc.

Pecorella (It). A red grape variety grown in Calabria.

Pecorino (It). A white grape variety grown in The Marche and Calabria regions.

Pecota Winery (USA). A winery based near Calistoga, Napa Valley, California. 16.5 ha. Grape varieties – Cabernet sauvignon, Colombard, Flora, Gamay and Sauvignon blanc. Produces varietal wines.

Pécoui-Touar (Fr). A red grape variety grown in the A.C. Bandol, Provence.

Pécs (Hun). A white wine made from the Olasrisling grape around the town of Pécs in the Mecsek Hills.

Pécs Brewery (Hun). A noted brewery based in south-western Hungary.

Pecsenyibór (Hun). A term that denotes dessert wine on a label.

Pécs Riesling (Hun). A sweet, white wine from the Pécs-Villàny region made from the Welschriesling grape.

Pécs-Villàny (Hun). Vineyards sited near the southern frontier on the right bank of the river Danube.

Pectic Enzymes (Eng). Enzymes found naturally in fruits which degrade pectin.

Pectin (Eng). A soluble substance found in ripe fruits. Can cause hazy wine (home-made wine). Is removed by using pectic enzymes.

Pectin-Methyl-Esterase (Eng). An enzyme that reduces pectin haze in wines. Known as P.M.E.

Pedernã (Port). A white grape variety grown in the Vinho Verde region.

Pedhoullas (Cyp). A wine village in the Troodos mountains on the north-west side in the region of Marathassa.

Pedicle (Eng). The name for the grape stem. Contains tannin.

Pedigree Bitter (Eng). A malty Bitter beer 1043 O.G. brewed by the Marston Brewery in Burton-on-Trent, Staffordshire.

Pedigreed Brewer's Yeast (USA). A yeast which is most suitable to the brewer to produce beer. The best strain to convert the wort sugars into alcohol.

Pediococcus (Lat). The alternative name for the lactobacillus.

Pedology (Eng). The study of the soil and its classification by type, age and origin.

Pedrizzetti Winery (USA). A winery based near Morgan Hill, Santa Clara, California. Grape varieties – Barbera, Chenin blanc, Colombard, Petite sirah and Zinfandel. Produces varietal wines.

Pedro II (Dom) (Port). Signed the Methuen Treaty in 1703 on behalf of Portugal.

Pedro Domecq (Sp). See Domecq.

Pedro Jimenez (Sp). An alternative spelling for the Pedro Ximénez grape.

Pedro Luis (Sp). A white grape variety grown in the Huelva region of south-western Spain.

Pedro Mole (Mad). Decomposed, yellow tufa soil found on Madeira.

Pedroncelli (USA). A winery in the Alexander Valley, Sonoma County, California. 56 ha. Grape varieties – Cabernet sauvignon, Chardonnay, Gewürztraminer and Zinfandel. Produces varietal wines.

Pedro Rodriguez (Sp). The brand-name of a range of young Sherries from Barbadillo in Sanlúcar de Barrameda.

Pedro Ximen (Sp). An alternative spelling of the Pedro Ximénez grape.

Pedro Ximénez (Sp). Also known as the P.X. A red grape variety grown in south-western Spain. Used in the making of Sherry, Málaga and Montilla. Also known in Germany, Alsace and Austria as the Elbling, Knipperlé, Räuschling and Grossriesling. Also spelt Pedro Jimenez, Pedro Ximen, Pedro Ximinez.

Pedro Ximinez (USA). An alternative spelling of Pedro Ximénez.

Peduncles (Lat). The flower/fruit stalk.

Peek Performance (Eng). A non-alcoholic, high-energy, glucose-rich, fruit and tropical fruit drink produced by Nabisco Food Service. Still and carbonated versions.

Peel Estate Winery (Austr). Address = Fletcher Road, Baldivis, P.O. Box 37, Mandurah 6210 Western Australia. 12.6 ha. Grape varieties – Cabernet sauvignon, Chardonnay, Chenin blanc, Sauvignon blanc, Shiraz, Verdelho and Zinfandel.

Peeterman (Bel). An ungarnished white wheat beer once brewed by Stella Artois Brasserie. See also Hoegaards Wit.

Peg (Eng). In early times drinking vessels would have small studs (pegs) on the inside which were used as measure marks. A customer would ask for a peg, 2 pegs etc. See also 'to drink a peg'.

Peggy Cocktail (Cktl). ⅔ measure dry Gin, ⅓ measure dry Vermouth, 2 dashes Ricard, 2 dashes Dubonnet. Stir over ice, strain into a cocktail glass.

Peissy (Switz). A wine-producing area in Geneva.

Pejo (It). A naturally sparkling mineral water from the Fonte Alpina in Pejo.

Pek (Eng) (abbr). Pekoe, tea grade.

Peket (Bel). The alternative name for Jenever.

Pek Ho (China). Lit – 'White hair'. Refers to the tip of the tea bush. See Pekoe. Also spelt Pak Ho.

Peking (China). Base for a branch of the China National Cereals, Oils and Foodstuffs Import and Export Corp. Produces a sparkling wine and a brandy.

Peking Beer (China). Beer brewed by the Peking Brewery, eastern China.

Peking Brewery (China). A noted brewery based in Peking, eastern China.

Pekko (Fin). The ancient God of beer and barley.

Pekoe (Asia). Tea grade. A large black leaf with twist. Derived from the Chinese Pak ho (white hairs). Describes the fine downy hairs on the young tea buds. See Orange Pekoe, Pekoe Souchong etc. See also Pek Ho.

Pekoe Souchong (Asia). A grade of unbroken tea leaf. Irregular in shape and smaller than Souchong.

Pelargonic Acid (Eng). An ester found in wines in small quantities.

Pelequen (Chile). A wine-producing area near Santiago.

Pelforth Brasserie (Fr). A brewery in Lille. Brews Pelforth Brune 1069 O.G. a top-fermented Brown ale and Killian's Irish Red which is brewed under licence.

Pelham Ale (Eng). A bottled Pale ale 1031 O.G. brewed by the Greene King Brewery in Bedford.

Pelhřimov Brewery (Czec). An old established brewery based in central-southern Czec.

Pelican Export (Fr). A Lager beer brewed by the Pelforth Brasserie in Lille.

Pelin (Bul). A style of bitters made from alcohol, herbs, quinces, apples, grapes and old wine.

Pelin (Rum). A herb-infused wine usually served 'iced'.

Pelješac (Yug). A small wine-producing area on the Dalmatian coast. Is noted for its Postup (a red wine).

Pellegrino (It). A carbonated, natural mineral water from Milan.

Pellejo (Sp). Wine skin/bag.

Pellicle (Eng). A membrane, film or skin that forms on a wine's surface.

Pellingen (Ger). Village. (Anb) = Mosel-Saar-Ruwer. (Ber) = Saar-Ruwer. (Gro) = Scharzberg. (Vins) = Herrgottsrock, Jesuitengarten.

Pelne (Pol). A well-hopped, dry pale Lager beer. (A Pilsener beer).

Peloponnese (Gre). The largest and most

important region of wine production in Greece.

Peloux (Les) (Fr). A wine-producing village in the commune of Solutré-Pouilly in A.C. Pouilly-Fuissé, Mâcon, Burgundy.

Pelure d'Oignon (Fr). Colour of onion skin. Applied to certain rosé and red wines as they gradually take on the colour due to their age.

Pelzerberger (Ger). Vineyard. (Anb) = Mosel-Saar-Ruwer. (Ber) = Zell/Mosel. (Gro) = Grafschaft. (Vil) = Beuren.

Pemartin (Sp). A noted Bodega based in Jerez. Was part of the Rumasa group.

Penadés (Sp). See Penedés. Alternative spelling.

Peñafiel (Port). A wine district of the Entre e Douro region. Produces both red and white Vinhos Verdes.

Peñaflor (Arg). The largest Argentinian wine company. Is based in the Mendoza region. Deals with bulk wines and Tio Quinto (a Sherry-style wine for export).

Penalva do Castelo (Port). A large cooperative based in the Dão region.

Pendant (Eng). A blended wine produced by the Elham Valley Vineyards in Barham, Kent.

Pendeli (Gre). A dry red table wine produced in Attica by Cambas.

Pendennis (Cktl). ⅕ gill dry Gin, ⅛ gill Apricot brandy, juice ½ lime, 2 dashes Peychaud bitters. Shake over ice, strain into a cocktail glass.

Pendennis Toddy (Cktl). Dissolve a sugar cube in a little water in a sour glass. Add 2 fl.ozs. Bourbon whiskey, stir, add ice and a slice of lemon.

Pendleton Winery (USA). A winery based in San Jose, Santa Clara, California. Grape varieties – Cabernet sauvignon, Chardonnay, Chenin blanc, Pinot noir and Zinfandel. Produces varietal wines.

Pendle Witches Brew (Eng). A cask conditioned Ale 1050 O.G. brewed by the Moorhouse Brewery in Burnley, Lancashire.

Pendura (Port). A white grape variety grown in the Alentejo region.

Penedés (Sp). A wine region of south-eastern Spain. Part of Cataluña. Has 3 sub-regions the Alto Penedés, Bajo Penedés and the Medio Penedés. Produces red, rosé and white wines. Main vines – Maccabéo, Parellada, Sumoll and Xarel-lo. See also Torres. Has 25,725 ha. under vines.

Penetrating (Eng). A term used to describe a powerful wine with a strong bouquet. Is usually high in alcohol.

Penfolds (Austr). Address = 634 Prince's Highway, Tempe, New South Wales 2004. 650 ha. in the Barossa Valley, Clare, Coonawarra and Morgon. Grape varieties – Cabernet sauvignon, Chardonnay, Muscat gordo, Rhine riesling, Shiraz and Traminer. Has wineries at Eden Vale, Barossa Valley and McLaren Vale Vineyard (New South Wales), Murrumbidgee Irrigation Area, plus Auldana near Magill, Modbuny and Kalimma in the Barossa Valley.

Penfolds (N.Z.). Address = 190 Lincoln Road, Henderson, Auckland. No vineyards, grapes bought in from Blenheim, Gisborne and Hawkes Bay. Varieties are – Cabernet sauvignon, Chardonnay, Chenin blanc, Gewürztraminer, Müller-Thurgau, Rhine riesling and Sauvignon blanc.

Penfolds Grandfather (Austr). The brandname of a Port-style wine produced by the Penfolds Winery.

Penguin Cocktail (Cktl). ⅓ measure Cointreau, ⅙ measure Cognac, ⅙ measure lemon juice, ⅙ measure orange juice, dash Grenadine. Stir well over ice, strain into an ice-filled balloon glass. Dress with a slice of orange, lemon and cherry.

Penguine Brewery (S.Am). A brewery based in Stanley in the Falkland Islands owned by Everards. Brews traditional cask conditioned Ales and Lager beer.

Pennine Bitter (Eng). A keg Bitter 1037 O.G. brewed by the Webster Brewery in Halifax, Yorkshire.

Penn's Ale (Eng). A cask conditioned Bitter 1045 O.G. brewed by the Hoskins Brewery in Leicester.

Penn Shore Vineyards (USA). A winery based in Erie County, north-east Pennsylvania. Produces Concord and American wines.

Pennsylvania Punch (Cktl). 1 quart water, juice of 12 lemons, 6 ozs. powdered sugar, ½ bottle Peach brandy, 1 bottle Brandy, 1 bottle Bourbon whiskey. Stir together with ice in a punch bowl. Garnish with orange slices.

Penny Black (Mad). A noted brand of Malmsey produced by Leacock.

Penny Universities (Eng). The nickname for the first coffee houses in the late seventeenth century. Stemmed from the habit of discussing business over coffee. Most of these coffee houses became the business institutions of the present day e.g. The Stock Exchange and Lloyds.

Penrhos Court (Eng). A small brewery based near Kington in Herefordshire. Brews cask conditioned Penrhos Bitter, Jones's Ale and an original Porter.

Pensans Brewery (Eng). A brewery based

in Penzance, Cornwall. Noted for its cask conditioned MSB 1050 O.G. and Caref Ertach Pensans 1055 O.G.

Penshurst Vineyards (Eng). A small vineyard based at Grove Road, Penshurst, Kent. Was first planted in 1972. 5 ha. Grape varieties – Müller-Thurgau, Reichensteiner and Seyval blanc.

Pentaploa (Gre). An ancient drink consisting of five ingredients (cheese, flour, honey, oil and wine).

Pentes (Fr). A term found on a wine label from Cahors. Lit – 'Slopes'. From the red soil slopes near the river Lot.

Pentland Beer (Scot). A cask conditioned heavy Ale 1036 O.G. brewed by the Drybrough Brewery in Edinburgh.

Pentland Fizz (Cktl). 2 fl.ozs. orange juice, 1 fl.oz. Glayva. Top up with iced Champagne.

Pentose (Eng). A monosaccharide found in wines.

Penukanda (Ind). A wine-producing area.

Pepi (It). A Chianti Classico producer based in Tuscany.

Pepi Winery (USA). A winery based between Yountville and Oakville in the Napa Valley, California. Grape variety – Sauvignon blanc.

Peplina Stepu (USSR). A table wine produced near Cherson in the Ukraine.

Peppermint Get (Fr). See Pippermint Get.

Peppermint Iceberg (Cktl). ¾ measure Vodka, ¼ measure Peppermint cordial. Mix together in an ice-filled highball. Dress with a sprig of mint.

Peppermint Paddy (Cktl). ⅓ measure Peppermint cordial, ⅓ measure Bourbon whiskey, ⅓ measure cream. Shake over ice, strain into a cocktail glass.

Peppermint Park (Cktl). ⅓ gill dry Gin, ⅙ gill lemon juice, dash Gomme syrup. Shake over ice, strain into a Champagne saucer. Top with iced Champagne. Serve with straws.

Peppermint Pastille (Fr). A green Crème de Menthe liqueur. 28% alc. by vol.

Peppermint Pattie (Cktl). ½ measure (white) Crème de Menthe, ½ measure (white) Crème de Cacao. Shake over ice, strain into an ice-filled old-fashioned glass.

Peppermint Pick Me Up (Cktl). Add ⅕ gill Crème de Menthe to a glass of hot, strong, black coffee. Stir, top with whipped cream and a few dashes of Crème de Menthe.

Peppermint Schnapps (USA). A mint liqueur. Lighter in body than Crème de Menthe. 30% alc. by vol.

Peppermint Stick (Cktl). ⅖ measure (white) Crème de Cacao, ⅕ measure Vodka, ⅕ measure cream, ⅕ measure

Peppermint cordial. Shake over ice, strain into a cocktail glass.

Peppermint Tea (Eng). A herbal tea which helps settle the stomach and aids digestion.

Pepper Vodka (USSR). See Okhotnichaya.

Peppery (Eng). A term used to describe the aroma and flavour of the Grenache-based wines of southern France. Also to young wines that are fierce and prickly on the nose.

Pepsi-Cola (USA). A brand-name for a carbonated soft drink. Red-brown in colour, it is produced by Pepsi-Cola Worldwide Beverages and drunk world-wide.

Pepsi-Cola Worldwide Beverages (USA). A large company that produces Pepsi-Cola. Partly owns Britvic Corona.

Pequea Valley Winery (USA). A large winery based in Willow Street, Pennsylvania. Produces hybrid wines.

Perbibere (Lat). Drink up.

Percolate (Eng). The action of wines and spirits as they are passed through herbs to extract flavours for Vermouths and liqueurs. Also applies to coffee when hot water is passed through the coffee grounds to extract colour and flavour.

Percolateur (Fr). Percolator.

Percolation (Eng). Is 'intensive maceration', where pure spirit is continuously passed through botanicals to extract flavours for liqueurs.

Percolator (Eng). A unit used in the making of coffee. Either automatic or manual. Near boiling water is passed over the grounds to extract the flavour and colour.

Perdeberg Co-operative (S.Afr). Based in Paarl. Address = Perdeberg Wynboere Koöperatiewe Box 214, Paarl 7621. Produces varietal wines.

Perdeberg Wynboere Koöperatiewe (S.Afr). See Perdeberg Co-operative.

Perdido Vineyard (USA). A bonded winery based in Alabama. Wines are produced mainly from the Muscadine grape.

Perdiz (Sp). A white grape variety grown in the León region.

Perdriel (Arg). The brand-name used by Bodegas Norton for their premium wines.

Père Blanc (Lux). A herb-flavoured liqueur.

Père et Fils (Fr). Father and son(s).

Père Hennepin (USA). A sparkling wine produced by the Thompson Winery in Michigan.

Perelada (Sp). A sparkling wine (Cava) producer of Penedés, Alto Ampurdán on the Costa Brava. Produces wines by the méthode champenoise. Gran Claustro is their top named wine.

Perelli-Minetti Winery (USA). A large winery based at Delano, Kern County, California. Produces most styles of wines under the California Wine Association Co. (Ambassador, Greystone, Guasti and Perelli-Minetti).

Père Marquete (USA). A sparkling wine produced by the Thompson Winery in Michigan.

Peré Palummo (It). Lit – 'Pigeon foot'. Refers to colour of the Piedirosso grape variety grown in the Campania region.

Pères Blancs (Fr). A Rum distillery based on the island of Guadeloupe.

Péret (Fr). A wine-producing commune in Clairette du Languedoc, southern France.

Pérez Barquero S.A. (Sp). A producer of Montilla wines based in Córdoba. (Was part of Rumasa).

Pérez Martin (Sp). A Sherry Bodega based in Sanlúcar de Barrameda.

Pérez Texeira (Sp). A producer and exporter of Málaga.

Perfect Affinity Cocktail (Cktl). ½ measure Scotch whisky, ¼ measure Italian vermouth, ¼ measure French vermouth, 2 dashes Angostura. Shake over ice, strain into a cocktail glass. Decorate with a spiral of lemon peel.

Perfect Cocktail (Cktl).(1). ½ measure dry Gin, ¼ measure sweet Vermouth, ¼ measure sweet Vermouth, dash Angostura. Stir with ice, strain into a cocktail glass. Add a twist of orange peel.

Perfect Cocktail (Cktl).(2). ½ gill Gin, ⅙ gill French vermouth, ⅙ gill Italian Vermouth, dash Absinthe. Shake over ice, strain into a wine glass. Serve with a slice of lemon and dash of lemon peel juice on top.

Perfection Pale (Eng). A medium-dry Sherry from Peter Dominic Wine Shops.

Perfect Lady (Cktl). ½ measure dry Gin, ¼ measure lemon juice, ¼ measure Peach brandy, 1 egg white. Shake over ice, strain into a cocktail glass.

Perfect Martini (Cktl). ⅔ measure Gin, ⅙ measure dry Vermouth, ⅙ measure sweet Vermouth. Stir over ice, strain into a cocktail glass, add a twist of lemon.

Perfect Match (Cktl). ½ measure Glayva, ¼ measure Cherry brandy, ¼ measure lemon juice, egg white. Shake over ice, strain into a cocktail glass.

Perfect Rob Roy (Cktl). ½ measure Scotch whisky, ¼ measure dry Vermouth, ¼ measure sweet Vermouth. Stir over ice,

strain into a cocktail glass. Dress with a lemon peel spiral.

Perfume (Eng). Description of the bouquet of a wine when it has a flowery scent. e.g. violets in Clarets.

Pergola (Port). A method of training vines to grow from a single trunk and trained on trellises with other crops underneath. Also used in Italy, Greece, Spain etc.

Pergola Torte (It). A red Vino da Tavola made from the Sangiovese grape in central-western Italy.

Pérignac-de-Pons (Fr). A commune in the Charente-Maritime Département whose grapes are classed Petite Champagne (Cognac).

Pérignon (Pierre) (Fr). The name of Dom Perignon before he took the monastic orders in 1658.

Perigord (Fr). A red grape variety grown in the Bergerac region.

Perikum-Snaps (Den). The brand-name of an Aquavit.

Perino (Bra). A spirit produced by the Indians from cassava root (the root is poisonous to eat).

Periquita (Port). A strong red wine produced in the Azeitão and Palmela districts in the Estremadura.

Perisco (Hol). A peach-flavoured bitters liqueur.

Perla (Czec). Lit – 'Pearl'. A special pale Ale brewed by the Ilava Brewery.

Perla de Tîrnave (Rum). A well-balanced, light, slightly sweet, blended wine from the Tîrnave region on the river Tîrnave. Is produced from the Fetească, Muskat-ottonel and Riesling grapes.

Perlan (Switz). The generic name given to the white wines produced in Geneva from the Chasselas grape.

Perlant (Fr). The term for very slightly sparkling wines.

Perlant Perlé (S.Afr). Pétillant.

Perlé (Fr). Beaded, light sparkle, pétillant.

Perle (Ger). A white grape variety. A cross between the Gewürztraminer and the Müller-Thurgau. Gives light fruity wines and resists low temperatures (-30°C in Winter and -5°C in the Spring).

Perlino Perlé (S.Afr). A slightly sparkling medium-sweet white wine made by the Stellenbosch Farmers' Winery from the Clairette blanche, Muscat d'Alexandrie and Steen grapes.

Perlwein (Ger). A term for light sparkling wine. Carbonic acid pressure must not be more than 2.5 atmospheres to qualify.

Perlwein (Lux). A term for a pétillant wine. Slightly sparkling.

Perlweizen (Ger). Pale wheat beer. A

well-matured Wheat beer 5% alc. by vol. Produced by the Riegele Brauerei in Augsburg.

Permezzo (Cktl). 1 oz. red Dubonnet, 1 oz. dry Dubonnet. Place in an old-fashioned glass. Serve 'On the rocks' with a slice of lemon.

Permitted Hours (Eng). The hours for which a person can consume alcoholic beverages on licensed premises. Vary from district to district. See also Drinking-Up Time.

Pernod (Fr). An un-sweetened aniseed-flavoured liqueur/spirit. A brand Pastis. 45% alc. by vol.

Pernod and Clementine (Cktl). 1 part Pernod, 1 part orange juice. Stir with ice in a highball glass. Top with Bitter lemon.

Pernod Caribbean (Cktl). 1 part Pernod, 1 part Malibu, 3 parts pineapple juice. Stir with ice in a highball glass, top with soda water.

Pernod Cocktail (Cktl). 1 measure Pernod, 1 measure water, dash Gomme syrup, dash Angostura. Shake over ice, strain into a cocktail glass.

Pernod Drip (Cktl). Pour 1 measure of Pernod onto a lump of ice in a small tumbler. Place 1 sugar lump on a French drip spoon, rest on the rim of the glass. Slowly pour cold water over the sugar lump until dissolved.

Pernod Jelly Bean (Cktl). 1 measure Pernod, 1 measure Vodka, 1 measure blackcurrant syrup. Stir into a highball glass with ice, top with lemonade.

Pernod Oriental (Cktl). 1 measure Pernod, ½ measure Midori, dash lime juice. Stir with ice into a highball glass, top with soda water.

Pernod-Ricard (Fr). A large company (merger of Pernod and Ricard Pastis companies). Produces Alize (pastis). Also own the Highland malt whiskies – Aberlour-Glenlivet and Edradour. Also owns Besserat de Bellefron.

Pernod Riviera (Cktl). ⅔ measure Pernod, ⅓ measure dry Gin, dash Angostura. Place into an ice-filled highball glass, top with lemonade and a slice of lemon.

Peroni Beer (It). An Italian brewed beer exported to the USA.

Peroni Brewery (It). A large brewing company. Has eight breweries in Italy.

Peronospora (Lat). Downy Mildew. Vine disease. Treated with copper sulphate.

Perpetua (It). A dessert wine produced by the Villa Fontna Winery in the Cerasuola di Vittoria, south-eastern Sicily.

Perpotatio (Lat). A heavy drinking bout.

Perpotare (Lat). To drink continuously.

Perquages (Les) (Ch.Isles). A vineyard based at Les Perquages Cottage, Mount Remon, St. Peter, Jersey. Was first planted in 1980–81. 1.2 ha. Grape varieties – Blauberger 20%, Regner 30% plus others.

Perréon (Le) (Fr). A commune in the Beaujolais. Has A.C. Beaujolais-Villages or Beaujolais-Le Perréon status.

Perricone (It). A black grape variety grown in Sicily. Is also known as the Piedirosso.

Perrier (Fr). A naturally sparkling mineral water from the spring at Vergeze in the Gard Département. Is also available in lemon and lime flavours.

Perrier (Joseph et Fils) (Fr). Champagne producer. Address = Avenue de Paris, BP 31, 51005 Chalons-sur-Marne. A Grande Marque. Produces – Vintage and non-vintage wines. Vintages – 1900, 1904, 1906, 1911, 1914, 1915, 1921, 1926, 1928, 1929, 1933, 1934, 1937, 1938, 1942, 1943, 1945, 1947, 1949, 1959, 1961, 1962, 1964, 1966, 1969, 1971, 1973, 1975, 1976, 1979, 1982, 1983.

Perrier Champagne (Fr). Three separate Champagne houses. See Perrier, Laurent Perrier Vine, Perrier (Joseph et Fils) and Perrier-Jouët & Co.

Perrière (La) (Fr). A Premier Cru vineyard [part] in the A.C. commune of Fixin, Côte de Nuits, Burgundy. 6.53 ha. Part also in Gevrey-Chambertin. Also known as Clos de la Perrière.

Perrière (La) (Fr). A Premier Cru vineyard [part] in the A.C. commune of Gevrey-Chambertin, Côte de Nuits, Burgundy. 2.47 ha. Part also in Fixin.

Perrière (La) (Fr). A Premier Cru vineyard in the A.C. commune of Nuits-Saint-Georges, Côte de Nuits, Burgundy. 4 ha.

Perrières (Les) (Fr). A Premier Cru vineyard in the A.C. commune of Beaune, Côte de Beaune, Burgundy. 3.18 ha.

Perrières (Les) (Fr). A wine-producing village in the commune of Fuissé in A.C. Pouilly-Fuissé, Mâcon, Burgundy.

Perrières (Les) (Fr). A Premier Cru vineyard in the A.C. commune of Meursault, Côte de Beaune, Burgundy. 17.8 ha.

Perrières (Les) (Fr). A vineyard in the A.C. commune of Montagny, Côte Chalonnaise, Burgundy.

Perrière-Noblet (Fr). A Premier Cru vineyard [part] in the A.C. commune of Nuits-Saint-Georges, Côte de Nuits, Burgundy. 2.2 ha.

Perrier-Jouët & Co (Fr). Champagne producer. Address = 26 Avenue de Champagne, 51201 Épernay. A Grande Marque. Produces – Vintage and non-vintage wines. Vintages – 1901, 1904,

1911, 1913, 1914, 1919, 1921, 1923, 1926, 1928, 1934, 1937, 1942, 1943, 1946, 1947, 1949, 1950, 1952, 1953, 1955, 1959, 1961, 1964, 1966, 1969, 1971, 1973, 1975, 1976, 1979, 1982, 1983. Part of G.H. Mumm. De Luxe vintage cuvée is Belle Époque. Also produces Blason de France Rosé (a non-vintage rosé).

Perrier-Jouët Belle Époque, Fleur de Champagne (Fr). The Perrier-Jouët house's top of the range Champagne. Vintages – 1966, 1969, 1971, 1973, 1975, 1976, 1979, 1982, 1983. 40–45% Chardonnay and 55–60% Pinot noir grapes.

Perrier Water (Fr). See Perrier.

Perrize (Eng). The brand-name for a sparkling Perry from Showerings.

Perroud (Fr). A noted producer of Beaujolais wine based in Lantignié. See Château du Basty.

Perroy (Switz). A wine-producing area in La Côte on the west bank of Lake Geneva.

Perrum (Port). A white grape variety grown in the Algarve region. Also known as the Palomino.

Perruno (Sp). A white grape variety.

Perry (Eng). An alcoholic beverage made from pear juice. Either still or sparkling and usually slightly sweet.

Perrys (Ire). A keg Beer brewed by the Irish Ale Breweries.

Perscheid (Ger). Village. (Anb) = Mittelrhein. (Ber) = Rheinburgengau. (Gro) = Schloss Schönburg. (Vin) = Rosental.

Persico (Hol). A brandy-based liqueur produced from almonds, peach stones, sugar and spices. 30% alc. by vol.

Persicot (Hol). See Persico.

Persigny de Bergerac (Fr). The Mähler-Besse Bordeaux négociants-éleveurs' label for their A.C. Bergerac wines sold in the U.K.

Personalidad (Sp). A term that denotes a wine of character and of breeding.

Perthuis (Le) (Fr). A vineyard in the A.C. commune of Montagny, Côte Chalonnaise, Burgundy.

Pertois-Lebrun (Fr). Champagne producer. Address = 399 Rue de la Libération, Cramant, 51200 Épernay. Récoltants-manipulants. Produces – Vintage and non-vintage wines. Vintages – 1971, 1973, 1975, 1976, 1979, 1982, 1983.

Pertsovka (USSR). A dark brown pepper-flavoured Vodka. Has a pleasant aroma and burning taste. Made from an infusion of Capsicum, cayenne and cubeb. 35% alc. by vol. Also spelt Pertsovka.

Pertsovka (USSR). See Pertsovaka.

Pertuisots (Les) (Fr). A Premier Cru vineyard in the A.C. commune of Beaune, Côte de Beaune, Burgundy. 5.16 ha. Also spelt Les Pertuizots.

Pertuizots (Les) (Fr). See Pertuisots (Les).

Perushtitza (Bul). A state wine co-operative.

Peruvian Coffee (S.Am). A light bodied, mild-flavoured coffee from Peru. Used mainly for blending with strong coffees as it is low in acidity.

Pescador (Sp). A sparkling wine produced using the cuve close method by Cavas del Ampurdàn.

Pesenti Winery (USA). A winery based in Templeton, San Luis Obispo County, California. 27 ha. Grape varieties – mainly Zinfandel.

Pessac (Fr). A commune within the A.C. Graves district. Has the Premier Grand Cru Château Haut Brion within its boundaries.

Pests (Eng). Insects which attack the vine and its fruit. Phylloxera, Red spider, Cochylis etc.

Petake Cocktail (Cktl). 2 fl.oz. golden Rum, 1 fl.oz. Cointreau, dash Van der Hum, dash pineapple juice, dash papaya juice, dash lime juice. Shake over ice, strain into a cocktail glass.

Petaluma (Austr). Vineyards. Address = Spring Gully Road, Piccadilly, South Australia. Vineyards in Coonawarra, Hanlin Hill at Clare and Piccadilly. Also own Old Bridgewater Mill. Grape varieties – Cabernet sauvignon, Chardonnay and Riesling. Produces varietal wines.

Pet Bottle (Eng). A moulded plastic bottle made from Polyethylene Terephthalate by the Metal Box Co. Ltd.

Petenara (Sp). A light, dry, Manzanilla sherry produced by Romate.

Peter Crau (Fr). A Vins de Pays area of the Bouches du Rhône Département, south-eastern France.

Peter Dominic (Eng). Part of IDV Ltd. under the Grand Metropolitain umbrella. Has a large chain of Off-licences around the U.K. Has taken over the Bottoms Up group.

Peter Pan (Cktl). ⅓ measure dry Gin, ⅓ measure French vermouth, ⅓ measure orange juice, 2 dashes Angostura. Shake over ice, strain into a cocktail glass.

Petersberg (Ger). Grosslage. (Anb) = Mittelrhein. (Ber) = Siebengebirge. (Vils) = Oberdollendorf, Niederdollendorf, Königswinter, Rhondorf.

Petersberg (Ger). Grosslage. (Anb) = Rheinhessen. (Ber) = Nierstein. (Vils) = Albig, Bechtolsheim, Biebelnheim, Framersheim, GauHeppenheim, Gau-Odernheim, Spiesheim.

Petersberg (Ger). Vineyard. (Anb) = Baden. (Ber) = Badische Bergstrasse/

Kraichgau. (Gro) = Hohenberg. (Vil) = Weingarten.

Petersberg (Ger). Vineyard. (Anb) = Mosel-Saar-Ruwer. (Ber) = Zell/Mosel (Gro) = Grafschaft. (Vil) = Neef.

Petersborn-Kabertchen (Ger). Vineyard. (Anb) = Mosel-Saar-Ruwer. (Ber) = Zell/Mosel. (Gro) = Schwarze Katz. (Vil) = Zell.

Peterstirn (Ger). Vineyard. (Anb) = Franken. (Ber) = Maindreieck. (Gro) = Not yet assigned. (Vil) = Schweinfurt.

Peters Val (Ger). A naturally sparkling spring water from the Black Forest mountains. Bottled at source.

Peter Thompson [Perth] Limited (Scot). Producers of the blended Scotch whisky Beneagles. Address = Box 22, Crieff Road, Perth.

Pétillant (Fr). The term for slightly sparkling wines. Especially those that have had a Malo-lactic fermentation in the bottle.

Pétillant de Savoie (Fr). See Vin de Savoie Pétillant.

Pétillant de Savoie-Ayze (Fr). See Vin de Savoie-Ayze Pétillant.

Pétillant du Bugey (Fr). See Vin du Bugey Pétillant.

Pétiller (Fr). To sparkle, fizz. See Pétillant.

Petit (Fr). Small.

Petit Bouschet (Afr). A local name for the Alicante bouschet in Tunisia. A cross between the Teinturier and the Aramon.

Petit Cabernet (Fr). The local Bordeaux name for the Cabernet Sauvignon.

Petit Calva (Un) (Fr). (slang). A small Calvados drunk in the morning as a pick-me-up.

Petit Chablis (Fr). The lowest grade of the Chablis wines A.C. It is much lighter than the Premiers Crus. Minimum alc. by vol. of 9.5%.

Petit Château (Fr). The name given to the lesser Châteaux that are not included in the Crus Classés.

Petit Clos de Brouard (Fr). A vineyard in the commune of Lalande de Pomerol. A.C. Lalande de Pomerol, Bordeaux.

Petit Clos Figeac (Fr). A vineyard in the commune of Saint-Émilion. A.C. Saint-Émilion, Bordeaux. 3 ha.

Petite Bouschet (USA). A white grape variety grown in California for the production of dessert wines.

Petite Champagne (Fr). The Cru of Cognac second only to Grande Champagne. 14.7 per cent of district. Jarnac is best known town. Communes = [Charente Département] – Angeac-Charente, Ars, Barbezieux, Barret, Birac, Bourg-Charente, Châteauneuf, Graves, Guimps, Jurignac, Lachaise, Ladiville, Lagarde-sur-le-Né,

Montchaude, Mosnac, Nonaville, Saint-Amant-de-Graves, Saint-Bonnet, Saint-Hilaire-de-Barbezieux, Saint-Médard-de-Barbezieux, Saint-Palais-du-Né, Salles-de-Barbezieux and Vignolles. [Charente-Maritime Département] – Allas-Champagne, Archiac, Arthenac, Biron, Bougneau, Brie-sous-Archiac, Brives-sur-Charente, Celles, Chadenac, Champagnac, Cierzac, Coulonges, Clam, Échebrune, Germignac, Jarnac-Champagne, Jonzac, Lonzac, Meux, Moings, Montils, Neuillac, Neulles, Perignac-de-Pons, Saint-Germain-de-Lusignan, Saint-Germain-de-Vibrac, Saint-Martial-de-Coculet, Saint-Martial-de-Vitaterne, Saint-Maurice-de-Tavernolles, Saint-Lheurine, Saint-Seurin-de-Palenne, Saint-Sever, Salignac-de-Pons.

Petite Chapelle (Fr). See Champitonnois.

Petite Crau (Fr). A red, rosé and dry white wine-producing area in the north of Bouches du Rhône.

Petite Dôle (Switz). A red wine from the Valais canton. Made from the Pinot noir grape.

Petite-Fer (Fr). The local name for the Cabernet franc in southern France.

Petite Flandre de Médoc (Fr). A lesser district of Bordeaux.

Petite Fleur (Cktl). ⅓ measure Cointreau, ⅓ measure white Rum, ⅓ measure fresh grapefruit juice. Shake over ice, strain into a cocktail glass.

Petite Liquorelle (Fr). A Pétillant rich dessert and sparkling wine with old Cognac produced by Moët et Chandon. 18% alc. by vol.

Petite-Sainte-Marie (Fr). The local name used in the Savoie region for the Chardonnay grape.

Petite Sirah (Fr). Another name for the Syrah grape.

Petite Sirah (USA). See California Petite Sirah.

Petites-Lolières (Les) (Fr). A Premier Cru vineyard in the commune of Ladoix-Serrigny, A.C. Aloxe-Corton, Côte de Beaune, Burgundy.

Petite Syrah (USA). An alternative spelling of Petite sirah

Petit Flute Cocktail (Cktl). ½ measure Bacardi White Label, ¼ measure dry Martini vermouth, ¼ measure Passion fruit liqueur, 2 dashes sweet Martini vermouth. Shake over ice, strain into a cocktail glass. Dress with mint and a spiral of lemon peel.

Petit Gamai (Fr). An alternative name for the Gamay noir à jus blanc.

Petit Manseng (Fr). A white grape variety grown in the Jurançon.

Petit Merle (Fr). An alternative name for

the Merlot grape.

Petit Meslier (Fr). A white grape variety grown in Champagne. Related to the Sémillon, produces a wine of great bouquet.

Petit Musigny (Fr). An old division together with Grand Musigny which divided the Grand Cru vineyard of Musigny in the commune of Chambolle-Musigny.

Petit Propriétaires (Fr). Small vineyard owners.

Petit-Rouge (It). A red grape variety grown in the Valle d'Aosta.

Petits Châteaux (Fr). See Petit Château.

Petits-Épenots (Les) (Fr). A Premier Cru vineyard in the A.C. commune of Pommard, Côte de Beaune, Burgundy. 20.2 ha.

Petits-Godeaux (Les) (Fr). A Premier Cru vineyard [part] in the A.C. commune of Savigny-lés-Beaune, Côte de Beaune, Burgundy.

Petits-Monts (Les) (Fr). A Premier Cru vineyard in the A.C. commune of Vosne-Romanée, Côte de Nuits, Burgundy. 3.7 ha.

Petits Vins Sucrés (Fr). A French description of the lesser German wines that have been sweetened with süssreserve.

Petits-Vougeots (Les) (Fr). A Premier Cru vineyard in the A.C. commune of Vougeot, Côte de Nuits, Burgundy. 5.8 ha.

Petit Verdot (Fr). A red grape variety grown in Bordeaux.

Petit Vidure (Fr). A local name for the Cabernet sauvignon in Bordeaux.

Petri Brandy (USA). The brand-name of a Brandy produced by the United Vintners, Lodi, California.

Petrovskaya (USSR). The method of distilling Vodka until it becomes a spirit. Either Pot or Continuous still or both.

Petrus (It). An apéritif wine produced in northern Italy.

Petrus Boonkamp (Hol). The full name of Boonkamp bitters.

Pettenthal (Ger). Vineyard. (Anb) = Rheinhessen. (Ber) = Nierstein. (Gro) = Rehbach. (Vil) = Nierstein.

Petures (Les) (Fr). A premier Cru vineyard in the A.C. commune of Meursault, Côte de Beaune, Burgundy. 11 ha.

Petures (Les) (Fr). A Premier Cru vineyard in the A.C. commune of Volnay. Côte de Beaune, Burgundy.

Peuillets (Les) (Fr). A Premier Cru vineyard [part] in the A.C. commune of Savigny-lès-Beaune, Côte de Beaune, Burgundy.

Peureux (Fr). A firm in the Haute-Savoie that produces fine fruit liqueurs.

Peverella (USA). A white grape variety grown in the San Joaquin Valley, California.

Pévy (Fr). A Cru Champagne village in the Canton de Fismes. District = Reims.

Pewsey Vale Rhine Riesling (Austr). A white wine produced by the Yalumba vineyard in South Australia.

Pewter (Eng). An alloy of tin, lead and copper used to make the Pewter pot-drinking vessels which are now illegal as they are not Government stamped.

Pewter (Eng). The old name for the draining board behind the bar in a public house.

Pewter Tankard (Eng). See Pewter.

Pexém (Port). A red grape variety grown in the Algarve region.

Péychaud's Bitters (USA). Aromatic bitters produced in New Orleans.

Peyote (Mex). The old local name for the Mescal cactus.

Peyote Cactus (Mex). The name for the small buds from the Mescal catus. The source of Mescalin.

Peza (Gre). A white wine produced by the co-operative of the same name on the island of Crete. Also the name of a red wine.

Peza Winery (Gre). A large co-operative winery on the island of Crete.

Pézenas (Fr). A Vins de Pays area in the Hérault Département. Produces red, rosé and dry white wines.

Pézerolles (Les) (Fr). A Premier Cru vineyard in the A.C. commune of Pommard, Côte de Beaune, Burgundy. 7.3 ha.

Pezinok (Czec). A wine-producing area which, together with the Modra area has the highest concentration of vines in the country.

Pfaffenberg (Ger). Vineyard. (Anb) = Ahr. (Ber) = Walporzheim/Ahrtal. (Gro) = Klosterberg. (Vil) = Walporzheim.

Pfaffenberg (Ger). Vineyard. (Anb) = Franken. (Ber) = Maindreieck. (Gro) = Not yet assigned. (Vil) = Würzburg.

Pfaffenberg (Ger). Vineyard. (Anb) = Mosel-Saar-Ruwer. (Ber) = Zell/ Mosel. (Gro) = Grafschaft. (Vil) = Ediger-Eller.

Pfaffenberg (Ger). Vineyard. (Anb) = Nahe. (Ber) = Schloss Böckelheim. (Gro) = Rosengarten. (Vil) = Burgsponheim.

Pfaffenberg (Ger). Vineyard. (Anb) = Rheingau. (Ber) = Johannisberg. (Gro) = Deutelsberg. (Vil) = Hattenheim.

Pfaffenberg (Ger). Vineyard. (Anb) = Rheinhessen. (Ber) = Bingen. (Gro) = Adelberg. (Vil) = Flonheim.

P

Pfaffenberg (Ger). Vineyard. (Anb) = Rheinpfalz. (Ber) = Südliche Weinstrasse. (Gro) = Herrlich. (Vil) = Mörzheim.

Pfaffenberg (Ger). Vineyard. (Anb) = Rheinpfalz. (Ber) = Südliche Weinstrasse. (Gro) = Kloster Liebfrauenberg. (Vil) = Billigheim-Ingenheim.

Pfaffengarten (Ger). Vineyard. (Anb) = Rheinhessen. (Ber) = Nierstein. (Gro) = Domherr. (Vil) = Saulheim.

Pfaffengrund (Ger). Grosslage. (Anb) = Rheinpfalz. (Ber) = Mittelhaardt-Deutsche Weinstrasse. (Vils) = Diedesfeld, Duttweiler, Geinsheim, Hambach, Lachen-Speyerdorf.

Pfaffenhalde (Ger). Vineyard. (Anb) = Rheinhessen. (Ber) = Wonnegau. (Gro) = Sybillenstein. (Vil) = Alzey.

Pfaffenhofen (Ger). Village. (Anb) = Württemberg. (Ber) = Württembergisch Unterland. (Gro) = Heuchelberg. (Vin) = Hohenberg.

Pfaffenkappe (Ger). Vineyard. (Anb) = Rheinhessen. (Ber) = Nierstein. (Gro) = Gutes Domtal. (Vil) = Nierstein.

Pfaffenmütze (Ger). Vineyard. (Anb) = Rheinhessen. (Ber) = Wonnegau. (Gro) = Pilgerpfad. (Vil) = Dittelsheim-Hessloch.

Pfaffenpfad (Ger). Vineyard. (Anb) = Nahe. (Ber) = Schloss Böckelheim. (Gro) = Paradiesgarten. (Vil) = Alsenz.

Pfaffen-Schwabenheim (Ger). Village. (Anb) = Rheinhessen. (Ber) = Bingen. (Gro) = Sankt Rochuskapelle. (Vins) = Hölle, Mandelbaum, Sonnenberg.

Pfaffensteig (Ger). Vineyard. (Anb) = Franken. (Ber) = Maindreieck. (Gro) = Hofrat. (Vil) = Segnitz.

Pfaffenstein (Ger). Vineyard. (Anb) = Nahe. (Ber) = Schloss Böckelheim. (Gro) = Burgweg. (Vil) = Niederhausen an der Nahe.

Pfaffenstück (Ger). Vineyard. (Anb) = Baden. (Ber) = Markgräflerland. (Gro) = Burg Neuenfels. (Vil) = Müllheim.

Pfaffenweg (Ger). Vineyard. (Anb) = Rheinhessen. (Ber) = Nierstein. (Gro) = Sankt Alban. (Vil) = Gau-Bischofsheim.

Pfaffenweiler (Ger). Village. (Anb) = Baden. (Ber) = Markgräflerland. (Gro) = Lorettoberg. (Vins) = Batzenberg, Oderdürrenberg.

Pfaffenwies (Ger). Vineyard. (Anb) = Rheingau. (Ber) = Johannisberg. (Gro) = Burgweg. (Vil) = Lorch.

Pfahlkultur (Aus). Stake culture. A cultivation system.

Pfalz (Ger). Lit – 'Palatinate'. See Rheinpfalz.

Pfälzer Landwein (Ger). One of the fifteen Deutsche Tafelwein zones.

Pfalzgrafenstein (Ger). Vineyard. (Anb) = Mittelrhein. (Ber) = Rheinburgengau. (Gro) = Herrenberg. (Vil) = Kaub.

Pfarrberg (Ger). Vineyard. (Anb) = Baden. (Ber) = Ortenau. (Gro) = Schloss Rodeck. (Vil) = Waldulm.

Pfarrgarten (Ger). Grosslage. (Anb) = Nahe. (Ber) = Kreuznach. (Vils) = Schoneberg, Spabrücken, Dalberg, Hergenfeld, Walhausen, Sommerloch, Gutenberg.

Pfarrgarten (Ger). Vineyard. (Anb) = Mittelrhein. (Ber) = Rheinburgengau. (Gro) = Marksberg. (Vil) = Filsen.

Pfarrgarten (Ger). Vineyard. (Anb) = Mosel-Saar-Ruwer. (Ber) = Zell/Mosel. (Gro) = Rosenhang. (Vil) = Bruttig-Fankel.

Pfarrgarten (Ger). Vineyard. (Anb) = Rheinhessen. (Ber) = Bingen. (Gro) = Sankt Rochuskapelle. (Vil) = Bingen.

Pfarrgarten (Ger). Vineyard. (Anb) = Rheinhessen. (Ber) = Nierstein. (Gro) = Petersberg. (Vil) = Gau-Heppenheim.

Pfarrgut (Ger). A vineyard owned by the church whose product is given to the priest, parson etc. as part of his renumeration.

Pfarrwingert (Ger). Vineyard. (Anb) = Ahr. (Ber) = Walporzheim/Ahrtal. (Gro) = Klosterberg. (Vil) = Dernau.

Pfedelbach (Ger). Village. (Anb) = Württemberg. (Ber) = Württembergisch Unterland. (Gro) = Lindelberg. (Vin) = Goldberg.

Pfeffrig (Aus). Denotes a wine with a peppery taste.

Pfirsichgarten (Ger). Vineyard. (Anb) = Mosel-Saar-Ruwer. (Ber) = Zell/ Mosel. (Gro) = Grafschaft. (Vil) = Ediger-Eller.

Pflingstweide (Ger). Vineyard. (Anb) = Nahe. (Ber) = Schloss Böckelheim. (Gro) = Burgweg. (Vil) = Niederhausen an der Nahe.

Pfülben (Ger). Vineyard. (Anb) = Franken. (Ber) = Maindreieck. (Gro) = Ewig Leben. (Vil) = Randersacker.

P.G. (Eng) (abbr). Polygalacturonase.

P.G. Tips (Eng). The famous brand-name for a tea produced by the Brooke Bond Oxo Ltd. Often called the 'Monkey tea' due to the use of chimpanzees in their advertising.

Pheasant and Firkin (Eng). A Bruce home-brew public house in London. Noted for its cask conditioned Pheasant Bitter 1036 O.G. Barbarian 1045 O.G. and Dogbolter 1060 O.G.

Phellos (Gre). Cork.

Phelps (USA). A small winery based in the Napa Valley, California. 83 ha. Grape varieties – Cabernet sauvignon, Gewürztraminer, Johannisberg riesling and

P

Syrah. Produces varietal wines under the Le Fleuron label.

Phénix (Fr). A noted Bière brand.

Phenols (Scot). Flavouring chemicals derived from the smoking of the barley during the malting process for whisky.

Phenylalanine (Eng). An Amino acid found in small traces in wine. Is formed by the yeasts.

Phileri (Gre). A red grape variety grown in Peloponnese.

Philippe Guillet Grande Fine Champagne (Fr). An 80 year old Cognac produced by Rouyer.

Philippe le Bon (Fr). Part of the vineyard Genevrières in the A.C. commune of Meursault, Côte de Beaune, Burgundy. Is owned by the Hospices de Beaune.

Philipponnat (Fr). Champagne producer. Address = 13 Rue du Pont, Mareuil-sur-Ay, 51160 Ay. Produces – Vintage and non-vintage wines. Vintages – 1971, 1973, 1975, 1976, 1979, 1980, 1982. Owned by Gosset. De Luxe vintage cuvée Clos des Goisses and also Royal Réserve (non-vintage).

Phillipine Ron (E.Ind). Rum.

Phillips (Captain Arthur, R.N.) (Eng). Naval officer who introduced vines to Australia in 1788. Vines were probably from South America and of the Cabernet sauvignon variety.

Phillips Brewery (Eng). A home-brew public house brewery in the Greyhound at Marsh Gibbon near Bicester, Buckinghamshire. Noted for its cask conditioned Heritage Bitter 1036 O.G. Ailric's Old Me 1045 O.G. and keg Hallerbrau Lager 1042 O.G.

Phillip the Bold (Fr). The fourteenth-century Duke of Burgundy who, because he was keen on wine-making, could be claimed as being responsible for its vineyards of today.

Philo (USA). A wine-producing area in the Anderson Valley, Mendocino County, California.

Philter (USA). See Philtre.

Philtre (Eng). A drink supposed to arouse sexual desire, love, etc. USA = Philter.

Phlegm Cutters (USA). Early American slang for cider or beer.

Phoebe Snow Cocktail (Cktl). ½ measure Cognac, ½ measure Dubonnet, 2 dashes Pernod. Stir over ice, strain into a cocktail glass.

Phoenix (Eng). A Watney owned company based in Brighton, Sussex. Tamplins Bitter 1038 O.G. is brewed for it in London.

Phoenix and Firkin (Eng). A Bruce home-brew public house in London. Noted for its cask conditioned Rail Ale 1036 O.G.

Phoenix Beer (Afr). A Pilsener-style beer brewed in Mauritius by the Mauritius Brewery.

Phoenix Bitter (Ire). A keg Bitter brewed by the Irish Ale Breweries.

Phoenix Gin Sling (Cktl). Place ½ measure Gin, ½ measure Cherry Heering, 2 dashes lemon juice, 2 dashes Gomme syrup in an ice-filled highball glass. Stir, decorate with a cherry and slice of lemon.

Phonicin 47 (Cktl). ½ measure Vodka, ¼ measure Mandarine Napoléon, ¼ measure sweet Vermouth, dash lemon juice. Stir over ice in a highball glass and decorate with slices of lemon, orange and a cherry.

Phosphotage (Fr). The addition of Phosphate of lime to wines to increase the acidity. As for Gypsum.

Phyllocoptes Vitis (Lat). The grape rust mite. See also Calepitrimerus Vitis and Acariosis.

Phylloxera Vastatrix (Lat). A vine louse from America which devastated the European vineyards from 1863–1890. Attacks the roots of the vine. Treatment by grafting Vitis Vinifera scions onto American vine root stock which is the only known cure in Europe.

Pian (Le) (Fr). A commune in the A.C. Haut-Médoc, north-western Bordeaux.

Pian-Médoc (Le) (Fr). See Pian (Le).

Piat (Fr). A measure of wine, now only associated with the Beaujolais. The bottle resembles an Indian club in shape and holds approximately 50 centilitres.

Piat d'Or (Fr). A popular brand of A.C. Bourgogne red and white wine produced by Piat Père et Fils.

Piat Père et Fils (Fr). Négociants-éleveurs of Mâcon and Beaujolais wines in Burgundy. Address = La Chapelle-de-Guinchay.

Piave Cabernet (It). D.O.C. red wine from Veneto. Made with the Cabernet grape. If minimum alc. content 12.5% by vol. and 3 years of age can be classed Riserva.

Piave Merlot (It). D.O.C. red wine from Veneto. Made from the Merlot and 10% Cabernet franc/sauvignon grape. If minimum alc. content 12% by vol. and aged 2 years can be classed Vecchio.

Piave Tocai (It). D.O.C. white wine from Veneto. Made from the Tocai grape.

Piave Verduzzo (It). D.O.C. white wine from Veneto. Made from the Verduzzo grape.

Picador Cocktail (Cktl). 1½ measures Kahlúa, 1½ measures Tequila. Stir over ice, strain into a cocktail glass. Dress with a spiral of lemon peel.

Picamoll (Sp). A white grape variety grown

in the Alella region of north-eastern Spain.

Picapoll (Sp). A red grape variety grown in the Tarragona region of south-eastern Spain. See Picapoll Blanco.

Picapoll Blanco (Sp). A white grape variety grown in the Tarragona region of south-eastern Spain. Also known as Folle blanche.

Pic à Pou (Fr). A local wine from the Pyrénées in south-east France.

Picarda (Fr). A red grape variety grown in the southern Rhône.

Picard et Cazot Fils (Fr). Major distillers of Élixers based in Lyons.

Picardin (Fr). A white grape variety grown in the southern Rhône.

Picardin Noir (Fr). The alternative name for the Cinsault grape.

Picard Père et Fils (Fr). A Burgundy négociant based at Chagny.

Picata (It). A black grape variety grown in Roman times. Produced a wine called Vinum Picatum which had a taste of pitch.

Picca (Cktl). 1 fl.oz. Scotch Whisky, ½ fl.oz. Punt-e-Mes, ½ fl.oz. Galliano. Stir over ice, strain into a cocktail glass. Decorate with a cherry.

Piccadilly (Cktl). ⅔ measure dry Gin, ⅓ measure dry Vermouth, dash Pastis, dash Grenadine. Stir over ice, strain into a cocktail glass.

Piccolit (It). A sweet dessert wine, straw yellow in colour and aromatic. 13–14% alc. by vol.

Picens (Lat). A white wine produced in eastern Italy in Roman times.

Pichet (Fr). An earthenware jug that holds ½ a litre.

Pichet d'Alsace (Fr). A popular Edelzwicker produced by Laugel. Grape varieties – Gewürztraminer 5%, 85% Pinot noir and 10% Riesling.

Pichia Membranaefaciens (Lat). A prolific 'Wild yeast' found on the grape bloom.

Pickett Brewery (USA). A brewery based in Dubuque, Iowa. Is noted for its Dubuque Star and Edelweiss beers.

Pickled (Eng) (slang). A term for intoxicated, very drunk.

Pick Me Up (Eng). A tonic, a drink to settle the stomach. Can be either alcoholic or non-alcoholic.

Pick-Me-Up (Cktl).(1). ⅓ measure Pastis, ⅓ measure Cognac, ⅓ measure dry Vermouth. Stir over ice, strain into a 5 oz. wine glass.

Pick-Me-Up (Cktl).(2). 1 measure Brandy, 4 fl.ozs. milk, 1 teaspoon sugar, dash Angostura. Shake over ice, strain into a highball glass. Add soda water.

Pick-Me-Up (Cktl).(3). ¾ measure Cognac, ¼ measure Grand Marnier, juice ½ orange, dash Grenadine. Shake over ice, strain into a balloon glass. Top with dry Champagne and decorate with a slice of orange, lemon and a cherry. Serve with straws.

Pick-Me-Up (Cktl).(4) (Non-alc). To settle the stomach. Juice of half lemon, 2 teaspoons Worcestershire sauce, mix with ice in a highball glass. Top up with soda water.

Pico (Port). A vineyard based in the Azores that once produced wines under the Fayal label.

Picolit (It). A white grape variety grown in the Udine district of the Friuli-Venezia Giulia region. Produces rich, sweet, botrytis wines. 13–15% alc. by vol.

Picon (Fr). See Amer Picon.

Picon (Cktl).(1). 2 ozs. Amer Picon in a highball with ice, top up with 4 ozs. soda water.

Picon (Cktl).(2). ½ measure Amer Picon, ½ measure sweet Vermouth. Stir over ice, strain into a cocktail glass.

Picon-Grenadine (Cktl). ½ gill Amer Picon, ⅙ gill Grenadine. Stir over ice in a highball glass. Top up with soda water.

Picon Punch (Cktl). Place some ice in a club goblet, add 1½ ozs. Amer Picon. Fill with soda water, top with a twist of lemon peel. Stir. Often has dash of Brandy on top.

Picotin (Cktl). ½ measure Vodka 72, ¼ measure Liqueur Santa Vittoria, ¼ measure Cinzano bianco, dash lemon juice. Stir over ice, strain into an ice-filled highball glass. Add a twist of orange peel.

Picoutener (It). The local name for the Nebbiolo grape in the Val d'Aosta region. Also spelt Picutener pugnet.

Picpouille (Fr). The alternative spelling of Picpoul.

Picpoul (Fr). The name given to the Folle blanche grape grown in the Armagnac and Cognac regions. It gives thin acid wine, but makes an outstanding brandy. See also Gros Plant, Picpouille and Piquepoul.

Picpoul-de-Pinet (Fr). A dry, white V.D.Q.S. wine produced in the Midi region of southern France.

Picquepoul (Fr). Alternative spelling of Picpoul.

Picquepoul du Gers (Fr). The local Armagnac name for the Folle blanche grape.

Picquepoul du Pays (Fr). A white grape variety grown in the Armagnac region.

Pic-Saint-Loup (Fr). A red, rosé and white A.C wine-producing region in the Hérault Département in southern France.

Picutener Pugnet (It). An alternative

P

spelling of the Picoutener.

Pidans (Les) (Fr). A vineyard in the A.C. commune of Montagny, Côte Chalonnaise, Burgundy.

Pie (Eng). A term sometimes used for the pulp left after the first pressing of the grapes.

Pièce (Fr). A hogshead, cask. Also known as a Fût. Côte d'Or = 228 litres, southern Burgundy = 216 litres, Bordeaux = 225 litres.

Pièce Sous le Bois (La) (Fr). A Premier Cru vineyard in the commune of Blagny, A.C. Meursault, Côte de Beaune, Burgundy. 11.2 ha.

Pied (Fr). A single vine stock.

Pied-d'Aloup (Fr). An A.C. Premier Cru Chablis. Sometimes reclassified as the Premier Cru Montée de Tonerre.

Pied de Cuve (Fr). The bottom of the vat (the lees) after the décuvage. Often used as a yeast starter.

Pied de Pedrix (Fr). An alternative name for the Malbec grape in southern France.

Piede di Palumbo (It). A red grape variety grown in Gragnano in the Campania region to produce a young red wine of the same name.

Piedirosso (It). A red grape variety grown in the Campania region. See also Perricone.

Piedmont (It). American spelling of Piemonte.

Piedmonte (It). English spelling of Piemonte.

Piedmont Vineyard (USA). A small winery based in Middleburg, Virginia. 10 ha. Grape varieties – Chardonnay and Sémillon. Produces varietal wines.

Pied Noir (Fr). An alternative name for the Malbec grape.

Pied Rouge (Fr). An alternative name for the Malbec grape.

Pied-Tendre (Fr). A white grape variety grown in the Charente region in western France. See also Bon Blanc, Blanquette and the Colombard.

Piemonte (It). Wine region. Lit – 'At the foot of the mountain'. Pennine, Graian, Cottian and Maritime Alps surround it to the north and south. East is the Po Valley. See also Piedmont, Piedmonte.

Piemontello (It). A slightly sparkling wine made from the Moscato grape in Piemonte.

Pieprozwka (Pol). A pepper-flavoured Vodka produced by Wodka Wyttrawna 45% alc. by vol.

Pierce's Disease (USA). A vine disease that occurs in California. The leaves become yellow along the veins, fruit wilts and dwarf shoots appear. The vine usually dies within 5 years. Is spread by insects.

Pierelle (La) (Fr). A vineyard in the A.C.

Hermitage, northern Rhône.

Pierian Spring (Gre). A sacred fountain in Pieria said to inspire anyone who drinks from it.

Pierlant Imperial (Fr). A lightly sparkling, medium-dry, white wine produced by Moët et Chandon from grapes grown in 9 different regions of France. 9.2% alc. by vol.

Pierlot (Jules) (Fr). Champagne producer. Address = 15 Rue Henry Martin, BP 129, 51200 Épernay. Produces – Vintage and non-vintage wine. Vintages – 1971, 1973, 1975, 1976, 1979, 1982, 1983.

Piermont (Eng). An apple-juice and natural water drink made by the Tauton Cider Co. Ltd.

Pierre-à-Fusil (Fr). Gun flint. Describes flinty wines.

Pierrefeu (Fr). A wine-producing village in the Côtes de Provence. Produces fine rosé wines.

Pierres (Fr). Stones (soil).

Pierres (Les) (Fr). A vineyard in the A.C. commune of Rully, Côte Chalonnais, Burgundy.

Pierres Dorées (Fr). An area where most of the Beaujolais Nouveau is produced.

Pierre Winery (N.Z.). A small winery based in Waikanae, Wellington, North Island. 3 ha. Grape varieties – Cabernet sauvignon, Chardonnay, Chenin blanc, Merlot, Müller-Thurgau and Pinot noir. Produces varietal wines.

Pierry (Fr). A Premier Cru Champagne village in the Canton d'Épernay. District = Épernay.

Piesport (Ger). Village. (Anb) = Mosel-Saar-Ruwer. (Ber) = Bernkastel. (Gro) = Michelsberg. (Vins) = Domherr, Falkenberg, Gärtchen, Goldtröpfchen, Gunterslay, Schubertslay, Treppchen.

Pietroasele (Rum). A wine-producing area, part of the Dealul-Mare vineyard.

Pig and Whistle (Eng). A home-brew public house at Privett, Hampshire. Noted for its cask conditioned BDS 1055 O.G. and Joshua Privett 1043 O.G.

Pig and Whistle (Scot). A home-brew public house in the Gorbals, Glasgow. Noted for its cask conditioned Pig Brew 1040 O.G. and Pig Light 1035 O.G.

Piganot (Switz). A red wine made from the Savagnin grape in the Vaud Canton.

Pigeon Holes (Fr). The term used in Armagnac for the resting of the casks in such a way that they do not touch one another, but rest in 'pigeon holes'.

Piggin (Eng). A cask of 2 gallons capacity. Rare now.

Piglio (It). A commune 40 miles from Rome in Latium. Gives its name to 2 types of red wine. See Cesanese del Piglio.

P

Pigment (Eng). The colouring matter in the skins of red grapes.

Pignatello (It). A black grape variety grown in Sicily. Used in the production of Marsala. Also known as the Perricone and Piedirosso.

Pignerol (Fr). A white grape variety grown in Bellet, Provence.

Pignola Valtellinese (It). A red grape variety.

Pignoletto (It). An alternative name for the Italian riesling and Welschriesling.

Pig's Ear (Eng) (slang). Cockney rhyming slang for beer.

Pig's Nose (Eng). A brand of blended Scotch whisky blended and bottled by M.J. Dowdeswell & Co. Ltd., Oldbury-on-Severn, Gloucestershire. See also Sheep Dip.

Pihlajanmarja (Fin). A rowanberry liqueur.

Pikant (Ger). Denotes an attractive, intriguing wine.

Pike's Peak Cooler (Cktl). 1 egg, 1 teaspoon powdered sugar, juice ½ lemon. Shake over ice, strain into an ice-filled highball glass. Top with dry Cider, stir, dress with an orange peel spiral.

Piketberg (S.Afr). A wine district of the west coast. Produces mainly dry white and dessert wines.

Pilarita Fino (Sp). A brand of Fino sherry produced by Lustau in Jerez de la Frontera.

Pilgerberg (Ger). Vineyard. (Anb) = Mosel-Saar-Ruwer. (Ber) = Obermosel. (Gro) = Königsberg. (Vil) = Liersberg.

Pilgerpfad (Ger). Grosslage. (Anb) = Rheinhessen. (Ber) = Wonnegau. (Vils) = Bechtheim, Dittelsheim-Hessloch, Frettenheim, Monzernheim, Osthofen.

Pilgerpfad (Ger). Vineyard. (Anb) = Mittelrhein. (Ber) = Rheinburgengau. (Gro) = Loreleyfelsen. (Vil) = Kamp-Bornhofen-Kestert.

Pilgerstein (Ger). Vineyard. (Anb) = Rheinhessen. (Ber) = Nierstein. (Gro) = Petersberg. (Vil) = Biebelnheim.

Pilgerweg (Ger). Vineyard. (Anb) = Rheinhessen. (Ber) = Nierstein. (Gro) = Gutes Domtal. (Vil) = Zornheim.

Pilgrim (USA). A brand of light Rum produced by Felton and Son in New England. 40% alc. by vol.

Pilgrim Brewery (Eng). Opened in 1982 in Woldingham, Surrey. Noted for its cask conditioned Surrey Bitter 1038 O.G. Progress 1042 O.G. and Talisman 1048 O.G.

Pilgrims Cyder (Eng). A Cider made by Badgers Farm in Chilham near Canterbury, Kent. Made from Kentish dessert and cider apples.

Piliers Chablisiens (Fr). A wine brotherhood of the Chablis, Burgundy.

Pillar Tap (Scot). See Tall Fount.

Pillot (Fr). A vineyard in the A.C. commune of Rully, Côte Chalonnaise, Burgundy.

Pilon (Le) (Fr). A wine-producing district in A.C. Bellet, Provence.

Pilongo (Port). An alternative name for the Alvarelhão grape.

Pils (Ger). Short for Pilsener. A strong bottled Lager beer.

Pilsator (Ger). A premium Beer brewed without the use of additives.

Pilsen (Czec). A town in Bohemia from which Pilsener Lager gets its name. The German spelling. See Plzen.

Pilsener (Euro). The name given to Lager beers on the style of the original beer from Plzen (Pilsen). See Pilsner Urquell.

Pils-Krone (Ger). A fine Pilsener beer. Light and delicate, with a malty flavour. Brewed by the Dortmunder Kronen Brauerei in Dortmund, Westphalia.

Pilsner (Czec). Other spelling of Pilsen. See Pilsner Urquell.

Pilsner (Eng). The English spelling of Pilsener.

Pilsner (Ger). A full-bodied Bavarian made 'hoppy' beer. Now made much lighter.

Pilsner Urquell (Czec). A famous old Lager from Plzen (Pilsen in German) known as Plzensky Prazdroi in Bohemia. Matured in wood casks for 3 months. Also the name of a brewery. Urquell means best.

Pils 27 (Afr). A Lager beer brewed in Benin 11.2° Plato.

Pilton Manor de Marsac (Eng). A sparkling wine made by the méthode champenoise from 66% Müller-Thurgau and 34% Seyval blanc grapes. Produced by the Pilton Manor Vineyards.

Pilton Manor Vineyard (Eng). Address = The Manor House, Pilton, near Shepton Mallet, Somerset. 2.7 ha. planted 1966. Soil – stoney marl overlying rock, clay, limestone and blue lias. Grape varieties – 87% Müller-Thurgau, 13% Seyval blanc (5276).

Piment (Fr). See Vin Piment.

Pimento (W.Ind). A liqueur made from dried, aromatic berries.

Pimento Dram (W.Ind). A dark red liqueur made by steeping green, ripe pimento berries in Rum. Made by the Caribbean Indians.

Piments (Eng). The name given to the flavourings used in wines in the Middle Ages (herbs and spices).

Pimms (Eng). A branded cocktail-type

P

mix. Spirit based. 6 varieties – N°1 Gin, N°2 Whisky, N°3 Brandy, N°4 Rum, N°5 Bourbon whiskey, N°6 Vodka. Only N°1 is now produced. 31% alc. by vol. Owned by the DCL group.

Pimm's Royal (Cktl). 1 measure Pimms N°1. 4 measures iced Champagne. Stir lightly together in a highball over ice.

Pimpeltjens (Hol). An orange Curaçao with selected herbs. See Nassau Orange. Produced by De Kuyper, Schiedam. 40% alc. by vol.

Pimpinella Anisum (Lat). The botanical name for the Anise plant used in the making of Pastis.

Pin (Eng). A beer cask/keg 4½ gallons capacity.

Pina (Mex). The name given to the bulbous core in the centre of the Maguey cactus. Weighs 80–175 lbs. Lit – 'Pineapple'.

Pina Colada (Cktl).(1). 1 fl.oz. Coconut cream, 1½ fl.ozs. white Rum, 2 fl.ozs. pineapple juice, 2 scoops crushed ice. Blend together. Pour into a large-bowled glass. Decorate with a slice of pineapple and a cherry. Serve with straws.

Pina Colada (Cktl).(2). 3 tots Malibu liqueur, a dash lemon juice. Top up with chilled pineapple juice. Mix well in blender, pour into a large-bowled glass. Serve with straws.

Pinard (Fr). The French army name for Vin Ordinaire. Also the name for their wine ration.

Pince à Champagne (Fr). Champagne cork pliers for the removal of the corks from sparkling wine bottles.

Pinceszet (Hun). The name given to the cellars used for the storage and maturation of Tokay aszú (in lava rock).

Pinchbottle (USA) (slang). The name for Haig's Dimple De Luxe Scotch Whisky. Refers to the bottle shape which is 3 cornered.

Pinching Back (Eng). The pruning or topping off of the ends of the leafy branches of the plant. Usually done by machine nowadays.

Pincota (Rum). A wine-producing area, part of the Banat vineyard.

Pineapple Cobbler (Cktl).(Non-alc). ⅓ pint pineapple juice, dash lime juice, 5 dashes Angostura. Shake well over ice, strain into a highball glass. Top with bitter lemon, cherry and a pineapple cube. Serve with straws.

Pineapple Cocktail (Cktl). 1½ fl.ozs. white Rum, ¾ fl.oz. pineapple juice, ½ teaspoon lime juice. Shake over ice, strain into a cocktail glass.

Pineapple Cooler (Cktl).(1). Place 2 fl.ozs.

pineapple juice, ½ teaspoon powdered sugar and 2 fl.ozs. soda water into a collins glass. Stir, add ice. Top with 2 fl.ozs. dry white wine, soda and an orange spiral.

Pineapple Cooler (Cktl).(2) (Non-alc). ⅓ pint pineapple juice, ½ fl.oz. lime juice, 3 fl.ozs. bitter lemon, 5 dashes Angostura. Stir over ice, strain into an ice-filled highball glass, dress with a pineapple cube, cherry and serve with straws.

Pineapple Fizz (Cktl). 2 fl.ozs. light Rum, 1½ fl.ozs. pineapple juice, 1 teaspoon Gomme syrup. Shake over ice, strain into an ice-filled highball glass. Top up with soda and lemonade. Serve with a muddler and straws.

Pineapple Liqueur (Fr). See Crème d'Ananas.

Pineapple Sparkle (Cktl). 1½ fl.ozs. dry Sherry, 3 fl.ozs. sweet Vermouth, 1 gill pineapple juice, 1 gill soda water, ½ pint sparkling Cider. Stir together in a large jug with ice, add ½ pint soda water prior to service.

Pineau (Fr). An alternative name for the Pinot noir grape.

Pineau (Fr). An apéritif. Muted wine. Wine fortified with brandy made from grapes grown in the A.C. Cognac area. Minimum strength of 60% alc. by vol. The proportion of grape must to Cognac is 3–1. No chaptalisation allowed. Must and Cognac aged on lees for 1 year. After ageing reduced to 16–22% alc. by vol. See Pineau des Charentes.

Pineau Blanc de la Loire (USA). The name for the Chenin blanc white grape variety.

Pineau d'Aunis (Fr). A red grape variety grown in the Anjou district of the Loire.

Pineau de la Loire (Fr). The local (Loire) name for the Chenin blanc grape variety.

Pineau de Loire (Fr). See Pineau de la Loire.

Pineau des Charentes (Fr). Local Charente wines blended with Cognac to produce a sweet apéritif wine. 18–22% alc. by vol. Matured 1 year in oak cask. White or rosé, must be made with grapes from the Départements of Charente and Charente-Maritime (white) = Colombard, Blanc ramé, Folle blanche, Jurançon blanc, Merlot blanc, Montils, Sauvignon blanc Sémillon and Ugni blanc. (rosé) = Cabernet franc, Cabernet sauvignon, Malbec and Merlot.

Pineau Meunier (Fr). A red grape variety. Also known in Germany as the Müllerrebe, Schwarzriesling. See also Wrotham Pinot.

Pinella (It). A white grape variety grown in the Veneto region.

Pinenc (Fr). A red grape variety grown in

the Pyrénées. Used in the production of Madiran.

Pine Ridge (USA). A winery based near Yountville, Napa Valley, California. Grape varieties – Cabernet sauvignon and Chardonnay. Produces varietal wines.

Pine Ridge Vineyard (Eng). A vineyard based at Staplecross, Robertsbridge, East Sussex. Was first planted in 1979. Grape varieties – Gutenborner, Huxelrebe, Kerner, Müller-Thurgau, Reichensteiner [50%] and Scheurebe.

Pinga (Bra). A fiery spirit produced from molasses.

Pinga (Port). Denotes a drop of wine (or other drink).

Ping Pong (Cktl). ½ measure Sloe gin, ½ measure Crème Yvette, 1 egg white, juice ¼ lemon. Shake over ice, strain into a cocktail glass.

Ping Pong Cocktail (Cktl). ¼ gill Sloe Gin, ¼ gill Italian vermouth, 2 dashes Angostura, 2 dashes Gomme syrup. Stir over ice, strain into a cocktail glass. Add a cherry and a squeeze lemon peel juice on top.

Pin Head (Asia). The name given to the small grade of Green Gunpowder teas.

Pinhel (Port). A district east of Dão that produces light pleasant wines.

Pink Camellia (Cktl). ³⁄₁₀ measure dry Gin, ²⁄₁₀ measure Apricot brandy, ¹⁄₁₀ measure Campari, ²⁄₁₀ measure orange juice, ²⁄₁₀ measure lemon juice, dash egg white. Shake well over ice, strain into a cocktail glass.

Pink Chablis (USA). A generic term used on labels to denote an off-dry, rosé wine.

Pink Champagne (Cktl). Iced Champagne with a dash of Angostura bitters added. Not to be confused with rosé Champagne.

Pink Champagne (USA). A generic term used on labels to denote sweet, rosé, sparkling wines.

Pink Cloves (Eng). An alcoholic cordial produced by Phillips, Avonmouth Way, Bristol. 6% alc. by vol.

Pink Creole Cocktail (Cktl). ½ measure white Rum, ⅙ measure lime juice, ⅙ measure Grenadine, ⅙ measure cream. Shake over ice, strain into a cocktail glass. Add a black cherry soaked in Rum.

Pinkers (Eng) (slang). The name given by the Royal Navy Officers for a Pink Gin.

Pink Explosion (Cktl). ½ measure Grand Marnier, ½ measure French vermouth, ⅙ measure Pernod, dash Angostura, dash Grenadine, 1 measure cream. Shake well over ice, strain into a Champagne saucer. Dress with a fresh strawberry.

Pink Gin (Cktl). A drink invented by Royal Naval Surgeons as a medicine. 1½ measures Plymouth Gin, 2 dashes Angostura.

Pink Grapefruit (Cktl). ⅓ measure Malibu, ⅔ measure grapefruit juice. Pour over crushed ice in an old-fashioned glass, add dash of Campari and cherry.

Pink Ice (USA). Ice cubes which have had Angostura bitters dripped onto them. Used in the making of cocktails.

Pink Lady (Cktl). ¾ oz. dry Gin, 1 egg white, ½ oz. Grenadine, dash lemon juice. Shake well over ice, strain into a cocktail glass.

Pink Lady (Eng). A brand of sparkling perry made by the Goldwell Co.

Pink Lady Cocktail (Cktl). As for a Pink Lady but with the addition of ½ oz. of cream.

Pink Melon Delight (Cktl). Blend a scoop of orange sorbet, 6 ozs. honeydew melon, 10 fresh strawberries together in a blender. Pour into a highball glass. Top with ginger ale and decorate with a strawberry and melon cube.

Pink Muscat (USSR). A red grape variety used to produce dessert wines in the Crimea.

Pink Panther (Cktl). ½ measure Pernod, ½ measure Vodka. Shake over ice, strain into an ice-filled highball, top with lemonade.

Pink Panther Flip (Cktl).(Non-alc). ⅙ gill Grenadine, 1 egg yolk, 2 dashes Angostura, ⅓ pint orange juice. Blend together with a scoop of crushed ice in a blender. Pour into a tulip glass, dress with a cherry.

Pink Pearl (Cktl). 1 measure Dry Cane Rum, 1 measure Cinzano bianco, ½ measure lemon juice, dash Grenadine, dash egg white. Shake well over ice, strain into a cocktail glass. Serve with a cherry and a slice of lemon.

Pink Pearl (Cktl).(Non-alc). 1 part Grenadine, 4 parts fresh grapefruit juice, 1 part lemon juice, 1 egg white. Shake over ice, strain into a wine glass.

Pink Pussy (Cktl). 1 fl.oz. Campari, ½ fl.oz. Peach brandy, dash egg white. Shake over ice, strain into an ice-filled highball glass, top with Bitter lemon.

Pink Pussy Cat (Cktl). 1 measure Vodka, 2 measures grapefruit juice, ¼ measure Grenadine. Shake over ice, strain into an ice-filled highball glass.

Pink Rose Fizz (Cktl). ⅕ gill dry Gin, ⅙ gill cream, 1 egg white, juice ¼ lemon, 2 dashes Gomme syrup. Shake over ice, strain into an ice-filled highball. Top with soda water.

Pink Squirrel (Cktl). 1 oz. Crème d'Almond, ½ oz. Crème de Cacao (white), 1 oz. light cream. Shake well over ice, strain into a cocktail glass.

Pink Tonic (Cktl).(Non-alc). Place the juice of ½ a lemon and three dashes Angostura bitters in an ice-filled highball glass. Top with tonic water and a lemon slice.

Pinkus Alt (Ger). A well-known Altbier from the Pinkus Müller Brauerei of Münster. Light in colour. 4.9% alc. by vol.

Pinkus Müller Brauerei (Ger). A brewery based in Münster in Western Germany. Produces a famous pale Altbier and exports to USA. See Pinkus Weizen, Alt and Pils.

Pinkus Pils (Ger). A fine Pilsener Lager beer from the Pinkus Müller Brauerei of Münster. 4.9% alc. by vol.

Pinkus Weizen (Ger). A top fermented Beer from the Pinkus Müller Brauerei of Münster. 4.9% alc. by vol.

Pinnacle Selection (Austr). The brand-name for a range of wines produced by the Saltram Winery in the Barossa Valley.

Pinnerkreuzberg (Ger). Vineyard. (Anb) = Mosel-Saar-Ruwer. (Ber) = Zell/ Mosel. (Gro) = Goldbäumchen. (Vil) = Cochem.

Pino (Fr). A full-bodied, red wine from St. Florent, Corsica.

Pinon (Claude) (Fr). A producer of Vouvray in the Touraine district of the Loire. Usually pétillant.

Pinot (Fr). One of the most distinguished of the wine grape families. Pinots noir, Chardonnay and Gris.

Pinotage (S.Afr). A red grape variety. A hybrid cross between the Pinot noir and Hermitage.

Pinot Auxerrois (Fr). Another name for the Auxerrois blanc in Alsace.

Pinot Beurot (Fr). A white grape variety. Also known as the Pinot gris. Grown in the Côte de Beaune in the production of Hautes-Côtes de Beaune and Bourgogne blanc.

Pinot Bianco (It). A white grape variety grown in the Veneto and Lombardy regions. Also known in Germany as the Weissburgunder.

Pinot Blanc (Fr). The name for a white grape variety. Also known as Pinot Chardonnay.

Pinot Blanc (S.Am). An alternative name of the Pinot Chardonnay grape.

Pinot Blanc (USA). See California Pinot Blanc.

Pinot Blanc Chardonnay (USA). The alternative name for the Chardonnay grape.

Pinot Blanche de Loire (USA). The Californian name for the Chenin blanc grape.

Pinot Blanc Vrai Clevner (Fr). An alternative name for the Pinot blanc grape.

Pinot Chardonnay (Fr). An alternative name for a white grape variety, more correctly known as Pinot blanc.

Pinot-Chardonnay-Mâcon (Fr). Dry white wines that are produced from Chardonnay or Pinot blanc grapes. May use this A.C. or just A.C. Mâcon.

Pinot de Juillet (Fr). A red grape variety (relation to the Pinot noir) grown by Moët et Chandon. It is an early ripener.

Pinot de la Loire (Fr). A white grape variety also known as the Chenin blanc.

Pinot de Loire (Fr). See Pinot de la Loire.

Pinot Grigio (It). A white grape variety grown in northern Italy. Produces wines of varying colours due to the copper pigment in the skin. Also known as the Ruländer in Germany and in the Südtirol. (Fr) = Pinot gris.

Pinot Gris (Fr). A white grape variety. A member of the Pinot family. Known as the Rülander in Germany, Pinot grigio in Italy and as the Tokay d'Alsace in Alsace. Also known as the Fauret, Pinot beurot and the Tocai in Yugoslavia.

Pinot Liebault (Fr). A black grape variety. Is closely related to the Pinot noir.

Pinot Maltais (Euro). A red grape variety grown on Malta which was grown in France in the Middle Ages. Also known as the Pinot morgeot.

Pinot Meslier (Fr). A red grape variety grown in the Burgundy region. Same as Pinot noir.

Pinot Meunier (Fr). A black grape variety grown in the Champagne region. Not as fine as the Pinot noir, but ripens later, therefore good assurance against frost. Related to the Gris meunier. Also known as the Auvernat gris, Blanche feuille, Dusty miller, Goujan, Morillon taconé, Müllerrebe, Müller rebe, Müller schwarzriesling, Plant de brie, Schwarzriesling and Wrotham pinot.

Pinot Morgeot (Euro). See Pinot Maltais.

Pinot Nero (It). The black Pinot noir in Italy. Known as the Bläuburgunder in the Südtirol.

Pinot Noir (Fr). The classical black grape of Burgundy and Champagne. One of the greatest red wine grapes. Known as the Pinot nero, Pinot vérot, Bläuburgunder, Nàgyburgundi, Pineau and Sauvignon noir.

Pinot Noir (USA). See California Pinot Noir.

Pinot Noir Rosé d'Alsace (Fr). A rosé wine of Alsace, drunk locally. Known as Schillerwein by the German speaking locals.

Pinot Oltrepo Pavese (It). A D.O.C. white wine from the Pinot grigio and Pinot nero grapes in north-western Italy.

Pinot St. George (USA). A red grape variety

P

grown in California to make red table wines.

Pinot Vérot (Fr). Another name for the Pinot noir grape.

Pint (Eng). Measure. 20 fl.ozs. 1.76 pints = 1 litre. ⅛ gallon. 0.568 litre.

Pint (USA). 16 fl.ozs. (0.473 litre).

Pinta (Eng) (slang). For a pint of milk.

Pinte (Fr). Pint.

Pinte (Ger). Denotes a rough, drinking place.

Pintos dos Santos [A] (Port). Vintage Port shippers. Vintages – 1955, 1957, 1958, 1960, 1963, 1970, 1974, 1975, 1977, 1978, 1979, 1980.

Pinwinnie (Scot). A De Luxe blended Scotch whisky 43% alc. by vol. Produced by Inver House Distillers in Airdrie, Lanarkshire.

Pio-Cesare (It). A noted winery based in Alba, Piemonte. Owns vineyards in Barbaresco and Barolo.

Pioneer Cocktail (Cktl). ⅓ measure Drambuie, ⅓ measure Vodka, ⅓ measure orange Curaçao. Shake over ice, strain into an ice-filled highball glass. Serve with straws.

Pipa (Port) (Sp). Butt or Pipe (cask) of wine.

Pipe (Mad). A cask of wine. 92 gallons.

Pipe (Port). A cask of Port. 115 gallons (522.5 litres) approximately. Douro pipe = 550 litres, Vila Nova de Gaia pipe = 547 litres and a Shipping pipe = 534 litres.

Pipe (Sp). A cask of wine in Marsala. 93 gallons.

Pipe Major (Scot). A blended Scotch whisky distributed by the Montrose Whisky Co. Ltd. Also De Luxe 12, 21 and 24 year old versions. 43% alc. by vol.

Piper (Scot). A fine keg Scotch Ale 1036 O.G. brewed by the Tennent Caledonian Brewery in Glasgow. Also produce a Piper Export 1042 O.G.

Piperdy (Fr). An alternative name for the Malbec grape.

Piper Export (Scot). See Piper.

Piper-Heidsieck (Fr). Champagne producer. Address = 51 Boulevard Henri Vasnier, 51100 Reims. A Grande Marque. Produces – Vintage and non-vintage wines. Vintages – 1902, 1906, 1910, 1912, 1916, 1918, 1921, 1926, 1929, 1933, 1937, 1943, 1947, 1949, 1952, 1953, 1955, 1957, 1959, 1961, 1963, 1967, 1969, 1971, 1973, 1975, 1976, 1979, 1982, 1983. De Luxe vintage cuvée is Champagne Rare. Now owns the Dolbec Champagne house.

Pipers (Scot). A blended Scotch whisky produced by Seagram. 40% alc. by vol.

Piper's Brook Winery (Austr). A winery based near Launceston, Tamar Valley, Tasmania. Grape varieties – Riesling and Pinot noir. Produces varietal wines.

Piper-Sonoma (USA). A sparkling (méthode champenoise) wine produced jointly by Piper Heidsieck of Champagne, France and Sonoma Vineyards, California.

Pipette (Eng). A long glass tube, narrowed at one end which is used to extract wine from the cask for testing during its maturation period.

Pipette (Pol). A drinking glass with a long narrow neck and a small bulb at the bottom. Used for drinking Vodka.

Pipkin (Eng). A species of barley malt from the Golden Promise variety. Gives medium sugar yields.

Pippermint Get (Fr). A peppermint liqueur produced by the Bénédictine company of monks. See also Peppermint Get. 28% alc. by vol.

Pippin Cocktail (Cktl). ½ measure Calvados, ½ measure Apricot brandy, juice ½ orange, ½ egg white. Shake well over ice, strain into a highball glass. Top with lemonade.

Pippins (Eng). An old English cider-making apple.

Pips (Eng). The seeds of the grapes. Contain unwanted tannins and bitter oils.

Piquant (Fr). A sharp-tasting wine.

Piqué (Fr). Pricked, pétillant wine. Can also be used to describe a wine with a slightly vinegary taste.

Piquepoult (Fr). The name given to wine produced in the Gers Département. Is distilled into Armagnac.

Piquetberg (S.Afr). See Piketberg.

Piquets-en-Rang (Fr). A method of vine training where posts 'in line' are used to train the vines up to two metres above the ground. See also Pachets-en-Rang.

Piquette (Fr). A common, ordinary wine used in certain parts of France. Is made from a fermentation of the marc from the 2nd or 3rd pressing and water.

Piqûre (Fr). Wine malady. See Acescence, Piqué.

Piranha (Cktl). 1 measure Bols Crème de Cacao, 1 measure Vodka. Stir over ice, strain into a cocktail glass.

Pirate Porter Beer (Eng). A cask conditioned Ale 1036 O.G. brewed by the home-brew public house at the Pier Hotel, Gravesend, Kent.

Pirate Porter Beer (Eng). A cask conditioned Ale 1036 O.G. brewed by the home-brew public house at the South-eastern Hotel, Strood, Kent.

Piros Cirfandli (Hun). A white grape variety.

Pirque (Chile). A wine-producing area.

Pirramimma Winery (Austr). A winery based in the McLaren Vale, Southern Vales, South Australia. Produces varietal wines.

Pirrone Winery (USA). A winery based in the Central Valley, California. Produces varietal wines.

Pisa (Sp). The name given to a small cistern into which Vino de Lágrima was run during the production of Málaga.

Pisador (Sp). A person who treads the grapes in the Sherry region.

Pisco (S.Am). A brandy made from Muscat wine. Colourless, with a slight oily consistency. Produced in Argentina, Bolivia, Chile and Peru. 45% alc. by vol.

Pisco Punch (Cktl). 2 fl.ozs. Pisco, 1 fl.oz lime juice, 1 fl.oz. fresh pineapple juice, 2 dashes Maraschino, 2 dashes Gomme syrup. Shake over ice, strain into 5 oz. goblet.

Pisco Sour (Cktl). 2½ fl.ozs. lime juice, 1½ fl.ozs. Pisco, ¼ fl.oz. Gomme syrup, 2 dashes Angostura, dash egg white. Shake well over ice, strain into 5 oz. goblet. Top with dash bitters.

Pisquero (Chile). A pot-still used in the production of Pisco.

Piss (Austr) (slang). A term for beer.

Piss Artist (Eng) (slang). An unsavoury term for a habitual drunkard.

Pissed (Eng) (slang). An unsavoury term for drunk, intoxicated.

Piss Up (Eng) (slang). An unsavoury term for a heavy drinking bout.

Pitcher (Eng). A container for water or wine. Made of clay, stone or glass.

Pitching (Eng). A name given to the adding of yeast to the cooled Wort to start the fermentation in brewing.

Piteşti (Rum). A wine-producing area in southern Rumania. Produces red and white wines.

Pitfield Brewery (Eng). A Brewery opened in 1981 in The Beer Shop (a London Off-Licence). Brews cask conditioned Hoxton Heavy 1048 O.G. and Dark Star 1050 O.G.

Pithoi (Gre). The name given to ancient fermenting jars.

Pitovske Plaže (Yug). A wine-producing region in Dalmatia.

Pits (Sri.L). A Pilsener-style beer 12.25° Balling brewed by the McCallum Brewery in Colombo.

Pitsilia (Cyp). A district in the north-west Troodos mountain range.

Pittara (Fr). A noted brand of Basque Cider produced in the Pyrénées.

Pittermännchen (Ger). Vineyard. (Anb) = Nahe. (Ber) = Kreuznach. (Gro) = Schlosskapelle. (Vil) = Dorsheim.

Pittersberg (Ger). Vineyard. (Anb) = Nahe. (Ber) = Kreuznach. (Gro) = Schlosskapelle. (Vil) = Münster-Sarmsheim.

Pittsburgh Brewing Co (USA). A noted brewery based in Pittsburgh, Pennsylvania.

Pittyvaich-Glenlivet (Scot). A single Malt whisky distillery based west of Dufftown, Banffshire. A Highland malt whisky. 43% alc. by vol.

Pitú (Bra). A well-known brand of Cachaça.

Pitures-Dessus (Les) (Fr). A Premier Cru vineyard in the A.C. commune of Volnay, Côte de Beaune, Burgundy.

Pivare (Yug). A Tavern specifically designed for beer drinking.

Pivniţă (Rum). Cellar.

Piwo (Port). Beer, ale.

Pixilated (Eng) (slang). A term for drunk, intoxicated.

Placer County (USA). A wine-producing county in the Sierra foothills, California.

Placerville (USA). A noted wine-producing town in Eldorado County, California.

Plafond Limité de Classement (Fr). P.L.C. 'Ceiling yield' which producers can produce for A.C. classification.

Plain (Ire). Word for Porter.

Plaine de L'Aude (Fr). A wine area within the Département of Aude of the Languedoc-Roussillon.

Plaine du Vidourle (Fr). A wine area within the Département of Gard of the Languedoc-Roussillon.

Plaine du Vistre (Fr). A wine area within the Département of Gard of the Languedoc-Roussillon.

Plaize (Fr). Cognac producer. Address = Denis Plaize et Fils, 17150 Mirambeau. 30 ha in the Fins Bois.

Planche à Égoutter (Fr). A draining board used for the cleaning of bottles. Made of metal, it has spikes so as to allow the placing of the necks of the bottles over the spikes so they can drain after cleaning.

Planèzes (Fr). A noted wine-producing village in the Côtes du Roussillon.

Planta de Elaboración y Ebotellado de Vinos (Sp). See VILE. Label Catedral de León. A modern winery based in León. Main grape varieties are the Picudo, Prieto, Mencia, Tempranillo and Verdejo.

Planta de Pedralba (Sp). An alternative name for the Planta fina grape.

Planta Fina (Sp). A white grape variety grown in southern Spain. Also known as the Planta de pedralba.

Plantagenet Winery (Austr). A winery based in Western Australia. Produces varietal wines.

Planta Nova (Sp). A white grape variety grown in southern Spain. Also known as the Tardania.

Plant d'Arles (Fr). The southern Rhône name for the Cinsault grape.

Plant de Brie (Fr). An alternative name for the Pinot meunier.

Plant de Grèce (Fr). A white grape variety grown in the Gers Département. Is used in the production of Armagnac. Also known as the Baco 22A.

Plant Doré (Fr). An alternative name for the Pinot noir.

Plateau Calcaire (Le) (Fr). A zone of production in Saint-Émilion, east Bordeaux. Lit – 'Limestone plateau'.

Planter's (Cktl). 1 measure Jamaican Rum, juice ½ lemon, 1 teaspoon Gomme syrup, dash Angostura. Shake over ice, strain into a cocktail glass, top with grated nutmeg.

Planter's Punch (Cktl).(1). 1 oz. lime juice, 1 teaspoon sugar, 2 ozs. Jamaican Rum. Dissolve sugar in lime juice. Shake Rum over ice and strain into a highball glass with ice, sugar and lime juice. Decorate with pineapple, cherry, sliced orange and mint. Serve with straws.

Planter's Punch (Cktl).(2). 1½ fl.ozs. lemon or lime juice, 1½ fl.ozs dark Rum, 2 barspoons Grenadine, dash Angostura. Build into an ice-filled highball glass. Stir with soda water added. Decorate with a slice of orange and lemon.

Planter's Punch (Cktl).(3). Put some ice into a highball glass, add 1 teaspoon orange Curaçao, 1 measure Jamaican Rum, 2 dashes Angostura, juice 1½ limes or lemons, 1 teaspoon Grenadine. Stir well, decorate with an orange slice, cherry, serve with straws.

Planter's Punch (Cktl).(4). 1 fl.oz. Bacardi White Label, juice ½ lemon, dash Curaçao, dash Maraschino, 2 dashes pineapple juice. Stir together in an ice-filled highball glass. Dress with a pineapple cube and a cherry soaked in white Rum.

Planter's Tea (Cktl). 2 parts strong tea, 1 part dark Rum, ½ pint orange juice, ¼ pint lemon juice. Heat, sweeten with sugar syrup. Decorate with slices of orange and lemon.

Planter's Tea Punch (Punch). As for Planter's Tea using Assam tea.

Plantes (Les) (Fr). A Premier Cru vineyard in the A.C. commune of Chambolle-Musigny, Côte de Nuits, Burgundy. 2.6 ha.

Plantes-de-Maranges (Les) (Fr). A Premier Cru vineyard [part] in the commune of Cheilly-lès-Maranges, A.C. Santenay, Côte de Beaune, Burgundy.

Plantin (Carl G.) & Co (Nor). A producer of Aquavit under the control of A/S Vinmonopolet.

Plant Liqueurs (USA). Liqueurs produced by either percolation or by distillation of the base spirit and plants.

Plant Médoc (Fr). Another name for the Merlot grape.

Plant Noble (Port). Noble grape (species). Noble vine.

Plaque (La) (Fr). The metal disc on the top of a Champagne or other sparkling wine bottle to stop the wire cage cutting the cork.

Plasmopara Viticola (Lat). Formerly known as Peronospora Viticola.

Plassac (Fr). A commune in the A.C. Côtes de Blaye, north-eastern Bordeaux.

Plastered (Eng) (slang). A term for drunk and incapable. Very intoxicated.

Plastering (Sp). The adding of Gypsum (calcium sulphate) to grape must to increase the acidity. Especially used in Sherry production. (Fr) = Plâtrage.

Plat (Fr). Flat or dull wine.

Platan (Czec). A 'Plant tree' Lager beer from the Provitín Brewery.

Platière (La) (Fr). A Premier Cru vineyard in the A.C. commune of Pommard, Côte de Beaune, Burgundy. 5.8 ha.

Platin Extra Fin (Swe). A Swedish Punsch 26% alc. by vol. produced by Aktiebolaget Vin & Spritcentralem.

Platinum Blonde Cocktail (Cktl). 1 fl.oz. Jamaican rum, 1 fl.oz. Grand Marnier, ½ fl.oz. cream. Shake over ice, strain into a cocktail glass. Dress with a slice of orange.

Plato (Euro). A measure used in beer production. 1 degree Plato equals 4.08 degrees of gravity.

Plâtrage (Fr). Plastering. The addition of Gypsum to the grape must to increase acidity.

Platres (Cyp). A wine village on the south-eastern slopes of the Troodos mountain in the Makheras region. Produce some of the island's finest red wines from the Mavron grape.

Platten (Ger). Village. (Anb) = Mosel-Saar-Ruwer. (Ber) = Bernkastel. (Gro) = Schwarzlay. (Vins) = Klosterberg, Rotlay.

Plattensee (Hun). Another name for Lake Balatòn.

Platzl Special (Ger). A sweet, full-bodied beer, light in colour 5% alc. by vol. brewed by the Aying Brauerei in Bavaria.

Plauelrain (Ger). Vineyard. (Anb) = Baden. (Ber) = Ortenau. (Gro) = Fürsteneck. (Vil) = Durbach.

Plavac (Yug). A red grape variety grown in Croatia and the Dalmatian Isles. Produces full-bodied and distinctive wines.

Plavina (Yug). The name given to light red wines produced on the Dalmatian coast.

Plavka (Yug). A red wine produced in Montenegro, southern Yugoslavia.

Playa Delight (Cktl). ½ measure dry Gin, ½ measure white Rum, juice ¼ lime, 1 measure orange juice. Shake over ice, strain into a cocktail glass. Dress with a slice of lime. Serve with straws.

Playmate (Cktl). ¼ measure Grand Marnier, ¼ measure Apricot brandy, ¼ measure Brandy, ¼ measure orange squash, 1 egg white, dash Angostura. Shake over ice, strain into a cocktail glass. Add a twist of orange peel.

Playtime (Cktl). ⅓ measure Grand Marnier, ⅓ measure Apricot brandy, ⅓ measure orange juice, dash egg white. Shake over ice, strain into a cocktail glass. Dress with a spiral of lemon and a cherry.

Plaza Cocktail (Cktl). ¼ gill dry Gin, ⅛ gill Italian vermouth, ⅛ gill French vermouth. Shake over ice, strain into a cocktail glass. Serve with a thin slice of pineapple on top.

P.L.C. (Fr) (abbr). See Plafond Limité de Classement.

Pleasanton (USA). A wine-producing town based in Alameda County, California.

Pleasant Valley Wine Company (USA). A leading wine producer of the Finger Lakes region of New York district. Lake Keuka. Produces fine sparkling wines under the Great Western label.

Pleasant Valley Winery (N.Z.). A winery based at Valley Road, Henderson, North Island. 24 ha. Grape varieties – Baco N°1, Baco 22A, Müller-Thurgau, Niagara, Palomino and Pinotage. Produces wines under the Château Yelas label.

Plein (Fr). A frank, forward, full-bodied wine.

Pleisweiler-Oberhofen (Ger). Village. (Anb) = Rheinpfalz. (Ber) = Südliche Weinstrasse. (Gro) = Kloster Liebfrauenberg. (Vin) = Schlossberg.

Pleitersheim (Ger). Village. (Anb) = Rheinhessen. (Ber) = Bingen. (Gro) = Rheingrafenstein. (Vin) = Sternberg.

Plemenka (Yug). A red wine from the Vojvodina region in northern Serbia. Made from the Bouvier (red and white) grapes.

Plemenka Ružica (Yug). A rosé wine produced near Kutjevo in eastern Croatia.

Pleňský Prazdroj (Czec). A golden Beer brewed by a brewery of the same name.

Plessac et Cie (Fr). A noted nineteenth-century Cognac producer.

Pletchistik (USSR). A white grape variety grown in the river Don area.

Pleudihen (Fr). A noted Cider from Brittany, north-western France.

Pleven (Bul). A demarcated wine-producing area of northern Bulgaria. Produces mainly red wines.

Plevna (Bul). The brand-name of a red wine from Pleven.

Pliny the Elder (Gre). An author who wrote a book devoted to a variety of wines and vines. A.D. 23–79.

Pliska (Bul). The trade-name used for Brandy produced in Preslav in the Balkan mountains for export.

Plješevica (Yug). A wine-producing area based in Croatia.

P.L.O. (Austr) (abbr). Penfolds, Lindemans and Orlando.

Plonk (Eng) (slang). A word which now denotes cheap ordinary wine. Derived from the English 'Tommies' in the First World War who could not say 'Blanc' (white wine).

Plonko (Austr) (slang). For an alcoholic who drinks mainly wine.

Ploughbottles (Eng). Wooden casks used by farmworkers to carry their daily ration of ale to the fields. Mainly in the Midlands.

Ploughman's Ale (Eng). A bottled XXX Bitter 1049 O.G. brewed by the Bateman Brewery in Wainfleet, Lincolnshire. Also an Export 1060 O.G.

Ploughman's Bitter (Eng). A canned Bitter 1032 O.G. brewed by the Watneys Brewery.

Ploughman's Lunch (Eng). Bitter ale, bread, cheese, pickles and fruit (usually apples).

Ploughman's Scrumpy (Eng). A dry Cider produced by Countryman in Devon.

Plovdic (Bul). A wine-producing region based in southern Bulgaria. Produces mainly red wines.

Plovdina (Yug). A red grape variety grown in Macedonia.

Ployez-Jacquemart (Fr). Champagne producer. Address = 8 Rue Astoin, 51500 Ludes. Produces – Vintage and non-vintage wines. Vintages – 1971, 1973, 1975, 1976, 1978, 1979, 1982. The De Luxe vintage cuvée is Cuvée Liesse d'Harbonville.

Plum Brandy (Euro). A colourless Eau-de-Vie produced from a variety of plums.

Plummer (W.Ind). A style of Rum produced in Jamaica. Also known as Wedderburn. See Grand Arôme.

Plummer Type (W.Ind). A Jamaican rum

P

using Dunder in the process. See Grand Arôme.

Plummy (Eng). A term used to describe wines that are rich and flavoursome.

Plum Shake (Cktl).(Non-alc). 3 fl.ozs. orange juice, 5 fl.ozs. plum juice, 2 scoops vanilla ice cream. Blend together in a blender. Pour into a large club goblet, serve with straws.

Plunger Coffee (Eng). A name given to the Cafétiere method of coffee-making.

Plus (W.Ind). A non-alcoholic drink produced in Barbados by Banks. Is rich in vitamin C, fructose and amino acids. Its make-up is similar to honey.

Plymouth (USA). A wine-producing town based in Amador County, California.

Plymouth Gin (Eng). See Blackfriars Distillery.

Plymouth Heavy (Eng). A Mild ale 1032 O.G. brewed by the Courage Brewery.

Plympton Brewery (Eng). Based in Plymouth, Devon. (Halls Brewery). Noted for its Plympton Pride 1045 O.G. and Plympton Best 1039 O.G.

Plzen (Czec). The Czec spelling of the town of Pilsen (the German spelling).

Plzeňský Prazdroi (Czec). The Czec spelling of Pilsner Urquell. Also the name of a large brewery based in Pilsen.

PM (Can). The brand-name of a Canadian whiskey produced by Canadian Gibson Distilleries. 40% alc. by vol.

PM Blended (USA). The brand-name of a blended Whiskey. 40% alc. by vol.

P.M.E. (Eng) (abbr). Pecti-Methyl-Esterase.

Pneumatic Press (Ger). Consists of a cylinder into which the grapes are placed. A deflated plastic or synthetic rubber bag is placed in the cylinder then inflated, pressing the grapes against the slatted sides of the drum.

Poacher Bitter (Eng). A keg Bitter 1032 O.G. brewed by Whitbread.

Poças Junior (Port). Vintage Port shippers. Vintages – 1960, 1963, 1967, 1970, 1975, 1977, 1978, 1980.

Pocholoa Manzanilla (Sp). A fine, pale, dry Manzanilla sherry from Domecq.

Pocillum (Lat). Small cup.

Pocket (Eng). A sack used to pack hops in for delivery to the brewery. 160 lbs.

Pocullum (Lat). Cup. See also Cymbium.

Poculum (Lat). Goblet. See also Cullulus.

Poda en Vaso (Sp). Low pruning of the vines. i.e. Goblet shaped. See also En Vaso.

Podar (Port). To prune (the vine).

Podensac (Fr). A commune within the district of A.C. Cérons in south-western Bordeaux. Produces sweet white wines.

Podensac (Fr). A commune within the district of A.C. Graves in south-western Bordeaux. Produces mainly dry white wines.

Podere di Cignano (It). A noted Chianti Putto producer based in the Tuscany region.

Podere Rocche dei Manzoni (It). A noted wine producer based in Monforte d'Alba, Piemonte. Produces sparkling (méthode champenoise) wines. Labels include Valentino Brut.

Poderi Marcarini (It). A noted winery based in La Morra (district of Barolo) in Piemonte.

Podersdorf (Aus). A wine-producing area in the Eisenstadt district.

Podkováň Brewery (Czec). A very old brewery c1434 in northern Czec.

Poggibonsi (It). An area of the Chianti in Tuscany. Outside the Classico district.

Poggio Guiseppe (It). A winery based at Roccagrimalda, Piemonte. 3 ha.

Poggio Reale (It). A Chianti Putto produced by Spalletti in Tuscany.

Poggio Romita (It). A Chianti Putto producer based in Tuscany.

Pohorje (Yug). A wine produced in Slovenia.

Poignettage (Fr). The gentle shaking of the bottles in Champagne. Given to those that have received their Dosage. To mix the contents.

Poilly (Fr). A Cru Champagne village in the Canton de Ville-en-Tardenois. District = Reims.

Poilly-sur-Serein (Fr). A commune in the A.C. Chablis, Burgundy.

Poinchy (Fr). A commune in the A.C. Chablis, Burgundy.

Poin de Pétillance (Fr). A hint of pétillance. Very slightly sparkling

Point (Eng). The acidity in coffee.

Point (A) (Fr). A term used to describe a wine which is ready for drinking. Is at its peak.

Point Brewery (USA). A brewery based in Stevens Point, Wisconsin. Brews beers under the Point label.

Point d'Angles (Fr). A Premier Cru vineyard in the A.C. commune of Volnay, Côte de Beaune, Burgundy. 1.5 ha. Also known as Les Point d'Angles.

Pointe (Fr). Punt. The depression in the bottom of most red wine bottles and some whites. Helps stacking. See Sur Pointe.

Pointe de Fraîcheur (Fr). An Alsatian term for a wine with a 'slight prickle' on the palate.

Pointouille (Fr). A term that denotes a wine with only a hint of oak from a short cask ageing.

Poio (Port). Terrace.

P

Poire au Cognac (Fr). A blend of natural extract of Poire Williams and Eau-de-vie-de-Cognac produced by Brillet.

Poire de Fer (Fr). A variety of pear used in the production of Calvados.

Poire de Grise (Fr). A variety of pear used in the production of Calvados.

Poire Williams (It). A pear spirit liqueur. Usually has a pear which is grown in the bottle from bud. (The bottle is tied over the set bud on the tree). 43% alc. by vol. See Williamine.

Poissenot (Fr). A Premier Cru vineyard in the A.C. commune Gevrey-Chambertin, Côte de Nuits, Burgundy. 2.19 ha.

Poitin (Ire). An alternative name for Poteen.

Pojer e Sandri (It). A small winery based at Faedo near San Michele all'Adige in the Trentino-Alto Adige region. Produces mainly white wines and sparkling (méthode champenoise) wine plus Grappa.

Pokal (Ger). A rotund ¼ litre, green-stemmed glass.

Pokale (Ger). A thick trunked glass used to serve Tafelwein in the Haardt region, close to the border with Alsace in France.

Pokal Wine (Ger). Tafelwein.

Poker (Cktl). ½ measure Bacardi White Label, ½ measure Italian vermouth. Stir over ice, strain into a cocktail glass.

Polaire (Jap). A brand-name wine of Sapporo Wines Ltd.

Poland (Pol). Noted for its Vodka. Has no wines of note. See also Slivovitch.

Polar (Fin). A cranberry liqueur produced by Chymos. Red in colour, 29% alc. by vol.

Polar (Ger). A brand of Rum produced at Hockheim. (Part of Seagram).

Polar Beer (Ice). A beer brewed by the Egill Skallagrimsson Brewery Ltd.

Polcevera (It). A white wine from Liguria. Made from the Bianchetta and Vermentino grapes.

Pol d'Argent (USA). A sparkling wine produced by Robin Fils in eastern America.

Polgazão (Port). A white grape variety grown in the Lafões region.

Pol Gessner (Fr). A Champagne producer based in Épernay. Wines sold only at Selfridges in London.

Pölich (Ger). Village. (Anb) = Mosel-Saar-Ruwer. (Ber) = Bernkastel. (Gro) = Sankt Michael. (Vins) = Held, Südlay.

Polichinelle (Cktl). ½ gill Cassis de Dijon, ⅙ gill Kirsch, soda water. Stir over ice, strain into a highball glass on ice. Also known as Cassis-Kirsch.

Polička Brewery (Czec). A brewery based in central Czec.

Polignac (Prince Hubert de) (Fr). Cognac producer. Address = Unicoop, 49 Rue Lohmeyer, 16102 Cognac. 5,200 ha. in the Co-op, sited mainly in the Fins Bois 49% and Bon Bois 36%. Produces – Dinasty Grande Champagne.

Poligny (Fr). A commune of the Jura Département, eastern France.

Polish (Eng). A brewery term used for the fine filtering of light-coloured beers to make them crystal clear, before bottling or kegging.

Polish Filtration (USA). The final filtration of wines, beers, etc. to give clarity prior to bottling.

Polish White Spirit (Pol). A potent Vodka-type spirit 80% alc. by vol.

Polisy (Fr). A Cru Champagne village in the Canton de l'Aube. District = Château Thierry.

Polito Vineyard (USA). A winery based in Vincentown, New Jersey.

Polja (Yug). A wine-producing area in Dalmatia.

Pollard's Brewery (Eng). A brewery based in Stockport, Cheshire. Brews John Barleycorn Bitter.

Pollino (It). D.O.C. red wine from Calabria. Made from the Gaglioppo, Greco nero, Guarnaccia bianca, Malvasia bianca and Montonico grapes. If minimum total alc. is 12.5% by vol. and aged 2 years then classed Superiore.

Polluted (USA) (slang). A term for intoxicated, drunk.

Polly (Eng). The nickname for Apollinaris mineral water. e.g. Scotch and Polly.

Pollyanna (Cktl). Crush 2 slices of fresh pineapple with 2 fl.ozs. dry Gin. Add ½ fl.oz. Italian vermouth, 2 dashes Grenadine, juice ½ orange. Shake over ice, strain into a large cocktail glass.

Polmassick Vineyard (Eng). A vineyard based at Polmassick, St. Ewe, St. Austell, Cornwall. 0.65 ha. Grape varieties – Müller-Thurgau and Seyve villard.

Polmos (Pol). Short for Panstwowy Monopol Spirytusowy. Polish State Vodka producers. Principal brand is Wyborowa.

Polnic (Cktl). 1 fl.oz. Polar liqueur, 1 fl.oz. Gin. Pour into an ice-filled highball glass. Stir in tonic water.

Polo Cocktail (Cktl). ⅗ measure dry Gin, ⅕ measure lemon juice, ⅕ measure orange juice. Shake over ice, strain into a cocktail glass.

Polonaise Cocktail (Cktl). ⅗ measure Brandy, ⅕ measure dry Sherry, ⅕ measure Blackberry brandy, dash lemon juice. Shake over ice, strain into an ice-filled old-fashioned glass.

Pol Roger (Fr). Champagne producer. Address = 1 Rue Henri Lelarge, 51200

P

Épernay. A Grande Marque. Produces – Vintage and non-vintage wines. Vintages – 1906, 1909, 1911, 1914, 1915, 1919, 1921, 1923, 1926, 1928, 1929, 1933, 1934, 1937, 1942, 1943, 1945, 1947, 1949, 1952, 1953, 1955, 1959, 1961, 1962, 1964, 1966, 1969, 1971, 1973, 1975, 1976, 1979, 1982, 1983.

Polsuho (Yug). Medium dry.

Polvillejo (Sp). The alternative name used in Sanlúcar de Barremeda for Lustrillo.

Polychrosis Viteana (Lat). A strain of the grape berry moth that produces larvae which feed on bunches of grapes leaving them susceptible to disease, especially rot.

Polyculture (Port). Mixed cropping. e.g. vines grown on high trellises with vegetables grown underneath.

Polyethylene Terephthalate (Eng). See Pet Bottle.

Polygalacturonase (Lat). P.G. A yeast enzyme that reduces pectic acid. Cleans wines that have a pectin haze.

Polynesian Cocktail (Cktl). ⅔ measure Vodka, ⅓ measure Cherry brandy, juice of a lime. Shake over ice, strain into a sugar (lime) rimmed cocktail glass. Top with a twist of lime peel juice.

Polynnaia (USSR). A wormwood Whiskey made around Odessa.

Poly Parrot (Cktl). 1 measure (green) Crème de Menthe, dash lime juice. Shake over ice, strain into a cocktail glass. Float double cream on top coloured with a 4 dashes of Grenadine.

Polyphenols (Eng). The substances that cause browning (tannins).

Polypin (Eng). A plastic insert inside a rigid cardboard container. Holds 4½ gallons of beer.

Polythene Drums (Eng). 240 litre containers for transporting wine. Often give the wines a slight plastic taint.

Polyvinylpyorolidone (Eng). P.V.P. A substance used to help stabilize wines and prevent them turning brown. Precipitates with excess tannin.

Pomace (Eng). The residue from apples after the juice has been extracted for cider. Pectin is then extracted from it, then it is used for cattle feed.

Pomace Brandy (USA). See California Brandy.

Pomagne (Eng). A brand-name sparkling cider made by the Bulmers company in Hereford. Allowed to ferment twice naturally.

Pombal (Marquis de) (Port). The man to whom is attributed the starting of the Port wine district in the Douro.

Pombe (Afr). An east African beer made from millet which has been germinated

and roasted, then mixed with Posho (maize flour) and fermented. Is usually drunk through tubes. High in alcohol. See also Pombo.

Pombo (Afr). The Bantu name for Pombe.

Pomeral (Fr). An old, established Cognac house who, with Antier, united in 1949 to form the house of Gaston de Lagrange.

Pomeranz (Ger). See Pomeranzen Bitters.

Pomeranzen Bitters (Ger) (Hol). Flavoured orange bitters made from unripe oranges.

Pomeranzen Liqueurs (Austr). Based on Pomeranzen oranges both green and orange coloured.

Pomeranzen Liqueurs (Ger). A Curaçao-type liqueur, green-gold in colour made on a base of unripe Pomeranzen oranges.

Pomerol (Fr). An area within the region of Bordeaux, on the east of the town of Libourne and Saint-Émilion. Produces fine red wines. Top growth Château Pétrus.

Pomino Bianco (It). A D.O.C. dry, white wine from Tuscany. Produced from the Pinot bianco, Pinot grigio and Trebbiano grapes.

Pommard (Fr). An A.C. village and commune of the Côte de Beaune, Burgundy. 300 ha. Has 27 Premier Cru vineyards – Clos de la Commaraine, Clos des Épenots, Clos du Verger, Derrière Saint-Jean, La Chanière, La Platière, La Refène, Le Clos Blanc, Le Clos Micot, Les Argillières, Les Arvelets, Les Bertins, Les Boucherottes, Les Chanlins-Bas, Les Chaponnières, Les Charmots, Les Combes-Dessus, Les Croix-Noires, Les Épenots, Les Fremiers, Les Jarollières, Les Petits-Épenots, Les Pézerolles, Les Poutures, Les Rugiens-Bas, Les Rugiens-Haut, Les Saussiles. 141.43 ha.

Pommeau (Fr). An apple juice muted with Calvados to produce a sweet, fortified drink. Made by the Drouin Co. in Normandy.

Pommeraie Vineyards (USA). A small winery based near Sebastopol, Sonoma County, California. Grape varieties – Cabernet sauvignon and Chardonnay. Produces varietal wines.

Pommeranzen Bitters (Ger) (Hol). The alternative spelling of Pomeranzen Bitters.

Pommeraye (La) (Fr). A commune in the A.C. Savennières, Anjou-Saumur, Loire.

Pommerell (Ger). Vineyard. (Anb) = Mosel-Saar-Ruwer. (Ber) = Zell/Mosel. (Gro) = Schwarze Katz. (Vil) = Zell.

P

Pommern (Ger). Village. (Anb) = Mosel-Saar-Ruwer. (Ber) = Zell/Mosel. (Gro) = Goldbäumchen. (Vins) = Goldberg, Rosenberg, Sonnenuhr, Zeisel.

Pommery (Fr). The new name for the old firm of Pommery et Gréno.

Pommery et Gréno (Fr). Champagne producer. Address = 5 Place du Général Gouraud, P.O. Box B7, 51100 Reims. A Grande Marque. Produces – Vintage and non-vintage wines. Vintages – 1904, 1906, 1911, 1915, 1921, 1926, 1928, 1929, 1934, 1937, 1941, 1943, 1947, 1949, 1952, 1953, 1955, 1959, 1961, 1962, 1964, 1966, 1969, 1973, 1975, 1976, 1978, 1979, 1980, 1981, 1982, 1983. De Luxe vintage cuvée is Louis Pommery. See also Pommery.

Pommie's Revenge (Eng). A cask conditioned Ale 1060 O.G. brewed by the Goose Eye Brewery in Yorkshire.

Pommy (Eng). A local Somerset word for the milled apple pulp before it is pressed. Short for Pomace.

Pompango Cocktail (Cktl). ½ measure dry Gin, ½ measure grapefruit juice, 2 dashes dry Vermouth. Shake over ice, strain into a cocktail glass.

Pompejaner (Ger). Vineyard. (Anb) = Franken. (Ber) = Mainviereck. (Gro) = Not yet assigned. (Vil) = Aschaffenburg.

Pomperjanum (Lat). A red wine produced in central-western Italy in Roman times.

Pompey Royal (Eng). A cask conditioned Bitter 1043 O.G. brewed by the Whitbread Brewery at Cheltenham for Wessex.

Pompier Daisy Cocktail (Cktl). 1 measure Crème de Cassis, 1½ measures Noilly Prat. Stir over ice, strain into an old-fashioned glass. Top with soda water.

Pompier Highball (Cktl). ½ measure Crème de Cassis, ½ measure French vermouth stirred over cracked ice in a highball glass.

Pomponette (Fr). A tall thin glass used for tasting and testing Champagnes.

Pomport (Fr). A commune in the A.C. Monbazillac in Bergerac. Produces sweet white (botrytised) wines.

Ponce (It). Punch drink.

Poncello (Sp). A ponche orange and brandy liqueur produced by the Caballero Co.

Ponche de Crema (S.Am). A drink, rum-based with eggs, milk and sugar Produced in Venezuela.

Ponches (Sp). A liqueur digestive that is brandy based. (A punch-type).

Ponches (Sp). Liqueur sherries.

Ponché Soto (Sp). A famous liqueur sold in a silver bottle. A blend of herbs, old sherries and brandy. Produced by Jose de Sóto in Jerez de la Frontera. 21% alc. by vol.

Ponferrada (Sp). A wine-producing area in the Galicia region. Produces red and white wines.

Poniatowski (Prince) (Fr). A noted producer of A.C. Vouvray in Touraine, Loire.

Poniente (Sp). A cool, humid wind, not very strong, that tends to bring on mildew in the Sherry region.

Ponnelle (Fr). A Burgundy négociant-éleveur based in Beaune, Côte de Beaune. Address = Abbaye St-Martin, 53 Avenue de l'Aigue, 21200 Beaune. Noted for their fine wines.

Ponoma Valley Claret (N.Z.). A full-bodied red wine produced by Abel and Co. in Kumeu.

Ponsigue (S.Am). A Rum-based cordial flavoured with Ponsigue cherries. Produced in Venezuela.

Pontac (S.Afr). A red grape variety.

Ponte da Barca (Port). An Aguardente produced by Adega Cooperativa de Ponte da Barca.

Pontet (Le) (Fr). A vineyard in the commune of St-Médard-d'Eyrans. A.C. Graves, Bordeaux. 5 ha. (red).

Pontevedra (Sp). A wine-producing region in north-western Spain. Is noted for a 'green wine' which is similar in style to the Vinhos Verdes of Portugal.

Pontil (Eng). An old name for the Punt at the bottom of the bottle. See also 'Kick'.

Pony (Eng). A brand-name cherry wine.

Pony (Eng). Small bottle, glass, ⅓ pint.

Pony (USA). A measure for cocktails. 1 fl.oz. US.

Pony Ales (Ch.Isles). Cask conditioned Bitter 1035–39 O.G. and Mild 1037.7 O.G. brewed by the Guernsey Brewery 1920. Ltd. St. Peter Port, Guernsey.

Pony Glass (USA). A small version of the Flip glass. 2 fl.ozs. (flute-shaped).

Pony Punch (Cktl). 1 bottle dry white wine, juice 3 lemons, ½ pint green tea, 1 teaspoon cinnamon oil, sugar syrup, 5 fl.ozs. of Rum, Brandy and Arrack. Mix all well together, heat gently and serve hot.

Ponzi Vineyards (USA). A small vineyard based in Oregon. Produces vinifera wines.

Poole Brewery (Eng). Opened in 1981 in Poole, Dorset. Noted for its cask conditioned Dolphin Best 1038 O.G. See also Brewhouse.

Poop Deck (Cktl). ⅔ measure Brandy, ⅔ measure Port wine, ⅕ measure

Blackberry brandy. Shake over ice, strain into a cocktail glass.

Poor (Eng). A term used to describe a wine that has little positive character or quality.

Poor Man's Champagne (S.Am). A term given to sparkling Cider.

Poor Man's Drink (Eng). A drink produced by infusing pearl barley in water over heat with figs, raisins and liquorice.

Poort Winery (Die) (S.Afr). A winery based in Klein Karoo. Address = P.O. Box 45, Albertina 6795. Produces varietal wines.

Pop (Eng) (slang). The name for any fizzy, non-alcoholic drink. i.e. Coke, Lemonade, 7-Up etc.

Pope (Cktl). Tokay wine heated with sugar and an orange studded with cloves.

Pope Clement V (Fr). See Clément V.

Pope's 1880 (Eng). A keg/bottled Ale 1041 O.G. brewed by the Eldridge Pope Brewery in Dorchester, Dorset.

Pope Valley Winery (USA). A winery based in the Napa Valley, California. Grape varieties – Cabernet sauvignon, Chardonnay, Chenin blanc, Johannisberg riesling, Petite sirah and Sauvignon blanc. Produces varietal wines.

Popoff (Eng). A proprietary brand of Vodka.

Po-Pomme Cocktail (Cktl). ⅔ measure Cherry brandy, ⅓ measure Calvados, 2 dashes Angostura. Stir over ice, strain into a highball glass. Top with dry Cider, 2 ice cubes and an apple slice.

Popovice Brewery (Czec). A brewery based in western Czec.

Poppenweiler (Ger). Village. (Anb) = Württemberg. (Ber) = Württembergisch Unterland. (Gro) = Schalkstein. (Vin) = Neckarhälde.

Poppy Cocktail (Cktl). ⅔ measure dry Gin, ⅓ measure Crème de Cacao. Shake over ice, strain into a cocktail glass.

Poprad Brewery (Czec). A brewery based in eastern Czec. Brews Tatran (a Lager beer).

Popular Troubador (Eng). A brand of Sherry shipped by Saccone and Speed.

Pop Wines (Can). Artificially carbonated wines. Have a full sparkle.

Pop Wines (USA). Natural wines which are flavoured with herbs, spices or fruit juices and other flavourings. Most are sweet.

Poretti Breweries (It). Breweries based in northern Italy.

Porous Peg (Eng). A soft wooden peg (spile) fitted into the Shive to allow a cask to breathe whilst it is working.

Porrets (Les) (Fr). A Premier Cru vineyards in the A.C. commune of Nuits-Saint-Georges, Côte de Nuits, Burgundy. 7 ha. Also known as Porrets.

Porrón (Sp). Decanter, flask or bottle with two cross-over spouts. Gives a stream of wine into the mouth.

Porsbrannvin (Den). A brand of Akvavit flavoured with Bog myrtle.

Port (Port). A fortified red wine produced in the upper Douro region of northern Portugal. Has many varieties including Vintage, Crusted, L.B.V., Wood, Dated, Tawny and Ruby. See also White Port.

Port à Binson (Fr). A Cru Champagne village in the Canton of Dormans. District = Épernay.

Portacask (Eng). 2650 litres container used for transporting wines. Made of fibre glass with a stainless steel liner.

Portador (Sp). Describes the wooden container used to transport the grapes from the vineyard.

Portainjerto (Sp). A resistant root stock onto which the vine is then grafted.

Port and Starboard (Pousse Café). ½ measure Grenadine and ½ measure (green) Crème de Menthe.

Port Carras (Gre). A sweet, red wine produced in Mount Vilia, Macedonia.

Port Cobbler (Cktl). ¾ gill Port, 2 dashes Brandy, 5 dashes plain syrup. Shake over ice, strain into a highball glass ½ full of crushed ice. Serve with slices of fresh fruit and a dash of lemon peel juice.

Port Cocktail (Cktl). 2 ozs. Port, dash Cognac. Stir over ice, strain into a cocktail glass. Squeeze of orange peel juice on top.

Port Dundas (Scot). A Grain whisky distillery based near the mouth of the river Clyde, western Scotland.

Porte-Bouchon (Fr). Cork-pin.

Porte-Fût (Fr). The name for the wooden trestles that support the wine casks.

Port Egg Nogg (Cktl). ¾ gill Port, ¼ gill Brandy, ¼ gill Rum, ⅓ gill milk, 1 egg, 1 teaspoon sugar. Shake over ice, strain into a tumbler. Serve with a dash of nutmeg on top.

Porte-Hotte (Fr). A Bordeaux hod carrier.

Port Ellen (Scot). A single Malt whisky distillery based on the Isle of Islay, western Scotland. An Islay malt whisky. 43% alc. by vol. (Part of the DCL group).

Porter (Eng). A Beer made from roasted unmalted barley. High hopping, very bitter, was popular in the seventeenth and eighteenth century. See Guinness.

Porter Gaff (Austr). A South Australian mixture of Stout and lemonade.

P

Porterhouse (Eng). An eighteenth-century Ale house where only Porter was served.

Porter 39 (Fr). A sweetish, dark, Stout-style beer 6.9% alc. by vol. brewed by the '33' Brasserie in the north of Maubeuge. (Part of the Union de Brasseries group).

Porterville (S.Afr). A wine and brandy-producing region based north of Tulbagh.

Porterville Co-operative (S.Afr). Based in Piketberg. Address = Porterville Koöperatiewe Keldermaatskappy, Box 52, Porterville 6810. Produces varietal wines.

Porterville Koöperatiewe Keldermaat-skappy (S.Afr). See Porterville Co-operative.

Portes-Greffes (Fr). Lit – 'Carry grafting'. American vine stocks are resistant to Phylloxera on which European stock is now grafted as a remedy against the pest.

Portet (Fr). A sweet (or dry) white wine from the Béarn region of south-western France. Grapes are often attacked by botrytis (known as Passerillage locally) in good years.

Portets (Fr). A commune in the A.C. Graves in south-western Bordeaux.

Porte Vecchio (Fr). An A.C. sub-region in southern Corsica.

Port Flip (Cktl). 1½ fl.ozs. Port, ½ fl.oz. Brandy, 1 egg yolk, 1 teaspoon sugar. Shake over ice, strain into a cocktail glass. Top with grated nutmeg.

Port-Greffes (Fr). See Portes-Greffes.

Port Highball (Cktl). As for Gin highball, substituting Port for Gin.

Portimão (Port). A co-operative based in the Algarve.

Portinhola (Port). A narrow entrance at the base of the head of the vat in which one can put one's head to smell that the inside is clean and sweet smelling.

Portland (USA). A white grape variety. A Labrusca cross. Little used now.

Port Light Cocktail (Cktl). 1 fl.oz. Bourbon whiskey, ½ fl.oz. lemon juice, 1 egg white, 2 teaspoons clear honey. Blend together with crushed ice in a blender. Pour into a highball glass. Dress with a sprig of mint.

Port Milk Punch (Cktl). 1 gill milk, ⅓ gill Port. Shake over ice, strain into a collins glass. Top with grated nutmeg.

Portnersberg (Ger). Vineyard. (Anb) = Mosel-Saar-Ruwer. (Ber) = Bernkastel. (Gro) = Schwarzlay. (Vil) = Wittlich.

Porto (Fr). Port wine.

Porto (Port). The Portuguese pronunciation of Oporto, the town situated on the mouth of the river Douro (north bank) from where Port gets its name. See Portus Cale.

Porto dos Cavaleiros (Port). A Dão red wine produced by Caves São João.

Portofino (It). A dry white wine from Liguria. Yellow in colour 10–11% alc. by vol.

Portos (USA). Port wines.

Porto-Vecchio (Fr). A wine-producing region in southern Corsica. Produces full-flavoured wines.

Port Phillip (Austr). The old name for Melbourne. A town where early wines were shipped from.

Portrait of a Winegrower (It). A famous eighteenth-century painting by Girlamo Forabosco. c1700.

Port Tilter (Eng). Another name for a mechanical decanter cradle made of brass or silver.

Port Tongs (Eng). An instrument to remove the neck and cork off old bottles of Port. The tongs are heated then applied to the neck. A wet feather is then used over the heated part to create a break.

Port Type (S.Afr). A designation given to fortified wines that are similar in style to Port.

Portugais Rouge (Fr). A red grape variety also known as the Limburger.

Portugal (Port). A wine-producing country on the west coast of the Iberian peninsular. Noted for its Port wine, Dão, Vinhos Verdes, Setúbal, Bucellas, Periquita etc.

Portugalin Kauppatoimisto (Fin). The Portuguese Wine Information Centre. Address = Runeberginkatu 29 a 16–100, Helsinki 10.

Portugals Handelskontor (Nor). The Portuguese Wine Information Centre. Address = Tollbugt, 25 – Oslo 1.

Portugieser (Ger). A red grape variety. Produces light red wines. Known in France as the Autrichen. Also known as the Blauer Portugieser.

Portugiesische Handelsdelegation (Aus). The Portuguese Wine Information Centre. Address = Stubenring, 24–1010 Wien.

Portugiesisches Handelsbuero (Ger). Portuguese Wine Information Centres. Addresses = Zentrale Bonn Ubierstrasse, 78–5300 Bonn 2. Zweigstelle Duesseldorf, Friedrichstrasse 20–4000 Duesseldorf 1. Zweigstelle Hamburg Am, Guensemarkt, 2L-20000 Hamburg 36.

Portugisiske Handelsbureau (Den). Portuguese Wine Information Centre. Address = Frederiksborggade, 1 MZ-1360 Copenhague K.

Portugizac (Yug). The name given to the Portugieser grape.

P

Portuguese Espresso Coffee (Port). See Uma Bica.

Portuguese Government Trade Office (Can). Portuguese Wine Information Centres. Addresses = 1801, McGill College Avenue, Suite 1150-Montreal, P.Q. H3A 2NA. ICEP MTL – 390, Bay Street. Suite 1718-Toronto, Ontario M5H 2Y2.

Portuguese Government Trade Office (Eng). Portuguese Wine Information Centre. Address = New Bond Street House, 4ᵗʰ Floor, 1–5 New Street, London W1Y 9PE.

Portuguese Government Trade Office (Jap). Portuguese Wine Information Centre. Address = Akabanebashi BLDG. 6ᵗʰ Floor-26–6 Higashi Azabu 1-Chome-Minato-Ku-Tokyo 106.

Portuguese Goverment Trade Office (S.Afr). Portuguese Wine Information Centre. Address = 6ᵗʰ Floor, Varig Centre, 134, Fox Street, Johannesberg-P.O. Box 70–2000 Johannesberg.

Portuguese Government Trade Office (USA). Portuguese Wine Information Centre. Address = 548, Fifth Avenue, New York 10036 N.Y.

Portuguese Handelsdelegate (Hol). Portuguese Wine Information Centre. Address = Groot Hertoginnenlaan, 22–2517 EG Den Haag.

Portus Cale (Lat). The Roman name for the old port on the river Douro. Was the centre of life and trade of ancient Lusitania. Gave its name to Portugal's Port.

Port-Vendres (Fr). A commune in the A.C. Banyuls, south-western France.

Portwein (Ger). Port wine.

Portwijn (Hol). Port wine.

Port Wine (Cktl). ⅔ measure Port, ⅓ measure Brandy. Stir over ice, strain into a cocktail glass. Add a twist of orange peel.

Port Wine Cobbler (Cktl). Dissolve a teaspoon of sugar in a little water in a highball glass. Add ice, 3 fl.ozs. Port. Top with fruit in season. Serve with straws.

Port Wine Eggnog (Cktl). 1 egg, 1 gill milk, 3 fl.ozs. Port, 2 dashes Gomme syrup. Shake well over ice, strain into a collins glass. Top with grated nutmeg.

Port Wine Flip (Cktl). 4 fl.ozs. Port, 1 egg yolk, 1 teaspoon powdered sugar. Shake well with ice, strain into a small tumbler. Top with grated cinnamon.

Port Wine Institute (Port). A body that governs the Port trade. Decides how much Must may be made.

Port Wine Negus (Cktl). Pour 3 fl.ozs. of hot water onto a sugar cube in an old-fashioned glass. Add 2 fl.ozs. Port and top with grated nutmeg.

Port Wine Sangaree (Cktl). 2¼ ozs. Port, ½

oz. Syrup. Stir with crushed ice, strain into a highball glass filled with ice. Add grated nutmeg.

Portwyn (S.Afr). Port-style wine.

Portz (Ger). Village. (Anb) = Mosel-Saar-Ruwer. (Ber) = Obermosel. (Gro) = Gipfel. (Vins) = Sites not yet chosen.

Porusots (Le) (Fr). See Poruzots (Le).

Porusots-Dessus (Le) (Fr). See Poruzots-Dessus (Le).

Poruzots (Le) (Fr). A Premier Cru vineyard in the A.C. commune of Meursault, Côte de Beaune, Burgundy. 1.6 ha. Also known as Le Porusots.

Poruzots-Dessus (Le) (Fr). A Premier Cru vineyard in the A.C. commune of Meursault, Côte de Beaune, Burgundy. 1.8 ha. Also known as Le Porusots-Dessus.

Posada (Sp). Inn, Tavern.

Posca (Lat). A cheap wine carried by the Roman soldiers.

Posho (Afr). Maize flour used in the making of Pombe beer.

Poshoote (Eng). The fifteenth- and sixteenth-century name for Posset.

Pošip (Yug). A white grape variety grown in Dalmatia.

Positano (It). A bitter-sweet apéritif wine.

Poso (Sp). Sediment, Lees.

Possenheim (Ger). Village. (Anb) = Franken. (Ber) = Steigerwald. (Gro) = Burgweg. (Vins) = Assorted parts of vineyards.

Posset (Eng). A Mediaeval drink of hot curdled milk with ale or wine. Is flavoured with spices, sugar and honey.

Possonnière (La) A commune in the A.C. Savennières, Anjou-Saumur, Loire.

Postel Brasserie (Bel). An Abbaye brewery based in north-eastern Belgium.

Posten (Ger). Vineyard. (Anb) = Mittelrhein. (Ber) = Bacharach. (Gro) = Schloss Stahleck. (Vil) = Bacharach.

Postup (Yug). A strong red wine from the Croatia region. Made from the Plavac grape, is high in alcohol and full-bodied.

Post Winery (USA). A small winery based in Altus.

Posum Trot Vineyards (USA). A small vineyard based in Unionville, Indiana. 2.5 ha. Produces French hybrid wines.

Pot (Eng) (slang). A name given to a pint tankard/mug.

Pot (Eng) (slang). A term used to denote that a customer has a drink bought for him by another customer in a public house which is 'in the pot' (held in stock) for him.

Pot (Fr). A specially shaped bottle containing 50 cls. Peculiar to the Burgundy region especially in the Beaujolais district.

Pot (Fr). Jug or tankard.

P

Pot (Fr). An old wine measure now no longer used.

Potabilis (Lat). Drinkable. (Potus = a drink).

Potable (Fr). Drinkable, fit to drink.

Potable Spirits (Eng). Drinkable spirits.

Potable Strength (Eng). The name given to spirits that passed the Gunpowder proofing test in the olden days. See Proof.

Pot Ale (Scot). The spent wash in Malt whisky production.

Pot Ale (Ire). The religious establishments' barley-based spirit. Earliest recorded spirit in the British Isles.

Potash Salts (Eng). Used in the rectification of spirits (purifying).

Potassium Bitartrate (Sp). A naturally occurring deposit sometimes found in bottles of sherry. Is removed by storage at low temperatures then filtering.

Potassium Carbonate (Eng). Used to reduce the acidity of wines that contain a high amount of tartaric acid.

Potassium Ferrocyanide (Eng). $K_4Fe(CN)_{6.3}H_2O$. Called Blue finings. Used to clear an excess of metallic salts from the wine. If these salts were left they would tend to oxidise with the air, leaving the wine cloudy and bitter. Must be used with caution.

Potassium Hydrogen Tartrate (Eng). Forms tartrate crystals which show when the wine is chilled to low temperatures. Are harmless and can be decanted off or will disappear when the wine is warmed.

Potassium Metabisulphide (Eng). $K_3S_2O_5$. Also known as Campden Tablets. Is added to the grape must or wine to inhibit the growth of micro organisms.

Pot à Thée (Ch.Isles). Teapot.

Potatio (Lat). A drinking bout.

Potation (Eng). The fifteenth- and sixteenth-century term for the drinking of alcoholic beverages.

Potatory (Eng). An old fifteenth-century word to denote a person who has succumbed to alcoholic drink.

Potàvel (Port). Drinkable.

Potàvel Água (Port). Drinking water.

Pot Boy (Austr). Barman. See also Potman.

Pot de Vin (Fr). See Vin du Marché.

Poteen (Ire). An illegal spirit made from either grain or potatoes. See Potscheen.

Potell (Eng). The old Mediaeval spelling of bottle.

Potensac (Fr). A commune in the Bas-Médoc, north-western Bordeaux. Has A.C. Médoc status.

Potential Alcohol (Eng). The amount of

alcohol that could be produced by fermentation from a certain amount of sugar.

Poterium (Lat). Goblet. See also Culullus.

Potferré (Fr). Armagnac producer. Address = Domaine de Jouanda de Jean du Haut, 40190 Arthez d'Armagnac, Villeneuve de Marsan. 38 ha. in the Bas Armagnac.

Pot Gascon (Fr). The traditional bottle used for Armagnac. Also called a Basquaise.

Potheen (Ire). See Poteen.

Potio (Lat). Drink.

Potion (Eng). Old word for a drink. e.g. 'Take a potion with me'. Usually spirits.

Potion (Eng). A drink made from a mixture of drinks, herbs and flavourings that was used as a medicine or élixer in the Middle Ages.

Potitare (Lat). To drink more.

Potitianum (Lat). A red wine produced in Sicily in Roman times.

Potman (Austr) (Eng). Barman. See also Pot Boy.

Potor (Lat). A drinker (of alcohol).

Potosi (Mex). The name given to a range of Rums (Anejo, Blanco and Oro) produced by Destileria Huasteca.

Potrix (Lat). A female drinker.

Potscheen (USA). A legal version of the illegal Irish whiskey (Poteen).

Pot Still (Scot). A copper still used for the distillation of Malt whisky. Also used in Ireland. See Cognac, Rum and Bergstrom. Also Alambic Armagnaçais, Alambic Charentais and Proquero.

Pott (Ger). A large Rum distiller based at Rinteln. Produces Rum under the Pott label.

Pöttelsdorf (Aus). A wine-producing area in the Mattersburg district.

Potter Distillery (Can). A distillery based in British Columbia. Produces Canadian whiskies.

Potter Drainer (USA). Equipment that drains the must through fine screens inside a tank, resulting in free-run juice.

Pottle (Eng). A fourteenth century wine measure of half a gallon capacity.

Pottsville Porter (USA). Yuengling of Pennsylvania's dark 'roasted beer' 5% alc. by vol.

Potulentus (Lat). Drinkable.

Potus (Lat). A drink. (Potare = to drink). Also denotes a drunken person. See also Vinolentus.

Pouançay (Fr). A commune in the Vienne Département. Has A.C. Saumur status.

Pougeoise (Charles) (Fr). Récoltants-manipulants in Champagne. Address =

P

21–23 Boulevard Paul Goerg, 51130 Vertus. Produces – Vintage and non-vintage wines.

Pouillon (Fr). A Cru Champagne village in the Canton de Bourgogne. District = Reims.

Pouilly Blanc Fumé (Fr). An A.C. dry white wine from the Central Vineyards of the Loire. Made with Sauvignon blanc.

Pouilly Fuissé (Fr). An A.C. dry white wine from the Mâconnais in the southern Burgundy. Made from the Chardonnay grape. Minimum alc. by vol. 11%.

Pouilly Fumé (Fr). An A.C. dry white wine from the Central Vineyards of the Loire. Made from the Sauvignon blanc grape.

Pouilly-Loché (Fr). An A.C. dry white wine from the Mâconnais in the southern Burgundy. Made from the Chardonnay grape from around the town of Loché.

Pouilly-sur-Loire (Fr). A commune in the Central Vineyards of the Loire. Produces a wine of the same name from the Chasselas grape.

Pouilly-Vinzelles (Fr). An A.C. white wine from the Mâconnais in the southern Burgundy. Made from the Chardonnay grape from around the town of Vinzelles.

Poulet Père et Fils (Fr). A Burgundy négociant based at 12 Rue Chaumergy, 21200 Beaune. Are old négociants. Noted for their heavy-styled wines.

Poulet Poulet (N.Z.). A sparkling wine produced by Montana Wines.

Poulettes (Les) (Fr). A Premier Cru vineyard in the A.C. commune of Nuits-Saint-Georges, Côte de Nuits, Burgundy. 2.4 ha.

Poulsard (Fr). A black grape variety grown in the Jura. Used to make the local Vin Gris of same name. A variety of the Pinot.

Poulsart (Fr). A white grape variety grown in the Jura.

Poulsen and Co's Distillation (Nor). A producer of Aquavits under the control of A/S Vinmonopolet.

Pourcy (Fr). A Cru Champagne village in the Canton de Châtillon-sur-Marne. District = Reims.

Pourridié (Lat). A family of fungi that attacks the vine roots. See Armillaria Root-Rot.

Pourriture Aigre (Fr). Bitter Rot. Occurs in sweet white wine-producing areas.

Pourriture Gris (Fr). Grey rot. Is botrytis cinerea (pourriture noble) in red wine areas. Attacks the skin colour and bouquet (aroma) of grapes and wines.

Pourriture Noble (Fr). Noble Rot. Botrytis Cinerea.

Pourriture Vulgaire (Fr). Describes both Aspergillus and Penicillium mould. Similar to Pourriture Aigre (bitter rot)

that occurs in sweet white wine-producing areas.

Pousada (Port). An inn, hotel.

Pousse (Fr). A malady of wine caused by a bacteria which attacks the tartaric acid in wine causing a brown deposit to appear. Treated with tartaric acid and bisulphates.

Pousse Café (Cktl). This is a cocktail made up of layers of different coloured liquids and of different densities which are gently floated on top of each other with the aid of a barspoon. Known in the USA as a floated liqueur.

Pousse Café (Pousse Café) (1). Place in layers as above in the following order. ⅙ each of Grenadine, Yellow Chartreuse, Crème Yvette, (white) Crème de Menthe, Green Chartreuse and Cognac.

Pousse Café (Pousse Café) (2). Place in layers as above in the following order. ⅙ each of Grenadine, (brown) Crème de Cacao, Maraschino, orange Curaçao, (green) Crème de Menthe, Parfait Amour, Liqueur Cognac.

Pousse Café American (Pousse Café). Place in order in a Pousse café glass. 1 teaspoon Raspberry syrup, ⅙ glass Maraschino, Crème Vanille, Curaçao, Yellow Chartreuse and liqueur Brandy. Also known as the Rainbow.

Pousse Café 81 (Pousse Café). Equal quantities of the following poured gently on top of each other in the following order. Grenadine, Crème de Menthe, Galliano, Kümmel and Brandy.

Pousse Café Glass (Fr). A thin narrow glass specially designed for Pousse cafés. ⅜ gill in capacity. Similar in style to an Elgin.

Pousse Café Parisien (Pousse Café). Place into a Pousse café glass gently in the following order ⅕ glass Sirop de Framboise, Marasquin de Zara, red Curaçao, Yellow Chartreuse and Champagne.

Pousse l'Amour (Pousse Café) (1). Into a Pousse café glass pour in order 3–4 dashes Grenadine, yolk of an egg, ⅙ gill Maraschino, ⅙ gill Champagne. Do not stir. Drink in one gulp.

Pousse l'Amour (Pousse Café) (2). Into a Pousse café glass pour in order ¼ measure Maraschino, egg yolk, Bénédictine and Cognac.

Pousse Rapière (Cktl). 1 oz. Armagnac topped up with Vin Sauvage. Serve chilled. Originates from the Pyrénées.

Poutures (Les) (Fr). A Premier Cru vineyard in the A.C. commune of Pommard, Côte de Beaune, Burgundy. 4.2 ha.

Poverella (Bra). A red grape variety.

Poverty Bay (N.Z.). A wine area of the central eastern part of the North Island.

Powdery Mildew (Eng). Oidium Tuckerii.

Powell (Wales). A beer, wines and spirits wholesaler based in Newtown, Powys, Mid-Wales. Operates under the name of Eagle Brewery. Took over the Powys Brewery in Newtown in 1983. Brews Samuel Powell's Traditional Bitter 1040 O.G.

Power Drury Lda (Mad). A shipping company formed in 1888. Is now part of the Madeira Wine Association (since 1925).

Powerful (Eng). Describes a red wine that has a forceful bouquet and flavour.

Powerhouse (Eng). A strong cask conditioned Bitter 1050 O.G. brewed by the Battersea Brewery in London.

Power's Distillery (Ire). A noted distiller based in Dublin. Produces Power's Gold Label. (Part of the Irish Distillers Group).

Powers Gold Label (Ire). A leading brand of Irish whiskey. A blend of Power's Pot-still whiskey and Grain whiskey.

Power's Special Dry (Ire). A brand of dry Gin distilled by the Power's Distillery in Dublin.

Poysdorf (Aus). A wine area in the Weinviertel. Produces red and white wines.

Pradel (Fr). A V.D.Q.S. wine from the Côtes de Provence.

Prädikatssekt (Ger). A grade of Sekt which must contain at least 60% of German wine.

Prädikatssekt mit Geographischer Bezeichung (Ger). The top appellation of Sekt. Only a limited amount made. e.g. Kupferberg Herringer.

Prädikatswein (Aus). Also known as Qualitätswein Besonderer Reife und Leseart.

Prädikatswein (Ger). Quality wine.

Prädikatsweinversteigerer (Ger). The name given to growers who sell their natural wine by auction. Formerly known as Naturweinversteigerer.

Prado (El) (Sp). A Sherry producer based in Jerez.

Prado Cocktail (Cktl). ⅔ measure Tequila silver, ⅓ measure lemon juice, ½ fl.oz. Maraschino, 3 dashes Grenadine, ½ egg white. Shake over ice, strain into a sour glass. Top with a slice of lemon and a cherry.

Prado Enea (Sp). A red wine produced by the Bodegas Muga S.A., Rioja. Made from 20–30% Garnacha, 10% Mazuelo and 60% Tempranillo. Matured for 1 year in oak vats of 18,000 litres and for 4 years in Barricas, then aged 2 years minimum in bottle.

Praenestinum (Lat). A red wine produced in central-western Italy in Roman times.

Praetutium (Lat). A white wine produced in north-eastern Italy in Roman times.

Prager Winery and Port Works (USA). A winery based near St. Helena, Napa Valley, California. Grape varieties – Cabernet sauvignon and Chardonnay. Produces varietal and dessert wines.

Prairie Chicken (Cktl). ⅙ gill dry Gin, 1 egg, pepper and salt. Place the egg in a wine glass (yolk unbroken) add Gin, pepper and salt.

Prairie Oyster (Cktl).(Non-alc). Equal measures of Worcestershire sauce, vinegar and tomato sauce (ketchup). Mix well together, add yolk of egg (unbroken) and red pepper. Do not stir. Also known as a Mountain Oyster.

Prairie Oyster Cocktail (Cktl). As for Prairie Oyster with the addition of ⅕ gill Brandy added. Top with cayenne pepper.

Prälat (Ger). Vineyard. (Anb) = Mosel-Saar-Ruwer. (Ber) = Bernkastel. (Gro) = Schwarzlay. (Vil) = Erden.

Pramnian Wine (Gre). A sweet, dessert wine produced in ancient Greece in Homer's time.

Prandell (It). A producer of sparkling (méthode champenoise) wines based in Lombardy.

Prås (Les) (Fr). A wine-producing village in the commune of Solutré-Pouilly in A.C. Pouilly/Fuissé, Mâcon, Burgundy.

Präsent (Ger). Vineyard. (Anb) = Nahe. (Ber) = Schloss Böckelheim. (Gro) = Paradiesgarten. (Vil) = Meddersheim.

Präsident (Ger). The brand-name for a Rum produced by Hansen in Flensburg.

Prayssac (Fr). A wine-producing area in northern Cahors, south-western France. (Red wines).

Pražanka (Czec). A dark, draught Beer brewed by the Holesovice Brewery in Prague.

Preakness Cocktail (Cktl). ⅔ measure Bourbon whiskey, ⅓ measure Italian vermouth, dash Angostura, 2 dashes Bénédictine. Stir over ice, strain into a cocktail glass. Top with a twist of lemon peel juice.

Preanger (E.Ind). A noted coffee-producing area in Java.

Préau (Fr). A vineyard in the A.C. commune of Rully, Côte Chalonnaise, Burgundy.

Prèchet (Fr). An alternative name for the Malbec grape.

Precipitated Chalk (USA). Used to cut down the acidity in grape must.

Precipitation (Eng). The action of tartrates forming crystals through exposure of the wine to low temperatures. Encouraged in some wines especially in Germany before the wine is bottled to remove excess acidity.

Précoce (Fr). A wine which has come forward too early. A precocious wine.

Précoce de Malingre (Fr). A lesser white grape variety.

Predigtstuhl (Ger). Vineyard. (Anb) = Franken. (Ber) = Mainviereck. (Gro) = Not yet assigned. (Vil) = Dorfprozelten.

Preferido (Sp). A red wine produced by the Bodegas Berberana S.A., Rioja. Produced from 80% minimum Tempranillo and has no ageing.

Préhy (Fr). A commune in the A.C. Chablis, northern Burgundy.

Preignac (Fr). A commune within the Sauternes district in south-western Bordeaux.

Preiselbeerlikoer (Ger). A cranberry liqueur.

Preiss Henny (Fr). An Alsace producer. Address = 68630 Mittelwhir. 33 ha.

Preiss Zimmer (Fr). A wine merchant based in Riquewihr, Alsace.

Prelude Cocktail (Cktl). ½ measure Noilly Prat, ¼ measure Peach Liqueur, ¼ measure peach juice, 2 dashes dry Gin, dash Crème de Framboise, ½ teaspoon clear honey. Shake well over ice, strain into a cocktail glass. Dress with a slice of peach and mint sprig.

Prelum (Lat). Wine press.

Prémeaux (Fr). A wine village within the A.C. commune of Nuits-Saint-Georges, Côte de Nuits. Its' vineyards are all classed Premier Cru (10 in all) – Aux Perdrix, Clos de la Maréchale, Clos des Argillières, Clos des Arlots, Clos des Corvées, Clos des Forêts, Clos des Grandes-Vignes, Les Clos Saint-Marc, Les Corvées-Paget, Les Didiers. 40.3 ha.

Premiat (Rum). The brand-name of high-quality wines that are produced for export.

Première Chauffe (Fr). The first distillate of Cognac.

Premier Écoulage (Fr). The first racking when wine is taken off the skins, pips etc. (This residue is then used as Vin de Presse.)

Premières Côtes de Blaye (Fr). A.C. wine-producing region based in north-eastern Bordeaux. (Red, demi-sec, sweet and dry white wines).

Premières Côtes de Bordeaux (Fr). A commune on the eastern bank of the river Garonne. Commences from opposite the town of Bordeaux to the Sauternes. Produces sweet white wines.

Premières Côtes de Gaillac (Fr). The designation for wines from Gaillac that have attained 12% alc. by vol.

Première Taille (Fr). The second pressing

of the Champagne grapes.

Premier Grand Cru (S.Afr). The maker's top classification for white wines only. Not an official classification.

Premier Grand Cru Classé (Fr). The top classification of the wines of the Médoc from the 1855 classification. Châteaux Lafite, Latour, Margaux, Haut Brion and in 1973 Mouton Rothschild. Also Château d'YQuem in Sauternes.

Premiers Crus (Fr). The second classification in Burgundy. Next to the Grands Crus.

Premiers Grands Crus (Fr). A classification of Pomerol wines in Bordeaux.

Premio Uropeo Mercurio d'Oro (It). An award presented for beers. (First presented in 1970).

Premium Bitter (Eng). A cask conditioned Bitter 1039 O.G. brewed by the Gibbs Mew Brewery in Salisbury, Wiltshire.

Premium Bitter (Eng). A cask conditioned Bitter 1036 O.G. brewed by the Moorhouses Brewery of Burnley.

Premium Verum Lager (Ger). A classification for a fine Lager (no additives or chemicals).

Prensa (Sp). The third pressing of the grapes in Jerez. The wine produced from this is usually made into brandy or vinegar. The pressing is usually done by hydraulic press. See also Espirraque.

Prensa de Lagar (Port). Wine press.

Prensar (Port). To press, to squeeze.

Prepared Cocktails (USA). These are cocktails that can be made and kept without losing their flavour or crystallising. Only certain cocktails will stand up to this. Usually finished by adding ice and a sparkling liquid (tonic, soda, Champagne etc).

Prepečenica (Pol). See Slivovitz.

Pre-Prandials (Eng). Another name for apéritif.

Přerov Brewery (Czec). A noted brewery based in central Czec.

Près (Fr). Near. e.g. Près Reims. (near Reims).

Presbyterian (Cktl). Place 1 measure Rye whiskey, dash Angostura into a tumbler. Add ice and top up with ½ soda water, ½ ginger ale.

President (Switz). The brand-name of a beer used by Feldschlösschen and Haldengut.

President Brut (It). A sparkling (cuve close) wine produced by Riccadonna in the Piemonte region.

President Cocktail (Cktl). 1 measure pineapple juice, 1 measure Rum, dash Grenadine. Shake over ice, strain into a cocktail glass.

Presidente (Cktl).(1). 1½ ozs. Bacardi

White Label, 1½ ozs. red Vermouth. Stir over ice, strain into a cocktail glass. Serve with a twist of orange peel.

Presidente (Cktl).(2). 2 ozs. Bacardi Gold Label, 1 oz. dry Vermouth, dash Grenadine. Stir together over ice, strain into a cocktail glass. Add a twist of orange peel and cherry.

Presidente (Mex). The brand-name of a noted Mexican brandy.

President's Sparkling Wines (The) (Isr). The brand-name of a sparkling wine produced by the méthode champenoise by Carmel in Richon-le-Zion and Zichron-Zacob.

Presque Isle Wine Cellars (USA). A winery based near Erie County, north-eastern Pennsylvania. Produces hybrid and vinifera wines.

Pressac (Fr). An alternative name for the Malbec grape.

Pressac-Malbec (Fr). A red grape variety (strain of the Malbec) in the Saint-Émilion district of Bordeaux.

Pressburg (Czec). An old wine region in the Bratislava. Produces mainly light, pleasant white wines.

Press Cake (Eng). After the first pressing of the grapes. The skins, pips and stalks. Usually used to make Vin de Presse.

Pressoir (Fr). Press house.

Pressurage (Fr). The pressing of the marc to produce Vin de Presse.

Pressure (Eng). The pressure inside a Champagne bottle measured in atmospheres. 1 at. = 14.7 lbs per sq.inch. The pressure of a bottle of Champagne is approximately 5.5 ats.

Press Wine (Fr). The wine made from the Press cake which has water added, is re-pressed and fermented. Either drunk locally or distilled.

Prestige (Fr). A De Luxe vintage cuvée Champagne produced by Roland Fliniaux.

Prestige Brut (Fr). A non-vintage Champagne produced by Cheurlin et Fils from 25% Chardonnay and 75% Pinot noir.

Prestige du Médoc (Fr). Address = Gaillan en Médoc, 33340 Lesparre. A.C. Médoc. Commune = Gaillan. Grape varieties – Cabernet sauvignon 50% and Merlot 50%.

Presto Cocktail (Cktl). 1 measure Brandy, ⅓ measure Italian vermouth, juice ¼ lemon, 2 dashes Pernod. Shake over ice, strain into a cocktail glass.

Preston Wine Cellars (USA). A winery based in Yakima Valley, Washington. 80 ha. Grape varieties – Chardonnay and Fumé blanc. Produces varietal wines.

Preston Winery (USA). A small winery based at Dry Creek Valley, Sonoma County, California. 33 ha. Grape varieties – Sauvignon blanc and Zinfandel. Produces varietal wines.

Preta (Port). A Münchner-style dark beer brewed by S.C.C.

Preto Martinho (Port). A red grape variety grown in Ribatejo.

Preto Mortàgua (Port). A red grape variety grown in the Dão region. Used to make medium red wines.

Pretti (It). The baby Bacchus. e.g. The emblem on the Chianti Putto label.

Pretty Perrier (Cktl).(Non-alc). ⅓ measure raspberry syrup, juice ½ lemon. Shake well over ice, strain into an ice-filled highball glass. Top with iced Perrier water, a cherry and a lemon peel spiral.

Preuses (Les) (Fr). A Grand Cru vineyard of A.C. Chablis, Burgundy.

Preuve (Fr). A small clear glass vessel on the end of a chain which is lowered into Cognac barrels in order to test the liquor. Also called a Taupette.

Preuze (Fr). A Premier Cru vineyard in the A.C. commune of Chablis, Burgundy.

Prévot (S.Am). One of two Rum distilleries based in French Guyana.

Prevoteau (Patrice) (Fr). Champagne producer. Address = 15 Rue A. Maginot, Damery, 51200 Épernay. Récoltants-manipulants. Produces – Vintage and non-vintage wines. Vintages – 1971, 1973, 1975, 1976, 1979, 1982, 1983.

Priapus (Lat). The classical God of vineyards.

Price Coffees (Eng). The bulk of the coffee produced especially from Brazil that is used to make cheap blends.

Pricked (Eng). A term to denote excessive volatile acidity.

Pricked Wine (Eng). The same as Piqué. A wine which has started to turn to vinegar.

Prickle (Eng). The term given to describe the sensation on the tongue from wines which are pétillant, spritzig, etc.

Prieto Picudo (Sp). A black grape variety grown in the León region.

Prieur (Ch. and A.) (Fr). Champagne producer. Address = 2, Rue de Villers-aux-Bois, 51130 Vertus. A Grande Marque. Produces vintage and non-vintage wines.

Prieur de Meyney (Fr). The second wine of Château Meyney, Cru Grand Bourgeois Exceptionnel, A.C. Saint-Estèphe.

Prieuré de Saint-Amand (Le) (Fr). A wine-producing domaine in Corbières, Languedoc, southern France.

Prignac (Fr). A commune in the Bas-Médoc. Has A.C. Médoc status.

Prignac-Marcamps (Fr). A commune in the A.C. Côtes de Bourg, north-eastern Bordeaux.

Prikkelbaar (Hol). Pétillant, prickling.

P

Primary Fermentation (Eng). The main fermentation of all beers in the fermentation vessels.

Primavera (Cktl). 1 part dry Gin, 1 part orange juice. Shake well over ice, strain into a cocktail glass. Add a dash of orange cordial and a twist of orange peel juice.

Prime (Eng). See Priming.

Prime Jamaica Washed (W.Ind). One of three grades of coffee produced on the island of Jamaica. Has fine body and acidity.

Primerberg (Lux). A vineyard site in the village of Remich.

Primerberg (Lux). A vineyard site in the village of Stadtbredimus.

Primer vi Novell (Sp). A light, fruity, white wine produced by Mont-Marça in the Penedés region.

Primeur (Fr). A term used to denote an early wine usually of Beaujolais origin, that can be drunk young.

Primings (Eng). A sugar and yeast solution added to cask conditioned ales to encourage a secondary fermentation in the cask (or tank if brewery conditioned). Usually has some dry hops added. See Dry Hopping.

Primitivo (It). A red grape variety grown in the Puglia region to produce a red wine of same name.

Primitivo di Manduria (It). D.O.C. red wine from Puglia. Made from the Primitivo grape grown in the commune of Manduria and others in the province of Taranto. Grapes are slightly dried. 3 types made – Dolce naturale, Liquoroso dolce naturale and Liquoroso secco. Liquoroso must be aged for a minimum of 2 years from time of fortification.

Primo (USA). A Beer brewed in Hawaii by the Schlitz Brewing Co. in Honolulu.

Primor (Isr). A dry, red table wine of Burgundy style.

Primus (Afr). A Beer brand brewed in Zaire with the technical assistance of Heineken. Is also brewed in Rwanda and Burundi.

Prince A. de Bourbon Parme (Fr). A De Luxe vintage cuvée Champagne produced by Abel Lepitre from 87% Chardonnay and 13% Pinot noir grapes.

Prince Albert (Fr). An 1834 distilled Cognac produced by A.E. Dor in Jarnac. 30% alc. by vol.

Prince Albert Vineyard (Austr). Address = Waurn Ponds, Victoria 3221. 2 ha. Grape variety – Pinot noir.

Prince Beer (Fr). A Bière brewed by the Sedan Brasserie in Lorraine.

Prince Charles (Cktl). ⅓ measure Drambuie, ⅓ measure Cognac, ⅓ measure lemon juice. Shake over ice, strain into a cocktail glass.

Prince Charles Coffee (Liq.Coffee). Using a measure of Drambuie. See also Highland Coffee.

Prince Charles Edward's Liqueur (Scot). The old name for Drambuie.

Prince Cocktail (Cktl). ⅓ measure Gin, ⅓ measure Italian vermouth, ⅓ measure (white) Crème de Menthe. Shake over ice, strain into a cocktail glass.

Prince Consort (Eng). The brand-name given to a range of spirits from Landmark Cash & Carry.

Prince de Cognac (Fr). A Cognac produced by Otard in Cognac. 40% alc. by vol.

Prince Imperial (Fr). An 1875 distilled Cognac produced by A.E. Dor in Jarnac. 36% alc. by vol.

Prince of Wales (China). A blend of tea from the Anhei province. Exclusive to the Twinings company. Full-flavoured and light coloured, it is one of the best teas.

Prince of Wales (Wales). A 10 year old Welsh malt whisky with herbs produced by the Brecon Brewery in Powys.

Prince's Ale (Eng). A strong beer 1100 O.G. that was brewed and bottled by the St. Austell Brewery, Cornwall. Produced to celebrate Prince Charles' 21ˢᵗ birthday.

Prince's Punch (Cktl) (Non-alc). Boil a cinnamon stick, 6 cloves and a piece of ginger together with a little water and sugar syrup for 5 minutes. Cool, add juice of 1 lemon and 2 oranges. Shake over ice with sprigs of mint. Strain into a highball glass and decorate with mint and slices of fruit in season. Serve with a spoon.

Princess Cocktail (Cktl). ⅔ measure Gin, ⅔ measure Crème de Cacao, ⅔ measure cream. Shake over ice, strain into a cocktail glass.

Princess Dania (Cktl). ⅓ measure Mandarine Napoléon, ⅓ measure Vodka, ⅓ measure iced Champagne, dash lime juice. Shake spirits and juice together, strain into a Champagne flute, add Champagne.

Princess Mary Cocktail (Cktl). ⅙ gill dry Gin, ⅙ gill Crème de Cacao, ⅙ gill fresh cream. Shake well over ice, strain into a cocktail glass.

Prince's Smile (Cktl). ½ measure Gin, ¼ measure Calvados, ¼ measure Apricot brandy, 2 dashes lemon juice. Shake over ice, strain into a cocktail glass.

Princess Pippin (Eng). A vintage Cider produced by the Symonds Cider Co. in Hereford, Herefordshire.

P

Princess Pousse Café (Pousse Café). 1 measure of Apricot brandy with a measure of cream on top.

Princess Pride (Cktl). ⅓ gill Calvados, ⅙ gill Dubonnet, ⅙ gill Italian vermouth. Shake well over ice, strain into a cocktail glass.

Princeton (Cktl). ⅓ measure Port, ⅔ measure dry Gin, dash Orange bitters. Stir over ice, strain into a cocktail glass. Add a twist of lemon peel juice.

Princeton Cocktail (Cktl). ½ measure dry Gin, ½ measure dry Vermouth, juice ½ lime. Stir over ice, strain into a cocktail glass.

Principauté de Franc Pineau (Fr). A wine brotherhood based in Cognac.

Principauté d'Orange (Fr). A Département in the southern Rhône. Communes of Bollerie, Orange, Vaison-la-Romaine and Valréas. Produces red and rosé wines.

Principe (Sp). The brand-name of a Manzanilla sherry produced by Barbadillo in Sanlúcar de Barrameda. Is around 60 years old (Solera).

Principe di Venosa (It). A wine-producer based in Latium. Noted for red wines.

Priniac (Eng). The seventeenth-century spelling for Preignac.

Prinzbrau Brauerei (It). A brewery owned by the German Oetker group.

Prior (Bel). See Abt.

Prior (USA). A dark Beer brewed by the Prior Brewery based in Pennsylvania.

Priorato (Sp). A red wine from the banks of the river Ebro in the Catalonia region. Known in the USA as Tarragona Port. See Bombonas.

Priorato (Sp). A Denominación de Origen region of Catalonia south-eastern Spain just north of Tarragona.

Prior Brewery (USA). A noted brewery based in Pennsylvnia.

Priory Brewers (Eng). A brewery based in Newark-on-Trent, Nottinghamshire. Formed in 1980. Brews Ned Belcher's Bitter 1040 O.G. and Priory Pride Bitter 1035 O.G.

Priory Pride (Eng). A Bitter beer 1035 O.G. brewed by the Priory Brewers in Newark-on-Trent, Nottinghamshire.

Pripps Brewery (Swe). A famous Swedish Brewery that exports to the USA. Has eight plants at Arboga, Bromma, Gällivare, Grötebug, Mora, Sundsvall, Tingsyd and Torsby. Is Sweden's largest brewing company.

Prirodno (Yug). Natural.

Pris de Boisson (Fr). Under the influence of alcohol. Drunk, intoxicated.

Prise de Mousse (Fr). The second fermentation in the bottle in Champagne production.

Prissey (Fr). A commune which is part of the Côte de Nuits Villages. Is not allowed to use the commune's name as its A.C. About 12.5 ha. of vineyards.

Private Hotel (Austr). A hotel that does not have a licence to sell alcoholic liquor.

Private Reserve (Scot). A bottled Ale 1056 O.G. brewed by the Drybrough Brewery in Edinburgh.

Private Stock Winery (USA). A winery based in Boone, Iowa. Produces mainly French hybrid wines.

Privé (S.Afr). A dry white wine produced from a blend of Colombard and Steen grapes from the Weltevrede Estate in Robertson.

Privé de Bois (S.Afr). A wood-matured, dry white wine produced from a blend of Colombard and Steen grapes by the Weltevrede Estate in Robertson.

Privilège d'Alexandre Bisquit (Fr). The world's most expensive Cognac. Produced by Bisquit and marketed by Saccone and Speed.

Privilegio (Sp). A red or dry white wine produced by SOGE-VIÑAS in the Rioja Alavesa.

Privilegio del Rey Sancho (Sp). A red wine from the Bodegas Domecq, S.A., Rioja. Made from the Tempranillo grape.

Privnitá (Rum). Cellar.

Prix du Base (Fr). The basic or top price for grapes upon which the lower qualities are based.

Prix du Raisin (Fr). The name given to the list of graded prices which are to be paid for the varieties of grapes of a Champagne vintage.

Prize Brew (Eng). A keg light Mild ale 1032 O.G. brewed by the Truman Brewery in London.

Prize Idiot (Cktl). 1 fl.oz. Vodka, 1 fl.oz. Crème de Banane, dash Grenadine, 2 dashes lemon juice. Pour into an ice-filled highball glass. Stir in Sinalco. Decorate with a green cherry, lemon wedge. Serve with a spoon and straws.

Prize Medal (Eng). A bottled Ale 1035 O.G. brewed by the Bass Charrington Brewery in London.

Prize Old Ale (Eng). A naturally-conditioned bottled Ale 1095 O.G. brewed by the Gales Brewery in Horndean, Hampshire. Sold in a corked bottle, it will improve with age.

Probar (Sp). To taste wine. Wine tasting.

Probstberg (Ger). Grosslage. (Anb) = Mosel-Saar-Ruwer. (Ber) = Bernkastel. (Vils) = Fell, Kenn, Longuich, Mehring, Riol, Schweich.

P

Probstberg (Ger). Vineyard. (Anb) = Württemberg. (Ber) = Kocher-Jagst-Tauber. (Gro) = Tauberberg. (Vil) = Elpersheim.

Probstberg (Ger). Vineyard. (Anb) = Württemberg. (Ber) = Kocher-Jagst-Tauber. (Gro) = Tauberberg. (Vil) = Markelsheim.

Probsteiberg (Ger). Vineyard. (Anb) = Mittelrhein. (Ber) = Rheinburgengau. (Gro) = Not yet assigned. (Vil) = Hirzenach.

Probstey (Ger). Vineyard. (Anb) = Rheinhessen. (Ber) = Nierstein. (Gro) = Domherr. (Vil) = Saulheim.

Procanico (It). The local Tuscan name for the Trebbiano grape. Also used in Elba.

Procedente (Sp). Found on a bottle label. Lit – 'Originating from'.

Procès (Les) (Fr). A Premier Cru vineyard in the A.C. commune of Nuits-Saint-Georges, Côte de Nuits, Burgundy. 1.9 ha.

Procurator (Fr). A name in the Middle Ages for an Abbaye cellarer.

Prodromos (Cyp). A wine village in the north-west region of Marathassa in the Troodos mountains.

Producteur (Fr). Producer.

Producteurs de Blanquette de Limoux (Fr). A group of producers of over 80% of A.C. Blanquette de Limoux. Labels include Alderic, Fleur de Lys and Sieur de Limoux.

Producteurs Directs (Fr). A term used to describe hybrid vines (banned in French A.C. areas).

Productos de Uva Aguascalientes (Mex). A winery based in Aguascalientes.

Productos Vinícola (Mex). A winery based in the Guadalupe area in the Baja California district. Produces wines under the Terrasda and Domecq (a division of the noted Sherry house).

Produit de Queue (Fr). The tailings, the end of the distillation in Cognac which is put back to be re-distilled. Only the heart, the 'Brouillis' is retained.

Produit de Tête (Fr). The headings, the start of the distillation in Cognac which is drawn off before the 'Brouillis' is collected. See Produit de Queue also.

Produttori di Barbaresco (It). A growers' co-operative based in Barbaresco, Piemonte.

Progress Bitter (Eng). A cask conditioned Best Bitter 1042 O.G. brewed by the Pilgrim Brewery in Woldingham, Surrey.

Prohibition (USA). The complete government ban on alcoholic drink between the years 1919 and 1933.

Prohibitionist (USA). The name for a person who favoured and supported the Prohibition.

Proizvedeno u Viastitoj Vinariji Poljoprivredne Zadruge (Yug). Denotes on a wine label – Made in the Co-operative cellars of the place named.

Proizvedeno u Vinariji (Yug). Produced at.

Prokupac (Yug). A red grape variety grown in Macedonia and southern Serbia. Produces wine of the same name and Ružica (a rosé wine).

Prokupac (Yug). A red wine from the Serbia region. Made from various grape varieties. Popular in Yugoslavia. Is a fresh, fruity wine that needs to be drunk young.

Proline (Eng). An amino acid found in wines. Is formed by the yeasts.

Prolongeau (Fr). An alternative name for the Malbec grape.

Prolonged Fermentation (Eng). The addition of small quantities of sugar to fermenting wines to extend or prolong the fermentation to obtain a high alcohol level (especially in home-made 'fruit' wines).

Promiscua (It). A method of planting vines with other crops planted between them. Produces good wines but a poor yield.

Proof (Eng). The British system of measuring alcohol content. Proof spirit contains 57.1% alcohol. A liquid containing less is deemed to be 'under-proof'; if more then deemed 'over-proof'. Was tested in the Middle Ages with a pan and gunpowder. The more gunpowder that was needed then the less alcohol the spirit contained.

Proof Gallon (Eng). The term used to describe a gallon of spirit at 'Proof' strength.

Proof Spirit (Eng). 57.1% alc. by vol. (49.28% alc. by weight) at 15.6°C (60°F).

Proof Spirit (USA). 50% alc. by vol. at 15.6°C (60°F).

Proosje Van Schiedam (Hol). A Golden Korenjenever produced by Nolet.

Propional-Dehyde (Eng). An Aldehyde found in wine which contributes to the bouquet and flavour of the wine.

Propionic Acid (Eng). An acid found in minute quantities.

Propriétaire-Récoltant (Fr). An independent wine grower. An owner-manager.

Propyl Alcohol (Eng). C_3H_7OH. A higher alcohol. Part of the Fusel Oils.

Prosecco (It). A white grape variety. Produces bitterish dry wines in the Treviso and Veneto regions.

Prosecco di Conegliano-Valdobbiadene (It). D.O.C. white wine from Veneto. Made from the Prosecco grape and up to 10% of Verdiso grapes. If grown in the restricted area called Cartizze then entitled to the special specification Superiore di Cartizze. Both produced by natural re-fermentation – Frizzante and Spumante.

Prosecco di Valdobbiadene (It). See Prosecco di Conegliano-Valdobbiadene.

Prošek Dioklecian (Yug). A medium-sweet dessert wine from Dalmatia. Has a unique aroma of ripe grapes.

Prosit (Ger). Good health, cheers.

Prost (Ger). Cheers, good health.

Prostějov Brewery (Czec). A brewery based in central Czec.

Prostel (Ger). A type of low-alcohol Lager brewed by Burgenbrau Bamberg Worner.

Prost Lager (Eng). A canned Lager beer 1031 O.G. brewed by the Higsons Brewery in Liverpool, Lancashire.

Protein Casse (Eng). A wine malady. A haze or brownish deposit. Unstable proteins in the wine. Cured by fining with Bentonite.

Protivín Brewery (Czec). A brewery based in south-western Czec.

Proton Nº1 (Cktl). ⅓ measure Triple Sec, ⅓ measure Vodka, ⅓ measure Galliano. Shake over ice, strain into a cocktail glass.

Protos (Sp). A 5 year old red wine produced by the Cooperativa de Ribero del Duero in Peñafiel.

Prouilly (Fr). A Cru Champagne village in the Canton of Fismes. District = Reims.

Provadya (Bul). A wine-producing area noted for its white wines.

Provence (Fr). A wine region in south-eastern France. Produces red, rosé and white wines, both A.C. and V.D.Q.S. mainly from the Mourvèdre and Ugni blanc grapes. Areas are Bandol, Bellet, Cassis, Côtes de Provence and Palette.

Provence (La) (S.Afr). A noted wine-producing estate based in the Franschhoek district.

Provenza Vineyards (USA). A small vineyard based in Brookeville, Maryland. 6 ha. Produces hybrid wines.

Provifin Winery (Bra). A large winery based in Rio Grande do Sol. 70 ha. A joint venture of Moët-Hennessy, Cinzano and Montero Aranha. Sparkling wines are produced under the Moët et Chandon label.

Provignage (Fr). The term given to the layering of vines so that over the years the roots contain the earth in a tangled mass. Used on hillside vineyards. Prevents erosion.

Provinci (It). Provinces. Equivalent of English counties.

Provins (Switz). A wine co-operative based in the Valais Canton.

Provisie (Bel). A beer made by Liefmans Brasserie. Classed as a vintage beer. Matures in the bottle in 2 years but will keep for 20 years plus.

Provisie (Bel). A top-fermented Bière 6% alc. by vol. brewed by the Oudenaarde Brasserie.

Prudence Island (USA). A wine-producing island based in the centre of the Naragansett Bay, Rhode Island. Produces Vinifera wines.

Prugna (It). A plum-based liqueur made by the Carmelite friars in Gethsemane.

Prugnolo Gentile (It). A red grape variety grown in central Italy. A species of the Sangiovese used for Chianti.

Pruht (W.Ind). A Rum-based proprietary apéritif.

Pruïmpje Prik In (Hol). A plum-based liqueur produced by Van Zuylekom Distillery, Amsterdam.

Pruliers (Les) (Fr). A Premier Cru vineyard in the A.C. commune of Nuits-Saint-Georges, Côte de Nuits, Burgundy. 7 ha.

Prune (Fr). Plum brandy.

Prunelle (Fr). A plum-flavoured liqueur. Purple in colour. 40% alc. by vol.

Prunelle (Fr). A green-coloured liqueur produced from sloe kernels by Garnier.

Prunelle Fine de Burgogne (Fr). A plum brandy produced in the Burgundy region.

Prunelle Savage (Fr). An alcool blanc made from sloes.

Prunellia (Fr). A green-coloured liqueur produced from sloe kernels by Cusenier.

Prunotto (Alfredo) (It). A winery based in Cassiano, Piemonte.

Prunier (Fr). Cognac producer. Address = Maison Prunier S.A, 16102.

Pruning (Eng). The process of cutting back the growth of a plant to encourage new growth and to prevent excessive foliage production so allowing better fruit.

Prunt (Ger). The name given to the raised globules on the sides of a Roemer glass stem and on the bowl of the glass.

Prussian-shaped (Eng). A decanter shape c1780. Is tapered similarly to a barrel and has 3 neck rings to provide a safe grip.

Pruzilly (Fr). A commune in the Beaujolais region. Has A.C. Beaujolais-Villages or Beaujolais-Pruzilly status. Can also produce grapes for A.C. Mâconnais blanc.

P.S. (Asia) (abbr). Pekoe Souchong. A tea grade.

Pschitt (Fr). A fizzy fruit drink.

Pseudococcus (Lat). A yellow insect that attacks vines. Is difficult to destroy. Hibernates underneath the bark of the vine. See Pulgón.

Pshenichnaya (USSR). A clean, pure wheat-distilled Vodka. 40% alc. by vol.

P

Psou (USSR). A white grape variety grown in Georgia. Used to produce dessert wines.

P'tit Barri (Ch.Isles). Keg. See also Fuste.

Ptolemées (Egy). See Cru des Ptolemées.

Ptolemy (Egy). A noted white wine-producing vineyard based in eastern Egypt.

Ptuj (Yug). A district of Slovenija region. Produces fine white wines.

Pub (Austr). A licensed hotel.

Pub (Eng). Short for Public house.

Pubbing (Austr) (slang). A drinking bout. See also Pub Crawl (Eng).

Pub Crawl (Eng). The term for a heavy drinking bout going from one public house (or hotel bar) to another and having a drink in each.

Pub Eighty [80] (Eng). A new style of public house that caters for the younger generation of drinkers.

Publican (Eng). The person who runs a Public house. Holds the Licence. Also called a Licensee, Landlord or Host.

Public Bar (Eng). A room in an inn or hotel for selling drinks to the general public. i.e. non-residents.

Public House (Eng). A building designed for selling alcoholic and other cold beverages under strict licensing laws. See Pub.

Public House (USA). An inn, tavern or small hotel.

Publicker (USA). A Philadelphian straight Whiskey distiller.

Publicker's White Duck (USA). The brand-name of a white Whiskey produced by the Publicker Distillery in Philadelphia.

Púcaro (Port). Mug (drinking).

Pucelles (Les) (Fr). A Premier Cru vineyard in the A.C. commune of Puligny-Montrachet, Côte de Beaune, Burgundy 6.8 ha.

Pudding Stones (Fr). The stones of the Rhône area which store the heat given off by the sun during the day to give warmth to the grapes at night. Used in the southern Rhône to combat the Mistral wind.

Pudding Wines (Eng) (slang). A term used to describe sweet white wines (usually botrytised).

Pueblo Hills (Mex). A noted coffee-producing region.

Puente Viejo (Sp). The brand-name used by Bodegas García Carrión in Jumilla for a range of red, rosé and white wines.

Puerta Viesa Blanco (Sp). A white wine from the Bodegas Riojanas S.A., Rioja. Made from 100% Viura grapes and matured for 1 year in oak vats.

Puerto Apple (Cktl). ⅔ measure Applejack brandy, ⅓ measure white Rum, juice ¼

lime, 2 dashes Orgeat syrup. Shake well over ice, strain into an ice-filled old-fashioned glass. Top with a slice of lime.

Puerto Cabello (Fr). A Bordeaux-based liqueur-producing company.

Puerto de Santa Maria (Sp). The Sherry town which together with Jerez and Sanlúcar, make the triangle of towns in Andalusia which is the Sherry Supérieur area.

Puerto Real (Sp). An area in the Jerez Supérieur district.

Puerto Rican Coffee (W.Ind). A full-flavoured, low acidity, sweetish coffee. Produced in Puerto Rico.

Puerto Rican Don (W.Ind). A light Rum.

Puerto Rican Rum (W.Ind). A light-bodied Rum made by the Patent still. A white Rum. Bacardi is the best known brand.

Puerto Rico Distilleries (W.Ind). A white Rum distillery based on the island of Puerto Rico.

Puff (USA). A drink consisting of Brandy, fresh milk and Schweppes tonic water served in a highball with ice.

Puffin Bitter (Eng). A Bitter beer 1040 O.G. brewed by the home-brew public house on Lundy Island using malt extract.

Puget Sound (USA). A wine district in the region of Washington.

Puget-Ville (Fr). A noted wine-producing village based in the Côtes de Provence.

Puglia (It). The 'heel' of Italy's boot. A region that produces the most wine in Italy. Most is used for Vermouth production and blending with weaker wines of the EEC as table wine.

Pugnac (Fr). A commune in the A.C. Côtes de Bourg, north-eastern Bordeaux.

Puisieulx (Fr). A Grand Cru Champagne village in the Canton de Verzy. District = Reims.

Puissant (Fr). Denotes a robust, powerful wine.

Puisseguin-Saint-Émilion (Fr). An A.C. commune in the Saint-Émilion region of eastern Bordeaux.

Pujols (Fr). A commune in the A.C. Graves region of south-western Bordeaux.

Pukhliakovski (USSR). A white grape variety grown in the river Don area.

Pulchen (Ger). Vineyard. (Anb) = Mosel-Saar-Ruwer. (Ber) = Saar-Ruwer. (Gro) = Scharzberg. (Vil) = Filzen.

Pulcianella (It). A 50 centilitre straw covered flask. Much of the Orvieto wine is bottled in these.

Pulcinculo (It). A white grape variety grown in Tuscany. See also the Grechetto Bianco.

Pulgar (Sp). See Thumb.

Pulgón (Sp). A yellow-green, oval insect that emerges from the bark of the vine

P

roots in the spring. The eggs hatch out on the vine and eat the tender leaves and shoots. See Pseudococcus.

Pulham Vineyard (Eng). Address = Mill Lane, Pulham Market, Diss, Norfolk. 2.5 ha. Soil – loam over clay. Grape varieties – Auxerrois, Bacchus, Cortaillod, Ebling, Kerner, Müller-Thurgau, Optima and Pinot noir. Wine sold under the Magdalen label.

Puligny Montrachet (Fr). A.C. village and commune which has the Grand Cru vineyards of Bâtard-Montrachet [part], Bienvenues-Montrachet [part], Chevalier-Montrachet [part] and Montrachet [part] 14.4 ha. plus the Premier Cru vineyards of Clovaillon, Garenne, Hameau de Blagny, Le Cailleret, Le Champ-Canet, Le Refert, Les Chalumeaux, Les Combettes, Les Folatières, Les Pucelles, Sous le Puits. 63.9 ha. See Montrachet, Côte de Beaune, Burgundy and Chassagne-Montrachet.

Pulkau (Aus). A wine-producing district in Weinviertel. Noted for its light-styled wines.

Pulliat (Fr). A Frenchman who developed the chart used to show the stages of grape maturation.

Pulp (Eng). A grape compound. 80% of the whole grape.

Pulp (Eng). The name for the flesh of the coffee cherry between the skin and the parchment.

Pulpito (Sp). A mechanical wine press.

Pulque (Mex). A beery liquid made from the Agave cactus from which Tequila is distilled. See also Maguey Cactus.

Pulqueria (Mex). An old bar that sells Pulque.

Pulse (USA). The alternative name for the Fever thermometer.

Pulteney (Scot). See Old Pulteney.

Pulverbuck (Ger). Vineyard. (Anb) = Baden. (Ber) = Kaiserstuhl-Tuniberg. (Gro) = Vulkanfelsen. (Vil) = Oberbergen.

Pulverised Coffee (Eng). A very fine ground coffee used to make Greek and Turkish coffees.

Pumping Percolator (USA). The name used for the Percolator coffee-making system.

Punch (Cktl). See Paantsch. An alcoholic drink made up of a number of beverages. Originally five, now any number. Originated in India in the eighteenth century. Was originally rum-based.

Puncheon (Eng). 72 gallon cask.

Puncheon (Fr). Cask for holding Brandy. Size varies between 327–545 litres.

Puncheon (W.Ind). A 110 gallon cask used for holding Rum.

Punch Martiniquais (W.Ind). A Rum-based drink also containing cane-sugar syrup and sliced lemon peel.

Puncia (Fr). A wine-producing district in A.C. Bellet, Provence.

Pünderich (Ger). Village. (Anb) = Mosel-Saar-Ruwer. (Ber) = Bernkastel. (Gro) = Vom Heissen Stein. (Vins) = Goldlay, Marienburg, Nonnengarten, Rosenberg.

Pundy (Scot). A seventeenth-century term for second mash, low-gravity beer. Now describes the free allowance of beer given to the Brewery workers.

Pungent (Eng). A term used to describe a wine that is spicy, heavily scented and powerful.

Punjéno u (Yug). Bottled at.

Punsch (Swe). A rum-based drink served hot or cold.

Punt (Eng). The depression in the bottom of bottles. Used for stacking by placing the neck of one into the Punt of the other.

Punt e Mes (It). A delicious apéritif produced by Carpano of Turin. A bitter sweet Vermouth flavoured with quinine. Lit – 'Point and a half'. It is traditionally drunk with piece of chocolate. 17% alc. by vol.

Puntigam Bier (Aus). A Beer brewed by the Reininghaus Brauerei for export to the USA.

Puntigam Märzen (Aus). A Beer 5% alc. by vol. brewed by the Reininghaus Brauerei in Graz.

Punty-Mark (Eng). This is left when the blown bottle is broken off the Punty rod. The 'Kick' was introduced to ensure that the bottle stood even and steady. See Kick and Punty-Rod.

Punty-Rod (Eng). In early glass bottle-making, a metal rod for carrying gathered glass at the tip, which was attached to the bottom of the bottle to enable the mouth to be reheated for shaping. This left a Punty-mark or rough scar when the bottle was broken off.

Punzante (Sp). Describes a Sherry with a sharp bouquet.

Pupillin (Fr). A wine-producing village in the Jura. Produces a dry white wine of same name.

Pupistras (Sp). Special racks to hold sparkling wines. See Pupîtres.

Pupîtres (Fr). Special racks in which Champagne bottles are placed for turning by the remueurs before dégorgement. Lit – 'desks'. See also Crécelle and Riddling Frames.

Pur (Fr). Unblended, undiluted.

Pur (Fr). A term applied to Kirsch that is a

natural distillation. Has no additives apart from cherries.

Pure Coffee (Eng). Unblended coffee beans from one area of a coffee-producing country. Is also known as Original coffee.

Purée (Fr). Another name for Absinthe Swiss-style where Grenadine is used instead of syrup to sweeten it. Also known as Tomate.

Pure Lincoln County Corn Whiskey (USA). A 21 year old N°7 Whiskey produced by the Jack Daniel Distillery in Tennessee.

Pure Love (Cktl). ¾ fl.oz. Framboise, 1½ fl.ozs. Gin, ¾ fl.oz. lime juice. Shake over ice, strain into an ice-filled high-ball glass. Stir in ginger ale. Decorate with a slice of lime.

Pure Strain (Eng). The native grape. Not a hybrid.

Purification Fining (Eng). A term given to the use of a fining agent to remove taint, tannins or colour from wine.

Purificator (Eng). A white cloth used to wipe the Chalice after Communion has been taken.

Purisima (La) (Sp). A large co-operative based in Yecla in the Levante. Produces wines under the Viña Montana label.

Purisima (La) (USA). A small winery based south of San Francisco, San Mateo, California, Grape varieties – Cabernet sauvignon, Pinot noire and Zinfandel. Produces varietal wines.

Purity Law (Ger). 1615. See Rein-heitsgebot.

Pur Jus (Fr). Pure juice.

Purl (Eng). An old-fashioned English drink of Gin, hot ale and bitters.

Purple Abbot (The) (Fr). A famous ninth-century monk of Angers who had a song written about his drinking habits saying that his skin was dyed with wine and his flesh became incorruptible through so much drink.

Purple Delight Cocktail (Cktl). ¼ measure Gin, ½ measure Parfait Amour, ¼ measure lemon juice. Shake over ice, strain into a cocktail glass.

Purple Kiss (Cktl). 1 measure dry Gin, ½ measure Crème de Noyau, ½ measure lemon juice, dash Cherry brandy, dash egg white. Shake over ice, strain into a cocktail glass.

Purple Mask Cocktail (Cktl). ⅖ measure Vodka, ⅖ measure grape juice, ⅕ measure (white) Crème de Cacao. Shake over ice, strain into a cocktail glass.

Pusser's (Eng). Producers of British Navy Rum 40% alc. by vol. from the sale of which a donation goes to the Sailors fund.

Pussy Cat Cocktail (Cktl).(Non-alc). 2 fl.ozs. pineapple juice, 2 fl.ozs. orange juice, 1 fl.oz. grapefruit juice, 3 dashes Grenadine. Shake over crushed ice, pour into a cocktail glass. Top with a slice of orange and grapefruit.

Pussyfoot (Cktl).(1) (Non-alc). ⅓ measure lime juice, ⅓ measure orange juice, ⅓ measure lemon juice, dash Grenadine. Shake over ice, strain into a large cocktail glass.

Pussyfoot (Cktl).(2) (Non-alc). Juice of a lemon and an orange, ⅙ gill Apricot syrup, white of egg, sprig of mint. Shake well over ice, strain into a 5 oz. goblet.

Pussyfoot (Cktl).(3). 1½ fl.ozs. white Rum, 1 fl.oz. cream, 1 fl.oz. pineapple juice, 1 fl.oz. lime juice, 1 fl.oz. cherry juice. Blend in a blender with a scoop of crushed ice. Pour into a collins glass. Dress with a cherry and slice of orange.

Pussyfoot Cocktail (Cktl). 2 fl.ozs. lime juice, 2 fl.ozs. lemon juice, 2 fl.ozs. orange juice, 1 egg yolk, dash of Gre-nadine. Shake over ice, strain into a tulip glass. Dress with a cherry and slice of orange.

Putachieside (Scot). A De Luxe blended Scotch whisky 12 years old. Produced by William Cadenhead in Aberdeen. 43% alc. by vol.

Putachieside Liqueur Whisky (Scot). A Vatted malt whisky produced by Wil-liam Cadenhead in Aberdeen. 43% alc. by vol.

P'u T'ao (China). Grapes. (Is often written Pu-Tao).

P'u T'ao Chiu (China). Grape wine.

Putt (Hun). See Puttonyos.

Putto (It). Tuscan dialect for the infant Bacchus. Used on the Chianti Putto neck label.

Puttony (Hun). See Puttonyos.

Puttonyos (Hun). A bucket for gathering grapes in the Tokay region. Holds about 13.5 kilos. Also used to denote the sweet-ness and quality in Tokay Aszú wines. Each puttonyos of botrytis affected grapes used is indicated on the bottle label.

Puvermächer (Ger). Vineyard. (Anb) = Württemberg. (Ber) = Remstal-Stuttgart. (Gro) = Wartbühl. (Vil) = Stetten i. R.

Puy de Dôme (Fr). A Vins de Pays area in the Puy de Dôme Département, central France. Is part of the Jardin de la France. Produces red, rosé and dry white wines. (Part of the Côte d'Auvergne region).

Puysegur (Fr). Armagnac producer. Based at Château de Puysegur.

Puysegur (Marquis de) (Fr). An Armagnac distiller of Labastide d'Armagnac.

Puzzle Jug (Eng). A joke jug. A jug/mug

with many holes which tests the drinker as to which is the correct hole to drink out of and which holes to cover with the fingers.

P.V.P. (Eng) (abbr). Polyvinylpyrolidone.

P.X. (Sp) (abbr). Pedro Ximénez.

Pyment (Eng). A mead made from honey and grape juice. (Similar to Madeira).

PYNC (Sp) (abbr). Penedés y Nort Cataluña.

Pynikki Brewery (Fin). A small family brewery based in Tampere, western Finland. Brews Admiral (labelled with a series of mariners from Nelson to Alfred Von Tirpitz).

Pyrenees (Austr). A wine-producing area in Victoria where a winery of the same name is based.

Pyrénées (Fr). A large area in south-western France on the Spanish border. Made up of the Ariège, Basses-Pyrénées, Hautes Pyrénées and Pyrénées-Orientales. Produces red, rosé, white and fortified (VdN) wines.

Pyrénées Atlantiques (Fr). A Vins de Pays area in the Basses-Pyrénées Département, south-western France.

Pyrénées Orientales (Fr). A département of the Languedoc-Roussillon. Based in the low valleys of rivers Agly and Tech.

Pyridine (Eng). The violet dye added to Methanol to produce Methylated spirits.

Pyridoxin (Eng). A vitamin found in wine in minute traces.

Pyrolysis (Lat). The chemical decomposition of sucrose in the coffee bean which is released when the bean is subjected to excessive heat (roasting). Occurs at 240°C.

Pyromucic Aldehyde (Lat). An Aldehyde formed at the beginning of spirit distillation which gradually disappears as it matures in the cask.

Qahwah (Arab). Coffee.

Qarabas (Iran). The name for the large wine jars used in Persian times.

Qat (Arab). A drink prepared with berries from a bush of the same name which has narcotic properties. See also Kat, Khat.

Q.b.a. (Ger) (abbr). Qualitätswein bestimmter Anbaugebiet.

Q.C. British Sherry (Eng). A brand-name British Sherry made from imported concentrated grape must by Vine Products Ltd.

Q Four Cocktail (Cktl). ¼ measure Scotch Whisky, ¼ measure Chartreuse, ¼ measure Royal Mint Chocolate Liqueur, ¼ measure Cinzano bianco. Shake over ice, strain into a cocktail glass.

Q Marchia di Qualità (It). The quality seal found on the label of Sicilian wines that have passed strict analysis and tasting tests. Is above D.O.C.

Q Mark (It). See Q Marchia di Qualità.

Q.m.p. (Ger) (abbr). Qualitätswein mit prädikat.

Qt (Eng) (abbr). Quart.

Quady Winery (USA). A winery based in Madera, California. Grape variety – Zinfandel. Noted for its port-style wines.

Quaff (Eng). To drink in large gulps.

Quaffing (Eng). Drinking in large gulps. Everyday drinking without care.

Quaich (Scot). Gaelic 'Cuach' means cup. Of Highlands origin it is like a small bowl with up to 4 handles on the sides. Made of wood or metal.

Quai des Chatrons (Fr). Where the négociants have their headquarters in Bordeaux.

Quail Ridge Winery (USA). A winery based in the Napa Valley, California. Grape varieties – Cabernet sauvignon and Chardonnay. Produces varietal wines.

Quaker's Cocktail (Cktl). ½ measure white Rum, ½ measure Brandy, juice ¼ lemon, 2 dashes raspberry syrup. Shake over ice, strain into a cocktail glass.

Qualitätsprüfung (Ger). Quality examination.

Qualitäts-Schaumwein (Aus). A sparkling wine produced by having the second fermentation in tank (or bottle then disgorged in tank). Also known as Qualitätssekt. Uses Austrian grapes only.

Qualitätsschaumwein (Ger). A classification of Sekt. Above Schaumwein it must be of 10% alcohol, have secondary fermentation, remain to the yeast at least 21 days and mature for 9 months. Also referred to as Qualitätssekt.

Qualitäts-Sekt (Aus). See Qualitätsschaumwein.

Qualitätssekt (Ger). See Qualitätsschaumwein.

Qualitätswein (Aus). Quality wine. Subject to strict conditions such as grapes used, quality and a minimum must weight of 15° KMW.

Qualitätswein (Ger). Quality wine (quality controlled).

Qualitätswein Besonderer Reife und Leseart (Aus). Also known as Prädikatswein. Has 6 possible designations – Spätlese, Auslese, Eiswein, Beerenauslese, Ausbruch and Trokenbeerenauslese.

Qualitätswein Bestimmter Anbaugebiet (Ger). Qba. Quality wines from specific areas.

Qualitätswein Kabinett (Aus). As for Qualitätswein but can be chaptalised or enriched and have a minimum must weight of 17° KMW.

Qualitätswein mit Prädikat (Ger). Qmp. Quality wine with predicate (distinction). i.e. made under superior quality control or specially harvested and quality controlled. See Kabinett, Spätlese, Auslese, Eiswein, Beerenauslese and Trokenbeerenauslese. See also Oeschle.

Qualité Anglaise (Fr). A name given to Claret wine in the eighteenth and nineteenth centuries for Claret that had the qualities the English liked.

Qualité Recomposée Chaque Année (Fr). Quality re-assessed annually. Found on a label or advert.

Quality Wine Produced in a Specific Region (EEC). Q.W.P.S.R.

Quancard (Fr). A Burgundy shipper based in Beaune in the Côte de Beaune.

Quarles Harris (Port). Vintage Port shippers. Vintages – 1927, 1934, 1945, 1947, 1950, 1955, 1958, 1960, 1963, 1966, 1970, 1975, 1977, 1980, 1983.

Quart (Eng). 2 Pints, 40 fl.ozs. ¼ Gallon (1.136 Litres). 1.2009 US Quarts. (abbr) = Qt.

Quart (USA). 2 Pints. (0.946 Litres). 0.8326 UK. Quarts. (abbr) = Qt.

Quart (USA). Bottle size. 32 fl.ozs. ¼ U.S. Gallon.

Quartaut (Fr). A barrel holding about 56 litres.

Quart de Chaume (Fr). See Quarts de Chaume.

Quarter (Eng). A measure of barley 448 lbs. Each quarter yields about 336 lbs of malt or 80–100 lbs of malt extract for the brewer.

Quarter Bottle (USA). A wine bottle containing 6–6½ fl.ozs. ¼ of a standard wine bottle.

Quarter Cask (Port). 134 litres.

Quarter Cask (USA). In cases where the standard cask, pipe or butt is too large for a merchant, casks containing one fourth the original are used. Quarter casks vary in contents, depending on the wine region where they are used.

Quarter Deck (Cktl). ⅓ measure dry Sherry, ⅔ measure dark Rum, dash lime cordial. Stir over ice, strain into a cocktail glass.

Quartern (Eng). Also known as a Noggin or a gill. A measure of 5 fl.ozs. ¼ pint.

Quarter Pipe (Port). 134 litres.

Quarter Round (Eng). An old-style spirits bottle (Brandy) of quarter bottle size. Was discontinued in 1981 in favour of the flask (retangular) bottle.

Quarters (Port). Cask. 28 gallons. (Port).

Quarters (Scot). Cask. 28 gallons. (Whisky).

Quarters (Sp). Cask. 28 gallons. (Sherry).

Quartet (Eng). A mandarine orange liqueur. 30% alc. by vol.

Quartiers (Fr). Plots (small vineyards) in the Rhône.

Quartino (It). A quarter litre of wine.

Quarts-de-Chaume (Fr). An A.C. wine made from the Chenin blanc grapes that have been attacked by botrytis cinerea. A sweet white wine from the Coteaux du Layon in the Anjou-Saumur district in the Loire region.

Quasi-Raisins (Fr). See Millerandage. Grapes that don't ripen but appear like raisins, hard, small and green.

Quass (USSR). A Rye beer made from stale black bread. See also Kvass and Kvas.

Quassen (Ger). A seventeenth-century term to denote excessive drinking.

Quatourze (Fr). A.C. district of the Aude Département in the Midi. Is classed as part of the Coteaux du Languedoc. Produces mainly red and dry white wines. Minimum alc. by vol. of 11%.

Quatre Coteaux (Les) (Fr). A.C. Côtes du Roussillon. A red wine by Les Grands Vignobles.

Quatrième Cru (Fr). The fourth growth Cru Classé of the Médoc of the 1855 classification.

Quawah (Afr). The old Arabic word used for coffee. See also Kahweh and Kahwa.

Quebec Cocktail (Cktl). 1 measure Canadian whisky, ¼ measure French vermouth, 2 dashes Amer Picon, 2 dashes Maraschino. Shake over ice, strain into a cocktail glass. Dress with a cherry.

Queen Adelaide (Austr). The label used by the Woodleys Winery for their Claret.

Queen Anne (Scot). A blended Scotch Whisky from Hill Thompson and Co. Ltd. Edinburgh. Part of the Glenlivet Distillers Ltd.

Queen Bee (Cktl). ⅓ measure Vodka, ⅓ measure Tia Maria, ⅙ measure lime juice, ⅙ measure sweet Sherry. Shake over ice, strain into a cocktail glass.

Queen Charlotte Cocktail (Cktl). ⅔ measure red wine, ⅓ measure Grenadine. Stir over ice, strain into a highball glass. Top with iced lemonade.

Queene Court Wine (Eng). A medium dry wine made from the Müller-Thurgau grapes. Produced at the Ospringe vineyards near Faversham. Made by Shepherd Neame.

Queen Elizabeth (Cktl).(1). ¾ measure dry Gin, ¼ measure dry Vermouth, 2 dashes Bénédictine. Stir over ice, strain into a cocktail glass.

Queen Elizabeth (Cktl).(2). ½ measure Cognac, ½ measure sweet Vermouth, dash Grand Marnier. Shake over ice, strain into a cocktail glass. Top with a cherry.

Queen Isabella (Sp). A dry apéritif wine produced by the Bodegas Los Curros and bottled in Rueda.

Queen Mary (Ind). A blend of Darjeeling teas. Made from fine Broken Orange Pekoe by Twinings for Queen Mary of England.

Queen's Cocktail (Cktl). ⅙ gill dry Gin, ⅙ gill French vermouth, ⅙ gill Italian vermouth. Shake well over ice, strain into a cocktail glass. Decorate with a slice of orange and a piece of pineapple.

Queen Victoria (Eng). A home-brew public house in London. Noted for its cask conditioned Sidekick 1047 O.G. and County 1036 O.G.

Queijeira (Port). Dairy.

Queimada (Sp). A drink made by pouring Aguardiente into an earthenware bowl, adding lemon slices, coffee beans and maraschino cherries. The spirit is then set alight.

Quel (Sp). A Zona de Crianza in the Rioja Baja.

Quelltaler Springvale Vineyard (Austr). Address = Main Road (P.O. Box 10) Watervale, South Australia 5452. 265 ha. Grape varieties – Chenin blanc, Rhine riesling, Sauvignon blanc, Sémillon and Traminer riesling. Noted for its Granfiesta South African Sherry.

Quench (Eng). To satisfy. e.g. 'To quench one's thirst'.

Quercia (It). Oak.

Quercus (Lat). Oak.

Quercus Pendonculus Albus (Lat). Monlezun oak.

Quercus Suber (Lat). The name for the Cork oak. The bark is used for bottle corks. Found in Portugal and Spain.

Quercus Vineyard (USA). A vineyard based in Lake County, California. Grape variety – Cabernet sauvignon. Vinified at the Carey Winery.

Quercy (Fr). An alternative name for the Malbec grape.

Querétaro (Mex). A wine-producing district that contains the Juan del Rio area.

Quetsch (Fr). An alcool blanc made from Switzen plums. 43–45% alc. by vol.

Quetsch d'Alsace (Fr). A plum liqueur brandy made in Alsace.

Queue (Fr). A Burgundy cask holding 2 hogsheads.

Queue de Hareng (Fr). A vineyard in the commune of Brochon, Côte d'Or, Burgundy.

Queue de Renard (Fr). An alternative name for the Ugni blanc grape.

Queue Tendre (Fr). An alternative name for the Colombard grape. Also called the Queue verte.

Queue Verte (Fr). An alternative name for the Colombard grape. Also called the Queue tendre.

Queyrac (Fr). A commune in the Bas-Médoc, north-western Bordeaux. Has A.C. Médoc status.

Quick Brew (Eng). A famous tea blend produced by Lyons Tetley.

Quickie (Eng). A term which refers to an acoholic drink (usually a tot of spirit or ½ pint of beer). A quick drink drunk without any ceremony or conversation. Also called a Quick one.

Quick One (Eng). See Quickie.

Quiet Sunday (Cktl). 1 fl.oz. Vodka, ½ fl.oz. Amaretto, 4 fl.ozs. fresh orange juice, 3 dashes Grenadine. Shake over ice (all except Grenadine), strain into an ice-filled highball glass. Add Grenadine.

Quila (E.Ind). See Quilang.

Quilang (E.Ind). A spirit distilled from cane juice in the Philippines. Also known as Quila.

Quillardet (Charles) (Fr). A négociant-éleveur. Address = 18, Route de Dijon, 21220 Gevrey-Chambertin, Côte de Nuits, Burgundy.

Quina Gris (Sp). Lit – 'Grey quinine'. An ingredient used to produce Vinos quinados.

Quina Roja (Sp). Lit – 'Red quinine'. An ingredient used to produce Vinos quinados.

Quincié (Fr). A commune in the Beaujolais region. Has A.C. Beaujolais-Villages or Beaujolais-Quincié status.

Quincy (Fr). An A.C. wine area of the Central Vineyards district in the eastern Loire. Produces steely, dry, well-perfumed white wines from the Sauvignon blanc grape. Communes = Brinay and Quincy. Mimimum alc. by vol. 10.5%.

Quincy Vin Noble (Fr). An A.C. white dry wine from Quincy in the Central Vineyards district of the Loire.

Quindto's Port (Fr). The brand-name of a Port.

Quinine (Eng). Chemical $C_2OH_{24}N_2O_2$ obtained from the Chinchona bark. Used in the making of Vermouth, Quinquina and Indian Tonic Water.

Quinine Wine (Fr). See Quinquina.

Quinn's Cooler (USA). A Cooler produced from red wine and natural citrus fruit. 6% alc. by vol. Also a white wine and natural citrus flavour. 6% alc. by vol.

Quinquina (Fr). An apéritif wine. Has a flavour of Quinine and was given to the soldiers who were fighting in the tropics to stave off Malaria.

Quinquina Bourin (Fr). A proprietary apéritif with a quinine flavour.

Quinta (Port). A vineyard or estate. It includes the actual vineyards and buildings. Lit – 'Farm'. See Vinha Vinhedo.

Quinta Amarela (Port). A noted Port wine quinta based south of the Vale de Mendiz in the Alto Douro.

Quinta Boa Vista (Port). A noted vineyard owned by Offley Forester. Based northeast of Peso da Pegua in the Alto Douro. Wine often sold as a single Quinta vintage Port. Vintages – 1900, 1904,

1908, 1910, 1912, 1919, 1920, 1922, 1924, 1925, 1927, 1929, 1935, 1947, 1950, 1954, 1955, 1960, 1962, 1963, 1966, 1967, 1970, 1972, 1975, 1977, 1980, 1982, 1983.

Quinta Crown (Port). A fine old Tawny Port from Balls Brothers of London.

Quinta da Agua Alta (Port). A single quinta vintage Port from Churchill Graham Lda based near Ferrão. Grape varities – Tinta barroca, Tinta roriz and Touriga nacional.

Quinta da Aguieira (Port). A vineyard based in the northern Bairrada region. 14 ha. Produces Garrafeira wines.

Quinta da Alegria (Port). A Port wine vineyard based north-east of São João da Pesqueira in the Alto Douro.

Quinta da Avelada (Port). A vineyard based in Peñafiel. 24 ha. Grape varieties – Loureiro, Pedernã and Trajadura. Produces Avelada and Casal Garcia.

Quinta da Bacalhôa (Port). A vineyard based near Setúbal in the Estremadura. Is American-owned.

Quinta da Baleira (Port). A Port-producing vineyard based north-east of São João de Pesqueira in the Alto Douro.

Quinta da Boa Vista (Port). See Quinta Boa Vista.

Quinta da Cabana (Port). A Port wine vineyard based east of Peso da Regua in the Alto Douro.

Quinta da Cachucha (Port). A Port wine vineyard based north of the river Douro in the Alto Douro.

Quinta da Carvalheira (Port). A Port wine vineyard based south-east of Pinhão in the Alto Douro.

Quinta da Corte (Port). A vintage Port from Delaforce. Grape varieties are Malvasia preta, Rufete, Tinta amarela, Tinta cão, Tinta roriz, Touriga francesa and Touriga nacional. Vintages – 1978, 1980.

Quinta da Costa (Port). A Port wine vineyard based north of the Vale de Mendiz in the Alto Douro.

Quinta da Costa de Bo (Port). A Port wine vineyard based north of the river Douro in the Alto Douro.

Quinta da Ferrad (Port). A Port wine vineyard based north of the river Douro near Peso da Regua in the Alto Douro.

Quinta da Ferradosa (Port). A Port wine vineyard based east of São João da Pesqueira in the Alto Douro.

Quinta da Foz (Port). A Port wine vineyard based near Pinhão in the Alto Douro. Produces vintage Port, owned by Cal'em. Grape varieties are Barroca, Tinta amarela, Tinta francisca, Tinta roriz, Touriga francesa and Touriga nacional. Vintages – 1927, 1931, 1934, 1935, 1938, 1949, 1954, 1955, 1958, 1960, 1963, 1966, 1970, 1975, 1977, 1978, 1982.

Quinta da Foz de Temjlobos (Port). A Port wine vineyard based south of the river Douro in the Alto Douro.

Quinta d'Aguieira (Port). Noted wine-producers based in Agueda.

Quinta da Lagoa Alta (Port). A Port wine vineyard based north of the river Douro in the Alto Douro.

Quinta da Malvedos (Port). See Quinta dos Malvedos.

Quinta da Pacheca (Port). A Port wine vineyard based south of Peso da Regua in the Alto Douro.

Quinta da Passadoura (Port). A Port wine vineyard based north of the Vale de Mendiz in the Alto Douro.

Quinta da Pilarrela (Port). A Port wine vineyard based near Santa Marta de Penaguião in the Alto Douro.

Quinta da Poca (Port). A Port wine vineyard based north of the river Douro in the Alto Douro.

Quinta da Portela (Port). A Port wine vineyard based south of the river Douro near Peso da Regua in the Alto Douro.

Quinta da Portela (Port). A producer of Vinho Verde. Address = Carreira, Barcelos.

Quinta da Quintão (Port). A noted producer of Vinho Verde wine from Loureiro and Trajadura grapes. Address = S. Tome Negreios, 4780 Santa Tirso.

Quinta da Ribeira (Port). A Port wine vineyard based near Pinhão in the Alto Douro.

Quinta da Roeda (Port). A quinta that belongs to Crofts. Based south of the Vale de Mendiz in the Alto Douro. Produces fine Ports. Vintages – 1967, 1970, 1978, 1980.

Quinta da Sapa de B (Port). A Port wine vineyard based north of the river Douro in the Alto Douro.

Quinta das Baratas (Port). A Port wine vineyard based south of Pinhão in the Alto Douro.

Quinta das Bouças (Port). A vineyard based near Braga. Grape varieties – Loureiro and Trajadura.

Quinta das Carvalhas [Royal Oporto] (Port). A Port wine vineyard based south of Pinhão in the Alto Douro. A single quinta Port. Vintages – 1952, 1954, 1958, 1960, 1962, 1963, 1967, 1970, 1977, 1978, 1980.

Quinta da Senhora da Ribeira (Port). A Port wine vineyard based east of São João de Pesqueira in the Alto Douro.

Quinta da Serra (Port). A Port wine vineyard based south-east of Pinhão in the Álto Douro.

Quinta das Lajes (Port). A Port wine vineyard based south-east of Pinhão in the Alto Douro.

Quinta das Manuelas (Port). A Port wine vineyard based north of the Vale de Mendiz in the Alto Douro.

Quinta da Sta Maria (Port). A single quinta estate that produces fine Vinho Verde wine.

Quinta da Teixeira (Port). A Port wine vineyard based east of Pinhão in the Alto Douro.

Quinta da Torre (Port). A Port wine vineyard based south-east of Peso da Regua in the Alto Douro.

Quinta da Vacaria (Port). A Port wine vineyard based east of Peso da Regua in the Álto Douro.

Quinta de Baguste (Port). A Port wine vineyard based south-east of Peso da Regua in the Alto Douro.

Quinta de Campanha (Port). A Port wine vineyard based north of Peso da Regua in the Álto Douro.

Quinta de Cavadinha (Port). A single quinta Port wine vineyard owned by Smith Woodhouse. Vintage – 1982.

Quinta de Cruzeiro (Port). A Port wine vineyard owned by Fonseca. 40 ha.

Quinta de Cruzeiro (Port). A single vineyard estate that produces fine Vinho Verde wines.

Quinta de Curvos (Port). A brand of Vinho Verde (is domaine bottled by Espasende).

Quinta de Eira Velha (Port). A single quinta vineyard based near Pinhão. The wine is produced by foot-treading in a lagar. Produced by Cockburn Smithies (was originally shipped as Tuke Holdsworth). Vintages – 1945, 1953, 1970, 1972, 1974, 1975, 1978.

Quinta de Nàpoles (Port). A Port wine vineyard based south of the river Douro in the Alto Douro.

Quinta de Pecheca (port). A vineyard estate based in Pemental in the Douro region. Produces red vintage wines.

Quinta de Romarigo (Port). A Port wine vineyard based south of Santa Marta de Penaguião in the Alto Douro.

Quinta de Santa Barbera (Port). A Port wine vineyard based south-east of Peso da Regua in the Alto Douro.

Quinta de São Claudio (Port). A famous Vinho Verde estate at Esposende in Braga, Vinho Verde. 4 ha. Grape variety – Loureiro.

Quinta de São Martinho (Port). A Port wine vineyard based north of São João de Pesqueira in the Alto Douro.

Quinta de S. Clàudio (Port). A fine Vinho Verde vineyard. Address = Curvos, 4740 Esposende. Grape variety – Loureiro.

Quinta de Seara (Port). A Vinho Verde producer based in Esposende. Brand-names include Montefaro.

Quinta de Terrafeita (Port). A Port wine vineyard based in the Pinhão Valley. 88 ha. Owned by Taylors.

Quinta de Tourais (Port). A Port wine vineyard based south of Peso da Regua in the Alto Douro.

Quinta de Vargellas (Port). A Port wine vineyard in the Alto Douro. 100 ha. Grape varieties are Tinto amarella, Tinta barroca, Tinto cão, Tinta roriz, Touriga francesa and Touriga nacional. Produces single vineyard vintage Ports. Owned by Taylors. Vintages – 1903, 1905, 1910, 1919, 1926, 1937, 1947, 1957, 1958, 1961, 1964, 1965, 1967, 1968, 1969, 1972, 1974, 1976, 1978.

Quinta de Ventozelo (Port). A Port wine vineyard based south-east of Pinhão in the Álto Douro.

Quinta de Vila Nova (Port). A single vineyard estate that produces Vinho Verde wines.

Quinta do Arnozelo (Port). A Port wine vineyard based east of the Vale de Figueira in the Alto Douro.

Quinta do Barão (Port). Vineyards owned by Raul Ferreira and Filho Lda, in Carcavelos.

Quinta do Barrilario (Port). A Port wine vineyard based south of the river Douro, near Peso da Regua in the Alto Douro.

Quinta do Bibio (Port). A Port wine vineyard based near Castedo in the Alto Douro.

Quinta do Bom Dia (Port). A Port wine vineyard based north of the river Douro in the Alto Douro.

Quinta do Bomfim (Port). A Port wine vineyard based south of the Vale de Mendiz in the Alto Douro. Belongs to Dow.

Quinta do Bom Retiro (Port). A Port wine vineyard based south of Pinhão in the Alto Douro. Owned by Ramos Pinto. Vintage – 1982.

Quinta do Bragão (Port). A Port wine vineyard based north of São Cristovão do Douro in the Alto Douro.

Quinta do Cachào (Port). A single quinta Port vineyard based at Ferradosa. Vintages – 1960, 1963, 1965, 1967, 1970, 1975, 1977, 1980.

Quinta do Canal (Port). A Port wine vineyard based near Peso da Regua in the Alto Douro.

Quinta do Carneiro (Port). A Port wine

vineyard based near Peso da Regua in the Alto Douro.

Quinta do Castelinho (Port). A Port wine vineyard based north of São João da Pesqueira in the Alto Douro.

Quinta do Castello Borges (Port). A Port wine vineyard based south of the river Douro in the Alto Douro.

Quinta do Cavalinho (Port). A single quinta Port produced by Warres.

Quinta do Charondo (Port). A Port wine vineyard based south-east of Pinhão in the Alto Douro.

Quinta do Cipreste (Port). A Port wine vineyard based east of Pinhão in the Alto Douro.

Quinta do Corval (Port). A vineyard based near Pinhão in Tràs-os-Montes. Produces light red wines.

Quinta do Cotto (Port). A single quinta vintage Port produced by Champali-maud at Cidadelhe near Régua. Vintage – 1982.

Quinta do Crasto (Port). A Port wine vineyard based north of the river Douro in the Alto Douro. Part of Ferreira.

Quinta do Crasto (Port). A Vinho Verde vineyard. Address = Travanca, 4690 Cinfães. Grape varieties – Avesso, Azal, Pedernã plus others.

Quinta do Cruzeiro (Port). A Vinho Verde vineyard. Address = Modelos, 4590 Paços de Ferreira. Grape varieties – Avesso, Loureiro and Trajadura.

Quinta do Dr. Christiano (Port). A Port wine vineyard based south-east of Pinhão in the Alto Douro.

Quinta do Eiravelha (Port). See Quinta da Eira Velha.

Quinta do Fojo (Port). A Port wine vineyard based north of the Vale de Mendiz in the Alto Douro.

Quinta do Garcia (Port). A Port wine vineyard based south-east of Peso da Regua in the Alto Douro.

Quinta do Junco (Port). A Port wine vineyard based south of São Cristovão do Douro (near Pinhão) in the Alto Douro. Grape varieties are Bastardo 5%, Donzelinho 10%, Mourisco tinto 5%, Tinta amarela 20%, Tinta barroca 20%, Tinta roriz 20%, Touriga francesa 5%. Produced by Borges.

Quinta do Lelo (Port). A Port wine vineyard based south-east of Pinhão in the Alto Douro.

Quinta do Loreiro (Port). A 'Vintage Port' of the nineteenth century bottled in 1971 by Cabral Port shippers. It is in fact a vintage 'Tawny' Port.

Quinta do Merouco (Port). A Port wine vineyard based south-east of the Vale de Mendiz in the Alto Douro.

Quinta do Miogo (Port). A Vinho Verde vineyard. Address = Campelos, 4800 Guimarães. Grape variety – Loureiro.

Quinta do Mourão (Port). A Port wine vineyard based near Peso da Regua in the Alto Douro.

Quinta do Noval (Port). A Port wine vineyard based south of the Vale de Mendiz in the Alto Douro. A single vintage Port shipper. Vintages – 1896, 1900, 1904, 1908, 1912, 1917, 1919, 1920, 1923, 1927, 1931, 1934, 1941, 1942, 1945, 1947, 1948, 1950, 1955, 1958, 1960, 1962, 1963, 1966, 1969, 1970, 1972, 1975, 1977, 1978, 1982.

Quinta do Outeiro de Baixo (Port). A Vinho Verde vineyard. Address = S. Goncalo, 4600 Amarante. Grape varieties – Azal, Espadeiro and Pedernã.

Quinta do Paço (Port). A single quinta estate that produces fine Vinho Verde wine.

Quinta do Panascal (Port). A Port wine vineyard based south of the river Douro in the Alto Douro. 80 ha.

Quinta do Pedrogão (Port). A Port wine vineyard based south-east of Pinhão in the Alto Douro.

Quinta do Pego (Port). A Port wine vineyard based south of the river Douro in the Alto Douro.

Quinta do Peso (Port). A Port wine vineyard based east of Peso da Pegua in the Alto Douro.

Quinta do Porto (Port). A 10 year old Tawny Port produced by A.A. Ferreira Port shippers.

Quinta do Roeda (Port). See Quinta da Roeda.

Quinta do Roriz (Port). A Port wine vineyard based east of Pinhão in the Alto Douro.

Quinta do Sagrado (Port). A Port wine vineyard based near Pinhão in the Alto Douro.

Quinta dos Canais (Port). A Port wine vineyard based east of São João da Pesqueira in the Alto Douro.

Quinta dos Currais (Port). A Port wine vineyard based east of Peso da Regua in the Alto Douro.

Quinta do Seixo (Port). A vintage Port single vineyard in the Rio Torto Valley. Owned by Ferreira.

Quinta dos Frades (Port). A Port wine vineyard based south of the river Douro near Peso da Regua in the Alto Douro.

Quinta do Sibio (Port). Vintage Port shipper. Owned by Real Vinícola. Vintages – 1945, 1947, 1950, 1955, 1960.

Quinta do Silval (Port). A Port wine vineyard based north of the Vale de Mendiz in the Alto Douro.

Quinta dos Lagares (Port). A Port wine vineyard based north of the Vale de Mendiz in the Alto Douro.

Quinta dos Malvedos (Port). A Port wine vineyard based near the river Tua in the Alto Douro. 128 ha. Grape varieties are Malvasia preta, Tinta barroca, Tinta roriz and Touriga nacional. Owned by Grahams. Vintages – 1954, 1957, 1958, 1961, 1962, 1964, 1965, 1968, 1982.

Quinta do Sol (Port). A Port wine vineyard based south of the river Douro in the Alto Douro.

Quinta do St. Antonio (Port). A Port wine vineyard owned by Taylors. 12 ha.

Quinta do Tamariz (Port). A noted Vinho Verde producer based at Barcelos. Run by the Soc. Agrícola da Quinta Santa Maria. Grape varieties – Loureiro and Trajadura.

Quinta do Tedo (Port). A Port wine vineyard based south of the river Douro in the Alto Douro.

Quinta do Val de Figueira (Port). A Port wine vineyard based near Pinhão in the Alto Douro.

Quinta do Vale de Dona Maria (Port). A single quinta Port wine vineyard owned by Smith Woodhouse.

Quinta do Vale de Sapos (Port). A Port wine vineyard based south of Peso da Regua in the Alto Douro.

Quinta do Vesúvio (Port). A Port wine vineyard based east of the Vale de Figueira in the Alto Douro.

Quinta do Zambujal (Port). A Port wine vineyard based near Peso da Regua in the Alto Douro.

Quinta do Zimbro (Port). A Port wine vineyard based near Ribalonga in the Alto Douro.

Quintal (Fr). Liquid measure of cask. 100 kgs.

Quintal (Sp). Liquid measure of cask. 100 lbs.

Quintale: (It). An expression used for grape yields per hectare. Quintals X Resa/100 = hl/ha.

Quinta Malvedos (Port). See Quinta dos Malvedos.

Quinta Milieu (Port). A Port wine vineyard based east of Pinhão in the Alto Douro.

Quinta Nova do Roncão (Port). A Port wine vineyard based south of the Vale de Mendiz in the Alto Douro.

Quintarelli (It). A noted Amarone wine-producer based in the north-east of Italy.

Quintas (Port). Vineyard and wineries.

Quinta St. Luiz (Port). A single quinta vintage Port produced by Kopke. Grape varieties are Tinta cão, Tinta roriz, Touriga francesa and Touriga nacional.

Quinta Velha (Port). A Port wine vineyard based east of Peso da Regua in the Alto Douro.

Quintessence (Fr). A 21 year old Cognac produced by L. Gourmel with a flavour and aroma of grapes.

Qui Sent le Bouchon (Fr). Corked.

Quizzling Glass (Eng). A seventeenth-century glass which is crazed to give a sparkle to the contents.

Quoique ce Soit (Fr). Lit – 'Whatever this may be'. The name given to a nineteenth-century French apéritif.

Quondyp Rhine Riesling (Austr). A fruity, aromatic wine from Château Barker in Western Australia.

Quosh (Eng). The brand-name of a whole fruit, non-alcoholic drink produced by Beecham.

Q.W.P.S.R. (EEC) (abbr). Quality Wine Produced in a Specific Region. The EEC classification for quality wines.

R

Rabaner (Ger). A white grape variety. A cross between the Riesling and a Riesling cross. Has a lower acidity than the Riesling.

Rabassa Morta System (Sp). An old system where vineyards were hired to the peasants by the marquis for a rent of part of the crop. Had a clause stating that if the vineyards were mis-run they could be reclaimed back. The system ended in the nineteenth century.

Rabat (Afr). A wine-producing area and capital of Morocco based on the west coast. Produces mainly red wines.

Rabat (José) (Chile). A noted wine exporter based in Santiago.

Rabat-Casablanca (Afr). A vineyard planted with imported vines in the Rabat area of Morocco.

Rabate Brandy (S.Afr). A Brandy produced in South Africa.

Rabat-Rharb (Afr). A wine-producing region on the western coast of Morocco.

Rabaud-Promis (Fr). See Château Rabaud-Promis.

Rabaud-Sigalas (Fr). See Château Rabaud-Sigalas.

Rabenkopf (Ger). Vineyard. (Anb) = Rheinhessen. (Ber) = Bingen. (Gro) = Kaiserpfalz. (Vil) = Ingelheim.

Rabenkopf (Ger). Vineyard. (Anb) = Rheinhessen. (Ber) = Bingen. (Gro) = Kaiserpfalz. (Vil) = Wackernheim.

Rabigato (Port). A white grape variety used in the production of white Port and Vinhos Verdes.

Rabinowka (USSR). A pink liqueur flavoured with rowanberries. Dry or sweet. Also produced in other eastern European countries.

Rablay-sur-Layon (Fr). A commune of the Coteaux du Layon in the Anjou-Saumur district of the Loire. Has its own A.C.

Rabo de Ovelho (Port). A white grape variety used in the making of white Port and Bairrada wines.

Rabosino (It). A dry white wine from the Piave Valley in Treviso. Has a Riesling character.

Raboso (It). D.O.C. red wine from the Treviso district of Veneto in the valley of the river Piave. A tough, tannic wine.

Raboso Piave (It). A red grape variety grown in the Veneto.

Raboso Piave (USA). A red grape variety grown in California. Used in the making of red table wines.

Raboso Veronese (It). A red grape variety grown in the Veneto.

Raboursay (Fr). A vineyard in the A.C. commune of Rully, Côte Chalonnaise, Burgundy.

Raca (Fr). The old word for the residue of grapes after they have been pressed in wine-making.

Racahout (Eng). A hot drink reconstituted with water. Produced from rice flour, cocoa, potato flour, sugar, vanilla, acorn flour and salep.

R.A.C. Cocktail (Cktl). ¼ gill Gin, ⅛ gill French vermouth, ⅛ gill Italian vermouth, dash Grenadine, dash Orange bitters. Stir well over ice, strain into a cocktail glass, add a cherry and a squeeze of orange peel juice on top.

Race (Fr). Breeding. A term to denote a wine of distinction.

Racemus (Lat). Bunch of grapes.

Rachis (Eng). The branch of the vine onto which the bunch of grapes is attached. (Fr) = Rafle.

Racimo (Sp). A bunch of grapes.

Racking (Eng). The changing of wine or beer from one cask to another, leaving the sediment (lees) behind in the old cask.

Raclet Festival (Fr). A festival celebrated in conjunction with the Beaujolais nouveau, Mâcon and Beaujolais celebrations in Burgundy.

Raclot (Fr). A vineyard in the A.C. commune of Rully, Côte Chalonnaise, Burgundy.

Racy (Eng). The term used to describe wines made from the Riesling grape that are lively, full of vitality, with a fresh acidity.

Radeberger-Pilsen (Ger). A Pilsener beer brewed at Radeberg near Dresden in Eastern Germany.

Radgona (Yug). A district within the

region of Slovenija. Famous for its sweet white wine Radgona Ranina, better known as Tiger Milk.

Radgona Ranina (Yug). See Tiger Milk.

Radgonska Ranina (Yug). The alternative spelling of Radgona Ranina.

Radis (It). A bitters apéritif made by the Stock Co.

Radkersburg (Aus). A wine-producing area in Klöch, southern Austria.

Radlermass (Ger). Lit – 'Cyclists' beer'. Ordinary beer and lemonade. A shandy (half and half).

Raeticum (Lat). A white wine produced in north-eastern Italy in Roman times.

Rafanelli Winery (USA). A winery based in Dry Creek Valley, Sonoma County, California. Grape varieties – Gamay and Zinfandel. Produces varietal wines.

Raffles Bar Sling (Cktl). 2 fl.ozs. Gin, 1 fl.oz. Cherry brandy, juice ½ lime, 2 dashes Angostura, 3 dashes Bénédictine. Put Brandy and Gin with the lime juice and bitters in an ice-filled highball glass. Stir in ginger beer. Top with the Bénédictine and decorate with the lime zest and some mint.

Rafle (Fr). See Rachis.

Rafle (Ger). A term used to denote a harsh, stemmy, green wine.

Rafsi (Afr). A white grape variety grown in North Africa.

Ragi (E.Ind). The name given to compressed balls of rice that are added to fermenting juice to give extra alcohol to the end spirit.

Ragnaud (Raymond) (Fr). Cognac producer. Address = Le Château Ambleville, 16300, Barbezieux. 50 ha. 50% in Grande Champagne and 50% in Petite Champagne. Produces Cognacs under the Château Ambleville label.

Ragnaud Sabourin (Fr). Cognac producer. Address = S.A. Ragnaud Sabourin Domaine de la Voute, Ambleville, 16300 Barbezieux. 50 ha in the Grande Champagne. Produces – Grande Champagne Fontvieille 35 year old, Grande Champagne Heritage Gaston Briand 1925, Heritage Gaston Briand la Paradis 90 year old, Heritage Mme Paul Ragnaud 1908.

Ragusa (It). A wine-producing area in Sicily.

Rail Ale (Eng). A cask conditioned Ale 1036 O.G. brewed by the Bruce home-brew public house the Phoenix and Firkin in London.

Railway (Eng). A Whitbread home-brew public house in Burgess Hill, Sussex. Noted for its cask conditioned Burgess Best 1036 O.G. Railway Special 1048 O.G. using malt extract.

Railway Cocktail (Eng). 1 measure dry Gin, 1 measure orange juice, dash Gomme syrup. Shake over ice, strain into an ice-filled highball glass. Top with Ashbourne water and an orange slice.

Railway Special (Eng). See Railway.

Raimat (Sp). A bodega based in Lérida. Produces a full range of wines. Grape varieties – Cabernet sauvignon, Chardonnay, Chenin blanc, Colombard, Garnacha, Macabeo, Merlot, Parellada and Tempranillo. Produces Cava and table wines. See Can Abadia, Can Casal, Can Clamor, Can Rius and Clos Casal.

Rain (Eng). Moisture falling as drops of water from clouds. Is free of any contamination except through air pollution or through pollution on contact with the earth. See Water, Mineral Water, Natural Spring Water.

Rainbow (Cktl). See Pousse Café Américan.

Rainbow Cocktail (Cktl). Place 1 fl.oz. Advocaat and 3 dashes orange juice into an ice-filled Paris goblet. Stir, carefully add ½ fl.oz. Cherry brandy, ½ fl.oz. blue Curaçao. Do not stir. Serve with straws.

Rainbow Cocktail (Pousse Café). Pour in order into a pousse café glass equal measures of Grenadine, Anisette, (green) Crème de Menthe, blue Curaçao, Parfait Amour, Goldwasser and Cognac.

Rainha Santa (Port). Vintage Port shippers based at Vila Nova de Gaia.

Rainier (USA). A Beer 7.25% alc. by vol. brewed in Seattle, Washington Also known as Green Death (has a green label).

Rainier Brewery (USA). A brewery based in Seattle, Washington. See Green Death.

Rainoldi (It). A fine producer of D.O.C. Valtellina and Sfursat wines in Lombardy. Noted for sparkling (méthode champenoise) wines.

Rainstorm Cocktail (Cktl). 1½ ozs. Beefeater Gin, ½ oz. Grand Marnier, 1½ ozs. pineapple juice, ½ oz. Jus de Citron, dash Grenadine. Shake well over ice, strain into an ice-filled highball glass, top up with soda water and decorate with half a pineapple slice and a cherry.

Rainwater (Eng). The accumulation of Rain.

Rainwater (Mad). The name given to blended Madeiras (Sercial and Verdelho) in the USA. So called because casks were stored outside like rainwater butts. First sold by a Mr. Habishan of Savannah in Georgia.

Raisin (Fr). Grape.

Raisin Blanc (S.Afr). A white grape variety cultivar used in the production of Vins de table (Vins ordinaires).

R

Raisin Bleu de Frankenthal (Fr). The name given to the red grape variety Trollinger.

Raisins Secs (Fr). Sun-dried grapes.

Rajika (Tur). The alternative spelling of Raki or Rakía.

Rajinski Rizling (Yug). The local name for the Rhine riesling grape grown in Ljutomer-Ormoz. See also Renski Riesling.

Raker Bitter (Eng). A keg Bitter 1030 O.G. brewed by the Wadworth Brewery in Devises, Wiltshire.

Raki (Tur). A spirit produced in the Balkans made from aniseed and liquorice. 34.5–40% alc. by vol. See also Lion's Milk and Arrack. Also spelt Rajika and Rakía.

Rakía (Tur). The alternative spelling of Raki or Rajika.

Rakija (Yug). The alternative name for Slivovitz in Bosnia and Serbia.

Rakovnik Brewery (Czec). An old established brewery based in north-western Czec. c1454.

Ralingen (Ger). Village. (Anb) = Mosel-Saar-Ruwer. (Ber) = Obermosel. (Gro) = Königsberg. (Vins) = Not yet chosen.

Rama (Port). A bamboo stick decorated with paper flowers which is presented to the lady of the Quinta at the end of the harvest to celebrate the vintage.

Rama Caida (Arg). A wine-producing area in southern Argentina.

Ramadas (Port). Tunnel trellises used to allow the growing grapes to be cooled by the winds.

Ramandolo (It). A sweet version of the wine Colli Orientali Fruili Verduzzo.

Ramato (It). The name given to white wine from the Pinot grigio grapes; its copper colour is due to a brief maceration on the skins.

Ramazzotti (It). A noted Brandy producer.

Rambooze (W.Ind). See Rumbooze.

Ram Cooler (Cktl). ⅓ gill white Rum, ⅛ gill Galliano, ⅔ gill lime juice. Shake over ice, strain into a cocktail glass, dress with a cherry and slice of lime.

Ramé (It). Pot-still.

Rameau (Fr). A commune in A.C. Chablis, Burgundy.

Rameau-Lamarosse (Fr). A cuvée in the Basses-Vergelesses vineyard in A.C. Pernand-Vergelesses, Côte de Beaune, Burgundy. Is owned by the Hospices de Beaune.

Ramillete (Sp). Bouquet.

Ramisco (Port). A red/black grape variety grown in 'The Ocean' Colares district of the Estremadura. Used to make red and white wines but getting rare because of the difficulties experienced in planting. See The Ocean.

Ramlösa (Swe). Scandinavia's leading natural mineral water. Carbonated and bottled at the Ramlösa Spa.

Rammersweier (Ger). Village. (Anb) = Baden. (Ber) = Ortenau. (Gro) = Fürsteneck. (Vin) = Kreuzberg.

Ramonet-Prudhon (Fr). Burgundy growers.

Ramos Fizz (Cktl). 2 measures Gin, 1 measure lemon juice, 3 dashes orange flower water, 1 egg white, 1 dash Gomme syrup, 1 dessertspoon cream. Shake over ice, strain into an ice-filled highball glass. Top with soda water, serve with straws and a muddler.

Ramos Pinto (Port). Vintage Port shippers. Vintages – 1924, 1927, 1945, 1955, 1963, 1970, 1975, 1982.

Ram Rod (Eng). A bottled Bitter beer 1046 O.G. brewed by the Young Brewery in Wandsworth, London.

Ramsthal (Ger). Village. (Anb) = Franken. (Ber) = Maindreieck. (Gro) = Burg. (Vin) = St. Klausen.

Ram Tam (Eng). A Winter ale 1043 O.G. brewed by the Timothy Taylor Brewery in Keighley, Yorkshire.

Ranchita Oaks Winery (USA). A winery based near Paso Robles, San Luis Obispo County, California. Grape varieties – Cabernet sauvignon, Petite syrah and Zinfandel. Produces varietal wines.

Rancho Alto Vista (USA). A vineyard based in Sonoma Valley, California. See Château St. Jean.

Rancho de Philo (USA). A small winery based in Cucamonga, California. Produces dessert wines.

Rancho dos Amigos (USA). A vineyard in Paso Robles, San Luis Obispo County, California. Produces grapes (Barbera bianca) for the Pedrizzetti Winery.

Rancho Sisquoc (USA). A winery based in Santa Barbara, California. 83 ha. Grape varieties – Cabernet sauvignon, Franken riesling and White riesling. Produces varietal wines.

Rancho Viejo (Mex). A wine-producing region in Baja California.

Rancio (Eng). A special flavour of some wines (especially fortified wines) acquired as they age in wood. Also Cognac which has a 'burnt' flavour.

Rancio (Sp). Rank or rancid. Usually denotes a dessert wine that has been kept for a long time in the bottle. Is deep-golden in colour with an aroma similar to Sherry. Now very rare.

Rancio (Tun). A noted wine-producing area. Produces fortified wines.

R

Randall Brewery (Ch.Isles). A family brewery based in St. Peter Port, Guernsey. Noted for its VB Bobby cask conditioned/keg beers. Bobby Ale 1036 O.G. Regal Lager 1045 O.G. Agents for Breda Lager. Not related to the Jersey Brewery.

Randall's Real Ale (Ch.Isles). A strong cask conditioned Bitter brewed by the Randalls Vautier Brewery in St. Helier, Jersey.

Randall's Reserve (Ch.Isles). The brand-name of a blended Scotch whisky 40% alc. by vol. from the Randall's Brewery, St. Peter Port, Guernsey.

Randalls Vautier (Ch.Isles). Based in St. Helier, Jersey. Brews Top Island Keg Bitter 1042 O.G. Randall's Real Ale and produces Grünhalle Lager which it also licenses to the Devenish and Greenall Whitley Breweries in England.

R and C Vintners (Eng). Producers of Wincarnis (a beef and malt-based tonic wine) based in Carrow, Norwich, Norfolk. 15% alc. by vol.

Randersacker (Ger). Village. (Anb) = Franken. (Ber) = Maindreieck. (Gro) = Ewig Leben. (Vins) = Marsberg, Pfülben, Sonnenstuhl, Teufelskeller.

Randersacker (Ger). Village. (Anb) = Franken. (Ber) = Maindreieck. (Gro) = Not yet assigned. (Vin) = Dabug.

Ranelagh (Eng). Eighteenth-century tea garden.

Ranina (Yug). A white grape variety grown in the Radogona district to produce Tiger's Milk. Also known as the Bouvier.

Ranina Radgona (Yug). A sweet white wine also known as Tiger's Milk.

Ranin Brewery (Fin). A small brewery based in Kuopio, central Finland. Noted for its alcohol-free beers.

Ranschbach (Ger). Village. (Anb) = Rheinpfalz. (Ber) = Südliche Weinstrasse. (Gro) = Königsgarten. (Vin) = Seligmacher.

Ranton (Fr). A commune in the A.C. Saumur district of the Anjou-Saumur, Loire. (Vienne Département).

Ranzau (N.Z.). A small vineyard based in Nelson, North Island. 1.5 ha. Grape varieties – Cabernet sauvignon, Gamay, Gewürztraminer, Müller-Thurgau and Rhine riesling. Produces varietal and table wines.

Ranzenberg (Ger). Vineyard. (Anb) = Württemberg. (Ber) = Württembergisch Unterland. (Gro) = Salzberg. (Vil) = Ellhofen.

Ranzenberg (Ger). Vineyard. (Anb) = Württemberg. (Ber) = Württembergisch Unterland. (Gro) = Salzberg. (Vil) = Weinsberg.

Rapazzini Winery (USA). A winery based in Gilroy, Santa Clara, California. Produces varietal, sparkling and dessert wines.

Rape (Eng). The name for the skins and stalks of grapes left after wine-making in the seventeenth century. (Fr) = Râpé.

Râpé (Fr). A name given to the Pomace which is fermented and used for vinegar. Also applied to the grapes removed during Triage in Châteauneuf-du-Pape that are used for the same purpose.

Rapet Père et Fils (Fr). A négociant-éleveur based in the Côte d'Or. Address = Pernand-Vergelesses, 21420, Savigny-lès-Beaune.

Rapid Ageing (Eng). The art of attempting to quickly bring wine to the peak of maturation in order for the wine-maker to have a faster turnover and less money tied up in wine stocks.

Rapid Fermentation (W.Ind). A method used in Rum production, takes a minimum of 12 hours to 1½ days. Produces light-styled Rums.

Rapier Lager (Eng). A Lager beer brewed in England and distributed by Linfood Cash and Carry, Northamptonshire.

Raposeira (Port). A sparkling wine produced by the méthode champenoise at Lamego, Beira Alta.

Rappe (Fr). A term used for the pulp left over after the first pressing of the grapes for Cognac. This is then pressed twice more and may be used for distillation.

Rappen (Ger). Vineyard. (Anb) = Württemberg. (Ber) = Württembergisch Unterland. (Gro) = Schozachtal. (Vil) = Ilsfeld.

Rappoltsweier (Fr). The German name for the town of Ribeauville in the Haut-Rhin, Alsace.

Rappu (Fr). A white VdN produced in Corsica from the Muscat grape.

Rapsani (Gre). A red wine produced in eastern Greece.

Rapsig (Ger). The term to denote a stalky-taste in wines where the must has a taste of grape pips, skins and stalks.

Rapsini (Gre). A dry red table wine made from the Xynomavro, Krassato and Stavroto grapes. Produced in northern Greece.

Raquet Club (Cktl). ⅔ measure Gin, ⅓ measure dry Vermouth, dash Campari. Stir over ice, strain into a cocktail glass.

Rara-Njagra (USSR). A red grape variety grown in Moldavia around the river Dnestr (lower reaches).

Rare (Fr). See Champagne Rare.

Rare Old Highland (Scot). A brand of blended Scotch whisky produced by Hiram Walker. 40% alc. by vol.

Rasiguères (Fr). A red wine from the Côtes du Roussillon-Villages.

R

Rasillo (Sp). A red wine produced by Faustino Rivero Ulecia, S.A., Rioja. Made from the Garnacha, Tempranillo and Viura grapes. Oak matured.

Raspail (Fr). A yellow liqueur made from herbs, invented by François Raspail in 1847.

Raspani (Gre). A red wine produced in Thessaly.

Raspberry Brandy (Euro). A fruit brandy made from raspberries in France, Germany and Switzerland.

Raspberry Cooler (Cktl). ¼ gill dry Gin, ¼ gill Raspberry syrup, ⅛ gill lime juice, 2 dashes Grenadine, ⅓ pint ginger ale. Stir well in a highball glass with an ice cube. Serve with a dash of Grenadine.

Raspberry Highball (Cktl). ½ gill Raspberry syrup, dash lemon juice, soda water. Stir in a highball glass with an ice cube.

Raspberry Leaf Tea (Eng). A herbal tea whose properties are as a settler of stomachs and labour smoother in pregnancy. Has a light astringency.

Raspberry Smash Cooler (Cktl).(Non-alc). ¼ gill Raspberry syrup, ¼ gill lemon juice, dash Angostura. Stir well over ice, strain into an ice-filled highball glass. Top with soda water. Serve with a few fresh raspberries.

Raspon (Sp). Vine stalk.

Rasputin's Revenge (Cktl). ½ measure Bols blue Curaçao, ½ measure Vodka. Stir over ice, strain into a cocktail glass.

Rassig (Ger). A wine with race and breeding.

Rasteau (Fr). A.C. district in the Côtes du Rhône. Noted for its Vin Doux Naturel made from the Grenache grape. Also produces red, rosé and white wines.

Rasteau Rancio (Fr). A special version of the Vin Doux Naturel which has obtained bottle age and has a Rancio taste.

Ratafee (Eng). The alternative spelling of Ratafia in the eighteenth century.

Ratafia (Fr). An apéritif wine made by adding brandy to grape juice, (see Muted Wine), produced in southern France. A sweet wine.

Ratafia (Pol). A fruit-flavoured Vodka produced by Polmos. 25% alc. by vol.

Ratafia de Bourgogne (Fr). A Ratafia made in the Burgundy region.

Ratafia de Champagne (Fr). A sweet apéritif that originates from Champagne. ⅔ grape juice (must) and ⅓ Brandy (Marc de Champagne).

Rathausberg (Ger). Vineyard. (Anb) = Mosel-Saar-Ruwer. (Ber) = Zell/Mosel. (Gro) = Rosenhang. (Vil) = Bruttig-Fankel.

Ratsch (Aus). A wine-producing town in Styria.

Ratsgrund (Ger). Vineyard. (Anb) = Nahe. (Ber) = Kreuznach. (Gro) = Pfarrgarten. (Vil) = Sommerloch.

Ratsherr (Ger). Vineyard. (Anb) = Franken. (Ber) = Maindreieck. (Gro) = Kirchberg. (Vil) = Volkach.

Ratskeller (Ger). A beer hall in a cellar/basement. The cellar is that of a town hall.

Ratskeller Edel-Pils (Ger). A bitter Pilsener Lager brewed by the Lindener-Gilde Brauerei in Hanover. Has a long lagering period. 5.5% alc. by vol.

Rattle Skull (Cktl). ½ measure Cognac, ½ measure Port wine. Stir over ice in a highball glass. Top with red wine.

Rattlesnake Cocktail (Cktl). 1½ measures Bourbon whiskey, 4 dashes lemon juice, 2 dashes Gomme, 1 dash Pastis, 1 egg white. Shake over ice, strain into a cocktail glass.

Rauchbiers (Ger). Smoked beer. Is made in much the same way as Malt whisky through the smoking of the barley (see Peat Reek) but using wood smoke. Produced in Bamburg, Bavaria.

Rauenberg (Ger). Village. (Anb) = Baden. (Ber) = Badische Bergstrasse/Kraichgau. (Gro) = Mannaberg. (Vin) = Burggraf.

Rauenthal (Ger). Village. (Anb) = Rheingau. (Ber) = Johannisberg. (Gro) = Steinmacher. (Vins) = Baiken, Gehrn, Langenstück, Nonnenberg, Rothenberg, Wülfen.

Rauh (Ger). Raw, harsh.

Rauhreif (Cktl). ⅖ measure Gin, ⅖ measure Curaçao, ⅕ measure Jamaican rum, 3 dashes Grenadine, 4 dashes lemon juice. Shake over ice, strain into a cocktail glass.

Raul (Ger). Vineyard. (Anb) = Mosel-Saar-Ruwer. (Ber) = Saar-Ruwer. (Gro) = Scharzberg. (Vil) = Oberemmel.

Rauli (Chile). A local wood used for wine and spirit casks.

Raumbach (Ger). Village. (Anb) = Nahe. (Ber) = Schloss Böckelheim. (Gro) = Paradiesgarten. (Vins) = Schlossberg, Schwalbennest.

Rauner and Sons Winery (USA). A small winery based in South Bend, Indiana. 1.25 ha. Produces hybrid wines.

Rausch (Ger). Drunkenness.

Rausch (Ger). Vineyard. (Anb) = Mosel-Saar-Ruwer. (Ber) = Saar-Ruwer. (Gro) = Scharzberg. (Vil) = Saarburg.

Rauschelay (Ger). Vineyard. (Anb) = Mittelrhein. (Ber) = Rheinburgengau. (Gro) = Herrenberg. (Vil) = Kaub.

Räuschling (Ger). A white grape variety. Also known as the Elbling, Kleinberger and Knipperlé.

Ravager (Fr). One of the nicknames for Phylloxera. See also Vastatrix.

Ravanello (Fr). A vanilla and coffee-flavoured liqueur produced by the Germain Co. in southern France.

Ravat (Fr). A famous hybridiser.

Ravel (Port). A Vinho Verde made at Farmalicão by Carvalho, Ribeiro and Ferreira in Ribatejo.

Ravello (It). A wine-producing area in Campania, southern Italy. Produces red, rosé and white wines.

Ravelsbach (Aus). A wine-producing district in the Weinviertel. Noted for its light-styled white wines.

Raven Brewery (Eng). Based in Brighton, Sussex. Reopened in 1983. Noted for its cask conditioned Old Master 1060 O.G.

Ravenhead (Eng). Famous glass producers based in Staines, Middlesex. Produce a fine, large range of beverage glassware.

Ravensburg (Ger). Grosslage. (Anb) = Franken. (Ber) = Mindreieck. (Vils) = Erlabrunn, Güntersleben, Retzbach, Thüngersheim, Veitshöchheim.

Ravenscroft (George) (Eng). A glassmaker who invented 'glass of lead' in 1675. Lead crystal glass.

Raventós (Don José) (Sp). The first Spaniard to produce Cava wines in Spain in 1872.

Ravenswood Winery (USA). A winery based in Sonoma County, California. Grape varieties – Cabernet sauvignon and Zinfandel. Produces varietal wines.

Raw Spirits (Eng). Undiluted spirits.

Raya (Sp). A system of classification of newly fermented wine for Sherry. A series of strokes (marks). 1 stroke denotes wines destined for Finos. See also Dos Rayas and Tres Rayas.

Raya Olorosa (Sp). A Sherry that has not quite made the grade of Oloroso.

Raya y Punto (Sp). A special mark on the side of a Sherry cask (one long stroke and one short stroke) that denotes that a new wine has not yet been finely classified. See Raya.

Rayment Brewery (Eng). Based in Furneaux Pelham, Hertfordshire. Is a subsidiary of the Greene King Brewery. Noted for its' cask conditioned BBA 1036 O.G. and Pelham Ale 1031 O.G.

Raymond Winery (USA). A vineyard and winery based near St. Helena, Napa Valley, California. 38 ha. Grape varieties – Cabernet sauvignon, Chardonnay, Chenin blanc, Sauvignon blanc and Zinfandel. Produces varietal wines.

Rcakzitelli (Bul). A white grape variety which produces strong, full-bodied dry wines. Also spelt Rcatzitelli.

Rcatzitelli (Bul). An alternative spelling of Rcakzitelli.

R.D. (Fr) (abbr). Récemment Dégorgé. Found on the label of Bollinger Champagne to denote that the wine has been recently disgorged. Shows date of vintage and dégorgement.

R.D. (Wales) (abbr). See Red Crown.

Real Ale (Eng). The term used for cask conditioned draught and bottle-conditioned beers. Cask ales dispensed with the natural CO_2 with no additional CO_2 added. The CAMRA name for Traditional ale.

Realbrut (It). A sparkling (méthode champenoise) wine produced by Calissano in the Piemonte region.

Real Cave do Cedro (Port). The producer of sparkling wines made by the méthode champenoise.

Real Companhía Vinícola do Norte de Portugal (Port). Produces wines under the Lagosta label and Cabido (a Dão wine) plus a wide range of other wines.

Real é Insigne Iglesia Colegial (Sp). On the steps of this building, hundreds of homing pigeons are released to announce the start of the Sherry vintage festival. See Fiesta de la Vendimia.

Realengo (Sp). The brand-name of a full-bodied, medium-dry, Oloroso sherry from the Diez Hermanos range produced by Diez Merito.

Real Mackenzie (The) (Scot). A blended Scotch whisky produced by P. Mackenzie and Co. (part of Arthur Bell and Sons, Perth).

Real McCoy (The) (Scot). The brand-name of a Scotch whisky and ginger wine drink.

Real Vinicola (Port). Quinta do Sibio. Vintage Port shippers. Vintages 1945, 1947, 1950, 1955, 1960.

Reaullt Hir (Wales). The monk who is purported to have introduced Whiskey to Wales in the fourth century (on Bardsey Island) as a medicine (pain killer).

Rebate Brandy (S.Afr). The name given to 3 year old Brandy that has been tasted by the Government Brandy Board. If acceptable will award a customs rebate to the distiller. Helps improve the quality of South African Brandy.

Rebe (Ger). Grape vine tendril.

Rebêche (Fr). The juice of the final pressing in Champagne. Used for the making of wine which is either distilled for Marc or is consumed by the vineyard workers.

Rebel Charge (Cktl). ⅔ measure Bourbon whiskey, ⅓ measure Triple Sec, ½ measure orange juice, ½ measure lemon juice, ½ egg white. Shake over ice, strain into an ice-filled highball glass. Top with a slice of orange.

Rebello Valente (Port). Vintage Port shippers. Vintages – 1870, 1875, 1878, 1881, 1884, 1887, 1890, 1892, 1894, 1896, 1897, 1900, 1904, 1908, 1911, 1912, 1917, 1920, 1922, 1924, 1927, 1931, 1935, 1942, 1955, 1960, 1963, 1966, 1967, 1970, 1975, 1977, 1980, 1983. Owned by Robertson.

Reblausgesetz (Ger). A Prussian law introduced on February 27th 1878 that was eventually extended in 1885. Contained procedures for destroying phylloxera-attacked vineyards. Was adopted by the whole of Germany in 1904.

Rebsorten (Ger). Vine varieties.

Rebstöckel (Ger). Grosslage. (Anb) = Rheinpfalz. (Ber) = Mittelhaardt-Deutsche Weinstrasse. (Vils) = Diedesfeld, Hambach, Neustadt an der Weinstrasse.

Rebtal (Ger). Vineyard. (Anb) = Baden. (Ber) = Kaiserstuhl-Tuniberg. (Gro) = Attilafelsen. (Vil) = Tiengen.

Rebula (Yug). A red wine produced in Vipava in north-western Slovenia.

Recaş (Rum). A wine-producing area (part of the Banat Vineyard). Main grapes are Cabernet sauvignon and Kadarka (red).

Recastra (Sp). The method of pruning in the Jerez district to remove any useless buds and so improve the chances of good buds on the vine.

Récemment Dégorgé (Fr). See R.D.

Recently Disgorged (Eng). See R.D.

Rech (Ger). Village. (Anb) = Ahr. (Ber) = Walporzheim/Ahrtal. (Gro) = Klosterberg. (Vins) = Blume, Hardtberg, Herrenberg.

Rechbächel (Ger). Vineyard. (Anb) = Rheinpfalz. (Ber) = Mittelhaardt-Deutsche Weinstrasse. (Gro) = Mariengarten. (Vil) = Wachenheim.

Rechberg (Ger). Village. (Anb) = Baden. (Ber) = Bodensee. See Klettgau.

Rechnitz (Aus). A wine-producing area in the district of south Burgenland.

Recia (It). Ear. See Recie.

Recie (It). Lit – 'Ears'. Adapted to Valpolicella Recioto where only the outer bunches of grapes that have had the most sun are used. Also known as Recia, Recioto.

Recioto (It). See Recie.

Recioto Amarone Della Valpolicella (It). D.O.C. red Valpolicella wine made in limited quantities. Produced from Recie grapes. High in alcohol up to 15½% by vol. See also Amarone.

Recioto Della Valpolicella (It). D.O.C. red wine from the Veneto. Made from the Barbera, Corvina veronese, Molinara, Rondinella, Rossignola negrara and Sangiovese grapes. Vinification can take place in Verona. If grapes are partially dried then the term Amarone can appear on the label. If produced in Valpantena then this appears on the label. The D.O.C. can also apply to sparkling wines vinified in Verona and also for fortified wines in Lombardy and Veneto.

Recioto di Gambellara (It). D.O.C. white wine from Veneto. Made from the Garganega and Trebbiano nostrano grapes which are partially dried. D.O.C. also applies to the sparkling wines produced according to current regulations by natural fermentation within 4 specific communes.

Recioto di Soave (It). D.O.C. white wine from Veneto. Made from the Garganega 70–90% and Trebbiano di soave 10–30%. Grapes are partially dried. Wine has a slight taste of bitter almonds. D.O.C. also applies to sparkling wines and to fortified wines if the preparation takes place in Lombardy and Veneto.

Recioto Nobile (It). A recioto wine in which the grapes have been attacked by botrytis cinerea (Muffa nobile). It is a sweet, sparkling red wine.

Réclame Trompeuse (Fr). Trade Descriptions Act. Lit – 'Misleading Advertisement'.

Recolta (Rum). Vintage.

Récoltants-Manipulants (Fr). Champagne producers who make their own Champagne and sell direct to the customer.

Récolte (Fr). Crop, vintage.

Record (Fr). A full-bodied beer brewed by the '33' Brasserie in Paris. 7.5% alc. by vol.

Re-cork (Eng). Many fine wines, after several years in the bottle, require their corks to be replaced with new ones. The wines are decanted and topped up with a sacrificial bottle of the same wine.

Recoulles (Les) (Fr). A vineyard of Coteaux de l'Hermitage, northern Rhône. (white wine).

Rectified Spirits (Eng). Purified spirits.

Rectifier (Eng). Part of the Continuous-still (Patent or Coffey still) which produces the pure spirit. Condenses a hot vapour (the spirits) to a liquid in distillation. See also Analyser.

Rectify (Eng). To change a natural spirit in some way. Either by redistilling or adding colour or flavourings. See Potash Salts.

Rectifying (Eng). The process of producing pure spirit. See Rectify.

Redalevn Liqueur (Eng). A liqueur made with a 100% Scotch whisky base. Produced by Savermo Ltd of London. 40% alc. by vol. Is sold only to the Manchester United Football club.

Red Apple Cocktail (Cktl). ⅙ gill Smirnoff Blue Label, ⅙ gill apple juice, ½ fl.oz. lemon juice, 2 dashes Grenadine. Shake over ice, strain into a cocktail glass.

Red Azur (Cktl). ½ measure Cointreau, ¼ measure Kirsch, ¼ measure dry Vermouth, dash Grenadine. Shake over ice, strain into a cocktail glass.

Red Band Export (N.Z.). The brand-name used for a range of beers brewed by the New Zealand Breweries.

Red Bank Winery (Austr). Address = Redbank, Victoria 3467. 10 ha. Grape varieties – Cabernet franc, Cabernet sauvignon, Malbec, Merlot, Pinot noir and Shiraz.

Red Beer (Bel). A top-fermented beer-style. The brew is blended with a beer which has been aged for at least 18 months in oak. Barley, maize grits, caramel, Vienna malts are added. Lactic acid is formed during the brewing process which gives the beer a sharp acidic flavour.

Red Biddy (Eng) (slang). A term for cheap red wine usually fortified with methylated spirits

Red Biddy (USA) (slang). Cheap red wine.

Redbrook Estate (Austr). Part of the Evans and Tate vineyards in Western Australia. 18 ha.

Red Bullet Cocktail (Cktl). 1 measure Gin, 2 measures redcurrant wine, 4 measures Cider. Mix together, chill well down, serve in a highball glass with an apple slice.

Red Cardinal Cup (Punch). 1 bottle Claret, ½ bottle soda water, 1 sliced lemon. Mix together with ice and serve.

Red Cloud Cocktail (Cktl). ¾ measure dry Gin, ¼ measure Apricot brandy, juice ¼ lemon, 2 dashes Grenadine. Shake well over ice, strain into a cocktail glass.

Red Corner (Fr). A *** Cognac brandy produced by A. Hardy. Average age of 3 years of Cognacs from the Borderies.

Red Crown (Eng). A bottled Pale ale 1034 O.G. brewed by the Everards Brewery, Leicester.

Red Crown [R.C] (Wales). A dark cask conditioned Mild ale 1035 O.G. brewed by the Brains Brewery in Cardiff.

Red Delicious (Gre). A sweet red liqueur (version of Mavrodaphne of Patras) wine produced by Tsantali.

Red E (USA). An early instant coffee brand which had a poor taste.

Red Eric (Den). A Beer once brewed by the Ceres Brewery that is now no longer produced.

Red Eye (Can). Drink of 3 parts beer, 1 part tomato juice.

Red Eye (USA) (slang). Cheap whiskey.

Redgate (Austr). Vineyard. Address = P.O. Box 117, Margaret River, Off Boodiscup Road, Western Australia. 12 ha. Grape varieties – Cabernet franc, Cabernet sauvignon, Chenin blanc, Riesling, Sauvignon blanc and Sémillon.

Red Hackle (Cktl). ¼ measure red Dubonnet, ¼ measure Brandy, ¼ measure Grenadine. Shake over ice, strain into a cocktail glass.

Red Hackle (Scot). A brand of blended Scotch whisky now owned by Highland Distilleries.

Red Hanepoot (S.Afr). A relation of the Muscat grape. See also Flame Muscat.

Red Head (Cktl). 3 parts Guinness and 1 part tomato juice.

Red Heart Rum (Eng). The brand-name for a Rum produced by U.R.M. 40% alc. by vol.

Red Hock (Eng). The eighteenth- and nineteenth-century name for German red wines.

Red Light Cocktail (Cktl).(Non-alc). ¼ measure pineapple juice, ¼ measure orange juice, ¼ measure Syrop de Fraises, ¼ measure lemon juice, 2 dashes Grenadine. Shake well over ice, strain into a cocktail glass. Dress with a slice of orange.

Red Lion (Cktl). ⅓ measure dry Gin, ⅓ measure Grand Marnier, ⅙ measure orange juice, ⅙ measure lemon juice. Shake well over ice, strain into a cocktail glass.

Red Lion Bitter (Eng). A Bitter beer 1038 O.G. distributed by Linfood Cash and Carry, Northamptonshire.

Red Lion Punch (Eng). An eighteenth-century recipe served hot or cold. Calves'-foot jelly, oranges, lemons, sugar syrup, Gin and white wine heated together.

Red Lips (Cktl). 1 fl.oz. Vodka, ¼ fl.oz. Campari, ¼ fl.oz. Grand Marnier, 2 dashes egg white, dash Angostura. Shake over ice, strain into a cocktail glass.

Redman (Austr). A winery in Coonawarra, South Australia. Produces varietal wines.

Red Misket (Bul). A red grape variety grown in northern Bulgaria.

Redmond (Austr). Vineyards. Address = P.O. Box 433, Albany, Western Australia 6330. 4.4 ha. Grape varieties – Cabernet sauvignon, Gewürztraminer, Rhine riesling and Sauvignon blanc. Produces varietal wines.

Red Mountain (Eng). The brand-name of a freeze-dried instant coffee produced by Brooke Bond Oxo Ltd.

Red Nose (Eng). A Beer brewed by the Reindeer Brewery in Derham Road, Norwich, Norfolk.

Redondo (Port). A co-operative based in Alentejo region. Produces mainly red wines.

Redondo (Sp). A round, well-balanced Sherry wine.

Redox Reactions (Eng). The collective name for the reductive and oxygen reactions that occur in wines which help it to age.

Red Pinot (USA). See California Red Pinot.

Red Raider Cocktail (Cktl). ⅖ measure Bourbon whiskey, ⅖ measure lemon juice, ⅕ measure Grand Marnier, dash Grenadine. Shake over ice, strain into a cocktail glass.

Redrescuts (Fr). A Premier Cru vineyard [part] in the A.C. commune of Savigny-lès-Beaune, Côte de Beaune, Burgundy.

Red Riesling (USA). A lesser grape variety grown in western America.

Red Rock Terrace (USA). The brand-name used by the Diamond Creek Winery for a style of wine from a specific section of their vineyards.

Red Rose (W.Ind). A noted brand of Jamaican rum produced by the Wray and Nephew Group on the island of Jamaica.

Red Rose Stout (Eng). A bottled Stout 1040 O.G. brewed by the Greenall Whitley Brewery in Warrington, Cheshire.

Red Santos (Bra). A grade of Pure coffee produced in the Santos region of north-eastern Brazil.

Red Seal Ale (I.O.M.). A bottled Pale ale 1036 O.G. brewed by the Castletown Brewery.

Red Sombrero Cocktail (Cktl).(Non-alc). ⅓ measure Grenadine, ⅓ measure pineapple juice, ⅓ measure orange juice. Shake over ice, strain into an ice-filled highball glass. Top with ginger ale. Dress with a cherry and lemon slice. Serve with straws.

Red Stripe Crucial Brew (W.Ind). A Jamaican Lager 1080–1086 O.G. brewed with American yeast and hops to a Jamaican recipe by the Charles Wells Brewery, Bedford.

Red Stripe Lager (W.Ind). A Jamaican Lager 1044 O.G. brewed in the U.K. under licence by the Charles Wells Brewery in Bedford, Bedfordshire.

Red Sumoll (Sp). A red grape variety

grown in Conca de Barbera in the province of Tarragona.

Red Sunset (Cktl). ⅖ measure white Rum, ⅖ measure Mansikka liqueur, ⅕ measure Lemon liqueur ⅕ measure lemon juice. Shake over ice, strain into a cocktail glass.

Red Swizzle (Cktl). As for a Gin Swizzle adding 1 fl.oz. Grenadine.

Red Traminer (USA). The alternative name for the Gewürztraminer grape (so named due to the red blush of the grapes as they are ripening).

Red Triangle Beer (Eng). The old name for the Sediment beer from the Worthington Brewery called White Shield.

Red Trollinger (Fr). An alternative name for the Trollinger grape.

Reducing (Eng). The term applied to the operation of lowering the alcoholic strength of a spirit by the addition of water.

Red Velvet (Can). A Canadian whisky produced by Gilbey Canada Ltd.

Red Vermouth (It). The sweet-flavoured, fortified wine which is now also produced in France.

Red Viking (Cktl). ⅓ measure Akvavit, ⅓ measure Maraschino, ⅓ measure lime juice cordial. Stir over ice, strain into an ice-filled highball glass.

Red, White and Blue (USA). A Lager beer brewed by the Pabst Brewery.

Red Wine (Eng). Any wine which has the red colouring obtained from the pigment in the grape skins by natural extraction. This is usually extracted during the fermentation process when the skins are left in the fermenting must. (Fr) = Vin rouge, (Ger) = Rotwein, (Gre) = Oinos erythros, (Hol) = Rood wijn. (It) = Vino rosso, (Port) = Vinho tinto, (Sp) = Vino tinto, (Wales) = Gwin coch.

Red Wine Island (Ger). The name given to Assmanshausen in the Rheingau because the vineyards produce red wines (from the Spätburgunder grape) and are surrounded by white grape vineyards.

Red Wine Path (Ger). Wine road of the Ahr Valley. Rotweinwanderweg.

Red Wine Punch (Cktl). 2 bottles red wine, 1 bottle Port, ½ bottle Cherry brandy, juice of 6 oranges and 4 lemons, ¼ lb. powdered sugar. Mix in a large bowl. Add contents of a soda syphon and ice, decorate with sliced fruit in season.

Reekin' (Scot) (slang). For 'smelling of drink'.

Reeling (Eng) (slang). A term used to denote being unsteady on one's feet through intoxication.

Reepham Brewery (Eng). Opened in 1983

in Reepham, Norfolk. Noted for its cask conditioned Brewhouse Ale 1055 O.G. and Granary Bitter 1038 O.G.

Refène (La) (Fr). A Premier Cru vineyard in the A.C. commune of Pommard, Côte de Beaune, Burgundy. 2.5 ha.

Referencia (Sp). The name given to the sample of wine the shipper retains.

Refert (Le) (Fr). A Premier Cru vineyard in the A.C. commune of Puligny-Montrachet, Côte de Beaune, Burgundy. 13.2 ha.

Reflets (Fr). A union of proprietors.

Reflets de Châteauneuf-du-Pape (Fr). A union of the leading estate proprietors in Châteauneuf-du-Pape, southern Rhône.

Reform Cocktail (Cktl). Another name for the Bamboo Cocktail.

Reform Cordial (USA). A Temperance name for Gin. Was placed in unusual shaped bottles to hide the fact that the contents were Gin.

Refosco (It). A red grape variety grown in the Aquileia region.

Refosco (USA). A red grape variety grown in California to make red table wines.

Refosco dal Penduncolo Rosso (It). A variety of the red Refosco grape variety grown in the Aquileia region.

Refosco Nostrano (It). A variety of the Refosco grape grown in the Aquileia region. Also the name of a red wine made from the same grape.

Refractometer (Eng). An instrument used to measure the sugar content of grape must. Measures the bending of light as it passes through the grape juice. A gram of sugar causes light to bend 1 degree Balling.

Refresco (Port). Denotes a refreshing cool drink.

Refresher (Eng). A cold drink. One that refreshes the thirst. i.e. iced lemonade, beer, water, etc.

Refresher Cocktail (Cktl). ½ lb. fresh ripe strawberries, juice of a lemon, 2 fl.ozs. water. Squeeze the juice from the fruit, mix with other ingredients over ice, strain into a highball glass. Other soft fruits may be substituted for strawberries.

Refreshing (Eng). The process of adding young wines to old to give added life to the old wine.

Refreshment of the Devil (Eng). The religious Temperance movement's nickname for alcoholic drink.

Règab (Afr). A Pilsener beer brewed by the Société des Brasseries du Haut Ogooué in Gabon.

Régalade (Fr). Describes the art of drinking out of a bottle without the bottle touching the lips.

Regal Bräu (USA). A Beer brewed by the Huber Brewery in Monroe, Wisconsin.

Regaleali (It). A region of Sicily producing red and white wines.

Regal Fizz (Cktl). ½ measure Bols Cherry brandy, ½ measure Kirsch. Shake over ice, strain into an ice-filled highball glass. Top with Champagne.

Regal Lager (Ch.Isles). A Lager-style beer 1045 O.G. brewed by the Randalls Brewery in St. Peter Port, Guernsey.

Regal Lager (Eng). A Lager beer 1039 O.G. brewed by the Holt Brewery in Manchester.

Regal Lager (Ind). A Lager beer produced by the Vinedale Brewery in Hyderabad. 1042 O.G.

Regar (Port). Drink with food. To wash down (the food) with a drink.

Regency (Eng). A beer brewed by the Wiltshire Brewery Company in Tisbury, Wiltshire.

Regency (Sp). A Sherry produced in Jerez de la Frontera.

Regency Cask (Eng). A light Bitter beer 1038 O.G. brewed by the Wiltshire Brewery Company in Tisbury, Wiltshire.

Regency Cocktail (Cktl). ½ measure dry Gin, ¼ measure Mandarine Napoléon, 2 dashes French vermouth, dash Crème de Banane. Stir over ice, strain into a cocktail glass. Top with a cherry and mint leaf.

Regency Star (Cktl). ¼ measure orange Curaçao, ½ measure dry Gin, ⅛ measure Passion fruit juice, ⅛ measure dry Vermouth. Shake over ice, strain into a cocktail glass.

Regensburger Landwein (Ger). A new Deutsche Tafelwein zone.

Rege Wine Co (USA). A winery based near Cloverdale, Sonoma County, California. Grape varieties – Barbera and Cabernet sauvignon. Produces varietal wines.

Rege Winery (USA). A winery based in the Russian River Valley, California.

Reggenhag (Ger). Vineyard. (Anb) = Baden. (Ber) = Markgräflerland. (Gro) = Burg Neuenfels. (Vil) = Müllheim.

Regiães Demarcadas (Port). Demarcated regions. Plural of Região Demarcada.

Região Demarcada (Port). Demarcated area. There are ten in total – Algarve, Bairrada, Bucelas, Carcavelos, Colares, Dão, Douro, Madeira, Moscatel de Setúbal and Vinho Verde.

Regimental Port (Austr). A Port-style wine from County Hamley in South Australia. Made from the Cabernet sauvignon grape and fortified with 2 year old brandy.

Reginum (Lat). A red wine produced in southern Italy in Roman times.

Regional (Eng). Denotes that a beverage has

R

been produced within a region as opposed to an individual village, district or vineyard.

Regional Bottling (Eng). On a label shows that the wines are made from grapes grown in the region named and are controlled by the local laws and customs.

Regional Designation (USA). In California, wines may obtain Regional Designation if at least 75% of the grapes are grown in that location. All the grapes though must be grown in California.

Regional Wine (Eng). A wine which takes its name from a district or region, not from a specific town or vineyard. Usually wines are blended.

Regione Siciliano (It). A Sicilian D.O.C. re-enforcement of their wines. Has a large Q encircling it. See Q Mark.

Regisseurs (Fr). Managers.

Regnard (A. et Fils) (Fr). A négociant based in Chablis, Burgundy. is noted for Grand Cru and Premier Cru wines. (Fr). A small Burgundy négociant-éleveur based in Chablis.

Regner (Ger). A white grape variety. A cross between the Luglianca bianca and the Gamay. Gives high sugar.

Regnié (Fr). An A.C. Cru Beaujolais-Villages, Burgundy.

Regnier (Fr). A subsidiary of Cointreau. Produces a large range of liqueurs.

Régua (Port). A Port-producing town in the Douro region.

Reguengos (Port). A sub-district in the Alentejo region. Produces full-bodied red wines.

Rehbach (Ger). Grosslage. (Anb) = Rheinhessen. (Ber) = Nierstein. (Vils) = Nachenheim, Nierstein.

Rehborn (Ger). Village. (Anb) = Nahe. (Ber) = Schloss Böckelheim. (Gro) = Paradiesgarten. (Vins) = Hahn, Herrenberg, Schikanenbukel.

Rehlingen (Ger). Village. (Anb) = Mosel-Saar-Ruwer. (Ber) = Obermosel. (Gro) = Gipfel. (Vin) = Kapellenberg.

Rehoboam (Fr). A bottle size. Equivalent of 6 standard bottles. Used mainly in Champagne. See also Champagne Bottle Sizes.

Rei (Port). A variety of the white grape Malvasia used in the making of white Port.

Reichelberg (Ger). Vineyard. (Anb) = Mosel-Saar-Ruwer. (Ber) = Bernkastel. (Gro) = Schwarzlay. (Vil) = Flussbach.

Reichenau (Ger). Village. (Anb) = Baden. (Ber) = Bodensee. (Gro) = Sonnenufer. (Vin) = Hochwart.

Reichenbach (Ger). Village. (Anb) =

Baden. (Ber) = Ortenau. (Gro) = Fürsteneck. (Vins) = Amselberg, Kinzigtäler.

Reichensteiner (Ger). A white grape variety. A cross between the Müller-Thurgau and the Madeleine angevine X Calabresi fröhlich.

Reichenweir (Fr). The German name for the town of Riquewihr in Alsace.

Reichesthal (Ger). Vineyard. (Anb) = Rheingau. (Ber) = Johannisberg. (Gro) = Daubhaus. (Vil) = Hochheim.

Reichesthal (Ger). Vineyard. (Anb) = Rheingau. (Ber) = Johannisberg. (Gro) = Daubhaus. (Vil) = Kostheim.

Reicholzheim (Ger). Village. (Anb) = Baden. (Ber) = Badische Frankenland. (Gro) = Tauberklinge. (Vins) = First, Kemelrain, Satzenberg.

Reichshalde (Ger). Vineyard. (Anb) = Württemberg. (Ber) = Württembergisch Unterland. (Gro) = Stromberg. (Vil) = Freudenstein.

Reichshalde (Ger). Vineyard. (Anb) = Württemberg. (Ber) = Württembergisch Unterland. (Gro) = Stromberg. (Vil) = Knittlingen.

Reichshalde (Ger). Vineyard. (Anb) = Württemberg. (Ber) = Württembergisch Unterland. (Gro) = Stromberg. (Vil) = Maulbronn.

Reichskeller (Ger). Vineyard. (Anb) = Rheinhessen. (Ber) = Bingen. (Gro) = Rheingrafenstein. (Vil) = Frei-Laubersheim.

Reichsrebsortiment (Ger). The official Government list of vines.

Reichsritterstift (Ger). Vineyard. (Anb) = Rheinhessen. (Ber) = Nierstein. (Gro) = Sankt Alban. (Vil) = Bodenheim.

Reif (Ger). Ripe, denotes a fine sweet wine.

Reifbräu Brauerei (Ger). A brewery owned by Patrizer.

Reifenbeisser (Aus). The name given to the very poor 1456 wine vintage. Wine produced was so acid that it penetrated the wood and hoops of the cask.

Reifenstein (Ger). Vineyard. (Anb) = Franken. (Ber) = Maindreieck. (Gro) = Not yet assigned. (Vil) = Sommerhausen.

Reifersley (Ger). Vineyard. (Anb) = Mittelrhein. (Ber) = Bacharach. (Gro) = Schloss Reichenstein. (Vil) = Niederheimbach.

Reigate Bitter (Eng). See Reigate Brewery.

Reigate Brewery (Eng). A brewery in the John Landregan Off-Licence in Reigate, Surrey. Brews cask conditioned Reigate Bitter 1042 O.G. using malt extract.

Reignots (Les) (Fr). A Premier Cru vineyard in the A.C. commune of Vosne-Romanée, Côte de Nuits, Burgundy. 1.7 ha.

R

Reil (Ger). Village. (Anb) = Mosel-Saar-Ruwer. (Ber) = Bernkastel. (Gro) = Vom Heissen Stein. (Vins) = Falklay, Goldlay, Moullay-Hofberg, Sorentberg.

Reims (Fr). A major town in the Champagne region. Has Cantons of Ay, de Beine, de Bourgogne, de Reims, de Verzy, de Châtillon-sur-Marne, de Fismes and de Ville-en-Tardenois. See Montagne de Reims.

Rein (Aus) (Ger). Pure, clean, natural.

Reindeer (Eng). A home-brew public house based at Dereham Road, Norwich. Brews cask conditioned Bill's Bevy, Reindeer Bitter and Red Nose.

Reina Verdelho (La) (Mad). A medium dry Madeira produced by Rutherford and Miles.

Reine (La) (S.Afr). An estate that produces mainly varietals.

Reine-Claude (Fr). A greengage plum spirit produced in Alsace. Noted for its strong bouquet.

Reine Cléopatre (Egy). A fine, white, full-flavoured wine produced by the Gianaclis Vineyards at Abú-Hummus.

Reine Juliana (Cktl). 1 fl.oz. Mandarine Napoléon, 1¾ fl.ozs. Vodka, 1 fl.oz. Sabra liqueur. Shake over ice, strain into an old-fashioned glass 'on the rocks'.

Reine Pédauque (Fr). A large wine-producer based in Aloxe-Corton, Côte de Beaune, Burgundy. Address = Corgolin, 21700 Nuits-Saint-Georges.

Reinheitsgebot (Ger). The oldest known food and drink law. The German Purity Law dated from 1516 to control the production of German beer (originally Bavarian beers but now amended to allow for wheat beers). Chemical additives and sugar are banned. Only pure water, hops, barley malt and yeast can be used in beer production.

Reinig auf der Burg (Ger). Vineyard. (Anb) = Mosel-Saar-Ruwer. (Ber) = Obermosel. (Gro) = Gipfel. (Vil) = Wasserliesch.

Reininghaus (Aus). A Beer brewed by the brewery of same name based in Graz.

Reininghaus Brauerei (Aus). A noted brewery based in Graz. Brews under its own and the Puntigam label.

Reinsbronn (Ger). Village. (Anb) = Württemberg. (Ber) = Kocher-Jagst-Tauber. (Gro) = Tauberberg. (Vin) = Röde.

Reinsortig (Aus). 'Only this particular type'.

Reintönig (Ger). Well-balanced, very good wine.

Reischklingeberg (Ger). Vineyard. (Anb) = Franken. (Ber) = Mainviereck. (Gro) = Heiligenthal. (Vil) = Grossostheim.

Reishu (Jap). Melon liqueur.

Reiterpfad (Ger). Vineyard. (Anb) =

Rheinpfalz. (Ber) = Mittelhaardt-Deutsche Weinstrasse. (Gro) = Hofstück. (Vil) = Ruppertsberg.

Reiterpfad (Ger). Vineyard. (Anb) = Rheinpfalz. (Ber) = Mittelhaardt-Deutsche Weinstrasse. (Gro) = Meerspinne. (Vil) = Königsbach.

Reitsteig (Ger). Vineyard. (Anb) = Franken. (Ber) = Steigerwald. (Gro) = Herrenberg. (Vil) = Castell.

Remain Sober (Cktl).(Non-alc). In a highball glass place an ice cube, 3 dashes Angostura, 1 wine glass lime juice cordial. Stir, top up with soda water.

Remelluri (Sp). A red wine produced by La Granja Nuestra Señora de Remelluri from a single vineyard.

Remerschen (Lux). A wine co-operative. Part of Vinsmoselle.

Remerschen (Lux). A wine-producing village on the river Moselle. Vineyard sites – Kreitzberg, Jongeberg.

Remeyerhof (Ger). Vineyard. (Anb) = Rheinhessen. (Ber) = Wonnegau. (Gro) = Liebfrauenmorgen. (Vil) = Worms.

Remich (Lux). A wine-producing village on the river Moselle. Vineyard sites – Primerberg, Hôpertsbour. Has a marl and chalk soil.

Remi Landier et Fils (Fr). A Cognac brandy producer. Address = GAEC Domaine du Carrefour, Cors, Foussignac, 162000 Jarnac. 50 ha. in the Fins Bois.

Remoissenet Père et Fils (Fr). Burgundy négociant-éleveur based at Beaune, Côte de Beaune.

Remontage (Fr). Denotes the piping of the fermenting must over the cap of skins.

Remontage (Fr). In Champagne denotes the carrying of eroded soil back up the hill.

Remounting (Fr). Pumping the fermenting must onto the cap of the must to extract the colour and break up the cap.

Remour (Fr). See Remueur. (mis-spelling of).

Removido (Sp). Remuage.

Remsen Cooler (Cktl). Dissolve ½ teaspoon of sugar in 2 fl.ozs. water in a highball glass. Add ice, 2 fl.ozs. dry Gin, top with ginger ale and a spiral of lemon peel over the rim of the glass.

Rems [River] (Ger). A tributary of the river Neckar in Württemberg. Has soil of red marl.

Remstal-Stuttgart (Ger). Bereich. (Anb) = Württemberg. (Gros) = Hoheneneuffen, Kopf, Sonnenbühl, Wartbühl, Weinsteige.

Remuage (Fr). The process of guiding the sediment down to the neck of a Champagne bottle so that it settles on the cork ready for dégorgement. See Remueur and Pupîtres.

R

Remueur (Fr). The person who performs Remuage in the méthode champenoise sparkling wine production.

Rémy (Austr). The brand-name of a Brandy locally blended by a Rémy Martin subsidiary. See Martin (Rémy) and Co.

Renaissance Cocktail (Cktl). ¾ measure dry Gin, ¼ measure dry sherry. ½ fl.oz. cream. Shake over ice, strain into a cocktail glass.

Renaissance Winery (USA). Vineyards and winery based in the Sierra foothills, Sacramento, California. Grape varieties – Cabernet sauvignon and Johannisberg riesling. Produces mainly table wines.

Renano (It). The northern Italian name for the Rhine riesling or True riesling.

Renarde (La) (Fr). A vineyard in the A.C. commune of Rully, Côte Chalonnaise, Burgundy.

Renat (Swe). Local pure spirit.

Renaud (Michel) (Fr). Armagnac producer. Address = Domaines de Jeanton Tauzia, Route de Sentex, 32150 Cazaubon. 13 ha in the Bas Armagnac.

Renaudin (R) (Fr). Champagne producer. Address = Domaine des Conardins, Moussy, 51200 Épernay. Récoltants-manipulants. Produces – Vintage and non-vintage wines. A member of the C.V.C. 22.5 ha. Vintages – 1973, 1974, 1975, 1976, 1978, 1979, 1981, 1983.

Renault (Alg). A wine-producing area in north-western Algeria. Produces mainly red wines.

Renault Cognac (Fr). Cognac producer. Address = Castillon Renault S.A., 22 Rue du Port, 16101 Cognac. Produces – Renault Carte Noire Extra 12–15 years old, Renault OVB 12–15 years old, Renault Age Unknown 40 years plus.

Renault Museum (USA). A wine-glass museum based at the Renault Winery in Egg Harbour, New Jersey.

Renault Winery (USA). A large winery based in Egg Harbour, New Jersey. 520 ha. Produces hybrid, native and vinifera wines. Also noted for its wine-glass museum.

Renchen (Ger). Village. (Anb) = Baden. (Ber) = Ortenau. (Gro) = Schloss Rodeck. (Vin) = Kreuzberg.

Renchtäler (Ger). Vineyard. (Anb) = Baden. (Ber) = Ortenau. (Gro) = Fürsteneck. (Vil) = Bottenau.

Renchtäler (Ger). Vineyard. (Anb) = Baden. (Ber) = Ortenau. (Gro) = Fürsteneck. (Vil) = Erlach.

Renchtäler (Ger). Vineyard. (Anb) = Baden. (Ber) = Ortenau. (Gro) = Fürsteneck. (Vil) = Lautenbach.

Renchtäler (Ger). Vineyard. (Anb) = Baden. (Ber) = Ortenau. (Gro) = Fürst-

eneck. (Vil) = Nesselried.

Renchtäler (Ger). Vineyard. (Anb) = Baden. (Ber) = Ortenau. (Gro) = Fürsteneck. (Vil) = Nussbach.

Renchtäler (Ger). Vineyard. (Anb) = Baden. (Ber) = Ortenau. (Gro) = Fürsteneck. (Vil) = Oberkirch.

Renchtäler (Ger). Vineyard. (Anb) = Baden. (Ber) = Ortenau. (Gro) = Fürsteneck. (Vil) = Oberkirch (ortsteil Haslach).

Renchtäler (Ger). Vineyard. (Anb) = Baden. (Ber) = Ortenau. (Gro) = Fürsteneck. (Vil) = Ödsbach.

Renchtäler (Ger). Vineyard. (Anb) = Baden. (Ber) = Ortenau. (Gro) = Fürsteneck. (Vil) = Ringelbach.

Renchtäler (Ger). Vineyard. (Anb) = Baden. (Ber) = Ortenau. (Gro) = Fürsteneck. (Vil) = Stadelhofen.

Renchtäler (Ger). Vineyard. (Anb) = Baden. (Ber) = Ortenau. (Gro) = Fürsteneck. (Vil) = Tiergarten.

Renchtäler (Ger). Vineyard. (Anb) = Baden. (Ber) = Ortenau. (Gro) = Fürsteneck. (Vil) = Ulm.

Rendement Annuel (Fr). The yield set each year. May be above or below the Rendement de base.

Rendement de Base (Fr). Basic yield. The amount of wine allowed to be produced at base level. See also Plafond de Classement.

Rendements (Fr). The amount of wine that is produced from a given area.

Rene Briand SpA (It). A noted brandy producer.

René Lalou (Fr). The top-of-the-range vintage Champagne from G.H. Mumm. Named after one of their first directors.

Rengo (Chile). A wine-producing area near Santiago.

Renishaw Vineyard (Eng). A vineyard based at Renishaw Hall, near Sheffield, Yorkshire. Was first planted in 1972. 0.85 ha. Grape varieties – Huxelrebe, Pinot meunier, Pinot noir, Reichensteiner, Schönberger and Seyval blanc.

Renmano Wines (Austr). Part of Berri Renmano, South Australia. Address = Renmark Avenue, Renmark, South Australia 5341.

Renmark (Austr). A wine district in New South Wales. Produces fine quality wines.

Renouard Larivière (Fr). A producer of Eau de Melisse des Carmes Boyer (an Élixer) in Paris.

Renski Riesling (Yug). A white grape also known as the Rhine riesling and Rajinski rizling.

Rentamt (Ger). Collecting office.

Renyshe (Eng). The old sixteenth-century name for Rhenish (Rhine) wines.

Renzo Tedeschi (It). A noted Recioto and Ripasso producer based in the Valpolicella region. Produces Ripasso – [Capitel San Rocco Rosso] and Recioto – [Cru Capitel Monte Fontana].

Repeal [The] (USA). The end of Prohibition 5th December 1933.

Repisa (Mad). Second pressing of the grapes.

Répouf et Fils (Fr). An Armagnac producer based in the Ténarèze. Address = 'Notre Dame' 32190-Vic-Fesensac.

Repperndorf (Ger). Village. (Anb) = Franken. (Ber) = Maindreieck. (Gro) = Hofrat. (Vin) = Kaiser Karl.

Reputed Pint (Eng). A half-bottle. An imperial gallon contains 12 half-bottles.

Reputed Quart (Eng). 1.33 imperial pints or 26.66 fl.ozs. The normal British bottle size.

Requeno (Sp). An alternative name for the Bobal grape.

Resaca (Sp). A hangover.

Resch's KB (Austr). A Lager beer brewed by the Tooths Brewery in Sydney.

Reserva (Sp). Mature quality wine.

Reservado (Chile). A wine that is 4 years old.

Reserva 904 (Sp). A red wine from La Rioja Alta.

Reservas (Port). The best wine from a particular year. See also Garrafeira (which is better).

Réserve (Fr). Found on Armagnac and Cognac labels and denotes a minumum of 4 years of age.

Réserve (Lux). The second from top grade for wine. (Top = Grande Réserve).

Réserve Ancestrale (Fr). A 50 year old Cognac brandy produced by Pierre Ferrand. Only 22 bottles are produced per year.

Réserve de Fondateur (Fr). A blend of rare Cognacs produced by Martell in Cognac. Limit of 2,160 bottles produced.

Réserve de la Comtesse (Fr). The second wine of Château Pinchon-Longueville-Lalande. Grand Cru Classé (2nd), A.C. Pauillac.

Réserve de l'Empéreur (Fr). A De Luxe cuvée Champagne produced by Mercier for the French market only.

Réserve des Ancestres (Fr). A 35 year old Cognac produced by Raymond Dudognon.

Reserved for England (Fr). Usually found on a Champagne label. Denotes the wine is dry.

Réserve Exceptionelle (Fr). Qualification

in Alsace. A phrase of quality used on some wines to denote a much better all round wine.

Reserve Madeira (Mad). Blended Madeira. The youngest wine must be a minimum of 5 years old after Estufagem. If the grape variety is stated it must contain 85% of named grape variety.

Réserve Nouvelle (Fr). R.N. After 5 years in cask the marking Cognac obtains. It is then left until it is used. Often stored in Paradis.

Réserve Royale (Fr). A Cognac produced by Croizet.

Réserve Saint Landelin (Fr). A full-bodied beer brewed by the Rimaux Brasserie based near Valenciennes.

Réserve Spéciale (Fr). Late gathered in Alsace. Has the same meaning as Spätlese in Germany.

Residential Licence (Eng). The liquor licence issued to certain Hotels, Boarding houses and Guest houses which only allows the sale of alcoholic beverages to residents of the establishment and their guests (providing the residents pay for them also).

Residual Sugar (USA). The natural grape sugar that remains unfermented in a wine. Measured usually in degrees Brix (from 0.1° to 27° the sweetest).

Resinated Wine (Gre). See Retsina.

Resinotte (Fr). An alternative name for the Muscadelle grape.

Resolute (Cktl). 1/6 gill dry Gin, 1/8 gill Apricot brandy, 1/8 gill lemon juice. Shake over ice, strain into a cocktail glass.

Resses (Les) (Fr). A vineyard in the A.C. commune of Montagny, Côte Chalonnaise, Burgundy.

Restanques (Fr). The name used in Bandol, Côtes de Provence for the terraced vineyards.

Restaurant Licence (Eng). A liquor licence issued to establishments to permit them to drink alcoholic beverages with a meal. Basic law allows 16–18 year olds to consume beer, cider or perry with a meal and the restaurant to be open during the afternoon (since May 1987). Drinking up time is 30 minutes. Opening hours differ from those of a full On licence.

Restsüsse (Ger). Lit – 'Residual sweetness'. An old term, that denotes the unfermented grape sugar in the wine which the yeasts fail to ferment.

Restzuckerbegrenzungen (Ger). The laws governing unfermented sugar retention in wines.

Reticent (Eng). A term used to describe wines that are holding back on the nose or palate due possibly to immaturity.

Retort (Eng). The name used for the base of a pot-still (the round tapering piece) that holds the liquid to be distilled.

Retour des Indes (Fr). A term used to describe the wines used as ballast (especially Madeira) in ships making the round trip to India and back during the eighteenth and nineteenth centuries. Ended soon after the Suez Canal was opened. See Estufada.

Retrate (Fr). The short spur found on the main arm of the Guyot method of vine training.

Retsina (Gre). Red and white wines which have the resin of the Aleppo pine (Calitris Quadrivalvis) added as a preservative and flavouring. One of the oldest methods of keeping wine. Grapes used are the Savatiano and Rhoditis.

Rettigheim (Ger). Village. (Anb) = Baden. (Ber) = Badische Bergstrasse/ Kraichgau. (Gro) = Mannaberg. (Vin) = Olbaum.

Retz (Aus). A wine-growing district in the region of Niederösterreich. Produces mainly white wines from the Grüner veltliner grape. See also Weinviertel.

Retzbach (Ger). Village. (Anb) = Franken. (Ber) = Maindreieck. (Gro) = Ravensburg. (Vin) = Benediktusberg.

Retzstadt (Ger). Village. (Anb) = Franken. (Ber) = Maindreieck. (Gro) = Rosstal. (Vin) = Langenberg.

Reugne (Fr). A Premier Cru vineyard in the A.C. commune of Auxey-Duresses, Côte de Beaune, Burgundy. Also known as La Chapelle. 7.8 ha.

Reugny (Fr). A commune of Vouvray in the Touraine district of the Loire.

Reuil (Fr). A Cru Champagne village in the Canton de Châtillon-sur-Maine. District = Reims.

Reuilly (Fr). A.C. area in the Central Vineyards district of the Loire. Produces a steely, dry, white wine made from the Sauvignon blanc grape variety.

Réunion Island (Afr). An island off the east coast of Africa (a Département of France) that produces mainly white Rum and a little cask aged Rum. Also produces some coffee.

Reuschberg (Ger). Grosslage. (Anb) = Franken. (Ber) = Mainviereck. (Vil) = Hörstein.

Reuter's Hill Vineyard (USA). A small vineyard based in Forest Grove, Oregon. 24 ha. Produces vinifera wines. Owned by the Charles Coury Vineyards since 1928.

Reuze (Fr). A Dortmunder-style beer 7%

alc. by vol. brewed by the Pelforth Brasserie in Lille.

Revat 51 (USA). A white hybrid grape variety.

Revenooers (USA). The name given to the Revenue agents who sought out the moonshiners after the 1791 Excise Tax Act. See Whiskey Rebellion

Reversées (Les). A Premier Cru vineyard in the A.C. commune of Beaune, Côte de Beaune, Burgundy. 4.97 ha.

Reverse Osmosis (Eng). A method of removing alcohol by passing the beer, wine, etc. through porous partitions.

Reynella (Austr). A region in Clare-Watervale, Southern Vales, South Australia. Noted for red table wines and brandies.

Reynella Flor (Austr). A fortified, pale, dry wine made by W. Reynell and Sons in South Australia.

Reynella Winery (Austr). A winery based in Reynella, Clare-Watervale, Southern Vales, South Australia. Produces varietal wines.

Reyniers (Eng). Eldridge Pope's Wine Library in Fleet Street, London, where its customers may purchase and sample wines. Opened in 1986.

Rèze (Switz). A white grape variety used in the production of Vin du Glacier (rare nowadays).

Rhacodium Cellare (Hun). A blue-grey velvety fungus that covers the walls of the cellars cut in the rocks to store Tokay Azsú wines. Also found elsewhere. Also spelt Rhacodium Celare. Aids the regulation of humidity.

Rhagoletis Pomonella (Lat). The apple maggot. A fruit fly larvae that feeds (bores) on the fruit of the apple tree. Family – Trypetidae.

Rheenen Vineyard (S.Afr). A small winery that sells its grapes to the Mooiuitsig Wynkelders.

Rhein (Ger). An Untergebiet of the Rhein und Mosel district.

Rheinberg (Ger). Vineyard. (Anb) = Mittelrhein. (Ber) = Bacharach. (Gro) = Schloss Stahleck. (Vil) = Oberdiebach.

Rheinberg (Ger). Vineyard. (Anb) = Nahe. (Ber) = Kreuznach. (Gro) = Schlosskapelle. (Vil) = Münster-Sarmsheim.

Rheinberg (Ger). Vineyard. (Anb) = Rheingau. (Ber) = Johannisberg. (Gro) = Steinmächer. (Vil) = Eltville.

Rheinberg (Ger). Vineyard. (Anb) = Rheinhessen. (Ber) = Wonnegau. (Gro) = Liebfrauenmorgen. (Vil) = Worms.

Rheinberg (Ger). Vineyard. (Anb) = Rheinhessen. (Ber) = Wonnegau. (Gro) = Pilgerpfad. (Vil) = Osthofen.

R

Rheinblick (Ger). Grosslage. (Anb) = Rheinhessen. (Ber) = Nierstein. (Vils) = Alsheim, Dorn-Dürkheim, Mettenheim.

Rheinbrohl (Ger). Village. (Anb) = Mittelrhein. (Ber) = Rheinburgengau. (Gro) = Burg Hammerstein. (Vins) = Monte Jup, Römerberg.

Rheinburgengau (Ger). Bereich. (Anb) = Mittelrhein. (Gros) = Burg Hammerstein, Burg Rheinfels, Gedeonseck, Herrenberg, Hahntal, Loreleyfelsen, Marksburg, Schloss Schönburg.

Rheinburger Landwein (Ger). One of 15 Deutsche Tafelwein zones.

Rheinfront (Ger). The finest part of the Rheinhessen that fringes the river Rhine on steep slopes. Has outcrops of sandstone.

Rheingasse (Ger). Vineyard. (Anb) = Nahe. (Ber) = Schloss Böckelheim. (Gro) = Paradiesgarten. (Vil) = Lettweiler.

Rheingau (Ger). Anbaugebiet. (Ber) = Johannisberg. Main grape varieties – Müller-Thurgau 10%, Riesling 75% and Silvaner 4%. plus others.

Rheingauer Riesling Route (Ger). A wine route through the Rheingau taking its name from the principal grape variety of the region.

Rheingauer Rieslings (Ger). High quality wines made from the Riesling vine in the Rheingau.

Rheingau Information Service (Ger). Der 'Rheingau-Der Weingau', Im altern Rathaus, 6225 Johannisberg Rheingau, Western Germany.

Rheingau Wine Festivals (Ger). Hilchenfest, Hochheimer Weinfest, Lindenfest, Weinfest-Rüdesheim, Weinfest-Hattenheim.

Rheingold (Fr). A full-bodied beer brewed by the Fischer-Pêcheur group at their Adelshoffen Brasserie.

Rheingoldberg (Ger). Vineyard. (Anb) = Mittelrhein. (Ber) = Rheinburgengau. (Gro) = Schloss Schönburg. (Vil) = Niederburg.

Rheingold Brewery (USA). A brewery based in Orange.

Rheingrafenberg (Ger). Vineyard. (Anb) = Nahe. (Ber) = Schloss Böckelheim. (Gro) = Paradiesgarten. (Vil) = Meddersheim.

Rheingrafenberg (Ger). Vineyard. (Anb) = Rheinhessen. (Ber) = Bingen. (Gro) = Adelberg. (Vil) = Wörrstadt.

Rheingrafenberg (Ger). Vineyard. (Anb) = Rheinhessen. (Ber) = Bingen. (Gro) = Rheinhessen. (Ber) = Bingen. (Gro) = Rheingrafenstein. (Vil) = Frei-Laubersheim.

Rheingrafenstein (Ger). Grosslage. (Anb)

= Rheinhessen. (Ber) = Bingen. (Vils) = Eckelsheim, Frei-Laubersheim, Fürfeld, Hackenheim, Neu-Bamberg, Pleitersheim, Siefersheim, Stein-Bockenheim, Tiefenthal, Volxheim, Wöllstein, Wonsheim.

Rheinhessen (Ger). Anbaugebiet. (Bers) = Bingen, Nierstein, Wonnegau.

Rheinhessen Information Service (Ger). Rheinhessenweine e. V. 117er Ehrenhof 5, 6500 Mainz, Western Germany.

Rheinhessen Wine Festivals (Ger). Winzerfest, Kellerwegfest, Bachfischfest, Mainzer Weinmarkt, Rotweinfest.

Rheinhöhe (Ger). Vineyard. (Anb) = Rheinhessen. (Ber) = Bingen. (Gro) = Kaiserpfalz. (Vil) = Ingelheim.

Rheinhöller (Ger). Vineyard. (Anb) = Mittelrhein. (Ber) = Rheinburgengau. (Gro) = Burg Hammerstein. (Vil) = Linz.

Rheinischer Landwein (Ger). One of 15 Deutsche Tafelwein zones.

Rheinnieder (Ger). Vineyard. (Anb) = Mittelrhein. (Ber) = Rheinburgengau. (Gro) = Marksburg. (Vil) = Urbar.

Rheinnieder (Ger). Vineyard. (Anb) = Mittelrhein. (Ber) = Rheinburgengau. (Gro) = Marksburg. (Vil) = Vallendar.

Rheinpfalz (Ger). Anbaugebiet. (Bers) = Mittelhaardt-Deutsche Weinstrasse, Südliche Weinstrasse. Main grape varieties are Müller-Thurgau, Portugieser, Riesling and Silvaner.

Rheinpfalz Information Service (Ger). 'Rheinpfalz-Weinpfalz' e. V. Friedrich-Ebert-Strasse 11–13, 6730 Neustadt/Weinstrasse, Western Germany.

Rheinpfalz Wine Festivals (Ger). Dürkheimer Wurstmarkt, Weinfest der Südlichen Weinstrasse, Deutsches Weinlesefest, Fest des Federweissen.

Rheinpforte (Ger). Vineyard. (Anb) = Rheinhessen. (Ber) = Nierstein. (Gro) = Gutes Domtal. (Vil) = Selzen.

Rhein-Riesling (Aus). The name given to the Riesling (white riesling) grape of Germany. Also known as the Riesling renano in the Südtirol in Italy.

Rhein Terrasse (Ger). The name for the vineyards in the Rheinhessen south of Mainz at Nierstein, Oppenheim and Dienheim.

Rhein und Mosel (Ger). A region which has three Untergebiete (table wine subareas) of the Rhein, Mosel and Saar.

Rheinweiler (Ger). Village. (Anb) = Baden. (Ber) = Margräflerland. (Gro) = Vogtei Rötteln. (Vin) = Kapellenberg.

Rhenania Brauerei (Ger). An Alt beer brewery based at Krefeld, near Düsseldorf.

Rhenish (Eng). An old name for Rhine

R

wines, mostly the red wines at the time of Shakespeare in the sixteenth/seventeenth century.

Rhenish Hesse (Ger). The Rheinhessen. Alternative name of.

Rhenish Palatinate (Ger). The Rheinpfalz. Alternative name of.

Rhens (Ger). Village. (Anb) = Mittelrhein. (Ber) = Rheinburgengau. (Gro) = Gedeonseck. (Vins) = König Wenzel, Sonnenlay.

Rhine (USA). A term used to describe generic white wines that are off-dry to sweet.

Rhine [River] (Ger). Germany's most famous river flows from the Bodensee in the south to Mainz in the north when it then flows east-west to the North Sea. Is the centre of its famous vineyards. Has the rivers – Ahr, Main, Mosel, Nahe and Neckar as its main tributaries.

Rhine Front (The) (Ger). An area of the Rheinhessen south of Mainz-Nachenheim, Nierstein and Oppenheim where the Riesling grape is grown.

Rhinewine Cobbler (Cktl). Place some ice into a large wine goblet. Add 4 dashes orange Curaçao, 1 teaspoon sugar syrup. Top up with a medium Rhine wine, stir and decorate with fruit in season and a sprig of mint. Serve with straws.

Rhine Wine Cup (Cktl). 1½ fl.ozs. sugar, small soda water, 1 fl.oz. Triple Sec, 2 fl.ozs. Brandy, 1 bottle Liebfraumilch. Stir together over ice, add fruits in season and mint sprigs.

Rhine Wines (Ger). The general term used to describe wines that are produced along the river Rhine. i.e. Rheinhessen, Rheinpalz, Mittelrhein, etc.

Rhiwlas St. Beuno (Wales). A table water brand produced in the late nineteenth century.

Rhodes (Gre). The main wine-producing island of the Dodecanese group of islands. Produces mainly white wines with some sparkling.

Rhodesian Breweries Limited (Afr). A brewery based in Zimbabwe that brews under the Castle and Lion brands.

Rhoditis (Gre). A pink grape variety used in the making of Retsina and Anchialos wines together with the Savatiano grape.

Rhodt (Ger). Village. (Anb) = Rheinpfalz. (Ber) = Südliche Weinstrasse. (Gro) = Ordensgut. (Vins) = Klosterpfad, Rosengarten, Schlossberg.

Rhom (Ch.Isles). Rum.

Rhöndorf (Ger). Village. (Anb) = Mittelrhein. (Ber) = Siebengebirge. (Gro) = Petersberg. (Vin) = Drachenfels.

Rhône (Fr). A major wine region which extends from south of Lyons in eastern France, southwards down to Avignon. Vineyards are sited mainly along the banks of the river Rhône. Most styles of wines are produced.

Rhône [River] (Fr). A major river that runs through eastern France to the Mediterranean sea. Has the rivers Saône and Isère as its main tributaries. Runs through the wine region of the Rhône (Côtes du Rhône).

Rhum (Fr). Rum.

Rhum Barbancourt (W.Ind). A Rum produced by the Damien Distillery in Haiti.

Rhum Black (Fr). Rum producers based in Bordeaux, south-western France.

Rhum Champion (W.Ind). The brand-name of a Rum produced by the Croix des Bouquets Distillery in Haiti.

Rhum Citadelle (W.Ind). A brand of Rum produced at Port au Prince, Haiti by Marie Colas.

Rhum Clément (W.Ind). A fine, full Rum from the Clément Distillery based in Martinique. Produces both a white and golden variety.

Rhum Duquesne (W.Ind). The name given to a white Rum produced on the southern part of Martinique. Sold under the Genippa label or if is aged 3 years then Grand Case (silver label) or 10 years then Val d'Or (gold label).

Rhum Marie Colas (W.Ind). The brand-name of a Rum produced in Haiti by the Cazeau Distillery.

Rhum Nazon (W.Ind). The brand-name of a Rum produced on Haiti.

Rhum Negrita (W.Ind). A fine, full Rum from Martinique.

Rhum Saint James (W.Ind). A fine, full Rum from Martinique. Made from cane juice syrup strengthened with dunder.

Rhum Tesserot (W.Ind). The brand-name of a Rum produced on Haiti.

Rhum Tropical (W.Ind). The brand-name of a Rum produced in Haiti by the Manège Distillery.

Rhum Verschnitt (Ger). Lit – 'Rum sandwich'. A blend of concentrated Pot-stilled Rums and local Corn spirits.

Rhyolite Rock (Hun). Rock from which the cellars of Tokay (for Aszú) are cut.

Rhyton (Gre). A drinking vessel used in ancient Greece. Was horn-shaped, the hole for drinking through being at the sharp (pointed) end.

Rialheim (S.Afr). See Clairvaux Co-operative.

Rialto Cocktail (Cktl). ¼ gill Calvados, ¼ gill Italian vermouth, 2 dashes orange squash, 2 sugar cubes. Crush sugar with squash, add remaining ingredients, stir over ice, strain into a cocktail glass, top with mint and an orange slice.

Rialtococo (Cktl). ⅓ measure Campari, ⅓ measure dry Gin, ⅓ measure Coconut cream, 1 scoop crushed ice. Blend together, serve in a large wine goblet with straws.

Ribatejo (Port). A wine district that produces low acidity, white wines and full-bodied, dark red wines of high alcohol.

Ribeauville (Fr). A wine town in the Haut-Rhin in Alsace. (Ger) = Rappoltsweiler.

Ribeiro (Sp). A Denominación de Origen wine producing area on the Portuguese border of north-western Spain. Grapes – Albariño, Brancellao, Cariño, Garnacha and Treixadura. Produces both red and white quality wines.

Ribeiro and Irmão (Port). Producers of Ribeiros (a brand of Vinho Verde).

Ribeiros (Port). A brand of Vinho Verde produced by Ribeiro and Irmão.

Ribena (Eng). The brand-name used by Beecham Products, Brentford, Middlesex for their famous non-alcoholic blackcurrant drink.

Ribera Alta (Sp). One of five wine-producing districts in the Navarra region. Divided into three sub-zones of Lerin, Marcilla and Olite.

Ribera Baja (Sp). One of five D.O. wine-producing districts in the Navarra region. A D.O. of Navarra.

Ribera de Ebro (Sp). One of three sub-zones in Tarragona. Grapes – Cariñena for red, Garnacha and Macabéo for white.

Ribero (Sp). The alternative spelling of the river Ribeiro and the region.

Riboflavin (Eng). A vitamin found in small traces in wines.

Ribolla (It). A white grape variety grown in north-eastern Italy. Produces dry white and sparkling wines.

Ribolla Gialla (It). A variety of the white Ribolla grape grown in north-eastern Italy.

Ribose (Eng). A Monosaccharide found in wine.

Ribote (Fr). A drunken bout, a booze-up.

Ricard (Fr). A famous French brand-name Pastis. 44.5% alc. by vol., nearly colourless.

Ricard-Bisquit Dubouché (Fr). A Cognac distillery based in Jarnac.

Ricardo (S.Afr). The brand-name of a dark Rum.

Ricasoli (It). A Tuscan family. The originators of Chianti at Brolio.

Riccadonna (It). A brand-name Italian vermouth made by the Gancia Co. of Turin. 15% alc. by vol. Also produces sparkling wines by both méthode champenoise and cuve close (see President Brut).

Ricciuti-Revolte (Fr). Champagne producer. Address = Avenay Val d'Or 51160 Ay. Récoltants-manipulants. Produces – Vintage and non-vintage wines.

Rice Beer (China) (Jap). Saké.

Rice Water (Eng). A non-alcoholic convalescent drink. Wash 2 ozs. rice and boil in 2 quarts water for 1½ hours, add sugar to taste and grated nutmeg, strain. Serve hot or cold.

Rice Wine (China) (Jap). Saké (rice beer). See Aspergillus Oryzae.

Riceys (Les) (Fr). A Cru Champagne village in the Canton de l'Aube. District = Château Thierry.

Rich (Eng). Denotes a wine having a generous bouquet, flavour and fullness of body.

Riche (Fr). A wine having a generous bouquet, flavour and fullness of body.

Richebourg (Fr). A Grand Cru vineyard in the A.C. commune of Vosne-Romanée, Côte de Nuits, Burgundy. 8 ha. Also known as Les Richebourg.

Richegude (Fr). A village in the A.C. Côtes du Rhône-Villages, south-eastern Rhône.

Richelieu Cocktail (Cktl). 1 measure Dubonnet, 1 measure Bourbon whiskey, 2 dashes Vieille Cure. Shake over ice, strain into an old-fashioned glass. Add a lemon peel spiral and an ice cube.

Richelieu's Infusion (Fr). A nickname given to Bordeaux wine in the eighteenth century after Cardinal Richelieu went to Aquitaine to retire after an active life. The wines of Bordeaux were said to give him a new lease of life.

Richemone (La) (Fr). A Premier Cru vineyard in the A.C. commune of Nuits-Saint-Georges, Côte de Nuits, Burgundy. 2.2 ha.

Richemont (Fr). A commune in the Charente-Maritime Département whose grapes are classed as Borderies.

Richert Cellars (USA).A winery based in Santa Clara, California. Grape varieties – Cabernet sauvignon and Chardonnay. Produces varietal and dessert wines.

Richis (Rum). An important wine-producing area (part of the Tîrnave Vine Vineyard).

Richlieu (S.Afr). The brand-name of a Brandy produced by Oude Meester.

Richmodis Kölsch (Ger). A beer brewed by the Richmodis Brauerei based in Cologne.

Richmond Grove Vineyard (Austr). Address = Sandy Hollow, New South

Wales, 2333. 150 ha. Grape varieties –
Cabernet sauvignon, Chardonnay,
Gewürztraminer, Merlot, Sauvignon
blanc and Sémillon.

Richon (Isr). A brand of medium-sweet
white wine produced by Carmel.

Richon-le-Zion (Isr). An important wine-
producing centre. Produces red, white
and sparkling wines from French grape
varieties.

Richter 110 (Sp). A rootstock used in the
regions of Alicante, Jumilla, Yecla and
Tarragona. A cross between the Vitis
Rupestris and Vitis Berlandieri.

Rick (USA). A constructed framework or
rack in a warehouse in which barrels of
distilled spirits are stored for ageing.

Ricketts (Thomas) (Eng). An early Bristol
glassmaker who patented in 1811 a
hinged butterfly mould which enabled
bottles to be blown in one operation.

Rickey (Cktl). A spirit, lime and soda
water served in a tall glass with ice.
Usually dry in taste. See Gin Rickey.

Ricking (USA). The process of stacking
Whiskey barrels on Ricks.

Ricoliano Cocktail (Cktl). 1¼ fl.ozs.
white Rum, ½ fl.oz. lime juice, ¼ fl.oz.
Galliano, dash Gomme syrup. Stir over
ice in a highball glass. Top with soda
water. Dress with a cherry, orange slice.
Serve with straws.

Ricour Brasserie (Fr). A small family
brewery based in St. Sylvestre Chappel.
Brews Du Moulin beers.

Riddar Cocktail (Cktl). 2 ozs. Mandarine
Napoléon, ½ oz. white Rum, ½ oz. dry
Gin, 1 oz. pineapple juice. Shake well
with ice, strain into a cocktail glass.

Ridder Pilsener (Bel). See De Ridder.

Riddling Bins (Eng). The name given to
the automatic Remueurs (Crécelles) for
sparkling wines.

Ridge Farm (Eng). Vineyard. Address =
Lamberhurst, Kent. 16.5 ha. Planted in
1972. Soil – clay on sandstone. Grape
varieties – Müller-Thurgau, Ortega,
Reichensteiner, Riesling, Schönburger
and Seyvre villard. Wines sold under
the Lamberhurst Priory label.

Ridge Vineyards (USA). A winery based
in Santa Cruz Mountains, Santa Clara,
California. Grape varieties – Cabernet
sauvignon, Petite syrah and Zinfandel.
Produces varietal wines.

Ridgways (Eng). Tea producers noted
especially for their Imperial blend.

Ridgway's Royal H.M.B. (Eng). A high
grown Ceylon, Chinese and Formosa
blend tea favoured by Queen Victoria
and others. Produced by Ridgway's.

Riding Brewery (Eng). North Country
Breweries of Hull, Yorkshire. Noted for

a cask conditioned Bitter 103

Ridley Brewery (Eng). Bo
Chelmsford, Essex. Noted for
ditioned HE Bitter 1045 O.G.
Ale 1080 O.G. Essex Ale 1030
Bob 1050 O.G. and Stock Ale 10

Riebeek-Wes (S.Afr). A table
producing region based w
Tulbagh.

Riebeek Wine Farmers' Co-op
(S.Afr). Based at Riebeek-K
Address = Riebeek Wynboere Ko
tiewe, Box 13, Riebeek-Kasteel,
Produces varietal wines.

Riebeek Wynboere Koöperatiewe (S
See Riebeek Wine Farmers' (
erative.

Riecine (It). A Chianti Classico proc
based in Tuscany.

Ried (Aus). Vineyard.

Riedersbückele (Ger). Vineyard. (An
Württemberg. (Ber) = Württemberg
Unterland. (Gro) = Kirchenwein
(Vil) = Lauffen.

Riedlingen (Ger). Village. (Anb) = Bac
(Ber) = Markgräflerland. (Gro) = Vo
Rötteln. (Vin) = Steingässle.

Rieffel (Pierre) (Fr). A noted Eau-de-
distiller in Breitenbach, in the E
Rhin, Alsace.

Riegel (Ger). Village. (Anb) = Baden.
(Ber) = Kaiserstuhl-Tuniberg. (Gro) =
Vulkanfelsen. (Vin) = St. Michaels-
berg.

Riegele Brauerei (Ger). A brewery base in
Augsburg that is noted for its' Perlweizen 5% alc. by vol. and Hefeweizen
5% alc. by vol. (both wheat beers),
Spezi 5% alc. by vol. (a malty Lager
beer) and Speziator 7.9% alc. by vol.

Riegelfeld (Ger). Vineyard. (Anb) = Ahr.
(Ber) = Walporzheim/Ahrtal. (Gro) =
Klosterberg. (Vil) = Ahrweiler.

Rieliel Distillerie (Fr). An Eau-de-vie
distillery based in Breitenbach, Bas
Rhin, Alsace.

Rielinghausen (Ger). Village. (Anb) =
Württemberg. (Ber) = Württembergisch
Unterland. (Gro) = Schalkstein. (Vin) =
Kelterberg.

Riemerschmied (Ger). A liqueur made
from figs.

Riemerschmied (Ger). A large distillery
based in Munich. Is noted for Enzian.

Rieschen (Ger). Vineyard. (Anb) = Baden.
(Ber) = Badensee. (Gro) = Sonnenufer.
(Vil) = Meersburg.

Rieslaner (Ger). A white grape variety. A
cross between the Sylvaner and the
Riesling. Gives fruity wines. Is also
known as the Main Riesling.

Riesling (Ger). One of the greatest white
grape varieties also grown in France,

Hungary, Yugoslavia etc. Produces superior quality white wines. Known also as the Johannisberg riesling, Rhine riesling, White riesling, Riesling renano etc. (No relation to the Welschriesling).

Riesling (USA). See California Riesling.

Riesling Cup (Cktl). 1 bottle Riesling, ½ bottle dry Cider, small bottle lemonade. Chill ingredients. Stir together, add slices of orange and lemon and a sprig of mint.

Riesling de Banat (Rum). See Creata.

Riesling de Caldas (Bra). See Duchesse.

Riesling de Dealulmare (Rum). A white wine from the Dealul Mare district.

Riesling de Italie (Rum). A name given to the white grape variety Welschriesling. See Riesling Italien (alternative spelling).

Riesling Doré (Fr). The name given to the Goldriesling of Germany.

Riesling-Italiano (It). See Riesling Italico.

Riesling Italico (It). A name given to the white grape variety Welschriesling in the Trentino-Alto Adige.

Riesling Italien (Rum). See Riesling de Italie.

Riesling Massandra (USSR). A dry white wine from the Crimean peninsula. Produced from the Riesling grape.

Riesling Renano (It). The name given to the true Riesling in the Trentino-Alto Adige region.

Riesling-Sylvaner (N.Z.). The name used for the Müller-Thurgau grape.

Riesling Talianski (Czec). A name given to the white grape variety Welschriesling.

Riesling Tea (Eng). An eighteenth- and nineteenth-century nickname for the wines of the Mosel-Saar-Ruwer made from the Riesling grape because of the reputed health-giving properties of the wine.

Riesling X Sylvaner (It). The Trentino-Alto Adige name for the Müller-Thurgau white grape variety.

Riet (Ger). Village. (Anb) = Württemberg. (Ber) = Württembergisch Unterland. (Gro) = Stromberg. (Vin) = Kirchberg.

Rietenau (Ger). Village. (Anb) = Württemberg. (Ber) = Württembergisch Unterland. (Gro) = Schalkstein. (Vin) = Güldenkern.

Rietrivier Co-operative (S.Afr). Based at Klein Karoo. Address = Rietrivier Wynkelder Koöperatief, Box 144, Montagu 6720. Produces – Chenel and varietal wines.

Rietrivier Wynkelder Koöperatief (S.Afr). See Rietrivier Co-operative.

Rietvallei Estate (S.Afr). Based at Robertson. Address = Box 368, Robertson, 6705. Produces varietal and some fortified wines.

Riex (Switz). A noted vineyard based in Lavaux.

Riffault (Pierre et Étienne) (Fr). Propriétaires-viticulteurs based at Verdigny-en-Sancerre, Cher.

Riga (USSR). A Pilsener-style beer brewed at the Yantar Brewery.

Right Arm (Eng) (slang). 'To exercise my right arm', to raise a glass of beer to the mouth.

Rignana (It). A Chianti Classico producer based in Tuscany.

Rigoverno (It). Occurs in March-April. The second operation which is similar to the Governo process (which occurs in December).

Rijckshof Wines (S.Afr). See Kango Co-operative.

Rijnwijn (Hol). Hock. Rhine wine.

Rikyu (Jap). The tea master who conducts the Chanoyu tea ceremony.

Rilly-la-Montagne (Fr). A Premier Cru Champagne village in the Canton de Verzy. District = Reims.

Rimaux Brasserie (Fr). A family-run brewery based near Valenciennes. Was formerly an Abbaye brewery. Brews Réserve Saint Landelin.

Rimavskà Brewery (Czec). A brewery based in eastern Czec.

Rimontaggio (It). The name given to the process of extracting the colour in red wine using the maceration technique.

Rimpar (Ger). Village. (Anb) = Franken. (Ber) = Maindreieck. (Gro) = Not yet assigned. (Vin) = Kobersberg.

Rimski (Can). A brand of Vodka produced by Hiram Walker. 40% alc. by vol.

Rinaldi (Guiseppe) (It). A small winery based in Barolo, Piemonte.

Rince Cochon (Fr) (slang). Lit – 'Pig's swill'. The old name for Nikita.

Rince Gueule (Fr). Lit – 'Mouth rinse'. Refers to a light wine drunk before a meal to refresh the palate. e.g. Beaujolais.

Rinces (Les) (Fr). A wine-producing village in the commune of Solutré-Pouilly in A.C. Pouilly-Fuissé, Mâcon, Burgundy.

Ringelbach (Ger). Village. (Anb) = Baden. (Ber) = Ortenau. (Gro) = Fürsteneck. (Vin) = Renchtäler.

Ringnes Brewery (Nor). A brewery based in Oslo. Produces Bock beers and Tuborg under licence. Exports to the USA.

Ringsheim (Ger). Village. (Anb) = Baden. (Ber) = Breisgau. (Gro) = Burg Lichteneck. (Vin) = Kaiserberg.

Ringtons Teas (Eng). An old established tea-blending company (1907) for the north-east of England based in Newcastle.

Ringwood Brewery (Eng). Based in Ringwood, Hampshire. Noted for its cask

conditioned Fortyniner 1049 O.G. and Old Thumper 1060 O.G.

Rinquinquin (Fr). A peach-flavoured liqueur. 14.8% alc. by vol.

Rinsol (Sp). A dry white wine produced by Federico Paternina S.A. in Rioja, north-western Spain.

Rio de Janeiro (Bra). A noted wine-producing state in central-western Brazil.

Rio Grande (Mad). A vitis vinifera cross white grape variety used in Madeira production.

Rio Grande do Sul (Bra). The main vine-yard area in southern Brazil which borders Uruguay.

Rioja (Sp). A Denominación de Origen of north-western Spain around the banks of the river Ebro and the tributary river Oja from which the region takes its name. Produces most styles of wines (dry) and is the best known of all the Spanish table wines. Grape varieties – Garnacha, Garnacha blanca, Graciano, Malvasia, Mazuela, Tempranillo and Viura. See Rioja Alavesa, Alta and Baja.

Rioja Alavesa (Sp). An area within the Rioja region of northern Spain. Lies north-west of the river Ebro.

Rioja Alta (Sp). An area within the Rioja region of northern Spain. Lies south-east of the river Ebro.

Rioja Alta (La) S.A. (Sp). Vineyard Address = Avenida de Vizcays s/n, Haro (La Rioja). 120 ha. Grape varieties – Garnacha, Graciano, Tempranillo and Viura. Wines – 96% red, 3% white and 1% rosé. Produces Viña Alberdi, Viña Ardanza, Reserva 904 and Metropol Extra (white).

Rioja Baja (Sp). An area within the Rioja region of northern Spain. Lies south-east of river Ebro.

Rioja Bordon (Sp). A red wine from the Bodegas Franco-Españolas. Made from Garnacha 40%, Mazuelo 10% and Tempranillo 50%. Matured in oak 2½ years and in bottle 1 year.

Rioja Ederra (Sp). A red wine produced by Bodegas Bilbainas, Haro, Rioja.

Rioja Information Bureau (Eng). Address = 140, Cromwell Road, London SW7.

Rioja Mark (Sp). A complicated series of lines put onto a wine cask to denote the style of wine.

Riojanas S.A. (Sp). See Bodegas Riojanas.

Rioja Santiago (Sp). A firm that exports Yago wines to the USA and most other countries. See Bodegas Rioja Santiago.

Rioja Vega (Sp). Red and white wines produced by the Bodegas Muerza S.A. Rioja.

Riol (Ger). Village. (Anb) = Mosel-Saar-Ruwer. (Ber) = Bernkastel. (Gro) = Prob-stberg. (Vin) = Römerberg.

Riomaggiore (It). One of five towns in the Cinque Terre, Liguria region.

Rio Negro (Arg). A wine-producing region south of Mendoza.

Rions (Fr). A commune in the Gironde Département. Produces red and white wines.

Rion Valley (USSR). A wine valley of the Georgia region. Noted for its white wines.

Rio Oja (Sp). A small river (a tributary of the river Ebro) in the Rioja Alta near Haro where the region gets its name.

Rio Plata (Mex). The brand-name of a noted Tequila.

Rio Segundo Beer (Arg). A Beer brewed for export to the USA.

Riotte (La) (Fr). A Premier Cru vineyard in the A.C. commune of Morey-Saint-Denis, Côte de Nuits, Burgundy. 2.47 ha.

Riottes (Les) (Fr). A Premier Cru vineyard in the A.C. commune of Monthélie, Côte de Beaune, Burgundy. 0.7 ha.

Rio Viejo (Sp). A brand of dry Oloroso sherry produced by Domecq at Jerez de la Frontera.

Ripaille Blanc (Fr). A dry white wine produced in Savoie.

Riparia (USA). See Vitis Riparia.

Riparia X Rupestris (Mad). A rootstock grown in Madeira.

Ripasso (It). A slow fermentation method used for wines similar in style to Valpo-licella. The finished wine is passed over the lees of Amarone or Recioto.

Ripe (Eng). The balance between the point of sugar and acid content.

Ripe (Eng). A term used to describe wines that have been made from ripe grapes (not necessarily mature).

Ripley (USA). A white hybrid grape variety that produces dry white wines.

Ripped (USA) (slang). Drunk.

Riquewihr (Fr). A wine town in the Haut-Rhin in Alsace. (Ger) = Reichenweir.

Riserva (It). A wine aged for a statutory period in cask. (Usually 3–4 years).

Riserva del Granduca (It). A Chianti Putto produced by Artimino in Tuscany.

Riserva di Montelera Brut (It). A sparkling (méthode champenoise) wine produced by Martini and Rossi in the Piemonte region.

Riserva Speciale (It). A wine aged for at least 5 years in cask.

Rishon-le-Zion (Isr). Lit – 'First in Zion'. The most important centre for viticulture in Israel which produces most styles of wines.

Risingsbo Brewery (Swe). A brewery based in Smadjebacken in eastern Sweden.

Risling Italianski (USSR). The name given to the white grape Welschriesling.

Risorgimento (It). Lit – 'Rebirth'. The term used for wine that has passito grapes added to the fermenting must.

Ristretto Coffee (It). Very strong, black Espresso coffee. See also Lungo Coffee.

Ritchie Creek (USA). A small winery based near St. Helena, Napa Valley, California. Grape variety – Cabernet sauvignon.

Ritsch (Ger). Vineyard. (Anb) = Mosel-Saar-Ruwer. (Ber) = Bernkastel. (Gro) = Sankt Michael. (Vil) = Thörinich.

Rittenhouse (USA). A brand of Rye whiskey.

Ritterberg (Ger). Vineyard. (Anb) = Rheinhessen. (Ber) = Nierstein. (Gro) = Domherr. (Vil) = Schornsheim.

Ritter Brauerei (Ger). A brewery based in Dortmund.

Ritter Export (Ger). A Dortmund export beer brewed by the Dortmunder Ritter Brauerei in Dortmund, Westphalia.

Rittergarten (Ger). Vineyard. (Anb) = Rheinpfalz. (Ber) = Mittelhaardt-Deutsche Weinstrasse. (Gro) = Hochmess. (Vil) = Bad Dürkheim.

Ritterhölle (Ger). Vineyard. (Anb) = Nahe. (Ber) = Kreuznach. (Gro) = Pfarrgarten. (Vil) = Dalberg.

Ritterpfad (Ger). Vineyard. (Anb) = Mosel-Saar-Ruwer. (Ber) = Saar-Ruwer. (Gro) = Scharzberg. (Vil) = Wawern.

Rittersberg (Ger). Grosslage. (Anb) = Baden. (Ber) = Badische Bergstrasse/Kraichgau. (Vils) = Dossenheim, Grossachsen, Heidelberg, Hemsbach, Hohensachsen, Laudenbach, Leutershausen, Lützelsachsen, Schriesheim, Sulzbach, Weinheim.

Rittersberg (Ger). Vineyard. (Anb) = Rheinpfalz. (Ber) = Südliche Weinstrasse. (Gro) = Herrlich. (Vil) = Ilbesheim.

Rittersheim (Ger). Village. (Anb) = Rheinpfalz. (Ber) = Mittelhaardt-Deutsche Weinstrasse. (Gro) = Schnepfenflug vom Zellertal. (Vin) = Am Hohen Stein.

Ritter von Dürnstein Trocken (Aus). A brand of Sekt produced by Inführ, from the Riesling grape.

Rittos, Irmãos. Lda (Port). A wine producer of Dão wines.

Ritz (Ire). The brand-name of a Perry produced by Showerings.

Ritz (The) (Eng). An old nineteenth-century tea blend.

Ritz Fizz (Cktl). 1 dash blue Curaçao, 1 dash Amaretto, 1 dash PLJ. Place into a Champagne flute, stir, top up with iced Champagne and decorate with a rose petal.

Riunite (It). The name of a growers' co-operative based in Emilia-Romagna that receives wine from other co-operatives and then blends, matures and bottles it.

Riva (La) (Sp). Sherry shippers based in Jerez de la Frontera. Produce the fino sherry – Tres Palmas, also Guadalupe and Royal Cream. Owned by Domecq.

Rivadavia (Arg). A wine-producing area based in the Mendoza region.

Rivaner (Lux). A name given to the Müller-Thurgau white grape variety.

Rivarey (Sp). Red and white wines produced by Bodegas Marqués de Cáceres S.A. Rioja, Spain. Red wines made from 85% Tempranillo and 20% of Garnacha, Graciano, Mazuelo and Viura. Oak matured for 6–12 months and 6 months in bottle. White made from the Viura grape.

Rivenich (Ger). Village. (Anb) = Mosel-Saar-Ruwer. (Ber) = Bernkastel. (Gro) = Michelsberg. (Vins) = Brauneberg, Geisberg, Niederberg, Rosenberg.

River City Brewery (USA). A brewery based in Sacramento, California. Is noted for its unpasteurised, dry-hopped Lager – River City Gold 4.8% alc. by vol.

River City Gold (USA). See River City Brewery.

River Don (USSR). A wine-producing region based near the Sea of Azov. Contains centres of Constantinovka, Novocherkassk and Tsimliansa. Produces mainly white wines.

River East Vineyard (USA). A vineyard owned by Sonoma Vineyards. Produces Johannisberg riesling grapes.

Riverettes (Les) (Switz). A white wine produced from the Fendant grape in the Valais region.

River Fly (Eng). A light-bodied Fino Sherry from Findlater.

Riverhead Wines Glenburn Limited (N.Z.). The brand-name used by the Glenburn Winery in Riverhead for a range of their wines.

Riverina (Austr). A wine area surrounding the towns of Riverina and Griffith in New South Wales. Noted for its white wines.

Riverina College Winery (Austr). See College Winery.

Riveris (Ger). Village. (Anb) = Mosel-Saar-Ruwer. (Ber) = Saar-Ruwer. (Gro) = Römerlay. (Vins) = Heiligenhäuschen, Kuhnchen.

Riverland (Austr). A wine area around the Murray region in South Australia/Victoria border.

Riverland Chardonnay (Austr). Part of Orlando Wines.

Riverlands Winery (N.Z.). Part of the Montana Wines.

R

Rivero (Sp). A Sherry house based in Jerez de la Frontera.

River Oaks Winery (USA). A winery based in the Alexander Valley, Sonoma County, California. 83 ha. Grape varieties – Cabernet sauvignon, Chardonnay, Chenin blanc, Colombard, Gamay and Gewürztraminer. Produces varietal and table wines.

River Road Winery (USA). A winery based in Forestville, Sonoma County, California. 50 ha. Grape varieties – Chardonnay, Johannisberg riesling and Zinfandel. Produces varietal wines.

River Run Vintners (USA). A winery based near Watsonville, Monterey County, California. Grape varieties – Cabernet sauvignon, Pinot noir, White riesling and Zinfandel. Produces varietal wines.

Riverside (USA). A Californian wine district within the region of Cucamonga. Produces table and dessert wines.

River West Vineyard (USA). A vineyard owned by Sonoma Vineyards. Produces Chardonnay grapes.

Rivesaltes (Fr). A fortified A.C. white Vin Doux Naturel from the Midi region. Made from the Muscat grape. Minimum age 1 year.

Riviera (Cktl). ¼ measure Regnier Framboise, ¼ measure Cointreau, ½ measure white Rum. Mix in a tumbler with ice, top with bitter lemon. Squeeze over with the juice of ¼ lemon.

Riviera Cocktail (Cktl).(Non-alc). ⅓ pint orange juice, ⅛ gill Angostura, ⅕ gill blackcurrant syrup. Shake over ice, strain into an ice-filled highball glass. Dress with an orange slice. Serve with straws.

Riviera del Garda Chiaretto (It). D.O.C. rosé wine from Lombardy. Made from the Barbera, Berzemino, Gropello and Sangiovese grapes.

Riviera del Garda Rosso (It). D.O.C. red wine from Lombardy. Made from the Barbera, Berzemino, Gropello and Sangiovese grapes. If the minimum alc. content is 12% by vol. and aged 1 year can be classed Superiore.

Rivière (Roland) (Fr). Cognac producer. Address = Domaine de St-Pardon, Mortiers, 17500 Jarnac. 160 ha. in the Fins Bois. Produces five different styles of Cognacs.

Rivolet (Fr). A commune in the Beaujolais district. Has A.C. Beaujolais-Villages or Beaujolais-Rivolet status.

Rizling (Hun). Riesling.

Rizling-Szemelt (Hun). A light, dry, white wine of Riesling character.

Rizlingszilvàni (Hun). A white grape variety also known as the Müller-Thurgau.

Rizling Vlassky (Czec). A name for the white grape variety Welschriesling. Lit – 'Riesling of Vlassos'.

Rkatsiteli (USA). A white grape variety originating in Georgia (USSR).

Rkatsiteli (USSR). A white grape variety. See Rka-ziteli.

Rka-ziteli (USSR). The name for a white grape variety grown in Georgia. See also Rkasiteli.

R.M. (Fr) (abbr). Récoltant-Manipulant. Champagne label initials which are registered by the C.I.V.C. for the name belonging to the proprietor of a vineyard who makes and sell his own wines.

R.N. (Fr) (abbr). Réserve Nouvelle. In Cognac production given to those Cognacs that had 5 years in cask.

Road House (Eng). A public house (pub) situated on a major highway. Usually incorporates a restaurant.

Road Runner (Cktl). 1 fl.oz. Vodka, ¼ fl.oz. Amaretto, ¼ fl.oz. Coconut milk. Shake over ice, strain into a cocktail glass. Top with nutmeg.

Roadster (Cktl). ⅓ measure Gin, ⅓ measure Grand Marnier, ⅓ measure orange juice. Shake over ice, strain into a cocktail glass. Add a twist of lemon.

Road Tanker (Eng). 16,000 litre containers usually of several compartments so that many different wines can be transported in bulk at the same time.

Roaillan (Fr). A commune in the A.C. Graves district in the south-western Bordeaux.

Roaix (Fr). An A.C. Côtes du Rhône-Villages red wine vineyard.

Roast and Grinders (Eng) (slang). Trader's term for people who make and grind fresh coffee.

Roasted Barley (Eng). Unmalted, kilned barley used to add colour to Porter and Stout beers.

Roasting (Eng). A process of heating the green coffee beans to 240°C to colour and release chemicals which give the coffee aroma and flavour. See Pyrolysis.

Rob (Eng). Describes a fruit juice that has been evaporated to a thick syrupy consistency.

Robardelle (Fr). A Premier Cru vineyard [part] in the A.C. commune of Volnay, Côte de Beaune, Burgundy.

Robe (Fr). The colour (purple) of wine.

Roberta (Cktl). ⅓ measure dry Vermouth, ⅓ measure Cherry brandy, ⅓ measure Vodka, dash Crème de Banane, dash

Campari. Shake over ice, strain into a cocktail glass. Add zest of an orange.

Roberta May (Cktl). ⅓ measure Aurum, ⅓ measure Vodka, ⅓ measure orange juice, dash egg white. Shake and strain into a cocktail glass.

Robert Brown (Jap). A brand of Whiskey produced by Seagram and the Kirin Brewery.

Robert Burns Cocktail (Cktl). 1 fl.oz. Scotch whisky, ½ fl.oz. sweet Vermouth, dash Pernod, dash Angostura. Stir over ice, strain into a cocktail glass.

Robert E. Lee Cooler (Cktl). Dissolve ½ teaspoon of sugar into the juice of ½ a lime and a little water in a highball glass. Add ice, 2 fl.ozs. Gin and 2 dashes Pernod. Top with ginger ale. Dress with a spiral of lemon peel.

Robert Keenan Winery (USA). See Keenan Winery.

Robert Mondavi Winery (USA). See Mondavi Winery.

Robert Pecota Winery (USA). See Pecota Winery.

Roberts (Eng). The trading name for a chain (229) of wine shops run by Imperial Retail Shops Ltd (a division of Courage Ltd).

Robert Setrakian Vineyards (USA). See Setrakian Vineyards.

Robertson (S.Afr). A district in the Breede River Valley. Noted for its Muscat dessert wines and Brandy.

Robertson and Baxter (Scot). A company founded in 1857, is one of the Lang Brothers subsidiaries. Were originally Whisky blenders.

Robertson Bros (Port). Vintage Port shippers. Vintages – 1942, 1945, 1947, 1955. Subsidiary of Sandemans. Ships Rebello Valente vintage Port, also Gamebird Ruby and Tawny Ports.

Robertson Co-operative (S.Afr). Based in Robertson. Address = Robertson Koöperatief Wynmakery, Box 37, Robertson 6705. Produces – Robroi and varietal wines.

Robertson Koöperatief Wynmakery (S.Afr). See Robertson Co-operative.

Robert Stemmler Winery (USA). See Stemmler Winery.

Robert Young Vineyards (USA). See Young Vineyards.

Robigato (Port). A white grape variety used in the making of Port.

Robin (Jules) (Fr). A Cognac producer. Address = 36, Rue Gabriel Jaulin, 16103 Cognac. Part of the Martell group.

Robin Fils (USA). Producers of sparkling wines based near New York. Labels include Pol d'Argent.

Robin Hood Ale (Eng). A bottled Pale ale 1045 O.G. brewed by the Home Brewery in Nottingham.

Robin's Nest Cocktail (Cktl). ⅖ measure Vodka, ⅖ measure cranberry juice, ⅕ measure (white) Crème de Menthe. Shake over ice, strain into a cocktail glass.

Robinson Brewery (Eng). Based in Stockport, Cheshire. Noted for its cask conditioned Old Tom 1080 O.G. and keg Cock Robin 1035 O.G. Einhorn Lager 1035 O.G. Took over the Hartley Brewery in Cumbria in 1982.

Robinsons (Eng). The brand-name used by Colman's of Norwich, Norfolk for a range of non-alcoholic soft fruit drinks.

Robinsons Barley Water (Eng). A famous non-alcoholic fruit drink made from citrus juice, sugar and cooked barley flour by Colman's of Norwich, Norfolk.

Robinsons Family Vineyard (Austr). Address = Lyra Church Road, Ballandean, Queensland. 18 ha. Grape varieties – Cabernet sauvignon, Chardonnay, Gewürztraminer, Malbec, Merlot, Pinot noir, Sauvignon blanc and Shiraz.

Robinvale Winery (Austr). Part of the McWilliams Vineyards in New South Wales. Also a winery in Murray River, Victoria.

Robiola (It). A white grape variety more commonly known as Ribolla.

Robka (Austr). The brand-name of an Australian Vodka.

Roble (Chile). Chilean oak casks.

Roble (Sp). Oak.

Robola (Gre). A white grape variety grown on the Isle of Cephalonia. Used to produce dry white wines of same name.

Robola (Gre). A dry, white wine made on Cephalonia Island. Also spelt Rombola.

Robola de Cephalonia (Gre). See Robola.

Robroi (S.Afr). A full-bodied red wine made from Cabernet 85% and Tinta barocca 15% grape varieties. Oak matured, produced by the Robertson Co-operative.

Rob Roy (Cktl).(1). 1½ measures Scotch whisky, ½ measure Italian Vermouth, dash Angostura. Stir over ice, strain into a cocktail glass.

Rob Roy (Cktl).(2). ¼ gill Scotch whisky, ¾ gill French vermouth, 2 dashes Angostura, 2 dashes Gomme syrup. Stir over ice, strain into a cocktail glass, add a cherry and a squeeze of lemon peel juice.

Rob Roy (Cktl).(3). ⅙ gill French vermouth, ⅙ gill Scotch whisky, 2 dashes Angostura, 1 dash Orange bitters, 2

R

dashes brown Curaçao. Stir over ice, strain into a cocktail glass. Serve with a cherry and dash of lemon peel juice.

Rob Roy (Scot). A blended Scotch whisky produced by Stanley P. Morrison. 40% alc. by vol.

Robson Cocktail (Cktl). ⅓ gill Jamaican rum, ⅓ gill orange juice, 4 dashes Grenadine, 4 dashes lemon juice. Shake over ice, strain into a cocktail glass.

Robson Vineyard (Austr). Address = Mount View, Hunter Valley, New South Wales. 5 ha. Grape varieties – Cabernet sauvignon, Chardonnay, Hermitage, Malbec, Merlot, Pinot noir, Sauvignon blanc and Traminer.

Robust (Eng). The term used by a wine taster to describe a sturdy, full-bodied wine.

Robusta Coffee (Afr). See Coffea Canephora.

Roc (Fr). A proprietary apéritif.

Roc Amadour (Fr). A liqueur made from Armagnac and juniper berries by Denoix of Brive.

Roc Blanquant (Fr). Address = 33330 Saint-Émilion, Commune = Saint-Émilion. A.C. Saint-Émilion, Bordeaux.

Roc Blanquet (Fr). The second wine of Château Belair Grand Cru Classé A.C. Saint-Émilion, Bordeaux.

Rocca (It). An honoury title awarded to the best wines annually.

Rocca dei Giorgi (It). A sparkling (méthode champenoise) wine produced by Gancia in the Piemonte region.

Rocca delle Macie (It). A Chianti Classico producer based in Tuscany.

Roche (La) (Ger). Vineyard. (Anb) = Rheinhessen. (Ber) = Bingen. (Gro) = Adelberg. (Vil) = Flonheim.

Roche-aux-Moines (La) (Fr). A famous vineyard in the A.C. Savennières. 25 ha. Produces sweet and dry white wines.

Rochecorbon (Fr). A commune in the A.C. Vouvray, Touraine district of the Loire.

Rochefort Brasserie (Bel). A Trappist abbaye brewery based near Dinant in south-east Belgium. Produces copper-coloured, bottle-conditioned Bières at 6, 8 and 10 ° Balling.

Rochefort-sur-Loire (Fr). A commune of the Coteaux du Layon, Anjou-Saumur district of the Loire. Sweet white wines.

Rochegude (Fr). An A.C. Côtes du Rhône-Villages. Drôme Département village.

Rochelle (La) (S.Afr). A wine and brandy company based in Bonnievale. Noted for its fortified wines.

Roche Pourrie (Fr). The name given to the disintergrating schist soil in the Mâcon district of Burgundy.

Roches (Les) (Fr). A vineyard in the A.C. Pouilly Fumé, Central Vineyards, Loire. Address = 58150 Pouilly-sur-Loire.

Roches-aux-Moines [La] (Fr). Dry white wines produced in the Savennières A.C. vineyards, Anjou-Saumur district in the Loire.

Rochusfels (Ger). Vineyard. (Anb) = Mosel-Saar-Ruwer. (Ber) = Obermosel. (Gro) = Gipfel. (Vil) = Köllig.

Rochusfels (Ger). Vineyard. (Anb) = Mosel-Saar-Ruwer. (Ber) = Obermosel. (Gro) = Gipfel. (Vil) = Nittel.

Rociador (Sp). The name for the perforated pipes used to refresh wine casks.

Rociar (Sp). To refresh an old Solera with young new wine.

Rock (Hugh) (Eng). A wine-producer based at Loddon Park Farm, Twyford, Berkshire.

Rock and Rum (USA). A liqueur based as for Rock and Rye.

Rock and Rye (USA). A liqueur with a Rye Whiskey base, but including grain neutral spirits, rock candy syrup and fruits (lemons, oranges and cherries). The sugar crystallises inside the bottle.

Rock and Rye Cooler (Cktl). ⅗ gill Vodka, ⅖ gill Rock and Rye, juice ¼ lime. Shake over ice, strain into an ice-filled highball glass. Top with bitter lemon and a slice of lime.

Rock Crystal (Eng). A type of glass from Thomas Webb.

Rock Lodge Vineyard (Eng). Address = Scaynes Hill, Sussex. 14.5 ha. planted in 1965. Soil – sandy loam. Grape varieties – Müller-Thurgau 95% and Reichensteiner 5%.

Rock's Country Wines (Eng). A range of wines produced by Hugh Rock, Loddon Park Farm, Twyford, Berkshire.

Rocky Cellar (Hun). The brand-name used for the Pilsener-style beers in Dreher.

Rocky Mountain Cooler (Cktl). Shake together over ice 1 egg, juice of a lemon and Gomme syrup to taste. Strain into a highball glass, top with iced Cider and a little grated nutmeg.

Rococo (Eng). A light and elegant glass c1725–45.

Rococo Cocktail (Cktl). ⅖ measure Kirsch, ⅖ measure orange juice, ⅕ measure Triple Sec. Shake over ice, strain into a cocktail glass.

Rödchen (Ger). Vineyard. (Anb) = Rheingau. (Ber) = Johannisberg. (Gro) = Steinmacher. (Vil) = Martinsthal.

R

Roddis Cellars (USA). A small winery based near Calistoga, Napa Valley, California. Grape variety – Cabernet sauvignon.

Röde (Ger). Vineyard. (Anb) = Württemberg. (Ber) = Kocher-Jagst-Tauber. (Gro) = Tauberberg. (Vil) = Reinsbronn.

Rödelsee (Ger). Village. (Anb) = Franken. (Ber) = Steigerwald. (Gro) = Schlossberg. (Vins) = Küchenmeister, Schwanleite.

Rodenbach (Bel). See Rodenbach Brasserie.

Rodenbach Brasserie (Bel). A brewery based in Roeselare. Is noted for its Rodenbach (Grand Cru) – a light-hopped, sour beer that's matured 2 years in which time a lactic fermentation occurs. Is blended with a younger version of Rodenbach. 5.25% alc. by vol.

Rodeorm (Swe). A brand of Mead produced by the Till Brewery.

Rödersheim-Gronau (Ger). Village. (Anb) = Rheinpfalz. (Ber) = Mittelhaardt-Deutsche Weinstrasse. (Gro) = Hofstück. (Vin) = Fuchsloch.

Rodet (Antonin) (Fr). A négociant-éleveur based in Mercurey, Côte Chalonnaise, Burgundy.

Rodet (Jacques) (Fr). Propriétaire-récoltant based in Tauriac, Gironde. Produces Château Brulesécaille.

Rode Wijn (Hol). Claret.

Roditis (Gre). A red grape variety used mainly in spirit production.

Roditys (Gre). A fairly dry, fragrant rosé wine.

Rodney Decanter (Eng). The name given to the Ship's decanter of the time of Admiral Rodney in the eighteenth century. Has a ringed neck.

Rodriguez y Berger (Sp). Noted wine-producers based in the La Mancha region.

Rød Tuborg (Den). A red label Tuborg Lager produced by Carlsberg. A Münchner-style beer.

Rødvin (Den). Red wine.

Roederer (Louis) (Fr). Champagne producer. Address = 21 Boulevard Lundy, 51100 Reims. Grande Marque. Produces – Vintage and non-vintage wines. Vintages – 1900, 1904, 1906, 1911, 1913, 1914, 1915, 1919, 1920, 1921, 1923, 1926, 1928, 1929, 1932, 1933, 1934, 1935, 1937, 1938, 1941, 1942, 1943, 1945, 1947, 1948, 1949, 1952, 1953, 1955, 1959, 1960, 1961, 1962, 1963, 1964, 1966, 1967, 1969, 1971, 1973, 1974, 1975, 1976, 1978, 1979, 1980, 1982, 1983. Produces Crystal Brut (in a white glass bottle).

Roederer (Théophile) (Fr). Champagne producer. Address = 20 Rue Andrieux, 51100 Reims. Produces – Vintage and non-vintage wines.

Roemer (Ger). A medium-stemmed decorated glass used for German wines. Not to be confused with the 'Hock' glass used for Mosel wines. See Prunt.

Roemer (Hol). A toasting glass used in the nineteenth century. Was egg-shaped and short-stemmed. See Rummer.

Roemerblut (Switz). A red (Grand Vin) produced by Martigny in the Valais from the Pinot noir.

Roero (It). D.O.C. red wine (introduced 1985) in central Piemonte. Made from the Nebbiolo grape. Pre 1985 was known as Nebbiolo d'Alba.

Roeselare Brasserie (Bel). A brewery based in western Flanders. Brews red beers.

Roetschelt (Lux). A vineyard site in the village of Bech-Kleinmacher.

Roffignac (Comte Ferdinand de) (Fr). Cognac producer. Address = Château Chesnel, B.P. 113, 16104. 35 ha. in Borderies. Produces – Vielle Fine Champagne 20 year old and Extra Grande Champagne 25–30 years old.

Roga (Port). A band of pruners who cut back the vines in the Douro in the Winter season.

Roger (Cktl). 1½ fl.ozs. Gin, 1½ fl.ozs. peach juice, 1½ fl.ozs. orange juice, 2 dashes lemon juice. Shake over ice, strain into an ice-filled highball glass.

Roger's Special Beer (Eng). A cask conditioned Ale 1065 O.G. brewed by the Frog and Parrot (Whitbread) home-brew public house in Sheffield, Yorkshire.

Rogge (Hol). Rye.

Roggen (Ger). Rye.

Rohracker (Ger). Village. (Anb) = Württemberg. (Ber) = Remstal-Stuttgart. (Gro) = Weinsteige. See Stuttgart.

Rohrbach (Ger). Village. (Anb) = Rheinpfalz. (Ber) = Südliche Weinstrasse. (Gro) = Herrlich. (Vin) = Schäfergarten.

Rohrbach (Ger). Village. (Anb) = Rheinpfalz. (Ber) = Südliche Weinstrasse. (Gro) = Kloster Liebfrauenberg. (Vin) = Mandelpfad

Rohrbach a Gr (Ger). Village. (Anb) = Baden. (Ber) = Badische Bergstrasse/Kraichgau. (Gro) = Stiftsberg. (Vil) = Lerchenberg.

Roi de Rome (Fr). An 1811 distilled Cognac 31% alc. by vol. produced by A.E. Dor in Jarnac.

Rois de France (Fr). A 30 year old Cognac produced by Rouyer.

Rojal Blanco (Sp). The alternative name used for Subirat/Malvasia riojana grape.

R

Rolande (La) (Fr). A vineyard in the A.C. Châteauneuf-du-Pape, southern Rhône.

Roliand (Bernard) (Fr). Récoltants-Manipulants in Champagne. Address = 21, Rue Corbier, Mareuil. Produces – Vintage and non-vintage wines.

Rolin (Nicholas) (Fr). The founder of the Hospices de Beaune, Beaune, Burgundy. Also name for certain cuvées in En Genêt 0.4 ha. Les Cents Vignes 1.5 ha. and Les Grèves 0.8 ha. (all Premier Cru Beaune vineyards) which are owned by the Hospices de Beaune.

Rolle (Fr). A white grape variety grown in A.C. Bellet, Provence.

Roller Disco (Cktl). Place ⅕ gill Cherry brandy into an ice-filled highball glass. Top with bitter lemon.

Rolling Rock (USA). A Lager beer brewed by the Latrobe Brewery in Pennsylvania.

Rolls-Royce (Cktl).(1). ⅓ measure Cointreau, ⅓ measure Brandy, ⅓ measure orange juice. Shake over ice, strain into a cocktail glass.

Rolls-Royce (Cktl).(2). ⅗ measure dry Gin, ⅕ measure dry Vermouth, ⅕ measure sweet Vermouth, 2 dashes Bénédictine. Stir over ice, strain into a cocktail glass.

Rolly-Gassmann (Fr). A wine-producer based in Alsace. Address = 1–2, Rue de l'Église, 68590 Rorschwihr.

Roma (Austr). A wine-producing area based in Queensland.

Roma (USA). A label used by the Guild of Wineries and Distilleries.

Roma Director's Choice Brandy (USA). The brand-name of a brandy bottled by the Guild of Wineries and Distilleries at Lodi, California.

Romagnano (It). A red wine produced by Bruno Colacicchi in the Latium region.

Roman Brasserie (Bel). A brewery based near Oudenaarde. Produces Mater (a Brown ale named after the village), Brunor (a Brown ale) and Dobbelen Bruinen (a double-Brown ale).

Romance Royale (Cktl). Into a large cocktail glass place some crushed ice, then in order, ½ oz. Rose's lime cordial, ½ oz. Coco-Ribe and 1 oz. Bols Parfait Amour. Serve with straws.

Romanèche-Thorins (Fr). A commune in the Beaujolais district. Has A.C. Beaujolais-Villages or Beaujolais-Romanèche-Thorins status.

Romanée (Fr). A Grand Cru vineyard in the A.C. commune of Vosne-Romanée, Côte de Nuits, Burgundy. 0.83 ha. Also known as La Romanée.

Romanée (La) (Fr). A Premier Cru vineyard [part] in the A.C. commune of Chassagne-Montrachet, Côte de Beaune, Burgundy. 3.16 ha.

Romanée-Conti (Fr). A Grand Cru vineyard in the A.C. commune of Vosne-Romanée, Côte de Nuits, Burgundy. 1.87 ha.

Romanée la Tâche (Fr). A Grand Cru vineyard in the A.C. commune of Vosne-Romanée, Côte de Nuits, Burgundy. Also known as La Tâche. 6 ha.

Romanée-Saint-Vivant (Fr). A Grand Cru vineyard in the A.C. commune of Vosne-Romanée, Côte de Nuits, Burgundy. 8.5 ha. Also known as La Romanée-Saint-Vivant.

Romanesti (USSR). A red wine from Moldavia. Produced in the Bordeaux style from Malbec, Merlot and Cabernet sauvignon grapes.

Roman Glass (It). The Romans were producing a crude form of drinking glasses c 100 BC.

Romania (Rum). Makes both red and white wines. Most esteemed wine is Cotnari, a white dessert wine.

Romano Cream (Sp). A brand of Cream sherry produced by Gonzalez Byass in Jerez de la Frontera.

Romanoff (Cktl). ⅓ measure Crème de Fraise, ⅓ measure Cointreau, ⅓ measure cream, dash lemon juice, dash egg white. Shake well over ice, strain into a flute glass, dress with a fresh strawberry and sprig of mint.

Romanoff (Eng). A brand-name British-made Vodka from Grants of St. James. 40% alc. by vol.

Romanoff Cocktail (Cktl).(Non-alc). ⅓ measure Sirop de Fraises, ⅓ measure orange juice, ⅓ measure cream, dash lemon juice, dash egg white. Shake well over ice, strain into a flute glass, dress with a fresh strawberry and mint sprig.

Roman Sling (Cktl). 1½ fl.ozs. dry Gin, ¼ fl.oz. Grand Marnier, ½ fl.oz. orange juice, ½ fl.oz. lemon juice, ¼ fl.oz. Brandy. Shake over ice, strain into an ice-filled highball glass, dress with an orange slice and a cherry.

Romansrivier Co-operative (S.Afr). Based at Breede river. Address = Romansrivier Koöperatiewe, P.O. Box 108, Wolseley 6830. Produces varietal wines.

Romansrivier Koöperatiewe (S.Afr). See Romansrivier Co-operative.

Romany (Eng). The old English name for the wines of Rumania. See also Rumney.

Romate (Sp). Brandy producer. Address = Sanchez Romate Tlnos S.A, Lealas. 26–28 P.O. Box 5, Jerez de la Frontera, Cadiz. Obtains wines from Jerez. Produces – Brandies under the labels of Cardenal Cisneros over 10 years old, Cardenal Mendoza over 10 years old.

R

Also produces a range of Sherries including Don José, Iberia Cream, Marismeno, N.P.U Amontillado and Petenara.

Roma Wines (S.Afr). A brand-name wine produced by the Stellenbosch Farmers' Winery.

Rombola (Gre). See Robola.

Rombouts (Ger). A coffee-producing company that produced the first individual (primed with ground coffee) disposable one cup filters.

Rome (Sp). A red grape variety once used in Málaga production.

Rome Anglais (W.Ind). A spirit derived from sugar cane. Superior to Guildhive. The name later altered to Rum.

Romefort (Fr). A Bourgeois Supérieur A.C. Médoc, Commune = Avensan, north-western Bordeaux.

Romeiko (Gre). A red grape variety grown on the island of Crete.

Romeral (Sp). A red wine produced by the A.G.E. Bodegas Unidas S.A., Rioja. Grape varieties – Garnacha 20%, Mazuelo 20% and Tempranillo 60%.

Römerberg (Ger). Lit – 'Roman hill'. A popular name for German vineyards. 23 individual sites have this name.

Römerberg (Ger). Vineyard. (Anb) = Baden. (Ber) = Markgräflerland. (Gro) = Burg Neuenfels. (Vil) = Badenweiler.

Römerberg (Ger). Vineyard. (Anb) = Baden. (Ber) = Markgräflerland. (Gro) = Burg Neuenfels. (Vil) = Niederweiler.

Römerberg (Ger). Vineyard. (Anb) = Mittelrhein. (Ber) = Bacharach. (Gro) = Schloss Reichenstein. (Vil) = Oberheimbach.

Römerberg (Ger). Vineyard. (Anb) = Mittelrhein. (Ber) = Bacharach. (Gro) = Burg Hammerstein. (Vil) = Rheinbrohl.

Römerberg (Ger). Vineyard. (Anb) = Mosel-Saar-Ruwer. (Ber) = Bernkastel. (Gro) = Kurfürstlay. (Vil) = Burgen.

Römerberg (Ger). Vineyard. (Anb) = Mosel-Saar-Ruwer. (Ber) = Bernkastel. (Gro) = Probstberg. (Vil) = Riol.

Römerberg (Ger). Vineyard. (Anb) = Mosel-Saar-Ruwer. (Ber) = Obermosel. (Gro) = Gipfel. (Vil) = Oberbillig.

Römerberg (Ger). Vineyard. (Anb) = Mosel-Saar-Ruwer. (Ber) = Zell/Mosel. (Gro) = Grafschaft. (Vil) = Nehren.

Römerberg (Ger). Vineyard. (Anb) = Mosel-Saar-Ruwer. (Ber) = Zell/Mosel. (Gro) = Goldbäumchen. (Vil) = Senheim.

Römerberg (Ger). Vineyard. (Anb) = Nahe. (Ber) = Kreuznach. (Gro) = Pfarrgarten. (Vil) = Gutenberg.

Römerberg (Ger). Vineyard. (Anb) =

Nahe. (Ber) = Kreuznach. (Gro) = Schlosskapelle. (Vil) = Bingen-Bingerbrück.

Römerberg (Ger). Vineyard. (Anb) = Nahe. (Ber) = Kreuznach. (Gro) = Schlosskapelle. (Vil) = Münster-Sarmsheim.

Römerberg (Ger). Vineyard. (Anb) = Nahe. (Ber) = Kreuznach. (Gro) = Schlosskapelle. (Vil) = Weiler.

Römerberg (Ger). Vineyard. (Anb) = Nahe. (Ber) = Kreuznach. (Gro) = Schlosskapelle. (Vil) = Windesheim.

Römerberg (Ger). Vineyard. (Anb) = Nahe. (Ber) = Schloss Böckelheim. (Gro) = Burgweg. (Vil) = Waldböckelheim.

Römerberg (Ger). Vineyard. (Anb) = Nahe. (Ber) = Schloss Böckelheim. (Gro) = Paradiesgarten. (Vil) = Merxheim.

Römerberg (Ger). Vineyard. (Anb) = Rheinhessen. (Ber) = Bingen. (Gro) = Kaiserpfalz. (Vil) = Engelstadt.

Römerberg (Ger). Vineyard. (Anb) = Rheinhessen. (Ber) = Bingen. (Gro) = Sankt Rochuskapelle. (Vil) = Badenheim.

Römerberg (Ger). Vineyard. (Anb) = Rheinhessen. (Ber) = Nierstein. (Gro) = Domherr. (Vil) = Essenheim.

Römerberg (Ger). Vineyard. (Anb) = Rheinhessen. (Ber) = Nierstein. (Gro) = Rheinblick. (Vil) = Alsheim.

Römerberg (Ger). Vineyard. (Anb) = Rheinhessen. (Ber) = Nierstein. (Gro) = Rheinblick. (Vil) = Dorn-Dürkheim.

Römerberg (Ger). Vineyard. (Anb) = Rheinhessen. (Ber) = Wonnegau. (Gro) = Sybillenstein. (Vil) = Alzey.

Römerberg (Ger). Vineyard. (Anb) = Rheinpfalz. (Ber) = Südliche Weinstrasse. (Gro) = Trappenberg. (Vins) = Alter Berg, Narrenberg, Schlittberg.

Römerbrunnen (Ger). Vineyard. (Anb) = Rheinpfalz. (Ber) = Mittelhaardt-Deutsche Weinstrasse. (Gro) = Pfaffengrund. (Vil) = Hambach.

Römergarten (Ger). Vineyard. (Anb) = Mosel-Saar-Ruwer. (Ber) = Zell/Mosel. (Gro) = Rosenhang. (Vil) = Briedern.

Römerhalde (Ger). Vineyard. (Anb) = Nahe. (Ber) = Kreuznach. (Gro) = Kronenberg. (Vil) = Bad Kreuznach (ortsteil Planig).

Römerkrug (Ger). Vineyard. (Anb) = Mittelrhein. (Ber) = Rheinburgengau. (Gro) = Schloss Schönburg. (Vil) = Dellhofen.

Römerkrug (Ger). Vineyard. (Anb) = Mittelrhein. (Ber) = Rheinburgengau. (Gro) = Schloss Schönburg. (Vil) = Oberwessel.

R

Römerlay (Ger). Grosslage. (Anb) = Mosel-Saar-Ruwer. (Ber) = Saar-Ruwer. (Vils) = Franzenheim, Hockweiler, Kasel, Korlingen, Mertesdorf, Mertesdorf (ortsteil Maximin Grünhaus), Morscheid, Riveris, Sommerau, Trier, Waldrach.

Römerpfad (Ger). Vineyard. (Anb) = Mosel-Saar-Ruwer. (Ber) = Bernkastel. (Gro) = Kurfüstlay. (Vil) = Maring-Noviand.

Römerpfad (Ger). Vineyard. (Anb) = Nahe. (Ber) = Schloss Böckelheim. (Gro) = Paradiesgarten. (Vil) = Unkenbach.

Römerquelle (Ger). Vineyard. (Anb) = Mosel-Saar-Ruwer. (Ber) = Zell/ Mosel. (Gro) = Schwarze Katz. (Vil) = Zell-Kaimt.

Römerschanze (Ger). Vineyard. (Anb) = Rheinhessen. (Ber) = Nierstein. (Gro) = Krötenbrunnen. (Vil) = Eimsheim.

Römersteg (Ger). Vineyard. (Anb) = Rheinhessen. (Ber) = Wonnegau. (Gro) = Liebfrauengarten. (Vil) = Worms.

Römerstich (Ger). Vineyard. (Anb) = Nahe. (Ber) = Schloss Böckelheim. (Gro) = Paradiesgarten. (Vil) = Auen.

Römerstrasse (Ger). Vineyard. (Anb) = Rheinpfalz. (Ber) = Mittelhaardt-Deutsche Weinstrasse. (Gro) = Schwarzerde. (Vil) = Kirchheim.

Römertor (Ger). An Untergebiet of the Oberrhein district.

Römerweg (Ger). Vineyard. (Anb) = Rheinpfalz. (Ber) = Südliche Weinstrasse. (Gro) = Mandelhöhe. (Vil) = Kirrweiler.

Romery (Fr). A Cru Champagne village in the Canton d'Ay. District = Reims.

Romford Brewery (Eng). A large brewery based in London and owned by Allied Breweries. Noted for its cask conditioned Benskins Bitter 1037 O.G. Taylor Walker 1037 O.G. Friary Meux 1037 O.G. keg John Bull 1036 O.G. canned Falcon Lager 1032 O.G.

Rommelshausen (Ger). Village. (Anb) = Württemberg. (Ber) = Remstal-Stuttgart. See Kernen.

Rommelshausen (Ger). Village. (Anb) = Württemberg. (Ber) = Remstal-Stuttgart. (Gro) = Wartbühl. (Vin) = Häder.

Romorantin (Fr). A white grape variety grown in the eastern Loire. Named after the town lying on a tributary of the river Cher.

Rom Ponche (Cktl). 2 dashes Angostura, teaspoon Grenadine, teaspoon sugar, juice ½ lemon. Build into an ice-filled highball glass. Fill with golden Rum, decorate with an orange, lemon and apple slice and a cherry.

Romy (Bel). The brand-name of a well-hopped Pilsener Lager beer.

Ron (Sp). Rum.

Ron (W.Ind). Rum.

Ronald Lamb Winery (USA). See Lamb Winery.

Ron Anejo Cacique (W.Ind). A brand of Rum produced in Costa Rica (is part of Seagram).

Ronceret (Fr). A Premier Cru vineyard in the A.C. commune of Volnay, Côte de Beaune, Burgundy.

Roncière (La) (Fr). A Premier Cru vineyard in the A.C. commune of Nuits-Saint-Georges, Côte de Nuits, Burgundy. 2.1 ha.

Roncières (Fr). A Premier Cru A.C. Chablis often is re-classified as the Premier Cru vineyard Mélinots.

Ronco (It). The Italian version of the French 'Cru'.

Ron Con Agua de Coco (S.Am). A local drink produced in Colombia drunk straight from a fresh coconut to which has been added a tot of Rum, crushed ice and sugar.

Rond (Fr). Denotes a full, supple, fleshy wine.

Rondeur (Fr). Roundness. A wine that drinks easily.

Rondibús (Fr). A term used in the Champagne region for a drunken person.

Rondinella (It). A red grape variety grown in the Veneto region. Used in the making of Bardolino.

Ron Guajiro (Sp). A brand of Rum produced by Cocal in Telde, Canary Isles.

Ron Llave (W.Ind). A white Rum produced in Puerto Rico and shipped for Seagram.

Ron Medellin (S.Am). The brand-name of a Rum that has been aged in Colombia to obtain a dark or yellowish colour.

Ron Montilla (Arg). A brand of Rum from Seagram.

Ronoro (W.Ind). A golden-coloured Rum produced on the island of Cuba.

Ron Peloeon (Sp). A primitive liquor. Lit – 'Drink of sailors'.

Ron Popular (S.Am). The brand-name of a Rum produced in Colombia by the State-owned Industria Licorera de Bolivar from molasses that have been distilled only once.

Ronrico (W.Ind). A white Rum shipped by Ronrico Rum Co. for Seagram.

Ron Viejo de Caldas (S.Am). The brand-name of a Rum produced in Colombia that has been aged to give a dark or yellowish colour.

Rood (Hol). Red.

Rood (S.Afr). A red wine blend of 80% Cabernet sauvignon and 20% Cinsault from the Lievland Estate.

R

Roodeberg (S.Afr). A red grape variety. A cross between the Hermitage and the Shiraz.

Roodeberg (S.Afr). A full-bodied red wine made from the Pinotage, Tinta barocca and Shiraz grapes. Made by the K.W.V.

Roodebloem (S.Afr). A smooth red wine made from the Cinsault based blended wine. Produced by the Stellenryck Wines.

Roodehof (S.Afr). A red wine made from the Pinotage grape by the De Doorns Co-operative.

Roode Huiswyn (S.Afr). A red wine made from 50% Cabernet sauvignon and 50% Tinta barocca. Produced by the Roodezandt Co-operative.

Roodendal (S.Afr). A rich red wine made by the SFW from the Cabernet sauvignon grape.

Rooderust (S.Afr). A blended red wine made from the Cabernet sauvignon, Pinotage and Shiraz grapes by SFW.

Roodewyn (S.Afr). Red wine.

Roodezandt Co-operative (S.Afr). Based in Robertson. Address = Roodezandt Koöperatiewe Wynmakery, Box 164, Robertson 6705. Produces varietal wines.

Roodezandt Koöperatiewe Wynmakery (S.Afr). See Roodezandt Co-operative.

Rooiberg Co-operative (S.Afr). Based in Robertson, Vinkrivier, Eilandia, Goree and Riverside. Address = Rooibergse Koöperatiewe Wynmakery, P.O. Box 358, Robertson 6705. Produces a vast range of varietal wines.

Rooibergse Koöperatiewe Wynmakery (S.Afr). See Rooiberg Co-operative.

Rooibos Tea [S.Afr]. A low tannin, caffeine free tea made from the indigenous Rooibos herb aspalathus linearis.

Rooiwyn (S.Afr). Red wine.

Room Temperature (Eng). The ideal temperature for red wines. 65°F to 68°F (18°C – 20°C). See also Chambré.

RO 15 4513 (Eng). A new drug that inhibits the intoxicating affect of alcohol (lasts approximately 30 minutes).

Roosje Zonder Doornen (Hol). Lit – 'Rose without thorns'. A liqueur made from rose essence.

Root Beer (USA). A carbonated drink made from ginger and other roots and herbs.

Rooty Hill (Austr). A vineyard based in the Murrumbidgee Irrigation Area, New South Wales.

Ropa (Gre). A red wine produced on the island of Corfu.

Rope (Eng). A bacterial infection that occurs in brewing. Zymamonas is an anaerobic bacteria that produces gelatinous threads in the beer. Ruins a cask in a few hours. See Ropey Beer. Can also be found in wine.

Rope and Anchor (W.Ind). A demerara Navy Rum producer. 40% alc. by vol.

Ropiness (Eng). See Graisse des Vins.

Ropiteau-Frères (Fr). A Burgundy négociant-éleveur based at Meursault, Côte de Beaune. Noted for the wines of Meursault and Monthélie.

Ropley Vineyard (Eng). A vineyard based at Ent House, Court Lane, Ropley, Hampshire. Was first planted in 1979. 0.4 ha. Grape varieties – Huxelrebe, Madeleine angevine, Müller-Thurgau and Reichensteiner.

Roquemaure (Fr). A commune of the A.C. Lirac in the southern Rhône. Produces white, rosé and red wines.

Roriz (Port). A red grape variety used in the making of Port. Used for its good colour and sugar. Also known as Tinto roriz.

Rory O'More Cocktail (Cktl). ⅔ measure Bushmills Irish Whiskey, ⅓ measure Italian vermouth, dash Orange bitters. Stir over ice, strain into a cocktail glass.

Rosa (Bul). A liqueur made from damascene rose petals.

Rosacki (Gre). A pink-red table grape sometimes used for making dessert wines in Crete.

Rosa de Perú (Mex). A red grape variety grown in Baja California.

Rosado (Port) (Sp). Rosé.

Rosado Fernandes (Port). A winery based in Reguengos, Alentejo. Produces red wines and pot-stilled brandies.

Rosales Distillery (Mex). A producer of Tequila of same name.

Rosa Muskat (Aus). A red grape variety also known as the Schönburger.

Rosati Winery (USA). A winery based in St. James, Missouri. Produces many different wines mainly based on the Concord grape.

Rosato (It). Pink, rosé wine.

Rosato del Salento (It). A non-D.O.C. rosé wine from the Puglia region. Made from the Negramaro and Malvasia grapes.

Rosbach Water (Fr). A naturally effervescent mineral water from Homburg.

Rosbercon (Austr). Part of the Tisdall Estate in Victoria. 80 ha.

Rosca (Port). The name for the spiral of a corkscrew. See Saca-Rolhas.

Roschbach (Ger). Village. (Anb) = Rheinpfalz. (Ber) = Südliche Weinstrasse. (Gro) = Bischofskreuz. (Vins) = Rosenkränzel, Simonsgarten.

Rosé (Fr). The term to denote a pink wine. Lit – 'Rosy'. See Vin Rosé.

Rosé (It). A sub-species of the Nebbiolo grape.

R

Rose and Crown (Eng). A Tetley Brewery home-brew public house in York. Noted for its cask conditioned Viking Bitter 1043 O.G.

Rosebank (Scot). A single Malt distillery near Falkirk, Stirlingshire. A Lowland malt. Produces an 8 year old Malt. Licence held by Distillers Agency Ltd. 43% alc. by vol.

Rosebower Vineyard (USA). A small vineyard based in Hampton-Sydney, Virginia. 1 ha. Produces French hybrid and vinifera wines.

Rose Cocktail (Cktl).(1). ¼ gill dry Gin, ⅛ gill French vermouth, ⅛ gill Dubonnet, 3 dashes Grenadine. Stir over ice, strain into a cocktail glass, add a cherry and a squeeze of lemon peel on top. (Orange peel can be used instead of lemon).

Rose Cocktail (Cktl).(2). ⅔ measure dry Vermouth, ⅓ measure Kirsch, teaspoon rose syrup. Stir over ice, strain into a cocktail glass. Top with a cherry.

Rose Cocktail (Cktl).(3). ½ measure Apricot brandy, 1 measure Gin, ½ measure dry Vermouth, dash lemon juice, 4 dashes Grenadine. Shake over ice, strain into a cocktail glass.

Rose Cocktail (Cktl).(4). ⅔ measure dry Gin, ⅙ measure orange juice, ⅙ measure Grenadine. Shake over ice, strain into a cocktail glass.

Rose Cocktail (Cktl).(5). 1 fl.oz. French vermouth, ¼ fl.oz. Cherry brandy, ¼ fl.oz. Kirsch. Stir well over ice, strain into a cocktail glass. Dress with a cherry.

Rose Cocktail (Cktl).(Non-alc). 4 strawberries cut into pieces, ½ slice pineapple cut into pieces, juice ½ lemon, juice ½ orange, few dashes orange cordial, Gomme syrup to taste. Shake all well over ice, strain into a 5 oz. wine glass. Decorate with rose petals.

Rose Cocktail Number One (Cktl). 1 measure Gin, ½ measure Cherry brandy, ½ measure dry Vermouth. Stir over ice, strain into a cocktail glass.

Rose Cocktail Number Two (Cktl). 1 measure Gin, ½ measure Kirsch, ½ measure Cherry brandy. Stir over ice, strain into a cocktail glass.

Rosé d'Anjou (Fr). An A.C. rosé wine from the Anjou-Saumur district of the Loire. Made from the Cot, Gamay, Groslot, Noble and Pinot d'Aunis grapes.

Rosé de Béarn (Fr). A V.D.Q.S. rosé wine from the south-west tip of France. Made from various grapes. See Irouléguy.

Rosé de Cabernet Anjou (Fr). An A.C. rosé wine from the Anjou-Saumur district of the Loire. Made from the Cabernet franc grape.

Rose de Chambertin (Cktl). 1½ fl.ozs.

Gin, ½ fl.oz. Crème de Cassis, ½ fl.oz. lime juice, dash egg white. Shake over ice, strain into a frosted cocktail glass (Crème de Cassis and castor sugar).

Rosé de Gamay (Switz). A dry rosé wine from the cantons of Geneva and Valais. Made from the Gamay grape.

Rosé de Loire (Fr). A recently created rosé wine of the Anjou-Saumur and the Touraine districts of the Loire. Has a minimum of 30% Cabernet grapes plus Gamay, Grolleau and Pineau d'Aunis.

Rosé de Marsannay (Fr). See Bourgogne Rosé de Marsannay.

Rosé de Riceys (Fr). A still rosé wine made in the Champagne region.

Rosé de Varsouie (Cktl). ⅙ measure Cointreau, ½ measure Vodka, ⅓ measure Cherry cordial, dash Angostura. Stir over ice, strain into an ice-filled highball glass. Add a cherry.

Rosé d'Orches (Fr). An Appellation Grand Ordinaire from the village of Orches near Auxey-Duresses. Made by La Cave Coopérative des Hautes-Côtes, Burgundy.

Roseewein (Ger). A rosé wine made from a blend of more than one type of red grape variety.

Rosé-Gris (Fr). A grade of rosé wine which is light and almost colourless.

Rosehill Vineyard (Austr). An estate belonging to the McWilliams Winery in Hunter Valley, New South Wales.

Rosehip Tea (Eng). A herbal tea rich in Vitamin C. Is sweet and astringent in taste.

Rosella (Cyp). A light, medium-dry, rosé wine produced by Keo in Limassol.

Rosellinia Necatrix (Lat). A fungus (family Pourridié) that attacks the vine roots. See Armillaria Root-Rot.

Roselyn (Cktl). Another name for the Rosington cocktail.

Rosé Millésimé (Fr). A vintage Champagne produced by Besserat de Bellefon from 70% Pinot noir and 30% Chardonnay.

Rosemount Estate (Austr). Address = Rosemount Road, Denman, Hunter Valley, New South Wales. 400 ha. in Coonawarra and Hunter Valley. Grape varieties – Cabernet sauvignon, Chardonnay, Sauvignon blanc, Sémillon, Shiraz and Traminer.

Rosenberg (Ger). Lit – 'Rosehill'. A popular name for vineyards in Germany. 42 individual vineyard sites are so named.

Rosenberg (Ger). Vineyard. (Anb) = Ahr. (Ber) = Walporzheim/Ahrtal. (Gro) = Klosterberg. (Vil) = Marienthal.

Rosenberg (Ger). Vineyard. (Anb) =

Baden. (Ber) = Badische Bergstrasse/ Kraichgau. (Gro) = Mannaberg. (Vil) = Dielheim.

Rosenberg (Ger). Vineyard. (Anb) = Baden. (Ber) = Badische Bergstrasse/ Kraichgau. (Gro) = Mannaberg. (Vil) = Tairnbach.

Rosenberg (Ger). Vineyard. (Anb) = Baden. (Ber) = Markgräflerland. (Gro) = Burg Neuenfels. (Vil) = Britzingen.

Rosenberg (Ger). Vineyard. (Anb) = Baden. (Ber) = Markgräflerland. (Gro) = Burg Neuenfels. (Vil) = Britzingen (ortsteil Dattingen).

Rosenberg (Ger). Vineyard. (Anb) = Baden. (Ber) = Markgräflerland. (Gro) = Burg Neuenfels. (Vil) = Zunzingen.

Rosenberg (Ger). Vineyard. (Anb) = Baden. (Ber) = Markgräflerland. (Gro) = Lorettoberg. (Vil) = Ehrenstetten.

Rosenberg (Ger). Vineyard. (Anb) = Franken. (Ber) = Maindreieck. (Gro) = Kirchberg. (Vil) = Sommerach.

Rosenberg (Ger). Vineyard. (Anb) = Franken. (Ber) = Maindreieck. (Gro) = Not yet assigned. (Vil) = Frankenwinheim.

Rosenberg (Ger). Vineyard. (Anb) = Mittelrhein. (Ber) = Rheinburgengau. (Gro) = Burg Hammerstein. (Vil) = Leutesdorf.

Rosenberg (Ger). Vineyard. (Anb) = Mittelrhein. (Ber) = Rheinburgengau. (Gro) = Burg Rheinfels. (Vil) = St. Goar-Werlau.

Rosenberg (Ger). Vineyard. (Anb) = Mosel-Saar-Ruwer. (Ber) = Bernkastel. (Gro) = Kurfürstlay. (Vil) = Bernkastel-Kues.

Rosenberg (Ger). Vineyard. (Anb) = Mosel-Saar-Ruwer. (Ber) = Bernkastel. (Gro) = Kurfürstlay. (Vil) = Osann-Monzel.

Rosenberg (Ger). Vineyard. (Anb) = Mosel-Saar-Ruwer. (Ber) = Bernkastel. (Gro) = Michelsberg. (Vil) = Minheim.

Rosenberg (Ger). Vineyard. (Anb) = Mosel-Saar-Ruwer. (Ber) = Bernkastel. (Gro) = Michelsberg. (Vil) = Rivenich.

Rosenberg (Ger). Vineyard. (Anb) = Mosel-Saar-Ruwer. (Ber) = Bernkastel. (Gro) = Schwarzlay. (Vil) = Kinheim.

Rosenberg (Ger). Vineyard. (Anb) = Mosel-Saar-Ruwer. (Ber) = Bernkastel. (Gro) = Schwarzlay. (Vil) = Wittlich.

Rosenberg (Ger). Vineyard. (Anb) = Mosel-Saar-Ruwer. (Ber) = Bernkastel. (Gro) = Vom Heissen Stein. (Vil) = Pünderich.

Rosenberg (Ger). Vineyard. (Anb) = Mosel-Saar-Ruwer. (Ber) = Obermosel. (Gro) = Gipfel. (Vil) = Wehr.

Rosenberg (Ger). Vineyard. (Anb) =

Mosel-Saar-Ruwer. (Ber) = Saar-Ruwer. (Gro) = Scharzberg. (Vil) = Oberemmel.

Rosenberg (Ger). Vineyard. (Anb) = Mosel-Saar-Ruwer. (Ber) = Saar-Ruwer. (Gro) = Scharzberg. (Vil) = Wiltingen.

Rosenberg (Ger). Vineyard. (Anb) = Mosel-Saar-Ruwer. (Ber) = Zell/Mosel. (Gro) = Goldbäumchen. (Vil) = Klotten.

Rosenberg (Ger). Vineyard. (Anb) = Mosel-Saar-Ruwer. (Ber) = Zell/Mosel. (Gro) = Goldbäumchen. (Vil) = Moselkern.

Rosenberg (Ger). Vineyard. (Anb) = Mosel-Saar-Ruwer. (Ber) = Zell/Mosel. (Gro) = Goldbäumchen. (Vil) = Pommern.

Rosenberg (Ger). Vineyard. (Anb) = Mosel-Saar-Ruwer. (Ber) = Zell/Mosel. (Gro) = Grafschaft. (Vil) = Neef.

Rosenberg (Ger). Vineyard. (Anb) = Mosel-Saar-Ruwer. (Ber) = Zell/Mosel. (Gro) = Rosenhang. (Vil) = Bruttig-Fankel.

Rosenberg (Ger). Vineyard. (Anb) = Mosel-Saar-Ruwer. (Ber) = Zell/Mosel. (Gro) = Rosenhang. (Vil) = Cochem.

Rosenberg (Ger). Vineyard. (Anb) = Mosel-Saar-Ruwer. (Ber) = Zell/Mosel. (Gro) = Rosenhang. (Vil) = Senheim.

Rosenberg (Ger). Vineyard. (Anb) = Mosel-Saar-Ruwer. (Ber) = Zell/Mosel. (Gro) = Weinhex. (Vil) = Oberfell.

Rosenberg (Ger). Vineyard. (Anb) = Nahe. (Ber) = Kreuznach. (Gro) = Kronenberg. (Vil) = Bad Kreuznach.

Rosenberg (Ger). Vineyard. (Anb) = Nahe. (Ber) = Kreuznach. (Gro) = Schlosskapelle. (Vil) = Windesheim.

Rosenberg (Ger). Vineyard. (Anb) = Nahe. (Ber) = Schloss Böckelheim. (Gro) = Burgweg. (Vil) = Niederhausen an der Nahe.

Rosenberg (Ger). Vineyard. (Anb) = Nahe. (Ber) = Schloss Böckelheim. (Gro) = Paradiesgarten. (Vil) = Mannweiler-Coelln.

Rosenberg (Ger). Vineyard. (Anb) = Nahe. (Ber) = Schloss Böckelheim. (Gro) = Paradiesgarten. (Vil) = Monzingen.

Rosenberg (Ger). Vineyard. (Anb) = Rheingau. (Ber) = Johannisberg. (Gro) = Burgweg. (Vil) = Lorchhausen.

Rosenberg (Ger). Vineyard. (Anb) = Rheinhessen. (Ber) = Nierstein. (Gro) = Petersberg. (Vil) = Biebelnheim.

Rosenberg (Ger). Vineyard. (Anb) = Rheinhessen. (Ber) = Nierstein. (Gro) = Spiegelberg. (Vil) = Nierstein.

Rosenberg (Ger). Vineyard. (Anb) =

R

Rheinpfalz. (Ber) = Südliche Wein-
strasse. (Gro) = Kloster Liebfrauenberg.
(Vil) = Billigheim-Ingenheim.
Rosenberg (Ger). Vineyard. (Anb) =
Rheinpfalz. (Ber) = Südliche Wein-
strasse. (Gro) = Kloster Liebfrauenberg.
(Vil) = Steinweiler
Rosenberg (Ger). Vineyard. (Anb) =
Rheinpfalz. (Ber) = Südliche Wein-
strasse. (Gro) = Königsgarten. (Vil) =
Arzheim.
Rosenberg (Ger). Vineyard. (Anb) =
Rheinpfalz. (Ber) = Südliche Wein-
strasse. (Gro) = Königsgarten. (Vil) =
Birkweiler.
Rosenberg (Ger). Vineyard. (Anb) =
Rheinpfalz. (Ber) = Südliche Wein-
strasse. (Gro) = Königsgarten. (Vil) =
Siebeldingen.
Rosenberg (Lux). A vineyard site in the
village of Grevenmacher.
Rosenblum Cellars (USA). A winery
based in Oakland, Alameda County,
California. Grape varieties – Cabernet
sauvignon, Chardonnay, Johannisberg
riesling, Petite syrah and Zinfandel.
Produces varietal wines.
Rosenbock (Ger). A Bock beer brewed by
the Rosenbrauerei based in Kauf-
beuren, western Munich.
Rosenborn (Ger). Vineyard. (Anb) =
Mosel-Saar-Ruwer. (Ber) = Zell/Mosel.
(Gro) = Schwarze Katz. (Vil) = Zell-
Kaimt.
Rosenbrauerei (Ger). A brewery based in
Kaufbeuren, western Munich. Uses the
symbol of a goat around the neck of the
bottle. Brews Rosenbock and Buro-
nator.
Rosenbühl (Ger). Grosslage. (Anb) =
Rheinpfalz. (Ber) = Mittelhaardt-
Deutsche Weinstrasse. (Vils) =
Erpolzheim, Freinsheim, Lambsheim,
Weisenheim/Sand.
Rosengärtchen (Ger). Vineyard. (Anb) =
Mosel-Saar-Ruwer. (Ber) = Bernkastel.
(Gro) = Michelsberg. (Vil) =
Neumagen-Dhron.
Rosengarten (Ger). Grosslage. (Anb) =
Nahe. (Ber) = Schloss Böckelheim.
(Vils) = Bockenau, Braunweiler, Burg-
sponheim, Hüffelsheim, Mandel, Rox-
heim, Rüdesheim, St. Katharinen,
Sponheim, Weinsheim.
Rosengarten (Ger). Vineyard. (Anb) =
Baden. (Ber) = Badische Bergstrasse/
Kraichgau. (Gro) = Hohenberg. (Vil) =
Hohenwettersbach.
Rosengarten (Ger). Vineyard. (Anb) =
Mosel-Saar-Ruwer. (Ber) = Bernkastel.
(Gro) = Schwarzlay. (Vil) = Traben-
Trarbach (ortsteil Starkenberg).
Rosengarten (Ger). Vineyard. (Anb) =

Rheingau. (Ber) = Johannisberg. (Gro)
= Burgweg. (Vil) = Rüdesheim.
Rosengarten (Ger). Vineyard. (Anb) =
Rheinhessen. (Ber) = Bingen. (Gro) =
Sankt Rochuskapelle. (Vil) = Bingen.
Rosengarten (Ger). Vineyard. (Anb) =
Rheinhessen. (Ber) = Nierstein. (Gro) =
Domherr. (Vil) = Gabsheim.
Rosengarten (Ger). Vineyard. (Anb) =
Rheinhessen. (Ber) = Wonnegau. (Gro)
= Domblick. (Vil) = Monsheim.
Rosengarten (Ger). Vineyard. (Anb) =
Rheinhessen. (Ber) = Wonnegau. (Gro)
= Gotteshilfe. (Vil) = Bechtheim.
Rosengarten (Ger). Vineyard. (Anb) =
Rheinpfalz. (Ber) = Mittelhaardt-
Deutsche Weinstrasse. (Gro) = Grafen-
stück. (Vil) = Obrigheim.
Rosengarten (Ger). Vineyard. (Anb) =
Rheinpfalz. (Ber) = Mittelhaardt-
Deutsche Weinstrasse. (Gro) = Hof-
stück. (Vil) = Freidelsheim.
Rosengarten (Ger). Vineyard. (Anb) =
Rheinpfalz. (Ber) = Südliche Wein-
strasse. (Gro) = Kloster Liebfrauenberg.
(Vil) = Kapellen-Drusweiler.
Rosengarten (Ger). Vineyard. (Anb) =
Rheinpfalz. (Ber) = Südliche Wein-
strasse. (Gro) = Ordensgut. (Vil) =
Edesheim.
Rosengarten (Ger). Vineyard. (Anb) =
Rheinpfalz. (Ber) = Südliche Wein-
strasse. (Gro) = Ordensgut. (Vil) =
Rhodt.
Rosengarten Brauerei (Switz). An
independent brewery based in Ein-
sieden.
Rosenhang (Ger). Grosslage. (Anb) =
Mosel-Saar-Ruwer. (Ber) = Zell/Mosel.
(Vils) = Beilstein, Bremm, Briedern,
Bruttig-Fankel, Cochem, Ellenz-
Poltersdorf, Mesenich, Senheim, Treis-
Karden, Valwig.
Rosenheck (Ger). Vineyard. (Anb) =
Nahe. (Ber) = Kreuznach. (Gro)
=Kronenberg. (Vil) = Bad Kreuznach
(ortsteil Winzenheim).
Rosenheck (Ger). Vineyard. (Anb) =
Nahe. (Ber) = Schloss Böckelheim.
(Gro) = Burgweg. (Vil) = Niederhausen
an der Nahe.
Rosenhügel (Ger). Vineyard. (Anb) = Mit-
telrhein. (Ber) = Siebengebirge. (Gro) =
Petersberg. (Vil) = Oberdollendorf.
Rosenkranz (Ger). Vineyard. (Anb) =
Baden. (Ber) = Kaiserstuhl-Tuniberg.
(Gro) = Vulkanfelsen. (Vil) = Bis-
choffingen.
Rosenkranz (Ger). Vineyard. (Anb) =
Rheinpfalz. (Ber) = Südliche Wein-
strasse. (Gro) = Bischofskreuz. (Vil) =
Böchingen.
Rosenkränzel (Ger). Vineyard. (Anb) =

Rheinpfalz. (Ber) = Südliche Weinstrasse. (Gro) = Bischofskreuz. (Vil) = Roschbach.

Rosenkranzweg (Ger). Vineyard. (Anb) = Baden. (Ber) = Badische Bergstrasse/Kraichgau. (Gro) = Mannaberg. (Vil) = Östringen.

Rosenlay (Ger). Vineyard. (Anb) = Mosel-Saar-Ruwer. (Ber) = Bernkastel. (Gro) = Beerenlay. (Vil) = Lieser.

Rosenmuskateller (It). The German name for the Moscato rosa grape variety in the Trentino-Alto Adige (Südtirol) region.

Rosental (Ger). Vineyard. (Anb) = Mittelrhein. (Ber) = Rheinburgengau. (Gro) = Schloss Schönburg. (Vil) = Perscheid.

Rosenteich (Ger). Vineyard. (Anb) = Nahe. (Ber) = Kreuznach. (Gro) = Schlosskapelle. (Vil) = Guldental.

Rosenthal (Ger). Vineyard. (Anb) = Ahr. (Ber) = Walporzheim/Ahrtal. (Gro) = Klosterberg. (Vil) = Ahrweiler.

Rosenthaler Riesling (Bul). A white wine produced from a blend of Riesling grapes grown in Karlovo.

Rosé of Cabernet Sauvignon (USA). The name given to a pink varietal wine made from the Cabernet sauvignon grape.

Rosé of Carmel (Isr). A semi-dry rosé wine produced for the USA market by the Carmel Co.

Rosé of Menes (Rum). See Menesi Rozsa.

Rosé of Pinot Noir (USA). The name given to a pink varietal wine made from the Pinot noir grape.

Rose of Warsaw (Cktl). ⅕ gill Vodka, ⅙ gill Wisniak Cherry liqueur, 3 dashes Cointreau, dash Angostura. Stir over ice, strain into a cocktail glass.

Rose Pauillac (La) (Fr). A vineyard in the commune of Pauillac. A.C. Pauillac, Haut-Médoc, Bordeaux.

Rose-Pauillac [La] (Fr). A blended wine from the Pauillac co-operative, Haut-Médoc, Bordeaux.

Rose Petal Tea (Eng). Freshly brewed tea, 3 dashes Angostura per cup, decorate with rose petals. Serve hot.

Rose Pouchong (China). A China tea flavoured with rose petals.

Rose's (Eng). The brand-name used by Schweppes for their famous lime juice cordial and High Juice orange squash.

Rose Street (Scot). A home-brew public house owned by the Alloa Brewery in Edinburgh. Noted for its cask conditioned Auld Reekie 1037 O.G.

Rosette (Fr). An A.C. district of the Bergerac region. Not a rosé! Produces medium-sweet white wines.

Rosé Vermouth (It). A base of rosé wine

flavoured with herbs and spices. Has a bitter-sweet flavour. Also produced by most major Vermouth manufacturers.

Rose Water (Eng). A perfumed water (oil of roses and of petals) used in certain cocktails.

Rosie Lee (Eng) (slang). Cockney rhyming slang for tea.

Rosington (Cktl). ⅓ gill dry Gin, ⅙ gill Italian vermouth. Shake over ice with a piece of orange zest. Strain into a cocktail glass, top with a squeeze of orange peel juice. Also known as the Roselyn Cocktail.

Rosita Cocktail (Cktl). ⅓ measure Tequila, ⅓ measure Campari, ⅙ measure Italian vermouth, ⅙ measure French vermouth. Stir over ice, strain into an ice-filled highball glass. Add a twist of lemon peel juice and serve with straws.

Rosnay (Fr). A Cru Champagne village in the Canton de Ville-en-Tardenois. District = Reims.

Rosoglio (USA). See Rosolio.

Rosolio (USA). A liqueur made from red rose petals, orange blossom water, cinnamon, clove, jasmine, sundew plant, alcohol and sugar. Also known as Rosoglio, Rossoll and Rossolis.

Ross (Can). The brand-name used by the Canadian Schenley Distilleries Ltd. for a range of liqueurs.

Rossanella (It). A red grape variety. Also known in Lombardy as the Molinara.

Rossara (It). A red grape variety grown in the Lake Garda distict.

Rossberg (Ger). Vineyard. (Anb) = Hessische Bergstrasse. (Ber) = Umstadt. (Gro) = None. (Vil) = Rossdorf.

Rossberg (Ger). Vineyard. (Anb) = Rheinpfalz. (Ber) = Südliche Weinstrasse. (Gro) = Trappenberg. (Vil) = Essingen.

Rossberg (Ger). Vineyard. (Anb) = Württemberg. (Ber) = Remstal-Stuttgart. (Gro) = Kopf. (Vil) = Winnenden.

Rossdorf (Ger). Vineyard. (Anb) = Hessische Bergstrasse. (Ber) = Umstadt. (Gro) = None. (Vil) = Rossberg.

Rossel (Ger). Vineyard. (Anb) = Nahe. (Ber) = Kreuznach. (Gro) = Schlosskapelle. (Vil) = Genheim.

Rosselli Mâté Rosso (S.Am). An apéritif, low in alcohol, made from Yerbe Mâté (a herbal tea).

Rossese (It). A red grape variety grown in Liguria.

Rossese di Dolceacqua (It). D.O.C. red wine from Liguria. Made from the Rossese grape. If total alc. content is 13% by vol. and is 10–11 months old then classed Superiore.

Rossetto (It). The local name for the Trebbiano giallo grape in Latium region.

Rossignol (Philippe) (Fr). A négociant-éleveur based at Gevrey-Chambertin, Côte de Nuits, Burgundy.

Rossignola (It). A red grape variety grown in the Veneto.

Rossiya (USSR). The name of a sparkling dry white wine.

Rosso (It). Red wine.

Rosso Antico (It). An apéritif wine produced and bottled by Gio Buton and G.S.P.A. in Trieste.

Rosso Barletta (It). A D.O.C. red wine from Apulia. Made from the Uva di Troia grape. 14% alc. by vol.

Rosso Conero (It). D.O.C. red wine from The Marches. Made from the Montepulciano and Sangiovese grapes in an area in the province of Ancona. The Governo all'Uso Toscano is recommended. Wine is named after Mount Conero.

Rosso della Quercia (It). D.O.C. red wine from the Chieti Hills. Made from 100% Montepulciano d'Abruzzo grapes.

Rosso delle Colline Lucchesi (It). D.O.C. red wine from Tuscany. Made from the Sangiovese 40–60% and Canaiolo, Ciliegiolo, Colorino, Malvasia, Trebbiano toscano and Verminto grapes.

Rosso di Cerignola (It). D.O.C. red wine from Puglia. Made from the Barbera, Malbec, Montepulciano, Nero amaro, Sangiovese, Trebbiano toscano and Uva di troia grapes. If aged minimum 2 years in cask and has total minimum alc. content of 13% by vol. then classed Riserva.

Rosso di Montalcino (It). A D.O.C. red wine from Montalcino, Siena in Tuscany. Produced mainly from the Sangiovese grape.

Rossola (It). A white grape variety also known as the Ugni blanc.

Rossolis (Fr). The French equivalent of Rosolio.

Rossoll (It). Also known as Rosolio.

Rosso Piceno (It). D.O.C. red wine from The Marches. Made from 40% Montepulciano and 60% Sangiovese grapes. Vinification can occur within the whole area of Ancona, Ascoli Piceno and Macerata. If total alc. content is 11.5% by vol. and aged 1 year minimum then classed Superiore (also grapes must be grown in the restricted area).

Ross Royal (Cktl). ⅓ measure Royal Mint Chocolate Liqueur, ⅓ measure Crème de Banane, ⅓ measure Brandy. Shake over ice, strain into a cocktail glass.

Rosstal (Ger). Grosslage. (Anb) = Fran-

ken. (Ber) = Maindreieck. (Vils) = Arnstein, Eussenheim, Gambach, Gössenheim, Himmelstadt, Karlburg, Karlstadt, Laudenbach, Mühlbach, Retzstadt, Stetten.

Rosstein (Ger). Vineyard. (Anb) = Mittelrhein. (Ber) = Rheinburgengau. (Gro) = Herrenberg. (Vil) = Kaub.

Rosswag (Ger). Village. (Anb) = Württemberg. (Ber) = Württembergisch Unterland. (Gro) = Stromberg. (Vins) = Forstgrube, Halde, Lichtenberg.

Rosy Cheeks (Cktl). ½ gill Ashbourne sparkling mineral water, ½ gill dry white wine. Place with ice in a highball glass, add dash of Grenadine, a slice of lime. Serve with straws.

Rot (Ger). Red.

Rota (Sp). Part of the Jerez Supérieur region.

Rota (Sp). The name given to the wine produced in the north of Spain. Usually used in blending.

Rotari Brut (It). A sparkling (méthode champenoise) wine produced by the Sociale Cooperativa di Mezzocorona.

Rota Tent (Sp). See Tintilla de Rota.

Rotberger (Ger). A red grape variety. A cross between the Trollinger and the Riesling. Produces fruity wines.

Rot Blanc (Fr). A white rot that attacks the ripening berries and splits them. Is treated using a copper solution or sodium bisulphite.

Rotclevener (Fr). A red grape variety grown in Alsace. Local name for the Pinot noir.

Rotclevner (Switz). See Rotclevener.

Rote Halde (Ger). Vineyard. (Anb) = Baden. (Ber) = Kaiserstuhl-Tuniberg. (Gro) = Vulkanfelsen. (Vil) = Sasbach.

Rote Kirsch (Ger). A bitter-sweet, deep red, cherry liqueur. Made by the Mampe Co.

Rotenberg (Ger). Village. (Anb) = Baden. (Ber) = Badische Bergstrasse/Kraichgau. (Gro) = Mannaberg. (Vin) = Schlossberg.

Rotenberg (Ger). Vineyard. (Anb) = Nahe. (Ber) = Schloss Böckelheim. (Gro) = Burgweg. (Vil) = Altenbamberg.

Rotenberg (Ger). Vineyard. (Anb) = Nahe. (Ber) = Schloss Böckelheim. (Gro) = Burgweg. (Vil) = Oberhausen an der Nahe.

Rotenberg (Ger). Vineyard. (Anb) = Rheinhessen. (Ber) = Wonnegau. (Gro) = Domblick. (Vil) = Wachenheim.

Rotenberg (Ger). Vineyard. (Anb) = Rheinpfalz. (Ber) = Südliche Weinstrasse. (Gro) = Trappenberg. (Vil) = Hochstadt.

Rotenberg (Ger). Village. (Anb) = Württemberg. (Ber) = Remstal-Stuttgart. (Gro) = Weinsteige. See Stuttgart.

Rotenbusch (Ger). Vineyard. (Anb) = Baden. (Ber) = Badische Bergstrasse/Kraichgau. (Gro) = Hohenberg. (Vil) = Söllingen.

Rotenfels (Ger). Vineyard. (Anb) = Nahe. (Ber) = Schloss Böckelheim. (Gro) = Burgweg. (Vil) = Traisen.

Rotenfels (Ger). Vineyard. (Anb) = Rheinhessen. (Ber) = Wonnegau. (Gro) = Sybillenstein. (Vil) = Alzey.

Rotenfelser im Winkel (Ger). Vineyard. (Anb) = Nahe. (Ber) = Schloss Böckelheim. (Gro) = Burgweg. (Vil) = Bad Münster a. St-Eburnburg.

Rotenpfad (Ger). Vineyard. (Anb) = Rheinhessen. (Ber) = Bingen. (Gro) = Adelberg. (Vil) = Flonheim.

Rotenstein (Ger). Vineyard. (Anb) = Rheinhessen. (Ber) = Wonnegau. (Gro) = Bergkloster. (Vil) = Westhofen.

Roter Berg (Ger). Vineyard. (Anb) = Baden. (Ber) = Breisgau. (Gro) = Burg Lichteneck. (Vil) = Kenzingen.

Roter Berg (Ger). Vineyard. (Anb) = Franken. (Ber) = Steigerwald. (Gro) = Schlosstück. (Vil) = Weimersheim.

Roter Berg (Ger). Vineyard. (Anb) = Württemberg. (Ber) = Württembergisch Unterland. (Gro) = Kirchenweinberg. (Vil) = Ilsfeld (ortsteil Schozach).

Roter Bur (Ger). Vineyard. (Anb) = Baden. (Ber) = Breisgau. (Gro) = Burg Zähringen. (Vil) = Glottertal.

Roterd (Ger). Vineyard. (Anb) = Mosel-Saar-Ruwer. (Ber) = Bernkastel. (Gro) = Michelsberg. (Vil) = Neumagen-Dhron.

Rotes Haus (Euro). Lit – 'Red house'. A wine from the Abtwingert vineyard in Liechtenstein.

Rotes Kreuz (Ger). Vineyard. (Anb) = Rheinhessen. (Ber) = Bingen. (Gro) = Kaiserpfalz. (Vil) = Ingelheim.

Rotfeld (Ger). Vineyard. (Anb) = Nahe. (Ber) = Schloss Böckelheim. (Gro) = Paradiesgarten. (Vil) = Nussbaum.

Rotgipfler (Aus). A white grape variety grown in southern Austria. Used for making Gumpoldskirchener.

Rotgrund (Ger). Vineyard. (Anb) = Baden. (Ber) = Kaiserstuhl-Tuniberg. (Gro) = Attilafelsen. (Vil) = Niederrimsingen.

Rot Gut (USA) (slang). A term for 'Bathtub Gin' or any other cheap inferior liquor.

Röth (Ger). Vineyard. (Anb) = Rheinpfalz. (Ber) = Mittelhaardt-Deutsche Weinstrasse. (Gro) = Höllenpfad. (Vil) = Grünstadt.

Rothbury Estate (Austr). Address = Broke Road, Pokolbin, New South Wales 2321. 185 ha. Grape varieties – Cabernet sauvignon, Chardonnay, Hermitage, Pinot noir, Sauvignon blanc and Sémillon. The second vineyard of Cowra.

Röthen (Ger). Vineyard. (Anb) = Baden. (Ber) = Markgräflerland. (Gro) = Burg Neuenfels. (Vil) = Niedereggenen.

Röthen (Ger). Vineyard. (Anb) = Baden. (Ber) = Markgräflerland. (Gro) = Burg Neuenfels. (Vil) = Obereggenen.

Rothenack (Ger). Vineyard. (Anb) = Mittelrhein. (Ber) = Rheinburgengau. (Gro) = Loreleyfelsen. (Vil) = Bornich.

Rothenberg (Ger). Vineyard. (Anb) = Nahe. (Ber) = Kreuznach. (Gro) = Schlosskapelle. (Vil) = Burg Layen.

Rothenberg (Ger). Vineyard. (Anb) = Nahe. (Ber) = Kreuznach. (Gro) = Schlosskapelle. (Vil) = Rümmelsheim.

Rothenberg (Ger). Vineyard. (Anb) = Nahe. (Ber) = Kreuznach. (Gro) = Sonnenborn. (Vil) = Langenlonsheim.

Rothenberg (Ger). Vineyard. (Anb) = Nahe. (Ber) = Schloss Böckelheim. (Gro) = Burgweg. (Vil) = Duchroth.

Rothenberg (Ger). Vineyard. (Anb) = Rheingau. (Ber) = Johannisberg. (Gro) = Burgweg. (Vil) = Geisenheim.

Rothenberg (Ger). Vineyard. (Anb) = Rheingau. (Ber) = Johannisberg. (Gro) = Steinmacher. (Vil) = Rauenthal.

Rothenberg (Ger). Vineyard. (Anb) = Rheinhessen. (Ber) = Bingen. (Gro) = Abtey. (Vil) = Gau-Algesheim.

Rothenberg (Ger). Vineyard. (Anb) = Rheinhessen. (Ber) = Nierstein. (Gro) = Rehbach. (Vil) = Nachenheim.

Rothschild (A. and Co) (Fr). A Champagne producer. Address = Epernay. Produces – Vintage and non-vintage wines. Vintages – 1900, 1904, 1906, 1911, 1914, 1921, 1926, 1928, 1934, 1937, 1941, 1943, 1945, 1947, 1952, 1953, 1955, 1959, 1961, 1962, 1964, 1966, 1969, 1970, 1971, 1975, 1976, 1979, 1982, 1983.

Rotlay (Ger). Vineyard. (Anb) = Mosel-Saar-Ruwer. (Ber) = Bernkastel. (Gro) = Michelsberg. (Vil) = Sehlem.

Rotlay (Ger). Vineyard. (Anb) = Mosel-Saar-Ruwer. (Ber) = Bernkastel. (Gro) = Schwarzlay. (Vil) = Platten.

Rotlay (Ger). Vineyard. (Anb) = Mosel-Saar-Ruwer. (Ber) = Saar-Ruwer. (Gro) = Römerlay. (Vil) = Trier.

Rotling (Ger). A pink wine made from red and white grapes mixed or musts. Is not made from mixed wines (red and white).

Roto System (Aus). A method of red wine vinification. A rotating inner container extracts the juice from the grapes leaving the pomace behind.

Rotsteig (Ger). Vineyard. (Anb) = Baden. (Ber) = Badische Bergstrasse/Kraichgau. (Gro) = Mannaberg. (Vil) = Malsch.

Rott (Ger). Grosslage. (Anb) = Hessische Bergstrasse. (Ber) = Starkenburg. (Vils) = Bensheim-Auerbach, Bensheim-Schönberg, Seeheim, Zwingenberg.

Rotten Egg Smell (Eng). See Hydrogen Sulphide.

Rotten Wood (Fr). A cask sickness that sometimes befalls Armagnac brandy between 8–14 months. Blending with older Armagnacs will hide this.

Rotter Muscateller (Ger). An alternative name for the Muscat rosé à petits grains grape variety.

Röttingen (Ger). Village. (Anb) = Franken. (Ber) = Maindreieck. (Gro) = Not yet assigned. (Vin) = Feuerstein.

Rottland (Ger). Lit – 'Red land'. An old vineyard near the town of Rudesheim in the Rheingau. Named after the colour of the Schistous soil. See Berg Rottland.

Rotunda (Gre). The name used by Boutari for a range of their cheaper wines.

Rotwein (Ger). Red wine.

Rotweinfest (Ger). Rheinhessen wine festival held at Ingelheim in September.

Rotweinwanderweg (Ger). The Ahr red wine road route.

Rocoules (Les) (Fr). A vineyard in the A.C. Hermitage, northern Rhône.

Roudey (Le) (Fr). A.C. Saint-Émilion, Commune = Saint-Sulpice-de-Faylrens. 4.44 ha. Grape varieties – Cabernet franc, Cabernet sauvignon and Merlot.

Roudnice (Czec). A wine-producing town based near Prague on the river Elbe.

Roudnice nad Labem Brewery (Czec). A brewery in northern Czec. based near Prague on the river Elbe.

Roudon-Smith Vineyards (USA). A winery based in Santa Cruz, California. Grape varieties – Cabernet sauvignon, Chardonnay, Gewürztraminer, Petite syrah, Pinot blanc and Zinfandel. Produces varietal wines.

Rouffach (Fr). A wine town in the Haut-Rhin region of Alsace. Known in German as either Rufach or Ruffach.

Rouffiac (Fr). A commune in the Charente-Maritime Département whose grapes are classed Petite Champagne (Cognac).

Rouffignac (Fr). A commune within the A.C. district of Monbazillac in Bergerac. Produces sweet (botrytis) white wines.

Rouge (Fr). Red. See Vin Rouge (red wine).

Rougeau (Fr). Lit – 'Leaf reddening'. Is caused by a wound in the plant stem that prevents the sap from rising from the roots. If it occurs above the ground the offending part is removed if possible.

Rouge d'Été (Fr). A brand label of J.C. Assemat in Roquemaure, Gard for a red A.C. Lirac produced by the semi-carbonique method from Cinsault and Grenache grapes.

Rouge Homme (Austr). Vineyard. Address = Coonawarra, South Australia. 60 ha. Grape varieties – Cabernet sauvignon, Chardonnay, Malbec, Pinot noir, Rhine riesling and Shiraz.

Rougemont Castle (Eng). A range of British wines from Whiteway's.

Rouge Noble (S.Afr). A red wine blend of 55% Tinta barocca and 35% Cinsault with some Pinotage. Produced by the Audacia Estate in Stellenbosch.

Rougeon (USA). A red grape variety also known as the Seibel 5898.

Rougeot (Fr). A fungus which causes sores to appear on the vines which eventually die and fall off. Not a regular hazard to vines. Treated by spraying with copper solution.

Rougets (Fr). The name for the light red (rosé) wines of the Anjou-Saumur district of the Loire.

Rough (Eng). A term used to describe a wine that is coarse and not balanced. Is heavy with tannin that will not soften with ageing.

Rough Elvot (Eng). An old Cider apple variety. See also Elvot.

Rouissillón Tinto (Sp). See Roussillon Tinto.

Roujolais (S.Afr). A soft red wine produced from the Cinsault grape in the coastal regions.

Roullet et Fils (Fr). Cognac producer. Address = Le Goulet de Foussignac, 16200, Jarnac. 21 ha. in the Fins Bois and 35 ha. in the Borderies. Produces Amber Gold *** and a wide range of other Cognac styles.

Round (Eng). A term used to describe drinks bought for those persons in drinking company. 'A round of drinks', 'Whose round is it?' 'My round' are some expressions used.

Round (Eng). A term used to describe a wine which is balanced and harmonious.

Round Hill Winery (USA). A winery based near St. Helena, Napa Valley, California. Grape varieties – Cabernet sauvignon, Chardonnay, Gewürztraminer, Petite syrah and Zinfandel. Produces varietal wines.

Round the World (Cktl). 1 oz. Gin, 2½

ozs. pineapple juice, 1½ ozs. Crème de Menthe. Shake over ice, strain into a large cocktail glass. Decorate with a pineapple piece on a cocktail stick.

Roupeiro (Port). A white grape variety grown in the Alentejo region.

Rousanne (Fr). See Roussanne and Ugni Blanc.

Rouse (Eng). A term used for a full measure of a drink (alcoholic) in the eighteenth century.

Rouse (Eng). A term used in brewing to describe the mixing of the Wort with large wooden paddles, air injection or by recycling the wort by spraying it back across the yeast head.

Roussan (Fr). An alternative spelling of Roussanne.

Roussanne (Fr). A white grape variety grown in the Rhône. See also Ugni Blanc.

Roussard, Rosé de Gamay Vaudois (Switz). A rosé wine produced in the Valais region from the Gamay grape.

Rousseau-Deslandes (Fr). A cuvée in the Cent-Vignes vineyard in the A.C. commune of Beaune, Côte de Beaune, Burgundy. Is owned by the Hospices de Beaune.

Rousselet de Béarn (Fr). A V.D.Q.S. district of the Pyrénées.

Rousset-les-Vignes (Fr). Drôme vineyards of the Côtes du Rhône-Villages.

Roussette (Fr). A white grape variety grown in the Bugey and Seyssel regions of eastern France. Also known as the Altesse.

Roussette d'Ayse (Fr). A white grape variety grown in the Ayse area of Savoie, south-eastern France.

Roussette de Bugey (Fr). A V.D.Q.S. wine-producing region. Produces wine of same name from the Altesse and Chardonnay grapes.

Roussette de Savoie (Fr). An A.C. of Savoie, south-eastern France. Includes the villages of Frangy, Marestrel, Montherminod and Monthoux.

Roussille (Fr). Cognac producer. Address = Roussille, Linars, 16290 Hiersac. 35 ha. in the Fins Bois. Produces a fine range of Cognac brandies. Also makes Pineau de Charentes

Roussillon (Fr). A wine region of south-western France which together with the Languedoc makes up part of the Midi.

Roussillonen (Fr). An alternative name for the Carignan grape.

Roussillon Tinto (Sp). An alternative name for the Grenache grape.

Routa Distillery (W.Ind). A Rum distillery based in Guadeloupe.

Route des Vins (Fr). The road through the Bordeaux vineyards.

Rouvrettes (Les) (Fr). A Premier Cru vineyard [part] in the A.C. commune of Savigny-lés-Beaune, Côte de Beaune, Burgundy.

Rouyer (Fr). Cognac producer. Address = Rouyer Guillet S.A., Château de la Roche, 17100 Saintes, Cognac. 86 ha. 42% in the Borderies and 58% in the Fins Bois. Produces – Rois de France 30 year old, Philippe Guillet Grande Fine Champagne 80 year old.

Rovalley Winery (Austr). A winery based in the Barossa Valley, South Australia.

Rowan Vineyard (USA). A vineyard based near Santa Maria, Santa Barbara County, California. Grape variety – Chardonnay.

Rowney Vineyard (Eng). A vineyard based at Rowney Farm, Chaseways, Sawbridgeworth, Herts. First planted in 1978. 1 ha. Grape varieties – Madeleine angevine, Müller-Thurgau and Seyval blanc.

Roxheim (Ger). Village. (Anb) = Nahe. (Ber) = Schloss Böckelheim. (Gro) = Rosengarten. (Vins) = Berg, Birkenberg, Höllenpfad, Hüttenberg, Mülhenberg, Sonnenberg.

Royal (Cktl). ⅓ measure dry Gin, ⅓ measure Port, ⅓ measure Grand Marnier, dash Angostura. Stir over ice, strain into a cocktail glass.

Royal (Eng). A Barley wine 1064 O.G. brewed by the Tolly Cobbold Brewery in Ipswich.

Royal (Jap). The brand-name for a Whiskey produced by Suntory.

Royal Altmunster (Lux). A Premium beer brewed by the Mousel et Clausen Brasserie.

Royal Ambassador Brut (It). A sparkling (méthode champenoise) wine produced by G & L Fratelli in the Piemonte region.

Royal Amber (USA). A beer brewed by the Wiedemann Brewery based in Newport, Kentucky.

Royal Ambrosante (Sp). A Palo Cortado sherry produced by Sandeman.

Royal Blanco (Sp). An alternative name for the Subirat-parent grape.

Royal Blend (It). A dry liqueur produced from imported Scottish malt whisky.

Royal Blush (Cktl). 1 measure Vodka, ½ measure Crème de Framboise, ½ measure cream, dash Grenadine. Shake over ice, strain into a 5 oz. goblet. Serve with a cherry.

Royal Blush Cocktail (Cktl). ⅓ measure Topaz, ⅓ measure blackberry liqueur, ⅓ measure lemon juice. Stir over ice, strain into an ice-filled highball glass, top with iced Champagne and dash of French vermouth.

Royal Brackla (Scot). A single Malt whisky

distillery near Nairn in Morayshire. A Highland malt. Produces a Vintage 1969 malt. 43% alc. by vol.

Royal Brewery (Eng). Based in Manchester. Owned by Scottish and Newcastle Breweries.

Royal Bronx (Cktl). 1 measure dry Gin, ½ measure dry Vermouth, ½ measure sweet Vermouth, 1 measure orange juice, dash dark Rum, dash orange Curaçao. Shake over ice, strain into a Champagne flute.

Royal Buchanan (Cktl). ⅓ measure Royal Mint Chocolate liqueur, ⅓ measure Scotch whisky, ⅓ measure cream. Stir gently with ice, strain into a 5 oz. goblet.

Royal Canadian (Can). A blended Canadian whisky produced by Jas Barclay and Co. (a subsidiary of Hiram Walker).

Royal Carlton (Sp). The brand-name of a Cava wine produced by the Bodegas Bilbainas.

Royal Charter (Can). A brand of Canadian whisky produced by the Hudson's Bay Co. (a subsidiary of Seagram).

Royal Cherry Chocolate (Eng). A cherry and chocolate-based liqueur from Hallgarten. 30% alc. by vol.

Royal Choice (Scot). A De Luxe blended Scotch whisky from the Long John Distillery, Glasgow. 21 year old. 43% alc. by vol.

Royal Cider (Eng). A brew of Cider distilled and often fortified with other spirits and sugar. Encouraged in 1703 to discourage smuggling.

Royal Clarence (Eng). A home-brew public house in Burnham-on-Sea, Somerset. Brews cask conditioned KC Bitter 1038 O.G.

Royal Clover Club Cocktail (Cktl). As for Clover Club Cocktail but with egg yolk instead of egg white.

Royal Cocktail (Cktl).(1). ⅓ gill dry Gin, ⅙ gill Dubonnet, dash Angostura, dash Orange bitters. Stir over ice, strain into a cocktail glass, add a cherry and a squeeze of lemon peel juice on top.

Royal Cocktail (Cktl).(2). ¾ measure dry Gin, ¼ measure lemon juice, 1 egg, 2 dashes Gomme syrup. Shake over ice, strain into a cocktail glass.

Royal Coco (Cktl). ⅓ measure Kahlúa, ⅓ measure golden Rum, ⅙ measure Crème de Cacao, ⅙ measure Cointreau, 2 dashes coconut cream. Shake over ice, strain into a flute glass. Top with grated chocolate, a slice of lime and a cherry.

Royal Coconut Liqueur (Fr). A coconut, cacao beans, French milk and spirit-based liqueur produced by Peter Hallgarten in Bordeaux. 21% alc. by vol.

Royal Coffee (Liq.Coffee). See Café Royale.

Royal Colmbier (Fr). A herb liqueur produced in Nantes, north-western France.

Royal Command (Can). A Canadian rye whisky produced by Canadian Park and Tilford (a subsidiary of Canadian Schenley Distilleries Ltd).

Royal Concquidor (Sp). A brand of Oloroso sherry produced by Sandeman in Jerez de la Frontera.

Royal Corregidor (Sp). A deep gold, old Oloroso sherry produced by Sandeman.

Royal Cream (Sp). A sweet, Cream sherry produced by La Riva in Jerez de la Frontera.

Royal Culross (Scot). An 8 year old Vatted malt produced by A. Gillies and Co. Glasgow. 40% alc. by vol. Part of Amalgamated Distilled Products.

Royal Decanter (Eng). A decanter of the 1820s named after George 1V.

Royal Denmark (Den). A strong Ale 7.75% alc. by vol. brewed by the Tuborg Brewery in Copenhagen. Also known as Fine Festival.

Royal Diana (The) (Cktl). ⅛ measure Brandy, ⅙ measure De Kuyper Nassau Orange, ¾ measure Kriter sparkling wine. Stir Cognac and liqueur together over ice, strain into a Champagne flute, top up with the wine and a slice of orange.

Royal Dutch (Cktl). ⅓ measure Mandarine Napoléon, ⅓ measure white Rum, ⅓ measure Cointreau, dash Orange bitters, dash lemon juice. Stir together with ice, strain into a cocktail glass.

Royal Dutch Lager (Hol). A brand of Lager beer 1030–1034 O.G. brewed by the Breda Brouwerij.

Royal Engagement (Cktl). ⅓ measure Scotch whisky, ⅓ measure Irish Mist, ⅓ measure Welsh cream, dash English Mead. Shake over ice, strain into a blue-frosted cocktail glass, garnish with a cherry.

Royal Esmeralda (Sp). A fine Amontillado sherry produced by Sandeman in Jerez de la Frontera.

Royal Fizz (Cktl). ¾ gill dry Gin, 1 whole egg, juice of a lemon, teaspoon Grenadine. Shake well over ice, strain into a highball glass, top with soda water.

Royal Framboise (Fr). A méthode champenoise raspberry apéritif with the addition of Cognac and fruit syrup produced by Gratien et Meyer. 15.2% alc. by vol.

Royal French Coffee-Chocolate Liqueur (Eng). A liqueur made from roasted coffee, chocolate and French milk by Hallgarten. 30% alc. by vol.

Royal Fruit and Nut Chocolate Liqueur (Eng). A fruit, nut and cocoa bean-based liqueur produced by Peter Hallgarten, London. 30% alc. by vol.

Royal Gin Fizz (Cktl). ⅓ gill Gin, 1 egg, juice ½ lemon, teaspoon powdered sugar. Shake over ice, strain into an ice-filled highball glass. Top with soda water and a slice of lemon.

Royal Ginger Chocolate (Eng). A liqueur made from ginger and cocoa beans. Produced by Hallgartens. 30% alc. by vol.

Royal Gold (S.Am). A 5 year old Demerara rum produced by Banks DIH. Ltd. Guyana.

Royal Host (USA). A label used by the East-Side Winery, California for their table, dessert wines and brandies.

Royal Household (Scot). A Whisky originally created for the exclusive use of the Royal Family by Buchanan and Company. Is now available more widely. 40% alc. by vol.

Royal Inn (Eng). A home-brew public house in Horsebridge, Devon. Noted for its cask conditioned Tamar Bitter 1039 O.G. Heller 1060 O.G. and Horsebridge Best 1045 O.G.

Royal Irish Distilleries (Ire). Was once one of the largest companies in Ireland. Has been closed since 1936.

Royal Irish Liqueur Co (Ire). Based under Tullamore centre. Makes Advocaat, Chocolate mint and Coffee-flavoured liqueurs.

Royalist (Cktl). ¼ measure Bénédictine, ¼ measure Bourbon whiskey, ½ measure dry Vermouth, dash Peach bitters. Stir over ice, strain into a cocktail glass.

Royal King (S.Afr). A sweet amber wine made from the white Cinsault and Hanepoot grapes by the SFW.

Royal Lemon Chocolate Liqueur (Eng). A lemon, cocoa bean-based liqueur produced by Peter Hallgarten, London. 30% alc. by vol.

Royal Liquid Gold (S.Am). A 10 year old Demerara rum produced by Banks DIH Ltd in Guyana.

Royal Lochnagar (Scot). A single Malt whisky distillery based in central-eastern Scotland. A Highland malt whisky. 43% alc. by vol.

Royal Love (Cktl). ⅓ measure Apricot brandy, ⅓ measure Mandarine Napoléon, ⅙ measure orange juice, ⅙ measure Crème de Cassis. Shake over ice, strain into a sugar-frosted (egg white and castor sugar) flute glass. Top with iced Champagne.

Royal Mail (Cktl). ¼ measure Van der Hum, ¼ measure Sloe Gin, ¼ measure orange juice, ¼ measure lemon juice, dash Pernod. Shake over ice, strain into a cocktail glass.

Royal Médoc Mousseux (Fr). A dry sparkling wine produced by Château Dauzac in the Médoc, north-western Bordeaux.

Royal Mint Ball (Cktl). ½ measure Royal Mint Chocolate liqueur, ½ measure Advocaat, 1½ measures lemonade. Stir over ice, strain into a 5 oz. goblet.

Royal Mint Chocolate Liqueur (Eng). A mint and chocolate liqueur made by Hallgartens. 30% alc. by vol.

Royal Mint Coffee (Liq.Coffee). Using a measure of Royal Mint Chocolate liqueur.

Royal Mousseux (Ind). A sparkling wine made by the méthode champenoise, south-east of Bombay in a new winery at Narayangaon. Made from the Chardonnay, Pinot meunier and Pinot noir grapes.

Royal Muscadine (Fr). An alternative name for the white Chasselas grape.

Royal Nut Chocolate Liqueur (Eng). A nut and cocoa bean-based liqueur produced by Peter Hallgarten, London. 30% alc. by vol.

Royal Oak (Eng). A cask conditioned Ale 1048 O.G. brewed by the Eldridge Pope Brewery in Dorchester, Dorset.

Royal Oak (S.Afr). The brand-name of a Brandy from Oude Meester.

Royal Oak Twelve (W.Ind). A 12 year old Rum produced by Trinidad Distillers Ltd. on the island of Trinidad.

Royal Oporto Wine Co (Port). Vintage Port shippers. Vintages – 1934, 1945, 1958, 1960, 1962, 1963, 1967, 1970, 1975, 1977, 1980, 1983.

Royal Orange Chocolate (Eng). A liqueur made from orange oil and cocoa beans by Hallgarten. 30% alc. by vol.

Royal Orchard (Eng). The brand-name of a Cider produced by the Weston's Cider Co. of Much Marcle, near Ledbury, Herefordshire.

Royal Palace (Sp). A brand-name of an Amontillado sherry produced by Wisdom and Warter in Jerez de la Frontera.

Royal Pale (Eng). A cask conditioned Ale 1035 O.G. brewed by the Kentish Ales Brewery in Tunbridge Wells, Kent.

Royal Pemartin (Sp). A brand of Oloroso sherry produced by Sandeman in Jerez de la Frontera.

Royal Pimms (Cktl). 1 part Pimm's N°1 and 3 parts Champagne served over ice in a highball glass.

Royal Porter (Eng). A cask conditioned Ale 1050 O.G. brewed by the Kentish Ales Brewery in Tunbridge Wells, Kent.

R

Royal Punch (Cktl). 2 glasses calves'-foot jelly, 1 measure Arrack, 1 measure Curaçao, 1 measure Brandy, 1 pint boiling green tea, 12 sugar cubes rubbed into rind of 2 limes, 12 slices of lemon. Add all together, serve hot, garnished with the slices of lemon.

Royal Purple (Punch). Place into a punch bowl some ice, 2 bottles Claret, 2 pints ginger ale, 1 sliced lemon and a whole lemon studded with 24 cloves. Stand for 10 minutes and serve.

Royal Raspberry Chocolate Liqueur (Eng). A raspberry and chocolate-flavoured liqueur produced by Peter Hallgarten, London. 30% alc. by vol.

Royal Réserve (Fr). The label used by Philipponnat for a range of vintage and non-vintage Champagnes (including a non-vintage rosé Champagne).

Royal Reserve (Scot). A 20 year old blended Scotch whisky produced by Bells.

Royal Romance (Cktl). ½ measure dry Gin, ¼ measure Grand Marnier, ¼ measure Passion fruit juice, dash Grenadine. Shake over ice, strain into a cocktail glass.

Royal Russian Cocktail (Cktl). 1 fl.oz. Vodka, 1 fl.oz. (white) Crème de Menthe, ½ fl.oz. cream, dash Grenadine. Shake over ice, strain into a Champagne saucer. Dress with a cherry.

Royal Salute (Scot). A 21 year old De Luxe blended Scotch whisky from Seagram. 43% alc. by vol.

Royal Shaker (Cktl). ½ pint milk, 1 oz. Royal Mint Chocolate liqueur, 1 scoop ice cream. Mix in a blender, serve in a tumbler.

Royal Smile (Cktl).(1). ¼ gill Calvados, ½ gill dry Gin, juice ½ lime (or lemon), 1 teaspoon Grenadine. Shake over ice, strain into a 5 oz. goblet. Top with a little cream.

Royal Smile (Cktl).(2). ³⁄₁₀ measure Bell's whisky, ⅕ measure Crème de Cassis, ⅕ measure pineapple juice, ⅕ measure grapefruit juice, ¹⁄₁₀ measure coconut cream. Shake over ice, strain into a cocktail glass. Dress with a cube of pineapple.

Royal Society of Harvesters of the Rioja (Sp). A society formed in 1790 to help improve viticulture and the developing market.

Royal Sovereign (Eng). A cask conditioned Best Bitter 1040 O.G. brewed by the Kentish Ales Brewery in Tunbridge Wells, Kent.

Royal Stag Ale (Eng). A bottled strong Ale 1052 O.G. brewed for export by the Paine Brewery in St. Neots, Cambridgeshire.

Royal St-Émilion (Fr). A cave coopérative. Is part of Côtes Rocheuses. Has 775 ha. in total under vines.

Royal Stewart (Scot). A 12 year old De Luxe blended Scotch whisky produced by Stewart and Son, Dundee.

Royal Stock (It). A Brandy produced by the Stock Co.

Royal Stout (W.Ind). A sweet Stout 1054 O.G. brewed by the Carib Brewery Co. in Trinidad.

Royal Tara Irish Cream Liqueur (Ire). An Irish whiskey and cream liqueur produced in Cork. 17% alc. by vol.

Royal Tawny (Port). A 10 year old dated Tawny Port from Sandeman Port shippers.

Royal Taylor Wine Company (USA). A large producer of sparkling wines based near New York.

Royal Toast (Eng). A specially brewed Barley wine 1086 O.G. brewed by the Mauldon Brewery in Suffolk to commemorate the engagement of HRH Prince Andrew to Miss Sarah Ferguson in the Spring of 1986.

Royal Triple Sec (Swe). A white Curaçao liqueur produced by the Aktiebolaget Vin & Spritcentralem.

Royalty (USA). A black grape variety introduced by UC-Davis for use in dessert wines. A cross between the Rubired X Trousseau.

Royal Victor (Cktl). ⅓ measure Liqueur d'Or, ⅓ measure Lemon Gin, ⅙ measure Cointreau, ⅙ measure lemon squash. Shake over ice, strain into a cocktail glass. Add a cherry.

Royal Wedding (Cktl). ¼ measure Kirsch, ¼ measure orange juice, ¼ measure Peach brandy. Shake well with ice, strain into a large goblet, top with iced Champagne.

Royal Wedding Cocktail (Cktl). ⅖ measure Cointreau, ⅖ measure Sirop de Fraises, ⅕ measure Cognac. Stir over ice, strain into a flute glass. Top with iced Champagne.

Royal Wedding Vintage Character Port (Eng). A Vintage Character Port introduced by Eldridge Pope to celebrate the wedding of the Prince of Wales in 1981.

Royat Cordon (Fr). One of the four methods of pruning permitted in the Champagne region.

Royé et Fils (Fr). A noted producer of Kosher Beaujolais-Villages wines. 8 ha. Address = La Salle, Lantignié, Beaujolais, Burgundy.

Royer (Louis) (Fr). Cognac producer. Address = Cognac Louis Royer, BP 12, 16200 Jarnac.

R

Roy René (Fr). Cognac producer. Address = Le Mas, Juillac-le-Coq, 16130 Segonzac. 30 ha. in Grande Champagne.

Roze (Gre). Rosé.

Roze (Tur). Rosé.

Rozenberg (Ger). Vineyard. (Anb) = Württemberg. (Ber) = Württembergisch Unterland. (Gro) = Schalkstein. (Vil) = Mundelsheim.

Rozendal Farm (S.Afr). Based at Stellenbosch. Address = Box 160, Stellenbosch 7600. Produces varietal wines.

Rozés (Port). The name given to the Moët-Hennessy Port shippers based in Vila Nova de Gaia.

Rozovoe Vino (USSR). Rosé wine.

Rozsa (Rum). Rosé.

RSVP (Eng). The brand-name used by Vine Products Ltd for a brand of their British Sherry.

Rub-a-dub (Eng) (slang). Cockney rhyming slang for a pub (public-house).

Rubberdy (Austr) (slang). For a pub. (From Rub-a-dub-dub). Also pronounced Rubbity or Rubidy.

Rubbity (Austr). See Rubberdy.

Rubby (Can) (slang). Used to denote an old drunkard (a down and out).

Rüberberger Domherrenberg (Ger). Vineyard. (Anb) = Mosel-Saar-Ruwer. (Ber) = Zell/Mosel. (Gro) = Goldbäumchen. (Vil) = Briedern.

Rüberberger Domherrenberg (Ger). Vineyard. (Anb) = Mosel-Saar-Ruwer. (Ber) = Zell/Mosel. (Gro) = Goldbäumchen. (Vil) = Ellenz-Poltersdorf.

Rüberberger Domherrenberg (Ger). Vineyard. (Anb) = Mosel-Saar-Ruwer. (Ber) = Zell/Mosel. (Gro) = Goldbäumchen. (Vil) = Senheim.

Rüberberger Domherrenberg (Ger). Vineyard. (Anb) = Mosel-Saar-Ruwer. (Ber) = Zell/Mosel. (Gro) = Schwarze Katz. (Vil) = Senheim.

Rubesco Torgiano Riserva (It). A D.O.C. single vineyard red wine produced by Lungarotti in Umbria.

Rubicon (S.Afr). A red wine made from the Cabernet franc, Cabernet sauvignon and Merlot grape. Produced by the Meerlust Estate.

Rubidy (Austr). See Rubberdy.

Rubiner (S.Afr). A light red wine made from the Cabernet grape by the Villiera estate in Paarl.

Rubino (It). Ruby.

Rubino (it). A style of Marsala from Sicily. See also Ambra and Oro.

Rubino di Cantavenna (It). D.O.C. red wine from Piemonte. Made from Barbera 75–90% and Grignolino/fresia up to 25%.

Rubinosa (Nor). A Sloe liqueur.

Rubion (USA). A hybrid red grape variety

developed by the University of California. Is grown in the Paul Masson Vineyard.

Rubired (USA). A red grape variety grown in California.

Rubis Cocktail (Cktl). 1 measure Noilly Prat, 4 dashes Cherry Heering, 3 dashes lime juice, 4 dashes Bourbon whiskey. Stir over ice, strain into a cocktail glass. Dress with a cherry and a slice of lime.

Ruby (Eng). The colour of certain red wines. Denotes a deep purple/red colour typical of a young wine.

Ruby Cabernet (USA). A varietal red grape grown in the Napa Valley, California. Cross between Cariñena and Cabernet sauvignon.

Ruby Cocktail (Cktl). ½ measure dry Vermouth, ½ measure Sloe Gin, 3 dashes raspberry syrup. Stir over ice, strain into a cocktail glass.

Ruby Fizz (Cktl). 2 fl.ozs. Sloe Gin, 1 egg white, juice ½ lemon, 3 dashes Grenadine, 3 dashes Gomme syrup. Shake over ice, strain into an ice-filled highball glass. Top with soda water.

Ruby Port (Port). A young deep red blended Port.

Ruby Wine (Eng). A British wine of a Port type. Sweet and rich.

Ruchots (Les) (Fr). A Premier Cru vineyard in the A.C. commune of Morey-Saint-Denis, Côte de Nuits, Burgundy. 2.6 ha.

Ruchottes-Chambertin (Fr). A Grand Cru vineyard in the A.C. commune of Gevrey-Chambertin, Côte de Nuits, Burgundy. 3.2 ha.

Rück (Ger). Village. (Anb) = Franken. (Ber) = Mainviereck. (Gro) = Not yet assigned. (Vins) = Jesuitenberg, Johannisberg.

Ruddles Brewery (Eng). A brewery based in Rutland (Leicestershire). Noted for its' cask conditioned Rutland Bitter 1032 O.G. County 1050 O.G. Ruddles Best 1037 O.G. and Barley Wine 1080 O.G.

Rude (Fr). Astringent.

Rüdesheim (Ger). Village. (Anb) = Nahe. (Ber) = Schloss Böckelheim. (Gro) = Rosengarten. (Vins) = Goldgrube, Wiesberg.

Rüdesheim (Ger). Village. (Anb) = Rheingau. (Ber) = Johannisberg. (Gro) = Burgweg. (Vins) = Berg Roseneck, Berg Rottland, Berg Schlossberg, Bischofsberg, Drachenstein, Kirchenpfad, Klosterberg, Klosterlay, Magdalenenkreuz, Rosengarten.

Rudežuša (Yug). A wine-producing area near the Dalmatian coast in south-western Yugoslavia.

Rudolfinger Beerli (Switz). A red wine produced from the Pinot noir grape.

Rudolfs Revenge (Eng). See Alford Arms.

R

Rueda (Sp). A Denominación de Origen district and wine town in the Valladolid region. Produces Sherry-style wines high in alcohol from the Verdejo blanco grape.

Rue-de-Chaux (Fr). A Premier Cru vineyard in the A.C. commune of Nuits-Saint-Georges, Côte de Nuits, Burgundy. 3 ha.

Ruedo (Sp). A dry, pale, light white wine at 14% alc. by vol. produced in Montilla-Moriles (not a Solera wine).

Rue Royale (Cktl). 2 measures dry Gin, 4 dashes Anisette, ½ egg white, 4 dashes milk. Shake over ice, strain into a cocktail glass.

Rufach (Fr). The German name of the town of Rouffach in the Haut-Rhin in Alsace. See also Ruffach.

Rufete (Port). An early ripening red grape variety used in the making of Port.

Ruffach (Fr). The German name for the town of Rouffach in the Haut-Rhin in Alsace. See also Rufach.

Ruffiac (Fr). A white grape variety used in the production of A.C. Pachérenc du Vic-Bilh in the Pyrénées.

Ruffino (It). A famous Chianti producer who belongs to neither the Classico or Putto consorzio.

Rufina (It). A commune of Chianti in Tuscany.

Rugenbrau Brauerei (Switz). An independent brewery based in Matten-Interlaken.

Ruggeri (L.) (It). A sparkling (méthode champenoise) wine producer based in the Veneto region.

Rugiens-Bas (Les) (Fr). A Premier Cru vineyard in the A.C. commune of Pommard, Côte de Beaune, Burgundy. 5.8 ha.

Rugiens-Haut (Les) (Fr). A Premier Cru vineyard in the A.C. commune of Pommard, Côte de Beaune, Burgundy. 7.6 ha.

Ruinart Père et Fils (Fr). Champagne producer. Address = 4 Rue des Crayères 51100, Reims. A Grande Marque. Produces – Vintage and non-wines. Vintages – 1900, 1904, 1911, 1914, 1919, 1921, 1923, 1926, 1928, 1929, 1934, 1937, 1941, 1943, 1945, 1947, 1949, 1952, 1953, 1955, 1959, 1961, 1964, 1966, 1969, 1971, 1973, 1975, 1976, 1978, 1979, 1981.

Ruiz (Mex). A well-known brand of Tequila.

Ruiz (José Garijo) (Sp). A noted producer and exporter of Málaga.

Ruiz (Luis Ortiz) (Sp). A producer of Montilla-Moriles wines.

Ruiz Hermanos (Sp). A second range of Sherries produced by Ruiz Mateos.

Ruiz Mateos (Sp). A Sherry Bodega and producer. Gives its name to the Rumasa group.

Ruju (It). Red (Sardinia).

Ruländer (Ger). A white grape variety grown mainly in Baden and Franconia. Also known as the Auxerrois gris, Fauvet, Grauer riesling, Grey burgundy, Pinot grigio, Pinot gris and the Tokayer.

Rulany (Czec). The local name used for a grape related to the Rülander.

Rule of Three (Eng). An unwritten rule that states that to be under the limit for the Drink Drive Laws (80 milligrammes of alcohol to 100 millilitres of blood), the average person can drink – 3 x glasses of table wine or 3 x ⅙ gill spirits or 3 x ⅓ gill sherries or 3 x ½ pint beer.

Rully (Fr). A district of the Côte Chalonnaise in southern Burgundy. Produces A.C. red, white and sparkling wines.

Rum (W.Ind). A spirit made from molasses distilled by the Pot-still or Patent-still methods. A light, clear spirit which is either matured in oak casks and coloured with caramel, e.g. Jamaican, Martinique. or left clear, e.g. Cuban and Puerto Rican.

Rum Alexander Cocktail (Cktl). ⅔ measure Crème de Cacao, ⅔ measure Rum, ⅔ measure cream. Shake well over ice, strain into a cocktail glass.

Rum and Rill Water (Cktl). An old name for the highball.

Rumania (Rum). A large wine-producing country in eastern Europe. Produces most styles of wines. Main regions are – Banat Vineyard, Cotnari Vineyard, Dealul-Mare Vineyard, Murfatler Vineyard, Tîrnave Vineyard and Vrancea Vineyard.

Rumasa Group (Sp). Was one of the largest Sherry producers in Spain. Run by the Government since 1983.

Rumbarricoe (Eng). A container (cask) for holding Rum on a ship. Was guarded by an officer until Rum rations were issued.

Rum Booze (Cktl). Beat 4 egg yolks and 2 tablespoons sugar. Heat ½ bottle of Sherry, grated peel of ½ lemon, 1 teaspoon grated nutmeg, stick of cinnamon. Bring to the boil, add 3 measures Rum. Add to the egg yolks, stir well. Serve in glasses with a drop of sweetened, beaten egg white on top.

Rumbooze (W.Ind). A term used to denote a good wine in Puerto Rico. Also spelt Rambooze.

Rumbullion (Eng). A name given to the Rum from which it got its name in the seventeenth century. See also Rumbustion.

Rumbustion (Eng). See Rumbullion.

Rum Cobbler (Cktl). 1 measure dark Rum, 1

barspoon sugar, 4 dashes orange Curaçao. Fill a medium sized goblet with ice, add the ingredients, stir. Decorate with sliced fruit and a sprig of mint. Serve with straws.

Rum Cocktail (Cktl). ⅓ gill Rum, 2 dashes Angostura, dash brown Curaçao. Stir over ice, strain into a cocktail glass. Serve with a cherry and dash of lemon peel juice.

Rum Cola (Cktl). See Cuba Libra.

Rum Collins (Cktl). ¾ gill Rum, sugar syrup to taste, juice of ½ lemon. Shake well together over ice, strain into an ice-filled highball. Top with soda water.

Rum Company [Jamaica] Ltd (W.Ind). A company first established in 1943 by a Swiss firm on the island of Jamaica. Produces Coruba and Sugar Mill rums.

Rum Cooler (Cktl). 1 measure dark Rum, 4 dashes Angostura, juice of lemon or lime. Shake over ice, strain into an ice-filled highball glass. Fill with soda water.

Rum Corps (The) (Austr). The nickname given to police in New South Wales (also known as Corps) to help enforce a ban on Rum distribution. They forced a stranglehold on the Rum trade.

Rum Daisy (Cktl).(1). 2 ozs. Bacardi White Label, ½ teaspoon yellow Chartreuse, juice ½ lime, dash Angostura, teaspoon Gomme syrup. Stir well together over ice, strain into an ice-filled highball glass. Garnish with mint, cherries and fruit in season.

Rum Daisy (Cktl).(2). ½ gill Rum, 2 dashes brown Curaçao, ⅛ gill Grenadine, ½ gill lemon juice. Shake over ice, strain into a highball glass. Top with soda, decorate with fresh fruit and a spoon.

Rum Domaci (Yug). A brand of Rum produced by Badel-Vinoprodukt in Zagreb.

Rum Dubonnet (Cktl). ⅘ measure white Rum, ⅕ measure Dubonnet, 2 dashes lemon juice. Shake over ice, strain into a cocktail glass.

Rum Egg Nogg (Cktl). ⅔ gill Rum, 1 egg, ¾ gill milk, 1 teaspoon sugar. Shake over ice, strain into a tumbler. Top with grated nutmeg.

Rum Egg Punch (Cktl). 12 beaten eggs, 1 bottle Jamaican Rum, ½ pint cream, ½ bottle Brandy, sugar to taste. Stir well in a punch bowl. Finish with grated nutmeg.

Rumeni Mŭskat (Yug). A medium-dry, white wine produced in north-east Slovenia.

Rum Fix (Cktl). ⅚ measure white Rum, ⅙

measure lemon juice, 1 teaspoon powdered sugar. Stir over ice in a highball glass. Top with soda water, slice of lemon. Serve with straws.

Rum Fizz (Cktl). 2 measures white Rum, juice of 2 lemons, 2 teaspoons sugar. Shake well over ice, strain into a highball glass. Top with soda water.

Rum Flip (Eng). An old drink that consisted of Ale, mulled Rum, cream, spices and beaten eggs. Mulled with a hot poker.

Rum Float (Cktl). 1 measure white Rum, juice ½ lime, 1 teaspoon sugar. In an ice-filled highball glass mix the juice and sugar. Top with soda, stir. Pour Rum in over the back of a spoon to float. Add slice of lime on rim of glass.

Rum Gimlet (Cktl). 1 fl.oz. white Rum, ½ fl.oz. lime juice, dash Gomme syrup. Stir over ice, strain into a cocktail glass. Dress with a slice of lime.

Rum Highball (Cktl). As for Gin Highball using Rum.

Rum Hospital (Austr). The name given to a hospital building built by contractors who were granted a 45,000 gallon monopoly to import Rum over 3 years in lieu of cash for their work.

Rumi (Yug). A red grape variety.

Rum Julep (Cktl). As for Mint Julep but substitute dark Rum for Brandy.

Rum Mac (Cktl). ½ measure dark Rum, ½ measure Ginger wine. Stir over ice, strain into a small wine glass. Can add a dash of water.

Rummager (Scot). 4 rotating arms carrying a copper mesh chain inside the Washstill in Malt Whisky production. Used to prevent solid particles in the Wash sticking and burning.

Rümmelsheim (Ger). Village. (Anb) = Nahe. (Ber) = Kreuznach. (Gro) = Schlosskapelle. (Vins) = Hölle, Johannisberg, Rothenberg, Schlossberg, Steinkopfchen.

Rummer (Eng). A name given to the Roemer glass in the nineteenth century.

Rum Milk Punch (Cktl). 1 gill milk, ⅕ gill Jamaican rum, dash Gomme syrup. Shake over ice, strain into a collins glass. Top with nutmeg.

Rümmingen (Ger). Village. (Anb) = Baden. (Ber) = Markgräflerland. (Gro) = Vogtei Rötteln. (Vin) = Sonnhohle.

Rummy (USA). The nickname for an alcoholic who likes Rum.

Rumney (Eng). The old Elizabethan name for Rumanian wines. See also Romany.

Rumona (W.Ind). A Rum liqueur produced on the island of Jamaica.

Rumor (Sp). The name used for a range of red and white wines from San Isidro in

Jumilla in the Levante.

Rum Orange Cocktail (Cktl). 1 fl.oz. white Rum into an ice-filled highball glass. Top with orange juice. Dress with orange slices.

Rumor-Bagaceira do Minho (Port). An Aguardente produced by Caves Dom Teodósio.

Rum Punch (Cktl). ¾ gill Rum, 1 tablespoon Gomme syrup, juice of ½ lemon, dash Brandy. Shake well over ice, strain into a 5 oz. wine glass. Top with soda water.

Rum Rickey (Cktl). ¾ measure Bacardi White Label, ¼ measure lime juice. Stir over ice in a highball glass. Top with soda and a slice of lime.

Rum Runner (USA). A person who brought in spirits from his boat anchored outside the 3 mile limit during Prohibition 1919–33.

Rum Runner Cocktail (Cktl). ⅗ measure dry Gin, ⅖ measure pineapple juice, juice of a lime, dash Angostura, 2 dashes Gomme syrup. Shake over ice, strain into a salt-rimmed cocktail glass.

Rum Screwdriver (Cktl). As for a Screwdriver Cocktail substituting white Rum for the Vodka.

Rum Shrub (Eng). 2 pints dark Rum, ¾ pint orange juice, ¼ lb. loaf sugar. Mix together and place in a covered container. Rest for six weeks.

Rum Smash (Cktl). As for Gin Smash but substitute Rum for Gin.

Rum Sour (Cktl). ¾ oz. lemon or lime juice, 1½ ozs. White Rum, 1 teaspoon powdered sugar. Shake over ice, strain into an old-fashioned glass with a slice of orange and a cherry.

Rum Swizzle (Cktl). As for Gin Swizzle but using white Rum in place of the Gin.

Rum Toddy (Cktl). 1 cube sugar, 1½ ozs. Jamaican Rum. Fill glass with boiling water, Rum and sugar. Stir with cinnamon stick, garnish with lemon and 4 cloves and twist of lemon peel juice.

Rum Verschnitt (Ger). See Rhum Verschnitt.

Rumverschnitt (Ger). See Rhum Verschnitt.

Rund (Ger). Round.

Rund um die Nahe-Weinstrasse (Ger). The Nahe region wine festival.

Runlet (Eng). A small cask used in mediaeval times for beer, wines and spirits.

Runnels (Fr). Woodens troughs from which the grape juice runs from the presses to vats in Champagne.

Runners (Eng). The bands on wine casks that keep the main staves off the floor when the cask is being moved (rolled).

Running Wine (USA). See Free Run Wine.

Rupert Group (S.Afr). A group that has links with the United Breweries of Denmark (Carlsberg and Tuborg) and Carling of Canada.

Rupestris du Lot (Fr). American root stock used for grafting in the Rhône at Châteauneuf-du-Pape.

Rupestris Martin (Mad). A rootstock found on Madeira.

Rupestris Monticola (Mad). A rootstock found on Madeira.

Rupestris St. George (USA). The basic root stock used for grafting to fight off Phylloxera.

Rupestris x Berlandieri (Mad). A cross American rootstock found on Madeira. Likes clay soil.

Ruppert Brewery (USA). A brewery based in New Bedford.

Ruppertsberg (Ger). Village. (Anb) = Rheinpfalz. (Ber) = Mittelhaardt-Deutsche Weinstrasse. (Gro) = Hofstück. (Vins) = Gaisböhl, Hoheburg, Linsenbusch, Nussbien, Reiterpfad, Spiess.

Rural-Method (Fr). See Méthode Rurale.

Rusalca (Sp). A brand of Vodka produced by Campeny in Barcelona.

Russ (Ger). A drink made from a top-fermented beer mixed with lemonade half and half (a Shandy).

Russet Ale (Eng). A bottled Mild ale 1032 O.G. brewed by the Elgood Brewery in Wisbech, Cambridgeshire.

Russia (R.S.F.S.R.) (USSR). Produces a range of spirits (especially Vodka), beers and wines. The main wine regions are the Don Valley and the Krasnodar area. See also U.S.S.R.

Russian Bear (Cktl). ½ measure Vodka, ¼ measure (white) Crème de Cacao, ¼ measure cream. Shake over ice, strain into a cocktail glass.

Russian Caravan (China). A blend of Anhwei province and Taiwan Oolong teas. Has excellent fragrance, named after the Camel caravans that crossed Russia.

Russian Champagne (USSR). Produced between Anapa and Gelendshipe districts. Has names such as Krasnodar, Tbilisi and Tsimlyanskoye.

Russian Cocktail (Cktl). ⅔ measure Vodka, ⅔ measure Gin, ⅔ measure Crème de Cacao. Shake over ice, strain into a cocktail glass.

Russian Coffee (Liq.Coffee). Using a measure of Vodka.

Russian Imperial (Eng). A bottled Stout 1098 O.G. brewed by Courage.

Russian River Valley (USA). A wine producing area north of San Francisco.

Wineries include Dry'Creek, Korbel and Simi.

Russian River Vineyards (USA). A winery based in the Russian River Valley, California. Produces varietal wines.

Russian Rum (USSR). Made from sugar cane grown around the area of Tashkent.

Russian Stout (Eng). An Ale originally brewed for the Russian Imperial family. A strong, vintage stout which is well matured. Courage now brew this. 1100 O.G. matured 1 year, sold in date stamped nip size bottles.

Russian Tea (USSR). A tea served without milk in a glass seated in a one- or two-handled silver holder. A slice of lemon is added and sugar to taste. Also known in England as Lemon tea.

Russin (Switz). A wine-producing area in Geneva.

Rüssingen (Ger). Village. (Anb) = Rheinpfalz. (Ber) = Mittelhaardt-Deutsche Weinstrasse. (Gro) = Schnepfenflug vom Zellertal. (Vin) = Breinsberg.

Russkaya (USSR). A clean, neutral Vodka 37.5% alc. by vol.

Russky Blazam (USSR). A bitter, spicy, dark brown Nastoika (high in alcohol).

Rüssling (Ger). An old eighteenth-century German name for the Riesling grape.

Rust (Aus). A wine growing area in Burgenland that is noted for its Ausbruch wines.

Rustenberg Estate (S.Afr). See Schoongezicht Estate.

Rustenberg Wines (S.Afr). Red wines produced by the Schoongezicht Estate.

Rust-en-Vrede (S.Afr). A vineyard based in Stellenbosch. Address = Box 473, Stellenbosch 7600. Produces varietal wines.

Ruster Ausbruch (Aus). A white wine produced from late-picked grapes in the Lake District, Burgenland.

Rusthof Wines (S.Afr). See Mooiuitsig Wynkelders. A brand-name for the varietals produced by them.

Rust Neusiedlersee (Aus). A wine district within the region of Burgenland. Produces mainly white wines.

Rusty Nail (Cktl). 1½ measures Scotch Whisky, ½ measure Drambuie. Stir 'on the rocks' in an old-fashioned glass. Add a twist of lemon.

Ruthe (Ger). Vineyard. (Anb) = Württemberg. (Ber) = Württembergisch Unterland. (Gro) = Heuchelberg. (Vil) = Nordheim.

Ruthe (Ger). Vineyard. (Anb) = Württemberg. (Ber) = Württembergisch Unterland. (Gro) = Heuchelberg. (Vil) = Schwaigern.

Rutherford (USA). A wine-producing town based in the central Napa Valley, California.

Rutherford and Miles (Mad). Madeira producer. Produces – Old Custom House Extra Pale Sercial, La Reina Verdelho, Old Trinity House Bual and Fine Old Malmsey.

Rutherford Hill Winery (USA). A winery based near Rutherford, Napa Valley, California. Grape varieties – Chardonnay, Gewürztraminer, Merlot, White riesling and Zinfandel. Produces varietal wines.

Rutherford Ranch (USA). A label owned by a Napa Valley grower in California.

Rutherford Vintners (USA). A winery based near Rutherford, Napa Valley, California. Grape varieties – Cabernet sauvignon, Johannisberg riesling and Pinot noir. Produces varietal wines.

Rutherglen (Austr). A vineyard in Victoria. 200 kms. north of Melbourne. Famous for its liqueur Muscats and Tokays.

Rutland Bitter (Eng). A cask conditioned Bitter 1032 O.G. brewed by the Ruddles Brewery in Rutland, Leicestershire.

Ruttgers (Ger). A large producer of Deutsche Sekt.

Ruwer (River) (Ger). A tributary of the river Mosel which joins it at the village of Ruwer in the upper Mosel.

Ružica (Yug). A rosé wine from Serbia. Lit – 'Little rosé'.

Rwanda Coffee (Afr). An Arabica pure coffee grown in Rwanda. Has good acidity and a full-flavour.

Ryan's Daughter (Cktl). 1 measure Irish Mist, ¾ measure Crème de Cacao. Pour into a small cocktail glass with crushed ice, float a little cream on top.

Ryan's Genuine Irish Cream Liqueur (Ire). A liqueur produced in Dublin from Irish cream and Irish whiskey. Was first produced in 1981.

Rye (USA). The earliest style of whiskey produced in America. Must contain 51% of rye grain. See Rye Whiskey.

Rye and Dry (Cktl). 2 ozs. Rye Whiskey poured over ice into an old-fashioned glass. Top with ginger ale.

Rye Cocktail (Cktl). 1 fl.oz. Rye whiskey, 2 dashes Angostura, 1 teaspoon Gomme syrup. Shake over ice, strain into a cocktail glass.

Rye Collins (Cktl). 1 fl.oz. Rye whiskey, ½ fl.oz. lemon juice, 1 teaspoon powdered sugar. Stir well over ice in a collins glass. Top with soda water and a slice of lemon.

Ryecroft (Austr). A McLaren Vale estate.

Rye Fizz (Cktl). ½ gill Canadian Club

Whisky, 1 teaspoon brown Curaçao, dash Grenadine, ¾ gill lemon juice, white of egg. Shake over ice, strain into a highball glass, fill with soda.

Rye Highball (Cktl). Pour 1 measure Rye Whisky into an ice-filled highball glass. Stir in dry ginger ale or soda water and add a twist of lemon.

Rye Lane (Cktl). ⅓ measure Rye whisky, ⅓ measure white Curaçao, ⅓ measure orange juice, 2 dashes Crème de Noyeau. Shake over ice, strain into a cocktail glass.

Rye Malt Whiskey (USA). Not exceeding 160° US Proof from fermented mash of not less than 51% corn, rye, wheat, malted barley or malted rye grain respectively and stored at not more than 125° US Proof in new charred oak. May be a blend of same whiskies of same type.

Rye Sour (Cktl). 1 fl.oz. Rye whiskey, ½ fl.oz. lemon juice, 1 teaspoon sugar. Shake over ice, strain into a cocktail glass. Dress with a cherry.

Rye Whiskey (USA). Made from a mash containing not less than 51% rye and aged in new charred oak barrels.

Rye Whiskey Cocktail (Cktl). ⅓ gill Canadian Club, 2 dashes Gomme syrup, dash Angostura. Shake over ice, strain into a cocktail glass. Top with a cherry.

Rye Whisky (Can). See Canadian Whisky.

Ryst-Dupeyron (Fr). An Armagnac brandy producer. Noted for its Dupeyron brand range.

Ryst Sarl (Jacques) (Fr). Armagnac producer based in Ténarèze. Address = 25, Rue de la République, 32100, Condom.

SA (Wales) (abbr). A malty Best Bitter 1042 O.G. brewed by the Brains Brewery in Cardiff. Is also known locally as 'Skull Attack'.

Saale (Ger). A wine valley in Thüringen, south of Jena. Produces acid wines.

Saaleck (Ger). Vineyard. (Anb) = Franken. (Ber) = Maindreieck. (Gro) = Burg. (Vil) = Schlossberg.

Saar (Ger). An Untergebiet of the Rhein und Mosel district.

Saarburg (Ger). Village. (Anb) = Mosel-Saar-Ruwer. (Ber) = Saar-Ruwer. (Gro) = Scharzberg. (Vins) = Antoniusbrunnen, Bergschlösschen, Fuchs, Klosterberg, Kupp, Rausch, Laurentiusberg, Schlossberg, Stirn.

Saarfeilser Marienberg (Ger). Vineyard. (Anb) = Mosel-Saar-Ruwer. (Ber) = Saar-Ruwer. (Gro) = Scharzberg. (Vil) = Schoden.

Saar [River] (Ger). A tributary of the river Mosel. See Mosel-Saar-Ruwer.

Saar-Ruwer (Ger). Bereich. (Anb) = Mosel-Saar-Ruwer. (Gros) = Römerlay, Scharzberg.

Saarweinfest (Ger). A Mosel-Saar-Ruwer wine festival held at Saarburg in September.

Saaz (Czec). A delicate strain of hops often used for 'dry-hopping' as it gives an excellent bouquet.

Sabatacha (Sp). The name given to a range of mature wines from San Isidro in the Jumilla district of the Levante.

Sabauda Riserva (It). A sparkling (méthode champenoise) wine produced by Contratto in the Piemonte region.

Sabbath Cooler (Cktl). ⅙ gill Cognac, ⅙ gill French vermouth, juice ¼ lime. Stir over ice, strain into an ice-filled highball glass. Top with soda and dress with a mint sprig.

Sabinum (Lat). A white wine produced in central Italy during Roman times.

Sablant (Fr). A brand-name used for fine Crémant de Loire sparkling wines.

Sablant (En) (Fr). An old Loire custom of filtering wines through fine sand. Now wines of the Loire use the names Sablant and Crémant de Loire.

Sables Anciens (Fr). Sandy soil. Applied to the Saint-Émilion district in eastern Bordeaux.

Sables du Golfe du Lion (Fr). A Vins de Pays area in the Languedoc-Roussillon region, southern France.

Sables du Golfe du Rhône (Fr). A Vins de Pays area of the Bouches du Rhône Département in south-eastern France.

Sables-Saint-Émilion (Fr). A commune within the A.C. Saint-Émilion, south-eastern Bordeaux.

Sablet (Fr). A noted wine-village in A.C. Vaucluse, Côtes du Rhône-Villages.

Sablo-Graveleux (Fr). A sandy, gravelly soil production zone in Saint-Émilion, eastern Bordeaux.

Sabotée Sancerroise et Comité de Propagande des Vins A.O.C. de Sancerre (Fr). A wine brotherhood based in the Central Vineyards district of the Loire. Promotes and improves the wines of Sancerre.

Sabra (Isr). An orange and Swiss chocolate liqueur. 30% alc. by vol. Name is thought to derive from the Sabra cactus. Produced by Seagram.

Sabra Sour (Cktl). 2 ozs. Sabra, 1 oz. lemon juice. Shake over ice, strain into a cocktail glass.

Sabre Cocktail (Cktl). ⅓ measure Sabra, ⅓ measure dry Gin, ⅓ measure cream, dash Syrop de Framboises. Shake over ice, strain into a cocktail glass.

Sabrita (Cktl). 2 ozs. Sabra, 1 oz. Brandy. Stir together with ice in a large balloon glass.

Sabrosa (Port). A wine-producing area north of Pinhão in the Alto Douro.

Saca (Sp). See also Sacar. Lit – 'To draw out'. Wine for export is designated Saca. See also Sacar.

Sacacorchos (Sp). Corkscrew.

Sacador (Sp). A worker who carries the grape baskets from the vineyard.

Sacar (Sp). Lit – 'To draw out'. Is suggested that 'Sack' derived from it. See also Vinos de Saca and Saca.

Saca-Rolhas (Port). Corkscrew. See also Rolhas.

Sac-à-Vin (Fr). A term used for a drunk in the Champagne region.

Saccharine Method (USA). The term given to the process of converting starch into fermentable sugars.

Saccharometer (Eng). An instrument for measuring the sugar content in the Wort for Beer or the Must for Wine.

Saccharomyces (Lat). The botanical name for yeast.

Saccharomyces Acidifaciens (Lat). A wine yeast.

Saccharomyces Apiculatus (Lat). A wild wine yeast.

Saccharomyces Baileii (Lat). A yeast that has a high alcohol tolerance and is highly resistant to SO_2.

Saccharomyces Bayanus (Lat). A wine yeast used in eastern Bordeaux for Pomerol and Saint-Émilion wines. Is fairly resistant to alcohol.

Saccharomyces Beticus (Lat). See Saccharomyces Ellipsoideus Beticus.

Saccharomyces Carlsbergensis (Lat). A bottom-fermenting yeast used in the making of Lager beer. See Saccharomyces Uvarum.

Saccharomyces Cerevisiae (Lat). A wine yeast. Also used as a top-fermenting wine yeast.

Saccharomyces Ellipsoideus (Lat). A wine yeast. The Bloom which settles on the grape skins and is used to convert grape sugar into CO_2 and alcohol when fermentation takes place.

Saccharomyces Ellipsoideus Beticus (Lat). Flor. The yeast used in the making of Fino Sherries, Vins de Paille etc.

Saccharomyces Oviformis (Lat). A yeast that has a high alcohol tolerance and is highly resistant to SO_2.

Saccharomyces Pastovianus (Lat). A wild wine yeast.

Saccharomyces Saké (Lat). A yeast strain used in the brewing of Saké.

Saccharomyces Uvarum (Lat). A bottom-fermenting Lager yeast. See Saccharomyces Carlsbergensis.

Saccharomyces Vordermanni (Lat). A wild yeast used in the making of Batavian Arak.

Saccharomycodes Ludwigii (Lat). A true yeast. If found in wines can cause problems because it is highly resistant to SO_2 and can carry on fermenting if residual sugar is present.

Saccharose (Lat). The sugar obtained from sugar beet. Used for Chaptalisation.

Saccharum Officiarum (Lat). Sugar cane from which Rum is produced.

Sacco (It). A peppermint liqueur produced in Turin.

Saccone and Speed (Eng). A large wine and spirit shippers owned by Courage.

Saccone and Speed (N.Z.). The brand-name used by McWilliams for their range of cask-aged, fortified wines.

Sache (Fr). A white wine produced in the Touraine district of the Loire.

Sachsenflur (Ger). Village. (Anb) = Baden. (Ber) = Badische Frankenland. (Gro) = Tauberklinge. (Vin) = Kailberg.

Sack (Eng). The Anglification of Spanish Seco, a dry fortified still wine. See Sacar.

Sack (Eng). The brewer's name for the hessian or plastic container used to package malt.

Sacke (Sp). Sherry. See Sack. As referred to in Pasquil's Palinodia in 1619.

Sack Mead (Eng). A sweet mead produced in the West Country in the seventeenth and eighteenth centuries.

Sack Metheglin (Eng). A sweet Metheglin-type mead produced in the seventeenth and eighteenth centuries.

Sackträger (Ger). Vineyard. (Anb) = Rheinhessen. (Ber) = Bingen. (Gro) = Sankt Rochuskapelle. (Vil) = Zotzenheim.

Sacotte (Fr). Champagne producer. Address = 13 Rue de la Verrière, B.P. 1017, Épernay, 51318. Produces vintage wines.

Sacramental Wine (Eng). Altar wine for the Eucharist. May be red or white and must be the natural grape juice.

Sacramento (USA). Lodi-Sacramento. A northern region of the Great Central Valley of California. Produces dessert and table wines.

Sacrarios (Sp). A tenth century name used in Catalonia for the Bodega.

Sacristia (Sp). 'The Chapel'. A part of Harveys' old Bodega where old butts of unblended Sherry are assembled from the best vintages.

Sacy (Fr). A Premier Cru Champagne village in the Canton de Ville-en-Tardenois. District = Reims.

Sacy (Fr). A white grape variety grown in the Burgundy region (in the Yonne). Also known as the Tressalier.

Sadana (Sp). A pale Cream Sherry produced by Bobadilla in Jerez de la Frontera.

Sadilly (USSR). A white table wine produced in Baku.

Sadova Rosé (Rum). A sweet rosé wine produced on the Danube plain.

Saemling 88 (Ger). An alternative name for the Scheurebe grape.

Saffron Cider Company (Eng). A small family-run Cider firm based at Radwinter, near Saffron Walden, Essex. Produces – Saffy's West Country Scrumpy, Black Bull, Cripple Cock and Sherston Scorcher.

Saffy's West Country Scrumpy (Eng). The brand-name of a bottled medium-dry, slightly carbonated, extra strong Cider produced by the Saffron Cider Company.

Safir (Bel). The brand-name of a well-hopped Pilsener Lager beer.

Safrap (Eng). 2,400 litre mild steel containers lined with expoxy resin. They are used for the transportation of wines. If the lining is damaged, iron contamination of the wine can occur.

Saftig (Ger). Juicy, fine wine of character.

Sage Canyon Winery (USA). A winery based at St. Helena, Napa Valley, California. Produces varietal wines.

Sagemoor Farms Vineyards (USA). A large vineyard based in the South Columbia River Basin, Washington. 200 ha. Sells grapes that it produces.

Sage's Milk (Eng). An old nineteenth-century nickname for coffee.

Sage Tea (Eng). Used in the old days to combat fever. Put ½ oz. dried sage leaves in a jug or pot. Add 1 quart of boiling water, sugar to taste and a dash of lemon juice. Infuse 5 minutes, strain and use as required.

Sağmak (Tur). Milk.

Sagrantino (It). A black grape variety grown in the Umbria region.

Sagres (Port). A Dortmunder-style beer 3.65% alc. by vol. brewed by S.C.C. Brewery.

Săhăteni (Rum). A wine-producing area. Is part of the Dealul-Mare Vineyard.

Sahel (Afr). An A.O.G. area in the wine-producing region of Casablanca, western Morocco.

Sahti (Fin). A festival beverage produced by female home-brewers consisting of barley, rye, malt, hops, juniper berries/branches and straw. (The branches act as a filter). Is fermented in milk churns.

Saibro (Mad). Decomposed red tufa mixed with stones found on the island of Madeira.

Saignée (Fr). The name given to the first pressing of Cinsault and Grenache grapes for the Rhône rosé of Tricastin in the Côtes du Rhône. Is also used in Touraine, Loire.

Saigon Brewery (S.E.Asia) A brewery based in Ho Chi Minh City (was Saigon) which brews Saigon Export Beer.

Saillans (Fr). A commune in the A.C. Côtes de Fronsac, eastern Bordeaux.

Saint-Amant-de-Graves (Fr). A commune in the Charente Département whose grapes are classed as Petite Champagne (Cognac).

Saint-Amour (Fr). An A.C. Cru Beaujolais-Villages, Burgundy. Has 240 ha. under vines.

Saint-Amour-de-Bellevue (Fr). A commune in the Beaujolais district. Has A.C. Beaujolais-Villages or Beaujolais-Saint-Amour-de-Bellevue status. Also as Mâconnais Blanc.

Saint Andelain (Fr). A commune in the Central Vineyards district of the Loire which produces A.C. Pouilly Fumé.

Saint-André (Fr). A commune in the Charente-Maritime Département whose grapes are classed Borderies and used for Cognac.

Saint-Aubin (Fr). An A.C. commune in the Côte de Beaune, Burgundy. Is also known as Saint-Aubin-Côte de Beaune. Has 8 Grand Cru vineyards – Champlot, En Remilly, La Chatenière, Les Combes, Les Frionnes, Les Murgers-des-Dents-de-Chien, Sur Gamay and Sur-le-Sentier-du-Clou. 65 ha. (red and white).

Saint Aubin (Fr). A commune in the A.C. Médoc, north-western Bordeaux. Produces red and white wines.

Saint-Aubin-Côte de Beaune (Fr). See Saint Aubin.

Saint-Aubin-de-Luigné (Fr). An A.C. commune in the Coteaux du Layon in the Anjou-Saumur district of the Loire.

Saint-Avertin (Fr). A white wine produced in the Touraine district of the Loire.

Saint Boes (Fr). See St. Boes.

Saint-Bonnet (Fr). A commune in the Charente Département whose grapes are classed as Petite Champagne (Cognac).

Saint Brendan's Irish Cream Liqueur (Eng). An Irish cream liqueur produced by the Saint Brendan's Irish Cream Liqueur Company.

Saint-Brice (Fr). A commune in the Charente Département whose grapes are classed as Grande Champagne (Cognac).

Saint-Catages (Les) (Fr). A vineyard in the A.C. commune of Montagny, Côte Chalonnaise, Burgundy.

Saint Chinian (Fr). A.C. red wine from the Béziers region in the Hérault Département.

Saint Christoly (Fr). A commune in the Bas-Médoc, A.C. Médoc, north western Bordeaux.

Saint-Christophe-des-Bardes (Fr). A commune in the A.C. Saint-Émilion, eastern Bordeaux.

Saint-Ciers-Champagne (Fr). A commune in the Charente-Maritime Département whose grapes are classed Petite Champagne (Cognac).

Saint-Cyprien (Afr). A noted wine-producing area in Tunisia.

Saint-Cyr-en-Bourg (Fr). A commune in the A.C. Saumur, Anjou-Saumur, Loire.

Saint-Cyr-sur-Mer (Fr). A commune in the Provence region of which Bandol is a part.

Saint-Drézery (Fr). A small A.C. wine-producing region in Languedoc near Pic-Saint-Loup. Minimum alc. 11% by vol. Grapes are mainly Carignan.

Sainte-Chapelle Vineyards (USA). Vineyards based near Caldwell, Idaho. 60 ha. Grape varieties – Chardonnay and Riesling. Produces varietal wines.

Sainte-Croix-du-Mont (Fr). An A.C. commune producing sweet white wines in southern Bordeaux.

Saint Edmund (Eng). A vineyard based in Bury St. Edmunds, Suffolk. Grape variety is Huxelrebe.

Sainte-Euphraise (Fr). A Cru Champagne village in the Canton of Ville-en-Tardenois. District = Reims.

Sainte-Foy-Bordeaux (Fr). An A.C. commune in the south-eastern Bordeaux. (South of the Entre-Deux-Mers). Produces sweet white and a little red wine.

Sainte-Gemme (Fr). A Cru Champagne village in the Canton de Châtillon sur-Marne. District = Reims.

Sainte-Jeoire-Prieuré (Fr). A village in the A.C. Savoie region that may use its own name to sell wine.

Sainte-Marie-d'Alloix (Fr). A village in the A.C. Savoie that may sell wines under its own name.

Saint-Émilion (Fr). An A.C. district in eastern Bordeaux. Produces fine red wines (Classified in 1955 and reviewed every ten years). Has eight communes – Saint-Christophe-des-Bardes, Saint-Émilion, Saint-Étienne-de-Lisse, Saint-Hippolyte, Saint Laurent des Combes, Saint Pey d'Armens, Saint-Sulpice-de-Faleyrens and Vignonet. See also St-Émilion and Saint-Émilion Classification.

Saint-Émilion (Fr). A white grape variety which is thick skinned and sturdy. Produces rather sour wines of about 8% alc. by vol. It is a smooth maturer and does not rot. Now more than 80% of the total yield for Cognac is this grape variety. Also known as the Ugni Blanc.

Saint-Émilion Classification (Fr). Wines were first classified in 1955. Are re-classified every ten years. Has 11 Premiers Grands Crus Classés, 63 Grands Crus Classés, 90 Grands Crus and numerous A.C. Saint-Émilion. The present reclassification comes into force in 1988 (two years late because of a court case).

Saint-Émilion des Charentes (Fr). A white grape variety, see Saint-Émilion.

Also known as the Trebbiano and Ugni blanc.

Saint-Émilion Grands Crus Classés Proprietors Association (Fr). The Association des Propriétaires de Grands Crus Classés de Saint-Émilion. Address = Les Templiers, Rue Guadet BP 46, 33330 Saint-Émilion.

Saint-Émilion Soils (Fr). The soils are divided into 5 zones as derived by Professor Enjalbert with Féret (13th edition) Bordeaux et Ses Vins. They are – [1] Le Plateau Calcaire, [2] Côtes et 'Pieds de Côtes', [3] Graves et Sables Anciens, [4] Sables Anciens, [5] Sablo-Graveleux.

Sainte-Odile (Fr). A wine village in the Bas-Rhin in Alsace. Known in German as Odilienberg.

Sainte Odile Distillerie (Fr). A liqueur producer based in Alsace. Address = 3, Rue de la Gare, 67210 Obernai.

Sainte-Radegonde (Fr). A commune in the A.C. Vouvray, Touraine district of the Loire.

Saint-Estèphe (Fr). An A.C. commune in the Haut-Médoc in Bordeaux. Wines come under the 1855 classification.

Saint-Estèphe (Marquis de) (Fr). Co-operative producing A.C. Saint-Estèphe. Commune = Saint-Estèphe. 350 ha. Grape varieties – Cabernet franc, Cabernet sauvignon, Malbec, Merlot and Petit verdot.

Saint-Étienne-de-Lisse (Fr). A commune of A.C. Saint-Émilion in eastern Bordeaux.

Saint-Étienne-des-Ouillières (Fr). A commune in the Beaujolais district. Has A.C. Beaujolais-Villages or Beaujolais-Saint-Étienne-des-Ouillières status.

Saint-Étienne-la-Varenne (Fr). A commune in the Beaujolais district. Has A.C. Beaujolais-Villages or Beaujolais-Saint-Étienne-la-Varenne status.

Saint-Eugène (Fr). A commune in the Charente-Maritime Département whose grapes are classed Petite Champagne (Cognac).

Saint-Féréon (Fr). A noted growth of Cider produced in Brittany.

Saint-Fiacre sur Maine (Fr). A commune in the A.C. Muscadet district of Pays Nantais, Loire.

Saint-Fort-sur-le-Né (Fr). A commune in the Charente Département whose grapes are classed Grande Champagne (Cognac).

Saint Gall (Fr). A fortified apéritif red wine.

Saint Galmier (Fr). An alkaline mineral

S

water bottled in a Burgundy-shaped, long-necked bottle.

Saint-Georges (Les) (Fr). A Premier Cru vineyard in the A.C. commune of Nuits-Saint-Georges, Côte de Nuits, Burgundy. 7.5 ha.

Saint-Georges-d'Orques (Fr). An A.C. red wine-producing area based near Montpellier in the Languedoc. Grape varieties – Carignan 50%, Cinsault 35% and Grenache 15%.

Saint-Georges [Les] (Fr). A commune in the Nuits-Saint-Georges, Côte de Nuits, Burgundy.

Saint-Georges-Saint-Émilion (Fr). A.C. Bordeaux red wine from the Saint-Émilion district.

Saint-Georges-sur-Loire (Fr). A commune in the A.C. Savennières, Anjou-Saumur, Loire.

Saint Germain (Cktl). See St. Germain.

Saint-Germain-de-Lusignan (Fr). A commune in the Charente-Maritime Département whose grapes are classed Petite Champagne (Cognac).

Saint-Germain-de-Vibrac (Fr). A commune in the Charente-Maritime Département whose grapes are classed Petite Champagne (Cognac).

Saint-Gervais (Fr). A wine-producing village in the Gard Département. Wines are of A.C. Côtes du Rhône-Villages.

Saint Ginés de la Jara (Sp). The patron saint of vintners. See Fiesta de la Vendimia.

Saint Helena (Fr). The patron saint of Champagne vineyard workers.

Saint-Hilaire-de-Barbezieux (Fr). A commune in the Charente Département whose grapes are classed Petite Champagne (Cognac).

Saint-Hippolyte (Fr). A wine town in the Bas-Rhin in Alsace. In German known as Sankt Pilt.

Saint-Jean-de-la-Porte (Fr). A.C. vineyard on the right bank of the river Isère in Savoie. Produces mainly red wines from the Mondeuse grape.

Saint-Jean-des-Mauvrets (Fr). An A.C. commune in the Coteaux de l'Aubance in the Anjou-Saumur district of the Loire.

Saint-Joseph (Fr). An A.C. district in the northern Rhône, west of the Hermitage district. Produces red and white wines. Communes – Glun, Lemps, Mauves, St. Jean-de-Muzels, Vion. Grape varieties are mainly the Syrah and Marsanne. Minimum alc. 10% by vol.

Saint-Julien (Fr). A.C. commune in the Haut-Médoc in Bordeaux. Wine comes under the 1855 classification. Red wines only. Minimum alc. 10.5% by vol.

Saint-Julien-en-Montmélas (Fr). A commune in the Beaujolais district. Has A.C. Beaujolais-Villages or Beaujolais-Saint-Julien-en-Montmélas status.

Saint-Lambert-du-Lattay (Fr). A commune in the A.C. Coteaux du Layon in the Anjou-Saumur district of the Loire. Produces sweet white (botrytis) wines.

Saint Landelin Brasserie (Fr). A brewery based in Crespin. Brews a Bière de Garde of same name.

Saint-Laurent (Aus). A red grape variety. Also grown in Czec.

Saint Laurent (Fr). A commune within the A.C. Médoc, Bordeaux.

Saint-Laurent-de-Cognac (Fr). A commune in the Charente-Maritime Département whose grapes (classed Borderies) are used in Cognac production.

Saint Laurent des Arbes (Fr). A commune in the A.C. Lirac, southern Rhône.

Saint-Laurent-des-Vignes (Fr). A commune in the A.C. Monbazillac district of the Bergerac. Produces sweet (botrytis) wines.

Saint-Leger (Fr). A commune in the Beaujolais district. Has A.C. Beaujolais-Villages or Beaujolais-Saint-Leger status.

Saint-Leger-de-Montbrillais (Fr). A commune in the A.C. Saumur, Anjou-Saumur, Vienne Département, Loire.

Saint Lheurine (Fr). A commune in the Charente-Maritime Département whose grapes are used in Cognac production.

Saint Marco (Fr). A lithiated mineral water.

Saint-Martial-de-Coculet (Fr). A commune in the Charente-Maritime Département whose grapes are classed Petite Champagne (Cognac).

Saint-Martial-de-Vitaterne (Fr). A commune in the Charente-Maritime Département whose grapes are classed Petite Champagne (Cognac).

Saint Martin (Fr). The Patron saint of wine in the Loire Valley. Discovered that vines flourished if they were pruned. See also St. Martin.

Saint-Martin-d'Ablois (Fr). A Cru Champagne village in the Canton d'Épernay. District = Épernay.

Saint Martin-le-Beau (Fr). A commune of A.C. Montlouis in the Touraine district of the Loire. Also spelt Saint Martin-les-Beaux.

Saint-Martin-sous-Montaigus (Fr). A commune in the A.C. Mercurey, Côte Chalonnaise, Burgundy.

Saint Maurice (Fr). A Champagne produced by Bruno Bocquet in Épernay. Part of the sales were donated to the British entry in the 1987 America's Cup race.

Saint Maurice (Fr). A Drôme vineyard of the A.C. Côtes du Rhône-Villages.

Saint-Maurice-de-Tavernolles (Fr). A commune in the Charente-Maritime Département whose grapes are classed Petite Champagne (Cognac).

Saint-Médard-de-Barbieux (Fr). A commune in the Charente Département whose grapes are classed Petite Champagne (Cognac).

Saint-Médard-en-Jalles (Fr). A commune in the A.C. Médoc, north-western Bordeaux.

Saint-Melaine (Fr). A commune in the A.C. Coteaux de l'Aubance in the Anjou-Saumur district of the Loire.

Saint-Même (Fr). A commune in the Charente Département whose grapes are classed Grande Champagne (Cognac).

Saint-Morille (Les) (Fr). A vineyard in the A.C. commune of Montagny, Côte Chalonnaise, Burgundy.

Saint Morillon (Fr). A commune in the A.C. Graves district of western Bordeaux. Produces red and white wines.

Saint Nectaire (Fr). A chalybeate mineral water.

Saint Nicolas de Bourgueil (Fr). An A.C. within the Touraine district of the Loire. Produces the finest red wines of the whole region from the Cabernet franc grape. Also some rosé produced.

Saint-Palais-du-Né (Fr). A commune in the Charente Département whose grapes are classed Petite Champagne (Cognac).

Saint Panteleimon (Cyp). A medium-sweet, white wine produced by Keo in Limassol.

Saint Pantaléon (Fr). A Drôme vineyard of the A.C. Côtes du Rhône-Villages.

Saint-Péray (Fr). An A.C. district of the central western Rhône. Produces good sparkling and still white wines from the Roussanne and Marsanne grape varieties.

Saint-Péray Mousseux (Fr). An A.C. sparkling white wine produced in the Côtes du Rhône from Roussanne and Marsanne grapes. Produced by the méthode champenoise it is considered by many as second only to Champagne. Minimum alc. by vol. 10%.

Saint Pey d'Armens (Fr). A commune of the A.C. Saint-Émilion in Bordeaux.

Saint-Pey-de-Langon (Fr). See Saint-Pierre-de-Mons.

Saint-Pierre-de-Bat (Fr). A commune in the Haut-Benauge, Entre-Deux-Mers, central Bordeaux.

Saint-Pierre-de-Mons (Fr). A commune in the A.C. Graves district. (Is also known as Saint-Pey-de-Langon). Produces sweet white wines.

Saint-Pierre-Doré (Fr). A white grape variety grown in the Loire region to produce wines of St-Pourçain-sur-Sioule.

Saint Pourçain (Fr). See St-Pourçain-sur-Sioule.

Saint-Preuil (Fr). A commune in the Charente Département whose grapes are classed Grande Champagne (Cognac).

Saint Raphaël (Fr). See St. Raphaël.

Saint Romain (Fr). A small A.C. commune in the southern Côte de Beaune, Burgundy. 100 ha. Produces red and white wines often sold as Côte de Beaune-Villages. Grape varieties – Chardonnay, Pinot blanc and Pinot noir.

Saint-Romain-de-Bellet (Fr). A wine-producing district in A.C. Bellet, Provence, south-eastern France.

Saints (Eng). There are a great number of Saints associated with the making of wines and spirits etc. some being general patrons whilst others have local associations. (Fr) = St. [Saint] (male) and Ste. [Sainte] (female), (Ger) = Sankt, (Hol) = Heilige, (It) = Santo, (Port) = São, (Sp) = Santa, (Tur) = Aziz.

Saint Saphorin (Switz). A Lavaux wine village. Produces dry white wines.

Saint-Sardon (Fr). A Vins de Pays area in the Tarn-et-Garonne Département in central-southern France.

Saint Saturnin (Fr). A small A.C. red wine-producing area in the Languedoc, southern France. Also produces Vin d'Une Nuit.

Saint-Sauveur (Fr). A wine-producing district in the A.C. Bellet, Provence, south-eastern France.

Saint-Sauveur (Fr). A commune in the A.C. Pécharmant in northern Bergerac. Produces red wines.

Saintsbury (USA). A winery based in the Napa Valley, California. Grape varieties – Chardonnay and Pinot noir. Produces varietal wines.

Saint Seurin-de-Cadourne (Fr). A commune within the A.C. Haut-Médoc, north-western Bordeaux.

Saint-Seurin-de-Palenne (Fr). A commune in the Charente-Maritime Département whose grapes are classed Petite Champagne (Cognac).

Saint-Sever (Fr). A commune in the Charente-Maritime Département whose grapes are classed Petite Champagne (Cognac).

Saint Simon (Fr). A non-vintage Champagne produced by the Le Crayère co-operative at Bethon in the southern Marne.

Saint Stefan (N.Z.). The brand-name

S

used by the Pacific Vineyards for their wines.

Saint Sulphice (Fr). A commune in the Charente-Maritime Département whose grapes are classed Borderies (Cognac).

Saint-Sulpice-de-Faleyrens (Fr). An A.C. commune within the Saint-Émilion district of eastern Bordeaux.

Saint-Symphorien-d'Ancelles (Fr). A commune in the Beaujolais district. Has A.C. Beaujolais-Villages or Beaujolais-Saint-Symphorien-d'Ancelles status.

Saint-Thierry (Fr). A Cru Champagne village in the Canton de Bourgogne. District = Reims.

Saint-Vallerin (Fr). A wine-producing town in the commune of A.C. Montagny, Côte Chalonnaise, Burgundy.

Saint-Véran (Fr). A commune in the Mâconnais district. Has A.C. Beaujolais-Villages or Beaujolais-Saint-Véran status (red wines). Also as A.C. Saint-Véran (white wine from the Chardonnay grape) minimum alc. 11% by vol. and A.C. Mâconnais Blanc (white wines).

Saint Victor-la-Coste (Fr). A commune in the A.C. Lirac, southern Rhône.

Saint Vincent (Fr). The patron saint of wine in Burgundy. A holiday on 22nd of January to celebrate his day (with processions).

Saint-Vivant (Fr). Armagnac producer. Address = Compagnie d'Armagnac, Saint Vivant, Route de Nérac, 32100 Condom.

Saint Vivien (Fr). A vineyard in the commune of Saint Vivien. A.C. Bourgeais et Blayais, Bordeaux.

Saint-Yzans (Fr). A commune in the Bas-Médoc. A.C. Médoc wines.

Saint-Yzans-de-Médoc (Fr). A noted cave coopérative based at Saint-Brice, Médoc, Bordeaux.

Saint Zeno (It). The patron saint of wine producers.

Sair (Eng). A home-brew public house in Linthwaite, Huddersfield, Yorkshire. Noted for its cask conditioned Linfit Mild 1032 O.G. Old Eli 1050 O.G. Leadboiler 1063 O.G. and Enoch's Hammer 1080 O.G.

Saïs (Afr). An A.O.G. area in the wine-producing region of Meknès-Fez, Morocco.

Saison (Bel). A top-fermented Bière from the French speaking region. Has a second fermentation in the bottle from a dosage of yeast. 5.6% alc. by vol. Saison Régal is the most popular.

Saison Dupont (Bel). A Bière brewed by the Dupont Brasserie in Tourpes.

Saison Régal (Bel). See Saison.

Saisons de Pipaix (Bel). A sharp Bière brewed by the Dupont Brasserie in Tourpes.

Saix (Fr). A region in the Saumur area of the Anjou-Saumur district in the Loire.

Saka (Tur). A water carrier.

Sakazuki (Jap). A small porcelain bowl into which Saké is poured from the Tokkuri. From this bowl the Saké is sipped.

Saké (Jap). A Beer made from rice. Named after the town of Osaka from where it was first produced. Served with seaweed biscuits. See also Koji and Suk.

Saké Collins (Cktl). 2 ozs. Saké, 1 oz. lemon juice, ½ teaspoon sugar. Mix juice and sugar together, add Saké and shake well over ice. Strain into a highball glass with ice, top up with soda. Dress with fruit in season.

Saké Gozenshu (Jap). The brand-name of a popular Saké.

Saké Manhattan (Cktl). 1 part Saké, 2 parts Rye whiskey. Stir well with ice, strain into a cocktail glass, top with a cherry.

Saké Martini (Cktl). 1 part Saké, 3 parts Gin. Stir well with ice, strain into a cocktail glass, top with an olive.

Saké Screwdriver (Cktl). Place 2–3 ice cubes in a tumbler. Pour in 2 ozs. Saké and 6 ozs. fresh orange juice. Stir, decorate with a slice of orange.

Saké Sour (Cktl). ½ oz. Saké, 1 oz. lemon juice, 1 teaspoon sugar. Mix in a mixing glass, add ice, then shake well together. Strain into a sour glass, add a dash of soda and a cherry.

Saké Tonic (Cktl). Place 2–3 ice cubes into a highball glass. Pour 2 ozs. Saké over the ice, top with tonic water.

Sakini (Cktl). 1 part Saké, 3 parts Gin. Stir over ice, serve 'On the rocks' with an olive.

Sakonnet Vineyards (USA). A winery based on Rhode Island. 14 ha. Produces vinifera and varietal hybrid wines.

Sakura Masamune (Jap). The brand-name of a popular brand of Saké.

Saladin Box (Scot). A large uncovered, open-ended, rectangular box used for modifying (germinating) barley during the malting process. For whisky and beer production.

Salage (Fr). The adding of sea water to wines to increase the mineral content. Up to 1 gramme per litre is permitted.

Salamanzar (Sp). A Salmonezah Cava wine bottle that equals 12 standard bottles.

Salaparuta-Corvo (It). A producer of sparkling (cuve close) wines in Sicily.

Salem [ortsteil Kirchberg] (Ger). Village. (Anb) = Baden. (Ber) = Bodensee. (Gro) = Sonnenufer. (Vin) = Schlossberg.

Salento Bianco Liquoroso (It). See Moscato di Salento.

Salep (Eng). See Saloop.

Salice Salentino Rosso (It). A D.O.C. red wine from Puglia. Produced mainly from the Negro amaro grape. Also made in rosato form.

Salignac (Fr). Cognac producer. Address = Domaine de Breuil, Rue Robert Daugas, 16100 Cognac. 7 ha. in the Grande Champagne. Produces – Très Vieille Grande Réserve 50 year old plus. (Part of the Hiram Walker group).

Salignac-de-Pons (Fr). A commune in the Charente-Maritime Département whose grapes are classed Petite Champagne (Cognac).

Salinas (USA). A new wine district in Monterey County, California.

Salins du Midi (Fr). A Vin de Pays. Has its own co-operative the Domaine Viticoles. Also has own grading – Cuvée Régence, Cuvée Gastronomique and Cuvée Centenaire.

Salisbury Bitter (Eng). A cask conditioned Bitter 1042 O.G. brewed by the Gibbs Mew Brewery, Salisbury, Wiltshire.

Salishan Vineyards (USA). A vineyard based in La Centre, Washington. 5 ha. Grape variety mainly Pinot noir.

Salkim (Tur). A bunch of grapes.

Salles (Fr). A commune in the Beaujolais district. Has A.C. Beaujolais-Villages or Beaujolais-Salles status.

Salles-d'Angles (Fr). A commune in the Charente Département whose grapes are classed Grande Champagne (Cognac).

Salles-de-Barbezieux (Fr). A commune in the Charente Département whose grapes are classed Petite Champagne (Cognac).

Sally's Paddock (Austr). A blended wine mainly of Cabernet sauvignon from the Redbank Estate, Victoria.

Salmanazar (Fr). A large bottle of 12 standard bottles capacity used in the Champagne region. See Champagne Bottle Sizes.

Salmen Brauerei (Switz). A brewery based in Rheinfelden (part of the Sibra group [Cardinal] Breweries).

Salome (Cktl). ⅓ measure dry Gin, ⅓ measure Dubonnet, ⅓ measure dry Vermouth. Stir over ice, strain into a cocktail glass.

Salon (Fr). Champagne producer. Address = B.P. 3, Le Mesnil-sur-Oger, 51190 Avize. Grande Marque. Produces – Vintage and non-vintage wines. Vintages – 1911, 1914, 1915, 1917, 1921, 1923, 1928, 1929, 1932, 1934, 1937, 1942, 1943, 1945, 1947, 1949, 1950, 1952, 1953, 1955, 1959, 1961, 1964, 1966, 1967, 1969, 1971, 1973, 1979.

Salón Rioja (Chile). The name given to red and white wine produced by Concha y Toro.

Saloon (USA). An old bar, especially in the old Western era. Now the equivalent of a U.K. lounge bar.

Saloop (Eng). A mediaeval tonic drink made from herbs and plants. Also spelt Salep.

Salta (Arg). A wine-producing region.

Saltana (S.Afr). A white grape variety.

Salters Winery (Austr). A winery based in the Barossa Valley, South Australia. Produces varietal and table wines.

Saltillo (Mex). A wine-producing area in the Coahuila district at the base of Nazario Ortiz Garza. Produces wines and brandies.

Saltram Winery (Austr). A winery in Southern Vales and Barossa Valley, South Australia. Owned by Seagram.

Salts (Eng). Minerals that are found in wines. See Mineral Salts.

Salty Dog (Cktl). 1½ fl.ozs. Vodka, 3½ fl.ozs. grapefruit juice. Salt the rim of a large wine glass, fill with ice. Add ingredients but do not stir.

Salus Brewery (S.Am). A brewery based in Uruguay.

Salva (La) (It). A producer of sparkling (cuve close) wines in the Lazio region.

Salvador (USA). A red grape variety grown in California for the making of dessert wines.

Salvador Coffee ($.Am). Produces mild, smooth coffees from high grade beans. Some of the coffees can be poor and thin and are used in blending. Grown in Salvador.

Salvador Poveda (Sp). A vineyard in Monóvar, Alicante. Produces 100% Monastrell wines. Fondillón is wood-aged for 15 years.

Salvagnin (Switz). A red wine from the Vaud of guaranteed quality. Made from a blend of Pinot noir and Gamay grapes. Deep in colour and high in alcohol.

Salvator (Ger). A lithiated mineral water.

Salvator (Ger). The brand-name of a Doppelbock beer brewed at the Paulaner-Thomas-Bräu Brauerei in Munich. See also St. Francis of Paula (the oldest Doppelbock). 7.51% alc. by vol.

Salvatore (Cktl). ⅕ measure Kirsch de Zoug, ⅖ measure Vodka, ⅕ measure Cointreau, ⅕ measure grapefruit juice. Shake over ice, strain into a cocktail glass, add a cherry.

Salzberg (Ger). Grosslage. (Anb) =

Württemberg. (Ber) = Württembergisch Unterland. (Vils) = Affaltrach, Eberstadt, Eichelberg, Ellhofen, Eschenau, Gellmersbach, Grantschen, Lehrensteinsfeld, Löwenstein, Löwenstein (ortsteil Hösslinsülz), Sulzbach, Weiler/Weinsberg, Weinsberg, Willsbach, Wimmental.

Salzberg (Fr). The German name for the wine town of Château-Salins in Alsace.

Sámago (Sp). A virus that turns the stem of the vine spongy and so prevents the production of fruit. The vine then dies.

Samalens (Fr). A noted Armagnac producer based in the Bas Armagnac.

Samaniego (Sp). A noted wine-producing village in the Rioja Alavesa.

Samarkand (Iran). A luscious white grape variety.

Sam Brown (Eng). A Brown ale 1035 O.G. brewed and bottled by the Mitchells and Butler Brewery in the Midlands.

Sam Brown (Eng). A Brown ale 1034 O.G. brewed and bottled by the Webster Brewery in Halifax, Yorkshire.

Sambuca (It). A liqueur made from an infusion of Witch elder bush and liquorice. Traditionally served ignited with 3 coffee beans floating on top. 40% alc. by vol. See also Sabucco (an alternative spelling).

Sambuca Cocktail (Cktl). Fill a liqueur glass with Sambuca, float 3 coffee beans (dark roasted) on top. Ignite, allow to burn for 30 seconds, douse and serve.

Sambuca Negra (It). A coffee-flavoured Sambuca liqueur. 40% alc. by vol.

Sambucco (It). A liqueur made from Elderberry and liquorice. See also Sambuca.

Samichlaus (Switz). A Beer brewed by the Hurlimann Brauerei. Lagered for 1 year. Purported to be the strongest beer in the World. 14.5% alc. by vol.

Samling 88 (Ger). A white grape cross variety.

Samogon (USSR). The name given to 'bootleg' Vodka.

Samonac (Fr). A commune in the A.C. Côtes de Bourg in north-eastern Bordeaux.

Samorodno (Yug). A medium-dry, white wine produced in north-eastern Yugoslavia near the Hungarian border.

Samos (Gre). An island in the Aegean Islands, eastern Greece. Produces mainly sweet, dessert wines of same name.

Samos Muscatel (Gre). A luscious dessert wine made from the Muscatel grape on the island of Samos.

Samotok (Yug). A white wine produced in southern Macedonia.

Samovar (USSR). An elaborate container used for the serving of tea.

Şampanya (Tur). Champagne, sparkling wine.

Sampigny-lès-Maranges (Fr). A vineyard in the A.C. commune of Sampigny, Côte de Beaune, Burgundy. 44 ha. Wines may be sold as Sampigny-lès-Maranges or Côte de Beaune-Villages. Has two vineyards that can use their name – Clos du Roi and Les Maranges both prefixed with Sampigny-lès-Maranges.

Sampson Ale (Eng). A cask conditioned Ale 1055 O.G. brewed by the Truman Brewery in London.

Samshoo (China). A liqueur made from distilled rice wine.

Samshu (China). See Samshoo.

Samsó (Sp). A red grape variety grown in Catalonia.

Samson Brewery (Czec). A brewery in the town of České Budějovice noted for its Dalila (a medium dark Lager). Founded in 1795.

Samson Strong Bitter (Eng). A Bitter beer 1042 O.G. brewed by the Vaux Brewery in Sunderland.

Samtrot (Ger). Lit – 'Velvet red'. A mutation of the red grape variety Schwarzriesling.

Samuel Port (Austr). A Port-style wine from the Wynvale vineyards, New South Wales.

Samuel Powell Traditional Bitter (Wales). See Powell.

Samuels [T.W.] (USA). A Bourbon whiskey distillery based south of Frankfort in Kentucky.

Samuel Whitbread Bitter (Eng). A cask conditioned Bitter 1044 O.G. brewed by the Whitbread Brewery in London. Also keg.

Samur (Fr). See Saumur. (mis-spelling of).

San Adrián (Sp). A Zona de Crianza in the Rioja Baja.

San Angelo Medium Amontillado (Sp). A brand of Amontillado sherry produced by Garvey's at Jerez de la Frontera.

San Antonio Winery (USA). A large winery based in Los Angeles, California. Produces table, sparkling and dessert wines.

Sanary (Fr). A commune in the Bandol district of Provence.

San Asensio (Sp). A wine-producing district in the Rioja Alta.

San Asensio (Sp). A red wine produced by Bodegas Campo Viejo in the district of same name in the Rioja Alta.

Sanatogen (Eng). A Tonic wine from the Whiteway company. Original formula or added iron formula.

San Benito Valley (USA). A new wine area of Central Coast, California. Produces

S

table, dessert and sparkling wines. See Almaden.

San Bernardino (USA). A wine district within the region of Cucamonga, California. Produces – table and dessert wines.

San Bernardino Winery (Austr). A winery based in Riverina, New South Wales.

San Carlos (Arg). A wine-producing area in central Argentina.

Sancerre (Fr). An A.C. dry white wine area within the Central Vineyards of the Loire. Wines produced from the Sauvignon blanc grape variety.

Sanchez de Alba (Sp). A Sherry producer based at Jerez de la Frontera. Labels include La Guita.

Sanchez-Romate (Sp). See Romate.

Sancocho (Sp). The action of boiling must down to ⅓ of its volume. This is used to sweeten and colour Sherries. See Paxarete.

San Cosma (It). A Chianti Classico producer based in Tuscany.

San Costanza Nouveau (It). A young red wine produced by Castello Villa Banfi from the Brunello grape.

San Cristobal (Cktl). ¼ measure golden Rum, ¼ measure Grenadine, ¼ measure pineapple juice, ¼ measure orange juice, dash Angostura, 2 dashes lime juice. Shake well over ice, strain into an ice-filled collins glass, dress with a slice of orange and pineapple cube.

Sanctified Wine (USA). A wine for religious service.

Sand (Ger). Vineyard. (Anb) = Rheinhessen. (Ber) = Nierstein. (Gro) = Sankt Alban. (Vil) = Mainz.

Sand (Eng). Soil that gives good drainage, is resistant to Phylloxera and is a good soil for vine cultivation. Occurs in the Côtes du Rhône and Armagnac.

Sandalera (Austr). A grape liqueur from the Sandalford winery in the Swan Valley, Western Australia. Made from the Pedro Ximénez (P.X.) grape. Has a raisiny flavour and aroma.

Sandalford Winery (Austr). Address = West Swan Road, Caversham, 6055, Western Australia. 175 ha. in the Margaret River and Swan Valley. Grape varieties – Cabernet sauvignon, Chardonnay, Chenin blanc, Verdelho, Pedro Ximénez, Riesling, Sémillon and Shiraz.

Sandanski Melnik (Bul). A delimited wine region based in south-western Bulgaria. Main grape varieties are Cabernet sauvignon, Chardonnay and Tamianka.

Sandberg (Ger). Vineyard. (Anb) = Mosel-Saar-Ruwer. (Ber) = Saar-Ruwer. (Gro) = Scharzberg. (Vil) = Wiltingen.

Sandeman (Port). Vintage Port shippers. Vintages – 1870, 1872, 1873, 1875, 1878, 1880, 1881, 1884, 1887, 1890, 1892, 1894, 1896, 1897, 1900, 1904, 1908, 1911, 1912, 1917, 1920, 1927, 1934, 1935, 1942, 1943, 1945, 1947, 1950, 1955, 1957, 1958, 1960, 1962, 1963, 1966, 1967, 1970, 1975, 1977, 1980, 1982, 1983.

Sandeman (Sp). A noted Sherry producer. Address = Calle Pizarro 10, Jerez de la Frontera. Over 675 ha of vineyards. Sherry brands include Don Fino, Royal Ambrosante, Royal Corregidor, Royal Esmeralda. Also a noted Port producer. Is famous for its 'Black Don' motif.

Sandeman and Son (Scot). A distillery based in Dundee, Perthshire. Produces King's Vat (a blended Scotch whisky) 40% alc. by vol. Also ships Madeira wine.

Sandeman Jubilee Port (Port). A vintage 1977 Port bottled to celebrate H.R.H. Queen Elizabeth II's Silver Jubilee.

Sandeman Silver Jubilee Port (Port). A vintage 1935 Port bottled to celebrate H.R.H. King George V's Silver Jubilee.

Sanderson (William and Son) (Scot). A noted Whisky distiller and blender based in Leith, Midlothian. Created the blend of VAT 69. Now part of DCL. Still hold the license of Glenesk Distillery Montrose.

S & G (Sp). A white wine produced in La Mancha by the Vinícola de Castilla.

Sandgrub (Ger). Vineyard. (Anb) = Rheingau. (Ber) = Johannisberg. (Gro) = Heiligenstock. (Vil) = Eltville.

Sandgrub (Ger). Vineyard. (Anb) = Rheingau. (Ber) = Johannisberg. (Gro) = Heiligenstock. (Vil) = Kiedrich.

Sandgrub (Ger). Vineyard. (Anb) = Rheingau. (Ber) = Johannisberg. (Gro) = Steinmacher. (Vil) = Eltville.

San Diego (USA). A wine district in southern California which produces table, sparkling and dessert wines.

Sand Martin (Cktl). ⅖ measure dry Gin, ⅖ measure Italian vermouth, ⅕ measure Green Chartreuse. Shake well over ice, strain into a cocktail glass.

Sando (Sri.L). A bitter Stout 13.8° Balling brewed by the McCallum Brewery in Colombo.

San Domingo (Sp). A sweet, pale, Cream sherry produced by Gonzalez Byass in Jerez de la Frontera.

S and P (Eng). A cask conditioned Bitter

S

1038 O.G. brewed by the Norwich Brewery, Norfolk.

Sandpitts Vineyard (Eng). A vineyard based near Gastard, Wiltshire. Was first planted in 1981. 0.25 ha. Grape varieties – Chambourcin, Leon Millot and Zweigeltrebe.

Sandro (Cktl). ½ fl.oz. Campari, ½ fl.oz. Bacardi White Rum, 1½ fl.ozs. Cinzano Rossi. Stir over ice, strain into a cocktail glass, add orange zest.

Sandrocken (Ger). Vineyard. (Anb) = Baden. (Ber) = Badische Bergstrasse/Kraichgau. (Gro) = Rittersberg. (Vil) = Grossachsen.

Sandrone (Luciano) (It). A small grower based in Barolo, Piemonte.

Sandstone Winery (USA). A winery based in Iowa. Produces mainly French hybrid wines.

Sandwald Weizen Krone (Ger). A Wheat beer 5.1% alc. by vol. brewed by the Dinkelacker Brauerei in Stuttgart.

Sandwalls Brewery (Swe). A brewery based in Boras, south-western Sweden.

Sandweine (Aus). The name given to wines of Burgenland grown on sandy soil (resistant to Phylloxera). See Winkel (is seen on label).

Sand Wines (Hun). The name given to the wines produced on the Transdanubian plain which has sandy soil.

Sandy Bottoms (Eng) (slang). A term used in the navy to obtain the rest of the Rum offered by a mate from his mug.

Sandy Soil (Eng). See Sand.

Sanel Valley Vineyard (USA). A vineyard based near Hopland, Mendocino County, California. 42 ha. Grape variety – Cabernet sauvignon. Vinified at the Milano Winery.

San Felice (It). A noted wine-producer based at San Gusmè, Siena, Tuscany.

San Felipe (Chile). A wine-producing area in the Aconcagua province.

San Félipe Bianco (Arg). A white wine produced in the Mendosa region from Pinot bianco and Riesling grapes.

San Félipe Traminer (Arg). An Alsace-type wine produced from the Traminer grape in the Mendosa region.

San Fernando (Chile). A wine-producing area in the Colchagua province.

Sanford and Benedict Vineyards (USA). A winery based near Buellton, Santa Barbara, California. 46 ha. Grape varieties – Chardonnay and Pinot noir. Produces varietal wines.

San Francisco (Cktl). ⅓ measure Sloe Gin, ⅓ measure Italian vermouth, ⅓ measure French vermouth, dash Angostura, dash Orange bitters. Shake over ice, strain into a cocktail glass. Top with a cherry.

San Francisco Brandy (USA). The brand-name of a 10 year old Brandy bottled by the Guild of Wineries and Distilleries in Lodi, California.

Sangarees (Cktl). Spirit, lemon slice, sugar syrup, fruit and nutmeg served in a tall glass over cracked ice. Can also be made with beer or wine in place of the spirits. Is similar to Sangría.

Sängerhalde (Ger). Vineyard. (Anb) = Baden. (Ber) = Bodensee. (Gro) = Sonnenufer. (Vil) = Stetten.

Sängerhalde (Ger). Vineyard. (Anb) = Baden. (Ber) = Bodensee. (Gro) = Sonnenufer. (Vil) = Markdorf.

Sängerhalde (Ger). Vineyard. (Anb) = Baden. (Ber) = Bodensee. (Gro) = Sonnenufer. (Vil) = Meersburg.

San Gil (Fr). The brand-name of an Armagnac brandy produced by the Domaine de Cassanel in Nérac. 40% alc. by vol.

San Ginés de la Jara (Sp). See Saint Ginés de la Jara.

San Giocondo (It). A Tuscany 'Nouveau' wine produced by Antinori.

San Giorgio (It). A red Vini da Tavola wine from 80–90% Sangiovese and 10–30% Cabernet grapes, produced in central Italy.

Sangiovese (It). A red grape variety grown mainly in the southern regions of Italy. Used in the making of full-bodied, well balanced wines. e.g. Chianti.

Sangiovese dei Colli Pesaresi (It). D.O.C. red wine from The Marches. Made from the Sangiovese, Ciliegiolo and Montepulciano grapes. Produced in an area around Pesaro.

Sangiovese di Aprilia (It). See Merlot di Aprilia. (Pink with orange reflections).

Sangiovese di Romagna (It). D.O.C. red wine from the Emilia-Romagna. Made from the Sangiovese grape. If aged minimum 2 years then classed Riserva. Cannot be sold to the consumer before 1st April following the vintage.

Sangiovese Grosso (It). A red grape variety grown in the Tuscany region for Chianti wines.

Sangiovese Toscano (It). The local Tuscany name for a variety of the Sangiovese grape.

Sangioveto (It). A red grape variety used in the making of Chianti.

Sangiovetto di Coltibuono (It). A red Vini da Tavola wine produced from the Sangiovese grape in central-western Italy.

Sangiovetto Piccolo (Arg). A red grape variety grown in the Mendoza region.

Sangre de Toro (Sp). The brand-name of a red wine produced by Torres in Penedés, Cataluña. Grape varieties – 60% Garnacha, 40% Cariñena and is oak aged.

S

Sangri (Eng). A drink made with Madeira, sugar, water and grated nutmeg. Served hot or cold.

Sangría (Sp). A wine cup made by adding fruit to red wine. 3 ozs. sugar, 1 gill water, 1 sliced orange, 1 sliced lime, 1 bottle red wine. Make a syrup with the water and sugar, whilst still hot add the thinly sliced fruit. Marinade for 4 hours, then add ice and red wine. Stir well and serve.

Sangria Punch (Cktl). 1 bottle dry red wine, 1 bottle apple juice, juice ½ small grapefruit, slices of orange, lemon, apple and pear, sugar syrup to taste. Combine together, stand in a cool place for 24 hours. Serve with ice.

Sangrita (Cktl). 1 measure Tequila, 1 measure tomato juice. Shake over ice, strain into a cocktail glass.

Sangue de Boi (Bra). A local named wine. Lit – 'Bull's blood'. Bares little resemblance to the Hungarian variety.

Sangue di Giuda (It). A red wine from Lombardy.

San Isidro (Sp). A large co-operative based in the Jumilla district in the Levante. Produces wines under names of Rumor, Sabatacha and Zambra.

San Joaquin Valley (USA). Fresno-San Joaquin Valley. Southern part of the Great Valley in California. Produces most of California's dessert wines with some table and sparkling wines.

San José (USA). A large city in Santa Clara, California. Has many wineries based there.

San Juan (Arg). A wine region based north of Mendoza.

San Juan del Río (Mex). A wine-producing region in the Querétaro district.

San Juan de Peteroa (Chile). A wine-producing area in central Chile.

Sanka (USA). A leading brand of decaffeinated coffee.

Sankt (Ger). Saint.

Sankt Alban (Ger). Grosslage. (Anb) = Rheinhessen. (Ber) = Nierstein. (Vils) = Bodenheim, Gau-Bischofsheim, Harxheim, Lörzweiler, Mainz.

Sankt Annaberg (Ger). Vineyard. (Anb) = Rheinhessen. (Ber) = Wonnegau. (Gro) = Liebfrauenmorgen. (Vil) = Worms.

Sankt Georgen (Ger). Vineyard. (Anb) = Rheinhessen. (Ber) = Bingen. (Gro) = Abtey. (Vil) = Partenheim.

Sankt Johann (Ger). Village. (Anb) = Rheinhessen. (Ber) = Bingen. (Gro) = Abtey. (Vins) = Geyersberg, Klostergarten, Steinberg.

Sankt Johännser (Ger). Vineyard. (Anb) = Württemberg. (Ber) = Württembergisch Unterland. (Gro) = Schalkstein. (Vil) = Markgröningen.

Sankt Julianenbrunnen (Ger). Vineyard. (Anb) = Rheinhessen. (Ber) = Nierstein. (Gro) = Krotenbrunnen. (Vil) = Guntersblum.

Sankt Kathrin (Ger). Vineyard. (Anb) = Rheinhessen. (Ber) = Bingen. (Gro) = Abtey. (Vil) = Wolfsheim.

Sankt Laurent (Aus). A red grape variety which produces full-bodied, fragrant red wines.

Sankt Margarethen (Aus). A Burgenland area which produces mainly white wines.

Sankt Martin (Ger). Village. (Anb) = Rheinphalz. (Ber) = Südliche Weinstrasse. (Gro) = Schloss Ludwigshöhe. (Vins) = Baron, Kirchberg, Zitadelle. (See St. Martin).

Sankt Michael (Ger). Grosslage. (Anb) = Mosel-Saar-Ruwer. (Ber) = Bernkastel. (Vils) = Bekond, Detzem, Ensch, Klusserath, Köwerich, Leiwen, Longen, Lörsch, Mehring, Pölich, Schleich, Thörnich.

Sankt Pilt (Fr). The German name for the wine village of Saint-Hippolyte in the Bas-Rhin, Alsace.

Sankt Rochuskapelle (Ger). Grosslage. (Anb) = Rheinhessen. (Ber) = Bingen. (Vils) = Aspisheim, Badenheim, Biebelsheim, Bingen, Dromersheim, Gensingen, Grolsheim, Ockenheim, Pfaffen-Schwabenheim, Sponsheim, Welgesheim, Zotzenheim.

San Leonino (It). A Chianti Classico producer based in Tuscany.

Sanlúcar de Barrameda (Sp). A seaport on the river Guadalquivir where Fino sherries are brought to mature into Manzanilla by absorbing the sea air which gives a salty tang to the wine. Part of the Jerez Supérieur region.

San Luis (Sp). A wine-producer based on Minorca in the Balearic Isles.

San Luis Obispo (USA). A wine-producing area in California.

San Luis Potosi (Mex). A wine-producing area in northern Mexico.

San Lunardo (It). A white grape variety grown on the island of Ischia.

San Marino (N.Z.). Vineyards. Address = 2 Highway 16, Kumeu, Auckland. 32 ha. at Kumeu, also grapes from Gisborne. Grape varieties – Cabernet franc, Cabernet sauvignon, Chardonnay, Gewürztraminer, Merlot, Müller-Thurgau, Pinot noir and Sauvignon blanc.

San Marino Trinity (N.Z.). A slightly spicy wine made from a blend of Chardonnay, Gewürztraminer and Müller-Thurgau grapes by San Marino in Kumeu.

San Martin (Arg). A wine-producing area based in the Mendoza region.

San Martin Cocktail (Cktl). ¼ gill Gin, ¼ gill Italian vermouth, 4 dashes Yellow Chartreuse. Shake well over ice, strain into a cocktail glass. Add a squeeze of lemon peel juice on top.

San Martino Della Battaglia (It). A small locality 2 miles south of Lake Garda in Lombardy. Tocai de San Martino della Battaglia is the white wine produced there.

San Martin Winery (USA). A winery based in Morgan Hill, Santa Clara, California. Grape varieties – Johannisberg riesling, Muscat and Petite syrah. Produces varietal wines.

San Mateo (USA). A small wine-producing county based near San Francisco, California.

San Matias (Mex). A producer of Tequila sold under the same name.

San Michele (Den). A tangerine-based liqueur produced by the Peter Heering Co.

San Miguel (Sp). A dry, Pilsener-style beer 5.4% alc. by vol. brewed by the San Miguel Brewery.

San Miguel Brewery (E.Ind). A brewery based in Manila which produces San Miguel Lager beers. Owned by a Spanish parent company.

San Miguel Brewery (Sp). A major brewing company in Spain. Has three breweries in Burgos, Lérida and Málaga. Brews San Miguel 1049–1055 O.G. and Selecta XV Lager beers.

San Pasqual Vineyards (USA). A winery based in Escondido, San Diego, California. 42 ha. Grape varieties – Gamay, Muscat canelli and Sauvignon blanc. Produces varietal and table wines.

San Patricio (Sp). A very dry, pale, Fino Sherry produced by Garvey in Jerez de la Frontera.

San Pedro Winery (Chile). A winery based in Talca province. Owned by Rumasa. Produces red and white wines.

San Pellegrino (It). A sparkling mineral water of Bergamo. Has added CO_2 gas.

San Rafael (Arg). A wine-producing area in southern Argentina.

San Rafael (USA). A wine town in Marin County, California. Has many wineries based there.

Sanraku Ocean (Jap). One of the largest whiskey and wine producers in Japan. Based in Yamanashi, Tokyo. Is noted for its Château Mercian (Grand Cru Classé) wine.

San Sadurní de Noya (Sp). The Penedés town where the sparkling wines of the region are made and stored.

Sans Année (Fr). Non-vintage.

San Sebastian Cocktail (Cktl). ⅗ measure dry Gin, ⅕ measure white Rum, ⅕ measure Triple Sec, ½ fl.oz. grapefruit juice, ½ fl.oz. lemon juice. Shake over ice, strain into a cocktail glass.

San Severo Bianco (It). D.O.C. white wine from the Puglia. Made from the Bombino bianco, Malvasia bianco, Trebbiano toscano and Verdeca grapes. The D.O.C. can also apply to naturally sparkling wines.

San Severo Rosato (It). D.O.C. rosé wine from the Puglia region. Made from the Montepulciano di Abruzzo and Sangiovese grapes. D.O.C. can also apply to the naturally sparkling wines.

San Severo Rosso (It). D.O.C. red wine from the Puglia region. Made from the Montepulciano di Abruzzo and Sangiovese grapes. D.O.C. can also apply to the naturally sparkling wines.

San Silvestro (It). A liqueur said to contain 100 herbs produced in the Abruzzi mountains. Also called Centerbe or Mentuccia. 40% alc. by vol.

San Simón (Sp). The brand-name used by Bodegas García Carrión in Jumilla for a range of their red, rosé and white wines.

San Souci (Cktl). ⅓ measure Tia Maria, ⅓ measure Jamaican rum, ⅓ measure Grand Marnier, 1 gill orange juice, 2 dashes lime juice. Stir over ice, strain into a highball glass.

Sans Thorn Rose (Yug). A light, fragrant, rosé wine.

Santa (It). Saint.

Santa Barbara (USA). A wine-producing county on the central-southern coast of California.

Santa Barbara Winery (USA). A small winery based near Buellton, Santa Barbara, California. 17 ha. Produces varietal and generic wines.

Santa Carolina (Chile). A bodega that produces wines mainly for home consumption.

Santa Catarina (Bra). A wine-producing state in south-eastern Brazil.

Santa Christina (It). A Chianti Classico produced by Antinori in Tuscany.

Santa Clara Valley (USA). A Californian valley which produces fine red and white wines plus dessert and sparkling wines.

Santa Croce (It). A small village in commune of Carpi in Emilia-Romagna. Lends its name to a red wine Lambrusco Salamino di S. Croce.

Santa Cruz (USA). A wine district sited south of San Francisco which produces table, sparkling and dessert wines.

Santa Cruz Mountain Vineyard (USA). A winery based in Santa Cruz, California.

5 ha. Grape varieties – Cabernet sauvignon and Pinot noir. Produces varietal wines.

Santa Daria (Sp). The brand-label for wines produced by the Co-operative Vinícola de Cenicero, Bodegas 'Santa Daría', Rioja.

Santa Digna (Chile). The name used by Torres of Spain for a range of wines produced in Chile. (Red, rosé and white).

Santa Emiliana (Chile). The name given to a red wine made from the Cabernet sauvignon and a white wine made from a blend of Sémillon and Sauvignon blanc. Produced by Concha y Toro.

Santa Giustina (It). See Leitacher.

Santa Helena (Chile). The brand-name of a range of wines produced by Rumasa Co.

Santa Helena (Gre). A silky dry white wine produced by the Achaia Clauss winery of Patras.

Santa Laura (Gre). A dry white wine.

Santa Lucia (It). A Chianti Classico producer based in Tuscany.

Santa Maddalena (It). D.O.C. red wine from the Trentino-Alto Adige. Made from the Schiava grigia, Schiava grossa, Schiava media and the Tschaggele grapes in the province of Bolzano. Classico designation is reserved to wine produced in the restricted area delimited by Ministerial decree.

Santa Margherita di Portogruaro (It). A producer of sparkling (cuve close) wines based in Veneto.

Santa Maria (Sp). A Cream sherry produced by Duff Gordon in Puerto de Santa Maria.

Santa Maria della Versa (It). A producer of sparkling (cuve close) wines based in Lombardy.

Santa Maura (Gre). A wine-producing area noted for its dark, red wines.

Santa Mavra (Gre). A red wine made from the Vertzami grape on the island of Levkas in the Ionian islands in western Greece.

Santa Rica (Eng). A freeze-dried instant coffee from the Nestlé Co. Made from 100% Arabica coffee beans.

Santa Rita Company (Chile). A wine-producing exporter of Santiago based in the Maipo Valley. Noted for Casa Real wine.

Santa Rosa (USA). A wine-producing area in the Russian River Valley, Sonoma County, California.

Santa Teresa (Chile). A winery based in the Colchagu province. Wines are produces in Santiago.

Santa Tirso (Port). A small district of the

Vinho Verde region that produces white Vinho Verde wines.

Santa Ynez Valley (USA). A wine area in Santa Barbara, southern California. Wineries include Firestone and Zaca Mesa.

Santa Ynez Valley Winery (USA). A small winery based near Solvang, Santa Barbara, California. Grape varieties – Cabernet sauvignon, Chardonnay, Gewürztraminer, White riesling and Sauvignon blanc. Produces varietal wines.

Santenay (Fr). An A.C. wine commune of the southern Côte de Beaune in the Burgundy region.

Santenots (Les) (Fr). A Premier Cru vineyard in the A.C. commune of Volnay, Côte de Beaune, Burgundy. Also known as Clos les Santenots.

Santenots-Blancs (Les) (Fr). A Premier Cru vineyard in the A.C. commune of Meursault, Côte de Beaune, Burgundy, 2.95 ha.

Santenots-du-Milieu (Les) (Fr). A Premier Cru vineyard in the A.C. commune of Meursault, Côte de Beaune, Burgundy. 7.7 ha.

Santerem-João Santarem (Port). A blue-black grape variety grown in Colares.

Santhagen's Original Cape Velvet Cream (S.Afr). A liqueur produced by Gilbey in Stellenbosch. Is similar in style to Bailey's Cream.

Santi (It). A D.O.C. white wine produced in Verona by a firm of the same name.

Santi (A.G.) (It). A noted producer of sparkling wines (by the méthode champenoise) in the Veneto region. Labels include – Durello Spumante Brut.

Santiago (Chile). A wine-producing area in the central zone.

Santiago (Cktl). 2 ozs. Bacardi White Label Rum, juice of ½ a lime, 4 dashes red Curaçao, ½ teaspoon sugar. Combine the juice and sugar, add other ingredients, shake well with ice, strain into a cocktail glass.

Santiago (W.Ind). The brand-name of a white Rum produced by U.R.M.

Santiago Ruiz (Sp). A bodega based in El Rosal, Galicia. Produces mainly white wines.

Santini (Pousse Café). Pour into a slim liqueur glass an equal measure of the following in order – Cognac, Maraschino, Grand Marnier and white Rum.

Santino Winery (USA). A winery based in the Shenandoah Valley, Amador County, California. Grape varieties – Cabernet sauvignon and Zinfandel. Produces varietal wines.

Sant Manel Brut Nature (Sp). A Cava

wine produced by Cavas Hill. Has a flinty, earthy flavour.

Santola (Port). A dry Vinho Verde produced by Vinhos Messias in Beira Alta.

Santonja (Vincente Simó) (Sp). A producer of fine wines from Valencia. Is noted for Foldillón (a fine red wine).

Santorin (Gre). A dry or sweet wine produced on the island of Santorin.

Santorini (Gre). A straw coloured wine, high in alcohol which is produced on the island of Thira in the Cyclades Islands in southern Greece. Made from the Assyrtiko and Aidani grapes. Also the name of a red wine.

Santos (Bra). A mild smooth coffee which produces a mild soft flavour with little acidity. Is the major coffee bean of Brazil. See Bourbon Santos, Flat Bean Santos and Red Santos (all are pure coffees).

Santo Steffano (It). A red wine produced in the Apulia province. Ages well.

Santo Tomàs (Mex). A wine-producing area in the Baja California.

Santys Port Wines (S.Afr). Port-style wines produced by the Gilbeys Co.

San Valentin (Sp). A semi-dry, white wine produced by Torres in the Penedés from the Parellada grape.

San Vincente (Sp). A wine-producing district in the Rioja Alta, north-western Spain.

San Vincente Vineyard (USA). A vineyard based near Soledad, Salinas Valley, Monterey County, California. Grape variety – Cabernet sauvignon. Vinified at the Staiger Winery.

Sanwald Brauerei (Ger). A brewery in Stuttgart which is noted for its top-fermented Weizen beers. Owned by the Dinkelacker Co.

Sanzay-le-Grand (Paul) (Fr). A wine-producer based at Varrains, Saumur, Anjou-Saumur, Loire. Noted for Saumur Mousseux.

San Zeno d'Oro (It). The annual awards given to the best wine producers. Saint Zeno is the patron saint of wine producers.

São Domingos (Port). An extra-dry, sparkling wine made by the méthode champenoise by Caves Solar de São Domingos.

São Domingos (Port). The brand-name of an Aguardente brandy produced by Caves Solar de São Domingos.

São Francisco (Bra). A locally, well-known brand of Cachaça.

São João (Mad). The name once given to a Madeira-style wine (the name is obtained from the district).

São Martinho (Mad). Name once given to a Madeira style (the name obtained from district).

Saône-et-Loire (Fr). A département between Mâcon and Chagny in the Burgundy region. Divided into Mercurey and Mâconnais.

Sâone [River] (Fr). River that runs through the Beaujolais in Burgundy to join the river Rhône.

Sap (Hol) (abbr). Juice. See Saprijk.

Sapa (Lat). A word used to describe a new wine.

Sapan d'Or (Fr). A green liqueur similar in style to Bénédictine.

Saparvi (USSR). A red grape variety grown in Moldavia. Produces light, sweet wines.

Saperavi (USSR). A red grape variety grown in Georgia and the Crimea.

Saperavi (USSR). A strong, dark red wine, high in alcohol. 14% alc. by vol. produced in the Tiflis district of Georgia.

Saperavi Massandra (USSR). A dry red wine from the Crimean peninsula.

Sapido (It). Spicy. A term applied to wines such as the Gewürztraminer in the Süd-tirol.

Sapin (Fr). See Sapindor.

Sapindor (Fr). A herb liqueur made at Pontarlier in the Jura since 1825. Sold in tree-trunk shaped bottles. Has a pine-needle extract flavour. Also known as Liqueur des Pins, Sapin and Extrait des Pins.

Sappig (Hol). Juicy.

Sapporo Brewery (Jap). A brewery based in Sapporo that brews Black Beer, Lager and Yebisu.

Sapporo Wines Limited (Jap). See Katsunuma Winery.

Saprijk (Hol). Juicy.

Saquier (Fr). A wine-producing district in A.C. Bellet, Provence, south-eastern France.

Sarabi (Tur). Sherry. See also Ispanyol Sarabi.

Sarah's Vineyard (USA). A winery based near Gilroy, Santa Clara, California. Grape varieties – Chardonnay, Chenin blanc, Petite syrah and Zinfandel. Produces varietal and table wines.

Şarap (Tur). Wine.

Şarap Beyaz (Tur). White wine.

Şarap Garson (Tur). Wine waiter.

Şarap Gül (Tur). Rosé wine.

Şarap Kirmizi (Tur). Red wine.

Saratoga (USA). A city based in eastern Santa Clara County, California. Has a large number of wineries based there.

Saratoga Cocktail (Cktl). 1 oz. Brandy, ½ oz. lemon juice, ½ oz. pineapple juice, 2 dashes Maraschino, 2 dashes Angostura. Shake over ice, strain into a cocktail glass.

S

Saratoga Cooler (Cktl).(Non-alc). Into a large tumbler place 2 ice cubes, juice of a lime, sugar syrup to taste. Top up with cold ginger ale. Stir and serve.

Sarcy (Fr). A Cru Champagne village in the Canton de Ville-en-Tardenois. District = Reims.

Sardegna (It). Sardinia.

Sardinia (It). The second largest island of Italy. Produces many fine wines. The vitis vinifera is indigenous to the island.

Sárgamuskotály (Hun). A minor white grape variety used in the making of Tokay wines.

Sarget de Gruaud-Larose (Fr). The second wine of Château Gruaud-Larose Grand Cru Classé (4th), A.C. Saint-Julien, north-western Bordeaux.

Sarhoş (Tur) (slang). Drunk, drink.

Sarica (Rum). A wine-producing region in the Dobrudja district.

Sarmento (Port). Vine-shoot.

Sarmientos (Sp). A term used to describe the two renewed spurs on the vine that will eventually bear grapes.

Saronno Cocktail (Cktl). ⅓ gill Amaretto, 1 gill milk, ½ oz. Galliano. Blend together with a scoop of crushed ice in a blender. Serve in a flute glass.

Saronno Sunset (Cktl). ⅙ measure Amaretto, ⅙ measure Drambuie, ⅔ measure orange juice, dash Grenadine. Shake over ice, strain into a cocktail glass. Dress with a cherry and orange slice.

Sàrospatak (Hun). A wine-producing area in the southern foothills.

Sarrau (Robert) (Fr). A Burgundy négociant-éleveur based at Saint Jean d'Ardières.

Sarsaparilla (USA). See Sasparella.

Sartène (Fr). An A.C. red and rosé wine produced around the town of same name on the south-west of the island of Corsica.

Sarum Special (Eng). A Pale ale 1048 O.G. brewed and bottled by the Gibbs Mew Brewery in Salisbury, Wiltshire.

SAS (Eng). A cask conditioned Anglian Special beer 1048 O.G. brewed by the Crouch Vale Brewery in Essex.

Sasbach (Ger). Village. (Anb) = Baden. (Ber) = Kaiserstuhl-Tuniberg. (Gro) = Vulkanfelsen. (Vins) = Limburg, Lützelberg, Rote Halde, Sceibenbuck.

Sasbachwalden (Ger). Village. (Anb) = Baden. (Ber) = Ortenau. (Gro) = Schloss Rodeck. (Vins) = Alter Gott, Klostergut Schelzberg.

Saskatchewan (Can). A small wine region.

Sasparella (USA). An old American soda pop. Also spelt Sarsaparilla.

Sassella (It). A sub district of Lombardy in the foothills of the Alps in the Valtellina Valley. Produces red wines of the same name from the Nebbiolo grape.

Sassicaia (It). D.O.C. red wine made from the Cabernet franc and Cabernet sauvignon grapes in the Tuscany region.

Sassumariello (It). A red grape variety grown in the Puglia region.

Satan's Brew (M.East). Early religious (Christian) nickname for coffee, because of its Islamic origins.

Satan's Whiskers (Cktl). ⅕ measure Grand Marnier, ⅕ measure Gin, ⅕ measure dry Vermouth, ⅕ measure sweet Vermouth, ⅕ measure orange juice, dash Orange bitters. Shake over ice, strain into a cocktail glass.

Satigny (Switz). A wine-producing area in Geneva.

Satoraljaujhely (Hun). A wine-producing town based in north-eastern Tokay.

Sattui Winery (USA). A winery based near St. Helena, Napa Valley, California. Grape varieties – Cabernet sauvignon, Johannisberg riesling and Zinfandel. Produces varietal and dessert wines.

Satul Marc (Rum). A wine-producing region based in the Siebenbürgen district.

Saturnus (Cktl). ⅛ measure Gin, ½ measure orange juice, ⅛ measure Bianco vermouth, ¼ measure Crème de Banane. Pour ingredients into an ice-filled high-ball glass. Stir, add a dash of iced Champagne.

Satyr (Gre). The mythylogical goat-like men who drank and danced in Dionysus's train.

Satyr Play (Gre). An ancient Greek drama with a ribald flavour performed at a Dionysian festival (has a choir of Satyrs).

Satzenbrau (Ire). A bottled Pils Lager 1047 O.G. brewed by the Harp Brewery in Dundalk. (Also brewed in London).

Satzenheim (Ger). Vineyard. (Anb) = Baden. (Ber) = Badische Frankenland. (Gro) = Tauberklinge. (Vil) = Reicholzheim.

Sätzler (Ger). Vineyard. (Anb) = Baden. (Ber) = Ortenau. (Gro) = Schloss Rodeck. (Vil) = Baden-Baden.

Sätzler (Ger). Vineyard. (Anb) = Baden. (Ber) = Ortenau. (Gro) = Schloss Rodeck. (Vil) = Sinzheim.

Sauber (Ger). A clean, pure wine.

Sauberg (Ger). Vineyard. (Anb) = Württemberg. (Ber) = Württembergisch Unterland. (Gro) = Stromberg. (Vil) = Ötisheim.

Sauce (USA) (slang). A name for alcoholic liquor.

Saucer (Eng). A round, concave china receptacle with a flattened base onto which a teacup is placed for ease of carrying.

Saucer (Fr). The name given to the glass used for Champagne cocktails. Is saucer-shaped on a thin stem and wide base. Often used mistakenly for serving Champagne. See Champagne Flute.

Saucy Sue (Cktl). ⅓ measure Calvados, 2 dashes Pernod, 2 dashes Apricot brandy. Stir over ice, strain into a cocktail glass.

Saudoy (Fr). A Cru Champagne village in the Canton de Sézanne. District = Épernay.

Saufen (Ger). Heavy drinking, to swill.

Saukopf (Ger). Vineyard. (Anb) = Nahe. (Ber) = Bad Kreuznach. (Gro) = Schlosskapelle. (Vil) = Windesheim.

Saukopf (Ger). Vineyard. (Anb) = Rheinhessen. (Ber) = Bingen. (Gro) = Kurfürstenstück. (Vil) = Gau-Bickelheim.

Saulcet (Fr). A white wine from Allier Département in central France. Usually uses the Saint Pourçain label.

Saulheim (Ger). Village. (Anb) = Rheinhessen. (Ber) = Nierstein. (Gro) = Domherr. (Vins) = Haubenberg, Heiligenhaus, Hölle, Pfaffengarten, Probstey, Schlossberg.

Saulo (Sp). The granitic soil based around Barcelona in the Alella D.O.

Sauloch (Ger). Vineyard. (Anb) = Rheinhessen. (Ber) = Wonnegau. (Gro) = Burg Rodenstein. (Vil) = Flörsheim-Dalsheim.

Saumagen (Ger). Grosslage. (Anb) = Rheinpfalz. (Ber) = Mittelhaardt-Deutsche Weinstrasse. (Vil) = Kallstadt.

Saumur (Fr). An A.C. wine area within the Anjou-Saumur district of the Loire. Produces red, rosé, white and sparkling wines.

Saumur-Champigny (Fr). An A.C. red wine area in the Anjou-Saumur district of the Loire. Wines made from the Cabernet franc.

Saumur-Mousseux (Fr). An A.C. sparkling wine from the Saumur area of the Anjou-Saumur district in the Loire. Is medium-sweet to dry.

Saumur Rosé de Cabernet (Fr). An A.C. rosé wine made from the Cabernet franc grape in the Saumur area of Anjou-Saumur district in the Loire. Now classed as Cabernet rosé.

Sausal-Leibnitz (Aus). A wine-producing area in Weststeiermark. Produces dark, spicy, fresh red wines.

Sausal Winery (USA). A winery based in Alexander Valley, Sonoma County, California. Grape varieties – Cabernet sauvignon, Chardonnay, Colombard and Zinfandel. Produces varietal wines.

Sauschwänzel (Ger). Vineyard. (Anb) = Rheinpfalz. (Ber) = Südliche Weinstrasse. (Gro) = Kloster Liebfrauenberg. (Vil) = Billigheim-Ingenheim.

Saussiles (Les) (Fr). A Premier Cru vineyard in the A.C. commune of Pommard, Côte de Beaune, Burgundy. 3.8 ha.

Saute Bouchon (Fr). 'Cork popper'. This is the name given to old sparkling wines that blew their cork.

Sauté Montagne (Le) (Fr). An orange and Cognac liqueur made by Logis de la Montagne (Cognac producer).

Sauternais (Fr). The people of the Sauternes district. Also to do with the Sauternes area.

Sauterne (USA). A Californian dry white wine. If Haut-Sauterne then medium-sweet.

Sauterne Cup (Cktl). 1 bottle Sauternes, ½ gill Brandy, ¼ gill brown Curaçao, 1 pint soda water, ¼ gill Bénédictine, ⅓ gill Yellow Chartreuse, ½ gill Maraschino, ⅛ gill Grenadine, ½ gill lemon juice. Stir in a bowl with ice, strain. Serve with a slice of lemon, cucumber and fresh fruit.

Sauternes (Fr). An area of southern Bordeaux, west of the river Garonne. Produces sweet botrytis-attacked wines. Communes of Barsac (also has separate A.C), Bommes, Fargues and Preignac. All come under the A.C. Sauternes. Wines must have a natural alcoholic content of 13% alc. by vol. to be classed A.C. Sauternes.

Sautomar (Port). An extra dry sparkling wine made by the méthode champenoise. Produced by Real Cave do Cedro.

Sauvignon (Fr). An excellent white grape variety used in the making of dry white wines in western France, Bordeaux and the Central Vineyards in the Loire. Is rich in sugar and extracts with moderate acidity. Also known as the Sauvignon blanc and Surin.

Sauvignon Blanc (Fr). See Sauvignon.

Sauvignon Blanc (USA). A white grape variety grown in California to make dry white wines.

Sauvignon de Banat (Rum). A white wine from the Banat Vineyards.

Sauvignon dei Colli Bolognesi (It). A D.O.C. dry, white wine from Bologna in Emilia Romagna. Produced from the Sauvignon and Trebbiano grapes.

Sauvignon de St. Bris (Fr). A V.D.Q.S. dry white wine from the Yonne Département in northern Burgundy. Made from the Sauvignon blanc. Minimum alc. by vol. of 9.5%.

Sauvignon Vert (USA). A white grape

S

variety grown in California to make dessert wines. Also known as the Colombard.

Sauza (Mex). A brand-name of Tequila produced by a distillery of same name. 38% alc. by vol.

Sauza Margarita (Cktl). 1½ fl.ozs. Sauza Tequila, ½ fl.oz. Triple Sec, 1 fl.oz. lime/lemon juice. Shake over ice, strain into a cocktail glass that has been rimmed with salt and lime juice.

Sauza Sour (Cktl). ⅔ measure Sauza Tequila, ⅓ measure lemon juice, 1 teaspoon powdered sugar. Shake over ice, strain into a cocktail glass. Dress with a cherry and lemon slice.

Savages Winery (Austr). A winery based in Riverina, New South Wales.

Savagnin (Fr). The local Jura name for the Sauvignon blanc grape. Used in the production of the Vins jaunes (See Château Chalon) and the Vins gris.

Savagnin (Switz). The local name for the Traminer grape. See also Païen.

Savagnin Noir (Fr). An alternative name for the Pinot noir grape.

Savagnin Noir Cortaillod (Fr). An alternative name in eastern France for the Pinot noir grape.

Savagnin Rosé (Fr). The alternative name for the Gewürztraminer grape in Alsace.

Savannah Cocktail (Cktl). ⅕ gill dry Gin, juice ½ orange, 1 egg white, dash (white) Crème de Cacao. Shake over ice, strain into a cocktail glass.

Savannah Gold (Eng). A brand of smooth Rum bottled by Saccone and Speed from Barbados rums.

Savatiano (Gre). A white grape variety used in the making of Retsina and Anchialos together with the Rhoditis.

Savennières (Fr). A.C. dry white wine from the vineyards in the Coteaux de la Loire area of the Anjou-Saumur district of the Loire. Produces fragrant, dry white wines from the Chenin blanc grape.

Saveur (Fr). Denotes a 'general taste'.

Savigny-lès-Beaunes (Fr). An A.C. commune of the Côte de Beaune in the Burgundy region.

Savigny-sur-Ardre (Fr). A Cru Champagne village in the Canton de Ville-en-Tardenois. District = Reims.

Savin (Sp). A large, noted Bodega based in Jumilla. Produces wines mainly from the Monastrell grape. Owns Campo Viejo and has a major share in Vinícola Navarra.

Savion (Isr). A Tokay-style, sweet, dessert wine.

Savoie (Fr). A wine region of eastern

France. Produces A.C. red, rosé, white and sparkling wines. A.C.'s are Crépy, Roussette de Savoie, Seyssel, Seyssel Mousseux and Vins de Savoie. Cru villages are – (Roussette de Savoie) = Frangy, Marestel, Monterminod and Monthoux. (Vins de Savoie) = Arbin, Abymes, Apremont, Ayze, Bergeron, Chantagne, Chaupignat, Chignin, Marignan, Montmélian, Ripaille, Saint Jeoire-Prieuré, Sante Marie d'Alloix and St. Jean-de-la-Porte. Also spelt Savoy.

Savoir Faire (Fr). The brand-name for a range of red and white table wines.

Savoy (Fr). An alternative spelling of Savoie.

Savoy Glasses (Eng). A brand-name for a range of glassware from the Dema Glass Co.

Savoy Ninety [90] (Cktl). ½ measure Amaretto, ½ measure lime juice, dash orange flower water. Shake over ice, strain into a sugar-frosted tulip glass. Top with iced Champagne.

Savoy Springbok (Cktl). ⅓ measure dry Sherry, ⅓ measure Lillet, ⅓ measure Van der Hum, 2 dashes Orange bitters. Stir over ice, strain into a cocktail glass.

Savuto (It). D.O.C. red or rosé wines from Calabria. Made from the Capuccio, Galioppo, Greco nero, Magliocco canino, Malvasia, Nerello, Percorino and Sangiovese grapes. Production area and vinification occur in 14 communes in provinces of Cosenza and Catanzaro. Classed Superiore if total alc. by vol. is 12.5% and aged 2 years.

Savuto du Rogliano (It). D.O.C. red wine of Calabria. See Savuto.

Sawanotsuru (Jap). A Saké produced in Nada, 657, Japan. 14.9% alc. by vol.

S.A.W.F.A. (S.Afr) (abbr). South African Wine Farmers' Association.

Saxenburg Wines (S.Afr). The producer of Buchu brandy.

Saxon Bitter (Eng). A keg Bitter 1033 O.G. brewed by the Devenish Brewery in Cornwall.

Saxon Cocktail (Cktl). ⅕ gill Bacardi White Label, juice ½ lime, 2 dashes Grenadine. Shake over ice, strain into a cocktail glass. Top with a twist of orange peel juice.

Saxon Cross (Eng). The trade-name used by the Winkles Brewery in Buxton, Derbyshire for their beers.

Saxon Mead (Eng). 12 gallons spring water, 20 lbs. honey, 6 beaten egg whites, 1 teaspoon ginger, 1 teaspoon cinnamon, 1 teaspoon nutmeg, 1 sprig rosemary, 1 oz. Brewer's yeast. Mix egg white with water, add honey, boil 1 hour. Skim, add herb and spices. When cool add yeast. Ferment, rack into bottles when fermentation has ceased, stand 6 months.

Saxonvale Winery (Austr). A winery based in the Hunter Valley, New South Wales. Grape varieties – Cabernet, Chardonnay, Sémillon and the Shiraz. Produces varietal wines.

Sax Winery (USA). A winery based in Altus.

Sazerac (Cktl). Add 1 cube to a teaspoon of water, 2 dashes Angostura, 3 dashes Pernod. Mix together, add 1½ ozs. Bourbon whiskey, ice cube, stir then strain into an old-fashioned glass. Add a twist of lemon.

SBA (Eng) (abbr). Special Bitter Ale 1042 O.G. brewed by the Donnington Brewery in the Cotswolds.

Sbarra (It). Bar.

SBB (Wales) (abbr). Special Bitter Beer 1036 O.G. brewed by the Crown Brewery in Pontyclun, Mid-Glamorgan.

S.B.G. (Swe) (abbr). Sveriges Bartenders Gille. The Swedish Bartenders' Association. Address = P.O. Box. 7579, S.E-103, 93 Stockholm.

S.B.H. (Hun) (abbr). Section of the Barmen of Hungary. Address = Hungar hotels, 1052 Budapest, Peköfi Sàndor U.14.

Sbornia (It). Intoxication, drunkenness.

S.B.U. (Switz) (abbr). Schweizer Barkeeper Union. The Swiss Bartenders' Association. Address = 16, Camille Martin, Ch. 1203, Genève.

Scaffa (The) (Cktl). ½ measure Cognac, ½ measure Green Chartreuse, 2 dashes Angostura. Shake over ice, strain into a cocktail glass.

Scalabrone (It). A single vineyard rosé wine produced by Antinori.

Scales (Sp). Part of the Solera system for Sherry. Each scale consists of those casks holding the same grades of wine.

Scandia Special (Den). An extra strong Lager beer 1078–1084 O.G. brewed exclusively for Cash & Carry outlets.

Scandinavian Akvavit (Scan). A caraway-flavoured Akvavit.

Scandinavian Coffee (Liq.Coffee). Using a measure of Akvavit.

Scanex (Cktl). ¼ measure Polar liqueur, ¼ measure Vodka, ¼ measure Gomme syrup, ¼ measure lemon juice, dash Grenadine. Shake over ice, strain into a cocktail glass.

Scantling (Fr). Wooden beams to support the casks in the cellars.

Scantling Pipes (Mad). Used for the storing of fine Madeira wines for Estufagem

and fermentation. 630–650 litres.

Scapa (Scot). A single Malt whisky distillery based in Kirkwall, in the Orkney Isles. Owned by the Hiram Walker Group. A Highland malt. 40% alc. by vol.

Scarlet Lady (Cktl).(1). 1 part dry Gin, 3 parts redcurrant wine. Stir together over ice, strain into a wine goblet.

Scarlet Lady (Cktl).(2). ¼ measure Mandarine liqueur, ¼ measure white Rum, ¼ measure Campari, ¼ measure lemon juice, 2 barspoons Maraschino. Shake over ice, strain into a cocktail glass. Dress with a spiral of orange peel.

Scarlet Lady (Cktl).(3). ⅓ measure Vodka, ⅓ measure Cherry brandy, ⅓ measure Tia Maria. Shake over ice, strain into a cocktail glass. Float a little cream on top and dress with a cherry and a slice of lemon.

Scarlet O'Hara Cocktail (Cktl). 1 fl.oz. Southern Comfort, juice ½ lime, ½ fl.oz. bilberry juice. Shake over ice, strain into a flute glass.

S.C.C. (Port) (abbr). Sociedade Central de Cervejas.

Scelto (It). The Italian word for Auslese in the Trentino-Alto Adige. Also known as Selezionato.

Scented (Eng). The term used to describe a wine with a grapey, flowery bouquet.

Scented Teas (Eng). Teas that have had flower scent added (either mixed in or impregnated). Such flowers as rose, jasmine, strawberry, camomile, mango, etc. See also China Teas.

Schaaner (Euro). The name given to the wines produced in Schaan, Liechtenstein.

Schaapskooi Abbaye Brouwerij (Hol). Lit – 'Sheep pen'. A Trappist Brewery based near Tilburg, north Brabant. Produces La Trappe (a bottle-conditioned Ale) 6.5% alc. by vol. and a Pilsener-style Lager beer.

Schaefer Brewery (USA). A brewery based in Baltimore.

Schaefer Horlacher Brewery (USA). A brewery based in Allentown.

Schäf (Ger). Vineyard. (Anb) = Baden. (Ber) = Markgräflerland. (Gro) = Burg Neuenfels. (Vil) = Auggen.

Schäf (Ger). Vineyard. (Anb) = Baden. (Ber) = Markgräflerland. (Gro) = Burg Neuenfels. (Vil) = Steinenstadt.

Schafberg (Ger). Vineyard. (Anb) = Rheinpfalz. (Ber) = Mittelhardt-Deutsche Weinstrasse. (Gro) = Schwarzerde. (Vil) = Grossniedesheim.

Schäfchen (Ger). Vineyard. (Anb) = Nahe. (Ber) = Kreuznach. (Gro) = Schlosskapelle. (Vil) = Windesheim.

Schäfergarten (Ger). Vineyard. (Anb) =

Rheinpfalz. (Ber) = Südliche Wein-strasse. (Gro) = Herrlich. (Vil) = Insheim.

Schäfergarten (Ger). Vineyard. (Anb) = Rheinpfalz. (Ber) = Südliche Wein-strasse. (Gro) = Herrlich. (Vil) = Rohrbach.

Schäferlay (Ger). Vineyard. (Anb) = Mosel-Saar-Ruwer. (Ber) = Bernkastel. (Gro) = Vom Heissen Stein. (Vil) = Briedel.

Schäfersley (Ger). Vineyard. (Anb) = Nahe. (Ber) = Kreuznach. (Gro) = Pfarr-garten. (Vil) = Schöneberg.

Schäffbräu (Ger). Company name of the Feuerfest Brewery of Treuchtlingen in Bavaria.

Schaffermahlzeit (Ger). A formal dinner/ceremony held on the second Friday of February (winter's end), traditionally to send the port's skippers off on a new season at sea. Drink Seefahrtbier.

Schaffhausen (Switz). A Swiss-German canton. Wines are produced from the Klevner grape. The village of Hallau has the finest vineyards.

Schafft (Afr). A strong Beer brewed by the South African Breweries.

Schafiser (Switz). The name given to a wine-producing area in Béarn and to a Chasselas-based wine (also known as Twanner).

Schafsteige (Ger). Vineyard. (Anb) = Württemberg. (Ber) = Kocher-Jagst-Tauber. (Gro) = Tauberberg. (Vil) = Haagen.

Schafsteige (Ger). Vineyard. (Anb) = Württemberg. (Ber) = Kocher-Jagst-Tauber. (Gro) = Tauberberg. (Vil) = Laudenbach.

Schafsteige (Ger). Vineyard. (Anb) = Württemberg. (Ber) = Kocher-Jagst-Tauber. (Gro) = Tauberberg. (Vil) = Niederstetten.

Schafsteige (Ger). Vineyard. (Anb) = Württemberg. (Ber) = Kocher-Jagst-Tauber. (Gro) = Tauberberg. (Vil) = Oberstetten.

Schafsteige (Ger). Vineyard. (Anb) = Württemberg. (Ber) = Kocher-Jagst-Tauber. (Gro) = Tauberberg. (Vil) = Vorbachzimmern.

Schafsteige (Ger). Vineyard. (Anb) = Württemberg. (Ber) = Kocher-Jagst-Tauber. (Gro) = Tauberberg. (Vil) = Wermutshausen.

Schal (Ger). Musty, a tired wine.

Schalkstein (Ger). Grosslage. (Anb) = Württemberg. (Ber) = Württembergisch Unterland. (Vils) = Affalterbach, All-mersbach a. W., Asperg, Beihingen, Benningen, Besigheim, Bietigheim, Bis-singen, Ermannhausen, Gemmrigheim,

Grossingersheim, Hessigheim, Höpfig-heim, Kirchberg, Kleinaspach, Kleinin-gersheim, Löchgau, Ludwigsburg (ortsteil Hoheneck), Marbach, Mark-gröningen, Mundelsheim, Murr, Neckarweihingen, Poppenweiler, Rielinghausen, Rietenau, Steinheim/Murr, Walheim.

Schallbach (Ger). Village. (Anb) = Baden. (Ber) = Markgräflerland. (Gro) = Vogtei Rötteln. (Vin) = Sonnhohle.

Schaller (Edgar) (Fr). Alsace wine pro-ducer. Address = 1, Rue du Château, 68630 Mittelwihr.

Schallstadt-Wolfenweile (Ger). Village. (Anb) = Baden. (Ber) = Markgräfler-land. (Gro) = Lorettoberg. (Vins) = Batzenberg, Durrenberg.

Schanderl (S.Afr). A fruity white wine from the Twee Jongegezellen Estate in Tulbagh. Made from the Muscat de Frontignac, Gewürztraminer and Weisser riesling grapes.

Schankbieres (Ger). Low-gravity draught beers with an O.G. range of 7–8% and 2–3% alc. by weight.

Schanzreiter (Ger). Vineyard. (Anb) = Württemberg. (Ber) = Württembergi-sch Unterland. (Gro) = Stromberg. (Vil) = Ensingen.

Schanzreiter (Ger). Vineyard. (Anb) = Württemberg. (Ber) = Württembergi-sch Unterland. (Gro) = Stromberg. (Vil) = Illingen.

Scharf (Ger). Fermentative. Wines that contain too much carbonic acid or contain unfermented sugar and have a second fermentation.

Scharlachberg (Ger). Lit – 'The scarlet mountain'.

Scharlachberg (Ger). A liqueur and Weinbrand producer based in Bingen, Western Germany.

Scharlachberg (Ger). Vineyard. (Anb) = Franken. (Ber) = Maindreieck. (Gro) = Ravensburg. (Vil) = Thüngersheim.

Scharlachberg (Ger). Vineyard. (Anb) = Rheinhessen. (Ber) = Bingen. (Gro) = Sankt Rochuskapelle. (Vil) = Bingen.

Scharlachberg Meisterbrand (Ger). A Weinbrand produced by the Scharl-achberg distillery in Bingen, Western Germany.

Scharrenberg (Ger). Vineyard. (Anb) = Württemberg. (Ber) = Remstal-Stuttgart. (Gro) = Weinsteige. (Vil) = Stuttgart (ortsteil Degerloch).

Scharzberg (Ger). Grosslage. (Anb) = Mosel-Saar-Ruwer. (Ber) = Saar-Ruwer. (Vils) = Ayl, Estate, Filzen, Hamm, Irsch, Kanzem, Kastel-Staadt, Könen, Konz, Mennig, Oberemmel, Ockfen, Pellingen, Saarburg, Schoden,

Serrig, Wawern, Wiltingen.

Scharzhofberger (Ger). Vineyard. (Anb) = Mosel-Saar-Ruwer. (Ber) = Saar-Ruwer. (Gro) = Scharzberg. (Vil) = Estate.

Schatzgarten (Ger). Vineyard. (Anb) = Mosel-Saar-Ruwer. (Ber) = Bernkastel. (Gro) = Schwarzlay. (Vil) = Traben-Trarbach (ortsteil Wolf).

Schatzkammer (Ger). Lit – 'Treasure room'. A cellar where old fine wines are kept in a winery or cellars.

Schaumwein (Ger). Lit – 'Foaming wine'. The lowest level of German sparkling wine. Either made by the cuve close method or by CO_2 injection. Uses cheap white wines from France, Italy etc.

Schaumwein mit Zugesetzter Kohlensaure (Ger). Cheap wines given a sparkle by CO_2 injection.

Schäwer (Ger). Vineyard. (Anb) = Rheinpfalz. (Ber) = Südliche Weinstrasse. (Gro) = Bischofskreuz. (Vil) = Burrweiler.

Schechar (Isr). A 'Bible wine'. An ancient wine that is mentioned in the Bible.

Scheibenbuck (Ger). Vineyard. (Anb) = Baden. (Ber) = Kaiserstuhl-Tuniberg. (Gro) = Vulkanfelsen. (Vil) = Sasbach.

Scheibkuern (Aus). An ancient vine variety that is rarely grown nowadays.

Scheidterberger (Ger). Vineyard. (Anb) = Mosel-Saar-Ruwer. (Ber) = Saar-Ruwer. (Gro) = Scharzberg. (Vil) = Ayl.

Scheinberg (Ger). Vineyard. (Anb) = Franken. (Ber) = Maindreieck. (Gro) =Burg. (Vil) = Wirmsthal.

Schekar (Isr). The Hebrew word for the fermented drink from which Cider originates.

Schelingen (Ger). Village. (Anb) = Baden. (Ber) = Kaiserstuhl-Tuniberg. (Gro) = Vulkanfelsen. (Vin) = Kirchberg.

Schell Brewery (USA). A brewery based in New Ulm, Minnesota. Noted for its Schells and Ulmer ales.

Schellenbrunnen (Ger). Vineyard. (Anb) = Baden. (Ber) = Badische Bergstrasse/Kraichgau. (Gro) = Stiftsberg. (Vil) = Tiefenbach.

Schelm (Ger). Vineyard. (Anb) = Mosel-Saar-Ruwer. (Ber) = Bernkastel. (Gro) = Vom Heissen Stein. (Vil) = Briedel.

Schelmen (Ger). Vineyard. (Anb) = Rheinhessen. (Ber) = Wonnegau. (Gro) = Sybillenstein. (Vil) = Wahlheim.

Schelmenklinge (Ger). Vineyard. (Anb) = Württemberg. (Ber) = Württembergisch Unterland. (Gro) = Kirchenweinberg. (Vil) = Ilsfeld (ortsteil Schozach).

Schelmenstück (Ger). Vineyard. (Anb) = Rheinhessen. (Ber) = Bingen. (Gro) = Sankt Rochuskapelle. (Vil) = Bingen.

Schelvispekel (Hol). A Brandewijn liqueur flavoured with herbs and cinnamon, served only to Vlaardingen fishermen in southern Schiedam.

Schemelsberg (Ger). Vineyard. (Anb) = Württemberg. (Ber) = Württembergisch Unterland. (Gro) = Salzberg. (Vil) = Weinsberg.

Schench (Eng). The sixteenth-century word for a drink.

Schengen Lux). A wine willage on the river Moselle.

Schenk (Sp). A Swiss-owned vineyard in Valencia. Noted for its Los Monteros (a red wine produced from the Monastrell grape).

Schenk (Switz). The largest wine-producing firm in the Vaud canton. Owns 237 ha. of vineyards. Also owns vineyards in Valencia, Spain.

Schenkenberg (Ger). Vineyard. (Anb) = Württemberg. (Ber) = Remstal-Stuttgart. (Gro) = Weinsteige. (Vil) = Esslingen.

Schenkenböhl (Ger). Grosslage. (Anb) = Rheinpfalz. (Ber) = Mittelhaardt-Deutsche Weinstrasse. (Vils) = Bad Dürkheim, Wachenheim.

Schenley Distillers (USA). Distillers of brandies at their Number One Distilling Company in California.

Schenley Distillery (USA). Bourbon whiskey distilleries based in Louisville and Frankfort, Kentucky.

Scheris (Sp). The original Moorish name for Jerez.

Scherisch (Sp). Moorish name for Sherry.

Scherisk (Arab). The Arabian spelling of Sherry.

Scherp Bier (Hol). Bitter beer.

Scherzingen (Ger). Village. (Anb) = Baden. (Ber) = Markgräflerland. (Gro) = Lorettoberg. (Vin) = Batzenberg.

Scheuerberg (Ger). Vineyard. (Anb) = Württemberg. (Ber) = Württembergisch Unterland. (Gro) = Staufenberg. (Vil) = Neckarsulm.

Scheurebe (Ger). A white grape variety. A cross between the Sylvaner and the Riesling. Named after Herr Scheu. Rebe is vine.

Schiava (It). See Schiave.

Schiava Gentile (It). A red grape variety also known as the Schiave piccola and Kleinvernatsch.

Schiava Grigia (It). A red grape variety grown in the Trentino-Alto Adige. Known as the Grauvernatsch in German.

Schiava Grossa (It). A red grape variety grown in the Trentino-Alto Adige. Known as the Grossvernatsch in German. Also known as the Trollinger.

S

Schiava Media (It). A red grape variety grown in the Trentino-Alto Adige. Known as the Mittervernatsch in German.

Schiava Piccola (It). A red grape variety grown in the Trentino-Alto Adige. Known as the Kleinvernatsch in German. Also known as the Schiava gentile.

Schiave (It). A red grape variety grown in the Trentino-Alto Adige. Known as the Vernatsch in German. Also known as Schiava.

Schiedam (Hol). A Gin distilling centre near Rotterdam.

Schiedam Gin (Hol). A very full-bodied Gin with a clean but pronounced malty aroma and flavour.

Schiefer (Ger). The name for the fossilised slate and shale which makes up the majority of Mosel ground on which the vines grow.

Schieferley (Ger). Vineyard. (Anb) = Ahr. (Ber) = Walporzheim/Ahrtal. (Gro) = Klosterberg. (Vil) = Bad Neuenahr.

Schieferley (Ger). Vineyard. (Anb) = Ahr. (Ber) = Walporzheim/Ahrtal. (Gro) = Klosterberg. (Vil) = Dernau.

Schieferley (Ger). Vineyard. (Anb) = Ahr. (Ber) = Walporzheim/Ahrtal. (Gro) = Klosterberg. (Vil) = Mayschoss.

Schiehallion Vineyards (USA). A vineyard based in Keysville, Virginia. Produces French hybrid and vinifera wines.

Schierstein (Ger). Village. (Anb) = Rheingau. (Ber) = Johannisberg. (Gro) = Steinmacher. (Vins) = Dachsberg, Hölle.

Schikanenbuckel (Ger). Vineyard. (Anb) = Nahe. (Ber) = Schloss Böckelheim. (Gro) = Paradiesgarten. (Vil) = Rehborn.

Schilcher (Aus). A red grape variety and rosé wine of the Styria region.

Schild (Ger). Grosslage. (Anb) = Franken. (Ber) = Steigerwald. (Vils) = Abtswind, Castell, Greuth.

Schildberg (Ger). Vineyard. (Anb) = Rheinhessen. (Ber) = Bingen. (Gro) = Adelberg. (Vil) = Sulzheim.

Schiller (John) (Can). A German who, in 1811, settled near Toronto, Ontario. Was a pioneer wine-producer in Canada.

Schillerfarbe (Ger). Lit – 'Iridescent or lustrous colour'. Used to describe the wines of Württemberg.

Schillerwein (Fr). The name given to the rosé wines of Alsace by the German speaking people of the region. Pinot noir rosé d'Alsace.

Schillerwein (Ger). The name given to the wine made from a blend of red and white grapes in the Württemberg. Only Qba. and Qmp. allowed. A rosé wine. Produced from grapes grown in same vineyard plot.

Schilscherwein (USA). The Austrian equivalent of the German Schillerwein.

Schimmel (Hol). Mildew.

Schimmelig (Ger). Denotes a wine that has a mouldy, musty smell.

Schinkenhäger (Ger). The brand-name used for a Steinhäger produced by König.

Schiopetto (It). A famous winery based at Capriva del Friuli in Friuli-Venezia Giulia.

Schioppettino (It). A red grape variety grown only in the Prepotto commune, near Udine in Friuli-Venezia Giulia.

Schiras (Euro). An alternative spelling of Syrah.

Schist (Eng). A soil consisting of foliated rock with mineral layers. See Schistous Rock.

Schistous Rock (Eng). This is formed of thin plates, formed from the splitting of foliated rock consisting of layers of different materials.

Schitterend (Hol). Brilliant. A brilliant wine.

Schladerer (Ger). A famous liqueur and spirits (Eau-de-vie) producer based in the Schwarzwald.

Schlagengraben (Ger). Vineyard. (Anb) = Mosel-Saar-Ruwer. (Ber) = Saar-Ruwer. (Gro) = Scharzberg. (Vil) = Estate.

Schlatt (Ger). Village. (Anb) = Baden. (Ber) = Markgräflerland. (Gro) = Lorettoberg. (Vins) = Maltesergarten, Steingrüble.

Schlehenschwarze (Aus). An ancient red vine variety now rarely grown.

Schleich (Ger). Village. (Anb) = Mosel-Saar-Ruwer. (Ber) = Bernkastel. (Gro) = Sankt Michael. (Vins) = Klosterberg, Sonnenberg.

Schleidberg (Ger). Vineyard. (Anb) = Mosel-Saar-Ruwer. (Ber) = Obermosel. (Gro) = Gipfel. (Vil) = Fellerich.

Schlemmertröpfchen (Ger). Vineyard. (Anb) = Mosel-Saar-Ruwer. (Ber) = Zell/Mosel. (Gro) = Grafschaft. (Vil) = Bremm.

Schlenkerla (Ger). A home-brew tavern in Bamberg, Bavaria. Produces Rauchbieres.

Schlettstadt (Fr). The German name for the town of Selestat in the Bas Rhin in Alsace.

Schlichte Distillery (Ger). A Steinhäger producer based in Steinhägen, Westphalia. Also producers of Alte Ernte (a Kornbranntwein).

Schliengen (Ger). Village. (Anb) = Baden. (Ber) = Markgräflerland. (Gro) = Burg

Neuenfels. (Vin) = Sonnenstück.

Schlierbach (Ger). Vineyard. (Anb) = Württemberg. (Ber) = Württembergisch Unterland. (Gro) = Salzberg. (Vil) = Weiler.

Schlipf (Ger). Vineyard. (Anb) = Baden. (Ber) = Markgräflerland. (Gro) = Vogtei Rötteln. (Vil) = Weil am Rhein.

Schlittberg (Ger). Vineyard. (Anb) = Rheinpfalz. (Ber) = Südliche Weinstrasse. (Gro) = Trappenberg. (Vil) = Römerberg.

Schlitz (USA). A Malt beer 1044 O.G. brewed by the Stroh Brewery in Milwaukee.

Schlitz Brewery (USA). A former brewery based in Milwaukee, Wisconsin. Has been taken over by the Stroh Brewery of Detroit.

Schloss (Ger). Castle.

Schloss (Ger). Vineyard. (Anb) = Rheinhessen. (Ber) = Nierstein. (Gro) = Krötenbrunnen. (Vil) = Dienheim.

Schloss (Ger). Vineyard. (Anb) = Rheinhessen. (Ber) = Nierstein. (Gro) = Krötenbrunnen. (Vil) = Oppenheim.

Schloss (Ger). Vineyard. (Anb) = Rheinhessen. (Ber) = Nierstein. (Gro) = Krötenbrunnen. (Vil) = Ülversheim.

Schloss (Ger). Vineyard. (Anb) = Rheinpfalz. (Ber) = Mittelhaardt-Deutsche Weinstrasse. (Gro) = Grafenstück. (Vil) = Obrigheim.

Schloss (Ger). Vineyard. (Anb) = Rheinpfalz. (Ber) = Mittelhaardt-Deutsche Weinstrasse. (Gro) = Höllenpfad. (Vil) = Grünstadt.

Schloss (Ger). Vineyard. (Anb) = Rheinpfalz. (Ber) = Südliche Weinstrasse. (Gro) = Ordensgut. (Vil) = Edesheim.

Schlossabfüllung (Ger). Estate bottled.

Schlossabzug (Ger). Estate bottled.

Schlossberg (Ger). Lit – 'Castle hill'. A popular vineyard name used in Germany. There are 87 individual vineyard sites with this name plus 2 Grosslagen.

Schlossberg (Ger). Grosslage. (Anb) = Franken. (Ber) = Steigerwald. (Vils) = Grosslangheim, Rödelsee, Sickershausen, Wiesenbronn.

Schlossberg (Ger). Grosslage. (Anb) = Hessische Bergstrasse. (Ber) = Starkenberg. (Vil) = Heppenheim (including Erbach and Hambach).

Schlossberg (Ger). Vineyard. (Anb) = Baden. (Ber) = Badische Bergstrasse/Kraichgau. (Gro) = Mannaberg. (Vil) = Rotenberg.

Schlossberg (Ger). Vineyard. (Anb) = Baden. (Ber) = Badische Bergstrasse/Kraichgau. (Gro) = Rittersberg. (Vil) = Schriesheim.

Schlossberg (Ger). Vineyard. (Anb) =

Baden. (Ber) = Badische Frankenland. (Gro) = Tauberklinge. (Vil) = Wertheim.

Schlossberg (Ger). Vineyard. (Anb) = Baden. (Ber) = Bodensee. (Gro) = Sonnenufer. (Vil) = Salem (ortsteil Kirchberg).

Schlossberg (Ger). Vineyard. (Anb) = Baden. (Ber) = Breisgau. (Gro) = Burg Lichteneck. (Vil) = Hecklingen.

Schlossberg (Ger). Vineyard. (Anb) = Baden. (Ber) = Breisgau. (Gro) = Burg Zähringen. (Vil) = Freiburg i. Br.

Schlossberg (Ger). Vineyard. (Anb) = Baden. (Ber) = Kaiserstuhl-Tuniberg. (Gro) = Vulkanfelsen. (Vil) = Achkarren.

Schlossberg (Ger). Vineyard. (Anb) = Baden. (Ber) = Kaiserstuhl-Tuniberg. (Gro) = Vulkanfelsen. (Vil) = Ihringen.

Schlossberg (Ger). Vineyard. (Anb) = Baden. (Ber) = Kaiserstuhl-Tuniberg. (Gro) = Vulkanfelsen. (Vil) = Oberrotweil.

Schlossberg (Ger). Vineyard. (Anb) = Baden. (Ber) = Markgräflerland. (Gro) = Lorettoberg. (Vil) = Grunern.

Schlossberg (Ger). Vineyard. (Anb) = Baden. (Ber) = Markgräflerland. (Gro) = Lorettoberg. (Vil) = Staufen.

Schlossberg (Ger). Vineyard. (Anb) = Baden. (Ber) = Ortenau. (Gro) = Fürsteneck. (Vil) = Diersburg.

Schlossberg (Ger). Vineyard. (Anb) = Baden. (Ber) = Ortenau. (Gro) = Fürsteneck. (Vil) = Durbach.

Schlossberg (Ger). Vineyard. (Anb) = Baden. (Ber) = Ortenau. (Gro) = Fürsteneck. (Vil) = Nesselried.

Schlossberg (Ger). Vineyard. (Anb) = Baden. (Ber) = Ortenau. (Gro) = Fürsteneck. (Vil) = Ortenberg.

Schlossberg (Ger). Vineyard. (Anb) = Baden. (Ber) = Ortenau. (Gro) = Schloss Rodeck. (Vil) = Neuweier.

Schlossberg (Ger). Vineyard. (Anb) = Franken. (Ber) = Maindreieck. (Gro) = Burg. (Vil) = Saaleck.

Schlossberg (Ger). Vineyard. (Anb) = Franken. (Ber) = Maindreieck. (Gro) = Not yet assigned. (Vil) = Hallburg.

Schlossberg (Ger). Vineyard. (Anb) = Franken. (Ber) = Maindreieck. (Gro) = Not yet assigned (Vil) = Würzburg.

Schlossberg (Ger). Vineyard. (Anb) = Franken. (Ber) = Mainviereck. (Gro) = Not yet assigned. (Vil) = Klingenberg.

Schlossberg (Ger). Vineyard. (Anb) = Franken. (Ber) = Mainviereck. (Gro) = Not yet assigned. (Vil) = Wasserlos.

Schlossberg (Ger). Vineyard. (Anb) = Franken. (Ber) = Seigerwald. (Gro) = Herrenberg. (Vil) = Castell.

S

Schlossberg (Ger). Vineyard. (Anb) = Mittelrhein. (Ber) = Rheinburgengau. (Gro) = Burg Hammerstein. (Vil) = Bad Hönningen.

Schlossberg (Ger). Vineyard. (Anb) = Mittelrhein. (Ber) = Rheinburgengau. (Gro) = Burg Hammerstein. (Vil) = Hammerstein.

Schlossberg (Ger). Vineyard. (Anb) = Mittelrhein. (Ber) = Rheinburgengau. (Gro) = Lahntal. (Vil) = Nassau.

Schlossberg (Ger). Vineyard. (Anb) = Mosel-Saar-Ruwer. (Ber) = Bernkastel. (Gro) = Kurfürstlay. (Vil) = Bernkastel-Kues.

Schlossberg (Ger). Vineyard. (Anb) = Mosel-Saar-Ruwer. (Ber) = Bernkastel. (Gro) = Kurfürstlay. (Vil) = Lieser.

Schlossberg (Ger). Vineyard. (Anb) = Mosel-Saar-Ruwer. (Ber) = Bernkastel. (Gro) = Münzlay. (Vil) = Zeltingen-Rachtig.

Schlossberg (Ger). Vineyard. (Anb) = Mosel-Saar-Ruwer. (Ber) = Bernkastel. (Gro) = Sankt Michael. (Vil) = Bekond.

Schlossberg (Ger). Vineyard. (Anb) = Mosel-Saar-Ruwer. (Ber) = Bernkastel. (Gro) = Schwarzlay. (Vil) = Burg.

Schlossberg (Ger). Vineyard. (Anb) = Mosel-Saar-Ruwer. (Ber) = Bernkastel. (Gro) = Schwarzlay. (Vil) = Traben-Trarbach.

Schlossberg (Ger). Vineyard. (Anb) = Mosel-Saar-Ruwer. (Ber) = Saar-Ruwer. (Gro) = Römerlay. (Vil) = Sommerau.

Schlossberg (Ger). Vineyard. (Anb) = Mosel-Saar-Ruwer. (Ber) = Saar-Ruwer. (Gro) = Scharzberg. (Vil) = Estate.

Schlossberg (Ger). Vineyard. (Anb) = Mosel-Saar-Ruwer. (Ber) = Saar-Ruwer. (Gro) = Scharzberg. (Vil) = Kanzem.

Schlossberg (Ger). Vineyard. (Anb) = Mosel-Saar-Ruwer. (Ber) = Saar-Ruwer. (Gro) = Scharzberg. (Vil) = Saarburg.

Schlossberg (Ger). Vineyard. (Anb) = Mosel-Saar-Ruwer. (Ber) = Zell/Mosel. (Gro) = Goldbäumchen. (Vil) = Cochem.

Schlossberg (Ger). Vineyard. (Anb) = Mosel-Saar-Ruwer. (Ber) = Zell/Mosel. (Gro) = Rosenhang. (Vil) = Beilstein.

Schlossberg (Ger). Vineyard. (Anb) = Mosel-Saar-Ruwer. (Ber) = Zell/ Mosel. (Gro) = Weinhex. (Vil) = Kobern-Gondorf.

Schlossberg (Ger). Vineyard. (Anb) = Nahe. (Ber) = Kreuznach. (Gro) = Pfarrgarten. (Vil) = Dalberg.

Schlossberg (Ger). Vineyard. (Anb) = Nahe. (Ber) = Kreuznach. (Gro) = Pfarrgarten. (Vil) = Gutenberg.

Schlossberg (Ger). Vineyard. (Anb) = Nahe. (Ber) = Kreuznach. (Gro) = Schlosskapelle. (Vil) = Burg Layen.

Schlossberg (Ger). Vineyard. (Anb) = Nahe. (Ber) = Kreuznach. (Gro) = Schlosskapelle. (Vil) = Rümmelsheim.

Schlossberg (Ger). Vineyard. (Anb) = Nahe. (Ber) = Schloss Böckelheim. (Gro) = Burgweg. (Vil) = Altenbamberg.

Schlossberg (Ger). Vineyard. (Anb) = Nahe. (Ber) = Schloss Böckelheim. (Gro) = Burgweg. (Vil) = Bad Münster a. St-Ebernburg.

Schlossberg (Ger). Vineyard. (Anb) = Nahe. (Ber) = Schloss Böckelheim. (Gro) = Paradiesgarten. (Vil) = Martinstein.

Schlossberg (Ger). Vineyard. (Anb) = Nahe. (Ber) = Schloss Böckelheim. (Gro) = Paradiesgarten. (Vil) = Obermoschel.

Schlossberg (Ger). Vineyard. (Anb) = Nahe. (Ber) = Schloss Böckelheim. (Gro) = Paradiesgarten. (Vil) = Raumbach.

Schlossberg (Ger). Vineyard. (Anb) = Nahe. (Ber) = Schloss Böckelheim. (Gro) = Rosengarten. (Vil) = Braunweiler.

Schlossberg (Ger). Vineyard. (Anb) = Nahe. (Ber) = Schloss Böckelheim. (Gro) = Rosengarten. (Vil) = Burgsponheim.

Schlossberg (Ger). Vineyard. (Anb) = Nahe. (Ber) = Schloss Böckelheim. (Gro) = Rosengarten. (Vil) = Mandel.

Schlossberg (Ger). Vineyard. (Anb) = Rheingau. (Ber) = Johannisberg. (Gro) = Burgweg. (Vil) = Lorch.

Schlossberg (Ger). Vineyard. (Anb) = Rheingau. (Ber) = Johannisberg. (Gro) = Deutelsberg. (Vil) = Erbach.

Schlossberg (Ger). Vineyard. (Anb) = Rheingau. (Ber) = Johannisberg. (Gro) = Honigberg. (Vil) = Winkel.

Schlossberg (Ger). Vineyard. (Anb) = Rheinhessen. (Ber) = Bingen. (Gro) = Kaiserpfalz. (Vil) = Gross-Winternheim.

Schlossberg (Ger). Vineyard. (Anb) = Rheinhessen. (Ber) = Bingen. (Gro) = Kaiserpfalz. (Vil) = Ingelheim.

Schlossberg (Ger). Vineyard. (Anb) = Rheinhessen. (Ber) = Bingen. (Gro) = Kaiserpfalz. (Vil) = Schwabenheim.

Schlossberg (Ger). Vineyard. (Anb) = Rheinhessen. (Ber) = Nierstein. (Gro) = Domherr. (Vil) = Saulheim.

Schlossberg (Ger). Vineyard. (Anb) = Rheinhessen. (Ber) = Nierstein. (Gro) = Krötenbrunnen. (Vil) = Oppenheim.

Schlossberg (Ger). Vineyard. (Anb) = Rheinhessen. (Ber) = Nierstein. (Gro) = Petersberg. (Vil) = Gau-Heppenheim.

Schlossberg (Ger). Vineyard. (Anb) = Rheinhessen. (Ber) = Nierstein. (Gro) = Rheinblick. (Vil) = Mettenheim.

S

Schlossberg (Ger). Vineyard. (Anb) =
Rheinhessen. (Ber) = Nierstein. (Gro) =
Sankt Alban. (Vil) = Harxheim.
Schlossberg (Ger). Vineyard. (Anb) =
Rheinpfalz. (Ber) = Mittelhaardt-
Deutsche Weinstrasse. (Gro) = Grafen-
stück. (Vil) = Bockenheim.
Schlossberg (Ger). Vineyard. (Anb) =
Rheinpfalz. (Ber) = Mittelhaardt-
Deutsche Weinstrasse. (Gro) = Hof-
stück. (Vil) = Niederkirchen.
Schlossberg (Ger). Vineyard. (Anb) =
Rheinpfalz. (Ber) = Mittelhaardt-
Deutsche Weinstrasse. (Gro) = Höl-
lenpfad. (Vil) = Battenberg.
Schlossberg (Ger). Vineyard. (Anb) =
Rheinfalz. (Ber) = Mittelhaardt-
Deutsche Weinstrasse. (Gro) = Höl-
lenpfad. (Vil) = Neuleiningen.
Schlossberg (Ger). Vineyard. (Anb) =
Rheinpfalz. (Ber) = Mittelhaardt-
Deutsche Weinstrasse. (Gro) = Reb-
stöckel. (Vil) = Hambach.
Schlossberg (Ger). Vineyard. (Anb) =
Rheinpfalz. (Ber) = Mittelhaardt-
Deutsche Weinstrasse. (Gro) =
Schenkenböhl. (Vil) = Wachenheim.
Schlossberg (Ger). Vineyard. (Anb) =
Rheinpfalz. (Ber) = Mittelhaardt-
Deutsche Weinstrasse. (Gro) =
Schnepenflug vom Zellertal. (Vil) =
Bolanden.
Schlossberg (Ger). Vineyard. (Anb) =
Rheinpfalz. (Ber) = Südliche Wein-
strasse. (Gro) = Kloster Liebfrauenberg.
(Vil) = Pleisweiler-Oberhofen.
Schlossberg (Ger). Vineyard. (Anb) =
Rheinpfalz. (Ber) = Südliche Wein-
strasse. (Gro) = Ordensgut. (Vil) =
Rhodt.
Schlossberg (Ger). Vineyard. (Anb) =
Rheinpfalz. (Ber) = Südliche Wein-
strasse. (Gro) = Trappenberg. (Vil) =
Weingarten.
Schlossberg (Ger). Vineyard. (Anb) =
Württemberg. (Ber) = Remstal-
Stuttgart. (Gro) = Kopf. (Vil) = Bürg.
Schlossberg (Ger). Vineyard. (Anb) =
Württemberg. (Ber) = Remstal-
Stuttgart. (Gro) = Weinsteige. (Vil) =
Stuttgart (ortsteil Rotenberg).
Schlossberg (Ger). Vineyard. (Anb) =
Württemberg. (Ber) = Remstal-
Stuttgart. (Gro) = Weinsteige. (Vil) =
Stuttgart (ortsteil Uhlbach).
Schlossberg (Ger). Vineyard. (Anb) =
Württemberg. (Ber) = Remstal-
Stuttgart. (Gro) = Weinsteige. (Vil) =
Stuttgart (ortsteil Untertürkheim).
Schlossberg (Ger). Vineyard. (Anb) =
Württemberg. (Ber) = Württembergisch
Unterland. (Gro) = Heuchelberg. (Vil)
= Brackenheim.

Schlossberg (Ger). Vineyard. (Anb) =
Württemberg. (Ber) = Württembergi-
sch Unterland. (Gro) = Heuchelberg.
(Vil) = Heilbronn (ortsteil
Klingenberg).
Schlossberg (Ger). Vineyard. (Anb) =
Württemberg. (Ber) = Württembergi-
sch Unterland. (Gro) = Heuchelberg.
(Vil) = Neipperg
Schlossberg (Ger). Vineyard. (Anb) =
Württemberg. (Ber) = Württembergi-
sch Unterland. (Gro) = Kirchenwein-
berg. (Vil) = Talheim.
Schlossberg (Ger). Vineyard. (Anb) =
Württemberg. (Ber) = Württembergi-
sch Unterland. (Gro) = Kirchenwein-
berg. (Vil) = Untergrappenbach.
Schlossberg (Ger). Vineyard. (Anb) =
Württemberg. (Ber) = Württembergi-
sch Unterland. (Gro) = Lindelberg.
(Vil) = Dimbach.
Schlossberg (Ger). Vineyard. (Anb) =
Württemberg. (Ber) = Württembergi-
sch Unterland. (Gro) = Lindelberg.
(Vil) = Schwabbach.
Schlossberg (Ger). Vineyard. (Anb) =
Württemberg. (Ber) = Württembergi-
sch Unterland. (Gro) = Lindelberg.
(Vil) = Siebeneich.
Schlossberg (Ger). Vineyard. (Anb) =
Württemberg. (Ber) = Württembergi-
sch Unterland. (Gro) = Lindelberg.
(Vil) = Waldbach.
Schlossberg (Ger). Vineyard. (Anb) =
Württemberg. (Ber) = Württembergi-
sch Unterland. (Gro) = Schalkstein.
(Vil) = Grossingersheim.
Schlossberg (Ger). Vineyard. (Anb) =
Württemberg. (Ber) = Württembergi-
sch Unterland. (Gro) = Schalkstein.
(Vil) = Kleiningersheim.
Schlossberg (Ger). Vineyard. (Anb) =
Württemberg. (Ber) = Württembergi-
sch Unterland. (Gro) = Schozachtal.
(Vil) = Auenstein.
Schlossberg-Schwätzerchen (Ger).
Vineyard. (Anb) = Rheinhessen. (Ber)
= Bingen. (Gro) = Sankt
Rochuskapelle. (Vil) = Bingen.
Schloss Böckelheim (Ger). Bereich.
(Anb) = Nahe. (Gros) = Burgweg, Para-
diesgarten, Rosengarten.
Schlossböckelheim (Ger). Village. (Anb)
= Nahe. (Ber) = Schloss Böckelheim.
(Gro) = Burgweg. (Vins) = Felsenberg,
Heimberg, Im den Felsen, Königsfels,
Kupfergrube, Mühlberg.
Schloss Boosenburg (Ger). A sparkling
alcohol-free wine from Rudesheim.
Produced by Carl Jung. Imported into
U.K. by Leisure Drinks of Derby.
Schlössel (Ger). Vineyard. (Anb) =
Rheinpfalz. (Ber) = Mittelhaardt-

Deutsche Weinstrasse. (Gro) = Meerspinne. (Vil) = Gimmeldingen.

Schloss Eltz (Ger). A noted Rheingau estate.

Schlösser Alt (Ger). An Altbier brewed by the Schlösser Brauerei in Düsseldorf.

Schlösser Brauerei (Ger). A brewery based in Düsseldorf. Is noted for its Altbier.

Schlossgarten (Ger). Vineyard. (Anb) = Baden. (Ber) = Kaiserstuhl-Tuniberg. (Gro) = Vulkanfelsen. (Vil) = Burkheim.

Schlossgarten (Ger). Vineyard. (Anb) = Baden. (Ber) = Markgräflerland. (Gro) = Burg Neuenfels. (Vil) = Hügelheim.

Schlossgarten (Ger). Vineyard. (Anb) = Nahe. (Ber) = Kreuznach. (Gro) = Kronenberg. (Vil) = Bretzenheim.

Schlossgarten (Ger). Vineyard. (Anb) = Nahe. (Ber) = Kreuznach. (Gro) = Schlosskapelle. (Vil) = Schweppenhausen.

Schlossgarten (Ger). Vineyard. (Anb) = Rheingau. (Ber) = Johannisberg. (Gro) = Erntebringer. (Vil) = Geisenheim.

Schlossgarten (Ger). Vineyard. (Anb) = Rheinhessen. (Ber) = Wonnegau. (Gro) = Domblick. (Vil) = Offstein.

Schlossgarten (Ger). Vineyard. (Anb) = Rheinpfalz. (Ber) = Mittelhaardt-Deutsche Weinstrasse. (Gro) = Schnepfenflug an der Weinstrasse. (Vil) = Friedelsheim.

Schlossgarten (Ger). Vineyard. (Anb) = Rheinpfalz. (Ber) = Mittelhaardt-Deutsche Weinstrasse. (Gro) = Schnepfenflug vom Kellertal. (Vil) = Kirchheimbolanden.

Schlossgarten (Ger). Vineyard. (Anb) = Rheinpfalz. (Ber) = Mittelhaardt-Deutsche Weinstrasse. (Gro) = Schwarzerde. (Vil) = Kleinniedesheim.

Schlossgarten (Ger). Vineyard. (Anb) = Rheinpfalz. (Ber) = Südliche Weinstrasse. (Gro) = Bischofskreuz. (Vil) = Burrweiler.

Schloss Grafenegg (Aus). A family-owned estate based near Krems. Is noted for its fine white wines.

Schloss Grohl (Ger). Vineyard. (Anb) = Baden. (Ber) = Ortenau. (Gro) = Fürsteneck. (Vil) = Durbach.

Schloss Gutenburg (Ger). Vineyard. (Anb) = Nahe. (Ber) = Kreuznach. (Gro) = Pfarrgarten. (Vil) = Gutenberg.

Schloss Hammerstein (Ger). Vineyard. (Anb) = Rheinhessen. (Ber) = Nierstein. (Gro) = Petersberg. (Vil) = Albig.

Schloss Hohenrechen (Ger). Vineyard. (Anb) = Rheinhessen. (Ber) = Nierstein. (Gro) = Spiegelberg. (Vil) = Nierstein.

Schloss Hohneck (Ger). Vineyard. (Anb)

= Mittelrhein. (Ber) = Bacharach. (Gro) = Schloss Reichenstein. (Vil) = Niederheimbach.

Schlosshölle (Ger). Vineyard. (Anb) = Rheinhessen. (Ber) = Bingen. (Gro) = Kurfürstenstück. (Vil) = Gumbsheim.

Schloss Johannisberg (Ger). Vineyard. (Anb) = Rheingau. (Ber) = Johannisberg. (Gro) = Erntebringer. (Vil) = Estate.

Schloss Kaltenburg (Ger). A brewery based in a castle in Bavaria. Beer brewed by the Von Bayern royal family.

Schlosskapelle (Ger). Grosslage. (Anb) = Nahe. (Ber) = Kreuznach. (Vils) = Bingen-Bingerbrück, Burg Layen, Dorsheim, Eckenroth, Genheim, Guldental, Laubenheim, Münster-Sarmsheim, Rümmelsheim, Schweppenhausen, Waldlaubersheim, Weiler, Windesheim.

Schloss Kauzenberg (Ger). Vineyard. (Anb = Nahe. (Ber) = Kreuznach. (Gro) = Kronenberg. (Vil) = Bad Kreuznach.

Schlosskellerei Schwanburg (It). A noted winery based in Nals, Südtirol (Trentino-Alto Adige).

Schloss Ludwigshöhe (Ger). Grosslage. (Anb) = Rheinpfalz. (Ber) = Südliche Weinstrasse. (Vils) = Edenkoben, St. Martin.

Schloss Neu-Windeck (Ger). Vineyard. (Anb) = Baden. (Ber) = Ortenau. (Gro) = Schloss Rodeck. (Vil) = Lauf.

Schloss Randeck (Ger). Vineyard. (Anb) = Nahe. (Ber) = Schloss Böckelheim. (Gro) = Paradiesgarten. (Vil) = Mannweiler-Coelln.

Schloss Reichenstein (Ger). Grosslage. (Anb) = Mittelrhein. (Ber) = Bacharach. (Vils) = Neiderheimbach, Oberheimbach, Trechtingshausen.

Schloss Reinhartshausen (Ger). A noted wine-producing estate in the Rheingau.

Schloss Rodeck (Ger). Grosslage. (Anb) = Baden. (Ber) = Ortenau. (Vils) = Achern (ortsteil Oberachern), Altschweier, Baden-Baden, Bühl (ortsteil Neusatz), Bühlertal, Eisental, Kappelrodeck, Lauf, Mösbach, Neuweier, Obersasbach, Obertsrot, Ottersweier, Renchen, Sasbachwalden, Sinzheim, Steinbach, Varnhalt, Waldulm, Weisenbach.

Schloss Saarfelser Schlossberg (Ger). Vineyard. (Anb) = Mosel-Saar-Ruwer. (Ber) = Saar-Ruwer. (Gro) = Scharzberg. (Vil) = Serrig.

Schloss Saarsteiner (Ger). Vineyard. (Anb) = Mosel-Saar-Ruwer. (Ber) = Saar-Ruwer. (Gro) = Scharzberg. (Vil) = Serrig.

Schloss Schönburg (Ger). Grosslage.

S

(Anb) = Mittelrhein. (Ber) = Rhein-burgengau. (Vils) = Damscheid, Dellhofen, Langscheid, Niederburg, Oberwessel, Perscheid, Urbar b. St. Goar.

Schloss Schwabsburg (Ger). Vineyard. (Anb) = Rheinhessen. (Ber) = Nierstein. (Gro) = Auflangen. (Vil) = Nierstein.

Schloss Stahlberg (Ger). Vineyard. (Anb) = Mittelrhein. (Ber) = Bacharach. (Gro) = Schloss Stahleck. (Vil) = Bacharach/Steeg.

Schloss Stahleck (Ger). Grosslage. (Anb) = Mittelrhein. (Ber) = Bacharach. (Vils) = Bacharach, Bacharach/Steeg, Mannbach, Oberdiebach.

Schloss Stolzenberg (Ger). Vineyard. (Anb) = Nahe. (Ber) = Schloss Böckelheim. (Gro) = Paradiesgarten. (Vil) = Bayerfeld-Steckweiler.

Schlossteige (Ger). Vineyard. (Anb) = Württemberg. (Ber) = Remstal-Stuttgart. (Gro) = Hohenneuffen. (Vil) = Beuren.

Schlossteige (Ger). Vineyard. (Anb) = Württemberg. (Ber) = Remstal-Stuttgart. (Gro) = Hohenneuffen. (Vil) = Frickenhausen.

Schlossteige (Ger). Vineyard. (Anb) = Württemberg. (Ber) = Remstal-Stuttgart. (Gro) = Hohenneuffen. (Vil) = Kappishäusern.

Schlossteige (Ger). Vineyard. (Anb) = Württemberg. (Ber) = Remstal-Stuttgart. (Gro) = Hohenneuffen. (Vil) = Kohlberg.

Schlossteige (Ger). Vineyard. (Anb) = Württemberg. (Ber) = Remstal-Stuttgart. (Gro) = Hohenneuffen. (Vil) = Linsenhofen.

Schlossteige (Ger). Vineyard. (Anb) = Württemberg. (Ber) = Remstal-Stuttgart. (Gro) = Hohenneuffen. (Vil) = Metzingen.

Schlossteige (Ger). Vineyard. (Anb) = Württemberg. (Ber) = Remstal-Stuttgart. (Gro) = Hohenneuffen. (Vil) = Neuffen.

Schlossteige (Ger). Vineyard. (Anb) = Württemberg. (Ber) = Remstal-Stuttgart. (Gro) = Hohenneuffen. (Vil) = Weilheim.

Schloss Thorner Kupp (Ger). Vineyard. (Anb) = Mosel-Saar-Ruwer. (Ber) = Obermosel. (Gro) = Gipfel. (Vil) = Kreuzweiler.

Schlosstück (Ger). Grosslage. (Anb) = Franken. (Ber) = Steigerwald. (Vils) = Bullenheim, Ergersheim, Frankenberg, Hüttenheim, Ippesheim, Seinsheim, Weimersheim.

Schloss Turmhof (It). A winery based in Entiklar in the Trentino-Alto Adige. 18 ha. Produces mainly red wines.

Schloss Vollrads (Ger). Vineyard. (Anb) = Rheingau. (Ber) = Johannisberg. (Gro) = Honigberg. (Vil) = Estate.

Schlosswengert (Ger). Vineyard. (Anb) = Württemberg. (Ber) = Württembergisch Unterland. (Gro) = Wunnenstein. (Vil) = Beilstein.

Schloss Westerhaus (Ger). Vineyard. (Anb) = Rheinhessen. (Ber) = Bingen. (Gro) = Kaiserpfalz. (Vil) = Ingelheim.

Schluck (Aus). Lit – 'A drop of wine'. The brand-name for a fresh, dry white wine from the Wachau district. Often spritzig. Made from the Grüner veltliner grape by Lenz Moser.

Schlumberger (Aus). A leading producer of sparkling (méthode champenoise) wines based in Vöslau. Produces Goldeck.

Schlumberger et Cie (Fr). A négociant-éleveur based in Guebwiller in Alsace.

Schlürfen (Ger). To sip.

Schlüsselberg (Ger). Vineyard. (Anb) = Württemberg. (Ber) = Kocher-Jagst-Tauber. (Gro) = Kocherberg. (Vil) = Bieringen.

Schmachtenberg (Ger). Village. (Anb) = Franken. (Ber) = Steigerwald. (Gro) = Kapellenberg. (Vin) = Eulengrund.

Schmecker (Ger). Vineyard. (Anb) = Württemberg. (Ber) = Kocher-Jagst-Tauber. (Gro) = Tauberberg. (Vil) = Weikersheim.

Schmidt Brewery (USA). A brewery based in Philadelphia, Cleveland. Is noted for its McSorley's, Prior Double Dark Beers, Ortlieb, Rheingold and Tiger Head beers.

Schmidt Winery (Austr). A winery based in north-eastern Victoria. Produces varietal and table wines.

Schmieheim (Ger). Village. (Anb) = Baden. (Ber) = Breisgau. (Gro) = Schutterlindenberg. (Vin) = Kirchberg.

Schmittskapellchen (Ger). Vineyard. (Anb) = Rheinhessen. (Ber) = Nierstein. (Gro) = Gutes Domtal. (Vil) = Nackenheim.

Schnait i. R. (Ger). Village. (Anb) = Württemberg. (Ber) = Remstal-Stuttgart. (Gro) = Wartbühl. (Vins) = Altenberg, Sonnenberg.

Schnait i. R. (Ger). Village. (Anb) = Württemberg. (Ber) = Remstal-Stuttgart. See Weinstaat.

Schnapps (Scan). See Schnaps.

Schnaps (Ger). Spirits, liquor. A rectified spirit.

Schnapsteufel (Ger). Lit – 'Drink of the devil'. A fifteenth-century term to describe a corn-based spirit.

S

Schneckenberg (Ger). Vineyard. (Anb) = Rheinhessen. (Ber) = Wonnegau. (Gro) = Liebfrauenmorgen. (Vil) = Worms.

Schneckenhof (Ger). Vineyard. (Anb) = Württemberg. (Ber) = Württembergisch Unterland. (Gro) = Lindelberg. (Vil) = Adolzfurt.

Schneckenhof (Ger). Vineyard. (Anb) = Württemberg. (Ber) = Württembergisch Unterland. (Gro) = Lindelberg. (Vil) = Geddelsbach.

Schneckenhof (Ger). Vineyard. (Anb) = Württemberg. (Ber) = Württembergisch Unterland. (Gro) = Lindelberg. (Vil) = Maienfels

Schneckenhof (Ger). Vineyard. (Anb) = Württemberg. (Ber) = Württembergisch Unterland. (Gro) = Lindelberg. (Vil) = Unterheimbach.

Schneewein (Ger). Snow wine. Another name for Eiswein.

Schneider Beers (Arg). Major brewers in Argentina.

Schneider Brauerei (Ger). A family brewery based in Munich. Is noted for its Aventinus 7.8% alc. by vol. and other Weizenbiers.

Schneider Weisse (Switz). A Berliner-style wheat beer brewed by the Hürlimann Brauerei.

Schneller (Ger). A seventeenth-century drinking tankard. Tall and tapered with a lid. Usually heavily ornamented with a Coat of Arms etc.

Schnepfenflug an der Weinstrasse (Ger). Grosslage. (Anb) = Rheinpfalz. (Ber) = Mittelhaardt-Deutsche Weinstrasse. (Vils) = Deidesheim, Forst, Friedelsheim, Wachenheim.

Schnepfenflug vom Zellertal (Ger). Grosslage. (Anb) = Rheinpfalz. (Ber) = Mittelhaardt-Deutsche Weinstrasse. (Vils) = Albisheim, Bolanden, Bubenheim, Einselthum, Gauersheim, Immesheim, Kerzenheim, Kirchheimbolanden, Morschheim, Niefernheim, Ottersheim/Zellertal, Rittersheim, Rüssingen, Stetten, Zell.

Schnepp (Ger). Vineyard. (Anb) = Rheinpfalz. (Ber) = Mittelhaardt-Deutsche-Weinstrasse. (Gro) = Schwarzerde. (Vil) = Obersülzen.

Schoden (Ger). Village. (Anb) = Mosel-Saar-Ruwer. (Ber) = Saar-Ruwer. (Gro) = Scharzberg. (Vins) = Geisberg, Herrenberg, Saarfeilser, Marienberg.

Schoenling Brewery (USA). A brewery based in Cincinnati. Brews Top Hat beer.

Schoffit (Robert) (Fr). A wine-producer based in Alsace. Address = 27 Rue des Aubépines 68000 Colmar.

Schollerbuckel (Ger). Vineyard. (Anb) = Baden. (Ber) = Badische Bergstrasse/Kraichgau. (Gro) = Stiftsberg. (Vil) = Eberbach.

Scholtz Hermanos (Sp). Dessert winemakers based in Málaga, southern Spain.

Schön (Ger). Lit – 'Lovely' A charming, pleasant, harmonious wine.

Schön (Ger). Vineyard. (Anb) = Württemberg. (Ber) = Württembergisch Unterland. (Gro) = Staufenberg. (Vil) = Duttenberg.

Schön (Ger). Vineyard. (Anb) = Württemberg. (Ber) = Württembergisch Unterland. (Gro) = Staufenberg. (Vil) = Offenau.

Schönauer (Ger). See Kornbrennerei Schönau GmbH.

Schönberg (Aus). A wine-producing area in the Klosterneuburg region.

Schönberg (Ger). Vineyard. (Anb) = Rheinhessen. (Ber) = Bingen. (Gro) = Adelberg. (Vil) = Bornheim.

Schönberg (Ger). Vineyard. (Anb) = Rheinhessen. (Ber) = Bingen. (Gro) = Adelberg. (Vil) = Lonsheim.

Schönborn [Graf von] (Ger). An estate at Hattenheim in the Rheingau.

Schönburger (Ger). A red grape variety. A cross between the Spätburgunder (Pinot noir) and the IP1 (Chasselas x Muscat Hamburg). Is also known as the Rosa muskat. Gives good bouquet and sugar.

Schöneberg (Ger). Village. (Anb) = Nahe. (Ber) = Kreuznach. (Gro) = Pfarrgarten. (Vins) = Schäferslay, Sonnenberg.

Schöne Blume (Ger). The name for the frothy head on a glass of beer or lager.

Schönhell (Ger). Vineyard. (Anb) = Rheingau. (Ber) = Johannisberg. (Gro) = Mehrhölzchen. (Vil) = Hallgarten.

Schönhölle (Ger). Vineyard. (Anb) = Rheinhessen. (Ber) = Bingen. (Gro) = Sankt Rochuskapelle. (Vil) = Ockenheim.

Schools of the Wise (Tur). The general name used for coffee houses in the seventeenth century due to the fact that much could be learned there.

Schooner (Austr). A large beer glass.

Schooner (Eng). A double Elgin glass ²/₃ gill capacity.

Schooner (USA). A large beer glass.

Schooner Beer (Ire). A Pale ale beer brewed by the Murphy & Co. Ltd. at their Ladywell Brewery, Cork.

Schoongezicht Estate (S.Afr). Based in Stellenbosch. Address = P.O. Box 33, Stellenbosch 7600. White wines sold under the Rustenberg wines label. Produces varietal wines.

S

Schoppen (Ger). A style of glass which is covered with a metal top. Used for drinking beer.

Schoppenwein (Ger). A term used to describe an everyday drinking wine.

Schoppenwein (Ger). A wine measure. Schoppen (measure), wein (wine).

Schoppenweine (Ger). 'Open wine'. A new wine drunk young from the Palatinate, sweet and heavy.

Schorle (Ger). A drink of ½ white table wine and ½ soda water. Also known as Spritzer.

Schorle-Morle (Ger). A mixture of ½ wine and ½ aerated mineral water.

Schorndorf (Ger). Village. (Anb) = Württemberg. (Ber) = Remstal-Stuttgart. (Gro) = Kopf. (Vin) = Grafenberg.

Schornsheim (Ger). Village. (Anb) = Rheinhessen. (Ber) = Nierstein. (Gro) = Domherr. (Vins) = Mönchspfad, Ritterberg, Sonnenhang.

Schots (Hol). Scotch (whisky).

Schou Brewery (Nor). A brewery based in Oslo. Produces Bock beers and Tuborg brewed under licence.

Schozach (Ger). Village. (Anb) = Württemberg. (Ber) = Württembergisch Unterland. (Gro) = Kirchenweinberg. See Ilsfeld.

Schozachtal (Ger). Grosslage. (Anb) = Württemberg. (Ber) = Württembergisch Unterland. (Vils) = Abstatt, Auenstein, Ilsfeld, Löwenstein, Unterheinriet.

Schramsberg (USA). A small winery based in the Napa Valley, northern California. 17 ha. Grape varieties – Chardonnay, Gamay, Muscat, Pinot noir and Pinot blanc. Is noted for its sparkling wines made by the méthode champenoise.

Schriesheim (Ger). Village. (Anb) = Baden. (Ber) = Badische Bergstrasse/ Kraichgau. (Gro) = Rittersberg. (Vins) = Kuhberg, Madonnenberg, Schlossberg, Staudenberg.

Schröder et Schyler (Fr). A famous négociant-éleveur of Bordeaux. Owns Château Kirwan.

Schubertslay (Ger). Vineyard. (Anb) = Mosel-Saar-Ruwer. (Ber) = Bernkastel. (Gro) = Michelsberg. (Vil) = Piesport.

Schug Winery (USA). A winery based in the Napa Valley, California. Is associated with Phelps Winery.

Schuigui (Afr). A co-operative winery based in Tunisia. Is owned by the UCCVT.

Schuim Manchet (Hol). The name for the creamy head on a beer or lager.

Schultheiss Brauerei (Ger). A major brewery in Berlin that is noted for its Weisse (white) beers.

Schulwein (Ger). The term parents use to threaten children with when they decide they don't want to attend school. They're given a dose of acidic wine.

Schumacher Altbier (Ger). A fine Altbier produced by the Ferdinand Schumacher Brauerei in Düsseldorf. Pale in colour, it has a good malty flavour.

Schuss (Ger). The term for the dash of raspberry juice that is sometimes added to Berliner Weisse.

Schuster (John and Son) (USA). A winery based in Egg Harbour, New Jersey. Produces hybrid wines.

Schutterlindenberg (Ger). Grosslage. (Anb) = Baden. (Ber) = Breisgau. (Vils) = Ettenheim (ortsteil Wallburg), Friesenheim, Heiligenzell, Hugsweier, Kippenheim, Lahr, Mahlberg, Mietersheim, Münchweiler, Oberschopfheim, Oberweier, Schmieheim, Sulz.

Schützenfest (Austr). The name given to a beer produced annually for the German club of South Australia.

Schützenfest (Ger). A beer festival held in Hanover.

Schützengarten Brauerei (Switz). A brewery based in St. Gall. Is part of the Interbeva group. Brews High Life beer.

Schützenhaus (Ger). Vineyard. (Anb) = Rheingau. (Ber) = Johannisberg. (Gro) = Deutelsberg. (Vil) = Hattenheim.

Schützenhütte (Ger). Vineyard. (Anb) = Rheinhessen. (Ber) = Bingen. (Gro) = Sankt Rochuskapelle. (Vil) = Zotzenheim.

Schützenhütte (Ger). Vineyard. (Anb) = Rheinhessen. (Ber) = Nierstein. (Gro) = Krötenbrunnen. (Vil) = Dolgesheim.

Schützenlay (Ger). Vineyard. (Anb) = Mosel-Saar-Ruwer. (Ber) = Zell/ Mosel. (Gro) = Grafschaft. (Vil) = Ediger-Eller.

Schützingen (Ger). Village. (Anb) = Württemberg. (Ber) = Württembergisch Unterland. (Gro) = Stromberg. (Vin) = Heiligenberg.

Schwabbach (Ger). Village. (Anb) = Württemberg. (Ber) = Württembergisch Unterland. (Gro) = Lindelberg. (Vin) = Schlossberg.

Schwabenheim (Ger). Village. (Anb) = Rheinhessen. (Ber) = Bingen. (Gro) = Kaiserpfalz. (Vins) = Klostergarten, Schlossberg, Sonnenberg.

Schwabischer Landwein (Ger). One of fifteen Deutsche Tafelwein zones.

Schwäbische Weinstrasse (Ger). The wine route through the Württemberg Anbaugebiet. The Swabian wine route.

Schwalber (Ger). An alternative name for the Sylvaner grape.

Schwaigern (Ger). Village. (Anb) = Württemberg. (Ber) = Württembergisch Unterland. (Gro) = Heuchelberg. (Vins)

= Grafenberg, Ruthe, Sonnenberg, Vogelsang.

Schwalben (Ger). Vineyard. (Anb) = Rheinhessen. (Ber) = Bingen. (Gro) = Kaiserpfalz. (Vil) = Wackernheim.

Schwalbennest (Ger). Vineyard. (Anb) = Nahe. (Ber) = Schloss Böckelheim. (Gro) = Paradiesgarten. (Vil) = Raumbach.

Schwanleite (Ger). Vineyard. (Anb) = Franken. (Ber) = Steigerwald. (Gro) = Schlossberg. (Vil) = Rödelsee.

Schwartzenstein (Ger). Vineyard. (Anb) = Rheingau. (Ber) = Johannisberg. (Gro) = Erntebringer. (Vil) = Estate.

Schwarze Katz (Ger). Grosslage. (Anb) = Mosel-Saar-Ruwer. (Ber) = Zell/ Mosel. (Vils) = Senheim, Zell, Zell-Kaimt, Zell-Merl.

Schwarzenberg (Ger). Vineyard. (Anb) = Mosel-Saar-Ruwer. (Ber) = Zell/ Mosel. (Gro) = Rosenhang. (Vil) = Valwig.

Schwarzenberg (Ger). Vineyard. (Anb) = Rheinhessen. (Ber) = Bingen. (Gro) = Sankt Rochuskapelle. (Vil) = Bingen.

Schwarzerde (Ger). Grosslage. (Anb) = Rheinpfalz. (Ber) = Mittelhaardt-Deutsche Weinstrasse. (Vils) = Bisserheim, Dirmstein, Gerolsheim, Grosskarlbach, Grossniedesheim, Hessheim, Heuchelheim/Frankenthal, Kirchheim, Kleinniedesheim, Laumersheim, Obersülzen.

Schwarzer Herrgott (Ger). Vineyard. (Anb) = Rheinpfalz. (Ber) = Mittelhaardt-Deutsche Weinstrasse. (Gro) = Schnepfenflug vom Zellertal. (Vil) = Zell.

Schwarzer Letten (Ger). Village. (Anb) = Rheinpfalz. (Ber) = Südliche Weinstrasse. (Gro) = Schloss Ludwigshöhe. (Vin) = Edenkoben.

Schwarzes Kreuz (Ger). Vineyard. (Anb) = Rheinpfalz. (Ber) = Mittelhaardt-Deutsche Weinstrasse. (Gro) = Kobnert. (Vil) = Freinsheim.

Schwarz Klevner (Ger). The local name for the Pinot noir grape.

Schwarzlay (Ger). Grosslage. (Anb) = Mosel-Saar-Ruwer. (Ber) = Bernkastel. (Vils) = Bausendorf, Bengel, Burg, Dreis, Enkirch, Erden, Flussbach, Hupperath, Kinheim, Lösnich, Platten, Traben-Trarbach, Traben-Trarbach (ortsteil Starkenburg), Traben-Trarbach (ortsteil Wolf), Ürzig, Wittlich.

Schwarzquell Spezial (Aus). A sweet, dark-brown Beer 13° Balling brewed by the Schwechat Brauerei.

Schwarzriesling (Ger). An erroneous varietal name of the red grape Müllerrebe. Also known as the Pinot meunier.

Schwarzwalder (Ger). A name for Kirsch or Kirschwasser.

Schwarzwald Kirschwasser (Ger). A cherry liqueur made with the fruit and crushed stones.

Schwebsingen (Lux). A wine village on the river Moselle. Vineyard sites of Kolteschberg and Letscheberg.

Schwechat Brauerei (Aus). A brewery based at Klein Schwechat near Vienna. Founded in 1632. Was the hub of the world's greatest brewing empire in the eighteenth century.

Schwechater (Aus). A noted Lager beer brewed by the Schwechat Brauerei.

Schwedenwein (Ger). A wine produced in the year that Sweden invaded Germany.

Schwefel (Ger). A sulphur smell in the bouquet of the wine.

Schwegenheim (Ger). Village. (Anb) = Rheinpfalz. (Ber) = Südliche Weinstrasse. (Gro) = Trappenberg. (Vin) = Bründelsberg.

Schweich (Ger). Village. (Anb) = Mosel-Saar-Ruwer. (Ber) = Bernkastel. (Gro) = Probstberg. (Vins) = Annaberg, Burgmauer, Herrenberg.

Schweigen-Rechtenbach (Ger). Village. (Anb) = Rheinpfalz. (Ber) = Südliche Weinstrasse. (Gro) = Guttenberg. (Vin) = Sonnenberg.

Schweighofen (Ger). Village. (Anb) = Rheinpfalz. (Ber) = Südliche Weinstrasse. (Gro) = Guttenberg. (Vins) = Sonnenberg, Wolfsberg.

Schweinfurt (Ger). Village. (Anb) = Franken. (Ber) = Maindreieck. (Gro) = Not yet assigned. (Vins) = Mainleite, Peterstirn.

Schweizer Barkeeper Union (Switz). S.B.U. The Swiss Bartenders' Union. Address = 16, Camille Martin, Ch. 1203, Genève.

Schweppenhausen (Ger). Village. (Anb) = Nahe. (Ber) = Kreuznach. (Gro) = Schlosskapelle. (Vins) = Schlossgarten, Steyerberg.

Schweppes (Eng). A famous soft-drinks manufacturer based at St. Albans in Hertfordshire. Products include – Malvern Water, Rose's Cordials, Slimline, Tropical Spring. Merged with the Coca Cola Co. in January 1987 and is now known as the 'Coca Cola and Schweppes Beverages Company'. CCSB.

Schweppes Green Ginger Wine (Eng). A green ginger wine produced by the CCSB Co.

Schweppes Italia (It). A brandy producer. Produces Cavallino Rosso.

Schwobajörgle (Ger). Vineyard. (Anb) = Württemberg. (Ber) = Württembergisch Unterland. (Gro) = Lindelberg. (Vil) = Eschelbach.

Schwobajörgle (Ger). Vineyard. (Anb) = Württemberg. (Ber) = Württembergisch

Unterland. (Gro) = Lindelberg. (Vil) = Kesselfeld.

Sciacarellu (Fr). A red grape variety grown in Corsica.

Sciacchetra (It). A sweet dessert white wine from the Liguria region at Cinqueterre.

Sciampagna (It). Champagne.

Sciascinoso (It). A red grape variety grown in Campania.

Scion (Eng). The part of the vine shoot or cane used for grafting onto root-stock. e.g. Vitis Vinifera scion onto Vitis Berlandieri root-stock.

Sclafani (It). A wine co-operative based near Palermo in Sicily.

Scolca (La) (It). A producer of sparkling (méthode champenoise) wines based in the Piemonte region, north-western Italy.

Sconce (Eng). An Oxbridge University student's beer drinking challenge (to drink a large quantity in one go) because of a misdemeanour. Also the name for the large mug used for Sconcing.

Sconcing (Eng). The drinking of a large quantity of beer through a challenge by university students. See Sconce.

Scooter Cocktail (Cktl). ⅓ measure Brandy, ⅓ measure Amaretto, ⅓ measure cream. Shake over ice, strain into a cocktail glass.

Scorched (Eng). A term applied to white wines that are made from grapes that have had too much sun and too little rain.

Scoresby Rare (USA). A blended Scotch whisky bottled in America by Long John International.

Scorpion (Cktl). ½ fl.oz. Brandy, 1½ fl.ozs. Golden Rum, 1 fl.oz. orange juice, 1 fl.oz. lemon juice, 2 dashes Orgeat. Blend altogether with a scoop of crushed ice. Pour into a large old-fashioned glass filled with ice cubes. Decorate with a slice of orange, sprig of mint. Serve with straws.

Scotch (Eng) (slang). A term for Scottish Whisky.

Scotch (Eng). Short for Scotch Ale (a mild style of beer).

Scotch Ale (Bel). A term used for a strong, dark, bottled beer.

Scotch Ale (Eng). The term used in the north of England for heavy beers.

Scotch Ale (Scot). An Export ale 1041 O.G. brewed and bottled by the Belhaven Brewery in Dunbar near Edinburgh. Produced for USA market.

Scotch Apple Liqueur (Scot). See Mrs. McGillvray's Scotch Apple Liqueur.

Scotch Bird Flyer (Cktl). ½ measure De Luxe Scotch whisky, ⅙ measure Cointreau, ⅓ measure cream, 1 egg yolk. Shake well over ice, strain into a flute glass.

Scotch Bishop (Cktl). ½ measure Scotch whisky, ¼ measure dry*Vermouth, ¼ measure orange juice, 2 dashes Cointreau, 2 dashes Gomme syrup. Shake over ice, strain into a cocktail glass. Add a twist of lemon peel juice.

Scotch Bounty (Cktl). 1 measure Malibu, 1 measure (white) Crème de Cacao, 1 measure Scotch whisky, 4 measures orange juice, dash egg white, dash Grenadine. Shake well over ice, strain into a highball glass. Add a slice of orange. Serve with straws.

Scotch Coffee (Liq.Coffee). Using a measure of Scotch whisky.

Scotch Collins (Cktl). 1 fl.oz. Scotch whisky, 1 fl.oz. lemon juice, ½ fl.oz. Gomme syrup. Stir over ice in a highball glass. Top with soda water. Serve with straws.

Scotch Cooler (Cktl). ⅓ gill Scotch whisky, 3 dashes (white) Crème de Menthe. Stir over ice in a highball glass. Top with soda.

Scotch Fir (Scot). A brand of Sherry once produced by Arthur Bell and Sons.

Scotch Frappé (Cktl). Place 1½ fl.ozs. Bell's Scotch whisky in an old-fashioned glass filled with crushed ice. Dress with a spiral of lemon peel.

Scotch Frog (Cktl). ¼ measure Galliano, ¼ measure Cointreau, ½ measure Vodka, juice of a lime, dash Angostura, barspoon Maraschino cherry juice. Shake over ice, strain into a cocktail glass.

Scotch Highball (Cktl). Place some ice in a highball glass and add ¾ gill Scotch whisky, fill with iced soda water. Top with a dash of lemon juice.

Scotch Holiday Sour (Cktl). ⅜ measure Scotch whisky, ¼ measure Cherry brandy, ¼ measure lemon juice, ⅛ measure Italian vermouth. Shake over ice, strain into an ice-filled old-fashioned glass. Add a slice of lemon.

Scotch Malt (Scot). Malt Whisky. See Malt Whisky.

Scotch Malt Whisky Society Ltd (Scot). Address = The Vaults, 87, Giles Street, Leith, Edinburgh EWH6 6B7. A club that blends and bottles its own whiskies for its members.

Scotch Milk Punch (Cktl). ⅓ gill Scotch whisky, 1 gill milk, 1 teaspoon Gomme syrup. Shake well over ice, strain into a collins glass. Top with grated nutmeg.

Scotch Mist (Cktl). Place some shaved ice in an old-fashioned glass. Pour in 1 jigger of Scotch whisky and a twist of lemon peel juice.

Scotch Mist (Eng). 3 parts Ceylon tea and 2 parts Scotch whisky, heated together. Add honey to taste. Pour into small coffee cups (demi-tasses), float cream on top.

Scotch Old Fashioned (Cktl). Moisten a cube of sugar with 2 dashes Angostura in an old-fashioned glass. Add sufficient water to dissolve the sugar, add 2 ice cubes and 1 fl.oz. Scotch whisky. Stir.

Scotch on the Rocks (Cktl). Scotch whisky served over ice in an old-fashioned glass.

Scotch Rickey (Cktl). ⅕ gill Scotch whisky, juice ½ lime. Stir over ice in a highball glass. Top with soda, add a twist of lemon peel.

Scotch Sour (Cktl).(1). 1½ measures Scotch whisky, ¾ oz. lemon or lime juice, 1 teaspoon powdered sugar. Shake over ice, strain into a cocktail glass. Add a slice of orange and cherry.

Scotch Sour (Cktl).(2). 1½ fl.ozs. Scotch whisky, 1 fl.oz. lemon juice, ½ fl.oz. Gomme syrup, dash egg white. Shake over ice, strain into a large cocktail glass. Decorate with a lemon slice.

Scotch Stinger (Cktl). As for Stinger Cocktail using Scotch whisky in place of brandy.

Scotch Whisky (Scot). A blend of Malt and Grain whiskies. The proportion varies from blend to blend but is approximately 40% Malts and 60% Grain. See De Luxe Scotch Whisky.

Scotch Whisky Association (Eng). Address = 17, Half Moon Street, London W1Y 7RB.

Scotch Whisky Brands Limited (Scot). Formed on the 1st April 1915 by the merger of Buchanan and Dewar. Name was then changed to Buchanan Dewar Ltd.

Scotia Royale (Scot). A 12 year old De Luxe blended Scotch whisky produced by Amalgamated Distillery Products.

Scots Dream (Scot). 1 measure Islay malt whisky, dash lime juice. Stir over ice, strain into a cocktail glass and float a teaspoon double cream on top.

Scots Grey (Scot). A De Luxe blended Scoth whisky produced by Invergordon Distilleries.

Scottish and Newcastle Brewery (U.K). Operates 4 breweries – Tyne in Newcastle, Royal in Manchester, Fountain and Holyrood in Edinburgh. Brews most styles of beer. See Scottish Brewers and Newcastle Brewers.

Scottish Brewers (Scot). The Scottish part of the Scottish and Newcastle Breweries. Formed in 1931. Noted for its cask conditioned McEwan 70/- 1036.5 O.G. (also known as Younger's Scotch), keg Tartan Bitter 1036 O.G. Harp Lager 1032 O.G. Kestrel Lager 1032 O.G. and bottled Blue Label 1032 O.G. Double Century 1054 O.G. Also produces a canned Monk Export 1042 O.G.

Scottish Cordial (Scot). A nickname for Whisky.

Scottish Hours (Scot). Licensing hours of Scotland. Vary within each region. Regular extension licenses may permit opening during the afternoon, prior to 11 am and after 11 pm. Differ from the hours in England and Wales.

Scottish Pride (Scot). A canned Lager beer 1032 O.G. brewed by the Drybrough Brewery in Edinburgh.

Scottish Wine (Scot). A nickname for Whisky.

Scott's Valley (USA). A small wine-producing area of Santa Cruz city, Santa Cruz, California. Has one winery sited there.

Screened (Eng). During the brewing process the term given to the removal of all impurities in the malted barley and to grade the corns into size.

Screwdriver (Cktl). 1 measure Vodka, 2 measures orange juice. Shake well over ice, strain into a cocktail glass.

Screwed (Eng) (slang). Drunk.

Screwpool (Fr). See Screwpull.

Screwpull (Eng). A modern style of corkscrew that has two side-pieces that slip between the cork and the bottle-neck together with a conventional corkscrew.

Screw Top (Eng). The bottle capping of inexpensive wines. Uses a metal cap with screw which can be refitted to keep contents fresh. Wines of this nature are meant to be drunk young. Is also applied to beers and carbonated soft drinks.

Scrumpy (Eng) (slang). The name for rough, draught Cider.

Scrumpy Jack (Eng). A strong, clear, traditional Cider produced by the Symonds Cider Co. in Herefordshire.

Scuddy (Eng). A thick and cloudy wine with a disturbed sediment.

Scuppernong (USA). Species of Vitis Rotundifolia found along the Atlantic seaboard from Maryland to Florida. Gives sweet, rich white wines. Also known as the Muscadine grape.

Scuttlebutt (Eng). An old eighteenth- and nineteenth-century cask of drinking water on a ship. Also the nickname for a modern drinking fountain.

Scyady (Arab). See Chadely.

Scyphus (Lat). Wine-cup.

Seaboard Cocktail (Cktl). ½ measure Bourbon whiskey, ½ measure Gin, ½ oz. lemon juice, 2 dashes Gomme syrup. Shake over ice, strain into an ice-filled highball glass. Dress with a sprig of mint.

Sea Breeze (Cktl). ½ measure Vodka, ⅙ measure blue Curaçao, ⅙ measure dry Vermouth, ⅙ measure Galliano. Stir over ice, strain into an ice-filled goblet, add a twist of orange.

Seagavin (Austr). The brand-name of a raisin-flavoured dessert wine.

Seagers Egg Flip (Eng). A drink produced from egg yolks and British wine by Seagers Wines Ltd., Isleworth, Middlesex. 17% alc. by vol.

Seagram (Can). The world's largest alcoholic beverage producer. Has interests in most countries and produces most styles of beverages including many top brands such The Glenlivet, Glen Grant, Chivas Regal, etc.

Seagram's Cooler (Cktl). 1 measure Bourbon Whiskey, ⅙ measure Martini vermouth, 3 dashes orange Curaçao, 1 dash Angostura. Place in an ice-filled tumbler with a slice of lemon and a strip of cucumber peel. Stir, top with ginger ale.

Seagram's Distillery (USA). A Bourbon whiskey distillery based in Louisville and near Frankfort, Kentucky.

Seagram's V.O. (Can). A 6 year old blended Canadian whisky produced by Seagram. 43% alc. by vol.

Seal (Eng). An early identification mark of a bottle's owner. Put onto the bottle because of the bottle's value (were re-used over and over). Bottles were used to carry the wine from the merchant's cask to the household.

Sealed Bottle (Eng). A bottle that had the owner's seal stamped on the bottle's side. Up to 1850. See Seal.

Sealord Ale (Eng). A strong Ale 1060 O.G. brewed by the Southsea Brewery near Portsmouth, Hampshire.

Sea Serpent Cocktail (Cktl). ½ measure Vodka, ½ measure (green) Crème de Menthe. Stir together in an ice-filled highball glass. Top with lemonade. Dress with a slice of lemon and a cherry.

Sea Side Cooler (Cktl).(Non-alc). 1½ fl.ozs. Grenadine, 1 pint soda water, juice of a lime. Stir gently over ice in a jug, serve in highball glasses with a slice of lime.

Sea Tossed Wines (Eng). A name given to Madeiras and old East India Sherries.

Seau à Bouteille (Fr). Wine cooler, wine bucket.

Seau à Glace (Fr). Ice bucket.

Seaview (Austr). Vineyard. Address = Chaffey's Road, McLaren Vale, South Australia. Vineyards in McLaren Vale

and Willunga, Clare Watervale, Southern Vales, Adelaide Hills.

Sea Water (Eng). Used to preserve and hide 'off' flavours in wine in the early ages.

Seaweed Extract (Eng). An ingredient of seaweed used to retain the 'head' on a glass of beer.

Seawitch (Cktl). 2 measures Strega, 1 measure blue Curaçao, 3 measures dry white wine. Stir over ice, strain into 5 oz. goblet, add a lemon slice.

Sebastiani (USA). A winery based in Sonoma County, California. Grape varieties – Barbera, Chenin blanc, Gewürztraminer, Pinot noir and Zinfandel. Produces varietal and dessert wines.

Sebastopol (USA). A winery town in the western Russian River Valley, Sonoma County, California.

Sec (Fr). Dry for still white wines. When applied to Champagne denotes not as dry as Brut.

Sec (Rum). Dry.

Sec (S.Afr). Dry.

Secano (Sp). A red grape variety grown in the Navarra region. Produces light red wines. Known as Ojo de Gallo.

Secco (It). Dry.

Secentenario (It). A wine produced by Antinori to commemorate the 600th anniversary. Made from Cabernet sauvignon 30% and Sangiovese 70%.

Séché (Fr). Denotes a flat, harsh wine that has a sharp aftertaste. Also spelt Séchet.

Séché (Fr). A Premier Cru Chablis. Often reclassified as the Premier Cru Vaillons.

Séchet (Fr). The alternative spelling of Séché.

Sechsamtertropfen (Ger). A herb liqueur produced by Eckes.

Secke (Eng). The sixteenth-century spelling of Sack.

Seco (Sp). A medium-dry grading for sparkling wines.

Sêco (Port). Dry.

Secoffex Water Process (Switz). A patented process of removing the caffeine from coffee using water only.

Secondary Fermentation (Eng). Presence of bubbles, cloudiness, blown cork, nasty smell and taste. These are all signs of secondary fermentation. Caused by bacterial infection, early bottling etc. See also Second Fermentation and Malo-Lactic Fermentation.

Second Fermentation (Fr). A part of méthode champenoise. The addition of yeast and grape must to new wine which is then bottled and allowed to ferment in the bottle.

Second Fermentation (Scot). The term used in Whisky production for the marrying of the malt and grain whiskies that occurs in the casks. Also known as the First marriage (the marrying of malts).

Second Wine (Fr). A wine produced by a top vineyard (classified crus). Usually produced from young vines or from grapes that are not up to the quality status for the vineyard's top wine.

Seco-Seco (Cktl). 1 measure Dubonnet, dash Rose's lime juice. Serve 'On the rocks' in an old-fashioned glass. Decorate with a slice of lime.

Sécrestat (Fr). Bitters.

Sécrestat Curaçao (Cktl). ½ measure Sécrestat, ½ measure Curaçao, ice, soda water. Stir together in a highball glass.

Secret Love (Cktl). A Cherry 'B' and bitter lemon.

Section of the Barmen of Hungary (Hun). S.B.H. Hungary's Bartenders' Association. Address = Hungarhotels, 1052 Budapest, Petöfi Sàndor u.14.

Secundo Año (Sp). Bottled in the second year.

Sedgewick Taylor (S.Afr). A producer of a range of brandies.

Sediment (Eng). A deposit in wine or beer. Caused through a secondary or other fermentation in bottle or, for red wines, the precipitation of colouring matter and tannins through age.

Sediment Beer (Eng). A beer sold either in cask or in bottle whilst still 'working'. Settles out by the addition of finings.

Sedimento (Sp). Lees, sediment, dregs.

Sedlmayr [Gabriel] (Ger). The man who, in the nineteenth century, pioneered the use of steam power in breweries. Associated with Pasteur in the study of fermentation. Based at the Spätenbrau Brauerei in Munich.

Seefahrtbier (Ger). A light, malty beer produced by the Haake-Beck Brauerei in Bremen. Originally brewed for seamen to take to sea, it fermented in the bottle, to be consumed later at sea. Now brewed for a maritime dinner in Bremen. See Schaffermahlzeit.

Seefelden (Ger). Village. (Anb) = Baden. (Ber) = Markgräflerland. (Gro) = Lorettoberg. (Vin) = Maltesergarten.

Seehalde (Ger). Vineyard. (Anb) = Franken. (Ber) = Bayer Bodensee. (Gro) = Lindauer Seegarten. (Vil) = Nonnenhorn.

Seeheim (Ger). Village. (Anb) = Hessische Bergstrasse. (Ber) = Starkenburg. (Gro) = Not yet assigned. (Vin) = Mundklingen.

See-it-Offers (Eng) (slang). A term used in the navy to empty the pot of Rum.

Seewein (Ger). Lit – 'Lake wine'. It is named after the Lake Constance (Konstanz) in the Bodensee (Baden) area. The vines grow on the banks of the lake.

Seewinkel (Aus). On a label denotes that the vines have been grown in sandy soil (resistant to Phylloxera). See Sandweine. Is also the alternative name for the Neusiedlersee in Burgenland, eastern Austria.

Segarcea Cabernet (Rum). A sweet, soft red wine produced in the Valea Cǎlugǎreascǎ region.

Segnana (It). The brand-name of a noted Grappa.

Segnitz (Ger). Village. (Anb) = Franken. (Ber) = Maindreieck. (Gro) = Hofrat. (Vins) = Pfaffensteig, Zobelsberg.

Segonzac (Fr). A commune in the Charente Département whose grapes are classed Grande Champagne (Cognac).

Segré Cidre (Fr). A fine Cider produced in the Anjou-Saumur district of the Loire.

Séguinot (Pierre et Gérard) (Fr). Cognac producers. Address = La Nerolle B.P. N°21, 16130 Segonzac. 47 ha. in the Grande Champagne. Produces a range of the Cognacs.

Segura (Guillermo Rein) (Sp). A producer and exporter of Málaga.

Segura Viudas (Sp). A cava sparkling wine producer based in the Penedés.

Séguret (Fr). A Vaucluse vineyard. An A.C. Côtes du Rhône-Villages.

Sehlem (Ger). Village. (Anb) = Mosel-Saar-Ruwer. (Ber) = Bernkastel. (Gro) = Michelsberg. (Vin) = Rotlay.

Sehr Herb (Ger). Very dry.

Seibel 5279 (Fr). A white hybrid grape variety that produces light, pale wines.

Siebel 5437 (N.Z.). A black hybrid grape variety also known as the Seibouchet and Tintara.

Seibel 5455 (N.Z.). A black hybrid grape variety also known as the Cinqua and Moya.

Seibel 5898 (USA). A red grape variety also known as the Rougeon.

Seibel 7053 (USA). A red hybrid grape variety. Also known as the Chancellor.

Seibel 9110 (USA). A white hybrid grape variety which produces a lightly perfumed wine.

Seibel 13053 (USA). A red hybrid grape variety which produces good red and rosé wines.

Seibouchet (N.Z.). The local name for the Seibel 5437 black hybrid grape variety. Also known as the Tintara.

Seicentario (It). A limited edition anniversary red wine from Antinori.

Seidenberg (Ger). Vineyard. (Anb) = Nahe. (Ber) = Schloss Böckelheim. (Gro) = Paradiesgarten. (Vil) = Mannweiler-Coelln.

S

Seidl (USA). A style of glass used for drinking beer. See Beer Seidl.

Seidlitz (Ger). An aperient mineral water.

Seigle (Fr). Rye.

Seigneur (Ger). The person who set the date for the harvest in feudal times. Also kept order in the vineyards so that no one pilfered others' grapes etc.

Seigneur's Delight (Cktl). 1 measure fine old Cognac, 1 measure fresh babaco juice, dash lime juice. Shake over ice, strain into a cocktail glass. Dress with a slice of lime.

Seilgarten (Ger). Vineyard. (Anb) = Rheinhessen. (Ber) = Wonnegau. (Gro) = Burg Rodenstein. (Vil) = Bermersheim/Worms.

Seine-et-Marne (Fr). A département in the Champagne region that adjoins the Marne Département.

Seinsheim (Ger). Village. (Anb) = Franken. (Ber) = Steigerwald. (Gro) = Schlosstück. (Vin) = Hohenbühl.

Seishu (Jap). A refined style of Saké exported to Europe.

Sekhor (Isr). An old Hebrew (Bible) word for strong drink.

Sekt (Ger). A term for sparkling wine. Derived from Sack of Falstaff's (Shakespeare) German actor Ludwig Devriant. He drank German sparkling wine instead of the Sherry (Sack) that he was meant to. So the name stuck. 1825.

Sekt (Ger). A sparkling wine that may be produced by the méthode champenoise, cuve close or transfer method. The lower grades are now known as Schaumwein. May not be bottled in quantities larger than 3.2 litres. 'Sekt' is only allowed for special Qualitätsschaumwein.

Selaks Vineyard (N.Z.). Address = Old North Road, Kumeu, Auckland. 28 ha. plus 34 ha. under contract from Kumeu, Gisborne and Hawkes Bay. Grape varieties – Cabernet sauvignon, Chardonnay, Chenin blanc, Müller-Thurgau, Pinot noir, Rhine riesling, Sauvignon blanc and Sémillon.

Selby Brewery (Eng). Based in Selby, Yorkshire. Noted for its cask conditioned Best Bitter 1039 O.G. which is bottled as Nº1. Also Brahms and Liszt (a special bottle-conditioned Pale ale).

Selecta XV (Sp). A Beer brewed by the San Miguel Brewery 5.1% alc. by vol.

Selected Late-Gathered (Fr). Auslesen grade in Alsace. No longer used.

Selected Madeira (Mad). May use a brand-name or word 'Madeira' and a description e.g. dry, medium, but not the name of the grape. Must be a minimum age of 3 years after Estufagem.

Sélection de Grains Nobles (Fr). Late picked over-ripe berries. As for Vendange Tardive but must have a higher minimum sugar content.

Sélection Deluxe (Fr). On an Armagnac label indicates a minimum age of 1 year old.

Sélection des Anges (Fr). A 25 year old Cognac produced by Pierre Ferrand.

Selenzhiz (Fr). An alternative name for the Sylvaner grape.

Selestat (Fr). A wine town in the Bas-Rhin in Alsace. Known in German as Schlettstadt.

Selezionato (It). The Italian for Auslese. Also Scelto.

Self Whiskies (Scot). A term used in the Scotch whisky trade to denote a 'straight' or an unblended Scotch Malt whisky.

Seligmacher (Ger). Vineyard. (Anb) = Rheingau. (Ber) = Johannisberg. (Gro) = Burgweg. (Vil) = Lorchheusen.

Seligmacher (Ger). Vineyard. (Anb) = Rheinpfalz. (Ber) = Südliche Weinstrasse. (Gro) = Königsgarten. (Vil) = Arzheim.

Seligmacher (Ger). Vineyard. (Anb) = Rheinpfalz. (Ber) = Südliche Weinstrasse. (Gro) = Königsgarten. (Vil) = Rauschbach.

Sella e Mosca (It). A winery based at Alghero in Sardinia.

Selo de Guarantia (Port). A seal of guarantee for Portuguese wines and Madeiras.

Selo de Origem (Port). Seal of origin. Guarantees the authenticity of a demarcated wine.

Selosse (Jacques) (Fr). Champagne producer. Address = Rue Ernest Valle, 51190, Avize. Récoltants-manipulants. Produces vintage and non-vintage wines. Member of the C.V.C.

Selters (Euro). An alkaline mineral water.

Seltzer (USA). A general term for sparkling non-alcoholic drinks.

Selvanella (It). A noted Chianti Classico producer based in Tuscany.

Selzen (Ger). Village. (Anb) = Rheinhessen. (Ber) = Nierstein. (Gro) = Gutes Domtal. (Vins) = Gottesgarten, Osterberg, Rheinpforte.

Séme (Fr). An alternative name for the Malbec grape.

Semele (Lat). The mother of Bacchus.

Semeli (Cyp). The name of a traditional red wine produced by the Haggipavlu Winery.

Semidano (It). A white grape variety grown in Sardinia.

Semi-Dry (S.Afr). A classification of sweetness in a wine 4–12 grammes per litre of grape sugar in the wine. Also known as Off-dry.

Semi-Dulce (Sp). Semi-sweet for sparkling wines.

Sémillon (Fr). An excellent white grape variety grown mainly in Bordeaux in the Sauternes and Graves districts. Has a thin skin so suitable for botrytis cinerea attack. Is also known as the Blanc doux, Chevier, Chevrier, Colombier, Malaga and the Cinsault riesling.

Sémillon du Soleil (USA). A white wine produced by the Stony Hill Vineyards, Napa Valley, California.

Sémillon Oreanda (USSR). A dry white wine from the Crimea, produced from the Sémillon grape.

Semi-Oscura (Mex). The name for Vienna-style beers.

Semi Seco (Sp). A term for medium to sweet (semi-dry) sparkling wines.

Semi Soet (S.Afr). Semi-sweet.

Semi-Sparkling (Eng). Describes those wines that have traces of effervescence but are not quite sparkling. (Fr) = Moustille.

Semi-Sweet (S.Afr). A classification of sweetness in a wine 4–30 grammes per litre of grape sugar in the wine.

Sempé (Fr). A famous Armagnac producer. Address = 32290 Aignan.

Sénancole (Fr). A yellow herb liqueur made by the monks of the Abbey of Sénanque.

Senard (Daniel) (Fr). A négociant based in Aloxe-Corton, Côte de Beaune, Burgundy.

Sencha Fukujyu (Jap). A brand of Green tea. See also Sencha Genmaicha and Kokeicha.

Sencha Genmaicha (Jap). A brand of Green tea. See also Sencha Fukujyu and Kokeicha.

Senheim (Ger). Village. (Anb) = Mosel-Saar-Ruwer. (Ber) = Zell/Mosel. (Gro) = Goldbäumchen. (Vins) = Römerberg, Rüberberger Domherrenberg.

Senheim (Ger). Village. (Anb) = Mosel-Saar-Ruwer. (Ber) = Zell/Mosel. (Gro) = Not yet assigned. (Vin) = Lay.

Senheim (Ger). Village. (Anb) = Mosel-Saar-Ruwer. (Ber) = Zell/Mosel. (Gro) = Rosenhang. (Vins) = Bienengarten, Rosenberg, Vogeilberg, Wahrsager.

Senheim (Ger). Village. (Anb) = Mosel-Saar-Ruwer. (Ber) = Zell/Mosel. (Gro) = Schwarze Katz. (Vin) = Rüberberger Domherrenberg.

Seniffeln (Aus). Denotes a foul smell and taste. See also Böckser.

Senior Service (Eng). The brand-name of a dark Rum bottled by Saccone and Speed. 40% alc. by vol.

Senn (Ger). Vineyard. (Anb) = Rheinpfalz. (Ber) = Mittelhaardt-Deutsche Weinstrasse. (Gro) = Höllenpfad. (Vil) = Kleinkarlbach.

Sennecey-le-Grand (Fr). A commune in the A.C. Mâcon where Mâcon Supérieur may be produced.

Sennheim (Fr). The German name for the town of Cernay in southern Alsace.

Señor Fabbri (It). A Brandy produced by the Fabbri Distillery.

Señorio Agos (Sp). A red wine produced by the Bodegas Lopez-Agos. Made from 100% Tempranillo grapes. Oak matured for 2 years and 2 years in bottle. Rioja.

Señorio Agos (Sp). A red wine produced by Bodegas Marqués del Puerto in Fuenmayor, Rioja. 12.5% alc. by vol.

Señorio de Guadianeja (Sp). A perfumed white wine produced by the Vinícola de Castilla in La Mancha.

Señorio de Prayla (Sp). A red wine produced by the Bodegas Faustino Rivero Ulecia S.A., Arnedo, Rioja. (Baja region). Made from the Garnacha, Tempranillo and Viura grapes. Oak matured for 2 years then bottle matured.

Señorio de Saraía (Sp). A bodega based in Navarra. Grape varieties – Garnacha, Graciano, Mazuelo and Tempranilla. Noted for its Ecoyen Tinto and Viña del Perdón.

Sensation Cocktail (Cktl). ⅙ gill dry Gin, ⅙ gill lemon juice, 3 dashes Maraschino, 3 sprigs fresh mint. Shake well over ice, strain into a cocktail glass.

Sensible Shoes (Eng). ½ Guinness and ½ Brown ale mixed.

Sensoric Tasting (Eng). A tasting of liquids using the three senses (sight, smell and taste) and assessing the recorded results.

Sentiers (Les) (Fr). A Premier Cru vineyard in the A.C. commune of Chambolle-Musigny, Côte de Nuits, Burgundy. 4.8 ha.

Séoules (Les) (Fr). A wine-producing district in Bellet, Provence.

Seppelts (Austr). Vineyards. Address = 181–187 Flinders Street, South Australia 5,000. 870 ha. at Barooga, Barossa, Coonawarra, Drumborg, Keppock, Mt. Pleasant, Qualco, Riverland, Western and Victoria. Grape varieties – Cabernet sauvignon, Chardonnay, Riesling, Shiraz. Produces varietal, sparkling and dessert wines.

Seppelt's Great Western Imperial Reserve (Austr). A sparkling wine made by the méthode champenoise from the Seppelts estates.

Seppelt's Para Vintage Tawny (Austr). A Port-style dessert wine made by the Seppelts estates.

Seppelt's Spritzig Rosé (Austr). A pétillant rosé wine produced by the Seppelts estates.

Sepphöld Winery (Aus). Based at St. Georgen in Burgenland. Produces a wide range of wines (mainly white) including Grüner Husar, Habsburg-Husar and Weisser Husar.

September Morn (Cktl). ½ gill Bacardi White Label, juice ½ lime, 4 dashes Grenadine, white of egg. Shake well over ice, strain into a cocktail glass.

Septemvri (Bul). A state wine-co-operative.

Septimer (Ger). A white grape variety. A cross between the Gewürztraminer and the Müller-Thurgau. Ripens early, has high sugar and a strong bouquet.

Sequoia Cellars (USA). A winery based in Woodland, Yolo, California. Grape varieties – Cabernet sauvignon, Carnelian, Gewürztraminer and Zinfandel. Produces varietal and table wines.

Sequoia Grove Vineyards (USA). A winery based between Rutherford and Oakville, Napa Valley, California. 9.5 ha. Grape varieties – Cabernet sauvignon and Chardonnay. Produces varietal wines.

Serbia (Yug). A wine region. Noted for its Smederevka (white wine), Prokupac (red) and Ružica (rosé).

Sercial (Mad). The driest of the Madeira dessert wines. Made from the Sercial grape.

Sercial (Port). A white grape variety used in the production of Madeira.

Seré (Sp). The local name for the Katabatic wind in Priorato.

Serègo Alighieri (It). A D.O.C. Valpolicella Classico produced by the Masi Winery. 12.5% alc. by vol.

Serein [River] (Fr). A river that runs through the district of Chablis in the Burgundy region. A tributary of the Seine.

Serenissima (Cktl). 1½ fl.ozs. Vodka, 1½ fl.ozs. grapefruit juice, dash Campari. Shake over ice, strain into an ice-filled goblet.

Sereno Winery (It). A winery based in Canelli. Produces Vermouths and sparkling wines.

Seret (Eng). An old name for Sherry. Corruption of Ceret. e.g. Xera-Ceret-Seret.

Sergi Karasi (Tur). A white grape variety.

Serimpi Brewery (E.Ind). A brewery based in Djakarta, Java which is noted for its Stout.

Serine (Eng). An Amino acid found in minute traces in wines. Is formed by the yeast.

Sérine (Fr). A red grape variety also known as the Syrah. Used in the northern Rhône.

Seris (Eng). An old name for Sherry. From Xera (Greek). Progressed from Ceret-Seret-Seris. Pronounced Sheris.

Seritium (Eng). An ancient spelling of Sherry.

Sermiers (Fr). A Cru Champagne village in the Canton de Verzy. District = Reims.

Serpentin (Fr). The name of the spiral tube used to cool the Cognac vapour back into liquid form during distillation. See Serpentine (Eng).

Serpentine (Eng). The name for the copper spiral tube used for the condensing of the alcoholic vapour in an Alambic Distillerie. (Fr) = Serpentin.

Serpent's Tooth (Cktl). 1 oz. Irish whiskey, ½ oz. Kümmel, 1 oz. lemon juice, 2 ozs. sweet Vermouth, dash Angostura. Stir well over ice, strain into a wine glass.

Serpette (Fr). Pruning knife.

Serpias (Sp). A method of trapping the rain water in the Sherry region by making a border around each vine.

Serprina (It). A white grape variety grown in northern Italy. Used for making grapey, medium wines with softness.

Serra (Friar Junipéro) (USA).. A Franciscan who introduced wine-making to California.

Serra and Sons Ltd (Port). A winery based in Lisbon. Produces red and white wines.

Serradayres (Port). The brand-name for red and white wines produced by Carvalho, Ribeiro and Ferreira in Ribatejo. The red is cask matured.

Serralles (W.Ind). A noted Rum distillery based in Ponce, Puerto Rico. Produces Don Q (a popular local Rum brand).

Serralunga d'Alba (It). A commune of Barolo in Piemonte.

Serre (Fr). High quality first pressing in Champagne. Vin de Cuvée.

Serre de Coiran (Fr). A Vins de Pays area of the Gard Département in south-western France.

Serre de Prieur (La) (Fr). A vineyard in the Côtes du Rhône, A.C. Côtes du Rhône. Address = Suze-la-Rousse, Drôme.

Serre-Long (Fr). A wine-producing district in A.C. Bellet, Provence, south-eastern France.

Serrenne (Fr). An alternative name for the Syrah grape.

Serres (Fr). A noted liqueur producer based in Toulouse. Produces Dojon, Eau de Noix Serres, Fine Pyrénées and Violette.

Serrig (Ger). Village. (Anb) = Mosel-Saar-Ruwer. (Ber) = Saar-Ruwer. (Gro) = Scharzberg. (Vins) = Antoniusberg,

S

Helligenborn, Herrenberg, Hoeppslei, König Johann Berg, Kupp, Schloss Saarfelser Schlossberg, Schloss Saarsteiner, Vogelsang, Würtzberg.

Serrigny (Fr). A commune in the Côte d'Or, Burgundy. Produces red wines.

Serrine (Fr). See Sérine.

Serschin Wodka (Ger). A Silver Vodka produced in Eastern Germany. 37.5% alc. by vol.

Servagnat (Henry) (Fr). An Armagnac producer and owner of Domaine de Toul at Dému in the Bas Armagnac.

Servatiusberg (Ger). Vineyard. (Anb) = Mosel-Saar-Ruwer. (Ber) = Zell/Mosel. (Gro) = Rosenhang. (Vil) = Briedern.

Serveuse (Fr). Barmaid.

Service de la Répression des Fraudes et du Contrôle de la Qualité (Fr). SRFCQ. A body that helps in controlling the quality of wines in France. May prosecute offending vintners.

Service des Contributions Indirectes (Fr). In Burgundy a body who have to be notified in advance by a written declaration prior to Chaptalisation.

Serviços de Cadastro da Região dos Vinhos do Dão (Port). A body that keeps a detailed vineyard register. Works with the Federação in Dão.

Servir à Buffet (Fr). The serving of watered down wine. See Buffeter.

Servir Frais (Fr). Serve cold, chilled.

Servir Gelado (Port). On a label denotes 'Serve chilled'.

Serzy-et-Prin (Fr). A Cru Champagne village in the Canton de Ville-en-Tardenois. District = Reims.

Sessa Aurunca (It). One of the areas in Campania where Falerno wine is produced.

Session (Eng) (slang). A term for a heavy drinking bout.

Setarah (Iran). A Lager beer produced by Sarkissian and Sahakians Brewing Company in Tehran. 11° Balling.

Setges (Sp). The alternative spelling of Sitges in south-eastern Spain.

Setine (It). A light red wine said to have been a favourite of Caesar. See Setinum.

Setinum (Lat). A red wine produced in central-western Italy during Roman times. See Setine.

Set Mash (Eng). Occurs during the brewing process when the Wort will not drain off properly due to a very sticky mash.

Setrakian Vineyards (USA). The brand-label produced at the California Growers Winery (owned by Setrakian) in Cutler, California.

Settesòli (It). A wine co-operative based in Menfi, near Palermo, Sicily.

Settlings (Eng). A rare word used for the lees of wine or beer.

Setúbal (Port). A port in southern Portugal where the wine Muscatel de Setúbal is made. A fortified sweet wine, it is produced by replacing the grape skins into the finished wine to obtain a strong Muscat aroma and flavour. Has a golden colour and is aged up to 25 years. See also Torna-Viagem.

Seuca (Rum). An important wine-producing area. Part of the Tîrnave Vineyard.

Seurey (Les) (Fr). A Premier Cru vineyard in the A.C. commune of Beaune, Côte de Beaune, Burgundy. 1.23 ha.

Sève (Fr). A Brandy-based, orange-flavoured herbal liqueur.

Sève (Fr). Refers to the strength and aroma when being tasted in the mouth. Differs from bouquet in that it will indicate the presence of spirit, or a sappy, woody spirit/wine. Is also applied to a deep, rich Sauternes.

Sève de Sapin (Bel). A pine sap-flavoured liqueur produced by the Distilleries Associées Belges.

Sève Fournier (Fr). A Sève liqueur produced by the Fournier Co.

Seven Crown (USA). A brand of single Whiskey produced by Seagram. 40% alc. by vol.

Sevenhill Monastry Winery (Austr). A Jesuit winery based near Clare, South Australia. Produces table and Sacramental wines.

Sevenoaks Brewery (Eng). A home-brew Brewery opened in 1981 at the Crown Point Inn, Seal Chart, Kent. Noted for its cask conditioned Crown Point B.B. 1038 O.G.

Seven Seas (S.Afr). A leading brand of double-distilled Cane spirit.

Seventeen-Sixty-One [1761] London Dry Gin (Eng). A fine, well-known dry Gin produced by Greenalls of Warrington, Lancashire. 40% alc. by vol.

Seventh Heaven (Cktl). 8 parts Gin, 1 part Maraschino, 2 parts grapefruit juice. Shake over ice, strain into a cocktail glass, add a twist of grapefruit peel.

Seventy-Five [75] (Cktl). 2 ozs. Gin, juice of lemon, 1 teaspoon powdered sugar, 2 dashes Angostura. Shake over ice, strain into a flute glass, top with iced Champagne.

Seventy Five Cocktail [75 Cocktail] (Cktl). ⅓ gill dry Gin, ⅙ gill Calvados, 4 dashes lemon juice, 2 dashes Grenadine. Shake over ice, strain into a cocktail glass.

Seventy Shilling Ale [70/-] (Scot). A term used for medium gravity beers, light in colour. Synonymous with 'Heavy'. See Shilling System.

Seven-Up [7-Up] (USA). A brand of carbonated, clear, non-alcoholic soft drink. Produced by the 7-Up Co., St. Louis, Missouri.

Severe (Eng). A term used to describe hard, immature wines, usually high in tannin.

Severn Bore (Eng). A Best Bitter beer 1045 O.G. brewed by the Jolly Roger Brewery in Upton-on-Severn, Worcs.

Sevilla Cocktail (Cktl). ⅙ gill white Rum, ⅙ gill Port wine, 1 egg, 2 dashes Gomme syrup. Shake over ice, strain into a cocktail glass.

Seville (Cktl). 1 part Mandarine Napoléon, ½ part Ginger wine, dash Grenadine, dash egg white, juice of an orange. Shake over ice, strain into a 10 oz. highball glass. Add a slice of orange.

Seville Estate (Austr). Address = Linwood Road, Seville, Victoria 3139. 3.1 ha. Grape varieties – Cabernet sauvignon, Chardonnay, Merlot, Pinot noir, Rhine riesling and Shiraz.

Seville Orange Bitters (Sp). A strong, orange-flavoured bitters made with Seville oranges.

Sèvre-et-Maine (Fr). Two rivers that are tributaries of the Loire. The best Muscadet is produced in the area. See Muscadet de Sèvre et Maine.

Sexau (Ger). Village. (Anb) = Baden. (Ber) = Breisgau. (Gro) = Burg Zähringen. (Vin) = Sonnhalde.

Sextarius (Lat). A measurement of liquid. Standard = Hogshead. Minor = ½ litre.

Seyarua Cabernet (Rum). A rosé wine, sweet in taste produced on the Danube plain.

Seymour Winery (Austr). A winery based in central Victoria. Produces fine varietal wines.

Seyssel (Fr). A wine-producing region in the upper Rhône Valley, Savoie in eastern France. Includes the communes of Corbonod and Seyssel (Ain Département) and Seyssel (Haute-Savoie Département). All are white wines (sparkling or still) made from the Roussette grape.

Seyssel Mousseux (Fr). An A.C. sparkling wine produced by a second fermentation in the bottle from Seyssel in Savoie, eastern France.

Seyval Blanc (Fr). A hardy white hybrid grape variety produced from European and American vines.

Seyval-Villard (Fr). A famous hybridiser. Is noted for many new varieties especially N° 5276 (also known as the Seyval blanc).

Seyve [Bertille] (Fr). A famous French hybridiser who has many grapes named after him.

Seyve [Joannes] (Fr). A famous French hybridiser.

Seyve Villard (Fr). See Seyval-Villard.

Sevye-Villard 5/276 (USA). A white grape variety grown in the eastern USA and GB.

Sézanne (Fr). A canton in the Épernay district. Villages of Barbonne Fayel, Fontaine Denis Nuisy, Saudoy, Sézanne and Vinedey.

Sézanne (Fr). A Cru Champagne village in the Canton de Sézanne. District = Épernay.

S.F.C. (Fr) (abbr). In Cognac denotes a Supérieur Fine Cognac.

Sforzato (It). See Sfursat.

Sfursat (It). A strong red wine produced in the Valtellina. The grapes are hung to dry over the winter and so concentrate the sugar. It has a curious, intense flavour and is high in alcohol. Is dry. Lit – 'Strained'. Also known as Sforzato.

S.F.W. (S.Afr) (abbr). Stellenbosch Farmers' Winery.

S.G. (Eng) (abbr). Specific Gravity.

Shady Grove Cooler (Cktl). 1 measure Gin, juice ½ lemon, 1 teaspoon Gomme syrup. Place in a highball with ice, stir, top with ginger beer.

Shafer Vineyards (USA). A winery based near Yountville, Napa Valley, California. Grape varieties – Cabernet sauvignon, Chardonnay and Zinfandel. Produces varietal wines.

Shaft and Globe (Eng). The name given to a type of decanter. c1630–1675. Has a long neck and round bowl. First bottle-shape of glass.

Shahoni (Iran). Known as the Royal grape. Grown in the Cashbia region.

Shake a Drink (USA). A literal request for a shaken cocktail. To shake over ice and strain into the required glass.

Shake Over Ice (Eng). See Shake a Drink.

Shaker (USA). Two styles – Boston and Standard. Consists of 2 metal plated containers which fit one in the other. The unit is held in both hands and shaken up and down (filled with ice and the cocktail ingredients) until the cocktail is well chilled and mixed.

Shaler Vineyard Cellars (USA). A winery based in Tualatin Valley, Oregon. Produces vinifera wines.

Shalom Cocktail (Cktl). ⅗ measure Blue Label Smirnoff Vodka, ⅖ measure Madeira, ½ oz. orange juice. Shake over ice, strain into an ice-filled old-fashioned glass. Add a slice of orange.

Shampanskoe (USSR). White sparkling

wines made by the méthode champenoise.

Shamrock (Ckt1). ½ measure Irish whiskey, ½ measure dry Vermouth, 3 dashes Green Chartreuse, 3 dashes (green) Crème de Menthe. Stir over ice, strain into a cocktail glass.

Shams (Iran). A Lager beer 11.5° Balling produced by the Sarkissian and Sahakians Brewery Company in Tehran.

Shandong (China). A noted wine-producing province.

Shandy (Eng). Equal quantities of Bitter beer and lemonade. A bottled version is available which is non-alcoholic.

Shandy Gaff (Eng). Equal parts of Bitter beer and Ginger ale.

Shanghai (China). A major Chinese city that has a branch of the China National Cereals, Oils and Foodstuffs Import and Export Corporation. Specialises in Rice wines.

Shanghai (Cktl).(1). ½ measure dark Rum, ⅛ measure Pastis, ⅜ measure lemon juice, 2 dashes Grenadine. Shake over ice, strain into a cocktail glass.

Shanghai (Cktl).(2). 1 fl.oz. Jamaican rum, juice ¼ lemon, 3 dashes Anisette, 2 dashes Grenadine. Shake over ice, strain into a cocktail glass.

Shanghai Beer (China). A bottled Lager-style beer 1043 O.G. brewed in Shanghai.

Shanghai Cocktail (Cktl). ⅓ gill Brandy, 1 teaspoon each of brown Curaçao, Angostura, Gomme syrup and Maraschino. Stir over ice, strain into a cocktail glass. Serve with a dash of lemon peel juice and a cherry.

Shanghai Cossack Punch (Cktl). 1 pint dark Rum, 1 quart hot tea, zest of 2 lemons, ½ pint Curaçao, strained juice of 4 lemons, 1½ teaspoons Orgeat syrup or Orange flower water. Bring slowly to the boil, strain into glasses.

Shanghai Gin Fizz (Cktl). 1 measure Gin, ¼ measure Bénédictine, ¼ measure Yellow Chartreuse. Shake over ice, strain into a large wine goblet. Top with lemonade.

Shan Niang (China). A noted brand of Rice wine. See Shaoh-Hsing Rice Wine.

Shannon Shandy (Cktl). 1 fl.oz. Irish Mist, dash Angostura. Pour over ice into a highball glass. Top with dry ginger ale.

Shantung (China). A major Chinese city that has a branch of the China National Cereals, Oils and Foodstuffs Import and Export Corporation. Sells Gin, Vodka and Whiskey under the Sunflower label. Also produces a Cider and Brandy.

Shantung (China). A province that is noted for its Rice wines. See Shaoh-Hsing Rice Wine.

Shanxi (China). A wine-producing province in eastern China.

Shao Chiu (China). Lit – 'Burning spirits'.

Shao-Hsing Rice Wine (China). A Generic rice wine made from glutinous rice. Served at 37°C in small cups. 11–15% alc. by vol. See Chia Fan, Hua Tiao and Yen Hung.

Shao-Hsing Shan Niang Chiew (China). A brand of Rice wine produced in Shanghai by the C.N.C.O.F.I.E.C.

Sharab (Arab). Mixed drink.

Shariba (Arab). To drink, drinking.

Sharir (Isr). A semi-dry golden wine produced in the Sherry-style for the USA market. Produced by Carmel.

Shark's Tooth Cocktail (Cktl).(1). 1 measure golden Rum, 3 dashes each of Sloe Gin, dry Vermouth, lemon juice and passion fruit juice, 1 dash Angostura. Shake well over ice, strain into a cocktail glass.

Shark's Tooth Cocktail (Cktl).(2). 1 fl.oz. golden Rum, dash Gomme, dash Grenadine, juice ½ lime. Stir over ice in a highball glass. Top with soda water and decorate with a slice of lime and mint sprig.

Sharpham Vineyard (Eng). A vineyard based at Sharpham House, Ashprington, Totnes, Devon. Was first planted in 1982. 1 ha. Grape varieties – Huxelrebe, Madeleine angevine, Pinot noir and Reichensteiner.

Sharpness (Eng). Describes a wine that has excessive acidity.

Sharpness (Switz). A quality peculiar to certain soils, giving the wine a much appreciated taste.

Shasha (USSR). A Vodka produced in Georgia that is distilled from wine.

Shavetail Cocktail (Cktl). ⅖ measure Vodka, ⅕ measure peppermint cordial, ⅕ measure pineapple juice, ⅕ measure cream. Shake over ice, strain into a cocktail glass.

Shaw Vineyards (USA). A winery based near St. Helena, Napa Valley, California. Grape varieties – Chenin blanc, Gamay and Sauvignon blanc. Produces varietal wines. (Chenin blanc sold under the Bale Mill Cellars label).

Sheaf Stout (Austr). A sweet Stout brewed by the Tooths Brewery in Sydney.

Shebean (USA). See Shebeen (alternative spelling).

Shebeen (Ire) (S.Afr) (Scot). A shop or bar where excise liquor is sold without a licence (illegally).

Shebeen (S.Afr). The name for a place where black Africans drink together.

Shebeen (USA) (Ire). A nickname for weak beer.

Shechem (Isr). A red Palestinian wine written about by the Romans.

Sheep Dip (Cktl). 1 oz. Tio Pepe, 2 ozs. Gin, 5 fl.ozs. sweet Merrydown Cider. Shake over ice, strain into a large goblet.

Sheep Dip (Eng). An 8 year old Highland malt whisky bottled by M.J. Dowdeswell and Co. Ltd. in Oldbury-on-Severn, Gloucestershire. Known as 'The original Oldbury Sheep Dip'. See also Pig's Nose.

Sheet Filters (Eng). Sheets of filter medium (See Kieselguhr) used for the coarse filtration of wines and beers.

Sheffield Best Bitter (Eng). A cask conditioned Bitter beer 1038 O.G. brewed by the Ward Brewery in Sheffield, Yorkshire. Also sold in a keg version.

Sheffield Stout (Eng). Equal quantities of Black beer and lemonade.

Sheffield Stout (Eng). An old English drink of Mineral water or Rum mixed with Spruce beer.

Shefford Bitter (Eng). A cask conditioned Bitter 1038 O.G. brewed by the Banks and Taylor Brewery in Shefford, Bedfordshire.

Shekhar (Isr). Lit – 'Strong drink'.

Shelf (Off the) (Eng). A term to denote a drink, usually bottled beer, that is not cold i.e. has not been in the cooler.

Shelf Life (Eng). A term to denote the length of time a product (wine, beer, etc) will last before starting to deteriorate.

Shell (USA). A style of beer glass. See Beer Shell.

Shell Creek Vineyards (USA). A vineyard based near Paso Robles, San Luis Obispo County, California. Grape varieties – Barbera, Cabernet sauvignon and Petite syrah. Produces varietal wines.

Shellisage (Fr). The illegal practice of adding glycerine to wines to improve the wine's body. Is easily detected.

Shenandoah Valley (USA). A wine-producing region based in the Amador County, California.

Shenandoah Vineyards (USA). A winery based in the Shenandoah Valley, Amador County, California. Grape varieties – Cabernet sauvignon, Chenin blanc and Zinfandel. Produces varietal and dessert wines.

Shen Nung (China). An Emperor 2737 BC who is often regarded as the founder of tea drinking.

Shepherd Neame Brewery (Eng). Based in Faversham, Kent. Noted for its cask conditioned Master Brew Bitter 1036 O.G. and Master Brew Mild 1031 O.G. Stock Ale 1036 O.G. Invicta Best Bitter 1044 O.G. keg Abbey 1039 O.G. Hurlimann Sternbrau Lager 1045 O.G. and Bottled Bishop's Finger 1053 O.G. Bourough Brown 1034 O.G. and Hurlimann Lager 1045 O.G.

Shepherd's Delight (Cktl). ⅓ gill red St. Raphaël, 1 small bitter lemon, dash Pernod. Stir in a highball with ice, decorate with a slice of orange.

Sherbet Glass (USA). A small tumbler holding ¾ gill.

Sheris (Sp). An old name and pronunciation of Seris (Sherry). From the Greek Xera (Jerez). Progressed from Ceret-Seret-Seris-Sheris.

Sherish (Sp). One of the many old Moorish names for Jerez that have been recorded.

Sherrill Cellars (USA). A small winery based near Saratoga, Santa Cruz Mountains, Santa Clara, California. Grape varieties–Cabernet sauvignon, Petite syrah and Zinfandel. Produces varietal wines.

Sherris Sack (Eng). The Shakespearian name for Sherry. See Sheris and Sack.

Sherry (Sp). The name given to the fortified wine produced in the Andalusian region of south eastern Spain. Name derives from the main town of Jerez de la Frontera. The region lies in a triangle of Jerez and the towns of Sanlúcar de Barrameda and Puerto de Santa Maria. See Criadera, Rayas, Solera, Flor, Oloroso, Amontillado, Manzanilla, Palo Cortado.

Sherry Butt (Sp). A 600 litre capacity storage butt. The shipping butt contains 516 litres.

Sherry Case (Sp). A lengthy court case in 1968 which decided that only the fortified wine from Andalusia could be called Sherry. All other copies must be known as British Sherry, Australian Sherry, Cyprus Sherry etc.

Sherry Circle (Eng). Address = 3–5 Duke Street, London W1M 6BA.

Sherry Cobbler (Cktl).(1). Fill a 5 oz. wine glass with ice, add dry Sherry until ½ full. Add 4 dashes Curaçao and 1 teaspoon Gomme syrup. Stir, decorate with fresh fruit and a sprig of mint. Serve with straws.

Sherry Cobbler (Cktl).(2). Half fill a tumbler with ice, add a dash of Orange bitters, 1 teaspoon orange Curaçao, 1 teaspoon Peach brandy, 4 ozs. dry sherry. Stir gently. Decorate with a piece of fresh pineapple.

Sherry Cobbler American Style (Cktl). 1 gill Sherry, 1 teaspoon pineapple syrup, 1 teaspoon sugar syrup. Shake well over ice, strain into an ice-filled highball glass. Decorate with fruit and top with a dash of Port. Serve with a spoon and straws.

Sherry Cobbler French Style (Cktl). As for American Style but change the pineapple syrup to Curaçao.
Sherry Cocktail (Cktl).(1). 1 measure dry Sherry, 1 dash Orange bitters, 2 dashes dry Vermouth. Stir over ice, strain into a cocktail glass.
Sherry Cocktail (Cktl).(2). ⅓ gill Sherry, 2 dashes Angostura, 2 dashes Orange bitters. Stir over ice, strain into a cocktail glass. Serve with a cherry and dash of orange peel juice on top.
Sherry Egg Nog (Cktl). 1 egg, ⅓ gill sweet Sherry, teaspoon sugar. Shake over ice, strain into a collins glass. Top with milk, stir, add grated nutmeg.
Sherry Exporters' Association (Sp). An association that includes producers and exporters of British firms.
Sherry Flip (Cktl). 1 egg, 1 teaspoon powdered sugar, 1½ ozs. Sherry. Shake over ice, strain into a small goblet. Grate nutmeg on top.
Sherry Highball (Cktl). As for Gin Highball but using Sherry instead of Gin.
Sherry Kina (Sp). A Spanish vermouth of Sherry flavoured with quinine.
Sherry Milk Punch (Cktl). ⅓ gill sweet Sherry, ½ pint milk, 1 teaspoon powdered sugar. Stir well over ice, strain into a large highball glass. Top with grated nutmeg.
Sherrys (Eng). The early English spelling of Jerez.
Sherry Sangaree (Cktl). 1 measure Sherry, barspoon sugar. Fill a glass with crushed ice, stir, sprinkle nutmeg on top. Decorate with a slice of lemon.
Sherry Style (Eng). The designation given to wines which have a sweet taste and are dark in colour with high alcohol. Usually of USA, South African or Australian origin.
Sherry Twist (Cktl). ⅖ measure dry Sherry, ⅖ measure orange juice, ⅕ measure Scotch whisky, 2 dashes Cointreau. Shake over ice, strain into a cocktail glass.
Sherry Twist Cocktail (Cktl). ⅖ measure dry Sherry, ⅕ measure Brandy, ⅕ measure French vermouth, ⅕ measure Cointreau, 2 dashes lemon juice. Shake over ice, strain into a cocktail glass. Top with a twist of lemon peel juice and a pinch of cinnamon.
Sherry Type (Eng). See Sherry Style.
Sherrywijn (Hol). Sherry.
Sherston Scorcher (Eng). The brand-name of a Cider produced by the Saffron Cider Company, Radwinter, Essex.
Sherston Wine Company (Eng). A franchised group of over 12 specialist wine shops in Sherston, Malmesbury and Cheltenham. Address = 12, Suffolk Parade, Cheltenham, Gloucestershire.
Shicker (Austr) (slang). Alcoholic drink, strong liquor.
Shickered (Austr) (slang). Drunk, intoxicated.
Shiel (Scot). The wooden shovel used to turn the barley during the malting process.
Shilling System (Scot). A method of grading beer in Scotland. Used in the c1870's to indicate the level of gravity. 70/-, 80/-, 90/-. Higher gravity beers have a higher beer duty. The higher the shilling mark the stronger the beer.
Shine (USA) (abbr). For moonshine.
Shiner Premium Beer (USA). A Beer brewed by the Spoetzl Brewery in Shiner, Texas.
Shinjiro Torii (Jap). The founder of Suntory Co. (The largest Whiskey producer in Japan) in 1899.
Shin-Neck Bottle (Fr). An old Champagne bottle with a thin, narrow neck.
Shipper (Eng). A person (company) that ships wines, spirits etc. from one country to another. May be in bulk or already bottled.
Shipper's Label (Eng). Denotes wines (usually generic) that are bottled by the shipper. e.g. Médoc, Côtes du Rhône, etc.
Shipping Butt (Sp). A Sherry cask of 110 gallons (516 litres) for shipping Sherry. Used afterwards for Malt Whisky maturation.
Shipping Pipe (Port). A Port cask of 534. litres used for the shipping of Port wine. See Pipe.
Ship's Decanter (Eng). Originally designed to be used at sea. Has a large flat base and tapered neck to prevent it falling over.
Shipstone Brewery (Eng). Based in Shipstone Nottinghamshire. Taken over by Greenall Whitley, Warrington, Lancs. Noted for its cask conditioned and keg beers, bottled Gold Star 1034 O.G. Ship Stout 1042 O.G.
Ship Stout (Eng). A bottled Stout 1042 O.G. brewed by the Shipstone Brewery in Nottinghamshire.
Shiraz (Austr) (S.Afr). The local name for the red Syrah grape variety.
Shiraz (Iran). The ancient city in southwestern Iran. Gave its name to the wines of Persia. Also the name for one of the oldest grape varieties.
Shirley Temple (Cktl).(Non-alc). Top an ice-filled highball glass with ginger ale. Add a dash of Grenadine, stir slightly. Decorate with cherries.
Shive (Eng). A flat cork used as a bung in a cask of wine.
Shive (Eng). A wooden bung which plugs

the beer cask where it has been filled. Has a central part (Tut) which is punched in when the cask of beer has been delivered to the public house and is vented. See Spile.

Shivowitza (Hun). A liqueur produced from the Shiva plum. 43% alc. by vol.

Shloer (Eng). A non-alcoholic apple juice drink produced by Beecham Products, Brentford, Middlesex. Also a sparkling grape juice. Red and white varieties.

Shochu (Jap). A white spirit distilled from rice wine or sweet potato. Is similar to Vodka.

Shomron (Isr). A wine-producing region in central Israel.

Shoot (The) (Cktl). ⅖ measure Scotch whisky, ⅖ measure Fino sherry, ⅒ measure orange juice, ⅒ measure lemon juice, 2 dashes Gomme syrup. Shake over ice, strain into a cocktail glass.

Shooting Lodge (Scot). A brand of blended Scotch whisky sold through Peter Dominic stores. 37.5% alc. by vol.

Short (Eng). The term used to describe a wine that has a good nose and flavour, but falls short on the finish. (The taste disappears quickly).

Short Berries (Eng). The alternative name for millerandage. Describes the condition of the vine after coulure. The grapes vary in size and resemble buckshot.

Shortridge Lawton (Mad). A producer of fine Madeiras.

Shot (USA). A single measure of spirit. Usually drunk neat.

Shot Glass (USA). A small glass that takes a single measure of spirits. Designed so that the spirit must be drunk neat.

Shotted Bottles (Port). In olden days Port bottles were pitted with shot from a cartridge shaken by hand. They were used as the crust thrown by vintage Port was said to adhere more firmly to the uneven surface.

Shoulders (Eng). The point on a bottle where the neck joins the body of the bottle. Most pronounced on a Bordeaux bottle.

Shoulder Shape (Eng). A style of decanter developed from the Mallet shaped decanter. Has pronounced shoulders at the join of the neck and body. The body is straight sided.

Shout (Eng) (slang). A term to denote whose turn it is to buy the next round of drinks. e.g. 'Whose shout is it?', 'Your shout', 'My shout', etc.

Showerings (Eng). A subsidiary of Allied Lyons. Noted for Babycham and Gaymer's Cider.

Shown and Sons (USA). A winery based near Rutherford, Napa Valley, California. 32 ha. Grape varieties – Cabernet sauvignon, Chenin blanc and Johannisberg riesling. Produces varietal wines.

Shrapnel Corkscrew (Eng). A rare corkscrew produced in 1839 by Henry Shrapnel which was operated by a cranked handle to turn the screw into the cork. The handle is then turned in reverse to extract the cork.

Shrewsbury (Earl of) (Eng). See (Talbot) John.

Shrewsbury and Wem Brewery (Eng). See Wem.

Shriner Cocktail (Cktl). ½ measure Brandy, ½ measure Sloe Gin, 2 dashes Angostura. Stir over ice, strain into a cocktail glass, top with a twist of lemon peel juice.

Shrub (Eng). An alcoholic cordial 9.5% alc. by vol. produced by Phillips of Bristol.

Shrub (Eng). A mixed drink made of Rum, sugar, spices and fruit juices.

Shrubs (USA). A special mixed drink made from spirits and fruit juices to special recipes. Mixed in jugs and served with ice. Often allowed to mature. Can be alcoholic or non-alcoholic.

Shumen (Bul). A demarcated wine-producing region in eastern Bulgaria.

Shurb (Arab). Drink.

Shypoo (Austr) (slang). Cheap, low quality liquor.

Shypoo Shanty (Austr). The nickname for a bar where poor quality drinks are sold.

Shyraz (Euro). An alternative name for the Syrah grape.

Sibarita (Sp). An 1863 vintage Amontillado sherry produced by Domecq.

Šibenik (Yug). A wine-producing area on the Dalmatian coast.

Sibin (Ire). The Gaelic for weak beer (low quality). See Shebeen.

Sibirskaya (USSR). A grain Vodka produced in Siberia. 45% alc. by vol.

Sibras (Afr). A Beer brewed by the Sibras Brewery in Senegal, West Africa.

S.I.C.A. (Fr) (abbr). Société d'Intérêt Collective Agricole. A local society based in the Languedoc. Interested in modernising equipment and technology.

Sica les Viticulteurs de Fort Médoc (Fr). Address = Les Caperans, Cussac-Fort-Médoc. A.C. Haut-Médoc. Commune = Cussac-Fort-Médoc. 55 ha. Grape varieties – Cabernet sauvignon 60% and Merlot 40%.

Sica Mouluc (Fr). A wine-producer based in Cognac in the Charente Département. Produces méthode champenoise wines. Noted for its' Vin sauvage.

Siccus (Lat). Thirsty, dry.

Sicera (Isr). The fermented juice of apples from which the word Cider derives. See also Schekar.

Sichel et Cie (Fr). Famous wine merchants of Bordeaux and Burgundy.

Sicilia (It). Sicily.

Sicily (It). The largest island in the Mediterranean which, together with Puglia, is the largest wine-producing region in Italy. Noted mainly for its' Marsala fortified wine. See Woodhouse (John) and Q Mark.

Sick (Eng). The general term used to describe diseased wines that are unfit for drinking.

Sickershausen (Ger). Village. (Anb) = Franken. (Ber) = Steigerwald. (Gro) = Schlossberg. (Vin) = Storchenbrünnle.

Sidamo (Afr). A coffee-producing region in Ethiopia. A pure coffee.

Sidecar (Cktl). ⅓ measure Cognac brandy, ⅓ measure Cointreau, ⅓ measure lemon juice. Shake over ice, strain into a cocktail glass.

Sidecar Cocktail (Cktl). ⅛ gill dry Gin, ¼ gill Brandy, juice ¼ lemon. Shake over ice, strain into a cocktail glass.

Sidekick Beer (Eng). A cask conditioned Ale 1047 O.G. brewed by the home-brew public house The Queen Victoria in London.

Sider (Eng). An old name for Cider.

Sidhu (Ind). The name given to a drink produced from pure cane juice in ancient India.

Sidi Larbi (Afr). A wine-producing area based near Rabat in Morocco. Produces fine red wines.

Sidi Raïs (Afr). The brand-name of a rosé wine produced by the UCCVT in Takelsa, Tunisia.

Sidi Thabet (Afr). A large co-operative winery belonging to the UCCVT in Tunisia.

Sidra (Port) (Sp). Cider.

Sidro (It). Cider.

Siebel 1000 (USA). A red hybrid grape variety grown in eastern USA.

Siebel 5278 (USA). A white hybrid grape variety grown in eastern USA.

Siebel 5279 (USA). A white grape variety grown in the eastern USA. Also known as Aurora.

Siebel 5409 (USA). A red hybrid grape variety grown in the eastern USA. Also known as the Cascade.

Siebel 8357 (USA). A red hybrid grape variety grown in the eastern USA. Also known as the Colobel.

Siebel 9110 (USA). A white hybrid grape variety grown in the eastern USA. Also known as the Verdlet.

Siebeldingen (Ger). Village. (Anb) = Rheinpfalz. (Ber) = Südliche Weinstrasse. (Gro) = Königsgarten. (Vins) = Im Sonnenschein, Mönchspfad, Rosenberg.

Siebeneich (Ger). Village. (Anb) = Württemberg. (Ber) = Württembergisch Unterland. (Gro) = Lindelberg. (Vins) = Himmelreich, Schlossberg.

Siebengebirge (Ger). Bereich. (Anb) = Mittelrhein. (Gro) = Petersberg. (Vils) = Königswinter, Niederdollendorf, Oberdollendorf, Rhöndorf.

Sieben Jungfrauen (Ger). Vineyard. (Anb) = Mittelrhein. (Ber) = Rheinburgengau. (Gro) = Schloss Schönburg. (Vil) = Oberwessel.

Siefersheim (Ger). Village. (Anb) = Rheinhessen. (Ber) = Bingen. (Gro) = Rheingrafenstein. (Vins) = Goldenes Horn, Heerkretz, Höllberg, Martinsberg.

Siegel Pils (Ger). A Pilsener lager beer brewed by the D.U.B. Brauerei of Dortmund, Westphalia. A dry Lager with a light bitterness.

Siegelsberg (Ger). Vineyard. (Anb) = Rheingau. (Ber) = Johannisberg. (Gro) = Deutelsberg. (Vil) = Erbach.

Siegerrebe (Ger). A white grape variety. A cross between the Riesling and the Traminer.

Siegersdorf Winery (Austr). Address = Sturt Highway, Dorrien, Barossa Valley, South Australia. Winery in McLaren Vale.

Siegert's Distillery (W.Ind). A Rum distillery based on the island of Trinidad.

Sieges (Sp). An alternative spelling of Sitges in south-eastern Spain.

Siemens (Peter) (Ger). A seventeenth-century German soldier reputed to have bought the Rhine riesling vine into Spain. Now known as the Pedro Ximénez.

Siena (It). A wine area in Tuscany that is outside Chianti Classico. A sub-area of Chianti Colli Senesi.

Sierk (Fr). A wine-producing area in the Vins de la Moselle district of Lorraine. Produces mainly white wines.

Sierra de Montilla (Sp). An area where the fine solera Montilla-Moriles are produced.

Sierra Foothills (USA). A wine-producing district consisting of a series of islands in California. Amador, Calaveras, Eldorado and Placer are counties.

Sierra Nevada Brewery (USA). A brewery based in Chico, California.

Sierra Vista Winery (USA). A winery based in Placerville, Eldorado, California. Grape varieties – Cabernet sauvignon, Chardonnay, Sauvignon blanc and Zinfandel. Produces varietal wines.

Sierre (Switz). A Valais vineyard pro-

S

ducing a Vin de Paille called Soleil de
Sierre.

Sietges (Sp). An alternative spelling of
Sitges in south-eastern Spain.

Sieur de Limoux (Fr). The name of a
Blanquette de Limoux produced by
Producteurs de Blanquette de Limoux.

Sievering (Aus). A famous white wine
produced in the Vienna region.

Si Fen (China). A grain spirit produced in
the Shensi province.

Sifi Flip (Cktl). 1 egg yolk, ½ fl.oz. Cointreau, 1 fl.oz. Gin, ½ fl.oz. Grenadine,
½ fl.oz. lemon juice. Shake well over
ice, strain into 5 oz. wine glass.

Sifon (Hol). Siphon.

Sifone (It). A name used in Sicily for
Mistella. Used in the making of
Marsala.

Sigerrebe (Ger). See Siegerrebe.

Siggiewi (Euro). A wine-producing area
on the island Malta.

Sigille de la Confrérie St. Étienne (Fr). A
red seal awarded to particularly good
wines by the growers' promotional
body in Alsace.

Sigl Brauerei (Aus). A brewery based in
Obertrum. Founded in 1601. Noted for
its top-fermented Weizenbier.

Siglingen (Ger). Village. (Anb) =
Württemberg. (Ber) = Kocher-Jagst-
Tauber. (Gro) = Kocherberg. (Vin) =
Hofberg.

Siglo Saco Red (Sp). A red wine produced
by A.G.E. Bodegas Unidas S.A., Rioja.
Made from 35% Garnacha, 15%
Mazuelo and 50% Tempranillo grapes.
Matured in oak for 2 years and bottle for
10 months. Sold in a hessian sacking-
covered bottle.

Siglo White (Sp). A dry white wine made
by the A.G.E. Bodegas Unidas S.A.,
Rioja. 100% Viura grapes used.

Signature (Fr). A Cognac brandy produced by Hine in Jarnac. Is of an
average age of 5 years old.

Signature (Fr). A vintage De Luxe cuvée
Champagne produced by Jacquesson et
Fils from 50% Chardonnay and 50%
Pinot noir.

Signature (USA). The American name
used for the Japanese Imperial Whiskey
produced by Suntory.

Signature (USA). A premium Lager beer
1046 O.G. produced by the Stroh
Brewery. Is imported into the U.K. by
Bass.

Signinum (Lat). A red wine produced in
central-western Italy in Roman times.

Sigtún Special (Cktl). ⅓ measure dry
Vermouth, ⅓ measure Lemon Gin, ⅓
measure Torres medium onion. Stir
over ice, strain into a cocktail glass.

Sikera (Gre). Strong drink (alcoholic).

Sikes (Eng). British inventor of the hydrometer used to ascertain the proof (alcohol content) of spirits. See Sykes
(Bartholomew).

Silberberg (Ger). Vineyard. (Anb) = Ahr.
(Ber) = Walporzheim/Ahrtal. (Gro) =
Klosterberg. (Vil) = Ahrweiler.

Silberberg (Ger). Vineyard. (Anb) = Ahr.
(Ber) = Walporzheim/Ahrtal. (Gro) =
Klosterberg. (Vil) = Mayschoss.

Silberberg (Ger). Vineyard. (Anb) =
Baden. (Ber) = Badische Bergstrasse/
Kraichgau. (Gro) = Stiftsberg. (Vil) =
Kraichtal (stadtteil Neuenbürg, Menz-
ingen and Münzesheim).

Silberberg (Ger). Vineyard. (Anb) =
Baden. (Ber) = Kaiserstuhl-Tuniberg.
(Gro) = Vulkanfelsen. (Vil) = Bah-
lingen.

Silberberg (Ger). Vineyard. (Anb) =
Mosel-Saar-Ruwer. (Ber) = Zell/Mosel.
(Gro) = Rosenhang. (Vil) = Ellenz-
Poltersdorf.

Silberberg (Ger). Vineyard. (Anb) =
Nahe. (Ber) = Schloss Böckelheim.
(Gro) = Paradiesgarten. (Vil) = Nieder-
moschel.

Silberberg (Ger). Vineyard. (Anb) =
Nahe. (Ber) = Schloss Böckelheim.
(Gro) = Paradiesgarten. (Vil) = Ober-
moschel.

Silberberg (Ger). Vineyard. (Anb) =
Rheinhessen. (Ber) = Nierstein. (Gro) =
Sankt Alban. (Vil) = Bodenheim.

Silberberg (Ger). Vineyard. (Anb) =
Rheinhessen. (Ber) = Wonnegau. (Gro)
= Domblick. (Vil) = Mölsheim.

Silberberg (Ger). Vineyard. (Anb) =
Rheinhessen. (Ber) = Wonnegau. (Gro)
= Domblick. (Vil) = Monsheim.

Silberberg (Ger). Vineyard. (Anb) =
Rheinpfalz. (Ber) = Südliche Wein-
strasse. (Gro) = Bischofskreuz. (Vil) =
Walsheim.

Silberberg (Ger). Vineyard. (Anb) =
Rheinpfalz. (Ber) = Südliche Wein-
strasse. (Gro) = Kloster Liebfrauenberg.
(Vil) = Niederhorbach.

Silbergrube (Ger). Vineyard. (Anb) =
Rheinhessen. (Ber) = Nierstein. (Gro) =
Gutes Domtal. (Vil) = Mommenheim.

Silberquell (Ger). Vineyard. (Anb) =
Baden. (Ber) = Badische Frankenland.
(Gro) = Tauberklinge. (Vil) = Tauber-
bischofsheim (ortsteil Impfingen).

Silberwasser (Ger). See Silverwasser.

Silent Spirit (Eng). The name given to the
colourless, odourless, tasteless rectified spirit used in spirit production.
Also called Neutral or Cologne spirit.

Silent Third (Cktl). ⅓ measure Scotch
whisky, ⅓ measure Cointreau, ⅓

measure lemon juice. Shake over ice, strain into a cocktail glass.

Silesian Goblet (Ger). A fine eighteenth-century bell-shaped, short knob-stemmed wine glass with a glass lid. Usually heavily engraved. See also Silesian Stem.

Silesian Stem (Eng). A pedestal-stemmed glass c1715. See Silesian Goblet.

Silicaceous Earth (Eng). A useful fining agent obtained from Spanish, American and South American soils.

Silic Acid (Ger). A compound used to help precipitate out the unwanted materials in wine.

Siliceous (Eng). A soil with a high quartz content. e.g. Sancerre in the Loire.

Siliusbrunnen (Ger). Vineyard. (Anb) = Rheinhessen. (Ber) = Nierstein. (Gro) = Güldenmorgen. (Vil) = Dienheim.

Silk Stockings (Cktl).(1). 1½ fl.ozs. Tequila, 1½ fl.ozs. cream, 1 fl.oz. Crème de Cacao (white), dash Grenadine. Blend with a scoop of ice. Serve in a tulip glass. Decorate with a cherry and a sprinkle of cinnamon on top. Serve with straws.

Silk Stockings (Cktl).(2). ⅕ gill Tequila, ⅓ gill evaporated milk, ⅙ gill (white) Crème de Cacao, ⅙ gill Grenadine. Stir over ice, strain into a goblet. Top with a cherry and powdered cinnamon.

Silk Stockings (Cktl).(3). 1 fl.oz. Tequila, ⅓ fl.oz. (white) Crème de Cacao, ⅓ fl.oz. Grenadine, 2 teaspoons milk powder. Blend together with scoop of crushed ice in a blender. Pour into a Paris goblet. Top with a cherry and powdered cinnamon.

Siller (Hun). Rosé or red wine.

Sillerwein (Ger). A deep rosé wine produced from red and white grapes that are mixed before vinification. The juice is only in contact with skins for a short length of time. See also Schillerwein and Schilscherwein.

Sillery (Fr). A Grand Cru Champagne village in the Canton de Verzy. District = Reims.

Sillery (Fr). A red wine produced in the Champagne region.

Sillery (Marquis de) (Fr). A seventeenth-century Champagne salesman. The first to ship Champagne to London.

Silva and Cosens (Port). A family group who own Dow, Graham and Warre brands of Port.

Silvaner (Fr). The alternative spelling of the Sylvaner grape.

Silvaner Feodosüsky (USSR). A dry white wine from the Crimean peninsula. Made from the Silvaner grape.

Silver Acquette (Eng). See Acquette d'Argent.

Silverado Cellars (USA). A winery based in Yountville, Napa Valley, California. Grape varieties – Cabernet sauvignon, Chardonnay and Sauvignon blanc. Produces varietal wines.

Silver Bronx (Cktl). 1 measure dry Gin, ½ measure dry Vermouth, ½ measure sweet Vermouth, juice ¼ orange, ¼ egg white. Shake well over ice, strain into a cocktail glass.

Silver Bullet (Cktl).(1). ½ measure dry Gin, ¼ measure Kümmel, ¼ measure lemon juice. Shake over ice, strain into a cocktail glass.

Silver Bullet (Cktl).(2). 1 fl.oz. Kümmel, 1½ fl.ozs. Vodka. Stir over ice, strain into a cocktail glass.

Silver Cocktail (Cktl).(1). ⅓ gill dry Gin, ⅙ gill Bianco vermouth, 1 teaspoon Maraschino, 1 teaspoon Orange bitters. Shake over ice, strain into a cocktail glass. Serve with a cherry and a squeeze of lemon peel juice.

Silver Cocktail (Cktl).(2). ¼ gill Gin, ¼ gill French vermouth, 2 dashes Orange bitters, 3 dashes Maraschino. Stir over ice, strain into a cocktail glass, add a squeeze of lemon peel juice.

Silver Crown (Ger). A Deutscher Sekt (produced by the cuve close method) from Langenbach as part of the Centenary celebrations of Stowells of Chelsea.

Silver Fizz (Cktl). Juice ½ lemon, ⅕ gill dry Gin, 1 teaspoon sugar, 1 egg white. Shake over ice, strain into a highball glass. Top with soda water and twist of lemon.

Silver Jubilee (Cktl). ½ measure Gin, ¼ measure cream, ¼ measure Crème de Banane. Shake over ice, strain into a cocktail glass.

Silver King (Cktl). ⅕ measure Gin, juice ¼ lemon, 1 egg white, 2 dashes Gomme syrup, 2 dashes Campari. Shake over ice, strain into a cocktail glass.

Silver Lady (Eng). A medium-sweet sparkling Perry produced by the Goldwells Company.

Silver Mountain Vineyards (USA). A winery based near Los Gatos, Santa Clara, California. Grape varieties – Chardonnay and Zinfandel. Produces varietal wines.

Silver Oak Cellars (USA). A winery based near Yountville, Napa Valley, California. Grape variety – Cabernet sauvignon.

Silver Peg (Scot). A brand of white Rum bottled by Scottish and Newcastle.

Silverskin (Eng). The inner skin of the coffee cherry which holds the beans (peaberries). Also known as the Testa.

Silver Snipe (Eng). A label used by the Snipe vineyard in Woodbridge, Suffolk for their wines.

Silver Special Mild (Eng). A keg Light Mild 1030 O.G. brewed by the Charles Wells

S

Brewery in Bedford.

Silver Stallion Fizz (Cktl). Blend 1 scoop of vanilla ice cream with ⅓ gill Gin. Pour into a highball glass. Top with soda water, stir. Serve with straws.

Silverstone (Cktl). Equal amounts of white Rum and dry Martini. Stir with ice, strain into a highball glass, add bitter lemon.

Silver Streak (Cktl). 1 measure Kümmel, 1 measure dry Gin. Pour the Kümmel through the Gin. Drink straight.

Silver Sunset (Cktl). 1 fl.oz. Vodka, ½ fl.oz. Apricot brandy, ½ fl.oz. lemon juice, 3 fl.ozs. orange juice, dash Campari, dash egg white. Shake over ice, strain into an ice-filled highball glass. Top with a cherry and an orange slice. Serve with straws.

Silver Tequila (Mex). Young Tequila not aged. Light matured in wax-lined vats so remains colourless. Bottled soon after distillation.

Silverthorne Brewery (Wales). A brewery opened in 1981 in Cwmbran, Gwent. Noted for its cask conditioned Druid's Ale 1072 O.G. Celtic Gold 1046 O.G. and keg Springvale Bitter 1033 O.G. The brewery was originally called the Gwent Brewery.

Silverwasser (Ger). A sweet, colourless liqueur, flavoured with aniseed and orange. Silver flakes float in it. See also Silberwasser.

Silvestro (It). See Mentuccia.

Simbureşti (Rum). A wine-producing vineyard noted for its red wines. Also produces medium-dry white wines.

Simferopol (USSR). A noted wine-producing area in the Ukraine.

Simi Winery (USA). A winery based in the Alexander Valley, Sonoma County, California. Grape varieties – Cabernet sauvignon, Chardonnay, Muscat canelli and Zinfandel. Produces varietal wines.

Simon (André) (Fr). A famous author, gourmet and wine entrepreneur. 1877–1970.

Simon Brasserie (Lux). A small brewery based in Wiltz.

Simon Brauerei (Ger). A brewery based in Bitburg in the Palatinate. Brews Bitburger Pils.

Simonds Bitter (Eng). A keg Light Bitter 1032 O.G. brewed by the Courage Brewery in Southern England.

Simonds Farsons Cisk (Euro). See Farsons Brewery.

Simonnet (W.Ind). A producer of Grosse Montagne (a popular local Rum brand) on the island of Guadeloupe.

Simonnet-Febvre (Fr). A producer of

Crémant de Bourgogne based at Chablis, Burgundy. Address = 9, Avenue d'Oberwesel, 89800 Chablis. A négociant-éleveur.

Simonsgarten (Ger). Vineyard. (Anb) = Rheinpfalz. (Ber) = Südliche Weinstrasse. (Gro) = Bischofskreuz. (Vil) = Roschbach.

Simonsig Estate (S.Afr). Based in Stellenbosch. Address = Box 6, Koelenhof 7605. Produces most styles of varietal wines including a sparkling wine made by the méthode champenoise.

Simonsvlei Co-operative (S.Afr). Based in Paarl. Address = Simonsvlei Koöperatiewe Wynkelders, Box 584, Suider Paarl 7624. Produces mainly varietal wines.

Simonsvlei Koöperatiewe Wynkelders (S.Afr). See Simonsvlei Cooperative.

Simpkiss Brewery (Eng). Based in Brierley Hill in the West Midlands. Noted for its cask conditioned AK 1036 O.G. Supreme 1043 O.G. TNT 1050 O.G. and bottled Black Country Old 1052 O.G.

Sin Crianza (Sp). Lit – 'Without ageing'. Applies to wines less than 3 years old. See Vinos de Crianza.

Sinday (Ind). A Hindustan wine made from the sap of palm trees.

Sinebrychoff Brewery (Fin). A brewery based in Pon, western Finland and Helsinki in southern Finland.

Singapore Gin Sling (Cktl). Place some ice in a tumbler. Add 1 measure of dry Gin, juice of ½ lemon, 1 teaspoon sugar, dash Angostura. Fill ⅔ soda water, stir, add ¼ measure Curaçao, ¼ measure Cherry brandy. Decorate with an orange slice.

Singapore Sling (Cktl).(1). Original. 2 ozs. Gin, juice 1 lemon, 1 teaspoon powdered sugar. Pour over ice in a highball glass. Add soda water, ½ oz. Cointreau, ½ oz. Cherry brandy, stir, decorate with a slice of lemon. Serve with straws.

Singapore Sling (Cktl).(2). 2 ozs. dry Gin, 1 oz. Cherry liqueur, 2 tablespoons lime juice. Stir together, pour onto ice in a highball glass. Add soda water.

Singapore Sling (Cktl).(3). ½ measure dry Gin, ¼ measure Cherry brandy, ¼ measure lemon juice, Stir over ice in a highball glass, top with soda water and a slice of orange.

Singapore Sling (Cktl).(4). ½ measure dry Gin, ½ measure Cherry Heering, dash Bénédictine, dash lemon juice. Shake over ice, strain into a highball glass. Top with soda water and slice of lemon.

Sing Beer (E.Ind). A strong malt beer brewed in Kuala Lumpur.

Singeing (Eng). An old method of roasting the coffee beans in which the beans are in direct contact with a naked flame.

Singen (Ger). Village. (Anb) = Baden. (Ber) = Bodensee. (Gro) = Sonnenufer. (Vins) = Elisabethenberg, Olgaberg.

Singha Lager Beer (E.Asia). A Lager beer brewed in Thailand by the Boon Rawd Brewery in Bangkok.

Singing Cups (Jap). See Singing Saké Cups.

Singing Ginger (Scot) (slang). For a Whisky Mac. (Also for ginger wine).

Singing Saké Cups (Jap). A special type of Sakazuki cup which has a tube from which the Saké is sipped. As you sip air is drawn in with the Saké into your mouth to give a whistling sound.

Single (Eng). A request for a 'single' measure of spirits (⅙ gill or ⅕ gill). Usually denotes a Whisky.

Single Malt (Scot). A Malt whisky from one distillery.

Single Whisky (Scot). See Single Malt.

Singlings (Eng). The name given to Brandy that has been distilled once and before its second distillation.

Sinker (Eng). The name given to the heavy perforated plate which is used for keeping the cap of the pulp and grape skins submerged below the must during fermentation.

Sinkiang (China). A noted wine-producing province.

Sinsheim [stadtteil Hilsbach] (Ger). Village. (Anb) = Baden. (Ber) = Badische Bergstrasse/Kraichgau. (Gro) = Stiftsberg. (Vin) = Eichelberg.

Sinsheim [stadtteil Weiler] (Ger). Village. (Anb) = Baden. (Ber) = Badische Bergstrasse/Kraichgau. (Gro) = Stiftsberg. (Vins) = Goldberg, Steinberg.

Sin-Yassus (Gre). Cheers (a toast), your good health.

Sinzheim (Ger). Village. (Anb) = Baden. (Ber) = Ortenau. (Gro) = Schloss Rodeck. (Vins) = Frühmessler, Fremersberger, Feigenwäldchen, Klostergut, Sätzler, Sonnenberg.

Sion (Switz). Centre of the Valais canton. Famous for Fendant.

Sion Brauerei (Ger). A brewery based in Cologne with its own tavern based at 5–12 Unter Taschen. Noted for its Kolschbier.

Sioner Klosterberg (Ger). Vineyard. (Anb) = Rheinhessen. (Ber) = Wonnegau. (Gro) = Sybillenstein. (Vil) = Mauchenheim.

Sionon (Ger). A diabetic Sekt from Sohnlein Rheingold cellars.

Sip (Eng). To drink a liquid by taking small mouthfuls.

Siphon Bottle (Eng). See Soda Syphon.

Siphon Vat (Port). A method of fermentation. Once fermentation begins the self-circulation system of the syphon starts. Grape juice is forced up into an open upper tank which, when full opens and lets fermenting juice fall back with considerable force on the 'Manta', beating colour out of it. Repeated many times. Also known as Autovinification.

Šipon (Yug). A white grape variety grown in the Maribor region. Known as the Furmint in Hungary. See also Mesler.

Sipp (Louis) (Fr). An Alsace wine-producer. Address = 68150 Ribeauville, Haut-Rhin.

Sippers (Eng) (slang). A term used in the navy to obtain a small sip of a shipmate's Rum ration.

Sira (Tur). Grape juice.

Sirac (Fr). An alternative spelling for the Syrah grape.

Sirah (Fr). An alternative spelling of the Syrah grape.

Sirály (Hun). A strong, pale Beer 6% alc. by vol. brewed by the Nagykanizsa Brewery.

Širavar (Czec). A strong dark, malty Lager beer brewed by the Michalovce Brewery.

Sir Frederick's Wild Strawberry (Fr). A liqueur Brandy based on Fraises des bois. Is pink in colour. 26% alc. by vol. Produced by Louis Baron.

Sirgis (Fr). A sweet muscatel wine produced in the Midi.

Şiria (Rum). A wine-producing area. Part of the Banat Vineyard.

Sirke (Tur). Vinegar.

Sirop (Fr). Syrup.

Sirop de Citron (Fr). Lemon syrup used for sweetening and flavouring. Is non-alcoholic.

Sirov Vodka (Hol). The brand-name of a Vodka produced by De Kuyper. 37.5% alc. by vol.

Sirrac (Fr). Another name for the red Syrah grape.

Sirrah (Fr). An alternative spelling of the Syrah grape.

Sirras (Fr). An alternative spelling of the Syrah grape.

Sir Robert Burnett and Co. Ltd (Eng). See Burnett Gin.

Sir Walter (Cktl). ½ measure Bacardi White Label, ½ measure old Brandy, 3 dashes Grenadine, 3 dashes Cointreau, 3 dashes lemon juice. Shake over ice, strain into a cocktail glass.

Sir Winston Churchill (Fr). A De Luxe vintage Champagne produced by Pol Roger. See Cuvée Sir Winston Churchill.

Sisca (Fr). The brand-name of a Crème de Cassis produced in Dijon. 26% alc. by vol.

Şişe (Tur). Bottle, flask.

Sisi (Ger). A cross white grape variety. A

S

cross between the Silvaner and Siegerrebe.

Sisies (Les) (Fr). A Premier Cru vineyard in the A.C. commune of Beaune, Côte de Beaune, Burgundy. 8.5 ha.

Siskiyou Vineyards (USA). A vineyard based near Siskiyou National Forest, Oregon. 5 ha. Produces vinifera wines.

Sistowa (Bul). The brand-name of a wine.

Sitges (Sp). An area on the coast of Cataluña, south-eastern Spain. Noted for its Malvasia and Moscatel sweet, dessert wines.

Sitges (Sp). An eighteenth-century sweet Muscatel wine produced in south-eastern Spain.

Sitia (Gre). A full, robust red wine produced on the isle of Crete from the Liatiko grape. Also a fortified version.

Six Bells (Cktl). ½ measure dark Rum, ¼ measure orange juice, ¼ measure lime juice, dash Gomme syrup, 2 dashes Angostura. Shake over ice, strain into a cocktail glass.

Six Étoiles (Fr). A standard litre 'returnable' bottle (wine) used in France. Is distinguished by the 6 [*] on the neck.

Sixex (Eng). A fine bottled Barley wine 1064 O.G. brewed by the Holt Brewery in Manchester.

Six o'Clock Swill (Austr). The title given to the time when pubs close at 6 p.m. The rush to drink from the time work closed (5 p.m.) until the pubs closed (6 p.m.) was hectic hence the name. Died out in the 1960s when laws changed.

Six Pack (USA) (slang). A term for the pack of six canned or bottled beers. See also Four Pack.

Six Row Barley (Eng). A strain of barley used in brewing. Produces heavy beers. The name refers to the number of rows of grain per ear of corn. See also Two Row and Four Row.

Sixteenth (Port). Size of cask in the Port (Douro) region.

Sixty Ale (Scot). A strong Ale 1060 O.G. brewed by the Alice Brewery in Inverness.

Sixty Shilling Ale [60/-] (Scot). A term for Mild beers, dark in colour 1030–1034 O.G. See Shilling System.

Sixty Shilling Light (Scot). A Beer brewed by the Belhaven Brewery in Dunbar, East Lothian.

Six X [XXXXXX] (Eng). A cask conditioned Bitter 1040 O.G. brewed by the Wadworth Brewery in Wiltshire.

Sizer (La) (Fr). A vineyard in the A.C. Hermitage, Coteaux de l'Hermitage, northern Rhône.

Sizeranne (La) (Fr). The name given to a red A.C. Hermitage wine from the firm of Charpoutier in Tain, Côtes du Rhône.

Sizzano (It). A small town 12 miles north-west of Navarra in Piemonte. Noted for a red wine of the same name.

Sizzano (It). D.O.C. red wine of Piemonte. Made from 40–60% Nebbiolo, 15–40% Vespolina and up to 25% Bonarda novarese grapes. Has to be aged 3 years of which 2 years must be in oak/chestnut cask.

Skaal (Scan). 'Good health'. A toast.

Skadarka (Yug). A red grape variety.

Skaling (Den). The term used when drinking Akvavit and a glass of ice cold Lager beer.

Skåne Aquavit (Swe). An Aquavit flavoured with aniseed, caraway, fennel and herbs.

Skerryvore (Scot). A blended Scotch whisky produced by Arthur Bell and Sons.

Skhou (USSR). The name given to a brand of Koumiss that is distilled in Siberia. Also produced in the Caucasus.

Skibsøl (Den). Lit – 'Ship's ale'. A tax-free, low-alcohol beer, dark in colour brewed by the Tuborg Brewery. 1.9% alc. by vol.

Ski Bunny (Punch). Heat ½ pint beer, pinch of cardamon, cinnamon and ginger, 1 fl.oz. Gin, ½ fl.oz. dark Rum until nearly boiling. Pour over 3 beaten egg yolks, whisking until smooth. Serve in mugs with a cinnamon stick.

Skier's Smoothie (Cktl). 2 measures Galliano, 1 cup hot strong tea. Pour tea onto Galliano in a wine goblet. Drink whilst hot.

Skim (Eng). In brewing, a term used for the removal of excess yeast from the top of the fermenting vessel. The surplus yeast is sold to make yeast products.

Skim (Eng). To remove the cream off the top of milk (or skin off the top of hot milk).

Skimmed Milk (Eng). Milk (fresh) which has had the cream removed.

Skinful (Eng) (slang). Denotes a large consumption of alcoholic beverage. Also used to describe a drunken person.

Skins (Eng). The skin of the grape. Contains colour and tannin (red varieties).

Skips (Scot). The alternative name for the long handled wooden shovels used to turn the barley during the malting process in Whisky production.

Skiraz (Austr). Another name for the red Sirah grape.

Ski Wasser Cocktail (Cktl).(Non-alc). 1 fl.oz. raspberry juice, 1 fl.oz. lemon juice. Pour into an ice-filled highball glass. Top with soda water. Dress with a slice of lemon and orange. Serve with straws.

Skokiaan (S.Afr). A highly alcoholic beverage which is consumed by the black Africans in their Shebeens.

Skol-Caracu (Bra). A brewing group linked with Labatt of Canada.

Skol Lager (Eng). First brewed in Holland in 1959. Now is brewed internationally. Owned by Allied Breweries who brew keg Skol 1037 O.G. in Alloa (Scot), Burton, Romford and Wrexham (Wales), bottled/canned 1035 O.G. Skol Special Strength 1046 O.G. and Extra Strength 1080 O.G.

Skona Lager (Eng). A canned Lager beer 1032 O.G. brewed by the Hall and Woodhouse Brewery in Dorset.

Skopelos (Gre). An eastern Mediterranean island that produces wines similar to Malmsey.

Skopje (Yug). A wine-producing region in southern Yugoslavia. Produces mainly red wines.

Skull Attack (Wales). A cask conditioned Best Bitter 1042 O.G. brewed by the Brains Brewery in Cardiff.

Skunky (USA). A description of the odour that a beer may have when opened if it has been stored in strong sunlight.

Skurkerabát (Hun). A white grape variety used in Tokay production.

Skyscraper Cocktail (Cktl). ⅜ measure Gin, ¼ measure dry Vermouth, ⅛ measure orange Curaçao, ⅛ measure lemon juice, ⅛ measure Grenadine, dash Angostura. Shake over ice, strain into a cocktail glass.

Sky Vineyards (USA). A winery based in the Sonoma County, California. Grape variety – Zinfandel.

Sladko Vino (Bul). Sweet wine.

Slàinte Mhath (Scot). Gaelic for 'Good health'. Used when drinking a toast with Whisky.

Slake (Eng). To satisfy, e.g. 'to slake one's thirst'.

Slalom (Cktl). ¼ measure Cointreau, ½ measure Bacardi White Label, ¼ measure lime juice. Shake over ice, strain into a cocktail glass. Add an olive.

Slalom Lager (Eng). A Lager beer 1036 O.G. brewed by Matthew Brown of Lakeland Lager Brewery in Workington, Cumbria. Produces keg/bottled Slalom D. 1045 O.G. and Slalom International 1068 O.G.

Slamnak (Yug). The name given to a late-harvested Riesling wine from a Lutomer estate.

Slanghoek Co-operative (S.Afr). Based in Slanghoek. Address = Slanghoek Koöperatiewe Wynkelder, Box 75, Rawsonville 6845. Produces varietal wines.

Slanghoek Koöperatiewe Wynkelder (S.Afr). See Slanghoek Co-operative.

Slankamenkarebe (Aus). An ancient red grape variety rarely grown nowadays.

Slantchev Birag (Bul). Lit – 'Sunshine coast'. A basic dry white wine made from the Rcakztelli grape. Strong and full-bodied.

Slate (Eng) (slang). A term used for obtaining drinks without payment (on tick, to be paid for at a later date). An illegal practice. The term derives from the nineteenth century when the debts would be chalked on a slate.

Slaterand Scott's Grassy Green (Scot). A John Walker and Sons light, fresh blended Scotch whisky produced for the French market.

Slate Square (Eng). See Square.

Slatko (Yug). Sweet.

Slavia (Fr). A Bière brewed by the Union des Brasseries group.

Slav Oak (USA) (abbr). Cooperage from European grown oak originating in Yugoslavia.

Slavonia (Yug). A wine region based on the Hungarian border in northern Croatia.

Slavonski Brod (Yug). A wine-producing town based in northern Croatia.

Slavyanskoye (USSR). A heavily-hopped beer brewed by the Yantar Brewery.

Sleeper (USA). The term given to a wine that is rather special but has not yet been fully recognised.

Sleepiness (Ger). A term used to describe grapes attacked by botrytis cinerea.

Sleeping Draught (Eng) (slang). For a strong bedtime drink or for any drink that contains a drug that induces sleep.

Sleeve (Eng). The name given to a straight glass with no handle.

Sleutel (Hol). See De Sleutel.

Sleutel Brouwerij (Hol). A brewery based at Dordrecht, southern Holland. No longer brews. Owned by Heineken, the name is still used. See De Sleutel.

Slewed (Eng) (slang). Drunk, intoxicated.

Slibovitza (Rum). Slivovitz. (plum brandy).

Slibowitz (Ger). Slivovitz.

Slim and Trim Cocktail (Cktl). 1½ measures dry Gin, 4 measures grapefruit juice, artificial sweetener to taste. Shake over ice, strain into a scooped out grapefruit shell with crushed ice, Serve with straws.

Slim Jane (Cktl).(Non-alc). Equal quantities of orange juice and tomato juice. Shake over ice with a dash of Worcestershire sauce. Strain into a goblet.

Slim Jim (Cktl).(Non-alc). Equal quantities of grapefruit juice and tomato juice. Shake over ice with a dash of Worcestershire sauce. Strain into a goblet.

Slim Jim (USA). Another name for a highball glass.

Slimline (Eng). A range of low-calorie,

non-alcoholic, soft 'mixer' drinks from the Coca Cola and Schweppes Beverages Company.

Slimmer's Breakfast (Cktl). 1 egg, ⅓ pint cold tea, 1 teaspoon honey. Shake over ice, strain into a goblet.

Slimsta (Eng). The brand-name used by Britvic for a range of fruit crushes and mixers.

Slings (USA). Spirit, fruit juice and cordials served in tall glasses with ice.

Slip Slop (Eng). A seventeenth-century term for a weak (unappetising) drink.

Slipstream (Cktl). ¼ measure Brandy, ¼ measure Grand Marnier, ¼ measure Lillet, ¼ measure orange juice, 1 egg white, 2 dashes Angostura. Shake over ice, strain into a cocktail glass.

Slivovica (Yug). An alternative spelling of Sljivovica.

Slivovitz (Pol). A plum brandy made from the dark-blue Sliva plum. Fermented, double-distilled, aged in oak. Either colourless or pale gold in colour. See Slivovica, Slibovitza, Sljivovica. Also made from the Pozega plum. 45% alc. by vol.

Slivovitza (Yug). An alternative spelling of Sljivovica.

Slivovo (Hun). The local name given for plum brandy.

Slivowitz (Yug). An alternative spelling of Sljivovica.

Sliwowica (Pol). A potato Vodka flavoured with plum spirit produced by Polmos. 45% alc. by vol.

Sljivovica (Yug). A single distilled plum brandy 26% alc. by vol. Also spelt Slivovica, Slivowitz.

Sljivovica-Prepečenia (Yug). A double distilled plum brandy 40–50% alc. by vol.

Slodowe (Pol). A low-alcohol, dark Beer.

Sloeberry Cocktail (Cktl). ⅓ gill Sloe Gin, 1 dash Angostura. Stir over ice, strain into a cocktail glass.

Sloe Comfortable Screw (Cktl). ½ fl.oz. Sloe Gin, 1 fl.oz. Vodka, ½ fl.oz. Southern Comfort, 4 fl.ozs. orange juice. Pour ingredients into an ice-filled highball glass. See also Slow Comfortable Screw.

Sloe Driver (Cktl). As for a Screwdriver but using a measure of Sloe Gin in place of the Vodka.

Sloe Gin (Eng). A Sloe-flavoured Gin. Made by steeping ripe Sloes that have been pricked with a pin in Gin with sugar. Strained and bottled. Traditional name is Stirrup cup. 25% plus alc. by vol.

Sloe Gin Cocktail (Cktl). ½ measure Sloe Gin, ¼ measure dry Vermouth, ¼ measure sweet Vermouth. Stir over ice, strain into a cocktail glass.

Sloe Gin Collins (Cktl). ⅓ gill Sloe Gin, juice ½ lemon. Shake over ice, strain into an ice-filled collins glass, top with soda, decorate with a lemon slice, orange slice and a cherry. Serve with straws.

Sloe Gin Fizz (Cktl). 1 teaspoon powdered sugar, 1½ fl.ozs. Sloe Gin. Shake over ice, strain into an ice-filled highball. Top with soda water.

Sloe Gin Flip (Cktl). 1 egg, teaspoon sugar, 1 fl.oz. Sloe Gin, 1 fl.oz. cream. Shake over ice, strain into a flip glass, top with grated nutmeg.

Sloe Gin Rickey (Cktl). Put 2 ice cubes into a highball glass. Add juice of ½ lime, ¾ gill Sloe Gin, stir, top with soda water.

Sloe Tequila Cocktail (Cktl). ⅔ measure Tequila, ⅓ measure Sloe Gin, juice ¼ lime. Blend together with scoop of crushed ice in a blender. Pour into an ice-filled old-fashioned glass. Dress with sliced cucumber.

Sloe Vermouth (Cktl). ½ measure Sloe Gin, ½ measure French vermouth, ½ oz. lemon juice. Shake over ice, strain into a cocktail glass.

Sloppen (Hol). To sip.

Sloppy Joe (Cktl). 1 oz. Brandy, 2 ozs. pineapple juice, 1 oz. Port, 2 dashes Cointreau. Shake over ice, strain into a cocktail glass.

Sloppy Joe Cocktail (Cktl). ⅙ gill Bacardi White Label, ⅙ gill French vermouth, 2 dashes Grenadine, 2 dashes Cointreau, juice of a lime. Shake over ice, strain into a cocktail glass.

Slops (Eng). Denotes waste or spilt beer either from a drip trap sited below the beer tap or from half consumed glasses of beer.

Slops (Eng) (slang). For poor quality drink.

Slops (Scot). A term sometimes used for the residue in the Pot-still after the first distillation.

Sloshed (Eng) (slang). Drunk, intoxicated.

Slotsmøllen Brewery (Den). A brewery based in Kolding.

Slovenia (Yug). An alternative spelling of Slovenija.

Slovenian Summer (Punch). 1 bottle Yugoslavian riesling, 3 measures Amontillado sherry, 1 sliced lemon, borage. Mix together, chill down for 2 hours. Add 1 pint soda water, stir and serve in highball glasses with ice.

Slovenija (Yug). The best wine region. Main town – Lutomer. Districts – Maribor, Ptuj, Radgona and Lutomer-Ormoz. See Tiger Milk.

Slovenske (Yug). A wine produced in Slovenia.

Slovin (Yug). A popular brand of Slivovitz.

Slow Comfortable Screw (Cktl). ⅓ measure Sloe Gin, ⅓ measure Southern Comfort, ⅓ measure orange juice. Shake over ice, strain into a cocktail glass. See also Sloe Comfortable Screw.

Slow Fermentation (W.Ind). A method used in Rum production. May take 12 days. Dunder is included and produces a heavy-style Rum.

Sludge Wines (Eng). A term given to denote blended wines with many varieties of wines contained in it. Has little or no character or individuality. They are completely unmemorable and totally without personality.

Slug (Eng) (slang). For a drink of spirits.

Slug (USA) (slang). For a single measure of spirit, usually served in a very small glass and drunk in one mouthful.

Slug of Blue Fish-Hooks (USA) (slang). A term used in local inns for a measure of Applejack.

Šluknov Brewery (Czec). An old brewery c1514 based in north-western Czec.

Slurp (Eng). To drink noisily.

Small Beer (Eng). See Strong Ale.

Small Beer (Eng) (ancient). An old term for a weak, low quality beer.

Small Beer (Eng) (modern). A half-pint of draught beer or a half-pint bottle of beer.

Small Bulls Bitter (Eng). A Bitter beer brewed by the Mouldon's Brewery in Sudbury, Suffolk.

Smash (Cktl). ¼ measure Vodka, ¼ measure Mandarine Napoléon, ¼ measure blackberry liqueur, ¼ measure lemon juice. Shake over ice, strain into a cocktail glass. Top with a twist of orange peel juice.

Smashed (Eng) (slang). Denotes a very drunken person.

Smashes (USA). Spirit, sugar cubes, mint and fruit served over ice in an old-fashioned glass.

Smederevka (Yug). A white wine from the Smederevo area of the Serbia region. Made from the Smederevka and Welschriesling grape. Is also produced in Macedonia.

Smederevo (Yug). A wine-producing region based on the south bank of the river Danube. Is noted for its white wines made from the Smerderevka and Wälschriesling grapes.

Smeets Distillerie (Bel). A large distillery based in Hasselt which produces a fine range of Jenevers, Advocaat, cocktail and fruit liqueurs.

Smile Cocktail (Cktl). ⅙ gill dry Gin, ⅙ gill Grenadine, 2 dashes lemon juice. Shake over ice, strain into a cocktail glass.

Smiler (Cktl). ½ measure dry Gin, ¼ measure Italian vermouth, ¼ measure French vermouth, dash Angostura, 2 dashes orange juice. Shake over ice, strain into a cocktail glass.

Smiles Brewery (Eng). Based in Bristol. Noted for its cask conditioned Exhibition Bitter 1051 O.G. and Brewery Bitter 1036 O.G.

Smiling Cocktail (Cktl). ⅔ measure dry white wine, ⅓ measure dry ginger ale, dash Cognac. Stir gently over ice, strain into a Champagne saucer. Add a cherry and an orange slice.

Smiling Duchess (Cktl). ⅓ measure Lillet, ⅓ measure dry Gin, ⅙ measure Apricot brandy, ⅓ measure Crème de Noyeau. Stir over ice, strain into a cocktail glass, add a cherry.

Smiling Ivy (Cktl). ⅓ measure dark Rum, ⅓ measure Peach brandy, ⅓ measure pineapple juice, 1 egg white, dash lemon juice. Shake over ice, strain into a cocktail glass.

Smiling Through (Cktl). ⅓ measure Grand Marnier, ⅓ measure dark Rum, ⅓ measure Maraschino, dash lemon juice, dash Grenadine. Shake over ice, strain into a cocktail glass. Add a cherry.

Smirnoff (Pol). A Vodka that is now produced in the U.K. and USA. Two styles – White Label 65.5° proof and Blue Label 80° proof.

Smith Bowman Distillery (USA). A Bourbon whiskey distillery based in Sunset Hills, Fairfax County, Virginia. Noted for its fine Virginia Gentleman 45% alc. by vol.

Smith (George and J.G.) (Scot). Highland malt whisky distillers. The only distillers allowed to have exclusive use of The Glenlivet. Other distilleries may only hyphenate their names with Glenlivet. Part of Seagram. See Glenlivet (The).

Smith [John] (Eng). Based in Tadcaster, Yorks. Taken over by Courage in 1970. Noted for its cask conditioned John Smith Bitter 1036 O.G. keg Chestnut 1033 O.G. Midland Mild 1036 O.G. Tawny Light 1032 O.G. Old Tom 1037 O.G. Magnet 1040 O.G. John Smith's Lager 1036 O.G. and bottled Double Brown 1041 O.G. Also cask conditioned Yorkshire Bitter.

Smith-Madrone Vineyards (USA). A winery based near St. Helena, Napa Valley, California. Grape varieties – Cabernet sauvignon, Chardonnay, Johannisberg riesling and Pinot noir. Produces varietal wines.

Smith [Samuel] (Eng). The oldest brewery in Yorkshire based in Tadcaster. Still uses wooden casks. Noted for its cask conditiond ales.

Smithwicks Ale (Ire). A keg/bottled Ale 1036 O.G. brewed by the Irish Ale Brewery in Kilkenny.

Smith Woodhouse (Port). Vintage Port shippers. Vintages – 1870, 1872, 1873, 1875, 1878, 1880, 1881, 1884, 1887, 1890, 1896, 1897, 1900, 1904, 1908, 1912, 1917, 1920, 1924, 1927, 1935, 1945, 1947, 1950, 1955, 1960, 1963, 1966, 1970, 1975, 1977, 1980, 1983, 1985.

Smith Woodhouse Vale D. Maria (Port). A single quinta of Smith Woodhouse. Vintages – 1978, 1979.

Smoke Cured (Scot). Refers to the malted barley for Malt whisky which is peat smoked as it is dried. See Peat Reek.

Smoked Beer (Ger). See Rauchbier.

Smoke-room (Eng). Originally a room in a public house where customers retired to smoke. Now known as the lounge.

Smoky (Eng). A term used to describe the bouquet on some Chardonnay and Sauvignon blanc wines.

Smooth (Eng). A term used to describe wines that are mature and have rounded off the tannin, acidity and extract especially on the finish on the palate.

Smothers Winery (USA). A winery based in Santa Cruz Mountains, Santa Cruz, California. Grape varieties – Cabernet sauvignon, Chardonnay, Gewürztraminer, Johannisberg riesling, Pinot noir and Zinfandel. Produces varietal and table wines.

Smouch (Eng). An old brew of Ash tree leaves boiled in Iron sulphate with Sheep's dung for an imitation of black tea because true tea was so scarce. For green tea, elder buds were used. Produced mainly in the late eighteenth century c1784.

Smudge Pots (USA). Stoves that are burned through the night to protect the vines against frost.

Smugglers (Eng). A dark Barley wine 1070 O.G. brewed and bottled by the St. Austell Brewery in Cornwall.

Snake Bite (Eng). ½ pint Guinness and ½ pint Cider mixed.

Snake Bite (USA). ½ pint Lager and ½ pint Cider mixed.

Snake-in-the-Grass (Cktl). ¼ measure dry Vermouth, ¼ measure dry Gin, ¼ measure Cointreau, ¼ measure lemon juice. Shake over ice, strain into a cocktail glass.

Snaps (Den). An alternative spelling of Schnapps.

Snaps (Eng). An old slang name for a

drink made from an equal quantity of Gin and Schnapps.

Snifter (Eng) (slang). A quick drink.

Snifter (USA). A name given to the Nosing glass (balloon glass).

Snipe Vineyard (Eng). A vineyard based at Snipe Farm Road, Clopton, Woodbridge, Suffolk. Was first planted in 1977. 0.65 ha. Grape variety – Müller-Thurgau. Uses the Silver Snipe label.

Snob Screen (Eng). Above the bar counter, a pivoted screen which allowed the upper classes to drink in private in the nineteenth century.

Snowball (Cktl). 1 fl.oz. Advocaat, dash lime cordial. Shake well over ice, strain into an ice-filled highball glass, stir in lemonade. Decorate with a cherry and orange slice and serve with straws.

Snowball (Eng). A commercially made bottled cocktail by the Goldwell Co. Contains Advocaat, lime juice and lemonade.

Snowball Cocktail (Cktl).(1). ⅓ measure Gin, ⅙ measure Anisette, ⅙ measure (white) Crème de Menthe, ⅙ measure Crème de Violette, ⅙ measure sweetened cream. Shake over ice, strain into a cocktail glass.

Snowball Cocktail (Cktl).(2). ¾ measure Gin, ¼ measure Anisette, 1 fl.oz. cream. Shake over ice, strain into a cocktail glass.

Snow Cap Lager (Afr). A Lager beer brewed by the Tanzania Breweries in Tanzania.

Snowflake (China). The brand-name of a Lager-style beer.

Snowflake Cocktail (Cktl). ⅖ measure Vodka, ⅕ measure Advocaat, ⅖ measure orange juice, 2 dashes Southern Comfort, 2 dashes Galliano. Shake over ice, strain into a highball glass. Top with lemonade and a little cream. Dress with a cherry and a slice of orange.

Snug (Eng). A small room in a public house. Usually used for private drinking.

Snyder Cocktail (Cktl). ¾ measure dry Gin, ¼ measure Anisette, 1 fl.oz. cream. Shake over ice, strain into cocktail glass.

SO₂ (Eng) (abbr). Sulphur-dioxide.

Soak (Eng) (slang). The term for a person who is always intoxicated (drunk), who drinks excessively, who drinks continuously.

Soave (It). A small town 15 miles east of Verona in the Veneto. Name is given to famous dry white wine of region.

Soave (It). D.O.C. white wine from Veneto. Made from 70–90% Garganega and 10–30% Trebbiano di Soave. D.O.C. also applies to sparkling wines. Also Soave Classico. (see Classico). Is classed Superiore if total alc. content is 11.5% by vol.

Sober (Eng). Not intoxicated.

Soberano (Sp). A 2 year old brandy produced by Gonzalez Byass. 38% alc. by vol.

Sobernheim (Ger). Village. (Anb) = Nahe. (Ber) = Schloss Böckelheim. (Gro) = Paradiesgarten. (Vins) = Domberg, Marbach.

Sobernheim-Steinhardt (Ger). Village. (Anb) = Nahe. (Ber) = Schloss Böckelheim. (Gro) = Paradiesgarten. (Vins) = Johannisberg, Spitalberg.

Sober Sundae (Cktl).(Non-alc). ⅓ pint freshly brewed (iced) coffee, ¼ lemon, 1 scoop vanilla ice cream. Blend in a blender, pour into a highball glass. Top with soda water and ground cinnamon.

Sobota Brewery (Czec). A brewery based in Eastern Czec.

Sobr (Wales). Sober.

Sobre (Fr). Sober.

Sobreira (Port). Cork oak.

Sobrero (Port). Oak.

Sobretabla (Sp). In the Sherry region new fortified racked wine which is placed into cleaned casks. Fortified on top of wood.

Socalcos (Sp). The Galician name for vineyard terraces.

Sochu (Jap). A neutral spirit made from grain or sweet potatoes.

Sociale Cooperativa di Mezzocorona (It). A producer of sparkling wine made by the méthode champenoise in Trentino-Alto Adige. Labels include Rotari.

Social Wine (Eng). A term used for any wine that is drunk socially without food, e.g. sparkling wine.

Sociedad Agrícola (Sp). A large co-operative winery based in La Seca, Rueda. Is noted for its Verdejo Palido (a light, fruity, white wine).

Sociedade Agrícola da Quinta da Avelada (Port). A small winery based in northern Portugal. Produces Vinhos Verdes.

Sociedade Agrícola da Quinta de Santa Maria (Port). A large Vinho Verde producer. Address = Carreira, 4750 Barcelos. Owns the Quinta do Tamariz and Quinta da Portela vineyards.

Sociedade Agrícola dos Vinhos Messias (Port). A noted Portuguese producer of a sparkling wine by the méthode champenoise.

Sociedade Brasileira de Vinhos, Ltda (Bra). A leading wine-producer in Brazil.

Sociedade Central de Cervejas (Port). S.C.C. A brewery group which has ⅔ of the Portuguese market with their Preta and Sagres beers. Has plants at Coimbra and Vialonga.

Sociedade Com. Abel Pereira da Fonseca (Port). A winery based in the Dão region. Produces Viriatus (a Dão wine).

Sociedade Comercial dos Vinhos de Mesa de Portugal (Port). SOGRAPE. Largest wine producer. Includes Aveleda (Vinho Verde) and Mateus Rosé.

Sociedade Constantino (Port). Vintage Port shippers. Vintages – 1912, 1927, 1935, 1941, 1945, 1947, 1950, 1958, 1966.

Sociedade da Quinta da Aveleda (Port). See Quinta da Aveleda.

Sociedade dos Vinhos do Porto Constantino (Port). Noted shippers of Dão wines in northern Portugal.

Sociedade dos Vinhos Vice-Rei (Port). A noted shipper of Dão wines in northern Portugal.

Sociedade Vinhos Unico, Ltda (Bra). A leading wine-producer based in southern Brazil.

Sociedad General de Vinos (Sp). A bodega based in Elciego in the Rioja Alavesa.

Sociedad Vinícola Laserna (Sp). Founded in 1974 by Viña Real S.A. Address = Finca San Rafael, Laserna Laguardia, Alva. 59 ha. in the Rioja Alavesa. Grape varieties – Garnacha 7%, Graciano 5%, Mazuela 5%, Tempranillo 70% and Viura 13%. Only red wine is produced. See Viñedos del Contino.

Société Anonyme de Magenta (Fr). A Champagne producer. Produces – Vintage and non-vintage wines sold under the Marguerite Christel label. Vintages – 1971, 1973, 1976, 1981.

Société Civile de La Romanée-Conti (Fr). A seal seen on the label and cork of all wines from the Romanée-Conti wines. Owners of La Romanée-Conti in Vosne-Romanée, Côte de Nuits, Burgundy. Also owns La Tâche, Côte de Nuits, Burgundy.

Société Coopérative de Saint Yzans de Médoc (Fr). Address = 33340 St. Yzans de Médoc. A.C. Médoc. Commune = St. Yzans. Grape varieties – Cabernet 45% and Merlot 55%.

Société Coopérative Vigneronne des Grandes Caves Richon-le-Zion et Zikhron-Yaacv (Isr). A co-operative formed in the early 1900s. Produces 75% of Israel's wine under name of Carmel.

S

Société des Brasseries du Haut Ogooué (Afr). A brewery based in Gabon which brews a Pilsener-style Lager beer 6% alc. by vol.

Société des Produits d'Armagnac [Marquis de Montesquiou] (Fr). An Armagnac producer. Address = Route de Cazaubon, 32800 Eauze.

Société de Viticulture du Jura (Fr). A society for the information and promotion of Jura wines.

Société d'Intérêt Collective Agricole (Fr). See S.I.C.A.

Société Hellenique des Vins et Spiritueux (Gre). A large winery based in Greece.

Société Socovin (Afr). A winery based in Casablanca, Morocco. Is noted for its Domaine de Ben Naceaur.

Société Vinicole de Perroy (Switz). A wine-producer based in the Vaud.

Society Cocktail (Cktl). ⅔ measure dry Gin, ⅓ measure French vermouth, 2 dashes Grenadine. Stir over ice, strain into a cocktail glass.

Socio (Sp). The name given to a partner in a co-operative winery.

Soda Fountain (USA). The American name for a soda syphon.

Soda Fountain (USA). The service area in drug stores, etc. where soda water and carbonated drinks are dispensed.

Soda Jerk (USA) (slang). An old name for a person that serves at a soda fountain in a drug store.

Sodap (Cyp). Vine Products Co-operative Marketing Union Ltd. Founded in 1947. Based in Limassol and near Paphos, it works on behalf of the growers. Produces most styles of wines.

Soda Pop (USA). The name given to any carbonated soft drink.

Soda Tonic (USA). Tonic water.

Soda Water (Eng). A sparkling water containing alkaline bicarbonate of soda.

Sodden (Eng) (slang). A term used to describe a person who is drunk (intoxicated). Usually a person who is perpetually drunk.

Sodium Benzoate (Eng). A form of Benzoic acid which is used to stop a fermentation.

Soest (Ger). Village. (Anb) = Mosel-Saar-Ruwer. (Ber) = Obermosel. (Gro) = Gipfel. (Vins) = Sites not yet chosen.

Soet Hanepoot (S.Afr). A sweet dessert, golden, honey-flavoured wine from the Koelenhof Co-operative.

Soetwynboere Co-operative (S.Afr). Based in Montagu. Address = Soetwynboere Koöperasie, Box 127, Montagu 6720. Produces varietal wines.

Soetwynboere Koöperaise (S.Afr). See Soetwynboere Co-operative.

Soft (Eng). A term used to describe wines that have plenty of fruit on the palate. If wines are too soft they become weak and flabby.

Soft Drinks (Eng). A term given to non-alcoholic fruit drinks. i.e. lemonade, Coca cola, squashes etc.

Softening Wine (Eng). A wine used to soften hard (tannic) wines so as to make them mature earlier.

Soft Water (Eng). A water that has a low mineral content. Whilst it is not ideal for brewing ales, tea and coffee infuse more easily (although some quality in the taste is lost).

Soft Wines (USA). Wines that have a very low alcohol content.

Soge-Vinas (Sp). A large bodega in the Rioja. Owned by Pedro Domecq. Has 571 ha. in the Rioja Alavesa.

SOGRAPE (Port) (abbr). Sociedade Comercial dos Vinhos de Mesa de Portugal.

Sohnlein (Ger). A noted producer of Sekt by the cuve close method.

Söhrenberg (Ger). Vineyard. (Anb) = Württemberg. (Ber) = Remstal-Stuttgart. (Gro) = Kopf. (Vil) = Neustadt.

Soif (Fr). Thirst. Avoir soif = 'To have thirst'.

Soilly (Fr). A Cru Champagne village in the Canton de Dormans. District = Épernay.

Soir (Le) (Eng). The brand-name of up-market table wines by Grants of St. James.

Sojuzplodoimport (USSR). The Soviet foreign trade organisation. Was established in 1966.

Sokol Blosser Vineyards (USA). A winery based in Dundee, Williamette Valley, Oregon. Produces varietal wines.

Solado (It). An orange-flavoured liqueur.

Solaia (It). A red Vino da Tavola produced by Antinori in the Chianti Classico region from 25% Cabernet franc and 75% Cabernet sauvignon grapes.

Solano Brewery (USA). A brewery based in Solano, California. Is noted for its Steam beer.

Solano County (USA). A wine district in northern California. Produces most styles of wines.

Solanos (Sp). The name given to the warm winds from the east that blow over the Rioja region in the Spring.

Solar (Port). Manor, manor house.

Solar das Bouças (Port). A Vinho Verde producer. Address = Prozelo, 4720 Amares. Grape variety – Loureiro.

Solar e Francesas (Port). A winery based in Bairrada. Produces red and white wines.

Solar de Ribeiro (Port). A Vinho Verde producer. Address = S. Lourenço do Douro, 4630 Marco de Canaveses.

Solar de Samaniego (Sp). From the Bodegas Alavesas S.A. in Rioja. All classes of wines are produced.

Solbaerrom (Den). A fruity liqueur.

Sol de Mayo (Cktl). ½ measure Scotch whisky, ³⁄₁₀ measure orange juice, ⅕ measure Cointreau. Shake over ice, strain into a cocktail glass.

Solear (Sp). A term meaning 'sunning'. Describes the exposure of the grapes to the sun (Sol) for 24–48 hours in the Sherry region.

Soledad (USA). A noted wine town based in the Salinas Valley, Monterey, California.

Soleil de Sierra (Switz). A Vin de Paille wine from Sierre in Valais made from the Fendant and Malvasia grapes.

Soleil du Valais (Switz). A white wine produced in Valais from the Fendant grape.

Solera (Sp). A system of blending and maturing Sherry. Gives a consistent standard product. Consists of a series of casks from which a measured amount of wine is removed from one cask and is replaced by younger wine from another cask and so on.

Solera Madeira (Mad). On a label the date must be the date of the original wine. May start drawing off 10% of wine after 5 years. Solera may exist for only 10 years, it must then all be bottled or returned to stock lotes.

Solera Manzanilla (Sp). A full, dry, Manzanilla Sherry produced Antonio Barbadillo.

Solera Manzanilla Pasada (Sp). An old, pale, dry 20 year old Manzanilla Sherry produced by Barbadillo in Sanlúcar de Barrameda.

Solera 1900 (Sp). A Brandy produced by De Terry.

Solera 1914 (Sp). A fine, rare Amontillado Sherry produced by Berisfords.

Solera Selecta Brandy (Sp). A Brandy aged in American oak for 5 years. Produced by Torres in the Penedés region.

Solicchiato (It). A dessert wine produced at the Vila Fontana winery in Cerasuola di Vittoria in south-eastern Sicily.

Solide (Fr). Denotes a full-bodied, well-balanced wine.

Solijans (N.Z.). A winery based in Lincoln Road, Henderson, North Island. Noted for its Sherry-style wines. Also has a vineyard at Riverlea.

Solimar (Sp). The name used by De Muller for their inexpensive range of table wines.

Solitaire (Eng). A deep finger bowl with two lips used for inserting glasses in order to clean them or to chill them before use.

Söllingen (Ger). Village. (Anb) = Baden. (Ber) = Badische Bergstrasse/Kraichgau. (Gro) = Hohenberg. (Vin) = Rotenbusch.

Solnechnaya Dolina (USSR). A sweet white, dessert wine from the Crimean peninsula.

Solomon Cocktail (Cktl). ⅓ measure Advocaat, ⅓ measure orange juice, dash Cointreau. Shake over ice, strain into a flute glass, top with iced Champagne and a cherry.

Solonis (Fr). An American vine used for grafting in the Rhône.

Solopaca Bianco (It). D.O.C. white wine from Campania. Made from the Coda di volpe, Malvasia di candia, Malvasia toscana, Trebbiano toscano and Uva cerreto grapes grown in the commune of Solpaca plus 3 others in the province of Benevento.

Solopaca Rosso (It). D.O.C. red wine from Campania. Made from the Aglianico, Piedirosso, Sangiovese and Sciascinoso grapes grown in the commune of Solpaca and part of 3 others in the province of Benevento.

Solotoje Polje (USSR). A table wine produced near Cherson in the Ukraine.

Soluble Coffee (Eng). The old name for instant coffee.

Solubles (USA). The nickname for instant coffee.

Soluble Tea (Eng). See Instant Tea.

Soluble Tea (Jap). The alternative name for green tea powder.

Solutré-Pouilly (Fr). A town in the Mâconnais, southern Burgundy. Vineyards in the communes of Pouilly-Fuissé and Saint Véran.

Sol y Sombra (Sp). ½ measure Gin and ½ measure Spanish brandy. Lit – 'Sun and shadow'. Drunk by Spanish sailors.

Sol y Sombra Cocktail (Cktl). ½ measure golden Rum, ¾ measure Apricot brandy, ¼ measure white Rum, 1 measure pineapple juice, dash Angostura, juice ¼ lemon. Blend with a scoop of crushed ice in a blender. Pour into a scooped out pineapple shell, replace the top. Serve with straws pushed through the top.

S.O.M. (It) (abbr). Superior Old Marsala. the old style name, denotes ageing for two years and 18% alc. by vol.

Som (Rum). The local name for the Furmint grape.

Soma (Ind). An alcoholic beverage used in the (Vedu) Hindu religious ceremonies. Made from various plants.

Sombrero (Sp). The alternative name for

S

the 'cap' of skins that forms at the top of the fermenting vat.

Sombrero Cocktail (Cktl). 1 measure Kahlúa served frappé in a flute glass with fresh cream floated on top.

Somers Distillers (W.Ind). A noted liqueur producer in Bermuda. Noted for its Bermuda Gold.

Somerset Cider (Eng). A medium-sweet Cider produced by Showerings.

Somerset Cooler (Cktl).(Non-alc). ⅓ gill apple juice, ⅓ gill Ceylon tea, dash lemon juice, dash Gomme syrup. Stir over ice in a highball glass. Top with a slice of lemon.

Somerset Special (Eng). A cask conditioned Bitter 1043 O.G. brewed by the Hardington Brewery in Somerset.

Somerset Spring (Eng). A natural spring water bottled for the East Indies market by a small family firm.

Somerset West (S.Afr). A wine-producing area in the Cape province.

Something Special (Scot). A De Luxe Scotch whisky produced by Hill Thompson and Co. in Edinburgh. 40% alc. by vol. (Part of Seagram).

Somlauer Auslese (Hun). The name used to market Somloi Furmint.

Somló (Hun). A small wine-producing district in north-eastern Hungary. Noted for its quality dry, white wines produced from the Riesling and Furmint grapes. Also spelt Somlyó.

Somlói Furmint (Hun). A fragrant dry white wine produced in Somlyó on lake Balaton. See Somlauer Auslese.

Somlyó (Hun). See Somló.

Sommelier (Fr). Wine waiter. Also the name of a style of corkscrew. See Waiter's Friend.

Sommelier Winery (USA). A winery based in Mountain View, Santa Clara, California. Grape varieties – Cabernet sauvignon, Chardonnay, Petite syrah and Zinfandel. Produces varietal wines.

Sommerach (Ger). Village. (Anb) = Franken. (Ber) = Maindreieck. (Gro) = Kirchberg. (Vins) = Katzenkopf, Rosenberg.

Sommerau (Ger). Village. (Anb) = Mosel-Saar-Ruwer. (Ber) = Saar-Ruwer. (Gro) = Römerlay. (Vin) = Schlossberg.

Sommerberg (Ger). Vineyard. (Anb) = Baden. (Ber) = Markgräflerland. (Gro) = Lorettoberg. (Vil) = Ebringen.

Sommerberg (Ger). Vineyard. (Anb) = Württemberg. (Ber) = Kocher-Jagst-Tauber. (Gro) = Kocherberg. (Vil) = Criesbach.

Sommerberg (Ger). Vineyard. (Anb) = Württemberg. (Ber) = Württembergisch

Unterland. (Gro) = Schozachtal. (Vil) = Abstatt.

Sommerberg (Ger). Vineyard. (Anb) = Württemberg. (Ber) = Württembergisch Unterland. (Gro) = Schozachtal. (Vil) = Löwenstein.

Sommerberg (Ger). Vineyard. (Anb) = Württemberg. (Ber) = Württembergisch Unterland. (Gro) = Schozachtal. (Vil) = Unterheinriet.

Sommerhalde (Ger). Vineyard. (Anb) = Baden. (Ber) = Breisgau. (Gro) = Burg Lichteneck. (Vil) = Bombach.

Sommerhalde (Ger). Vineyard. (Anb) = Baden. (Ber) = Ortenau. (Gro) = Schloss Rodeck. (Vil) = Eisental.

Sommerhalde (Ger). Vineyard. (Anb) = Württemberg. (Ber) = Remstal-Stuttgart. (Gro) = Kopf. (Vil) = Korb.

Sommerhalde (Ger). Vineyard. (Anb) = Württemberg. (Ber) = Württembergisch Unterland. (Gro) = Salzberg. (Vil) = Eberstadt.

Sommerhausen (Ger). Village. (Anb) = Franken. (Ber) = Maindreieck. (Gro) = Not yet assigned. (Vins) = Reifenstein, Steinbach.

Sommerheil (Ger). Vineyard. (Anb) = Rheingau. (Ber) = Johannisberg. (Gro) = Daubhaus. (Vil) = Hochheim.

Sommerloch (Ger). Village. (Anb) = Nahe. (Ber) = Kreuznach. (Gro) = Pfarrgarten. (Vins) = Birkenberg, Ratsgrund, Sonnenberg, Steinrossel.

Sommerstuhl (Ger). Vineyard. (Anb) = Franken. (Ber) = Maindreieck. (Gro) = Ravensburg. (Vil) = Güntersleben.

Sommerwende (Ger). Vineyard. (Anb) = Rheinhessen. (Ber) = Wonnegau. (Gro) =˙ Bergkloster. (Vil) = Hangen-Weisheim.

Somontano (Sp). A Denominación de Origen based in western Spain.

Somosierra (Sp). The name of a still mineral water sourced at La Cabrera in the Somosierra mountains, central Spain. Bottled by Fonsana.

Songoularé Misket (Bul). A dry white wine from the Black Sea coast. Produced from the Misket grape.

Songurlare (Bul). A delimited wine-producing area in the eastern region of Bulgaria.

Sonne (Ger). Vineyard. (Anb) = Mittelrhein. (Ber) = Bacharach. (Gro) = Schloss Reichenstein. (Vil) = Oberheimbach.

Sonneck (Ger). Vineyard. (Anb) = Mosel-Saar-Ruwer. (Ber) = Zell/Mosel. (Gro) = Grafschaft. (Vil) = Bullay.

Sonneck (Ger). Vineyard. (Anb) = Mosel-Saar-Ruwer. (Ber) = Zell/Mosel. (Gro) = Schwarze Katz. (Vil) = Zell-Merl.

Sonnelle (Eng). A producer of a range of canned wines.

Sonnema (Hol). A producer of Beerenburg, an aromatic bitters.

Sonnenberg (Ger). Lit – 'Sunny hill'. A popular name for south facing vineyards in Germany. There are 71 individual sites within the wine regions.

Sonnenberg (Ger). Vineyard. (Anb) = Ahr. (Ber) = Walporzheim/Ahrtal. (Gro) = Klosterberg. (Vil) = Bad Neuenahr.

Sonnenberg (Ger). Vineyard. (Anb) = Baden. (Ber) = Badische Bergstrasse/Kraichgau. (Gro) = Hohenberg. (Vil) = Berghausen.

Sonnenberg (Ger). Vineyard. (Anb) = Baden. (Ber) = Badische Bergstrasse/Kraichgau. (Gro) = Rittersberg. (Vil) = Laudenbach.

Sonnenberg (Ger). Vineyard. (Anb) = Baden. (Ber) = Badische Bergstrasse/Kraichgau. (Gro) = Stiftsberg. (Vil) = Eichtersheim.

Sonnenberg (Ger). Vineyard. (Anb) = Baden. (Ber) = Badische Bergstrasse/Kraichgau. (Gro) = Stiftsberg. (Vil) = Eschelbach.

Sonnenberg (Ger). Vineyard. (Anb) = Baden. (Ber) = Badische Bergstrasse/Kraichgau. (Gro) = Stiftsberg. (Vil) = Michelfeld.

Sonnenberg (Ger). Vineyard. (Anb) = Baden. (Ber) = Badische Bergstrasse/Kraichgau. (Gro) = Stiftsberg. (Vil) = Waldangelloch.

Sonnenberg (Ger). Vineyard. (Anb) = Baden. (Ber) = Badische Frankenland. (Gro) = Tauberklinge. (Vil) = Dertingen.

Sonnenberg (Ger). Vineyard. (Anb) = Baden. (Ber) = Badische Frankenland. (Gro) = Tauberklinge. (Vil) = Kembach.

Sonnenberg (Ger). Vineyard. (Anb) = Baden. (Ber) = Breisgau. (Gro) = Burg Zähringen. (Vil) = Wildtal.

Sonnenberg (Ger). Vineyard. (Anb) = Baden. (Ber) = Kaiserstuhl-Tuniberg. (Gro) = Attilafelsen. (Vil) = Opfingen.

Sonnenberg (Ger). Vineyard. (Anb) = Baden. (Ber) = Ortenau. (Gro) = Schloss Rodeck. (Vil) = Sinzheim.

Sonnenberg (Ger). Vineyard. (Anb) = Baden. (Ber) = Ortenau. (Gro) = Schloss Rodeck. (Vil) = Varnhalt.

Sonnenberg (Ger). Vineyard. (Anb) = Franken. (Ber) = Maindreieck. (Gro) = Hofrat. (Vil) = Marktbreit.

Sonnenberg (Ger). Vineyard. (Anb) = Franken. (Ber) = Maindreieck. (Gro) = Kirchberg. (Vil) = Untereisenheim.

Sonnenberg (Ger). Vineyard. (Anb) = Mittelrhein. (Ber) = Rheinburgengau. (Gro) = Burg Hammerstein. (Vil) = Unkel.

Sonnenberg (Ger). Vineyard. (Anb) = Mosel-Saar-Ruwer. (Ber) = Bernkastel. (Gro) = Sankt Michael. (Vil) = Schleich.

Sonnenberg (Ger). Vineyard. (Anb) = Mosel-Saar-Ruwer. (Ber) = Saar-Ruwer. (Gro) = Römerlay. (Vil) = Trier.

Sonnenberg (Ger). Vineyard. (Anb) = Mosel-Saar-Ruwer. (Ber) = Saar-Ruwer. (Gro) = Römerlay. (Vil) = Waldrach.

Sonnenberg (Ger). Vineyard. (Anb) = Mosel-Saar-Ruwer. (Ber) = Saar-Ruwer. (Gro) = Scharzberg. (Vil) = Irsch.

Sonnenberg (Ger). Vineyard. (Anb) = Mosel-Saar-Ruwer. (Ber) = Saar-Ruwer. (Gro) = Scharzberg. (Vil) = Kanzem.

Sonnenberg (Ger). Vineyard. (Anb) = Mosel-Saar-Ruwer. (Ber) = Saar-Ruwer. (Gro) = Scharzberg. (Vil) = Mennig.

Sonnenberg (Ger). Vineyard. (Anb) = Mosel-Saar-Ruwer. (Ber) = Zell/Mosel. (Gro) = Goldbäumchen. (Vil) = Cochem.

Sonnenberg (Ger). Vineyard. (Anb) = Nahe. (Ber) = Kreuznach. (Gro) = Pfarrgarten. (Vil) = Dalberg.

Sonnenberg (Ger). Vineyard. (Anb) = Nahe. (Ber) = Kreuznach. (Gro) = Pfarrgarten. (Vil) = Hergenfeld.

Sonnenberg (Ger). Vineyard. (Anb) = Nahe. (Ber) = Kreuznach. (Gro) = Pfarrgarten. (Vil) = Schöneberg.

Sonnenberg (Ger). Vineyard. (Anb) = Nahe. (Ber) = Kreuznach. (Gro) = Pfarrgarten. (Vil) = Sommerloch.

Sonnenberg (Ger). Vineyard. (Anb) = Nahe. (Ber) = Kreuznach. (Gro) = Schlosskapelle. (Vil) = Guldental.

Sonnenberg (Ger). Vineyard. (Anb) = Nahe. (Ber) = Schloss Böckelheim. (Gro) = Burgweg. (Vil) = Norheim.

Sonnenberg (Ger). Vineyard. (Anb) = Nahe. (Ber) = Schloss Böckelheim. (Gro) = Paradiesgarten. (Vil) = Nussbaum.

Sonnenberg (Ger). Vineyard. (Anb) = Nahe. (Ber) = Schloss Böckelheim. (Gro) = Rosengarten. (Vil) = Roxheim.

Sonnenberg (Ger). Vineyard. (Anb) = Rheingau. (Ber) = Johannisberg. (Gro) = Steinmacher. (Vil) = Eltville.

Sonnenberg (Ger). Vineyard. (Anb) = Rheinhessen. (Ber) = Bingen. (Gro) = Abtey. (Vil) = Sprendlingen.

Sonnenberg (Ger). Vineyard. (Anb) = Rheinhessen. (Ber) = Bingen. (Gro) = Kaiserpfalz. (Vil) = Ingelheim.

Sonnenberg (Ger). Vineyard. (Anb) = Rheinhessen. (Ber) = Bingen. (Gro) = Kaiserpfalz. (Vil) = Schwabenheim.

Sonnenberg (Ger). Vineyard. (Anb) = Rheinhessen. (Ber) = Bingen. (Gro) = Kurfürstenstück. (Vil) = Vendersheim.

Sonnenberg (Ger). Vineyard. (Anb) = Rheinhessen. (Ber) = Bingen. (Gro) = Eheingrafenstein. (Vil) = Hackenheim.

Sonnenberg (Ger). Vineyard. (Anb) = Rheinhessen. (Ber) = Bingen. (Gro) = Rheingrafenstein. (Vil) = Stein-Bockenheim.

Sonnenberg (Ger). Vineyard. (Anb) = Rheinhessen. (Ber) = Bingen. (Gro) = Rheingrafenstein. (Vil) = Wonsheim.

Sonnenberg (Ger). Vineyard. (Anb) = Rheinhessen. (Ber) = Bingen. (Gro) = Sankt Rochuskapelle. (Vil) = Aspisheim.

Sonnenberg (Ger). Vineyard. (Anb) = Rheinhessen. (Ber) = Bingen. (Gro) = Sankt Rochuskapelle. (Vil) = Pfaffen-Schwabenheim.

Sonnenberg (Ger). Vineyard. (Anb) = Rheinhessen. (Ber) = Nierstein. (Gro) = Domherr. (Vil) = Udenheim.

Sonnenberg (Ger). Vineyard. (Anb) = Rheinhessen. (Ber) = Nierstein. (Gro) = Gutes Domtal. (Vil) = Nieder-Olm.

Sonnenberg (Ger). Vineyard. (Anb) = Rheinhessen. (Ber) = Nierstein. (Gro) = Krötenbrunnen. (Vil) = Guntersblum.

Sonnenberg (Ger). Vineyard. (Anb) = Rheinhessen. (Ber) = Nierstein. (Gro) = Petersberg. (Vil) = Bechtolsheim.

Sonnenberg (Ger). Vineyard. (Anb) = Rheinhessen. (Ber) = Nierstein. (Gro) = Rheinblick. (Vil) = Alsheim.

Sonnenberg (Ger). Vineyard. (Anb) = Rheinhessen. (Ber) = Wonnegau. (Gro) = Bergkloster. (Vil) = Gundheim.

Sonnenberg (Ger). Vineyard. (Anb) = Rheinhessen. (Ber) = Wonnegau. (Gro) = Domblick. (Vil) = Hohen-Sülzen.

Sonnenberg (Ger). Vineyard. (Anb) = Rheinhessen. (Ber) = Wonnegau. (Gro) = Sybillenstein. (Vil) = Heimersheim.

Sonnenberg (Ger). Vineyard. (Anb) = Rheinpfalz. (Ber) = Mittelhaardt-Deutsche Weinstrasse. (Gro) = Feuerberg. (Vil) = Ellerstadt.

Sonnenberg (Ger). Vineyard. (Anb) = Rheinpfalz. (Ber) = Mittelhaardt-Deutsche Weinstrasse. (Gro) = Grafenstück. (Vil) = Bockenheim.

Sonnenberg (Ger). Vineyard. (Anb) = Rheinpfalz. (Ber) = Mittelhaardt-Deutsche Weinstrasse. (Gro) = Grafenstück. (Vil) = Kindenheim.

Sonnenberg (Ger). Vineyard. (Anb) = Rheinpfalz. (Ber) = Mittelhaardt-Deutsche Weinstrasse. (Gro) = Grafenstück. (Vil) = Obrigheim.

Sonnenberg (Ger). Vineyard. (Anb) = Rheinpfalz. (Ber) = Mittelhaardt-Deutsche Weinstrasse. (Gro) = Hofstück. (Vil) = Gönnheim.

Sonnenberg (Ger). Vineyard. (Anb) =

Rheinpfalz. (Ber) = Mittelhaardt-Deutsche Weinstrasse. (Gro) = Höllenpfad. (Vil) = Neuleiningen.

Sonnenberg (Ger). Vineyard. (Anb) = Rheinpfalz. (Ber) = Mittelhaardt-Deutsche Weinstrasse. (Gro) = Kobnert. (Vil) = Weisenheim am Berg.

Sonnenberg (Ger). Vineyard. (Anb) = Rheinpfalz. (Ber) = Südliche Weinstrasse. (Gro) = Guttenberg. (Vil) = Oberotterbach.

Sonnenberg (Ger). Vineyard. (Anb) = Rheinpfalz. (Ber) = Südliche Weinstrasse. (Gro) = Guttenberg. (Vil) = Schweigen-Rechtenbach.

Sonnenberg (Ger). Vineyard. (Anb) = Rheinpfalz. (Ber) = Südliche Weinstrasse. (Gro) = Guttenberg. (Vil) = Schweighofen.

Sonnenberg (Ger). Vineyard. (Anb) = Rheinpfalz. (Ber) = Südliche Weinstrasse. (Gro) = Herrlich. (Vil) = Leinsweiler.

Sonnenberg (Ger). Vineyard. (Anb) = Rheinpfalz. (Ber) = Südliche Weinstrasse. (Gro) = Trappenberg. (Vil) = Essingen.

Sonnenberg (Ger). Vineyard. (Anb) = Württemberg. (Ber) = Remstal-Stuttgart. (Gro) = Wartbühl. (Vil) = Beutelsbach.

Sonnenberg (Ger). Vineyard. (Anb) = Württemberg. (Ber) = Remstal-Stuttgart. (Gro) = Wartbühl. (Vil) = Geradstetten.

Sonnenberg (Ger). Vineyard. (Anb) = Württemberg. (Ber) = Remstal-Stuttgart. (Gro) = Wartbühl. (Vil) = Kleinheppach.

Sonnenberg (Ger). Vineyard. (Anb) = Württemberg. (Ber) = Remstal-Stuttgart. (Gro) = Wartbühl. (Vil) = Schnait i. R.

Sonnenberg (Ger). Vineyard. (Anb) = Württemberg. (Ber) = Württembergisch Unterland. (Gro) = Heuchelberg. (Vil) = Schwaigern.

Sonnenberg (Ger). Vineyard. (Anb) = Württemberg. (Ber) = Württembergisch Unterland. (Gro) = Heuchelberg. (Vil) = Stetten a. H.

Sonnenberg (Ger). Vineyard. (Anb) = Württemberg. (Ber) = Württembergisch Unterland. (Gro) = Kirchenweinberg. (Vil) = Flein.

Sonnenberg (Ger). Vineyard. (Anb) = Württemberg. (Ber) = Württembergisch Unterland. (Gro) = Kirchenweinberg. (Vil) = Heilbronn.

Sonnenberg (Ger). Vineyard. (Anb) = Württemberg. (Ber) = Württembergisch Unterland. (Gro) = Kirchenweinberg. (Vil) = Talheim.

Sonnenberg (Ger). Vineyard. (Anb) = Württemberg. (Ber) = Württembergisch Unterland. (Gro) = Stromberg. (Vil) = Bönnigheim.

Sonnenborn (Ger). Grosslage. (Anb) = Nahe. (Ber) = Kreuznach. (Vil) = Langenlonsheim.

Sonnenbräu Brauerei (Switz). A brewery based in Rebstein. Is part of the Interbeva group.

Sonnenbrunnen (Ger). Vineyard. (Anb) = Baden. (Ber) = Markgräflerland. (Gro) = Vogtei Rötteln. (Vil) = Lörrach.

Sonnenbückel (Ger). Vineyard. (Anb) = Franken. (Ber) = Bayer Bodensee. (Gro) = Lindauer Seegarten. (Vil) = Nonnenhorn.

Sonnenbühl (Ger). Grosslage. (Anb) = Württemberg. (Ber) = Remstal-Stuttgart. (Vils) = Beutelsbach, Schnait i. R, Endersbach, Rommelshausen Stetten i. R, Strümpfelbach.

Sonnengarten (Ger). Vineyard. (Anb) = Rheinpfalz. (Ber) = Mittelhaardt-Deutsche Weinstrasse. (Gro) = Schwarzerde. (Vil) = Laumersheim.

Sonnengold (Ger). Vineyard. (Anb) = Mosel-Saar-Rower. (Ber) = Zell/Mosel. (Gro) = Goldbäumchen. (Vil) = Klotten.

Sonnengold (N.Z.). The brand-name of a Chasselas varietal wine produced by the Glenvale Winery, Hawkes Bay.

Sonnenhalde (Ger). Vineyard. (Anb) = Baden. (Ber) = Bodensee. (Gro) = Sonnenufer. (Vil) = Konstanz.

Sonnenhalden (Ger). Vineyard. (Anb) = Württemberg. (Ber) = Kocher-Jagst-Tauber. (Gro) = Tauberberg. (Vil) = Kressbronn am Bodensee Tubingen (ortsteil Hirschau, Unterjesingen).

Sonnenhang (Ger). Vineyard. (Anb) = Rheinhessen. (Ber) = Bingen. (Gro) = Kaiserpfalz. (Vil) = Ingelheim.

Sonnenhang (Ger). Vineyard. (Anb) = Rheinhessen. (Ber) = Nierstein. (Gro) = Domherr. (Vil) = Schornsheim.

Sonnenhang (Ger). Vineyard. (Anb) = Rheinhessen. (Ber) = Nierstein. (Gro) = Krötenbrunnen. (Vil) = Eimsheim.

Sonnenhang (Ger). Vineyard. (Anb) = Rheinhessen. (Ber) = Nierstein. (Gro) = Krötenbrunnen. (Vil) = Guntersblum.

Sonnenköpfchen (Ger). Vineyard. (Anb) = Rheinhessen. (Ber) = Bingen. (Gro) = Rheingrafenstein. (Vil) = Eckelsheim.

Sonnenküste (Bul). The brand-name of a medium-sweet white wine produced from the Rcatzitelli grape and sold in Germany.

Sonnenlauf (Ger). Vineyard. (Anb) = Nahe. (Ber) = Kreuznach. (Gro) = Pfarrgarten. (Vil) = Gutenberg.

Sonnenlay (Ger). Vineyard. (Anb) = Mittelrhein. (Ber) = Rheinburgengau. (Gro) = Gedeonseck. (Vil) = Rhens.

Sonnenlay (Ger). Vineyard. (Anb) = Mosel-Saar-Ruwer. (Ber) = Bernkastel. (Gro) = Kurfürsylay. (Vil) = Mülheim.

Sonnenlay (Ger). Vineyard. (Anb) = Mosel-Saar-Ruwer. (Ber) = Bernkastel. (Gro) = Sankt Michael. (Vil) = Ensch.

Sonnenlay (Ger). Vineyard. (Anb) = Mosel-Saar-Ruwer. (Ber) = Bernkastel. (Gro) = Schwarzlay. (Vil) = Traben-Trarbach (ortsteil Wolf).

Sonnenleite (Ger). Vineyard. (Anb) = Franken. (Ber) = Maindreieck. (Gro) = Honigberg. (Vil) = Dettelbach.

Sonnenleite (Ger). Vineyard. (Anb) = Franken. (Ber) = Maindreieck. (Gro) = Kirchberg. (Vil) = Krautheim.

Sonnenmorgen (Ger). Vineyard. (Anb) = Nahe. (Ber) = Kreuznach. (Gro) = Schlosskapelle. (Vil) = Windesheim.

Sonnenplätzchen (Ger). Vineyard. (Anb) = Nahe. (Ber) = Schloss Böckelheim. (Gro) = Paradiesgarten. (Vil) = Obermoschel.

Sonnenring (Ger). Vineyard. (Anb) = Mosel-Saar-Ruwer. (Ber) = Zell/Mosel. (Gro) = Goldbäumchen. (Vil) = Münden.

Sonnenring (Ger). Vineyard. (Anb) = Mosel-Saar-Ruwer. (Ber) = Zell/Mosel. (Gro) = Weinhex. (Vil) = Löf.

Sonnenschein (Ger). Vineyard. (Anb) = Ahr. (Ber) = Walporzheim/Ahrtal. (Gro) = Klosterberg. (Vil) = Bachem.

Sonnenschein (Ger). Vineyard. (Anb) = Franken. (Ber) = Maindreieck. (Gro) = Not yet assigned. (Vil) = Veitshöchheim.

Sonnenseite (Ger). Vineyard. (Anb) = Mosel-Saar-Ruwer. (Ber) = Bernkastel. (Gro) = Kurfürstlay. (Vil) = Wintrich.

Sonnenseite ob der Bruck (Ger). Vineyard. (Anb) = Baden. (Ber) = Badische Bergstrasse/Kraichgau. (Gro) = Rittersberg. (Vil) = Heidelberg.

Sonnenstock (Ger). Vineyard. (Anb) = Mittelrhein. (Ber) = Rheinburgengau. (Gro) = Schloss Schönburg. (Vil) = Damscheid.

Sonnenstück (Ger). Vineyard. (Anb) = Baden. (Ber) = Markgräflerland. (Gro) = Burg Neuenfels. (Vil) = Bad Bellingen.

Sonnenstück (Ger). Vineyard. (Anb) = Baden. (Ber) = Markgräflerland. (Gro) = Burg Neuenfels. (Vil) = Liel.

Sonnenstück (Ger). Vineyard. (Anb) = Baden. (Ber) = Markgräflerland. (Gro) = Burg Neuenfels. (Vil) = Mauchen.

Sonnenstück (Ger). Vineyard. (Anb) = Baden. (Ber) = Markgräflerland. (Gro)

= Burg Neuenfels. (Vil) = Niedereggenen.

Sonnenstück (Ger). Vineyard. (Anb) = Baden. (Ber) = Markgräflerland. (Gro) = Burg Neuenfels. (Vil) = Schliengen.

Sonnenstück (Ger). Vineyard. (Anb) = Baden. (Ber) = Markgräflerland. (Gro) = Burg Neuenfels. (Vil) = Steinenstadt.

Sonnenstück (Ger). Vineyard. (Anb) = Rheinpfalz. (Ber) = Mittelhaardt-Deutsche Weinstrasse. (Gro) = Schnepfenflug vom Kellertal. (Vil) = Immesheim.

Sonnenstuhl (Ger). Vineyard. (Anb) = Franken. (Ber) = Maindreieck. (Gro) = Ewig Leben. (Vil) = Randersacker.

Sonnenufer (Ger). Grosslage. (Anb) = Baden. (Ber) = Bodensee. (Vils) = Bermatingen, Bodman, Hagnau, Hilzingen, Immenstaad, Kippenhausen, Konstanz, Markdorf, Meersburg, Oberuhldingen, Reichenau, Salem (ortsteil Kirchberg), Singen, Stetten, Überlingen.

Sonnenuhr (Ger). Vineyard. (Anb) = Mosel-Saar-Ruwer. (Ber) = Bernkastel. (Gro) = Kurfürstlay. (Vil) = Maring-Noviand.

Sonnenuhr (Ger). Vineyard. (Anb) = Mosel-Saar-Ruwer. (Ber) = Bernkastel. (Gro) = Michelsberg. (Vil) = Neumagen-Dhron.

Sonnenuhr (Ger). Vineyard. (Anb) = Mosel-Saar-Ruwer. (Ber) = Bernkastel. (Gro) = Münzlay. (Vil) = Wehlen.

Sonnenuhr (Ger). Vineyard. (Anb) = Mosel-Saar-Ruwer. (Ber) = Bernkastel. (Gro) = Münzlay. (Vil) = Zeltingen-Rachtig.

Sonnenuhr (Ger). Vineyard. (Anb) = Mosel-Saar-Ruwer. (Ber) = Zell/Mosel. (Gro) = Goldbäumchen. (Vil) = Pommern.

Sonnenweg (Ger). Vineyard. (Anb) = Nahe. (Ber) = Kreuznach. (Gro) = Pfarrgarten. (Vil) = Wallhausen.

Sonnenweg (Ger). Vineyard. (Anb) = Rheinhessen. (Ber) = Nierstein. (Gro) = Krötenbrunnen. (Vil) = Gimbsheim.

Sonnenwinkel (Ger). Vineyard. (Anb) = Franken. (Ber) = Steigerwald. (Gro) = Not yet assigned. (Vil) = Altmannsdorf.

Sonnhalde (Ger). Vineyard. (Anb) = Baden. (Ber) = Breisgau. (Gro) = Burg Zähringen. (Vil) = Buchholz.

Sonnhalde (Ger). Vineyard. (Anb) = Baden. (Ber) = Breisgau. (Gro) = Burg Zähringen. (Vil) = Denzlingen.

Sonnhalde (Ger). Vineyard. (Anb) = Baden. (Ber) = Breisgau. (Gro) = Burg Zähringen. (Vil) = Sexau.

Sonnhalde (Ger). Vineyard. (Anb) = Baden. (Ber) = Markgräflerland. (Gro) = Burg Neuenfels. (Vil) = Müllheim.

Sonnheil (Ger). Vineyard. (Anb) = Rheinhessen. (Ber) = Nierstein. (Gro) = Krötenbrunnen. (Vil) = Hillesheim.

Sonnhohle (Ger). Vineyard. (Anb) = Baden. (Ber) = Markgräflerland. (Gro) = Burg Neuenfels. (Vil) = Britzingen.

Sonnhohle (Ger). Vineyard. (Anb) = Baden. (Ber) = Markgräflerland. (Gro) = Burg Neuenfels. (Vil) = Britzingen (ortsteil Dattingen).

Sonnhohle (Ger). Vineyard. (Anb) = Baden. (Ber) = Markgräflerland. (Gro) = Lorettoberg. (Vil) = Heitersheim.

Sonnhohle (Ger). Vineyard. (Anb) = Baden. (Ber) = Markgräflerland. (Gro) = Vogtei Rötteln. (Vil) = Binzen.

Sonnhohle (Ger). Vineyard. (Anb) = Baden. (Ber) = Markgräflerland. (Gro) = Vogtei Rötteln. (Vil) = Sfringen-Kirchen.

Sonnhohle (Ger). Vineyard. (Anb) = Baden. (Ber) = Markgräflerland. (Gro) = Vogtei Rötteln. (Vil) = Egringen.

Sonnhohle (Ger). Vineyard. (Anb) = Baden. (Ber) = Markgräflerland. (Gro) = Vogtei Rötteln. (Vil) = Eimeldingen.

Sonnhohle (Ger). Vineyard. (Anb) = Baden. (Ber) = Markgräflerland. (Gro) = Vogtei Rötteln. (Vil) = Fischingen.

Sonnhohle (Ger). Vineyard. (Anb) = Baden. (Ber) = Markgräflerland. (Gro) = Vogtei Rötteln. (Vil) = Hertingen.

Sonnhohle (Ger). Vineyard. (Anb) = Baden. (Ber) = Markgräflerland. (Gro) = Vogtei Rötteln. (Vil) = Ötlingen.

Sonnhohle (Ger). Vineyard. (Anb) = Baden. (Ber) = Markgräflerland. (Gro) = Vogtei Rötteln. (Vil) = Rummingen.

Sonnhohle (Ger). Vineyard. (Anb) = Baden. (Ber) = Markgräflerland. (Gro) = Vogtei Rötteln. (Vil) = Schallbach.

Sonntagsberg (Ger). Vineyard. (Anb) = Württemberg. (Ber) = Württembergisch Unterland. (Gro) = Heuchelberg. (Vil) = Heilbronn (ortsteil Klingenberg).

Sonntagsberg (Ger). Vineyard. (Anb) = Württemberg. (Ber) = Württembergisch Unterland. (Gro) = Heuchelberg. (Vil) = Nordhausen.

Sonntagsberg (Ger). Vineyard. (Anb) = Württemberg. (Ber) = Württembergisch Unterland. (Gro) = Heuchelberg. (Vil) = Nordheim.

Sonny Boy (Cktl). ½ fl.oz. orange Curaçao, ½ fl.oz. Peach brandy, 2 dashes Angostura. Shake over ice, strain into a Champagne flute. Fill with iced Champagne.

Sonoma (USA). A county in northern California producing fine, full-bodied red wines from the Cabernet sauvignon and Pinot noir, with the white wines from the Pinot Chardonnay.

Sonoma-Cutrer Vineyards, Inc (USA). A specialist estate based in Sonoma

County, California. Grape varieties – Cabernet sauvignon, Chardonnay and Colombard. Produces varietal and sparkling wines.

Sonoma Riesling (USA). An alternative name for the Green sylvaner grape in California.

Sonoma Vineyards (USA). Vineyards based in Sonoma County, California. Wines are produced from Cabernet sauvignon, Chardonnay and the French colombard. Owns Alexander's Crown.

Sonora (Mex). A district that contains the wine-producing area of Hermosillo.

Sonsón (Sp). A red grape variety grown in Galicia. Produces fine, perfumed wines.

Soonecker Schlossberg (Ger). Vineyard. (Anb) = Mittelrhein. (Ber) = Bacharach. (Gro) = Schloss Reichenstein. (Vil) = Niederheimbach.

Soonwald (Ger). A series of hills in the Nahe Anbaugebiet.

Soortelijk Gewicht (Hol). Specific Gravity.

Soother Cocktail (Cktl). ⅓ measure Brandy, ⅓ measure Calvados, ⅓ measure Grand Marnier, juice ½ lemon, 2 dashes Gomme syrup. Shake over ice, strain into a cocktail glass.

Sophistiquer (Fr). To falsify a wine or to ameliorate a defective wine with anything which will cover up its defects.

Soplica (Pol). A Brandy and apple-flavoured Vodka produced by Polmos. 40% alc. by vol.

Sopra Ceneri (Switz). A wine-producing area in Ticino. Includes the vineyards of Bellinzonese and Locarnese.

Sopron (Hun). A wine-producing district in north-western Hungary. Noted for its red wines from the Gamay grape.

Sopron Brewery (Hun). A brewery based in north-western Hungary. Is noted for its Löver Lager.

Soquel (USA). A noted winery town based in Santa Cruz, California.

Sorbés (Les) (Fr). A Premier Cru vineyard in the A.C. commune of Morey-Saint-Denis, Côte de Nuits, Burgundy. 3 ha.

Sorbet and Tea Punch (Cktl).(Non-alc). 2 fl.ozs. cold tea, 1 fl.oz. orange juice, ¼ fl.oz. lemon juice, ½ fl.oz. Gomme syrup, 2 scoops orange sorbet. Blend together in a blender. Pour into a flute glass.

Sorbic Acid (Eng). An additive to wine. Inhibits yeast, but does not kill it. No effect on bacteria. Efficiency depends on the presence of alcohol and SO_2. A stabiliser. See Garlic.

Sorbino (Fin). A cherry-flavoured liqueur.

Sorbitio (Lat). A drink.

Sorbitol (Eng). A sugar that wine yeasts cannot ferment. A useful agent for sweetening home-made wines.

Sorciéres (Les) (Fr). A vineyard of Dopff & Irion in Alsace. Named after the site where witches and unfaithful wives were burnt at the stake in the Middle Ages. Produces Gewürztraminer wines.

Sorentberg (Ger). Vineyard. (Anb) = Mosel-Saar-Ruwer. (Ber) = Bernkastel. (Gro) = Vom Heissen Stein. (Vil) = Reil.

Sorgenbrecher (Ger). The local name for the red wine of Stumpfelbach in Württemberg. Lit – 'Breaker of cares'.

Sörgenloch (Ger). Vineyard. (Anb) = Rheinhessen. (Ber) = Nierstein. (Gro) = Gutes Domtal. (Vin) = Moosberg.

Sorni (It). A D.O.C. red wine produced in Trentino-Alto Adige. Made from the Lagrein, Schiava and Teroldego grapes.

Sorrentine (It). A red wine produced in Roman times from Minean grapes.

SOS (Eng) (abbr). Shefford Old Strong 1050 O.G. brewed by the Banks and Taylor Brewery in Shefford, Bedfordshire.

Sot (Eng) (slang). For a person who is consistently intoxicated (drunk).

Sotatachna Zahar (Bul). Denotes semi-sweet with residual grape sugar.

Soto (Sp). The name given to a range of Sherries (Amontillado, Oloroso and Cream) produced by Sandeman.

Sotoyome Winery (USA). A winery based in Healdsburg, Sonoma County, California. Grape varieties – Cabernet sauvignon, Petite syrah and Zinfandel. Produces varietal wines.

Sotto Ceneri (Switz). A wine-producing area in Ticino. Includes the vineyards of Luganese and Mendrisiotto.

Sottodenominazioni Geografiche (It). Geographical sub-district names.

Sottosuolo (It). Sub-soil.

Sottozona (It). Denotes a single vineyard.

Souche (Fr). Cep or vine root stock.

Souchong (China). Comes from the Chinese 'Sian ching' (little plant). Describes the size of tea bush. i.e. Pekoe Souchong, Lapsang Souchong etc. Large coarse leaf.

Soucoupe (Fr). Saucer.

Sou-Dag (USSR). A white grape variety grown in the Crimea. Produces Port-style and red wines.

Soudak (USSR). An alternative spelling of Sou-Dag, a rich, red wine.

Soulaines (Fr). A commune in the A.C. Coteaux de l'Aubance in the Anjou-Saumur district of the Loire. Produces light red wines.

Soulières (Fr). A Cru Champagne village in the Canton de Vertus. District = Châlons.

Soulignac (Fr). A commune in the Haut-Benauge, Entre-Deux-Mers, central Bordeaux.

Soul Kiss (Cktl). 1 part French vermouth, 1 part Italian vermouth, 1 part Dubonnet, 2 teaspoons orange juice. Mix over ice, strain into an ice-filled highball glass.

Soul Kiss Cocktail (Cktl). ⅙ gill French vermouth, ⅙ gill Bourbon whiskey, ½ fl.oz. orange juice, ½ fl.oz. Dubonnet. Shake over ice, strain into a cocktail glass.

Soul of the Wine (Hol). The old Dutch description of brandy (Cognac) which was imported to Holland. Concentrated to reduce bulk and save freight charges that would have been levied.

Soultz-les-Bains (Fr). A village in Alsace. Known as Sulzbach in German.

Soumoll (Sp). See Sumoll.

Sound (Eng). A wine-tasting term for a wine which has no defects and shows no abnormal qualities.

Souped-Up (Eng). A term used to describe a wine that has been blended with something more robust or richer (may be done legally) to improve the quality.

Souple (Fr). Describes a supple, well-balanced wine, soft and easy to drink.

Sour (Cktl). 1 measure of desired spirit, juice ¾ lemon, 1 teaspoon castor sugar, dash Angostura, white of egg. Shake well over ice, strain into a small wine glass.

Sour (Eng). Used to describe a wine which is spoiled and unfit to drink. Acidic, bitter or vinegary. Usually caused through bacterial infection or too much acid.

Source of the Nile (Afr). A Lager beer 1040· O.G. brewed by the Nile Breweries in Jinja, Uganda.

Sourire de Reims (Fr). A non-vintage Champagne produced by Abele from 10–30% Chardonnay and 40–60% Pinot noir grapes.

Sour Mash (USA). In Whiskey production the adding of ¼ spent beer from previous fermentation to the fresh mash and fresh yeast.

Sourness (Eng). Taste of sourness. Like lemon or vinegar. Tart.

Sourteq (Cktl). 2 fl.ozs. Tequila, 1 fl.oz. lemon juice, 2 dashes Gomme syrup, dash egg white. Shake over ice, strain into a large cocktail glass. Decorate with a lemon slice and a cherry.

Sousan (Sp). A black grape variety grown in Ribeiro.

Sousão (Port). A red grape variety grown in the Douro for the production of Port. Used mainly for colour.

Soused (Eng) (slang). The term for a person who is consistently intoxicated (drunk).

Sous-le-Dos-d'Âne (Fr). A Premier Cru vineyard in the commune of Blagny, A.C. Meursault, Côte de Beaune, Burgundy. 5.6 ha.

Sous le Puits (Fr). A Premier Cru vineyard

in the A.C. commune of Puligny-Montrachet, Côte de Beaune, Burgundy. 6.9 ha.

Sous-lès-Roches (Fr). A vineyard in the A.C. commune of Montagny, Côte Chalonnaise, Burgundy.

Sous-Marques (Fr). The name given to the lesser wines of the Champagne houses.

Sous-Noms (Fr). Under-names. Names given to wines especially in Bordeaux to Châteaux that don't exist.

Soussans (Fr). A commune in the A.C. Haut-Médoc, north-western Bordeaux.

South Africa (S.Afr). A wine and brandy-producing country that was first planted with vines in 1654 by Johan Van Riebeeck. Produces most styles of wines including fine fortified Port and Sherry-styles. Planted mainly with Vitis vinifera and Vitis vinifera crosses, the main regions are – Coastal Area [Constantia Valley, Durbanville, Malmesbury, Paarl, Stellenbosch, Tulbagh and Wellington] and Klein Karoo [Breede River, Ladismith, Montagu, Oudtshoorn, Robertson and Worcester]. See SFW, KWV, Nederburg and Wine of Origin Superior.

South African Breweries (S.Afr). A brewery founded in 1895. Brews most styles of beer.

South African Riesling (S.Afr). A lesser name for the Crouchon grape of France.

South African Sherry (S.Afr). Sherry-type wines made in most styles from Finos to Creams.

South African Viticultural and Oenological Research Institute (S.Afr). V.O.R.I. A body that conducts clonal experiments etc. Produces new grape varieties. Also referred to as the Nietvoorbij.

Southard (Port). Vintage Port shippers. Vintage – 1927.

South Australia (Austr). State that includes the wine regions of Barossa Valley, Clare Watervale, Coonawarra, Keppoch Valley, McLaren Vale, Reynella and Riverland. ⅔ of Australia's annual wine production comes from this state.

South Australian Brewing (Austr). A brewery based in Adelaide. Brews Southwark Bitter and uses the brand-name of Southwark. Is also noted for its Lager beers.

South Burgenland (Aus). A wine-producing district based near Rechnitz and Eisenberg. Produces soft red wines.

South Carolina (USA). A small wine-producing State. Produces mainly wines from the Catawba, Concord and Muscadine grapes.

Southcott House (Eng). Vineyard. Address

S

= Pewsey, Wiltshire. 0.5 ha. Grape varieties – Müller-Thurgau 80%, Ortega 10% and Septima 10%.

South County Vineyards (USA). A winery based in Slocum, Rhode Island. Produces Vinifera wines.

Southdown Bitter (Eng). A keg Bitter 1040 O.G. brewed by the Gales Brewery in Horndean, Hampshire.

South-East English Wine Festival (Eng). A wine festival held annually in September in East Sussex.

South-Eastern Seaboard (USA). The wine region which stretches from Virginia to Florida along the coastal plain.

Southern Belle Cocktail (Cktl). ½ measure Bourbon whiskey, ⅓ measure cream, dash (white) Crème de Cacao, dash (green) Crème de Menthe. Shake over ice, strain into a cocktail glass.

Southern Bride (Cktl). ¾ measure dry Gin, ¼ measure grapefruit juice, dash Maraschino. Shake over ice, strain into a cocktail glass.

Southern California (USA). A general descriptive term used for the wine-producing districts based south and east of Los Angeles in California.

Southern Comfort (USA). An orange and peach-flavoured Whiskey. Produced by the Southern Comfort Corporation. 50% alc. by vol.

Southern Gin Cocktail (Cktl). ⅓ gill dry Gin, 3 dashes Cointreau, 2 dashes Campari. Stir over ice, strain into a cocktail glass. Top with a twist of lemon peel juice.

Southern Ginger Cocktail (Cktl). 1 fl.oz. Bourbon whiskey, ½ fl.oz. lemon juice. Shake over ice, strain into an ice-filled highball glass. Top with ginger ale.

Southern Liqueur Co (S.Afr). A liqueur producing company. See Amarula.

Southern Mint Julep (Cktl). The same as an Old Georgia Julep but using liqueur brandy instead of Brandy.

Southern Style (Eng). A term used to describe a full-bodied, full-flavoured red wine with a peppery character from southern France. In white wines denotes a flabby wine with excess alcohol and too little acidity and freshness.

Southern Ukraine (USSR). The main wine district north of the Black Sea.

Southern U.S.S.R. (USSR). The largest wine region of the Soviet Union. Contains the republics of Armenia, Azerbaijan and Georgia.

Southern Vales (Austr). A wine area of South Australia that includes McClaren Vale and Reynella.

Southern Vales Co-operative (Austr). A

winery based in McClaren Vale in Southern Vales, South Australia. Produces varietal wines.

Southern Viking Cocktail (Cktl). ⅓ measure Kahlúa, ⅓ measure Akvavit, ⅓ measure double cream. Shake over ice, strain into a cocktail glass, decorate with grated nutmeg on top.

Southfield Vineyard (Eng). Based at the Huntley vineyard in Gloucestershire.

South of the Border (Cktl). 1 oz. Kahlúa, 1½ ozs. Gin, 1 oz. lemon juice, 1 egg white. Shake well over ice, strain into a cocktail glass. Decorate with a cherry.

South of the Border Cocktail Cock). ⅕ measure Tequila, ⅛ measure Tia Maria, juice ½ lime. Shake over ice, strain into a cocktail glass. Top with a slice of lime.

South Pacific (Cktl). 1 fl.oz. Gin, ½ fl.oz. blue Curaçao, ½ fl.oz. Galliano. Pour Gin and Galliano into an ice-filled highball glass, top with lemonade. Splash in the Curaçao. Decorate with a slice of lemon and a cherry. Serve with straws.

Southsea Brewery (Eng). Opened in 1982 in the Old Lion Brewery in Portsmouth. Noted for its cask conditioned Bosun Dark 1032 O.G. Captain's Bitter 1037 O.G. Admiral's Ale 1048 O.G. and Sealord 1060 O.G.

Southside (Mad). A blend of Madeira (medium-sweet) sold in America.

South-Side Cocktail (Cktl). ⅕ gill Gin, juice ½ lemon, 2 dashes Gomme syrup. Shake over ice, strain into a cocktail glass. Top with a sprig of mint.

South-Side Fizz (Cktl). As for South-Side Cocktail but place in an ice-filled highball glass and top with soda.

South Tyrol (Aus). See Südtirol and Trentino-Alto Adige.

South Wales Clubs (Wales). A brewery based in Pontyclun, Mid-Glamorgan. See CPA and SBB.

Southwark (Austr). The brand-name used by the South Australian Brewing Co. for their range of beers.

Southwark Beer (Austr). A pasteurised, bottom-fermented Bitter beer brewed by Cooper's Brewery in Southwark, South Australia.

South-West Breweries Limited (Afr). A brewery based in Windhoek, Namibia.

Soutirage (Fr). Racking, the drawing off of the wine from the lees.

Soutiran (Gérard et Fils) (Fr). Champagne producer. Address = Ambonnay, 51150 Tours-sur-Marne. Produces vintage and non-vintage wines.

Soutirer (Fr). To rack, to draw off wine.

Souto Vedro (Port). A brand of sharp, dry, pétillant Vinho Verde produced by Amarante.

Souverain (USA). A winery based in the Alexander Valley Sonoma County, California. Grape varieties – Cabernet sauvignon, Chardonnay, Chenin blanc, Colombard, Johannisberg riesling and Zinfandel. Produces varietal and table wines.

Souverain Cellars (USA). A winery based near Lake Henessey, Napa Valley, California. Produces varietal wines.

Souverain Vineyards (USA). A winery based in Geyersville, California. Grape varieties – Cabernet sauvignon and Chardonnay. Produces varietal wines.

Souzão (S.Afr). A red grape variety used in the making of Port-type fortified wines.

Souzy-Champigny (Fr). A commune in the Saumur area of the Anjou-Saumur district, Loire region.

Soveh (Isr). A 'Bible wine'.

Sovelle (N.Z.). A white, wood-treated, Burgundy-style wine produced by Montana Wines.

Sovereign Bitter (Eng). A keg Bitter 1037 O.G. brewed by the Samuel Smith Brewery in Tadcaster, Yorkshire.

Soviet Cocktail (Cktl). ¾ measure Vodka, ¼ measure medium Sherry, ¼ measure dry Vermouth. Shake over ice, strain into an ice-filled old-fashioned glass. Top with a twist of lemon peel juice.

Soyeux (Fr). Smooth, silky wine.

Sozzled (Eng) (slang). Drunk, intoxicated.

SPA (Eng) (abbr). Special Pale Ale 1041 O.G. brewed by the Wethered Brewery in Marlow, Buckinghamshire.

Spa (Bel). A still and sparkling mineral water of Spa. Still comes from the Reine Springs in the Ardenne hills whilst the sparkling comes from the Marie-Henriette Springs.

Spa Barisart (Bel). A sparkling mineral water from Spadel. Distributed by Crombie Eustace.

Spabrücken (Ger). Village. (Anb) = Nahe. (Ber) = Kreuznach. (Gro) = Pfarrgarten. (Vin) = Höll.

Spaceman (Cktl). 1½ measures Vodka, ½ measure dry Vermouth, dash Pernod, dash Grenadine. Stir over ice, strain into a cocktail glass.

Spade (Sp). A name given in the Sherry region to the long branch left during pruning together with the Thumb. Also known as the Espada.

Spadel (Bel). A mineral water bottler. Bottles both still and sparkling.

Spain (Sp). A large wine-producing country on the Iberian peninsula. Produces most styles of wines. Noted for Sherry and Cava wines. Regions are – Alella, Alicante, Ampurdán Costa Brava, Aragón, Balearic Islands, Canaries, Cataluña, Cheste, Estremadura, Gandesa Terralta, Galicia, Huelva, Jerez, Jumilla, La Mancha, León, Levante, Montilla-Moriles, Navarra, Penedés, Priorato, Rioja, Rueda, Tarragona, Utiel-Requena, Valencia and Yecla. See also Denominación de Origen, Cava.

Spalato (It). The name given to red table and dessert wines from the vineyards of central Italy.

Spalletti (It). A Chianti Putto producer based in Tuscany. See Poggio Reale.

Spalletti di Montalbano (It). A Chianti Putto producer based in Tuscany.

Spalliera (It). A method of vine training (similar to the Guyot system).

Spalt (Ger). A strain of hops that produces pronounced bitterness in beers.

Spanish Brandy (Sp). A pot-distilled Brandy distilled from the wines of La Mancha and Valdepeñas. Produced mainly in Jerez and Penedés.

Spanish Captain (Cktl). ⅓ measure dry Sherry, ⅔ measure white Rum, teaspoon lime juice. Shake over ice, strain into a cocktail glass. Decorate with a cherry.

Spanish Cocktail (Cktl). ½ gill Italian vermouth, 4 dashes Angostura, ½ egg white. Shake well over ice, strain into a cocktail glass, top with a twist of lemon peel juice. Also known as Spanish Delight.

Spanish Delight (Cktl). See Spanish Cocktail.

Spanish Earth (Sp). A diatomaceous soil found in Lebrija, northern Andalusia. Used to remove proteins etc. out of Sherry. See also Silicaceous Earth.

Spanish Fly (Eng). The name for any drink that has been laced with a soft drug (or with a very high alcohol content).

Spanish Oyster (Cktl). 1 egg yolk (unbroken) in a goblet, add 2 fl.ozs. dry Sherry, salt and pepper. Do not stir.

Spanish Punch (Sp). Sangría. Based with wine and fruit.

Spanish Town (Cktl). ⅓ gill white Rum, 3 dashes Triple Sec. Stir over ice, strain into a cocktail glass.

Spanish Wax (Euro). Wax mixed with a little added fat, used to seal the corks in the bottles in the nineteenth and early twentieth centuries to prevent insects, etc. getting at the cork.

Spanna (It). Another name used for the red Nebbiolo grape.

Spanna (It). A red wine from the Vercelli province in Piemonte. Made from the Spanna (Nebbiolo) grape.

S

Spa Reine (Bel). A sparkling mineral water from Spadel. Distributed by Crombie Eustace.

Sparging (Eng). In brewing, the process of spraying (sparging) the Grist with hot Liquor to extract the sugar.

Sparkler (Cktl).(Non-alc). 2 dashes Angostura in an ice-filled highball glass. Top with mineral water and dress with a cherry.

Sparkler (Eng). A device attached to the beer engine outlet. The beer is forced through small holes to produce a Head and to aerate it. This can be varied by altering the setting of the sparkler).

Sparkling Aerobic (Cktl). 2 parts Johnny Walker Red Label Scotch whisky, 1 part Cointreau, 1 part lime juice, 6 parts soda water. Mix over ice, strain into an ice-filled highball glass. Add a slice of lemon or lime.

Sparkling Ale (Eng). An old term used by brewers to denote that their bottled ales have been filtered.

Sparkling Bordeaux (Fr). Usually white or rosé wines from vineyards in the Garonne.

Sparkling Burgundy (Fr). Denotes red wine made from the Gamay grape and white wine from the Aligoté. See Bourgogne Mousseux.

Sparkling Burgundy (USA). See Californian Sparkling Burgundy.

Sparkling Cider (Eng). A still Cider injected with CO_2 gas.

Sparkling Golden Lexia (Austr). A clean, Muscat-sweet, non-alcoholic grape juice from Bonnonee, Victoria.

Sparkling Kir (Cktl). In a highball glass place ⅙ gill blackcurrant cordial, ice and top with ⅓ gill white wine, ⅓ gill Ashbourne mineral water.

Sparkling Malvasia Bianca (USA). See California Sparkling Malvasia bianca.

Sparkling Moselle (USA). See California Sparkling Moselle.

Sparkling Muscat (USA). See California Sparkling Muscat.

Sparkling Sauterne (USA). See California Sparkling Sauterne.

Sparkling Wines (Eng). Wines that contain CO_2 gas which has been put in either by the méthode champenoise, cuve close, Charmat or injection.

Sparr (Fr). An Alsace wine-producer. Address = 2, Rue de la Première Armée, 68240 Sigolsheim.

Spätburgunder (Ger). A red grape variety flourishing on the Rhine and the Ahr and also in Baden. It produces a dark, strong and finely spiced wine. Known in France as the Pinot noir.

Spatenbräu Brauerei (Ger). A large, noted brewery in Munich. Brews Spatengold.

Spatengold (Ger). A pale Beer 5.4% alc. by vol. brewed in Munich by the Spatenbräu Brauerei.

Spätlese (Aus). A wine made from grapes picked after the main harvest which are completely ripe. Minimum must weight of 19°KMW.

Spätlese (Ger). Lit – 'Late-harvest'. Denotes a style of wine made from grapes gathered after the official harvest date. Have a higher sugar content, are made naturally without additives and are of Qmp quality.

Spätrot (Aus). See Zierfändler.

Spatzendreck (S.Afr). A brand-name used by Delheim Wines.

Spaulding Vineyard (USA). A vineyard based in the Napa Valley, California. 8.5 ha. Grape variety – Chardonnay. Also owns the Stonegate Vineyard.

Spauna (It). An alternative name for the Nebbiolo grape in northern Italy.

Spa Water (Bel). See Spa.

Spay (Ger). Village. (Anb) = Mittelrhein. (Ber) = Rheinburgengau. (Gro) = Gedeonseck. (Vin) = Engelstein.

Speakeasy (USA). An outlet for the sale of illicit beverages during the Prohibition period. Gets its name from the New York Irish saloon keepers who used to ask their clients to 'Speak-easy' when drinking after hours so as not to be heard by any passing police officers.

Special (Chile). Denotes a wine that is 2 years old.

Special (Eng). A term used to describe above average beers.

Special Chun Mee (Taiwan). See Chun Mee.

Special Club Brut (Fr). A vintage De Luxe cuvée Champagne produced from 26% Chardonnay and 74% Pinot noir by Henri Goutorbe.

Special d'Avignon (Bel). A dark, sweet Ale brewed in Nismes, southern Belgium.

Special Dutch (Hol). A sweet, premium Beer brewed by a Stella Artois subsidiary brewery.

Speciale Aerts (Bel). A top-fermented Beer traditionally sold in Burgundy bottles.

Special Late Harvest (S.Afr). A wine classification. Must have 20–50 grammes per litre of grape sugar. 22° Balling minimum.

Special Marsala (It). An early Marsala of the twentieth century produced in northern Italy and abroad using additives, chemicals and colouring.

Special Old (Can). A blended Canadian whisky produced by Hiram Walker.

Special R (Eng). A range of non-alcoholic

fruit drinks containing fruit and 'Nutra-sweet' (an artificial sweetener) produced by Robinsons.

Special Red Ale (Eng). A strong bottled Ale 1052 O.G. brewed by the Paine Brewery, St. Neots, Cambridgeshire for export.

Special Rough Cocktail (Cktl). ½ measure Calvados, ½ measure Cognac, 2 dashes Pernod. Stir over ice, strain into a cocktail glass.

Special Variety Madeira (Mad). Blended, the youngest wine must be a minimum of 10 years old after Estufagem. If grape variety is stated then it must contain 85% of that named variety.

Specific Gravity (Eng). S.G. The ratio of the density of a substance to that of water. Water being 1000. See also O.G. (the S.G. prior to fermentation),

Spectrum (USA). The brand-name for a range of 'Coolers' in cans that are produced by Paul Masson in California. Flavours include white wine, lemon juice and soda, white wine and soda, red wine, redcurrant juice and soda, mango and orange juice.

Speight's (N.Z.). The brand-name used by the New Zealand Breweries in Dunedin.

Spencer Cocktail (Cktl). ⅔ measure dry Gin, ⅓ measure Apricot brandy, 2 dashes orange juice, 1 dash Campari. Shake over ice, strain into a cocktail glass. Top with a cherry and twist of orange peel juice.

Spence's Vineyard (N.Z.). A former vineyard. Now closed.

Spent Grains (Eng). In brewing the term for left-over malt grains after mashing. Usually sold for cattle food.

Spent Liquor (Eng). A term used for the leftover residue after distillation has occurred.

Spergola (It). The name used in Emilia Romagna for the Sauvignon blanc grape. Also known as the Spergolina.

Spergolina (It). See Spergola.

Sperone (It). A producer of Moscato spumante wins in Piemonte.

Sperr (Aus). A term that describes a wine that leaves a drying taste in the mouth. Caused by sulphur or woodiness.

Spetsat (Swe). A herb beer brewed by the Till Brewery.

Speyburn (Scot). A single Malt whisky distillery based north of Inverness. A Highland malt whisky. 43% alc. by vol.

Spey Cast (Scot). A De Luxe blended Scotch whisky blended by Gordon and MacPhail of Elgin. 40% alc. by vol.

Spey (River) (Scot). See Speyside.

Spey Royal (Scot). A blended Scotch whisky. 40% alc. by vol.

Speyside (Scot). A famous area of eastern Scotland on the river Spey which produces many of the Highland malt whiskies.

Spezi (Ger). A malty, Bavarian Lager beer 5% alc. by vol. brewed by the Riegele Brauerei in Augsburg.

Spezia (La) (It). A coastal region of Liguria from which Clinque Terre is part. Many vineyards only accessible by boat as they rise straight out of the sea.

Speziator (Ger). A Doppelbock beer 7.9% alc. by vol. brewed by the Riegele Brauerei in Augsburg.

Sphinx (Cktl). 2 fl.ozs. Gin, ½ fl.oz. Italian vermouth, ½ fl.oz. French vermouth. Stir over ice, strain into a cocktail glass. Top with a slice of lemon.

Spiagga de Lesina (It). The name given to the white, dessert wines from Dalmatia in Yugoslavia.

Spiced Tea (Sri.L.). A blend of high grown Ceylon teas. Pekoe leaf, mixed with cloves and dried orange peel which gives a full, heady aroma.

Spiced Tea Punch (Cktl). 1½ pints tea, juice of a lemon, 1 pint red wine, 4 cloves, 1 cinnamon stick, sugar syrup. Heat together, strain and serve hot in glasses with a slice of lemon.

Spice Imperial (Eng). A clove and orange peel-flavoured tea produced by Whittards of Chelsea.

Spicy (Eng). The term used to describe a varietal characteristic e.g. Gewürztraminer, Scheurebe, or a complex bouquet or palate derived from cask and bottle ageing.

Spider Cocktail (Cktl). Place 1 fl.oz. Crème de Café in a highball glass, top with Coca Cola and a scoop of vanilla ice cream. Stir, serve with straws.

Spider Mite (Eng). Family – Tetranychidae. The vine pest (Lat) = Panonychus ulmi. See Red Spider.

Spiegel (Ger). Mirror.

Spiegel (Ger). Vineyard. (Anb) = Rheinpfalz. (Ber) = Mittelhaardt-Deutsche Weinstrasse. (Gro) = Meerspinne. (Vil) = Mussbach.

Spiegel (Hol). Glass.

Spiegelberg (Ger). Grosslage. (Anb) = Rheinhessen. (Ber) = Nierstein. (Vils) = Nackenheim, Nierstein.

Spiegelberg (Ger). Vineyard. (Anb) = Baden. (Ber) = Badische Bergstrasse/Kraichgau. (Gro) = Stiftsberg. (Vil) = Elsenz.

Spiegelberg (Ger). Vineyard. (Anb) = Baden. (Ber) = Badische Bergstrasse/Kraichgau. (Gro) = Stiftsberg. (Vil) = Kraichtal (stadtteil Landshausen and Menzingen).

Spiegelberg (Ger). Vineyard. (Anb) =

Baden. (Ber) = Badische Bergstrasse/Kraichgau. (Gro) = Stiftsberg. (Vil) = Tiefenbach.

Spiel (Ger). Denotes a balanced wine.

Spielberg (Ger). Village. (Anb) = Württemberg. (Ber) = Württembergisch Unterland. (Gro) = Stromberg. (Vin) = Liebenberg.

Spielberg (Ger). Vineyard. (Anb) = Rheinpfalz. (Ber) = Mittelhaardt-Deutsche Weinstrasse. (Gro) = Hochmess. (Vil) = Bad Dürkheim.

Spielberg (Ger). Vineyard. (Anb) = Rheinpfalz. (Ber) = Mittelhaardt-Deutsche Weinstrasse. (Gro) = Hofstück. (Vil) = Meckenheim.

Spielbühl (Ger). Vineyard. (Anb) = Württemberg. (Ber) = Württembergisch Unterland. (Gro) = Lindelberg. (Vil) = Harsberg (ortsteil Neuholz).

Spier Estate (S.Afr). Based in Stellenbosch. Address = Box 28, Vlottenburg 7604. Produces mainly varietal wines.

Spiesheim (Ger). Village. (Anb) = Rheinhessen. (Ber) = Nierstein. (Gro) = Petersberg. (Vin) = Osterberg.

Spiess (Ger). Vineyard. (Anb) = Rheinpfalz. (Ber) = Mittelhaardt-Deutsche Weinstrasse. (Gro) = Hofstück. (Vil) = Ruppertsberg.

Spigot (Eng). Cask bung hole. Also the old name for a tap (cask).

Spigot (USA). The name for a cask tap.

Spike a Drink (Eng). To lace a drink with a strong alcoholic liquor. Is usually done without the knowledge of the drinker.

Spiked (USA) (slang). Similar to fortified. A drink that has had alcohol added to it. Especially in the Prohibition era.

Spiked Beer (USA). A glass of beer to which a measure of spirits has been added to it. Usually not in the knowledge of the drinker.

Spiked Lemonade (USA). Lemonade with spirit (usually Whiskey) added to it.

Spiked Wine (Sp). A wine that has been fermented with the mother stock.

Spile (Eng). A small wood/cane peg (hard/soft spile) which is inserted into the Shive through the Tut hole. Is used either to allow the escape of CO_2 gas (soft cane spile) or prevent the escape of CO_2 gas (hard wooden spile).

Spillare (It).To tap a cask or barrel.

Spingo (Eng). The collective name of Blue Anchor beers brewed by the Helston Brewery in Cornwall.

Spinster's Dream (Cktl). 1 measure Gin, ½ measure Brandy, ½ measure Passion fruit juice, 4 dashes orange Curaçao. Shake over ice, strain into a cocktail glass.

Spiral (Eng). For cocktails the complete peel of fruit cut in spiral fashion.

Spiral Cellar (The) (Eng). See Caves Harnois. Address = 27, Grafton Park Road, Worcester Park, Surrey.

Spirit (Eng). The name given to the alcohol removed from a fermented beverage during distillation. See Rectified Spirit.

Spirit Beverages (USA). Lit – The result from a pure distillation of fermented beverages

Spirit Frame (Eng). Victorian silver or plate cruet stand type holder for spirit bottles.

Spirits (USA). The generic term for distilled liquors, neutral spirits and Cologne spirits. A spirit distilled out at 95% alc. by vol. or more. Used for blending and the preparation of rectified products.

Spirit Safe (Scot). In Whisky distilling, a Customs and Excise glass case where the new distillate passes through under lock and key. The distiller can separate the Foreshots and Feints by the operation of levers.

Spirits of Wine (Eng). The distillate from wine. Eau-de-vie-de-vin. (Brandy).

Spirits Receiver (Scot). A container to receive the newly distilled spirit in Malt whisky production.

Spiritueux (Fr). Spirity, a wine high in alcohol.

Spirituous (Eng). Lit – 'Containing alcohol'. An alcoholic beverage.

Spiritus Vini de Gallice (Lat). The medical term for Brandy used in England during Roman times.

Spirit Whiskey (USA). A mixture of neutral spirits and not less than 5% on a proof gallon (US) basis of Whiskey, or Straight Whiskey and Whiskey, if the Straight Whiskey component is less than 20% on a proof gallon (US) basis.

Spirity (Eng). Having a taste of spirits, applied to wine especially a fortified wine. e.g. Port.

Spital (Ger). Hospital.

Spitalberg (Ger). Vineyard. (Anb) = Nahe. (Ber) = Schloss Böckelheim. (Gro) = Paradiesgarten. (Vil) = Sobernheim-Steinhardt.

Spittoons (USA). A metal container (urn) used in the nineteenth century in Saloon bars for customers to spit tobacco juice from the habit of chewing a tobacco plug.

Spitz (Ger). Denotes a thin wine, deteriorating.

Spitzberg (Ger). Vineyard. (Anb) = Rheinhessen. (Ber) = Nierstein. (Gro) = Domherr. (Vil) = Stadecken-Elsheim.

Spitzenberg (Ger). Vineyard. (Anb) = Baden. (Ber) = Badische Bergstrasse/Kraichgau. (Gro) = Mannaberg. (Vil) = Wiesloch.

Spitzengewächs (Ger). An old term used to denote best growths. Now no longer used.

Spitzenlagen (Ger). Peak growths. These vineyards almost always produce outstanding wines.

Spitzenweins (Aus) (Ger). Best wines, quality wines. Lit – 'Peak wines'.

Splash (Eng). An informal request for a dash of one beverage into another. e.g. a 'splash' of soda into a measure of Whisky.

Splice the Mainbrace (Eng). The term used in the Royal Navy for the issue of the crew's daily Rum ration.

Split (USA). Same as a quarter bottle. 6 fl.ozs. U.S. 187 mls.

Spoetzl Brewery (USA). A brewery based in Shiner, Texas. Brews Shiner Premium Beer.

Spoiled Beer (Eng). A beer that has spoiled whilst at the brewery. Excise duty can be reclaimed.

Spoletinum (Lat). A red wine produced in central Italy in Roman times.

Sponheim (Ger). Village. (Anb) = Nahe. (Ber) = Schloss Böckelheim. (Gro) = Rosengarten. (Vins) = Abtei, Grafenberg, Klostergarten, Mühlberg.

Sponsheim (Ger). Village. (Anb) = Rheinhessen. (Ber) = Bingen. (Gro) = Sankt Rochuskapelle. (Vin) = Palmenstein.

Spontaneous Fermentation (W.Ind). Wild fermentation in Rum production.

Spore (Eng). The condition a yeast cell (or certain bacteria cells) can adopt when deprived of moisture. Will lie dormant until moisture is restored e.g. dried yeast.

Sporen (Fr). A lesser white grape variety grown in eastern France.

Sporting House (Eng). An eighteenth- and nineteenth-century name for an inn or public house where gambling took place or sportsmen frequented

Sport Lager (Eng). A keg Lager beer 1036 O.G. brewed by the Leicester Brewery.

Sportsman Lager (S.Afr). A Lager beer brewed by the Intercontinental Breweries.

Spot (Eng). An informal request for a small amount of one beverage to be added to the main drink. e.g. Whisky and a 'spot' of soda.

Spots Farm (Eng). A vineyard, also known as the Tenterden Vineyards. Address = Small Hythe, Tenterden, Kent. Grape varieties – Gutenborner, Müller-Thurgau, Reichensteiner, Seyval blanc and others.

Spottswoode Winery (USA). A winery based in St. Helena, Napa Valley, California. Produces varietal wines.

Spotykach (USSR). A cherry-based spirit.

Spraying (Eng). Vines sprayed to protect against mildew, Oiidium, insects, etc.

See Bordeaux Mixture. Also with water to protect against frost in the Spring.

Spread Eagle (Eng). Home-brew public house in Erpingham, Norfolk. Home of the Woodeforde Brewery. Opened in 1983. Brews Spread Eagle Bitter.

Spread Eagle Bitter (Eng). A cask conditioned Bitter 1036 O.G. brewed by the Spread Eagle public house in Woodeforde, Norfolk.

Sprendlingen (Ger). Village. (Anb) = Rheinhessen. (Ber) = Bingen. (Gro) = Abtey. (Vins) = Hölle, Honigberg, Klostergarten, Sonnenberg, Wissberg.

Springbank (Scot). A single Malt whisky distillery in the centre of Campbeltown. Owned and operated by J. and A. Mitchell and Co. of Argyll. A Campbelltown malt. Produces a 12 year old Malt 45% alc. by vol. and at 57% alc. by vol. Also a 21 year old 46% alc. by vol.

Springbok (Cktl).(1). 1 measure white Rum, 1 measure Van der Hum, 1 measure fresh cream. Shake well over ice, strain into a cocktail glass. Serve with straws and a twist of orange peel juice on top.

Springbok (Cktl).(2). ⅓ measure Van der Hum, ⅓ measure Lillet, ⅓ measure medium Sherry, 2 dashes Orange bitters. Stir well over ice, strain into a cocktail glass.

Springdale Winery (USA). A winery based in Granby, Connecticut. Produces mainly French hybrid wines.

Spring Farm Vineyard (Eng). A vineyard based at Moorlynch, Bridgewater, Somerset. Was first planted in 1981. 6.5 ha. Grape varieties – Madeleine angevine 25%, Müller-Thurgau 20%, Seyval blanc 20%, Schönberger 10% and others. Sells wines under the Moorlynch label.

Spring Feeling (Cktl). ½ measure dry Gin, ¼ measure lime juice, ¼ measure Green Chartreuse. Shake over ice, strain into a cocktail glass.

Springfield Bitter (Eng). A Bitter beer 1036 O.G. brewed by Bass, Mitchells and Butlers in Wolverhampton, Staffs. Also brewed by Bass Charrington.

Springfield Bitter (Eng). A Bitter beer brewed by the White Swan, a home-brew public house in Netherton, Lancashire.

Springfield Brewery (Eng). A brewery belonging to Bass, Mitchells and Butlers based in Wolverhampton, Staffs.

Springland Wines (S.Afr). Are varietal wines bottled by the Drop-Inn Group in Cape Town. Address = 42 Main Road, Diep River 7800.

Spring Mountain (USA). A small producer of fine wines in the Napa Valley, northern California. Grape varieties – Cabernet sauvignon, Chardonnay, Pinot noir and Sauvignon blanc.

Spring Time Cocktail (Cktl). 1½ fl.ozs. Vodka, 1 fl.oz. orange juice, ½ fl.oz. Cointreau. Shake over ice, strain into an ice-filled highball glass. Top with ginger ale, dress with lemon and orange peel spirals and a cherry. Serve with straws.

Springtime Cocktail (Cktl). ⅔ measure Bacardi White Label Rum, ⅓ measure (green) Crème de Menthe. Shake over ice, strain into an ice-filled highball glass. Top with ginger ale. Serve with straws.

Springvale (Austr). A dry white wine produced by the Berri Estates, South Australia.

Springvale Bitter (Wales). A keg Bitter 1033 O.G. brewed by the Silverthorne Brewery in Cwmbran, Gwent.

Spritz (Switz). A pétillant wine, slightly sparkling.

Spritzer (Ger). A drink of ½ white table wine, ½ soda water. Pour into an ice-filled highball glass. Add a twist of lemon. Also known as a Schorle. Mineral water may be used in place of soda water.

Spritzer (N.Z.). A Hock wine, lime juice and soda water drink once produced by Cooks, Te Kauwata.

Spritzer Highball (USA). The American name for Spritzer.

Spritzig (Ger). A term given to semi-sparkling wines. Wines which have a slight sparkle or prickle caused by a malo-lactic fermentation in the bottle. (Fr) = Pétillant.

Spritzigkeit (Ger). The name given to German pétillant wines.

Spruce Beer (Eng). A Black Beer brewed from fermented Spruce fir shoots, sugar and Malted barley.

Spruitdrift Co-operative (S.Afr). Based in Spruitdrift. Address = Spruitdrift Koöperatiewe Wynkelders Bpk., Box 129, Vredendal 8160. Produces varietal wines.

Spruitdrift Koöperatiewe Wynkelders Bpk (S.Afr). See Spruitdrift Co-operative.

Sprung (Ger). Vineyard. (Anb) = Mosel-Saar-Ruwer. (Ber) = Saar-Ruwer. (Gro) = Scharzberg. (Vil) = Konz.

Spuitwater (Hol). Soda water.

Spumante (It). Sparkling. Applied to a wine that is truly sparkling. Gran spumante is made by the méthode champenoise. Others are made by the cuve close method.

Spumante Naturale (It). The name for sparkling wines made by the méthode champenoise. See also Gran Spumante.

Spumare (It). To sparkle or foam.

Spumos (Rum). Sparkling.

Spumoso (Port). Sparkling.

Sputacchiera (It). A spittoon.

Sputnik (Cktl). 1 measure Vodka, 1 measure cream, 1 teaspoon Maraschino. Shake over ice, strain into a cocktail glass. Decorate with 2 cocktail sticks stuck crossways through a cherry.

Squadron (S.Afr). The brand-name of a Rum marketed by Gilbeys.

Square (Eng). Traditional form of fermenting vessel, square in shape. Now made of stainless steel.

Square Bottle (Hol). The early name for Jenever (Gin).

Squareface (Eng). The nickname given to the square bottles of Dutch Geneva Gin in the nineteenth century.

Squash (Eng). A fruit drink which is usually diluted with water to drink. Is non-alcoholic.

Squeeze (USA). Another name for Red Eye.

Squiffy (Eng) (slang). A term used to denote a person who is partially intoxicated.

Squinzano (It). A red wine from the Puglia. Non D.O.C., made from the Malvasia and Negramaro grapes.

Squires Beer (Eng). A cask conditioned Bitter 1044 O.G. brewed by the Blackawton Brewery in Devon.

Sremski Karlovici (Yug). A wine-producing area in Fruška Gora, Vojvodina. Is noted for Carlowitz (a red full-bodied wine).

SRFCQ (Fr) (abbr). Service de la Répression des Fraudes et du Contrôle de la Qualité.

SSS (Eng) (abbr). Subalterns' Soothing Syrup. (An old name used in England for Madeira wines).

Staaliche Domaene (Ger). State-owned viticultural domaines.

Staatliche Hofkeller (Ger). A Bavarian State Domaine. 119 ha. vineyards based in Franken.

Staatliche Weinbaudomäne Rheinhessia (Ger). State-owned vineyards based in the Rheinhessen. Wines marketed by Jakob Gerhardt.

Staatsweingut (Ger). A vineyard owned by the State.

Staatsweinkellerei (Hun). State wine cellars.

Stabilise (Eng). Wines are stabilised by passing them through filters to remove all the yeast cells or by pasteurisation.

Stabilisierungsfonds Für Wein (Ger). Overseers for the promulgation of the 1971 German Wine Laws. A fund set up to help pay for Flurbereinigung. Created by a per litre sales tax paid four times a year.

S

Stachelberg (Ger). Vineyard. (Anb) = Hessische Bergstrasse. (Ber) = Umstadt. (Gro) = Not yet assigned. (Vil) = Klein-Umstadt.

Stadecken-Elsheim (Ger). Village. (Anb) = Rheinhessen. (Ber) = Nierstein. (Gro) = Domherr. (Vins) = Blume, Bockstein, Lenchen, Spitzberg, Tempelchen.

Stadelhofen (Ger). Village. (Anb) = Baden. (Ber) = Ortenau. (Gro) = Fürsteneck. (Vin) = Renchtäler.

Stadtbredimus (Lux). A wine co-operative owned by Vinsmoselle.

Stadtbredimus (Lux). A wine village on the river Moselle. Vineyard sites – Primerberg, Dieffert.

Stadtbühl Brauerei (Switz). An independent brewery based in Gossau.

Stadtteil (Ger). In the district of.

Stag Beer (Eng). A cask conditioned Bitter 1044 O.G. brewed by the Watney Brewery. Named after their Stag Brewery in Mortlake. Also a canned version.

Staggers (Eng) (slang). The term to denote a person who is unsteady on their feet when under the influence of alcohol.

Stag Lager (Austr). A Lager beer brewed by the Toohey's Brewery in New South Wales.

St. Agnes (Austr). The brand-name of a Brandy. Varieties = V.O. aged not less than 20 years. Old brandy minimum age 5 year old, *** must be aged at least 2 years in wood.

Stag's Leap (USA). A small producer of fine wines in the Napa Valley, northern California. Grape varieties – Cabernet sauvignon and Merlot. Wines vinified at the Stag's Leap Wine Cellars.

Stag's Leap Wine Cellars (USA). A winery based in Napa Valley, California. Grape varieties – Cabernet sauvignon, Chardonnay, Johannisberg riesling and Merlot. Produces varietal wines.

Stag's Leap Winery (USA). A winery and vineyard based in the Napa Valley, California. Grape varieties – Chenin blanc and Petite syrah. Produces varietal wines.

Stahlberg (Ger). Vineyard. (Anb) = Baden. (Ber) = Badische Frankenland. (Gro) = Tauberklinge. (Vil) = Uissigheim.

Stahlbühl (Ger). Vineyard. (Anb) = Württemberg. (Ber) = Württembergisch Unterland. (Gro) = Staufenberg. (Vil) = Heilbronn.

Stahlig (Ger). Steely or sour lesser wines of the Mosel.

Staig (Ger). Vineyard. (Anb) = Württemberg. (Ber) = Württembergisch Unterland. (Gro) = Heuchelberg. (Vil) = Hausen/Z.

Staiger Winery (USA). A small winery based near Boulder Creek, Santa Cruz, California. 2.5 ha. Grape varieties–Cabernet sauvignon, Chardonnay, Pinot noir and Zinfandel. Produces varietal wines.

St-Aignan (Fr). A commune in the A.C. Côtes de Fronsac, Bordeaux.

Stainless Dry (Cktl). ⅔ measure Gin, ⅓ measure grapefruit juice. Pour over ice into a tall glass. Add a teaspoon of Cointreau, dash Angostura. Top with lemonade.

Stainless Steel (Eng). Used in the lining of vats especially for white wines to exclude air. Fermenting vessels for beer are also made of this.

Stake Culture (Aus). Pfahlkultur. A cultivation system.

Staked Plains Winery (USA). A winery based in the South Plains, Lubbock, western Texas. Produces American and vinifera wines.

St. Aldegund (Ger). Village. (Anb) = Mosel-Saar-Ruwer. (Ber) = Zell/Mosel. (Gro) = Grafschaft. (Vins) = Himmelreich, Klosterkammer, Palmberg-Terrassen.

Stalk (Eng). The stem of the grape. Attaches the fruit to the plant. Removed before the grapes are crushed as stalks contain tannin. See Égrappage and Pedicule.

Stalky (Eng). The term used to describe the characteristics of the Cabernet grapes. Can also apply to wines made where grapes were pressed with the stalks. May also indicate a corked wine.

Stallard (Port). Vintage Port shippers. Vintage – 1927.

Stallion Bitter (Eng). See Stallion Brewery.

Stallion Brewery (Eng). Based in Chippingham, Berkshire. Noted for its' cask conditioned Barnstormer 1048 O.G. and Stallion Bitter 1037 O.G.

St. Amant Vineyard (USA). An independent vineyard based in Amador County, California. Grape variety – Zinfandel.

Stammheim (Ger). Village. (Anb) = Franken. (Ber) = Maindreieck. (Gro) = Kirchberg. (Vin) = Eselsberg.

Stammtische (Ger). Drinking tables found in Weinstüben (bars). Are usually reserved for various drinking fraternities' ritual drinking. The best table in the house.

Stanbridge Estate (Austr). A winery based in Riverina, New South Wales. Produces varietal wines.

Standard Bitter (Wales). A cask conditioned Bitter 1032 O.G. brewed by the Buckley Brewery in Llanelli. Also a keg version.

Standard Panel [The] (M.East). One of the earliest finds from Ur. Depicts wine drinking and is dated from about 2,500 B.C.

Standard Shaker (Eng). A 3 piece utensil, stainless steel or silver plate. Has a cone-shaped base, dumpy top and built in strainer with a fitted cap.
Standfast (Scot). A blended Scotch whisky produced by Grant and Sons. 40% alc. by vol.
St-André-de-Cubzac (Fr). A town in eastern Bordeaux. Produces A.C. Bordeaux red and white wines.
St. Andrews (USA). A small estate based near Napa City, Napa Valley, California. Is noted for its Chardonnay wines.
St. Androny (Fr). A commune in the A.C. Côtes de Blaye, north-eastern Bordeaux.
Stanislaus (USA). A wine-producing county in the San Joaquin Valley, California.
Staňkov Brewery (Czec). A noted brewery based in western Czec.
Stanley Cocktail (Cktl). ¾ measure dry Gin, ¼ measure Bacardi White Label, juice ¼ lemon, 3 dashes Grenadine. Shake over ice, strain into a cocktail glass.
Stanley Wine Company (Austr). A winery in the Claire-Watervale district. Grape varieties – Cabernet and Rhine riesling. Sells wines under Leasingham label.
St. Annaberg (Ger). Vineyard. (Anb) = Rheinpfalz. (Ber) = Südliche Weinstrasse. (Gro) = Bischofskreuz. (Vil) = Burrweiler.
St. Anna Schloss (S.Afr). A medium sweet, white wine made from the Steen and Sémillon grapes by the Douglas Green Cellars label of Paarl.
St. Anne's Vineyard (Eng). A vineyard based at Wainhouse, Oxenhall, Newent, Gloucestershire. Was first planted in 1979. 0.8 ha. Grape varieties – Madeleine angevine 50%, Müller-Thurgau 25%, Triomphe d'Alsace 30% and Wrotham pinot.
St. Antoine Distillery (Afr). A Rum distillery based at Goodlands on the island of Mauritius, western Africa.
Stanton and Killeen (Austr). Vineyard. Address = Gracerray Vineyards, Rutherglen, Victoria 3685. 22 ha. Grape varieties – Cabernet sauvignon, Durif, Frontignan rouge, Muscadelle and Touriga.
Stanton Estate (USA). A vineyard based near Rutherford, Napa Valley, California. Grape variety – Johannisberg riesling. Is owned jointly by the Phelps and Burgess Cellars.
St. Antoniusweg (Ger). Vineyard. (Anb) = Nahe. (Ber) = Kreuznach. (Gro) = Sonnenborn. (Vil) = Langenlonsheim.
Staple (Eng). An estate near Canterbury, Kent. Produces dry white wines from the Müller-Thurgau, Huxelrebe and Reichensteiner grapes. 3 ha.
Staplegrove Vineyard (Eng). A vineyard based at Burlands Farm, Staplegrove, Taunton, Somerset. Was first planted in 1981. 2 ha. Grape varieties – Huxelrebe, Madeleine angevine, Reichensteiner, Siegerrebe and others.
Stappare (It). To uncork a bottle/cask.
Star (The) (Switz). A name the Swiss give to pétillant wines.
Stara Zagora (Bul). A delimited wine-producing area based in southern Bulgaria. Produces mainly red wines.
Starboard Light (Cktl). ½ measure dry Gin, ¼ measure Crème de Menthe, ¼ measure lemon juice. Shake over ice, strain into a cocktail glass.
Star-Bright (Eng). A descriptive term used for wines that are brilliantly clear.
Starbright IPA (Eng). A Pale ale 1039 O.G. brewed and bottled by the Hardys and Hanson Brewery in Nottingham.
Starch (Eng). $C_6H_{10}O_5$. Unfermentable by wine yeasts and may cause a haze in home-made wines.
Star Cocktail (Cktl). ¼ gill Apple brandy, ¼ gill French vermouth, 3 dashes Orange bitters, 3 dashes orange Curaçao. Stir over ice, strain into a cocktail glass. Add an olive and a squeeze of lemon peel juice on top.
Star Daisy (Cktl). 1 fl.oz. Calvados, 1 fl.oz. Gin, ½ fl.oz. lemon juice, ½ barspoon powdered sugar, 2 dashes Grenadine. Shake well over ice, strain into a wine glass containing cracked ice. Top with soda water and fresh fruit.
Star Hill (USA). A Bourbon whiskey distillery based in Loretta, south of Frankfort, Kentucky. Produces Maker's Mark. 50% alc. by vol.
Starico (Cktl). ½ measure Puerto Rican Rum, ⅕ measure Apricot brandy, ⅕ measure pineapple juice, ⅒ measure blue Curaçao. Shake over ice, strain into a cocktail glass.
Stark (Eng). A term used to denote a strong, vigorous wine that is high in alcohol.
Starka (Pol). A Vodka aged 10 years in oak giving it a rich brown colour and a kick like a mule. Made with an infusion of leaves from the Crimean apple tree with Port and Brandy added. See Polmos.
Starkbieres (Ger) (Switz). Strong beers with an O.G. of 18–20%.
Starkenburg (Ger). Bereich. (Anb) = Hessische Bergstrasse. (Gros) = Rott, Wolfsmagen, Schlossberg.

Starkenburg Brauerei (Aus). A small independent brewery based in the Tyrol.

Starkenburger Landwein (Ger). One of fifteen Deutsche Tafelwein zones.

Star Lager (Afr). A Lager beer 1047 O.G. brewed by the Nigerian Breweries Limited in Nigeria. Is also brewed by the Kumasi Brewery in Ghana.

Starlight Beer (Eng). A keg Bitter 1033 O.G. brewed by the Watney Combe Reid Brewery in London.

Starlight Cocktail (Cktl). ⅓ measure dry Gin, ⅓ measure Apricot brandy, ⅓ measure French vermouth. Shake over ice, strain into an ice-filled highball glass. Top with grapefruit juice.

Starobrno (Czec). Lit – 'Old Brno beer'. Brewed by the Brno Brewery.

Staropolski (Pol). A blended-honey mead sold in earthenware jars.

Staropramen (Czec). Lit – 'Old Spring beer'. Brewed by a brewery based in Prague of the same name.

Staropramen Brewery (Czec). The largest of Prague's Breweries. Produces fine Lager beers.

Starovar (Czec). Lit – 'Old brew'. Brewed by the Žatec Brewery.

Stars and Stripes (Pousse Café). Pour in order into an Elgin liqueur glass ⅓ measure Grenadine, ⅓ measure cream and ⅓ measure Crème Yvette.

Star System (Fr). An old system introduced by Maurice Hennessy in 1865 to show the ages of Cognac. *, **, ***, ****, ***** etc. which showed how many years Brandy had spent in wood. Now only the *** is used.

Starter (Eng). Added to wine yeasts to start the must fermenting (a selected wine yeast).

Starter's Orders (Cktl). ⅕ gill Midori in an ice-filled highball glass. Top with 1 gill sparkling wine.

State Domain (Ger). Possesses important holdings. Many are the top vineyards and it is the largest single owner of these famous vineyard properties. Headquarters are at Eltville.

Statianum (Lat). A red wine produced in central Italy in Roman times.

Station (Eng). A Tetley home-brew public house based in Guiseley, Leeds, Yorkshire. Noted for its cask conditioned Guiseley Gyle 1045 O.G. using Malt extract.

Statute of Vines, Wines and Spirits (Sp). Spanish wine laws introduced in 1970 by the Ministerio de Agricultura. See Consejos.

St. Aubyns Claret (N.Z.). A red wine from the Vidal winery. Is full-flavoured and dry with a soft after-taste.

Staudenberg (Ger). Vineyard. (Anb) = Baden. (Ber) = Badische Bergstrasse/ Kraichgau. (Gro) = Rittersberg. (Vil) = Leutershausen.

Staudenberg (Ger). Vineyard. (Anb) = Baden. (Ber) = Badische Bergstrasse/ Kraichgau. (Gro) = Rittersberg. (Vil) = Schriesheim.

Stauder Brauerei (Ger). A brewery based in Essen. Noted for its Stauder Pilsener Lager.

Staudernheim (Ger). Village. (Anb) = Nahe. (Ber) = Schloss Böckelheim. (Gro) = Paradiesgarten. (Vins) = Goldgrube, Herrenberg.

Staufen (Ger). Village. (Anb) = Baden. (Ber) = Markgräflerland. (Gro) = Lorettoberg. (Vin) = Schlossberg.

Staufenberg (Ger). Grosslage. (Anb) = Württemberg. (Ber) = Württembergish Unterland. (Vils) = Brettach, Cleversulzbach, Duttenberg, Erlenbach, Gundelsheim, Heilbronn, Horkheim, Neckarsulm, Oedheim, Offenau, Talheim, Untereisesheim.

Staufen [ortsteil Wettelbrunn] (Ger). Village. (Anb) = Baden. (Ber) = Markgräflerland. (Gro) = Lorettoberg. (Vin) = Maltesergarten.

St. Augustine (S.Afr). A blended red wine from the Douglas Green Group in the Paarl. Made from the Pinotage, Shiraz and Tinta barocca grapes. It is the KWV export red Roodeberg, cask aged for 2 years.

St. Austell Brewery (Eng). Based in St. Austell, Cornwall. Noted for its cask conditioned Tinners Ale 1038 O.G. Hicks Special 1050 O.G. keg Duchy 1037 O.G. and bottled Smugglers 1070 O.G. Prince's Ale 1100 O.G. Also brews Crippledick.

Staves (Eng). The sections of a cask.

Stavropol (USSR). A wine-producing region based near the Caucasus mountains. Produces dry white and dessert wines.

Stavroto (Gre). A red grape variety grown in northern Greece to make dry red wines.

St. Bernadus Brauerei (Bel). A commercial brewery that brews Bernadus Pater (a dark-brown, strong, top-fermented, bottle-conditioned Trappist-style beer) for St. Sixtus to enable them to meet demands.

St. Blaise (Switz). A principal vineyard based in the Neuchâtel.

St. Boes (Fr). A sulphurous mineral water.

St-Bris-le-Vineux (Fr). A village near Irancy (Chablis) which produces dry, white wines from the Sauvignon grape and some minor red wines.

S

St. **Castorhöhle** (Ger). Vineyard. (Anb) = Mosel-Saar-Ruwer. (Ber) = Zell/ Mosel. (Gro) = Goldbäumchen. (Vil) = Müden.

St. **Catherines** (Can). A wine district between Niagara and Crystal Beach.

St. **Cedd's Vineyard** (Austr). A part of the Lindemans estate, New South Wales. 24 ha. of mixed grape varieties, mainly Gewürztraminer.

St. **Charle's Punch** (Cktl). ½ gill Port, ½ gill Brandy, juice ½ lemon, sugar syrup, 4 dashes Curaçao. Shake over ice, strain into an ice-filled highball glass, decorate with fruit and serve with straws.

St. **Chinian** (Fr). An A.C. red wine from Minervois. Is produced by the Nicolas Co.

St-**Christ-de-Blaye** (Fr). A commune in the A.C. Côtes de Blaye, north-eastern Bordeaux.

St. **Christoly** (Fr). See Saint Christoly.

St. **Christopher Lager** (Eng). An alcohol-free Lager brewed and bottled by Allied Breweries.

St-**Ciers-de-Canesse** (Fr). A commune in the A.C. Côtes de Bourg, north-eastern Bordeaux.

St. **Clements** (Eng). A range of sparkling, non-alcoholic, soft drinks produced by Mandora (part of the Mansfield Brewery). Available in a variety of flavours. Also a range of fruit squashes.

St. **Clement Vineyards** (USA). A winery based near St. Helena, Napa Valley, California. Grape varieties – Cabernet sauvignon and Chardonnay. Produces varietal wines.

St. **Croix Rum** (USA). A light Rum produced in the eastern states.

St. **Cyriakusstift** (Ger). Vineyard. (Anb) = Rheinhessen. (Ber) = Wonnegau. (Gro) = Liebfrauenmorgen. (Vil) = Worms.

St. **David's Porter** (Wales). A Brown ale 1036 O.G. brewed and bottled by the Felinfoel Brewery for export to the USA.

Steam Beer (USA). A Californian method of brewing using bottom-fermenting yeasts at Ale temperatures (rare). See Anchor Steam. 5% alc. by vol.

Steaming (Scot) (slang). A term for very intoxicated (drunk).

Steap (Eng). A mediaeval type of jug or flagon.

Ste. Chapelle (USA). A major winery based in Idaho, Pacific North-West. See Sainte-Chapelle Vineyards.

Sté. Delord (Fr). An Armagnac producer. Address = 32520 Lannepax.

St. **Edmunds Ale** (Eng). A bottled Ale 1060 O.G. brewed by the Greene King Brewery in East Anglia.

Steel's Masher (Eng). A rotary device which ensures a correct balance of Liquor and Grist and runs the mixture into the Mash tun.

Steely (Eng). A term to describe a wine that is hard, though not harsh. White wines.

Steen (S.Afr). A white grape variety. Known as the Chenin blanc in France. Also known as the Steendruif.

Steendruif (S.Afr). See Steen.

Steep (Eng). To soak. Applied to barley that is soaked in water (known as the liquor) for germination. Also for solids to be steeped in liquids to extract flavour. i.e. Tea, herbs in alcohol or wine, etc.

Steep (Scot). A stone trough in which the barley is soaked before being spread on the floor to germinate.

Steeped (Eng). The term used for soaking the barley prior to the germination period.

Steeps (Scot). Tanks in which the grain (barley) is soaked before it is allowed to germinate for Malt whisky production.

Stefaneşti (Rum). A wine-producing area. Produces mainly white wines.

Stefansberg (Ger). Vineyard. (Anb) = Mosel-Saar-Ruwer. (Ber) = Zell/Mosel. (Gro) = Schwarze Katz. (Vil) = Zell-Merl.

Stefanslay (Ger). Vineyard. (Anb) = Mosel-Saar-Ruwer. (Ber) = Bernkastel (Gro) = Kurfürstlay. (Vil) = Wintrich.

Sté. Fermière du Château de Malliac (Fr). An Armagnac producer. Address = Château de Malliac, 32250 Montréal du Gers.

Steffensberg (Ger). Vineyard. (Anb) = Mosel-Saar-Ruwer. (Ber) = Bernkastel. (Gro) = Nacktarsch. (Vil) = Kröv.

Steffensberg (Ger). Vineyard. (Anb) = Mosel-Saar-Ruwer. (Ber) = Bernkastel. (Gro) = Schwarzlay. (Vil) = Enkirch.

Steffl (Aus). The first Lager beer ever brewed in 1841. Produced by Anton Dreher. Known generally as the original 'Vienna Lager'.

Steffl Export (Aus). A Lager beer 5.4% alc. by vol. brewed by the Schwechat Brauerei in Vienna. Conditioned for 3 months. (Is part of Bräu A.G).

Sté-Foy-Bordeaux (Fr). An A.C. red and white wine commune in southern Bordeaux.

Stehlerberg (Ger). Vineyard. (Anb) = Mittelrhein. (Ber) = Rheinburgengau. (Gro) = Burg Hammerstein. (Vil) = Kasbach.

Steichling (Ger). Vineyard. (Anb) = Hessische Bergstrasse. (Ber) = Starkenburg. (Gro) = Wolfsmagen. (Vil) = Bensheim.

Steiermark (Aus). A wine region which contains the districts of Kloch-Ost-Steiermark, Südsteiermark and Weststeiermark.

Steig (Ger). Vineyard. (Anb) = Baden. (Ber)

= Badische Bergstrasse/Kraichgau. (Gro) = Hohenberg. (Vil) = Eisingen.

Steig (Ger). Vineyard. (Anb) = Rheingau. (Ber) = Johannisberg. (Gro) = Daubhaus. (Vil) = Kostheim.

Steig (Ger). Vineyard. (Anb) = Rheinhessen. (Ber) = Wonnegau. (Gro) = Burg Rodenstein. (Vil) = Flörsheim-Dalsheim.

Steig (Ger). Vineyard. (Anb) = Rheinpfalz. (Ber) = Mittelhaardt-Deutsche Weinstrasse. (Gro) = Schwarzerde. (Vil) = Bisserheim.

Steige (Ger). Vineyard. (Anb) = Baden. (Ber) = Markgräflerland. (Gro) = Vogtei Rötteln. (Vil) = Haltingen.

Steige (Ger). Vineyard. (Anb) = Baden. (Ber) = Markgräflerland. (Gro) = Vogtei Rötteln. (Vil) = Ötlingen.

Steige (Ger). Vineyard. (Anb) = Rheinhessen. (Ber) = Bingen. (Gro) = Rheingrafenstein. (Vil) = Fürfeld.

Steigerberg (Ger). Vineyard. (Anb) = Rheinhessen. (Ber) = Bingen. (Gro) = Adelberg. (Vil) = Wendelsheim.

Steigerdell (Ger). Vineyard. (Anb) = Nahe. (Ber) = Schloss Böckelheim. (Gro) = Burgweg. (Vil) = Bad Münster a. St-Ebernburg.

Steigerwald (Ger). Bereich. (Anb) = Franken. (Gros) = Burgweg, Herrenberg, Kapellenberg, Schild, Schlossberg, Schlosstück. Has a soil of Marl which gives an earthly taste to the wines.

Steig-Terrassen (Ger). Vineyard. (Anb) = Rheinhessen. (Ber) = Nierstein. (Gro) = Vogelsgärten. (Vil) = Guntersblum.

Steil (Ger). Grosslage. (Anb) = Rheingau. (Ber) = Johannisberg. (Vils) = Assmannshausen, Assmannshausen-Aulhausen.

Stein (Ger). A beer mug (earthenware) of between a ½ litre and 2 litre capacity. Often has a lid.

Stein (Ger). Lit – 'Stone'.

Stein (Ger). Vineyard. (Anb) = Franken. (Ber) = Maindreieck. (Gro) = Not yet assigned. (Vil) = Würzburg.

Stein (Ger). Vineyard. (Anb) = Franken. (Ber) = Maindreieck. (Gro) = Rosstal. (Vil) = Stetten.

Stein (Ger). Vineyard. (Anb) = Rheingau. (Ber) = Johannisberg. (Gro) = Daubhaus. (Vil) = Hochheim.

Stein (Ger). Vineyard. (Anb) = Rheingau. (Ber) = Johannisberg. (Gro) = Daubhaus. (Vil) = Wicker.

Stein (Ger). Vineyard. (Anb) = Rheinhessen. (Ber) = Wonnegau. (Gro) = Gotteshilfe. (Vil) = Bechtheim.

Stein (S.Afr). A medium-sweet wine produced from a blend of Steen and other white grape varieties.

Stein (**Robert**) (Scot). The pioneer, inventor of the continuous still which was perfected by Aeneas Coffey in 1826.

Steinacker (Ger). Vineyard. (Anb) = Baden. (Ber) = Markgräflerland. (Gro) = Vogtei Rötteln. (Vil) = Herten.

Steinacker (Ger). Vineyard. (Anb) = Rheinhessen. (Ber) = Bingen. (Gro) = Abtey. (Vil) = Nieder-Hilbersheim.

Steinacker (Ger). Vineyard. (Anb) = Rheinhessen. (Ber) = Bingen. (Gro) = Kaiserpfalz. (Vil) = Heidesheim.

Steinacker (Ger). Vineyard. (Anb) = Rheinhessen. (Ber) = Bingen. (Gro) = Kaiserpfalz. (Vil) = Ingelheim.

Steinacker (Ger). Vineyard. (Anb) = Rheinpfalz. (Ber) = Mittelhaardt Deutsche Weinstrasse. (Gro) = Kobnert. (Vil) = Kallstadt.

Steinacker (Ger). Vineyard. (Anb) = Rheinpfalz. (Ber) = Mittelhaardt-Deutsche Weinstrasse. (Gro) = Schwarzerde. (Vil) = Kirchheim.

Steinacker (Ger). Vineyard. (Anb) = Württemberg. (Ber) = Württembergisch Unterland. (Gro) = Salzberg. (Vil) = Lehrensteinsfeld.

Stein-am-Rhein (Switz). A wine-producing area based in Schauffhausen, northern Switzerland. Famous for its white wines.

Steinbach (Ger). Village. (Anb) = Baden. (Ber) = Ortenau. (Gro) = Schloss Rodeck. (Vins) = Stich den Buben, Yburgberg.

Steinbach (Ger). Village. (Anb) = Franken. (Ber) = Steigerwald. (Gro) = Kapellenberg. (Vin) = Nonnenberg.

Steinbach (Ger). Vineyard. (Anb) = Franken. (Ber) = Maindreieck. (Gro) = Not yet assigned. (Vil) = Sommerhausen.

Steinbachhof (Ger). Vineyard. (Anb) = Württemberg. (Ber) = Württembergisch Unterland. (Gro) = Stromberg. (Vil) = Gründelbach.

Steinberg (Ger). Vineyard. (Anb) = Baden. (Ber) = Markgräflerland. (Gro) = Lorettoberg. (Vil) = Bollschweil.

Steinberg (Ger). Vineyard. (Anb) = Baden. (Ber) = Ortenau. (Gro) = Fürsteneck. (Vil) = Durbach.

Steinberg (Ger). Vineyard. (Anb) = Franken. (Ber) = Maindreieck. (Gro) = Not yet assigned. (Vil) = Michelbach.

Steinberg (Ger). Vineyard. (Anb) = Nahe. (Ber) = Kreuznach. (Gro) = Kronenberg. (Vil) = Bad Kreuznach.

Steinberg (Ger). Vineyard. (Anb) = Nahe. (Ber) = Schloss Böckelheim. (Gro) = Burgweg. (Vil) = Niederhausen an der Nahe.

Steinberg (Ger). Vineyard. (Anb) = Rheingau. (Ber) = Johannisberg. (Gro) = Deutelsberg. (Vil) = Estate.

Steinberg (Ger). Vineyard. (Anb) = Rheinhessen. (Ber) = Bingen. (Gro) = Abtey. (Vil) = Partenheim.

Steinberg (Ger). Vineyard. (Anb) = Rheinhessen. (Ber) = Bingen. (Gro) = Abtey. (Vil) = Sankt Johann.

Steinberg (Ger). Vineyard. (Anb) = Rheinhessen. (Ber) = Bingen. (Gro) = Kaiserpfalz. (Vil) = Wackernheim.

Steinberg (Ger). Vineyard. (Anb) = Rheinhessen. (Ber) = Nierstein. (Gro) = Gutes Domtal. (Vil) = Dalheim.

Steinberg (Ger). Vineyard. (Anb) = Rheinhessen. (Ber) = Nierstein. (Gro) = Krötenbrunnen. (Vil) = Guntersblum.

Steinberg (Ger). Vineyard. (Anb) = Rheinpfalz. (Ber) = Mittelhaardt-Deutsche Weinstrasse. (Gro) = Feuerberg. (Vil) = Bad Dürkheim.

Steinberg (Ger). Vineyard. (Anb) = Württemberg. (Ber) = Württembergisch Unterland. (Gro) = Wunnenstein. (Vil) = Beilstein.

Steinberger (Ger). Vineyard. (Anb) = Mosel-Saar-Ruwer. (Ber) = Saar-Ruwer. (Gro) = Scharzberg. (Vil) = Filzen.

Steinbock (Eng). A draught Lager beer 1034 O.G. brewed by the Shepherd Neame Brewery in Faversham, Kent.

Stein-Bockenheim (Ger). Village. (Anb) = Rheinhessen. (Ber) = Bingen. (Gro) = Rheingrafenstein. (Vin) = Sonnenburg.

Steinböhl (Ger). Vineyard. (Anb) = Rheinhessen. (Ber) = Wonnegau. (Gro) = Pilgerpfad. (Vil) = Monzernheim.

Steinbuck (Ger). Vineyard. (Anb) = Baden. (Ber) = Kaiserstuhl-Tuniberg. (Gro) = Vulkanfelsen. (Vil) = Bischoffingen.

Steinchen (Ger). Vineyard. (Anb) = Mosel-Saar-Ruwer. (Ber) = Zell/Mosel. (Gro) = Weinhex. (Vil) = Kattenes.

Steinchen (Ger). Vineyard. (Anb) = Nahe. (Ber) = Kreuznach. (Gro) = Sonnenborn. (Vil) = Langenlonsheim.

Steinenstadt (Ger). Village. (Anb) = Baden. (Ber) = Markgräflerland. (Gro) = Burg Neuenfels. (Vins) = Schäf, Sonnenstück.

Steiner Hund (Aus). A dry white wine from the Wachau district. Made from the Riesling grape.

Steinert (Ger). Vineyard. (Anb) = Rheinhessen. (Ber) = Bingen. (Gro) = Abtey. (Vil) = Gau-Algesheim.

Steiner Vineyard (USA). A vineyard based near Glen Ellen, Sonoma Valley, California. Grape variety – Cabernet sauvignon. See Crema Vinera (La).

Steinfeld (Ger). Village. (Anb) = Rheinpfalz. (Ber) = Südliche Weinstrasse. (Gro) = Guttenberg. (Vin) = Herrenwingert.

Steinfelsen (Ger). Vineyard. (Anb) = Baden. (Ber) = Kaiserstuhl-Tuniberg. (Gro) = Vulkanfelsen. (Vil) = Bickensohl.

Steinfelsen (Ger). Vineyard. (Anb) = Baden. (Ber) = Kaiserstuhl-Tuniberg. (Gro) = Vulkanfelsen. (Vil) = Ihringen.

Steingarten (Austr). The label used by the Orlando Winery in the Barossa Valley for their Riesling-based wines.

Steingässle (Ger). Vineyard. (Anb) = Baden. (Ber) = Markgräflerland. (Gro) = Vogtei Rötteln. (Vil) = Efringen-Kirchen.

Steingässle (Ger). Vineyard. (Anb) = Baden. (Ber) = Markgräflerland. (Gro) = Vogtei Rötteln. (Vil) = Feuerbach.

Steingässle (Ger). Vineyard. (Anb) = Baden. (Ber) = Markgräflerland. (Gro) = Vogtei Rötteln. (Vil) = Holzen.

Steingässle (Ger). Vineyard. (Anb) = Baden. (Ber) = Markgräflerland. (Gro) = Vogtei Rötteln. (Vil) = Riedlingen.

Steingässle (Ger). Vineyard. (Anb) = Baden. (Ber) = Markgräflerland. (Gro) = Vogtei Rötteln. (Vil) = Tannenkirch.

Steingässle (Ger). Vineyard. (Anb) = Baden. (Ber) = Markgräflerland. (Gro) = Vogtei Rötteln. (Vil) = Welmlingen.

Steingässle (Ger). Vineyard. (Anb) = Baden. (Ber) = Markgräflerland. (Gro) = Vogtei Rötteln. (Vil) = Wintersweiler.

Steingässle (Ger). Vineyard. (Anb) = Baden. (Ber) = Markgräflerland. (Gro) = Vogtei Rötteln. (Vil) = Wollbach.

Steingebiss (Ger). Vineyard. (Anb) = Rheinpfalz. (Ber) = Südliche Weinstrasse. (Gro) = Kloster Liebfrauenberg. (Vil) = Billigheim-Ingenheim.

Steingeröll (Ger). Vineyard. (Anb) = Hessische Bergstrasse. (Ber) = Starkenburg. (Gro) = Rott. (Vil) = Zwingenberg.

Steingerück (Ger). Vineyard. (Anb) = Hessische Bergstrasse. (Ber) = Umstadt. (Gro) = Not yet assigned. (Vil) = Gross-Umstadt.

Steingold Lager (Eng). A Lager beer 1042 O.G. brewed by the McMullen Brewery in Hertford.

Steingrube (Ger). Vineyard. (Anb) = Baden. (Ber) = Kaiserstuhl-Tuniberg. (Gro) = Vulkanfelsen. (Vil) = Endingen.

Steingrube (Ger). Vineyard. (Anb) = Baden. (Ber) = Kaiserstuhl-Tuniberg. (Gro) = Vulkanfelsen. (Vil) = Jechtingen.

Steingrube (Ger). Vineyard. (Anb) = Baden. (Ber) = Kaiserstuhl-Tuniberg. (Gro) = Vulkanfelsen. (Vil) = Neuershausen.

Steingrube (Ger). Vineyard. (Anb) = Baden. (Ber) = Kaiserstuhl-Tuniberg. (Gro) = Vulkanfelsen. (Vil) = Nimburg.

Steingrube (Ger). Vineyard. (Anb) = Rheinhessen. (Ber) = Wonnegau. (Gro) = Bergkloster. (Vil) = Westhofen.

Steingrube (Ger). Vineyard. (Anb) = Württemberg. (Ber) = Remstal-Stuttgart. (Gro) = Weinsteige. (Vil) = Stuttgart (ortsteil Ulhbach).

Steingrube (Ger). Vineyard. (Anb) = Württemberg. (Ber) = Württembergisch Unterland. (Gro) = Heuchelberg. (Vil) = Neipperg.

Steingrüble (Ger). Vineyard. (Anb) = Baden. (Ber) = Markgräflerland. (Gro) = Lorettoberg. (Vil) = Bad Krotzingen.

Steingrüble (Ger). Vineyard. (Anb) = Baden. (Ber) = Markgräflerland. (Gro) = Lorettoberg. (Vil) = Schlatt.

Steingrüble (Ger). Vineyard. (Anb) = Baden. (Ber) = Kaiserstuhl-Tuniberg. (Gro) = Vulkanfelsen. (Vil) = Königschaffhausen.

Steingrüble (Ger). Vineyard. (Anb) = Württemberg. (Ber) = Remstal-Stuttgart. (Gro) = Wartbühl. (Vil) = Grossheppach.

Steingrüble (Ger). Vineyard. (Anb) = Württemberg. (Ber) = Remstal-Stuttgart. (Gro) = Wartbühl. (Vil) = Kleinheppach.

Steingrüble (Ger). Vineyard. (Anb) = Württemberg. (Ber) = Remstal-Stuttgart. (Gro) = Wartbühl. (Vil) = Korb.

Steingrüble (Ger). Vineyard. (Anb) = Württemberg. (Ber) = Remstal-Stuttgart. (Gro) = Wartbühl. (Vil) = Waiblingen.

Steingrübler (Ger). Vineyard. (Anb) = Baden. (Ber) = Ortenau. (Gro) = Schloss Rodeck. (Vil) = Varnhalt.

Steingrübler (Ger). Vineyard. (Anb) = Franken. (Ber) = Mainviereck. (Gro) = Not yet assigned. (Vil) = Miltenberg.

Steinhaeger (Ger). A Gin, colourless and juniper-flavoured. Sold in stone jars. Produced in Steinhägen, Westphalia. 38% alc. by vol.

Steinhäger (Ger). See Steinhaeger.

Steinhalde (Ger). Vineyard. (Anb) = Baden. (Ber) = Kaiserstuhl-Tuniberg. (Gro) = Vulkanfelsen. (Vil) = Amoltern.

Steinhalde (Ger). Vineyard. (Anb) = Württemberg. (Ber) = Remstal-Stuttgart. (Gro) = Weinsteige. (Vil) = Stuttgart (ortsteil Cannstatt).

Steinhalde (Ger). Vineyard. (Anb) = Württemberg. (Ber) = Remstal-Stuttgart. (Gro) = Weinsteige. (Vil) = Stuttgart (ortsteil Mühlhausen).

Steinhalde (Ger). Vineyard. (Anb) = Württemberg. (Ber) = Remstal-Stuttgart. (Gro) = Weinsteige. (Vil) = Stuttgart (ortsteil Münster).

Stein/Harfe (Ger). Vineyard. (Anb) = Franken. (Ber) = Maindreieck. (Gro) = Not yet assigned. (Vil) = Würzburg.

Steinhaus (USA). The brand-name used by Schell Brewery in New Ulm, Minnesota for their range of light-style beers.

Steinheim (Ger). Village. (Anb) = Württemberg. (Ber) = Württembergisch Unterland. (Gro) = Schalkstein. (Vin) = Burgberg.

Steinheim (Ger). Village. (Anb) = Württemberg. (Ber) = Württembergisch Unterland. (Gro) = Wunnenstein. (Vin) = Lichtenberg.

Steinkaul (Ger). Vineyard. (Anb) = Ahr. (Ber) = Walporzheim/Ahrtal. (Gro) = Klosterberg. (Vil) = Bachem.

Steinkaut (Ger). Vineyard. (Anb) = Nahe. (Ber) = Schloss Böckelheim. (Gro) = Rosengarten. (Vil) = Weinsheim.

Steinklinge (Ger). Vineyard. (Anb) = Baden. (Ber) = Badische Frankenland. (Gro) = Tauberklinge. (Vil) = Oberlauda.

Steinkopf (Ger). Vineyard. (Anb) = Hessische Bergstrasse. (Ber) = Starkenburg. (Gro) = Schlossberg. (Vil) = Heppenheim including Erbach and Hambach.

Steinkopf (Ger). Vineyard. (Anb) = Nahe. (Ber) = Kreuznach. (Gro) = Schlosskapelle. (Vil) = Münster-Sarmsheim.

Steinkopf (Ger). Vineyard. (Anb) = Rheinpfalz. (Ber) = Mittelhaardt-Deutsche Weinstrasse. (Gro) = Schwarzerde. (Vil) = Heuchelheim/Frankenthal.

Steinköpfchen (Ger). Vineyard. (Anb) = Nahe. (Ber) = Kreuznach. (Gro) = Schlosskapelle. (Vil) = Rümmelsheim.

Steinkreuz (Ger). Vineyard. (Anb) = Nahe. (Ber) = Schloss Böckelheim. (Gro) = Rosengarten. (Vil) = St. Katharinen.

Stein Lager (Ch.Isles). A Lager beer 1048 O.G. brewed by the Guernsey Brewery 1920 Ltd., St. Peter Port, Guernsey. Previously known as Hi-Brau.

Stein Lager (Eng). A Lager beer 1036 O.G. brewed by the Thwaites Brewery in Blackburn, Lancashire.

Steinlager (N.Z.). A full-bodied Lager beer 1052 O.G. brewed by the New Zealand Breweries.

S

Steinler (Ger). Vineyard. (Anb) = Baden. (Ber) = Bodensee. (Gro) = Not yet assigned. (Vil) = Lottstetten (ortsteil Nack).

Steinler (Ger). Vineyard. (Anb) = Baden. (Ber) = Markgräflerland. (Gro) = Lorettoberg. (Vil) = Freiburg.

Steinmächer (Ger). Grosslage. (Anb) = Rheingau. (Ber) = Johannisberg. (Vils) = Dotzheim, Eltville, Frauenstein, Martinsthal, Niederwalluf, Oberwalluf, Rauenthal, Schierstein.

Steinmauer (Ger). Vineyard. (Anb) = Baden. (Ber) = Kaiserstuhl-Tuniberg. (Gro) = Attilafelsen. (Vil) = Waltershofen.

Steinmorgen (Ger). Vineyard. (Anb) = Rheingau. (Ber) = Johannisberg. (Gro) = Deutelsberg. (Vil) = Erbach.

Steinrossel (Ger). Vineyard. (Anb) = Nahe. (Ber) = Kreuznach. (Gro) = Pfarrgarten. (Vil) = Sommerloch.

Steinsberg (Ger). Vineyard. (Anb) = Baden. (Ber) = Badische Bergstrasse/Kraichgau. (Gro) = Stiftsberg. (Vil) = Sinsheim (stadtteil Weiler).

Steinsberg (Ger). Vineyard. (Anb) = Baden. (Ber) = Badische Bergstrasse/Kraichgau. (Gro) = Stiftsberg. (Vil) = Steinsfurt.

Steinschiller (Rum). A white grape variety grown in the Banat Vineyard for the production of white wines in Teremia Mare and Tomnatec.

Steinsfurt (Ger). Village. (Anb) = Baden. (Ber) = Badische Bergstrasse/Kraichgau. (Gro) = Stiftsberg. (Vin) = Steinsberg.

Steinweg (Ger). Vineyard. (Anb) = Nahe. (Ber) = Kreuznach. (Gro) = Kronenberg. (Vil) = Bad Kreuznach.

Steinweiler (Ger). Village. (Anb) = Rheinpfalz. (Ber) = Südliche Weinstrasse. (Gro) = Kloster Liebfrauenberg. (Vin) = Rosenberg.

Steinwein (Ger). A term used to denote the wines of Franconia, which are white, dry and steely in flavour. Lit – 'Stone wine'. Named after the vineyard.

Steinwein 1540 (Ger). The longest living wine recorded. Is still drinkable. Discovered in Wurzberg in the twentieth century.

Steinwengert (Ger). Vineyard. (Anb) = Baden. (Ber) = Badische Bergstrasse/Kraichgau. (Gro) = Hohenberg. (Vil) = Wöschbach.

Steinwingert (Ger). Vineyard. (Anb) = Nahe. (Ber) = Schloss Böckelheim. (Gro) = Burgweg. (Vil) = Niederhausen an der Nahe.

Steirisch Pils (Aus). A light, well-hopped Pilsener Lager brewed by the Gösser Brauerei at Leoben.

Stella Artois (Bel). The largest brewery in Belgium. Its Lager 1047 O.G. is brewed in Britain under licence by the Whitbread Brewery, London.

Stella Pils (Afr). A Pilsener Lager beer brewed by the Mauritius Brewery on the island of Mauritius.

Stellenbosch (S.Afr). Wine town and region of the western Cape. Produces most of the Cape's finest wines. Estates include – Goede Houp, Jacobsdal, Meerlust, Middelvlei, Simonsig and Uitkyk.

Stellenbosch Farmers' Winery (S.Afr). SFW. Address = P.O. Box 46, Stellenbosch 7600. The largest wine wholesaler. Instituted the Nederburg Wine Auction. Labels include – Château Libertas, La Gratitude, Lanzerac, Oom Tas, Oude Libertas, Tasheimer, Taskelder and Zonnebloem.

Stellenrood (S.Afr). A light red wine produced from the Cabernet, Cinsault and Shiraz grapes by Bertrams Wines, Stellenbosch.

Stellenryck Collection (S.Afr). A range of varietal wines produced by the Die Bergkelder.

St. Elmo (Port). A brand of sweet white wine produced by SOGRAPE.

Steltzer Vineyard (USA). A vineyard based near Yountville, California. Grape varieties – Cabernet sauvignon and Johannisberg riesling. Produces varietal wines.

Sté-Michelle Winery (Can). A vineyard based in Okanagin. Produces Labrusca-type and French hybrid wines.

St. Emiliana (Chile). The brand-name of a red wine produced by Concha y Toro.

St-Émilion (Fr). A.C. wine region of eastern Bordeaux. Red wines only. Classified in 1955. Cabernet franc, Merlot and Cabernet sauvignon main grape varieties. See also Saint-Émilion and Saint-Émilion Classification.

Stemmed Glass (Eng). A glass with a long stem between the bowl and the foot. It enables the glass to be held without the drink being heated by the hand.

Stemming (Eng). The name given to the process of removing stalks from grapes using an Égrappoir or Foulograppe.

Stemmler (Ger). Vineyard. (Anb) = Hessische Bergstrasse. (Ber) = Starkenburg. (Gro) = Schlossberg. (Vil) = Heppenheim including Erbach and Hambach.

Stemmler Winery (USA). A winery based in the Dry Creek Valley, Sonoma County, California. Grape varieties – Cabernet sauvignon, Chardonnay and Fumé blanc. Produces varietal wines.

Stephanoderes Hamjei (Lat). The Coffee Berry Borer. A parasite that attacks the berries of the coffee bush.

Stephansberg (Ger). Vineyard. (Anb) =

Baden. (Ber) = Badische Bergstrasse/ Kraichgau. (Gro) = Rittersberg. (Vil) = Hohensachsen.

Stephansberg (Ger). Vineyard. (Anb) = Baden. (Ber) = Badische Bergstrasse/ Kraichgau. (Gro) = Rittersberg. (Vil) = Lützelsachsen.

Stephansberg (Ger). Vineyard. (Anb) = Nahe. (Ber) = Schloss Böckelheim. (Gro) = Burgweg. (Vil) = Bad Münster a. St-Ebernburg.

Stephanus-Rosengärtchen (Ger). Vineyard. (Anb) = Mosel-Saar-Ruwer. (Ber) = Bernkastel. (Gro) = Kurfürstlay. (Vil) = Bernkastel-Kues.

Stephen Zellerbach Winery (USA). A winery based in the Napa Valley, northern California. Produces varietal wines.

Sterke Drank (Hol). Beverage, alcoholic liquor, spirits.

Sterken (Hol). To fortify with spirits.

Sterling Vineyards (USA). A large winery in Calistoga, Napa Valley, northern California. Grape varieties – Cabernet sauvignon, Chardonnay, Merlot and Sauvignon blanc. Produces varietal wines. Owned by the Coca Cola Company.

Sternberg (Ger). Vineyard. (Anb) = Rheinhessen. (Ber) = Bingen. (Gro) = Rheingrafenstein. (Vil) = Pleitersheim.

Sternbrau (Switz). A Lager beer 1045 O.G. brewed by the Hurlimann Brauerei. Brewed under licence by the Shepherd Neame Brewery in Faversham, Kent.

Sternenberg (Ger). Vineyard. (Anb) = Baden. (Ber) = Ortenau. (Gro) = Schloss Rodeck. (Vil) = Altschweier.

Sternenberg (Ger). Vineyard. (Anb) = Baden. (Ber) = Ortenau. (Gro) = Schloss Rodeck. (Vil) = Bühl (ortsteil Neusatz).

Sternenfels (Ger). Village. (Anb) = Württemberg. (Ber) = Württembergisch Unterland. (Gro) = Stromberg. (Vin) = König.

Stert Vineyard (Eng). A vineyard based at Barn Cottage, Stert, Devizes, Wiltshire. 0.5 ha. Was first planted in 1976. Grape varieties – Müller-Thurgau and Wrotham pinot (Pinot meunier).

St-Estèphe (Fr). A.C. wine commune within the Haut-Médoc. Has vineyards in the 1855 classification. Cabernet sauvignon, Cabernet franc and Merlot are the main grape varieties. Red wines only.

St. Etheldreda (Eng). A dry white, table wine produced by the Isle of Ely vineyard in Cambridgeshire.

St. Étienne-de-Baïgorry (Fr). A V.D.Q.S. district in south-western Irouléguy.

Home to the co-operative that controls all the Irouléguy wines.

Stetten (Ger). Village. (Anb) = Baden. (Ber) = Bodensee. (Gro) = Sonnenufer. (Vins) = Fohrenberg, Lerchenberg, Sängerhalde.

Stetten (Ger). Village. (Anb) = Franken. (Ber) = Maindreieck. (Gro) = Rosstal. (Vin) = Stein.

Stetten (Ger). Village. (Anb) = Rheinpfalz. (Ber) = Mittelhaardt-Deutsche Weinstrasse. (Gro) = Schnepfenflug vom Zellertal. (Vin) = Heilighäuschen.

Stetten a. H. (Ger). Village. (Anb) = Württemberg. (Ber) = Württembergisch Unterland. (Gro) = Heuchelberg. (Vin) = Sonnenberg.

Stetten i. R. (Ger). Village. (Anb) = Württemberg. (Ber) = Remstal-Stuttgart. See Kernen.

Stetten i. R. (Ger). Village. (Anb) = Württemberg. (Ber) = Remstal-Stuttgart. (Gro) = Wartbühl. (Vins) = Brotwasser, Häder, Lindhälder, Puvermächer.

Stettfeld (Ger). See Ubstadt-Weiher.

Stettyn Co-operative (S.Afr). A winery based in Worcester. Address = Stettyn Wynkelders Koöperatief, Private Bag 3011, Worcester 6850. Produces varietals.

Stettyn Wynkelders Koöperatief (S.Afr). See Stettyn Co-operative.

Steuk Wine Company (USA). A winery based near Cleveland, Ohio. Produces Concord, vinifera and French-American hybrid wines.

Stevenot Winery (USA). A winery based at Murphy's, Calaveras County, California. Grape varieties – Cabernet sauvignon, Chardonnay, Chenin blanc, White riesling and Zinfandel. Produces varietal and table wines.

Stewart and Son (Scot). A noted blender and exporter of Scotch whiskies based in Dundee and Glasgow. Noted for its Stewarts Cream of the Barley and Royal Stewart. Now part of the Allied Group. Was formerly part of William Teacher and Sons.

Stewart's Cream of the Barley (Scot). A blended Scotch whisky produced by Stewart and Son of Dundee, Glasgow. Has a high proportion of single Malt whiskies (30) in the blend. Sold in a distinctive square-shaped bottle.

Stewed (Eng) (slang). Intoxicated (drunk).

Stewed (Eng). A term used to denote a tea that has been brewed too long and has a bitter taste through too much tannin and caffeine.

Stewed (Eng). The term used to describe

S

coffee brewed from freshly ground beans that has been kept hot for a long time. Has a bitter flat taste.

Steyer (Ger). Vineyard. (Anb) = Nahe. (Ber) = Schloss Böckelheim. (Gro) = Rosengarten. (Vil) = Hüffelsheim.

Steyerberg (Ger). Vineyard. (Anb) = Nahe. (Ber) = Kreuznach. (Gro) = Schlosskapelle. (Vil) = Schweppenhausen.

St. Felician (Arg). A Cabernet-based wine produced by Esmeralda at Córdoba.

St. Feuillion (Bel). A golden Abbaye beer brewed by the Roeulx Brasserie in central Belgium.

St. Fiacre (Fr). A village in the A.C. district of Muscadet de Sèvre et Maine, Loire. Produces some of the finest Muscadets.

St. Francis of Paula Brauerei (Ger). The first Doppelbock created in Germany in Munich (in a monastery) named Salvator. Now known as the Paulaner-Thomas-Bräu Brauerei.

St. Francis Winery (USA). A winery based in Kenwood, Sonoma County, California. 46 ha. Grape varieties – Chardonnay, Gewürztraminer, Johannisberg riesling, Merlot and Pinot noir. Produces varietal and table wines.

St-Gall (Fr). The label used by the Champagne Growers' Co-operative at Avize, Union-Champagne.

St. Galmier (Fr). See Saint Galmier.

St-Genès-de-Blaye (Fr). A commune in the A.C. Côtes de Blaye in north-eastern Bordeaux.

St. Genies-de-Comolas (Fr). A commune in the district of A.C. Lirac in the southern Rhône. Produces white, rosé and red wines.

St. George Brewery (Afr). A brewery based in Addis Ababa, Ethiopia. Brews a fine Pilsener lager beer.

St. Georgen (Aus). A wine-producing area in the Eisenstadt district.

St. Georgenberg (Ger). Vineyard. (Anb) = Rheinhessen. (Ber) = Bingen. (Gro) = Kaiserpfalz. (Vil) = Jugenheim.

St. Georgenberg (Ger). Vineyard. (Anb) = Rheinhessen. (Ber) = Wonnegau. (Gro) = Liebfrauengarten. (Vil) = Worms.

St. Georges (Gre). A red grape variety. See Agiorgitiko.

St. Georges d'Orques (Fr). See Saint-Georges d'Orques.

St. George's English Wines (Eng). See Waldron Vineyards.

St. Georges Saint-Émilion (Fr). An A.C. commune within the Saint-Émilion district in eastern Bordeaux.

St. George's Vineyard (Austr). Part of the Lindemans estate in New South Wales. 12 ha. of mainly Cabernet sauvignon grapes.

St. Georgshof (Ger). Vineyard. (Anb) = Mosel-Saar-Ruwer. (Ber) = Obermosel. (Gro) = Gipfel. (Vil) = Temmels.

St. Germain (Cktl). ⅓ measure Green Chartreuse, ⅓ measure grapefruit juice, ⅓ measure lemon juice, 1 egg white. Shake over ice, strain into a cocktail glass.

St. Germain d'Esteuil (Fr). A commune in the northern (Bas) Médoc, north-western Bordeaux.

St-Gervais (Fr). Part of the A.C. Côtes du Rhône-Villages, Gard Département.

St. Gilbert (Austr). A blended red wine from the Botobolar vineyards in New South Wales. 50% Cabernet sauvignon and 50% Shiraz.

St-Girons (Fr). A commune in the A.C. Côtes de Blaye, north-eastern Bordeaux.

St. Goarshausen (Ger). Village. (Anb) = Mittelrhein. (Ber) = Rheinburgengau. (Gro) = Loreleyfelsen. (Vins) = Burg Katz, Burg Maus, Hessern, Loreley-Edel.

St. Goar-Werlau (Ger). Village. (Anb) = Mittelrhein. (Ber) = Rheinburgengau. (Gro) = Burg Rheinfels. (Vins) = Ameisenberg, Frowingert, Kuhstall, Rosenberg.

St. Gualtier of Pontoise (Fr). The patron saint of vine-dressers.

St. Hallett's Winery (Austr). A winery based near Tanunda in the Barossa Valley, South Australia. Produces varietal and table wines.

St. Hallvard (Nor). A herb-flavoured liqueur. Has a base of spirit distilled from potatoes.

St. Helena (USA). A wine-producing town in the upper Napa Valley, California. Has many wineries based there.

St. Helena Wine Estate (N.Z.). A winery based at Coutts Island, South Island. 25 ha. Grape varieties – Cabernet sauvignon, Chardonnay, Gewürztraminer, Merlot, Müller-Thurgau, Pinot blanc, Pinot noir and Rhine riesling. Produces varietal and table wines.

St. Henri South Australian Cabernet (Austr). A red wine produced by the Penfolds Estate in South Australia.

St. Hillary Winery (USA). A winery based in North Grosvenor, Connecticut. Produces mainly French hybrid wines.

St. Hubertswein (Ger). The name for a wine produced from grapes harvested on 3rd November each year. A pre 1971 name.

St. Hubert's Winery (Austr). A winery based in the Yarra Valley, Victoria.

St. Hubertus Vlassky Riesling (Czec). A dry Vlassky riesling wine produced near Bratislava in southern Czec.

Sticciano (It). A Chianti Putto producer based in Tuscany.

Stichcombe (Eng). A village in Wiltshire in which the Mildenhall vineyard is situated.

Stich den Buben (Ger). Vineyard. (Anb) = Baden. (Ber) = Ortenau. (Gro) = Schloss Rodeck. (Vil) = Steinbach.

Stichtig (Ger). Denotes a wine that is turning sour due to the presence of acetic acid.

Sticke Alt (Ger). The name given to a strong version of Altbier from Düsseldorf. 7.5% alc. by vol. it is brewed in March or September. It is also known as Latzenbier.

Sticking Temperature (Eng). The point at which wine ceases to ferment either because the temperature is too low or too high.

Stiege (Ger). Vineyard. (Anb) = Baden. (Ber) = Markgräflerland. (Gro) = Vogtei Rötteln. (Vil) = Weil am Rhein.

Stiegl Brauerei (Aus). A brewery based in Salzburg. Is noted for its Columbus, Goldbräu and Paracelsus beers.

Stielweg (Ger). Vineyard. (Anb) = Rheingau. (Ber) = Johannisberg. (Gro) = Daubhaus. (Vil) = Hochheim.

Stiff Horse's Neck (Cktl). As for Horse's Neck but ¾ gill of spirit instead of ½ gill.

Stift (Ger). Vineyard. (Anb) = Rheinpfalz. (Ber) = Mittelhaardt-Deutsche Weinstrasse. (Gro) = Schnepfenflug an der Weinstrasse. (Vil) = Forst.

Stift Heiligenkreuz (Aus). A wine-producing monastery based at Thallern that produces some fine wines under the label of Thallern.

Stiftsberg (Ger). Grosslage. (Anb) = Baden. (Ber) = Badische Bergstrasse/Kraichgau. (Vils) = Bauerbach, Binau, Diedesheim, Eberbach, Eichelberg, Eichtersheim, Elsenz, Eppingen, Eschelbach, Flehingen, Gemmingen, Hassmersheim, Heinsheim, Herbolzheim, Kirchardt (ortsteil Berwangen), Kraichtal (stadtteil Bahnbrücken, stadtteil Gochsheim, stadtteil Oberacker), Kraichtal (stadtteil Neuenbürg, stadtteil Menzingen, stadtteil Münzesheim), Kraichtal (stadtteil Landshausen, stadtteil Menzingen), Kürnbach, Michelfeld, Mühlbach, Neckarmühlbach, Neckarzimmern, Neudenau, Odenheim, Rohrbach a. G., Sinsheim (stadtteil Hilsbach), Sinsheim (stadtteil Weiler), Steinsfurt, Sulzfeld, Tiefenbach, Waldangelloch, Zaisenhausen.

Stiftsberg (Ger). Vineyard. (Anb) = Ahr. (Ber) = Walporzheim/Ahrtal. (Gro) = Klosterberg. (Vil) = Marienthal.

Stiftsberg (Ger). Vineyard. (Anb) = Württemberg. (Ber) = Württembergisch Unterland. (Gro) = Staufenberg. (Vil) = Heilbronn.

Stiftsberg (Ger). Vineyard. (Anb) = Württemberg. (Ber) = Württembergisch Unterland. (Gro) = Staufenberg. (Vil) = Horkheim.

Stiftsberg (Ger). Vineyard. (Anb) = Württemberg. (Ber) = Württembergisch Unterland. (Gro) = Staufenberg. (Vil) = Talheim.

Stiftsbräu (Aus) (Ger). A Trappist-style beer. High in alcohol.

Stifts Export (Ger). A Dortmunder Export beer brewed by the Dortmund Westphalia Brauerei of Dortmund Stifts.

Stiletto Cocktail (Cktl). ⅘ measure Bourbon whiskey, ⅕ measure Amaretto, juice ½ lemon. Stir over ice in an old-fashioned glass.

Still (Eng). An apparatus either of the 'Pot' or 'Patent' variety where fermented beverages are distilled into spirits.

Stillage (Eng). Also known as Thralls or Horsing. A wooden framework on which the beer casks are set up on in a public house cellar. Held in position with Scotches.

Stillage (USA). The name given to the residue after the alcohol has been distilled out of the beer in Whiskey production. Is fed to cattle etc. Contains grain residue, yeasts and minerals.

Stillare (Lat). To distil.

Still Man (Scot). The man who tends the Stills and stokes the furnaces.

Still Wine (Eng). A non-sparkling wine. Has no trace of CO_2 present.

Stinger (Cktl). ⅕ gill Bourbon whiskey served over crushed ice with an equal quantity of soda.

Stinger Cocktail (Cktl). ¾ oz. Brandy, ¾ oz. Crème de Menthe (white), Shake over ice, strain into a cocktail glass. Add a twist of lemon peel juice on top.

Stingo (Eng). A highly hopped, semi-sweet, Barley wine brewed in Yorkshire. Was served when flat and stale after a long maturation period.

Stingo (Eng). A Barley wine 1066 O.G. brewed and bottled by the Hall and Woodhouse Brewery in Blandford Forum, Dorset.

Stingo (Eng). A Barley wine 1078 O.G. brewed and bottled by the Higsons Brewery in Liverpool, Lancashire.

Stingo (Eng). A Barley wine 1076 O.G. brewed and bottled by the Watney Combe Reid Brewery in London.

Stinray (Cktl). ⅓ measure Pastis, ⅓ measure Apricot brandy, ⅓ measure orange juice, dash egg white. Shake well with ice, strain into a cocktail glass.

Štip (Yug). A wine-producing area in Macedonia.

Stir (Eng). In cocktail-making denotes to mix the ingredients together with ice until well chilled and blended. To stir in a mixing glass with the ice and then strain into the required glass.

Stir In (Eng). In cocktail-making denotes the stirring in with a barspoon of the final ingredient.

Stirn (Ger). Vineyard. (Anb) = Mosel-Saar-Ruwer. (Ber) = Saar-Ruwer. (Gro) = Scharzberg. (Vil) = Saarburg.

Stir Over Ice (Eng). In cocktail-making denotes the stirring over ice cubes in a mixing jug (or in the glass) with a barspoon, stirring rod etc.

Stirrers (Eng). Assorted shaped spoons used to stir the drinks in either a glass or jug. Can have a Muddler attachment. Often now made of disposable plastic.

Stirring Rod (USA). A glass rod used for mixing cocktails over ice in a mixing jug or glass. Is also used for making Pousse cafés.

Stirrup Cup (Eng). The parting drink. The name comes from the custom in the olden days of having the last drink with the guests either to help him to his saddle or after he has mounted his horse before his journey. Now served to members of a Hunting Party before they set off. Served in a special glass without a base. Drink has to be finished as glass must be inverted to stand. See Sloe Gin and Coup de l'Étrier.

Stirrup Cup Cocktail (Cktl). ½ measure Brandy, ½ measure Cherry brandy, 2 dashes lemon juice, dash Gomme syrup. Shake over ice. Strain into an ice-filled old-fashioned glass.

Stir up a Drink (USA). Make a mixed drink by using a Mixing glass and barspoon. Stir over ice.

St. Ismier (Fr). A vineyard based in Vienne, Isère Département. Produces red wines.

St. Jakobsberg (Ger). Vineyard. (Anb) = Rheinhessen. (Ber) = Bingen. (Gro) = Sankt Rochuskapelle. (Vil) = Ockenheim.

St. James (Afr). A de-caffeinated tea.

St. James (W.Ind). A Martinique Rum made by the Pot-still method using sugar cane sap. Has a dry, burnt flavour. Is very dark.

St. James' Gate (Ire). The Guinness Brewery based in Dublin.

St. James Winery (USA). A small winery based in St. James, Missouri. Produces Vinifera and French hybrid wines.

St-Jean-de-la-Porte (Fr). See Saint-Jean-de-la-Porte.

St. Jean-de-Minervois (Fr). An A.C. wine-producing district near Minervois in Roussillon, southern France.

St. Jean de Moirans (Fr). A vineyard based in Vienne, Isère Département, central-western France.

St. Jean-de-Muzels (Fr). A commune in the A.C. district of Saint-Joseph in the northern Rhône.

St. Jeoire-Prieuré (Fr). An A.C. Cru village of Savoie, south-eastern France.

St-Joseph (Fr). See Saint-Joseph.

St. Jost (Ger). Vineyard. (Anb) = Mittelrhein. (Ber) = Bacharach. (Gro) = Schloss Stahleck. (Vil) = Bacharach/Steeg.

St. Julien (Fr). An A.C. wine commune in the Haut-Médoc in the western Bordeaux. Red wines only. Classified in the 1855 Médoc classification.

St. Julien Wine Company (USA). A winery based in Paw Paw, Michigan. Produces French/American hybrid wines.

St. Katharinen (Ger). Village. (Anb) = Nahe. (Ber) = Schloss Böckelheim. (Gro) = Rosengarten. (Vins) = Fels, Klostergarten, Steinkreuz.

St. Katharinenwein (Ger). The name for a wine made from grapes that are harvested on 25th November annually. A pre 1971 name.

St. Katherine (Cktl). 1 part Bacardi White Label, 1 part white Crème de Cacao. Mix well together over ice, strain into a cocktail glass. Top with whipped cream and grated nutmeg.

St. Kilian (Ger). An Irish missionary. Patron saint of vintagers in Franconia. Lived in the seventh century.

St. Klausen (Ger). Vineyard. (Anb) = Franken. (Ber) = Maindreieck. (Gro) = Burg. (Vil) = Ramsthal.

St-Laurent (Aus). A red grape variety. Is not permitted in the EEC.

St. Laurent (Fr). A commune within the A.C. Médoc district in western Bordeaux.

St. Laurent-Ausstich (Aus). A red wine produced from the St-Laurent grape by the Augustine monks at Klosterneuburg, Vienna.

St. Laurent de Médoc (Fr). A commune in the A.C. Médoc. See St. Laurent.

St. Laurent des Arbes (Fr). A commune in the A.C. district of Lirac. Produces red, rosé and white wines.

St. Laurent des Combes (Fr). An A.C. commune in the Saint-Émilion district of eastern Bordeaux. Red wines only.

St. Laurenzikapelle (Ger). Vineyard. (Anb) = Rheinhessen. (Ber) = Bingen. (Gro) = Abtey. (Vil) = Gau-Algesheim.

St. Leger (Eng). A brand-name drink, low

in alcohol, made from mineral water, orange juice and white wine. 3.5% alc. by vol.

St. Leonard (Fr). A Bierè de Garde from Boulogne.

St. Leonards Winery (Austr). A winery based in north-eastern Victoria. Produces varietal wines.

St. Lucia Distillereies Ltd (W.Ind). A major Rum distiller based on St. Lucia. Produces Bounty.

St. Macaire (USA). A red grape variety grown in California to make red table wines.

St. Magdalene (Scot). A single Malt whisky distillery sited at Linlithgow. Owned by John Hopkins and Co. (Whiskies bottled by Gordon MacPhail). A Highland malt. Produces a Vintage malt 1964 and a 15 year old Malt 45% alc. by vol.

St. Magdalener (Ger). See Santa Maddalena.

St. Marco (Fr). See Saint Marco.

St. Margarethan (Aus). A wine-producing area based in the Lake District, Burgenland.

St. Mark Brandy (USA). The brand-name of a Brandy bottled by the Guild of Wineries and Distillers at Lodi, California. 40% alc. by vol.

St. Martin (Fr). A fourth-century monk who brought wine-making to the central Loire. Is reputed to have invented the art of pruning by cutting the vines low which produced better wines. Is also the patron saint of the Mosel vine growers.

St. Martin (Ger). Village. (Anb) = Rheinpfalz. (Ber) = Südliche Weinstrasse. (Gro) = Schloss Ludwigshöhe. (Vins) = Baron, Kirchberg, Zitadelle.

St. Martin (Ger). Vineyard. (Anb) = Mosel-Saar-Ruwer. (Ber) = Bernkastel. (Gro) = Sankt Michael. (Vil) = Ensch.

St. Martin (Ger). Vineyard. (Anb) = Nahe. (Ber) = Kreuznach. (Gro) = Kronenberg. (Vil) = Bad Kreuznach.

St. Martin (Ger). Vineyard. (Anb) = Nahe. (Ber) = Kreuznach. (Gro) = Schlosskapelle. (Vil) = Guldental.

St-Martin-Caussaude (Fr). A commune in the A.C. Côtes de Blaye in north-eastern Bordeaux.

St. Martiner Hofberg (Ger). Vineyard. (Anb) = Mosel-Saar-Ruwer. (Ber) = Saar-Ruwer. (Gro) = Römerlay. (Vil) = Trier.

St. Martinsberg (Ger). Vineyard. (Anb) = Mittelrhein. (Ber) = Rheinburgengau. (Gro) = Schloss Schönburg. (Vil) = Oberwessel.

St. Martinskreuz (Ger). Vineyard. (Anb)

= Rheinpfalz. (Ber) = Mittelhaardt-Deutsche Weinstrasse. (Gro) = Höllenpfad. (Vil) = Mertesheim.

St. Martin's Sickness (Fr). A term for intoxication in the Tours area (Touraine) of the Loire from a fourth century monk St. Martin who introduced wine-making to the area.

St. Martinswein (Ger). A wine produced from grapes harvested on the 11th November annually. A pre 1971 name.

St. Matheiser (Ger). Vineyard. (Anb) = Mosel-Saar-Ruwer. (Ber) = Saar-Ruwer. (Gro) = Römerlay. (Vil) = Trier.

St. Maurice-sur-Eygues (Fr). A village in the Côtes du Rhône-Villages.

St. Maximiner Kreuzberg (Ger). Vineyard. (Anb) = Mosel-Saar-Ruwer. (Ber) = Saar-Ruwer. (Gro) = Römerlay. (Vil) = Trier.

St-Médard d'Eyrans (Fr). A commune in the A.C. Graves district in south-western Bordeaux.

St. Michaelsberg (Ger). Vineyard. (Anb) = Baden. (Ber) = Kaiserstuhl-Tuniberg. (Gro) = Vulkanfelsen. (Vil) = Riegel.

St. Michael's Fino (Sp). The brand-name of a Fino sherry produced by Fernando A. de Terry in Puerto de Santa Maria.

St-Michel (Fr). A commune in the A.C. Canon-Fronsac, eastern Bordeaux.

St. Morandus (Fr). The Alsatian patron saint of wine growers. A Bénédictine monk who lived in the twelfth century.

St Morillon (Fr). A commune in the A.C. Graves district in south-western Bordeaux. Produces red and white wines.

St. Moritz (Cktl). ⅓ measure Marc du Valais, ⅓ measure Cointreau, ⅓ measure lemon juice, 5 dashes Pastis. Shake over ice, strain into a cocktail glass.

St. Nazarius (Ger). See Codex Laureshamensis.

St. Nectaire (Fr). See Saint Nectaire.

St. Neots Bitter (Eng). A cask conditioned Bitter 1041 O.G. brewed by the Paines Brewery in St. Neots, Cambridgeshire. Also as keg.

St-Nicaise Abbey (Fr). The cellars of Taittinger Champagne.

St. Nicholas de Bourgueil (Fr). An A.C. red wine in the Touraine district of the Loire. Wines made from the Cabernet franc.

St. Nicholas Vineyard (Eng). A vineyard based at Moat Lane, Canterbury, Kent. Was first planted in 1979. 1 ha. Grape varieties – Müller-Thurgau and Schönburger.

St. Nicolas Tawny Port (Austr). A wood-matured Tawny port produced by Sandalford in Western Australia.

St. Nikolaus (Ger). Vineyard. (Anb) = Rheingau. (Ber) = Johannisberg. (Gro) = Erntebringer. (Vil) = Mittelheim.

St. Nikolaus (Ger). Vineyard. (Anb) = Rheingau. (Ber) = Johannisberg. (Gro) = Honigberg. (Vil) = Mittelheim.

St. Nikolaus Wein (Ger). The pre 1971 name given to wine made from grapes harvested on 6th December (the Saint's day).

St. Nikolaus Wine (Ger). See St. Nikolaus Wein.

Stoat Beer (Eng). A cask conditioned Bitter 1036 O.G. brewed by the Ferret and Firkin home-brew public house owned by Bruce in London.

Stock (It). Noted brandy, liqueur and vermouth producers based in Trieste, Piemonte, north-western Italy. See Bora Sambuca, Gala Caffé and Grappa Julia.

Stock Ale (Eng). A Beer brewed over a long period, usually dark, well-hopped with a characteristic bitterness.

Stock Ale (Eng). A cask conditioned Ale 1085 O.G. brewed by the Godson Brewery in London. Also a bottled variety.

Stock Ale (Eng). An Ale 1050 O.G. brewed and bottled by the Ridley Brewery in Chelmsford, Essex.

Stock Ale (Eng). A draught Ale 1036 O.G. brewed by the Shepherd Neame Brewery in Faversham, Kent.

Stock Brandy (It). See Distilline Stock.

Stock Ferment (Eng). The name given to a yeast that has been activated in a starter solution.

Stockheim (Ger). Village. (Anb) = Württemberg. (Ber) = Württembergisch Unterland. (Gro) = Heuchelberg. (Vin) = Altenberg.

Stocks Brewery (Eng). A brewery based at the Hall Cross public house in Doncaster, Yorkshire. Noted for its cask conditioned Select 1044 O.G. and Old Horizontal 1054 O.G.

Stocks Vineyard (Eng). Address = Suckley, Worcestershire. 4 ha. Planted 1972. Grape varieties – Reichensteiner 80% and Riesling sylvaner 20%.

Stockton Distillers (USA). A winery based near Lodi, Central Valley, California.

Stod Brewery (Czec). A brewery based in western Czec.

St. Odile (Fr). The name given to Perle (a cuve close) and Crémant F. Kobus (a méthode champenoise) sparkling wines fron Union Vinicole Divinal at Obernai, Alsace.

Stolichnaya (USSR). A Vodka made from 100% grain spirits. 40% alc. by vol. Produced in Leningrad.

Stollberg (Ger). Vineyard. (Anb) = Franken. (Ber) = Steigerwald. (Gro) = Not yet assigned. (Vil) = Handthal.

Stollenberg (Ger). Vineyard. (Anb) = Nahe. (Ber) = Schloss Böckelheim. (Gro) = Burgweg. (Vil) = Niederhausen an der Nahe.

Stolno Vino (Yug). Table wine.

Stolovaya (USSR). A brand of Vodka. 48% alc. by vol.

Stolovoe Vino (USSR). Table wine.

Stolzenberg (Ger). Vineyard. (Anb) = Mosel-Saar-Ruwer. (Ber) = Zell/Mosel. (Gro) = Weinhex. (Vil) = Hatzenport.

Stolz Winery (USA). A large winery and vineyard based in St. James, Missouri. 52 ha. Produces a large variety of wines.

Stomsdorfer (Ger). A herb-flavoured, digestive liqueur.

Stone Cocktail (Cktl). ¼ measure white Rum, ¼ measure sweet Vermouth, ½ measure sweet Sherry. Stir over ice, strain into a cocktail glass.

Stonecrop Vineyards (USA). A vineyard based in Stonington, Connecticut. Produces mainly French hybrid wines.

Stoned (Eng) (slang). Highly intoxicated. e.g. 'stoned out of his mind'.

Stone Face (Cktl). 1 measure Whisky, ice, 2 dashes Angostura. Stir in a highball glass, top up with dry Cider. Also known as a Stone Fence Cocktail.

Stone Fence Cocktail (Cktl). See Stone Face.

Stonegate Winery (USA). A winery based near Calistoga, Napa Valley, California. Grape varieties – Cabernet sauvignon, Chardonnay, Pinot noir and Sauvignon blanc. Produces varietal wines.

Stonehenge Bitter (Eng). A Bitter beer 1041 O.G. brewed by the Wiltshire Brewery Company, Tisbury, Wiltshire.

Stone Hill Wine Company (USA). A small winery based in Hermann, Missouri. 16 ha. Produces fruit, berry, generic and sparkling wines.

Stone Quarry Winery (USA). A winery with vineyards based in Waterford, Ohio. Produces American and French hybrid wines.

Stoneridge Winery (USA). A small winery based near Sutter Creek, Amador County, California. Grape varieties – Ruby cabernet and Zinfandel. Produces varietal wines.

Stones Best Bitter (Eng). A cask conditioned Bitter 1038 O.G. brewed by the Bass Worthington (Stones) Brewery in Sheffield, Yorkshire.

Stone's Mac (Eng). A ginger wine and Scotch whisky drink produced by Whiskymac Ltd. of Moorland Street, London.

Stone's Original Green Ginger Wine (Eng). A wine made from dried grapes fermented then fined and fortified. Powdered pure root ginger is added and it is then matured for 9 months in oak vats. Produced at the Finsbury Distillery.

Stone Square (Eng). Another name for a square. Stone denoted the material from which it was made.

Stonewall Jackson (Cktl). 1½ measures Applejack brandy mixed with ½ pint dry Cider.

Stone Wines (Ger). The old name that was given to the wines of Franconia (Stein wines) because they were placed in 'Bocksbeutels' stone bottles.

Stoneyfell (Austr). An Adelaide Co. famous for Metala wines. (Cabernet and Shiraz blend).

Stoney's (USA). A Beer brewed by the Jones Brewery in Smithton, Pennsylvania.

Stonsdorfer (Ger). A dark, bitter, herb liqueur. 32% alc. by vol.

Stonsdorferei (Die) (Ger). A distillery owned by Koerner. Produces Enzian.

Stony Hill Vineyards (USA). A winery based in the St. Helena, Napa Valley, California. 14.5 ha. Grape varieties – Chardonnay, Gewürztraminer and White riesling. Produces varietal wines.

Stony Ridge Winery (USA). A winery based in Livermore Valley, Alameda, California. Grape varieties – Chardonnay, Petite syrah and Zinfandel. Produces varietal wines.

Stoop (Eng). An alternative spelling of Stoup (a cup/mug used in the religious ceremonies in the Middle Ages). See Stoup.

Stopper (Eng). A cork, plastic or cork and plastic bottle closure unit that excludes air, bacteria etc. from the contents of the bottle and also prevents the contents escaping.

Storchenbrünnle (Ger). Vineyard. (Anb) = Franken. (Ber) = Steigerwald. (Gro) = Schlossberg. (Vil) = Sickershausen.

Stormonth Tait (Port). Vintage Port shippers. Vintages – 1896, 1900, 1904, 1908, 1912, 1920, 1922, 1927.

Storybook Mountain Winery (USA). A winery and vineyard based near Calistoga, Napa Valley, California. 17 ha. Grape variety – Zinfandel.

Story Vineyards (USA). A winery based in the Sierra Foothills, Amador County, California. Grape varieties – Mission and Zinfandel. Produces table and varietal wines.

St. Oswald (Ger). Vineyard. (Anb) = Mittelrhein. (Ber) = Bacharach. (Gro) = Schloss Stahleck. (Vil) = Manubach.

Stotious (Ire). A term used to describe an intoxicated person.

Stoup (Eng). An old name used to describe a flagon, tankard, cup, mug or other drinking vessel. Usually used for religious ceremonies. Is also used to describe a draught of wine. See Stoop.

Stout (U.K). A strong, rich style of Porter. 2 styles = a dry, Irish version e.g. Guinness and Murphy's, a sweet English version e.g. Mackeson. The barley is roasted to a dark colour and it has a high proportion of Malt and Hops.

Stoves (Eng). Used to ward off late frosts in the vineyards in the Spring and so protect the young shoots. Placed between the vine rows. See Smudge Pots.

Stowford Press (Eng). The brand-name of a Cider produced by Westons of Hereford.

St. Pantaleimon (Gre). A monastery on Athos, a self-governing State. Tend the vines supplied by Tsantalis and harvest them under Tsantalis supervision.

St. Pantaléon-les-Vignes (Fr). A part of the A.C. Côtes du Rhône-Villages.

St. Panteleimon (Cyp). A sweet white wine produced by the Keo Co. Limassol.

St-Pardon-de-Conques (Fr). A commune of the A.C. Graves district, south-western Bordeaux.

St. Patrick's Day Cocktail (Cktl). ⅓ measure (white) Crème de Menthe, ⅓ measure Irish whiskey, ⅓ measure Green Chartreuse, dash Angostura. Stir over ice, strain into a cocktail glass.

St-Paul (Fr). A commune in the A.C. Côtes de Blaye in north-eastern Bordeaux.

St. Pauli Girl (Ger). A Bier produced by the Becks Brauerei in Bremen for the USA market.

St-Péray (Fr). See Saint-Péray.

St. Peters Winery (Austr). A winery based in Riverina, New South Wales. Produces varietal wines.

St. Petrusberg (Ger). Vineyard. (Anb) = Mosel-Saar-Ruwer. (Ber) = Saar-Ruwer. (Gro) = Römerlay. (Vil) = Trier.

St-Pierre-de-Mons (Fr). A commune in the A.C. Graves district of south-western Bordeaux. See also Saint-Pierre-de-Mons.

St. Pierre Smirnoff Fils (Fr). A Paris based firm. The original Smirnoff plant. Now owned by Heublein of USA. The most popular Vodka in the World.

St. Pourçain (Fr). See St. Pourçain-sur-Sioule.

St. Pourçain-sur-Sioule (Fr). A V.D.Q.S. red, rosé and white wine-producing region in the Allier Département in central France. Grape varieties – Chardonnay, Gamay, Pinot noir, Sauvignon blanc and Tressalier (Sacy).

Straccali (It). A Chianti Classico producer based in Tuscany.

Strade del Vino (It). 'Wine roads'. Signposted itineraries through the vineyards.

Straight (Eng). A term used to imply that the customer wants a measure of spirits (usually Whisky) without the addition of other ingredients.

Straight Blonde (Cktl). Fill a Paris goblet with chilled Dubonnet Blonde, add a twist of lemon peel juice and a slice of lemon.

Straight Bourbon (USA). The produce of one distillery.

Straight Highball (USA). As for Highball. Another name for.

Straight Law Cocktail (Cktl). ⅔ measure dry Sherry, ⅓ measure Gin. Stir over ice, strain into a cocktail glass.

Straight Rye and Water Back (USA). A straight Whiskey with a jug of water.

Straight-Siders (Eng). Early name 1715–1730 given to the Bladder bottle that had its sides flattened for storage. The forerunner of the bottle as we know it today.

Straight Up (Eng). A term used to denote a request for a drink with no ice.

Straight Whiskey (USA). An unblended Whiskey aged for 2 years in new charred oak casks. Distilled at 80% alc. by vol. Corn whiskey may be aged in uncharred casks.

Straight Whisky (Scot). See Straight.

Strain a Drink (USA). To strain after mixing or shaking a drink. Usually done through a Hawthorne strainer.

Strainer (Eng). Composed of a metal ring, covered with gauze and a handle attached. After the ingredients have been shaken or stirred the mixture is poured through it to strain out the pieces of ice, fruit pulp etc. See Hawthorne Strainer.

Straining (Eng). A term used for the removal of pulp from a fermenting liquid or must. Removes large particles and pulp.

Straits Sling (Cktl). ½ gill dry Gin, ⅛ gill dry Cherry brandy, ⅙ gill Bénédictine, juice of ½ lemon, 2 dashes Orange bitters, 2 dashes Angostura. Pour all the ingredients into a large highball with ice. Top with soda water. Add a slice of lemon.

Strakonice Brewery (Czec). An old established brewery c1659 based in south-western Czec.

St. Rambert (Fr). A vineyard based in the Grésivaudan Valley, Vienne Département. Produces red wines.

St. Raphaël (Fr). An apéritif wine made from wine, quinine, bark and herbs. 17% alc. by vol. Red and white versions.

St. Raphael (S.Afr). A dry red wine blended from the Cabernet, Pinotage and Cinsault grapes made by the Douglas Green Group in Paarl.

St. Raphaël-Citron (Cktl). ½ gill St. Raphaël, ½ gill Sirop de Citron, soda water. Stir gently together in an ice-filled highball glass.

Strass (Aus). A wine-producing district based in the Kamp Valley, north-western Austria.

Strasswirtschaften (Ger). The right of the vintner to sell his wines directly to the public for a set period of time each year on his own property at the roadside. Originates from the Rheingau.

Stratford Glasses (Eng). The brand-name used by the Dema Glass Co. for a range of glasses.

Strathalbyn Brewery (Scot). Opened in 1982. Noted for its cask conditioned Ales.

Strathclyde (Scot). A Grain whisky distillery based near the river Clyde.

Strathconon (Scot). A 12 year old Vatted malt whisky produced by Buchanan and Company. 57% alc. by vol.

Strathisla (Scot). A single Malt whisky distillery in Keith, Banffshire. Owned by Seagram. A Highland malt. Built in 1786. Produces a 15 year old Whisky. 43% alc. by vol.

Strathisla-Glenlivet (Scot). See Strathisla.

Strathmill (Scot). A single Malt whisky distillery based east of Keith. A Highland malt whisky. 43% alc. by vol.

Strathmore Scottish Water (Scot). A sparkling mineral water from the Strathmore Water Company, Forfar, Angus.

Strathspey (Scot). A Vatted malt whisky from International Distillers and Vintners.

Stratos (Cktl). ¼ measure Cinzano dry Vermouth, ¼ measure Drambuie, ⅜ measure dry Gin, ⅛ measure Crème de Banane. Stir over ice, strain into a cocktail glass. Add a cherry and a twist of lemon peel juice.

Stratospheric Tags (USA) (slang). Very high prices for rare wines.

Straub Brewery (USA). A brewery based in St Mary's, Pennsylvania. Noted for its Straub beer.

Straussberg (Ger). Vineyard. (Anb) = Nahe. (Ber) = Kreuznach. (Gro) = Kronenberg. (Vil) = Hargesheim.

Stravecchia (It). Grappa that has had extra maturation.

Stravecchio (It). A term to denote very old, ripe or mellow wines.

Stravecchio Branca (It). A Brandy produced by Fratelli Branca of Milan.

Strawberry Blonde Cocktail (Cktl). 1 fl.oz. Irish Mist, 3 fresh strawberries. Blend together with a scoop of crushed ice in a blender. Pour into a flute glass, top with Champagne. Dress with a strawberry.

Strawberry Brandy (Euro). A fruit brandy made from strawberries. 44.5% alc. by vol.

Strawberry Daiquiri (Cktl). ½ fl.oz. Fraise liqueur, 1½ fl.ozs. white Rum, juice ½ lemon, 3 strawberries. Blend on high speed with 2 scoops crushed ice. Pour into a tall glass unblended. Serve with short thick straws and a fresh strawberry.

Strawberry Dawn (Cktl). 2–3 fresh strawberries, 1 fl.oz. Gin, 1 fl.oz. Coconut cream, 2–3 scoops crushed ice. Blend well together, serve in a saucer-type glass. Decorate with a strawberry and short straws.

Strawberry Liqueur (Fr). A liqueur made from strawberries steeped in spirit. 30% alc. by vol.

Strawberry Martini (Cktl). Chambraise and a fresh strawberry with a twist of lemon peel juice.

Strawberry Vermouth (Fr). A Chambéry vermouth flavoured with Alpine strawberries. Brand-name in U.K. is Chambéryzette.

Straw Wines (Fr). See Vins de Paille. Wine produced from grapes that have been dried on straw mats.

Strega (It). A spring herb liqueur, yellow in colour. 40% alc. by vol.

Strega Crossword (Cktl). 2 measures Strega, 2 measures white Rum, 2 measures Gin, 4 measures grapefruit juice. Shake over ice, strain into a highball glass with ice. Decorate with mint and an orange slice.

Strega Flip (Cktl). ½ measure Strega, ½ measure Cognac, juice ¼ orange, 2 dashes lemon juice, 1 egg. Shake well over ice, strain into a cocktail glass. Top with grated nutmeg.

Strega Shake (Cktl). 2 measures Strega, 3 measures orange juice, 1 measure Vodka, 1 scoop vanilla ice cream. Stir all well together, serve in goblets with straws.

St. Remigiusberg (Ger). Vineyard. (Anb) = Nahe. (Ber) = Kreuznach. (Gro) = Schlosskapelle. (Vil) = Laubenheim.

Strength (Eng). Strength is limited by regulations governing the wines and spirits by where they were made and by British Customs and Excise. See also Gay Lussac, Sykes, OIML and US Proof.

Stretched (Eng). The term sometimes used to describe a good wine that has been increased by the addition of stronger, cheaper wines.

Stretched Wine (Eng). See Stretched.

Striep (Bel). A Flemish drink composed of a glass of Lager of which half is froth.

Strike (Cktl). ⅙ measure Cinzano dry vermouth, ⅙ measure Dubonnet, ⅙ measure Sève Fournier, ⅓ measure Canadian rye whisky. Stir over ice, strain into a cocktail glass. Add a twist of orange peel and a cherry.

Stringbag (Cktl). ⁷⁄₁₀ measure dry Gin, ¹⁄₁₀ measure La Ina sherry, dash Angostura, dash Rose's lime juice. Stir well together over ice. Strain into an old-fashioned glass with ice.

String Neck Bottle (Eng). A seventeenth-century bottle with a thick band of glass around the neck to stop the string loop which held the wooden cork or plug in place from slipping off.

Strip Back (Aus). The passing of grape must that has started to ferment before reaching the fermenting vats through charcoal to remove any oxidation.

St. Roch (Ger). The patron saint of vine growers in the Rhine and Nahe regions. A Franciscan friar who lived in the fourteenth century.

Stroganoff (Ger). A brand of Vodka produced by Schlichte Distillery of Steinhägen.

Stroh (Aus). A brand of Rum produced by the Stroh Distillery based in Klagenfurt.

Stroh Beer (USA). See Stroh Brewery.

Stroh Brewery (USA). A brewery that produces Schlitz beer 1045 O.G. Is based in Detroit.

Strohwein (Ger). Straw wine.

Stromberg (Ger). Grosslage. (Anb) = Württemberg. (Ber) = Württembergisch Unterland. (Vils) = Bönnigheim, Diefenbach, Ensingen, Erligheim, Freudenstein, Freudental, Gründelbach, Häfnerhaslach, Hofen, Hohenhaslach, Hohenstein, Horrheim, Illingen, Kirchheim, Kleinsachsenheim, Knittlingen, Lienzingen, Maulbronn, Mühlhausen, Obererdingen, Ochsenbach, Ötisheim, Riet, Rosswag, Schützingen, Spielberg, Sternenfels, Vaihingen.

Stromberg (Ger). Vineyard. (Anb) = Nahe. (Ber) = Schloss Böckelheim. (Gro) = Rosengarten. (Vil) = Bockenau.

Strong Ale (Eng). An Ale with an average

O.G. of 1055. Can be dark or light in colour and sweet or dry. A common characteristic is the strength, which is higher than normal beers.

Strong Amber (Eng). See Alford Arms.

Strong Arm (Eng). A Bitter beer 1040 O.G. brewed by the Camerons Brewery in Hartlepool. Also bottled 1046 O.G.

Strongbiers (Ger). A strong beer 18%+ O.G. Originally made to celebrate Christmas or Lent. Names usually end in -ator or in a saint's name.

Strongbow (Eng). The flagship Cider of Bulmers, Hereford. Dry, strong and sparkling. Sold as draught or in bottle.

Strongbow 1080 (Eng). A bottled Cider, double-fermented 1080 O.G. produced by Bulmers of Hereford, Herefordshire.

Strong Brown (Eng). A Brown ale 1045 O.G. brewed and bottled by the Samuel Smith Brewery in Tadcaster, Yorkshire.

Strong Country Bitter (Eng). A cask conditioned Bitter 1037 O.G. brewed by the Whitbread Brewery for the Essex region.

Strong Drink (Eng). The alternative name for alcoholic drink. Applies especially to spirits.

Strong Golden (Eng). A Barley wine 1100 O.G. brewed and bottled by the Samuel Smith Brewery in Tadcaster, Yorkshire.

Strong Pale Ale (Eng). A Pale ale 1045 O.G. brewed and bottled by the Samuel Smith Brewery in Tadcaster, Yorkshire.

Strongs (Scot). The name given to the Low Wines at the Auchentoshan distillery in Dalmuir, Glasgow. See also Weaks.

Strong Suffolk Ale (Eng). A bottled dark Old ale 1056 O.G. brewed and bottled by the Greene King Brewery in East Anglia. Is matured in sealed oak vats for 1 year.

Strong Waters (Eng). The mediaeval name for alcoholic beverages.

Stroumf (Cktl). ⅔ measure Gin, ⅔ measure Apricot brandy, ⅓ measure Amaretto di Saronno, dash lemon juice. Shake over ice, strain into an ice-filled highball glass. Add a dash of orange juice.

Strugure (Rum). Grape.

Strümpfelbach (Ger). Village. (Anb) = Württemberg. (Ber) = Remstal-Stuttgart. (Gro) = Wartbühl. (Vins) = Gastenklinge, Nonnenberg.

Strümpfelbach (Ger). Village. (Anb) = Württemberg. (Ber) = Remstal-Stuttgart. See Weinstadt.

Strumpfwein (Ger). The name for any wine that is so sour (acidic) that it may rot your stockings.

St. Ruppertsberg (Ger). Vineyard. (Anb) = Nahe. (Ber) = Kreuznach. (Gro) = Pfarrgarten. (Vil) = Gutenberg.

St-Saphorin (Switz). A wine-producing region based near Lavaux in central Vaud. Produces dry white wines.

St. Saturnin (Fr). An A.C. red wine from the Grenache grape. Produced north of Montpellier in the Languedoc.

St-Sauveur (Fr). A commune in the A.C. Haut-Médoc, north-western Bordeaux.

St. Savin (Fr). A vineyard based in the Grésivaudan Valley, Vienne Département. Produces red wines.

St-Selve (Fr). A commune in the A.C. Graves district of south-western Bordeaux.

St-Seurin-Bourg (Fr). A commune in the A.C. Côtes de Bourg, north-eastern Bordeaux.

St-Seurin-Cursac (Fr). A commune in the A.C. Côtes de Bourg, north-eastern Bordeaux.

St-Seurin-de-Cadourne (Fr). A commune in the A.C. Haut-Médoc, north-western Bordeaux.

St. Sixtus (Bel). A Westvleteren Abbaye which produces Abt beer 12% alc. by vol. the strongest beer in Belgium.

St. Stephan (Ger). Vineyard. (Anb) = Rheinpfalz. (Ber) = Mittelhaardt-Deutsche Weinstrasse. (Gro) = Höllenpfad. (Vil) = Grünstadt.

St. Thomas Burgundy (Austr). A red wine from the Old Mill winery in South Australia.

Stuart Highway (Austr). A part of the Bilyara Vineyards, Nurioopta, South Australia.

Stubby (Austr) (slang). The term for a small beer bottle.

Stück (Ger). Cask of the Rhineland holding 1,200 litres.

Stückfasser (Ger). See Stück.

Stuck Ferment (Eng). The name given to a fermenting must or wine in which the fermentation has prematurely stopped because it is too cold (or hot).

Stuck Wine (Eng). Describes a wine that has stopped fermenting before all the sugar has been converted into alcohol.

Stud (The) (Cktl). 1 part Vodka, 1 part Cinzano Rosé. Stir together in an ice-filled highball glass.

Studenà Brewery (Czec). An old established brewery based in central-southern Czec.

Stuffing (Eng). A wine drinker's term for meaty wines that have body and alcohol. e.g. Châteauneuf-du-Pape.

Stum (Eng). A partially-fermented grape must drink that was popular in the seventeenth century. Also drunk unfermented.

Stumpf (Ger). Denotes a lifeless wine.

Sturare (It). To uncork, or tap a cask.

St. Urbain (Switz). A white wine produced in Johannisberg in the Valais Canton.

St. Urban (Ger). The Patron saint of the grape. 25th May is the Saint's day. A French monk.

Sturm (Aus). A term that describes a wine that is still fermenting.

Sturn (Eng). A seventeenth-century name for unfermented or partly fermented grape juice.

St. Ursula (Ger). A noted wine merchant based at Bingen.

Stuttgart (Ger). Village. (Anb) = Württemberg. (Ber) = Remstal-Stuttgart. (Gro) = Weinsteige. (Vins) = Kreigsberg, Mönchberg, Mönchhalde.

Stuttgart [ortsteil Bad Cannstatt] (Ger). Village. (Anb) = Württemberg. (Ber) = Remstal-Stuttgart. (Gro) = Weinsteige. (Vins) = Berg, Halde, Herzongenberg, Mönchberg, Mönchhalde, Steinhalde, Zuckerle.

Stuttgart [ortsteil Degerloch] (Ger). Village. (Anb) = Württemberg. (Ber) = Remstal-Stuttgart. (Gro) = Weinsteige. (Vin) = Scharrenberg.

Stuttgart [ortsteil Feuerbach] (Ger). Village. (Anb) = Württemberg. (Ber) = Remstal-Stuttgart. (Gro) = Weinsteige. (Vin) = Berg.

Stuttgart [ortsteil Gaisburg] (Ger). Village. (Anb) = Württemberg. (Ber) = Remstal-Stuttgart. (Gro) = Weinsteige. (Vin) = Abelsberg.

Stuttgart [ortsteil Hedelfingen] (Ger). Village. (Anb) = Württemberg. (Ber) = Remstal-Stuttgart. (Gro) = Weinsteige. (Vin) = Lenzenberg.

Stuttgart [ortsteil Hofen] (Ger). Village. (Anb) = Württemberg. (Ber) = Remstal-Stuttgart. (Gro) = Weinsteige. (Vin) = Zuckerle.

Stuttgart [ortsteil Mühlhausen] (Ger). Village. (Anb) = Württemberg. (Ber) = Remstal-Stuttgart. (Gro) = Weinsteige. (Vins) = Steinhalde, Zuckerle.

Stuttgart [ortsteil Münster] (Ger). Village. (Anb) = Württemberg. (Ber) = Remstal-Stuttgart. (Gro) = Weinsteige. (Vins) = Berg, Steinhalde, Zuckerle.

Stuttgart [ortsteil Obertürkheim] (Ger). Village. (Anb) = Württemberg. (Ber) = Remstal-Stuttgart. (Gro) = Weinsteige. (Vins) = Ailenberg, Kirchberg.

Stuttgart [ortsteil Rohracker] (Ger). Village. (Anb) = Württemberg. (Ber) = Remstal-Stuttgart. (Gro) = Weinsteige. (Vin) = Lenzenberg.

Stuttgart [ortsteil Rotenberg] (Ger). Village. (Anb) = Württemberg. (Ber) = Remstal-Stuttgart. (Gro) = Weinsteige. (Vin) = Schlossberg.

Stuttgart [ortsteil Uhlbach] (Ger). Village. (Anb) = Württemberg. (Ber) = Remstal-Stuttgart. (Gro) = Weinsteige. (Vins) = Götzenberg, Schlossberg, Steingrube.

Stuttgart [ortsteil Untertürkheim] (Ger). Village. (Anb) = Württemberg (Ber) = Remstal-Stuttgart. (Gro) = Weinsteige. (Vins) = Altenberg, Gips, Herzogenberg, Mönchberg, Schlossberg, Wetzenstein.

Stuttgart [ortsteil Wangen] (Ger). Village. (Anb) = Württemberg. (Ber) = Remstal-Stuttgart. (Gro) = Weinsteige. (Vin) = Berg.

Stuttgart [ortsteil Zuffenhausen] (Ger). Village. (Anb) = Württemberg. (Ber) = Remstal-Stuttgart. (Gro) = Weinsteige. (Vin) = Berg.

St. Véran (Fr). An A.C. dry white wine from the Mâconnais.

St. Victor Lacoste (Fr). A commune of the Laudun district in the south-western Rhône. Produces red, rosé and white wines.

St. Vincent of Saragossa (S.Afr). A dry white wine from the Douglas Green Group in Paarl.

St. Vivien (Fr). A commune in Prignac in the Médoc, western Bordeaux.

St. Wernerberg (Ger). Vineyard. (Anb) = Mittelrhein. (Ber) = Rheinburgengau. (Gro) = Schloss Schönburg. (Vil) = Dellhofen.

Stylish (Eng). A term used to describe wines which possess charm, finesse and elegance.

Styll (Eng). The sixteenth-century spelling of Still (distillation).

Styria (Aus). A wine region. Has volcanic soil. See Steiermark.

St-Yzans (Fr). A commune in the Bas Médoc, north-western Bordeaux. Wines have A.C. Médoc.

Su (Tur). Fruit juice. Can also denote water.

Suave (Port). Sweet.

Subalterns' Soothing Syrup (Ind). The old name used for Madeira wine in India.

Suber (Lat). Cork.

Subercaseaux (Chile). The name given to brut and demi-sec sparkling wines produced by Concha y Toro (made by the méthode champenoise).

Suberin (Eng). The waxy element in cork that makes it water impermeable and decay resistant.

Subirat-Parent (Sp). A white grape variety used in the making of Cava wines. Also known as the Malvasia riojana and Rojal blanco.

Submarino (Mex). A glass of Tequila immersed in a glass of beer.

S

Subotička Peščara (Yug). A wine-producing area in Vojvodina. Produces red and white wines. Also spelt Subotica.

Subrouska (Pol). A green Vodka. See Zubrówka.

Subrowka (Pol). See Zubrówka.

Subsoil (Eng). Denotes the soil found under the top soil (3 metres in depth or more). Is rich in minerals.

Succinic Acid (Eng). A wine acid produced through the result of fermentation. The principal acid in the form of esters. Gives the wine its flavour and aroma.

Succo (It). Juice, sap.

Succo d'Arancia (It). Orange juice.

Succo di Frutta (It). Fruit juice.

Succo di Limone (It). Lemon juice.

Succo di Mele (It). Cider.

Succo di Pomodori (It). Tomato juice.

Succo d'Uva (It). Grape juice.

Succus (Lat). Juice, sap.

Suc de Monbazillac (Fr). A green liqueur produced from wine and herbs. Produced in the Perigord region. Also a yellow (sweet) version.

Sucesores de Alfonso Abellán (Sp). A winery based in Almanza. Produces wines mainly from the Monastrell grape.

Suchots (Les) (Fr). A Premier Cru vineyard in the A.C. commune of Vosne-Romanée, Côte de Nuits, Burgundy. 13.1 ha.

Sucio (Sp). A word used to describe an unclean Sherry.

Suckering (USA). The removal of all shoots that originate either below the ground or on the trunk of the vine if they are not fruit bearing.

Suckers (Eng). The excessive growth on the vine. Removed so as to give the grapes increased nutrition.

Sucrage (Fr). A term used for the addition of sugar to the grape must during fermentation. See also Chaptalisation and Sugaring.

Sucré (It). Usually denotes the addition of sugar to the must.

Sucrose (Eng). Cane sugar used for Chaptalisation. Also the name of the sugar found in green coffee beans.

Sucu (Tur). Water (drinking) seller.

Sudbadischer Landwein (Ger). One of the 15 Deutsche Tafelwein zones.

Südlay (Ger). Vineyard. (Anb) = Mosel-Saar-Ruwer. (Ber) = Bernkastel. (Gro) = Sankt Michael. (Vil) = Pölich.

Südliche-Weinstrasse (Ger). Southern Wine Route.

Südliche Weinstrasse (Ger). Bereich. (Anb) = Rheinpfalz. (Gros) = Bischofskreuz, Guttenberg, Herrlich, Kloster Liebfrauenberg, Königsgarten, Mandelhöhe,

Ordensgut, Schloss Ludwigshöhe, Trappenberg.

Suds (USA) (slang). A term for the frothy head on a glass of beer.

Südsteiermark (Aus). South Styria. A wine district within the region of Steiermark. Produces mainly white wines.

Südtirol (It). South Tyrol. The German name for the Trentino-Alto Adige region. Produces fine wines. Labels can be written in German or Italian or mixture of both. Often written Süd Tirol.

Süd Tirol (It). See Südtirol.

Südtiroler (It). An appellation on the label of South Tyrolean wines. Appears in front of the grape variety.

Suelo (Sp). Lit – 'The Butt nearest the ground'. In the Sherry region. See Solera.

Süffig (Ger). Denotes a light, young, supple wine.

Sugar (Eng). $C_6H_{12}O_6$. The food that yeast needs to reproduce by binary fission. Is converted into alcohol and CO_2. i.e. grape sugar, Maltose, Sucrose etc.

Sugar Cane Juice (W.Ind). Extracted by pressing sugar cane through successive roller mills. Contains 10–12% sugar. Rum is distilled from this fermented juice. Results in a lightly flavoured Rum.

Sugar Cane Syrup (W.Ind). Produced by evaporating water from sugar cane juice in a vacuum distillation process. A brown viscous liquid. See Molasses.

Sugar Frosting (Eng). In cocktails the method of sugaring the rim of the glass by dipping the rim in egg white or fruit juice and then in sugar. See Frosted Glass.

Sugaring (Eng). The alternative name for Chaptalisation.

Sugar Mill (W.Ind). The brand-name of Rum produced by the Rum Company (Jamaica) Ltd. on the island of Jamaica. 43% alc. by vol.

Sugar of Milk (Eng). Lactose.

Sugar Wine (Eng). Produced by fermenting together water, sugar and grape husks.

Sughero (It). Cork, corktree.

Suhindol (Bul). A delimited wine-producing area in the northern region which is also the site of the first co-operative cellar for Cabernet, Gamza and Pamid grapes.

Suho (Bul) (Yug). Dry.

Suippes (Fr). A canton in the Châlons district in Champagne. Has the villages of Billy-le-Grand, Marne and Vaudemanges.

Suissesse (Cktl). ½ measure Pastis, ½ measure lemon juice, 1 egg white. Shake well over ice, strain into a small tumbler, add a splash of soda water.

Suissesse Cocktail (Cktl). 1 fl.oz. Pernod, 1 egg, dash Anisette, dash (white) Crème de Menthe, dash Orange flower water. Shake over ice, strain into a cocktail glass.

Suk (E.Asia). Equivalent of Saké. A type of rice beer made in Korea.

Sukhoe Vino (USSR). Dry wine.

Sukkar (Arab). See Muscavado.

Sukur Ziada (Tur). Sweet coffee. Is also known as Belon.

Sulak (Tur). A term to describe a watery, thin drink.

Sulfurous Acid (USA). See Sulphurous Acid.

Sullivan County (USA). A wine region in the New York district. The Highland is the best.

Sullivan Vineyards (USA). A winery and vineyard based near Rutherford, Napa Valley, California. Grape varieties – Cabernet sauvignon, Chardonnay and Chenin blanc. Produces varietal wines.

Sulmoniense (Lat). A red wine produced in central-eastern Italy during Roman times.

Sulm [River] (Ger). A tributary of the river Neckar in Württemberg.

Sulphur (Eng). The principal use of Sulphur in wine production is as a general preservative and safeguard against oxidation. This is especially true for white wines but also to a lesser extent for red wines. Sulphur is often added to the Must to prevent Aerobic yeasts from working before the wine yeasts.

Sulphur Candles (Fr). Used in Burgundy. They are burnt in the casks that new wine is to be racked into. Produces SO_2.

Sulphur-dioxide (Eng). SO_2. See Sulphur.

Sulphurisation (Eng). Excessive use of Sulphur as a preservative. Normally harmless but the smell is unpleasant. Will disperse eventually if left to the air.

Sulphurous Acid (Eng). The result of SO_2 gas after being added to wine. Reacts with water to form Sulphurous acid. See also Sulphur.

Sulphurous Anhydride (Eng). A chemical added to the must of white wines and to red wine grapes. Destroys any biological disorders present but does not harm the wine yeasts.

Sulphurous Water (Eng). A mineral water impregnated with Hydrogen. e.g. Challes, Harrogate and St. Boes.

Sultamine (Gre). A white grape variety grown mainly on the Isle of Crete and made mainly into raisins and dessert wines.

Sultana (Austr). A white grape variety grown in the Riverland, South Australia to make Australian brandy and sweet dessert wines. Also grown in Crete.

Sultanina (USA). A white table grape variety which is grown in the Central Valley. Also known as the Thompson Seedless.

Sulz (Ger). Village. (Anb) = Baden. (Ber) = Breisgau. (Gro) = Schutterlindenberg. (Vin) = Haselstaude.

Sulzbach (Ger). Village. (Anb) = Baden. (Ber) = Badische Bergstrasse/Kraichgau. (Gro) = Rittersberg. (Vin) = Herrnwingert.

Sülzbach (Ger). Village. (Anb) = Württemberg. (Ber) = Württembergisch Unterland. (Gro) = Salzberg. (Vin) = Altenberg.

Sulzbach (Fr). The German name for the village of Soultz-les-Bains in Alsace.

Sulzburg (Ger). Village. (Anb) = Baden. (Ber) = Markgräflerland. (Gro) = Burg Neuenfels. (Vin) = Altenberg.

Sülzenberg (Ger). Vineyard. (Anb) = Mittelrhein. (Ber) = Johannisberg. (Gro) = Petersberg. (Vil) = Oberdollendorf.

Sulzfeld (Ger). Village. (Anb) = Baden. (Ber) = Badische Bergstrasse/ Kraichgau. (Gro) = Stiftsberg. (Vins) = Burg Ravensburger Dicker Franz, Burg Ravensburger Husarenkappe, Burg Ravensburger Löchle, Lerchenberg.

Sulzfeld (Ger). Village. (Anb) = Franken. (Ber) = Maindreieck. (Gro) = Hofrat. (Vins) = Cyriakusberg, Maustal.

Sulzheim (Ger). Village. (Anb) = Rheinhessen. (Ber) = Bingen. (Gro) = Adelberg. (Vins) = Greifenberg, Honigberg, Schildberg.

Sumatra Coffee (E.Ind). An Indonesian coffee which produces a mellow flavour with a full musty aroma and full flavour.

Su-Mi-Re (Jap). A violet-coloured, spicy, liqueur cordial with a citric aroma. Contains vanilla, almond, spices, fruit etc. 30% alc. by vol.

Summer Cocktail (Cktl).(Non-alc). Mash some blackcurrants, raspberries and strawberries with a muddler and sugar. Add juice of ½ a lemon and same quantity of water. Shake well over ice, strain into a 5 oz. wine glass.

Summer Cooler (Cktl).(Non-alc). ⅓ pint orange juice, ½ fl.oz. Angostura, 1 fl.oz. blackcurrant cordial. Shake well over ice, strain into an ice-filled highball glass.

Summer Dream (Cktl). 1 part Cherry 'B' and 1 part orange juice.

Summerfield Winery (Austr). A winery based in the Pyrenees, Victoria. Produces varietal wines.

Summer Fun Cocktail (Cktl). ½ measure Brandy, ½ measure Crème de Banane, 1½ measures orange juice, 1½ measures pineapple juice. Shake well over ice, strain into a highball glass. Serve with straws.

S

Summer Mint Cocktail (Cktl). ⅓ measure Galliano, ⅓ measure (green) Crème de Menthe, ⅓ measure Cointreau, ½ measure grapefruit juice, ½ measure lemon juice. Blend together with a scoop of crushed ice in a blender, pour into a flute glass. Dress with mint and a cherry. Serve with straws.

Summer Pruning (Eng). The cutting back of the excess growth tendrils on the vine. This allows the vine's energy to be concentrated on the grapes.

Summer Reverie Cocktail (Cktl). 1 fl.oz. Beefeater Gin, ½ fl.oz. Cointreau, 1 fl.oz. French vermouth, ½ fl.oz. grapefruit juice, ⅓ fl.oz. Apricot brandy. Mix well together over ice. Strain into a cocktail glass, decorate with a ½ apricot and a cherry.

Summerskill Brewery (Eng). Opened in 1983 in Kingsbridge, Devon then moved to Plymouth in 1985. Noted for its cask conditioned Bigbury Best Bitter 1044 O.G.

Summer Sparkler (Cktl). 1 part Mardi Gras, 2 parts sparkling dry white wine. Stir gently over ice in a highball glass.

Summertime (Cktl). In a tall glass with ice pour 1 oz. Vodka, 1 oz. dry Vermouth, juice ½ grapefruit. Stir, top with tonic water.

Summertime Cocktail (Cktl). 1¼ measures Bacardi rum, ½ measure pineapple juice, ½ measure orange juice, 3 dashes golden Rum, juice ¼ lemon. Stir over ice, strain into an ice-filled collins glass. Dress with mint and an orange slice. Serve with straws.

Summit (USA). A label used by the Geyser Peak Winery in California for their generic and varietal wines.

Sumoll (Sp). A white grape variety grown in the Penedés region. The main grape for Spanish Cava. See also Soumoll.

Sumoll Negro (Sp). A red grape variety grown in the Penedés region.

Sun Country Refresher (USA). A proprietary drink of white wine, fruit juice and carbonated spring water. 5% alc. by vol.

Sunderland Bitter (Eng). A cask conditioned Bitter 1040 O.G. brewed by the Vaux Brewery in Sunderland. Also a keg version.

Sun Dew Cocktail (Cktl).(Non-alc). ½ gill orange juice, ¼ gill grapefruit juice, ¼ gill Gomme syrup, dash Angostura. Stir well over ice, strain into an ice-filled highball glass. Top with soda water and a slice of orange.

Sundowner (Cktl). 1 fl.oz. Brandy, ¼ fl.oz. Van der Hum, ¼ fl.oz. lemon juice, ¼ fl.oz. orange juice. Shake over ice, strain into a cocktail glass.

Sundowner (S.Afr). A brand of Rum produced in South Africa.

Sunflower (China). A brand-name used by the Shantung C.N.C.O.F.I.E.C. for their dry Gin, Whiskey and Vodka.

Sungurlare (Bul). A wine-producing town that produces a medium-dry white wine from the Misket grape.

Sun Lik (S.E.Asia). A Lager beer 4.75% alc. by vol. brewed by the San Miguel Brewery in Hongkong.

Sunny Brook (USA). The brand-name of a blended Whiskey. 40% alc. by vol.

Sunnycliff Winery (Austr). A winery based in the Murray River area, Victoria. Produces varietal and table wines.

Sunny Dream (Cktl). 3 fl.ozs. orange juice, 1 fl.oz. Apricot brandy, ½ fl.oz. Cointreau, 1 scoop ice cream. Blend together, serve in a goblet with straws and an orange slice.

Sunquick (Eng). The brand-name of a fruit concentrate which is drunk diluted. Is available in apple, grapefruit, orange and tangerine flavours.

Sunraku Ocean (Jap). A large winery based in Japan.

Sunrise (Cktl).(1). ⅕ measure Crème de Banane, ⅕ measure Galliano, ⅖ measure Tequila, ⅕ measure cream, dash Grenadine, dash lemon juice. Shake over ice, strain into a cocktail glass.

Sunrise (Cktl).(2). ⅓ wine glass Brandy, ¾ wine glass Port, 2 dashes Angostura, 1 oz. Vanilla syrup. Shake well over ice, strain into a chilled tumbler, dress with lemon rind.

Sunrise Winery (USA). A winery based in Santa Cruz, California. Grape varieties – Cabernet sauvignon, Chardonnay and Pinot noir. Produces varietal wines.

Sunset (Cktl). 2 fl.ozs. golden Tequila, 1 fl.oz. lemon juice, ½ oz. light honey. Stir well together, serve in a cocktail glass with shaved ice.

Sunset Club (Eng). A lightly sparkling British wine and citrus-fruit Cooler. Low in alcohol.

Sunset Tea (Cktl). Heat 2 fl.ozs. orange juice, 1 fl.oz. Curaçao and ½ fl.oz. light Rum until nearly boiling. Pour into a heatproof glass containing ⅓ pint hot tea. Decorate with a clove (6) studded orange piece, cinnamon stick.

Sunshine Cocktail (Cktl).(1). ¼ gill Gin, ⅛ gill Italian vermouth, ¼ gill orange squash, 1 teaspoon Orange bitters, 1 teaspoon Grenadine. Stir over ice, strain into a small wine glass, serve with a cherry.

Sunshine Cocktail (Cktl).(2). ⅙ gill Old

Tom Gin, ⅙ gill French vermouth, ⅙ gill Italian vermouth, 2 dashes Orange bitters. Stir well over ice, strain into a cocktail glass, add lemon peel juice on top.

Suntip Fruit Juices (Eng). The name given to frozen concentrated fruit juices. Distributed by Moccomat U.K. Ltd.

Suntory (Jap). A large Whiskey producer based at Hakushu. Use Scotch malt whisky in their blends. Produces a range of whiskies under the Suntory label. Also a large wine producer.

Suntory Brewery (Jap). A brewery based in Osaka which is noted for its Suntory beer.

Suntory Chiyoda (Jap). A popular brand of Saké produced by the Suntory company.

Suntory Whisky Custom (Jap). The brand-name of a light-style Whiskey first produced in 1967 by the Suntory Distillery in Hakushu.

Suntory Whisky Excellence (Jap). The brand-name of a premium Whiskey first produced in 1971 by the Suntory Distillery in Hakushu.

Suntory Whisky Gold Label (Jap). The brand-name of a light-styled Whiskey first produced in 1965 by the Suntory Distillery in Hakushu.

Suntory Whisky Imperial (Jap). The brand-name of a premium Whiskey first produced in 1964 by the Suntory Distillery in Hakushu.

Suntory Whisky Rawhide (Jap). The brand-name of a Bourbon-flavoured Whiskey produced by the Suntory Distillery in Hakushu.

Suntory Whisky Red Label (Jap). The brand-name of a light-styled Whiskey first produced by the Suntory Distillery in Hakushu.

Suntory Whisky Royal (Jap). The brand-name of a premium Whiskey first produced in 1960 by the Suntory Distillery in Hakushu.

Suntory Whisky Special Reserve (Jap). The brand-name of a premium Whiskey first produced in 1969 by the Suntory Distillery in Hakushu.

Sun Worship Cocktail (Cktl). 1 oz. Beefeater Gin, ½ oz. French vermouth, ¼ oz. Campari, ¼ oz. Liqueur de Framboise. Stir together over ice, strain into a cocktail glass, add a twist of orange.

Suomurrain (Fin). A liqueur made from cloudberries similar to Lakka. Produced by Lignell and Piispanen.

Supalitre (Eng). A Pale ale 1031 O.G. brewed by the Gibbs Mews Brewery in Salisbury, Wiltshire. Sold in litre bottles.

Super Ale (Eng). A Brown ale 1032 O.G. brewed and bottled by the Burtonwood Brewery in Cheshire.

Super Brew (Eng). A cask conditioned Bitter 1047 O.G. brewed by the Baileys Brewery in Malvern, Worcestershire.

Superior (S.Afr). A wine classification. Must have at least 30 grammes per litre of residual grape sugar and be harvested at 28 or more degrees Baume of sugar.

Superiore (It). Superior. To a wine means being from a clearly defined area and of defined quality. Usually it is aged for not less than 1–3 years and has a minimum alcoholic content.

Superiore di Cartizze (It). D.O.C. white wine from the Veneto region. Made from the Prosecco and Verdiso grapes in the restricted area of Cartizze. Also produced by natural refermentation as Frizzante – semi-sparkling and Spumante – sparkling.

Superiore Naturalmente Amabile (It). A term meaning a naturally semi-sweet wine. Must be aged minimum 2 years in oak/chestnut casks.

Superiore Naturalmente Dolce (It). A term meaning a naturally sweet wine. Must be aged minimum 2 years in oak/chestnut casks.

Superiore Naturalmente Secco (It). A term meaning a naturally dry wine. Must be aged minimum 2 years in oak/chestnut casks.

Superior Old Marsala (It). See S.O.M.

Superior Ruby (Port). A deep-coloured Ruby Port produced by Ferreira Port shippers.

Super Lager (Scot). A Lager beer 1081 O.G. brewed and bottled by the Tennent Caledonian Brewery.

Super Leeuw (Hol). A slightly bitter beer brewed by the De Leeuw Brouwerij based in Valkenburg, Limburg.

Super Mild (Eng). A keg Dark Mild 1031 O.G. brewed by the Gibbs Mew Brewery in Salisbury, Wiltshire.

Super Nikka (Jap). A brand of Whiskey produced by the Nikka Distilleries.

Super White (S.Am). A light-styled Rum, aged for 12 months and produced by Banks DIH in Guyana.

Supple (Eng). A term used to describe an easy-to-drink wine. With age the tannin becomes supple.

Supreme Bitter (Eng). A cask conditioned Bitter 1043 O.G. brewed by the Abbey Brewery in Retford, Nottinghamshire.

Supreme Bitter (Eng). A cask conditioned Bitter 1043 O.G. brewed by the Simpkiss Brewery in Brierley Hill, Staffordshire.

Supreme Coffee (S.Am). A grade of Colombian coffee. Produces a rich, smooth, strong brew.
Sur (Wales). Acidic, sour.
Sura (Ind). A spirit made from rice starch.
Surdo (Mad). A sweet wine fortified with grape alcohol after being fermented for only a short time.
Suresnes (Fr). Ancient vineyards planted by priests in the tenth century.
Surfboard (Cktl). 2 measures Malibu poured over an ice cube in a large high-ball glass. Add 1 measure blue Curaçao, then fresh cream until the ice cube surfaces.
Surfers (W.Ind). A Rum and coconut liqueur.
Surfer's Paradise (Cktl). Build 3 dashes Angostura and 1 fl.oz. lime juice in an ice-filled highball glass, stir in lemonade, decorate with a slice of orange.
Surfing Cocktail (Cktl). ½ measure light Rum, ½ measure Apricot brandy, dash Gomme syrup, 1 egg yolk. Shake well over ice, strain into a cocktail glass. Top with grated nutmeg.
Surf Sailor Splash (Cktl). ⅕ gill Cherry Heering placed in an ice-filled highball glass. Top with ½ gill orange juice and soda water.
Sur Gamay (Fr). A Premier Cru vineyard in the A.C. commune of Saint Aubin, Côte de Beaune, Burgundy. 14 ha.
Surin (Fr). The alternative name used for the Sauvignon blanc grape in the Loire Valley.
Sur Lattes (Fr). Bottles laid Lit – 'Head in Punt' on wooden racks for maturation especially in Champagne.
Sur Lavelle (Fr). A Premier Cru vineyard in the A.C. commune of Monthélie, Côte de Beaune, Burgundy. 6.1 ha.
Sur-le-Sentier-du-Clou (Fr). A Premier Cru vineyard in the A.C. commune of Saint Aubin, Côte de Beaune, Burgundy. 12 ha.
Sur-les-Grèves (Fr). A Premier Cru vineyard in the A.C. commune of Beaune, Côte de Beaune, Burgundy. 4.02 ha.
Sur Lie (Fr). Lit – 'Bottled off the Lees'. e.g. Muscadet. Placed into the bottle without firstly racking.
Surmaturité (Fr). Over ripe, over maturity.
Surni (Wales). Acidity.
Sur Plaque (Fr). The term to describe filtering. The wine is run through cellulose filters before being bottled.
Sur Pointe (Fr). On its head. The name for Champagne bottles that are stored upside down with the head of one bottle in the Punt of the one below after the 2nd fermentation and before Dégorgement.
Surrentinum (Lat). A red wine produced in central-western Italy in Roman times.
Surrey Bitter (Eng). A cask conditioned Bitter 1038 O.G. brewed by the Pilgrim Brewery in Woldingham, Surrey.
Sur Souche (Fr). The term given when there is a great demand for wine and the merchants buy the wine when the grapes are still on the vine!
Sur Terre (Fr). The name for a type of filtration where the wine is passed through a powdered shell screen before going into casks. Used in Bordeaux.
Şurup (Tur). Fruit juice, cordial, syrup.
Susa Don Ramón (Sp). A noted wine-producer based in the Cariñena region.
Susie Taylor Cocktail (Cktl). ⅕ gill Bacardi White Label, juice ½ lime. Stir over ice in a highball glass. Top with ginger ale.
Suso y Pérez (Vincente) (Sp). The largest wine producer in Cariñena, north-eastern Spain. See Don Ramon, Duque de Sevilla, Mosen Cleto and Old Duque de Sevilla brandy.
Suspension (Cktl). ⅓ measure Scotch whisky, ⅓ measure orange juice, ⅓ measure ginger wine. Shake well together over ice, strain into a cocktail glass.
Süss (Ger). Sweet.
Süssdruck (Switz). A rosé (and light red wine) produced from the Pinot noir grape.
Süsse (Ger). Grape sugar. See also Süesse.
Sussex Beers (Eng). The name of Ales brewed by the Harvey Brewery in Lewes, Sussex.
Sussex Beers (Eng). The name of Ales brewed by the King and Barnes Brewery in Horsham, Sussex.
Sussex Punch (Cktl). 3/6 measure dark Rum, 2/6 measure elderberry wine, ⅙ measure dry Cider, 1 dash lemon juice. Stir well over ice, strain into a cocktail glass. Top with a spiral of lemon peel.
Sussex Tap Water (Eng). A still water, filtered or un-filtered. Sparkling water is carbonated by Soda Stream.
Süsskopf (Ger). Vineyard. (Anb) = Rheinpfalz. (Ber) = Mittelhaardt-Deutsche Weinstrasse. (Gro) = Schepfenflug an der Weinstrasse. (Vil) = Forst.
Sussling (Fr). An alternative name for the Chasselas grape in eastern France.
Süssmund (Ger). Vineyard. (Anb) = Württemberg. (Ber) = Württembergisch Unterland. (Gro) = Wunnenstein. (Vil) = Kleinbottwar.
Süssreserve (Ger). Unfermented grape juice which has been centrifuged to remove all yeasts. Used to sweeten Tafel and Qba. wines.
Süssung (Ger). The name given to the process of adding Süssreserve to wine

S

prior to bottling. May only be practised by growers and wholesalers.

Süsswasser (Ger). Fresh water.

Süsswein (Ger). Grape must where the yeasts are removed or killed without use of alcohol so further fermentation is possible.

Sütçü (Tur). Milkman.

Süthane (Tur). Dairy.

Sutherland Water (Scot). A natural spring water from the Scottish highlands.

Sutter Basin Vineyard (USA). A vineyard based in the Yolo County, California. Grape variety – Zinfandel. Vinified at the Carneros Creek Winery.

Sutterer (Ger). A noted Eau-de-vie producer based in Mösbach, Schwarzwald.

Sutter Home (USA). A winery in the Napa Valley in northern California. Grape variety – Zinfandel.

Suzão Teroldico (USA). A red grape variety grown in California to make dessert wines.

Suze (Fr). A bitter gentian-flavoured apéritif made by J.R. Parkinson (Pernod). 17% alc. by vol.

Svagdricka (Swe). A dark, sweet Beer that is low in alcohol 1.8% alc. by weight and with added yeast.

Svart-Vinbärs (Swe). A blackcurrant-flavoured Brannvin used to make Kir.

Svenzka (Eng). The brand-name of a Vodka bottled by Thomas Shaw of London and Glasgow. 37.2% alc. by vol.

Sveriges Bartenders' Gille (Swe). S.B.G. Swedish Bartenders' Guild. Address = P.O. Box 7579, S.E. 103, 93 Stockholm.

Sveta Nedelja (Yug). A wine-producing region in Dalmatia.

Světlé (Czec). Pale (beer).

Světovar (Czec). A Pilsener-type lager produced by the Gambrinus Brewery.

Svijany Brewery (Czec). An old established brewery based in north-western Czec. c1546.

S. Vincente (Port). A Dão wine produced by the Caves Borlida.

Svishtov (Bul). A noted winery that produces Cabernet-based wines in a delimited area of the same name in the northern region.

Svitavy Brewery (Czec). A brewery based in central Czec.

Swabian Wine Route (Ger). See Schwäbische Weinstrasse.

Swacked (Eng) (slang). In a very intoxicated state. Very drunk.

Swan Brewery (Austr). A large brewery based in Perth, Western Australia. Brews Swan and Emu Lagers.

Swan Hill (Austr). A wine district of New South Wales. Produces good quality wines.

Swanky (Austr). A Beer brewed by the Cooper's Brewery in South Australia.

Swan Premium Export Lager (Austr). A fine Lager beer 5% alc. by vol. brewed by the Swan Brewery in Perth. Distributed in the U.K. by Courage and Bass.

Swan's Neck (Eng). See Col du Cygne.

Swan Special Light (Austr). A low-alcohol Lager 0.9% alc. by vol. brewed in Western Australia.

Swan Special Lite Lager (Austr). See Swan Special Light.

Swan Throat (Fr). The curve of copper tubing which connects the Still to a Condenser in Cognac production.

Swan Valley (Austr). A wine region of Western Australia. Is noted for dessert wines.

Swan Vineyards (USA). A winery based near Forestville, Russian River Valley, California. Grape varieties – Chardonnay, Pinot noir and Zinfandel. Produces varietal wines.

Swartberg Aristaat (S.Afr). A brand-name of the Ladismith Co-operative.

Swartland (S.Afr). A district on the west coast near the town of Malmesbury.

Swartland Co-operative (S.Afr). Based in Swartland. Address = Die Swartland Koöperatiewe Wynmaatskappy, Box 95, Malmesbury 7300. Produces varietal wines.

Swartland Koöperatiewe Wynmaatskappy (Die) (S.Afr). See Swartland Cooperative.

Swedish Punsch (Swe). Based on Batavian Arak, Akvavit, spices, tea, lemon and sugar. Wine is added after a few months' maturation. 30% alc. by vol.

Sweet (Eng). Fine wines obtain their sweetness from excess grape sugar after fermentation. (see Botrytis Cinerea). Others are fortified with spirit to stop fermentation before all the sugar has been fermented out. Finally some wines have residual sweetness from unfermentable sugars remaining in the wine.

Sweet and Low (Cktl).(Non-alc). ⅓ measure Grenadine, ⅓ measure lemon juice, ⅓ measure orange juice. Shake over ice, strain into a cocktail glass.

Sweet Beer (USA). A combination of beer with a fruit juice (lemon, lime or grape) to give a sweeter drink.

Sweet Blondy (Cktl). ⅓ measure sweet white Vermouth, ⅓ measure Royal Mint Chocolate liqueur, ⅓ measure light Rum, dash orange juice. Shake over ice, strain, add a slice of orange peel.

Sweet Cider (USA). Unfermented apple juice. See also Hard Cider.

Sweet Desire (Cktl). ⅓ measure dry Gin, ⅓ measure red Dubonnet, ⅙ measure

Kirsch, ⅙ measure Parfait Amour. Shake over ice, strain into a cocktail glass.

Sweet Dreams (Cktl). Place ½ gill Crème de Cacao into a highball glass, top with hot milk, stir, add grated nutmeg.

Sweetened Spirits (Eng). H.M. Customs and Excise technical definition of Liqueurs.

Sweetheart (Scot). A bottled sweet Stout 1035 O.G. brewed by the Tennent Caledonian Brewery.

Sweet Maria Cocktail (Cktl). ½ measure Vodka, ¼ measure Amaretto, ¼ measure cream. Shake over ice, strain into a cocktail glass.

Sweet Martini Cocktail (Cktl). ¼ gill Gin, ¼ gill Italian vermouth. Stir over ice, strain into a cocktail glass, add a squeeze of lemon peel juice on top.

Sweet Mash (USA). Yeasting process in the production of Whiskey. Also known as the 'Yeast Mash Process'. Is the adding of fresh yeast to the Mash and no spent beer. See Sour Mash.

Sweet Memories (Cktl). ⅓ measure dry Vermouth, ⅓ measure white Rum, ⅓ measure orange Curaçao. Stir over ice, strain into a cocktail glass.

Sweet Millenary (Cktl). ⅓ measure Rosé Cinzano, ⅓ measure Galliano, ⅓ measure Aperol Aperitivo. Stir over ice, strain into a cocktail glass, add a twist of orange peel juice.

Sweet Nancy (USA). A sweet, botrytised white wine made from the Chenin blanc grape by Callaway Winery in Temecula, California.

Sweet Patootie (Cktl). ⅔ measure dry Gin, ⅓ measure Triple Sec, ⅙ measure orange juice. Shake over ice, strain into a cocktail glass.

Sweet Permain (Eng). An old English cider-making apple.

Sweet Sauterne (USA). A Californian sweet white wine made from the Sauvignon blanc, Sémillon and Muscadelle grapes.

Sweet Stout (Eng). An English stout. Sometimes flavoured with Oyster essence and oatmeal.

Sweet Stout (Eng). A processed Stout 1043 O.G. brewed and bottled by the Federation Brewery in Dunston, Newcastle-upon-Tyne.

Sweetwater (Austr). An alternative name for the Palomino grape.

Sweet Wort (Eng). The name given to the liquid run off from the Mash tun to the Copper.

Sweet Young Thing (Cktl). ½ measure Malibu, ½ measure Crème de Fraises, 2 dashes Gomme syrup. Shake well over ice, strain into an ice-filled highball glass. Top with iced Champagne and a fresh strawberry.

Swellendam (S.Afr). A district which stretches from the south coast inland to the town of Bonnievale.

Swift Half (Eng). A term to denote a quick drink. Usually a ½ pint of beer and denotes that a person cannot stay long (drinking).

Swifty (Eng) (slang). 'A quick drink'.

Swill (Eng) (slang). To drink quickly. Guzzle.

Swilling (Eng) (slang). A term used to denote heavy, fast drinking.

Swing (Scot). A De Luxe blended Scotch whisky produced by Johnnie Walker. Sold in a dumpy bottle. 40% alc. by vol.

Swinger Cocktail (Cktl).(1). 1 part Glayva, 5 parts orange juice. Shake well together over ice, strain into an ice-filled highball. Decorate with a slice of lime.

Swinger Cocktail (Cktl).(2) (Non-alc). 1 fl.oz. pineapple syrup, ½ fl.oz. Gomme syrup, ⅓ pint grapefruit juice. Shake over ice, strain into a highball glass. Add a grapefruit segment and a cherry.

Swiss (Cktl). ½ measure Pastis, ½ measure fresh cream, teaspoon Grenadine Shake over ice, strain into a cocktail glass.

Swiss Colony (USA). See United Vintners.

Swiss Family (Cktl). ⅔ measure Bourbon whiskey, ⅓ measure French vermouth, 2 dashes Pastis, 2 dashes Angostura. Stir over ice, strain into a cocktail glass.

Swiss Valley (USA). A small vineyard based in Vevay, Indiana. 1.25 ha. Produces French hybrid wines.

Switz (Euro) (abbr). Switzerland.

Switzerland (Switz). A small wine-producing country situated between the borders of France, Germany and Italy. Its wines are influenced by the three countries in their styles (vines and wines). The major regions are French – (Chablais Vaudois, Geneva, La Côte, Lavaux, Neuchâtel, Northern Vaudois, Valais and Vaud). German–Argovia, Basle, Schaffhausen, Thurgau and Zurich). Italian – (Ticino).

Swizzles (USA). A drink of spirits, sugar or other sweetening agent and soda. Made in pitchers with ice then served in ice-filled highball glasses.

Swizzle Stick (USA). A gadget used to remove the bubbles from sparkling wines. Popular in the 1930s.

Swizzle Stick (W.Ind). A device used to 'Swizzle' ice and liquor together in a jug or glass to create a frost on the outside. Originally made from the dried stem of a tropical plant with a few small branches left on one end. Now often made of plastic. Up to two foot long.

Swn y Don (Wales). The rebirth of Welsh Whiskey. Lit – 'Sound of the waves'. Made by Powys Promotions Ltd.

Swn y Mor (Wales). A Whiskey produced in Mid-Wales from a Scottish malt grain blend, then steeped in local herbs. Produced by the Brecon Brewery Ltd. 40% alc. by vol. See Chwisgi. Lit – 'Sound of Sea'.

SW1 (Cktl). ⅓ measure Campari, ⅓ measure Vodka, ⅓ measure orange juice, dash egg white. Shake over ice, strain into a cocktail glass.

SW1 (Eng). A cask conditioned Bitter brewed by the Clifton Inns home-brew public house in London.

SW2 (Eng). A cask conditioned Bitter brewed by the Clifton Inns home-brew public house in London.

Sybillenstein (Ger). Grosslage. (Anb) = Rheinhessen. (Ber) = Wonnegau. (Vils) = Alzey, Bechenheim, Dautenheim, Freimersheim, Heimersheim, Mauchenheim, Offenheim, Wahlheim, Weinheim.

SYC (N.Z.). A producer of Sherry-style wines.

Sycamore Creek Vineyards (USA). A winery based in Hecker Pass, Santa Clara, California. 6 ha. Grape varieties – Cabernet sauvignon, Carignane, Chenin blanc, Johannisberg riesling and Zinfandel. Produces varietal wines.

Sychedig (Wales). Thirsty. (Sychedu = to thirst).

Sydney Sunset (Cktl). 1 oz. Glayva, 2 ozs. orange juice, ½ oz. orange Curaçao, dash egg white. Shake well over ice, strain into a large cocktail glass. Decorate with a cherry, orange slice and serve with straws.

Sydoon-Gezer (Isr). The second largest wine-producing region. Noted for fine red and white wines.

Sykes Hydrometer (Eng). An instrument for measuring alcoholic strengths. Named after the man who invented it.

Sylhet (Asia). A tea-producing area in Bangladesh.

Sylikou (Cyp). A wine village on the south eastern side of the island. Produces mainly red grapes for the making of Commandaria.

Syllabub (Eng). An old drink of fresh milk (full-cream), wine (or spirits) and spices. The milk should be as fresh as possible and warm. Whisk in the wine and spices. Drink as soon as possible. Is also served as a dessert (modern).

Sylvaner (Ger). A superior white grape variety which gives fresh, fruity wines. Grown extensively in Austria, France, Switzerland and the USA. See also Silvaner (alternative spelling). Also known as the Gruber, Grünling, Gros rhin, Johannisberg and Oesterreicher.

Sylvaner Bechtau (USSR). A white grape variety used in the production of dry white wines in Stavropol.

Sylvatica (It). Wild chestnut casks made from forest of same name and used in the Chianti region.

Sylvester Wine (Ger). A wine made on New Year's Eve. Usually of either Trokenbeerenauslesen or Eiswein quality. Illegal since 1971.

Sylvia Cocktail (Cktl). ⅓ measure Grand Marnier, ⅓ measure Bacardi White Label, ⅓ measure pineapple juice, 1 egg yolk, juice ¼ orange, 2 dashes Grenadine. Shake over ice, strain into an ice-filled highball. Serve with straws.

Sylvius (Hol). A doctor in Leyden who produced the first Jenever in the sixteenth century. See also De la Boe (Dr Franciscus).

Symonds (Eng). A noted Cider-making company based in Hereford. Produces – Drystone (medium-sweet), Princess Pippin (a vintage Cider) and Scrumpy Jack. Address = Stoke Lacy, Bromyard, Hereford. Part of Greenhall Whitley.

Syndale Valley Vineyards (Eng). Vineyards based at Newsham, near Faversham, Kent. Soil = chalk. Grape varieties – Müller-Thurgau, Reichensteiner, Seyval blanc and others.

Syndicat de Défense des Vins des Côtes de Provence (Fr). A body for the protection of the wines of the Côtes de Provence. Formed by a group of growers.

Syndicat des Crus Classés du Médoc (Fr). Address = 1, Cours du XXX Juliet, 33000 Bordeaux. A group that represents many of the great châteaux.

Syndicat des Producteurs de Vins Mousseux Méthode Champenoise de Bourgogne (Fr). A body that represents over 30 firms in the Burgundy region regarding Crémant de Bourgogne and sparkling Burgundy.

Syndicat du Commerce des Vins de Champagne (Fr). A body founded in the late nineteenth century by Paul Krug to help deal with Phylloxera. Consisted of a group of Champagne shippers.

Syndicat du Cru de Bonnezeaux (Fr). A body of the A.C. Bonnezeaux wine producers based in Thouarcé, Anjou-Saumur, Loire.

Syndicat National des Fabricants de

Liqueurs (Fr). Produce a selection of liqueurs from 90 members. Has an inner court called the Groupement des Grandes Liqueurs de France.

Syndicat Viticole de Fronsac (Fr). Les Gentilshommes de Fronsac. Address = Maison des Vins, B.P. N°7, 33126 Fronsac.

Synthetic Wine (Eng). A 'wine' made of glucose, glycerine, spirit, water and colouring. An artificial wine.

Syra (Fr). An alternative spelling of the Syrah grape.

Syrac (Fr). An alternative spelling of the Syrah grape.

Syracuse (It). A Muscat wine produced on the island of Sicily.

Syrah (Fr). A red grape variety. Grown mainly in the Rhône (especially in the northern Rhône where it is the only red variety used). Gives deep colour, tannin and a distictive bouquet of blackberries. Also known as the Chira, Entournerier, Hignan, Hignan noir, Petite syrah, Schiras, Sérine, Serrenne, Shiraz, Shyraz, Sirac, Sirah, Sirrah, Sirras, Syra, Syrac and Syras.

Syras (Euro). An alternative spelling of the Syrah grape in eastern Europe.

Syrberg (Lux). A vineyard site in the village of Nertert.

Syrgis (Eng). An eighteenth-century name for the wines of Sitges.

Syria (M.East). A lesser wine-producing country. Vineyard areas are in the regions of Aleppo, Damascus and Homs.

Syrrah (Fr). Another spelling of the Syrah.

Syrupy (Eng). A term used to describe wines that are excessively rich, e.g. Sauternes or very sweet Sherry, Madeira, Port.

System 24 (Eng). A patented unit produced by the Nestlé Co. which dispenses their instant coffees. Is similar to the automatic drip filter method. Produces up to 22 x 3 pint carafes per filling.

Szamorodni (Hun). Found on Tokay wine labels. Denotes a dry or sweet wine (depending on year). The wine is made from ripe or over-ripe grapes which are pressed together indiscriminately. See also Aszú. Lit – 'As it comes'.

Szàraz (Hun). Dry. Pronounced Shah-rahsh.

Szàraz Szamorodni (Hun). A dry tasting Szamorodni wine from Tolna.

Sze Chuan Dah Poo Chiew (China). A medicinal wine said to help expectant mothers. From Hwarto.

Szekszàrd (Hun). A wine-producing district in southern Transdanubia. Is noted for its red wines.

Szekszàrdi Kardarka (Hun). A full-bodied red wine produced in the Szekszàrd district.

Szekszàrdi Vörós (Hun). A strong, dark red wine from the Szekszàrd district.

Szemelt (Hun). Selected berries. Similar to Auslese.

Szilva (Hun). A spirit distilled from plums.

Szilvàni (Hun). An alternative name for the Sylvaner grape. See also Szilvanyi.

Szilvàni Zöld (Hun). See Szilvanyi Zöld.

Szilvany (Hun). Sylvaner.

Szilvanyi Zöld (Hun). Lit – 'Green Sylvaner'. A medium-dry, white wine which has a soft bouquet and a green tinge. Made from the Sylvaner grape.

Szilva Pàlinka (Hun). A plum brandy produced in Szatmar County. Is also known as Szilvorium.

Szilvorium (Hun). See Szilva Pàlinka.

Szomerodny (Hun). White table wine.

Szürkebaràt (Hun). A white grape variety grown around lake Balatòn in the Badacsonyi area. Produces sweetish wines of the same name. Lit – 'Grey Friar'. Known as the Pinot gris in France.

T

Tabanon Distillery (W.Ind). A noted Rum distillery based on the island of Guadeloupe.

Tabereiro (Port). Publican, tavern-owner.

Taberna (Sp). Tavern, inn, public house.

Table Beer (Eng). A term for Dinner ale. Bottled beers.

Tablespoon (USA). A bar-measure which equals ½ fl.oz. Imp = ⅜ fl.oz. USA = 3 level teaspoons.

Table Water (Eng). Natural or manufactured mineral waters. Drunk on their own (or as mixers). Usually low in minerals and alkaline. e.g. Aix-le-Chapelle, Apollinaris, Buxton, Malvern, Perrier and St. Galmier.

Table Wines (Eng). Wines for everyday drinking. Not for laying down. Usually light and of no quality status. Are suitable for drinking at the table with food. See Vin de Table, Tafelwein, Tafelwyn, Vino do Mesa, Vino de Tavola.

Taboo (Eng). An exotic fruit, white wine and Vodka-based drink produced jointly by William Grant and Bulmers subsidiaries. 14.9% alc. by vol.

Tàbor Brewery (Czec). An old established brewery c1612 based in western Czec.

Tabor Hill Vineyard (USA). A vineyard based in Berrien County, Michigan. Produces vinifera and hybrid wines.

Tachar (Port). Lit – 'To get drunk'. To go on a binge.

Taché (Fr). A malady found in white wines when they obtain a slight rosé colour. Lit – 'Stained'. Are treated with sulphuric acid.

Tâche [La] (Fr). A Grand Cru vineyard in the A.C. commune of Vosne-Romanée, Côte de Nuits, Burgundy. 6 ha.

Ta Chu (China). A grain spirit produced in Szechwan.

Tacoronte (Sp). A red wine, strong in alcohol (12–14% by vol) that is produced on the Canary Islands.

Tacorontes (Sp). Another name used for the 'Mountain' wines.

Tadcaster Bitter (Eng). A cask conditioned Bitter beer 1035 O.G. brewed by the Samuel Smith Brewery in Tadcaster, Yorkshire.

Taddy Ales (Eng). A name used by the Samuel Smith Brewery in Tadcaster, Yorkshire for their beers.

Tadzhikistan (USSR). A wine-producing area in central Asia. Is noted for its dessert wines. Is also the name for a red, Port-style wine.

Taeniotic (Egy). An aromatic, sweet, greenish-white wine produced in the second century A.D. near Alexandria. Was enjoyed by Athenaeus.

Taetta (Scan). An alcoholic beverage fermented from milk. Is similar to Koumiss.

Tafarn (Wales). Inn.

Tafarnwr (Wales). Innkeeper.

Tafel Akvavit (Scan). A clean tasting, caraway-flavoured Akvavit. 45% alc. by vol.

Tafelaquavit (Scan). See Tafel Akvavit.

Tafelstein (Ger). Vineyard. (Anb) = Rheinhessen. (Ber) = Nierstein. (Gro) = Güldenmorgen. (Vil) = Dienheim.

Tafelwein (Aus). Table wine. Must have a minimum must weight of 13° KMW.

Tafelwein (Ger). A blend of wines from E.E.C. countries. See Aus Ländern der EWG. Deutscher Tafelwein is from German wines only.

Tafelweinanbaugebiet (Ger). Table wine region.

Tafelwyn (S.Afr). Table wine.

Taffea (W.Ind). The alternative spelling of Tafia.

Taffia (W.Ind). The alternative spelling of Tafia.

Tafia (Egy). A spirit distilled from sugar, usually high in alcohol (over 60% by vol).

Tafia (S.Am). The ancient Negro word for Rum. Nowadays it is a dark spirit produced from inferior molasses (impure) in Guyana.

Tafia Habitant (W.Ind). A local fiery spirit made from sugar cane juice.

Tafia Industriel (W.Ind). A spirit obtained from molasses.

Tafski (Wales). A Vodka produced by the Brecon Brewery, Powys, Mid-Wales. Made with local spring water.

Taglio (It). Blended wine.

Tagus (River) (Port). See River Tejo.

Tahammür (Tur). Fermentation.

Tahbilk (Austr). An estate in Victoria. Produces red and white wines. See Château Tahbilk.

Tahiti Club Cocktail (Cktl). ½ measure white Rum, ⅙ measure lemon juice, ⅙ measure lime juice, ⅙ measure pineapple juice, 2 dashes Maraschino. Shake well over ice, strain into an ice-filled old-fashioned glass. Add a slice of lemon.

Tahsiang-Pin-Chiu (China). A sparkling wine.

Taifi (USSR). A red grape variety grown in Tadzhikistan. Produces fine Port-style wines.

Tail Box (USA). Part of a Gin still. Retains the 'Tails', the unwanted congeners from the spirit.

Tailings (Fr). The ends of the distillation which are removed after the 'Heart' of the distillation has been taken. See also Heads.

Taillan (Le) (Fr). A commune in the A.C. Haut-Médoc, north-western Bordeaux.

Taille à Quarante (Fr). A style of vine training on the 'Double Guyot' line used in the Hérault Département. Is used to produce large crops of grapes.

Taille Chablis (Fr). A method of vine training in which 3, 4 or 5 main branches are trained parallel to the ground. Each is pruned to either 4 or 5 buds.

Taille-Genre Bordelaise (Fr). A method of vine training which consists of forming a stem with 2 main branches each bearing at least 2 short shoots. (Cocques Courtes).

Taille Guyot (Fr). See Guyot.

Taille-Pieds (Fr). A Premier Cru vineyard in the A.C. commune of Volnay, Côte de Beaune, Burgundy.

Tailles (Fr). Pressings in Champagne after the Tête de Cuvée has been removed.

Tails (Fr). See Tailings.

Tailspin (Cktl). ⅓ measure dry Gin, ⅓ measure Italian vermouth, ⅓ measure Green Chartreuse, 1 dash Campari. Stir over ice, strain into a cocktail glass. Top with a twist of lemon peel juice and a cherry.

Taión (Sp). A style of Albariza soil in the Sherry region. Has a high lime content.

Tairnbach (Ger). Village. (Anb) = Baden. (Ber) = Badische Bergstrasse/ Kraichgau. (Gro) = Mannaberg. (Vin) = Rosenberg.

Taissy (Fr). A Premier Cru Champagne village in the Canton de Reims. District = Reims.

Taittinger (Fr). Champagne producer. Address = 9 Place Saint Nicaise, 51100 Reims. A Grande Marque. Produces – Vintage and non-vintage wines. Vintages – 1934, 1937, 1941, 1943, 1945, 1947, 1949, 1950, 1952, 1953, 1955, 1959, 1961, 1962, 1964, 1966, 1969, 1970, 1971, 1973, 1975, 1976, 1978, 1979, 1980, 1982. De Luxe vintage cuvée iş Comte de Champagne. The second label is Irroy.

Taiwan Brewery (E.Asia). A brewery based on the island of Taiwan that brews Taiwan beer.

Tajón (Sp). A type of Albariza soil in Jerez. Is high in limestone. The soil is too hard for the vines which suffer from Chlorosis if grown in it.

Tajo [River] (Port). See River Tejo.

Tajut (It). An apéritif from Friuli.

Takara Shuzo (Jap). A company who, along with the Okura Co., have acquired the Tomatin Distillery in Scotland.

Takelsa (Afr). A co-operative winery based in Tunisia. Belongs to the UCCVT. Is noted for its rosé wines.

Taketia (USSR). A wine-producing region in Georgia. Produces fine red and white wines.

Take to Drink (Eng), **Take to the Bottle** (Eng). A term to denote a person who has resigned themselves to drinking alcoholic liquor to try and forget their problems.

Taki-Taki Spicy Tomato Cocktail (Mex). A brand of alcohol-free cocktail imported by Leisure Drinks in the U.K.

Talagante (Chile). A wine-producing area based near Santiago.

Talbot (John) (Eng). Earl of Shrewsbury. Commander of the English Expeditionary force who were defeated at the battle of Castillion in 1453 when the English lost Bordeaux.

Talca (Chile). A province and wine-producing area in the Central Zone.

Talence (Fr). A commune within the A.C. Graves district of south-western Bordeaux.

Talheim (Ger). Village. (Anb) = Württemberg. (Ber) = Württembergisch Unterland. (Gro) = Kirchenweinberg. (Vins) = Hohe Eiche, Schlossberg, Sonnenberg.

Talheim (Ger). Village. (Anb) = Württemberg. (Ber) = Württembergisch Unterland. (Gro) = Staufenberg. (Vin) = Stiftsberg.

Talisker (Scot). A single Malt whisky distillery in Carbost, Isle of Skye. Owned by John Walker and Sons (part of the DCL group). A Highland malt. Produces an 8 year old Malt. 45% alc. by vol.

Talisman (Eng). A Winter ale 1048 O.G.

brewed by the Pilgrim Brewery in Woldingham, Surrey.

Talisman Cocktail (Cktl). ¼ measure white Rum, ¼ measure golden Rum, ¼ measure Grand Marnier, ¼ measure Vodka, juice ¼ lime, 1 measure pear juice. Shake over ice, strain into a cocktail glass. Dress with a cherry, slice of lime and mint sprig.

Taljanska Graševina (Yug). A local name for the Welschriesling grape.

Tall Fount (Scot). A tall pillar-tap situated on a bar counter which dispenses most traditional beers in Scotland. The beer is driven to the fount by either air pressure or electric pump.

Tall Sour (Cktl). As for Sour but is served in a highball glass with ice and topped with soda water.

Tàllya (Hun). A noted wine-producing village based in the southern foothills.

Tally Ho (Eng). A cask conditioned summer Ale 1046 O.G. brewed by the Palmer Brewery in Bridport, Dorset.

Tally Ho Barley Wine (Eng). A Barley wine 1075 O.G. brewed and bottled by Adnams' Sole Bay Brewery in Southwold, Suffolk.

Talmettes (Les) (Fr). A Premier Cru vineyard in the A.C. commune of Savigny-lès-Beaune, Côte de Beaune, Burgundy.

Taltarni Vineyard (Austr). Address = Moonambel, Victoria 3478. 110 ha. Grape varieties – Cabernet franc, Cabernet sauvignon, Chardonnay, Chenin blanc, Malbec, Merlot, Rhine riesling and the Shiraz. Produces varietal and sparkling wines.

Talus-Saint-Prix (Fr). A Cru Champagne village in the Canton de Montmort. District = Épernay.

TAM (Eng) (abbr). Tea After Meals.

Tamagozake (Cktl). 6 ozs. Saké, 1 egg, 1 teaspoon sugar. Boil Saké, ignite, remove from heat. Stir in beaten egg and sugar, pour into a mug.

Tamar (Eng). A cask conditioned Ale 1039 O.G. brewed by the home-brew public house The Royal Inn in Horsebridge, Devon.

Tamara (Isr). A liqueur made from dates.

Tamarez (Port). A white grape variety grown in Lafões and Alentejo.

Tamar Valley Vineyard (Austr). Address = Foreshore Road, Deviot, Tasmania 7251. 35 ha. Grape varieties – Cabernet sauvignon, Chardonnay, Müller-Thurgau and Pinot noir.

Tamburlaine (Austr). A small vineyard based in New South Wales.

Tamdhu (Scot). A single Malt whisky distillery based at Knockando, Banffshire. Owned by the Highland Distilleries Co. PLC. A Highland malt. Produces a 10 year old Malt. 43% alc. by vol.

Tamdhu-Glenlivet (Scot). See Tamdhu.

Tâmega (Port). A brand of full-flavoured Vinho Verde.

Tamianka (Bul). A very sweet white wine.

Tǎmiîoasa Romînească (Rum). A white grape variety also known as the Muscat of Hamburg.

Taminick Cellars (Austr). Address = Taminick via Glenrowan, Victoria 3675. 17 ha. Grape varieties – Alicante bouschet, Cabernet sauvignon, Shiraz and Trebbiano.

Tamnavulin-Glenlivet (Scot). A single Malt whisky distillery based in Ballindalloch, Banffshire. Operated by Longman Distillers of Glasgow (part of Invergordon group). A Highland malt. Produces an 8 year old 43% alc. by vol. and a 10 year old 40% alc. by vol.

Tampico (Cktl). ½ measure Cointreau, ½ measure Campari, 2 dashes lemon juice. Stir over ice, strain into a Paris goblet. Top with tonic water, a cherry and an orange slice.

Tamplins Bitter (Eng). A cask conditioned Bitter 1038 O.G. brewed by the Watney Mann, Truman Breweries.

Tañama (Mex). A wine-producing region in the Baja California.

Tanat (Fr). An alternative spelling for the Tannat grape.

Tanchão (Port). The name for a stake used to support a vine.

Tanduay (E.Ind). A leading brand of Rum produced in the Philippine Islands.

Tangerinette (Fr). A tangerine-flavoured liqueur, red in colour.

Tanglefoot Ale (Eng). A cask conditioned strong Ale 1048 O.G. brewed by the Hall and Woodhouse Brewery in Blandford Forum, Dorset.

Tango (Cktl). ½ measure Gin, ¼ measure sweet Vermouth, ¼ measure dry Vermouth, 2 dashes orange juice, dash orange Curaçao. Shake over ice, strain into a cocktail glass.

Tangy (Eng). A descriptive term for wines with a zesty bouquet and an after-taste of an old Sherry or Madeira.

Tanisage (Fr). The practice of adding tannin to wines to increase the astringency.

Tankard (Eng). A jug or mug made out of glass, pewter or other material for beers. ½ pint, 1 pint, ½ litre or 1 litre capacity.

Tankard Bitter (Austr). A high gravity Lager beer 4.4% alc. by vol. brewed by the Courage Brewery in Victoria.

T

Tankard Bitter (Eng). A keg Bitter 1037 O.G. brewed by the Whitbread Breweries.

Tank Beer (Eng). Brewery-conditioned beers delivered by road tanker to the public house and pumped into large disposable polythene bag-lined tanks in the cellar. (90 or 180 gallon capacity). Beer is dispensed to the bar pumps by air pressure.

Tannacker (Ger). Vineyard. (Anb) = Baden. (Ber) = Kaiserstuhl-Tuniberg. (Gro) = Vulkanfelsen. (Vil) = Endingen.

Tannat (Fr). A local red grape variety grown in the Madiran district of southwest France. Gives full-bodied wines. Known in Uruguay as the Harriague. See also Bordeleza, Belch, Moustrou and Tanat.

Tannate Film (Eng). Finings and Tannin which together form an insoluble film which slowly precipitates, acting as a filter which cleans the wine as it sinks to the bottom of the cask or vat.

Tannenberg (Ger). Vineyard. (Anb) = Franken. (Ber) = Steigerwald. (Gro) = Schlosstück. (Vil) = Hüttenheim.

Tannenkirch (Ger). Village. (Anb) = Baden. (Ber) = Markgräflerland. (Gro) = Vogtei Rötteln. (Vin) = Steingässle.

Tanners Wine Ltd (Eng). Noted, old established wine merchants based in Shrewsbury, Shropshire. Has outlets in England and Wales. Deals in fine wines, spirits and beers. See Mariscal.

Tannic (Eng). The term to describe a red wine that has excessive Tannin.

Tànnico (It). Tannic.

Tannin (Eng). $C_{76}H_{52}O_{46}$. Tannic acid. An astringent acid in red wine found in the stalk, pips and skin of the grapes. Also found in tea giving colour and bitterness.

Tannisage (Fr). An alternative spelling of Tanisage.

Tanqueray (Eng). The brand-name of a dry Gin produced by Charles Tanqueray and Co., Groswell Road, London. Part of the Distillers Co. Ltd.

Tansy (Eng). See Mugwort.

Tantalus (Eng). A case for holding decanters. Usually the decanters are visable but are locked so that the contents are secure. Eighteenth and nineteenth century.

Tantalus Cocktail (Cktl). ⅓ measure Brandy, ⅓ measure Forbidden fruit liqueur, ⅓ measure lemon juice. Shake over ice, strain into a cocktail glass.

Tanunda (Austr). A winery, part of the Masterton Estate in South Australia.

Tanus Mountains (Ger). A mountain range that protects the Rheinhessen and southern Rheingau from the northerly winds.

Tanzania (Afr). Has a wine-producing region at Dodoma. Two vintages each year; August/September and December/January.

Tanzania Breweries (Afr). A brewery based in Tanzania. Noted for its Snow Cap Lager.

Tanzanian Coffee (Afr). Produces a fruity-flavoured coffee from a mixture of Robustas and Arabicas. Most are coarse and low in acidity. Used for blending. Light bodied. See also Kibo Chagga.

Tanzanian Teas (Afr). African teas used mainly for blending.

Tap (Eng). Found on beer casks. Is driven into the Keystone. Made of wood or metal. (See Beer-Tap). Also an expression used for connections to any form of beer container.

Tapadura (Sp). Stopper.

Tap Ales (Eng). Beers drawn from a cask or keg.

Tapas (Sp). Lids of bread placed over wine glasses to keep out flies. (Also snacks served in bars).

Tap Beer (USA). Draught beer.

Tap Bitter (Eng). A Bitter brewed by the Truman's Brewery in Brick Lane. (Part of Watney Mann, Truman Brewers).

Tapestry Wines Ltd (Eng). Vineyards based at Wells Farm, Appurley, Gloucestershire and The Vineyard, Ampney Crucis, Gloucestershire. Were first planted in 1979. 2.2 ha. Grape varieties – Madeleine angevine, Müller-Thurgau, Reichensteiner and Seyval blanc.

Tap House (Eng). The name in the eighteenth and nineteenth centuries for an inn, bar or public house.

Tapio (Fin). A herb and juniper-flavoured liqueur. 29% alc. by vol. Produced by Lignell and Piispanen.

Tapón (Sp). Cork, stopper.

Tappaie (Ch.Isles). A drinking bout.

Tappare (It). To cork or plug a bottle or cask.

Tapping (Eng). See Broach.

Tappit-Hen (Scot). A bottle which holds 3 imperial quarts which is equivalent to 4½ reputed quarts. Used for Whisky.

Tappit Hen (Scot). The name for a pewter tankard in the nineteenth century which had a lid with a distinctive knob on top.

Tappo (It). Cork, stopper.

Tap Room (Eng). A public bar where the customers were able to buy beers drawn from the cask stillaged behind the bar.

T

Tapster (Afr). A person who makes and sells Palm wine.

Tapster (Eng). The name for a barman in the nineteenth century.

Taps Too (Eng). See Tattoo.

Taptemelk (Hol). Skimmed milk.

Taptoe (Hol). A seventeenth-century military command to stop serving beer. Lit – 'Shut taps'. See Tattoo.

Tapuy (E.Ind). A spirit distilled from rice and corn.

Tapuzza Coffee (W.Ind). A mild type of coffee produced in Costa Rica. Popular at breakfast time.

Tap Water (Eng). Denotes water from the domestic supply. Drinking water.

Tap Water Cocktail (Cktl). ½ measure dry Gin, ½ measure Triple Sec. Shake well over ice, strain into an ice-filled highball glass. Top with lemonade and slice of lemon.

Tap Wine (Austr). House wine. Served from the cask.

Tap Wine (Eng). Cask wines sold from the cask in Cafés, Inns etc.

Tar (Eng). Used to preserve and hide 'off' flavours in wines in early times.

Tarcal (Hun). A noted wine-producing village based in the southern foothills.

Tarcoola Winery (Austr). A winery based in Geelong, Victoria. Produces varietal and table wines.

Tardania (Sp). An alternative name for the white Planta nova grape.

Tarefa de Barro (Port). A large earthenware container for fermenting wine.

Tarentinum (Lat). A red wine produced in south-eastern Italy in Roman times.

Target (Eng). A hop variety high in acids. Disease resistant.

Targon (Fr). A commune in Haut-Benauge, Entre-Deux-Mers, central Bordeaux.

Târgovichte (Bul). A delimited wine-producing area in the eastern region. Mainly white wines.

Tarik (Afr). A full-bodied red wine produced in the A.O.G. region of Beni M'Tir, Morocco. Made from Carignan, Cinsault and Grenache grapes. Bottled by CVM.

Tarnavale (Rum). A wine-producing region based in the Siebenbürgen district.

Tarn-et-Garonne (Fr). A Vins de Pays area in the Tarn-et-Garonne Département of south-western France. Includes the area of Saint Sardos.

Tarniówka (Pol). A sloe-flavoured spirit.

Tarouca (Port). A white grape variety grown in the Dão region.

Tarquinio Lomelino (Mad). Madeira shippers that are noted for their antique wines. Use the label Dom Henriques for their standard range of Madeiras.

Tarragone (Fr). A name for Green Chartreuse which the Carthusian monks used in Spain whilst in exile 1903.

Tarragona (Sp). A Denominación de Origen wine district of south-eastern Spain. Grape varieties – Garnacha, Macabeo, Malvasia, Moscatell, Pansa, Picapoll blanco and Picapoll cariñena. Produce fortified Port-style wines, also an over-sweet non-red wine. 3 sub-regions (Comarca de Falset, Ribera de Ebro and Tarragona Campo).

Tarragona Campo (Sp). Red and white table wines from the Tarragona district. Made by natural fermentation which differs to the Classico.

Tarragona Classico (Sp). A dessert white wine from Tarragona district. Made by subjecting the must to very high temperatures. This quickly oxidises it. The wine is then stored in glass vessels open to the air.

Tarragona Port (Sp). A fortified wine from the Tarragona district. Was sold as Tarragona Port in the USA but now the use of the word Port is banned by international law. In Spain is known as Priorato.

Tarrango (Austr). A red grape variety developed by the CSIRO. A cross between the Touriga and Sultana. Grown mainly in south-eastern Australia.

Tarrango (Austr). A white wine produced by Brown Brothers from a cross between the Touriga and Sultana grapes.

Tart (Eng). Term to describe sharp, acid wines.

Tartan Bitter (Scot). A keg/canned Bitter beer 1036 O.G. brewed by the William Younger Brewery. (Part of Scottish and Newcastle).

Tartar (Eng). Potassium hydrogen. Also known as Argol. Is the deposit left behind during the fermentation of wine.

Tartaric Acid (Eng). COOH (CHOH)$_3$. The main acid found in wine. See Tartrate Crystals.

Tartarophtorum (Lat). A wine spoilage bacteria. See Toume.

Tartrate Crystals (Eng). Found in wines that have been stored at very cold temperatures. The crystals (Potassium Hydrogen Tartrate) are harmless and will usually disappear if the wine is brought to room temperature. Tend to soften the wine if removed by lowering the wine's acidity.

Tarula Farms (USA). A vineyard based in Clarksville, Ohio. Produces hybrid and varietal wines.

Tascas (Sp). Bars where food and drink are sold in the Andalusian region of south-west Spain.

Tasche 1888 (Ger). A Steinhäger produced by Tasche GmbH., Steinhägen.

Tasheimer Goldtröpfchen (S.Afr). A medium-sweet, fruity white wine made from a blend of the Clairette blanche and Steen grapes. Produced by the S.F.W.

Taskelder Wines (S.Afr). A range of varietal wines produced by the Stellenbosch Farmers' Winery.

Tasse (Fr). Cup.

Tasse à Vin (Fr). A Bordeaux tastevin. A plain cup with a bulge in the middle for the wine to run over to observe the colour.

Tassenberg (S.Afr). A very popular table wine made from a blend of Cinsault and Pinotage grapes. See Tassie.

Tassie (S.Afr). The nickname for Tassenberg.

Taste (Eng). There are 4 taste sensations – bitter, sour, salt and sweet.

Taste Buds (Eng). An area of the mouth that experiences taste.

Tastevin (Fr). A silver tasting cup that is common in the Burgundy region and other regions in France. Used mainly for checking the colour, clarity and taste of red wines.

Tastevinage (Fr). A wine tasting by the Confrérie des Chevaliers du Tastevin who judge and award a seal to the top wines of Burgundy.

Tasting (Eng). Applied to the sampling of wines on offer for sale or to a pre-taste of the bottle of wine purchased by the customer in the restaurant to drink with the meal.

Tasting Cup (Eng). Tastevin. A utensil for tasting wine.

Tasting Glass (Eng). See I.S.O. Glass.

Tasting Notes (Eng). The record made of a tasting of wine. Each is recorded and used as a reference to check on a wine's progress to maturity or quality.

Tatachilla Winery (Austr). A winery based in McClaren Vale, South Australia. Sell wines in the U.K. under the Keystone label.

Tate Brewery (Eng). A brewery that was founded in 1985. Brews four types of beer using natural spring water with no additives.

Tâte-Vin (Fr). An alternative name for Tastevin.

Tatizinho (Bra). Lit – 'Little Armadillo'. The brand-name of a Cachaça.

Tatran (Czec). A Lager beer brewed by the Poprad Brewery.

Tatra Vodka Tatrzanska (Pol). A light green-coloured, herb Vodka produced by Polmos in the Kraków area. 45% alc. by vol.

Tattoo (Eng). From the old military bugle call of 'Taps too'. Used to call soldiers back to barracks and tell the landlords to turn off the beer taps. See Taps Too and Taptoe.

Taubenberg (Ger). Vineyard. (Anb) = Rheingau. (Ber) = Johannisberg. (Gro) = Steinmächer. (Vil) = Eltville.

Taubenhaus (Ger). Vineyard. (Anb) = Mosel-Saar-Ruwer. (Ber) = Bernkastel. (Gro) = Schwarzlay. (Vil) = Traben-Trarbach.

Tauberberg (Ger). Grosslage. (Anb) = Württemberg. (Ber) = Kocher-Jagst-Tauber. (Vils) = Elpersheim, Wermutshausen.

Tauberbischofsheim (Ger). Village. (Anb) = Baden. (Ber) = Badische Frankenland. (Gro) = Tauberklinge. (Vin) = Edelberg.

Tauberbischofsheim [ortsteil Impfingen] (Ger). Village. (Anb) = Baden. (Ber) = Badische Frankenland. (Gro) = Tauberklinge. (Vin) = Silberquell.

Tauberklinge (Ger). Grosslage. (Anb) = Baden. (Ber) = Badische Frankenland. (Vils) = Beckstein, Boxberg (stadtteil Unterschüpf), Dertingen, Gerlachsheim, Grossrinderfeld, Höhenfeld, Kembach, Königheim, Königshofen, Krautheim, Krautheim (stadtteil Klepsau), Külsheim, Lauda, Lindelbach, Marbach, Oberlauda, Oberschüpf, Reicholzheim, Sachsenflur, Tauberbischofsheim, Tauberbischofsheim (ortsteil Impfingen), Uissigheim, Werbach, Wertheim.

Tauberrettersheim (Ger). Village. (Anb) = Franken. (Ber) = Maindreieck. (Gro) = Not yet assigned. (Vin) = Königin.

Tauber [River] (Ger). A tributary of the river Neckar in Württemberg. Has a soil of shell limestone.

Taunton Cider Company Limited (Eng). Cider makers based in Norton Fitzwarren, Taunton, Somerset, TA2 6RD. Noted for their Dry Blackthorn draught and bottled/canned Cider.

Taupette (Fr). See Preuve.

Taupine [La] (Fr). A Premier Cru vineyard in the A.C. commune of Monthélie, Côte de Beaune, Burgundy. 4.3 ha.

Taurasi (It). D.O.C. red wine from the Campania region. Made from the Aglianico, Barbera, Piedirosso and Sangiovese grapes grown in the commune of Taurasi and others. Vinification can occur in province of Avellino. Must be aged 3 years (1 year in wood). If aged 4 years classed Riserva.

Tauriac (Fr). A commune in the A.C. Côtes de Bourg, north-eastern Bordeaux.

Tauromenitanum (Lat). A red wine produced on Sicily during Roman times.

Täuscherspfad (Ger). Vineyard. (Anb) = Rheinhessen. (Ber) = Bingen. (Gro) = Kaiserpfalz. (Vil) = Ingelheim.

Tauxières (Fr). A Premier Cru Champagne village in the Canton d'Ay. District = Reims.

Tavel (Fr). An A.C. rosé wine from the southern Rhône. Made from the Bourboulenc, Clairette and Grenache grapes. High in alcohol, minimum 11% by vol. Noted for its onion skin colour. Sold in flûte bottles

Tavern (Eng). A hostelry which caters for local custom. Different to an Inn.

Tavern (Eng). The old name for keg Beer from the Courage Brewery.

Taverna (It). Pub, tavern.

Taverna (Port). An alternative spelling of Taberna.

Taverna (S.Afr). An everyday full red wine produced mainly from the Pinotage grape. Often oak aged.

Tavern Bottle (Eng). Early bottles that had the seal of the Tavern embossed on them. c1657–1750.

Tavistock Beer (Eng). A cask conditioned Bitter 1036 O.G. brewed by the homebrew Bruce public house in London.

Tavola (USA). A label used by the Guild of Wineries and Distilleries, California for table wines.

Tawern (Ger). Village. (Anb) = Mosel-Saar-Ruwer. (Ber) = Obermosel. (Gro) = Gipfel. (Vins) = Sites not yet chosen.

Tawny (Port). The quality of paleness or golden tinge which Ports acquire when matured in wood. See Tawny Port.

Tawny Bitter (Eng). A cask conditioned Bitter 1040 O.G. brewed by the Cotleigh Brewery in Somerset.

Tawny Mild (Eng). A keg light Mild 1032 O.G. brewed by the John Smith Brewery in Tadcaster, Yorkshire.

Tawny Port (Port). Blended young Ports (non-vintage) that have been aged in casks for 6 years plus. Obtains a golden tinge as it ages. See Dated Ports.

Tay (China). The pronunciation of tea in China from which the word 'tea' derives. See T'é.

Taylor (Port). Vintage Port shippers. Vintages – 1870, 1872, 1873, 1875, 1878, 1881, 1884, 1887, 1890. 1892, 1896, 1900, 1904, 1906, 1908, 1912, 1917, 1920, 1924, 1927, 1935, 1940, 1942,

1945, 1948, 1955, 1960, 1963, 1966, 1970, 1975, 1977, 1980, 1982, 1983, 1985. Full name is Taylor, Fladgate and Yeatman. Single quinta is the Quinta da Vargellas.

Taylor California Cellars (USA). A winery owned by the Coca Cola Co.

Taylor, Fladgate and Yeatman (Port). See Taylor.

Taylor's VO (S.Afr). A brand of Brandy produced by Sedgewick Taylor.

Taylors Wines (Austr). A winery based in Clare Valley, South Australia. Grape varieties – Cabernet sauvignon and Hermitage. Produces varietal wines.

Taylor [Timothy] (Eng). A brewery based in Keighley, Yorkshire. Noted for its cask conditioned Golden Best 1033 O.G. Bitter Ale 1033 O.G. Landlord 1042 O.G. Ram Tam 1043 O.G. and bottled Northerner 1033 O.G. Blue Label 1043 O.G. Black Bess Stout 1043 O.G.

Taylor-Walker (Eng). Ind Coope's London company beers are brewed at Burton and Romford. Brews most styles of beers.

Taylor Wine Company (USA). A leading wine-producer of the Finger Lakes region of the New York district [Lake Keuka]. Sells wines under Lake County and Great Western labels. Are noted for their pink (rosé) wines.

Taza (Sp). Cup.

Tazza (It). Cup.

Tbilisi (USSR). Soviet Champagne. Produced in Tbilisi (Tiflis), Georgia and between the regions of Anapa and Gelendshik in the Crimean peninsula.

Tcha (China). A Cantonese dialect word for tea from which Cha (English slang) is derived.

Tchkhavéri (USSR). A white grape variety grown in Georgia. Produces dessert wines.

Tchoung-Tchoung (E.Asia). A digestive liqueur made from fermented rice in Vietnam. See Choum.

Tchuve (Ch.Isles). Vat.

T'é (China). Tea.

Tè (It). Tea.

Te (Wales). Tea.

Tea (Eng). Denotes a beverage made from the dried leaves of the tea bush grown between the latitudes of 42°N to 29°S. Main tea-producing countries are – Africa, Caucasia (USSR, Turkey and Iran), China, India, Indonesia, Japan, Malaya, Pakistan, South America and Taiwan.

Téa (Sp). A wine-producing area on the river Miño in western Spain. Grape varieties – Caíño, Espadeiro and Tintarrón. Produces mainly red wines.

Tea Act (Eng). Passed in 1773. Allowed the

East India Company to sell tea to the USA. Caused the famous Boston Tea Party.

Tea After Meals (Eng). TAM. An idea introduced by the Twining Co. A package containing two teabags. The idea being that the customer hands over teabags and host provides the water.

Tea Auctions (Eng). Occur every Monday at Sir John Lyon House, London. Buying brokers bid for the tea available.

Tea Ball (USA). A round, perforated metal infuser, filled with tea leaves for making tea. Is suspended in a jug, pot, etc. The forerunner of the tea bag. Was invented in the nineteenth century.

Tea Break (Eng). The name given to the rest period from working duties when workers would consume a cup/mug of tea in the morning and afternoon.

Tea Breeze (Fr). A liqueur with a subtle taste of tea. 25% alc. by. vol.

Tea Brick (China). An ancient way of transporting tea. Compressed into bricks. Was also used as currency. Still made by the Tsaiao Liu China Tea Brick Factory.

Tea Bush (Asia). Botanical name – Camellia Sinensis. The plant from which the leaves are dried and used for making tea. There are 2 varieties – Cambodia and China with many hybrids and crosses.

Tea Caddy (Eng). A container for keeping/storing tea. Derived from the Chinese Catty which means weight. Was also used for mixing tea. Often locked, especially in the eighteenth century when tea was a valuble commodity.

Tea Camellia (Eng). Tea Bush. See Camellia Sinensis.

Tea Cart (USA). Tea trolley.

Tea Ceremonies (E.Asia). Developed in the twelfth century by Hsu Ching, a Chinese envoy in Korea. Used teas from the Chiri mountains. See Tea of Bamboo Dew and Tea of Peacock's Tongue.

Tea Ceremony (China). Evolved in the fourteenth century by a Buddhist priest called Shuko. Lasts 2 hours and uses green teas. See Cha No Yu.

Teacher (William and Sons) (Scot). A famous Malt whisky distillery. Owns Ardmore and Glendronach distilleries in Aberdeenshire. Took over Stewart and Sons in Dundee. Now owned by the Allied Group.

Tea Council (Eng). Address = Sir John Lyon House, 5, High Street, London EC4V 3NJ.

Teacher's Highland Cream (Scot). A blended Scotch whisky produced by William Teacher and Sons. (part of Allied Breweries). Has 45% Malt whiskies in the blend. 43% alc. by vol.

Teacher's Sixty [60] (Scot). A De Luxe blended Scotch whisky by William Teacher and Sons. (part of Allied Breweries). Has 60% Malt whiskies in the blend. 43% alc. by vol.

Tea Clipper (Eng). Nineteenth-century ships, 3 masted Schooners that were used to transport tea from East to West. Cutty Sark was the most famous.

Tea Cobbler (Cktl). ⅓ gill Jamaican Rum, few dashes sugar syrup, fresh brewed tea, (cooled). Stir over ice, strain into an ice-filled highball glass. Top with a little Port wine, serve with straws and fruit in season.

Tea Cosy (Eng). Cover for a Teapot to keep the pot and its' contents hot. Made of wool or other good insulating material.

Tea Council of the USA (USA). Address = 230 Park Avenue, New York, NY 10017.

Tea Dance (Eng). An afternoon function practised in the late nineteenth century where dancing took place during afternoon tea in hotels, restaurants. The idea was introduced and supported by the Temperance movements of the day. Has been revived in the 1970s.

Tea Egg (Eng). See Tea Maker.

Tea Flushes (Eng). See Flushes.

Tea For Two Cup (Cup). 1 pint freshly brewed tea, ½ pint Dubonnet, juice ½ lemon, 1½ tablespoons redcurrant jelly, 1 tablespoon soft brown sugar. Heat together, serve with black grape halves which have been deseeded.

Tea Gardens (Eng). Mid-eighteenth-century gardens where people met to drink tea and be entertained with music and fireworks. The most popular was at Ranelagh near Chelsea, London.

Tea Kettle (Eng). See Kettle.

Tea Leaves (Eng). The name given to the dried cut tea leaf that is ready for brewing.

Tea Liqueur (Jap). A liqueur made from 2 types of tea.

Tea Maker (Eng). A spoon (of teaspoon size) with a perforated top and bottom in which tea leaves are placed to infuse in a cup of boiling water to make 1 cup of tea. Also known as a Tea egg or Infuser.

Tea Making (Eng). Bring to the boil some freshly drawn cold water. Heat the teapot, place the correct measure of good quality tea (1 level teaspoonful per ¼ pint of water) into the warmed teapot. When the water has come to a rapid boil, pour straight onto the tea leaves. Allow to infuse for 3–4 minutes (hard water requires a longer infusion time), stir and pour. Note the strength of the brew depends on the quantity of tea used. Many advocate the addition of one extra measure of tea per pot. (Three cups of tea are obtainable from 1 pint of brewed tea). Brewed tea should never be allowed to 'stew' as this will give the tea a bitter flavour.

Tea Mosquito (Eng). See Helopeltis Theivora.

Teaninich (Scot). A single Malt whisky distillery owned by R.W. Thompson and Co. A Highland malt. Produces a 22 year old Malt whisky. 45% alc. by vol.

Tea of Bamboo Dew (E.Asia). Tea from the Chiri mountains in Korea, used in ancient tea ceremonies.

Tea of Peacock's Tongues (E.Asia). Tea grown in the Chiri mountains, Korea. Used in ancient tea ceremonies.

Tea Parcel (Eng). A large quantity of tea usually associated with tea auctions.

Tea Plant (Eng). See Tea Bush.

Teapot (Eng). A utensil used for the making (brewing) of tea. Made of china, pottery or metal (silver, stainless steel or aluminium).

Tea Poy (Eng) (Ind). A three-legged stand and tea caddy of the eighteenth and nineteenth centuries.

Tea Punch (Punch). ½ bottle Cognac, ½ bottle Jamaican Rum, juice and rind of a lemon, ½ lb. sugar. Heat together in a metal punch bowl, flame, add hot tea and serve.

Tears (Eng). A term used to describe the ethyl alcohol and glycerine lines which run down the glass when it is being drunk. Also known as 'Legs'.

Tea Scripture (The) (China). 'The Ch'a Ching of Lu Yu'. Written in A.D. 800 it was the book on how to make and serve tea.

Tea Service (Eng). Teapot, hot water jug, teacup, saucer, teaspoon, strainer, slop-bowl, sugar bowl, sugar tongs and milk jug.

Teaspoon (Eng). An implement made of metal, china or plastic used for the stir-ring of tea that has had sugar/milk added. 1 fluid dram.

Teaspoon (USA). A bar measure that equals ⅛ fl.oz. US. ⅙ fl.oz. Imp.

Tea Strainer (Eng). A sieve or perforated dish to remove the spent tea leaves from brewed tea as it is poured into the teacup.

Tea Tipple (Cktl). ⅓ pint freshly brewed tea, ⅕ gill Cointreau. Add the liqueur to the tea, dress with a slice of orange.

Tea Towel (Eng). A cotton/linen cloth used for the drying of crockery, glassware, etc.

Tea Tree (N.Z.). Leptospermum. A native tree of New Zealand and of Australia which is used as a tea substitute.

Tea Trolley (Eng). A trolley which is used to serve tea in factories, offices or in the home. Known as a Tea Cart or Tea Wagon in the USA.

Tea Wagon (USA). See Tea Trolley.

Tebot (Wales). Teapot.

Tébourba (Afr). A noted wine-producing area in Tunisia.

Tecali (The) (Cktl). 3 parts Silver Tequila, 1 level teaspoon of coffee, 1 part lemon juice, 2 parts mineral water. Shake well with ice, strain into an ice-filled highball glass.

Tecate (Mex). A strong Beer brewed with a low mineral salt content. Imported to the U.K. by Mexican Beer Import Co., Glasgow.

Tech [River] (Fr). A river in the Pyrénées Orientales wine Département of the Languedoc-Roussillon area.

Teddy Bear (Eng). ⅚ measure Stout, ⅙ measure Port wine. Stir gently.

Tedeschi Vineyard (USA). A winery based on the island of Maui in Hawaii. 8 ha. Produces grape and fruit wines (pine-apple).

Tè di Camomilla (It). Camomile tea.

Tedge (Afr). An Ethiopean drink made from honey.

Teetotal (USA). The name that derived from a meeting of the Temperance Society of Laingsbury, Michigan in the 1830s. Had 2 pledges. 1) – for moderate drinking, O.P. [Old Pledge]. and 2) – for complete abstinence. T. [Total Pledge]. People who took the Total pledge became known as 'T' totallers.

Teetotaller (USA). See Teetotal.

Tegea (Gre). A fragrant dry rosé wine.

Tegestologist (Eng). A collector of beer (drip) mats.

Teheran (Iran). A wine-producing province in northern Iran.

Tehigo (Sp). An area within Andalusia whose vineyards produce grapes for Sherry production.

Teiera (It). Teapot.

Teinturiers (Fr). Also known as 'Dyers'. Black grapes with red juice. The only red grapes that cannot be used for white wines. e.g. Malbec.

Teissedre (Fr). A Bordeaux-based firm that produces fine fruit-based liqueurs.

Teixeira (Tristao Vaz) (Mad). A Portuguese man who, together with João Goncalves Zarco, discovered Madeira in 1418.

Tejo [River] (Port). See Tajo River.

Te Kauwhata (N.Z.). A wine area on the mid-west coast of the North Island.

Te Kauwhata Viticultural Research Station (N.Z.). A research centre that

T

has played an important role in the New Zealand commercial wine industry.

Tekel (Tur). On the neck label of a wine bottle guarantees quality. Awarded by the state monopoly.

Tekel Brewery (Tur). A brewery based in Ankara. Produces Pilsener and Münchener-style beers.

Tekirdağ (Tur). A vineyard based in the region of Marmara and Thrace. Produces both red and white wines.

Tekirdağ-Canakkale (Tur). A vineyard based in the Marmara and Thrace region. Produces red wines.

Teldeschi Vineyard (USA). A small vineyard based in Dry Creek, Sonoma County, California. Grape varieties – Cabernet sauvignon and Zinfandel.

Television Cocktail (Cktl). ⅓ measure dry Gin, ⅙ measure dry Vermouth, ⅙ measure sweet Vermouth, ⅙ measure Crème de Noyeau. Shake over ice, strain into a cocktail glass.

Téliani (USSR). A red grape variety grown in Georgia. A variety of the Cabernet.

Telve (Tur). Coffee grounds.

Te Mata Winery (N.Z.). Address = P.O. Box. 335, Havelock North, Hawkes Bay. 23 ha. Grape varieties – Cabernet sauvignon, Chardonnay, Merlot and Sauvignon blanc.

Temecula (USA). A wine-producing district in southern California.

Temmels (Ger). Village. (Anb) = Mosel-Saar-Ruwer. (Ber) = Obermosel. (Gro) = Gipfel. (Vins) = Münsterstatt, St. Georgshof.

Te Moana (N.Z.). The brand-name used by Vidal Wine Producers in Hawkes Bay for their white Riesling-Sylvaner wines.

Tempelchen (Ger). Vineyard. (Anb) = Rheinhessen. (Ber) = Nierstein. (Gro) = Domherr. (Vil) = Stadecken-Elsheim.

Temperance (USA). The abstinence from alcohol. See Teetotal.

Tempérance (De) (Fr). Teetotal.

Temperance Mocktail (Cktl). (Non-alc). 3 ozs. lemon juice, 1 oz. sugar syrup, 1 egg yolk. Shake well over ice, strain into a large cocktail glass.

Temperance Society (N.Z.). Founded in 1853. Tried to stop drinking and the establishment of breweries. Now part of New Zealand Breweries.

Temperance Special (Cktl). (Non-alc). 2 teaspoons Grenadine, 1 egg yolk, 1 gill lemon juice. Shake well over ice, strain into a cocktail glass.

Temperate Zone (Eng). An area where vines that are best for wines are grown.

Latitudes 30°-50°N and 30°-50°S.

Temperature (Eng). Important in wine and beer production, storage and service.

Templar (To Drink Like a) (Eng). A mediaeval saying which denotes a great thirst. (The Knights Templar were noted drinkers of wines).

Templeton (USA). A wine town in the San Luis Obispo County, California. Is the home to many wineries.

Templiers (Bel). An Abbaye-produced beer.

Temprana (Sp). The alternative name for the Palomino grape.

Tempranillo (Sp). The top red grape variety grown in the Rioja region. Also known as the Ojo de Llebre (in Cataluña), Cencibel and the Tinto fino.

Temptation (Cktl).(1). 1 measure Nassau Orange Liqueur, 2 measures Scotch whisky, juice ½ lemon, dash Grenadine. Shake well over ice, strain into an ice-filled highball glass, top with chilled orange juice. Add a slice of orange and a cherry.

Temptation (Cktl).(2). ⁷⁄₁₀ measure Rye whiskey, ¹⁄₁₀ measure Dubonnet, ¹⁄₁₀ measure Pastis, ¹⁄₁₀ measure orange Curaçao. Shake over ice, strain into a cocktail glass. Add a twist of orange and lemon peel juice.

Temptation Cocktail (Cktl). ¾ measure Bourbon whiskey, 2 dashes each of Cointreau, Pastis and Dubonnet. Shake over ice, strain into a cocktail glass. Top with a twist of orange and lemon peel juice.

Tempter (Cktl). ½ measure Apricot Liqueur, ½ measure Port wine. Stir over ice, strain into a cocktail glass.

Temulentus (Lat). Drunken, intoxicated.

Tenant (Eng). A licensee of a brewery-owned public house. Held under a tenancy agreement.

Tenant Streams (Eng). Denotes the tenancies of one brewery.

Ténarèze (Fr). A town in the Gers Département where Armagnac is made. Gives its name to one of the appellations of Armagnac.

Tenderfoot Mint Cocktail (Cktl).(Non-alc). ½ fl.oz. lemon juice, 1 fl.oz. mint syrup, dash lime juice, ¼ fl.oz. Gomme syrup. Shake over ice, strain into a Champagne saucer.

Tendone (It). A high method of vine training. Gives a high grape yield.

Tendre (Fr). A rather light and delicate wine, usually a young wine.

Tendrils (Eng). The part of the vine which attaches it to the stakes, wires etc. for anchorage.

Tenementi (It). Holding or estate. See Tenimenti.

Tenerife (Sp). Spanish-owned islands off the coast of western Africa that produce average quality red and white wines.

Ten High (USA). The brand-name of a Bourbon whiskey.

Tenimenti (It). Denotes either a holding or estate. See Tenementi.

Tennent Caledonian (Scot). Bass's Scottish Company. Has breweries in Glasgow and Edinburgh. Has brewed Lager beers since 1885. Produces many fine beers.

Tenner Brothers Winery (USA). A winery based in Patrick, South Carolina. Grape varieties – Catawba, Concord and Muscadine.

Tennessee Sunrise (Cktl). ⅓ gill Rye whiskey, 4 dashes Maraschino, 4 dashes lime juice. Shake over ice, strain into an ice-filled old-fashioned glass.

Tennessee Whiskey (USA). A straight Whiskey distilled in Tennessee with no specific grain criteria. 45% alc. by vol.

Tennessee Wine (USA). A nickname for Moonshine whiskey in the 1920s.

Teno (Chile). A wine-producing area in the Curicó region.

Ten o'Clock Swill (Eng). Due to longer hours, more civilised drinking habits have occurred and this has now practically disappeared. Denoted the fact that the drinker tried to get as much drink as possible before the bar closed at 10 o'clock.

Ten Penny Stock Ale (Can). A dark Ale 5.3% alc. by vol. brewed by the Moosehead Brewery.

Ten Sixty Six [1066] (Eng). A draught Winter ale 1066 O.G. brewed by the Goacher Brewery in Maidstone, Kent.

Ten Sixty Six [1066] (Eng). A keg Beer 1064 O.G. brewed by the Alexander Brewery in Brighton.

Tent (Eng). An old Elizabethan corruption of the red wine Tinto produced in Spain and the Canaries.

Tent (Sp). A sweet red wine from Alicante.

Tent (Sp). See Tintilla de Rota.

Tenterden Vineyards (Eng). A vineyard based at Small Hythe, Kent. 4.25ha. Grape variety – Gutenborner. Wine sold under the Spots Farm label.

Tenth (USA). Bottle size. 12.68 fl.ozs. (⅘ quart). 375 mls.

Tenuta (It). Estate.

Tenuta Amalia (It). A winery based in Emilia-Romagna. Produces sparkling wines by the cuve close method.

Tenuta di Lilliano (It). A noted Chianti Classico winery based in Tuscany.

Tenuta Pegazzera (It). A winery based in Oltrepo Pavese, Lombardy.

Tenuta Regaleali (It). A large winery based at Vallelunga, Sicily. 500 ha. Wines sold under the Regaleal label.

Teobar (Port). The brand-name of a red wine blended and bottled by Caves Dom Teodosio.

Teplice Brewery (Czec). A brewery based in north-western Czec.

Tequador (Cktl). 1½ fl.ozs. Tequila, 2 fl.ozs. pineapple juice, dash lime juice. Shake over ice, pour over ice into a large goblet. Add few drops Grenadine. Serve with short straws.

Tequila (Mex). A spirit made from distilled Pulque (a beer made from fermented Agave cactus). Tequila is properly known as Mezcal, Tequila is the Mezcal from Tequila county. Two styles – Silver and Golden. See Tequila [Straight Drink].

Tequila Anejo (Mex). The grading of Golden Tequila. Is graded by the amount of time the spirit spends in wood.

Tequila Cocktail (Cktl). 1 fl.oz. Tequila, dash Grenadine, dash Gomme syrup, juice of a lime. Blend with scoop of crushed ice in a blender. Strain into a cocktail glass. Dress with a slice of lime.

Tequila Collins (Cktl). As for a Gin Collins using a measure of Tequila in place of the Gin.

Tequila Daisy (Cktl). 1 fl.oz. Tequila, juice ½ lime, 2 dashes Grenadine. Shake over ice, strain into an ice-filled Paris goblet. Top with soda water.

Tequila Especial (Mex). A brand of Tequila produced by Gavilan of Jalisco. 40% alc. by vol.

Tequila Fizz (Cktl). ⅕ gill Tequila, ⅕ gill Grenadine, juice ¼ lime, 1 egg white. Shake well over ice, strain into an ice-filled highball glass. Top with ginger ale, stir.

Tequila Manhattan (Cktl). ⅔ measure Tequila Silver Label, ⅓ measure Italian vermouth, dash lime juice. Shake over ice, strain into an ice-filled old-fashioned glass. Top with an orange slice and a cherry.

Tequila Matador (Cktl). 1½ measures Tequila, 3 fl.ozs. pineapple juice, juice ½ lime. Shake over ice, strain into a flute glass.

Tequila Mockingbird (Cktl). ⅔ measure Tequila, ⅓ measure (white) Crème de Menthe, juice of a lime. Shake over ice, strain into a cocktail glass. Top with a slice of lime.

Tequila Old Fashioned (Cktl). ⅓ gill Tequila, 2 dashes Gomme syrup, dash Angostura. Stir over ice in a highball glass, add a splash of soda and a pineapple cube.

Tequila Orange (Cktl). ⅓ gill Tequila placed over ice in a highball glass. Top with orange juice and a slice of orange.

Tequila Pink Cocktail (Cktl). ⅗ measure Tequila, ⅖ measure French vermouth, dash Grenadine. Shake over ice, strain into a cocktail glass.

Tequila Punch (Punch). 1 bottle Tequila, 1 bottle Champagne, 3 bottles Sauternes, 1 melon cut into balls. Mix together over ice, serve in flute glasses.

Tequila Sour (Cktl). 1½ ozs. Tequila, ¾ oz. lemon or lime juice, 1 teaspoon powdered sugar. Shake over ice, strain into an old-fashioned glass. Add a cherry and slice of orange.

Tequila [Straight Drink] (Cktl). 1 measure Tequila, wedge lime (or of lemon), pinch of salt. Put the salt between the thumb and index finger on the back of the left hand. Hold the glass of Tequila in the right hand together with the lime wedge. Taste salt, drink Tequila then suck the lime.

Tequila Sunrise (Cktl). 2 parts Silver Tequila, 6 parts orange juice, 2 parts Grenadine. Place ice into a highball glass, add all the ingredients, stir gently.

Tequila Sunset (Cktl).(1). 4 parts Golden Tequila, 2 parts lemon juice, 1 part honey. Mix well until blended, serve in a highball glass over ice.

Tequila Sunset (Cktl).(2). Into an ice-filled highball glass place 1 measure Tequila, ½ measure lemon juice. Top with soda water. Add 2 dashes Crème de Cassis and 2 dashes Grenadine. Do not stir. Place a slice of lemon on the glass rim. Serve with straws.

Tequila Zapata (Sp). The brand-name used by Campeny in Barcelona for their Tequila.

Tequini (Cktl). ¾ measure Tequila, ¼ measure French vermouth, dash Angostura. Stir over ice, strain into a cocktail glass. Top with a twist of lemon peel and an olive.

Tequonic (Cktl). ⅓ gill Tequila, juice ½ lime. Stir over ice in a highball glass. Top with tonic water and a squeeze of lemon peel juice.

Teran (Yug). The local name for the Italian red Refosco grape. Produces a wine of same the name from Istria.

Térbache (USSR). A white grape variety grown in Turkmenistan. Produces dessert wines.

Tercher Año (Sp). A red wine produced by the Bodegas Carlos Serres, Rioja. Made from the Garnacha, Tempranillo and Viura grapes. Matured in oak for 15 months and 1 year in bottle. Produced by carbonic maceration.

Tercia (La) (Sp). A noted vineyard based in the Montilla-Moriles region.

Tercier (Hol). The brand-name for a French cream liqueur made with Cognac and dry Curaçao. Produced by Cooymans. 14.9% alc. by vol. Also brand-name for fruit brandies from same company.

Terme (Marquis de) (Fr). See Château Marquis de Terme.

Teremia Mare (Rum). A wine-producing area. Part of the Banat Vineyard. Grape varieties – Creata, Majarca and Steinschiller. Produces mainly white wines.

Terreno (El) (Sp.) A Sherry producer based in Jerez.

Terlaner (It). A white grape variety grown in the Trentino-Alto Adige.

Terlaner Edel Muskateller (It). A sweet white wine from the Trentino-Alto Adige.

Terlano (It). D.O.C. white wine from Trentino-Alto Adige. Made from the Pinot bianco, Riesling italico, Riesling renano, Sauvignon and Sylvaner grapes. Also Terlano Pinot bianco, Terlano Riesling italico, Terlano Riesling renano and Terlano Sauvignon. All D.O.C.

Terminus (Fr). A noted Absinthe producer.

Termo (Port). White table wine.

Ternay (Fr). A commune in the Vienne Département. Wines are produced under the A.C. Saumur, Anjou-Saumur, Loire.

Terne (Fr). A dull, ordinary wine that lacks quality.

Teroldego (It). A red grape variety grown in the Trentino-Alto Adige.

Teroldego (It). A red wine from the Trentino-Alto Adige. Made from a grape of the same name.

Teroldego Rotaliano (It). D.O.C. red or rosé wine from the Trentino-Alto Adige. Made from the Lagrein and Pinot grapes. Red can have Rubino (ruby) on the label.

Teroldego Rotaliano Superiore (It). D.O.C. red wine from the Trentino-Alto Adige. Made from the Lagrein and Pinot grapes. Minimum alcohol content 12% by vol.

Terpenes (Eng). Chemicals that along with other substances make up tertiary constituents and add to spirits' character.

Terra Alta (Sp). A Denominación de Origen region based west of Tarragona. Produces red and white wines mainly from the Garnacha and Macabeo grapes.

Terraces (Port). A name given to the ledge-type vineyards of the Douro area. Blasted out of the rocks in the upper Douro valley.

Terracina (It). A noted wine-producing city based south of Rome in the Latium region. Noted for its Muscat wines.

Terran (Yug). A red grape variety grown in Istia, Croatia.

T

Terranis (Fr). An alternative name for the Malbec grape.

Terrantez (Mad). A lesser known Madeira with a dry, bitter finish. Also the name of a white grape variety.

Terrantez Preto (Mad). A noble black grape variety.

Terra Rosa (Austr). A strip of red soil 1 km wide by 9 kms long in the Coonawarra district of South Australia. Produces Australia's premium red wines in good years.

Terras Altas (Port). The name given to the Dão wines produced by Fonseca in Bierra Alta.

Terrasola (Mex). The brand-name used by Productos Vinícola in Guadalupe, Baja California for a range of their wines.

Terre dei Rotari (It). A well-known wine-producer of the Arneis grape in southern Piemonte.

Terre del Barolo (It). A growers' co-operative based in Barolo, Piemonte, north-western Italy.

Terres Blanches (Fr). The Loire name for the Kimmeridge clay soil in and around Sancerre in the Central Vineyards.

Terres Blanches (Fr). An A.C. Coteaux des Baux-en-Provence, Saint-Remy-de-Provence.

Terres Fortes (Fr). Heavy clay soil.

Terret-Bourret (Fr). A white grape variety grown in the Palette district of Provence.

Terret Noir (Fr). A red grape variety grown in the southern Rhône for Châteauneuf-du-Pape.

Terroir de Caunes (Fr). An A.C. red wine from the Minervois district in the Midi.

Terry (Sp). Brandy and Sherry producer. Address = Fernando A. de Terry S.A., Santissima Trinidad P.O. Box 30, Puerto de Santa Maria, Cadiz. Source of base wine – La Mancha. Produces – Terry 1° Special Reserve not less than 6 years old, Imperio brandy and Centenario brandy. Sherry brands include – Solera 1900 and Maruja Fino.

Terskoye (USSR). A dessert wine produced near Machackala on the Caspian Sea.

Tertiary Constituents (Eng). See Tertiary Deposits.

Tertiary Deposits (Eng). The name used to cover substances such as terpenes, essential oils which add to the character of the spirits. Also known as Tertiary Constituents.

Tertiary Fermentation (Eng). Third fermentation.

Tesseydre (Fr). A noted grower based in the A.C. Cahors region who bottles his own wines.

Tessons (Les) (Fr). A vineyard in the A.C.

commune of Meursault, Côte de Beaune, Burgundy.

Testa (Eng). See Silverskin.

Test Achats (Bel). A consumer journal that reports on types of commodities including beers. Organises tastings.

Testerbranntwein (Ger). Marc brandy.

Testi (Tur). Pitcher, urn.

Testuz (Switz). Noted négociant-éleveurs based at Dézaley, Lavaux.

Tête (Louis) (Fr). A négociant-éleveur based in Beaujolais-Villages. Address = 69430 Beaujeu, Lantignié, Rhône.

Tête de Cuvée (Fr). The best growth, best wines from any vineyard.

Tetero (Cktl). 1 measure Ponche Crema, 1 teaspoon Grenadine. Place ice in an old-fashioned glass, add ingredients, do not mix. Serve with straws.

Tetley Brewery (Eng). Joined with Ansells and Ind Coope to form Allied Breweries in 1961. Public houses have the Huntsman sign. Noted for its cask conditioned Falstaff 1032 O.G. and keg Imperial 1042 O.G.

Tetley Tea (Eng). A famous brand-name for a range of teas produced by the Lyons Tetley Co.

Tetley Walker (Eng). A brewery based in Warrington, Lancs. Produces most styles of beers.

Tetovo (Yug). A wine-producing area based in Macedonia.

Tetra (USSR). A white grape variety grown in Georgia. Produces white dessert wines.

Tetra-Brik (Eng). Small 125 ml. Tetrapacks used to sell fruit juices. Easy to store, need minimum space. Also known as the Combi-Blok.

Tetraethylthiuram disulphide (Eng). See Antibuse.

Tetra Pack (Eng). Cardboard package for wines similar to fruit juice cartons, soft, 1 litre capacity, usually foil lined.

Tettnang (Ger). A Bavarian hop variety and growing region.

Te Tui Vineyard (N.Z.). The name of an old vineyard that now no longer exists.

Teufel (Ger). Vineyard. (Anb) = Franken. (Ber) = Steigerwald. (Gro) = Not yet assigned. (Vil) = Kammerforst.

Teufelsburg (Ger). Vineyard. (Anb) = Baden. (Ber) = Kaiserstuhl-Tuniberg. (Gro) = Vulkanfelsen. (Vil) = Kiechlinsbergen.

Teufelskeller (Ger). Vineyard. (Anb) = Franken. (Ber) = Maindreieck. (Gro) = Ewig Leben. (Vil) = Randersacker.

Teufelskopf (Ger). Vineyard. (Anb) = Baden. (Ber) = Badische Bergstrasse/Kraichgau. (Gro) = Mannaberg. (Vil) = Dielheim.

T

Teufelskopf (Ger). Vineyard. (Anb) = Rheinhessen. (Ber) = Nierstein. (Gro) = Vogelsgärten. (Vil) = Ludwigshöhe.

Teufelsküche (Ger). Vineyard. (Anb) = Nahe. (Ber) = Kreuznach. (Gro) = Schlosskapelle. (Vil) = Guldental.

Teufelspfad (Ger). Vineyard. (Anb) = Rheinhessen. (Ber) = Nierstein. (Gro) = Domherr. (Vil) = Essenheim.

Teufelstein (Ger). Vineyard. (Anb) = Mittelrhein. (Ber) = Rheinburgengau. (Gro) = Loreleyfelsen. (Vil) = Patersberg.

Teug (Hol). Draught, drink.

Teuillac (Fr). A commune in the A.C. Côtes de Bourg in north-eastern Bordeaux.

Teurons (Les) (Fr). A Premier Cru vineyard [part] in the A.C. commune of Beaune, Côte de Beaune, Burgundy. 7.32 ha.

Te Whare Ra (N.Z.). A small winery in based in Renwick, Marlborough, South Island.

Texas Ale (Scot). A bottled Ale 1056 O.G. brewed by the Belhaven Brewery in Dunbar. Brewed for export to Texas, USA.

Texas Fizz (Cktl). 1 gill Gin, 1 fl.oz. lemon juice, 1 fl.oz. orange juice, ½ egg white, 4 dashes Gomme syrup. Shake over ice, strain into an ice-filled highball glass. Top with soda water. Serve with straws and a muddler.

Texas Tea (USA) (slang). Crude oil.

Teixeira Loureiro (Antonio) (Port). A producer of fine Vinho Verde wines. Address = Lapas, Real, 4605 Vila Real.

Texture (Eng). The chemical reaction between protein found in the mucous membrane in the mouth and the tannin in the wine.

T.G. Bright (Can). See Bright.

Thai Amarit Brewery (E.Asia). A brewery based in Bangkok, Thailand. Produces Amarit (a Lager beer).

Thai Wine (E.Asia). Red, rosé and white wines produced by United Products Co. Ltd. Nakornpathorn, Thailand.

Thallern (Aus). The brand-name used by Stift Heiligenkreuz for their range of wines. Is also the name of a village near Gumpoldskirchen.

Thanksgiving Cocktail (Cktl). See Thanksgiving Special.

Thanksgiving Special (Cktl). ⅓ measure dry Gin, ⅓ measure Apricot brandy, ⅓ measure French vermouth, 2 dashes lemon juice. Shake over ice, strain into a cocktail glass. Top with a cherry. Also known as a Thanksgiving Cocktail.

Thann (Fr). A town and wine commune in Alsace.

Thasian (Gre). A sweet wine produced in ancient Greece that was mixed with honeyed dough. It was strained before it was served.

Thatcher's Ruin (Wales). A brand of Cider produced by the Dragon Cider Company, Hirwaun, West Glamorgan.

Thatcher's Third (Cktl). 1 measure blue Curaçao, stir over ice and strain into a cocktail glass. Float double cream on top and sprinkle with powdered chocolate.

Thé (Fr). Tea.

Thea (Lat). Tea.

Theaflavins (Eng). Chemicals which are an important part of tea. They give it life and are produced during the processing of the tea leaves.

Theakston Brewery (Eng). Based in Masham, North Yorkshire. Purchased the Carlisle State Brewery in 1974 and was taken over itself in 1984 by the Matthew Brown Brewery. Noted for its cask conditioned Old Peculier 1058.5 O.G. Black Bull 1035 O.G. and bottled Scotch Ale 1035 O.G.

Thearubigins (Eng). Chemicals which are an important part of tea. They give the tea briskness and brightness. Are produced during the processing of the tea leaves.

Thée (Ch.Isles). Tea.

Thee (Hol). Tea.

Theepot (Hol). Teapot.

Théière (Fr). Teapot.

Theine (Eng). A name often used for the caffeine in tea.

Theobroma Cacao (Lat). The cacao tree from which cocoa and chocolate is produced from its seeds.

Theobromine (Eng). A constituent of coffee, stimulates the heart, acts as a muscle relaxant and stimulates the nervous system. Also helps to promote diuresis.

Theophylline (Eng). A constituent of coffee. Stimulates the nervous system, acts as a muscle relaxant, promotes diuresis and stimulates the heart.

Thera (Gre). A wine-producing area on the island of Santorin. Also the name of a white wine from the area.

Thermomètre à Vin (Fr). Wine thermometer. Is used to test the temperature of wines to be drunk.

Thermotic Bottling (Eng). A method of bottling wine. Hot bottling at a temperature of 52°C – 54°C.

Thessaly (Gre). A wine region of central Greece. Produces medium quality red and white table wines from the Krassato, Stavroto and Xynomavro grapes.

Theuniskraal Estate (S.Afr). Based in Tulbagh. Address = Theuniskaal, Tulbagh 6820. Produces varietal wines.

Thévenin [Roland] (Fr). A négociant-éleveur and owner of Château Puligny-Montrachet, Côte de Beaune, Burgundy. Address = Domaine du Château, Haut de Santenay, 21590 Santenay.

Thévenot (Fr). A Frenchman who opened the first coffee house in Paris in 1647. Was known as the Petit-Châtelet. See Cahouet.

Thi (La) (Fr). A vineyard in the A.C. commune of Montagny, Côte Chalonnaise, Burgundy.

Thiaucourt (Fr). A red wine produced in Lorraine, north-eastern France.

Thibar (Afr). The brand-name for a wine produced by the Domaine de Thibar in Tunisia. 12% alc. by vol. (minimum).

Thief Tube (Fr). The nickname for a Pipette. See Valinch.

Thier Export (Ger). A Dortmunder Export Lager produced by the Dortmunder Thier Brauerei in Dortmund, Westphalia.

Thiergarten Felsköpfchen (Ger). Vineyard. (Anb) = Mosel-Saar-Ruwer. (Ber) = Saar-Ruwer. (Gro) = Römerlay. (Vil) = Trier.

Thiergarten Unterm Kreuz (Ger). Vineyard. (Anb) = Mosel-Saar-Ruwer. (Ber) = Saar-Ruwer. (Gro) = Römerlay. (Vil) = Trier.

Thier Pils (Ger). A Pilsener beer brewed by the Dortmunder Thier Brauerei in Dortmund, Westphalia.

Thil (Fr). A Cru Champagne village in the Canton de Bourgogne. District = Reims.

Thilles (Les) (Fr). A vineyard in the A.C. commune of Montagny, Côte Chalonnaise, Burgundy.

Thillonnes (Les) (Fr). A vineyard in the A.C. commune of Montagny, Côte Chalonnaise, Burgundy.

Thimble (USA). An alternative name for a spirit measure.

Thin (Eng). A term used to describe a wine that lacks body and taste, almost wanting. (Ger) = Duenn.

Thins (Eng). A brewing term used by Maltsters for rootlets and waste shed by barley during the malting process.

Thíra (Gre). An island in the Cyclades group of islands. Produces red and dessert wines, also a straw wine. See Santorini and Nycteri.

Third Degree (Cktl). A Martinez cocktail with a dash of Absinthe and an olive, but with ⅓ gill Gin, ⅙ gill French vermouth used instead.

Third Rail (Cktl). ⅓ measure white Rum, ⅓ measure Applejack, ⅓ measure Brandy, 2 dashes Pastis. Shake over ice, strain into a cocktail glass.

Thirion (Achille) (Fr). Alsace wine producer. Address = 67, Route du Vin, 68580 St-Hippolite.

Thirty Three [33] Brasserie (Fr). A brewery based in Paris. Noted for Record and Porter 39 beers.

Thisted Brewery (Den). A brewery based in North Jutland.

Thistle (Cktl). ½ measure Scotch whisky, ½ measure sweet Vermouth, dash Angostura. Stir over ice, strain into a cocktail glass.

Thistle Glass (Eng). A specific shaped (thistle) glass used mainly for Whisky-based liqueurs.

Thitarine (Afr). A sweet north African liqueur made from figs, herbs and liquorice.

Thomas Adams Distillers Ltd (Can). A subsidiary of Seagram. Produces Antique, Homestead, Gold Stripe and Private Stock brands of Canadian whiskies.

Thomasberg (Ger). Vineyard. (Anb) = Mosel-Saar-Ruwer. (Ber) = Bernkastel. (Gro) = Schwarzlay. (Vil) = Burg.

Thomas Hardy Ale (Eng). A naturally-conditioned, bottled beer, the strongest produced in Britain 1125 O.G. Brewed annually by the Eldridge Pope Brewery in Dorchester, Dorset since 1968. Needs to be matured in bottle for up to 4 years before it is at its peak. 12% alc. by vol. all bottles are individually numbered and dated.

Thomas Hardy Winery (Austr). A winery based in the Southern Vales, South Australia. Produces varietal and table wines.

Thomas Lund (Eng). A nineteenth-century corkscrew producer who patented the Rack and Pinion corkscrew.

Thomas Vineyards (USA). A winery based in Cucamonga, Southern California. Produces varietal, table, sparkling and dessert wines.

Thomas Winery (Austr). A winery based in the Margaret River area of Western Australia.

Thompson (USA). See Thompson Seedless.

Thompson Brewery (Eng). Opened in 1981 in Ashburton, Devon. Produces cask conditioned Bitter 1040 O.G. Mild 1034 O.G. IPA 1045 O.G. keg Dartmoor Bitter 1037 O.G. Dartmoor Lager 1036 O.G. and bottled Pale ale 1045 O.G. IPA 1050 O.G.

Thompson Seedless (USA). A high yielding white grape variety used for blending with cheap table wines. See Wuhebai.

Thompson Winery (USA). A winery based in Michigan. Produces sparkling wines under the labels of Père Hennepin and Père Marquete.

Thor Brewery (Den). A brewery based in Randers, North Jutland. Brews Thunder beer (light-coloured Lager beer) and Kastel Karl Lager 10.7% alc. by weight.

Thorin (Fr). A large noted négociant-éleveur based in the Beaujolais region in Burgundy at Pontaneveaux, 71570 La Chapelle-de-Guinchay.

Thorins (Fr). The name given to wine from the Saône-et-Loire Département in the Burgundy region.

Thornbury (Eng). Address = Bristol. 0.5 ha. Planted 1972. Grape variety – Müller-Thurgau. Produces Thornbury Castle wines.

Thornbury Castle (Eng). See Thornbury.

Thorne (Eng). A cask conditioned Bitter 1038 O.G. brewed by the Darley Brewery in Thorne, South Yorkshire.

Thörnich (Ger). Village. (Anb) = Mosel-Saar-Ruwer. (Ber) = Bernkastel. (Gro) = Sankt Michael. (Vins) = Enggass, Ritsch.

Thoroughbreds (Eng). A term used to describe wines which have turned out as expected of wines of their class.

Thorp Cocktail (Cktl). 1 measure dry Gin, ¼ measure Maraschino, ½ measure Gomme syrup, ½ measure Campari. Stir over ice in a highball glass. Top with a dash lemon peel juice.

Thouarcé (Fr). A commune on the right bank of the river Layon in the Coteaux du Layon in the Anjou-Saumur district of the Loire. Produces Bonnezeaux.

Thousand Oaks Winery (USA). A vineyard and winery based in Starkville, Mississippi. 10 ha. Produces French-American hybrids, Muscadine and vinifera wines.

Thrace (Gre). A wine region of north-eastern Greece.

Thralls (Eng). See Stillage.

Thrash (Eng) (slang). A term for a heavy drinking bout.

Three Choirs Vineyard (Eng). Based in Gloucester. 8.5 ha. Was first planted in 1973. Grape varieties – Huxelrebe, Müller-Thurgau, Reichensteiner, Ortega, Riesling and Seyval blanc.

Three Coins (Sri.L). A Lager beer 12° Balling, brewed by the McCallum Brewery in Colombo.

Three Corners Vineyard (Eng). A vineyard based at Beacon Lane, Woodnesborough, Kent. Was first planted in 1981. 0.5 ha. Grape varieties – Madeleine angevine, 10%, Reichensteiner 40% and Siegerrebe 50%.

Three Counties Brewery (Eng). Opened in 1984 in Gloucester. Produces cask conditioned Three Counties Bitter 1040 O.G. Related to the Jolly Roger Brewery

in Worcester. Covers the counties of Gloucester, Hereford and Worcester.

Three-Country-Corner (Euro). The area of France, Germany and Luxembourg which all have vineyards there.

Three Crowns (Eng). A home-brew public house based in Ashurstwood, Sussex. Noted for its cask conditioned Session Bitter 1038 O.G. Strong Ale 1050 O.G. A Phoenix Co. public house.

Three D Cocktail (Cktl). 1 part Vodka, 1 part Dubonnet, 1 part orange juice. Shake over ice, strain into a cocktail glass.

Three Feathers (Can). A Canadian rye whisky produced by Canadian Park and Tilford (a subsidiary of Canadian Schenley Distillers Ltd).

Three Horse Shoes Brewery (Afr). A brewery based in Cameroon that brews Breda Lager under licence.

Three Kings' Wine (Ger). An old designation for wines made from grapes gathered on the 6th January (Twelfth night). No longer used since 1971. See Dreikönigswein.

Three Lancers (Can). The name for a Canadian whisky produced by Canadian Park and Tilford (a subsidiary of Canadian Schenley Distillers Ltd).

Three Miller (Cktl). ⅓ measure white Rum, ⅔ measure Brandy, 1 barspoon Grenadine, dash of lemon juice. Shake over ice, strain into a cocktail glass.

Three Palms Vineyard (USA). A vineyard based near Calistoga, Napa Valley, California. 41.5 ha. Grape variety – Merlot. Vinified at the Duckhorn Winery.

Three Sheets to the Wind (Eng) (slang). A term for being intoxicated. Is likened to the sails (sheets) of a ship that are flapping around in a variable wind.

Three Stars Cognac [***] (Fr). A Cognac rating. Under British law must be three years old. French law at least 18 months old.

Three Stripes Cocktail (Cktl). ⅔ measure Gin, ⅓ measure French vermouth, juice ¼ orange. Shake over ice, strain into a cocktail glass.

Three Thirds (Eng). See Entire.

Three Three Three [333] Cocktail (Cktl). ⅓ measure Cointreau, ⅓ measure Calvados, ⅓ measure grapefruit juice. Shake over ice, strain into a tulip glass. Dress with a cherry and a slice of lemon.

Three Threads (Eng). A mixture consisting of stale Brown ale and Pale ale.

Three Towns Export (Swe). A full-bodied Beer 5.6% alc. by vol. brewed by the Pripps Brewery.

Three Tuns (Eng). Based at Bishop's

Castle, Shropshire. A home-brew public house of long standing. Noted for its cask conditioned Castle Steamer 1045 O.G. Mild 1035 O.G. and XXX 1042 O.G.

Threonine (Eng). An Amino acid found in minute traces in wines. Is formed by the yeasts.

Thresher (Eng). A large chain of wine shops owned by the Whitbread group.

Thumb (Sp). A short stub on the vine in the Sherry region which bears one or two buds, left after winter pruning. Also known as the Pulgar.

Thunder and Lightning (Cktl). ⅕ gill Cognac, 1 egg yolk, 2 dashes Gomme syrup. Shake over ice, strain into a cocktail glass.

Thunderbird (USA). See Gallo's Thunderbird.

Thunderclap (Cktl). ⅓ measure dry Gin, ⅓ measure Bourbon whiskey, ⅓ measure Brandy. Shake over ice, strain into a cocktail glass.

Thunder Cocktail (Cktl). ⅕ gill Cognac, 1 egg yolk, 1 teaspoon powdered sugar, dash Tabasco sauce. Shake well over ice, strain into a cocktail glass.

Thüngersheim (Ger). Village. (Anb) = Franken. (Ber) = Maindreieck. (Gro) = Ravensburg. (Vins) = Johannisberg, Scharlachberg.

Thüringen (Ger). See Saarle.

Thurinum (Lat). A red wine produced in southern Italy in Roman times.

Thwaites Brewery (Eng). Based in Blackburn, Lancashire. Noted for its cask conditioned Bitter 1036 O.G. Best Mild 1034 O.G. Mild 1032 O.G. (also in keg). keg Stein Lager 1036 O.G. bottled Big Ben 1050 O.G. Danny Brown 1034 O.G. East Lancs. 1036 O.G. and Old Dan 1075 O.G.

Thyoneus (Lat). A word used for Bacchus. See also Bassareus, Bromius, Dionysus, Euhan, Euan, Euhius, Euius, Lacchus and Lyaeus.

Thyrsta (Eng). The mediaeval word for 'to thirst'.

Thyrsus (Gre). The staff (stick) of Dionysus (has a pine cone on top).

Tia Eggnogg (Cktl). 2 ozs. Tia Maria, 1 oz. Cognac, 2 ozs. milk, 1 egg, 1 teaspoon sugar. Shake over ice, strain into a highball glass, top with nutmeg.

Tia Lola (Sp). The brand-name of a Fino sherry produced by Findlater.

Tia Maria (W.Ind). A coffee-flavoured liqueur from Jamaica. Rum based with Blue mountain coffee extract and spices. 26.5% alc. by vol.

Tibaani (USSR). A white grape variety grown in Georgia. Produces dry white wines.

Tibouren (Fr). A red grape variety grown in the Bandol district of Provence.

Tiburtinum (Lat). A red wine produced in central western Italy in Roman times.

Ticino (Switz). An Italian speaking wine region in the south-east. The Canton is famous for the production of Merlot wines. Grapes–Bondola, Nebbiolo and Nostrano.

Tico (Sp). A light style of Sherry. Produced by Harvey in Jerez de la Frontera. Used as a mixer.

Tidal Wave (Cktl). 1 measure Mandarine Napoléon, juice of a lemon. Shake over ice, strain into a cocktail glass, add a dash of bitter lemon and a slice of lemon.

Tidbit Cocktail (Cktl). ⅕ gill dry Gin, dash dry Sherry, scoop vanilla ice cream. Blend together in a blender. Serve in a highball glass.

Tiddly (Eng). An eighteenth- and nineteenth-century term for a small drink. Usually of Gin.

Tiddly (Eng) (slang). Applied to a person, usually female, under the influence of alcohol.

Tiddy (Can). A Canadian Whisky-based liqueur.

Tie (Eng). A Tied public-house where a brewery insists that they sell the brewery's wares either because the brewery owns the pub or has a contract with the pub.

Tied House (Eng). See Tie.

Tiefenbach (Ger). Village. (Anb) = Baden. (Ber) = Badische Bergstrasse/Kraichgau. (Gro) = Stiftsberg. (Vins) = Schellenbrunnen, Spiegelberg.

Tiefenthal (Ger). Village. (Anb) = Rheinhessen. (Ber) = Bingen. (Gro) = Rheingrafenstein. (Vin) = Graukatz.

Tiegs Winery (USA). A winery based in Lenoir City, Tennessee. Produces French hybrid wines.

Tiélandry (Fr). A Premier Cru vineyard in the A.C. commune of Beaune, Côte de Beaune, Burgundy. 1.98 ha.

T'ien-Chin (China). A branch of the China National Cereals, Oils and Foodstuffs, Import and Export Corporation. Has a Golden Star branch.

Tiengen (Ger). Village. (Anb) = Baden. (Ber) = Kaiserstuhl-Tuniberg. (Gro) = Attilafelsen. (Vin) = Rebstal.

Tientan Beer (China). A beer brewed in T'ien Chin by C.N.C.O.F.I.E.C.

Tierce (Eng). A cask holding a ⅓ of a Butt/Pipe. See (Fr) = Tierçon and (Ger) = Tierze.

Tierçon (Fr). A cask holding ⅓ of a Butt or Pipe.

Tiergarten (Ger). Village. (Anb) = Baden.

(Ber) = Ortenau. (Gro) = Fürsteneck. (Vin) = Renchtäler.

Tierra Blanca (Sp). Albariza soil. See also Tierra de Anafas.

Tierra de Anafas (Sp). Albariza soil. See also Tierra Blanca.

Tierra de Lebrija (Sp). Diatomaceous earth used for fining wines. See Tierra de Vino.

Tierra de Vino (Sp). Diatomaceous earth. See Tierra de Lebrija.

Tierra Estella (Sp). One of five D.O. wine-producing districts in the Navarra, north-eastern Spain.

Tierze (Ger). A cask holding ⅓ of a Butt or Pipe.

Tietericus (Lat). A word used to describe the festival of Bacchus.

Tiff (Eng). An eighteenth-century word for a small drink. See also Tiffin.

Tiff (Eng). A mediaeval word for 'to sip'. See Tiffing.

Tiffin (Eng). An eighteenth-century name for a short (little) drink.

Tiffing (Eng). A mediaeval term meaning sipping (a drink).

Tiffon (Fr). A Cognac producer based in Jarnac. Produces *** (aged 7 years in cask) and V.S.O.P. (aged 12 years in cask).

Tiflis (USSR). A district of Georgia where strong red wines are made. See Saperavi and Mukuzani.

Tig (Eng). A wooden tankard used in Elizabethan times.

Tiger (S.E.Asia). The brand-name used by the Malayan Breweries based in Singapore for Stout and Lager beers.

Tiger Ale (Eng). An Ale 1038 O.G. brewed by the Brewing Up Shop in Leyland, Lancashire.

Tiger Beer (S.E.Asia). See Tiger Lager.

Tiger Bitter (Eng). A full-flavoured Bitter 1041 O.G. brewed by the Everards Brewery of Leicester.

Tigerbone Wine (China). A wine sold in small earthenware jars.

Tiger Head (USA). A top-fermented Ale 4.6% alc. by vol. brewed by the Schmidt Brewery in Pennsylvania.

Tiger Lager (S.E.Asia). A strong Lager beer brewed by the Malayan Breweries in Singapore. Also known as Tiger Beer.

Tiger Lillet (Cktl). ⅓ measure Lillet, ⅓ measure Van der Hum, ⅙ measure Maraschino, ⅙ measure dry Vermouth. Stir over ice, strain into a cocktail glass. Add a twist of orange peel.

Tiger Milk (Yug). A sweet white wine from the Radgona district of Slovenija. Made from the Ranina grape. Also known as Radgona Ranina.

Tiger Rag (Punch). 1 bottle Tiger Milk, ½ bottle lemonade, ⅗ gill dry Gin, ⅓ gill Port. Serve well-chilled with sliced fruit in season.

Tiger Scotch (Fr). A well-known Bière brewed by the BSN Bières.

Tiger's Eye Pinot Noir (Austr). A red Burgundy-style wine from the Château Barker vineyards, Western Australia.

Tiger's Milk (Cktl). 1 egg, ½ measure Crème de Cacao, ½ measure Cherry brandy, ½ measure Bénédictine, 1 measure Italian vermouth. Shake over ice, strain into a goblet. Sprinkle with nutmeg.

Tiger's Tail (Cktl). ⅓ measure Pastis, ⅔ measure fresh orange juice. Pour into an ice-filled old-fashioned glass. Add a slice of orange.

Tight (Eng) (slang). Drunk, intoxicated.

Tight Head (Eng). Obtained by forcing beer through small holes in the sparkler on a beer pump. A stiff creamy foam appears.

Tigmandru (Rum). An important wine-producing area. Part of the Tîrnave Vineyard.

Tignanello (It). A red wine produced by Antinori in Tuscany from Canaiolo and Sangiovese grapes.

Tigrovo Mljeko (Yug). A sweet 'Tiger Milk' wine produced from the Ranina grape.

Tikveš (Yug). A wine-producing district in Macedonia.

Tilgesbrunnen (Ger). Vineyard. (Anb) = Nahe. (Ber) = Kreuznach. (Gro) = Kronenberg. (Vil) = Bad Kreuznach.

Till Breweries (Swe). A large brewing company with breweries based in Bollnas, Gävle, Lulea, Ostersund and Umea. Produces Rodeorm mead and Spetsat herb beer.

Tilth (Eng). Cultivated (tilled) land.

Tilts (USA). Bars used for adjusting casks or scantlings to the desired position. Known in England as Scotches.

Time (Eng). See 'Call Time'.

Timişoara (Rum). A wine-producing area noted mainly for its white wines with some red from the Cabernet sauvignon.

Timmermans Brasserie (Bel). Brewers of wild Lambic beers from Itterbeek, central Belgium. Their bottled Gueze is produced in naturelle and filtered forms. Also brew Lambic and Cherry beers.

Timor Coffee (E.Ind). An Indonesian coffee of the Arabica type. Produces a good aroma and mellow flavour.

Timothy Taylor (Eng). See Taylor.

Timpert (Ger). Vineyard. (Anb) = Mosel-Saar-Ruwer. (Ber) = Saar-Ruwer. (Gro) = Römerlay. (Vil) = Kasel.

Tinaja (Sp). A large earthenware jar used in the Montilla-Moriles region in southern Spain.

Tinas (Sp). Earthenware containers used to hold Sherry must. Can also denote a large oak cask in the Rioja region.

Tincture of Tiger Bone (China). A medicinal drink taken by people who have 'aches in their bones'.

Tinetas (Sp). Baskets used for carrying the grapes from harvest to the vinery in the Sherry region.

Tinglewood (Austr). A wine-maker based in the Great Southern area of Western Australia.

Tinners Bitter (Eng). A cask conditioned Bitter 1038 O.G. brewed by the St. Austell Brewery in Cornwall.

Tinny (Austr) (slang). A term for a can of beer.

Tino (It). Vat, tub.

Tino (Sp). A large oak vat that is used during the secondary fermentation process and racking of wine.

Tinta Amarela (Port). A red grape variety used in the production of Port. Gives colour to the wine. Also used in the Dão region.

Tinta Baroca (Port). A red grape variety grown in the the Port region.

Tinta Barocca (S.Afr). A vintage red wine produced by the Landskroon Estate in Paarl and the Rust-en-Verde Wine Estates in the Stellenbosch.

Tinta Caida (Port). A grape variety grown in the Alentejo district.

Tinta Cão (Port). A red grape variety.

Tinta Carvalha (Port). A red grape variety grown in the Dão region to make red wines.

Tinta da Madeira (Mad). A red grape variety used in the production of Madeira. Is a vinifera cross variety.

Tinta das Baroccas (S.Afr). A red grape variety used in the making of Port-type fortified wines.

Tinta de Toro (Sp). A red grape variety grown in the Galicia region.

Tinta Fina (Sp). A red grape variety grown in Galicia.

Tinta Francesa (Port). A red grape variety used in the production of Port.

Tinta Francesca (Port). See Tinta Francisca.

Tinta Francisca (Port). A red grape variety used in the making of Port. Gives colour to the wine. Known in France as the Teinturier.

Tintaine [La] (Fr). A herb liqueur with aniseed. Sold with a sprig of fennel inside the bottle.

Tinta Madeira (USA). A red grape variety grown in California to make dessert wines.

Tinta Miuda (Port). A red grape variety grown in the Torres Vedras district.

Tinta Muera (Port). A black grape variety grown in the Alenquer district.

Tinta Nascida (Port). A red grape variety used in the production of Port to give colour to the wine.

Tinta Negra Mole (Mad). A black grape variety used in the production of Madeira. A vinifera cross between the Pinot noir and Grenache.

Tinta Pinheira (Port). A red grape variety grown near Viseu in the Dão region. Has Pinot noir connections.

Tinta Pomar (Port). A red grape variety used in the production of Port to give colour to the wine.

Tinta Port (USA). Denotes a ruby Port made from Portuguese grapes instead of non-Portuguese varieties.

Tinta Portuguesa (Port). A red grape variety used in the production of Port to give colour to the wine.

Tintara (N.Z.). The local name used for the Siebel 5437 red grape variety.

Tintara Vineyard (Austr). A vineyard based in McLaren Vale, South Australia.

Tinta Roriz (Port). A red grape variety used in the production of Port to give colour to the wine.

Tintarrón (Sp). A red grape variety grown in Galicia.

Tintilla (Sp). A deep-brown Sherry with a raisiny aroma produced by Williams and Humbert.

Tintilla de Rota (Sp). A dark, red wine, often used for blending. Is also known as Tent.

Tintillo de Málaga (Sp). A red-style of Málaga.

Tinto (Port). Red (wine).

Tinto (Sp). Red (wine). Also the name used for the Mourvèdre grape.

Tinto Aragonés (Sp). The alternative name for the red Garnacho grape in the Rioja.

Tinto Cão (Port). A red grape variety used in the production of Port to give colour to the wine. See also Tinta Cão.

Tinto Cazador (Sp). A red wine (aged 3 years in cask) produced by the Cavas del Ampurdán near Barcelona.

Tinto Mazuela (Port). Another name for the Carignan grape.

Tinto de País (Sp). A red grape variety grown in central Spain.

Tinto de Requena (Sp). An alternative name for the Bobal grape.

Tinto Femia (Sp). A red grape variety grown in Galicia.

Tinto Fino (Sp). The alternative name for the Cencibel, Tempranillo or Ull de Llebre grape.

Tinto Francisca (Port). See Tinta Francisca.

Tintometer (Port). An instrument for measuring the colour in wine.

Tintorera (Sp). A red grape variety grown in Galicia. Is also known as the Mencía.

Tinto Seco (Bra). Dry red wine.

Tinto Suave (Bra). Mellow red wine.

Tintourier (Port). A grape variety used for colouring. Has colour right through to the pips.

Tio Diego (Sp). A brand of dry Amontillado sherry produced by Valdespino at Jerez de la Frontera.

Tio Guillermo (Sp). A dry, full-bodied Amontillado Sherry produced by Garvey in Jerez de la Frontera.

Tio Mateo (Sp). A brand of Fino sherry produced from the Palomino y Vergara in Jerez de la Frontera.

Tio Pepe (Sp). A brand-name Fino sherry from Gonzalez Byass.

Tio Quinto (Arg). A Sherry produced for export by Peñaflor.

Tipa (Tur). To cork, seal or plug a cask or bottle.

Tipicità (It). Denotes a wine that conforms to that expected from its origin and style.

Tipicity (Eng). A grading of how typical the wine is to the original style in wine tasting.

Tip Lady Cocktail (Cktl). ⅕ gill Bacardi White Label, ⅙ gill lemon juice, ⅛ gill lime juice, 2 dashes Gomme syrup. Shake over ice, strain into an ice-filled highball glass. Dress with a cherry.

Tipo de la Bordeos (Sp). Once found on the labels of Riojan wines to denote that the wine was of a Bordeaux-type.

Tipo de la Borgoña (Sp). Once found on the labels of Riojan wines to denote that the wine was of a Burgundy-type.

Tippeny (Scot). A term for ale used by Robbie Burns.

Tipperary Cocktail (Cktl).(1). ⅓ gill Gin, ⅙ gill Italian vermouth, ⅙ gill Grenadine, ⅙ gill orange juice, 2 sprigs mint. Shake well over ice, strain into a cocktail glass.

Tipperary Cocktail (Cktl).(2). ⅓ measure Irish whiskey, ⅓ measure Green Chartreuse, ⅓ measure Italian vermouth. Stir over ice, strain into a cocktail glass.

Tipple (Ch.Isles). The brand-name of a Guernsey and Jersey cream liqueur sold in single cup-size individual vacuum packed portions. Served with coffee in lieu of milk or cream.

Tipple (Eng) (slang). A term for a drink. Usually denotes a persons favourite drink.

Tippler (Eng) (slang). The term for a consistent drinker, one who drinks small quantities of alcoholic beverages regularly.

Tipsy (Eng) (slang). The term used to describe a person who is under the influence of alcohol.

Tipsy Guava (Cktl).(Non-alc). ⅓ pint Guava syrup, ½ fl.oz. lime juice, 5 dashes rum essence (non-alc), 2 dashes blackcurrant syrup. Blend together with scoop of crushed ice in a blender. Strain into a highball glass. Dress with a slice of Guava.

Tip Top Punch (Cktl). A Brandy punch filled with Champagne instead of soda water.

Tiquira (S.Am). A white spirit made from the Tapioca root. 40–45.5% alc. by vol.

Tirabuzón (Sp). Corkscrew.

Tirador (Sp). Denotes the man who works the wooden screw used in the second pressing of the grapes.

Tirage (Fr). Bottling, drawing wine from casks.

Tirajas (Sp). See Tinajas.

Tirbuşon (Tur). Corkscrew.

Tire-Bouchon (Ch.Isles). Corkscrew.

Tire-Bouchon (Fr). Corkscrew.

Tire-Bouchon à Champagne (Fr). A Champagne corkscrew. Used to extract corks from Champagne bottles (whose heads have broken off). It fits over the top of the bottle neck to retain the cork.

Tire-Bouchon avec Plumeau (Fr). A corkscrew with a horsehair brush in the handle for the removal of verdigris from the top of the cork.

Tiré Sur Lie au Château (Fr). Bottled off its lees at the Château.

Tîrnave (Rum). A wine region in the heart of the Carpathian mountains. Named after the river that runs through the region. White wines are the best. Welschriesling and Perla.

Tîrnaveni (Rum). Quality vineyards situated in the Tîrnaveni in the central province of Transylvania.

Tîrnave Perla (Rum). A medium white wine from the Tîrnave region made with the Perla grape.

Tîrnave Riesling (Rum). A medium sweet white wine from the Tîrnave region made with the Welschriesling grape.

Tirnovo (Bul). A very sweet red wine from south-western Bulgaria. A dessert wine.

Tirollinger (Aus). See Trollinger.

Tiros (Isr). An old Hebrew (Bible) word for strong medium-sweet wines. Also spelt Tirosh.

Tirosh (Isr). See Tiros.

Tisane (Fr). Infusion. (Eng). Herbal tea. Non 'tea' tea. e.g. Camomile tea, Mint tea, Maté, etc.

Tisane de Champagne (Fr). A term that denotes a light-style Champagne.

Tisbury Brewery (Eng). Opened in 1980

in Tisbury, Wiltshire by the Sussex Leisure Co. Noted for its cask conditioned Old Grumble 1060 O.G. Also a keg/bottled version.

Tischwein (Aus). Table wine.

Tisdall (Austr). Address = Cornelia Creek Road, Echuca, Victoria 3625. 80 ha. at Rosbercon. Grape varieties – Cabernet, Chardonnay, Chenin blanc, Colombard, Merlot and Sauvignon blanc. 50 ha. at Mount Helen. Grape varieties – Cabernet, Chardonnay, Merlot, Pinot noir, Rhine riesling, Sauvignon blanc and Traminer.

Titoki Liqueur (N.Z.). A green-coloured liqueur made from the leaves and berries of the titoki bush and manuka honey. Produced by Balic in Henderson, North Island.

Titration (Eng). The total acid quantity of a wine is determined by titration.

Titten Tei (Cktl). ⅔ measure Smirnoff Red Label Vodka, ⅓ measure Bénédictine, dash orange juice, dash Grenadine. Shake over ice, strain into a cocktail glass. Fill with iced sparkling wine. Dress with a slice of orange and a cherry.

Tivon (Isr). A Tokay-style, sweet, dessert wine.

Tiziano (Cktl). 1 fl.oz. freshly squeezed grape juice topped with iced Spumante, served in Champagne flutes.

Tizzano (It). A Chianti Classico producer based in Tuscany.

T.J. (S.Afr) (abbr). Initials for the Twee Jongegezellen Estate.

TJ 39 (S.Afr). A dry white wine produced by the Twee Jongegezellen Estate from over 17 different grape varieties.

Tlaxcala (Mex). A wine-producing area in southern Mexico.

Tlemcen (Alg). A noted V.D.Q.S. wine-producing area based near the Moroccan border.

Tmavé (Czec). Dark (beer).

Tmavé (Czec). A dark beer produced by the Branik Brewery in Prague.

T.N.T. (Cktl).(1). Montezuma Silver Tequila over ice in a highball glass topped with iced tonic water.

T.N.T. (Cktl).(2). Place the juice of ½ a lime together with the spent shell into an ice-filled highball glass. Add ⅓ gill Tequila, top with tonic water. Stir well.

TNT (Cktl). ⅔ measure Brandy, ⅓ measure orange Curaçao, dash Pastis, dash Angostura. Stir over ice, strain into a cocktail glass.

TNT Ale (Eng). A cask conditioned Ale 1050 O.G. brewed by the Simpkiss Brewery in Brierley Hill, Staffordshire.

T.N.T. Cocktail (Cktl). 1 measure Pernod, 1 measure Rye whisky. Shake over ice, strain into a cocktail glass.

Toad's Eyes (Fr). A term to denote sparkling wines that have large bubbles. Often wines that have been charged with CO_2 gas.

Toast (Eng). The process of drinking to the health or future of a person. Usually made with Champagne or other sparkling wine especially at a wedding, christening, birthday etc. See Alla Sua (It), Cheers (Eng).

Toast and Ale (Eng). Ale and ginger root heated together, poured into a tankard and a piece of toasted bread floated on top.

Toasting Glass (Eng). A thin stemmed glass of the eighteenth century. After drinking the toast the stem was snapped to prevent anyone else's health being drunk from the same glass.

Toast Master (Eng). A person who proposes and announces after-dinner speakers and toasts at formal dinners. Is dressed in a red jacket. Female = Toast Mistress.

Toast Mistress (Eng). A female Toast Master.

Toast Water (Eng). An old invalid remedy drink. Break a few slices of thin toast into a jug and cover with 1 pint boiling water. When cool, strain and sweeten, add a little grated nutmeg to taste.

Tobacco (Eng). A term applied to the wines of Bordeaux in wine tasting. Wines that have been oak matured.

Tobago Punch (Punch). 1 pint white Rum, juice of a lemon, ¼ pint sugar syrup, ¼ pint pineapple juice, small can lychees. Stir over ice, decorate with 2 sliced bananas and serve.

Tobermory (Scot). A single Malt whisky distillery on the Isle of Mull. A Highland malt. Also called Ledaig. 43% alc. by vol.

Tobía (Sp). The alternative name for the white grapes Blanca-Roja, Blanquirroja and Malvasia.

Toby (Eng). The name of Bass Charrington beers. A Toby jug sign. Keg Toby Light 1032 O.G.

Toby Light (Eng). See Toby.

Tocai (It). A white grape variety grown in the Friulia region. Also a wine of the same name.

Tocai (Yug). The alternative name for the Pinot gris grape in the Slovenia region.

Tocai di Lison (It). D.O.C. white wine from Veneto. Made from 95% Tocai and 5% other grape varieties. If produced in a confined restricted area is entitled to the additional specification of Classico.

T

Tocai di San Martino Della Battaglia
(It). D.O.C. white wine from Lombardy.
Made from the Tocai Friulano grapes.

Tocai Friulano (It). A white grape variety
grown in Lombardy. Also known as the
Trebbianello.

Tocane (Fr). The name given to new
Champagne that is produced from the
first pressing of the grapes.

Tocjai Aszú (Hun). The alternative spelling of Tokay Aszú.

Tocornal [José] (Chile). A noted exporter
of wines to Canada and Venezuela.

Toddies (USA). A drink served either hot
or cold of spirit, lemon slice, sugar,
cloves and hot/cold water. Served in an
old-fashioned glass (cold) or mug (hot).

Toddy (E.Ind). The sap of wine palms
used as a non-alcoholic (or fermented)
beverage.

Toddy (Eng) (Cock). 1 measure spirit, 1
barspoon sugar. Dissolve sugar in a
little water, add spirit. Build in an
old-fashioned glass. Add a twist of
lemon, serve with a stirrer.

Toddy (Eng). Old name for a measure (nip).

Toddy (Ind). A spirit that is obtained from
the fermented Jaggery. Also the alternative name for Raki and Arrack.

Toddy (S.E.Asia). An alcoholic drink
made from coconut milk. Has a sour
after-taste. Produced in Malaya by the
Indians.

Toddy (Sri.L). A spirit made from fermented palm sap.

Toddy (USA). Originally the fermented
sap of palm trees. Now classed for a tot
of spirit.

Toddy Glass (USA). A special handled
glass or mug for serving hot Toddies in.

Toddy Lifter (Eng). An implement made
of glass or metal consisting of a cup on a
long handle used to draw a 'Toddy'
from a cask or barrel. Also a bottle-
shaped glass with a hole at the base so
that when placed in a cask of spirit the
thumb is placed over the top to prevent
the contents returning to the cask.

Toddy Mug (USA). See Toddy Glass.

Toddy Palm (E.Ind). See Wine Palm. (Fr)
= Arbre à liqueur.

To Drink a Peg (Eng). An old English
request in the Middle Ages for a
measure of drink. See Peg.

Tod's Cooler (Cktl). Place into a large
tumbler – 2 ice cubes, ½ gill dry Gin, ⅙
gill Cassis, juice of ½ lemon. Top up
with soda water, stir well.

Togal (Sp). A red wine made from mainly
Garnacha grapes by the Bodegas
Bardón in Ribera Baja.

Tohani (Rum). A wine-producing area.
Part of the Dealul-Mare Vineyard.

Toio (Cktl). ⅓ measure Triple Sec, ⅓
measure dry Gin, ⅓ measure Apricot
brandy, 3 dashes lemon juice. Stir well
over ice, strain into a cocktail glass, add
a twist of lemon peel juice.

Toison de Oro (Sp). A Brandy produced
by Agustín Blázquez.

Tokaier (Fr). An alternative name in eastern France for the Pinot gris.

Tokaj-Aszú (Hun). See Tokay Aszú.

Tokaj Essence (Hun). See Tokay Essenz.

Tokaj Furmint (Hun). See Tokay
Furmint.

Tokaj-Hegyalja (Hun). Hilly wine-
producing region in northern Hungary
which produces fine Tokay wines. Also
spelt Tokaj-Hegyalya.

Tokaj-Hegyalya (Hun). An alternative
spelling of Tokaj-Hegyalja.

Tokaji (Hun). An alternative spelling of
Tokaj-Hegyalja made from the Furmint
grape with Muskotály and Hárslevelü
grapes used to a small degree.

Tokaji Édes (Hun). Describes a sweet
Tokay wine.

Tokaji Muskotályos (Hun). Dry Muscat
wine made in the Tokay region.

Tokaji Pecsenyebor (Hun). The lowest
quality Tokay wine that is available.

Tokaji Szàeaz (Hun). Describes a dry
Tokay wine.

Tokaj Szamorodni (Hun). See Tokay
Szamorodni.

Tokay (Austr). The alternative name for
the white Muscadelle grape.

Tokay (Hun). A small village in north-
east Hungary near the Russian border.
Produces the famous Tokay wines.

Tokay Aszú (Hun). A wine made in the
Tokay region from grapes that have
been attacked by botrytis cinerea. The
grapes attacked by the botrytis cinerea
are kept separate from the unaffected
grapes and placed into tubs called Puttonyos. The number of Puttonyos
added to the wine made from the non-
affected grapes are recorded on the
bottle neck-label. (3, 4, 5 or 6).

Tokay Aztali (Hun). A wine made from
the Marc or lees of the Tokay Aszú
wines. Not usually shipped but consumed locally. See also Tokay Forditàs
and Tokay Màslàs.

Tokay d'Alsace (Fr). The Alsace name for
the white Pinot Gris grape.

Tokay Édes Szamorodni (Hun). The
description used on Tokay Szamorodni
if it is fairly rich in style.

Tokayer (Ger). The name used in the
Palatinate for the Ruländer or Grauer
Burgunder grape.

Tokay Essenz (Hun). The juice from the
botrytis-attacked grapes. Is extracted by

the grape's own weight on themselves. It is rich, sweet and is now rarely sold but used to improve Aszú variety wines. From the Furmint grape.

Tokay Eszencia (Hun). See Essenz. Produced only in exceptional years from individually selected grapes from the best areas in the vineyard. Fermented with a special yeast (Tokay 22) and matured for a minimum of 10 years. Is richer than a 6 Puttonyos Tokay.

Tokay Forditàs (Hun). A wine made from the Marc or lees of the pressing of Aszú. Usually consumed locally. See also Tokay Aztali and Tokay Màslàs.

Tokay Furmint (Hun). A rich white table wine with a flavour of raisins sold in the flûte bottle. Made from the Furmint grape in the Tokaj-Hegyalja region.

Tokay Màslàs (Hun). A wine made from the Marc or lees of the Aszú pressings. Consumed locally. See Tokay Aztali and Tokay Forditàs.

Tokay Szamorodni (Hun). Lit – ' Tokay born of itself'. Is a wine made from botrytis attacked and ordinary grapes pressed together. Wine is a little drier than Aszú.

Tokay 22 (Hun). A special strain of yeast used in the fermenting of Tokay Essencia.

Tokeah (Isr). A sweet, Tokay-style, dessert wine.

Tokier (Hun). See Tokay Aszú.

Tokkuri (Jap). Small ceramic bottles (flasks) from which Saké is traditionally served. It is served from these into Sakazuki.

Tolaga Bay (N.Z.). Part of the Corbans.

Tolcsva (Hun). A noted wine-producing village based in the southern foothills.

Toledo (Sp). A wine-producing area in the La Mancha region.

Toledo Punch (Punch). In a large Punch bowl place 2 lbs. sugar, 4 large bottles soda water, juice of 4 lemons, ¾ bottle Brandy, 4 oranges, 1 pineapple cut up, 6 bottles Champagne, 2 bottles Claret, 4 bottles Perrier water. Mix well with ice and serve.

Tollana (Austr). A winery in the Barossa Valley, South Australia. Is noted for its Brandy.

Tolley, Scott and Tolley's Winery (Austr). A winery based south of Nuriootpa in South Australia.

Tolleys Pedare (Austr). A winery in the Barossa Valley in South Australia. Produces varietal and table wines, also Tolleys TST Brandy.

Tolly Cobbold Brewery (Eng). A brewery based in Ipswich noted for its cask conditioned Bitter 1034 O.G. Mild 1032

O.G. Original 1036 O.G. Old Strong 1046 O.G. (also keg versions), bottled Light 1032 O.G. Dark 1032 O.G. Export 1036 O.G. 250 1073 O.G. Royal 1064 O.G. Is linked with the Camerons Brewery in Hartlepool (both owned by Ellerman Lines) which brews under licence DAB Lager 1046 O.G. and Hansa keg Lager 1036 O.G.

Tom and Jerry (USA). ⅙ gill Jamaican Rum, ⅙ gill Brandy, 1 beaten egg, hot water or milk and sugar. Serve in a Tom and Jerry mug or coffee cup.

Tom and Jerry Mug (USA). A special mug for serving Tom and Jerry cocktails in. Tall and slim. A demi-tasse (coffee cup can be used as a substitute.)

Tomasello Winery (USA). A winery based in Hammonton, New Jersey. 40 ha. Produces hybrid wines.

Tomate (Fr). See Purée.

Tomatin (Scot). A single Malt whisky distillery in Tomatin, Inverness. A Highland malt. Taken over by 2 Japanese Companies (Okura and Takara Shuzo). Produces – a 5 year old Malt 43% alc. by vol. and a 10 year old 40% alc. by vol.

Tomato Cocktail (Cktl). ⅕ gill Pernod, 3 dashes Grenadine. Pour into a small tumbler. Top with iced water and a cherry.

Tomato Juice Cocktail (Cktl). 4 fl.ozs. tomato juice, ½ fl.oz. lemon juice, 2 dashes Worcestershire sauce, 2 dashes celery salt. Shake over ice, strain into 5 oz. goblet or an ice-filled highball glass.

Tomato Wine (Ch.Isles). See Aztecato.

Tomboladero (Port). A white enamel or porcelain saucer, similar to a tastevin, used in the Port trade to check the wine's colour.

Tomboy (Cktl). 1 part tomato juice, 1 part bitter beer.

Tom Collins (Cktl). ¾ oz. lime or lemon juice, 1 teaspoon powdered sugar, 1½ ozs. Old Tom dry Gin. Shake over ice, strain into a highball glass, top with mineral water. Stir.

Tomelloso (Sp). Centre of production of Brandy and Industrial alcohol in the La Mancha region of central Spain.

Tomintoul-Glenlivet (Scot). A single Malt whisky distillery based south of Ballindalloch, Banffshire. Owned by Whyte and MacKay. A Highland malt. 40% alc. by vol.

Tømmermaend (Den) (slang). A hangover.

Tomnatec (Rum). A wine-producing area. Part of the Banat Vineyard. Noted for its white wines produced from the Creaţa, Majarca and Steinschiller grapes.

Tom Sayer (Cktl). 2 parts Southern Comfort, 1 part Galliano, dash Orange bitters. Shake over ice, strain into an ice-filled highball glass. Top with lemonade, add an orange slice, serve with straws.

Tom's Coffee House (Eng). A coffee-house bought by Thomas Twining in 1706. Sold tea as well in an effort to attract customers. Also sold dry tea for home use.

Ton (Hol). Cask.

Tona (It). A fine wine-producer based in Lombardy. Produces D.O.C. Valtellina and Sforzato wines.

Tondeña (La) (E.Ind). Leading Rum producers in the Philippines. Well-known brand is Manila.

Tondonia (Sp). A cask-aged white wine produced by López de Heredia.

Toneis (Port). Large maturing casks used in the Douro for maturing Port.

Tonel (Fr). An old French word for a cask.

Tonel (Port) (Sp). A large Barrel, Pipe, Cask.

Tonelada (Sp). 10 hectolitres of wine.

Tonelero (Sp). Cask maker, Cooper.

Toneles (Port). Vats.

Tongerlo Brasserie (Bel). An Abbaye brewery based in north-eastern Belgium.

Tonica (Mad). A bottom-fermented, sweet black beer.

Tonic Water (Eng). A carbonated water which contains a small amount of quinine. See Indian Tonic Water.

Toni Kola (Afr) (Fr). Aromatic bitters made from the Kola nut.

Tonmergel (Lux). Type of soil.

Tonna (Lat). Barrel, cask. See Tunna.

Tonne (Euro). 1,000 kilogrammes. (0.98 tons).

Tonneau (Fr). Measurement of wine. Wines are bought by the Tonneau in Bordeaux. Equal to 4 hogsheads. 1 tonneau = 96 to 100 dozen bottles.

Tonnelier (Fr). Cask maker, Cooper.

Tonnellerie (Fr). Cooperage.

Tonnerre (Fr). A wine town in the Yonne Département in Burgundy. Produces fine red and white wines.

Toohey's Breweries (Austr). Breweries in Grafton, Sydney.

Toohey's Old (Austr). A fruity beer brewed by the Toohey's Brewery in New South Wales. Also known as Hunter Ale.

Tooley Street Brewery (Eng). Opened in 1984 in London. Serves the Dickens Inn, St Katherine's Dock. Noted for its cask conditioned Dickens Own (or TSB) 1040 O.G. and Archway 1042 O.G.

Tooths Brewery (Austr). A brewery known for its Resch's KB Lager.

Top (Afr). A Lager beer brewed by the West African Breweries.

Top (Switz). A beer brewed by the Cardinal Brewery in Fribourg.

Topaz (Isr). A rich, sweet, golden wine produced for the USA market.

Topaz (W.Ind). A brand-name for a drink of white Rum and passion drink. 28% alc. by vol.

Top Banana (Cktl). ⅙ gill Vodka, ⅙ gill Crème de Banane, juice ½ orange. Shake over ice, strain into an ice-filled old-fashioned glass.

Top Brass Lager (Eng). A bottled/canned Lager 1033 O.G. brewed by the Wilson Brewery in Manchester.

Top Brew Ale (Eng). A dark strong Ale 1071 O.G. brewed and bottled by the Davenports Brewery in Birmingham.

Top Brew De Luxe (Eng). A dark extra strong Ale 1075 O.G. brewed and bottled by the Davenports Brewery in Birmingham.

Topedo Cocktail (Cktl). ⅔ measure Calvados, ⅓ measure Cognac, dash dry Gin. Shake over ice, strain into a cocktail glass.

Topette (Fr). Lit – 'Cheers'. A toast in the Pays Nantais region.

Top Fermentation (Eng). In brewing, applied to ferments (yeasts) that stay on top of the brew. (Ales, Porter and Stout). Saccharomyces Cerevisiae.

Top Hat (Eng). ½ Guinness and ½ ginger beer mixed.

Top Hat Ale (Eng). A keg/bottled strong Ale 1046 O.G. brewed by the Burtonwood Brewery in Warrington, Cheshire.

Topicos (Gre). Country wines. (Fr) = Vins de Pays.

Top Island Bitter (Ch.Isles). A keg Best Bitter 1042 O.G. brewed by the Randalls Vautier Brewery in St. Helier, Jersey.

Top Notch Cocktail (Cktl). ¼ gill Sloe Gin, ¼ gill French vermouth, 1 teaspoon raspberry syrup. Stir over ice, strain into a cocktail glass. Serve with a cherry.

Top of the World (Cktl). 1 oz. Mandarine Napoléon, 1 oz. Tequila, 1 oz. grapefruit juice, 1 oz. orange juice, white of egg. Shake over ice, strain into a highball glass, top with soda water. Dress with mint, orange and lemon slices.

Topolčany Brewery (Czec). A brewery based in south-eastern Czec.

Topolos at Russian River Vineyards (USA). A winery based in Forestville, Sonoma County, California. Grape varieties – Cabernet sauvignon, Chardonnay, Petite syrah, Pinot noir and Zinfandel. Produces varietal wines.

Toppe-au-Vert (La) (Fr). A Premier Cru vineyard in the commune of Ladoix-Serrigny, A.C. Aloxe-Corton, Côte de Beaune, Burgundy.

Toppedt Szölöböl Keszült Bor (Hun). Denotes a wine produced from botrytis cinerea affected grapes (white).

Toppette (Afr). An alternative name for Grog on Mauritius off the west African coast.

Topping Smile (Cktl). ⅘ measure Cognac, ⅕ measure Drambuie, dash Anisette, dash Cherry brandy, dash lemon and orange juice. Stir over ice, strain into a cocktail glass.

Topping-Up (Eng). The filling of casks or jars with wine in order to fill the air space to prevent contamination.

Top Pressure (Eng). A method of forcing beer up from the cellar to the bar tap using CO_2 gas under pressure.

Topsy Turvy Ale (Eng). A strong Ale 1055 O.G. brewed by the Berrow Brewery in Burnhan-on-Sea, Somerset.

Top Tory (Cktl). ⅖ measure Scotch whisky, ⅖ measure Peachtree liqueur, ⅕ measure (white) Crème de Menthe, dash egg white, ½ measure Schweppes Tropical Juice. Shake well over ice, strain into a goblet, add a dash of blue Curaçao and a cherry.

Top-Up (Eng). A request for a glass of beer to be filled up after the head has settled and ended below the prescribed measure. e.g. 'Top it up' or 'Would you like a top up?'.

Torbato (It). A white grape variety grown in Sardinia. (Is related to the Malvasia).

Torcerse (Sp). Sour wine.

Torchiati (It). Vin de Presse.

Torchio (It). A traditional method of grape pressing used in the Tuscany region (Brunello di Montalcino).

Torconal (Chile). A wine-producing area of northern Chile near the Maipo river.

Toreador (Cktl). ⅔ measure Brandy, ⅓ measure Kahlúa, dash egg white. Shake over ice, serve 'on the rocks' in an old-fashioned glass.

Toreador Cocktail (Cktl). ¾ measure Tequila, ¼ measure (white) Crème de Cacao, 1 measure cream. Shake over ice, strain into a cocktail glass. Top with whipped cream and dust with cocoa powder.

Torera (La) (Sp). A brand of Manzanilla sherry from the Diez Hermanos range produced by Diez Merito.

Torgaio (It). A young, fruity, light Chianti from Ruffino. D.O.C.G.

Torgiano (It). An area of Umbria in which the town of Assisi is found. Produces red and white wines.

Torgiano Bianco (It). D.O.C. white wine from Umbria. Made from the Grechetto, Malvasia di candia, Malvasia toscano, Trebbiano toscano and Verdelho grapes in the commune of Torgiano.

Torgiano Rosso (It). D.O.C. red wine from Umbria. Made from the Ciliegiolo, Montepulciano, Sangiovese and Trebbiano toscano grapes grown within the commune of Torgiano.

Torgiano Torre di Giano (It). See Torgiano Bianco.

Tormore (Scot). A single Malt whisky distillery at Advie, 7 miles north of Grantown-on-Spey, Morayshire. Owned by Long John Distilleries. A Highland malt. Produces a 10 year old malt. 43% alc. by vol.

Tornado (Hol). A pineapple liqueur using Hawaiian fruit. 43% alc. by vol.

Tornado (Sp). The equivalent to the (Fr) = Tourne.

Torna-Viagem (Port). The name given to a Setúbal wine which has been shipped to and from the tropics like the old Madeiras. Was used as the ship's ballast. Lit – 'Back from a journey'

Tornay (Bernard) (Fr). Récoltants-manipulants in Champagne. Address = 51150 Bouzy, Tours sur Marne. Produces – Vintage and non-vintage wines.

Toro (Sp). A wine-producing area in northern Spain. Grape varieties – Albillo, Aragonés, Jaén, Tempranillo and Valencia. Produces mainly red wines.

Toro (Sp). A full-bodied red wine from La Nava, Castile.

Torontel (Chile). A white grape variety.

Toronto Cocktail (Cktl). ⅛ gill Scotch whisky, ⅛ gill Dubonnet, ¼ gill Gin. Stir over ice, strain into a cocktail glass. Serve with a cherry and a dash of lemon peel juice.

Torrar (Port). Denotes the roasting of the green coffee beans.

Torre à Decima (It). A Chianti Putto producer based in Tuscany.

Torre a Mosciano (Le) (It). A noted Chianti Putto producer based in Tuscany.

Torrebreba (Sp). Area within Andalusia whose grapes go to make Sherry.

Torre Ercolana (It). A red wine produced by Bruno Colacicchi in Latium.

Torre Giulia (It). A full-bodied white wine produced by the Foggia Vineyards in Puglia.

Torremilanos (Sp). A brand-name used by Bodegas Peñalba López in Ribera del Duero.

Torrentés (Sp). A white grape variety grown in Galicia. Also spelt Torrontés.

Torres (Sp). Brandy producer. Address = Bodegas Miguel Torres, Apartado 13 – Commercio 22, Vilafranca del Penedés, Barcelona. Source of base wine is 2nd pressing of Parellada vines in Penedés.

Torres (Sp). A large wine producer in the

Penedés region of south-eastern Spain. Address = Bodegas Miguel Torres, Apartado 13 Commercio 22, Vilafranca del Penedés, Barcelona. Produces fine wines – Viña Sol, Gran Viña Sol, Gran Sangre de Toro, Viña Magdala, Tres Torres Sangredetoro, De Casta Rosado, San Valentin, Viña Esmeralda, Coronas and Gran Coronas. Also brandies.

Torres de Serrano (Sp). A range of wines produced by VINIVAL based in Valencia.

Torresella (It). A winery that produces Vino da Tavola wines. Noted for their labels depicting endangered bird species. Wines made from grapes grown in the Trentino-Alto Adige and Friuli Venezia Giulia regions of north-eastern Italy.

Torres Miguel Winery (Chile). Associated with Torres of Spain. Noted wines produced from Cabernet and Sauvignon grapes.

Torres Vedras (Port). A white wine area in the region of Estremadura on the plains of the river Tejo. Grape varieties – Alicanté, Fernão Pires, Garnpal, Grand noir and João de Santarém.

Torre Vinaria (Sp). The name given to a modern gravity-fed tower that is used in wine production.

Torridora (Cktl). ⅗ measure white Rum, ⅕ measure Kahlúa, ⅕ measure cream. Shake over ice, strain into a cocktail glass. Float ½ fl.oz. dark Rum on top.

Torri Syched (Wales). To quench one's thirst.

Torrontés (Sp). See Torrentés.

Tortosi (Sp). A white grape variety grown in Valencia. Also known as the Bobal blanco.

Tórula (Sp). An inactive yeast present on grape skins.

Torula Compniacensis (Lat). A black fungus that lives off the alcohol fumes and grows on the roof and walls of spirit warehouses.

Torulaspora (Sp). See Tórula.

Torys (Jap). The brand-name of a Whiskey produced by Suntory.

Tosca (Eng). A bitter-sweet apéritif (orange bitters) produced by Matthew Clark. 17% alc. by vol.

Toscana (It). Tuscany. A wine region of central Italy. Noted for its Chianti wines.

Toscana Bianca (It). The Vino da Tavola of Tuscany. Used to be known as white Chianti before red Chianti became well-known.

Toscanello (It). The 2 litre wicker-covered flask used for white wines of Orvieto.

Toso (Jap). A sweet, spicy style of Saké that is usually drunk at the New Year.

Toso Pascual Winery (Arg). A winery based at San José. Is noted for its Cabernet toso, Riesling and sparkling wines.

Toss Off (Eng) (slang). A term to denote the drinking of a drink in one gulp.

Tosti (It). Noted producers of a range of Vermouths, Marsala and sparkling wines. Based in Canelli.

Tot (Eng). A measure. No specific capacity. Depends on the region and laws. Denotes a measure of spirits, fortified wines or cordial.

Total Acidity (Eng). The sum of fixed acids and volatile acids usually expressed in terms of grammes per litre (g/litre).

Total Acids (Eng). The sum of all the acids found in grape must.

Total Extract (Eng). See Extract.

Total Pledge (USA). See T. Pledge.

Totara Fu Gai (N.Z.). A white wine blend of Chasselas, Chenin blanc, Müller-Thurgau and Muscat grapes produced by the Totara SYC.

Totara SYC (N.Z.). A winery near Te Kauwhata. Unique in that it is owned by the Chinese.

Totara Vineyards (N.Z.). A winery based in Thames, North Island.

Tou Brewery (Nor). A brewery based in Stavanger, south-west Norway. Brews Tuborg Lager under licence.

Toul (Fr). A vin gris (rosé wine) of Toul in Lorraine in eastern France.

Toulenne (Fr). A commune in the A.C. Graves district in south-western Bordeaux.

Toulon-la-Montagne (Fr). A Cru Champagne village in Canton de Verzy. District = Châlons.

Touniller (Ch.Isles). Cooper.

Tour (La) (Fr). A wine-producing district of A.C. Bellet, provence, southern France.

Touraine (Fr). A.C. wine district of the central Loire. Produces red, rosé, white (still and sparkling) wines. See Vouvray, Chinon, Bourgueil. Minimum alc. by vol. (red) = 9% and (white) = 9.5%. Grape varieties – Arbois, Breton, Cabernet sauvignon, Chardonnay, Chenin blanc, Cot, Gamay, Groslôt, Pinot d'Aunis, Pinot meunier and Sauvignon blanc.

Touraine-Amboise (Fr). A.C. area of the Touraine district in the Loire. Red, rosé and white wines are produced.

Touraine Azay-le-Rideau (Fr). An A.C. red, rosé and white wine area within the district of the Touraine in the central Loire.

Touraine-Mesland (Fr). An area of the Touraine in the central Loire. Produces red, rosé and white wines.

Touraine Mousseux (Fr). An old designation of the sparkling wines of the Touraine district in the central Loire.

Touraine Pétillant (Fr). An old designation of the slightly sparkling wines of the Touraine district in the central Loire.

Tour Blanche [La] (Fr). A vineyard belonging to the French government at the commune of Bommes (Sauternes) making sweet white wines.

Tour Carnet (La) (Fr). Address = Saint Laurent de Médoc, Médoc. A.C. Haut-Médoc. Commune = Saint Laurent. 31 ha. Grape varieties – Cabernet franc, Cabernet sauvignon, Merlot and Petit verdot.

Tour de Mons [La] (Fr). Cru Bourgeois. A.C. Margaux.

Tour des Combes (Fr). Grand Cru Classé. A.C. Saint-Émilion. Commune = Saint Laurent des Combes. 17 ha. Grape varieties – Cabernet franc, Cabernet sauvignon and Merlot.

Tour du Vatican (Fr). A red wine produced by Château Hanteillon in the commune of Cissac, Médoc, north-western Bordeaux.

Touriga (Port). A red grape variety similar to the Cabernet franc of France used in the making of Port.

Touriga Francesa (Port). A red grape variety used in the production of Port.

Touriga Nacional (Port). A red grape variety used in the production of Port and Dão wines to give body and fruit.

Tourigão (Port). A red grape variety used in the production of Port to give body.

Tourigo (Port). See Touriga.

Tourigo-do-Dão (Port). A red grape variety grown in the Dão region to make red wines.

Tourinio (Fr). A medium-dry white wine produced in Corsica.

Tourlopsis (Lat). A slime-forming spoilage yeast. Attacks low-acid musts and wines that have not been sulphated.

Tour Martillac [La] (Fr). A vineyard in the commune of Martillac. A.C. Graves, Bordeaux.

Tourne (Fr). Bacterial spoilage of wine by the bacteria Tartarophtorum. The wine loses colour and acidity. Tartaric acid and Glycerol being totally lost. (Sp) = Tornado.

Tourne-Bride (Fr). Referred to a country inn situated near a Château. Servants of visitors would be lodged here.

Tournée (Fr). A round (of drinks).

Tournon (Fr). A small district on the right bank of the Rhône. Produces red and white wines.

Tournus (Fr). A wine-producing area in the Saône-et-Loire Département, central-eastern France.

Tours-sur-Marne (Fr). A Grand Cru Champagne village in the Canton d'Ay. District = Reims. (Red grapes).

Tours-sur-Marne (Fr). A Premier Cru Champagne village in the Canton d'Ay. District = Reims. (White grapes).

Toussaints (Les) (Fr). A Premier Cru vineyard in the A.C. commune of Beaune, Côte de Beaune, Burgundy. 6.43 ha.

Tout Court (Fr). Simple wine.

Touzac (Fr). A commune in the Charente Département whose grapes are classed Grande Champagne (Cognac).

Tovarich Cocktail (Cktl). ⅔ measure Vodka, ⅓ measure Kümmel, juice ½ lime. Shake over ice, strain into a cocktail glass.

Tow (Eng). Wax used to plug the necks of wine bottles in the seventeenth century.

Tower Bitter (Eng). A cask conditioned Bitter 1036 O.G. brewed by the Bass Brewery. Formerly known as Brew Ten.

Tower Brewery (Eng). A nineteenth-century style of brewery designed so that after the malt and water are raised to the top of the building, the materials flow downwards with gravity.

Towerkop (S.Afr). A brand-name of the Ladismith Co-operative, Klein Karoo.

Tower of London (Sp). A brand of dry Gin produced by Cocal in Telde, Canary Islands.

Townend (Eng). A producer of a large range of egg-based drinks based in Hull, Humberside.

Towngate Special (Eng). A cask conditioned Ale 1043 O.G. brewed by the Crouch Vale Brewery, Essex.

T. Pledge (USA). Total Pledge. Taken in the nineteenth century by people who vowed to abstain from all types of alcohol.

Trabalhadores (Port). The name given to the grape treaders.

Traben-Trarbach (Ger). Village. (Anb) = Mosel-Saar-Ruwer. (Ber) = Bernkastel. (Gro) = Schwarzlay. (Vils) = Burgweg, Gaispfad, Huhnerberg, Königsberg, Kräuterhaus, Kreuzberg, Schlossberg, Taubenhaus, Ungsberg, Würzgarten, Zollturm.

Traben-Trarbach [ortsteil Starkenburg] (Ger). Village. (Anb) = Mosel-Saar-Ruwer. (Ber) = Bernkastel. (Gro) = Schwarzlay. (Vin) = Rosengarten.

Traben-Trarbach [ortsteil Wolf] (Ger). Village. (Anb) = Mosel-Saar-Ruwer.

T

(Ber) = Bernkastel. (Gro) = Schwarz-lay. (Vins) = Auf der Heide, Goldgrube, Klosterberg, Schatzgarten, Sonnenlay.

Trace Elements (Eng). Elements in the soil that go to produce fine wines. Iodine, Manganese, Molybedenum, Nickel, Vanadium, Zinc.

Trachyte (Hun). Volcanic rock on which the grapes for Tokay are grown.

Tracy (Fr). A commune in the Central Vineyards district of the Loire which produces A.C. Pouilly Fumé.

Trade Descriptions Act (Eng). An Act of Parliament passed in 1968 to protect the purchaser from inferior goods or goods that are sold different to the sales description. e.g. Scotch whisky being sold as Malt whisky, Vins de Pays wines being sold as A.C. wines, etc. (Fr) = Réclame Trompeuse. (Ger) = Unlauterer Wettbewerb. (Hol) = Misleidende Reklame.

Trader Vic's Broadway Bar (Eng). The only L.V.A. – owned public house in the U.K. Based in Huddersfield, Yorkshire.

Trader Vic's Punch (Cktl). 1¼ ozs. light Rum, 1¼ ozs. Jamaican Rum, ½ teaspoon Orgeat syrup, teaspoon sugar, slice pineapple, juice of ½ orange and ½ lemon. Shake over ice, pour unstrained into a highball glass. Add pineapple and straws.

Traditional (Eng). A term applied to beer that has been brewed using a mash tun, open fermenters and no filtration, pasteurisation or re-carbonation.

Tradition Impériale (Fr). A 20–25 year old Cognac produced by Menard.

Trago (S.Am). The local name in Colombia given to Rum that is drunk neat in a single shot (measure).

Traisen (Ger). Village. (Anb) = Nahe. (Ber) = Schloss Böckelheim. (Gro) = Burgweg. (Vins) = Bastei, Kickelskopf, Nonnengarten, Rotenfels.

Traiskirchen (Aus). A wine village near Gumpoldskirchen. Produces mainly medium-sweet and dry white wines.

Traismauer-Carnuntum (Aus). A wine-producing district in the Nieder-österreich region.

Trait (Eng). Describes a small quantity of liquor (approx. 1 teaspoonful) used in cocktail preparations.

Trajadura (Port). A white grape variety used in the making of Vinhos Verdes.

Trakia (Bul). A red wine produced from a blend of 60% Mavrud and 40% Pamid grapes.

Trakia (Rum). Well-balanced red and white wines shipped to the USA.

Trakya (Tur). The alternative name for Thrace in north-western Turkey. A major wine-producing region.

Trakya (Tur). Red and white wines, the red light and dry, the white (from the Sémillon grape) dry and medium bodied.

Tralles (It). A scale used for measuring the strength of alcohol in wines and spirits. Similar to Gay Lussac.

Tramery (Fr). A Cru Champagne village in the Canton de Ville-en-Tardenois. District = Reims.

Traminac (Yug). The local name for the Traminer grape grown in the Slovenia and Vojvodina regions.

Traminer (Euro). A white grape variety grown in eastern Europe. Low in acidity. The best is the Gewürztraminer.

Traminer Aromatico (It). A name for the white Gewürztraminer grape in the Trentino-Alto Adige.

Traminer Musqué (Fr). An alternative name for the Gewürztraminer.

Tramini (Hun). A local name for the Traminer grape.

Tramontana (Sp). The north wind that blows through the Penedés region in the winter months.

Tranchette (Fr). A cone-shaped glass that evolved from French Inns. Travellers had to drink up before they could set the glass (inverted) on the table.

Trancy (Fr). A red wine area in Auxerre, Yonne Département, Burgundy.

Tranksteuer (Aus). Wine taxes introduced in 1780 by the Empress Maria Theresa.

Tranquillity Tea (Cktl). 1 measure Brandy, 1 pint hot tea, 1 teaspoon instant coffee, 1 teaspoon lemon juice, 1 tablespoon milk powder (mixed with a little water), dash vanilla essence, sugar syrup to taste. Whisk milk and lemon juice together, heat remaining ingredients, pour into glasses, add the topping in a swirl.

Transcaucasia (Asia). The place where the genius Vitis is thought to have originated.

Transdanubia (Hun). A wine-producing region that stretches between the rivers Danube and Drava.

Transetcom S.A. (Gre). A noted wine merchant based near Patras in the Peloponnese.

Transfer Method (Eng). A process of making sparkling wine where the second fermentation takes place in the bottle and then is filtered in a tank under pressure and re-bottled.

Transfusion (Eng) (slang). A term often used for the 'Hair of the dog'.

Transvasage (Fr). See Transvasion.

Transvasée (Fr). The method of transferring Champagne off its lees (sediment) into another bottle. Most of the bubbles were destroyed. This method was used before Dégorgement was introduced.

Transvasion (Fr). Second fermentation in bottle then dégorgement under pressure into refrigerated tanks, dosage added, clarified and filtered then re-bottled under pressure at 3°C. (Eng) = Transfer method.

Trappe (La) (Hol). Trappist ale 6.5% alc. by vol. brewed by Schaapskooi Abbaye Brouwerij, Tilburg, Brabant.

Trapiche (Arg). A premium wine produced by Peñaflor.

Trapiche Syrup (Cktl). A cocktail ingredient. ½ lb. cane sugar, ½ teaspoon ground cinnamon, ½ teaspoonful ground cloves, ¾ pint heated orange juice. Stir together, cool, strain into bottles.

Trappenberg (Ger). Grosslage. (Anb) = Rheinpfalz. (Ber) = Südliche Weinstrasse. (Vils) = Altdorf, Bellheim, Böbingen, Bornheim, Essingen, Freimersheim, Gross u. Kleinfischlingen, Hochstadt, Knittelsheim, Lustadt, Ottersheim, Römerberg, Schwegenheim, Venningen, Weingarten, Zeiskam.

Trappist Beers (Bel). Belgian real draught beers. Top fermented ales (not lagers), bottle conditioned, vary in strength from 5.7% to 12% alc. by vol. From the Belgian Trappist abbayes of Chimay, Orval, Rochefort, St. Sixtus, Westmalle. Also from Schaapskool in the Netherlands.

Trappistine (Fr). A herb liqueur with a base of Armagnac brandy. Yellow green in colour. From the Abbaye de la Grâce de Dieu, Doubs.

Traquair House Brewery (Scot). Based near Innerleithen, Peeblesshire. Noted for its cask conditioned Bear Ale 1050 O.G. and Tranquair House Ale 1075 O.G.

Trasanejas (Sp). The name given to a special Málaga which has been produced from Solera wines that contain casks of over 200 years of age.

Trasfegar (Port). To decant. Trasfega = The decanting or racking of the wine off its lees.

Trasiego (Sp). Decanting or racking of the wine off its lees.

Tras os Montes (Port). Lit – 'Across the mountains'. North-east from river Douro. Produces red, rosé and pétillant wines.

Trattore (It). Innkeeper, landlord.

Trattoria (It). Inn.

Traube (Ger). Grape.

Traubenmaische (Ger). Unfermented grape mash containing less than 5 grams of grape sugar.

Traubenmost (Aus) (Ger). Grape must.

Traubenmost-Konzentrat (Ger). Grape must concentrate (the dehydrated juice of Traubenmost or Traubenmaische).

Traubensaft (Ger). Grape juice, Must.

Traubensaftkonzentrat (Ger). Concentrated grape must.

Traubisoda (Aus). A carbonated nonalcoholic grape juice drink for export to Muslim countries.

Trauersdorf (Aus). A wine-producing area in the Mattersburg district.

Trautberg (Ger). Vineyard. (Anb) = Franken. (Ber) = Steigerwald. (Gro) = Herrenberg. (Vil) = Castell.

Trautlestal (Ger). Vineyard. (Anb) = Franken. (Ber) = Maindreieck. (Gro) = Burg. (Vil) = Hammelburg.

Travaglini (It). A top wine producer based in Piemonte. Produces D.O.C. Gattinara.

Travarice (Yug). A generic name for fruit brandies with herbs added.

Trawal Wynkelders (S.Afr). Based in the Olifants River area. Address = Box 2, Klawer 8145. Does not bottle, but sells wine to other co-operatives.

Trbjan (Yug). The name of a red wine produced on the west Croatian coast.

Trboljan (Yug). A red wine produced on the north-western Dalmatian coast.

Treading (Eng). An old method of crushing grapes with the feet using spiked shoes or bare feet. Now little used except in Portugal and Madeira. Very labour intensive.

Treaty of Windsor (Port). 1353.

Trebbianello (It). A white grape variety grown in Lombardy. Also known as the Tocai friulano.

Trebbiano (It). A white grape variety which produces fine dry white wines. Many varieties. Known in France as the Ugni blanc.

Trebbiano d'Abruzzo (It). A white grape variety grown in Abruzzi. Also known as the Bombino bianco.

Trebbiano d'Abruzzo (It). D.O.C. white wine from Abruzzi. Made from the Trebbiano d'Abruzzo, Trebbiano toscano, Coccocciola, Malvasia toscana and Passerina grapes. Produced throughout the Abruzzi region.

Trebbiano di Aprilia (It). See Merlot di Aprilia.

Trebbiano di Lugana (It). A white grape variety grown in the Lombardy region.

Trebbiano di Romagna (It). A white grape variety grown in the Emilia-Romagna region.

Trebbiano di Romagna (It). D.O.C. white wine from the Emilia-Romagna. Made from the Trebbiano di Romagna grape. D.O.C. also applies to the Spumante wine (dry, semi-sweet and sweet) produced within a defined area in accordance to regulations.

Trebbiano di Soave (It). A white grape variety grown in the Lombardy region. Also known as the Trebbiano nostrano.

Trebbiano Giallo (It). A white grape variety grown in the Lazio region. Also known as the Castelli romani in Lombardy.

Trebbiano Nostrano (It). See Trebbiano di Soave.

Trebbiano Romagnolo (It). A white grape variety grown in the Emilia-Romagna. See Trebbiano di Romagna.

Trebbiano Toscano (It). A white grape variety grown in northern Italy. Also known as the Castelli romani.

Trebbiano Val Trebbia (It). D.O.C. white wine from the Emilia-Romagna region. Made from the Trebbiano romagnolo, Malvasia di candia, Moscato bianco, Ortrugo and Sauvignon grapes. Vinification can take place throughout the 4 communes.

Trebbiano Verde (It). A white grape variety grown in the Latium region.

Trebellicanum (Lat). A red wine produced in central-western Italy in Roman times.

Trebern (Aus). A spirit distilled from apples.

Treble Gold Ale (Eng). A strong Ale 1052 O.G. brewed and bottled by the Ind Coope Brewery in Burton-on-Trent for Friary Meux.

Treble Gold Cocktail (Cktl). 1 measure Avocaat, ½ measure Crème de Banana, dash orange juice. Shake over ice, strain into an ice-filled highball glass. Top with tonic water.

Treble Seven Mild (Eng). A keg dark Mild 1034 O.G. brewed by the Gales Brewery in Horndean, Hampshire.

Třeboň Brewery (Czec). An ancient brewery based in south-western Czec.

Trebujena (Sp). An area in the Jerez Supérieur district.

Trechtingshausen (Ger). Village. (Anb) = Mittelrhein. (Ber) = Bacharach. (Gro) = Schloss Reichenstein. (Vin) = Morgenbachtaler.

Trefethen Winery (USA). A winery based in the Napa Valley, northern California. 300 ha. Grape varieties – Cabernet sauvignon, Chardonnay, Johannisberg riesling, Merlot and Pinot noir. Produces varietal and table wines.

Tre Fontane (It). A liqueur produced by the Cistercian monks just outside Rome. Produce both a green and yellow variety. Flavoured with Eucalyptus leaves.

Tregnum (Scot). A bottle of Whisky containing 3 standard bottles. 80 fl.ozs. Used by Long John Whisky only.

Tregrehan Claret (Austr). A red wine from Angoves, South Australia. A blend of Cabernet and Shiraz grapes.

Treilles (Fr). A commune in the region of Fitou, southern France.

Treis-Karden (Ger). Village. (Anb) = Mosel-Saar-Ruwer. (Ber) = Zell/ Mosel. (Gro) = Goldbäumchen. (Vins) = Dechantsberg, Juffermauer, Münsterberg.

Treiso (It). A commune in the D.O.C. Barbaresco, Piemonte.

Treixadura (Sp). A white grape variety grown in the Ribeiro area of northwestern Spain.

Trellis-Training (Fr). See Palissage.

Trelou-sur-Marne (Fr). A Cru Champagne village in the Canton de Condéen-Brie. District = Château Thierry.

Tren (Sp). The name given to the bottling line where bottles are filled.

Trentadue Winery (USA). A winery and vineyard based in the Alexander Valley, Sonoma County, California. 83 ha. Grape varieties – Aleatico, Carignane, Early burgundy, French colombard, Ruby cabernet and Sémillon. Produces varietal and table wines.

Trent Bitter (Eng). A bottled/canned takehome Bitter 1032 O.G. brewed by Allied Breweries.

Trentino-Alto Adige (It). The northernmost region of Italy. Situated on the Austrian and Swiss border. Also known as the Südtirol in German. See Venezia Tridentina. Became Italian in 1919. See also Süd-Tirol.

Trentino Cabernet (It). D.O.C. red wine from the Trentino-Alto Adige. Made from the Cabernet franc and Cabernet sauvignon grapes. Must be aged 2 years. (If 3 years classed Riserva).

Trentino Lagrein (It). D.O.C. red wine from the Trentino-Alto Adige. Made from the Lagrein grape. Must be aged 1 year. (If 2 years then classed Riserva).

Trentino Marzemino (It). D.O.C. red wine from the Trentino-Alto Adige. Made from the Marzemino grape. Must be aged 1 year minimum. (If 2 years then classed Riserva).

Trentino Merlot (It). D.O.C. red wine from the Trentino-Alto Adige. Made from the Merlot grape. Must be aged 1 year minimum. (If aged 2 years then classed Riserva).

Trentino Moscato (It). D.O.C. white wine from the Trentino-Alto Adige. Made from the Moscato giallo and Moscato rosa grapes. Must be aged 1 year minimum. (If aged 2 years then classed Riserva). D.O.C. also applies to fortified wines.

Trentino Pinot (It). D.O.C. white wine from the Trentino-Alto Adige. Made from the Pinot bianco and Pinot grigio grapes. Must be aged 1 year minimum. (2 years then classed Riserva). D.O.C. also applies to the sparkling wines made from the Pinot bianco grapes.

Trentino Pinot Nero (It). D.O.C. red wine from the Trentino-Alto Adige. Made from the Pinot nero grape. Must be aged 1 year minimum. (If 2 years then classed Riserva).

Trentino Riesling (It). D.O.C. red wine from the Trentino-Alto Adige. Made from the Riesling italico, Riesling renano and Riesling sylvaner grapes.

Trentino Traminer Aromatico (It). D.O.C. white wine from the Trentino-Alto Adige. Made from the Gewürztraminer grape.

Trentino Vino Santo (It). D.O.C. white wine from the Trentino-Alto Adige. Made from the Pinot bianco grape (partly dried to raise the grape sugar level). D.O.C. also applies to fortified wines Must be aged 1 year minimum. (If 2 years then classed Riserva).

Trent Mild (Eng). A bottled 'Take-home' Mild beer 1033 O.G. brewed by Allied Breweries.

Trepat (Sp). A white grape variety grown in south-eastern Spain.

Treppchen (Ger). Vineyard. (Anb) = Mosel-Saar-Ruwer. (Ber) = Bernkastel. (Gro) = Michelsberg. (Vil) = Piesport.

Treppchen (Ger). Vineyard. (Anb) = Mosel-Saar-Ruwer. (Ber) = Bernkastel. (Gro) = Schwarzlay. (Vil) = Erden.

Treppchen (Ger). Vineyard. (Anb) = Mosel-Saar-Ruwer. (Ber) = Zell/Mosel. (Gro) = Rosenhang. (Vil) = Treis-Karden.

Tresbolillo (Sp). The name for the diagonal pattern used when planting vines.

Tres Castillos (W.Ind). A sweet, aniseed-flavoured liqueur produced in Puerto Rico.

Tres Cepas (Sp). A 2 year old Brandy produced by Domecq.

Très Esquinas (S.Am). Lit – 'Three corners'. The brand-name of a Rum produced by the state-owned Industria Licorera de Bolivar Distillery in Colombia. Made from molasses distilled twice. Is sold in a triangular bottle.

Treslon (Fr). A Cru Champagne village in the Canton of Ville-en-Tardenois. District = Reims.

Tres Magueyes (Mex). A noted Tequila producer and brand-name of their Tequila.

Tres Marias (Port). A brand of slightly sweet Vinho Verde produced in Vizela.

Trésor de Famille (Fr). An Armagnac produced by La Croix de Salles.

Tres Palmas (Sp). A brand of Fino sherry produced by La Riva.

Tresques (Fr). A commune of the region Laudun in the south-west Rhône. Produces red, rosé and white wines.

Très Rare Heritage (Fr). A 30–35 year old Cognac produced by Brillet. 45% alc. by vol.

Tres Rayas (Sp). Lit – 'Three strokes'. Used in Sherry production. Marks on a Sherry butt to denote that the wine is destined as ordinary wine to be used for cleaning and seasoning casks. See Raya.

Tressalier (Fr). The name given to the Sacy grape in Bourbonnais, eastern France. Used in the making of St. Pourçain.

Tressat (Fr). See Tressot.

Très Sec (Fr). Very dry.

Tressler Process (USA). The method of making Sherry-type wines. After fortification the wines are stored in special vats at temperatures of over 125°F for several weeks during which time oxygen is bubbled through the wine. When the Sherry flavour is obtained they are aged in vats for set times.

Tressot (Fr). A red grape variety grown in the Yonne to make Bourgogne rouge.

Tresterbranntwein (Ger). A Brandy made from distilling the residue of grape pressings after wine-making. Also known as Tresterschnapps.

Trestergeschmack (Aus). A term to describe a wine that tastes of grape cap (from being left too long in the mash or pressed too late). See also Tresterln.

Tresterhut (Ger). The name given to the cap of pulp, skins and pips.

Tresterln (Aus). See Trestergeschmack.

Tresterschnapps (Ger). A style of Brandy distilled from grape skins. Similar to French Marc. See Tresterbranntwein.

Tres Torres Sangredetoro (Sp). An oak (American) aged red wine produced by Torres in Penedés from 60% Garnacha and 40% Cariñena.

Très Vieille Grande Réserve (Fr). A 50 year old Cognac produced by Salignac.

Très Vieux Dillon (W.Ind). The brand-name of a dark Rum produced by Bardinet in north-western Martinique.

Treuenfels (Ger). Vineyard. (Anb) = Nahe. (Ber) = Schloss Böckelheim. (Gro) = Burgweg. (Vil) = Altenbamberg.

T

Treviris Glass (Ger). Made in Trier. Have shallow bowls with a particular pattern of cutting on them. Used to serve Mosel wines.

Treviso (It). A wine town north of Venice noted for its Prosecco wine.

Tri (Fr). The 'sorting out' of the grapes. Selecting those that have botrytis cinerea, occurs in Sauternes.

Tria Corda (S.Afr). A red Médoc-style wine made from 70% Cabernet and 30% Merlot grapes by the Overgaauw Estate in Stellenbosch.

Triage (Eng). A grade of Coffee bean. One that is broken or too short.

Triage (Fr). The separation of unsound grapes at harvest time. Used in the southern Rhône. (Châteauneuf-du-Pape and Tavel).

Trialcohols (Eng). An alcohol that has 3 carbon atoms attached to the hydroxyl group.

Trial Finings (Eng). The name given to a quantity of fining agent used to ascertain the minimum amount of fining agent needed to clear a wine.

Tricastin (Fr). See Coteaux de Tricastin.

Tricorne (Eng). A wine label used by the Three Corners Vineyard in Kent.

Trier (Ger). Village. (Anb) = Mosel-Saar-Ruwer. (Ber) = Saar-Ruwer. (Gro) = Römerlay. (Vins) = Altenberg, Andreasberg, Augenscheiner, Benediktinerberg, Burgberg, Deutschherrenberg, Deutschherrenköpfchen, Domherrenberg, Hammerstein, Herrenberg, Jesuitenwingert, Karthäuserhofberg Burgberg, Karthäuserhofberg Kronenberg, Karthäuserhofberg Orthsberg, Karthäuserhofberg Sang, Karthauserhofberg Stirn, Kupp, Kurfürstenhofberg, Leikaul, Marienholz, Maximiner, Rotlay, St. Martiner Hofberg, St. Matheiser, St. Maxitheiser, St. Maximiner Kreuzberg, St Petrusberg, Sonnenberg, Thiergarten, Felsköpfchen, Thiergarten unterm Kreuz.

Tries-Karden (Ger). Village. (Anb) = Mosel-Saar-Ruwer. (Ber) = Zell/Mosel. (Gro) = Rosenhang. (Vins) = Greth, Kapellenberg, Treppchen.

Triesner (Euro). The name given to the wines produced from Triesen in Liechtenstein.

Trifalter (Aus). A light, spicy white wine from the Traminer grape, produced in the Wachau district.

Trifesti (USSR). A dessert wine made from the Pinot gris grape in the Moldavia region.

Trigny (Fr). A Cru Champagne village in the Canton de Fismes. District = Reims.

Trilby Cocktail (Cktl). ⅔ measure Bourbon whiskey, ⅓ measure Italian vermouth, 2 dashes Campari. Stir over ice, strain into a cocktail glass.

Trimbach (Fr). An Alsace wine négociant-éleveur. Address = 15 Route de Bergheim, 68150 Ribeauville. Also produces Eau-de-vie. 28 ha.

Trincadeira (Port). A red grape variety grown in Ribatejo.

Trincadeira Branca (Port). A white grape variety grown near Bucelas.

Trincar (Sp). To drink a toast, to good health.

Trinchieri (It). Tonic wine.

Trinidad Distillers Ltd (W.Ind). A large Rum distillery based at Lavenville, Trinidad. Produces – Kairi, Limbo Drummer, Old Oak, Royal Oak Twelve and White Drummer Rums.

Trinidad Punch (Cktl). 1½ fl.ozs. dark Rum, 1 fl.oz. lime juice, 2 dashes Angostura, teaspoon Gomme syrup. Shake over ice, strain into an ice-filled goblet. Top with grated nutmeg and a twist of lemon.

Trinidad Rum (W.Ind). A light, medium-coloured Rum from Trinidad which is light in flavour with a slight sweet taste.

Trinity (Cktl). ⅓ measure Gin, ⅓ measure French vermouth, ⅓ measure Italian vermouth. Stir over ice, strain into a cocktail glass.

Trinity Vine (USA). An old vine grown in the western region in the eighteenth and nineteenth centuries.

Trinquer (Fr). To touch glasses in a toast.

Triomphe (Fr). A 40 year old Cognac produced by Hine in Jarnac.

Tripel (Bel). A Golden Trappist Ale 8% alc. by vol. from the Abbaye of Westmalle Brasserie on the Dutch border.

Triple Alliance (Cktl). ½ measure French vermouth, ¼ measure Gin, ¼ measure Glayva. Stir over ice, strain into a 5 oz. cocktail glass.

Triple B-Boons Birthday Beer (Eng). Produced by Clarks Brewery in Wakefield, Yorkshire to commemorate the birthday of their founder Henry Boon who was born in 1906.

Triple Crown (Can). A Canadian rye whiskey produced by Gilbey Canada Ltd.

Triple Crown Bitter (Eng). A keg Bitter 1033 O.G. brewed by the Usher Brewery in Trowbridge, Wiltshire. Also sold under the Manns Brewery label.

Triple Distilled (U.K). Refers to Irish whiskey which differs from the Scottish Malt whisky which is only double distilled (except the Auchentoschen Distillery which is triple distilled).

Triple Or (Fr). An orange and Cognac liqueur.

Triple Sec (Fr). A very sweet, white Curaçao.

Triplex (Eng). A Bitter 1044 O.G. brewed by the Hermitage Brewery in West Sussex.

Tris (Fr). A term used to describe the continuous picking of the vineyard to obtain the ripest grapes.

Trittenheim (Ger). Village. (Anb) = Mosel-Saar-Ruwer. (Ber) = Bernkastel. (Gro) = Michelsberg (Vins) = Altärchen, Apotheke, Felsenkopf, Leiterchen.

Triumph (Fr). A variety of Barley malt which gives high sugar. Carmargue, Corgi, Doublet and Heriot are species.

Triumphator (Ger). The name of the Doppelbock beer brewed by the Löwenbräu Brauerei in Munich.

Triunfo (Mad). A black Vitis vinifera grape variety used in the production of Madeira.

Trnava Brewery (Czec). A brewery based in south-eastern Czec.

Trnovo (Bul). A wine region of northern Bulgaria. Produces red, white, dessert and sparkling wines.

Trocadero Cocktail (Cktl). ¼ gill Italian vermouth, ¼ gill French vermouth, 1 dash Orange bitters, 1 dash Grenadine. Stir over ice, strain into a cocktail glass. Add a cherry and a squeeze of lemon peel juice on top.

Trocken (Ger). Dry.

Trockenbeerenauslese (Aus). Produced from botrytis attacked grapes. Must have a mimimum must weight of 30° KMW.

Trockenbeerenauslese (Ger). A wine that has been made from Edelfäule (Noble rot) attacked grapes. 150° Oechsle minimum.

Trockenverbessert (Ger). Equivalent to Chaptalisation.

Troesmes (Fr). A Premier Cru Chablis vineyard. Often reclassified as the Premier Cru vineyard Beauroy.

Troika Cocktail (Cktl). ⅔ measure orange Chartreuse, ⅓ measure Vodka, juice ½ lime. Shake over ice, strain into a cocktail glass.

Trois Ceps (Les) (Fr). The local Chablis wine growers' fraternity founded in 1965. Meets in November and January.

Trois Glorieuses (Fr). The name given to the Hospices de Beaune sales held in November (3ʳᵈ Sunday) in Beaune, Burgundy.

Troisième Cru (Fr). Third growths of the 1855 classification of the Médoc in western Bordeaux.

Troisième Taille (Fr). Fourth pressing of Champagne grapes. 266 litres of grape must is produced.

Trois-Puits (Fr). A Premier Cru Champagne village in the Canton de Reims. District = Reims.

Trois Rivières (Cktl). ⅔ measure Canadian rye whiskey, ⅙ measure red Dubonnet, ⅙ measure Cointreau. Shake over ice, strain into an ice-filled old-fashioned glass. Top with a twist of orange peel juice.

Trois-Six (Fr). Lit – 'Three six'. A term often used for alcohol at 85% by volume as 3 parts of this alcohol with 3 parts of pure water produces 6 parts of Eau-de-vie.

Troissy-Bouquigny (Fr). A Cru Champagne village in the Canton de Dormans. District = Épernay.

Trojan Horse (Eng). ½ Guinness and ½ Cola.

Trokenbeerenauslese (Aus) (Ger). An alternative spelling of Trockenbeerenauslese.

Trokendiabetiker (Ger). A dry white wine produced by Bénédictine monks around Klosterberg in the Rheingau.

Trokenwein (Ger). Dry wine.

Trollberg (Ger). Vineyard. (Anb) = Nahe. (Ber) = Kreuznach. (Gro) = Schlosskapelle. (Vil) = Dorsheim.

Trollberg (Ger). Vineyard. (Anb) = Nahe. (Ber) = Kreuznach: (Gro) = Schlosskapelle. (Vil) = Münster-Sarmsheim.

Trollinger (Ger). Red grape variety grown in the Württemberg Anbaugebiet. Came originally from the Tirol, Austria. (Called the Tirollinger). Also known as the Black Hamburg, Black muscat, Blauer malvasier and Frankenthaler.

Tromel (Arg). The brand-name of a wine produced by Bodegas Gonzales Videla.

Tronçais (Fr). An oak used for casks in the Cognac brandy maturation.

Tronche (La) (Fr). A vineyard based in Vienne, Isère Département. Produces dry white wines.

Troödos (Cyp). A mountain where grape vines are grown in Cyprus. Best regions Makheras, Marathassa and Pitsilia. The Kokkineli red wine from the Mavron grape is the most widely produced.

Trophy Bitter (Eng). A keg Bitter 1035 O.G. brewed by the Whitbread Brewery. Brewed by Fremlins, Salford, Samlesbury and Sheffield Breweries. At the Cheltenham Brewery 1033 O.G. At Castle Eden Brewery a Special Trophy Bitter 1040 O.G. and in the north of England a cask Trophy Bitter 1037 O.G.

Tropical Cocktail (Cktl). ⅓ measure Maraschino, ⅓ measure (white) Crème de Cacao, ⅓ measure Noilly Prat, dash

Angostura. Stir over ice, strain into a cocktail glass.

Tropical Dawn (Cktl). ⅖ measure Gin, ⅕ measure Campari, ⅖ measure orange juice. Shake orange and Gin over ice, strain into an 8 fl.oz. goblet containing a ball of crushed ice. Add a dash of Campari, serve with straws.

Tropical Fruit Lotus Light (Eng). A blend of sparkling mineral water, British wine and tropical fruits. 4.5% alc. by vol.

Tropical Kiss Cocktail (Cktl). ⅕ measure Maraschino, ⅕ measure white Rum, ⅗ measure pineapple juice, dash Grenadine. Shake well over ice, strain into a scooped-out pineapple shell. Dress with a mint sprig and a cherry. Serve with straws.

Tropical Mimosa Cocktail (Cktl). ⅕ gill white Rum, ⅗ gill orange juice, dash Grenadine. Stir over ice, strain into a flute glass. Top with iced Champagne and a spiral of orange peel.

Tropical Spring (Eng). A sparkling, non-alcoholic soft drink produced by Schweppes. A blend of nine different fruits. Has 55% juice and 45% natural spring water with no sugar or preservatives.

Tropical Storm (Cktl). 1½ fl.oz. golden Rum, 1 fl.oz. orange juice, ½ fl.oz. Vodka, ½ fl.oz. lime juice, ½ fl.oz. pineapple juice, dash Angostura, dash Grenadine. Blend together with a scoop of crushed ice in a blender. Pour into a highball glass. Dress with an orange slice, cherry and banana slice. Serve with straws.

Tropical Tonic Cocktail (Cktl). ⅔ measure Malibu, ⅓ measure Mandarine Napoléon. Stir over ice in a highball glass. Top with ginger ale. Dress with a slice of orange and a cherry.

Tropicana (Cktl). ⅓ measure dry white wine, ⅔ measure grapefruit juice, 1 teaspoon Bénédictine, 1 teaspoon lemon juice. Shake over ice, strain into a goblet.

Tropicana (W.Ind). A white Caribbean Rum.

Tropicana (S.Am). The brand-name of a Rum produced in Guyana for Seagram. 40% alc. by vol.

Tropic of Capricorn (Cktl). 1½ fl.ozs. white Rum, ¾ fl.oz. (white) Crème de Cacao, 4 fl.ozs. orange juice, 1 egg white. Shake well over ice, strain into a highball glass. Top with a dash of blue Curaçao, orange slice and a cherry.

Trotsky (Eng). The brand-name used by Davis and Co. for a range of their liqueurs.

Trottevieille (Fr). See Château Trottevieille.

Troubador (Sp). The brand-name of a Sherry range produced by Cuesta in Puerto de Santa Maria.

Troublé (Fr). Lit – 'Troubled'. Denotes a hazy, cloudy wine.

Trouffières (Les) (Fr). A vineyard in the A.C. commune of Montagny, Côte Chalonnaise, Burgundy.

Trough Brewery (Eng). Opened in 1981 in Bradford, Lancashire. Noted for its cask conditioned Wild Boar 1039 O.G.

Trough Withering (Afr). A method of drying tea using a trough that has air forced through the tea leaf.

Trou Normand (Fr). Lit – 'Norman hole'. The name given to a glass of Calvados during a meal to stimulate the appetite and make more room for food.

Trou Normand (Un) (Fr). An A.C. Calvados 40% alc. by vol.

Trousseau (Fr). Local Jura name for the black Pinot grape. Used in the making of Vin gris.

Trovador (Port). A brand of light, rosé wine produced by Soc. Vinhos Borges & Irmão, Porto-Portugal.

Trub (Eng). During the brewing process a solid malt protein formed during the boiling of the Wort. It is removed before fermentation.

Truchard Vineyard (USA). A vineyard based in the Napa Valley, California. 6.5 ha. Grape variety – Cabernet sauvignon. Vinified at Carneros Creek.

True Blue Witches' Brew (Cktl). 2 measures Vodka, 1 measure Sambuca, 1 measure Bols blue Curaçao. Stir over ice, strain into a cocktail glass with a twist of lemon. Stand the glass in a bowl of dry ice.

Trug Baskets (Fr). Wooden baskets used by the grape pickers of Champagne to gather the grapes.

Truluck Winery (USA). A winery based in Lake City, South Carolina. Produces French hybrid and vinifera wines.

Truman Brewery (Eng). Based in Brick Lane, London. A partner of Watneys. noted for its cask conditioned Sampson 1055 O.G. keg Ben Truman 1038 O.G. Prize Brew 1032 O.G. bottled Barley Wine 1086 O.G. and Brewer's Gold 1078 O.G.

Trustees' Choice (Eng). A fine Tawny Port bottled by Howells of Bristol.

Trutnov Brewery (Czec). An old established brewery based in northern Czec.

Tryptophan (Eng). An Amino acid found in small traces in wines. Is formed by the yeasts.

Tsantali Winery (Gre). A winery based in

Agios Pavlos, Halkidiki. 90 ha. Produces a wide range of table wines under the names of – Aspro, Blue Boy, Country Girl, Golden Delicious and Grecian Urn. Grape varieties – Cabernet sauvignon, Limnio and Xinomavro.

Tsarina Cocktail (Cktl). ½ measure Vodka, ¼ measure dry Vermouth, ¼ measure Apricot brandy, dash Angostura. Stir over ice, strain into a cocktail glass.

Tsar Mandarine (Cktl). 1 oz. Mandarine Napoléon, ⅔ oz. Vodka, 1 tablespoon cream, dash Grenadine. Shake over ice, strain into a cocktail glass.

TSB (Cktl). ⅓ gill Golden Heart liqueur, juice ¼ lemon, 2 dashes pineapple juice. Stir over ice in a highball glass, dress with a spiral of lemon peel.

TSB (Eng) (abbr). Tooley Street Bitter 1040 O.G. a cask conditioned Bitter brewed by the Tooley Street Brewery in London.

Tschaggele (It). A red grape variety grown in the Trentino-Alto Adige. Known as the Tschaggelervernatsch in Germany.

Tschaggelervernatsch (Ger). A red grape variety from the Südtirol in Italy. Known as the Tschaggele in Italy.

Tselinnoe (USSR). A white grape variety grown in Kazakhstan. Produces dessert and fortified wines.

Tsen Gon (China). A brand of rice wine from the Fukien branch of the C.N.C.O.F.I.E.C.

Tsimlianska (USSR). A wine-producing centre in the river Don area. Produces mainly white wines.

Tsimlyanskoye (USSR). A Champagne-type wine produced between the district of Anapa and Gelendshik in the Crimean peninsula in a district of the same name. Also produces table wines.

Tsinandali (USSR). A white table wine from the Rion Valley district in the Georgia region.

Tsindali N°1 (USSR). A dry white wine produced in the Alazan Valley in the Georgia region from the Mtsvane and Rkatsiteli grapes.

Tsing Tao (China). The name given to red or white wines produced in northern China.

Tsing Tao Brewery (China). A brewery based in northern China that brews a Pilsener-style beer of same name.

Tsipouri (Gre). A strong form of Ouzo.

Tsolikohouri (USSR). A white grape variety grown in Georgia to produce dry white wines.

Tsun (China). A large old Chinese wine vessel. c1,000 B.C. Used as a Chalice.

Tuaca (It). A sweet, citrus-flavoured liqueur. 40% alc. by vol.

Tualatin Vineyards (USA). A winery based in Tualatin, Oregon. 27.5 ha. Produces varietal wines.

Tuba (E.Ind). A wine produced in the Philippines from coconuts and nipa rice. When distilled is known as Lambanog.

Tube (Austr) (slang). The name for a can of beer.

Tübingen (Ger). Village. (Anb) = Württemberg. (Ber) = Jagst-Kocher-Tauber. (Gro) = Not yet assigned. See Kressbronn am Bodensee Tübingen.

Tuborg (Den). A brewery in Copenhagen which together with the Carlsberg Brewery makes up the United Breweries. Noted for its Tuborg Pilsener 1030 O.G. and Tuborg Gold 1045 O.G. brewed in the U.K. at Carlsberg's Northampton Brewery.

Tuchan (Fr). A commune in the A.C. Fitou region in southern France.

Tuchen (Fr). A noted wine-producing village based in Corbières in the Languedoc.

Tucher Brauerei (Ger). A brewery based in Nürnberg. Produces a dry double-hopped beer of the same name.

Tucquan Vineyards (USA). Vineyards based in Holtwood, Pennsylvania. Produces hybrid wines.

Tudal Winery (USA). A winery based north of St. Helena, Napa Valley, California. Grape varieties – Cabernet sauvignon and Chardonnay. Produces varietal wines.

Tudelilla (Sp). A Zona de Crianza in the Rioja Baja, north-western Spain.

Tudor Ale (Eng). A Beer 1051 O.G. brewed and bottled by the Gales Brewery in Horndean, Hampshire. A bottled version of HSB is brewed for the French market.

Tudor Ale (Eng). A cask conditioned Bitter 1044 O.G. brewed by the Liddington Brewery in Rugby, Warwickshire.

Tudor Rose (Cktl). 3 parts Merrydown Mead, 1 part Bourbon whiskey, dash Angostura. Shake over crushed ice, strain, serve with lemon zest and splash of soda.

Tudor Rose (Eng). An oak-aged, dry, rosé wine produced by the St. George's Vineyard from Pinot noir grapes.

Tufa (Fr). A rock of vulcanized chalk (boiled limestone). Easy to work for cellars, full of minerals, is porous and water retentive. Is found in the Touraine distict of the Loire and in parts of Italy. See Calctufa and Calctuff.

Tuffeau (Fr). A chalk-clay soil found in the Touraine district in the Loire region. Produces good red wines. Also found in Saumur.

Tuica (Rum). A Plum brandy, Plum liqueur. Green-yellow in colour.

Tuilé (Fr). Denotes a wine of brick-red colour that has lost its youthful purple.

Tuinwingerd (S.Afr). A white, dry wine from the Riesling grape made by the Montpellier Estate in Tulbagh.

Tuke Holdsworth (Port). The original name used to ship Quinta de Eira Velha (prior to 1943).

Tuke Holdsworth Hunt, Roope and Co (Port). Vintage Port shippers. Vintages – 1870, 1873, 1874, 1875, 1881, 1884, 1887, 1890, 1892, 1894, 1896, 1900, 1904, 1908, 1912, 1917, 1920, 1922, 1924, 1927, 1934, 1935, 1943, 1945, 1947, 1950, 1955, 1960, 1963, 1966.

Tulare (USA). A wine district within the Great Central Valley in California. Produces sweet, dessert wines.

Tulbagh (S.Afr). A wine region which produces fine white wines and Sherry-style wines. 3 Estates – Montpellier, Theuniskraal and Twee Jongegezellen. Home of the Drostdy Co-operative.

Tulip Cocktail (Cktl). ⅓ measure Applejack, ⅓ measure Italian vermouth, ⅙ measure lemon juice, ⅙ measure Apricot brandy. Shake over ice, strain into a cocktail glass.

Tulip Lager (Eng). A Lager beer 1034 O.G. brewed and bottled by the Lees Brewery in Manchester.

Tulip Tumbler (Eng). A tulip-shaped beer glass of ½ pint and 1 pint capacity produced by Dema Glass.

Tullamore Dew (Ire). A blended Irish whiskey from the Tullamore Dew Co. Midleton, Dublin. Sold in a stone crock. 40% alc. by vol.

Tullibardine (Scot). A single Malt whisky distillery in Blackford, Perthshire. Operated by Longman Distillers of Glasgow (part of the Invergordon group). A Highland malt. Produces a 10 year old malt. 43% alc. by vol.

Tullins (Fr). A vineyard based in Vienne, Isère Département. Produces white wines.

Tulloch Winery (Austr). Address = Allied Vintners, De Beyers Road, Pol-kolbin, New South Wales 2321. Grape varieties – Cabernet sauvignon, Hermitage and Sémillon.

Tulocay Vineyards (USA). A winery based in Napa Valley, California. Grape varieties – Cabernet sauvignon, Pinot noir and Zinfandel. Produces varietal wines.

Tulun Valley (Arg). One of the country's main wine-producing areas.

Tumbler (Eng). A straight-sided drinking glass of 6–12 fl.ozs capacity.

Tumbril (Cktl). Guinness, Port, Brandy and Champagne all in the same glass.

Tuminton (Scot). A brand of blended Scotch whisky. 43% alc. by vol.

Tumultuous Fermentation (Eng). The first violent fermentation usually from the wild yeasts.

Tun (Eng). A container for beer brewing. e.g. Mash tun.

Tun (Eng). An old cask of 250 gallons.

Tun (Eng). A wine cask. 9454 litres, 210 Imp. gallons. 252 US gallons.

Tun Bitter (Eng). A cask conditioned Ale 1041 O.G. brewed by the Creedy Valley Brewery in Crediton, Devon.

Tungusian Arrack (USSR). An arrack distilled from fermented mare's milk by the Tartars in Tungusia.

Tunisia (Afr). A north African country that has made wine since before Roman times. Produces all types of wines especially Muscat. Red wines are the best styles for export.

Tunna (Lat). Cask, tun. See Tonna.

Tunne (Eng). The mediaeval spelling of tun (cask).

Tunsel (Ger). Village. (Anb) = Baden. (Ber) = Markgräflerland. (Gro) = Lorettoberg. (Vin) = Maltesergarten.

Tunuyán (Arg). A wine-producing area in central Argentina.

Tuplàk (Czec). A boot-glass used for festive occasions and drinking contests.

Tupungato (Arg). A wine-producing area based south of the Mendoza region.

Tura (It). A light, dry, sparkling white and rosé wine produced in the Veneto region.

Turacciolo (It). Stopper, cork.

Turbar (Port). A cloudy wine. A wine that has turned cloudy through being shaken.

Turbid (Eng). Denotes a cloudy (not clear) liquid. Has suspended particles in it. e.g. a shaken old red wine.

Turbios (Sp). Wine lees (not lias – must lees).

Turckheim (Fr). A commune in Alsace, north-eastern France.

Turf Cocktail (Cktl). ¼ gill Plymouth Gin, ¼ gill French vermouth, 2 dashes each of Absinthe, Orange bitters and Maraschino. Stir over ice, strain into a cocktail glass, add an olive.

Turgeon and Lohr Winery (USA). A large winery based in San Jose, Salinas Valley, California. 116 ha. Grape varieties – Cabernet sauvignon, Chardonnay, Johannisberg riesling, Petite syrah,

Pinot blanc and Sauvignon blanc. Produces varietal wines.

Turiga (Port). A red grape variety used in the making of Port.

Turkey (Euro). Produces red, rosé and white wines. Little is exported. Red Buzbağ and white Trakya are the best.

Turkish Blood (Eng). In a pint tankard mix ½ pint Burton XXX Ale and ½ pint red Burgundy.

Turkish Coffee (Tur). Coffee made from finely ground, dark roasted beans. Is boiled with sugar in small pans and served in small cups traditionally with iced water and a tot of Ouzo. See Ibrik. Also known as Byzantine Coffee.

Turkish State Monopoly (Tur). Has control of 17 wineries and has most exports of Turkish wines.

Turkmenistan (USSR). A noted wine-producing area.

Turmberg (Ger). Vineyard. (Anb) = Baden. (Ber) = Badische Bergstrasse/ Kraichgau. (Gro) = Hohenberg. (Vil) = Grötzingen.

Turmberg (Ger). Vineyard. (Anb) = Baden. (Ber) = Badische Bergstrasse/ Kraichgau. (Gro) = Hohenberg. (Vil) = Karlsruhe-Durlach.

Turmberg (Ger). Vineyard. (Anb) = Baden. (Ber) = Badische Frankenland. (Gro) = Tauberklinge. (Vil) = Königshofen.

Turned Over (W.Ind). A term used in Rum production when the new Rum is taken from a non-wood container to a wooden container to start its 3 years maturation (legal minimum). Most have more.

Turner (Can). A noted wine-producer based south of Toronto.

Turner Winery (USA).A winery based in San Joaquin and Lake County, California. 241 ha. Grape varieties – Cabernet sauvignon, Chardonnay, Chenin blanc, Gamay, Johannisberg riesling and Zinfandel. Produces varietal wines.

Turning the Piece (Scot). The term used by the maltsters for the turning of the germinating barley corns to aerate them.

Turquant (Fr). A commune in the Coteaux du Saumur, Anjou-Saumur, Loire.

Turrentés (Sp). A black grape variety grown in the central regions of Spain.

Tursan (Fr). A V.D.Q.S. region in south-western France. Produces red, rosé and white wines. Minimum alc. 10.5% by vol.

Turtucaia (Rum). A wine-producing region in the Dobruja district.

Tuscan (It). Good quality red and white wines made in Tuscany. Have to be labelled 'Red Tuscan' or 'White Tuscan'.

Tuscany (It). A region south of Emilia-Romagna, it borders Liguria to the north-west, to the west is the Tyrrhenian Sea. Is famous for its red wines. Chianti, Brunello di Montalcino, Vino Nobile di Montepulciano (all D.O.C.G).

Tusker Bitter (Eng). A dry, special Bitter 1046 O.G. brewed by the Whitbread brewery in London.

Tusker Lager (Afr). A Lager beer brewed by the Kenyan Breweries in Kenya.

Tusker Lager (Afr). A Lager beer 1038 O.G. brewed by the East African Breweries in Tanzania.

Tut (Eng). The central part of the Shive.

Tutela (It). Guardian. Protective body of wines.

Tutschfelden (Ger). Village. (Anb) = Baden. (Ber) = Breisgau. (Gro) = Burg Lichteneck. (Vin) = Kaiserberg.

Tutti Frutti (Fr). An Alcool blanc made from a mixture of fruits.

Tuvilains (Les) (Fr). A Premier Cru vineyard in the A.C. commune of Beaune, Côte de Beaune, Burgundy. 8.73 ha.

Tuxedo Cocktail (Cktl). ¼ gill Burnett Gin, ¼ gill French vermouth, (or Italian vermouth for a sweet version), 2 dashes Maraschino, 2 dashes Orange bitters, 1 dash Absinthe. Stir over ice, strain into a cocktail glass, add a squeeze of lemon peel juice on top.

Tvichi (USSR). A white grape variety grown in Georgia. Produces dessert wines of same name. See also Tvishi.

Tvishi (USSR). An alternative spelling of Tvichi.

Twadell Scale (USA). A scale used to measure the gravity of liquids. 1° Twadell = 5° S.G. (on British scale).

Twankey (Eng). A grade of China tea.

Twann (Switz). A vineyard based in Berne. Noted for its deep, golden-coloured wines.

Twanner (Switz). The name given to a light Chasselas wine from Schafiser, Bern. Also called Schafiser.

Tweed (Eng). A species of Barley malt from the Golden Promise variety. Gives medium sugar yields.

Twee Jongegezellen Estate (S.Afr). Vineyards based in Tulbagh. Address = Box 16, Tulbagh 6820. Produces mainly white varietal wines from the Riesling and Steen grapes. Labels include TJ 39 and Scandert. Also produces Sherries.

Twelfth Night (Cktl). 1 apple, 1 bottle red wine. Stick the apple full of cloves and float in a bowl of the red wine (heated).

Add hot water to dilute according to taste. Add sugar syrup to taste.

Twelve Horse Ale (USA). An Ale 5% alc. by vol. brewed by the Genesee Brewery of Rochester, New York. Top-fermented.

Twentieth Century (Cktl). ⅕ measure Lillet, ⅖ measure Gin, ⅕ measure Crème de Cacao, ⅕ measure lemon juice. Shake over ice, strain into a cocktail glass.

Twiggy (Eng). A term which is similar to Stalky.

Twin Hills Cocktail (Cktl). ⅕ gill Bourbon whiskey, ½ fl.oz. lemon juice, ½ fl.oz. lime juice, ½ fl.oz. Bénédictine. Shake over ice, strain into a sour glass. Add a slice of lime and lemon.

Twinings (Eng). An old well-established tea and coffee company that produces many fine and famous tea blends. Address = R. Twining & Co. South Way, Andover, Hampshire. See also Tom's Coffee House.

Twinings Tea Punch (Cktl). 5 measures strong tea, 2 measures Sherry, 2 measures Rum, 4 dashes lime juice cordial, juice ¼ lemon, sugar syrup to taste. Mix together over ice, strain into a punch bowl, float orange slices on top.

Twinkle of the Polestar (Cktl). ⅓ measure dry Gin, ⅙ measure dry Vermouth, ⅙ measure Drambuie, ⅓ measure Green Chartreuse, dash Orange bitters. Stir over ice, strain into a cocktail glass.

Twin Six (Cktl). ½ measure dry Gin, ¼ measure Italian vermouth, ¼ measure orange juice, 1 egg white, 2 dashes Grenadine. Shake over ice, strain into a cocktail glass.

Twist [A] (Eng). In cocktails denotes a twist of citrus fruit zest.

Twister (Cktl). 1½ fl.ozs. Vodka, teaspoon lime juice. Pour over ice into a highball glass, top with 7-Up.

Twists (USA). Another name for a Collins.

Two Diamonds (Port). A fine Tawny Port produced by Pocas Junior Port shippers.

Two Hundred (Eng). A bottled Beer 1055 O.G. brewed at the Berkshire Brewery, Reading, Berkshire to celebrate the 200th anniversary of Courage 1787–1987.

Two Hundred and Fifty [250] (Eng). A Pale ale 1072 O.G. brewed and bottled by the Tolly Cobbold Brewery in Ipswich to celebrate 250 years of brewing in East Anglia.

225 Anniversary Cuvée (Fr). A vintage De Luxe cuvée Champagne produced by Lanson. 57% Chardonnay and 43% Pinot noir.

Two Lane Blacktop (Eng). ½ Guinness and ½ dry ginger.

Two Row Barley (Eng). The finest quality barley that is used in beer making. Refers to the 2 rows of grain on each ear of barley. See also Four Row and Six Row.

Two Shot (USA). A method of making Gin.

Twyford Amber Ale (Eng). A bottled Ale for export only brewed by the Guinness Park Royal Brewery in London.

Txacoliñ Gorri (Sp). One of the two varieties of Chacolí wine produced from Ondarrubi beltza and Ondarrubi zuria grapes. See also Txacoliñ Zuri.

Txacoliñ Zuri (Sp). One of the two varieties of Chacolí wine produced from Ondarrubi beltza and Ondarrubi zuria grapes. See also Txacoliñ Gorri.

Tyke Bitter (Eng). A Best Bitter 1041 O.G. brewed by the West Riding Brewery in Huddersfield, Yorkshire.

Tyland Vineyards (USA). A winery based in Mendocino County, California. 14.5 ha. Grape varieties – Cabernet sauvignon, Chardonnay, Chenin blanc, Gamay, Johannisberg riesling and Zinfandel. Produces varietal wines.

Tyna (Afr). The brand-name of a wine produced in Tunisia.

Typhoo (Eng). A famous brand of blended tea produced by Kenco-Typhoo Ltd.

Typhoon Cocktail (Cktl). ⅖ measure dry Gin, ⅖ measure lime juice, ⅕ measure Anisette. Shake over ice, strain into an ice-filled highball glass. Top with Champagne.

Tyrells (Austr). Vineyards. Address = Broke Road, Pokolbin, New South Wales 2321. 83 ha. owned (plus 83 ha. leased). Grape varieties – Blanquette, Cabernet, Chardonnay, Hermitage, Merlot, Pinot noir, Rhine riesling, Sauvignon blanc, Sémillon, Traminer and Trebbiano. The winery is known as Ashman's Winery.

Tyrni (Fin). See Buckthorn Berry Liqueur, produced by Marli.

Tyrol (Aus). A vine-growing area of southern Austria.

Tyrosine (Eng). An Amino acid found in small traces in wines. Is formed by the yeasts.

Tysk Vin Information (Swe). German Wine Information Service. Address = Sagaavägen 14, S-18142 Lidingö.

Tywallt (Wales). To decant, to pour.

Tzuica (Rum). A fruit Brandy made from a distillate of plums and almonds.

U

UAC (Sp) (abbr). Unión Cooperativa Agria.

Ubbriacare (It). To get drunk, tipsy.

Ubbriachezza (It). Drunkenness, intoxication.

Übereltzer (Ger). Vineyard. (Anb) = Mosel-Saar-Ruwer. (Ber) = Zell/Mosel. (Gro) = Goldbäumchen. (Vil) = Moselkern.

Überlingen (Ger). Village. (Anb) = Baden. (Ber) = Bodensee. (Gro) = Sonnenufer. (Vin) = Felsengarten.

Übigberg (Ger). Vineyard. (Anb) = Ahr. (Ber) = Walporzheim/Ahrtal. (Gro) = Klosterberg. (Vil) = Altenahr.

Ubriaco (It). Drunk. Excess of alcohol.

Ubriacone (It). Drunkard.

Ubstadt (Ger). See Ubstadt-Weiher.

Ubstadt-Weiher [ortsteil Stettfeld] (Ger). Village. (Anb) = Baden. (Ber) = Badische Bergstrasse/Kraichgau. (Gro) = Mannaberg. (Vin) = Himmelreich.

Ubstadt-Weiher [ortsteil Ubstadt] (Ger). Village. (Anb) = Baden. (Ber) = Badische Bergstrasse/Kraichgau. (Gro) = Mannaberg. (Vin) = Weinhecke.

UCCVT (Afr) (abbr). Union des Caves Coopératives Vinicoles de Tunisie. A large wine co-operative in Tunisia. Has 14 individual co-operatives.

UC-Davis (USA) (abbr). University of California at Davis. Base for the Department of Viticulture and Ecology which conducts research and a teaching programme.

UCOVIP (Fr) (abbr). Union des Coopératives Vinicoles du Pic Saint-Loup.

U.C.V.A. (Fr) (abbr). Union des Caves de Vinification de l'Armagnac. A union of 10 Co-operatives from Gers for Armagnac.

Udan (Ind). An old Indian (Sanskrit) word for water.

Udenheim (Ger). Village. (Anb) = Rheinhessen. (Ber) = Nierstein. (Gro) = Domherr. (Vins) = Goldberg, Kirchberg, Sonnenberg.

Udine (It). A district within the area of Friuli-Venezia Giulia.

Ueberschwefelt (Ger). A term used to describe a wine that contains too much sulphur.

Ueli Brauerei (Switz). A brewery based in Basel.

Ufficio Commerciale del Portogallo (It). The Portuguese Wine Information Centre. Address = Piazzale de Agostini, 3–20146, Milano.

U Flèkû Brewery (Czec). An old brewery in Prague north-western Czec. which brews beers for its own house. Is a sweet, dark Lager 5.4% alc. by vol.

Ugandan Coffee (Afr). The best is from the Bugisu district. Robustas produce a mild, low grade coffee.

Ugandan Teas (Afr). African teas used mainly for blending.

Ughetta (It). A red grape variety.

Ugni Blanc (Fr). A white grape variety grown in the Cognac and Armagnac regions for making Brandy. Gives low alcohol, acidic wines. Also known as the Clairette à grains ronds, Clairette de Venice, Grasse rousanne, Queue de renard, Saint-Émilion and Trebbiano.

Ugni Blanc (USA). See California Ugni Blanc.

Uherský Brod (Czec). A brewery based in Eastern Czec.

Uhlbach (Ger). Vineyard. (Anb) = Württemberg. (Ber) = Remstal-Stuttgart. (Gro) = Weinsteige. See Stuttgart.

Uhlen (Ger). Vineyard. (Anb) = Mosel-Saar-Ruwer. (Ber) = Zell/Mosel. (Gro) = Weinhex. (Vil) = Kobern-Gondorf.

Uhlen (Ger). Vineyard. (Anb) = Mosel-Saar-Ruwer. (Ber) = Zell/Mosel. (Gro) = Weinhex. (Vil) = Winningen.

U.H.T. (Eng) (abbr). Ultra High Temperature. Denotes milk or cream that has been heated to a high temperature (132°C) for 1 second to prolong its keeping qualities.

Uisage Beatha (Ire). A Tullamore Dew Whiskey that is bottled in a crock bottle.

Uisce Baugh (Eng). Old English for Whisky (Usquebaugh).

Uisce Beatha (Ire). Irish (Gaelic) for Whiskey. Lit – 'Water of life'.

Uisce Beathadh (Ire). The sixteenth-century spelling of Water of life.

Uisce Beatha Malt Whisky Company (Scot). Produce limited editions of Uisce Beatha Malt Whisky in specially designed flagons and containers. Address = 33/34 Alfred Place, London WC1E 7DP.

Uisge Baugh (Ire). Water of life. Alt. spelling of Uisque beatha.

Uisge Beatha (Ire). 'Water of life'. Celtic spelling. (Whisky).

Uisquebaugh (Scot). 'The water of life'. The Gaelic word from which Whisky derives.

Uissigheim (Ger). Village. (Anb) = Baden. (Ber) = Badische Frankenland. (Gro) = Tauberklinge. (Vin) = Stahlberg.

Uiterwyk Estate (S.Afr). Vineyards based in Stellenbosch. Address = Box 15, Vlottenburg 7604. Produces varietal wines.

Uitkyk Estate (S.Afr). Vineyards based in Stellenbosch. Address = Box 3, Muldersvlei 7606. Produces varietal wines. 166 ha.

Uitvlugt (S.Am). A noted Rum distillery based in Guyana.

U.I.V.B. (Fr) (abbr). Union Interprofessionnelle des Vins du Beaujolais.

U.K.B.G. (Eng) (abbr). United Kingdom Bartenders' Guild. United Kingdom Bartenders' Association. Address = 70, Brewer Street, London W1R 3PJ.

Ukiah (USA). A wine-producing valley and town based in Mendocino County, California.

Ukraine (USSR). A large vineyard area which includes the Crimea. The river Dneipr is the centre for sparkling wine production.

Ukrainian (USSR). A dark Beer 13° Balling brewed by the Yantar Brewery.

UKRIG (U.K.) (abbr). United Kingdom Rum Importers Group.

Ulanda Cocktail (Cktl). ⅔ measure dry Gin, ⅓ measure Cointreau, 2 dashes Pastis. Stir over ice, strain into a cocktail glass.

Ulander (Cktl). Same as for Ulanda Cocktail but 1 dash Pastis only and is shaken not stirred.

Uley Brewery (Eng). A brewery based in Uley, Gloucestershire. Re-opened in 1985. Brews Uley Bitter and Old Spot Prize Ale.

Ullage (Eng). The space between the liquid and the stopper in a bottle of wine, spirit or beer when improperly filled. Also when wine seeps through the cork to leave an air gap. Also a term given to beer that is drawn off from the cask during pipe cleaning or through bad service. See Ullage Allowance.

Ullage Allowance (Eng). The allowance a brewery gives to public houses for beer which is lost due to the finings contaminating the last few pints in a cask.

Ull de Llebre (Sp). The alternative spelling of Ojo de Llebre.

Ullun Valley (Arg). A major wine-producing zone.

Ulm (Ger). Village. (Anb) = Baden. (Ber) = Ortenau. (Gro) = Fürsteneck. (Vin) = Renchtäler.

Ulmer (USA). A premium light Beer brewed by the Schell Brewery in New Ulm, Minnesota.

Ulrichsberg (Ger). Vineyard. (Anb) = Baden. (Ber) = Badische Bergstrasse/Kraichgau. (Gro) = Mannaberg. (Vil) = Östringen.

Ultima Thule (Austr). A late-picked Riesling from the Hickinbotham Family Vineyard in Victoria.

Ülversheim (Ger). Village. (Anb) = Rheinhessen. (Ber) = Nierstein. (Gro) = Krötenbrunnen. (Vins) = Aulenberg, Schloss.

Umalak (USSR). A white grape variety grown in Uzbekistan. Produces dessert wines.

Umani Ronchi (It). A noted Verdicchio and sparkling wine producer based in Osimo, The Marches.

Um Bongo (Eng). A brand-name for a style of fruit juices from Libby's.

Umbrella (Eng). In brewing, a mushroom-like structure in the Copper. The boiling Wort rises up the central column and cascades over the domed top ensuring the contents are mixed well.

Umbria (It). A small internal region surrounded by Tuscany to the north, The Marches to the east, Latium to the southwest. Is noted for its Orvieto. Produces both red and white wines.

Umechu (Jap). See Umeshu.

Umeshu (Jap). A plum wine made by infusion. A medicinal wine.

Umhali Water (Afr). A style of Rum produced in the nineteenth century on the island of Madagascar.

Umor (Lat). Liquid, fluid.

Umstadt (Ger). Bereich. (Anb) = Hessische Bergstrasse. (Gro) = Nil. (Vils) = Dietzenbach, Gross Umstadt, Klein-Umstadt, Rossdorf.

Una Raya (Sp). Lit – 'One stroke'. A mark used in the Sherry region to denote the first classification of new wines.

Unbalanced (Eng). The term used to describe a wine that is either lacking in fruit or has too much tannin or acid.

Unbroken Tea (Eng). A grade of large tea. Is graded by passing through vibrating sieves. Such examples are – Orange Pekoe, Flowering Orange Pekoe and Pekoe Souchong.

Unchair (Fr). A Premier Cru Champagne village in the Canton de Fismes. District = Reims.

Uncinula Necator (Lat). A disease of the vine. See Oiidium.

Uncinula Spiralis (Lat). The former name for Oidium Tuckerii.

Unclassified (Fr). Not in the official wine classifications of the Médoc 1855, Saint-Émilion 1955 and Graves 1959.

Uncle Ben's Tartan Breweries (Can). Noted breweries based in British Columbia. Taken over in 1976 by new owners.

Uncle Sam (Cktl). ³⁄₁₀ measure Glayva, ⁴⁄₁₀ measure Bourbon whiskey, ¹⁄₁₀ measure lemon juice, ¹⁄₁₀ measure orange juice, ¹⁄₁₀ measure Martini (dry). Shake over ice, strain into a 6 oz. cocktail glass.

Uncle Sam (Eng). Cherry 'B' and American dry ginger ale.

Uncle Sam Cocktail (Cktl). 1 measure Peachtree liqueur, 1 measure Bourbon whiskey. Stir over ice in a highball glass. Top with soda water and a spiral of lemon peel.

Uncork (Eng). To remove the cork from a bottle of wine, beer, spirits, etc. (Fr) = Déboucher.

Undenheim (Ger). Village. (Anb) = Rheinhessen. (Ber) = Nierstein. (Gro) = Gutes Domtal. (Vin) = Goldberg.

Under Age (Eng). Denotes a juvenile who has not reached the age of eighteen years and who cannot, by law, consume alcoholic liquor on licensed premises. They can though be on the premises if fourteen years of age.

Under-Age Drinking (U.K). The illegal drinking of alcoholic liquor by those under 18 years of age on licensed premises.

Underback (Eng). In brewing a vessel that does some filtering of the Wort and is also used to dissolve invert (brewer's) sugar if it is to be added to the brew.

Underberg (Ger). A digestif of herbs and roots, hot macerated with distilled water and alcohol then aged in oak casks. Invented in 1846 and sold in single portion bottles.

Under Proof (Eng). A spirit whose alcoholic content is below proof. See Proof.

Under Strength (Eng). The term that applies mainly to spirits. If Whisky, Brandy, Gin, Rum or Vodka have a strength of below 40% alc. by vol. (Vodka below 37.2% alc. by vol.) must be descrribed on the label as 'under strength'.

Undertone (Eng). A term used to describe wines that are subtle and supporting but not dominating.

Underwood (Eng). A chemist who discovered the 13 minerals present in wine necessary for life – calcium, chlorine, copper, cobalt, iron, iodine, magnesium, manganese, potassium, phosphorus, sodium, sulphur and zinc.

Undurraga Winery (Chile). A family-owned winery. Produces Gran Vino Tinto, Viejo Roble and white wines.

Unfermented Grape Juice (Eng). The juice of freshly gathered grapes. Is known as Verjuice in France.

Unfermented Wine (Eng). A grape juice that has not been fermented. Is known in France as Moût.

U.N.G.C. (Fr) (abbr). Union Normande des Grands Calvados. Producers of Berneroy Calvados. Address = 14130 Blangy le Château, France.

Ungegorener Traubenmost (Ger). Unfermented grape must that has less than 5g alc. per litre.

Ungeheuer (Ger). Vineyard. (Anb) = Rheinpfalz. (Ber) = Mittelhaardt-Deutsche Weinstrasse. (Gro) = Mariengarten. (Vil) = Forst.

Ungezuckert (Ger). Unsugared, pure wine.

Ungsberg (Ger). Vineyard. (Anb) = Mosel-Saar-Ruwer. (Ber) = Bernkastel. (Gro) = Schwarzlay. (Vil) = Traben-Trarbach.

Ungstein (Ger). Village. (Anb) = Rheinpfalz. (Ber) = Mittelhaardt-Deutsche Weinstrasse. (Gro) = Hochmess. (Vin) = Michelsberg.

Ungstein (Ger). Village. (Anb) = Rheinpfalz. (Ber) = Mittelhaardt-Deutsche Weinstrasse. (Gro) = Honigsäckel. (Vins) = Herrenberg, Nussriegel, Weilberg.

Ungstein (Ger). Village. (Anb) = Rheinpfalz. (Ber) = Mittelhaardt-Deutsche Weinstrasse. (Gro) = Kobnert. (Vins) = Bettelhaus, Osterberg.

Unharmonisch (Ger). Opposite to harmonious, an unbalanced wine.

União Comercial da Beira (Port). A noted Dão wine producer based in Oliveirinha.

União das Adegas Cooperativas do Dão (Port). A co-operative based in Dão. Produces wines under the Dão Adegas Cooperativas.

União Vinícola Regional de Bucelas (Port). A body now absorbed by the Junta Nacional do Vinho.

União Vinícola Regional de Carcavelos (Port). A body now absorbed by the Junta Nacional do Vinho.

União Vinícola Regional de Moscatel de Setúbal (Port). A body now absorbed by the Junta Nacional do Vinho.

Unicellular (Eng). Having a single cell. Applied to yeast.

Unicognac (Fr). A Cognac co-operative. Address = BP N°2, 17500, Jonzac. 5,000 ha. owned by 3,500 growers. Distils, ages and blends Cognacs.

Unicorn (Eng). The brand sign for Robinsons Brewery in Stockport.

Unicum (It). Aromatised bitters made by the Zwack Co.

Unidor (Fr). A Dordogne-based union of co-operatives.

Uniewyn (S.Afr). A noted producer of a range of brandies.

Uni-Médoc (Fr). A co-operative based at Gaillan-en-Médoc. A group of four co-operatives in Bégadan, Ordonnac, Prignac and Queyrac.

Union (Yug). A Beer brewed by the Ljubljana Brewery in Slovenia.

Union Agricole du Pays de Loire (Fr). A co-operative based in the Loire region. Address = 49380 Brissac.

Union Camerounaise de Brasseries (Afr). A brewery based in Cameroun which brews Bock beers, a Pilsener and a Breda beer.

Unión Cooperativa Agria (Sp). UCA. Based in Tarragona. Deals with the wines vinified by the co-operatives.

Union de Brasseries (Afr). A branch of the French brewery of same name that is active in north-west Africa.

Union de Brasseries (Fr). A brewery which has 6 plants. The largest near Paris at Drancy. Brews Slavia and Porter 39 (a dark Stout-type beer).

Union des Caves Coopératives Vinicoles de Tunisie (Afr). UCCVT. The top wine exporter in Tunisia. Has 14 co-operatives as members – Bejaoua, Bou Arkoub, Borj El Armi, Ghezala, Grombalia, Bir Drassen, Kélibia, Khledia, Mornag, Mrira, Nahli, Sidi Tabet, Takelsa and Schuigui.

Union des Caves de Vinification de L'Armagnac (Fr). See U.C.V.A.

Union des Coopératives de l'Armagnac [Marquis de Caussade] (Fr). Armagnac producer. Address = Avenue de l'Armagnac, 32800 Eauze.

Union des Coopératives Vinicoles du Pic Saint-Loup (Fr). A body that market the Le Pic range of red and white wines. UCOVIP.

Union des Grands Crus de Bordeaux (Fr). A body dedicated to maintaining quality standards in Bordeaux. Member-properties may be from the whole of the Médoc.

Union des Producteurs de Saint-Émilion (Fr). Grand Cru. A.C. Saint-Émilion. Commune – Saint-Émilion. 851 ha. Grape varieties – Cabernet franc, Cabernet sauvignon and Merlot. The largest co-operative in Saint-Émilion, has 350 members. Address = BP 27, 33330 Saint-Émilion. Wines are sold under labels – Bois Royal, Côtes Rocheuses, Royal Saint-Émilion, Haut Quercus, Cuvée Galius and Saint-Émilion. Also vinifies many to Château wines.

Union des Propriétaires (Fr). Co-operative.

Union Interprofessionnelle des Vins du Beaujolais (Fr). A body based at 210, Boulevard Vermorel, 69400 Villefranche-sur-Saône, Beaujolais, Burgundy. U.I.V.B.

Union Jack (Cktl). ²⁄₃ measure Gin, ¹⁄₃ measure Crème Yvette, 2 dashes Grenadine. Shake over ice, strain into a cocktail glass.

Union Jack Cocktail (Pousse Café). Pour into a tall liqueur glass in order ¹⁄₃ measure Green Chartreuse, ¹⁄₃ measure Maraschino and ¹⁄₃ Grenadine.

Union Normande des Grands Calvados (Fr). See UNGC.

Union of Rheingau Wine-Growers (Ger). A body which has 35 members.

Unión Territorial de Co-operativas del Campo (Sp). UTECO. A body on the Register of Exporters. This permits the Bodegas to export directly if they wish to.

Union Vinicole Divinal (Fr). A co-operative based in Obernai, Alsace. Produces Crémant d'Alsace and wines under the St. Odile label.

Union Vinicole Pour la Diffusion des Vins d'Alsace (Fr). A body formed by a merger of small proprieters. Controls over 15% of the market.

Union Voison (Bel). A Bière brewed by the Dupont Brasserie in Tourpes.

Union Wine Limited (S.Afr). Wine merchants based in Wellington. Wines sold under Bellingham, Culemborg and Val du Charron labels. Address = P.O. Box 246 Wellington 7655.

United Breweries (Den). A giant company that includes Carlsberg and Tuborg Breweries. Is linked with the Rupert group of South Africa.

United Breweries (Ind). A brewery based in Bangalore. Produces Lagers and bitter Stouts.

United Distilleries Company of Belfast and Londonderry (Ire). An old distilling company in Northern Ireland that closed down in 1929.

United Distillers (Austr). A subsidiary of the British-based DCL. Produces Gin under the Vickers label.

United Kingdom Bartenders' Guild (U.K.). U.K.B.G. The United Kingdom Bartenders' Association. Address = 70, Brewer Street, London, W1R 3 PJ.

United Kingdom Rum Importers Group (U.K.). UKRIG. An important body that maintains close links with the WIRSPA.

United Rum Merchants (Eng). U.R.M. Formed by the merger of 3 companies in 1946. Based in London. Brands include – Black Heart Rum, Lamb's Navy Rum, Lemon Hart Rum, Red Heart Rum and Santiago White Rum.

United States Bartenders' Guild (USA).

U.S.B.G. American Bartenders' Association. Address = 4805 Lindley Avenue, Tarzana, California 91356, USA.

United States of America (USA). See America.

United States of America Pint (USA). 16½ fl.ozs.

United Vintners (USA). U.V. Inglenook and Swiss Colony's operating company of distillers. Uses patent and pot-stills to produce a range of brandies under the labels of – Petri, Lejon, Hartley and Jacques Bonet. Also produces wines (see Bali-Hai).

Universal Order of the Knights of the Vine of California (USA). A wine brotherhood based in California for the promotion of the region's wines.

Univitis (Fr). A co-operative based in Bordeaux. Address = Société Coopérative, Les Leves, 33220, Sainte Foy la Grande. A large producer of A.C. Bordeaux white wine and V.D.Q.S. wines.

Unkel (Ger). Village. (Anb) = Mittelrhein. (Ber) = Rheinburgengau. (Gro) = Burg Hammerstein. (Vins) = Berg, Sonnenberg.

Unkenbach (Ger). Village. (Anb) = Nahe. (Ber) = Schloss Böckelheim. (Gro) = Paradiesgarten. (Vins) = Römerpfad, Würzhölle.

Unlauterer Wettbewerb (Ger). Trade Description Act. (Fr) = Réclame Trompeuse. (Hol) = Misleidende Reklame.

Unlicensed (Eng). Denotes having no licence to sell alcoholic liquor.

Unrein (Ger). Refers to an unclean wine.

Unsauber (Ger). Denotes a defective, dirty tasting wine due to bad storage.

Unter Ausbrausen (Aus). Lit – 'An effervescent manner'. Refers to the opening of a bottle of sparkling wine where the contents bubble up.

Unterbadischer Landwein (Ger). One of fifteen Deutsche Tafelwein zones.

Unterberg (Ger). Vineyard. (Anb) = Mosel-Saar-Ruwer. (Ber) = Saar-Ruwer. (Gro) = Scharzberg. (Vil) = Filzen.

Untereisenheim (Ger). Village. (Anb) = Franken. (Ber) = Maindreieck. (Gro) = Kirchberg. (Vin) = Sonnenberg.

Untereisesheim (Ger). Village. (Anb) = Württemberg. (Ber) = Württembergisch Unterland. (Gro) = Staufenberg. (Vin) = Vogelsang.

Untergebiete (Ger). Table wine sub-areas. There are eight in total – Burgengau, Donau, Lindau in Bayern, Mosel, Rhein, Romertor in Oberrhein and Saar in Rhein and Mosel.

Untergruppenbach (Ger). Village. (Anb) = Württemberg. (Ber) = Württembergisch Unterland. (Gro) = Kirchenweinberg. (Vin) = Schlossberg.

Unterheimbach (Ger). Village. (Anb) = Württemberg. (Ber) = Württembergisch Unterland. (Gro) = Lindelberg. (Vin) = Schneckenhof.

Unterheinriet (Ger). Village. (Anb) = Württemberg. (Ber) = Württembergisch Unterland. (Gro) = Schozachtal. (Vin) = Sommerberg.

Unterjesingen (Ger). Village. (Anb) = Württemberg. See Kressbronn am Bodensee Tübingen.

Unterlagen (Aus). Root stock.

Untermosel (Ger). Another name for the Bereich Zell in the Mosel-Saar-Ruwer.

Unteröwisheim (Ger). See Kraichtal.

Untersteinbach (Ger). Village. (Anb) = Württemberg. (Ber) = Württembergisch Unterland. (Gro) = Lindelberg. (Vin) = Dachsteiger.

Untertürkheim (Ger). Village. (Anb) = Württemberg. (Ber) = Remstal-Stuttgart. (Gro) = Weinsteige. See Stuttgart.

Unusual Cocktail (Cktl). ⅓ measure Gin, ⅓ measure Swedish Punsch, ⅓ measure Cherry brandy, dash lemon juice. Shake over ice, strain into a cocktail glass.

Unwins (Eng). A family-owned group of specialist wine shops. 300 outlets in the south-east of England and East Anglia.

Up Front (Eng). A term applied to wines that have an attractive, simple quality which is easily recognisable.

U Pinkasû (Czec). An Ale-house in Prague.

Upper Corgo (Port). The higher region of the river Douro where the grapes are grown for Port.

Upper Hunter (Austr). A wine region based in New South Wales. The vineyards are irrigated. Produces mainly white wines.

Uppington (S.Afr). A wine region based north of Stellenbosch.

Upstairs (Cktl). ⅓ measure Port wine, ⅓ measure Vodka, ⅙ measure Lakka liqueur, ⅙ measure lime juice. Shake over ice, strain into a cocktail glass.

Upstairs Cocktail (Cktl). ⅓ gill Dubonnet, juice ½ lemon. Stir over ice in a highball glass, top with soda water and a slice of lemon.

Up-To-Date (Cktl). ⅖ measure dry Vermouth, ⅖ measure Rye whiskey, ⅕ measure Grand Marnier, dash Angostura. Stir over ice, strain into a cocktail glass, add a twist of lemon peel.

Upton Ranch (USA). A vineyard based in

Amador County, California. Grape variety – Zinfandel. Vinified at the Lamb Winery.

Ur (Ger). 'Original'. Used by breweries that have adopted a beer-style such as Spaten Ur-Marzen, Pilsner Urquell. Also known as Urtyp.

Urbana Wine Company (USA). The former name for the Gold Seal Winery on Lake Keuka.

Urbar (Ger). Village. (Anb) = Mittelrhein. (Ber) = Rheinburgengau. (Gro) = Marksburg. (Vin) = Rheinnieder.

Urbar [St. Goar] (Ger). Village. (Anb) = Mittelrhein. (Ber) = Rheinburgengau. (Gro) = Schloss Schönburg. (Vin) = Beulsberg.

Urbeis (Fr). The German name for the district of Orbey in Alsace.

Urbelt (Ger). Vineyard. (Anb) = Mosel-Saar-Ruwer. (Ber) = Saar-Ruwer. (Gro) = Scharzberg. (Vil) = Filzen.

Urceus (Lat). Pitcher.

Urébères (Fr). A vine pest of early times now no longer found. Also spelt Uribères.

Urfé (Fr). A Vins de Pays area in the northern Loire. Produces red, rosé and dry white wines from the Aligoté, Chardonnay, Gamay, Pinot gris, Pinot noir and Viognier grapes.

Uribères (Fr). See Urébères.

Uricani (Rum). A wine-producing area noted for its red and white wines.

Urlaţi (Rum). A wine-producing area. Part of the Dealul-Mare Vineyard.

U.R.M. (Eng) (abbr). United Rum Merchants.

Ursulinengarten (Ger). Vineyard. (Anb) = Ahr. (Ber) = Walporzheim/Ahrtal. (Gro) = Klosterberg. (Vil) = Ahrweiler.

Urtyp (Ger). The name given to describe an ordinary beer of the Astra brand produced by the Bavaria-St Pauli Brauerei in Hamburg.

Uruguay (S.Am). Makes all styles of wine and spirits but for local consumption, little is exported.

Ürzig (Ger). Village. (Anb) = Mosel-Saar-Ruwer. (Ber) = Bernkastel. (Gro) = Schwarzlay. (Vin) = Würzgarten.

Usak (Tur). A wine-producing region in western Turkey. Produces mainly white wines.

U Salzmanů (Czec). A famous beer taproom in Pilsen.

U.S.B.G. (USA) (abbr). The United States Bartenders' Guild. American Bartenders' Association. Address = 4805 Lindley Avenue, Tarzana, California 91356. USA.

Usé (Fr). Applied to a wine past its best.

Usher (Andre) (Scot). A noted Whisky distiller (part of DCL). Brands include Usher's Green Stripe.

Usher Brewery (Eng). Watneys West Country Brewery. Noted for its' cask conditioned Founder's Ale 1045 O.G. keg Triple Crown 1033 O.G. Country Bitter 1036 O.G. and canned Ploughman's Bitter 1032 O.G.

Usher's Green Stripe (Scot). A brand of blended Scotch whisky produced by Andrew Usher. 40% alc. by vol. (Part of DCL).

Usher's O.V.G. (Scot) (abbr). Old Vatted Glenlivet. One of the first blended Malt whiskies introduced in 1853.

U.S. Proof (USA). A measurement of alcoholic proof. Works as water = 0° and pure alcohol = 200°.

Usquaebach, The Grand Whisky of the Highlands (Scot). A blended De Luxe Scotch Whisky, produced by Douglas Laing for the American Co. Twelve Stone Flagons, comes in stone flagon facsimile bottles with a cork stoppered closure.

Usquebaugh (Ire). A liqueur Whiskey flavoured with coriander.

Usquebaugh (Scot). Gaelic for 'Water of life' from which the name Whisky derives.

U.S.S.R. [The Soviet Union] The third largest producer of wines in the world. Produces most styles of beers, spirits (especially vodka) and wines (many produced from hybrid vines). Is noted for its méthode champenoise wines. Main wine regions are – Armenia, Azerbaijan, Crimea, Georgia, Krasnodar, Moldavia, River Don, Stavropol, and the Ukraine generally. Also produces some teas in the Southern Republics.

Uster Brauerei (Switz). A brewery based in Uster. Part of the Interbeva group.

Ústí nad Labem Brewery (Czec). A brewery based in north-western Czec.

Ususha (Jap). The name given to a thin whipped tea made during the Chonoyu ceremony. The second stage of Chonoyu is held in another room.

U Svatého Tomáse (Czec). An Ale house in Prague.

UTECO (Sp) (abbr). Unión Territorial de Co-operativas del Campo.

Utero (Sp). Red wines produced by the Bodegas José Palacios in Rioja. Made from the Garnacha, Mazuelo and Tempranillo grapes. Matured in cask and aged in bottle. Produces Reservas and Gran Reservas.

Utica Club Cream Ale (USA). A well-hopped, top-fermented Beer brewed by the West End Brewing Co. in Utica.

Utica Club Pilsener (USA). A light, dry Pilsener Lager brewed by the West End Brewing Co. in Utica.

Utiel-Requena (Sp). A Denominación de Origen region within the wine province of Valencia in southern Spain. Grape varieties – Bobal, Crujidera and Garnacha. Produces red and rosé wines.

Uto Mij (Hol). A noted distiller of Jenever.

U.V. (USA). See United Vintners.

Uva (It). Grape.

Uva (Lat). Berry.

Uva (Port). Berry (grape).

Uva (Sp). Grape.

Uva Cerreto (It). The Campania name for the white grape variety Malvasia di candia.

Uva de Mesa (Sp). A red dessert (table) grape.

Uva di Spagna (Sp). An alternative name for the Garnacha grape.

Uva di Troia (It). A red grape variety grown in the Puglia region.

Uva d'Oro (It). A red grape variety.

Uva Francesca (It). The Tuscany name for the Cabernet grape.

Uvaggio (It). The name given to a wine made from a mixture of grape varieties.

Uval (Fr). Pertaining to grapes.

Uva Rara (Sp). A red grape variety known as the Bonarda novarese in Italy.

Uvas Pasa (Sp). Raisin-like grapes.

Uveira (Port). Tree vine.

Uzbekistan (USSR). A wine-producing area based north of Turkmenistan. Also the name for a red grape variety.

Uzège (Fr). A Vins de Pays area in the Gard Département in south-western France. Produces red, rosé and dry white wines.

Üzüm (Tur). Grape.

Üzüm Baği (Tur). Vineyard.

Üzüm Suyu (Tur). Grape juice.

V.A. (Fr) (abbr). Vintage Appellation.

Vaalharts Co-operative (S.Afr). Vineyards based at Vaalharts and Andalusia. Address = Vaalharts Landboukoöperasie, Box 4, Hartswater 8750. Produces varietal wines under Overvaal Wines and Andalusia Wines labels.

Vaalharts Landboukoöperasie (S.Afr). See Vaalharts Co-operative.

Vaapukka (Fin). A raspberry liqueur.

Vaatje (Hol). Keg.

Vaccarèse (Fr). A red grape variety grown in the southern Rhône for Châteauneuf-du-Pape.

Vacio (Sp). A term used to describe a Sherry with a dumb bouquet.

Vacqueyras (Fr). An A.C. Côtes du Rhône-Villages. Produces full-bodied red wines.

Vacuum-Distilled Gin (USA). A Gin distilled in a glass-lined vacuum still at a low temperature (90°F). Produces only a light Gin with little bitterness and a light flavour.

Vacuum Method (Eng). A method of making coffee. Boiling water is drawn up through expansion from one container into another, holding the coffee grounds where infusion takes place. After the heat source has been removed from the bottom container, a vacuum is created which draws the infused coffee (liquid) back into the bottom container. (The grounds are retained in the top unit by a special valve). The 'Cona' coffee system works on such a principal.

Vacuum Packed (Eng). Ground or instant coffee that is packed in a vacuum package (tin, glass or cellophane) to retain freshness.

Vacuum Still (USA). A glass-lined still which distills at approx. 90°F instead of 212°F (100°C). Produces light flavoured spirits.

Vaduzer (Euro). The name given in Liechtenstein to ⅔ of red wine produced. Is light in colour and made with the Blauburgunder.

Vaegne (Ch.Isles). Vine.

Vaihingen (Ger). Village. (Anb) = Württemberg. (Ber) = Württembergisch Unterland. (Gro) = Stromberg. (Vin) = Höllisch Feuer.

Vaillons (Fr). A Premier Cru Chablis vineyard. Often has the Premier Cru vineyards of Beugnons, Châtains, Les Lys and Séché sold as its vintage.

Vaison-la-Romaine (Fr). A commune of the Principauté d'Orange Département in southern Rhône.

Vais Vista (USA). A vineyard based in the Alexander Valley, Sonoma County, California. 7.5 ha. Grape varieties – Cabernet sauvignon and Chardonnay. Produces varietal wines.

Vajda, S.L. (Sp). A major wine-producer based in Rioja, north-western Spain.

Vakche (USSR). A red grape variety grown in Tadzhikistan. Produces dessert wines.

Valagarina (It). A wine-producing area in the Trentino-Alto Adige. Produces red wines.

Valais (Switz). A wine area producing dry white, dessert and red wines. Dôle is the most famous red wine. Grapes varieties – Chasselas, Johannisberg riesling, Gamay and Pinot noir.

Valaisanne (Switz). A Brewery in Sion. Is part of the Feldschlösschen group.

Valbuena (Sp). A red wine produced by Bodegas Vega Sicilia, Old Castile, Valladolid. Sold as 3 or 5 years old. Vega Sicilia is the best quality. Valbuena is the second quality.

Valcalepio (It). A D.O.C. red wine from Pavia, Lombardy. Produced from the Cabernet sauvignon and Merlot grapes.

Valcalepio Bianco (It). A D.O.C. white wine from Bergamo, Lombardy. Produced from the Pinot bianco and Pinot grigio grapes.

Valcarcelia (Sp). A black grape variety grown in Rioja. Also known as the Mechín, Ministrel, Monastel, Monastrel, Moraster and Negralejo. Also grown in Aragón and Cataluña.

Val d'Adige Bianco (It). D.O.C. white wine from the Trentino-Alto Adige. Made from a wide variety of grapes including the Blanchetta trevigiana, Müller-Thurgau, Pinot bianco, Nosiola, Pinot grigio, Riesling italico, Sylvaner veltliner bianco, Trebbiano toscano and Vernacchia.

Val d'Adige Rosso (It). D.O.C. red wine from the Trentino-Alto Adige. Made from the Lagrein, Lambrusco, Merlot, Negrara, Pinot nero, Schiave and Teroldego.

Val d'Agly (Fr). A Vins de Pays area in the Côtes de Roussillon, Midi region. Produces red, rosé and dry white wines.

Val d'Aosta (It). A small region between Piemonte and the French/Swiss borders. 2 D.O.C. wines produced – Donnaz and Enfer d'Arvier. Both red wines.

Val de Cesse (Fr). A Vins de Pays area in the Aude Département in southern France.

Val de Dagne (Fr). A Vins de Pays area in the Aude Département in southern France.

Val de Loire (Fr). Loire Valley. Section of the river between Nantes and Bec d'Ambes. In this region all the important vineyards are found.

Valdemar (Sp). See Bodegas Martinez Bujanda.

Valdemontan Tinto Cosecha (Sp). Wines produced by the Co-operative Vinícola de Cenicero, Bodegas Santa Daria, Rioja. (Alta region).

Val de Montferrand (Fr). A Vins de Pays area in the Gard Département in south-western France.

Valdeorras (Sp). A Denominación de Origen region in north-western Spain. Grape varieties – Alicante, Bodello, Garnacha and Mencía. Produces red and white wines.

Valdepeñas (Sp). A Denominación de Origen region of La Mancha, central-southern Spain. Grape varieties – Aragón, Airén, Bobal, Castellana, Cencibel, Cirial, Garnacha, Jaén, Monastrel, Pardillo and Tinto Basto. Produces red, rosé and white wines that are high in alcohol.

Valdepeñas (USA). A red grape variety used in the making of red and dessert wines in California.

Val de Rance (Fr). A brut sparkling Cider from Normandy.

Val des Desmoiselles (Fr). A vintage rosé Champagne produced by André Drappier. Produced from the Pinot noir grape.

Valdespino (Sp). A Jerez de la Frontera Sherry Bodega. Labels include – Machanudo Fino Inocente and Matador Manzanilla.

Val di Lupo (It). A producer of red and white wines at Catania, Sicily.

Valdizarbe (Sp). One of 5 D.O. wine-producing districts in the Navarra region of north-eastern Spain.

Valdobbiadene (It). A fine dry white wine from the province of Treviso in Venetia. Made from the Prosecco grape.

Valdo Cantina Sociale di Valdobbiadene (It). A producer of Prosecco di Conegliano-Valdobbiadene (a méthode champenoise produced sparkling wine), also a cuve close variety. Is based in the Veneto region.

Val d'Or (W.Ind). A 'gold label' Rum that has been aged for 10 years on the island of Martinique. Is derived from Rhum Dusquesne production.

Val d'Orbieu (Fr). A Vins de Pays area in the Aude Département in southern France.

Valdoro (Sp). A 'cold-fermented' white wine produced by the Bodegas Felix Solis in the Valdepeñas region.

Valdouro (Sp). A red wine produced from the Garnacha and Vencia grapes by the Cooperativa Jesus Nazareno.

Val du Charron Wines (S.Afr). A brand-name label for Union Wines Ltd.

Val du Torgan (Fr). A Vins de Pays area in the Aude Département in southern France.

Valea Călugărească (Rum). A wine region on the Black Sea. Lit – 'Valley of the monks'. Part of the Dealul Mare vineyard. Produces fine sweet wines. See Muscat Ottonel and Segarcea Cabernet.

Valea-Lungă (Rum). A wine-producing area, part of the Tîrnave vineyard.

Valeccito (Cktl). 1½ fl.ozs. Pisco, ¾ fl.oz. Curaçao, 1 fl.oz. dry Vermouth, 1 fl.oz. lemon juice. Shake over ice, strain into an ice-filled highball glass.

Valençay (Fr). A V.D.Q.S. area near Chevernay in the Indre Département. Produces red, rosé and dry white wines. Minimum alc. of 9% by vol. Grape varieties are Arbois, Cabernet franc, Cabernet sauvignon, Gamay and Pinot d'Aunis.

Valencia (Cktl). ⅔ measure Apricot brandy, ⅓ measure orange juice, 4 dashes Angostura. Shake over ice, strain into a cocktail glass.

Valencia (Sp). Wine area of southern Spain. Has the Denominación de Origen regions of Cheste, Utiel-Requena and Valencia. Grape varieties – Garnacha, Macabeo, Malvasia, Merseguera, Monastrell, Pedro Ximénez, Planta fina, Planta nova and Tintorera.

Valencia Cocktail (Cktl). ⅔ measure

Apricot brandy, ⅓ measure orange juice, 4 dashes Orange bitters. Shake over ice, strain into a flute glass. Top with iced Champagne. Also known as a Valencia Smile.

Valenciana (Sp). A white grape variety grown in the Galicia region.

Valencia Smile (Cktl). See Valencia Cocktail.

Valencia Winery (Austr). A winery based in the Swan Valley, Western Australia. Produces varietal wines.

Valentino Brut (It). A méthode champenoise sparkling wine produced by Podere Rocche dei Manzoni in the Piemonte region.

Valeria (Switz). A red wine produced in Sion, Valais.

Valeric Acid (Eng). An ester that is present in wine in minute traces.

Valesa Târnavelor (Rum). A noted white wine-producing vineyard.

Valeyrac (Fr). A commune in the Bas-Médoc, north-western Bordeaux. Has A.C. Médoc status.

Valfieri (It). A noted producer of Moscato d'Asti Spumante in the Piemonte region.

Valgella (It). A sub-district of the Lombardy in the foothills of the Alps in the Valtellina Valley. Produces red wines of the same name from the Nebbiolo grape.

Valinch (Fr). Pipette or 'Thief tube' for drawing samples from a cask.

Valine (Eng). An amino acid found in small traces in wines. Is formed by the yeasts.

Valladolid (Sp). A D.O. wine-producing area in north-western Spain.

Valle d'Aosta (It). A small wine region of north-west Italy. Has two D.O.C's. See Val d'Aosta

Valle de Monterrey (Sp). A Denominación de Origen area based near the Portuguese border. Grape varieties – Alicante, Bodello, Garnacha and Mencía. Produces red and white wines.

Valle de Rosal (Sp). A noted rosé wine-producing area in north-western Spain. Is famous for Albariño grapes.

Valle d'Isarco (It). A valley north-east of Bolzano in the Trentino-Alto Adige. Produces 5 white wines – Valle Isarco Müller-Thurgau, V.I. Pinot grigio, V.I. Silvaner, V.I. Traminer aromatico and V.I. Veltliner. If produced within part of the communes of Bressanone and Varna then has Bressanone on label. See Eisack Valley.

Valle d'Oro Winery (Austr). A winery based in McLaren Vale, Southern Vales, South Australia.

Vallée d'Auge (Cktl). Heat ⅓ gill Calvados and ⅓ pint milk until almost boiling. Pour over 1 oz. sugar that has been beaten with an egg yolk. Stir until smooth. Dress with a slice of apple and ground cinnamon.

Vallée de la Marne (Fr). A vineyard area of Champagne around the town of Épernay. Grapes give fruit and body to the wines.

Vallée du Paradis (Fr). A Vins de Pays area in the Aude Département in southern France.

Vallendar (Ger). Village. (Anb) = Mittelrhein. (Ber) = Rheinburgengau. (Gro) = Marksburg. (Vin) = Rheinnieder.

Valle Renondo (Mex). A wine-producing region based in the Baja California.

Vallerots (Les) (Fr). A Premier Cru vineyard [part] in the A.C. commune of Nuits-Saint-Georges, Côte de Beaune, Burgundy. 9.7 ha.

Vallet (Fr). Village in the Pays Nantais district of the Loire. From here some of the finest Muscadets are produced in the Sèvre et Maine A.C. Have excellent acidity and fruit.

Valley of the Moon (USA). A Californian valley between the Napa Valley and Sonoma Valley which produces fine table wines.

Valley of the Moon Winery (USA). A winery based in the valley of the same name in the Sonoma County, California. Grape varieties – Colombard, Pinot noir, Sémillon and Zinfandel. Produces varietal wines.

Valley View Vineyard (USA). A vineyard based in south-western Oregon. 12 ha. Produces hybrid wines vinified in the Jacksonville Winery.

Valley Vineyards (USA). A vineyard based in Morrow, Ohio. 16 ha. Produces hybrid and varietal wines.

Valley Vista (USA). The label used by Lytton Springs Winery's home vineyard in Alexander Valley, Sonoma County, California.

Valley Wines (S.Afr). Varietal brand-name wines from Gilbeys Limited.

Valley Wines (USA). Wines from the valleys of California – Alexander, Napa, Naples, Russian River, Sonoma, etc.

Valmur (Fr). A Grand Cru vineyard in the A.C. Chablis, Burgundy.

Valmy (Cktl). 1 oz. Mandarine Napoléon, 1 oz. dark Rum, 3 ozs. orange juice, 1 teaspoon sugar. Shake over ice, strain into a cocktail glass.

Valorisation (Eng). A name given to the process by which countries try to regulate coffee prices (buying the crop and

V

keeping it until the prices are favourable).

Valorization (Eng). A term used to denote the elements of assessment in wine tasting. i.e. colour, aroma, flavour, etc with grades i.e. Excellent, good, average, passable, poor, etc.

Valozières (Les) (Fr). A Premier Cru vineyard [part] in the A.C. commune of Aloxe-Corton, Côte de Beaune, Burgundy.

Valpantena (It). A dry red wine from the Veneto region.

Valpolicella (It). D.O.C. red wine from the Veneto region. Made from the Barbera, Corvina veronese, Molinara, Negrara, Rondinella, Rossignola and Sangiovese grapes. Vinification can take place in Verona. If produced in Valpantena can add this name to the label. Also Valpolicella Classico (see Classico). If total alc. content is 12% by vol. and aged minimum 1 year then is classed Superiore.

Valpolicella Recioto (It). D.O.C. red wine from the Veneto region. Wine is made from the Recie ('ears') or outer bunches of grapes that have had the most sun. See also Amarone della Recioto Valpolicella.

Valporaiso (Chile). A province and wine-producing area in the Central Zone.

Valréas (Fr). A village in the Vaucluse, A.C. Côtes du Rhône-Villages. See Principauté d'Orange.

Vals d'Agly (Fr). A Vins de Pays area in the Pyrénées Orientales Département in south-western France.

Vals St. Jean (Fr). A slightly pétillant mineral water.

Valtellina (It). Wine area in the valley of the river Adda in northern Lombardy under the Alps. Produces mostly red wines from the Nebbiolo grape (known locally as the Chiavennasca).

Valtellina (It). D.O.C. red wine from the Lombardy region. Made from the Nebbiolo 70% and 30% Brugnola, Merlot, Pinot noir and Rossola grapes. Can add specification Sfursat or Sforzato (strained) if obtained from slightly dried grapes and has an alc. content of 14.5% by vol. minimum.

Valtellina Superiore (It). D.O.C. red wine from the Lombardy region. Made from the Nebbiolo grape. If aged 4 years (1 year in wood) can be classed Riserva.

Val Verde Winery (USA). A winery based south of Lubbock, Texas. Produces European and hybrid wines.

Valwig (Ger). Village. (Anb) = Mosel-Saar-Ruwer. (Ber) = Zell/Mosel. (Gro) = Rosenhag. (Vins) = Herrenberg, Palmberg, Schwarzenberg.

Van Damme Distillerie (Bel). A farm-based distillery near Balagem. Produces Jenevers.

Vanden Hautte (Bel). A brewery based in Groot Bijgaarden in northern Belgium.

Vanderbilt Cocktail (Cktl). ¼ gill Cherry brandy, ¼ gill Liqueur Cognac, 2 dashes Angostura, 3 dashes Gomme syrup. Stir over ice, strain into a cocktail glass. Add a cherry and a twist of lemon peel.

Van Der Hum (S.Afr). A liqueur made from mandarine oranges, Brandy, plants, seeds and barks. 30% alc. by vol.

Van Der Hum Cocktail (Cktl). 1 measure Brandy, 1 measure Van der Hum, 1 measure Port, ½ yolk of egg, ½ teaspoon sugar, ½ teaspoon whipped cream. Shake over ice (all except cream), strain into a 5 oz. goblet, top with the cream.

Vanderlinden Brasserie (Bel). A brewery based in Halle, central Belgium.

Vandermint (Hol). A mint chocolate liqueur. 30% alc. by vol. Produced by Bols.

Vanderpan Vineyards (USA). A vineyard based near Greenfield, Salinas Valley, Monterey, California. Grape variety – Chardonnay.

Vanderspritz (Cktl). Pour 2 ozs. Vandermint over ice in a highball glass. Top with soda water.

Van der Stel (Simon) (S.Afr). A Dutchman who together with Jan Van Riebeech started the vineyards in South Africa in the late seventeenth century.

Vandervelden Brasserie (Bel). A brewery based in Beersel. Is noted for its dry, acidic Lambic beers.

Vandeuil (Fr). A Cru Champagne village in the Canton de Fismes. District = Reims.

Vandières (Fr). A Cru Champagne village in the Canton de Châtillon-sur-Marne. District = Reims.

Van Donck (S.Afr). The brand-name of an Advockaat (Advocaat).

Van Gent (Pieter) (Austr). Address = Black Spring Road, P.O. Box 222, Mudgee, New South Wales 2850. Specialises in Chardonnay wines.

Vanilchina (It). A quinine and vanilla-flavoured Vermouth produced by the Carpano company.

Vanilla (Eng). A term in wine-tasting often used to describe the nose and palate of oak-aged wines. Originates from the aldehyde vanillin found in oak.

Vanilla de Mexico (Mex). A vanilla-flavoured liqueur produced by Vreez.

Vanillen-Geschmack (Ger). The vanilla taste found in many fine red wines.

Vanillin (Eng). Obtained from wooden casks and into the wine. See Aldehyde and Vanillin.

Van Loveren Vineyard (S.Afr). Based at Robertson. Address = Box 97, Robertson 6705. Produces varietal wines.

Van Lubbeek (Bel). A sweet Brown ale, low in alcohol from the Leuven district.

Van Malder Brasserie (Bel). A brewery based in Anderlecht, Brussels.

Van Merritt (USA). A brand of beer brewed by the Peter Hand Brewery.

Van Offlen (Hol). A company that is owned by Heineken. Sells under the Zwarte Kip (black hen) label.

Van Ostade (Hol). A noted liqueur producer based in Zaandam.

Van Riebeck Co-operative (S.Afr). A co-operative winery based at Riebeck, Kasteel, Malmesbury. Noted for its white wines.

Van Riebeeck (Jan) (S.Afr). A Dutchman who, together with Simon Van der Stel, started the vineyards of South Africa in 1655. First wine was produced in 1659.

Vantogrio (Czec). A non-alcoholic syrup.

Van Vleet Cocktail (Cktl). ⅗ measure Bacardi rum, ⅕ measure orange juice, ⅕ measure maple syrup. Shake well over ice, strain into an ice-filled old-fashioned glass.

Van Vollenhoven's Stout (Hol). A Stout produced by bottom-fermentation from the Heineken Brouwerij 6.4% alc. by vol.

Van Wyck Cocktail (Cktl). ½ measure dry Gin, ½ measure Sloe gin, dash Orange bitters. Shake over ice, strain into a cocktail glass.

Van Zeller (Port). Vintage Port shippers. Vintages – 1878, 1881, 1884, 1887, 1890, 1892, 1896, 1904, 1908, 1912, 1917, 1922, 1924, 1927, 1935.

Van Zondt Cocktail (Cktl). ½ measure dry Gin, ½ measure French vermouth, dash Apricot brandy. Stir over ice, strain into a cocktail glass.

Van Zuylekom (Hol). A noted Jenever producer.

Vappa (Lat). Describes a wine that has gone flat, lifeless.

Vaqueyras (Fr). See Vacqueyras.

Var (Fr). A Département in south-eastern France. Has the Provence wine-producing region in its boundaries.

Vara (Sp). A unit of measurement equivalent to 1.74 metres.

Vara y Pulgar (Sp). The traditional method of pruning in the Jerez region.

Varazdin (Yug). A wine-producing area in Croatia.

Varela (Sp). Sherry and Brandy producing bodega and shippers based in Puerto de Santa Maria.

Varichon et Clerc (Fr). A négociant-éleveur of sparkling wines based in Savoie.

Varietal (Eng). A grape which is slightly different to the main known varietal such as Welschriesling to the Riesling.

Varietal (Eng). A term applied to a wine which has a predominance of one grape variety and uses that grape's name for the name of the wine.

Varietal Bottling (USA). This indicates the grape from which the wine is produced. Must be from at least 51% of single variety but local laws may require much higher proportions.

Varignus (Le) (Fr). A vineyard in the A.C. commune of Montagny, Côte Chalonnaise, Burgundy.

Varil (Tur). A small cask, barrel.

Varna (Bul). A small delimited wine-producing area in the eastern region of Bulgaria. Produces white wines.

Varna Dimiot (Bul). A dry, fruity wine made from the Dimiot grape in the Varna region of the Black Sea.

Varnenski Misket (Bul). A white grape variety.

Varnhalt (Ger). Village. (Anb) = Baden. (Ber) = Ortenau. (Gro) = Schloss Rodeck. (Vins) = Klosterbergfelsen, Sonnenberg, Steingrübler.

Varogne (La) (Fr). A vineyard in the A.C. Hermitage, southern Rhône.

Varoilles (Les) (Fr). A Premier Cru vineyard [part] in the A.C. commune of Gevrey-Chambertin in the Côte de Nuits. 7.4 ha. It belongs entirely to the Domaine des Varoilles.

Varrains (Fr). A commune in the A.C. Saumur district, Anjou-Saumur, Loire. Produces red and white wines.

Varsilaki (Tur). A red grape variety grown in the Thrace and Marmara region.

Varsity Bitter (Eng). A cask conditioned Bitter 1041 O.G. brewed by the Morrells Brewery of Oxford.

Varsity Blues Cocktail (Cktl). ½ measure Gin, ¼ measure Vodka, ¼ measure blue Curaçao, dash Maraschino. Stir over ice, strain into a cocktail glass.

Vasija R.F.N. (Arg). A Bordeaux-style red wine made from the Sangiovetto piccolo and Merlot grapes in the Mendosa region.

Vasilha (Port). Cask, barrel.

Vaslin Press (Sp). A horizontal, rotating press that enables the number of pressings and amount of pressure to be controlled.

Vaso (Sp). Tumbler, glass.

Vaso (En) (Sp). The local name for the Goblet method of vine-training.

Vasse Felix Winery (Austr). Address = Cowaramup 6284 Western Australia 10 ha. Grape varieties – Cabernet sauvignon, Gewürztraminer, Hermitage, Malbec and Riesling.

V

Vastatrix (Fr). One of the nicknames used in France for the Phylloxera vine louse. See also Ravager.

V.A.T. (Cktl).(abbr). Vodka And Tonic.

Vat (Eng). Usually an open vessel used in the brewing process for beer fermentation.

Vat (Fr). Large casks used for the blending and maturing of wines and spirits.

Vat (Hol). A container holding 100 litres (22 Imp. gallons), 26.4 US gallons.

Vat 1884 (Egy). A Brandy produced from local grapes by the Egyptian Vineyards and Distilleries Co.

Vaticanum (Lat). A red wine produced in central-western Italy during Roman times.

Vat 69 (Scot). A famous blended Scotch whisky from William Sanderson and Son Ltd. Named after the original vat blend. 40% alc. by vol.

Vat 69 Reserve (Scot). A blended De Luxe Scotch whisky 12 year old from William Sanderson and Son Ltd. at Queensferry. 40% alc. by vol.

Vatted Malt (Scot). A blend of pure Malt (single) whiskies. Up to 6 individual malts may be used. e.g. Speyside, Concannon, etc.

Vatting (Eng). Mixing or blending in a vat.

Vat 20 (Egy). A Brandy produced from local grapes by the Egyptian Vineyards and Distilleries Co.

Vauchrétien (Fr). An A.C. commune in the Coteaux de l'Aubance in the Anjou-Saumur district of the Loire.

Vauciennes (Fr). A Cru Champagne village in the Canton d'Épernay. District = Épernay.

Vaucluse (Fr). A département in the north-eastern Rhône. See Roaix.

Vaucoupains (Fr). See Vaucoupan.

Vaucoupin (Fr). A Premier Cru vineyard in the A.C. Chablis, Burgundy. Also spelt Vaucoupains.

Vaucrains (Les) (Fr). A Premier Cru vineyard in the A.C. commune of Nuits-Saint-George, Côte de Nuits, Burgundy. 6 ha.

Vaud (Switz). A famous wine area producing mainly dry white wines. Has three districts – Chablais, La Côte and Lavaux. Produces white wines from the Chasselas and Riesling grapes and red wines from the Gamay and Pinot noir grapes.

Vaud Dorin (Switz). The local name for the white Chasselas grape in the Vaud region.

Vaudemanges (Fr). A Premier Cru Champagne village in the Canton de Suippes. District = Châlons.

Vaudésir (Fr). A Grand Cru Chablis vineyard.

Vaudevey (Fr). A Premier Cru vineyard in the A.C. Chablis, Burgundy.

Vaudois Chablais (Switz). Strong, smooth white wines with a flavour of gunflint made at Aigle on Lake Leman in the canton of Vaud.

Vaugiraut (Fr). A Premier Cru vineyard in the A.C. Chablis, Burgundy. Is often reclassified as the Premier Cru vineyard Vosgros.

Vaulorent (Fr). A Premier Cru vineyard in the A.C. Chablis, Burgundy. Is often reclassified as the Premier Cru vineyard Fourchaume.

Vault (Eng). A cellar. Originally a room where casks were stored especially in the north of England. Name is now used as an alternative to the public bar.

Vaunage (Fr). A Vins de Pays area in Provence, south-eastern France. Produces red, rosé and dry white wines.

Vaupulent (Fr). A Premier Cru vineyard in the A.C. Chablis, Burgundy. Is often reclassified as the Premier Cru vineyard Fourchaume.

Vauvert (Fr). An area of vinification for V.D.Q.S. wines of Costières du Gard, Languedoc.

Vauvry (Fr). A vineyard based in the A.C. commune of Rully, Côte Chalonnaise, Burgundy.

Vaux (Eng). Large brewing group with many public houses and breweries in Scotland, south Yorkshire, Sunderland and Belgium. Noted for its cask conditioned Sunderland Draught 1040 O.G. Samson 1042 O.G. plus many keg and bottled beers.

Vaux-en-Beaujolais (Fr). A commune in the Beaujolais district. Has A.C. Beaujolais-Villages or Beaujolais-Vaux-en-Beaujolais status.

Vauxhall Nectar (Eng). A mixture of Rum, syrup and bitter almond, drunk diluted with water in the nineteenth century.

Vauxrenard (Fr). A commune in the Beaujolais district. Has A.C. Beaujolais-Villages or Beaujolais-Vauxrenard status.

Vayres (Fr). A region of west Saint-Émilion in the Gironde on the river Dordogne. Produces red and white wines. Best known is the Graves de Vayres (white wine).

VB (Ch.Isles) (abbr). For the Vauxlaurens Brewery owned by Randalls of St. Peter Port, Guernsey. Initials are used on beer labels. e.g. VB Bitter.

V.B. Bruzzone (It). A noted producer of sparkling wines (produced by the méthode champenoise) based in the Piemonte region.

V.C.C. (Fr) (abbr). Stands for Vins Ordinaires de Consommation Courante. These are wines for everyday drinking.

V.d.L. (Fr) (abbr). Vins de Liqueur.

V.d.N. (Fr) (abbr). Vin doux natural.

V.D.P.V. (Ger) (abbr). Verband Deutscher Prädikatswein Versteigerer.

V.D.Q.S. (Fr) (abbr). Vins Délimités de Qualité Supérieure. Second from top classification of wines in France. Was introduced in 1949.

Vecchia Romagna (It). A Brandy made by the firm of Buton of Romagna.

Vecchio (It). Old. Denotes a wine with cask age. e.g. Chianti must have minimum of 2 years in cask.

Vecchio Piemonte (It). A Brandy produced by Martini and Rossi in Turin.

Vedel System (S.Afr). A Wine circle tasting system of using asterisks instead of numbers to rate wines. ***** = excellent, **** = very good, *** = good, ** = acceptable and * = poor.

Vedin (USSR). A wine-producing centre in Armenia.

Veedercrest Winery (USA). A winery based in Emeryville, Alameda, California. Grape varieties – Cabernet sauvignon, Chardonnay, Gewürztraminer, Johannisberg riesling and Merlot. Produces varietal wines. Also has a vineyard on Mount Veeder in the Napa Valley.

Veeport (Can). A red grape variety established by the Ontario Department of the Agricultural Experimental Station. Is used in Port-style wine production.

Vega Sicilia (Sp). A red wine from Old Castile. Up to 16% alc. by volume. Produced by the Bodegas Vega Sicilia. (Valbuena is the second quality wine). Wine is produced from a 60 ha. area of the estate. Grape varieties Albiño, Cabernet sauvignon, Malbec, Merlot and Tinto fino. D.O. Ribera de Duero.

Vega Winery (USA). A winery and vineyard based in the Santa Ynez Valley, Santa Barbara, California. Grape varieties – Gewürztraminer and White riesling. Produces varietal and table wines.

Vegetal (Eng). Wine-tasting term denoting a vegetable taste or aroma.

Vehissima (Port). When seen on a label denotes 'old'.

Veiga Franca and Co. Ltd (Mad). A noted Madeira wine shipper.

Veiling (Eng). A term used when one part of the wine masks or veils another part. e.g. the bouquet may veil part of the taste.

Veitshöchheim (Ger). Village. (Anb) = Franken. (Ber) = Maindreick. (Gro) =

Not yet assigned. (Vin) = Sonnenschein.

Veitshöchheim (Ger). Village. (Anb) = Franken. (Ber) = Maindreieck. (Gro) = Ravensburg. (Vin) = Wölflein.

Velazquez (Sp). Red wines produced by Bodegas Velazquez S.A. from 80% Tempranillo and 20% Garnacha grapes. All classes are produced.

Veldenz (Ger). Village. (Anb) = Mosel-Saar-Ruwer. (Ber) = Bernkastel. (Gro) = Kurfürstlay. (Vins) = Carlsberg, Elisenberg, Grafschafter Sonnenberg, Kirchberg, Mühlberg.

Veldt (Fr). A measure once used in the Cognac region. 27 veldts was equal to a 205 litre cask. 35 veldts equals 60 Imp. gallons (72 US gallons).

Velenche (Sp). Pipette or Sonde used for drawing wine from the cask. Can be metal or glass, looks like a big syringe. Is plunged into the cask, filled, then the finger is placed over the top whilst it is lifted out. When the finger is removed the wine is released into the glass.

Velho (Port). Old wine.

Veliternum (Lat). A red wine produced in central-western Italy during Roman times.

Veliterra (Sp). A white wine produced from the Palomino, Verdejo and Viura grapes by Cooperative La Seca in La Rueda.

Velké Březno Brewery (Czec). An old brewery based in north-western Czec.

Velké Pavlovice (Czec). A wine district within the region of Bohemia. Produces some of the best wines of the region.

Velké Popvice Brewery (Czec). A large, noted brewery based in western Czec.

Velké Šariš Brewery (Czec). A brewery which is noted for a special Pale ale of same name.

Velké Zernoseky (Czec). A wine-producing town based north of Prague.

Velletri Bianco (It). D.O.C. white wine from the Latium region. Made from the Bellone, Bonvino, Malvasia and Trebbiano grapes grown in commune of Velletri and Lariano and part of commune of Cisterna di Latina.

Velletri Rosso (It). D.O.C. red wine from the Latium region. Made from the Cesanese comune/di affile, Montepulciano and Sangiovese grapes grown in communes of Velletri and Lariano and part of the Cisterna di Latina commune.

Vellutato (It). Denotes wine with a velvety character.

Velluto Rosso (N.Z.). A red table wine produced by Corbans in the Henderson Valley, North Island.

Velocity Cocktail (Cktl). ⅓ gill Gin, ⅙ gill Italian vermouth. Shake well over ice, strain into a cocktail glass, add a slice of orange.
Velo de Flor (Sp). 'Veil of Flor'. The Flor yeasts that float on the top of the new Sherry like a film (veil). See Flor.
Velouté (Fr). Used to describe a wine which has a soft, rich, mellow, velvety softness. Has no roughness whatsoever.
Veltelini (Hun). A white grape variety grown in north-western Hungary.
Veltliner (Aus). A white grape variety used in the production of Gumpoldskirchener. 3 variations – red, green (Grüner) and early red Veltiner.
Veltliner Bianco (It). A white grape variety grown in northern Italy.
Velvet (Can). A name for the English drink Black Velvet. (½ Stout and ½ Champagne).
Velvet Cocktail (Cktl). ½ measure Scotch whisky, ⅓ measure dry Vermouth, ⅙ measure Parfait Amour, dash Absinthe, dash Wormwood bitters. Shake over ice, strain into a cocktail glass.
Velvet Hammer (Cktl).(1). ⅓ measure Tia Maria, ⅓ measure Cointreau, ⅓ measure fresh cream. Shake over ice, strain into a cocktail glass.
Velvet Hammer (Cktl).(2). ⅗ measure Strega, ⅕ measure (white) Crème de Cacao, ⅕ measure cream. Shake over ice, strain into a cocktail glass.
Velvet Hammer Cocktail (Cktl). ⅕ gill Vodka, ⅛ gill (white) Crème de Cacao, ⅛ gill cream. Shake over ice, strain into a cocktail glass.
Velvet Hill (USA). The name used by the Llords and Elwood Winery in Livermore, California for a range of their wines.
Velvet Stout (Eng). A Stout 1042 O.G. brewed and bottled by the Courage Brewery in London.
Velvet Stout (Eng). A Stout 1042 O.G. brewed and bottled by the Webster Brewery in Halifax, Yorkshire.
Velvety (Eng). Denotes a wine or beer that is very smooth and has no roughness.
Vemagering (Hol). Maceration.
Venčac-Oplenac (Yug). A wine-producing region noted for its red and rosé wines produced from the Gamay, Pinot noir and Prokupac grape varieties.
Vencia (Sp). A red grape variety grown in Galicia.
Vendage (Fr). See Vendange. Mis-spelling of.
Vendange (Fr). Harvest, Vintage.
Vendangeoirs (Fr). Buildings in Champagne where the grapes are pressed also used to house the grape pickers.
Vendange Tardive (Fr). Late harvested. In Alsace replaced the Spätlese designation. Grapes are usually attacked by botrytis cinerea. Denotes a finer wine.
Vendangeur (Fr). Grape picker, harvester, vintage worker.
Vendemia (Sp). See Vendimia.
Vendémiarire (Fr). The month of the grape harvest. 23rd September to 22nd October. (The first month of the French Revolutionary Calender).
Vendemmia (It). Harvest, vintage.
Vendersheim (Ger). Village. (Anb) = Rheinhessen. (Ber) = Bingen. (Gro) = Kurfürstenstück. (Vins) = Goldberg, Sonnenberg.
Vendimia (Sp). Vintage, Harvest.
Vendimia Especial Reserve (Sp). Wines produced by Bodegas Bilbainas, S.A. (Alta region) Rioja.
Vendramino Vineyards (USA). A winery based in Paw Paw, Michigan. Is noted for its quality table wines.
Venecia (Sp). See Venencia.
Veneciador (Sp). See Venenciador.
Venencia (Sp). A metal cup which is on a long handle of bone or wood and is used to dip into Sherry casks to take out a sample of wine from the centre of the cask.
Venenciador (Sp). The man who uses a Venencia to draw wine from the centre of the Sherry cask. Usually demonstrates his skill by pouring the wine into a number of Copitas from a height at the same time without any spillage.
Venetian Cream (It). A Brandy-based cream liqueur. 17% alc. by vol.
Venetian Glass (It). Early drinking glasses. Soda glass. Thin, light and fragile.
Venetian Sunset (Cktl). ⅖ measure dry Gin, ⅕ measure Campari, ⅕ measure dry Vermouth, ⅕ measure Grand Marnier. Stir over ice, strain into a cocktail glass. Add a cherry on top.
Veneto (It). A region in north-eastern Italy. It borders Trentino-Alto Adige, Venezia, Friulia, Emilia-Romagna, The Adriatic Sea, Lombardy and Austria. Lies between Lake Garda and River Po. See Venezia-Euganea.
Venezia-Euganea (It). The alternative name for the Veneto region.
Venezia Tridentina (It). The pre 1947 name for the Trentino-Alto Adige (Süd Tirol) region.
Venezuelan Coffee (S.Am). Coffee used mainly for blending. Produces a light style of coffee with medium flavour and acidity. Has three main regions – Caracas, Maracibos and Meridas.
Venningen (Ger). Village. (Anb) = Rheinpfalz. (Ber) = Südliche Weinstrasse. (Gro) = Trappenberg. (Vin) = Doktor.

Vensac (Fr). A commune in the A.C. Médoc, north-western Bordeaux.

Vent (Eng). Allowing the escape of a CO_2 gas build up in a beer cask owing to the secondary fermentation during conditioning. Is released through the soft Spile.

Ventana Vineyards (USA). A winery based near Soledad, Monterey County, California. 125 ha. Grape varieties – Chardonnay, Chenin blanc, Gamay, Johannisberg riesling, Muscat blanc, Petite sirah, Pinot noir, Sauvignon blanc and Zinfandel. Produces varietal, botrytised and table wines.

Vente Directe (Fr). On the outside of a Château. Denotes that wines can be bought from the Château.

Ventes sur Place (Fr). A term that denotes that the wines are sold on the premises.

Vente sur Souches (Fr). Describes the sale of wines made prior to the harvest. Based on the amount of alcohol that should be produced, therefore the price may be fixed. It is altered if the amount of alcohol eventually produced is higher or lower.

Venteuil (Fr). A Cru Champagne village in the Canton d'Épernay. District = Épernay.

Venusbuckel (Ger). Vineyard. (Anb) = Rheinpfalz. (Ber) = Südliche Weinstrasse. (Gro) = Kloster Liebfrauenberg. (Vil) = Billigheim-Ingenheim.

V.E.P. (Fr) (abbr). Vieillissement Exceptionnellement Prolongé. A liqueur.

Véraison (Fr). The ripening of the grapes.

Verband der Südtiroler Kellereigenossenschaften (It). The Union of Südtirol Co-operatives. A body that markets for 21 of the co-operatives in the Südtirol. Based at Crispistr.

Verband Deutscher Naturwein Versteigerer (Ger). German natural wine auction-sellers' association. See V.D.P.V. (new name).

Verband Deutscher Prädikatswein Versteigerer (Ger). V.D.P.V. A winegrowers' association. The new name given to the Verband Deutscher Naturwein Versteigerer.

Verbena (Fr). A herb liqueur produced in south-western France. There are two styles' yellow (sweet) and green (dry).

Verbesco (It). A lightly sparkling white wine produced from Barbera, Freisa and Grignolino grapes by Gallo d'Oro.

Verbessert (Ger). The sugaring of the must in poor years to increase the alcohol content. (Fr) = Chaptalisation.

Verbesserung (Ger). The process of adding sugar to the grape must. See Verbessert. See Anreicherung.

Verboten Cocktail (Cktl). ⅙ gill dry Gin, ¹⁄₁₀ measure orange juice, ¹⁄₁₀ measure lemon juice, ¹⁄₁₀ measure Forbidden fruit. Shake well over ice, strain into a cocktail glass. Top with a cherry that has been soaked in old Cognac.

Vercoope (Port). A group of thirteen farmers who blend, bottle and market their wines. Produce Verdegar, a noted white Vinho Verde.

Verdana (It). The Pollino, Calabria name for the Malvasia bianca grape.

Verde (Port). Lit – 'Green'. Used for Vinho Verde wines coming from the delimited area of Minho in northern Portugal. Wines are low in alcohol and are characterised by the slight prickle on the tongue (pétillance) from malo-lactic fermentation in the bottle. The green denotes age (young) and not colour.

Verdea (Gre). A white pungent wine from the island of Zante in western Greece (Ionian Isles). Made from a large variety of grape species.

Verdeca (It). A white grape variety grown in the Puglia region.

Verdegar (Port). The brand-name of a Vinho Verde produced by Vercoope and an Aguardente produced in the Minho.

Verdejo (Sp). A white grape variety grown in the central regions of Spain.

Verdejo Palido (Sp). A light, white wine produced by Sociedad Agrícola in La Seca, Rueda.

Verdelho (Mad). A white grape variety used in the production of a fortified wine of same name. Also used in the making of a white Port wine.

Verdelho (Mad). A medium dry fortified wine from the island of Madeira.

Verdelho Tinto (Mad). A black grape variety used in the production of Madeira wines.

Verdello (It). A white grape variety used in minor quantities to make Orvieto wine.

Verdenay (N.Z.). A dry, bottle-fermented, sparkling wine produced from the Chardonnay and Pinot noir grape varieties by Penfolds.

Verdencho (Sp). A white grape variety grown in the southern central regions.

Verdepino (Port). A noted Vinho Verde produced by C. Vinhas, S.A.R.L. P.O. Box 2422, Lisbon.

Verdet (Alain) (Fr). A noted producer of Crèmont de Bourgogne based at Arcrenat, Burgundy.

Verdicchio (It). A white grape variety grown in the central regions of Italy. See Verdicchio dei Castelli di Jesi.

Verdicchio dei Castelli di Jesi (It). D.O.C.

white wine from The Marches region. Made from the Verdicchio, Malvasia and Trebbiano toscano grapes. Sold in amphora-shaped bottles. D.O.C. also applies to naturally sparkling wines produced according to regulations. Also a Classico.

Verdicchio di Matelica (It). D.O.C. white wine from The Marches region Made from the Verdicchio, Malvasia and Trebbiano toscano grapes. D.O.C. also applies to a sparkling wine made with musts or wines produced in accordance to regulations.

Verdier (Fr). A French gentleman who, in 1850, perfected the Alambic Armagnaçais invented by Edouard Adam.

Verdil (Sp). A white grape variety grown in the Alicante region.

Verdiso (It). A white grape variety grown in the Veneto.

Verdiso (It). A white, dry wine of the Treviso province of Venetia made from a grape of the same name.

Verdlet (USA). A white hybrid grape variety also known as the Seibel 9110.

Verdoncho (Sp). A white grape variety grown in the La Mancha region. Is also known as the Verducho.

Verdosilla (Sp). An alternative name for the Merseguera grape.

Verdot (Fr). See Petit Verdot.

Verdot (USA). A red grape variety used for making red wines in California.

Verducho (Sp). A white grape variety grown in the La Mancha region. Is also known as the Verdoncho.

Verdun Estate (S.Afr). Vineyards based in Stellenbosch. Address = Verdun Kelders, Box 22, Vlottenburg 7604. Produces varietal wines.

Verdunnen (Hol). Dilute.

Verduzzo (It). A white grape variety grown in the Veneto region.

Verduzzo Friulano (It). A variety of the white Verduzzo grape grown in the Friuli-Venezia Giulia.

Vered (Isr). A Port-style, sweet dessert wine.

Vereinigte Hospitien (Ger). The German equivalent of the French Hospices de Beaune. Sited on the river Mosel at Trier.

Verenberg (Ger). Vineyard. (Anb) = Württemberg. (Ber) = Württembergisch Unterland. (Gro) = Lindelberg. (Vil) = Verrenberg.

Vereots (Les) (Fr). A Premier Cru vineyard in the A.C. commune of Aloxe-Corton, Côte de Beaune, Burgundy.

Vergara (Sp). A Sherry and Brandy producer based in Jerez de la Frontera.

Vergelesses (Fr). An A.C. district of the Côte de Beaune which contains the Île de Vergelesses and Les Basses-Vergelesses with an area of 9.75 and 18.5 ha. respectively in the parish of Pernand. White wines are renowned for their finesse and distinction.

Verge Longue (Fr). The long shoot found on each arm of the Guyot method of vine training.

Vergennes (USA). A lesser red grape variety of the Vitis Labrusca used in the making of varietal wines.

Vergenoegd Estate (S.Afr). Vineyards based in Stellenbosch. Address = Vergenoegd Langoed (Faure and Faure) Box 1, Faure 7131. Produces varietal wines.

Vergenoegd Langoed (S.Afr). See Vergenoegd Estate.

Vergers (Les) (Fr). A Premier Cru vineyard [part] in the commune of Chassagne-Montrachet, Côte de Beaune, Burgundy. 9.54 ha. (white and red).

Vergine (It). A style of Marsala in Sicily. Wine is kept 5 years in Solera. It emerges lighter and drier.

Vergisson (Fr). A commune in the A.C. Pouilly-Fuissé, Mâconnais, Burgundy.

Verhoeven (Hol). A small Jenever-producing distillery.

Verín (Sp). A noted wine-producing town on the Portuguese border in Galicia. Produces high alcohol (14% by vol) red wines.

Verin Valley (Sp). A naturally sparkling mineral water from a valley of the same name in north-eastern Spain. Bottled by Fontenova.

Veritas Winery (Austr). A winery based near Tanunda, Barossa Valley, South Australia. Produces varietal wines.

Verjuice (Eng). Unripe grape juice.

Verjus (Fr). The juice from unripe grapes. Usually the result of second or late flowering. Is very high in acidity.

Vermentino (It). A white grape variety grown in northern Italy and in Sardinia to produce light, dry wines. Known in Corsica as the Malvoisie de Corse.

Vermentino (It). A dry white wine from the Liguria region from a grape of same name.

Vermentino di Gallura (It). D.O.C. white wine from Sardinia. Made from the Vermentino grape. Area of production is Gallura and 17 communes in province of Sassari and 2 in the province of Nuoro. If minimum total alc. content is 14% by vol. then classed as Superiore.

Vermentino Ligure (It). A white wine made from Vermentino grape in the Liguna region. May be sparkling.

Vermouté (Fr). Vermouth.

Vermouth (Euro). A fortified wine flavoured with herbs, spices, barks and flowers by either infusion, maceration or distillation. Name derives from the German 'Wermut' (Wormwood, an ingredient of Vermouth). Originally the French variety was white and dry and the Italian red and sweet. Now firms from both countries as well as others produce all styles including sweet white, dry red and rosé.

Vermouth Achampanado (Cktl). ⅓ gill French vermouth placed over ice in a highball glass, piece of lime peel and teaspoon castor sugar. Top with soda water, stir.

Vermouth Apéritif (Cktl). ⅓ gill French vermouth, ⅓ gill soda, 3 dashes brown Curaçao. Place the Curaçao in a wine goblet, add Vermouth and soda, serve with a lump of ice.

Vermouth Cassis (Cktl). 1½ ozs. dry Vermouth, ¼ oz. Crème de Cassis. Place in a 5 oz. goblet with 2 ice cubes. Stir, top with mineral water.

Vermouth Cocktail (Cktl). ½ measure sweet Vermouth, ½ measure French vermouth, dash Campari. Stir over ice, strain into a cocktail glass. Top with a cherry.

Vermouth Curaçao (Cktl). ½ gill French vermouth, ⅙ gill Curaçao. Stir over ice, strain into an ice-filled highball glass, top with soda water.

Vermouth Highball (Cktl). As for Gin Highball using Vermouth instead of Gin. French = dry, Italian = sweet.

Vermouth Hour (Bra). See Copetin.

Vermut (Port) (Sp) (Tur). Vermouth.

Vernaccia (It). A white grape variety grown in Sardinia.

Vernaccia (It). A dry golden-yellow wine, high in alcohol with a Sherry taste. Unfortified, it has an almond blossom bouquet. Made from grapes of the same name. Drunk as an apéritif or digestive. Made in Sardinia.

Vernaccia del Campidano (It). See Vernaccia.

Vernaccia di Oristano (It). A white grape variety grown in Sardinia to make a wine of same name.

Vernaccia di Oristano (It). D.O.C. white wine from Sardinia. Made from the Vernaccia di oristano grape. Aged for 2 years minimum in wood. If minimum alc. content is 15.5% by vol. and aged 3 years then classed Superiore. Liquoroso – fortified and aged 2 years in wood. Superiore Riserva when wine has aged for minimum of 4 years in wood.

Vernaccia di San Gimignano (It). A white grape variety grown in the Tuscany region imported from Greece in the twelfth century.

Vernaccia di San Gimignano (It). D.O.C. white wine from the Tuscany region. Made from the Vernaccia di San Gimignano grapes. Vinification must occur within the production area. (Siena). Wine is taken quickly off the skins. If aged minimum 1 year then classed Riserva. D.O.C. also applies to fortified wines according to specific regulation.

Vernaccia di Serrapetrona (It). A red grape variety grown in The Marches region.

Vernaccia di Serrapetrona (It). D.O.C. red sparkling wine from The Marches. Made from the Vernaccia di Serrapetrona, Ciliegiolo, Montepulciano and Sangiovese grapes. Grapes are partially dried. Classed either as Amabile (semi-sweet) or Dolce (sweet).

Vernaccia Sarda (USA). A white grape variety grown in California to produce white wines.

Vernage (Eng). Chaucer's way of spelling Vernaccia wine from Tuscany in his *Canterbury Tales*.

Vernatsch (It). A red grape variety grown in the Trentino-Alto Adige region. Also known as the Schiave and the Trollinger in German.

Vernazza (It). One of the five towns in the Cinque Terre district of Liguna.

Verneuil (Fr). A Cru Champagne village in the Canton de Dormans. District = Épernay.

Vernon (Admiral) (Eng). See 'Old Rummy'.

Vernou (Fr). A commune in the Touraine district of the Loire. Produces A.C. Vouvray white and sparkling wines.

Véron (Fr). The local Loire name for the Breton (Cabernet franc) grape.

Véronique (Cktl). 1 measure Batida de Coco, 1 measure Cointreau, 1 measure Cognac, ½ measure Vodka, ½ measure orange juice. Shake over ice, strain into a club goblet. Dress with an orange slice.

Véronique Bottle (Fr). Elongated bottle, usually clear in colour, with triple ring of ridges around the neck, used for certain French white wines such as Tavel.

Verpelet (Hun). A noted wine-producing village in Debrö that produces Hárslevelü (a sweet white wine).

Verre (Fr). Glass, drinking glass.

Verre à Bordeaux (Fr). A bell-shaped glass for drinking red Bordeaux wines.

Verre à INAO (Fr). INAO glass. Full-bowled with a tapered rim. Recommended as the most suitable glass for the tasting of wines

Verre Ancien (Fr). Antique drinking glass.

Vèrre à Pid (Ch.Isles). Wine glass. See also Vèrre à Vin.

Vèrre à Vin (Ch.Isles). Wine glass. See also Vèrre à Pid.

Verre à Vin du Moselle (Fr). German Mosel wine drinking glass.

Verre à Vin du Rhin (Fr). Hock glass.

Verre Ballon (Fr). Balloon glass, nosing glass.

Verre Couché (Fr). Cut glass, crystal glass.

Verre de Cognac (Fr). Cognac glass.

Verre Gravé (Fr). Engraved drinking glass.

Verrenberg (Ger). Village. (Anb) = Württemberg. (Ber) = Württembergisch Unterland. (Gro) = Lindelberg. (Vins) = Goldberg, Verenberg.

Verre Ordinaire de Paris (Fr). Paris goblet.

Verrerie (Fr). Drinking glasses.

Verre Vaudois (Switz). A straight-sided drinking glass for wines.

Verrières (Fr). A commune in the Charente Département whose grapes are classed Grande Champagne (Cognac).

Vers (Fr). A commune in the Mâconnais whose grapes may be used to produce Mâcon Supérieur.

Versa Cantina Sociale (La) SpA (It). A noted producer of sparkling (méthode champenoise) wines. Address = Via Crispi 15, 27047 S. Maria della Versa, P.V.

Versailles Distillerie (S.Am). A noted Rum distillery based in Guyana.

Versarmières (Fr). A vineyard in the commune of Fuissé, A.C. Pouilly-Fuissé, Mâconnais, Burgundy.

Verschnitt (Ger). The general term used for different spirits that are blended together, one spirit being dominant in flavour. See Rhum Verschnitt.

Versetzte (Aus). A wine-based beverage. e.g. Vermouth, Aromatised wine.

Versetzte Wein (Aus). A fortified wine, (one that has been manufactured).

Versieden (Aus). A term that describes the action of stopping a fermentation before all the sugar in the must has been converted into alcohol.

Versterk (S.Afr). Fortified (wine).

Vert (Fr). Green, young wine.

Vert Doré (Fr). An alternative name used for the Pinot noir grape.

Vertheuil (Fr). A wine-producing commune in the A.C. Haut-Médoc, Bordeaux.

Vertical Tasting (Eng). A term to denote the tasting of wines of different vintages.

Verticillium Wilt (Eng). A disease which affects hops. New wilt-resistant varieties have now almost eradicated it. e.g. Target.

Vert Jus (Fr). Lit - 'Green juice'. Unripe grape juice. See Verjus.

Vert-la-Gravelle (Fr). A Cru Champagne village in the Canton de Vertus. District = Châlons.

Vertou (Fr). A noted wine village in the Muscadet de Sèvre-et-Maine, Loire.

Vertus (Fr). A canton in the district of Châlons in the Champagne region. Has the Premier Cru villages of – Bergères-les-Vertus, Etrechy, Vertus and Villeneuve-Renneville.

Vertus (Fr). A Premier Cru Champagne village in the Canton de Vertus. District = Châlons.

Vertzami (Gre). A red grape variety grown mainly in central and western Greece.

Verveine du Rouverge (Fr). A herb liqueur both green (dry) and yellow (sweet) based on the herb vervein produced by Germain in southern France.

Verveine du Vélay (Fr). A digestive, herb liqueur made in both green and yellow versions. Based on the herb vervein, honey and Brandy. Produced by Pages.

Verwaltung (Ger). Administration (property).

Verwaltung der Staatsweinguter (Ger). A state wine domaine manager.

Very Dry Gin (USA). The term on a label to denote a Gin that has a dry (botanical) taste.

Very Old (Fr). V.O. (Cognac). V.O. (Armagnac).

Very Old Tokay (Austr). A wine from the Brown Brothers in Milawa, Victoria. A pale, tawny-coloured dessert wine.

Very Rare Âge Inconnu (Fr). A fine Cognac brandy produced by Château Paulet.

Very Specially Recommended (Fr). V.S.R. Awarded to certain merchants if the quality of their wines merits it.

Very Superior Extra Pale (Fr). See V.S.E.P.

Very Superior Old Pale (Fr). See V.S.O.P. (Cognac). and V.S.O.P. (Armagnac).

Very Very Pale (Sp). V.V.P. colour grading for Manzanilla and Fino sherries.

Verzenay (Fr). A Grand Cru Champagne village in the Canton de Verzy. District = Reims.

Verzy (Fr). A canton of the Reims district in the Champagne region. Has the Grand Cru villages of – Beaumont-sur-Vesle, Mailly-Champagne, Sillery, Verzenay and Verzy. Also the Premier Cru villages of – Chigny-les-Roses, Ludes, Montbré, Puisieulx, Rilly-la-Montagne, Trépail, Villers-Allerand and Villers-Marmery.

Verzy (Fr). A Grand Cru Champagne village in the Canton de Verzy. District = Reims.

Vescovato (Fr). A noted red wine produced on the island of Corsica.

Ves Heill (Scan). The old Norse toast for 'Good health'. See also Wassail.

Vespaiola (It). A dry white wine from the

Venetia region. Also known as Bresparolo.

Vespere (Fr). Beetle. See Hanneton.

Vespétro (Fr). An ancient liqueur once produced in Grenoble from angelica, anise, coriander and fennel.

Vespitro (It). A herb flavoured liqueur made from sugar, Brandy, aniseed, lemon, angelica, fennel and coriander.

Vespolina (It). A red grape variety.

Vesselle (Alain) (Fr). Champagne producer. Address = 8 Rue de Louvois, Bouzy 51150 Tours-sur-Marne, Récoltants-Manipulants. Produces – Non-vintage wine.

Vestfyen Brewery (Den). A noted brewery based in Assens.

Vesuvio (Cktl). ⅖ measure Bacardi White Label, ⅖ measure lemon juice, ⅕ measure Italian vermouth, ½ egg white, 2 dashes Gomme syrup. Shake well over ice, strain into an ice-filled old-fashioned glass.

Vesuvio (It). A red wine from the foot of Vesuvius in Campania. 11% alc. by vol. is dry and normally sparkling. A white version is also produced.

Veterano (Sp). A 3 year old Brandy produced by Osborne. 37% alc. by vol.

Vetrice (It). A Chianti Putto producer based in Tuscany.

Vétroz (Switz). A noted wine-producing village based near Sion in the Valais. Is noted for its Fendant wines.

Vetter (Ger). A noted liqueur and Aquavit producer based in Wunsiedel.

Veuve Aimot Cuvée Haute Tradition (Fr). A brut méthode champenoise sparkling wine from the Anjou-Saumur district of the Loire. Owned by Martini & Rossi. U.K. agents – Stowells of Chelsea.

Veuve Ambal (Fr). A wine-producer based in Burgundy. Is noted for its méthode champenoise sparkling Burgundies.

Veuve Clicquot Ponsardin (Fr). Champagne producer. Address = 12 Rue du Temple, 51100 Reims. A Grande Marque. Produces – Vintage and non-vintage wines (La Grande Dame – de luxe vintage cuvée and Clicquot Rosé – vintage rosé). Vintages – 1904, 1906, 1911, 1915, 1919, 1920, 1921, 1923, 1926, 1928, 1929, 1937, 1942, 1943, 1945, 1947, 1949, 1952, 1953, 1955, 1959, 1961, 1962, 1964, 1966, 1969, 1970, 1973, 1975, 1976, 1979, 1980, 1982, 1983. See Grande Dame (La).

Veuve de Vernay (Fr). A sparkling wine from the Bordeaux region. Produced by the tank method. Brut and demi-sec.

Veuve J. Goudoulin (Fr). Armagnac producer. Address = Domaine du Bigor,

Courrensan, 32330 Gondrin. 20 ha. in the Bas Armagnac.

Vevey Festival (Switz). A famous wine festival held in the town of Vevey near Montreaux since the seventeenth century. Held every 25–30 years. The last held in 1977. See Fête des Vignerons.

Vézelay (Fr). A red and white wine area in Avallon, Yonne Département.

Vézélise Brasserie (Fr). A brewery that is part of the Stella Artois Brasserie of Belgium.

Vhrunsko (Yug). Highest quality wine.

Viana (Port). The original port from which Port wine was shipped to England. Is 60 miles north of Oporto.

Viano Winery (USA). A winery based in Martinez, Contra Costa County, California. Grape varieties – Barbera, Cabernet sauvignon and Zinfandel. Produces varietal wines.

Vibert Chasselas (Fr). A white grape variety which is used for both wine production and eating.

Vibrisat (Sp). A term used to describe wines that are macerated on the skins. Vi verge = 'off the skins'.

Vibrona (Eng). An alcoholic British Tonic wine 17% alc. by vol. Produced by Vine Products Ltd., Kingston-Upon-Thames, London.

Vicente (Sp). A bodega based near Sarragossa, Aragón. Is noted for its fine Cariñena wines.

Viceroy (S.Afr). The brand-name of a Brandy produced by Castle Wine and Green.

Vichon Winery (USA). A winery based in the Napa Valley, California. Grape varieties – Cabernet sauvignon, Chardonnay, Sauvignon blanc and Sémillon. Produces varietals and Chevrier Blanc (a Sauvignon and Sémillon blend).

Vichy Boussange (Fr). A sparkling mineral water from Vichy.

Vichy-Célestins (Fr). A still mineral water (slightly pétillant) from Vichy. Eau Minérale Naturelle designation.

Vichy Grande Grille (Fr). A medicinal water from Vichy.

Vichy Hôpital (Fr). A medicinal water from Vichy.

Vichy Saint-Yorre (Fr), A naturally sparkling mineral water bottled at Saint-Yorre.

Vichy Water (Fr). The English name for Vichy-Célestins water.

Vickers (Austr). The brand-name for a Gin produced by the United Distillers.

Vicomte Champagne Liqueur (Fr). A liqueur produced by the De Castellane Champagne house.

Vicomte d'Aumelas (Fr). A Vins de Pays area in the Hérault Département in southern France.

Vicomte Stephane de Castelbajac (Fr). A 12 year old Cognac produced by Logis de la Montagne.

Vic-sur-Seille (Fr). A wine-producing area in the Vins de la Moselle, Lorraine. Produces Vin gris.

Victor Cocktail (Cktl). ½ measure sweet Vermouth, ¼ measure dry Gin, ¼ measure Cognac. Shake over ice, strain into a cocktail glass.

Victor Hugo Brandy (USA). The brand-name of a Brandy produced by the California Wine Association, Delano, California. 40% alc. by vol.

Victoria (Austr). A wine State in southern Australia. Areas include Goulburn Valley, Great Western and Rutherglen.

Victoria (Mex). A highly-carbonated 'Clara' beer brewed by the Modelo Brewery in Mexico City.

Victoria Bitter (Austr). A light Lager beer brewed by the Carlton and United Brewery in Melbourne.

Victoria Brewery (Eng). A brewery based in Ware, Hertfordshire. Opened in 1981. Brews cask conditioned Special 1043 O.G. Bitter 1037 O.G. and Hellfire 1063 O.G.

Victoria Regina (Sp). A brand of Oloroso sherry produced by Diez Merito (part of their Diez Hermanos range).

Victoria Sour (Cktl). ¼ gill Whisky, ¼ gill Sherry, dash Rum, dash Pineapple syrup, dash Apricot syrup. Shake well over ice, strain into a wine glass, top with a dash of soda water.

Victoria Wine Company (Eng). A large chain of Off-Licences owned by Allied Lyons.

Victory Ale (Eng). A rich Ale 1070 O.G. brewed by the Paradise Brewery in Hayle, Cornwall.

Victory Collins (Cktl). 1 fl.oz. Vodka, 2 fl.ozs. grape juice, 2 fl.ozs. lemon juice, 2 dashes Gomme syrup. Shake over ice, strain into an ice-filled highball glass. Dress with a slice of orange.

Victory Winery (N.Z.). A small winery near Blenheim, Main Road, South Stoke, Nelson, South Island. 1 ha.

Victualler (Eng). Lit – 'Purveyor of food'. Licensed victualler is a purveyer of food and alcoholic beverages.

Vid (Sp). Vine.

Vidal-Fleury (Fr). A négociant-éleveur based in the Rhône.

Vidal Winery (N.Z.). Address = St. Aubyn Street, P.O. Box 48, Hastings, Hawkes Bay, North Island. 125 ha. Grape varieties – Cabernet sauvignon,

Chardonnay, Chenin blanc, Gewürztraminer, Merlot, Müller-Thurgau, Muscat, Pinot noir, Sémillon and Sauvignon blanc. Produces varietal wines and a unique 100% Cabernet sauvignon sparkling wine.

Vidange (Fr). The gap between the wine and the cask top. If allowed, can cause Acescence (spoilage). See also Ullage.

Vide (Port). Vine shoot.

Vidiella (S.Am). A red grape variety grown in Uruguay.

Vidigueira (Port). A wine-producing area based south of Évora in Alentejo. Produces mainly white wines.

Vidonia (Sp). A popular eighteenth-century sweet dessert wine from the island of Tenerife. (Popular in England).

Vidueno (Sp). A white wine produced in the Canary Islands.

Vidure (Fr). The alternative name for the Cabernet franc grape.

Vie (Rum). Vine.

Vie (La) (S.Afr). A low-alcohol pétillant, Muscat white wine made by the Stellenbosch Farmers' Winery. Labelled Jules Grillet and Fils.

Vieil (Fr). Old. See also Vieille, Vieux.

Vieille (Fr). Old. See also Vieil, Vieux.

Vieille Cure (Fr). A herb liqueur made at Cenon in the Gironde. Has a base of Armagnac and Cognac. Produced by Intermarque, Gironde. 43% alc. by vol.

Vieille Eau de Vie de Marc du Château Grancy (Fr). A Fine Bourgogne Marc made by Louis Latour which is matured for 4–5 years in oak casks.

Vielle Ferme (La) (Fr). A vineyard in the A.C. Côtes du Ventoux, southern France.

Vieille Récolte Fine (Egy). A Brandy made from local grapes by the Egyptian Vineyards and Distilleries Co.

Vieille Relique (Fr). A 15 year old Armagnac produced by Samalens.

Vieille Réserve (Fr). A class of fine old Cognac a minimum of 5 years of age. Also a class of Armagnac a minimum age of 5 years.

Vieilles Vignes (Fr). Old vines which give the finest fruit.

Vieilles Vignes Françaises (Fr). A vintage 'Blanc de Noir' Champagne made from ungrafted Pinot noir vines by Bollinger from two small vineyards in Ay and Bouzy.

Vieillissement Exceptionnellement Prolongé (Fr). V.E.P. A superior Green Chartreuse, 12 year old, only available in Voiron or Fanchon in Paris.

Viejas Reservas (Sp). A grade of old fine matured wines of the Rioja region.

Viejisimo (Sp). Very old.

Viejo (Sp). Old.

Viejo Roble (Chile). A dry white wine produced by Undurraga.

Vien de Nus (It). A red grape variety.

Vienna (Aus). A town of Gumpoldskirchen. Gives its name to a sweet white wine. See Wien.

Vienna (Aus). A full-bodied, malty, copper coloured Lager. Style used at the Oktoberfest. Known as Marzen in Germany.

Vienna Lager (Aus). See Steffl.

Vienne (Fr). A noted wine-producing Département which includes part of Saumur, Anjou-Saumur, Loire.

Vienne (Fr). A wine-producing city in Dauphiny, Isère Département, south-eastern France. Produces red and white wines.

Viennese Apricot 'Old Glory' Liqueur (Aus). A liqueur made by the firm of J. Zwack using whole apricots fermented and distilled 34% alc. by vol.

Viennese Café (Aus). A coffee-flavoured liqueur made by the firm of J. Zwack.

Viennese Coffee (Aus). A blend of coffees which have had roasted figs added. Gives coffee a stronger, sweeter taste with a more bitter flavour.

Viennese Iced Coffee (Aus). Iced coffee with a swirl of whipped cream on top or a topping of coffee ice cream.

Viennese Pear (Aus). A Pear liqueur made by the firm of J. Zwack. 34% alc. by vol.

Viennese Velvet (Aus). Into a highball glass place some vanilla ice cream. Pour on some double strength hot black coffee. Top with whipped cream, grated chocolate and serve with straws.

Viénot (Fr). A négociant-éleveur based at Nuits-Saint-Georges in the Burgundy region. Address = 5 Quai Dumorey, 21700, Nuits-Saint-Georges.

Viertel (Ger). A special glass, shaped like a tulip with a handle like a Punch glass. ¼ litre capacity. Used in Württemberg, west Germany.

Viertelstück (Ger). A round cask holding 300 litres.

Viesch (Switz). A dry white wine produced in the upper Rhône Valley.

Vietti (It). A noted wine-producer based in the village of Castiglione Falletto, Piemonte.

Vieux (Fr). Old. See Vieille, Vielle.

Vieux Cahors (Fr). A Cahors wine that has been kept to mature. Lit – 'Old Cahors'. Has no legal meaning but denotes aged in wood for 3 years.

Vieux-Château (Le) (Fr). A vineyard in the A.C. commune of Montagny, Côte Chalonnaise, Burgundy.

Vieux-Château-Boënot (Fr). A part of Château Bel-Air in the A.C. Pomerol, Bordeaux.

Vieux-Château-Bourgueneuf (Fr). A vineyard in the commune of Pomerol. A.C. Pomerol, Bordeaux.

Vieux Château-Certan (Fr). A vineyard in the commune of Pomerol. A.C. Pomerol. 13 ha. Grape varieties – Cabernet franc, Cabernet sauvignon, Malbec.

Vieux-Château-Calon (Fr). A vineyard in the commune of Montagne-Saint-Émilion. A.C. Montagne-Saint-Émilion, Bordeaux. 5 ha.

Vieux-Château-Chauvin (Fr). A vineyard in the A.C. Saint-Émilion, Bordeaux. 4 ha.

Vieux-Château-Cloquet (Fr). A vineyard in the commune of Pomerol. A.C. Pomerol, Bordeaux. 2 ha.

Vieux-Château-Fortin (Fr). A vineyard in the A.C. Saint-Émilion, Bordeaux. 6 ha.

Vieux-Château-Goujon (Fr). A vineyard in the commune of Montagne-Saint-Émilion. A.C. Montagne-Saint-Émilion, Bordeaux. 2 ha.

Vieux-Château-la-Beyesse (Fr). A vineyard in the commune of Puisseguin-Saint-Émilion. A.C. Puisseguin-Saint-Émilion, Bordeaux. 4 ha.

Vieux Château Landon (Fr). Address = Bégadan 33340 Médoc. Cru Bourgeois A.C. Médoc. Commune = Bégadan. Grape varieties – Cabernet franc, Cabernet sauvignon, Malbec and Merlot.

Vieux-Château-l'Angélus (Fr). A vineyard in the commune of Pomerol. A.C. Pomerol, Bordeaux. 1 ha.

Vieux-Château-Mazerat (Fr). A part of Clos Haut-Mazerat in the A.C. Saint-Émilion, Bordeaux.

Vieux Château Negrit (Fr). A vineyard in the commune of Montagne-Saint-Émilion. A.C. Montagne-Saint-Émilion, Bordeaux. 10 ha.

Vieux-Château-Palon (Fr). A vineyard in the commune of Montagne-Saint-Émilion. A.C. Montagne-Saint-Émilion, Bordeaux. 5 ha.

Vieux-Château-Peymouton (Fr). A vineyard in the A.C. Saint-Émilion, Bordeaux. 3 ha.

Vieux-Château-Peyrou (Fr). A vineyard in the A.C. Saint-Émilion, Bordeaux. 9 ha.

Vieux-Château-Tropchaud (Fr). A vineyard in the commune of Pomerol. A.C. Pomerol, Bordeaux. 2 ha.

Vieux Clos (Fr). A vineyard in the commune of Avensa. A.C. Médoc, Bordeaux. Bourgeois Supérieur.

Vieux-Domaine-Menuts (Fr). A vineyard in the A.C. Saint-Émilion, Bordeaux. 3 ha.

Vieux Pays (Switz). Lit – 'Old country'. The other name for the Valais canton.

Vieux Rafiot (Cktl). ⅓ measure Mandarine Napoléon, ⅔ measure Cognac. Stir over ice, strain into a balloon glass, decorate with a slice of tangerine.

Vieux Réserve du Vigneron (Fr). A 30 year old plus Cognac produced by Destreilles.

Vieux Rouge du Valais (Switz). A red Vin de Pays wine from the Valais.

Vieux Rum (W.Ind). The term given to a Rum that has been aged for more than 6 years. See Liqueur Rum.

Vieux Temps (Bel). A Belgian-style Ale brewed by the Artois Brasserie based in Louvain.

Viewpoint of the German Wine-Route (Ger). Aussichtsterrasse der Deutsche Weinstrasse.

Views Land Co (USA). A winery based in Sonoma County, California. Grape varieties – Cabernet sauvignon, Chardonnay and Gewürztraminer. Produces varietal wines.

Vif (Fr). A lively, brisk wine.

Vigevanese (It). Producers of Millefiori liqueur.

Vigna (It). The Italian equivalent to the French Cru.

Vignacourt (Austr). A winery in Swan Valley, Western Australia.

Vignaioli Piemontesi (It). Producer of Moscato d'Asti Spumante in the Piemonte region.

Vignaiolo (It). Wine grower.

Vigne (Fr). Vine.

Vigneau et Chevreau (Fr). A noted sparkling Vouvray producer based at Chancay, Touraine, Loire.

Vigne de l'Enfant Jésus (La) (Fr). See Les Grèves.

Vigne-Devant (La) (Fr). A vineyard in the A.C. commune of Montagny, Côte Chalonnaise, Burgundy.

Vignée (La) (Fr). The brand-name for red and white wines from Bouchard Père et Fils in Burgundy.

Vigne en Fleur (Fr). Lit – 'Vine in flower'. Denotes new spirit after the wine has been distilled for Cognac. The spirit as it matures in cask.

Vigneron (Fr). A vine grower who may be working for himself or not.

Vigneron à Moitié (Fr). A vine grower who does not work for himself but receives part of the production for tending the vineyard.

Vigneronnage (Fr). In Burgundy is to a vineyard what a Tenant farmer is to an agricultural estate. Used only in the Beaujolais.

Vignerons de Franschhoek (S.Afr). A body based in the Franschhoek Valley east of Stellenbosch. Founded due to the Huguenot refugees who settled there to escape persecution in France. The vignerons planted vines there.

Vignerons de Oisly et Thesée (Fr). A noted co-operative based in the Touraine district of the Loire.

Vignerons de Saint-Vincent (Fr). Started in 1950 for the Mâconnais and Chalonnaise. Meets at Château d'Aine in the Mâcon.

Vignerons Réunis des Côtes de Buzet (Fr). A partnership of 150 vintners formed in 1955 in Buzet. Co-operative which now has over 500 members.

Vignes-Blanches (Les) (Fr). A vineyard in the A.C. commune of Montagny, Côte Chalonnaise, Burgundy.

Vignes-Blanches (Les) (Fr). A wine-producing village in the commune of Fuissé in A.C. Pouilly-Fuissé, Mâcon, Burgundy.

Vignes-Couland (Les) (Fr). A vineyard in the A.C. commune of Montagny, Côte Chalonnaise, Burgundy.

Vignes-Derrière (Les) (Fr). A vineyard in the A.C. commune of Montagny, Côte Chalonnaise, Burgundy.

Vignes-Dessous (Les) (Fr). A vineyard in the A.C. commune of Montagny, Côte Chalonnaise, Burgundy.

Vignes-du-Puits (Les) (Fr). A vineyard in the A.C. commune of Montagny, Côte Chalonnaise, Burgundy.

Vignes-du-Soliel (Les) (Fr). A vineyard in the A.C. commune of Montagny, Côte Chalonnaise, Burgundy.

Vignes Franches (Les) (Fr). A Premier Cru vineyard in the A.C. commune of Beaune, Côte de Beaune, Burgundy. 8.56 ha.

Vignes Hautes (Fr). A method of vine training used in the Côte d'Or, Burgundy. Vines are widely spaced and are grown very high to obtain the maximum sunshine.

Vignes-Longues (Les) (Fr). A vineyard in the A.C. commune of Montagny, Côte Chalonnaise, Burgundy.

Vignes Rondes (Les) (Fr). A Premier Cru vineyard in the A.C. commune of Monthélie, Côte de Beaune, Burgundy. 2.7 ha.

Vignes-Saint-Pierre (Les) (Fr). A vineyard in the A.C. commune of Montagny, Côte Chalonnaise, Burgundy.

Vignes-sur-le-Clou (Fr). A vineyard in the A.C. commune of Montagny, Côte Chalonnaise, Burgundy.

Vigneto (It). Vineyard.

Vignoble (Fr). Vineyard.

Vignolles (Fr). A commune in the

V

Charente Département whose grapes are used in Petite Champagne (Cognac).

Vigorous (Eng). The term used to describe wines with a lively, healthy, full flavour.

Viguerie du Madrian (La) (Fr). A wine society based in Béarn, southern France.

Viguerie Royale du Jurançon (Fr). A wine fraternity based in the Jurançon district, south-western France.

Viile (Rum). Vineyard.

Viking (Cktl). ½ fl.oz. Aquavit, ½ fl.oz. lime juice, 1½ fl.ozs. Swedish Punsch. Shake over ice, strain into an old-fashioned glass 'on the rocks'.

Viking (S.Afr). The brand-name of a Brandy produced by Huguenot Wine Farmers.

Viking Ale (Eng). An old name of a Devenish Brewery Lager beer.

Viking Ale (Eng). A Pale ale 1042 O.G. brewed and bottled by the Morland Brewery in Abingdon, Oxfordshire.

Viking Bitter (Eng). A cask conditioned Bitter 1043 O.G. brewed by the Rose and Crown home-brew public house in York. Owned by the Tetley Brewery.

Viktoriaberg (Ger). A famous vineyard of the village of Hochheim in the Rheingau. Named after Queen Victoria. See Königin Viktoriaberg and Hock.

Vilafranca del Penedés (Sp). The name given to the mainly dry wines from Barcelona.

Vilàgos (Hun). An unpasteurised, mild Lager beer.

Vilamoura Marina (Cktl). ⁵/₁₀ measure Smirnoff Vodka, ²/₁₀ measure Yellow Chartreuse, ²/₁₀ measure blue Curaçao, ¹/₁₀ measure Galliano, 2 drops lemon juice. Shake over ice, strain into a cocktail glass. Add 2 cherries.

Vilana (Gre). A white grape variety grown in Crete.

Vila Nova de Gaia (Port). A town opposite Oporto on the river Douro estuary (southern bank) where Port is stored in the Lodges to mature.

Vila Nova de Gaia Pipe (Port). A cask of 547 litres capacity. See Pipe.

Vilàny (Hun). A wine-producing city in Mecsek, southern Hungary. Is noted for Vilànyi Burgundi (a red wine produced from the Pinot noir grape).

Vilànyi Burgundi (Hun). See Vilàny.

Vila Real (Port). A port town of the Alto Douro.

VILE (Sp). A León group of merchants who form the Planta de Elaboración y Embotellado de Vinos S.A. See Catedral de León.

Villa Antinori (It). Trade-name of the Antinori family who produce non D.O.C. or Chianti Classico. Instead is sold as Gran Vino (No designation, just a message).

Villa Armando (USA). A winery based in the Livermore Valley, Alameda, California. 25 ha. Grape varieties – Chardonnay and Pinot blanc. Produces varietal wines.

Villa Atuel (Arg). A wine-producing area in southern Argentina.

Villa Banfi (It). A noted producer of sweet, slightly sparkling Moscato wines.

Villa Bianchi (USA). A large winery based in Fresno, California. Grape varieties – French colombard and Zinfandel. Produces varietal and table wines.

Villabuena (Sp). A noted wine-producing village in the Rioja Alavesa.

Villa Cafaggio (It). A noted Chianti Classico producer based in Tuscany.

Villa Calcinaia (It). A Chianti Classico producer based in Tuscany.

Villa Cerna (It). A Chianti Classico producer based in Tuscany.

Villa Costa (It). A sparkling wine producer based in Piemonte. Wines are made by the méthode champenoise.

Villa di Capezzana (It). A winery based in Carmignano, Tuscany. 100 ha.

Villa di Corte (It). A dry rosé wine produced by Frescobaldi. Has an 'onion skin' colour.

Villa d'Ingianni Winery (USA). A winery based in Dundee, Finger Lakes, New York. 60 ha. Produces American varietal wines.

Villa Dolores (Arg). A small wine region in the province of Córdoba which produces fine table wines.

Villa Doluca (Tur). A full-bodied, dry, red wine produced in Thrace.

Village (Le) (Fr). A Premier Cru vineyard in the A.C. commune of Saint-Aubin, Côte de Beaune, Burgundy.

Village Bitter (Eng). A cask conditioned Bitter 1035 O.G. brewed by the Archers Brewery in Swindon, Wiltshire.

Village-de-Volnay (Fr). A Premier Cru vineyard [part] in the A.C. commune of Volnay, Côte de Beaune, Burgundy.

Village Saint-Jacques (Fr). A Premier Cru vineyard in the A.C. commune of Gevrey-Chambertin, Côte de Nuits, Burgundy. Also sold as Clos Saint-Jacques. 6.92 ha.

Villa Grande (It). A winery based near Etna in Sicily.

Villa Maria Winery (N.Z.). Address = Kirkbridge Road, Mangere, Auckland. 6 ha. owned, 600 ha. under contract.

Grape varieties – Cabernet sauvignon, Chardonnay, Chenin blanc, Gewürztraminer, Müller-Thurgau, Pinot noir, Rhine riesling and Sauvignon blanc. Produces varietal and table wines.

Villa Medeo Vineyards (USA). A vineyard based in Madison, Indiana. Grows French hybrid vines.

Villa Mount Eden (USA). A vineyard estate in the Napa Valley, northern California. Grape varieties – Cabernet sauvignon, Chardonnay, Chenin blanc, Gewürztraminer and Pinot noir. Produces varietal wines.

Villana (Gre). A white grape variety grown in Crete. Produces straw-coloured wines with a grapey bouquet.

Villànyer (Hun). The brand-name used by Villany-Pécs (a wine-producing area) for its red and white wines.

Villany-Pécs (Hun). A red and white wine-producing district in south-western Hungary. See Villànyer.

Villàny-Siklós (Hun). A wine-producing district based in southern Transdanubia. Produces top quality red wines.

Villa Pigna (It). A winery based in The Marche. 300 ha. Produces D.O.C. wines. See Rosso Piceno.

Villa Sachsen (Ger). A 28 ha. estate based in Bingen. Is owned by St. Ursula.

Villa Terciona (It). A Chianti Classico producer based in Tuscany.

Villaudric (Fr). A small V.D.Q.S. wine-producing area in the Haut-Garonne, south-western France.

Villedommange (Fr). A Premier Cru Champagne village in the Canton de Ville-en-Tardenois. District = Reims.

Ville-en-Tardenois (Fr). A Canton of the Reims district in the Champagne region. Has the Premier Cru villages of – Écueil, Les Mesneux, Sacy and Villedommange. And Cru villages of Bligny, Bouilly, Bouleuse, Branscourt, Brouillet, Chambrecy, Chaumuzy, Coulommes-la-Montagne, Courcelles-Sapicourt, Courmas, Faverolles, Germigny, Gueux, Janvry, Jouy-les-Reims, Lagery, Marfaux, Paigny-les-Reims, Poilly, Rosnay, Sainte-Euphraise, Sarcy, Savigny-sur-Ardre, Serzy-et-Prin, Tramery, Treslon, Ville-en-Tardenois and Vrigny.

Ville-en-Tardenois (Fr). A Cru Champagne village in the Canton de Ville-en-Tardenois. District = Reims.

Villenave-d'Ornon (Fr). A commune within the A.C. district of Graves in south-western Bordeaux.

Villeneuve (Fr). A commune in the A.C. Côtes de Bourg, north-eastern Bordeaux.

Villeneuve-lès-Corbières (Fr). A commune in the A.C. Fitou district of southern France.

Villeneuve-Renneville (Fr). A Premier Cru Champagne village in the Canton de Vertus. District = Châlons.

Villenkeller (Ger). Vineyard. (Anb) = Rheinhessen. (Ber) = Nierstein. (Gro) = Domherr. (Vil) = Klein-Winternhaus.

Villers-Allerand (Fr). A Premier Cru Champagne village in the Canton de Verzy. District = Reims.

Villers-Franqueux (Fr). A Cru Champagne village in the Canton de Bourgogne. District = Reims.

Villers-Marmery (Fr). A Premier Cru Champagne village in the Canton de Verzy. District = Reims.

Villers-sous-Châtillon (Fr). A Cru Champagne village in the Canton de Châtillon-sur-Marne. District = Reims.

Villette (Switz). A noted vineyard based in Lavaux.

Villevenard (Fr). A Premier Cru Champagne village in the Canton de Montmort. District = Épernay.

Villié-Morgon (Fr). A commune in the Beaujolais district. Has A.C. Beaujolais-Villages or Beaujolais-Villié-Morgon status.

Villiera Estate (S.Afr). A vineyard based in Paarl. Address = Box 66, Koelenhof 7605. Produces varietal wines including Gavotte, Minuet and Operette.

Villiersdorp (S.Afr). A wine-producing region based east of Cape Town.

Villiersdorp Co-operative (S.Afr). Vineyards based in Overberg. Address = Villiersdorp-Koöperasie Bpk., Box 14, Villiersdorp 7170. Produces varietal wines.

Villiersdorp-Koöperasie (S.Afr). See Villiersdorp Co-operative.

Villman (Fin). Raspberry-flavoured liqueurs produced by Chymos.

Villum (Lat). A drop of wine.

Villy (Fr). A commune in the A.C. Chablis, Burgundy.

Vimto (Eng). A branded sparkling soft drink. Produced by J.N. Nichols.

Vin (Fr). Wine.

Viña (Sp). Vine, vineyard.

Viña Albali (Sp). An oak-matured red wine produced by the Bodegas Felix Solis in the Valdepeñas district.

Viña Alberdi (Sp). A red wine from La Rioja Alta, S.A., Rioja. Made from the Garnacha, Graciano, Tempranillo and Viura grapes. Matured in oak casks for 1½ years minimum and for 3 years in bottle.

Viña Albina (Sp). A red wine produced by the Bodegas Riojanas in the Rioja region.

Viña Arana (Sp). A light-styled red wine from Rioja.

Viña Ardanza (Sp). A red wine from La Rioja Alta, Rioja. Made from the Tempranillo and Mazuelo grapes. Oak-matured for 3½ years and for 2 years in bottle.

Viña Berceo (Sp). Red and white wines of various grades produced by the Bodegas Gurpegui, Rioja.

Viña Bosconia (Sp). A red wine produced by López de Heredia.

Viña Carossa (Sp). A white wine-producing vineyard based in the Penedés region.

Vinaccia (It). The name given to the residue grape pulp left after the pressing.

Vinaccio (It). Grape brandy, the equivalent of French Marc.

Vinacea (Lat). Grape brandy, the equivalent of French Marc.

Vinaceous (Eng). Pertaining to wine.

Vinaceus (Lat). Grape. See also Uva. Also denotes anything relating to wine.

Viña Cubillo (Sp). A red wine produced by López de Heredia.

Viña Cumbrero (Sp). Red and white wines produced by the Bodegas El Montecillo, Alto region, Rioja. Red wines from Tempranillo 100% and white wines from Viura 100%.

Viña del Calar (Sp). A red wine produced by the Bodegas Princesa in the Valdepeñas region.

Viña del Perdón (Sp). A fruity red wine produced by Señorio de Sarría in the Navarra region.

Viña de Santa Ynez (USA). A vineyard based in Santa Ynez, Santa Barbara, California. Grape variety – Chardonnay.

Vinadri (It). Wine merchants of Italy in the Middle Ages.

Viña Eguia (Sp). A wine produced by the Bodegas Domecq S.A., Rioja. Red wine from the Tempranillo grape.

Viña Esmeralda (Sp). A semi-dry white wine produced by Torres in the Penedés region from 40% Gewürztraminer and 60% Muscat d'Alsace.

Viña Franca (Sp). A fruity white wine produced by Mascaró in Vilafranca del Penedés, Cataluña.

Viña Fresca (Sp). A light white wine from Mascaró in Vilafranca del Penedés, Cataluña.

Vinage (Fr). The term used for the addition of alcohol to wine in order to raise the alccholic strength.

Viña Gravonia (Sp). An extra dry, white wine produced by Lopez de Heredia.

Viña Herminia (Sp). A red wine produced by the Bodegas Lagunilla in Rioja. Made from the Tempranillo grape. Oak-matured for 3 years and for 2 years in bottle.

Vinaigre (Fr). Vinegar. Lit – 'Sour wine'.

Viña (La) (USA). A vineyard based near Roswell, Mesilla Valley, New Mexico. 20 ha. Produces Vinifera wines.

Viña Lanciano (Sp). A red wine produced by the Bodegas Landalan in Rioja. Oak and bottle matured.

Viña Laranda Blanco (Sp). A white wine produced by Ferret y Mateu.

Vin Alb (Rum). White wine.

Vinalia (Lat). Wine festival.

Viña Linderos (Chile). A winery based in the Maipo Valley. Is noted for its Cabernet-based wines.

Viña Madre (USA). A vineyard based near Roswell, Mesilla Valley, New Mexico. 16 ha. Grape varieties – Barbera, Cabernet sauvignon, Napa gamay, Ruby cabernet and Zinfandel. Produces varietal and table wines.

Viña Magdala (Sp). A fine red wine produced by Torres in the Penedés region from the Cariñena and Pinot noir grapes. Oak-aged for 2 years.

Viña Montana (Sp). The name given to the red and white wines from La Purisima in the Yecla region.

Viña Monty (Sp). A red wine produced by the Bodegas El Montecillo in Rioja. Made from 90% Tempranillo and 10% Mazuelo grapes. Is oak-matured then bottle-matured for 1½–2 years.

Viña Pomal (Sp). A red wine produced by the Bodegas Bilbainas S.A. in Haro, Rioja. (Alta region).

Viña Q (Sp). A white wine produced by Bodegas Ayuso in the La Mancha region.

Viña Real (Sp). A red wine produced by the C.V.N.E. in the Alta region Rioja. Is oak and bottle-matured. Also a Viña Real Reserve.

Viña Real Reserve (Sp). See Viña Real.

Viña Rebelde (Sp). A dry white wine produced by Alfonso Maldonaldo in the Rueda region.

Vinarius (Lat). Vintner.

Vinaroz (Sp). A wine-producing area in the Levante near Tarragona. Produces mainly red wines.

Viña Salceda (Sp). Vineyards. Address = Viña Salceda S.A., Carretera de Cenicero, km-3, Elciego, Alavesa, Rioja. 15 ha. Grape variety – Tempranillo 100%. All wines oak and bottle-matured.

Viña San Felipe Borgono Tinto (Arg). A Burgundy-style red wine from the Mendosa region made from the Cabernet sauvignon grape.

Viña San Pedro (Chile). The name of a

V

noted winery that produces wines under the same name.

Viña Santa Digna (Chile). The name of a Cabernet-based wine produced by Torres.

Viña Santa Marta (Sp). A range of red and white wines produced by Bodegas J. Freixedas.

Viña Santa Rita (Chile). A large vineyard from Santiago in the Maipo district.

Vinas de Orfila (Arg). The brand-name of a white wine produced by Orfila in the Mendoza region.

Viña Sol (Sp). A dry white wine produced by Torres in the Penedés region from 100% Parellada grapes.

Viña Soledad (Sp). A white wine produced by the Bodegas Franco-Españolas S.A., Alta region, Rioja. Made from 50% Malvasia and 50% Viura grapes.

Vinasse (Fr). The residue after distillation of wine into brandy.

Vinate (Sp). The label used in Spain for a range of wines from José López Bertran. See also Corrida.

Viña Tesos (Sp). A red wine produced by the Bodegas Lopez-Agos in the Rioja. Made from 80% Tempranillo and 20% Garnacha grapes. Is oak matured for 2 years and bottle matured for 4 years.

Viña Tondonia (Sp). Red and white wines produced by R. López de Heredia, Viña Tondonia S.A. Rioja. Are oak and bottle matured.

Vinattieri (It). Wine merchants of ancient Florence. 1200–1282. The earliest controlling body for the production and sale of wine.

Viña Turzaballa (Sp). A red wine produced by the Bodegas Ramón Bilbao S.A., Rioja. Is matured 2–4 years in oak and 10 years in bottle.

Viña Umbral (Sp). A red wine produced by the Bodegas Ramón Bilbao S.A., Rioja. Is oak matured 2–4 years then bottle matured for 1–10 years.

Viña Undurraga (Chile). The label used by a winery based in the Maipo Valley.

Viña Valoria (Sp). A red wine produced by Gustillo, Alto region in Rioja. Made from 80% Tempranillo, 5% Garnacha and 15% Viura grapes. Is oak matured for 3–6 months and 1 year in bottle.

Viña Vial (Sp). A red wine produced by Federico Paternina, Rioja. Is oak and bottle matured.

Viña Vista (USA). A winery based in Sonoma County, California. Grape varieties – Cabernet sauvignon, Chardonnay, Johannisberg riesling, Petite sirah and Zinfandel. Produces varietal wines.

Vinay (Fr). A Cru Champagne village in the Canton d'Épernay. District = Épernay.

Viña Zaco (Sp). A red wine produced by the Bodegas Bilbainas S.A. in the Alta region, Rioja.

Viña Zaconia (Sp). A white wine produced by R. López de Heredia, Viña Tondonia S.A., Rioja. Made from 50% Malvasia and 50% Viura grapes. Oak matured for 5 years and 6 months in bottle.

Vin Blanc Cassis (Fr). An apéritif made from white wine with Cassis. Not to be confused with Vin blanc de Cassis.

Vin Blanc de Cassis (Fr). An A.C. white wine from the Cassis district in the Côtes de Provence. Not to be confused with Vin blanc Cassis.

Vin Bourro (Fr). A term used for new wine. See also Bourro (spiced wine). Refers to the spicy nature of some new wines.

Vin Bourru (Fr). The name used for wines which have just been drawn from the barrel or are still on the original lees.

Vin Brulaï (Ch.Isles). Mulled wine, hot spiced wine.

Vin Brûlé (Fr). An alternative name for the Dutch term Brandewijn.

Vin Capiteux (Fr). A spirity, heady wine.

Vincelles (Fr). A Cru Champagne village in the Canton de Dormans. District = Épernay.

Vincelli (Dom Bernado) (Fr). The name of the Bénédictine monk who invented the liqueur Bénédictine in 1510.

Vin Chaud (Fr). Mulled wine.

Vin Ché (N.Z.). A dry white wine produced by Balic, Sturges Road, Henderson, North Island.

Vin Choisi (Fr). Simple wines. V.C.C. that are used for everyday drinking. Ordinary drinking wines.

Vin Classé (Lux). Classification of wines. See Marque Nationale.

Vincool Wine Pump System (Eng). A patent pump that pours out chilled wine at 1 fl.oz. per second from a dispenser. Marketed by Gilbeys.

Vin Cuit (Fr). A concentrated wine used to improve thin wines.

Vin d'Absinthe (Fr). A nineteenth-century wine that was flavoured with wormwood.

Vin d'Alsace (Fr). A name given to wines that are not made from noble grape varieties in Alsace. e.g. Chasselas. If noble variety and gathered after certain date also called this.

Vin d'Alsace Zwicker (Fr). Blended Alsace wine from noble grape varieties.

Vindara (Austr). A winery in the Swan Valley in Western Australia.

Vin de Blanquette (Fr). A still white wine from Limoux, south-western France.

Made from 90% Mauzac and 10% Clairette blanche grapes. Also a sparkling version produced known as Limoux or Blanquette de Limoux. (Originally created by monks in 1531 at the abbey of St-Hilaire. Produced by the 'Ruralmethod' which results in a slight sediment occurring).

Vin de Bourgeoise (Fr). A wine offered during the Middle Ages to any citizen or mayor who was elected town Burgher.

Vin de Campagne (Fr). Country wine. Vin ordinaire of the Jura (Arbois).

Vin de Café(Fr). 'One night's wine'. Term used in the Côtes du Ventoux for lightstyled A.C. wines that are removed from the vat and pressed before the end of fermentation.

Vin de Carafe (Fr). Carafe wine, house wine.

Vin de Consommation Courante (Fr). Denotes 'everyday drinking'. Is often used to refer to the vins ordinaires or non-vintage and inexpensive wine. The term also applies to wines made from 'Producteurs directs' (hybrid vines) and to the declassified wines in Bordeaux. (abbr) = V.C.C.

Vin de Corse (Fr). The name used in Corsica for Tout Court.

Vin de Corse (Fr). A.C. VdN red, rosé and white (semi-sweet or dry) wines. Produced in Corsica from Carignan, Cinsault, Mourvèdre, Niellucio, Sciacarello, Syrah and Vermentino grapes. Minimum alc. by vol. 11.5%.

Vin de Corse Calvi (Fr). A.C. red, demi-sec and dry white wines produced in Corsica. Grapes – Niellucio, Sciacarello and Vermentino.

Vin de Côtes (Fr). A term used for wine obtained from vineyards sited on hillsides.

Vin de Coucher (Fr). Lit – 'Nuptial wine'. Wine offered by a newly married couple to their guests who attend the wedding feast just before they retire.

Vin de Coule (Fr). The name given to wine obtained from the first pressing of the grapes.

Vin de Cru (Fr). Wine that is produced from grapes of a single vineyard.

Vin de Cuvée (Fr). In Champagne, the first juice of the Marc. 2,000 litres.

Vin de Garde (Fr). Wine for laying down to mature.

Vin de Gingembre (Fr). Ginger wine.

Vin de Glacé (Fr). German and Austrian Eiswein (Ice-wine).

Vin de Glacier (Switz). Young wine from the valley vineyards taken to the cellars of high, cool villages to finish its fermentation very slowly. Develops a hard,

almost bitter taste. Matured in Larchwood casks for up to 15 years. The wine originally comes from the Valais canton. Rarely found outside Switzerland. Made usually from the Rèze grape.

Vin de Goutte (Fr). Poor quality wine from the last pressing of the grapes. Also denotes the first pressing of the grapes in the Cognac region.

Vin de la Moselle Luxembourgeoise (Lux). Common wines. Put on the label together with the grape variety. e.g. Vin de la Moselle Luxembourgeoise Riesling.

Vin de l'Année (Fr). Wine of the year, most recent vintage.

Vin de la Région (Fr). Wine from a specific region. e.g. Champagne from the Champagne region.

Vin de Lavilledieu (Fr). A V.D.Q.S. wine-producing district in the Tarn-et-Garonne Département. Main grape variety is the Negrette.

Vin de l'Étrier (Fr). Lit – 'Stirrup cup'. A drink offered to departing guests.

Vin Délimité de Qualité Supérieure (Fr). See V.D.Q.S.

Vin de Liqueur (Fr). A naturally sweet wine made by adding grape brandy to the unfermented must.

Vin de Lune (Fr). The name given to Chaptalised wines.

Vin de Macadam (Fr). A term used to describe a sweet white wine that has been rushed to Paris straight from the fermenting vat.

Vin de Marc (Fr). Grape brandy. See Marc.

Vin de Marcillac (Fr). A V.D.Q.S. wine-producing district in the Aveyron Département.

Vin de Masǎ (Rum). Table wine.

Vin de Messe (Fr). Altar wine.

Vindemia (Lat). Vintage, grape harvest. See also Vindemiator.

Vindemiator (Lat). Vintage, grape harvest. See also Vindemia.

Vindemiolo (Lat). Small vintage.

Vin de Noix (Fr). A walnut-flavoured liqueur 14.8% alc. by vol.

Vin d'Entraygues et du Fel (Fr). A V.D.Q.S. wine-producing district in the Aveyron Département and Cantal Département.

Vin de Nuits (S.Afr). On a label denotes that the grapes were harvested during the night.

Vin de Paille (Fr). Straw wine. Named from the fact that the grapes are spread upon straw to dry for a period of time before they are pressed to concentrate the sugar. Occur in the Jura. See Château Châlon and Château d'Arlay. Usually sold in 60 cls. bottles called Clavelins.

Vin de Pays (Fr). Country wine, small local wine.

Vin de Paysan (Fr). The name used for poor quality Vin de Pays.

Vin de Plaine (Fr). The name given to inferior wine from ordinary vineyards as opposed to wine from hillsides.

Vin de Porto (Fr). Port wine.

Vin de Première Presse (Fr). Wine from the wet solids after the first Écoulage (racking). If good, will be used for blending.

Vin de Presse (Fr). The wine made from the pressed marc (after fermentation). Used to give the workman as a daily ration.

Vin de Primeur (Fr). The name given to wine that is drunk the same year that it was made, usually 3 months after the harvest.

Vin de Queue (Fr). A poor quality, inferior wine made from the pressing of the stalks.

Vin de Réserve (Fr). Fine old wine used in the dosage of Champagnes to sweeten them (the sugar is first dissolved in the old wine). Also applies to the old vintage Champagnes used in blending in poor years.

Vin de Sable (Fr). A Vin de Pays wine produced in the Midi region of southern France.

Vin de Saint-Pourçain-sur-Sioule (Fr). A V.D.Q.S. wine-producing district in the Allier Département in central France.

Vin de Savoie (Fr). A.C. red, rosé and dry white wines produced in Ain, Haute-Savoie, Isère and Savoie Départements. Minimum alc. by vol. 9%.

Vin de Savoie-Ayze Mousseux (Fr). See Mousseux de Savoie-Ayze.

Vin de Savoie-Ayze Pétillant (Fr). Also known as Pétillant de Savoie-Ayze. A.C. sparkling wines produced by the méthode gaillaçoise.

Vin de Savoie Mousseux (Fr). See Mousseux de Savoie.

Vin de Savoie-Pétillant (Fr). Also known as Pétillant de Savoie. A.C. sparkling wine produced by the méthode gaillaçoise.

Vin des Dieux (Fr). Lit – 'Wine of the Gods'. A term used to describe sweet, botrytised wines.

Vin des Matines (Fr). A red wine from the A.C. Saumur, Anjou-Saumur, Loire.

Vin des Noces (Fr). Lit – 'Marriage wine'. Wine offered as a gift to the priest who performed the ceremony.

Vin d'Estaing (Fr). A V.D.Q.S. wine-producing district in the Aveyron Département. Also known as Vins d'Estaing.

Vin de Table (Fr). The lowest classification of French table wine.

Vin de Taille (Fr). In Champagne after the Vin de Cuvée. The next 666 litres of juice.

Vin de Tête (Fr). An abbreviated form of Tête de Cuvée meaning best cuvée

Vin de Thourasais (Fr). A V.D.Q.S. red wine made from the Gamay grape in the south of the Saumur area in the Anjou-Saumur, Loire.

Vin de Veille (Fr). A night cap of wine placed beside the King's bed in case he required a drink during the night in the Middle Ages. Lit – 'Vigil wine'.

Vin de Vierge (Fr). Lit – 'Wine of the virgin'. An old term for new wine.

Vin d'Honneur (Fr). Signifies a drink on a moderately formal occasion to honour a guest.

Vin Diable (Fr). Lit – 'Devil wine'. The name given to a bottle of Champagne which has burst through too much pressure.

Vindima (Port). Vintage, grape harvest.

Vindimador (Port). Grape picker.

Vindimar (Port). The gathering (harvesting) of the grapes.

Vin d'Neuches (Ch.Isles). Marriage wine.

Vin d'Orange (Fr). An orange-flavoured liqueur 14.8% alc. by vol.

Vin Doré (USA). A sweet 'Altar wine' produced by the Novitiate Vineyards of Los Gatos, California. Is a Sauternes-style wine.

Vin Doux (Fr). Sweet wine.

Vin Doux Muté (Fr). A liqueur wine produced by adding alcohol to partially fermented grape must after extraction.

Vin Doux Naturel (Fr). A fortified wine produced in southern France where fermentation has been arrested by the addition of grape brandy to retain some of the natural sugar in the wine. Brandy can be added at an early stage of fermentation or later. Much depends on the style of wine. See Muscat de Beaumes de Venise. Banyuls, Frontignan, Rivesaltes etc.

Vin Doux Passerillé (Fr). Liqueur wines produced from musts with high sugar contents and from raisin grapes. 13%-15% alc. by vol. (part of the sugar remains).

Vin Doux Semi-Muté (Fr). A liqueur wine produced by adding alcohol to the partially fermented musts to raise the alcohol to 15% by vol.

Vin du Bugey (Fr). A V.D.Q.S. district near Savoie. Produces white wine from the Roussette grape. Also light-styled, red, rosé and sparkling white wines. Includes A.C. Roussette de Bugey and Vin de Bugey (plus name of Cru). 9.5% alc. by vol. minimum.

Vin du Bugey-Cerdon Mousseux (Fr). A.C. sparkling wines produced in the Savoie region by the méthode champenoise.

Vin du Bugey-Cerdon Pétillant (Fr). A.C. sparkling wines produced in the Savoie region by the méthode gaillaçoise.

Vin du Bugey Mousseux (Fr). See Mousseux du Bugey.

Vin du Bugey Pétillant (Fr). Also known as Pétillant du Bugey. A.C. sparkling wines produced by the méthode gaillaçoise in the Savoie region.

Vin du Clerc (Fr). A wine offered to the clerk of the court by the defendant if the verdict of the tribunal was found in his favour.

Vin du Coucher (Fr). Night cap.

Vin du Curé (Fr). A wine offered after Baptism to the priest who performed the service.

Vin du Glacier (Switz). See Vin de Glacier.

Vin du Haut-Poitou (Fr). A V.D.Q.S. wine-producing district in the Vienne Département. Produces red (minimum alc. by vol. 9%), rosé and white wines (minimum alc. by vol. 9.5%).

Vin du Marché (Fr). Wine originally given to someone as a gift for helping in a business transaction. Also known as Pot de Vin.

Vin d'Une Nuit (Fr). St. Saturnin (rosé). So called because the grape skins were left in contact with the must for 1 night. Now are usually left in for longer periods.

Vin du Rhin Français (Fr). Alsatian wines. Wines from the French Rhine in Alsace. See Vins d'Alsace.

Vin du Thoursais (Fr). A V.D.Q.S. wine-producing region in the Deux-Sèvres Département, western France.

Vin du Tursan (Fr). A V.D.Q.S. wine-producing region in the Landes Département, south-western France.

Vin Dynamique (Fr). A herb-flavoured, Tonic wine produced by the Bénédictine monks in the Middle Ages. See Buckfast (an offspring of).

Vine (Eng). The plant on which grapes grow. See Vitis.

Viné (Fr). The illegal practice of adding alcohol to wine to increase its alcoholic strength. Not to be confused with fortification.

Vinea (Eng). An old British name for monastery vineyards.

Vinea (Lat). Vineyard, See also Vinetum.

Vinedale Brewery (Ind). A brewery based in Hyderabad. Produces Black Beard 1044 O.G. Crazy 1064 O.G. and Regal 1042 O.G.

Vinedey (Fr). A Cru Champagne village in the Canton de Sézanne. District = Épernay.

Viñedo (Sp). Vineyard.

Viñedos del Contino (Sp). Wines produced by the Sociedad Vinícola Laserna, Rioja. Oak matured.

Viñedos San Marcos (Mex). A noted vineyard based in Aguascalientes. Is owned by Don Nazario Ortiz Garza.

Vine Dresser (Eng). A person who tends the vines, a vineyard worker.

Vine Dresser (USA). Old name for vineyard cultivators.

Vin Effervescent (Fr). Sparkling wine. A term used in Vouvray in the Touraine district of the Loire.

Vine Flow (USA). The label used by the Bella Napoli Winery.

Vinegar (Eng). The result of the vinegar bacterium Acetobacter when it feeds upon the alcohol in wine or beer etc. The alcohol is converted into Acetic acid which turns the wine/beer to vinegar. Prevented by excluding air. CH_3COOH. Acetic acid.

Vinegar Eel (Eng). Anguillula Aceti. A nematode worm that feeds on the organisms that cause the fermentation in vinegar, etc. Also known as the Vinegar worm.

Vinegar Fly (Eng). Drosophila Melanogaster or fruit fly. Is attracted by the smell of fruit. Carries vinegar bacteria which in turn may infect the wine in the winery.

Vinegar Taint (Eng). The smell caused by Lactic acid bacteria which produce acetic acid which gives wine a smell. Also caused by wild yeasts. Wine has not turned to vinegar.

Vinegar Worm (Eng). See Vinegar Eel.

Vine Hill Vineyard (USA). A vineyard based in Santa Cruz, California. Grape varieties – Chardonnay and Johannisberg riesling. Owned by Smothers. See also Felton Empire.

Vine Leaf (Eng). The brand-name used by Lamb and Watt of Liverpool, Merseyside for Sherry.

Vinello (It). The Italian diminutive for wine. Always poor, thin vin ordinaire. See also Vinetto and Vinettino.

Vine Louse (Eng) (slang). For the Phylloxera Vastatrix.

Vinenca (Bul). A noted wine-producing area.

Vine Products Commission (Cyp). A body set up in 1968 to help maintain the quality and standard of wines.

Vine Products Cooperative Marketing Union Ltd (Cyp). See SODAP.

Vine Products Ltd (Eng). Address =

Kingston-Upon-Thames, London. Producers of British Wines including Hudson & Cooper Sherries, Lord Ducane, QC, RSVP, VP, Vibrona and Votrix.

Viner (Fr). To add alcohol to a wine.

Vinery (Eng). A place where grapes are grown.

Vinetarius (Lat). Wine merchant.

Vinetier (Fr). An old French word for a wine merchant.

Vinettino (It). Poor, thin wine. Vin ordinaire. See also Vinello and Vinetto.

Vinetto (It). Poor, thin wine. Vin ordinaire. See also Vinello and Vinettino.

Vinetum (Lat). Vineyard. See also Vinea.

Vineus (Lat). Belonging to wine.

Vineux (Fr). Vinosity.

Vine-Vivarium (It). A vine museum opened in the Asti district of Piemonte in the eighteenth and nineteenth centuries by the Rocchetta family at Rocchetta Tanaro. Had over 300 vine species growing.

Vinexport (Rum). A government-run body which controls wine production. Headquarters in Bucharest.

Vineyard (Eng). The name given to an area that is planted with vines.

Vineyards (The) (Eng). Address = Cricks Green, Felsted, Essex. 4.5 ha. Soil – clay and loam. Grape varieties – Madeleine angevine, Madeleine sylvaner, Müller-Thurgau, Pinot chardonnay, Pinot noir. Scheurebe, Seyval blanc and Wrotham pinot.

Vin Fin (Fr). A loosely applied term meaning 'fine wine' or 'wine of quality'.

Vin Fin d'Alsace (Fr). A denomination that Edelzwicker wines could use in Alsace.

Vin Fin des Hautes Côtes (Fr). The general term used for any wine that is from the specified area of Burgundy.

Vin Flétri (Switz). The Swiss name for Vin de Paille (straw wine).

Vin Fou (Fr). The Jura name for the local sparkling wine.

Vin Fumé (S.Afr). A wood-matured, white wine produced by the Simonsig Estate Wines.

Vingarthr (Scan). Vineyard.

Vingrau (Fr). Côtes du Roussillon-Villages wines.

Vin Gris (Fr). A cheap wine made in the eastern part of France from a mixture of red and white grapes.

Vinha (Port). Vineyard (also vine).

Vinhão (Port). A black grape variety grown in the Entre Minho e Douro to produce deep red wines.

Vinhateiro (Port). Wine-producer (vine-grower).

Vinhedo (Port). A large vineyard.

Vinho (Port). Wine.

Vinho Branco (Port). White wine.

Vinho Claro (Mad). The name given to the new wine after fermentation and before fortification.

Vinho Consumo (Port). The term used to describe an ordinary everyday wine.

Vinho Criado (Port). Wine waiter.

Vinho da Roda (Mad). Lit – 'Wine of the round voyage'. The old nickname for Madeira wines.

Vinho de Mesa (Port). Table wine from no particular region.

Vinho de Mesa Regional (Port). Denotes table wines from a specified region. One of five – Alentejo, Beiras, Estremadura, Ribatejo and Tras-os-Montes.

Vinho de Pasto (Port). Denotes quality table wine. See also Vinho de Mesa.

Vinho Doce (Port). Sweet wine.

Vinho do Porto (Port). Port wine. Port.

Vinho do Rodo (Port). Sparkling wine.

Vinho Espumante (Port). Sparkling wine. See also Vinho Spumoso.

Vinho Estufado (Mad). The name given to Madeira wine after it leaves the Estufada. After resting becomes Vinho Transfugado.

Vinho Garrafeira (Port). See Garrafeira.

Vinho Generoso (Mad). Madeira wine that has been fortified and is ready to go into the Solera system for blending.

Vinho Licoroso (Port). Fortified wine. See also Vinho Liquoroso.

Vinho Liquoroso (Port). Fortified wine. See also Vinho Licoroso.

Vinho Maduro (Port). Wine which comes from the 4 regions of Bucelas, Colares, Dão and Douro. A normal mature table wine.

Vinho Qinado (Port). A Tonic wine that contains quinine.

Vinho Regional (Port). A category of quality wines from one of five named (not demarcated) regions. These are – Região das Beiras, Região de Tras-os-Montes, Região de Estremadura, Região do Ribatejo and Região do Alentejo.

Vinho Reserva (Port). An old wine from a good (vintage) year.

Vinho Rosado (Port). Rosé wine.

Vinhos Barbeito (Mad). A noted Madeira wine shipper based in Funchal.

Vinhos de Monção Lda (Port). One of 3 producers of Alvarinho. All the wine is fermented and matured in wood. Also produce Cepa Velha (a Marc brandy).

Vinhos de Qualidade (Port). Denotes quality wines from specified areas and produced from specified grapes.

Vinho Seco (Port). Dry wine.

Vinho Spumoso (Port). Sparkling wine. See also Vinho Espumante.

Vinho Surdo (Mad). The name given to grape juice which is prevented from fermenting by the addition of alcohol. Is added to the Madeira wine as a sweetening wine.

Vinho Surdo (Port). Fortified wine. According to Portuguese law, Port wine must be a vinho surdo.

Vinho Tinto (Port). Red wine.

Vinho Trasfegado (Mad). See Vinho Trasfugado.

Vinho Trasfugado (Mad). Madeira wine that has been through the Estufada system and has been racked and is ready to be fortified when it becomes vinho generoso.

Vinho Verde (Port). A light, young wine (white or red) produced in the Minho district. Is a pétillant wine produced by having the malo-lactic fermentation take place in the bottle. Verde denotes 'young' and *not* 'green'. Sub-regions – Barcelas, Moncão, Penafiel and Guimarães. See APEVV.

Vini (It). Wines.

Vini Bianchi (It). White wines.

Vinic (Eng). Containing or relating to wine.

Vinica (Yug). A wine-producing area in Croatia.

Vinícola (Port). Wine-producing.

Vinicola Abbazia-Santero (It). A noted producer of Moscato Spumante in the Piemonte region.

Vinícola Andalucía (Sp). A producer and exporter of Málaga.

Vinícola de Castilla (Sp). A winery based in Manzanares, La Mancha. Produces Señorio de Guadianeja (a white perfumed wine). Also produce oak-aged red wine.

Vinícola del Marqués de Aguyo (Mex). A winery based at Parras de la Fuente, Coahuila. Produces table and sparkling wines.

Vinícola del Vergel (Mex). A winery and vineyard based west of Parras de la Fuente.

Vinícola de Nelas (Port). A producer of Dão wines based in Nelas.

Vinícola de Sangalhos (Port). A noted shipper of Dão wines.

Vinícola do Vale do Dão (Port). A modern winery producing Dão wines based near Viseu. Owned by SOGRAPE.

Vinícola Hildago (Sp). A Sherry producer based at Sanlúcar de Barrameda. Labels include – Jerez Cortado Hildago and La Gitana.

Vinícola Ibérica (Sp). Wineries (owns no vineyards) based in Utiel, Valencia and Tarragona.

Vinícola Navarra (Sp). A winery based Las Campanas in Navarra. Noted for Castillo de Tiebas (a full-bodied, red

wine) and Las Campanas. Is partially owned by Savin.

Vinícola Ribalonga (Port). Noted producers of red Dão wines based in the Bierra Alta.

Vinícola Vizcaina, Rojas y Cía (Sp). A noted wine-producer based in Rioja.

Vinicultor (Sp). Wine grower.

Viniculture (Eng). The making and maturing of wine.

Vini da Banco (It). Table wine.

Vini da Tavola (It). Table wines. Lowest classification of table wine.

Vini dei Castelli (It). Wines from the Alban hills near Rome. e.g. Est! Est!! Est!!! and Frascati.

Vini dei Castelli Romani (It). The name of the wine consumed by the Romans. Now known as Frascati.

Vini del Piave (It). See Piave.

Vinifera (Lat). Part of the genus Vitis. Includes European vines which are cultivated all over the world. See Vitis Vinifera.

Vinifera Vineyard (USA). A winery based near the west shore on Lake Keuka, Finger Lakes, New York. Grape varieties – Chardonnay, Pinot noir and Riesling. Produces varietal wines.

Vinifera Wine Growers' Association (USA). An experimental winery and vineyard based in Highbury, Virginia.

Vinification (Eng). The making of wine at all stages. Fermentation, ageing, etc. (excluding vineyard work).

Vinification à Chaud (Fr). The fermentation method where a higher temperature than normal is used. Mainly used in the southern Rhône.

Vinificato Fuori Zona (It). A term denoting 'Vinified outside the production area'.

Vinificato in Bianco (It). Taken quickly off the skins. Used in the Tuscany region.

Vinificator (Eng). In distillation a condenser that collects escaping alcoholic vapours.

Vinifié (Fr). Vinified, made into wine.

Vinified (Eng). A term to denote that grape juice has been fermented into wine.

Vinifier (Fr). The process where the grape juice is turned (fermented) into wine.

Viniloire Chasam (Fr). Address = Boulevard de l'Industrie, Zide Nazelles Amboise, Touraine, Loire. A wine company that filters and bottles wines.

Vinimpex (Bul). 'State Commercial Enterprise for Export and Import of Wines and Spirits'. A monopoly that controls all wine exports.

Vini Rosati (It). Rosé wine.

Vini Rossi (It). Red wines.

Vinitaly (It). The world's largest, annual, specialty wine trade exhibition. Held in Verona.

Vinitech (Euro). An annual international exhibition for vinification, oenology and cellar equipment.

Vini Tipici (It). Standard, ordinary wines.

Vinitor (Lat). Vine dresser.

VINIVAL (Sp). A large winery based in Valencia. Is noted for its Torres de Serrano (red and white wines).

Vinjak (Yug). Brandy.

Vinjak Cezar (Yug). A brand of local grape brandy.

Vin Jaune (Fr). Lit – 'Yellow wine'. Wine produced in the Jura region eastern France where the wine is exposed to the air and Flor is encouraged to grow, See Flor and Château Châlon. Produced from the Savagnin grape.

Vinkrivier Wines (S.Afr). A brand-name for the wines of the Rooiberg Co-operative.

Vinland (USA). The Vikings' name for the North Americas because of the vines there. Also known as Vinland the Good. See Vitis Labrusca.

Vinmark (USA). A label used by the Markham Winery for wines produced from bought in grapes.

Vin Medecin (Fr). Basic Bordeaux wine made a little more palatable by a little wine from elsewhere other than Bordeaux.

Vinmonopolet (Nor). See A/S Vinmonopolet.

Vin Mousseux (Fr). Sparkling wine.

Vin Mousseux Gazéifié (USA). Sparkling wine carbonated artificially. Must have this term on the label.

Vin Nature (Fr). Natural, unsweetened (chaptalised) wine.

Vin Nature de Champagne (Fr). Still wine made in the Champagne region. Also known as Coteaux Champenois.

Vin Nobile di Montepulciano (It). D.O.C.G. red wine from the Tuscany region. See Vino Nobile di Montepulciano.

Vin Nobile du Minervois (Fr). A V.D.Q.S. sweet white wine produced from the Grenache, Maccabéo, Malvoisie and Muscat grapes in the Minervois district, southern France. 13% minimum alc. by vol.

Vin Non-Mousseux (Fr). The name given to still wine.

Vin Nouveau (Fr). New wine. See Beaujolais Nouveau.

Vino (It). Wine.

Vino (Sp). Wine.

Vino Aloque (Sp). The name given to wine produced in Valdepeñas from a blend of red and white grapes.

Vino Bevanda (It). An ordinary beverage wine.

Vino Bianco (It). White wine.

Vino Blanco (Sp). White wine.

Vino Caldo (It). Mulled Claret wine.

Vino Clarete (Sp). Light red wine.

Vino Comun (Sp). An ordinary wine. See also Vino Corriente.

Vino Corriente (Sp). Vin ordinaire. Lit – 'Current or running wine'. Usually red carafe wine. Also known as Vino Comun.

Vino Cotto (It). Lit – 'cooked wine'. Made by boiling down grape must and adding brandy. e.g. in Marsala. For colouring and sweetening.

Vino Crudo (Sp). Young, immature wine.

Vino da Arrosto (It). Describes a fine wine with breeding.

Vino da Meditazione (It). Lit – 'For meditation'. A great, fine wine which should be drunk with consideration, in peace and quiet and usually without food.

Vino da Tavola (It). Table wine.

Vino da Tavola con Indicazione Geografica (It). Denotes a table wine from a defined area.

Vino de Agujas (Sp). A pétillant, dry, white wine produced in the Galicia region.

Vino de Añada (Sp). A young wine of one vintage ready for the Criadera reservas.

Vino de Arrosto (It). See Vino da Arrosto.

Vino de Calidad (Sp). Quality wines produced from free-run or lightly pressed juice which has undergone a controlled fermentation.

Vino de Color (Sp). Pedro ximénez grape must boiled down and fortified with brandy to darken it. Used for enriching and adding colour to Sherries mainly for the British market. See Paxerete and Cuytes.

Vino de Corazón (Sp). The wine produced in Rioja after the Vino de Lágrima has been removed. The remaining grapes are aroused with a fork, fermented, and the resulting wine is then mixed with the Vino de Lágrima.

Vino de Cosecha Propria (Sp). A wine made by the owner of the vineyard.

Vino de Crianza (Sp). A suitable wine destined to become Sherry.

Vino de Cuarte (Sp). The name given to a Valencian rosé wine.

Vino de Doble Pasta (Sp). A Vino de Lágrima that has had crushed grapes added. It ferments yielding a wine at 18% alc. by vol.

Vino de Gran Reserva (Sp). Red wines,

aged for 2 years in oak, then 3 years in bottle. White and rosé wines aged for 4 years of which 6 months minimum should be in cask.

Vino de Jerez (Sp). Sherry. The wine from the Jerez district in Andalusia.

Vino de Lágrima (Sp). The wine after the first light pressing of the grapes. See Vino de Corazón. Produced in Rioja. Can also be made from the 'free-run juice'.

Vino de la Tierra (Sp). An ordinary or a Vin de Pays wine of the region.

Vino della Riviera (It). Describes a wine as having originated from the Lombardy region of Lake Garda.

Vino de Mesa (Sp). Table wine.

Vino de Pasto (Sp). Table wine.

Vino de Prensa (Sp). A term used to refer to the wine that has been obtained by hydraulic pressing. Is rich in tannin, dark and undrinkable unless blended.

Vino de Reserva (Sp). Red wines aged a minimum of 1 year in oak, then 2 years in bottle. White and rosé wines aged in cask and bottled for a minimum of 24 months including 6 months in oak.

Vino de Yema (Sp). Lit – 'Yolk of the wine'. The name given to wine that is drawn off the vat first.

Vino di Famiglia (It). Mellow wine, soft, with no acidity or tannin.

Vino di Lusso (It). The term used for an expensive, fine, dessert wine (fortified).

Vino Dolce Naturale (It). Naturally sweet wine. Has no added sugar.

Vinodolsko (Yug). A red wine produced off the north-western Croatian coast.

Vino Dulce (Sp). Sweet wine used for blending.

Vino Esperanto (Eng). A dry white wine produced by the St. Georges Vineyard to celebrate 100 years of the Esperanto language in 1984. The label written in Esperanto.

Vino Espumoso (Sp). Sparkling wine. Authorised vines are – Garnacha, Maccabéo, Malvasia, Monastrell, Parellada and Xarel-lo. Cava wine. Only 100 litres of must may be extracted from 150 kgs. of grapes. If the second fermentation is carried out in sealed containers (tanks), the wine is known as Granvas.

Vino Frizzante (It). A lightly sparkling-style of wine that is usually consumed locally.

Vino Generoso (Sp). Fortified wine.

Vinolentia (Lat). Wine drinking.

Vinolentus (Lat). Drunk, intoxicated. See also Potus.

Vino Liquoroso (It). Fortified wine.

Vino Maestro (Sp). Master wine. A sweet full wine used to lend character and body to a weaker, thin wine.

Vinometer (Eng). An implement used to test the alcohol content of a dry wine (not one with residual sugar).

Vino Naturalmente Dolce (It). A naturally sweet wine. Has no added sugar.

Vino Nobile di Montepulciano (It). D.O.C.G. red wine from the Tuscany region. Made from 50–70% Prugnolo gentile plus Canaiolo, Malvasia del Chianti, Mammolo, Pulcinculo and Trebbiano toscano grapes. Vinification and ageing must occur in Montepulciano. Must be aged 2 years in wood. If aged 3 years then classed Riserva. If 4 years then is classed Riserva Speciale.

Vino Novello (It). Italy's answer to France's Beaujolais nouveau. Released on November 14th.

Vino Ordinario (It). Ordinary wine. Not usually bottled.

Vino Passito (It). See Passito.

Vinophile (Eng). A wine lover.

Vinoproizvoditel (Bul). Wine-producer.

Vino di Qualitá Produtto in Regione Determinata (It). See V.Q.P.R.D.

Vino Rancio (Sp). Denotes a white wine that has maderised or has been fortified.

Vin Ordinaire (Fr). Ordinary cheap wine for general consumption.

Vino Rosado (Sp). Rosé wine.

Vino Rosso (It). Red wine.

Vino Santo (It). A wine made from grapes dried indoors over the winter.

Vino Santo di Gambellara (It). See Vin Santo di Gambellara.

Vinos Blancos de Castilla (Sp). A noted winery based in Rueda.

Vinos Corrientes (Sp). The equivalent to the French Vins Ordinaires.

Vinos de Aguja (Sp). Lit – 'Needle wines'. Produced from Prieto picudo grapes. Is a bone-dry and slightly pétillant wine.

Vinos de Año (Sp). Red Rioja wines that are neither aged in cask or bottle.

Vinos de Castilla (Sp). A large private bodega based in the La Mancha region. Produces Castillo de Manza wines.

Vinos de Chile (Chile). A noted winery and exporter of Chilean wines based in Santiago.

Vinos de Crianza (Sp). Wines of the Rioja region which have been aged for a minimum of 2 complete years of which at least 1 year must be in oak cask with a capacity of 225 litres.

Vinos de España (Can). The Spanish Wine Office. Address = Suite 1204, 55, Bloor Street, Toronto, M4W 1AF, Ontario.

Vinos de España (Eng). The Spanish

Wine Office. Address = 22, Manchester Square, London W1M 5AP.

Vinos de España (Ger). The Spanish Wine Office. Address = Jägerhofsler, 30,4000 Düsseldorf.

Vinos de León (Sp). The alternative name for VILE.

Vinos de Los Herederos del Marqués de Riscal (Sp). Vineyards. Address = Torrea, 1 – Elciego (Alava). 300 ha. Grape varieties – Cabernet 5%, Merlot 5%, Tempranillo 80% and Viura 10%. Produces 95% red wine and 5% rosé wine.

Vinos de Saca (Sp). Export wines. From the word 'Sacar' = To draw from. Sack may have derived from this word.

Vino Seco (S.Am). A mixture of red and white wines, fortified with alcohol which are allowed to maderise in the sun. Produced in Uruguay.

Vino Seco (Sp). Dry wine.

Vinosity (Eng). Refers to the 'Wine-like' smell and taste of the beverage.

Vino Spumante (It). Sparkling wine.

Vino Spumoso (Sp). The term for any sparkling wine. See also Cava and Granvas.

Vinos Quinados (Sp). The name given to Tonic wines that contain quinine extract. e.g. Calisay.

Vinos Sanz (Sp). A winery based in La Seca and Medina del Campo, Rueda.

Vinosul S/A (Bra). See Central Vinícola do Sul.

Vinosus (Lat). Wine-bibber. Someone who is fond of wine.

Vinoteka (Yug). Wine library.

Vinothèque (Fr). Wine library.

Vino Tierno (Sp). A sweet wine made from dried out grapes. Is used in the making of Málaga.

Vino Tintillo (Sp). Pale red wine.

Vino Tinto (Sp). Red wine.

Vinous (Eng). Pertaining to wine.

Vinous Orders (Eng). Denotes Chapters and Brotherhoods whose rules are for the promotion, quality maintenance etc. of wines. See Chevaliers.

Vino Virgen (Sp). Wine fermented from grapes without the skins or pips.

Vinozavod (USSR). Wine factory.

Vin Piment (Fr). A red wine produced in early times usually flavoured with herbs.

Vin Pimentaï (Ch.Isles). Mulled or spiced wine.

Vinprom (Bul). State marketing organisation. Owns 10% of vineyards, runs research institutes.

Vin Rafraîchisseur (Fr). Wine cooler.

Vin Rosé (Fr). A pink coloured wine of varying shades made from red grapes,

the wines being left on the skins for a short time only.

Vin Rose (Rum). Rosé wine.

Vin Rosu (Rum). Red wine.

Vin Rouge (Fr). Red wine.

Vins Amers (Fr). Bitter wines. See Absinthe, Gentian and Quinquina.

Vinsanti (It). See Vino Santo.

Vin Santo (It). See Vino Santo.

Vin Santo di Gambellara (It). D.O.C. white wine from the Veneto region. Made from partially dried Garganega, Nostrano and Trebbiano grapes. Must be aged for 2 years minimum.

Vin Sauvage (Fr). A sparkling white wine of the Gers region of south-east France. Has a powerful mousse and is very acidic. Often used for the making of Pousse rapière.

Vins Clairs (Fr). Base wines (after the first fermentation in Champagne) before blending.

Vins d'Alsace (Fr). Alsatian wines. The wines of Alsace in north-eastern France. Also Vins du Rhin Français.

Vins de Base (Fr). Base wines. A term used in sparkling wine production to denote what the base wine was.

Vins de Bugey (Fr). V.D.Q.S. wine-producing district in Savoie, south-eastern France.

Vins de Café (Fr). Everyday drinking wines often not bottled but served straight from the cask.

Vins de Comptoir (Fr). Denotes everyday, pleasant drinking wines.

Vins de Consommation Courante (Fr). V.C.C. Everyday drinking wines. Also referred to as Vins Ordinaires de Consommation Courante.

Vins de Diable (Fr). 'Wines of the Devil'. An early term used to describe Champagnes that burst the bottles because of too much pressure.

Vins de Haut-Poitou (Fr). V.D.Q.S. wine-producing district in the Vienne Département in western France.

Vins de la Moselle (Fr). V.D.Q.S. white wines produced in the valley of the river Moselle in Lorraine, north-eastern France. Three regions – Metz, Sierk and Vic-sur-Seille.

Vins de l'Étoile (Fr). Dry white and sparkling wines of the Arbois area in the Jura region.

Vins Délimités de Qualité Supérieure (Fr). See V.D.Q.S.

Vins de Liqueur (Fr). See Vin de Liqueur.

Vins de l'Orléanais (Fr). V.D.Q.S. wines from the region around Orléans in the Touraine district of the Loire. Red, rosé and white wines.

Vins de Marcillac (Fr). A small V.D.Q.S.

red wine-producing area in south-western France.

Vins de Marque (Fr). Everyday wines, one up from V.C.C. wines though still for everyday drinking only.

Vins de Négoce (Fr). Shippers' wines. Wines, usually generic, that are blended by the négociant.

Vins d'Entraygues et du Fel (Fr). A small V.D.Q.S. light red and rosé wine-producing area in the Cantal and Aveyron Départements in south-western France. Minimum alc. by vol. red 9% and white 10%.

Vins de Paille (Fr). Straw wines. See Vin de Paille.

Vins de Pays de Cher (Fr). See Jardin de la France.

Vins de Pays de Corse (Fr). See Île de Beauté.

Vins de Pays de Drôme (Fr). See Coteaux de Baronnies.

Vins de Pays de Gard (Fr). Includes areas of – Coteaux Cévenols, Coteaux Flaviens, Coteaux du Pont du Gard, Coteaux du Salavès, Coteaux du Vidourle, Mont Bouquet, Serve de Coiran, Uzège, Val de Montferrand, Vistrenque, La Vaunage and Coteaux de Cèze.

Vins de Páys de Gers (Fr). Includes areas of – Côtes du Condomois, Côtes de Gascogne, Côtes de Montestruc and Côtes de Saint-Mont.

Vins de Pays de Hérault (Fr). Includes the areas of – Bessan, Caux, Cessenon, Collines de la Moure, Coteaux d'Enserune, Coteaux de Laurens, Coteaux de Libron, Coteaux de Murviel, Coteaux du Salagou, Côtes du Brian, Côtes de Thau, Côtes de Thongue, Gorges de l'Hérault, Haute Vallée de l'Orb, Vicomté d'Aulmelas, Mont Baudile and Côtes de Céressou.

Vins de Pays de l'Île de Beauté (Fr). Corsican table wines.

Vins de Pays de Jura (Fr). See Franche-Comté.

Vins de Pays de l'Ain (Fr). A small Vins de Pays area in the Ain Département, eastern France. Mainly dry white wines.

Vins de Pays de la Meuse (Fr). A white and Gris wine-producing area in Lorraine, north-eastern France.

Vins de Pays de l'Ardèche (Fr). See Coteaux de l'Ardèche.

Vins de Pays de l'Aude (Fr). A wine-producing area in the Aude Département of southern France. Produces red, rosé and dry white wines. Main grapes are Carignan, Cinsault and Grenache.

Vins de Pays de l'Isère (Fr). See Balmes Dauphinoises and Coteaux du Grésivaudan.

Vins de Pays de Loire Atlantique (Fr). See Pays de Retz and Marches de Bretagne.

Vins de Pays de Lot (Fr). See Coteaux de Glanes and Coteaux de Quercy.

Vins de Pays de Lot-et-Garonne (Fr). See Agenais and Côte du Brulhois.

Vins de Pays de l'Yonne (Fr). Describes the white wines from regions of Chablis, Coulange-la-Vineuse, Irancy and Saint-Bris in the Yonne Département. Minimum alc. by vol. 9%.

Vins de Pays de Pyrénées-Orientales (Fr). See Coteaux de Fenouillèdes, Pays Catalan, Vals d'Agley and Côte Catalane.

Vins de Pays des Alpes-de-Haute-Provence (Fr). A wine-producing area in the Hautes Alpes Département of south-eastern France. Produces red, rosé and dry white wines.

Vins de Pays des Alpes-Maritimes (Fr). A wine-producing area in the Alpes Maritimes Département of south-eastern France. Produces red, rosé and white wines.

Vins de Pays de Savoie et Haute-Savoie (Fr). See Allogrogie.

Vins de Pays des Bouches du Rhône (Fr). See Petite Crau and Sables du Golfe du Lion.

Vins de Pays de Tarn (Fr). See Côtes du Tarn.

Vins de Pays de Tarn-et-Garonne (Fr). See Saint-Sardos.

Vins de Pays de Var (Fr). See Les Maures, Coteaux Varois and Mont Caume.

Vins de Pays de Vendée (Fr). See Fiefs Vendéens.

Vins de Pays d'Oc (Fr). A group of eight Vins de Pays Départements – Ardèche, Aude, Bouches-du-Rhône, Drôme, Gard, Hérault, Var and Vaucluse.

Vins de Pays du Vaucluse (Fr). A wine-producing area in the Vaucluse Département of south-eastern France. Produces red, rosé and dry white wines. Grape varieties mainly Cinsault and Grenache.

Vins de Qualité Produits dans des Regions Déterminées (E.E.C.). The grading for all quality wines in the E.E.C. V.Q.P.R.D.

Vins de Renaison (Fr). The alternative name for Côtes Roannaises wines in the Loire.

Vins d'Estaing (Fr). A V.D.Q.S. wine-producing district in the Aveyron Département in central-southern France. Produces red and white wines.

Vins Doux Mistelles (Fr). See Vins Doux Mûtes.

Vins Doux Mûte (Fr). Fortified wines made

by adding Brandy to slightly fermented grape must. A Vin Doux Naturel, Vin Doux Liqueur. Are also known as Vins Doux Mistelles.

Vins Doux Passerillés (Fr). Sweet fortified wines made from dried grapes. 13%–15% alc. by vol.

Vins Doux Semi-Mûte (Fr). A medium-sweet, fortified wine of around 15% alc. by vol.

Vins du Lyonnais (Fr). A mainly red V.D.Q.S. wine-producing region based near Lyon in the Rhône. Wines produced from the Gamay and Syrah grape varieties.

Vins d'Une Nuit (Fr). See Vins Souples.

Vins du Thouarsis (Fr). V.D.Q.S. sweet white, rosé and light red wine-producing region based south of the Loire region.

Vin Sec (Fr). Dry wine.

Vins Fins de la Côte de Nuits (Fr). The old appellation for the Côte de Nuits-Villages.

Vins Jaunes (Fr). Yellow wines of the Jura. See Jura.

Vins Liquoreux (Fr). See Straw Wines.

Vinsmoselle (Lux). An association that consists of five of the six co-operatives in Luxembourg. (Grenenmacher, Greivel-dange, Remerschen, Stadtbredimus and Wellenstein).

Vins Nouveaux (Fr). New wines. See Beaujolais Nouveau.

Vinsobres (Fr). An A.C. Côtes du Rhône-Villages. Produces full red wines.

Vinsol, S.A. (Sp). A noted producer of Montilla wines based in the Montilla-Moriles region.

Vins Ordinaires (Fr). Simple ordinary wines for everyday drinking.

Vins Pétillants (Fr). Slightly sparkling wines produced by allowing the malo-lactic fermentation to take place in the bottle instead of in the cask.

Vins Souples (Fr). Wines made from free-run must with pressed grape must added. Also known as Vins d'Une Nuit.

Vins Tournés (Fr). Lit – 'Turned wines'. A wine that has deteriorated because of its poor quality. The wine has usually been left on the lees too long, turns cloudy and has a rotten vegetable smell. Is treated with citric acid and pasteurisation. Is not caused by Acetobacter!

Vin Supérieur (Fr). Wines for everyday drinking. They are controlled by regulations but not as strict as A.C.

Vin Superioare (Rum). Superior top quality wine.

Vins Vieux (Fr). Wines of the previous years.

Vintage (Eng). The gathering of the grapes. The harvest.

Vintage Appellation (Switz). V.A. Are subject to supervision by the authorities which grant or withhold entitlement to such appellations. (Fendant and Dôle for the Valais, Dorin and Sauvignon for the Vaud).

Vintage Beers (Eng). A term used to denote a beer that needs bottle age, that is conditioned in the bottle. e.g. Bière de Garde, Chimay Trappiste, Worthington White Shield, etc.

Vintage Character (Port). A term given to older blended good quality Ruby Ports that show Vintage Port characteristics.

Vintage Cider (Eng). A slightly sparkling Cider produced by Merrydown in Essex. Also produce a Vintage Dry Cider.

Vintage Darjeeling (Ind). A tea from Darjeeling, bordering the Himalayas. Blended from Darjeeling flowery Orange Pekoe leaves. Has a superb aroma and flavour.

Vintage Madeira (Mad). A Madeira produced from 100% noble grape varieties from a single year, kept in cask for a minimum of 20 years after Estufagem and 2 years in bottle before sale.

Vintage Port (Port). Port wine from a single year. Blended and bottled in Portugal between the 2nd and 3rd year after the vintage. Not produced every year but is declared by some or all of the Port shippers on good years. Recent vintages are – 1960, 1963, 1966, 1970, 1975, 1977, 1980, 1982, 1983, 1985. Must now all be bottled in Oporto (since 1975).

Vintage Royale (Eng). A cider cocktail produced by Symonds of Hereford, Herefordshire. Contains Cider, Brandy and ginger wine.

Vintagers (Eng). Workers of the harvest and wine-making.

Vintage Wine (Eng). A wine of a single year.

Vintitulist (Eng). A wine label collector.

Vintner (Fr). Wine seller, merchant.

Vintner (The) (Eng). The trading name for a specialist shop in Kensington Church Street, London. Belongs to Arthur Rackham. Is home of the Vintner wine club.

Vintners' Choice (S.Afr). See Drop Inn Group.

Vin Tranquille (Fr). Still wine. Designation for the still wines of Vouvray in the Touraine district of the Loire.

Vinueño (Sp). A wine made from grapes grown on Albariza soil. Not from Palomino grapes.

Vinum (Lat). Wine. See also Merum.

Vinum Bonum Est (It). 'The wine is good'. See Est! Est!! Est!!!

Vinum Claratum (Lat). Clarified wine.

Vinum Clarum (Lat). Light, clear wine.

Vinum Picatum (Lat). A Roman wine

which was made from the black Picata grape which had a taste of pitch. Was produced in the Rhône region of southern France.

Vinum Theologicum (Lat). 'The best wine'.

Vin-Union-Genève (Switz). A large growers' co-operative based at Satigny.

Vin Uşoare (Rum). Light wine.

Vin Veneto (Cktl). 1 measure Grappa, ¼ measure Sambuca, ¼ measure Gomme syrup, juice ¼ lemon, ½ egg white. Shake over ice, strain into a cocktail glass.

Vin Vert (Fr). A young wine from the Roussillon made from the Maccabéo grape.

Vin Vieux (Fr). A wine of the previous year.

Vin Vif (Fr). The name used for sparkling wines in the Touraine district of the Loire.

Vin Viné (Fr). Fortified wine.

Vinzel (Switz). A wine-producing village in La Côte, western Switzerland.

Viognier (Fr). A white grape variety grown mainly in the northern Rhône. Used for making Château Châlon, Condrieu and Hermitage.

Violet Fizz (Cktl). ⅕ measure dry Gin, ⅕ measure Crème Yvette, 2 dashes Gomme syrup, juice ¼ lemon. Shake over ice, strain into an ice-filled highball glass. Top with soda water.

Violet Frères (Fr). A noted producer of Byrrh at Thuir, Pyrénées-Orientales.

Violette (Fr). A liqueur made by the infusion of violet roots and leaves. Is produced by Serres in Toulouse.

Violland (Léon) (Fr). A Burgundy shipper based in Beaune.

Vion (Fr). A commune of the A.C. Saint-Joseph in the northern Rhône.

Vionnier (USA). The USA spelling of the Viognier grape.

Viosinho (Port). A white grape variety grown in the Douro region for Port production.

VIP (Cktl). ⅓ measure Cointreau, ⅓ measure dry Cinzano, ⅓ measure Rye whisky. Stir over ice, strain into a cocktail glass, add a twist of orange peel.

V.I.P. (Cktl). 1½ ozs. Gin, 1 oz. Pimms N°1, 2 ozs. Passion fruit juice, ½ oz. dry Vermouth, ½ oz. fresh lemon juice. Shake over ice, strain into 5 oz. glass, decorate with a white water lotus nut on a cocktail stick.

Viré (Fr). An A.C. Mâconnais white wine. See Château de Viré.

Virelade (Fr). A commune in the A.C. Graves, central-western Bordeaux.

Virgen (En) (Port). A term given to the Vinho Verde wine prior to fermentation when the stalks, pips and skins are removed. Bottled 3–4 months after fermentation and before the Malo-lactic fermentation.

Virgin (Sp). A term to denote the driest of the Málagas.

Virgin Brandy (Fr). A term applied to unblended Cognac brandies.

Virgin Cocktail (Cktl). ⅓ measure Gin, ⅓ measure (white) Crème de Menthe, ⅓ measure Forbidden Fruit liqueur. Shake over ice, strain into a cocktail glass.

Virgin Hills Winery (Austr). A winery based in Bendigo/Ballarat. Produces varietal and table wines.

Virginia (S.Afr). A medium sweet white wine from the SFW. Made from the Steen and Clairette blanche grapes.

Virginia Drams (USA). An early Peach brandy that was probably the forerunner of Southern Comfort.

Virginia Gentleman (USA). The brand-name of a Bourbon whiskey at 45% alc. by vol. produced by the Smith Bowman Distillery in Sunset Hills, Fairfax County, Virginia.

Virgin Islands Rum (W.Ind). A light bodied Rum, fairly dry and flavoured with a slightly sweet after-taste. Produced by the Virgin Islands Rum Industries Ltd.

Virgin Islands Rum Industries Ltd (W.Ind). A noted Rum producer based in the Virgin Islands. Sold under Old St-Croix and Cruzan labels.

Virgin Mary (Cktl). See Tomato Juice Cocktail.

Viriatus (Port). A Dão wine produced by Sociedade Com. Abel Pereira da Fonseca.

Virreyes (Mex). A well-known brand of Tequila.

Vis (Yug). A pale white wine produced on the island of Vugava, off the Dalmatian coast.

Visable Fermentation (Eng). The first sign of visible CO_2 gas during fermentation which bubbles to the surface.

Visan (Fr). A wine village of Vaucluse. The A.C. is Côtes du Rhône-Villages.

Viscosity (Eng). A term used to describe, albeit loosely, the body of the wine through the alcohol and glycerine content. Is usually judged by the 'tears' or 'legs' left on the side of the glass after the wine has been swirled around the glass.

Viseu (Port). The principal wine town of the Dão region.

Vishnyovaya Nalivka (USSR). A Cherry-flavoured liqueur.

Visitor (The) (Cktl). ⅓ measure Cointreau, ⅓ measure Crème de Banane. ⅓ measure dry Gin, dash orange juice, 1 egg white. Shake over ice, strain into a cocktail glass.

Viski (Tur). Whiskey.

Vislijm (Hol). Isinglass.

Visokokvalitetno (Yug). High quality wine.

Visperterminen (Switz). Wines from the Valais canton. At 12,000 feet above sea level are amongst the highest vineyards in the World.

Vistrenque (Fr). A Vins de Pays area of the Gard Département in south-western France.

Vitaceae (Lat). A botanical family of which Vitis is part.

Vital (Port). A white grape variety grown in Torres Vedras.

Vitamalz (Ger). A Malzbier.

Vitamins (Eng). Essential to all life forms. Many found in wines. Vitamin B1 is needed by yeast during fermentation. Vitamin C used as the reducing agent (Ascorbic acid) which prevents oxidation (the browning of wines).

Vita-Stout (N.Z.). A Stout brewed by the Dominion Brewery.

Vite (It). Grape vine.

Viteus (Lat). Denotes that it is 'Of the vine'.

Viteus Vitifolii (Lat). Phylloxera vastatrix.

Viti (Switz). A red wine produced in the Ticino canton from the Merlot grape.

Viticcio (It). A noted Chianti Classico producer based in Tuscany.

Viticula (Lat). A small vine.

Viticulteur (Fr). A person who cultivates vineyards of which they are the owner.

Viticultura (It) (Port). Vine-growing. Viticulture.

Viticultura (Sp). Vine-growing. Viticulture.

Viticultural and Oenological Research Advisory Council (N.Z.). VORAC. Comprises of a number of representatives from other associated bodies including the Wine Institute and Grape Growers' Council.

Viticultural and Oenological Research Institute (S.Afr). V.O.R.I. The institute for the improvement of vine species. Also known as Nievoorbij.

Viticultural Association of New Zealand (N.Z.). An organisation formed by wine growers to respond to adversities facing the industry in the 1920s.

Viticultural Ecology (Eng). The study of the vine, soil and climate in which it grows. Examines the quality of fruit and wine produced.

Viticulture (Fr). The cultivation of the vine from the planting to the harvest.

Vitigenus (Lat). Produced from the vine, originating from the vine.

Vitis (Lat). Vine genus.

Vitis Aestivalis (USA). An American root stock grown in the north-eastern states. Gives high acidity and a little foxiness.

Vitis Amurensis (Asia). A vine root stock that originated from Japan, Mongolia and Sakhalin Islands.

Vitis Argentifolia (USA). The alternative name for Vitis Bicolor under the Bailey classification.

Vitis Arizonica (USA). A vine root stock that originated from the western zone.

Vitis Armata (Asia). A vine root stock that originated in China.

Vitisator (Lat). Vine planter.

Vitis Balansaeana (Asia). A vine root stock that originated in Tonkin.

Vitis Berlandieri (USA). An American root stock. Native of the state of Texas.

Vitis Bicolor (USA). A vine root stock that originated from the eastern zone.

Vitis Bourgoeana (USA). A vine root stock that originated from the tropical zones.

Vitis California (USA). A vine root stock that originated from the western zone.

Vitis Candicans (USA). A vine root stock that originated from the central zone.

Vitis Cariboea (USA). A vine root stock that originated from the tropical zones. See Vitis Sola.

Vitis Chasselas (Lat). A vine root stock crossed with Vitis Berlandieri to produce Millardet de Grasset.

Vitis Cinerea (USA). A vine root stock that originated from the central zone.

Vitis Coegnetiae (Euro). Table grapes.

Vitis Coignetiae (Asia). A vine root stock that originated from Japan, Korea and Sakhalin Islands.

Vitis Cordifolia (USA). A vine root stock that originated from the central zone.

Vitis Coriacea (USA). A vine root stock that originated from Florida and the Bahamas.

Vitis Davidii (Asia). A vine root stock that originated from China.

Vitis Elevenea (Ger). A vine similar to the Elbling. Was planted by the Romans in the Mosel.

Vitis Flexuosa (Asia). A vine root stock that originated in Cochin-China, India, Japan, Korea and Nepal.

Vitis Gigas (USA). A vine root stock that originated from Florida and the Bahamas.

Vitis Labrusca (USA). An American vine species grown in the north-east states. A wild grape variety is used extensively for grafting in Europe because of its Phylloxera resistance.

Vitis Lanata (Asia). A vine root stock that originated from Burma, Dekkan, India, Nepal and southern China.

Vitis Licecunici (USA). A vine root stock that originated from the eastern zone.

Vitis Monticola (USA). A vine root stock that originated from the central zone.

Vitis Munsoniana (USA). A vine root stock that originated from northern USA.

Vitis Pagnucii (Asia). A vine root stock that originated in China.

Vitis Pedicellata (Asia). A vine root stock that originated in the Himalayan mountains.

Vitis Pentagona (Asia). A vine root stock that originated in China.

Vitis Piasezkii (Asia). A vine root stock that originated in China.

Vitis Popenoei (USA). A vine root stock that originated in northern USA.

Vitis Retordi (Asia). A vine root stock that originated in Tonkin.

Vitis Riparia (USA). An American vine species grown in the Riverbank area. Is used extensively for grafting in Europe because of its Phylloxera resistance. See Vitis Vulpina.

Vitis Romaneti (Asia). A vine root stock that originated in China.

Vitis Romanetia (Asia). See Vitis Romaneti.

Vitis Rotundifolia (USA). An early American grape variety of Florida in southern American.

Vitis Rubra (USA). A vine stock that originated from the central zone.

Vitis Rupestris (USA). An American vine species grown in the Rock region. Is used extensively in Europe for grafting because of its resistance to Phylloxera.

Vitis Rutilans (Asia). A vine root stock that originated in China.

Vitis Silvestris (Euro). Old vine species from which it is thought the Riesling and Sylvaner grape varieties derived.

Vitis Sola (USA). Along with Vitis Cariboea the alternative name for Vitis Tilioefolia. Under the Bailey classification the two species are recognised. See also Vitis Tilioefolia.

Vitis Thunbergii (Asia). A vine root stock that originated from Formosa, Japan, Korea and south-western China.

Vitis Tilioefolia (USA). Along with Vitis Sola the alternative names for Vitis Cariboea. Under the Bailey classification the two species are recognised.

Vitis Vinifera (Euro). The European vine species from which all of the European quality wines are made. After the Phylloxera epidemic of the late nineteenth century, with just a few exceptions, all the vines are grafted onto American vine root stocks.

Vitis Vulpina (USA). The alternative name for the Vitis Riparia under the Bailey classification.

Vitis Wilsonae (Asia). A vine root stock that originated in China.

Vitiviniculture (Eng). The study of grape growing and wine-making.

Vitraille (Fr). An alternative name for the Merlot grape.

Vittel Grande Source (Fr). A still mineral water from the Vosges mountains.

Vittel Hepar (Fr). A Chalybeate mineral water from the Vosges mountains, 4 miles from Contrexville. A still mineral water.

Vitteloise (Fr). A very effervescent mineral water from the Vosges mountains. Is similar to soda water.

Viura (Sp). The principal white grape variety grown in the Rioja region. Also known as the Alcañol, Alcanón and the Macabeo.

Viuva Rosado Fernandes (Port). A small firm that produces full-bodied red wines in Alentejo.

Vivace (Fr). The term used to denote a lively, fresh and slightly tart wine.

Viva Maria (Cktl). ¼ measure Tia Maria, ¼ measure Galliano, ¼ measure Brandy, ¼ measure blackcurrant juice. Shake over ice, strain into a cocktail glass. Top with a cherry.

Vivasti (It). The name given to registered nurseries that sell vines.

Viva Villa Cocktail (Cktl). ⅓ gill Tequila, juice of a lime, 3 dashes Gomme syrup. Shake over ice, strain into a salt-rimmed, ice-filled, old-fashioned glass.

Vive (W.Ind). The brand-name of a Rum produced only from molasses by Bardinet on the island of Martinique.

Vivency (Fr). A wine-producer based at Saumur, Anjou-Saumur, Loire. Owned by Piper-Heidsieck. Noted for its Saumur Mousseux.

Vi Verge (Sp). A term that describes wines that are macerated off the skins. Vi Brisat = 'On the skins'.

Viviers (Fr). A commune in the A.C. Chablis, Burgundy.

Viville (Fr). A commune in the Charente Département whose grapes are classed Grande Champagne (Cognac).

Vixen Beer (Eng). A cask conditioned Bitter 1036 O.G. brewed by the Fox and Firkin home-brew public house in London. A Bruce house.

Vladimarvellous (Cktl). 2 measures Vladivar vodka, 1 measure Pernod, juice of lemon, juice of orange. Shake over ice, strain into an ice-filled highball glass.

V

Dress with a sprig of mint.

Vladivar (Eng). A British Vodka distilled by Greenalls in Warrington, Cheshire. 40% alc. by vol.

Vladivar Imperial Gold (Eng). A brand of Vodka produced by Greenall in Warrington, Cheshire. 43% alc. by vol.

Vlasotinci (Yug). A wine-producing area based south of Serbia. Produces mainly rosé wines from the Plovdina and Prokupac grapes.

Vloeistof (Hol). Liquid.

Vlottenburg Co-operative (S.Afr). Vineyards based in Stellenbosch. Address = Vlottenburg Wynkelder Koöperatief Bpk., Box 40, Vlottenburg 7604. Has 29 members.

Vlottenburg Wynkelder Koöperatief (S.Afr). See Vlottenburg Co-operative.

V.O. (Can). The top selling, straight Rye whisky produced by Seagram.

V.O. (Fr). A Cognac term found on a bottle label. Denotes that the brandy is Very Old. At least 10–12 years in cask. Must have a minimum age of 4½ years. (4 years in U.K). For Armagnac 4 years minimum. (Also for Calvados).

Vocht (Hol). Liquor, liquid.

Voda (USSR). Water. The word from which Vodka is a diminutive.

Vodka (USSR). A pure spirit, charcoal-filtered which removes certain oils and congenerics. Various sorts. Name drives from Zhiznennia voda = 'Water of life'. The word Vodka or Wodka means 'little water'.

Vodka Collins (Cktl). As for Gin Collins but using Vodka in place of the Gin.

Vodka Cooler (Cktl). As for Gin Cooler but using Vodka in place of the Gin.

Vodka Daisy (Cktl). ⅓ gill Vodka, juice ½ lemon, 2 dashes Gomme syrup, 4 dashes Grenadine. Shake over ice, strain into an old-fashioned glass. Dress with fruit in season.

Vodka Gibson (Cktl). ⅕ gill Vodka, dash dry Vermouth. Stir over ice, strain into a cocktail glass. Dress with an olive.

Vodka Gimlet (Cktl). As for Gin Gimlet but using Vodka in place of the Gin.

Vodka Grasshopper (Cktl). ⅔ measure Vodka, ⅓ measure Bénédictine, dash Angostura. Stir over ice, strain into a cocktail glass.

Vodka Mac (Cktl). 1 fl.oz. ginger wine, 1 fl.oz. Vodka. Shake over ice, strain into a 5 oz. goblet.

Vodka Martini (Cktl). ⅞ measure Vodka, ⅛ measure dry Martini. Shake over ice, strain into a cocktail glass. Top with a twist of lemon peel juice.

Vodka Pippin (Cktl). ⅕ gill Vodka on ice in a highball glass. Top with dry Cider, stir.

Dress with an apple slice.

Vodka-Polar Cocktail (Cktl). ½ measure Vodka, ½ measure Polar liqueur. Shake over ice, strain into a cocktail glass.

Vodka Salty Dog (Cktl). ⅙ gill Vodka, 1 gill grapefruit juice, ¼ teaspoon salt. Stir over ice in a highball glass.

Vodka Seven [7] (Cktl). ⅓ gill Vodka, juice ½ lime. Stir over ice in a highball glass. Top with lemonade and the rind of lime.

Vodka Sling (Cktl). As for Gin Sling but using Vodka in place of the Gin.

Vodka Sour (Cktl). 1½ measures Vodka, ¾ oz. lemon or lime juice, 1 teaspoon powdered sugar. Shake over ice, strain into an old-fashioned glass, add a slice of orange and a cherry.

Vodka Stinger (Cktl). ½ measure Vodka, ½ measure (white) Crème de Menthe. Shake over ice, strain into a cocktail glass.

Vodkatini (Cktl). ⅓ gill Vodka, ⅙ gill sweet Martini (or dry). Mix together over ice, strain into a cocktail glass, dress with a twist of lemon peel juice.

V.O. Estilo Fine Marivaux (Sp). A Brandy produced by Mascaró.

Vögelein (Ger). Vineyard. (Anb) = Franken. (Ber) = Maindreieck. (Gro) = Kirchberg. (Vil) = Nordheim.

Vogelsang (Ger). Lit – 'Birdsong'. A popular name for German vineyards. 23 individual sites have this name.

Vogelsang (Ger). Vineyard. (Anb) = Baden. (Ber) = Badische Bergstrasse/Kraichgau. (Gro) = Stiftsberg. (Vil) = Gemmingen.

Vogelsang (Ger). Vineyard. (Anb) = Baden. (Ber) = Badische Bergstrasse/Kraichgau. (Gro) = Stiftsberg. (Vil) = Kirchhardt (ortsteil Berwangen).

Vogelsang (Ger). Vineyard. (Anb) = Franken. (Ber) = Steigerwald. (Gro) = Burgweg. (Vil) = Markt Einersheim.

Vogelsang (Ger). Vineyard. (Anb) = Mosel-Saar-Ruwer. (Ber) = Saar-Ruwer. (Gro) = Scharzberg. (Vil) = Irsch.

Vogelsang (Ger). Vineyard. (Anb) = Mosel-Saar-Ruwer. (Ber) = Saar-Ruwer. (Gro) = Scharzberg. (Vil) = Serrig.

Vogelsang (Ger). Vineyard. (Anb) = Nahe. (Ber) = Kreuznach. (Gro) = Kronenberg. (Vil) = Bad Kreuznach.

Vogelsang (Ger). Vineyard. (Anb) = Nahe. (Ber) = Kreuznach. (Gro) = Kronenberg. (Vil) = Bretzenheim.

Vogelsang (Ger). Vineyard. (Anb) = Nahe. (Ber) = Kreuznach. (Gro) = Schlosskapelle. (Vil) = Laubenheim.

Vogelsang (Ger). Vineyard. (Anb) = Nahe. (Ber) = Schloss Böckelheim. (Gro) = Paradiesgarten. (Vil) = Merxheim.

Vogelsang (Ger). Vineyard. (Anb) = Rheingau. (Ber) = Johannisberg. (Gro) =

Erntebringer. (Vil) = Estate.

Vogelsang (Ger). Vineyard. (Anb) = Rheinhessen. (Ber) = Bingen. (Gro) = Kurfürstenstück. (Vil) = Wallertheim.

Vogelsang (Ger). Vineyard. (Anb) = Rheinhessen. (Ber) = Nierstein. (Gro) = Gutes Domtal. (Vil) = Zornheim.

Vogelsang (Ger). Vineyard. (Anb) = Rheinhessen. (Ber) = Nierstein. (Gro) = Petersberg. (Vil) = Gau-Odernheim.

Vogelsang (Ger). Vineyard. (Anb) = Rheinpfalz. (Ber) = Mittelhaardt-Deutsche Weinstrasse. (Gro) = Feuerberg. (Vil) = Weisenheim am Berg.

Vogelsang (Ger). Vineyard. (Anb) = Rheinpfalz. (Ber) = Mittelhaardt-Deutsche Weinstrasse. (Gro) = Grafenstück. (Vil) = Bockenheim.

Vogelsang (Ger). Vineyard. (Anb) = Rheinpfalz. (Ber) = Mittelhaardt-Deutsche Weinstrasse. (Gro) = Grafenstück. (Vil) = Kindenheim.

Vogelsang (Ger). Vineyard. (Anb) = Württemberg. (Ber) = Württembergisch Unterland. (Gro) = Heuchelberg. (Vil) = Hausen/Z.

Vogelsang (Ger). Vineyard. (Anb) = Württemberg. (Ber) = Württembergisch Unterland. (Gro) = Heuchelberg. (Vil) = Kleingartach.

Vogelsang (Ger). Vineyard. (Anb) = Württemberg. (Ber) = Württembergisch Unterland. (Gro) = Heuchelberg. (Vil) = Leingarten.

Vogelsang (Ger). Vineyard. (Anb) = Württemberg. (Ber) = Württembergisch Unterland. (Gro) = Heuchelberg. (Vil) = Neipperg.

Vogelsang (Ger). Vineyard. (Anb) = Württemberg. (Ber) = Württembergisch Unterland. (Gro) = Heuchelberg. (Vil) = Niederhofen.

Vogelsang (Ger). Vineyard. (Anb) = Württemberg. (Ber) = Württembergisch Unterland. (Gro) = Heuchelberg. (Vil) = Schwaigern.

Vogelsang (Ger). Vineyard. (Anb) = Württemberg. (Ber) = Württembergisch Unterland. (Gro) = Staufenberg. (Vil) = Untereisesheim.

Vogelsang (Lux). A vineyard site in the village of Ahn.

Vogelschlag (Ger). Vineyard. (Anb) = Nahe. (Ber) = Schloss Böckelheim. (Gro) = Burgweg. (Vil) = Duchroth.

Vogelsgärten (Ger). Grosslage. (Anb) = Rheinhessen. (Ber) = Nierstein. (Vils) = Guntersblum, Ludwigshöhe.

Vogelsprung (Ger). Vineyard. (Anb) = Rheinpfalz. (Ber) = Südliche Weinstrasse. (Gro) = Bischofskreuz. (Vil) = Flemlingen.

Vogensen's Vineyard (USA). A vineyard

based in the Dry Creek Valley, Sonoma County, California. Grape variety – Zinfandel.

Vogiras (Fr). An alternative to Vosgros.

Vogteilberg (Ger). Vineyard. (Anb) = Mosel-Saar-Ruwer. (Ber) = Zell/Mosel. (Gro) = Rosenhang. (Vil) = Senheim.

Vogtei Rötteln (Ger). Grosslage. (Anb) = Baden. (Ber) = Markgräflerland. (Vils) = Bamlach, Binzen, Blansingen, Efringen-Kirchen, Egringen, Eimeldingen, Feuerbach, Fischingen, Grenzach, Haltingen, Herten, Hertingen, Holzen, Huttingen, Istein, Kleinkems, Lörrach, Ötlingen, Rheinweiler, Riedlingen, Rümmingen, Schallbach, Tannenkirch, Weil am Rhein, Welmlingen, Wintersweiler, Wollbach.

Voile [Le] (Fr). The name used in the Jura region for Flor, the fungus which form on the surface of certain wines. See Mycodermae Vini.

Voiura (Sp). See Viura.

Vojvodina (Yug). A wine region based in northern Serbia. Produces Plemenka and P.W. Berniet (a red Vermouth).

Vok (Austr). A noted liqueur producer.

Volari (It). A brand-name red or white Frizzante wine.

Volatile (Eng). Being able to change from liquid to vapour at low temperatures. e.g. acids, alcohol.

Volatile Acid (Eng). Acetic acid (vinegar). A normal by-product of alcoholic fermentation. Acceptable in wine up to 0.6–0.8 grms. per litre. 600–800 parts per million.

Volatile Matter (Eng). In wine the Acids, Alcohol, Aldehydes and Esters.

Volcano Hill (USA). The brand-name used by the Diamond Creek Winery for one of their wines from a specific section of their property.

Volée (A la) (Fr). The old method of dégorgement in Champagne which uses the pressure in the bottle to push out the sediment from the second fermentation together with a small amount of the wine. See also Glace (A la).

Volkach (Ger). Village. (Anb) = Franken. (Ber) = Maindreieck. (Gro) = Kirchberg. (Vin) = Ratsherr.

Volker Eisele Vineyard (USA). See Eisele Vineyard.

Voll (Ger). Full. Denotes a wine that has a high percentage of alcohol.

Vollbieres (Ger). Beer with an O.G. of 11–14%.

Vollburg (Ger). Vineyard. (Anb) = Franken. (Ber) = Steigerwald. (Gro) = Not yet assigned. (Vil) = Michelau i. Steigerwald.

Vollereaux (Fr). Champagne producer.

Address = 48 Rue Léon Bourgeois. Pierry, 51200 Épernay. 40 ha. Produces – Vintage and non-vintage wines. Vintages – 1973, 1976, 1979, 1982.

Vollmersweiler (Ger). Village. (Anb) = Rheinpfalz. (Ber) = Südliche Weinstrasse. (Gro) = Guttenberg. (Vin) = Krapfenberg.

Volnay (Fr). A.C. red wine commune in the Côte de Beaune, Burgundy. The Premier Cru vineyards are – Clos des Ducs, La Barre, La Bousse d'Or, Le Clos des Chênes, Les Angles, Les Brouillards, Les Caillerets, Les Caillerets-Dessus, Les Champans, Les Chevrets, Les Fremiets, Les Mitans, Les Pointes d'Angles, L'Ormeau. 84.2 ha.

Volonté (Bel). The brand-name used for a range of fruit juices imported into U.K. by Leisure Drinks, Derby.

Volsoet Rooi Muskadel (S.Afr). A red, rich, full dessert wine from the Boere Co-operative. Made with the Montagu muskadel grape.

Volstead (Cktl). 1½ fl.ozs. Swedish Punsch, ½ fl.oz. Rye whiskey, ¼ fl.oz. Raspberry syrup, ¼ fl.oz. orange juice. Shake over ice, serve 'on the rocks' in an old-fashioned glass.

Volstead Act (USA). 1919–1933. Senator Volstead prohibited wine-making altogether except for use in churches.

Voltipe (S.Afr). Full-bodied.

Voluptuous (Eng). In relation to wines, denotes one that gives feelings of luxurious pleasure and taste.

Volvic (Fr). A still mineral water from Puy-de-Dome. Eau minérale naturelle designation. Bottled at source at Clairvic, Auvergne.

Volxheim (Ger). Village. (Anb) = Rheinhessen. (Ber) = Bingen. (Gro) = Rheingrafenstein. (Vins) = Alte Römerstrasse, Liebfrau, Mönchberg.

Vom Heissen Stein (Ger). Grosslage. (Anb) = Mosel-Saar-Ruwer. (Ber) = Bernkastel. (Vils) = Briedel, Pünderich, Reil.

Von der Hölle (Ger). Vineyard. (Anb) = Nahe. (Ber) = Schloss Böckelheim. (Gro) = Paradiesgarten. (Vil) = Desloch.

Vonkel (S.Afr). A medium-dry sparkling wine made by the Boplaas Estate from the Colombard grape using the cuve close method.

Vonkelwyn (S.Afr). Sparkling wine.

Von Plettenberg (Ger). An estate in the Nahe at Bad Kreuznach.

Von Schubert (Ger). Owner of Maximin Grünhaus.

Von Simmern (Ger). A family estate at Hattenheim in the Rheingau.

Voorburg (Hol). A citrus-flavoured Brandewijn.

VORAC (N.Z.) (abbr). Viticultural and Oenological Research Advisory Council.

Vorbachzimmern (Ger). Village. (Anb) = Württemberg. (Ber) = Kocher-Jagst-Tauber. (Gro) = Tauberberg. (Vin) = Schafsteige.

Vorderberg (Ger). Vineyard. (Anb) = Rheinpfalz. (Ber) = Mittelhaardt-Deutsche Weinstrasse. (Gro) = Schwarzerde. (Vil) = Kleinniedesheim.

V.O.R.I. (S.Afr) (abbr). South African Viticultural and Oenological Research Institute. Also known as Nievoorbij.

Vorlese (Ger). The early gathering of the grapes before the main harvest that takes place when adverse weather conditions occur.

Vornehm (Ger). Exquisite, delightful wine.

Vörös (Hun). Red.

Vörösbor (Hun). Red wine.

Vose Vineyards (USA). A winery based near Oakville, Napa Valley, California. 14.5 ha. Grape varieties – Cabernet sauvignon, Chardonnay and Zinfandel. Produces varietal wines. (Zinfandel wine is known as Zinblanca).

Vosges (Fr). A range of mountains that separate Lorraine from Alsace on which some of the famous Alsace vineyards are situated. Also Vittel mineral waters.

Vosgros (Fr). A Premier Cru A.C. Chablis vineyard. Often has the Premier Cru vineyard Vaugiraut used as a vintage wine under its name.

Vöslau (Aus). A district of the Niederösterreich south of Vienna that produces mainly red wines from the Blaufränkisch and Portugieser grapes.

Vöslauer Rotwein (Aus). A fine red wine from the Vöslau district.

Vosne Romanée (Fr). An A.C. commune within the Côte de Nuits, Burgundy. Has the Grand Cru vineyards of La Richebourg, La Romanée, La Romanée-Conti, La Romanée Saint-Vivant and La Tâche 25.13 ha. and the Premier Cru vineyards of Aux Brûlées, Aux Petits-Monts, Aux Reignots, Clos des Réas, La Chaume, La Grande Rue, Les Beaux-Monts, Les Malconsorts and Les Suchots. 47.5 ha.

Votka (Tur). Vodka.

Votrix (Eng). British-made Vermouth. Produced from concentrated grape juice fermented in England by Vine Products Ltd.

Vougeot (Fr). An A.C. commune of the Côte de Nuits. Has the Grand Cru Clos

V

de Vougeot within the commune plus the Premiers Crus of Clos Blanc de Vougeot, Les Cras and Les Petits-Vougeots 11.8 ha.

Vouvray (Fr). An A.C. sweet/dry pétillant, sparkling or still wine from the Touraine district of the Loire. Made from the Chenin blanc and Arbois grapes. Produced on Tufa soil. Mimimum alc. by vol. of 11%.

Vouvray Mousseux (Fr). An A.C. sparkling wine from the Touraine district of the Loire. Sweet, medium and dry varieties. Minimum alc. by vol. of 9.5%.

Vouvray Pétillant (Fr). A white dry wine with a slight prickle, made from the Chenin blanc grape in Touraine in the Loire.

Vov (It). A light 'egg-zabaglione' style of liqueur.

Voyens (Les) (Fr). A vineyard in the A.C. commune of Mercurey, Côte Chalonnaise, Burgundy. Also known as Clos Voyen.

V.P. (Eng) (abbr). Vine Products Ltd. Also the name of a popular brand of British sherry produced by Vine Products Ltd.

V.P.A. (Eng) (abbr). Ventnor Pale Ale. A Best Bitter 1040 O.G. brewed by the Burt Brewery on the Isle of Wight.

V.Q.P.R.D. (EEC) (abbr) (Fr). Vins de Qualité Produits dans des Régions Déterminées.

V.Q.P.R.D. (EEC) (abbr) (It). Vino di Qualitá Produtto in Regione Determinata.

Vrac (Fr). Price of wine sold. Includes the cork and bottle but not normally the label and capsule. Never includes the case price. Lit – 'Bulk', 'wholesale'.

Vrachanski Misket (Bul). A white grape variety. Produces strong muscat-flavoured wines.

Vracs (Fr). Plastic containers to hold 'draught' wine.

Vrai Auxerrois (Fr). An alternative name for the Pinot blanc grape.

Vranac (Yug). A red wine made from a local red grape variety in Montenegro on the Dalmatian coast in Croatia.

Vrancea Vineyard (Rum). The largest area of vineyards. Contains areas of Coteşti, Nicoreşti, Odobeşti and Panciu. See also Focsani.

Vratislavice nad Nisou Brewery (Czec). A noted brewery based in northern Czec. Brews Kapucín.

Vrdnik (Yug). A wine-growing area in Fruška Gora, Vojvodina.

Vredenburg Wines (S.Afr). Varietal wines produced by Gilbeys Limited for export.

Vredendal (S.Afr). A brandy and dessert wine-producing area based north of Tulbagh.

Vredenheim Estate Wines (S.Afr). Vineyard based in Stellenbosch. Address = P.O. Box 7, Vlottenburg 7604. Produces varietal wines.

Vreez (Mex). Producers of liqueurs. Noted for Vanilla de Mexico (a vanilla-flavoured liqueur).

Vriesenhof Vineyard (S.Afr). A vineyard based in Stellenbosch. Address = P.O. Stellenbosch 7600. Produces varietal wines.

Vrigny (Fr). A Cru Champagne village in the Canton de Ville-en-Tardenois. District = Reims.

Vrillon (Jean) (Fr). A producer of sparkling Touraine wines based at Faverolles-sur-Cher, Touraine, Loire.

Vrnicka Zlahtina (Yug). A white wine produced in north-western Croatia.

Vršac (Yug). A wine-producing centre in Banat. Produces mainly white wines.

V.S. (Eng) (abbr). Designation on a Cognac brandy label. Denotes Very Superior.

V.S.E.P. (Eng) (abbr). Designation on a Cognac brandy label. Denotes Very Superior Extra Pale. Mainly for the USA market.

V.S.O. (Eng) (abbr). Designation on a Cognac brandy label. Denotes Very Superior Old. 12–17 years in cask.

V.S.O.P. (Eng) (abbr). Designation of a Cognac brandy label. Denotes Very Superior Old Pale. The youngest Cognac must be 4 years old. New law. Old designations were for 20–30 years in cask. (Also for Armagnac which must have a minimum age of 4 years).

V.S.R. (Fr) (abbr). Very Specially Recommended.

Vuelta (Sp). An alternative word used for Tourne.

Vugava (Yug). A small wine-producing island on the Dalmatian coast. Produces high alcohol (Sherry-style) wines. Also noted for Vis wine.

Vugava (Yug). A white grape variety grown in the Dalmatian area.

Vuida de Romero (Mex). The brand-name of a popular local Tequila.

Vukovar (Yug). A noted wine-producing town in Croatia.

Vulcan (The) (Eng). A patent corkscrew based on the 1802 Thomason patent. Has a brush in the handle and cylinder that fits over the screw. Made by Westol Wine Consultants, 16, King Street, Bristol BS1 4EF.

Vulkanfelsen (Ger). Grosslage. (Anb) = Baden. (Ber) = Kaiserstuhl-Tuniberg. (Vils) = Achkarren, Amoltern, Bahlingen, Bickensohl, Bischoffingen, Bötzingen, Breisach a. Rh., Burkheim, Eichstetten, Endingen, Ihringen,

Ihringen (ortsteil Blankenhornsberg, Jechtingen, Kiechlinsbergen, Königschaffhausen, Leiselheim, Neuershausen, Nimburg, Oberbergen, Oberrotweil, Riegel, Sasbach, Schelingen, Wasenweiler.

Vully (Switz). A wine-producing area in northern Vaud. Produces white, pétillant wines.

V.V.P. (Sp) (abbr). Very, Very, Pale. A colour grading of Sherries. Finos to the Manzanillas.

V.V.S.O.P. (Eng) (abbr). Designation of Cognac brandy. Denotes Very, Very, Superior Old Pale. An old designation.

Denotes that it has spent 40 years in cask.

VWB Winery Co (USA). A winery based near St. Helena, Napa Valley, California. Grape varieties – Cabernet sauvignon, Chardonnay and Sauvignon blanc. Produces varietal wines.

Vyborova (Pol). A brand of Vodka. Also spelt Wyborowa.

Vyhne Brewery (Czec). An old established brewery based in eastern Czec.

Vyškov Brewery (Czec). An old brewery based in central Czec.

Vysoký Chlumec Brewery (Czec). An old brewery based in western Czec.

Waboomsrivier Co-operative (S.Afr). Vineyards based at Worcester. Address = Waboomsrivier Koöperatiewe Wynkelder. Box 24, Breërivier 6858. Produces varietal wines under the Wageboom Wines label.

Waboomsrivier Koöperatiewe Wynkelder (S.Afr). See Waboomsrivier Co-operative.

Wachau (Aus). A wine area of the Niederösterreich district. The best known of all Austrian wine areas, produces fresh, light dry white wines, often pétillant. Best known is Schluck.

Wachauer Marillen (Aus). A liqueur made from apricots.

Wachelter Water (Bel). Juniper water. Produced in Hasselt in the province of Limburg in 1610.

Wachenheim (Ger). Village. (Anb) = Rheinpfalz. (Ber) = Mittelhaardt-Deutsche Weinstrasse. (Gro) = Mariengarten. (Vins) = Altenburg, Belz, Böhlig, Gerümpel, Goldbächel, Rechbächel.

Wachenheim (Ger). Village. (Anb) = Rheinpfalz. (Ber) = Mittelhaardt-Deutsche Weinstrasse. (Gro) = Schenkenböhl. (Vins) = Fuchsmantel, Königswingert, Mandelgarten, Odinstal, Schlossberg.

Wachenheim (Ger). Village. (Anb) = Rheinpfalz. (Ber) = Mittelhaardt-Deutsche Weinstrasse. (Gro) = Schnepfenflug an der Weinstrasse. (Vins) = Bischofsgarten, Luginsland.

Wachenheim (Ger). Village. (Anb) = Rheinhessen. (Ber) = Wonnegau. (Gro) = Romblick. (Vins) = Horn, Rotenberg.

Wachhügel (Ger). Vineyard. (Anb) = Franken. (Ber) = Steigerwald. (Gros) = Schlossberg. Wiesenbronn.

Wacholder (Ger). A juniper-flavoured neutral spirit (similar to Gin). The generic name for Steinhäger.

Wacholderkorn-Brannt (Ger). A juniper-flavoured whiskey.

Wachstum (Ger). Growth, grown by own vineyard.

Wachtkopf (Ger). Vineyard. (Anb) = Württemberg. (Ber) = Württembergisch Unterland. (Gro) = Stromberg. (Vil) = Gründelbach.

Wackernheim (Ger). Village. (Anb) = Rheinhessen. (Ber) = Bingen. (Gro) = Kaiserpfalz. (Vins) = Rabenkopf, Schwalben, Steinberg.

Wädenswil Brauerei (Switz). A brewery based in Wädenswil. Is part of the Sibra Group (Cardinal) Breweries.

Wadworth Brewery (Eng). Opened in 1885 at the Northgate Brewery in Devizes, Wiltshire. Noted for its cask conditioned Devizes Bitter 1030 O.G. XXXXXX 1040 O.G. Farmers Glory 1046 O.G. Old Timer 1055 O.G. keg Northgate Bitter 1036 O.G. Raker Bitter 1030 O.G. and bottled Green Label 1040 O.G.

Wageboom Wines (S.Afr). See Waboomsrivier Co-operative.

Wagenstadt (Ger). Village. (Anb) = Baden. (Ber) = Breisgau. (Gro) = Burg Lichteneck. (Vin) = Hummelberg.

Wager Cup (Eng). An eighteenth-century cup which consisted of a girl holding a cup in her arms (on a swivel) above her head. She was also full-skirted. The cup was filled with an alcoholic beverage and one had to drink from the cup whilst upending the girl. Her skirt would then be filled and this had to be drunk to win the wager (bet).

Wagner Stein (Chile). A leading wine exporter based in Santiago.

Waggon (Off the) (Eng). Denotes a person who has started drinking alcohol after a period of abstention. See On The Waggon.

Wahlheim (Ger). Village. (Anb) = Rheinhessen. (Ber) = Wonnegau. (Gro) = Sybillenstein. (Vin) = Schelmen.

Wahrheit (Ger). Vineyard. (Anb) = Mittelrhein. (Ber) = Bacharach. (Gro) = Schloss Reichenstein. (Vil) = Oberheimbach.

Wahrsager (Ger). Vineyard. (Anb) = Mosel-Saar-Ruwer. (Ber) = Zell/Mosel. (Gro) = Rosenhang. (Vil) = Senheim.

Waiblingen (Ger). Village. (Anb) = Württemberg. (Ber) = Remstal-Stuttgart. (Gro) = Kopf. (Vin) = Hörnle.

W

Waiblingen (Ger). Village. (Anb) = Württemberg. (Ber) = Remstal-Stuttgart. (Gro) = Wartbühl. (Vin) = Steingrüble.

Waihirere Winery (N.Z.). The old name used for the Ormond Vineyards. 40 ha.

Waikato (N.Z.). The brand-name given to beers brewed by New Zealand Breweries in Hamilton. Waikato Draught 1039 O.G. and Waikato XXXX 1036 O.G.

Waikato (N.Z.). A wine-producing area in the northern part of the North Island.

Waikerie (Austr). A district along the river Murray in New South Wales. Produces fine quality wines.

Waikiki Beachcomer (Cktl). ½ measure dry Gin, ½ measure Cointreau, ¼ measure pineapple juice. Shake over ice, strain into a cocktail glass.

Waikiki Cocktail (Cktl). 1 measure Bourbon whiskey, ¼ measure Curaçao, ½ measure lemon juice, 3 dashes Grenadine. Blend together with a scoop of crushed ice in a blender. Pour into a Champagne saucer.

Wairau Valley (N.Z.). A wine area in the South Island. The Marlborough vineyards are planted here.

Waitemata (N.Z.). A Beer brewed by the Dominion Brewery under licence from the Scottish Brewery.

Wakefield Ale (Eng). See Henry Boon's Wakefield Ale.

Waldangelloch (Ger). Village. (Anb) = Baden. (Ber) = Badische Bergstrasse/Kraichgau. (Gro) = Stiftsberg. (Vin) = Sonnenberg.

Waldbach (Ger). Village. (Anb) = Württemberg. (Ber) = Württembergisch Unterland. (Gro) = Lindelberg. (Vin) = Schlossberg.

Waldböckelheim (Ger). Village. (Anb) = Nahe. (Ber) = Schloss Böckelheim. (Gro) = Burgweg. (Vins) = Drachenbrunnen, Hamm, Kirchberg, Kronenfels, Marienpforter Klosterberg, Muckerhölle, Muhlberg, Römerberg.

Waldböckelheim (Ger). Village. (Anb) = Nahe. (Ber) = Schloss Böckelheim. (Gro) = Paradiesgarten. (Vins) = Johannesberg, Kastell.

Waldlaubersheim (Ger). Village. (Anb) = Nahe. (Ber) = Kreuznach. (Gro) = Schlosskapelle. (Vins) = Alteburg, Bingerweg, Domberg, Hörnchen, Lieseberg, Otterberg.

Waldmeister (Ger). Essence of woodruff which is sometimes added to Berliner Weisse beer for flavour.

Waldmeisterlikoer (Ger). A pale green liqueur based on woodruff.

Waldrach (Ger). Village. (Anb) = Mosel-Saar-Ruwer. (Ber) = Saar-Ruwer. (Gro)

= Römerlay. (Vins) = Doktorberg, Ehrenberg, Heiligenhauschen, Hubertusberg, Jesuitengarten, Jungfernberg, Krone, Kurfürstenberg, Laurentiusberg, Meisenberg, Sonnenberg.

Waldron Vineyards (Eng). A vineyard based in Waldron, Heathfield, East Sussex. 2 ha. Grape varieties – Kerner, Müller-Thurgau, Ortega, Reichensteiner and Seyval blanc. Produces wines under the St. George's label. See Vino Esperanto.

Waldulm (Ger). Village. (Anb) = Baden. (Ber) = Ortenau. (Gro) = Schloss Rodeck. (Vins) = Kreuzberg, Pfarrberg.

Wales (U.K). A principality that produces a little wine. Is too far north for any major production. See Croffta and Llanrhystud.

Walheim (Ger). Village. (Anb) = Württemberg. (Ber) = Württembergisch Unterland. (Gro) = Schalkstein. (Vins) = Neckarberg, Wurmberg.

Walkenberg (Ger). Vineyard. (Anb) = Rheingau. (Ber) = Johannisberg. (Gro) = Steinmacher. (Vil) = Niederwalluf.

Walker (John and Sons) (Scot). Noted Scotch and Malt whisky distillers (part of DCL) based at Kilmarnock, Ayrshire. Brands include Cardhu, Johnnie Walker (Red and Black Label), Swing, Talisker and Old Harmony (for Japanese market).

Walker [Peter] (Eng). A subsidiary Brewery of the Tetley Walker group. Opened in 1981. Noted for its cask conditioned beers and keg Bergman's Lager 1033 O.G. and bottled Brown Peter 1034 O.G.

Walker Valley Vineyards (USA). A vineyard based in Hudson Valley, New York. 6 ha. Produces white hybrid grapes.

Walker Winery (USA). A small winery based near Santa Cruz mountains, Santa Clara, California. Grape varieties – Barbera, Chardonnay and Petite sirah. Produces varietal wines.

Walker Winter Warmer (Eng). A dark, rich, extra-strong Ale 1058–1062 O.G. brewed by the Walker Brewery in Warrington, Cheshire. (A subsidiary of Allied-Lyons).

Wallbury (Ger). See Ettenheim.

Wallertheim (Ger). Village. (Anb) = Rheinhessen. (Ber) = Bingen. (Gro) = Kurfürstenstück. (Vins) = Heil, Vogelsang.

Wallhausen (Ger). Village. (Anb) = Nahe. (Ber) = Kreuznach. (Gro) = Pfarrgarten. (Vins) = Backöfchen, Felseneck, Hasensprung, Höllenpfad, Hörnchen, Johannisberg, Kirschheck, Laurentiusberg, Mühlenberg, Pastorenberg, Sonnenweg.

Wallick Cocktail (Cktl). ½ measure French vermouth, ½ measure dry Gin, 4 dashes Grand Marnier. Stir over ice, strain into a cocktail glass.

Wallis Blue (Cktl). ½ measure Cointreau, ½ measure dry Gin, juice of a lime. Shake over ice, strain into a sugar-rimmed (lime juice), ice-filled, old-fashioned glass.

Wallmauer (Ger). Vineyard. (Anb) = Baden. (Ber) = Badische Bergstrasse/Kraichgau. (Gro) = Stiftsberg. (Vil) = Neckarzimmern.

Wallop (Eng) (slang). An old term for beer.

Wallop (Eng). A Winter ale 1056 O.G. brewed by the Bourne Valley Brewery, Andover, Hampshire.

Walluf (Ger). The oldest wine-producing town in the Rheingau in the Steinmächer grosslagen. (See Oberwalluf and Neiderwalluf).

Wallup (Eng) (slang). Cockney for Mild beer. See also Wallop.

Walnut Brown (Sp). An old Oloroso sherry produced by Williams and Humbert.

Walporzheim (Ger). Village. (Anb) = Ahr. (Ber) = Walporzheim/Ahrtal. (Gro) = Klosterberg. (Vins) = Alte Lay, Domlay, Gärkammer, Himmelchen, Krauterberg, Pfaffenberg.

Walporzheim/Ahrtal (Ger). Bereich. (Anb) = Ahr. (Gro) = Klosterberg.

Walsheim (Ger). Village. (Anb) = Rheinpfalz. (Ber) = Südliche Weinstrasse. (Gro) = Bischofskreuz. (Vins) = Forstweg, Silberberg.

Wälshriesling (Aus) (Ger). The alternative pronunciation of the Welschriesling grape.

Walter Brewery (USA). A brewery in Eau Claire, Wisconsin.

Walter's Cocktail (Cktl). ⅕ gill Scotch whisky, ⅛ gill orange juice, ⅛ gill lemon juice. Shake over ice, strain into a cocktail glass.

Waltershofen (Ger). Village. (Anb) = Baden. (Ber) = Kaiserstuhl-Tuniberg. (Gro) = Attilafelsen. (Vin) = Steinmauer.

Walterstal (Ger). Vineyard. (Anb) = Baden. (Ber) = Badische Frankenland. (Gro) = Tauberklinge. (Vil) = Königshofen.

Walton's Diamond (Cktl). 1 measure dry Vermouth, 1 measure Vodka, ⅓ measure Grand Marnier. Mix well over ice, strain 'on the rocks' in an old-fashioned glass. Add a twist of orange.

Waltraud (Sp). A medium white wine made from the Riesling grape by Miguel Torres in Vilafranca del Penedés.

Walzbachtal [ortsteil Jöhlingen] (Ger). Village. (Anb) = Baden. (Ber) = Badische Bergstrasse/Kraichgau. (Gro) = Hohenberg. (Vin) = Hasensprung.

Wamakersvallei Co-operative (S.Afr). Vineyards based at Wellington. Address = Wamakersvallei Co-operative, Box 509, Wellington 7657. Produces varietal wines.

Wana Tallinn (USSR). A dark orange-brown, vanilla and cinnamon-flavoured spirit with a Rum-like taste.

Wandalusia (Sp). The name given to the Sherry region in the eighth century A.D. by the Goths, from which the present day name Andalusia derived.

Wanderhaufen (Ger). An automatic malting process known as the 'moving couch'. The barley is turned automatically during germination and drying. Is similar to the Saladin Box system.

Wanderhausen (Ger). See Wanderhaufen.

Wangaratta (Austr). A wine-producing area in north-eastern Victoria.

Wangen (Ger). Village. (Anb) = Württemberg. (Ber) = Remstal-Stuttgart. (Gro) = Weinsteige. See Stuttgart.

Wangford Arms (Eng). A home-brew public house opened in 1985 in Wangford, Suffolk. Noted for its cask conditioned Wangle 1040 O.G.

Wangle (Eng). See Wangford Arms.

Wanne (Ger). Vineyard. (Anb) = Württemberg. (Ber) = Remstal-Stuttgart. (Gro) = Kopf. (Vil) = Grossheppach.

Wantirna Winery (Austr). Address = Bushy Park Lane, Wantirna South, Victoria 3152. 4 ha. Grape varieties – Cabernet sauvignon, Chardonnay, Merlot and Pinot noir.

Wappen (Ger). Lit – 'Coat of arms'. Found on a wine label.

Waratam Cocktail (Cktl). 1½ measures white Rum, ¾ measure dry Vermouth, ¼ measure Grenadine. Stir over ice, strain into a tulip glass. Dress with a slice of lemon.

Wårby Brewery (Swe). A co-operative brewery in Solleftea, central Sweden. Also a co-operative in Varby eastern Sweden.

Ward Eight (Cktl). 1 jigger Whiskey, 1 oz. lemon juice, 1 teaspoon Grenadine. Shake over ice, strain into an ice-filled highball glass, top with soda.

Ward Eight Cocktail (Cktl). 1 fl.oz. Rye whiskey, ½ fl.oz. orange juice, ½ fl.oz. lemon juice, 4 dashes Grenadine. Shake over ice, strain into a cocktail glass.

Wards Brewery (Eng). Based in Sheffield, Yorkshire. Part of the Vaux Group. Best noted for its Sheffield Best Bitter 1038 O.G.

Ward's Frappé (Cktl). ½ measure Brandy, ½ measure Green Chartreuse, rind of lemon in a large cocktail glass. Pour the Brandy in last over crushed ice. Do not mix.

Warmth (Eng). A term used to describe southern-styled French wines. e.g. the Côtes du Rhône. These wines are high in alcohol and have a good flavour.

Warner Vineyards (USA). A winery based in Michigan (formerly known as the Michigan Winery). Produces hybrid and sparkling wines.

Warneton Brasserie (Bel). An Abbaye brewery in West Flanders.

Warnink (Hol). A noted Advocaat-producing company owned by Allied Breweries.

Warramate Winery (Austr). Address = Lot 4, Macklen's Lane, Gruyere, Victoria 3770. 2 ha. Grape varieties − Cabernet sauvignon, Rhine riesling and Shiraz.

Warre (Port). Vintage Port shippers. Vintages − 1870, 1872, 1875, 1878, 1881, 1884, 1887, 1890, 1894, 1896, 1899, 1900, 1904, 1908, 1912, 1917, 1920, 1922, 1924, 1927, 1931, 1934, 1945, 1947, 1950, 1955, 1958, 1960, 1963, 1966, 1970, 1975, 1977, 1980, 1982, 1983. The oldest English Port Lodge c1670.

Warre Cavadinha (Port). A single quinta Port of Warre. Vintages − 1978, 1979.

Warrenmang Vineyard (Austr). Mountain Creek Road, Moonambel, via Avoca, Victoria. 11 ha. Grape varieties − Cabernet sauvignon, Chardonnay, Merlot and Shiraz.

Warren Sublette Winery (USA). A winery based in Cincinnati, Ohio. Produces French hybrid wines.

Warrington Brown (Eng). The export name for Old Chester 1067 O.G. the strong dark ale brewed by the Greenall Whitley Brewery in Warrington, Cheshire.

Warrior (Eng). A home-brew public house in Brixton, London. Noted for its cask conditioned Brixton Bitter 1036 O.G. and Warrior 1050 O.G.

Warrior Port (Port). The brand-name for a vintage character Port from the Port shippers Warre.

Warsaw Cocktail (Cktl). ⅗ measure Vodka, ⅕ measure French vermouth, ⅕ measure Blackberry brandy, 2 dashes lemon juice. Shake over ice, strain into a cocktail glass.

Warsteiner Brauerei (Ger). A noted producer of a premium Pilsener Lager beer (of same name) that contains no additives.

Wartberg (Ger). Vineyard. (Anb) = Rheinhessen. (Ber) = Wonnegau. (Gro) = Sybillenstein. (Vil) = Alzey.

Wartberg (Ger). Vineyard. (Anb) =

Württemberg. (Ber) = Württembergisch Unterland. (Gro) = Staufenberg. (Vil) = Heilbronn.

Wartberg (Ger). Vineyard. (Anb) = Württemberg. (Ber) = Württembergisch Unterland. (Gro) = Wunnenstein. (Vil) = Beilstein.

Wartbühl (Ger). Grosslage. (Anb) = Württemberg. (Ber) = Remstal-Stutt (Vils) = Aichelberg, Baach, Beutelsbach, Breuningsweiler, Endersbach, Geradstetten, Grossheppach, Grunbach, Hanweiler, Hebsack, Hertmannsweiler, Kleinheppach, Korb, Rommelshausen, Schnait i. R., Stetten i. R., Strümpfelbach, Waiblingen, Winnenden.

Warteck Brauerei (Switz). An independent brewery in Basle.

Warteck Lager (Switz). A low-alcohol Lager beer brewed by the Warteck Brauerei in Basle. 0.5% alc. by vol.

Wasenweiler (Ger). Village. (Anb) = Baden. (Ber) = Kaiserstuhl-Tuniberg. (Gro) = Vulkanfelsen. (Vins) = Kreuzhalde, Lotberg.

Wash (Scot). The name for the fermented liquor before it goes for distillation into Whisky.

Wash (W.Ind). The mixture of molasses, water and fermenting agents ready for fermentation in Rum production.

Wash Back (Scot). The fermenting vessel in the production of Malt Scotch Whisky.

Wash Down (Eng) (slang). To take a drink after eating to help swallow the food.

Washed Coffee (Eng). Another name for the coffee beans prepared by the Wet Method.

Washington (Cktl). ⅔ measure French vermouth, ⅓ measure Brandy, 2 dashes Angostura, 2 dashes Gomme syrup. Stir over ice, strain into a cocktail glass.

Washington (USA). A wine region in the Yakima Valley area around Puget Sound. Produces Labrusca, vinifera and hybrid wines.

Washington (G.) (Eng). An Englishman who lived in Guatemala and invented Instant coffee.

Wash Still (Scot). In Malt whisky production the first copper still which distils the Wash into Low wines.

Waspsting (Eng). Guinness and orange juice. Equal quantities.

Wassail (Eng). Derives from the Anglo-Saxon Wes Hal − 'be of good health'. An old English seventeenth-century drink of spiced beer.

Wassail (Eng). A seventeenth-century festivity (party) where heavy drinking takes place.

Wassail (Eng). A strong ale 1060 O.G. brewed by the Ballards Brewery in Sussex.

Wassail Bowl (Cktl). A hot punch containing many spices, eggs, Sherry or Madeira, garnished with whole cored and roasted apples. Is slightly frothy due to the beaten eggs.

Wasser (Ger). A term which may be added to certain types of liqueurs made from fully-fermented fruits or berries. e.g. Kirsch.

Wasserbillig (Lux). A wine village on the river Moselle. Vineyard site is Bocksberg.

Wasserliesch (Ger). Village. (Anb) = Mosel-Saar-Ruwer. (Ber) = Obermosel. (Gro) = Gipfel. (Vins) = Albachtaler, Reinig auf der Burg.

Wasserlos (Ger). Village. (Anb) = Franken. (Ber) = Maindreieck. (Gro) = Not yet assigned. (Vin) = Schlossberg.

Wasseros (Ger). Vineyard. (Anb) = Rheingau. (Ber) = Johannisberg. (Gro) = Heiligenstock. (Vil) = Kiedrich.

Water [H₂O] (Eng). (Fr) = Eau. (Ger) = Wasser. (Hol) = Water. (It) = Acqua. (Lat) = Aqua. (Port) = Ãgua. (Sp) = Agua. (Tur) = Sulamak. (Wales) = Dwfr. See also Distilled Water, Mineral Water.

Waterbury Cocktail (Cktl). ⅓ gill Brandy, juice ¼ lemon, ½ teaspoon sugar, 2 dashes Grenadine, 1 egg white. Shake over ice, strain into a cocktail glass.

Water Cooler (USA). A unit which cools and dispenses drinking water. Is usually made of glass.

Water Engine (U.K.). An old method of dispensing beer using water pressure which is converted into air pressure. Now little used except in parts of Scotland.

Waterfill Frazier (USA). A Bourbon whiskey distillery based in south-western Frankfurt, Kentucky.

Waterford (Ire). An Irish Whiskey and cream liqueur. 17% alc. by vol.

Waterford (Ire). The Irish glass-making centre. Famous for its cut crystal glass especially for drinking glasses and decanters.

Water Fountain (Fr). A nineteenth-century glass bowl which is on a stand and has four taps from which can be drawn iced water. Was used for watering Absinthe. Invented by Pernod.

Watering Hole (Eng) (slang). The name for a public house, inn, hotel or licensed bar.

Waterloo (Cktl). 1 fl.oz. Mandarine Napoléon, 4 fl.ozs. fresh orange juice. Build into an ice-filled highball glass.

Waterloo Cocktail (Cktl). 1 fl.oz. white Rum, 3 fl.ozs. orange juice. Stir over ice in a highball glass, float ½ fl.oz. of Mandarine Napoléon on top.

Water of Life (Eng). The early name given to spirits. (Fr) = Eau de vie. (It) = Acqua vitae.

Watervale (Austr). A wine region in the northern part of South Australia.

Watervale Shiraz-Cabernet (Austr). A red wine from Château Leonay in South Australia. Owned by Leo Buring Co.

Watervale Spätlese Rhine Riesling (Austr). A light, medium-sweet white wine from the Lindemans Winery in New South Wales.

Watery (Eng). Denotes a wine that lacks body. A thin wine.

Watney Combe Reid (Eng). Part of Grand Metropolitan, is a company that runs 1,500 public houses in the south-east of England. Owns the Stag Brewery in Mortlake. Brews many cask conditioned, keg and bottled beers.

Watney Mann, Truman (Eng). The Hotel and Leisure giant Grand Metropolitan's brewing division. Formed after 1972 when they took over Watneys. Operates 6 breweries, runs 5,000 public houses and 1,800 managed houses. Owns 2 breweries abroad, the Maes Brewery in Belgium and the Stern Brewery in West Germany.

WATP (USA) (abbr). Wine And The People.

Waukon Corporation (USA). A winery based in Waukon, Iowa. Produces mainly French hybrid wines.

Wawel (Pol). A mead made from honey and pasteurised fruit juices in the Royal Castle Wawel in Cracow. Sold in squat bottles. 12–14% alc by vol.

Wawern (Ger). Village. (Anb) = Mosel-Saar-Ruwer. (Ber) = Saar-Ruwer. (Gro) = Scharzberg. (Vins) = Goldberg, Herrenberger, Jesuitenberg, Ritterpfad.

Wax (Eng). Used for the sealing of bottles in the eighteenth and nineteenth centuries. Bottle necks were dipped in molten wax after they had been corked to prevent air contamination. Used for vintage Ports until the 1970s.

Wax Cocktail (Cktl).(1). ½ gill Plymouth gin, 3 dashes Orange bitters. Stir over ice, strain into a cocktail glass, add a cherry and a squeeze of orange peel juice.

Wax Cocktail (Cktl).(2). ½ measure Pastis, ½ measure Gin, 1 egg white, 3 dashes Gomme syrup. Shake over ice, strain into a cocktail glass.

WB (Eng). A cask conditioned Bitter 1037 O.G. brewed by the Cotleigh Brewery in Somerset. Brewed mainly for the New Inn public house in Waterley Bottom, Glos.

Weak (Eng). A term used to describe a wine or beer that has little alcohol or flavour.

Weaks (Scot). The name given to the

W

'feints' at the Auchentoshan Distillery in Dalmuir, Glasgow. See also Strongs.

Weardale Bitter (Eng). A cask conditioned Bitter 1038 O.G. brewed by the King's Arms, a home-brew public house in Bishop Auckland, County Durham.

Weathering (USA). A method used in the making of Vermouths to maderise the wine by exposing the casks to the sun.

Weather Weights (Eng). Small brass washers used on early hydrometers to compensate for the weather conditions. Marked – cold, hot, coldish, etc.

Weavers Bitter (Eng). A cask conditioned Bitter 1037 O.G. brewed by the Bourne Valley Brewery in Andover, Hampshire.

Webster (Cktl). ½ measure dry Gin, ¼ measure French vermouth, ⅛ measure Apricot brandy, ⅛ measure lemon juice. Shake well over ice, strain into a cocktail glass.

Webster Brewery (Eng). Watney's brewery in Halifax, Yorkshire. Has a Lager brewing plant for Budweiser, Carlsberg and Fosters. Also brews cask conditioned Yorkshire Bitter 1037.5 O.G. (also a keg version 1037.5 O.G.). bottled Sam Brown 1034 O.G. Green Label 1038 O.G. and Velvet Stout 1042 O.G.

Wedderburn (W.Ind). The local name in Jamaica for the dark traditional Rums made from cane grown south on the island. Also called Plummer.

Wedding Belle (Cktl). ⅓ measure dry Gin, ⅓ measure Dubonnet, ⅙ measure orange juice, ⅙ measure Cherry brandy. Shake over ice, strain into a cocktail glass.

Wedding Champagne (Eng). Old disparaging name for B.O.B. Champagnes.

Wedding Winner (Cktl). ⅕ measure Cointreau, ⅕ measure Syrop de Fraises, ⅒ measure Cognac, dash Calvados. Stir over ice, strain into a flute glass. Top with iced Champagne.

Weedkiller (Eng). A Bitter beer brewed by the Wiltshire Brewery Company in Tisbury, Wiltshire.

Wee Heavy (Scot). A term for nip-sized bottles of Strong ale. See Fowler's Wee Heavy.

Weepers (Eng). Bottles that show leakage through the cork. Applies mostly to Champagne and other sparkling wines.

Weeping (Eng). The loss of wine seeping out through a bottle of wine which has a poor cork that doesn't fit the bottle properly or is too small.

Weep-No-More (Cktl). ½ measure red Dubonnet, ½ measure Cognac, 2 dashes

Maraschino, juice ½ lime. Shake over ice, strain into a cocktail glass.

Wee Willie Ale (Scot). A Brown and Pale ale 1032 O.G. brewed and bottled by the William Younger Brewery in Edinburgh. Is sold mainly in Ulster.

Wegeler Erben (Ger). A 58 ha. estate owned by Deinhard in the Rheingau. Vineyards are – Geisenheim, Mittelheim, Oestrich, Rüdesheim and Winkel.

Wehlen (Ger). Village. (Anb) = Mosel-Saar-Ruwer. (Ber) = Bernkastel. (Gro) = Münzlay. (Vins) = Klosterberg, Nonnenberg, Sonnenuhr.

Wehr (Ger). Village. (Anb) = Mosel-Saar-Ruwer. (Ber) = Obermosel. (Gro) = Gipfel. (Vin) = Rosenberg.

Weibel Champagne Vineyards (USA). A winery based in California. Grape varieties – Cabernet sauvignon, Chardonnay, Pinot noir and Zinfandel. Produces sparkling and table wines.

Weich (Ger). Denotes soft. A wine that is low in acid and alcohol.

Weidlinger Predigtstuhl (Aus). A white wine made from the Muskat ottonel grape by the Augustine monks at Klosterneuburg, Vienna.

Weight (Eng). The term used to describe body in a wine.

Weihenstephan (Ger). A Brewery based at Freising in Bavaria. Brews Weizen beers. Was opened in the eleventh century. Is also linked with the state-owned Hofbrauhaus Brauerei.

Weikersheim (Ger). Village. (Anb) = Württemberg. (Ber) = Kocher-Jagst-Tauber. (Gro) = Tauberberg. (Vins) = Hardt, Karlsberg, Schmecker.

Weil am Rhein (Ger). Village. (Anb) = Baden. (Ber) = Markgräflerland. (Gro) = Vogtei Rötteln. (Vins) = Schlipf, Stiege.

Weilberg (Ger). Vineyard. (Anb) = Rheinpfalz. (Ber) = Mittelhaardt-Deutsche Weinstrasse. (Gro) = Honigsäckel. (Vil) = Ungstein.

Weiler (Ger). See Sinsheim.

Weiler (Ger). Village. (Anb) = Nahe. (Ber) = Kreuznach. (Gro) = Schlosskapelle. (Vins) = Abtei Ruppertsberg, Klostergarten, Römerberg.

Weiler (Ger). Village. (Anb) = Württemberg. (Ber) = Württembergisch Unterland. (Gro) = Salzberg. (Vins) = Handsberg, Schlierbach.

Weiler bei Monzingen (Ger). Village. (Anb) = Nahe. (Ber) = Schloss Böckelheim. (Gro) = Paradiesgarten. (Vins) = Heiligenberg, Herrenzehntel.

Weiler/Z (Ger). Village. (Anb) = Württemberg. (Ber) = Württembergisch

Unterland. (Gro) = Heuchelberg. (Vin) = Hohenberg.

Weilheim (Ger). Village. (Anb) = Württemberg. (Ber) = Remstal-Stuttgart (Gro) = Hohenneuffen. (Vin) = Schlossteige.

Weimersheim (Ger). Village. (Anb) = Franken. (Ber) = Steigerwald. (Gro) = Schlosstück. (Vin) = Roter Berg.

Wein (Ger). Wine.

Weinachts Christmas Beer (Ger). A fine Beer brewed by the Riegele Brauerei in Augsburg.

Weinähr (Ger). Village. (Anb) = Mittelrhein. (Ber) = Rheinburgengau. (Gro) = Lahntal. (Vin) = Giebelhöll.

Weinaufsicht (Aus). Wine control. Inspectors who enter cellars, vineyards, press-houses, inspect books and ledgers, also take samples of wines. Control the making and distribution of wines and vinous beverages.

Weinbau (Ger). The cultivation of the grapes.

Weinbauer (Ger). Wine-grower.

Weinbaugebiet (Aus). Wine area.

Weinbaugebiet (Ger). A large area of production such as the Rhein, Mosel, Main, Nekar, Oberrhein.

Weinbaukataster (Ger). Land register. Established 1961 to help with the control of viticulture.

Weinbauort (Ger). Wine village. See also Gemeinde, Gemarkung.

Weinbauschule (Aus) (Ger). Wine college, wine school.

Weinbauverein (Aus). Association of vine-growers.

Weinberg (Ger). Hillside vineyard.

Weinbergrecht (Aus). Vineyard law. (Viticultural law).

Weinbergslage (Ger). Vineyard site.

Weinbergsrolle (Ger). The official register of vineyards as required by the 1971 German Wine Laws.

Weinbesserungs-Gesellschaft (Ger). A society for the improvement of wine. Founded in 1823 in Württemberg.

Weinblütenfest (Ger). Mittelrhein wine festival held in Bacarach in June.

Weinbrand (Ger). Brandy. Also spelt Weinbrannt.

Weinbrannt (Ger). See Winbrand.

Weinfass (Ger). Wine cask.

Weinfelden Brauerei (Switz). A small brewery based in Weinfelden.

Weinfest (Ger). Lit – Wine festival.

Weinfest (Ger). A Mittelrhein wine festival held at Boppard in September.

Weinfest (Ger). A Rheingau wine festival held at Rüdesheim in August.

Weinfest (Ger). A Rheingau wine festival held at Hattenheim in August.

Weinfest der Mittelmosel (Ger). A Mosel-Saar-Ruwer wine festival held at Bernkastel in September.

Weinfest der Südlichen Weinstrasse (Ger). A Rheinpfalz wine festival held at Edenkoben in September.

Weingarten (Ger). Village. (Anb) = Baden. (Ber) = Badische Bergstrasse/Kraichgau. (Gro) = Hohenberg. (Vins) = Katzenberg, Petersberg.

Weingarten (Ger). Village. (Anb) = Rheinpfalz. (Ber) = Südliche Weinstrasse. (Gro) = Trappenberg. (Vin) = Schlossberg.

Weingau (Ger). A nickname for the Rheingau.

Weingeist (Ger). Wine spirit (ghost).

Weingrube (Ger). Vineyard. (Anb) = Mittelrhein. (Ber) = Rheinburgengau. (Gro) = Gedeonseck. (Vil) = Boppard.

Weingut (Ger). Vineyard.

Weingütesiegal (Aus). Seal of guarantee of the Austrian Wine Board. Wines of Spätlese quality and above must have the seal to be exported.

Weingut Hochheimer Königin Victoria Berg (Ger). A unique estate based in the Rheingau that has only one parcel of land unlike most other estates. Name is guaranteed by Queen Victoria.

Weingut Siegfried (N.Z.). A small winery near Blenheim, Upper Mourere, Nelson. 12 ha. Produces table wines.

Weinhauer (Aus). Vine grower.

Weinheber (Aus). A wine dispenser made of wrought iron with a stainless steel dispenser. Has a stand and cluster of grapes. Some have a candle and an ice-tube for cooling white wines.

Weinhecke (Ger). Vineyard. (Anb) = Baden. (Ber) = Badische Bergstrasse/Kraichgau. (Gro) = Mannaberg. (Vil) = Bruchsal (stadtteil Untergrombach).

Weinhecke (Ger). Vineyard. (Anb) = Baden. (Ber) = Badische Bergstrasse/Kraichgau. (Gro) = Mannaberg. (Vil) = Ubstadt-Weiher (ortsteil Ubstadt).

Weinheim (Ger). Village. (Anb) = Baden. (Ber) = Badische Bergstrasse/Kraichgau. (Gro) = Rittersberg. (Vins) = Hubberg, Wüstberg.

Weinheim (Ger). Village. (Anb) = Rheinhessen. (Ber) = Wonnegau. (Gro) = Sybillenstein. (Vins) = Heiliger Blutberg, Hölle, Kapellenberg, Kirchenstück, Mandelberg.

Weinhex (Ger). Grosslage. (Anb) = Mosel-Saar-Ruwer. (Ber) = Zell/Mosel. (Vils) = Alken, Burgen, Dieblich, Güls, Hatzenport, Kattenes, Kobern-Gondorf, Koblenz (ortsteil

Lay), Koblenz (ortsteil Moselweiss), Lehmen, Löf, Moselsürsch, Niederfell, Oberfell, Winningen.

Weinig (Ger). Denotes high in alcohol.

Weiningenieur (Ger). Lit – 'Wine engineer'. The highest qualification for viticulture in Germany.

Weininstitut (Ger). Oenological college.

Weinkammer (Ger). Vineyard. (Anb) = Mosel-Saar-Ruwer. (Ber) = Bernkastel. (Gro) = Schwarzlay. (Vil) = Enkirch.

Weinkarte (Ger). Wine list.

Weinkeller (Ger). Vineyard. (Anb) = Rheinhessen. (Ber) = Nierstein. (Gro) = Sankt Alban. (Vil) = Mainz.

Weinkellerei (Ger). Wine cellars.

Weinkelter (Ger). The vintage.

Weinkühler (Ger). Wine cooler.

Weinlehrpfad (Ger). A nature trail or wine education walk. Usually ends at a wine cellar for tastings.

Weinlesefest (Ger). Mittelrhein wine festival held at Bacharach in September.

Weinolsheim (Ger). Village. (Anb) = Rheinhessen. (Ber) = Nierstein. (Gro) = Gutes Domtal. (Vins) = Hohberg, Kehr.

Weinpfalz (Ger). A nickname for the Rheinpfalz.

Weinprobe (Ger). Wine tasting.

Weinrebe (Ger). Grape vine.

Weinsack (Ger). Vineyard. (Anb) = Nahe. (Ber) = Schloss Böckelheim. (Gro) = Paradiesgarten. (Vil) = Odernheim.

Weinsberg (Ger). Village. (Anb) = Württemberg. (Ber) = Württembergisch Unterland. (Gro) = Salzberg. (Vins) = Altenberg, Ranzenberg, Schemelsberg.

Weinsheim (Ger). Village. (Anb) = Nahe. (Ber) = Schloss Böckelheim. (Gro) = Rosengarten. (Vins) = Katergrube, Kellerberg, Steinkaut

Weinstadt [ortsteil Beutelsbach] (Ger). Village. (Anb) = Württemberg. (Ber) = Remstal-Stuttgart. (Gro) = Sonnenbühl. (Vin) = Burghalde.

Weinstadt [ortsteil Endersbach] (Ger). Village. (Anb) = Württemberg. (Ber) = Remstal-Stuttgart. (Gro) = Sonnenbühl. (Vin) = Hintere Klinge.

Weinstadt [ortsteil Rommelshausen] (Ger). Village. (Anb) = Württemberg. (Ber) = Remstal-Stuttgart. (Gro) = Sonnenbühl. (Vins) = Mönchhalde, Mönchberg.

Weinstadt [ortsteil Schnait i. R.] (Ger). Village. (Anb) = Württemberg. (Ber) = Remstal-Stuttgart. (Gro) = Sonnenbühl. (Vin) = Burghalde.

Weinstadt [ortsteil Strümpfelbach] (Ger). Village. (Anb) = Württemberg.

(Ber) = Remstal-Stuttgart. (Gro) = Sonnenbühl. (Vin) = Altenberg.

Weinsteig (Ger). Vineyard. (Anb) = Franken. (Ber) = Maindreieck. (Gro) = Ravensburg. (Vil) = Erlabrunn.

Weinsteige (Ger). Grosslage. (Anb) = Württemberg. (Ber) = Remstal-Stuttgart. (Vils) = Esslingen, Fellbach, Gerlingen, Stuttgart (ortsteil Gaisburg), Stuttgart (ortsteil Untertürkheim), Stuttgart (ortsteil Uhlbach), Stuttgart (ortsteil Obertürkheim), Stuttgart (ortsteil Bad Cannstatt, Feuerbach, Münstewr, Wangen, Zuffenhausen), Stuttgart (ortsteil Bad Cannstatt), Stuttgart (ortsteil Bad Cannstatt, Untertürkheim), Stuttgart (ortsteil Obertürkheim), Stuttgart (ortsteil Hedelfingen, Rohracker), Stuttgart (ortsteil Bad Cannstatt, Untertürkheim), Stuttgart (ortsteil Degerloch), Stuttgart (ortsteil Rotenberg, Uhlbach, Untertürkheim), Stuttgart (ortsteil Uhlbach), Stuttgart (ortsteil Bad Cannstatt, Mühlhausen, Münster), Stuttgart (ortsteil Untertürkheim), Stuttgart (ortsteil Bad Cannstatt, Hofen, Mühlhausen, Münster).

Weinstein (Ger). Tartrate deposits.

Weinstrassen (Ger). Wine roads for the touring motorist to follow.

Weinstübe (Ger). A wine bar in the Württemberg Anbaugebiet.

Weinstüble (Ger). See Weinstübe.

Weinverordnung (Aus). Wine decree. Used to renew and enlarge on part of the Austrian wine law.

Weinviertel (Ger). A wine-producing district based near Wien. Divided Falkenstein, Matzen and Retz.

Weinwirtschaftsfond (Aus). Wine industry institute.

Weinwirtschaftsgesetz (Ger). See Gesetz über Massnahmen auf dem Gebiete der Weinwirtschaft.

Weinwoche (Ger). Mittelrhein wine festival held at St. Goarshausen in September.

Weisbaden (Ger). A town on the north bank of the Rhine in the area of the Rheingau. Noted for such wines as Schloss Vollrads.

Weischler GmbH (Aus). A noted producer of Brandies and fruit spirits. Part of Seagram.

Weisenbach (Ger). Village. (Anb) = Baden. (Ber) = Ortenau. (Gro) = Schloss Rodeck. (Vin) = Kestelberg.

Weisenheim am Berg (Ger). Village. (Anb) = Rheinpfalz. (Ber) = Mittelhaardt-Deutsche Weinstrasse. (Gro) = Feuerberg. (Vin) = Vogelsang.

Weisenheim am Berg (Ger). Village. (Anb) = Rheinpfalz. (Ber) = Mittelhaardt-Deutsche Weinstrasse. (Gro) = Kobnert. (Vins) = Mandelgarten, Sonnenberg.

W

Weisenheim/Sand (Ger). Village. (Anb) = Rheinpfalz. (Ber) = Mittelhaardt-Deutsche Weinstrasse. (Gro) = Rosenbühl. (Vins) = Altenberg, Burgweg, Goldberg, Hahnen, Halde, Hasenzeile.

Weissarbstwein (Ger). The nineteenth-century name for a rosé wine made mainly from the Spätburgunder grape. Is now known as Weissherbst.

Weissbach (Ger). Village. (Anb) = Württemberg. (Ber) = Kocher-Jagst-Tauber. (Gro) = Kocherberg. (Vins) = Altenberg, Engweg.

Weissbier (Ger). White beer. A weak, frothy beer served in Munich usually with a slice of lemon. A version of Weizenbier.

Weissburgunder (Ger). A white grape variety. Also known as the Pinot blanc in France and the Pinot bianco in Italy. Produces light neutral wines. Also known as the Muscadet in western France.

Weiss-Clevner (Ger). Local name for the Weissburgunder (Pinot blanc).

Weisse (Ger). A shortened term for Weissbier. Refers mainly to the top-fermented pale brews of Berlin. See Berliner Weisse.

Weisse Bier (Ger). See Weissbier.

Weisse Muskateller (Ger). An alternative name for the Muscat blanc à petits grains.

Weissenberg (Ger). Vineyard. (Anb) = Mosel-Saar-Ruwer. (Ber) = Zell/Mosel. (Gro) = Weinhex. (Vil) = Kobern-Gondorf.

Weissenkirchen (Aus). A wine-producing area based in western Austria.

Weissenstein (Ger). Vineyard. (Anb) = Mosel-Saar-Ruwer. (Ber) = Bernkastel. (Gro) = Kurfürstlay. (Vil) = Bernkastel-Kues.

Weissenstein (Ger). Vineyard. (Anb) = Nahe. (Ber) = Schloss Böckelheim. (Gro) = Paradiesgarten. (Vil) = Mannweiler-Coelln.

Weissenstein (Ger). Vineyard. (Anb) = Nahe. (Ber) = Schloss Böckelheim. (Gro) = Paradiesgarten. (Vil) = Oberndorf.

Weisserberg (Ger). Vineyard. (Anb) = Mosel-Saar-Ruwer. (Ber) = Bernkastel. (Gro) = Vom Heissen Stein. (Vil) = Briedel.

Weisser Bruch (Ger). Lit – 'White turbidity'. Describes wines with a cloudy, bluish-white appearance.

Weisser Burgunder (Aus). See Weissburgunder.

Weiss Erd (Ger). Vineyard. (Anb) = Rheingau. (Ber) = Johannisberg. (Gro) = Daubhaus. (Vil) = Kostheim.

Weisser Gutedel (Ger). A white grape variety grown mainly in the Baden region. Has high sugar and gives light, pleasant wines.

Weisser Husa (Aus). A white wine produced from the Muscat grape by Sepp Höld in St. Georgen.

Weisser Klevner (Ger). A white grape variety, known as the Pinot chardonnay in France.

Weisser Kreuz (Ger). Vineyard. (Anb) = Mittelrhein. (Ber) = Rheinburgengau. (Gro) = Burg Hammerstein. (Vil) = Leubsdorf.

Weisser Pressburger (Ger). A white grape variety.

Weisser Riesling (S.Afr). A white grape variety, known as the Riesling in Germany.

Weissherbst (Ger). Local rosé wine of Kaiserstuhl in Baden. Made from the Blauer Spätburgunder, Portugieser and Trollinger grapes. Grapes are pressed as for white wine. The name of the grape on the label must be the same size as Weissherbst. See also Weissarbstwein.

Weisslack (Ger). A Qba. wine from the Herrgottströpfchen range of wines from Jakob Gerhardt.

Weisswein (Ger). White wine.

Weitheimer (S.Afr). A label used by the Weltevrede Estate in Robertson for a range of their wines.

Weitraumkulturen (Aus). A term used to describe the wide-spaced training used in vine growing.

Weizenbier (Ger). Lit – 'Wheat beer'. Made with a high proportion of wheat. Is low in alcohol, light in colour and with a strong flavour. Served in tall narrow glasses.

Weizenbock (Ger). A strong version of Weizenbier. 6.25% alc. by vol.

Weizenkorn (Ger). A Whiskey made from a wheat base.

Weizenthaler (Ger). A low alcohol Lager beer brewed in West Germany. Is not allowed to ferment.

Weldra (S.Afr). A white grape variety. Gives good acidity and bouquet.

Welgemeend Estate (S.Afr). Vineyard based at Paarl. Address = P.O. Box 69, Klapmuts 7625. Produces Amadé and varietal wines.

Welgesheim (Ger). Village. (Anb) = Rheinhessen. (Ber) = Bingen. (Gro) = Sankt Rochuskapelle. (Vin) = Kirchgärtchen.

Well (Eng). A hole sunk into the ground so that water can be drawn from natural reservoirs under the surface.

Welland (Can). A wine region between Niagara and Crystal Beach.

W

Well-Balanced (Eng). A term used to describe a harmonious wine.
Wellen (Ger). Village. (Anb) = Mosel-Saar-Ruwer. (Ber) = Obermosel. (Gro) = Gipfel. (Vin) = Altenberg.
Wellenstein (Lux). A wine village on the river Moselle. Vineyard sites are Fulschette, Kourschels. Also the name of a co-operative that is part of Vinsmoselle.
Welling's Bitters (Hol). Aromatic bitters.
Wellington (S.Afr). A wine-producing region based south of Tulbagh in Paarl. Produces table wines.
Wellington (N.Z.). A small wine-producing area on the southern tip of the North Island.
Wellington Distilleries Ltd (Afr). A noted distillery based in Sierra Leone, western Africa. Produces a range a spirits.
Wellington Glass (Eng). A beer glass 12 fl.oz. capacity, specially made for bottled top-fermented beers. Has a wide base, short stem and a bell-shaped bowl.
Wellington Wynboere Co-operative (S.Afr). Vineyards based in Paarl. Address = Die Wellington Wynboere Co-operative, P.O. Box 520, Wellington 7655. Produces varietal wines.
Well-Knit (Eng). A wine term used to denote a strong, sturdy and firm wine (in body).
Well-Oiled (Eng) (slang). A term for intoxicated. Usually applied to a person who talks a lot (with slurred speech) and is not fully comprehensible.
Wells Brewery (Eng). Situated in Bedford. Produces cask conditioned Eagle Bitter 1035 O.G. Bombadier 1042 O.G. keg Silver Special 1030 O.G. Gold Eagle 1034 O.G. Noggin 1039 O.G. Red Stripe 1044 O.G. and a range of bottled beers.
Wells Drinks (Eng). A soft drinks company based in Tenbury Wells, Worcestershire. Produces a range of soft drinks under the Wells Wonderful World label.
Well-Succeeded (Eng). A term which denotes a wine that displays the best characteristics of its growth. (Fr) = Très Réussi.
Wells Wonderful World (Eng). See Wells Drinks.
Welmlingen (Ger). Village. (Anb) = Baden. (Ber) = Margräflerland. (Gro) = Vogtei Rötteln. (Vin) = Steingässle.
Welmoed Co-operative (S.Afr). Vineyards in Stellenbosch. Address = Welmoed Koöpertiewe Wynkelders, Box 23, Lynedock 7603. Produces varietal wines.

Welmoed Koöperatiewe Wynkelders (S.Afr). See Welmoed Co-operative.
Welschriesling (Euro). A white grape variety. (Welsch means foreign in German). Used in most countries. Known as the Riesling italico in Italy.
Welsh Bitter (Wales). A keg Bitter 1032 O.G. brewed by the Whitbread Brewery at Magor.
Welsh Brewers (Wales). A brewery belonging to Bass in Cardiff. Has some 500 public houses in the principality. Brews cask conditioned Worthington Pale 1033 O.G. Hancock's PA 1033 O.G. Fussell's Best 1038 O.G. and keg Albright 1033 O.G.
Welsh Connection (Pousse Café). In an Elgin liqueur glass pour in order ½ measure Midori, ½ measure red Maraschino.
Welsh Connexion (Cktl). 1 fl.oz. Malibu, ¾ fl.oz. blue Curaçao, 2 fl.ozs. orange juice, dash egg white. Shake well over ice, strain into a cocktail glass. Top with a cherry.
Welsh Mist (Wales). A herb-flavoured liqueur, yellow-gold in colour. 40% alc. by vol.
Welsh Whiskey (Wales). Distilled near Frongoch near Bala, Powys. Made by Richard John Lloyd Price in 1898. See also Swn y Don and Swn y Mor.
Weltevrede Estate (S.Afr). A vineyard based at Robertson. Address = Weltevrede Langoed Box 6, Bonnievale 6730. Produces varietal and fortified wines. Labels include Privé and Weitheimer.
Weltevrede Langoed (S.Afr). See Weltevrede Estate.
Wembley (Cktl). ⅓ measure Scotch whisky, ⅓ measure dry Vermouth, ⅓ measure pineapple juice. Shake over ice, strain into a cocktail glass.
Wembley Ale (Eng). A Pale ale 1036 O.G. brewed and bottled by the Wilson Brewery in Manchester.
Wembley Cocktail (Cktl). ⅔ measure dry Gin, ⅓ measure French vermouth, 2 dashes Apricot brandy, 2 dashes Calvados. Stir over ice, strain into a cocktail glass.
Wem Brewery (Eng). The Shropshire subsidiary of Greenall Whitley which produces cask conditioned and other beers near Shrewsbury.
Wench's Quiver (Cktl). 1 fl.oz. Mandarine Napoléon, ½ fl.oz. Galliano, 2 fl.ozs. pineapple juice, ½ fl.oz. lemon juice, 1 egg white. Shake over ice, strain into a 10 fl.oz. goblet with crushed ice. Float ¼ fl.oz. blue Curaçao on top.
Wendelsheim (Ger). Village. (Anb) = Rheinhessen. (Ber) = Bingen. (Gro) =

Adelberg. (Vins) = Heiligenpfad, Steigerberg.

Wendelstück (Ger). Vineyard. (Anb) = Mosel-Saar-Ruwer. (Ber) = Bernkastel. (Gro) = Schwarzlay. (Vil) = Burg.

Wenden (Eng). Vineyard. Address = Duddenhoe End, Near Saffron Walden, Essex. 1.25 ha. Soil – clay loam on chalk. Grape variety – Müller-Thurgau. Vinification at Chilford Hundred Wine Co.

Wendewein (Ger). A wine made in the Bodensee. It is so acidic that consumers have to keep turning over in bed at night so that it does not eat a hole through their stomachs!

Wenigumstadt (Ger). Village. (Anb) = Franken. (Ber) = Maindreieck. (Gro) = Heiligenthal. (Vins) = Assorted parts of vineyards.

Wente Bros Winery (USA). A winery based in Livermore Valley, Alameda, California. Grape varieties – Chardonnay, Chenin blanc, Sauvignon blanc, Sémillon and Ugni blanc. Produces varietal and table wines.

Werbach (Ger). Village. (Anb) = Baden. (Ber) = Badische Frankenland. (Gro) = Tauberklinge. (Vins) = Beilberg, Hirschberg.

Wermod (Eng). The Anglo-Saxon name for wormwood. See Wermut.

Wermut (Ger). Wormwood. The name from which Vermouth derives. See Wermod.

Wermutshausen (Ger). Village. (Anb) = Württemberg. (Ber) = Kocher-Jagst-Tauber. (Gro) = Tauberberg. (Vin) = Schafsteige.

Wernersgrüner Brauerei (Ger). A brewery based in the Vogtland district in Eastern Germany.

Wernersgrüner Pils (Ger). A Pilsener lager beer brewed in the Wernersgrüner Brauerei in the Vogtland district of East Germany.

Wernig (Ger). Vinious, vinosity.

Wertheim (Ger). Village. (Anb) = Baden. (Ber) = Badische Frankenland. (Gro) = Tauberklinge. (Vin) = Schlossberg.

Wesh (Tur). The name given to the foam on the top of a cup of Turkish coffee. Lit – 'Face'.

Wes Hal (Eng). An Anglo-Saxon word meaning 'be of good health'. See Wassail.

Wessex Best Bitter (Eng). A cask conditioned Best Bitter 1042 O.G. brewed by the Cornish Brewery in Weymouth, Dorset. Also sold as bottled Wessex Pale Ale.

Wessex Pale Ale (Eng). See Wessex Best Bitter.

West African Breweries (Afr). A large brewery in Nigeria. Produces Top Lager beer.

Westbury Farm Vineyard (Eng). Address = Purley, near Reading in the Thames Valley, Berkshire. 6.7 ha. Planted 1968. Grape varieties – Madeleine angevine, Müller-Thurgau, Pinot meunier, Pinot noir, Reichensteiner, Seibel, Siegerrebe and Seyval blanc.

West Coast Cooler (Eng). A commercial blend of Pacific fruits and white wine. 3.5% alc. by vol.

West Country Ale (Eng). A cask conditioned Pale ale 1030 O.G. brewed by the Whitbread Brewery in Cheltenham, Glos.

West Country Cider (Eng). A fine Cider produced by Landons at Hewish, Near Weston-Super-Mare, Avon.

West Crown Brewery (Eng). A brewery based in Newark, Nottinghamshire. Brews Regal Bitter, Greenwood's N°8 and Greenwood's N°10.

West End (Eng). A brand of coffee produced by Kenco-Typhoo Catering. Blend of Arabica coffees.

West End and Southwark Brewery (Austr). A brewery based in Adelaide.

West End Beer (Austr). A pasteurised, bottom-fermented Bitter beer brewed by the Coopers Brewery in the West End district of South Australia.

West End Bitter (Austr). A Lager beer brewed by the South Australian Brewing Co. in Adelaide.

West End Brewery (USA). A brewery based in Utica. See West End Brewing Company.

West End Brewing Company (USA). A brewery based at Utica. Brews Maximus Super, Matt's Premium, Utica Club Cream Ale and Utica Club Pilsener.

West End Wines (Austr). Vineyard. Address = 1283 Brayne Road, Griffith, New South Wales 2680. 12.5 ha. Grape varieties – Cabernet sauvignon, Chardonnay, Hermitage, Rhine riesling, Sémillon, Traminer. One of the smaller wineries of the M.I.A.

Western Australia (Austr). A state with nearly 60 wineries concentrated in a 20 kilometre strip. See Swan Valley, Margaret River, Frankland and Mount Barker.

Western Electric (Cktl). 1 fl.oz. Claret, 1 fl.oz. Cointreau, 1 fl.oz. Cognac. Shake over ice, strain into a highball glass. Top with iced Champagne.

Western Rose (Cktl). ½ measure dry Gin, ¼ measure Apricot brandy, ¼ measure dry Vermouth, dash lemon juice. Shake over ice, strain into a cocktail glass.

Western Vineyards (N.Z). A former vineyard. Is now no longer in operation.

Westfield (Austr). A winery in the Swan Valley in Western Australia.

Westfield-Fredonia (USA). A wine district along Lake Erie in the New York region.

West Highland Malt Whisky (Scot). The old name for Islay Malt Whisky.

Westhofen (Ger). Village. (Anb) = Rheinhessen. (Ber) = Wonnegau. (Gro) = Bergkloster. (Vins) = Aulerde, Benn, Brunnenhäuschen, Kirchspiel, Morstein, Rotenstein, Steingrube.

West Indian Punch (Punch). Into a large punch bowl place 1 pint each of Bacardi rum, pineapple juice, orange juice and lemon juice, ¼ pint Crème de Banane, 4 ozs. castor sugar, grated nutmeg, cinnamon and cloves. Stir well, chill down in a refrigerator. Dress with sliced bananas and serve.

West Indian Rum Refinery (W.Ind). A noted Rum distillery based on the island of Barbados.

West Indies Distilleries Ltd (W.Ind). A Rum distillery based in the Virgin Islands.

West Indies Rum and Spirits Producers Association (W.Ind). WIRSPA. A group of West Indian islands – Antigua, Bahamas, Barbados, Guyana, Jamaica and Trinidad formed to promote and protect Rum.

West Indies Swizzle (Cktl). ½ bottle Jamaican Rum, 6 teaspoons sugar, 6 sprigs mint, 6 fl.ozs. lime juice. Fill a jug with ice, add ingredients, place between feet, use a swizzle stick until the outside of the jug is frosted.

Westmalle (Bel). An Abbaye which brews Trappist beer. Based at Tripel on the Dutch border. Also brews a dark Dubbel beer. 7% alc. by vol.

Westminster (Cktl). ½ measure French vermouth, ½ measure Canadian rye whisky, 3 dashes Arum, dash Angostura. Stir over ice, strain into a cocktail glass.

Westminster Pure Coffee (Eng). The brand-name of a ground coffee produced by Kenco-Typhoo Catering Services.

Westons (Eng). Famous cider makers of Much Marcle in Herefordshire.

Weston Winery (USA). A noted winery based in Idaho, Pacific North-West.

West Riding Brewery (Eng). Opened in 1980 in Huddersfield, Yorkshire. Now based in Meltham, Yorkshire (due to a fire). Brews cask conditioned Tyke Bitter 1041 O.G.

Westrum (Ger). Vineyard. (Anb) = Rheinhessen. (Ber) = Nierstein. (Gro) = Sankt Alban. (Vil) = Bodenheim.

Weststeiermark (Aus). West Styria. A wine district within the region of Steiermark. Produces both red and white wines.

Wet (Eng) (slang). A term for a drink. 'To have a wet'.

Wet (USA). A person who advocates the free sale of alcoholic liquor.

Wethered Brewery (Eng). Whitbread's Brewery in Marlow, Buckinghamshire. Noted for its cask conditioned beers.

Wet Method (Eng). The process of removing the coffee beans from the coffee cherries using water. Beans are soaked in tanks, fermented and the pulp washed away. See Washed Coffee and Dry Method.

Wet One's Whistle (Eng) (slang). To have a drink. See Wet.

Wet Rent (Eng). The method of renting a public house to a tenant. The rent to the tenant was low and the brewery's income was from a surcharge on the wholesale price of the drink.

Wets Brasserie (Bel). A brewery based in St. Genisius-Rode, Central Belgium.

Wet Smell (Eng). The name given to the process of aroma testing (sniffing) of the coffee. Also known as the Crust Test.

Wet State (USA). The name for a State that permits the free sale of alcoholic liquor.

Wettelbrunn (Ger). Village. (Anb) = Baden. See Staufen.

Wetterkreuz (Ger). Vineyard. (Anb) = Nahe. (Ber) = Schloss Böckelheim. (Gro) = Rosengarten. (Vil) = Braunweiler.

Wetzstein (Ger). Vineyard. (Anb) = Württemberg. (Ber) = Remstal-Stuttgart. (Gro) = Wartbühl. (Vil) = Endersbach.

Wetzstein (Ger). Vineyard. (Anb) = Württemberg. (Ber) = Remstal-Stuttgart. (Gro) = Weinsteige. (Vil) = Fellbach.

Wetzstein (Ger). Vineyard. (Anb) = Württemberg. (Ber) = Remstal-Stuttgart. (Gro) = Weinsteige. (Vil) = Stuttgart (ortsteil Untertürkheim).

Weyher (Ger). Village. (Anb) = Rheinpfalz. (Ber) = Südliche Weinstrasse. (Gro) = Ordensgut. (Vins) = Heide, Michelsberg.

WGS (Aus). Öesterreichisches Weingutesiegel. The Austrian wine seal of quality.

Whale Ale (Eng). A cask conditioned Ale 1045 O.G. brewed by the Bruce homebrew public house, the Flounder and Firkin in London.

Wharfdale Ale (Eng). A cask conditioned Special Ale 1045 O.G. brewed by the Goose Eye Brewery in Keighley, Yorkshire.

Whatiri Wines (N.Z.). A winery based in Poroti, west of Whangarei, Northland. 2 ha. Closed in 1983.

What's Yours? (Eng). An informal request to know what you would like to drink. An offer to buy a person a drink.

What the Hell (Cktl). ⅓ measure dry Gin, ⅓ measure French vermouth, ⅓ measure Apricot brandy, dash lemon juice. Stir over ice in an old-fashioned glass.

Wheat Whiskey (USA). A Whiskey produced at not exceeding 160° US proof from not less than 51% of wheat mash and stored in charred oak casks at not more than 125° US proof.

Wherry Bitter (Eng). A Best Bitter 1039 O.G. brewed by the Woodforde Brewery in Norwich, Norfolk.

Whip and Tongue (Eng). A method of grafting used in France that consists of cutting the scion and stock at the same angle and then splitting them so that they lock into each other.

Whip Cocktail (Cktl). ⅛ gill Pernod, ⅛ gill Brandy, ⅛ gill French vermouth, ⅛ gill Curaçao. Shake over ice, strain into a cocktail glass. Also known as a Kurbag Cocktail.

Whipkull (Scot). A mixed drink of egg yolks, sugar, cream, Rum which is traditionally served in the Shetland Islands at Yuletide (January 6th). Is considered to be of Scandinavian origin.

Whirlpool (Eng). Another name for the Centrifuge.

Whiskey (Eng). The spelling of Whiskies other than Scotch Whisky and the Canadian Rye Whisky.

Whiskey Cobbler (Cktl). Place ⅓ gill Bourbon whiskey into an old-fashioned glass over ice. Add 2 dashes of Gomme syrup and a splash of soda. Decorate with fruits in season and serve with straws.

Whiskey Cocktail (Cktl). ⅕ gill Bourbon whiskey, 4 dashes Gomme syrup, dash Angostura. Stir over ice, strain into a cocktail glass. Add a cherry.

Whiskey Collins (Cktl). 2 fl.ozs. Bourbon whiskey, juice ½ lemon, 1 teaspoon powdered sugar. Shake over ice, strain into an ice-filled collins glass. Top with soda water, lemon slice, orange slice and a cherry. Serve with straws.

Whiskey Daisy (Cktl). 2 ozs. Bourbon or Rye whiskey, juice of ½ lemon or lime, 3 dashes Gomme syrup. Shake over ice, strain into a small tumbler. Top with soda water and a dash of Grenadine.

Whiskey Eggnog (Cktl). ⅕ gill Bourbon whiskey, 1 egg, 1 teaspoon powdered sugar. Shake well over ice, strain into a collins glass. Top with milk, stir, add grated nutmeg.

Whiskey Fix (Cktl). Dissolve 1 teaspoon of powdered sugar in the juice of ½ lemon in a highball glass. Add ice, ½ gill Bourbon whiskey. Stir, top with a slice of lemon. Serve with straws.

Whiskey Fizz (Cktl). 2 measures Bourbon whiskey, 1 teaspoon sugar, juice of a lemon. Shake over ice, strain into an ice-filled highball glass. Top with soda water.

Whiskey Flip (Cktl). ⅕ gill Bourbon whiskey, 1 egg, ⅛ gill cream, 1 teaspoonful powdered sugar. Shake well over ice, strain into a flip glass. Top with grated nutmeg.

Whiskey Glass (USA). The alternative name for a Nip glass. Holds a single measure.

Whiskey Highball (Cktl). As for Gin Highball but using Whiskey instead of Gin.

Whiskey Julep (Cktl). In a large glass dissolve 1 teaspoon of sugar in a little water. Fill with crushed ice. Top with Bourbon whiskey to within ½ inch of top. Decorate with mint. The mint can be crushed with the sugar if desired.

Whiskey Milk Punch (Cktl). ⅓ gill Bourbon whiskey, 1½ gills milk, 1 teaspoonful powdered sugar. Shake over ice, strain into a highball glass. Top with grated nutmeg.

Whiskey Mist (Cktl). In an old-fashioned glass place some shaved ice, add 1 jigger of Bourbon or Rye whiskey and a twist of lemon peel juice.

Whiskey Orange (Cktl). ⅕ gill Bourbon whiskey, juice ½ orange, 1 teaspoon powdered sugar, 2 dashes Pernod. Shake well over ice, strain into an ice-filled highball glass. Top with a slice of lemon and orange.

Whiskey Rebellion (USA). 15th September 1794. Distillers revolted against the Excise tax of 1791. Led to the first making of Moonshine.

Whiskey Rickey (Cktl). ⅓ gill Bourbon whiskey, juice ½ lime. Stir over ice, strain into a highball glass. Top with soda water and a squeeze of lime peel juice.

Whiskey Sangaree (Cktl). Dissolve ½ teaspoonful of powdered sugar in a little water in a highball glass. Add ice and ⅕ gill Bourbon whiskey. Top with 2 fl.ozs. soda water, dash of Port and grated nutmeg.

Whiskey Skin (Cktl). Into an old-fashioned glass place a sugar cube and 2 fl.ozs. boiling water. Stir, add ⅕ gill Bourbon whiskey and a twist of lemon peel. Stir.

Whiskey Sling (Cktl). Dissolve 1 teaspoonful powdered sugar in the juice of ½ lemon and 1 fl.oz. water in an old-fashioned glass. Add ⅓ gill Rye whiskey, stir, add a twist of lemon peel.

Whiskey Smash (Cktl). Muddle a cube of sugar with ½ jigger of water and some mint. Add ice, 1 jigger of Whiskey. Serve decorated with mint and top with Club soda.

Whiskey Sour (Cktl). ¾ oz. lemon or lime juice, 1½ ozs. Bourbon or Rye whiskey, 1 teaspoon powdered sugar. Shake well over ice, strain into a cocktail glass, add a cherry and a slice of orange.

Whiskey Squirt (Cktl). ⅕ gill Bourbon whiskey, 2 dashes Grenadine. Shake over ice, strain into an ice-filled highball glass. Top with a pineapple cube and fresh strawberry.

Whiskey Swizzle (Cktl). As for Gin Swizzle but using Bourbon whiskey in place of the Gin.

Whiskey Toddy (Cktl). ⅓ gill Bourbon (or Rye) whiskey, ½ teaspoon powdered sugar, ⅙ gill boiling water. Stir sugar in the water in an old-fashioned glass. Add Whiskey, stir and top with a twist of lemon peel.

Whisky (Eng). The spelling of Whiskies that come from Scotland only with the exception of Canadian Rye whisky. See Whiskey.

Whisky (The) (Jap). A special Whiskey produced by Suntory. Only 6,000 bottles are produced annually.

Whisky Cobbler (Cktl). 1 gill Whisky, ¼ gill brown Curaçao. Shake over ice, strain into an ice-filled highball glass. Serve with a dash of lemon peel juice, slices of fresh fruit, spoon and straws.

Whisky Cobbler (Cktl). 1 measure Scotch whisky, 1 teaspoon sugar, 4 dashes orange Curaçao. Fill a 5 oz. wine glass with ice. Add Whisky, sugar and Curaçao, stir. Decorate with fruit, mint sprig. Serve with straws.

Whisky Cocktail (Cktl).(1). ⅘ measure Scotch whisky, ⅕ measure orange Curaçao, 2 dashes Angostura. Stir over ice, strain into a cocktail glass. Add a cherry.

Whisky Cocktail (Cktl).(2). ⅓ gill Scotch whisky, 2 dashes brown Curaçao, 1 dash Angostura, 1 lump sugar. Stir over ice, strain into a cocktail glass. Serve with a cherry and a dash lemon peel juice on top.

Whisky Collins (Cktl). ¾ gill Scotch whisky, dash lemon juice, sugar syrup to taste. Shake well over ice, strain into a highball glass, top with soda water.

Whisky Cooler (Cktl). ½ gill Scotch whisky, ½ pint soda water, 2 dashes Orange bitters. Stir in a tall glass with an ice cube. Serve with a slice of orange on top.

Whisky Crusta (Cktl). ⅓ gill Scotch whisky, ⅙ gill lemon juice, 1 teaspoon sugar syrup, 1 teaspoon Maraschino, dash Angostura, dash Orange bitters, ½ teaspoon powdered sugar. Moisten wine glass with lemon and add sugar, place in a spiral of lemon peel. Shake ingredients over ice, strain into a crusta glass. Serve with slices of fruit.

Whisky Daisy (Cktl). ½ gill Scotch whisky, ¼ gill orange juice, ½ gill lime juice, ½ gill lemon juice, dash Grenadine. Shake over ice, strain into a highball. Top with soda water. Serve with slices of fresh fruit and add 2 dashes brown Curaçao.

Whisky Egg Nogg (Cktl). ⅔ gill Scotch whisky, 1 egg, dash Rum, 1 teaspoon sugar, ¾ gill milk. Shake over ice, strain into a tumbler, serve with a dash of nutmeg on top.

Whisky Elsie (Cktl). 1 teaspoon sugar, juice ½ lemon, 1 measure Scotch whisky, dash Angostura. Shake well over ice, strain into a wine glass.

Whisky Jug (Scot). An alternative name for old Whisky bottles.

Whisky-Lime Grog (Cktl). 1 measure Scotch whisky, dash vanilla essence, 2 teaspoons sugar. Add to ½ pint lime tea. Serve in a heat-proof glass. Decorate with a slice of lime.

Whisky Mac (Cktl). 1½ fl.ozs. Scotch whisky, 1 fl.oz. Ginger wine. Build into an old-fashioned glass.

Whisky-Mint Cocktail (Cktl). 2 fl.ozs. mint tea, 1 fl.oz. Scotch whisky, juice of ½ lime. Shake well over ice, strain into a cocktail glass. Dress with mint leaves.

Whisky Punch (Cktl). 2 measures Scotch whisky, 1 measure Jamaican rum, ½ measure lemon juice, 1 teaspoon sugar, dash Angostura. Shake well over ice, strain into an ice-filled highball glass. Dress with an orange slice soaked in Curaçao and a dash of soda water.

Whisky Safe (Scot). A glass case through which Scotch Malt whisky runs during the second distillation. Is locked by the Customs and Excise. The distiller controls the flow (of Foreshots and Feints etc) by remote control.

Whisky Sangaree (Cktl). Dissolve ½ oz.

sugar in 5 fl.ozs. water in a tumbler. Add 1 oz. Scotch whisky and 2 ice cubes. Top with grated nutmeg.

Whisky Sling [Hot] (Cktl). 2 measures Scotch whisky in an old-fashioned glass. Top with boiling water and grated nutmeg.

Whisky Smash (Cktl). As for Gin Smash but substituting Scotch whisky for the Gin.

Whisky Toddy (Cktl). 2 ozs. Scotch whisky, 1 oz. water, 1 teaspoon sugar. Stir until sugar dissolves, serve in a 5 oz. wine glass.

Whispers-of-the-Past (Cktl). ⅓ measure Bourbon whiskey, ⅓ measure Port, ⅓ measure dry Sherry, 1 teaspoon powdered sugar. Stir over ice, strain into a cocktail glass. Dress with a slice of lemon and orange.

Whist Cocktail (Cktl). ⅓ measure dark Rum, ⅓ measure Italian vermouth, ⅓ measure Calvados. Shake over ice, strain into a cocktail glass.

Whitbread (Eng). A National Brewer. Has over 6,800 public houses. Has 6 breweries and 2 keg brewing plants in England and Wales. Noted for its cask conditioned Trophy Bitter 1035 O.G. (also keg). Tankard 1037 O.G. (also keg). Stella Artois 1047 O.G. bottled Forest Brown 1032 O.G. Mackeson 1042 O.G.

Whitbread Investments (Eng). The shares that Whitbreads have in some of the independent breweries. These are Border 17%, Boddington 22%, Brakspear 27%, Buckley 18%, Devenish 26%, Marston 35% and Morland 40%.

Whitbread Shires (Eng). The shire horses used by the Whitbread Brewery in London to pull their dray. They are working shire horses.

White (R) (Eng). A noted producer of soft drinks based in Northamptonshire.

White and Mackay (Scot). A blended Scotch whiskey 43% alc. by vol.

White Beer (Ger). See Weisse, and Weizen.

White Blend (Austr). A white wine made from the Chenin blanc and Sémillon grapes by the Freycinet Estate in Western Australia.

White Cap (W.Ind). A brand of white Rum produced by the Hansen Caribbean Rum Co., Ariba. 38% alc. by vol.

White Cap Lager (Afr). A Lager beer 1038 O.G. brewed by the East African Breweries in Tanzania.

White Cargo (Cktl). ⅕ gill dry Gin, scoop of vanilla ice cream. Blend together in a blender with 2 dashes Sauternes. Pour into a flute glass.

White Chianti (USA). See California White Chianti.

White Cocktail (Cktl). ½ gill dry Gin, ⅛ gill Anisette, 2 dashes Orange bitters. Stir well over ice, strain into a cocktail glass, add an olive and a squeeze of lemon peel juice on top.

White Cooler (Cktl). 1 measure Scotch whisky, ½ pint ginger ale, juice of ½ orange, dash Angostura. Stir over ice, strain into a large highball glass. Dress with strips of orange zest.

White Delight Retsina (Gre). The name given to white Retsina produced by Tsantali.

White Diamond (S.Afr). A leading brand of double-distilled cane spirit.

White Drummer (W.Ind). A brand of Rum produced on the island of Trinidad by the Trinidad Distillers Ltd.

White Elephant Cocktail (Cktl). ⅓ gill dry Gin, ⅕ gill French vermouth, 1 egg white. Shake over ice, strain into a cocktail glass.

White Flash (Port). The name given to the paint mark placed on vintage Port bottles to denote the position the bottles should be binned.

White Frontignan (Eng). An alternative name for the Muscat blanc à petits grains.

Whitehall Lane Winery (USA). A winery based between Rutherford and St. Helena, Napa Valley, California. Grape varieties – Cabernet sauvignon, Chardonnay, Chenin blanc and Sauvignon blanc. Produces varietal wines.

White Hanepoot (S.Afr). An alternative name for the Muscat of Alexandria grape.

White Heather (Scot). An 8 year old blended Scotch whisky produced by Campbell's (Distillery) Ltd., part of Pernod-Ricard. The company also owns the Aberlour-Glenlivet Malt distillery. Also produce a 15 year old Whisky 43% alc. by vol.

White Heather Cocktail (Cktl). ½ measure Gin, ⅙ measure Curaçao, ⅙ measure dry Vermouth, ⅙ measure pineapple juice, dash Pernod. Shake over ice, strain into a cocktail glass.

White Horse (Scot). A famous blended Scotch whisky produced by the White Horse Distillers Ltd. Glasgow. 43% alc. by vol.

White Horse America's Cup Limited Edition (Scot). A 12 year old blended Scotch whisky produced by the White Horse Distillers for the 1987 America's Cup. 43% alc. by vol.

White Horse Daisy (Cktl). ½ gill White Horse Scotch whisky, 1 teaspoon

Pernod, 2 dashes Grenadine, ½ gill lemon juice, egg white. Shake over ice, strain into a highball glass, top with soda water. Serve with slices fresh fruit and a spoon.

White Horse Distillers (Scot). Owns 3 distilleries – Craigellachie, Glen Elgin and Lagavulin. Now part of DCL. Produces White Horse (a noted blended Scotch whisky).

White Label Rum (W.Ind). A light-coloured neutral Rum, dry in taste with a very slight molasses flavour.

White Lady (Austr). The Aborigine name for Methylated spirits.

White Lady (Cktl). 1 measure Gin, ½ measure Cointreau, ½ measure lemon juice, dash egg white. Shake well over ice, strain into a cocktail glass.

White Lady Cocktail (Cktl). ⅓ gill Gin, ½ fl.oz. cream, 1 egg white, 2 dashes Gomme syrup. Shake over ice, strain into a cocktail glass.

White Lightning (USA). The nickname for Moonshine liquor. Also the name for the Patent still for Corn whiskey.

White Lily (Cktl). ⅓ measure Gin, ⅓ measure white Rum, ⅓ measure Cointreau, dash Pastis. Stir over ice, strain into a cocktail glass.

White Lion (Cktl). ¾ gill white Rum, ¼ gill Raspberry syrup, ¼ gill Curaçao, juice ½ lemon. Shake over ice, strain into an ice-filled highball glass. Decorate with fruits in season.

White Lion Bitter (Eng). A cask conditioned Bitter 1036 O.G. brewed by the Woodforde Brewery, Norfolk for the White Lion Inn in Norwich.

White Liquor (USA). Another name for Moonshine.

Whitely (William) (Scot). A Scotch whisky distillery based at Pitlochry. Produces House of Lords and King's Ransom blended Scotch whiskies. Owned by Pernod-Ricard.

White Mountain Vineyards (USA). A winery based in New Hampshire. Produces varietal and French hybrid wines.

White Pinot (Austr). The local name for the Pinot chardonnay grape of France.

White Pinot (S.Afr). The name for the Chenin blanc. See also Steen.

White Plush Cocktail (Cktl). ⅓ gill Bourbon whiskey, 1 gill milk, 2 dashes Gomme syrup. Shake over ice, strain into a collins glass.

White Port (Port). A Port wine made from white grapes only. Always blended (non-vintage). Sweet or dry varieties produced.

White Riesling (Euro). The name often given to the true Riesling grape to distinguish it from all other hybrids and varietals.

White Riesling (USA). The true Riesling grape. Also known as the Johannisberger riesling.

White Rose (Cktl). ½ measure Gin, ½ measure Kirsch, dash Gomme syrup, white of egg. Shake well over ice, strain into a cocktail glass.

White Rose Cocktail (Cktl). ⅙ gill dry Gin, juice ½ lime, ⅛ gill orange juice, 2 dashes Maraschino, 1 egg white. Shake over ice, strain into a cocktail glass.

White Rot (Eng). Disease that affects the ripening berries by splitting them. Treated with a copper/sodium bisulphide solution. (Fr) = Pourriture blanc.

White Rum (W.Ind). A colourless Rum, is light in body, produced in patent stills. 40% alc. by vol. Produced in Cuba, Puerto Rico and other islands.

White Russian (Cktl). ¾ fl.oz. Kahlúa, ½ fl.oz. Vodka. Build into an ice-filled old fashioned glass. Float cream on top.

White Satin (Cktl).(1). ³⁄₁₀ measure Gin, ⁶⁄₁₀ measure white Curaçao, ¹⁄₁₀ measure lemon juice. Shake over ice, strain into a cocktail glass.

White Satin (Cktl).(2). ⅓ measure Tia Maria, ⅓ measure Galliano, ⅓ measure cream. Shake over ice, strain into a cocktail glass.

White Satin (Eng). A popular dry Gin produced by Burnett of London. 40% alc. by vol. (Part of Seagram).

White Scotch (The) (Scot). A colourless Scotch whisky.

White Shield (Eng). A bottle-conditioned Ale 1051 O.G. brewed by the Bass Worthington Brewery. A Sediment beer.

Whitestone Vineyards (Eng). A vineyard based in Bovey Tracey, near Newton Abbot, south Devon. 0.7 ha. Grape varieties – Madeleine angevine 25% and Müller-Thurgau 75%.

White Swan (Can). A brand of dry Gin produced by Hiram Walker. 40% alc. by vol.

White Swan (Fr). A well-known brand of Brandy.

White Tequila (Mex). A colourless Tequila. It has been matured in wax-lined vats. Also known as Silver Tequila.

White Velvet (Cktl). ⅙ measure white Curaçao, ⅔ measure dry Gin, ⅙ measure pineapple juice. Shake over ice, strain into a cocktail glass.

Whitewash (Eng). The ideal covering for cellars. Will not inhibit the mould Rhacodium Celare.

White Way Cocktail (Cktl). ⅔ measure dry

Gin, ⅓ measure (white) Crème de Menthe. Shake over ice, strain into a cocktail glass.

Whiteways (Eng). A subsidiary of Allied-Lyons based at Whimple, Exeter, Devon. Has a wide range of apple-based drinks which includes Cider. Also produce British Sherry. Closed July 1989.

White Wheat Whiskey (Can). A grain Whiskey produced in Ontario by Seagram. 40% alc. by vol.

White Whiskey (USA). An uncoloured Whiskey which still has a Whiskey taste.

White Wine (Eng). Wine which may be made from white or red grapes or a mixture of both. (All grape juice is colourless). In (Bul) = Bjalo vino. (Fr) = Vin blanc. (Ger) = Weisse wein. (Gre) = Oenos. (It) = Vino bianco. (Port) = Vinho branco. (Sp) = Vino blanco. (USSR) = Belloe vino. (Wales) = Gwyn gwin.

White Wine Cup (Cup). 3 bottles dry white wine, 1 bottle dry Vermouth, 1 bottle lemonade, 1 orange and lemon (sliced). Chill all ingredients, mix together, add fruit and mint.

White Wine Punch (Punch). 3 bottles dry white wine, ½ bottle Brandy, 1 bottle dry Sherry, ¾ pint lemon juice, ½ pint Gomme syrup, ½ pint strong tea. Mix with ice in a large Punch bowl. Add a syphon of soda water, decorate with slices of cucumber.

White Wing (W.Ind). A noted brand of Rum produced in Jamaica by the Wray and Nephew Group.

White Witch (Cktl).(Non-alc). Dissolve 1 teaspoon of honey in a little hot water. Add ⅓ measure lemon juice, ⅓ measure grapefruit juice, ⅓ measure pineapple juice, ½ egg white. Shake well over ice, strain into a cocktail glass. Top with a slice of lemon.

White Witch Cocktail (Cktl). 1 fl.oz. white Rum, ½ fl.oz. (white) Crème de Cacao, ½ fl.oz. Cointreau, juice ½ lime. Shake over ice, strain into an ice-filled highball glass. Top with soda. Stir, decorate with a slice of lime and mint sprig.

White Zinfandel (USA). A Blanc de Noir. The name given to a varietal white wine produced from the black Zinfandel grape by preventing skin contact with the juice.

Whittards of Chelsea (Eng). An old tea firm. Produces a wide range of fine teas including – Spice Imperial (clove, orange peel flavour), Lotus Flower (Lotus blossom flavour) and Mango Indica (Mango blossom flavour).

Whizbang Cooler (Cktl). ½ gill dry Gin, ½ pint Ginger ale. Stir in a highball glass with lump of ice, top with a dash of peppermint and sprig of mint.

Whizz Bang Cocktail (Cktl). ⅓ gill Scotch whisky, ⅙ gill French vermouth, 2 dashes Orange bitters, 2 dashes Grenadine, 2 dashes Pernod. Stir well over ice, strain into a cocktail glass with a squeeze of lemon peel juice.

Whole Milk (Eng). Denotes milk which has had nothing removed. See Skimmed Milk.

Wholesale Dealer's Licence (U.K.). A licence needed to sell, at any time, wines or spirits in quantities of 2 gallons (1 case) or more, or beers in quantities of 4½ gallons or more. Is supplied by H.M. Customs and Excise.

Why Not Cocktail (Cktl). ⅖ measure dry Gin, ⅖ measure Apricot brandy, ⅕ measure French vermouth, dash lemon juice. Shake over ice, strain into a cocktail glass.

Whyte and Mackay (Scot). A blended Scotch whisky produced by a company of same name. Also a 12 year old De Luxe Scotch whisky version produced in a gold pot-still decanter, a 21 year old in a 'Harrods' whisky decanter 40% alc. by vol. and Whyte and Mackay Supreme. 43% alc. by vol.

Whyte and Mackay Distillers (Scot). Scotch whisky producers. Own three distilleries – Fettercairn, Dalmore and Toumintoul.

Wickenden Vineyard (Eng). A vineyard based at Cliveden Road, Taplow, Buckinghamshire. 1.2 ha. Grape varieties – Müller-Thurgau 49%, Reichensteiner 39%, Sauvignon 11% and Schreurebe 1%.

Wicker (Ger). Village. (Anb) = Rheingau. (Ber) = Johannisberg. (Gro) = Daubhaus. (Vins) = Goldene Luft, König Wilhelmsberg, Nonnberg, Stein.

Wickford Vineyards (USA). A winery based in North Kingstown. Produces French hybrid wines.

Widdern (Ger). Village. (Anb) = Württemberg. (Ber) = Kocher-Jagst-Tauber (Gro) = Kocherberg. (Vin) = Hofberg.

Widerkomm (Ger). A large glass used for ceremonial feasts in the Middle Ages.

Widmer's Wine Cellars (USA). Leading wine producers of the Finger Lakes region of the New York district.

Widow Clicquot (Fr). Invented the art of removing the sediment from a bottle of Champagne by remuage and dégorgement. See Veuve Clicquot.

Widow's Dream (Cktl). ⅕ gill Bénédictine, 1 egg. Shake over ice, strain into a cocktail glass. Float a little cream on top.

Widow's Kiss Cocktail (Cktl). ¼ measure Bénédictine, ¼ measure Chartreuse, ½ measure Calvados, dash Angostura. Shake over ice, strain into a cocktail glass.

Wiedemann Brewery (USA). A brewery in Newport. Brews Royal Amber beer.

Wiedeman Vineyard (USA). A vineyard based west of Santa Clara County, California. Grape variety – Zinfandel.

Wiederkehr Winery (USA). A winery based in Altus. Produces French hybrid wines.

Wielemans Brasserie (Bel). A brewery based in Brussels. Brews Coronation Ale.

Wiemer Winery (USA). A winery based in the Finger Lakes region. Grape varieties – Chardonnay and Riesling. Produces varietal wines.

Wien (Aus). Vienna. A wine region which produces mainly white wines.

Wiener (Ger). A copper-coloured beer produced in Munich.

Wiener Ale (Den). A low alcohol, light Beer brewed by the Wiibroe Brewery in Elsinore.

Wiers Patent Lazy Tongs (Eng). A patent nineteenth-century corkscrew that operated on the expanding arm method.

Wiesbaden (Ger). An old vineyard region around the town of the same name in the Rheingau.

Wiesberg (Ger). Vineyard. (Anb) = Nahe. (Ber) = Schloss Böckelheim. (Gro) = Rosengarten. (Vil) = Rüdesheim.

Wiese and Krohn (Port). Vintage Port shippers. Vintages – 1927, 1934, 1935, 1947, 1950, 1952, 1960, 1967, 1970.

Wiesenbronn (Ger). Village. (Anb) = Franken. (Ber) = Steigerwald. (Gro) = Schlossberg. (Vin) = Wachhügel.

Wiesloch (Ger). Village. (Anb) = Baden. (Ber) = Badische Bergstrasse/Kraichgau. (Gro) = Mannaberg. (Vins) = Bergwäldle, Hagenich, Spitzenberg.

Wigwam (Fr). A method of planting vines in the Rhône to withstand the Mistral winds. Also known as the Gobelet system.

Wiibroe Brewery (Den). Is based in Elsinore. Owned by the United Breweries. Noted for its Nanok 6.5% alc. by vol. Wiener Ale and Dansk L.A. a full-bodied, low alcohol Lager 0.9% alc. by volume.

Wijn (Hol). Wine.

Wijnfles (Hol). Wine bottle.

Wijngaard (Hol). Vineyard.

Wijnhandel (Hol). Wine shop.

Wijnkaart (Hol). Wine list.

Wijnkoeler (Hol). Wine cooler, Champagne bucket.

Wijnkooperij (Hol). Wine merchants.

Wijnoogst (Hol). Vintage. See also Jaargang.

Wijnstok (Hol). Vine. See also Wingerd.

Wijnwater (Hol). Holy water.

Wild Beer (Bel). See Lambic Beer.

Wild Beer (USA). Description of the condition when beer is served too warm and CO_2 gas escapes from the beer too quickly causing it to foam violently.

Wild Boar Bitter (Eng). A Best Bitter beer 1039 O.G. brewed by the Trough Brewery in Bradford, Yorkshire.

Wild Chicory Coffee (Eng). Roots are roasted in an oven, ground finely and then brewed for ten minutes.

Wildenberg (Ger). Vineyard. (Anb) = Württemberg. (Ber) = Württembergisch Unterland. (Gro) = Salzberg. (Vil) = Grantschen.

Wild Ferment (Eng). Is caused by a must with natural yeasts (no extra added) or other micro-organisms present either on the raw material present in the fermentation vessel or those that have landed on the must during fermentation.

Wild Fermentation (W.Ind). A very quick fermentation caused when dunder is added to the molasses. Causes natural yeasts to multiply rapidly. Also called Spontaneous fermentation.

Wildgrafenberg (Ger). Vineyard. (Anb) = Nahe. (Ber) = Schloss Böckelheim. (Gro) = Paradiesgarten. (Vil) = Kirschroth.

Wild Irish Rose (USA). A 'Pop wine' from the Canadaigua Wine Company in New York State.

Wildsau (Ger). Vineyard. (Anb) = Rheingau. (Ber) = Johannisberg. (Gro) = Steinmacker. (Vil) = Martinsthal.

Wild Strawberry Brandy (Euro). A French, German or Swiss fruit Brandy made from wild mountain strawberries 44.5% alc. by vol.

Wild Strawberry Liqueur (Fr). A liqueur made by steeping wild strawberries in Brandy. 30% alc. by vol.

Wildtal (Ger). Village. (Anb) = Baden. (Ber) = Breisgau. (Gro) = Burg Zähringen. (Vin) = Sonnenberg.

Wild Turkey (USA). The brand-name of a straight Bourbon whiskey at 50.5% alc. by vol. and a liqueur Bourbon whiskey at 40% alc. by vol. produced by Austin Nichols, Lawrenceburg, Kentucky.

Wildwood Vineyard (USA). A vineyard based near Kenwood, Sonoma Valley, California. 125 ha. Grape varieties – Cabernet sauvignon and Chardonnay. Produces varietal wines.

Wild Yeasts (Eng). The prolific micro-flora that are present in the bloom of the grape.

They are aerobic and start the first violent fermentation. Destroyed by SO_2 or heat treatment. Kloeckera Apiculata and Pichia Membranaefaciens.

Wilhelmsberg (Ger). Vineyard. (Anb) = Baden. (Ber) = Badische Bergstrasse/ Kraichgau. (Gro) = Mannaberg. (Vil) = Nussloch.

Wilhelmsberg (Ger). Vineyard. (Anb) = Franken. (Ber) = Maindreieck. (Gro) = Hofrat. (Vin) = Kitzingen.

Willamette Valley (USA). A cool, hilly region in Oregon. Has many fine wineries based there.

Willet Distillery (USA). A Bourbon whiskey distillery based southwest of Frankfort, Kentucky.

William and Robin (Cktl). ⅓ measure William Christ, ⅓ measure orange Curaçao, ⅓ measure lemon juice, dash Orange bitters. Shake over ice, strain into a cocktail glass, decorate with a slice of lemon and a cherry.

William Hill Winery (USA). See Hill Winery.

Williamine (Fr) (Switz). A pear-flavoured liqueur. Usually an Alcool blanc (Eau-de-vie).

William Lawson's (Scot). A blended Scotch whisky produced by the William Lawson Distillery Ltd., Coatbridge and MacDuff.

William of Orange (Hol). 1688. Dutch king who became King of England and so made Gin popular to the English.

Williams and Humbert (Sp). A Sherry house that belongs to the Rumasa organisation. Bodega is at Nuno del Canas 1, Jerez de la Frontera. Sherry brands include – Canasta Cream, Dos Cortados, Dry Sack, Pando, Tintilla and Walnut Brown.

Williamsbirnen (Ger). A liqueur made from Poire Williams.

Willm (Fr). A noted wine-producing family based in Alsace.

Willmes Press (Euro). A computerised press that works using an inflatable bag which presses the grapes against the slatted sides of the press. Also rotates.

Willmes Schlauchpresse (Ger). See Willmes Press.

Willow Creek Vineyard (USA). A vineyard based near Paso Robles, San Luis Obispo, California. Grape variety – Zinfandel. Vinified at the Monterey Peninsula Winery.

Willowside Vineyards (USA). A winery based in Santa Rosa, Sonoma County, California. Grape varieties – Chardonnay, Gewürztraminer, Pinot noir and Zinfandel. Produces varietal wines.

Will Rogers Cocktail (Cktl). ⅕ gill dry Gin,

3 dashes orange juice, 2 dashes French vermouth, dash Cointreau. Shake well over ice, strain into a cocktail glass.

Willsbach (Ger). Village. (Anb) = Württemberg. (Ber) = Württembergisch Unterland. (Gro) = Salzberg. (Vins) = Dieblesberg, Zeilberg.

Willyabrup (Austr). A winery based in the Margaret River district of Western Australia.

Willy Gisselbrecht et Fils (Fr). An Alsace wine producer. Address = 67650 Dambach-la-Ville. 15.5 ha.

Wilmont Wines (USA). A winery based in Schwenksville, Pennsylvania. Produces hybrid wines.

Wilmot's Hop Cone (Eng). A cask conditioned Bitter 1042 O.G. brewed by the Godson-Chudley Brewery in London.

Wilsford Winery (Austr). A winery based in the Barossa Valley, South Australia. Produces varietal wines.

Wilson Brewery (Eng). Watney's Manchester brewery. Has 720 public houses. Noted for its cask conditioned beers and keg Newton Bitter 1032 O.G. Grand Northern 1036 O.G. and bottled Wembley 1036 O.G. Top Brass Lager 1033 O.G.

Wilson Distillers (N.Z.). A distillery based at Dunedin. Produces 45 South and Wilsons Matured Blend whiskies.

Wilt (Eng). See Verticillium Wilt.

Wilting (Ind). A term used to describe the drying out of the tea leaf. Also known as Withering.

Wiltingen (Ger). Village. (Anb) = Mosel-Saar-Ruwer. (Ber) = Saar-Ruwer. (Gro) = Scharzberg. (Vins) = Braune Kupp, Braunfels, Gottesfuss, Hölle, Klosterberg, Kupp, Rosenberg, Sandberg.

Wiltshire Bitter (Eng). A cask conditioned Special Bitter 1036 O.G. brewed by the Gibbs Mew Brewery in Salisbury, Wiltshire. Also a keg version.

Wiltshire Brewery Company (Eng). A brewery based in Tisbury, Wiltshire. Is noted for its Old Stonehenge Bitter 1041 O.G. Regency and Weedkiller beers.

Wilyabrup Winery (Austr). A winery based in Western Australia. Produces varietal and dessert wines.

Wimbledon (Cktl). 1 measure Gin, ½ measure Bénédictine, 1 measure lemon juice, dash Grenadine, dash Fraise, dash egg white. Shake over ice, strain into a cocktail glass. Dress the rim of glass with sugar and a sugar-frosted strawberry.

Wimbledon Winner (Cktl). 1 pint iced tea, juice ½ lemon, 2 ozs. sliced strawberries. Leave to stand overnight, strain, decorate with strawberries rolled in castor sugar.

Wimmental (Ger). Village. (Anb) = Württemberg. (Ber) = Württembergisch Unterland. (Gro) = Salzberg. (Vin) = Altenberg.

Wincarnis Tonic Wine (Eng). The brand-name of a beef and malt-based Tonic wine 14% alc. by vol. Produced by R & C Vintners, Carrow, Norwich.

Wincheringen (Ger). Village. (Anb) = Mosel-Saar-Ruwer. (Ber) = Obermosel. (Gro) = Gipfel. (Vins) = Burg Warsberg, Fuchsloch.

Winchester Quart (USA). An imperial quart measure used in the USA.

Wind Chimes Cocktail (Cktl). 1½ ozs. Beefeater Gin, ½ oz. Crème de Menthe, 2 ozs. grapefruit juice. Mix well together over ice in a mixing glass. Top with soda water, strain into a highball glass. Decorate with segments of grapefruit and a cherry.

Winden (Ger). Village. (Anb) = Rheinpfalz. (Ber) = Südliche Weinstrasse. (Gro) = Kloster Liebfrauenberg. (Vin) = Narrenberg.

Windesheim (Ger). Village. (Anb) = Nahe. (Ber) = Kreuznach. (Gro) = Schlosskapelle. (Vins) = Breiselberg, Fels, Hausgiebel, Hölle, Römerberg, Rosenberg, Saukopf, Schäfchen, Sonnenmorgen.

Windhoek Extra Stout (Afr). A bitter Stout 1050 O.G. brewed and bottled by the South-West Breweries in Windhoek, Namibia.

Windhoek Mai-Bock (Afr). A Bock Beer 1072 O.G. brewed by the South-West Breweries in Windhoek, Namibia.

Windischenbach (Ger). Village. (Anb) = Württemberg. (Ber) = Württembergisch Unterland. (Gro) = Lindelberg. (Vin) = Goldberg.

Windjammer (Scot). The brand-name for a Rum bottled by Scottish and Newcastle Breweries.

Windjammer (W.Ind). A dark Jamaican Rum produced by MacKinlay and McPherson. 43% alc. by vol.

Windmeul Co-operative (S.Afr). Vineyards based in Paarl. Address = Windmeul Koöperatiewe Wynkelders, Box 2013, Windmeul 7630. Produces varietal wines.

Windmeul Koöperatiewe Wynkelders (S.Afr). See Windmeul Co-operative.

Winds (Eng). Winds that affect grape production and need special protective precautions. Either warm or cold. See Bora, Katabatic Wind, Levante, Llebeig, Mistral, Poniente, Seré and Solanos.

Windsor (Austr). The brand-name used by Mildara Wines, Coonawarra, South Australia.

Windsor Glasses (Eng). A brand-name used by the Dema Glass Co. Ltd. for a range of shaped cocktail glasses and a Champagne saucer.

Windsor Vineyards (USA). The label used by the Sonoma Vineyards for their range of wines usually sold by mail order.

Windsurfer (The) (Cktl). 2 parts Johnny Walker Red Label, 2 parts blue Curaçao, 3 parts Passion Fruit, 3 parts orange juice, 1 egg white. Shake over ice, strain into an ice-filled highball glass. Decorate with a slice of kiwi fruit.

Windy Corner Cocktail (Cktl). ⅓ gill Blackberry brandy stirred over ice. Strain into a cocktail glass, top with grated nutmeg.

Windy Hill (N.Z.). A small vineyard based at Simpson Road, Henderson, North Island. 3 ha. Grape varieties – Cabernet sauvignon, Gamay and Pinotage. Produces table wines and sherries.

Wine (Eng). The juice of freshly gathered grapes vinified according to the customs and traditions from region to region. (Fr) = Vin. (Ger) = Wein. (Hol) = Wijn. (It) = Vino. (Port) = Vinho. (Sp) = Vino. (Tur) = Sarap. (USSR) = Vino. (Wales) = Gwin. See also British Wine and Fortified Wine.

Wine Aid (Fr). A specific wine made in Burgundy (Beaujolais) and Bordeaux with a Wine Aid label. Proceeds go to the starving African countries.

Wine and Food Society (Eng). A society founded by André L. Simon. See International Wine and Food Society.

Wine and Spirit Association of Great Britain (Eng). Address = Five Kings House, Kennet Wharf Lane, Upper Thames Street, London EC4V 3BH. (abbr) = W.S.A.

Wine and Spirit Board (S.Afr). Government appointed body who award a seal about the size of a postage stamp which guarantees the authenticity of the wine in the bottle. The code is in the form of a series of coloured bands. Blue band = Origin, Red band = Vintage, Green band = Grape variety. If the seal is in gold then classed Superior. See Bus Ticket.

Wine and Spirit Education Trust Limited (Eng). Address = Five Kings House, Kennet Wharf Lane, Upper Thames Street, London EC4V 3AJ. Runs wine courses – Certificate, Higher Certificate and Diploma grades. (abbr) = W.S.E.T.

Wine And The People (USA). WATP. A

winery based in Alameda, California. Grape varieties – Chardonnay, Merlot and Zinfandel. Produces varietal wines under the Berkeley Wine Cellars label.

Wine Bar (Eng). Licensed premises where the main drink is wine. The licence may be a full On-Licence or have restrictions to the type of drink sold. Many are Restaurant/Wine bars.

Wine Basket (USA). A wine cradle.

Wine Bibber (Eng). The name for a person who drinks mostly wine in any quantity.

Wine Brokers (Fr). See Courtiers.

Wine Bucket (Eng). A container for holding ice and water into which wine bottles (especially sparkling wines) are placed to be cooled down. Also known as a wine cooler.

Wine Butler (Eng). A person who is in charge of everything involving a wine-cellar. It is usually he who decides the wines to be consumed with each course at a banquet.

Wine by Syphon (Eng). A silver pump syphon used in the nineteenth century to draw wine out of casks at the table. Has a key-type tap.

Wine Cooler (Cktl). 1 measure red or white wine, 4 dashes Grenadine. Add ice and Grenadine to the wine in a highball glass. Top with soda water.

Wine Cooler (Eng). See Wine Bucket.

Wine Cradle (Eng). A wicker basket used for carrying mature red wines that have thrown a sediment from the cellar to the decanter. Used so that the bottle can be carried horizontally and the sediment remain undisturbed. It should not be used as a pouring unit at the table as the sediment becomes mixed with the wine after approximately two thirds of the contents have been poured. Is also known as the Wine Basket or Burgundy Basket.

Wine Emperor (It). Emperor Probus A.D.260. Promoted German wines.

Wine Equity Act (USA). A law introduced in 1983 as a measure against wine trade barriers.

Wine Fountains (Gre) (It). A fountain where wine flowed instead of water in ancient Greek and Roman times.

Wine From Germany Information Service (Eng). Address = 15, Thayer Street, London W.1.

Wine Funnel (Eng). A device for decanting wines from the bottle into a decanter. Has a curved tip to allow wine to run down the side of the decanter and not gather air.

Wine Gallon (Eng). An old English measure of 231 cubic inches.

Wineglass (USA). A measure of 4 fl.ozs. (US).

Wine Gods (Euro). See Bacchus, Fufluns and Dionysus.

Wine Guild of the United Kingdom (Eng). Address = Islington House, Puddletown, Dorchester, Dorset DT2 8TO.

Wine Herb Cooler (Cktl). 1 gill rosé wine, 2 teaspoons tarragon vinegar, 2 sprigs fresh oregano, 2 gills Apricot syrup. Make a syrup with wine, vinegar and herbs, heat, simmer 5 minutes, strain and cool. Add apricot syrup and ice then top with 4 gills iced rosé wine and decorate with fresh herbs.

Wine Institute (USA). A California-based voluntary trade association of wineries situated in San Francisco. Researches wine and grape technology.

Wine Lake (Euro). A new term invented to describe the surplus cheap wine that E.E.C. countries have due to increased production. Most is made into industrial alcohol or vinegar.

Wineland (Eng). A company belonging to Arthur Rackham and trading name for a retail outlet in Upper Richmond Road, Putney, London.

Wine Library (Eng). A library of bottles of wine for reference of colour, taste etc. Popular in Italy. See (Fr) = Vinothèque, (It) = Enoteca, (Sp) = Biblioteca, (Yug) = Vinoteka.

Wine List (Eng). The list of wines offered by a restaurant for sale to their customers for consumption on the premises with a meal. Also the list of a wine merchant which is sent to customers at their homes for their perusal.

Winemaster (USA). The label used by the Guild of Wineries and Distilleries in Lodi, California.

Winemaster's Guild Brandy (USA). The brand-name of a Brandy bottled by the Guild of Wineries and Distillers at Lodi, California.

Wine Memory (Eng). The art of storing information from tastings of wines and recalling the sensations at future tastings.

Wine Menu (Eng). See Wine List.

Wine Museum (USA). A winery based in the Finger Lakes region.

Wine of Araby (Euro). The sixteenth-century name for coffee. So called because the Muslims were forbidden to drink any wine or alcoholic beverage and so drank coffee as a substitute for stimulation.

Wine of Friendship (Eng). The term applied to Sherry because of its use as a meeting drink for centuries.

Wine of Origin Superior (S.Afr). W.O.S.

Seal of control board. See W.O.S. and Wine and Spirit Board.

Wine Pack (Austr). A container for selling wines in plastic bags within cardboard boxes. See Bag in the Box.

Wine Palm (Eng). Also known as the Toddy Palm. Various species of palm trees whose sap is used as a drink. See Toddy.

Wine Press (Eng). An implement used to extract the juice from the grapes by crushing. Various types are used.

Winery (USA). The name given to the buildings used for making wine.

Winery Lake Vineyard (USA). A winery based in Carneros, Napa Valley, California. 50 ha. Grape varieties – Chardonnay, Johannisberg riesling, Merlot and Pinot noir. Produces varietal wines.

Winery of the Abbey (USA). A winery based in Cuba, Missouri. Produces hybrid wines.

Winery Rushing (USA). A winery based in Merigold, Mississippi. 9 ha. Produces Muscadine wines.

Wine Sangaree (Cktl). 1 teaspoon of powdered sugar into a highball glass. Add chosen wine, 2 ice cubes, stir well, top with more of the same wine.

Wine Sellers (Eng). A retail chain of 140 shops belonging to the Bass group (who also own Augustus Barnett and Galleon Wine).

Wine Skin (Eng). The skin of an animal (goats or sheep) which is cured, sewn up and used to hold wine.

Wineskin (Eng). An old skin bottle which monks hung from their girdle. The German Bocksbeutel is modelled on it.

Wines of Spain (USA). Spanish Wine promotion office. Address = 405, Lexington Avenue, New York 10017. N.Y.

Winespeak (Eng). A word to denote the terms used by wine drinkers to describe wines.

Wines [UK] Ltd (Eng). An organisation formed by 4 English vineyards – Adgestone, Astley, Wickenden and Wooton. Pool resources to help develop markets at home and abroad.

Wine State (The) (Austr). A designation given to the State of South Australia.

Wine Waiter (Eng). A person who sells and serves wines in a restaurant. See also Sommelier and Wine Butler.

Wingeard (Eng). The mediaeval name for a vineyard.

Wingeardnaem (Eng). The Anglo-Saxon word used for the vintage (harvest time). Lit – 'Wine gathering'.

Wingerd (Hol). Vine. See also Vijnstok.

Wingertsberg (Ger). Vineyard. (Anb) = Hessische Bergstrasse. (Ber) = Umstadt. (Gro) = None assigned. (Vil) = Dietzenbach.

Wingertsberg (Ger). Vineyard. (Anb) = Rheinhessen. (Ber) = Bingen. (Gro) = Adelberg. (Vil) = Nieder-Weisen.

Wingertstor (Ger). Vineyard. (Anb) = Rheinhessen. (Ber) = Nierstein. (Gro) = Petersberg. (Vil) = Bechtolsheim.

Winiak Luksusowy (Pol). Matured brandy.

Winkel (Ger). Village. (Anb) = Rheingau. (Ber) = Johannisberg. (Gro) = Erntebringer. (Vin) = Dachsberg.

Winkel (Ger). Village. (Anb) = Rheingau. (Ber) = Johannisberg. (Gro) = Honigberg. (Vins) = Bienengarten, Gutenberg, Hasensprung, Jesuitengarten, Klaus, Schlossberg.

Winklerberg (Ger). Vineyard. (Anb) = Baden. (Ber) = Kaiserstuhl-Tuniberg. (Gro) = Vulkanfelsen. (Vil) = Ihringen.

Winkles Brewery (Eng). A brewery opened in 1979 in Buxton, north Derbyshire. Brews cask conditioned BVA 1037 O.G. and Saxon Cross Mild 1037 O.G.

Winnenden (Ger). Village. (Anb) = Württemberg. (Ber) = Remstal-Stuttgart. (Gro) = Kopf. (Vins) = Berg, Holzenberg, Rossberg.

Winnenden (Ger). Village. (Anb) = Württemberg. (Ber) = Remstal-Stuttgart. (Gro) = Wartbühl. (Vin) = Haselstein.

Winnie-the-Pooh (Cktl). ½ measure Egg flip, ¼ measure fresh cream, ⅛ measure Crème de Cacao, ⅛ measure Chocolate liqueur. Shake over ice, strain into a cocktail glass.

Winningen (Ger). Village. (Anb) = Mosel-Saar-Ruwer. (Ber) = Zell/Mosel. (Gro) = Weinhex. (Vins) = Brückstück, Domgarten, Hamm, Im Röttgen, Uhlen.

Winnowing (Eng). The method used in coffee production to remove dust, leaves, twigs from coffee cherries.

Wino (Eng) (USA) (slang). An alcoholic who drinks mainly cheap wines.

Wins Sangria (Sp). The brand-name of Sangría. 2 versions – an alcoholic one consisting of red wine and citrus juices and a non-alcoholic one (sparkling) made from pure red grape juice and citrus juices. Both are free of preservatives, sugar or colourings. Marketed by Helvita Sangría.

Winston (Bel). A Bière 7.5% alc. by vol. brewed by the Marbaix Brasserie.

Winston (Bel). A pale-style Ale 7.5% alc. by vol. brewed by the Du Bocq Brasserie Centrale.

Winston Pale Ale (Bel). A Pale ale brewed by the Marbaix Brasserie.

Winston's Stout (Scot). A Stout 1053 O.G. brewed and bottled for export to Italy by the Belhaven Brewery in Dunbar.

Winter Ale (Eng). Ales produced and sold from November to February. Usually dark, rich, high-gravity draught Ales.

Winterbach ' (Ger). Village. (Anb) = Württemberg. (Ber) = Remstal-Stuttgart. (Gro) = Kopf. (Vin) = Hungerberg.

Winterborn (Ger). Village. (Anb) = Nahe. (Ber) = Schloss Böckelheim. (Gro) = Paradiesgarten. (Vin) = Graukatz.

Winterhoek (S.Afr). A brand of wine produced in Tulbagh.

Winter Reserve (Ire). A Winter ale 1044 O.G. brewed by the Hilden Brewery in Ulster.

Winter Royal (Eng). A Winter ale 1056 O.G. brewed by the Wethered Brewery in Marlow, Buckinghamshire.

Wintersdorf (Ger). Village. (Anb) = Mosel-Saar-Ruwer. (Ber) = Obermosel. (Gro) = Königsberg. (Vins) = Sites not yet chosen.

Wintersheim (Ger). Village. (Anb) = Rheinhessen. (Ber) = Nierstein. (Gro) = Krotenbrunnen. (Vin) = Frauengarten.

Winter's Tale (Cktl). 2 parts Merrydown mead, 4 parts red Burgundy, cloves and cinnamon stick. Heat together, strain and serve.

Wintersweiler (Ger). Village. (Anb) = Baden. (Ber) = Markgräflerland. (Gro) = Vogtei Rötteln. (Vin) = Steingässle.

Winter Warmer (Cktl). Heat ½ pint of milk with 1½ fl.ozs. Scotch whisky until nearly boiling. Pour over 1 egg yolk beaten with 1 oz. sugar, whisk until smooth. Serve in a heat-proof glass.

Winter Warmer (Eng). An Old ale 1055 O.G. brewed by the Youngs Brewery in Wandsworth, London.

Winter Warmer (Punch). Boil ¾ pint of water with 10 cloves, 1 teaspoon mixed spice, 2 ozs. sugar for 5 minutes. Strain, add 1 bottle Malmsey wine, juice of a lemon and a whole lemon that has been studded with 12 cloves and roasted in the oven for 1 hour. Reheat and serve in glasses.

Winter Warmer (USA). A dark, strong, brown Ale 7.25% alc. by vol. brewed by the Newman Brewery in Albany, New York.

Wintrange (Lux). A wine village on the river Moselle. Vineyard sites are – Felsberg and Hommelsberg.

Wintrich (Ger). Village. (Anb) = Mosel-Saar-Ruwer. (Ber) = Bernkastel. (Gro)

= Kurfürstlay. (Vins) = Grosser Herrgott, Ohligsberg, Sonnenseite, Stefanslay.

Winy (Eng). Denotes having a taste of wine or is intoxicating, heady.

Winzenheim (Ger). An old wine parish in the Nahe.

Winzer (Ger). Wine-grower.

Winzerfest (Ger). A wine festival held in Dernau in the Ahr in September.

Winzerfest (Ger). A wine festival held in Klingenberg in the Franken in the middle of August.

Winzerfest (Ger). A wine festival held in Nierstein in the Rheinhessen in August.

Winzerfest (Ger). A wine festival held in Würzburg in the Franken in September-October.

Winzergenossenschaft (Aus) (Ger). Wine growers' co-operative.

Winzerhausen (Ger). Village. (Anb) = Württemberg. (Ber) = Württembergisch Unterland. (Gro) = Wunnenstein. (Vins) = Harzberg, Lichtenberg.

Winzersekt (Ger). A recently formed association of over 500 growers who produce vintage (méthode champenoise) Sekt.

Winzerverband (Aus). A regional co-operative.

Winzerverein (Ger). Wine growers' co-operative.

Wipfeld (Ger). Village. (Anb) = Franken. (Ber) = Maindreieck. (Gro) = Kirchberg. (Vin) = Zehntgraf.

Wire Mesh (Sp). See Arame, Alambre and Alambrado.

Wirmsthal (Ger). Village. (Anb) = Franken. (Ber) = Maindreieck. (Gro) = Burg. (Vin) = Scheinberg.

Wirranirra Winery (Austr). A winery based in McLaren Vale, Southern Vales, South Australia. Produces varietal and table wines.

Wirra Wirra (Austr). A winery in the Clare-Watervale and Southern Vales regions of South Australia.

WIRSPA (W.Ind) (abbr). West Indies Rum and Spirits Producers Association.

Wirt (Ger). Host or Landlord.

Wirtschaft (Ger). The term for any style of drinking establishment.

Wirthaus (Ger). A drinking house, pub or inn.

Wisdom and Warter (Sp). A Sherry producer owned by Gonzalez Byass and based in Jerez de la Frontera. Brands include – Cream of the Century, Feliciano, Olivar and Royal Palace.

Wishniak (Pol). A liqueur made from cherries and spices.

Wisniak (Pol). A cherry-flavoured liqueur 25% alc. by vol.

Wisniówka (Pol). A cherry-flavoured

Vodka. 25–40% alc. by vol. Made from wild cherries. Also produced in USSR and Czec.

Wissberg (Ger). Vineyard. (Anb) = Rheinhessen. (Ber) = Bingen. (Gro) = Abtey. (Vil) = Sprendlingen.

Wissberg (Ger). Vineyard. (Anb) = Rheinhessen. (Ber) = Bingen. (Gro) = Kurfürstenstück. (Vil) = Gau-Weinheim.

Wisselbrunnen (Ger). Vineyard. (Anb) = Rheingau. (Ber) = Johannisberg. (Gro) = Deutelsberg. (Vil) = Hattenheim.

Wit (S.Afr). White.

Witblits (S.Afr). Lit – 'White lightning'. The alternative name for Poteen or Moonshine.

Withered (Ind). A term to denote the method of drying the tea leaves to reduce moisture and make them soft and flexible.

Withering (Ind). The controlled method of drying tea. See also Wilting.

Withies (Eng). The old name for willow trees that were used for binding the vines.

Witkampff (Hol). A Moutwijnjenever from Schiedam.

Witkap Pater (Bel). A light-coloured, bottle-conditioned, top-fermented beer from the Brasschaat Brasserie.

Witney Bitter (Eng). A cask conditioned Bitter 1037 O.G. brewed by the Glenny Brewery in Witney, Oxon.

Wittlich (Ger). Village. (Anb) = Mosel-Saar-Ruwer. (Ber) = Bernkastel. (Gro) = Schwarzlay. (Vins) = Bottchen, Felsentreppche, Klosterweg, Kupp, Lay, Portnersberg, Rosenberg.

Wittnau (Ger). Village. (Anb) = Baden. (Ber) = Markgräflerland. (Gro) = Lorettoberg. (Vin) = Kapuzinerbuck.

Wit Wyn (S.Afr). White wine.

WKK (Aus) (abbr). Amtliche Weinkostkommission.

Woda (Pol). Water.

Wodka (USSR). Lit – 'Little water'. The original name for Vodka.

Wodka Luksusowa (Pol). A luxury Vodka produced from double-distilled potato spirits. 45% alc. by vol.

Wodka Mysliwska (Pol). See Hunter Vodka.

Woerdemann Winery (USA). A small winery based in Temecula, Southern California. Grape varieties – Cabernet sauvignon and Sauvignon blanc. Produces varietal wines.

Wohlfahrtsberg (Ger). Vineyard. (Anb) = Württemberg. (Ber) = Württembergisch Unterland. (Gro) = Salzberg. (Vil) = Löwenstein.

Wolf Blass (Austr). A winery in the Barossa Valley, South Australia. Produces varietal and sparkling wines.

Wolfer (Ger). Vineyard. (Anb) = Baden. (Ber) = Markgräflerland. (Gro) = Vogtei Rötteln. (Vil) = Blansingen.

Wolfer (Ger). Vineyard. (Anb) = Baden. (Ber) = Markgräflerland. (Gro) = Vogtei Rötteln. (Vil) = Kleinkems.

Wolfhag (Ger). Vineyard. (Anb) = Baden. (Ber) = Ortenau. (Gro) = Schloss Rodeck. (Vil) = Bühl (ortsteil Neusatz).

Wolfhag (Ger). Vineyard. (Anb) = Baden. (Ber) = Ortenau. (Gro) = Schloss Rodeck. (Vil) = Ottersweier.

Wölflein (Ger). Vineyard. (Anb) = Franken. (Ber) = Maindreieck. (Gro) = Ravensburg. (Vil) = Veitshöchheim.

Wolfsaugen (Ger). Vineyard. (Anb) = Württemberg. (Ber) = Württembergisch Unterland. (Gro) = Heuchelberg. (Vil) = Brackenheim.

Wolfsberg (Ger). Vineyard. (Anb) = Rheinpfalz. (Ber) = Südliche Weinstrasse. (Gro) = Guttenberg. (Vil) = Schweighofen.

Wolfschmidt (Eng). A brand-name of a Vodka. 40% alc. by vol. Produced by Seagram.

Wolfschmidt (Den). The name for a Kümmel 43% alc. by vol. Produced in Copenhagen.

Wolfschmidt Royal (Cktl). 2 parts Wolfschmidt Kümmel, 3 parts Scotch whisky. Shake over ice, strain into an old fashioned glass 'on the rocks'.

Wolfsdarm (Ger). Vineyard. (Anb) = Rheinpfalz. (Ber) = Mittelhaardt-Deutsche Weinstrasse. (Gro) = Hofstück. (Vil) = Meckenheim.

Wolfsheim (Ger). Village. (Anb) = Rheinhessen. (Ber) = Bingen. (Gro) = Abtey. (Vins) = Götzenborn, Osterberg, Sankt Kathrin.

Wolfshöhle (Ger). Vineyard. (Anb) = Mittelrhein. (Ber) = Bacharach. (Gro) = Schloss Stahleck. (Vil) = Bacharach.

Wolfsmagen (Ger). Grosslage. (Anb) = Hessische Bergstrasse. (Ber) = Starkenburg. (Vil) = Bensheim.

Wolfsnack (Ger). Vineyard. (Anb) = Mittelrhein. (Ber) = Rheinburgengau. (Gro) = Herrenberg. (Vil) = Dörscheid.

Wolkersdorf (Aus). A district in the Weinviertel. Produces light-styled white wines.

Wollbach (Ger). Village. (Anb) = Baden. (Ber) = Markgräflerland. (Gro) = Vogtei Rötteln. (Vin) = Steingässle.

Wollersheim Winery (USA). A small winery based at Prairie du Sac, Wisconsin. 8 ha. Produces vinifera and French hybrid wines.

Wollmesheim (Ger). Village. (Anb) = Rheinpfalz. (Ber) = Südliche Weinstrasse. (Gro) = Herrlich. (Vin) = Müt-terle.

Wollombi Brook Estate (Austr). A vineyard in the Hunter Valley in the South Australia. Owned by Leo Buring Co.

Wöllstein (Ger). Village. (Anb) = Rheinhessen. (Ber) = Bingen. (Gro) = Rheingrafenstein. (Vins) = Affchen, Haarberg-Katzensteg, Hölle, Ölberg.

Wolverhampton and Dudley (Eng). W & D. See Banks Brewery and Hansons Brewery.

Women's Petition Against Coffee (Eng). A campaign started in 1674 as a revolt against coffee houses. Resulted in King Charles the Second passing an Act of Parliament banning coffee houses in 1675.

Wonder Bar Cocktail (Cktl). ⅓ gill dry Gin, ⅛ gill French vermouth, ⅛ gill Italian vermouth, dash Absinthe, 3 dashes Orange bitters, 3 dashes Angostura. Stir over ice, strain into a 5 oz. wine glass. Serve with cherry and a dash of lemon peel juice.

Wonneberg (Ger). Vineyard. (Anb) = Rheinpfalz. (Ber) = Südliche Weinstrasse. (Gro) = Guttenberg. (Vil) = Bad Bergzabern.

Wonneberg (Ger). Vineyard. (Anb) = Rheinpfalz. (Ber) = Südliche Weinstrasse. (Gro) = Guttenberg. (Vil) = Dörrenbach.

Wonnegau (Ger). Bereich. (Anb) = Rheinhessen. (Gros) = Bergkloster, Burg Rodenstein, Domblick, Gotteshilfe, Liebfrauenmorgen, Pilgerpfad, Sybillenstein.

Wonsheim (Ger). Village. (Anb) = Rheinhessen. (Ber) = Bingen. (Gro) = Rheingrafenstein. (Vins) = Hölle, Sonnenberg.

Wood Aged (Austr). Matured in cask.

Wood Aged Chenin Blanc (Austr). A dry white wine which has been aged in German oak Puncheons, produced by the Jane Brook Estate in Western Australia.

Wood Aged Sémillon (Austr). A full-bodied dry white wine from the Quelltaler Estate, South Australia.

Wood Alcohol (Eng). Methanol.

Woodbourne Cabernet Sauvignon (N.Z.). A red wine produced by Montana Wines Ltd, Marlborough.

Woodbury Vineyards (USA). A winery based in Chautauqua, New York. Noted for their Chardonnay and Riesling wines.

Woodbury Winery (USA). A winery based in San Rafael, Marin, California. Grape varieties – Cabernet sauvignon, Petite syrah and Zinfandel. Produces varietal wines.

Wood Chips (Ger). Used for fining Lager beers.

Woodcock (Eng). An old English cider-making apple.

Woodforde Brewery (Eng). Opened in Norwich in 1981. Now moved to the Spread Eagle public house, Erpingham since 1983. Noted for its cask conditioned Norfolk Pride 1036 O.G. Wherry 1039 O.G. and Phoenix XXX 1047 O.G. See also White Lion Bitter.

Woodham Bitter (Eng). A cask conditioned Bitter 1035.5 O.G. brewed by the Crouch Vale Brewery in Chelmsford, Essex.

Woodhay (Eng). A label used by the Holt Vineyard for a range of their wines.

Woodhill (N.Z.). Brand-name used by Penfolds for a selection of their wines.

Woodhouse (John) (Eng). A British importer of Marsala and Sicilian wines in the eighteenth century. Operated from Liverpool, Lancs.

Woodland Claret (N.Z.). A light, dry red wine from the Ormind Vineyard.

Woodleys (Austr). A winery in the Barossa Valley and Adelaide Hills South Australia. Noted for Queen Adelaide label Claret.

Woodman Bitter (Eng). An own-label canned Bitter beer from the Booker Cash and Carry. Address = Malt House, P.O. Box 65, Field End Road, Eastcote, Ruislip, Middlesex HA4 9LA.

Wood Matured Chenin Blanc (Austr). A full-bodied, fruity wine, oak matured from the Peel estate in Western Australia.

Woodpecker Cider (Eng). A leading brand-name Cider from Bulmers of Hereford. Dry or sweet.

Wood Port (Port). Denotes Port wines matured in cask. L.B.V. Tawny, Ruby and White Ports.

Wood's (W.Ind). Producers of a fine old Navy Demerara Rum 57% alc. by vol.

Woods Brewery (Eng). Opened in 1980 behind the Plough Inn in Winstanstow, Shropshire. Noted for its cask conditioned Parish 1040 O.G. and Christmas Cracker 1060 O.G.

Woodside Vineyards (USA). A small winery based in San Mateo, California. 3.25 ha. Produces varietal wines.

Woodsman Mild (Eng). A keg dark Mild ale 1034 O.G. brewed by the New Forest Brewery in Cadnam, Hampshire.

Wood's Old Navy Rum (W.Ind). See Wood's.

Wood Spirit (USA). Methanol.

Woodstock (Austr). A winery in Clare-Watervale, South Australia.

Woodstock Cocktail (Cktl). ⅔ measure dry Gin, ⅓ measure lemon juice, 1 oz. maple syrup, dash Cointreau. Shake well over ice, strain into a cocktail glass.

Wood Tannins (Eng). Tannins obtained

from the wooden casks used to mature wines. Gives the wine flavour. Hydrolyzable tannins, Gallic and Egallic acids, Aldehydes, Vanillin and Lignins.

Woodward Cocktail (Cktl). ⅓ gill Scotch whisky, ⅛ gill French vermouth, ⅛ gill grapefruit juice. Shake over ice, strain into a cocktail glass.

Woody (Eng). A term used to describe a wine with a smell and taste of the cork or cask.

Woogberg (Ger). Vineyard. (Anb) = Mosel-Saar-Ruwer. (Ber) = Zell/Mosel. (Gro) = Rosenhang. (Vil) = Ellenz-Poltersdorf.

Wootton (Eng). Vineyard. Address = North Wootton, Shepton Mallet, Somerset. 2.5 ha. Planted 1971. Soil – medium clay loam. Grape varieties – Müller-Thurgau 40%, Schönburger 30% and Seyval 30%.

Worcester (S.Afr). A wine district around the town of Worcester. Produces mainly dry and dessert wines.

Working (Eng). A term used in brewing and wine production to describe an active fermentation.

Working Man's Drink (Eng). A nickname for beer.

World's Largest Brewery (USA). See Anheuser-Busch Brewery, St. Louis, Missouri.

Worm (Scot). The condensing copper tube which is used in the production of Malt whisky.

Wormeldange (Lux). A wine village on the river Moselle. Vineyard sites are Elterberg, Koeppchen (Koepp) and Nussbaum. Also the name of a co-operative in the village.

Worms (Ger). Village. (Anb) = Rhein-hessen. (Ber) = Wonnegau. (Gro) = Liebfrauenmorgen. (Vins) = Affenberg, Am Heiligen Häuschen, Bildstock, Burgweg, Goldberg, Goldpfad, Hochberg, Kapellenstück, Klausenberg, Kreuzblick, Lerchelsberg, Liebfrauenstift-Kirchenstück, Nonnenwingert, Remeyerhof, Rheinberg, Römersteg, Sankt Annaberg, St. Cyriakusstif, St. Georgenberg, Schneckenberg.

Wormseed (Mex) (USA). A style of tea produced from the Ambroissier shrub.

Wormser Liebfrauenstifte (Ger). The original Liebfraumilch which now can't be called Liebfraumilch without losing its original name.

Wormwood (Eng). The main herb flavour in Vermouth from which it gets its name. From the German Wermut = Wormwood.

Wormwood Bitters (Eng). Place 3–4 sprigs of wormwood into a container. Pour over a bottle of Gin, cover. Stand for 3 weeks, strain, bottle and use as required.

Wörrstadt (Ger). Village. (Anb) = Rhein-hessen. (Ber) = Bingen. (Gro) = Adelberg. (Vins) = Kachelberg, Rheingrafenberg.

Wort (Eng). In brewing the name given to the liquid which holds the malt extract from the malted barley. In beer production hops are added. See Sweet Wort, Hopped Wort.

Worthington BB (Wales). A Best Bitter 1037 O.G. brewed by the Welsh Brewers in Cardiff.

Worthington Brewery (Eng). Merged in 1927 with Bass. Brews cask conditioned beers in South Wales. Keg 'E' 1041 O.G. See also Welsh Breweries.

Worthington Dark (Wales). A dark Mild Ale 1034 O.G. brewed by the Welsh Brewers, Cardiff.

Worthington E (Eng). A keg Bitter 1041 O.G. brewed by the Worthington Brewery in Burton-on-Trent, Staffs.

Worthington Glass (Eng). Another name used for the Wellington glass.

Worthington M (Wales). A light Mild ale 1033 O.G. brewed by the Welsh Brewers in Cardiff.

Worthington White Shield (Eng). A bottle conditioned Ale 1051 O.G. brewed by the Worthington Brewery, Burton-on-Trent, Staffs.

W.O.S. (S.Afr) (abbr). See Wine of Origin Superior.

Wöschbach (Ger). Village. (Anb) = Baden. (Ber) = Badische Bergstrasse/Kraichgau. (Gro) = Hohenberg. (Vin) = Steinwengert.

Wousselt (Lux). A vineyard site in the village of Ehnen.

Wowser (Austr) (slang). For a non-drinker. A fanatical teetotaller.

Wraxall (Eng). Vineyard. Address = Shepton Mallet, Somerset. 2.5 ha. Grape varieties – Müller-Thurgau and Seyval blanc.

Wray and Nephew Group (W.Ind). A Rum distiller based in St. Ann, Jamaica. Produces Black Seal, Green Seal, Red Rose and White Wing.

Wrexham Brewery (Wales). The oldest Lager brewery in U.K. Brews Skol and Wrexham Lager 1033 O.G. Taken over by Ind Coope in 1949. Brews keg, bottled and canned lagers under licence for Allied Breweries.

Wrights (Austr). A winery in the Margaret River district of Western Australia.

Wrotham Pinot (Eng). A black grape

W

variety also known as the Pinot meunier.

W.S.A. (Eng) (abbr). Wine and Spirit Association.

Wuchtig (Ger). Potent, high in alcohol.

Wuhebai (China). The ancient name for the Thompson seedless grape variety.

Wuhrer Group (It). A company that has 4 breweries in northern Italy.

Wülfel Brauerei (Ger). Co-operative owned brewery based in Hanover.

Wülfen (Ger). Vineyard. (Anb) = Rheingau. (Ber) = Johannisberg. (Gro) = Steinmacker. (Vil) = Rauenthal.

Wu Liang Yu (China). A grain spirit produced in Szechuan.

Wu Lung (China). Lit – 'Black dragon'. A semi-fermented large leaf tea with a flavour of ripe peaches.

Wunderbar (Ger). The brand-name of a de-alcoholised red wine.

Wunnenstein (Ger). Grosslage. (Anb) = Württemberg. (Ber) = Württembergisch Unterland. (Vils) = Beilstein, Gronau, Grossbottwar, Hof und Lembach, Ilsfeld, Kleinbottwar, Ludwigsburg (ortsteil Hoheneck), Oberstenfeld, Steinheim, Winzerhausen.

Wurmberg (Ger). Vineyard. (Anb) = Franken. (Ber) = Maindreieck. (Gro) = Not yet assigned. (Vil) = Böttigheim.

Wurmberg (Ger). Vineyard. (Anb) = Württemberg. (Ber) = Württembergisch Unterland. (Gro) = Schalkstein. (Vil) = Besigheim.

Wurmberg (Ger). Vineyard. (Anb) = Württemberg. (Ber) = Württembergisch Unterland. (Gro) = Schalkstein. (Vil) = Gemmrigheim.

Wurmberg (Ger). Vineyard. (Anb) = Württemberg. (Ber) = Württembergisch Unterland. (Gro) = Schalkstein. (Vil) = Walheim.

Württemberg (Ger). Anbaugebiet. (Bers) = Kocher-Jagst-Tauber, Remstal-Stuttgart, Württembergisch Unterland. Main grape varieties – Portugieser, Riesling, Silvaner and Trollinger.

Württemberg Information Service (Ger). Werbegemeinschaft Württembergischer Weingärtnergenossenschaft. Heilbronnersstrasse 41, 7000 Stuttgart 1.

Württembergisch Unterland (Ger). Bereich. (Anb) = Württemberg. (Gros) = Heuchelberg, Kirchenweinberg, Lindelberg, Salzberg, Schalkstein, Schozachtal, Stauffenberg, Stromberg, Wunnenstein

Württemberg Wine Festivals (Ger). Heilbronner Herbst and Fellbacher Herbst.

Würtzberg (Ger). Vineyard. (Anb) = Mosel-Saar-Ruwer. (Ber) = Saar-Ruwer. (Gro) = Scharzberg. (Vil) = Serrig.

Wurzburg (Ger). Village. (Anb) = Franken. (Ber) = Maindreieck. (Gro) = Not yet assigned. (Vins) = Abtsleite, Innere Leiste, Kirchberg, Pfaffenberg, Schlossberg, Stein, Stein/Harfe.

Würzburger Hofbräu (Ger). A Bier brewed in Würzberg.

Würzburger Perle (Ger). A white grape variety. A cross between the Gewürztraminer and the Müller-Thurgau. Is more resistant to frost.

Würzburger Stein (Ger). A famous vineyard in the Franconia region. Gave its name to the 'Steinweine'.

Würzer (Ger). A white grape variety. A cross between the Gewürztraminer and the Müller-Thurgau. Gives a strong bouquet.

Würzgarten (Ger). Vineyard. (Anb) = Mosel-Saar-Ruwer. (Ber) = Bernkastel. (Gro) = Sankt Michel. (Vil) = Detzem.

Würzgarten (Ger). Vineyard. (Anb) = Mosel-Saar-Ruwer. (Ber) = Bernkastel. (Gro) = Schwarzlay. (Vil) = Traben-Trarbach.

Würzgarten (Ger). Vineyard. (Anb) = Mosel-Saar-Ruwer. (Ber) = Bernkastel. (Gro) = Schwarzlay. (Vil) = Ürzig.

Würzgarten (Ger). Vineyard. (Anb) = Rheingau. (Ber) = Johannisberg. (Gro) = Mehrholzchen. (Vil) = Hallgarten.

Würzhölle (Ger). Vineyard. (Anb) = Nahe. (Ber) = Schloss Böckelheim. (Gro) = Paradiesgarten. (Vil) = Unkenbach.

Würzig (Ger). Spicy wine.

Würzlay (Ger). Vineyard. (Anb) = Mosel-Saar-Ruwer. (Ber) = Zell/Mosel. (Gro) = Weinhex. (Vil) = Lehmen.

Wüstberg (Ger). Vineyard. (Anb) = Baden. (Ber) = Badische Bergstrasse/ Kraichgau. (Gro) = Rittersberg. (Vil) = Weinheim.

Wutschenberg (Ger). Vineyard. (Anb) = Franken. (Ber) = Steigerwald. (Gro) = Not yet assigned. (Vil) = Kleinlangheim.

Wyborowa (Pol). A brand of Vodka produced by the Polish State. Panstwowy Monopol Spirytusowy. Distilled from pure grain. Red Label 38% alc. by vol. Blue label 42% alc. by vol. Also spelt Vyborova.

Wychwood Bitter (Eng). A cask conditioned Premium Bitter 1044 O.G. brewed by the Glenny Brewery in Witney, Oxfordshire.

Wye Valley Brewery (Eng). A noted brewery based in Herefordshire. Is noted for its cask conditioned beers.

Wylandgoed (S.Afr). Wine estate.

Wynberg (S.Afr). A wine-producing region of the Cape Peninsula.

Wynboer (S.Afr). A bi-monthly wine paper produced in southern Paarl.

Wyndham Estate (Austr). Address = Dalwood via Branxton, New South Wales 2335. 400 ha. Grape varieties –

Blanquette, Cabernet sauvignon, Chardonnay, Frontignac, Malbec, Merlot, Pinot noir, Rhine riesling, Ruby cabernet, Ruby red, Sauvignon blanc, Sémillon, Shiraz, Tokay, Traminer and Verdelho.

Wyne (Eng). A word for wine in the sixteenth century.

Wyne Seck (Eng). The sixteenth-century word for dry wine.

Wynkelders (S.Afr). Wine cellars.

Wynmaker (S.Afr). Wine producer, wine maker.

Wynmakery (S.Afr). Winery.

Wyn Moneth (Eng). The Anglo-Saxon name for October when the grapes were harvested in England.

Wynns (Austr). A winery in the Barossa Valley and Coonawarra in South Australia. Address = Coonawarra, South Australia 5263. Produces mainly red wines.

Wyn Seck (Eng). The mediaeval name for the dry Spanish wine 'Vino Seco'.

Wynvale Winery (Austr). Address = Miroul Avenue, Yenda, New South Wales 2681. No vineyards, grapes bought in from High Eden, Hunter Valley, Mclaren Vale, M.I.A. and Padthaway.

Wyn Van Oorsprong (S.Afr). Wine of Origin.

Wyoming Swing (Cktl). ½ measure Italian vermouth, ½ measure French vermouth, juice ½ orange, dash Gomme syrup. Stir over ice, strain into an ice-filled highball glass. Top with soda and a slice of orange.

X

X (Eng). The seventeenth-century method of showing the strength of beer. X = standard, XX = double strength Wort. Today the N° of X's has no meaning and is only to the brewer's own classification

Xampan (Sp). Champagne.

Xanath (Mex). A Cream of vanilla liqueur produced by Montini.

Xanthia (Cktl). ⅓ measure Yellow Chartreuse, ⅓ measure Cherry-brandy, ⅓ measure Gin. Stir over ice, strain into a cocktail glass.

Xarab al Maqui (Arab). An ancient Arabian sweet Málaga-style wine.

Xarello (Sp). See Xarel-lo.

Xarel-lo (Sp). A white grape variety grown in the Penedés and Alella regions. Also spelt Xarello, Xerel-lo and Xerello. Also known as the Cartoixa and Pansa blanca.

XB (Eng). A Bitter beer 1036 O.G. brewed by the Bateman Brewery in Wainfleet, Lincolnshire.

XB (Eng). A Best Bitter beer 1040 O.G. brewed by the Hartley Brewery in Ulverston, Cumbria.

XB (Eng). A premium Ale 1045 O.G. brewed by the Theakston Brewery in Masham, Yorkshire.

XB (Scot). A heavy Ale 1036 O.G. brewed by the Devanta Brewery in Aberdeen.

Xeito (Sp). The name given to white and red wines produced by Bodega Cooperativa de Ribeiro.

Xera (Sp). The Phoenician/Greek name for Jerez.

Xerello (Sp). See Xarel-lo.

Xerel-lo (Sp). See Xarel-lo.

Xeres (Hol). Sherry.

Xérès (Fr). Sherry.

Xeres (USA). A white grape variety used in the making of dessert wines in California.

Xeres Cocktail (Cktl).(1). ⅓ gill Fino sherry, dash Campari. Stir over ice, strain into a cocktail glass.

Xeres Cocktail (Cktl).(2). ⅓ gill dry Sherry, dash Peach bitters, dash Orange bitters. Stir over ice, strain into a cocktail glass.

Xerez (Sp). Sherry.

Xeriñac (Sp). The alternative spelling of Jeriñac.

Xeros (Gre). Dry. See also Xiros.

Xinomavro (Gre). A local red grape variety grown in the Salonica district. See also Xynomavro.

Xiros (Gre). Dry. See also Xeros.

Xithum (Egy). A drink produced in ancient Egypt. A cross between wine and beer produced from fermented barley.

XM Standard (S.Am). The name given to light and dark Rums produced by Banks DIH in Guyana.

X.O. (Fr). On Armagnac and Cognac labels, indicates a minimum of 6 years of age.

X.O. (Fr). An old designation on Armagnac and Cognac labels. Denoted that the brandy was Extra Old. 45 years in cask.

Xochimilco (Pousse Café). Pour 1 fl.oz. of Kahlúa into a liqueur glass. Float 1 fl.oz. cream on top.

Xocoatl (C.Am). An Aztec Indian beverage made from the Cacao plant. The modern chocolate beverage drink derived from this.

X-Pert (Hol). An all-malt, unpasteurised Beer 5% alc. by vol. brewed by the Gulpen Brouwerij in Gulpen, Limburg.

XS (Eng). A Winter ale 1052 O.G. brewed by the Clark Brewery in Wakefield, Yorkshire.

XX (Eng). A cask conditioned dark Mild 1031 O.G. brewed by the Greene King Brewery in East Anglia.

XX (Eng). A cask conditioned Mild ale 1030 O.G. brewed by the Harvey Brewery in Lewes, Sussex.

XX (Eng). A light keg Mild ale 1033 O.G. brewed by the Shepherd Neame Brewery in Faversham, Kent.

XXX (Eng). A cask conditioned Mild ale 1030 O.G. brewed by the Brakspear Brewery in Henley-on-Thames, Oxfordshire.

XXX (Eng). A cask conditioned Mild ale 1034 O.G. brewed by the Donnington Brewery in Stow-on-the-Wold.

XXX (Eng). A cask conditioned Bitter 1036 O.G. brewed by the Paine Brewery in St. Neots, Cambridgeshire.

XXX (Eng). A cask conditioned Mild ale 1034 O.G. brewed by the Ridley Brewery in Chelmsford, Essex.

XXX (Eng). A cask conditioned Bitter 1042

O.G. brewed by the Three Tuns home-brew public house in Bishop's Castle, Shropshire.

XXX (Scot). A dark malty Bitter 1042 O.G. brewed by the Devanha Brewery in Aberdeen.

XXXB (Eng). A cask conditioned malty Bitter 1048 O.G. brewed by the Bateman's Brewery in Wainfleet, near Skegness, Lincolnshire. Also sold in bottles as Ploughman's Ale.

XXXD (Eng). A cask conditioned dark Mild 1032 O.G. brewed by the Gales Brewery in Horndean, Hampshire.

XXXL (Eng). A cask conditioned light Mild 1030 O.G. brewed by the Gales Brewery in Horndean, Hampshire.

XXXX (Eng). A cask conditioned Mild ale 1031 O.G. brewed by the Bass Brewery in London.

XXXX (Eng). A cask conditioned Ale 1043 O.G. brewed by the Brakspear Brewery in Henley-on-Thames, Oxfordshire.

XXXX (Eng). A cask conditioned old Ale 1043 O.G. brewed by the Harvey Brewery in Lewes, Sussex.

XXXX (Eng). A cask conditioned old Ale 1046 O.G. brewed by the King and Barnes Brewery in Horsham, Sussex.

XXXX (Eng). A cask conditioned Mild 1033 O.G. brewed by the Samuel Smith Brewery in Tadcaster, Yorkshire.

XXXX (Eng). A cask conditioned Mild ale 1034 O.G. brewed by the St. Austell Brewery in Cornwall.

XXXXX (Eng). A Winter ale 1044 O.G. brewed by the Gales Brewery in Horndean, Hampshire.

XXXXXX (Eng). A Barley wine 1064 O.G. brewed and bottled by the Holt Brewery in Manchester.

Xylose (Eng). A monosaccharide found in wine.

Xynisteri (Cyp). A white grape variety grown to produce dry white wines.

Xynomavro (Gre). A red grape variety grown in northern Greece.

X.Y.Z. (Cktl). ½ measure white Rum, ½ measure Cointreau, ¼ measure lemon juice. Shake over ice, strain into a cocktail glass.

Y

Yacht Club (Cktl). ⅓ measure Gin, ⅓ measure Italian vermouth, ⅓ measure orange juice, 2 dashes Campari, 2 dashes Gomme syrup. Shake over ice, strain into a cocktail glass.

Yago Condal (Sp). A white wine produced by Bodegas Rioja Santiago in the Haro region.

Yago Sant'gria (USA). A brand-name of a Sangría. One of the largest selling brands. See Sangría, Rioja Santiago Co.

Yağsiz (Tur). Skimmed milk.

Yakenet (Isr). The name given to a rich, red dessert wine produced by Carmel from the Alicante grape.

Yakima River Winery (USA). A winery based in Prosser, Washington. Produces mainly white wines.

Yakima Valley (USA). A wine region in the Washington district.

Yaldara Winery (Austr). A winery based in the Barossa Valley, South Australia. Produces varietal wines.

Yale Cocktail (Cktl).(1). ½ measure Italian vermouth, ½ measure dry Gin. Shake over ice, strain into a highball glass. Top with soda water and a squeeze of lemon peel juice.

Yale Cocktail (Cktl).(2). ¾ measure dry Gin, ¼ measure French vermouth, dash Angostura, 3 dashes Crème Yvette. Stir over ice, strain into a cocktail glass.

Yalta (USSR). A wine district of the Crimea. Produces good red, rosé and white wines.

Yalumba Vineyards (Austr). Address = Angaston, South Australia 5353. 400 ha. Grape varieties – Cabernet sauvignon, Merlot, Riesling and Shiraz.

Yamagata (Jap). A small wine-producing province in southern Japan.

Yamanashi (Jap). A large wine-producing province based in Tokyo.

Yamazaki (Jap). A distillery built in the Vale of Yamazaki in 1923 by Shinjiro Torii.

Yam Wine (Afr) (S.Am). A fermented beverage produced from the roots of the yam plant.

Yankee-Doodle Cocktail (Cktl). ⅙ gill Crème de Banane, ⅙ gill Cognac, ⅙ gill Royal Mint Chocolate Liqueur. Shake well over ice, strain into a cocktail glass.

Yankee-Dutch (Cktl). ¼ measure Bourbon whiskey, ¼ measure Cherry brandy, ¼ measure Triple sec, ¼ measure Vodka. Stir over ice, strain into a cocktail glass, add a twist of orange peel.

Yankee Invigorator (Cktl). Add ¾ pint cold strong coffee, 1 oz. Brandy, ½ wine glass Port to a beaten egg and sugar to taste. Add ice, Shake, strain into a tumbler.

Yantar (USSR). 'Amber'. Brewery at Nikolayev. Brews Zhiguli (unmalted barley and corn brew), Riga, Slavyanskoye, Moscow and Amber.

Yapincak (Tur). A derivative of the white Sémillon grape.

Yapp Brothers (Eng). Noted wine merchants based at The Old Brewery, Mere, Wiltshire. Specialise in the wines of the Loire, Rhône and Midi of France.

Yarck Winery (Austr). A winery in Central Victoria.

Yarden (Isr). The name given to a range of Israeli wines imported into the U.K. by the House of Hallgarten, London. Are Kosher wines produced from French vines on the Golan Height. 160 ha.

Yard of Ale (Eng). A long glass vessel used mainly for drinking contests. Holds between 2¼ and 4½ pints. Has a bulbous end. The drinker must be careful as, if it is tipped too sharply, the beer may flow too quickly and drench the drinker.

Yard of Flannel (Eng). Old English drink of sugar, eggs and Brandy heated. This is then added to hot ale and mixed until smooth. Drunk hot.

Yard of Flannel (USA). Traditionally a hot toddy of Cider, cream and Rum mixed with spices and beaten egg.

Yarra Valley Wines (Austr). Cabernet sauvignon, Rhine riesling and Shiraz wines from Fergussons, Yarra Glen, Victoria.

Yarra Yering Vineyard (Austr). Address = Briarty Road, via Coldstream, Victoria 3770. 12 ha. Grape varieties – Cabernet sauvignon, Chardonnay, Malbec, Merlot, Pinot noir and Shiraz.

Yashan Noshan (Isr). A sweet, dessert wine.

Yasman-Salik (USSR). A fortified wine produced in Turkmenistan.
Yasti (Ind). The old name for yeast.
Yates and Jackson (Eng). A brewery based in Lancaster. Brews a sharp, dark Mild and medium Bitter.
Yava (E.Ind). See Ava and Kava.
Yawa (Afr). A palm wine produced in west Africa.
Yayin (Isr). An old Hebrew (Bible) word for wine described as having originated from Noah's vineyard.
Yburgberg (Ger). Vineyard. (Anb) = Baden. (Ber) = Ortenau. (Gro) = Schloss Rodeck. (Vil) = Steinbach.
Yeadstone (Eng). Vineyard. Address = Bickleigh, Tiverton, Devon. 0.75 ha. Planted 1976.
Yearlstone Vineyard (Eng). A vineyard based at Bickley, Tiverton, Devon. 1.5 ha. Grape varieties – Chardonnay, Madeleine angevine and Siegerrebe.
Yeast (Eng). The organism Saccharomyces which converts sugars into alcohol and carbon-dioxide. Many strains (see Saccharomyces) of yeasts are used for various styles of alcoholic beverages.
Yeast Cultures (Eng). Preparations made for adding to Musts to encourage Yeast growth, such as Potassium Phosphate, Ammonium Phosphate, Vitamin B1 etc.
Yeasting (USA). The adding of pure yeast culture to the Mash in the production of Whiskey for fermentation.
Yeasty (Eng). Describes a wine with a smell of yeast, possibly due to a secondary fermentation in the bottle.
Yebisu (Jap). An all-malt Beer 4.5% alc. by vol. brewed by the Sapporo Brewery in Sapporo.
Yebisu Beer (Jap). A Beer brewed by the Sapporo Breweries Ltd. in Tokyo.
Yecla (Sp). A Denominación de Origen region of Levante in southern Spain. Grape varieties – Garnacha and Monastrell.
Yeisai (Jap). A Zen Buddhist abbot who promoted tea drinking in Japan in the thirteenth century.
Yellow Bird (Cktl). 1½ fl.ozs. white Rum, ½ fl.oz. Cointreau, ½ fl.oz. Galliano, ½ fl.oz. lime juice. Shake well over ice, pour unstrained into a goblet, dress with a slice of lime.
Yellow Chartreuse (Fr). A slightly sweeter version of Green Chartreuse produced 6 years later in 1838. 56% alc. by vol.
Yellow Daisy (Cktl). ⅖ measure dry Gin, ⅖ measure dry Vermouth, ⅕ measure Grand Marnier. Stir over ice, strain into a cocktail glass.
Yellow Dwarf (Cktl).(Non-alc). 1 egg yolk, ½ measure cream, ½ measure Gomme syrup. Shake over ice, strain into an ice-filled highball glass, top with soda water.
Yellow Dwarf Cocktail (Cktl).(Non-alc). 3 fl.ozs. cream, 1 egg yolk, dash almond essence, 1 fl.oz. passion fruit syrup. Stir over ice, strain into a Champagne saucer. Add a splash of soda.
Yellow Fever (Cktl). Mix ½ fl.oz. Vodka with ½ teaspoon of sugar in a highball glass until dissolved. Add 2 fl.ozs. lemon juice, 2 fl.ozs. Vodka and ice. Stir, top with soda water and a slice of orange.
Yellowglen Vineyard (Austr). Address = White's Road, Smythesdale, Victoria 3351. 18 ha. Grape varieties – Cabernet sauvignon, Chardonnay and Pinot noir. Noted for sparkling wines.
Yellow Label Red (Austr). A red wine blend of Cabernet sauvignon and Shiraz. Produced by the Bilyara Vineyards in South Australia.
Yellow Parrot Cocktail (Cktl). ⅙ gill Yellow Chartreuse, ⅙ gill Apricot brandy, ⅙ gill Pernod. Shake well over ice, strain into a cocktail glass.
Yellow Rattler (Cktl). ⅛ gill dry Gin, ⅛ gill French vermouth, ⅛ gill Italian vermouth, ⅛ gill fresh orange juice. Shake well over ice, strain into a cocktail glass, dress with a small crushed yellow pickled onion.
Yellow Sea (Cktl). ¼ measure light Rum, ¼ measure Galliano, ⅛ measure Maraschino, ⅜ measure Vodka, juice of a lime, 1 teaspoon sugar. Shake over ice, strain into a cocktail glass.
Yellowstone (USA). A 6 year old Kentucky Bourbon whiskey produced by the Yellowstone Distilleries Co. in Owensboro and Louisville, Kentucky. 43%, 45% and 50% alc. by vol.
Yema (Sp). The first pressing of the Sherry grapes to which Gypsum is added.
Yemen Coffee (Arab). See Moka Coffee.
Yenda Winery (Austr). Part of the McWilliams Estate, New South Wales.
Yen Hung (China). A noted brand of Rice wine. See Shao-Hsing Rice Wine.
Yenon (Isr). A sweet, dessert wine.
Yeoman (Eng). A noted hop variety grown in the county of Kent.
Yeoman Bitter (Eng). A keg Bitter 1038 O.G. brewed by the Greene King Brewery in East Anglia. (Is named after a hop variety).
Yeradjes (Cyp). A wine village in the region of Marathassa in the north-west Troodos.
Yerasa (Cyp). See Yerassa.
Yerassa (Cyp). A wine village in the south-east of the island that grows the grapes used in the production of Commandaria. Also spelt Yarasa.

Y

Yerba Maté (S.Am). A herbal tea from Paraguay. Contains tannin, is good for slimmers. Traditionally drunk in hollowed out gourds known as Culhas or Matés in Brazil and sucked with straws known as Bombillas. See Maté.

Yeringberg (Austr). A winery in the Yarra Valley, Victoria.

Yesca (Sp). A fungus which attacks faulty vine prunings in the Málaga region.

Yeso (Sp). Calcium Sulphate (Gypsum) which is sprinkled on the grapes during the first pressing (Yema) to slow down fermentation and increase acidity.

Ye'-Ye' (Cktl). 1 oz. Mandarine Napoléon, 1¾ ozs. grapefruit juice, ¾ oz. Rum. Shake over ice, strain into a highball glass, top with Bitter lemon. Decorate with 2 cherries, slice of lemon and cucumber.

Yfed (Wales). To quaff, drink easily.

Y Grec (Fr). The brand-name of the dry wine from Château d'Yquem. Is very rare.

Ynocente (Sp). A brand of Fino sherry produced by Valdespino.

Yokohama Cocktail (Cktl). ⅙ gill Crème de Menthe, ⅙ gill dry Gin, ⅙ gill Italian vermouth. Shake over ice, strain into a cocktail glass. Serve with an olive and dash of lemon peel juice.

Yolanda (Cktl). ⅓ measure Cognac, ⅓ measure dry Gin, ⅓ measure Anisette, 1 oz. Italian vermouth, dash Grenadine. Shake well over ice, strain into a cocktail glass. Top with a twist of orange peel juice.

Yolo (USA). A small wine-producing district and county in Sacramento Valley, California.

Yonne (Fr). A wine-producing Département in central France. Was originally part of Burgundy.

Yop (Fr). A yoghurt fruit-flavoured drink from Joplait.

York Brewery (Eng). Based in Boroughbridge. Produces malty beers.

York Cocktail (Cktl). Another name for the Thistle Cocktail.

York Creek (USA). A vineyard based near St. Helena, Napa Valley, California. 41.5 ha. Grape varieties – Cabernet sauvignon, Petite sirah and Zinfandel. Produces varietal wines.

York Mountain Winery (USA). A winery based near Templeton, San Luis Obispo County, California. Grape varieties – Cabernet sauvignon, Chardonnay, Merlot, Pinot noir and Zinfandel. Produces varietal, dessert and sparkling wines.

Yorkshire Bitter (Eng). A cask conditioned Bitter 1036 O.G. brewed by the John Smith Brewery in Tadcaster, Yorkshire. (Also a keg version produced).

Yorkshire Bitter (Eng). A cask conditioned Bitter 1037.5 O.G. brewed by the Webster Brewery in Halifax, Yorkshire. (Also a keg version produced). Sold in the south of England.

Yorkshire Grey (Eng). A Clifton home-brew public house owned by Clifton Inns. Noted for its cask conditioned Headline Bitter 1037 O.G. and Holborn Best 1047 O.G.

Yorkshire Square (Eng). A term used in the north for fermenting vessels used in the brewing process. See Square.

York Springs Winery (USA). A winery based in York Springs, Pennsylvania. Produces hybrid wines.

Young (Eng). A term used to denote a wine which is not fully matured or one which remains fruity and lively despite its age.

Young Blade (Cktl). 1 measure Cherry brandy, juice of an orange, cube of sugar. Shake well over ice, strain into a flute glass. Top with iced Champagne.

Young Brewery (Eng). Based in Wandsworth, London. Noted for its cask conditioned and keg Ales, also for bottled London Lager 1037 O.G. Old Nick 1084 O.G. and Ram Rod 1046 O.G.

Younger (Scot). The brand-name used by the Fountain Brewery in Edinburgh. Is part of the Scottish and Newcastle Breweries.

Younger (William) (Eng). Scottish and Newcastle's southern England and south Wales marketing company.

Young Hyson (China). A type of unfermented Green tea from China.

Young Man Cocktail (Cktl). See Diabolo Cocktail.

Young's Brewery (Eng). Based in Wandsworth, London. Noted for its cask conditioned traditional beers.

Young Vineyards (USA). A large winery based in the Alexander Valley, Sonoma County, California. 114 ha. Grape varieties – Chardonnay, Gewürztraminer, Johannisberg riesling and White riesling. Produces varietal and table wines.

Yountville (USA). A noted wine town in the Napa Valley, California. Is the home to many wineries.

Your Shout (Eng). See Shout.

Youthful (Eng). A term used to describe a wine with a fresh acidity.

Yovac (Yug). A wine district.

Ypioca (Bra). See Ypiocha.

Ypiocha (Bra). The brand-name of a Cachaça that has a slight yellow colour due to wood ageing. Also spelt Ypioca.

Yuba (USA). A small wine-producing

county based in the Sacramento Valley, California.

Yubileyneya Osobaya (Pol). A Vodka also known as Jubilee Vodka. Contains honey, Brandy and botanicals.

Yucateca Brewery (Mex). An independent brewery which produces Montejo and Leon Negra beers.

Yudumlamak (Tur). To sip a drink.

Yuengling Brewery (USA). The oldest brewery in the USA. Based in Pottsville, Pennsylvania. Dates back to 1829.

Yugoslav Amselfelder Spätburgunder (Yug). A red wine from the 'Kosovo Pilje' vineyards. Also called by that name. See also Burgomer Burgundec.

Yugoslavia (Euro). A wine-producing country that includes the regions of – Croatia, Kosmet, Krajina, Macedonia, Serbia, Slovenia (Ljutomer), Smederevo, Vencac-Oplenac, Vlasotinci and Vojvodina. Also spelt Jugoslavia.

Yukon Gold (Can). A Pilsener-style beer brewed by the Old Fort Brewery, British Columbia.

Yuma Jana Cocktail (Pousse Café). ⅓ measure each of the following in order in an Elgin glass – Crème de Cacao, Apricot brandy, Prunée cordial, Regina cordial and cream.

Yunnan (China). A delicate, flavoured tea produced in western China.

Yuntero (Sp). A full, dry, white wine produced by Nuestro Padre Jesus del Perdon in La Mancha.

Yverdon Vineyards (USA). A winery based near St. Helena, Napa Valley, California. Grape varieties – Cabernet sauvignon, Chenin blanc, Johannisberg riesling and Gamay. Produces varietal and table wines.

Yvon (M.) (Fr). A famous Frenchman who managed to make Cognac during the Phylloxera epidemic in the nineteenth century by finding a way of beating the louse. His company is owned by Hennessy.

Yvon Mau et Fils (Fr). A noted négociant based in south-western France. Address = Rue de la Gare, 33190 Gironde-sur-Dropt.

Yvorne (Switz). A dry white wine from the Vaud canton.

Zaberfeld (Ger). Village. (Anb) = Württemberg. (Ber) = Württembergisch Unterland. (Gro) = Heuchelberg. (Vin) = Hohenberg.

Zaber [River] (Ger). A tributary of the river Neckar in Württemberg.

Zaca Mesa Winery (USA). A large winery based in Santa Barbara, California. Grape varieties – Cabernet sauvignon, Chardonnay, Johannisberg riesling, Pinot noir and Zinfandel. Produces varietal and table wines.

Zaca Vineyard (La) (USA). A large vineyard on Zaca Mesa, Santa Barbara, California. 42 ha. Grape varieties – Cabernet sauvignon, Chardonnay and Johannisberg riesling. Produces varietal wines.

Zacatecas (Mex). An area where grapes are grown.

Zaccagnini (It). A noted producer of cuve close sparkling wines from the Marche region.

Začinka (Yug). A red wine produced in eastern Serbia.

Zaco (Sp). Light, dry, red and white wines produced by Bodegas Bilbainas in Haro, Rioja Alta, north-western Spain.

Zaeh (Ger). Denotes a ropy, oily, thick wine.

Zaer (Afr). An A.O.G. area in Morocco in the wine-producing region of Gharb.

Zagarese (It). A ruby-red sweet wine from the Apulia region. 17–18% alc. by vol.

Zagarolo (It). D.O.C. white wine from the Latium region. Made from the Malvasia and Trebbiano grapes in the communes of Gallicano and Zagarolo. Vinification has to occur within the delimited territory. If total alc content is 12.5% by vol. then classed Superiore.

Zagarrón (Sp). A label used by Cooperativa de Manjavacas in the La Mancha region.

Zagreb (Yug). A wine-producing area in northern Yugoslavia. Produces mainly white wines.

Zähe (Aus). Denotes a wine that is thick and full-bodied.

Zaire (Afr). A major coffee-producing country in southern Africa. Produces high acidity coffees which are used mainly in blending. Ituri and Kivi are the main producing areas.

Zaisenhausen (Ger). Village. (Anb) = Baden. (Ber) = Badische Bergstrasse/ Kraichgau. (Gro) = Stiftsberg. (Vin) = Lerchenberg.

Zakkelweiss (Rum). A white grape variety also known as the Banater riesling, Kriacza, Kreaca and Creaca.

Zalema (Sp). A white grape variety grown in Condado de Huelva.

Zambra (Sp). The name given to a range of mature wines produced by San Isidro in Jumilla, Levante.

Zamora (Sp). A wine-producing province based near Salamanca. Is noted for its dark Toro vines.

Zandvliet Estate (S.Afr). A vineyard based in Robertson. Address = P.O. Box 36, Aston 6715. Produces varietal wines.

Zanjan (Iran). A wine-producing province in northern Iran.

Zante (Gre). An Ionian island in western Greece that produces wines mainly for local consumption.

Zapatos de Pisar (Sp). Special boots used for treading the grapes in the Sherry region.

Zapekanka (USSR). A cherry-based spirit. 40% alc. by vol.

Zapfeter (Aus). An alternative name for the Furmint grape.

Zapoi (USSR). Drunkard.

Zapple (Eng). A non-alcoholic sparkling apple juice drink produced by Showerings. Contains no artificial colouring or preservatives.

Zara Cocktail (Cktl). The alternative name for the Zaza Cocktail.

Zarco [João Gonçalves] (Mad). Rediscovered the island of Madeira in 1418.

Zardetto (It). A noted producer of Prosecco di Conegliano-Valdobbiadene in Veneto.

Zarf (Arab). A glass where the bowl fits into an ornate holder made of precious metal. Used for drinking Turkish-style coffee. Was also made of porcelain.

Zarragon (Sp). A dry white wine produced by the Bodega Cooperative del Campo Nuestra Señora in La Mancha.

Z

Zartchin (Bul). A wine-producing area noted for its red wines.

Zat (Hol). Drunk, inebriated.

Žatec Brewery (Czec). Based in north west Czech. Founded in 1801.

Žatec Red (Czec). A variety of Bohemian hop. Derives from an 1865 strain.

Zauner (Aus). A famous coffee house in Bad Ischl.

Zaza (Cktl).(1). 1 measure dry Gin, 1 measure Dubonnet, dash Angostura. Stir over ice, strain into a cocktail glass.

Zaza (Cktl).(2). ⅓ measure Old Tom Gin, ⅔ measure Dubonnet, dash Orange bitters. Stir over ice, strain into a cocktail glass. Also known as a Zara Cocktail.

Zazie (Cktl). ⅓ measure Curaçao, ⅓ measure Gin, ⅓ measure Stock Apéritif. Stir over ice, strain into a cocktail glass, add a twist of orange peel.

Z.B.W. (Ger) (abbr). Zentralkellerei Badischer Winzergenossenschaften. EG., Breisach, Kaiserstuhl. See ZKW.

Z-D Wines (USA). A winery based near Rutherford, Napa Valley, California. Grape varieties – Chardonay, Gewürztraminer, Pinot noir, White riesling and Zinfandel. Produces varietal and table wines.

Zebibi (Arab). An ancient Arabian, sweet, Málaga-style wine produced from grapes that have been partially dried in the sun.

Zechberg (Ger). Vineyard. (Anb) = Rheinhessen. (Ber) = Nierstein. (Gro) =Petersberg. (Vil) = Framersheim.

Zechpeter (Ger). Vineyard. (Anb) = Rheinpfalz. (Ber) = Südliche Weinstrasse. (Gro) = Bischofskreuz. (Vil) = Flemlingen.

Zechwein (Ger). Lit – 'The drinker's wine'. Made from the Trollinger grape in the Württemberg. A fruity, light, ruby red wine.

Zeer Oude (Hol). Z.O. Very old. Refers to old Jenever.

Zehnmorgen (Ger). Vineyard. (Anb) = Rheinhessen. (Ber) = Nierstein. (Gro) = Auflangen. (Vil) = Nierstein.

Zehntgraf (Ger). Vineyard. (Anb) = Franken. (Ber) = Maindreieck. (Gro) = Kirchberg. (Vil) = Wipfeld.

Zehnt-Wein (Ger). A charge paid by a tenant to a landlord (a tenth of his grape harvest or must). The time to pick the grapes is decided by the landlord.

Zeil (Ger). Village. (Anb) = Franken. (Ber) = Steigerwald. (Gro) =Kapellenberg. (Vin) = Kronberg.

Zeil a. Main (Ger). Village. (Anb) = Franken. (Ber) = Steigerwald. (Gro) = Not yet assigned. (Vin) = Mönchshang.

Zeilberg (Ger). Vineyard. (Anb) = Württemberg. (Ber) = Württembergisch Unterland. (Gro) = Salzberg. (Vil) = Affaltrach.

Zeilberg (Ger). Vineyard. (Anb) = Württemberg. (Ber) = Württembergisch Unterland. (Gro) = Salzberg. (Vil) = Löwenstein (ortsteil Hösslinsülz).

Zeilberg (Ger). Vineyard. (Anb) = Württemberg. (Ber) = Württembergisch Unterland. (Gro) = Salzberg. (Vil) = Willsberg.

Zeisel (Ger). Vineyard. (Anb) = Mosel-Saar-Ruwer. (Ber) = Zell/Mosel. (Gro) = Goldbäumchen. (Vil) = Pommern.

Zeiskam (Ger). Village. (Anb) = Rheinpfalz. (Ber) = Südliche Weinstrasse. (Gro) = Trappenberg. (Vin) = Klostergarten.

Zell (Ger). Village. (Anb) = Mosel-Saar-Ruwer. (Ber) = Zell/Mosel. (Gro) = Schwarze Katz. (Vins) = Burglay-Felsen, Domherrenberg, Geisberg, Kreuzlay, Nussberg, Petersborn-Kabertchen, Pommerell.

Zell (Ger). Village. (Anb) = Rheinpfalz. (Ber) = Mittelhaardt-Deutsche Weinstrasse. (Gro) = Schnepfenflug vom Zellertal. (Vins) = Königsweg, Kreuzberg, Klosterstück, Schwarzer Herrgott.

Zellerberg (Ger). Vineyard. (Anb) = Mosel-Saar-Ruwer. (Ber) = Bernkastel. (Gro) = Sankt Michael. (Vil) = Longen.

Zellerberg (Ger). Vineyard. (Anb) = Mosel-Saar-Ruwer. (Ber) = Bernkastel. (Gro) = Sankt Michael. (Vil) = Lörsch.

Zellerberg (Ger). Vineyard. (Anb) = Mosel-Saar-Ruwer. (Ber) = Bernkastel. (Gro) = Sankt Michael. (Vil) = Mehring.

Zeller Schwarze Katz (Ger). A wine from the Mosel-Saar-Ruwer. A type of wine of which 75% of the grapes must come from the village of Zell. See Schwarze Katz.

Zellerweg am Schwarzen Herrgott (Ger). Vineyard. (Anb) = Rheinhessen. (Ber) = Wonnegau. (Gro) = Domblick. (Vil) = Mölsheim.

Zell-Kaimt (Ger). Village. (Anb) = Mosel-Saar-Ruwer. (Ber) = Zell/Mosel. (Gro) = Schwarze Katz. (Vins) = Marienburger, Römerquelle, Rosenborn.

Zell-Merl (Ger). Village. (Anb) = Mosel-Saar-Ruwer. (Ber) = Zell/Mosel. (Gro) = Grafshaft. (Vins) = Sites not yet chosen.

Zell-Merl (Ger). Village. (Anb) = Mosel-Saar-Ruwer. (Ber) = Zell/Mosel. (Gro) = Schwarze Katz. (Vins) = Adler, Fettgarten, Klosterberg, Königslay-Terrassen, Stefansberg, Sonneck.

Zell/Mosel (Ger). Bereich. (Anb) = Mosel-Saar-Ruwer. (Gros) = Goldbäumchen,

Z

Grafschaft, Rosenhang, Schwarze Katz, Weinhex.

Zell-Weierbach (Ger). Village. (Anb) = Baden. See Offenburg.

Zeltingen-Rachtig (Ger). Village. (Anb) = Mosel-Saar-Ruwer. (Ber) = Bernkastel. (Gro) = Münzlay. (Vins) = Deutscherrenberg, Himmelreich, Schlossberg, Sonnenuhr.

Zemmour (Afr). An A.O.G. area in Morocco in the wine-producing region of Gharb.

Zenata (Afr). An A.O.G. area in Morocco in the wine-producing region of Casablanca.

Zeni (Roberto) (It). A small winery based at Grumo near San Michele all'Adige in Trentino-Alto Adige. 7 ha.

Zenith Cooler (Cktl). Crush a slice of fresh pineapple into a shaker, add ice, ¾ gill Gin, dash sugar syrup. Shake well, strain into a tumbler with ice, top with soda water. Decorate with pieces of pineapple.

Zentgericht (Ger). Vineyard. (Anb) = Hessische Bergstrasse. (Ber) = Starkenberg. (Gro) = Schlossberg. (Vil) = Heppenheim (including Erbach and Hambach). Also spelt Centgericht.

Zentralkellerei Badischer Winzergenossenschaften (Ger). Z.B.W. The central winery of Baden wine-growers co-operatives. The largest wine co-operative in Europe.

Zeppwingert (Ger). Vineyard. (Anb) = Mosel-Saar-Ruwer. (Ber) = Bernkastel. (Gro) = Schwarzlay. (Vil) = Enkirch.

Zerhoun (Afr). An A.O.G. area in Morocco in the wine-producing region of Meknès-Fez.

Zero (Nor). A non-alcoholic beer.

Zero Hour Cocktail (Cktl). ¼ gill Brandy, ⅛ gill Apricot brandy, 3 dashes Crème de Menthe, 2 dashes Absinthe. Shake over ice, strain into a cocktail glass. Serve with an olive and 2 dashes Absinthe on top.

Zero Mint Cocktail (Cktl). Blend ⅓ gill of (green) Crème de Menthe which has been stirred over ice with ⅙ gill of iced water. Serve in a cocktail glass.

Zest (Eng). For cocktails, thin pieces of citrus peel (the white pith excluded). Essential oil is squeezed on top of a drink.

Zeta River Valley (Yug). A noted wine-producing area in Montenegro, south-eastern Yugoslavia. Produces red wines mainly from the Vranac grape.

Zeutern (Ger). Village. (Anb) = Baden. (Ber) = Badische Bergstrasse/ Kraichgau. (Gro) = Mannaberg. (Vin) = Himmelreich.

Zevenwacht Vineyard (S.Afr). Based in

Stellenbosch. Address = P.O. Box 387, Kuilsriver 7580. Produces varietal wines.

Zgarolo (It). A D.O.C. white wine from the Lazio region.

Zhiguli (USSR). A light Beer brewed by the Yantar Brewery using unmalted barley and cornflour.

Zhitomiraskaya Vodka (USSR). The main Vodka-style produced in Zhitomir, Ukraine.

Zibeben (Aus). The name given to sun-dried grapes used in wine production. Derives from the Arabic Zabib (dried raisin).

Zibib (Egy). A fiery spirit distilled from dates.

Zibibbo (It). A white grape variety grown in southern Italy. Used in the production of Moscato Passito di Pantelleria. Also known as the Muscat of Alexandria.

Zichron-Jacob (Isr). Israel viticultural centre which produces most styles of wines from French grape varieties.

Zickelgarten (Ger). Vineyard. (Anb) = Mosel-Saar-Ruwer. (Ber) = Saar-Ruwer. (Gro) = Scharzberg. (Vil) = Ockfen.

Zickend (Aus). A term that describes a wine with a taste of rancid butter.

Ziegelanger (Ger). Village. (Anb) = Franken. (Ber) = Steigerwald. (Gro) = Kapellenberg. (Vin) = Olschnabel.

Ziegelhof Brauerei (Switz). An independent brewery based in Liestal.

Ziegler Winery (USA). A winery based in Cuba, Missouri. Produces Concord grape wines.

Ziem Vineyards (USA). A small winery based in Fairplay, Maryland. Produces hybrid wines.

Zierfändler (Aus). A white grape variety grown in the Baden area.

Zikhron-Yaacov (Isr). The largest wine-producing region based around the slopes of Mount Carmel. Produces most styles of wines.

Žilavka (Yug). A white grape variety grown in Macedonia to make Mostarska Žilavka, a dry, white, fruity, perfumed wine.

Zimbabwe (Afr). A coffee, tea and wine-producing country of central-eastern Africa. See Mateppe.

Zinblanca (USA). The name given to the white Zinfandel-based wine produced by Vose Vineyards, California.

Zind-Humbrecht (Fr). A wine producer of Alsace. Address = 34, Rue du Maréchal-Joffre, Wintzenheim, 68000 Colmar.

Zinfandel (It). A purple-red grape variety grown in Bari.

Zinfandel (USA). See California Zinfandel.

Zinfandel Essence (USA). A wine made from botrytised grapes in San Benito,

California by the Calera Wine Co.

Zinfandel Rosé (USA). A rosé wine made from the Zinfandel grape in California.

Zingy (Eng). Term applied to wines that are refreshing, vital and lively, resulting from a high balance of acidity, fruit or pétillance. See also Zippy.

Ziolowy (Pol). A herb-flavoured liqueur produced by Polmos.

Zipf Brauerei (Aus). A brewery that is a subsidiary of Bräu AG.

Zipfer Stefanibock (Aus). A pale Bock beer 6.75% alc. by vol. brewed by the Zipf Brauerei.

Zipfer Urtyp (Aus). A dry, pale premium Lager brewed by the Zipf Brauerei.

Zippy (Eng). See Zingy.

Zirpass Brewery (Switz). An independent brewery in Buchs.

Zistersdorf (Aus). A wine-producing district in the Weinviertel region. Produces light, white wines.

Zitadelle (Ger). Vineyard. (Anb) = Rheinpfalz. (Ber) = Südliche Weinstrasse. (Gro) = Schloss Ludwigshöhe. (Vil) = St. Martin.

Zitsa (Gre). A sweet, white, pétillant wine from the Debina grape produced in the region of Ipiros.

Zivania (Cyp). The name used for grape alcohol.

ZKW (Ger). The former initials of the ZBW formed in 1952. Changed to present name in 1954.

Zlatoroc Pivo (Yug). A pale Lager 12% alc. by vol. brewed at Lasko in Slovenia.

Zlatý Kuň (Czec). Lit – 'Golden horse' A Lager beer from Beroun.

Zleni Veltlinac (Yug). A white grape variety grown in Serbia. Is also known as the Grüner veltliner.

Zlota Woda (Pol). A style of Goldwasser.

Znojmo Brewery (Czec). A brewery based in southern Czec. Founded in 1720.

Z.O. (Hol) (abbr). Zeer Oude.

Zobelsberg (Ger). Vineyard. (Anb) = Franken. (Ber) = Maindreieck. (Gro) = Hofrat. (Vil) = Segnitz.

Zöbing (Aus). A wine-producing area noted for its Riesling wines.

Zoilo Ruiz-Mateos (Sp). A Sherry bodega and producer based in Jerez de la Frontera.

Zöld (Hun). Green.

Zöldszilváni (Hun). A variety of Sylvaner grape, has green skin grown near Lake Balatòn.

Zollturm (Ger). Vineyard. (Anb) = Mosel-Saar-Ruwer. (Ber) = Bernkastel. (Gro) = Schwarzlay. (Vil) = Traben-Trarbach.

Zollverein (Ger). The nineteenth-century customs union organised to raise and standardise the German wines including a register of the vineyards.

Zolotaya Osen (USSR). Lit – 'Golden Autumn'. A liqueur made from quinces, apples and Caucasian damsons.

Zombie (Cktl). ¾ oz. lime juice, ¾ oz. pineapple juice, 1 teaspoon Falernum (or sugar syrup), 1 oz. White Label Rum, 2 ozs. Gold Label Rum, 1 oz. Jamaican Rum, ½ oz. 100° proof Rum, ½ oz. Apricot liqueur. Shake well over ice, strain into a Zombie glass with ice, garnish with an orange slice and mint sprig. Serve with straws.

Zombie Cocktail (Cktl). ¾ measure golden Rum, ¾ measure lemon juice, ½ measure white Rum, 1 measure orange juice, dash Grenadine, dash lime juice, 2 dashes Grand Marnier, 2 dashes Crème de Noyau. Stir over crushed ice, pour into a Zombie glass. Dress with an orange slice, mint leaves and serve with straws.

Zombie Glass (USA). A specially large glass (14 fl.ozs.) used for the serving of Zombie cocktails.

Zona de Crianza (Sp). An area within the Denominación de Origen where quality wines may be matured and blended.

Zona de Jerez Superior (Sp). Zone of superior Sherry. Lies between the towns of Puerto de Santa Maria, Jerez de la Frontera and Sanlúcar de Barrameda. Soil is of chalk. See Albariza.

Zona del Albariño (Sp). A noted Vinos Verdes wine producer based in Galicia.

Zona del Albero (Sp). The name given to Moriles Altos in southern Spain.

Zona d'Origine (It). In the growing area.

Zonda Valley (Arg). A major wine-producing area in central Argentina.

Zones (Ger). The 'Table wine' zones of Germany = Ahrtaler Landwein, Rheinburger Landwein, Altrheingauer Landwein, Nahegauer Landwein, Rheinischer Landwein, Starkenburger Landwein, Pfalzer Landwein, Landwein der Mosel, Landwein der Saar, Unterbadischer Landwein, Südbadischer Landwein, Schwäbischer Landwein, Frankischer Landwein, Regensburger Landwein and Bayerischer Bodensee Landwein.

Zonnebloem (S.Afr). Large estates in Simondium, Driesprong, Muratie and Rustenburg.

Zonnebloem Wines (S.Afr). Varietal wines made by the S.F.W.

Zonnheimer (S.Afr). A white wine made from the Steen, Hanepoot and Clairette blanche grapes.

Zoom (USA). Spirit, honey dissolved in boiling water and fresh cream. Shaken over ice, strained and served in a wine glass.

Z

Zoopiyi (Cyp). A wine village in the south-east of the island. Produces the grapes used in the making of Commandaria.

Zornheim (Ger). Village. (Anb) = Rheinhessen. (Ber) = Nierstein. (Gro) = Gutes Domtal. (Vins) = Dachgewann, Güldenmorgen, Mönchbäumchen, Pilgerweg, Vogelsang.

Zotzenheim (Ger). Village. (Anb) = Rheinhessen. (Ber) = Bingen. (Gro) = Sankt Rochuskapelle. (Vins) = Johannisberg, Klostergarten, Sackträger, Schützenhütte, Zuckerberg.

Zoute (Le) (Cktl). 1½ ozs. Vodka, ½ oz. Mandarine Napoléon, 3 ozs. grapefruit juice. Mix with ice, strain into 5 oz. goblet.

Zsiráf (Hun). An export Beer marketed in Africa.

Zuber (Switz). An Eau-de-vie distillery based in Arisdorf, Basel.

Zubrovka (USSR). See Zubrówka.

Zubrówka (Pol). A Bison grass Vodka. Each bottle has a blade of Bison grass (Hierochloe Odorata) in it. Is lemon coloured and has a grassy taste. Also spelt Subrouska. Produced by Polmos.

Zubrówka Grass (Hun). Hierochloe Odorata. Also known as Bison grass. See Zubrówka.

Zucco (It). A noted dessert wine produced in Sicily.

Zuckerberg (Ger). Vineyard. (Anb) = Rheinhessen. (Ber) = Bingen. (Gro) = Sankt Rochuskapelle. (Vil) = Zotzenheim.

Zuckerhütl (Aus). A wine that has a slight amount of residual sugar left after fermentation.

Zuckerkulor (Ger). On a label denotes that a spirit has been sweetened and coloured with colouring sugar (caramel).

Zucherle (Ger). Vineyard. (Anb) = Württemberg. (Ber) = Remstal-Stuttgart. (Gro) = Weinsteige. (Vil) = Stuttgart (ortsteil Cannstatt).

Zuckerle (Ger). Vineyard. (Anb) = Württemberg. (Ber) = Remstal-Stuttgart. (Gro) = Weinsteige. (Vil) = Stuttgart (ortsteil Hofen).

Zuckerle (Ger). Vineyard. (Anb) = Württemberg. (Ber) = Remstal-Stuttgart. (Gro) = Weinsteige. (Vil) = Stuttgart (ortsteil Mühlhausen).

Zuckerle (Ger). Vineyard. (Anb) = Württemberg. (Ber) = Remstal-Stuttgart. (Gro) = Weinsteige. (Vil) = Stuttgart (ortsteil Münster).

Zuckerung (Ger). The old name for Anreicherung/Verbesserung.

Zuffenhausen (Ger). Village. (Anb) = Württemberg. (Ber) = Remstal-Stuttgart. (Gro) = Weinsteige. See Stuttgart.

Zügernberg (Ger). Vineyard. (Anb) = Württemberg. (Ber) = Remstal-Stuttgart. (Gro) = Wartbühl. (Vil) = Grossheppach.

Zuijlekom (Hol). A small distillery based in Amsterdam.

Zukunft (Ger). Lit – 'For the future'. A wine that will lay down for keeping.

Zumbo Cocktail (Cktl). ½ measure dry Gin, ⅙ measure Grand Marnier, ⅙ measure Italian vermouth, ⅙ measure French vermouth, 2 dashes Fernet Branca. Shake over ice, strain into a cocktail glass.

Zummy Cocktail (Cktl). ⅓ measure Gin, ½ measure Bénédictine, ¼ measure French vermouth, ¼ measure Italian vermouth, dash Campari. Shake over ice, strain into a cocktail glass.

Zum Schlüssel (Ger). A fine brewery of Bolkerstrasse in Düsseldorf. Produces fine Altbiers. See Zum Schlüssel Alt and Gatzweiler Alt.

Zum Schlüssel Alt (Ger). An Altbier produced by the Zum Schlüssel Brewery of Düsseldorf. A bitter, slightly acidic, light beer.

Zum Uerige (Ger). A brewery in the Bergerstrasse in Düsseldorf. Noted for its Altbier. See Zum Uerige Altbier.

Zum Uerige Altbier (Ger). A fine, full hop-flavoured and bitter Altbier brewed by the Zum Uerige Brewery in Düsseldorf.

Zunsweier (Ger). Village. (Anb) = Baden. (Ber) = Ortenau. (Gro) = Fürsteneck. (Vin) = Kinzigtäler.

Zunzingen (Ger). Village. (Anb) = Baden. (Ber) = Markgräflerland. (Gro) = Burg Neuenfels. (Vin) = Rosenhang.

Župa (Yug). A wine-producing district based in Central Serbia. Noted for red and rosé wines produced from the Plovdina and Prokupac grapes.

Zupsko Crno (Yug). A red wine produced in the Župa district of central Serbia from a blend of Plovdina and Prokupac grapes.

Zupsko Ruzica (Yug). A rosé wine produced in the Župa district of central Serbia from a blend of Plovdina and Prokupac grapes.

Zürich (Switz). A wine-producing region in north-eastern Switzerland. Produces sweet red and dry white wines.

Zurrapa (Port). A rough, poor wine.

Zusammenschluss (Ger). Describes an association or co-operative who produce wines from their own members' grapes.

Zuur (Hol). Acid.

Zuurheid (Hol). Acidity. Zuur = acid.

Zwack (Aus). A noted liqueur producer. Produces a fine range of liqueurs including Viennese Café, Viennese Pear and Barack Pálinka.

Zwack Unicum (It). An Eau-de-vie based bitter-flavoured liqueur produced from 40 herbs and roots. 40% alc. by vol. Produced in Milan and Genoa. An orange and mint-flavoured variety also produced.

Zwartbier (Hol). Stout.

Zwarte Kip (Hol). Lit – 'Black hen'. A label used by the Heineken-owned Van Offlen Company.

Zweifelberg (Ger). Vineyard. (Anb) = Württemberg. (Ber) = Württembergisch Unterland. (Gro) = Heuchelberg. (Vil) = Brackenheim.

Zweigeltrebe (Aus). A red grape variety. A cross between the St. Laurent and Blaufränkischer varieties. Can withstand frosts.

Zwetgenwasser (Ger). A fruit Brandy made from Switzen plums 44.5% alc. by vol. Also known as Zwetschenwasser.

Zwetgenwasser (Switz). A fruit Brandy made from Quetsch plums. 45% alc. by vol.

Zwetschenwasser (Ger). See Zwetgenwasser.

Zwetschenwasser (Switz). A Zwetgenwasser made from Mirabelle plums.

Zwicker (Fr). An Alsatian word which denotes a blend. See Edelzwicker.

Zwingenberg (Ger). Village. (Anb) = Hessische Bergstrasse. (Ber) = Starkenburg. (Gro) = Rott. (Vins) = Steingeröll, Alte Burg.

Zymamonas (Lat). See Rope.

Zymase (Eng). The specific enzyme in yeast cells which causes vinous fermentation and whose catalytic action converts sugars into alcohol and CO_2.

Zymotechnology (Eng). The technology of yeast fermentation.

Zymurgy (USA). The name of an American home-brewers' magazine. Art and science of brewing.

Zytnia (Pol). A dry, flavoured Vodka 40% alc. by vol. produced by Polmos. Has an aromatic, fruit (apple and cherry added to give it a yellowish tint) flavour.

Zywiec Brewery (Pol). A brewery based south of Cracow.

Z.Y.X. (Cktl). 1 measure Sambuca, 1 measure orange juice, dash lemon juice. Shake over ice, strain into an ice-filled highball glass. Top with bitter lemon.

NOTES